A London
Bibliography of the
Social Sciences

BRITISH LIBRARY OF POLITICAL AND ECONOMIC SCIENCE

A London Bibliography of the Social Sciences

Fourteenth Supplement

1979

VOLUME XXXVII

MANSELL, LONDON, 1980

*This Bibliography has been computer typeset from
the machine-readable subject catalogue of the
British Library of Political and Economic Science by*
Mansell Publishing, a part of Bemrose UK Limited,
3 Bloomsbury Place, London WC1A 2QA

ISBN 0 7201 1594 9
ISSN 0076-051X
Library of Congress Card Number 31-9970

*Printed and bound in Great Britain by
The Scolar Press Ilkley West Yorkshire*

© 1980 *The British Library of Political and Economic Science*

British Library Cataloguing in Publication Data

British Library of Political and Economic Science
   A London bibliography of the social sciences.
   Vol.37: 1979: 14th supplement
   1. Social sciences – Bibliography
   I. Title
   016.3   Z7161   31-9970

ISBN 0-7201-1594-9
ISSN 0076-051X

Prefatory Note

Readers are reminded that the 'List of subject headings used in the Bibliography arranged under topics' is an essential guide to related headings in their field. This is to be found at the end of the volume.

D. A. Clarke   *September* 1980

Contents

VOLUMES I-XXXVII

VOLUMES I–IV   *Original Compilation*
Holdings up to 1929 of the
British Library of Political and Economic Science
Edward Fry Library of International Law
Goldsmith's Library of Economic Literature,
  University of London
National Institute of Industrial Psychology
Royal Anthropological Institute
Royal Institute of International Affairs
Royal Statistical Society

Special collections in the libraries of
The Reform Club (*political and historical pamphlets*)
University College, London (*the Hume, Ricardo and other economic and political collections*)
The University of London (*works on economics and related subjects*)

VOLUME V   *First Supplement*
Additions from 1929 to 1931 to the collections included in Volumes I–IV

VOLUME VI   *Second Supplement*
Additions from 1931 to 1936 to the
British Library of Political and Economic Science
Edward Fry Library of International Law
Goldsmith's Library of Economic Literature

VOLUMES VII–IX   *Third Supplement*
Additions from 1936 to 1950, other than works in the Russian language, to the
British Library of Political and Economic Science
Edward Fry Library of International Law

VOLUMES X–XI   *Fourth Supplement*
Additions from 1950 to 1955 in all languages, and also from 1936 to 1950 in Russian, to the
British Library of Political and Economic Science
Edward Fry Library of International Law

VOLUMES XII–XIV   *Fifth Supplement*
Additions from 1955 to 1962 to the
British Library of Political and Economic Science
Edward Fry Library of International Law

VOLUMES XV–XXI   *Sixth Supplement*
Additions from 1962 to 1968 to the
British Library of Political and Economic Science
Edward Fry Library of International Law
Volume XXI contains indexes to Volumes XV–XXI

VOLUMES XXII–XXVIII   *Seventh Supplement*
Additions from 1969 to 1972 to the
British Library of Political and Economic Science
Edward Fry Library of International Law
Volume XXVIII contains an index to
Volumes XXII–XXVIII

VOLUMES XXIX–XXXI   *Eighth Supplement*
Additions from 1972 to 1973 to the
British Library of Political and Economic Science
Edward Fry Library of International Law
Volume XXXI contains an index to
Volumes XXIX–XXXI

VOLUME XXXII   *Ninth Supplement*
Additions during 1974 to the
British Library of Political and Economic Science
Edward Fry Library of International Law
with index

VOLUME XXXIII   *Tenth Supplement*
Additions during 1975 to the
British Library of Political and Economic Science
Edward Fry Library of International Law
with index

VOLUME XXXIV   *Eleventh Supplement*
Additions during 1976 to the
British Library of Political and Economic Science
Edward Fry Library of International Law
with index

VOLUME XXXV   *Twelfth Supplement*
Additions during 1977 to the
British Library of Political and Economic Science
Edward Fry Library of International Law
with index

VOLUME XXXVI   *Thirteenth Supplement*
Additions during 1978 to the
British Library of Political and Economic Science
Edward Fry Library of International Law
with index

VOLUME XXXVII   *Fourteenth Supplement*
Additions during 1979 to the
British Library of Political and Economic Science
Edward Fry Library of International Law
with index

PERIODICALS LISTS

An alphabetical list of the periodicals in the British Library of Political and Economic Science in 1929 is given in Volume IV; supplementary lists up to 1936 are given in Volumes V and VI, after which they have been discontinued.

AUTHOR INDEX

Author indexes are given in Volumes IV (for Volumes I–III), V, and VI, but not in later volumes.
Volumes I–XIV were published by the
British Library of Political and Economic Science,
Houghton Street, London WC2

A London
Bibliography of the
Social Sciences

ADMINISTRATION.

AARGAU (CANTON)

— Constitution.

AARGAU (CANTON). Constitution, 1885. Staatsverfassung des Kantons Aargau vom 23. April 1885...mit den bis 1. Januar 1972 erfolgten Abänderungen. Aarau, Staatskanzlei, 1972. pp. 41.

ABAELARDUS (PETRUS).

LUSCOMBE (D.E.) Peter Abelard. London, [1979]. pp. 40. *bibliog. (Historical Association. General Series. G.95)*

ABDALLAH, King of Jordan.

ABDALLAH, King of Jordan. My memoirs completed: al-Takmilah; translated from the Arabic by Harold W. Glidden. London, 1978. pp. 102. *Reprint, with extensive introduction by King Hussein of Jordan of work published in Amman, Jordan, in 1951.*

ABELARD (PETER).

See ABAELARDUS (PETRUS).

ABILITY.

The STUDY of real skills vol. 1. The analysis of practical skills; edited by W.T. Singleton. Lancaster, [1978]. pp. 333. *bibliogs.*

ABILITY GROUPING IN EDUCATION.

YATES (ALFRED) The organization of schooling: a study of educational grouping practices. London, 1971. pp. 104. *bibliog.*

ABOLITIONISTS.

HERSH (BLANCHE GLASSMAN) The slavery of sex: feminist-abolitionists in America. Urbana, Ill., [1978]. pp. 280. *bibliog.*

— United States.

DILLON (MERTON LYNN) The abolitionists: the growth of a dissenting minority. De Kalb, 1974 repr. 1975. pp. 298. *bibliog.*

WALKER (PETER F.) Moral choices: memory, desire, and imagination in nineteenth- century American abolition. Baton Rouge, [1978]. pp. 387. *bibliog.*

ABORTION.

FRANCKE (LINDA BIRD) The ambivalence of abortion. London, 1979. pp. 261.

— Law and legislation.

WORLD HEALTH ORGANIZATION. 1971. Abortion laws: a survey of current world legislation. Geneva, 1971. pp. 78. *bibliog. Originally published in International Digest of Health Legislation, v. 21, 1970.*

— Denmark.

USSING (JYTTE) Om abort; (with an English summary) Facts about legally induced abortion. København, 1979. pp. 83. *(Socialforskningsinstituttet. Publikationer. 87)*

— Italy.

BERLINGUER (GIOVANNI) La legge sull'aborto: (dalle prime proposte al voto del parlamento; il testo commentato della legge e le sue applicazioni). Roma, 1978. pp. 187. *bibliog.*

— United Kingdom — Commonwealth.

THREE studies of abortion laws in the Commonwealth;...by Mostyn P. Embrey [and others]. London, Commonwealth Secretariat, [1977]. 1 vol. (various pagings). *bibliog.*

ABSENTEEISM (LABOUR).

ALBANI (PAOLO) L'assenteismo operaio: una forma di non collaborazione. Roma, 1976. pp. 157.

— Bibliography.

SHEA (MARNIE) compiler. Absenteeism and lates; a selected bibliography. [Toronto], Ontario Ministry of Labour Research Library, 1975. fo. 6.

ABSTRACTING AND INDEXING SERVICES.

HARZFELD (LOIS A.) Periodical indexes in the social sciences and humanities: a subject guide. Metuchen, N.J., 1978. pp. 174.

ABUSE OF ADMINISTRATIVE POWER

— United States.

SHELDON (CHARLES P.) The bolshevization of the USA. New York, [1978]. pp. 725.

THEOHARIS (ATHAN G.) Spying on Americans: political surveillance from Hoover to the Huston Plan. Philadelphia, 1978. pp. 331. *bibliog.*

ABUSED WIVES

— Services for — United Kingdom.

NATIONAL WOMEN'S AID FEDERATION. Battered women, refugees and women's aid. [London, 1977]. pp. 54.

ACCOUNTANTS

— Sri Lanka.

SRI LANKA. Committee on Duties, Responsibilities and Standards of Professional Accountants and Auditors. 1974. Report...to the Public Acco[u]nts Committee; [P.M.W. Wijesuriya, chairman]. Colombo, 1974. pp. 120. *(Sri Lanka. Parliament. Sessional Papers. 1974. No. 11)*

ACCOUNTING.

MATTESSICH (RICHARD) Accounting and analytical methods: measurement and projection of income and wealth in the micro- and macro-economy. Houston, 1977. pp. 556. *bibliog. Reprint of book first published 1964.*

WOOD (FRANK) Business accounting. 2nd ed. London, 1972-73 repr. 1977. 2 vols.

IJIRI (YUJI) Theory of accounting measurement. [Sarasota], 1975. pp. 210. *bibliog. (American Accounting Association. Studies in Accounting Research. 10)*

CURRENT issues in accounting;...[edited by] Bryan Carsberg and Tony Hope. Deddington, Oxon., 1977. pp. 293.

BIERMAN (HAROLD) and DREBIN (ALLAN RICHARD) Financial accounting: an introduction. 3rd ed. Philadelphia, 1978. pp. 452.

INTERNATIONAL CONGRESS OF ACCOUNTANTS, 11TH, MUNICH, 1977. Accounting and auditing in one world; proceedings of the ... congress. Düsseldorf, 1978. pp. 511.

TAMARI (M.) Financial ratios: analysis and prediction. London, 1978. pp. 182. *bibliog.*

TRENDS in managerial and financial accounting: income determination and financial reporting; Cees van Dam, editor. Leiden, 1978. pp. 221. *bibliogs. 11 papers from a research seminar 'Decision-making in business', held at Nijenrode, 1976.*

— History.

YAMEY (BASIL SELIG) Essays on the history of accounting. New York, 1978. 1 vol. (various pagings).

— Measurement.

NAKANO (ISAO) Accounting measurement under uncertainties. Kobe, [1977]. pp. 214. *(Kobe. University. Research Institute for Economics and Business Administration. Kobe Economic and Business Research Series. No. 5)*

— Research.

The IMPACT of accounting research on practice and disclosure; [edited by] A. Rashad Abdel-khalik and Thomas F. Keller. Durham, N.C., 1978. pp. 222. *bibliog. Symposium held at Duke University, 1975.*

READINGS in accounting and business research, 1970-1977; edited by R. H. Parker. [London], 1978. pp. 184.

FINANCIAL information requirements for security analysis; edited by A. Rashad Abdel-khalik and Thomas F. Keller. [Durham, N.C., 1979?]. pp. 164. *bibliogs. Duke Second Accounting Symposium, 1976.*

— Social aspects.

GAMBLING (TREVOR) Beyond the conventions of accounting. London, 1978. pp. 182. *bibliog.*

— United Kingdom.

INSTITUTE OF CHARTERED ACCOUNTANTS IN ENGLAND AND WALES. Accounting Standards Committee. Accounting standards, 1979; prepared by members of the staff of the Technical Directorate. London, [1979]. pp. 320.

ACCULTURATION.

MINTZ (SIDNEY WILFRED) and PRICE (RICHARD) Anthropologist. An anthropological approach to the Afro-American past: a Caribbean perspective. Philadelphia, [1976]. pp. 64. *bibliog. (Institute for the Study of Human Issues. ISHI Occasional Papers in Social Change. No. 2)*

ALVERSON (HOYT) Mind in the heart of darkness: value and self-identity among the Tswana of southern Africa. New Haven, 1978. pp. 299. *bibliog.*

RECK (GREGORY G.) In the shadow of Tlaloc: life in a Mexican village. Harmondsworth, 1978. pp. 224.

ACT (PHILOSOPHY).

JOHN PAUL II., Pope [Karol WOJTYŁA]. The acting person; translated from the Polish by Andrzej Potocki; this definitive text of the work established in collaboration with the author by Anna-Teresa Tymieniecka. Dordrecht, [1979]. pp. 367. *(Analecta Husserliana. vol. 10)*

ADAM, of Orleton, Bishop of Winchester.

HAINES (ROY MARTIN) The church and politics in fourteenth-century England: the career of Adam Orleton, c.1275-1345. Cambridge, 1978. pp. 303. *bibliog.*

ADAPTATION (BIOLOGY).

EXTINCTION and survival in human populations; edited by Charles D. Laughlin, Jr., and Ivan A. Brady. New York, 1978. pp. 327. *bibliog.*

ADAT LAW

— Borneo.

NORTH BORNEO. Native Affairs Bulletins. No.7. Dusun custom in Putatan district; compiled by Pangeran Osman bin O.K.K. Pangeran Haji Omar; with a translation by G.C. Woolley. Jesselton, [1932] repr. 1962. pp. 55. *In English and Malay.*

ADDIS ABABA

— Population.

ETHIOPIA. Central Statistical Office. 1972. Population of Addis Ababa: results from the population sample survey of October 1967. Addis Ababa, 1972. pp. 84, (14). *(Statistical Bulletins. 8)*

ADMINISTRATION.

MILLETT (JOHN DAVID) Organization for the public service. Princeton, [1966]. pp. 159.

HILL (MICHAEL J.) The sociology of public administration. New York, [1975]. pp. 278. *bibliog. First published in 1972.*

ADMINISTRATION.(Cont.)

KEELING (DESMOND) Management in government. London, 1972. pp. 210. *bibliog.*

HOOD (CHRISTOPHER C.) The limits of administration. London, [1976]. pp. 213.

NIGRO (FELIX A.) and NIGRO (LLOYD G.) Modern public administration. 4th ed. New York, [1977]. pp. 492. *bibliogs.*

ORGANIZATION development in public administration...; edited by Robert T. Golembiewski and William B. Eddy. New York, [1978] in progress. *bibliogs.*

DUNSIRE (ANDREW) Control in a bureaucracy. Oxford, 1978. pp. 263. *bibliog. (The execution process. vol.2)*

DUNSIRE (ANDREW) Implementation in a bureaucracy. Oxford, 1978. pp. 260. *bibliog. (The execution process. vol.1)*

HODGKINSON (CHRISTOPHER) Towards a philosophy of administration. Oxford, [1978]. pp. 244. *bibliog.*

SHAFRITZ (JAY M.) and HYDE (ALBERT C.) eds. Classics of public administration. Oak Park, Ill., [1978]. pp. 446.

— Decision making.

URBAN PROGRAMME RESEARCH. Working Papers. 4. Urban programme decision making: the phase 7 exercise. Leeds, [1974?]. fo. 42.

STRUCTURE of decision: the cognitive maps of political elites; edited by Robert Axelrod. Princeton, N.J., [1976]. pp. 404. *bibliog.*

INTERNATIONAL INSTITUTE FOR STRATEGIC STUDIES. Adelphi Papers. No. 147, 148. Decision-making in Soviet weapons procurement; by Arthur J. Alexander. London, 1978-79. pp. 64.

CALCUL économique et décisions publiques:...l'oeuvre d'un groupe de travail...(J.C. Milleron) [chairman]. Paris, 1979. pp. 157. *(France. Commissariat Général du Plan. Economie et Planification)*

— — Mathematical models.

GEARY (K.) Treatment of multiple objectives for programming problems: a review with reference to possible public sector application. London, 1978. pp. 25. *bibliog. (Planning Research Applications Group. PRAG Technical Papers. TP 25)*

— Study and teaching — United Kingdom.

RHODES (R.A.W.) Public administration and policy analysis: recent developments in Britain and America. Farnborough, [1979]. pp. 122.

— — United States.

RHODES (R.A.W.) Current developments in the study of public administration in the United States. Birmingham, 1976. pp. 128, 9. *bibliog. (Birmingham. University. Institute of Local Government Studies. Discussion Papers. New Series. No. 1)*

RHODES (R.A.W.) Public administration and policy analysis: recent developments in Britain and America. Farnborough, [1979]. pp. 122.

ADMINISTRATIVE AGENCIES

— Australia — Queensland.

QUEENSLAND. Department of the Co-ordinator-General of Public Works. 1975. State of regional planning, public works organization and environmental control in Queensland. [Brisbane, 1975?]. pp. 16.

— France.

REMOND (BRUNO) Les OREAM et l'aménagement du territoire, 1966-76. [Paris, Documentation Française, 1977]. pp. 215. *bibliog. 11 maps in end pocket.*

— India — Goa, Daman and Diu.

GOA, DAMAN AND DIU. Bureau of Economics, Statistics and Evaluation. 1976. An evaluation of the Marginal Farmers and Agricultural Labourers Development Agency, Goa, 1974-75. Panaji, 1976. pp. 131. *(Evaluation Reports. No.16)*

— United Kingdom.

BOWEN (GORDON) Survey of fringe bodies; report;...assisted by B.V. Lindsay. London, Civil Service Department, [1978]. pp. 151.

SHERMAN (ALFRED V.) The newest profession. [London, 1978]. pp. 16.

— United States.

COLE (BARRY G.) and OETTINGER (MAL) Reluctant regulators: the FCC and the broadcast audience. Reading, Mass., [1978]. pp. 310.

ADMINISTRATIVE AND POLITICAL DIVISIONS.

SENFTLEBEN (WOLFGANG) Studies in electoral geography. Taipei, 1977. pp. 113. *bibliog.*

See also the subdivision Administrative and political divisions under names of countries, cities, etc.

ADMINISTRATIVE COURTS

— Germany.

EUROPEAN COURT OF HUMAN RIGHTS. Publications. Series A: Judgments and Decisions. [A27]. ...König case: 1. Decision of 23 April 1977; 2. Judgment of 28 June 1978. Strasbourg, Council of Europe, 1978. pp. 52bis. *In English and French.*

— Spain.

PEREZ HERNANDEZ (ANTONIO) El Consejo de Estado. Madrid, Centro de Formacion y Perfeccionamiento de Funcionarios, 1965. pp. 130. *(Estudios Administrativos. Serie A.26)*

— United Kingdom.

FLICK (GEOFFREY A.) Natural justice: principles and practical application. Sydney, 1979. pp. 175. *bibliog.*

ADMINISTRATIVE LAW

— Canada.

REID (ROBERT F.) and DAVID (HILLEL) Administrative law and practice. 2nd ed. Toronto, [1978]. pp. 504.

— Europe.

NEDJATI (ZAIM M.) and TRICE (J.E.) English and continental systems of administrative law. Amsterdam, 1978. pp. 211.

— France.

DEMICHEL (ANDRÉ) Le droit administratif: essai de réflexion théorique. Paris, 1978. pp. 220.

LAUBADÈRE (ANDRÉ DE) Manuel de droit administratif. 11th ed. Paris, 1978. pp. 399.

— Germany.

WESSEL (HELGA) Zweckmässigkeit als Handlungsprinzip in der deutschen Regierungs- und Verwaltungslehre der frühen Neuzeit. Berlin, 1978. pp. 169. *bibliog.*

— Italy.

ITALY. Statutes, etc. 1850-1977. Codice amministrativo; a cura di E. Guicciardi [and others]. 5th ed. Padova, 1977. pp. 3052.

— Russia.

EREMIN (ALEKSANDR IVANOVICH) Akty mestnykh organov narodnogo kontrolia. Moskva, 1976. pp. 111.

PROBLEMY upravleniia i grazhdanskogo prava. Moskva, 1976. pp. 185.

METODY i formy gosudarstvennogo upravleniia. Moskva, 1977. pp. 334.

KORENEV (ALEKSEI PROKOF'EVICH) Normy administrativnogo prava i ikh primenenie. Moskva, 1978. pp. 142.

SOTSIAL'NYE i gosudarstvenno-pravovye aspekty upravleniia v SSSR. Kiev, 1978. pp. 427.

— United Kingdom.

NEDJATI (ZAIM M.) and TRICE (J.E.) English and continental systems of administrative law. Amsterdam, 1978. pp. 211.

PHILLIPS (OWEN HOOD) Constitutional and administrative law; sixth edition by O.H. Phillips and Paul Jackson. London, 1978. pp. 746.

GARNER (JOHN FRANCIS) Administrative law. 5th ed. London, 1979. pp. 525. *bibliog.*

ADMINISTRATIVE PROCEDURE

— Canada.

REID (ROBERT F.) and DAVID (HILLEL) Administrative law and practice. 2nd ed. Toronto, [1978]. pp. 504.

— Poland.

POLAND. Statutes, etc. 1966. Loi du 17 juin 1966 sur les voies d'exécution administrative. Warszawa, 1968. pp. 61-94. *Reprinted from Droit Polonais Contemporain, No. 9, 1968.*

— United States.

FREEDMAN (JAMES O.) Crisis and legitimacy: the administrative process and American government. Cambridge, 1978. pp. 324. *bibliog.*

ADMINISTRATIVE RESPONSIBILITY

— Russia — White Russia.

WHITE RUSSIA. Statutes, etc., 1929-1970. Sbornik zakonodatel'nykh aktov ob administrativnoi otvetstvennosti. Minsk, 1970. pp. 318.

ADOLESCENCE.

ODLUM (DORIS MAUDE) Journey through adolescence. London, 1957. pp. 186.

IS anyone there?; edited by Monica Dickens and Rosemary Sutcliff. [Harmondsworth, 1978]. pp. 204.

CORRIGAN (PAUL) Schooling the Smash Street Kids. London, 1979. pp. 158. *bibliog.*

ADOLESCENT PSYCHOLOGY.

LIVESLEY (WILLIAM JOHN) and BROMLEY (DENNIS BASIL) Person perception in childhood and adolescence. London, [1973]. pp. 320. *bibliog.*

— United Kingdom.

LOUDEN (DELROY M.) West Indian adolescents in school: towards a typology of behaviour patterns. [Bristol, Social Science Research Council Research Unit on Ethnic Relations, 1976?]. fo. 14.

— United States.

BRENNAN (TIM) and others. The social psychology of runaways. Lexington, Mass., [1978]. pp. 346. *bibliog.*

ADOPTION

— France.

L'ADOPTION: effectivité de la loi du 11 juillet 1966; par Marie Pierre Marmier-Champenois [and others]. [Paris, 1978]. pp. 275. *(France. Ministère de la Justice. Service de Coordination de la Recherche. Etude[s] de Sociologie Juridique)*

ADOPTION, INTERRACIAL.

See INTERRACIAL ADOPTION.

ADORNO (THEODOR WIESENGRUND).

ROSE (GILLIAN) The melancholy science: an introduction to the thought of Theodor W. Adorno. London, 1978. pp. 212. *bibliog.*

ADVERTISING.

WILLIAMSON (JUDITH) Decoding advertisements: ideology and meaning in advertising. London, 1978. pp. 180. *bibliog.*

— Psychological aspects.

WILLIAMSON (JUDITH) Decoding advertisements: ideology and meaning in advertising. London, 1978. pp. 180. *bibliog.*

— United States.

EDWARDS (PAUL KENNETH) The southern urban negro as a consumer. New York, 1932; New York, 1969. pp. 323. *bibliog. Facsimile reprint.*

ADYGEI

— Statistics.

ADYGEI. Statisticheskoe Upravlenie. Sovetskaia Adygeia k 50-letiiu obrazovaniia SSSR: statisticheskii sbornik. Maikop, 1973. pp. 175.

ADZHARIA

— History — 1917-1921, Revolution.

MARGVELASHVILI (VLADIMIR I.) Iz istorii angliiskoi okkupatsii Adzharii, 1918-1920 gg. Batumi, 1973. pp. 52.

AERIAL PHOTOGRAMMETRY.

LUCHTATLAS van Nederland; onder auspiciën van het Koninklijk Nederlands Aardrijkskundig Genootschap. Bussum, [1978]. pp. 229. *bibliog.*

AERONAUTICS

— New Zealand — History.

ALEXANDER (RONALD TREVOR) High adventure: from balloons to Boeings in New Zealand. [Wellington, Natural Airways Corporation, 1968]. pp. 93.

— United Kingdom — Laws and regulations.

SHAWCROSS (CHRISTOPHER NYHOLE) and BEAUMONT (KENNETH MACDONALD) Air law; fourth edition [by] Peter Martin [and others]. London, 1977. 2 vols. *Vol. 2 is a looseleaf binder containing noter-up, treaties and legislation.*

AERONAUTICS, COMMERCIAL.

HAMMARSKJÖLD (KNUT OLOF HJALMAR AKESSON) The state of the air transport industry. Montreal, [1978]. pp. 36. *Report for the 34th annual meeting at Geneva in 1978 of the International Air Transport Association. Actual verbal report attached as separate item.*

AERONAUTICS, MILITARY

— Russia.

The SOVIET air and rocket forces; edited by Asher Lee. Westport, Conn., [1959]. pp. 311.

— United States.

COULAM (ROBERT F.) Illusions of choice: the F-111 and the problem of weapons acquisition reform. Princeton, [1977]. pp. 432. *bibliog.*

LEHMAN (JOHN) Aircraft carriers: the real choices. Beverly Hills, [1978]. pp. 83. *(Georgetown University. Center for Strategic and International Studies. Washington Papers. vol. 6/52)*

AEROPLANE INDUSTRY AND TRADE

— France.

COSTELLO (JOHN) and HUGHES (TERRY) Concorde: the international race for a supersonic passenger transport. London, 1976. pp. 302.

— United Kingdom.

COSTELLO (JOHN) and HUGHES (TERRY) Concorde: the international race for a supersonic passenger transport. London, 1976. pp. 302.

BRITISH AEROSPACE. Annual report and accounts. a., 1977(1st)- Weybridge.

AEROPLANES, MILITARY.

LEHMAN (JOHN) Aircraft carriers: the real choices. Beverly Hills, [1978]. pp. 83. *(Georgetown University. Center for Strategic and International Studies. Washington Papers. vol. 6/52)*

AESTHETICS.

PLEKHANOV (GEORGII VALENTINOVICH) Estetika i sotsiologiia iskusstva: [sbornik statei, 1897-1913]. Moskva, 1978. 2 vols. *With introductory article by M. Lifshits.*

CASSIRER (ERNST) Symbol, myth, and culture: essays and lectures of Ernst Cassirer, 1935-1945; edited by Donald Phillip Verene. New Haven, 1979. pp. 304.

AETAS (PHILIPPINE NIGRITOS).

PETERSON (JEAN TRELOGGEN) The ecology of social boundaries: Agta foragers of the Philippines. Urbana, [1978]. pp. 141. *bibliog. (Illinois University. Illinois Studies in Anthropology. No. 11)*

AFAN VALLEY

— Social conditions.

GLAMORGAN-GLYNCORRWG COMMUNITY DEVELOPMENT PROJECT. A report to the Minister about the work of the Glamorgan/Glyncorrwg Community Development Project, to be read in conjunction with the Director's report to the Project Management Committee, July 1972. [Port Talbot, 1972]. 1 pamphlet (various foliations).

GLAMORGAN-GLYNCORRWG COMMUNITY DEVELOPMENT PROJECT. The Upper Afan Community Development Project. [Port Talbot], 1975. pp. 19.

— Social policy.

GLAMORGAN-GLYNCORRWG COMMUNITY DEVELOPMENT PROJECT. Director's report to the Community Development Project Management Committee, June 1973. [Port Talbot, 1973]. 1 pamphlet (various foliations).

GLAMORGAN-GLYNCORRWG COMMUNITY DEVELOPMENT PROJECT. Director's report to the Management Committee, 2..., July 1974. [Port Talbot], 1974. fo. 12.

GLAMORGAN-GLYNCORRWG COMMUNITY DEVELOPMENT PROJECT. Director's report to the Project Management Committee..., March 1974. [Port Talbot], 1974. pp. (60).

GLAMORGAN-GLYNCORRWG COMMUNITY DEVELOPMENT PROJECT. Technical report 2. [Port Talbot], 1974. 1 pamphlet (various foliations).

GLAMORGAN-GLYNCORRWG COMMUNITY DEVELOPMENT PROJECT. Director's report to the Management Committee, 4..., March 1975. Port Talbot, 1975. pp. (26).

AFFIRMATIVE ACTION PROGRAMMES

— United States.

BENOKRAITIS (NIJOLE V.) and FEAGIN (JOE R.) Affirmative action and equal opportunity: action, inaction, reaction. Boulder, Colo., 1978. pp. 255. *bibliog.*

FEAGIN (JOE R.) and FEAGIN (CLAIRECE BOOHER) Discrimination American style: institutional racism and sexism. Englewood Cliffs, [1978?]. pp. 190.

JACKSON (JESSE) and others. A conversation with the Reverend Jesse Jackson: the quest for economic and educational parity. Washington, [1978]. pp. 27. *(American Enterprise Institute for Public Policy Research. AEI Studies. 209)*

AFGHANISTAN.

AFGANISTAN: voprosy istorii, ekonomiki i filologii. Tashkent, 1978. pp. 123.

— Boundaries — Pakistan.

PAZHWAK (RAHMAN) An article on Pakhtunistan, a new state in central Asia. London, Royal Afghan Embassy, [1960]. pp. 28.

AFRICA

— Armed forces — Political activity.

BIENEN (HENRY) Armies and parties in Africa. New York, [1978]. pp. 278. *bibliogs.*

— Bibliography.

STANDING CONFERENCE ON LIBRARY MATERIALS ON AFRICA. Theses on Africa, 1963-1975, accepted by universities in the United Kingdom and Ireland; compiled by J.H.St.J. McIlwaine. London, 1978. pp. 123.

— Boundaries.

BROWNLIE (IAN) African boundaries: a legal and diplomatic encyclopaedia; with the assistance of Ian R. Burns. London, [1979]. pp. 1355. *bibliog.*

— Colonization.

AFRICAN proconsuls: European governors in Africa; [edited by] L.H. Gann and Peter Duignan. New York, [1978]. pp. 548. *bibliog.*

EXPANSION and reaction: essays on European expansion and reaction in Asia and Africa; edited by H.L. Wesseling. Leiden, 1978. pp. 200.

GANN (LEWIS H.) and DUIGNAN (PETER) The rulers of British Africa, 1870-1914. London, [1978]. pp. 406. *bibliog.*

KNOLL (ARTHUR J.) Togo under imperial Germany, 1884-1914: a case study in colonial rule. Stanford, Calif., [1978]. pp. 224. *bibliog. (Stanford University. Hoover Institution on War, Revolution and Peace. Hoover Institution Publications. 190)*

— Commerce — France.

FRANCE. Ministère de la Coopération. Sous-Direction des Etudes Economiques et de la Planification. 1975. Bilan global des échanges commerciaux entre la France et les EAM. Paris, 1975. pp. 26. *(Etudes et Documents. No. 20)*

— Economic conditions.

SURVEY OF ECONOMIC CONDITIONS IN AFRICA, A; [pd.by] Economic Commission for Africa, United Nations. 1960/1964[1st issue]; a., 1967[2nd]- New York.

AFRICA (Cont.)

STATISTICAL INFORMATION BULLETIN FOR AFRICA (formerly Statistical and Economic Information Bulletin for Africa) [pd. by Economic Commission for Africa] United Nations. [in English and French]. irreg., [Je 1972] (no.1)- , with gaps (1974, nos.5-6). Addis Ababa. *Supersedes Statistical bulletin for Africa, (N 1965 - Mr 1967).*

INTERNATIONAL MONETARY FUND. Surveys of African Economies. Vol. 7. Algeria, Mali, Morocco, and Tunisia. Washington, 1977. pp. 374.

HUMAN resources and African development; edited by Ukandi G. Damachi and Victor P. Diejomaoh. New York, [1978]. pp. 378. *bibliog.*

SEIDMAN (ROBERT BENJAMIN) The state, law and development. London, [1978]. pp. 483.

— — Statistics.

UNITED STATES. Agency for International Development. Statistics and Reports Division. 1976. Africa: economic growth trends. [Washington], 1976. pp. 46.

— Economic integration.

NANA-SINKAM (SAMUEL C.) Monetary integration and theory of optimum currency areas in Africa. The Hague, [1978]. pp. 315. *bibliog.*

— Economic policy.

DEMOGRAPHIC aspects of socio-economic development in some Arab and African countries; edited by S. A. Huzayyin and T. E. Smith. Cairo, 1974. pp. 427. *bibliogs. (Cairo Demographic Centre. Research Monograph Series. No. 5)*

INTERNATIONAL MONETARY FUND. Surveys of African Economies. Vol. 7. Algeria, Mali, Morocco, and Tunisia. Washington, 1977. pp. 374.

— Foreign economic relations — Communist countries.

INTERNATIONAL CONFERENCE OF THE SOCIALIST COUNTRIES' AFRICANISTS, BUDAPEST, 1976. Economic relations of Africa with the socialist countries; proceedings of the 5th...conference, etc. Vol.1: Hungarian contributions. Budapest, 1978. pp. 167. *bibliogs. (Magyar Tudományos Akadémia. Világgazdasági Kutató Intézet. Studies on Developing Countries. No. 95)*

— — United Kingdom.

BANGURA (YUSUF) The politics of economic relations between Britain and Commonwealth Africa, 1951-1975. 1978. fo. 526. *bibliog.* Typescript. Ph.D. (London) thesis: unpublished. This thesis is the property of London University and may not be removed from the Library.

— Foreign relations.

WAYAS (JOSEPH) Nigeria's leadership role in Africa. London, 1979. pp. 132.

— — Arab countries.

OJO (MATTHEW OLUSOLA) The Africa states and the Arab world: the development of Afro-Arab relations, with special reference to the O.A.U. and the League of Arab States. 1977 [or rather 1978]. fo. 444. *bibliog.* Typescript. Ph.D. (London) thesis: unpublished. This thesis is the property of London University and may not be removed from the Library.

— — Russia.

JANKE (PETER F.) Marxist statecraft in Africa: what future? London, 1978. pp. 18. *(Institute for the Study of Conflict. Conflict Studies. No.95)*

— History.

AFRICAN labor history; Peter C.W. Gutkind [and others], editors. Beverly Hills, [1978]. pp. 280. *bibliogs.*

CURTIN (PHILIP DEARMOND) and others. African history. London, 1978. pp. 612.

— — Maps.

FAGE (JOHN DONNELLY) An atlas of African history. 2nd ed. London, 1978. 1 vol. (unpaged). *Contains 71 maps.*

— History, Military.

SMITH (ROBERT SYDNEY) Warfare and diplomacy in pre-colonial West Africa. London, 1976. pp. 240. *bibliog.*

— Politics and government.

AFRICAN FREEDOM ANNUAL, 1977; edited by F.R. Metrowich [and others]. Sandton, 1977. pp. 165.

AFRICAN labor history; Peter C.W. Gutkind [and others], editors. Beverly Hills, [1978]. pp. 280. *bibliogs.*

AKE (CLAUDE) Revolutionary pressures in Africa. London, 1978. pp. 109.

AUSTIN (DENNIS) Politics in Africa. Manchester, [1978]. pp. 202. *bibliog.*

AWOLOWO (OBAFEMI) The problems of Africa: the need for ideological reappraisal. London, 1978. pp. 78. *(University of Cape Coast. Kwame Nkrumah Memorial Lectures. First Series)*

BIENEN (HENRY) Armies and parties in Africa. New York, [1978]. pp. 278. *bibliogs.*

BOATENG (ERNEST AMANO) A political geography of Africa. Cambridge, 1978. pp. 292. *bibliog.*

BRETON (JEAN MARIE) Le contrôle d'état sur le continent africain: contribution à une théorie des contrôles administratifs et financiers dans les pays en voie de développement. Paris, 1978. pp. 532. *bibliog.*

GONIDEC (PIERRE FRANÇOIS) Les systèmes politiques africains. 2nd ed. Paris, 1978. pp. 431. *bibliog.*

HODDER (BRAMWELL WILLIAM) Africa today: a short introduction to African affairs. London, 1978. pp. 166. *bibliog.*

MUNFORD (CLARENCE J.) Production relations, class and black liberation: a marxist perspective in Afro-American studies. Amsterdam, 1978. pp. 235. *bibliog.*

— — Abstracts.

AFRICAN ADMINISTRATIVE ABSTRACTS: a q. jl.; ([pd. by] African Training and Research Centre in Administration for Development). q., 1974(v.1)- Tangier.

— — Bibliography.

SOLOMON (ALAN C.) compiler. A bibliography for the study of African politics, vol. 2. Waltham, Mass., [1977]. pp. 193.

— Population.

DEMOGRAPHIC aspects of socio-economic development in some Arab and African countries; edited by S. A. Huzayyin and T. E. Smith. Cairo, 1974. pp. 427. *bibliogs. (Cairo Demographic Centre. Research Monograph Series. No. 5)*

— Relations (general) with China.

BOGOSLOVSKII (VIKTOR VASIL'EVICH) Proiski Pekina v Afrike. Kiev, 1978. pp. 175.

— Religion.

RAY (BENJAMIN C.) African religions: symbol, ritual and community. Englewood Cliffs, [1976]. pp. 238. *bibliog.*

The NEW religions of Africa; edited by Bennetta Jules-Rosette. Norwood, N.J., [1979]. pp. 248. *bibliog.*

— Social conditions.

AKE (CLAUDE) Revolutionary pressures in Africa. London, 1978. pp. 109.

— Statistics — Directories.

HARVEY (JOAN M.) Statistics Africa: sources for social, economic and market research. 2nd ed. Beckenham, 1978. pp. 374.

AFRICA, CENTRAL

— Economic conditions.

PERRINGS (CHARLES) Black mineworkers in Central Africa: industrial strategies and the evolution of an African proletariat in the copperbelt 1911-41. London, 1979. pp. 302. *bibliog.*

— Industries.

PERRINGS (CHARLES) Black mineworkers in Central Africa: industrial strategies and the evolution of an African proletariat in the copperbelt 1911-41. London, 1979. pp. 302. *bibliog.*

— Rural conditions.

The ROOTS of rural poverty in central and southern Africa; edited by Robin Palmer and Neil Parsons. Berkeley, Calif., 1977. pp. 430. *bibliogs.*

— Social conditions.

PERRINGS (CHARLES) Black mineworkers in Central Africa: industrial strategies and the evolution of an African proletariat in the copperbelt 1911-41. London, 1979. pp. 302. *bibliog.*

AFRICA, EAST

— Commerce.

STEIN (LESLIE) The growth of East African exports and their effect on economic development. London, [1979]. pp. 272. *bibliog.*

— Economic history.

STEIN (LESLIE) The growth of East African exports and their effect on economic development. London, [1979]. pp. 272. *bibliog.*

— Population.

MONSTED (METTE) and WALJI (PARVEEN) A demographic analysis of East Africa: a sociological interpretation. Uppsala, 1978. pp. 211. *bibliogs.*

AFRICA, NORTH

— History.

HESS (ANDREW C.) The forgotten frontier: a history of the sixteenth-century Ibero-African frontier. Chicago, 1978. pp. 278. *bibliog. (Chicago. University. Center for Middle Eastern Studies. Publications. 10)*

— Relations (general) with Spain.

HESS (ANDREW C.) The forgotten frontier: a history of the sixteenth-century Ibero-African frontier. Chicago, 1978. pp. 278. *bibliog. (Chicago. University. Center for Middle Eastern Studies. Publications. 10)*

AFRICA, SUBSAHARAN

— Economic conditions.

EGELAND (LEIF) Interdependence in Southern Africa. Braamfontein, 1978. pp. 4. *(South African Institute of International Affairs. Occasional Papers)*

— Foreign relations — Russia.

WALKER (Sir WALTER) The bear at the back door: the Soviet threat to the West's lifeline in Africa. Richmond, Surrey, 1978. pp. 246.

— History.

RASMUSSEN (R. KENT) Migrant kingdom: Mzilikazi's Ndebele in South Africa. London, 1978. pp. 262. *bibliog.*

— Politics and government.

WEST (RICHARD LEAF) The white tribes of Africa. New York, 1965. pp. 281.

CONFLICT and change in Southern Africa: papers from a Scandinavian-Canadian conference [held in Ottawa in 1978]; edited by Douglas G. Anglin [and others]. Washington, [1978]. pp. 269.

EGELAND (LEIF) Interdependence in Southern Africa. Braamfontein, 1978. pp. 4. (*South African Institute of International Affairs. Occasional Papers*)

WALKER (Sir WALTER) The bear at the back door: the Soviet threat to the West's lifeline in Africa. Richmond, Surrey, 1978. pp. 246.

WEST (RICHARD LEAF) The white tribes revisited. London, 1978. pp. 199.

MANGOPE (LUCAS) Trends in Southern Africa and the role of Bophuthatswana. Braamfontein, 1979. pp. 8. (*South African Institute of International Affairs. Occasional Papers*)

SOCIALISM in Sub-Saharan Africa: a new assessment; edited by Carl G. Rosberg and Thomas M. Callaghy. Berkeley, [1979]. pp. 426. *bibliog.* (*California University. Institute of International Studies. Research Series. No.38*)

SOUTHERN Africa: the continuing crisis; edited by Gwendolen M. Carter and Patrick O'Meara. Bloomington, [1979]. pp. 404. *bibliog.*

— Relations (general) with South Africa.

CILLIE (PIET) Vision of the seventies: evolving relationships in southern Africa. [London, Department of Information, South African Embassy, 1969]. pp. (7). *Reprinted from January 1969 Report from South Africa.*

— Rural conditions.

The ROOTS of rural poverty in central and southern Africa; edited by Robin Palmer and Neil Parsons. Berkeley, Calif., 1977. pp. 430. *bibliogs.*

AFRICA, WEST

— Economic conditions.

CONFEDERATION OF BRITISH INDUSTRY. West African visit report: Nigeria, Ivory Coast, Liberia, Senegal. London, 1978. pp. 45. *bibliog.*

UDO (REUBEN K.) A comprehensive geography of West Africa. Ibadan, 1978. pp. 304. *bibliog.*

— History.

CROWDER (MICHAEL) Colonial West Africa: collected essays. London, 1978. pp. 341.

— — Sources.

MATTHEWS (NOEL) compiler. Materials for West African history in the archives of the United Kingdom. London, 1973. pp. 225.

— Industries.

CONFEDERATION OF BRITISH INDUSTRY. West African visit report: Nigeria, Ivory Coast, Liberia, Senegal. London, 1978. pp. 45. *bibliog.*

— Social conditions.

UDO (REUBEN K.) A comprehensive geography of West Africa. Ibadan, 1978. pp. 304. *bibliog.*

AFRICA IN LITERATURE.

BERGHAHN (MARION) Images of Africa in black American literature. London, [1977]. pp. 230. *bibliog.*

AFRICAN LITERATURE

— History and criticism.

GRIFFITHS (GARETH) A double exile: African and West Indian writing between two cultures. London, 1978. pp. 205. *bibliog.*

AFRICAN NATIONAL CONGRESS (SOUTH AFRICA).

GERHART (GAIL M.) Black Power in South Africa: the evolution of an ideology. Berkeley, Calif., [1978]. pp. 364. *bibliog.*

AFRICAN STUDIES

— United Kingdom — Bibliography.

STANDING CONFERENCE ON LIBRARY MATERIALS ON AFRICA. Theses on Africa, 1963-1975, accepted by universities in the United Kingdom and Ireland; compiled by J.H.St.J. McIlwaine. London, 1978. pp. 123.

AFRICANS IN FRANCE.

Le PROLETARIAT africain noir en France; témoignages recueillis et présentés par Michel Samuel. Paris, 1978. pp. 262. *bibliog.*

AFRIKAANS LANGUAGE.

SOUTH AFRICA. Embassy (London). Department of Information. 196-. The story of Afrikaans. [London, 196-]. pp. 7.

AFRIKAANS LITERATURE.

SOUTH AFRICA. Embassy (London). Department of Information. 196-. The story of Afrikaans. [London, 196-]. pp. 7.

AFRIKANER-BROEDERBOND.

PELZER (A.N.) Die Afrikaner-Broederbond: eerste 50 jaar. Kaapstad, 1979. pp. 193.

AFRO-AMERICAN CLERGY.

BURKETT (RANDALL K.) Garveyism as a religious movement: the institutionalization of black civil religion. Metuchen, 1978. pp. 216. (*American Theological Library Association. ATLA Monograph Series. No.13*)

AFRO-AMERICAN FAMILIES.

DAVIS (LENWOOD G.) compiler. The black family in the United States: a selected bibliography of annotated books, articles, and dissertations on black families in America. Westport, Conn., 1978. pp. 129.

AFRO-AMERICAN LAWYERS.

WOODSON (CARTER GODWIN) The negro professional man and the community, with special emphasis on the physician and the lawyer. [Washington, D.C.], 1934; New York, 1969. pp. 365. *Facsimile reprint.*

AFRO-AMERICAN PHYSICIANS.

WOODSON (CARTER GODWIN) The negro professional man and the community, with special emphasis on the physician and the lawyer. [Washington, D.C.], 1934; New York, 1969. pp. 365. *Facsimile reprint.*

AFRO-AMERICAN STUDENTS

— Political activity.

McCLAIN (J. DUDLEY) Political profiles of black college students in the South: sociopolitical attitudes, preferences, personality and characteristics. Atlanta, [1977]. pp. 316.

— Southern States.

McCLAIN (J. DUDLEY) Political profiles of black college students in the South: sociopolitical attitudes, preferences, personality and characteristics. Atlanta, [1977]. pp. 316.

AFRO-AMERICAN YOUTH.

REID (IRA DE AUGUSTINE) In a minor key: negro youth in story and fact. Westport, 1971. pp. 134. *Reprint of work originally published in Washington, D.C., 1940.*

AFRO-AMERICANS.

SOUTHERN SOCIETY FOR THE PROMOTION OF THE STUDY OF RACE CONDITIONS AND PROBLEMS IN THE SOUTH. Annual Conference, 1st, 1900. Race problems of the south: report of the proceedings of the... conference...at Montgomery, Alabama, etc. [Richmond, Va.], 1900; New York, 1969. pp. 240. *bibliog. Facsimile reprint.*

HUGGINS (NATHAN IRVIN) Black Odyssey: the ordeal of slavery in America. London, 1979. pp. 250. *bibliog.*

— Bibliography.

DAVIS (LENWOOD G.) compiler. The black family in the United States: a selected bibliography of annotated books, articles, and dissertations on black families in America. Westport, Conn., 1978. pp. 129.

— Charities.

BLACK heritage in social welfare, 1860-1930; compiled and edited by Edyth L. Ross. Metuchen, N.J., 1978. pp. 488. *bibliogs.*

— Civil rights.

COHN (DAVID LEWIS) Where I was born and raised. Notre Dame, 1967. pp. 380. *Part 1 of this book was published in 1935 under the title God shakes creation.*

The AGE of segregation: race relations in the South, 1890-1945; essays by Derrick Bell [and others]; edited by Robert Haws. Jackson, Miss., 1978. pp. 156.

SITKOFF (HARVARD) A new deal for blacks: the emergence of civil rights as a national issue. New York, 1978. pp. 397.

— Diseases.

SAVITT (TODD L.) Medicine and slavery: the diseases and health care of blacks in antebellum Virginia. Urbana, 1978. pp. 332.

— Economic conditions.

VICKERY (WILLIAM EDWARD) The economics of the negro migration, 1900-1960. New York, 1977. pp. 223. *bibliog.*

JACKSON (JESSE) and others. A conversation with the Reverend Jesse Jackson: the quest for economic and educational parity. Washington, [1978]. pp. 27. (*American Enterprise Institute for Public Policy Research. AEI Studies. 209*)

— Education.

EDWARDS (WILLIAM JAMES) Twenty-five years in the black belt. Boston, Mass., 1918; Westport, Conn., 1970. pp. 143. *Facsimile reprint.*

— Education, Higher — Bibliography.

CHAMBERS (FREDRICK) compiler. Black higher education in the United States: a selected bibliography on negro higher education and historically black colleges and universities. Westport, Conn., 1978. pp. 268. *bibliog.*

— Employment.

HILL (HERBERT) Black labor and the American legal system. vol. 1. Race, work, and the law. Washington D.C., [1977]. pp. 455.

EMPLOYMENT of blacks in the South: a perspective on the 1960s; edited by Ray Marshall and Virgil L. Christian, Jr. Austin, [1978]. pp. 247. *bibliogs.*

LEIGH (DUANE E.) An analysis of the determinants of occupational upgrading. New York, [1978]. pp. 185. *bibliog.* (*Wisconsin University, Madison. Institute for Research on Poverty. Monograph Series*)

PEARN (M.A.) Employment testing and the goal of equal opportunity: the American experience. [London], 1978. pp. 38.

AFRO-AMERICANS.(Cont.)

— History.

The AGE of segregation: race relations in the South, 1890-1945; essays by Derrick Bell [and others]; edited by Robert Haws. Jackson, Miss., 1978. pp. 156.

BELZ (HERMAN) Emancipation and equal rights: politics and constitutionalism in the Civil War era. New York, [1978]. pp. 171.

LITTLEFIELD (DANIEL F.) The Cherokee freedmen from emancipation to American citizenship. Westport, Conn., 1978. pp. 281. *bibliog.*

MOSES (WILSON JEREMIAH) The golden age of black nationalism, 1850-1925. Hamden, 1978. pp. 345. *bibliog.*

MUNFORD (CLARENCE J.) Production relations, class and black liberation: a marxist perspective in Afro-American studies. Amsterdam, 1978. pp. 235. *bibliog.*

NOVAK (DANIEL A.) The wheel of servitude: black forced labor after slavery. Lexington, Ky., [1978]. pp. 126. *bibliog.*

SITKOFF (HARVARD) A new deal for blacks: the emergence of civil rights as a national issue. New York, 1978. pp. 397.

TROTSKII (LEV DAVYDOVICH) Leon Trotsky on black nationalism and self-determination. 2nd ed. New York, 1978. pp. 95.

— Legal status, laws, etc.

HIGGINBOTHAM (A. LEON) In the matter of color: race and the American legal process; the colonial period. New York, 1978. pp. 512. *bibliog.*

— Politics and suffrage.

AMERICAN ACADEMY OF POLITICAL AND SOCIAL SCIENCE. Annals. vol. 439. Urban black politics; special editors of this volume John R. Howard and Robert C. Smith. Philadelphia, 1978. pp. 201.

— Psychology.

WILKINSON (DORIS Y.) and TAYLOR (RONALD L.) The black male in America: perspectives on his status in contemporary society. Chicago, [1977]. pp. 375. *bibliog.*

WALLACE (MICHELE) Black macho and the myth of the superwoman. London, 1979. pp. 182.

— Religion.

BURKETT (RANDALL K.) Garveyism as a religious movement: the institutionalization of black civil religion. Metuchen, 1978. pp. 216. (*American Theological Library Association. ATLA Monograph Series. No.13*)

RABOTEAU (ALBERT J.) Slave religion: the "invisible institution" in the antebellum South. New York, 1978. pp. 382.

SIMPSON (GEORGE EATON) Black religions in the New World. New York, 1978. pp. 415. *bibliog.*

— Social conditions.

WOODSON (CARTER GODWIN) The negro professional man and the community, with special emphasis on the physician and the lawyer. [Washington, D.C.], 1934; New York, 1969. pp. 365. *Facsimile reprint.*

COHN (DAVID LEWIS) Where I was born and raised. Notre Dame, 1967. pp. 380. *Part 1 of this book was published in 1935 under the title God shakes creation.*

LAMON (LESTER C.) Black Tennesseans 1900-1930. Knoxville, [1977]. pp. 320.

WILKINSON (DORIS Y.) and TAYLOR (RONALD L.) The black male in America: perspectives on his status in contemporary society. Chicago, [1977]. pp. 375. *bibliog.*

BLACK heritage in social welfare, 1860-1930; compiled and edited by Edyth L. Ross. Metuchen, N.J., 1978. pp. 488. *bibliogs.*

DU BOIS (WILLIAM EDWARD BURGHARDT) W.E.B. Du Bois on sociology and the Black community; edited... by Dan S. Green and Edwin D. Driver. Chicago, 1978. pp. 320. *bibliog.*

MUNFORD (CLARENCE J.) Production relations, class and black liberation: a marxist perspective in Afro-American studies. Amsterdam, 1978. pp. 235. *bibliog.*

TROTSKII (LEV DAVYDOVICH) Leon Trotsky on black nationalism and self-determination. 2nd ed. New York, 1978. pp. 95.

WALLACE (MICHELE) Black macho and the myth of the superwoman. London, 1979. pp. 182.

— California.

BEASLEY (DELILAH LEONTIUM) The Negro trail blazers of California: a compilation of records, etc. New York, 1969. pp. 317. *bibliog. Reprint of work originally published in Los Angeles, 1919.*

— Detroit.

GESCHWENDER (JAMES A.) Class, race and worker insurgency: the League of Revolutionary Black Workers. Cambridge, 1977. pp. 250. (*American Sociological Association. Arnold and Caroline Rose Monograph Series in Sociology*)

— Tennessee.

LAMON (LESTER C.) Black Tennesseans 1900-1930. Knoxville, [1977]. pp. 320.

— Virginia.

SAVITT (TODD L.) Medicine and slavery: the diseases and health care of blacks in antebellum Virginia. Urbana, 1978. pp. 332.

AFRO-AMERICANS AS CONSUMERS.

EDWARDS (PAUL KENNETH) The southern urban negro as a consumer. New York, 1932; New York, 1969. pp. 323. *bibliog. Facsimile reprint.*

AFRO-ASIAN PEOPLE'S SOLIDARITY ORGANIZATION.

RUEBENSAAL (JACK DWIGHT) The impact of the Sino-Soviet dispute on the Afro-Asian People's Solidarity Organization. 1978. fo.237. *bibliog. Typescript. M.Phil. (London)thesis: unpublished. This thesis is the property of London University and may not be removed from the Library.*

AGE (PSYCHOLOGY).

GUBRIUM (JABER F.) and BUCKHOLDT (DAVID R.) Toward maturity: the social processing of human development. San Francisco, 1977. pp. 224. *bibliog.*

SEX and age as principles of social differentiation; edited by J. S. La Fontaine. London, 1978. pp. 188. *bibliogs.* (*Association of Social Anthropologists of the Commonwealth. A.S.A. Monographs. 17*)

AGE GROUPS.

AGE, generation and time: some features of East African age organisations; edited by P.T.W. Baxter and Uri Almagor. London, [1978]. pp. 276. *bibliogs.*

AGE OF CONSENT

— United Kingdom.

U.K. Policy Advisory Committee on Sexual Offences. 1979. Working party [sic., i.e. paper] on the age of consent in relation to sexual offences; [Lord Justice Waller, chairman]. London, 1979. pp. 31.

AGENCY (LAW)

— United Kingdom.

MARKESINIS (BASIL SPYRIDONOS) and MUNDAY (RODERICK JOHN CORBETT) An outline of the law of agency. London, 1979. pp. 252.

AGING.

ROSENFELD (JEFFREY P.) The legacy of aging: inheritance and disinheritance in social perspective. Norwood, N.J., [1979]. pp. 151. *bibliog.*

— Research.

IMPLICATIONS for social security of research on aging and retirement: report of round table meeting, The Hague, 27-29 April 1976. Geneva, 1977. pp. 74. (*International Social Security Association. Studies and Research. No.9*)

AGRICULTURAL ASSISTANCE, NORWEGIAN

— India.

INDO-NORWEGIAN PROJECT. Souvenir issued on the occasion of the ceremony held on 1-4-1972 to mark the conclusion of the Indo-Norwegian Project agreement. [Cochin, 1972?]. pp. 122.

AGRICULTURAL COLONIES

— Israel.

JEWISH AGENCY. Agricultural Settlement Department and Information Department. 16 years of agricultural settlement in Israel. Jerusalem, 1964. 1 vol. (unpaged).

AGRICULTURAL CREDIT

— Netherlands.

LANDBOUW-ECONOMISCH INSTITUUT. Het landbouwkrediet in Nederland. Den Haag, 1975. pp. 123.

— Russia.

KOCHKAREV (VIKTOR VASIL'EVICH) Rol' v povyshenii effektivnosti kolkhoznogo proizvodstva. Moskva, 1977. pp. 176.

— Sri Lanka.

WEERAWARDENA (I.K.) and COLLONNEGE (I.) A short history on credit for peasant agriculture in Sri Lanka. [Colombo], 1974. pp. 291. (*Sri Lanka. Rural Institutions and Agricultural Productivity Laws Division. Evaluation Studies. 2*)

AGRICULTURAL EDUCATION

— Canada.

A NATIONAL statement by the faculties of agriculture and veterinary medicine at Canadian universities. [Ottawa, Science Council of Canada, 1974?]. pp. 22.

— France.

FRANCE. Comité du Travail Féminin. 1974. La formation des femmes en milieu rural. Paris, 1974. pp. 79.

— India.

CHAUDHRI (D.P.) Education, innovations and agricultural development: a study of North India (1961-72). London, [1979]. pp. 127. *bibliog.*

— Russia.

VESELOV (ANATOLII PAVLOVICH) Bor'ba Kommunisticheskoi partii za provedenie kul'turnoi revoliutsii v derevne v gody kollektivizatsii. Leningrad, 1978. pp. 128.

AGRICULTURAL EXPERIMENT STATIONS

— Canada — Saskatchewan.

CAMPBELL (J. BADEN) The Swift Current Research Station, 1920-70. [Ottawa, 1971]. pp. 79. *bibliog.* (*Canada. Department of Agriculture. Historical Series. No. 6*)

AGRICULTURE.

AGRICULTURAL GEOGRAPHY.

POLSKA AKADEMIA NAUK. Instytut Geografii. Geographia Polonica. 40. Agricultural typology: proceedings of the eighth meeting of the Commission on Agricultural Typology, International Geographical Union, Odessa, 20-26 July, 1976; edited by Jerzy Kostrowicki and Wiesława Tyszkiewicz. Warszawa, 1979. pp. 260. *bibliog. In English or French.*

AGRICULTURAL INDUSTRIES

— Russia.

KARLIUK (IPPOLIT IAKOVLEVICH) and VASIL'EV (ANATOLII NESTEROVICH) Razvitie agrarno-promyshlennogo kompleksa. Moskva, 1976. pp. 61.

PTUSHCHENKO (VOLODYMYR OLEKSANDROVYCH) Zakonomernosti stanovleniia i razvitiia mezhkhoziaistvennoi kooperatsii. Kiev, 1977. pp. 207.

— — Latvia.

EFFEKTIVNOST' ekonomiki v usloviiakh industrializatsii sel'skogo khoziaistva. Riga, 1978. pp. 157.

— — Siberia.

SOTRUDNICHESTVO rabochikh i krest'ian Sibiri v usloviiakh razvitogo sotsializma: materialy k "Istorii rabochego klassa Sibiri". Novosibirsk, 1978. pp. 158.

AGRICULTURAL INNOVATIONS.

UNITED NATIONS RESEARCH INSTITUTE FOR SOCIAL DEVELOPMENT. UNRISD Reports. No. 74.1. The social and economic implications of large-scale introduction of new varieties of foodgrain: summary of conclusions of a global research project. (UNRISD 74/27). Geneva, 1974. pp. 55. *([Studies on the Green Revolution. No. 6])*

INTERNATIONAL CONFERENCE ON ECONOMIC ANALYSIS IN THE DESIGN OF NEW TECHNOLOGY FOR SMALL FARMERS, 1975. Economics and the design of small-farmer technology; edited by Alberto Valdés [and others]. Ames, 1979. pp. 211. *bibliog.*

— Brazil.

CONTADOR (CLAUDIO ROBERTO) Tecnologia e rentabilidade na agricultura brasileira. Rio de Janeiro, 1975. pp. 257. *bibliog.* (Brazil. *Instituto de Planejamento Econômico e Social. Instituto de Pesquisas. Relatorios de Pesquisa. No. 28*)

— India.

DASGUPTA (BIPLAB KUMAR) Agrarian change and the new technology in India. (UNRISD Report No. 77.2). Geneva, United Nations Research Institute for Social Development, 1977. pp. 408. *bibliog.* *([Studies on the Green Revolution. No. 16])*

— Philippine Islands.

PALMER (INGRID) The new rice in the Philippines (UNRISD Report No. 75.2) (UNRISD/75/C.38). Geneva, United Nations Research Institute for Social Development, 1975. pp. 200. *bibliog.* *([Studies on the Green Revolution. No. 10])*

AGRICULTURAL LABOURERS

— China.

ULLERICH (CURTIS) Rural employment and manpower problems in China. New York, [1979]. pp. 130. *bibliog.*

— Colombia.

El AGRO en el desarrollo historico colombiano: ensayos de economia politica; [by] F. Leal Buitrago [and others]. Bogota, 1977. pp. 395. *Papers presented at the Primer Seminario Nacional de Desarrollo Rural held at the Universidad de los Andes, 29-31 July 1976.*

— France.

FRANCE. Ministère de l'Agriculture et du Développement Rural. 1974. Pour les professions agricoles un régime autonome et décentralisé de protection sociale. [Paris, 1974]. pp. 115. (*Bulletin d'Information. Numéros spéciaux*) *Cover title: Point 74: la protection sociale agricole.*

— Germany — Prussia.

LAGE und Kampf der Landarbeiter im ostelbischen Preussen, vom Anfang des 19. Jahrhunderts bis zur Novemberrevolution 1918/19...: Quellen; Einleitung: Hans Hübner; Auswahl und Bearbeitung: Hans Hübner und Heinz Kathe. Vaduz, 1977. 2 vols. (*Akademie der Wissenschaften der DDR. Zentralinstitut für Geschichte. Archivalische Forschungen zur Geschichte der Deutschen Arbeiterbewegung. Band 8*)

— India.

INDIA. Labour Bureau. 1964. Agricultural labour in India. [Delhi, 1964]. pp. 34. (*Pamphlet Series. 7*)

— — Maharashtra.

MAHARASHTRA. Study Group on Landless Agricultural Labourers. 1961. Report. Bombay, 1961. pp. 24,xvi.

— Italy.

AGRICOLTURA e movimento operaio: documenti di analisi e di proposta politica; a cura di Giovanni Mottura e Enrico Pugliese. Roma, [1977]. pp. 158.

— Malaysia.

BARNUM (H.N.) and SQUIRE (LYN) Consistent aggregation of family and hired labor in agricultural production functions. Ann Arbor, Mich., 1978. pp. 12. (*Michigan University. Center for Research on Economic Development. Discussion Papers. No. 73*)

— Pakistan.

DARLING (Sir MALCOLM LYALL) Report...on labour conditions in agriculture in Pakistan, etc. Karachi, Manager of Publications, [1955]. pp. 160.

— Russia.

DIUKOV (VIKTOR VLADIMIROVICH) Sovershenstvovanie material'nykh uslovii vosproizvodstva rabochei sily v kolkhozakh. Kazan', 1977. pp. 166.

— — Siberia.

TONAEVSKAIA (NELLI SERGEEVNA) Rabochie sovkhozov Zapadnoi Sibiri, 1959-1965 gg.; otvetstvennyi redaktor V.T. Aniskov. Novosibirsk, 1978. pp. 191.

— Tanzania.

TANGANYIKA. Non-Plantation Agricultural Workers Minimum Wages Board. 1963. Report; [F. Mfundo, chairman]. Dar es Salaam, 1963. pp. 15.

— United States.

VAN DEBURG (WILLIAM L.) The slave drivers: black agricultural labor supervisors in the antebellum South. Westport, 1979. pp. 202.

— — California.

GALARZA (ERNESTO) Farm workers and agri-business in California, 1947-1960. Notre Dame, [1977]. pp. 405.

AGRICULTURAL PRICE SUPPORTS

— European Economic Community countries.

FEARN (HOWARD A.) The evolution and basic concepts of the green currency system. London, Ministry of Agriculture, Fisheries and Food, 1978. pp. 10. (*Government Economic Service Working Papers. No. 12*)

— United Kingdom — Mathematical models.

DICKINSON (SHEILA) and WILDGOOSE (JAMES) A framework for assessing the economic effects of a green pound devaluation. London, Ministry of Agriculture, Fisheries and Food, 1979. pp. 14. (*Government Economic Service Working Papers. No. 23*)

AGRICULTURAL PRICES.

DISTORTIONS of agricultural incentives; edited by Theodore W. Schultz. Bloomington, [1978]. pp. 343. *bibliogs.*

— Brazil.

BRAZIL. Conselho Nacional de Estatistica. Laboratorio de Estatistica. 1960. Numeros indices das quantidades e dos preços do agricultor de 36 produtos agricolas nos anos de 1952 a 1958. Rio de Janeiro, [1960?]. fo. 17. (*Estudos sôbre as Quantidades e os Preços das Mercadorias Produzidas ou Negociadas. No. 91*)

BRAZIL. Conselho Nacional de Estatistica. Laboratorio de Estatistica. 1960. Numeros indices das quantidades e dos preços do agricultor de 36 produtos agricolas, classificados segundo grandes grupamentos, nos anos de 1952 a 1958. Rio de Janeiro, [1960?]. fo. 15. (*Estudos sôbre as Quantidades e os Preços das Mercadorias Produzidas ou Negociadas. No. 91 bis*)

— European Economic Community countries.

EUROPEAN COMMUNITIES. Statistical Office. Purchase prices of the means of production, (formerly Purchase prices of agriculture). q., 1977(v.1 no.1)- Luxembourg. *[in Community languages].*

EUROPEAN COMMUNITIES. Statistical Office. EC-index of producer prices of agricultural products. bi-m., 1978(no. 4/5)- Luxembourg. *[in Community languages]*

EUROPEAN COMMUNITIES. Statistical Office. Selling prices of animal products. bi-m., 1978(no.5/6)- Luxembourg. *[in Community languages]*

EUROPEAN COMMUNITIES. Statistical Office. Selling prices of vegetable products. bi-m., 1978(no.5)- Luxembourg. *[in Community languages]*

— India.

INDIA. Ministry of Agriculture and Irrigation. Directorate of Economics and Statistics. 1975. Farm (harvest) prices of principal crops in India, 1965-66 to 1970-71. [Delhi], 1975. pp. 172.

INDIA. Ministry of Agriculture and Irrigation. Directorate of Economics and Statistics. 1978. Farm (harvest) prices of principal crops in India, 1970-71 to 1974-75. New Delhi, [1978]. pp. 118.

AGRICULTURAL RESEARCH

— Africa, Subsaharan.

ANTHONY (KENNETH R.M.) Agricultural change in tropical Africa. Ithaca, 1979. pp. 326. *bibliog.*

— Canada.

A NATIONAL statement by the faculties of agriculture and veterinary medicine at Canadian universities. [Ottawa, Science Council of Canada, 1974?]. pp. 22.

— Underdeveloped areas.

See UNDERDEVELOPED AREAS — Agricultural research.

AGRICULTURE.

FOOD AND AGRICULTURE ORGANIZATION. FAO Statistics Series. No.1. Programme for the 1980 World Census of Agriculture. Rome, 1976. pp. 80.

INTERNATIONAL CONFERENCE OF AGRICULTURAL ECONOMISTS, 16TH, NAIROBI, KENYA, 1976. Decision-making and agriculture: papers and reports; edited by Theodor Dams and Kenneth E. Hunt. Lincoln, Neb., [1977]. pp. 603. *bibliogs.*

AGRICULTURE.(Cont.)

— Bibliography.

SOUTH AFRICA. Division of Library Services. 1978. Bibliography of South African government publications. Vol. 2. Department of Agricultural Technical Services, Department of Agricultural Economics and Marketing publications: 1910- 1972. Pretoria, 1978. pp. 610.

— Economic aspects.

ORGANIZATION FOR ECONOMIC CO-OPERATION AND DEVELOPMENT. Agricultural Policy Reports. Paris, 1964 in progress.

INTERNATIONAL CONFERENCE OF AGRICULTURAL ECONOMISTS, 16TH, NAIROBI, KENYA, 1976. Decision-making and agriculture: papers and reports; edited by Theodor Dams and Kenneth E. Hunt. Lincoln, Neb., [1977]. pp. 603. *bibliogs.*

BRADING (DAVID A.) Haciendas and ranchos in the Mexican Bajío, Leon 1700-1860. Cambridge, 1978. pp. 258. *bibliog.*

DISTORTIONS of agricultural incentives; edited by Theodore W. Schultz. Bloomington, [1978]. pp. 343. *bibliogs.*

DOLL (JOHN P.) and ORAZEM (FRANK) Production economics: theory with applications. Columbus, Ohio, [1978]. pp. 406. *bibliogs.*

FOOD and population: priorities in decision making...; edited by T.Dams [and others]. Farnborough, [1978]. pp. 192. *bibliogs. Report of a meeting of the International Conference of Agricultural Economists, Nairobi, 1976.*

HILLMAN (JIMMYE S.) Nontariff agricultural trade barriers. Lincoln, Neb., [1978]. pp. 236. *bibliog.*

McCLINTOCK (DAVID W.) U.S. food: making the most of a global resource. Boulder, Colo., 1978. pp. 122. *bibliog.*

OELHAF (ROBERT C.) Organic agriculture: economic and ecological comparisons with conventional methods. Montclair, N.J., [1978]. pp. 271. *bibliog.*

TRIBE (KEITH) Land, labour and economic discourse. London, 1978. pp. 182. *bibliog.*

INTERNATIONAL CONFERENCE ON ECONOMIC ANALYSIS IN THE DESIGN OF NEW TECHNOLOGY FOR SMALL FARMERS, 1975. Economics and the design of small-farmer technology; edited by Alberto Valdés [and others]. Ames, 1979. pp. 211. *bibliog.*

— History.

FUSSELL (GEORGE EDWIN) Farms, farmers and society: systems of food production and population numbers. Lawrence, Kan., 1976. pp. 332. *bibliog.*

— Statistical methods.

FOOD AND AGRICULTURE ORGANIZATION. FAO Statistics Series. No.10. Report on the 1970 World Census of Agriculture. Rome, 1977. pp. 289.

— Africa, Subsaharan — Productivity.

ANTHONY (KENNETH R.M.) Agricultural change in tropical Africa. Ithaca, 1979. pp. 326. *bibliog.*

— Algeria.

JÖNSSON (LARS) La révolution agraire en Algérie: historique, contenu et problèmes. Uppsala, 1978. pp. 84. *(Nordiska Afrikainstitutet. Research Reports. No. 47)*

— Asia.

ASIAN DEVELOPMENT BANK. 1978. Rural Asia: challenge and opportunity. New York, 1978. pp. 489. *Report of the Second Asian Agricultural Survey.*

— Australia.

QUARTERLY REVIEW OF THE RURAL ECONOMY; [pd.by] Bureau of Agricultural Economics [Australia]. q., N 1978[introductory issue]- Canberra. *Supersedes QUARTERLY REVIEW OF AGRICULTURAL ECONOMICS.*

— — Northern Territory.

AUSTRALIA. Northern Territory Administration. Animal Industry and Agriculture Branch. Annual report. a., 1965/66-1967/68(1st-3rd). [Alice Springs].

AUSTRALIA. Northern Territory Administration. Animal Industry and Agriculture Branch. Production statistics (formerly Pastoral production, previously Pastoral and agricultural production statistics). a., 1968/69- [Alice Springs].

— — Queensland.

BEREZOVSKY (C.A.) The relative dependence of the Queensland economy on the rural sector. [Brisbane], Marketing Services Branch, Department of Primary Industries, 1975. pp. 61. *bibliog.*

— Bangladesh.

BANGLADESH. Agro-Economic Research Section. 1977. Bangladesh agriculture in 1978: a survey report on expected crop acreage and inputs use. [Dacca], 1977. 1 vol. (various foliations).

— — Statistics.

AGRICULTURAL STATISTICS OF BANGLADESH; [pd. by] Bureau of Statistics. a., 1972-73/1974-75(4th)- Dacca.

BANGLADESH. Agro-Economic Research Section. 1974. Bangladesh agriculture in statistics. Dacca, [1974]. pp. 156. *(Statistical Series. No. 1)*

BANGLADESH. Agro-Economic Research Section. 1975. Basic statistics of Bangladesh agriculture. Dacca, 1975. pp. 203. *(Statistical Series. No.2)*

— Bolivia.

PRESTON (DAVID ANTHONY) Farmers and towns: rural-urban relations in highland Bolivia. Norwich, [1978]. pp. 196. *bibliog.*

— Botswana.

BOTSWANA. Agricultural Statistics Unit. 1972. Technical report on the sample design for the annual agricultural survey. Gaborone, 1972. pp. 60.

— — Statistics.

BOTSWANA. Ministry of Agriculture. Planning and Statistics Unit. 1978. Agricultural statistics, 1977: summary of results from agricultural surveys 1974/75, 1975/76 and 1976/77, sample census of cattle 1976, and other administrative statistics. Gaborone, [1978]. pp. 49.

— Brazil.

CONTADOR (CLAUDIO ROBERTO) Tecnologia e rentabilidade na agricultura brasileira. Rio de Janeiro, 1975. pp. 257. *bibliog. (Brazil. Instituto de Planejamento Econômico e Social. Instituto de Pesquisas. Relatorios de Pesquisa. No. 28)*

— — Economic aspects.

TAYLOR (KIT SIMS) Sugar and the underdevelopment of northeastern Brazil, 1500-1970. Gainesville, Fla., 1978. pp. 167. *bibliog. (Florida University. Monographs. Social Sciences. No. 63)*

— Canada.

TOSINE (TONU P.) The physical base for agriculture in central Canada. Toronto, 1978. pp. 59. *bibliog. (Ontario. Ministry of Agriculture and Food. Economics Branch. Economics Information)*

— — British Columbia — Statistics.

BRITISH COLUMBIA. Ministry of Agriculture. 1978. Census of agriculture for all agricultural holdings: British Columbia, 1971 and 1976. [Victoria], 1978. pp. 36.

— — Ontario.

CAMPBELL (BLAIR) Trends in Ontario agriculture. Toronto, 1974. pp. 29. *(Ontario. Ministry of Agriculture and Food. Economics Branch. Economics Information)*

ONG (K.T.) An agriculturally orientated input-output analysis of the Ontario economy. Toronto, 1977. pp. 33. *bibliog. (Ontario. Ministry of Agriculture and Food. Economics Branch. Economic Research)*

ONTARIO. Ministry of Agriculture and Food. Economics Branch. 1977. Outlook for Ontario agriculture, 1977. Toronto, [1977]. pp. 17. *(Economics Information)*

— — Prince Edward Island.

CAMPBELL (ELIZABETH) An economic profile of the agricultural industry of Prince Edward Island. Charlottetown, Department of Agriculture and Forestry, 1977. pp. 39.

— Chile — Statistics.

CHILE. Departamento de Estadisticas Agropecuarias. Encuesta nacional agropecuaria. a., 1975- with gap (1976). Santiago.

— China — History.

ULLERICH (CURTIS) Rural employment and manpower problems in China. New York, [1979]. pp. 130. *bibliog.*

— Communist countries.

SUSLOV (IVAN FEDOROVICH) Agrarnyi sektor ekonomiki stran sotsializma: mesto i rol' v stroitel'stve i funktsionirovanii razvitoi ekonomiki. Moskva, 1978. pp. 254.

— — Productivity.

BUKH (MIKHAIL EFIMOVICH) Problemy effektivnosti sel'skogo khoziaistva v evropeiskikh stranakh SEV. Moskva, 1978. pp. 167.

— Ecuador — Statistics.

ECUADOR. Oficina de los Censos Nacionales. Censo Agropecuario, 1974. II censo agropecuario, 1974: resultados provisionales. Quito, 1976. pp. 53.

— El Salvador.

CAMBRIDGE. University. Centre of Latin American Studies. Working Papers. No. 32. Agricultural modernisation in El Salvador, Central America; by T.J. Downing. Cambridge, 1978. fo. 54. *bibliog.*

— Europe, Eastern.

SPROTT (D.C.) and HEARN (S.E.) Agricultural developments and the prospect for trade with the Comecon countries. Canberra, 1974. pp. 34. *(Australia. Bureau of Agricultural Economics. Occasional Papers. No.24)*

— — History.

WAEDEKIN (KARL EUGEN) Sozialistische Agrarpolitik in Osteuropa. Berlin, 1974-78. 2 vols. *(Giessen. Universität. Zentrum für Kontinentale Agrar- und Wirtschaftsforschung. Giessener Abhandlungen zur Agrar- und Wirtschaftsforschung des Europäischen Ostens. Bände 63, 67) With English summaries.*

— European Economic Community countries.

GALLI (ROSEMARY ELIZABETH) and TORCASIO (SAVERIO) La partecipazione italiana alla politica agricola comunitaria. Roma, [1976]. pp. 260. *(Istituto Affari Internazionali. Collana dello Spettatore Internazionale. 37)*

— France.

BERGMANN (DENIS) Matériaux et réflexions pour une réorientation de la politique agricole. Paris, 1975. pp. 57. *bibliog. (Institut National de la Recherche Agronomique [France]. Département d'Economie et Sociologie Rurales. Série Economie et Sociologie Rurales)*

— — Accounting.

COMPTES DE L'AGRICULTURE FRANÇAISE, LES (formerly Comptes de l'agriculture); [pd. by] Ministère de l'Agriculture. a., 1976- Paris. *(Statistique agricole. Supplément. Série Etudes)*

AGRICULTURE.(Cont.)

—— History.

GOREUX (LOUIS M.) Agricultural productivity and economic development in France 1852- 1950 [and] Les migrations agricoles en France depuis un siècle et leur relation avec certains facteurs économiques. New York, 1977. pp. 376. *bibliog.*

NEWELL (WILLIAM HENRY) Population change and agricultural development in nineteenth century France. New York, 1977. pp. 199. *bibliog.*

—— Mathematical models.

GOREUX (LOUIS M.) Agricultural productivity and economic development in France 1852- 1950 [and] Les migrations agricoles en France depuis un siècle et leur relation avec certains facteurs économiques. New York, 1977. pp. 376. *bibliog.*

—— Statistics.

FRANCE. Ministère de l'Agriculture. Statistique agricole. Supplément. Série Etudes. No. 150. Recensement général de l'agriculture 1970-71: résultats France entière: tableaux structures complémentaires, dans les domaines démographie, main d'oeuvre, équipements des exploitations agricoles. [Paris], 1977. pp. 96.

FRANCE. Ministère de l'Agriculture. Statistique agricole. Supplément. (Série Etudes. No. 151. Approche des résultats économiques des exploitations agricoles en 1970: resultats définitifs: résultats détaillés France entière, récapitulations régionales, résultats généraux par région agricole. [Paris], 1977. 2 vols.

FRANCE. Ministère de l'Agriculture. Statistique agricole. Supplément. Série Etudes. No. 153. Résultats de l'enquête sur les exploitations agricoles en location en 1970: campagne agricole 1968-1969. [Paris], 1977. pp. 152.

— Germany.

KRUEGER (HANS) Stadtrat, and BAADE (FRITZ) Sozialdemokratische Agrarpolitik: Erläuterungen zum sozialdemokratischen Agrarprogramm. Berlin, [1927]. pp. 99.

—— History.

FRANZ (GUENTHER) Der Dreissigjährige Krieg und das deutsche Volk: Untersuchungen zur Bevölkerungs- und Agrargeschichte. 4th ed. Stuttgart, 1979. pp. 140.

—— Prussia — History.

SCHISSLER (HANNA) Preussische Agrargesellschaft im Wandel: gesellschaftliche und politische Transformationsprozesse von 1763 bis 1847. Göttingen, 1978. pp. 285. *bibliog.*

— Germany, Eastern — Magdeburg — History.

LANDWIRTSCHAFT und Kapitalismus: zur Entwicklung der ökonomischen und sozialen Verhältnisse in der Magdeburger Börde...; herausgegeben von Hans-Jürgen Rach und Bernhard Weissel. Berlin, 1978-79. 2 vols. *bibliogs. (Akademie der Wissenschaften der DDR. Zentralinstitut für Geschichte. Veröffentlichungen zur Volkskunde und Kulturgeschichte. Band 66)*

— Guyana.

GUYANA. Division of Agricultural Education and Information. 1960. A brochure on agriculture in British Guiana. [Georgetown], 1960. fo. 14.

— Honduras — Statistics.

HONDURAS. Direccion General de Estadistica y Censos 1977- . Censo nacional agropecuario 1974. Tegucigalpa, 1977 in progress.

— India.

TAGORE (RONENDRA MOHAN) Rural reconstruction. Calcutta, [1937?]. pp. 76.

SEN (SUDHIR) Land and its problems. volume 1. Some regional investigations with a special study on paddy cultivation. Santiniketan, 1943. pp. 166. *(Visva-Bharati University. Economic Research Publications. No. 3)*

RURAL economy and municipal problems of India; by K.P. Bhatnagar [and others]. Kanpur, 1953. pp. 392.

THIRUMALAI (S.) Post-war agricultural problems and policies in India. Bombay, 1954. pp. 280. *bibliog.*

SEN (SUDHIR) A richer harvest: new horizons for developing countries. New York, [1974]. pp. 573. *bibliog.*

SEN (SUDHIR) Reaping the green revolution: food and jobs for all. New York, [1975]. pp. 397. *bibliog.*

INDIA. National Commission on Agriculture. 1976. Report; [C. Subramaniam, B. Sivaraman, Nathu Ram Mirdha, successively chairman]. [Delhi], 1976. 15 pts.

DASGUPTA (BIPLAB KUMAR) Agrarian change and the new technology in India. (UNRISD Report No. 77.2). Geneva, United Nations Research Institute for Social Development, 1977. pp. 408. *bibliog. ([Studies on the Green Revolution. No. 16])*

JOHNSON (BASIL LEONARD CLYDE) India: resources and development. London, 1979. pp. 211. *bibliog.*

—— Economic aspects.

CHAUDHRI (D.P.) Education, innovations and agricultural development: a study of North India (1961-72). London, [1979]. pp. 127. *bibliog.*

—— Bengal — History.

ISLAM (M. MUFAKHARUL) Bengal agriculture, 1920-1946: a quantitative study. Cambridge, 1978. pp. 283. *bibliog. (Cambridge. University. Centre of South Asian Studies. Cambridge South Asian Studies. 22)*

—— Bengal, West.

RAY (DEBIDAS) Studies in the economics of farm management in Hooghly district, West Bengal: three year consolidated report, 1970-71 to 1972-73. [Delhi, Controller of Publications, 1977]. pp. 55.

RUDRA (ASHOK) and others. Studies in the economics of farm management in Hooghly district, West Bengal: report for the year 1970-71. [Delhi, Controller of Publications], 1977. pp. 129.

—— Rajasthan — Statistics.

RAJASTHAN. Directorate of Economics and Statistics. 1976. 19 years of agriculture statistics, Rajasthan, 1956-57 to 1974-75. Jaipur, [1976]. pp. 229.

— Indonesia — Sumatra — Statistics.

INDONESIA. Kantor Sensus dan Statistik Propinsi Sumatera Utara. 1976. Production of food crops in north Sumatra, 1968-1974. [Medan, 1976]. fo. 27.

— Italy.

GALLI (ROSEMARY ELIZABETH) and TORCASIO (SAVERIO) La partecipazione italiana alla politica agricola comunitaria. Roma, [1976]. pp. 260. *(Istituto Affari Internazionali. Collana dello Spettatore Internazionale. 37)*

—— History.

GIORGETTI (GIORGIO) Capitalismo e agricoltura in Italia. Roma, 1977. pp. 591.

SCIACCA (MARISA) Le terre del Sud: la formazione del paesaggio agrario meridionale moderno. Cosenza, [1977]. pp. 112.

ZANGHERI (RENATO) Agricoltura e contadini nella storia d'Italia: discussioni e ricerche. Torino, [1977]. pp. 290.

— Japan.

SAXON (ERIC ALFRED) Farm production in Japan: determinants, performance and prospects. Canberra, 1976. pp. 63. *bibliog. (Australia. Bureau of Agricultural Economics. Occasional Papers. No.35)*

SAXON (ERIC ALFRED) Japan's food gap and trade in farm products. Canberra, 1977. pp. 63. *bibliog. (Australia. Bureau of Agricultural Economics. Occasional Papers. No.42)*

SMITH (THOMAS CARLYLE) Nakahara: family farming and population in a Japanese village, 1717-1830. Stanford, 1977. pp. 183. *bibliog.*

— Mexico.

FEDER (ERNEST) Agronomist. Strawberry imperialism: an enquiry into the mechanisms of dependency in Mexican agriculture. The Hague, 1977. pp. 199. *(Hague. Institute of Social Studies. Research Report Series. No. 1)*

FRANK (ANDRE GUNDER) Mexican agriculture, 1521-1630: transformation of the mode of production. Cambridge, 1979. pp. 91. *bibliog.*

— Netherlands — History.

SLICHER VAN BATH (BERNARD HENDRIK) Bijdragen tot de agrarische geschiedenis. Utrecht, 1978. pp. 331.

— New Zealand.

NEW ZEALAND. Ministry of Agriculture and Fisheries. Information Services. 1974. Facts and figures on New Zealand agriculture. rev. ed. Wellington, 1974. pp. 28.

NEW ZEALAND. Ministry of Agriculture and Fisheries. Information Services. 1976. Facts and figures on New Zealand agriculture. 2nd ed. Wellington, 1976. pp. 28.

NEW ZEALAND. Agricultural Review Committee. 1979. Report...to the Minister of Agriculture. [Wellington], 1979. pp. 56.

— Poland — History.

SŁABEK (HENRYK) Polityka agrarna PPR: geneza, realizacja, konsekwencje. 2nd ed. Warszawa, 1978. pp. 639. *bibliog.*

—— Productivity.

ROLNICTWO a wy'zywienie w Polsce: pobudzanie, efekty, koszty produkcji; pod redakcją E. Gorzelaka. Warszawa, 1978. pp. 429.

—— Silesia.

HAINES (MICHAEL R.) Economic-demographic interrelations in developing agricultural regions: a case study of Prussian Upper Silesia, 1840-1914. New York, 1977. pp. 499. *bibliogs.*

— Reunion Island.

FRANCE. Ministere de l'Agriculture. Statistique agricole. Supplément. Série Etudes. No. 154. Le recensement général de l'agriculture 1973 à la Réunion. [Paris], 1977. pp. 128.

— Romania — History.

LAPADATU (AUREL) Über die Genesis der rumänischen Agrargesellschaft bis zum Aufgang des 18. Jahrhunderts, etc. Köln, 1978. pp. 142. *bibliog.*

— Rome, Ancient.

FRAYN (JOAN M.) Subsistence farming in Roman Italy. Fontwell, 1979. pp. 168. *bibliog.*

— Russia — Historiography.

SOVETSKAIA istoriografiia agrarnoi istorii SSSR, do 1917 g. Kishinev, 1978. pp. 262.

—— History.

GINEV (VLADIMIR NIKOLAEVICH) Agrarnyi vopros i melkoburzhuaznye partii v Rossii v 1917 g.: k istorii bankrotstva neonarodnichestva. Leningrad, 1977. pp. 295.

OKTIABR' i sovetskoe krest'ianstvo, 1917-1927 gg. Moskva, 1977. pp. 295.

PETROV (ALEKSANDR PETROVICH) Kritika fal'sifikatsii agrarno-krest'ianskogo voprosa v trekh russkikh revoliutsiiakh. Moskva, 1977. pp. 399. *bibliog.*

AGRICULTURE.(Cont.)

HARRISON (MARK) Peasant economy, subordinate Marxism and the struggle for socialised agriculture in the USSR in the 1920s. Coventry, 1978. pp. 22. (*University of Warwick. Department of Economics. Warwick Economic Research Papers. No. 131*)

VOPROSY metodologii i istorii istoricheskoi nauki. vyp.2. Moskva, 1978. pp. 206.

— — Productivity.

EFIMOV (VIL'GEL'M PAVLOVICH) and MANIAKIN (VIKTOR IVANOVICH) Effektivnost' sel'skokhoziaistvennogo proizvodstva v SSSR: ekonomiko-statisticheskii analiz. Moskva, 1977. pp. 239.

— — Kirghizia — History.

SAPELKIN (ALEKSEI ALEKSANDROVICH) Agrarnye otnosheniia v Kirgizii v nachale XX veka, 1900-1917 gg. Frunze, 1977. pp. 281. *bibliog.*

— — Leningrad (Oblast') — History.

KURSOM intensifikatsii sel'skogo khoziaistva: iz opyta raboty Leningradskoi partiinoi organizatsii v 1965-1975 gg. Leningrad, 1977. pp. 192.

— — Moldavian Republic — History.

SOTSIALISTICHESKOE i kommunisticheskoe stroitel'stvo v Moldavskoi SSR: voprosy istorii; mezhvuzovskii sbornik. Kishinev, 1978. pp. 89.

— — Moscow (Oblast') — History.

CHERNOBAEV (ANATOLII ALEKSANDROVICH) Kombed. Moskva, 1978. pp. 127. *bibliog.*

— — Russia (RSFSR).

SEL'SKOE khoziaistvo Rossii: desiataia piatiletka. Moskva, 1977. pp. 255.

— — Siberia.

GEOGRAFICHESKIE problemy pri sel'skokhoziaistvennom osvoenii Sibiri. Novosibirsk, 1977. pp. 160. *bibliog.*

LADENKOV (VASILII NIKOLAEVICH) and NOSKOV (ALEKSEI ANATOL'EVICH) Problemy razvitiia sel'skogo khoziaistva Zapadnoi Sibiri; otvetstvennyi redaktor A.I. Tianutov. Novosibirsk, 1977. pp. 205.

— — — History.

PROBLEMY istorii sovetskoi sibirskoi derevni. Novosibirsk, 1977. pp. 302.

GUSHCHIN (NIKOLAI IAKOVLEVICH) and others. Soiuz rabochego klassa i krest'ianstva Sibiri v period postroeniia sotsializma, 1917-1937 gg. Novosibirsk, 1978. pp. 430.

SOTRUDNICHESTVO rabochikh i krest'ian Sibiri v usloviiakh razvitogo sotsializma: materialy k "Istorii rabochego klassa Sibiri". Novosibirsk, 1978. pp. 158.

— — Ukraine.

MAL'KO (OLEH OLEKSIIOVYCH) Robitnychyi klas - trudivnykam sela. Kyïv, 1978. pp. 135.

— São Tome e Principe.

RODRIGUES (FRANCISCO MANUEL DE CARVALHO) S. Tome e Principe sob o ponto de vista agricola. Lisboa, 1974. pp. 180; 25 plates. *bibliog.* (*Portugal. Junta de Investigaçoes Cientificas do Ultramar. Estudos, Ensaios e Documentos. 130*) 3 maps in end pocket.

— Sardinia.

ANGIONI (GIULIO) Sa laurera: il lavoro contadino in Sardegna. Cagliari, [1976]. pp. 294.

— Senegal.

MAINTENANCE sociale et changement économique au Sénégal. 2. Pratique du travail et rééquilibres sociaux en milieu Serer; [by] B. Delpech [and others]. Paris, 1974. pp. 155. *bibliog.* (*France. Office de la Recherche Scientifique et Technique Outre-Mer. Travaux et Documents. No. 34*) Vol. 1 published as Travaux et Documents. No. 15.

— Spain.

ALVAREZ GOMEZ (SANTIAGO) El Partido Comunista y el campo: la evolucion del problema agrario y la posicion de los comunistas. Madrid, [1977]. pp. 265.

— — Statistics.

SPAIN. Instituto Nacional de Estadistica. 1974. Censo agrario de España, 1972. Serie B. Cuadernos provinciales. Madrid, 1974. 30 vols. (in 3).

— Sweden — Gothenburg and Bohus County.

GOTHENBURG AND BOHUS (COUNTY). Lantbruksnämnden. Lantbruket i Göteborgs och Bohus län. Stockholm, 1975. pp. 185. (*Sweden. Lantbruksstyrelsen. Meddelanden. 1975.5*) Maps in end pocket.

— — Jämtland (County).

JÄMTLAND (COUNTY). Länsstyrelsen. Lantbruket i Jämtlands län. Stockholm, 1978. pp. 192. (*Sweden. Lantbruksstyrelsen. Meddelanden. 1978.2*)

— — Norrbotten (County).

NORRBOTTEN (COUNTY). Lantbruksnämnden. Jord och skog i Norrbottens län. Stockholm, 1974. pp. 136. (*Sweden. Lantbruksstyrelsen. Meddelanden. 1974. 2*) Map in end pocket.

— — Örebro (County).

ÖREBRO (COUNTY). Lantbruksnämnden. Lantbruket i Örebro län: produktion, ekonomi, utveckling; [edited by Per-Olof Esbjörner]. Stockholm, 1974. pp. 244. (*Sweden. Lantbruksstyrelsen. Meddelanden. 1974.3*) Maps in end pocket.

— — Södermanland (County).

SÖDERMANLAND (COUNTY). Lantbruksnämnden. Sörmländskt lantbruk. Stockholm, 1978. pp. 102. (*Sweden. Lantbruksstyrelsen. Meddelanden. 1978.5*)

— — Uppsala (County).

UPPSALA (COUNTY). Lantbruksnämnden. Lantbruket i Uppsala län. Stockholm, 1975. pp. 103. (*Sweden. Lantbruksstyrelsen. Meddelanden. 1975.7*)

— Switzerland — History.

BRUGGER (HANS) Die schweizerische Landwirtschaft, 1850 bis 1914. Frauenfeld, [1978]. pp. 423. *bibliog.*

— — Ticino (Canton).

TICINO (CANTON). Ufficio delle Ricerche Economiche. 1968. L'agricoltura ticinese. Bellinzona, 1968. pp. 112.

— Taiwan — Statistics.

FORMOSA. Food Bureau. 1960. Food production and activities of Taiwan Provincial Food Bureau. [Taipei], 1960. pp. 66. *In English and Chinese.*

FORMOSA. Joint Commission on Rural Reconstruction. Rural Economics Division. 1977. Taiwan agricultural statistics, 1961-1975. Taipei, 1977. pp. 208. (*Joint Commission on Rural Reconstruction. Economic Digest Series. No. 22*)

— Tanzania.

DUMONT (RENÉ) Tanzanian agriculture after the Arusha declaration. [Dar es Salaam, Ministry of Economic Affairs and Development Planning, 1969]. pp. 62.

UNITED REPUBLIC OF TANZANIA. Information Services Division. 1979. Agriculture in Tanzania. Dar es Salaam, 1979. pp. 51.

— Thailand — Statistics.

THAILAND. National Statistical Office. 1974. Final report, crop cutting survey, 1971. [Bangkok, 1974]. pp. 69. *In English and Thai.*

— Tropics.

KAMARCK (ANDREW M.) The tropics and economic development: a provocative inquiry into the poverty of nations...; published for the World Bank. Baltimore, [1976]. pp. 113. *bibliog.*

— Uganda.

UGANDA. Department of Agriculture. Agricultural production programme 1964. Entebbe, 1964. pp. 24.

— Underdeveloped areas.

See UNDERDEVELOPED AREAS — Agriculture.

— United Kingdom.

CAMBRIDGE. University. Department of Land Economy. Agricultural Economics Unit. Reports. No. 67. Report on farming: harvest year 1976: changes in the production and profitability of farming with standards for farm business analysis. Eastern counties of England; [by] M.C. Thompson. Cambridge, 1977. 1 pamphlet (unpaged).

U.K. Ministry of Agriculture, Fisheries and Food. 1977. The changing structure of agriculture, 1968-1975. London, 1977. pp. 78.

FOOD, health and farming: reports of panels on the implications for U.K. agriculture; edited by C.J. Robbins. rev. ed. Reading, 1978. pp. 119. *bibliogs.* (*Reading. University. Centre for Agricultural Strategy. CAS Papers. 7*)

WORMELL (PETER) Anatomy of agriculture: a study of Britain's greatest industry. London, 1978. pp. 571.

— — Productivity.

U.K. Ministry of Agriculture, Fisheries and Food. 1979. Possible patterns of agricultural production in the United Kingdom by 1983. London, 1979. pp. 20.

— — Ireland.

AALEN (F.H.A.) Man and the landscape in Ireland. London, 1978. pp. 343. *bibliog.*

— — Ireland, Northern — Statistics.

IRELAND, NORTHERN. Department of Agriculture. Economics and Statistics Division. 1977. Ninth report on the agricultural statistics of Northern Ireland: economic trends in Northern Ireland agriculture: 1966-67 to 1973-74. Belfast, 1977. pp. 194.

— — Scotland.

SCOTTISH CONSERVATIVE AND UNIONIST ASSOCIATION. "Food for thought": a policy for food and farming in Scotland. [Edinburgh, 1978?]. pp. 7.

CARTER (IAN) Farmlife in northeast Scotland, 1840-1914: the poor man's country. Edinburgh, [1979]. pp. 258. *bibliog.*

— — Wales — Statistics.

WELSH AGRICULTURAL STATISTICS; [pd. by] the Welsh Office. a., 1979(no.1)- Cardiff. Partly supersedes U.K. Ministry of Agriculture, Fisheries and Food. Agricultural statistics, England and Wales.

— United States.

KLEPPER (ROBERT) The economic bases for agrarian protest movements in the United States, 1870-1900. New York, 1978. pp. 378. *bibliog. Originally presented as a thesis, University of Chicago, 1973.*

BONNIFIELD (PAUL) The dust bowl: men, dirt, and depression. Albuquerque, [1979]. pp. 232. *bibliog.*

— — History.

GRAY (LEWIS CECIL) and THOMPSON (ESTHER KATHERINE) History of agriculture in the southern United States to 1860. Gloucester, Mass., 1958. 2 vols. *bibliog. First published in 1933.*

DANBOM (DAVID B.) The resisted revolution: urban America and the industrialization of agriculture, 1900-1930. Ames, Iowa, 1979. pp. 195. *bibliog.*

— — Iowa — History.

COGSWELL (SEDDIE) Tenure, nativity and age as factors in Iowa agriculture, 1850-1880. Ames, Iowa, 1975. pp. 170. *bibliog.*

— Zambia.

DODGE (DORIS JANSEN) Agricultural policy and performance in Zambia: history, prospects, and proposals for change. Berkeley, [1977]. pp. 285. *(California University. Institute of International Studies. Research Series. No. 32)*

AGRICULTURE, COOPERATIVE

— Law and legislation — Europe.

ISSERT (J.) The legal status of (agricultural) cooperatives in European countries...; translated by J.A.E. Morley. [Oxford, 1978]. pp. 112. *(Horace Plunkett Foundation. Occasional Papers. No. 44)*

— Europe — Bibliography.

COMMONWEALTH AGRICULTURAL BUREAUX and HORACE PLUNKETT FOUNDATION. Annotated Bibliographies. No. CP 1. Agricultural co-operatives in Europe. Slough, 1976. pp. 150,6.

— Israel.

JEWISH AGENCY. Agricultural Settlement Department and Information Department. 16 years of agricultural settlement in Israel. Jerusalem, 1964. 1 vol. (unpaged).

— Poland.

ROMANOWSKI (TADEUSZ) Spółdzielczość wiejska a przemiany wsi i rolnictwa. Warszawa, 1978. pp. 159. *bibliog.*

— Russia.

OKTIABR' i sovetskoe krest'ianstvo, 1917-1927 gg. Moskva, 1977. pp. 295.

PTUSHCHENKO (VOLODYMYR OLEKSANDROVYCH) Zakonomernosti stanovleniia i razvitiia mezhkhoziaistvennoi kooperatsii. Kiev, 1977. pp. 207.

VESELOV (ANATOLII PAVLOVICH) Bor'ba Kommunisticheskoi partii za provedenie kul'turnoi revoliutsii v derevne v gody kollektivizatsii. Leningrad, 1978. pp. 128.

— — Kirghizia.

OSUSHCHESTVLENIE leninskogo kooperativnogo plana v Kirgizii. Frunze, 1976. pp. 232.

— Tanzania.

UNITED REPUBLIC OF TANZANIA. Presidential Special Committee of Enquiry into Co-operative Movement and Marketing Boards. 1966. Report; [J.A.Mhaville, chairman]. Dar es Salaam, 1966. pp. 84.

AGRICULTURE AND STATE.

ORGANIZATION FOR ECONOMIC CO-OPERATION AND DEVELOPMENT. Agricultural Policy Reports. Paris, 1964 in progress.

DISTORTIONS of agricultural incentives; edited by Theodore W. Schultz. Bloomington, [1978]. pp. 343. *bibliogs.*

— Bulgaria.

WIEDEMANN (PAUL PAT) The organisation of Bulgarian agriculture. Glasgow, 1976. fo. 58.

— Colombia.

El AGRO en el desarrollo historico colombiano: ensayos de economia politica; [by] F. Leal Buitrago [and others]. Bogota, 1977. pp. 395. *Papers presented at the Primer Seminario Nacional de Desarrollo Rural held at the Universidad de los Andes, 29-31 July 1976.*

— European Economic Community countries.

AVERYT (WILLIAM F.) Agropolitics in the European Community: interest groups and the common agricultural policy. New York, 1977. pp. 128. *bibliog.*

EUROPEAN COMMUNITIES. Press and Information [Service], Brussels Office. Newsletter on the common agricultural policy. m. (approx.). Brussels. *Current issues only kept.*

— Germany.

GESSNER (DIETER) Agrardepression und Präsidialregierungen in Deutschland, 1930 bis 1933: Probleme des Agrarprotektionismus am Ende der Weimarer Republik. Düsseldorf, [1977]. pp. 209. *bibliog.*

— Germany, Eastern.

HOFFMANN (MANFRED) Instrumente zur Lenkung der landwirtschaftlichen Bodennutzung in der DDR. Berlin, 1977. pp. 162. *bibliog. (Giessen. Universität. Zentrum für Kontinentale Agrar- und Wirtschaftsforschung. Giessener Abhandlungen zur Agrar- und Wirtschaftsforschung des Europäischen Ostens. Band 86)*

— India.

APPU (P.S.) Agrarian structure and rural development. New Delhi, 1975. pp. 34. *(India. Department of Personnel and Administrative Reforms. Training Division. Occasional Papers. No. 7)*

INDIA. Department of Rural Development. 1978. Drought prone areas programme. New Delhi, 1978. pp. 19.

— — Goa, Daman and Diu.

GOA, DAMAN AND DIU. Bureau of Economics, Statistics and Evaluation. 1976. An evaluation of the Marginal Farmers and Agricultural Labourers Development Agency, Goa, 1974-75. Panaji, 1976. pp. 131. *(Evaluation Reports. No.16)*

— Ireland (Republic).

SHEEHY (SEAMUS J.) and O'CONNELL (JOHN J.) Policies to accelerate agricultural development. Dublin, Stationery Office, [1978]. pp. 141. *(National Economic and Social Council [Eire]. [Reports]. No. 40)*

— Jamaica.

JAMAICA. Ministry of Agriculture. 1973. Green paper on agricultural development strategy. [Kingston, 1973]. pp. 46.

— Malawi.

NYASALAND. Legislative Council. Select Committee appointed to Report upon the Desirability or otherwise of a Native Agricultural Board. 1930. Report; [Keith Tucker, chairman]. Zomba, 1930. pp. 14. *(Sessional Papers. 1930. No. 1)*

BANDA (HASTINGS KAMUZU) His Excellency the Life President's speeches: mass rally at Chingale, Zomba district, August 22, 1976. [Blantyre, Department of Information, 1976?]. pp. 9.

— Malaysia.

SENFTLEBEN (WOLFGANG) Background to agricultural land policy in Malaysia. Wiesbaden, [1978]. pp. 347. *bibliog. (Hamburg. Institut für Asienkunde. Schriften. Band 44)*

— Norfolk Island.

AUSTRALIA. Bureau of Agricultural Economics. 1978. The prospects for rural development on Norfolk Island. Canberra, 1978. pp. 20. *(Occasional Papers. No. 46)*

— Poland.

TOMCZAK (FRANCISZEK) and GORZELAK (EUGENIUSZ) Agrarian policy and agricultural planning. Warsaw. 1977. pp. 128. *(Instytut Gospodarki Krajów Rozwijających Się. Teaching Papers: Advanced Course in National Economic Planning. vol. 24)*

— Russia.

SOLOMON (SUSAN GROSS) The Soviet agrarian debate: a controversy in social science, 1923-1929. Boulder, Colo., 1977. pp. 309. *bibliog. (Columbia University. Russian Institute. Studies)*

— South Africa.

SOUTH AFRICA. Department of Agriculture and Forestry. Reconstruction Committee. 1944. Reconstruction of agriculture; report. Pretoria, [1944]. pp. 47.

— Thailand.

THAILAND. Ministry of Agriculture and Co-operatives. Division of Agricultural Economics. 1976. Thailand's fourth five-year agricultural development plan, B.E. 2520-2524 [i.e. A.D. 1977-1981]: guidelines;...on behalf of the National Economic and Social Development Board, etc. [Bangkok], 1976. 1 vol. (various pagings). *(Agricultural Economics Research Bulletins. No. 114)*

— United Kingdom.

ECONOMIC DEVELOPMENT COMMITTEE FOR THE AGRICULTURAL INDUSTRY. Agriculture into the 1980s: progress on recommendations. [London, National Economic Development Office, 1978]. pp. 20.

LIBERAL PARTY. Agriculture and Food Panel. A new deal for British farming; edited by Roger Pincham. London, 1979. pp. 22.

— United States.

KLEPPER (ROBERT) The economic bases for agrarian protest movements in the United States, 1870-1900. New York, 1978. pp. 378. *bibliog. Originally presented as a thesis, University of Chicago, 1973.*

McCLINTOCK (DAVID W.) U.S. food: making the most of a global resource. Boulder, Colo., 1978. pp. 122. *bibliog.*

The NEW politics of food; edited by Don F. Hadwiger and William P. Browne. Lexington, Mass., [1978]. pp. 267. *bibliogs. (Policy Studies Organization. Policy Studies Organization Series. 19)*

— Zambia.

DIXON (CAROLE L.) The development of agricultural policy in Zambia, 1964-1971. Aberdeen, 1977. pp. 44. *bibliog. (Aberdeen. University. Department of Geography. O'Dell Memorial Monographs. No.5)*

AGTA (PHILIPPINE PEOPLE).

See AETAS (PHILIPPINE NIGRITOS).

AGUIRRE Y LECUBE (JOSÉ ANTONIO DE).

AGUIRRE Y LECUBE (JOSÉ ANTONIO DE) Freedom was flesh and blood. London, 1945. pp. 288.

AIR

— Pollution.

BACH (WILFRID) Atmospheric pollution. New York, [1972]. pp. 144. *bibliogs.*

AIR LINES

AIR LINES

— United States.

O'CONNOR (WILLIAM E.) An introduction to airline economics. New York, [1978]. pp. 254. *bibliog.*

AIR POWER.

The SOVIET air and rocket forces; edited by Asher Lee. Westport, Conn., [1959]. pp. 311.

AIR power in the next generation; [edited by] E.J. Feuchtwanger and R.A. Mason. London, 1979. pp. 151. *bibliog. Papers presented at a symposium, University of Southampton, 1977.*

AIR RAID SHELTERS

— United Kingdom.

BAKER (JOHN FLEETWOOD) Baron Baker. Enterprise versus bureaucracy: the development of structural air-raid precautions during the 2nd World War. Oxford, 1978. pp. 123.

AIRCRAFT CARRIERS.

LEHMAN (JOHN) Aircraft carriers: the real choices. Beverly Hills, [1978]. pp. 83. *(Georgetown University. Center for Strategic and International Studies. Washington Papers. vol. 6/52)*

AIRPORTS

— Environmental aspects — United States — New Jersey.

CAVANAUGH (CAM) Saving the Great Swamp: the people, the power brokers, and an urban wilderness. Frenchtown, N.J., [1978]. pp. 240.

— Planning.

FAHIM (MOHAMMED ESSAM EL-DIN) The planning of airport departure systems using computer simulation models. 1978. fo. 286. *bibliog.* Typescript. Ph.D. (London) thesis: unpublished. *This thesis is the property of London University and may not be removed from the Library.*

— United Kingdom.

ASSOCIATION OF BRITISH CHAMBERS OF COMMERCE. Airports in Great Britain: time for government to act;... response to the Department of Trade's two-part consultation document An airport strategy for Great Britain. London, 1977. pp. 24.

WORRALL (A.R.) Heathrow sub-regional study: (the first draft of a thesis). [1977]. fo. 106. *bibliog.*

AIT WARYAGHAR (BERBER PEOPLE).

See WARYAGHAR (BERBER PEOPLE).

AIX-EN-PROVENCE.

FRANCE. Direction de la Documentation. La Documentation Française. Notes et Etudes Documentaires. Nos. 4,108-4, 109. Les villes françaises: Aix-en-Provence; [par M. Wolkowitsch]. [2nd ed.]. [Paris], 1977. pp. 92. *bibliog.*

— Politics and government.

KETTERING (SHARON) Judicial politics and urban revolt in seventeenth-century France: the Parlement of Aix, 1629-1659. Princeton, N.J., [1978]. pp. 370. *bibliog.*

AKADEMIE DER WISSENSCHAFTEN DER DDR.

Die BERLINER Akademie der Wissenschaften in der Zeit des Imperialismus;...von Conrad Grau [and others]; Leitung der Arbeiten und Gesamtredaktion: Leo Stern. Berlin, 1975-79. 3 vols. *(Akademie der Wissenschaften der DDR. Forschungsstelle für die Geschichte der Akademie. Studien zur Geschichte der Akademie der Wissenschaften der DDR. Band 2)*

AKHUNDOV (MIRZA FATALI).

MAMEDOV (SHEIDABEK FARADZHIEVICH) Mirza-Fatali Akhundov. Moskva, 1978. pp. 166. *bibliog.*

ALABAMA

— Social conditions.

WIENER (JONATHAN M.) Social origins of the new South: Alabama, 1860-1885. Baton Rouge, [1978]. pp. 247.

ALASKA

— Economic conditions.

WEEDEN (ROBERT B.) Alaska: promises to keep. Boston, Mass., 1978. pp. 254.

— History.

TIKHMENEV (PETR ALEKSANDROVICH) A history of the Russian-American Company; translated and edited by Richard A. Pierce and Alton S. Donnelly. Seattle, 1978. pp. 522.

— Social conditions.

WEEDEN (ROBERT B.) Alaska: promises to keep. Boston, Mass., 1978. pp. 254.

ALBANIA

— Economic history.

RUSS (WOLFGANG) Der Entwicklungsweg Albaniens: ein Beitrag zum Konzept autozentrierter Entwicklung. Meisenheim am Glan, 1979. pp. 350. *bibliog.*

— History.

PRIFTI (PETER R.) Socialist Albania since 1944: domestic and foreign developments. Cambridge, Mass., [1978]. pp. 311. *(Massachusetts Institute of Technology. Center for International Studies. Studies in Communism, Revisionism, and Revolution. 23)*

— Maps.

BREU (JOSEF) ed. Atlas der Donauländer; Atlas of the Danubian countries. Wien, 1970 in progress.

ALBERTA

— Administrative agencies.

ALBERTA. Treasury. 1977. Manual of organization structure. [Edmonton, 1977]. pp. 99.

ALBERTA. Treasury. 1978. Organization of the government of Alberta, October 1978. [Edmonton], 1978. pp. 103.

— Department of Business Development and Tourism.

ALBERTA. Department of Business Development and Tourism. Annual report. a., 1976/77- Edmonton.

— Department of Labour.

ALBERTA. Department of Labour. Annual report. a., 1974/75- Edmonton.

— Economic conditions.

ALBERTA. Department of Federal and Intergovernmental Affairs. 1976. Alberta human settlement policies...; report prepared for United Nations Habitat Conference, Vancouver, Canada, May 31-June 11, 1976. Edmonton, 1976. pp. 31.

ALBERTA. Department of Business Development and Tourism. Industry and resources. a., 1978/79- Edmonton.

— Economic policy.

ALBERTA. Department of Federal and Intergovernmental Affairs. 1976. Alberta human settlement policies...; report prepared for United Nations Habitat Conference, Vancouver, Canada, May 31-June 11, 1976. Edmonton, 1976. pp. 31.

— Executive departments.

ALBERTA. Department of Labour. Annual report. a., 1974/75- Edmonton.

ALBERTA. Department of Business Development and Tourism. Annual report. a., 1976/77- Edmonton.

ALBERTA. Treasury. 1977. Manual of organization structure. [Edmonton, 1977]. pp. 99.

ALBERTA. Treasury. 1978. Organization of the government of Alberta, October 1978. [Edmonton], 1978. pp. 103.

— Government publications.

BACKHAUS (CHRISTINE E.) compiler. Royal commissions and commissions of inquiry in Alberta, 1905-1976. Edmonton, Legislative Library, 1977. 1 vol. (unpaged). *bibliog.*

— Industries.

ALBERTA. Department of Business Development and Tourism. Industry and resources. a., 1978/79- Edmonton.

— Politics and government.

BETTISON (DAVID G.) The politics of Canadian urban development. Edmonton, 1975. pp. 337. *bibliog.*

— Population.

ALBERTA. Department of Municipal Affairs. Municipal Inspection and Advisory Services Branch. 1977. Population 1977. Edmonton, 1977. fo.7.

— Social policy.

ALBERTA. Department of Federal and Intergovernmental Affairs. 1976. Alberta human settlement policies...; report prepared for United Nations Habitat Conference, Vancouver, Canada, May 31-June 11, 1976. Edmonton, 1976. pp. 31.

— Statistics, Vital.

ALBERTA. Department of Social Services and Community Health. Vital Statistics Division. Vital statistics annual review. a., 1975/1976- Edmonton.

ALBERTA OPPORTUNITY COMPANY.

ALBERTA OPPORTUNITY COMPANY. Annual report. a., 1977/78- Edmonton.

ALCOHOL AND CHILDREN

— United Kingdom — Scotland.

AITKEN (PHILIP P.) Ten-to-fourteen-year-olds and alcohol: a developmental study in the Central Region of Scotland: vol. 3; an enquiry conducted by the Department of Psychology, University of Strathclyde for the Scottish Health Education Unit. Edinburgh, H.M.S.O., [1978]. pp. 88. *bibliog.*

ALCOHOL AND YOUTH

— United Kingdom.

HAWKER (ANN) Adolescents and alcohol: report of an enquiry into adolescent drinking patterns carried out from October 1975 to June 1976. London, [1978]. pp. 98. *bibliog.*

ALCOHOLICS ANONYMOUS.

ROBINSON (DAVID) 1941- . Talking out of alcoholism: the self-help process of Alcoholics Anonymous. London, [1979]. pp. 152. *bibliog.*

ALCOHOLISM

— Treatment — United Kingdom.

ROBINSON (DAVID) 1941- . Talking out of alcoholism: the self-help process of Alcoholics Anonymous. London, [1979]. pp. 152. *bibliog.*

— — United States.

SCHRAMM (CARL J.) and others. Workers who drink: their treatment in an industrial setting. Lexington, Mass., [1978]. pp. 153. *bibliog.*

REGIER (MARILYN C.) Social policy in action: perspectives on the implementation of alcoholism reforms. Lexington, Mass., [1979]. pp. 177. *bibliog.*

— United Kingdom.

PLANT (MARTIN A.) Drinking careers: occupations, drinking habits and drinking problems. London, 1979. pp. 167. *bibliog.*

ALCOHOLISM AND EMPLOYMENT.

SCHRAMM (CARL J.) and others. Workers who drink: their treatment in an industrial setting. Lexington, Mass., [1978]. pp. 153. *bibliog.*

ALENCAR (JOSE DE).

ALENCAR (JOSE DE) Discursos parlamentares; obra comemorativa, etc. Brasilia, 1977. pp. 680. *(Brazil. Congresso. Câmara dos Deputados. Perfis Parlamentares. 1)*

ALGEBRA.

BIRKHOFF (GARRETT) and BARTEE (THOMAS C.) Modern applied algebra. New York, [1970]. pp. 431. *bibliog.*

WHIPKEY (KENNETH L.) and others. The power of mathematics: applications to management and the social sciences. New York, [1978]. pp. 452.

ALGEBRA, BOOLEAN.

BELL (JOHN LANE) Boolean-valued models and independence proofs in set theory. Oxford, 1977. pp. 126. *bibliog.*

ALGEBRA, HOMOLOGICAL.

MACLANE (SAUNDERS) Homology. New York, 1963 repr. 1975. pp. 422. *bibliog.*

NORTHCOTT (DOUGLAS GEOFFREY) Finite free resolutions. Cambridge, 1976. pp. 271. *bibliog.*

ALGEBRAIC NUMBER THEORY.

EDWARDS (HAROLD M.) Fermat's last theorem: a genetic introduction to algebraic number theory. New York, [1977]. pp. 410. *bibliog.*

ALGEBRAS, LINEAR.

DIEUDONNÉ (JEAN A.) Linear algebra and geometry; translated from the original French text. London, 1969. pp. 207. *bibliog.*

STOER (JOSEF) and WITZGALL (CHRISTOPH) Convexity and optimization in finite dimensions I. Berlin, 1970. pp. 293. *bibliog.*

GREUB (WERNER H.) Multilinear algebra. 2nd ed. New York, [1978]. pp. 294.

CAMPBELL (STEPHEN LA VERN) and MEYER (CARL DEAN) Generalized inverses of linear transformations. London, 1979. pp. 272. *bibliog.*

ALGERIA

— Economic conditions.

BOURDIEU (PIERRE) Algeria 1960: The disenchantment of the world; The sense of honour; The Kabyle house or the world reversed; translated by Richard Nice. Cambridge, 1979. pp. 158.

— Foreign relations — France.

SMITH (TONY) The French stake in Algeria, 1945-1962. Ithaca, 1978. pp. 199. *bibliog.*

— History — 1945-1962.

HUTCHINSON (MARTHA CRENSHAW) Revolutionary terrorism: the FLN in Algeria, 1954-1962. Stanford, [1978]. pp. 178. *(Stanford University. Hoover Institution on War, Revolution and Peace. Hoover Institution Publications. 196)*

SMITH (TONY) The French stake in Algeria, 1945-1962. Ithaca, 1978. pp. 199. *bibliog.*

— Industries.

ALGERIA. Direction des Statistiques. Bureau des Statistiques Industrielles. 1971. Données sur l'industrie algérienne en 1969. Tomes 2-3. Alger, 1971. 2 vols. *Tome 1 out of print.*

— Nationalism.

BOURGUIBA (HABIB) Towards peace in Algeria. [Tunis, Secretariat of State for Information, 1960]. pp. 60. *(Publications)*

— Politics and government.

BOURGUIBA (HABIB) Towards peace in Algeria. [Tunis, Secretariat of State for Information, 1960]. pp. 60. *(Publications)*

ALGORITHMS.

CARNAHAN (BRICE) and others. Applied numerical methods. New York, 1969. pp. 604. *bibliog.*

LAWLER (EUGENE L.) Combinatorial optimization: networks and matroids. New York, [1976]. pp. 374.

EISELT (HORST A.) and FRAJER (HELMUT VON) Operations research handbook: standard algorithms and methods with examples. London, 1977. pp. 398. *bibliog.*

MINIEKA (EDWARD) Optimization algorithms for networks and graphs. New York, [1978]. pp. 356. *bibliogs.*

NIJENHUIS (ALBERT) and WILF (HERBERT S.) Combinatorial algorithms for computers and calculators. 2nd ed. New York, 1978. pp. 302. *bibliog.*

ALIANZA POPULAR REVOLUCIONARIA AMERICANA.

HAYA DE LA TORRE (VICTOR RAUL) Obras completas. Lima, [1977]. 7 vols.

ALIBI

— United Kingdom.

GOODERSON (RICHARD NORMAN) Alibi. London, 1977. pp. 269. *bibliog. (Cambridge. University. Institute of Criminology. Cambridge Studies in Criminology. vol. 37)*

ALIEN LABOUR

— United States.

SCHACHTER (JOSEPH) Capital value and relative wage effects of immigration into the United States, 1870-1930. New York, 1977. pp. 125. *bibliog. Facsimile reprint of Ph.D. thesis, City University of New York, submitted in 1969.*

ALIEN LABOUR, AFRICAN

— France.

Le PROLETARIAT africain noir en France; témoignages recueillis et présentés par Michel Samuel. Paris, 1978. pp. 262. *bibliog.*

ALIEN LABOUR, MEXICAN

— United States.

IMMIGRANTS - and immigrants: perspectives on Mexican labor migration to the United States; edited by Arthur F. Corwin. Westport, 1978. pp. 378.

ALIEN LABOUR, POLISH

— Germany.

KLESSMANN (CHRISTOPH) Polnische Bergarbeiter im Ruhrgebiet, 1870-1945: soziale Integration und nationale Subkultur einer Minderheit in der deutschen Industriegesellschaft. Göttingen, 1978. pp. 306. *bibliog.*

ALIENATION (PHILOSOPHY).

FEUERLICHT (IGNACE) Alienation: from the past to the future. Westport, Conn., [1978]. pp. 273. *bibliog.*

ALIENATION (SOCIAL PSYCHOLOGY).

LONDON. University. London School of Economics and Political Science. Graduate School of Geography. Discussion Papers. No. 63. Alienation and explanation in human geography; [by] Simon Duncan. London, 1977. pp. 40. *bibliog.*

SIEGAL (HARVEY A.) Outposts of the forgotten: socially terminal people in slum hotels and single room occupancy tenements. New Brunswick, N.J., [1978]. pp. 211. *bibliog.*

ALIENS

— Germany.

AMNESTY INTERNATIONAL. Sektion der Bundesrepublik Deutschland. Politisches Asyl in der Bundesrepublik Deutschland: Grundlagen und Praxis, Erfahrungsbericht und Dokumentation. Baden-Baden, 1977. pp. 335. *bibliog.*

— Switzerland.

BORY-LUGON (VALERIE) Immigration et xénophobie dans la société suisse. Lausanne, 1977. pp. 117. *bibliog.*

— United States.

AMERICAN ENTERPRISE INSTITUTE FOR PUBLIC POLICY RESEARCH. Legislative Analyses. 95th Congress. No. 32. Illegal aliens: problems and policies. Washington, 1978. pp. 33.

ALLEMAND-LAVIGERIE (CHARLES MARTIAL) Cardinal.

O'DONNELL (JOSEPH DEAN) Lavigerie in Tunisia: the interplay of imperialist and missionary. Athens, Ga., [1979]. pp. 300. *bibliog.*

ALLENDE (SALVADOR).

SIGMUND (PAUL E.) The overthrow of Allende and the politics of Chile, 1964-1976. Pittsburgh, [1977]. pp. 326.

WILLIAMS (LEE H.) compiler. The Allende years. Boston, Mass., [1977]. pp. 339.

ALLGEMEINER DEUTSCHER GEWERKSCHAFTSBUND.

BRAUNTHAL (GERARD) Socialist labor and politics in Weimar Germany: the General Federation of German Trade Unions. Hamden, Conn., 1978. pp. 253. *bibliog.*

ALLIANCE PARTY.

McALLISTER (IAN) and WILSON (BRIAN) Political scientist. Bi-confessionalism in a confessional party system: the Northern Ireland Alliance Party. Glasgow, [1977]. pp. 24. *bibliog. (Glasgow. University of Strathclyde. Centre for the Study of Public Policy. Studies in Public Policy. No. 8)*

ALLIED MENTAL HEALTH PERSONNEL.

GERSHON (MICHAEL) and BILLER (HENRY B.) The other helpers: paraprofessionals and nonprofessionals in mental health. Lexington, Mass., [1977]. pp. 268. *bibliog.*

ALLSPICE.

RODRIQUEZ (D.W.) Pimento: a short economic history. [Kingston, 1969]. pp. 52. *bibliog. (Jamaica. Agricultural Planning Unit. Commodity Bulletins. No 3)*

ALTHUSSER (LOUIS).

LOUIS Althusser: marxistische Kritik am Stalinismus?; ([by] Projekt Klassenanalyse). Westberlin, [1975]. pp. 175.

ALTITUDE, INFLUENCE OF.

The BIOLOGY of high-altitude peoples; edited by P.T. Baker. Cambridge, 1978. pp. 357. *bibliogs. (International Council of Scientific Unions. International Biological Programme. 14)*

ALTRUISM.

ALTRUISM, morality, and economic theory; edited by Edmund S. Phelps. New York, [1975]. pp. 232. *bibliogs.*

ALUMINIUM INDUSTRY AND TRADE.

ORGANISATION FOR ECONOMIC CO-OPERATION AND DEVELOPMENT. Environment Directorate. 1977. Pollution control costs in the primary aluminium industry. Paris, 1977. pp. 151. *bibliog.*

AMADO (GILBERTO).

See FARIA (GILBERTO DE LIMA AZEVEDO SOUZA FERREIRA AMADO DE).

AMAZON VALLEY

— Colonization.

TAVARES (VANIA PORTO) and others. Colonização dirigida no Brasil: suas possibilidades na região amazônica. Rio de Janeiro, 1972. pp. 202. *bibliog. (Brazil. Instituto de Planejamento Econômico e Social. Instituto de Pesquisas. Relatorios de Pesquisa. No. 8)*

— Economic conditions.

MAHAR (DENNIS J.) Desenvolvimento econômico da Amazônia: una analise das politicas governamentais. Rio de Janeiro, 1978. pp. 259. *bibliog. (Brazil. Instituto de Planejamento Econômico e Social. Instituto de Pesquisas. Relatorios de Pesquisa. No. 39)*

AMBULATORY MEDICAL CARE.

STEPHEN (WILLIAM JOHN) An analysis of primary medical care: an international study. Cambridge, 1979. pp. 401. *bibliog.*

AMERICA

— Emigration and immigration.

MARTINEZ CACHERO (LUIS ALFONSO) La emigracion asturiana a America. Salinas, Oviedo, [1976]. pp. 153. *bibliog.*

— Statistics.

STATISTICAL BULLETIN OF THE OAS; [pd.by] Program of Development Programming, Organization of American States. q., Ja/Mr 1979(v.1, no.1)- Washington, D.C..

AMERICA, LATIN.

ADAMS (RICHARD NEWBOLD) Cultural surveys of Panama, Nicaragua, Guatemala, El Salvador, Honduras. Washington, Pan American Sanitary Bureau, 1957; Detroit, 1976. pp. 669. *bibliogs. (Pan American Sanitary Bureau. Scientific Publications. No.33) Facsimile reprint.*

— Antiquities.

WEAVER (MURIEL PORTER) The Aztecs, Maya, and their predecessors. New York, 1972. pp. 347. *bibliog. (Northwestern University. Studies in Archaeology)*

— Armed forces.

The POLITICS of antipolitics: the military in Latin America; edited by Brian Loveman and Thomas M. Davies. Lincoln, Nebr., [1978]. pp. 309.

— Bibliography.

LEVY (KURT L.) ed. Book list on Latin America for Canadians. [Ottawa], Canadian Commission for Unesco, [1969]. pp. 51. *Introduction and notes in English and French.*

DEAL (CARL W.) compiler. Latin America and the Caribbean: a dissertation bibliography. Ann Arbor, [1978]. pp. 164.

LATIN American bibliography: a guide to sources of information and research;...edited by Laurence Hallewell. London, 1978. pp. 227.

— Civilization.

RIVERA (JULIUS) Latin America: a sociocultural interpretation. new ed. New York, [1978]. pp. 246. *bibliogs.*

— Economic conditions.

STOEHR (WALTER) Regional development experiences and prospects in Latin America. Paris, [1975]. pp. 186. *bibliog.*

FURTADO (CELSO) Economic development of Latin America: historical background and contemporary problems...; translated by Suzette Macedo. 2nd ed. Cambridge, 1976. pp. 317. *bibliog.*

QUIJANO (ANÍBAL) Dependencia, urbanización y cambio social en Latinoamerica. Lima, 1977. pp. 242.

SILVERT (KALMAN HIRSCH) Essays in understanding Latin America. Philadelphia, [1977]. pp. 240.

SYNTHESIS OF ECONOMIC PERFORMANCE IN LATIN AMERICA; [pd. by] Program of Development Programming, Organization of American States. a., 1978 (1st issue)- Washington, D.C.

CLINE (WILLIAM R.) and DELGADO (ENRIQUE) eds. Economic integration in Central America. Washington, D.C., [1978]. pp. 712.

ODELL (PETER R.) and PRESTON (DAVID ANTHONY) Economies and societies in Latin America: a geographical interpretation. 2nd ed. Chichester, 1978. pp. 289. *bibliogs.*

TECHNOLOGICAL progress in Latin America: the prospects for overcoming dependency; edited by James H. Street and Dilmus D. James. Boulder, Colo., 1979. pp. 257.

— — Abstracts.

CLADINDEX: resumen de documentos CEPAL/ILPES; [pd. by] Centro Latinoamericano de Documentacion Economica y Social, Economic Commission for Latin America. s-a., 1977 (v.1, no.1)- Santiago. *In 2 pts.; pt.1 Resumenes, pt.2 Indice.*

— — Indexes.

CLADINDEX: resumen de documentos CEPAL/ILPES; [pd. by] Centro Latinoamericano de Documentacion Economica y Social, Economic Commission for Latin America. s-a., 1977 (v.1, no.1)- Santiago. *In 2 pts.; pt.1 Resumenes, pt.2 Indice.*

— — Statistics.

UNITED STATES. Agency for International Development. Statistics and Reports Division. 1975. Latin America: economic growth trends. [Washington], 1975. pp. 31.

— Economic history.

SIMPOSIO DE HISTORIA ECONOMICA LATINOAMERICANA, 1o, LIMA, 1970. La historia economica en America Latina;...XXXIX Congreso Internacional de Americanistas,...Comision de Historia Economica del Consejo Latinoamericano de Ciencias Sociales. Mexico, Secretaria de Educacion Publica, 1972. 2 vols. (in 1). *bibliog. (Sep/Setentas. 37, 47)*

MARTINIERE (GUY) Les Amériques latines, une histoire économique. Grenoble, 1978. pp. 362.

— — Bibliography.

SIMPOSIO DE HISTORIA ECONOMICA LATINOAMERICANA, 1o LIMA, 1970. La historia economica en America Latina;...XXXIX Congreso Internacional de Americanistas,...Comision de Historia Economica del Consejo Latinoamericano de Ciencias Sociales. Mexico, Secretaria de Educacion Publica, 1972. 2 vols. (in 1). *bibliog. (Sep/Setentas. 37, 47)*

— Economic integration.

DERECHO DE LA INTEGRACION; [pd.by] Instituto para la Integracion de America Latina, Banco Interamericano de Desarrollo. 3 a yr. (formerly s-a), Oc 1967(no.1)- Buenos Aires.

REVISTA DE LA INTEGRACION: economia, politica, sociologia; ([pd. by] Banco Interamericano de Desarrollo, Instituto para la Integracion de America Latina). 3 a yr. (formerly s-a.), My 1968 - My 1975 (nos.2 - 19/20) . Buenos Aires. *Superseded by INTEGRACION LATINOAMERICANO.*

BACH (LUIS) El Pacto Andino y la integracion latinoamericana. Buenos Aires, 1976. pp. 147.

REVISTA DE LA INTEGRACION Y EL DESARROLLO DE CENTRO-AMERICA; [pd. by] Central American Bank for Economic Integration. irreg., [1977, (no.24)]- [Tegucigalpa].

LATIN-AMERICAN INTEGRATION; [ed. bi-m. by the Institute for Latin-American Integration...Inter-American Development Bank). bi-m. Buenos Aires. *Current issues only kept.*

— Economic policy.

GUZMAN FERRER (MARTIN LUIS) La inflacion y el desarrollo en la America Latina. Mexico, 1976. pp. 653. *bibliog.*

WYNIA (GARY W.) The politics of Latin American development. Cambridge, 1978. pp. 335. *bibliogs.*

CARDOSO (FERNANDO HENRIQUE) and FALETTO (ENZO) Dependency and development in Latin America...; translated by Marjory Mattingly Urquidi. Berkeley, [1979]. pp. 227. *An expanded and amended version of 'Dependencia y desarrollo en América Latina'.*

— Foreign economic relations.

QUIJANO (ANÍBAL) Dependencia, urbanización y cambio social en Latinoamerica. Lima, 1977. pp. 242.

— — United States.

FISHLOW (ALBERT) The mature neighbor policy: a new United States economic policy for Latin America. Berkeley, [1977?]. pp. 56. *bibliog. (California University. Institute of International Studies. Policy Papers in International Affairs. No. 3).*

— Foreign relations.

AMERICA Latina: unidos o dominados; [texts by Bolivar and others]; introduccion y seleccion Norberto Galasso. Buenos Aires, 1975. pp. 166.

— — Israel.

KAUFMAN (EDY) and others. Israel-Latin American relations. New Brunswick, [1979]. pp. 256.

— — Russia.

BARTLEY (RUSSELL H.) Imperial Russia and the struggle for Latin American independence, 1808-1828. Austin, [1978]. pp. 236. *bibliog. (Texas University. Institute of Latin American Studies. Latin American Monographs. No. 43)*

— — United States.

SCOTT (JACK) Yankee unions, go home!: how the AFL helped the U.S. build an empire in Latin America. Vancouver, [1978]. pp. 287. *bibliog.*

— Historiography.

SOVIET historians on Latin America: recent scholarly contributions; edited and translated by Russell H. Bartley. Madison, 1978. pp. 345. *bibliog. (Conference on Latin American History. Publications. No.5)*

— History.

SHAFER (ROBERT JONES) A history of Latin America. Lexington, Mass., [1978]. pp. 843. *bibliog.*

SOVIET historians on Latin America: recent scholarly contributions; edited and translated by Russell H. Bartley. Madison, 1978. pp. 345. *bibliog. (Conference on Latin American History. Publications. No.5)*

— — 1806-1830, Wars of Independence.

BARTLEY (RUSSELL H.) Imperial Russia and the struggle for Latin American independence, 1808-1828. Austin, [1978]. pp. 236. *bibliog. (Texas University. Institute of Latin American Studies. Latin American Monographs. No. 43)*

— Politics and government.

KAPLAN (MARCOS) Formacion del Estado nacional en America Latina. Buenos Aires, 1969 repr. 1976. pp. 356. *bibliog.*

FERNANDES (FLORESTAN) Circuito fechado: cuatro ensaios sobre o "poder institucional". São Paulo, 1976. pp. 224. *bibliogs.*

HAYA DE LA TORRE (VICTOR RAUL) Obras completas. Lima, [1977]. 7 vols.

SILVERT (KALMAN HIRSCH) Essays in understanding Latin America. Philadelphia, [1977]. pp. 240.

SOLARI (ALDO E.) ed. Poder y desarrollo: America Latina; estudios sociologicos en homenaje a Jose Medina Echavarria. Mexico, 1977. pp. 429.

The BREAKDOWN of democratic regimes; edited by Juan J. Linz and Alfred Stepan. Baltimore, [1978]. pp. 168.

CAMBRIDGE. University. Centre of Latin American Studies. Working Papers. No. 31. On the characterisation of authoritarian regimes in Latin America; by F.H. Cardoso. Cambridge, 1978. pp. 32.

The POLITICS of antipolitics: the military in Latin America; edited by Brian Loveman and Thomas M. Davies. Lincoln, Nebr., [1978]. pp. 309.

RIVERA (JULIUS) Latin America: a sociocultural interpretation. new ed. New York, [1978]. pp. 246. *bibliogs.*

WYNIA (GARY W.) The politics of Latin American development. Cambridge, 1978. pp. 335. *bibliogs.*

— Population.

CENTRO PARA EL DESARROLLO ECONOMICO Y SOCIAL DE AMERICA LATINA. Poblacion y familia en una sociedad en transicion. Buenos Aires, 1970. pp. 375.

CENTRO LATINOAMERICANO DE DEMOGRAFIA. Boletin demografico. s-a., Ja 1973(año 6, no.11)- Santiago.

NOTAS DE POBLACION: revista latinoamericana de demografia; [pd. by] Centro Latinoamericano de Demografia. 3 a yr., Ap 1973 (año 1, v.1)- Santiago.

POPULATION growth and human productivity; Manuel J. Carvajal, editor. Gainesville, 1976. pp. 296. *Papers given at a symposium held at the University of Florida, February 17-20, 1974 and sponsored by the Center for Latin American Studies of the University of Florida. Text in English or Spanish.*

— Relations (general) with Russia.

SOVIET historians on Latin America: recent scholarly contributions; edited and translated by Russell H. Bartley. Madison, 1978. pp. 345. *bibliog. (Conference on Latin American History. Publications. No.5)*

— Relations (general) with the United States.

REID (JOHN TURNER) Spanish American images of the United States, 1790-1960. Gainesville, 1977. pp. 298. *bibliog.*

— Religion.

NIDA (EUGENE A.) Understanding Latin Americans, with special reference to religious values and movements. South Pasadena, Calif., 1974 repr. 1976. pp. 165. *bibliog.*

DUSSEL (ENRIQUE) History and the theology of liberation: a Latin American perspective...; translated by John Drury. New York, [1976]. pp. 189. *bibliog.*

— Rural conditions.

ALEXANDER (ROBERT JACKSON) Agrarian reform in Latin America. New York, [1974]. pp. 118.

— Social conditions.

FURTADO (CELSO) Economic development of Latin America: historical background and contemporary problems...; translated by Suzette Macedo. 2nd ed. Cambridge, 1976. pp. 317. *bibliog.*

QUIJANO (ANÍBAL) Dependencia, urbanización y cambio social en Latinoamerica. Lima, 1977. pp. 242.

SOLARI (ALDO E.) ed. Poder y desarrollo: America Latina; estudios sociologicos en homenaje a Jose Medina Echavarria. Mexico, 1977. pp. 429.

ODELL (PETER R.) and PRESTON (DAVID ANTHONY) Economies and societies in Latin America: a geographical interpretation. 2nd ed. Chichester, 1978. pp. 289. *bibliogs.*

RIVERA (JULIUS) Latin America: a sociocultural interpretation. new ed. New York, [1978]. pp. 246. *bibliogs.*

CARDOSO (FERNANDO HENRIQUE) and FALETTO (ENZO) Dependency and development in Latin America...; translated by Marjory Mattingly Urquidi. Berkeley, [1979]. pp. 227. *An expanded and amended version of 'Dependencia y desarollo en América Latina'.*

— — Abstracts.

CLADINDEX: resumen de documentos CEPAL/ILPES; [pd. by] Centro Latinoamericano de Documentacion Economica y Social, Economic Commission for Latin America. s-a., 1977 (v.1, no.1)- Santiago. *In 2 pts.; pt.1 Resumenes, pt.2 Indice.*

— — Indexes.

CLADINDEX: resumen de documentos CEPAL/ILPES; [pd. by] Centro Latinoamericano de Documentacion Economica y Social, Economic Commission for Latin America. s-a., 1977 (v.1, no.1)- Santiago. *In 2 pts.; pt.1 Resumenes, pt.2 Indice.*

— Social policy.

RIVERA (JULIUS) Latin America: a sociocultural interpretation. new ed. New York, [1978]. pp. 246. *bibliogs.*

— Statistics.

STATISTICAL YEARBOOK FOR LATIN AMERICA; [pd. by] Economic Commission for Latin America, United Nations. a., 1976- New York. *[in Spanish and English]. Supersedes STATISTICAL BULLETIN FOR LATIN AMERICA.*

AMERICAN ASSOCIATION FOR THE ADVANCEMENT OF SCIENCE.

KOHLSTEDT (SALLY GREGORY) The formation of the American scientific community: the American Association for the Advancement of Science, 1848-60. Urbana, Ill., [1976]. pp. 330. *bibliog.*

AMERICAN FEDERATION OF LABOR.

SCOTT (JACK) Yankee unions, go home!: how the AFL helped the U.S. build an empire in Latin America. Vancouver, [1978]. pp. 287. *bibliog.*

AMERICAN FICTION

— History and criticism.

SMITH (HENRY NASH) Democracy and the novel: popular resistance to classic American writers. New York, [1978]. pp. 204.

AMERICAN INSTITUTE FOR FREE LABOR DEVELOPMENT.

BLAKE (WALTER) El sindicalismo libre en el Peru. Lima, 1975. pp. 70. *bibliog. (Pontificia Universidad Catolica del Peru. Taller de Estudios Urbano Industriales. Estudios Sindicales. No.2)*

AMERICAN LITERATURE

— Afro-American authors.

BERGHAHN (MARION) Images of Africa in black American literature. London, [1977]. pp. 230. *bibliog.*

AMERICAN LOYALISTS.

HANCOCK (HAROLD BELL) The loyalists of revolutionary Delaware. Newark, Del., [1977]. pp. 159. *bibliog.*

AMERICAN PERIODICALS.

BELFRAGE (CEDRIC) and ARONSON (JAMES) Something to guard: the stormy life of the National Guardian, 1948-1967. New York, 1978. pp. 362.

— Bibliography.

CARNAHAN (DON) compiler. Guide to alternative periodicals. 2nd ed. St. Petersburg Beach, Fla., 1977. pp. 76.

AMERICAN TELEPHONE AND TELEGRAPH COMPANY.

STEHMAN (JONAS WARREN) The financial history of the American Telephone and Telegraph Company. New York, 1967. pp. 339. *bibliog. Reprint of work originally published Boston, 1925.*

AMERICANIZATION.

The KOREAN diaspora: historical and sociological studies of Korean immigration and assimilation in North America; Hyung- chan Kim, editor. Santa Barbara, [1977]. pp. 268.

AMERICANS IN THE FAR EAST.

WAR-wasted Asia: letters, 1945-46;... [by] Donald Keene [and others]; (edited by Otis Cary). Tokyo, 1975. pp. 322.

AMIN (IDI).

KYEMBA (HENRY) State of blood: the inside story of Idi Amin. London, 1977. pp. 288.

AMNESTY INTERNATIONAL.

AMNESTY INTERNATIONAL. A.I. in quotes. London, 1976. pp. 25.

AMSTERDAM

— Economic history.

HEIJDER (M.) Amsterdam: korenschuur van Europa: historische schets van de Amsterdamse graanhandel. Amsterdam, 1979. pp. 104.

ANALYSIS OF VARIANCE.

BOX (GEORGE E.P.) and others. Statistics for experimenters: an introduction to design, data analysis and model building. New York, [1978]. pp. 653.

ANARCHISM AND ANARCHISTS.

BAKUNIN (MIKHAIL ALEKSANDROVICH) Gesammelte Werke. Bände 1-3, Vaduz, 1978. 3 vols. (in 1). *Reprint of a work originally published in Berlin, 1921-24.*

ARMAND (EMILE) pseud. [i.e. Ernest Lucien JUIN] Qu'est-ce qu'un anarchiste? Paris, 1925. pp. 28. *bibliog.*

ANARCHISM AND ANARCHISTS.(Cont.)

FURTH (RENE) Formes et tendances de l'anarchisme. Paris, 1967. pp. 97.

BALKANSKI (GR.) L'anarchisme et le problème de l'organisation. Toulouse, 1969. pp. 36.

POLIANSKII (FEDOR IAKOVLEVICH) Kritika ekonomicheskikh teorii anarkhizma. Moskva, 1976. pp. 301.

TARIZZO (DOMENICO) L'anarchia: storia dei movimenti libertari nel mondo. [Verona, 1976]. pp. 323. *bibliog.*

JOLL (JAMES) The anarchists. 2nd ed. London, 1979. pp. 299. *bibliog.*

REINVENTING anarchy: what are anarchists thinking these days?; edited by Howard J. Ehrlich [and others]. London, 1979. pp. 371.

— **Belgium.**

DAY (HEM) pseud. [i.e. Marcel DIEU] Elisée Reclus en Belgique: sa vie, son activité, 1894- 1905. Paris, 1956. pp. 32.

— **France.**

FLEMING (MARIE) The anarchist way to socialism: Elisée Reclus and nineteenth- century European anarchism. London, 1979. pp. 299. *bibliog.*

— **Germany.**

RICHTER (ARMIN) Der Ziegelbrenner: das individualanarchistische Kampforgan des frühen B. Traven. Bonn, 1977. pp. 442. *bibliog.*

VOGEL (ANGELA) Der deutsche Anarcho-Syndikalismus: Genese und Theorie einer vergessenen Bewegung. Berlin, 1977. pp. 312. *bibliog.*

BECKER (JILLIAN) Hitler's children. rev. ed. London, 1978. pp. 415. *bibliog.*

— **Italy.**

GOSI (ROSELLINA) Il socialismo utopistico: Giovanni Rossi e la colonia anarchica Cecilia. Milano, [1977]. pp. 179. *bibliog.*

— **Mexico.**

FLORES MAGON (RICARDO) Land and liberty: anarchist influences in the Mexican Revolution. Sanday, 1977. pp. 156. *bibliog.*

— **Netherlands.**

RAMAER (HANS) compiler. De piramide der tirannie: anarchisten in Nederland. Amsterdam, 1977. pp. 223. *bibliog.*

WELCKER (J.M.) Heren en arbeiders in de vroege Nederlandse arbeidersbeweging, 1870-1914. Amsterdam, 1978. pp. 681. *bibliog. (International Institute of Social History. De Nederlandse Arbeidersbeweging. 3)* With summary in English.

— **Russia.**

POMPER (PHILIP) Sergei Nechaev. New Brunswick, [1979]. pp. 273. *bibliog.*

— **Spain.**

FRANCISCO Ferrer anarchiste: la grève générale; articles écrits par Ferrer ou en collaboration avec Anselmo Lorenzo. Paris, 1934. pp. 28.

GARCIA (FELIX) Colectivizaciones campesinas y obreras en la Revolucion española. Bilbao, 1977. pp. 266. *bibliog.*

BERNECKER (WALTHER L.) Anarchismus und Bürgerkrieg: zur Geschichte der sozialen Revolution in Spanien, 1936-1939. Hamburg, 1978. pp. 372. *bibliog.* With English summary.

A NEW world in our hearts: the faces of Spanish anarchism; edited by Albert Meltzer. Sanday, 1978. pp. 100.

— **United Kingdom.**

STOKE NEWINGTON FIVE SOLIDARITY COMMITTEE. Release the five; statement of the...committee. London, [1973?]. pp. 8.

QUAIL (JOHN) The slow burning fuse: the lost history of the British anarchists. London, 1978. pp. 350. *bibliog.*

— **United States.**

DELEON (DAVID) The American as anarchist: reflections on indigenous radicalism. Baltimore, 1978. pp. 242. *bibliog.*

ANDALUSIA

— **Industries.**

CAMPS GARCIA (CARLES) La industria andaluza. Barcelona, 1978. pp. 303. *bibliog.*

— **Politics and government.**

RAMOS ESPEJO (ANTONIO) Andalucia: campo de trabajo y represion. Granada, [1978]. pp. 501. *bibliog.*

— **Social conditions.**

RAMOS ESPEJO (ANTONIO) Andalucia: campo de trabajo y represion. Granada, [1978]. pp. 501. *bibliog.*

ANDEAN GROUP.

BACH (LUIS) El Pacto Andino y la integracion latinoamericana. Buenos Aires, 1976. pp. 147.

FONTAINE (ROGER W.) The Andean pact: a political analysis. Beverly Hills, [1977]. pp. 72. *bibliog. (Georgetown University. Center for Strategic and International Studies. Washington Papers. vol. 5/45)*

— **Economic integration.**

GRUPO ANDINO: carta informativa oficial de la Junta del Acuerdo de Cartagena. m., F 1973(no.21)- Lima.

ANDHRA PRADESH

— **Department of Social Welfare.**

ANDHRA PRADESH. Department of Social Welfare. 1975. Note on the activities of the Social Welfare Department. Hyderabad, [1975?]. fo. 50.

— **Economic conditions — Maps.**

ANDHRA PRADESH. Department of Finance and Planning. 1974. Planning atlas of Andhra Pradesh; [editor, S. Manzoor Alam]. Hyderabad, [1974]. fo. 96.

— **Executive departments.**

ANDHRA PRADESH. Department of Social Welfare. 1975. Note on the activities of the Social Welfare Department. Hyderabad, [1975?]. fo. 50.

— **Social conditions — Maps.**

ANDHRA PRADESH. Department of Finance and Planning. 1974. Planning atlas of Andhra Pradesh; [editor, S. Manzoor Alam]. Hyderabad, [1974]. fo. 96.

— **Social policy.**

ANDHRA PRADESH. Department of Social Welfare. 1974. Towards greater social justice to the weaker sections in Andhra Pradesh. Hyderabad, 1974. pp. 48.

ANDRÁSSY (GYULA) Gróf.

DECSY (JÁNOS) Prime Minister Gyula Andrássy's influence on Habsburg foreign policy during the Franco-German War of 1870-1871. Boulder, 1979. pp. 177. *(East European Quarterly. East European Monographs. 52) (City University of New York. Brooklyn College. Department of History. Studies on Society in Change. No. 8)*

ANDRONICUS II PALAEOLOGUS, Emperor of the East.

LAIOU-THOMADAKIS (ANGELIKI E.) Constantinople and the Latins: the foreign policy of Andronicus II, 1282-1328. Cambridge, Mass., 1972. pp. 388. *bibliog. (Harvard University. Harvard Historical Studies. vol. 88)*

ANGLICAN PACIFIST FELLOWSHIP.

ANGLICAN PACIFIST FELLOWSHIP. Annual report. a., 1977/78- Oxford.

ANGLO-SAXON LITERATURE.

SISAM (KENNETH) Studies in the history of Old English literature. Oxford, 1953 repr. 1967. pp. 314.

ANGOLA

— **Foreign relations — United States.**

STOCKWELL (JOHN) In search of enemies: a CIA story. London, 1978. pp. 285.

— **History.**

MARCUM (JOHN) The Angolan revolution. Cambridge, Mass., [1969-78]. 2 vols. *bibliog. (Massachusetts Institute of Technology. Center for International Studies. Studies in Communism, Revisionism and Revolution. 15,22)*

BENDER (GERALD J.) Angola under the Portuguese: the myth and the reality. London, 1978. pp. 287. *bibliog.*

— **Nationalism.**

MARCUM (JOHN) The Angolan revolution. Cambridge, Mass., [1969-78]. 2 vols. *bibliog. (Massachusetts Institute of Technology. Center for International Studies. Studies in Communism, Revisionism and Revolution. 15,22)*

— **Race relations.**

BENDER (GERALD J.) Angola under the Portuguese: the myth and the reality. London, 1978. pp. 287. *bibliog.*

ANIMAL COMMUNICATION.

LANGUAGE learning by a chimpanzee: the LANA project; edited by Duane M. Rumbaugh. New York, [1977]. pp. 312. *bibliogs.*

ANIMAL INDUSTRY.

WORLD ANIMAL REVIEW: a q. jl. devoted to world developments in animal production, animal health and animal products; (pd. by the Food and Agriculture Organization of the United Nations). q. Rome. *Current issues only kept.*

— **United Kingdom — Law.**

SANDYS-WINSCH (GODFREY) Animal law. London, 1978. pp. 216.

ANIMAL POPULATIONS

— **Statistical methods.**

ENGEN (S.) Stochastic abundance models with emphasis on biological communities and species diversity. London, 1978. pp. 126. *bibliog.*

ANIMAL PRODUCTS.

WORLD ANIMAL REVIEW: a q. jl. devoted to world developments in animal production, animal health and animal products; (pd. by the Food and Agriculture Organization of the United Nations). q. Rome. *Current issues only kept.*

— **Brazil.**

BRAZIL. Conselho Nacional de Estatistica. Laboratorio de Estatistica. 1960. Numeros indices das quantidades e dos preços do produtor de 18 produtos de origem animal nos anos de 1950 a 1958. Rio de Janeiro, [1960?]. fo. 14. *(Estudos sôbre as Quantidades e os Preços das Mercadorias Produzidas ou Negociadas. No. 93)*

— **European Economic Community countries.**

EUROPEAN COMMUNITIES. Statistical Office. Selling prices of animal products. bi-m., 1978(no.5/6)- Luxembourg. *[in Community languages]*

ANIMALS, HABITS AND BEHAVIOUR OF.

TINBERGEN (NICHOLAS) The animal in its world: explorations of an ethologist, 1932-1972. London, 1972-73. 2 vols. *bibliogs.*

ANIMALS, TREATMENT OF

— **United Kingdom.**

LABOUR PARTY. Policy Background Papers. Living without cruelty: Labour's charter for animal protection. [London], 1978. pp. 53.

ANIMISM.

BEST (ELSDON) Spiritual and mental concepts of the Maori. Wellington, [1922] repr. 1954. pp. 57. *(New Zealand. Dominion Museum. Monographs. No. 2)*

ANNUNZIO (GABRIELE D').

LEDEEN (MICHAEL ARTHUR) The first duce: D'Annunzio at Fiume. Baltimore, [1977]. pp. 225.

ANTARCTIC REGIONS.

FRIEDRICH (CHRISTOF) Germany's Antarctic claim: secret Nazi polar expeditions. Toronto, [1978?]. pp. 128.

ANTHROPOGEOGRAPHY.

GOULD (PETER R.) and WHITE (RODNEY) Mental maps. Harmondsworth, [1974]. pp. 203. *bibliog.*

ABLER (RONALD) and others. Human geography in a shrinking world. North Scituate, Mass., [1975]. pp. 307. *bibliogs.*

RELPH (EDWARD) Place and placelessness. London, [1976]. pp. 156. *bibliog.*

LONDON. University. London School of Economics and Political Science. Graduate School of Geography. Discussion Papers. No. 63. Alienation and explanation in human geography; [by] Simon Duncan. London, 1977. pp. 40. *bibliog.*

SCUDAMORE (C.N.J.) Settlement problems. [Exeter, 1977]. pp. 73.

ATLAS of world population history, by Colin McEvedy and Richard Jones. Harmondsworth, 1978. pp. 368. *bibliog.*

HUMANISTIC geography: prospects and problems; edited by David Ley and Marwyn S. Samuels. London, 1978. pp. 337. *bibliogs.*

KING (LESLIE J.) and GOLLEDGE (REGINALD G.) Cities, space, and behavior: the elements of urban geography. Englewood Cliffs, [1978]. pp. 393. *bibliogs.*

RADICAL geography: alternative viewpoints on contemporary social issues; [edited by] Richard Peet. London, 1978. pp. 387. *A collection of essays drawn mainly from "Antipode".*

— **America, Latin.**

ODELL (PETER R.) and PRESTON (DAVID ANTHONY) Economies and societies in Latin America: a geographical interpretation. 2nd ed. Chichester, 1978. pp. 289. *bibliogs.*

— **Russia.**

DEWDNEY (JOHN CHRISTOPHER) A geography of the Soviet Union. 3rd ed. Oxford, 1979. pp. 175. *bibliog.*

— **United Kingdom.**

PRE-INDUSTRIAL England: geographical essays; edited with an introduction by John Patten. Folkstone, [1979]. pp. 245. *bibliogs.*

— **United States.**

WATSON (JAMES WREFORD) Social geography of the United States. London, 1979. pp. 290. *bibliogs.*

ANTHROPOLOGICAL LINGUISTICS.

COLLOQUIUM ON NEW WAYS OF ANALYZING VARIATION, 3RD, GEORGETOWN UNIVERSITY, 1974. Studies in language variation: semantics, syntax, phonology, pragmatics, social situations, ethnographic approaches; [edited by] Ralph W. Fasold [and] Roger W. Shuy. Washington, D.C., [1977]. pp. 311. *bibliogs.*

GEORGETOWN UNIVERSITY ROUNDTABLE ON LANGUAGES AND LINGUISTICS, 1977. Linguistics and anthropology; Muriel Saville-Troike, editor. Washington, D.C., [1977]. pp. 309. *bibliogs.*

INTERNATIONAL CONGRESS OF ANTHROPOLOGICAL AND ETHNOLOGICAL SCIENCES. 9th Congress, 1973. Approaches to language: anthropological issues; [papers and discussion of a session of the congress]; edited by William C. McCormack [and] Stephen A. Wurm. The Hague, [1978]. pp. 672. *bibliogs.*

INTERNATIONAL CONGRESS OF ANTHROPOLOGICAL AND ETHNOLOGICAL SCIENCES. 9th Congress, 1973. Language and society: anthropological issues; [papers and discussion of a session of the congress]; edited by William C. McCormack [and] Stephen A. Wurm. The Hague, [1979]. pp. 771. *bibliog.*

ANTHROPOLOGY.

APPLIED anthropology in America; [edited by] Elizabeth M. Eddy and William L. Partridge. New York, 1978. pp. 484. *bibliog.*

The NEW economic anthropology; edited by John Clammer. New York, 1978. pp. 260. *bibliogs.*

SLOBODIN (RICHARD) W.H.R. Rivers; [includes selections from his writings]. New York, 1978. pp. 295. *bibliog.*

POLITICAL anthropology: the state of the art; editors S. Lee Seaton, Henri J.M. Claessen. The Hague, [1979]. pp. 411. *bibliogs.*

RATIONALITY; edited by Bryan R. Wilson. Oxford, 1979. pp. 275. *bibliog.*

TOWARD a Marxist anthropology: problems and perspectives; editor, Stanley Diamond. The Hague, [1979]. pp. 492. *bibliogs.*

— **Field work.**

MEAD (MARGARET) Letters from the field, 1925-1975. New York, [1977]. pp. 343. *bibliog.*

RABINOW (PAUL) Reflections on fieldwork in Morocco. Berkeley, [1977]. pp. 164. *bibliog.*

APPELL (GEORGE N.) Ethical dilemmas in anthropological inquiry: a case book. Waltham, Mass., [1978]. pp. 291. *bibliog.*

— **Methodology.**

APPELL (GEORGE N.) Ethical dilemmas in anthropological inquiry: a case book. Waltham, Mass., [1978]. pp. 291. *bibliog.*

The POLITICS of anthropology: from colonialism and sexism toward a view from below; [edited by] Gerrit Huizer and Bruce Mannheim. The Hague, [1979]. pp. 520. *bibliogs.*

ANTIFASCHISTISCHE AKTION.

LEIN (ALBRECHT) Antifaschistische Aktion 1945: die "Stunde Null" in Braunschweig. Göttingen, [1978]. pp. 480. *bibliog. (Göttingen. Universität. Seminar für die Wissenschaft von der Politik. Göttinger Politikwissenschaftliche Forschungen. Band 2)*

ANTINAZI MOVEMENT.

DEUTSCH (HAROLD C.) Hitler and his generals: the hidden crisis, January-June 1938. Minneapolis, [1974]. pp. 452. *bibliog.*

YOUNG (ARTHUR PRIMROSE) The 'X' documents; edited by Sidney Aster. London, 1974. pp. 253. *bibliog.*

HOFFMANN (PETER) The history of the German resistance, 1933-1945. London, 1977. pp. 847. *bibliog. Translation of 2nd ed., München, 1970.*

JAHNKE (KARL HEINZ) Jungkommunisten im Widerstandskampf gegen den Hitlerfaschismus. Dortmund, 1977. pp. 431. *bibliog.*

ZEUGEN des Widerstandes: eine Dokumentation über die Opfer des Nationalsozialismus in Nord-, Ost- und Südtirol von 1938 bis 1945; bearbeitet von Johann Holzner [and others] . Innsbruck, [1977]. pp. 112.

ZORN (GERDA) Widerstand in Hannover: gegen Reaktion und Faschismus, 1920- 1946. Frankfurt am Main, [1977]. pp. 276. *bibliog.*

DREXEL (JOSEPH EDUARD) Rückkehr unerwünscht: Joseph Drexels "Reise nach Mauthausen" und der Widerstandskreis Ernst Niekisch; herausgegeben von Wilhelm Raimund Beyer. Stuttgart, [1978]. pp. 332.

FINKER (KURT) Graf Moltke und der Kreisauer Kreis. Berlin, [1978]. pp. 336. *bibliog.*

Die FRONT war überall: (Erlebnisse und Berichte vom Kampf des Nationalkomitees "Freies Deutschland"; herausgegeben von Else und Bernt von Kügelgen). 2nd ed. Berlin, 1978. pp. 507. *bibliog.*

KONRAD (HELMUT) Widerstand an Donau und Moldau: KPÖ und KSČ zur Zeit des Hitler-Stalin-Paktes. Wien, [1978]. pp. 348. *bibliog. (Ludwig Boltzmann Institut für Geschichte der Arbeiterbewegung. Veröffentlichungen)*

PIKARSKI (MARGOT) Jugend im Berliner Widerstand: Herbert Baum und Kampfgefährten. Berlin, [1978]. pp. 236. *bibliog.*

PIOCH (KARL) Nie im Abseits. Berlin, [1978]. pp. 204.

SCHRAMM (WILHELM VON) Aufstand der Generale: der 20. Juli 1944 in Paris. München, [1978]. pp. 365. *bibliog.*

TIDL (MARIE) Frauen im Widerstand: Frauen im Kampf gegen Faschismus und Krieg. [Vienna, 1978]. pp. 52. *bibliog.*

HOFFMANN (PETER) Widerstand gegen Hitler: Probleme des Umsturzes. München, [1979]. pp. 104. *bibliog.*

WIDERSTAND und Verfolgung im Burgenland, 1934-1945: eine Dokumentation; Auswahl, Bearbeitung und Zusammenstellung: Wolfgang Neugebauer; unter Mitarbeit von Erica Fischer [and others]. Wien, Österreichischer Bundesverlag, [1979]. pp. 487.

— **Bibliography.**

DOHMS (PETER) compiler. Flugschriften in Gestapo-Akten: Nachweis und Analyse der Flugschriften in den Gestapo-Akten des Hauptstaatsarchivs Düsseldorf, etc. Siegburg, 1977. pp. 683. *bibliog. (Veröffentlichungen der Staatlichen Archive des Landes Nordrhein-Westfalen. Reihe C. Quellen und Forschungen. Band 3)*

ANTIQUARIAN BOOKSELLERS

— **United Kingdom — Directories.**

LEWIS (ROY HARLEY) compiler. The book browser's guide: Britain's secondhand and antiquarian bookshops. Newton Abbot, [1975]. pp. 184.

ANTISEMITISM

— **France.**

JUSSEM-WILSON (NELLY) Bernard-Lazare: antisemitism and the problem of Jewish identity in late nineteenth-century France. Cambridge, 1978. pp. 348. *bibliog.*

— **Russia.**

SOVIET Jewry and the Australian Communist Party: documents. Caulfield, Victoria, [1966]. pp. 79.

ANTISEMITISM (Cont.)

— United Kingdom.

HOLMES (COLIN) Anti-semitism in British society, 1876-1939. London, 1979. pp. 328. *bibliog.*

— United States.

SPIVAK (JOHN L.) Plotting America's pogroms: a documented exposé of organized anti-semitism in the United States. [New York], 1934. pp. 95. *(Reprinted from The New Masses, October-December, 1934)*

ANTITRUST LAW

— United States.

BORK (ROBERT H.) The antitrust paradox: a policy at war with itself. New York, [1978]. pp. 462.

GOOLRICK (ROBERT M.) Public policy toward corporate growth: the ITT merger cases. Port Washington, N.Y., [1978]. pp. 212. *bibliog.*

KAUFMAN (BURTON IRA) The oil cartel case: a documentary study of antitrust activity in the Cold War era. Westport, Conn., 1978. pp. 217.

OWEN (BRUCE M.) and BRAEUTIGAM (RONALD) The regulation game: strategic uses of the administrative process. Cambridge, Mass., [1978]. pp. 270. *bibliog.*

ANXIETY.

EYSENCK (HANS JÜRGEN) The dynamics of anxiety and hysteria: an experimental application of modern learning theory to psychiatry. London, 1957. pp. 311. *bibliog.*

APARTMENT HOUSES

— France.

REYNAUD (PAUL) La copropriété dans les grands ensembles immobiliers: essai d'analyse des fondements socio-économiques et juridiques. [Paris, 1978]. pp. 333. *bibliog. (France. Ministère de la Justice. Collection Ministère de la Justice)*

— India — Maharashtra.

MAHARASHTRA. Ownership Flats Enquiry Committee. 1962. Report. Bombay, 1962. pp. 75.

APHASIA.

LANGUAGE acquisition and language breakdown; parallels and divergencies; edited by Alfonso Caramazza and Edgar B. Zurif. Baltimore, [1978]. pp. 339. *bibliogs.*

APPALACHIAN MOUNTAINS.

McKINNEY (GORDON B.) Southern mountain Republicans 1865-1900: politics and the Appalachian community. Chapel Hill, N.C., [1978]. pp. 277. *bibliog.*

— History.

ROHRBOUGH (MALCOLM JUSTIN) The trans-Appalachian frontier: people, societies, and institutions, 1775-1850. New York, 1978. pp. 444. *bibliog.*

APPELLATE PROCEDURE

— United Kingdom.

STEVENS (ROBERT BOCKING) Law and politics: the House of Lords as a judicial body, 1800- 1976. London, 1979. pp. 701. *bibliog.*

THOMAS (DAVID ARTHUR) Principles of sentencing: the sentencing policy of the Court of Appeal, Criminal Division. 2nd ed. London, 1979. pp. 410. *(Cambridge. University. Institute of Criminology. Cambridge Studies in Criminology. vol. 27)*

APPRENTICES

— Canada — Quebec.

HARDY (JEAN PIERRE) and RUDDEL (DAVID THIERY) Les apprentis artisans à Québec, 1660-1815. Montréal, 1977. pp. 220. *bibliog.*

— Denmark.

LARSEN (HELGE) Apprenticeships in Denmark. Brussels, European Communities, [1977]. pp. 54. *(European Economic Community. Studies. Social Policy Series. 32)*

— Ireland (Republic).

McCARTHY (THOMAS) Apprenticeships in Ireland. Brussels, European Communities, [1977]. pp. 82. *(European Economic Community. Studies. Social Policy Series. 33)*

APPROXIMATION THEORY.

MITRINOVIC (DRAGOSLAV S.) Analytic inequalities. New York, 1970. pp. 400.

WOLFE (MICHAEL ANTHONY) Numerical methods for unconstrained optimization: an introduction. New York, 1978. pp. 312. *bibliog.*

AQUITAINE

— Economic policy.

AQUITAINE (REGION). Préfecture. 1977. Programme de développement et d'aménagement..., 1976-1980. [Bordeaux], 1977. pp. 178.

— Social policy.

AQUITAINE (REGION). Préfecture. 1977. Programme de développement et d'aménagement..., 1976-1980. [Bordeaux], 1977. pp. 178.

ARAB COUNTRIES

— Biography.

WHO's who in the Arab world...1978-1979: [edited by] Gabriel M. Bustros. 5th ed. Beirut, [1978?]. pp. 2058. *bibliog.*

— Directories.

WHO's who in the Arab world...1978-1979: [edited by] Gabriel M. Bustros. 5th ed. Beirut, [1978?]. pp. 2058. *bibliog.*

— Economic conditions.

FRANCE. Direction de la Documentation. La Documentation Française. Notes et Etudes Documentaires. No. 4481. Pétrole et développement au Moyen-Orient; [by] Mahmoud Montazer-Zohour. [Paris], 1978. pp. 96.

ARAB industrialisation and economic integration; edited by Roberto Aliboni. London, [1979]. pp. 196. *bibliogs.*

— Economic policy.

DEMOGRAPHIC aspects of socio-economic development in some Arab and African countries; edited by S. A. Huzayyin and T. E. Smith. Cairo, 1974. pp. 427. *bibliogs. (Cairo Demographic Centre. Research Monograph Series. No. 5)*

PUBLIC enterprises and development in the Arab countries: legal and managerial aspects; (papers presented at a seminar held in Kuwait, 1976). New York, [1977]. pp. 236.

— Foreign relations — Africa.

OJO (MATTHEW OLUSOLA) The Africa states and the Arab world: the development of Afro-Arab relations, with special reference to the O.A.U. and the League of Arab States. 1977 [or rather 1978]. fo. 444. *bibliog.* Typescript. Ph.D. (London) thesis: unpublished. This thesis is the property of London University and may not be removed from the Library.

— History.

AMIN (SAMIR) The Arab nation; translated [from the French] by Michael Pallis. London, 1978. pp. 116.

— Industries.

ARAB industrialisation and economic integration; edited by Roberto Aliboni. London, [1979]. pp. 196. *bibliogs.*

— Nationalism.

AMIN (SAMIR) The Arab nation; translated [from the French] by Michael Pallis. London, 1978. pp. 116.

— Politics and government.

BOURGUIBA (HABIB) The path to Arab unity: memorandum sent...to the heads of state attending the 3rd Arab Summit Meeting, held at Casablanca on 13th September 1965. [Tunis, Secretariat of State for Information and Orientation, 1965]. pp. 41.

KAZZIHA (WALID W.) Palestine in the Arab dilemma. London, [1979]. pp. 111.

— Population.

DEMOGRAPHIC aspects of socio-economic development in some Arab and African countries; edited by S. A. Huzayyin and T. E. Smith. Cairo, 1974. pp. 427. *bibliogs. (Cairo Demographic Centre. Research Monograph Series. No. 5)*

ARABIA

— Social life and customs.

AHSAN (MUHAMMAD MANAZIR) Social life under the Abbasids, 170-289 AH, 786-902 AD. London, 1979. pp. 316. *bibliog.*

ARABIC LITERATURE.

NICHOLSON (REYNOLD ALLEYNE) A literary history of the Arabs. 2nd ed. Cambridge, 1969. pp. 506. *bibliog.*

ARAUCANIAN INDIANS.

BERGLUND (STAFFAN) The national integration of Mapuche: ethnical minority in Chile...; (English translation: Bernard Wolves). Stockholm, [1977]. pp. 228. *bibliog.*

ARAWAK INDIANS.

MIGLIAZZA (ERNEST C.) The integration of the indigenous peoples of the territory of Roraima, Brazil. Copenhagen, 1978. pp. 29. *bibliog. (International Work Group for Indigenous Affairs. Documents. 32)*

ARBITRATION, INDUSTRIAL

— Australia.

AUSTRALIA. Department of Labor and Immigration. 1974. Conciliation and arbitration in Australia. Canberra, 1974. pp. 32.

— United Kingdom.

U.K. Central Arbitration Committee. Annual report. a., 1976(1st)- London.

ADVISORY, CONCILIATION AND ARBITRATION SERVICE [U.K.]. Arbitration in trade disputes. London, [1977?]. pp. 7.

ADVISORY, CONCILIATION AND ARBITRATION SERVICE [U.K.]. An industrial relations service to industry. London, [1977]. pp. 7.

ADVISORY, CONCILIATION AND ARBITRATION SERVICE [U.K.]. The ACAS role: (the ACAS role in conciliation, arbitration and mediation). [London, 1979]. pp. 24. *An extract from the ACAS annual report 1978.*

ARBITRATION, INTERNATIONAL.

LOCKHART (CHARLES) Bargaining in international conflicts. New York, 1979. pp. 205. *bibliog.*

RESTRAINTS on war: studies in the limitation of armed conflict; edited by Michael Howard. Oxford, 1979. pp. 173. *bibliog.*

ARBITRATION AND AWARD.

The DISPUTING process: law in ten societies; Laura Nader and Harry F. Todd Jr., editors. New York, 1978. pp. 372. *bibliog.*

LEW (JULIAN DAVID MATHEW) Applicable law in international commercial arbitration: a study in commercial arbitration awards. Dobbs Ferry, N.Y., 1978. pp. 633.

ARBITRATION AND AWARD, INTERNATIONAL.

HUDEC (ROBERT E.) Adjudication of international trade disputes. London, 1978. pp. 88. *(Trade Policy Research Centre. Thames Essays. No. 16)*

ARCHAEOLOGY.

ARCHAEOLOGY and the landscape: essays for L.V. Grinsell; edited by P.J. Fowler. London, 1972. pp. 263. *bibliog.*

— Methodology.

STEANE (JOHN M.) and DIX (BRIAN F.) Peopling past landscapes: a handbook introducing archaeological fieldwork techniques in rural areas. London, 1978. pp. 94. *bibliog.*

— Scandinavia.

SHETELIG (HAAKON) and FALK (HJALMAR) Scandinavian archaeology. New York, 1978. pp. 458.

ARCHAEOLOGY, INDUSTRIAL.

HUDSON (KENNETH) World industrial archaeology. Cambridge, 1979. pp. 247. *bibliog.*

— United Kingdom.

SHERLOCK (ROBERT) The industrial archaeology of Staffordshire: [a survey made on behalf of Staffordshire County Council]. Newton Abbot, [1976]. pp. 216. *bibliog.*

ARCHAEOLOGY, MEDIEVAL.

EUROPEAN towns: their archaeology and early history; edited by M. W. Barley. London, 1977. pp. 523. *bibliogs.*

ARCHITECTURE

— Human factors.

LERUP (LARS) Building the unfinished: architecture and human action. Beverly Hills, [1977]. pp. 169.

— Psychological aspects.

CANTER (DAVID VICTOR) The psychology of place. London, 1977. pp. 198. *bibliog.*

— France — History — Sources.

SUGER, Abbot of Saint-Denis, 1081-1151. Abbot Suger on the abbey church of St. Denis and its art treasures; edited...by Erwin Panofsky; second edition by Gerda Panofsky-Soergel. 2nd ed. Princeton, [1979]. pp. 285. *bibliog.*

— United Kingdom.

TAYLOR (HAROLD M.) and TAYLOR (JOAN) Anglo-Saxon architecture. Cambridge, 1965. 2 vols. *bibliogs.*

— — Conservation and restoration.

BATH. Department of Architecture and Planning. Saving Bath: a programme for conservation; (conservation study, stage 2: final report). Bath, [1978]. 1 vol. (various pagings).

ARCHITECTURE, ANGLO-SAXON.

TAYLOR (HAROLD M.) and TAYLOR (JOAN) Anglo-Saxon architecture. Cambridge, 1965. 2 vols. *bibliogs.*

ARCHITECTURE, CARLOVINGIAN.

CONANT (KENNETH JOHN) Carolingian and Romanesque architecture, 800 to 1200. rev.ed. Harmondsworth, 1978. pp. 522. *bibliog.*

ARCHITECTURE, DOMESTIC.

CHERMAYEFF (SERGE) and ALEXANDER (CHRISTOPHER) Community and privacy: toward a new architecture of humanism. Garden City, N.Y., 1965. pp. 255.

— United Kingdom.

WORSDALL (FRANK) The tenement: a way of life: a social, historical and architectural study of housing in Glasgow. [Edinburgh], 1979. pp. 165. *bibliog.*

ARCHITECTURE, ROMANESQUE.

CONANT (KENNETH JOHN) Carolingian and Romanesque architecture, 800 to 1200. rev.ed. Harmondsworth, 1978. pp. 522. *bibliog.*

ARCHITECTURE AND SOCIETY.

BAUM (ANDREW) and VALINS (STUART) Architecture and social behavior: psychological studies of social density. Hillsdale, N.J., 1977. pp. 112. *bibliog.*

ARCHIVES.

UNESCO JOURNAL OF INFORMATION SCIENCE, LIBRARIANSHIP AND ARCHIVE ADMINISTRATION; [pd. by] Unesco. q., Ja/Mr 1979 (v.1, no.1)- Paris. *Supersedes UNESCO BULLETIN FOR LIBRARIES.*

— France.

FRANCE. Archives Nationales. 1978. Les archives nationales: état général des fonds; publié sous la direction de Jean Favier. (Tome II. 1789-1940; sous la direction de Rémi Mathieu). Paris, 1978. pp. 656.

— United Kingdom.

MANDER JONES (PHYLLIS) compiler. Manuscripts in the British Isles relating to Australia, New Zealand and the Pacific. Honolulu, [1972]. pp. 697.

MATTHEWS (NOEL) compiler. Materials for West African history in the archives of the United Kingdom. London, 1973. pp. 225.

BOTT (MICHAEL) and EDWARDS (J.A.) Records management in British universities: a survey with some suggestions. Reading, 1978. pp. 38.

COOK (CHRISTOPHER PIERS) and WEEKS (JEFFREY) compilers. Sources in British political history, 1900-1951: compiled for the British Library of Political and Economic Science; vol. 5. London, 1978. pp. 221.

LONDON. University. University College. Library. Occasional Publications. No. 1. Manuscript collections in the library of University College, London: a handlist. 2nd ed. London, 1978. pp. 21.

PERCIVAL (JANET) compiler. The Society for the Diffusion of Useful Knowledge, 1826-1848: a handlist of the society's correspondence and papers. London, 1978. pp. 120. *(London. University College. Library. Occasional Publications. No. 5)*

— — Scotland.

MacDOUGALL (IAN) compiler. A catalogue of some labour records in Scotland and some Scots records outside Scotland. Edinburgh, 1978. pp. 598.

— United States.

McCOY (DONALD RICHARD) The National Archives: America's ministry of documents, 1934-1968. Chapel Hill, [1978]. pp. 437. *bibliog.*

ARCTIC REGIONS

— Defences.

BACH (H.C.) and TAAGHOLT (JØRGEN) Greenland and the Arctic region in the light of defence policies: defence aims. Copenhagen, Information and Welfare Service of the Danish Defence, 1977. pp. 55. *bibliog.*

ARGENTINE REPUBLIC

— Armed forces.

JAURETCHE (ARTURO) Ejercito y politica. Buenos Aires, [1976]. pp. 217.

— Boundaries — Chile.

U.K. 1977. Award of Her Britannic Majesty's Government pursuant to the agreement for arbitration, compromiso, of a controversy between the Argentine Republic and the Republic of Chile concerning the region of the Beagle Channel; [Sir Gerald Fitzmaurice, president of the Court of Arbitration]. London, 1977. pp. 152, 4 maps.

— Economic conditions.

CECONI (TULIO ALBERTO) La economia argentina: un analisis de su funcionamiento. Buenos Aires, 1975. pp. 76.

— Economic history.

FRIZZI DE LONGONI (HAYDEE E.) Rivadavia y la economia argentina. Buenos Aires, [1947 repr. 1976]. pp. 209. *bibliog.*

ALEN LASCANO (LUIS C.) Dependencia y liberacion en los origenes argentinos. Buenos Aires, [1974]. pp. 193.

— Economic policy.

POLITICA ECONOMICA ARGENTINA: discursos del Ministro de Economia y Trabajo; [pd. by] Ministerio de Economia y Trabajo, Republica Argentina. a., 1967/8- Buenos Aires.

UNIVERSIDAD DE BELGRANO. Catedra del Pensamiento Argentino. La Argentina posible; vista por Jose Luis de Imaz [and others]. Buenos Aires, 1976. pp. 335.

WYNIA (GARY W.) Argentina in the postwar era: politics and economic policy making in a divided society. Albuquerque, [1978]. pp. 289. *bibliog.*

— Foreign relations.

MONTEMAYOR (MARIANO) Proyeccion latinoamericana de la politica petrolera nacional. Buenos Aires, 1958. pp. 79.

JAURETCHE (ARTURO) Ejercito y politica. Buenos Aires, [1976]. pp. 217.

— — Spain.

FRABOSCHI (ROBERTO O.) La Comision regia española al Rio de la Plata, 1820-1821. Buenos Aires, 1945. pp. 57,xx. *(Buenos Aires. Universidad. Instituto de Investigaciones Historicas. Publicaciones. No. 89)*

— Historiography.

CUCCORESE (HORACIO JUAN) Historia critica de la historiografia socioeconomica argentina del siglo XX. [La Plata, 1975]. pp. 438. *(La Plata. Universidad Nacional. Facultad de Humanidades y Ciencias de la Educacion. Departamento de Historia. Monografias y Tesis.9)*

— History.

CUTOLO (VICENTE OSVALDO) Manual de historia economica y social. Buenos Aires, 1976. pp. 530.

JAURETCHE (ARTURO) Ejercito y politica. Buenos Aires, [1976]. pp. 217.

BRAVO (OMAR A.) Historia de las instituciones argentinas. Buenos Aires, 1977. pp. 279. *bibliog.*

— — 1810- .

FAGALDE (LAURO) El interior al poder: de Caseros a Roca. Buenos Aires, [1975]. pp. 129. *bibliog.*

LOPEZ ROSAS (JOSE RAFAEL) Entre la monarquia y la republica, 1815-1820. Buenos Aires, [1976]. pp. 388. *bibliog.*

ARGENTINE REPUBLIC (Cont.)

— — 1817-1860.

GALMARINI (HUGO R.) Del fracaso unitario al triunfo federal, 1824-1830. Buenos Aires, [1977]. pp. 214. *bibliog.*

— — 1860-1910.

GARCIA HOLGADO (BENJAMIN) De Mitre a Roca: politica, sociedad y economia, 1860-1904. Buenos Aires, [1976]. pp. 348. *bibliog.*

IRAZUSTA (JULIO) El transito del siglo XIX al XX, 1896-1904. Buenos Aires, [1977]. pp. 248. *bibliog.*

— — 1910-1943.

ALEN LASCANO (LUIS C.) La Argentina ilusionada, 1922-1930. Buenos Aires, [1977]. pp. 391. *bibliog.*

— — 1943- .

MARTINEZ CONSTANZO (PEDRO SANTOS) La nueva Argentina, 1946-1955. Buenos Aires, [1976]. 2 vols. *bibliog.*

— Industries.

MINSBURG (NAUM) Multinacionales en la Argentina. Buenos Aires, 1976. pp. 189.

— Politics and government.

CIRIA (ALBERTO) Partidos y poder en la Argentina moderna, 1930-1946. 3rd ed. Buenos Aires, 1975. pp. 414. *bibliog.*

BRAVO (OMAR A.) Historia de las instituciones argentinas. Buenos Aires, 1977. pp. 279. *bibliog.*

LANUSSE (ALEJANDRO AGUSTIN) Mi testimonio. Lima, [1977]. pp. 353.

WYNIA (GARY W.) Argentina in the postwar era: politics and economic policy making in a divided society. Albuquerque, [1978]. pp. 289. *bibliog.*

ZINN (RICARDO) Argentina: a nation at the crossroads of myth and reality. New York, [1979]. pp. 211. *bibliog.*

— Population.

ARGENTINE REPUBLIC. Instituto Nacional de Planificacion Economica. 1978. Republica Argentina: proyeccion de poblacion por departamentos, 1970-2000. Buenos Aires, 1978. pp. 226.

— Social policy.

UNIVERSIDAD DE BELGRANO. Catedra del Pensamiento Argentino. La Argentina posible; vista por Jose Luis de Imaz [and others]. Buenos Aires, 1976. pp. 335.

ARID REGIONS

— Brazil.

BENTON (PEGGIE) Fight for the drylands: struggle and achievement in Brazil. London, 1977. pp. 188. *First published in 1972.*

— United States.

BOWDEN (CHARLES) Killing the hidden waters. Austin, [1977]. pp. 174. *bibliog.*

ARISTOCRACY.

DRAYER (EDWARD HARRY) Problems in the analysis of social prestige, with special reference to aristocracy at six formative periods. 1978. fo. 407. *bibliog. Typescript. Ph.D. (London) thesis: unpublished. This thesis is the property of London University and may not be removed from the Library.*

ARISTOTLE.

CONTOGIORGIS (GEORGES D.) La théorie des révolutions chez Aristote. Paris, 1978. pp. 288. *bibliog.*

KENNY (ANTHONY JOHN PATRICK) The Aristotelian ethics: a study of the relationship between the Eudemian and Nicomachean ethics of Aristotle. Oxford, 1978. pp. 250. *bibliog.*

WOOD (ELLEN MEIKSINS) and WOOD (NEAL) Class ideology and ancient political theory: Socrates, Plato and Aristotle in social context. Oxford, 1978. pp. 275. *bibliog.*

LANGHOLM (ODD) Price and value in the Aristotelian tradition: a study in scholastic economic sources. Bergen, [1979]. pp. 175. *bibliog.*

ARMAMENTS.

STOCKHOLM INTERNATIONAL PEACE RESEARCH INSTITUTE. Anti-personnel weapons. London, 1978. pp. 299. *bibliog.*

— Data processing.

EXPLORING competitive arms processes: applications of mathematical modeling and computer simulation in arms policy analysis; editor: W. Ladd Hollist. New York, [1978]. pp. 279.

— Economic aspects.

SIVARD (RUTH LEGER) Military budgets and social needs: setting world priorities. New York, 1977. pp. 24. *bibliog. (Public Affairs Committee. Public Affairs Pamphlets. No. 551)*

— Mathematical models.

EXPLORING competitive arms processes: applications of mathematical modeling and computer simulation in arms policy analysis; editor: W. Ladd Hollist. New York, [1978]. pp. 279.

— Social aspects.

SIVARD (RUTH LEGER) Military budgets and social needs: setting world priorities. New York, 1977. pp. 24. *bibliog. (Public Affairs Committee. Public Affairs Pamphlets. No. 551)*

ARMENIA

— History.

SARKISYANZ (EMANUEL) A modern history of Transcaucasian Armenia: social, cultural and political. Leiden, 1975. pp. 413. *bibliog.*

— — 1917-1921, Revolution.

EL'CHIBEKIAN (AMBARTSUM MELKONOVICH) Ot revkomov k Sovetam: sozdanie Sovetov v Armenii. Erevan, 1978. pp. 144.

ARMIES.

RUSSIA (USSR). Ministerstvo Oborony. 1977. Voina i armiia: filosofsko-sotsiologicheskii ocherk; pod redaktsiei D.A. Volkogonova [and others]. Moskva, 1977. pp. 415. *bibliog.*

ARMS CONTROL.

CONGRESS and arms control; edited by Alan Platt and Lawrence D. Weiler. Boulder, Colo., [1978]. pp. 227.

NEGOTIATING security: an arms control reader; edited by William H. Kincade and Jeffrey D. Porro. Washington, D.C., [1979]. pp. 321. *bibliog.*

RANGER (ROBIN) Arms and politics, 1958-1978: arms control in a changing political context. Toronto, [1979]. pp. 280. *bibliog.*

ARONSON (JAMES).

BELFRAGE (CEDRIC) and ARONSON (JAMES) Something to guard: the stormy life of the National Guardian, 1948-1967. New York, 1978. pp. 362.

ART

— Canada — Galleries and museums.

CANADA. Statistics Canada. Culture statistics: museums, art galleries and related institutions, large institutions. a., 1976(1st)- Ottawa. *[in English and French]*

— France — History — Sources.

SUGER, Abbot of Saint-Denis, 1081-1151. Abbot Suger on the abbey church of St. Denis and its art treasures; edited...by Erwin Panofsky; second edition by Gerda Panofsky-Soergel. 2nd ed. Princeton, [1979]. pp. 285. *bibliog.*

ART, CARLOVINGIAN.

HINKS (ROGER) Carolingian art: a study of early medieval painting and sculpture in Western Europe. Ann Arbor, Mich., 1962. pp. 226. *bibliog. First published in 1935.*

ART, ENGLISH.

FARINGTON (JOSEPH) The diary of Joseph Farington; edited by Kenneth Garlick and Angus Macintyre. New Haven, 1978 in progress. *(Paul Mellon Centre for Studies in British Art. Studies in British Art)*

ART, MODERN

— 20th century.

SHAPIRO (THEDA) Painters and politics: the European avant-garde and society, 1900-1925. New York, [1976]. pp. 341. *bibliog.*

ART, RENAISSANCE.

GOMBRICH (Sir ERNST HANS) Norm and form: studies in the art of the Renaissance. 3rd ed. London, 1978. pp. 168.

ART AND SOCIETY.

SHAPIRO (THEDA) Painters and politics: the European avant-garde and society, 1900-1925. New York, [1976]. pp. 341. *bibliog.*

ART AND STATE

— United Kingdom.

JENKINS (HUGH) The culture gap: an experience of government and the arts. London, 1979. pp. 271.

ART COMMISSIONS

— United States.

NETZER (DICK) The subsidized muse: public support for the arts in the United States. Cambridge, 1978. pp. 289. *bibliog. Twentieth Century Fund study.*

ART PATRONAGE

— United Kingdom.

ECONOMIST INTELLIGENCE UNIT. Q[arterly] E[conomic] R[eview] Specials. No. 41. Sponsorship. London, [1977]. pp. 82.

ARTHROPODA.

HASSELL (MICHAEL P.) The dynamics of arthropod predator-prey systems. Princeton, N.J., 1978. pp. 237. *bibliog.*

ARTIFICIAL INTELLIGENCE.

BODEN (MARGARET A.) Artificial intelligence and natural man. Hassocks, 1977. pp. 537. *bibliog.*

ARTIFICIAL SATELLITES.

STOCKHOLM INTERNATIONAL PEACE RESEARCH INSTITUTE. Outer space: battlefield of the future?; [written by Bhupendra M. Jasani]. London, 1978. pp. 202. *bibliog.*

ASIA

ARTIFICIAL SATELLITES IN TELECOMMUNICATION.

GARMIER (JACQUES) L'UIT et les télécommunications par satellites. Bruxelles, 1975. pp. 341. *bibliog.*

ARTISANS

— Canada — Quebec.

HARDY (JEAN PIERRE) and RUDDEL (DAVID THIERY) Les apprentis artisans à Québec, 1660-1815. Montréal, 1977. pp. 220. *bibliog.*

— Germany.

GERMANY (BUNDESREPUBLIK). Statistisches Bundesamt. Kostenstruktur im Handwerk (formerly Handwerk). quadrennial, 1970- Wiesbaden. *(Unternehmen und Arbeitsstätten. Reihe 1.1)*

— — Political activity.

VOLKOV (SHULAMIT) The rise of popular antimodernism in Germany: the urban master artisans, 1873-1896. Princeton, N.J., [1978]. pp. 399. *bibliog.*

— — Hesse.

HESSE. Statistisches Landesamt. 1978- . Ergebnisse der Handwerkszählung, 1977. Wiesbaden, 1978 in progress. *(Statistische Berichte. Handwerkszählung 1977-1, etc.)*

— United Kingdom — Political activity.

PROTHERO (IORWERTH J.) Artisans and politics in early nineteenth-century London: John Gast and his times. Folkestone, 1979. pp. 418. *bibliog.*

ARTISTS, EUROPEAN.

SHAPIRO (THEDA) Painters and politics: the European avant-garde and society, 1900-1925. New York, [1976]. pp. 341. *bibliog.*

ARTOIS

— History.

PIERRARD (PIERRE) Histoire du Nord: Flandre, Artois, Hainaut, Picardie. [Paris, 1978]. pp. 404. *bibliog.*

ARTS.

BRONOWSKI (JACOB) The visionary eye: essays in the arts, literature, and science;.. .selected and edited by Piero E. Ariotti in collaboration with Rita Bronowski. Cambridge, Mass., [1978]. pp. 185.

— Germany.

CAMPBELL (JOAN) The German Werkbund: the politics of reform in the applied arts. Princeton, [1978]. pp. 350. *bibliog.*

— Russia.

SOTSIALISTICHESKAIA revoliutsiia i iskusstvo. Moskva, 1977. pp. 319.

— South Africa.

SOUTH AFRICA. Information Service of South Africa, New York. 1970. South African tradition: a brief survey of culture and art in the Republic of South Africa. [New York, 1970]. pp. 128.

— United Kingdom.

GOODMAN (ARNOLD ABRAHAM) Baron Goodman. How much paternalism? [Colchester], 1977. pp. 19. *(University of Essex. Noel Buxton Lectures. 1977)*

ELSOM (JOHN) The arts: change and choice. London, [1978]. pp. 29.

JENKINS (HUGH) The culture gap: an experience of government and the arts. London, 1979. pp. 271.

— United States — Finance.

NETZER (DICK) The subsidized muse: public support for the arts in the United States. Cambridge, 1978. pp. 289. *bibliog. Twentieth Century Fund study.*

ARTS AND SOCIETY.

PLEKHANOV (GEORGII VALENTINOVICH) Art and society and other papers in historical materialism. New York, [1974]. pp. 187.

PLEKHANOV (GEORGII VALENTINOVICH) Estetika i sotsiologiia iskusstva: [sbornik statei, 1897-1913]. Moskva, 1978. 2 vols. *With introductory article by M. Lifshits.*

CHANEY (DAVID C.) Fictions and ceremonies: representations of popular experience. London, 1979. pp. 156. *bibliog.*

JOHNSON (LESLEY) The cultural critics: from Matthew Arnold to Raymond Williams. London, 1979. pp. 235. *bibliog.*

ARUNPUR

— Politics and government.

SHARMA (MIRIAM) The politics of inequality: competition and control in an Indian village. [Honolulu, 1978]. pp. 258. *bibliog.* (Hawaii University. Asian Studies Program. *Asian Studies at Hawaii.* 22)

— Social conditions.

SHARMA (MIRIAM) The politics of inequality: competition and control in an Indian village. [Honolulu, 1978]. pp. 258. *bibliog.* (Hawaii University. Asian Studies Program. *Asian Studies at Hawaii.* 22)

ASHBOURNE INVESTMENTS.

AULD (ROBIN ERNEST) and others. Ashbourne Investments Limited: investigation under sections 164 and 172 of the Companies Act 1948; report. London, H.M.S.O., 1979. pp. 602.

ASIA

— Bibliography.

SOUTH Asian bibliography: a handbook and guide; compiled by the South Asia Library Group; general editor: J.D. Pearson. Hassocks, 1979. pp. 381.

— Commerce — Australia.

AUSTRALIA. Bureau of Industry Economics. 1978. Industrialisation in Asia: some implications for Australian industry. Canberra, 1978. pp. 130. *bibliog. (Research Reports. 1)*

— Defences.

ASIA'S nuclear future; William H. Overholt, editor; contributors: Lewis A. Dunn [and others]. Boulder, Colo., [1977]. pp. 285. *(Columbia University. Research Institute on International Change. Studies)*

— Economic conditions.

BLACKMORE (W.H.) and others. Impact: tradition, change and problems in Asia. South Melbourne, 1970 repr. 1972. pp. 336.

AUSTRALIA. Bureau of Industry Economics. 1978. Industrialisation in Asia: some implications for Australian industry. Canberra, 1978. pp. 130. *bibliog. (Research Reports. 1)*

— — Bibliography.

LEE (MOLLY KYUNG SOOK CHANG) compiler. East Asian economics: a guide to information sources. Detroit, [1979]. pp. 326.

— Economic integration.

UNITED NATIONS. Economic Commission for Asia and the Far East. Regional Economic Cooperation Series. No. 7. Regional economic cooperation in Asia and the Far East: report of the meeting of government and central bank officials on trade and monetary cooperation; consideration and proposals for trade and monetary cooperation in the ECAFE region. (E/CN.11/958). New York, 1971. pp. 84.

— Foreign relations.

The ORIGINS of the Cold War in Asia; edited by Yonosuke Nagai and Akira Iriye. New York, [1977]. pp. 448. *bibliogs.*

The SUBCONTINENT in world policies: India, its neighbors, and the great powers; edited by Lawrence Ziring. New York, [1978]. pp. 238. *bibliogs.*

— — Europe.

The AGE of partnership: Europeans in Asia before Dominion; edited by Blair B. Kling and M.N. Pearson. Honolulu, [1979]. pp. 247. *bibliogs.*

— — United Kingdom.

INGRAM (EDWARD) The beginning of the great game in Asia, 1828-1834. Oxford, 1979. pp. 361. *bibliog.*

— — United States.

UNITED States foreign policy in Asia: an appraisal; edited by Yung-Hwan Jo. Santa Barbara, [1978]. pp. 488. *bibliogs.*

JAPAN, Korea, and China: American perceptions and policies; [by] William Watts. Lexington, Mass., [1979]. pp. 154.

— History.

BLACKMORE (W.H.) and others. Impact: tradition, change and problems in Asia. South Melbourne, 1970 repr. 1972. pp. 336.

— Industries.

AUSTRALIA. Bureau of Industry Economics. 1978. Industrialisation in Asia: some implications for Australian industry. Canberra, 1978. pp. 130. *bibliog. (Research Reports. 1)*

— Politics and government.

BLACKMORE (W.H.) and others. Impact: tradition, change and problems in Asia. South Melbourne, 1970 repr. 1972. pp. 336.

RELIGION and the legitimation of power in South Asia; edited by Bardwell L. Smith. Leiden, 1978. pp. 186. *bibliogs.*

The SUBCONTINENT in world policies: India, its neighbors, and the great powers; edited by Lawrence Ziring. New York, [1978]. pp. 238. *bibliogs.*

— Religion.

RELIGION and the legitimation of power in South Asia; edited by Bardwell L. Smith. Leiden, 1978. pp. 186. *bibliogs.*

— Social conditions.

BLACKMORE (W.H.) and others. Impact: tradition, change and problems in Asia. South Melbourne, 1970 repr. 1972. pp. 336.

— Statistics.

QUARTERLY BULLETIN OF STATISTICS FOR ASIA AND THE PACIFIC (formerly Quarterly Bulletin of Statistics for Asia and the Far East) ([pd.by] Economic and Social Commission for Asia and the Pacific) United Nations. q., S 1971(v.1, no.1)- Bangkok.

ASIA, SOUTHEAST

ASIA, SOUTHEAST
— Bibliography.
LONDON. University. School of Oriental and African Studies. Centre of South East Asian Studies. List of theses and dissertations concerned with South East Asia accepted for higher degrees of the University of London, 1965-1977. London, [1978]. fo. 11.

— Commerce — Japan.
KATANO (HIKOJI) and others. Japan's direct investment to ASEAN countries. Kobe, [1978]. pp. 152. *bibliog.* (Kobe. University. Research Institute for Economics and Business Administration. Kobe Economic and Business Research Series. No. 6)

— Economic conditions.
ECONOMIC problems and prospects in Asean countries; edited by Saw Swee-Hock and Lee Soo Ann. Singapore, [1977]. pp. 194.

FRYER (DONALD W.) Emerging Southeast Asia: a study in growth and stagnation. 2nd ed. London, [1979]. pp. 540. *bibliog.*

— History.
OSBORNE (MILTON E.) Southeast Asia: an introductory history. Sydney, 1979. pp. 205. *bibliog.*

— Neutrality.
PATHMANATHAN (MURUGESU) Conflict management in Southeast Asia: a neutralized Malaysia? Kuala Lumpur, 1977. pp. 32,4. *(University of Malaya. Faculty of Economics and Administration. Occasional Papers on Malaysian Socio-Economic Affairs. No. 7)*

— Politics and government.
LEE (YONG LENG) Southeast Asia and the law of the sea: some preliminary observations on the political geography of Southeast Asian seas. Singapore, [1978]. pp. 44. *bibliog.*

SOUTHEAST Asian transitions: approaches through social history; edited by Ruth T. McVey with the assistance of Adrienne Suddard. New Haven, 1978. pp. 242. *(Yale University. Yale Southeast Asia Studies. 8) Essays in honour of Harry J. Benda.*

— Social conditions.
SOUTHEAST Asian transitions: approaches through social history; edited by Ruth T. McVey with the assistance of Adrienne Suddard. New Haven, 1978. pp. 242. *(Yale University. Yale Southeast Asia Studies. 8) Essays in honour of Harry J. Benda.*

— Social history.
SOUTHEAST Asian transitions: approaches through social history; edited by Ruth T. McVey with the assistance of Adrienne Suddard. New Haven, 1978. pp. 242. *(Yale University. Yale Southeast Asia Studies. 8) Essays in honour of Harry J. Benda.*

ASIATICS IN THE UNITED KINGDOM.
KANNAN (C.T.) Cultural adaptation of Asian immigrants: first and second generation. Greenford, 1978. pp. 246. *bibliog.*

LLEWELYN-DAVIES WEEKS [AND PARTNERS]. Inner area study: Birmingham: Birmingham Community Relations Council: Small Heath fieldworker. [London], Department of the Environment, [1978]. pp. 38.

WANDSWORTH COUNCIL FOR COMMUNITY RELATIONS. Asians and the health service: a directory of measures implemented by area health authorities to meet the needs of the Asian community. London, 1978. pp. 30.

WILSON (AMRIT) Finding a voice: Asian women in Britain. London, [1978]. pp. 179.

REX (JOHN ARDERNE) and TOMLINSON (SALLY) Colonial immigrants in a British city: a class analysis. London, 1979. pp. 357. *bibliog.*

ASIATICS IN THE UNITED STATES.
MELENDY (HOWARD BRETT) Asians in America: Filipinos, Koreans, and East Indians. Boston, Mass., [1977]. pp. 340. *bibliog.*

ASSAM
— Social life and customs.
BAHADUR (K.P.) Caste, tribes and culture of India: Assam. Delhi, 1977. pp. 137.

ASSASSINATION
— Dominican Republic.
DIEDERICH (BERNARD) Trujillo: the death of the goat. Boston, Mass., 1978. pp. 265.

ASSIMILATION (SOCIOLOGY).
BASH (HARRY H.) Sociology, race and ethnicity: a critique of American ideological intrusions upon sociological theory. New York, [1979]. pp. 252. *bibliog.*

ASSISTANCE IN EMERGENCIES
— United States.
SHAPO (MARSHALL S.) The duty to act: tort law, power and public policy. Austin, [1977]. pp. 203.

ASSOCIATION OF COUNTY COUNCILS.
ASSOCIATION OF COUNTY COUNCILS. Brief outline of the activities of the Committees of the Association. a., 1975/77- London.

ASSOCIATION OF SOUTHEAST ASIAN NATIONS.
ECONOMIC problems and prospects in Asean countries; edited by Saw Swee-Hock and Lee Soo Ann. Singapore, [1977]. pp. 194.

FEDERATION OF MALAYSIA. Ministry of Foreign Affairs. 1977. Facts on A[ssociation of] S[outh] E[ast] A[sian] N[ations]. [Kuala Lumpur, 1977?]. pp. 132.

The FUTURE of Singapore: the global city; edited by Wee Teong-Boo. [Singapore, 1977]. pp. 219. *Includes papers delivered at the seminar "Political and economic trends in Singapore", 1975, organized by the Democratic Socialist Club, University of Singapore.*

KATANO (HIKOJI) and others. Japan's direct investment to ASEAN countries. Kobe, [1978]. pp. 152. *bibliog.* (Kobe. University. Research Institute for Economics and Business Administration. Kobe Economic and Business Research Series. No. 6)

ASSOCIATIONS, INSTITUTIONS, ETC.
KRAMER (RALPH M.) The voluntary service agency in Israel. Berkeley, [1976]. pp. 94. *bibliog.* (California University. Institute of International Studies. Research Series. No.26)

SMITH (GILBERT) Social work and the sociology of organizations. rev. ed. London, 1979. pp. 108. *bibliog.*

— Germany.
RITTER (ERNST) German historian. Das Deutsche Ausland-Institut in Stuttgart, 1917-1945: ein Beispiel deutscher Volkstumsarbeit zwischen den Weltkriegen. Wiesbaden, 1976. pp. 168. *bibliog.*

RASCHKE (PETER) Vereine und Verbände: zur Organisation von Interessen in der Bundesrepublik Deutschland. München, [1978]. pp. 272. *bibliog.*

SCHARPF (FRITZ W.) Autonome Gewerkschaften und staatliche Wirtschaftspolitik: Probleme einer Verbändegesetzgebung. Köln, [1978]. pp. 50. *(Otto Brenner Stiftung. Schriftenreihe. 12)*

— Russia.
SHCHIGLIK (ARON ISAAKOVICH) Zakonomernosti stanovleniia i razvitiia obshchestvennykh organizatsii v SSSR: politiko-pravovoe issledovanie. Moskva, 1977. pp. 253.

— United Kingdom.
COOK (CHRISTOPHER PIERS) and WEEKS (JEFFREY) compilers. Sources in British political history, 1900-1951: compiled for the British Library of Political and Economic Science; vol. 5. London, 1978. pp. 221.

U.K. 1978. The government and the voluntary sector: a consultative document. [London, 1978]. pp. 53.

BOEHM (KLAUS) and MORRIS (BRIAN) Civil servant. Who decides what: the citizen's handbook. London, 1979. pp. 472.

— — Directories.
OVERSEAS DEVELOPMENT INSTITUTE. Development guide: a directory of non-commercial organisations in Britain actively concerned in overseas development and training. 3rd ed. London, 1978. pp. 216.

— United States.
POPULATION COUNCIL. The Population Council: a chronicle of the first twenty-five years, 1952-1977. New York, [1978]. pp. 210.

— — Dictionaries and encyclopedias.
ENCYCLOPEDIA of associations;...Nancy Yakes [and] Denise Akey, co-editors. 13th ed. Detroit, [1979 in progress].

ASTRONAUTICS
— International cooperation.
KHOZIN (GRIGORII SERGEEVICH) SSSR - SShA: orbity kosmicheskogo sotrudnichestva. Moskva, 1976. pp. 160.

VERESHCHETIN (VLADLEN STEPANOVICH) Mezhdunarodnoe sotrudnichestvo v kosmose: pravovye voprosy. Moskva, 1977. pp. 264. *bibliog.*

ASTRONOMY.
HOYLE (Sir FRED) Astronomy and cosmology: a modern course. San Francisco, [1975]. pp. 729. *bibliogs.*

BRANDT (JOHN C.) and MARAN (STEPHEN P.) The new astronomy and space science reader. San Francisco, [1977]. pp. 371. *bibliogs.*

— History.
DRAKE (STILLMAN) Galileo at work: his scientific biography. Chicago, 1978. pp. 536.

ASTURIAS
— Emigration and immigration.
MARTINEZ CACHERO (LUIS ALFONSO) La emigracion asturiana a America. Salinas, Oviedo, [1976]. pp. 153. *bibliog.*

ASYLUM, RIGHT OF.
AMNESTY INTERNATIONAL. Sektion der Bundesrepublik Deutschland. Politisches Asyl in der Bundesrepublik Deutschland: Grundlagen und Praxis, Erfahrungsbericht und Dokumentation. Baden-Baden, 1977. pp. 335. *bibliog.*

ASYMPTOTIC EXPANSIONS.
ERDELYI (ARTHUR) Asymptotic expansions. New York, [1956]. pp. 108. *bibliog.*

BHATTACHARYA (RABINDRA NATH) and RAO (RAMASWAMY RANGA) Normal approximation and asymptotic expansions. New York, [1976]. pp. 274. *bibliog.*

ATHEISM.

PLEKHANOV (GEORGII VALENTINOVICH) Ob ateizme i religii v istorii obshchestva i kul'tury: izbrannye proizvedeniia i izvlecheniia iz trudov. Moskva, 1977. pp. 355.

KOBETSKII (VLADIMIR DMITRIEVICH) Sotsiologicheskoe izuchenie religioznosti i ateizma. Leningrad, 1978. pp. 118. *bibliog.*

KOLESNIKOV (ANATOLII SERGEEVICH) Svobodomyslie Bertrana Rassela [i.e. Bertrand Russell]. Moskva, 1978. pp. 133. *bibliog.*

ATLANTA

— Politics and government.

WATTS (EUGENE J.) The social bases of city politics: Atlanta, 1865-1903. Westport, Conn., 1978. pp. 188. *bibliog.*

ATLANTIC, THE

— Defences.

NEW strategic factors in the North Atlantic; edited by Christoph Bertram and Johan Jørgen Holst. Oslo, [1977]. pp. 193. *(Norsk Utenrikspolitisk Institutt. Norwegian Foreign Policy Studies. Nr. 21)*

— Economic history.

DAVIS (RALPH) Professor of Economic History, Leicester University. The rise of the Atlantic economies. London, [1973]. pp. 352. *bibliog.*

ATLANTIC COMMUNITY

— Bibliography.

GORDON (COLIN) compiler. The Atlantic Alliance; a bibliography. London, 1978. pp. 216.

ATLANTIC INSTITUTE FOR INTERNATIONAL AFFAIRS.

ATLANTIC INSTITUTE. Statement of purpose and programs. Paris, 1979. pp. 31.

ATOMIC BOMB.

GOWING (MARGARET MARY) Science and politics. London, [1977]. pp. 16. *(London. University. Birkbeck College. Bernal Lectures. 1977)*

ATOMIC ENERGY.

GOWING (MARGARET MARY) Reflections on atomic energy history. Cambridge, 1978. pp. 26. *(Cambridge. University. Rede Lectures. 1978)*

ROBERTS (ALAN) The self-managing environment. London, [1979]. pp. 189. *bibliog.*

— International cooperation.

SYMPOSIUM ON INTERNATIONAL CO-OPERATION IN THE NUCLEAR FIELD: PERSPECTIVES AND PROSPECTS, PARIS, 1978. Proceedings. Paris, Nuclear Energy Agency, Organisation for Economic Co-operation and Development, [1978]. pp. 137.

— Social aspects.

NUCLEAR or not: choices for our energy future: a Royal Institute forum; edited by Gerald Foley and Ariane van Buren. London, 1978. pp. 205. *bibliogs.*

ATOMIC ENERGY INDUSTRIES

— United States.

AHMED (S. BASHEER) Nuclear fuel and energy policy. Lexington, Mass., [1979]. pp. 158. *bibliog.*

ATOMIC POWER.

KLEMA (ERNEST D.) and WEST (ROBERT L.) compilers. Public regulation of site selection for nuclear power plants: present procedures and reform proposals; an annotated bibliography. Washington, 1977. pp. 129. *(Resources for the Future, Inc. Research Papers. R-2)*

— Law and legislation — United States.

KLEMA (ERNEST D.) and WEST (ROBERT L.) compilers. Public regulation of site selection for nuclear power plants: present procedures and reform proposals; an annotated bibliography. Washington, 1977. pp. 129. *(Resources for the Future, Inc. Research Papers. R-2)*

— United States — Security measures.

EDELHERTZ (HERBERT) and WALSH (MARILYN) The white-collar challenge to nuclear safeguards. Lexington, Mass., [1978]. pp. 101.

ATOMIC POWER INDUSTRY

— Environmental aspects.

STOCKTON (BAYARD) and JANKE (PETER F.) Nuclear power: protest and violence. London, 1978. pp. 20. *bibliog. (Institute for the Study of Conflict. Conflict Studies. No.102)*

— France.

FRANCE. Commission Consultative pour la Production d'Electricité d'Origine Nucléaire. 1973. Rapport. [Paris], 1973. 2 vols.

— Italy.

Una STRATEGIA per lo sviluppo energetico italiano; [by] G. Cozzi [and others]. Milano, [1977]. pp. 356.

— United Kingdom.

BREACH (IAN) Windscale fallout: a primer for the age of nuclear controversy. Harmondsworth, 1978. pp. 192.

ATOMIC POWER-PLANTS

— Safety measures — United Kingdom.

U.K. Health and Safety Executive. Health and safety: nuclear establishments. a., 1975/76(1st)- London.

— United States — Location.

KLEMA (ERNEST D.) and WEST (ROBERT L.) compilers. Public regulation of site selection for nuclear power plants: present procedures and reform proposals; an annotated bibliography. Washington, 1977. pp. 129. *(Resources for the Future, Inc. Research Papers. R-2)*

ATOMIC WEAPONS.

STEINBRUNER (JOHN D.) The cybernetic theory of decision: new dimensions of political analysis. Princeton, N.J. [1974]. pp. 366. *bibliog.*

ASIA'S nuclear future; William H. Overholt, editor; contributors: Lewis A. Dunn [and others]. Boulder, Colo., [1977]. pp. 285. *(Columbia University. Research Institute on International Change. Studies)*

HAGEN (LAWRENCE S.) Civil defence: the case for reconsideration. Kingston, Ont., 1977. pp. 88. *bibliog. (Kingston, Ontario. Queen's University. Center for International Relations. National Security Series. No. 7/77)*

SMART (IAN) The future of the British nuclear deterrent: technical, economic and strategic issues. London, [1977]. pp. 82. *(Royal Institute of International Affairs. British Foreign Policy to 1985)*

COURTEIX (SIMONE) Exportations nucléaires et non-prolifération. Paris, 1978. pp. 263. *bibliog. (Paris. Université de Paris I (Panthéon- Sorbonne). Recherches Panthéon-Sorbonne. Série Sciences Juridiques. Droit des Relations Internationales)*

STOCKHOLM INTERNATIONAL PEACE RESEARCH INSTITUTE. Tactical nuclear weapons: European perspectives; [edited by Frank Barnaby]. London, 1978. pp. 371.

VAN CLEAVE (WILLIAM R.) and COHEN (S.T.) Tactical nuclear weapons: an examination of the issues. London, [1978]. pp. 119. *bibliog.*

LEFEVER (ERNEST WARREN) Nuclear arms in the Third World: U.S. policy dilemma. Washington, D.C., [1979]. pp. 154.

— Testing.

DIVINE (ROBERT A.) Blowing on the wind: the nuclear test ban debate, 1954-1960. New York, 1978. pp. 393. *bibliog.*

ATOMIC WEAPONS AND DISARMAMENT.

COX (ARTHUR MACY) The dynamics of détente: how to end the arms race. New York, [1976]. pp. 256. *bibliog.*

NUCLEAR proliferation and safeguards; [report prepared by] Office of Technology Assessment Energy Program staff. New York, 1977. pp. 270.

COURTEIX (SIMONE) Exportations nucléaires et non-prolifération. Paris, 1978. pp. 263. *bibliog. (Paris. Université de Paris I (Panthéon- Sorbonne). Recherches Panthéon-Sorbonne. Série Sciences Juridiques. Droit des Relations Internationales)*

DISARM or die: a disarmament reader for the leaders and the peoples of the world; published on behalf of the Non-Partisan Fund for World Disarmament and Development. London, 1978. pp. 108.

DIVINE (ROBERT A.) Blowing on the wind: the nuclear test ban debate, 1954-1960. New York, 1978. pp. 393. *bibliog.*

RAMBERG (BENNETT) The seabed arms control negotiations: a study of multilateral arms control conference diplomacy. Denver, [1978]. pp. 135. *bibliog. (Denver. University. Graduate School of International Studies. Monograph Series in World Affairs. vol. 15, no. 2)*

STOCKHOLM INTERNATIONAL PEACE RESEARCH INSTITUTE. Tactical nuclear weapons: European perspectives; [edited by Frank Barnaby]. London, 1978. pp. 371.

MENAUL (STEWART WILLIAM BLACKER) Salt II: the Eurostrategic imbalance. London, 1979. pp. 17. *(Institute for the Study of Conflict. Conflict Studies. No.104)*

STOCKHOLM INTERNATIONAL PEACE RESEARCH INSTITUTE. Postures for non-proliferation: arms limitation and security policies to minimize nuclear proliferation. London, 1979. pp. 168.

ATOMISM.

BOLTZMANN (LUDWIG) Theoretical physics and philosophical problems: selected writings [translated from the German by Paul Foulkes]; edited by Brian McGuinness. Dordrecht, [1974]. pp. 280. *bibliog.*

ATTACHMENT AND GARNISHMENT.

PUCKETT (THOMAS COLLIN) Wage garnishment: a study of the problem in a Canadian metropolis. 1978. fo. 443. *bibliog.* Typescript. Ph.D. (London) thesis: unpublished. Copy of questionnaire in end pocket. *This thesis is the property of London University and may not be removed from the Library.*

ATTACK AND DEFENCE (MILITARY SCIENCE).

CRITCHLEY (JULIAN) Warning and response: a study of surprise attack in the twentieth century and an analysis of its lessons for the future. London, 1978. pp. 123.

ATTITUDE (PSYCHOLOGY).

CHISMAN (FORREST P.) Attitude psychology and the study of public opinion. University Park, Pa., [1976]. pp. 253. *bibliog.*

OSKAMP (STUART) Attitudes and opinions. Englewood Cliffs, [1977]. pp. 466. *bibliogs.*

ATTITUDE CHANGE.

ATTITUDE change: the competing views; edited by Peter Suedfeld. Chicago, 1971. pp. 259. *bibliogs.*

ATTRIBUTION (SOCIAL PSYCHOLOGY).

NEW directions in attribution research; volume 1; edited by John H. Harvey [and others]. Hillsdale, N.J., 1976. pp. 467. *bibliogs.*

AUCKLAND

— Industries.

TAYLOR (MICHAEL J.) Behavioural considerations in the location of industry in Auckland. [Auckland, Auckland Regional Authority], 1977. pp. 70.

AUCTIONS.

CONFERENCE ON BIDDING AND AUCTIONING, NEW YORK UNIVERSITY, 1975. Bidding and auctioning for procurement and allocation: proceedings of a conference at the Center for Applied Economics, New York University; edited by Yakov Amihud. New York, 1976. pp. 220. *bibliogs.*

AUDITING.

CYPRUS. Audit Office. Audit review. s-a., My 1978 (v. 1, no. 1)- Nicosia.

EUROPEAN COMMUNITIES. Commission. 1978. Proposal for an Eighth Directive pursuant to Article 54(3)(g) of the EEC Treaty concerning the approval of persons responsible for carrying out statutory audits of the annual accounts of limited liability companies: presented...to the Council on 24 April 1978. [Brussels, 1978]. pp. 23. *(Bulletin of the European Communities. Supplements. [1978/4]) Includes an explanatory memorandum.*

INTERNATIONAL CONGRESS OF ACCOUNTANTS, 11TH, MUNICH, 1977. Accounting and auditing in one world; proceedings of the ... congress. Düsseldorf, 1978. pp. 511.

AUDITORS

— Legal status, laws, etc. — European Economic Community countries.

EUROPEAN COMMUNITIES. Commission. 1978. Proposal for an Eighth Directive pursuant to Article 54(3)(g) of the EEC Treaty concerning the approval of persons responsible for carrying out statutory audits of the annual accounts of limited liability companies: presented...to the Council on 24 April 1978. [Brussels, 1978]. pp. 23. *(Bulletin of the European Communities. Supplements. [1978/4]) Includes an explanatory memorandum.*

— Sri Lanka.

SRI LANKA. Committee on Duties, Responsibilities and Standards of Professional Accountants and Auditors. 1974. Report...to the Public Acco[u]nts Committee; [P.M.W. Wijesuriya, chairman]. Colombo, 1974. pp. 120. *(Sri Lanka. Parliament. Sessional Papers. 1974. No. 11)*

AUSTRALIA

— Australian Government Rehabilitation Service.

LE SUEUR (EDDIE J.) The Australia Government Rehabilitation Service. Canberra, 1977. pp. 108. *(Australia. Commission of Inquiry into Poverty. Social/Medical Aspects of Poverty Series)*

— Civilization.

WINDEYER (Sir WILLIAM JOHN VICTOR) Australia in the Commonwealth. London, 1978. pp. 32. *(Cambridge. University. Commonwealth Lectures. 1977)*

— Commerce.

AUSTRALIA. Department of Overseas Trade. 1976. Information on the operation of the Australian generalised system of preferences in 1974/75. [Canberra, 1976]. 1 pamphlet (various pagings).

AUSTRALIA. Department of Overseas Trade. 1977. Australia's overseas trade: an introduction. [Canberra, 1977]. pp. 28.

— — Asia.

AUSTRALIA. Bureau of Industry Economics. 1978. Industrialisation in Asia: some implications for Australian industry. Canberra, 1978. pp. 130. *bibliog. (Research Reports. 1)*

— — Europe, Eastern.

SPROTT (D.C.) and HEARN (S.E.) Agricultural developments and the prospect for trade with the Comecon countries. Canberra, 1974. pp. 34. *(Australia. Bureau of Agricultural Economics. Occasional Papers. No.24)*

— Constitution.

WILSON (L.G.) A new start in a new state?: is an aboriginal new state movement the way towards rehabilitation of the aboriginal people? Brisbane, 1973. pp. 33.

LANE (PATRICK HARDING) An introduction to the Australian constitution. 2nd ed. Sydney, 1977. pp. 350.

— Constitutional law.

LANE (PATRICK HARDING) An introduction to the Australian constitution. 2nd ed. Sydney, 1977. pp. 350.

— Economic conditions.

SURVEYS of Australian economics; edited by F.H. Gruen for the Academy of the Social Sciences in Australia. Sydney, 1978. pp. 296. *bibliog.*

BRAIN (PETER J.) and others. Population, immigration and the Australian economy. London, [1979]. pp. 404. *bibliog.*

— — Mathematical models.

CONFERENCE IN APPLIED ECONOMIC RESEARCH, RESERVE BANK OF AUSTRALIA, 1977. [Papers of the conference]. [Sydney, 1978?]. pp. 347. *bibliogs.*

— — Statistics.

AUSTRALIA. Commonwealth Bureau of Census and Statistics. Monthly review of business statistics. m., N 1937(no.2)- , with gaps (Ap 1968, no. 365; D 1973, no. 433). Canberra.

ROUND-UP OF ECONOMIC STATISTICS; pd. for the Treasury [Australia]. m., F 1973(no.1)- Canberra.

— Emigration and immigration.

MARTIN (JEAN I.) The migrant presence: Australian responses, 1947-1977. Sydney, 1978. pp. 261. *bibliog. Research report for the National Population Inquiry.*

SALTER (MOIRA JOAN) Studies in the immigration of the highly skilled. Canberra, 1978. pp. 208. *bibliog. (Academy of the Social Sciences in Australia. Immigrants in Australia. 7)*

BRAIN (PETER J.) and others. Population, immigration and the Australian economy. London, [1979]. pp. 404. *bibliog.*

— Exiles.

RUDÉ (GEORGE E.) Protest and punishment: the story of the social and political protesters transported to Australia 1788-1868. Oxford, 1978. pp. 270. *bibliog.*

— Foreign relations.

MILLAR (THOMAS BRUCE) Australia in peace and war: external relations, 1788-1977. London, 1978. pp. 578. *bibliog.*

— History.

CLARKE (FRANCIS GORDON) The land of contrarieties: British attitudes to the Australian colonies, 1828-1835. Melbourne, 1977. pp. 223. *bibliog.*

WINDEYER (Sir WILLIAM JOHN VICTOR) Australia in the Commonwealth. London, 1978. pp. 32. *(Cambridge. University. Commonwealth Lectures. 1977)*

— — Sources.

MANDER JONES (PHYLLIS) compiler. Manuscripts in the British Isles relating to Australia, New Zealand and the Pacific. Honolulu, [1972]. pp. 697.

— Industries.

AUSTRALIA. Department of Urban and Regional Development. 1975. The inter-relation of manufacturing industry policy and urban and regional development policy: a discussion paper based on a submission to the Committee to Advise on Policies for Manufacturing Industry, Jackson Committee. [Canberra], 1975. pp. 109.

— Parliament.

SOLOMON (DAVID HARRIS) Inside the Australian parliament. Sydney, 1978. pp. 211. *bibliog.*

— — Elections.

AUSTRALIA at the polls: the national elections of 1975; edited by Howard R. Penniman. Washington, [1977]. pp. 373. *(American Enterprise Institute for Public Policy Research. Studies in Political and Social Processes)*

— Politics and government.

LANG (JOHN THOMAS) Communism in Australia. Sydney, [1944?]. pp. 142.

WINDEYER (Sir WILLIAM JOHN VICTOR) Australia in the Commonwealth. London, 1978. pp. 32. *(Cambridge. University. Commonwealth Lectures. 1977)*

KERR (Sir JOHN ROBERT) Matters for judgment: an autobiography. London, 1979. pp. 468. *bibliog. First published in Australia in 1978.*

— Population.

AUSTRALIA. Department of Immigration. 1973. Australia's human resources: an address to the Australian and New Zealand Association for the Advancement of Science; by...A.J. Grassby, etc. Canberra, 1973. pp. 10. *(Immigration Reference Papers)*

HICKS (NEVILLE) 'This sin and scandal': Australia's population debate, 1891-1911. Canberra, 1978. pp. 208. *bibliog.*

— Race relations.

WHO are our enemies?: racism and the Australian working class; edited by Ann Curthoys and Andrew Markus. Neutral Bay, 1978. pp. 211.

MARKUS (ANDREW) Fear and hatred: purifying Australia and California, 1850-1901. Sydney, 1979. pp. 95.

— Rural conditions.

AUSTRALIA. Industries Assistance Commission. 1978. Rural income fluctuations. Canberra, 1978. pp. 121. *(Reports. No. 161)*

— Social conditions.

AUSTRALIA. Department of Immigration. 1973. A multi-cultural society for the future: a paper prepared for the Cairnmillar Institute's symposium 'Strategy 2000: Australia for Tomorrow'; by...A.J. Grassby, etc. Canberra, 1973. pp. 15. *(Immigration Reference Papers)*

ABORIGINES and change: Australia in the '70s; edited by R.M. Berndt. Canberra, [1977]. pp. 424. *bibliogs. (Australian Institute of Aboriginal Studies. Social Anthropology Series. No. 11) Papers presented to a symposium at the 1974 meeting of the Australian Institute of Aboriginal Studies.*

— Statistics, Vital.

AUSTRALIA. Commonwealth Bureau of Census and Statistics. 1976. Australian life tables, 1970-1972. [Canberra, 1976]. pp. 16.

AUSTRALIAN ABORIGINES.

WILSON (L.G.) A new start in a new state?: is an aboriginal new state movement the way towards rehabilitation of the aboriginal people? Brisbane, 1973. pp. 33.

ABORIGINES and change: Australia in the '70s; edited by R.M. Berndt. Canberra, [1977]. pp. 424. *bibliogs.* (Australian Institute of Aboriginal Studies. Social Anthropology Series. No. 11) *Papers presented to a symposium at the 1974 meeting of the Australian Institute of Aboriginal Studies.*

COOMBS (HERBERT COLE) Australia's policy towards Aborigines, 1967-1977. London, 1978. pp. 20. *bibliog.* (Minority Rights Group. Reports. No.35)

ROBERTS (JANINE) From massacres to mining: the colonization of aboriginal Australia. London, [1978]. pp. 212. *bibliog.*

SCHEFFLER (HAROLD WALTER) Australian kin classification. Cambridge, 1978. pp. 567. *bibliog.*

AUSTRALIAN INFORMATION SERVICE. The Australian aboriginals. [Canberra], 1979. pp. 19. (Reference Papers)

— Economic conditions.

ALTMAN (JON C.) and NIEUWENHUYSEN (JOHN PETER) The economic status of Australian aborigines. Cambridge, 1979. pp. 230. *bibliog.*

AUSTRALIAN PERIODICALS
— Bibliography.

CURRENT AUSTRALIAN SERIALS: a select list; [pd. by] National Library of Australia. irreg. Canberra. *Current issue only kept.*

AUSTRIA
— Constitutional history.

ROSDOLSKY (ROMAN) Die Bauernabgeordneten im konstituierenden österreichischen Reichstag, 1848-1849. Wien, 1976. pp. 234. *bibliog.* (Ludwig Boltzmann Institut für Geschichte der Arbeiterbewegung. Materialien zur Arbeiterbewegung. Nr. 5)

— Constitutional law.

BERCHTOLD (KLAUS) ed. Die Verfassungsreform von 1929: Dokumente und Materialien zur Bundes-Verfassungsgesetz-Novelle von 1929. Wien, [1979]. 2 vols.

— Economic history.

HUERTAS (THOMAS F.) Economic growth and economic policy in a multinational setting: the Habsburg Monarchy, 1841-1865. New York, 1977. pp. 114. *bibliog.*

BRANDT (HARM HINRICH) Der österreichische Neoabsolutismus: Staatsfinanzen und Politik, 1848-1860. Göttingen, 1978. 2 vols. *bibliog.* (Bayerische Akademie der Wissenschaften. Historische Kommission. Schriftenreihe. Schrift 15)

SCHULMEISTER (OTTO) Der zweite Anschluss: Österreichs Verwandlung seit 1945. Wien, [1979]. pp. 256.

— Economic policy.

SCHMIDJELL (R.) Die Wirtschaftspolitik der Bundesländer. Wien, 1976. pp. 213. *bibliog.* (Institut für Angewandte Sozial- und Wirtschaftsforschung. Schriftenreihe. Heft 27)

HUERTAS (THOMAS F.) Economic growth and economic policy in a multinational setting: the Habsburg Monarchy, 1841-1865. New York, 1977. pp. 114. *bibliog.*

— Foreign economic relations.

Der KLEINSTAAT in der europäischen wirtschaftlichen Zusammenarbeit, aus der Sicht Ungarns und Österreichs; wissenschaftliche Gesamtleitung: Wilhelm Weber. Wien, 1975. pp. 165. (Österreichisches Ost- und Südosteuropa-Institut. Schriftenreihe. Band 5)

— Foreign relations.

JELAVICH (BARBARA) The Habsburg Empire in European affairs, 1814-1918. Hamden, Conn., 1975. pp. 190. *First published in Chicago in 1969.*

KIRCHSCHLAEGER (RUDOLF) Reden, 1974-1977; herausgegeben von Karl Heinz Ritschel. [Salzburg, 1978]. pp. 418.

KLENNER (FRITZ) Eine Renaissance Mitteleuropas: die Nationwerdung Österreichs. Wien, [1978]. pp. 272. *bibliog.*

— — Treaties.

Das JULIABKOMMEN von 1936: Vorgeschichte, Hintergründe und Folgen: Protokoll des Symposiums in Wien am 10. und 11. Juni 1976; (herausgegeben von Ludwig Jedlicka und Rudolf Neck). Wien, 1977. pp. 480. (Theodor-Körner-Stiftungsfonds, and Leopold-Kunschak-Preis. Wissenschaftliche Kommission zur Erforschung der Österreichischen Geschichte der Jahre 1927 bis 1938. Veröffentlichungen. Band 4)

— — Germany.

Das JULIABKOMMEN von 1936: Vorgeschichte, Hintergründe und Folgen: Protokoll des Symposiums in Wien am 10. und 11. Juni 1976; (herausgegeben von Ludwig Jedlicka und Rudolf Neck). Wien, 1977. pp. 480. (Theodor-Körner-Stiftungsfonds, and Leopold-Kunschak-Preis. Wissenschaftliche Kommission zur Erforschung der Österreichischen Geschichte der Jahre 1927 bis 1938. Veröffentlichungen. Band 4)

— — Italy.

JENKS (WILLIAM ALEXANDER) Francis Joseph and the Italians, 1849-1859. Charlottesville, 1978. pp. 206. *bibliog.*

— History.

STADLER (KARL RUDOLF) Austria. London, 1971. pp. 346. *bibliog.*

KLENNER (FRITZ) Eine Renaissance Mitteleuropas: die Nationwerdung Österreichs. Wien, [1978]. pp. 272. *bibliog.*

— — 1789-1918.

JELAVICH (BARBARA) The Habsburg Empire in European affairs, 1814-1918. Hamden, Conn., 1975. pp. 190. *First published in Chicago in 1969.*

— — 1848-1867.

BRANDT (HARM HINRICH) Der österreichische Neoabsolutismus: Staatsfinanzen und Politik, 1848-1860. Göttingen, 1978. 2 vols. *bibliog.* (Bayerische Akademie der Wissenschaften. Historische Kommission. Schriftenreihe. Schrift 15)

— — 1848-1849, Revolution.

ROSDOLSKY (ROMAN) Die Bauernabgeordneten im konstituierenden österreichischen Reichstag, 1848-1849. Wien, 1976. pp. 234. *bibliog.* (Ludwig Boltzmann Institut für Geschichte der Arbeiterbewegung. Materialien zur Arbeiterbewegung. Nr. 5)

STEINER (HERBERT) 1923- . Karl Marx in Wien: die Arbeiterbewegung zwischen Revolution und Restauration, 1848. Wien, [1978]. pp. 223.

— — 1867-1918.

JEDLICKA (LUDWIG) Vom alten zum neuen Österreich: Fallstudien zur österreichischen Zeitgeschichte, 1900-1975. St. Pölten, 1977. pp. 496. *bibliog.*

— — 1900- .

JEDLICKA (LUDWIG) Vom alten zum neuen Österreich: Fallstudien zur österreichischen Zeitgeschichte, 1900-1975. St. Pölten, 1977. pp. 496. *bibliog.*

— — 1918-1938.

Das JULIABKOMMEN von 1936: Vorgeschichte, Hintergründe und Folgen: Protokoll des Symposiums in Wien am 10. und 11. Juni 1976; (herausgegeben von Ludwig Jedlicka und Rudolf Neck). Wien, 1977. pp. 480. (Theodor-Körner-Stiftungsfonds, and Leopold-Kunschak-Preis. Wissenschaftliche Kommission zur Erforschung der Österreichischen Geschichte der Jahre 1927 bis 1938. Veröffentlichungen. Band 4)

FINIS Austriae: Österreich, März 1938; (Franz Danimann, Hrsg.). Wien, [1978]. pp. 287. *bibliog.*

HOLTMANN (EVERHARD) Zwischen Unterdrückung und Befriedung: sozialistische Arbeiterbewegung und autoritäres Regime in Österreich, 1933- 1938. Wien, [1978]. pp. 328. *bibliog.* (Theodor-Körner-Stiftungsfonds, and Leopold- Kunschak-Preis. Wissenschaftliche Kommission zur Erforschung der Österreichischen Geschichte der Jahre 1918 bis 1938. Studien und Quellen zur Österreichischen Zeitgeschichte. Band 1)

INTERNATIONALE TAGUNG DER HISTORIKER DER ARBEITERBEWEGUNG, 1975. Einheits- und Volksfrontpolitik, 1935-1939; Klassenkampf und nationale Frage zur Zeit der II. Internationale; (bearbeitet von Hans Hautmann). Wien, 1978. pp. 335. (Internationale Tagung der Historiker der Arbeiterbewegung. ITH-Tagungsberichte. Band 10)

KOCH (HANNSJOACHIM WOLFGANG) Der deutsche Bürgerkrieg: eine Geschichte der deutschen und österreichischen Freikorps, 1918-1923. Berlin, [1978]. pp. 487. *bibliog.*

WEST (FRANZ) Die Linke im Ständestaat Österreich: Revolutionäre Sozialisten und Kommunisten, 1934-1938. Wien, [1978]. pp. 353. (Ludwig Boltzmann Institut für Geschichte der Arbeiterbewegung. Schriftenreihe. 8)

WIEN 1938; [by the Kommission Wien 1938; edited by Felix Czeike]. Wien, 1978. pp. 326. *bibliog.* (Vienna. Verein für Geschichte der Stadt Wien. Forschungen und Beiträge zur Wiener Stadtgeschichte. Band 2)

Die EREIGNISSE des 15. Juli 1927: Protokoll des Symposiums in Wien am 15. Juni 1977; (herausgegeben von Rudolf Neck und Adam Wandruszka). München, 1979. pp. 256. (Theodor-Körner-Stiftungsfonds, and Leopold-Kunschak- Preis. Wissenschaftliche Kommission zur Erforschung der Österreichischen Geschichte der Jahre 1918 bis 1938. Veröffentlichungen. Band 5)

— — 1934, Socialist Uprising, February.

INTERNATIONALE TAGUNG DER HISTORIKER DER ARBEITERBEWEGUNG, 1974. Arbeiterbewegung und Faschismus; Der Februar 1934 in Österreich; (bearbeitet von Gerhard Botz). Wien, 1976. pp. 464. (Internationale Tagung der Historiker der Arbeiterbewegung. ITH-Tagungsberichte. Band 9)

DUCZYNSKA (ILONA) Workers in arms: the Austrian Schutzbund and the civil war of 1934. New York, [1978]. pp. 256. *bibliog. An abridged version of Der demokratische Bolschewik, published in Munich, 1945.*

— — 1938-1945.

BOTZ (GERHARD) Wien vom "Anschluss" zum Krieg: nationalsozialistische Machtübernahme und politisch-soziale Umgestaltung am Beispiel der Stadt Wien, 1938/39; mit einem einleitenden Beitrag von Karl R. Stadler. Wien, [1978]. pp. 646. *bibliog.*

FINIS Austriae: Österreich, März 1938; (Franz Danimann, Hrsg.). Wien, [1978]. pp. 287. *bibliog.*

WIEN 1938; [by the Kommission Wien 1938; edited by Felix Czeike]. Wien, 1978. pp. 326. *bibliog.* (Vienna. Verein für Geschichte der Stadt Wien. Forschungen und Beiträge zur Wiener Stadtgeschichte. Band 2)

— — 1945-1955, Allied occupation.

SCHULMEISTER (OTTO) Der zweite Anschluss: Österreichs Verwandlung seit 1945. Wien, [1979]. pp. 256.

— — 1955- .

SCHULMEISTER (OTTO) Der zweite Anschluss: Österreichs Verwandlung seit 1945. Wien, [1979]. pp. 256.

AUSTRIA (Cont.)

— Industries.

BEIRAT FÜR WIRTSCHAFTS- UND SOZIALFRAGEN. [Publikationen. 32]. Vorschläge zur Industriepolitik II. Wien, 1978. pp. 107.

— Intellectual life.

FUCHS (ALBERT) Geistige Strömungen in Österreich, 1867-1918. Wien, [1978]. pp. 320. *bibliog. Nachdruck der Ausgabe 1949.*

— Konstituierender Reichstag.

ROSDOLSKY (ROMAN) Die Bauernabgeordneten im konstituierenden österreichischen Reichstag, 1848-1849. Wien, 1976. pp. 234. *bibliog. (Ludwig Boltzmann Institut für Geschichte der Arbeiterbewegung. Materialien zur Arbeiterbewegung. Nr. 5)*

— Politics and government.

FUCHS (ALBERT) Geistige Strömungen in Österreich, 1867-1918. Wien, [1978]. pp. 320. *bibliog. Nachdruck der Ausgabe 1949.*

KIRCHSCHLAEGER (RUDOLF) Reden, 1974-1977; herausgegeben von Karl Heinz Ritschel. [Salzburg, 1978]. pp. 418.

RIEDLSPERGER (MAX E.) The lingering shadow of Nazism: the Austrian Independence Party Movement since 1945. Boulder, Colo., 1978. pp. 214. *bibliog. (East European Quarterly. East European Monographs. 42)*

— Population.

FINDL (PETER) and HELCZMANOVSZKI (HEIMOLD) The population of Austria. Vienna, 1977. pp. 245. *bibliog. (Committee for International Coordination of National Research in Demography. C.I.C.R.E.D. Series)*

— Social history.

BELKE (INGRID) Die sozialreformerischen Ideen von Josef Popper-Lynkeus, 1838-1921, im Zusammenhang mit allgemeinen Reformbestrebungen des Wiener Bürgertums um die Jahrhundertwende. Tübingen, 1978. pp. 296. *bibliog.*

BEWEGUNG und Klasse: Studien zur österreichischen Arbeitergeschichte...; (G. Botz [and others], Hrsg.). Wien, [1978]. pp. 841. *(Ludwig Boltzmann Institut für Geschichte der Arbeiterbewegung. Veröffentlichungen)*

AUSTRIA-HUNGARY

— Foreign relations.

DECSY (JÁNOS) Prime Minister Gyula Andrássy's influence on Habsburg foreign policy during the Franco-German War of 1870-1871. Boulder, 1979. pp. 177. *(East European Quarterly. East European Monographs. 52) (City University of New York. Brooklyn College. Department of History. Studies on Society in Change. No. 8)*

— History.

INTERUNIVERSITY CENTRE FOR EUROPEAN STUDIES. International Colloquium, 2nd, 1976. Situations révolutionnaires en Europe, 1917-1922: Allemagne, Italie, Autriche-Hongrie; Revolutionary situations in Europe, 1917-1922: Germany, Italy, Austria-Hungary...edited by Charles L. Bertrand. Montreal, 1977. pp. 251. *bibliog.*

MACARTNEY (CARLILE AYLMER) The house of Austria: the later phase 1790-1918. Edinburgh, [1978]. pp. 309.

AUSTRIAN SCHOOL OF ECONOMISTS.

LITTLECHILD (STEPHEN CHARLES) Change rules, O.K.? Birmingham, 1977. pp. 23. *Inaugural lecture given at the University of Birmingham in 1977.*

EBELING (RICHARD M.) ed. The Austrian theory of the trade cycle and other essays; by Ludwig von Mises [and others]. New York, 1978. pp. 44. *(Centre for Libertarian Studies. Occasional Papers Series. 8)*

NEW directions in Austrian economics; edited by Louis M. Spadaro. Kansas City, [1978]. pp. 239. *bibliogs. Papers sponsored by the Institute for Humane Studies and presented at a symposium.*

AUSTRIANS IN THE UNITED KINGDOM.

GOLDNER (FRANZ) Die österreichische Emigration, 1938 bis 1945. 2nd ed. Wien, [1977]. pp. 364. *bibliog.*

AUSTRIANS IN THE UNITED STATES.

GOLDNER (FRANZ) Die österreichische Emigration, 1938 bis 1945. 2nd ed. Wien, [1977]. pp. 364. *bibliog.*

AUTHORITARIANISM.

CAMBRIDGE. University. Centre of Latin American Studies. Working Papers. No. 31. On the characterisation of authoritarian regimes in Latin America; by F.H. Cardoso. Cambridge, 1978. pp. 32.

AUTHORITY.

CAPOGRASSI (GIUSEPPE) Riflessioni sull'autorità e la sua crisi...; a cura di Mario D'Addio. Milano, [1977]. pp. 290.

CARTER (APRIL) Authority and democracy. London, 1979. pp. 93.

AUTHORS, AFRICAN.

GRIFFITHS (GARETH) A double exile: African and West Indian writing between two cultures. London, 1978. pp. 205. *bibliog.*

AUTHORS, AMERICAN.

O'BRIEN (MICHAEL) The idea of the American South, 1920-1941. Baltimore, [1979]. pp. 273. *(Johns Hopkins University. Studies in Historical and Political Science. Series 97. No. 1)*

AUTHORS, ENGLISH.

BONHAM-CARTER (VICTOR) Authors by profession. London, 1978 in progress. *bibliog.*

JOHNSON (LESLEY) The cultural critics: from Matthew Arnold to Raymond Williams. London, 1979. pp. 235. *bibliog.*

AUTHORS, GERMAN.

WIESAND (ANDREAS JOHANNES) and FOHRBECK (KARLA) Literature and the public in the Federal Republic of Germany. Munich, [1976]. pp. 103.

AUTHORS, WEST INDIAN.

GRIFFITHS (GARETH) A double exile: African and West Indian writing between two cultures. London, 1978. pp. 205. *bibliog.*

AUTHORS AND PUBLISHERS

— United Kingdom.

MANN (PETER HENRY) Author-publisher relationships in scholarly publishing. London, 1978. pp. 79. *bibliog. (British Library. Research and Development Department. Reports. 5416)*

PATTEN (ROBERT LOWRY) Charles Dickens and his publishers. Oxford, [1978]. pp. 502. *bibliog.*

— United States.

BERG (A. SCOTT) Max Perkins: editor of genius. London, 1979. pp. 498.

AUTHORS AND READERS.

WIESAND (ANDREAS JOHANNES) and FOHRBECK (KARLA) Literature and the public in the Federal Republic of Germany. Munich, [1976]. pp. 103.

AUTISM.

CHURCHILL (DON W.) Language of autistic children. Washington, D.C., 1978. pp. 139. *bibliog.*

AUTOMATIC CONTROL.

ROBINSON (ENDERS ANTHONY) Random wavelets and cybernetic systems. London, 1962. pp. 125. *bibliog.*

ATHANS (MICHAEL) and FALB (PETER L.) Optimal control: an introduction to the theory and its applications. New York, [1966]. pp. 879. *bibliog. (Massachusetts Institute of Technology. Lincoln Laboratory. Publications)*

AUTOMATION

— Social aspects — United Kingdom.

FREEMAN (CHRISTOPHER) Government policies for industrial innovation. London, 1978. pp. 18. *(London. University. Birkbeck College. Bernal Lectures. 1978)*

AUTOMOBILE INDUSTRY AND TRADE.

BLOOMFIELD (GERALD) The world automotive industry. Newton Abbot, 1978. pp. 368.

— France.

BERTRAND (OLIVIER) and others. L'évolution des emplois et la main-d'oeuvre dans l'industrie automobile: problèmes et perspectives. Paris, 1977. pp. 233. *bibliog. (Centre d'Etudes et de Recherches sur les Qualifications. Dossiers. 15)*

— Turkey.

PEKARUN (IZZET) Research on the automotive industry: supply and demand in automotive products. Section 1:...sectoral research. Istanbul, 1977. pp. 274. *bibliog. (Türkiye Sınaî Kalkınma Bankası. Sector Research Publications. No.11)*

— United Kingdom.

FOREMAN-PECK (JAMES STANLEY) Economies of scale and the development of the British motor industry before 1938. 1978. fo. 234. *bibliog. Typescript. Ph.D. (London) thesis: unpublished. This thesis is the property of London University and may not be removed from the Library.*

LLOYD (IAN) Rolls-Royce: the growth of a firm. London, 1978. pp. 164.

— United States.

KENNEDY (EDWARD D.) The automobile industry: the coming of age of capitalism's favorite child. Clifton, N.J., 1972. pp. 333. *Reprint of work first published New York, 1941.*

KATZ (HAROLD) The decline of competition in the automobile industry, 1920-1940. New York, 1977. pp. 504. *bibliog.*

MAY (GEORGE SMITH) R.E. Olds: auto industry pioneer. Grand Rapids, Mich., [1977]. pp. 458.

ABERNATHY (WILLIAM J.) The productivity dilemma: roadblock to innovation in the automobile industry. Baltimore, [1978]. pp. 267. *bibliog.*

TODER (ERIC J.) and others. Trade policy and the U.S. automobile industry. New York, 1978. pp. 243. *(Charles River Associates. Research Reports).*

AUTOMOBILE INDUSTRY WORKERS

— Germany.

OPEL streikt: Ausbeutung und Kämpfe bei Opel; [by] Redaktionskollektiv in der Projektgruppe Ruhrgebietsanalyse, Bochum. Bochum, [1973?]. pp. 196.

STREIK bei Ford, Köln, Fr. 24-Do. 30. August 1973; herausgegeben von der Betriebszelle Ford der Gruppe Arbeiterkampf. Gaiganz/Ofr., 1973. pp. 236.

AUTOMOBILE OWNERSHIP.

MASSACHUSETTS. Metropolitan Area Planning Council. 1967. Affluence and mobility: a discussion of the automobile and the future of the Boston region. [Boston], 1967. fo. 13. *(Working Papers. 2)*

AUTOMOBILES

— Apparatus and supplies.

AMADUZZI (ANTONIO) and others. Studio sull'evoluzione della concentrazione industriale in Italia, 1968-1974: pneumatici, candele, accumulatori. [Brussels], Comunità Europee, 1976. pp. 341.

KIENBAUM UNTERNEHMENSBERATUNG. Untersuchung der Konzentrationsentwicklung in der Reifenindustrie sowie ein Branchenbild der Kraftfahrzeug-Elektrikindustrie in Deutschland. [Brussels], Europäischen Gemeinschaften, 1976. pp. 190.

FISHWICK (FRANCIS) A study of the evolution of concentration in the manufacture and supply of tyres, sparking plugs, and motor-vehicle accumulators for the United Kingdom. [Brussels], European Communities, 1977. pp. 119.

— Registration — New Hebrides.

NEW HEBRIDES. Condominium Bureau of Statistics. Statistical bulletin: New registrations of motor vehicles and motor vehicles on the register. a., 1962/1972- Vila. *[in English and French]*

— Service stations — United Kingdom.

U.K. Committee of Inquiry into Motorway Service Areas. 1978. Report; (with Appendices); [Peter J. Prior, chairman]. London, 1978. 2 pts.

— Statistics — Australia.

AUSTRALIA. Commonwealth Bureau of Census and Statistics. 1978. Census of motor vehicles, 30 September 1976: final statement. Canberra, 1978. pp. 2.

— — — New South Wales.

NEW SOUTH WALES. Commonwealth Bureau of Census and Statistics. New South Wales Office. 1978. Motor vehicle census, 30 September 1976: New South Wales. [Sydney, 1978]. pp. 31.

AUTOMOBILES, STEAM.

JAMES (FRANCIS) Walter Hancock and his common road steam carriages. Alresford, 1975. pp. 131, 104. *Includes a facsimile reprint of Narrative of twelve years' experiments, 1824-1836 by Walter Hancock published in London in 1838.*

AYMARA INDIANS.

LEWELLEN (TED) Peasants in transition: the changing economy of the Peruvian Aymara: a general systems approach. Boulder, Colo., [1978]. pp. 195. *bibliog.*

AZERBAIJAN

— Nationalism.

DASHDAMIROV (AFRAND FIRUDINOV) Sovetskii narod: nekotorye filosofsko-sotsiologicheskie problemy edinstva novoi istoricheskoi obshchosti. Baku, 1977. pp. 156.

AZORES

— Description and travel.

FOWLER (JOHN) Traveller. Journal of a tour through the State of New York in the year 1830 with remarks on agriculture in those parts most eligible for settlers. New York, 1970. pp. 333. *Reprint of work first published London, 1831.*

AZTEC LITERATURE

— History and criticism.

LEON-PORTILLA (MIGUEL) Pre-Columbian literatures of Mexico. Norman, 1969. pp. 191.

AZTECS.

WEAVER (MURIEL PORTER) The Aztecs, Maya, and their predecessors. New York, 1972. pp. 347. *bibliog.* (Northwestern University. Studies in Archaeology)

DUVERGER (CHRISTIAN) L'esprit du jeu chez les Aztèques. Paris, 1978. pp. 298. *bibliog.* (Paris. Ecole des Hautes Etudes en Sciences Sociales. Centre de Recherches Historiques. Civilisations et Sociétés. 59)

— Religion and mythology.

CASO (ALFONSO) The Aztecs: people of the sun;...translated [from the Spanish] by Lowell Dunham. Norman, Okla., 1958, repr. 1970. pp. 123.

LEON-PORTILLA (MIGUEL) Aztec thought and culture: a study of the ancient Nahuatl mind; translated from the Spanish by Jack Emory Davis. Norman, Okla., 1963, repr. 1975. pp. 237. *bibliog.*

BAADER (ANDREAS).

BECKER (JILLIAN) Hitler's children. rev. ed. London, 1978. pp. 415. *bibliog.*

BABEUF (FRANÇOIS NOEL).

ROSE (ROBERT BARRIE) Gracchus Babeuf: the first revolutionary communist. Stanford, 1978. pp. 434. *bibliog.*

BADEN

— Politics and government.

ELSAESSER (KONRAD) Die badische Sozialdemokratie, 1890 bis 1914: zum Zusammenhang von Bildung und Organisation. Marburg, [1978]. pp. 323. *bibliog.* (Studiengesellschaft für Sozialgeschichte und Arbeiterbewegung, Marburg. Schriftenreihe für Sozialgeschichte und Arbeiterbewegung. Band 14)

BADEN-WUERTTEMBERG

— History.

SAUER (PAUL) Demokratischer Neubeginn in Not und Elend: das Land Württemberg-Baden von 1945 bis 1952. Ulm, 1978. pp. 504. *bibliog.*

— Politics and government.

Die CDU in Baden-Württemberg und ihre Geschichte; herausgegeben von Paul-Ludwig Weinacht. Stuttgart, [1978]. pp. 399. *bibliog.*

BAGDAD RAILWAY.

WOLF (JOHN BAPTIST) The diplomatic history of the Bagdad railroad. New York, 1973. pp. 107. *bibliog.* (Missouri University. Studies. vol. 11, no. 2) *Reprint of work originally published Columbia, 1936.*

BAHAMAS

— Politics and government.

BAHAMAS. Cabinet Office. 1972. Independence for the commonwealth of the Bahamas; presented to Parliament 8th March, 1972. Nassau, [1972]. pp. 32.

— Statistics, Vital.

OSWALD (R.R.) Report on Bahamas life tables 1962-1964 and 1969-1971. Nassau, Department of Statistics, [1973]. pp. 36.

BAHAMAS ELECTRICITY CORPORATION.

BAHAMAS ELECTRICITY CORPORATION. Annual report and accounts. a., 1962/63- , with gaps (1964/65, 1966/67). Nassau.

BAHRO (RUDOLF).

BAHRO (RUDOLF) Eine Dokumentation. Köln, [1977]. pp. 111.

SOLIDARITAET mit Rudolf Bahro: Briefe in die DDR; (Hannes Schwenger, Hg.). Reinbek bei Hamburg, 1978. pp. 138.

BAHUSHEVICH (FRANTSISHAK).

MAIKHROVICH (AL'FRED STEPANOVICH) Belorusskie revoliutsionnye demokraty: vazhneishie aspekty mirovozzreniia; redaktory N.S. Kupchin, V.M. Konon. Minsk, 1977. pp. 207.

BAIL

— Australia — New South Wales.

NEW SOUTH WALES. Bureau of Crime Statistics and Research. 1977. Bail. [Sydney], 1977. pp. 27. (Research Reports. 1)

— New Zealand.

OXLEY (PRUE) Remand and bail decisions in a magistrate's court. [Wellington], 1979. pp. 135. *bibliog.* (New Zealand. Department of Justice. Research Section. Research Series. No. 7)

BAKERS AND BAKERIES

— United Kingdom.

HILL (HOWARD) Secret ingredient: the story of Fletchers' seven bakeries. Wakefield, 1978. pp. 94.

BAKUNIN (MIKHAIL ALEKSANDROVICH).

POLIANSKII (FEDOR IAKOVLEVICH) Kritika ekonomicheskikh teorii anarkhizma. Moskva, 1976. pp. 301.

BAKUNIN (MIKHAIL ALEKSANDROVICH) Michel Bakounine sur la guerre franco-allemande et la révolution sociale en France, 1870-1871. Leiden, 1977. pp. 455. (International Institute of Social History. Archives Bakounine. 6) *In French or Russian.*

DZHANGIRIAN (VLADIMIR GURGENOVICH) Kritika anglo-amerikanskoi burzhuaznoi istoriografii M.A. Bakunina i bakunizma. Moskva, 1978. pp. 181. *bibliog.*

BALANCE OF PAYMENTS.

HELLER (HEINZ ROBERT) International monetary economics. Englewood Cliffs, N.J., [1974]. pp. 230. *bibliogs.*

MINFORD (ANTHONY PATRICK LESLIE) Substitution effects, speculation and exchange rate stability. Amsterdam, 1978. pp. 222. *bibliog.*

RIECHEL (KLAUS-WALTER) Economic effects of exchange-rate changes. Lexington, [1978]. pp. 155. *bibliog.*

— Austria.

BEIRAT FÜR WIRTSCHAFTS- UND SOZIALFRAGEN. [Publikationen. 35]. Die statistische Differenz in der österreichischen Zahlungsbilanz. Wien, 1979. pp. 67.

— Singapore.

SINGAPORE. Sessional Papers. 1958. Cmd. 3. The external trade and balance of payments of Singapore, 1956. [Singapore, 1958]. pp. 13.

— Underdeveloped areas.

See UNDERDEVELOPED AREAS — Balance of payments.

— United Kingdom.

MINFORD (ANTHONY PATRICK LESLIE) Substitution effects, speculation and exchange rate stability. Amsterdam, 1978. pp. 222. *bibliog.*

— United States.

BERGSTEN (C. FRED) The dilemmas of the dollar: the economics and politics of United States international monetary policy. New York, [1975]. pp. 584.

KENEN (PETER BAIN) A model of the U.S. balance of payments. Lexington, Mass., [1978]. pp. 422.

BALANCE OF POWER.

BALANCE OF POWER.

HEURLIN (BERTEL) The threat as a concept in international politics. Copenhagen, Information and Welfare Service of the Danish Defence, 1977. pp. 32. *bibliog.*

INTERNATIONAL perceptions of the superpower military balance; edited by Donald C. Daniel. New York, [1978]. pp. 198. *bibliogs.*

DEPORTE (ANTON WILLIAM) Europe between the superpowers: the enduring balance. New Haven, 1979. pp. 256. *bibliog.*

BALANCE OF TRADE
— Egypt.

GIRGIS (MAURICE) Industrialization and trade patterns in Egypt. Tübingen, [1977]. pp. 261. *bibliog. (Kiel. Universität. Institut für Weltwirtschaft. Kieler Studien. 143)*

BALKAN STATES
— Foreign relations — United Kingdom.

MILLMAN (RICHARD) Britain and the Eastern question, 1875-1878. Oxford, 1979. pp. 613. *bibliog.*

— Historical geography.

An HISTORICAL geography of the Balkans; edited by Francis W. Carter. London, 1977. pp. 599. *bibliog.*

— Relations (general) with Russia.

BALKANSKIE strany v novoe i noveishee vremia: sbornik statei. Kishinev, 1977. pp. 178.

— Social history.

BALKANSKIE strany v novoe i noveishee vremia: sbornik statei. Kishinev, 1977. pp. 178.

BALTIC STATES
— History.

The BALTIC states in peace and war, 1917-1945; edited by V. Stanley Vardys and Romuald J. Misiunas. University Park, [1978]. pp. 240. *bibliog.*

BALUCHISTAN.

BALUCHISTAN. Information Directorate. 1970. Baluchistan: an introduction. Quetta, 1970. pp. 28. *Cover title: Baluchistan: the youngest and largest province of Pakistan.*

— Economic policy.

BALUCHISTAN. Information Directorate. 1970. Baluchistan begins: 1970-71 development plan. [Quetta, 1970]. pp. 21.

— Social policy.

BALUCHISTAN. Information Directorate. 1970. Baluchistan begins: 1970-71 development plan. [Quetta, 1970]. pp. 21.

BANACH SPACES.

BARBU (VIOREL) Nonlinear semigroups and differential equations in Banach spaces. Bucureşti, 1976. pp. 352. *bibliog.*

PROBABILITY on Banach spaces; edited by James Kuelbs. New York, [1978]. pp. 521. *bibliog.*

BANBURY
— Politics and government.

HODGKINS (JOHN R.) Over the hills to glory: radicalism in Banburyshire, 1832-1945. Southend, [1978]. pp. 218.

BANCA D'ITALIA.

GATTONI (ROMANO) Come funziona la Banca d'Italia e il sistema delle banche. Roma, [1977]. pp. 105.

BANCO INDUSTRIAL DEL PERU.

PERU. Direccion General de Asuntos Financieros. 1976. g actividad del Banco Industrial del Peru: el fomento del desarrollo industrial en provincias, 1970-1974. Lima, 1976. 3 vols. (in 1).

BANDA (HASTINGS KAMUZU).

WILLIAMS (T. DAVID) Malawi: the politics of despair. Ithaca, 1978. pp. 339. *bibliog.*

BANDA ISLANDS
— Colonization.

HANNA (WILLARD A.) Indonesian Banda: colonialism and its aftermath in the Nutmeg Islands. Philadelphia, [1978]. pp. 164. *bibliog.*

— History.

HANNA (WILLARD A.) Indonesian Banda: colonialism and its aftermath in the Nutmeg Islands. Philadelphia, [1978]. pp. 164. *bibliog.*

BANG CHAN.

SHARP (LAURISTON W.) and HANKS (LUCIEN MASON) Bang Chan: social history of a rural community in Thailand. Ithaca, 1978. pp. 314. *bibliog.*

BANGLADESH.

BANGLADESH. External Publicity Division. 1972. Introducing Bangladesh. [Dacca], 1972. pp. 38.

— Census.

BANGLADESH. Census, 1974. Population census of Bangladesh, 1974: national volume: report and tables. [Dacca, 1977]. pp. 673.

— Commerce.

BANGLADESH. Provincial Statistical Board and Bureau of Commercial and Industrial Intelligence. Trade supplement: an account relating to the foreign trade, coastal trade, navigation, East Bengal railway. Statistics and balance of trade of East Pakistan. m., Je 1958. Dacca.

— Constitution.

BANGLADESH. Constitution. 1976. The constitution of the People's Republic of Bangladesh, as modified up to 28th May, 1976. Dacca, [1976]. pp. 203. *Original printed text of constitution to 25th January, 1975 with manuscript and inserted printed revisions to 28th May, 1976.*

— Economic conditions.

BANGLADESH ECONOMIC SURVEY; [pd. by] Economic Adviser's Wing, Ministry of Finance. a., 1971/73 (1st)- , with gap (1974/75, 3rd) Dacca.

BANGLADESH. Planning Commission. 1974. Memorandum for the Bangladesh consortium, 1974-75. [Dacca], 1974. pp. 101.

OSMANI (SIDDIQUR RAHMAN) Economic inequality and group welfare: theory and application to Bangladesh. 1978. fo. 329. *bibliog. Typescript. Ph.D. (London) thesis: unpublished. This thesis is the property of London University and may not be removed from the Library.*

STEPANEK (JOSEPH F.) Bangladesh - equitable growth? New York, [1979]. pp. 191. *bibliog.*

— Economic policy.

BANGLADESH. Department of Publications. 1972. Bangladesh forges ahead: policies and measures. [Dacca, 1972?]. pp. 39.

BANGLADESH. Planning Commission. 1973. The first five year plan, 1973-78. [Dacca], 1973. pp. 549.

BANGLADESH. Planning Commission. 1974. Memorandum for the Bangladesh consortium, 1974-75. [Dacca], 1974. pp. 101.

BANGLADESH. Planning Commission. 1978. The two-year plan, 1978-80. [Dacca],1978. pp. 303.

— Industries.

BANGLADESH. Department of Industries. 1976. Industrial investment schedule for two years, 1976-1978, for private sector. [Dacca, 1976]. pp. 163.

— Politics and government.

BANGLADESH. Prime Minister. 1972. 7 June: English translation of speech delivered by Bangabandhu Sheikh Mujibur Rahman on June 7, 1972 at Suhrawardy Uddyan, Dacca. [Dacca], 1972. pp. 22.

— Rural conditions.

STEPANEK (JOSEPH F.) Bangladesh - equitable growth? New York, [1979]. pp. 191. *bibliog.*

— Social conditions.

OSMANI (SIDDIQUR RAHMAN) Economic inequality and group welfare: theory and application to Bangladesh. 1978. fo. 329. *bibliog. Typescript. Ph.D. (London) thesis: unpublished. This thesis is the property of London University and may not be removed from the Library.*

— Social policy.

BANGLADESH. Department of Publications. 1972. Bangladesh forges ahead: policies and measures. [Dacca, 1972?]. pp. 39.

BANGLADESH. Planning Commission. 1973. The first five year plan, 1973-78. [Dacca], 1973. pp. 549.

BANGLADESH. Planning Commission. 1974. Memorandum for the Bangladesh consortium, 1974-75. [Dacca], 1974. pp. 101.

BANGLADESH. Planning Commission. 1978. The two-year plan, 1978-80. [Dacca],1978. pp. 303.

BANK FUER GEMEINWIRTSCHAFT.

LOESCH (ACHIM VON) The Bank für Gemeinwirtschaft: development, structure, tasks. 2nd ed. Frankfurt am Main, [1977]. pp. 62. *bibliog. (Bank für Gemeinwirtschaft. Series Commonweal Economy. No. 20)*

BANKERS
— United Kingdom.

GREEN (EDWIN) Debtors to their profession: a history of the Institute of Bankers, 1879-1979. London, 1979. pp. 245.

BANKING LAW
— Germany.

DIESSNER (REINHARD) Die Sozialisierung der Banken nach Art. 15 GG. Erlangen-Nürnberg, 1979. pp. [305]. *bibliog.*

— United States.

The DEREGULATION of the banking and securities industries; edited by Lawrence G. Goldberg, Lawrence J. White. Lexington, Mass., [1979]. pp. 356. *Papers of a conference sponsored by the Salomon Brothers Center for the Study of Financial Institutions.*

— — New York (State).

NEW YORK (STATE). Statutes, etc. 1914-1976. Banking law. New York, [1976]. pp. [862].

BANKS AND BANKING.

INTER-BANK RESEARCH ORGANISATION. Banking systems abroad: the role of large deposit banks in the financial systems of Germany, France, Italy, the Netherlands, Switzerland, Sweden, Japan and the United States. London, [1978?]. pp. 347. *bibliog.*

THOMPSON (THOMAS W.) and others. Banking tomorrow: managing markets through planning. New York, [1978]. pp. 304.

THOMAS (LLOYD BREWSTER) Money, banking, and economic activity. Englewood Cliffs, N.J., [1979]. pp. 626.

— Argentine Republic.

FRIZZI DE LONGONI (HAYDEE E.) Rivadavia y la economia argentina. Buenos Aires, [1947 repr. 1976]. pp. 209. *bibliog.*

— Brazil.

PELAEZ (CARLOS MANUEL) and SUZIGAN (WILSON) Historia monetaria do Brasil: analise da politica, comportamento e instituições monetarias. Rio de Janeiro, 1976. pp. 487. *(Brazil. Instituto de Planejamento Econômico e Social. Instituto de Pesquisas. Monografias. No.23)*

— Canada.

BLYTHE (L.N.) Banking in Canada. Plymouth, 1978. pp. 70. *bibliog.*

— Europe.

ORGANISATION FOR ECONOMIC CO-OPERATION AND DEVELOPMENT. 1978. Regulations affecting international banking operations of banks and non-banks in France, Germany, the Netherlands, Switzerland, the United Kingdom. Paris, 1978. pp. 108.

— Europe, Eastern.

BANKING and sources of finance in COMECON; edited by A.H. Hermann. London, [1978?]. pp. 137.

— European Economic Community countries.

IMMENGA (ULRICH) Participation by banks in other branches of the economy: an opinion on the economic, competitive and operational advantages and disadvantages of such participation on the basis of the statutory provisions of the member states of the European Communities. Brussels, European Communities, 1975. pp. 190. *bibliog. (European Economic Community. Studies. Competition: Approximation of Legislation Series. 25)*

BANKER RESEARCH UNIT. Banking and sources of finance in the European Community; edited by Philip Thorn [and] Jean M. Lack. London, 1977. pp. 313.

MASTROPASQUA (SALVATORE) The banking system in the countries of the EEC: institutional and structural aspects. Alphen aan den Rijn, 1978. pp. 155.

The REGULATION of banks in the member states of the EEC; edited by IBRO (Inter-Bank Research Organisation). Alphen aan den Rijn, 1978. pp. 321.

— Finland.

FINLAND. Tilastokeskus. Pankit: pankki- ja laitoskohtaisia tietoja, etc. a., 1977- Helsinki.

— Germany.

DIESSNER (REINHARD) Die Sozialisierung der Banken nach Art. 15 GG. Erlangen-Nürnberg, 1979. pp. [305]. *bibliog.*

— Italy.

CAROLEO (ANNA) Le banche cattoliche dalla prima guerra mondiale al fascismo. Milano, 1976. pp. 194. *bibliog.*

GATTONI (ROMANO) Come funziona la Banca d'Italia e il sistema delle banche. Roma, [1977]. pp. 105.

— Japan.

BANK OF JAPAN. Economic Research Department. The Japanese financial system. [Tokyo?], 1978. pp. 154.

— New Hebrides — Statistics.

NEW HEBRIDES. Condominium Bureau of Statistics. Statistical bulletin: Banking statistics. q., D 1977- Vila.

— Norway.

NORWAY. Statistiske Centralbyrå. Forretnings- og sparebanker: balanser og resultatregnskaper for de enkelte banker. a., 1975/1976- Oslo. *[in Norwegian with English preface and table of contents] Data previously pd. in NORWAY. Statistiske Centralbyrå. Finansinstitusjoner.*

— Pakistan.

MEENAI (SAID AHMAD) Banking system of Pakistan. Karachi, [1964?]. pp. 147. *bibliog.*

— Qatar.

QATAR NATIONAL BANK S.A.Q. Annual report and accounts. a., 1977- Doha. *[in English and Arabic]*

— Russia.

LAVRUSHIN (OLEG IVANOVICH) Ekonomicheskaia rol' bankovskogo protsenta. Moskva, 1977. pp. 70.

— Singapore.

CHEW (DAVID B.H.) Banking and finance. 2nd ed. [Singapore, 1973]. pp. 107.

— South Africa.

SOUTH AFRICA. Committee of Inquiry into a Giro System. 1976. Report. [Pretoria, 1976?]. pp. 11.

— Sudan — Mathematical models.

KHALIL (KHALIL SALAMA) A computer-based economic model for the Bank of Sudan utilizing data base management systems. 1978. fo. 340. *bibliog.* Typescript. Ph.D. (London) thesis: unpublished. Five microfiches in end pocket. This thesis is the property of London University and may not be removed from the Library.

— United Kingdom.

INSTITUTE OF BANKERS. Questions on banking practice. 11th ed. London, 1978. pp. 349.

HANSON (DERRICK G.) Service banking: a commentary on bank services in the United Kingdom. London, [1979]. pp. 325. *bibliogs.*

— — Wales.

JONES (REG CHAMBERS) Arian: the story of money and banking in Wales. Swansea, 1978. pp. 170. *bibliog.*

— United States.

CAREY (MATTHEW) Essays on banking...; with a selection of his other writings on banking and [a new] introduction by Herman E. Krooss. Clifton, N.J., 1972. 1 vol. (various pagings). *Reprint of works originally published Philadelphia, 1810-19.*

ADAMS (DONALD R.) Finance and enterprise in early America: a study of Stephen Girard's Bank 1812-1831. [Philadelphia, 1978]. pp. 163.

JAMES (JOHN A.) Money and capital markets in postbellum America. Princeton, N.J., [1978]. pp. 293. *bibliog.*

KOTZ (DAVID M.) Bank control of large corporations in the United States. Berkeley, [1978]. pp. 217. *bibliog.*

COCHRAN (JOHN A.) Money, banking, and the economy. 4th ed. New York, [1979]. pp. 588. *bibliogs.*

— — Texas.

GRANT (JOSEPH M.) and CRUM (LAWRENCE L.) The development of state-chartered banking in Texas from predecessor systems until 1970. Austin, Tex., [1978]. pp. 281.

BANKS AND BANKING, AMERICAN.

ARONSON (JONATHAN DAVID) Money and power: banks and the world monetary system. Beverly Hills, [1977]. pp. 224. *bibliog.*

BANKS AND BANKING, CENTRAL

— Netherlands.

ZIJLSTRA (JELLE) Gesprekken en geschriften; samengesteld door G. Puchinger met bijdrage van W. Drees. Naarden, [1978]. pp. 383.

— United States.

TIMBERLAKE (RICHARD HENRY) The origins of central banking in the United States. Cambridge, Mass., 1978. pp. 272. *bibliog.*

BANKS AND BANKING, COOPERATIVE

— Law and legislation — United States.

AMERICAN ENTERPRISE INSTITUTE FOR PUBLIC POLICY RESEARCH. Legislative Analyses. 95th Congress. No. 31. The National Consumer Cooperative Bank Bill. Washington, 1978. pp. 23.

— Germany.

LOESCH (ACHIM VON) The Bank für Gemeinwirtschaft: development, structure, tasks. 2nd ed. Frankfurt am Main, [1977]. pp. 62. *bibliog. (Bank für Gemeinwirtschaft. Series Commonweal Economy. No. 20)*

— Italy.

MOTTA (LUCIO) Credito popolare e sviluppo economico: l'esperienza di una banca locale lombarda fra il 1874 e il 1907. Milano, 1976. pp. 201.

BANKS AND BANKING, INTERNATIONAL.

BEAUFORT WIJNHOLDS (J.A.H. DE) Developments in international banking since 1973. Amsterdam, [1979?]. pp. 18. *(Nederlandsche Bank. Reprints. No. 40)*

BANTUS.

SOUTH AFRICA. Embassy (London). Department of Information. 1969. The golden magnet: why S.A. gold mines annually attract 220,000 foreign Bantu. [London, 1969]. pp. (7).

— Bibliography.

VILJOEN (R.A.) compiler. Bibliography on the Bantu in the republic of South Africa. Pretoria, 1966. pp. 45. *(South Africa. National Bureau of Educational and Social Research. Information Series. No. 12)* In English and Afrikaans.

BARANYA

— History.

TIHANY (LESLIE CHARLES) The Baranya dispute, 1918-1921: diplomacy in the vortex of ideologies. New York, 1978. pp. 138. *bibliog. (East European Quarterly. East European Monographs. 35)*

BARBADOS

— Bibliography.

HANDLER (JEROME S.) compiler. A guide to source materials for the study of Barbados history, 1627-1834. Carbondale, Ill., [1971]. pp. 205.

— Economic conditions — Statistics.

CENTRAL BANK OF BARBADOS. Annual statistical digest. a., 1976(2nd)- Bridgetown.

— History.

HOYOS (F.A.) Barbados: a history from the Amerindians to Independence. London, 1978. pp. 293. *bibliog.*

— — Sources.

HANDLER (JEROME S.) compiler. A guide to source materials for the study of Barbados history, 1627-1834. Carbondale, Ill., [1971]. pp. 205.

BARDINI (VITTORIO).

BARDINI (VITTORIO) Storia di un comunista. Firenze, 1977. pp. 121.

BARNARDO (THOMAS JOHN).

WAGNER (GILLIAN) Barnardo. London, [1979]. pp. 344. *bibliog.*

BARODA
— Politics and government.

PANTHAM (THOMAS) Political parties and democratic consensus: a study of party organisations in an Indian city. Delhi, 1976. pp. 215. *bibliogs.*

BARTH (KARL).

PROLINGHAUER (HANS) Der Fall Karl Barth, 1934-1935: Chronographie einer Vertreibung. Neukirchen-Vluyn, [1977]. pp. 410. *bibliog.*

BAS-RHIN (DEPARTMENT).

FRANCE. Direction de la Documentation. La Documentation Française. Notes et Etudes Documentaires. No. 4458. Les départements français. 67. Bas-Rhin, Alsace. Paris, 1978. pp. 202.

BASEL (CITY)
— Economic history.

STRITMATTER (ROBERT) Die Stadt Basel während des Dreissigjährigen Krieges: Politik, Wirtschaft, Finanzen. Bern, [1977]. pp. 293. *bibliog.*

BASEL-LAND (CANTON)
— Politics and government.

BLUM (ROGER MAX) Die politische Beteiligung des Volkes im jungen Kanton Baselland, 1832-1875. Liestal, 1977. pp. 782. *(Basel-Land (Canton). Quellen und Forschungen zur Geschichte und Landeskunde des Kantons Baselland. Bd. 16)*

BASHKIR REPUBLIC
— Economic conditions.

MEZHOTRASLEVYE kompleksy Bashkirskoi ASSR. Ufa, 1975. pp. 159.

GUBAIDULLIN (MANSUR SADYKOVICH) Ekonomicheskie problemy razvitiia zhivotnovodstva v usloviiakh nauchno-tekhnicheskogo progressa: na primere Bashkirskoi ASSR. Moskva, 1978. pp. 144. *(Akademiia Nauk SSSR. Problemy Sovetskoi Ekonomiki)*

BASIC (COMPUTER PROGRAM LANGUAGE).

LOTT (RICHARD W.) BASIC with business applications. New York, [1979]. pp. 284. *bibliog.*

BASQUE PROVINCES
— History.

AGUIRRE Y LECUBE (JOSÉ ANTONIO DE) Freedom was flesh and blood. London, 1945. pp. 288.

— Industries.

HARRISON (ROBERT JOSEPH) The origins of modern industrialism in the Basque country. Sheffield, 1977. pp. 18. *(Sheffield. University. Department of Economic and Social History. Studies in Economic and Social History. 2)*

— Social conditions.

NUÑEZ ASTRAIN (LUIS C.) Clases sociales en Euskadi. San Sebastian, [1977]. pp. 217.

NUÑEZ ASTRAIN (LUIS C.) La sociedad vasca actual. San Sebastian, [1977]. pp. 213.

BASSE-NORMANDIE
— Economic policy.

BASSE-NORMANDIE. Conseil Régional. Liaisons, informations, région: revue d'information économique de Basse-Normandie. No. 8. VIIe plan Basse-Normandie: rapport d'orientation générale. [Caen], 1975. pp. 100.

BASSE-NORMANDIE. Conseil Régional. Liaisons, informations, région: revue d'information économique de Basse-Normandie. No. 12. VIIe plan: les programmes d'action prioritaires Bas-Normands [and] budget régional 1977. [Caen], 1977. pp. 119.

— Population.

BASSE-NORMANDIE. Conseil Régional. Liaisons, informations, région: revue d'information économique de Basse-Normandie. No. 13. Recensement. [Caen], 1977. pp. 99.

BATH
— Civic improvement.

BATH. Department of Architecture and Planning. Saving Bath: a programme for conservation; (conservation study, stage 2: final report). Bath, [1978]. 1 vol. (various pagings).

BATLEY
— Poor.

FINNEGAN (FRANCES) and SIGSWORTH (ERIC M.) Poverty and social policy: an historical study of Batley. [York, 1978]. pp. 127. *(Papers in Community Studies. No. 19)*

— Social history.

FINNEGAN (FRANCES) and SIGSWORTH (ERIC M.) Poverty and social policy: an historical study of Batley. [York, 1978]. pp. 127. *(Papers in Community Studies. No. 19)*

BATTERED WIVES.
See ABUSED WIVES.

BATTERSEA
— City planning — Citizen participation.

BERESFORD (PETER) and BERESFORD (SUZIE) A say in the future: planning, participation and meeting social need: a new approach: North Battersea: a case study. London, 1978. pp. 210. *bibliog. (Battersea Community Action. Reports. No.1)*

— Politics and government.

ROEBUCK (JANET) Urban development in 19th-century London: Lambeth, Battersea and Wandsworth, 1838-1888. London, 1979. pp. 211. *bibliog.*

— Social policy.

BERESFORD (PETER) and BERESFORD (SUZIE) A say in the future: planning, participation and meeting social need: a new approach: North Battersea: a case study. London, 1978. pp. 210. *bibliog. (Battersea Community Action. Reports. No.1)*

BAUER (BRUNO).

LAUFNER (RICHARD) and KOENIG (KARL LUDWIG) Bruno Bauer, Karl Marx und Trier: ein unbekannter Brief von Bruno Bauer an Karl Marx und radikale Vormärzliteratur in der Stadtbibliothek Trier. Trier, [1978]. pp. 28. *(Karl-Marx-Haus. Schriften. 20)*

BAVARIA
— History.

BAYERN in der NS-Zeit...; herausgegeben von Martin Broszat [and others]. München, 1977 in progress. *bibliog.*

— Landtag.

SCHOSSER (ERICH) Presse und Landtag in Bayern von 1850 bis 1918. München, 1968. pp. 127. *bibliog. (Munich. Stadtarchiv. Neue Schriftenreihe. Band 22)*

— Politics and government.

SCHOSSER (ERICH) Presse und Landtag in Bayern von 1850 bis 1918. München, 1968. pp. 127. *bibliog. (Munich. Stadtarchiv. Neue Schriftenreihe. Band 22)*

SCHWARZE (JOHANNES) Die bayerische Polizei und ihre historische Funktion bei der Aufrechterhaltung der öffentlichen Sicherheit in Bayern von 1919-1933. München, 1977. pp. 292. *bibliog. (Munich. Stadtarchiv. Neue Schriftenreihe. Band 92)*

HIRSCHFELDER (HEINRICH) Die bayerische Sozialdemokratie, 1864-1914. Erlangen, 1979. 2 vols.(in 1). *bibliog.*

— Social history.

Die JUEDISCHEN Gemeinden in Bayern, 1918-1945: Geschichte und Zerstörung; herausgegeben und bearbeitet von Baruch Z. Ophir und Falk Wiesemann. München, 1979. pp. 525. *bibliog. Based on the section on Bavaria in Pinkas Hakehillot, Encyclopaedia of Jewish Communities from their Foundation till after the Holocaust, published in Hebrew, Jerusalem 1972.*

BAXTER (RICHARD).

LAMONT (WILLIAM MONTGOMERIE) Richard Baxter and the millennium: Protestant imperialism and the English revolution. London, 1979. pp. 340.

BAYESIAN STATISTICAL DECISION THEORY.

LINDLEY (DENNIS VICTOR) Bayesian statistics: a review. Philadelphia, 1972 repr. 1978. pp. 83. *bibliog. (Conference Board of the Mathematical Sciences. Regional Conference Series in Applied Mathematics. No 2)*

BEDFORDSHIRE
— Economic conditions.

BEDFORDSHIRE. County Council. County structure plan: annual monitory report. a., 1978- Bedford.

BEEF
— Prices — Australia.

AUSTRALIA. Bureau of Agricultural Economics. 1979. Beef price stabilisation. Canberra, 1979. pp. 86. *(Beef Research Reports. No. 21)*

— — Canada.

CANADA. Food Prices Review Board. 1974. Beef pricing. [Ottawa, 1974]. pp. 29,29. *In English and French.*

— — United States.

CANADA. Food Prices Review Board. 1974. Beef pricing. [Ottawa, 1974]. pp. 29,29. *In English and French.*

BEEF CATTLE
— Economic aspects — United States.

AUSTRALIA. Bureau of Agricultural Economics. 1977. An econometric model of the United States beef market. Canberra, 1977. pp. 149. *bibliog. (Beef Research Reports. No. 20)*

— Australia — Prices.

WILLIAMS (L.E.) and MOORHOUSE (W.) Fat cattle prices at Cannon Hill saleyards: trends and relationships, 1-7-1966 to 30-6-76. Brisbane, 1976. pp. 26. *(Queensland. Department of Primary Industries. Economic Services Branch. Miscellaneous Bulletins. No.6)*

BEGIN (MENACHEM).

BEGIN (MENACHEM) The revolt. rev. ed. New York, [1977]. pp. 386.

GERVASI (FRANK) The life and times of Menahem Begin: rebel to statesman. New York, 1979. pp. 382. *bibliog.*

BEHAVIOUR MODIFICATION.

BEHAVIOUR modification with the severely retarded...; edited by C.C. Kiernan and F. Peter Woodford. Amsterdam, 1975. pp. 332. *bibliogs. (Institute for Research into Mental and Multiple Handicap. Study Groups. No. 8)*

PACKARD (VANCE OAKLEY) The people shapers. London, 1978. pp. 395. *bibliog.*

BEHAVIOURISM (PSYCHOLOGY).

SKINNER (BURRHUS FREDERIC) Reflections on behaviorism and society. Englewood Cliffs, N.J., [1978]. pp. 209.

BELFAST

— Transit systems.

IRELAND, NORTHERN. Department of the Environment. 1978. Belfast urban area plan: review of transportation strategy; statement by the Department, etc. Belfast, [1978]. pp. 30.

LAVERY (C.M.) Belfast urban area plan: review of transportation strategy: report on public inquiry. Belfast, H.M.S.O., 1978. pp. 241.

BELFRAGE (CEDRIC).

BELFRAGE (CEDRIC) and ARONSON (JAMES) Something to guard: the stormy life of the National Guardian, 1948-1967. New York, 1978. pp. 362.

BELGIUM

— Civilization.

DEMEY (J.) De historische twee-eenheid der Nederlanden: bestendige kloof in toenadering. Nijmegen, [1978]. pp. 214. *bibliogs.*

— Colonies.

EMERSON (BARBARA) Leopold II of the Belgians: king of colonialism. London, 1979. pp. 324. *bibliog.*

— Constitution.

SENELLE (ROBERT) The reform of the Belgian state. Brussels, Ministry of Foreign Affairs, External Trade and Cooperation in Development, 1978. pp. 378. *(Memo from Belgium. No.179)*

— Economic conditions.

BELGIQUE: pays en voie de sous-développement; pour une restructuration démocratique de l'économie; précédé du manifeste du G.E.M., [by] M. Alle [and others]. Bruxelles, [1977]. pp. 149. *bibliog.*

— — Statistics.

BELGIUM. Institut National de Statistique. 1978. Enquête socio-économique, avril 1977. Bruxelles, 1978. 3 vols. (in 1).

— Economic history.

GILLINGHAM (JOHN BENNETT) Belgian business in the Nazi new order. Ghent, 1977. pp. 237. *bibliog.*

— Foreign relations.

BELGIUM. Ministère des Affaires Etrangères, du Commerce Extérieur et de la Coopération au Développement. 1972. Stability through co-operation; by Pierre Harmel, Minister for Foreign Affairs: (speech made...at the 27th session of the United Nations General Assembly in New York, 5 October 1972). [Brussels], 1972. pp. 12. *(Memo from Belgium. No. 154-155)*

— History.

DEMEY (J.) De historische twee-eenheid der Nederlanden: bestendige kloof in toenadering. Nijmegen, [1978]. pp. 214. *bibliogs.*

— — 1940-1945, German occupation.

GILLINGHAM (JOHN BENNETT) Belgian business in the Nazi new order. Ghent, 1977. pp. 237. *bibliog.*

— Kings and rulers.

INSTITUT BELGE D'INFORMATION ET DE DOCUMENTATION. A contempory monarchy; [text, François Jacqmot]. Brussels, 1970. pp. 92. *(Belgian Review)*

EMERSON (BARBARA) Leopold II of the Belgians: king of colonialism. London, 1979. pp. 324. *bibliog.*

— Parliament.

SMETS (PAUL F.) Les traités internationaux devant le Parlement, 1945-1955. Bruxelles, 1978. pp. 565. *bibliog.* *(Centre Interuniversitaire de Droit Public. Travaux et Etudes. 14)*

— Population.

DOOGHE (GILBERT) De bevolking in Belgie: demografisch overzicht. [Brussels], 1976. pp. 135. *(Centre d'Etude de la Population et de la Famille [Belgium]. Technische Rapporten. 10)*

BELGIUM. Institut National de Statistique. 1978. Enquête socio-économique, avril 1977. Bruxelles, 1978. 3 vols. (in 1).

BELGIUM. Institut National de Statistique. 1978. Population des communes fusionnées. Bruxelles, 1978. pp. 99.

POPULATION and family in the Low Countries, II; edited by H. G. Moors [and others]. Leiden, 1978. pp. 153. *bibliogs.* *(Nederlands Interuniversitair Demografisch Instituut and Centre d'Etude de la Population et de la Famille [Belgium]. Publications. vol. 6)*

— Social conditions — Statistics.

BELGIUM. Institut National de Statistique. 1978. Enquête socio-économique, avril 1977. Bruxelles, 1978. 3 vols. (in 1).

— Social policy.

DELEECK (HERMAN) Ongelijkheden in de welvaartsstaat: opstellen over sociaal beleid: tweede bundel. Antwerpen, [1977]. pp. 319.

BELIZE.

BELIZE. 1976. Belize: new nation in Central America. Belmopan, 1976. pp. 41. *bibliog.*

— Economic conditions.

BELIZE. 1967. Investment opportunities. [Belize City], 1967. pp. 34.

— Statistics.

BELIZE. British Honduras through the fifties. [Belize, 1961]. pp. 34.

BELL (ALEXANDER GRAHAM).

FIELD (KATE) ed. The history of Bell's telephone. London, 1878. pp. 71.

BENARES

— History.

NARAIN (V.A.) Jonathan Duncan and Varanasi. Calcutta, 1959. pp. 240. *bibliog.*

BENEDICTINES.

BENEDICT, Saint, Abbot of Monte Cassino. The rule of Saint Benedict. London, 1978. pp. 79.

BENGAL

— Economic history.

ISLAM (M. MUFAKHARUL) Bengal agriculture, 1920-1946: a quantitative study. Cambridge, 1978. pp. 283. *bibliog.* *(Cambridge. University. Centre of South Asian Studies. Cambridge South Asian Studies. 22)*

BENGAL, WEST

— Economic conditions.

WEST Bengal: an analytical study; sponsored by the Bengal Chamber of Commerce and Industry, Calcutta. New Delhi, [1971]. pp. 208.

— Social conditions.

WEST Bengal: an analytical study; sponsored by the Bengal Chamber of Commerce and Industry, Calcutta. New Delhi, [1971]. pp. 208.

BEN-GURION (DAVID).

BAR-ZOHAR (MICHEL) Ben-Gurion; translated by Peretz Kidron. London, [1978]. pp. 334.

BENIN

— History.

IGBAFE (PHILIP AIGBONA) Benin under British administration: the impact of colonial rule on an African kingdom, 1897-1938. London, 1979. pp. 432. *bibliog.*

— Statistics.

GERMANY (BUNDESREPUBLIK). Statistisches Bundesamt. Länderkurzbericht: Benin. a., 1978- Wiesbaden.

BENN (ANTHONY NEIL WEDGWOOD).

LEWIS (W. RUSSELL) Tony Benn: a critical biography. London, 1978. pp. 203.

BENTHAM (JEREMY).

GRAHAM (JOHN FREELE) The political and moral thought of Jeremy Bentham: a revaluation. 1978. fo. 432. *bibliog.* Typescript. Ph.D. (London) thesis: unpublished. This thesis is the property of London University and may not be removed from the Library.

BENTHAM (THOMAS) Bishop of Lichfield and Coventry.

CAMDEN SOCIETY. [Publications]. 4th Series. vol.22. Camden miscellany. vol.27. London, 1979. pp. 248.

BEOWULF.

CHAMBERS (RAYMOND WILSON) Beowulf: an introduction to the study of the poem with a discussion of the stories of Offa and Finn;...with a supplement by C.L. Wrenn. 3rd ed. Cambridge, 1959 repr. 1972. pp. 628. *bibliogs.*

BERARD (ARMAND).

BERARD (ARMAND) Un ambassadeur se souvient: au temps du danger allemand. [Paris, 1976]. pp. 554.

BERBERS.

For a related heading see WARYAGHAR (BERBER PEOPLE).

BERDIAEV (NIKOLAI ALEKSANDROVICH).

UCHENYE ZAPISKI KAFEDR OBSHCHESTVENNYKH NAUK VUZOV LENINGRADA. Filosofiia. vyp.17. Filosofskie i sotsiologicheskie issledovaniia. Leningrad, 1977. pp. 200.

BERKSHIRE

— Economic conditions.

BERKSHIRE. Planning Department. Central Berkshire structure plan: report of survey. [Reading, Berks.], 1976. pp. 260.

BERKSHIRE. Planning Department. The first structure plan for West Berkshire: consultation document. [Reading, Berks.], 1976. pp. 141.

— Economic policy.

BERKSHIRE. Planning Department. Berkshire: record of planning policies. [Reading, Berks.], 1973. pp. 28.

BERKSHIRE. Planning Department. East Berkshire structure plan: issues report. [Reading, Berks., 1974]. pp. 39.

BERKSHIRE (Cont.)

BERKSHIRE. Planning Department. The first structure plan for West Berkshire: consultation document. [Reading, Berks.], 1976. pp. 141.

BERKSHIRE. Planning Department. Central Berkshire structure plan: consultation document. [Reading, Berks.], 1977. pp. 169.

BERKSHIRE. Planning Department. East Berkshire structure plan: consultation document. [Reading, Berks.], 1977. pp. 151.

BERKSHIRE. Planning Department. West Berkshire structure plan: report of public participation. [Reading, Berks.], 1977. 1 vol. (various pagings).

BERKSHIRE. Planning Department. West Berkshire structure plan, submitted to the Secretary of State for the Environment, August 1977. [Reading, Berks., 1977]. pp. 109.

BERKSHIRE. Planning Department. Central Berkshire structure plan: report of public participation. [Reading, Berks.], 1978. pp. 113.

BERKSHIRE. Planning Department. Central Berkshire structure plan, submitted to the Secretary of State for the Environment, June 1978. [Reading, Berks., 1978]. pp. 119.

BERKSHIRE. Planning Department. East Berkshire structure plan: report of public participation. [Reading, Berks.], 1978. pp. 67,40.

BERKSHIRE. Planning Department. East Berkshire structure plan, submitted to the Secretary of State for the Environment, June 1978. [Reading, Berks., 1978]. pp. 115.

BERKSHIRE. Planning Department. West Berkshire structure plan: monitoring process report. [Reading, Berks.], 1978. pp. 41.

— Social conditions.

BERKSHIRE. Planning Department. Central Berkshire structure plan: report of survey. [Reading, Berks.], 1976. pp. 260.

BERKSHIRE. Planning Department. The first structure plan for West Berkshire: consultation document. [Reading, Berks.], 1976. pp. 141.

— Social policy.

BERKSHIRE. Planning Department. Berkshire: record of planning policies. [Reading, Berks.], 1973. pp. 28.

BERKSHIRE. Planning Department. East Berkshire structure plan: issues report. [Reading, Berks., 1974]. pp. 39.

BERKSHIRE. Planning Department. The first structure plan for West Berkshire: consultation document. [Reading, Berks.], 1976. pp. 141.

BERKSHIRE. Planning Department. Central Berkshire structure plan: consultation document. [Reading, Berks.], 1977. pp. 169.

BERKSHIRE. Planning Department. East Berkshire structure plan: consultation document. [Reading, Berks.], 1977. pp. 151.

BERKSHIRE. Planning Department. West Berkshire structure plan: report of public participation. [Reading, Berks.], 1977. 1 vol. (various pagings).

BERKSHIRE. Planning Department. West Berkshire structure plan, submitted to the Secretary of State for the Environment, August 1977. [Reading, Berks., 1977]. pp. 109.

BERKSHIRE. Planning Department. Central Berkshire structure plan: report of public participation. [Reading, Berks.], 1978. pp. 113.

BERKSHIRE. Planning Department. Central Berkshire structure plan, submitted to the Secretary of State for the Environment, June 1978. [Reading, Berks., 1978]. pp. 119.

BERKSHIRE. Planning Department. East Berkshire structure plan: report of public participation. [Reading, Berks.], 1978. pp. 67,40.

BERKSHIRE. Planning Department. East Berkshire structure plan, submitted to the Secretary of State for the Environment, June 1978. [Reading, Berks., 1978]. pp. 115.

BERKSHIRE. Planning Department. West Berkshire structure plan: monitoring process report. [Reading, Berks.], 1978. pp. 41.

BERLIN
— Economic history.

JERSCH-WENZEL (STEFI) Juden und "Franzosen" in der Wirtschaft des Raumes Berlin/Brandenburg zur Zeit des Merkantilismus. Berlin, 1978. pp. 290. *bibliog.* (*Historische Kommission zu Berlin. Einzelveröffentlichungen. Band 23*)

— Economic policy.

DEUTSCHES INSTITUT FÜR WIRTSCHAFTSFORSCHUNG. Sonderhefte. [Neue Folge]. 124. Forschung und Entwicklung in der Berliner Industrie: Ergebnisse einer Befragung; ([by] Burkhard Dreher). Berlin, 1978. pp. 112.

— Foreign population.

JERSCH-WENZEL (STEFI) Juden und "Franzosen" in der Wirtschaft des Raumes Berlin/Brandenburg zur Zeit des Merkantilismus. Berlin, 1978. pp. 290. *bibliog.* (*Historische Kommission zu Berlin. Einzelveröffentlichungen. Band 23*)

— History.

PIKARSKI (MARGOT) Jugend im Berliner Widerstand: Herbert Baum und Kampfgefährten. Berlin, [1978]. pp. 236. *bibliog.*

— — 1945- , Allied occupation.

COLLIER (RICHARD) Bridge across the sky: the Berlin blockade and airlift, 1948- 1949. London, 1978. pp. 239. *bibliog.*

NELSON (DANIEL J.) Wartime origins of the Berlin dilemma. University, Ala., [1978]. pp. 219. *bibliog.*

— Industries.

DEUTSCHES INSTITUT FÜR WIRTSCHAFTSFORSCHUNG. Sonderhefte. [Neue Folge]. 124. Forschung und Entwicklung in der Berliner Industrie: Ergebnisse einer Befragung; ([by] Burkhard Dreher). Berlin, 1978. pp. 112.

BERLIN, TREATY OF, 1878.

CONGRESS OF BERLIN, 1878. Der Berliner Kongress 1878: Protokolle und Materialien; herausgegeben von Imanuel Geiss. Boppard am Rhein, [1978]. pp. 428. *bibliog.* (*Germany (Bundesrepublik). Bundesarchiv. Schriften. 27*)

BERLIN QUESTION (1945-).

CATUDAL (HONORE MARC) The diplomacy of the Quadripartite Agreement on Berlin: a new era in East-West politics. Berlin, [1978]. pp. 335. *bibliog.*

COLLIER (RICHARD) Bridge across the sky: the Berlin blockade and airlift, 1948- 1949. London, 1978. pp. 239. *bibliog.*

NELSON (DANIEL J.) Wartime origins of the Berlin dilemma. University, Ala., [1978]. pp. 219. *bibliog.*

BERNARD-LAZARE.
See LAZARE (BERNARD).

BERNSTEIN (EDUARD).

BERNSTEIN und der demokratische Sozialismus: Bericht über den wissenschaftlichen Kongress "Die historische Leistung und aktuelle Bedeutung Eduard Bernsteins"; Horst Heimann, Thomas Meyer, Hrsg. Berlin, [1978]. pp. 578.

BERRY (CHARLES ACKERMAN).

BERRY (CHARLES ACKERMAN) Gentleman of the road. London, 1978. pp. 216.

BESSARABIA
— Nationalism.

ESAULENKO (ALEKSANDR SERGEEVICH) Sotsialisticheskaia revoliutsiia v Moldavii i politicheskii krakh burzhuaznogo natsionalizma, 1917-1918. Kishinev, 1977. pp. 212. *bibliog.*

BEVAN (ANEURIN).

JENKINS (MARK) Bevanism: Labour's high tide: the cold war and the democratic mass movement. Nottingham, 1979. pp. 323. *bibliogs.*

BEVERAGES.

MARKETING DEVELOPMENT BUREAU [UNITED REPUBLIC OF TANZANIA] and COLLEGE OF BUSINESS EDUCATION [UNITED REPUBLIC OF TANZANIA]. Distribution patterns of food and beverages in Dar es Salaam. Dar es Salaam, 1973. fo. (61).

BHAVE (VINOBA).

MISRA (BABU RAM) V for Vinoba: the economics of the Bhoodan movement. Bombay, 1956. pp. 70.

BHOODAN MOVEMENT.

MISRA (BABU RAM) V for Vinoba: the economics of the Bhoodan movement. Bombay, 1956. pp. 70.

BATTERSBY (OLWEN) Bhoodan-Gramden: the gentle revolution. London, [1973?]. pp. 8. (*Marr-Munning Trust. Edwina Mountbatten Papers. No. 2*)

BHUTAN
— Politics and government.

RUSTOMJI (NARI) Bhutan: the Dragon Kingdom in crisis. Delhi, 1978. pp. 150.

BHUTTO (ZULFIKAR ALI).

PAKISTAN. Supreme Court. 1978. Order...on application by Zulfikar Ali Bhutto, Rawalpindi, May 20, 1978. Rawalpindi, 1978. pp. 15.

PUNJAB (PAKISTAN). High Court. 1978. Summary of judgement in murder trial: state vs Zulfikar Ali Bhutto and others. [Lahore, 1978?]. pp. 23.

BIBB (HENRY).

BIBB (HENRY) Narrative of the life and adventures of Henry Bibb, an American slave, written by himself. New York, 1850; New York, 1969. pp. 204. *Facsimile reprint.*

BIBBY (J.) AND SONS.

BIBBY (JOHN BENJAMIN) and BIBBY (CHARLES LESLIE) A miller's tale: a history of J. Bibby and Sons Ltd., Liverpool. Liverpool, [1978]. pp. 218.

BIBLE.
— Prophecies.

OLIVER (WILLIAM HALDANE) Prophets and millennialists: the uses of biblical prophecy in England from the 1790s to the 1840s. Auckland, 1978. pp. 269. *bibliog.*

BIBLE, OLD TESTAMENT.
— Criticism, interpretation, etc.

[WILLIS (ROBERT) M.D.] The Pentateuch and book of Joshua in face of the science and moral sense of our age; by a physician. London, 1875. pp. 490.

BIBLIOGRAPHICAL SERVICES.

BEAUDIQUEZ (MARCELLE) compiler. Bibliographical services throughout the world, 1970-74. Paris, Unesco, 1977. pp. 419. (*Documentation, Libraries and Archives: Bibliographies and Reference Works. 3*)

BIBLIOGRAPHY

— Bibliography — America, Latin.

GROPP (ARTHUR E.) compiler. A bibliography of Latin American bibliographies published in periodicals. Metuchen, 1976. 2 vols.

BIBLIOGRAPHY, NATIONAL

— Australian — Periodicals.

CURRENT AUSTRALIAN SERIALS: a select list; [pd. by] National Library of Australia. irreg. Canberra. *Current issue only kept.*

— Brazilian.

BOLETIM BIBLIOGRAFICO DA BIBLIOTECA NACIONAL [BRAZIL] (formerly Boletim bibliografico). q. (formerly s-a.), 1956 (v.6)-, with gap (1.semestre 1964: v. 14, no.1); susp. pbln. 1968-1972. Rio de Janeiro.

— English.

BRITISH NATIONAL BIBLIOGRAPHY, THE; [pd. by] the Council of the British National Bibliography Ltd. w., with q., a. and quadrennial cumulative vols., 1950[vol.1]- London. *Cumulative v. only kept permanently: Cumulated indexes: 1950/1954, 1955/1959, 1960/1964, 1965/1967. Cumulated subject indexes: 1951/1954, 1955/1959, 1960/1964, 1965/1967.*

— Jamaican.

JAMAICAN NATIONAL BIBLIOGRAPHY; [pd. by] Institute of Jamaica, West India Reference Library. q., Ja/Mr 1975(v.1, no.1)- Kingston.

BIG BUSINESS

— Germany.

ENGELMANN (BERNT) Das Reich zerfiel, die Reichen blieben: Deutschlands Geld- und Machtelite; mit Rangliste der 500 grossen alten Vermögen. München, 1975 repr.1978. pp. 402. *bibliog.*

— Sweden.

LINDSTRÖM (SVERKER) and NORDIN (STEN) Vem äger storföretagen? [Stockholm, 1977]. pp. 202. *bibliog.*

BIHAR

— Economic conditions.

BIHAR. Directorate of Information and Public Relations. 1975. Changing face of Bihar. [Patna, 1975?]. pp. 28.

BIHAR. Directorate of Information and Public Relations. 1976. Bihar makes phenomenal progress. [Patna, 1976]. pp. 45.

— Economic policy.

BIHAR. Directorate of Information and Public Relations. 1975. Changing face of Bihar. [Patna, 1975?]. pp. 28.

BIHAR. Directorate of Information and Public Relations. 1976. Bihar makes phenomenal progress. [Patna, 1976]. pp. 45.

BIHAR. Directorate of Information and Public Relations. 1976. Prime minister's 20pt. programme: towards a better Bihar. [Patna, 1976?]. pp. 11.

— Politics and government.

BARIK (RADHAKANTA) Politics of the JP movement. New Delhi, 1977. pp. 120. *bibliog.*

SHAH (GHANSHYAM) Protest movements in two Indian states: a study of the Guyarat and Bihar movements. Delhi, 1977. pp. 171. *bibliogs. (Centre for Social Studies, Surat. Publications. No. 8)*

— Social conditions.

BIHAR. Directorate of Information and Public Relations. 1975. Changing face of Bihar. [Patna, 1975?]. pp. 28.

BIHAR. Directorate of Information and Public Relations. 1976. Bihar makes phenomenal progress. [Patna, 1976]. pp. 45.

— Social policy.

BIHAR. Directorate of Information and Public Relations. 1975. Changing face of Bihar. [Patna, 1975?]. pp. 28.

BIHAR. Directorate of Information and Public Relations. 1976. Bihar makes phenomenal progress. [Patna, 1976]. pp. 45.

BIHAR. Directorate of Information and Public Relations. 1976. Prime minister's 20pt. programme: towards a better Bihar. [Patna, 1976?]. pp. 11.

BIKO (STEVEN).

BIKO (STEVEN) The testimony of Steve Biko; [edited by Millard Arnold]. London, 1979. pp. 298.

BILINGUALISM.

BILINGUALISM: psychological, social and educational implications; [proceedings of a conference held at Plattsburgh, New York in 1976]; edited by Peter A. Hornby. New York, 1977. pp. 167. *bibliog.*

GEORGETOWN UNIVERSITY ROUND TABLE ON LANGUAGES AND LINGUISTICS, 1978. International dimensions of bilingual education; James E. Alatis, editor. Washington, D.C., [1978]. pp. 668. *bibliogs.*

McLAUGHLIN (BARRY) Second-language acquisition in childhood. Hillsdale, N.J., 1978. pp. 239. *bibliog.*

— Austria — Oberwart.

GAL (SUSAN) Language shift: social determinants of linguistic change in bilingual Austria. New York, [1979]. pp. 20a1. *bibliog.*

— Canada.

CANADA. Statistics Canada. Minority and second language education: elementary and secondary levels. a., 1975-76/1976-77(1st)- Ottawa. *[in English and French]*

— United Kingdom — Scotland.

McKINNON (KENNETH M.) Language shift and education: conservation of ethnolinguistic culture amongst schoolchildren of a Gaelic community. Hatfield, 1978. pp. 25. *bibliog. (Hatfield Polytechnic. School of Social Sciences. Social Sciences Occasional Papers. No.2)*

BILL DRAFTING.

THORNTON (G.C.) Legislative drafting. 2nd ed. London, 1979. pp. 350.

BIOGRAPHY.

The BIOGRAPHICAL process: studies in the history and psychology of religion; edited by Frank E. Reynolds and Donald Capps. The Hague, [1976]. pp. 436. *bibliog.*

BIOLINGUISTICS.

MASSACHUSETTS INSTITUTE OF TECHNOLOGY WORK GROUP IN THE BIOLOGY OF LANGUAGE. Explorations in the biology of language; [essays] edited by Edward Walker. Montgomery, Vt., [1978]. pp. 247. *bibliog.*

BIOLOGICAL ASSAY.

ASHTON (WINIFRED DIANA) The logit transformation with special reference to its uses in bioassay. London, 1972. pp. 88. *bibliog.*

BIOLOGICAL SYSTEMS.

MILLER (JAMES GRIER) Living systems. New York, 1978. pp. 1102. *bibliog.*

BIOLOGICAL WARFARE.

RANGER (ROBERT JOHN) The Canadian contribution to the control of chemical and biological warfare. Toronto, [1976]. pp. 66. *(Canadian Institute of International Affairs. Wellesley Papers. 5)*

BIOLOGY

— History.

ALLEN (GARLAND E.) Life science in the twentieth century. Cambridge, 1978. pp. 257. *bibliog. Reprint of work originally published, New York, 1975.*

— Philosophy.

THORPE (WILLIAM HOMAN) Purpose in a world of chance: a biologist's view. Oxford, [1978]. pp. 124.

BIRMINGHAM

— Foreign population.

LLEWELYN-DAVIES WEEKS [AND PARTNERS]. Inner area study: Birmingham: Birmingham Community Relations Council: Small Heath fieldworker. [London], Department of the Environment, [1978]. pp. 38.

— Race relations.

FLETT (HAZEL) Black council tenants in Birmingham. Bristol, Social Science Research Council Research Unit on Ethnic Relations, [1979]. pp. 79. *bibliog. (Working Papers on Ethnic Relations. No. 12)*

BIRMINGHAM AND MIDLAND CANAL CARRYING COMPANY.

BELCHAMBERS (ANTHONY MURRAY) and MANN (JACK) The Birmingham and Midland Canal Carrying Company Limited: investigation under section 165b of the Companies Act, 1948; report. [London, Department of Trade], 1978. pp. (42).

BIRMINGHAM POLITICAL UNION.

FLICK (CARLOS) The Birmingham Political Union and the movements for reform in Britain, 1830-1839. Hamden, Conn., 1978. pp. 206. *bibliog.*

BIRSE (ARTHUR HERBERT).

BIRSE (ARTHUR HERBERT) Memoirs of an interpreter. London, 1967. pp. 254.

BIRTH CONTROL.

SRIKANTAN (K.S.) The family planning program in the socioeconomic context. New York, [1977]. pp. 240.

— Evaluation.

ORGANISATION FOR ECONOMIC CO-OPERATION AND DEVELOPMENT. Development Centre. Studies. Measuring the impact of family planning: a short guide. Paris, [1977]. pp. 73. *bibliog.*

— Law and legislation — Lebanon.

DIB (GEORGE MOUSSA) Law and population in Lebanon. Medford, Mass., 1975. pp. 47. *(Tufts University. Fletcher School of Law and Diplomacy. Law and Population Monograph Series. No. 29)*

— — United Kingdom — Commonwealth.

THREE studies of abortion laws in the Commonwealth;...by Mostyn P. Embrey [and others]. London, Commonwealth Secretariat, [1977]. 1 vol. (various pagings). *bibliog.*

— Religious aspects.

POPULATION problems and Catholic responsibility...; edited by L.H. Janssen. Rotterdam, 1975. pp. 196. *(Tilburg. Katholieke Hogeschool. Tilburg Institute of Development Research. Studies on Development Research. 2) Proceedings of the international symposium on population problems in developing countries and worldwide Catholic responsibility.*

— Societies — Directories.

TRZYNA (THADDEUS C.) and SMITH (JOAN DICKSON) Population: an international directory of organizations and information resources. Claremont, Calif., 1976. pp. 132.

BIRTH CONTROL.(Cont.)

— Study and teaching — Sri Lanka.

WANIGARATNE (RANJIT D.) A study of communication flow in selected villages in Sri Lanka: case study 1. the Medagama village. Colombo, Agrarian Research and Training Institute and the Communication Strategy Project, Ministry of Information and Broadcasting, 1975. pp. 62. bibliog.

— America, Latin.

CENTRO PARA EL DESARROLLO ECONOMICO Y SOCIAL DE AMERICA LATINA. Poblacion y familia en una sociedad en transicion. Buenos Aires, 1970. pp. 375.

— Australia.

HICKS (NEVILLE) 'This sin and scandal': Australia's population debate, 1891-1911. Canberra, 1978. pp. 208. bibliog.

— Bangladesh — Bibliography.

BANGLADESH. Directorate of Population Control and Family Planning. Research, Evaluation, Statistics and Planning Unit. 1977. A bibliography on research and evaluation reports of Bangladesh from 1964; research and evaluation reports of official family planning programme under erstwhile Pakistan Family Planning Council, Family Planning Board, E[ast P[akistan] R[esearch and] E[valuation] C[entre] and agencies under the Population Control and Family Planning Directorate. [Dacca], 1977. fo. 7.

— Belgium.

POPULATION and family in the Low Countries, II; edited by H. G. Moors [and others]. Leiden, 1978. pp. 153. bibliogs. (Nederlands Interuniversitair Demografisch Instituut and Centre d'Etude de la Population et de la Famille [Belgium]. Publications. vol. 6)

— Fiji.

FIJI. 1966. Family planning in Fiji, 1966. [Suva, 1966]. pp. 31.

— India.

DAYAL (JOHN) and BOSE (AJOY) For reasons of state: Delhi under emergency. Delhi, 1977. pp. 239.

INDIA. Department of Family Welfare. 1978. Family welfare programme in India: a brief account. New Delhi, 1978. pp. 22.

— — Kerala.

KERALA. Demographic Research Centre. 1973. The characteristics of the population of Kerala and the impact of the family planning programme. Trivandrum, 1973. pp. 20. (Papers. No 79)

KERALA. Demographic Research Centre. 1977. A study of sterilised persons in Kerala, 1971-74. Trivandrum, 1977. pp. 30.

— Malaysia.

MALAYSIA FAMILY PLANNING ANNUAL STATISTICAL REPORT; [pd. by] National Family Planning Board. a., 1967/1970- Kuala Lumpur.

NATIONAL FAMILY PLANNING BOARD, MALAYSIA. Facts about the N[ational] F[amily] P[lanning] programme. Kuala Lumpur, 1977. 1 vol. (unpaged). *In English and Malay.*

— Netherlands.

POPULATION and family in the Low Countries, II; edited by H. G. Moors [and others]. Leiden, 1978. pp. 153. bibliogs. (Nederlands Interuniversitair Demografisch Instituut and Centre d'Etude de la Population et de la Famille [Belgium]. Publications. vol. 6)

— South Africa.

LÖTTER (JOHANN MORGENDALL) and VAN TONDER (JAN LOUIS) Fertility and family planning among blacks in South Africa: 1974;...translated by C.P. Kleyn. Pretoria, 1976. pp. 111. bibliog. (Human Sciences Research Council [South Africa] . Institute for Sociological, Demographic and Criminological Research. Reports. No S-39)

— Taiwan.

TAIWAN PROVINCIAL INSTITUTE OF FAMILY PLANNING. Annual report. a., Jl 1976/Je 1977- Taichung.

— Underdeveloped areas.

See UNDERDEVELOPED AREAS — Birth control.

— United Kingdom.

LEATHARD (AUDREY MARY) The development of family planning services in Britain. 1977 [or rather 1978]. fo. 564. bibliog. Typescript. Ph.D. (London) thesis: unpublished. *This thesis is the property of London University and may not be removed from the Library.*

— United States — Michigan.

CARTER (REGINALD) and NELL (CATHY) Family planning services provided to AFDC recipients in ichigan, January-June 1974. [Lansing], 1975. pp. 92. bibliog. (Michigan. Department of Social Services. Studies in Welfare Policy. No. 6)

BIRTH WEIGHT, LOW

— United Kingdom.

NEWCOMBE (ROBERT) Perinatal mortality and low birthweight, 1965-73: an analysis for administrative areas of England and Wales. [London], 1978. pp. 16. bibliog. (U.K. Office of Population Censuses and Surveys. Occasional Papers. 7)

BISHOPS

— United Kingdom.

HAINES (ROY MARTIN) The church and politics in fourteenth-century England: the career of Adam Orleton, c.1275-1345. Cambridge, 1978. pp. 303. bibliog.

— United States.

MILLS (FREDERICK V.) Writer on church history. Bishops by ballot: an eighteenth-century ecclesiastical revolution. New York, 1978. pp. 367. bibliog.

BISMARCK-SCHOENHAUSEN (OTTO EDUARD LEOPOLD VON) Prince.

TAYLOR (ALAN JOHN PERCIVALE) Bismarck: the man and the statesman. London, 1955, repr. 1978. pp. 286. bibliog.

PALMER (ALAN WARWICK) Bismarck. London, [1976]. pp. 326. bibliog.

KENT (GEORGE O.) Bismarck and his times. Carbondale, Ill., [1978]. pp. 184. bibliog.

BLACK NATIONALISM

— South Africa.

BIKO (STEVEN) Steve Biko: I write what I like: a selection of his writings; edited with a personal memoir by Aelred Stubbs. London, 1978. pp. 216.

GERHART (GAIL M.) Black Power in South Africa: the evolution of an ideology. Berkeley, Calif., [1978]. pp. 364. bibliog.

— United States.

MOSES (WILSON JEREMIAH) The golden age of black nationalism, 1850-1925. Hamden, 1978. pp. 345. bibliog.

TROTSKII (LEV DAVYDOVICH) Leon Trotsky on black nationalism and self-determination. 2nd ed. New York, 1978. pp. 95.

BLACK POWER.

BOESAK (ALLAN AUBREY) Black theology, black power. London, 1978. pp. 185. bibliog. *First published in the Netherlands in 1976.*

BLACK THEOLOGY.

BOESAK (ALLAN AUBREY) Black theology, black power. London, 1978. pp. 185. bibliog. *First published in the Netherlands in 1976.*

BLACKHEATH

— History.

RHIND (NEIL) Blackheath centenary, 1871-1971: short history of Blackheath from earliest times. [London], Greater London Council, [1971]. pp. 32.

BLACKS

— Education — Rhodesia.

TAYLOR (R.) Education Officer, Rhodesia. African education: the historical development and organization of the system. [Salisbury, Ministry of Information, Immigration and Tourism, 1970]. pp. 31.

— Brazil.

FERNANDES (FLORESTAN) Circuito fechado: cuatro ensaios sobre o "poder institucional". São Paulo, 1976. pp. 224. bibliogs.

NINA RODRIGUES (RAIMUNDO) Os africanos no Brasil; revisão e prefacio de Homero Pires; notas bibliograficas de Fernando Sales. São Paulo, 1977. pp. 283. bibliog. *Reprint, with addition of biographical notes and bibliography by Fernando Sales, of first edition published in 1932.*

BASTIDE (ROGER) The African religions of Brazil: toward a sociology of the interpenetration of civilizations; translated by Helen Sebba. Baltimore, [1978]. pp. 494. bibliog.

— Caribbean Area.

MINTZ (SIDNEY WILFRED) and PRICE (RICHARD) Anthropologist. An anthropological approach to the Afro-American past: a Caribbean perspective. Philadelphia, [1976]. pp. 64. bibliog. (Institute for the Study of Human Issues. ISHI Occasional Papers in Social Change. No. 2)

AFRICA and the Caribbean: the legacies of a link; edited by Margaret E. Crahan and Franklin W. Knight. Baltimore, [1979]. pp. 159. bibliog. (Johns Hopkins University. Johns Hopkins Studies in Atlantic History and Culture)

— Mozambique.

SITHOLE (NDABANINGI) and INGWANE (JULIUS PAUNDE SHIMANGANE) Frelimo militant: the story of Ingwane from Mozambique, an ordinary, yet extraordinary man, awakened. Nairobi, 1977. pp. 187.

— Rhodesia.

RHODESIA. Ministry of Information, Immigration and Tourism. 1969. The man - and his ways: an introduction to the customs and beliefs of Rhodesia's African people. [Salisbury, 1969 repr. 1970]. pp. 43.

RHODESIA. Ministry of Information, Immigration and Tourism. 1969. A people's progress. [Salisbury, 1969]. 1 pamphlet (unpaged).

PARTRIDGE (MARK) Minister speaks on community development and the urban African;...text of an address by the Minister of Local Government and Housing...to the Associate Member Council of the Associated Members of Commerce of Rhodesia. [Salisbury, 1972]. fo.9. (Rhodesia. Ministry of Information, Immigration and Tourism. Press Statements) Xerox copy.

— South Africa.

LÖTTER (JOHANN MORGENDALL) and VAN TONDER (JAN LOUIS) Fertility and family planning among blacks in South Africa: 1974;...translated by C.P. Kleyn. Pretoria, 1976. pp. 111. *bibliog*. *(Human Sciences Research Council [South Africa]. Institute for Sociological, Demographic and Criminological Research. Reports. No. S-39)*

SITHOLE (NDABANINGI) and INGWANE (JULIUS PAUNDE SHIMANGANE) Frelimo militant: the story of Ingwane from Mozambique, an ordinary, yet extraordinary man, awakened. Nairobi, 1977. pp. 187.

DEANE (DEE SHIRLEY) Black South Africans: a Who's who: 57 profiles of Natal's leading blacks. Cape Town, 1978. pp. 210.

RAEDEL (FRITZ E.) Progress or exploitation? Cape Town, 1978. pp. 55. *Translated from the German*.

— United States — Religion.

SIMPSON (GEORGE EATON) Black religions in the New World. New York, 1978. pp. 415. *bibliog*.

BLADEN (VINCENT WHEELER).

BLADEN (VINCENT WHEELER) Bladen on Bladen: memoirs of a political economist. Toronto, 1978. pp. 218. *bibliog*.

BLAGOEV (DIMITUR).

DIMITR Blagoev - vydaiushchiisia teoretik i revoliutsioner: sbornik statei k 120-letiiu so dnia rozhdeniia; [perevod s bolgarskogo]. Moskva, 1977. pp. 303.

BLANK (JOOST DE) Archbishop of Capetown.

See DE BLANK (JOOST) Archbishop of Capetown.

BLASSINGAME (JOHN W.)

REVISITING Blassingame's The slave community: the scholars respond; edited by Al-Tony Gilmore. Westport, Conn., 1978. pp. 204.

BLIND

— South Africa.

VAN DER BURGH (CHRIS) The socio-economic position of Indian blind persons in Natal. Pretoria, 1976. pp. 65. *bibliog*. *(Human Sciences Research Council [South Africa]. Institute for Sociological, Demographic and Criminological Research. Reports. No. S-42)*

BOCHUM

— Automobile industry workers' strike, 1973.

OPEL streikt: Ausbeutung und Kämpfe bei Opel; [by] Redaktionskollektiv in der Projektgruppe Ruhrgebietsanalyse, Bochum. Bochum, [1973?]. pp. 196.

BODIN (JEAN).

KRAUTHEIM (ULRIKE) Die Souveränitätskonzeption in den englischen Verfassungskonflikten des 17. Jahrhunderts: eine Studie zur Rezeption der Lehre Bodins in England, etc. Frankfurt am Main, [1977]. pp. 597. *bibliog*.

BOERS.

FARRELLY (MICHAEL JAMES) The settlement after the war in South Africa. London, 1900. pp. 321.

RUSSELL (MARGO) and RUSSELL (MARTIN) Afrikaners of the Kalahari: white minority in a black state. Cambridge, 1979. pp. 167. *bibliog*.

BOESCHENSTEIN (HERMANN).

BOESCHENSTEIN (HERMANN) Vor unsern Augen: Aufzeichnungen über das Jahrzehnt 1935-1945. Bern, 1978. pp. 334.

BOGDANOV (ALEKSANDR ALEKSANDROVICH) pseud.

JENSEN (KENNETH MARTIN) Beyond Marx and Mach: Aleksandr Bogdanov's philosophy of living experience. Dordrecht, [1978]. pp. 189. *bibliog*. *(Freiburg (Switzerland). Universität. Ost-Europa Institut. Sovietica. vol. 41)*

BOGUSHEVICH (FRANTISHEK).

See BAHUSHEVICH (FRANTSISHAK).

BOILER-MAKERS

— Canada.

MacINTOSH (ROBERT) Boilermakers in British Columbia. [Vancouver?], 1976. pp. 124.

BOLIVIA

— Census.

BOLIVIA. Census. 1976. (Censo nacional de poblacion y viviendas); resultados provisionales (departmental series). La Paz, 1977. 9 vols. (in 1)

BOLIVIA. Census. 1976. (Censo nacional de poblacion y vivienda, 1976): resultados anticipados por muestreo. [La Paz, 1977]. pp. 77.

— Economic conditions.

ZONDAG (CORNELIUS HENRY) The Bolivian economy, 1952-65: the revolution and its aftermath. New York, [1966]. pp. 262. *bibliog*.

BOLIVIA. President, 1971-1978 (Banzer Suarez). 1976. Cuatro años de creacion: (1971-1975, orden, paz, trabajo). [La Paz, 1976]. PP. 389.

— Economic history.

ZONDAG (CORNELIUS HENRY) The Bolivian economy, 1952-65: the revolution and its aftermath. New York, [1966]. pp. 262. *bibliog*.

— Politics and government.

BOLIVIA. Junta Militar de Gobierno. 1966. Informe a la nacion por el General Alfredo Ovando Candia... 6 de Agosto de 1966. La Paz, 1966. pp. 161.

BOLIVIA. President, 1971-1978 (Banzer Suarez). 1976. Cuatro años de creacion: (1971-1975, orden, paz, trabajo). [La Paz, 1976]. PP. 389.

— Rural conditions.

PRESTON (DAVID ANTHONY) Farmers and towns: rural-urban relations in highland Bolivia. Norwich, [1978]. pp. 196. *bibliog*.

— Social conditions.

BOLIVIA. President, 1971-1978 (Banzer Suarez). 1976. Cuatro años de creacion: (1971-1975, orden, paz, trabajo). [La Paz, 1976]. PP. 389.

BOMBAY (STATE)

— Economic policy.

BOMBAY (STATE). Political and Services Department. Study Group on Statistics and Intelligence. 1959. Third Five Year Plan, 1961-62 to 1965-66, Bombay State: report. Baroda, 1959. pp. 34.

— Social policy.

BOMBAY (STATE). Political and Services Department. Study Group on Statistics and Intelligence. 1959. Third Five Year Plan, 1961-62 to 1965-66, Bombay State: report. Baroda, 1959. pp. 34.

BOMBERS.

CULVER (JOHN C.) and McLUCAS (JOHN L.) Prospects for the strategic bomber: two views. Washington, [1978]. pp. 24. *(American Enterprise Institute for Public Policy Research. AEI Defense Reviews. Vol. 2. No. 1)*

BONNIERES

— History.

ACKERMAN (EVELYN BERNETTE) Village on the Seine: tradition and change in Bonnières, 1815-1914. Ithaca, 1978. pp. 185. *bibliog*.

BOOK INDUSTRIES AND TRADE

— United Kingdom.

UNWIN (PHILIP) The Stationers' Company 1918-1977: a livery company in the modern world. London, 1978. pp. 144.

BOOKKEEPING.

KOJIMA (OSAMU) ed. Historical studies of double-entry bookkeeping; edited on behalf of Institute of Industrial Research, Kwansei Gakuin University. Kyoto, 1975. pp. 305. *In Japanese with English summary. Articles previously published in other books or journals*.

BOOKS

— History — Poland.

ALEKSIEWICZ (ANNA) Drukarstwo w Rzeczypospolitej Krakowskiej i Galicji Zachodniej w latach 1815-1860. Warszawa, 1976. pp. 179. *bibliog*. *(Wrocław. Uniwersytet. Acta Universitatis Wratislaviensis. No. 300. Bibliotekoznawstwo. 8) With German summary*.

BOOKSELLERS AND BOOKSELLING

— France.

MARTIN (HENRI JEAN) and LECOCQ (M.) Les registres du libraire Nicolas, 1645-1668. Genève, 1977. 2 vols. *bibliog*. *(Paris. Ecole Pratique des Hautes Etudes. Section des Sciences Historiques et Philologiques. Centre de Recherches d'Histoire et de Philologie. Publications. 6. Histoire et Civilisation du Livre. 10)*

BOOTH (WILLIAM).

COUTTS (FREDERICK) Bread for my neighbour: an appreciation of the social influence of William Booth. London, 1978. pp. 192. *bibliog*.

BOOTHBY (ROBERT JOHN GRAHAM) Baron Boothby.

BOOTHBY (ROBERT JOHN GRAHAM) Baron Boothby. Boothby: recollections of a rebel. London, 1978. pp. 272.

BOPHUTHATSWANA

— Politics and government.

MANGOPE (LUCAS) Trends in Southern Africa and the role of Bophuthatswana. Braamfontein, 1979. pp. 8. *(South African Institute of International Affairs. Occasional Papers)*

BORDEAUX

— History.

MALINO (FRANCES) The Sephardic Jews of Bordeaux: assimilation and emancipation in Revolutionary and Napoleonic France. University, Ala., [1978]. pp. 166. *bibliog*.

BOREDOM.

GUEST (DAVID) and others. Job design and the psychology of boredom;...a paper presented at the nineteenth International Congress of Applied Psychology, Munich, August 1978. London, Department of Employment, Work Research Unit, [1979]. pp. 10. *bibliog*.

BORGIA FAMILY.

MALLETT (MICHAEL EDWARD) The Borgias: the rise and fall of a Renaissance dynasty. London, 1969. pp. 351. *bibliog*.

BORNEO.

STUDIES in Borneo societies: social process and anthropological explanation; G.N. Appell, editor; contributors: G.N. Appell [and others]. [DeKalb, Ill.], 1976. pp. 156. *bibliog.* (Northern Illinois University. Center for Southeast Asian Studies. Special Reports. No.12)

— **Economic conditions.**

NORTH BORNEO. 1959. Invest in North Borneo. Jesselton, 1959. pp. 59, 1 map.

BOSANQUET (BERNARD).

STEVENS (LESLIE MALCOLM) The political thought of Bernard Bosanquet. 1977. fo.157. *bibliog.* Typescript. M. Phil. (London) thesis: unpublished. This thesis is the property of London University and may not be removed from the Library.

BÖSCHENSTEIN (HERMANN).

See BOESCHENSTEIN (HERMANN).

BOSTON, MASSACHUSETTS

— **Economic conditions.**

WARNER (SAM BASS) the Younger. The way we really live: social change in metropolitan Boston since 1920. Boston, Mass., 1977. pp. 108.

— **Police Strike, 1919.**

RUSSELL (FRANCIS) 1910- . A city in terror: the 1919 Boston police strike. Harmondsworth, 1977. pp. 256. *bibliog.* First published in 1975 by Viking Press.

— **Population.**

SWEETSER (FRANK L.) Patterns of change in the social ecology of metropolitan Boston, 1950-1960. [Boston], Division of Mental Hygiene, 1962. pp. 158.

SWEETSER (FRANK L.) The social ecology of metropolitan Boston: 1960. [Boston], Division of Mental Hygiene, 1962. pp. 239.

— **Social conditions.**

SWEETSER (FRANK L.) Patterns of change in the social ecology of metropolitan Boston, 1950-1960. [Boston], Division of Mental Hygiene, 1962. pp. 158.

SWEETSER (FRANK L.) The social ecology of metropolitan Boston: 1960. [Boston], Division of Mental Hygiene, 1962. pp. 239.

WARNER (SAM BASS) the Younger. The way we really live: social change in metropolitan Boston since 1920. Boston, Mass., 1977. pp. 108.

— **Social history.**

WARNER (SAM BASS) the Younger. The way we really live: social change in metropolitan Boston since 1920. Boston, Mass., 1977. pp. 108.

BOTANY

— **United Kingdom.**

PENNINGTON (WINIFRED) The history of British vegetation. 2nd ed. London, [1974]. pp. 152. *bibliog.*

BOTANY, MEDICAL

— **Mexico.**

ROYS (RALPH LOVELAND) The ethno-botany of the Maya; with a new introduction and supplemental bibliography by Sheila Cosminsky. Philadelphia, 1976. pp. 380. *bibliog.* (Institute for the Study of Human Issues. ISHI Reprints on Latin America and the Caribbean) Reprint of the edition of 1931.

BOTSWANA

— **Economic conditions.**

BOTSWANA. Tenth Anniversary Co-ordinating Unit. 1976. Botswana: ten years of progress, 1966-1976. [Gaborone, 1976]. pp. 55.

ALVERSON (HOYT) Mind in the heart of darkness: value and self-identity among the Tswana of southern Africa. New Haven, 1978. pp. 299. *bibliog.*

HARTLAND-THUNBERG (PENELOPE) Botswana: an African growth economy. Boulder, Colo., 1978. pp. 151.

— **Executive departments.**

BOTSWANA. Tenth Anniversary Co-ordinating Unit. 1976. Botswana: ten years of progress, 1966-1976. [Gaborone, 1976]. pp. 55.

— **Foreign relations.**

BOTSWANA. President, 1966- (Khama). Address to the General Assembly of the United Nations... September 1969. Gaborone, [1969]. pp. (7).

— **History.**

CHIRENJE (J. MUTERO) A history of Northern Botswana, 1850-1910. Rutherford, N.J., 1977. pp. 316. *bibliog.*

— **Politics and government.**

BOTSWANA. Tenth Anniversary Co-ordinating Unit. 1976. Botswana: ten years of progress, 1966-1976. [Gaborone, 1976]. pp. 55.

— **Race relations.**

RUSSELL (MARGO) and RUSSELL (MARTIN) Afrikaners of the Kalahari: white minority in a black state. Cambridge, 1979. pp. 167. *bibliog.*

— **Relations (general) with Kenya.**

KHAMA (Sir SERETSE) Dr. Moi in Botswana: speech of welcome by His Excellency the President of Botswana...at a state banquet in honour of the Vice-President of Kenya Dr. Daniel Arap Moi, during his official visit to Botswana in July 1970, and Dr. Moi's reply. [Gaborone, Information Services, 1970]. pp. 9.

— **Social conditions.**

BOTSWANA. Tenth Anniversary Co-ordinating Unit. 1976. Botswana: ten years of progress, 1966-1976. [Gaborone, 1976]. pp. 55.

BOTTLES.

GRACE (RICHARD) and FISHER (JONATHAN) Beverage containers: re-use or recycling. Paris, Organisation for Economic Co-operation and Development, 1978. pp. 159. *bibliog.*

BOUAKE

— **Economic conditions.**

ANCEY (G.) and others. L'économie de l'espace rural de la région de Bouaké. Paris, 1974. pp. 251. *bibliog.* (France. Office de la Recherche Scientifique et Technique Outre-Mer. Travaux et Documents. No. 38)

— **Rural conditions.**

ANCEY (G.) and others. L'économie de l'espace rural de la région de Bouaké. Paris, 1974. pp. 251. *bibliog.* (France. Office de la Recherche Scientifique et Technique Outre-Mer. Travaux et Documents. No. 38)

BOUNDARIES.

STUDYING boundary conflicts: a theoretical framework; [by] Sven Tägil [and others]. Lund, 1977. pp. 215. *bibliog.* (Lund. Universitet. Historiska Institutionen. Lund Studies in International History. 9)

BROWNLIE (IAN) African boundaries: a legal and diplomatic encyclopaedia; with the assistance of Ian R. Burns. London, [1979]. pp. 1355. *bibliog.*

BOURBAKI (NICOLAS).

DIEUDONNÉ (JEAN) Panorama des mathématiques pures: le choix bourbachique. [Paris, 1977]. pp. 302. *bibliog.*

BOURGUIBA (HABIB).

BOURGUIBA (HABIB) Electoral campaign speeches, October 26-November 5, 1959. [Tunis, Secretariat of State for Information, 1960]. pp. 100. (Publications)

BOXERS.

COMPILATION GROUP FOR THE "HISTORY OF MODERN CHINA" SERIES. The Yi Ho Tuan Movement of 1900. Peking, 1976. pp. 133.

BRABANT (DUCHY)

— **Population.**

BRUNEEL (CLAUDE) La mortalité dans les campagnes: le duché de Brabant aux XVIIe et XVIIIe siècles. Louvain, 1977. pp. 777. *bibliog.* (Louvain. Université. Recueil de Travaux d'Histoire et de Philologie. 6e Série. Fasc. 10)

BRABAZON (REGINALD) 12th Earl of Meath.

BRABAZON (REGINALD) 12th Earl of Meath. Memories of the twentieth century. London, 1924. pp. 310.

BRACKEN (BRENDAN) Viscount Bracken of Christchurch.

LYSAGHT (CHARLES EDWARD) Brendan Bracken. London, 1979. pp. 327.

BRAHMS (JOHANNES).

GAY (PETER) Freud, Jews and other Germans: masters and victims in modernist culture. Oxford, 1978. pp. 289.

BRAIN.

POPPER (Sir KARL RAIMUND) and ECCLES (Sir JOHN CAREW) The self and its brain. Berlin, [1977]. pp. 597. *bibliogs.*

BRAIN DAMAGE.

GARDNER (HOWARD) The shattered mind: the person after brain damage. New York, 1975. pp. 481,viii.

BRANCHING PROCESSES.

ATHREYA (KRISHNA B.) and NEY (PETER E.) Branching processes. New York, 1972. pp. 287. *bibliog.*

BRANDENBURG

— **Economic history.**

JERSCH-WENZEL (STEFI) Juden und "Franzosen" in der Wirtschaft des Raumes Berlin/Brandenburg zur Zeit des Merkantilismus. Berlin, 1978. pp. 290. *bibliog.* (Historische Kommission zu Berlin. Einzelveröffentlichungen. Band 23)

— **Foreign population.**

JERSCH-WENZEL (STEFI) Juden und "Franzosen" in der Wirtschaft des Raumes Berlin/Brandenburg zur Zeit des Merkantilismus. Berlin, 1978. pp. 290. *bibliog.* (Historische Kommission zu Berlin. Einzelveröffentlichungen. Band 23)

BRASCHI (GIOVANNI).

TRONCONI (GABRIELLA MEDRI) Giovanni Braschi e il partito popolare nel forlivese. Roma, [1975]. pp. 194. *bibliog.*

BRAYHEAD LIMITED.

DILLON (THOMAS MICHAEL) and GARRETT (DENNIS) Burnholme and Forder Limited, in liquidation; Brayhead Limited, in liquidation: investigation under section 165b of the Companies Act 1948; report. London, H.M.S.O., 1979. 1 vol.(various pagings).

BRAZIL.

BRAZIL. Ministerio das Relações Exteriores. Departamento de Administração. Grupo de Trabalho para a Elaboração do Livro 'Brasil'. 1973. Brasil. [Brasilia, 1973?]. pp. 1107. *3rd Spanish edition. Map and pamphlet in end pocket.*

BRAZIL. Ministerio das Relações Exteriores. Departamento de Administração. Grupo de Trabalho para a Elaboração do Livro 'Brasil'. 1977. Brazil.[Brasilia, 1977]. pp. *Map and pamphlet in end pocket.*

— Armed forces.

OLIVEIRA (ELIEZER RIZZO DE) As forças armadas: politica e ideologia no Brasil, 1964-1969. Petropolis, 1976. pp. 133. *bibliog.*

— — Political activity.

ROETT (RIORDAN) Brazil: politics in a patrimonial society. New York, [1978]. pp. 189. *bibliog.*

— Commerce.

TRANSFORMAÇÃO da estrutura das exportações brasileiras 1964/70; [by] Carlos von Doellinger [and others]. Rio de Janeiro, 1973. pp. 268. *bibliog. (Brazil. Instituto de Planejamento Econômico e Social. Instituto de Pesquisas. Relatorios de Pesquisa. No. 14)*

DOELLINGER (CARLOS VON) and others. Politica e estrutura das importações brasileiras. Rio de Janeiro, 1977. pp. 171. *(Brazil. Instituto de Planejamento Econômico e Social. Instituto de Pesquisas. Relatorios de Pesquisa. No. 38)*

— Economic conditions.

BENTON (PEGGIE) Fight for the drylands: struggle and achievement in Brazil. London, 1977. pp. 188. *First published in 1972.*

The FUTURE of Brazil; edited by William H. Overholt. Boulder, Colo., 1978. pp. 289.

HOWE (GARY NIGEL) Pentecostalism, Umbanda and the Brazilian socio-economic order: from 1945 to the present day. 1978. fo. 409. *bibliog.* Typescript. Ph.D. (London) thesis: unpublished. This thesis is the property of London University and may not be removed from the Library.

TAYLOR (KIT SIMS) Sugar and the underdevelopment of northeastern Brazil, 1500-1970. Gainesville, Fla., 1978. pp. 167. *bibliog. (Florida University. Monographs. Social Sciences. No. 63)*

— Economic history.

PEREIRA (JOSE EDUARDO DE CARVALHO) Financiamento externo e crescimento econômico no Brasil, 1966/73. Rio de Janeiro, 1974. pp. 273. *bibliog. (Brazil. Instituto de Planejamento Econômico e Social. Instituto de Pesquisas. Relatorios de Pesquisa. No. 27)*

ESSAYS concerning the socioeconomic history of Brazil and Portuguese India; edited by Dauril Alden and Warren Dean. Gainesville, 1977. pp. 247.

— Economic policy.

SUDENE INFORMA: orgão mensal da Superintendência do Desenvolvimento do Nordeste [Brazil]. s-m. (formerly m.), 1968 (v.6)- , with gaps (1968: nos. 5, 7-8). Recife.

PESQUISA PLANEJAMENTO ECONOMICO: revista do Instituto de Planejamento Econômico e Social [Brazil]. s-a., Je 1971 (v.1, no.1)- Rio de Janeiro. *Index: 1971/1975(v. 1-5)*

FIGUEIREDO (NUNO FIDELINO DE) A transferência de tecnologia no desenvolvimento industrial do Brasil. Rio de Janeiro, 1972. pp. 360. *(Brazil. Instituto de Planejamento Econômico e Social. Instituto de Pesquisas. Monografias. No. 7)*

CRESCIMENTO industrial no Brazil: incentivos e desempenho recente; [by] Wilson Suzigan [and others]. Rio de Janeiro, 1974. pp. 281. *bibliog. (Brazil. Instituto de Planejamento Econômico e Social. Instituto de Pesquisas. Relatorios de Pesquisa. No. 26)*

GOODMAN (DAVID EDWIN) and ALBUQUERQUE (ROBERTO CAVALCANTI DE) Incentivos a industrialização e desenvolvimento do nordeste. Rio de Janeiro, 1974. pp. 397. *(Brazil. Instituto de Planejamento Econômico e Social. Instituto de Pesquisas. Relatorios de Pesquisa. No. 20)*

VELHO (OTAVIO GUILHERME) Capitalismo autoritario e campesinato: um estudo comparativo a partir da fronteira em movimento. São Paulo, 1976. pp. 261. *bibliog.*

DOELLINGER (CARLOS VON) and others. Politica e estrutura das importações brasileiras. Rio de Janeiro, 1977. pp. 171. *(Brazil. Instituto de Planejamento Econômico e Social. Instituto de Pesquisas. Relatorios de Pesquisa. No. 38)*

POLITICA econômica externa e industrialização no Brasil 1939/52; [by] Pedro S. Malan [and others]. Rio de Janeiro, 1977. pp. 535. *bibliog. (Brazil. Instituto de Planejamento Econômico e Social. Instituto de Pesquisas. Relatorios de Pesquisa. No. 36)*

MAHAR (DENNIS J.) Desenvolvimento econômico da Amazônia: una analise das politicas governamentais. Rio de Janeiro, 1978. pp. 259. *bibliog. (Brazil. Instituto de Planejamento Econômico e Social. Instituto de Pesquisas. Relatorios de Pesquisa. No. 39)*

— — Mathematical models.

PLANEJAMENTO regional: metodos e aplicação ao caso brasileiro;...Paulo Roberto Haddad, editor. Rio de Janeiro, 1974. pp. 244. *bibliog. (Brazil. Instituto de Planejamento Econômico e Social. Instituto de Pesquisas. Monografias. No. 8)*

— Foreign relations.

RESENHA DE POLITICA EXTERIOR DO BRAZIL; [pd. by] Ministerio das Relações Exteriores [Brazil]. q., Je 1974 (ano 1, no.1)- Brasilia.

— History.

TAYLOR (KIT SIMS) Sugar and the underdevelopment of northeastern Brazil, 1500-1970. Gainesville, Fla., 1978. pp. 167. *bibliog. (Florida University. Monographs. Social Sciences. No.63)*

— — 1889-1930.

LEVINE (ROBERT M.) Pernambuco in the Brazilian federation, 1889-1937. Stanford, Calif., 1978. pp. 236. *bibliog.*

— Industries.

BARROS (FREDERICO JOSE O. ROBALINHO DE) and MODENESI (RUI LYRIO) Pequenas e medias industrias: analise dos problemas, incentivos, e sua contribuição ao desenvolvimento. Rio de Janeiro, 1973. pp. 192. *bibliog. (Brazil. Instituto de Planejamento Econômico e Social. Instituto de Pesquisas. Relatorios de Pesquisa. No.17)*

BOISIER (SERGIO) and others. Desenvolvimento regional e urbano: diferenciais de produtividade e salarios industriais. Rio de Janeiro, 1973. pp. 151. *(Brazil. Instituto de Planejamento Econômico e Social. Instituto de Pesquisas. Relatorios de Pesquisa. No.15)*

CRESCIMENTO industrial no Brazil: incentivos e desempenho recente; [by] Wilson Suzigan [and others]. Rio de Janeiro, 1974. pp. 281. *bibliog. (Brazil. Instituto de Planejamento Econômico e Social. Instituto de Pesquisas. Relatorios de Pesquisa. No. 26)*

DIFUSÃO de inovações na industria brasileira: três estudos de caso; [edited by] Jose Tavares de Araujo Jr. Rio de Janeiro, 1976. pp. 246. *bibliog. (Brazil. Instituto de Planejamento Econômico e Social. Instituto de Pesquisas. Monografias. No.24)*

POLITICA econômica externa e industrialização no Brasil 1939/52; [by] Pedro S. Malan [and others]. Rio de Janeiro, 1977. pp. 535. *bibliog. (Brazil. Instituto de Planejamento Econômico e Social. Instituto de Pesquisas. Relatorios de Pesquisa. No. 36)*

— Politics and government.

SKIDMORE (THOMAS E.) Politics in Brazil, 1930-1964: an experiment in democracy. London, [1967]. pp. 446. *bibliog.*

ALENCAR (JOSE DE) Discursos parlamentares; obra comemorativa, etc. Brasilia, 1977. pp. 680. *(Brazil. Congresso. Câmara dos Deputados. Perfis Parlamentares. 1)*

CHRISTO (CARLOS ALBERTO LIBANIO) Letters from a prisoner of conscience...; translated by John Drury. Guildford, 1978. pp. 241.

FIGUEIREDO (AFONSO CELSO DE ASSIS) Visconde de Ouro Preto. Discursos parlamentares; seleção, introdução e comentarios de Costa Porto. Brasilia, 1978. pp. 516. *(Brazil. Congresso. Câmara dos Deputados. Perfis Parlamentares. 5)*

FONTOURA (JOÃO NEVES DA) Discursos parlamentares; seleção e introdução de Helgio Trindade. rasilia, 1978. pp. 722. *(Brazil. Congresso. Câmara dos Deputados. Perfis Parlamentares. 8)*

The FUTURE of Brazil; edited by William H. Overholt. Boulder, Colo., 1978. pp. 289.

MANGABEIRA (OTAVIO) Discursos parlamentares; seleção e introdução de Josephat Marinho. Brasilia, 1978. pp. 557. *(Brazil. Congresso. Câmara dos Deputados. Perfis Parlamentares. 10)*

NUNES MACHADO (FRANCISCO) Discursos parlamentares; seleção e introdução de Vamireh Chacon. Brasilia, 1978. pp. 201. *(Brazil. Congresso. Câmara dos Deputados. Perfis Parlamentares. 3)*

PEIXOTO (CARLOS) Discursos parlamentares; seleção, introdução e comentarios de David V. Fleischer. Brasilia, 1978. pp. 759. *bibliog. (Brazil. Congresso. Câmara dos Deputados. Perfis Parlamentares. 2)*

PESSOA (EPITACIO) Discursos parlamentares; seleção e introdução, Jose Octavio. Brasilia, 1978. pp. 453. *(Brazil. Congresso. Câmara dos Deputados. Perfis Parlamentares. 7)*

ROETT (RIORDAN) Brazil: politics in a patrimonial society. New York, [1978]. pp. 189. *bibliog.*

SARAIVA (JOSE ANTÔNIO) Discursos parlamentares; seleção e introdução, Alvaro Valle. Brasilia, 1978. pp. 661. *(Brazil. Congresso. Câmara dos Deputados. Perfis Parlamentares. 4)*

CAMPOS (FRANCISCO LUIS DA SILVA) Discursos parlamentares; seleção e introdução Paulo Bonavides. Brasilia, 1979. pp. 153. *Brazil. Congresso. Câmara dos Deputados. Perfis Parlamentares. 6)*

FARIA (GILBERTO DE LIMA AZEVEDO SOUZA FERREIRA AMADO DE) Discursos parlamentares; seleção e introdução Homero Senna. Brasilia, 1979. pp. 336. *(Brazil. Congresso. Câmara dos Deputados. Perfis Parlamentares. 11)*

VASCONCELOS (ZACARIAS DE GOIS E) Discursos parlamentares; seleção e introdução de Alberto Venancio Filho. Brasilia, 1979. pp. 588. *(Brazil. Congresso. Câmara dos Deputados. Perfis Parlamentares. 9)*

— Religion.

BASTIDE (ROGER) The African religions of Brazil: toward a sociology of the interpenetration of civilizations; translated by Helen Sebba. Baltimore, [1978]. pp. 494. *bibliog.*

— Social conditions.

BENTON (PEGGIE) Fight for the drylands: struggle and achievement in Brazil. London, 1977. pp. 188. *First published in 1972.*

HOWE (GARY NIGEL) Pentecostalism, Umbanda and the Brazilian socio-economic order: from 1945 to the present day. 1978. fo. 409. *bibliog.* Typescript. Ph.D. (London) thesis: unpublished. This thesis is the property of London University and may not be removed from the Library.

BRAZIL.(Cont.)

TAYLOR (KIT SIMS) Sugar and the underdevelopment of northeastern Brazil, 1500-1970. Gainesville, Fla., 1978. pp. 167. bibliog. (Florida University. Monographs. Social Sciences. No. 63)

— Social history.

ESSAYS concerning the socioeconomic history of Brazil and Portuguese India; edited by Dauril Alden and Warren Dean. Gainesville, 1977. pp. 247.

— Social policy.

ALMEIDA (WANDERLY JOSE MANSO DE) and CHAUTARD (JOSE LUIZ) FGTS: uma politica de bem-estar social. Rio de Janeiro, 1976. pp. 159. (Brazil. Instituto de Planejamento Econômico e Social. Instituto de Pesquisas. Relatorios de Pesquisa. No. 30)

— Statistics.

REVISTA BRASILEIRA DE ESTATISTICA: orgão oficial do IBGE [Instituto Brazileiro de Geografia e Estatistica, Brazil] e Sociedade Brasileira de Estatistica). q., 1940 (ano 1)- , with gaps (nos. 11, 16, 106). Rio de Janeiro.

BREAD.

MAURITIUS. Commission of Enquiry as to the aspects of the Manufacture, Distribution and Sale of Bread in the Island of Mauritius, 1975. Findings; [Joseph Philippe de Ravel, chairman]. Port Louis, 1975. pp. 25.

— Law and legislation.

BARLOW (KENNETH) The law and the loaf: how the government has been wrong in legislating about bread, etc. Marlow, 1978. pp. 70.

— Prices — Canada.

CANADA. Food Prices Review Board. 1974. Report on bread prices [Ottawa], 1974. pp. 33, 40. In English and French.

BREMEN

— Metal workers' strike, 1974.

KOMMUNISTISCHER BUND WESTDEUTSCHLAND. Ortsgruppe Bremen. Der Streik der Metallarbeiter, Bremen, März 74: Analyse und Dokumentation. Heidelberg, 1974. pp. 118.

BRETON (ANDRE).

ROSEMONT (FRANKLIN) André Breton and the first principles of surrealism. London, 1978. pp. 147.

BREWING INDUSTRIES

— Belgium.

JACQUEMIN (ALEXIS) and GHELLINCK (ELIZABETH DE) L'évolution de la concentration dans l'industrie de la brasserie et des boissons en Belgique. [Brussels], Communautés Européennes, 1976. pp. 108.

— France.

RASTOIN (J.-L.) and others. L'évolution de la concentration dans l'industrie de la brasserie en France. [Brussels], Communautés Européennes, 1975. pp. 99.

BOULET (D.) and LAPORTE (J.P.) Etude sur l'évolution de la concentration dans les industries des boissons et des boissons non alcoolisées en France. [Brussels], Communautés Européennes, 1976. pp. 284.

— Germany.

BREITENACHER (MICHAEL) Untersuchung zur Konzentrationsentwicklung in der Getränke Industrie in Deutschland. [Brussels], Europäischen Gemeinschaften, 1976. pp. 156.

— Italy.

BALLIANO (PIERA) and LANZETTI (RENATO) Studio sull'evoluzione della concentrazione nell'industria delle bevande in Italia. [Brussels], Comunità Europee, 1976. pp. 143.

— Netherlands.

BROUWER (MARIA) and PIJNAPPEL (THEO) A study of the evolution of concentration in the Dutch beverages industry. [Brussels], European Communities, 1976. pp. 149.

— United Kingdom.

NATIONAL ECONOMIC DEVELOPMENT COUNCIL. Brewing Sector Working Group. Investment and efficiency in the brewing industry; report. [London, National Economic Development Office, 1978]. 1 pamphlet (various pagings).

HAWKINS (KEVIN H.) and PASS (CHRISTOPHER L.) The brewing industry: a study in industrial organisation and public policy. London, 1979. pp. 169. bibliog.

BREZHNEV (LEONID IL'ICH).

BREZHNEV (LEONID IL'ICH) Ob aktual'nykh problemakh partiinogo stroitel'stva: (rechi, stat'i i vystupleniia s 1964 po oktiabr' 1976 g.). 2nd ed. Moskva, 1976. pp. 775.

BREZHNEV (LEONID IL'ICH) How it was: the war and post-war reconstruction in the Soviet Union. Oxford, 1979. pp. 115. Translation of his "Malaia zemlia" and "Vozrozhdenie".

BRIBERY

— United States.

BOULTON (DAVID) The Lockheed papers. London, 1978. pp. 289.

BRIDGEWATER (FRANCIS EGERTON) 3rd Duke of.

See EGERTON (FRANCIS) 3rd Duke of Bridgewater.

BRIGANDS AND ROBBERS

— Colombia.

BUITRAGO SALAZAR (EVELIO) Zarpazo the bandit: memoirs of an undercover agent of the Colombian Army;...translated by M. Murray Lasley; edited.. .by Russell W. Ramsey. University, Ala., [1977]. pp. 169.

BRIGHT (JOHN).

ROBBINS (KEITH GILBERT) John Bright. London, 1979. pp. 288. bibliog.

BRISBANE

— Population.

QUEENSLAND. Commonwealth Bureau of Census and Statistics. Queensland Office. 1973. Population growth within the Brisbane statistical division, 1856- 1971. Brisbane, [1973]. pp. 33.

BRISTOL

— Church history — Sources.

BRISTOL. Bristol Record Society. Publications. vol. 30. Minute book of the Men's Meeting of the Society of Friends in Bristol 1686-1704; edited by Russell Mortimer. Bristol, 1977. pp. 310. bibliog.

— Docks.

BRISTOL. City Planning Department. Bristol city docks local plan: draft district plan report. Bristol, 1979. 1 vol. (various pagings). Map in end pocket.

BRISTOL. City Planning Department. Bristol city docks local plan: the opportunities. [Bristol], 1977. 1 vol. (various pagings).

BRITAIN, BATTLE OF, 1940.

WOOD (DEREK) and DEMPSTER (DEREK) The narrow margin: the Battle of Britain and the rise of air power, 1930-40. Westport, Conn., [1961]. pp. 536.

BRITISH AEROSPACE.

BRITISH AEROSPACE. Annual report and accounts. a., 1977(1st)- Weybridge.

BRITISH AIRWAYS.

TAUSSIG (WILLIAM M.) British Airways: an analysis of efficiency and cost levels. Washington, D.C., Department of Transportation, 1977. pp. 66. Photocopy.

BRITISH BROADCASTING CORPORATION.

SWANN (Sir MICHAEL MEREDITH) The BBC's external services under threat? London, [1978]. pp. 12.

BRITISH COLUMBIA

— Administrative and political divisions.

BRITISH COLUMBIA. Royal Commission on Electoral Reform. 1978. Interim report on the redefinition of electoral districts for the province of British Columbia; L.S. Eckardt, commissioner. [Victoria], 1978. pp. 77. 5 maps in end pocket.

— Economic conditions.

BRITISH COLUMBIA. Premier. 1978. A report on the economy, incorporating the financial report for the nine months April-December, 1977; by William R. Bennett, etc. [Victoria], 1978. pp. 26.

— Executive departments.

BRITISH COLUMBIA. Ministry of the Environment. Annual report. a., 1976(1st)- Victoria.

— Industries.

BRITISH COLUMBIA. Ministry of Economic Development. 1978. Industrial expansion in British Columbia by economic regions, 1977. Vancouver, [1978]. pp. (63).

— Ministry of the Environment.

BRITISH COLUMBIA. Ministry of the Environment. Annual report. a., 1976(1st)- Victoria.

BRITISH FISHERIES SOCIETY.

DUNLOP (JEAN) The British Fisheries Society 1786-1893. Edinburgh, [1978]. pp. 239. bibliog.

BRITISH IN BENIN.

IGBAFE (PHILIP AIGBONA) Benin under British administration: the impact of colonial rule on an African kingdom, 1897-1938. London, 1979. pp. 432. bibliog.

BRITISH IN INDIA.

TEMPLE (Sir RICHARD) Bart., G.C.S.I. India in 1880. London, 1880. pp. 524.

PANCKRIDGE (H. R.) A short history of the Bengal Club, 1827-1927. Calcutta, 1927. pp. 64.

DYSON (KETAKI KUSHARI) A various universe: a study of the journals and memoirs of British men and women in the Indian subcontinent, 1765-1856. Delhi, 1978. pp. 406. bibliog.

BRITISH IN THE NEAR EAST.

SEARIGHT (SARAH) The British in the Middle East. rev. ed. London, 1979. pp. 290. bibliog.

BRITISH IN WEST AFRICA.

GOLDIE (Sir GEORGE DASHWOOD TAUBMAN) Empire builder extraordinary: Sir George Goldie, his philosophy of government and empire; [selected articles, letters, etc.; edited by] D.J.M. Muffett. Douglas, 1978. pp. 334. bibliog.

BRITISH LEYLAND.

NATIONAL ENTERPRISE BOARD [U.K.]. Report...on the British Leyland corporate plan, up to 1981, and business plan for 1978. [London], 1978. fo. 13.

BRITISH LIBRARY OF POLITICAL AND ECONOMIC SCIENCE.

JOHN (ARTHUR HENRY) The British Library of Political and Economic Science: a brief history. London, 1971. pp. 15.

BRITISH SHIPBUILDERS.

BRITISH SHIPBUILDERS. Report and accounts. a., 1977/78(1st)- London.

BROADCASTING

— United Kingdom.

CURRAN (Sir CHARLES J.) A seamless robe: broadcasting: philosophy and practice. London, 1979. pp. 358.

— — Political aspects.

TRETHOWAN (IAN) Broadcasting and politics. London, [1977]. pp. 13.

BROADCASTING POLICY

— United States.

COLE (BARRY G.) and OETTINGER (MAL) Reluctant regulators: the FCC and the broadcast audience. Reading, Mass., [1978]. pp. 310.

BRONCHITIS.

REPORT on a second retrospective mortality study in North-East England;...[by] G. Dean [and others]. London, 1977-78. 2 pts. (in 1 vol.). bibliogs. (Tobacco Research Council. Research Papers. 14) Report of the first study published as Research Paper 8.

BRONFMAN FAMILY.

NEWMAN (PETER CHARLES) Bronfman dynasty: the Rothschilds of the New World. Toronto, [1978]. pp. 318.

BRONZE AGE

— Europe.

BRIARD (JACQUES) The Bronze Age in barbarian Europe: from the megaliths to the Celts; translated [from the French] by Mary Turton. London, 1979. pp. 246. bibliog.

BROOKE (Sir CHARLES ANTHONI) Rajah of Sarawak.

CRISSWELL (COLIN N.) Rajah Charles Brooke, monarch of all he surveyed. Kuala Lumpur, 1978. pp. 253. bibliog.

BROWN (LUCIUS POLK).

WOLFE (MARGARET RIPLEY) Lucius Polk Brown and progressive food and drug control: Tennessee and New York City 1908-1920. Lawrence, Kan., [1978]. pp. 194.

BRUNSWICK

— Politics and government.

LEIN (ALBRECHT) Antifaschistische Aktion 1945: die "Stunde Null" in Braunschweig. Göttingen, [1978]. pp. 480. bibliog. (Göttingen. Universität. Seminar für die Wissenschaft von der Politik. Göttinger Politikwissenschaftliche Forschungen. Band 2)

BRUSSELS

— Intellectual life.

BELGIUM. Ministerie van Nederlandse Cultuur. 1970. 21 maanden Nederlands cultuurbeleid voor Brussel-hoofdstad. [Brussel, 1970]. 1 vol. (unpaged).

BRYDGES (CHARLES JOHN).

HUDSON'S BAY RECORD SOCIETY. Publications. 31. The letters of Charles John Brydges, 1879-1882, Hudson's Bay Company Land Commissioner; edited by Hartwell Bowsfield. Winnipeg, 1977. pp. 346.

BUDDHA AND BUDDHISM

— Sri Lanka.

MALALGODA (KITSIRI) Buddhism in Sinhalese society, 1750-1900: a study of religious revival and change. Berkeley, 1976. pp. 300. bibliog.

SENEVIRATNE (H.L.) Rituals of the Kandyan State. Cambridge, 1978. pp. 190. bibliog.

— United Kingdom.

HUMPHREYS (CHRISTMAS) Both sides of the circle: the autobiography of Christmas Humphreys. London, 1978. pp. 269.

BUDDHIST RITES AND CEREMONIES

— Sri Lanka.

SENEVIRATNE (H.L.) Rituals of the Kandyan State. Cambridge, 1978. pp. 190. bibliog.

BUDGET.

ORGANISATION FOR ECONOMIC CO-OPERATION AND DEVELOPMENT. Department of Economics and Statistics. 1978. Budget indicators; [by the Monetary and Fiscal Policy Division; and] The international competitiveness of selected OECD countries; [by the Balance of Payments Division]. Paris, 1978. pp. 52. (OECD Economic Outlook. Occasional Studies)

WEBER (LUC) L'analyse économique des dépenses publiques: fondements et principes de la rationalisation des choix budgétaires. Paris, [1978]. pp. 312. bibliog.

— Australia.

KNIGHT (KENNETH W.) and WILTSHIRE (KENNETH W.) Formulating government budgets: aspects of Australian and North American experience. St. Lucia, [1977]. pp. 179. bibliog.

— Canada.

KNIGHT (KENNETH W.) and WILTSHIRE (KENNETH W.) Formulating government budgets: aspects of Australian and North American experience. St. Lucia, [1977]. pp. 179. bibliog.

— India — Orissa.

ORISSA. Finance Department. Fiscal Analysis and Statistical Section. 1976. Conspectus of Orissa budgets, 1936-37 - 1973-74. [Bhubaneswar, 1976?]. pp. 308.

— Nigeria.

GOWON (YAKUBU) 1973-74 federal budget broadcast. [Lagos, 1973]. pp. 20. Cover title: Progress in stability.

GOWON (YAKUBU) 1974-75 national budget broadcast. [Lagos, 1974?]. pp. 20. Cover title: A better life for the people.

NIGERIA. Federal Ministry of Information. 1974. Caring for the people: answers on the 1974/75 federal budget. [Lagos, 1974?]. pp. 23.

— Pakistan.

SYED (HASAB ALI) An economic analysis of the annual budgets of the Punjab, Sind, North-West Frontier and Baluchistan provinces, 1972-73. Lahore, [1973]. pp. 174. (Punjab (Pakistan). Board of Economic Inquiry. Publications. No.155)

— Spain.

BELTRAN VILLALVA (MIGUEL) Ideologias y gasto publico en España, 1814-1860. [Madrid], Instituto de Estudios Fiscales, [1977]. pp. 522. bibliog.

— United Kingdom.

POND (CHRIS) The wages free fall: a submission to the chancellor and the TUC. London, 1977. fo. 8. (Low Pay Unit. Low Pay Papers. No. 14)

CONFEDERATION OF BRITISH INDUSTRY. The Budget 1978: CBI representations to the Chancellor of the Exchequer. London, 1978. pp. 35.

HAWKINS (ANGUS B.) A forgotten crisis: Gladstone and finance during the 1850's. London, 1978. fo. 39. (London. University. London School of Economics and Political Science. Gladstone Memorial Trust Prize Essays. 1978) Typescript.

WARD (T.S.) and NEILD (R.R.) The measurement and reform of budgetary policy. London, 1978. pp. 118.

— United States.

KNIGHT (KENNETH W.) and WILTSHIRE (KENNETH W.) Formulating government budgets: aspects of Australian and North American experience. St. Lucia, [1977]. pp. 179. bibliog.

HAVEMANN (JOEL) Congress and the budget. Bloomington, [1978]. pp. 247. bibliog.

IPPOLITO (DENNIS S.) The budget and national politics. San Francisco, [1978]. pp. 217. bibliogs.

BUENOS AIRES

— Harbour.

HISTORIAS del puerto de Buenos Aires. Buenos Aires, [1975]. 1 vol. (unpaged).

— History.

SOCOLOW (SUSAN MIGDEN) The merchants of Buenos Aires 1778-1810: family and commerce. Cambridge, 1978. pp. 253. bibliog.

— Social life and customs.

ARNAUDO (LIDIA) Del Buenos Aires de ayer: de como se vivia en el barrio de Palermo a fines del siglo pasado y principios de 1900. Buenos Aires, [1976]. pp. 96.

BUFFALO CREEK

— Flood, 1972.

ERIKSON (KAI T.) Everything in its path: destruction of community in the Buffalo Creek flood. New York, [1976]. pp. 284. bibliog.

ERIKSON (KAI T.) In the wake of the flood. London, [1979]. pp. 220. bibliog.

BUILDING

— Canada — Alberta.

ALBERTA. Department of Business Development and Tourism. Research and Analysis Branch. List of construction projects. s-a., Ja/Je 1978- Edmonton. Supersedes ALBERTA. Business Services Branch. List of industrial projects.

— Jamaica — Statistics.

JAMAICA. Department of Statistics. 1978. Abstract of building and construction statistics, 1977. [Kingston, 1978]. pp. 32.

— United Kingdom — Contracts and specifications.

HUDSON (ALFRED) Building and engineering contracts, including the duties and liabilities of architects, engineers and surveyors; tenth edition by I.N. Duncan Wallace. London, 1970. pp. 921.

BUILDING AND LOAN ASSOCIATIONS

— Finland.

FINLAND. Tilastokeskus. Asuntoyhteisöjen yritystilasto. a., 1974- Helsinki. [in Finnish and Swedish]

BUILDING AND LOAN ASSOCIATIONS (Cont.)

— United Kingdom.

BIRMINGHAM. University. Centre for Urban and Regional Studies. Housing Monitoring Team. The structure and functioning of building societies: a head office view. Birmingham, 1978. pp. 53. *(Birmingham. University. Centre for Urban and Regional Studies. Research Memoranda. No. 64)*

BUILDING FITTINGS

— Trade and manufacture — Norway.

INNSTILLING om innredningsindustriens strukturelle omstilling; fra et utvalg oppnevnt av Industridepartementet i juni 1967. Oslo, 1970. pp. 51.

BUILDING MATERIALS INDUSTRY

— Russia — Ukraine.

PEDAN (MIKHAIL PETROVICH) and others. Problemy razvitiia i razmeshcheniia promyshlennosti stroitel'nykh materialov. Kiev, 1977. pp. 245.

BUILDING TRADES

— United States.

GLOVER (ROBERT W.) Minority enterprise in construction. New York, 1977. pp. 174. *bibliog.*

BUITRAGO SALAZAR (EVELIO).

BUITRAGO SALAZAR (EVELIO) Zarpazo the bandit: memoirs of an undercover agent of the Colombian Army;...translated by M. Murray Lasley; edited.. .by Russell W. Ramsey. University, Ala., [1977]. pp. 169.

BUKHARIN (NIKOLAI IVANOVICH).

VAGANOV (FEDOR MIKHAILOVICH) Pravyi uklon v VKP(b) i ego razgrom, 1928-1930 gg. 2nd ed. Moskva, 1977. pp. 328.

COATES (KEN) The case of Nikolai Bukharin. Nottingham, 1978. pp. 104. *bibliogs.*

BUKHARIN (NIKOLAI IVANOVICH) The politics and economics of the transition period; edited with an introduction by Kenneth J. Tarbuck. London, 1979. pp. 261. *bibliog.*

BUKOVSKII (VLADIMIR KONSTANTINOVICH).

BUKOVSKII (VLADIMIR KONSTANTINOVICH) To build a castle: my life as a dissenter. London, 1978. pp. 352.

BUKUSU.

WOLF (JAN J. DE) Differentiation and integration in Western Kenya: a study of religious innovation and social change among the Bukusu. The Hague, [1977]. pp. 231. *bibliog. (Afrika-Studiecentrum. Change and Continuity in Africa. 10)*

BULGARIA

— Constitution.

BULGARIA. Constitution, 1971. Constitution of the People's Republic of Bulgaria, adopted by a national referendum on May 16, 1971. Sofia, 1971. pp. 47.

— Dictionaries and encyclopedias.

ENTSIKLOPEDIIA A - Ia. Sofiia, 1974. pp. 975.

— Economic conditions.

SHABUNINA (VALENTINA IVANOVNA) Ekonomika Narodnoi Respubliki Bolgarii: na etape stroitel'stva razvitogo sotsialisticheskogo obshchestva. Moskva, 1977. pp. 191.

— History — 1876, Uprising.

ULUNIAN (AKOP ARUTIUNOVICH) Aprel'skoe vosstanie 1876 goda v Bolgarii i Rossiia: ocherki. Moskva, 1978. pp. 214. *bibliog.* With English table of contents.

— Politics and government.

DIMITR Blagoev - vydaiushchiisia teoretik i revoliutsioner: sbornik statei k 120-letiiu so dnia rozhdeniia; [perevod s bolgarskogo]. Moskva, 1977. pp. 303.

— Relations (general) with Russia.

ULUNIAN (AKOP ARUTIUNOVICH) Aprel'skoe vosstanie 1876 goda v Bolgarii i Rossiia: ocherki. Moskva, 1978. pp. 214. *bibliog.* With English table of contents.

— Statistics.

SBORNIK TRUDOVE PO STATISTIKA; [pd. by] Nauchnoizsledovatelski Institut po Statistika [Bulgaria]. irreg., 1976(no.1)- Sofia. *[with Russian and English summaries].*

BULGARIANS IN MACEDONIA.

MACDERMOTT (MERCIA) Freedom or death: the life of Gotsé Delchev. London, 1978. pp. 405. *bibliog.*

BUND DER GEÄCHTETEN.

GRANDJONC (JACQUES) and WERNER (MICHAEL) Wolfgang Strähls "Briefe eines Schweizers aus Paris", 1835: zur Geschichte des Bundes der Geächteten in der Schweiz und zur Rezeption Heines unter deutschen Handwerkern in Paris. Trier, [1978]. pp. 85. *bibliog. (Karl-Marx-Haus. Schriften. 21)*

BUREAUCRACY.

WOLL (PETER) American bureaucracy. 2nd ed. New York, [1977]. pp. 260.

DUNSIRE (ANDREW) Control in a bureaucracy. Oxford, 1978. pp. 263. *bibliog. (The execution process. vol.2)*

DUNSIRE (ANDREW) Implementation in a bureaucracy. Oxford, 1978. pp. 260. *bibliog. (The execution process. vol.1)*

NACHMIAS (DAVID) and ROSENBLOOM (DAVID H.) Bureaucratic culture: citizens and administrators in Israel. London, [1978]. pp. 212. *bibliog.*

SPROULL (LEE) and others. Organizing an anarchy: belief, bureaucracy, and politics in the National Institute of Education. Chicago, 1978. pp. 282. *bibliog.*

BUREAUCRACY: the career of a concept; edited by Eugene Kamenka and Martin Krygier. London, 1979. pp. 165.

CAMPBELL (EDWIN COLIN) and SZABLOWSKI (GEORGE J.) The superbureaucrats: structure and behaviour in central agencies. Toronto, [1979]. pp. 286. *bibliog.*

PRESTHUS (ROBERT V.) The organizational society. rev.ed. London, 1979. pp. 288.

BURGLARY

— Canada.

WALLER (IRVIN) and OKIHIRO (NORMAN) Burglary: the victim and the public. Toronto, [1978]. pp. 190. *bibliog. (Toronto. University. Centre of Criminology. Canadian Studies in Criminology. 4)*

BURGUNDY

— History.

VAUGHAN (RICHARD) Professor of Medieval History, University of Hull. Charles the Bold: the last Valois duke of Burgundy. London, 1973. pp. 491. *bibliog.*

VAUGHAN (RICHARD) Professor of Medieval History, University of Hull. Valois Burgundy. London, 1975. pp. 254. *bibliog.*

BURKE (EDMUND).

KRAMNICK (ISAAC) The rage of Edmund Burke: portrait of an ambivalent conservative. New York, [1977]. pp. 225. *bibliogs.*

BURN (JAMES DAWSON).

BURN (JAMES DAWSON) The autobiography of a beggar boy;...edited with an introduction by David Vincent. London, [1978]. pp. 205. *bibliog.* Reprint of the first edition published in London, 1855.

BURNHOLME AND FORDER LIMITED.

DILLON (THOMAS MICHAEL) and GARRETT (DENNIS) Burnholme and Forder Limited, in liquidation; Brayhead Limited, in liquidation: investigation under section 165b of the Companies Act 1948; report. London, H.M.S.O., 1979. 1 vol.(various pagings).

BURTON-UPON-TRENT

— Industries.

OWEN (C.C.) The development of industry in Burton upon Trent. Chichester, 1978. pp. 279. *bibliog.*

BURYAT REPUBLIC

— Economic conditions.

RADNAEV (GOMBO SHIRAPOVICH) Narodnokhoziaistvennyi kompleks Buriatskoi ASSR: struktura, ispol'zovanie resursov, problemy razvitiia; otvetstvennyi redaktor B.P. Orlov. Novosibirsk, 1979. pp. 253.

— Economic policy.

PROBLEMY osvoeniia severa Buriatskoi ASSR. Novosibirsk, 1978. pp. 109.

— History.

KRAVTSOV (VASILII TIKHONOVICH) Kiakhta revoliutsionnaia: iz istorii goroda Kiakty i iuzhnogo Pribaikal'ia v 1905-1923 gg. Ulan-Ude, 1977. pp. 239.

BUSINESS.

BRANDEIS (LOUIS DEMBITZ) Business: a profession. New York, 1971. pp. 327. *Reprint of work originally published Boston, 1914.*

The BUSINESS system: a bicentennial view; [by] Milton Friedman [and others]. Hanover, N.H., 1977. pp. 91. *Symposium to celebrate the 75th anniversary of the Amos Tuck School of Business Administration, Dartmouth College.*

BUSINESS and businessmen: studies in business, economic and accounting history; edited by Sheila Marriner. Liverpool, [1978]. pp. 300. *bibliogs.*

READINGS in accounting and business research, 1970-1977; edited by R. H. Parker. [London], 1978. pp. 184.

DREW (JOHN) Writer on international affairs. Doing business in the European Community. London, 1979. pp. 280. *bibliogs.*

ETHICAL theory and business; edited by Tom L. Beauchamp, Norman E. Bowie. Englewood Cliffs, N.J., [1979]. pp. 642. *bibliogs.*

— Data processing.

BRESLIN (JUDSON) and TASHENBERG (C. BRADLEY) Distributed processing systems: end of the mainframe era? New York, [1978]. pp. 228.

McKEONE (DERMOT H.) Small computers for business and industry. Farnborough, Hants., [1979]. pp. 209.

BUSINESS CYCLES.

CONTADOR (CLAUDIO ROBERTO) Ciclos econômicos e indicadores de atividade no Brasil. Rio de Janeiro, 1977. pp. 237. *bibliog. (Brazil. Instituto de Planejamento Econômico e Social. Instituto de Pesquisas. Relatorios de Pesquisa. No. 35)*

IN search of economic indicators: essays on business surveys; edited by Werner H. Strigel. Berlin, 1977. pp. 198.

ECKSTEIN (OTTO) The great recession, with a postscript on stagflation. Amsterdam, 1978. pp. 213.

HEILBRONER (ROBERT LOUIS) Beyond boom and crash. New York, [1978]. pp. 111.

KINDLEBERGER (CHARLES POOR) The aging economy. Kiel, 1978. pp. 17. *bibliog. (Kiel. Universität. Institut für Weltwirtschaft. Bernhard-Harms-Vorlesungen. 8)*

SPREE (REINHARD) Wachstumstrends und Konjunkturzyklen in der deutschen Wirtschaft von 1820 bis 1913: quantitativer Rahmen für eine Konjunkturgeschichte des 19. Jahrhunderts. Göttingen, [1978]. pp. 215. *bibliog.*

WETTERGREEN (KJELL) Konjunkturbølger fra utlandet i Norsk økonomi: international cycles in the Norwegian economy. Oslo, 1978. pp. 138. *(Norway. Statistiske Centralbyrå. Samfunnsøkonomiske Studier. 36)*

BUSINESS ETHICS.

ISSUES in business and society;...[edited by] George A. Steiner [and] John F. Steiner. 2nd ed. New York, [1977]. pp. 560.

ETHICS, free enterprise, and public policy: original essays on moral issues in business; edited by Richard T. de George and Joseph A. Pichler. New York, 1978. pp. 329. *bibliogs.*

ETHICAL theory and business; edited by Tom L. Beauchamp, Norman E. Bowie. Englewood Cliffs, N.J., [1979]. pp. 642. *bibliogs.*

BUSINESS FORECASTING.

The FUTURE of business: global issues in the 80s and 90s; edited by Max Ways. New York, [1979]. pp. 99.

BUSINESS LAW

— Netherlands.

DUTCH business law: legal, accounting and tax aspects of business in the Netherlands; by Steven R. Schuit [and others]. Deventer, 1978. pp. 567.

BUSINESS MATHEMATICS.

KOO (DELIA) Elements of optimization with applications in economics and business. New York, [1977]. pp. 220. *bibliog.*

BUSINESS RELOCATION

— United Kingdom.

TOWNROE (P.M.) Industrial movement: experience in the US and the UK. Farnborough, [1979]. pp. 250. *bibliog.*

— United States.

TOWNROE (P.M.) Industrial movement: experience in the US and the UK. Farnborough, [1979]. pp. 250. *bibliog.*

BUSINESSMEN.

BUSINESS and businessmen: studies in business, economic and accounting history; edited by Sheila Marriner. Liverpool, [1978]. pp. 300. *bibliogs.*

— Canada.

BLISS (MICHAEL) A living profit: studies in the social history of Canadian business, 1883-1911. Toronto, [1974]. pp. 160. *bibliog.*

NEWMAN (PETER CHARLES) Bronfman dynasty: the Rothschilds of the New World. Toronto, [1978]. pp. 318.

— United States.

MAY (GEORGE SMITH) R.E. Olds: auto industry pioneer. Grand Rapids, Mich., [1977]. pp. 458.

BUSTAMANTE (Sir ALEXANDER).

JAMAICA INFORMATION SERVICE. Sir Alexander Bustamante. Kingston, [1969]. pp. 19. *(Facts on Jamaica. No. 25)*

BUTTINGER (JOSEPH).

GARDINER (MURIEL) and BUTTINGER (JOSEPH) Damit wir nicht vergessen: unsere Jahre 1934-1947 in Wien, Paris und New York. Wien, [1978]. pp. 168. *bibliog.*

BYZANTINE EMPIRE

— Civilization.

BROWN (PETER ROBERT LAMONT) The world of late antiquity: from Marcus Aurelius to Muhammad. London, 1976. pp. 216. *bibliog.*

— Foreign relations.

GEANAKOPLOS (DENO JOHN) Emperor Michael Palaeologus and the west, 1258-1282: a study in Byzantine-Latin relations. Hamden, Conn., 1973. pp. 434. *bibliog. First published in Cambridge, Massachusetts, in 1959.*

— History.

PROCOPIUS, of Caesarea. History of the wars; (with an English translation by H.B. Dewing). London, 1914-28 repr. 1962-71. 5 vols. *bibliog. Parallel Greek and English texts.*

GEANAKOPLOS (DENO JOHN) Emperor Michael Palaeologus and the west, 1258-1282: a study in Byzantine-Latin relations. Hamden, Conn., 1973. pp. 434. *bibliog. First published in Cambridge, Massachusetts, in 1959.*

LAIOU-THOMADAKIS (ANGELIKI E.) Constantinople and the Latins: the foreign policy of Andronicus II, 1282-1328. Cambridge, Mass., 1972. pp. 388. *bibliog. (Harvard University. Harvard Historical Studies. vol. 88)*

— Intellectual life.

RUNCIMAN (Sir STEVEN) The last Byzantine renaissance. Cambridge, 1970. pp. 112. *bibliog. (Belfast. Queen's University. Wiles Lectures. 1968)*

CABINET MINISTERS

— Africa.

BIDWELL (ROBIN LEONARD) ed. Guide to African ministers. London, 1978. pp. 79.

— United Kingdom.

U.K. Civil Service Department. List of ministerial responsibilities. q., Oc 1978- London.

— United States.

BIOGRAPHICAL directory of the United States executive branch, 1774-1977; Robert Sobel, editor in chief. Westport, 1977. pp. 503.

CAKCHIKEL INDIANS.

WARREN (KAY B.) The symbolism of subordination: Indian identity in a Guatemalan town. Austin, [1978]. pp. 209. *bibliog.*

CALABRIA

— Social history.

PEZZINO (PAOLO) La riforma agraria in Calabria: intervento pubblico e dinamica sociale in un'area del Mezzogiorno, 1950-1970. Milano, 1977. pp. 253. *(Istituto Nazionale per la Storia del Movimento di Liberazione in Italia. [Publications])*

CALCULUS.

SPIVAK (MICHAEL) Calculus on manifolds: a modern approach to classical theorems of advanced calculus. Menlo Park, Calif., 1965. pp. 146. *bibliog.*

CALCULUS, DIFFERENTIAL.

SCHREIBER (MORRIS) Differential forms: a heuristic introduction. New York, [1977]. pp. 147. *bibliog.*

CALCULUS OF VARIATIONS.

EKELAND (IVAR) and TEMAM (ROGER) Convex analysis and variational problems. Amsterdam, 1976. pp. 402. *bibliog.*

CALCUTTA

— City planning.

CALCUTTA METROPOLITAN PLANNING ORGANISATION. First report, 1962. [Calcutta, 1963]. pp. 80.

— Clubs.

PANCKRIDGE (H. R.) A short history of the Bengal Club, 1827-1927. Calcutta, 1927. pp. 64.

CALDERA (MIGUEL).

POWELL (PHILIP WAYNE) Mexico's Miguel Caldera: the taming of America's first frontier, 1548-1597. Tucson, 1977. pp. 322. *bibliog.*

CALENDAR, RUSSIAN SECTARIAN.

BOLONEV (FIRS FEDOSOVICH) Narodnyi kalendar' semeiskikh Zabaikal'ia, vtoraia polovina XIX - nachalo XX v.; otvetstvennyi redaktor E.A. Ashchepkov. Novosibirsk, 078. pp. 159.

CALIFORNIA

— History.

BEASLEY (DELILAH LEONTIUM) The Negro trail blazers of California: a compilation of records, etc. New York, 1969. pp. 317. *bibliog. Reprint of work originally published in Los Angeles, 1919.*

POWELL (RICHARD ROY BELDEN) Compromises of conflicting claims: a century of California law; 1760 to 1860. Dobbs Ferry, N.Y., 1977. pp. 332.

— Race relations.

MARKUS (ANDREW) Fear and hatred: purifying Australia and California, 1850-1901. Sydney, 1979. pp. 95.

— Social life and customs.

ORD (EDWARD OTHO CRESAP) The city of the angels and the city of the saints; or, A trip to Los Angeles and San Bernardino in 1856;...edited by Neal Harlow. San Marino, 1978. pp. 56. *bibliog.*

CALVIN (JEAN).

WENDEL (FRANÇOIS) Calvin: the origins and development of his religious thought; translated [from the French] by Philip Mairet. London, 1965 repr. 1978. pp. 383. *bibliog.*

CAMARA (HELDER) Archbishop of Olinda and Recife.

CAMARA (HELDER) Archbishop of Olinda and Recife. The conversions of a bishop: an interview with José de Broucker; translated by Hilary Davies. London, 1979. pp. 222.

CAMBODIA

— Foreign relations — China.

BOUCHER (JEAN-MARIE) The relationship between Cambodia and China, 1954-1970: a study of the changing bases of political accommodation. 1978. fo. 355. *bibliog. Typescript. Ph.D. (London) thesis: unpublished. This thesis is the property of London University and may not be removed from the Library.*

— — United States.

SHAWCROSS (WILLIAM) Sideshow: Kissinger, Nixon and the destruction of Cambodia. London, 1979. pp. 467. *bibliog.*

CAMBODIA(Cont.)

— Politics and government.

SHAWCROSS (WILLIAM) Sideshow: Kissinger, Nixon and the destruction of Cambodia. London, 1979. pp. 467. *bibliog.*

CAMBRIDGE

— Economic conditions.

CAMBRIDGESHIRE. County Planning Department. Cambridgeshire structure plan: Cambridge sub-area: report of the joint study team. Cambridge, 1977. pp. 77.

— Economic policy.

CAMBRIDGESHIRE. County Planning Department. Cambridgeshire structure plan: Cambridge sub-area: report of the joint study team. Cambridge, 1977. pp. 77.

— Social conditions.

CAMBRIDGESHIRE. County Planning Department. Cambridgeshire structure plan: Cambridge sub-area: report of the joint study team. Cambridge, 1977. pp. 77.

— Social policy.

CAMBRIDGESHIRE. County Planning Department. Cambridgeshire structure plan: Cambridge sub-area: report of the joint study team. Cambridge, 1977. pp. 77.

CAMBRIDGESHIRE

— Economic conditions.

CAMBRIDGESHIRE. County Planning Department. Cambridgeshire structure plan: report of survey: consultation draft. Cambridge, 1976. pp. 160.

CAMBRIDGESHIRE. County Planning Department. Cambridgeshire structure plan: draft written statement. Cambridge, 1977. pp. 182.

CAMBRIDGESHIRE. County Planning Department. Cambridgeshire structure plan: supplement to report of survey: consultation draft. Cambridge, 1977. pp. 93.

CAMBRIDGESHIRE. County Planning Department. Cambridgeshire structure plan: report on public participation and consultations. Cambridge, 1979. pp. 60, 89.

CAMBRIDGESHIRE. County Planning Department. Cambridgeshire structure plan: supplement to report of survey. Cambridge, 1979. pp. 176.

CAMBRIDGESHIRE. County Planning Department. Cambridgeshire structure plan: written statement. Cambridge, 1979. pp. 197.

— Economic policy.

CAMBRIDGESHIRE. County Planning Department. Cambridgeshire structure plan: draft written statement. Cambridge, 1977. pp. 182.

CAMBRIDGESHIRE. County Planning Department. Cambridgeshire structure plan: report on alternative strategies. Cambridge, 1977. pp. 74.

CAMBRIDGESHIRE. County Planning Department. Cambridgeshire structure plan: report on public participation and consultations. Cambridge, 1979. pp. 60, 89.

CAMBRIDGESHIRE. County Planning Department. Cambridgeshire structure plan: written statement. Cambridge, 1979. pp. 197.

— Social conditions.

CAMBRIDGESHIRE. County Planning Department. Cambridgeshire structure plan: report of survey: consultation draft. Cambridge, 1976. pp. 160.

CAMBRIDGESHIRE. County Planning Department. Cambridgeshire structure plan: draft written statement. Cambridge, 1977. pp. 182.

CAMBRIDGESHIRE. County Planning Department. Cambridgeshire structure plan: supplement to report of survey: consultation draft. Cambridge, 1977. pp. 93.

CAMBRIDGESHIRE. County Planning Department. Cambridgeshire structure plan: report on public participation and consultations. Cambridge, 1979. pp. 60, 89.

CAMBRIDGESHIRE. County Planning Department. Cambridgeshire structure plan: supplement to report of survey. Cambridge, 1979. pp. 176.

CAMBRIDGESHIRE. County Planning Department. Cambridgeshire structure plan: written statement. Cambridge, 1979. pp. 197.

— Social policy.

CAMBRIDGESHIRE. County Planning Department. Cambridgeshire structure plan: draft written statement. Cambridge, 1977. pp. 182.

CAMBRIDGESHIRE. County Planning Department. Cambridgeshire structure plan: report on alternative strategies. Cambridge, 1977. pp. 74.

CAMBRIDGESHIRE. County Planning Department. Cambridgeshire structure plan: report on public participation and consultations. Cambridge, 1979. pp. 60, 89.

CAMBRIDGESHIRE. County Planning Department. Cambridgeshire structure plan: written statement. Cambridge, 1979. pp. 197.

CAMPOS (FRANCISCO LUIS DA SILVA).

CAMPOS (FRANCISCO LUIS DA SILVA) Discursos parlamentares; seleção e introdução Paulo Bonavides. Brasilia, 1979. pp. 153. *Brazil. Congresso. Câmara dos Deputados. Perfis Parlamentares. 6)*

CANADA.

DROUIN (MARIE JOSÉE) and BRUCE-BRIGGS (B.) Canada has a future. Toronto, [1978]. pp. 282. *Published for the Hudson Institute of Canada.*

— Appropriations and expenditures.

CANADA. Treasury Board. Federal expenditure plan. a., 1979/80- Ottawa. *[in English and French].*

— Census.

CANADA. Census, 1971. 1971 census catalogue: population, housing, agriculture, employment; Publications du recensement de 1971: population, logement, agriculture, emploi. Final ed. [Ottawa], 1974. pp. 72. *In English and French.*

— Commerce — Statistics.

CANADA. Statistics Canada. Trade of Canada: imports: merchandise trade: commodity detail. a., 1976/1977(1st)- Ottawa. *[in English and French]*

— — France.

MIQUELON (DALE) Dugard of Rouen: French trade to Canada and the West Indies, 1729-1770. Montreal, [1978]. pp. 282. *bibliog.*

— Constitution.

BRITISH COLUMBIA. Premier. 1976. What is British Columbia's position on the constitution of Canada?; presented by William R. Bennett, etc.. Victoria, 1976. 1 pamphlet (unpaged).

BRITISH COLUMBIA. 1978. British Columbia's constitutional proposals. [Victoria, Queen's Printer], 1978. 9 vols. (in 1)

COLAS (EMILE) La troisième voie: une nouvelle constitution. [Ottawa, 1978]. pp. 246. *bibliog.*

— Constitutional law.

SCOTT (FRANCIS REGINALD) Essays on the constitution: aspects of Canadian law and politics. Toronto, [1977]. pp. 422. *bibliog.*

— Defences.

HAGEN (LAWRENCE S.) Civil defence: the case for reconsideration. Kingston, Ont., 1977. pp. 88. *bibliog.* *(Kingston, Ontario. Queen's University. Center for International Relations. National Security Series. No. 7/77).*

PRESTON (RICHARD ARTHUR) The defence of the undefended border: planning for war in North America, 1867-1939. Montreal, 1977. pp. 300.

— Department of Industry, Trade and Commerce.

CANADA. Department of Industry, Trade and Commerce. 1973. Industry, Trade and Commerce at your service. Ottawa, 1973. pp. 62.

— Economic conditions.

CANADA in transition; edited by Grant S. McClellan. New York, 1977. pp. 224. *bibliog.*

DROUIN (MARIE JOSÉE) and BRUCE-BRIGGS (B.) Canada has a future. Toronto, [1978]. pp. 282. *Published for the Hudson Institute of Canada.*

— — Bibliography.

CLEMENT (WALLACE) and DRACHE (DANIEL) A practical guide to Canadian political economy. Toronto, 1978. pp. 183. *bibliog.*

— Economic history.

BLISS (MICHAEL) A living profit: studies in the social history of Canadian business, 1883-1911. Toronto, [1974]. pp. 160. *bibliog.*

— — Bibliography.

DICK (TREVOR J.O.) compiler. Economic history of Canada: a guide to information sources. Detroit, [1978]. pp. 174.

— Economic policy.

PHIDD (RICHARD W.) and DOERN (G. BRUCE) The politics and management of Canadian economic policy. Toronto, [1978]. pp. 598. *bibliog.*

POLICY review and outlook, 1978: a time for realism; edited by Judith Maxwell. [Montreal], [1978]. pp. 157.

— Emigration and immigration.

CANADA. Department of Citizenship and Immigration. Statistics Section. 1956. Origine ethnique des immigrants par province de destination, années civiles 1946-1955. Ottawa, 1956. fo. (12).

CANADA. Department of Employment and Immigration. Annual report. a., 1977/78- Ottawa. *[in English and French] Supersedes CANADA. Department of Manpower and Immigration. Annual report and CANADA. Unemployment Insurance Commission. Annual report.*

MUNRO (IAIN R.) Immigration. Toronto, [1978]. pp. 96.

— Executive departments.

CANADA. Department of Industry, Trade and Commerce. 1973. Industry, Trade and Commerce at your service. Ottawa, 1973. pp. 62.

CANADA. Department of Employment and Immigration. Annual report. a., 1977/78- Ottawa. *[in English and French] Supersedes CANADA. Department of Manpower and Immigration. Annual report and CANADA. Unemployment Insurance Commission. Annual report.*

CAMPBELL (EDWIN COLIN) and SZABLOWSKI (GEORGE J.) The superbureaucrats: structure and behaviour in central agencies. Toronto, [1979]. pp. 286. *bibliog.*

— Foreign economic relations — European Economic Community countries.

CONFERENCE ON CANADA AND THE EUROPEAN COMMUNITY, QUEEN'S UNIVERSITY, KINGSTON, ONTARIO, 1977. Report...; by Nils Ørvik, editor. Kingston, Ont., [1978?]. pp. 225. *bibliogs*. (Kingston, Ontario. Queen's University. Centre for International Relations. European Studies Series. No. 1/77)

VALASKAKIS (KIMON) "L'option Europe": analyse de la plausibilité d'une association Québec/Canada/Europe; préparé pour le compte du Ministère des Affaires Intergouvernementales du Québec. [Québec, 1979]. pp. 176.

— — Scandinavia.

TELLIER (LUC-NORMAND) Etude des possibilités de rapprochement économique entre le Québec, le Canada et les pays scandinaves; préparé pour le compte du Ministère des Affaires Intergouvernementales du Québec. [Québec, 1979]. pp. 139. *bibliog*.

— — United States.

CUFF (ROBERT D.) and GRANATSTEIN (JACK LAWRENCE) American dollars - Canadian prosperity: Canadian-American economic relations, 1945-1950. Toronto, 1978. pp. 286. *bibliog*.

FRANK (HELMUT J.) and SCHANZ (JOHN J.) U.S.-Canadian energy trade: a study of changing relationships. Boulder, [1978]. pp. 136.

— Foreign relations.

CANADA in transition; edited by Grant S. McClellan. New York, 1977. pp. 224. *bibliog*.

A FOREMOST nation: Canadian foreign policy and a changing world; edited by Norman Hillmer and Garth Stevenson. Toronto, [1977]. pp. 296.

— — United States.

PRESTON (RICHARD ARTHUR) The defence of the undefended border: planning for war in North America, 1867-1939. Montreal, 1977. pp. 300.

— History.

WINKS (ROBIN WILLIAM) The relevance of Canadian history: U.S. and imperial perspectives. Toronto, [1979]. pp. 99. *bibliog*. *The 1977 Joanne Goodman lectures delivered at the University of Western Ontario.*

— Industries.

GORECKI (PAUL KAROL) Economies of scale and efficient plant size in Canadian manufacturing industries. [Ottawa, 1976?]. pp. 111. *bibliog*. (Canada. Bureau of Competition Policy. Research Branch. Research Monographs. No. 1)

CANADA. Statistics Canada. Capital and repair expenditures, manufacturing sub-industries, Canada. a., 1978(1st)- Ottawa. *[in English and French] Data previously included in CANADA. Statistics Canada. Service bulletin: Investment statistics.*

TRAVES (TOM) The state and enterprise: Canadian manufacturers and the Federal government, 1917-1931. Toronto, [1979]. pp. 175. *Revision of author's thesis, York University.*

— Military policy.

RANGER (ROBERT JOHN) The Canadian contribution to the control of chemical and biological warfare. Toronto, [1976]. pp. 66. *(Canadian Institute of International Affairs. Wellesley Papers. 5)*

— Nationalism.

CANADA'S third option; edited by S.D. Berkowitz and Robert K. Logan. Toronto, [1978]. pp. 282.

— Parliament — Senate.

CAMPBELL (EDWIN COLIN) The Canadian Senate: a lobby from within. Toronto, [1978]. pp. 184. *bibliogs*.

— Politics and government.

CANADA in transition; edited by Grant S. McClellan. New York, 1977. pp. 224. *bibliog*.

LAZARUS (MORDEN) The long winding road: Canadian labour in politics. Vancouver, [1977]. pp. 103. *bibliog*.

RANKIN (T. MURRAY) Freedom of information in Canada: will the doors stay shut? [Victoria?], 1977. pp. 155.

SCOTT (FRANCIS REGINALD) Essays on the constitution: aspects of Canadian law and politics. Toronto, [1977]. pp. 422. *bibliog*.

APPROACHES to Canadian politics; editor: John H. Redekop. Scarborough, Ontario, [1978]. pp. 377. *bibliogs*.

CANADA'S third option; edited by S.D. Berkowitz and Robert K. Logan. Toronto, [1978]. pp. 282.

CANADIAN provincial politics: the party systems of the ten provinces...; edited by Martin Robin. 2nd ed. Scarborough, Ont., [1978]. pp. 316. *bibliogs*.

COLAS (EMILE) La troisième voie: une nouvelle constitution. [Ottawa, 1978]. pp. 246. *bibliog*.

FIDLER (RICHARD) RCMP: the real subversives. Toronto, [1978]. pp. 91. *bibliog*.

HUMPHREYS (DAVID L.) Joe Clark: a portrait. [Ottawa], 1978. pp. 276.

POLICY review and outlook, 1978: a time for realism; edited by Judith Maxwell. [Montreal], [1978]. pp. 157.

RADWANSKI (GEORGE) Trudeau. Toronto, [1978]. pp. 372. *bibliog*.

STURSBERG (PETER) Lester Pearson and the dream of unity. Toronto, 1978. pp. 456.

The CANADIAN political process; edited by Richard Schultz [and others]. 3rd ed. Toronto, [1979]. pp. 416.

CHANDLER (MARSHA) and CHANDLER (WILLIAM M.) Public policy and provincial politics. Toronto, [1979]. pp. 325. *bibliog*.

CLIPPINGDALE (RICHARD) Laurier: his life and world. Toronto, [1979]. pp. 224. *bibliog*.

— Population.

CANADA. Statistics Canada. Estimates of population for Canada and the provinces. a., Je 1977- Ottawa. *[in English and French]*

— Race relations.

BASHAM (RICHARD DALTON) Crisis in blanc and white: urbanization and ethnic identity in French Canada. Boston, Mass., [1978]. pp. 287. *bibliog*.

KRAUTER (JOSEPH F.) and DAVIS (MORRIS) Minority Canadians: ethnic groups. Toronto, [1978]. pp. 120.

WARD (W. PETER) White Canada forever: popular attitudes and public policy toward Orientals in British Columbia. Montreal, [1978]. pp. 205.

— Social conditions.

MARSDEN (LORNA R.) and HARVEY (EDWARD B.) Fragile federation: social change in Canada. Toronto, [1979]. pp. 242. *bibliog*.

— Social policy.

TAYLOR (MALCOLM G.) Health insurance and Canadian public policy: the seven decisions that created the Canadian Health Insurance System. Montreal, [1978]. pp. 473. *bibliog*. *(Institute of Public Administration of Canada. Canadian Public Administration Series)*

— Statistics.

INFORMAT: w. bulletin; [pd. by] Statistics Canada. w. Ottawa. *Current issues only kept.*

CANADIAN LITERATURE

— Exhibitions.

CANADA. National Library of Canada. 1970. Manitoba authors. Ottawa, 1970. 1 vol. (unpaged). *In English and French.*

CANADIAN UNION OF POSTAL WORKERS.

DAVIDSON (JOE) and DEVERELL (JOHN) Joe Davidson. Toronto, 1978. pp. 192.

CANALS

— United Kingdom.

MALET (HUGH) Bridgewater: the canal Duke, 1736-1803. Manchester, [1977]. pp. 208. *bibliog*.

GRANT (RODERICK) The great canal. London, [1978]. pp. 156. *bibliog*.

— United States.

DUANE (WILLIAM JOHN) Letters addressed to the people of Pennsylvania respecting the internal improvement of the commonwealth by means of roads and canals. Philadelphia, 1811; New York, 1968. pp. 125.

POOR (HENRY VARNUM) History of the railroads and canals of the United States of America. New York, 1970. pp. 612. *Reprint of work originally published in New York, 1860.*

CANCER

— Europe.

CONFERENCE ON COMPREHENSIVE CANCER CONTROL, COPENHAGEN, 1977. Comprehensive cancer control; report, etc. Copenhagen, World Health Organization, Regional Office for Europe, 1978. pp. 52.

— Sweden.

SWEDEN. Socialstyrelsen. Cancer Registry. 1971. Cancer incidence in Sweden, 1959-1965; [by Nils Ringertz and others]. Stockholm, 1971. pp. 197.

— United Kingdom — Statistics.

U.K. Office of Population Censuses and Surveys. Cancer statistics: registrations: cases of diagnosed cancer registered in England and Wales. a., 1971- London.

CANNIBALISM.

ARENS (W.) The man-eating myth: anthropology and anthropophagy. New York, 1979. pp. 206. *bibliog*.

CANNING TOWN

— Industries.

CANNING TOWN COMMUNITY DEVELOPMENT PROJECT. Canning Town to North Woolwich: the aims of industry?: a study of industrial decline in one community. 2nd ed. [London, 1977]. pp. 76.

CANNING TOWN COMMUNITY DEVELOPMENT PROJECT. Growth and decline: Canning Town's economy, 1846-1976. [London], 1977. pp. 31. *bibliog*.

CANVEY ISLAND.

U.K. Health and Safety Executive. 1978. Canvey: an investigation of potential hazards from operations in the Canvey Island/Thurrock area, London, 1978. pp. 192, 1 map.

CAPE OF GOOD HOPE

— Government publications — Bibliography.

MUSIKER (NAOMI) compiler. Guide to Cape of Good Hope official publications, 1854-1910; edited by Reuben Musiker. Boston, Mass., [1976]. pp. 466.

CAPITAL.

CAPITAL.

HARCOURT (GEOFFREY COLIN) Theoretical controversy and social significance: an evaluation of the Cambridge controversies. Nedlands, W. Austr., 1975. pp. 29. *bibliog. (Western Australia, University of. Edward Shann Memorial Lectures in Economics. 1975)*

TESTA (VICTOR) El capital imperialista. Buenos Aires, 1975. pp. 460.

BOCCARA (PAUL) Sur la mise en mouvement du "Capital": premiers essais. [Paris, 1978]. pp. 334.

CAPITAL shortage and unemployment in the world economy: symposium 1977; edited by Herbert Giersch. Tübingen, [1978]. pp. 348. *bibliogs.*

The MEASUREMENT of capital: theory and practice; edited by K. D. Patterson and Kerry Schott. London, 1979. pp. 290. *bibliogs.*

— Canada.

NIOSI (JORGE) Le contrôle financier du capitalisme canadien. Montréal, 1978. pp. 217. *bibliog.*

— Kenya.

LEITNER (KERSTIN) Workers, trade unions and peripheral capitalism in Kenya after independence. Frankfurt am Main, [1977]. pp. 182. *bibliog.*

— Portugal.

PEREIRA (JOÃO MARTINS) Industria, ideologia e quotidiano: ensaio sobre o capitalismo em Portugal. Porto, 1974. pp. 254.

— Russia.

KULAZHENKO (VLADIMIR ANDREEVICH) Ekonomicheskie usloviia vosproizvodstva osnovnykh fondov v kolkhozakh. Minsk, 1978. pp. 158.

RYNDZIUNSKII (PAVEL GRIGOR'EVICH) Utverzhdenie kapitalizma v Rossii, 1850-1880 gg. Moskva, 1978. pp. 295.

— Underdeveloped areas.

See UNDERDEVELOPED AREAS — Capital.

— United Kingdom.

CITY CAPITAL MARKETS COMMITTEE. Written evidence to the Royal Commission on the Distribution of Income and Wealth. [London], 1975. fo.12.

KING (J.R.) Realisations and accruals of capital gains, with particular reference to company securities. London, Inland Revenue, 1978. pp. 29. *(Government Economic Service Working Papers. No. 15)*

— United States.

JAMES (JOHN A.) Money and capital markets in postbellum America. Princeton, N.J., [1978]. pp. 293. *bibliog.*

CAPITAL BUDGET

— United Kingdom.

The TEST discount rate and the required rate of return on investment: proceedings of a seminar held at the Civil Service College, Sunningdale, 16/17 June 1978. London, Treasury, 1979. pp. 57. *(Government Economic Service Working Papers. No. 22)*

CAPITAL GAINS TAX

— United Kingdom.

BUTTERWORTH AND CO. LTD. Handbook on the Capital Gains Tax Act 1979. London, 1979. pp. 276.

CAPITAL INVESTMENTS.

FITZGERALD (EDMUND VALPY KNOX) Public sector investment planning for developing countries. London, 1978. pp. 200. *bibliog.*

KING (PAUL FREDERICK) An investigation of the process of large scale capital investment decision making in diversified hierarchical organisations. 1978. fo. 510. *bibliog. Typescript. Ph.D. (London) thesis: unpublished. This thesis is the property of London University and may not be removed from the Library.*

SEKIGUCHI (SUEO) Japanese direct foreign investment. London, 1979. pp. 153. *bibliogs.*

— Decision making.

TRENDS in financial decision-making: planning and capital investment decisions; Cees van Dam, editor. Leiden, 1978. pp. 283. *bibliogs. (Instituut voor Bedrijfskunde. Nijenrode Studies in Business. vol. 2)*

— Bangladesh.

BANGLADESH. Department of Industries. 1976. Industrial investment schedule for two years, 1976-1978, for private sector. [Dacca, 1976]. pp. 163.

— Canada.

CANADA. Statistics Canada. Capital and repair expenditures, manufacturing sub-industries, Canada. a., 1978(1st)- Ottawa. *[in English and French] Data previously included in CANADA. Statistics Canada. Service bulletin: Investment statistics.*

— — Ontario.

ONTARIO. Economic Council. 1978. Business investment. [Toronto], 1978. pp. 137. *bibliog. (Issues and Alternatives, 1978)*

— Fiji.

FIJI. Bureau of Statistics. 1969. A survey of private sector capital investment expenditure in Fiji in 1968. [Suva], 1969. pp. 43.

— Germany — North Rhine-Westphalia.

NORTH RHINE-WESTPHALIA. Landesamt für Datenverarbeitung und Statistik. Beiträge zur Statistik des Landes Nordrhein- Westfalen. Heft 388. Investitionen der Industrie in Nordrhein- Westfalen 1966 bis 1975. Düsseldorf, 1978. pp. 169.

— Russia.

CHERNIAVSKII (VASILII OSIPOVICH) Voprosy effektivnosti i optimal'nosti. Moskva, 1977. pp. 171. *(Akademiia Nauk SSSR. Problemy Sovetskoi Ekonomiki)*

— United Kingdom.

CARRINGTON (JOHN C.) and EDWARDS (GEORGE T.) Financing industrial investment. London, 1979. pp. 283. *bibliog.*

— United States.

CAPITAL INVESTMENT CONFERENCE, UNIVERSITY OF PITTSBURGH, 1976. Health care capital: competition and control; editors: Gordon K. Macleod, Mark Perlman. Cambridge, Mass., [1978]. pp. 412.

EISNER (ROBERT) Factors in business investment. Cambridge, Mass., 1978. pp. 219. *bibliog. (National Bureau of Economic Research. Publications. No. 102)*

CAPITAL MOVEMENTS

— United Kingdom — Mathematical models.

A FINANCIAL sector for the Treasury model. Part 1. The model of the domestic monetary system; by Peter Spencer and Colin Mowl. Part 2. The model of external capital flows; by Rachel Lomax and Michael Denham. London, Treasury, 1978. pp. 115. *bibliogs. (Government Economic Service Working Papers. No. 17)*

CAPITAL PUNISHMENT

— United Kingdom.

MORRIS (TERENCE PATRICK) and BLOM-COOPER (LOUIS JACQUES) Murder in England and Wales since 1957. [London], 1979. pp. 16.

— United States.

CARRINGTON (FRANK G.) Neither cruel nor unusual. New Rochelle, N.Y., [1978]. pp. 223.

CAPITAL STOCK

— United Kingdom.

REES (R.D.) and MIALL (R.H.C.) The effects of regional policy on manufacturing investment and capital stock within the UK. London, Department of Industry, 1979. pp. 22. *(Government Economic Service Working Papers. No. 26)*

CAPITALISM.

FIELDHOUSE (DAVID KENNETH) ed. The theory of capitalist imperialism. London, 1967, repr. 1977. pp. 202. *bibliog.*

BOCCARA (PAUL) Etudes sur le capitalisme monopoliste d'État, sa crise et son issue. 3rd ed. [Paris, 1974]. pp. 504.

HABERMAS (JUERGEN) Legitimation crisis. London, 1976. pp. 166. *bibliog.*

KAPITALISTISCHE Ausbeutung heute: Autorenkollektiv DDR-UdSSR; (verantwortliche Redaktion: Günter Fabiunke [and others]). Berlin, [1977]. pp. 264.

NOVOSELOV (SERGEI PAVLOVICH) Obostrenie ekonomichskikh i sotsial'no-politicheskikh protivorechii kapitalizma. Moskva, 1977. pp. 199.

QUINNEY (RICHARD) Class, state and crime: on the theory and practice of criminal justice. New York, 1977 repr. 1978. pp. 179.

RIPALDA (JOSÉ MARÍA) The divided nation: the roots of a bourgeois thinker: G.W.F. Hegel. Assen, 1977. pp. 221. *bibliog.*

AMIN (SAMIR) The law of value and historical materialism...; (translated by Brian Pearce). New York, [1978]. pp. 133.

RUNHOFF (SUZANNE DE) The state, capital and economic policy; translated by Mike Sonenscher. London, 1978. pp. 152.

FRANK (ANDRE GUNDER) World accumulation, 492-1789. New York, [1978]. pp. 303. *bibliog.*

HEILBRONER (ROBERT LOUIS) Beyond boom and crash. New York, [1978]. pp. 111.

NOVAK (MICHAEL) The American vision: an essay on the future of democratic capitalism. Washington, [1978]. pp. 60. *(American Enterprise Institute for Public Policy Research. AEI Studies. 222)*

POLITICS, ideology and the state: papers from the Communist University of London, [9th session, 1977]; edited by Sally Hibbin. London, 1978. pp. 143.

ROTH (MIKE) and ELDRED (MICHAEL) Guide to Marx's "Capital". London, 1978. pp. 127. *(Conference of Socialist Economists. CSE Books)*

SOCIAL change in the capitalist world economy; edited by Barbara Hockey Kaplan. Beverly Hills, Calif., [1978]. pp. 239. *bibliogs. (American Sociological Association. Political Economy of the World-System Annuals. vol. 1)*

BELL (DANIEL) The cultural contradictions of capitalism. 2nd ed. London, 1979. pp. 301.

The CASE for private enterprise; editor: Cecil Turner. London, 1979. pp. 111.

DETHLOFF (HENRY C.) Americans and free enterprise. Englewood Cliffs, [1979]. pp. 336. *bibliogs.*

KAY (GEOFFREY B.) The economic theory of the working class. London, 1979. pp. 140. *bibliog.*

KUCZYNSKI (JUERGEN) Gesammelte Studien zur Geschichte und Theorie des Kapitalismus. Berlin, 1979. pp. 362.

LIS (CATHARINA) and SOLY (HUGO) Poverty and capitalism in pre-industrial Europe. Hassocks, 1979. pp. 267. *bibliog.*

ROGGE (BENJAMIN A.) Can capitalism survive? Indianapolis, [1979]. pp. 329.

ROUSSEAS (STEPHEN W.) Capitalism and catastrophe: a critical appraisal of the limits to capitalism. Cambridge, 1979. pp. 139. *bibliog.*

STATE and economy in contemporary capitalism; edited by Colin Crouch. London, [1979]. pp. 264. *bibliog.*

STEPHENS (JOHN D.) The transition from capitalism to socialism. London, 1979. pp. 231. *bibliog.*

WALLERSTEIN (IMMANUEL) The capitalist world-economy. Cambridge, 1979. pp. 305. *bibliogs.*

CAPITALISTS AND FINANCIERS

— Canada.

NIOSI (JORGE) The economy of Canada: a study of ownership and control; translated by Penelope Williams. Montréal, [1978]. pp. 179. *bibliog.*

— Egypt.

GRAN (PETER) Islamic roots of capitalism: Egypt, 1760-1840. Austin, [1979]. pp. 278. *bibliog. (Texas University. Center for Middle Eastern Studies. Modern Middle Eastern Series. No. 4)*

— Russia.

ARKHIPOV (VLADIMIR ANDREEVICH) and MOROZOV (LEONID FEDOROVICH) Bor'ba protiv kapitalisticheskikh elementov v promyshlennosti i torgovle, 20-e - nachalo 30-kh godov. Moskva, 1978. pp. 263. *bibliog.*

— United Kingdom.

BENWELL COMMUNITY DEVELOPMENT PROJECT. The making of a ruling class: two centuries of capital development on Tyneside. Newcastle-upon-Tyne, 1978. pp. 121. *(Final Report Series. No. 6)*

CLAY (CHRISTOPHER) Public finance and private wealth: the career of Sir Stephen Fox, 1627-1716. Oxford, 1978. pp. 362. *bibliog.*

— United States.

STURM (JAMES LESTER) Investing in the United States 1798-1893: upper wealth-holders in a market economy. New York, 1977. pp. 196. *bibliog.*

BLUME (MARSHALL E.) and FRIEND (IRWIN) The changing role of the individual investor. New York, [1978]. pp. 243. *bibliogs.*

CAPRIVI (LEO VON) Graf.

WEITOWITZ (ROLF GUNTER) Deutsche Politik und Handelspolitik unter Reichskanzler Leo von Caprivi, 1890-1894. Düsseldorf, [1978]. pp. 406. *bibliog.*

CARIB INDIANS.

MIGLIAZZA (ERNEST C.) The integration of the indigenous peoples of the territory of Roraima, Brazil. Copenhagen, 1978. pp. 29. *bibliog. (International Work Group for Indigenous Affairs. Documents. 32)*

CARIBBEAN AREA

— Bibliography.

DEAL (CARL W.) compiler. Latin America and the Caribbean: a dissertation bibliography. Ann Arbor, [1978]. pp. 164.

— Civilization — African influences.

AFRICA and the Caribbean: the legacies of a link; edited by Margaret E. Crahan and Franklin W. Knight. Baltimore, [1979]. pp. 159. *bibliog. (Johns Hopkins University. Johns Hopkins Studies in Atlantic History and Culture)*

— Commerce — Statistics.

EAST CARIBBEAN COMMON MARKET. Secretariat. Digest of external trade statistics. a., 1976(1st)- Antigua.

— Economic conditions.

PALMER (RANSFORD W.) Caribbean dependence on the United States economy. New York, [1979]. pp. 173. *bibliog.*

— Economic integration.

CARICOM BULLETIN; [pd. by] Caribbean Community Secretariat. irreg., Ag 1978(no. 1)- Georgetown.

AXLINE (W. ANDREW) Caribbean integration: the politics of regionalism. London, 1979. pp. 233. *bibliog.*

— Economic policy.

MOHAMMED (KAMALUDDIN) Caribbean integration; a review. [Port-of-Spain, Government Printery], 1969. pp. 26.

—Foreign economic relations — United States.

PALMER (RANSFORD W.) Caribbean dependence on the United States economy. New York, [1979]. pp. 173. *bibliog.*

— Foreign relations — United States.

CARTER (PURVIS M.) Congressional and public reaction to Wilson's Caribbean policy, 1913-1917. New York, [1977]. pp. 164. *bibliog.*

MARTIN (JOHN BARTLOW) U.S. policy in the Caribbean. Boulder, Colo., [1978]. pp. 420. *bibliog. A Twentieth Century Fund essay.*

— Politics and government.

MOHAMMED (KAMALUDDIN) Caribbean integration; a review. [Port-of-Spain, Government Printery], 1969. pp. 26.

GARCIA ZAMOR (JEAN-CLAUDE) The bureaucratic framework of development administration in the Caribbean. Austin, Tex., 1970. fo. 99. *bibliog.*

MARTIN (JOHN BARTLOW) U.S. policy in the Caribbean. Boulder, Colo., [1978]. pp. 420. *bibliog. A Twentieth Century Fund essay.*

— Religion.

AFRICA and the Caribbean: the legacies of a link; edited by Margaret E. Crahan and Franklin W. Knight. Baltimore, [1979]. pp. 159. *bibliog. (Johns Hopkins University. Johns Hopkins Studies in Atlantic History and Culture)*

CARIBBEAN COMMUNITY.

CARICOM BULLETIN; [pd. by] Caribbean Community Secretariat. irreg., Ag 1978(no. 1)- Georgetown.

CARLOVINGIANS.

GANSHOF (FRANÇOIS LOUIS) The Carolingians and the Frankish monarchy: studies in Carolingian history; translated by Janet Sondheimer. London, 1971. pp. 314. *bibliog.*

CARLYLE (THOMAS).

HARRIS (KENNETH MARC) Carlyle and Emerson: their long debate. Cambridge, Mass., 1978. pp. 194.

CARRANZA (VENUSTIANO).

GILDERHUS (MARK T.) Diplomacy and revolution: U.S.-Mexican relations under Wilson and Carranza. Tucson, Ariz., [1977]. pp. 159. *bibliog.*

CARRIAGE AND WAGON MAKING

— United Kingdom.

NOCKOLDS (HAROLD) ed. The coachmakers: a history of the Worshipful Company of Coachmakers and Coach Harness Makers, 1677-1977. London, [1977]. pp. 239. *bibliog.*

CARRIERS

— United Kingdom.

RIDLEY (JASPER) Barrister-at-Law. The law of the carriage of goods by land, sea and air...; fifth edition by Geoffrey Whitehead. London, 1978. pp. 297.

CARROLL (JOHN) Archbishop of Baltimore.

CARROLL (JOHN) Archbishop of Baltimore. The John Carroll papers: Thomas O'Brien Hanley, editor, under the auspices of the American Catholic Historical Association. Notre Dame, Ind., [1976]. 3 vols.

CARTER (JAMES EARL) President of the United States.

MILLER (WILLIAM LEE) Yankee from Georgia: the emergence of Jimmy Carter. New York, [1978]. pp. 247.

THOMAS (SUNNY) Jimmy Carter: from peanuts to presidency. Cornwall, Ont., [1978]. pp. 101.

WOOTEN (JAMES) Dasher: the roots and the rising of Jimmy Carter. London, [1978]. pp. 377.

CARTOGRAPHY

— Computer programs.

LONDON. University. London School of Economics and Political Science. Graduate School of Geography. Discussion Papers. No. 67. The construction of computer produced views of three-dimensional data; [by] Christopher Worth. London, 1978. pp. 41. *bibliog.*

— United States — Ohio.

SMITH (THOMAS H.) The mapping of Ohio. [Kent, Ohio], [1977]. pp. 252. *bibliogs.*

CASO (ALFONSO).

KRAUZE (ENRIQUE) Caudillos culturales en la Revolucion mexicana. Mexico, 1976. pp. 340.

CASSIRER (ERNST).

LIPTON (DAVID R.) Ernst Cassirer: the dilemma of a liberal intellectual in Germany, 1914-1933. Toronto, [1978]. pp. 212. *bibliog.*

CASTE

— India.

CASTE, class and power-structure; by Mumtaz Ali Khan [and others]. Bangalore, 1974. pp. 96. *Special issue of 'Religion and Society', vol. 21, no.3, September 1974.*

— — Hyderabad.

LEONARD (KAREN ISAKSEN) Social history of an Indian caste: the Kayasths of Hyderabad. Berkeley, 1978. pp. 353. *bibliog.*

CASTILE

— Commerce — United Kingdom.

CHILDS (WENDY R.) Anglo-Castilian trade in the later Middle Ages. Manchester, 1978. pp. 264. *bibliog.*

CASTRO LEAL (ANTONIO).

KRAUZE (ENRIQUE) Caudillos culturales en la Revolucion mexicana. Mexico, 1976. pp. 340.

CATALOGUES, LIBRARY.

EUROPEAN COMMUNITIES. Bibliothèque [Luxembourg]. Acquisitions récentes de la Bibliothèque. [in French and German]. bi-m. Luxembourg. *Current issues only kept.*

CATASTROPHES (MATHEMATICS).

POSTON (TIM) and STEWART (IAN) Catastrophe theory and its applications. London, 1978. pp. 491. *bibliog.*

CATERERS AND CATERING

— Germany.

WIEDENHOFER (HARALD) Probleme gewerkschaftlicher Interessenvertretung: das Beispiel der Gewerkschaft Nahrung, Genuss, Gaststätten. Bonn, [1979]. pp. 166. *bibliog.* (*Friedrich-Ebert-Stiftung. Forschungsinstitut. Reihe: Arbeit. Band 3*)

— United Kingdom.

MEDLIK (S.) and AIREY (D.W.) Profile of the hotel and catering industry. 2nd ed. London, 1978. pp. 282. *bibliog.*

THOMAS (CERI) and ERLAM (ANDREW) Unequal portions: a survey of pay in the hotel and catering industry. London, 1978. pp. 18. (*Low Pay Unit. Low Pay Papers. No.23*)

CATHEDRALS

— Design and construction — Finance.

KRAUS (HENRY) Gold was the mortar: the economics of cathedral building. London, 1979. pp. 292.

CATHOLIC CHURCH.

PIGOTT (ADRIAN) Freedom's foe - the Vatican: a collection of danger-signals for those who value liberty. London, [1956?]. pp. 128.

— History — Sources.

LUNT (WILLIAM EDWARD) Accounts rendered by papal collectors in England, 1317-1378; transcribed with annotations and introduction by William E. Lunt; edited with additions and revisions by Edgar B. Graves. Philadelphia, 1968. pp. 579. (*American Philosophical Society. Memoirs. vol. 70*)

— Relations (diplomatic) with Communist countries.

DUNN (DENNIS J.) Détente and papal-communist relations, 1962-1978. Boulder, [1979]. pp. 216. *bibliog.*

CATHOLIC CHURCH IN BRAZIL.

CAMARA (HELDER) Archbishop of Olinda and Recife. The conversions of a bishop: an interview with José de Broucker; translated by Hilary Davies. London, 1979. pp. 222.

CATHOLIC CHURCH IN COMMUNIST COUNTRIES.

DUNN (DENNIS J.) Détente and papal-communist relations, 1962-1978. Boulder, [1979]. pp. 216. *bibliog.*

CATHOLIC CHURCH IN EUROPE.

BENELLI (GIOVANNI) L'âme de l'Europe: contribution de L'Église et des chrétiens à l'édification d'une nouvelle Europe. Lausanne, 1978. pp. 27. (*Lausanne. Université. Centre de Recherches Européennes. Publications. 1. Histoire, Précurseurs et Promoteurs de l'Union de l'Europe*)

ACQUAVIVA (SABINO SAMELE) The decline of the sacred in industrial society; translated by Patricia Lipscomb. Oxford, 1979. pp. 289. *bibliog.*

CHURCH and society in Catholic Europe of the eighteenth century; edited by William J. Callahan and David Higgs. Cambridge, 1979. pp. 168. *bibliog.*

CATHOLIC CHURCH IN FRANCE.

QUENIART (JEAN) Les hommes, l'Église et Dieu dans la France du XVIIIe siècle. [Paris], 1978. pp. 358. *bibliog.*

CATHOLIC CHURCH IN IRELAND.

LARKIN (EMMET) The historical dimensions of Irish Catholicism. New York, 1976. 1 vol. (various pagings). *Essays previously published in the American historical review, 1967-1975.*

CATHOLIC CHURCH IN ITALY.

PENCO (GREGORIO) Storia della chiesa in Italia. Milano, 1978 in progress.

CATHOLIC CHURCH IN SPAIN.

LINEHAN (PETER) The Spanish Church and the Papacy in the thirteenth century. Cambridge, 1971. pp. 389. *bibliog.*

CATHOLIC CHURCH IN THE NETHERLANDS.

COLEMAN (JOHN A.) The evolution of Dutch Catholicism, 1958-1974. Berkeley, 1978. pp. 328.

CATHOLIC CHURCH IN THE UNITED KINGDOM.

NEWMAN and Gladstone: centennial essays; edited by James D. Bastable. Dublin, 1978. pp. 324. *bibliogs. Selection of papers presented at the International Newman Conference, Dublin, 1975.*

CATHOLIC CHURCH IN THE UNITED STATES.

CARROLL (JOHN) Archbishop of Baltimore. The John Carroll papers: Thomas O'Brien Hanley, editor, under the auspices of the American Catholic Historical Association. Notre Dame, Ind., [1976]. 3 vols.

CATHOLICS IN ITALY.

CAROLEO (ANNA) Le banche cattoliche dalla prima guerra mondiale al fascismo. Milano, 1976. pp. 194. *bibliog.*

ROSSI (MARIO G.) Le origini del partito cattolico: movimento cattolico e lotta di classe nell'Italia liberale. Roma, 1977. pp. 466.

CATHOLICS IN THE UNITED KINGDOM.

PRITCHARD (ARNOLD) Catholic loyalism in Elizabethan England. London, 1979. pp. 243. *bibliog.*

CATHOLICS IN THE UNITED STATES.

WROBEL (PAUL) Our way: family, parish, and neighborhood in a Polish-American community. Notre Dame, Ind., [1979]. pp. 192.

CATTLE STEALING.

CONVEGNO INTERNAZIONALE SULL' ABIGEATO, CAGLIARI, 1966. Atti del Convegno...Cagliari, 16-18 dicembre 1966; edizione a cura del Centro Regionale di Profilassi della Criminalita sotto gli auspici della Regione Autonoma Sarda, Assessorato all' Istruzione. [Cagliari, 1967]. pp. 303. (*Rivista Sarda di Criminologia. Vol. 3. fasc. 1-2. 1967*)

CAUCASUS

— History.

BIHL (WOLFDIETER) Die Kaukasus-Politik der Mittelmächte. Wien, 1975 in progress. *bibliog.* (*Kommission für Neuere Geschichte Österreichs. Veröffentlichungen. 61*)

CAVOUR (CAMILLO BENSO DI) Conte.

EIMER (BIRGITTA) Cavour and Swedish politics. Stockholm, [1978]. pp. 457. *bibliog.* (*Lund. Universitet. Historiska Institutionen. Lund Studies in International History. 12*)

CELSO (AFONSO).

See FIGUEIREDO (AFONSO CELSO DE ASSIS) Visconde de Ouro Preto.

CENSORSHIP

— Bibliography.

GARLING (MARGUERITE) compiler. Human rights research guide: library holdings in London on human rights, censorship and freedom of expression. London, 1978. pp. 77. *Compiled for the Writers and Scholars Educational Trust.*

— Malawi.

MALAWI. 1975. Catalogue of banned publications, cinematograph pictures and records from 1st August, 1968 to 1st October, 1975. Zomba, [1975?]. pp. 16.

— United Kingdom.

DEFENCE OF LITERATURE AND THE ARTS SOCIETY. Evidence to the Committee on Obscenity and Film Censorship. London, 1978. pp. 13.

ROBERTSON (GEOFFREY) Obscenity: an account of censorship laws and their enforcement in England and Wales. London, [1979]. pp. 364.

— United States.

FOWLER (DOROTHY GANFIELD) Unmailable: Congress and the Post Office. Athens, Ga., [1977]. pp. 266. *bibliog.*

CENSUS.

FOOD AND AGRICULTURE ORGANIZATION. FAO Statistics Series. No.1. Programme for the 1980 World Census of Agriculture. Rome, 1976. pp. 80.

FOOD AND AGRICULTURE ORGANIZATION. FAO Statistics Series. No.10. Report on the 1970 World Census of Agriculture. Rome, 1977. pp. 289.

CENTERPRISE TRUST.

CENTERPRISE TRUST. Local publishing and local culture: an account of the work of the Centerprise publishing project, 1972-1977. London, [1977]. pp. 22.

CENTRAL AMERICAN COMMON MARKET.

CLINE (WILLIAM R.) and DELGADO (ENRIQUE) eds. Economic integration in Central America. Washington, D.C., [1978]. pp. 712.

CENTRAL AND SHERWOOD.

GRINYER (PETER HUGH) and SPENDER (J.C.) Turnaround: managerial recipes for strategic success; the fall and rise of the Newton Chambers group. London, 1979. pp. 211.

CENTRAL BANK OF KENYA.

CENTRAL BANK OF KENYA. The first ten years; [a souvenir brochure]. Nairobi, [1977]. pp. 34.

CENTRAL BUSINESS DISTRICTS.

Le COMMERCE dans la cité. Bruxelles, [1967]. pp. 63. (*Cahiers d'Urbanisme et d'Aménagement du Territoire. Nos. 57,58,59*)

CENTRAL LIMIT THEOREM.

BHATTACHARYA (RABINDRA NATH) and RAO (RAMASWAMY RANGA) Normal approximation and asymptotic expansions. New York, [1976]. pp. 274. *bibliog.*

CENTRAL LIMIT THEORY.

PROBABILITY on Banach spaces; edited by James Kuelbs. New York, [1978]. pp. 521. *bibliog.*

CENTRAL PLACES

— Mathematical models.

GUNNARSON (JAN) Production systems and hierarchies of centres: the relationship between spatial and economic structures. Leiden, 1977. pp. 140. *bibliog.*

— Germany — Hesse.

VOGLER (LUTZ) Hierarchie und Einzugsbereiche zentraler Orte auf Grund der Verbrauchernachfrage: empirische Untersuchung für die Planungsregion Nordhessen anhand von 39,000 Interviews. Bonn, 1978. 1 vol. (various pagings). *bibliog. (Germany (Bundesrepublik). Bundesforschungsanstalt für Landeskunde und Raumordnung. Forschungen zur Raumentwicklung. 7)*

CENTRAL PUBLIC HEALTH ENGINEERING RESEARCH INSTITUTE.

WORLD HEALTH ORGANIZATION. 1968. The Central Public Health Engineering Research Institute, Nagpur, India: report prepared for the Government of India by the World Health Organization acting...for the United Nations Development Programme. Geneva, 1968. pp. 56.

CENTRE PARTIES

— Europe.

Die EUROPAEISCHEN Parteien der Mitte: Analysen und Dokumente zur Programmatik christlich-demokratischer und konservativer Parteien Westeuropas; mit Beiträgen von: Werner Allemeyer [and others], etc. Bonn, [1978]. pp. 740. *(Politische Akademie Eichholz. Handbücher. Band 6)*

— European Economic Community countries.

IRVING (RONALD ECKFORD MILL) The Christian Democratic parties of Western Europe. London, 1979. pp. 338. *bibliog.*

— Germany.

ZEENDER (JOHN K.) The German Center Party, 1890-1906. Philadelphia, 1976. pp. 125. *bibliog. (American Philosophical Society. Transactions. New Series. vol.66, part 1)*

Die CDU in Baden-Württemberg und ihre Geschichte; herausgegeben von Paul-Ludwig Weinacht. Stuttgart, [1978]. pp. 399. *bibliog.*

— Italy.

BERTOCCI (SILVIO) Dossier Baia Domizia: uno scandalo democristiano. Roma, 1977. pp. 180.

ROSSI (MARIO G.) Le origini del partito cattolico: movimento cattolico e lotta di classe nell'Italia liberale. Roma, 1977. pp. 466.

CERAMIC AND ALLIED TRADES UNION.

BURCHILL (FRANK) and ROSS (RICHARD) A history of the potter's union. Stoke-on-Trent, 1977. pp. 292. *bibliog.*

CEREBRAL DOMINANCE.

LANGUAGE development and neurological theory; edited by Sidney J. Segalowitz, Frederic A. Gruber. New York, 1977. pp. 376. *bibliogs.*

CHAD

— Politics and government.

BUIJTENHUIJS (ROBERT) Le Frolinat et les révoltes populaires du Tchad, 1965-1976. The Hague, [1978]. pp. 526. *bibliog. (Afrika-Studiecentrum. Change and Continuity in Africa)*

CHAIANOV (ALEKSANDR VASIL'EVICH).

HARRISON (MARK) Peasant economy, subordinate Marxism and the struggle for socialised agriculture in the USSR in the 1920s. Coventry, 1978. pp. 22. *(University of Warwick. Department of Economics. Warwick Economic Research Papers. No. 131)*

CHAMBERLAIN (JOSEPH).

MACKINTOSH (Sir ALEXANDER) The story of Mr. Chamberlain's life. London, 1914. pp. 144.

CHAMPAGNE-ARDENNE

—Economic conditions.

ECONOMIE CHAMPENOISE; [pd. by] Direction Régionale de Reims, Institut National de la Statistique et des Etudes Economiques. q., 1978(no.1)- Reims.

CHARENTE (DEPARTMENT).

FRANCE. Direction de la Documentation. La Documentation Française. Notes et Etudes Documentaires. No. 4477. Les départements français. 16. Charente, Poitou-Charentes. [Paris], 1978. pp. 133.

CHARITABLE USES, TRUSTS AND FOUNDATIONS

— United Kingdom.

CHESTERMAN (MICHAEL) Charities, trusts and social welfare. London, [1979]. pp. 490.

CHARITIES

— United Kingdom.

AGE CONCERN ENGLAND. Policy Publications. No. 2. Age Concern policy: focus on the future. London, 1977. pp. 29.

HEBDITCH (SIMON) Age Concern: the national policy. London, [1978]. pp. 20.

TOMPSON (RICHARD S.) The Charity Commission and theage of reform. London, 1979. pp. 379. *bibliog.*

— — Directories.

CHARITIES AID FOUNDATION. Directory of grant-making trusts; Elizabeth Skinner, editor. 6th ed. Tonbridge, [1978]. pp. 973.

— United States.

TRATTNER (WALTER I.) From poor law to welfare state: a history of social welfare in America. 2nd ed. London, [1979]. pp. 290. *bibliogs.*

— — Directories.

SOCIAL service organisations; editor-in-chief Peter Romanofsky; advisory editor Clarke A. Chambers. Westport, Conn., 1978. 2 vols.

CHARLES, Duke of Burgundy, called the Bold.

VAUGHAN (RICHARD) Professor of Medieval History, University of Hull. Charles the Bold: the last Valois duke of Burgundy. London, 1973. pp. 491. *bibliog.*

CHARLES, the Great.

The SONG OF ROLAND; translated by Dorothy L. Sayers. Harmondsworth, 1957. pp. 206.

EGINHARDUS, Abbot of Seligenstadt. The life of Charlemagne; (translated...by Samuel Epes Turner). Ann Arbor, Mich., 1960 repr. 1975. pp. 74.

— Coronation.

FOLZ (ROBERT) The coronation of Charlemagne, 25 December 800; translated [from the French] by J.E. Anderson. London, 1974. pp. 266. *bibliog.*

CHARTISM.

MATHER (FREDERICK CLARE) Chartism. London, 1965 repr. 1977. pp. 35. *(Historical Association. General Series. G. 61)*

FLICK (CARLOS) The Birmingham Political Union and the movements for reform in Britain, 1830-1839. Hamden, Conn., 1978. pp. 206. *bibliog.*

CHATTERJI (BANKIM CHANDRA).

CHATTERJI (BANKIM CHANDRA) Bankim on equality: an English translation of Bankim Chandra Chattopadhyay's Bengali article, Samya [with an essay on its background] by M.K. Haldar. Nedlands, W.A., 1974. pp. 38, 124. *(Western Australia, University of. Centre for Asian Studies. Working Papers in Asian Studies. No. 5)*

CHEMICAL INDUSTRIES

— France.

FRANCE. Direction de la Documentation. La Documentation Française. Notes et Etudes Documentaires. No.4454. L'industrie chimique en France; par Louis Marthey. [Paris], 1978. pp. 171. *bibliog.*

— United Kingdom.

NORTHERN REGION STRATEGY TEAM. The chemicals industry in the Northern Region: trends and prospects; (draft technical report). Newcastle-upon-Tyne, 1976. 1 vol. (various foliations). *([Working Papers. No. 1])*

— Zambia.

ZAMBIA. Central Statistical Office. 1976. Chemicals, rubber and plastics industries. Lusaka, 1976. pp. 64. *(Industry Monographs. No.5)*

CHEMICAL WARFARE.

RANGER (ROBERT JOHN) The Canadian contribution to the control of chemical and biological warfare. Toronto, [1976]. pp. 66. *(Canadian Institute of International Affairs. Wellesley Papers. 5)*

CHEMICAL weapons and chemical arms control; papers and discussions from a conference at...Boston...1977; Matthew Meselson, editor. New York, [1978]. pp. 128.

CHEROKEE INDIANS.

LITTLEFIELD (DANIEL F.) The Cherokee freedmen from emancipation to American citizenship. Westport, Conn., 1978. pp. 281. *bibliog.*

PERDUE (THEDA) Slavery and the evolution of Cherokee society, 1540-1866. Knoxville, 1979. pp. 207. *bibliog.*

CHESHIRE

— History.

VICTORIA HISTORY OF THE COUNTIES OF ENGLAND. Cheshire. A history of the county of Chester; edited by B.E. Harris. London, 1979 in progress.

CHICAGO

— City planning.

BURNHAM (DANIEL HUDSON) and BENNETT (EDWARD HERBERT) Plan of Chicago (prepared under the direction of the Commercial Club);...edited by Charles Moore; new introduction by Wilbert R. Hasbrouck. New York, 1970. pp. 164. *Facsimile reprint of the first edition, Chicago, 1909.*

— Maps.

BURNHAM (DANIEL HUDSON) and BENNETT (EDWARD HERBERT) Plan of Chicago (prepared under the direction of the Commercial Club);...edited by Charles Moore; new introduction by Wilbert R. Hasbrouck. New York, 1970. pp. 164. *Facsimile reprint of the first edition, Chicago, 1909.*

— Politics and government.

RAKOVE (MILTON L.) Don't make no waves, don't back no losers: an insider's analysis of the Daley machine. Bloomington, [1975]. pp. 296. *bibliog.*

CHICHIMECS.

POWELL (PHILIP WAYNE) Mexico's Miguel Caldera: the taming of America's first frontier, 1548-1597. Tucson, 1977. pp. 322. *bibliog.*

CHILD ABUSE.

CHILD ABUSE.

FAMILY violence: an international and interdisciplinary study; [proceedings of a conference held in Montreal in 1977]; edited by John M. Eekelaar [and] Sanford N. Katz. Toronto, [1978]. pp. 572. *bibliog.*

— Bibliography.

KALISCH (BEATRICE J.) compiler. Child abuse and neglect: an annotated bibliography. Westport, 1978. pp. 535.

— United States.

COSTA (JOSEPH J.) and NELSON (GORDON KENNETH) Child abuse and neglect: legislation, reporting, and prevention. Lexington, Mass., [1978]. pp. 417. *bibliogs.*

CHILD DEVELOPMENT.

CHILD alive: new insights into the development of young children; edited by Roger Lewin. London, 1975. pp. 230. *bibliog. Based on a series of articles first published in the magazine "New Scientist" during 1974.*

GREVEN (PHILIP J.) The protestant temperament: patterns of child-rearing, religious experience, and the self in early America. New York, 1977. pp. 431.

KENISTON (KENNETH) and others. All our children: the American family under pressure. New York, [1977]. pp. 255. *Published under the auspices of the Carnegie Council on Children, Carnegie Corporation of New York.*

SMART (MOLLIE STEVENS) and SMART (RUSSELL COOK) Children: development and relationships. 3rd ed. New York, [1977]. pp. 705. *bibliog.*

SOCIAL development in childhood: day-care programs and research; edited by Roger A. Webb. Baltimore, [1977]. pp. 196. *bibliogs. Papers from the 4th Hyman Blumberg Symposium on Research in Early Childhood Education, held Mar. 7-9, 1974.*

CHILDREN'S thinking: what develops?; edited by Robert S. Siegler. Hillsdale, N.J., 1978. pp. 371.

ISSUES in childhood social development; edited by Harry McGurk. London, 1978. pp. 270. *bibliogs.*

PILLING (DORIA) and PRINGLE (MIA LILLY KELLMER) Controversial issues in child development. London, 1978. pp. 424. *bibliog.*

BOWER (THOMAS GILLIE RUSSELL) Human development. San Francisco, [1979]. pp. 473. *bibliog.*

LIGHT (PAUL) The development of social sensitivity: a study of social aspects of role-taking in young children. Cambridge, 1979. pp. 123. *bibliog.*

CHILD MOLESTING.

SEXUAL assault of children and adolescents; [by] Ann Wolbert Burgess [and others]. Lexington, Mass., [1978]. pp. 245.

CHILD PSYCHIATRY.

SEGAL (HANNA) Klein. [London], 1979. pp. 189. *bibliog.*

CHILD PSYCHOLOGY.

PIAGET (JEAN) The child's conception of number; [translated by C. Gattegno and F.M. Hodgson]. London, 1952. pp. 248.

BLURTON-JONES (N.G.) ed. Ethological studies of child behaviour. London, 1972. pp. 400. *bibliogs.*

LIVESLEY (WILLIAM JOHN) and BROMLEY (DENNIS BASIL) Person perception in childhood and adolescence. London, [1973]. pp. 320. *bibliog.*

PHILLIPS (JOHN L.) The origins of intellect: Piaget's theory. 2nd ed. San Francisco, [1975]. pp. 205. *bibliog.*

The STRUCTURING of experience; edited by Ina Č. Užgiris and Fredric Weizmann. New York, [1977]. pp. 449. *bibliogs.*

WORKING GROUP ON PROBLEMS OF CHILDREN OF SCHOOL AGE II (10-13 YEARS). Problems of children of school age: 10-13 years: report on a working group [held in] Moscow, 30 November-3 December, 1976. Copenhagen, World Health Organization, Regional Office for Europe, 1977. pp. 39.

DONALDSON (MARGARET) Children's minds. London, [1978]. pp. 156. *bibliog.*

LIPSITT (LEWIS PAEFF) and REESE (HAYNE W.) Child development. Glenview, Ill., [1979]. pp. 152. *bibliog.*

CHILD WELFARE.

HERON (ALASTAIR) Early childhood care and education: objectives and issues. Paris, Organisation for Economic Co-operation and Development, 1977. pp. 61.

— Cuba.

RANDALL (MARGARET) Child care in Cuba. Toronto, [1975]. pp. 9.

WALD (KAREN) Children of Che: childcare and education in Cuba. Palo Alto, Calif., [1978]. pp. 399.

— Hong Kong.

FIELD (C. ELAINE) and BABER (FLORA M.) Growing up in Hong Kong: a preliminary report on a study of the growth, development and rearing of Chinese children in Hong Kong. Hong Kong, 1973. pp. 178. *bibliog.*

— Poland.

ZIEMSKA (MARIA) Early child care in Poland. London, [1978]. pp. 148. *bibliog. (International Study Group for Early Child Care. International Monograph Series on Early Child Care. vol. 8)*

— United Kingdom.

NATIONAL UNION OF TEACHERS. The report of the Committee on Child Health Services, Fit for the future: the NUT view. London, [1977]. pp. 22. *The report itself is Cmnd. 6684 in the Parliamentary Papers for Session 1976-77*

WAGNER (GILLIAN) Barnardo. London, [1979]. pp. 344. *bibliog.*

— — Scotland.

SCOTLAND. Scottish Education Department. Social Work Services Group. Children in care or under supervision: Scotland. a., 1976/77(1st)- Edinburgh. *Supersedes in part SCOTTISH SOCIAL WORK STATISTICS.*

— United States.

COSTA (JOSEPH J.) and NELSON (GORDON KENNETH) Child abuse and neglect: legislation, reporting, and prevention. Lexington, Mass., [1978]. pp. 417. *bibliogs.*

— — New York.

NEW YORK (CITY). Youth Board. Youth Board Monographs. No. 4. Reaching the group: an analysis of group work methods used with teenagers. New York, 1956. pp. 75.

CHILDBIRTH.

The PLACE of birth: a study of the environment in which birth takes place with special reference to home confinements; edited by Sheila Kitzinger and John A. Davis. Oxford, 1978. pp. 265. *bibliogs.*

— Psychology.

BREEN (DANA) The birth of a first child: towards an understanding of femininity. London, 1975. pp. 262. *bibliog.*

— France.

LEVY (CLAUDE) L'accouchement prématuré: compte-rendu d'une enquête socio- démographique. [Paris], 1978. pp. 166. *(France. Institut National d'Etudes Démographiques. Travaux et Documents. Cahiers. No. 84)*

CHILDLESSNESS

— United States.

NASON (ELLEN MARA) and POLOMA (MARGARET M.) Voluntarily childless couples: the emergence of a variant lifestyle. Beverly Hills, [1976]. pp. 54. *bibliog.*

CHILDREN.

The CHILD in the world of tomorrow: a window into the future; [edited by] Spyros Doxiadis [and others]. Oxford, 1979. pp. 549. *bibliogs.*

— Care and hygiene — Hong Kong.

FIELD (C. ELAINE) and BABER (FLORA M.) Growing up in Hong Kong: a preliminary report on a study of the growth, development and rearing of Chinese children in Hong Kong. Hong Kong, 1973. pp. 178. *bibliog.*

— — United Kingdom.

NATIONAL UNION OF TEACHERS. The report of the Committee on Child Health Services, Fit for the future: the NUT view. London, [1977]. pp. 22. *The report itself is Cmnd. 6684 in the Parliamentary Papers for Session 1976-77*

TRADES UNION CONGRESS. TUC charter on facilities for the under-fives. London, [1979?]. pp. 16.

— Death and future state.

SLATER (PETER GREGG) Children in the New England mind in death and in life. Hamden, Conn., 1977. pp. 248. *bibliog.*

— Employment — United Kingdom.

FORSTER (ERIC) The pit children. Newcastle, [1978]. pp. 48.

— Hospital care.

BEYOND separation: further studies of children in hospital; edited by David Hall and Margaret Stacey. London, 1979. pp. 243. *bibliog.*

— Institutional care — Denmark.

LIHME (BENNY) and PALSVIG (KURT) Effekten af behandling på børne- og ungdomshjem: en analyse af foreliggende undersøgelser, etc. København, 1977. pp. 387. *bibliog. (Socialforskningsinstituttet. Publikationer. 78) With English summary.*

— Language.

VYGOTSKII (LEV SEMENOVICH) Thought and language; edited and translated by Eugenia Hanfmann and Gertrude Vakar. Cambridge, Mass., 1962. pp. 168. *bibliog.*

DALE (PHILIP S.) Language development: structure and functions. 2nd ed. New York, 1976. pp. 358. *bibliog.*

LANGUAGE development and neurological theory; edited by Sidney J. Segalowitz, Frederic A. Gruber. New York, 1977. pp. 376. *bibliogs.*

LANGUAGE learning and thought; edited by John Macnamara. New York, 1977. pp. 296. *bibliogs.*

MENYUK (PAULA) Language and maturation. Cambridge, Mass., [1977]. pp. 180. *bibliog.*

MILLS (ANNE E.) First and second language acquisition in German: a parallel study. Ludwigsburg, 1977. pp. 209. *bibliog.*

WIDDOWSON (JOHN D.A.) If you don't be good: verbal social control in Newfoundland. St. John's, 1977. pp. 345. *bibliog. (St. John's. Memorial University of Newfoundland. Institute of Social and Economic Research. Newfoundland Social and Economic Papers. No. 21)*

ACTION, gesture and symbol: the emergence of language; edited by Andrew Lock. London, 1978. pp. 588. *bibliog.*

BLOOM (LOIS) and LAHEY (MARGARET) Language development and language disorders. New York, [1978]. pp. 689. *bibliog.*

CHURCHILL (DON W.) Language of autistic children. Washington, D.C., 1978. pp. 139. *bibliog.*

The DEVELOPMENT of communication; edited by Natalie Waterson and Catherine Snow. Chichester, [1978]. pp. 498. *bibliogs. Papers presented at the Third International Child Language Symposium of the International Association for the Study of Child Language.*

DEVELOPMENTAL dysphasia; edited by Maria A. Wyke. London, 1978. pp. 179. *bibliogs.*

DE VILLIERS (JILL G.) and DE VILLIERS (PETER A.) Language acquisition. Cambridge, Mass., 1978. pp. 312. *bibliog.*

McLAUGHLIN (BARRY) Second-language acquisition in childhood. Hillsdale, N.J., 1978. pp. 239. *bibliog.*

MENN (LISE) Pattern, control and contrast in beginning speech: a case study in the development of word form and word function. Bloomington, Ind., 1978. pp. 291.

PAPERS on linguistics and child language; [the] Ruth Hirsch Weir Memorial Volume; edited by Vladimir Honsa [and] M.J. Hardman-de-Bautista. The Hague, [1978]. pp. 298. *bibliogs.*

CRUTTENDEN (ALAN) Language in infancy and childhood: a linguistic introduction to language acquisition. Manchester, [1979]. pp. 193. *bibliog.*

— — Bibliography.

ABRAHAMSEN (ADELE A.) compiler. Child language: an interdisciplinary guide to theory and research. Baltimore, [1977]. pp. 381. *bibliogs.*

— Law.

The CHILD and the courts: [essays; edited by] Ian F.G. Baxter and Mary A. Eberts. Toronto, 1978. pp. 429.

— — Australia.

FOULSHAM (JOHN) Legal sanctions and the rights of the child: a paper delivered at the Rights of the Child Conference in Canberra, November 1974. Queanbeyan, 1975. pp. 16. *(Australia. Social Welfare Commission. Reference Papers)*

MURRAY (K.A.) Children and the courts: ideals and reality; a paper delivered at the Rights of the Child Conference in Canberra, 1974. Queanbeyan, 1975. pp. 25. *(Australia. Social Welfare Commission. Reference Papers)*

— — Russia.

RUSSIA (USSR). Statutes, etc. 1918-1977. Molodezh' i sovetskoe zakonodatel'stvo: sbornik dokumentov. Moskva, 1977. pp. 686.

— — United States.

COSTA (JOSEPH J.) and NELSON (GORDON KENNETH) Child abuse and neglect: legislation, reporting, and prevention. Lexington, Mass., [1978]. pp. 417. *bibliogs.*

WILSON (JOHN PASLEY) The rights of adolescents in the mental health system. Lexington, Mass., [1978]. pp. 321.

— Management.

SLATER (PETER GREGG) Children in the New England mind in death and in life. Hamden, Conn., 1977. pp. 248. *bibliog.*

— Mortality.

NEW ZEALAND. Department of Health. National Health Statistics Centre. 1976. A review of mortality rates of children aged between one and under five years, in New Zealand and in selected countries, 1972. Wellington, [1976]. pp. 6.

NEW ZEALAND. Department of Health. National Health Statistics Centre. 1978. A review of mortality rates of children aged between 1 and under 5 years, in New Zealand and in selected countries, 1972-74. Wellington, [1978]. pp. 6.

— Netherlands.

NETHERLANDS. Centraal Bureau voor de Statistiek. 1977- . De Nederlandse jeugd: een inventarisatie van statistische gegevens. 's- Gravenhage, 1977 in progress.

NETHERLANDS. Centraal Bureau voor de Statistiek. 1978. Het kind in tel: cijfers over kinderen in Nederland in de zeventiger jaren: uitgave ter gelegenheid van het Internationaal Jaar van het Kind, 1979. 's-Gravenhage, 1978. pp. 44. *bibliog.*

— Underdeveloped areas.

See UNDERDEVELOPED AREAS — Children.

— United Kingdom.

WEDGE (PETER) and PROSSER (HILARY) Born to fail? London, 1973 repr. 1977. pp. 64.

— United States.

DAVIS (GLENN) Childhood and history in America. New York, [1976]. pp. 281. *bibliogs.*

KENISTON (KENNETH) and others. All our children: the American family under pressure. New York, [1977]. pp. 255. *Published under the auspices of the Carnegie Council on Children, Carnegie Corporation of New York.*

— — New England.

AXTELL (JAMES L.) The school upon a hill: education and society in colonial New England. New Haven, Conn., 1974. pp. 298.

CHILDREN (CHRISTIAN THEOLOGY).

SLATER (PETER GREGG) Children in the New England mind in death and in life. Hamden, Conn., 1977. pp. 248. *bibliog.*

CHILDREN, FIRSTBORN.

BREEN (DANA) The birth of a first child: towards an understanding of femininity. London, 1975. pp. 262. *bibliog.*

CHILDREN AND POLITICS.

O'DELL (FELICITY ANN) Socialisation through children's literature: the Soviet example. Cambridge, 1978. pp. 278. *bibliog. (National Association for Soviet and East European Studies. Soviet and East European Studies)*

CHILDREN AS WITNESSES

— Israel.

NEW ZEALAND. Criminal Law Reform Committee. 1977. Report on the position of young witnesses in cases involving a sexual offence. Wellington, 1977. pp. 8.

— New Zealand.

NEW ZEALAND. Criminal Law Reform Committee. 1977. Report on the position of young witnesses in cases involving a sexual offence. Wellington, 1977. pp. 8.

CHILDREN OF IMMIGRANTS

— Education — United Kingdom.

U.K. Commission for Racial Equality. 1977. Education of ethnic minorities: comments on the consultative document issued by the Department of Education and Science on the report on the West Indian community issued by the Select Committee on Race Relations and Immigration. London, 1977. pp. 6. *(Occasional Papers. No. 1)*

TEACHER education for a multi-cultural society: (the report of a joint working party of the Community Relations Commission and the Association of Teachers in Colleges and Departments of Education; [Beryl Paston-Brown, chairman]). 2nd ed. London, Commission for Racial Equality, 1978. pp. 71.

CHILE

U.K. Commission for Racial Equality. 1978. Schools and ethnic minorities: comments on Education in schools: a consultative document issued by the Department of Education and Science. London, 1978. pp. 8. *(Occasional Papers. No. 3)*

— United Kingdom.

LOUDEN (DELROY M.) West Indian adolescents in school: towards a typology of behaviour patterns. [Bristol, Social Science Research Council Research Unit on Ethnic Relations, 1976?]. fo. 14.

LOBO (EDWIN DE H.) Children of immigrants to Britain: their health and social problems. London, 1978. pp. 116. *(National Children's Home and Orphanage. Convocation Lectures. 1977)*

CHILDREN OF WORKING MOTHERS

— Canada.

CANADA. Women's Bureau. 1970. Working mothers and their child-care arrangements. Ottawa, 1970. pp. 58.

— United Kingdom.

NURSERY ACTION GROUP and BENWELL COMMUNITY DEVELOPMENT PROJECT. Work and play in Benwell. [Newcastle-upon-Tyne, 1977?]. pp. 29.

U.K. Central Policy Review Staff. 1978. Services for young children with working mothers; report. London, 1978. pp. 89.

TRADES UNION CONGRESS. TUC charter on facilities for the under-fives. London, [1979?]. pp. 16.

CHILDREN'S ACCIDENTS

— United Kingdom.

U.K. Consumer Safety Unit. 1979. The home accident surveillance system: analysis of domestic accidents to children. London, 1979. pp. 66.

CHILDREN'S LITERATURE, RUSSIAN.

O'DELL (FELICITY ANN) Socialisation through children's literature: the Soviet example. Cambridge, 1978. pp. 278. *bibliog. (National Association for Soviet and East European Studies. Soviet and East European Studies)*

CHILDREN'S RIGHTS.

GRUNSEIT (F.) The child: rights and wrongs; a paper delivered at the Rights of the Child Conference in Canberra, November 1974. Queanbeyan, 1975. pp. 20. *(Australia. Social Welfare Commission. Reference Papers)*

— Australia.

FOULSHAM (JOHN) Legal sanctions and the rights of the child: a paper delivered at the Rights of the Child Conference in Canberra, November 1974. Queanbeyan, 1975. pp. 16. *(Australia. Social Welfare Commission. Reference Papers)*

CHILE

— Bibliography.

WILLIAMS (LEE H.) compiler. The Allende years. Boston, Mass., [1977]. pp. 339.

— Boundaries — Argentine Republic.

U.K. 1977. Award of Her Britannic Majesty's Government pursuant to the agreement for arbitration, compromiso, of a controversy between the Argentine Republic and the Republic of Chile concerning the region of the Beagle Channel; [Sir Gerald Fitzmaurice, president of the Court of Arbitration]. London, 1977. pp. 152, 4 maps.

— Census.

CHILE. Census, 1970. (XIV censo de poblacion y III de vivienda, 1970: resultados definitivos); poblacion [provincial results]. Santiago, 1977. 18 vols. *Library lacks Aysen, Cautin, Llanquihue, Malleco, Maule, Valdivia, Valparaiso, which are out of print.*

CHILE(Cont.)

— Economic conditions.

ADVANCES OF CHILEAN ECONOMY; [pd. by] Oficina de Planificacion Nacional. s-a., 1976- Santiago.

STALLINGS (BARBARA) Class conflict and economic development in Chile, 1958-1973. Stanford, Calif., 1978. pp. 295. *bibliog.*

— Economic policy.

CHILE. [Oficina de Planificacion Nacional]. Programas ministeriales. a., 1977- Santiago.

— History.

HISTORIA de Chile; [by] Sergio Villalobus R. [and others]. Santiago de Chile, [1974 in progress].

LOVEMAN (BRIAN) Chile: the legacy of Hispanic capitalism. New York, 1979. pp. 429. *bibliog.*

— — 1973, Coup d'état.

SIGMUND (PAUL E.) The overthrow of Allende and the politics of Chile, 1964-1976. Pittsburgh, [1977]. pp. 326.

ALEXANDER (ROBERT JACKSON) The tragedy of Chile. Westport, Conn., 1978. pp. 509. *bibliog.*

— Politics and government.

FREI MONTALVA (EDUARDO) The mandate of history and Chile's future; translated [from the Spanish] by Miguel d'Escoto; edited...by Thomas W. Walker. Athens, Ohio., 1977. pp. 79. *(Ohio University. Center for International Studies. Papers in International Studies. Latin American Series. No. 1)*

SIGMUND (PAUL E.) The overthrow of Allende and the politics of Chile, 1964-1976. Pittsburgh, [1977]. pp. 326.

WILLIAMS (LEE H.) compiler. The Allende years. Boston, Mass., [1977]. pp. 339.

ALEXANDER (ROBERT JACKSON) The tragedy of Chile. Westport, Conn., 1978. pp. 509. *bibliog.*

The BREAKDOWN of democratic regimes; edited by Juan J. Linz and Alfred Stepan. Baltimore, [1978]. pp. 168.

CARRIERE (JEAN) The "Sociedad Nacional de Agricultura" in Chilean politics: 1932-1970. 1978. fo. 235. *bibliog. Typescript. Ph.D. (London) thesis: unpublished. This thesis is the property of London University and may not be removed from the Library.*

STALLINGS (BARBARA) Class conflict and economic development in Chile, 1958-1973. Stanford, Calif., 1978. pp. 295. *bibliog.*

— Social conditions.

BERGLUND (STAFFAN) The national integration of Mapuche: ethnical minority in Chile...; (English translation: Bernard Wolves). Stockholm, [1977]. pp. 228. *bibliog.*

— Social policy.

CHILE. [Oficina de Planificacion Nacional]. Programas ministeriales. a., 1977- Santiago.

— Statistics.

CHILE. Instituto Nacional de Estadisticas. Anuario estadistico. a., 1976- Santiago.

CHILE. Instituto Nacional de Estadisticas. Informativo estadistico. irreg., Ja 1976- Santiago.

CHIMBUS.

BROWN (PAULA) Highland peoples of New Guinea. Cambridge, 1978. pp. 258. *bibliog.*

CHIMPANZEES.

LANGUAGE learning by a chimpanzee: the LANA project; edited by Duane M. Rumbaugh. New York, [1977]. pp. 312. *bibliogs.*

CHINA.

The PEOPLE'S Republic of China: a handbook; edited by Harold C. Hinton. Boulder, [1979]. pp. 443. *bibliog.*

— Armed forces — History.

SEMENOV (GEORGII GAVRILOVICH) Tri goda v Pekine: zapiski voennogo sovetnika. Moskva, 1978. pp. 296.

— Army.

SMEDLEY (AGNES) China's Red Army marches. New York, [1934]. pp. 311.

— Boundaries — Russia.

ROBINSON (THOMAS W.) The Sino-Soviet border dispute: background, development and the March 1969 clashes. Santa Monica, Ca., 1970. pp. 74. *(Rand Corporation. Research Memoranda. 6171)*

ROBINSON (THOMAS W.) The border negotiations and the future of Sino-Soviet-American relations. [Santa Monica, Calif., 1971]. pp. 48. *(Rand Corporation. [Papers]. 4661)*

GINSBURGS (GEORGE) and PINKELE (CARL F.) The Sino-Soviet territorial dispute, 1949-64. New York, [1978]. pp. 145. *bibliog.*

— Civilization.

LIN (YU-SHENG) The crisis of Chinese consciousness: radical antitraditionalism in the May Fourth era. Madison, Wis., 1979. pp. 201. *bibliog.*

— Commerce — United States.

GOLDSTEIN (JONATHAN) Philadelphia and the China trade, 1682-1846: commercial, cultural and attitudinal effects. University Park, Pa., [1978]. pp. 121. *bibliog.*

— Constitution.

FRANCE. Direction de la Documentation. La Documentation Française. Notes et Etudes Documentaires. Nos. 4,501-4, 502. Les institutions chinoises et la constitution de 1978; [by] Tsien Tche-hao. Paris, 1979. pp. 174. *bibliog.*

— Defences.

MIDDLETON (DREW) The duel of the giants: China and Russia in Asia. New York, 1978. pp. 241.

— Description and travel.

SMEDLEY (AGNES) China's Red Army marches. New York, [1934]. pp. 311.

SMEDLEY (AGNES) Chinese destinies: sketches of present-day China. London, 1934. pp. 284.

SEMENOV (GEORGII GAVRILOVICH) Tri goda v Pekine: zapiski voennogo sovetnika. Moskva, 1978. pp. 296.

— Dictionaries and encyclopedias.

KAPLAN (FREDRIC M.) and others. Encyclopedia of China today. London, 1979. pp. 336. *bibliog.*

— Economic conditions.

EVANS (LES) China after Mao. New York, 1978. pp. 191. *bibliog.*

LARDY (NICHOLAS R.) Economic growth and distribution in China. Cambridge, 1978. pp. 244. *bibliog.*

— Economic history.

FEUERWERKER (ALBERT) Economic trends in the Republic of China, 1912-1949. Ann Arbor, 1977. pp. 123. *(Michigan University. Center for Chinese Studies. Michigan Papers in Chinese Studies. No. 31)*

SOTSIAL'NO-ekonomicheskii stroi i ekonomicheskaia politika KNR, 1949-1975. Moskva, 1978. pp. 261. *bibliog.*

— Economic policy.

CHINA'S finance and trade: a policy reader; edited by Gordon Bennett. London, 1978. pp. 249. *bibliog.*

CHINESE economic planning: translations from Chi-hua ching-chi; edited with an introduction by Nicholas R. Lardy; translated by K.K. Fung. White Plains, N.Y., 1978. pp. 268.

HENNICKE (PETER) Die entwicklungstheoretischen Konzeptionen Mao Tse-tungs: historische Grundlagen und sozialökonomische Bedingungen der Entwicklungspolitik der Volksrepublik China, 1927-1957. München, [1978]. pp. 609. *bibliog.*

LARDY (NICHOLAS R.) Economic growth and distribution in China. Cambridge, 1978. pp. 244. *bibliog.*

SOTSIAL'NO-ekonomicheskii stroi i ekonomicheskaia politika KNR, 1949-1975. Moskva, 1978. pp. 261. *bibliog.*

CHINESE communist modernization problems; (by Wei Yung and others). Taipei, [1979]. pp. 122.

ELLMAN (MICHAEL JOHN) Socialist planning. Cambridge, 1979. pp. 300. *bibliog.*

— Foreign economic relations — Russia.

SLADKOVSKII (MIKHAIL IOSIFOVICH) Istoriia torgovo-ekonomicheskikh otnoshenii SSSR s Kitaem, 1917-1974. Moskva, 1977. pp. 368. *bibliog.*

— Foreign relations.

ROBINSON (THOMAS W.) The border negotiations and the future of Sino-Soviet-American relations. [Santa Monica, Calif., 1971]. pp. 48. *(Rand Corporation. [Papers]. 4661)*

HALPERIN (MORTON H.) Contemporary military strategy. new ed. London, 1972. pp. 149. *bibliog.*

CHINA and the three worlds: a foreign policy reader; edited by King C. Chen. London, 1979. pp. 381. *bibliog.*

HARRIS (NIGEL) The mandate of heaven: Marx and Mao in modern China. London, 1978. pp. 307.

FOREIGN policy making in Communist countries: a comparative approach; edited by Hannes Adomeit and Robert Boardman. Farnborough, [1979]. pp. 164. *bibliogs.*

HOXHA (ENVER) Reflections on China...: extracts from the political diary. Tirana, 1979 in progress.

KIM (SAMUEL S.) China, the United Nations and world order. Princeton, 1979. pp. 581. *bibliog.*

See also UNITED NATIONS — China.

— — Cambodia.

BOUCHER (JEAN-MARIE) The relationship between Cambodia and China, 1954-1970: a study of the changing bases of political accommodation. 1978. fo. 355. *bibliog. Typescript. Ph.D. (London) thesis: unpublished. This thesis is the property of London University and may not be removed from the Library.*

— — France.

BARLOW (JEFFREY G.) Sun Yat-Sen and the French, 1900-1908. Berkeley, [1979]. pp. 93. *(California University. Center for Chinese Studies. China Research Monographs. No.14)*

— — Germany.

LIANG (HSI-HUEY) The Sino-German connection: Alexander von Falkenhausen between China and Germany, 1900-1941. Assen, 1978. pp. 229. *bibliog.*

— — Japan.

NOSOV (MIKHAIL GRIGOR'EVICH) Iapono-kitaiskie otnosheniia, 1949-1975. Moskva, 1978. pp. 216. *bibliog.*

CHINA.

— — Pakistan.

PAKISTAN. Department of Films and Publications. 1978. New era of Pak-China friendship. [Islamabad, 1978]. pp. 53.

— — Russia.

MIDDLETON (DREW) The duel of the giants: China and Russia in Asia. New York, 1978. pp. 241.

RUEBENSAAL (JACK DWIGHT) The impact of the Sino-Soviet dispute on the Afro-Asian People's Solidarity Organization. 1978. fo.237. *bibliog. Typescript. M.Phil. (London)thesis: unpublished. This thesis is the property of London University and may not be removed from the Library.*

— — United Kingdom.

GRAHAM (GERALD SANDFORD) The China station: war and diplomacy, 1830-1860. Oxford, 1978. pp. 444. *bibliog.*

OSTRIKOV (PETR IVANOVICH) Imperialisticheskaia politika Anglii v Kitae v 1900-1914 godakh. Moskva, 1978. pp. 227. *bibliog.*

— — United States.

SYMPOSIUM ON CHINESE-AMERICAN RELATIONS, 1976. Our China prospects; [proceedings of the] symposium...; edited by John K. Fairbank. Philadelphia, 1977. pp. 51. *(American Philosophical Society. Memoirs. vol. 121)*

CLOUGH (RALPH N.) Island China. Cambridge, Mass., 1978. pp. 264. *bibliog.*

DRAGON and eagle: United States-China relations; past and future; edited by Michel Oksenberg, Robert B. Oxnam. New York, [1978]. pp. 384. *bibliog.*

TWO Chinese states: U.S. foreign policy and interests; edited by Ramon H. Myers. Stanford, [1978]. pp. 81. *(Stanford University. Hoover Institution on War, Revolution and Peace. Hoover Institution Publications. 200)*

FAIRBANK (JOHN KING) The United States and China. 4th ed. Cambridge, Mass., 1979. pp. 606. *bibliog.*

SCHALLER (MICHAEL) The U.S. crusade in China, 1938-1945. New York, 1979. pp. 364. *bibliog.*

— Historiography.

DIRLIK (ARIF) Revolution and history: the origins of Marxist historiography in China, 1919-1937. Berkeley, Calif., [1978]. pp. 299. *bibliog.*

— History.

FAIRBANK (JOHN KING) The United States and China. 4th ed. Cambridge, Mass., 1979. pp. 606. *bibliog.*

PERSPECTIVES on a changing China: essays in honor of Professor C. Martin Wilbur...; edited by Joshua A. Fogel and William T. Rowe. Boulder, 1979. pp. 325. *bibliog.*

— — 1800-1899.

CHESNEAUX (JEAN) and others. China from the Opium Wars to the 1911 revolution; translated from the French by Anne Destenay. Hassocks, 1977. pp. 412.

GRAHAM (GERALD SANDFORD) The China station: war and diplomacy, 1830-1860. Oxford, 1978. pp. 444. *bibliog.*

— — 1857-1861, Foreign intervention.

COMPILATION GROUP FOR THE "HISTORY OF MODERN CHINA" SERIES. The Taiping revolution. Peking, 1976. pp. 188.

— — 1898, Reform movement.

COMPILATION GROUP FOR THE 'HISTORY OF MODERN CHINA' SERIES. The Reform Movement of 1898. Peking, 1976. pp. 136.

— — 1900.

COMPILATION GROUP FOR THE "HISTORY OF MODERN CHINA" SERIES. The Yi Ho Tuan Movement of 1900. Peking, 1976. pp. 133.

— — 1900- .

CHESNEAUX (JEAN) and others. China from the Opium Wars to the 1911 revolution; translated from the French by Anne Destenay. Hassocks, 1977. pp. 412.

BARLOW (JEFFREY G.) Sun Yat-Sen and the French, 1900-1908. Berkeley, [1979]. pp. 93. *(California University. Center for Chinese Studies. China Research Monographs. No.14)*

— — 1912-1949, Republic.

CHESNEAUX (JEAN) and others. China from the 1911 revolution to liberation...; translated from the French by Paul Auster and Lydia Davis. Hassocks, [1977]. pp. 372. *bibliogs.*

KEENAN (BARRY) The Dewey experiment in China: educational reform and political power in the early republic. Cambridge, Mass., 1977. pp. 335. *bibliog.*

SAPOZHNIKOV (BORIS GRIGOR'EVICH) Kitai v ogne voiny, 1931-1950. Moskva, 1977. pp. 351.

TONG (TE-KONG) and LI (TSUNG-JEN) The memoirs of Li Tsung-jen. Boulder, Colo., 1979. pp. 636. *(Columbia University. East Asian Institute. Studies)*

— — 1912-1937.

The STRENUOUS decade: China's nation-building efforts, 1927- 1937; [papers given at a symposium held in New York in 1970]; edited...by Paul K.T. Sih. New York, [1970]. pp. 385. *(New York (City). St. John's University. Center of Asian Studies. Asia in the Modern World. No. 9)*

McDONALD (ANGUS W.) The urban origins of rural revolution: elites and the masses in Hunan Province, China, 1911-1927. Berkeley, Calif., [1978]. pp. 369. *bibliog.*

LIN (YU-SHENG) The crisis of Chinese consciousness: radical antitraditionalism in the May Fourth era. Madison, Wis., 1979. pp. 201. *bibliog.*

— — 1937-1945.

SCHALLER (MICHAEL) The U.S. crusade in China, 1938-1945. New York, 1979. pp. 364. *bibliog.*

— — 1945- .

FALCONER (ALUN) New China: friend or foe? London, 1950. pp. 128.

HARRIS (NIGEL) The mandate of heaven: Marx and Mao in modern China. London, 1978. pp. 307.

TERRILL (ROSS) The future of China: after Mao. London, 1978. pp. 331.

CHESNEAUX (JEAN) China: the People's Republic, 1949-1976...; translated from the French by Paul Auster and Lydia Davis. Hassocks, 1979. pp. 255.

CHINA'S road to development; edited by Neville Maxwell. 2nd ed. Oxford, 1979. pp. 365.

— History, Military.

TONG (TE-KONG) and LI (TSUNG-JEN) The memoirs of Li Tsung-jen. Boulder, Colo., 1979. pp. 636. *(Columbia University. East Asian Institute. Studies)*

— Intellectual life.

ALITTO (GUY S.) The last Confucian: Liang Shu-ming and the Chinese dilemma of modernity. Berkeley, 1979. pp. 396. *bibliog.*

— Politics and government.

The CHINESE Communists; [edited] by Stuart Gelder. London, 1946. pp. 290.

FALCONER (ALUN) New China: friend or foe? London, 1950. pp. 128.

BLOFELD (JOHN) Red China in perspective. London, 1951. pp. 242.

IASHCHENKO (GEORGII NIKOLAEVICH) Ideologicheskaia bor'ba v KNR, 1957-1964. Moskva, 1977. pp. 107. *bibliog.*

BETTELHEIM (CHARLES) and BURTON (NEIL G.) China since Mao. New York, [1978]. pp. 130.

CHANG (PARRIS H.) Power and policy in China. 2nd ed. University Park, Pa, [1978]. pp. 331. *bibliog.*

CHINESE communism in the 1970s. Taipei, Taiwan, [1978]. pp. 209. *bibliog. Papers presented to the seventh Sino-American Conference held in Taipei, 1978.*

EVANS (LES) China after Mao. New York, 1978. pp. 191. *bibliog.*

HARRIS (NIGEL) The mandate of heaven: Marx and Mao in modern China. London, 1978. pp. 307.

ALITTO (GUY S.) The last Confucian: Liang Shu-ming and the Chinese dilemma of modernity. Berkeley, 1979. pp. 396. *bibliog.*

CHINESE communist modernization problems; by Wei Yung and others). Taipei, [1979]. pp. 122.

FRANCE. Direction de la Documentation. La Documentation Française. Notes et Etudes Documentaires. Nos. 4,501-4, 502. Les institutions chinoises et la constitution de 1978; [by] Tsien Tche-hao. Paris, 1979. pp. 174. *bibliog.*

HOXHA (ENVER) Reflections on China...: extracts from the political diary. Tirana, 1979 in progress.

PERSPECTIVES on a changing China: essays in honor of Professor C. Martin Wilbur...; edited by Joshua A. Fogel and William T. Rowe. Boulder, 1979. pp. 325. *bibliog.*

WILSON (RICHARD GARRATT) Mao: the people's emperor. London, 1979. pp. 480. *bibliog.*

— Population policy.

CHAI (SUNGLIN) Population and population policy in mainland China. Taipei, 1977. pp. 90. *(Asia and the World Forum. Asia and the World Monographs. 6)*

— Relations (general) with Africa.

BOGOSLOVSKII (VIKTOR VASIL'EVICH) Proiski Pekina v Afrike. Kiev, 1978. pp. 175.

— Rural conditions.

The RUSTICATION of urban youth in China: a social experiment; edited by Peter J. Seybolt. White Plains, 1977. pp. 199.

PARISH (WILLIAM L.) and WHYTE (MARTIN KING) Village and family in contemporary China. Chicago, [1978]. pp. 419. *bibliog.*

SU (JING) and LUN (LUO) Landlord and labor in late imperial China: case studies from Shandong...; translated from the Chinese with an introduction by Endymion Wilkinson. Cambridge, Mass., 1978. pp. 310. *bibliog. (Harvard University. East Asian Research Center. Harvard East Asian Monographs. 80)*

ULLERICH (CURTIS) Rural employment and manpower problems in China. New York, [1979]. pp. 130. *bibliog.*

— Social conditions.

SMEDLEY (AGNES) Chinese destinies: sketches of present-day China. London, 1934. pp. 284.

PARISH (WILLIAM L.) and WHYTE (MARTIN KING) Village and family in contemporary China. Chicago, [1978]. pp. 419. *bibliog.*

CHINA'S road to development; edited by Neville Maxwell. 2nd ed. Oxford, 1979. pp. 365.

CHINA.(Cont.)

— Social history.

SOTSIAL'NO-ekonomicheskii stroi i ekonomicheskaia politika KNR, 1949-1975. Moskva, 1978. pp. 261. *bibliog.*

— Social life and customs.

FREEDMAN (MAURICE) The study of Chinese society: essays by Maurice Freedman; selected and introduced by G. William Skinner. Stanford, 1979. pp. 491. *bibliog.*

CHINESE IN AFRICA.

BOGOSLOVSKII (VIKTOR VASIL'EVICH) Proiski Pekina v Afrike. Kiev, 1978. pp. 175.

CHINESE IN AUSTRALIA.

MARKUS (ANDREW) Fear and hatred: purifying Australia and California, 1850-1901. Sydney, 1979. pp. 95.

CHINESE IN CANADA.

WARD (W. PETER) White Canada forever: popular attitudes and public policy toward Orientals in British Columbia. Montreal, [1978]. pp. 205.

CHINESE IN INDONESIA.

SURYADINATA (LEO) Peranakan Chinese politics in Java, 1917-42. [Singapore, 1976]. pp. 184. *bibliog.*

SURYADINATA (LEO) The Chinese minority in Indonesia. Singapore, 1978. pp. 175.

CHINESE IN PAPUA NEW GUINEA.

INGLIS (CHRISTINE BRENDA) Social structure and patterns of economic action: the Chinese in Papua New Guinea. 1977 [or rather 1978]. fo.529. *bibliog. Typescript. Ph.D. (London) thesis: unpublished. This thesis is the property of London University and may not be removed from the Library.*

CHINESE IN SINGAPORE.

LEE POH PING. Chinese society in nineteenth century Singapore. Kuala Lumpur, 1978. pp. 139. *bibliog.*

FREEDMAN (MAURICE) The study of Chinese society: essays by Maurice Freedman; selected and introduced by G. William Skinner. Stanford, 1979. pp. 491. *bibliog.*

CHINESE IN SOUTH AFRICA.

SMEDLEY (LINDA NORA) and GROENEWALD (DIRK CORNELIS) The Chinese community in South Africa: phase 1: background and attitudes of the white population group towards the Chinese minority group. Pretoria, 1976. pp. 103. *bibliog. (Human Sciences Research Council [South Africa] . Institute for Sociological, Demographic and Criminological Research. Reports. No. S-44)*

CHINESE IN SOUTHEAST ASIA.

FREEDMAN (MAURICE) The study of Chinese society: essays by Maurice Freedman; selected and introduced by G. William Skinner. Stanford, 1979. pp. 491. *bibliog.*

CHINESE IN THE UNITED STATES.

MARKUS (ANDREW) Fear and hatred: purifying Australia and California, 1850-1901. Sydney, 1979. pp. 295.

CHINESE-JAPANESE WAR, 1937-1945.

SAPOZHNIKOV (BORIS GRIGOR'EVICH) Kitai v ogne voiny, 1931-1950. Moskva, 1977. pp. 351.

CHIRADZULU

— Census.

MALAWI. National Statistical Office. 1974. Chiradzulu population pilot census, August 1973. Zomba, 1974. pp. 39.

CHOCO

— Population.

COLOMBIA. Census, 1964. XIII censo de poblacion y II de edificios y viviendas, julio 15 de 1964: Choco. Bogota, 1970. pp. 96.

CHOICE (PSYCHOLOGY).

STRUCTURE of decision: the cognitive maps of political elites; edited by Robert Axelrod. Princeton, N.J., [1976]. pp. 404. *bibliog.*

SCHELLING (THOMAS CROMBIE) Micromotives and macrobehavior. New York, [1978]. pp. 252. *(Pennsylvania University. Fels Center of Government. Fels Lectures on Public Policy Analysis)*

CHOMSKY (NOAM).

SAMPSON (GEOFFREY) Liberty and language. Oxford, 1979. pp. 251. *bibliog.*

CHRISTIAN ANTIQUITIES

— United Kingdom.

CONFERENCE ON CHRISTIANITY IN ROMAN AND SUB-ROMAN BRITAIN, NOTTINGHAM, 1967. Christianity in Britain, 300-700; papers presented to the conference...; edited by M.W. Barley and R.P.C. Hanson. Leicester, 1968. pp. 221.

CHRISTIAN LABOUR ASSOCIATION OF CANADA.

A CHRISTIAN union in labour's wasteland; edited by Edward Vanderkloet. Toronto, 1978. pp. 139. *bibliog.*

CHRISTIANITY.

MONTEFIORE (HUGH WILLIAM) Bishop of Birmingham. Taking our past into our future. [London], 1978. pp. 287.

— Controversial literature.

VIA catholica: or, Passages from the autobiography of a country parson; (by E.P.). London, [1872?]. pp. 302.

— Africa.

HASTINGS (ADRIAN) A history of African Christianity, 1950-1975. Cambridge, 1979. pp. 336. *bibliog.*

— Europe.

LITTLE (LESTOR K.) Religious poverty and the profit economy in medieval Europe. London, 1978. pp. 267. *bibliog.*

— India.

SOCIETY and religion: essays in honour of M.M. Thomas; edited by Richard W. Taylor. Madras, 1976. pp. 193.

— Russia.

BOURDEAUX (MICHAEL) and others, eds. Religious liberty in the Soviet Union: W[orld] C[ouncil of] C[hurches] and USSR: a post-Nairobi documentation. West Wickham, Kent, [1976]. pp. 96. *(Centre for the Study of Religion and Communism. Keston Books. No.7)*

— United States — Southern States.

MATHEWS (DONALD G.) Religion in the Old South. Chicago, [1977]. pp. 274. *bibliog.*

CHRISTIANITY AND ECONOMICS.

WOGAMAN (J. PHILIP) Christians and the great economic debate. London, 1977. pp. 182.

LITTLE (LESTOR K.) Religious poverty and the profit economy in medieval Europe. London, 1978. pp. 267. *bibliog.*

PRESTON (RONALD H.) Religion and the persistence of capitalism; the Maurice Lectures for 1977 and other studies in Christianity and social change. London, 1979. pp. 182. *bibliog. (Maurice Lectures, 1977)*

CHRISTIANITY AND INTERNATIONAL AFFAIRS.

HUDSON (DARRIL) The World Council of Churches in international affairs. Leighton Buzzard, Beds., 1977. pp. 336.

CHRISTIANITY AND OTHER RELIGIONS.

MARTIN (DAVID ALFRED) The dilemmas of contemporary religion. Oxford, [1978]. pp. 104.

MUSLIM-Christian conflicts: economic, political and social origins; edited by Suad Joseph and Barbara L.K. Pillsbury. Boulder, Colo., 1978. pp. 245. *bibliogs.*

CHRISTIANITY AND POLITICS.

WARD (WILLIAM) Author of "How can I help England?". How can I help England?; and other addresses on the relationship of Christianity to social and political problems of today. London, 1906. pp. 168.

DUSSEL (ENRIQUE) History and the theology of liberation: a Latin American perspective...; translated by John Drury. New York, [1976]. pp. 189. *bibliog.*

BIGO (PIERRE) The Church and third world revolution. Maryknoll, N.Y., 1977. pp. 316.

DESMOND (COSMAS) Christians or capitalists?: Christianity and politics in South Africa. London, 1978. pp. 160. *bibliog.*

HAMMOND (JOHN L.) The politics of benevolence: revival religion and American voting behavior. Norwood, N.J., [1979]. pp. 243. *bibliog.*

NORMAN (EDWARD ROBERT) Christianity and the world order. Oxford, 1979. pp. 105. *(British Broadcasting Corporation. Reith Lectures. 1978)*

PRESTON (RONALD H.) Religion and the persistence of capitalism; the Maurice Lectures for 1977 and other studies in Christianity and social change. London, 1979. pp. 182. *bibliog. (Maurice Lectures, 1977)*

CHRISTIANS IN INDIA.

CHRISTIAN participation in nation-building: the summing up of a corporate study on rapid social change; compiled by M. M. Thomas. Bangalore, 1960. pp. 325. *bibliog.*

CHRISTIANS IN THE NEAR EAST.

BETTS (ROBERT BRENTON) Christians in the Arab East: a political study. London, 1979. pp. 318. *bibliog.*

CHRISTO (CARLOS ALBERTO LIBANIO).

CHRISTO (CARLOS ALBERTO LIBANIO) Letters from a prisoner of conscience...; translated by John Drury. Guildford, 1978. pp. 241.

CHRONOLOGY, MAORI.

BEST (ELSDON) The Maori division of time. Wellington, [1922] repr. 1959. pp. 52. *(New Zealand. Dominion Museum. Monographs. No. 4)*

CHURCH AND LABOUR

— Canada.

A CHRISTIAN union in labour's wasteland; edited by Edward Vanderkloet. Toronto, 1978. pp. 139. *bibliog.*

— United Kingdom.

CHURCH OF ENGLAND. National Assembly. Board for Social Responsibility. Industrial Committee. Understanding closed shops: a Christian enquiry into compulsory trade union membership. London, [1977]. pp. 31. *bibliog. (Church of England. National Assembly. Board for Social Responsibility. Occasional Papers)*

CHURCH AND RACE PROBLEMS.

See CHURCH AND RACE RELATIONS.

CHURCH AND RACE RELATIONS.

AUSTIN (GEORGE) World Council of Churches' Programme to Combat Racism. London, 1979. pp. 20. *bibliog. (Institute for the Study of Conflict. Conflict Studies. No. 105)*

— South Africa.

DESMOND (COSMAS) Christians or capitalists?: Christianity and politics in South Africa. London, 1978. pp. 160. *bibliog.*

TURNER (RICHARD) The eye of the needle: toward participatory democracy in South Africa. Maryknoll, 1978. pp. 173.

CHURCH AND SOCIAL PROBLEMS.

WARD (WILLIAM) Author of "How can I help England?". How can I help England?; and other addresses on the relationship of Christianity to social and political problems of today. London, 1906. pp. 168.

BIGO (PIERRE) The Church and third world revolution. Maryknoll, N.Y., 1977. pp. 316.

— Kenya.

WOLF (JAN J. DE) Differentiation and integration in Western Kenya: a study of religious innovation and social change among the Bukusu. The Hague, [1977]. pp. 231. *bibliog.* (Afrika-Studiecentrum. *Change and Continuity in Africa.* 10)

— South Africa.

DESMOND (COSMAS) Christians or capitalists?: Christianity and politics in South Africa. London, 1978. pp. 160. *bibliog.*

— United Kingdom.

MONTEFIORE (HUGH WILLIAM) Bishop of Birmingham. Taking our past into our future. [London], 1978. pp. 287.

CHURCH AND STATE

— Catholic Church.

PIGOTT (ADRIAN) Freedom's foe - the Vatican: a collection of danger-signals for those who value liberty. London, [1956?]. pp. 128.

CHURCH AND STATE IN GERMANY.

GURIAN (WALDEMAR) Hitler and the Christians; translated by E.F. Peeler. London, 1936. pp. 175.

SCHOLDER (KLAUS) Die Kirchen und das Dritte Reich. Frankfurt/M, 1977 in progress. *bibliog.*

CHURCH AND STATE IN ITALY.

MOLINARI (FRANCO) and NERI (VITO) Olio santo e olio di ricino: rapporto su Chiesa e fascismo. Torino, 1976. pp. 143. *bibliogs.*

LEZIROLI (GIUSEPPE) Aspetti della libertà religiosa, nel quadro dell'attuale sistema di relazione fra Stato e confessioni religiose. Milano, 1977. pp. 240. *bibliog.* (Ferrara. Università. Facoltà Giuridica. *Pubblicazioni. 2a Serie.* 10)

SETTEMBRINI (DOMENICO) La Chiesa nella politica italiana, 1944-1963: alle origini del compromesso storico. [2nd ed.] Milano, 1977. pp. 509.

CHURCH AND STATE IN MALAWI.

BANDA (HASTINGS KAMUZU) His Excellency the Life President's speeches: Blantyre synod centenary church service in St. Michael and All Angels church, Blantyre, October 24, 1976. [Blantyre, Department of Information, 1976?]. pp. 10.

CHURCH AND STATE IN MEXICO.

COSTELOE (MICHAEL P.) Church and state in independent Mexico: a study of the patronage debate, 1821-1857. London, 1978. pp. 207. *bibliog.* (Royal Historical Society. *Studies in History*)

CHURCH AND STATE IN SPAIN.

LINEHAN (PETER) The Spanish Church and the Papacy in the thirteenth century. Cambridge, 1971. pp. 389. *bibliog.*

CHURCH AND STATE IN TUNISIA.

O'DONNELL (JOSEPH DEAN) Lavigerie in Tunisia: the interplay of imperialist and missionary. Athens, Ga., [1979]. pp. 300. *bibliog.*

CHURCH AND STATE IN YUGOSLAVIA.

ALEXANDER (STELLA) Church and state in Yugoslavia since 1945. Cambridge, 1979. pp. 351. *bibliog.* (National Association for Soviet and East European Studies. *Soviet and East European Studies*)

CHURCH HISTORY.

DUSSEL (ENRIQUE) History and the theology of liberation: a Latin American perspective...; translated by John Drury. New York, [1976]. pp. 189. *bibliog.*

ACQUAVIVA (SABINO SAMELE) The decline of the sacred in industrial society; translated by Patricia Lipscomb. Oxford, 1979. pp. 289. *bibliog.*

— Methodology.

ECCLESIASTICAL HISTORY SOCIETY. Summer Meeting, 16th, and Winter Meeting, 17th, 197-. Religious motivation: biographical and sociological problems for the church historian: papers read at the...meeting[s]...; edited by Derek Baker. Oxford, 1978. pp. 516. (*Studies in Church History.* vol.15)

— 600-1500, Middle Ages.

FLICK (ALEXANDER CLARENCE) The decline of the medieval church. New York, 1967. 2 vols. *bibliog. Reprint of 1930, New York, ed.*

KNOWLES (DAVID) and OBOLENSKY (DIMITRI) Prince. The Middle Ages. London, 1969 repr. 1978. pp. 519. *bibliog.*

LINEHAN (PETER) The Spanish Church and the Papacy in the thirteenth century. Cambridge, 1971. pp. 389. *bibliog.*

LITTLE (LESTOR K.) Religious poverty and the profit economy in medieval Europe. London, 1978. pp. 267. *bibliog.*

WHITE (LYNN T.) Medieval religion and technology: collected essays. Berkeley, Calif., [1978]. pp. 360. (California University. Center for Medieval and Renaissance Studies. *Publications.* 13)

— — Sources.

CROWDER (C.M.D.) compiler. Unity, heresy and reform, 1378-1460: the conciliar response to the Great Schism. London, 1977. pp. 212. *bibliog.*

CHURCH LANDS

— Russia.

ZIMIN (ALEKSANDR ALEKSANDROVICH) Krupnaia feodal'naia votchina i sotsial'no-politicheskaia bor'ba v Rossii, konets XV - XVI v. Moskva, 1977. pp. 356.

— United Kingdom.

HARVEY (BARBARA F.) Westminster Abbey and its estates in the Middle Ages. Oxford, 1977. pp. 499. *bibliog.*

CHURCH OF ENGLAND.

ANGLICAN PACIFIST FELLOWSHIP. Annual report. a., 1977/78- Oxford.

CHURCH OF ENGLAND IN AMERICA.

MILLS (FREDERICK V.) Writer on church history. Bishops by ballot: an eighteenth-century ecclesiastical revolution. New York, 1978. pp. 367. *bibliog.*

CHURCHILL (JOHN) 1st Duke of Marlborough.

CHANDLER (DAVID) Marlborough as military commander. 2nd ed. London, 1979. pp. 368. *bibliog.*

CHURCHILL (Sir WINSTON LEONARD SPENCER).

FEIS (HERBERT) Churchill, Roosevelt, Stalin: the war they waged and the peace they sought. 2nd ed. Princeton, N.J., 1967 repr. 1974. pp. 702.

BARKER (ELISABETH) Churchill and Eden at war. London, 1978. pp. 346. *bibliog.*

CIESZKOWSKI (AUGUST VON) Graf.

CIESZKOWSKI (AUGUST VON) Graf. Selected writings...; edited and translated...by André Liebich. Cambridge, 1979. pp. 172.

LIEBICH (ANDRE) Between ideology and utopia: the politics and philosophy of August Cieszkowski. Dordrecht, [1979]. pp. 390. (Freiburg (Switzerland). Universität. Ost-Europa Institut. *Sovietica.* vol. 39)

CINCINNATI

— Politics and government.

TAFT (CHARLES PHELPS) City management: the Cincinnati experiment. Port Washington, N.Y., 1933, repr. 1971. pp. 275. *With a new introduction.*

CISTERCIANS.

LEKAI (LOUIS JULIUS) The Cistercians: ideals and reality. [Kent, Ohio, 1977]. pp. 524. *bibliog.*

CISTERCIANS IN THE UNITED KINGDOM.

DONKIN (ROBIN A.) The Cistercians: studies in the geography of medieval England and Wales. Toronto, 1978. pp. 242. *bibliog.* (Pontifical Institute of Mediaeval Studies. *Studies and Texts.* 38)

CITIES AND TOWNS.

SJOBERG (GIDEON) The preindustrial city: past and present. New York, 1960 repr. 1965. pp. 353.

BIRMINGHAM. University. Centre for Urban and Regional Studies. Papers in urban and regional studies. Birmingham. 1977 in progress.

HABITAT FOUNDATION NEWS; [pd. by] United Nations Habitat and Human Settlements Foundation. q., Je 1977(no.2)- Nairobi.

SCHEMA général d'aménagement de la France: villes internationales, villes mondiales; [by Colette Durand and others]. Paris, 1977. pp. 105. (France. Délégation à l'Aménagement du Territoire et à l'Action Régionale. *Travaux et Recherches de Prospective.* 72)

HUMAN settlement systems: international perspectives on structure, change and public policy; editor Niles M. Hansen. Cambridge, Mass., [1978]. pp. 292. *bibliogs. Based on a conference organized by the Human Settlements and Services Area of the International Institute for Applied Systems Analysis, Luxemburg, Austria.*

KING (LESLIE J.) and GOLLEDGE (REGINALD G.) Cities, space, and behavior: the elements of urban geography. Englewood Cliffs, [1978]. pp. 393. *bibliogs.*

The MATURE metropolis; edited by Charles L. Leven. Lexington, [1978]. pp. 317. *bibliogs. Contains essays commissioned by the Institute for Urban and Regional Studies, Washington University, St. Louis for a symposium held June 6-8, 1977.*

BLUMENFELD (HANS) Metropolis and beyond: selected essays;... edited by Paul D. Spreiregen. New York, [1979]. pp. 420.

COUSINS (ALBERT N.) and NAGPAUL (HANS) Urban life: the sociology of cities and urban society. New York, [1979]. pp. 608. *bibliog.*

NORTHAM (RAY M.) Urban geography. 2nd ed. New York, [1979]. pp. 512.

CITIES AND TOWNS.(Cont.)

— Growth.

BURCHELL (ROBERT WILLIAM) and LISTOKIN (DAVID) The fiscal impact handbook: estimating local costs and revenues of land development. New Brunswick, [1978]. pp. 480. *bibliog.*

INTERNATIONAL urban growth policies: new-town contributions; Gideon Golany, editor. New York, [1978]. pp. 460.

— Research — Canada.

CANADA. Ministry of State for Urban Affairs. 1973. Inner city research. [Ottawa, 1973]. pp. 61. *(Urban Research Themes. No. 2) In English and French.*

— America, Latin.

LATIN American urban researchs; [series editors] Francine F. Rabinovitz and Felicity M. Trueblood. Beverly Hills, [1971 in progress]. *bibliog.*

HARDOY (JORGE) and SCHAEDEL (RICHARD P.) eds. Las ciudades de America Latina y sus areas de influencia a traves de la historia. Buenos Aires, 1975. pp. 448.

— Australia.

KILMARTIN (LESLIE) and THORNS (DAVID C.) Cities unlimited: the sociology of urban development in Australia and New Zealand. Sydney, 1978. pp. 195. *bibliog.*

— Europe.

ENNEN (EDITH) The medieval town; translated by Natalie Fryde. Amsterdam, 1979. pp. 287. *bibliog.*

— Europe, Eastern.

The SOCIALIST city: spatial structure and urban policy; edited by R.A. French and F.E. Ian Hamilton. Chichester, [1979]. pp. 541. *bibliogs.*

— France.

DAGNAUD (MONIQUE) Le mythe de la qualité de la vie et la politique urbaine en France: enquête sur l'idéologie urbaine de l'élite technocratique et politique, 1945-1975. Paris, [1978]. pp. 326. *bibliog.*

La FRANCE des villes; (sous la direction de Jacqueline Beaujeu-Garnier [and others]): vol. 1. Le Bassin parisien. [Paris, La Documentation Française, 1978]. pp. 221.

La FRANCE des villes; (sous la direction de Jacqueline Beaujeu-Garnier [and others]): vol. 2. Ouest et Centre-Ouest. [Paris, La Documentation Française, 1978]. pp. 176.

— Italy.

MARTINES (LAURO) Power and imagination: city-states in Renaissance Italy. New York, 1979. pp. 368. *bibliog.*

— Kenya.

HENNING (PETER H.) The urban popular economy and informal sector productions. Ann Arbor, Mich., 1978. pp. 67. *(Michigan University. Center for Research on Economic Development. Discussion Papers. No. 69)*

— Netherlands — History — Bibliography.

HERWIJNEN (G. VAN) compiler. Bibliografie van de stedengeschiedenis van Nederland;...met medewerking van W.G. van der Moer [and others]. Leiden, 1978. pp. 355.

— New Zealand.

KILMARTIN (LESLIE) and THORNS (DAVID C.) Cities unlimited: the sociology of urban development in Australia and New Zealand. Sydney, 1978. pp. 195. *bibliog.*

— Palestine — History.

COHEN (AMNON) and LEWIS (BERNARD) Population and revenue in the towns of Palestine in the sixteenth century. Princeton, N.J., [1978]. pp. 199. *bibliog.*

— Russia.

KIZEVETTER (ALEKSANDR ALEKSANDROVICH) Posadskaia obshchina v Rossii XVIII stoletiia...; with a new introduction by Gilbert Rozman, Princeton University. Newtonville, Mass., 1978. pp. 810. *bibliog. Xerographic reprint of 1st ed., Moscow, 1903, with additional new title page.*

CHISTIAKOV (EVGENII GAVRILOVICH) and SEMENOV (AL'BERT KONSTANTINOVICH) Balansovye modeli khoziaistva goroda. Moskva, 1977. pp. 192. *bibliog.*

ZANIATOST' v nebol'shikh gorodakh: ekonomiko-demograficheskii aspekt; pod redaktsiei A.E. Kotliara. Moskva, 1978. pp. 207.

The SOCIALIST city: spatial structure and urban policy; edited by R.A. French and F.E. Ian Hamilton. Chichester, [1979]. pp. 541. *bibliogs.*

— — Siberia.

ISTORIIA gorodov Sibiri dosovetskogo perioda, XVII - nachalo XX v. Novosibirsk, 1977. pp. 303.

GORODA Sibiri: epokha feodalizma i kapitalizma. Novosibirsk, 1978. pp. 335.

— Tasmania.

TASMANIA. Commonwealth Bureau of Census and Statistics. Tasmanian Office. 1975. Index of towns, localities and standard area codes. [Hobart, 1975]. pp. 51.

— Underdeveloped areas.

See UNDERDEVELOPED AREAS — Cities and towns.

— United Kingdom.

The HEART of the Empire: discussions of problems of modern city life in England; [edited by] C.F.G. Masterman; [facsimile reprint of the edition of 1901] edited with an introduction by Bentley B. Gilbert. Brighton, 1973. pp. 415,xlvii.

NORTHERN REGION STRATEGY TEAM. Urban environment in the Northern Region. Newcastle-upon-Tyne, 1977. pp. 125. *(Working Papers. No. 16)*

The IDEAL city; edited with an introduction by Helen E. Meller. Leicester, [1979]. pp. 183. *Contains 'The ideal city' by Canon Barnett, and, 'Civics: as applied sociology', by Patrick Geddes.*

LAWLESS (PAUL) Urban deprivation and government initiative. London, 1979. pp. 251. *bibliog.*

SOCIAL problems and the city: geographical perspectives; edited by David T. Herbert and David M. Smith. Oxford, 1979. pp. 2717. *bibliogs.*

TREBLE (JAMES H.) Urban poverty in Britain 1830-1914. London, 1979. pp. 216.

URBAN deprivation and the inner city; edited by Colin Jones. London, [1979]. pp. 218. *bibliogs.*

— — Growth.

OPEN UNIVERSITY. Arts A322 [Course Team]. Block 3, units 9-12. English urban history, 1500-1780: the traditional community under stress; ([with] Supplementary material). Milton Keynes, 1977. 2 pts. (in 1 vol.) *bibliogs.*

OPEN UNIVERSITY. Arts A322 [Course Team]. Block 4, units 13-16. English urban history, 1500-1780: the rise of the new urban society. Milton Keynes, 1977. pp. 120. *bibliogs.*

LONDON. University. London School of Economics and Political Science. Graduate School of Geography. Discussion Papers. No. 70. Exploding the myth of rapidly expanding urban systems in Britain: implications for the adoption of functional areas in the 1981 census; [by] Stephen Kennett. London, 1978. pp. 20. *bibliog.*

— — Wales — History.

BOROUGHS of medieval Wales; edited by R.A. Griffiths (in memory of John Goronwy Edwards). Cardiff, 1978. pp. 338. *Published on behalf of the History and Law Committee of the Board of Celtic Studies, University of Wales.*

— United States.

GOODALL (LEONARD E.) and SPRENGEL (DONALD P.) The American metropolis. 2nd ed. Columbus, Ohio, [1975]. pp. 277. *bibliogs.*

The AGE of urban reform: new perspectives on the progressive era; [edited by] Michael H. Ebner and Eugene M. Tobin. Port Washington, N.Y., 1977. pp. 213. *bibliog.*

LEVIN (MELVIN R.) The urban prospect: planning, policy, and strategies for change. North Scituate, Mass., [1977]. pp. 305. *bibliog.*

COUSINS (ALBERT N.) and NAGPAUL (HANS) Urban life: the sociology of cities and urban society. New York, [1979]. pp. 608. *bibliog.*

NORTHAM (RAY M.) Urban geography. 2nd ed. New York, [1979]. pp. 512.

REES (P.H.) Residential patterns in American cities: 1960. Chicago, 1979. pp. 405. *bibliog. (Chicago. Unversity. Department of Geography. Research Papers. No. 189)*

— — Growth.

BOYER (PAUL S.) Urban masses and moral order in America, 1820-1920. Cambridge, Mass., 1978. pp. 387. *bibliogs.*

MILLER (ROBERTA BALSTAD) City and hinterland: a case study of urban growth and regional development. Westport, Conn., 1979. pp. 179.

TOLLEY (GEORGE STANFORD) and others. Urban growth policy in a market economy. New York, 1979. pp. 220. *bibliogs.*

— — The West — History.

LARSEN (LAWRENCE HAROLD) The urban West at the end of the frontier. Lawrence, [1978]. pp. 173. *bibliog.*

CITIES AND TOWNS, MEDIEVAL

— Europe.

EUROPEAN towns: their archaeology and early history; edited by M.W. Barley. London, 1977. pp. 523. *bibliogs.*

ENNEN (EDITH) The medieval town; translated by Natalie Fryde. Amsterdam, 1979. pp. 287. *bibliog.*

CITIZENS' ADVISORY COMMITTEES IN EDUCATION

— United States.

PUBLIC participation in local school districts: the dissatisfaction theory of democracy; edited by Frank W. Lutz [and] Laurence Iannaccone. Lexington, Mass., [1978]. pp. 135. *bibliogs.*

CITIZENSHIP

— Puerto Rico.

CABRANES (JOSÉ A.) Citizenship and the American Empire: notes on the legislative history of the United States citizenship of Puerto Ricans. New Haven, 1979. pp. 101. *Reprinted from University of Pennsylvania Law Review, 1978*

— United States.

CABRANES (JOSÉ A.) Citizenship and the American Empire: notes on the legislative history of the United States citizenship of Puerto Ricans. New Haven, 1979. pp. 101. *Reprinted from University of Pennsylvania Law Review, 1978*

CITY PLANNING.

CITY PLANNERS

— United Kingdom.

McLOUGHLIN (PETE) Regional policy and the inner areas: a study of planners' attitudes. Reading, 1978. pp. 26. bibliog. (Reading. University. Department of Geography. Reading Geographical Papers. No. 64).

CITY PLANNING.

HUMAN SETTLEMENTS; issued by the Centre for Housing, Building and Planning. Department of Economic and Social Affairs, United Nations. q., Ja 1971 (v.1, no.1)- New York.

LANE (ROBERT) and others. Analytical transport planning. London, 1971 repr. 1974. pp. 283.

The OREGON experiment; [by] Christopher Alexander [and others]. New York, 1975. pp. 190. (Center for Environmental Structure. Center for Environmental Structure Series. vol.3)

STATISTICS and urban planning....; edited by Ken Williams. London, [1975]. pp. 189. *Based on papers presented at the 8th general meeting of the International Association of Municipal Statisticians, held at Helsinki, 1972.*

The ENVIRONMENT of human settlements: human well-being in cities: proceedings of the conference held in Brussels, Belgium, April 1976; editor in chief P. Laconte, etc. Oxford, 1976. 2 vols.

SOCIAL areas in cities; edited by D.T. Herbert and R.J. Johnston. London, [1976]. 2 vols. bibliogs.

AD HOC EXPERT GROUP MEETING ON HUMAN SETTLEMENTS PERFORMANCE STANDARDS, [NEW YORK], 1975. Report of...[the] Meeting [held at] United Nations Headquarters, 15-19 December 1975. (ST/ESA/61). New York, United Nations, 1977. pp. 83.

CAMHIS (MATHIEU MARIOS) Planning theory and philosophy: a comparative analysis. 1977. fo. 313. bibliog. *Typescript. Ph.D. (London) thesis: unpublished. This thesis is the property of London University and may not be removed from the Library.*

CHADWICK (GEORGE F.) A systems view of planning: towards a theory of the urban and regional planning process. 2nd ed. Oxford, [1978]. pp. 432. bibliogs.

The MATURE metropolis; edited by Charles L. Leven. Lexington, [1978]. pp. 317. bibliogs. *Contains essays commissioned by the Institute for Urban and Regional Studies, Washington University, St. Louis for a symposium held June 6-8, 1977.*

PEARCE (BARRY J.) and others. Land, planning and the market. Cambridge, 1978. pp. 101. bibliog. (Cambridge. University. Department of Land Economy. Occasional Papers. No. 9)

HARTOG (HUGO HENDRIK WOUTER DEN) Leefbare stedebouw: stedebouwkundige kwaliteit, sociale integratie, democratisering. Alphen aan den Rijn, 1979. pp. 415. *Proefschrift (doctor in de sociale wetenschappen) - Erasmus Universiteit Rotterdam. With English summary.*

NEW trends in urban planning: studies in housing, urban design and planning...; edited by Dan Soen. Oxford, [1979]. pp. 357. bibliogs.

RESOURCES and planning; edited by Brian Goodall and Andrew Kirby. Oxford, 1979. pp. 373. bibliogs.

U.K. Department of the Environment. Library. Bulletin. fortn. London. *Current issues only kept.*

— Bibliography.

BODDAERT (JACQUELINE) compiler. Bibliographie sélective: aménagement du territoire, environnement, urbanisme. 3rd ed. Paris, Délégation à l'Aménagement du Territoire et à l'Action Régionale, 1978. pp. 38.

— Congresses.

URBAN, regional and national planning (UNRENAP): proceedings of the IFAC Workshop, Kyoto, Japan, 5-6 August 1977; edited by T. Hasegawa and K. Inoue. Oxford, 1978. pp. 233.

— Data processing.

FOOT (DAVID H.S.) Urban models I: a computer program for the Garin-Lowry model. Reading, 1978. pp. 47. (Reading. University. Department of Geography. Reading Geographical Papers. No. 65)

— Information services.

BARRICK (JOHN) compiler. Town and country planning: sources of information on town and country planning. [London, 1979]. pp. 64. bibliog. (U.K. Department of the Environment. Library. Information Series)

— — United Kingdom.

BARRICK (JOHN) compiler. Town and country planning: sources of information on town and country planning. [London, 1979]. pp. 64. bibliog. (U.K. Department of the Environment. Library. Information Series)

— Mathematical models.

LEE (COLIN) Models in planning: an introduction to the use of quantitative models in planning. Oxford, [1973]. pp. 142.

MORRISON (W.I.) and SMITH (P.N.) Input-output methods in urban and regional planning: a practical guide. London, 1976. pp. 122. bibliog. (Planning Research Applications Group. PRAG Technical Papers. TP6)

MODELS of cities and regions: theoretical and empirical developments; edited by A.G. Wilson [and others]. Chichester, [1977]. pp. 536. bibliogs.

FOOT (DAVID H.S.) Urban models I: a computer program for the Garin-Lowry model. Reading, 1978. pp. 47. (Reading. University. Department of Geography. Reading Geographical Papers. No. 65)

— Australia.

AUSTRALIA. Department of Urban and Regional Development. 1975. The inter-relation of manufacturing industry policy and urban and regional development policy: a discussion paper based on a submission to the Committee to Advise on Policies for Manufacturing Industry, Jackson Committee. [Canberra], 1975. pp. 109.

NEUTZE (MAX) Australian urban policy. Sydney, 1978. pp. 252. bibliog.

— — Queensland.

MORETON REGION GROWTH STRATEGY INVESTIGATIONS. Urban land-use and commitment. [Brisbane], Co-ordinator-General's Department and Cities Commission, 1976. 1 vol. (various pagings). bibliog. (Tasks. 2)

— Canada.

BETTISON (DAVID G.) The politics of Canadian urban development. Edmonton, 1975. pp. 337. bibliog.

PLUNKETT (THOMAS J.) and BETTS (GEORGE M.) The management of Canadian urban government: a basic text for a course in urban management. Kingston, Ontario, [1978]. pp. 304. bibliog.

— — Alberta.

ALBERTA. Task Force on Urbanization and the Future. 1972. Task committee reports. [Edmonton, 1972]. pp. 91.

— — Nova Scotia.

LANG (R.S.) Nova Scotia municipal and regional planning in the seventies: report/evaluation of the Town Planning Act review...; prepared and published under an agreement between the Nova Scotia Department of Municipal Affairs and Central Mortgage and Housing Corporation. [Halifax], 1972. pp. 470.

— — Ontario.

ONTARIO. Planning Act Review Committee. 1977. Report; [Eli Comay, chairman]. [Toronto], 1977. pp. 186.

— Europe.

KONVITZ (JOSEF W.) Cities and the sea: port city planning in early modern Europe. Baltimore, [1978]. pp. 235.

— France.

MICHAUD (CLAUDE) La décision dans l'action collective: application à l'urbanisme. [Paris, 1976]. pp. 322. bibliog.

HOUSE (JOHN WILLIAM) France: an applied geography. London, 1978. pp. 478. bibliogs.

RUBENSTEIN (JAMES M.) The French new towns. Baltimore, [1978]. pp. 165.

FRANCE. Mission des Villes du Massif Central. 1979. Le Massif Central: politique des villes et des pays. Paris, [1979]. pp. 112. (France. Délégation à l'Aménagement du Territoire et à l'Action Régionale. Massif Central. Dossiers. 5)

— Germany.

GERMANY (BUNDESREPUBLIK). Bundesforschungsanstalt für Landeskunde und Raumordnung. Informationen zur Raumentwicklung. m., Ja 1973 (Heft 1)- Bonn-Bad Godesberg. *Supersedes Rundbrief des Instituts für Landeskunde [of which the Library has no file] and Informationen; [pd. by] Institut für Raumordnung (N 1950 - 1973).*

LINDER (WOLF) and others. Erzwungene Mobilität: Alternativen zur Raumordnung, Stadtentwicklung und Verkehrspolitik. Köln, [1975]. pp. 167. bibliog.

— Ireland (Republic).

NATIONAL HOUSING CONFERENCE, LEOPARDSTOWN, CO. DUBLIN, 1974. Living in town, conserving the future: a summary of the papers presented at the...conference; (sponsored jointly by the Department of Local Government and the Royal Institute of the Architects of Ireland). [Dublin, An Foras Forbartha], 1975. pp. 26.

— Netherlands.

HARTOG (HUGO HENDRIK WOUTER DEN) Leefbare stedebouw: stedebouwkundige kwaliteit, sociale integratie, democratisering. Alphen aan den Rijn, 1979. pp. 415. *Proefschrift (doctor in de sociale wetenschappen) - Erasmus Universiteit Rotterdam. With English summary.*

— Nicaragua.

NICARAGUA. Statutes, etc. 1958. Ley de urbanizaciones; con las reformas y adiciones aprobadas por las honorables camaras legislativas en septiembre de 1958. [Managua, Oficina Nacional de Urbanismo, 1958]. pp. xxxii.

— United Kingdom.

U.K. Department of the Environment. 1977. Local plans: public local inquiries: a guide to procedure. [London, 1977]. pp. 31.

WHITBREAD (MICHAEL) Programmes for inner city regeneration: the search for priorities. London, Department of the Environment, [1977]. fo. 14.

LONDON. University. London School of Economics and Political Science. Graduate School of Geography. Discussion Papers. No. 68. Urban planning: theory, practice and ideology; [by] Eleftheria Karnavou. London, 1978. pp. 28. bibliog.

U.K. Inner Cities Directorate. 1978. Industry in the inner city: case studies in mixed-use development. [London, 1978]. pp. 39.

McKAY (DAVID H.) and COX (ANDREW W.) The politics of urban change. London, 1979. pp. 297. bibliog.

CITY PLANNING.(Cont.)

— — Citizen participation.

COMMUNITY involvement and leisure; edited by John T. Haworth. London, [1979]. pp. 205.

— — — Bibliography.

COCKETT (IEN) compiler. Public participation in planning: the British experience. 2nd ed. London, 1976. pp. 42. *(London. Greater London Council. Research Library. Research Bibliographies. No. 55)*

— — Information services.

KIDD (SUSAN) compiler. New towns in the U.K. London, 1977. pp. 124. *(U.K. Department of the Environment. Library. Information Series)*

— United States.

The AGE of urban reform: new perspectives on the progressive era; [edited by] Michael H. Ebner and Eugene M. Tobin. Port Washington, N.Y., 1977. pp. 213. *bibliog.*

LEVIN (MELVIN R.) The urban prospect: planning, policy, and strategies for change. North Scituate, Mass., [1977]. pp. 305. *bibliog.*

CENTRAL city economic development; edited by Benjamin Chinitz. Cambridge, Mass., [1979]. pp. 198. *bibliogs.*

CITY PLANNING AND REDEVELOPMENT LAW

— Africa, East.

URBAN legal problems in eastern Africa: (papers presented at a workshop held in Nairobi, April 1976); edited by G.W. Kanyeihamba and J.P.W.B. McAuslan. Uppsala, 1978. pp. 298. *(Nordiska Afrikainstitutet and International Center for Law in Development. Studies of Law in Social Change and Development. No. 2)*

— United Kingdom.

TELLING (ARTHUR EDWARD) Planning law and procedure. 5th ed. London, 1977. pp. 392.

CITY TRAFFIC

— South Africa.

SOUTH AFRICA. Planning Advisory Council. 1975. An investigation into a system of staggered working hours for Pretoria to help alleviate traffic problems; by a standing committee of a subsidiary committee of the Planning Advisory Council, etc. [Pretoria], 1975. pp. 25.

CIUDAD JUAREZ

— Economic conditions.

MARTÍNEZ (OSCAR J.) Border boom town: Ciudad Juárez since 1848. Austin, [1978]. pp. 231. *bibliog.*

— Social conditions.

MARTÍNEZ (OSCAR J.) Border boom town: Ciudad Juárez since 1848. Austin, [1978]. pp. 231. *bibliog.*

CIUDAD REAL (CITY)

— Economic history.

PHILLIPS (CARLA RAHN) Ciudad Real, 1500-1750: growth, crisis, and readjustment in the Spanish economy. Cambridge, Mass., 1979. pp. 190. *bibliog.*

CIUDAD REAL (PROVINCE)

— Economic history.

PHILLIPS (CARLA RAHN) Ciudad Real, 1500-1750: growth, crisis, and readjustment in the Spanish economy. Cambridge, Mass., 1979. pp. 190. *bibliog.*

CIVIL ENGINEERS

— Australia — Western Australia.

TAUMAN (MERAB) The chief: C.Y. O'Connor. Nedlands, 1978. pp. 290.

CIVIL LAW

— Austria.

GSCHNITZER (FRANZ) Allgemeiner Teil des bürgerlichen Rechts. Wien, 1966. pp. 282.

KOZIOL (HELMUT) and WELSER (RUDOLF) Grundriss des bürgerlichen Rechts. Band 1. Allgemeiner Teil und Schuldrecht. 4th ed. Wien, 1976. pp. 384.

— France.

JOBERT (ANNETTE) and others. Les étrangers et la justice civile: analyse sociologique de la différenciation des pratiques judiciaires. [Paris], 1976. pp. 262. *(France. Ministère de la Justice. Service de Coordination de la Recherche. Etude[s] de Sociologie Juridique)*

— Italy.

SANTORO-PASSARELLI (FRANCESCO) Libertà e autorità nel diritto civile. Padova, 1977. pp. 433. *bibliog.*

— Russia.

OIGENZIKHT (VIKTOR ARKAD'EVICH) Prezumptsii v sovetskom grazhdanskom prave. Dushanbe, 1976. pp. 190.

PROBLEMY upravleniia i grazhdanskogo prava. Moskva, 1976. pp. 185.

ZENIN (IVAN ALEKSANDROVICH) Nauka i tekhnika v grazhdanskom prave. Moskva, 1977. pp. 208.

CIVIL PROCEDURE.

ACCESS to justice; general editor, Mauro Cappelletti. Alphen aan den Rijn, 1978-79. 4 vols. (in 6). *bibliogs.*

— Russia.

KOMMENTARII sudebnoi praktiki za 1975 god. Moskva, 1976. pp. 223.

KOMMENTARII sudebnoi praktiki za 1976 god. Moskva, 1977. pp. 134.

— United Kingdom — Ireland, Northern.

IRELAND, NORTHERN. Enforcement of Judgments Office. Master's report under Section 5(4) of the Act and statement of expenses and fees; certified by the Comptroller and Auditor-General for Northern Ireland. a., 1970/73- Belfast.

CIVIL RIGHTS.

HUMAN rights: a compilation of international instruments of the United Nations. (A/CONF.32/4). New York, United Nations, 1967. pp. 94.

UNITED NATIONS. Office of Public Information. 1968. The United Nations and human rights. New York, 1968. pp. 93.

HUMAN rights: a compilation of international instruments of the United Nations. (ST/HR/1). [2nd ed.] New York, United Nations, 1973. pp. 106.

AMNESTY INTERNATIONAL. A.I. in quotes. London, 1976. pp. 25.

WORLD HEALTH ORGANIZATION. 1976. Health aspects of human rights: with special reference to developments in biology and medicine. Geneva, 1976. pp. 48.

GASTIL (RAYMOND D.) Freedom in the world: political rights and civil liberties, 1978. Boston, Mass., [1978]. pp. 335.

HAAS (ERNST BERNARD) Global evangelism rides again: how to protect human rights without really trying. Berkeley, [1978]. pp. 49. *(California University. Institute of International Studies. Policy Papers in International Affairs. No. 5)*

HUMAN rights and world order; edited by Abdul Aziz Said. New York, 1978. pp. 170. *bibliogs.*

HUMAN rights: a compilation of international instruments. (ST/HR/1/Rev.1). [3rd ed.] New York, United Nations, 1978. pp. 132.

MOURGEON (JACQUES) Les droits de l'homme. [Paris, 1978]. pp. 127. *bibliog.*

PARTRIDGE (A.C.) Human rights: their origin, validity and implementation. Braamfontein, 1978. pp. 14. *bibliog. (South African Institute of International Affairs. Ocasional Papers)*

GLASER (KURT) and POSSONY (STEFAN THOMAS) Victims of politics: the state of human rights. New York, 1979. pp. 614. *bibliog.*

HENKIN (LOUIS) The rights of man today. London, 1979. pp. 173. *bibliog.*

HUMAN rights: problems, perspectives and texts...; edited by F. E. Dowrick. Farnborough, [1979]. pp. 223. *bibliog. A series of lectures and seminar papers delivered in the University of Durham in 1978, with supporting texts.*

RIGHTS; [selected essays edited by] David Lyons. Belmont, Calif., [1979]. pp. 188. *bibliog.*

— Bibliography.

GARLING (MARGUERITE) compiler. Human rights research guide: library holdings in London on human rights, censorship and freedom of expression. London, 1978. pp. 77. *Compiled for the Writers and Scholars Educational Trust.*

— Societies, etc.

GARLING (MARGUERITE) compiler. The human rights handbook: a guide to British and American international human rights organisations; compiled...for the Writers and Scholars Educational Trust. London, 1979. pp. 299. *bibliog.*

— Canada.

HUMAN RIGHTS IN CANADA; [pd. by] Legislative Analysis, Department of Labour. a., 1977- Ottawa.

— — New Brunswick.

NEW BRUNSWICK. Human Rights Commission. 1976. The human rights code of New Brunswick: a continuing program of education in human rights. Fredericton, [1976]. pp. 13, 15. *In English and French.*

— — Ontario.

ONTARIO. Human Rights Commission. 1977. Life together: a report on human rights in Ontario. [Toronto, 1977]. pp. 139.

— — Quebec.

QUEBEC (PROVINCE). Civil Code Revision Office. Civil Rights Committee. 1966. Report; [F.R. Scott, président]. Montréal, 1966. pp. 29. *(Quebec (Province). Civil Code Revision Office. [Reports]. 2) In English and French.*

— Europe.

NEDJATI (ZAIM M.) Human rights under the European Convention. Amsterdam, 1978. pp. 298. *(London. University. King's College. Centre of European Law. European Studies in Law. vol. 8)*

— Europe, Eastern.

BEAMISH (TUFTON VICTOR HAMILTON) Baron Chelwood and HADLEY (GUY) The Kremlin's dilemma: the struggle for human rights in Eastern Europe. London, 1979. pp. 285. *bibliog.*

— Iran.

BUTLER (WILLIAM J.) and LEVASSEUR (GEORGES) Human rights and the legal system in Iran. Geneva, 1976. pp. 72. *bibliog.*

— Italy.

GREVI (VITTORIO) Libertà personale dell'imputato e costituzione. [Milan, 1976]. pp. 400.

— Poland.

POLISH GOVERNMENT IN EXILE. In defence of Poland's freedom: facts and documents. London, 1977. pp. 32.

— Russia.

SHINDLER (COLIN) Exit visa: detente, human rights and the Jewish emigration movement in the USSR. London, 1978. pp. 291. *bibliog.*

— South Africa.

SOUTH AFRICA. Information Service of South Africa, New York. 1967. Setting the record straight. New York, [1967]. pp. 24.

DUGARD (JOHN) Human rights and the South African legal order. Princeton, N.J., [1978]. pp. 470. *bibliog.*

— Switzerland.

MASTRONARDI (PHILIPPE) Der Verfassungsgrundsatz der Menschenwürde in der Schweiz: ein Beitrag zu Theorie und Praxis der Grundrechte. Berlin, 1978. pp. 331. *bibliog.*

— United Kingdom.

U.K. Central Office of Information. Reference Division. Reference Pamphlets. 162. Human rights in the United Kingdom. London, 1978. pp. 50. *bibliog.*

— — Ireland, Northern.

EUROPEAN COURT OF HUMAN RIGHTS. Series A: Judgments and Decisions. [A25]. ...Case of Ireland v. The United Kingdom: 1. Decision of 29 April 1976; 2. Judgment of 18 January 1978. Strasbourg, Council of Europe, 1978. pp. 141 [bis]. *In English and French.*

NORTHERN IRELAND CIVIL RIGHTS ASSOCIATION. "We shall overcome"...; the history of the struggle for civil rights in Northern Ireland 1968-1978. Belfast, [1978?]. pp. 47.

— United States.

BELZ (HERMAN) Emancipation and equal rights: politics and constitutionalism in the Civil War era. New York, [1978]. pp. 171.

FEAGIN (JOE R.) and FEAGIN (CLAIRECE BOOHER) Discrimination American style: institutional racism and sexism. Englewood Cliffs, [1978?]. pp. 190.

FISS (OWEN M.) The civil rights injunction. Bloomington, [1978]. pp. 117. *(Indiana University. School of Law. Addison C. Harris Lectures. 1976)*

GARROW (DAVID J.) Protest at Selma: Martin Luther King, Jr., and the Voting Rights Act of 1965. New Haven, 1978. pp. 346.

NUNN (CLYDE Z.) and others. Tolerance for nonconformity: a national survey of Americans' changing commitment to civil liberties. San Francisco, 1978. pp. 212. *bibliog.*

POLLACK (HARRIET) and SMITH (ALEXANDER B.) Civil liberties and civil rights in the United States. St. Paul, Minn., 1978. pp. 299.

SHELDON (CHARLES P.) The bolshevization of the USA. New York, [1978]. pp. 725.

CIVIL RIGHTS (INTERNATIONAL LAW).

BENNETT (GORDON IRVINE) Aboriginal rights in international law. London, 1978. pp. 88. *bibliog. (Royal Anthropological Institute of Great Britain and Ireland. Occasional Papers. No. 37)*

CIVIL SERVICE.

BUREAUCRACY and political development; edited by Joseph La Palombara. 2nd ed. Princeton, N.J., [1967]. pp. 513. *bibliog. (Social Science Research Council. Committee on Comparative Politics. Studies in Political Development. 2)*

— Canada — Quebec (Province).

O'NEILL (PIERRE) and BENJAMIN (JACQUES) Les mandarins du pouvoir au Québec de Jean Lesage à René Lévesque. Montréal, 1978. pp. 285.

— France.

FRANCE. Ecole Nationale d'Administration. 1955. Recruitment and training for the higher civil service in France. [Paris, 1955?]. pp. 134.

— India.

SAY not the struggle: essays in honour of A.D. Gorwala; [edited by H.M. Patel]. Delhi, 1976. pp. 328.

— — Examinations.

INDIA. Committee on Recruitment Policy and Selection Methods. 1978. Civil services examination: report...; [D.S. Kothari, chairman] . [New Delhi, 1978]. pp. 235.

— Ireland (Republic).

DOONEY (SÉAN) The Irish civil service. Dublin, 1976. pp. 201. *bibliog.*

EIRE. Civil Service Commission. Report. a., 1977(1st)- Dublin.

— Israel.

NACHMIAS (DAVID) and ROSENBLOOM (DAVID H.) Bureaucratic culture: citizens and administrators in Israel. London, [1978]. pp. 212. *bibliog.*

— Malaysia.

PUTHUCHEARY (MAVIS) The politics of administration: the Malaysian experience. Kuala Lumpur, 1978. pp. 170. *bibliog.*

— Nigeria.

NIGERIA. Public Service Review Commission. 1974. Main report; [J.O. Udoji, chairman]. Lagos, 1974. pp. 228.

NIGERIA (OYO STATE). Public Service Commission. Report. a., 1976/77(1st)- [Ibadan]. *Supersedes in part NIGERIA (WESTERN STATE). Public Service Commission. Report.*

— Sierra Leone.

SIERRA LEONE. Committee set up to Consider the Appointment of Africans to the Senior Service of Government. 1949. Reports; [G.E. Mercer, chairman]. Freetown, 1949. pp. 16. *(Sierra Leone. Sessional Papers. 1949. No. 4)*

— Spain.

GARRIDO FALLA (FERNANDO) La nueva legislacion sobre funcionarios publicos en España. [Madrid, 1964]. pp. 52. *(Centro de Formacion y Perfeccionamiento de Funcionarios [Spain]. Conferencias y Documentos. No.6)*

— Sudan.

SUDAN. 1951. Memorandum on the recommendations of the Terms of Service Commission. Khartoum, 1951. pp. 27.

— United Kingdom.

DALE (HAROLD EDWARD) The higher Civil Service of Great Britain. [London], 1941. pp. 232.

WALKER (NIGEL) Morale in the civil service: a study of the desk worker. Westport, Conn., 1977. pp. 302. *Reprint of work originally published Edinburgh, 1962.*

KEELING (DESMOND) Management in government. London, 1972. pp. 210. *bibliog.*

HILL (MICHAEL J.) The sociology of public administration. New York, [1975]. pp. 278. *bibliog. First published in 1972.*

INTERCHANGE between the home civil service and the diplomatic service; report of a Working Group; [Sir John Herbecq, chairman]. [London], Civil Service Department, 1978. pp. 17.

U.K. Civil Service Department. 1979. Guide for new managers. London, 1979. pp. 34. *First issued as a CSD departmental publication in 1975.*

— — Minority employment.

TAVISTOCK INSTITUTE OF HUMAN RELATIONS. Application of race relations policy in the civil service. London, H.M.S.O., 1978. pp. 275.

— — Ireland, Northern.

OLIVER (JOHN ANDREW) Working at Stormont: memoirs. Dublin, 1978. pp. 251.

— United States.

DAVID (PAUL THEODORE) and POLLOCK (ROSS) Executives for government: central issues of federal personnel administration. Westport, Conn., 1976. pp. 196. *bibliog. Reprint of work originally published Washington, 1957, with 1958 supplement.*

STAHL (OSCAR GLENN) Public personnel administration. 7th ed. New York, [1976]. pp. 575. *bibliog.*

PERSONNEL management in government: politics and process; [by] Jay M. Shafritz [and others]. New York, [1978]. pp. 305. *bibliogs.*

CIVIL SUPREMACY OVER THE MILITARY

— Communist countries.

CIVIL-military relations in communist systems; edited by Dale R. Herspring and Ivan Volgyes. Boulder, Colo., 1978. pp. 273.

— Russia.

COLTON (TIMOTHY J.) Commissars, commanders, and civilian authority: the structure of Soviet military politics. Cambridge, Mass., 1979. pp. 365. *(Harvard University. Russian Research Center. Studies. 79)*

— Sudan.

ABDEL-RAHIM (MUDDATHIR) Changing patterns of civilian-military relations in the Sudan. Uppsala, 1978. pp. 32. *(Nordiska Afrikainstitutet. Research Reports. No. 46)*

CIVIL WAR.

LOMBARDI (ALDO VIRGILIO) Bürgerkrieg und Völkerrecht: die Anwendbarkeit völkerrechtlicher Normen in nicht-zwischenstaatlichen bewaffneten Konflikten. Berlin, 1976. pp. 416. *bibliog.*

CIVILIZATION.

SIBLEY (MULFORD QUICKERT) Nature and civilization: some implications for politics. Itasca, Ill., [1977]. pp. 319. *bibliogs.*

WADDINGTON (CONRAD HAL) Tools for thought. St. Albans, 1977. pp. 250. *bibliog.*

CASSIRER (ERNST) Symbol, myth, and culture: essays and lectures of Ernst Cassirer, 1935-1945; edited by Donald Phillip Verene. New Haven, 1979. pp. 304.

— History.

WOLFENDALE (WILFRID) History has tongues: a study of the comparative development of ancient and modern civilizations. London, 1946. pp. 152.

ELIAS (NORBERT) The civilizing process: the history of manners; translated by Edmund Jephcott. Oxford, 1978. pp. 314.

CIVILIZATION, MEDIEVAL.

ESSAYS on medieval civilization; by Richard E. Sullivan [and others]; edited by Bede Karl Lackner and Kenneth Roy Philp. Austin, Texas, [1978]. pp. 178. *(Texas University. Walter Prescott Webb Memorial Lectures. 12)*

MURRAY (ALEXANDER) M.A., B.Phil. Reason and society in the Middle Ages. Oxford, 1978. pp. 511.

CIVILIZATION, MEDIEVAL.(Cont.)

— **Arab influences.**

DANIEL (NORMAN) The Arabs and mediaeval Europe. 2nd ed. London, 1979. pp. 385.

CIVILIZATION, MODERN.

TOURAINE (ALAIN) La société invisible: regards 1974-1976. Paris, 1977. pp. 289.

DEBUS (ALLEN G.) Man and nature in the Renaissance. Cambridge, 1978. pp. 159.

GLUBB (Sir JOHN BAGOT) The fate of empires; and Search for survival. Edinburgh, 1978. pp. 46.

SATIN (MARK IVOR) New age politics: healing self and society: the emerging new alternative to Marxism and liberalism. West Vancouver, 1978. pp. 240. *bibliog.*

BELL (DANIEL) The cultural contradictions of capitalism. 2nd ed. London, 1979. pp. 301.

CIVILIZATION, MOHAMMEDAN.

BURCKHARDT (TITUS) Moorish culture in Spain; translated by Alisa Jaffa. London, [1972]. pp. 219. *bibliog.*

CHEJNE (ANWAR G.) Muslim Spain: its history and culture. Minneapolis, [1974]. pp. 559. *bibliog.*

CIVILIZATION, OCCIDENTAL.

SOLZHENITSYN (ALEKSANDR ISAEVICH) Alexander Solzhenitsyn speaks to the West. London, 1978. pp. 100.

WESSON (ROBERT GALE) State systems: international pluralism, politics, and culture. New York, [1978]. pp. 296. *bibliog.*

CLARK (JOE).

HUMPHREYS (DAVID L.) Joe Clark: a portrait. [Ottawa], 1978. pp. 276.

NOLAN (MICHAEL) Journalist. Joe Clark: the emerging leader. Toronto, [1978]. pp. 139.

CLASSROOM MANAGEMENT.

METZ (MARY HAYWOOD) Classrooms and corridors: the crisis of authority in desegregated secondary schools. Berkeley, Calif., [1978]. pp. 275. *bibliog.*

CLEATOR MOOR

— **Playgrounds.**

DANBY (SIMON) The Big Hill adventure playground, 1972-1976. [Cleator Moor], Cumbria Community Development Project, [1976?]. pp. 30.

CLEAVER (ELDRIDGE).

CLEAVER (ELDRIDGE) Soul on fire. London, 1979. pp. 220.

CLEMENCEAU (GEORGES EUGENE BENJAMIN).

McCABE (JOSEPH) Georges Clemenceau: France's grand old man; his life and opinions. London, 1919. pp. 88.

CLERGY

— **United Kingdom.**

METCALFE (FRANCIS JAMES) Colliers and I; or, Thirty years' work among Derbyshire colliers. Manchester, 1903. pp. 218.

HEENEY (WILLIAM BRIAN DANFORD) A different kind of gentleman: parish clergy as professional men in early and mid-Victorian England. Hamden, Conn., 1976. pp. 169. *bibliog.* (*Conference on British Studies and Wittenberg University [Ohio]. Studies in British History and Culture. vol. 5*)

CLEVELAND, UNITED KINGDOM

— **Economic conditions.**

CLEVELAND [COUNTY]. Planning Department. Cleveland (Hartlepool) structure plan: report of survey: draft document for consultation: stud[ies]. Middlesbrough, 1975. 19 pts. (in 1 vol.).

CLEVELAND [COUNTY]. Planning Department. Cleveland (Hartlepool) structure plan: report of survey. [Middlesbrough], 1977-78. 2 vols. (*Reports. No. 115*)

— **Economic policy.**

CLEVELAND [COUNTY]. County Council. Cleveland (Teesside) structure plan, Cleveland (East Cleveland) structure plan, Cleveland (West Cleveland) structure plan: examination in public, June 1975: County Council statement. [Middlesbrough], 1975. fo 84, xxxiii.

CLEVELAND [COUNTY]. Planning Department. Cleveland (Hartlepool) structure plan: report of survey: draft document for consultation: stud[ies]. Middlesbrough, 1975. 19 pts. (in 1 vol.).

CLEVELAND [COUNTY]. Planning Department. (Cleveland (Hartlepool) structure plan): public participation, stage 1. [Middlesborough], 1976. pp. 33,x. (*Reports. No. 61*)

CLEVELAND [COUNTY]. Planning Department. (Cleveland (Hartlepool) structure plan): public participation, stage 2. [Middlesbrough], 1976. pp. 91. (*Reports. No. 79*)

CLEVELAND [COUNTY]. Planning Department. Cleveland (Hartlepool) structure plan: report of survey. [Middlesbrough], 1977-78. 2 vols. (*Reports. No. 115*)

CLEVELAND [COUNTY]. [Planning Department]. Cleveland (East Cleveland) structure plan. [Middlesbrough], 1974 [or rather 1977]. pp. 199. *Map in end pocket.*

CLEVELAND [COUNTY]. [Planning Department]. Cleveland (West Cleveland) structure plan. [Middlesbrough], 1974 [or rather 1977]. pp. 193. *Map in end pocket.*

CLEVELAND [COUNTY]. Planning Department. Cleveland (East Cleveland) structure plan: proposals for alterations. [Middlesbrough], 1978. 3 pts. (in 1 vol.). (*Reports. Nos. 125-127*)

CLEVELAND [COUNTY]. Planning Department. (Cleveland (Hartlepool) structure plan): public participation, stage 3: public and formal consultations. [Middlesbrough], 1978. 1 vol. (various pagings). (*Reports. No. 100*)

CLEVELAND [COUNTY]. Planning Department. (Cleveland (Hartlepool) structure plan): public participation, stage 3: response and recommended changes. [Middlesbrough], 1978. pp. 164. (*Reports. No. 101*)

CLEVELAND [COUNTY]. Planning Department. Cleveland (Hartlepool) structure plan: written statement. [Middlesbrough], 1978. pp. 285. (*Reports. No. 114*) *Map in end pocket.*

CLEVELAND (COUNTY]. Planning Department. Cleveland (West Cleveland) structure plan: proposals for alterations. [Middlesbrough], 1978. 3 pts. (in 1 vol.) (*Reports. Nos. 128-130*)

— **Social conditions.**

CLEVELAND [COUNTY]. Planning Department. Cleveland (Hartlepool) structure plan: report of survey: draft document for consultation: stud[ies]. Middlesbrough, 1975. 19 pts. (in 1 vol.).

CLEVELAND [COUNTY]. Planning Department. Cleveland (Hartlepool) structure plan: report of survey. [Middlesbrough], 1977-78. 2 vols. (*Reports. No. 115*)

— **Social policy.**

CLEVELAND [COUNTY]. County Council. Cleveland (Teesside) structure plan, Cleveland (East Cleveland) structure plan, Cleveland (West Cleveland) structure plan: examination in public, June 1975: County Council statement. [Middlesbrough], 1975. fo 84, xxxiii.

CLEVELAND [COUNTY]. Planning Department. Cleveland (Hartlepool) structure plan: report of survey: draft document for consultation: stud[ies]. Middlesbrough, 1975. 19 pts. (in 1 vol.).

CLEVELAND [COUNTY]. Planning Department. (Cleveland (Hartlepool) structure plan): public participation, stage 1. [Middlesborough], 1976. pp. 33,x. (*Reports. No. 61*)

CLEVELAND [COUNTY]. Planning Department. (Cleveland (Hartlepool) structure plan): public participation, stage 2. [Middlesbrough], 1976. pp. 91. (*Reports. No. 79*)

CLEVELAND [COUNTY]. Planning Department. Cleveland (Hartlepool) structure plan: report of survey. [Middlesbrough], 1977-78. 2 vols. (*Reports. No. 115*)

CLEVELAND [COUNTY]. [Planning Department]. Cleveland (East Cleveland) structure plan. [Middlesbrough], 1974 [or rather 1977]. pp. 199. *Map in end pocket.*

CLEVELAND [COUNTY]. [Planning Department]. Cleveland (West Cleveland) structure plan. [Middlesbrough], 1974 [or rather 1977]. pp. 193. *Map in end pocket.*

CLEVELAND [COUNTY]. Planning Department. Cleveland (East Cleveland) structure plan: proposals for alterations. [Middlesbrough], 1978. 3 pts. (in 1 vol.). (*Reports. Nos. 125-127*)

CLEVELAND [COUNTY]. Planning Department. (Cleveland (Hartlepool) structure plan): public participation, stage 3: public and formal consultations. [Middlesbrough], 1978. 1 vol. (various pagings). (*Reports. No. 100*)

CLEVELAND [COUNTY]. Planning Department. (Cleveland (Hartlepool) structure plan): public participation, stage 3: response and recommended changes. [Middlesbrough], 1978. pp. 164. (*Reports. No. 101*)

CLEVELAND [COUNTY]. Planning Department. Cleveland (Hartlepool) structure plan: written statement. [Middlesbrough], 1978. pp. 285. (*Reports. No. 114*) *Map in end pocket.*

CLEVELAND [COUNTY]. Planning Department. Cleveland (West Cleveland) structure plan: proposals for alterations. [Middlesbrough], 1978. 3 pts. (in 1 vol.) (*Reports. Nos. 128-130*)

CLOCK AND WATCH MAKING

— **Russia.**

PIPUNYROV (VASILII NIKOLAEVICH) and CHERNIAGIN (BORIS MIKHAILOVICH) Razvitie khronometrii v Rossii. Moskva, 1977. pp. 215. *bibliog.* (*Akademiia Nauk SSSR. Seriia "Istoriia Nauki i Tekhniki"*)

CLOTHING TRADE

— **Malta.**

GRECH (JOHN C.) Threads of dependence. Msida, Malta, 1978. pp. 200. *bibliog.*

— **United Kingdom.**

CLOTHING AND ALLIED PRODUCTS INDUSTRY TRAINING BOARD [U.K.]. Self-organised groups: a study of their introduction in one clothing company and what it might mean for others. [Leeds, 1978]. pp. 28.

CLUNIACS IN FRANCE.

EVANS (JOAN) Monastic life at Cluny 910-1157. Hamden, Conn., 1968. pp. 137. *bibliog. Reprint of work first published in 1931.*

CLUSTER ANALYSIS.

CLASSIFICATION and clustering; (proceedings of an advanced seminar conducted by the Mathematics Research Center, the University of Wisconsin at Madison...1976); edited by J. van Ryzin. New York, 1977. pp. 467. *bibliogs*. (*Wisconsin University, Madison. Mathematics Research Center, United States Army. Publications. No. 37*)

CLYRO, WALES

— Social conditions.

LE QUESNE (A. LAURENCE) After Kilvert. Oxford, 1978. pp. 233.

COAL

— Canada — British Columbia.

BRITISH COLUMBIA. Northeast Coal Study. Resource Sub- committee on Northeast Development. 1977. Report on coal resource evaluation studies, January 1977. [Victoria], 1977. pp. 126.

— European Economic Community countries.

EZRA (Sir DEREK JOSEPH) European Community coal policy; paper. [London, 1978]. pp. 5. (*Energy Commission [U.K.]. Papers. No. 14*)

EUROPEAN COMMUNITIES. Statistical Office. Coal: press notice. [in German, English and French]. m., Luxembourg.

— United States.

NATIONAL ACADEMY OF SCIENCES. Academy Forum, 1977. Coal as an energy resource: conflict and consensus. Washington, 1977. pp. 326.

ROSENBAUM (WALTER A.) Coal and crisis: the political dilemmas of energy management. New York, [1978]. pp. 107. *bibliogs*.

TYNER (WALLACE E.) and others. Western coal: promise or problem. Lexington, Mass., [1978]. pp. 181. *bibliog*.

COAL MINERS

— Belgium — Personal narratives.

MALVA (CONSTANT) Ma nuit au jour le jour. Paris, 1978. pp. 203.

— Canada — British Columbia.

PEAT, MARWICK AND PARTNERS. Manpower development and promotion in the coal mining industry: report to the Federal-Provincial Manpower Sub-Committee on North East Coal Development. [Victoria, B.C.?], 1978. fo. 78. *bibliog*.

— France.

HAINSWORTH (RAYMOND EDWIN) The trade union movements and labour-management relations in the coal mines of the Nord and Pas-de-Calais departments of France during the depression of 1930-1936. 1978. fo. 587. *bibliog*. Typescript. Ph.D. (London) thesis: unpublished. This thesis is the property of London University and may not be removed from the Library.

— Germany.

KLESSMANN (CHRISTOPH) Polnische Bergarbeiter im Ruhrgebiet, 1870-1945: soziale Integration und nationale Subkultur einer Minderheit in der deutschen Industriegesellschaft. Göttingen, 1978. pp. 306. *bibliog*.

— Poland.

JOŃCZYK (JAN) Der Bergarbeiterstreik im Jahre 1871 in Königshütte auf dem Hintergrund der Arbeiterklasse in Oberschlesien; übersetzt aus dem Polnischen von Anne-Marie Griese. Bremen, 1977. pp. 63.

— United Kingdom.

INDEPENDENT collier: the coal miner as archetypal proletarian reconsidered; edited by Royden Harrison. Hassocks, 1978. pp. 276. *bibliog*.

McCORMICK (BRIAN JOSEPH) Industrial relations in the coal industry. London, 1979. pp. 263. *bibliog*.

— United States — Kentucky.

HEVENER (JOHN W.) Which side are you on?: the Harlan County coal miners, 1931- 1939. Urbana, [1978]. pp. 216. *bibliogs*.

COAL MINES AND MINING

— Environmental aspects — United Kingdom.

HAIGH (MARTIN J.) Evolution of slopes on artificial landforms: Blaenavon, U.K. Chicago, 1978. pp. 293. *bibliog*. (*Chicago. University. Department of Geography. Research Papers. No. 183*)

— Canada — British Columbia.

PEAT, MARWICK AND PARTNERS. Manpower development and promotion in the coal mining industry: report to the Federal-Provincial Manpower Sub-Committee on North East Coal Development. [Victoria, B.C.?], 1978. fo. 78. *bibliog*.

— France.

HAINSWORTH (RAYMOND EDWIN) The trade union movements and labour-management relations in the coal mines of the Nord and Pas-de-Calais departments of France during the depression of 1930-1936. 1978. fo. 587. *bibliog*. Typescript. Ph.D. (London) thesis: unpublished. This thesis is the property of London University and may not be removed from the Library.

— Germany — Ruhr.

JANKOWSKI (MANFRED DIETER) Public policy in industrial growth: the case of Ruhr mining region, 1776-1865. New York, 1977. pp. 299. *bibliog*.

— India.

GHOSH (AMIYA BHUSHAN) Coal industry in India: an historical and analytical account. New Delhi, [1978]. pp. 312. *bibliog*.

— — Fires and fire prevention.

INDIA. Committee on Coal Mine Fires. 1971. Report. [Delhi], 1969 [or rather 1971]. pp. 130.

— United Kingdom.

FORSTER (ERIC) The pit children. Newcastle, [1978]. pp. 48.

WILCOCK (DON) The Durham coalfield. part 1. The "sea cole" age. Durham, 1979. pp. 89. *bibliog*. (*Durham County Library. Local History Publications. No. 14*)

— — Government ownership.

ARNOT (ROBERT PAGE) The miners: one union, one industry: a history of the National Union of Mineworkers, 1939-46. London, 1979. pp. 212.

McCORMICK (BRIAN JOSEPH) Industrial relations in the coal industry. London, 1979. pp. 263. *bibliog*.

— — Wales.

SYMONS (MALCOLM V.) Coal mining in the Llanelli area. Llanelli, Borough Council, [1979 in progress]. (*Llanelli. Public Library. Local History Research Group Series. No.1*)

— United States.

KRUTILLA (JOHN V.) and others. Economic and fiscal impacts of coal development: Northern Great Plains. Baltimore, [1978]. pp. 208. *bibliog*. Published for Resources for the Future, Inc.

COAL TRADE

— United States.

GORDON (RICHARD L.) Coal in the U.S. energy market: history and prospects. Lexington, Mass., [1978]. pp. 224. *bibliog*.

TYNER (WALLACE E.) and others. Western coal: promise or problem. Lexington, Mass., [1978]. pp. 181. *bibliog*.

COALITION (SOCIAL SCIENCES).

SCHNEIDER (JERROLD E.) Ideological coalitions in Congress. Westport, Conn., 1979. pp. 270. *bibliog*.

COALITION GOVERNMENTS

— Germany.

KIESINGER (KURT GEORG) Die Grosse Koalition, 1966-1969: Reden und Erklärungen des Bundeskanzlers; herausgegeben von Dieter Oberndörfer. Stuttgart, [1979]. pp. 420. *bibliog*.

— India.

The COALITION government: a critical examination of the concept of coalition, the performance of some coalition governments and the future prospects of coalition in India; by Omprakash Deepak [and others]; edited by Saral K. Chatterji. Madras, 1974. pp. 145.

— United States.

EMERGING coalitions in American politics; [by] Jack Bass [and others]; Seymour Martin Lipset, editor. San Francisco, 1978. pp. 524. *bibliog*.

COCA-COLA COMPANY.

WATTERS (PAT) Coca-Cola: an illustrated history. New York, 1978. pp. 288.

COCOA

— Ghana.

GUNNARSSON (CHRISTER) The Gold Coast cocoa industry, 1900-1939: production, prices and structural change. Lund, 1978. pp. 184. *bibliog*. Akademisk avhandling (doktorsexamen) - Lunds Universitet.

COCONUT INDUSTRY

— Tanzania.

MARKETING DEVELOPMENT BUREAU [UNITED REPUBLIC OF TANZANIA]. The current state of the coconut industry in Tanzania and proposals for the establishment of a Coconut Development Authority. Dar es Salaam, 1976. fo. (56).

COFFEE

— Colombia.

El AGRO en el desarrollo historico colombiano: ensayos de economia politica; [by] F. Leal Buitrago [and others]. Bogota, 1977. pp. 395. *Papers presented at the Primer Seminario Nacional de Desarrollo Rural held at the Universidad de los Andes, 29-31 July 1976.*

BERGQUIST (CHARLES W.) Coffee and conflict in Colombia, 1886-1910. Durham, N.C., 1978. pp. 277. *bibliog*.

COFFEE TRADE.

QUARTERLY STATISTICAL BULLETIN ON COFFEE; [pd. by] International Coffee Organization. q., Ja/Mr 1977 (v.1,no.1)- London.

BERGQUIST (CHARLES W.) Coffee and conflict in Colombia, 1886-1910. Durham, N.C., 1978. pp. 277. *bibliog*.

COGNITION.

NEISSER (ULRIC) Cognitive psychology. Englewood Cliffs, N.J., [1967]. pp. 351. *bibliog*.

NEISSER (ULRIC) Cognition and reality: principles and implications of cognitive psychology. San Francisco, [1976]. pp. 230. *bibliog*.

SPIVACK (GEORGE) and others. The problem-solving approach to adjustment. San Francisco, 1976. pp. 318. *bibliog*.

COGNITION.(Cont.)

STRUCTURE of decision: the cognitive maps of political elites; edited by Robert Axelrod. Princeton, N.J., [1976]. pp. 404. *bibliog.*

BROWN (JASON) Mind, brain, and consciousness: the neuropsychology of cognition. New York, 1977. pp. 190. *bibliog.*

SYMPOSIUM ON COGNITION, 12TH, CARNEGIE-MELLON UNIVERSITY, 1976. Cognitive processes in comprehension; edited by Marcel Adam Just [and] Patricia A. Carpenter. Hillsdale, N.J., 1977. pp. 329. *bibliogs.*

COGNITION and categorization; sponsored by the Social Science Research Council; edited by Eleanor Rosch [and] Barbara B. Lloyd. Hillsdale, N.J., 1978. pp. 328. *bibliogs.*

SEMANTIC factors in cognition; edited by John W. Cotton, Roberta L. Klatzky. Hillsdale, N.J., 1978. pp. 239. *Papers presented at a conference held on May 26 and 27, 1976 at the University of California, Santa Barbara.*

STRATEGIES of information processing; edited by Geoffrey Underwood. London, 1978. pp. 455. *bibliog.*

STREUFERT (SIEGFRIED) and STREUFERT (SUSAN C.) Behavior in the complex environment. New York, 1978. pp. 316. *bibliogs.*

BOWER (THOMAS GILLIE RUSSELL) Human development. San Francisco, [1979]. pp. 473. *bibliog.*

BRANSFORD (JOHN D.) Human cognition: learning, understanding and remembering. Belmont, Calif., [1979]. pp. 300. *bibliog.*

WICKELGREN (WAYNE A.) Cognitive psychology. Englewood Cliffs, N.J., [1979]. pp. 436. *bibliog.*

COGNITION (CHILD PSYCHOLOGY).

PERSPECTIVES on the development of memory and cognition; edited by Robert V. Kail [and] John W. Hagen. Hillsdale, 1977. pp. 498. *bibliogs.*

CHILDREN'S thinking: what develops?; edited by Robert S. Siegler. Hillsdale, N.J., 1978. pp. 371.

O'CONNOR (NEIL) and HERMELIN (BEATE) Seeing and hearing and space and time. London, 1978. pp. 157. *bibliog.*

ROSENTHAL (TED L.) and ZIMMERMAN (BARRY J.) Social learning and cognition. New York, 1978. pp. 338. *bibliog.*

COHN (DAVID LEWIS).

COHN (DAVID LEWIS) Where I was born and raised. Notre Dame, 1967. pp. 380. *Part 1 of this book was published in 1935 under the title God shakes creation.*

COHORT ANALYSIS.

HART (P. L.) A cohort analysis of changes in the distribution of incomes, United Kingdom, 1963-73. Reading, 1975. pp. 52. *bibliog. (Reading. University. Department of Economics. Discussion Papers in Economics. No. 74)*

COINAGE
— **France.**

BISSON (THOMAS NOEL) Conservation of coinage: monetary exploitation and its restraint in France, Catalonia, and Aragon (c.A.D.1000-c.1225). Oxford, 1979. pp. 250. *bibliog.*

— **Spain.**

BISSON (THOMAS NOEL) Conservation of coinage: monetary exploitation and its restraint in France, Catalonia, and Aragon (c.A.D.1000-c.1225). Oxford, 1979. pp. 250. *bibliog.*

COKE (Sir EDWARD).

WHITE (STEPHEN D.) Sir Edward Coke and "the grievances of the Commonwealth", 1621- 1628. Chapel Hill, [1979]. pp. 327. *bibliog.*

COKE INDUSTRY
— **Canada.**

CHRISMAS (L.P.) and McMULLEN (M.K.) Coking coal in Canada. Ottawa, 1973. pp. 28. *bibliog. (Canada. Mineral Resources Division. Mineral [Information] Bulletins. 135)*

COLBY (BAINBRIDGE).

SMITH (DANIEL MALLOY) Aftermath of war: Bainbridge Colby and Wilsonian diplomacy, 1920-1921. Philadelphia, 1970. pp. 173. *bibliog. (American Philosophical Society. Memoirs. vol. 80)*

COLE (ARTHUR CHARLES).

TOWARD a new view of America; essays in honor of Arthur C. Cole; edited by Hans L. Trefousse. [New York, 1977]. pp. 230.

COLINS (JEAN GUILLAUME CESAR ALEXANDRE HIPPOLYTE).

GUIZART (MAURICE) Science sociale selon la pensée de Hippolyte Colins. Paris, [1971]. pp. 75.

COLLECTIVE BARGAINING.

INTERNATIONAL LABOUR OFFICE. 1973. Collective bargaining in industrialised market economies. Geneva, 1973. pp. 415. *bibliog. ([Studies and Reports. New Series. No. 80!)*

— **United Kingdom.**

HULL (DARYLL) The shop stewards' guide to work organisation. Nottingham, 1978. pp. 130.

— **United States.**

TAYLOR (BENJAMIN J.) and WITNEY (FRED) Labor relations law. 3rd ed. Englewood Cliffs, N.J., 1979. pp. 834. *bibliog.*

COLLECTIVISM.

GARCIA (FELIX) Colectivizaciones campesinas y obreras en la Revolucion española. Bilbao, 1977. pp. 266. *bibliog.*

BELOFF (MAX) The tide of collectivism: can it be turned? London, 1978. pp. 23. *(Conservative Political Centre. [Publications]. No. 629)*

COLLEGE ADMINISTRATORS
— **United Kingdom.**

PIPER (DAVID WARREN) and GLATTER (RON) The changing university: a report on the Staff Development in Universities programme 1972/4. Windsor, 1977. pp. 410. *bibliog.*

COLLEGE COSTS
— **United Kingdom.**

U.K. Social Survey. 1979. Postgraduate income and expenditure: a survey commissioned by the Department of Education and Science and the Scottish Education Department of postgraduates' sources of income and patterns of expenditure during the academic year 1975/6; [by] Susan Dight [and] Peter Bush. [London], 1979. pp. 107.

U.K. Social Survey. [Reports. New Series]. 1039. Undergraduate income and expenditure: a survey commissioned by the Department of Education and Science and the Scottish Education Department of undergraduates' and trainee teachers' sources of income and patterns of expenditure for the academic year 1974/5; [by] Peter Bush [and] Susan Dight. London, 1979. pp. 70.

COLLEGE LIBRARIANS
— **United Kingdom — Directories.**

GUY (SUSANNA) compiler. Directory of humanities librarians in British academic libraries. [London], 1978. pp. 74.

COLOGNE
— **Automobile industry workers' strike, 1973.**

STREIK bei Ford, Köln, Fr. 24-Do. 30. August 1973; herausgegeben von der Betriebszelle Ford der Gruppe Arbeiterkampf. Gaiganz/Ofr., 1973. pp. 236.

COLOMBIA
— **Census.**

COLOMBIA. Census, 1951. Censo de poblacion de Colombia, 1951, mayo 9: resumen. [Bogota, 1955?]. pp. 191. *Photocopy.*

— **Economic policy.**

REVISTA DE PLANEACION Y DESARROLLO; publicada por el Departamento Nacional de Planeación,...Colombia. [articles in English or Spanish]. q., 1969 (v.1)- Bogota.

COLOMBIA. Departamento Nacional de Planeacion. 1976. Para cerrar la brecha: plan de desarrollo social, economico y regional 1975-1978. [Bogota, 1976]. pp. 205.

WOGART (JAN PETER) Industrialization in Colombia: policies, patterns, perspectives. Tübingen, [1978]. pp. 176. *bibliog. (Kiel. Universität. Institut für Weltwirtschaft. Kieler Studien. 153)*

— **History.**

BUITRAGO SALAZAR (EVELIO) Zarpazo the bandit: memoirs of an undercover agent of the Colombian Army;...translated by M. Murray Lasley; edited.. .by Russell W. Ramsey. University, Ala., [1977]. pp. 169.

— — **Sources.**

El EMPRESTITO de Mexico a Colombia; recopilacion de documentos con una introduccion y notas; por Joaquin Ramirez Cabañas. Mexico, 1930. pp. 247. *(Archivo Historico Diplomatico Mexicano. [Serie 1]. Num. 33)*

— **Politics and government.**

BERGQUIST (CHARLES W.) Coffee and conflict in Colombia, 1886-1910. Durham, N.C., 1978. pp. 277. *bibliog.*

GOMEZ BUENDIA (HERNANDO) Alfonso Lopez Michelsen: un examen critico de su pensamiento y de su obra de gobierno. Bogota, 1978. pp. 367.

— **Rural conditions.**

El AGRO en el desarrollo historico colombiano: ensayos de economia politica; [by] F. Leal Buitrago [and others]. Bogota, 1977. pp. 395. *Papers presented at the Primer Seminario Nacional de Desarrollo Rural held at the Universidad de los Andes, 29-31 July 1976.*

— **Social policy.**

COLOMBIA. Departamento Nacional de Planeacion. 1976. Para cerrar la brecha: plan de desarrollo social, economico y regional 1975-1978. [Bogota, 1976]. pp. 205.

COLONIES.

UNITED NATIONS. Office of Public Information. 1969. Foreign economic interests and decolonization: a report. (OPI/370). New York, 1969. pp. 32.

— **History.**

WILLIAMS (GLYNDWR) The expansion of Europe in the eighteenth century: overseas rivalry, discovery and exploitation. London, 1968. pp. 309. *bibliog.*

COLONIES IN AFRICA.

CROWDER (MICHAEL) Colonial West Africa: collected essays. London, 1978. pp. 341.

EXPANSION and reaction: essays on European expansion and reaction in Asia and Africa; edited by H.L. Wesseling. Leiden, 1978. pp. 200.

COLONIES IN ASIA.

EXPANSION and reaction: essays on European expansion and reaction in Asia and Africa; edited by H.L. Wesseling. Leiden, 1978. pp. 200.

COLONIZATION.

COLONIALISM and change: essays presented to Lucy Mair; edited by Maxwell Owusu. The Hague, [1975]. pp. 264. *bibliogs.*

COLOURED PEOPLE (SOUTH AFRICA).

SOUTH AFRICA. Commission of Inquiry into Matters relating to the Coloured Population Group. 1976. Report; [E. Theron, chairman] (R.P.38/1976). in SOUTH AFRICA. Parliament. House of Assembly. Votes and proceedings; (with Printed annexures).

SOUTH AFRICA. Department of Coloured, Rehoboth and Nama Relations. 1977. Witskrif oor die verslag van die Kommissie van Ondersoek na Aangeleenthede rakende die Kleurlingbevolkingsgroep. [Pretoria, 1977]. pp. 110. *(South Africa. W[hite] P[aper Series]. 1977. [No.] D) Afrikaans text.*

QUISLINGS or realists?: a documentary study of "Coloured" politics in South Africa; [edited by] Pierre Hugo. Johannesburg, 1978. pp. 744.

COLUMBUS (CHRISTOPHER).

MORISON (SAMUEL ELIOT) Christopher Columbus, mariner. Boston, Mass., [1955]. pp. 224.

COMBINATORIAL ANALYSIS

— Computer programs.

NIJENHUIS (ALBERT) and WILF (HERBERT S.) Combinatorial algorithms for computers and calculators. 2nd ed. New York, 1978. pp. 302. *bibliog.*

COMINES (PHILIPPE DE).

LINIGER (JEAN) Philippe de Commynes. [Paris, 1978]. pp. 432. *bibliog.*

COMMERCE.

REVIEW OF INTERNATIONAL TRADE AND DEVELOPMENT: report by the Secretariat of UNCTAD. [title varies]. a., 1967- , with gap (1971,1972). New York.

AHMAD (JALEEL) Import substitution, trade and development. Greenwich, Conn., [1978]. pp. 128. *bibliog.*

CHACHOLIADES (MILTIADES) International trade theory and policy. [2nd ed.] New York, [1978]. pp. 614. *bibliogs. First ed. published in 1973 under title: The pure theory of international trade.*

GARLAND (RANSLEY VICTOR) Some thoughts on developments in the international trading system: an Australian perspective. London, 1978. pp. 15.

HAZARI (BHARAT R.) The pure theory of international trade distortions. London, [1978]. pp. 206.

KINDLEBERGER (CHARLES POOR) Government and international trade. Princeton, 1978, pp. 19. *bibliog. (Princeton University. Department of Economics and Sociology. International Finance Section. Essays in International Finance. No. 129)*

WHITING (D.P.) International trade and payments. Plymouth, 1978. pp. 145.

BALASSA (BELA A.) and others. World trade: constraints and opportunities in the 80's. Paris, [1979]. pp. 70. *(Atlantic Institute. Atlantic Papers. 1979.36)*

KOSTIUKHIN (DMITRII IVANOVICH) The world market today. Moscow, 1979. pp. 215.

The NEWLY industrialising countries and the adjustment problem; report by a Working Group. London, Foreign and Commonwealth Office, 1979. pp. 57, 39. *(Government Economic Service Working Papers. No. 18)*

ROM (MICHAEL) The role of tariff quotas in commercial policy. London, 1979. pp. 258. *bibliog.*

SNIDER (DELBERT ARTHUR) Introduction to international economics. 7th ed. Homewood, Ill., 1979. pp. 454. *bibliogs.*

— Mathematical models.

CLAUDON (MICHAEL P.) International trade and technology: models of dynamic comparative advantage. Washington, D.C., [1977]. pp. 179. *bibliog.*

COMMERCE, PRIMITIVE.

RUBEL (PAULA G.) and ROSMAN (ABRAHAM) Your own pigs you may not eat: a comparative study of New Guinea societies. Chicago, 1978. pp. 368. *bibliog.*

COMMERCIAL AGENTS

— South Africa.

SOUTH AFRICA. Bureau of Statistics. 1976. Census of wholesale and retail trade, 1970-71: part 3: commercial agents and allied services. [Pretoria, 1976]. pp. 40. *(Reports. No. 04-11-02) In English and Afrikaans.*

COMMERCIAL FINANCE COMPANIES

— Norway.

NORWAY. Statistiske Centralbyrå. Kredittmarkedstatistikk: private kredittforetak og finansieringsselskaper. a., 1974/1976- Oslo. *[in English and Norwegian] Supersedes in part NORWAY. Statistiske Centralbyrå. Kredittmarkedstatistikk.*

— United States.

NORRIS (JAMES D.) R.G. Dun Co. 1841-1900: the development of credit-reporting in the nineteenth century. Westport, Conn., 1978. pp. 206. *bibliog.*

COMMERCIAL LAW

— European Economic Community countries.

COMMERCIAL operations in Europe; edited by R.M. Goode and K. R. Simmonds. Leyden, 1978. pp. 448. *bibliogs.*

— Germany, Eastern — Dictionaries and encyclopedias.

LEXIKON der Wirtschaft: Wirtschaftsrecht; (Herausgeber: Gerhart Görner [and others]). Berlin, 1978. pp. 441.

— Italy.

TRATTATO di diritto commerciale e di diritto pubblico dell'economia. vol. 2. L'impresa; [by] Francesco Galgano [and others]. Padova, 1978. pp. 695. *bibliog.*

— United Kingdom.

BALL (BRIAN) and ROSE (FRANK W.) Principles of business law. London, 1979. pp. 569.

COMMERCIAL POLICY.

UNITED NATIONS. Conference on Trade and Development, 4th, Nairobi, 1976. Proceedings of the...Conference..., fourth session, Nairobi, 5- 31 May 1976. (TD/218). New York, 1977-78. 3 vols. (in 1).

CHACHOLIADES (MILTIADES) International trade theory and policy. [2nd ed.] New York, [1978]. pp. 614. *bibliogs. First ed. published in 1973 under title: The pure theory of international trade.*

BALASSA (BELA A.) and others. World trade: constraints and opportunities in the 80's. Paris, [1979]. pp. 70. *(Atlantic Institute. Atlantic Papers. 1979.36)*

KRAUSS (MELVYN B.) The new protectionism: the welfare state and international trade. Oxford, [1979]. pp. 119. *bibliogs.*

MAYRZEDT (HANS M.) Multilaterale Wirtschaftsdiplomatie zwischen westlichen Industriestaaten als Instrument zur Stärkung der multilateralen und liberalen Handelspolitik. Bern, [1979]. pp. 625. *bibliog. (Hochschule St. Gallen. Veröffentlichungen. Schriftenreihe Volkswirtschaft. Band 4)*

COMMERCIAL PRODUCTS.

— Underdeveloped areas.

See UNDERDEVELOPED AREAS — Commercial products.

COMMISSIONS OF INQUIRY

— Canada — Alberta.

BACKHAUS (CHRISTINE E.) compiler. Royal commissions and commissions of inquiry in Alberta, 1905-1976. Edmonton, Legislative Library, 1977. 1 vol. (unpaged). *bibliog.*

COMMODITY CONTROL.

The COMMON fund: papers prepared for Commonwealth Technical Group. London, Commonwealth Secretariat, 1977. 2 vols. *bibliog. (Commonwealth Economic Papers. No. 8)*

COMMONWEALTH TECHNICAL GROUP ON THE COMMON FUND. The common fund: report of the Commonwealth Technical Group; [Lord Campbell of Eskan, chairman]. London, Commonwealth Secretariat, 1977. pp. 84.

MICHALOPOULOS (CONSTANTINE) U.S. commodity trade policy and the developing countries. [Washington], 1977. pp. 40. *(United States. Agency for International Development. Bureau for Program and Policy Coordination. A.I.D. Discussion Papers. No. 37)*

ECONOMETRIC modeling of world commodity policy...; edited by F. Gerard Adams and Jere R. Behrman. Lexington, Mass, [1978]. pp. 223. *bibliog.*

McNICOL (DAVID L.) Commodity agreements and price stabilization: a policy analysis. Lexington, Mass., [1978]. pp. 142. *bibliog.*

REYNOLDS (PAUL DONOVAN) International commodity agreements and the common fund: a legal and financial analysis. New York, 1978. pp. 233.

STABILIZING world commodity markets: analysis, practice, and policy; edited by F. Gerard Adams and Sonia A. Klein. Lexington, Mass., [1978]. pp. 335. *bibliogs. Representative selection of papers presented at a conference held at Airlie, Va., 1977, and sponsored by the Ford Foundation.*

COMMODITY EXCHANGES.

The ECONOMICS of futures trading; readings selected, eited and introduced by B.A. Goss and B.S. Yamey. 2nd ed. London, 1978. pp. 239. *bibliogs.*

HARRIS (STUART) and others. Analysis of commodity markets for policy purposes. London, 1978. pp. 81. *(Trade Policy Research Centre. Thames Essays. No. 17)*

COMMUNES (CHINA).

CROOK (ISABEL JOY) and CROOK (DAVID) Ten mile Inn: mass movement in a Chinese village. New York, [1979]. pp. 291.

COMMUNICABLE DISEASES.

DOWLING (HARRY FILMORE) Fighting infection: conquests of the twentieth century. Cambridge, Mass., [1977]. pp. 339. *bibliog.*

COMMUNICATION.

The USES of mass communications: current perspectives on gratifications research; Jay G. Blumler and Elihu Katz, editors. Beverly Hills, [1974]. pp. 318. *bibliogs.*

WOLD (ASTRI HEEN) Decoding oral language. London, 1978. pp. 214. *bibliog.*

— Psychological aspects.

KLAPP (ORRIN E.) Opening and closing: strategies of information adaptation in society. Cambridge, 1978. pp. 226. *bibliog. (American Sociological Association. Arnold and Caroline Rose Monograph Series in Sociology)*

COMMUNICATION.(Cont.)

— Social aspects.

WILSON (DAVID) Science correspondent. The communicators and society. Oxford, 1968. pp. 121. *bibliog.*

KLAPP (ORRIN E.) Opening and closing: strategies of information adaptation in society. Cambridge, 1978. pp. 226. *bibliog. (American Sociological Association. Arnold and Caroline Rose Monograph Series in Sociology)*

— Sri Lanka.

WANIGARATNE (RANJIT D.) A study of communication flow in selected villages in Sri Lanka: case study 1. the Medagama village. Colombo, Agrarian Research and Training Institute and the Communication Strategy Project, Ministry of Information and Broadcasting, 1975. pp. 62. *bibliog.*

COMMUNICATION AND TRAFFIC.

VARIS (TAPIO) The impact of transnational corporations on communication. Tampere, 1975. fo. 58. *bibliog. (Tampere Peace Research Institute. Research Reports. No. 10)*

— Asia.

TRANSPORT AND COMMUNICATIONS BULLETIN FOR ASIA AND THE PACIFIC (formerly TRANSPORT AND COMMUNICATIONS BULLETIN FOR ASIA AND THE FAR EAST previously Transport bulletin); ([pd.by] Economic and Social Commission for Asia and the Pacific) United Nations. irreg., Oc 1951(v.1, no.4)- with gaps. New York (formerly Bangkok).

— Pacific, The.

TRANSPORT AND COMMUNICATIONS BULLETIN FOR ASIA AND THE PACIFIC (formerly TRANSPORT AND COMMUNICATIONS BULLETIN FOR ASIA AND THE FAR EAST previously Transport bulletin); ([pd.by] Economic and Social Commission for Asia and the Pacific) United Nations. irreg., Oc 1951(v.1, no.4)- with gaps. New York (formerly Bangkok).

— Sudan.

SUDAN. Ministry of National Planning. Transport and Communications Section. 1977. Six year plan: transport and communications sector, 1977-1983. Khartoum, [1977] repr. 1978. fo. 71.

COMMUNICATION IN AGRICULTURE.

OTTAVIANI (OBERDAN) Sant'Agata dei Goti: l'informazione mancata; la comunicazione nella società agricola del Mezzogiorno: ricerca in un comune campione. Urbino, [1977]. pp. 319. *bibliog.*

COMMUNICATION IN MANAGEMENT.

HILTON (ANTHONY) Employee reports: how to communicate financial information to employees. Cambridge, 1978. pp. 113.

COMMUNICATIONS RESEARCH.

COMMUNICATION research: a half-century appraisal; edited by Daniel Lerner and Lyle M. Nelson. Honolulu, [1977]. pp. 348. *bibliog.*

COMMUNISM.

ZILLIACUS (KONNI) the Younger. A new birth of freedom?: world communism after Stalin. London, 1957. pp. 286.

ALLEN (GARY) None dare call it conspiracy. Seal Beach, Calif., [1972]. pp. 141.

LEONHARD (WOLFGANG) Three faces of Marxism: the political concepts of Soviet ideology, Maoism, and humanist Marxism; (translated [from the German] by Ewald Osers). New York, [1974]. pp. 497. *bibliog.*

PROGRESUL istoric și contemporaneitatea. București, 1976. pp. 538. *With English, French, German and Russian tables of contents.*

KOSESKI (ADAM) Budowa rozwiniętego społeczeństwa socjalistycznego: zarys koncepcji politycznej. Warszawa, 1977. pp. 391. *bibliog.*

KRASIN (IURII ANDREEVICH) Teoriia sotsialisticheskoi revoliutsii: leninskoe nasledie i sovremennost'. Moskva, 1977. pp. 292.

MIDWEST MARXIST SCHOLARS CONFERENCE, 1ST, UNIVERSITY OF MINNESOTA, 1976. Marxism and new left ideology; Ileana Rodríguez and William L. Rowe, editors. Minneapolis, [1977]. pp. 102.

XXV s"ezd KPSS o sovremennom mirovom revoliutsionnom protsesse. Kiev, 1978. pp. 191.

BREZHNEV (LEONID IL'ICH) Mir sotsializma - torzhestvo velikikh idei: (rechi, stat'i i vystupleniia za period 1964-1978 gg.). Moskva, 1978. pp. 656.

CHERTKOV (VIKTOR PETROVICH) Dialektika revoliutsionnogo protsessa. Moskva, 1978. pp. 144.

COMMUNISM: end of the monolith?; edited by Evelyn Geller. New York, 1978. pp. 243. *bibliog.*

DOCUMENTS in communist affairs, 1977; edited by Bogdan Szaikowski. Cardiff, 1978. pp. 363.

LEONHARD (WOLFGANG) Was ist Kommunismus?: Wandlungen einer Ideologie. [Munich], 1978. pp. 271. *bibliog.*

The MANY faces of communism; edited by Morton A. Kaplan. New York, 1978. pp. 366.

MOLYNEUX (JOHN) Marxism and the party. London, 1978. pp. 192.

REVEL (JEAN FRANÇOIS) The totalitarian temptation; (translated by David Hapgood). Harmondsworth, 1978. pp. 332.

SETON-WATSON (GEORGE HUGH NICHOLAS) The imperialist revolutionaries: trends in world communism in the 1960s and 1970s. Stanford, [1978]. pp. 157. *(Stanford University. Hoover Institution on War, Revolution and Peace. Hoover Institution Publications. 193)*

SHAKHNAZAROV (GEORGII KHOSROEVICH) Sotsialisticheskaia sud'ba chelovechestva. Moskva, 1978. pp. 462.

BUKHARIN (NIKOLAI IVANOVICH) The politics and economics of the transition period; edited with an introduction by Kenneth J. Tarbuck. London, 1979. pp. 261. *bibliog.*

CORRIGAN (PHILIP R.D.) and others. For Mao: essays in historical materialism. London, 1979. pp. 207. *bibliog.*

PERSPECTIVES for change in communist societies; edited by Teresa Rakowska-Harmstone. Boulder, Colo., 1979. pp. 194.

ULAM (ADAM BRUNO) The unfinished revolution: marxism and communism in the modern world. rev. ed. Boulder, Colo., 1979. pp. 287.

— History.

BRAVO (GIAN MARIO) ed. Da Weitling a Marx: la Lega dei Comunisti; [a collection of documents]. Milano, [1977]. pp. 307. *bibliog.*

LUEBBE (PETER) Kommunismus und Sozialdemokratie: eine Streitschrift. Berlin, [1978]. pp. 299.

VYGODSKII (VITALII SOLOMONOVICH) Das Werden der ökonomischen Theorie von Marx und der wissenschaftliche Kommunismus; (aus dem Russischen übersetzt von G. Rieske). Berlin, 1978. pp. 312.

— Africa.

RHODESIA. Ministry of Information, Immigration and Tourism. 1967. Red for danger. [Salisbury, 1967]. pp. 8.

JANKE (PETER F.) Marxist statecraft in Africa: what future? London, 1978. pp. 18. *(Institute for the Study of Conflict. Conflict Studies. No.95)*

— Canada.

BENOIT (JACQUES) Journalist. L'extrême gauche. Ottawa, 1977. pp. 137.

PENNER (NORMAN) The Canadian left: a critical analysis. Scarborough, Ont., [1977]. pp. 287. *bibliog.*

— China.

SMEDLEY (AGNES) China's Red Army marches. New York, [1934]. pp. 311.

SMEDLEY (AGNES) Chinese destinies: sketches of present-day China. London, 1934. pp. 284.

The CHINESE Communists; [edited] by Stuart Gelder. London, 1946. pp. 290.

FALCONER (ALUN) New China: friend or foe? London, 1950. pp. 128.

BLOFELD (JOHN) Red China in perspective. London, 1951. pp. 242.

SOVETSKIE raiony Kitaia: zakonodatel'stvo Kitaiskoi Sovetskoi Respubliki, 1931-1934. Moskva, 1977. pp. 141.

CHINESE communism in the 1970s. Taipei, Taiwan, [1978]. pp. 209. *bibliog. Papers presented to the seventh Sino-American Conference held in Taipei, 1978.*

DIRLIK (ARIF) Revolution and history: the origins of Marxist historiography in China, 1919-1937. Berkeley, Calif., [1978]. pp. 299. *bibliog.*

HARRIS (NIGEL) The mandate of heaven: Marx and Mao in modern China. London, 1978. pp. 307.

HENNICKE (PETER) Die entwicklungstheoretischen Konzeptionen Mao Tse-tungs: historische Grundlagen und sozialökonomische Bedingungen der Entwicklungspolitik der Volksrepublik China, 1927-1957. München, [1978]. pp. 609. *bibliog.*

INNOVATION in communist systems; edited by Andrew Gyorgy and James A. Kuhlman. Boulder, Colo., 1978. pp. 224.

McDONALD (ANGUS W.) The urban origins of rural revolution: elites and the masses in Hunan Province, China, 1911-1927. Berkeley, Calif., [1978]. pp. 369. *bibliog.*

SMITH (BRUCE) Sinologist. Mao's last battle: the next stage. London, [1978]. pp. 32.

HOXHA (ENVER) Reflections on China...: extracts from the political diary. Tirana, 1979 in progress.

— — Tibet.

BOGOSLOVSKII (VASILII ALEKSEEVICH) Tibetskii raion KNR, 1949-1976. Moskva, 1978. pp. 199. *bibliog.*

— Europe.

NOCE (AUGUSTO DEL) L'eurocomunismo e l'Italia. [Rome, 1976]. pp. 141.

CLAUDIN (FERNANDO) L'eurocommunisme; traduit de l'espagnol par Anne Valier. Paris, 1977. pp. 151.

EUROCOMMUNISM and détente; edited by Rudolf L. Tokés. Oxford, 1978. pp. 578.

GODSON (ROY) and HASELER (STEPHEN MICHAEL ALAN) "Eurocommunism": implications for East and West. London, 1978. pp. 144.

GOMBIN (RICHARD) The radical tradition: a study in modern revolutionary thought; translated by Rupert Swyer. London, 1978. pp. 153. *bibliog.*

INNOVATION in communist systems; edited by Andrew Gyorgy and James A. Kuhlman. Boulder, Colo., 1978. pp. 224.

KRIEGEL (ANNIE) Eurocommunism: a new kind of communism?; (translated from the French by Peter S. Stern). Stanford, [1978]. pp. 131. *(Stanford University. Hoover Institution on War, Revolution and Peace. Hoover Institution Publications. 194)*

COMMUNISM.

MANDEL (ERNEST) Critique de l'eurocommunisme. Paris, 1978. pp. 323.

MANDEL (ERNEST) From Stalinism to Eurocommunism: the bitter fruits of 'socialism in one country'; translated by Jon Rothschild. London, 1978. pp. 223.

POLITICS, ideology and the state: papers from the Communist University of London, [9th session, 1977]; edited by Sally Hibbin. London, 1978. pp. 143.

SCHAPIRO (LEONARD BERTRAM) The Soviet Union and Eurocommunism. London, 1978. pp. 21. *(Institute for the Study of Conflict. Conflict Studies. No.99)*

TANNAHILL (R. NEAL) The communist parties of Western Europe: a comparative study. Westport, 1978. pp. 299. *bibliog.*

BELL (DAVID SCOTT) Eurocommunism. London, 1979. pp. 28. *(Fabian Society. Research Series. [No.] 342)*

BLANK (FRANK VON) Rote Werwölfe: Volksfront gegen die Völker Europas. Rosenheim, [1979]. pp. 192.

COMMUNISM and political systems in Western Europe; edited by David E. Albright. Boulder, Colo., 1979. pp. 379.

EUROCOMMUNISM and Eurosocialism: the left confronts modernity; edited by Bernard E. Brown. New York, [1979]. pp. 408.

EUROKOMMUNISMUS: ein dritter Weg für Europa?; (Helmut Richter, Günter Trautmann, Hrsg.). Hamburg, [1979]. pp. 352. *bibliog.*

GRUJIĆ (PREDRAG M.) Von Marx bis Berlinguer: klassischer Marxismus und Eurokommunismus. Würzburg, [1979]. pp. 126.

— **Europe, Eastern.**

VII kongress Kominterna i bor'ba za sozdanie narodnogo fronta v stranakh Tsentral'noi i Iugo-Vostochnoi Evropy. Moskva, 1977. pp. 375.

VELIKII Oktiabr' i revoliutsii 40-kh godov v stranakh Tsentral'noi i Iugo-Vostochnoi Evropy: opyt sravnitel'nogo izucheniia sotsial'no-ekonomicheskikh preobrazovanii v revoliutsionnom protsesse. Moskva, 1977. pp. 541.

BAHRO (RUDOLF) The alternative in Eastern Europe; translated by David Fernbach. [London], 1978. pp. 463.

INNOVATION in communist systems; edited by Andrew Gyorgy and James A. Kuhlman. Boulder, Colo., 1978. pp. 224.

IZ istorii Velikogo Oktiabria i posleduiushchikh sotsialisticheskikh revoliutsii: sbornik statei. Moskva, 1978. pp. 542.

COMMUNISM in Eastern Europe; edited by Teresa Rakowska-Harmstone and Andrew Gyorgy. Bloomington, 1979. pp. 338.

PERSPECTIVES for change in communist societies; edited by Teresa Rakowska-Harmstone. Boulder, Colo., 1979. pp. 194.

— **Finland.**

KORONEN (MATVEI MATVEEVICH) V.I. Lenin i Finliandiia. Leningrad, 1977. pp. 311. *bibliog.*

— **France.**

LABBE (DOMINIQUE) Le discours communiste. [Paris, 1977]. pp. 204.

LECOEUR (AUGUSTE) Le PCF: continuité dans le changement. Paris, [1977]. pp. 237.

ALTHUSSER (LOUIS) Ce qui ne peut plus durer dans le Parti communiste. Paris, 1978. pp. 125.

— **Germany, Eastern.**

BAHRO (RUDOLF) Eine Dokumentation. Köln, [1977]. pp. 111.

SOLIDARITAET mit Rudolf Bahro: Briefe in die DDR; (Hannes Schwenger, Hg.). Reinbek bei Hamburg, 1978. pp. 138.

McCAULEY (MARTIN) Marxism-Leninism in the German Democractic Republic: the Socialist Unity Party (SED). London, 1979. pp. 267. *bibliog.*

— **Hungary.**

ANTAL (ENDRE) Grundlagen und reformpolitische Einordnung des ungarischen Wirtschaftssystems. Berlin, 1978. pp. 170. *bibliog. (Giessen. Universität. Zentrum für Kontinentale Agrar- und Wirtschaftsforschung. Giessener Abhandlungen zur Agrar- und Wirtschaftsforschung des Europäischen Ostens. Band 93)* With English summary.

POWER, liberty, democracy: speeches and articles of leading Hungarian politicians, 1974-1977. Budapest, 1978. pp. 223.

— **India.**

WIELENGA (BASTIAAN) Marxist views on India in historical perspective. Madras, 1976. pp. 155. *(Christian Institute for the Study of Religion and Society. Studies on Indian Marxism. No. 2)*

CHOWDHURI (SATYABRATA RAI) Leftist movements in India: 1917-1947. Columbia, 1977. pp. 313. *bibliog.*

— **Iran.**

MOSS (ROBERT) The campaign to destabilise Iran. London, 1978. pp. 18. *(Institute for the Study of Conflict. Conflict Studies. No.101)*

— **Italy.**

NOCE (AUGUSTO DEL) L'eurocomunismo e l'Italia. [Rome, 1976]. pp. 141.

— **Korea.**

MATERIALS on Korean communism 1945-1947; translated and edited by Chong-Sik Lee. Honolulu, [1977]. pp. 268.

KIM (IL-SUNG) On the work of the United Front: excerpts. Pyongyang, 1978. pp. 208.

— **Malaysia.**

FEDERATION OF MALAYSIA. 1971. The resurgence of armed communism in west Malaysia. Kuala Lumpur, 1971. pp. 30.

— **Mongolia.**

MATVEEVA (GALINA SERGEEVNA) Sozdanie material'no-tekhnicheskoi bazy sotsializma v MNR. Moskva, 1978. pp. 278. *bibliog.*

— **Poland.**

SCAEVOLA, pseud. A study in forgery: (the Lublin Committee and its rule over Poland). London, [1945]. pp. 123.

KLEVCHENIA (ALEKSANDR SEMENOVICH) Ocherki po istorii marksistsko-leninskoi filosofskoi mysli v Pol'she. Minsk, 1978. pp. 198. *bibliog.*

— **Russia.**

GLUCKSMANN (ANDRE) La cuisinière et le mangeur d'hommes: essai sur les rapports entre l'Etat, le marxisme et les camps de concentration. Paris, [1975]. pp. 223.

MEDVEDEV (ROI ALEKSANDROVICH) Political essays. Nottingham, 1976. pp. 151.

BOVSH (VIKTOR IVANOVICH) Futurologiia i antikommunizm; nauchnyi redaktor F.T. Konstantinov. Minsk, 1977. pp. 270. *(Akademiia Nauk Belorusskoi SSR. Institut Filosofii i Prava. Ideologicheskaia Bor'ba v Sovremennom Mire)*

KAMAEV (VLADIMIR DOROFEEVICH) Razvitoi sotsializm: tempy i kachestvo ekonomicheskogo rosta. Moskva, 1977. pp. 210.

SEMENOV (VADIM SERGEEVICH) Dialektika razvitiia sotsial'noi struktury sovetskogo obshchestva. Moskva, 1977. pp. 215.

SOTSIALISTICHESKII obraz zhizni i voprosy ideologicheskoi raboty: po materialam Vsesoiuznoi nauchno-prakticheskoi konferentsii v Kieve, 18-20 maia 1977 g. Moskva, 1977. pp. 383.

RAZVITOI sotsializm. Moskva, 1978. pp. 432.

SOVIET society and the Communist Party; edited by Karl W. Ryavec; contributors, Karl W. Ryavec [and others]. Amherst, Mass., 1978. pp. 220.

YANOV (ALEXANDER) The Russian new right: right-wing ideologies in the contemporary USSR. Berkeley, [1978]. pp. 185. *(California University. Institute of International Studies. Research Series. No. 35)*

BELLIS (PAUL) Marxism and the U.S.S.R.: the theory of proletarian dictatorship and the Marxist analysis of Soviet society. London, 1979. pp. 267. *bibliog.*

BENNIGSEN (ALEXANDRE) and WIMBUSH (S. ENDERS) Muslim national communism in the Soviet Union: a revolutionary strategy for the colonial world. Chicago, [1979]. pp. 267. *bibliog. (Chicago. University. Center for Middle Eastern Studies. Publications. 11)*

MASNATA (ALBERT) Le monde marxiste soviétique par lui-même: connaître et juger. Lausanne, 1979. pp. 90. *(Lausanne. Université. Centre de Recherches Européennes. Publications. 4. L'Europe et les Pays Tiers)*

— — **Bibliography.**

GRIN (TSILIA IOSIFOVNA) compiler. K. Marks, F. Engel's i revoliutsionnaia Rossiia: k 160- letiiu so dnia rozhdeniia K. Marksa: rekomendatel'nyi ukazatel' literatury; nauchnyi redaktor S.S. Volk. Moskva, 1978. pp. 95.

— — **Study and teaching.**

SOLOV'EV (OLEG FEDOROVICH) Triumf Lenina i bankrotstvo ego kritikov. Moskva, 1978. pp. 159.

— — **Buryat Republic — History.**

KRAVTSOV (VASILII TIKHONOVICH) Kiakhta revoliutsionnaia: iz istorii goroda Kiakty i iuzhnogo Pribaikal'ia v 1905-1923 gg. Ulan-Ude, 1977. pp. 239.

— — **Moldavian Republic.**

SOVETSKOE stroitel'stvo v levoberezhnykh raionakh Moldavii, 1921-1924: sbornik dokumentov i materialov; redaktsionnaia kollegiia B.K. Vizer [and others]. Kishinev, 1977. pp. 378.

— — **Turkestan.**

INOIATOV (KHAMID SHARAPOVICH) Pobeda Sovetskoi vlasti v Turkestane. Moskva, 1978. pp. 364. *bibliog.*

— **Spain.**

NIN (ANDRES) Por la unificacion marxista. Madrid, [1978]. pp. 623. *bibliog.*

BOLLOTEN (BURNETT) The Spanish revolution: the left and the struggle for power during the Civil War. Chapel Hill, N.C., [1979]. pp. 665. *bibliog.*

— **Sudan.**

WARBURG (GABRIEL) Islam, nationalism and communism in a traditional society: the case of Sudan. London, 1978. pp. 253. *bibliog.*

— **United States.**

CHILDS (JOHN LAWRENCE) and COUNTS (GEORGE SYLVESTER) America, Russia and the Communist Party in the postwar world. New York, [1943]. pp. 92.

ALLEN (GARY) None dare call it conspiracy. Seal Beach, Calif., [1972]. pp. 141.

SHELDON (CHARLES P.) The bolshevization of the USA. New York, [1978]. pp. 725.

COMMUNISM.(Cont.)

— Yugoslavia.

The BELGRADE revisionist clique - renegades from Marxism- Leninism and agents of imperialism. Tirana, 1964. pp. 325.

COMMUNISM AND ANTHROPOLOGY.

The NEW economic anthropology; edited by John Clammer. New York, 1978. pp. 260. *bibliogs.*

TOWARD a Marxist anthropology: problems and perspectives; editor, Stanley Diamond. The Hague, [1979]. pp. 492. *bibliogs.*

COMMUNISM AND CHRISTIANITY.

STOCKWOOD (MERVYN) Bishop of Southwark. The cross and the sickle. London, 1978. pp. 98. *bibliog.*

— Catholic Church.

DUNN (DENNIS J.) Détente and papal-communist relations, 1962-1978. Boulder, [1979]. pp. 216. *bibliog.*

— — India.

VADAKKAN (JOSEPH) A priest's encounter with revolution: an autobiography. Bangalore, 1974. pp. 159.

— — Italy.

PER una storia della sinistra cristiana: documenti, 1937-1945; a cura di Mario Cocchi e Pio Montesi. Roma, 1975. pp. 278.

SALERNO (MICHELE) Il compromesso storico. [Roma, 1977]. pp. 128.

— Yugoslavia.

ALEXANDER (STELLA) Church and state in Yugoslavia since 1945. Cambridge, 1979. pp. 351. *bibliog.* (*National Association for Soviet and East European Studies. Soviet and East European Studies*)

COMMUNISM AND CULTURE.

LUKIN (IURII ANDREEVICH) Mnogogrannaia sotsialisticheskaia kul'tura: XXV s"ezd KPSS o glavnykh napravleniiakh kul'turnoi politiki partii. Moskva, 1977. pp. 155.

COMMUNISM AND ISLAM.

TURNER (BRYAN STANLEY) Marx and the end of Orientalism. London, 1978. pp. 98. *bibliog.*

BENNIGSEN (ALEXANDRE) and WIMBUSH (S. ENDERS) Muslim national communism in the Soviet Union: a revolutionary strategy for the colonial world. Chicago, [1979]. pp. 267. *bibliog.* (*Chicago. University. Center for Middle Eastern Studies. Publications. 11*)

COMMUNISM AND LITERATURE.

BISZTRAY (GEORGE) Marxist models of literary realism. New York, 1978. pp. 247. *bibliog.*

BENNETT (TONY) Formalism and marxism. London, 1979. pp. 200. *bibliog.*

COMMUNISM AND RELIGION.

MORRA (GIANFRANCO) Marxismo e religione. Milano, 1976 repr. 1977. pp. 317.

COMMUNISM AND SCIENCE.

WERSKEY (GARY) The visible college. London, 1978. pp. 376.

COMMUNISM AND SOCIAL SCIENCES.

MARX: sociology/social change/capitalism; edited by Donald McQuarie. London, 1978. pp. 327. *bibliogs.*

POLISH essays in the methodology of the social sciences; edited by Jerzy J. Wiatr. Dordrecht, [1979]. pp. 260. (*Boston Colloquium for the Philosophy of Science. Boston Studies in the Philosophy of Science. vol. 29*)

WESOŁOWSKI (WŁODZIMIERZ) Classes, strata and power; translated and with an introduction by George Kolankiewicz. London, 1979. pp. 159. *bibliog.*

WONG (SIU-LUN) Sociology and socialism in contemporary China. London, 1979. pp. 147. *bibliog.*

COMMUNISM AND SOCIETY.

GOULD (CAROL C.) Marx's social ontology: individuality and community in Marx's theory of social reality. Cambridge, Mass., [1978]. pp. 208. *bibliog.*

PONZIO (AUGUSTO) Marxismo, scienza e problema dell'uomo, con un'intervista dell'autore ad Adam Schaff. Verona, [1978]. pp. 270.

KILMINSTER (RICHARD) Praxis and method: a sociological dialogue with Lukács, Gramsci and the early Frankfurt school. London, 1979. pp. 334. *bibliog.*

PARKIN (FRANK IORWETH) Marxism and class theory: a bourgeois critique. London, 1979. pp. 217. *bibliog.*

POLISH essays in the methodology of the social sciences; edited by Jerzy J. Wiatr. Dordrecht, [1979]. pp. 260. (*Boston Colloquium for the Philosophy of Science. Boston Studies in the Philosophy of Science. vol. 29*)

COMMUNISM AND THE ARTS.

SOTSIALISTICHESKAIA revoliutsiia i iskusstvo. Moskva, 1977. pp. 319.

COMMUNISM AND ZIONISM.

The LEFT against Zion: communism, Israel and the Middle East; edited by Robert S. Wistrich. London, 1979. pp. 309.

COMMUNIST COUNTRIES

— Commercial policy.

LEVINSON (CHARLES) Vodka Cola. [London, 1978]. pp. 328.

— Economic conditions.

MARQUIT (ERWIN) The socialist countries: general features of political, economic, and cultural life. Minneapolis, 1978. pp. 208. *bibliog.*

SOTSIAL'NO-ekonomicheskoe razvitie stran sotsializma v 1971-1975 gg. Moskva, 1978. pp. 277.

— Economic integration.

LADYGIN (BORIS NIKOLAEVICH) and others. Sotsialisticheskoe sodruzhestvo na novom etape. Moskva, 1976. pp. 192.

KOMPLEKSNYE programmy razvitiia v stranakh SEV. Moskva, 1977. pp. 223. *bibliog.*

The MULTILATERAL economic co-operation of socialist states: a collection of documents. Moscow, 1977. pp. 588.

KHEIFETS (BORIS ARONOVICH) Sovershenstvovanie otraslevoi struktury i sotsialisticheskaia integratsiia: voprosy strukturnoi politiki evropeiskikh stran SEV. Moskva, 1978. pp. 120.

SZAWLOWSKI (RICHARD) Political, security and economic relations in the Eastern bloc. Braamfontein, 1978. pp. 11. (*South African Institute of International Affairs. Occasional Papers*)

— Economic policy.

KOMPLEKSNYE programmy razvitiia v stranakh SEV. Moskva, 1977. pp. 223. *bibliog.*

Die WIRTSCHAFT Osteuropas und der VR China, 1970-1980: Bilanz und Perspektiven; (Hans-Hermann Höhmann, Hrsg.). Stuttgart, [1978]. pp. 380. *bibliog.*

— Foreign economic relations.

LEVINSON (CHARLES) Vodka Cola. [London, 1978]. pp. 328.

— — Africa.

INTERNATIONAL CONFERENCE OF THE SOCIALIST COUNTRIES' AFRICANISTS, BUDAPEST, 1976. Economic relations of Africa with the socialist countries; proceedings of the 5th...conference, etc. Vol.1: Hungarian contributions. Budapest, 1978. pp. 167. *bibliogs.* (*Magyar Tudományos Akadémia. Világgazdasági Kutató Intézet. Studies on Developing Countries. No. 95*)

— Politics and government.

MARQUIT (ERWIN) The socialist countries: general features of political, economic, and cultural life. Minneapolis, 1978. pp. 208. *bibliog.*

SZAWLOWSKI (RICHARD) Political, security and economic relations in the Eastern bloc. Braamfontein, 1978. pp. 11. (*South African Institute of International Affairs. Occasional Papers*)

— Population.

VOSPROIZVODSTVO naseleniia sotsialisticheskikh stran: na primere Sovetskogo Soiuza i Pol'shi; pod redaktsiei D.I. Valenteia i M. Liatukha. Moskva, 1977. pp. 360.

— Social conditions.

MARQUIT (ERWIN) The socialist countries: general features of political, economic, and cultural life. Minneapolis, 1978. pp. 208. *bibliog.*

SOTSIAL'NO-ekonomicheskoe razvitie stran sotsializma v 1971-1975 gg. Moskva, 1978. pp. 277.

— Statistics.

STATISTICAL YEARBOOK OF MEMBER STATES OF THE COUNCIL FOR MUTUAL ECONOMIC ASSISTANCE. a., 1976- London.

COMMUNIST EDUCATION

— Russia.

MOSTOVOI (STEPAN NIKOLAEVICH) Leninskie printsipy ideino-vospitatel'noi raboty. 2nd ed. Moskva, 1977. pp. 316.

VOPROSY metodiki prepodavaniia istorii KPSS v universitete: mezhvuzovskii sbornik. Leningrad, 1978. pp. 150.

— — Ukraine.

KOMMUNISTICHESKAIA PARTIIA UKRAINY. Tsentral'nyi Komitet. Plenum, noiabr', 1977. Materialy, etc. Kiev, 1977. pp. 52.

COMMUNIST ETHICS.

GRIER (PHILIP TODD) Marxist ethical theory in the Soviet Union. Dordrecht, 1978. pp. 276. *bibliog.* (*Freiburg (Switzerland). Universität. Ost- Europa Institut. Sovietica. vol. 40*)

COMMUNIST PARTIES.

GODSON (ROY) The Kremlin and labor: a study in national security policy. New York, 1977. pp. 79.

EUROCOMMUNISM and détente; edited by Rudolf L. Tökés. Oxford, 1978. pp. 578.

GODSON (ROY) and HASELER (STEPHEN MICHAEL ALAN) "Eurocommunism": implications for East and West. London, 1978. pp. 144.

The MANY faces of communism; edited by Morton A. Kaplan. New York, 1978. pp. 366.

MOLYNEUX (JOHN) Marxism and the party. London, 1978. pp. 192.

TANNAHILL (R. NEAL) The communist parties of Western Europe: a comparative study. Westport, 1978. pp. 299. *bibliog.*

COMMUNISM and political systems in Western Europe; edited by David E. Albright. Boulder, Colo., 1979. pp. 379.

COMMUNIST PARTY

— Europe, Eastern.

PERSPECTIVES for change in communist societies; edited by Teresa Rakowska-Harmstone. Boulder, Colo., 1979. pp. 194.

COMMUNIST PARTY

— Australia.

LANG (JOHN THOMAS) Communism in Australia. Sydney, [1944?]. pp. 142.

SOVIET Jewry and the Australian Communist Party: documents. Caulfield, Victoria, [1966]. pp. 79.

— Austria.

KONRAD (HELMUT) Widerstand an Donau und Moldau: KPÖ und KSČ zur Zeit des Hitler-Stalin-Paktes. Wien, [1978]. pp. 348. *bibliog.* (Ludwig Boltzmann Institut für Geschichte der Arbeiterbewegung. Veröffentlichungen)

WEST (FRANZ) Die Linke im Ständestaat Österreich: Revolutionäre Sozialisten und Kommunisten, 1934-1938. Wien, [1978]. pp. 353. (Ludwig Boltzmann Institut für Geschichte der Arbeiterbewegung. Schriftenreihe. 8)

— — History.

KOMMUNISTISCHE PARTEI ÖSTERREICHS. Historische Kommission. Geschichte der Kommunistischen Partei Österreichs, 1918- 1955: kurzer Abriss; von einem Autorenkollektiv...unter Leitung von Friedl Fürnberg. Wien, [1977]. pp. 302.

— China.

The CHINESE Communists; [edited] by Stuart Gelder. London, 1946. pp. 290.

— — History.

IASHCHENKO (GEORGII NIKOLAEVICH) Ideologicheskaia bor'ba v KNR, 1957-1964. Moskva, 1977. pp. 107. *bibliog.*

— Czechoslovakia.

KONRAD (HELMUT) Widerstand an Donau und Moldau: KPÖ und KSČ zur Zeit des Hitler-Stalin-Paktes. Wien, [1978]. pp. 348. *bibliog.* (Ludwig Boltzmann Institut für Geschichte der Arbeiterbewegung. Veröffentlichungen)

— France.

LECOEUR (AUGUSTE) Le PCF: continuité dans le changement. Paris, [1977]. pp. 237.

ALTHUSSER (LOUIS) Ce qui ne peut plus durer dans le Parti communiste. Paris, 1978. pp. 125.

— Germany.

JAHNKE (KARL HEINZ) Jungkommunisten im Widerstandskampf gegen den Hitlerfaschismus. Dortmund, 1977. pp. 431. *bibliog.*

PIKARSKI (MARGOT) Jugend im Berliner Widerstand: Herbert Baum und Kampfgefährten. Berlin, [1978]. pp. 236. *bibliog.*

FISCH (GERHARD) and KRAUSE (FRITZ) Writer on politics. SPD und KPD, 1945/46: Einheitsbestrebungen der Arbeiterparteien, dargestellt an Beispielen aus Südhessen. Frankfurt am Main, 1978. pp. 169. *bibliog.*

— Germany, Eastern.

McCAULEY (MARTIN) Marxism-Leninism in the German Democratic Republic: the Socialist Unity Party (SED). London, 1979. pp. 267. *bibliog.*

— — History.

GESCHICHTE der Freien Deutschen Jugend: Chronik; (Redaktionskollegium: K.H. Jahnke [and others]; Autoren: W. Arlt [and others]). 2nd ed. Berlin, 1978. pp. 391.

— Greece — History.

AVEROFF-TOSSIZZA (EVANGELOS) By fire and axe: the Communist Party and the civil war in Greece, 1944-1949; translated [from the French] by Sarah Arnold Rigos. New Rochelle, N.Y., 1978. pp. 438. *bibliog.*

— Hungary — History.

MOLNÁR (MIKLÓS) A short history of the Hungarian Communist Party. Boulder, Colo., [1978]. pp. 168. *bibliog.*

— Italy.

BAGNOLATI (LUIGI) Origini della Federazione Comunista Ferrarese: memorie e documenti; a cura dell'Istituto di Storia Contemporanea del Movimento Operaio e Contadino di Ferrara. Modena, [1976]. pp. 159.

La SINISTRA Comunista nel cammino della rivoluzione: (nella linea marxista di Bordiga). Roma, 1976. pp. 247.

CASTELLACCI (CLAUDIO) Mani pulite. Milano, [1977]. pp. 175.

GRAZIANI (PIER ANTONIO) Il PCI ieri e oggi. Roma, [1977]. pp. 535.

Il P.C.I. e la questione giovanile: [an anthology]; a cura di Walter Veltroni. Roma, 1977. pp. 353.

SALERNO (MICHELE) Il compromesso storico. [Roma, 1977]. pp. 128.

SPRIANO (PAOLO) Gramsci in carcere e il partito. Roma, 1977. pp. 166.

AMENDOLA (GIORGIO) Il rinnovamento del PCI: intervista di Renato Nicolai. Roma, 1978. pp. 208.

— — History.

VOPROSY metodologii i istorii istoricheskoi nauki. vyp.2. Moskva, 1978. pp. 206.

— Korea.

KIM (IL-SUNG) On the building of the Workers' Party of Korea. 2. Pyongyang, 1978. pp. 643.

— Poland.

KOŁODZIEJ (EDWARD) Komunistycna Partia Robotnicza Polski w ruchu zawodowym, 1918- 1923. Warszawa, 1978. pp. 254. *bibliog.*

— — History.

SŁABEK (HENRYK) Polityka agrarna PPR: geneza, realizacja, konsekwencje. 2nd ed. Warszawa, 1978. pp. 639. *bibliog.*

— Portugal.

PARTIDO COMUNISTA PORTUGUÊS. Conferência Nacional, 1976. Conferência Nacional do PCP: 14 de Março de 1976. Lisboa, 1976. pp. 216.

— Russia.

BREZHNEV (LEONID IL'ICH) Ob aktual'nykh problemakh partiinogo stroitel'stva: (rechi, stat'i i vystupleniia s 1964 po oktiabr' 1976 g.). 2nd ed. Moskva, 1976. pp. 775.

DAL'NEISHEE vozrastanie rukovodiashchei roli partii v kommunisticheskom stroitel'stve. Kiev, 1976. pp. 315.

DUDUKALOV (VIKTOR IVANOVICH) Deiatel'nost' partiinykh organizatsii Sibiri po razvitiiu sovetskoi torgovli v pervye gody nepa, 1921-1923 gg. Tomsk, 1976. pp. 185. *bibliog.*

KURSOM intensifikatsii sel'skogo khoziaistva: iz opyta raboty Leningradskoi partiinoi organizatsii v 1965-1975 gg. Leningrad, 1977. pp. 192.

LISETSKII (ANATOLII MIKHAILOVICH) Voprosy natsional'noi politiki KPSS v usloviiakh razvitogo sotsializma: na materialakh Moldavskoi SSR. Kishinev, 1977. pp. 159.

BOR'BA partii i rabochego klassa za vosstanovlenie i razvitie narodnogo khoziaistva SSSR, 1943-1950 gg. Moskva, 1978. pp. 324.

KUNAEV (DINMUKHAMED AKHMEDOVICH) Izbrannye rechi i stat'i, [1965-78]. Moskva, 1978. pp. 511.

PEL'SHE (ARVID IANOVICH) Izbrannye rechi i stat'i, [1940-77]. Moskva, 1978. pp. 671.

RUKOVODIASHCHAIA i organizuiushchaia rol' KPSS v period razvitogo sotsializma. Leningrad, 1978. pp. 304.

SOVIET society and the Communist Party; edited by Karl W. Ryavec; contributors, Karl W. Ryavec [and others]. Amherst, Mass., 1978. pp. 220.

COLTON (TIMOTHY J.) Commissars, commanders, and civilian authority: the structure of Soviet military politics. Cambridge, Mass., 1979. pp. 365. (Harvard University. Russian Research Center. Studies. 79)

— — Congresses.

IZUTKIN (ANATOLII MAKSIMOVICH) and TSAREGORODTSEV (GENNADII IVANOVICH) Sotsialisticheskii obraz zhizni i zdorov'e naseleniia v svete reshenii XXV s"ezda KPSS. Moskva, 1977. pp. 232. *bibliog.*

XXV s"ezd KPSS o sovremennom mirovom revoliutsionnom protsesse. Kiev, 1978. pp. 191.

VNESHNEPOLITICHESKAIA programma XXV s"ezda KPSS v deistvii. Kiev, 1978. pp. 307.

— — Historiography.

RODIONOV (PETR ALEKSANDROVICH) Osnovnye problemy istoriko-partiinoi nauki na sovremennom etape: lektsiia. Moskva, 1976. pp. 72. (Kommunisticheskaia Partiia Sovetskogo Soiuza. Tsentral'nyi Komitet. Vysshaia Partiinaia Shkola. Aktual'nye Voprosy Marksistsko-Leninskoi Teorii)

— — History.

OCHERKI istorii Volgogradskoi organizatsii KPSS. Volgograd, 1977. pp. 703.

SHUSHKIN (NIKOLAI NIKITICH) and ULITIN (S.D.) Soiuz rabochikh i krest'ian v Velikoi Otechestvennoi voine: na materialakh respublik i oblastei Severo-Zapada RSFSR. Leningrad, 1977. pp. 182.

VAGANOV (FEDOR MIKHAILOVICH) Pravyi uklon v VKP(b) i ego razgrom, 1928-1930 gg. 2nd ed. Moskva, 1977. pp. 328.

ISTORIIA Kommunisticheskoi partii Sovetskogo Soiuza. 5th ed. Moskva, 1978. pp. 792.

JAROSLAWSKI (JAN) Soziologie der kommunistischen Partei; (aus dem Polnischen übersetzt von Edda Werfel). Frankfurt/Main, [1978]. pp. 561. *bibliog.*

MOLETOTOV (IVAN AFANAS'EVICH) Sibkraikom: partiinoe stroitel'stvo v Sibiri, 1924-1930 gg.; otvetstvennyi redaktor B.M. Shereshevskii. Novosibirsk, 1978. pp. 366. *bibliog.*

VESELOV (ANATOLII PAVLOVICH) Bor'ba Kommunisticheskoi partii za provedenie kul'turnoi revoliutsii v derevne v gody kollektivizatsii. Leningrad, 1978. pp. 128.

SERVICE (ROBERT) The Bolshevik party in revolution: a study in organisational change, 1917-1923. London, 1979. pp. 246.

— — — Study and teaching.

VOPROSY metodiki prepodavaniia istorii KPSS v universitete: mezhvuzovskii sbornik. Leningrad, 1978. pp. 150.

— — Party work.

PETRENKO (FEDOR FEDOROVICH) and SHAPKO (VALERII MAKAROVICH) Partiinoe stroitel'stvo na sovremennom etape. Moskva, 1977. pp. 213.

COMMUNIST PARTY (Cont.)

AKADEMIIA OBSHCHESTVENNYKH NAUK. Kafedra Teorii i Metodov Ideologicheskoi Raboty. Voprosy Teorii i Metodov Ideologicheskoi Raboty. vyp.9. Problemy kompleksnogo podkhoda k ideologicheskoi rabotes; Propaganda preimushchestv sotsializma v usloviiakh sovremennoi ideologicheskoi bor'by. Moskva, 1978. pp. 280.

— — Ukraine.

KOMMUNISTICHESKAIA PARTIIA UKRAINY. Tsentral'nyi Komitet. Plenum, noiabr', 1977. Materialy, etc. Kiev, 1977. pp. 52.

— — Uzbekistan.

OCHERKI istorii Tashkentskoi gorodskoi partiinoi organizatsii. Tashkent, 1976. pp. 446.

— Spain.

ALVAREZ GOMEZ (SANTIAGO) El Partido Comunista y el campo: la evolucion del problema agrario y la posicion de los comunistas. Madrid, [1977]. pp. 265.

PARTIDO COMUNISTA DE ESPAÑA. PCE en sus documentos, 1920-1977. Madrid, 1977. pp. 260. bibliog.

— Thailand.

THAILAND: roots of conflict; edited by Andrew Turton [and others]. Nottingham, 1978. pp. 196.

— United Kingdom.

MATHER (GRAHAM) The Communist Party of Great Britain: freedom's foremost enemy. London, [1978]. pp. 17. (Aims for Freedom and Enterprise. Studies of the Left. No. 2)

COMMUNIST REVISIONISM.

BERNSTEIN und der demokratische Sozialismus: Bericht über den wissenschaftlichen Kongress "Die historische Leistung und aktuelle Bedeutung Eduard Bernsteins"; Horst Heimann, Thomas Meyer, Hrsg. Berlin, [1978]. pp. 578.

COMMUNIST STATE.

KOSITSYN (ALEKSANDR PAVLOVICH) Sotsializm i gosudarstvo. Moskva, 1976. pp. 144.

INNOVATION in communist systems; edited by Andrew Gyorgy and James A. Kuhlman. Boulder, Colo., 1978. pp. 224.

SOVETSKOE gosudarstvo v usloviiakh razvitogo sotsialisticheskogo obshchestva. Moskva, 1978. pp. 327.

UCHENIE K. Marksa, F. Engel'sa, V.I. Lenina o sotsialisticheskom gosudarstve i prave: istoriia razvitiia i sovremennost'. Moskva, 1978. pp. 431. Continuation of Marksistsko-leninskoe uchenie o gosudarstve i prave, Moskva, 1977.

COMMUNIST STRATEGY.

SOLZHENITSYN (ALEKSANDR ISAEVICH) Alexander Solzhenitsyn speaks to the West. London, 1978. pp. 100.

COMMUNISTIC SETTLEMENTS

— Brazil.

GOSI (ROSELLINA) Il socialismo utopistico: Giovanni Rossi e la colonia anarchica Cecilia. Milano, [1977]. pp. 179. bibliog.

— United Kingdom.

HARDY (DENNIS) Alternative communities in nineteenth century England. London, 1979. pp. 268. bibliog.

— United States.

EGERTON (JOHN) Historian. Visions of Utopia: Nashoba, Rugby, Ruskin and the new communities in Tennessee's past. Knoxville, [1977]. pp. 95. bibliog.

— — Bibliography.

STEINMETZ (ASTRID) compiler. Kommunitarische Experimente in den USA im 19. Jahrhundert: Verzeichnis des Bestandes im Karl-Marx-Haus Trier. Trier, [1977]. pp. 38. (Karl-Marx-Haus. Schriften. 19)

COMMUNISTS

— Germany.

GOODE (PATRICK) Karl Korsch: a study in western marxism. London, 1979. pp. 239. bibliog.

— Spain.

SEMPRUN (JORGE) Autobiographie de Federico Sánchez; traduit de l'espagnol par Claude et Carmen Durand. Paris, 1978. pp. 319.

COMMUNITY.

BENDER (THOMAS) Community and social change in America. New Brunswick, [1978]. pp. 159.

FROM contract to community: political theory at the crossroads; edited by Fred R. Dallmayr. New York, [1978]. pp. 172. Based on a lecture series held at Purdue University's Department of Political Science during the academic year 1974- 1975.

COMMUNITY AND SCHOOL.

NATIONAL UNION OF STUDENTS. Student Community Action. Action education kit. London, [1974?]. pp. 150. bibliog.

COMMUNITY CENTRES

— Canada.

CANADA. Department of Regional Economic Expansion. 1973. Who knows?: hundreds of programs to serve the disadvantaged, but who knows about them? To what extent is failure to communicate information a factor in disadvantage? Ottawa, 1973. pp. 55. bibliog.

— United Kingdom.

CENTERPRISE TRUST. Local publishing and local culture: an account of the work of the Centerprise publishing project, 1972-1977. London, [1977]. pp. 22.

CROUSAZ (DIONE) and others. Towards participation: a study of self-management in a neighbourhood community centre. London, 1978. pp. 82. bibliog. (U.K. Department of Halth and Social Security. Research Reports. No. 3)

LLEWELYN-DAVIES WEEKS [AND PARTNERS]. Inner area study: Birmingham: Small Heath Information and Advice Centre. [London], Department of the Environment, [1978]. pp. 46.

— — Scotland.

PAISLEY COMMUNITY DEVELOPMENT PROJECT. The Information and Action Centre; (by Barbara Jackson and Pam Davidson). Paisley, 1978. pp. 30.

COMMUNITY DEVELOPMENT.

ROBERTS (HAYDEN) Community development: learning and action. Toronto, [1979]. pp. 201. bibliog.

— Research.

UNITED NATIONS RESEARCH INSTITUTE FOR SOCIAL DEVELOPMENT. Research notes: a review of recent and current studies conducted at the Institute. a., Je 1968(no.1)- Geneva.

— Thailand.

THAILAND. Delegation to a Six Country Seminar on Planning and Administration in Community Development, Bangkok, 1959. Report. [Bangkok, 1959]. fo. 12.

— United Kingdom.

GLAMPSON (ANN) and others. A guide to the assessment of community needs and resources. London, 1975 repr. 1977. pp. 80. bibliog. (National Institute for Social Work. Papers. No. 1)

SPECHT (HARRY) The Community Development Project: national and local strategies for improving the delivery of services. London, 1976. pp. 70. bibliog. (National Institute for Social Work. Papers. No. 2)

GLEN (ANDREW) and others. Resources for social change. [York], 1977. pp. 148. (Papers in Community Studies. No. 14)

COMMUNITY participation and poverty: the final report of Cumbria C[ommunity] D[evelopment] P[roject]; [by] Hu Butcher [and others]. [York], 1979. pp. 265. bibliog. (Papers in Community Studies. No. 22)

— — Wales.

GLAMORGAN-GLYNCORRWG COMMUNITY DEVELOPMENT PROJECT. A report to the Minister about the work of the Glamorgan/Glyncorrwg Community Development Project, to be read in conjunction with the Director's report to the Project Management Committee, July 1972. [Port Talbot, 1972]. 1 pamphlet (various foliations).

GLAMORGAN-GLYNCORRWG COMMUNITY DEVELOPMENT PROJECT. Director's report to the Community Development Project Management Committee, June 1973. [Port Talbot, 1973]. 1 pamphlet (various foliations).

GLAMORGAN-GLYNCORRWG COMMUNITY DEVELOPMENT PROJECT. Director's report to the Management Committee, 2..., July 1974. [Port Talbot], 1974. fo. 12.

GLAMORGAN-GLYNCORRWG COMMUNITY DEVELOPMENT PROJECT. Director's report to the Project Management Committee..., March 1974. [Port Talbot], 1974. pp. (60).

GLAMORGAN-GLYNCORRWG COMMUNITY DEVELOPMENT PROJECT. Technical report 2. [Port Talbot], 1974. 1 pamphlet (various foliations).

GLAMORGAN-GLYNCORRWG COMMUNITY DEVELOPMENT PROJECT. Director's report to the Management Committee, 4..., March 1975. Port Talbot, 1975. pp. (26).

GLAMORGAN-GLYNCORRWG COMMUNITY DEVELOPMENT PROJECT. The Upper Afan Community Development Project. [Port Talbot], 1975. pp. 19.

COMMUNITY DEVELOPMENT, URBAN

— Rhodesia.

PARTRIDGE (MARK) Minister speaks on community development and the urban African;.. .text of an address by the Minister of Local Government and Housing...to the Associate Member Council of the Associated Members of Commerce of Rhodesia. [Salisbury, 1972]. fo.9. (Rhodesia. Ministry of Information, Immigration and Tourism. Press Statements) Xerox copy.

— United Kingdom.

COMMUNITY DEVELOPMENT PROJECT. Political Economy Collective. C[ommunity] D[evelopment] P[roject]: community work or class politics. [North Shields, 1976]. pp. 8.

LLEWELYN-DAVIES WEEKS [AND PARTNERS]. Inner area study: Birmingham: SHAPE housing and community project. [London], Department of the Environment, [1978]. pp. 52.

LLEWELYN-DAVIES WEEKS [AND PARTNERS]. Inner area study: Birmingham: Small Heath Community Federation: a study in local influence. [London], Department of the Environment, [1978]. pp. 43.

NORTH TYNESIDE COMMUNITY DEVELOPMENT PROJECT. North Shields: organising for change in a working class area. [Newcastle-upon-Tyne, 1978]. 2 pts. (Final Reports. Vols. 3-4)

CORINA (LEWIS) and others. Oldham C[ommunity] D[evelopment] P[roject]: the final report. [York], 1979. pp. 86. bibliog. (Papers in Community Studies. No. 23)

— — Scotland.

PAISLEY COMMUNITY DEVELOPMENT PROJECT. The C[ommunity] D[evelopment] P[roject] Management Committee: an analysis of its role; (by Barbara Jackson). [Paisley, 1978]. pp. 25.

COMMUNITY HEALTH SERVICES.

GERSHON (MICHAEL) and BILLER (HENRY B.) The other helpers: paraprofessionals and nonprofessionals in mental health. Lexington, Mass., [1977]. pp. 268. *bibliog.*

LEWIS (JUDITH A.) and LEWIS (MICHAEL D.) Community counseling: a human services approach. New York, [1977]. pp. 382. *bibliogs.*

HEALTH care in big cities; edited by Leslie H.W. Paine. New York, 1978. pp. 368.

COLLABORATION in community care: a discussion document; [Dame Albertine Winner, chairman of the Working Party]. London, H.M.S.O., 1978. pp. 64. *bibliog.*

JORDAN (WILLIAM STONE) Community medicine in the United Kingdom: medical education and an emerging specialty within the reorganized National Health Service. New York, [1978]. pp. 310.

HANNAY (DAVID RAINSFORD) The symptom iceberg: a study of community health. London, 1979. pp. 218. *bibliogs.*

SIMPSON (ROBIN) Access to primary care. London, 1979. pp. 62. *bibliog.* (*U.K. Royal Commission on the National Health Service, 1976. Research Papers. No.6*)

— — Wales.

WELSH CONSUMER COUNCIL. Getting primary care on the NHS: a sample survey carried out in the Merthyr and Cynon Valley Health District of parents of children under 10 and people aged over 60. Cardiff, 1979. pp. 43, 22.

COMMUNITY HEALTH SERVICES FOR THE AGED.

An AGEING population: a reader and sourcebook; edited by Vida Carver and Penny Liddiard. Sevenoaks, [1978]. pp. 434. *bibliogs.*

COMMUNITY LIFE.

NATIONAL UNION OF STUDENTS. Student Community Action. Action education kit. London, [1974?]. pp. 150. *bibliog.*

COMMUNITY MENTAL HEALTH SERVICES.

ALTERNATIVES to mental hospital treatment; edited by Leonard I. Stein and Mary Ann Test. New York, [1978]. pp. 327. *bibliogs. Papers from the Conference on Alternatives to Mental Hospital Treatment, Madison, Wis., 1975.*

— United Kingdom.

COMMUNITY care for the mentally disabled; edited by J.K. Wing and Rolf Olsen. Oxford, 1979. pp. 188. *bibliogs.*

FABIAN SOCIETY. Fabian Tracts. [No.] 460. A family service for the mentally handicapped; [by] Walter Jaehnig. London, 1979. pp. 24.

NEW methods of mental health care; edited by Molly Meacher. Oxford, 1979. pp. 233. *bibliog.*

— United States.

An ASSESSMENT of the community mental health movement; edited by Walter E. Barton and Charlotte J. Sanborn. Lexington, Mass., [1977]. pp. 194. *bibliogs.*

EVALUATION of human service programs; edited by C. Clifford Attkisson [and others]. New York, 1978. pp. 492. *bibliogs.*

COMMUNITY ORGANIZATION.

MASSACHUSETTS. Department of Community Affairs. 1972. Report...relative to community and environmental development and governmental roles and responsibilities. [Boston], 1972. pp. 39.

TAYLOR (MARILYN) and others. Principles and practice of community work in a British town. London, 1976. pp. 81. (*Young Volunteer Force Foundation. Community and Youth Work Papers*)

COMMUNITY PSYCHOLOGY.

LEWIS (JUDITH A.) and LEWIS (MICHAEL D.) Community counseling: a human services approach. New York, [1977]. pp. 382. *bibliogs.*

COMMUTERS

— Japan.

JAPAN. Census, 1975. Commuting population. [Tokyo, 1978]. 1 vol. (various pagings). (*Reference Report Series. No. 1*) *In English and Japanese.*

COMMUTING

— Australia.

MANNING (IAN) The journey to work. Sydney, 1978. pp. 194. *bibliog.*

— — New South Wales.

NEW SOUTH WALES. Planning and Environment Commission. 1976. Work places and work trips, 1971. [Sydney], 1976. pp. 32. (*Research Studies. 2*)

COMMYNES (PHILIPPE DE).

See COMINES (PHILIPPE DE).

COMPARATIVE LAW.

LAWSON (FREDERICK HENRY) Selected essays. Amsterdam, 1977. 2 vols. (*London. University. King's College. Centre of European Law. European Studies in Law. vols. 4, 5*)

COMPENSATION (LAW)

— United Kingdom — Ireland, Northern.

IRELAND, NORTHERN. Committee to Review the Principles and Operation of the Criminal Injuries to Property (Compensation Act) (Northern Ireland) 1971. 1976. Report...; chairman: Sir James Waddell. Belfast, [1976]. pp. 63.

COMPETENCE AND PERFORMANCE (LINGUISTICS).

MENYUK (PAULA) Language and maturation. Cambridge, Mass., [1977]. pp. 180. *bibliog.*

COMPETITION.

GRIBBIN (J.D.) The post-war revival of competition as industrial policy. London, Price Commission, 1978. pp. 58, 2. (*Government Economic Service Working Papers. No. 19*)

KOTTKE (FRANK JOSEPH) The promotion of price competition where sellers are few. Lexington, Mass., [1978]. pp. 227. *bibliogs.*

NATIONAL ECONOMIC DEVELOPMENT OFFICE. Competition policy; including a research annex by Alan Hughes: Competition policy and economic performance in the UK. London, 1978. pp. 102.

The CASE for private enterprise; editor: Cecil Turner. London, 1979. pp. 111.

COMPETITION policy, profitability and growth; [by] D.P. O'Brien. London, 1979. pp. 154. *bibliog.*

GRIBBIN (J.D.) The role of competition in the 1977 Price Commission Act. London, Price Commision, 1979. pp. (34). (*Government Economic Service Working Papers. No. 21*)

— Mathematical models.

CASE (JAMES H.) Economics and the competitive process. New York, 1979. pp. 295. *bibliogs.*

COMPETITION, INTERNATIONAL.

Le DEFI économique de tiers monde; rapport du groupe de travail animé par Yves Berthelot et Gérard Tardy; préface par Michel Albert; [with] Annexes. Paris, La Documentation Française, [1978]. 2 vols. *bibliog.*

ORGANISATION FOR ECONOMIC CO-OPERATION AND DEVELOPMENT. Department of Economics and Statistics. 1978. Budget indicators; [by the Monetary and Fiscal Policy Division; and] The international competitiveness of selected OECD countries; [by the Balance of Payments Division]. Paris, 1978. pp. 52. (*OECD Economic Outlook. Occasional Studies*)

COMPREHENSION.

SYMPOSIUM ON COGNITION, 12TH, CARNEGIE-MELLON UNIVERSITY, 1976. Cognitive processes in comprehension; edited by Marcel Adam Just [and] Patricia A. Carpenter. Hillsdale, N.J., 1977. pp. 329. *bibliogs.*

COMPULSORY LICENSING OF PATENTS

— United States.

SCHERER (FREDERIC M.) The economic effects of compulsory patent licensing. New York, 1977. pp. 88. (*New York (City). University. Salomon Brothers Center for the Study of Financial Institutions. Monograph Series in Finance and Economics. 1977. No. 2*)

COMPUTER ARCHITECTURE.

MYERS (GLENFORD J.) Advances in computer architecture. New York, [1978]. pp. 314. *bibliogs.*

COMPUTER GRAPHICS.

CAD 78: third international conference and exhibition on computers in engineering and building design, Brighton, 14-16 March 1978; organized by the journal "Computer aided design". Guildford, [1978]. pp. 803.

COMPUTER INTERFACES.

STECHER (PETER) On the interface between business systems and data processing systems. 1978. fo. 226. *bibliog.* Typescript. *Ph.D. (London) thesis: unpublished. This thesis is the property of London University and may not be removed from the Library.*

COMPUTER NETWORKS.

ABRAMS (MARSHALL D.) and others, eds. Computer networks; text and references for a tutorial. New York, 1978. 1 vol. (various pagings). *bibliogs. Sponsored by the IEEE Computer Society.*

BLEAZARD (G.B.) Teleprocessing monitor packages for ICL 2903/04. Manchester, 1978. pp. 55.

HEBDITCH (DAVID L.) Teleprocessing monitor packages for IBM 370. Manchester, 1978. pp. 89.

COMPUTER OUTPUT MICROFILM DEVICES.

GILDENBERG (ROBERT F.) Computer-output-microfilm systems. Los Angeles, [1974]. pp. 199.

COMPUTER PROGRAMS.

METRA INTERNATIONAL. Investigation on the development of software: report of the synthesis. Brussels, European Communities, 1973. pp. 21. (*European Economic Community. Studies. Industry Series. 7*)

BLEAZARD (G.B.) Teleprocessing monitor packages for ICL 2903/04. Manchester, 1978. pp. 55.

HEBDITCH (DAVID L.) Teleprocessing monitor packages for IBM 370. Manchester, 1978. pp. 89.

COMPUTER PROGRAMS. (Cont.)

HUZAN (EVA) Investigation and modelling of indexed sequential files on exchangeable disc stores. 1979. fo. 239. *bibliog. Typescript. Ph.D. (London) thesis: unpublished. This thesis is the property of London University and may not be removed from the Library.*

— Evaluation.

SPIRN (JEFFREY R.) Program behavior: models and measurements. New York, [1977]. pp. 277. *bibliog.*

BEIZER (BORIS) Micro-analysis of computer system performance. New York, [1978]. pp. 404. *bibliog.*

— Testing.

VAN TASSEL (DENNIS) Program style, design, efficiency, debugging, and testing. 2nd ed. Englewood Cliffs, N.J., [1978]. pp. 323. *bibliogs.*

COMPUTER SIMULATION.

SMITH (JOHN UPHAM MURRAY) Computer simulation models. New York, 1968. pp. 112.

COMPUTERS.

SOUTH AFRICA. Bureau of Statistics. Computer survey. bien., 1975(1st)- Pretoria. *[in English and Afrikaans]*

NATIONAL COMPUTER CONFERENCE, 1976. National Computer Conference, June 7-10, 1976, New York; [edited by] Stanley Winkler. Montvale, N.J., [1976]. pp. 1109. *bibliogs. (American Federation of Information Processing Societies. Conference Proceedings. vol. 45) Microfiche containing the paper The integration of microfilm and the computer by D.R. Neary enclosed in pocket on back end-paper.*

NATIONAL COMPUTER CONFERENCE, 1977. National Computer Conference, June 13-16, 1977, Dallas, Texas; [edited by] Robert R. Korfhage. Montvale, N.J., [1977]. pp. 1025. *bibliogs. (American Federation of Information Processing Societies. Conference Proceedings. vol. 46)*

EUROPEAN COMPUTING CONGRESS, 1978. Eurocomp 78: proceedings of the...congress, [London], 1978. London, [1978]. pp. 1088. *bibliogs.*

INTERNATIONAL CONFERENCE ON THE PERFORMANCE OF COMPUTER INSTALLATIONS, GARDONE RIVIERA, ITALY, 1978. Performance of computer installations: evaluation and management: proceedings...; edited by Domenico Ferrari. Amsterdam, 1978. pp. 351. *bibliogs.*

MARTIN (JAMES THOMAS) The wired society. Englewood Cliffs, N.J., [1978]. pp. 300.

NATIONAL COMPUTER CONFERENCE, 1978. National Computer Conference, June 5-8, 1978, Anaheim, California; [edited by] Sakti P. Ghosh and Leonard Y. Liu. Montvale, N.J., [1978]. pp. 1300. *bibliogs. (American Federation of Information Processing Societies. Conference Proceedings. vol. 47)*

— Law and legislation.

SEIPEL (PETER) Computing law: perspectives on a new legal discipline. Stockholm, [1977]. pp. 375. *bibliog.*

— Public opinion.

CANADA. Department of Communications. 1973. Survey of public attitudes towards the computer. Ottawa, 1973. pp. 40,40. *(Studies) In English and French.*

— Social aspects.

JAMOUS (HAROUN) and GREMION (PIERRE) L'ordinateur au pouvoir: essai sur les projets de rationalisation du gouvernement des hommes. Paris, [1978]. pp. 254.

CONCENTRATION CAMPS

— Austria.

DREXEL (JOSEPH EDUARD) Rückkehr unerwünscht: Joseph Drexels "Reise nach Mauthausen" und der Widerstandskreis Ernst Niekisch; herausgegeben von Wilhelm Raimund Beyer. Stuttgart, [1978]. pp. 332.

— Europe.

KOGON (EUGEN) Der SS-Staat: das System der deutschen Konzentrationslager. München, 1979. pp. 431.

— Germany.

ROTHE (WOLF DIETER) Die Endlösung der Judenfrage. Band 1. Zeugen. Frankfurt/Main, 1974. pp. 208. *No more published.*

NATIONALSOZIALISTISCHE Konzentrationslager im Dienst der totalen Kriegsführung: sieben württembergische Aussenkommandos des Konzentrationslagers Natzweiler/Elsass; herausgegeben von Herwart Vorländer. Stuttgart, 1978. 1 vol. (various pagings). *bibliog. (Kommission für Geschichtliche Landeskunde in Baden-Württemberg. Veröffentlichungen. Reihe B: Forschungen. Band 91)*

PINGEL (FALK) Häftlinge unter SS-Herrschaft: Widerstand, Selbstbehauptung und Vernichtung im Konzentrationslager. Hamburg, 1978. pp. 338. *bibliog. With English summary.*

— Poland.

MUELLER (FILIP) Auschwitz inferno: the testimony of a Sonderkommando...; edited and translated by Susanne Flatauer. London, 1979. pp. 180.

PAWEŁCZYŃSKA (ANNA) Values and violence in Auschwitz: a sociological analysis; translated with an introduction by Catherine S. Leach. Berkeley, 1979. pp. 170.

STAEGLICH (WILHELM) Der Auschwitz-Mythos: Legende oder Wirklichkeit?: eine kritische Bestandsaufnahme. Tübingen, 1979. pp. 467. *bibliog. (Institut für Deutsche Nachkriegsgeschichte. Veröffentlichungen. Band 9)*

— Russia.

GLUCKSMANN (ANDRE) La cuisinière et le mangeur d'hommes: essai sur les rapports entre l'Etat, le marxisme et les camps de concentration. Paris, [1975]. pp. 223.

CONCILIAR THEORY.

CROWDER (C.M.D.) compiler. Unity, heresy and reform, 1378-1460: the conciliar response to the Great Schism. London, 1977. pp. 212. *bibliog.*

CONCORDE (JET TRANSPORTS).

COSTELLO (JOHN) and HUGHES (TERRY) Concorde: the international race for a supersonic passenger transport. London, 1976. pp. 302.

CONCUBINAGE

— France.

ROUSSEL (LOUIS) Demographer, and BOURGUIGNON (ODILE) Générations nouvelles et mariage traditionnel: enquête auprès de jeunes de 18-30 ans. [Paris], 1978. pp. 283. *(France. Institut National d'Etudes Démographiques. Travaux et Documents. Cahiers. No. 86)*

CONDOTTIERI.

MALLETT (MICHAEL EDWARD) Mercenaries and their masters: warfare in Renaissance Italy. London, [1974]. pp. 284. *bibliog.*

CONDUCT OF COURT PROCEEDINGS

— United Kingdom.

ATKINSON (JOHN MAXWELL) and DREW (PAUL) Order in court: the organisation of verbal interaction in judicial settings. London, 1979. pp. 275. *bibliog. (U.K. Social Science Research Council. Centre for Socio-Legal Studies. Oxford Socio-Legal Studies)*

CONDUCT OF LIFE.

DAVISON (IAN) b. 1939. Values, ends, and society. St. Lucia, [1977]. pp. 257. *bibliog.*

CONFEDERACION ESPAÑOLA DE DERECHAS AUTONOMAS.

MONTERO (JOSE R.) La CEDA: el catolicismo social y politico en la II republica. Madrid, Ediciones de la Revista de Trabajo, Ministerio de Trabajo, [1977]. 2 vols. *bibliog.*

CONFEDERATE STATES OF AMERICA

— History.

ESCOTT (PAUL D.) After secession: Jefferson Davis and the failure of confederate nationalism. Baton Rouge, [1978]. pp. 295. *bibliog.*

CONFEDERAZIONE GENERALE ITALIANA DEL LAVORO.

PISTILLO (MICHELE) Giuseppe Di Vittorio, 1944-1957: la costruzione della CGIL; la lotta per la rinascita del paese e l'unità dei lavoratori. Roma, 1977. pp. 361.

CONFIDENTIAL COMMUNICATIONS.

WILSON (SUANNA J.) Confidentiality in social work: issues and principles. New York, [1978]. pp. 274. *bibliog.*

— Census — United Kingdom.

HAKIM (C.) Census confidentiality, microdata and census analysis. [London], 1978. pp. 18. *bibliog. (U.K. Office of Population Censuses and Surveys. Occasional Papers. 3)*

CONFLICT OF GENERATIONS.

MEAD (MARGARET) Culture and commitment: the new relationships between the generations in the 1970s. [rev. ed.] New York, 1978. pp. 178. *bibliog.*

CONFLICT OF INTERESTS (PUBLIC OFFICE)

— Canada — New Brunswick.

NEW BRUNSWICK. Premier. 1977. Conflicts of interest: outline of government policy pertaining to conflicts of interest affecting elected persons and appointive public servants. [Fredericton], 1977. fo.27.

CONFLICT OF LAWS

— Matrimonial actions — Ireland (Republic).

NORTH (PETER MACHIN) The private international law of matrimonial causes in the British Isles and the Republic of Ireland. Amsterdam, 1977. pp. 465. *bibliog.*

— — United Kingdom.

NORTH (PETER MACHIN) The private international law of matrimonial causes in the British Isles and the Republic of Ireland. Amsterdam, 1977. pp. 465. *bibliog.*

— Taxation.

CARROLL (MITCHELL BENEDICT) Global perspectives of an international tax lawyer. Hicksville, N.Y., [1978]. pp. 151.

— Argentine Republic.

BOGGIANO (ANTONIO) Professor of Private International Law. Derecho internacional privado. Buenos Aires, 1978. pp. 933.

— Canada.

CASTEL (JEAN GABRIEL) Introduction to conflict of laws. Toronto, [1978]. pp. 189. *bibliog.*

— United Kingdom.

CHESHIRE (GEOFFREY CHEVALIER) and NORTH (PETER MACHIN) Private international law; tenth edition by P.M. North. London, 1979. pp. 755. *bibliog.*

CONFUCIUS AND CONFUCIANISM.

ALITTO (GUY S.) The last Confucian: Liang Shu-ming and the Chinese dilemma of modernity. Berkeley, 1979. pp. 396. *bibliog.*

CONGO (BRAZZAVILLE)

— Politics and government.

L'INDEPENDANCE de la république du Congo: textes des discours prononcés à la session solennelle de l'Assemblée Nationale et à la proclamation publique de l'indépendance. Brazzaville, Ministère de l'Information de la République du Congo, 1960. pp. 22.

— Social life and customs.

MOTLEY (MARY) pseud. [i.e. Mary Margaret Motley de RENEVILLE] Devils in waiting. London, 1959. pp. 224.

CONGRESS OF BERLIN, 1878.

CONGRESS OF BERLIN, 1878. Der Berliner Kongress 1878: Protokolle und Materialien; herausgegeben von Imanuel Geiss. Boppard am Rhein, [1978]. pp. 428. *bibliog.* *(Germany (Bundesrepublik). Bundesarchiv. Schriften. 27)*

CONGRESS OF VIENNA.

NICOLSON (Sir HAROLD) The Congress of Vienna: a study in allied unity, 1812-1822. London, 1961 repr. 1970. pp. 312. *bibliog.*

CONIC SECTIONS.

OPEN UNIVERSITY. Linear Mathematics Course Team. Unit 15: Affine geometry and convex cones. Milton Keynes, 1972, repr. 1976. pp. 40. *(Open University. Mathematics: a second level course: linear mathematics. Unit 15)*

CONJUGAL VIOLENCE.

FAMILY violence: an international and interdisciplinary study; [proceedings of a conference held in Montreal in 1977]; edited by John M. Eekelaar [and] Sanford N. Katz. Toronto, [1978]. pp. 572. *bibliog.*

VIOLENCE and responsibility: the individual, the family and society; [edited by] Robert L. Sadoff. New York, [1978]. pp. 139.

— United Kingdom.

FREEMAN (MICHAEL D.A.) Violence in the home. Farnborough, [1979]. pp. 257. *bibliogs.*

— — Ireland, Northern.

IRELAND, NORTHERN. Inter-departmental Committee on Family Problems. 1977. Family problems: a commentary on the implementation in Northern Ireland of the recommendations of the Finer report on one parent families and of the report of the Select Committee on Violence in Marriage. [Belfast], 1977. fo. 11.

CONNECTICUT

— Politics and government.

JEFFRIES (JOHN W.) Testing the Roosevelt coalition: Connecticut society and politics in the era of World War II. Knoxville, [1979]. pp. 312.

— Social history.

JEFFRIES (JOHN W.) Testing the Roosevelt coalition: Connecticut society and politics in the era of World War II. Knoxville, [1979]. pp. 312.

CONNOLLY (JAMES).

FALIGOT (ROGER) James Connolly et le mouvement révolutionnaire irlandais. Paris, 1978. pp. 333. *bibliog.*

CONSCIOUSNESS.

BROWN (JASON) Mind, brain, and consciousness: the neuropsychology of cognition. New York, 1977. pp. 190. *bibliog.*

CONSERVATION OF NATURAL RESOURCES.

O'RIORDAN (TIMOTHY) ed. Environmentalism. London, [1976]. pp. 373. *bibliog.*

FRIENDS OF THE EARTH. Progress as if survival mattered: a handbook for a conserver society, by Friends of the Earth; edited by Hugh Nash. San Francisco, [1977]. pp. 319. *bibliog.*

— Study and teaching — Asia, Southeast.

ROMM (JEFF) Higher education and natural resources management in Southeast Asia. Washington, 1978. pp. 47. *(American Council on Education. Overseas Liaison Committee. Papers. No. 13)*

CONSERVATISM.

REKONSTRUKTION des Konservatismus;...(Gerd-Klaus Kaltenbrunner, Hrsg.). Bern, [1978]. pp. 614. *bibliog.*

— European Economic Community countries.

TUGENDHAT (CHRISTOPHER) Conservatives in Europe: a personal view. London, 1979. pp. 23. *(Conservative Political Centre. [Publications]. No. 636)*

— Germany.

POEHLS (JOACHIM) Die "Tägliche Rundschau" und die Zerstörung der Weimarer Republik, 1930 bis 1933. Münster, 1975. 2 vols. (in 1). *bibliog. (Münster in Westfalen. Westfälische Wilhelms-Universität. Institut für Publizistik. Arbeiten. Band 14)*

BAMBERG (HANS DIETER) Die Deutschland-Stiftung e.V.: Studien über Kräfte der "demokratischen Mitte" und des Konservatismus in der Bundesrepublik Deutschland. Meisenheim am Glan, 1978. pp. 563. *bibliog.*

— United Kingdom.

THATCHER (MARGARET) and others. The right angle: three studies in conservatism. London, [1978]. pp. 32.

— United States.

LIPSET (SEYMOUR MARTIN) and RAAB (EARL) The politics of unreason: right-wing extremism in America, 1790-1977. 2nd ed. Chicago, [1978]. pp. 581.

CONSERVATIVE PARTY (UNITED KINGDOM).

CONSERVATIVE AND UNIONIST PARTY. The campaign guide, 1977; [edited by Anthony Greenland]. London, [1977]. pp. 789.

CONSERVATIVE AND UNIONIST PARTY. Pamphlets and leaflets. [Hassocks, Sussex, 1978 in progress]. *Microfiche. (Conservative and Unionist Party. Archives of the British Conservative Party. Series 1)*

AUGHEY (ARTHUR) Conservative party attitudes towards the Common Market. Hull, 1978. fo. 29. *(Hull. University. Department of Politics. Hull Papers in Politics. No.2)*

RAMSDEN (JOHN) b. 1947. The age of Balfour and Baldwin, 1902-1940. London, 1978. pp. 413. *bibliog.*

CONSERVATIVE AND UNIONIST PARTY. The Conservative manifesto 1979. London, 1979. pp. 32.

CRUICKSHANKS (EVELINE) Political untouchables: the Tories and the '45. London, 1979. pp. 166. *bibliog.*

TUGENDHAT (CHRISTOPHER) Conservatives in Europe: a personal view. London, 1979. pp. 23. *(Conservative Political Centre. [Publications]. No. 636)*

CONSOLIDATION AND MERGER OF CORPORATIONS

— Ireland (Republic).

EIRE. Restrictive Practices Commission. 1976. Report of studies into industrial concentration and mergers in Ireland. Dublin, [1976]. pp. 132. *bibliog.*

— United Kingdom.

GRINYER (PETER HUGH) and SPENDER (J.C.) Turnaround: managerial recipes for strategic success; the fall and rise of the Newton Chambers group. London, 1979. pp. 211.

CONSTITUTIONAL COURTS

— Germany.

GRUND (HENNING) "Preussenschlag" und Staatsgerichtshof im Jahre 1932. Baden-Baden, 1976. pp. 167. *bibliog.*

— Italy.

La CORTE Costituzionale tra norma giuridica e realtà sociale: bilancio di vent'anni di attività [proceedings of a Convegno di Studio held at Parma in 1976]; a cura di Nicola Occhiocupo. Bologna, [1978]. pp. 528.

CONSTITUTIONAL LAW.

MIAILLE (MICHEL) L'état du droit: introduction à une critique du droit constitutionnel. Grenoble, 1978. pp. 267.

CADART (JACQUES) Institutions politiques et droit constitutionnel. 2nd ed. Paris, 1979 in progress.

— Germany.

KNEBEL (JUERGEN) Koalitionsfreiheit und Gemeinwohl: zur verfassungsrechtlichen Zulässigkeit staatlicher Einwirkung auf die tarifautonome Lohngestaltung. Berlin, 1978. pp. 179. *bibliog.*

CONSTRUCTION INDUSTRY.

HUMAN SETTLEMENTS; issued by the Centre for Housing, Building and Planning. Department of Economic and Social Affairs, United Nations. q., Ja 1971 (v.1, no.1)- New York.

— Canada — Statistics.

CANADA. Statistics Canada. Special trades contracting industry. a., 1975(1st)- Ottawa. *[in English and French]*

CANADA. Statistics Canada. Service bulletin: Construction statistics. irreg., Ap 1978(v. 1, no. 1)- Ottawa. *[in English and French]*

— France — Finance.

FRANCE. Bureau des Enquêtes sur la Construction. 1974. Deuxième enquête sur les coûts prévisionnels des immeubles à usage d'habitation: résultats sur les logements mis en chantier en 1969 et 1970. Paris, 1974. pp. 64. *(France. Ministère de l'Equipement. Statistiques de la Construction. Suppléments. No. 15)*

— Ireland (Republic) — Labour productivity.

NATIONAL INSTITUTE FOR PHYSICAL PLANNING AND CONSTRUCTION RESEARCH. [Construction Division]. An examination of labour content in house building; [by] L.F. Shanley and B.J. Kearney). Dublin, 1970. pp. 49.

NATIONAL INSTITUTE FOR PHYSICAL PLANNING AND CONSTRUCTION RESEARCH. Construction Division. A productivity study of housebuilding; [by] Pierce T. Pigott. Dublin, 1972. pp. 37.

— Jamaica — Statistics.

JAMAICA. Department of Statistics. 1976. Building activity in Jamaica, 1967-1975. [Kingston, 1976]. pp. 60.

JAMAICA. Department of Statistics. 1978. Abstract of building and construction statistics, 1977. [Kingston, 1978]. pp. 32.

— Russia — Ukraine.

GANCHEV (IVAN DMITRIEVICH) Rezervy brigadnogo podriada. Moskva, 1978. pp. 80. *(Bibliotechka Profsoiuznogo Aktivista. 31)*

— South Africa.

SOUTH AFRICA. Bureau of Statistics. Census of township developers. a., 1974- Pretoria. *[in English and Afrikaans]*

CONSTRUCTION INDUSTRY.(Cont.)

— Uganda.

UGANDA. Ministry of Planning and Community Development. Statistics Division. 1966. Survey of industrial production: building and construction, 1964. [Entebbe], 1966. pp. (34).

— United States.

GLOVER (ROBERT W.) Minority enterprise in construction. New York, 1977. pp. 174. *bibliog.*

CONSTRUCTION WORKERS

— Brazil.

WERNECK (DOROTHEA FONSECA FURQUIM) Emprego e salarios na industria de construção. Rio de Janeiro, 1978. pp. 160. *bibliog. (Brazil. Instituto de Planejamento Econômico e Social. Instituto de Pesquisas. Relatorios de Pesquisa. No. 40)*

— India.

INDIA. Labour Bureau. 1979. Report on the working and living conditions of workers in the building construction industry in Delhi, 1977-78. Chandigarh, [1979]. pp. 81. *(Unorganised Sector Survey Series. No. 1)*

— New Zealand.

TURKINGTON (DON) Industrial conflict: a study of three New Zealand industries. Wellington, N.Z., 1976. pp. 324.

— United Kingdom.

HOPPÉ (MALCOLM) Direct labour: how councils waste our money. [London, 1978]. pp. 11.

CONSULTING ENGINEERS

— India.

INDIA. Committee on Technical Consultancy Services. 1971. Report. [Delhi], 1970 [or rather 1971]. pp. 125.

CONSUMER COOPERATIVES

— Law and legislation — United States.

AMERICAN ENTERPRISE INSTITUTE FOR PUBLIC POLICY RESEARCH. Legislative Analyses. 95th Congress. No. 31. The National Consumer Cooperative Bank Bill. Washington, 1978. pp. 23.

CONSUMER CREDIT

— Law and legislation — United Kingdom.

ISON (TERENCE G.) Credit marketing and consumer protection. London, [1979]. pp. 522.

— United Kingdom.

GOODE (ROYSTON MILES) The Consumer Credit Act: a students' guide. London, 1979. pp. 415.

CONSUMER EDUCATION.

MAURIZI (ALEX R.) and KELLY (THOM) Prices and consumer information: the benefits from posting retail gasoline prices. Washington, D.C., [1978]. pp. 76. *(American Enterprise Institute for Public Policy Research. AEI Studies. 193)*

CONSUMER PROTECTION.

MILLER (ROGER LEROY) Economics today and tomorrow. San Francisco, [1978]. pp. 416.

— Law and legislation — European Economic Community countries.

SYMPOSIUM ON THE JUDICIAL AND QUASI-JUDICIAL MEANS OF CONSUMER PROTECTION, MONTPELLIER, 1975. ...Symposium...[held at] Montpellier...December 10, 11, 12 1975. [Brussels], European Communities, [1976]. pp. 318.

— — United Kingdom.

CRANSTON (ROSS) Regulating business: law and consumer agencies. London, 1979. pp. 186.

MICKLEBURGH (JOHN) Consumer protection. Abingdon, 1979. pp. 689.

— United Kingdom.

HARRIES (JOHN V.) Consumers: know your rights. London, [1978]. pp. 213.

ISON (TERENCE G.) Credit marketing and consumer protection. London, [1979]. pp. 522.

CONSUMERS.

KATONA (GEORGE) and STRUEMPEL (BURKHARD) A new economic era. New York, [1978]. pp. 176. *bibliog.*

— Europe.

CAO-PINNA (VERA) and SHATALIN (STANISLAV SERGEEVICH) Consumption patterns in Eastern and Western Europe. Oxford, 1979. pp. 190.

— United Kingdom.

NATIONAL CONSUMER COUNCIL. Real money, real choice: consumer priorities in economic policy: a document for discussion. London, 1978. pp. 68.

CONSUMERS' PREFERENCES

— United Kingdom.

BRITISH MARKET RESEARCH BUREAU. B[ritish] M[arket] R[esearch] B[ureau] housing consumer survey: a survey of attitudes towards current and alternative housing policies, January 1976: supplementary table volume. London, H.M.S.O., 1977. pp. 290.

CONSUMPTION (ECONOMICS).

DECAILLOT (M.) and others. Besoins et mode de production: du capitalisme en crise au socialisme. [Paris, 1977]. pp. 285.

WONG (STANLEY) The foundations of Paul Samuelson's revealed preference theory: a study by the method of rational reconstruction. London, 1978. pp. 148. *bibliog.*

— Europe.

CAO-PINNA (VERA) and SHATALIN (STANISLAV SERGEEVICH) Consumption patterns in Eastern and Western Europe. Oxford, 1979. pp. 190.

— Germany — Hesse.

VOGLER (LUTZ) Hierarchie und Einzugsbereiche zentraler Orte auf Grund der Verbrauchernachfrage: empirische Untersuchung für die Planungsregion Nordhessen anhand von 39,000 Interviews. Bonn, 1978. 1 vol. (various pagings). *bibliog. (Germany (Bundesrepublik). Bundesforschungsanstalt für Landeskunde und Raumordnung. Forschungen zur Raumentwicklung. 7)*

— India — Kerala.

KERALA. Bureau of Economics and Statistics. 1976. Consumer expenditure on selected items in Kerala. Trivandrum, 1976. fo. 16.

— Russia.

ABALKIN (LEONID IVANOVICH) Konechnye narodnokhoziaistvennye rezul'taty: sushchnost', pokazateli, puti povysheniia. Moskva, 1978. pp. 151.

AKADEMIIA NAUK SSSR. Nauchnyi Sovet po Probleme "Ekonomicheskie Zakonomernosti Razvitiia Sotsializma i Ego Pererastaniia v Kommunizm". Potrebitel'naia stoimost' produktov truda pri sotsializme: materialy nauchnoi sessii. Moskva, 1978. pp. 247.

— — Mathematical models.

DIFFERENTSIROVANNYI balans dokhodov i potrebleniia naseleniia. Moskva, 1977. pp. 223. *bibliog. (Akademiia Nauk SSSR. Problemy Sovetskoi Ekonomiki)*

BARANOVA (LIANA IAKOVLEVNA) and LEVIN (ALEKSANDR IVANOVICH) Modelirovanie i prognozirovanie sprosa naseleniia. Moskva, 1978. pp. 208.

— South Africa.

RAEDEL (FRITZ E.) Progress or exploitation? Cape Town, 1978. pp. 55. *Translated from the German.*

CONTIGUOUS ZONES (MARITIME LAW).

EXTAVOUR (WINSTON CONRAD) The exclusive economic zone: a study of the evolution and progressive development of the international law of the sea. Genève, 1979. pp. 369. *bibliog. (Geneva. Graduate Institute of International Studies. Collection de Droit International.5)*

CONTINENTAL SHELF.

McQUILLIN (R.) and ARDUS (D.A.) Exploring the geology of shelf seas. London, 1977. pp. 234. *bibliog.*

CONTINGENCY TABLES.

GOKHALE (DATTAPRABHAKAR V.) and KULLBACK (SOLOMON) The information in contingency tables. New York, [1978]. pp. 365. *bibliog.*

UPTON (GRAHAM J.G.) The analysis of cross-tabulated data. Chichester, [1978]. pp. 148. *bibliog.*

CONTRACEPTION

— South Africa.

LÖTTER (JOHANN MORGENDALL) and VAN TONDER (JAN LOUIS) Fertility and family planning among blacks in South Africa: 1974;...translated by C.P. Kleyn. Pretoria, 1976. pp. 111. *bibliog. (Human Sciences Research Council [South Africa] . Institute for Sociological, Demographic and Criminological Research. Reports. No. S-39)*

CONTRACTS

— Austria.

GSCHNITZER (FRANZ) Schuldrecht: besonderer Teil und Schadenersatz. Wien, 1963. pp. 223.

GSCHNITZER (FRANZ) Schuldrecht: allgemeiner Teil. Wien, 1965. pp. 169.

KOZIOL (HELMUT) and WELSER (RUDOLF) Grundriss des bürgerlichen Rechts. Band 1. Allgemeiner Teil und Schuldrecht. 4th ed. Wien, 1976. pp. 384.

— France.

KAHN-FREUND (Sir OTTO) and others. A source-book on French law: system, methods, outlines of contract. 2nd ed. Oxford, 1979. pp. 550. *bibliog. In French or English.*

— United Kingdom.

BRAZIER (RODNEY JOHN) Cases and statutes on contract. 2nd ed. London, 1976. pp. 179.

CHITTY (JOSEPH) the Younger. On contracts; twenty-fourth edition (by A.G. Guest [and others]). London, 1977. 2 vols.

THOMPSON (PETER KENNETH JAMES) Unfair Contract Terms Act 1977. London, 1978. pp. 97.

ATIYAH (PATRICK SELIM) The rise and fall of freedom of contract. Oxford, 1979. pp. 791.

TREITEL (GUENTER HEINZ) The law of contract. 5th ed. London, 1979. pp. 799.

TREITEL (GUENTER HEINZ) An outline of the law of contract. 2nd ed. London, 1979. pp. 385.

— United States.

KRONMAN (ANTHONY T.) and POSNER (RICHARD A.) The economics of contract law. Boston, Mass., [1979]. pp. 274.

CONTRACTS, LETTING OF.

CONFERENCE ON BIDDING AND AUCTIONING, NEW YORK UNIVERSITY, 1975. Bidding and auctioning for procurement and allocation: proceedings of a conference at the Center for Applied Economics, New York University; edited by Yakov Amihud. New York, 1976. pp. 220. *bibliogs.*

CONTRACTS, MARITIME

— United Kingdom.

PAYNE (WILLIAM) Barrister-at-Law, and IVAMY (EDWARD RICHARD HARDY) Carriage of goods by sea: eleventh edition by E.R.H. Ivamy. London, 1979. pp. 332.

CONTROL THEORY.

BROGAN (WILLIAM L.) Modern control theory. New York, [1974]. pp. 393. *bibliog.*

MODELLING economic change: the recursive programming approach; [edited by] Richard H. Day and Alessandro Cigno. Amsterdam, 1978. pp. 447. *bibliog.*

OPTIMAL control for econometric models: an approach to economic policy formulation; edited by Sean Holly [and others]. London, 1979. pp. 303. *bibliogs.*

CONTROLLERSHIP.

CENTRALIZATION vs. decentralization in organizing the controller's department: a research study and report prepared for Controllership Foundation, Inc., by Herbert A. Simon [and others]. Houston, Tex., 1978. pp. 106. *Reprint of the edition originally published by the Foundation in 1954.*

CONVERGENCE.

BHATTACHARYA (RABINDRA NATH) and RAO (RAMASWAMY RANGA) Normal approximation and asymptotic expansions. New York, [1976]. pp. 274. *bibliog.*

CONVERSATION.

STUDIES in the organization of conversational interaction; edited by Jim Schenkein. New York, [1978]. pp. 275. *bibliog.*

CONVERSION

— Psychology.

DOWNTON (JAMES V.) Sacred journeys: the conversion of young Americans to Divine Light Mission. New York, 1979. pp. 245. *bibliog.*

CONVEX FUNCTIONS.

EKELAND (IVAR) and TEMAM (ROGER) Convex analysis and variational problems. Amsterdam, 1976. pp. 402. *bibliog.*

CONVICT LABOUR.

MELOSSI (DARIO) and PAVARINI (MASSIMO) Carcere e fabbrica: alle origini del sistema penitenziario (16- 19 secolo). Bologna, [1977]. pp. 252. *(La Questione Criminale. Quaderni. 1)*

COOPERATION.

KAGAWA (TOYOHIKO) Brotherhood economics. London, 1937. pp. 224. *bibliog.*

FRAUCHIGER (FRIEDRICH) and others. Genossenschaft und Gemeinschaft: vier Aufsätze. Basel, [1939]. pp. 80. *(Verband Schweizerischer Konsumvereine. Genossenschaftliche Volksbibliothek. Nr. 44)*

UNITED for freedom: co-operatives and Christian democracy; edited by Leo R. Ward. Milwaukee, [1945]. pp. 264. *bibliog.*

YOUNGJOHNS (B.A.) Co-operative organisation: an introduction. London, [1977]. pp. 34.

— Belgium.

BELGIUM. Conseil National de la Coopération. 1977. La coopération en Belgique. [Brussels, 1977]. pp. 121.

— India — Orissa.

ORISSA. Office of the Registrar, Co-operative Societies. tatistics Section. 1975. A decade of progress, 1965-75: co-operation. [Bhubaneswar, 1975?]. pp. 43.

— Italy.

SERENI (UMBERTO) Il movimento cooperativo a Parma tra riformismo e sindacalismo. Bari, [1977]. pp. 326.

— Kenya.

MBITHI (PHILIP M.) and RASMUSSON (RASMUS) Self reliance in Kenya: the case of harambee. Uppsala, 1977. pp. 175. *bibliog.*

— Nigeria.

ADEYEYE (SAMUEL OLADELE) The co-operative movement in Nigeria: yesterday, today and tomorrow. Göttingen, 1978. pp. 221. *bibliog. (Marburg. Universität. Institut für Kooperation in Entwicklungsländern. Marburger Schriften zum Genossenschaftswesen. Reihe B. Band 16)*

— Russia.

TSENTRAL'NYI SOIUZ POTREBITEL'SKIKH OBSHCHESTV SSSR. Potrebitel'skaia kooperatsiia SSSR, 1930-1933. Moskva, 1934. 43 plates. *In Russian and English.*

COOPERATIVE MARKETING OF FARM PRODUCE

— Tanzania.

MARKETING DEVELOPMENT BUREAU [UNITED REPUBLIC OF TANZANIA]. Co-operative marketing in Tanzania: its costs, present situation and proposals for improvement. Dar es Salaam, 1974. fo. 117.

— United Kingdom — Wales.

LE VAY (CLARE) and LEWIS (M.R.) Farmer participation in cooperatives: a study of the Brecon and Radnor area. Aberystwyth, 1977. pp. 129. *bibliog.*

COOPERATIVE SOCIETIES.

OAKESHOTT (ROBERT) The case for workers' co-ops. London, 1978. pp. 272.

— Law.

ISSERT (J.) The legal status of (agricultural) cooperatives in European countries...; translated by J.A.E. Morley. [Oxford, 1978]. pp. 112. *(Horace Plunkett Foundation. Occasional Papers. No. 44)*

— Tanzania.

UNITED REPUBLIC OF TANZANIA. Presidential Special Committee of Enquiry into Co-operative Movement and Marketing Boards. 1966. Report; [J.A.Mhaville, chairman]. Dar es Salaam, 1966. pp. 84.

— Underdeveloped areas.

See UNDERDEVELOPED AREAS — Cooperative societies.

— United Kingdom.

INDUSTRIAL common ownership and co-operative production: report of a seminar held at the Co-operative College, Loughborough, 21 April 1977. [London, Department of Industry, 1977]. pp. 19.

U.K. Working Party on Kirkby Manufacturing and Engineering Co. Ltd. 1978. Report; [D.C. Hague, chairman]. [London], 1978. fo. 22.

— — Law.

U.K. Registry of Friendly Societies. 1978. Guide to the law relating to industrial and provident societies. London, 1978. pp. 90.

— — Scotland.

PAISLEY COMMUNITY DEVELOPMENT PROJECT. Concentrated unemployment and a local initiative; (by Mike Martin). Paisley, 1978. pp. 47.

— United States.

CHAZANOF (WILLIAM) Welch's grape juice: from corporation to co-operative. New York, [1977]. pp. 407. *bibliog.*

— — San Francisco.

PERRY (STEWART E.) Sociologist. San Francisco scavengers: dirty work and the pride of ownership. Berkeley, [1978]. pp. 236.

COPPER INDUSTRY AND TRADE.

NAVIN (THOMAS RANDALL) Copper mining and management. Tucson, [1978]. pp. 426. *bibliog.*

— United States.

NAVIN (THOMAS RANDALL) Copper mining and management. Tucson, [1978]. pp. 426. *bibliog.*

COPPERSMITHING

— Mexico.

HORCASITAS DE BARROS (MARIA LUISA) La artesania con raices prehispanicas de Santa Clara del Cobre. Mexico, Secretaria de Educacion Publica, 1973. pp. 188. *bibliog. (Sep/Setentas. 87)*

COPYRIGHT

— Russia.

LEIDEN. Rijks Universiteit. Documentation Office for East European Law. Law in Eastern Europe. No. 22(1). Copyright, defamation, and privacy in Soviet civil law: De lege lata ac ferenda; by Serge L. Levitsky. Alphen aan den Rijn, 1979. pp. 487.

— United States.

JOHNSTON (DONALD F.) Copyright handbook. New York, 1978. pp. 309.

CORDOBA (CITY)

— Industries.

CASADO RAIGON (JOSE MARIA) La politica de accion regional en España: los polos de desarrollo y especial referencia al caso de Cordoba. Sevilla, 1977. pp. 227. *bibliog.*

CORDOBA (PROVINCE, ARGENTINE REPUBLIC)

— Emigration and immigration.

CORDOBA (PROVINCE, ARGENTINE REPUBLIC). Direccion General de Estadistica, Censos e Investigaciones. 1968. Movimientos migratorios, Provincia de Cordoba, 1947-1960. Cordoba, 1968. pp. (16). *bibliog.*

— Industries.

CORDOBA (PROVINCE, ARGENTINE REPUBLIC). Direccion General de Estadistica, Censos e Investigaciones. 1962. Industrias. [Cordoba, 1962]. pp. 90. *(Publicaciones Especiales. No. 4)*

CORIGLIANO

— Economic history.

MERZARIO (RAUL) Signori e contadini di Calabria: Corigliano Calabro dal XVI al XIX secolo. Milano, 1975. pp. 142. *(Università degli Studi della Calabria. Ricerche di Storia ed Economia)*

CORN LAWS

CORN LAWS

— United Kingdom.

ELLIOT (JOHN EDMOND) Letter to the Teviotside farmer. London, [imprint], 1841. pp. 8.

METROPOLITAN ANTI-CORN LAW ASSOCIATION. Address...to the public; [signed by Francis Place]. London, [imprint], 1841. pp. 8.

CORNISH IN SOUTH AFRICA.

DICKASON (G.B.) Cornish immigrants to South Africa: the Cousin Jacks' contribution to the development of mining and commerce, 1820-1920. Cape Town, 1978. pp. 122. *bibliog.*

CORNWALL

— Nationalism.

CORNISH NATIONALIST PARTY. Program an Party Kenethlegek Kernow/ Programme of the Cornish Nationalist Party. St. Austell, [1977?]. 1 pamphlet (unpaged). *In Cornish and English.*

CORPORAL PUNISHMENT

— United Kingdom — Isle of Man.

EUROPEAN COURT OF HUMAN RIGHTS. Publications. Series A: Judgments and Decisions. [A26]. ... Tyrer case: judgment of 25 April 1978. Strasbourg, Council of Europe, 1978. pp. 32[bis]. *In English and French.*

CORPORATE DIVESTITURE

— United States.

CONFERENCE ON HORIZONTAL DIVESTITURE IN THE OIL INDUSTRY, WASHINGTON, 1977. Horizontal divestiture in the oil industry: proceedings of a conference addressing the question: should oil companies be prohibited from owning nonpetroleum energy resources?; edited by Edward J. Mitchell. Washington, D.C., [1978]. pp. 111. *(American Enterprise Institute for Public Policy Research. AEI Symposia. 78E)*

CORPORATE PLANNING.

CHANNON (DEREK F.) and JALLAND (MICHAEL) Multinational strategic planning. London, 1979. pp. 344.

— United Kingdom.

SKITT (JOHN) ed. Practical corporate planning in local government. Leighton Buzzard, 1975. pp. 260.

IBM UK SCIENTIFIC CENTRE SEMINAR ON CORPORATE PLANNING IN LOCAL GOVERNMENT, PETERLEE, 1977. Proceedings of the...seminar; edited by B.V. Wagle. Peterlee, 1978. pp. 128. *bibliog. (IBM United Kingdom Limited. UK Scientific Centre. [Technical Reports]. 0092)*

CORPORATE STATE.

The CORPORATE state: reality or myth?; a symposium. London, 1976. pp. 160. *Papers from a symposium organised by the Centre for Studies in Social Policy held in London on 24th September, 1976.*

— Italy.

ROBERTS (DAVID D.) The syndicalist tradition and Italian fascism. Chapel Hill, N.C., [1979]. pp. 410. *bibliog.*

— Peru.

STEPAN (ALFRED C.) The state and society: Peru in comparative perspective. Princeton, [1978]. pp. 348. *bibliog.*

CORPORATION LAW

— Africa.

MEISSONNIER (GEORGES) Droit des sociétés en Afrique (Afrique noire francophone, Maroc et Madagascar). Paris, 1978. pp. 863. *bibliog.*

— Canada.

IACOBUCCI (FRANK) and others. Canadian business corporations: an analysis of recent legislative developments. Agincourt, Ont., 1977. pp. 532. *bibliog.*

— — Newfoundland.

BARRY (LEO D.) Proposals for a new company law for Newfoundland: report...; supplement by James W. Ryan. St. John's, 1978. 1 vol. (various pagings).

— Europe.

MEINHARDT (PETER) Company law in Europe. 2nd ed. Farnborough, 1978. Loose-leaf. *bibliogs.*

The HARMONISATION of European company law; edited by Clive M. Schmitthoff. London, 1973. pp. 243. *(United Kingdom National Committee of Comparative Law. United Kingdom Comparative Law Series. vol. 1)*

— Netherlands.

NETHERLANDS. Commissie van Advies inzake de Uitvoering. 1970. Richtlijnen voor het beoordelen van oprichtingen en van statutenwijzigingen van naamloze vennootschappen. 's-Gravenhage, 1970. pp. 36.

— United Kingdom.

HORNBY (JAMES ANGUS) An introduction to company law. 5th ed. London, 1975. pp. 216. *bibliog.*

GOWER (LAURENCE CECIL BARTLETT) Principles of modern company law; fourth edition by L.C.B. Gower [and others]. London, 1979. pp. 770.

PENNINGTON (ROBERT ROLAND) Company law. 4th ed. London, 1979. pp. 874.

CORPORATIONS.

GALBRAITH (JOHN KENNETH) The new industrial state. 3rd ed. Boston, Mass., 1978. pp. 438.

WILLIAMS (PHILIP LAURENCE) The emergence of the theory of the firm: from Adam Smith to Alfred Marshall. London, 1978. pp. 207.

ETHICAL theory and business; edited by Tom L. Beauchamp, Norman E. Bowie. Englewood Cliffs, N.J., [1979]. pp. 642. *bibliogs.*

KAY (NEIL M.) The innovating firm: a behavioural theory of corporate R D. London, 1979. pp. 266. *bibliog.*

— Charitable contributions — United States.

KOCH (FRANK) The new corporate philanthropy: how society and business can profit. New York, [1979]. pp. 305.

— Finance.

STAPLETON (R.C.) and BURKE (C.M.) Tax systems and corporate financing policy. New York, 1978. pp. 51. *bibliog. (New York (City). University. Salomon Brothers Center for the Study of Financial Institutions. Monograph Series in Finance and Economics. 1978. No. 1)*

TRENDS in financial decision-making: planning and capital investment decisions; Cees van Dam, editor. Leiden, 1978. pp. 283. *bibliogs. (Instituut voor Bedrijfskunde. Nijenrode Studies in Business. vol. 2)*

VICKERS (DOUGLAS WILLIAM) Financial markets in the capitalist process. Philadelphia, 1978. pp. 180.

— — Bibliography.

LISTER (ROGER JEFFREY) and LISTER (EVA) compilers. Annotated bibliography of corporate finance. London, 1979. pp. 240.

— Taxation.

DRESCH (STEPHEN P.) and others. Substituting a value-added tax for the corporate income tax: first-round analysis. Cambridge, Mass., 1977. pp. 213. *bibliog. (National Bureau of Economic Research. Fiscal Studies. 15)*

STAPLETON (R.C.) and BURKE (C.M.) Tax systems and corporate financing policy. New York, 1978. pp. 51. *bibliog. (New York (City). University. Salomon Brothers Center for the Study of Financial Institutions. Monograph Series in Finance and Economics. 1978. No. 1)*

McLURE (CHARLES E.) Must corporate income be taxed twice? Washington, D.C., [1979]. pp. 262. *(Brookings Institution. Studies of Government Finance) A report of a conference sponsored by the Fund for Public Policy Research and the Brookings Institution.*

— Brazil — Taxation.

CONTADOR (CLAUDIO ROBERTO) A transferência do imposto de renda e incentivos fiscais no Brasil. Rio de Janeiro, 1976. pp. 178. *bibliog. (Brazil. Instituto de Planejamento Econômico e Social. Instituto de Pesquisas. Relatorios de Pesquisa. No. 33)*

— Canada.

NIOSI (JORGE) The economy of Canada: a study of ownership and control; translated by Penelope Williams. Montréal, [1978]. pp. 179. *bibliog.*

— Europe — Accounting.

LAFFERTY (MICHAEL) and others. 1979 Financial Times survey of 100 major European companies' reports and accounts. London, [1979]. pp. 341.

— France — Accounting.

FRANCE. Institut National de la Statistique et des Etudes Economiques. Les comptes régionaux des branches industrielles. a., 1971/1972- Paris.

— — Finance.

DELESTRE (HENRI) and MAIRESSE (JACQUES) La rentabilité des sociétés privées en France de 1956 à 1975. Paris, Institut National de la Statistique et des Etudes Economiques, 1978. pp. 154.

— Ireland (Republic).

KELLY (AIDAN) and BOURKE (PHILIP) Business enterprise: its structure in Ireland. Dublin, 1977. pp. 60.

— Japan.

SHIMIZU (RYUEI) Appraisal of organization effectiveness: referring mainly to a survey...on 260 firms in Japan. Tokyo, 1978. pp. 89.

CLARK (RODNEY C.) The Japanese company. New Haven, 1979. pp. 282. *bibliog.*

— Singapore — Finance.

GRUNDY (PHILIP GERALD) Haw Par Brothers International Limited: investigation under sections 195 and 196 of the Companies Act, 1967, as amended; interim (and second and final) report(s). [Singapore, 1976]. 2 vols.

— United Kingdom.

NORTHERN REGION STRATEGY TEAM. Changes in the corporate structure of manufacturing industry in the Northern Region; (project A.9). Newcastle-upon-Tyne, 1976. pp. 41. *(Working Papers. [No.5])*

BENWELL COMMUNITY DEVELOPMENT PROJECT. Multinationals in Tyne and Wear; (compiled by Benwell and North Tyneside Community Development Projects in conjunction with the Tyne Conference of Shop Stewards); (with Amendments). [Newcastle-upon-Tyne, 1977 in progress]. 2 vols. (vol.2 loose- leaf).

JORDAN DATAQUEST LTD. Britain's quoted industrial companies, 1977. London, [1978]. 1 vol. (various pagings).

UTTON (MICHAEL A.) Diversification and competition. Cambridge, 1979. pp. 113. *(National Institute of Economic and Social Research. Occasional Papers. 31)*

— — Accounting.

PLATT (C.J.) Survey of company reports: an analysis of current practices in presenting information. Farnborough, [1978]. pp. 125.

COST AND STANDARD OF LIVING

— — Finance.

JEFFERYS (JAMES BAVINGTON) Business organisation in Great Britain, 1856-1914. New York, 1977. pp. 476. *bibliog.*

RANKIN (ANDREW) and WHITE (THOMAS) F.C.A. New Brighton Association Football and Athletic Club Company Limited: investigation under section 165b of the Companies Act, 1948; report. London, H.M.S.O., 1977. pp. 112.

RAW (CHARLES) Slater Walker: an investigation of a financial phenomenon. London, 1977. pp. 368.

BELCHAMBERS (ANTHONY MURRAY) and MANN (JACK) The Birmingham and Midland Canal Carrying Company Limited: investigation under section 165b of the Companies Act, 1948; report. [London, Department of Trade], 1978. pp. (42).

HEILBRON (Dame ROSE) and SAMWELL (STANLEY DAVID) Kuehne and Nagel Limited: investigation under section 165(b) of the Companies Act 1948; report. London, H.M.S.O., 1978. 1 vol.(various pagings).

McCOWAN (ANTHONY JAMES DENYS) and HUMPHRIES (ALAN PETER) Electermination Limited: in liquidation: formerly known as APT Electronic Industries Ltd.: investigation under section 165(b) of the Companies Act 1948; report. London, H.M.S.O., 1978. pp. 96,xvi.

NOURSE (MARTIN CHARLES) and DUBUISSON (PETER WILLIAM GROSTETE) Land and General Developments Limited; Napet Securities Limited: investigation under sections 164 and 172 of the Companies Act, 1948; interim and final reports. [London], Department of Trade, 1978. 1 vol. (various pagings)

STANLEY (RONALD ARTHUR TERENCE) and BUTTIMER (JAMES MICHAEL) Rajawella Produce Holdings Limited: investigation under section 165b of the Companies Act 1948; report . [London], Department of Trade, 1978. 1 vol. (various pagings).

THOMAS (W.A.) The finance of British industry, 1918-1976. London, 1978. pp. 351. *bibliog.*

AULD (ROBIN ERNEST) and others. Ashbourne Investments Limited: investigation under sections 164 and 172 of the Companies Act 1948; report. London, H.M.S.O., 1979. pp. 602.

DILLON (THOMAS MICHAEL) and GARRETT (DENNIS) Burnholme and Forder Limited, in liquidation; Brayhead Limited: in liquidation: investigation under section 165b of the Companies Act 1948; report. London, H.M.S.O., 1979. 1 vol.(various pagings).

HOOPER (BRIAN MICHAEL) and BUTTIMER (JAMES MICHAEL) North Devon Railway Company Limited; Words in Action Limited: investigations under section 165b of the Companies Act, 1948; reports. London, Department of Trade, 1979. 1 vol. (various pagings).

KIDWELL (RAYMOND INCLEDON) and SAMWELL (STANLEY DAVID) Peachey Property Corporation Limited: investigation under section 165(b) of the Companies Act 1948; report. London, H.M.S.O., 1979. pp. (205).

— — Taxation.

CHOWN (JOHN F.) and HUMBLE (JOHN WILLIAM) Tax strategy for general management: economic and social issues. London, [1978]. pp. 25.

BRAMWELL (RICHARD MERVYN) and DICK (JOHN) Taxation of companies. 2nd ed. London, 1979. pp. 236.

— United States.

QUANTE (WOLFGANG) The exodus of corporate headquarters from New York city. New York, 1976. pp. 209.

POST (JAMES E.) Corporate behavior and social change. Reston, Va., [1978]. pp. 294.

— — Finance.

KOTZ (DAVID M.) Bank control of large corporations in the United States. Berkeley, [1978]. pp. 217. *bibliog.*

CORPORATIONS, AMERICAN

— America, Latin.

LEDOGAR (ROBERT J.) Hungry for profits: U.S. food and drug multinationals in Latin America. New York, [1975]. pp. 206.

CORPORATIONS, FOREIGN

— Argentine Republic.

MINSBURG (NAUM) Multinacionales en la Argentina. Buenos Aires, 1976. pp. 189.

— Canada.

MARCHAK (PATRICIA) In whose interests: an essay on multinational corporations in a Canadian context. Toronto, [1979]. pp. 317. *bibliog.*

— East (Near East).

INTERNATIONAL business in the Middle East: case studies; edited by Ashok Kapoor. Boulder, Colo., 1979. pp. 134. *bibliog.*

— Nigeria.

BIERSTEKER (THOMAS J.) Distortion or development?: contending perspectives on the multinational corporation. Cambridge, Mass., [1978]. pp. 199. *bibliog.*

— United States — Taxation.

McDANIEL (RONALD) and AULT (HUGH J.) Introduction to United States international taxation. Deventer, [1977]. pp. 183. *(Erasmus Universiteit Rotterdam. Fiscaal-Economisch Instituut. International Series. no 2)*

CORPORATIONS, JAPANESE.

YOUNG (ALEXANDER K.) The Sogo Shosha: Japan's multinational trading companies. Boulder, Colo., 1979. pp. 247. *bibliog.*

CORPORATIONS, PUBLIC

— Arab countries.

PUBLIC enterprises and development in the Arab countries: legal and managerial aspects; (papers presented at a seminar held in Kuwait, 1976). New York, [1977]. pp. 236.

— Bahamas.

BAHAMAS ELECTRICITY CORPORATION. Annual report and accounts. a., 1962/63- , with gaps (1964/65, 1966/67). Nassau.

— Kenya.

NATIONAL HOUSING CORPORATION OF KENYA. Annual report. a., 1970- Nairobi.

— Malawi.

MALAWI HOUSING CORPORATION. Annual reports and accounts. a., 1977- Blantyre.

— United Kingdom.

BRITISH SHIPBUILDERS. Report and accounts. a., 1977/78(1st)- London.

HOLLAND (PHILIP WELSBY) and FALLON (MICHAEL) The quango explosion: public bodies and ministerial patronage. London, 1978. pp. 28. *(Conservative Political Centre. [Publications]. No. 627)*

— — Finance.

The TEST discount rate and the required rate of return on investment: proceedings of a seminar held at the Civil Service College, Sunningdale, 16/17 June 1978. London, Treasury, 1979. pp. 57. *(Government Economic Service Working Papers. No. 22)*

CORRELATION (STATISTICS).

THORNDIKE (ROBERT M.) Correlational procedures for research. New York, [1978]. pp. 340. *bibliog.*

CORRUPTION (IN POLITICS).

ROSE-ACKERMAN (SUSAN) Corruption: a study in political economy. New York, [1978]. pp. 258. *bibliog.*

— Sierra Leone.

SIERRA LEONE. Percy Davies Commission of Inquiry into the Activities of the Sierra Leone Produce Marketing Board from January, 1961 to March, 1967. 1968. Report...: canteen accounts, and government statement thereon; [Percy R. Davies, commissioner]. [Freetown, 1968?]. pp. 12.

— South Africa.

SOUTH AFRICA. Commission of Inquiry into Alleged Irregularities in the former Department of Information. 1978. Report; [R.P.B. Erasmus, chairman] (R.P. 113/1978). in SOUTH AFRICA. Parliament. House of Assembly. Votes and proceedings; (with Printed annexures).

— United States.

BRAXTON (BERNARD) Sexual, racial and political faces of corruption: a view on the high cost of institutional evils. Washington, [1977]. pp. 278. *bibliog.*

BENSON (GEORGE CHARLES SUMNER) and others. Political corruption in America. Lexington, Mass., [1978]. pp. 339. *bibliog.*

— — Washington (State).

CHAMBLISS (WILLIAM J.) On the take: from petty crooks to presidents. Bloomington, 1978. pp. 269.

COSMOLOGY.

HOYLE (Sir FRED) Astronomy and cosmology: a modern course. San Francisco, [1975]. pp. 729. *bibliogs.*

COST ACCOUNTING.

DEMSKI (JOEL S.) and FELTHAM (GERALD A.) Cost determination: a conceptual approach. Ames, Iowa, 1976. pp. 272. *bibliog.*

HORNGREN (CHARLES T.) Cost accounting: a managerial emphasis. 4th ed. London, [1977]. pp. 934. *bibliogs.*

COST AND STANDARD OF LIVING

— Australia.

AUSTRALIA. Commonwealth Bureau of Census and Statistics. Household expenditure survey: bulletin[s]. a., 1974/75(1st survey)- Canberra. *In 8 pts. Bulletin 1, An outline of concepts, methodology and procedures; Bulletin 2, Preliminary results; Bulletin 3, Standard errors; Bulletin 4, Expenditure classified by income of household; Bulletin 5, Quarterly expenditure patterns; Bulletin 6, Expenditure classified by household composition; Bulletin 7, Income distribution; Bulletin 8, Expenditure classified by selected household characteristics.*

— Bahamas.

BAHAMAS. Department of Statistics. 1975. The Grand Bahama household budgetary survey and retail price index report. Nassau, [1975?]. fo.60.

— Bangladesh.

BANGLADESH. Bureau of Statistics. 1978- . A report on the household expenditure survey of Bangladesh, 1973- 74. Dacca, 1978 in progress.

COST AND STANDARD OF LIVING (Cont.)

RABBANI (ABUL KALAM MOHAMMED GHULAM) and HOSSAIN (SHAHADAT) Rural and urban consumption patterns in contemporary Bangladesh. Dacca, Bureau of Statistics, 1978. pp. 47. *bibliog.*

— France.

FRANCE. Centre d'Etude des Revenus et des Coûts. 1978. Connaissances et opinions des Français sur les prix: ce qu'ils perçoivent des évolutions de prix: analyse de résultats d'enquêtes 1970, 1972, 1974, 1976; [by] Raymond Jaulent and Jacques Antoine. [Paris], 1978. pp. 152. *(Documents. Nos. 43-44)*

— Germany, Eastern.

LIVING in security: a report from the GDR. Berlin, 1978. pp. 64. *At foot of title page: Panorama DDR.*

— India — Goa, Daman and Diu.

GOA, DAMAN AND DIU. General Statistics Department. 1967. Report on the middle class family living survey in Panaji town, 1964-65. [Panaji], 1967. pp. 85.

— — Kerala.

KERALA. Bureau of Economics and Statistics. 1976. Consumer expenditure on selected items in Kerala. Trivandrum, 1976. fo. 16.

— Japan.

JAPAN. Bureau of Statistics. 1977. Family income and expenditure survey, 1963-1975. [Tokyo], 1977. pp. 508. *In English and Japanese.*

— Morocco.

MOROCCO. Service Central des Statistiques. 1961. La consommation et les dépenses des ménages Marocains Musulmans: résultats de l'enquête 1959-60; (rédigée par [P.] Dubois). [Rabat], 1961. pp. 206.

— Russia.

ANCHISHKIN (IVAN ALEKSANDROVICH) Ekonomicheskie usloviia rosta blagosostoianiia sovetskogo naroda. Moskva, 1977. pp. 199.

— United Kingdom.

McCLEMENTS (LESLIE D.) Some experiments with the Singh-Nagar method of estimating equivalence scales. [London, Department of Health and Social Security, 1979]. pp. 27. *bibliog. (Government Economic Service Working Papers. No. 20)*

COST EFFECTIVENESS.

MISHAN (EDWARD JOSHUA) Cost-benefit analysis: an informal introduction. 2nd ed. London, 1975 repr. 1979. pp. 454.

SELF (PETER J.O.) Econocrats and the policy process: the politics and philosophy of cost-benefit analysis. London, 1975. pp. 212. *bibliog.*

SQUIRE (LYN) and TAK (HERMAN G. VAN DER) Economic analysis of projects...; published for the World Bank. Baltimore, [1975]. pp. 153. *bibliog. (International Bank for Reconstruction and Development. World Bank Research Publications)*

U.K. Ministry of Overseas Development. 1977. A guide to the economic appraisal of projects in developing countries. rev. ed. London, 1977. pp. 160. *bibliog.*

ANDERSON (LEE G.) and SETTLE (RUSSELL F.) Benefit-cost analysis: a practical guide. Lexington, Mass., 1978. pp. 140. *bibliog.*

ASSOCIATION OF METROPOLITAN AUTHORITIES. Value for money: local authorities and cost effectiveness. London, [1978]. pp. 19.

The VALUATION of social cost; edited by David W. Pearce. London, 1978. pp. 197. *bibliogs.*

ABELSON (PETER) Cost benefit analysis and environmental problems. Farnborough, [1979]. pp. 202. *bibliogs.*

EICHNER (ALFRED S.) and BRECHER (CHARLES) Controlling social expenditures: the search for output measures. Montclair, 1979. pp. 210. *bibliogs.*

SENECA (JOSEPH J.) and TAUSSIG (MICHAEL K.) Environmental economics. 2nd ed. Englewood Cliffs, N.J., [1979]. pp. 379. *bibliogs.*

COSTA RICA

— Population.

FERNANDEZ ARIAS (MARIO E.) and SCHMIDT DE ROJAS (ANABELLE) La poblacion de Costa Rica. [San Jose, 1976]. pp. 199. *(Committee for International Coordination of National Research in Demography. C.I.C.R.E.D. Series)*

COSTS, INDUSTRIAL.

HORNGREN (CHARLES T.) Cost accounting: a managerial emphasis. 4th ed. London, [1977]. pp. 934. *bibliogs.*

— United States.

WEIDENBAUM (MURRAY L.) and DE FINA (ROBERT) The cost of federal regulation of economic activity. Washington, 1978. pp. 33. *(American Enterprise Institute for Public Policy Research. Reprints. No. 88)*

COTTAGE INDUSTRIES

— India.

SEMINAR ON FINANCING OF SMALL-SCALE INDUSTRIES IN INDIA, HYDERABAD, 1959. Report of proceedings ([and] background papers). Bombay, [1960?]. 2 vols.

COTTON GROWING

— Malawi.

CHILIVUMBO (ALIFEYO) Chikwawa Cotton Development Project: a sociological study. [Ngabu, Chikwawa Cotton Development Project, 1970?]. pp. 67.

— United States.

CHRISTY (DAVID) Cotton is king: or the culture of cotton and its relation to agriculture, manufactures and commerce. 2nd ed. Clifton, N. J., 1975. pp. 298. *Reprint of work originally published New York, 1856.*

COTTON MANUFACTURE.

JEREMY (DAVID JOHN) The transmission of cotton and woollen manufacturing technologies between Britain and the U.S.A. from 1790 to the 1830s. 1978. fo. 344. *bibliog. Typescript. Ph.D. (London) thesis: unpublished. This thesis is the property of London University and may not be removed from the Library.*

— China.

CHAO (KANG) The development of cotton textile production in China. Cambridge, Mass., 1977. pp. 151. *bibliog. (Harvard University. East Asian Research Center. Harvard East Asian Monographs. 74)*

— Italy.

BALLIANO (PIERA) and others. Studio sull'evoluzione della concentrazione nell'industria cotoniera Italiana, etc. [Brussels], Comunità Europee, 1975. pp. 149.

— United Kingdom.

FARNIE (DOUGLAS ANTONY) The English cotton industry and the world market, 1815-1896. Oxford, 1979. pp. 399. *bibliog.*

— United States.

BATCHELDER (SAMUEL) Introduction and early progress of the cotton manufacture in the United States. Clifton, N.J., 1972. pp. 108. *Reprint of work originally pblished in Boston, Mass., 1863.*

STETTLER (HENRY LOUIS) Growth and fluctuations in the ante-bellum textile industry. New York, 1977. pp. 283. *bibliog.*

COTTON TRADE

— India — Maharashtra.

MAHARASHTRA. Study Group on Forward Markets in Cotton. 1967. Report. [Bombay], 1966 [or rather 1967]. pp. 38, 19.

— United Kingdom.

TATTERSALL'S TRADE REVIEW OF THE COTTON AND ALLIED TEXTILE INDUSTRIES: annual review. a., 1970- Manchester. *Earlier annual reviews bound in with TATTERSALL'S TRADE REVIEW OF THE COTTON AND ALLIED INDUSTRIES.*

FARNIE (DOUGLAS ANTONY) The English cotton industry and the world market, 1815-1896. Oxford, 1979. pp. 399. *bibliog.*

— United States.

BATCHELDER (SAMUEL) Introduction and early progress of the cotton manufacture in the United States. Clifton, N.J., 1972. pp. 108. *Reprint of work originally published in Boston, Mass., 1863.*

WRIGHT (GAVIN) The political economy of the cotton South: households, markets, and wealth in the nineteenth century. New York, [1978]. pp. 205. *bibliog.*

COUNCIL FOR MUTUAL ECONOMIC ASSISTANCE.

COUNCIL FOR MUTUAL ECONOMIC ASSISTANCE. 1976. Charter of the Council for Mutual Economic Assistance [as amended in 1974]. Moscow, 1976. pp. 24.

COUNCIL FOR MUTUAL ECONOMIC ASSISTANCE. 1977. Communique on the 79th meeting of the Executive Committee of the Council for Mutual Economic Assistance. Moscow, 1977. pp. 5.

COUNCIL FOR MUTUAL ECONOMIC ASSISTANCE. 1977. Co-operation of CMEA member countries in the field of forecasting. Moscow, 1977. pp. 15.

COUNCIL FOR MUTUAL ECONOMIC ASSISTANCE. 1977. Information on cooperation of state labour bodies of the CMEA member countries in 1976-1977. Moscow, 1977. pp. 6.

COUNCIL FOR MUTUAL ECONOMIC ASSISTANCE. 1977. Information on cooperation of the CMEA member countries in planning. Moscow, 1977. pp. 13.

COUNCIL FOR MUTUAL ECONOMIC ASSISTANCE. 1977. Information on the activities of the CMEA in the elaboration of long-term specific programmes of cooperation of the CMEA member countries. Moscow, 1977. pp. 12.

COUNCIL FOR MUTUAL ECONOMIC ASSISTANCE. 1977. Information on the CMEA activities in developing co-operation with the United Nations Economic Commission for Europe in 1976-1977. Moscow, 1977. pp. 13.

COUNCIL FOR MUTUAL ECONOMIC ASSISTANCE. 1977. Information on the CMEA activities on co-operation in manufacturing equipment for protecting the environment against pollution: prepared...for the ECE Ad Hoc Meeting on Production of Engineering Equipment for Preventing Pollution...Geneva, February 1-2, 1977. Moscow, 1977. pp. 9.

The MULTILATERAL economic co-operation of socialist states: a collection of documents. Moscow, 1977. pp. 588.

BANKING and sources of finance in COMECON; edited by A.H. Hermann. London, [1978?]. pp. 137.

The EEC and Eastern Europe; (editors: Avi Shlaim and G. N. Yannopoulos). Cambridge, 1978. pp. 251.

LASCELLES (DAVID) Comecon mid-plan report. London, [1978]. pp. 303.

BYSTRICKÝ (RUDOLF) Le droit de l'intégration économique socialiste. Genève, 1979. pp. 471. *bibliog. (Geneva. Graduate Institute of International Studies. Collection de Droit International. 6)*

COUNCILS AND SYNODS.

CROWDER (C.M.D.) compiler. Unity, heresy and reform, 1378-1460: the conciliar response to the Great Schism. London, 1977. pp. 212. *bibliog.*

COUNSELLING.

FRIEND (JEANNETTE G.) and HAGGARD (ERNEST ALEXANDER) Work adjustment in relation to family background: a conceptual basis for counseling; a report of an investigation sponsored by the Family Society of Greater Boston. Stanford, 1948. pp. 150. *bibliog.* (American Psychological Association. Applied Psychology Monographs. No. 16)

LEWIS (JUDITH A.) and LEWIS (MICHAEL D.) Community counseling: a human services approach. New York, [1977]. pp. 382. *bibliogs.*

STUDENTS in need: essays in memory of Nicolas Malleson. Guildford, 1978. pp. 230. *bibliogs.* (Society for Research into Higher Education. Occasional Papers)

COUNTER-REFORMATION.

O'CONNELL (MARVIN R.) The Counter Reformation, 1560-1610. New York, 1974. pp. 390. *bibliog.*

COUNTERFACTUALS (LOGIC).

LEWIS (DAVID KELLOGG) Counterfactuals. Oxford, 1973. pp. 150.

COUNTERFEITS AND COUNTERFEITING

— Germany.

HOETTL (WILHELM) Hitler's paper weapon;...translated from the German by Basil Creighton. London, 1955. pp. 187.

COUNTERPART FUNDS.

EXCHANGE of expertise: the counterpart system in the new international order; edited by Irving J. Spitzberg, Jr. Boulder, Colo., [1978]. pp. 257. *bibliogs.*

COUNTRY HOMES

— United Kingdom.

GIROUARD (MARK) Life in the English country house: a social and architectural history. New Haven, 1978. pp. 344.

— — Wales.

BOLLOM (CHRIS) Attitudes and second homes in rural Wales. Cardiff, 1978. pp. 126. (Wales. University. Board of Celtic Studies. Social Science Monographs. No. 3)

COURT LINE LIMITED.

COMYN (JAMES P.) and others. Court Line Limited: investigation under section 165b of the Companies Act 1948: final report. London, H.M.S.O., 1978. pp. 188, 167.

COURT OF JUSTICE OF THE EUROPEAN COMMUNITIES.

EUROPEAN COMMUNITIES. Court of Justice. Judicial and Academic Conference, Luxembourg, 1976. Judicial and Academic Conference, 27-28 September 1976: reports. Luxembourg, 1976. 1 vol. (various pagings). *bibliog.*

EUROPEAN COMMUNITIES. Court of Justice. Documentation Branch. Synopsis of case-law: the EEC convention of 27 September 1968 on jurisdiction and the enforcement of judgments in civil and commercial matters. a., 1977(no.1)- Luxembourg.

INFORMATION ON THE COURT OF JUSTICE OF THE EUROPEAN COMMUNITIES; [pd. by] Information Office, Court of Justice of the European Communities. q., 1977(4th q.)- Luxembourg.

— Bibliography.

BULLETIN BIBLIOGRAPHIQUE DE JURISPRUDENCE COMMUNAUTAIRE; [pd. by] Court of Justice, European Communities. a., 1977(no. 1)- Luxembourg. *Supersedes EUROPEAN COMMUNITIES. Court of Justice. 1965-. Bibliographie de jurisprudence européenne.*

COURT RECORDS

— United Kingdom.

U.K. Public Record Office. Calendar of Assize Records. Essex indictments, Elizabeth I; edited by J.S. Cockburn. London, 1978. pp. 761.

COURT RULES

— United Kingdom.

WILLIAMS (EMLYN) A.B.C. guide to the practice of the Supreme Court. 39th ed. London, 1978. pp. 200.

— — Ireland, Northern.

IRELAND, NORTHERN. Supreme Court. 1979. Rules of the Supreme Court, Northern Ireland, 1979. [Belfast, 1979]. 1 vol. (loose-leaf). *Issued as Statutory Rules of Northern Ireland.*

COURTS

— Russia — White Russia.

MARTINOVICH (IZABELLA IVANOVNA) and PLIUTA (EFIM FEDOTOVICH) Sud i pravosudie v BSSR. Minsk, 1977. pp. 166.

— United Kingdom.

BLATCHER (MARJORIE) The Court of King's Bench, 1450-1550: a study in self-help. London, 1978. pp. 181. *bibliog.* (London. University. Institute of Advanced Legal Studies. University of London Legal Series. 12)

— United States.

BALL (HOWARD) Judicial craftsmanship or fiat?: direct overturn by the United States Supreme Court. Westport, Conn., 1978. pp. 160. *bibliog.*

BERKSON (LARRY CHARLES) The Supreme Court and its publics: the communication of policy decisions. Lexington, Mass., 1978. pp. 145.

MILLER (ARTHUR SELWYN) The Supreme Court: myth and reality. Westport, Conn., 1978. pp. 388. *bibliog.*

SEMONCHE (JOHN E.) Charting the future: the Supreme Court responds to a changing society, 1890-1920. Westport, Conn., 1978. pp. 470. *bibliog.*

— — Florida.

HAYS (STEVEN W.) Court reform: ideal or illusion? Lexington, Mass., [1978]. pp. 151.

— — Kentucky.

TACHAU (MARY K. BONSTEEL) Federal courts in the early Republic: Kentucky, 1789-1816. Princeton, N.J., [1978]. pp. 234. *bibliog.*

COVENANTERS.

MAKEY (WALTER H.) The church of the Covenant, 1637-1651: revolution and social change in Scotland. Edinburgh, [1979]. pp. 216. *bibliog.*

COVENT GARDEN.

RICHARDSON (JOHN) Chairman of the Camden History Society. Covent Garden. New Barnet, 1979. pp. 112.

CREATIVE ABILITY.

CREATIVITY: selected readings; edited by P.E. Vernon. Harmondsworth, 1970. pp. 400. *bibliogs.*

WESSON (ROBERT GALE) State systems: international pluralism, politics, and culture. New York, [1978]. pp. 296. *bibliog.*

CREDIT

— Communist countries.

LIUBSKII (MIKHAIL SERGEEVICH) and others. Valiutnye i kreditnye otnosheniia stran SEV. Moskva, 1978. pp. 160.

— European Economic Community countries.

BANKER RESEARCH UNIT. Banking and sources of finance in the European Community; edited by Philip Thorn [and] Jean M. Lack. London, 1977. pp. 313.

— India.

SEMINAR ON FINANCING OF SMALL-SCALE INDUSTRIES IN INDIA, HYDERABAD, 1959. Report of proceedings ([and] background papers). Bombay, [1960?]. 2 vols.

INDIA. Expert Committee on Consumption Credit. 1976. Report; [B. Sivaraman, chairman]. [Delhi], 1976. pp. 32.

INDIA. Banking Laws Committee. 1978. Report on personal property security law; [P.V. Rajamannar, chairman]. [Delhi, 1978]. pp. 407,2.

INDIA. Banking Laws Committee. 1978. Report on real property security law; [P.V. Rajamannar, chairman]. [Delhi, 1978]. pp. 356,4.

— Pakistan.

PAKISTAN. Credit Enquiry Commission. 1960. Report; [Abdul Qadir, chairman]. Karachi, 1960. pp. 218.

— Peru.

PERU. Direccion General de Asuntos Financieros. 1976. La actividad del Banco Industrial del Peru: el fomento del desarrollo industrial en provincias, 1970-1974. Lima, 1976. 3 vols. (in 1).

— Russia.

ROGOVA (OL'GA LEONIDOVNA) Denezhnoe obrashchenie i kratkosrochnyi kredit: issledovanie sviazei i proportsii. Moskva, 1978. pp. 158.

ZAIDENVARG (VIKTOR ALEKSANDROVICH) and GERASIMENKO (GALINA PETROVNA) Pokazateli effektivnosti kratkosrochnogo kredita. Moskva, 1978. pp. 96.

— United States.

NORRIS (JAMES D.) R.G. Dun Co. 1841-1900: the development of credit-reporting in the nineteenth century. Westport, Conn., 1978. pp. 206. *bibliog.*

REDISTRIBUTION through the financial system: the grants economics of money and credit; [edited by] Kenneth E. Boulding and Thomas Frederick Wilson. New York, [1978]. pp. 301. *bibliogs.*

CREOLE DIALECTS.

PIDGINS and creoles: current trends and prospects; [papers presented at the pidgin and creole interest group session which met at the Georgetown University Round Table on Languages and Linguistics in 1972]; edited by David DeCamp [and] Ian F. Hancock. Washington, [1974]. pp. 137. *bibliogs.*

PIDGIN and creole linguistics; edited by Albert Valdman. Bloomington, [1977]. pp. 399. *bibliogs.*

EDWARDS (V.K.) The West Indian language issue in British schools: challenges and responses. London, 1979. pp. 168. *bibliog.*

CRIME AND AGE.

JUSTICE and older Americans; [edited by] Marlene A. Young Rifai. Lexington, Mass., [1977]. pp. 201.

CRIME AND CRIMINALS.

CRIME and delinquency: a reader; edited by Carl A. Bersani. New York, [1970]. pp. 575. *bibliogs.*

CRIME AND CRIMINALS.(Cont.)

MANNHEIM (HERMANN) Group problems in crime and punishment, and other studies in criminology and criminal law. 2nd ed. Montclair, N.J., 1971. pp. 328.

VAN DEN HAAG (ERNEST) Punishing criminals: concerning a very old and painful question. New York, [1975]. pp. 283. *bibliog.*

ECONOMIC models of criminal behavior; [edited by] J.M. Heineke. Amsterdam, 1978. pp. 391. *bibliog.*

BOTTOMLEY (A. KEITH) Criminology in focus: past trends and future prospects. Oxford, 1979. pp. 181.

DEVIANT interpretations; edited by David Downes and Paul Rock. Oxford, 1979. pp. 176. *bibliog.*

GIBBONS (DON C.) The criminological enterprise: theories and perspectives. Englewood Cliffs, [1979]. pp. 226.

— Canada.

CRIME and delinquency in Canada; edited by Edmund W. Vaz and Abdul Q. Lodhi. Scarborough, Ont., [1979]. pp. 390.

— Europe.

WEISSER (MICHAEL R.) Crime and punishment in early modern Europe. Hassocks, 1979. pp. 193. *bibliog.*

— Fiji.

FIJI. Royal Commission of Inquiry into Crime. 1976. Report; [Clifford H. Grant, commissioner]. Suva, 1976. pp. 41. *bibliog.*

— France.

REPONSES à la violence...Recherches sur l'urbanisation, l'habitat et la violence. Paris, [1977] pp. 424. *bibliog.* *(France. Comité d'Etudes sur la Violence, la Criminalité et la Délinquance. Annexes. 3)*

REPONSES à la violence...Recherches sur les aspects péenaux et pénitentiaires. Paris, [1977]. pp. 202. *bibliog.* *(France. Comité d'Etudes sur la Violence, la Criminalité et la Délinquance. Annexes. 6)*

— Switzerland — Basel-Stadt (Canton).

SUTTER (WERNER A.) Die Kriminalität im Kanton Basel-Stadt: Querschnittsuntersuchung zur Soziologie der Delinquenz. Basel, 1970. pp. 139. *bibliog.* *(Basel-Stadt (Canton). Statistisches Amt. Mitteilungen. Nr. 81)*

— United Kingdom.

TOBIAS (JOHN JACOB) Crime and police in England, 1700-1900. London, 1979. pp. 194.

— — Identification.

U.K. Home Office. Circulars. No. 109/1978. Identification parades and the use of photographs for identification. London, 1978. pp. 23.

— United States.

QUINNEY (RICHARD) Class, state and crime: on the theory and practice of criminal justice. New York, 1977 repr. 1978. pp. 179.

HASKELL (MARTIN R.) and YABLONSKY (LEWIS) Crime and delinquency. Chicago, [1978]. pp. 780.

GIBBONS (DON C.) The criminological enterprise: theories and perspectives. Englewood Cliffs, [1979]. pp. 226.

— — Washington (State).

CHAMBLISS (WILLIAM J.) On the take: from petty crooks to presidents. Bloomington, 1978. pp. 269.

CRIME FORECASTING

— United States — Mathematical models.

FOX (JAMES ALAN) Forecasting crime data: an econometric analysis. Lexington, Mass., [1978]. pp. 140. *bibliog.*

CRIME PREVENTION.

A POLICY approach to planning in social defence. (ST/SOA/114). New York, United Nations, 1972. pp. 306.

VAN DEN HAAG (ERNEST) Punishing criminals: concerning a very old and painful question. New York, [1975]. pp. 283. *bibliog.*

— Russia.

TEORETICHESKIE osnovy preduprezhdeniia prestupnosti. Moskva, 1977. pp. 255.

— United Kingdom — Citizen participation.

CRIME in public view; by P.Mayhew [and others]; a Home Office Research Unit report. London, 1979. pp. 33. *bibliog.* *(U.K. Home Office. Home Office Research Studies. No. 49)*

CROFT (IVOR JOHN) Crime and the community; a Home Office Research Unit report. London, 1979. pp. 12. *(U.K. Home Office. Home Office Research Studies..No. 50)*

— United States.

SORRENTINO (ANTHONY) Organizing against crime: redeveloping the neighborhood. New York, [1977]. pp. 272. *bibliog.*

CRIMEAN WAR, 1853-1856

— Causes.

MONNIER (LUC) Etude sur les origines de la Guerre de Crimée. Genève, 1977. pp. 146.

CRIMINAL BEHAVIOUR, PREDICTION OF.

JOHNSON (RICHARD E.) Juvenile delinquency and its origins: an integrated theoretical approach. Cambridge, 1979. pp. 182. *bibliog.*

CRIMINAL COURTS

— United Kingdom.

JACKSON (STANLEY) The Old Bailey. London, 1978. pp. 234. *bibliog.*

— United States.

LEVIN (MARTIN A.) Urban politics and the criminal courts. Chicago, 1977. pp. 332.

CRIMINAL JUSTICE, ADMINISTRATION OF.

A POLICY approach to planning in social defence. (ST/SOA/114). New York, United Nations, 1972. pp. 306.

CRELINSTEN (RONALD D.) and others. Terrorism and criminal justice: an international perspective. Lexington, Mass., [1978]. pp. 131. *Based on a conference held in 1976 in Rochester, Michigan.*

— United States.

JUSTICE and older Americans; [edited by] Marlene A. Young Rifai. Lexington, Mass., [1977]. pp. 201.

QUINNEY (RICHARD) Class, state and crime: on the theory and practice of criminal justice. New York, 1977 repr. 1978. pp. 179.

ROSSUM (RALPH A.) The politics of the criminal justice system: an organizational analysis. New York, [1978]. pp. 287. *bibliogs.*

GORECKI (JAN) A theory of criminal justice. New York, 1979. pp. 185. *bibliog.*

REIMAN (JEFFREY H.) The rich get richer and the poor get prison: ideology, class, and criminal justice. New York, [1979]. pp. 214.

CRIMINAL LAW.

GROSS (HYMAN) A theory of criminal justice. New York, 1979. pp. 521. *bibliog.*

— France.

FRANCE. Commission de Révision du Code Pénal. 1978. Avant-projet définitif de code pénal. Livre 1. Dispositions générales. Paris, 1978. pp. 171.

— United Kingdom.

WILLIAMS (GLANVILLE LLEWELLYN) Textbook of criminal law. London, 1978. pp. 973.

— — Scotland.

GORDON (GERALD H.) The criminal law of Scotland. 2nd ed. Edinburgh, 1978. pp. 1174.

— United States.

ALIX (ERNEST KAHLAR) Ransom kidnapping in America, 1874-1974: the creation of a capital crime. Carbondale, [1978]. pp. 222. *bibliog.*

WICE (PAUL B.) Criminal lawyers: an endangered species. Beverly Hills, 1978. pp. 233. *bibliog.*

CRIMINAL LIABILITY

— United Kingdom.

KENNY (ANTHONY JOHN PATRICK) Freewill and responsibility. London, 1978. pp. 101. *(Trent University. Ryle Lectures. 1976).*

CRIMINAL PROCEDURE

— Italy.

GREVI (VITTORIO) Libertà personale dell'imputato e costituzione. [Milan, 1976]. pp. 400.

MAGISTRATURA DEMOCRATICA. Il codice Bonifacio: il progetto di riforma del codice di procedura penale. Torino, 1978. pp. 221.

— Russia.

KOMMENTARII sudebnoi praktiki za 1975 god. Moskva, 1976. pp. 223.

KOMMENTARII sudebnoi praktiki za 1976 god. Moskva, 1977. pp. 134.

— United Kingdom.

JUSTICES' CLERKS SOCIETY. Evidence to the Royal Commission on Criminal Procedure. Coventry, 1978. pp. 38.

U.K. Commission for Racial Equality. 1978. Evidence and recommendations to the Royal Commission on Criminal Procedure. [London], 1978. pp. 48.

U.K. [Home Office]. Metropolitan Police Force. 1978. The Royal Commission on Criminal Procedure:...written evidence of the Commissioner of Police of the Metropolis. London, 1978. 2 pts.

U.K. Home Office. 1979. Evidence to the Royal Commission on Criminal Procedure: memorandum no. 7: preparation for trial and disclosure of evidence. London, 1979. pp. 50.

CRIMINAL STATISTICS

— Chile.

CHILE. Instituto Nacional de Estadisticas. Justicia y policia. a., 1967, 1971, 1974- Santiago.

— United Kingdom.

U.K. Home Office. Statistical bulletin. irreg., Mr 15 1979 (no.1)- Surbiton.

CRISES.

HABERMAS (JUERGEN) Legitimation crisis. London, 1976. pp. 166. *bibliog.*

NOVOSELOV (SERGEI PAVLOVICH) Obostrenie ekonomichskikh i sotsial'no-politicheskikh protivorechii kapitalizma. Moskva, 1977. pp. 199.

WATERS (JOSEPH PAUL) Technological acceleration and the Great Depression. New York, 1977. pp. 250. *bibliog.*

ECKSTEIN (OTTO) The great recession, with a postscript on stagflation. Amsterdam, 1978. pp. 213.

HEILBRONER (ROBERT LOUIS) Beyond boom and crash. New York, [1978]. pp. 111.

KINDLEBERGER (CHARLES POOR) Manias, panics, and crashes: a history of financial crises. London, 1978. pp. 271.

MANDEL (ERNEST) The second slump: a marxist analysis of recession in the seventies; translated by Jon Rothschild. London, 1978. pp. 212.

ROTHSTEIN (ARTHUR) The depression years as photographed. New York, [1978]. pp. 119.

WEINTRAUB (SIDNEY) b. 1914. Capitalism's inflation and unemployment crisis: beyond monetarism and Keynesianism. Reading, Mass., [1978]. pp. 242.

AGLIETTA (MICHEL) A theory of capitalist regulation: the U.S. experience; translated by David Fernbach. London, 1979. pp. 390.

BONNIFIELD (PAUL) The dust bowl: men, dirt, and depression. Albuquerque, [1979]. pp. 232. *bibliog.*

CRISIS INTERVENTION (PSYCHIATRY).

GOLAN (NAOMI) Treatment in crisis situations. New York, [1978]. pp. 266. *bibliog.*

CRITICISM.

BLEICH (DAVID) Subjective criticism. Baltimore, Md., [1978]. pp. 309.

CRITICISM (PHILOSOPHY).

McCARTHY (THOMAS A.) The critical theory of Jürgen Habermas. Cambridge, Mass., [1978]. pp. 466. *bibliog.*

CROATIA

— **Nationalism.**

CLISSOLD (STEPHEN) Croat separatism: nationalism, dissidence and terrorism. London, 1979. pp. 21. (*Institute for the Study of Conflict. Conflict Studies. No.103*)

— **Politics and government.**

CLISSOLD (STEPHEN) Croat separatism: nationalism, dissidence and terrorism. London, 1979. pp. 21. (*Institute for the Study of Conflict. Conflict Studies. No.103*)

CROFT (Sir HERBERT).

HAM (R.E.) The county and the Kingdom: Sir Herbert Croft and the Elizabethan state. Washington, D.C., [1977]. pp. 304.

CROFTERS

— **Norway.**

COULL (JAMES R.) Crofter-fishermen in Norway and Scotland. Aberdeen, 1971. pp. 15. *bibliog.* (*Aberdeen. University. Department of Geography. O'Dell Memorial Monographs. No.2*)

— **United Kingdom — Scotland.**

COULL (JAMES R.) Crofter-fishermen in Norway and Scotland. Aberdeen, 1971. pp. 15. *bibliog.* (*Aberdeen. University. Department of Geography. O'Dell Memorial Monographs. No.2*)

CROMARTY PETROLEUM COMPANY.

ROSIE (GEORGE) The Ludwig initiative: a cautionary tale of North Sea oil. Edinburgh, 1978. pp. 147.

CROP YIELDS.

PALMER (INGRID) The new rice in Indonesia. (UNRISD Reports. No. 77.1) (UNRISD/76/C.44). Geneva, United Nations Research Institute for Social Development, 1976. pp. 198. (*Studies on the Green Revolution. No. 15.]*)

CROWDING STRESS.

BAUM (ANDREW) and VALINS (STUART) Architecture and social behavior: psychological studies of social density. Hillsdale, N.J., 1977. pp. 112. *bibliog.*

HUMAN response to crowding; edited by Andrew Baum and Yakov M. Epstein. Hillsdale, N.J., 1978. pp. 418. *bibliogs.*

INSEL (PAUL M.) and LINDGREN (HENRY CLAY) Too close for comfort: the psychology of crowding. Englewood Cliffs, [1978]. pp. 180. *bibliog.*

CROWDS.

HOERDER (DIRK) Crowd action in revolutionary Massachusetts, 1765-1780. New York, [1977]. pp. 394.

CRUSADES.

MAYER (HANS EBERHARD) The crusades;...translated by John Gillingham. Oxford, 1972 repr. 1978. pp. 339.

CRYSTAL CITY

— **Race relations.**

HIRSCH (HERBERT) and GUTIERREZ (ARMANDO) Learning to be militant: ethnic identity and the development of political militance in a Chicano community. San Francisco, 1977. pp. 146.

CUBA

— **Description and travel.**

BREMER (FREDRIKA) The homes of the new world: impressions of America;... translated by Mary Howitt. New York, 1853; New York, 1968. 2 vols. *Facsimile reprint.*

— **Economic conditions.**

CUBA: the second decade; edited by John Griffiths and Peter Griffiths. London, 1979. pp. 268. *bibliog.*

— **Foreign relations — Russia.**

LEVESQUE (JACQUES) The USSR and the Cuban revolution: Soviet ideological and strategical perspectives 1959-77; translated from the French by Deanna Drendel Leboeuf. New York, [1978]. pp. 215. *bibliog.*

— — **Venezuela.**

VENEZUELA. Oficina Central de Informacion. 1967. Six years of aggression. [Caracas, 1967]. pp. 95.

— **History — 1895- .**

DOMINGUEZ (JORGE I.) Cuba: order and revolution. Cambridge, Mass., 1978. pp. 683. *bibliog.*

— — **1933, Revolution.**

BENJAMIN (JULES ROBERT) The United States and Cuba: hegemony and dependent development, 1880-1934. Pittsburgh, [1977]. pp. 266. *bibliog.*

— — **1959- .**

LEVESQUE (JACQUES) The USSR and the Cuban revolution: Soviet ideological and strategical perspectives 1959-77; translated from the French by Deanna Drendel Leboeuf. New York, [1978]. pp. 215. *bibliog.*

— **Politics and government.**

DOMINGUEZ (JORGE I.) Cuba: order and revolution. Cambridge, Mass., 1978. pp. 683. *bibliog.*

HANSEN (JOSEPH) Marxist. Dynamics of the Cuban revolution: the Trotskyist view. New York, [1978]. pp. 393.

CUBA: the second decade; edited by John Griffiths and Peter Griffiths. London, 1979. pp. 268. *bibliog.*

— **Relations (general) with the United States.**

BENJAMIN (JULES ROBERT) The United States and Cuba: hegemony and dependent development, 1880-1934. Pittsburgh, [1977]. pp. 266. *bibliog.*

— **Social conditions.**

CUBA: the second decade; edited by John Griffiths and Peter Griffiths. London, 1979. pp. 268. *bibliog.*

— **Social life and customs.**

BREMER (FREDRIKA) The homes of the new world: impressions of America;... translated by Mary Howitt. New York, 1853; New York, 1968. 2 vols. *Facsimile reprint.*

CUESMES

— **Social conditions.**

GAUPIN (MICHEL) Projet de plan d'animation sociale pour une commune fusionnée: Cuesmes;...sous la direction de Pierre Mory. Bruxelles, 1972. pp. 78. *bibliog.* (*Belgium. Direction Générale des Arts et des Lettres. Documentation et Enquêtes. No.5*)

CULLODEN, BATTLE OF, 1746.

PREBBLE (JOHN) Culloden. Harmondsworth, 1967 repr. 1978. pp. 360. *bibliog.*

CULTS

WALLIS (ROY) Salvation and protest: studies of social and religious movements. New York, 1979. pp. 231.

— **Africa.**

The NEW religions of Africa; edited by Bennetta Jules-Rosette. Norwood, N.J., [1979]. pp. 248. *bibliog.*

— **United States.**

SIMPSON (GEORGE EATON) Black religions in the New World. New York, 1978. pp. 415. *bibliog.*

ELLWOOD (ROBERT S.) Alternative altars: unconventional and eastern spirituality in America. Chicago, [1979]. pp. 192.

CULTURAL PROPERTY, PROTECTION OF.

EUROPEAN COMMUNITIES. Commission. 1978. Community action in the cultural sector:...communication to the Council, sent on 22 November 1977. [Brussels, 1978]. pp. 26. (*Bulletin of the European Communities. Supplements. [1977/6]*)

CULTURE.

EUROPEAN COMMUNITIES. Commission. 1978. Community action in the cultural sector:...communication to the Council, sent on 22 November 1977. [Brussels, 1978]. pp. 26. (*Bulletin of the European Communities. Supplements. [1977/6]*)

KRAUS (WOLFGANG) Kultur und Macht: die Verwandlung der Wünsche. München, 1978. pp. 156. *bibliog.*

JOHNSON (LESLEY) The cultural critics: from Matthew Arnold to Raymond Williams. London, 1979. pp. 235. *bibliog.*

MERQUIOR (JOSE GUILHERME) The veil and the mask: essays on culture and ideology. London, 1979. pp. 161. *bibliog.*

CULTURE CONFLICT.

MEAD (MARGARET) Culture and commitment: the new relationships between the generations in the 1970s. [rev. ed.] New York, 1978. pp. 178. *bibliog.*

CULTUS.

See CULTS.

CUMBRIA

CUMBRIA
— Social policy.

COMMUNITY participation and poverty: the final report of Cumbria C[ommunity] D[evelopment] P[roject]; [by] Hu Butcher [and others]. [York], 1979. pp. 265. *bibliog.* *(Papers in Community Studies. No. 22)*

CUNNINGHAME-GRAHAM (ROBERT BONTINE).

WATTS (CEDRIC THOMAS) and DAVIES (LAURENCE) 1943- . Cunninghame Graham: a critical biography. Cambridge, 1979. pp. 333. *bibliog.*

CURAÇAO
— Economic conditions.

CURAÇAO. Eilandsdienst Economische Zaken en Welvaartszorg. 1962. Guide for the establishment of enterprises in Curaçao. Curaçao, 1962. pp. 69.

CUSTODY OF CHILDREN.

WYLAND (FRANCIE) Motherhood, lesbianism and child custody. Toronto, 1977. pp. 34.

CUSTOMARY LAW.

The DISPUTING process: law in ten societies; Laura Nader and Harry F. Todd Jr., editors. New York, 1978. pp. 372. *bibliog.*

CUSTOMS UNIONS.

EEC customs union: what's the form?; proceedings of a joint conference held at the Café Royal, London, 28 September 1977 by the Confederation of British Industry and the British Shippers Council. London, 1977. pp. 76.

CYBERNETICS.

ROBINSON (ENDERS ANTHONY) Random wavelets and cybernetic systems. London, 1962. pp. 125. *bibliog.*

STEINBRUNER (JOHN D.) The cybernetic theory of decision: new dimensions of political analysis. Princeton, N.J. [1974]. pp. 366. *bibliog.*

COMMUNICATION and control in society; edited by Klaus Krippendorff. New York, [1979]. pp. 529. *bibliogs.*

CYPRUS.

CYPRUS. Public Information Office. 1978. Cyprus in brief. Nicosia, [1978]. pp. 112.

— Constitutional history.

TORNARITES (KRITON G.) Cyprus and its constitutional and other legal problems. Nicosia, 1977. pp. 142.

— Economic conditions.

CYPRUS. Audit Office. Audit review. s-a., My 1978 (v. 1, no. 1)- Nicosia.

— Economic policy.

CYPRUS. Planning Bureau. 1977. Second emergency economic action plan, 1977-1978. Nicosia, [1977?]. pp. 196.

— History.

CYPRUS. Public Information Office. 1974. Cyprus report on the Attila "peacemakers", July 20-October 1, 1974. [Nicosia, 1974?]. 1 vol. (unpaged).

CYPRUS. Public Information Office. 1976. Proposals of Greek Cypriot side on the various aspects of the Cyprus problem. Nicosia, 1976. pp. 9. *(Political Documents)*

STERN (LAURENCE) The wrong horse: the politics of intervention and the failure of American diplomacy. New York, [1977]. pp. 170.

KYPRIANOU (SPYROS) Speech...in the House of Representatives on his investiture as President of the Republic of Cyprus on February 28, 1978. [Nicosia, 1978]. pp. 16.

SALIH (HALIL IBRAHIM) Cyprus: the impact of diverse nationalism on a state. Alabama, [1978]. pp. 203. *bibliog.*

— Nationalism.

SALIH (HALIL IBRAHIM) Cyprus: the impact of diverse nationalism on a state. Alabama, [1978]. pp. 203. *bibliog.*

— Politics and government.

CYPRUS. Public Information Office. 1976. Proposals of Greek Cypriot side on the various aspects of the Cyprus problem. Nicosia, 1976. pp. 9. *(Political Documents)*

TORNARITES (KRITON G.) Cyprus and its constitutional and other legal problems. Nicosia, 1977. pp. 142.

KYPRIANOU (SPYROS) Speech...in the House of Representatives on his investiture as President of the Republic of Cyprus on February 28, 1978. [Nicosia, 1978]. pp. 16.

— Population.

CYPRUS. Ministry of Labour and Social Insurance. Statistics and Research Section. 1971. Report on the sample survey of the 1968/1969 social insurance cards. Nicosia, 1971. pp. 78.

— Social conditions.

CYPRUS. Audit Office. Audit review. s-a., My 1978 (v. 1, no. 1)- Nicosia.

— Social policy.

CYPRUS. Planning Bureau. 1977. Second emergency economic action plan, 1977-1978. Nicosia, [1977?]. pp. 196.

CZECH NEWSPAPERS.

KAPLAN (FRANK L.) Winter into spring: the Czechoslovak press and the reform movement, 1963-1968. New York, 1977. pp. 208. *bibliog. (East European Quarterly. East European Monographs. 29)*

CZECHOSLOVAKIA
— Economic conditions.

ECONOMIC discussion in Czechoslovakia. Prague, [1964]. 1 vol. (various pagings). *A collection of papers previously published elsewhere republished by Pragopress.*

HÄUFLER (VLASTISLAV) Ekonomická geografie Československa. Praha, 1978. pp. 685. *bibliog.*

— Foreign relations — Germany.

HENCKE (ANDOR) Augenzeuge einer Tragödie: Diplomatenjahre in Prag, 1936- 1939. München, 1977. pp. 351. *bibliog. (Sudetendeutsches Archiv. Veröffentlichungen. 11)*

— — Russia.

KAPLAN (KAREL) Dans les archives du comité central: trente ans de secrets du bloc soviétique. [Paris, 1978]. pp. 365.

VALENTA (JIRI) Soviet intervention in Czechoslovakia, 1968: anatomy of a decision. Baltimore, [1979]. pp. 208. *bibliog.*

— — United States.

ULLMAN (WALTER) The United States in Prague, 1945-1948. New York, 1978. pp. 205. *bibliog. (East European Quarterly. East European Monographs. 36).*

— History.

KROFTA (KAMIL) A short history of Czechoslovakia; with a foreword by J.G. Masaryk; translated by William Beardmore. London, 1935. pp. 200.

CZECHOSLOVAKIA: the heritage of ages past: essays in memory of Josef Korbel; edited by Hans Brisch and Ivan Volgyes. Boulder, 1979. pp. 239. *(East European Quarterly. East European Monographs. 51)*

— — Sources.

DOLEŽAL (JIŘÍ) and KŘEN (JAN) eds. Czechoslovakia's fight: documents on the resistance movement of the Czechoslovak people, 1938-1945. Prague, 1964. pp. 210.

— — 1848, Revolution.

ORTON (LAWRENCE D.) The Prague Slav Congress of 1848. Boulder, 1978. pp. 187. *bibliog. (East European Quarterly. East European Monographs. 46) (Columbia University. East Central European Studies)*

— — 1918-1938.

HENCKE (ANDOR) Augenzeuge einer Tragödie: Diplomatenjahre in Prag, 1936- 1939. München, 1977. pp. 351. *bibliog. (Sudetendeutsches Archiv. Veröffentlichungen. 11)*

— — 1938-1945.

WOYTAK (RICHARD A.) On the border of war and peace: Polish intelligence and diplomacy in 1937-1939 and the origins of the ultra secret. Boulder, 1979. pp. 141. *bibliog. (East European Quarterly. East European Monographs. 49)*

— — 1945- .

SCHROEDER-LASKOWSKI (SIBYLLE) Der Kampf um die Macht in der Tschechoslowakei, 1945-1948. Berlin, 1978. pp. 230. *(Akademie der Wissenschaften der DDR. Zentralinstitut für Geschichte. Schriften. Band 59)*

ULLMAN (WALTER) The United States in Prague, 1945-1948. New York, 1978. pp. 205. *bibliog. (East European Quarterly. East European Monographs. 36).*

— — 1968- , Intervention.

HAJEK (JIRI) Dix ans après: Prague 1968-1978. Paris, [1978]. pp. 205. *bibliog.*

MLYNAR (ZDENEK) Nachtfrost: Erfahrungen auf dem Weg vom realen zum menschlichen Sozialismus. Köln, 1978. pp. 366.

PACHMAN (LUDĚK) Was in Prag wirklich geschah: Illusionen und Tatsachen aus der Ära Dubček; (aus dem Tschechischen übersetzt: Carmen Dragan). Freiburg im Breisgau, [1978]. pp. 128.

STEPANEK-STEMMER (MICHAEL) Der wahre Dubček: woran der Prager Frühling scheiterte; herausgegeben und mit einem Vorwort von Werner Anrod. Köln, [1978]. pp. 182. *bibliog.*

VALENTA (JIRI) Soviet intervention in Czechoslovakia, 1968: anatomy of a decision. Baltimore, [1979]. pp. 208. *bibliog.*

— — — Sources.

ČSSR: fünf Jahre "Normalisierung", 21.8.1968/21.8.1973: Dokumentation...; Herausgeber: R. Crusius [and others]. Hamburg, [1973]. pp. 348.

— Intellectual life.

PREČAN (VILÉM) Die sieben Jahre von Prag, 1969-1976: Briefe und Dokumente aus der Zeit der "Normalisierung"; übersetzt von Ilse Löffler. Frankfurt am Main, 1978. pp. 254.

— Nationalism.

PAUL (DAVID W.) The cultural limits of revolutionary politics: change and continuity in socialist Czechoslovakia. Boulder, 1979. pp. 361. *(East European Quarterly. East European Monographs. 48)*

— Politics and government.

HAJEK (JIRI) Dix ans après: Prague 1968-1978. Paris, [1978]. pp. 205. *bibliog.*

MLYNAR (ZDENEK) Nachtfrost: Erfahrungen auf dem Weg vom realen zum menschlichen Sozialismus. Köln, 1978. pp. 366.

PREČAN (VILÉM) Die sieben Jahre von Prag, 1969-1976: Briefe und Dokumente aus der Zeit der "Normalisierung"; übersetzt von Ilse Löffler. Frankfurt am Main, 1978. pp. 254.

BLOOMFIELD (JON) Passive revolution: politics and the Czechoslovak working class, 1945-1948. London, 1979. pp. 290. *bibliog.*

CZECHOSLOVAKIA: the heritage of ages past: essays in memory of Josef Korbel; edited by Hans Brisch and Ivan Volgyes. Boulder, 1979. pp. 239. *(East European Quarterly. East European Monographs. 51)*

PAUL (DAVID W.) The cultural limits of revolutionary politics: change and continuity in socialist Czechoslovakia. Boulder, 1979. pp. 361. *(East European Quarterly. East European Monographs. 48)*

DAGHESTAN

— Economic history.

OSMANOV (AKHMED IBRAGIMOVICH) Osushchestvlenie novoi ekonomicheskoi politiki v Dagestane, 1921- 1925 gg. Moskva, 1978. pp. 215. *bibliog.*

DAIRYING

— Australia.

AUSTRALIA. Bureau of Agricultural Economics. 1977. Structural adjustment in the Australian dairy processing sector. Canberra, 1977. pp. 39. *(Industry Economics Monographs. No. 17)*

— Canada.

MACFARLANE (DAVID L.) and FISCHER (LEWIS ANTHONY) Canadian dairy industry: short term perspectives. [Ottawa, Food Prices Review Board, 1974]. pp. 107, 135. *In English and French.*

— New Zealand.

NEW ZEALAND. Dairy Board. 1977. A brief account of the organisation and operations of the New Zealand dairy industry, supplier of quality milk food products to the world. [Wellington, 1977]. pp. 24.

DAKOTA INDIANS.

EASTMAN (ELAINE GOODALE) Sister to the Sioux: the memoirs of Elaine Goodale Eastman, 1885-91; edited by Kay Graber. Lincoln, Neb., 1978. pp. 175.

DALEY (RICHARD J.).

RAKOVE (MILTON L.) Don't make no waves, don't back no losers: an insider's analysis of the Daley machine. Bloomington, [1975]. pp. 296. *bibliog.*

DAMAGES

— Austria.

GSCHNITZER (FRANZ) Schuldrecht: besonderer Teil und Schadenersatz. Wien, 1963. pp. 223.

DAMS

— Africa, Subsaharan.

OLIVIER (HENRY) Great dams in southern Africa. Cape Town, [1978?]. pp. 232.

DANGEROUS GOODS.

See HAZARDOUS SUBSTANCES.

DANUBE VALLEY

— Maps.

BREU (JOSEF) ed. Atlas der Donauländer; Atlas of the Danubian countries. Wien, 1970 in progress.

DAR ES SALAAM

— Commerce.

MARKETING DEVELOPMENT BUREAU [UNITED REPUBLIC OF TANZANIA] and COLLEGE OF BUSINESS EDUCATION [UNITED REPUBLIC OF TANZANIA]. Distribution patterns of food and beverages in Dar es Salaam. Dar es Salaam, 1973. fo. (61).

MARKETING DEVELOPMENT BUREAU [UNITED REPUBLIC OF TANZANIA]. Food marketing systems in Dar es Salaam. Dar es Salaam, 1974. fo. (42).

DARLINGTON

— Economic conditions.

DURHAM (COUNTY). County Council. Darlington urban structure plan: report of survey. [Durham], 1977. pp. 172.

— Economic policy.

DURHAM (COUNTY). County Council. Darlington urban structure plan: report of survey. [Durham], 1977. pp. 172.

DURHAM (COUNTY). County Council. Darlington urban structure plan: (written statement). Durham, [1979]. pp. 55. *Map in end pocket.*

— Social conditions.

DURHAM (COUNTY). County Council. Darlington urban structure plan: report of survey. [Durham], 1977. pp. 172.

— Social policy.

DURHAM (COUNTY). County Council. Darlington urban structure plan: report of survey. [Durham], 1977. pp. 172.

DURHAM (COUNTY). County Council. Darlington urban structure plan: (written statement). Durham, [1979]. pp. 55. *Map in end pocket.*

DASANETCH (AFRICAN PEOPLE).

ALMAGOR (URI) Pastoral partners: affinity and bond partners among the Dassanetch of south-west Ethiopia. Manchester, 1978. pp. 258. *bibliog.*

DATA BASE MANAGEMENT.

CODASYL. Systems Committee. Selection and acquisition of data base management systems: a report of the...committee. Amsterdam, 1976. pp. 252. *bibliog.*

INTERNATIONAL IFIP CONFERENCE ON VERY LARGE DATA BASES, 3RD., TOKYO, 1977. Proceedings [of the]...conference. New York, [1977]. pp. 570. *bibliogs.*

SHARE WORKING CONFERENCE ON DATA BASE MANAGEMENT SYSTEMS, 2ND, MONTREAL, 1976. The ANSI/SPARC DBMS model; proceedings of the...conference...; edited by Donald A. Jardine. Amsterdam, [1977]. pp. 225. *bibliogs.*

INTERNATIONAL IFIP CONFERENCE ON VERY LARGE DATA BASES, 4TH, WEST-BERLIN, 1978. [Proceedings]; edited by S. Bing Yao. New York, [1978]. pp. 555. *bibliog.*

KHALIL (KHALIL SALAMA) A computer-based economic model for the Bank of Sudan utilizing data base management systems. 1978. fo. 340. *bibliog. Typescript. Ph.D. (London) thesis: unpublished. Five microfiches in end pocket. This thesis is the property of London University and may not be removed from the Library.*

ROSS (RONALD G.) Data base systems: design, implementation and management. New York, [1978]. pp. 229. *bibliog.*

DAURA

— History.

SMITH (MICHAEL GARFIELD) The affairs of Daura. Berkeley, [1978]. pp. 532.

DAVIDSON (JOE).

DAVIDSON (JOE) and DEVERELL (JOHN) Joe Davidson. Toronto, 1978. pp. 192.

DAVIS (JEFFERSON).

ESCOTT (PAUL D.) After secession: Jefferson Davis and the failure of confederate nationalism. Baton Rouge, [1978]. pp. 295. *bibliog.*

DAY NURSERIES

— United States.

CHILD care and public policy: studies of the economic issues; edited by Philip K. Robins, Samuel Weiner. Lexington, Mass., [1978]. pp. 237. *bibliog.*

KAGAN (JEROME) and others. Infancy: its place in human development. Cambridge, Mass., 1978. pp. 462. *bibliog.*

DEAF

— Means of communication.

SIGN language of the deaf: psychological, linguistic, and sociological perspectives; edited by I.M. Schlesinger and Lila Namir. New York, 1978. pp. 380. *bibliog.*

DEATH.

ARIÈS (PHILIPPE) L'homme devant la mort. Paris, [1977]. pp. 642. *bibliog.*

PASSING: the vision of death in America; edited by Charles O. Jackson. Westport, Conn., 1977. pp. 258. *bibliog.*

RELIGIOUS encounters with death: insights from the history and anthropology of religions; edited by Frank E. Reynolds and Earle H. Waugh. University Park, Pa., [1977]. pp. 247. *Includes papers prepared for the convention of the American Academy of Religion held in Chicago in 1973.*

STANNARD (DAVID E.) The Puritan way of death: a study in religion, culture and social change. New York, 1977. pp. 236.

DEATH and decision; edited by Ernan McMullin. Boulder, Colo., 1978. pp. 154. *(American Association for the Advancement of Science. Selected Symposia Series. 18)*

SCHUMANN (MAURICE) Angoisse et certitude: de la mort - de la vie - de la liberté. [Paris, 1978]. pp. 204.

— Causes.

U.K. Office of Population Censuses and Surveys. Medical Statistics Division. Social and biological factors in infant mortality. a., 1975/76(3rd)- London.

DEBENHAMS LIMITED.

CORINA (MAURICE) Fine silks and oak counters: Debenhams, 1778-1978. London, 1978. pp. 200.

DE BLANK (JOOST) Archbishop of Capetown.

DE BLANK (BARTHA) Joost de Blank: a personal memoir. Ipswich, [1977]. pp. 209. *bibliog.*

DEBRAY (REGIS).

RAMM (HARTMUT) The Marxism of Régis Debray: between Lenin and Guevara. Lawrence, Kan., [1978]. pp. 240. *bibliog.*

DEBTOR AND CREDITOR

— Australia.

KELLY (DAVID ST. L.) Debt recovery in Australia. Canberra, 1977. pp. 167. *(Australia. Commission of Inquiry into Poverty. Law and Poverty Series)*

DEBTOR AND CREDITOR(Cont.)

— **United States.**

COLEMAN (PETER J.) Debtors and creditors in America: insolvency, imprisonment for debt, and bankruptcy, 1607-1900. Madison, 1974. pp. 303.

DEBTS, EXTERNAL

— **France.**

SCHRECKER (ELLEN) The hired money: the French debt to the United States, 1917- 1929. New York, 1979. pp. 383. *bibliog.*

— **Underdeveloped areas.**

See UNDERDEVELOPED AREAS — Debts, External.

DEBTS, PUBLIC

— **Brazil.**

SILVA (MARIA DA CONCEICÃO) A divida do setor publico brasileiro: seu papel no financiamento dos investimentos publicos. Rio de Janeiro, 1976. pp. 201. *bibliog.* (Brazil. Instituto de Planejamento Econômico e Social. Instituto de Pesquisas. Relatorios de Pesquisa. No. 32)

— **France.**

FRANCE. Direction de la Comptabilité Publique. Compte de la dette publique rendu...par le Ministre de l'Economie et des Finances. a., 1976- Paris.

— **Germany.**

DIECKHEUER (GUSTAV) Staatsverschuldung und wirtschaftliche Stabilisierung: eine theoretische Analyse und eine ökonometrische Studie für die Bundesrepublik Deutschland. Baden-Baden, 1978. pp. 327. *bibliog.* With summaries in various languages.

DEBUGGING IN COMPUTER SCIENCE.

VAN TASSEL (DENNIS) Program style, design, efficiency, debugging, and testing. 2nd ed. Englewood Cliffs, N.J., [1978]. pp. 323. *bibliogs.*

DECEMBRISTS.

LITERATURNO-kriticheskie raboty dekabristov. Moskva, 1978. pp. 381.

DECENTRALIZATION IN GOVERNMENT

— **Algeria.**

La CHARTE communale, la charte de Wilaya [and] la charte de la gestion socialiste des entreprises, et textes réglementaires. Alger, 1979. 1 vol. (pag.var.). (Algeria. Direction de la Documentation et des Publications. Dossiers Documentaires. 27) In English and Arabic.

— **France.**

Le DEVELOPPEMENT des initiatives financières locales et régionales: rapport à Monsieur le Premier Ministre du Groupe de réflexion presidé par Jacques Mayoux. Paris, [1979]. pp. 300.

— **Italy.**

Il SOCIALISMO dal basso: le autonomie locali nella transizione al socialismo; [by] Francesco De Martino [and others]. Venezia, 1976. pp. 392.

— **Netherlands.**

BERGE (J.B.J.M. TEN) Decentraliseren met commissies: binnengemeentelijke organisatiestructuren op basis van artikel 61 gemeentewet. 's-Gravenhage, 1978. pp. 343. *bibliog.*

— **United Kingdom.**

NEWTON (KENNETH) Is small really so beautiful?: is big really so ugly? Glasgow, [1978]. pp. 31. (Glasgow. University of Strathclyde. Centre for the Study of Public Policy. Studies in Public Policy. No. 18)

OGDANOR (VERNON) Devolution. Oxford, 1979. pp. 246. *bibliog.*

KERMODE (D.G.) Devolution at work: a case study of the Isle of Man. Farnborough, [1979]. pp. 180. *bibliogs.*

SCOTLAND: the framework for change; [edited by] Donald I. Mackay. Edinburgh, 1979. pp. 196.

— **Yugoslavia.**

DRULOVIĆ (MILOJKO) Self-management on trial. Paris, 1973. pp. 246.

BURGER (WILLEM) and others. Self-management and investment control in Yugoslavia: an exploratory investigation. The Hague, [1977]. pp. 336. *bibliog.* (Hague. Institute of Social Studies. Research Report Series. No. 2)

DECENTRALIZATION IN MANAGEMENT

— **Yugoslavia.**

DRULOVIC (MILOJKO) Self-management on trial. Paris, 1973. pp. 246.

BURGER (WILLEM) and others. Self-management and investment control in Yugoslavia: an exploratory investigation. The Hague, [1977]. pp. 336. *bibliog.* (Hague. Institute of Social Studies. Research Report Series. No. 2)

DECISION-MAKING.

KEENEY (RALPH L.) and RAIFFA (HOWARD) Decisions with multiple objectives: preferences and value tradeoffs;...with a contribution by Richard F. Meyer. New York, [1976]. pp. 569. *bibliog.*

ENDERUD (HARALD GJESSING) Four faces of leadership in an academic organization: a study of joint decision making in a Scandinavian university. København, 1977. pp. 484. *bibliog.* (Copenhagen. Handelshøjskolen. Skriftraekke O. 7)

INTERNATIONAL CONFERENCE OF AGRICULTURAL ECONOMISTS, 16TH, NAIROBI, KENYA, 1976. Decision-making and agriculture: papers and reports; edited by Theodor Dams and Kenneth E. Hunt. Lincoln, Neb., [1977]. pp. 603. *bibliogs.*

BOWEN (KEN C.) Research games: an approach to the study of decision processes;...with contributions by Janet I. Harris. London, 1978. pp. 126. *bibliog.* (Operational Research Society. ORASA Texts. No. 3)

CALABRESI (GUIDO) and BOBBITT (PHILIP) Tragic choices. New York, [1978]. pp. 252. *bibliog.*

DECISION theory and social ethics: issues in social choice; edited by Hans W. Gottinger and Werner Leinfellner. Dordrecht, [1978]. pp. 329. *bibliogs.*

JUDGEMENT and decision in public policy formation; edited by Kenneth R. Hammond. Boulder, Colo., [1978]. pp. 175. *bibliog.* (American Association for the Adavancement of Science. Selected Symposia Series. 1)

KICKERT (WALTER J.M.) Fuzzy theories on decision-making: a critical review. Leiden, 1978. pp. 182. *bibliog.*

KING (PAUL FREDERICK) An investigation of the process of large scale capital investment decision making in diversified hierarchical organisations. 1978. fo. 510. *bibliog.* Typescript. Ph.D. (London) thesis: unpublished. This thesis is the property of London University and may not be removed from the Library.

KUNREUTHER (HOWARD) Disaster insurance protection: public policy lessons. New York, [1978]. pp. 400.

WHITE (DOUGLAS JOHN) Finite dynamic programming: an approach to finite Markov decision processes. Chichester, [1978]. pp. 204. *bibliog.*

UNCERTAIN outcomes; edited by C.R. Bell. Lancaster, [1979]. pp. 204. *bibliogs.*

— **Mathematical models.**

ADVANCED SEMINAR ON MARKOV DECISION, AMSTERDAM, 1976. Markov decision theory: proceedings of the...seminar...; edited by H.C. Tijms and J. Wessels. Amsterdam, 1977. pp. 220. *bibliog.* (Mathematical Centre. Tracts. [No.] 93)

TAPIERO (CHARLES S.) Managerial planning: an optimum and stochastic control approach. New York, [1977]. 2 vols. *bibliogs.*

HEMMING (TOM) Multiobjective decision making under certainty. Stockholm, 1978. pp. 180. *bibliog.* Akademisk avhandling (doktor) - Handelshögskolan i Stockholm.

DECISION-MAKING, GROUP.

MICHAUD (CLAUDE) La décision dans l'action collective: application à l'urbanisme. [Paris, 1976]. pp. 322. *bibliog.*

DYNAMICS of group decisions; edited by Hermann Brandstätter and others. Beverly Hills, [1978]. pp. 276. *bibliogs.*

HAGLUND (STIG) Effektivitet i beslutsfattande grupper...: Effectiveness in decision making groups, etc. Helsingfors, 1978. pp. 285. *bibliog.* (Svenska Handelshögskolan. Ekonomi och Samhälle. Nr. 26) With English summary.

DE CLEYRE (VOLTAIRINE).

AVRICH (PAUL HENRY) An American anarchist: the life of Voltairine de Cleyre. Princeton, [1978]. pp. 266. *bibliog.*

DEFENCES, NATIONAL.

HAGEN (LAWRENCE S.) Civil defence: the case for reconsideration. Kingston, Ont., 1977. pp. 88. *bibliog.* (Kingston, Ontario. Queen's University. Center for International Relations. National Security Series. No. 7/77).

DEFOE (DANIEL).

DEFOE (DANIEL) The versatile Defoe: an anthology of uncollected writings by Daniel Defoe; edited and introduced by Laura Ann Curtis. London, 1979. pp. 469. *bibliog.*

DE LA GARDIE (MAGNUS GABRIEL).

REVERA (MARGARETA) Gods och gård, 1650-1680: Magnus Gabriel De la Gardies godsbildning och godsdrift i Västergötland. Uppsala, 1975 in progress. *bibliog.* (Uppsala. Universitet. Historiska Institutionen. Studia Historica Upsaliensia. 70) With English summary.

DELAVAL (Lady ELIZABETH).

SURTEES SOCIETY. Publications. vol. 190. The meditations of Lady Elizabeth Delaval, written between 1662 and 1671; edited by Douglas G. Greene. Gateshead, 1978. pp. 223.

DELAWARE

— **History.**

HANCOCK (HAROLD BELL) The loyalists of revolutionary Delaware. Newark, Del., [1977]. pp. 159. *bibliog.*

DELCEV (GOCE).

MACDERMOTT (MERCIA) Freedom or death: the life of Gotsé Delchev. London, 1978. pp. 405. *bibliog.*

DELCHEV (GOTSÉ).

See DELCEV (GOCE).

DELEGATED LEGISLATION

— **United States.**

AMERICAN ENTERPRISE INSTITUTE FOR PUBLIC POLICY RESEARCH. Special Analyses. No. 78-3. Regulation and regulatory reform: a survey of proposals of the 95th Congress. Washington, [1978]. pp. 59.

KOSTERS (MARVIN H.) and MILLER (JAMES CLIFFORD) Major regulatory initiatives during 1978: the agencies, the courts and the Congress. Washington, [1978]. pp. 26. *(American Enterprise Institute for Public Policy Research. Special Analyses. No. 78-4)*

WEIDENBAUM (MURRAY L.) and DE FINA (ROBERT) The cost of federal regulation of economic activity. Washington, 1978. pp. 33. *(American Enterprise Institute for Public Policy Research. Reprints. No. 88)*

DE LEON (DANIEL).

SERETAN (L. GLEN) Daniel DeLeon: the odyssey of an American Marxist. Cambridge, Mass., 1979. pp. 302. *bibliog.*

DELHI (UNION TERRITORY)

— Economic conditions — Statistics.

DELHI AT A GLANCE; [pd.by] Bureau of Economics and Statistics. a., 1978- Delhi.

— Economic policy.

DELHI (UNION TERRITORY). Delhi Administration. 1975. New era of progress. [Delhi, 1975]. pp. 41.

DELHI (UNION TERRITORY). Delhi Administration. 1976. New horizons. [Delhi, 1976]. pp. 41.

— History.

DAYAL (JOHN) and BOSE (AJOY) For reasons of state: Delhi under emergency. Delhi, 1977. pp. 239.

— Social conditions — Statistics.

DELHI AT A GLANCE; [pd.by] Bureau of Economics and Statistics. a., 1978- Delhi.

— Social policy.

DELHI (UNION TERRITORY). Delhi Administration. 1975. New era of progress. [Delhi, 1975]. pp. 41.

DELHI (UNION TERRITORY). Delhi Administration. 1976. New horizons. [Delhi, 1976]. pp. 41.

DEMOCRACY.

PENNAN (JOHN SIMPSON) The irresistible movement of democracy. New York, 1923. pp. 729.

BEDREIGDE democratie?: parlementaire democratie en overheidsbemoeienis in de economie; onder redactie van H. Daudt en E. van der Wolk; met bijdragen van F. Bolkestein [and others]. Assen, 1978. pp. 142.

GOLDRING (MAURICE) Démocratie, croissance zéro. [Paris, 1978]. pp. 187.

NOVAK (MICHAEL) The American vision: an essay on the future of democratic capitalism. Washington, [1978]. pp. 60. *(American Enterprise Institute for Public Policy Research. AEI Studies. 222)*

CARTER (APRIL) Authority and democracy. London, 1979. pp. 93.

MARGOLIS (MICHAEL) Viable democracy. London, 1979. pp. 211. *bibliog.*

DEMOCRATIC PARTY (UNITED STATES).

CROTTY (WILLIAM J.) Decision for the Democrats: reforming the party structure. Baltimore, [1978]. pp. 318.

SHEPSLE (KENNETH A.) The giant jigsaw puzzle: Democratic committee assignments in the modern House. Chicago, [1978]. pp. 333. *bibliog.*

— History.

COHN (DAVID LEWIS) The fabulous Democrats: a history of the Democratic Party in text and pictures. New York, [1956]. pp. 192.

DEMOGRAPHY.

TUNCER (BARAN) The impact of population growth on the Turkish economy. [Ankara, 1968]. pp. 66.

The DEMOGRAPHIC and social pattern of emigration from the Southern European countries; edited by Massimo Livi Bacci. Firenze, 1972. pp. 393. *General report and studies...in connection with the iv. theme of the Second European Population Conference, Strasbourg, 1971.*

IMHOF (ARTHUR ERWIN) Einführung in die historische Demographie. München, [1977]. pp. 149.

KEYFITZ (NATHAN) Applied mathematical demography. New York, [1977]. pp. 388. *bibliog.*

KOZLOV (VIKTOR IVANOVICH) Etnicheskaia demografiia. Moskva, 1977. pp. 240.

PANKRAT'EVA (NINA VIKTOROVNA) Naselenie i sotsialisticheskoe vosproizvodstvo; pod redaktsiei A. Ia. Boiarskogo. Moskva, 1977. pp. 223.

SMITH (THOMAS CARLYLE) Nakahara: family farming and population in a Japanese village, 1717-1830. Stanford, 1977. pp. 183. *bibliog.*

THRUPP (SYLVIA LETTICE) Society and history: essays...; edited by Raymond Grew and Nicholas H. Steneck. Ann Arbor, [1977]. pp. 363. *bibliog.*

CONFERENCE ON SOCIAL DEMOGRAPHY, MADISON, 1975. Social demography; edited by Karl E. Taeuber, Larry L. Bumpass, James A. Sweet. New York, [1978]. pp. 336. *bibliogs.*

WACHTER (KENNETH W.) and others. Statistical studies of historical social structure. New York, [1978]. pp. 229. *bibliog.*

EUROPEAN demography and economic growth; edited by W.R. Lee. London, [1979]. pp. 413. *bibliogs.*

— Mathematical models.

ROGERS (ANDREI) The aggregation problem in demography. Ljubljana, 1967. 2 pts. (in 1 vol.). *bibliog. Appendix entitled An analysis of the aggregation problem in demography: data for Yugoslavia; by Silvo Kranjec and Andrei Rogers. A study of the American- Yugoslav Project in Regional and Urban Planning Studies.*

MATHEMATICAL demography: selected papers; [edited by] David Snmith, Nathan Keyfitz. Berlin, 1977. pp. 514. *bibliogs.*

DENIKIN (ANTON IVANOVICH).

SUPRUNENKO (NIKOLAI IVANOVICH) Borot'ba trudiashchykh Ukraïny proty denikinshchyny. Kyïv, 1979. pp. 287.

DENMARK

— Commerce — India.

FELDBAEK (OLE) India trade under the Danish flag, 1772-1808: European enterprise and Anglo-Indian remittance and trade. [Copenhagen], [1969]. pp. 359. *bibliog. (Scandinavian Institute of Asian Studies. Monograph Series. No. 2) Summary in Danish.*

— Defences.

BACH (H.C.) and TAAGHOLT (JØRGEN) Greenland and the Arctic region in the light of defence policies: defence aims. Copenhagen, Information and Welfare Service of the Danish Defence, 1977. pp. 55. *bibliog.*

— Population.

MOGENSEN (GUNNAR VIBY) and others. Småbyer i landdistrikter; (with an English summary) Villages in rural areas: population development and living conditions. København, 1979. pp. 421. *bibliog. (Socialforskningsinstituttet. Publikationer. 86)*

— Rural conditions.

MOGENSEN (GUNNAR VIBY) and others. Småbyer i landdistrikter; (with an English summary) Villages in rural areas: population development and living conditions. København, 1979. pp. 421. *bibliog. (Socialforskningsinstituttet. Publikationer. 86)*

DEPARTMENT STORES

— United Kingdom.

CORINA (MAURICE) Fine silks and oak counters: Debenhams, 1778-1978. London, 1978. pp. 200.

DEPRESSION, MENTAL.

SELIGMAN (MARTIN E.P.) Helplessness: on depression, development, and death. San Francisco, [1975]. pp. 250. *bibliog.*

DESAI (MORARJI RANCHHODJI).

DESAI (MORARJI RANCHHODJI) The story of my life. Delhi, 1974 repr. 1977. 2 vols.

DESCARTES (RENE).

DESCARTES: critical and interpretive essays; edited by Michael Hooker. Baltimore, 1978. pp. 322. *bibliog.*

DESERTIFICATION

DESERTIFICATION CONTROL BULLETIN: half-yearly bulletin on on-going and planned activities; [pd. by] United Nations Environment Programme. s-a., Je 1978(v. 1, no. 1)- Nairobi.

— Sudan.

SUDAN. General Administration for Natural Resources. 1974. Desert encroachment control: project proposed by Sudan government, 1975-80. Khartoum, 1974. fo. 68.

DESERTION, MILITARY

— United States.

BASKIR (LAWRENCE M.) and STRAUSS (WILLIAM A.) Chance and circumstance: the draft, the war, and the Vietnam generation. New York, 1978. pp. 312. *bibliog.*

DESIGN, INDUSTRIAL.

CAD 78: third international conference and exhibition on computers in engineering and building design, Brighton, 14-16 March 1978; organized by the journal "Computer aided design". Guildford, [1978]. pp. 803.

DESIGN PROTECTION

— United Kingdom.

MYRANTS (GEORGE) The protection of industrial designs: a practical guide for businessmen and industrialists. London, [1977]. pp. 211.

DETENTE.

COX (ARTHUR MACY) The dynamics of détente: how to end the arms race. New York, [1976]. pp. 256. *bibliog.*

MEDVEDEV (ROI ALEKSANDROVICH) Political essays. Nottingham, 1976. pp. 151.

YANOV (ALEXANDER) Détente after Brezhnev: the domestic roots of Soviet foreign policy; translation by Robert Kessler. Berkeley, [1977]. pp. 87. *(California University. Institute of International Studies. Policy Papers in International Affairs. No. 2)*

DIMENSIONS of detente; edited by Della W. Sheldon. New York, 1978. pp. 221.

EUROCOMMUNISM and détente; edited by Rudolf L. Tokés. Oxford, 1978. pp. 578.

LABOUR PARTY. Cold peace: Soviet power and Western security. [London], 1978. pp. 54.

The SOVIET threat: myths and realities; edited by Grayson Kirk and Nils Wessell. New York, 1978. pp. 182.

BREZHNEV (LEONID IL'ICH) Peace, détente, and Soviet-American relations: a collection of public statements. New York, [1979]. pp. 235.

DUNN (DENNIS J.) Détente and papal-communist relations, 1962-1978. Boulder, [1979]. pp. 216. *bibliog.*

DETENTION OF PERSONS

— United Kingdom.

U.K. Home Office. 1978. Evidence to the Royal Commission on Criminal Procedure: memorandum no. 4: the law and procedures relating to the detention and treatment of persons in police custody. London, 1978. pp. 51.

— — Ireland, Northern.

EUROPEAN COURT OF HUMAN RIGHTS. Series A: Judgments and Decisions. [A25]. ...Case of Ireland v. The United Kingdom: 1. Decision of 29 April 1976; 2. Judgment of 18 January 1978. Strasbourg, Council of Europe, 1978. pp. 141 [bis]. *In English and French.*

DETROIT

— Social conditions.

WROBEL (PAUL) Our way: family, parish, and neighborhood in a Polish-American community. Notre Dame, Ind., [1979]. pp. 192.

DEUTSCHE AKADEMIE DER WISSENSCHAFTEN ZU BERLIN.

Die BERLINER Akademie der Wissenschaften in der Zeit des Imperialismus;...von Conrad Grau [and others]; Leitung der Arbeiten und Gesamtredaktion: Leo Stern. Berlin, 1975-79. 3 vols. (Akademie der Wissenschaften der DDR. Forschungsstelle für die Geschichte der Akademie. Studien zur Geschichte der Akademie der Wissenschaften der DDR. Band 2)

DEUTSCHE DEMOKRATISCHE PARTEI.

POIS (ROBERT A.) The bourgeois democrats of Weimar Germany. Philadelphia, 1976. pp. 117. *bibliog.* (American Philosophical Society. Transactions. New Series. vol 66 Pt. 4)

SCHNEIDER (WERNER) Political historian. Die Deutsche Demokratische Partei in der Weimarer Republik, 1924-1930. München, 1978. pp. 278. *bibliog.*

DEUTSCHER GEWERKSCHAFTSBUND.

PIRKER (THEO) Die blinde Macht: die Gewerkschaftsbewegung in Westdeutschland. Berlin, 1979. 2 vols (in 1). *Reprint, with new introduction, of work originally published Munich, 1960.*

HOCHGUERTEL (GERHARD) and STIEGLER (BARBARA) Die Aufgaben des DGB an der Basis: zum Berufsbild des DGB-Sekretärs. Bonn, [1978]. pp. 238. *bibliog.* (Friedrich-Ebert-Stiftung. Forschungsinstitut. Reihe: Arbeit)

INSTITUT FÜR MARXISTISCHE STUDIEN UND FORSCHUNGEN. DGB wohin?: Dokumente zur Programm-Diskussion; eingeleitet von Frank Deppe. Frankfurt am Main, [1978]. pp. 280. *bibliog.*

DEUTSCHER WERKBUND.

CAMPBELL (JOAN) The German Werkbund: the politics of reform in the applied arts. Princeton, [1978]. pp. 350. *bibliog.*

DEUTSCHES AUSLAND-INSTITUT.

RITTER (ERNST) German historian. Das Deutsche Ausland-Institut in Stuttgart, 1917-1945: ein Beispiel deutscher Volkstumsarbeit zwischen den Weltkriegen. Wiesbaden, 1976. pp. 168. *bibliog.*

DEUTSCHLAND-STIFTUNG.

BAMBERG (HANS DIETER) Die Deutschland-Stiftung e.V.: Studien über Kräfte der "demokratischen Mitte" und des Konservatismus in der Bundesrepublik Deutschland. Meisenheim am Glan, 1978. pp. 563. *bibliog.*

DEVELOPMENT BANKS

— Africa.

FRANCE. Ministère de la Coopération. Service des Etudes Economiques et [des] Questions Internationales. 1976. Nouvelles ressources financières pour l'Afrique. Paris, 1976. pp. 79. *(Etudes et Documents. No. 24)*

— Salvador.

INSTITUTO SALVADOREÑO DE FOMENTO INDUSTRIAL. What is INSAFI. [San Salvador, 1968?]. pp. 5.

DEVELOPMENT CREDIT CORPORATIONS.

DEVELOPMENT finance companies: aspects of policy and operation; edited by William Diamond; essays by E.T. Kuiper [and others]...; published...for the World Bank Group. [Baltimore, 1968]. pp. 119.

— Canada — Alberta.

ALBERTA OPPORTUNITY COMPANY. Annual report. a., 1977/78- Edmonton.

— — Newfoundland.

NEWFOUNDLAND AND LABRADOR DEVELOPMENT CORPORATION LTD. Annual report. a., 1976/77- St. John's.

— Kenya.

INDUSTRY IN KENYA: newsletter of the Development Finance Company of Kenya. m., current issues only. Nairobi.

DEVELOPMENT FINANCE COMPANY OF KENYA.

INDUSTRY IN KENYA: newsletter of the Development Finance Company of Kenya. m., current issues only. Nairobi.

DEVELOPMENTAL PSYCHOLOGY.

LANGER (JONAS) Theories of development. New York, [1969]. pp. 191. *bibliog.*

WOHLWILL (JOACHIM F.) The study of behavioral development. New York, 1973. pp. 413. *bibliog.*

GUBRIUM (JABER F.) and BUCKHOLDT (DAVID R.) Toward maturity: the social processing of human development. San Francisco, 1977. pp. 224. *bibliog.*

EVANS (ELLIS D.) and McCANDLESS (BOYD R.) Children and youth: psychosocial development. 2nd ed. New York, [1978]. pp. 568. *bibliogs.*

DEVELOPMENTALLY DISABLED CHILDREN.

DEVELOPMENTAL dysphasia; edited by Maria A. Wyke. London, 1978. pp. 179. *bibliogs.*

DEVIANT BEHAVIOUR.

CRIME and delinquency: a reader; edited by Carl A. Bersani. New York, [1970]. pp. 575. *bibliogs.*

PEARSON (GEOFFREY) The deviant imagination: psychiatry, social work and social change. London, 1975. pp. 258. *bibliog.*

BECKER (GEORGE) The mad genius controversy: a study in the sociology of deviance. Beverly Hills, [1978]. pp. 151. *bibliog.*

DEVIANCE and mass media; edited by Charles Winick. Beverly Hills, [1978]. pp. 309. *bibliogs.*

MILLER (GALE) Odd jobs: the world of deviant work. Englewood Cliffs, N.J., [1978]. pp. 260. *bibliog.*

SOCIAL deviance in Eastern Europe; edited by Ivan Volgyes. Boulder, Colo., [1978]. pp. 198. *bibliogs.*

DITTON (JASON) Controlology: beyond the new criminology. London, 1979. pp. 124. *bibliog.*

DEVONSHIRE

— Economic conditions.

DEVON IN FIGURES; [pd. by] Central Information Service, Devon County Council. a., 1977(3rd)- Exeter.

— Economic policy.

GLYN-JONES (ANNE) Village into town: a study of transition in south Devon. [Exeter], Devon County Council and the University of Exeter, [1977]. pp. 88.

— Social conditions.

DEVON IN FIGURES; [pd. by] Central Information Service, Devon County Council. a., 1977(3rd)- Exeter.

— Social policy.

GLYN-JONES (ANNE) Village into town: a study of transition in south Devon. [Exeter], Devon County Council and the University of Exeter, [1977]. pp. 88.

DEVOTIO MODERNA.

HYMA (ALBERT) The Christian Renaissance: a history of the devotio moderna. 2nd ed. Hamden, Conn., 1965. pp. 617.

DEWEY (JOHN).

KEENAN (BARRY) The Dewey experiment in China: educational reform and political power in the early republic. Cambridge, Mass., 1977. pp. 335. *bibliog.*

DICKENS (CHARLES).

PATTEN (ROBERT LOWRY) Charles Dickens and his publishers. Oxford, [1978]. pp. 502. *bibliog.*

POPE (NORRIS) Dickens and charity. London, 1978. pp. 303.

DICTATORSHIP OF THE PROLETARIAT.

KOSITSYN (ALEKSANDR PAVLOVICH) Sotsializm i gosudarstvo. Moskva, 1976. pp. 144.

McCARTHY (TIMOTHY) Marx and the proletariat: a study in social theory. Westport, 1978. pp. 102 *bibliog.*

DIEDERICHS (GEORG).

VOGT (HANNAH) Georg Diederichs. Hannover, Niedersächsische Landeszentrale für Politische Bildung, 1978. pp. 175. *bibliog.*

DIET

— United Kingdom.

U.K. Department of Health and Social Security. 1978. Eating for health: a discussion booklet prepared by the health departments of Great Britain and Northern Ireland. London, 1978. pp. 83. *bibliog.* At head of title: *Prevention and health.*

DIFFERENCE EQUATIONS.

BENDER (CARL M.) and ORSZAG (STEVEN A.) Advanced mathematical methods for scientists and engineers. New York, [1978]. pp. 593. *bibliog.*

DIFFERENTIAL EQUATIONS.

SIMMONS (GEORGE FINLAY) Differential equations, with applications and historical notes. New Delhi, 1974 repr. 1978. pp. 465.

BENDER (CARL M.) and ORSZAG (STEVEN A.) Advanced mathematical methods for scientists and engineers. New York, [1978]. pp. 593. *bibliog.*

BIRKHOFF (GARRETT) and ROTA (GIAN-CARLO) Ordinary differential equations. 3rd ed. New York, [1978]. pp. 342. *bibliog.*

DERRICK (WILLIAM R.) and GROSSMAN (STANLEY I.) Elementary differential equations with applications. Reading, Mass., 1978. pp. 598.

DIFFERENTIAL EQUATIONS, PARTIAL.

MITCHELL (ANDREW R.) and WAIT (R.) The finite element method in partial differential equations. Chichester, 1977. pp. 198. *bibliog.*

SHOWALTER (R.E.) Hilbert space methods for partial differential equations. London, [1977]. pp. 196. *bibliog.*

DIFFERENTIAL TOPOLOGY.

SPIVAK (MICHAEL) Calculus on manifolds: a modern approach to classical theorems of advanced calculus. Menlo Park, Calif., 1965. pp. 146. *bibliog.*

CHILLINGWORTH (DAVID R.J.) Differential topology with a view to applications. London, 1978. pp. 291. *bibliog.*

DIFFUSION OF INNOVATIONS.

DAVIES (STEPHEN) The diffusion of process innovations. Cambridge, 1979. pp. 193. *bibliog.*

DIFFUSION PROCESSES.

WILLIAMS (DAVID) 1938- . Diffusions, Markov processes and martingales. vol.1. Foundations. Chichester, [1979]. pp. 237. *bibliog.*

DIGITAL COMPUTER SIMULATION.

LEWIS (THEODORE GYLE) Distribution sampling for computer simulation. Lexington, Mass., [1975]. pp. 150. *bibliog.*

DILTHEY (WILHELM).

RICKMAN (H.P.) Wilhelm Dilthey: pioneer of the human studies. London, 1979. pp. 197. *bibliog.*

DIPLOMACY.

SATOW (Sir ERNEST MASON) A guide to diplomatic practice; edited by Lord Gore-Booth; assistant editor Desmond Pakenham. 5th ed. London, [1979]. pp. 544. *bibliog.*

DIPLOMATIC AND CONSULAR SERVICE.

SATOW (Sir ERNEST MASON) A guide to diplomatic practice; edited by Lord Gore-Booth; assistant editor Desmond Pakenham. 5th ed. London, [1979]. pp. 544. *bibliog.*

DIPLOMATIC NEGOTIATIONS IN INTERNATIONAL DISPUTES.

RAMBERG (BENNETT) The seabed arms control negotiations: a study of multilateral arms control conference diplomacy. Denver, [1978]. pp. 135. *bibliog.* *(Denver. University. Graduate School of International Studies. Monograph Series in World Affairs. vol. 15, no. 2)*

DIPLOMATS

— France — Correspondence, reminiscences, etc.

BERARD (ARMAND) Un ambassadeur se souvient: au temps du danger allemand. [Paris, 1976]. pp. 554.

— United Kingdom.

ROSE (NORMAN ANTHONY) Vansittart: study of a diplomat. London, 1978. pp. 308. *bibliog.*

DIPLOMATS, AMERICAN

— Correspondence, reminiscences, etc.

EMMERSON (JOHN K.) The Japanese thread: a life in the U.S. foreign service. New York, 1978. pp. 465.

DISABILITY EVALUATION.

SIMKINS (JEAN) and TICKNER (VINCENT) Whose benefit: an examination of the existing system of cash benefits and related provisions for intrinsically handicapped adults and their families. London, [1978]. pp. 245. *bibliog.*

DISARMAMENT.

AKTUAL'NYE problemy razoruzheniia. Moskva, 1976. pp. 175.

GALTUNG (JOHAN) Peace, war and defence; essays in peace research. Copenhagen, 1976. pp. 472. *(International Peace Research Institute. PRIO Monographs. No.5)*

RANGER (ROBERT JOHN) The Canadian contribution to the control of chemical and biological warfare. Toronto, [1976]. pp. 66. *(Canadian Institute of International Affairs. Wellesley Papers. 5)*

JOHANSEN (ROBERT C.) The disarmament process: where to begin. New York, [1977]. pp. 22.

PROBLEMELE păcii şi ale războiului în condiţiile revoluţiei ştiinţifice şi tehnice: necesitatea istorică a dezarmării: sesiunea ştiinţifică din 21 ianuarie 1977. Bucureşti, 1977. pp. 488. *With English, French, German, Italian, Russian and Spanish tables of contents and identifications of authors.*

BARNABY (CHARLES FRANK) Global armaments and disarmament. New Malden, [1978]. pp. 19. *(Fellowship of Reconciliation. Alex Wood Memorial Lectures. 1978)*

CHEMICAL weapons and chemical arms control; papers and discussions from a conference at...Boston...1977; Matthew Meselson, editor. New York, [1978]. pp. 128.

CONGRESS and arms control; edited by Alan Platt and Lawrence D. Weiler. Boulder, Colo., [1978]. pp. 227.

DISARM or die: a disarmament reader for the leaders and the peoples of the world; published on behalf of the Non-Partisan Fund for World Disarmament and Development. London, 1978. pp. 108.

JOHANSEN (ROBERT C.) Toward a dependable peace: a proposal for an appropriate security system. New York, [1978]. pp. 58.

OPPORTUNITIES for disarmament: a preview of the 1978 United Nations Special Session on Disarmament; edited by Jane M. O. Sharp. New York, [1978]. pp. 146. *bibliog.*

STOCKHOLM INTERNATIONAL PEACE RESEARCH INSTITUTE. Arms control: a survey and appraisal of multilateral agreements. London, 1978. pp. 238.

INTERNATIONAL INSTITUTE FOR STRATEGIC STUDIES. Adelphi Papers. No. 149. The future of arms control: part III: confidence-building measures; edited by Jonathan Alford. London, 1979. pp. 39.

NOEL-BAKER (PHILIP JOHN) Baron Noel-Baker. The first world disarmament conference, 1932-1933, and why it failed. Oxford, 1979. pp. 147.

RANGER (ROBIN) Arms and politics, 1958-1978: arms control in a changing political context. Toronto, [1979]. pp. 280. *bibliog.*

SIMS (NICHOLAS A.) Approaches to disarmament; an introductory analysis. rev.ed. London, 1979. pp. 180.

— Bibliography.

LLOYD (LORNA) and SIMS (NICHOLAS A.) compilers. British writing on disarmament from 1914 to 1978: a bibliography. London, 1979. pp. 171.

DISASTER RELIEF

— Botswana.

G.P. McGOWAN AND ASSOCIATES. A study of drought relief and contingency measures relating to the livestock sector of Botswana: final report. volume 1. Executive report;...carried out for the government of Botswana. Albury, 1979. pp. 70, 4 maps.

— United Kingdom.

MEADS (R.) A preliminary study on emergency planning and the involvement of volunteers in England and Wales. n.p., [1975]. pp. 26. *Typescript: unpublished.*

— United States.

KUNREUTHER (HOWARD) Disaster insurance protection: public policy lessons. New York, [1978]. pp. 400.

DISASTERS

— Psychological aspects.

ERIKSON (KAI T.) Everything in its path: destruction of community in the Buffalo Creek flood. New York, [1976]. pp. 284. *bibliog.*

ERIKSON (KAI T.) In the wake of the flood. London, [1979]. pp. 220. *bibliog.*

DISCOUNT

— United Kingdom.

The TEST discount rate and the required rate of return on investment: proceedings of a seminar held at the Civil Service College, Sunningdale, 16/17 June 1978. London, Treasury, 1979. pp. 57. *(Government Economic Service Working Papers. No. 22)*

DISCOVERIES (IN GEOGRAPHY).

CHAUNU (PIERRE) European expansion in the later Middle Ages; translated by Katharine Bertram. Amsterdam, 1979. pp. 326. *bibliog.*

DISCRIMINANT ANALYSIS.

CLASSIFICATION and clustering; (proceedings of an advanced seminar conducted by the Mathematics Research Center, the University of Wisconsin at Madison...1976); edited by J. van Ryzin. New York, 1977. pp. 467. *bibliogs.* *(Wisconsin University, Madison. Mathematics Research Center, United States Army. Publications. No. 37)*

GOLDSTEIN (MATTHEW) and DILLON (WILLIAM R.) Discrete discriminant analysis. New York, [1978]. pp. 186. *bibliog.*

DISCRIMINATION.

GLASER (KURT) and POSSONY (STEFAN THOMAS) Victims of politics: the state of human rights. New York, 1979. pp. 614. *bibliog.*

— United States.

DIMOND (PAUL R.) and others. A dilemma of local government: discrimination in the provision of public services. Lexington, Mass., [1978]. pp. 319. *bibliogs.*

FEAGIN (JOE R.) and FEAGIN (CLAIRECE BOOHER) Discrimination American style: institutional racism and sexism. Englewood Cliffs, [1978?]. pp. 190.

DISCRIMINATION IN EDUCATION.

RACE, education and identity; edited by Gajendra K. Verma and Christopher Bagley. London, 1979. pp. 268. *bibliog.*

DISCRIMINATION IN EMPLOYMENT

— Law and legislation — United States.

EQUAL rights and industrial relations; [by] Farrell E. Bloch [and others]. Madison, [1977]. pp. 281. *bibliogs.*

HILL (HERBERT) Black labor and the American legal system. vol. 1. Race, work, and the law. Washington D.C., [1977]. pp. 455.

EMPLOYMENT discrimination: the impact of legal and administrative remedies; [by] Ray Marshall [and others]. New York, [1978]. pp. 153.

— United Kingdom.

PEARN (M.A.) Employment testing and the goal of equal opportunity: the American experience. [London], 1978. pp. 38.

DISCRIMINATION IN EMPLOYMENT(Cont.)

U.K. Commission for Racial Equality. 1978. Looking for work: black and white school leavers in Lewisham; a short report of a survey carried out for the Commission for Racial Equality in conjunction with Lewisham Borough Council and Lewisham Council for Community Relations. London, 1978. pp. 16. bibliog.

— — Ireland, Northern.

FAIR EMPLOYMENT AGENCY FOR NORTHERN IRELAND. An industrial and occupational profile of the two sections of the population in Northern Ireland: an analysis of the 1971 population census. [Belfast, 1978]. pp. 15. bibliog. ([Research Papers. 1])

— United States.

EMPLOYMENT, income, and welfare in the rural South; by Brian Rungeling [and others]. New York, 1977. pp. 355. bibliog.

BENOKRAITIS (NIJOLE V.) and FEAGIN (JOE R.) Affirmative action and equal opportunity: action, inaction, reaction. Boulder, Colo., 1978. pp. 255. bibliog.

PEARN (M.A.) Employment testing and the goal of equal opportunity: the American experience. [London], 1978. pp. 38.

DISCRIMINATION IN HOUSING

— South Africa.

MAASDORP (GAVIN G.) and PILLAY (P. NESEN) Urban relocation and racial segregation: the case of Indian South Africans. Durban, 1977. pp. 206. bibliog. (Natal University. Department of Economics. Research Monographs)

— United Kingdom.

HATCH (J.C.S.) Estate agents as urban gatekeepers: [a talk given to the] B[ritish] S[ociological] A[ssociation] Urban Sociology Group, University of Stirling, 6th October 1973. [Bristol, Social Science Research Council Research Unit on Ethnic Relations, 1973]. fo. 19.

— United States.

AFTER Mount Laurel: the new suburban zoning; edited by Jerome G. Rose and Robert E. Rothman. New Brunswick, N.J., [1977]. pp. 354.

DISEASES

— Causes and theories of causation.

TOTMAN (RICHARD) Social causes of illness. London, 1979. pp. 263. bibliog.

DISINFECTION AND DISINFECTANTS.

PALFREYMAN (DAVID) John Jeyes...: the making of a household name. Thetford, [1977]. pp. 127. bibliog.

DISSENTERS.

The TECHNOLOGY of political control; by Carol Ackroyd [and others]. Harmondsworth, 1977. pp. 320.

— Europe, Eastern.

BAHRO (RUDOLF) The alternative in Eastern Europe; translated by David Fernbach. [London], 1978. pp. 463.

SOCIAL deviance in Eastern Europe; edited by Ivan Volgyes. Boulder, Colo., [1978]. pp. 198. bibliogs.

BEAMISH (TUFTON VICTOR HAMILTON) Baron Chelwood and HADLEY (GUY) The Kremlin's dilemma: the struggle for human rights in Eastern Europe. London, 1979. pp. 285. bibliog.

OPPOSITION in Eastern Europe; edited by Rudolf L. Tökés. London, 1979. pp. 306.

POWER and opposition in post-revolutionary societies; translated from the French by Patrick Camiller and the Italian by Jon Rothschild. London, 1979. pp. 281. bibliogs. Papers of a conference organised by Il Manifesto and held in Venice, 1977.

— Poland.

La POLOGNE: une société en dissidence; textes rassemblés par Z. Erard et G.M. Zygier. Paris, 1978. pp. 195.

— Russia.

BUKOVSKII (VLADIMIR KONSTANTINOVICH) To build a castle: my life as a dissenter. London, 1978. pp. 352.

— United States — Bibliography.

HOERDER (DIRK) compiler. Protest, direct action, repression: dissent in American society from colonial times to the present: a bibliography. München, 1977. pp. 434.

DISSENTERS, RELIGIOUS

— United Kingdom — Wales.

LEWIS (HOWELL ELVET) Nonconformity in Wales. London, 1904. pp. 117. (National Council of the Evangelical Free Churches. Eras of Nonconformity. 4)

DISSERTATIONS, ACADEMIC

— Canada.

DEAL (CARL W.) compiler. Latin America and the Caribbean: a dissertation bibliography. Ann Arbor, [1978]. pp. 164.

— United Kingdom — Bibliography.

UNIVERSITIES TRANSPORT STUDY GROUP. Occasional Publications. No. 1. Doctoral theses in transport from Great Britain: first issue, 1960-1975; edited by Howard R. Kirby. London, 1977. pp. 24.

LONDON. University. School of Oriental and African Studies. Centre of South East Asian Studies. List of theses and dissertations concerned with South East Asia accepted for higher degrees of the University of London, 1965-1977. London, [1978]. fo. 11.

STANDING CONFERENCE ON LIBRARY MATERIALS ON AFRICA. Theses on Africa, 1963-1975, accepted by universities in the United Kingdom and Ireland; compiled by J.H.St.J. McIlwaine. London, 1978. pp. 123.

— United States.

DEAL (CARL W.) compiler. Latin America and the Caribbean: a dissertation bibliography. Ann Arbor, [1978]. pp. 164.

DISTILLING INDUSTRIES

— Belgium.

JACQUEMIN (ALEXIS) and GHELLINCK (ELIZABETH DE) L'évolution de la concentration dans l'industrie de la brasserie et des boissons en Belgique. [Brussels], Communautés Européennes, 1976. pp. 108.

— Canada.

NEWMAN (PETER CHARLES) Bronfman dynasty: the Rothschilds of the New World. Toronto, [1978]. pp. 318.

— France.

BOULET (D.) and LAPORTE (J.P.) Etude sur l'évolution de la concentration dans l'industrie des spiritueux en France, etc. [Brussels], Communautés Européennes, 1976. pp. 163.

BOULET (D.) and LAPORTE (J.P.) Etude sur l'évolution de la concentration dans les industries des boissons et des boissons non alcoolisées en France. [Brussels], Communautés Européennes, 1976. pp. 284.

— Germany.

BREITENACHER (MICHAEL) Untersuchung zur Konzentrationsentwicklung in der Getränke Industrie in Deutschland. [Brussels], Europäischen Gemeinschaften, 1976. pp. 156.

— Italy.

BALLIANO (PIERA) and LANZETTI (RENATO) Studio sull'evoluzione della concentrazione nell'industria delle bevande in Italia. [Brussels], Comunità Europee, 1976. pp. 143.

— Netherlands.

BROUWER (MARIA) and PIJNAPPEL (THEO) A study of the evolution of concentration in the Dutch beverages industry. [Brussels], European Communities, 1976. pp. 149.

— United Kingdom.

WEIR (RONALD B.) The history of the Malt Distillers' Association of Scotland. [York?, 1974?]. pp. 177.

DISTRIBUTION (ECONOMIC THEORY).

FETTER (FRANK ALBERT) Capital, interest, and rent: essays in the theory of distribution; edited...by Murray N. Rothbard. Kansas City, [1977]. pp. 400. bibliog.

JUSTICE and economic distribution; edited by John Arthur [and] William H. Shaw. Englewood Cliffs, [1978]. pp. 262.

RANADIVE (K.R.) Income distribution: the unsolved puzzle. Bombay, 1978. pp. 353.

DISTRIBUTION (PROBABILITY THEORY).

JOHNSON (NORMAN LLOYD) and KOTZ (SAMUEL) Distributions in statistics: discrete distributions. New York, [1969]. pp. 328. bibliogs.

JOHNSON (NORMAN LLOYD) and KOTZ (SAMUEL) Distributions in statistics: continuous univariate distributions. New York, [1970]. 2 vols. bibliog.

JOHNSON (NORMAN LLOYD) and KOTZ (SAMUEL) Distributions in statistics: continuous multivariate distributions. New York, [1972]. pp. 333. bibliog.

HABERMAN (SHELBY J.) The analysis of frequency data. Chicago, [1974]. pp. 419. bibliog.

MILLER (KENNETH SIELKE) Multivariate distributions. [2nd ed.]. Huntington, N.Y., 1975. pp. 167. bibliog.

JOHNSON (NORMAN LLOYD) and KOTZ (SAMUEL) Urn models and their application: an approach to modern discrete probability theory. New York, [1977]. pp. 402. bibliogs.

GALAMBOS (JANOS) The asymptotic theory of extreme order statistics. New York, [1978]. pp. 352. bibliog.

MARDIA (K.V.) and ZEMROCH (P.J.) Tables of the F- and related distributions with algorithms. London, 1978. pp. 256. bibliog.

DIVERSIFICATION IN INDUSTRY

— United Kingdom.

UTTON (MICHAEL A.) Diversification and competition. Cambridge, 1979. pp. 113. (National Institute of Economic and Social Research. Occasional Papers. 31)

DIVIDENDS

— Taxation.

McLURE (CHARLES E.) Must corporate income be taxed twice? Washington, D.C., [1979]. pp. 262. (Brookings Institution. Studies of Government Finance) A report of a conference sponsored by the Fund for Public Policy Research and the Brookings Institution.

— United Kingdom — Taxation.

ORHNIAL (ANTONY J. H.) Estimates of marginal tax rates for dividends and bond interest 1970- 75. London, 1977. pp. 18. bibliog. (Papers on Capital and Risk. No. 5)

DIVINE LIGHT MISSION.

DOWNTON (JAMES V.) Sacred journeys: the conversion of young Americans to Divine Light Mission. New York, 1979. pp. 245. bibliog.

DIVORCE

— France.

FRANCE. Direction de la Documentation. La Documentation Française. Notes et Etudes Documentaires. No. 4478. Le divorce en France: de la réforme de 1975 à la sociologie du divorce; [by] Jacques Commaille. [Paris], 1978. pp. 148. *bibliog.*

— United Kingdom.

LEETE (RICHARD) Changing patterns of family formation and dissolution in England and Wales, 1964-76. London, 1979. pp. 130. *bibliog. (U.K. Office of Population Censuses and Surveys. Studies on Medical and Population Subjects. No. 39)*

THORNES (BARBARA) and COLLARD (JEAN) of the Marriage Research Centre. Who divorces? London, 1979. pp. 223. *bibliog.*

— United States — California.

CALIFORNIA. Department of Health. 1977. Marriage and marriage dissolution in California: marriages and final decrees of dissolution of marriage, judgment of nullity and legal separation, 1966-1973. [Sacramento], 1977. pp. 110. *bibliog.*

DJILAS (MILOVAN).

DJILAS (MILOVAN) Wartime; translated [from the Serbo-Croat] by Michael B. Petrovich. New York, [1977]. pp. 470.

DOCK WORKERS

— Canada — Newfoundland.

TRADE DISPUTE BOARD [NEWFOUNDLAND]. Settlement of Trade Dispute Board appointed under the Defence, control and conditions of employment and disputes settlement, regulations, 1941, for the settlement of a dispute between the Employers' Association and the Longshoremen's Protective Union of St. John's. St. John's, Office of the King's Printer, 1942. pp. 62.

— United Kingdom.

[U.K. Department of Employment. 1978]. Dock labour scheme 1978: draft dock labour scheme laid before Parliament under the Dock Work Regulation Act 1976, etc. [London, 1978]. pp. 23.

DOLLAR.

The DOLLAR abroad, inflation at home;...[an AEI Public Policy Forum] held on August 31, 1978...[in] Washington; (John Charles Daly, moderator). Washington, [1978]. pp. 27. *(American Enterprise Institute for Public Policy Research. Public Policy Forums. 22)*

ROSE (HAROLD BERTRAM) and others. The U.S. dollar and its role as a reserve currency. London, 1978. fo. 20. *(British North-American Research Association. Occasional Papers. 4)*

DOMESTIC ANIMALS

— United Kingdom — Law.

SANDYS-WINSCH (GODFREY) Animal law. London, 1978. pp. 216.

DOMESTIC RELATIONS

— Austria.

GSCHNITZER (FRANZ) Familienrecht. Wien, 1963 repr. 1971. pp. 135.

— Canada — Quebec.

QUEBEC (PROVINCE). Civil Code Revision Office. Committee on the Law on Persons and on the Family. 1974-75. Report on the family; [Claire L'Heureux-Dubé, présidente] . Montréal, 1974-75. 2 pts. *(Quebec (Province). Civil Code Revision Office. [Reports]. 26, 36) In English and French.*

— Europe.

The REFORM of family law in Europe: the equality of the spouses, divorce, illegitimate children; a seminar of the University Institute of Luxembourg; editor: A.G. Chloros. Deventer, 1978. pp. 349.

— Hungary.

PRAVOVOE regulirovanie obshchestvennykh otnoshenii. Moskva, 1976. pp. 120.

— United Kingdom.

PINDER (JOHN S.) and PACE (P.J.) Cases and statutes on family law. London, 1979. pp. 174.

— — Scotland.

NICHOLS (DAVID IAN) Marriage, divorce and the family in Scotland. 3rd ed. Edinburgh, 1978. pp. 40.

DOMINICA

— House of Assembly — Elections.

DOMINICA. 1970. Report on the House of Assembly general elections, 1970. [Roseau, 1970?]. pp. 25.

— Politics and government.

DOMINICA. Speech from the throne. a., Jl 1978- Dominica.

DOMINICAN REPUBLIC

— History — 1961- .

GLEIJESES (PIERO) The Dominican crisis: the 1965 constitutionalist revolt and American intervention...; translated by Lawrence Lipson. Baltimore, [1978]. pp. 460. *bibliog.*

— Politics and government.

DIEDERICH (BERNARD) Trujillo: the death of the goat. Boston, Mass., 1978. pp. 265.

— Relations (general) with the United States.

GLEIJESES (PIERO) The Dominican crisis: the 1965 constitutionalist revolt and American intervention...; translated by Lawrence Lipson. Baltimore, [1978]. pp. 460. *bibliog.*

DOMINICANS.

BENNETT (RALPH FRANCIS) The early Dominicans: studies in thirteenth-century Dominican history. New York, 1971. pp. 189. *bibliog. First published in 1937.*

DONETS BASIN

— Social conditions.

PONOMAR'OV (ANATOLII PETROVYCH) Suchasna sim'ia i simeinyi pobut robitnykiv Donbasu, 1950-1975. Kyïv, 1978. pp. 143.

DOUBLE CROPPING

— Malaysia.

FREDERICKS (L. J.) and others. Patterns of labour utilization and income distribution in rice double cropping systems: policy implications. Kuala Lumpur, 1977. pp. 66. *bibliog. (University of Malaya. Faculty of Economics and Administration. Occasional Papers on Malaysian Socio-Economic Affairs. No. 8)*

DRAINAGE.

GREGORY (KENNETH JOHN) and WALLING (D.E.) Drainage basin form and process: a geomorphological approach. [2nd ed.] London, 1979. pp. 458. *bibliog. Reprint of the work first published in 1973, with an additional bibliography.*

DREAMS.

RYCROFT (CHARLES) The innocence of dreams. London, 1979. pp. 184.

DRENTHE

— Economic conditions.

HOEK (SIETSE VAN DER) Hopend op een vrijer leven: Drentse veenarbeiders/sters verhalen. 's-Gravenhage, 1978 repr. 1979. pp. 89. *bibliog.*

— Social history.

HOEK (SIETSE VAN DER) Hopend op een vrijer leven: Drentse veenarbeiders/sters verhalen. 's-Gravenhage, 1978 repr. 1979. pp. 89. *bibliog.*

DREXEL (JOSEPH EDUARD).

DREXEL (JOSEPH EDUARD) Rückkehr unerwünscht: Joseph Drexels "Reise nach Mauthausen" und der Widerstandskreis Ernst Niekisch; herausgegeben von Wilhelm Raimund Beyer. Stuttgart, [1978]. pp. 332.

DRIEU LA ROCHELLE (PIERRE).

DESANTI (DOMINIQUE) Drieu la Rochelle: le séducteur mystifié. Paris, 1978. pp. 476. *bibliog.*

DRINKING CUSTOMS

— United Kingom.

PLANT (MARTIN A.) Drinking careers: occupations, drinking habits and drinking problems. London, 1979. pp. 167. *bibliog.*

DRINKING WATER

— Contamination.

WORKING GROUP ON HEALTH HAZARDS FROM DRINKING-WATER. Health hazards from drinking-water: report on a working group [held in] London, 26-30 September, 1977. Copenhagen, World Health Organization, Regional Office for Europe, 1978. pp. 13.

— Standards.

WORKING GROUP ON HEALTH HAZARDS FROM DRINKING-WATER. Health hazards from drinking-water: report on a working group [held in] London, 26-30 September, 1977. Copenhagen, World Health Organization, Regional Office for Europe, 1978. pp. 13.

WORKING GROUP ON TREATMENT AGENTS AND PROCESSES FOR DRINKING-WATER AND THEIR EFFECTS ON HEALTH. Treatment agents and processes for drinking-water and their effects on health: report on a working group [held in] Brussels, 6-9 December 1977. Copenhagen, World Health Organization, Regional Office for Europe, 1978. pp. 22. *bibliog.*

— United States.

SAFE drinking water: current and future problems; [edited by] Clifford S. Russell. Washington, D.C., [1978]. pp. 641. *bibliogs. Resources for the Future, Inc. (Research Papers. R-12) Proceedings of a national conference in Washington, D.C.*

DROUGHTS

— Botswana.

G.P. McGOWAN AND ASSOCIATES. A study of drought relief and contingency measures relating to the livestock sector of Botswana: final report. volume 1. Executive report;...carried out for the government of Botswana. Albury, 1979. pp. 70, 4 maps.

— India.

INDIA. Department of Rural Development. 1978. Drought prone areas programme. New Delhi, 1978. pp. 19.

— United States.

BONNIFIELD (PAUL) The dust bowl: men, dirt, and depression. Albuquerque, [1979]. pp. 232. *bibliog.*

DRUG ABUSE

— Law and legislation — Australia.

TOMASIC (ROMAN ALEXANDER) Drugs, alcohol and community control. Sydney, 1977. pp. 248. *bibliog.* (*Law Foundation of New South Wales. Criminal Justice Monograph Series. No.3*)

— Treatment — United States.

DRUGS, crime and politics; edited...by Arnold S. Trebach. New York, 1978. pp. 178. *bibliogs.*

— France.

FRANCE. Mission d'Étude sur l'Ensemble des Problèmes de la Drogue. 1978. Rapport à M. le Président de la République; présenté par Monique Pelletier. Paris, 1978. pp. 284. *bibliog.*

— Ireland (Republic).

MACKEN (ULTAN) Drug abuse in Ireland. Cork, [1975]. pp. 132. *bibliog.*

— South Africa.

ENGELBRECHT (SCHALK WILLEM HENDRIK) Drug abuse as an educational problem; translated by R.F. Purchase. Pretoria, 1977. pp. 175. *bibliog.* (*Human Sciences Research Council [South Africa]. Institute for Educational Research. Reports. No. O-55*)

— Trinidad and Tobago.

TRINIDAD AND TOBAGO. Commission of Inquiry into Drug Addiction. 1972. Report; [Anthony Pantin, chairman]. [Port of Spain], 1972. pp. 109. (*Trinidad and Tobago. House of Representatives. House Papers. 1971. No. 6*)

DRUG ABUSE AND CRIME.

AULD (JOHN RICHARD MANSON) Deviant behaviour and social change: the case of marijuana use. 1978. fo. 340. *bibliog.* Typescript. Ph.D. (London) thesis: unpublished. *This thesis is the property of London University and may not be removed from the Library.*

DRUGS, crime and politics; edited...by Arnold S. Trebach. New York, 1978. pp. 178. *bibliogs.*

DRUG TRADE.

REEKIE (W.DUNCAN) and WEBER (MICHAEL H.) Profits, politics and drugs. London, 1979. pp. 185. *bibliog.*

— Belgium.

SOCIÉTÉ STUDIA. Etude sur l'évolution de la concentration dans l'industrie pharmaceutique en Belgique. [Brussels], Communautés Européennes, 1975. pp. 111.

— France.

BLUNDEN (KATHERINE) Etude sur l'évolution de la concentration dans l'industrie pharmaceutique en France. [Brussels], Communautés Européennes, 1975. pp. 126.

— India.

INDIA. Tariff Commission. Drugs. Report on the fair selling prices of drugs and pharmaceuticals, 1968. [Delhi, 1971]. pp. 753.

— Netherlands.

JONG (HENDRIK WOUTER DE) and LANGE (R. DE) A study of the evolution of concentration in the pharmaceutical industry in the Netherlands. [Brussels], European Communities, 1975. pp. 115.

— United Kingdom.

A STUDY of the evolution of concentration in the pharmaceutical industry for the United Kingdom; by...J.B. Heath and [others], etc. [Brussels], European Communities, 1975. pp. 168.

— United States.

WOLFE (MARGARET RIPLEY) Lucius Polk Brown and progressive food and drug control: Tennessee and New York City 1908-1920. Lawrence, Kan., [1978]. pp. 194.

DRUGS.

SUFFER the children: the story of thalidomide; [by] Phillip Knightley [and others]. London, 1979. pp. 309. *bibliog.*

— Prices — India.

INDIA. Tariff Commission. Drugs. Report on the fair selling prices of drugs and pharmaceuticals, 1968. [Delhi, 1971]. pp. 753.

DRUMMOND (Sir ERIC).

See DRUMMOND (JAMES ERIC) 16th Earl of Perth.

DRUMMOND (JAMES ERIC) 16th Earl of Perth.

BARROS (JAMES) Office without power: Secretary-General Sir Eric Drummond, 1919-1933. Oxford, 1979. pp. 423.

DRY-DOCKS.

BALDWIN (LOAMMI) Thoughts on the study of political economy as connected with the population, industry and paper currency of the United States;... to which is added an appendix, Dry docks, etc. New York, 1968. pp. 105. *Reprint of work first published in Cambridge, Mass., 1809, with appendix of articles first published in the Columbian Centinel, 1804.*

DUBCEK (ALEXANDER).

STEPANEK-STEMMER (MICHAEL) Der wahre Dubček: woran der Prager Frühling scheiterte; herausgegeben und mit einem Vorwort von Werner Anrod. Köln, [1978]. pp. 182. *bibliog.*

DUEHRING (EUGEN KARL).

"ANTI-Diuring" F. Engel'sa i sovremennost'. Moskva, 1978. pp. 192. *bibliog.*

VOLODIN (ALEKSANDR IVANOVICH) "Anti-Diuring" F.Engel'sa i obshchestvennaia mysl' Rossii XIX veka: istoriko-filosofskie ocherki. Moskva, 1978. pp. 252.

DUGARD (ROBERT).

MIQUELON (DALE) Dugard of Rouen: French trade to Canada and the West Indies, 1729-1770. Montreal, [1978]. pp. 282. *bibliog.*

DUISBURG

— Economic history.

SCHULZ (MANFRED) Die Entwicklung Duisburgs und der mit ihm vereinigten Gemeinden bis zum Jahre 1962. Duisburg, 1977. pp. 269. *bibliog.* (*Duisburg. Stadtarchiv. Duisburger Forschungen. Band 24/25*) *7 plans and tables in end pocket.*

DULLES (JOHN FOSTER).

GOOLD-ADAMS (RICHARD JOHN MORTON) The time of power: a reappraisal of John Foster Dulles. London, [1962]. pp. 320.

DUN (R.G.) AND COMPANY.

NORRIS (JAMES D.) R.G. Dun Co. 1841-1900: the development of credit-reporting in the nineteenth century. Westport, Conn., 1978. pp. 206. *bibliog.*

DUNCAN (JONATHAN) 1756-1811.

NARAIN (V.A.) Jonathan Duncan and Varanasi. Calcutta, 1959. pp. 240. *bibliog.*

DUNCAN (WALTER) AND GOODRICKE.

DUNCAN (WALTER) AND GOODRICKE. The Duncan Group: being a short history of Duncan Brothers and Co. Ltd., Calcutta and Walter Duncan and Goodricke Ltd., London, 1859-1959. London, 1959. pp. 184. *The first ten chapters were originally printed for private circulation in 1931.*

DUNGANS.

IUSUPOV (IL'IAS ISMAILOVICH) Sovetskie dungane v period stroitel'stva sotsializma. Frunze, 1977. pp. 262.

DUNSTAN, Saint, Archbishop of Canterbury.

ROBINSON (JOSEPH ARMITAGE) The times of Saint Dunstan. Oxford, 1923 repr. 1969. pp. 188. (*Oxford. University. Ford Lectures. 1922*)

DU PLESSIS (ARMAND JEAN) Cardinal, Duc de Richelieu.

TREASURE (G.R.R.) Cardinal Richelieu and the development of absolutism. London, 1972. pp. 316. *bibliog.*

DUPONT (CLIFFORD W.).

DUPONT (CLIFFORD W.) The reluctant president: the memoirs of...Clifford Dupont. Bulawayo, 1978. pp. 246.

DURHAM (CITY)

— Economic policy.

DURHAM (COUNTY). County Council. County structure plan: report of survey. vol. 3. Choosing the policies; ([with] Supplement: City of Durham: choosing the policies). [Durham], 1978. 2 vols. (in 1).

— Social policy.

DURHAM (COUNTY). County Council. County structure plan: report of survey. vol. 3. Choosing the policies; ([with] Supplement: City of Durham: choosing the policies). [Durham], 1978. 2 vols. (in 1).

DURHAM (COUNTY)

— Economic conditions.

DURHAM (COUNTY). County Council. Durham county structure plan: (public participation: survey stage). [Durham, 1978?]. pp. 168. (*Technical Papers. No. 23*)

DURHAM (COUNTY). County Council. Durham county structure plan: (written statement). Durham, [1979]. pp. 194. *Map in end pocket.*

— Economic history.

McCORD (NORMAN) North East England: an economic and social history. London, 1979. pp. 267.

WILCOCK (DON) The Durham coalfield. part 1. The "sea cole" age. Durham, 1979. pp. 89. *bibliog.* (*Durham County Library. Local History Publications. No. 14*)

— Economic policy.

DURHAM (COUNTY). County Council. County structure plan: report of survey. vol. 2. Resolving the issues. [Durham], 1977. pp. 145.

DURHAM (COUNTY). County Council. County structure plan: report of survey. vol. 3. Choosing the policies; ([with] Supplement: City of Durham: choosing the policies). [Durham], 1978. 2 vols. (in 1).

DURHAM (COUNTY). County Council. Durham county structure plan: (public participation: aims stage). [Durham, 1978?]. pp. 161. (*Technical Papers. No. 25*)

DURHAM (COUNTY). County Council. Durham county structure plan: (public participation: survey stage). [Durham, 1978?]. pp. 168. (*Technical Papers. No. 23*)

DURHAM (COUNTY). County Council. Durham county structure plan: comments on "Choosing the policies". [Durham], 1979. pp. 132.

DURHAM (COUNTY). County Council. Durham county structure plan: (public participation: policy stage). [Durham, 1979?]. pp. 172. (Technical Papers. No. 26)

DURHAM (COUNTY). County Council. Durham county structure plan: (written statement). Durham, [1979]. pp. 194. Map in end pocket.

— Social conditions.

DURHAM (COUNTY). County Council. Durham county structure plan: (public participation: survey stage). [Durham, 1978?]. pp. 168. (Technical Papers. No. 23)

DURHAM (COUNTY). County Council. Durham county structure plan: (written statement). Durham, [1979]. pp. 194. Map in end pocket.

— Social history.

McCORD (NORMAN) North East England: an economic and social history. London, 1979. pp. 267.

— Social policy.

DURHAM (COUNTY). County Council. County structure plan: report of survey. vol. 2. Resolving the issues. [Durham], 1977. pp. 145.

DURHAM (COUNTY). County Council. County structure plan: report of survey. vol. 3. Choosing the policies; ([with] Supplement: City of Durham: choosing the policies). [Durham], 1978. 2 vols. (in 1).

DURHAM (COUNTY). County Council. Durham county structure plan: (public participation: aims stage). [Durham, 1978?]. pp. 161. (Technical Papers. No. 25)

DURHAM (COUNTY). County Council. Durham county structure plan: (public participation: survey stage). [Durham, 1978?]. pp. 168. (Technical Papers. No. 23)

DURHAM (COUNTY). County Council. Durham county structure plan: comments on "Choosing the policies". [Durham], 1979. pp. 132.

DURHAM (COUNTY). County Council. Durham county structure plan: (public participation: policy stage). [Durham, 1979?]. pp. 172. (Technical Papers. No. 26)

DURHAM (COUNTY). County Council. Durham county structure plan: (written statement). Durham, [1979]. pp. 194. Map in end pocket.

DURKHEIM (EMILE).

KOENIG (RENÉ) Emile Durkheim zur Diskussion: jenseits von Dogmatismus und Skepsis. München, [1978]. pp. 364. bibliog.

DUSUNS.

NORTH BORNEO. Native Affairs Bulletins. No.7. Dusun custom in Putatan district; compiled by Pangeran Osman bin O.K.K. Pangeran Haji Omar; with a translation by G.C. Woolley. Jesselton, [1932] repr. 1962. pp. 55. In English and Malay.

DUTCH EAST INDIA COMPANY.

SMITH (GEORGE VINAL) The Dutch in seventeenth-century Thailand. Detroit, [1977]. pp. 203. bibliog. (Northern Illinois University. Center for Southeast Asian Studies. Special Reports. No. 16)

DUTCH GUIANA

— Politics and government.

DEW (EDWARD) The difficult flowering of Surinam: ethnicity and politics in a plural society. The Hague, 1978. pp. 234. bibliog.

— Race relations.

DEW (EDWARD) The difficult flowering of Surinam: ethnicity and politics in a plural society. The Hague, 1978. pp. 234. bibliog.

— Statistics.

DUTCH GUIANA. Economic Information Service. 1975. A statistic survey of Surinam. Paramaribo, 1975. pp. 36.

DUTCH IN INDONESIA.

INDONESIA: selected documents on colonialism and nationalism, 1830- 1942; edited and translated by Chr. L.M. Penders. St. Lucia, Queensland, 1977. pp. 367.

DUTCH IN SRI LANKA.

BROHIER (RICHARD LESLIE) Links between Sri Lanka and the Netherlands: a book of Dutch Ceylon. Colombo, [1978?]. pp. 165. bibliog.

DUTCH IN THE UNITED STATES.

STOKVIS (PIETER RUDOLF DEGENHARD) De Nederlandse trek naar Amerika, 1846-1847. Leiden, 1977. pp. 251. bibliog. (Leiden. Rijks Universiteit. Leidse Historische Reeks. Deel 21) With summary in English.

DUTCH REFORMED CHURCH IN AFRICA.

BREYER (KARL) My brother's keeper: a picture report on the mission of the Dutch Reformed Church in Southern Africa. Johannesburg, 1977. pp. 163.

DUTCH WEST INDIA COMPANY.

WINTER (PIETER JAN VAN) De Westindische Compagnie ter kamer Stad en Lande. 's-Gravenhage, 1978. pp.280. (Nederlandsch Economisch-Historisch Archief. Werken. 15)

DUTHIERS (GERARD DE LACAZE-).

See LACAZE-DUTHIERS (GERARD DE).

DWELLINGS

— Prices — United Kingdom — London.

JACHNIAK (DANUTA) House prices in the G.L.C. area 1939-1971. Reading, 1978. pp. 78. bibliog. (Reading. University. Department of Geography. Reading Geographical Papers. No. 62)

— European Economic Community countries — Maintenance and repair.

REPORT on the ECSC experimental programme of modernization of housing. [Brussels], European Communities, 1975. pp. 368.

— United Kingdom — Maintenance and repair.

U.K. Department of the Environment. 1977. Housing policy review: statutory housing repairs account: consultation paper. [London, 1977]. pp. 4.

— — Statistics.

U.K. Department of the Environment. 1979. National dwelling and housing survey. London, 1979. pp. 317. Form in end pocket.

— — Scotland — Maintenance and repair.

PAISLEY COMMUNITY DEVELOPMENT PROJECT. Westmarch action group: a fight for improvements; (by Barbara Jackson). [Paisley, 1978]. pp. 59.

DYNAMIC PROGRAMMING.

DREYFUS (STUART ERNEST) and LAW (AVERILL M.) The art and theory of dynamic programming. New York, 1977. pp. 284.

LARSON (ROBERT EDWARD) and CASTI (JOHN L.) Principles of dynamic programming. pt. 1. Basic analytic and computational methods. New York, [1978]. pp. 330. bibliog.

WHITE (DOUGLAS JOHN) Finite dynamic programming: an approach to finite Markov decision processes. Chichester, [1978]. pp. 204. bibliog.

DZERZHINSKII (FELIKS EDMUNDOVICH).

O Felikse Edmundoviche Dzerzhinskom: vospominaniia, stat'i, ocherki sovremennikov. Moskva, 1977. pp. 303.

EARTH SCIENCES.

MENARD (HENRY W.) Geology, resources, and society: an introduction to earth science. San Francisco, [1974]. pp. 621. bibliogs.

EAST (FAR EAST)

— Civilization.

FAIRBANK (JOHN KING) and others. East Asia: tradition and transformation. Boston, [Mass.], 1978. pp. 982.

— Economic integration.

UNITED NATIONS. Economic Commission for Asia and the Far East. Regional Economic Cooperation Series. No. 7. Regional economic cooperation in Asia and the Far East: report of the meeting of government and central bank officials on trade and monetary cooperation; consideration and proposals for trade and monetary cooperation in the ECAFE region. (E/CN.11/958). New York, 1971. pp. 84.

— Foreign economic relations — United Kingdom.

STEEDS (DAVID) and NISH (IAN HILL) compilers. China, Japan and 19th century Britain; [commentaries on British parliamentary papers]. Dublin, [1977]. pp. 136. bibliog.

— Foreign relations — Germany.

STINGL (WERNER) Der Ferne Osten in der deutschen Politik vor dem Ersten Weltkrieg, 1902-1914. Frankfurt/Main, [1978]. 2 vols. bibliog.

— — United Kingdom.

STEEDS (DAVID) and NISH (IAN HILL) compilers. China, Japan and 19th century Britain; [commentaries on British parliamentary papers]. Dublin, [1977]. pp. 136. bibliog.

— History.

FAIRBANK (JOHN KING) and others. East Asia: tradition and transformation. Boston, [Mass.], 1978. pp. 982.

EAST (NEAR EAST)

— Economic conditions.

MIDDLE EAST CONTEMPORARY SURVEY; vol.1, 1976-77; Colin Legum, editor; [pd. by] Shiloah Center for Middle Eastern and African Studies, Tel Aviv University. New York, 1978. pp. 684.

DUNCAN (ANDREW) Money rush. London, 1979. pp. 384. bibliog.

WILSON (RODNEY) The economies of the Middle East. London, 1979. pp. 209. bibliog.

— Foreign relations.

McLAURIN (RONALD D.) and others. Foreign policy making in the Middle East: domestic influences on policy in Egypt, Iraq, Israel, and Syria. New York, 1977. pp. 313. bibliog.

MIDDLE EAST CONTEMPORARY SURVEY; vol.1, 1976-77; Colin Legum, editor; [pd. by] Shiloah Center for Middle Eastern and African Studies, Tel Aviv University. New York, 1978. pp. 684.

— — France.

PURYEAR (VERNON JOHN) Napoleon and the Dardanelles. Berkeley, 1951. pp. 437. bibliog.

— — Russia.

FREEDMAN (ROBERT OWEN) Soviet policy toward the Middle East since 1970. rev. ed. New York, 1978. pp. 373. bibliog.

HEIKAL (MOHAMED) Sphinx and commissar: the rise and fall of Soviet influence in the Arab world. London, 1978. pp. 303.

EAST (NEAR EAST)(Cont.)

KASS (ILANA) Soviet involvement in the Middle East: policy formulation, 1966-1973. Boulder, 1978. pp. 273.

The LIMITS to power: Soviet policy in the Middle East; edited by Yaacov Ro'i. London, [1979]. pp. 376. *bibliogs.*

— — United States.

CHURBA (JOSEPH) The politics of defeat: America's decline in the Middle East. New York, [1977]. pp. 224. *bibliog.*

CONGRESSIONAL QUARTERLY INC. The Middle East: U.S. policy, Israel, oil and the Arabs. 3rd ed. Washington, D.C., [1977]. pp. 196.

QUANDT (WILLIAM B.) Decade of decisions: American policy toward the Arab-Israeli conflict, 1967-1976. Berkeley, [1977]. pp. 313. *bibliog.*

— History.

CONGRESSIONAL QUARTERLY INC. The Middle East: U.S. policy, Israel, oil and the Arabs. 3rd ed. Washington, D.C., [1977]. pp. 196.

The PALESTINIANS and the Middle East conflict; [edited by] Gabriel Ben-Dor. Ramat Gan, 1978. pp. 575. *bibliog. Proceedings of an international conference held at the Institute of Middle Eastern Studies, University of Haifa, 1976.*

— Military policy.

MILITARY aspects of the Israeli-Arab conflict; [edited by] Louis Williams. Tel Aviv, [1975]. pp. 265.

— Politics and government.

BOURGUIBA (HABIB) The path to Arab unity: memorandum sent...to the heads of state attending the 3rd Arab Summit Meeting, held at Casablanca on 13th September 1965. [Tunis, Secretariat of State for Information and Orientation, 1965]. pp. 41.

CONGRESSIONAL QUARTERLY INC. The Middle East: U.S. policy, Israel, oil and the Arabs. 3rd ed. Washington, D.C., [1977]. pp. 196.

MIDDLE EAST CONTEMPORARY SURVEY; vol.1, 1976-77; Colin Legum, editor; [pd. by] Shiloah Center for Middle Eastern and African Studies, Tel Aviv University. New York, 1978. pp. 684.

— Relations (general) with the United Kingdom.

SEARIGHT (SARAH) The British in the Middle East. rev. ed. London, 1979. pp. 290. *bibliog.*

EAST ANGLIA

— Economic conditions.

EAST Anglia regional strategy: monitoring report no. 1. [London, Department of the Environment], 1977. pp. 64.

— Population.

EAST Anglia regional strategy: monitoring report no. 1. [London, Department of the Environment], 1977. pp. 64.

EAST ANGLIA ECONOMIC PLANNING COUNCIL. Future population of East Anglia; a report. [London, 1978]. pp. 52. *bibliog.*

— Social conditions.

EAST Anglia regional strategy: monitoring report no. 1. [London, Department of the Environment], 1977. pp. 64.

EAST INDIA COMPANY.

CHAUDHURI (K.N.) The trading world of Asia and the English East India Company, 1660-1760. Cambridge, 1978. pp. 629. *bibliog.*

EAST INDIAN STUDENTS IN THE UNITED STATES.

GANDHI (RAJNIKANT SURESH) Locals and cosmopolitans of Little India: a sociological study of the Indian student community at Minnesota, U.S.A. Bombay, 1974. pp. 216. *bibliog.*

EAST INDIANS IN CANADA.

WARD (W. PETER) White Canada forever: popular attitudes and public policy toward Orientals in British Columbia. Montreal, [1978]. pp. 205.

EAST INDIANS IN FIJI.

NORTON (ROBERT) Race and politics in Fiji. New York, [1977]. pp. 210. *bibliog.*

EAST INDIANS IN NATAL.

VAN DER BURGH (CHRIS) The socio-economic position of Indian blind persons in Natal. Pretoria, 1976. pp. 65. *bibliog. (Human Sciences Research Council [South Africa]. Institute for Sociological, Demographic and Criminological Research. Reports. No. S-42)*

EAST INDIANS IN SOUTH AFRICA.

LÖTTER (JOHANN MORGENDALL) and VAN TONDER (JAN LOUIS) Aspects of fertility of Indian South Africans. Pretoria, 1975. pp. 37. *bibliog. (Human Sciences Research Council [South Africa]. Institute for Sociological, Demographic and Criminological Research. Reports. No. S-40)*

MEER (FATIMA) The ghetto people: a study of the uprooting of the Indian people of South Africa. London, 1975. pp. 33. *(Africa Publications Trust. Studies in the Mass Removal of Population in South Africa. No. 6)*

SOUTH AFRICA. Department of Information. 1975. The Indian South African. Pretoria, 1975. pp. 80.

MAASDORP (GAVIN G.) and PILLAY (P. NESEN) Urban relocation and racial segregation: the case of Indian South Africans. Durban, 1977. pp. 206. *bibliog. (Natal University. Department of Economics. Research Monographs)*

EAST INDIANS IN THE UNITED KINGDOM.

WARD (ROBIN W.) Ugandan Asians in Britain: some local variations in the potential for resettlement; paper presented [to] (Seminar [on] Ugandan Asians, London, 2 December 1976). [Bristol], Social Science Research Council Research Unit on Ethnic Relations, [1976?]. fo. (11).

EAST INDIANS IN THE UNITED STATES.

MELENDY (HOWARD BRETT) Asians in America: Filipinos, Koreans, and East Indians. Boston, Mass., [1977]. pp. 340. *bibliog.*

EAST KILBRIDE

— Growth.

SMITH (ROGER) East Kilbride: the biography of a Scottish new town, 1947-1973. London, H.M.S.O., 1979. pp. 165.

EAST MIDLAND ALLIED PRESS.

NEWTON (DAVID) Men of mark: makers of East Midland Allied Press. Peterborough, 1977. pp. 239.

EAST SUSSEX

— Economic conditions.

EAST SUSSEX. Planning Department. County structure plan [1978]: first alteration; ([with] County structure plan [1978]: first alteration: report of survey). Lewes, 1978. 2 pts. (in 1 vol.).

— Economic policy.

EAST SUSSEX. Planning Department. The altered county structure plan 1978: the approved county structure plan 1978 as amended by the County Council in the submitted first alteration: informal draft. Lewes, 1978. pp. 121.

EAST SUSSEX. Planning Department. County structure plan 1978, as approved by the Secretary of State for the Environment, May 1978. Lewes, 1978. pp. 86.

EAST SUSSEX. Planning Department. County structure plan [1978]: first alteration; ([with] County structure plan [1978]: first alteration: report of survey). Lewes, 1978. 2 pts. (in 1 vol.).

— Social conditions.

EAST SUSSEX. Planning Department. County structure plan [1978]: first alteration; ([with] County structure plan [1978]: first alteration: report of survey). Lewes, 1978. 2 pts. (in 1 vol.).

— Social policy.

EAST SUSSEX. Planning Department. The altered county structure plan 1978: the approved county structure plan 1978 as amended by the County Council in the submitted first alteration: informal draft. Lewes, 1978. pp. 121.

EAST SUSSEX. Planning Department. County structure plan 1978, as approved by the Secretary of State for the Environment, May 1978. Lewes, 1978. pp. 86.

EAST SUSSEX. Planning Department. County structure plan [1978]: first alteration; ([with] County structure plan [1978]: first alteration: report of survey). Lewes, 1978. 2 pts. (in 1 vol.).

EAST-WEST TRADE (1945-).

INDUSTRIAL policies and technology transfers between East and West; edited by C.T. Saunders. Wien, 1977. pp. 316. *(Wiener Institut Für Internationale Wirtschaftsvergleiche. East-West European Economic Interaction. Workshop Papers. vol.3)*

LEVINSON (CHARLES) Vodka Cola. [London, 1978]. pp. 328.

NOVE (ALEXANDER) East-west trade: problems, prospects, issues. Beverley Hills, [1978]. pp. 76. *bibliog. (Georgetown University. Center for Strategic and International Studies. Washington Papers. vol. 6/53)*

KOSTECKI (M.M.) East-West trade and the GATT system. London, 1979. pp. 157. *bibliog.*

LEVČÍK (FRIEDRICH) and STANKOVSKY (JAN) Industrial cooperation between east and west; translated by Michel Vale. White Plains, N.Y., [1979]. pp. 287. *bibliog.*

EAST YORK WORKERS' ASSOCIATION.

SCHULZ (PATRICIA V.) The East York Workers' Association: a response to the great depression. Toronto, [1975]. pp. 74.

EASTERN QUESTION (BALKAN).

ULUNIAN (AKOP ARUTIUNOVICH) Aprel'skoe vosstanie 1876 goda v Bolgarii i Rossiia: ocherki. Moskva, 1978. pp. 214. *bibliog. With English table of contents.*

MILLMAN (RICHARD) Britain and the Eastern question, 1875-1878. Oxford, 1979. pp. 613. *bibliog.*

EASTMAN (ELAINE GOODALE).

EASTMAN (ELAINE GOODALE) Sister to the Sioux: the memoirs of Elaine Goodale Eastman, 1885-91; edited by Kay Graber. Lincoln, Neb., 1978. pp. 175.

EASTMAN (MAX).

O'NEILL (WILLIAM LAWRENCE) The last romantic: a life of Max Eastman. New York, 1978. pp. 339. *bibliog.*

EC-121 CRISIS, 1969.

SIMMONS (ROBERT R.) The Pueblo, EC-121, and Mayaguez incidents: some continuities and changes. Baltimore, 1978. pp. 51. *(Maryland University. School of Law. Occasional Papers/Reprints Series in Contemporary Asian Studies. No.20)*

ECCLES (MARRINER STODDARD).

HYMAN (SIDNEY) Marriner S. Eccles: private entrepreneur and public servant. Stanford, Calif., 1976. pp. 456.

ECCLESIASTICAL COURTS

— United Kingdom.

HOULBROOKE (RALPH ANTHONY) Church courts and the people during the English Reformation, 1520-1570. Oxford, 1979. pp. 304. *bibliog.*

ECOLOGY.

MAN and the ecosphere. San Francisco, 1971. pp. 307. *bibliog. Readings from Scientific American.*

ARAB-OGLY (EDVARD ARTUROVICH) Demograficheskie i ekologicheskie prognozy: kritika sovremennykh burzhuaznykh kontseptsii; Demographic and ecological forecasts: critical survey of modern bourgeois conceptions. Moskva, 1978. pp. 319. *With Russian and English tables of contents.*

GIARINI (ORIO) and LOUBERGÉ (HENRI) The diminishing returns of technology: an essay on the crisis in economic growth. Oxford, 1978. pp. 122.

HENDERSON (HAZEL) Creating alternative futures: the end of economics. New York, [1978]. pp. 403. *bibliogs.*

HOLDGATE (M.W.) A perspective of environmental pollution. Cambridge, 1979. pp. 278. *bibliog.*

ROSZAK (THEODORE) Person/planet: the creative disintegration of industrial society. London, 1979. pp. 347. *bibliog.*

SOCIAL and ecological systems; edited by P.C. Burnham and R.F. Ellen. London, 1979. pp. 314. *bibliogs. (Association of Social Anthropologists of the Commonwealth. A.S.A. Monographs. 18)*

— Canada.

ECOLOGY versus politics in Canada; edited by William Leiss. Toronto, [1979]. pp. 282. *bibliogs.*

ECOLOGY PARTY

— United Kingdom.

ECOLOGY PARTY. The real alternative: Ecology Party 1979 election manifesto. Birmingham, 1979. pp. 16.

ECONOMIC ASSISTANCE.

WILSON (Sir HAROLD) The first Edwina Mountbatten Memorial Lecture. London, [1973?]. 1 pamphlet (unpaged). *(Marr-Munning Trust. Edwina Mountbatten Papers. No. 1)*

ANOTHER development: approaches and strategies; [by] Fernando Henrique Cardoso [and others]; edited by Marc Nerfin. Uppsala, 1977. pp. 265..

EXCHANGE of expertise: the counterpart system in the new international order; edited by Irving J. Spitzberg, Jr. Boulder, Colo., [1978]. pp. 257. *bibliogs.*

HOOLE (FRANCIS W.) Evaluation research and development activities. Beverly Hills, [1978]. pp. 205. *bibliog.*

PARSONS (CHRISTOPHER) Finance for development or survival?: the debt crisis of developing countries. London, 1978. pp. 27. *(Fabian Society. Research Series. [No.] 336)*

REPORT: news of the World Bank. bi-m. Washington. *Current issues only kept.*

ECONOMIC ASSISTANCE, AMERICAN.

ATLANTIC COUNCIL OF THE UNITED STATES. The Atlantic Council Working Group on the United States and the Developing Countries. The United States and the developing countries. Boulder, Colo., [1977]. pp. 150.

HARRINGTON (MICHAEL) b. 1928. The vast majority: a journey to the world's poor. New York, [1977]. pp. 281. *bibliog.*

— Europe.

BAILEY (THOMAS ANDREW) The Marshall Plan summer: an eyewitness report on Europe and the Russians in 1947. Stanford, Calif., [1977]. pp. 246.

The ORIGINS of the cold war and contemporary Europe; edited with an introduction by Charles S. Maier. New York, 1978. pp. 254. *bibliog.*

— Greece.

AMEN (MICHAEL MARK) American foreign policy in Greece, 1944/1949: economic, military and institutional aspects. Frankfurt am Main, 1978. pp. 310.

— Palestine.

TERRY (JANICE J.) Attitudes of United States congressmen toward aid to the Palestinians and arms to Israel. Beirut, [1973]. pp. 78. *(Palestine Research Center. Palestine Essays. No. 37)*

ECONOMIC ASSISTANCE, BRITISH.

McQUEEN (MATTHEW) Britain, the EEC and the developing world. London, 1977. pp. 119. *bibliog.*

U.K. Ministry of Overseas Development. 1978. United Kingdom memorandum to the Development Aid Committee of the OECD. [London], 1978. 1 pamphlet (various pagings).

U.K. Ministry of Overseas Development. Study Group on Urban Poverty. 1979. Urban poverty: report; [E.C. Burr, chairman]. London, [1979]. pp. 44. *(Overseas Development Papers. No. 19)*

— Directories.

OVERSEAS DEVELOPMENT INSTITUTE. Development guide: a directory of non-commercial organisations in Britain actively concerned in overseas development and training. 3rd ed. London, 1978. pp. 216.

— Public opinion.

BOWLES (T.S.) Survey of attitudes towards overseas development; submitted to the Central Office of Information...by the Schlackman Research Organisation Ltd. (on behalf of the Ministry of Overseas Development). London, H.M.S.O., 1978. pp. 158.

ECONOMIC ASSISTANCE, DOMESTIC

— United States.

EMPLOYMENT, income, and welfare in the rural South; by Brian Rungeling [and others]. New York, 1977. pp. 355. *bibliog.*

ECONOMIC ASSISTANCE, EUROPEAN.

McQUEEN (MATTHEW) Britain, the EEC and the developing world. London, 1977. pp. 119. *bibliog.*

ECONOMIC ASSISTANCE, FRENCH.

FRANCE. Ministère de la Coopération. Service des Etudes Economiques et des Questions Internationales. 1978. Contributions du Ministère de la Coopération au mémorandum de la France, 1977, au Comité d'Aide au Développement de l'O.C.D.E. Paris, 1978. pp. 54. *(Etudes et Documents. No. 31)*

ECONOMIC ASSISTANCE, RUSSIAN.

MAKSIMOVA (MARGARITA MATVEEVNA) SSSR i mezhdunarodnoe ekonomicheskoe sotrudnichestvo. Moskva, 1977. pp. 196.

ECONOMIC ASSISTANCE IN AFRICA.

FRANCE. Ministère de la Coopération. Service des Etudes Economiques et [des] Questions Internationales. 1976. Nouvelles ressources financières pour l'Afrique. Paris, 1976. pp. 79. *(Etudes et Documents. No. 24)*

ARNOLD (GUY) Aid in Africa. London, 1979. pp. 240. *bibliog.*

ECONOMIC DEVELOPMENT.

ECONOMIC COMMUNITY OF WEST AFRICAN STATES.

CAMPBELL (R. KEITH) Nigerian foreign policy and the Economic Community of West African states (ECOWAS). Braamfontein, 1978. pp. 10. *bibliog. (South African Institute of International Affairs. Occasional Papers)*

ECONOMIC CONDITIONS.

KULKARNI (GANESH BHAURAO) Economic organization. Bombay, 1950 repr. 1951. pp. 262.

PROGRESUL istoric și contemporaneitatea. București, 1976. pp. 538. *With English, French, German and Russian tables of contents.*

BANCA D'ITALIA. Research Department. Economic papers. irreg., 1977(no. 1)- Roma.

NOVOSELOV (SERGEI PAVLOVICH) Obostrenie ekonomichskikh i sotsial'no-politicheskikh protivorechii kapitalizma. Moskva, 1977. pp. 199.

TOWARDS full employment and price stability: a report to the OECD by a group of independent experts. Paris, Organisation for Economic Co-operation and Development, 1977. pp. 341.

KOSTIUKHIN (DMITRII IVANOVICH) The world market today. Moscow, 1979. pp. 215.

— Statistics.

WORLD STATISTICS IN BRIEF; [pd. by] Statistical Office [United Nations]. a., 1977(2nd)- New York.

ECONOMIC COUNCILS

— United Kingdom — Ireland, Northern.

IRELAND, NORTHERN. Working Party on Future of Northern Ireland Economic Council. 1977. Report; [John Waddell, chairman]. Belfast, 1977. pp. 11.

ECONOMIC DEVELOPMENT.

FINANCE AND DEVELOPMENT (formerly The Fund and Bank review): a publication of the International Monetary Fund and the World Bank Group. q., Je 1964(v.1, no.1)- Washington.

WARD (BARBARA) Baroness Jackson. Towards a world of plenty? [Toronto, 1964]. pp. 79. *(Toronto. University. Falconer Lectures. 1963)*

REVIEW OF INTERNATIONAL TRADE AND DEVELOPMENT: report by the Secretariat of UNCTAD. [title varies]. a., 1967- , with gap (1971,1972). New York.

NOWICKI (JÓZEF) Development theory of the less advanced economies. [new ed.] Warsaw, 1972. pp. 127. *bibliog. (Instytut Gospodarki Krajów Rozwijających Się. Teaching Papers: Advanced Course in National Economic Planning. vol. 14)*

BARAN (PAUL A.) The political economy of growth; with an introduction by R.B. Sutcliffe. Harmondsworth, [1973]. pp. 475.

UNITED NATIONS. Centre for Development Planning, Projections and Policies. 1973. Implementation of the international development strategy: papers for the first over-all review and appraisal of progress during the second United Nations development decade. (E/5267) (ST/ECA/178). New York, 1973. 2 vols. (in 1).

WILSON (Sir HAROLD) The first Edwina Mountbatten Memorial Lecture. London, [1973?]. 1 pamphlet (unpaged). *(Marr-Munning Trust. Edwina Mountbatten Papers. No. 1)*

INTERNATIONAL BANK FOR RECONSTRUCTION AND DEVELOPMENT. 1974. Environmental, health, and human ecologic considerations in economic development projects. Washington, 1974. pp. 142. *bibliog.*

NYERERE (JULIUS KAMBARAGE) The economic challenge: dialogue or confrontation. London, [1976]. pp. 12. *Address given to the Royal Commonwealth Society in London in 1975.*

ECONOMIC DEVELOPMENT.(Cont.)

ANOTHER development: approaches and strategies; [by] Fernando Henrique Cardoso [and others]; edited by Marc Nerfin. Uppsala, 1977. pp. 265..

KAMAEV (VLADIMIR DOROFEEVICH) Razvitoi sotsializm: tempy i kachestvo ekonomicheskogo rosta. Moskva, 1977. pp. 210.

LUKINOV (IVAN ILLARIONOVICH) Vosproizvodstvo i tseny. Moskva, 1977. pp. 431.

MORAWETZ (DAVID) Twenty-five years of economic development 1950 to 1975. Washington, D.C., International Bank for Reconstruction and Development, 1977. pp. 125.

SHIELDS (ROGER ELWOOD) Economic growth with price deflation, 1873-1896. New York, 1977. pp. 346. bibliog.

SOCIETY and change: essays in honour of Sachin Chaudhuri; edited by K.S. Krishnaswamy [and others]. Bombay, 1977. pp. 327.

ZEYLSTRA (WILLEM GUSTAAF) Aid or development: the relevance of development aid to problems of developing countries. 2nd ed. Leyden, 1977. pp. 269. bibliog.

AHMAD (JALEEL) Import substitution, trade and development. Greenwich, Conn., [1978]. pp. 128. bibliog.

BINSWANGER (HANS P.) and RUTTAN (VERNON WESLEY) Induced innovation: technology, institutions, and development. Baltimore, [1978]. pp. 423.

GEOGRAPHY and development: a world regional approach; edited by Don R. Hoy. New York, [1978]. pp. 728.

GESELLSCHAFT FÜR SOZIAL- UND WIRTSCHAFTSGESCHICHTE. 6. Arbeitstagung, 1975. Wirtschaftliches Wachstum, Energie und Verkehr vom Mittelalter bis ins 19. Jahrhundert: Bericht...; herausgegeben von Hermann Kellenbenz. Stuttgart, 1978. pp. 248.

GIARINI (ORIO) and LOUBERGÉ (HENRI) The diminishing returns of technology: an essay on the crisis in economic growth. Oxford, 1978. pp. 122.

LEIBENSTEIN (HARVEY) General x-efficiency theory and economic development. New York, 1978. pp. 189.

SCIENCE, technology, and economic development: a historical and comparative study; edited by William Beranek, Jr. [and] Gustav Ranis. New York, [1978]. pp. 347. bibliogs.

SEIDMAN (ROBERT BENJAMIN) The state, law and development. London, [1978]. pp. 483.

TEUNE (HENRY) and MLINAR (ZDRAVKO) The developmental logic of social systems. Beverly Hills, [1978]. pp. 175.

TORRES (JAMES F.) Success in smallness: a self-help plan for developing countries. [River Falls, Wis., 1978]. pp. 54.

WILKINSON (JOHN CRAVEN) Problems of oasis development. Oxford, 1978. pp. 40. bibliog. (Oxford. University. School of Geography. Research Papers. No.20)

ZOLLSCHAN (GEORGE K.) A critical examination of theories of "development" with special reference to underlying motivational assumptions. 1978. 2 vols. bibliog. Typescript. Ph.D.(London) thesis: unpublished. This thesis is the property of London University and may not be removed from the Library.

TRADE AND DEVELOPMENT: an UNCTAD review; [pd.by] United Nations Conference on Trade and Development. q.?, spring 1979 (no.1)- Geneva.

BOURDIEU (PIERRE) Algeria 1960: The disenchantment of the world; The sense of honour; The Kabyle house or the world reversed; translated by Richard Nice. Cambridge, 1979. pp. 158.

DEVELOPMENT theory: four critical studies; edited by David Lehmann. London, 1979. pp. 106. bibliog.

KNOX (FRANK) Labour supply in economic development. Farnborough, [1979]. pp. 114. bibliogs.

ROXBOROUGH (IAN) Theories of underdevelopment. London, 1979. pp. 175. bibliog.

— Congresses.

UNITED NATIONS. Conference on Trade and Development, 4th, Nairobi, 1976. Proceedings of the...Conference..., fourth session, Nairobi, 5- 31 May 1976. (TD/218). New York, 1977-78. 3 vols. (in 1).

— Research.

UNITED NATIONS RESEARCH INSTITUTE FOR SOCIAL DEVELOPMENT. Research notes: a review of recent and current studies conducted at the Institute. a., Je 1968(no.1)- Geneva.

DEVELOPMENT STUDIES: register of research in the United Kingdom; [pd. by] Institute of Development Studies at the University of Sussex. bien., 1977/78- Brighton.

— Social aspects.

ALBIN (PETER S.) Progress without poverty: socially responsible economic growth. New York, [1978]. pp. 229. bibliog.

ECONOMIC DEVELOPMENT COUNCIL OF NEW YORK CITY.

ROGERS (DAVID) Can business management save the cities?: the case of New York. New York, [1978]. pp. 276.

ECONOMIC FORECASTING.

PACHAURI (RAJENDRA KUMAR) The dynamics of electrical energy supply and demand: an economic analysis. New York, 1975. pp. 171.

The FUTURE of the Soviet economy, 1978-1985: edited by Holland Hunter; contributors: David W. Carey [and others]. Boulder, Colo., [1978]. pp. 177. bibliogs.

HENDERSON (HAZEL) Creating alternative futures: the end of economics. New York, [1978]. pp. 403. bibliogs.

MAKRIDAKIS (SPYROS) and WHEELWRIGHT (STEVEN C.) Interactive forecasting: univariate and multivariate methods. 2nd ed. San Francisco, [1978]. pp. 650. bibliog.

RESOURCES for an uncertain future: papers presented at a forum marking the 25th anniversary of Resources for the Future, October 13, 1977, Washington, D.C.; Charles J. Hitch, editor. Baltimore, [1978]. pp. 105.

WORLD index of economic forecasts; edited by George Cyriax. Farnborough, [1978]. pp. 379.

— Mathematical models.

SWEDEN. Finansdepartementet. Langtidsutredningen. 1976. [Langtidsutredningen 1975. Bilaga 7]. Modeller för samhällsekonomiske perspektivplanering; av Tomas Restad. Stockholm, 1976. pp. 149. bibliog. (Sweden. Statens Offentliga Utredningar. 1976.51) With English summary.

SWEDEN. Finansdepartementet. Långtidsutredningen. 1976. (Långtidsutredningen 1975. Bilaga 8). Långtidsutredningens modellsystem;...[by] Finansdepartementets Ekonomiska Avdelning. Stockholm, 1976. pp. 143. (Sweden. Statens Offentliga Utredningar. 1976.42)

NATIONAL Institute model II;... [by] George Fane [and others]. London, [1977]. 4 vols. (National Institute of Economic and Social Research. Discussion Papers. No. 10)

DAVIES (STEPHEN GETHYN) The Treasury world economic prospects model. London, Treasury, 1979. pp. 68. (Government Economic Service Working Papers. No. 25)

— Netherlands.

NETHERLANDS. Centraal Planbureau. 1978. Omvang en samenstelling van het trendmatige arbeidsaanbod tussen 1975 en 2000. 's-Gravenhage, 1978. pp. 77. (Monografieën. No. 22)

— New Zealand — Mathematical models.

MORGAN (G.H.T.) and others. Topics in econometric model research. Wellington, 1978. pp. 48. bibliogs. (Reserve Bank of New Zealand. Research Papers. No.24)

— Russia.

SOTSIAL'NO-ekonomicheskoe prognozirovanie razvitiia regiona. Leningrad, 1977. pp. 214. bibliog.

— United Kingdom.

NORTHERN REGION STRATEGY TEAM. Future trends and prospects in the United Kingdom economy; interim draft report; (project no.A.5.a). Newcastle-upon-Tyne, 1976. 1 vol. (various pagings). ([Working Papers. No.2])

RAY (GEORGE F.) Energy and transport: problems of medium-term assessment: a post- mortem on the Energy and Inland Transport chapters of The British economy in 1975. London, 1978. pp. 31. (National Institute of Economic and Social Research. Discussion Papers. No. 14)

— — Mathematical models.

A FINANCIAL sector for the Treasury model. Part 1. The model of the domestic monetary system; by Peter Spencer and Colin Mowl. Part 2. The model of external capital flows; by Rachel Lomax and Michael Denham. London, Treasury, 1978. pp. 115. bibliogs. (Government Economic Service Working Papers. No. 17)

SAVAGE (DAVID) The monetary sector of the NIESR model: preliminary results. London, [1978]. pp. 24. bibliog. (National Institute of Economic and Social Research. Discussion Papers. No.21)

ECONOMIC HISTORY.

KULKARNI (GANESH BHAURAO) Economic organization. Bombay, 1950 repr. 1951. pp. 262.

WIRTSCHAFTS- und sozialgeschichtliche Probleme der frühen Industrialisierung; mit Beiträgen von Pierre Ayçoberry [and others]; herausgegeben von Wolfram Fischer. Berlin, 1968. pp. 542. (Historische Kommission zu Berlin. Einzelveröffentlichungen. Band 1)

DAVIS (RALPH) Professor of Economic History, Leicester University. The rise of the Atlantic economies. London, [1973]. pp. 352. bibliog.

LEON (PIERRE) Histoire économique et sociale du monde. Paris, [1977-78]. 6 vols. bibliog.

BUSINESS and businessmen: studies in business, economic and accounting history; edited by Sheila Marriner. Liverpool, [1978]. pp. 300. bibliogs.

DOEHAERD (RENEE) The early Middle Ages in the West: economy and society; translated by W.G. Deakin. Amsterdam, 1978. pp. 307. bibliog.

FRANK (ANDRE GUNDER) World accumulation, 1492-1789. New York, [1978]. pp. 303. bibliog.

GEOGRAPHY and development: a world regional approach; edited by Don R. Hoy. New York, [1978]. pp. 728.

KATONA (GEORGE) and STRUEMPEL (BURKHARD) A new economic era. New York, [1978]. pp. 176. bibliog.

KERNPROBLEMEN der economische geschiedenis; onder redactie van H. Baudet en H. van der Meulen. Groningen, [1978]. pp. 404. bibliogs.

KINDLEBERGER (CHARLES POOR) Manias, panics, and crashes: a history of financial crises. London, 1978. pp. 271.

HUTTON (JOHN) The mystery of wealth: political economy - its development and impact on world events. Cheltenham, 1979. pp. 412. bibliog.

WALLERSTEIN (IMMANUEL) The capitalist world-economy. Cambridge, 1979. pp. 305. bibliogs.

— **Bibliography.**

KERNPROBLEMEN der economische geschiedenis; onder redactie van H. Baudet en H. van der Meulen. Groningen, [1978]. pp. 404. *bibliogs.*

— **Congresses.**

INTERNATIONAL CONFERENCE OF ECONOMIC HISTORY, 7TH, EDINBURGH, 1978. Proceedings...; edited by Michael Flinn. Edinburgh, [1978]. 2 vols.

ECONOMIC INDICATORS.

IN search of economic indicators: essays on business surveys; edited by Werner H. Strigel. Berlin, 1977. pp. 198.

HART (P.E.) Redundant inequalities. London, [1978]. pp. 22. *bibliog.* (*National Institute of Economic and Social Research. Discussion Papers. No. 18*)

— **Belize.**

BELIZE. British Honduras through the fifties. [Belize, 1961]. pp. 34.

— **Brazil.**

CONTADOR (CLAUDIO ROBERTO) Ciclos econômicos e indicadores de atividade no Brasil. Rio de Janeiro, 1977. pp. 237. *bibliog.* (*Brazil. Instituto de Planejamento Econômico e Social. Instituto de Pesquisas. Relatorios de Pesquisa. No. 35*)

— **Dutch Guiana.**

DUTCH GUIANA. Economic Information Service. 1975. A statistic survey of Surinam. Paramaribo, 1975. pp. 36.

— **France — Picardy.**

OBSERVATOIRE ECONOMIQUE DE PICARDIE. Indicateurs économiques et sociaux. a., 1978- Amiens.

— **India — Madras.**

MADRAS. Finance Department. 1976. Tamil Nadu: an economic appraisal, 1976. Madras, 1976. pp. 223.

— **Indonesia.**

INDONESIA. Biro Pusat Statistik. Indikator ekonomi: buletin statistik bulanan: monthly statistical bulletin. m., Ja 1978- Jakarta. *[in English and Indonesian]*

— **Pacific, The.**

KEY ECONOMIC INDICATORS OF THE SOUTH PACIFIC; [pd. by] South Pacific Commission. irreg., D 1977(no.1)- Noumea. *[in English and French]*

ECONOMIC LEGISLATION

— **Germany.**

BRUEGGEMEIER (GERT) Entwicklung des Rechts im organisierten Kapitalismus: Materialien zum Wirtschaftsrecht. Frankfurt am Main, [1977]-1979. 2 vols.

— **Germany, Eastern — Dictionaries and encyclopedias.**

LEXIKON der Wirtschaft: Wirtschaftsrecht; (Herausgeber: Gerhart Görner [and others]). Berlin, 1978. pp. 441.

— **Italy.**

GUALTIEROTTI (PIERO) L'impresa artigiana. Milano, 1977. pp. 465. *bibliog.*

TRATTATO di diritto commerciale e di diritto pubblico dell'economia. vol. 2. L'impresa; [by] Francesco Galgano [and others]. Padova, 1978. pp. 695. *bibliog.*

— **Russia.**

PROBLEMY upravleniia i grazhdanskogo prava. Moskva, 1976. pp. 185.

RAZNATOVS'KYI (IVAN MYTROFANOVYCH) Pravovoe regulirovanie planirovaniia narodnogo khoziaistva SSSR. Kiev, 1977. pp. 259.

DOZORTSEV (VIKTOR ABRAMOVICH) Zakonodatel'stvo i nauchno-tekhnicheskii progress. Moskva, 1978. pp. 191.

LAPTEV (VLADIMIR VIKTOROVICH) Pravovaia organizatsiia khoziaistvennykh sistem. Moskva, 1978. pp. 168.

— **United Kingdom.**

JULIAN (MARK ROBERT) English economic legislation 1660-1714. 1979. fo. 376. *bibliog.* Typescript. M.Phil. (London) thesis: unpublished. *This thesis is the property of London University and may not be removed from the Library.*

ECONOMIC POLICY.

MEILAN (JOSE LUIS) La organización administrativa de los planes de desarrollo. [Madrid], 1966. pp. 65. (*Centro de Formacion y Perfeccionamiento de Funcionarios [Spain]. Conferencias y Documentos. No. 15*)

GALBRAITH (JOHN KENNETH) Economics and the public purpose. London, 1974. pp. 334.

ALTRUISM, morality, and economic theory; edited by Edmund S. Phelps. New York, [1975]. pp. 232. *bibliogs.*

INDIVIDUAL freedom: selected works of William H. Hutt; edited by Svetozar Pejovich and David Klingaman. Westport, Conn., 1975. pp. 250. *bibliog.*

ROSE (RICHARD) Governing and ungovernability: a sceptical inquiry. Glasgow, [1977]. pp. 29. (*Glasgow. University of Strathclyde. Centre for the Study of Public Policy. Studies in Public Policy. No. 1*)

ROSE (RICHARD) and PETERS (B. GUY) The political consequences of economic overload: on the possibility of political bankruptcy. Glasgow, 1977. pp. 27,5. *bibliog.* (*Glasgow. University of Strathclyde. Centre for the Study of Public Policy. Studies in Public Policy. No. 4*)

TOWARDS full employment and price stability: a report to the OECD by a group of independent experts. Paris, Organisation for Economic Co-operation and Development, 1977. pp. 341.

BEDREIGDE democratie?: parlementaire democratie en overheidsbemoeienis in de economie; onder redactie van H. Daudt en E. van der Wolk; met bijdragen van F. Bolkestein [and others]. Assen, 1978. pp. 142.

BEYOND capitalist planning; edited by Stuart Holland. Oxford, [1978]. pp. 222. *Based on a conference held in 1976 at the University of Sussex.*

BROOKS (JOHN) and EVANS (ROBERT W.) Macroeconomic policy in theory and practice. London, 1978. pp. 140. *bibliog.*

BROWN (CHARLES VICTOR) and JACKSON (PETER McLEOD) Public sector economics. Oxford, 1978. pp. 452. *bibliog.*

CARNEGIE-ROCHESTER CONFERENCE ON PUBLIC POLICY, 1977. November Conference. Public policies in open economies; editors Karl Brunner [and] Allan H. Meltzer. Amsterdam, 1978. pp. 273. *bibliogs.* (*Journal of Monetary Economics. Carnegie- Rochester Conference Series on Public Policy. vol. 9*)

CARSON (ROBERT B.) Economic issues today: alternative approaches. New York, [1978]. pp. 241. *bibliog.*

The ECONOMICS of politics;...[by] James M. Buchanan [and others]. [London], 1978. pp. 192. *bibliogs.* (*Institute of Economic Affairs. Readings. 18*)

EIDEM (ROLF) and VIOTTI (STAFFAN) Economic systems. Oxford, 1978. pp. 111. *bibliog.*

FLEMING (JOHN MARCUS) Essays on economic policy. New York, 1978. pp. 381.

HARROD (DOMINICK) The politics of economics. London, 1978. pp. 80. *Based on a series of six radio programmes, first broadcast by the BBC 1977/78.*

HAYEK (FRIEDRICH AUGUST) Economic progress in an open society. Seoul, 1978. pp. 53. (*Korea International Economic Institute. Seminar Series. No.16*)

INTERORGANIZATIONAL policy making: limits to coordination and central control; [edited by] Kenneth Hanf and Fritz W. Scharpf. London, [1978]. pp. 373. *bibliogs.*

KINDLEBERGER (CHARLES POOR) The aging economy. Kiel, 1978. pp. 17. *bibliog.* (*Kiel. Universität. Institut für Weltwirtschaft. Bernhard-Harms-Vorlesungen. 8*)

KRISE der Wirtschaftspolitik; herausgegeben von Heinz Markmann und Diethard B. Simmert. Köln, [1978]. pp. 611. *bibliogs.*

BAUMOL (WILLIAM JACK) and OATES (WALLACE E.) Economics, environmental policy, and the quality of life. Englewood Cliffs, [1979]. pp. 377.

BOWLES (ROGER A.) and WHYNES (DAVID K.) Macroeconomic planning. London, 1979. pp. 202. *bibliog.*

ELLMAN (MICHAEL JOHN) Socialist planning. Cambridge, 1979. pp. 300. *bibliog.*

POST-INDUSTRIAL society: proceedings of an international symposium held in Uppsala from 22 to 25 March 1977 to mark the occasion of the 500th anniversary of Uppsala University; edited by Bo Gustafsson. London, [1979]. pp. 238. *bibliogs.*

ROSE (RICHARD) and PETERS (B. GUY) Can government go bankrupt? London, 1979. pp. 283.

RUBNER (ALEXANDER) The price of a free lunch: the perverse relationship between economists and politicians. London, 1979. pp. 256.

TSUKUI (JINKICHI) and MURAKAMI (YASUSUKE) Turnpike optimality in input-output systems: theory and application for planning. Amsterdam, 1979. pp. 260. *bibliog.*

WIRTSCHAFTS- und Gesellschaftspolitik in kritischen Zeiten: Festschrift zum 80. Geburtstag von Heinrich Dräger; herausgegeben von Walter Petwaidic; mit Beiträgen von Reinhard Blum [and others]. Frankfurt am Main, [1979]. pp. 176. *bibliog.*

— **Congresses.**

INTERNATIONAL ECONOMIC ASSOCIATION. Conference, 1976, Urbino. Econometric contributions to public policy: proceedings of a conference...; edited by Richard Stone and William Peterson. London, 1978. pp. 474. *bibliogs.*

ECONOMIC RESEARCH

— **Bibliography.**

BIBLIOGRAPHY OF...PUBLICATIONS OF UNIVERSITY BUREAUS OF BUSINESS AND ECONOMIC RESEARCH; [pd. for] Association for University Business and Economic Research. a., 1977(v.21)- Knoxville.

— **Germany.**

DEUTSCHES INSTITUT FÜR WIRTSCHAFTSFORSCHUNG. Sonderhefte. [Neue Folge]. 124. Forschung und Entwicklung in der Berliner Industrie: Ergebnisse einer Befragung; ([by] Burkhard Dreher). Berlin, 1978. pp. 112.

— **United Kingdom — Directories.**

OVERSEAS DEVELOPMENT INSTITUTE. Development guide: a directory of non-commercial organisations in Britain actively concerned in overseas development and training. 3rd ed. London, 1978. pp. 216.

ECONOMIC STABILIZATION.

HANSEN (ALVIN HARVEY) Economic stabilization in an unbalanced world. New York, 1971. pp. 384. *Reprint of work originally published in New York, 1932.*

ECONOMIC STABILIZATION.(Cont.)

MAMMEN (GERHARD) Grundzüge differenzierter Stabilisierungspolitik in der Bundesrepublik Deutschland. Göttingen, [1978]. pp. 237. *bibliog. (Hamburg. Hansische Universität. Institut für Europäische Wirtschaftspolitik. Wirtschaftspolitische Studien. 47)*

ECONOMIC SURVEYS.

IN search of economic indicators: essays on business surveys; edited by Werner H. Strigel. Berlin, 1977. pp. 198.

ECONOMIC ZONING

— Russia.

BELOUSOV (IVAN IVANOVICH) Osnovy ucheniia ob ekonomicheskom raionirovanii: razmeshchenie i raionirovanie proizvoditel'nykh sil. Moskva, 1976. pp. 320. *bibliog.*

ADAMESKU (ALEKO ALEKSANDROVICH) and BELORUSOV (DMITRII VASIL'EVICH) Razvitie i razmeshchenie proizvoditel'nykh sil SSSR v desiatoi piatiletke. Moskva, 1977. pp. 192.

SOTSIAL'NO-ekonomicheskoe prognozirovanie razvitiia regiona. Leningrad, 1977. pp. 214. *bibliog.*

KOZHUKHAR' (PAVEL VASIL'EVICH) Voprosy kompleksnogo planirovaniia khoziaistva soiuznoi respubliki. Moskva, 1979. pp. 179. *bibliog. (Akademiia Nauk SSSR. Problemy Sovetskoi Ekonomiki)*

METODOLOGICHESKIE i metodicheskie problemy razmeshcheniia otraslei material'nogo proizvodstva. Moskva, 1979. pp. 263. *(Akademiia Nauk SSSR. Problemy Sovetskoi Ekonomiki)*

— — Ukraine.

PALAMARCHUK (MAKSIM MARTYNOVICH) and others. Mineral'nye resursy i formirovanie promyshlennykh territorial'nykh kompleksov. Kiev, 1978. pp. 219. *bibliog.*

ECONOMICS.

WALKER (FRANCIS AMASA) Discussions in economics and statistics; edited by Davis R. Dewey; with an introduction by Joseph Dorfman. New York, 1971. 2 vols. *Reprint of work first published New York, 1899.*

GUYOT (YVES) Economic prejudices; translated by Fred Rothwell. London, 1910. pp. 166.

SPANN (OTHMAR) Gesamtausgabe; Herausgeber: Walter Heinrich [and others]. Graz, 1963-79. 21 vols. *bibliogs.*

WEBER (MAX) Critique of Stammler;...translated, with an introductory essay, by Guy Oakes. New York, [1977]. pp. 184.

BRUNHOFF (SUZANNE DE) The state, capital and economic policy; translated by Mike Sonenscher. London, 1978. pp. 152.

NEW directions in Austrian economics; edited by Louis M. Spadaro. Kansas City, [1978]. pp. 239. *bibliogs. Papers sponsored by the Institute for Humane Studies and presented at a symposium.*

UNCERTAINTY in economics: readings and exercises; edited by Peter Diamond, Michael Rothschild. New York, [1978]. pp. 574. *bibliogs.*

ROGGE (BENJAMIN A.) Can capitalism survive? Indianapolis, [1979]. pp. 329.

SOCIOLOGICAL economics; edited by Louis Lévy-Garboua. London, [1979]. pp. 306. *bibliogs. Papers presented at a seminar held in Paris, 1977, sponsored by the Centre National de la Recherche Scientifique, Maison des Sciences de l'Homme and the National Science Foundation.*

WARD (BENJAMIN N.) The ideal worlds of economics; liberal, radical, and conservative economic world views. London, 1979. pp. 482. *bibliog.*

See also KEYNESIAN ECONOMICS.

— Abstracts.

KEY TO ECONOMIC SCIENCE (formerly ECONOMIC ABSTRACTS): s-m review of abstracts on economics, finance, trade, industry, foreign aid, management, marketing, labour; (compiled by the Library of the Economic Information Service, Ministry of Economic Affairs [Netherlands], etc.). s-m., Je 1953(v.1, no.1)- The Hague.

— Graduate work.

JOHNSON (HARRY GORDON) The uneasy case for universal graduate programmes in economics. n.p., [c. 1975]. fo. 11.

— History.

LEBENSBILDER grosser Nationalökonomen: Einführung in die Geschichte der Politischen Ökonomie; herausgegeben von Horst Claus Recktenwald. Köln, [1965]. pp. 666.

KIRZNER (ISRAEL MAYER) The economic point of view: an essay in the history of economic thought...; edited with an introduction by Laurence S. Moss. [2nd ed]. Kansas City, [1976]. pp. 228. *bibliog.*

BERTRAND (MICHELE) Histoire et théories économiques. [Paris, 1978]. pp. 223.

BLAUG (MARK) Economic theory in retrospect. 3rd ed. Cambridge, 1978. pp. 756.

DEANE (PHYLLIS) The evolution of economic ideas. Cambridge, 1978. pp. 236. *bibliogs.*

DEHEM (ROGER) Précis d'histoire de la théorie économique. Québec, 1978. pp. 252.

FRANTZEN (PIETER) Histoire de la pensée économique: une analyse marxiste. Bruxelles, [1978]. pp. 504. *bibliog.*

GESCHICHTE der politischen Ökonomie: Grundriss; (herausgegeben von Herbert Meissner). Frankfurt am Main, 1978. pp. 683.

HUTCHISON (TERENCE WILMOT) On revolutions and progress in economic knowledge. Cambridge, 1978. pp. 349. *bibliog.*

RIMA (INGRID HAHNE) Development of economic analysis. 3rd ed. Homewood, Ill., 1978. pp. 507. *bibliogs.*

TRIBE (KEITH) Land, labour and economic discourse. London, 1978. pp. 182. *bibliog.*

HUNT (E.K.) History of economic thought: a critical perspective. Belmont, Calif., [1979]. pp. 478. *bibliog.*

HUTTON (JOHN) The mystery of wealth: political economy - its development and impact on world events. Cheltenham, 1979. pp. 412. *bibliog.*

LANGHOLM (ODD) Price and value in the Aristotelian tradition: a study in scholastic economic sources. Bergen, [1979]. pp. 175. *bibliog.*

— — Italy.

MUELLER (JOHANN ANTON) Chronologische Darstellung der italienischen Klassiker über National-Ökonomie. Vaduz, 1978. pp. 316. *Reprint of work originally published in Pest in 1820.*

— — United States.

PARKS (ROBERT JAMES) European origins of the economic ideas of Alexander Hamilton. New York, 1977. pp. 170.

— Methodology.

BAHADIR (SEFIK ALP) Allokation der Produktivkräfte und gesamtwirtschaftliche Stabilität: ein Beitrag zur Analyse ihrer Zusammenhänge. Berlin, [1978]. pp. 234. *bibliog.*

HUTCHISON (TERENCE WILMOT) On revolutions and progress in economic knowledge. Cambridge, 1978. pp. 349. *bibliog.*

MISES (LUDWIG VON) The ultimate foundation of economic science: an essay on method. 2nd ed. Kansas City, [1978]. pp. 148.

— Psychological aspects.

BENSUSAN-BUTT (DAVID MILES) On economic man: an essay on the elements of economic theory. Canberra, 1978. pp. 188.

KATONA (GEORGE) and STRUEMPEL (BURKHARD) A new economic era. New York, [1978]. pp. 176. *bibliog.*

— Study and teaching.

JOHNSON (HARRY GORDON) The uneasy case for universal graduate programmes in economics. n.p., [c. 1975]. fo. 11.

— Before 1776.

[CARRER (LUIGI) ed.] Notizie mercantili delle monete e de'cambi; [extracts from works by Francesco Dino di Iacopo, Bernardo Davanzati, Giovanni Botero, and John Locke]. Venezia, [imprint], 1840. pp. 226. *(Biblioteca Classica Italiana di Scienza, Lettere ed Arti. Classe 5, vol. 6)*

— 1776-1876.

SEDGWICK (THEODORE) Public and private economy...in three parts, 1836-1839 with an introduction: Theodore Sedgwick: from federalism to Jacksonianism, by Joseph Dorfman. Clifton, N. J., 1974. pp. 490. *Reprint of work originally published in New York, 1836-1839.*

LONGFIELD (MOUNTIFORT) The economic writings...; with an introduction and bibliography by R.D. Collison Black. New York, 1971. 1 vol. (various pagings). *bibliog.*

— 1876-1976.

ROBINSON (JOAN) Collected economic papers. Oxford, 1951-79. 5 vols.

PESQUISA PLANEJAMENTO ECONOMICO: revista do Instituto de Planejamento Econômico e Social [Brazil]. s-a., Je 1971 (v.1, no.1)- Rio de Janeiro. *Index: 1971/1975(v. 1-5)*

STANLAKE (GEORGE FREDERICK) Introductory economics. 2nd ed. London, 1971 repr. 1972. pp. 373. *bibliog.*

ECONOMIC theory and planning: essays in honour of A.K. Das Gupta; edited by Ashok Mitra. Calcutta, 1974. pp. 326.

GALBRAITH (JOHN KENNETH) Economics and the public purpose. London, 1974. pp. 334.

NARANG (S.D.) An introduction to the theory of bio-economics. Bombay, 1974. pp. 176.

ALTRUISM, morality, and economic theory; edited by Edmund S. Phelps. New York, [1975]. pp. 232. *bibliogs.*

KRITIKA burzhuaznoi politicheskoi ekonomii. vyp.5. Moskva, 1977. pp. 118.

NEISSER (HANS) Selected papers. El Cerrito, 1977. pp. 232.

BREADTH and depth in economics: Fritz Machlup: the man and his ideas; edited by Jacob S. Dreyer. Lexington, Mass., [1978]. pp. 316. *bibliog.*

FLEMING (JOHN MARCUS) Essays on economic policy. New York, 1978. pp. 381.

HAYEK (FRIEDRICH AUGUST) A tiger by the tail: a 40-years' running commentary on Keynesianism...; compiled and introduced by Sudha R. Shenoy; with an essay on The outlook for the 1970s: open or repressed inflation?; by F.A. Hayek. 2nd ed. London, 1978. pp. 145. *bibliog. (Institute of Economic Affairs. Hobart Paperbacks. 4)*

LIPSEY (RICHARD GEORGE) An introduction to positive economics. 5th ed. London, 1979. pp. 810.

PRESLEY (JOHN R.) Robertsonian economics: an examination of the work of Sir D.H. Robertson on industrial fluctuation. London, 1979. pp. 320.

— 1976- .

SOCIETY and change: essays in honour of Sachin Chaudhuri; edited by K.S. Krishnaswamy [and others]. Bombay, 1977. pp. 327.

ACKLEY (GARDNER) Macroeconomics: theory and policy. New York, [1978]. pp. 738.

ALLPORT (J.A.) and STEWART (C.M.N.) Economics. 2nd ed. Cambridge, 1978. pp. 418. *bibliog.*

ASSOCIATION OF UNIVERSITY TEACHERS OF ECONOMICS. Annual Conference, 1977. Contemporary economic analysis...; edited by M.J. Artis and A.R. Nobay. London, [1978]. pp. 448. *bibliogs.*

BEARE (JOHN BARRINGTON) Macroeconomics: cycles, growth, and policy in a monetary economy. New York, [1978]. pp. 499. *bibliogs.*

BORDES (CHRISTIAN) Analyse macroéconomique. Paris, [1978]. pp. 239.

BROOKS (JOHN) and EVANS (ROBERT W.) Macroeconomic policy in theory and practice. London, 1978. pp. 140. *bibliog.*

CARSON (ROBERT B.) Economic issues today: alternative approaches. New York, [1978]. pp. 241. *bibliog.*

EIDEM (ROLF) and VIOTTI (STAFFAN) Economic systems. Oxford, 1978. pp. 111. *bibliog.*

GORDON (ROBERT J.) Macroeconomics. Boston, [Mass.], [1978]. pp. 585, liii.

HANSON (JOHN LLOYD) Economics for students. 8th ed. Plymouth, 1978. pp. 226. *bibliog.*

HEILBRONER (ROBERT LOUIS) and THUROW (LESTER C.) Understanding macroeconomics. 6th ed. Englewood Cliffs, [1978]. pp. 353.

HOMMAGE à François Perroux; (by Maurice Allais and others). Grenoble, 1978. pp. 748. *bibliog. In French or English.*

McKENZIE (RICHARD B.) and TULLOCK (GORDON) The new world of economics: explorations into the human experience. rev.ed. Homewood, Ill., 1978. pp. 331.

MILLER (ROGER LEROY) Economics today and tomorrow. San Francisco, [1978]. pp. 416.

MISES (LUDWIG VON) The ultimate foundation of economic science: an essay on method. 2nd ed. Kansas City, [1978]. pp. 148.

NÄSLUND (BERTIL) and SELLSTEDT (BO) Neo-Ricardian theory: with applications to some current economic problems. Berlin, 1978. pp. 165. *bibliog.*

SCHMID (ALFRED ALLAN) Property, power, and public choice: an inquiry into law and economics. New York, [1978]. pp. 316. *bibliog.*

UNDERSTANDING economics: an introduction for students; [by] Paul Bennett [and others]; edited by David Burningham. London, 1978. pp. 388. *bibliog.*

VEREIN FÜR SOZIALPOLITIK. Schriften. Neue Folge. Band 98. Neuere Entwicklungen in den Wirtschaftswissenschaften: (Verhandlungen auf der Arbeitstagung...in Münster vom 19.-21. September 1977; herausgegeben von Ernst Helmstädter). Berlin, [1978]. pp. 922.

CREW (MICHAEL A.) and KLEINDORFER (PAUL R.) Public utility economics. London, 1979. pp. 246. *bibliog.*

GALBRAITH (JOHN KENNETH) and SALINGER (NICOLE) Almost everyone's guide to economics. London, 1979. pp. 162.

HEY (JOHN DENIS) Uncertainty in microeconomics. Oxford, 1979. pp. 261. *bibliog.*

KOUTSOGIANNES (A.) Modern microeconomics. 2nd ed. London, 1979. pp. 581. *bibliog.*

KRONMAN (ANTHONY T.) and POSNER (RICHARD A.) The economics of contract law. Boston, Mass., [1979]. pp. 274.

LEONARD (FRED H.) Macroeconomic theory: static and dynamic analyses. New York, [1979]. pp. 436. *bibliogs.*

RUBNER (ALEXANDER) The price of a free lunch: the perverse relationship between economists and politicians. London, 1979. pp. 256.

SIVEN (CLAES-HENRIC) A study in the theory of inflation and unemployment. Amsterdam, 1979. pp. 372. *bibliog.*

TSUKUI (JINKICHI) and MURAKAMI (YASUSUKE) Turnpike optimality in input-output systems: theory and application for planning. Amsterdam, 1979. pp. 260. *bibliog.*

ECONOMICS, COMPARATIVE.

SVERIGES INDUSTRIFÖRBUND. Economic Affairs Directorate. The Nordic economic outlook: a survey prepared [by Eva Christina Horwitz]...; [with] special studies [by various authors]. [Stockholm], 1975. pp. 86.

KRITIKA burzhuaznoi politicheskoi ekonomii. vyp.5. Moskva, 1977. pp. 118.

EIDEM (ROLF) and VIOTTI (STAFFAN) Economic systems. Oxford, 1978. pp. 111. *bibliog.*

INTERNATIONAL economics: comparisons and interdependences: Internationale Wirtschaft: Vergleiche und Interdependenzen; edited by...F. Levcik; (Festschrift für Franz Nemschak). Wien, 1978. pp. 528. *bibliogs.* (Wiener Institut für Internationale Wirtschaftsvergleiche. Studien über Wirtschafts- und Systemvergleiche. Band 9) *In English or German.*

MUELLER (HANS) Ph.D. and KAWAHITO (KIYOSHI) Steel industry economics: a comparative analysis of structure, conduct and performance. New York, 1978. pp. 63.

BORNSTEIN (MORRIS) ed. Comparative economic systems: models and cases. 4th ed. Homewood, Ill., 1979. pp. 489.

ELLMAN (MICHAEL JOHN) Socialist planning. Cambridge, 1979. pp. 300. *bibliog.*

ROSE (RICHARD) and PETERS (B. GUY) Can government go bankrupt? London, 1979. pp. 283.

ECONOMICS, MATHEMATICAL.

NIKAIDO (HUKUKANE) Introduction to sets and mappings in modern economics; translated by Kazuo Sato. Amsterdam, [1970]. pp. 343. *bibliog.*

STAFFORD (LEONARD W.T.) Mathematics for economists. London, 1971. pp. 371.

ECONOMETRIC studies of macro and monetary relations; edited by Alan A. Powell and Ross A. Williams. Amsterdam, 1973. pp. 358. *bibliog. Papers presented at the second Australasian Conference of Econometricians held at Monash University, 1971.*

TAKAYAMA (AKIRA) Mathematical economics. Hinsdale, Ill., [1974]. pp. 744. *bibliogs.*

STUDIES in nonlinear estimation; [including papers given at a seminar at Princeton University in 1974]; edited by Stephen M. Goldfeld and Richard E. Quandt. Cambridge, Mass., [1976]. pp. 278. *bibliog.*

TODD (MICHAEL J.) The computation of fixed points and applications. Berlin, [1976]. pp. 129. *bibliog.*

JUNIUS (T.) Shephard technologies and neoclassical production functions. Leiden, 1977. pp. 128. *bibliog.* (Tilburg. Katholieke Hogeschool. Tilburg Institute of Economics. Tilburg Studies in Econometrics. vol. 2)

KLEIN (LAWRENCE ROBERT) Project link. Athens, 1977. pp. 56. (Center of Planning and Economic Research [Athens]. Lecture Series. 30)

KOO (DELIA) Elements of optimization with applications in economics and business. New York, [1977]. pp. 220. *bibliog.*

MAKAROV (VALERII LEONIDOVICH) and RUBINOV (ALEKSANDR MOISEEVICH) Mathematical theory of economic dynamics and equilibria; translated from the Russian by Mohamed El-Hodiri. New York, [1977]. pp. 252. *bibliog.*

MURATA (YASUO) Mathematics for stability and optimization of economic systems. New York, 1977. pp. 418. *bibliog.*

ASSOCIATION OF UNIVERSITY TEACHERS OF ECONOMICS. Annual Conference, 1977. Contemporary economic analysis...; edited by M.J. Artis and A.R. Nobay. London, [1978]. pp. 448. *bibliogs.*

BHATTACHARYYA (D.K.) Demand for financial assets: an econometric study of the U.K. personal sector. Farnborough, [1978]. pp. 197. *bibliogs.*

BOWDEN (ROGER JOHN) The econometrics of disequilibrium. Amsterdam, 1978. pp. 324. *bibliog.*

DUBBELMAN (CORNELIS) Disturbances in the linear model, estimation and hypothesis testing. Leiden, 1978. pp. 113. *bibliog.*

ECONOMETRIC modeling of world commodity policy...; edited by F. Gerard Adams and Jere R. Behrman. Lexington, Mass, [1978]. pp. 223. *bibliog.*

EICHHORN (WOLFGANG) Functional equations in economics. Reading, Mass., 1978. pp. 260. *bibliog.*

HALVORSEN (ROBERT) Econometric models of U.S. energy demand. Lexington, Mass., [1978]. pp. 171. *bibliog.*

HART (P.E.) Redundant inequalities. London, [1978]. pp. 22. *bibliog.* (National Institute of Economic and Social Research. Discussion Papers. No. 18)

MODELIROVANIE v ekonomicheskikh issledovaniiakh; otvetstvennye redaktory E.L. Berliand i B.G. Mirkin. Novosibirsk, 1978. pp. 184. (Akademiia Nauk SSSR. Sibirskoe Otdelenie. Institut Ekonomoki i Organizatsii Promyshlennogo Proizvodstva. Matematicheskii Analiz Ekonomicheskikh Modelei)

MODELLING economic change: the recursive programming approach; [edited by] Richard H. Day and Alessandro Cigno. Amsterdam, 1978. pp. 447. *bibliog.*

PRASKI (SVERKER) Econometric investment functions and an attempt to evaluate the investment policy in Sweden, 1960-1973. Uppsala, 1978. pp. 131. *bibliog.* (Uppsala. Universitet. Acta Universitatis Upsaliensis. Studia Oeconomica Upsaliensia. 5)

WOODS (JOHN E.) Mathematical economics. London, 1978. pp. 364. *bibliogs.*

MODELI sotsial'no-ekonomicheskikh protsessov i sotsial'noe planirovanie. Moskva, 1979. pp. 213. *bibliog.* (Akademiia Nauk SSSR. Problemy Sovetskoi Ekonomiki)

OPTIMAL control for econometric models: an approach to economic policy formulation; edited by Sean Holly [and others]. London, 1979. pp. 303. *bibliogs.*

— Bibliography.

ZAREMBA (JOSEPH M.) compiler. Mathematical economics and operations research: a guide to information sources. Detroit, [1978]. pp. 606.

— Congresses.

INTERNATIONAL ECONOMIC ASSOCIATION. Conference, 1976, Urbino. Econometric contributions to public policy: proceedings of a conference...; edited by Richard Stone and William Peterson. London, 1978. pp. 474. *bibliogs.*

ECONOMICS, PRIMITIVE.

ECONOMIC anthropology: readings in theory and analysis; edited by Edward E. Leclair, Jr. and Harold K. Schneider. New York, [1968]. pp. 523. *bibliog.*

ECONOMISTS.

ECONOMISTS.

LEBENSBILDER grosser Nationalökonomen: Einführung in die Geschichte der Politischen Ökonomie; herausgegeben von Horst Claus Recktenwald. Köln, [1965]. pp. 666.

RUBNER (ALEXANDER) The price of a free lunch: the perverse relationship between economists and politicians. London, 1979. pp. 256.

— Italy.

MUELLER (JOHANN ANTON) Chronologische Darstellung der italienischen Klassiker über National-Ökonomie. Vaduz, 1978. pp. 316. *Reprint of work originally published in Pest in 1820.*

— United Kingdom.

JAMES (PATRICIA) Population Malthus: his life and times. London, 1979. pp. 524.

ECUADOR

— Census.

ECUADOR. Census, 1974. III censo de poblacion, II de vivienda, 1974: resultados anticipados por muestreo. Quito, 1975. pp. 66.

— Officials and employees.

ECUADOR. Oficina de los Censos Nacionales. Censo Nacional de Servidores Publicos, 1975. Primer censo nacional de servidores publicos, 1975: resultados provisionales. Quito, 1976. 1 vol. (unpaged).

EDEN (ROBERT ANTHONY) 1st Earl of Avon.

ASTER (SIDNEY) Anthony Eden. London, 1976. pp. 176. *bibliog.*

BARKER (ELISABETH) Churchill and Eden at war. London, 1978. pp. 346. *bibliog.*

EDUCATION.

SAY not the struggle: essays in honour of A.D. Gorwala; [edited by H.M. Patel]. Delhi, 1976. pp. 328.

LYNCH (JAMES) Education for community: a cross-cultural study in education. Basingstoke, 1979. pp. 212. *bibliogs.*

— Aims and objectives.

EDUCATIONAL DEVELOPMENT CONFERENCE, NEW ZEALAND, 1974. Working Party on Aims and Objectives. Educational aims and objectives: report...; [J.R. Osborne, chairman]. Wellington, 1974. pp. 36.

O'TOOLE (JAMES) Work, learning, and the American future. San Francisco, 1977. pp. 238. *bibliog.*

EDUCATION for uncertainty; edited by Edmund J. King. London, [1979]. pp. 250. *bibliogs.*

HARRIS (KEVIN) Education and knowledge: the structured misrepresentation of reality. London, 1979. pp. 214. *bibliog.*

WARNOCK (HELEN MARY) Education: a way ahead. Oxford, [1979]. pp. 106.

— Congresses.

MYLONAS (DENIS) La genèse de l'Unesco: la Conférence des Ministres alliés de l'Education (1942-1945). Bruxelles, 1976. pp. 495. *bibliog.*

— Curricula.

EGGLESTON (S. JOHN) The sociology of the school curriculum. London, 1977. pp. 171. *bibliog.*

BECHER (TONY) and MACLURE (JOHN STUART) The politics of curriculum change. London, 1978. pp. 192. *bibliogs.*

REID (WILLIAM ARBUCKLE) Thinking about the curriculum: the nature and treatment of curriculum problems. London, 1978. pp. 132.

WARING (MARY) Social pressures and curriculum innovation: a study of the Nuffield Foundation Science Teaching Project. London, 1979. pp. 263. *bibliog.*

— Economic aspects.

LUNDGREEN (PETER) Bildung und Wirtschaftswachstum im Industrialisierungsprozess des 19. Jahrhunderts: methodische Ansätze, empirische Studien und internationale Vergleiche. Berlin, [1973]. pp. 182. *bibliog.*

SCHOOLING and capitalism: a sociological reader; edited by Roger Dale [and others]. London, 1976. pp. 232. *bibliogs.*

— — Bibliography.

BLAUG (MARK) Economics of education: a selected annotated bibliography. 3rd ed. Oxford, 1978. pp. 421.

BRIGHTON. University of Sussex. Institute of Development Studies. Library. Occasional Guides. No. 12. Labour market backwash and the educational process: an annotated bibliography. Brighton, [1978]. pp. 68.

— — Africa.

HUMAN resources and African development; edited by Ukandi G. Damachi and Victor P. Diejomaoh. New York, [1978]. pp. 378. *bibliog.*

— — India.

CHAUDHRI (D.P.) Education, innovations and agricultural development: a study of North India (1961-72). London, [1979]. pp. 127. *bibliog.*

— — Ireland (Republic).

TUSSING (A. DALE) Irish educational expenditures: past, present and future. Dublin, [1978]. pp. 187. *bibliog. (Economic and Social Research Institute. Papers. No. 92)*

— — United States.

LEIGH (DUANE E.) An analysis of the determinants of occupational upgrading. New York, [1978]. pp. 185. *bibliog. (Wisconsin University, Madison. Institute for Research on Poverty. Monograph Series)*

SQUIRES (GREGORY D.) Education and jobs: the imbalancing of the social machinery. New Brunswick, N.J., [1979]. pp. 235. *bibliog.*

— Finance — Bibliography.

BLAUG (MARK) Economics of education: a selected annotated bibliography. 3rd ed. Oxford, 1978. pp. 421.

— History.

LUNDGREEN (PETER) Bildung und Wirtschaftswachstum im Industrialisierungsprozess des 19. Jahrhunderts: methodische Ansätze, empirische Studien und internationale Vergleiche. Berlin, [1973]. pp. 182. *bibliog.*

ARCHER (MARGARET SCOTFORD) Social origins of educational systems. London, [1979]. pp. 315. *bibliogs.*

— Philosophy.

PATERSON (R.W.K.) Values, education and the adult. London, 1970. pp. 306. *bibliog.*

ROBINSON (MARGARET) Schools and social work. London, 1978. pp. 268.

CASTLES (STEPHEN) and WÜSTENBERG (WIEBKE) The education of the future: an introduction to the theory and practice of socialist education. London, 1979. pp. 220. *bibliog.*

GORDON (PETER) and WHITE (JOHN PONSFORD) Philosophers as educational reformers: the influence of idealism on British educational thought and practice. London, 1979. pp. 314. *bibliog.*

— Africa.

MAZRUI (ALI AL'AMIN) Political values and the educated class in Africa. Berkeley, 1978. pp. 392.

— America, Latin.

CARNOY (MARTIN) Can educational policy equalise income distribution in Latin America?;...with the collaboration of José Lobo [and others]; a study prepared for the International Labour Office within the framework of the Research Programmes on Income Distribution and Employment and on Education and Employment of the World Employment Programme. Farnborough, [1979]. pp. 110. *bibliog.*

— Australia — Finance.

AUSTRALIA. Schools Commission. 1978. Some aspects of school finance in Australia. Canberra, 1978. pp. 100.

— — History.

MUSGRAVE (PETER WILLIAM) Society and the curriculum in Australia. Sydney, 1979. pp. 160. *bibliogs.*

— — New South Wales — Statistics.

NEW SOUTH WALES. Commonwealth Bureau of Census and Statistics. New South Wales Office. Education. a., 1976- Sydney.

— Bangladesh.

BANGLADESH. Planning Commission. Manpower Section. 1974. An educational geography of Bangladesh: locational availability against ideal requirement. [Dacca], 1974. pp. 142.

— Brazil — Finance.

SOUZA (ALBERTO DE MELLO E) Financiamento da educação e acesso a escola no Brasil. Rio de Janeiro, 1979. pp. 200. *bibliog. (Brazil. Instituto de Planejamento Econômico e Social. Instituto de Pesquisas. Relatorios de Pesquisa. No. 42)*

— Canada.

MARTIN (WILFRED B.W.) and MACDONELL (ALLAN J.) Canadian education: a sociological analysis. Scarborough, Ont., [1978]. pp. 354. *bibliog.*

— — Newfoundland.

NEWFOUNDLAND. Task Force on Education. 1979. Improving the quality of education: challenge and opportunity; final report, etc. St. John's, 1979. pp. 239. *bibliog.*

— — Ontario.

BUTTRICK (JOHN A.) Educational problems in Ontario and some policy options. [Toronto, 1977]. pp. 135. *bibliog. (Ontario. Economic Council. Occasional Papers. 4)*

ONTARIO. Commission on Declining School Enrolments in Ontario. 1978. Implications of declining enrolment for the schools of Ontario: a statement of effects and solutions: final report; [R.W.B. Jackson, commissioner]. Toronto, 1978. pp. 331.

— China — History.

KEENAN (BARRY) The Dewey experiment in China: educational reform and political power in the early republic. Cambridge, Mass., 1977. pp. 335. *bibliog.*

— Egypt — History.

HYDE (GEORGIE D.M.) Education in modern Egypt: ideals and realities. London, 1978. pp. 245. *bibliog.*

— Europe — History.

RINGER (FRITZ FRANZ KLAUS) Education and society in modern Europe. Bloomington, [1979]. pp. 370. *bibliog.*

— France.

FRANCE. Institut National de la Statistique et des Etudes Economiques. 1958. Coût et développement de l'enseignement en France. Paris, 1958. pp. 99. *(Etudes Economiques, No.3)*

— — Finance.

FRANCE. Institut National de la Statistique et des Etudes Economiques. 1958. Coût et développement de l'enseignement en France. Paris, 1958. pp. 99. *(Etudes Economiques, No.3)*

— Germany.

WENDORFF (WERNER) Schule und Bildung in der Politik von Wilhelm Liebknecht: ein Beitrag zur Geschichte der deutschen Arbeiterbewegung im 19. Jahrhundert. Berlin, [1978]. pp. 334. *bibliog.*

— — History.

STRAUSS (GERALD) Luther's house of learning: indoctrination of the young in the German Reformation. Baltimore, 1978. pp. 390.

— Guinea-Bissau.

FREIRE (PAULO) Pedagogy in process: the letters to Guinea-Bissau. London, 1978. pp. 178. *Translated by Carman St. John Hunter.*

— India — History.

CHATTERJI (BANKIM CHANDRA) Bankim on equality: an English translation of Bankim Chandra Chattopadhyay's Bengali article, Samya [with an essay on its background] by M.K. Haldar. Nedlands, W.A., 1974. pp. 38, 124. *(Western Australia, University of. Centre for Asian Studies. Working Papers in Asian Studies. No. 5)*

— Ireland (Republic) — Finance.

TUSSING (A. DALE) Irish educational expenditures: past, present and future. Dublin, [1978]. pp. 187. *bibliog. (Economic and Social Research Institute. Papers. No. 92)*

— Malaya.

FOOK-SENG (PHILIP LOH) Seeds of separatism: educational policy in Malaya, 1874-1940. Kuala Lumpur, 1975. pp. 165. *bibliog.*

— New Zealand.

NEW ZEALAND. Department of Education. 1973. Public education in New Zealand. Wellington, [1973]. pp. 39.

— Nigeria.

GOWON (YAKUBU) Vital role for universities; [two significant addresses...on university occasions]. [Lagos, 1973?]. pp. 18.

DUROJAIYE (M.O.A.) Investment in man. Lagos, 1978. pp. 35. *bibliog. (Lagos. University. Inaugural Lecture Series)*

— Rhodesia.

TAYLOR (R.) Education Officer, Rhodesia. African education: the historical development and organization of the system. [Salisbury, Ministry of Information, Immigration and Tourism, 1970]. pp. 31.

— Romania — History.

STANCIU (ION GH.) O istorie a pedagogiei universale şi româneşti pînă la 1900. Bucureşti, 1977. pp. 395. *bibliog.*

— Russia.

SAMOILOVA (ELENA STEPANOVNA) Naselenie i obrazovanie. Moskva, 1978. pp. 143. *bibliog.*

— Singapore — History.

WILSON (H.E.) Social engineering in Singapore: educational policies and social change, 1819-1972. Singapore. [1978]. pp. 300. *bibliog.*

— South Africa.

REPORTS ON THE STATE OF SOUTH AFRICA. No. 28. Education for success. London, Department of Information, South African Embassy, 1965. 1 pamphlet (unpaged).

ENGELBRECHT (SCHALK WILLEM HENDRIK) Drug abuse as an educational problem; translated by R.F. Purchase. Pretoria, 1977. pp. 175. *bibliog. (Human Sciences Research Council [South Africa]. Institute for Educational Research. Reports. No. O-55)*

BEHR (A.L.) New perspectives in South African education: a blueprint for the last quarter of the twentieth century. Durban, 1978. pp. 283.

— Tanzania.

UNITED REPUBLIC OF TANZANIA. Information Services Division. 1979. Tanzania: educational development. [Dar es Salaam, 1979?]. pp. 12.

— Underdeveloped areas.

See UNDERDEVELOPED AREAS — Education.

— United Kingdom.

NATIONAL UNION OF STUDENTS. Student Community Action. Action education kit. London, [1974?]. pp. 150. *bibliog.*

RICHMOND (WILLIAM KENNETH) Education in Britain since 1944: a personal retrospect. London, 1978. pp. 168.

— — History.

GOSDEN (PETER HENRY JOHN HEATHER) and SHARP (PAUL R.) The development of an education service: the West Riding, 1889- 1974. Oxford, 1978. pp. 273.

RODERICK (GORDON W.) and STEPHENS (MICHAEL D.) Education and industry in the nineteenth century: the English disease? London, 1978. pp. 196. *bibliog.*

GORDON (PETER) and WHITE (JOHN PONSFORD) Philosophers as educational reformers: the influence of idealism on British educational thought and practice. London, 1979. pp. 314. *bibliog.*

— United States.

COONS (JOHN E.) and SUGARMAN (STEPHEN D.) Education by choice: the case for family control. Berkeley, Calif., [1978]. pp. 249. *bibliog.*

— — History.

ALTSCHULER (GLENN C.) Andrew D. White: educator, historian, diplomat. Ithaca, 1979. pp. 300. *bibliog.*

NASAW (DAVID) Schooled to order: a social history of public schooling in the United States. New York, 1979. pp. 03. *bibliog.*

— — New England.

AXTELL (JAMES L.) The school upon a hill: education and society in colonial New England. New Haven, Conn., 1974. pp. 298.

EDUCATION, COMPARATIVE.

RINGER (FRITZ FRANZ KLAUS) Education and society in modern Europe. Bloomington, [1979]. pp. 370. *bibliog.*

EDUCATION, COOPERATIVE

— Cuba.

WALD (KAREN) Children of Che: childcare and education in Cuba. Palo Alto, Calif., [1978]. pp. 399.

EDUCATION, ELEMENTARY

— Canada.

CANADA. Statistics Canada. Minority and second language education: elementary and secondary levels. a., 1975-76/1976-77(1st)- Ottawa. *[in English and French]*

— Rhodesia.

RHODESIA. Committee of Inquiry into African Primary Education. 1974. Report; [L.J. Lewis, chairman]. [Salisbury], 1974. pp. 36.

— United Kingdom — History.

HURT (JOHN S.) Elementary schooling and the working classes 1860-1918. London, 1979. pp. 241.

— — London.

SHEPHERD (JOHN WILLIAM) Education and the urban environment: geographical perspectives on primary school data in inner London. 1977 [or rather 1978]. fo. 273. *bibliog.* Typescript. Ph.D. (London) thesis: unpublished. *This thesis is the property of London University and may not be removed from the Library.*

EDUCATION, HIGHER.

SEMINAR ON NEW MODELS IN HIGHER EDUCATION, HONOLULU, 1970. Trends in external higher education: case studies from Australia, Japan, New Zealand and western Europe; by R. D. Goodman [and others]. [Honolulu, 1970]. 1 vol. (various pagings). *bibliogs.*

MEREDITH MEMORIAL LECTURES. 1977. The role of universities today. Bundoora, Victoria, [1977]. pp. 73. *bibliogs.*

— Asia, Southeast.

ROMM (JEFF) Higher education and natural resources management in Southeast Asia. Washington, 1978. pp. 47. *(American Council on Education. Overseas Liaison Committee. Papers. No. 13)*

— Belgium.

VANDEKERCKHOVE (LIEVEN) and HUYSE (LUCIEN) In de buitenbaan: arbeiderskinderen, universitair onderwijs en sociale ongelijkheid. 2nd ed. Antwerpen, [1977]. pp. 207. *bibliog.*

— Canada — Ontario.

SEMINAR ON EMERGING ISSUES AND ALTERNATIVES IN POST-SECONDARY EDUCATION, SCARBOROUGH, ONTARIO, 1977. Emerging problems in post-secondary education. [Toronto, 1977]. pp. 135. *(Ontario. Economic Council. Discussion Paper Series)*

— India.

INDIA. University Grants Commission. 1977. Third all-India educational survey: higher education, 1973-74. [New Delhi, 1977]. pp. 503.

INDIA. National Review Committee on Higher Secondary Education with Special Reference to Vocationalisation. 1978. Learning to do: towards a learning and working society: report.. .; [M.S. Adiseshiah, chairman]. New Delhi, 1978. pp. 60.

— Japan — Bibliography.

HIGHER education and the student problem: K.B.S. bibliography of standard reference books for Japanese studies with descriptive notes. Tokyo, 1972. pp. 309.

— Russia — Curricula.

VOPROSY metodiki prepodavaniia istorii KPSS v universitete: mezhvuzovskii sbornik. Leningrad, 1978. pp. 150.

— United Kingdom.

WILLIAMS (SHIRLEY) Robbins plus twenty: which way for higher education? London, 1977. pp. 22. *(London. University. Birkbeck College. Foundation Orations. 1977)*

LIBERAL PARTY. Higher education. London, [1978]. pp. 9. *(Liberal Publication Department. Study Papers. No.9)*

NORRIS (GRAEME) Justifying research and teaching objectives in universities. Farnborough, [1979]. pp. 219. *bibliogs.*

EDUCATION, HIGHER.(Cont.)

U.K. Department of Education and Science. 1979. 16-18: education and training for 16-18 year olds: a consultative paper. [London, 1979]. pp. 16.

—— Economic aspects.

PRATT (JOHN) and others. Costs and control in further education. Windsor, 1978. pp. 242. *bibliog.*

—— Finance.

PRATT (JOHN) and others. Costs and control in further education. Windsor, 1978. pp. 242. *bibliog.*

—— Statistics.

U.K. Department of Education and Science. 1978. Higher education into the 1990s: a discussion document. London, 1978. 1 pamphlet (various pagings).

FUTURE trends in higher education: a one-day conference organised by The Times Higher Education Supplement in association with the Department of Education and Science, 5 March 1979, at the University of London Institute of Education: a follow-up report on Higher education into the 1990s, presented to the conference by the Department of Education and Science. [London, Department of Education and Science, 1979]. pp. 7.

— United States.

BOWEN (HOWARD ROTHMANN) Investment in learning: the individual and social value of American higher education. San Francisco, 1977. pp. 507. *bibliog. A report prepared with the support of the Sloan Foundation and issued by the Carnegie Council on Policy Studies in Higher Education.*

The STATES and private higher education: problems and policies in a new era; a report of the Carnegie Council on Policy Studies in Higher Education. San Francisco, 1977. pp. 206. *bibliog.*

—— Curricula.

MAYHEW (LEWIS B.) Legacy of the seventies: experiment, economy, equality, and expediency in American higher education. San Francisco, 1977. pp. 366. *bibliog.*

—— Economic aspects.

MAYHEW (LEWIS B.) Legacy of the seventies: experiment, economy, equality, and expediency in American higher education. San Francisco, 1977. pp. 366. *bibliog.*

EDUCATION, PRESCHOOL.

HERON (ALASTAIR) Early childhood care and education: objectives and issues. Paris, Organisation for Economic Co-operation and Development, 1977. pp. 61.

— Denmark.

PLATZ (MERETE) Velkommen til børnehaveklasserne: en undersøgelse af familier der bruger, og familier der ikke bruger børnehaveklasseordningen, etc. København, 1977. pp. 280. *bibliog. (Socialforskningsinstituttet. Publikationer. 76) With English summary.*

— United States.

SOCIAL development in childhood: day-care programs and research; edited by Roger A. Webb. Baltimore, [1977]. pp. 196. *bibliogs. Papers from the 4th Hyman Blumberg Symposium on Research in Early Childhood Education, held Mar. 7-9, 1974.*

EDUCATION, RURAL.

— Underdeveloped areas.

See UNDERDEVELOPED AREAS — Education, Rural.

EDUCATION, SECONDARY.

McMULLEN (TIM) Innovative practices in secondary education: the lower secondary stage; problems and possibilities. Paris, Organisation for Economic Co-operation and Development, 1978. pp. 100.

— Canada.

CANADA. Statistics Canada. Minority and second language education: elementary and secondary levels. a., 1975-76/1976-77(1st)- Ottawa. *[in English and French]*

— Malawi.

MALAWI. Ministry of Education. Planning Section. 1965. Education project, International Development Association: secondary technical education and teacher training. [Zomba, 1965]. pp. 202.

— United Kingdom.

SIMON (BRIAN) Intelligence, psychology and education: a Marxist critique. rev. ed. London, [1971]. pp. 286.

COMPREHENSIVE education: report of a conference held at the invitation of the Secretary of State for Education and Science at the University of York on 16/17 December 1977. London, H.M.S.O., 1978. pp. 177.

—— Ireland, Northern.

IRELAND, NORTHERN. Department of Education. 1978. Reorganisation of secondary education in Northern Ireland: resume of contributions received in response to the consultative document. Belfast, 1978. pp. 34.

OPPORTUNITIES at sixteen; report of a study group; [Derek Birley, chairman]. Belfast, H.M.S.O., 1978. pp. 110. *bibliog.*

OSBORNE (ROBERT D.) and MURRAY (RUSSELL C.) Educational qualifications and religious affiliation in Northern Ireland: an examination of G.C.E.'O' and 'A' levels. Belfast, 1978. pp. 42. *bibliog. (Fair Employment Agency for Northern Ireland. Research Papers. 3)*

EDUCATION, URBAN

— United Kingdom.

GRACE (GERALD) Teachers, ideology and control: a study in urban education. London, 1978. pp. 264. *bibliog.*

— United States.

WILLIE (CHARLES VERT) The sociology of urban education: desegregation and integration. Lexington, Mass., [1978]. pp. 184. *bibliogs.*

EDUCATION AND STATE.

APPLE (MICHAEL W.) Ideology and curriculum. London, 1979. pp. 203.

ARCHER (MARGARET SCOTFORD) Social origins of educational systems. London, [1979]. pp. 315. *bibliogs.*

— Australia.

MUSGRAVE (PETER WILLIAM) Society and the curriculum in Australia. Sydney, 1979. pp. 160. *bibliogs.*

— Egypt.

HYDE (GEORGIE D.M.) Education in modern Egypt: ideals and realities. London, 1978. pp. 245. *bibliog.*

— India.

NAIK (J.P.) Educational reform in India: a historical review. [Poona], 1978. pp. 17. *(Gokhale Institute of Politics and Economics. R.R. Kale Memorial Lectures. 1978)*

—Nigeria.

NIGERIA. 1977. Federal Republic of Nigeria national policy on education. [Lagos], 1977. pp. 36.

— South Africa.

SOUTH AFRICA. Information Service of South Africa, New York. 1967. Setting the record straight. New York, [1967]. pp. 24.

— United Kingdom.

GOODMAN (ARNOLD ABRAHAM) Baron Goodman. How much paternalism? [Colchester], 1977. pp. 19. *(University of Essex. Noel Buxton Lectures. 1977)*

U.K. Department of Education and Science. 1978. Progress in education: a report on recent initiatives. London, 1978 repr. 1979. pp. 40.

— United States.

FINN (CHESTER E.) Scholars, dollars, and bureaucrats. Washington, D.C., [1978]. pp. 238. *(Brookings Institution. Studies in Higher Education Policy. 2)*

EDUCATION OF ADULTS.

PATERSON (R.W.K.) Values, education and the adult. London, 1970. pp. 306. *bibliog.*

KALLEN (DENIS) and BENGTSSON (JARL) Recurrent education: a strategy for lifelong learning. Paris, Organisation for Economic Co-operation and Development, 1973. pp. 91.

CENTRE FOR EDUCATIONAL RESEARCH AND INNOVATION. 1978. Alternation between work and education: a study of educational leave of absence at enterprise level. Paris, Organisation for Economic Co-operation and Development, 1978. pp. 97.

— Australia.

LIFELONG education and poor people: three studies. Canberra, 1976. pp. 71. *bibliog. (Australia. Commission of Inquiry into Poverty. Poverty and Education Series)*

— Belgium.

Les ORGANISATIONS d'éducation permanente pour adultes; par Axel Gryspeerdt [and others]. [Bruxelles, 1977]. pp. 119. *bibliog. (Cahiers JEB. 1977.7)*

— Canada.

VERNER (COOLIE) and DICKINSON (GARY) Union education in Canada: a report of the educational activities of labour organizations...; submitted to the Canadian Labour Congress and the Canada Department of Labour. Vancouver, Adult Research Centre, University of British Columbia, 1974. pp. 224.

— Denmark.

BUNNAGE (DAVID) and HEDEGAARD (BIRTHE) Voksenuddannelse: uddannelsesaktivitet, uddannelsesbaggrund og uddannelsesønsker hos den voksne danske befolkning ved midten af 1970-erne, etc. København, 1978. pp. 306. *bibliog. (Socialforskningsinstituttet. Publikationer. 81) With English summary.*

— United Kingdom.

MOHR (DIANA H.) Research monograph on adult education and the physically handicapped person. London, [1977]. pp. 143. *bibliog.*

NEWMAN (MICHAEL) The poor cousin: a study of adult education. London, 1979. pp. 249.

EDUCATION OF CHILDREN.

WORKING GROUP ON PROBLEMS OF CHILDREN OF SCHOOL AGE II (10-13 YEARS). Problems of children of school age: 10-13 years: report on a working group [held in] Moscow, 30 November-3 December, 1976. Copenhagen, World Health Organization, Regional Office for Europe, 1977. pp. 39.

EDUCATION OF PRISONERS

— United States.

SEASHORE (MARJORIE J.) and HABERFELD (STEVEN) Prisoner education: project NewGate and other college programs. New York, 1976. pp. 329. *bibliog.*

EDUCATION OF WOMEN

— France.

FRANCE. Comité du Travail Féminin. 1974. La formation des femmes en milieu rural. Paris, 1974. pp. 79.

FRANCE. Comité du Travail Féminin. 1976. La formation professionnelle continue des femmes;...mise à jour:juillet 1976. [Paris, Centre pour le Développement de l'Information sur la Formation Permanente, 1976]. pp. 68.

— United Kingdom.

BYRNE (EILEEN M.) Women and education. London, 1978. pp. 285. *bibliog.*

EDUCATIONAL ACCOUNTABILITY

— United Kingdom.

ACCOUNTABILITY in education; edited by Tony Becher and Stuart Maclure. Windsor, 1978. pp. 256. *bibliogs.*

EDUCATIONAL ASSISTANCE, BRITISH.

GRANTLEY (DAVID) Practical training in Britain of students from the developing countries. London, [1973?]. pp. 7. *(Marr-Munning Trust. Edwina Mountbatten Papers. No. 3)*

EDUCATIONAL EQUALIZATION.

BISSERET (NOELLE) Education, class language and ideology. London, 1979. pp. 145. *bibliogs.*

— Belgium.

VANDEKERCKHOVE (LIEVEN) and HUYSE (LUCIEN) In de buitenbaan: arbeiderskinderen, universitair onderwijs en sociale ongelijkheid. 2nd ed. Antwerpen, [1977]. pp. 207. *bibliog.*

— United States.

JACKSON (JESSE) and others. A conversation with the Reverend Jesse Jackson: the quest for economic and educational parity. Washington, [1978]. pp. 27. *(American Enterprise Institute for Public Policy Research. AEI Studies. 209)*

EDUCATIONAL INNOVATIONS.

McMULLEN (TIM) Innovative practices in secondary education: the lower secondary stage; problems and possibilities. Paris, Organisation for Economic Co-operation and Development, 1978. pp. 100.

WHITESIDE (TOM) The sociology of educational innovation. London, 1978. pp. 125. *bibliog.*

EDUCATIONAL LAW AND LEGISLATION

— United Kingdom.

BARRELL (GEOFFREY RICHARD) Teachers and the law. 5th ed. London, 1978. pp. 543. *bibliog.*

EDUCATIONAL PLANNING.

KALLEN (DENIS) and BENGTSSON (JARL) Recurrent education: a strategy for lifelong learning. Paris, Organisation for Economic Co-operation and Development, 1973. pp. 91.

— India.

NAIK (J.P.) Educational reform in India: a historical review. [Poona], 1978. pp. 17. *(Gokhale Institute of Politics and Economics. R.R. Kale Memorial Lectures. 1978)*

— Pakistan.

RUUD (KAARE) Manpower and educational requirements of Pakistan, 1961-90. [Karachi], 1970. pp. 89. *bibliog. (Pakistan. National Commission on Manpower and Education. Research Studies. No. 1)*

EDUCATIONAL PSYCHOLOGY.

SIMON (BRIAN) Intelligence, psychology and education: a Marxist critique. rev. ed. London, [1971]. pp. 286.

PIAGET, psychology and education: papers in honour of Jean Piaget; edited by Ved P. Varma and Philip Williams. London, [1976]. pp. 233. *bibliog.*

RECONSTRUCTING educational psychology; edited by Bill Gillham. London, [1978]. pp. 197. *bibliog.*

EDUCATIONAL RESEARCH

— United States.

SPROULL (LEE) and others. Organizing an anarchy: belief, bureaucracy, and politics in the National Institute of Education. Chicago, 1978. pp. 282. *bibliog.*

EDUCATIONAL SOCIOLOGY.

HOPPER (EARL ISSER) ed. Readings in the theory of educational systems. London, 1971 repr. 1972. pp. 336.

SCHOOLING and capitalism: a sociological reader; edited by Roger Dale [and others]. London, 1976. pp. 232. *bibliogs.*

EDUCATION in a changing society; edited by Antonina Kloskowska and Guido Martinotti. London, [1977]. pp. 311.

LAWTON (DENIS) Education and social justice. London, [1977]. pp. 198. *bibliog.*

PLATZ (MERETE) Velkommen til børnehaveklasserne: en undersøgelse af familier der bruger, og familier der ikke bruger børnehaveklasseordningen, etc. København, 1977. pp. 280. *bibliog. (Socialforskningsinstituttet. Publikationer. 76)* With English summary.

GRACE (GERALD) Teachers, ideology and control: a study in urban education. London, 1978. pp. 264. *bibliog.*

MORRISH (IVOR) The sociology of education: an introduction. 2nd ed. London, 1978. pp. 308. *bibliogs.*

PARSONS (TALCOTT) Action theory and the human condition. New York, [1978]. pp. 464. *bibliogs.* Collected essays.

SARUP (MADAN) Marxism and education. London, 1978. pp. 224.

WHITESIDE (TOM) The sociology of educational innovation. London, 1978. pp. 125. *bibliog.*

APPLE (MICHAEL W.) Ideology and curriculum. London, 1979. pp. 203.

ARCHER (MARGARET SCOTFORD) Social origins of educational systems. London, [1979]. pp. 315. *bibliogs.*

BISSERET (NOELLE) Education, class language and ideology. London, 1979. pp. 145. *bibliogs.*

WILLIAMSON (BILL) Education, social structure and development: a comparative analysis. London, 1979. pp. 238. *bibliog.*

— Australia.

MUSGRAVE (PETER WILLIAM) Society and the curriculum in Australia. Sydney, 1979. pp. 160. *bibliogs.*

— Canada.

MARTIN (WILFRED B.W.) and MACDONELL (ALLAN J.) Canadian education: a sociological analysis. Scarborough, Ont., [1978]. pp. 354. *bibliog.*

— Europe.

RINGER (FRITZ FRANZ KLAUS) Education and society in modern Europe. Bloomington, [1979]. pp. 370. *bibliog.*

— United Kingdom.

EGGLESTON (S. JOHN) The sociology of the school curriculum. London, 1977. pp. 171. *bibliog.*

ROBINSON (MARGARET) Schools and social work. London, 1978. pp. 268.

SCHOOLING in decline; edited by Gerald Bernbaum. London, 1979. pp. 240. *bibliog.*

— United States.

BOWEN (HOWARD ROTHMANN) Investment in learning: the individual and social value of American higher education. San Francisco, 1977. pp. 507. *bibliog. A report prepared with the support of the Sloan Foundation and issued by the Carnegie Council on Policy Studies in Higher Education.*

WILLIE (CHARLES VERT) The sociology of urban education: desegregation and integration. Lexington, Mass., [1978]. pp. 184. *bibliogs.*

NASAW (DAVID) Schooled to order: a social history of public schooling in the United States. New York, 1979. pp. 303. *bibliog.*

EDWARD II, King of England.

FRYDE (NATALIE) The tyranny and fall of Edward II, 1321-1326. Cambridge, 1979. pp. 301. *bibliog.*

EDWARDS (WILLIAM JAMES).

EDWARDS (WILLIAM JAMES) Twenty-five years in the black belt. Boston, Mass., 1918; Westport, Conn., 1970. pp. 143. *Facsimile reprint.*

EFFICIENCY, INDUSTRIAL.

CENTRE FOR INTERFIRM COMPARISON. Management policies and practices and business performance. Colchester, [1977]. 3 vols.

CHERNIAVSKII (VASILII OSIPOVICH) Voprosy effektivnosti i optimal'nosti. Moskva, 1977. pp. 171. *(Akademiia Nauk SSSR. Problemy Sovetskoi Ekonomiki)*

EKONOMICHESKAIA effektivnost' obshchestvennogo proizvodstva v period razvitogo sotsializma: metodologicheskie voprosy. Moskva, 1977. pp. 359. *(Akademiia Nauk SSSR. Problemy Sovetskoi Ekonomiki)*

ERMOLOVICH (LIDIIA LUKINICHNA) Sovershenstvovanie ekonomicheskogo analiza effektivnosti proizvodstva. Minsk, 1978. pp. 119.

NATIONAL ECONOMIC DEVELOPMENT COUNCIL. Brewing Sector Working Group. Investment and efficiency in the brewing industry; report. [London, National Economic Development Office, 1978]. 1 pamphlet (various pagings).

VECHKANOV (VASILII SERGEEVICH) Mera effektivnosti sotsialisticheskogo vosproizvodstva: voprosy teorii i metodologii. Moskva, 1978. pp. 188.

EGERTON (FRANCIS) 3rd Duke of Bridgewater.

MALET (HUGH) Bridgewater: the canal Duke, 1736-1803. Manchester, [1977]. pp. 208. *bibliog.*

EGG TRADE

— European Economic Community countries.

EUROPEAN COMMUNITIES. Statistical Office. Monthly statistics of eggs (formerly Agriculture: monthly statistics: eggs. (Internal Information)). m., 1975/1- Luxembourg.

EGGS

— Production.

BURTON (DAVID A.) The economics of egg production: a study of production and marketing on 70 farms. Manchester, 1978. pp. 96. *bibliog. (Agricultural Enterprise Studies in England and Wales. [Economic Reports]. No. 63)*

— South Africa — Production.

KRUGER (CARL DAVID) An investigation into the cost structure of the egg industry in three areas of the republic. [Pretoria, 1968]. pp. 18. *(South Africa. Department of Agricultural Economics and Marketing. Economic Series. No. 66)*

EGO (PSYCHOLOGY).

LOEVINGER (JANE) Ego development. San Francisco, [1976]. pp. 504. *bibliog.*

EGYPT.

EGYPT.

GROUPE DE RECHERCHES ET D'ETUDES SUR LE PROCHE ORIENT. L'Egypte d'aujourd'hui: permanence et changements 1805-1976; par M.C. Aulas (and others). Paris, 1977. pp. 388. *bibliog.*

— Census.

EGYPT. Census, 1976. The preliminary results of the general population and housing census. 22/23 November 1976 in Egypt. [Cairo, 1977]. pp. 57.

— Commerce.

GIRGIS (MAURICE) Industrialization and trade patterns in Egypt. Tübingen, [1977]. pp. 261. *bibliog. (Kiel. Universität. Institut für Weltwirtschaft. Kieler Studien. 143)*

— Economic conditions.

WATERBURY (JOHN) Egypt: burdens of the past, options for the future. Bloomington, [1978]. pp. 318. *bibliogs.*

— Economic history.

GRAN (PETER) Islamic roots of capitalism: Egypt, 1760-1840. Austin, [1979]. pp. 278. *bibliog. (Texas University. Center for Middle Eastern Studies. Modern Middle Eastern Series. No. 4)*

— Foreign relations.

McLAURIN (RONALD D.) and others. Foreign policy making in the Middle East: domestic influences on policy in Egypt, Iraq, Israel, and Syria. New York, 1977. pp. 313. *bibliog.*

— — Russia.

HEIKAL (MOHAMED) Sphinx and commissar: the rise and fall of Soviet influence in the Arab world. London, 1978. pp. 303.

DAWISHA (KAREN) Soviet foreign policy towards Egypt. London, 1979. pp. 271.

— History — 1882-1936, British occupation.

DEEB (MARIUS) Party politics in Egypt: the Wafd and its rivals, 1919-1939. London, 1979. pp. 451. *bibliog.*

— — 1952- .

BAKER (RAYMOND WILLIAM) Egypt's uncertain revolution under Nasser and Sadat. Cambridge, Mass., 1978. pp. 290. *bibliog.*

— — 1956, Intervention.

FULLICK (ROY) and POWELL (GEOFFREY) Suez: the double war. London, 1979. pp. 227. *bibliog.*

— Industries.

GIRGIS (MAURICE) Industrialization and trade patterns in Egypt. Tübingen, [1977]. pp. 261. *bibliog. (Kiel. Universität. Institut für Weltwirtschaft. Kieler Studien. 143)*

— Nationalism.

BAKER (RAYMOND WILLIAM) Egypt's uncertain revolution under Nasser and Sadat. Cambridge, Mass., 1978. pp. 290. *bibliog.*

DEEB (MARIUS) Party politics in Egypt: the Wafd and its rivals, 1919-1939. London, 1979. pp. 451. *bibliog.*

— Politics and government.

BURRELL (R.M.) and KELIDAR (ABBAS) Egypt: the dilemmas of a nation, 1970-1977. Beverly Hills, [1977]. pp. 78. *bibliog. (Georgetown University. Center for Strategic and International Studies. Washington Papers. vol. 5/48)*

BINDER (LEONARD) In a moment of enthusiasm: political power and the second stratum in Egypt. Chicago, [1978]. pp. 437. *bibliog.*

WATERBURY (JOHN) Egypt: burdens of the past, options for the future. Bloomington, [1978]. pp. 318. *bibliogs.*

— Rural conditions.

BINDER (LEONARD) In a moment of enthusiasm: political power and the second stratum in Egypt. Chicago, [1978]. pp. 437. *bibliog.*

— Social conditions.

HYDE (GEORGIE D.M.) Education in modern Egypt: ideals and realities. London, 1978. pp. 245. *bibliog.*

EINAUDI (LUIGI).

LUIGI Einaudi nel centenario della nascita. [Reggio Emilia, 1977]. pp. 191. *(Istituto per la Storia del Movimento Liberale. Quaderni. 1]*

EINSTEIN (ALBERT).

CLARK (RONALD WILLIAM) Einstein: the life and times. London, 1979. pp. 672. *bibliog.*

EISENHOWER (DWIGHT DAVID) President of the United States.

EISENHOWER (DWIGHT DAVID) President of the United States. The papers of Dwight David Eisenhower...; Alfred D. Chandler ([and] Louis Galambos) editor[s]. Baltimore, [1970 in progress]. *bibliogs.*

ELEANOR, Queen Consort of Henry II, King of England.

SEWARD (DESMOND) Eleanor of Aquitaine, the mother queen. Newton Abbot, [1978]. pp. 264. *bibliog.*

ELECTERMINATIONS LIMITED.

McCOWAN (ANTHONY JAMES DENYS) and HUMPHRIES (ALAN PETER) Electerminations Limited: in liquidation: formerly known as APT Electronic Industries Ltd.: investigation under section 165(b) of the Companies Act 1948; report. London, H.M.S.O., 1978. pp. 96,xvi.

ELECTION LAW

— Botswana.

BOTSWANA. Statutes, etc. 1974. Laws of Botswana. Electoral. Chapter O2:07. Gaborone, 1974. pp. 77.

— Canada — British Columbia.

BRITISH COLUMBIA. Royal Commission on Electoral Reform. 1978. [Final report; L.S. Eckhardt, commissioner]. [Victoria], 1978. 6 vols. (in 1).

— Peru.

PERU. Statutes, etc. 1962-66. Legislacion electoral del Peru, anotada y concordada. [Lima], 1966. pp. 255.

— Tanzania.

UNITED REPUBLIC OF TANZANIA. Statutes, etc. 1965. An Act to amend the National Assembly, Elections, Act, 1964. [Dar es Salaam], 1965. pp. 285-302.

UNITED REPUBLIC OF TANZANIA. Statutes, etc. 1965. An Act to make provision for presidential elections. [Dar es Salaam], 1965. pp. 269-276.

UNITED REPUBLIC OF TANZANIA. 1965. Report on rules for the nomination process and conduct of election campaigns for the National Assembly. Dar es Salaam, 1965. pp. 10.

ELECTIONS.

SENFTLEBEN (WOLFGANG) Studies in electoral geography. Taipei, 1977. pp. 113. *bibliog.*

NOHLEN (DIETER) Wahlsysteme der Welt: Daten und Analysen: ein Handbuch. München, [1978]. pp. 449. *bibliog.*

— Botswana.

BOTSWANA. 1974. Botswana elections: a guide to presiding officers in the parliamentary and local government elections, 1974. Gaborone, 1974. pp. 32.

— Canada — Prince Edward Island.

PRINCE EDWARD ISLAND. Chief Electoral Officer. 1974. Report...on the 1974 general provincial election. Charlottetown, 1974. fo.7. *Photocopy.*

— — Quebec (Province).

DUPONT (PIERRE) How Levesque won;...translated by Sheila Fischman. Toronto, 1977. pp. 136.

— Finland.

FINLAND. Tilastokeskus. Valtiolliset vaalit: tasavallan presidentin valitsijamiesten vaalit. a., 1978- Helsinki. *[in Finnish and Swedish with English summary and table headings].*

— India.

INDIA. Election Commission. 1978. Biennial elections brochure: an analysis: Council of States and Legislative Councils, 1974-1975. [Delhi, 1978]. pp. 226. *In English and Hindi.*

— — Kerala.

KERALA. Department of Public Relations. 1977. Kerala election reportage, 1977. [Trivandrum], 1977. pp. 96.

— — Uttar Pradesh.

U.P. politics and elections; by B. Jhunjhunwala [and others] Bangalore, 1974. pp. 99. *Special issue of 'Religion and Society', vol. 21, no. 2, June 1974.*

— Italy.

Le ELEZIONI del 20 giugno. Milano, [1976]. pp. 144.

GHINI (CELSO) Il terremoto del 15 giugno. Milano, 1976. pp. 282.

— Russia.

RUSSIA (USSR). Verkhovnyi Sovet. Prezidium. Otdel po Voprosam Raboty Sovetov. 1973. Itogi vyborov i sostav deputatov mestnykh Sovetov deputatov trudiashchikhsia, 1973 g.: statisticheskii sbornik. Moskva, 1973 g. pp. 254.

— Spain.

RAMIREZ (PEDRO J.) Asi se ganaron las elecciones. Barcelona, 1977. pp. 372.

— Sweden.

SÄRLVIK (BO) and PETERSSON (OLOF) Rikspolitik och lokalpolitik i valet 1973. [Stockholm, 1976]. pp. 60. *(Sweden. Statistiska Centralbyrån. Valundersökningar. Rapporter. 1)*

PETERSSON (OLOF) Väljarna och valet 1976. [Stockholm, 1977]. pp. 295. *(Sweden. Statistiska Centralbyrån. Valundersökningar. Rapporter. 2)*

PETERSSON (OLOF) Valundersökning 1976. Teknisk rapport. [Stockholm, 1978]. pp. 259. *(Sweden. Statistiska Centralbyrån. Valundersökningar. Rapporter. 3)*

— Underdeveloped areas.

See UNDERDEVELOPED AREAS — Elections.

— United States.

POMPER (GERALD M.) and others. The election of 1976: reports and interpretations; Marlene M. Pomper, editor. New York, [1977]. pp. 184.

HADLEY (ARTHUR TWINING) 1924- . The empty polling booth. Englewood Cliffs, [1978]. pp. 179. *bibliog.*

PARTIES and elections in an anti-party age: American politics and the crisis of confidence; edited with an introduction by Jeff Fishel. Bloomington, [1978]. pp. 350.

KLEPPNER (PAUL) The third electoral system, 1853-1892: parties, voters and political cultures. Chapel Hill, N.C., [1979]. pp. 424. *bibliog.*

ELECTRIC INDUSTRIES

— Germany.

WEISS (FRANK DIETMAR) Electrical engineering in West Germany: adjusting to imports from less developed countries. Tübingen, [1978]. pp. 115. *bibliog.* (Kiel. Universität. Institut für Weltwirtschaft. Kieler Studien. 155)

— Netherlands.

TEULINGS (AD) Philips: geschiedenis en praktijk van een wereldconcern. Amsterdam, 1977. pp. 325. *bibliog.*

— United Kingdom.

BYATT (I.C.R.) The British electrical industry, 1875-1914: the economic returns to a new technology. Oxford, 1979. pp. 228. *bibliog.*

ELECTRIC POWER-PLANTS.

DEYOUNG (JOHN H.) and TILTON (JOHN E.) Public policy and the diffusion of technology: an international comparison of large fossil-fueled generating units. University Park, Pa., [1978]. pp. 102. *bibliog.* (Pennsylvania State University. Penn State Studies. No. 43)

— Load.

UNITED NATIONS. Economic and Social Commission for Asia and the Pacific. Energy Resources Development Series. No. 17. Peak-load coverage with particular reference to gas turbines and hydroelectric plants. (ST/ESCAP/45). New York, 1977. pp. 129. *bibliog.*

ELECTRIC POWER TRANSMISSION

— New Zealand.

NEW ZEALAND. Electricity Department. 1967. Electric power transmission. [Wellington, 1967]. 1 pamphlet (unpaged).

ELECTRICITY SUPPLY

— Law and legislation — United States.

AMERICAN ENTERPRISE INSTITUTE FOR PUBLIC POLICY RESEARCH. Legislative Analyses. 95th Congress. No. 11. Electric utility rate reform. Washington, 1977. pp. 27.

— Bahamas.

BAHAMAS ELECTRICITY CORPORATION. Annual report and accounts. a., 1962/63- , with gaps (1964/65, 1966/67). Nassau.

— Colombia.

COLOMBIA. Departamento Administrativo Nacional de Estadistica. Censo de Energia Electrica, 1970. Censo de energia electrica. Bogota, [1970?]. pp. 19.

— European Economic Community countries.

EUROPEAN COMMUNITIES. Statistical Office. Electrical energy statistics. a., 1977- Luxembourg. [in English and French]

— United Kingdom.

NUCLEAR or not: choices for our energy future: a Royal Institute forum; edited by Gerald Foley and Ariane van Buren. London, 1978. pp. 205. *bibliogs.*

BYATT (I.C.R.) The British electrical industry, 1875-1914: the economic returns to a new technology. Oxford, 1979. pp. 228. *bibliog.*

HANNAH (LESLIE) Electricity before nationalisation: a study of the development of the electricity supply industry in Britain to 1948. London, 1979. pp. 467.

— United States.

PACHAURI (RAJENDRA KUMAR) The dynamics of electrical energy supply and demand: an economic analysis. New York, 1975. pp. 171.

HALVORSEN (ROBERT) Econometric models of U.S. energy demand. Lexington, Mass., [1978]. pp. 171. *bibliog.*

— — Rates.

AMERICAN ENTERPRISE INSTITUTE FOR PUBLIC POLICY RESEARCH. Legislative Analyses. 95th Congress. No. 11. Electric utility rate reform. Washington, 1977. pp. 27.

PUBLIC utility rate making in an energy-conscious environment; edited by Werner Sichel. Boulder, Colo., 1979. pp. 145.

ELECTRONIC DATA PROCESSING.

GILDERSLEEVE (THOMAS ROBERT) Design of sequential file systems. New York, [1971]. pp. 49.

LEWIS (THEODORE GYLE) Distribution sampling for computer simulation. Lexington, Mass., [1975]. pp. 150. *bibliog.*

NATIONAL COMPUTER CONFERENCE, 1976. National Computer Conference, June 7-10, 1976, New York; [edited by] Stanley Winkler. Montvale, N.J., [1976]. pp. 1109. *bibliogs.* (American Federation of Information Processing Societies. Conference Proceedings. vol. 45) Microfiche containing the paper The integration of microfilm and the computer by D.R. Neary enclosed in pocket on back end-paper.

CHAMBERS (JOHN M.) Computational methods for data analysis. New York, [1977]. pp. 268. *bibliog.*

NATIONAL COMPUTER CONFERENCE, 1977. National Computer Conference, June 13-16, 1977, Dallas, Texas; [edited by] Robert R. Korfhage. Montvale, N.J., [1977]. pp. 1025. *bibliogs.* (American Federation of Information Processing Societies. Conference Proceedings. vol. 46)

GILDERSLEEVE (THOMAS ROBERT) Successful data processing system analysis. Englewood Cliffs, [1978]. pp. 309.

INTERNATIONAL CONFERENCE ON THE PERFORMANCE OF COMPUTER INSTALLATIONS, GARDONE RIVIERA, ITALY, 1978. Performance of computer installations: evaluation and management: proceedings...; edited by Domenico Ferrari. Amsterdam, 1978. pp. 351. *bibliogs.*

MOORE (RICHARD W.) Introduction to the use of computer packages for statistical analyses. Englewood Cliffs, N.J., [1978]. pp. 115.

NATIONAL COMPUTER CONFERENCE, 1978. National Computer Conference, June 5-8, 1978, Anaheim, California; [edited by] Sakti P. Ghosh and Leonard Y. Liu. Montvale, N.J., [1978]. pp. 1300. *bibliogs.* (American Federation of Information Processing Societies. Conference Proceedings. vol. 47)

NORTON (DAVID P.) and RAU (KENNETH G.) A guide to EDP performance management, systems development, computer performance operations. Wellesley, Mass., [1978]. pp. 310. *bibliog.*

STECHER (PETER) On the interface between business systems and data processing systems. 1978. fo. 226. *bibliog.* Typescript. Ph.D. (London) thesis: unpublished. This thesis is the property of London University and may not be removed from the Library.

— Distributed processing.

BRESLIN (JUDSON) and TASHENBERG (C. BRADLEY) Distributed processing systems: end of the mainframe era? New York, [1978]. pp. 228.

EXPERTISE INTERNATIONAL. Distributed processing: current practice and future developments: vol. 1: management report. Wellesley, Mass., [1978]. pp. 80.

LIEBOWITZ (BURT H.) and CARSON (JOHN H.) Distributed processing. 2nd ed. New York, [1978]. pp. 445. *bibliogs.* Sponsored by the IEEE Computer Society.

THIERAUF (ROBERT J.) Distributed processing systems. Englewood Cliffs, N.J., [1978]. pp. 305. *bibliogs.*

ELECTRONIC DATA PROCESSING DEPARTMENTS.

— Security measures.

TUTORIAL on computer security and integrity; [by] Marshall D. Abrams [and others]. Long Beach, Calif., [1977]. 1 vol. (various pagings). *bibliogs.*

ELECTRONIC DIGITAL COMPUTERS.

DIGITAL systems design; proceedings of the Joint IBM University of Newcastle upon Tyne Seminar held in the University Computing Laboratory 6th-9th September 1977; edited by B. Shaw. Newcastle upon Tyne, 1978. pp. 201.

— Evaluation.

INTERNATIONAL SYMPOSIUM ON COMPUTER PERFORMANCE MODELING, MEASUREMENT AND EVALUATION, YORKTOWN HEIGHTS, NEW YORK, 1977. Computer performance; proceedings of the...symposium...; edited by K. Mani Chandy and Martin Reiser. Amsterdam, [1977]. pp. 564. *bibliogs.*

ELECTRONIC INDUSTRIES.

MATTELART (ARMAND) Multinational corporations and the control of culture: the ideological apparatuses of imperialism; translated from the French by Michael Chanan. Brighton, 1979. pp. 304. *bibliogs.*

ELITE.

Les DOMINATIONS socio-politiques dans le monde, [by] Michel Rocard [and others]. Paris, [1975]. pp. 147. *bibliog.* (Institut Oecuménique pour le Développement des Peuples. Cahiers. 2)

WELSH (WILLIAM A.) Leaders and elites. New York, 1979. pp. 209.

— Egypt.

BINDER (LEONARD) In a moment of enthusiasm: political power and the second stratum in Egypt. Chicago, [1978]. pp. 437. *bibliog.*

— France.

SULEIMAN (EZRA N.) Elites in French society: the politics of survival. Princeton, N.J., [1978]. pp. 299. *bibliog.*

— Pakistan.

HUSSAIN (ASAF) Elite politics in an ideological state: the case of Pakistan. Folkestone, 1979. pp. 212. *bibliog.*

— Russia.

BAILES (KENDALL E.) Technology and society under Lenin and Stalin: origins of the Soviet technical intelligentsia, 1917-1941. Princeton, 1978. pp. 469. *bibliog.* (Columbia University. Russian Institute. Studies)

MATTHEWS (MERVYN) Privilege in the Soviet Union: a study of elite life-styles under communism. London, 1978. pp. 197. *bibliog.*

— United Kingdom.

CROSSICK (GEOFFREY) An artisan elite in Victorian society: Kentish London, 1840- 1880. London, [1978]. pp. 306.

SHRIMSLEY (ANTHONY) The new establishment: an inquiry into who really governs Britain in 1978. [London], 1978. pp. 44.

— United States.

LEADERSHIP in America: consensus, corruption and charisma; edited by Peter Dennis Bathory. New York, [1978]. pp. 200.

EMERGENCY MEDICAL SERVICES.

EMERGENCY medical systems analysis: papers on the planning and evaluation of services; edited by Thomas R. Willemain and Richard C. Larson. Lexington, Mass., [1977]. pp. 181. *(Innovative Resource Planning in Urban Public Safety Systems. [Publications]. vol. 4)*

EMERSON (RALPH WALDO).

HARRIS (KENNETH MARC) Carlyle and Emerson: their long debate. Cambridge, Mass., 1978. pp. 194.

EMIGRATION AND IMMIGRATION.

MUKERJEE (RADHAKAMAL) Races, lands, and food: a program for world subsistence. New York, 1946. pp. 107.

PEOPLE FOR PROGRESS: Les Hommes du progrès; [pd.by] Intergovernmental Committee for European Migration. [in English and French]. irreg., 1967(3)- Geneva.

The DEMOGRAPHIC and social pattern of emigration from the Southern European countries; edited by Massimo Livi Bacci. Firenze, 1972. pp. 393. *General report and studies...in connection with the iv. theme of the Second European Population Conference, Strasbourg, 1971.*

GENDT (RIEN VAN) and GARCIA PASSIGLI (G.) Return migration and reintegration services. Paris, Organisation for Economic Co-operation and Development, 1977. pp. 64.

HUMAN migration: patterns and policies; edited by William H. McNeill and Ruth S. Adams. Bloomington, [1978]. pp. 442. *Proceedings of a conference held in 1976 by the Midwest Council of the American Academy of Arts and Sciences and Indiana University, at New Haven, Indiana.*

EMIGRATION AND IMMIGRATION LAW
— European Economic Community countries.

HARTLEY (TREVOR C.) EEC immigration law. Amsterdam, 1978. pp. 335. *bibliog.*

EMILIA-ROMAGNA
— Economic policy.

EMILIA-ROMAGNA. Giunta Regionale. 1973. Progetto di programma degli interventi della regione Emilia- Romagna: tesi di discussione, etc. [Bologna], 1973. pp. 97. *(Informazioni. N.16-17)*

— Social policy.

EMILIA-ROMAGNA. Giunta Regionale. 1973. Progetto di programma degli interventi della regione Emilia- Romagna: tesi di discussione, etc. [Bologna], 1973. pp. 97. *(Informazioni. N.16-17)*

EMINENT DOMAIN
— America, Latin.

CASAD (ROBERT C.) and MONTAGNÉ (ROGELIO SOTELA) Expropriation in Central America and Panama: processes and procedures. Buffalo, N.Y., 1975. pp. 188. *bibliog.*

— Germany.

GERMANY. Statistisches Reichsamt. Statistik des Deutschen Reichs. Neue Folge. Band 332. Volksbegehren und Volksentscheid "Enteignung der Fürstenvermögen". Anhang: Die Vorabstimmung in Hannover am 18.Mai 1924. Berlin, 1926; Osnabrück, 1978. pp. 38. *Photographic reprint.*

EMMERSON (JOHN K.)

EMMERSON (JOHN K.) The Japanese thread: a life in the U.S. foreign service. New York, 1978. pp. 465.

EMPLOYEE-MANAGEMENT RELATIONS IN GOVERNMENT
— United States — California.

CROUCH (WINSTON WINFORD) Organized civil servants: public employer-employee relations in California. Berkeley, [1978]. pp. 302. *bibliog.*

EMPLOYEE MORALE.

WALKER (NIGEL) Morale in the civil service: a study of the desk worker. Westport, Conn., 1977. pp. 302. *Reprint of work originally published Edinburgh, 1962.*

EMPLOYEE RIGHTS
— United States.

EWING (DAVID WALKLEY) Freedom inside the organization: bringing civil liberties to the workplace. New York, [1977]. pp. 246.

EMPLOYEE THEFT
— Bibliography.

SHEA (MARNIE) compiler. Sabotage and pilferage: a selected bibliography. [Toronto], Ontario Ministry of Labour Research Library, 1975. fo. 5. *Photocopy.*

— United Kingdom.

HENRY (STUART) The hidden economy: the context and control of borderline crime. London, 1978. pp. 194. *bibliog.*

EMPLOYEES, DISMISSAL OF
— United Kingdom.

McGLYNE (JOHN E.) Unfair dismissal cases. 2nd ed. London, 1979. pp. 362.

EMPLOYEES, REPORTING TO.

HILTON (ANTHONY) Employee reports: how to communicate financial information to employees. Cambridge, 1978. pp. 113.

EMPLOYEES, TRAINING OF
— Australia.

AUSTRALIAN TRADE UNION TRAINING AUTHORITY. Annual report. a., 1975/76(1st)- Canberra. Included in AUSTRALIA. Parliament. [Parliamentary papers].

— United Kingdom.

NORTHERN REGION STRATEGY TEAM. Industrial training in the Northern Region. Newcastle-upon-Tyne, 1977. pp. 114. *(Technical Reports. No. 17)*

ZIDERMAN (ADRIAN) Manpower training: theory and policy. London, 1978. pp. 90. *bibliog.*

TRANSPORT TRAINING: the newspaper of the Road Transport Industry Training Board. m. Wembley. *Current issues only kept.*

EMPLOYEES' MAGAZINES, HANDBOOKS, ETC.

ZANDEGIACOMI (NINETTA) Autonomia operaia: esperienze di giornalismo operaio. Verona, [1974]. pp. 319.

EMPLOYEES' REPRESENTATION IN MANAGEMENT.

AGENDA for dealing with the Bullock proposals. London, [1977]. pp. 189. *(Rabvale Limited. Special Studies. No. 1)*

INTERNATIONAL CONFERENCE ON INDUSTRIAL DEMOCRACY, CAMBRIDGE, 1977. Industrial democracy: international views; papers given at the...Conference, etc. Coventry, Social Science Research Council Industrial Relations Research Unit, 1978. pp. 305. *bibliogs.*

KING (CHARLES D.) Writer on industrial relations, and VALL (MARINUS VAN DE) Models of industrial democracy: consultation, co-determination and workers' management. The Hague, [1978]. pp. 218. *bibliog.*

The CONTROL of work; edited by John Purcell and Robin Smith. London, 1979. pp. 184. *bibliogs.*

INDUSTRIAL democracy today: a new role for labour; [edited by] George Sanderson and Frederick Stapenhurst. Toronto, [1979]. pp. 243. *bibliog.*

PUTTING participation into practice; edited by David Guest and Kenneth Knight. Farnborough, [1979]. pp. 333. *bibliog.*

TOWARDS industrial democracy: Europe, Japan and the United States; edited by Benjamin C. Roberts. London, [1979]. pp. 287.

— Australia.

AUSTRALIA. Department of Productivity. 1978. Commonwealth government's policy on employee participation. [Canberra], 1978. pp. 13.

— Canada.

LEVANT (VICTOR) Capital and labour: partners: two classes - two views. Toronto, 1977. pp. 276. *bibliog.*

INDUSTRIAL democracy today: a new role for labour; [edited by] George Sanderson and Frederick Stapenhurst. Toronto, [1979]. pp. 243. *bibliog.*

— Europe.

KOLVENBACH (WALTER) Employee councils in European companies. Kluwer, 1978. pp. 334,

— France.

FRANCE. Direction de la Documentation. La Documentation Française. Notes et Etudes Documentaires. Nos. 4488-4489. Institutions représentatives du personnel dans l'entreprise; par Albert Arseguel. [Paris], 1978. pp. 175. *bibliog.*

MARSDEN (DAVID) Industrial democracy and industrial control in West Germany, France and Great Britain. [London], 1978. pp. 70. *(U.K. Department of Employment. Research Papers. No. 4)*

— Germany.

MARSDEN (DAVID) Industrial democracy and industrial control in West Germany, France and Great Britain. [London], 1978. pp. 70. *(U.K. Department of Employment. Research Papers. No. 4)*

— United Kingdom.

INDUSTRIAL democracy: the implications of the Bullock report; proceedings of a conference held at...Leicester...1977; edited by Roger Benedictus, Colin ourn and Alan C. Neal. Leicester, 1977. 1 vol. (various pagings).

CLIFTON (RICHARD) The economic implications of industrial democracy. [London, Department of Employment, 1978]. pp. 27. *bibliog. (Government Economic Service Working Papers. No. 7)*

FOX (ALAN) Socialism and shop floor power. London, 1978. pp. 20. *(Fabian Society. Research Series. [No.] 338)*

MARSDEN (DAVID) Industrial democracy and industrial control in West Germany, France and Great Britain. [London], 1978. pp. 70. *(U.K. Department of Employment. Research Papers. No. 4)*

TRADES UNION CONGRESS. Industrial democracy: TUC policy statement, 1974: supplementary evidence to the Bullock Committee of Inquiry, 1976: report of the Bullock Committee, 1977: government white paper and congress resolution, 1978. 3rd ed. London, 1979. pp. 61.

TRADES UNION CONGRESS. Conference, 1978. Report of the...conference...to mark the 30th anniversary of the establishment of the National Health Service. London, [1979?]. pp. 48.

— United States.

LEVANT (VICTOR) Capital and labour: partners: two classes - two views. Toronto, 1977. pp. 276. *bibliog.*

— Zambia.

ZAMBIA. Department of Industrial Participatory Democracy. Annual report. a., 1976- Lusaka.

EMPLOYMENT (ECONOMIC THEORY)

— Mathematical models.

MORGAN (PHILLIP L.) Employment functions in manufacturing industry. [London, Department of Employment, 1979]. pp. 32. bibliog. (Government Economic Service Working Papers. No. 24)

EMPLOYMENT FORECASTING.

ALLEN (KEVIN J.) and YUILL (DOUGLAS M.) Small area employment forecasting: data and problems. Farnborough, Hants., [1978]. pp. 248.

— Canada — Nova Scotia.

COFFEY (WILLIAM J.) Nova Scotia population, household, family and labour force projections, 1977-1986; prepared for Nova Scotia [Department of] Development. [Halifax], 1979. fo. 87. bibliog.

— — Ontario.

FOOT (DAVID K.) Public policy and future population in Ontario. [Toronto, 1979]. pp. 57. bibliog. (Ontario. Economic Council. Discussion Paper Series)

— Pakistan.

RUUD (KAARE) Manpower and educational requirements of Pakistan, 1961-90. [Karachi], 1970. pp. 89. bibliog. (Pakistan. National Commission on Manpower and Education. Research Studies. No. 1)

— United Kingdom.

NORTHERN REGION STRATEGY TEAM. Preparation of projections of employment: projection of employment in the Northern Region and sub-regions to 1991; (project no.B. 1.b). Newcastle-upon-Tyne, 1976. 1 vol (various foliations). (Working Papers. No.4)

MAYNARD (ALAN K.) and WALKER (ARTHUR) Doctor manpower 1975-2000: alternative forecasts and their resource implications. London, 1978. pp. 60. bibliog. (U.K. Royal Commission on the National Health Service, 1976. Research Papers. No.4)

U.K. Department of Employment. 1978. Manpower requirements of the energy industries; paper. [London, 1978]. pp. 57. (Energy Commission [U.K.]. Papers. No. 18)

U.K. Department of Health and Social Security. 1978. Medical manpower: the next twenty years; a discussion paper. London, 1978 repr. 1979. pp. 84.

— United States — Massachusetts.

MASSACHUSETTS. Division of Employment Security. Occupation/Industry Research Department. 1976. Employment requirements for Massachusetts by occupation, by industry, 1970-1985. Boston, 1976. fo. 36.

EMPLOYMENT MANAGEMENT.

See PERSONNEL MANAGEMENT.

EMPLOYMENT SUBSIDIES

— United States.

CREATING jobs: public employment programs and wage subsidies: a study sponsored jointly by the Institute for Research on Poverty and the Brookings Institution; John L. Palmer, editor. Washington, D.C., [1978]. pp. 379. (Brookings Institution. Studies in Social Economics) (Wisconsin University, Madison. Institute for Research on Poverty. Monograph Series) Based on a conference held in 1977.

EMPLOYMENT TESTING

— United Kingdom.

PEARN (M.A.) Employment testing and the goal of equal opportunity: the American experience. [London], 1978. pp. 38.

— United States.

PEARN (M.A.) Employment testing and the goal of equal opportunity: the American experience. [London], 1978. pp. 38.

ENCYCLOPEDIAS AND DICTIONARIES.

ENTSIKLOPEDIIA A - Ia. Sofiia, 1974. pp. 975.

ENDOWMENTS.

WHITAKER (BENJAMIN CHARLES GEORGE) The foundations: an anatomy of philanthropic societies. rev. ed. Harmondsworth, 1979. pp. 287. bibliog.

ENERGY

— Canada — Manitoba.

ECONOMIC DEVELOPMENT ADVISORY BOARD OF MANITOBA. Energy and manufacturing in Manitoba: report. [Winnipeg], 1978. pp. 160. bibliog.

ENERGY CONSERVATION

— France.

COMMENT économiser l'énergie dans les transports: (étude interministerielle de rationalisation des choix budgetaires); [by] (Pierre Merlin). Paris, La Documentation Française, 1976. 2 vols (in 1).

Les ECONOMIES d'énergie dans l'industrie. [Paris, 1977]. pp. 86. (France. Ministère de l'Industrie, du Commerce et de l'Artisanat. Les Dossiers de l'Energie. 16)

— Sweden.

SWEDEN. Industridepartementet. Energiprogramkommittén. 1974. Energiforskning: expertmaterial utarbetat på uppdrag av Energiprogramkommittén. Avdelning C. Energianvändning för transporter och samfärdsel. Stockholm, 1974. pp. 77. bibliog. (Sweden. Statens Offentliga Utredningar. 1974. 75)

— United Kingdom.

ADVISORY COUNCIL ON ENERGY CONSERVATION [U.K.]. Report to the Secretary of State for Energy. London, 1978. pp. 28. (U.K. Department of Energy. Energy Papers. No. 31)

U.K. Department of Energy. 1978. Energy conservation research, development and demonstration: an initial strategy for industry. London, 1978. pp. 51. (Energy Papers. No.32)

— United States.

CONGRESSIONAL QUARTERLY INC. Continuing energy crisis in America. Washington, D.C., [1975]. pp. 124. bibliog.

CONSERVATION and the changing direction of economic growth; edited by Bernhard J. Abrahamsson. Boulder, Colo., 1978. pp. 151. bibliogs. Revisions of papers presented at a conference, sponsored by the Rocky Mountain Oil and Gas Association and the Denver Research Institute.

ENERGY CONSUMPTION.

INTERNATIONAL ENERGY AGENCY. 1979. Workshops on energy supply and demand. Paris, 1978 [or rather 1979]. pp. 501. bibliogs.

— Canada — Manitoba.

ECONOMIC DEVELOPMENT ADVISORY BOARD OF MANITOBA. Energy and manufacturing in Manitoba: report. [Winnipeg], 1978. pp. 160. bibliog.

— Sweden.

SWEDEN. Industridepartementet. Energiprogramkommittén. 1974. Energiforskning: expertmaterial utarbetat på uppdrag av Energiprogramkommittén. Avdelning B. Näringslivets energianvändning. Stockholm, 1974. pp. 381. (Sweden. Statens Offentliga Utredningar. 1974. 74)

SWEDEN. Industridepartementet. Energiprogramkommittén. 1974. Energiforskning: expertmaterial utarbetat på uppdrag av Energiprogramkommittén. Avdelning D. Energianvändning för lokalkomfort och hushåll. Stockholm, 1974. pp. 164. (Sweden. Statens Offentliga Utredningar. 1974. 76)

SWEDEN. Industridepartementet. Energiprogramkommittén. 1974. Energiforskning: program för forskning och utveckling: betänkand avgivet av Energiprogramkommittén. Stockholm, 1974. pp. 225. bibliog. (Sweden. Statens Offentliga Utredningar. 1974.72)

ENERGY INDUSTRIES

— United Kingdom.

U.K. Department of Employment. 1978. Manpower requirements of the energy industries; paper. [London, 1978]. pp. 57. (Energy Commission [U.K.]. Papers. No. 18)

ENERGY POLICY.

ENERGY COMMISSION [U.K.]. [Background information papers: ENCOM series]. irreg., 1977(no.1)- London.

GOALS in a global community: the original background papers for Goals for mankind: a report to the Club of Rome; edited by Ervin Laszlo and Judah Bierman. New York, [1977 in progress]. bibliogs.

DARMSTADTER (JOEL) and others. How industrial societies use energy: a comparative analysis. Baltimore, [1977]. pp. 282.

ENERGY: global prospects, 1985-2000: report of the Workshop on Alternative Energy Strategies: a project sponsored by the Massachusetts Institute of Technology. New York, [1977]. pp. 291.

WONDER (EDWARD F.) Nuclear fuel and American foreign policy: multilateralization for uranium enrichment. Boulder, Colo., 1977. pp. 72.

DEYOUNG (JOHN H.) and TILTON (JOHN E.) Public policy and the diffusion of technology: an international comparison of large fossil-fueled generating units. University Park, Pa., [1978]. pp. 102. bibliog. (Pennsylvania State University. Penn State Studies. No. 43)

ENERGY policy; edited by J.S. Aronofsky [and others]. Amsterdam, 1978. pp. 260. bibliogs.

EZZATI (ALI) World energy markets and OPEC stability. Lexington, Mass., [1978]. pp. 205. bibliog.

MIHAILOVITCH (LIOUBOMIR) and PLUCHART (JEAN JACQUES) Energie mondiale: les nouvelles stratégies. Paris, [1978]. pp. 288. bibliog.

U.K. Department of Energy. 1978. International energy questions; paper. [London, 1978]. pp. 13. (Energy Commission [U.K.]. Papers. No. 13)

AHMED (S. BASHEER) Nuclear fuel and energy policy. Lexington, Mass., [1979]. pp. 158. bibliog.

— Environmental aspects — United States.

MEAD (WALTER J.) Energy and the environment: conflict in public policy. Washington, 1978. pp. 36. (American Enterprise Institute for Public Policy Research. Special Analyses. No. 78-1)

— Mathematical models.

BLAIR (PETER D.) Multiobjective regional energy planning: application to the energy park concept. Boston, Mass., [1979]. pp. 163. bibliog.

— Social aspects — United Kingdom.

NUCLEAR or not: choices for our energy future: a Royal Institute forum; edited by Gerald Foley and Ariane van Buren. London, 1978. pp. 205. bibliogs.

— — United States.

KRUTILLA (JOHN V.) and others. Economic and fiscal impacts of coal development: Northern Great Plains. Baltimore, [1978]. pp. 208. bibliog. Published for Resources for the Future, Inc.

ENERGY POLICY.(Cont.)

— Asia.

UNITED NATIONS. Economic and Social Commission for Asia and the Pacific. Energy Resources Development Series. No. 15. Proceedings of the second session of the Committee on Natural Resources. (E/CN.11/1259). New York, 1976. pp. 113.

— Canada.

FRANK (HELMUT J.) and SCHANZ (JOHN J.) U.S.-Canadian energy trade: a study of changing relationships. Boulder, [1978]. pp. 136.

— Europe.

SIMEONS (CHARLES) Energy research and development programmes in western Europe. Amsterdam, 1978. pp. 323. *bibliog.*

— Europe, Eastern.

PARK (DANIEL) Oil and gas in COMECON countries. London, 1979. pp. 240. *bibliog.*

— France.

FRANCE. Commission Consultative pour la Production d'Electricité d'Origine Nucléaire. 1973. Rapport. [Paris], 1973. 2 vols.

COMMENT économiser l'énergie dans les transports: (étude interministerielle de rationalisation des choix budgetaires); [by] (Pierre Merlin). Paris, La Documentation Française, 1976. 2 vols (in 1).

FRANCE. Commission d'Etude de la Production d'Electricité d'Origine Hydraulique et Marémotrice. 1976. La production d'électricité d'origine hydraulique: rapport Paris, 1976. pp. 120. *(France. Ministère de l'Industrie et de la Recherche. Les Dossiers de l'Energie. 9)*

— Germany.

EVANS (DOUGLAS) Western energy policy: the case for competition. London, 1978. pp. 198. *bibliog.*

— India.

TYNER (WALLACE EDWARD) Energy resources and economic development in India. Leiden, 1978. pp. 139. *bibliog.*

— New Zealand.

NEW ZEALAND. Ministry of Energy. 1978. Goals and guidelines: an energy strategy for New Zealand. Wellington, 1978. pp. 111.

— North Sea.

The EFFECTIVE management of resources: the international politics of the North Sea; edited by C.M. Mason. London, 1979. pp. 268. *bibliogs.*

— Pacific, The.

UNITED NATIONS. Economic and Social Commission for Asia and the Pacific. Energy Resources Development Series. No. 15. Proceedings of the second session of the Committee on Natural Resources. (E/CN.11/1259). New York, 1976. pp. 113.

— Philippine Islands.

ENERGY DEVELOPMENT BOARD [PHILIPPINE ISLANDS]. Annual report. a., 1976- Manila.

— Russia — Siberia.

TOPLIVNO-energeticheskii kompleks Sibiri: sostoianie i napravleniia razvitiia. Novosibirsk, 1978. pp. 255.

— Sweden.

SWEDEN. Industridepartementet. Energiprogramkommittén. 1974. Energiforskning: expertmaterial utarbetat på uppdrag av Energiprogramkommittén. Avdelning A. Utvinning av energiråvaror och industriell energiproduktion. Stockholm, 1974. pp. 482. *(Sweden. Statens Offentliga Utredningar. 1974. 73)*

SWEDEN. Industridepartementet. Energiprogramkommittén. 1974. Energiforskning: program för forskning och utveckling: betänkande avgivet av Energiprogramkommittén. Stockholm, 1974. pp. 225. *bibliog. (Sweden. Statens Offentliga Utredningar. 1974.72)*

SWEDEN. Finansdepartementet. Långtidsutredningen. 1975. (Långtidsutredningen 1975. Bilaga 3). Energiförsörjningen, 1975-1980;...rapport av Statens Industriverk. Stockholm, 1975. pp. 48. *(Statens Offentliga Utredningar. 1975. 96)*

BERGMAN (LARS) Energy and economic growth in Sweden: an analysis of historical trends and present choices. Stockholm, [1977]. pp. 321. *bibliog.*

— United Kingdom.

U.K. Department of Energy. Corporate Planning Conference. Report of proceedings. a., 1975- London.

ENERGY COMMISSION [U.K.]. [Background information papers: ENCOM series]. irreg., 1977(no.1)- London.

BAILEY (RICHARD) Energy: the rude awakening. London, [1977]. pp. 241. *bibliog.*

WATT COMMITTEE ON ENERGY. Deployment of national resources in the provision of energy in the United Kingdom, 1975-2025. London, [1977]. pp. 60. *(Watt Committee on Energy. Reports. No. 2)*

WATT COMMITTEE ON ENERGY. Energy research and development in the United Kingdom. London, [1977]. pp. 68. *(Watt Committee on Energy. Reports. No. 1)*

EVANS (DOUGLAS) Western energy policy: the case for competition. London, 1978. pp. 198. *bibliog.*

WATT COMMITTEE ON ENERGY. The rational use of energy. London, 1978. pp. 71. *(Watt Committee on Energy. Reports. No. 3)*

— United States.

NATIONAL ACADEMY OF SCIENCES. Academy Forum, 1977. Coal as an energy resource: conflict and consensus. Washington, 1977. pp. 326.

TAVOULAREAS (WILLIAM) and KAYSEN (CARL) A debate on A time to choose. Cambridge, Mass., 1977. pp. 107.

UNITED States and world energy resources: prospects and priorities...; edited by Ragaei El Mallakh and Carl McGuire. Boulder, Colo., [1977]. pp. 272. *Proceedings of the third international conference of the International Research Center for Energy and Economic Development held at Boulder, Colorado, 1976.*

AMERICAN ENTERPRISE INSTITUTE FOR PUBLIC POLICY RESEARCH. High School Debate Series. The Federal government's energy policies, 1978-1979. Washington, 1978. pp. 79. *bibliog.*

BOHI (DOUGLAS R.) and RUSSELL (MILTON) Limiting oil imports: an economic history and analysis. Baltimore, [1978]. pp. 356. *Report of a project initiated by Resources for the Future, Inc.*

CONSERVATION and the changing direction of economic growth; edited by Bernhard J. Abrahamsson. Boulder, Colo., 1978. pp. 151. *bibliogs. Revisions of papers presented at a conference, sponsored by the Rocky Mountain Oil and Gas Association and the Denver Research Institute.*

ENERGY analysis: a new public policy tool; edited by Martha W. Gilliland. Boulder, Colo., [1978]. pp. 110. *bibliogs. (American Association for the Advancement of Science. Selected Symposia Series. 9)*

EVANS (DOUGLAS) Western energy policy: the case for competition. London, 1978. pp. 198. *bibliog.*

FRANK (HELMUT J.) and SCHANZ (JOHN J.) U.S.-Canadian energy trade: a study of changing relationships. Boulder, [1978]. pp. 136.

GORDON (RICHARD L.) Coal in the U.S. energy market: history and prospects. Lexington, Mass., [1978]. pp. 224. *bibliog.*

HALVORSEN (ROBERT) Econometric models of U.S. energy demand. Lexington, Mass., [1978]. pp. 171. *bibliog.*

HOW energy affects the economy; edited by A. Bradley Askin. Lexington, Mass., [1978]. pp. 133. *bibliogs.*

ROSENBAUM (WALTER A.) Coal and crisis: the political dilemmas of energy management. New York, [1978]. pp. 107. *bibliogs.*

TYNER (WALLACE E.) and others. Western coal: promise or problem. Lexington, Mass., [1978]. pp. 181. *bibliog.*

ENERGY future: report of the energy project at the Harvard Business School. New York, [1979]. pp. 353.

PHILLIPS (OWEN M.) The last chance energy book. Baltimore, 1979. pp. 142.

PUBLIC utility rate making in an energy-conscious environment; edited by Werner Sichel. Boulder, Colo., 1979. pp. 145.

ENGELS (FRIEDRICH).

KUCZYNSKI (JUERGEN) Studien zu einer Geschichte der Gesellschaftswissenschaften. Berlin, 1975-78. 10 vols.

MOLNÁR (MIKLÓS) Marx, Engels et la politique internationale. Paris, 1975. pp. 385. *bibliog.*

MARX-ENGELS JAHRBUCH; hrsg. vom Institut für Marxismus- Leninismus (Berlin). a., [1977] (no.1)- Berlin.

ENGELS (FRIEDRICH) Dokumente seines Lebens, 1820-1895; (zusammengestellt und erläutert von Manfred Kliem). Frankfurt am Main, 1977. pp. 693. *bibliog.*

"ANTI-Diuring" F. Engel'sa i sovremennost'. Moskva, 1978. pp. 192. *bibliog.*

KARL Marx und Friedrich Engels: ihr Leben und ihre Zeit; (Herausgeber:...Karl-Heinz Mahlert, Leitung). Berlin, [1978]. pp. 352.

ROSE (MARGARET A.) Reading the young Marx and Engels: poetry, parody and the censor. London, 1978. pp. 165. *bibliog.*

UCHENIE K. Marksa, F. Engel'sa, V.I. Lenina o sotsialisticheskom gosudarstve i prave: istoriia razvitiia i sovremennost'. Moskva, 1978. pp. 431. *Continuation of Marksistsko-leninskoe uchenie o gosudarstve i prave, Moskva, 1977.*

VOLODIN (ALEKSANDR IVANOVICH) "Anti-Diuring" F.Engel'sa i obshchestvennaia mysl' Rossii XIX veka: istoriko-filosofskie ocherki. Moskva, 1978. pp. 252.

— Bibliography.

EUBANKS (CECIL L.) compiler. Karl Marx and Friedrich Engels: an analytical bibliography. New York, 1977. pp. 163.

GRIN (TSILIA IOSIFOVNA) compiler. K. Marks, F. Engel's i revoliutsionnaia Rossiia: k 160- letiiu so dnia rozhdeniia K. Marksa: rekomendatel'nyi ukazatel' literatury; nauchnyi redaktor S.S. Volk. Moskva, 1978. pp. 95.

ENGINEERING

— Management.

MANAGEMENT of large capital projects: proceedings of the conference held [by the Institution of Civil Engineers] in London, 17-18 May, 1978. London, 1978. pp. 239.

— India.

INDIA. Labour Bureau. 1978. Report on survey of labour conditions in general and jobbing engineering, manufacture of machinery except electrical, industry, 1974-75. [Delhi, 1978]. pp. 72.

— United Kingdom.

NORTHERN REGION STRATEGY TEAM. Trends and prospects in the shipbuilding and heavy engineering industries. Newcastle-upon-Tyne, 1977. pp. 247. *(Working Papers. No. 11)*

— — Contracts and specifications.

HUDSON (ALFRED) Building and engineering contracts, including the duties and liabilities of architects, engineers and surveyors; tenth edition by I.N. Duncan Wallace. London, 1970. pp. 921.

ENGINEERING MATHEMATICS.

BENDER (CARL M.) and ORSZAG (STEVEN A.) Advanced mathematical methods for scientists and engineers. New York, [1978]. pp. 593. *bibliog.*

ENGINEERS

— India.

INDIA. Labour Bureau. 1977. Report on survey of labour conditions in general and jobbing engineering, manufacture of electrical machinery, apparatus, appliances and supplies industry, 1974-75. [Delhi, 1977]. pp. 80.

INDIA. Labour Bureau. 1978. Report on survey of labour conditions in general and jobbing engineering, manufacture of machinery except electrical, industry, 1974-75. [Delhi, 1978]. pp. 72.

— Rhodesia.

RHODESIA. Department of Labour. 1976. Survey of engineering manpower in Rhodesia, 1974/75. Salisbury, 1976. pp. 26,2.

— Russia — Soviet Far East.

DEREVIANKO (ALEKSEI PANTELEVICH) Inzhenerno-tekhnicheskie kadry Dal'nego Vostoka SSSR, 1959- 1965 gg. Moskva, 1978. pp. 150.

— United States — Biography — Indexes.

ROYSDON (CHRISTINE) and KHATRI (LINDA A.) compilers. American engineers of the nineteenth century: a biographical index. New York, 1978. pp. 247.

ENGLISH FICTION

— History and criticism.

CUNNINGHAM (GAIL) The new woman and the Victorian novel. London, 1978. pp. 172. *bibliog.*

ENGLISH LANGUAGE

— Accents and accentuation.

HUGHES (ARTHUR) and TRUDGILL (PETER) English accents and dialects: an introduction to social and regional varieties of British English. London, 1979. pp. 90. *bibliog.*

— Dialects.

HUGHES (ARTHUR) and TRUDGILL (PETER) English accents and dialects: an introduction to social and regional varieties of British English. London, 1979. pp. 90. *bibliog.*

— Dictionaries.

The OXFORD paperback dictionary; compiled by Joyce M. Hawkins. Oxford, 1979. pp. 770.

— Grammar, Generative.

PULLUM (GEOFFREY K.) Rule interaction and the organization of a grammar. New York, 1979. pp. 413. *bibliog.*

— Semantics.

KEENAN (EDWARD L.) and FALTZ (LEONARD M.) Logical types for natural language. [Los Angeles, 1978]. pp. 338. *bibliog. (California University. Occasional Papers in Linguistics. No.3)*

— Study and teaching — Spanish students.

SCHUMANN (JOHN H.) The pidginization process: a model for second language acquisition. Rowley, Mass., [1978]. pp. 190. *bibliog.*

— Syntax.

JACKENDOFF (RAY S.) X syntax: a study of phrase structure. Cambridge, Mass., [1977]. pp. 248. *bibliog.*

ENGLISH LITERATURE

— History and criticism.

WILSON (RICHARD MIDDLEWOOD) The lost literature of medieval England. New York, 1969. pp. 272. *First published in 1952.*

INGLE (STEPHEN) Socialist thought in imaginative literature. London, 1979. pp. 211.

ENGLISH NEWSPAPERS.

NEWTON (DAVID) Men of mark: makers of East Midland Allied Press. Peterborough, 1977. pp. 239.

TELEN' (EL'MIRA FEDOROVNA) Sotsial'naia mimikriia burzhuaznykh massovykh gazet Velikobritanii. Moskva, 1978. pp. 96.

ENGLISH PERIODICALS

— Bibliography.

NOYCE (JOHN LEONARD) compiler. The directory of British alternative periodicals, 1965-1974. Hassocks, Sussex, 1979. pp. 359.

ENGLISH PHILOLOGY

— Study and teaching.

BLEICH (DAVID) Subjective criticism. Baltimore, Md., [1978]. pp. 309.

ENGLISH POETRY.

The EARLIEST English poems; translated and introduced by Michael Alexander. 2nd ed. Harmondsworth, 1977. pp. 160.

— History and criticism.

FEINGOLD (RICHARD) Nature and society: later eighteenth-century uses of the pastoral and georgic. Hassocks, 1978. pp. 209.

— Translations from Latin.

WADDELL (HELEN JANE) Mediaeval Latin lyrics. 5th ed. London, 1948 repr. 1975. pp. 342. *Parallel Latin and English texts.*

ENLIGHTENMENT.

RIPALDA (JOSÉ MARÍA) The divided nation: the roots of a bourgeois thinker: G.W.F. Hegel. Assen, 1977. pp. 221. *bibliog.*

COMMAGER (HENRY STEELE) The empire of reason: how Europe imagined and America realized the enlightenment. Garden City, 1978. pp. 381.

RENDALL (JANE) The origins of the Scottish Enlightenment. London, 1978. pp. 257. *bibliog.*

ANCHOR (ROBERT) The enlightenment tradition. Berkeley, 1979. pp. 167. *bibliog.*

ENTREPRENEUR.

PALMER (JOHN CARRINGTON) Entrepreneurs and economic development in a small town in Kenya. 1978. fo. 384. *bibliog. Typescript. Ph.D. (London) thesis: unpublished. This thesis is the property of London University and may not be removed from the Library.*

ENVIRONMENTAL ENGINEERING.

DUNNE (THOMAS) and LEOPOLD (LUNA BERGERE) Water in environmental planning. San Francisco, [1978]. pp. 818. *bibliogs.*

ENVIRONMENTAL IMPACT ANALYSIS.

ENVIRONMENTAL assessment approaching maturity; [edited by] Selina Bendix [and] Herbert R. Graham. Ann Arbor, [1978]. pp. 288. *Proceedings of a seminar, held in Washington D.C. in 1977, sponsored by the National Association of Environmental Professionals.*

ENVIRONMENTAL IMPACT STATEMENTS.

ENVIRONMENTAL assessment approaching maturity; [edited by] Selina Bendix [and] Herbert R. Graham. Ann Arbor, [1978]. pp. 288. *Proceedings of a seminar, held in Washington D.C. in 1977, sponsored by the National Association of Environmental Professionals.*

ENVIRONMENTAL LAW.

ENVIRONMENTAL pollution and individual rights: an international symposium; edited by Stephen C. McCaffrey...and Robert E. Lutz. Deventer, 1978. pp. 213. *Four tables in pocket.*

ENVIRONMENTAL POLICY.

HUMAN SETTLEMENTS; issued by the Centre for Housing, Building and Planning. Department of Economic and Social Affairs, United Nations. q., Ja 1971 (v.1, no.1)- New York.

ENLOE (CYNTHIA H.) The politics of pollution in a comparative perspective: ecology and power in four nations. New York, [1975]. pp. 342.

The ENVIRONMENT of human settlements: human well-being in cities: proceedings of the conference held in Brussels, Belgium, April 1976; editor in chief P. Laconte, etc. Oxford, 1976. 2 vols.

O'RIORDAN (TIMOTHY) ed. Environmentalism. London, [1976]. pp. 373. *bibliog.*

UNITED NATIONS ENVIRONMENT PROGRAMME. State of the environment: selected topics. a., 1977(1st)- [Nairobi].

ENVIRONMENTAL improvement through economic incentives; [by] Frederick R. Anderson [and others]. Baltimore, [1977]. pp. 195. *A joint project of Resources for the Future and the Environmental Law Institute.*

DESERTIFICATION CONTROL BULLETIN: half-yearly bulletin on on-going and planned activities; [pd. by] United Nations Environment Programme. s-a., Je 1978(v. 1, no. 1)- Nairobi.

MILLS (EDWIN S.) The economics of environmental quality. New York, [1978]. pp. 304. *bibliogs.*

RESOURCES for an uncertain future: papers presented at a forum marking the 25th anniversary of Resources for the Future, October 13, 1977, Washington, D.C.; Charles J. Hitch, editor. Baltimore, [1978]. pp. 105.

URBAN, regional and national planning (UNRENAP): proceedings of the IFAC Workshop, Kyoto, Japan, 5-6 August 1977; edited by T. Hasegawa and K. Inoue. Oxford, 1978. pp. 233.

ABELSON (PETER) Cost benefit analysis and environmental problems. Farnborough, [1979]. pp. 202. *bibliogs.*

AMERICAN ACADEMY OF POLITICAL AND SOCIAL SCIENCE. Annals. vol. 444. The environment and the quality of life: a world view; special editor of this volume Marvin E. Wolfgang. Philadelphia, 1979. pp. 201.

BAUMOL (WILLIAM JACK) and OATES (WALLACE E.) Economics, environmental policy, and the quality of life. Englewood Cliffs, [1979]. pp. 377.

ROBERTS (ALAN) The self-managing environment. London, [1979]. pp. 189. *bibliog.*

ROSZAK (THEODORE) Person/planet: the creative disintegration of industrial society. London, 1979. pp. 347. *bibliog.*

ENVIRONMENTAL POLICY.(Cont.)

— Citizen participation.

NATURAL resources for a democratic society: public participation in decision-making; edited by Albert E. Utton [and others]. Boulder, 1976. pp. 236. *(Reprinted from Natural Resources Journal, vol.16, 1976. no. 1)*

— Asia, Southeast.

DEVELOPING economies and the environment: the southeast Asian experience; edited by Colin MacAndrews and Chia Lin Sien. Singapore, [1979]. pp. 299.

— Australia — New South Wales.

NEW SOUTH WALES. Planning and Environment Commission. 1975. Second report: proposals for a new environmental planning system for New South Wales. [Sydney], 1975. pp. 44.

— — Queensland.

QUEENSLAND. Department of the Co-ordinator-General of Public Works. 1975. State of regional planning, public works organization and environmental control in Queensland. [Brisbane, 1975?]. pp. 16.

— Canada.

ECOLOGY versus politics in Canada; edited by William Leiss. Toronto, [1979]. pp. 282. *bibliogs.*

— — British Columbia.

BRITISH COLUMBIA. Ministry of the Environment. Annual report. a., 1976(1st)- Victoria.

— Caribbean area.

ENVIRONMENTAL planning and development in the Caribbean; [based on a workshop held in May 1974, directed by] Charles Frankenhoff. 2nd ed. [Rio Pedras], 1977. pp. 51. *(Puerto Rico University. Graduate School of Planning. Series on Environmental Planning. No. 1)*

— Czechoslovakia.

LANDSCAPE and man in socialist Czechoslovakia; five studies edited by O. Vidlakova; [translated from the Czech by E. Kovanda]. Prague, 1977. pp. 111.

— France — Basse-Normandie.

BASSE-NORMANDIE. Conseil Régional. Liaisons, informations, région: revue d'information économique de Basse-Normandie. No. 14. Spécial environnement. [Caen], 1978. pp. 136. *Map in end pocket.*

— Japan.

PRUD'HOMME (RÉMY) Environmental policies in Japan. Paris, Organisation for Economic Co-operation and Development, 1977. pp. 94.

— Sweden.

SWEDEN. Utrikesdepartementet. Aktstycken. Ny Serie II. 21. Svenska regeringens svar på FN-sekretariatets enkät i samband med 1972 års konferens om den mänskliga miljön. Stockholm, 1969. pp. 39.

SWEDEN. Finansdepartementet. Långtidsutredningen. 1975. (Långtidsutredningen 1975. Bilaga 6). Miljövård i Sverige, 1975-1980;...rapport av Utredningen om Kostnaderna för Miljövården. Stockholm, 1975. pp. 104. *bibliog. (Statens Offentliga Utredningar. 1975.98) With English summary.*

— United Kingdom.

DRAPER (PAUL) Creation of the D.O.E.: (a study of the merger of three departments to form the Department of the Environment). London, 1977. pp. 239. *(U.K. Civil Service Department. Civil Service Studies. No. 4)*

NORTHERN REGION STRATEGY TEAM. Urban environment in the Northern Region. Newcastle-upon-Tyne, 1977. pp. 125. *(Working Papers. No. 16)*

U.K. Central Office of Information. Reference Division. Reference Pamphlets. 9. Environmental planning in Britain. London, 1979. pp. 65. *bibliog.*

— — Citizen participation.

HAMPTON (WILLIAM) Providing the posh words...: two experiments in community participation: ...an evaluation of the appointment of Environmental Liaison Officers in Birmingham and Loughborough. [Loughborough, Department of the Environment], 1978. pp. 60.

— United States.

CURRENT issues in U.S. environmental policy; [edited by] Paul R. Portney. Baltimore, [1978]. pp. 207.

SPROUT (HAROLD HANCE) and SPROUT (MARGARET TUTTLE) The context of environmental politics: unfinished business for America's third century. Lexington, [1978]. pp. 216. *bibliog.*

SENECA (JOSEPH J.) and TAUSSIG (MICHAEL K.) Environmental economics. 2nd ed. Englewood Cliffs, N.J., [1979]. pp. 379. *bibliogs.*

ENVIRONMENTAL PROTECTION.

INTERNATIONAL BANK FOR RECONSTRUCTION AND DEVELOPMENT. 1974. Environmental, health, and human ecologic considerations in economic development projects. Washington, 1974. pp. 142. *bibliog.*

CONSTANTINESCU (N.N.) Economia protecţiei mediului natural. Bucureşti, 1976. pp. 369. *With English, French, Russian and Spanish tables of contents.*

UNITED NATIONS ENVIRONMENT PROGRAMME. State of the environment: selected topics. a., 1977(1st)- [Nairobi].

FRIENDS OF THE EARTH. Progress as if survival mattered: a handbook for a conserver society, by Friends of the Earth; edited by Hugh Nash. San Francisco, [1977]. pp. 319. *bibliog.*

INDUSTRY AND ENVIRONMENT; pd. by the United Nations Environment Programme. q., Oc/D 1978(v.1, no.1)- Paris.

AMERICAN ACADEMY OF POLITICAL AND SOCIAL SCIENCE. Annals. vol. 444. The environment and the quality of life: a world view; special editor of this volume Marvin E. Wolfgang. Philadelphia, 1979. pp. 201.

— Bibliography.

BODDAERT (JACQUELINE) compiler. Bibliographie sélective: aménagement du territoire, environnement, urbanisme. 3rd ed. Paris, Délégation à l'Aménagement du Territoire et à l'Action Régionale, 1978. pp. 38.

— Communist countries.

COUNCIL FOR MUTUAL ECONOMIC ASSISTANCE. 1977. Information on the CMEA activities on co-operation in manufacturing equipment for protecting the environment against pollution: prepared...for the ECE Ad Hoc Meeting on Production of Engineering Equipment for Preventing Pollution...Geneva, February 1-2, 1977. Moscow, 1977. pp. 9.

— Denmark.

DENMARK. Udenrigsministeriet. 1972. Environment Denmark: Denmark's national report to the United Nations on the human environment. [Copenhagen, 1972]. pp. 57.

— United Kingdom — Citizen participation.

BREACH (IAN) Windscale fallout: a primer for the age of nuclear controversy. Harmondsworth, 1978. pp. 192.

ENVIRONMENTAL PSYCHOLOGY.

CANTER (DAVID VICTOR) and STRINGER (PETER) Environmental interaction: psychological approaches to our physical surroundings. London, [1975]. pp. 374. *bibliog.*

BAUM (ANDREW) and VALINS (STUART) Architecture and social behavior: psychological studies of social density. Hillsdale, N.J., 1977. pp. 112. *bibliog.*

CANTER (DAVID VICTOR) The psychology of place. London, 1977. pp. 198. *bibliog.*

TUAN (YI-FU) Space and place: the perspective of experience. London, 1977. pp. 235. *bibliog.*

FARBSTEIN (JAY) and KANTROWITZ (MIN) People in places: experiencing, using, and changing the built environment. Englewood Cliffs, N.J., [1978]. pp. 182.

INSEL (PAUL M.) and LINDGREN (HENRY CLAY) Too close for comfort: the psychology of crowding. Englewood Cliffs, [1978]. pp. 180. *bibliog.*

EPHEMERAL STREAMS.

LONDON. University. London School of Economics and Political Science. Graduate School of Geography. Discussion Papers. No. 71. Flow depth monitoring in an ephemeral channel and its relationship to channel changes; [by] Geoff Butcher and John Thornes. London, 1978. pp. 26. *bibliog.*

EPIDEMICS

— United Kingdom.

GOTTFRIED (ROBERT S.) Epidemic disease in fifteenth century England: the medical response and the demographic consequences. Leicester, 1978. pp. 262. *bibliog.*

— United States.

CROSBY (ALFRED W.) Epidemic and peace, 1918. Westport, Conn., 1976. pp. 337. *bibliogs.*

EQUAL PAY FOR EQUAL WORK.

EQUAL PAY/EQUAL OPPORTUNITY CONFERENCE, TORONTO, 1978. Issues and options: equal pay/equal opportunity; papers presented at the Equal Pay/Equal Opportunity Conference etc. Toronto, Ministry of Labour, 1978 repr. 1979. pp. 76.

EQUALITY.

CHATTERJI (BANKIM CHANDRA) Bankim on equality: an English translation of Bankim Chandra Chattopadhyay's Bengali article, Samya [with an essay on its background] by M.K. Haldar. Nedlands, W.A., 1974. pp. 38, 124. *(Western Australia, University of. Centre for Asian Studies. Working Papers in Asian Studies. No. 5)*

WORLD inequality: origins and perspectives on the world system; edited by Immanuel Wallerstein. Nottingham, [1975]. pp. 169.

LEWIS (MICHAEL) 1937- . The culture of inequality. Amherst, 1978. pp. 207.

BRAKEL (ARIE) Gelijk is niet gelijk: over het veranderen van organisaties. Meppel, [1979]. pp. 344. *bibliog. Proefschrift - Doctor in de Sociale Wetenschappen - Erasmus Universiteit Rotterdam. With English summary.*

JOSEPH (Sir KEITH SINJOHN) and SUMPTION (JONATHAN) Equality. London, [1979]. pp. 130. *bibliog.*

McAULEY (ALASTAIR) Economic welfare in the Soviet Union: poverty, living standards, and inequality. Madison, [1979]. pp. 389. *bibliog.*

— America, Latin.

CARNOY (MARTIN) Can educational policy equalise income distribution in Latin America?;...with the collaboration of José Lobo [and others]; a study prepared for the International Labour Office within the framework of the Research Programmes on Income Distribution and Employment and on Education and Employment of the World Employment Programme. Farnborough, [1979]. pp. 110. *bibliog.*

EQUATIONS.

PROESSDORF (SIEGFRIED) Some classes of singular equations; translated by Siegfried Dümmel. Amsterdam, 1978. pp. 417. *bibliog.*

EQUILIBRIUM.

HILDENBRAND (WERNER) and KIRMAN (A.P.) Introduction to equilibrium analysis: variations on themes by Edgeworth and Walras. Amsterdam, 1976. pp. 216. *bibliog.*

EQUILIBRIUM (ECONOMICS).

MAKAROV (VALERII LEONIDOVICH) and RUBINOV (ALEKSANDR MOISEEVICH) Mathematical theory of economic dynamics and equilibria; translated from the Russian by Mohamed El-Hodiri. New York, [1977]. pp. 252. *bibliog.*

NÄSLUND (BERTIL) An analysis of economic size distributions. Berlin, 1977. pp. 100. *bibliog.*

BOWDEN (ROGER JOHN) The econometrics of disequilibrium. Amsterdam, 1978. pp. 324. *bibliog.*

KALMAN (PETER JASON) Some aspects of the foundations of general equilibrium theory: the posthumous papers...; edited by Jerry Green. Berlin, 1978. pp. 167. *bibliogs.*

TOPICS in disequilibrium economics; edited by Steinar Strøm and Lars Werin. London, 1978. pp. 124. *bibliogs.*

ENGLUND (PETER) Profits and market adjustment: a study in the dynamics of production, productivity and rates of return. Stockholm, 1979. pp. 260. *bibliog.*

EQUITY
— United Kingdom.

PETTIT (PHILIP HENRY) Equity and the law of trusts. 4th ed. London, 1979. pp. 594.

ERASMUS (DESIDERIUS).

TRACY (JAMES D.) The politics of Erasmus: a pacifist intellectual and his political milieu. Toronto, [1978]. pp. 216. *bibliog.*

ERICSSON (L.M.) TELEFONAKTIEBOLAGET.

L.M. Ericsson 100 years; [by] Artur Attman [and others]. [Stockholm?, 1977]. 3 vols.

ESKIMOS.

MAUSS (MARCEL) Seasonal variations of the Eskimo: a study in social morphology...; translated, with a foreword, by James J. Fox. London, 1979. pp. 138. *bibliog.*

ESPIONAGE
— Bibliography.

BLACKSTOCK (PAUL W.) and SCHAF (FRANK L.) compilers. Intelligence, espionage, counterespionage, and covert operations: a guide to information sources. Detroit, [1978]. pp. 255.

ESPIONAGE, GERMAN
— Ireland (Republic).

STEPHAN (ENNO) Spies in Ireland;...translated from the German by Arthur Davidson. London, 1963. pp. 311. *bibliog.*

ESPIONAGE, RUSSIAN
— United Kingdom.

BOYLE (ANDREW) The climate of treason: five who spied for Russia. London, 1979. pp. 504.

ESSEX
— Economic policy.

ESSEX. County Planning Department. Development plan scheme [1975]. [Chelmsford], 1975. pp. 88.

ESSEX. County Planning Department. Development plan scheme [1977]. [Chelmsford], 1977. pp. 72. *Looseleaf.*

— Social policy.

ESSEX. County Planning Department. Development plan scheme [1975]. [Chelmsford], 1975. pp. 88.

ESSEX. County Planning Department. Development plan scheme [1977]. [Chelmsford], 1977. pp. 72. *Looseleaf.*

ESTATE PLANNING
— United States.

COOPER (GEORGE) A voluntary tax?: new perspectives on sophisticated estate tax avoidance. Washington, D.C., [1979]. pp. 115. *(Reprinted from Columbia Law Review, 1977) (Brookings Institution. Studies of Government Finance. 2nd Series)*

ROSENFELD (JEFFREY P.) The legacy of aging: inheritance and disinheritance in social perspective. Norwood, N.J., [1979]. pp. 151. *bibliog.*

ESTIMATION THEORY.

GRAY (HENRY L.) and SCHUCANY (W.R.) The generalized jackknife statistic. New York, [1972]. pp. 308. *bibliog.*

STUDIES in nonlinear estimation; [including papers given at a seminar at Princeton University in 1974]; edited by Stephen M. Goldfeld and Richard E. Quandt. Cambridge, Mass., [1976]. pp. 278. *bibliog.*

LINEAR least-squares estimation; edited by Thomas Kailath. Stroudsburg, [1977]. pp. 318.

ESTONIA
— Relations (general) with other countries.

K stoletiiu russko-turetskoi voiny 1877-1878 godov; pod redaktsiei V. Maamiagi. Tallin, 1977. pp. 120.

ESTONIAN LITERATURE
— History and criticism.

K stoletiiu russko-turetskoi voiny 1877-1878 godov; pod redaktsiei V. Maamiagi. Tallin, 1977. pp. 120.

ETHICS.

MACKINTOSH (Sir JAMES) Barrister-at-Law. Dissertation on the progress of ethical philosophy chiefly during the seventeenth and eighteenth centuries; with a preface by William Whewell. 3rd ed. Edinburgh, 1862. pp. 385.

ALTRUISM, morality, and economic theory; edited by Edmund S. Phelps. New York, [1975]. pp. 232. *bibliogs.*

FACIONE (PETER A.) and others. Values and society: an introduction to ethics and social philosophy. Englewood Cliffs, N.J., [1978]. pp. 294.

VALUES and morals: essays in honor of William Frankena, Charles Stevenson, and Richard Brandt; edited by Alvin I. Goldman and Jaegwon Kim. Dordrecht, [1978]. pp. 331. *bibliogs.*

BRANDT (RICHARD BOOKER) A theory of the good and the right. Oxford, 1979. pp. 362. *bibliog.*

LANGHOLM (ODD) Price and value in the Aristotelian tradition: a study in scholastic economic sources. Bergen, [1979]. pp. 175. *bibliog.*

NAGEL (THOMAS) Mortal questions. Cambridge, 1979. pp. 215.

— History — Russia.

GRIER (PHILIP TODD) Marxist ethical theory in the Soviet Union. Dordrecht, 1978. pp. 276. *bibliog. (Freiburg (Switzerland). Universität. Ost- Europa Institut. Sovietica. vol. 40)*

ETHIOPIA
— History.

IAG'IA (VATANIAR SAIDOVICH) Efiopiia v noveishee vremia. Moskva, 1978. pp. 327.

— Politics and government.

IAG'IA (VATANIAR SAIDOVICH) Efiopiia v noveishee vremia. Moskva, 1978. pp. 327.

OTTAWAY (MARINA) and OTTAWAY (DAVID) Ethiopia: empire in revolution. New York, 1978. pp. 250.

VALDÉS VIVÓ (RAÚL) Ethiopia's revolution. New York, 1978. pp. 124.

ETHNIC ATTITUDES.

LANGUAGE, ethnicity and intergroup relations; edited by Howard Giles. London, 1977. pp. 370. *bibliog.*

ETHNIC GROUPS.

LANGUAGE, ethnicity and intergroup relations; edited by Howard Giles. London, 1977. pp. 370. *bibliog.*

MINORITIES in history; edited by A.C. Hepburn. London, 1978. pp. 251. *Papers read before the Thirteenth Irish Conference of Historians at the New University of Ulster, 1977.*

ETHNICITY.

STONE (JOHN) D. Phil. Race, ethnicity, and social change: readings in the sociology of race and ethnic relations. North Scituate, Mass., [1977]. pp. 399. *bibliog.*

BURKEY (RICHARD M.) Ethnic and racial groups: the dynamics of dominance. Menlo Park, Calif., [1978]. pp. 510. *bibliog.*

ETHNIC leadership in America; edited by John Higham. Baltimore, [1978]. pp. 214. *(Johns Hopkins University. Department of History. Johns Hopkins Symposia in Comparative History. 9) Based on a symposium held at the Johns Hopkins University in 1976.*

GROSS (FELIKS) Ethnics in a borderland: an inquiry into the nature of ethnicity and reduction of ethnic tensions in a one-time genocide area. Westport, Conn., 1978. pp. 193. *bibliog.*

MAMAK (ALEXANDER) Colour, culture and conflict: a study of pluralism in Fiji. Rushcutters Bay, 1978. pp. 203. *bibliog.*

The MIXING of peoples: problems of identity and ethnicity; edited by Robert I. Rotberg. [Stamford, Conn., 1978]. pp. 197. *bibliogs.*

ETHNICITY at work; edited by Sandra Wallman. London, 1979. pp. 252. *bibliog.*

RUSSELL (MARGO) and RUSSELL (MARTIN) Afrikaners of the Kalahari: white minority in a black state. Cambridge, 1979. pp. 167. *bibliog.*

ETHNOBOTANY.

ROYS (RALPH LOVELAND) The ethno-botany of the Maya; with a new introduction and supplemental bibliography by Sheila Cosminsky. Philadelphia, 1976. pp. 380. *bibliog. (Institute for the Study of Human Issues. ISHI Reprints on Latin America and the Caribbean) Reprint of the edition of 1931.*

ETHNOCENTRISM.

BOOTH (KEN) Strategy and ethnocentrism. London, [1979]. pp. 191. *bibliogs.*

ETHNOLOGICAL JURISPRUDENCE.

CROSS-EXAMINATIONS: essays in memory of Max Gluckman; edited by P.H. Gulliver. Leiden, 1978. pp. 169.

STARR (JUNE) Dispute and settlement in rural Turkey: an ethnography of law. Leiden, 1978. pp. 304. *bibliog.*

ETHNOLOGY.

MUSEU DE ETNOLOGIA DO ULTRAMAR. Peoples and cultures: exhibition, National Gallery of Modern Art, April-June 1972. Lisbon, Junta de Investigações do Ultramar, [1972]. pp. 616. *bibliog.*

KOZLOV (VIKTOR IVANOVICH) Etnicheskaia demografiia. Moskva, 1977. pp. 240.

ADAPTATION and symbolism: essays on social organization; presented to Sir Raymond Firth...; edited by Karen Ann Watson-Gegeo and S. Lee Seaton. Honolulu, [1978]. pp. 228. *bibliogs.*

ETHNOLOGY.(Cont.)

— Methodology.

JOHNSON (ALLEN WILLARD) Research methods in social anthropology. London, 1978. pp. 231. *bibliog.*

— Africa.

SPIRIT mediumship and society in Africa...; edited by John Beattie and John Middleton. New York, 1969. pp. 310. *bibliogs.*

COLONIALISM and change: essays presented to Lucy Mair; edited by Maxwell Owusu. The Hague, [1975]. pp. 264. *bibliogs.*

SLAVERY in Africa: historical and anthropological perspectives; edited by Suzanne Miers and Igor Kopytoff. Madison, Wis., [1977]. pp. 473. *bibliogs.*

— Africa, East.

KESBY (JOHN D.) The cultural regions of East Africa. London, [1977]. pp. 320. *bibliog.*

AGE, generation and time: some features of East African age organisations; edited by P.T.W. Baxter and Uri Almagor. London, [1978]. pp. 276. *bibliogs.*

— Africa, Subsaharan.

NURSE (G.T.) and JENKINS (T.) Health and the hunter-gatherer: biomedical studies on the hunting and gathering populations of southern Africa. Basel, 1977. pp. 126. *bibliog.*

ETHNICITY in modern Africa; edited by Brian M. du Toit. Boulder, Colo., 1978. pp. 319. *bibliog.*

SOCIAL system and tradition in southern Africa: essays in honour of Eileen Krige; edited by John Argyle [and] Eleanor Preston-Whyte. Cape Town, 1978. pp. 251. *bibliogs.*

— Asia, Southeast.

CULTURAL-ecological perspectives on Southeast Asia; a symposium [held in 1976 at Ohio University]; edited by William Wood. Athens, Ohio, 1977. pp. 192. *bibliog.* (Ohio University. Center for International Studies. Papers in International Studies. Southeast Asia Series. No. 41)

— Bengal.

INDEN (RONALD B.) and NICHOLAS (RALPH W.) Kinship in Bengali culture. Chicago, [1977]. pp. 139. *bibliog.*

— Borneo.

STUDIES in Borneo societies: social process and anthropological explanation; G.N. Appell, editor; contributors: G.N. Appell [and others]. [DeKalb, Ill.], 1976. pp. 156. *bibliog.* (Northern Illinois University. Center for Southeast Asian Studies. Special Reports. No.12)

ESSAYS on Borneo societies; edited by Victor T. King. Oxford, 1978. pp. 256. *bibliog.* (Hull. University. Centre for South-East Asian Studies. Monographs on South-East Asia. No. 7)

— Canada.

KRAUTER (JOSEPH F.) and DAVIS (MORRIS) Minority Canadians: ethnic groups. Toronto, [1978]. pp. 120.

—Guatemala — San Andrés.

WARREN (KAY B.) The symbolism of subordination: Indian identity in a Guatemalan town. Austin, [1978]. pp. 209. *bibliog.*

— India.

ARCHER (WILLIAM GEORGE) The hill of flutes: life, love and poetry in tribal India: a portrait of the Santals. London, 1974. pp. 375. *bibliog.*

SCHERMERHORN (RICHARD ALONZO) Ethnic plurality in India. Tucson, [1978]. pp. 369. *bibliogs.*

WEINER (MYRON) Sons of the soil: migration and ethnic conflict in India. Princeton, N.J., [1978]. pp. 383. *bibliogs.*

— — Andhra Pradesh.

FUERER-HAIMENDORF (CHRISTOPH VON) Freiherr and FUERER- HAIMENDORF (ELIZABETH VON) The Gonds of Andhra Pradesh: tradition and change in an Indian tribe. London, 1979. pp. 569. *bibliog.*

— — Assam.

BAHADUR (K.P.) Caste, tribes and culture of India: Assam. Delhi, 1977. pp. 137.

— Iraq.

THESIGER (WILFRED) The Marsh Arabs. Harmondsworth, 1967 repr. 1978. pp. 233. *First published by Longmans, Green, 1964.*

— Ireland (Republic).

FOX (ROBIN) The Tory Islanders: a people of the Celtic fringe. Cambridge, 1978. pp. 210. *bibliog.*

— Italy.

GROSS (FELIKS) Ethnics in a borderland: an inquiry into the nature of ethnicity and reduction of ethnic tensions in a one-time genocide area. Westport, Conn., 1978. pp. 193. *bibliog.*

— Kenya.

PARKIN (DAVID J.) The cultural definition of political response: lineal destiny among the Luo. London, 1978. pp. 347. *bibliog.*

— Mohammedan countries.

MUSLIM peoples: a world ethnographic survey; edited by Richard V. Weekes. Westport, Conn., 1978. pp. 546. *bibliogs.*

— Morocco.

RABINOW (PAUL) Reflections on fieldwork in Morocco. Berkeley, [1977]. pp. 164. *bibliog.*

See also WARYAGHAR (BERBER PEOPLE).

— Nepal.

GABORIEAU (MARC) Le Népal et ses populations. [Paris, 1978]. pp. 312. *bibliog.*

— New Guinea.

RUBEL (PAULA G.) and ROSMAN (ABRAHAM) Your own pigs you may not eat: a comparative study of New Guinea societies. Chicago, 1978. pp. 368. *bibliog.*

— Nigeria.

ARONSON (DAN R.) The city is our farm: seven migrant Ijebu Yoruba families. Cambridge, Mass., [1978]. pp. 208. *bibliog.*

SMITH (MICHAEL GARFIELD) The affairs of Daura. Berkeley, [1978]. pp. 532.

PEACE (ADRIAN J.) Choice, class and conflict: a study of Southern Nigerian factory workers. Brighton, 1979. pp. 204. *bibliog.*

— Papua New Guinea.

SCHIEFFELIN (EDWARD L.) The sorrow of the lonely and the burning of the dancers. New York, [1976]. pp. 243. *bibliog.*

BROWN (PAULA) Highland peoples of New Guinea. Cambridge, 1978. pp. 258. *bibliog.*

— Peru.

LEWELLEN (TED) Peasants in transition: the changing economy of the Peruvian Aymara: a general systems approach. Boulder, Colo., [1978]. pp. 195. *bibliog.*

— Rhodesia.

RHODESIA. Ministry of Information, Immigration and Tourism. 1969. The man - and his ways: an introduction to the customs and beliefs of Rhodesia's African people. [Salisbury, 1969 repr. 1970]. pp. 43.

— Russia.

SOVREMENNYE etnicheskie protsessy v SSSR. 2nd ed. Moskva, 1977. pp. 562. *With English, French, German and Spanish summaries.*

— Sierra Leone.

JACKSON (MICHAEL) Anthropologist. The Kuranko: dimensions of social reality in a West African society. New York, 1977. pp. 256. *bibliog.*

— Singapore.

HASSAN (RIAZ) Interethnic marriage in Singapore: a study in interethnic relations. Singapore, 1974. pp. 85. *bibliog.* (Institute of Southeast Asian Studies. Occasional Papers. No. 21)

— Thailand.

SHARP (LAURISTON W.) and HANKS (LUCIEN MASON) Bang Chan: social history of a rural community in Thailand. Ithaca, 1978. pp. 314. *bibliog.*

— Trinidad and Tobago.

NEWSON (LINDA A.) Aboriginal and Spanish colonial Trinidad: a study in culture contact. London, 1976. pp. 268. *bibliog.*

— Trobriand Islands.

MALINOWSKI (BRONISLAW) The ethnography of Malinowski: the Trobriand Islands, 1915- 18; edited by Michael W. Young. London, 1979. pp. 254. *bibliog.*

— Uganda.

MWAMULA-LUBANDI (E.D.) Transitional socio-economic clan relations among Basoga. [Uppsala], 1978. pp. 182. *bibliog.*

ROBERTSON (ALEXANDER FOSTER) Community of strangers: a journal of discovery in Uganda. London, 1978. pp. 252. *bibliog.*

— Upper Volta.

RIESMAN (PAUL) Freedom in Fulani social life: an introspective ethnography; translated by Martha Fuller. Chicago, [1977]. pp. 297. *bibliog.*

— Venezuela.

DUMONT (JEAN PAUL) The headman and I: ambiguity and ambivalence in the fieldworking experience. Austin, [1978]. pp. 211. *bibliog.*

EUGENICS.

EUGENICS SOCIETY. Annual Symposium, 14th, 1978. Perimeters of social repair: proceedings...; edited by W.H.G. Armytage and John Peel. London, 1978. pp. 157. *bibliogs.*

EUROBOND MARKET.

DUFEY (GUNTER) and GIDDY (IAN H.) The international money market. Englewood Cliffs, [1978]. pp. 283.

EURODOLLAR MARKET.

DUFEY (GUNTER) and GIDDY (IAN H.) The international money market. Englewood Cliffs, [1978]. pp. 283.

EUROPE

— Civilization — Arab influences.

DANIEL (NORMAN) The Arabs and mediaeval Europe. 2nd ed. London, 1979. pp. 385.

EUROPE

— **Colonies.**

AFRICAN proconsuls: European governors in Africa; [edited by] L.H. Gann and Peter Duignan. New York, [1978]. pp. 548. *bibliog.*

— **Commerce — United Kingdom.**

EXPORTING to western Europe, 1977: case studies; a B[ritish] O[verseas] T[rade] B[oard] national conference, November 29, 1977,...Wembley. [London], British Overseas Trade Board, [1977]. pp. 52.

— **Defences.**

STOCKHOLM INTERNATIONAL PEACE RESEARCH INSTITUTE. Tactical nuclear weapons: European perspectives; [edited by Frank Barnaby]. London, 1978. pp. 371.

— **Description and travel.**

MELLOR (ROY EGERTON HENDERSON) and SMITH (E. ALISTAIR) Europe: a geographical survey of the continent. London, 1979. pp. 180. *bibliog.*

— **Economic conditions.**

LAQUEUR (WALTER ZE'EV) A continent astray: Europe, 1970-1978. New York, 1979. pp. 293.

UNDERDEVELOPED Europe: studies in core-periphery relations; edited by Dudley Seers [and others]. Hassocks, 1979. pp. 325. *bibliogs.*

— **Economic history.**

GESELLSCHAFT FÜR SOZIAL- UND WIRTSCHAFTSGESCHICHTE. 6. Arbeitstagung, 1975. Wirtschaftliches Wachstum, Energie und Verkehr vom Mittelalter bis ins 19. Jahrhundert: Bericht...; herausgegeben von Hermann Kellenbenz. Stuttgart, 1978. pp. 248.

EUROPEAN demography and economic growth; edited by W.R. Lee. London, [1979]. pp. 413. *bibliogs.*

LIS (CATHARINA) and SOLY (HUGO) Poverty and capitalism in pre-industrial Europe. Hassocks, 1979. pp. 267. *bibliog.*

— **Economic integration.**

VLERICK (ANDRE J.) European monetary union. [Brussels], Ministry of Foreign Affairs, External Trade and Cooperation in Development, 1972. pp. 14. *(Memo from Belgium. No. 153)*

EUROPEAN economic integration; [edited by] Bela Balassa [and others]. Amsterdam, 1975. pp. 416. *bibliog.*

A COMMON man's guide to the Common Market: the European Community; edited by Hugh Arbuthnott and Geoffrey Edwards. London, 1979. pp. 213. *bibliogs. Published for the Federal Trust for Education and Research.*

UNDERDEVELOPED Europe: studies in core-periphery relations; edited by Dudley Seers [and others]. Hassocks, 1979. pp. 325. *bibliogs.*

— **Emigration and immigration.**

The DEMOGRAPHIC and social pattern of emigration from the Southern European countries; edited by Massimo Livi Bacci. Firenze, 1972. pp. 393. *General report and studies...in connection with the iv. theme of the Second European Population Conference, Strasbourg, 1971.*

— **Foreign economic relations — United States.**

KAISER (KARL) Europe and the United States: the future of the relationship. Washington, 1973. pp. 146.

— **Foreign population — Civil rights.**

WIHTOL DE WENDEN (CATHERINE) Les immigrés dans la cité: la représentation des immigrés dans la vie publique en Europe; ...avec la participation, pour la partie documentaire et bibliographique d'Anne Françoise Beylier. Paris, 1978. pp. 136. *bibliog. (France. Direction de la Population et des Migrations. Migrations et Sociétés. 3)*

— **Foreign relations.**

THORNE (CHRISTOPHER) The approach of war, 1938-1939. London, 1967 repr. 1977. pp. 232. *bibliog.*

VO imia mira: mezhdunarodno-pravovye problemy evropeiskoi bezopasnosti. Moskva, 1977. pp. 191.

FOREIGN policy making in western Europe; edited by William Wallace [and] W.E. Paterson. Farnborough, Hants., [1978]. pp. 161.

— — **Asia.**

The AGE of partnership: Europeans in Asia before Dominion; edited by Blair B. Kling and M.N. Pearson. Honolulu, [1979]. pp. 247. *bibliogs.*

— — **Russia.**

SCHAPIRO (LEONARD BERTRAM) The Soviet Union and Eurocommunism. London, 1978. pp. 21. *(Institute for the Study of Conflict. Conflict Studies. No.99)*

DEPORTE (ANTON WILLIAM) Europe between the superpowers: the enduring balance. New Haven, 1979. pp. 256. *bibliog.*

— — **Turkey.**

VAUGHAN (DOROTHY MARGARET) Europe and the Turk: a pattern of alliances, 1350-1700. Liverpool, 1954; New York, 1976. pp. 305. *bibliog. Facsimile reprint.*

— — **United States.**

KAISER (KARL) Europe and the United States: the future of the relationship. Washington, 1973. pp. 146.

BAILEY (THOMAS ANDREW) The Marshall Plan summer: an eyewitness report on Europe and the Russians in 1947. Stanford, Calif., [1977]. pp. 246.

DEPORTE (ANTON WILLIAM) Europe between the superpowers: the enduring balance. New Haven, 1979. pp. 256. *bibliog.*

LEFFLER (MELVYN P.) The elusive quest: America's pursuit of European stability and French security, 1919-1933. Chapel Hill, [1979]. pp. 409. *bibliog.*

— **Historical geography.**

MELLOR (ROY EGERTON HENDERSON) and SMITH (E. ALISTAIR) Europe: a geographical survey of the continent. London, 1979. pp. 180. *bibliog.*

— **Historiography.**

ANDERSON (MATTHEW SMITH) Historians and eighteenth-century Europe, 1715-1789. Oxford, 1979. pp. 251.

— **History.**

BRABAZON (REGINALD) 12th Earl of Meath. Memories of the twentieth century. London, 1924. pp. 310.

— — **392-814.**

MUSSET (LUCIEN) The Germanic invasions: the making of Europe, AD 400-600;.. .translated by Edward and Columba James. London, 1975. pp. 287. *bibliog.*

— — **476-1492.**

BROOKE (CHRISTOPHER NUGENT LAWRENCE) Europe in the central middle ages, 962-1154. London, 1977. pp. 403.

LOCKYER (ROGER) Habsburg and Bourbon Europe, 1470-1720. London, 1977. pp. 594.

— — **1492-1648.**

CUTOLO (VICENTE OSVALDO) Manual de historia economica y social. Buenos Aires, 1976. pp. 530.

LOCKYER (ROGER) Habsburg and Bourbon Europe, 1470-1720. London, 1977. pp. 594.

— — **1517-1648.**

SUTHERLAND (NICOLA MARY) The massacre of St. Bartholomew and the European conflict, 1559-1572. London, 1973. pp. 373. *bibliog.*

O'CONNELL (MARVIN R.) The Counter Reformation, 1560-1610. New York, 1974. pp. 390. *bibliog.*

EVANS (ROBERT JOHN WESTON) The making of the Habsburg monarchy, 1550-1700: an interpretation. Oxford, 1979. pp. 531.

— — **1600-1699.**

PURITANS and revolutionaries: essays in seventeenth-century history presented to Christopher Hill; edited by Donald Pennington and Keith Thomas. Oxford, 1978. pp. 149. *bibliog.*

EVANS (ROBERT JOHN WESTON) The making of the Habsburg monarchy, 1550-1700: an interpretation. Oxford, 1979. pp. 531.

The SATELLITE state in the 17th and 18th centuries: [papers from a conference held at the University of Bergen, 1-4 September, 1977; edited by Ståle Dyrvik [and others]. Bergen, [1979]. pp. 192.

— — **1648-1789.**

WILLIAMS (ERNEST NEVILLE) The Ancien Régime in Europe: government and society in the major states, 1648-1789. London, 1970. pp. 599. *bibliog.*

— — **1648-1715.**

LOCKYER (ROGER) Habsburg and Bourbon Europe, 1470-1720. London, 1977. pp. 594.

DOYLE (WILLIAM) D.Phil. The old European order, 1660-1800. Oxford, 1978. pp. 420. *bibliog.*

— — **1700-1799.**

WILLIAMS (GLYNDWR) The expansion of Europe in the eighteenth century: overseas rivalry, discovery and exploitation. London, 1968. pp. 309. *bibliog.*

DOYLE (WILLIAM) D.Phil. The old European order, 1660-1800. Oxford, 1978. pp. 420. *bibliog.*

ANDERSON (MATTHEW SMITH) Historians and eighteenth-century Europe, 1715-1789. Oxford, 1979. pp. 251.

The SATELLITE state in the 17th and 18th centuries: [papers from a conference held at the University of Bergen, 1-4 September, 1977; edited by Ståle Dyrvik [and others]. Bergen, [1979]. pp. 192.

— — **1789-1900.**

McMANNERS (JOHN) Lectures on European history, 1789-1914: men, machines and freedom. Oxford, 1966 repr. 1977. pp. 420.

— — **1789-1815.**

CONNELLY (OWEN) Napoleon's satellite kingdoms. New York, [1965] repr. 1969. pp. 389. *bibliog.*

— — **1900- .**

McMANNERS (JOHN) Lectures on European history, 1789-1914: men, machines and freedom. Oxford, 1966 repr. 1977. pp. 420.

TAYLOR (ALAN JOHN PERCIVALE) From Sarajevo to Potsdam. London, [1966 repr. 1974]. pp. 216. *bibliog.*

INTERUNIVERSITY CENTRE FOR EUROPEAN STUDIES. International Colloquium, 2nd, 1976. Situations révolutionnaires en Europe, 1917-1922: Allemagne, Italie, Autriche-Hongrie; Revolutionary situations in Europe, 1917-1922: Germany, Italy, Austria-Hungary...edited by Charles L. Bertrand. Montreal, 1977. pp. 251. *bibliog.*

VAUGHAN (RICHARD) Professor of Medieval History, University of Hull. Twentieth-century Europe: paths to unity. London, [1979]. pp. 261.

EUROPE(Cont.)

The WAR plans of the great powers, 1880-1914; edited by Paul M. Kennedy. London, 1979. pp. 282. *bibliog.*

— — 1918-1945.

BOESCHENSTEIN (HERMANN) Vor unsern Augen: Aufzeichnungen über das Jahrzehnt 1935- 1945. Bern, 1978. pp. 334.

— — 1945- .

BAILEY (THOMAS ANDREW) The Marshall Plan summer: an eyewitness report on Europe and the Russians in 1947. Stanford, Calif., [1977]. pp. 246.

— Intellectual life.

COMMAGER (HENRY STEELE) The empire of reason: how Europe imagined and America realized the enlightenment. Garden City, 1978. pp. 381.

MANDROU (ROBERT) From humanism to science, 1480-1700...; translated by Brian Pearce. Hassocks, 1978. pp. 329. *bibliog.*

MURRAY (ALEXANDER) M.A., B.Phil. Reason and society in the Middle Ages. Oxford, 1978. pp. 511.

KOENIGSBERGER (DOROTHY) Renaissance man and creative thinking: a history of concepts of harmony, 1400-1700. Hassocks, [1979]. pp. 282. *bibliogs.*

— Languages.

STEPHENS (MEIC) Linguistic minorities in western Europe. [Llandysul], 1976 repr. 1978. pp. 796. *bibliog.*

— Military policy.

The WAR plans of the great powers, 1880-1914; edited by Paul M. Kennedy. London, 1979. pp. 282. *bibliog.*

— Politics and government.

KOLINSKY (A. MARTIN) Continuity and change in European society: Germany, France and Italy since 1870. London, 1974. pp. 234. *bibliog.*

POLITICS in Europe: structures and processes in some postindustrial democracies; edited by Martin O. Heisler. New York, [1974]. pp. 415.

The BREAKDOWN of democratic regimes; edited by Juan J. Linz and Alfred Stepan. Baltimore, [1978]. pp. 168.

CRISES of political development in Europe and the United States; edited by Raymond Grew; contributors: David D. Bien [and others]. Princeton, [1978]. pp. 434. *bibliogs.*

DIRTY work: the CIA in Western Europe; edited by Philip Agee and Louis Wolf. Secaucus, N.J., [1978]. pp. 734.

The ORIGINS of the cold war and contemporary Europe; edited with an introduction by Charles S. Maier. New York, 1978. pp. 254. *bibliog.*

TANNAHILL (R. NEAL) The communist parties of Western Europe: a comparative study. Westport, 1978. pp. 299. *bibliog.*

A COMMON man's guide to the Common Market: the European Community; edited by Hugh Arbuthnott and Geoffrey Edwards. London, 1979. pp. 213. *bibliogs.* Published for the Federal Trust for Education and Research.

COMMUNISM and political systems in Western Europe; edited by David E. Albright. Boulder, Colo., 1979. pp. 379.

DAHRENDORF (RALF) Intervista sul liberalismo e l'Europa; [translated from the English]; a cura di Vincenzo Ferrari. Roma, 1979. pp. 173.

DEPORTE (ANTON WILLIAM) Europe between the superpowers: the enduring balance. New Haven, 1979. pp. 256. *bibliog.*

LAQUEUR (WALTER ZE'EV) A continent astray: Europe, 1970-1978. New York, 1979. pp. 293.

STATE and society in contemporary Europe; edited by Jack Hayward and R.N. Berki. Oxford, 1979. pp. 269. *bibliogs.*

— Population.

The DEMOGRAPHIC and social pattern of emigration from the Southern European countries; edited by Massimo Livi Bacci. Firenze, 1972. pp. 393. *General report and studies...in connection with the iv. theme of the Second European Population Conference, Strasbourg, 1971.*

EUROPEAN demography and economic growth; edited by W.R. Lee. London, [1979]. pp. 413. *bibliogs.*

— — Congresses.

SEMINAR ON THE IMPLICATIONS OF A STATIONARY OR DECLINING POPULATION IN EUROPE, STRASBOURG, 1976. Population decline in Europe: implications of a declining or stationary population;...(proceedings of a Seminar held by the Council of Europe...6-10 September 1976). London, 1978. pp. 254. *bibliogs.*

— Race relations.

MOSSE (GEORGE L.) Toward the final solution: a history of European racism. London, 1978. pp. 277.

— Relations (general) with the Pacific.

RALSTON (CAROLINE) Grass huts and warehouses: Pacific beach communities of the nineteenth century. Canberra, 1977. pp. 268. *bibliog.*

— Rural conditions.

BLUM (JEROME) The end of the old order in rural Europe. Princeton, 1978. pp. 505. *bibliog.*

EUROPE, EASTERN.

HANDBOOK OF CENTRAL AND EAST EUROPE. a., 1932/33. Zurich.

— Biography.

WHO'S WHO IN CENTRAL AND EAST-EUROPE. bien., 1935/36(2nd). Zurich.

— Commerce — Australia.

SPROTT (D.C.) and HEARN (S.E.) Agricultural developments and the prospect for trade with the Comecon countries. Canberra, 1974. pp. 34. *(Australia. Bureau of Agricultural Economics. Occasional Papers. No.24)*

— Description and travel.

POUNDS (NORMAN JOHN GREVILLE) Eastern Europe. London, 1969. pp. 912. *bibliogs.*

— Economic conditions.

POUNDS (NORMAN JOHN GREVILLE) Eastern Europe. London, 1969. pp. 912. *bibliogs.*

EASTERN Europe's uncertain future: a selection of Radio Free Europe Research Reports; edited by Robert R. King [and] James F. Brown. New York, 1977. pp. 359. *bibliog.*

The SOVIET Union and East Europe into the 1980's: multidisciplinary perspectives: [papers from a conference held at Laval University, May 1976]; edited by Simon McInnes, William McGrath and Peter J. Potichnyj. [Ontario, 1978]. pp. 340. *bibliog.*

Die WIRTSCHAFTLICHE Entwicklung in Osteuropa zur Jahreswende 1978/79; herausgegeben von Klaus Bolz; mit Beiträgen [by] Albrecht Iwersen [and others]. Hamburg, 1979. pp. 292. *(Hamburg. Hamburgisches Welt-Wirtschafts-Archiv. Veröffentlichungen)*

— Foreign economic relations.

EASTERN Europe's uncertain future: a selection of Radio Free Europe Research Reports; edited by Robert R. King [and] James F. Brown. New York, 1977. pp. 359. *bibliog.*

See also EUROPEAN ECONOMIC COMMUNITY — Europe, Eastern.

— Foreign relations.

EASTERN Europe's uncertain future: a selection of Radio Free Europe Research Reports; edited by Robert R. King [and] James F. Brown. New York, 1977. pp. 359. *bibliog.*

FOREIGN policy making in Communist countries: a comparative approach; edited by Hannes Adomeit and Robert Boardman. Farnborough, [1979]. pp. 164. *bibliogs.*

LINDEN (RONALD HALY) Bear and foxes: the international relations of the East European states, 1965-1969. Boulder, 1979. pp. 328. *bibliog. (East European Quarterly. East European Monographs. 50)*

ORLIK (IGOR' IVANOVICH) Politika zapadnykh derzhav v otnoshenii vostochnoevropeiskikh sotsialisticheskikh gosudarstv, 1965-1975. Moskva, 1979. pp. 367. *bibliog.*

— — Germany.

"DRANG nakh Osten" i narody Tsentral'noi, Vostochnoi i Iugo-Vostochnoi Evropy 1871-1918 gg. Moskva, 1977. pp. 317.

GRIFFITH (WILLIAM E.) The Ostpolitik of the Federal Republic of Germany. Cambridge, Mass., [1978]. pp. 325.

— — Russia.

HOENSCH (JOERG K.) Sowjetische Osteuropa-Politik, 1945-1975. Kronberg/Ts., 1977. pp. 512. *bibliog.*

— History.

HALECKI (OSKAR VON) Ritter von Chalecki-Halecki. Borderlands of Western civilization: a history of East Central Europe. New York, [1952]. pp. 503. *bibliog.*

— Politics and government.

ZILLIACUS (KONNI) the Younger. A new birth of freedom?: world communism after Stalin. London, 1957. pp. 286.

VII kongress Kominterna i bor'ba za sozdanie narodnogo fronta v stranakh Tsentral'noi i Iugo-Vostochnoi Evropy. Moskva, 1977. pp. 375.

FRANCE. Direction de la Documentation. La Documentation Française. Notes et Etudes Documentaires. Nos. 4467-4468. L'URSS et l'Europe de l'Est en 1977; [by] Thomas Schreiber and others]. [Paris], 1978 in progress. *bibliog.*

BAHRO (RUDOLF) The alternative in Eastern Europe; translated by David Fernbach. [London], 1978. pp. 463.

The SOVIET Union and East Europe into the 1980's: multidisciplinary perspectives: [papers from a conference held at Laval University, May 1976]; edited by Simon McInnes, William McGrath and Peter J. Potichnyj. [Ontario, 1978]. pp. 340. *bibliog.*

OPPOSITION in Eastern Europe; edited by Rudolf L. Tökés. London, 1979. pp. 306.

POWER and opposition in post-revolutionary societies; translated from the French by Patrick Camiller and the Italian by Jon Rothschild. London, 1979. pp. 281. *bibliogs. Papers of a conference organised by Il Manifesto and held in Venice, 1977.*

— Relations (general) with the United States.

EAST Central European perceptions of early America; edited by Béla K. Király and George Barany. Lisse, 1977. pp. 139. *(City University of New York. Brooklyn College. Department of History. Studies on Society in Change. No. 5)*

— Social conditions.

SOCIAL deviance in Eastern Europe; edited by Ivan Volgyes. Boulder, Colo., [1978]. pp. 198. *bibliogs.*

EUROPEAN COMMUNITIES.

EUROPEAN COMMUNITIES. Commission. 1977. The European Community, international organisations and multilateral agreements. [Brussels, 1977]. pp. 298.

EUROPEAN ECONOMIC COMMUNITY COUNTRIES.

EIRE. Oireachtas. Joint Committee on the Secondary Legislation of the European Communities. 1978- . Reports...together with proceedings; [Mark Clinton, chairman]. [Dublin, 1978 in progress].

AMERICAN ACADEMY OF POLITICAL AND SOCIAL SCIENCE. Annals. vol. 440. The European Community after twenty years; special editor of this volume Pierre-Henri Laurent. Philadelphia, 1978. pp. 229.

BELGIUM. Ministère des Affaires Etrangères, du Commerce Extérieur et de la Coopération au Développement. 1978. Bilan de la présidence belge du Conseil des Communautés Européennes du 1er juillet au 31 décembre 1977. Bruxelles, 1978. pp. 51. *(Textes et Documents. Collection "Idées et Etudes". No. 313)*

EUROPEAN COMMUNITIES. Commission. 1978. Commission report on the establishment of a European Foundation: sent to the European Council on 17 November 1977. [Brussels, 1978]. pp. 23. *(Bulletin of the European Communities. Supplements. [1977/5])*

EUROPEAN COMMUNITIES. Commission. 1978. Community action in the cultural sector:...communication to the Council, sent on 22 November 1977. [Brussels, 1978]. pp. 26. *(Bulletin of the European Communities. Supplements. [1977/6])*

EUROPEAN COMMUNITIES. Commission. 1978. Economic and sectoral aspects: Commission analyses supplementing its views on enlargement; communication...sent to the Council on 20 April 1978. [Brussels, 1978]. pp. 55. *(Bulletin of the European Communities. Supplements. [1978/3])*

EUROPEAN COMMUNITIES. Commission. 1978. European union: report[s] for 1977 by the Ministers of Foreign Affairs [and] by the Commission. [Brussels, 1978]. pp. 16. *(Bulletin of the European Communities. Supplements. [1977/8])*

EUROPEAN COMMUNITIES. Commission. 1978. General considerations on the problems of enlargement: communication sent...to the Council on 20 April 1978. [Brussels, 1978]. pp. 17. *(Bulletin of the European Communities. Supplements. [1978/1])*

EUROPEAN COMMUNITIES. Commission. 1978. The transitional period and the institutional implications of enlargement:...communication to the Council further to the communication sent on 20 April 1978. [Brussels, 1978]. pp. 17. *(Bulletin of the European Communities. Supplements. [1978/2])*

SEMAINE DE BRUGES, 1978. A Community of twelve?: the impact of further enlargement on the European Communities; [by] M. Abad [and others]; edited by W. Wallace and I. Herreman; Une Communauté à douze?, etc. Bruges, 1978. pp. 442. *(College of Europe. Cahiers de Bruges. Nouvelle Série. 37) In English or French.*

EUROFORUM: Europe day by day. (formerly Industry and society); pd. by the Commission of the European Communities, Directorate General of Information, Division for Industrial Information and Consumers. w. Brussels. *Current issues only kept.*

EUROPEAN COMMUNITIES. Press and Information [Service], Brussels Office. Information. [in English or French]. irreg. Bruxelles. *Current issues only kept.*

EUROPEAN FILE; [pd. by] Directorate General for Information, Commission of the European Communities. fortn., current issues only. Brussels.

— Appropriations and expenditures.

EUROPEAN COMMUNITIES. Commission. 1978. Preliminary draft general budget of the European Communities for the financial year 1979: general introduction; sent to the Council...on 13 June 1978, and subsequently amended by the letter of amendment of 18 September 1978. [Brussels, 1978]. pp. 98. *(Bulletin of the European Communities. Supplements. [1978/6])*

— Bibliography.

BULLETIN BIBLIOGRAPHIQUE DE JURISPRUDENCE COMMUNAUTAIRE; [pd. by] Court of Justice, European Communities. a., 1977(no. 1)- Luxembourg. *Supersedes EUROPEAN COMMUNITIES. Court of Justice. 1965-. Bibliographie de jurisprudence européenne.*

COLLESTER (J. BRYAN) compiler. The European Communities: a guide to information sources. Detroit, [1979]. pp. 265.

SOURCES of information on the European Communities; edited by Doris M. Palmer. London, 1979. pp. 230. *bibliogs.*

— Ireland (Republic).

EIRE. Oireachtas. Joint Committee on the Secondary Legislation of the European Communities. 1978- . Reports...together with proceedings; [Mark Clinton, chairman]. [Dublin, 1978 in progress].

— Portugal.

EUROPEAN COMMUNITIES. Commission. 1978. Opinion on Portuguese application for membership: transmitted to the Council...on 19 May 1978. [Brussels, 1978]. pp. 50. *(Bulletin of the European Communities. Supplements. [1978/5])*

EUROPEAN CONVENTION ON HUMAN RIGHTS.

NEDJATI (ZAIM M.) Human rights under the European Convention. Amsterdam, 1978. pp. 298. *(London. University. King's College. Centre of European Law. European Studies in Law. vol. 8)*

EUROPEAN ECONOMIC COMMUNITY.

CAMPS (MIRIAM) European unification in the sixties: from the veto to the crisis. London, 1967. pp. 273. *bibliog.*

CAPORASO (JAMES A.) The structure and function of European integration. Pacific Palisades, Calif., [1974]. pp. 214. *bibliog.*

EUROPE right ahead; [by] Peter Blaker [and others]; edited by Lord O'Hagan...[and] Simon May. London, 1978. pp. 35. *(Conservative Political Centre. [Publications]. No. 631)*

SWANN (DENNIS) The economics of the Common Market. 4th ed. Harmondsworth, 1978. pp. 332. *bibliog.*

A COMMON man's guide to the Common Market: the European Community; edited by Hugh Arbuthnott and Geoffrey Edwards. London, 1979. pp. 213. *bibliogs. Published for the Federal Trust for Education and Research.*

ECONOMIC policies of the Common Market; edited by Peter Coffey. London, 1979. pp. 212.

HALLSTEIN (WALTER) Europäische Reden; herausgegeben von Thomas Oppermann. Stuttgart, [1979]. pp. 707. *In various languages.*

TUGENDHAT (CHRISTOPHER) Conservatives in Europe: a personal view. London, 1979. pp. 23. *(Conservative Political Centre. [Publications]. No. 636)*

— Foreign economic relations.

EUROPE and the north-south dialogue; edited by W. Wessels. Paris, [1978]. pp. 78. *(Atlantic Institute. Atlantic Papers. No. 35)*

— Maps.

EUROPEAN COMMUNITIES. Service de Presse et Information. 1968. The European Community in maps; compiled by I.B.F. Kormoss. [Brussels, 1968]. pp. 8. *12 loose-leaf maps in cover with explanatory text.*

— Politics and government.

COOMBES (DAVID) Politics and bureaucracy in the European Community: a portrait of the commission of the E.E.C. Beverly Hills, [1970]. pp. 343.

— Europe, Eastern.

The EEC and Eastern Europe; (editors: Avi Shlaim and G. N. Yannopoulos). Cambridge, 1978. pp. 251.

— Germany.

BELLERS (JUERGEN) Reformpolitik und EWG-Strategie der SPD: die innen- und aussenpolitischen Faktoren der europapolitischen Integrationswilligkeit einer Oppositionspartei, 1957-63. München, [1979]. pp. 570. *bibliog.*

— Greece.

GREECE and the European Community: edited by Loukas Tsoukalis. Farnborough, Hants., [1979]. pp. 172. *Based on a conference held in Oxford in 1977 under the auspices of the University Association for Contemporary European Studies and St. Catherine's College, Oxford.*

— New Zealand.

NEW ZEALAND. Planning Council. 1978. New Zealand and the European Community. Wellington, 1978. pp. 82.

— United Kingdom.

CAMPS (MIRIAM) European unification in the sixties: from the veto to the crisis. London, 1967. pp. 273. *bibliog.*

AUGHEY (ARTHUR) Conservative party attitudes towards the Common Market. Hull, 1978. fo. 29. *(Hull. University. Department of Politics. Hull Papers in Politics. No. 2)*

LEWIS (D.E.S.) Britain and the European Economic Community. London, 1978. pp. 125. *bibliog.*

NICHOLLS (J.R.) The impact of the EEC on the UK food industry: effects on the strategies of UK food, drink and tobacco manufacturing companies. Farnborough, Hants., [1978]. pp. 349.

POCOCK (GERRY) The Common Market fraud. London, [1978]. pp. 27. *(Communist Party of Great Britain. Communist Party Pamphlets)*

EUROPEAN ECONOMIC COMMUNITY ASSOCIATED COUNTRIES

— Commerce — European Economic Community countries.

EUROPEAN COMMUNITIES. Statistical Office. EC trade with the: ACP states: South Mediterranean states. q., 1978 (preliminary issue)- Luxembourg. *[in Community languages]*

EUROPEAN ECONOMIC COMMUNITY COUNTRIES.

EUROPEAN COMMUNITY STUDIES: for teachers and students (formerly EUROPEAN STUDIES: teachers' series): pr. under the auspices of the Centre for Contemporary European Studies, University of Sussex in association with the European Community Information Service. irreg. London. *Current issues only kept.*

— Commerce.

CROWSON (PHILLIP) Non-fuel minerals and foreign policy. London, [1977]. 2 vols. *(Royal Institute of International Affairs. British Foreign Policy to 1985)*

McQUEEN (MATTHEW) Britain, the EEC and the developing world. London, 1977. pp. 119. *bibliog.*

— — Statistics.

EUROPEAN COMMUNITIES. Statistical Office. Foreign trade analytical tables (NIMEXE). [in German and French]. a. (in pts. A-L) (formerly q.), 1966- Luxembourg.

— — European Economic Community associated countries.

EUROPEAN COMMUNITIES. Statistical Office. EC trade with the: ACP states: South Mediterranean states. q., 1978 (preliminary issue)- Luxembourg. *[in Community languages]*

EUROPEAN ECONOMIC COMMUNITY COUNTRIES.(Cont.)

— — Mediterranean.

EUROPEAN COMMUNITIES. Statistical Office. EC trade with the: ACP states: South Mediterranean states. q., 1978 (preliminary issue)- Luxembourg. *[in Community languages]*

— Economic conditions.

EUROPEAN COMMUNITIES. Statistical Office. Regional statistics: main regional indicators. a., 1970/1977- Luxembourg. *[in English and French]*

EUROPEAN ECONOMY; [pd.by] Directorate-General for Economic and Financial Affairs, Commission of the European Communities. q., N 1978(no.1)- Brussels. *File includes supplements: Supplement A, Recent economic trends; Supplement B, Economic prospects - business survey results; Supplement C, Economic prospects - consumer survey results. Supersedes ECONOMIC SITUATION IN THE COMMUNITY and GRAPHS AND NOTES OF THE ECONOMIC SITUATION IN THE COMMUNITY. Fourth quarter includes Annual economic review.*

PARKER (GEOFFREY) The countries of Community Europe: a geographical survey of contemporary issues. London, 1979. pp. 211. *bibliog.*

— — Statistics.

EUROPEAN COMMUNITIES. Statistical Office. Regional statistics: main regional indicators. a., 1970/1977- Luxembourg. *[in English and French]*

— Economic policy.

SCOTTISH COUNCIL (DEVELOPMENT AND INDUSTRY). E.E.C. Committee. The future of regional policy in the enlarged European Economic Community. [Edinburgh], [1973]. fo. 14.

EUROPEAN REGIONAL DEVELOPMENT FUND. Annual report. a., 1976(2nd)- Brussels.

— Foreign economic relations.

FELD (WERNER J.) The European Community in world affairs: economic power and political influence. [Port Washington, 1976]. pp. 352.

— — Canada.

CONFERENCE ON CANADA AND THE EUROPEAN COMMUNITY, QUEEN'S UNIVERSITY, KINGSTON, ONTARIO, 1977. Report...; by Nils Ørvik, editor. Kingston, Ont., [1978?]. pp. 225. *bibliogs.* (Kingston, Ontario. Queen's University. Centre for International Relations. European Studies Series. No. 1/77)

VALASKAKIS (KIMON) "L'option Europe": analyse de la plausibilité d'une association Québec/Canada/Europe; préparé pour le compte du Ministère des Affaires Intergouvernementales du Québec. [Québec, 1979]. pp. 176.

— — — Quebec.

VALASKAKIS (KIMON) "L'option Europe": analyse de la plausibilité d'une association Québec/Canada/Europe; préparé pour le compte du Ministère des Affaires Intergouvernementales du Québec. [Québec, 1979]. pp. 176.

— — Scandinavia.

ØRVIK (NILS) and BJØL (ERLING) The Scandinavian allies and the European Community. Kingston, Ont., 1978. pp. 98. (Kingston, Ontario. Queen's University. Centre for International Relations. European Studies Series. No. 1/78)

— Foreign relations.

FELD (WERNER J.) The European Community in world affairs: economic power and political influence. [Port Washington, 1976]. pp. 352.

Les POLITIQUES extérieures européennes dans la crise. [Paris, 1976]. pp. 198. (Fondation Nationale des Sciences Politiques. Travaux et Recherches de Science Politique. 43)

— — Mediterranean.

PETIT-LAURENT (PHILIPPE) Les fondements politiques des engagements de la Communauté Européenne en Méditerranée. Paris, [1976]. pp. 168. *bibliog.* (Paris. Université de Paris II. Travaux et Recherches. Série Science Politique. 7)

— Politics and government.

EUROPEAN PARLIAMENT. Background note. irreg. London. *Current issues only kept.*

— Social conditions.

RIFFAULT (HELENE) and RABIER (JACQUES RENE) The perception of poverty in Europe: report on a public opinion survey carried out in the member countries of the European Community as part of the programme of pilot projects to combat poverty. Brussels, European Communities, 1977. 1 vol. (various pagings). *Working document for the Commission of the European Communities.*

— Social policy.

FABIAN SOCIETY. Fabian Tracts. [No.] 461. Creating a caring Community; [by] Roy Manley [and others]. London, 1979. pp. 28.

— Statistics.

EUROSTATISTICS: data for short-term economic analysis; [pd. by] Statistical Office of the European Communities. m., Ja 1979(no.1)- Luxembourg. *[in Community languages] Supersedes EUROPEAN COMMUNITIES. Statistical Office. Monthly general statistics bulletin.*

EUROPEAN FEDERATION.

CAMPS (MIRIAM) European unification in the sixties: from the veto to the crisis. London, 1967. pp. 273. *bibliog.*

CAPORASO (JAMES A.) The structure and function of European integration. Pacific Palisades, Calif., [1974]. pp. 214. *bibliog.*

SCHWEITZER (MICHAEL) Dauernde Neutralität und europäische Integration. Wien, 1977. pp. 347. *bibliog.*

CONFOEDERATIO Europaea. Lausanne, 1978. pp. 39. (Lausanne. Université. Centre de Recherches Européennes. Publications. 1. Histoire, Précurseurs et Promoteurs de l'Union de l'Europe)

EUROPEAN COMMUNITIES. Commission. 1978. Commission report on the establishment of a European Foundation: sent to the European Council on 17 November 1977. [Brussels, 1978]. pp. 23. (Bulletin of the European Communities. Supplements. [1977/5])

EUROPEAN COMMUNITIES. Commission. 1978. European union: report[s] for 1977 by the Ministers of Foreign Affairs [and] by the Commission. [Brussels, 1978]. pp. 16. (Bulletin of the European Communities. Supplements. [1977/8])

EUROPEAN integration, regional devolution and national parliaments; [by] D. Coombes [and others]. London, 1979. pp. 45. (Policy Studies Institute. Studies in European Politics. 3)

VAUGHAN (RICHARD) Professor of Medieval History, University of Hull. Twentieth-century Europe: paths to unity. London, [1979]. pp. 261.

EUROPEAN INVESTMENT BANK.

EUROPEAN INVESTMENT BANK. Information. irreg. Luxembourg. *Current issues only kept.*

EUROPEAN PARLIAMENT.

STEPHENS (WILLIAM) and LLEWELLYN (TREFOR) A parliament is born: the European Parliament after direct elections. London, [1977]. pp. 20.

COOMBES (DAVID) The future of the European Parliament. London, [1979]. pp. 136. (Policy Studies Institute. Studies in European Politics. 1)

The EUROPEAN Parliament and the national parliaments; edited by Valentine Herman and Rinus van Schendelen. Farnborough, [1979]. pp. 304. *bibliog.*

JACKSON (ROBERT VICTOR) and FITZMAURICE (JOHN) The European Parliament: a guide for the European elections. Harmondsworth, 1979. pp. 174. *bibliog.*

MARQUAND (DAVID) Parliament for Europe. London, 1979. pp. 147. *bibliog.*

TUGENDHAT (CHRISTOPHER) Conservatives in Europe: a personal view. London, 1979. pp. 23. (Conservative Political Centre. [Publications]. No. 636)

EUROPEAN PARLIAMENT. Background note. irreg. London. *Current issues only kept.*

EUROPEAN PARLIAMENT. Newsletter. irreg. London. *Current issues only kept.*

EUROPEAN PARLIAMENT. Report. irreg. London. *Current issues only kept.*

— Elections.

LABOUR COMMITTEE FOR EUROPE. Direct elections to the European Parliament: what the Labour Party should say. London, [1977]. pp. 6.

COOK (CHRISTOPHER PIERS) and FRANCIS (MARY) The first European elections: a handbook and guide. London, 1979. pp. 193.

EUROPEAN REGIONAL DEVELOPMENT FUND.

EUROPEAN REGIONAL DEVELOPMENT FUND. Annual report. a., 1976(2nd)- Brussels.

[U.K. Department of Industry. 1978.] Regional development programme, United Kingdom, 1978-1980. [London, 1978]. pp. 91.

EUROPEAN WAR, 1914-1918

— Campaigns — Western.

JOFFRE (JOSEPH JACQUES CESAIRE) Mémoires du Maréchal Joffre, 1910-1917. Paris, [1932]. 2 vols.

— — Turkey and the Near East.

PRICE (MORGAN PHILIPS) War and revolution in Asiatic Russia. London, 1918. pp. 296.

— Causes.

TURNER (LEONARD CHARLES FREDERICK) Origins of the First World War. London, 1970. pp. 120. *bibliog.*

The WAR plans of the great powers, 1880-1914; edited by Paul M. Kennedy. London, 1979. pp. 282. *bibliog.*

— Diplomatic history.

BIHL (WOLFDIETER) Die Kaukasus-Politik der Mittelmächte. Wien, 1975 in progress. *bibliog.* (Kommission für Neuere Geschichte Österreichs. Veröffentlichungen. 61)

QUELLEN zur Entstehung des Ersten Weltkrieges: internationale Dokumente, 1901-1914; herausgegeben von Erwin Hölzle. Darmstadt, 1978. pp. 497. *bibliog.*

WEST (RACHEL) The Department of State on the eve of the First World War. Athens, Ga., [1978]. pp. 183. *bibliog.*

— Finance.

SCHRECKER (ELLEN) The hired money: the French debt to the United States, 1917- 1929. New York, 1979. pp. 383. *bibliog.*

— Food question.

HOOVER (HERBERT CLARK) and WILSON (THOMAS WOODROW) Two peacemakers in Paris: the Hoover-Wilson post-armistice letters, 1918-1920; edited and with commentaries by Francis William O'Brien. College Station, [1978]. pp. 254. *bibliog.*

— Peace.

DEBENEDETTI (CHARLES) Origins of the modern American peace movement, 1915-1929. New York, [1978]. pp. 281. *bibliog.*

HOOVER (HERBERT CLARK) and WILSON (THOMAS WOODROW) Two peacemakers in Paris: the Hoover-Wilson post-armistice letters, 1918-1920; edited and with commentaries by Francis William O'Brien. College Station, [1978]. pp. 254. *bibliog.*

KRAFT (BARBARA S.) The peace ship: Henry Ford's pacifist adventure in the First World War. New York, [1978]. pp. 367. *bibliog.*

— Personal narratives, French.

GALLIENI (JOSEPH SIMON) Mémoires du Général Galliéni: défense de Paris, 25 Août-11 Septembre 1914. Paris, 1920. pp. 271.

JOFFRE (JOSEPH JACQUES CESAIRE) Mémoires du Maréchal Joffre, 1910-1917. Paris, [1932]. 2 vols.

— Propaganda.

OWEN (DAVID) b. 1939. Battle of wits: a history of psychology and deception in modern warfare. London, 1978. pp. 207.

— Sources.

QUELLEN zur Entstehung des Ersten Weltkrieges: internationale Dokumente, 1901-1914; herausgegeben von Erwin Hölzle. Darmstadt, 1978. pp. 497. *bibliog.*

— Supplies.

HAMILTON (PEGGY) Lady. Three years or the duration: the memoirs of a munition worker, 1914-1918. London, 1978. pp. 125.

— Women's work.

GERSDORFF (URSULA VON) Frauen im Kriegsdienst, 1914-1945. Stuttgart, 1969. pp. 572. *bibliog. (Militärgeschichtliches Forschungsamt. Beiträge zur Militär- und Kriegsgeschichte. Band 11)*

HAMILTON (PEGGY) Lady. Three years or the duration: the memoirs of a munition worker, 1914-1918. London, 1978. pp. 125.

— France.

GALLIENI (JOSEPH SIMON) Mémoires du Général Galliéni: défense de Paris, 25 Août-11 Septembre 1914. Paris, 1920. pp. 271.

GROSSHEIM (HEINRICH) Sozialisten in der Verantwortung: die französischen Sozialisten und Gewerkschafter im ersten Weltkrieg, 1914-17. Bonn, [1978]. pp. 286. *bibliog. (Friedrich-Ebert-Stiftung. Forschungsinstitut. Schriftenreihe. Band 140)*

— Germany.

FARRAR (L.L.) Divide and conquer: German efforts to conclude a separate peace, 1914-1918. New York, 1978. pp. 180. *bibliog. (East European Quarterly. East European Monographs. 45)*

GEISS (IMANUEL) Das Deutsche Reich und der Erste Weltkrieg. München, [1978]. pp. 243. *bibliog.*

QUIDDE (LUDWIG) Der deutsche Pazifismus während des Weltkrieges 1914-1918; aus dem Nachlass Ludwig Quiddes herausgegeben von Karl Holl unter Mitwirkung von Helmut Donat. Boppard am Rhein, 1979. pp. 416. *bibliog. (Germany (Bundesrepublik). Bundesarchiv. Schriften. 23)*

— Russia.

PRICE (MORGAN PHILIPS) War and revolution in Asiatic Russia. London, 1918. pp. 296.

— — Caucasus.

BIHL (WOLFDIETER) Die Kaukasus-Politik der Mittelmächte. Wien, 1975 in progress. *bibliog. (Kommission für Neuere Geschichte Österreichs. Veröffentlichungen. 61)*

— United States.

PARSONS (EDWARD B.) Wilsonian diplomacy: Allied-American rivalries in war and peace. St. Louis, Miss., [1978]. pp. 213. *bibliog.*

EUROPEANS IN ASIA.

The AGE of partnership: Europeans in Asia before Dominion; edited by Blair B. Kling ånd M.N. Pearson. Honolulu, [1979]. pp. 247. *bibliogs.*

EUROPEANS IN SOUTH AFRICA.

GRUNDY (KENNETH W.) Defense legislation and communal politics: the evolution of a white South African nation as reflected in the controversy over the assignment of armed forces abroad, 1912-1976. Athens, Ohio, 1978. pp. 51. *(Ohio University. Center for International Studies. Papers in International Studies. Africa Series. No. 33)*

EUROPEANS IN SUBSAHARAN AFRICA.

WEST (RICHARD LEAF) The white tribes of Africa. New York, 1965. pp. 281.

WEST (RICHARD LEAF) The white tribes revisited. London, 1978. pp. 199.

EUROPEANS IN THE PACIFIC.

RALSTON (CAROLINE) Grass huts and warehouses: Pacific beach communities of the nineteenth century. Canberra, 1977. pp. 268. *bibliog.*

EUTHANASIA.

EUTHANASIA; [papers presented at a symposium held in Durban in 1978]; edited by G.C. Oosthuizen [and others]. Cape Town, 1978. pp. 241. *(Human Sciences Research Council [South Africa]. Publication Series. No. 65)*

GRISEZ (GERMAIN GABRIEL) and BOYLE (JOSEPH M.) Life and death with liberty and justice: a contribution to the euthanasia debate. Notre Dame, [1979]. pp. 521.

EVALUATION RESEARCH (SOCIAL ACTION PROGRAMMES).

METHODS of evaluating the effectiveness of social security programmes: report of research conference Vienna, 10-13 September 1975. Geneva, 1976. pp. 107. *bibliog. (International Social Security Association. Studies and Research. No. 8)*

EVALUATION research methods: a basic guide; edited by Leonard Rutman. Beverly Hills, [1977]. pp. 238.

EVALUATION and accountability in human service programs...; edited by William C. Sze [and] June G. Hopps. 2nd ed. Cambridge, Mass., [1978]. pp. 222. *bibliog.*

EVALUATION of human service programs; edited by C. Clifford Attkisson [and others]. New York, 1978. pp. 492. *bibliogs.*

HOOLE (FRANCIS W.) Evaluation research and development activities. Beverly Hills, [1978]. pp. 205. *bibliog.*

ORENSTEIN (ALAN) and PHILLIPS (WILLIAM R.F.) Understanding social research: an introduction. Boston, Mass., 1978. pp. 428.

TRIPODI (TONY) and others. Differential social program evaluation. Itasca, Ill., [1978]. pp. 173. *bibliogs.*

— United States.

REGIER (MARILYN C.) Social policy in action: perspectives on the implementation of alcoholism reforms. Lexington, Mass., [1979]. pp. 177. *bibliog.*

EVANGELICAL REVIVAL.

KENT (JOHN) 1923- . Holding the fort: studies in Victorian revivalism. London, 1978. pp. 381.

EVANGELICALISM.

MATHEWS (DONALD G.) Religion in the Old South. Chicago, [1977]. pp. 274. *bibliog.*

CARWARDINE (RICHARD) Transatlantic revivalism: popular evangelicalism in Britain and America, 1790-1865. Westport, [1978]. pp. 249. *bibliog.*

EVICTION

— United Kingdom — Scotland.

PAISLEY COMMUNITY DEVELOPMENT PROJECT. Against eviction; (by Barbara Jackson [and others]). [Paisley, 1978]. pp. (91).

EVIDENCE, CRIMINAL

— United Kingdom.

U.K. Home Office. 1978. Evidence to the Royal Commission on Criminal Procedure: memorandum no.9: the law of evidence in criminal proceedings. London, 1978. pp. 43.

U.K. Home Office. 1979. Evidence to the Royal Commission on Criminal Procedure: memorandum no. 7: preparation for trial and disclosure of evidence. London, 1979. pp. 50.

EVOLUTION.

BOULDING (KENNETH EWART) Ecodynamics: a new theory of societal evolution. Beverly Hills, [1978]. pp. 367. *bibliog.*

POLSKA AKADEMIA NAUK. Instytut Geografii. Geografia Polonica. 38. Rural landscape and settlement evolution in Europe: proceedings of the conference, Warsaw, September 1975; edited by Maria Kiełczewska-Zaleska. Warsaw, 1978. pp. 304. *bibliogs.* 2 maps in end pocket.

EXAMINATIONS

— France.

PIGELET (JEAN LUC) and PHAM-KHAC (KHANG) L'échec au baccalauréat: ses conséquences dans l'éducation et la vie active. [Paris], 1978. pp. 114. *(Centre d'Etudes et de Recherches sur les Qualifications. Dossiers. 18)*

— Germany.

GERMANY (BUNDESREPUBLIK). Statistisches Bundesamt. Prüfungen an Hochschulen. a., 1974/75- Wiesbaden. *(Bildung und Kultur. Reihe 4.2)*

— Trinidad and Tobago.

TRINIDAD AND TOBAGO. Central Statistical Office. Education Statistics Section. 1978. Report on London G.C.E. examination results, 1973-1977. [Port of Spain, 1978]. pp. 43.

TRINIDAD AND TOBAGO. Central Statistical Office. Education Statistics Section. 1979. Report on Cambridge G.C.E. examination results, 1973-1977. [Port of Spain, 1979]. pp. 85.

EXECUTIVE POWER.

MOULIN (RICHARD) Le présidentialisme et la classification des régimes politiques. Paris, 1978. pp. 389. *bibliog.*

— United Kingdom.

JOHNSON (PAUL) Britain's own road to serfdom. London, 1978. pp. 15. *(Conservative Political Centre. [Publications]. No. 633)*

SHRIMSLEY (ANTHONY) The new establishment: an inquiry into who really governs Britain in 1978. [London], 1978. pp. 44.

EXECUTIVE POWER.(Cont.)

— United States.

JOHNSTONE (ROBERT M.) Jefferson and the Presidency: leadership in the young republic. Ithaca, 1978. pp. 332. *bibliog.*

EXECUTIVES.

The INTERNATIONAL executive; papers from a Princeton University conference, April 26-29, 1977; edited by Leon Gordenker. Princeton, 1978. pp. 60. *(Princeton University. Center of International Studies. World Order Studies Program. Occasional Papers. No.6)*

— United States — Retirement.

WIKSTROM (WALTER S.) The productive retirement years of former managers. New York, [1978]. pp. 45. *(National Industrial Conference Board. Conference Board Reports. No. 747)*

EXMOOR NATIONAL PARK.

EXMOOR NATIONAL PARK COMMITTEE. Exmoor National Park plan; ([with] Supplement). Dulverton, 1977. 2 pts. (in 1 vol.) *bibliog.*

EXPENDITURES, PUBLIC.

SQUIRE (LYN) and TAK (HERMAN G. VAN DER) Economic analysis of projects...; published for the World Bank. Baltimore, [1975]. pp. 153. *bibliog. (International Bank for Reconstruction and Development. World Bank Research Publications)*

SINGER (NEIL M.) Public microeconomics: an introduction to government finance. 2nd ed. Boston, Mass., [1976]. pp. 447.

SIVARD (RUTH LEGER) World military and social expenditures, 1977. Leesburg, Va., [1977]. pp. 31.

CLARKE (Sir RICHARD WILLIAM BARNES) Public expenditure, management and controls: the development of the Public Expenditure Survey Committee (PESC). London, 1978. pp. 212.

WEBER (LUC) L'analyse économique des dépenses publiques: fondements et principes de la rationalisation des choix budgétaires. Paris, [1978]. pp. 312. *bibliog.*

BROWNING (EDGAR K.) and BROWNING (JACQUELENE M.) Public finance and the price system. New York, [1979]. pp. 464. *bibliogs.*

POST-INDUSTRIAL society: proceedings of an international symposium held in Uppsala from 22 to 25 March 1977 to mark the occasion of the 500th anniversary of Uppsala University; edited by Bo Gustafsson. London, [1979]. pp. 238. *bibliogs.*

EXPERIENCE.

SOCIAL behaviour and experience: multiple perspectives; edited by Hedy Brown and Richard Stevens. Sevenoaks, [1975]. pp. 627. *bibliogs.*

TUAN (YI-FU) Space and place: the perspective of experience. London, 1977. pp. 235. *bibliog.*

JENSEN (KENNETH MARTIN) Beyond Marx and Mach: Aleksandr Bogdanov's philosophy of living experience. Dordrecht, [1978]. pp. 189. *bibliog. (Freiburg (Switzerland). Universität. Ost- Europa Institut. Sovietica. vol. 41)*

EXPERIENCE (RELIGION).

GREVEN (PHILIP J.) The protestant temperament: patterns of child-rearing, religious experience, and the self in early America. New York, 1977. pp. 431.

EXPERIMENTAL DESIGN.

DAVID (HERBERT ARON) The method of paired comparisons. London, 1963 repr. 1969. pp. 124. *bibliog.*

ANDERSON (VIRGIL L.) and McLEAN (ROBERT A.) Design of experiments: a realistic approach. New York, [1974]. pp. 418. *bibliogs.*

DANIEL (CUTHBERT) Applications of statistics to industrial experimentation. New York, [1976]. pp. 294. *bibliog.*

JOHN (J.A.) and QUENOUILLE (MAURICE HENRY) Experiments: design and analysis. 2nd ed. New York, 1977. pp. 296.

BOX (GEORGE E.P.) and others. Statistics for experimenters: an introduction to design, data analysis and model building. New York, [1978]. pp. 653.

KEMPTHORNE (OSCAR) The design and analysis of experiments. Huntington, N.Y., 1979. pp. 631.

EXPORT CREDIT.

UNITED NATIONS. Department of Economic and Social Affairs. Fiscal and Financial Branch. 1967. Export credits and development financing: part one, current practices and problems; part two, national export credit systems. (E/4274) (ST/ECA/95-96). New York, 1967. pp. 122.

ROUND TABLE ON EXPORT CREDIT AS A MEANS OF PROMOTING EXPORTS FROM DEVELOPING COUNTRIES, NEW YORK, 1969. Report of the Round Table...[held at] New York 24 to 28 March 1969. (E/4661)(ST/ECA/116). New York, United Nations, 1969. pp. 27.

— United Kingdom.

EXPORT finance in foreign currencies: a look at the problems associated with obtaining medium and long term finance for larger projects and associated matters; conference addresses [at a conference in 1977 organized by the Confederation of British Industry]. London, 1977. pp. 36.

EXPORT finance: the short end: a look at some of the problems facing exporters in undertaking overseas sales and financing them on credit terms of up to two years; addresses given at a conference held by the CBI...[in London], 1977. London, 1978. pp. 44.

EXPORT MARKETING.

INTERNATIONAL TRADE FORUM; [pd.by] International Trade Centre UNCTAD/GATT. q., D 1964(v.1, no.1)- ; with gaps (Ap-D 1973, v.9, nos. 2-4; 1974 v.10). Geneva. *File includes q. suppl., Ag 1965(no.1)-Supersedes General Agreement on Tariffs and Trade. Developments in commercial policy (Ja/Je 1960 - Ja/Je 1963).*

NEW ZEALAND. Department of Trade and Industry. 1975. How to export. Wellington, 1975. pp. 80.

EXPORTING to western Europe, 1977: case studies; a B[ritish] O[verseas] T[rade] B[oard] national conference, November 29, 1977,...Wembley. [London], British Overseas Trade Board, [1977]. pp. 52.

EXPORT PREMIUMS.

— Underdeveloped areas.

See UNDERDEVELOPED AREAS — Export premiums.

EXSERVICEMEN

— Canada.

SCHULL (JOHN JOSEPH) Veneration for valor: an assessment of the Veterans Charter: its impact on Canada as a whole. Ottawa, Information Canada, 1973. pp. 108.

EXSERVICEMEN, DISABLED

— Rehabilitation.

UNITED NATIONS. Department of Economic and Social Affairs. 1971. Study on rehabilitation of the war disabled in selected countries. (ST/SOA/108). New York, 1971. pp. 193. *bibliog.*

— — Israel.

ISRAEL. Ministry of Defence. Rehabilitation Department. 1968. Rehabilitation programs and benefits for disabled veterans and dependents. [Tel Aviv], 1968. pp. 20.

EXTERNALITIES (ECONOMICS).

PUBLIC goods and public policy; edited by William Loehr and Todd Sandler. Beverly Hills, [1978]. pp. 240. *bibliogs.*

The VALUATION of social cost; edited by David W. Pearce. London, 1978. pp. 197. *bibliogs.*

EXTREME VALUE THEORY.

GALAMBOS (JANOS) The asymptotic theory of extreme order statistics. New York, [1978]. pp. 352. *bibliog.*

FABIAN SOCIETY.

STUART (JAMES GIBB) The mind benders: the gradual revolution and Scottish independence. Glasgow, 1978. pp. 180. *bibliog.*

FACIAL EXPRESSION.

GRAHAM (JEAN ANN) Aspects of gaze, facial expression and gesture in dyadic interactions. 1978. fo. 433. *bibliog. Typescript. Ph.D. (London) thesis: unpublished. This thesis is the property of London University and may not be removed from the Library.*

FACTOR ANALYSIS.

THEORY construction and data analysis in the behavioral sciences: a volume in honor of Louis Guttman; [edited by] Samuel Shye. San Francisco, 1978. pp. 426. *bibliog.*

FACTORIES

— Europe — Location.

LILLY (W. GORDON) Plant location in Europe. London, [1974]. fo. 65.

— United Kingdom.

JONES (D.T.) Plant size and efficiency in the production of metalworking machine tools. London, [1978]. pp. 26. *bibliog. (National Institute of Economic and Social Research. Discussion Papers. No. 19)*

FACTORY INSPECTION

— Ireland (Republic).

EIRE. Department of Labour. Labour inspection: report...of Industrial Inspectorate and General Inspectorate. a., 1977- Dublin.

FAIRBANKS

—Social conditions.

DIXON (MIM) What happened to Fairbanks?: the effects of the trans-Alaska oil pipeline on the community of Fairbanks, Alaska. Boulder, Colo., 1978. pp. 337. *bibliog.*

FALKENHAUSEN (ALEXANDER VON).

LIANG (HSI-HUEY) The Sino-German connection: Alexander von Falkenhausen between China and Germany, 1900-1941. Assen, 1978. pp. 229. *bibliog.*

FAMILY.

The FAMILY and change; edited by John N. Edwards. New York, [1969]. pp. 492. *bibliog.*

BOTT (ELIZABETH JANE) Family and social network: roles, norms and external relationships in ordinary urban families. 2nd ed. New York, [1971]. pp. 363. *bibliog.*

IZMENENIE polozheniia zhenshchiny i sem'ia: [sbornik statei]. Moskva, 1977. pp. 214.

POSTER (MARK) Critical theory of the family. New York, 1978. pp. 233. *bibliog.*

SCANZONI (JOHN H.) Sex roles, women's work and marital conflict: a study of family change. Lexington, Mass., [1978]. pp. 175. *bibliog.*

LESLIE (GERALD RONNELL) The family in social context. 4th ed. New York, 1979. pp. 637. *bibliogs.*

— Economic aspects.

TILLY (LOUISE) and SCOTT (JOAN WALLACH) Women, work, and family. New York, [1978]. pp. 274. *bibliog.*

— History.

The FAMILY in history; edited by Charles E. Rosenberg. [Philadelphia, 1975 repr. 1978]. pp. 207.

FLANDRIN (JEAN-LOUIS) Families in former times: kinship, household and sexuality...; translated by Richard Southern. Cambridge, 1979. pp. 265. *bibliog.*

— Belgium.

POPULATION and family in the Low Countries, II; edited by H. G. Moors [and others]. Leiden, 1978. pp. 153. *bibliogs. (Nederlands Interuniversitair Demografisch Instituut and Centre d'Etude de la Population et de la Famille [Belgium]. Publications. vol. 6)*

— Canada — Quebec.

QUEBEC (PROVINCE). Conseil des Affaires Sociales et de la Famille. 1978. La situation des familles québécoises. [Québec, 1978]. pp. 108. *(Etudes et Avis)*

— China.

BAKER (HUGH D.R.) Chinese family and kinship. London, 1979. pp. 243. *bibliog.*

— France.

FLANDRIN (JEAN-LOUIS) Families in former times: kinship, household and sexuality...; translated by Richard Southern. Cambridge, 1979. pp. 265. *bibliog.*

— India.

MUKHERJEE (RAMKRISHNA) West Bengal family structures, 1946-1966: an example of viability of joint family. Delhi, 1977. pp. 267. *bibliog.*

— Italy.

BELMONTE (THOMAS) The broken fountain. New York, 1979. pp. 151.

— Netherlands.

MOOK (BERTHA) The Dutch family in the 17th and 18th centuries: an explorative- descriptive study. Ottawa, 1977. pp. 100. *bibliog.*

POPULATION and family in the Low Countries, II; edited by H. G. Moors [and others]. Leiden, 1978. pp. 153. *bibliogs. (Nederlands Interuniversitair Demografisch Instituut and Centre d'Etude de la Population et de la Famille [Belgium]. Publications. vol. 6)*

— New Zealand.

NEW ZEALAND. Social Development Council. 1978-79. Families in special circumstances. [Wellington], 1978-79. 5 vols.

— — Statistics.

NEW ZEALAND. Department of Statistics. 1978. Family statistics in New Zealand. [Wellington], 1978. pp. 143. *(Miscellaneous Bulletin Series. No. 10)*

— Russia.

The FAMILY in imperial Russia: new lines of historical research; [papers presented at a symposium held at the University of Illinois, Urbana-Champaign, Oct. 1976]; edited by David L. Ransel. Urbana, 1978. pp. 342. *bibliog.*

— — Kazakstan.

SEM'IA i semeinye obriady u narodov Srednei Azii i Kazakhstana. Moskva, 1978. pp. 215.

— — Soviet Central Asia.

SEM'IA i semeinye obriady u narodov Srednei Azii i Kazakhstana. Moskva, 1978. pp. 215.

— — Ukraine.

PONOMAR'OV (ANATOLII PETROVYCH) Suchasna sim'ia i simeinyi pobut robitnykiv Donbasu, 1950-1975. Kyïv, 1978. pp. 143.

— — Singapore.

KUO (EDDIE C.Y.) Families under economic stress: the Singapore experience. [Singapore, 1976]. pp. 72. *bibliog. (Institute of Southeast Asian Studies. Field Reports. No. 11)*

— United Kingdom.

HEASMAN (KATHLEEN J.) Home, family and community. London, 1978. pp. 151. *bibliog.*

TRUMBACH (RANDOLPH) The rise of the egalitarian family: aristocratic kinship and domestic relations in eighteenth-century England. New York, [1978]. pp. 324. *bibliog.*

WACHTER (KENNETH W.) and others. Statistical studies of historical social structure. New York, [1978]. pp. 229. *bibliog.*

— — Ireland, Northern.

EVASON (EILEEN) Family poverty in Northern Ireland. London, 1978. pp. 36. *(Child Poverty Action Group. Poverty Research Series. 6)*

— United States.

McGOVERN (JAMES R.) Yankee family. New Orleans, 1975. pp. 191.

RUBIN (LILLIAN B.) Worlds of pain: life in the working-class family. New York, [1976]. pp. 268.

KENISTON (KENNETH) and others. All our children: the American family under pressure. New York, [1977]. pp. 255. *Published under the auspices of the Carnegie Council on Children, Carnegie Corporation of New York.*

The AMERICAN family in social-historical perspective;...Michael Gordon, editor. 2nd ed. New York, [1978]. pp. 580. *bibliogs.*

GITTLEMAN (SOL) From shtetl to suburbia: the family in Jewish literary imagination. Boston, [Mass.], [1978]. pp. 209. *bibliog.*

SEWARD (RUDY RAY) The American family: a demographic history. Beverly Hills, [1978]. pp. 222. *bibliog.*

DYER (EVERETT D.) The American family: variety and change. New York, [1979]. pp. 478. *bibliogs.*

FARAGHER (JOHN MACK) Women and men on the overland trail. New Haven, 1979. pp. 281. *bibliog. (Yale University. Yale Historical Publications. Miscellany. 121)*

FAMILY ALLOWANCES

— New Zealand.

NEW ZEALAND. Social Development Council. 1977. Family finances: can the community do better? [Wellington], 1977. 1 vol.(various pagings). *bibliog.*

NEW ZEALAND. Social Development Council. 1977. Family finances: can we do better? [Wellington, 1977]. 1 pamphlet (unpaged).

FAMILY PLANNING ASSOCIATION.

LEATHARD (AUDREY MARY) The development of family planning services in Britain. 1977 [or rather 1978]. fo. 564. *bibliog.* Typescript. Ph.D. (London) thesis: unpublished. This thesis is the property of London University and may not be removed from the Library.

FAMILY PSYCHOTHERAPY.

TECHNIQUES of family psychotherapy: a primer; edited by D.A. Bloch. New York, [1973]. pp. 124. *bibliogs. (Reprinted from the May 1973 issue, vol. 5, no. 2, of Seminars in Psychiatry)*

WALROND-SKINNER (SUE) Family therapy: the treatment of natural systems. London, 1976. pp. 164. *bibliog.*

HALEY (JAY) Problem-solving therapy: new strategies for effective family therapy. San Francisco, 1978. pp. 275.

FAMILY RESEARCH.

CENTRE D'ETUDE DE LA POPULATION ET DE LA FAMILLE. Annual report. a., 1976- Brussels.

— United States.

SEWARD (RUDY RAY) The American family: a demographic history. Beverly Hills, [1978]. pp. 222. *bibliog.*

FAMILY SIZE.

ASTEL (KARL) and WEBER (ERNA) Die Kinderzahl der 29000 politischen Leiter des Gaues Thüringen der NSDAP und die Ursachen der ermittelten Fortpflanzungshäufigkeit; 4. Untersuchung über die unterschiedliche Fortpflanzung in Thüringen (aus dem Thüringischen Landesamt für Rassewesen, Weimar und Jena). Berlin, 1943. pp. 187.

— Bibliography.

PECK (GRAHAM) compiler. Family planning and integration: the inclusion of family planning in comprehensive programmes for the alleviation of poverty deprivation. London, 1978. pp. 23. *(International Planned Parenthood Federation. Bibliography Series)*

— Brazil.

NAGELSCHMIDT (ANNA MATHILDE PACHECO E CHAVES) Social-psychological variables related to women's use of contraception in a society in transition: the case of Sao Paulo, Brazil. 1978. fo. 298. *bibliog.* Typescript. Ph.D. (London) thesis: unpublished. This thesis is the property of London University and may not be removed from the Library.

— Mohammedan countries.

WOMEN'S status and fertility in the Muslim world; edited by James Allman. New York, [1978]. pp. 378. *bibliog.*

FAMILY SOCIAL WORK

— Australia.

LIFFMAN (MICHAEL) Power for the poor: the Family Centre Project: an experiment in self-help. Sydney, 1978. pp. 160. *bibliog.*

— Canada — Quebec.

QUEBEC (PROVINCE). Conseil des Affaires Sociales et de la Famille. 1974. Contribution à une politique des affaires sociales et de la famille: les propositions et recommandations du Conseil des Affaires Sociales et de la Famille. [Québec], 1974. pp. 85.

FARIA (GILBERTO DE LIMA AZEVEDO SOUZA FERREIRA AMADO DE).

FARIA (GILBERTO DE LIMA AZEVEDO SOUZA FERREIRA AMADO DE) Discursos parlamentares; seleção e introdução Homero Senna. Brasilia, 1979. pp. 336. *(Brazil. Congresso. Câmara dos Deputados. Perfis Parlamentares. 11)*

FARINGTON (JOSEPH).

FARINGTON (JOSEPH) The diary of Joseph Farington; edited by Kenneth Garlick and Angus Macintyre. New Haven, 1978 in progress. *(Paul Mellon Centre for Studies in British Art. Studies in British Art)*

FARM EQUIPMENT.

BARTHOLOMEW (R.B.) The economics of acquiring farm machinery. Brisbane, 1976. pp. 27. *bibliog. (Queensland. Department of Primary Industries. Economic Services Branch. Technical Bulletins. No.9)*

FARM INCOME

FARM INCOME
— Australia.
AUSTRALIA. Industries Assistance Commission. 1978. Rural income fluctuations. Canberra, 1978. pp. 121. *(Reports. No. 161)*

— United Kingdom.
AGRICULTURAL DEVELOPMENT AND ADVISORY SERVICE [U.K.]. Farm resources and non-agricultural income; report of an ADAS Working Party; chairman: M.D. Brooke. [London, 1974]. pp. 54. *(Socio-Economics Papers. 1)*

FARM LIFE
— Rome, Ancient.
FRAYN (JOAN M.) Subsistence farming in Roman Italy. Fontwell, 1979. pp. 168. *bibliog.*

— United Kingdom — Scotland.
CARTER (IAN) Farmlife in northeast Scotland, 1840-1914: the poor man's country. Edinburgh, [1979]. pp. 258. *bibliog.*

FARM MANAGEMENT.
RAY (DEBIDAS) Studies in the economics of farm management in Hooghly district, West Bengal: three year consolidated report, 1970-71 to 1972-73. [Delhi, Controller of Publications, 1977]. pp. 55.

RUDRA (ASHOK) and others. Studies in the economics of farm management in Hooghly district, West Bengal: report for the year 1970-71. [Delhi, Controller of Publications], 1977. pp. 129.

— Bibliography.
CHRISTIAN (PORTIA) compiler. Agricultural enterprises management in an urban-industrial society: a guide to information sources. Detroit, [1978]. pp. 314. *(Gale Research Company. Management Information Guides. 34)*

— Malawi.
MALAWI. Agro-Economic Survey. 1972. Agro-economic survey: 9th report: Lake Chilwa: a sample farm management survey among rice and maize growers at the northern end of Lake Chilwa in Kasupe district, Malawi; prepared by T.W. Bieze. Zomba, 1972. fo. 63.

MALAWI. Agro-Economic Survey. 1973. Agro-economic survey: 11th report: Mbawa: a sample farm management survey among oriental tobacco, maize and groundnut growers in the Mbawa area in the southern part of Mzimba district, Malawi, with special reference to oriental tobacco; prepared by T.W. Bieze. Lilongwe, 1973. fo. 87. *bibliog.*

MALAWI. Agro-Economic Survey. 1978. Agro-economic survey: report no. 24: Thiwi-Lifidzi: a farm management survey of smallholder rural farmers in the Thiwi- Lifidzi area of Dedza district, Malawi. Lilongwe, 1978. fo. 97.

FARM OWNERSHIP
— United Kingdom.
AGRICULTURAL MORTGAGE CORPORATION and ECONOMIC DEVELOPMENT COMMITTEE FOR THE AGRICULTURAL INDUSTRY. The ownership of land by agricultural landlords in England and Wales; a survey. London, National Economic Development Office, 1977. pp. 26.

FARM PRODUCE
— Brazil.
BRAZIL. Conselho Nacional de Estatistica. Laboratorio de Estatistica. 1960. Numeros indices das quantidades e dos preços do agricultor de 36 produtos agricolas nos anos de 1952 a 1958. Rio de Janeiro, [1960?]. fo. 17. *(Estudos sôbre as Quantidades e os Preços das Mercadorias Produzidas ou Negociadas. No. 91)*

BRAZIL. Conselho Nacional de Estatistica. Laboratorio de Estatistica. 1960. Numeros indices das quantidades e dos preços do agricultor de 36 produtos agricolas, classificados segundo grandes grupamentos, nos anos de 1952 a 1958. Rio de Janeiro, [1960?]. fo. 15. *(Estudos sôbre as Quantidades e os Preços das Mercadorias Produzidas ou Negociadas. No. 91 bis)*

— European Economic Community countries.
EUROPEAN COMMUNITIES. Statistical Office. Selling prices of vegetable products. bi-m., 1978(no.5)- Luxembourg. *[in Community languages]*

— France — Marketing.
FRANCE. Institut National de la Statistique et des Etudes Economiques. Division Agriculture. 1977. Industries agricoles et alimentaires: données économiques 1970 à 1976. [Paris], 1977. pp. 119.

FRANCE. Direction de la Documentation. La Documentation Française. Notes et Etudes Documentaires. No. 4487. Les échanges agro-alimentaires de la France. [Paris], 1978. pp. 88.

— Japan.
SAXON (ERIC ALFRED) Japan's food gap and trade in farm products. Canberra, 1977. pp. 63. *bibliog.* *(Australia. Bureau of Agricultural Economics. Occasional Papers. No.42)*

— Poland.
ROLNICTWO a wy'zywienie w Polsce: pobudzanie, efekty, koszty produkcji; pod redakcją E. Gorzelaka. Warszawa, 1978. pp. 429.

— Russia — Marketing.
BAKHOVKINA (LIDIIA NIKOLAEVNA) Gosudarstvennoe upravlenie zakupkami sel'skokhoziastvennykh produktov. Moskva, 1978. pp. 135.

— Tanzania — Marketing.
UNITED REPUBLIC OF TANZANIA. Presidential Special Committee of Enquiry into Co-operative Movement and Marketing Boards. 1966. Report; [J.A.Mhaville, chairman]. Dar es Salaam, 1966. pp. 84.

FARM TENANCY
— China.
SU (JING) and LUN (LUO) Landlord and labor in late imperial China: case studies from Shandong...; translated from the Chinese with an introduction by Endymion Wilkinson. Cambridge, Mass., 1978. pp. 310. *bibliog.* *(Harvard University. East Asian Research Center. Harvard East Asian Monographs. 80)*

— United States — Iowa.
COGSWELL (SEDDIE) Tenure, nativity and age as factors in Iowa agriculture, 1850-1880. Ames, Iowa, 1975. pp. 170. *bibliog.*

FARMERS
— Malawi.
CHILIVUMBO (ALIFEYO) Chikwawa Cotton Development Project: a sociological study. [Ngabu, Chikwawa Cotton Development Project, 1970?]. pp. 67.

FARMS
— Canada — Ontario.
NOBLE (HENRY F.) Farmland purchases and financing in Ontario, 1968 to 1971. Toronto, 1975. pp. 14. *(Ontario. Ministry of Agriculture and Food. Economics Branch. Economics Information)*

— Italy.
CONVEGNO SULLA PROPRIETÀ COLTIVATRICE, UDINE, 1972. Convegno sulla proprietà coltivatrice. [Udine, Regione Autonoma Friuli-Venezia Giulia, 1972]. pp. 94.

— United Kingdom.
U.K. Ministry of Agriculture, Fisheries and Food. 1977. The changing structure of agriculture, 1968-1975. London, 1977. pp. 78.

FARMS, COLLECTIVE
— Russia.
DIUKOV (VIKTOR VLADIMIROVICH) Sovershenstvovanie material'nykh uslovii vosproizvodstva rabochei sily v kolkhozakh. Kazan', 1977. pp. 166.

KOCHKAREV (VIKTOR VASIL'EVICH) Rol' v povyshenii effektivnosti kolkhoznogo proizvodstva. Moskva, 1977. pp. 176.

DOLOTOV (ALEKSANDR PAVLOVICH) and SELEZNEV (SERGEI NIKOLAEVICH) Tovarno-denezhnye otnosheniia v kolkhoznom proizvodstve: osobennosti proiavleniia i ispol'zovaniia na sovremennom etape. Moskva, 1978. pp. 167.

KULAZHENKO (VLADIMIR ANDREEVICH) Ekonomicheskie usloviia vosproizvodstva osnovnykh fondov v kolkhozakh. Minsk, 1978. pp. 158.

— — Moldavian Republic.
NOVAKOV (SAVELII ZAKHAROVICH) Ukrupnenie kolkhozov Moldavskoi SSR, 1950-1965. Kishinev, 1978. pp. 176.

FARMS, SIZE OF.
INTERNATIONAL CONFERENCE ON ECONOMIC ANALYSIS IN THE DESIGN OF NEW TECHNOLOGY FOR SMALL FARMERS, 1975. Economics and the design of small-farmer technology; edited by Alberto Valdés [and others]. Ames, 1979. pp. 211. *bibliog.*

— Europe.
HIRSCH (GUENTHER PAUL HERMANN) and MAUNDER (ALLEN HOWARD) Farm amalgamation in Western Europe. Farnborough, Hants., [1978]. pp. 120. *bibliogs.*

FASCISM.
WEBER (EUGEN) Varieties of fascism: doctrines of revolution in the twentieth century. New York, [1964]. pp. 191. *bibliog.*

INTERNATIONALE TAGUNG DER HISTORIKER DER ARBEITERBEWEGUNG, 1974. Arbeiterbewegung und Faschismus; Der Februar 1934 in Österreich; (bearbeitet von Gerhard Botz). Wien, 1976. pp. 464. *(Internationale Tagung der Historiker der Arbeiterbewegung. IH-Tagungsberichte. Band 9)*

BILLIG (MICHAEL) Fascists: a social psychological view of the National Front. London, 1978. pp. 393. *bibliog.* *(European Association of Experimental Social Psychology. European Monographs in Social Psychology. 15)*

— Austria.
RIEDLSPERGER (MAX E.) The lingering shadow of Nazism: the Austrian Independence Party Movement since 1945. Boulder, Colo., 1978. pp. 214. *bibliog.* *(East European Quarterly. East European Monographs. 42)*

— Germany.
FREIER DEUTSCHER GEWERKSCHAFTSBUND. Bundesvorstand. Trade union enemies in judges' robes: a documentation, etc. [Berlin, 1962-63]. 2 vols. (in 1).

THEWELEIT (KLAUS) Männerphantasien. Frankfurt am Main, 1977-78. 2 vols. *bibliog.*

BRODER (HENRYK M.) Deutschland erwacht; mit Beiträgen von: Ossip K. Flechtheim [and others]. Köln, 1978. pp. 135.

POMORIN (JUERGEN) and JUNGE (REINHARD) 1946- . Die Neonazis, und wie man sie bekämpfen kann. Dortmund, 1978. pp. 154.

WAS verschweigt Fest?: Analysen und Dokumente zum Hitler- Film von J.C. Fest; ([edited by] Jörg Berlin [and others]). Köln, [1978]. pp. 217.

— Italy.

GAY (HARRY NELSON) Strenuous Italy: solving a perilous problem. Boston [Mass.], 1927. pp. 217. *bibliog.*

DELZELL (CHARLES F.) Mussolini's enemies: the Italian anti-fascist resistance. New York, 1974. pp. 620. *bibliog.* Reprint of work originally published at Princeton, 1961.

ROSENBAUM (PETRA) Neofaschismus in Italien. Frankfurt, [1975]. pp. 117. *bibliog.*

AMENDOLA (GIOVANNI) L'Aventino contro il fascismo: scritti politici, 1924-1926; a cura di Sabato Visco. Milano, 1976. pp. 402.

MOLINARI (FRANCO) and NERI (VITO) Olio santo e olio di ricino: rapporto su Chiesa e fascismo. Torino, 1976. pp. 143. *bibliogs.*

MICHAELIS (MEIR) Mussolini and the Jews: German-Italian relations and the Jewish question in Italy, 1922-1945. Oxford, 1978. pp. 472. *bibliog.*

ROBERTS (DAVID D.) The syndicalist tradition and Italian fascism. Chapel Hill, N.C., [1979]. pp. 410. *bibliog.*

— United Kingdom.

MOSLEY (Sir OSWALD ERNALD) The greater Britain. new ed. London, [1934]. pp. 191.

RACISM and political action in Britain; edited by Robert Miles and Annie Phizacklea. London, 1979. pp. 246. *bibliogs.* Papers from the Conference on Racism and Political Action in Britain, held by the Social Science Research Council Research Unit on Ethnic Relations, 1977.

— — Bibliography.

REES (PHILIP) compiler. Fascism in Britain: [an annotated bibliography]. Hassocks, 1979. pp. 243.

FATHER-SEPARATED CHILDREN.

CASSETTY (JUDITH) Child support and public policy: securing support from absent fathers. Lexington, Mass., [1978]. pp. 171.

FEAR.

TRESEMER (DAVID WARD) Fear of success. New York, [1977]. pp. 245. *bibliog.*

FEDERAL AID TO HIGHER EDUCATION

— United States.

FINN (CHESTER E.) Scholars, dollars, and bureaucrats. Washington, D.C., [1978]. pp. 238. *(Brookings Institution. Studies in Higher Education Policy. 2)*

FEDERAL AID TO THE ARTS

— United States.

NETZER (DICK) The subsidized muse: public support for the arts in the United States. Cambridge, 1978. pp. 289. *bibliog.* Twentieth Century Fund study.

FEDERAL-CITY RELATIONS

— United States.

FUNIGIELLO (PHILIP J.) The challenge to urban liberalism: federal-city relations during World War II. Knoxville, [1978]. pp. 273. *bibliog.*

FEDERAL GOVERNMENT.

POLITICAL and administrative federalism; [by] R.M. Burns [and others]. Canberra, 1976. pp. 113. *(Australian National University. Centre for Research on Federal Financial Relations. Research Monographs. No. 14)* Papers presented at seminars at the Centre for Research on Federal Financial Relations, 1975.

HICKS (URSULA KATHLEEN) Federalism: failure and success: a comparative study. London, 1978. pp. 205.

— Canada.

BETTISON (DAVID G.) The politics of Canadian urban development. Edmonton, 1975. pp. 337. *bibliog.*

FEDERALISM: central/regional relations. Edinburgh, [1975?]. 1 vol. (various foliations). *(Edinburgh. University. Centre of Canadian Studies. Seminar Papers. No. 1)*

ALBERTA. 1978. Harmony in diversity: a new federalism for Canada; Alberta government position paper on constitutional change. [Edmonton], 1978. pp. 40.

COLAS (EMILE) La troisième voie: une nouvelle constitution. [Ottawa, 1978]. pp. 246. *bibliog.*

OUTLOOK AND ISSUES SEMINAR, KINGSTON, ONTARIO, 1977. Issues in intergovernmental relations. Toronto, [1978]. pp. 32. *(Ontario. Economic Council. Discussion Paper Series)*

ONTARIO. Advisory Committee on Confederation. 1979. Second report...: the federal-provincial distribution of powers; [H.I. Macdonald, chairman]. [Toronto], 1979. pp. 77,85. *In English and French.*

RAWLYK (GEORGE A.) and others. Regionalism in Canada: flexible federalism or fractured nation? Scarborough, Ont., [1979]. pp. 244. *bibliog.*

— Germany.

TEPPE (KARL) Provinz, Partei, Staat: zur provinziellen Selbstverwaltung im Dritten Reich, untersucht am Beispiel Westfalens. Münster in Westfalen, 1977. pp. 300. *bibliog.* *(Historische Kommission für Westfalen. Veröffentlichungen. 38)*

— Malaysia.

HOLZHAUSEN (WALTER) Federal finance in Malaysia: the theory and problems of federal/state government financial relations in a developing country. Kuala Lumpur, 1974. pp. 196. *bibliog.*

— United States.

BURNS (JAMES MACGREGOR) and others. State and local politics: government by the people. 2nd ed. Englewood Cliffs, N.J., [1978]. pp. 289.

FEDERAL PARTY.

BROUSSARD (JAMES H.) The Southern Federalists, 1800-1816. Baton Rouge, [1978]. pp. 438. *bibliog.*

FEDERAL RESERVE BANKS.

HYMAN (SIDNEY) Marriner S. Eccles: private entrepreneur and public servant. Stanford, Calif., 1976. pp. 456.

FEDERATION OF RHODESIA AND NYASALAND.

RHODESIA AND NYASALAND IN BRIEF [pd. by] Federal Public Relations Division. a., 1959, 1963. Salisbury.

FEES, PROFESSIONAL

— Canada — Quebec.

QUEBEC (PROVINCE). Office des Professions. 1978. Professional fees in private practice: the question of regulation; report etc. [Quebec, 1978]. 2 vols.

FEMINISM.

FRIEDAN (BETTY) The feminine mystique. London, 1971. pp. 410. *bibliog.*

EASTMAN (CRYSTAL) On women and revolution; edited by Blanche Wiesen Cook. New York, 1978. pp. 388.

WOMEN united, women divided: cross-cultural perspectives on female solidarity; edited by Patricia Caplan and Janet M. Bujra. London, 1978. pp. 288. *bibliogs.*

SEX roles and social policy: a complex social science equation; edited by Jean Lipman-Blumen and Jessie Bernard. London, [1979]. pp. 404. *bibliogs.*

— Bibliography.

KRICHMAR (ALBERT) and others, compilers. The women's movement in the seventies: an international English-language bibliography. Metuchen, N.J., 1977. pp. 875.

— Europe.

SOCIALIST women: European socialist feminism in the nineteenth and early twentieth centuries; edited by Marilyn J. Boxer and Jean H. Quataert. New York, [1978]. pp. 260. *bibliog.*

— France.

LAOT (JEANNETTE) Stratégie pour les femmes; en collaboration avec Dominique Pélegrin. [Paris, 1977]. pp. 250.

ZYLBERBERG-HOCQUARD (MARIE HELENE) Féminisme et syndicalisme en France. Paris, 1978. pp. 199.

— Russia.

CLEMENTS (BARBARA EVANS) Bolshevik feminist: the life of Aleksandra Kollontai. Bloomington, 1979. pp. 352. *bibliog.*

— United Kingdom.

MALMGREEN (GAIL) Neither bread nor roses: Utopian feminists and the English working class, 1800-1850. Brighton, 1978. pp. 44.

HOLLIS (PATRICIA) Women in public, 1850-1900: documents of the Victorian women's movement. London, 1979. pp. 331.

PANKHURST (RICHARD KEIR PETHICK) Sylvia Pankhurst: artist and crusader. New York, [1979]. pp. 224.

— United States.

HERSH (BLANCHE GLASSMAN) The slavery of sex: feminist-abolitionists in America. Urbana, Ill., [1978]. pp. 280. *bibliog.*

WOMEN'S studies: an interdisciplinary collection; edited by Kathleen O'Connor Blumhagen and Walter D. Johnson. Westport, Conn., [1978]. pp. 142. *bibliogs.*

SCHRAMM (SARAH SLAVIN) Plow women rather than reapers: an intellectual history of feminism in the United States. Metuchen, N.J., 1979. pp. 441. *bibliog.*

FERMAT'S THEOREM.

EDWARDS (HAROLD M.) Fermat's last theorem: a genetic introduction to algebraic number theory. New York, [1977]. pp. 410. *bibliog.*

FERRARA (PROVINCE)

— History.

BAGNOLATI (LUIGI) Origini della Federazione Comunista Ferrarese: memorie e documenti; a cura dell'Istituto di Storia Contemporanea del Movimento Operaio e Contadino di Ferrara. Modena, [1976]. pp. 159.

FERRER Y GUARDIA (FRANCISCO).

FRANCISCO FERRER anarchiste: la grève générale; articles écrits par Ferrer ou en collaboration avec Anselmo Lorenzo. Paris, 1934. pp. 28.

FERTILITY, HUMAN.

FORTY years of research in human fertility: retrospect and prospect; [edited by] Clyde V. Kiser. New York, [1971]. pp. 254. *bibliogs.* Published as Vol. XLIX, No.4, Part 2 of the Milbank Memorial Fund Quarterly.

WORLD FERTILITY SURVEY. Annual report. a., 1972/75 (1st issue)- Voorburg.

WORLD FERTILITY SURVEY. Occasional Papers. Voorburg, 1973 in progress.

FERTILITY, HUMAN.(Cont.)

SIMON (JULIAN LINCOLN) The effects of income on fertility. Chapel Hill, [1974]. pp. 210. *bibliog.* (*North Carolina University. Carolina Population Center. Monographs. [No.] 19*)

WORLD FERTILITY SURVEY. Basic Documentation. Voorburg, 1975 in progress.

WORLD FERTILITY SURVEY. Technical Bulletins. Voorburg, 1976 in progress.

WORLD FERTILITY SURVEY. Scientific Reports. Voorburg, 1977 in progress.

WORLD FERTILITY SURVEY. Summary of Findings. Voorburg, 1977 in progress.

CONFERENCE ON SOCIAL DEMOGRAPHY, MADISON, 1975. Social demography; edited by Karl E. Taeuber, Larry L. Bumpass, James A. Sweet. New York, [1978]. pp. 336. *bibliogs.*

— Bangladesh.

BANGLADESH. Population Control and Family Planning Division. 1978. World Fertility Survey: Bangladesh Fertility Survey, 1975- 1976: first report. [Dacca], 1978. 1 vol. (various pagings)

— Belgium.

LESTHAEGHE (RON J.) The decline of Belgian fertility, 1800-1970. Princeton, N.J., [1977]. pp. 259. *bibliogs.*

— Fiji.

FIJI. Bureau of Statistics, 1976. Fiji fertility survey, 1974: principal report. Suva, 1976. pp. 563.

— India — Bombay.

SOVANI (NILKANTH VITHAL) and DANDEKAR (KUMUDINI) Fertility survey of Nasik, Kolaba and Satara (North) districts. Poona, 1955. pp. 167. (*Gokhale Institute of Politics and Economics. Publications. No.31*) With ms. review by Vera Anstey.

— Indonesia.

INDONESIA. Biro Pusat Statistik. 1978. Indonesia fertility survey, 1976: principal report. Jakarta, 1978. 2 vols. (in 1).

— Korea.

KOREA (REPUBLIC). National Bureau of Statistics. 1977. The Korean national fertility survey: first country report. Seoul, 1977. 1 vol. (various pagings).

— Nepal.

NEPAL FAMILY PLANNING AND MATERNAL CHILD HEALTH PROJECT. Nepal fertility survey, 1976: first report. Kathmandu, 1977. pp. 347.

— Netherlands.

NETHERLANDS. Centraal Bureau voor de Statistiek. 1974. Regionale huwelijksvruchtbaarheidsverschillen, 1959/1961, 1967/1968, 1971/1972. 's-Gravenhage, 1974. pp. 21. *Map transparency and list of economic-geographical regions in end pocket.*

— Pakistan.

PAKISTAN. Population Planning Council. 1976. World fertility survey: Pakistan fertility survey: first report. [Islamabad], 1976. 1 vol. (various pagings). *bibliog.*

— South Africa.

HIGGINS (EDWARD) A study of some norms and values pertaining to fertility in an urban white population. [Johannesburg], 1960. pp. 266. *bibliog. Dissertation presented to the University of the Witwatersrand for the degree of Master of Arts, 1960.*

LÖTTER (JOHANN MORGENDALL) and VAN TONDER (JAN LOUIS) Aspects of fertility of Indian South Africans. Pretoria, 1975. pp. 37. *bibliog.* (*Human Sciences Research Council [South Africa] . Institute for Sociological, Demographic and Criminological Research. Reports. No. S-40*)

LÖTTER (JOHANN MORGENDALL) and VAN TONDER (JAN LOUIS) Fertility and family planning among blacks in South Africa: 1974;...translated by C.P. Kleyn. Pretoria, 1976. pp. 111. *bibliog.* (*Human Sciences Research Council [South Africa] . Institute for Sociological, Demographic and Criminological Research. Reports. No. S-39*)

— Sri Lanka.

SRI LANKA. Department of Census and Statistics. 1978. World Fertitlity Survey, Sri Lanka, 1975: first report. [Colombo], 1978. pp. 713.

— Thailand.

CHULALONGKORN UNIVERSITY. Institute of Population Studies. The survey of fertility in Thailand: country report; a joint project of [the] Institute...[and] Population Survey Division, National Statistical Office. Bangkok, 1977. 2 vols. (in 1) (*World Fertility Survey. Reports. No. 1*)

— United Kingdom.

U.K. Census, 1971. Census, 1971: England and Wales: fertility tables. London, 1979. 3 vols.(in 1).

U.K. Social Survey. [Reports. New Series]. 1080. Family formation 1976: a survey carried out on behalf of Population Statistics Division 1 of the Office of Population Censuses and Surveys of a sample of women, both single and ever married, aged 16-49 in Great Britain; [by] Karen Dunnell. London, 1979. pp. 117.

— United States.

ZERO population growth - for whom?: differential fertility and minority group survival; edited by Milton Himmelfarb and Victor Baras. Westport, 1978. pp. 213. *Proceedings of a conference held by the American Jewish Committee in 1975, in New York.*

FERTILIZERS AND MANURES

— Prices — India.

NATIONAL COUNCIL OF APPLIED ECONOMIC RESEARCH. The impact of the price rise in petroleum based agricultural inputs on the production of wheat and rice in India; a study prepared for the Commonwealth Secretariat;...[directed by] I.Z. Bhatty. London, Commonwealth Secretariat, [1976]. pp. 74. (*Commonwealth Economic Papers. No. 6*)

FEST (JOACHIM).

WAS verschweigt Fest?: Analysen und Dokumente zum Hitler- Film von J.C. Fest; ([edited by] Jörg Berlin [and others]). Köln, [1978]. pp. 217.

FEUDALISM.

SLAVIANE v epokhu feodalizma: k stoletiiu akademika V.I. Pichety. Moskva, 1978. pp. 343.

— Europe.

BLUM (JEROME) The end of the old order in rural Europe. Princeton, 1978. pp. 505. *bibliog.*

— Russia.

ZIMIN (ALEKSANDR ALEKSANDROVICH) Krupnaia feodal'naia votchina i sotsial'no-politicheskaia bor'ba v Rossii, konets XV - XVI v. Moskva, 1977. pp. 356.

FIBRES.

TISDELL (CLEMENT ALLAN) and McDONALD (PAUL W.) Economics of fibre markets: a global view of the interdependence between man-made fibres, wool and cotton. Oxford, 1979. pp. 261. *bibliogs.*

FIGUEIREDO (AFONSO CELSO DE ASSIS) Visconde de Ouro Preto.

FIGUEIREDO (AFONSO CELSO DE ASSIS) Visconde de Ouro Preto. Discursos parlamentares; seleção, introdução e comentarios de Costa Porto. Brasilia, 1978. pp. 516. (*Brazil. Congresso. Câmara dos Deputados. Perfis Parlamentares. 5*)

FIJI.

FIJI. 1957. Colony of Fiji: a handbook; revised and edited by Ravuama Vunivalu. 6th ed. Suva, 1957. pp. 122, 1 map. *bibliog.*

— Administrative and political divisions.

FIJI. Constituency Boundaries Commission. 1971. An account of the work of the Commission, March-July 1971. Suva, 1971. pp. 47.

— Politics and government.

NORTON (ROBERT) Race and politics in Fiji. New York, [1977]. pp. 210. *bibliog.*

— Race relations.

NORTON (ROBERT) Race and politics in Fiji. New York, [1977]. pp. 210. *bibliog.*

MAMAK (ALEXANDER) Colour, culture and conflict: a study of pluralism in Fiji. Rushcutters Bay, 1978. pp. 203. *bibliog.*

— Social conditions.

MAMAK (ALEXANDER) Colour, culture and conflict: a study of pluralism in Fiji. Rushcutters Bay, 1978. pp. 203. *bibliog.*

FILMER (Sir ROBERT).

DALY (JAMES) Sir Robert Filmer and English political thought. Toronto, [1979]. pp. 212. *bibliog.*

FINANCE.

FEDOROWICZ (ZDZISŁAW) Financial planning. Warsaw, 1977. pp. 70. (*Instytut Gospodarki Krajów Rozwijających Się. Teaching Papers: Advanced Course in National Economic Planning. vol. 25*)

BROWN (CHARLES VICTOR) and JACKSON (PETER McLEOD) Public sector economics. Oxford, 1978. pp. 452. *bibliog.*

CONFERENCE ON FEDERAL FISCAL RESPONSIBILITY, HOT SPRINGS, VIRGINIA, 1976. Fiscal responsibility in constitutional democracy; [papers and discussion presented at the conference; edited by] James M. Buchanan and Richard E. Wagner. Leiden, 1978. pp. 180. (*Center for Study of Public Choice. Studies in Public Choice. 1*)

ESSAYS in public economics: the Kiryat Anavim papers; edited by Agnar Sandmo. Lexington, Mass., [1978]. pp. 367. *bibliogs. Papers of a conference held at Kibbutz Kiryat Anavim, 1975.*

LINDHOLM (RICHARD WADSWORTH) Money management and institutions. Totowa, N.J., 1978. pp. 434. *bibliogs.*

ORGANISATION FOR ECONOMIC CO-OPERATION AND DEVELOPMENT. Department of Economics and Statistics. 1978. Budget indicators; [by the Monetary and Fiscal Policy Division; and] The international competitiveness of selected OECD countries; [by the Balance of Payments Division]. Paris, 1978. pp. 52. (*OECD Economic Outlook. Occasional Studies*)

THAVARAJ (M.J.K.) Financial management of government. New Delhi, [1978]. pp. 928. *bibliog.*

VICKERS (DOUGLAS WILLIAM) Financial markets in the capitalist process. Philadelphia, 1978. pp. 180.

CARGILL (THOMAS F.) Money, the financial system, and monetary policy. Englewood Cliffs, [1979]. pp. 552. *bibliogs.*

CURRENT issues in fiscal policy; edited by S.T. Cook and P.M. Jackson. Oxford, 1979. pp. 230. *bibliog.*

PREST (ALAN RICHMOND) and BARR (NICHOLAS A.) Public finance in theory and practice. 6th ed. London, 1979. pp. 552. *bibliogs.*

THOMAS (LLOYD BREWSTER) Money, banking, and economic activity. Englewood Cliffs, N.J., [1979]. pp. 626.

FINANCE.

— **Mathematical models.**

ZIEMBA (W.T.) and VICKSON (R.G.) eds. Stochastic optimization models in finance. New York, [1975]. pp. 719. *bibliogs.*

STOCHASTIC dominance: an approach to decision-making under risk; edited by G.A. Whitmore [and] M.C. Findlay. Lexington, Mass., [1978]. pp. 401. *bibliog.*

— **Africa.**

INTERNATIONAL MONETARY FUND. Surveys of African Economies. Vol. 7. Algeria, Mali, Morocco, and Tunisia. Washington, 1977. pp. 374.

BRETON (JEAN MARIE) Le contrôle d'état sur le continent africain: contribution à une théorie des contrôles administratifs et financiers dans les pays en voie de développement. Paris, 1978. pp. 532. *bibliog.*

— **Australia.**

AUSTRALIA. Department of the Capital Territory. 1973. Inquiry into the proportion of municipal and state-type costs which should be met by the A[ustralian] C[apital] T[erritory] community: supplementary statement of evidence for presentation to the Joint Committee on the Australian Capital Territory. [Canberra], 1973. pp. 65.

— **Austria.**

BRANDT (HARM HINRICH) Der österreichische Neoabsolutismus: Staatsfinanzen und Politik, 1848-1860. Göttingen, 1978. 2 vols. *bibliog.* (Bayerische Akademie der Wissenschaften. Historische Kommission. Schriftenreihe. Schrift 15)

— **Barbados — Statistics.**

CENTRAL BANK OF BARBADOS. Annual statistical digest. a., 1976(2nd)- Bridgetown.

— **Bermuda.**

BERMUDA MONETARY AUTHORITY. Report and accounts (formerly Final accounts and annual report). a., 1972, 1975- Hamilton.

— **Brazil — Rio de Janeiro (City).**

ARAUJO (ALOISIO BARBOSA DE) Aspectos fiscais das areas metropolitanas. Rio de Janeiro, 1974. pp. 125. *(Brazil. Instituto de Planejamento Econômico e Social. Instituto de Pesquisas. Monografias. No. 15)*

— — **São Paulo (City).**

ARAUJO (ALOISIO BARBOSA DE) Aspectos fiscais das areas metropolitanas. Rio de Janeiro, 1974. pp. 125. *(Brazil. Instituto de Planejamento Econômico e Social. Instituto de Pesquisas. Monografias. No. 15)*

— **Canada.**

NIOSI (JORGE) Le contrôle financier du capitalisme canadien. Montréal, 1978. pp. 217. *bibliog.*

PATTISON (JOHN CHARLES) Financial markets and foreign ownership. [Toronto, 1978]. pp. 143. *bibliog.* (Ontario. Economic Council. Occasional Papers. 8)

— — **Accounting.**

CANADA. Statistics Canada. System of national accounts: provincial economic accounts: experimental data: the annual estimates. a., 1961/1976(1st)- Ottawa. *[in English and French]*

— — **Ontario.**

FOOT (DAVID K.) Provincial public finance in Ontario: an empirical analysis of the last twenty-five years. Toronto, [1977]. pp. 213. *bibliog.* (Ontario. Economic Council. Research Studies. 12)

— — — **Mathematical models.**

FOOT (DAVID K.) Provincial public finance in Ontario: an empirical analysis of the last twenty-five years. Toronto, [1977]. pp. 213. *bibliog.* (Ontario. Economic Council. Research Studies. 12)

— **Chile.**

CHILE. Superintendencia de Bancos e Instituciones Financieras. Informacion financiera. m., Oc 1978- Santiago. *Supersedes CHILE. Superintendencia de Bancos. Boletin estadistico and CHILE. Superintendencia de Bancos. Estadistica bancaria.*

— **European Economic Community countries.**

MORGAN (EDWARD VICTOR) and HARRINGTON (RICHARD) Capital markets in the EEC: the sources and uses of medium- and long-term finance. Farnborough, 1977. pp. 495. *bibliog. Published for the Economists Advisory Group.*

EUROPEAN COMMUNITIES. Commission. 1978. Preliminary draft general budget of the European Communities for the financial year 1979: general introduction; sent to the Council...on 13 June 1978, and subsequently amended by the letter of amendment of 18 September 1978. [Brussels, 1978]. pp. 98. *(Bulletin of the European Communities. Supplements. [1978/6])*

— **France.**

HARRIS (ROBERT D.) Necker: reform statesman of the ancien régime. Berkeley, Calif., [1979]. pp. 259. *bibliog.*

— **Hong Kong.**

HO (H.C.Y.) The fiscal system of Hong Kong. London, [1979]. pp. 182. *bibliogs.*

— **India.**

MISRA (BABU RAM) Indian federal finance. 3rd ed. Bombay, 1960. pp. 463. *bibliog.*

SEMINAR ON FINANCING OF SMALL-SCALE INDUSTRIES IN INDIA, HYDERABAD, 1959. Report of proceedings ([and] background papers). Bombay, [1960?]. 2 vols.

THAVARAJ (M.J.K.) Financial management of government. New Delhi, [1978]. pp. 928. *bibliog.*

— — **Madhya Pradesh.**

SIVARAMAN (M.R.) and CHAUBAL (C.T.) A study of the finances of the government of Madhya Pradesh. [Bhopal], Finance Department, [1977]. 2 vols. (in 1) *bibliog.*

— **Ireland (Republic).**

FANNING (RONAN) The Irish Department of Finance, 1922-58. Dublin, [1978]. pp. 707. *bibliog.*

— **Israel.**

GLASS (MOSES MICHAEL) Die Beeinflussung der israelischen Volkswirtschaft durch die Fiskalpolitik in den Jahren 1960-1974: Versuch einer strukturell-quantitativen Analyse. [Zürich], 1977. pp. 270. *bibliog. Dissertation - Universität Zürich.*

— **Italy.**

VANONI (EZIO) Scritti di finanza pubblica e di politica economica; a cura di Antonino Tramontana. Padova, 1976. pp. 219. *(Perugia. Università. Facoltà di Giurisprudenza. Pubblicazioni)*

— **Ivory Coast.**

REVUE ECONOMIQUE ET FINANCIERE IVOIRIENNE; [pd.by] Ministère de l'Economie, des Finances et du Plan [Ivory Coast]. bi-m., Jl 1978(no.1)- Abidjan.

— **Japan.**

BANK OF JAPAN. Economic Research Department. The Japanese financial system. [Tokyo?], 1978. pp. 154.

— **Mexico — Bibliography.**

SIERRA BRABATA (CARLOS J.) and MARTINEZ VERA (ROGELIO) compilers. Bibliografia de la hacienda publica. Mexico, 1972-74. 3 vols. (in 1)

— **Norway — Accounting.**

NORWAY. Statistiske Centralbyrå. Kredittmarkedstatistikk: finansielle sektorbalanser. a., 1971/1976- Oslo. *[in English and Norwegian] Supersedes in part NORWAY. Statistiske Centralbyrå. Kredittmarkedstatistikk.*

— **Peru.**

MELENA G. (GERMAN DE LA) La reforma financiera, octubre 1968 - octubre 1973. Lima, 1973. pp. 312.

PERU. Comision del Estudio de Fuentes y Usos de Fondos de la Economia del Peru. 1973. Estudio de fuentes y usos de fondos: avances y evaluacion a diciembre de 1972. [Lima], 1973. 3 vols. *bibliog.*

— **Qatar.**

QATAR MONETARY AGENCY. Monetary and financial report. a., 1977(1st)- Doha. *[in English and Arabic]*

— **Russia.**

FINANSOVAIA GAZETA (formerly Ekonomicheskaia zhizn'); [pd.by] Ministerstvo Finansov [Russia (USSR)]. d., N 11 1918 - Je 13 1941, with gaps. Moskva.

PROBLEMY razvitiia sotsialisticheskikh finansov. Moskva, 1977. pp. 414.

— **Singapore.**

CHEW (DAVID B.H.) Banking and finance. 2nd ed. [Singapore, 1973]. pp. 107.

— **Spain.**

CANSECO CANSECO (JOSE EMILIO) Politica fiscal de España: estudio de la politica economica publica española desde el plan de estabilizacion. Madrid, Instituto de Estudios Fiscales, 1978. pp. 691. *bibliog.*

— **Underdeveloped areas.**

See UNDERDEVELOPED AREAS — Finance.

— **United Kingdom.**

HUGHES (DOROTHY) A study of social and constitutional tendencies in the early years of Edward III, as illustrated more especially by the events connected with the ministerial inquiries of 1340 and the following years. Philadelphia, 1978. pp. 245. *bibliog. Reprint of work originally published London, 1915.*

The ECONOMICS of politics;...[by] James M. Buchanan [and others]. [London], 1978. pp. 192. *bibliogs. (Institute of Economic Affairs. Readings. 18)*

PREST (ALAN RICHMOND) Intergovernmental financial relations in the United Kingdom. Canberra, 1978. pp. 118. *bibliog. (Australian National University. Centre for Research on Federal Financial Relations. Research Monographs. No. 23)*

HOCKLEY (GRAHAM CHARLES) Public finance: an introduction. rev. ed. London, 1979. pp. 448. *bibliog.*

PREST (ALAN RICHMOND) and BARR (NICHOLAS A.) Public finance in theory and practice. 6th ed. London, 1979. pp. 552. *bibliogs.*

U.K. Home Office. 1977. The Home Office. [London, 1977]. fo. 29. *Photocopy.*

— — **Bibliography.**

U.K. Treasury. 1979. Guide to public sector financial information. No.1, 1979; editors: part 1: P.R. Money; part 2: E.A. Thomas. London, 1979. pp. 108. *bibliog.*

— — **Mathematical models.**

PRICE (R.W.R.) Modelling fiscal policy: the personal income tax system. London, [1978]. pp. 22. *bibliog. (National Institute of Economic and Social Research. Discussion Papers. No. 22)*

FINANCE.(Cont.)

— — London.

CANNING TOWN COMMUNITY DEVELOPMENT PROJECT. How important are industrial rates? [London, 1976?]. pp. 27.

— United States.

HENDERSHOTT (PATRIC H.) and others. Understanding capital markets. Lexington, Mass., [1977]. 2 vols. *bibliogs.*

WINTER (PIETER JAN VAN) American finance and Dutch investment, 1780-1805; with an epilogue to 1840;...English adaptation of the revised version of the original Dutch edition...by James C. Riley. New York, 1977. 2 vols. *bibliog.*

JAMES (JOHN A.) Money and capital markets in postbellum America. Princeton, N.J., [1978]. pp. 293. *bibliog.*

JONES (FRANK JOSEPH) Macrofinance: the financial system and the economy. Cambridge, Mass., [1978]. pp. 310. *bibliogs.*

SAMETZ (ARNOLD WILLIAM) Prospects for capital formation and capital markets: financial requirements over the next decade. Lexington, Mass., [1978]. pp. 145. *bibliog.*

COCHRAN (JOHN A.) Money, banking, and the economy. 4th ed. New York, [1979]. pp. 588. *bibliogs.*

— — New York (State).

The DECLINING Northeast: demographic and economic analyses; edited by Benjamin Chinitz. New York, [1978]. pp. 182. *bibliogs.*

— Upper Volta.

UPPER VOLTA. Ministère des Finances et du Commerce. 1972. Qu'est-ce que le Ministère des Finances et du Commerce? Ouagadougou, 1972. pp. 112. *(Opération Portes Ouvertes. Documents. 1)*

FINANCIAL INSTITUTIONS.

LINDHOLM (RICHARD WADSWORTH) Money management and institutions. Totowa, N.J., 1978. pp. 434. *bibliogs.*

— Canada.

NIOSI (JORGE) The economy of Canada: a study of ownership and control; translated by Penelope Williams. Montréal, [1978]. pp. 179. *bibliog.*

— France.

HAUMONT (BERNARD) Le tertiaire financier à Paris. [Paris], 1968. 2 vols.

— United Kingdom.

U.K. Committee to Review the Functioning of Financial Institutions. 1979- . Second stage evidence; (chairman: Sir Harold Wilson). London, 1979 in progress.

FINANCIAL INSTITUTIONS, INTERNATIONAL.

The COMMON fund: papers prepared for Commonwealth Technical Group. London, Commonwealth Secretariat, 1977. 2 vols. *bibliog. (Commonwealth Economic Papers. No. 8)*

COMMONWEALTH TECHNICAL GROUP ON THE COMMON FUND. The common fund: report of the Commonwealth Technical Group; [Lord Campbell of Eskan, chairman]. London, Commonwealth Secretariat, 1977. pp. 84.

FINANCIAL STATEMENTS.

FOSTER (GEORGE) Financial statement analysis. Englewood Cliffs, [1978]. pp. 581.

TAMARI (M.) Financial ratios: analysis and prediction. London, 1978. pp. 182. *bibliog.*

TRENDS in managerial and financial accounting: income determination and financial reporting; Cees van Dam, editor. Leiden, 1978. pp. 221. *bibliogs. 11 papers from a research seminar 'Decision-making in business', held at Nijenrode, 1976.*

— United Kingdom.

PLATT (C.J.) Survey of company reports: an analysis of current practices in presenting information. Farnborough, [1978]. pp. 125.

— United States.

FINANCIAL ACCOUNTING STANDARDS BOARD. Tentative conclusions on objectives of financial statements of business enterprises. Stamford, Conn., 1976. pp. 78.

FINANCIAL ACCOUNTING STANDARDS BOARD. Discussion Memoranda. An analysis of issues related to conceptual framework for financial accounting and reporting: elements of financial statements and their measurement. Stamford, Conn., 1976. pp. 360. *Includes a book on Scope and implications of the conceptual framework project.*

FINITE ELEMENT METHOD.

MITCHELL (ANDREW R.) and WAIT (R.) The finite element method in partial differential equations. Chichester, 1977. pp. 198. *bibliog.*

FINLAND.

— Commerce.

ÖLLER (LARS ERIK) Time series analysis of Finnish foreign trade. Helsinki, 1978. 1 vol.(various pagings). *bibliog. (Suomen Tilastoseura. Tilastotieteellisiä Tutkimuksia. 3)*

— Constitutional history.

THIBAUT (FRANÇOISE) La Finlande. Paris, [1978]. pp. 382. *bibliog.*

— Economic conditions.

SOCIAL structure and change: Finland and Poland: comparative perspective; edited by Erik Allardt and Włodzimierz Wesołowski. Warszawa, 1978. pp. 392.

— Foreign relations — Germany.

UEBERSCHAER (GERD R.) Hitler und Finnland, 1939-1941: die deutsch-finnischen Beziehungen während des Hitler-Stalin-Paktes. Wiesbaden, 1978. pp. 376. *bibliog.*

— — Russia.

PUNASALO (V.I.) The reality of Finlandisation: living under the Soviet shadow. London, 1978. pp. 15. *bibliog. (Institute for the Study of Conflict. Conflict Studies. No.93)*

— Government publications — Bibliography.

FINLAND. Tilastokeskus. Valtion tilastojulkaisut. a., 1977- Helsinki. *[in English, Finnish and Swedish]*

— History.

KIRBY (DAVID G.) Finland in the twentieth century. London, 1979. pp. 253. *bibliog.*

— Industries.

FINLAND. Tilastokeskus. Teollisuuden yritystilasto: TOL 2,3,4. a., 1974- Helsinki. *[in Finnish and Swedish with English summary]*

— Politics and government.

PUNASALO (V.I.) The reality of Finlandisation: living under the Soviet shadow. London, 1978. pp. 15. *bibliog. (nstitute for the Study of Conflict. Conflict Studies. No.93)*

SOCIAL structure and change: Finland and Poland: comparative perspective; edited by Erik Allardt and Włodzimierz Wesołowski. Warszawa, 1978. pp. 392.

THIBAUT (FRANÇOISE) La Finlande. Paris, [1978]. pp. 382. *bibliog.*

— Population.

FINLAND. Tilastokeskus. Väesto. a., 1976- Helsinki. *In 2 parts, v.1, Väestorake ne ja väestönmuutokset: Koko maa ja laänit, v.2, Väestorakenne ja väestonmuutokset kunnittain. Supersedes FINLAND. Tilastokeskus. Väestönmuutokset.*

— Presidents — Election.

FINLAND. Tilastokeskus. Valtiolliset vaalit: tasavallan presidentin valitsijamiesten vaalit. a., 1978- Helsinki. *[in Finnish and Swedish with English summary and table headings].*

— Relations (general) with Russia.

KORONEN (MATVEI MATVEEVICH) V.I. Lenin i Finliandiia. Leningrad, 1977. pp. 311. *bibliog.*

BARTEN'EV (T.) and KOMISSAROV (IU.) SSSR - Finliandiia: orientiry sotrudnichestva. Moskva, 1978. pp. 118.

— Social conditions.

MIEMOIS (KARL JOHAN) Changes in the social structure of the Swedish-speaking population of Finland, 1950-1970. Helsinki, 1978. pp. 37. *bibliog. (Helsinki. Yliopisto. Research Group for Comparative Sociology. Research Reports. No. 19)*

SOCIAL structure and change: Finland and Poland: comparative perspective; edited by Erik Allardt and Włodzimierz Wesołowski. Warszawa, 1978. pp. 392.

— Statistics — Bibliography.

FINLAND. Tilastokeskus. Valtion tilastojulkaisut. a., 1977- Helsinki. *[in English, Finnish and Swedish]*

— Statistics, Vital.

FINLAND. Tilastokeskus. Väesto. a., 1976- Helsinki. *In 2 parts, v.1, Väestorake ne ja väestönmuutokset: Koko maa ja laänit, v.2, Väestorakenne ja väestonmuutokset kunnittain. Supersedes FINLAND. Tilastokeskus. Väestönmuutokset.*

FINNESBURH.

CHAMBERS (RAYMOND WILSON) Beowulf: an introduction to the study of the poem with a discussion of the stories of Offa and Finn;...with a supplement by C.L. Wrenn. 3rd ed. Cambridge, 1959 repr. 1972. pp. 628. *bibliogs.*

FINNISH AMERICANS.

KARNI (MICHAEL G.) and others. For the common good: Finnish immigrants and the radical response to industrial America. Superior, Wis., [1977]. pp. 235. *bibliogs.*

FIRE DEPARTMENTS

— Hong Kong.

HONG KONG. Fire Services. Annual departmental report by the Director. a., 1976- Hong Kong.

— United Kingdom — Ireland, Northern.

FIRE AUTHORITY FOR NORTHERN IRELAND. Statement of accounts. a., 1973/74 [1st]- Belfast.

FIRMS.

PARENT (JEAN) Les firmes industrielles. Paris, [1975-78]. 2 vols. *bibliog.*

TIVEY (LEONARD J.) The politics of the firm. Oxford, 1978. pp. 196. *bibliog.*

WILLIAMS (PHILIP LAURENCE) The emergence of the theory of the firm: from Adam Smith to Alfred Marshall. London, 1978. pp. 207.

— History — India.

DUNCAN (WALTER) AND GOODRICKE. The Duncan Group: being a short history of Duncan Brothers and Co. Ltd., Calcutta and Walter Duncan and Goodricke Ltd., London, 1859-1959. London, 1959. pp. 184. *The first ten chapters were originally printed for private circulation in 1931.*

— — Netherlands.

TEULINGS (AD) Philips: geschiedenis en praktijk van een wereldconcern. Amsterdam, 1977. pp. 325. *bibliog.*

— — Sweden.

L.M. Ericsson 100 years; [by] Artur Attman [and others]. [Stockholm?, 1977]. 3 vols.

— — United Kingdom.

DUNCAN (WALTER) AND GOODRICKE. The Duncan Group: being a short history of Duncan Brothers and Co. Ltd., Calcutta and Walter Duncan and Goodricke Ltd., London, 1859-1959. London, 1959. pp. 184. *The first ten chapters were originally printed for private circulation in 1931.*

RAW (CHARLES) Slater Walker: an investigation of a financial phenomenon. London, 1977. pp. 368.

HILL (HOWARD) Secret ingredient: the story of Fletchers' seven bakeries. Wakefield, 1978. pp. 94.

GRINYER (PETER HUGH) and SPENDER (J.C.) Turnaround: managerial recipes for strategic success; the fall and rise of the Newton Chambers group. London, 1979. pp. 211.

— — United States.

STEHMAN (JONAS WARREN) The financial history of the American Telephone and Telegraph Company. New York, 1967. pp. 339. *bibliog. Reprint of work originally published Boston, 1925.*

NEWCOMEN SOCIETY IN NORTH AMERICA. Newcomen Addresses. [Histories of businesses in the United States]. New York, 1947-1974. 610 parts.

GALLAGHER (EDWARD A.) Getting the message across: the story of Western Union International, Inc. New York, 1971. pp. 24. (Newcomen Society in North America. Newcomen Addresses. 1971)

— European Economic Community countries.

DREW (JOHN) Writer on international affairs. Doing business in the European Community. London, 1979. pp. 280. *bibliogs.*

— Sweden.

ERIKSSON (GÖRAN) Growth and finance of the firm: models of firm behavior tested on data from Swedish industrial firms. Stockholm, [1978]. pp. 176. *bibliog.*

FISHER (Sir RONALD AYLMER).

BOX (JOAN FISHER) R.A. Fisher: the life of a scientist. New York, [1978]. pp. 512. *bibliog.*

FISHERIES.

FISHERIES ECONOMICS NEWSLETTER; [pd. by] Fishery Economics Research Unit, White Fish Authority. s-a., 1976(no.1)- Edinburgh.

— Abstracts.

FISHERIES ECONOMICS NEWSLETTER; [pd. by] Fishery Economics Research Unit, White Fish Authority. s-a., 1976(no.1)- Edinburgh.

— Economic aspects.

ECONOMIC impacts of extended fisheries jurisdiction: proceedings of a symposium sponsored by the University of Delaware Sea Grant College Program and the National Marine Fisheries Service; edited by Lee G. Anderson. Ann Arbor, Mich., [1977]. pp. 428.

HANNESSON (RÖGNVALDUR) Economics of fisheries: an introduction. Bergen, [1978]. pp. 156. *bibliog.*

— Australia.

The 200 mile Australian fishing zone: a report of the working group established by the Australian Fisheries Council. Canberra, Australian Government Publishing Service, 1978. pp. 137.

— Canada — Newfoundland.

OMNIFACTS RESEARCH LIMITED. Report on selected aspects of the fishing industry in Newfoundland. [St. John's], 1978. pp. 70. *(Newfoundland. Fishing Industry Advisory Board. Special Reports)*

— Europe.

WHITE FISH AUTHORITY [U.K.]. Fishery Economics Research Unit. F.E.R.U. Occasional Papers Series. Edinburgh, 1977 in progress.

— European Economic Community countries.

EUROPEAN COMMUNITIES. Statistical Office. Fisheries: fishery products and fishing fleet. a., 1974/75- Luxembourg. *[in Community languages] Earlier data included in EUROPEAN COMMUNITIES. Statistical Office. Agricultural statistics, 1975 (no.1).*

EUROPEAN COMMUNITIES. Statistical Office. Quarterly bulletin of fisheries. q., 1978(no. 1/2)- Luxembourg. *[in Community languages]*

— India.

INDO-NORWEGIAN PROJECT. Souvenir issued on the occasion of the ceremony held on 1-4-1972 to mark the conclusion of the Indo-Norwegian Project agreement. [Cochin, 1972?]. pp. 122.

— — Mysore.

MYSORE. Directorate of Project Formulation, Evaluation and Manpower. Project Formulation Unit. 1973. Project for the development of the off shore and deep sea fishing Industry of the Mysore coast. Bangalore, 1973. pp. 177.

— United Kingdom.

WHITE FISH AUTHORITY [U.K.]. Fishery Economics Research Unit. F.E.R.U. Occasional Papers Series. Edinburgh, 1977 in progress.

DUNLOP (JEAN) The British Fisheries Society 1786-1893. Edinburgh, [1978]. pp. 239. *bibliog.*

— — Scotland.

GRAY (MALCOLM) The fishing industries of Scotland, 1790-1914: a study in regional adaptation. Oxford, [1978]. pp. 230. *bibliog. (Aberdeen. University. Studies. No.155)*

FISHERMEN

— Norway.

COULL (JAMES R.) Crofter-fishermen in Norway and Scotland. Aberdeen, 1971. pp. 15. *bibliog. (Aberdeen. University. Department of Geography. O'Dell Memorial Monographs. No.2)*

— Portugal.

OLIVEIRA (CARLOS MANUEL GRAÇA RAMOS DE) Fuzeta: uma abordagem antropologica. [Lisbon, 1974]. pp. 230. *bibliog. Includes summary in English.*

— United Kingdom — Scotland.

COULL (JAMES R.) Crofter-fishermen in Norway and Scotland. Aberdeen, 1971. pp. 15. *bibliog. (Aberdeen. University. Department of Geography. O'Dell Memorial Monographs. No.2)*

— United States.

ORBACH (MICHAEL K.) Hunters, seamen, and entrepreneurs: the tuna seinermen of San Diego. Berkeley, [1977]. pp. 304. *bibliog.*

FISHERY LAW AND LEGISLATION

— Iceland.

GILCHRIST (Sir ANDREW) Cod wars and how to lose them. Edinburgh, 1977. pp. 122.

— United Kingdom.

GILCHRIST (Sir ANDREW) Cod wars and how to lose them. Edinburgh, 1977. pp. 122.

— United States.

BROWDER (JOAN A.) The Fishery Act of 1976: a summary; the management councils: a description. Miami, 1977. pp. 19. *bibliog. (Miami (Florida). University. Sea Grant Program. Sea Grant Special Reports. No. 12)*

FISHERY MANAGEMENT.

ECONOMIC impacts of extended fisheries jurisdiction: proceedings of a symposium sponsored by the University of Delaware Sea Grant College Program and the National Marine Fisheries Service; edited by Lee G. Anderson. Ann Arbor, Mich., [1977]. pp. 428.

BROWDER (JOAN A.) The Fishery Act of 1976: a summary; the management councils: a description. Miami, 1977. pp. 19. *bibliog. (Miami (Florida). University. Sea Grant Program. Sea Grant Special Reports. No. 12)*

FISHERY PRODUCTS

— European Economic Community countries.

EUROPEAN COMMUNITIES. Statistical Office. Fisheries: fishery products and fishing fleet. a., 1974/75- Luxembourg. *[in Community languages] Earlier data included in EUROPEAN COMMUNITIES. Statistical Office. Agricultural statistics, 1975 (no.1).*

FISHING BOATS

— Russia.

FRANCE. Direction de la Documentation. La Documentation Française. Notes et Etudes Documentaires. No. 4479-4480. La marine soviétique; [by] Claude Huan [and] Jürgen Rohwer. [Paris], 1978. pp. 157.

FISHING VILLAGES

— Portugal.

OLIVIERA (CARLOS MANUEL GRAÇA RAMOS DE) Fuzeta: uma abordagem antropologica. [Lisbon, 1974]. pp. 230. *bibliog. Includes summary in English.*

FITZPATRICK (JOHN).

FITZPATRICK (JOHN) c.1737-1791. The merchant of Manchac: the letterbooks of John Fitzpatrick, 1768-1790; edited with an introduction by Margaret Fisher Dalrymple. Baton Rouge, [1978]. pp. 451. *bibliog.*

FIXED POINT THEOREMS (TOPOLOGY).

TODD (MICHAEL J.) The computation of fixed points and applications. Berlin, [1976]. pp. 129. *bibliog.*

FLANDERS

— Economic history.

De VLAAMSE gemeenschap. 2. Bevolking, economie, sociaal- economische ontwikkeling, vernederlandsing van het bedrijfsleven; [by] Gilbert Dooghe [and others]. Hasselt, [1978]. pp. 387. *bibliogs. (Twintig eeuwen Vlaanderen. Deel 8)*

— History.

PIERRARD (PIERRE) Histoire du Nord: Flandre, Artois, Hainaut, Picardie. [Paris, 1978]. pp. 404. *bibliog.*

— Nationalism.

De VLAAMSE gemeenschap. 2. Bevolking, economie, sociaal- economische ontwikkeling, vernederlandsing van het bedrijfsleven; [by] Gilbert Dooghe [and others]. Hasselt, [1978]. pp. 387. *bibliogs. (Twintig eeuwen Vlaanderen. Deel 8)*

FLANDERS (Cont.)

— Social history.

De VLAAMSE gemeenschap. 2. Bevolking, economie, sociaal- economische ontwikkeling, vernederlandsing van het bedrijfsleven; [by] Gilbert Dooghe [and others]. Hasselt, [1978]. pp. 387. *bibliogs. (Twintig eeuwen Vlaanderen. Deel 8)*

FLAVELLE (Sir JOSEPH WESLEY).

BLISS (MICHAEL) A Canadian millionaire: the life and business times of Sir Joseph Flavelle, Bart., 1858-1939. Toronto, [1978 repr. 1979]. pp. 562.

FLEMISH MOVEMENT.

DEMEY (J.) De historische twee-eenheid der Nederlanden: bestendige kloof in toenadering. Nijmegen, [1978]. pp. 214. *bibliogs.*

FLETCHER (CALVIN).

FLETCHER (CALVIN) The diary of Calvin Fletcher, vol.5, 1853-1856, including letters to and from Calvin Fletcher; edited by Gayle Thornbrough [and others]. Indianapolis, 1977. pp. 662.

FLETCHERS' BAKERIES.

HILL (HOWARD) Secret ingredient: the story of Fletchers' seven bakeries. Wakefield, 1978. pp. 94.

FLOOD CONTROL.

UNITED NATIONS. Economic Commission for Europe. Committee on Water Problems. 1976. Rational methods of flood control planning in river basin development: a report, etc. (ECE/WATER/17). New York, 1976. pp. 71.

SMITH (KEITH) Ph.D., and TOBIN (GRAHAM A.) Human adjustment to the flood hazard. London, 1979. pp. 130. *bibliog.*

FLOOD DAMAGE PREVENTION.

UNITED NATIONS. Department of Economic and Social Affairs. Natural Resources/Water Series. No. 5. Guidelines for flood loss prevention and management in developing countries. (ST/ESA/45). New York, 1976. pp. 183. *bibliog.*

FLOODS

— United Kingdom.

SMITH (KEITH) Ph.D., and TOBIN (GRAHAM A.) Human adjustment to the flood hazard. London, 1979. pp. 130. *bibliog.*

— United States.

ERIKSON (KAI T.) Everything in its path: destruction of community in the Buffalo Creek flood. New York, [1976]. pp. 284. *bibliog.*

ERIKSON (KAI T.) In the wake of the flood. London, [1979]. pp. 220. *bibliog.*

FLOOR SPACE, INDUSTRIAL.

U.K. Department of the Environment. Commercial and industrial floorspace statistics, England and Wales. a., 1974/1977(no. 6)- London.

FLORENCE

— History.

HALE (JOHN RIGBY) Florence and the Medici: the pattern of control. London, [1977]. pp. 208. *bibliog.*

— Population.

HERLIHY (DAVID) and KLAPISCH-ZUBER (CHRISTIANE) Les Toscans et leurs familles: une étude du catasto florentin de 1427. [Paris, 1978]. pp. 703. *bibliog.*

— Social conditions.

HERLIHY (DAVID) and KLAPISCH-ZUBER (CHRISTIANE) Les Toscans et leurs familles: une étude du catasto florentin de 1427. [Paris, 1978]. pp. 703. *bibliog.*

FLOUR-MILLS

— United Kingdom.

BIBBY (JOHN BENJAMIN) and BIBBY (CHARLES LESLIE) A miller's tale: a history of J. Bibby and Sons Ltd., Liverpool. Liverpool, [1978]. pp. 218.

— United States.

KUHLMANN (CHARLES BYRON) The development of the flour-milling industry in the United States with special reference to the industry in Minneapolis. Clifton, N.J., 1973. pp. 349. *bibliog. Reprint of work first published Boston, Mass., 1929.*

— — Minneapolis.

KUHLMANN (CHARLES BYRON) The development of the flour-milling industry in the United States with special reference to the industry in Minneapolis. Clifton, N.J., 1973. pp. 349. *bibliog. Reprint of work first published Boston, Mass., 1929.*

FLOW OF FUNDS

— United States.

HENDERSHOTT (PATRIC H.) and others. Understanding capital markets. Lexington, Mass., [1977]. 2 vols. *bibliogs.*

SAMETZ (ARNOLD WILLIAM) Prospects for capital formation and capital markets: financial requirements over the next decade. Lexington, Mass., [1978]. pp. 145. *bibliog.*

FOGGIA (PROVINCE)

— Economic conditions.

GIORGIO (MARIO) La sconfitta del Subappennino Dauno. Matera, [1977]. pp. 101.

FOLK LORE

— Europe.

ZIPES (JACK) Breaking the magic spell: radical theories of folk and fairy tales. London, 1979. pp. 201.

FOLK LORE, MAORI.

BEST (ELSDON) The Maori division of time. Wellington, [1922] repr. 1959. pp. 52. *(New Zealand. Dominion Museum. Monographs. No. 4)*

FOLK LORE OF CHILDREN.

WIDDOWSON (JOHN D.A.) If you don't be good: verbal social control in Newfoundland. St. John's, 1977. pp. 345. *bibliog. (St. John's. Memorial University of Newfoundland. Institute of Social and Economic Research. Newfoundland Social and Economic Papers. No. 21)*

FOLK MEDICINE

— United States.

MEDICINE without doctors: home health care in American history; edited by Guenter B. Risse [and others]. New York, 1977. pp. 124. *bibliogs.*

FONTOURA (JOÃO NEVES DE).

FONTOURA (JOÃO NEVES DA) Discursos parlamentares; seleção e introdução de Helgio Trindade. Brasilia, 1978. pp. 722. *(Brazil. Congresso. Câmara dos Deputados. Perfis Parlamentares. 8)*

FOOD (IN RELIGION, FOLK-LORE, ETC.).

GASTRONOMY: the anthropology of food and food habits; [edited by] Margaret L. Arnott. The Hague, [1975]. pp. 354. *bibliogs.*

FOOD ADULTERATION AND INSPECTION

— United States.

WOLFE (MARGARET RIPLEY) Lucius Polk Brown and progressive food and drug control: Tennessee and New York City 1908-1920. Lawrence, Kan., [1978]. pp. 194.

FOOD CONSERVATION.

ROY (ROBIN) Wastage in the UK food system. London, 1976. pp. 42. *bibliog.*

WALKER (ADRIAN) Food from waste: a plan to enable the UK to save money, conserve resources and improve the world food situation. London, [1977]. pp. 18. *bibliog. (Oxfam. Public Affairs Unit. Oxfam Public Affairs Action Papers. 1)*

FOOD CONSUMPTION.

ENZER (SELWYN) and others. Neither feast nor famine: food conditions to the year 2000. Lexington, Mass., [1978]. pp. 185. *bibliog.*

— Bangladesh.

RABBANI (ABUL KALAM MOHAMMED GHULAM) and HOSSAIN (SHAHADAT) Rural and urban consumption patterns in contemporary Bangladesh. Dacca, Bureau of Statistics, 1978. pp. 47. *bibliog.*

— United Kingdom.

ROY (ROBIN) Wastage in the UK food system. London, 1976. pp. 42. *bibliog.*

WALKER (ADRIAN) Food from waste: a plan to enable the UK to save money, conserve resources and improve the world food situation. London, [1977]. pp. 18. *bibliog. (Oxfam. Public Affairs Unit. Oxfam Public Affairs Action Papers. 1)*

FOOD CONTAMINATION

— United Kingdom.

U.K. Steering Group on Food Surveillance. 1978. The surveillance of food contamination in the United Kingdom; the first report of the Steering Group. London, 1978. pp. 38. *(Food Surveillance Papers. No.1)*

FOOD HABITS.

GASTRONOMY: the anthropology of food and food habits; [edited by] Margaret L. Arnott. The Hague, [1975]. pp. 354. *bibliogs.*

FOOD INDUSTRY AND TRADE

— Bibliography.

CHRISTIAN (PORTIA) compiler. Agricultural enterprises management in an urban-industrial society: a guide to information sources. Detroit, [1978]. pp. 314. *(Gale Research Company. Management Information Guides. 34)*

— Belgium.

HALLET (M. JACQUES) Etude sur l'évolution de la concentration dans l'industrie alimentaire en Belgique. [Brussels], Communautés Européennes, 1975. pp. 93.

— Canada — Bibliography.

MATTHEWS (CATHERINE J.) and ARMSTRONG (DOUGLAS) compilers. The food processing industry in Canada; a selected bibliography, with particular emphasis on Ontario food processing. [Toronto], Ontario Ministry of Labour Research Library, 1975. fo. 23.

— Denmark.

INSTITUTE FOR FUTURES STUDIES. A study of the evolution of concentration in the Danish food distribution industry, etc. [Brussels], European Communities, 1976. pp. 292.

— **France.**

FRANCE. Ministère de l'Agriculture. Service Central des Enquêtes et Etudes Statistiques. 1970. Industries agricoles, alimentaires de Lorraine et d'Alsace. [Metz, 1970?]. pp. 37.

RASTOIN (J.L.) and others. Etude sur l'évolution de la concentration dans l'industrie alimentaire en France...(tableaux de concentration). [Brussels], Communautés Européennes, 1975. 2 vols.(in 1) .

ETUDE sur l'évolution de la concentration dans la distribution des produits alimentaires en France. [Bruxelles], Communautés Européennes, 1976. pp. 213.

FRANCE. Institut National de la Statistique et des Etudes Economiques. Division Agriculture. 1977. Industries agricoles et alimentaires: données économiques 1970 à 1976. [Paris], 1977. pp. 119.

— **Germany.**

BREITENACHER (MICHAEL) Untersuchung zur konzentrationsentwicklung in ausgewählten Branchen und Produktgruppen der Ernährungsindustrie in Deutschland. [Brussels], Europäischen Gemeinschaften, 1976. pp. 331.

GREIPL (ERICH) and WUERL (DIETER) Untersuchung zur Konzentrationsentwicklung in der Nahrungsmitteldistribution in Deutschland. [Brussels], Europäischen Gemeinschaften, 1976. pp. 307.

— **India — Bengal, West.**

WEST BENGAL. Bureau of Applied Economics and Statistics. 1974. Economic survey of small industries, 1965 and 1966, West Bengal. No. 2. Report on food manufacturing industries. [Calcutta], 1974. pp. 127.

— **Italy.**

BALLIANO (PIERA) and LANZETTI (RENATO) Studio sull'evoluzione della concentrazione dei prodotti alimentari in Italia, etc. [Brussels], Comunità Europee, [1977]. pp. 189.

— **Tanzania.**

MARKETING DEVELOPMENT BUREAU [UNITED REPUBLIC OF TANZANIA] and COLLEGE OF BUSINESS EDUCATION [UNITED REPUBLIC OF TANZANIA]. Distribution patterns of food and beverages in Dar es Salaam. Dar es Salaam, 1973. fo. (61).

MARKETING DEVELOPMENT BUREAU [UNITED REPUBLIC OF TANZANIA]. Food marketing systems in Dar es Salaam. Dar es Salaam, 1974. fo. (42).

— **United Kingdom.**

NICHOLLS (J.R.) The impact of the EEC on the UK food industry: effects on the strategies of UK food, drink and tobacco manufacturing companies. Farnborough, Hants., [1978]. pp. 349.

— **United States.**

McCLINTOCK (DAVID W.) U.S. food: making the most of a global resource. Boulder, Colo., 1978. pp. 122. bibliog.

FOOD PRICES

— **Canada.**

CANADA. Food Prices Review Board. 1974. Food price trends in Canada and the United States: report with special reference to the U.S. price and income control program. [Ottawa], 1974. pp. 26,26. In English and French.

— **European Economic Community countries.**

U.K. Ministry of Agriculture, Fisheries and Food. Economics Division. 1974. Retail food prices in the EEC, 1973 and 1974. London, 1974. pp. 99.

— **India — Orissa.**

ORISSA. State Civil Supplies Price Enquiry Committee. 1969. Final report; Radhanath Rath, chairman. Cuttack, 1969. pp. 150.

— **United States.**

CANADA. Food Prices Review Board. 1974. Food price trends in Canada and the United States: report with special reference to the U.S. price and income control program. [Ottawa], 1974. pp. 26,26. In English and French.

FOOD RELIEF

— **Africa.**

STEVENS (CHRISTOPHER ANTHONY) Food aid and the developing world: four African case studies. London, [1979]. pp. 224. bibliog.

— **United States.**

MACDONALD (MAURICE) Food, stamps, and income maintenance. New York, [1977]. pp. 155. bibliog. (Wisconsin University, Madison. Institute for Research on Poverty. Poverty Policy Analysis Series)

FOOD SUPPLY.

MUKERJEE (RADHAKAMAL) Races, lands, and food: a program for world subsistence. New York, 1946. pp. 107.

FOOD AND NUTRITION; [pd. q. by the Nutrition Division of] Food and Agriculture Organization of the United Nations. q., 1975(v.1, no.1)- Rome.

BROWN (LESTER RUSSELL) Redefining national security. Washington, 1977. pp. 46. (Worldwatch Institute. Worldwatch Papers. No. 14)

ENZER (SELWYN) and others. Neither feast nor famine: food conditions to the year 2000. Lexington, Mass., [1978]. pp. 185. bibliog.

FOOD and population: priorities in decision making...; edited by T.Dams [and others]. Farnborough, [1978]. pp. 192. bibliogs. Report of a meeting of the International Conference of Agricultural Economists, Nairobi, 1976.

The GLOBAL political economy of food; edited by Raymond F. Hopkins and Donald J. Puchala. Madison, [1978]. pp. 339. bibliog. Contents of the Summer 1978 issue of International Organization, (vol. 32, no.3). sponsored by the World Peace Foundation.

McCLINTOCK (DAVID W.) U.S. food: making the most of a global resource. Boulder, Colo., 1978. pp. 122. bibliog.

The WORLD food problem: consensus and conflict; edited by Radha Sinha. Oxford, 1978. pp. 676. bibliog. First published as a special issue of World Development, vol. 5., nos. 5-7.

WORTMAN (STERLING) and CUMMINGS (RALPH WALDO) To feed this world: the challenge and the strategy. Baltimore, [1978]. pp. 440. bibliogs.

GILLAND (BERNARD) The next seventy years: population, food and resources. Tunbridge Wells, 1979. pp. 133. bibliog.

MORGAN (DAN) Merchants of grain. New York, 1979. pp. 387.

— **Political aspects.**

CALDWELL (DAN) Food crises and world politics. Beverly Hills, [1977]. pp. 82. bibliog.

— **France.**

FRANCE. Ministère de l'Agriculture. Statistique agricole. Supplément. Série Etudes. No. 164. Bilans alimentaires et autres bilans, 1974-1975-1976; [étude réalisée par Melle Ferran]. Paris, 1978. pp. 47.

— **India.**

SEN (SUDHIR) Reaping the green revolution: food and jobs for all. New York, [1975]. pp. 397. bibliog.

— **Poland.**

ROLNICTWO a wy'zywienie w Polsce: pobudzanie, efekty, koszty produkcji; pod redakcją E. Gorzelaka. Warszawa, 1978. pp. 429.

— **Taiwan.**

FORMOSA. Food Bureau. 1960. Food production and activities of Taiwan Provincial Food Bureau. [Taipei], 1960. pp. 66. In English and Chinese.

— **Underdeveloped areas.**

See UNDERDEVELOPED AREAS — Food supply.

— **United Kingdom.**

ROY (ROBIN) Wastage in the UK food system. London, 1976. pp. 42. bibliog.

WALKER (ADRIAN) Food from waste: a plan to enable the UK to save money, conserve resources and improve the world food situation. London, [1977]. pp. 18. bibliog. (Oxfam. Public Affairs Unit. Oxfam Public Affairs Action Papers. 1)

FOOT (PAUL).

COMMUNIST WORKERS' MOVEMENT. Why Paul Foot should be a socialist: the case against the Socialist Workers' Party. Liverpool, 1978. pp. 198.

FOOTBALL

— **Social aspects.**

DUNNING (ERIC) and SHEARD (KENNETH) Barbarians, gentlemen and players: a sociological study of the development of rugby football. Oxford, 1979. pp. 321. bibliog.

FORCED LABOUR

— **America, Latin.**

SHERMAN (WILLIAM L.) Forced native labor in sixteenth-century Central America. Lincoln, Neb., 1979. pp. 496. bibliog.

FORD (HENRY).

KRAFT (BARBARA S.) The peace ship: Henry Ford's pacifist adventure in the First World War. New York, [1978]. pp. 367. bibliog.

FORD FOUNDATION.

MAGAT (RICHARD) The Ford Foundation at work: philanthropic choices, methods and styles. New York, [1979]. pp. 207.

FORECASTING.

COLSTON RESEARCH SOCIETY. Symposium, 22nd, 1971. Regional forecasting: proceedings...; edited by Michael Chisholm [and others]. Hamden, Conn., 1971. pp. 470. (Colston Research Society and Bristol. University. Colston Papers. vol. 22)

BOVSH (VIKTOR IVANOVICH) Futurologiia i antikommunizm; nauchnyi redaktor F.T. Konstantinov. Minsk, 1977. pp. 270. (Akademiia Nauk Belorusskoi SSR. Institut Filosofii i Prava. Ideologicheskaia Bor'ba v Sovremennom Mire)

COUNCIL FOR MUTUAL ECONOMIC ASSISTANCE. 1977. Co-operation of CMEA member countries in the field of forecasting. Moscow, 1977. pp. 15.

FERKISS (VICTOR CHRISTOPHER) Futurology: promise, performance, prospects. Beverly Hills, [1977]. pp. 66. bibliog. (Georgetown University. Center for Strategic and International Studies. Washington Papers. vol. 5/50)

METODOLOGICHESKIE problemy sotsial'nogo predvideniia. Kiev, 1977. pp. 347.

ANTICIPATORY democracy: people in the politics of the future; edited by Clement Bezold. New York, [1978]. pp. 405. bibliog.

ENZER (SELWYN) and others. Neither feast nor famine: food conditions to the year 2000. Lexington, Mass., [1978]. pp. 185. bibliog.

FORECASTING.(Cont.)

FORECASTING in international relations: theory, methods, problems, prospects; edited by Nazli Choucri and Thomas W. Robinson. San Francisco, [1978]. pp. 468. *bibliog.*

SHAKHNAZAROV (GEORGII KHOSROEVICH) Sotsialisticheskaia sud'ba chelovechestva. Moskva, 1978. pp. 462.

VOPROSY prognozirovaniia obshchestvennykh iavlenii. Kiev, 1978. pp. 194. *(Akademiia Nauk Ukraïns'koï RSR. Instytut Filosofii. Istoricheskii Materializm kak Teoriia Sotsial'nogo Poznaniia i Deistviia)*

THOMPSON (ALAN E.) Futurologist. Understanding futurology: an introduction to futures study. Newton Abbott, [1979]. pp. 96. *bibliog.*

FOREIGN EXCHANGE.

SVERIGES INDUSTRIFÖRBUND. Economic Affairs Directorate. The Nordic economic outlook: a survey prepared [by Eva Christina Horwitz]...; [with] special studies [by various authors]. [Stockholm], 1975. pp. 86.

BEENSTOCK (MICHAEL CHARLES) The foreign exchanges: theory, modelling and policy. London, 1978. pp. 163. *bibliog.*

FRANCE. Direction de la Documentation. La Documentation Française. Notes et Etudes Documentaires. No. 4459. Le marché des changes; par Jacques Blanc. [Paris], 1978. pp. 99. *bibliog.*

FRENKEL (JACOB A.) and JOHNSON (HARRY GORDON) eds. The economics of exchange rates: selected studies. Reading, Mass., [1978]. pp. 218. *bibliogs.*

KOHLHAGEN (STEVEN W.) The behavior of foreign exchange markets: a critical survey of the empirical literature. New York, 1978. pp. 52. *bibliog.* *(New York (City). University. Salomon Brothers Center for the Study of Financial Institutions. Monograph Series in Finance and Economics. 1978. No. 3)*

SZASZ (ANDRE) Monetary policy and exchange rate stability. Amsterdam, [1978?]. pp. 33. *(Nederlandsche Bank. Reprints. No. 39)*

— Law — Tanzania.

UNITED REPUBLIC OF TANZANIA. Statutes, etc. 1969. Exchange control: chapter 294 of the laws, principal legislation. Dar es Salaam, 1969. pp. 50. *(Gazette. Special Supplements. 1969. No.1)*

— — United Kingdom.

U.K. Statutes, etc. 1947- . Exchange control: the Act and the Instruments as in operation on 1st March 1979; (with Supplements). London, 1979 in progress. 1 vol. (loose-leaf).

MILLER (ROBERT) Writer on money and WOOD (JOHN B.) Exchange control for ever? London, 1979. pp. 78. *bibliog.* *(Institute of Economic Affairs. Research Monographs. 33)*

— Mathematical models.

KAREKEN (JOHN H.) and WALLACE (NEIL) Samuelson's consumption-loan model with county-specific fiat monies. [Minneapolis], 1977. fo. 61. *bibliog.* *(Federal Reserve Bank of Minneapolis. Research Department. Staff Reports. [No.] 24)*

— Communist countries.

LIUBSKII (MIKHAIL SERGEEVICH) and others. Valiutnye i kreditnye otnosheniia stran SEV. Moskva, 1978. pp. 160.

— European Economic Community countries.

FEARN (HOWARD A.) The evolution and basic concepts of the green currency system. London, Ministry of Agriculture, Fisheries and Food, 1978. pp. 10. *(Government Economic Service Working Papers. No. 12)*

— France.

FRANCE. Groupe d'Economie Monétaire Appliquée. 1978. Crédit, change et inflation: rapport du groupe d'économie monétaire appliquée. [Paris, 1978]. 2 vols. *(France. Commissariat Général du Plan. Economie et Planification)*

— Switzerland.

LEUTWILER (FRITZ) Swiss monetary and exchange rate policy in an inflationary world; translated [from the German] by Herbert Zassenhaus. Washington, [1978]. pp. 14. *(American Enterprise Institute for Public Policy Research. AEI Studies. 218)*

— Underdeveloped areas.

See UNDERDEVELOPED AREAS — Foreign exchange.

— United Kingdom.

BUSINESS views on exchange-rate policy: an independent study by a group of leading economists; (Peter Oppenheimer, chairman). London, 1978. pp. 36.

HILLIARD (B.C.) Exchange flows and the gilt-edged security market: a causality study. London, 1979. pp. 31. *bibliog.* *(Bank of England. Discussion Papers. No. 2)*

— — Mathematical models.

DICKINSON (SHEILA) and WILDGOOSE (JAMES) A framework for assessing the economic effects of a green pound devaluation. London, Ministry of Agriculture, Fisheries and Food, 1979. pp. 14. *(Government Economic Service Working Papers. No. 23)*

FOREIGN EXCHANGE PROBLEM.

The NEW international monetary system; Robert A. Mundell and Jacques J. Polak, editors. New York, 1977. pp. 244. *Proceedings of a conference held by the I.M.F. in Washington D.C. in 1976, jointly sponsored by Columbia University.*

JACQUE (LAURENT L.) Management of foreign exchange risk: theory and praxis. Lexington, Mass., [1978]. pp. 285. *bibliogs.*

MINFORD (ANTHONY PATRICK LESLIE) Substitution effects, speculation and exchange rate stability. Amsterdam, 1978. pp. 222. *bibliog.*

RIECHEL (KLAUS-WALTER) Economic effects of exchange-rate changes. Lexington, [1978]. pp. 155. *bibliog.*

— Brazil.

SAVASINI (JOSÉ AUGUSTO ARANTES) Export promotion: the case of Brazil. New York, [1978]. pp. 141. *bibliog.*

— United Kingdom.

MINFORD (ANTHONY PATRICK LESLIE) Substitution effects, speculation and exchange rate stability. Amsterdam, 1978. pp. 222. *bibliog.*

— United States.

BERGSTEN (C. FRED) The dilemmas of the dollar: the economics and politics of United States international monetary policy. New York, [1975]. pp. 584.

FOREIGN NEWS.

SUSSMAN (LEONARD R.) Mass news media and the third world challenge. Beverly Hills, [1977]. pp. 80. *bibliog.* *(Georgetown University. Center for Strategic and International Studies. Washington Papers. vol. 5/46)*

FOREIGN TRADE PROMOTION

— Australia.

AUSTRALIA. Department of Overseas Trade. 1977. Australia's overseas trade: an introduction. [Canberra, 1977]. pp. 28.

— Brazil.

SAVASINI (JOSÉ AUGUSTO ARANTES) Export promotion: the case of Brazil. New York, [1978]. pp. 141. *bibliog.*

— Salvador.

SALVADOR. Statutes, etc. 1970. Export Development Law. [San Salvador], 1971. fo. 16.

— Underdeveloped areas.

See UNDERDEVELOPED AREAS — Foreign trade promotion.

— United Kingdom.

BRITISH OVERSEAS TRADE BOARD. Report. a., 1972(initial report)- London.

FOREIGN TRADE REGULATION.

RHYNE (CHARLES S.) and others. Law-making activities of the United Nations Conference on Trade and Development. Washington, D.C., 1976. pp. 120.

— United Statess.

STERN (PAULA) Water's edge: domestic politics and the making of American foreign policy. Westport, Conn., 1979. pp. 265. *bibliog.*

FOREST MANAGEMENT

— Thailand.

DUSIT PHATNITCHAPHAT. The management of forests in Thailand. Bangkok, 1962. pp. 12. *(Thailand. Forest Department. [Publications]. No. R. 49)*

FOREST POLICY.

SYMPOSIUM ON RESEARCH IN FOREST ECONOMICS AND FOREST POLICY, WASHINGTON, 1977. Research in forest economics and forest policy;...papers...from... [the] symposium; [edited by] Marion Clawson. Washington, 1977. pp. 555. *bibliogs.* *(Resources for the Future, Inc. Research Papers. R-3)*

FOREST PRODUCTS

— Prices.

MONTHLY PRICES FOR FOREST PRODUCTS; [pd. by] Economic Commission for Europe, United Nations. q., F 1979(no.1)- Geneva.

— European Economic Community countries.

EUROPEAN COMMUNITIES. Statistical Office. Forest statistics. a., 1970/1975(1st)- Luxembourg. *[in Community languages] Data previously included in EUROPEAN COMMUNITIES. Statistical Office. Agricultural statistics; 1965 (no. 8), 1966 (no.8), 1968 (nos. 2 and 11), 1969 (no.6), 1970 (no.5), 1972 (no.2) and 1973 (no.6).*

FOREST RANGERS

— United States.

KAUFMAN (HERBERT) The forest ranger: a study in administrative behavior. Baltimore, 1960 repr.1967. pp. 259.

FORESTS AND FORESTRY

— Economic aspects.

SYMPOSIUM ON RESEARCH IN FOREST ECONOMICS AND FOREST POLICY, WASHINGTON, 1977. Research in forest economics and forest policy;...papers...from... [the] symposium; [edited by] Marion Clawson. Washington, 1977. pp. 555. *bibliogs.* *(Resources for the Future, Inc. Research Papers. R-3)*

— Canada — British Columbia.

BRITISH COLUMBIA. Royal Commission on Forest Resources. 1976. Synopsis of timber rights and forest policy in British Columbia: report...; Peter H. Pearse, commissioner. Victoria, 1976. pp. 55.

— **European Economic Community countries.**

EUROPEAN COMMUNITIES. Statistical Office. Forest statistics. a., 1970/1975(1st)- Luxembourg. *[in Community languages] Data previously included in* EUROPEAN COMMUNITIES. *Statistical Office. Agricultural statistics; 1965 (no. 8), 1966 (no.8), 1968 (nos. 2 and 11), 1969 (no.6), 1970 (no.5), 1972 (no.2) and 1973 (no.6).*

— **France.**

FRANCE. Délégation à l'Aménagement du Territoire et à l'Action Régionale. 1978. Le Massif Central: [forests; by J. le Ray and others]. [Paris, 1978]. pp. 126. *(Massif Central. Dossiers. 4)*

— — **Aquitaine.**

CAQUET (PAUL) Les forêts d'Aquitaine: structures et organisation. [Bordeaux, Service Régional d'Aménagement Forestier d'Aquitaine, 1977]. pp. 190.

— **Nigeria.**

ONOCHIE (C.F.A.) Some considerations for a forest policy in the East Central State. Ibadan, Federal Department of Forestry, 1973. pp. 13. *(Nigeria Forestry Information Bulletins. New Series. No. 26) Reprinted from pages 150-160 of the Proceedings of the Inaugural Conference of the Forestry Association of Nigeria, October 6-9, 1970.*

— **Thailand.**

SAMAPUDDHI (KRIT) The forests of Thailand and forestry programs. [2nd ed.] Bangkok, 1957. pp. 35. *bibliog. (Thailand. Forest Department. [Publications]. No. R.20)*

DUSIT PHATNITCHAPHAT. Brief note on forests and forestry problems in Thailand. Bangkok, 1962. pp. 7. *(Thailand. Forest Department. [Publications]. No. R. 48)*

RATANAPRASIDHI (METH) Forest industries and forestry of Thailand. Bangkok, 1963. fo. 31. *(Thailand. Forest Department. [Publications]. No. R. 59)*

FORMALISM (RUSSIAN LITERATURE).

BENNETT (TONY) Formalism and marxism. London, 1979. pp. 200. *bibliog.*

FORNANDER (ABRAHAM).

DAVIS (ELEANOR HARMON) Abraham Fornander: a biography. Honolulu, [1979]. pp. 322. *bibliog.*

FORT-LAMY

— **Census.**

CHAD. Bureau de la Statistique. 1963. Recensement démographique de Fort-Lamy, mars-juillet 1962: résultats provisoires; [by] Marcel Lafarge [and] Jean-Philippe Schneider. [Paris, 1963]. pp. 78.

FORWARDING MERCHANTS.

See FREIGHT FORWARDERS.

FOUR-COLOUR PROBLEM.

SAATY (THOMAS L.) and KAINEN (PAUL C.) The four-color problem: assaults and conquest. New York, [1977]. pp. 217. *bibliog.*

FOURAH BAY COLLEGE

— **Finance.**

SIERRA LEONE. Triennial Grants Committee appointed to consider the Estimates of Fourah Bay College. 1964. Report...for the period 1st September, 1964 to 31st August, 1967 and the government statement thereon; [Sir James Cook, chairman]. [Freetown, 1964]. pp. 9.

FOURIER (FRANÇOIS CHARLES MARIE).

GODWIN (PARKE) A popular view of the doctrines of Charles Fourier;...with the addition of Democracy, constructive and pacific. New York, 1844; Philadelphia, 1972. 2 vols. (in 1). *Facsimile reprint.*

FOURIER ANALYSIS.

BLOOMFIELD (PETER) Fourier analysis of time series: an introduction. New York, [1976]. pp. 258. *bibliog.*

FOX (Sir STEPHEN).

CLAY (CHRISTOPHER) Public finance and private wealth: the career of Sir Stephen Fox, 1627-1716. Oxford, 1978. pp. 362. *bibliog.*

FRANCE

— **Armed forces.**

FRANCE. Direction de la Documentation. La Documentation Française. Notes et Etudes Documentaires. Nos. 4,503-4, 504. Le statut des militaires; par Jean Claude Roqueplo. Paris, 1979. pp. 162. *bibliog.*

— **Census.**

FRANCE. Census, 1968. Recensement général de la population de 1968; résultats du sondage au ¼: population, ménages, logements, immeubles; fascicules départementaux. Paris, 1971. 95 pts. in 10 vols. *Pt. 45, Loiret, out of print.*

FRANCE. Census, 1968. Recensement général de la population de 1968; résultats du sondage au ¼: population, ménages, logements, immeubles; agglomération de Paris. Paris, 1971. pp. 186.

FRANCE. Census, 1975. Recensement général de la population de 1975; résultats du sondage au 1/5: population, ménages, logements, immeubles; [fascicules départementaux]. [Paris, 1976]. 95 pts. in 10 vols. *Pt. 20, Corsica, not published.*

FRANCE. Census, 1975. Recensement général de la population de 1975; résultats du sondage au 1/5: population, ménages, logements, immeubles; [fascicules départementaux]; agglomération de Paris. [Paris, 1976]. pp. 91.

FRANCE. Census, 1975. Recensement général de la population de 1975: villes et agglomérations urbaines : délimitation 1975: évolutions démographiques 1968-1975 et 1962-1968. [Paris, 1977]. pp. 780.

SAMMAN (MOUNA LILIANE) Les étrangers au recensement de 1975. Paris, [1977]. pp. 141. *(France. Direction de la Population et des Migrations. Migrations et Sociétés. 2)*

FRANCE. Census, 1975. Recensement général de la population de 1975; résultats du sondage au 1/5: population, ménages, logements, immeubles: [regional fascicules and] (France entière). [Paris, 1978]. 22 pts. (in 3 vols.).

— **Colonies.**

AGERON (CHARLES ROBERT) France coloniale ou parti colonial? Paris, [1978]. pp. 302.

— — **Economic conditions.**

UNION GENERALE DES TRAVAILLEURS SENEGALAIS EN FRANCE. Notre Afrique: débats sur le tiers monde. Paris, 1978. pp. 123.

— — **History.**

SMITH (TONY) The French stake in Algeria, 1945-1962. Ithaca, 1978. pp. 199. *bibliog.*

— **Commerce.**

FRANCE. Département des Statistiques des Transports. 1976. Système d'information sur les transports de marchandises: comment évaluer la part du trafic maritime né de notre commerce extérieur qui échappe aux ports français. Paris, 1976. pp. 38.

FRANCE. Direction de la Documentation. La Documentation Française. Notes et Etudes Documentaires. No. 4487. Les échanges agro-alimentaires de la France. [Paris], 1978. pp. 88.

— — **Statistics.**

FRANCE. Commission des Comptes Commerciaux de la Nation. Rapport. a., 1976- Paris.

— — **Africa.**

FRANCE. Ministère de la Coopération. Sous-Direction des Etudes Economiques et de la Planification. 1975. Bilan global des échanges commerciaux entre la France et les EAM. Paris, 1975. pp. 26. *(Etudes et Documents. No. 20)*

— — **Canada.**

MIQUELON (DALE) Dugard of Rouen: French trade to Canada and the West Indies, 1729-1770. Montreal, [1978]. pp. 282. *bibliog.*

— — **West Indies.**

MIQUELON (DALE) Dugard of Rouen: French trade to Canada and the West Indies, 1729-1770. Montreal, [1978]. pp. 282. *bibliog.*

— **Constitution.**

GICQUEL (JEAN) Essai sur la pratique de la Ve République: bilan d'un septennat. Paris, 1977. pp. 398. *bibliog. Reprint of 1968 ed. with supplement, "Reflexions sur la seconde décennie du régime."*

MAUS (DIDIER) ed. Textes et documents sur la pratique institutionnelle de la Ve République. Paris, La Documentation Française, [1978]. pp. 436.

— **Constitutional history.**

CHABANNE (ROBERT) Les institutions de la France de la fin de l'ancien régime à l'avènement de la IIIème République, 1789-1875. Lyon, 1977. pp. 416.

CHEVALLIER (JEAN JACQUES) Histoire des institutions et des régimes politiques de la France de 1789 à nos jours. 5th ed. Paris, 1977. pp. 846. *bibliog.*

— **Constitutional law.**

FRANCK (CLAUDE) Droit constitutionnel: (les grandes décisions de la jurisprudence). Paris, 1978. pp. 371.

— **Defences.**

YOUNG (ROBERT J.) Historian. In command of France: French foreign policy and military planning, 1933-1940. Cambridge, Mass., 1978. pp. 346. *bibliog.*

— **Economic conditions.**

HANSEN (NILES M.) France in the modern world. New York, [1969]. pp. 167. *bibliog.*

SALLEZ (ALAIN) Polarisation et sous-traitance: conditions du développement régional. Paris, 1972. pp. 237. *bibliog.*

REPONSES à la violence... Recherches sur la violence et l'économie. Paris, [1977]. pp. 457. *(France. Comité d'Etudes sur la Violence, la Criminalité et la Délinquance. Annexes. 4)*

SCHEMA général d'aménagement de la France: le scenario de l'inacceptable: sept ans après; [by Bernard Cuneo and others]. [Paris], 1977. pp. 144. *(France. Délégation à l'Aménagement du Territoire et à l'Action Régionale. Travaux et Recherches de Prospective. 68)*

BACHELARD (PAUL) L'industrialisation de la région Centre: transformations économiques et socio-politiques. [Tours, 1978]. pp. 473. *bibliog. 19 maps in end pocket.*

BROST (FRANZ FRIEDRICH) and VILLOT (JEAN GERARD) Analyse comparative de l'évolution structurelle des systèmes productifs français et ouest-allemands: une étude statistique pour la période de 1960 à 1974. Frankfurt am Main, [1978]. pp. 259. *bibliog.*

HOUSE (JOHN WILLIAM) France: an applied geography. London, 1978. pp. 478. *bibliogs.*

SAUVY (ALFRED) La tragédie du pouvoir: quel avenir pour la France? Paris, [1978]. pp. 287.

FRANCE(Cont.)

SCHEMA général d'aménagement de la France: le grand Sud-Ouest: diagnostics par l'avenir; [by Florence Bas and others]. [Paris, 1979]. pp. 215. (France. Délégation à l'Aménagement du Territoire et à l'Action Régionale. Travaux et Recherches de Prospective. 76)

— Economic history.

CARON (FRANÇOIS) An economic history of modern France; translated by Barbara Bray. London, 1979. pp. 384.

— Economic policy.

FRANCE. Commissariat General du Plan de l'Equipement et de la Productivité. 1966. Fifth Plan: economic and social development plan, 1966-1970. Paris, [1966]. pp. 106.

SALLEZ (ALAIN) Polarisation et sous-traitance: conditions du développement régional. Paris, 1972. pp. 237. bibliog.

SCHEMA général d'aménagement de la France: restructuration de l'appareil productif française: prospectives. Paris, 1976. 2 vols. (France. Délégation à l'Aménagement du Territoire et à l'Action Régionale. Travaux et Recherches de Prospective. 65-66)

Le REDEPLOIEMENT industriel; [by Alain Cotta and others]. Paris, [1977]. pp. 131. bibliog. (France. Ministère de l'Industrie, du Commerce et de l'Artisanat. Etudes de Politique Industrielle. 17)

SAUVY (ALFRED) La tragédie du pouvoir: quel avenir pour la France? Paris, [1978]. pp. 287.

CALCUL économique et décisions publiques:...l'oeuvre d'un groupe de travail...(J.C. Milleron) [chairman]. Paris, 1979. pp. 157. (France. Commissariat Général du Plan. Economie et Planification)

HUITIEME plan: rapport sur les principales options du VIIIe plan: projet soumis par le gouvernement à l'avis du Conseil Economique et Social. Paris, La Documentation Française, 1979. pp. 84. Map in end pocket.

— Executive departments.

QUIVAUX (ROBERT) Le tertiaire public et semi-public dans l'agglomération et la région parisiennes;... sous la direction du Professeur Jean Bastié. [Paris], Atelier Parisien d'Urbanisme, [1969?]. pp. 84.

ANDERSON (MALCOLM) Government in France: an introduction to the executive power. Oxford, [1970]. pp. 217.

— Foreign economic relations —
   Underdeveloped areas.

Le DEFI économique de tiers monde; rapport du groupe de travail animé par Yves Berthelot et Gérard Tardy; préface par Michel Albert; [with] Annexes. Paris, La Documentation Française, [1978]. 2 vols. bibliog.

— Foreign population.

JOBERT (ANNETTE) and others. Les étrangers et la justice civile: analyse sociologique de la différenciation des pratiques judiciaires. [Paris], 1976. pp. 262. (France. Ministère de la Justice. Service de Coordination de la Recherche. Etude[s] de Sociologie Juridique)

SAMMAN (MOUNA LILIANE) Les étrangers au recensement de 1975. Paris, [1977]. pp. 141. (France. Direction de la Population et des Migrations. Migrations et Sociétés. 2)

FEMMES et immigrées: l'insertion des femmes immigrées en France; [by Isabel Taboada Leonetti [and others]. [Paris, 1978]. pp. 286. (France. Direction de la Population et des Migrations. Migrations et Sociétés. 4)

— Foreign relations.

NOEL (LEON) Les illusions de Stresa: l'Italie abandonnée à Hitler. Paris, [1975]. pp. 206.

BERARD (ARMAND) Un ambassadeur se souvient: au temps du danger allemand. [Paris, 1976]. pp. 554.

YOUNG (ROBERT J.) Historian. In command of France: French foreign policy and military planning, 1933-1940. Cambridge, Mass., 1978. pp. 346. bibliog.

— — Algeria.

SMITH (TONY) The French stake in Algeria, 1945-1962. Ithaca, 1978. pp. 199. bibliog.

— — China.

BARLOW (JEFFREY G.) Sun Yat-Sen and the French, 1900-1908. Berkeley, [1979]. pp. 93. (California University. Center for Chinese Studies. China Research Monographs. No.14)

— — East (Near East).

PURYEAR (VERNON JOHN) Napoleon and the Dardanelles. Berkeley, 1951. pp. 437. bibliog.

— — Germany.

HEINEMANN (IRMGARD) Le Traité franco-allemand du 22 janvier 1963 et sa mise en oeuvre sous le général de Gaulle, 1963-1969; (thèse... présentée...à la Faculté de Droit et des Sciences Economiques de l'Université de Nice). Nice, 1977. pp. 475. bibliog.

SEYDOUX (FRANÇOIS) Dans l'intimité franco-allemande: une mission diplomatique. Paris, 1977. pp. 184.

McDOUGALL (WALTER A.) France's Rhineland diplomacy, 1914-1924: the last bid for a balance of power in Europe. Princeton, [1978]. pp. 420. bibliog.

— — Lebanon.

SPAGNOLO (JOHN P.) France and Ottoman Lebanon, 1861-1914. London, 1977. pp. 339. bibliog. (Oxford. University. St. Antony's College. Middle East Centre. St. Antony's Middle East Monographs. No. 7).

— — Saar Territory.

SAARGEBIET. Treaties. 1953. Die neuen Staatsverträge zwischen Frankreich und dem Saarland: Text der am 20. Mai 1953 in Paris unterzeichneten Verträge mit Anlagen und Zusatzprotokollen in den beiden amtlichen Sprachen. Saarbrücken, [1953?]. pp. 215. In German and French.

— — United Kingdom.

LECA (DOMINIQUE) La rupture de 1940. [Paris, 1978]. pp. 353.

THOMAS (R.T.) Britain and Vichy: the dilemma of Anglo-French relations, 1940-42. London, 1979. pp. 230. bibliog.

— — United States.

DUROSELLE (JEAN BAPTISTE) France and the United States: from the beginnings to the present...; (translated by Derek Coltman). Chicago, 1978. pp. 276. bibliog.

STRAUSS (DAVID) Historian. Menace in the West: the rise of French anti-Americanism in modern times. Westport, Conn., 1978. pp. 317. bibliog.

SULLIVAN (MARIANNA P.) France's Vietnam policy: a study in French-American relations. Westport, Conn., 1978. pp. 165. bibliog.

LEFFLER (MELVYN P.) The elusive quest: America's pursuit of European stability and French security, 1919-1933. Chapel Hill, [1979]. pp. 409. bibliog.

— — Vietnam.

SULLIVAN (MARIANNA P.) France's Vietnam policy: a study in French-American relations. Westport, Conn., 1978. pp. 165. bibliog.

— Government publications.

FRANCE. Commission Chargée de Favoriser la communication au Public des Documents Administratifs. 1978. Rapport au Premier Ministre: premier rapport; [Pierre Ordonneau, chairman]. Paris, 1978. pp. 43.

— Historiography.

GEYL (PIETER) Napoleon for and against; translated from the Dutch by Olive Renier. Harmondsworth, 1965. pp. 431. First published in Great Britain in 1949.

— History — Sources.

FRANCE. Archives Nationales. 1978. Les archives nationales: état général des fonds; publié sous la direction de Jean Favier. (Tome II. 1789-1940; sous la direction de Rémi Mathieu). Paris, 1978. pp. 656.

— — To 1515, Medieval period.

The SONG OF ROLAND; translated by Dorothy L. Sayers. Harmondsworth, 1957. pp. 206.

DUBY (GEORGES) The chivalrous society; translated by Cynthia Postan. London, 1977. pp. 246.

— — 1589-1789, Bourbons.

GOUBERT (PIERRE) Louis XIV and twenty million Frenchmen; translated from the French by Anne Carter. New York, [1966]. pp. 350. bibliog.

— — 1789-1799, Revolution.

CONTRIBUTIONS à l'histoire paysanne de la révolution française; sous la direction d'Albert Soboul. [Paris, 1977]. pp. 407.

FAILEVIC (MAURICE) and LA ROCHEFOUCAULD (JEAN DOMINIQUE DE) 1788: luttes révolutionnaires pour une propriété paysanne. [Paris, 1978]. pp. 303.

HUNT (LYNN AVERY) Revolution and urban politics in provincial France: Troyes and Reims, 1786-1790. Stanford, Ca., 1978. pp. 187. bibliog.

LEWIS (GWYNNE) The second Vendée: the continuity of counter-revolution in the Department of the Gard, 1789-1815. Oxford, 1978. pp. 250. bibliog.

ROSE (ROBERT BARRIE) Gracchus Babeuf: the first revolutionary communist. Stanford, 1978. pp. 434. bibliog.

— — — Influence.

LINKSRHEINISCHE deutsche Jakobiner: Aufrufe, Reden, Protokolle; Briefe und Schriften, 1794-1801; [edited by] Axel Kuhn. Stuttgart, [1978]. pp. 353. bibliog.

GOODWIN (ALBERT) The friends of liberty: the English democratic movement in the age of the French revolution. London, 1979. pp. 594. bibliog.

— — 1799-1815, Consulate and Empire.

CONNELLY (OWEN) Napoleon's satellite kingdoms. New York, [1965] repr. 1969. pp. 389. bibliog.

— — 1852-1870, Second Empire.

IMAGES of the Commune; edited by James A. Leith. Montreal, 1978. pp. 349.

— — 1870-1940, Third Republic.

BAKUNIN (MIKHAIL ALEKSANDROVICH) Michel Bakounine sur la guerre franco-allemande et la révolution sociale en France, 1870-1871. Leiden, 1977. pp. 455. (International Institute of Social History. Archives Bakounine. 6) In French or Russian.

IMAGES of the Commune; edited by James A. Leith. Montreal, 1978. pp. 349.

— — 1940-1945, German occupation.

SYDNOR (CHARLES W.) Soldiers of destruction: the SS Death's Head Division, 1933-1945. Princeton, N.J., [1977]. pp. 371. bibliog.

DEBU-BRIDEL (JACQUES) De Gaulle et le CNR. Paris, [1978]. pp. 278. bibliog.

LECA (DOMINIQUE) La rupture de 1940. [Paris, 1978]. pp. 353.

MICHEL (HENRI) Pétain et le régime de Vichy. [Paris, 1978]. pp. 128. bibliog.

FRANCE(Cont.)

MALRAUX (CLARA) Et pourtant j'étais libre. Paris, [1979]. pp. 262. *(Le bruit de nos pas. 6)*

—— 1945- .

MALRAUX (CLARA) Et pourtant j'étais libre. Paris, [1979]. pp. 262. *(Le bruit de nos pas. 6)*

— Industries.

FRANCE. Institut National de la Statistique et des Etudes Economiques. Les comptes régionaux des branches industrielles. a., 1971/1972- Paris.

DUMARD (JEAN) and LETABLIER (MARIE THERESE) L'emploi industriel en France, fin 1968 - fin 1971: modifications spatiales et structurelles. [Paris, 1976]. pp. 211. *(France. Centre d'Etudes de l'Emploi. Cahiers. 9)* With English summary.

J.R.R.S. INTERNATIONAL. Déconcentration industrielle et productivité [et si on produisait mieux en concentrant moins...; etude réalisée pour le Ministère de l'Industrie, du Commerce et de l'Artisanat]. [Paris, 1977]. pp. 113. *(Etudes de Politique Industrielle. 19)*

Le REDEPLOIEMENT industriel; [by Alain Cotta and others]. Paris, [1977]. pp. 131. *bibliog. (France. Ministère de l'Industrie, du Commerce et de l'Artisanat. Etudes de Politique Industrielle. 17)*

BACHELARD (PAUL) L'industrialisation de la région Centre: transformations économiques et socio-politiques. [Tours, 1978]. pp. 473. *bibliog.* 19 maps in end pocket.

FRANCE. Ministère de l'Industrie. Service du Traitement de l'Information et des Statistiques Industrielles. 1978. Enquête annuelle d'entreprise: résultats définitifs 1975. Paris, [1978]. pp. 61. *(Traits Fondamentaux du Système Industriel Français. Recueils Statistiques. Publication no. 10)*

FRANCE. Ministère de l'Industrie. Service du Traitement de l'Information et des Statistiques Industrielles. 1978. L'implantation étrangère dans l'industrie au 1er janvier 1976. Paris, [1978]. pp. 183. *(Traits Fondamentaux du Système Industriel Français. Recueils Statistiques. Publication no.9)*

KING (MERVYN A.) and MAIRESSE (JACQUES) Profitability in Britain and France: a comparative study, 1956- 1975. Paris, Institut National de la Statistique et des Etudes Economiques, 1978. pp. 80.

— Intellectual life — Maps.

FRANCE. Ministère de la Culture et de l'Environnement. Service des Etudes et de la Recherche. Atlas culturel, 1977. Paris, 1977. pp. 543.

— Maps.

FRANCE. Ministère de la Culture et de l'Environnement. Service des Etudes et de la Recherche. Atlas culturel, 1977. Paris, 1977. pp. 543.

— Occupations.

FRANCE. Institut National de la Statistique et des Etudes Economiques. 1962. Code des catégories socio-professionnelles; (code[s] no[s]. 3 [-6] du recensement de la population de 1962). 4th ed. Paris, 1962. 1 vol. (various pagings).

— Officials and employees.

QUIVAUX (ROBERT) Le tertiaire public et semi-public dans l'agglomération et la région parisiennes;... sous la direction du Professeur Jean Bastié. [Paris], Atelier Parisien d'Urbanisme, [1969?]. pp. 84.

— Parliament — Elections.

FRANCE. Ministère de l'Intérieur. 1978. Les élections législatives de 1978: 12 et 19 mars 1978. Paris, 1978. pp. 1125.

—— Assemblée Nationale — Elections.

FREARS (JOHN RUSSELL) and PARODI (JEAN LUC) War will not take place: the French parliamentary elections, March 1978. London, 1979. pp. 147. *bibliog.*

——— History.

FRANCE. Direction de la Documentation. La Documentation Française. Notes et Etudes Documentaires. No. 4463-4464. Les assemblées parlementaires sous la Ve République; [by] Jean Bourdon. [Paris], 1978. pp. 235. *bibliog.*

——— Rules and practice.

FRANCE. Assemblée Nationale, [1958-]. 1978. Règlement de l'Assemblée Nationale: instruction général du Bureau de l'Assemblée: constitution. 7th ed. [Paris], 1978. pp. 381.

—— Parlement — History.

COLLINS (IRENE) Napoleon and his parliaments, 1800-1815. London, 1979. pp. 193. *bibliog.*

— Politics and government.

LAUGEL (AUGUSTE) La France politique et sociale. Paris, 1877. pp. 349.

PENNAN (JOHN SIMPSON) The irresistible movement of democracy. New York, 1923. pp. 729.

KOLINSKY (A. MARTIN) Continuity and change in European society: Germany, France and Italy since 1870. London, 1974. pp. 234. *bibliog.*

HAUSS (CHARLES) The new left in France: the Unified Socialist Party. Westport, Conn., 1978. pp. 283. *bibliog.*

—— To 987.

McKEON (PETER R.) Hincmar of Laon and Carolingian politics. Urbana, [1978]. pp. 327. *bibliog.*

—— 1328-1589.

HARDING (ROBERT R.) Anatomy of a power elite: the provincial governors of early modern France. New Haven, 1978. pp. 310. *bibliog.*

LINIGER (JEAN) Philippe de Commynes. [Paris, 1978]. pp. 432. *bibliog.*

—— 1589-1789.

KETTERING (SHARON) Judicial politics and urban revolt in seventeenth-century France: the Parlement of Aix, 1629-1659. Princeton, N.J., [1978]. pp. 370. *bibliog.*

HARRIS (ROBERT D.) Necker: reform statesman of the ancien régime. Berkeley, Calif., [1979]. pp. 259. *bibliog.*

—— 1789- .

CHEVALLIER (JEAN JACQUES) Histoire des institutions et des régimes politiques de la France de 1789 à nos jours. 5th ed. Paris, 1977. pp. 846. *bibliog.*

—— 1789-1900.

CHABANNE (ROBERT) Les institutions de la France de la fin de l'ancien régime à l'avènement de la IIIème République, 1789-1875. Lyon, 1977. pp. 416.

—— 1799-1815.

COLLINS (IRENE) Napoleon and his parliaments, 1800-1815. London, 1979. pp. 193. *bibliog.*

—— 1870-1940.

McDOUGALL (WALTER A.) France's Rhineland diplomacy, 1914-1924: the last bid for a balance of power in Europe. Princeton, [1978]. pp. 420. *bibliog.*

UDT (TONY) Socialism in Provence, 1871-1914: a study in the origins of the modern French left. Cambridge, 1979. pp. 370. *bibliog.*

—— 1945- .

HANSEN (NILES M.) France in the modern world. New York, [1969]. pp. 167. *bibliog.*

ANDERSON (MALCOLM) Government in France: an introduction to the executive power. Oxford, [1970]. pp. 217.

GIROUD (FRANÇOISE) La comédie du pouvoir. [Paris, 1977]. pp. 361.

McINNES (NEIL) French politics today: the future of the Fifth Republic. Beverly Hills, [1977]. pp. 69. *(Georgetown University. Center for Strategic and International Studies. Washington Papers. vol. 5/51)*

POUJADE (PIERRE) A l'heure de la colère. [Paris, 1977]. pp. 253.

SUR (SERGE) La vie politique en France sous la Ve République. Paris, 1977. pp. 496.

LECOMTE (BERNARD) and SAUVAGE (CHRISTIAN) Les Giscardiens. [Paris, 1978]. pp. 217.

MITTERRAND (FRANÇOIS) L'abeille et l'architecte: chronique. [Paris, 1978]. pp. 403.

WRITING on the wall: May 1968: a documentary anthology; edited by Vladimir Fišera; translated from the French. London, 1978. pp. 327. *bibliog.*

CONFLICT and consensus in France; edited by Vincent Wright. London, 1979. pp. 150.

FREARS (JOHN RUSSELL) and PARODI (JEAN LUC) War will not take place: the French parliamentary elections, March 1978. London, 1979. pp. 147. *bibliog.*

HANLEY (DAVID L.) and others. Contemporary France: politics and society since 1945. London, 1979. pp. 325. *bibliog.*

— Population.

NEWELL (WILLIAM HENRY) Population change and agricultural development in nineteenth century France. New York, 1977. pp. 199. *bibliog.*

FRANCE. Institut National de la Statistique et des Etudes Economiques. Service Conditions de Vie des Ménages, Prix de Détail. 1978. Projection du nombre de ménages, 1975-2000. Paris, 1978. pp. 91.

— Relations (general) with Germany.

LAPIE (PIERRE OLIVIER) and SCHMID (CARLO) La coopération franco-allemande. Paris, La Documentation Française, [1973]. pp. 63.

— Religion.

QUENIART (JEAN) Les hommes, l'Eglise et Dieu dans la France du XVIIIe siècle. [Paris], 1978. pp. 358. *bibliog.*

— Rural conditions.

FRANCE. Ministère de l'Agriculture. Région Bourgogne. Atelier Régional d'Etudes Economiques et d'Aménagement Rural. 1975. La dévitalisation de l'espace rural: l'exemple de quatre cantons du plateau de Langres, Côte d'Or; [edited by J. Bellet]. Paris, 1975. pp. 113. Annexe au bulletin no.5.

— Social conditions.

HANSEN (NILES M.) France in the modern world. New York, [1969]. pp. 167. *bibliog.*

SCHEMA général d'aménagement de la France: le scenario de l'inacceptable: sept ans après; [by Bernard Cuneo and others]. [Paris], 1977. pp. 144. *(France. Délégation à l'Aménagement du Territoire et à l'Action Régionale. Travaux et Recherches de Prospective. 68)*

BACHELARD (PAUL) L'industrialisation de la région Centre: transformations économiques et socio-politiques. [Tours, 1978]. pp. 473. *bibliog.* 19 maps in end pocket.

HANLEY (DAVID L.) and others. Contemporary France: politics and society since 1945. London, 1979. pp. 325. *bibliog.*

—— Maps.

FRANCE. Ministère de la Culture et de l'Environnement. Service des Etudes et de la Recherche. Atlas culturel, 1977. Paris, 1977. pp. 543.

FRANCE(Cont.)

— — Statistics.

FRANCE. Institut National de la Statistique et des Etudes Economiques. 1978. Données sociales. 3rd ed. [Paris, 1978]. pp. 424.

— Social history.

DUBY (GEORGES) The chivalrous society; translated by Cynthia Postan. London, 1977. pp. 246.

GUIRAL (PIERRE) and THUILLIER (GUY) La vie quotidienne des domestiques en France au XIXe siècle. [Paris, 1978]. pp. 281. *bibliog.*

— Social life and customs.

LAUGEL (AUGUSTE) La France politique et sociale. Paris, 1877. pp. 349.

— Social policy.

FRANCE. Commissariat General du Plan de l'Equipement et de la Productivité. 1966. Fifth Plan: economic and social development plan, 1966-1970. Paris, [1966]. pp. 106.

HUITIEME plan: rapport sur les principales options du VIIIe plan: projet soumis par le gouvernement à l'avis du Conseil Economique et Social. Paris, La Documentation Française, 1979. pp. 84. *Map in end pocket.*

— Territories and possessions — Economic conditions.

FRANCE. Secrétariat Général pour l'Administration des Départements d'Outre-Mer. Service des Affaires Economiques et des Investissements. 1977. L'Économie des DOM en 1976. [Paris], 1977. pp. 85.

— — Social policy.

FRANCE. Secrétariat Général des Départements d'Outre-Mer. Service des Affaires Administratives Financières et Sociales. 1976. La politique sociale dans les départements d'outre-mer. [Paris], 1976. fo. 54.

FRANCIS JOSEPH I, Emperor of Austria.

HERRE (FRANZ) Kaiser Franz Joseph von Österreich: sein Leben, seine Zeit. Köln, [1978]. pp. 502. *bibliog.*

JENKS (WILLIAM ALEXANDER) Francis Joseph and the Italians, 1849-1859. Charlottesville, 1978. pp. 206. *bibliog.*

FRANCO BAHAMONDE (FRANCISCO).

RAMIREZ (LUIS) Franco: la obsesión de ser, la obsesión de poder. Paris, 1976. pp. 324.

MAY (HARRY S.) Francisco Franco: the Jewish connection. Washington, D.C., [1978]. pp. 187. *bibliog.*

FRANCO-GERMAN WAR, 1870-1871.

BAKUNIN (MIKHAIL ALEKSANDROVICH) Michel Bakounine sur la guerre franco-allemande et la révolution sociale en France, 1870-1871. Leiden, 1977. pp. 455. *(International Institute of Social History. Archives Bakounine. 6) In French or Russian.*

DECSY (JÁNOS) Prime Minister Gyula Andrássy's influence on Habsburg foreign policy during the Franco-German War of 1870-1871. Boulder, 1979. pp. 177. *(East European Quarterly. East European Monographs. 52) (City University of New York. Brooklyn College. Department of History. Studies on Society in Change. No. 8)*

FRAUD

— Ghana.

GHANA. 1976. White Paper on the report of the Committee of Enquiry into the Affairs of R.T. Briscoe (Ghana) Limited. Accra, [1976]. pp. 12. *(W[hite] P[apers]. 1976. No. 4) Bound with report.*

GHANA. Committee of Enquiry into the Affairs of R.T. Briscoe (Ghana) Limited. 1976. Report; [Joe Appiah, chairman]. Accra, [1976]. pp. 229. *Bound with the White Paper on the report.*

— Russia.

PANOV (NIKOLAI IVANOVICH) Ugolovnaia otvetstvennost' za prichinenie imushchestvennogo ushcherba putem obmana ili zloupotrebleniia doveriem. Khar'kov, 1977. pp. 127. *bibliog.*

FRAUDULENT CONVEYANCES

— New Zealand.

NEW ZEALAND. Property Law and Equity Reform Committee. 1977. Report...on the decision in Frazer v. Walker; [C.P. Hutchinson chairman]. Wellington, 1977. pp. 21.

FREDERICK II, called the Great, King of Prussia.

REDDAWAY (WILLIAM FIDDIAN) Frederick the Great and the rise of Prussia. New York, 1904; New York, 1969. pp. 368.

PARET (PETER) ed. Frederick the Great: a profile. London, 1972. pp. 244. *bibliog.*

FREE CHOICE OF EMPLOYMENT

— Germany.

RADÜ (FRIEDRICH WILHELM) Die Konkretisierung der Berufsfreiheit im Arbeitsrecht der Bundesrepublik Deutschland und der Schweiz. Basel, 1978. pp. 171. *bibliog. (Basel. Universität. Juristische Fakultät. Institut für Internationales Recht und Internationale Beziehungen. Schriftenreihe. Heft 26)*

FREE TRADE AND PROTECTION.

GUYOT (YVES) Economic prejudices; translated by Fred Rothwell. London, 1910. pp. 166.

KRAUSS (MELVYN B.) The new protectionism: the welfare state and international trade. Oxford, [1979]. pp. 119. *bibliogs.*

FREE WILL AND DETERMINISM.

KENNY (ANTHONY JOHN PATRICK) Freewill and responsibility. London, 1978. pp. 101. *(Trent University. Ryle Lectures. 1976).*

FREEDMEN IN THE UNITED STATES.

LITTLEFIELD (DANIEL F.) The Cherokee freedmen from emancipation to American citizenship. Westport, Conn., 1978. pp. 281. *bibliog.*

OUBRE (CLAUDE F.) Forty acres and a mule: the Freedmen's Bureau and black land ownership. Baton Rouge, [1978]. pp. 212. *bibliog.*

FREEDOM OF ASSOCIATION

— Germany.

KNEBEL (JUERGEN) Koalitionsfreiheit und Gemeinwohl: zur verfassungsrechtlichen Zulässigkeit staatlicher Einwirkung auf die tarifautonome Lohngestaltung. Berlin, 1978. pp. 179. *bibliog.*

FREEDOM OF INFORMATION.

ROWAT (DONALD CAMERON) Public access to government documents. [Toronto], 1978. pp. 116. *(Ontario. Commission on Freedom of Information and Individual Privacy. Research Publications. 3)*

— Canada.

RANKIN (T. MURRAY) Freedom of information in Canada: will the doors stay shut? [Victoria?], 1977. pp. 155.

— — New Brunswick.

NEW BRUNSWICK. Premier. 1977. Freedom of information: outline of government policy pertaining to a legislated right of access by the public to government documents. [Fredericton], 1977. fo.35.

— France.

FRANCE. Commission Chargée de Favoriser la Communication au Public des Documents Administratifs. 1978. Rapport au Premier Ministre: premier rapport; [Pierre Ordonneau, chairman]. Paris, 1978. pp. 43.

— United Kingdom.

SWANN (Sir MICHAEL MEREDITH) Are the lamps going out? London, [1977]. pp. 15. *(Claysemore Lectures. 1977)*

BENN (ANTHONY NEIL WEDGWOOD) The right to know: the case for freedom of information to safeguard our basic liberties. Nottingham, 1978. pp. 15. *(Institute for Workers' Control. Pamphlet Series. No. 62)*

JUSTICE (BRITISH SECTION OF THE INTERNATIONAL COMMISSION OF JURISTS). Freedom of information: (a report); chairman of committee, Anthony Lincoln. London, 1978. pp. 18.

— United States.

RANKIN (T. MURRAY) Freedom of information in Canada: will the doors stay shut? [Victoria?], 1977. pp. 155.

FREEDOM OF MOVEMENT

— Hungary.

SOLYOM-FEKETE (WILLIAM) Travel abroad and emigration under new rules adopted by the government of Hungary. Washington, Library of Congress, 1979. pp. 104.

FREEMASONS

— United States.

LIPSON (DOROTHY ANN) Freemasonry in Federalist Connecticut. Princeton, 1977. pp. 380. *bibliog.*

FREETOWN

— Politics and government.

HARRELL-BOND (BARBARA E.) and others. Community leadership and the transformation of Freetown (1801- 1976). The Hague, [1978]. pp. 416. *bibliog.*

FREGE (GOTTLOB).

CURRIE (GREGORY PAUL) The objectivism of Frege and Popper: an historical and critical investigation. 1978. fo. 294. *bibliog. Typescript. Ph.D. (London) thesis: unpublished. This thesis is the property of London University and may not be removed from the Library.*

FREIE DEMOKRATISCHE PARTEI.

WAGNER (DIETRICH) FDP und die Wiederbewaffnung: die wehrpolitische Orientierung der Liberalen in der Bundesrepublik Deutschland, 1949-1955. Boppard am Rhein, 1978. pp. 182. *bibliog. (Militärgeschichtliches Forschungsamt. Militärgeschichte seit 1945. 5)*

FREIE LEHRERGEWERKSCHAFT DEUTSCHLANDS.

STOEHR (WOLFGANG) Lehrer und Arbeiterbewegung: Entstehung und Politik der ersten Gewerkschaftsorganisation der Lehrer in Deutschland, 1920 bis 1923. Marburg, [1978]. 2 vols. *bibliog. (Studiengesellschaft für Sozialgeschichte und Arbeiterbewegung, Marburg. Schriftenreihe für Sozialgeschichte und Arbeiterbewegung. Band 13)*

FREIER GEWERKSCHAFTSBUND HESSEN.

WEISS-HARTMANN (ANNE) Der Freie Gewerkschaftsbund Hessen, 1945-1949. Marburg, 1977 repr. 1978. pp. 417. *bibliog. (Studiengesellschaft für Sozialgeschichte und Arbeiterbewegung, Marburg. Schriftenreihe für Sozialgeschichte und Arbeiterbewegung. Band 2)*

FREIGHT AND FREIGHTAGE.

IMAKITA (JUNICHI) A techno-economic analysis of the port transport system. Farnborough, Hants., [1978]. pp. 206. *bibliog.*

— Australia.

AUSTRALIA. Bureau of Transport Economics. 1978. Estimates of Australian interregional freight movements, 1975-76. Canberra, 1978. pp. 74.

— France.

FRANCE. Département des Statistiques des Transports. Système d'information sur les transports de marchandises: résultats généraux; trafic intérieur et international. a., 1975- Paris.

— India.

KERALA. Bureau of Economics and Statistics. 1977. Report on the survey of interstate movement of goods by road. Trivandrum, 1977. pp. 22.

— United Kingdom.

RIDLEY (JASPER) Barrister-at-Law. The law of the carriage of goods by land, sea and air...; fifth edition by Geoffrey Whitehead. London, 1978. pp. 297.

PAYNE (WILLIAM) Barrister-at-Law, and IVAMY (EDWARD RICHARD HARDY) Carriage of goods by sea: eleventh edition by E.R.H. Ivamy. London, 1979. pp. 332.

FREIGHT FORWARDERS

— United Kingdom.

HEILBRON (Dame ROSE) and SAMWELL (STANLEY DAVID) Kuehne and Nagel Limited: investigation under section 165(b) of the Companies Act 1948; report. London, H.M.S.O., 1978. 1 vol.(various pagings).

FREIRE (PAULO).

WORLD COUNCIL OF CHURCHES. Commission on the Churches' Participation in Development. Conscientization: [a dossier including separately published articles]. Geneva, 1975. 1 vol. (various pagings). *bibliog.* (CCPD Documents. 7)

FRENCH CANADIANS.

BASHAM (RICHARD DALTON) Crisis in blanc and white: urbanization and ethnic identity in French Canada. Boston, Mass., [1978]. pp. 287. *bibliog.*

FRENCH GUIANA

— Economic conditions.

FRANCE. Direction de la Documentation. La Documentation Française. Notes et Etudes Documentaires. Nos. 4,497-4, 498. La Guyane française: un bilan de trente années; [by] Gérard Brasseur. Paris, 1978. pp. 183. *bibliog.*

— Social conditions.

FRANCE. Direction de la Documentation. La Documentation Française. Notes et Etudes Documentaires. Nos. 4,497-4, 498. La Guyane française: un bilan de trente années; [by] Gérard Brasseur. Paris, 1978. pp. 183. *bibliog.*

— Statistics.

GERMANY (BUNDESREPUBLIK). Statistisches Bundesamt. Länderkurzbericht: Franz[ösisch]-Guayana. a., 1977- Wiesbaden.

FRENCH IN GERMANY.

JERSCH-WENZEL (STEFI) Juden und "Franzosen" in der Wirtschaft des Raumes Berlin/Brandenburg zur Zeit des Merkantilismus. Berlin, 1978. pp. 290. *bibliog.* (Historische Kommission zu Berlin. Einzelveröffentlichungen. Band 23)

FRENCH LANGUAGE.

GORDON (DAVID CROCKETT) The French language and national identity (1930-1975). The Hague, [1978]. pp. 225. *bibliog.*

— Discourse analysis.

LABBE (DOMINIQUE) Le discours communiste. [Paris, 1977]. pp. 204.

— Syntax.

HARRIS (MARTIN) The evolution of French syntax: a comparative approach. London, 1978. pp. 268. *bibliog.*

FRENCH LANGUAGE IN CANADA.

QUEBEC (PROVINCE). Department of Cultural Development. 1977. Québec's policy on the French language. [Quebec], 1977. pp. 109.

QUEBEC (PROVINCE). Statutes, etc. 1977. Bill 101: charter of the French language. Québec, 1977. pp. 45.

FRENCH POETRY

— To 1500.

The SONG OF ROLAND; translated by Dorothy L. Sayers. Harmondsworth, 1957. pp. 206.

FRENTE DE LIBERTAÇÃO DE MOÇAMBIQUE.

SITHOLE (NDABANINGI) and INGWANE (JULIUS PAUNDE SHIMANGANE) Frelimo militant: the story of Ingwane from Mozambique, an ordinary, yet extraordinary man, awakened. Nairobi, 1977. pp. 187.

FREQUENCY CURVES.

HABERMAN (SHELBY J.) The analysis of frequency data. Chicago, [1974]. pp. 419. *bibliog.*

FREUD (SIGMUND).

CUDDIHY (JOHN MURRAY) The ordeal of civility: Freud, Marx, Lévi-Strauss, and the Jewish struggle with modernity. New York, [1974]. pp. 272.

BOCOCK (ROBERT) Freud and modern society: an outline and analysis of Freud's sociology. New York, 1978. pp. 200. *bibliog.*

GAY (PETER) Freud, Jews and other Germans: masters and victims in modernist culture. Oxford, 1978. pp. 289.

FRIENDLY SOCIETIES

— United Kingdom.

U.K. Registry of Friendly Societies. 1978. Guide to the law relating to industrial and provident societies. London, 1978. pp. 90.

FRIENDS, SOCIETY OF.

BELL (JOHN HYSLOP) British folks and British India fifty years ago: Joseph Pease and his contemporaries, containing letters by Thomas Clarkson,...and others. London, [1891]. pp. 207.

YARROW (C.H. MIKE) Quaker experiences in international conciliation. New Haven, 1978. pp. 308.

— History — Sources.

BRISTOL. Bristol Record Society. Publications. vol. 30. Minute book of the Men's Meeting of the Society of Friends in Bristol 1686-1704; edited by Russell Mortimer. Bristol, 1977. pp. 310. *bibliog.*

FRIULI-VENEZIA GIULIA

— History.

GROSS (FELIKS) Ethnics in a borderland: an inquiry into the nature of ethnicity and reduction of ethnic tensions in a one-time genocide area. Westport, Conn., 1978. pp. 193. *bibliog.*

FROEBEL (JULIUS).

KOCH (RAINER) Demokratie und Staat bei Julius Fröbel, 1805-1893: liberales Denken zwischen Naturrecht und Sozialdarwinismus. Wiesbaden, 1978. pp. 298. *bibliog.* (Institut für Europäische Geschichte. Veröffentlichungen. Band 84)

FROLINAT.

BUIJTENHUIJS (ROBERT) Le Frolinat et les révoltes populaires du Tchad, 1965-1976. The Hague, [1978]. pp. 526. *bibliog.* (Afrika-Studiecentrum. Change and Continuity in Africa)

FRONT DE LIBERATION NATIONALE.

HUTCHINSON (MARTHA CRENSHAW) Revolutionary terrorism: the FLN in Algeria, 1954-1962. Stanford, [1978]. pp. 178. *(Stanford University. Hoover Institution on War, Revolution and Peace. Hoover Institution Publications. 196)*

FRONT DE LIBERATION NATIONALE [CHAD].

See FROLINAT.

FRONTIER AND PIONEER LIFE

— Brazil.

VELHO (OTAVIO GUILHERME) Capitalismo autoritario e campesinato: um estudo comparativo a partir da fronteira em movimento. São Paulo, 1976. pp. 261. *bibliog.*

— Mexico.

POWELL (PHILIP WAYNE) Mexico's Miguel Caldera: the taming of America's first frontier, 1548-1597. Túcson, 1977. pp. 322. *bibliog.*

— United States.

BILLINGTON (RAY ALLEN) America's frontier culture: three essays. College Station, Tex., [1977]. pp. 97.

DAVIS (JAMES E.) Frontier America, 1800-1840: a comparative demographic analysis of the settlement process. Glendale, Calif., 1977. pp.220. *bibliog.*

HARDEMAN (NICHOLAS PERKINS) Wilderness calling: the Hardeman family in the American westward movement, 1750-1900. Knoxville, [1977]. pp. 357. *bibliog.*

ROHRBOUGH (MALCOLM JUSTIN) The trans-Appalachian frontier: people, societies, and institutions, 1775-1850. New York, 1978. pp. 444. *bibliog.*

BOYER (LARRY M.) Frontier justice. Washington, Library of Congress, 1979. pp. 102. *bibliog.*

FARAGHER (JOHN MACK) Women and men on the overland trail. New Haven, 1979. pp. 281. *bibliog. (Yale University. Yale Historical Publications. Miscellany. 121)*

UNRUH (JOHN DAVID) The plains across: the overland emigrants and the Trans- Mississippi West, 1840-60. Urbana, 1979. pp. 565. *bibliog.*

— — Louisiana.

FITZPATRICK (JOHN) c.1737-1791. The merchant of Manchac: the letterbooks of John Fitzpatrick, 1768-1790; edited with an introduction by Margaret Fisher Dalrymple. Baton Rouge, [1978]. pp. 451. *bibliog.*

FRUIT

— Marketing — Australia.

WEISSEL (D.A.) and WHITTINGHAM (R.B.) Price information in the fresh fruit and vegetable industries in Australia: an exploratory analysis of its effectiveness of transmission. Canberra, 1978. pp. 46. *(Australia. Bureau of Agricultural Economics. Occasional Papers. No.47)*

FRUIT TRADE.

COMMONWEALTH SECRETARIAT. Fruit and tropical products. s-a., D 1978(no.1)- London.

FRUIT TRADE.(Cont.)

— America, Latin.

KARNES (THOMAS L.) Tropical enterprise: the Standard Fruit and Steamship Company in Latin America. Baton Rouge, [1978]. pp. 332. *bibliog.*

FUEL.

INTERNATIONAL ENERGY AGENCY. 1979. Workshops on energy supply and demand. Paris, 1978 [or rather 1979]. pp. 501. *bibliogs.*

— Russia — Siberia.

TOPLIVNO-energeticheskii kompleks Sibiri: sostoianie i napravleniia razvitiia. Novosibirsk, 1978. pp. 255.

— United Kingdom — Prices.

RICHARDSON (PAUL) Fuel poverty: a study of fuel expenditure among low income council tenants. [York], 1978. pp. 56. *(Papers in Community Studies. No. 20)*

FUERSTENBERG (WILHELM EGON) Graf von, Cardinal.

O'CONNOR (JOHN T.) Negotiator out of season: the career of Wilhelm Egon von Fürstenberg, 1629 to 1704. Athens, Ga., [1978]. pp. 263. *bibliog.*

FULAHS.

RIESMAN (PAUL) Freedom in Fulani social life: an introspective ethnography; translated by Martha Fuller. Chicago, [1977]. pp. 297. *bibliog.*

FULL EMPLOYMENT POLICIES

— India — Maharashtra.

MAHARASHTRA COMMERCIAL AND INDUSTRIAL CONFERENCE, 5TH, BOMBAY, 1972. Development through employment. [Bombay, Maharashtra Economic Development Council, 1972?]. pp. 59.

— United Kingdom.

POCOCK (C.C.) More jobs: a small cure for a big problem. [Berkhamsted, 1977]. pp. 16. *(Ashridge Management College. Ashridge Lectures. 1977)*

FULLERTON (DOUGLAS H.).

FULLERTON (DOUGLAS H.) The dangerous delusion: Quebec's independence obsession, as seen by former adviser to René Lévesque and Jean Lesage. Toronto, [1978]. pp. 240.

FUNCTIONAL ANALYSIS.

HOLMES (RICHARD B.) Geometric functional analysis and its applications. New York, [1975]. pp. 246. *bibliog.*

FUNCTIONAL ANALYSIS (SOCIAL SCIENCES).

FEBBRAJO (ALBERTO) Funzionalismo strutturale e sociologia del diritto nell'opera di Niklas Luhmann. Milano, 1975. pp. 226. *bibliog.* (Milan. Università. Istituto di Filosofia e Sociologia del Diritto. Studi di Sociologia del Diritto. 2)

FUNCTIONAL EQUATIONS.

EICHHORN (WOLFGANG) Functional equations in economics. Reading, Mass., 1978. pp. 260. *bibliog.*

FUNCTIONS.

LUKACS (EUGENE) Characteristic functions. 2nd ed. London, 1970. pp. 350. *bibliog.*

FUNCTIONS, HYPERGEOMETRIC.

EXTON (HAROLD) Handbook of hypergeometric integrals: theory, applications, tables, computer programs. Chichester, 1978. pp. 316. *bibliog.*

FUNERAL RITES AND CEREMONIES

— United States.

PASSING: the vision of death in America; edited by Charles O. Jackson. Westport, Conn., 1977. pp. 258. *bibliog.*

FUR TRADE

— Canada.

MITCHELL (ELAINE ALLAN) Fort Timiskaming and the fur trade. Toronto, [1977]. pp. 306. *bibliog.*

RAY (ARTHUR J.) and FREEMAN (DONALD B.) 'Give us good measure': an economic analysis of relations between the Indians and the Hudson's Bay Company before 1763. Toronto, [1978]. pp. 298. *bibliog.*

— United States.

WISHART (DAVID J.) The fur trade of the American west, 1807-1840: a geographical synthesis. London, 1979. pp. 237. *bibliog.*

— — Alaska.

TIKHMENEV (PETR ALEKSANDROVICH) A history of the Russian-American Company; translated and edited by Richard A. Pierce and Alton S. Donnelly. Seattle, 1978. pp. 522.

GAELIC LANGUAGE.

McKINNON (KENNETH M.) Language shift and education: conservation of ethnolinguistic culture amongst schoolchildren of a Gaelic community. Hatfield, 1978. pp. 25. *bibliog.* (Hatfield Polytechnic. School of Social Sciences. Social Sciences Occasional Papers. No.2)

GAITSKELL (HUGH TODD-NAYLOR).

WILLIAMS (PHILIP MAYNARD) Hugh Gaitskell: a political biography. London, 1979. pp. 1007. *bibliog.*

GALATINA

— History.

CAGGIA (CARLO) Cronache fra due secoli: lotte politiche e sociali dal 1896 al 1909 in una città del Salento attraverso la stampa socialista. [Napoli, 1976]. pp. 179.

GALBRAITH (JOHN KENNETH).

FIRESTONE (OTTO JOHN) Canada's anti-inflation program and Kenneth Galbraith. Ottawa, 1977. pp. 259. *(Ottawa. Université. Collection Sciences Sociales. No. 5)*

GALICIA (SPAIN)

— Economic conditions.

PRADA BLANCO (ALBINO) and LOPEZ RODRIGUEZ (ABEL) A outra economia galega. La Coruña, 1979. pp. 213. *bibliog.*

— Rural conditions.

PRADA BLANCO (ALBINO) and LOPEZ RODRIGUEZ (ABEL) A outra economia galega. La Coruña, 1979. pp. 213. *bibliog.*

— Social conditions.

PRADA BLANCO (ALBINO) and LOPEZ RODRIGUEZ (ABEL) A outra economia galega. La Coruña, 1979. pp. 213. *bibliog.*

GALILEI (GALILEO).

DRAKE (STILLMAN) Galileo at work: his scientific biography. Chicago, 1978. pp. 536.

GALLAND (ADOLF).

GALLAND (ADOLF) The first and the last: the German fighter force in World War II. London, 1955 repr. 1973. pp. 368.

GALLIENI (JOSEPH SIMON).

GALLIENI (JOSEPH SIMON) Mémoires du Général Galliéni: défense de Paris, 25 Août-11 Septembre 1914. Paris, 1920. pp. 271.

GALLOWAY (JOSEPH).

FERLING (JOHN E.) The Loyalist mind: Joseph Galloway and the American Revolution. University Park, [1977]. pp. 157. *bibliog.*

GAMBIA

— Foreign relations.

MOMEN (WENDY C.) The foreign policy and relations of the Gambia. 1978. fo. 339. *bibliog.* Typescript. Ph.D. (London) thesis: unpublished. This thesis is the property of London University and may not be removed from the Library.

GAMES, THEORY OF.

BOWEN (KEN C.) Research games: an approach to the study of decision processes;.. .with contributions by Janet I. Harris. London, 1978. pp. 126. *bibliog.* (Operational Research Society. ORASA Texts. No. 3)

GAME theory and political science; edited by Peter C. Ordeshook. New York, 1978. pp. 627. *bibliogs.* Papers based on a Mathematical Social Science Board sponsored Conference on Game Theory and Political Science, Hyannis, 1977.

HAGLUND (STIG) Effektivitet i beslutsfattande grupper...: Effectiveness in decision making groups, etc. Helsingfors, 1978. pp. 285. *bibliog.* (Svenska Handelshögskolan. Ekonomi och Samhälle. Nr. 26) With English summary.

TELSER (LESTER G.) Economic theory and the core. Chicago, [1978]. pp. 407. *bibliog.*

CASE (JAMES H.) Economics and the competitive process. New York, 1979. pp. 295. *bibliogs.*

GANDHI (INDIRA).

LAMB (BEATRICE PITNEY) The Nehrus of India: three generations of leadership. New York, [1967]. pp. 276. *bibliog.*

SOCIALIST INDIA. Republic Day Number, 1976. The Indira Gandhi decade, 1966-1976. Delhi, 1976. 1 vol. (various pagings). *bibliog.*

GANDHI (MOHANDAS KARAMCHAND).

SHAHANI (RANJEE GURDASING) Mr. Gandhi. New York, 1961. pp. 211. *With ms. comments by Vera Anstey on end paper and a typescript copy of her review in end pocket.*

BIRLA (GHANSHYAM DASS) Bapu: a unique association. Bombay, 1977. 4 vols. *Correspondence between M.K. Gandhi, G.D. Birla, and others, 1924-1947.*

GANGS

— United States — California.

CALIFORNIA. Legislature. Senate Subcommittee on Civil Disorder. 1974. Executive session...: gang violence in penal institutions. Los Angeles, 1974. pp. 104.

GARD

— Politics and government.

LEWIS (GWYNNE) The second Vendée: the continuity of counter-revolution in the Department of the Gard, 1789-1815. Oxford, 1978. pp. 250. *bibliog.*

— Religion.

LEWIS (GWYNNE) The second Vendée: the continuity of counter-revolution in the Department of the Gard, 1789-1815. Oxford, 1978. pp. 250. *bibliog.*

GARDIE (MAGNUS GABRIEL DE LA).

See DE LA GARDIE (MAGNUS GABRIEL).

GARDINER (MURIEL).

GARDINER (MURIEL) and BUTTINGER (JOSEPH) Damit wir nicht vergessen: unsere Jahre 1934-1947 in Wien, Paris und New York. Wien, [1978]. pp. 168. *bibliog.*

GARNISHMENT.

See ATTACHMENT AND GARNISHMENT.

GARVEY (MARCUS).

BURKETT (RANDALL K.) Garveyism as a religious movement: the institutionalization of black civil religion. Metuchen, 1978. pp. 216. *(American Theological Library Association. ATLA Monograph Series. No.13)*

GAS, NATURAL

— Canada — British Columbia.

BRITISH COLUMBIA. Energy Commission. 1977. 1977 petroleum and natural gas price and incentives hearing. [Vancouver], 1977. pp. 99.

— Norway.

JOHNSON (CHRISTOPHER) 1931- . North Sea energy wealth 1965-1985: oil and gas in the British and Norwegian economies. London, [1978]. 2 vols. *bibliog.*

— United Kingdom.

BARNES (MICHAEL CECIL JOHN) and others. U.K. oil and natural gas depletion. [London, 1978]. pp. 4. *(Energy Commission [U.K.]. Papers. No. 20)*

JOHNSON (CHRISTOPHER) 1931- . North Sea energy wealth 1965-1985: oil and gas in the British and Norwegian economies. London, [1978]. 2 vols. *bibliog.*

— United States — Rates.

PUBLIC utility rate making in an energy-conscious environment; edited by Werner Sichel. Boulder, Colo., 1979. pp. 145.

GAS, NATURAL, IN SUBMERGED LANDS

— Canada — Newfoundland.

SCARLETT (MAURICE) ed. Consequences of offshore oil and gas: Norway, Scotland and Newfoundland; a selection of background papers prepared for a colloquium (November, 1974) on the potential impact on the province of future commercial oil/gas discovery offshore Newfoundland. St. John's, 1977. pp. 264. *(St. John's. Memorial University of Newfoundland. Institute of Social and Economic Research. Newfoundland Social and Economic Papers. No.6)*

— North Sea.

JOHNSON (CHRISTOPHER) 1931- . North Sea energy wealth 1965-1985: oil and gas in the British and Norwegian economies. London, [1978]. 2 vols. *bibliog.*

— Norway.

SCARLETT (MAURICE) ed. Consequences of offshore oil and gas: Norway, Scotland and Newfoundland; a selection of background papers prepared for a colloquium (November, 1974) on the potential impact on the province of future commercial oil/gas discovery offshore Newfoundland. St. John's, Nfld., 1977. pp. 264. *(St. John's. Memorial University of Newfoundland. Institute of Social and Economic Papers. No.6)*

— United Kingdom — Scotland.

SCARLETT (MAURICE) ed. Consequences of offshore oil and gas: Norway, Scotland and Newfoundland; a selection of background papers prepared for a colloquium (November, 1974) on the potential impact on the province of future commercial oil/gas discovery offshore Newfoundland. St. John's, Nfld., 1977. pp. 264. *(St. John's. Memorial University of Newfoundland. Institute of Social and Economic Papers. No.6)*

GAST (JOHN).

PROTHERO (IORWERTH J.) Artisans and politics in early nineteenth-century London: John Gast and his times. Folkestone, 1979. pp. 418. *bibliog.*

GAULLE (CHARLES DE).

DEBU-BRIDEL (JACQUES) De Gaulle et le CNR. Paris, [1978]. pp. 278. *bibliog.*

GDANSK

— History.

WÓJCICKI (JÓZEF) Wolne Miasto Gdańsk, 1920-1939. Warszawa, 1976. pp. 355. *bibliog.*

— Politics and government.

DRZYCIMSKI (ANDRZEJ) Polacy w Wolnym Mieście Gdańsku, 1920-1933: polityka Senatu gdańskiego wobec ludności polskiej. Wrocław, 1978. pp. 367. *bibliog.* With English summary.

GENERAL AGREEMENT ON TARIFFS AND TRADE.

HUDEC (ROBERT E.) Adjudication of international trade disputes. London, 1978. pp. 88. *(Trade Policy Research Centre. Thames Essays. No. 16)*

GENERAL AGREEMENT ON TARIFFS AND TRADE. 1979. The Tokyo Round of multilateral trade negotiations: report by the Director-General of GATT. Geneva, 1979. pp. 196.

KOSTECKI (M.M.) East-West trade and the GATT system. London, 1979. pp. 157. *bibliog.*

GENERATIVE GRAMMAR.

D'AGOSTINO (FREDERICK BRUCE) A philosophical examination of transformational linguistics. 1978. fo. 246. *bibliog.* Typescript. Ph.D. (London) thesis: unpublished. This thesis is the property of London University and may not be removed from the Library.

KAC (MICHAEL B.) Corepresentation of grammatical structure. Minneapolis, [1978]. pp. 168. *bibliog.*

CHOMSKY (NOAM) Language and responsibility: based on conversations with Mitsou Ronat; translated from the French by John Viertel. Hassocks, 1979. pp. 212. *bibliog.*

PULLUM (GEOFFREY K.) Rule interaction and the organization of a grammar. New York, 1979. pp. 413. *bibliog.*

GENETIC ENGINEERING.

GOODFIELD (JUNE) Playing God: genetic engineering and the manipulation of life. New York, [1977]. pp. 218.

PACKARD (VANCE OAKLEY) The people shapers. London, 1978. pp. 395. *bibliog.*

GENEVA (CANTON)

— History.

REY (MICHEL) Genève 1930-1933: la révolution de Léon Nicole. Berne, [1978]. pp. 309. *bibliog.*

GENIUS.

BECKER (GEORGE) The mad genius controversy: a study in the sociology of deviance. Beverly Hills, [1978]. pp. 151. *bibliog.*

GEOGRAPHICAL PERCEPTION.

CANTER (DAVID VICTOR) and STRINGER (PETER) Environmental interaction: psychological approaches to our physical surroundings. London, [1975]. pp. 374. *bibliog.*

RELPH (EDWARD) Place and placelessness. London, [1976]. pp. 156. *bibliog.*

BURGESS (JACQUELIN A.) Image and identity: a study of urban and regional perception with particular reference to Kingston upon Hull. Hull, 1978. pp. 97. *bibliog. (Hull. University. Department of Geography. Occasional Papers in Geography. No. 23)*

LONDON. University. London School of Economics and Political Science. Graduate School of Geography. Discussion Papers. No. 69. Measures of spatial opportunity: the use of urban images in constructing subjective indicators of spatial opportunity; [by] Lefteris Tsoulouvis. London, 1978. pp. 58. *bibliog.*

GEOGRAPHY.

CHANGE and tradition: geography's new frontiers; a collection of papers discussed at a conference...held in the Department of Geography at Queen Mary College on 30 June and 1st July 1977; [edited by Roger Lee]. London, 1977. pp. 75.

DE BLIJ (HARM J.) Geography: regions and concepts; with a chapter by Stephen S. Birdsall. 2nd ed. New York, [1978]. pp. 593.

RADICAL geography: alternative viewpoints on contemporary social issues; [edited by] Richard Peet. London, 1978. pp. 387. *A collection of essays drawn mainly from "Antipode".*

TIMING space and spacing time; edited by Tommy Carlstein [and others]. London, 1978. 3 vols. *bibliogs.*

SETTLEMENTS; [by] Iain R. Meyer and Richard J. Huggett. London, 1979. pp. 201. *(Geography: theory in practice. Book 1)*

— Congresses.

NEW ZEALAND GEOGRAPHY CONFERENCE, 9TH, DUNEDIN, 1977. Proceedings of the...conference; edited by T.J. Hearn and R.P. Hargreaves. Dunedin, 1977. pp. 133. *bibliogs. (New Zealand Geographical Society. Conference Series. No. 9)*

— Methodology.

LONDON. University. London School of Economics and Political Science. Graduate School of Geography. Discussion Papers. No. 64. Some questions of philosophy, methodology and explanation in geography; [by] Bernard Harris. London, 1978. pp. 16.

— Philosophy.

LONDON. University. London School of Economics and Political Science. Graduate School of Geography. Discussion Papers. No. 64. Some questions of philosophy, methodology and explanation in geography; [by] Bernard Harris. London, 1978. pp. 16.

GEOGRAPHY, ECONOMIC.

GEOGRAPHY and development: a world regional approach; edited by Don R. Hoy. New York, [1978]. pp. 728.

GEOGRAPHY, HISTORICAL

— Maps.

The TIMES atlas of world history; edited by Geoffrey Barraclough. London, 1978. pp. 360.

GEOGRAPHY, POLITICAL.

KASPERSON (ROGER E.) and MINGHI (JULIAN VINCENT) eds. The structure of political geography. Chicago, 1969 repr. 1971. pp. 527.

BOATENG (ERNEST AMANO) A political geography of Africa. Cambridge, 1978. pp. 292. *bibliog.*

GEOGRAPHY, POLITICAL.(Cont.)

COLE (JOHN PETER) Geography of world affairs. 5th ed. Harmondsworth, 1979. pp. 471. *bibliog.*

GEOLOGY.

MENARD (HENRY W.) Geology, resources, and society: an introduction to earth science. San Francisco, [1974]. pp. 621. *bibliogs.*

PRESS (FRANK) and SIEVER (RAYMOND) Earth. 2nd ed. San Francisco, [1978]. pp. 649. *bibliogs.*

— Atlases.

DIXON (COLIN J.) Atlas of economic mineral deposits. London, 1979. pp. 143. *bibliog.*

— Canada — Nova Scotia.

NOVA SCOTIA. Department of Mines. 1974. A brief history of mining and geology in Nova Scotia. [Halifax, 1974?]. 1 vol. (unpaged).

NOVA SCOTIA. Department of Mines. 1976. Geology, minerals and mining in Nova Scotia. Halifax, [1976]. 1 pamphlet (unpaged). *bibliog.* (Information Series. No.1)

— Ghana.

JUNNER (NORMAN ROSS) and HIRST (TOM) The geology and hydrology of the Voltaian basin. Accra, 1946. pp. 51, 4 maps. *(Ghana. Geological Survey. Memoirs. No.8)*

— Nigeria.

JACOBSON (R.R.E.) and MACLEOD (W.N.) Geology of the Liruei, Banke and adjacent younger granite ring-complexes. [Lagos], 1977. pp. 117. *bibliog.* (Nigeria. Geological Survey of Nigeria. Bulletins. No. 33) 5 maps in end pocket.

— Uganda.

UGANDA. Geological Survey. Memoirs. No.10. Pleistocene stratigraphy in Uganda; by W. W. Bishop. Entebbe, 1969. pp. 128. *bibliog.* 7 maps etc. in end pocket.

UGANDA. Geological Survey. Memoirs. No. 11. Problems of structure and correlation in the Precambrian systems of central and western Uganda; by B.C. King and A.M.J. de Swardt. [Entebbe, 1970]. pp. 133. *bibliog.*

— United Kingdom.

U.K. Geological Survey. Memoirs. [Sheet Memoirs. New Series]. 32. Geology of the country around Barnard Castle: explanation of one-inch geological sheet 32, new series; by D.A.C. Mills and J. H. Hull; with contributions by C.R. Burch [and others]. London, 1976. pp. 385. *bibliogs.*

BRITISH Quaternary studies: recent advances; edited by F.W. Shotton. Oxford, [1977]. pp. 298. *bibliogs.*

U.K. Geological Survey. Memoirs. [Sheet Memoirs. New Series]. 251. Geology of the Malmesbury District: explanation of one-inch geological sheet 251, new series; by R. Cave [and others]. London, 1977. pp. 343. *bibliog.*

GEOLOGY, ECONOMIC.

INDUSTRIAL geology; edited by J. L. Knill. Oxford, 1978. pp. 344. *bibliog.*

DIXON (COLIN J.) Atlas of economic mineral deposits. London, 1979. pp. 143. *bibliog.*

GEOLOGY, STRATIGRAPHIC

— Pleistocene.

UGANDA. Geological Survey. Memoirs. No.10. Pleistocene stratigraphy in Uganda; by W. W. Bishop. Entebbe, 1969. pp. 128. *bibliog.* 7 maps etc. in end pocket.

— Quaternary.

BRITISH Quaternary studies: recent advances; edited by F.W. Shotton. Oxford, [1977]. pp. 298. *bibliogs.*

GEOMETRIC PROBABILITIES.

SOLOMON (HERBERT) Geometric probability. Philadelphia, 1978. pp. 174. *bibliog.* (Conference Board of the Mathematical Sciences. Regional Conference Series in Applied Mathematics. No. 28)

GEOMETRY.

DIEUDONNÉ (JEAN A.) Linear algebra and geometry; translated from the original French text. London, 1969. pp. 207. *bibliog.*

GEOMETRY, AFFINE.

OPEN UNIVERSITY. Linear Mathematics Course Team. Unit 15: Affine geometry and convex cones. Milton Keynes, 1972, repr. 1976. pp. 40. (Open University. Mathematics: a second level course: linear mathematics. Unit 15)

GEOMORPHOLOGY.

CARSON (MICHAEL ANTHONY) and KIRKBY (M.J.) Hillslope form and process. London, 1972 repr. 1975. pp. 475. *bibliog.*

THEORIES of landform development; Wilton N. Melhorn, Ronald C. Flemal, editors. Binghamton, [1976?]. pp. 306. (New York State University. State University of New York at Binghamton. Publications in Geomorphology)

THORNES (JOHN B.) and BRUNSDEN (DENYS) Geomorphology and time. London, 1977. pp. 208. *bibliog.*

GEOPHYSICS.

McQUILLIN (R.) and ARDUS (D.A.) Exploring the geology of shelf seas. London, 1977. pp. 234. *bibliog.*

GEORGE I, King of Great Britain and Ireland.

HATTON (RAGNHILD) George I, Elector and King. Cambridge, Mass., 1978. pp. 416. *bibliog.*

GEORGE III, King of Great Britain and Ireland.

BROOKE (JOHN) 1920- . King George III. London, [1972]. pp. 411.

GEORGE (DAVID LLOYD) 1st Earl Lloyd George.

GRIGG (JOHN EDWARD POYNDER) Lloyd George: the people's champion, 1902-1911. Berkeley, 1978. pp. 391.

GEORGE (HENRY).

HARRISON (FRED) B.A., M.Sc. Marx, economic growth and land taxation. London, 1975. pp. 27. (Economic and Social Science Research Association. Discussion Papers. No. 2)

GERIATRIC NURSING.

WEINER (MARCELLA BAKUR) and others. Working with the aged: practical approaches in the institution and community. Englewood Cliffs, N.J., [1978]. pp. 231.

GERIATRIC PSYCHIATRY

— United Kingdom — Scotland.

MENTAL DISORDER PROGRAMME PLANNING GROUP [SCOTLAND]. Report on services for the elderly with mental disability in Scotland; a report by a Programme Planning Group of the Scottish Health Service Planning Council and the Advisory Council on Social Work; [G.C. Timbury, chairman of the Sub- Committee]. Edinburgh, H.M.S.O., 1979. pp. 61.

GERMAN LANGUAGE

— Dictionaries.

WOERTERBUCH der deutschen Gegenwartssprache; herausgegeben von Ruth Klappenbach und Wolfgang Steinitz. Berlin, 1977-78. 6 vols. *bibliog.* Vol.1 is of the 9th ed., vol. 2 of the 5th, vol.3 of the 4th; vols 4-6 are of the 2nd ed.

— Study and teaching.

MILLS (ANNE E.) First and second language acquisition in German: a parallel study. Ludwigsburg, 1977. pp. 209. *bibliog.*

— — Foreign students.

MILLS (ANNE E.) First and second language acquisition in German: a parallel study. Ludwigsburg, 1977. pp. 209. *bibliog.*

GERMAN LITERATURE

— History and criticism.

THEWELEIT (KLAUS) Männerphantasien. Frankfurt am ain, 1977-78. 2 vols. *bibliog.*

GERMAN NEWSPAPERS.

POEHLS (JOACHIM) Die "Tägliche Rundschau" und die Zerstörung der Weimarer Republik, 1930 bis 1933. Münster, 1975. 2 vols. (in 1). *bibliog.* (Münster in Westfalen. Westfälische Wilhelms- Universität. Institut für Publizistik. Arbeiten. Band 14)

SCHWARZ (ROBERT) 1921- . "Sozialismus" der Propaganda: das Werben des "Völkischen Beobachters" um die österreichische Arbeiterschaft, 1938/1939; mit einer Einleitung von Gerhard Botz, etc. Wien, 1975. pp. 159. *bibliog.* (Ludwig Boltzmann Institut für Geschichte der Arbeiterbewegung. Materialien zur Arbeiterbewegung. Nr.2)

WALLRAFF (GUENTER) Wallraff: the undesirable journalist; [a selection of articles] translated by Steve Gooch and Paul Knight. London, 1978. pp. 180.

GERMAN PERIODICALS.

RICHTER (ARMIN) Der Ziegelbrenner: das individualanarchistische Kampforgan des frühen B. Traven. Bonn, 1977. pp. 442. *bibliog.*

GERMAN REUNIFICATION QUESTION (1949-).

EINHEIT der Nation: Diskussionen und Konzeptionen zur Deutschlandpolitik der grossen Parteien seit 1945; ([by] Wolfgang Benz [and others]). Stuttgart-Bad Cannstatt, [1978]. pp. 399. *bibliog.*

MOERSCH (KARL) Kurs-Revision: deutsche Politik nach Adenauer. Frankfurt am Main, [1978]. pp. 325.

GERMANIC TRIBES.

MUSSET (LUCIEN) The Germanic invasions: the making of Europe, AD 400-600;.. .translated by Edward and Columba James. London, 1975. pp. 287. *bibliog.*

GERMANS IN EASTERN EUROPE.

HACKER (WERNER) Auswanderungen aus Oberschwaben im 17. und 18. Jahrhundert, archivalisch dokumentiert. Stuttgart, [1977]. pp. 799. *bibliog.*

GERMANS IN FOREIGN COUNTRIES.

RITTER (ERNST) German historian. Das Deutsche Ausland-Institut in Stuttgart, 1917-1945: ein Beispiel deutscher Volkstumsarbeit zwischen den Weltkriegen. Wiesbaden, 1976. pp. 168. *bibliog.*

GERMANS IN HUNGARY.

HACKER (WERNER) Auswanderungen aus Oberschwaben im 17. und 18. Jahrhundert, archivalisch dokumentiert. Stuttgart, [1977]. pp. 799. *bibliog.*

GERMANS IN RUSSIA.

HOFFMANN (JOACHIM) 1930- . Deutsche und Kalmyken, 1942 bis 1945. Freiburg, [1974]. pp. 214. *bibliog.* (Militärgeschichtliches Forschungsamt. Einzelschriften zur Militärischen Geschichte des Zweiten Weltkrieges. 14)

KOCH (FRED C.) The Volga Germans in Russia and the Americas, from 1763 to the present. University Park, Pa., 1977. pp. 365. *bibliog.*

GERMANY.

FACTS about Germany: the Federal Republic of Germany; (editor: Karl Römer...for the Press and Information Office of the Government of the Federal Republic of Germany). Bonn, 1979. pp. 383.

— Air force.

GALLAND (ADOLF) The first and the last: the German fighter force in World War II. London, 1955 repr. 1973. pp. 368.

— Appropriations and expenditures.

GERMANY (BUNDESREPUBLIK). Statistisches Bundesamt. Rechnungsergebnisse des öffentlichen Gesamthaushalts. a., 1974- Wiesbaden. *(Finanzen und Steuern. Reihe 3.1) Supersedes GERMANY (BUNDESREPUBLIK). Statistisches Bundesamt. Jahresabschlüsse: Öffentliche Finanzwirtschaft.*

— Army — History.

DEUTSCH (HAROLD C.) Hitler and his generals: the hidden crisis, January-June 1938. Minneapolis, [1974]. pp. 452. *bibliog.*

GUDERIAN (HEINZ) Panzer leader:...translated from the German by Constantine Fitzgibbon. London, 1974 repr. 1979. pp. 528. *First published in Great Britain in 1952.*

MAJEWSKI (RYSZARD) Waffen SS: mity i rzeczywistość. Wrocław, 1977. pp. 302. *bibliog.*

COOPER (MATTHEW) The German Army, 1933-1945: its political and military failure. London, 1978. pp. 598. *bibliog.*

— — Officers.

DEUTSCH (HAROLD C.) Hitler and his generals: the hidden crisis, January-June 1938. Minneapolis, [1974]. pp. 452. *bibliog.*

MILITARISMUS und Opportunismus gegen die Novemberrevolution; ([edited by] Lothar Berthold [and] Helmut Neef). 2nd ed. Frankfurt am Main, 1978. pp. 468.

SCHRAMM (WILHELM VON) Aufstand der Generale: der 20. Juli 1944 in Paris. München, [1978]. pp. 365. *bibliog.*

— — Panzerdivision Grossdeutschland.

LUCAS (JAMES) Germany's elite panzer force: Grossdeutschland. London, 1978. pp. 152. *bibliog.*

— Bundesrat.

RAUH (MANFRED) Die Parlamentarisierung des Deutschen Reiches. Düsseldorf, [1977]. pp. 533. *bibliog. (Germany (Bundesrepublik). Kommission für Geschichte des Parlamentarismus und der Politischen Parteien. Beiträge zur Geschichte des Parlamentarismus und der Politischen Parteien. Band 60)*

— Bundestag.

GERMANY (BUNDESREPUBLIK). Deutscher Bundestag. Presse- und Informationszentrum. 1979. 30 Jahre Deutscher Bundestag: Dokumentation, Statistik, Daten; bearbeitet von Peter Schindler. Bonn, 1979. pp. 504.

— Census.

GERMANY. Statistisches Reichsamt. Statistik des Deutschen Reichs. Neue Folge. Bände 150-151. Die Volkszählung am 1. Dezember 1900 im Deutschen Reich. Berlin, 1903; Osnabrück, 1976. 2 vols. *Photographic reprint.*

GERMANY. Statistisches Reichsamt. Statistik des Deutschen Reichs. Neue Folge. Band 240. Die Volkszählung im Deutschen Reiche am 1. Dezember 1910. Berlin, 1914-1915; Osnabrück, 1976. 1 vol. (various pagings) *Photographic reprint.*

— Church history.

GURIAN (WALDEMAR) Hitler and the Christians; translated by E.F. Peeler. London, 1936. pp. 175.

— Civilization.

CAMPBELL (JOAN) The German Werkbund: the politics of reform in the applied arts. Princeton, [1978]. pp. 350. *bibliog.*

Der NATIONALSOZIALISTISCHE Alltag: so lebte man unter Hitler; ([edited by] George L. Mosse; aus dem Englischen von Renate Becker). Königstein/Ts., 1978. pp. 389.

— Colonies.

KNOLL (ARTHUR J.) Togo under imperial Germany, 1884-1914: a case study in colonial rule. Stanford, Calif., [1978]. pp. 224. *bibliog. (Stanford University. Hoover Institution on War, Revolution and Peace. Hoover Institution Publications. 190)*

SMITH (WOODRUFF D.) The German colonial empire. Chapel Hill, N.C., [1978]. pp. 274. *bibliog.*

SCHROEDER (HANS CHRISTOPH) Gustav Noske und die Kolonialpolitik des Deutschen Kaiserreichs. Berlin, [1979]. pp. 107.

— Commerce — Statistics.

GERMANY (BUNDESREPUBLIK). Statistisches Bundesamt. Einfuhr nach Herstellungs- und Einkaufsländern und Warengruppen. a., 1976- Wiesbaden. *(Aussenhandel. Reihe 3.1) Supplementary volume to GERMANY (BUNDESREPUBLIK). Statistisches Bundesamt. Aussenhandel nach Ländern und Warengruppen: Spezialhandel.*

GERMANY (BUNDESREPUBLIK). Statistisches Bundesamt. Ausfuhr nach Verbrauchs- und Käuferländern und Warengruppen. a., 1977- Wiesbaden. *(Aussenhandel. Reihe 3.2) Supplementary volume to GERMANY (BUNDESREPUBLIK). Statistisches Bundesamt. Aussenhandel nach Ländern und Warengruppen (Spezialhandel)*

— — United Kingdom.

KRAWEHL (OTTO ERNST) Hamburgs Schiffs- und Warenverkehr mit England und den englischen Kolonien, 1814-1860. Köln, 1977. pp. 536. *bibliog. With summary and table of contents in English.*

— Commercial policy.

WEITOWITZ (ROLF GUNTER) Deutsche Politik und Handelspolitik unter Reichskanzler Leo von Caprivi, 1890-1894. Düsseldorf, [1978]. pp. 406. *bibliog.*

— Constitutional history.

RAUH (MANFRED) Die Parlamentarisierung des Deutschen Reiches. Düsseldorf, [1977]. pp. 533. *bibliog. (Germany (Bundesrepublik). Kommission für Geschichte des Parlamentarismus und der Politischen Parteien. Beiträge zur Geschichte des Parlamentarismus und der Politischen Parteien. Band 60)*

— Constitutional law.

GRUND (HENNING) "Preussenschlag" und Staatsgerichtshof im Jahre 1932. Baden-Baden, 1976. pp. 167. *bibliog.*

SCHIER (ROLF) Standesherren: zur Auflösung der Adelsvorherrschaft in Deutschland, 1815-1918. Heidelberg, 1977. pp. 157. *bibliog.*

WESSEL (HELGA) Zweckmässigkeit als Handlungsprinzip in der deutschen Regierungs- und Verwaltungslehre der frühen Neuzeit. Berlin, 1978. pp. 169. *bibliog.*

WITTKOWSKI (WOLFRAM) Der Schutz der Arbeitskraft durch das Grundgesetz: zugleich ein Beitrag zum Sozialstaatsprinzip. Frankfurt am Main, 1979. pp. 249. *bibliog.*

— Defences.

[SCHREINER (ALBERT)] Hitler rearms: an exposure of Germany's war plans; edited by Dorothy Woodman. London, 1934. pp. 336. *Translation of Hitler treibt zum Krieg.*

SPEIDEL (HANS) Aus unserer Zeit: Erinnerungen. Frankfurt/M, 1977. pp. 512.

WAGNER (DIETRICH) FDP und die Wiederbewaffnung: die wehrpolitische Orientierung der Liberalen in der Bundesrepublik Deutschland, 1949-1955. Boppard am Rhein, 1978. pp. 182. *bibliog. (Militärgeschichtliches Forschungsamt. Militärgeschichte seit 1945. 5)*

— Economic conditions.

BROST (FRANZ FRIEDRICH) and VILLOT (JEAN GERARD) Analyse comparative de l'évolution structurelle des systèmes productifs français et ouest-allemands: une étude statistique pour la période de 1960 à 1974. Frankfurt am Main, [1978]. pp. 259. *bibliog.*

DEUTSCHES INSTITUT FÜR WIRTSCHAFTSFORSCHUNG. Sonderhefte. [Neue Folge]. 122. Konzeption einer Strukturberichterstattung für die Bundesrepublik Deutschland: Möglichkeiten und Grenzen der Analyse sektoraler Strukturentwicklungen; ([by] Bernd Görzig und Wolfgang Kirner). Berlin, 1978. pp. 68.

— Economic history.

MELLOR (ROY EGERTON HENDERSON) The two Germanies: a modern geography. London, 1978. pp. 461. *bibliogs.*

SPREE (REINHARD) Wachstumstrends und Konjunkturzyklen in der deutschen Wirtschaft von 1820 bis 1913: quantitativer Rahmen für eine Konjunkturgeschichte des 19. Jahrhunderts. Göttingen, [1978]. pp. 215. *bibliog.*

WEISBROD (BERND) Schwerindustrie in der Weimarer Republik: Interessenpolitik zwischen Stabilisierung und Krise. Wuppertal, [1978]. pp. 552. *bibliog.*

FRANZ (GUENTHER) Der Dreissigjährige Krieg und das deutsche Volk: Untersuchungen zur Bevölkerungs- und Agrargeschichte. 4th ed. Stuttgart, 1979. pp. 140.

— — Sources.

ARCHIVBESTÄNDE zur Wirtschafts- und Sozialgeschichte der Weimarer Republik: Übersicht über Quellen in Archiven der Bundesrepublik Deutschland; bearbeitet von Thomas Trumpp und Renate Köhne; mit Beiträgen von Jens Flemming [and others]. Boppard am Rhein, [1979]. pp. 380. *bibliog. (Germany (Bundesrepublik). Bundesarchiv. Schriften. 29)*

— Economic policy.

Der STAAT in der BRD: ökonomische Basis und Entwicklungstendenzen, 1950-1976; ([by] Projekt Klassenanalyse). Hamburg, [1977]. pp. 183.

GIERSCH (HERBERT) Im Brennpunkt: Wirtschaftspolitik: kritische Beiträge, 1967 bis 1977; herausgegeben von Karl Heinz Frank. [Stuttgart, 1978]. pp. 310.

KRACK (JUERGEN) and NEUMANN (KARL) Konjunktur, Krise, Wirtschaftspolitik: die wirtschaftliche Entwicklung in der Bundesrepublik, etc. Köln, [1978]. pp. 384. *bibliog.*

MAMMEN (GERHARD) Grundzüge differenzierter Stabilisierungspolitik in der Bundesrepublik Deutschland. Göttingen, [1978]. pp. 237. *bibliog. (Hamburg. Hansische Universität. Institut für Europäische Wirtschaftspolitik. Wirtschaftspolitische Studien. 47)*

OTT (ERICH) Die Wirtschaftskonzeption der SPD nach 1945. Marburg, [1978]. pp. 298. *bibliog. (Studiengesellschaft für Sozialgeschichte und Arbeiterbewegung, Marburg. Schriftenreihe für Sozialgeschichte und Arbeiterbewegung. Band 12)*

STABILITAET im Wandel: Wirtschaft und Politik unter dem evolutionsbedingten Diktat: Festschrift für Bruno Gleitze zum 75. Geburtstage; herausgegeben von Bodo B. Gemper. Berlin, [1978]. pp. 645. *bibliogs.*

GERMANY.(Cont.)

— — Mathematical models.

DIECKHEUER (GUSTAV) Staatsverschuldung und wirtschaftliche Stabilisierung: eine theoretische Analyse und eine ökonometrische Studie für die Bundesrepublik Deutschland. Baden-Baden, 1978. pp. 327. *bibliog*. With summaries in various languages.

— Emigration and immigration.

HACKER (WERNER) Auswanderungen aus Oberschwaben im 17. und 18. Jahrhundert, archivalisch dokumentiert. Stuttgart, [1977]. pp. 799. *bibliog*.

— Executive departments.

HUNDERT Jahre Patentamt: Festschrift herausgegeben vom Deutschen Patentamt. München, 1977. pp. 476.

— Foreign economic relations.

See also EUROPEAN ECONOMIC COMMUNITY — Germany.

— — South Africa.

CERVENKA (ZDENEK) and ROGERS (BARBARA) The nuclear axis: secret collaboration between West Germany and South Africa. London, 1978. pp. 464.

— — Sweden.

WITTMANN (KLAUS) Schwedens Wirtschaftsbeziehungen zum Dritten Reich, 1933-1945. München, 1978. pp. 479. *bibliog*. (Hamburg. Hansische Universität. Studien zur Modernen Geschichte. Band 23)

— Foreign opinion, Russian.

METTIG (VOLKER) Russische Presse und Sozialistengesetz: die deutsche Sozialdemokratie und die Entstehung des Sozialistengesetzes aus russischer Sicht, 1869-1878. Bonn, [1979]. pp. 476. *bibliog*. (Friedrich-Ebert-Stiftung. Forschungsinstitut. Reihe: Politik- und Gesellschaftsgeschichte. Band 4)

— Foreign relations.

CALLEO (DAVID PATRICK) The German problem reconsidered: Germany and the world order, 1870 to the present. Cambridge, 1978. pp. 239. *bibliog*.

FARRAR (L.L.) Divide and conquer: German efforts to conclude a separate peace, 1914-1918. New York, 1978. pp. 180. *bibliog*. (East European Quarterly. East European Monographs. 45)

KENT (GEORGE O.) Bismarck and his times. Carbondale, Ill., [1978]. pp. 184. *bibliog*.

MOERSCH (KARL) Kurs-Revision: deutsche Politik nach Adenauer. Frankfurt am Main, [1978]. pp. 325.

MORGAN (ROGER P.) West Germany's foreign policy agenda. Beverly Hills, [1978]. pp. 80. *bibliog*. (Georgetown University. Center for Strategic and International Studies. Washington Papers. vol. 6/54)

NATIONALSOZIALISTISCHE Aussenpolitik; herausgegeben von Wolfgang Michalka. Darmstadt, 1978. pp. 579. *bibliog*.

GREWE (WILHELM GEORG) Rückblenden, 1976-1951. [Frankfurt/Main, 1979]. pp. 813.

KIESINGER (KURT GEORG) Die Grosse Koalition, 1966-1969: Reden und Erklärungen des Bundeskanzlers; herausgegeben von Dieter Oberndörfer. Stuttgart, [1979]. pp. 420. *bibliog*.

See also EUROPEAN ECONOMIC COMMUNITY — Germany.

— — Treaties.

Das JULIABKOMMEN von 1936: Vorgeschichte, Hintergründe und Folgen: Protokoll des Symposiums in Wien am 10. und 11. Juni 1976; (herausgegeben von Ludwig Jedlicka und Rudolf Neck). Wien, 1977. pp. 480. (Theodor-Körner-Stiftungsfonds, and Leopold-Kunschak-Preis. Wissenschaftliche Kommission zur Erforschung der Österreichischen Geschichte der Jahre 1927 bis 1938. Veröffentlichungen. Band 4)

— — Austria.

Das JULIABKOMMEN von 1936: Vorgeschichte, Hintergründe und Folgen: Protokoll des Symposiums in Wien am 10. und 11. Juni 1976; (herausgegeben von Ludwig Jedlicka und Rudolf Neck). Wien, 1977. pp. 480. (Theodor-Körner-Stiftungsfonds, and Leopold-Kunschak-Preis. Wissenschaftliche Kommission zur Erforschung der Österreichischen Geschichte der Jahre 1927 bis 1938. Veröffentlichungen. Band 4)

— — China.

LIANG (HSI-HUEY) The Sino-German connection: Alexander von Falkenhausen between China and Germany, 1900-1941. Assen, 1978. pp. 229. *bibliog*.

— — Czechoslovakia.

HENCKE (ANDOR) Augenzeuge einer Tragödie: Diplomatenjahre in Prag, 1936- 1939. München, 1977. pp. 351. *bibliog*. (Sudetendeutsches Archiv. Veröffentlichungen. 11)

— — East (Far East).

STINGL (WERNER) Der Ferne Osten in der deutschen Politik vor dem Ersten Weltkrieg, 1902-1914. Frankfurt/Main, [1978]. 2 vols. *bibliog*.

— — Europe, Eastern.

"DRANG nakh Osten" i narody Tsentral'noi, Vostochnoi i Iugo-Vostochnoi Evropy 1871-1918 gg. Moskva, 1977. pp. 317.

GRIFFITH (WILLIAM E.) The Ostpolitik of the Federal Republic of Germany. Cambridge, Mass., [1978]. pp. 325.

— — Finland.

UEBERSCHAER (GERD R.) Hitler und Finnland, 1939-1941: die deutsch-finnischen Beziehungen während des Hitler-Stalin-Paktes. Wiesbaden, 1978. pp. 376. *bibliog*.

— — France.

HEINEMANN (IRMGARD) Le Traité franco-allemand du 22 janvier 1963 et sa mise en oeuvre sous le général de Gaulle, 1963-1969; (thèse... présentée...à la Faculté de Droit et des Sciences Economiques de l'Université de Nice). Nice, 1977. pp. 475. *bibliog*.

SEYDOUX (FRANÇOIS) Dans l'intimité franco-allemande: une mission diplomatique. Paris, 1977. pp. 184.

McDOUGALL (WALTER A.) France's Rhineland diplomacy, 1914-1924: the last bid for a balance of power in Europe. Princeton, [1978]. pp. 420. *bibliog*.

— — Italy.

MICHAELIS (MEIR) Mussolini and the Jews: German-Italian relations and the Jewish question in Italy, 1922-1945. Oxford, 1978. pp. 472. *bibliog*.

SCHREIBER (GERHARD) Revisionismus und Weltmachtstreben: Marinefuhrung und deutsch- italienische Beziehungen, 1919 bis 1944. Stuttgart, 1978. pp. 428. *bibliog*. (Militärgeschichtliches Forschungsamt. Beiträge zur Militär- und Kriegsgeschichte. Band 20)

— — Japan.

PRESSEISEN (ERNST L.) Germany and Japan: a study in totalitarian diplomacy, 1933-1941. New York, 1969. pp. 368. *bibliog*. Reprint of work first published in The Hague, 1958.

— — Sweden.

KARLSSON (RUNE) Så stoppades tysktågen: den tysktågen: den tyska transiteringstrafiken i svensk politik, 1942-1943. Stockholm, 1974. pp. 363. *bibliog*. With English summary.

— — Turkey.

WEBER (FRANK G.) The evasive neutral: Germany, Britain and the quest for a Turkish alliance in the Second World War. Columbia, Mo., 1979. pp. 244. *bibliog*.

— — United Kingdom.

YOUNG (ARTHUR PRIMROSE) The 'X' documents; edited by Sidney Aster. London, 1974. pp. 253. *bibliog*.

— — United States.

TREVERTON (GREGORY F.) The dollar drain and American forces in Germany: managing the political economics of alliance. Athens, Ohio, [1978]. pp. 226. *bibliog*.

— Historiography.

HITLER heute: Gespräche über ein deutsches Trauma; herausgegeben und bearbeitet von Guido Knopp; (Aschaffenburger Gespräche, 1978). Aschaffenburg, 1979. pp. 256.

— History.

DIWALD (HELLMUT) Geschichte der Deutschen. Frankfurt am Main, [1978]. pp. 764.

— — 1618-1648 — Sources.

BENECKE (GERHARD) ed. Germany in the Thirty Years War. London, 1978. pp. 108. *bibliog*.

— — 1789-1900.

CARR (WILLIAM) b. 1921. A history of Germany 1815-1945. [rev. ed.] London, 1972 repr. 1977. pp. 462. *bibliog*.

— — 1848-1849, Revolution.

BLUM (ROBERT) Politiker. Politische Schriften; hrsg. von Sander L. Gilman. Nendeln, Liechtenstein, 1979. 6 vols.

— — 1866-1871.

CRAIG (GORDON ALEXANDER) Germany, 1866-1945. Oxford, [1978]. pp. 825. *bibliog*.

— — 1871- .

CALLEO (DAVID PATRICK) The German problem reconsidered: Germany and the world order, 1870 to the present. Cambridge, 1978. pp. 239. *bibliog*.

CRAIG (GORDON ALEXANDER) Germany, 1866-1945. Oxford, [1978]. pp. 825. *bibliog*.

— — 1871-1918.

GEISS (IMANUEL) Das Deutsche Reich und der Erste Weltkrieg. München, [1978]. pp. 243. *bibliog*.

METTIG (VOLKER) Russische Presse und Sozialistengesetz: die deutsche Sozialdemokratie und die Entstehung des Sozialistengesetzes aus russischer Sicht, 1869-1878. Bonn, [1979]. pp. 476. *bibliog*. (Friedrich-Ebert-Stiftung. Forschungsinstitut. Reihe: Politik- und Gesellschaftsgeschichte. Band 4)

— — 1900- .

CARR (WILLIAM) b. 1921. A history of Germany 1815-1945. [rev. ed.] London, 1972 repr. 1977. pp. 462. *bibliog*.

INTERUNIVERSITY CENTRE FOR EUROPEAN STUDIES. International Colloquium, 2nd, 1976. Situations révolutionnaires en Europe, 1917-1922: Allemagne, Italie, Autriche-Hongrie; Revolutionary situations in Europe, 1917-1922: Germany, Italy, Austria-Hungary...edited by Charles L. Bertrand. Montreal, 1977. pp. 251. *bibliog*.

GERMANY.(Cont.)

TAMPKE (JÜRGEN) The Ruhr and revolution: the revolutionary movement in the Rhenish-Westphalian industrial region, 1912-1919. London, [1979]. pp. 209. *bibliog.*

—— 1918-1933.

POEHLS (JOACHIM) Die "Tägliche Rundschau" und die Zerstörung der Weimarer Republik, 1930 bis 1933. Münster, 1975. 2 vols. (in 1). *bibliog.* (Münster in Westfalen. Westfälische Wilhelms- Universität. Institut für Publizistik. Arbeiten. Band 14)

POIS (ROBERT A.) The bourgeois democrats of Weimar Germany. Philadelphia, 1976. pp. 117. *bibliog.* (American Philosophical Society. Transactions. New Series. vol. 66. Pt. 4)

ENGELMANN (BERNT) Einig gegen Recht und Freiheit: deutsches Anti- Geschichtsbuch, 2. Teil. Frankfurt am Main, 1977. pp. 296. *bibliog.*

GESSNER (DIETER) Agrardepression und Präsidialregierungen in Deutschland, 1930 bis 1933: Probleme des Agrarprotektionismus am Ende der Weimarer Republik. Düsseldorf, [1977]. pp. 209. *bibliog.*

GESSNER (DIETER) Das Ende der Weimarer Republik: Fragen, Methoden und Ergebnisse interdisziplinärer Forschung. Darmstadt, 1978. pp. 131.

HENTSCHEL (VOLKER) Weimars letzte Monate: Hitler und der Untergang der Republik. Düsseldorf, [1978 repr. 1979]. pp. 180. *bibliog.*

KOCH (HANNSJOACHIM WOLFGANG) Der deutsche Bürgerkrieg: eine Geschichte der deutschen und österreichischen Freikorps, 1918-1923. Berlin, [1978]. pp. 487. *bibliog.*

LUDEWIG (HANS ULRICH) Arbeiterbewegung und Aufstand: eine Untersuchung zum Verhalten der Arbeiterparteien in den Aufstandsbewegungen der frühen Weimarer Republik, 1920-1923. Husum, [1978]. pp. 267. *bibliog.*

NICHOLLS (ANTHONY JAMES) Weimar and the rise of Hitler. 2nd ed. London, 1979. pp. 151. *bibliog.*

—— — Sources.

GERMANY. Reichskanzlei. 1923. Die Kabinette Stresemann I u. II: 13. August bis 6. Oktober 1923; 6. Oktober bis 30. November 1923; bearbeitet von Karl Dietrich Erdmann und Martin Vogt. Boppard am Rhein, [1978]. 2 vols. *bibliog.* (Akten der Reichskanzlei, Weimarer Republik)

— — 1918-1919, Revolution.

TOLLER (ERNST) I was a German: an autobiography;...translated by Edward Crankshaw. London, 1934. pp. 298.

ILLUSTRIERTE Geschichte der deutschen Novemberrevolution, 1918/1919; (Autorenkollektiv: Günter Hortzschansky [and others]). Berlin, 1978. pp. 454. *bibliog.*

MATERNA (INGO) Der Vollzugsrat der Berliner Arbeiter- und Soldatenräte, 1918/19. Berlin, 1978. pp. 294. *bibliog.*

MILITARISMUS und Opportunismus gegen die Novemberrevolution; [edited by] Lothar Berthold [and] Helmut Neef). 2nd ed. Frankfurt am Main, 1978. pp. 468.

MILLER (SUSANNE) Die Bürde der Macht: die deutsche Sozialdemokratie, 1918- 1920. Düsseldorf, [1978]. pp. 532. *bibliog.* (Germany (Bundesrepublik). Kommission für Geschichte des Parlamentarismus und der Politischen Parteien. Beiträge zur Geschichte des Parlamentarismus und der Politischen Parteien. Band 63)

—— 1933-1945.

REED (DOUGLAS) The burning of the Reichstag. London, 1934. pp. 352.

DEUTSCH (HAROLD C.) Hitler and his generals: the hidden crisis, January-June 1938. Minneapolis, [1974]. pp. 452. *bibliog.*

ENGELMANN (BERNT) Einig gegen Recht und Freiheit: deutsches Anti- Geschichtsbuch, 2. Teil. Frankfurt am Main, 1977. pp. 296. *bibliog.*

FRIEDRICH (CHRISTOF) Germany's Antarctic claim: secret Nazi polar expeditions. Toronto, [1978?]. pp. 128.

Die FRONT war überall: (Erlebnisse und Berichte vom Kampf des Nationalkomitees "Freies Deutschland"; herausgegeben von Else und Bernt von Kügelgen). 2nd ed. Berlin, 1978. pp. 507. *bibliog.*

IRVING (DAVID J.) The war path: Hitler's Germany, 1933-9. London, [1978]. pp. 301.

SCHRAMM (WILHELM VON) Aufstand der Generale: der 20. Juli 1944 in Paris. München, [1978]. pp. 365. *bibliog.*

— — 1945- .

BAUMANN (MICHAEL) Wie alles anfing: how it all began; translated by Helene Ellenbogen and Wayne Parker. Vancouver, [1977]. pp. 121.

—— 1945-1955, Allied occupation.

BACKER (JOHN H.) The decision to divide Germany: American foreign policy in transition. Durham, N.C., 1978. pp. 212. *bibliog.*

—— — Pictorial works.

TREES (WOLFGANG) and others. Drei Jahre nach Null: Geschichte der britischen Besatzungszone, 1945-1948: ein Bild/Text-Band. Düsseldorf, 1978 repr. 1979. pp. 221.

GRUBE (FRANK) and RICHTER (GERHARD) Die Schwarzmarktzeit: Deutschland zwischen 1945 und 1948. [Hamburg, 1979]. pp. 156. *Pictorial record.*

— History, Naval.

SCHREIBER (GERHARD) Revisionismus und Weltmachtstreben: Marineführung und deutsch- italienische Beziehungen, 1919 bis 1944. Stuttgart, 1978. pp. 428. *bibliog.* (Militärgeschichtliches Forschungsamt. Beiträge zur Militär- und Kriegsgeschichte. Band 20)

— Industries.

GERMANY. Statistisches Reichsamt. Statistik des Deutschen Reichs. Neue Folge. Bände 202-222. Berufs- und Betriebszählung vom 12 Juni 1907: Berufsstatistik [and] (Gewerbliche Betriebsstatistik). Berlin, 1909-12; Osnabrück, 1976. 22 vols. *Photographic reprint.*

GERMANY (BUNDESREPUBLIK). Statistisches Bundesamt. 1979. Beschäftigte, Lohn- und Gehaltsumme twie Umsatz der Unternehmen im Bergbau und im Verarbeitenden Gewerbe, 1977. Wiesbaden, [1979]. pp. 142. (Produzierendes Gewerbe. Reihe S. 4)

— Intellectual life.

GAY (PETER) Freud, Jews and other Germans: masters and victims in modernist culture. Oxford, 1978. pp. 289.

LIPTON (DAVID R.) Ernst Cassirer: the dilemma of a liberal intellectual in Germany, 1914-1933. Toronto, [1978]. pp. 212. *bibliog.*

SONTHEIMER (KURT) Die verunsicherte Republik: die Bundesrepublik nach 30 Jahren. München, [1979]. pp. 149.

— Kings and rulers.

GERMANY. Statistisches Reichsamt. Statistik des Deutschen Reichs. Neue Folge. Band 332. Volksbegehren und Volksentscheid "Enteignung der Fürstenvermögen". Anhang: Die Vorabstimmung in Hannover am 18.Mai 1924. Berlin, 1926; Osnabrück, 1978. pp. 38. *Photographic reprint.*

— Learned institutions and societies.

Die BERLINER Akademie der Wissenschaften in der Zeit des Imperialismus;...von Conrad Grau [and others]; Leitung der Arbeiten und Gesamtredaktion: Leo Stern. Berlin, 1975-79. 3 vols. (Akademie der Wissenschaften der DDR. Forschungsstelle für die Geschichte der Akademie. Studien zur Geschichte der Akademie der Wissenschaften der DDR. Band 2)

— Nationalism.

RITTER (ERNST) German historian. Das Deutsche Ausland-Institut in Stuttgart, 1917-1945: ein Beispiel deutscher Volkstumsarbeit zwischen den Weltkriegen. Wiesbaden, 1976. pp. 168. *bibliog.*

SONTHEIMER (KURT) Antidemokratisches Denken in der Weimarer Republik: die politischen Ideen des deutschen Nationalismus zwischen 1918 und 1933. München, 1978. pp. 331. *bibliog.*

— Nobility.

SCHIER (ROLF) Standesherren: zur Auflösung der Adelsvorherrschaft in Deutschland, 1815-1918. Heidelberg, 1977. pp. 157. *bibliog.*

— Occupations.

GERMANY. Statistisches Reichsamt. Statistik des Deutschen Reichs. Neue Folge. Bände 202-222. Berufs- und Betriebstatistik vom 12 Juni 1907: Berufsstatistik [and] (Gewerbliche Betriebsstatistik). Berlin, 1909-12; Osnabrück, 1976. 22 vols. *Photographic reprint.*

— Patentamt.

HUNDERT Jahre Patentamt: Festschrift herausgegeben vom Deutschen Patentamt. München, 1977. pp. 476.

— Politics and government.

KOLINSKY (A. MARTIN) Continuity and change in European society: Germany, France and Italy since 1870. London, 1974. pp. 234. *bibliog.*

—— 1789-1900.

KENT (GEORGE O.) Bismarck and his times. Carbondale, Ill., [1978]. pp. 184. *bibliog.*

LINKSRHEINISCHE deutsche Jakobiner: Aufrufe, Reden, Protokolle; Briefe und Schriften, 1794-1801; ([edited by] Axel Kuhn). Stuttgart, [1978]. pp. 353. *bibliog.*

BLUM (ROBERT) Politician. Politische Schriften; hrsg. von Sander L. Gilman. Nendeln, Liechtenstein, 1979. 6 vols.

—— 1871-1918.

ZEENDER (JOHN K.) The German Center Party, 1890-1906. Philadelphia, 1976. pp. 125. *bibliog.* (American Philosophical Society. Transactions. New Series. vol.66, part 1)

SMITH (WOODRUFF D.) The German colonial empire. Chapel Hill, N.C., [1978]. pp. 274. *bibliog.*

WEITOWITZ (ROLF GUNTER) Deutsche Politik und Handelspolitik unter Reichskanzler Leo von Caprivi, 1890-1894. Düsseldorf, [1978]. pp. 406. *bibliog.*

—— 1900- .

HITLER (ADOLF) Mein Kampf...: unexpurgated edition; [translated and annotated by James Murphy]. London, [1939]. pp. 584. *Published in 18 parts by Hutchinson and Co.*

—— 1918-1945.

SOHN-RETHEL (ALFRED) Economy and class structure of German fascism...; translated [from the German] by Martin Sohn-Rethel. London, 1978. pp. 159.

SONTHEIMER (KURT) Antidemokratisches Denken in der Weimarer Republik: die politischen Ideen des deutschen Nationalismus zwischen 1918 und 1933. München, 1978. pp. 331. *bibliog.*

—— 1945- .

BARZEL (RAINER) Auf dem Drahtseil. München, [1978]. pp. 247.

CONRADT (DAVID P.) The German polity. New York, [1978]. pp. 235. *bibliog.*

MOERSCH (KARL) Kurs-Revision: deutsche Politik nach Adenauer. Frankfurt am Main, [1978]. pp. 325.

GERMANY.(Cont.)

MORGAN (ROGER P.) West Germany's foreign policy agenda. Beverly Hills, [1978]. pp. 80. *bibliog. (Georgetown University. Center for Strategic and International Studies. Washington Papers. vol. 6/54)*

WALLRAFF (GUENTER) Wallraff: the undesirable journalist; [a selection of articles] translated by Steve Gooch and Paul Knight. London, 1978. pp. 180.

KIESINGER (KURT GEORG) Die Grosse Koalition, 1966-1969: Reden und Erklärungen des Bundeskanzlers; herausgegeben von Dieter Oberndörfer. Stuttgart, [1979]. pp. 420. *bibliog.*

SONTHEIMER (KURT) Die verunsicherte Republik: die Bundesrepublik nach 30 Jahren. München, [1979]. pp. 149.

— Population.

FRANZ (GUENTHER) Der Dreissigjährige Krieg und das deutsche Volk: Untersuchungen zur Bevölkerungs- und Agrargeschichte. 4th ed. Stuttgart, 1979. pp. 140.

— Presidents — Election.

GERMANY. Statistisches Reichsamt. Statistik des Deutschen Reichs. Neue Folge. Band 321. Die Wahl des Reichspräsidenten am 29. März und 26. April 1925. Berlin, 1925; Osnabrück, 1977. pp. 49. *Photographic reprint.*

— Reichstag.

RAUH (MANFRED) Die Parlamentarisierung des Deutschen Reiches. Düsseldorf, [1977]. pp. 533. *bibliog. (Germany (Bundesrepublik). Kommission für Geschichte des Parlamentarismus und der Politischen Parteien. Beiträge zur Geschichte des Parlamentarismus und der Politischen Parteien. Band 60)*

GERMANY. Statistisches Reichsamt. Statistik des Deutschen Reichs. Neue Folge. Band 315. Die Wahlen zum Reichstag am 4. Mai 1924 und am 7. Dezember 1924, zweite und dritte Wahlperiode. Berlin, 1925; Osnabrück, 1977. 6 vols(in 1). *Photographic reprint.*

GERMANY. Statistisches Reichsamt. Statistik des Deutschen Reichs. Neue Folge. Band 372. Die Wahlen zum Reichstag am 20. Mai 1928, vierte Wahlperiode. Berlin, 1931; Osnabrück, 1978. 3 vols.(in 1). *Photographic reprint.*

GERMANY. Statistisches Reichsamt. Statistik des Deutschen Reichs. Neue Folge. Band 382. Die Wahlen zum Reichstag am 14. September 1930, fünfte Wahlperiode. Berlin, 1932; Osnabrück, 1978. 3 vols.(in 1). *Photographic reprint.*

— Relations (general) with France.

LAPIE (PIERRE OLIVIER) and SCHMID (CARLO) La coopération franco-allemande. Paris, La Documentation Française, [1973]. pp. 63.

— Social conditions.

BOEHME (HELMUT) An introduction to the social and economic history of Germany: politics and economic change in the nineteenth and twentieth centuries. Oxford, [1978]. pp. 171. *Translated by W.R. Lee.*

WALLRAFF (GUENTER) Wallraff: the undesirable journalist; [a selection of articles] translated by Steve Gooch and Paul Knight. London, 1978. pp. 180.

— Social history — Bibliography.

WEHLER (HANS ULRICH) compiler. Bibliographie zur modernen deutschen Sozialgeschichte, 18.-20. Jahrhundert. Göttingen, [1976]. pp. 269.

— — Sources.

ARCHIVBESTÄNDE zur Wirtschafts- und Sozialgeschichte der Weimarer Republik: Übersicht über Quellen in Archiven der Bundesrepublik Deutschland; bearbeitet von Thomas Trumpp und Renate Köhne; mit Beiträgen von Jens Flemming [and others]. Boppard am Rhein, [1979]. pp. 380. *(Germany (Bundesrepublik). Bundesarchiv. Schriften. 29)*

— Social life and customs.

Der NATIONALSOZIALISTISCHE Alltag: so lebte man unter Hitler; ([edited by] George L. Mosse; aus dem Englischen von Renate Becker). Königstein/Ts., 1978. pp. 389.

— Statistics.

GERMANY (BUNDESREPUBLIK). Bundesministerium für innerdeutsche Beziehungen. 1978. Zahlenspiegel Bundesrepublik Deutschland, Deutsche Demokratische Republik: ein Vergleich. [Bonn, 1978]. pp. 105.

— — Bibliography.

QUELLEN für statistische Marktdaten: Führer durch die amtliche Statistik der Bundesrepublik Deutschland; (Veröffentlichung des HWW, Institut für Wirtschaftsforschung, Hamburg und des Landesamtes für Datenverarbeitung und Statistik, Nordrhein-Westfalen. Hamburg, [1976]. pp. 140. *(Hamburg. Hamburgisches Welt-Wirtschafts-Archiv. Veröffentlichungen)*

GERMANY, EASTERN

— Biography.

BUCH (GUENTHER) Namen und Daten wichtiger Personen der DDR. 2nd ed. Berlin, [1979]. pp. 386.

— Commerce — New Zealand.

NEW ZEALAND. Department of Trade and Industry. Trade Services Division. 1978. German Democratic Republic: [a market profile]. [Wellington, 1978]. fo. 34. *(Background to Export)*

— Economic conditions.

ARNOLD (KARL HEINZ) Socialist economy - aim and strategy. Berlin, 1977. pp. 64. *At foot of title page: Panorama DDR.*

NEW ZEALAND. Department of Trade and Industry. Trade Services Division. 1978. German Democratic Republic: [a market profile]. [Wellington, 1978]. fo. 34. *(Background to Export)*

— Economic history.

MELLOR (ROY EGERTON HENDERSON) The two Germanies: a modern geography. London, 1978. pp. 461. *bibliogs.*

— Economic policy.

BIERMANN (WOLFGANG) Demokratisierung in der DDR?: ökonomische Notwendigkeiten, Herrschaftsstrukturen, Rolle der Gewerkschaften, 1961-1977. Köln, [1978]. pp. 170. *bibliog.*

LEPTIN (GERT) and MELZER (MANFRED) Economic reform in East German industry. Oxford, 1978. pp. 200. *(Glasgow. University. Institute of Soviet and East European Studies. Economic Reforms in East European Industry) Translated from the German by Roger A. Clarke.*

ROESLER (JOERG) Die Herausbildung der sozialistischen Planwirtschaft in der DDR, etc. Berlin, 1978. pp. 355.

Die VOLKSWIRTSCHAFT der DDR;...Autoren: Gerd Friedrich [and others]. Berlin, 1979. pp. 296.

— Foreign relations.

AGAINST racism, apartheid and colonialism: documents published by the GDR, 1949-1977; [edited by Alfred Babing]. Berlin, 1978. pp. 664. *Facing title page: GDR Institute for International Politics and Economics; GDR Committee for the Decade of Action to Combat Racism and Racial Discrimination.*

— Industries.

LEPTIN (GERT) and MELZER (MANFRED) Economic reform in East German industry. Oxford, 1978. pp. 200. *(Glasgow. University. Institute of Soviet and East European Studies. Economic Reforms in East European Industry) Translated from the German by Roger A. Clarke.*

— Learned institutions and societies.

Die BERLINER Akademie der Wissenschaften in der Zeit des Imperialismus;...von Conrad Grau [and others]; Leitung der Arbeiten und Gesamtredaktion: Leo Stern. Berlin, 1975-79. 3 vols. *(Akademie der Wissenschaften der DDR. Forschungsstelle für die Geschichte der Akademie. Studien zur Geschichte der Akademie der Wissenschaften der DDR. Band 2)*

— Politics and government.

The GDR today. Dresden, 1977. pp. 175.

McCAULEY (MARTIN) Marxism-Leninism in the German Democractic Republic: the Socialist Unity Party (SED). London, 1979. pp. 267. *bibliog.*

— Social conditions.

LIVING in security: a report from the GDR. Berlin, 1978. pp. 64. *At foot of title page: Panorama DDR.*

SOCIALIST life and its values: aspects of advanced socialist society in the GDR. Berlin, 1978. pp. 87. *At foot of title page: Panorama DDR.*

— Social policy.

The GDR today. Dresden, 1977. pp. 175.

— Statistics.

GERMANY (BUNDESREPUBLIK). Bundesministerium für innerdeutsche Beziehungen. 1978. Zahlenspiegel Bundesrepublik Deutschland, Deutsche Demokratische Republik: ein Vergleich. [Bonn, 1978]. pp. 105.

GERSHUN (ALEKSANDR L'VOVICH).

IVANOV (NIKOLAI IVANOVICH) Aleksandr L'vovich Gershun, 1868-1915. Leningrad, 1976. pp. 135. *bibliog. (Akademiia Nauk SSSR. Nauchno-Biograficheskaia Seriia)*

GESTURE.

GRAHAM (JEAN ANN) Aspects of gaze, facial expression and gesture in dyadic interactions. 1978. fo. 433. *bibliog. Typescript. Ph.D. (London) thesis: unpublished. This thesis is the property of London University and may not be removed from the Library.*

GEWERKSCHAFT NAHRUNG, GENUSS, GASTSTÄTTEN.

WIEDENHOFER (HARALD) Probleme gewerkschaftlicher Interessenvertretung: das Beispiel der Gewerkschaft Nahrung, Genuss, Gaststätten. Bonn, [1979]. pp. 166. *bibliog. (Friedrich-Ebert-Stiftung. Forschungsinstitut. Reihe: Arbeit. Band 3)*

GEWERKSCHAFT ÖFFENTLICHE DIENSTE, TRANSPORT UND VERKEHR.

WEISS (GERHARD) Die ÖTV: Politik und gesellschaftspolitische Konzeptionen der Gewerkschaft Ö[ffentliche Dienste], T[ransport und] V[erkehr] von 1966 bis 1976. Marburg, 1978. pp. 533. *bibliog. (Studiengesellschaft für Sozialgeschichte und Arbeiterbewegung, Marburg. Schriftenreihe für Sozialgeschichte und Arbeiterbewegung. Band 7)*

GHANA

— Economic conditions.

GHANA'S ECONOMY AND AID REQUIREMENTS. a., 1968. Accra.

— Politics and government.

GHANA. Ministry of Information. 1970. One year of progress. [Accra, 1970]. pp. 27.

CROOK (RICHARD CHARLES) Local elites and national politics in Ghana: a case study of political centralization and local politics in Offinso, Ashanti (1945-1966). 1977 [or rather 1978]. 2 vols. *bibliog. Typescript. Ph.D. (London) thesis: unpublished. This thesis is the property of London University and may not be removed from the Library.*

GILCHRIST (Sir ANDREW).

GILCHRIST (Sir ANDREW) Cod wars and how to lose them. Edinburgh, 1977. pp. 122.

GILMAN CITY
— History.

REID (LOREN) Hurry home Wednesday: growing up in a small Missouri town, 1905-1921. Columbia, 1978. pp. 291.

GINGER.

RODRIQUEZ (D.W.) Ginger: (a short economic history). [Kingston, 1971]. pp. 36. bibliog. (Jamaica. Agricultural Planning Unit. Commodity Bulletins. No. 4)

GIRARD (STEPHEN).

ADAMS (DONALD R.) Finance and enterprise in early America: a study of Stephen Girard's Bank 1812-1831. [Philadelphia, 1978]. pp. 163.

GIRARD BANK.

ADAMS (DONALD R.) Finance and enterprise in early America: a study of Stephen Girard's Bank 1812-1831. [Philadelphia, 1978]. pp. 163.

GISCARD D'ESTAING (VALERY).

LECOMTE (BERNARD) and SAUVAGE (CHRISTIAN) Les Giscardiens. [Paris, 1978]. pp. 217.

GLADSTONE (WILLIAM EWART).

SMITH (GOLDWIN) My memory of Gladstone. London, 1904. pp. 88.

GLADSTONE (WILLIAM EWART) Autobiographical memoranda, 1845-1866; edited by John Brooke and Mary Sorensen. London, 1978. pp. 292. (U.K. Historical Manuscripts Commission. The Prime Ministers' Papers. W.E. Gladstone. 3)

HAWKINS (ANGUS B.) A forgotten crisis: Gladstone and finance during the 1850's. London, 1978. fo. 39. (London. University. London School of Economics and Political Science. Gladstone Memorial Trust Prize Essays. 1978) Typescript.

NEWMAN and Gladstone: centennial essays; edited by James D. Bastable. Dublin, 1978. pp. 324. bibliogs. Selection of papers presented at the International Newman Conference, Dublin, 1975.

GLASGOW
— Social conditions.

WORSDALL (FRANK) The tenement: a way of life: a social, historical and architectural study of housing in Glasgow. [Edinburgh], 1979. pp. 165. bibliog.

GLASS WORKERS
— India — Maharashtra.

MAHARASHTRA. Minimum Wages Committee for Employment in Glass Industry. 1970. Report...1969; [Adam Adil, chairman]. [Bombay, 1970]. pp. 50.

GOA, DAMAN AND DIU
— Appropriations and expenditures.

GOA, DAMAN AND DIU. Bureau of Economics, Statistics and Evaluation. An abstract of public finance. a., 1970-71/1977-78- Panaji.

GOBETTI (PIERO).

SPRIANO (PAOLO) Gramsci e Gobetti: introduzione alla vita e alle opere. Torino, [1977]. pp. 182.

GOD.

GUTKIND (ERICH) The absolute collective: a philosophical attempt to overcome our broken state;...translated from the original German text by Marjorie Gabain. London, 1937. pp. 120.

GODWIN (MARY).

TAYLOR (GEORGE ROBERT STIRLING) Mary Wollstonecraft: a study in economics and romance. London, 1911. pp. 210.

GODWIN (MARY) Collected letters of Mary Wollstonecraft; edited by Ralph M. Wardle. Ithaca , 1979. pp. 439.

GOEBBELS (JOSEPH).

GOEBBELS (JOSEPH) Tagebücher, 1945: die letzten Aufzeichnungen; Einführung: Rolf Hochhuth; (Redaktion: Peter Stadelmayer). Hamburg, [1977]. pp. 608.

GOERDELER (CARL FRIEDRICH).

YOUNG (ARTHUR PRIMROSE) The 'X' documents; edited by Sidney Aster. London, 1974. pp. 253. bibliog.

GOLD.

SUTTON (ANTONY C.) The war on gold. Sandton, South Africa, 1977. pp. 238. bibliog.

GOLD MINES AND MINING
— Canada — British Columbia.

TRIMBLE (WILLIAM JOSEPH) The mining advance into the Inland Empire;...with an introduction...by Rodman W. Paul. New York, 1972. pp. 254. bibliog. (Wisconsin University, Madison. Bulletins. History Series. vol. 3, no. 2) Reprint of work originally published Madison, Wis., 1914.

— South Africa.

SOUTH AFRICA. Embassy (London). Department of Information. 1969. The golden magnet: why S.A. gold mines annually attract 220,000 foreign Bantu. [London, 1969]. pp. (7).

PHILLIPS (Sir LIONEL) All that glittered: selected correspondence...1890-1924; [edited by] Maryna Fraser and Alan Jeeves. Cape Town, 1977. pp. 428. bibliog.

KUBICEK (ROBERT V.) Economic imperialism in theory and practice: the case of South African gold mining finance 1886-1914. Durham, 1979. pp. 239. bibliog. (Duke University. Center for Commonwealth and Comparative Studies. [Publications]. No. 45)

— United States.

TRIMBLE (WILLIAM JOSEPH) The mining advance into the Inland Empire;...with an introduction...by Rodman W. Paul. New York, 1972. pp. 254. bibliog. (Wisconsin University, Madison. Bulletins. History Series. vol. 3, no. 2) Reprint of work originally published Madison, Wis., 1914.

GOLDEN (CLINTON STRONG).

BROOKS (THOMAS R.) Clint: a biography of a labor intellectual: Clinton S. Golden. New York, 1978. pp. 377. bibliog.

GOLDIE (Sir GEORGE DASHWOOD TAUBMAN).

GOLDIE (Sir GEORGE DASHWOOD TAUBMAN) Empire builder extraordinary: Sir George Goldie, his philosophy of government and empire; [selected articles, letters, etc.; edited by] D.J.M. Muffett. Douglas, 1978. pp. 334. bibliog.

GOMEZ MORIN (MANUEL).

KRAUZE (ENRIQUE) Caudillos culturales en la Revolucion mexicana. Mexico, 1976. pp. 340.

GONDS.

FUERER-HAIMENDORF (CHRISTOPH VON) Freiherr and FUERER- HAIMENDORF (ELIZABETH VON) The Gonds of Andhra Pradesh: tradition and change in an Indian tribe. London, 1979. pp. 569. bibliog.

GOVERNMENT, COMPARATIVE.

GOOD AND EVIL.

DOOB (LEONARD WILLIAM) Panorama of evil: insights from the behavioral sciences. Westport, Conn., 1978. pp. 186. bibliog.

GOOD FAITH (LAW).

ZOLLER (ELISABETH) La bonne foi en droit international public. Paris, [1977]. pp. 392. bibliog. (Revue Générale de Droit International Public. Publications. Nouvelle série. No. 28) With English summary.

GORDON (GEORGE HAMILTON) 4th Earl of Aberdeen.

IREMONGER (LUCILLE) Lord Aberdeen: a biography of the fourth Earl of Aberdeen, K.G., K.T., prime minister 1852-1855. London, 1978. pp. 384. bibliog.

GORTER (HERMAN).

HERMAN Gorter en Henriette Roland Holst in hun tijd; (samengesteld en verzorgd door het Nederlands Letterkundig Museum en Documentatiecentrum). Amsterdam, 1978. pp. 135.

PANNEKOEK (ANTON) and GORTER (HERMAN) Pannekoek and Gorter's Marxism; (edited and introduced by D. A. Smart). London, 1978. pp. 176.

GORWALA (ASTAD DINSHAW).

SAY not the struggle: essays in honour of A.D. Gorwala; [edited by H.M. Patel]. Delhi, 1976. pp. 328.

GOSSIP.

HAVILAND (JOHN BEARD) Gossip, reputation, and knowledge in Zinacantan. Chicago, 1977. pp. 260. bibliog.

GOTHENBURG
— Statistics.

STATISTIKA MEDDELANDEN FRÅN GÖTEBORGS STADSKONTOR (sometime Meddelanden från Göteborgs Stads Statistiska Kontor). q., 1953(årg.1)- Göteborg.

GOTHS IN ITALY.

PROCOPIUS, of Caesarea. History of the wars; (with an English translation by H.B. Dewing). London, 1914-28 repr. 1962-71. 5 vols. bibliog. Parallel Greek and English texts.

GOVERNMENT, COMPARATIVE.

BENDIX (REINHARD) Nation-building and citizenship: studies of our social changing order. Berkeley, 1977. pp. 449.

ROSE (RICHARD) and PETERS (B. GUY) The political consequences of economic overload: on the possibility of political bankruptcy. Glasgow, 1977. pp. 27,5. bibliog. (Glasgow. University of Strathclyde. Centre for the Study of Public Policy. Studies in Public Policy. No. 4)

COMPARING public policies: new concepts and methods; Douglas E. Ashford, editor. Beverly Hills, [1978]. pp. 254. bibliogs.

CRISES of political development in Europe and the United States; edited by Raymond Grew; contributors: David D. Bien [and others]. Princeton, [1978]. pp. 434. bibliogs.

FACTION politics: political parties and factionalism in comparative perspective; Frank P. Belloni [and] Dennis C. eller, editors. Santa Barbara, [1978]. pp. 471. bibliogs.

GOVERNMENTS and leaders: an approach to comparative politics; [by] Edward Feit, contributing editor [and others]. Boston, [Mass., 1978]. pp. 552. bibliogs.

HAGOPIAN (MARK N.) Regimes, movements, and ideologies: a comparative introduction to political science. New York, [1978]. pp. 508. bibliogs.

TERRITORIAL politics in industrial nations; edited by Sidney Tarrow [and others]. New York, 1978. pp. 328.

GOVERNMENT, COMPARATIVE.(Cont.)

WESSON (ROBERT GALE) State systems: international pluralism, politics, and culture. New York, [1978]. pp. 296. *bibliog.*

GOVERNMENT AND THE PRESS.

GOREN (DINA) Secrecy and the right to know. Ramat Gan, Israel, 1979. pp. 194. *bibliog.*

— United Kingdom.

PINCHER (CHAPMAN) Inside story: a documentary of the pursuit of power. London, 1978. pp. 400.

— United States.

HOHENBERG (JOHN) A crisis for the American press. New York, 1978. pp. 316.

MORGAN (DAVID R.) The capitol press corps: newsmen and the governing of New York State. Westport, Conn., 1978. pp. 177. *bibliog.*

GOVERNMENT BUSINESS ENTERPRISES.

L'ENTREPRISE publique et l'intérêt public: compte rendu d'un colloque international; public enterprise and the public interest: proceedings of an international seminar; André Gélinas, editor. Toronto, [1978]. pp. 268. *bibliog. In French or English, with introductory matter in French and English.*

— Law and legislation — Africa.

LAW in the political economy of public enterprise: African perspectives; edited by Yash Ghai. Uppsala, 1977. pp. 351. *bibliog. (Nordiska Afrikainstitutet and International Legal Center. Studies of Law in Social Change and Development. 1)*

— Arab countries.

PUBLIC enterprises and development in the Arab countries: legal and managerial aspects; (papers presented at a seminar held in Kuwait, 1976). New York, [1977]. pp. 236.

— Botswana.

BOTSWANA. Tenth Anniversary Co-ordinating Unit. 1976. Botswana: ten years of progress, 1966-1976. [Gaborone, 1976]. pp. 55.

— Sierra Leone.

SIERRA LEONE. Percy Davies Commission of Inquiry into the Activities of the Sierra Leone Produce Marketing Board from January, 1961 to March, 1967. 1968. Report...: canteen accounts, and government statement thereon; [Percy R. Davies, commissioner]. [Freetown, 1968?]. pp. 12.

— Underdeveloped areas.

See UNDERDEVELOPED AREAS — Government business enterprises.

— United Kingdom — Scotland.

SCOTLAND. Scottish Economic Planning Department. 1976. Scottish Development Agency: industrial investment guidelines. Edinburgh, 1976. fo. 11, 2.

GOVERNMENT CONSULTANTS.

GOLDHAMER (HERBERT) The adviser. New York, [1978]. pp. 195. *bibliog.*

— United States.

ROGERS (DAVID) Can business management save the cities?: the case of New York. New York, [1978]. pp. 276.

GOVERNMENT EXECUTIVES

— United States.

DAVID (PAUL THEODORE) and POLLOCK (ROSS) Executives for government: central issues of federal personnel administration. Westport, Conn., 1976. pp. 196. *bibliog. Reprint of work originally published Washington, 1957, with 1958 supplement.*

GOVERNMENT INFORMATION.

ROWAT (DONALD CAMERON) Public access to government documents: a comparative perspective. [Toronto], 1978. pp. 116. *(Ontario. Commission on Freedom of Information and Individual Privacy. Research Publications. 3)*

— Canada — Ontario.

FLAHERTY (DAVID) Research and statistical uses of Ontario government personal data. [Toronto], 1979. pp. 188. *(Ontario. Commission on Freedom of Information and Individual Privacy. Research Publications. 5)*

— France.

FRANCE. Commission Chargée de Favoriser la Communication au Public des Documents Administratifs. 1978. Rapport au Premier Ministre: premier rapport; [Pierre Ordonneau, chairman]. Paris, 1978. pp. 43.

GOVERNMENT LAWYERS

— United Kingdom.

ARCHER (PETER) The role of the law officers. London, 1978. pp. 32. *(Fabian Society. Research Series. [No.] 339)*

GOVERNMENT OWNERSHIP.

The NATIONALISATION of multinationals in peripheral economies; edited by Julio Faundez and Sol Picciotto. London, 1978. pp. 238.

— Underdeveloped areas.

See UNDERDEVELOPED AREAS— Government ownership.

— United Kingdom.

BOARDMAN (TOM) and RIDLEY (NICHOLAS) The future of nationalized industries. [London, 1979]. pp. 14.

GOVERNMENT PUBLICATIONS.

CHERNS (J.J.) Official publishing: an overview: an international survey and review of the role, organisation and principles of official publishing. Oxford, 1979. pp. 527.

GOVERNMENT PUBLICITY

— Germany.

WIPPERMANN (KLAUS W.) Politische Propaganda und staatsbürgerliche Bildung: die Reichszentrale für Heimatdienst in der Weimarer Republik. Köln, [1976]. pp. 584. *bibliog.*

GOVERNMENT PURCHASING

— France.

FRANCE. Ministère de l'Industrie et de la Recherche. Service du Traitement de l'Information et des Statistiques Industrielles. 1975. Les marchés publics en 1974 dans l'industrie. Paris, 1977. pp. 89. *(Traits Fondamentaux du Système Industriel Français. Recueils Statistiques. Publication no. 2)*

— Russia.

BAKHOVKINA (LIDIIA NIKOLAEVNA) Gosudarstvennoe upravlenie zakupkami sel'skokhoziastvennykh produktov. Moskva, 1978. pp. 135.

GOVERNMENT SPENDING POLICY.

SCHULTZE (CHARLES L.) The politics and economics of public spending. Washington, D.C., [1968]. pp. 143. *(System Development Corporation. H. Rowan Gaither Lectures in Systems Science. No. 2)*

PUBLIC expenditure and policy analysis; [edited by] Robert H. Haveman and Julius Margolis. 2nd ed. Chicago, [1977]. pp. 591.

— Mathematical models.

COLLETTE (JEAN MICHEL) L'allocation des ressources dans les secteurs sociaux: étude sur les systèmes de décision. Paris, 1975. pp. 130. *bibliog.*

— United Kingdom.

OUTRAM (QUENTIN) The significance of public expenditure plans. [London], 1975. pp. 105. *bibliog. (Centre for Studies in Social Policy. Working Papers)*

CLARKE (Sir RICHARD WILLIAM BARNES) Public expenditure, management and controls: the development of the Public Expenditure Survey Committee (PESC). London, 1978. pp. 212.

ROBINSON (ANN) Parliament and public spending: the Expenditure Committee of the House of Commons, 1970-76. London, 1978. pp. 184. *bibliog.*

— United States.

PUBLIC expenditure and policy analysis; [edited by] Robert H. Haveman and Julius Margolis. 2nd ed. Chicago, [1977]. pp. 591.

GRADUATES

— India.

INDIA. Directorate General of Employment and Training. 1977. Report on the employment pattern of graduates. New Delhi, [1977]. pp. 111.

— Italy.

I GIOVANI ad elevato livello di istruzione e i mercati del lavoro in Italia; di Andrea Cafarelli [and others]. Milano, [1977]. pp. 166.

— Norway.

KOBBERSTAD (TOR) and MEIER (KNUT) Arbeidsmarkedet for nye akademikere, etc. [Oslo, 1973]. pp. 128. *(Utredninger om Forskning og Høyere Utdanning. 1973.5) With English summary.*

— United Kingdom.

BANKS (JOSEPH AMBROSE) and WEBB (DAVID) Ideas or people: the vocational dilemma for sociology graduates. London, [1977]. pp. 111.

U.K. Social Survey. 1979. Postgraduate income and expenditure: a survey commissioned by the Department of Education and Science and the Scottish Education Department of postgraduates' sources of income and patterns of expenditure during the academic year 1975/6; [by] Susan Dight [and] Peter Bush. [London], 1979. pp. 107.

GRAHAM (ROBERT BONTINE CUNNINGHAME-).

See CUNNINGHAME-GRAHAM (ROBERT BONTINE).

GRAIN.

UNITED NATIONS RESEARCH INSTITUTE FOR SOCIAL DEVELOPMENT. UNRISD Reports. No. 74.1. The social and economic implications of large-scale introduction of new varieties of foodgrain: summary of conclusions of a global research project. (UNRISD 74/27). Geneva, 1974. pp. 55. *([Studies on the Green Revolution. No. 6])*

GRAIN TRADE.

MUELLER (JOHANN ANTON) Chronologische Darstellung der italienischen Klassiker über National-Ökonomie. Vaduz, 1978. pp. 316. *Reprint of work originally published in Pest in 1820.*

MORGAN (DAN) Merchants of grain. New York, 1979. pp. 387.

— Netherlands.

HEIJDER (M.) Amsterdam: korenschuur van Europa: historische schets van de Amsterdamse graanhandel. Amsterdam, 1979. pp. 104.

GRAMMAR, COMPARATIVE AND GENERAL

— Interrogative.

QUESTIONS; edited by Henry Hiz. Dordrecht, [1978]. pp. 366. *bibliogs.*

— Phonology.

READINGS in historical phonology: chapters in the theory of sound change; edited by Philip Baldi and Ronald N. Werth. University Park, [1978]. pp. 376. *bibliogs.*

RECENT developments in historical phonology; edited by Jacek Fisiak. The Hague, [1978]. pp. 455. *bibliogs. Papers prepared for the International Conference on Historical Phonology held at Ustronie (Poland), 1976.*

— Syntax.

JACKENDOFF (RAY S.) X syntax: a study of phrase structure. Cambridge, Mass., [1977]. pp. 248. *bibliog.*

SYNTACTIC typology: studies in the phenomenology of language; edited by Winfred P. Lehmann. Austin, [1978]. pp. 463. *bibliog.*

PULLUM (GEOFFREY K.) Rule interaction and the organization of a grammar. New York, 1979. pp. 413. *bibliog.*

GRAMSCI (ANTONIO).

SPRIANO (PAOLO) Gramsci e Gobetti: introduzione alla vita e alle opere. Torino, [1977]. pp. 182.

SPRIANO (PAOLO) Gramsci in carcere e il partito. Roma, 1977. pp. 166.

SASSOON (ANNE SHOWSTACK) The political thought of Antonio Gramsci with special reference to the revolutionary party and the founding of a new state. 1978. fo. 347. *bibliog.* Typescript. Ph.D. (London) thesis: unpublished. This thesis is the property of London University and may not be removed from the Library.

KILMINSTER (RICHARD) Praxis and method: a sociological dialogue with Lukács, Gramsci and the early Frankfurt school. London, 1979. pp. 334. *bibliog.*

GRANELLI (GIUSEPPE).

MANZINI (GIORGIO) Una vita operaia. Torino, [1977]. pp. 148.

GRANTS-IN-AID

— United Kingdom.

URBAN PROGRAMME RESEARCH. Working Papers. 4. Urban programme decision making: the phase 7 exercise. Leeds, [1974?]. fo. 42.

— United States.

REDISTRIBUTION through the financial system: the grants economics of money and credit; [edited by] Kenneth E. Boulding and Thomas Frederick Wilson. New York, [1978]. pp. 301. *bibliogs.*

GRAPH THEORY.

BIGGS (NORMAN L.) and others. Graph theory, 1736-1936. Oxford, 1976. pp. 239. *bibliogs.*

BONDY (JOHN ADRIAN) and MURTY (UPPALURI SIVA RAMACHANDRA) Graph theory with applications. London, [1976]. pp. 264. *bibliogs.*

SAATY (THOMAS L.) and KAINEN (PAUL C.) The four-color problem: assaults and conquest. New York, [1977]. pp. 217. *bibliog.*

MINIEKA (EDWARD) Optimization algorithms for networks and graphs. New York, [1978]. pp. 356. *bibliogs.*

GREAT PLAINS

— Economic conditions.

KRUTILLA (JOHN V.) and others. Economic and fiscal impacts of coal development: Northern Great Plains. Baltimore, [1978]. pp. 208. *bibliog. Published for Resources for the Future, Inc.*

BONNIFIELD (PAUL) The dust bowl: men, dirt, and depression. Albuquerque, [1979]. pp. 232. *bibliog.*

— History.

BONNIFIELD (PAUL) The dust bowl: men, dirt, and depression. Albuquerque, [1979]. pp. 232. *bibliog.*

GREAT SWAMP.

CAVANAUGH (CAM) Saving the Great Swamp: the people, the power brokers, and an urban wilderness. Frenchtown, N.J., [1978]. pp. 240.

GREECE

— Commerce.

PRODROMIDIS (KYPRIANOS P.) Foreign trade of Greece: a quantitative analysis at a sectoral level. Athens, 1976. pp. 369. *bibliog. (Center of Planning and Economic Research [Athens]. Special Studies Series. A. 6)*

— Economic conditions.

GREECE. Ministry of Governmental Policy. Public Relations Service. 1972. Five years of economic progress, (1967-1972). [Athens, 1972]. pp. 136.

GREECE. Dieuthynsis Ethnikon Logariasmon. 1978. Input-output table of the Greek economy, year 1970. Athens, 1978. pp. 121. *In Greek and English.*

— — Mathematical models.

VERNARDAKIS (NIKOS) Econometric models for the developing economies: a case study of Greece. Farnborough, Hants., [1978]. pp. 143. *bibliog.*

— Economic policy.

GREECE. Ministry of Governmental Policy. Public Relations Service. 1972. Five years of economic progress, (1967-1972). [Athens, 1972]. pp. 136.

ZOLOTAS (XENOPHON) The dollar crisis and other papers. Athens, 1979. pp. 69. *bibliog. (Bank of Greece. Papers and Lectures. 41)*

— Foreign economic relations.

For a related heading see EUROPEAN ECONOMIC COMMUNITY — Greece.

— Foreign relations.

See also EUROPEAN ECONOMIC COMMUNITY — Greece.

— — United States.

STERN (LAURENCE) The wrong horse: the politics of intervention and the failure of American diplomacy. New York, [1977]. pp. 170.

AMEN (MICHAEL MARK) American foreign policy in Greece, 1944/1949: economic, military and institutional aspects. Frankfurt am Main, 1978. pp. 310.

— History.

CLOGG (RICHARD) A short history of modern Greece. Cambridge, 1979. pp. 242. *bibliog.*

— — 1863-1913.

AUGUSTINOS (GERASIMOS) Consciousness and history: nationalist critics of Greek society, 1897-1914. New York, 1977. pp. 182. *bibliog. (East European Quarterly. East European Monographs. 32)*

— — 1944-1949.

AVEROFF-TOSSIZZA (EVANGELOS) By fire and axe: the Communist Party and the civil war in Greece, 1944-1949; translated [from the French] by Sarah Arnold Rigos. New Rochelle, N.Y., 1978. pp. 438. *bibliog.*

— Nationalism.

AUGUSTINOS (GERASIMOS) Consciousness and history: nationalist critics of Greek society, 1897-1914. New York, 1977. pp. 182. *bibliog. (East European Quarterly. East European Monographs. 32)*

— Social life and customs.

McNEILL (WILLIAM HARDY) The metamorphosis of Greece since World War II. Oxford, 1978. pp. 264.

GREECE, ANCIENT

— Commerce.

HOPPER (ROBERT JOHN) Trade and industry in Classical Greece. London, 1979. pp. 240. *bibliog.*

— Economic conditions.

HOPPER (ROBERT JOHN) Trade and industry in Classical Greece. London, 1979. pp. 240. *bibliog.*

— History — 395-386 B.C., Corinthian War.

HAMILTON (CHARLES DANIEL) Sparta's bitter victories: politics and diplomacy in the Corinthian war. Ithaca, 1979. pp. 346. *bibliog.*

— — 431-404 B.C., Peloponnesian War.

HAMILTON (CHARLES DANIEL) Sparta's bitter victories: politics and diplomacy in the Corinthian war. Ithaca, 1979. pp. 346. *bibliog.*

— Industries.

HOPPER (ROBERT JOHN) Trade and industry in Classical Greece. London, 1979. pp. 240. *bibliog.*

GREEK LANGUAGE

— Syntax.

JOSEPH (BRIAN DANIEL) Morphology and universals in syntactic change: evidence from medieval and modern Greek. Bloomington, Ind., 1978. pp. 293. *bibliog.*

— Word formation.

JOSEPH (BRIAN DANIEL) Morphology and universals in syntactic change: evidence from medieval and modern Greek. Bloomington, Ind., 1978. pp. 293. *bibliog.*

GREEN REVOLUTION.

DAHLBERG (KENNETH A.) Beyond the green revolution: the ecology and politics of global agricultural development. New York, [1979]. pp. 256. *bibliog.*

GRIFFIN (KEITH) The political economy of agrarian change: an essay on the green revolution. 2nd ed. London, [1979]. pp. 268.

GREENLAND

— Defences.

BACH (H.C.) and TAAGHOLT (JØRGEN) Greenland and the Arctic region in the light of defence policies: defence aims. Copenhagen, Information and Welfare Service of the Danish Defence, 1977. pp. 55. *bibliog.*

GREEN'S FUNCTIONS.

KEILSON (JULIAN) Green's function methods in probability theory. London, 1965. pp. 220.

GRENVILLE FAMILY.

SACK (JAMES J.) The Grenvillites, 1801-29: party politics and factionalism in the age of Pitt and Liverpool. Urbana, [1979]. pp. 244. *bibliog.*

GREWE (WILHELM GEORG).

GREWE (WILHELM GEORG) Rückblenden, 1976-1951. [Frankfurt/Main, 1979]. pp. 813.

GREY (EDWARD) 1st Viscount Grey of Fallodon.

WELLS (SHERRILL PERKINS BROWN) The influence of Sir Cecil Spring Rice and Sir Edward Grey on the shaping of Anglo- American relations, 1913-1916. 1978. fo. 416. bibliog. Typescript. Ph.D. (London) thesis: unpublished. This thesis is the property of London University and may not be removed from the Library.

GROMYKO (ANDREI ANDREEVICH).

GROMYKO (ANDREI ANDREEVICH) Only for peace: selected speeches and writings. Oxford, 1979. pp. 277.

GROSS DOMESTIC PRODUCT

— Canada — Nova Scotia.

NOVA SCOTIA. Department of Development. Economic Analysis Section. 1977. Employment and gross domestic product by sector, Nova Scotia: 1964-1975 estimated, 1976-1984 projected; highlights, tables, charts and detailed description. Halifax, 1977. fo. 53.

— Indonesia.

INDONESIA. Biro Pusat Statistik. 1973. Regional income from several provinces in Indonesia, [1969, 1970, 1971]. Jakarta, 1973. fo. 26. bibliog. (Statistik Pendapatan Nasional)

— Trinidad and Tobago.

TRINIDAD AND TOBAGO. Central Statistical Office. 1977. The gross domestic product of the republic of Trinidad and Tobago, 1966-1976. [Port of Spain, 1977]. pp. 55.

GROSS NATIONAL PRODUCT.

BECKERMAN (WILFRED) Measures of leisure, equality and welfare. Paris, Organisation for Economic Co-operation and Development, 1978. pp. 63.

INTERNATIONAL comparisons of real product and purchasing power: (United Nations International Comparison Project, phase II); produced by the Statistical Office of the United Nations and the World Bank...; published for the World Bank. Baltimore, [1978]. pp. 264.

— Russia.

DVA podrazdeleniia obshchestvennogo produkta: metodologiia deleniia; pod redaktsiei A.I. Zalkinda. Moskva, 1976. pp. 191. bibliog.

— — Kirghizia.

KOICHUEV (TURAR KOICHUEVICH) Vosproizvodstvo obshchestvennogo produkta v Kirgizskoi SSR. Frunze, 1977. pp. 112.

— Spain.

SCHWARTZ (PEDRO) ed. El producto nacional de España en el siglo XX: seleccion de textos. Madrid, Instituto de Estudios Fiscales, 1977. pp. 690.

GROUP PSYCHOTHERAPY.

WHITELEY (J. STUART) and GORDON (JOHN) Psychotherapist. Group approaches in psychiatry. London, 1979. pp. 245. bibliog.

GROUP RELATIONS TRAINING.

KATZ (JUDY H.) White awareness: handbook for anti-racism training. Norman, [1978]. pp. 211. bibliog.

GRUNWICK STRIKE, 1976.

DROMEY (JACK) and TAYLOR (GRAHAM) of Brent Trades Council. Grunwick: the workers' story. London, 1978. pp. 207.

GUARDIAN AND WARD

— United Kingdom.

LOWE (NIGEL VAUGHAN) and WHITE (RICHARD A.H.) Wards of court. London, 1979. pp. 413.

GUATEMALA

— Foreign relations — United States.

SOTO (JOSÉ M. AYBAR DE) Dependency and intervention: the case of Guatemala in 1954. Boulder, Colo., 1978. pp. 374. bibliog.

— Politics and government.

SOTO (JOSÉ M. AYBAR DE) Dependency and intervention: the case of Guatemala in 1954. Boulder, Colo., 1978. pp. 374. bibliog.

— Population.

BARRERA TUNCHEZ (J. ANTONIO) and others. Aspectos generales de la situacion demografica de Guatemala: trabajo presentado por la Direccion General de Estadistica, Departamento de Estudios Especiales y Estadisticas Continuas;...colaboracion Luis Efrain de Leon Robles [and] Carlos Guillermo Herrera. [Guatemala, 1968]. pp. 31. At head of title: Seminario sobre "El Crecimiento de la Poblacion y Desarrollo Economico de Guatemala"...1968.

— Statistics, Vital.

BARRERA TUNCHEZ (J. ANTONIO) and others. Aspectos generales de la situacion demografica de Guatemala: trabajo presentado por la Direccion General de Estadistica, Departamento de Estudios Especiales y Estadisticas Continuas;...colaboracion Luis Efrain de Leon Robles [and] Carlos Guillermo Herrera. [Guatemala, 1968]. pp. 31. At head of title: Seminario sobre "El Crecimiento de la Poblacion y Desarrollo Economico de Guatemala"...1968.

GUAYAQUI INDIANS.

ARENS (RICHARD) Writer on law, ed. Genocide in Paraguay. Philadelphia, 1976. pp. 171.

GUDERIAN (HEINZ).

GUDERIAN (HEINZ) Panzer leader:...translated from the German by Constantine Fitzgibbon. London, 1974 repr. 1979. pp. 528. First published in Great Britain in 1952.

GUERRILLAS.

INTERNATIONAL WORKING CONFERENCE ON VIOLENCE AND NON-VIOLENT ACTION IN INDUSTRIALIZED SOCIETIES, 1ST, BRUSSELS, 1974. Part 1. Urban guerilla: studies on the theory, strategy and practice of political violence in modern societies; (proceedings of the...conference); edited by Johan Niezing. Rotterdam, 1974. pp. 149. bibliogs. (Vrije Universiteit Brussel. Polemological Centre. Publications. vol. 4)

GUIDED MISSILES.

YANARELLA (ERNEST J.) The missile defense controversy: strategy, technology, and politics, 1955-1972. Lexington, [1977]. pp. 236.

GUJARAT

— Legislative Assembly — Elections.

GUJARAT. Chief Electoral Officer. 1975. Report on the general elections to the Gujarat Legislative Assembly, June 1975: statistical review. [Gandhinagar], 1975. pp. 253.

— Politics and government.

SHAH (GHANSHYAM) Protest movements in two Indian states: a study of the Guyarat and Bihar movements. Delhi, 1977. pp. 171. bibliogs. (Centre for Social Studies, Surat. Publications. No. 8)

GURO MAHARAJ JI.

DOWNTON (JAMES V.) Sacred journeys: the conversion of young Americans to Divine Light Mission. New York, 1979. pp. 245. bibliog.

GUSII.

WIPPER (AUDREY) Rural rebels: a study of two protest movements in Kenya. Nairobi, 1977. pp. 363. bibliog.

GUTTMAN (LOUIS).

THEORY construction and data analysis in the behavioral sciences: a volume in honor of Louis Guttman; [edited by] Samuel Shye. San Francisco, 1978. pp. 426. bibliog.

GUYANA.

GUYNEWS: m. magazine of the Co-operative Republic of Guyana; produced by the Ministry of Information and Culture. m., N 1971 (v.1, no.1)- Georgetown.

— Constitution.

GUYANA. Constitutional Committee. 1959. Report; [Donald Jackson, chairman]. Georgetown, 1959. 1 vol. (various pagings).

— Economic conditions.

GUYANA. Ministry of Information. 1968. Two years of independence and progress. [Georgetown, 1968]. pp. 41.

GUYANA. Ministry of Information and Culture. 1974. Guyana: a decade of progress; 10th anniversary of People's National Congress in government. Georgetown, 1974. pp. 127.

— Economic policy.

GUYANA. Prime Minister. 1975. Onward to socialism: Prime Minister's address to the nation on the occasion of the celebration of the fifth anniversary of the Co-operative Republic of Guyana...February 23, 1975. [Georgetown, 1975]. pp. 20.

GUYANA. Prime Minister. 1976. On the road to socialism; [address by...L.F.S. Burnham on the occasion of the celebration of the sixth anniversary of the Co- operative Republic of Guyana...February 22, 1976]. [Georgetown, 1976]. pp. 24.

GUYANA. Prime Minister. 1976. The pursuit of perfection; [address to the nation by L.F.S. Burnham on the occasion of the 10th anniversary of independence, National Park, May 25, 1976]. [Georgetown, 1976]. pp. 44.

— Foreign relations.

GUYANA JOURNAL; (issued by the Ministry of External Affairs, Guyana). irreg., Ap 1968 (v. 1, no.1)- with gap (1970, v.1,no.4). Georgetown.

GUYANA. Prime Minister. 1976. On the road to socialism; [address by...L.F.S. Burnham on the occasion of the celebration of the sixth anniversary of the Co- operative Republic of Guyana...February 22, 1976]. [Georgetown, 1976]. pp. 24.

— History — 1803-1966.

WAGNER (MICHAEL JOHN) Structural pluralism and the Portuguese in nineteenth century British Guiana: a study in historical geography. Montreal, 1975. pp. 346. Microfiche copy.

— Politics and government.

GUYANA. Ministry of Information. 1968. Two years of independence and progress. [Georgetown, 1968]. pp. 41.

LUTCHMAN (HAROLD ALEXANDER) From colonialism to co-operative republic: aspects of political development in Guyana. Puerto Rico, 1974. pp. 291. bibliog. (Puerto Rico University. Institute of Caribbean Studies. Caribbean Monograph Series. No. 9)

GUYANA. Prime Minister. 1976. The pursuit of perfection; [address to the nation by L.F.S. Burnham on the occasion of the 10th anniversary of independence, National Park, May 25, 1976]. [Georgetown, 1976]. pp. 44.

— Social conditions.

GUYANA. Ministry of Information. 1968. Two years of independence and progress. [Georgetown, 1968]. pp. 41.

GUYANA. Ministry of Information and Culture. 1974. Guyana: a decade of progress; 10th anniversary of People's National Congress in government. Georgetown, 1974. pp. 127.

— Social policy.

GUYANA. Prime Minister. 1975. Onward to socialism: Prime Minister's address to the nation on the occasion of the celebration of the fifth anniversary of the Co-operative Republic of Guyana...February 23, 1975. [Georgetown, 1975]. pp. 20.

HABERMAS (JUERGEN).

McCARTHY (THOMAS A.) The critical theory of Jürgen Habermas. Cambridge, Mass., [1978]. pp. 466. *bibliog.*

SENSAT (JULIUS) Habermas and Marxism: an appraisal. Beverly Hills, [1979]. pp. 176. *bibliog.*

HABSBURG FAMILY.

EVANS (ROBERT JOHN WESTON) The making of the Habsburg monarchy, 1550-1700: an interpretation. Oxford, 1979. pp. 531.

HACIENDAS

— Mexico.

BAZANT (JAN) Cino haciendas mexicanas: tres siglos de vida rural en San Luis Potosí, 1600-1910. Mexico, 1975. pp. 226. *(Mexico City. Colegio de Mexico. Centro de Estudios Historicos. Nueva Serie. 20)*

BOORTEIN COUTURIER (EDITH) La hacienda de Hueyapan, 1550-1936; traduccion de Carlos E. Guerrero. Mexico, Secretaria de Educacion Publica, 1976. pp. 199. *bibliog. (Sep/Setentas. 310)*

BRADING (DAVID A.) Haciendas and ranchos in the Mexican Bajío, Leon 1700-1860. Cambridge, 1978. pp. 258. *bibliog.*

— Peru.

MACERA (PABLO) ed. Poblacion rural en haciendas, 1876. Lima, 1976. pp. 82.

HACKNEY

— Social conditions.

CENTERPRISE TRUST. Local publishing and local culture: an account of the work of the Centerprise publishing project, 1972-1977. London, [1977]. pp. 22.

HAGUE

— International Court of Justice.

FONTES JURIS GENTIUM. Series A. Sectio 1. Tomus 6. Digest of the decisions of the International Court of Justice, 1959-1975; bearbeitet im Max-Planck-Institut für ausländisches öffentliches Recht und Völkerrecht von Rudolf Bernhardt [and others]. Berlin, 1978. 2 vols. *In French and English.*

HAGUE. International Court of Justice. [Series D.] Acts and Documents concerning the Organization of the Court. No. 4. Charter of the United Nations, statute and rules of Court and other documents. [4th. ed.] [The Hague], 1978. pp. 268. *In English and French.*

HAINAUT

— History.

PIERRARD (PIERRE) Histoire du Nord: Flandre, Artois, Hainaut, Picardie. [Paris, 1978]. pp. 404. *bibliog.*

HAITI.

FRANCE. Direction de la Documentation. La Documentation Française. Notes et Etudes Documentaires. Nos. 4,436-4, 438. La république d'Haiti; par Robert Lacombe. [Paris], 1977. pp. 96. *bibliog.*

— Economic conditions.

LUNDAHL (MATS) Peasants and poverty: a study of Haiti. London, 1979. pp. 699. *bibliog.*

— History.

HEINL (ROBERT DEBS) and HEINL (NANCY GORDON) Written in blood: the story of the Haitian people, 1492-1971. Boston, [Mass.], 1978. pp. 785. *bibliog.*

HALLAND

— Economic conditions.

JÖNSSON (BENGT) and WADENSJÖ (ESKIL) Industriell miljö i Halland: (en undersökning om de mindre och medelstora företagens problem och utvecklingsbetingelser). [Falkenberg, imprint, 1972]. pp. 176. *bibliog.*

HAMBURG

— Commerce.

HANDEL UND SCHIFFAHRT DES HAFEN HAMBURG (formerly Hamburgs Handel und Schiffahrt); (hrsg. vom Statistischen Landesamt der Freien und Hansestadt Hamburg). a., 1846-1913, with gaps; 1948/1949- Hamburg.

KRAWEHL (OTTO ERNST) Hamburgs Schiffs- und Warenverkehr mit England und den englischen Kolonien, 1814-1860. Köln, 1977. pp. 536. *bibliog. With summary and table of contents in English.*

HAMILTON (ALEXANDER).

PARKS (ROBERT JAMES) European origins of the economic ideas of Alexander Hamilton. New York, 1977. pp. 170.

HAMILTON (PEGGY) Lady.

HAMILTON (PEGGY) Lady. Three years or the duration: the memoirs of a munition worker, 1914-1918. London, 1978. pp. 125.

HAMPSHIRE

— Economic conditions.

HAMPSHIRE. County Council. (North East Hampshire structure plan): report of survey: summary and conclusions; ([with] Supplement). [Winchester], 1977-8. 2 pts. (in 1 vol.)

— Economic policy.

HAMPSHIRE. County Council. (North East Hampshire structure plan): report of survey: summary and conclusions; ([with] Supplement). [Winchester], 1977-8. 2 pts. (in 1 vol.)

HAMPSHIRE. County Council. (North East Hampshire structure plan): choice and policy. [Winchester], 1977. pp. 38.

HAMPSHIRE. County Council. Mid Hampshire structure plan, submitted 1978. [Winchester], 1978. pp. 121. *Map in end pocket.*

HAMPSHIRE. County Council. Mid Hampshire structure plan: report on publicity and consultations. [Winchester], 1978. 3 vols. (in 1).

HAMPSHIRE. County Council. North East Hampshire structure plan, submitted 1978. [Winchester], 1978. pp. 108. *Map in end pocket.*

HAMPSHIRE. County Council. (North East Hampshire structure plan): report on publicity and consultations; ([with] Representations [and] Technical comments). [Winchester], 1978. 3 vols. (in 1).

— Social conditions.

HAMPSHIRE. County Council. (North East Hampshire structure plan): report of survey: summary and conclusions; ([with] Supplement). [Winchester], 1977-8. 2 pts. (in 1 vol.)

— Social policy.

HAMPSHIRE. County Council. (North East Hampshire structure plan): report of survey: summary and conclusions; ([with] Supplement). [Winchester], 1977-8. 2 pts. (in 1 vol.)

HAMPSHIRE. County Council. (North East Hampshire structure plan): choice and policy. [Winchester], 1977. pp. 38.

HAMPSHIRE. County Council. Mid Hampshire structure plan, submitted 1978. [Winchester], 1978. pp. 121. *Map in end pocket.*

HAMPSHIRE. County Council. Mid Hampshire structure plan: report on publicity and consultations. [Winchester], 1978. 3 vols. (in 1).

HAMPSHIRE. County Council. North East Hampshire structure plan, submitted 1978. [Winchester], 1978. pp. 108. *Map in end pocket.*

HAMPSHIRE. County Council. (North East Hampshire structure plan): report on publicity and consultations; ([with] Representations [and] Technical comments). [Winchester], 1978. 3 vols. (in 1).

HAMPSTEAD HEATH

— History.

IKIN (CHRISTOPHER WOODROFFE) Hampstead Heath centenary, 1871-1971: how the heath was saved for the public. [London], Greater London Council, [1971]. pp. 24. *Map in end pocket.*

HANCOCK (WALTER).

JAMES (FRANCIS) Walter Hancock and his common road steam carriages. Alresford, 1975. pp. 131, 104. *Includes a facsimile reprint of Narrative of twelve years' experiments, 1824-1836 by Walter Hancock published in London in 1838.*

HANDICAPPED.

HAMMERMAN (SUSAN R.) Rehabilitation for the disabled: the social and economic implications of investments for this purpose. (ST/ESA/35). New York, United Nations, 1977. pp. 70.

ROESSLER (RICHARD) and BOLTON (BRIAN) Psychosocial adjustment to disability;...with the assistance of Daniel Cook [and others]. Baltimore, [1978]. pp. 184. *bibliog.*

— Employment — United Kingdom.

FIELD (FRANK) 1942- . Unfair shares: the disabled and unemployment. London, 1977. fo.5. *(Low Pay Unit. Low Pay Papers. No. 20)*

— Housing — United Kingdom.

SOCIAL SERVICES RESEARCH AND INTELLIGENCE UNIT [PORTSMOUTH]. Information Sheets. No.31. Housing for the disabled. Portsmouth, 1977. fo. 11. *Notes on a conference organised by the Southampton Branch of the Disablement Income Group, 1977.*

— Law and legislation.

UNITED NATIONS. Department of Economic and Social Affairs. 1976. Comparative study on legislation, organization and administration of rehabilitation services for the disabled: prepared jointly by the United Nations, the International Labour Organisation and the World Health Organization. (ST/ESA/28). New York, 1976. pp. 183.

— Psychology.

ROESSLER (RICHARD) and BOLTON (BRIAN) Psychosocial adjustment to disability;...with the assistance of Daniel Cook [and others]. Baltimore, [1978]. pp. 184. *bibliog.*

— Denmark.

HÜBBE (PER) Invalidepensionistundersøgelserne 4. Ansøgere til invalide pension...; Surveys of disability pensioners 4. Applicants for disability pensions, etc. København, 1978. pp. 175. *bibliog. (Socialforskningsinstituttet. Publikationer. 84) With English summary.*

HANDICAPPED.(Cont.)

HÜBBE (PER) and WESTERGÅRD (POUL) Invalidepensionistundersøgelserne 3. Materiale og metoder; Surveys of disability pensioners 3. Material and methods. København, 1978. pp. 216. *bibliog.* *(Socialforskningsinstituttet. Publikationer. 83)* With English summary.

HÜBBE (PER) Invalidepensionistundersøgelserne 5. Forhold efter første ansøgning; Surveys of disability pensioners 5. Situation after the first application. København, 1979. pp. 167. *bibliog.* *(Socialforskningsinstituttet. Publikationer. 85)* With English summary.

— **United Kingdom.**

OSWIN (MAUREEN) Holes in the welfare net. London, 1978. pp. 168. *bibliog.*

SIMKINS (JEAN) and TICKNER (VINCENT) Whose benefit: an examination of the existing system of cash benefits and related provisions for intrinsically handicapped adults and their families. London, [1978]. pp. 245. *bibliog.*

— — **Wales.**

U.K. Welsh Office. Residential accommodation for the elderly and younger physically handicapped. a., 1975/76- Cardiff.

HANDICAPPED CHILDREN.

O'CONNOR (NEIL) and HERMELIN (BEATE) Seeing and hearing and space and time. London, 1978. pp. 157. *bibliog.*

— **Care and treatment — United Kingdom.**

OSWIN (MAUREEN) Holes in the welfare net. London, 1978. pp. 168. *bibliog.*

— **New Zealand.**

CHILDREN with handicaps; [H.J.H. Hiddlestone, chairman]. [Wellington], 1975. pp. 40. *(New Zealand. Board of Health. Report Series. No. 24)*

HANDICRAFT

— **Italy.**

GUALTIEROTTI (PIERO) L'impresa artigiana. Milano, 1977. pp. 465. *bibliog.*

— **Netherlands.**

BOUMA (HANS) Leve het oude ambacht; met foto's van Cas Oorthuys en Ernst Niewenhuis. Laren, [1978]. pp. 119.

HANOVER

— **History.**

ZORN (GERDA) Widerstand in Hannover: gegen Reaktion und Faschismus, 1920- 1946. Frankfurt am Main, [1977]. pp. 276. *bibliog.*

HANSLICK (EDUARD).

GAY (PETER) Freud, Jews and other Germans: masters and victims in modernist culture. Oxford, 1978. pp. 289.

HARBOURS

— **Maps.**

LLOYD'S maritime atlas, including a comprehensive list of ports and shipping places of the world. 10th ed. London, 1975. pp. 160.

— **Belgium.**

SUYKENS (F.) The future of port development in the Rhine, Meuse and Scheldt delta. 1978. fo. 49.

— **Europe.**

KONVITZ (JOSEF W.) Cities and the sea: port city planning in early modern Europe. Baltimore, [1978]. pp. 235.

— **Netherlands.**

SUYKENS (F.) The future of port development in the Rhine, Meuse and Scheldt delta. 1978. fo. 49.

— **United Kingdom.**

LONDON. University. London School of Economics and Political Science. Graduate School of Geography. Discussion Papers. No. 65. Modelling the process of the development of seaports in Great Britain and the formulation of a comprehensive future port planning policy; [by] David K.Y. Chu. London, [1978]. fo. 8. *bibliog.*

HARDEMAN FAMILY.

HARDEMAN (NICHOLAS PERKINS) Wilderness calling: the Hardeman family in the American westward movement, 1750-1900. Knoxville, [1977]. pp. 357. *bibliog.*

HARNESS MAKING AND TRADE

— **United Kingdom.**

NOCKOLDS (HAROLD) ed. The coachmakers: a history of the Worshipful Company of Coachmakers and Coach Harness Makers, 1677-1977. London, [1977]. pp. 239. *bibliog.*

HARON (ABDULLA).

DESAI (BARNEY) and MARNEY (CARDIFF) The killing of the Imam. London, 1978. pp. 146.

HARRINGTON (JAMES).

COTTON (JAMES STEPHEN) James Harrington's political thought and its context. 1978. fo. 243. *bibliog.* Typescript. Ph.D. (London) thesis: unpublished. This thesis is the property of London University and may not be removed from the Library.

HARRISON (BYRON PATTON).

See HARRISON (PAT).

HARRISON (PAT).

SWAIN (MARTHA H.) Pat Harrison: the New Deal years. Jackson, Miss., 1978. pp. 316. *bibliog.*

HAUSAS.

SMITH (MICHAEL GARFIELD) The affairs of Daura. Berkeley, [1978]. pp. 532.

HAUSHOFER (KARL).

JACOBSEN (HANS ADOLF) Karl Haushofer: Leben und Werk. Boppard am Rhein, 1979. 2 vols. *(Germany (Bundesrepublik). Bundesarchiv. Schriften. 24)*

HAUT-RHIN (DEPARTMENT).

FRANCE. Direction de la Documentation. La Documentation Française. Notes et Etudes Documentaires. No. 4466. Les départements français. 68. Haut-Rhin, Alsace; [by Arsène Matty]. [Paris], 1978. pp. 186.

HAUTE-LOIRE (DEPARTMENT).

FRANCE. Direction de la Documentation. La Documentation Française. Notes et Etudes Documentaires. Nos. 4415-4417. Les départements français. 43. Haute-Loire, Auvergne. [Paris], 1977. pp. 104.

HAUTE-SAVOIE.

FRANCE. Direction de la Documentation. La Documentation Française. Notes et Etudes Documentaires. Nos. 4,505-4, 506. Les départements français. 74. Haute-Savoie, Rhône- Alpes; (par Simone Chabert). Paris, 1979. pp. 162.

HAW PAR BROTHERS INTERNATIONAL.

GRUNDY (PHILIP GERALD) Haw Par Brothers International Limited: investigation under sections 195 and 196 of the Companies Act, 1967, as amended; interim (and second and final) report(s). [Singapore, 1976]. 2 vols.

HAWAIIAN ISLANDS

— **Economic conditions.**

HAWAI'I (formerly Hawaii economic review); [pd by] Department of Planning and Economic Development, State of Hawaii. q. (formerly bi-m.), S/Oc 1970 (v.8, no.2)- , with gap (Ja/F 1971: v.8, no.4). Honolulu.

— **Politics and government.**

DAVIS (ELEANOR HARMON) Abraham Fornander: a biography. Honolulu, [1979]. pp. 322. *bibliog.*

HAY (JOHN).

CLYMER (KENTON J.) John Hay: the gentleman as diplomat. Ann Arbor, [1975]. pp. 314. *bibliog.*

HAYA DE LA TORRE (VICTOR RAUL).

HAYA DE LA TORRE (VICTOR RAUL) Obras completas. Lima, [1977]. 7 vols.

HAYEK (FRIEDRICH AUGUST).

LIBERTY and the rule of law: [papers from a conference held in San Francisco in 1976]; edited...by Robert L. Cunningham. College Station, Texas, [1979]. pp. 349.

HAZARDOUS SUBSTANCES

— **Transportation.**

U.K. Standing Advisory Committee on the Carriage of Dangerous Goods in Ships. 1978- . Carriage of dangerous goods in ships; report..., 1978: the Blue Book; (with Amendments); [R. K. Roberts, chairman]. 3rd ed. London, 1978 in progress. 1 vol.(loose-leaf)

EUROPEAN AGREEMENT CONCERNING THE INTERNATIONAL CARRIAGE OF DANGEROUS GOODS BY ROAD (ADR). European agreement concerning the international carriage of dangerous goods by road; (with Annex A: provisions concerning dangerous substances and articles; annex B: provisions concerning transport equipment and transport operations;...includes all amendments which came into force on and before 1st October, 1978). 4th ed. London, H.M.S.O., 1978. pp. 523.

— **United Kingdom.**

U.K. Health and Safety Executive. 1978. Canvey: an investigation of potential hazards from operations in the Canvey Island/Thurrock area. London, 1978. pp. 192, 1 map.

HEALTH BOARDS

— **United Kingdom — Scotland.**

SCOTLAND. Working Party on Relationships between Health Boards and Local Authorities. 1977. Report; [J.A.M. Mitchell, chairman]. Edinburgh, 1977. pp. 26.

HEALTH EDUCATION

— **New Zealand.**

POPE (JAMES H.) Health for the Maori: a manual for use in native schools. 3rd ed, Wellington, Government Printer, 1901. pp. 152.

HEALTH OFFICERS

— **Training of — Europe.**

WORKING GROUP ON THE EDUCATION AND TRAINING OF PUBLIC HEALTH MEDICAL OFFICERS. The education and training of public health medical officers: report on a working group [held in] Copenhagen, 23-25 February, 1976. Copenhagen, World Health Organization, Regional Office for Europe, 1977. pp. 34.

HEALTH PLANNING.

WORKING GROUP ON THE ROLE OF HEALTH ECONOMICS IN NATIONAL HEALTH PLANNING AND POLICY-MAKING. The role of health economics in national health planning and policy-making; report on a working group [held in] Cologne, 7-10 June 1977. Copenhagen, World Health Organization, Regional Office for Europe, 1978. pp. 31.

ECONOMICS and health planning; edited by Kenneth Lee. London, [1979]. pp. 195. *bibliog.*

— **United Kingdom.**

BUXTON (MARTIN J.) and KLEIN (RUDOLF EWALD) Allocating health resources: a commentary on the report of the Resource Allocation Working Party. London, 1978. pp. 27. *(U.K. Royal Commission on the National Health Service, 1976. Research Papers. No.3)*

HEALTH SERVICES ADMINISTRATION.

HEALTH care in big cities; edited by Leslie H.W. Paine. New York, 1978. pp. 368.

The HEALTH service administrator: innovator or catalyst?: selected papers from a King's Fund international seminar; edited, with commentaries, by Leslie Paine. London, [1978]. pp. 198. *bibliog.*

— **Study and teaching.**

WORKING GROUP ON THE EDUCATION OF MANAGERS IN HEALTH SERVICES. Education of managers in health services: report on a working group [held in] Düsseldorf, 29 November-2 December 1977. Copenhagen, World Health Organization, Regional Office for Europe, 1978. pp. 40. *bibliog.*

— **Europe.**

WORLD HEALTH ORGANIZATION. Regional Office for Europe. 1975. Health services in Europe. 2nd ed. Copenhagen, 1975. pp. 299.

— **United Kingdom.**

REVIEW COMMITTEE FOR THE OXFORD REGION. Report on the management functions of the regional and area health authorities: discussion document; [G.J. Roberts, chairman]. [Oxford, Oxford Regional Health Authority], 1977. pp. (38).

HEALTH services: their nature and organization, and the role of patients, doctors, nurses, and the complementary professions; editor Elliott Jaques, with members of the Brunel Health Services Organization Research Unit. London, 1978. pp. 346. *bibliog. A report of the main findings arising from the Brunel Health Services Organization Research Unit.*

HEALTH SURVEYS.

NORD-LARSEN (MOGENS) At måle helbred: en litteraturstudie; (with an English summary) Measurement of health: a study of present literature. København, 1979. pp. 197. *bibliog.* *(Socialforskningsinstituttet. Studier. 38)*

HECKFORD (SARAH).

ALLEN (VIVIEN) Lady trader: a biography of Mrs. Sarah Heckford. London, 1979. pp. 243.

HEGEL (GEORG WILHELM FRIEDRICH).

PITKETHLY (LAWRENCE) Hegel in modern France (1900-1950). 1975. fo. 401. *bibliog. Typescript. Ph.D. (London) thesis: unpublished. This thesis is the property of London University and may not be removed from the Library.*

FEL'DMAN (DAVID ISAAKOVICH) and BASKIN (IURII IAKOVLEVICH) Uchenie Kanta i Gegelia o mezhdunarodnom prave i sovremennost'. Kazan', 1977. pp. 127.

RIPALDA (JOSÉ MARÍA) The divided nation: the roots of a bourgeois thinker: G.W.F. Hegel. Assen, 1977. pp. 221. *bibliog.*

SOCIETÀ, politica e stato in Hegel, Marx e Gramsci; [by] Remo Bodei [and others]. Padova, 1977. pp. 111.

MACGREGOR (DAVID EDWARD STEPHEN) Studies in the concept of ideology: from the Hegelian dialectic to western Marxism. 1978. fo. 504. *bibliog. Typescript. Ph.D. (London) thesis: unpublished. This thesis is the property of London University and may not be removed from the Library.*

TAYLOR (CHARLES) Hegel and modern society. Cambridge, 1979. pp. 180. *bibliog.*

HEIDEGGER (MARTIN).

STEINER (GEORGE) Heidegger. [London], 1978. pp. 157. *bibliog.*

HELPLESSNESS (PSYCHOLOGY).

SELIGMAN (MARTIN E.P.) Helplessness: on depression, development, and death. San Francisco, [1975]. pp. 250. *bibliog.*

HERANGI (TE PUEA).

See **PUEA HERANGI (TE).**

HEREDITY.

HEREDITY and environment; edited by A.H. Halsey. London, 1977. pp. 337. *bibliog.*

HEREFORDSHIRE

— **Economic conditions.**

[HEREFORDSHIRE. County Planning Department]. County of Herefordshire county structure plan: study report: green papers, nos. 1-10, 12-15, 17-20. [Hereford, 1974?]. 18 pts. (in 3 vols.) *Nos. 11. Minerals, and 16. Shopping out of print.*

— **Economic policy.**

[HEREFORDSHIRE. County Planning Department]. County of Herefordshire county structure plan: study report: green papers, nos. 1-10, 12-15, 17-20. [Hereford, 1974?]. 18 pts. (in 3 vols.) *Nos. 11. Minerals, and 16. Shopping out of print.*

— **Social conditions.**

[HEREFORDSHIRE. County Planning Department]. County of Herefordshire county structure plan: study report: green papers, nos. 1-10, 12-15, 17-20. [Hereford, 1974?]. 18 pts. (in 3 vols.) *Nos. 11. Minerals, and 16. Shopping out of print.*

— **Social policy.**

[HEREFORDSHIRE. County Planning Department]. County of Herefordshire county structure plan: study report: green papers, nos. 1-10, 12-15, 17-20. [Hereford, 1974?]. 18 pts. (in 3 vols.) *Nos. 11. Minerals, and 16. Shopping out of print.*

HERMENEUTICS.

BAUMAN (ZYGMUNT) Hermeneutics and social science: approaches to understanding. London, 1978. pp. 263.

HESSE

— **Politics and government.**

FISCH (GERHARD) and KRAUSE (FRITZ) Writer on politics. SPD und KPD, 1945/46: Einheitsbestrebungen der Arbeiterparteien, dargestellt an Beispielen aus Südhessen. Frankfurt am Main, 1978. pp. 169. *bibliog.*

HIDES AND SKINS INDUSTRY.

COMMONWEALTH SECRETARIAT. Hides and skins. s-a., D 1978- London.

HIGHER EDUCATION AND STATE

— **United Kingdom.**

PRATT (JOHN) and others. Costs and control in further education. Windsor, 1978. pp. 242. *bibliog.*

U.K. Department of Education and Science. 1978. Higher education into the 1990s: a discussion document. London, 1978. 1 pamphlet (various pagings).

FUTURE trends in higher education: a one-day conference organised by The Times Higher Education Supplement in association with the Department of Education and Science, 5 March 1979, at the University of London Institute of Education: a follow-up report on Higher education into the 1990s, presented to the conference by the Department of Education and Science. [London, Department of Education and Science, 1979]. pp. 7.

— **United States.**

GOVERNMENT and academia: the uneasy bond; (a Round Table held on April 13, 1978...); John Charles Daly, moderator, etc. Washington, [1978]. pp. 28. *(American Enterprise Institute for Public Policy Research. Round Tables)*

The UNIVERSITY and the state: what role for government in higher education?: edited by Sidney Hook [and others]. New York, [1978]. pp. 296. *bibliogs.*

The HIDDEN professoriate: credentialism, professionalism, and the tenure crisis; edited by Arthur S. Wilke. Westport, Conn., [1979]. pp. 290. *bibliog.*

HIGHWAY RESEARCH.

INTERNATIONAL ROAD FEDERATION. A report covering an international survey of current research and development on roads and road transport prepared for the Federal Highway Administration; (prepared... in cooperation with the Organization for Economic Cooperation and Development and the Transportation Research Board). Washington, D.C., 1978. pp. 566. *Cover title: 1978 world survey of current research and development on roads and road transport.*

HILBERT (DAVID).

REID (CONSTANCE) Hilbert; with an appreciation of Hilbert's mathematical work, by Hermann Weyl. New York, 1970 repr. 1978. pp. 290.

HILBERT SPACE.

SHOWALTER (R.E.) Hilbert space methods for partial differential equations. London, [1977]. pp. 196. *bibliog.*

SLEEMAN (BRIAN D.) Multiparameter spectral theory in Hilbert space. London, 1978. pp. 118. *bibliogs.*

HILL (JAMES JEROME).

MARTIN (ALBRO) James J. Hill and the opening of the Northwest. New York, 1976. pp. 676.

HILL FARMING

— **Thailand.**

FARMERS in the forest: economic development and marginal agriculture in northern Thailand; edited by Peter Kunstadter [and others]. Honolulu, [1978]. pp. 402. *bibliog.*

HILLQUIT (MORRIS).

PRATT (NORMA FAIN) Morris Hillquit: a political history of an American Jewish socialist. Westport, Conn., 1979. pp. 272. *bibliog.*

HILLS (DENIS).

HILLS (DENIS) Rebel people. London, 1978. pp. 248.

HINCMARUS, Bishop of Laon.

McKEON (PETER R.) Hincmar of Laon and Carolingian politics. Urbana, [1978]. pp. 327. *bibliog.*

HIROTA (KOKI).

SHIROYAMA (SABURO) War criminal: the life and death of Hirota Koki; translated by John Bester. Tokyo, 1977. pp. 301. *bibliog.*

HISTORIANS.

HISTORIANS.

KUCZYNSKI (JUERGEN) Studien zu einer Geschichte der Gesellschaftswissenschaften. Berlin, 1975-78. 10 vols.

— Argentine Republic.

CUCCORESE (HORACIO JUAN) Historia critica de la historiografia socioeconomica argentina del siglo XX. [La Plata, 1975]. pp. 438. *(La Plata. Universidad Nacional. Facultad de Humanidades y Ciencias de la Educacion. Departamento de Historia. Monografias y Tesis.9)*

— France.

LEFEBVRE (GEORGES) Réflexions sur l'histoire. Paris, 1978. pp. 282.

— Japan.

BROWN (DELMER MYERS) and ISHIDA (ICHIRO) The future and the past: a translation of the Gukansho, an interpretative history of Japan written in 1219. Berkeley, 1979. pp. 479. *bibliog.*

— Peru.

GIRON DE VILLASEÑOR (NICOLE) Peru: cronistas indios y mestizos en el siglo XVI; traduccion de Roberto Gomez Ciriza. Mexico, Secretaria de Educacion Publica, 1975. pp. 183. *(Sep/Setentas. 199)*

— Russia.

ENTEEN (GEORGE M.) The Soviet scholar-bureaucrat: M.N. Pokrovskii and the Society of Marxist Historians. University Park, Penn., 1978. pp. 236. *bibliog.*

HISTORICAL FILMS.

McARTHUR (COLIN) Television and history. London, 1978. pp. 60. *(British Film Institute. Television Monographs. 8)*

HISTORICAL MATERIALISM.

WEBER (MAX) Critique of Stammler;...translated, with an introductory essay, by Guy Oakes. New York, [1977]. pp. 184.

AMIN (SAMIR) The law of value and historical materialism...; (translated by Brian Pearce). New York, [1978]. pp. 133.

McCARTHY (TIMOTHY) Marx and the proletariat: a study in social theory. Westport, 1978. pp. 102 *bibliog.*

HISTORICAL SOCIOLOGY.

BATRA (RAVEENDRA NATH) The downfall of capitalism and communism: a new study of history. London, 1978. pp. 283.

HISTORIOGRAPHY.

MURPHEY (MURRAY G.) Our knowledge of the historical past. Indianapolis, 1973. pp. 209.

KUCZYNSKI (JUERGEN) Studien zu einer Geschichte der Gesellschaftswissenschaften. Berlin, 1975-78. 10 vols.

ATKINSON (RONALD) Knowledge and explanation in history: an introduction to the philosophy of history. London, 1978. pp. 229. *bibliog.*

BATRA (RAVEENDRA NATH) The downfall of capitalism and communism: a new study of history. London, 1978. pp. 283.

VOPROSY metodologii i istorii istoricheskoi nauki. vyp.2. Moskva, 1978. pp. 206.

HISTORY.

ROBINSON (JAMES HARVEY) The new history: essays illustrating the modern historical outlook. New York, [1965]. pp. 266. *Reprint of work first published in 1912.*

GLUBB (Sir JOHN BAGOT) The fate of empires; and Search for survival. Edinburgh, 1978. pp. 46.

LEFEBVRE (GEORGES) Réflexions sur l'histoire. Paris, 1978. pp. 282.

McARTHUR (COLIN) Television and history. London, 1978. pp. 60. *(British Film Institute. Television Monographs. 8)*

— Bibliography.

POULTON (HELEN J.) and HOWLAND (MARGUERITE S.) compilers. The historian's handbook: a descriptive guide to reference works. Norman, Okla., 1972 repr. 1974. pp. 304.

— Methodology.

THRUPP (SYLVIA LETTICE) Society and history: essays...; edited by Raymond Grew and Nicholas H. Steneck. Ann Arbor, [1977]. pp. 363. *bibliog.*

BERINGER (RICHARD E.) Historical analysis: contemporary approaches to Clio's craft. New York, [1978]. ppi 317.

— Philosophy.

MURPHEY (MURRAY G.) Our knowledge of the historical past. Indianapolis, 1973. pp. 209.

CASTRO (AMÉRICO) An idea of history: selected essays; translated from the Spanish and edited by Stephen Gilman and Edmund L. King. Columbus, Ohio, [1977]. pp. 343.

MANDELBAUM (MAURICE) The anatomy of historical knowledge. Baltimore, [1977]. pp. 230.

MARTIN (REX) Historical explanation: re-enactment and practical inference. Ithaca, N.Y., 1977. pp. 267. *bibliog.*

ARON (RAYMOND) Politics and history: selected essays...; collected, translated, and edited by Miriam Bernheim Conant. New York, [1978]. pp. 274.

ATKINSON (RONALD) Knowledge and explanation in history: an introduction to the philosophy of history. London, 1978. pp. 229. *bibliog.*

COHEN (G.A.) Karl Marx's theory of history: a defence. Oxford, 1978. pp. 369. *bibliog.*

ERIC Voegelin's search for order in history; edited by Stephen A. McKnight. Baton Rouge, [1978]. pp. 209. *bibliog.*

WILKINS (BURLEIGH TAYLOR) Has history any meaning: a critique of Popper's philosophy of history. Hassocks, [1978]. pp. 251.

HISTORY, MODERN

— 20th century.

RIFORME e rivoluzione nella storia contemporanea; [by] Aldo Zanardo [and others]; a cura di Guido Quazza. Torino, [1977]. pp. 342.

— — Bibliography.

HARCOURT (FREDA) and ROBINSON (FRANCIS) compilers. Twentieth-century world history: a select bibliography. London, [1979]. pp. 154.

HISTORY, UNIVERSAL.

The TIMES atlas of world history; edited by Geoffrey Barraclough. London, 1978. pp. 360.

HISTORY (THEOLOGY).

BUTTERFIELD (Sir HERBERT) Writings on Christianity and history; edited...by C.T. McIntire. New York, 1979. pp. 273. *bibliog.*

HITLER (ADOLF).

HITLER (ADOLF) Mein Kampf...: unexpurgated edition; [translated and annotated by James Murphy]. London, [1939]. pp. 584. *Published in 18 parts by Hutchinson and Co.*

DEUTSCH (HAROLD C.) Hitler and his generals: the hidden crisis, January-June 1938. Minneapolis, [1974]. pp. 452. *bibliog.*

CARR (WILLIAM) b.1921. Hitler: a study in personality and politics. London, 1978. pp. 200. *bibliog.*

GOERLITZ (WALTER) Geldgeber der Macht: wie Hitler, Lenin, Mao Tse-tung, Mussolini, Stalin und Tito finanziert wurden. Frankfurt am Main, 1978. pp. 256. *bibliog.*

RECKERT (WILFRIED) Die Wahrheit über Hitler; Kurt Bachmann im Gespräch mit Wilfried Reckert. Dortmund, [1978]. pp. 195.

WAGENER (OTTO) Hitler aus nächster Nähe: Aufzeichnungen eines Vertrauten [Otto Wagener], 1929-1932; herausgegeben von H.A. Turner, Jr. Frankfurt/Main, [1978]. pp. 509.

WAS verschweigt Fest?: Analysen und Dokumente zum Hitler- Film von J.C. Fest; ([edited by] Jörg Berlin [and others]). Köln, [1978]. pp. 217.

HITLER heute: Gespräche über ein deutsches Trauma; herausgegeben und bearbeitet von Guido Knopp; (Aschaffenburger Gespräche, 1978). Aschaffenburg, 1979. pp. 256.

NICHOLLS (ANTHONY JAMES) Weimar and the rise of Hitler. 2nd ed. London, 1979. pp. 151. *bibliog.*

POOL (JAMES) and POOL (SUZANNE) Who financed Hitler: the secret funding of Hitler's rise to power, 1919-1933. London, 1979. pp. 535. *bibliog.*

HOBBES (THOMAS).

THOMAS Hobbes in his time; edited by Ralph Ross [and others]. Minneapolis, [1974]. pp. 150. *bibliog.*

LEMOS (RAMON M.) Hobbes and Locke: power and consent. Athens, [1978]. pp. 185.

HOBHOUSE (LEONARD TRELAWNEY).

COLLINI (STEFAN) Liberalism and sociology: L. T. Hobhouse and political argument in England, 1880-1914. Cambridge, 1979. pp. 281. *bibliog.*

HOEGNER (WILHELM).

KRITZER (PETER) Wilhelm Hoegner: politische Biographie eines bayerischen Sozialdemokraten. München, [1979]. pp. 480. *bibliog.*

HOFFA (JAMES RIDDLE).

MOLDEA (DAN E.) The Hoffa wars: teamsters, rebels, politicians and the mob. New York, [1978]. pp. 450.

HOLDING COMPANIES

— United Kingdom — Finance.

NICHOLLS (DONALD JAMES) and WRIGHT (EDMUND KENNETH) Larkfold Holdings Limited: investigation under section 165(b) of the Companies Act 1948; report. London, H.M.S.O., 1979. pp. (246).

HOLIDAYS

— Jamaica.

JAMAICA. Ministry of Labour and National Insurance. 1970. Holidays with pay for all. [Kingston, 1970?]. pp. (13).

HOLLAND, MICHIGAN

— Foreign population.

KIRK (GORDON W.) The promise of American life: social mobility in a nineteenth century immigrant community, Holland, Michigan, 1847-1894. Philadelphia, 1978. pp. 164. *bibliog. (American Philosophical Society. Memoirs. vol. 124)*

— Social history.

KIRK (GORDON W.) The promise of American life: social mobility in a nineteenth century immigrant community, Holland, Michigan, 1847-1894. Philadelphia, 1978. pp. 164. *bibliog. (American Philosophical Society. Memoirs. vol. 124)*

HOLLOWAY TENANT COOPERATIVE.

POWER (ANNE) Holloway Tenant Cooperative: five years on. London, 1977. pp. 135.

HOLOCAUST, JEWISH (1939-1945).

MORSE (ARTHUR D.) While six million died. London, [1968]. pp. 420.

ROTHE (WOLF DIETER) Die Endlösung der Judenfrage. Band 1. Zeugen. Frankfurt/Main, 1974. pp. 208. *No more published.*

The CATASTROPHE of European Jewry: antecedents, history, reflections: selected papers; edited by Yisrael Gutman and Livia Rothkirchen. Jerusalem, 1976. pp. 757. *bibliog.*

SHONFELD (REB MOSHE) The holocaust victims accuse: documents and testimony on Jewish war criminals. Part 1. New York, [1977]. pp. 124.

BAUER (YEHUDA) The holocaust in historical perspective. Seattle, [1978]. pp. 181.

FACKENHEIM (EMIL L.) The Jewish return into history: reflections in the age of Auschwitz and a New Jerusalem. New York, 1978. pp. 296.

BETTELHEIM (BRUNO) Surviving and other essays. New York, 1979. pp. 432.

FEIN (HELEN) Accounting for genocide: national responses and Jewish victimization during the holocaust. London, [1979]. pp. 468. *bibliog.*

STAEGLICH (WILHELM) Der Auschwitz-Mythos: Legende oder Wirklichkeit?: eine kritische Bestandsaufnahme. Tübingen, 1979. pp. 467. *bibliog. (Institut für Deutsche Nachkriegsgeschichte. Veröffentlichungen. Band 9)*

WASSERSTEIN (BERNARD) Britain and the Jews of Europe, 1939-1945. Oxford, 1979. pp. 389. *bibliog.*

— Poland.

RINGELBLUM (EMMANUEL) Polish-Jewish relations during the Second World War; edited...by Joseph Kermish [and] Shmuel Krakowski; translated from Polish by Dafna Allon [and others]. Jerusalem, Yad Vashem, 1974. pp. 330.

HOLY ROMAN EMPIRE

— History — 1648-1804.

O'CONNOR (JOHN T.) Negotiator out of season: the career of Wilhelm Egon von Fürstenberg, 1629 to 1704. Athens, Ga., [1978]. pp. 263. *bibliog.*

HOME ACCIDENTS

— United Kingdom.

U.K. Consumer Safety Unit. 1979. The home accident surveillance system: analysis of domestic accidents to children. London, 1979. pp. 66.

HOME AND SCHOOL.

COONS (JOHN E.) and SUGARMAN (STEPHEN D.) Education by choice: the case for family control. Berkeley, Calif., [1978]. pp. 249. *bibliog.*

HOME ECONOMICS.

NEW ZEALAND. Social Development Council. 1977. Housework and caring work: can men do better? [Wellington], 1977. 1 vol. (various pagings). *bibliog.*

— Malaysia.

FEDERATION OF MALAYSIA. Department of Agriculture. Development Branch. 1973. Report on home economic surveys in Tanjong Karang, Beranang and Muda. Kuala Lumpur, 1973. pp. 58. *In Malay and English.*

HOME HELPS.

NATIONAL SOCIAL SERVICE COUNCIL [EIRE]. Report on home help service. [Dublin], 1978. pp. 19.

HOWELL (NEIL) and others. Allocating the home help services. London, 1979. pp. 110. *(Social Administration Research Trust. Occasional Papers on Social Administration. No.63)*

— United States — Michigan.

EMLING (DIANE CARPENTER) Adult chore services: a profile of in-home assistance, October 1975-February 1976. [Lansing], 1976. pp. 144. *bibliog. (Michigan. Department of Social Services. Studies in Welfare Policy. No. 10)*

HOME LABOUR

— Italy.

CUTRUFELLI (MARIA ROSA) Operaie senza fabbrica: inchiesta sul lavoro a domicilio. Roma, 1977. pp. 150. *bibliog.*

HOME OIL COMPANY.

SMITH (PHILIP) 1925- . The treasure-seekers: the men who built Home Oil. Toronto, [1978]. pp. 310.

HOME RULE

— Ireland.

WICKS (PEMBROKE) The truth about home rule. London, 1913. pp. 238.

SHORT (K.R.M.) The dynamite war: Irish-American bombers in Victorian Britain. Dublin, 1979. pp. 278. *bibliog.*

HOMELESSNESS

— Australia.

AUSTRALIA. Department of Social Security. 1978. A place of dignity: report of a survey of homeless people and homeless persons assistance centres. Canberra, 1978. pp. 75.

— United Kingdom.

A GUIDE to the Housing (Homeless Persons) Act 1977; [by] Catholic Housing Aid Society [and others]. London, [1977]. pp. 49.

PHILLIPS (MARK) Homelessness and tenants' control: struggles for council housing in Tower Hamlets, 1974-1976. London, 1977. pp. 123.

HOMESTEAD STRIKE, 1892.

BURGOYNE (ARTHUR GORDON) Homestead: a complete history of the struggle between the Carnegie Steel Company and the Amalgamated Association of Iron and Steel Workers, July 1892. New York, 1971. pp. 298. *Reprint of work originally published Pittsburgh, 1893.*

HOMICIDE

— New Zealand.

NEW ZEALAND. Property Law and Equity Reform Committee. 1976. The effect of culpable homicide on rights of succession: report... presented to the Minister of Justice in October 1976; [C.P. Hutchinson, chairman]. [Wellington], 1976. pp. 30.

HOMOLOGY THEORY.

MACLANE (SAUNDERS) Homology. New York, 1963 repr. 1975. pp. 422. *bibliog.*

HOMOSEXUALITY.

PLUMMER (KENNETH JOHN) Sexual stigma: an interactionist account. London, 1975. pp. 258. *bibliog.*

— United Kingdom.

GAYPRINTS and RATSTUDIES. The joke's over. London, [1973]. pp. 24.

— United States.

WARREN (CAROL A.B.) Identity and community in the gay world. New York, [1974]. pp. 191. *bibliog.*

HONG KONG

— Census.

HONG KONG. Census, 1976. Hong Kong by-census, 1976: main report. Hong Kong, [1979]. 2 vols. (in 1).

— Economic conditions.

HONG KONG. Half-yearly economic report. s-a., 1978- Hong Kong.

— Economic policy.

HO (H.C.Y.) The fiscal system of Hong Kong. London, [1979]. pp. 182. *bibliogs.*

— Executive departments.

HONG KONG. Public Works Department. 1978. Public Works Department: organisation and functions. [Hong Kong, 1978]. pp. 22. *In English and Chinese.*

— History.

SAYER (GEOFFREY ROBLEY) Hong Kong 1862-1919: years of discretion. Hong Kong, 1975. pp. 166.

CAMERON (NIGEL) Hong Kong: the cultural pearl. Hong Kong, 1978. pp. 281. *bibliog.*

— Industries.

HONG KONG'S ECONOMIC PROSPECTS; [pd. by] Industrial Production Statistics Section, Census and Statistics Department. a., 1977- Hong Kong.

— Public works.

HONG KONG. Public Works Department. 1978. Public Works Department: organisation and functions. [Hong Kong, 1978]. pp. 22. *In English and Chinese.*

— Public Works Department.

HONG KONG. Public Works Department. 1978. Public Works Department: organisation and functions. [Hong Kong, 1978]. pp. 22. *In English and Chinese.*

— Siege, 1941.

LINDSAY (OLIVER) The lasting honour: the fall of Hong Kong, 1941. London, 1978. pp. 226. *bibliog.*

— Social conditions.

FIELD (C. ELAINE) and BABER (FLORA M.) Growing up in Hong Kong: a preliminary report on a study of the growth, development and rearing of Chinese children in Hong Kong. Hong Kong, 1973. pp. 178. *bibliog.*

HOOVER (HERBERT CLARK) President of the United States.

HOOVER (HERBERT CLARK) and WILSON (THOMAS WOODROW) Two peacemakers in Paris: the Hoover-Wilson post-armistice letters, 1918-1920; edited and with commentaries by Francis William O'Brien. College Station, [1978]. pp. 254. *bibliog.*

BURNER (DAVID) Herbert Hoover: a public life. New York, 1979. pp. 433. *bibliog.*

HOPE (VICTOR ALEXANDER JOHN) 2nd Marquess of Linlithgow.

RIZVI (GOWHER) Linlithgow and India: a study of British policy and the political impasse in India, 1936-43. London, 1978. pp. 261. *bibliogs.*

HOPI INDIANS.

WATERS (FRANK) Book of the Hopi. New York, 1977 repr. 1978. pp. 345. *Reprint of work first published in 1963.*

HOPTON (CHARLES).

CHARLES Hopton and the founding of the almshouses. [London, 1977]. pp. 32.

HORTICULTURE

HORTICULTURE

— Norway.

NORWAY. Statistiske Centralbyrå. 1975. Hagebruksteljing, 1974, etc. Oslo, 1975. pp. *(Norges Offisielle Statistik. Rekke A. 751)* In Norwegian and English.

NORWAY. Statistiske Centralbyrå. 1977. Norsk hagebruk, 1969-1974: ein analyse på grunnlag av jordbruksteljinga 1969 og hagebruksteljinga, 1974, etc. Oslo, 1977. pp. 98. *(Statistiske Analyser. 32)* With English summary.

HOSPITAL CARE

— United States — Costs.

AMERICAN ENTERPRISE INSTITUTE FOR PUBLIC POLICY RESEARCH. Legislative Analyses. 95th Congress. No. 29. Proposals for the regulation of hospital costs. Washington, 1978. pp. 76.

HOSPITAL PATIENTS

— United Kingdom — Attitudes.

GREGORY (JANET) Patients' attitudes to the hospital service. London, 1978. pp. 257. *(U.K. Royal Commission on the National Health Service, 1976. Research Papers. No.5)*

HOSPITALS

— Netherlands — Staff.

NETHERLANDS. Ziekenhuiscommissie. 1969. Rapport inzake personeelshuisvesting. ['s-Gravenhage, 1969]. pp. 13. *(Netherlands. Ministerie van Sociale Zaken. Verslagen en Mededelingen betreffende de Volksgezondheid. 1969.9)*

— New Zealand.

NEW ZEALAND. Department of Health. National Health Statistics Centre. 1979. Bed occupation survey 1976: public, private and maternity hospital patients and old people's homes. Wellington, 1979. pp. 47. *(Department of Health. Special Report Series. No. 54)*

— South Africa.

SOUTH AFRICA. Bureau of Statistics. Census of hospitals and establishments for in-patients. a., 1976- Pretoria. *[in English and Afrikaans]*

— Switzerland — Basel-Stadt (Canton).

BASEL-STADT (CANTON). Regierungsrat. 1969. Ratschlag betreffend Bürgerspital 3. Bauetappe, Programm, Baukonzept, Projektierungskredit...: [Anhang: Bericht des Sanitätsdepartementes über die Spitalplanung in regionaler und kantonaler Sicht]. [Basel?, 1969?]. pp. 152. *16 plans in end pocket.*

— — Vaud (Canton).

VAUD (CANTON). Conseil d'Etat. 1966. Rapport...au Grand Conseil sur le plan hospitalier cantonal vaudois. [Lausanne, 1966]. pp. 81.

— United Kingdom.

ALLEN (DAVID E.) Writer on health services. Hospital planning: the development of the 1962 hospital plan: a case study in decision making. Tunbridge Wells, 1979. pp. 191. *bibliog.*

HAYNES (R.M.) and BENTHAM (C.G.) Community hospitals and rural accessibility. Farnborough, [1979]. pp. 200. *bibliog.*

— — Laws and legislation.

SPELLER (SYDNEY REGINALD) Law relating to hospitals and kindred institutions; sixth edition.. .by Joe Jacob. London, 1978. pp. 805.

— United States — Cost of operation.

REINHOLDS (HAROLD) Hospital incentive reimbursement: an institutional overview. [Lansing], 1976. pp. 30. *(Michigan. Department of Social Services. Studies in Welfare Policy. No. 9)*

— — Laws and legislation.

AMERICAN ENTERPRISE INSTITUTE FOR PUBLIC POLICY RESEARCH. Legislative Analyses. 95th Congress. No. 29. Proposals for the regulation of hospital costs. Washington, 1978. pp. 76.

— — Massachusetts.

MASSACHUSETTS. Metropolitan Area Planning Council. 1967. Hospital and health facilities in eastern Massachusetts. [Boston], 1967. fo. 43.

HOTELS, TAVERNS, ETC.

— Fiji.

FIJI. Bureau of Statistics. 1973. A report on the survey of the hotel industry and the travel agencies in Fiji. Suva, 1973. fo. (14).

— Tasmania.

TASMANIA. Commonwealth Bureau of Census and Statistics. Tasmanian Office. 1975. Census of tourist accommodation establishments, 1973-74. [Hobart, 1975]. pp. 19.

— United Kingdom.

MEDLIK (S.) and AIREY (D.W.) Profile of the hotel and catering industry. 2nd ed. London, 1978. pp. 282. *bibliog.*

— — Employees.

THOMAS (CERI) and ERLAM (ANDREW) Unequal portions: a survey of pay in the hotel and catering industry. London, 1978. pp. 18. *(Low Pay Unit. Low Pay Papers. No.23)*

HOURS OF LABOUR

— Australia.

AUSTRALIA. Commonwealth Bureau of Census and Statistics. Earnings and hours of employees. a., 1977- Canberra.

— Canada — British Columbia.

BRITISH COLUMBIA. Board of Industrial Relations. 969. Summary of orders and regulations made pursuant to Male Minimum Wage Act, Female Minimum Wage Act, Annual and General Holidays Act, Hours of Work Act, Payment of Wages Act; compiled as at May 31, 1969. [Victoria], 1969. pp. 52.

— Denmark.

HILLESTRØM (KARSTEN) and KOCH-NIELSEN (INGER) Ønsker om fleksibel pensionsalder og nedsat arbejdstid. København, 1977. pp. 55. *(Socialforskningsinstituttet. Meddelelser. 23)*

— Guyana.

GUYANA. National Working Hours Commission. 1971. Report; [Dennis H. Irvine, chairman]. [Georgetown], 1971. 1 pamphlet (various pagings).

— Italy.

IOVANE (ANDREA) and PALA (GIANFRANCO) Lavoro salariato e tempo libero: un'analisi dell'economia del tempo. Milano, [1977]. pp. 192. *(Istituto per gli Studi sullo Sviluppo Economico e il Progresso Tecnico. Collana Isvet. n. 32)*

— Jamaica — Statistics.

JAMAICA. Department of Statistics. 1978. Employment, earnings and hours in large establishments, 1977. [Kingston, 1978]. pp. 45.

— Russia.

PATRUSHEV (VASILII DMITRIEVICH) Ispol'zovanie sovokupnogo vremeni obshchestva: problemy balansa vremeni naseleniia. Moskva, 1978. pp. 216. *bibliog.*

— South Africa.

SOUTH AFRICA. Planning Advisory Council. 1975. An investigation into a system of staggered working hours for Pretoria to help alleviate traffic problems; by a standing committee of a subsidiary committee of the Planning Advisory Council, etc. [Pretoria], 1975. pp. 25.

— United Kingdom.

U.K. Equal Opportunities Commission. 1979. Health and safety legislation: should we distinguish between men and women?; report and recommendations of the...Commission. [Manchester], 1979. pp. 153.

— United States.

OWEN (JOHN D.) Working hours: an economic analysis. Lexington, Mass., [1979]. pp. 206. *bibliog.*

HOUSE BUYING.

MAYES (DAVID G.) The property boom: the effects of building society behaviour on house prices. Oxford, 1979. pp. 146. *bibliog.*

HOUSING.

HUMAN SETTLEMENTS; issued by the Centre for Housing, Building and Planning. Department of Economic and Social Affairs, United Nations. q., Ja 1971 (v.1, no.1)- New York.

HABITAT FOUNDATION NEWS; [pd. by] United Nations Habitat and Human Settlements Foundation. q., Je 1977(no.2)- Nairobi.

UNITED NATIONS. Department of Economic and Social Affairs. 1978. The role of housing in promoting social integration. (ST/ESA/72). New York, 1978. pp. 197. *bibliogs.*

— Information services — United Kingdom.

CONNOLLY (KATHLEEN) compiler. Housing: sources of information on housing. rev. ed. [London], 1979. pp. 58. *(U.K. Department of the Environment. Library. Information Series)*

— Africa, East — Law.

URBAN legal problems in eastern Africa: (papers presented at a workshop held in Nairobi, April 1976); edited by G.W. Kanyeihamba and J.P.W.B. McAuslan. Uppsala, 1978. pp. 298. *(Nordiska Afrikainstitutet and International Center for Law in Development. Studies of Law in Social Change and Development. No. 2)*

— Australia.

SOCIAL indicators in Australia: health and housing. [Canberra, 1977?]. 2 vols. *bibliogs. Papers presented at a conference at the Research School of Social Sciences, Australian National University, Canberra, 1977.*

— Bolivia — Statistics.

BOLIVIA. Census, 1976. (Censo nacional de poblacion y vivienda, 1976): resultados anticipados por muestreo. [La Paz, 1977]. pp. 77.

— Brazil — Finance.

ALMEIDA (WANDERLY JOSE MANSO DE) and CHAUTARD (JOSE LUIZ) FGTS: uma politica de bem-estar social. Rio de Janeiro, 1976. pp. 159. *(Brazil. Instituto de Planejamento Econômico e Social. Instituto de Pesquisas. Relatorios de Pesquisa. No. 30)*

— Colombia — Statistics.

COLOMBIA. Census, 1964. XIII censo de poblacion y II de edificios y viviendas, julio 15 de 1964: Choco. Bogota, 1970. pp. 96.

COLOMBIA. Departamento Administrativo Nacional de Estadistica. Censo nacional de Edificios y Viviendas, 1964. II censo nacional de edificios y viviendas, julio 15 de 1964: Cundinamarca. Bogota, 1970. pp. 127.

HOUSING.

— Ecuador — Statistics.

ECUADOR. Census, 1974. III censo de poblacion, II de vivienda, 1974: resultados anticipados por muestreo. Quito, 1975. pp. 66.

— Egypt — Statistics.

EGYPT. Census, 1976. The preliminary results of the general population and housing census. 22/23 November 1976 in Egypt. [Cairo, 1977]. pp. 57.

— European Economic Community countries.

REPORT on the ECSC experimental programme of modernization of housing. [Brussels], European Communities, 1975. pp. 368.

— France.

FRANCE. Bureau des Enquêtes sur le Marché du Bâtiment. Deuxième enquête sur les prix de revient des logements neufs mis en chantier en 1969 et 1970: quelques caractéristiques des logements neufs selon leur prix de revient. Paris, 1975. pp. 99. (France. Ministère de l'Equipement. Statistiques de la Construction. Suppléments. No. 19)

FRANCE. Bureau des Enquêtes sur le Marché du Bâtiment. 1975. Deuxième enquête sur les prix de revient des logements neufs: résultats sur les logements mis en chantier en 1969 et 1970: résultats régionaux. Paris, 1975. pp. 125. (France. Ministère de l'Equipement. Statistiques de la Construction. Suppléments. No. 17)

— — Finance.

FRANCE. Bureau des Enquêtes sur la Construction. 1974. Deuxième enquête sur les coûts prévisionnels des immeubles à usage d'habitation: résultats sur les logements mis en chantier en 1969 et 1970. Paris, 1974. pp. 64. (France. Ministère de l'Equipement. Statistiques de la Construction. Suppléments. No. 15)

— — Statistics.

FRANCE. Census, 1968. Recensement général de la population de 1968; résultats du sondage au $\frac{1}{4}$: population, ménages, logements, immeubles; fascicules départementaux. Paris, 1971. 95 pts. in 10 vols. *Pt. 45, Loiret, out of print.*

FRANCE. Census, 1968. Recensement général de la population de 1968; résultats du sondage au $\frac{1}{4}$: population, ménages, logements, immeubles; fascicules départementaux; agglomération de Paris. Paris, 1971. pp. 186.

FRANCE. Census, 1975. Recensement général de la population de 1975; résultats du sondage au 1/5: population, ménages, logements, immeubles; [fascicules départementaux]. [Paris, 1976]. 95 pts. in 10 vols. *Pt. 20, Corsica, not published.*

FRANCE. Census, 1975. Recensement général de la population de 1975; résultats du sondage au 1/5: population, ménages, logements, immeubles; [fascicules départementaux]; agglomération de Paris. [Paris, 1976]. pp. 91.

FRANCE. Census, 1975. Recensement général de la population de 1975; résultats du sondage au 1/5: population, ménages, logements, immeubles: [regional fascicules and] (France entière). [Paris, 1978]. 22 pts. (in 3 vols.).

— — Paris.

ATELIER PARISIEN D'URBANISME. Vingt ans d'évolution de Paris: données statistiques 1954- 1975, Paris et arrondissements: population, logement, ménages. Paris, [1976?]. 1 vol. (unfoliated).

— Germany — Statistics.

GERMANY. Statistisches Reichsamt. Statistik des Deutschen Reichs. Neue Folge. Band 287. Reichswohnungszählung im Mai 1918. Berlin, 1919-20; Osnabrück, 1977. 2 vols(in 1). *Photographic reprint.*

— Iran — Statistics.

IRAN. Census, 1976. National census of population and housing, November 1976: [reports for shahrestans, ostans and total country]. [Tehran, 1978 in progress]. *In English and Persian.*

— Ireland (Republic).

NATIONAL HOUSING CONFERENCE, LEOPARDSTOWN, CO. DUBLIN, 1974. Living in town, conserving the future: a summary of the papers presented at the...conference; (sponsored jointly by the Department of Local Government and the Royal Institute of the Architects of Ireland). [Dublin, An Foras Forbartha], 1975. pp. 26.

— Jamaica.

JAMAICA. Department of Statistics. 1974. Population trends and housing needs. [Kingston, 1974]. pp. 43.

JAMAICA. Department of Statistics. 1976. Building activity in Jamaica, 1967-1975. [Kingston, 1976]. pp. 60.

JAMAICA. Department of Statistics. 1978. Abstract of building and construction statistics, 1977. [Kingston, 1978]. pp. 32.

— Kenya.

NATIONAL HOUSING CORPORATION OF KENYA. Annual report. a., 1970- Nairobi.

— — Mombasa.

STREN (RICHARD E.) Housing the urban poor in Africa: policy, politics and bureaucracy in Mombasa. Berkeley, Calif., [1978]. pp. 330. *bibliog.* (California University. Institute of International Studies. Research Series. No. 34)

— Malawi.

MALAWI HOUSING CORPORATION. Annual reports and accounts. a., 1977- Blantyre.

— Malaysia.

CHANDER (R.) Housing needs vs effective demand in Malaysia, 1976-1990. Kuala Lumpur, 1977. pp. 39. (Federation of Malaysia. Department of Statistics. Research Papers. No. 12) *In English and Malay.*

— New Zealand.

NEW ZEALAND. National Housing Commission. 1978. Housing in New Zealand: five yearly report, March 1978. Wellington, 1978. pp. 175.

— Niue — Statistics.

NEW ZEALAND. Department of Justice. 1973. Census of population and dwellings, Niue Island, 1971. [Alofi], 1973. pp. 48.

— Pakistan — Statistics.

PAKISTAN. Census, 1972-73. Housing, economic and demographic survey, 1973. volume 2. Islamabad, [197-]. 5 pts.

— Portugal — Statistics.

PORTUGAL. Instituto Nacional de Estatistica. Serviços Centrais. 1975. I recenseamento da habitação, 1970: continente e ilhas adjacentes; estimativa a 20 [per cent]. [Lisbon, 1975]. pp. 320.

— Russia — Kirghizia — Law.

KIRGHIZIA. Statutes, etc. 1976. Zhilishchnoe zakonodatel'stvo Kirgizskoi SSR: sbornik normativnykh aktov. Frunze, 1976. pp. 268.

— Sweden — Statistics.

SWEDEN. Statistiska Centralbyrån. 1979. Lägenheter och hushåll enligt folk- och bostadsräkningarna 1965, 1970 och 1975 kommunvis enligt indelningen 1976-01-01; Dwellings and households according to the 1965, 1970 and 1975 population and housing censuses, by communes, etc. Stockholm, 1979. pp. 76. (Statistiska Meddelanden. Be 1979: 6) *With English summary.*

— Underdeveloped areas.

See UNDERDEVELOPED AREAS — Housing.

— United Kingdom.

JOHNSON (ALEC) This housing question. London, 1954. pp. 119.

The HISTORY of working class housing: a symposium; edited by Stanley D. Chapman. Totowa, N.J., [1971]. pp. 307. *bibliogs.*

The SALE of council houses: papers presented at a one-day conference on the sale of council houses...on 5th October 1976; edited by John English and Colin Jones. Glasgow, 1977. pp. 100. *bibliogs.* (Glasgow. University. Department of Economic and Social Research. Discussion Papers in Social Research. No.18)

SHELTER. The future of private rented housing: evidence to the review of the Rent Acts. London, 1977. pp. 34.

CORNFORD (A.J.) The market for owned houses in England and Wales since 1945: prices, building and finance. Farnborough, [1979]. pp. 323. *bibliog.*

— — Bibliography.

ELLENDER (PAT) Housing in Britain: a select list relating to housing in Britain based on the material contained in the D[epartment] o[f the] E[nvironment] D[epartment of] T[ransport] Library Bulletin, 1976-1978. [London], 1979. pp. 312. (U.K. Department of the Environment. Library. Bibliographies. No. 132)

— — Finance.

HOUSING CENTRE TRUST. Green paper response: 1: housing finance memorandum submitted to the Secretary of State for the Environment. London, 1977. fo.8.

MAYES (DAVID G.) The property boom: the effects of building society behaviour on house prices. Oxford, 1979. pp. 146. *bibliog.*

— — Law.

TIPLADY (DAVID) Housing welfare law. London, 1975. pp. 162.

A GUIDE to the Housing (Homeless Persons) Act 1977; [by] Catholic Housing Aid Society [and others]. London, [1977]. pp. 49.

ARDEN (ANDREW) Housing: security and rent control. London, 1978. pp. 231. *bibliogs.*

WEST (WILLIAM ALEXANDER) The law of housing; fourth edition by Keith Davies. 4th ed. London, 1979. pp. 345. *bibliog.*

— — Statistics.

U.K. Department of the Environment. 1978. English house condition survey, 1976. Part 1. Report of the physical condition survey. London, 1978. pp. 30. (Housing Survey Reports. No. 10)

U.K. Department of the Environment. 1979. National dwelling and housing survey. London, 1979. pp. 317. *Form in end pocket.*

— — Batley.

NINER (PAT) Homes to let: a review of housing need and waiting list policy in Batley and Copeland, Cumbria. [York], 1978. pp. 56. (Papers in Community Studies. No. 18)

— — Birmingham.

LLEWELYN-DAVIES WEEKS [AND PARTNERS]. Inner area study: Birmingham: SHAPE housing and community project. [London], Department of the Environment, [1978]. pp. 52.

BIRMINGHAM COMMUNITY DEVELOPMENT PROJECT. Leasehold loopholes. Oxford, 1979. pp. 36. (Final Reports. No. 5: the Problems of Owner- Occupation in Inner Birmingham)

HOUSING.(Cont.)

— — Copeland.

NINER (PAT) Homes to let: a review of housing need and waiting list policy in Batley and Copeland, Cumbria. [York], 1978. pp. 56. *(Papers in Community Studies. No. 18)*

— — London.

UNION PLACE COMMUNITY RESOURCE CENTRE. As things are: women, work and family in South London. London, 1976. pp. 52. *Reprint of 4 articles appearing in 1975 and 1976 in Knuckle.*

TAYLOR (G.H.) Writer on Housing. A review of housing in London, 1966-1976. London, [1978]. pp. 72. *bibliog. (London. Greater London Council. Research Memoranda. 534)*

— — Newcastle-upon-Tyne.

BENWELL COMMUNITY DEVELOPMENT PROJECT. Private housing and the working class. Newcastle-upon-Tyne, 1978. pp. 111. *(Final Report Series. No. 3)*

— — — Finance.

BENWELL: news and views from Benwell Community Project. Special issue on housing finance, December 1976. [Newcastle-upon Tyne, Benwell Community Development Project], 1976. pp. 12.

— — North Shields.

NORTH TYNESIDE COMMUNITY DEVELOPMENT PROJECT. North Shields: working class politics and housing, 1900-1977. [Newcastle-upon-Tyne, 1978]. pp. 72. *(Final Reports. Vol.1)*

— — Scotland.

DARTINGTON AMENITY RESEARCH TRUST. Second homes in Scotland; a report to Countryside Commission for Scotland, Scottish Tourist Board, Highlands and Islands Development Board, Scottish Development Department. Totnes, 1977. pp. 88. *bibliog. (Publications. No. 22)*

— — — Glasgow.

WORSDALL (FRANK) The tenement: a way of life: a social, historical and architectural study of housing in Glasgow. [Edinburgh], 1979. pp. 165. *bibliog.*

— — Tyne and Wear.

An END to private landlordism: a response to the D[epartment] o[f the] E[nvironment] consultation paper on the review of the rent acts, April 1977; (by Benwell Community Development Project and others). [Newcastle-upon-Tyne, Benwell Community Development Project, 1977]. 1 pamphlet (various pagings).

— — Wales — Finance.

U.K. Working Party on Housing Finance in Wales. 1977. Housing finance in Wales; first report; [P.J. Hosegood, chairman]. [Cardiff], 1977. pp. (15).

U.K. Working Party on Housing Finance in Wales. 1978. Housing finance in Wales; second report; [P.J. Hosegood, chairman]. [Cardiff], 1978. pp. 13, 3.

— — — Statistics.

U.K. Welsh Office. 1978. Welsh house condition survey, 1976. Cardiff, 1978. pp. 99.

— — — — Afan Valley.

[GLAMORGAN-GLYNCORRWG COMMUNITY DEVELOPMENT PROJECT]. Housing in Glyncorrwg. [Port Talbot, 1973]. pp. (10).

— — West Midlands.

CLARK (DAVID) Immigrant responses to the British housing market: a case study in the West Midlands conurbation. Bristol, Social Science Research Council Research Unit on Ethnic Relations, [1977]. pp. 65. *bibliog. (Working Papers on Ethnic Relations. No. 7)*

— United States.

FRIEDEN (BERNARD J.) and SOLOMON (ARTHUR P.) The nation's housing: 1975 to 1985. Cambridge, Mass., 1977. pp. 155.

LINDAMOOD (SUZANNE) and HANNA (SHERMAN D.) Housing, society, and consumers: an introduction. St. Paul, Minn., [1979]. pp. 498.

— — Finance.

HENDERSHOTT (PATRIC H.) and VILLANI (KEVIN E.) Regulation and reform of the housing finance system. Washington, D.C., [1977]. pp. 135. *(American Enterprise Institute for Public Policy Research. AEI Studies. 210)*

HOUSING, COOPERATIVE

— France.

REYNAUD (PAUL) La copropriété dans les grands ensembles immobiliers: essai d'analyse des fondements socio-économiques et juridiques. [Paris, 1978]. pp. 333. *bibliog. (France. Ministère de la Justice. Collection Ministère de la Justice)*

— United Kingdom.

GORRIE (DONALD) Tenants' cooperatives. Manchester, [1977?]. pp. 15.

HAYHOW (DAVID) and others. Streets ahead: impressions from a survey of tenants' co-operatives. London, [1977]. pp. 89.

PHILLIPS (MARK) Homelessness and tenants' control: struggles for council housing in Tower Hamlets, 1974-1976. London, 1977. pp. 123.

POWER (ANNE) Holloway Tenant Cooperative: five years on. London, 1977. pp. 135.

SHELTER. Street by street: improvement and tenant control in Islington: North Islington Housing Rights Project. London, [1977]. pp. 64.

U.K. Housing Association Subsidy Working Group. 1977. Report. [London], 1977. pp. 23.

U.K. Housing Services Advisory Group. 1978. Housing Associations and their part in current housing strategies; [T.L. Jones, chairman]. [London, 1978]. pp. 19.

HOUSING MANAGEMENT.

SINGH (SATWANT B.) Report on housing management in the U.K. and its applicability to India. n.p., [1962?]. 1 vol. (various pagings). *bibliog.*

NATIONAL CONSUMER COUNCIL. Social Policy Unit. Housing policy review: housing management: a tenants' charter: the...Council's response to the Department of the Environment consultation paper. London, [1978]. pp. 18.

RICHARDSON (ANN WICKENDEN) The politics of participation: a study of schemes for tenant participation in council housing management. 1978. fo. 430. *bibliog. Typescript. Ph.D. (London) thesis: unpublished. This thesis is the property of London University and may not be removed from the Library.*

HOUSING POLICY.

HEADEY (BRUCE WYNDHAM) Housing policy in the developed economy: the United Kingdom, Sweden and the United States. London, [1978]. pp. 276.

— Sweden.

HEADEY (BRUCE WYNDHAM) Housing policy in the developed economy: the United Kingdom, Sweden and the United States. London, [1978]. pp. 276.

— Underdeveloped areas.

See UNDERDEVELOPED AREAS — Housing policy.

— United Kingdom.

GOUGH (JULIAN) Housing policy and the distribution of income and wealth in the U.K. Cardiff, 1976. fo.28,ii. *bibliog. (Wales. University. University College, Cardiff. Institute of Science and Technology. Research and Discussion Papers in Economics, Finance and Politics. No. 1)*

BRITISH MARKET RESEARCH BUREAU. B[ritish] M[arket] R[esearch] B[ureau] housing consumer survey: a survey of attitudes towards current and alternative housing policies, January 1976: supplementary table volume. London, H.M.S.O., 1977. pp. 290.

The SALE of council houses: papers presented at a one-day conference on the sale of council houses...on 5th October 1976; edited by John English and Colin Jones. Glasgow, 1977. pp. 100. *bibliogs. (Glasgow. University. Department of Economic and Social Research. Discussion Papers in Social Research. No.18)*

SHELTER. Housing policy in the 1980's: Shelter's response to the Housing Green Paper. London, 1977. pp. 72.

HEADEY (BRUCE WYNDHAM) Housing policy in the developed economy: the United Kingdom, Sweden and the United States. London, [1978]. pp. 276.

U.K. Central Policy Review Staff. 1978. Housing and social policies: some interactions; report. London, 1978. pp. 50.

U.K. Housing Services Advisory Group. 1978. Housing Associations and their part in current housing strategies; [T.L. Jones, chairman]. [London, 1978]. pp. 19.

U.K. Housing Services Advisory Group. 1978. Organising comprehensive housing service; [T.L. Jones, chairman]. [London, 1978]. pp. 22.

CULLINGWORTH (JOHN BARRY) Essays on housing policy: the British scene. London, 1979. pp. 188. *bibliog.*

LANSLEY (STEWART) Housing and public policy. London, [1979]. pp. 246. *bibliogs.*

ROBINSON (RAY) Housing economics and public policy. London, 1979. pp. 166. *bibliog.*

— — London.

YOUNG (KENNETH GEORGE) and KRAMER (JOHN) Strategy and conflict in metropolitan housing: suburbia versus the Greater London Council, 1965-75. London, 1978. pp. 306.

— — Scotland.

SCOTLAND. Working Party on Assessment of Housing Need. 1977. Assessing housing need: a manual of guidance; [C.J. Watson, chairman]. [Edinburgh], 1977. pp. 106. *bibliog. (Scottish Housing Handbooks. 1)*

— United States.

HEADEY (BRUCE WYNDHAM) Housing policy in the developed economy: the United Kingdom, Sweden and the United States. London, [1978]. pp. 276.

TREND (M.G.) Housing allowances for the poor: a social experiment. Boulder, Colo., [1978]. pp. 369. *bibliog.*

HOUSING REHABILITATION

— United Kingdom.

BARR (ALAN) Housing improvement and the multi-racial community: a report on action and research strategies in Oldham C[ommunity] D[evelopment] P[roject]. [York], 1978. pp. 99. *(Papers in Community Studies. No. 16)*

HADDEN (TOM) Compulsory repair and improvement: a study of the operation of the Housing Acts 1957-1974. Oxford, 1978. pp. 126. *(U.K. Social Science Research Council. Centre for Socio-Legal Studies. Research Studies. No. 1)*

U.K. Department of the Environment. Housing Improvement Group. 1978. General improvement areas, 1969-1976: a report of a comprehensive study of progress achieved in the rehabilitation of older housing in general improvement areas; [by] Audrey Williamson [and] Elizabeth Wrigley. London, 1978. 1 vol. (various pagings). *bibliog. (Improvement Research Notes. 77-3)*

— United States.

WOMEN'S CITY CLUB OF NEW YORK. With love and affection: a study of building abandonment. New York, 1977. pp. 69.

— Zambia.

PASTEUR (DAVID) The management of squatter upgrading: a case study of organisation, procedures and participation. Farnborough, [1979]. pp. 232. *bibliog.*

HOUSING SUBSIDIES

— Ireland (Republic).

NATIONAL INSTITUTE FOR PHYSICAL PLANNING AND CONSTRUCTION RESEARCH. Construction Division. Public subventions to housing in Ireland; [by] J. McKeon [and] R. Jennings. Dublin, 1978. pp. 68. *bibliog.*

— United Kingdom.

U.K. Department of the Environment. 1977. Housing policy review: proposed new housing subsidy system for local authorities: consultation paper. [London, 1977]. fo. (12). *Photocopy.*

U.K. Department of the Environment. 1977. Housing policy review: proposed new housing subsidy system for local authorities: increase in local contribution: consultation paper. [London, 1977]. fo. 4. *Photocopy.*

U.K. Department of the Environment. 1977. Housing policy review: proposed new housing subsidy system for local authorities: loan repayment periods and associated matters: consultation paper. [London, 1977]. pp. 5.

U.K. Department of the Environment. 1977. Housing policy review: proposed new housing subsidy system for local authorities: rate of subsidy: consultation paper. [London, 1977]. pp. 3.

U.K. Department of the Environment. 1977. Housing policy review: statutory housing repairs account: consultation paper. [London, 1977]. pp. 4.

U.K. Housing Association Subsidy Working Group. 1977. Report. [London], 1977. pp. 23.

— United States.

TREND (M.G.) Housing allowances for the poor: a social experiment. Boulder, Colo., [1978]. pp. 369. *bibliog.*

HOUSING SURVEYS.

U.K. Department of the Environment. 1979. National dwelling and housing survey. London, 1979. pp. 317. *Form in end pocket.*

HUDSON'S BAY COMPANY.

HUDSON'S BAY RECORD SOCIETY. Publications. 31. The letters of Charles John Brydges, 1879-1882, Hudson's Bay Company Land Commissioner; edited by Hartwell Bowsfield. Winnipeg, 1977. pp. 346.

MITCHELL (ELAINE ALLAN) Fort Timiskaming and the fur trade. Toronto, [1977]. pp. 306. *bibliog.*

RAY (ARTHUR J.) and FREEMAN (DONALD B.) 'Give us good measure': an economic analysis of relations between the Indians and the Hudson's Bay Company before 1763. Toronto, [1978]. pp. 298. *bibliog.*

HUGENBERG (ALFRED).

HONIGMANN (GEORG) Kapitalverbrechen; oder, Der Fall des Geheimrats Hugenberg. Berlin, [1976 repr. 1978]. pp. 365. *bibliog.*

HUGH, Saint, Abbot of Cluny.

HUNT (NOREEN) Cluny under Saint Hugh 1049-1109. Notre Dame, Ind., 1968. pp. 228. *bibliog.*

HULL UNIVERSITY.

BAMFORD (THOMAS WILLIAM) The University of Hull: the first fifty years. Oxford, 1978. pp. 290. *(Hull. University. Publications)*

HUMAN BEHAVIOUR.

TINBERGEN (NICHOLAS) The animal in its world: explorations of an ethologist, 1932-1972. London, 1972-73. 2 vols. *bibliogs.*

SOCIAL behaviour and experience: multiple perspectives; edited by Hedy Brown and Richard Stevens. Sevenoaks, [1975]. pp. 627. *bibliogs.*

REYNOLDS (VERNON) The biology of human action. San Francisco, [1976]. pp. 269. *bibliog.*

SKINNER (BURRHUS FREDERIC) Reflections on behaviorism and society. Englewood Cliffs, N.J., [1978]. pp. 209.

CHOROVER (STEPHAN L.) From genesis to genocide: the meaning of human nature and the power of behavior control. Cambridge, Mass., [1979]. pp. 238.

HUMAN ECOLOGY.

CULTURAL-ecological perspectives on Southeast Asia; a symposium [held in 1976 at Ohio University]; edited by William Wood. Athens, Ohio, 1977. pp. 192. *bibliog. (Ohio University. Center for International Studies. Papers in International Studies. Southeast Asia Series. No. 41)*

ASHBY (ERIC) Baron Ashby. Reconciling man with the environment. London, [1978]. pp. 104. *(Stanford University. Leon Sloss Junior Memorial Lectures in Humanities. 1977)*

HUMAN settlement systems: international perspectives on structure, change and public policy; editor Niles M. Hansen. Cambridge, Mass., [1978]. pp. 292. *bibliogs. Based on a conference organized by the Human Settlements and Services Area of the International Institute for Applied Systems Analysis, Luxemburg, Austria.*

PHILIP, Prince of the United Kingdom of Great Britain and Northern Ireland, Duke of Edinburgh, Consort of Elizabeth II, Queen of Great Britain. The environmental revolution; speeches on conservation 1962-1977. London, 1978. pp. 156.

RADICAL geography: alternative viewpoints on contemporary social issues; [edited by] Richard Peet. London, 1978. pp. 387. *A collection of essays drawn mainly from "Antipode".*

The SOCIAL ecology of change: from equilibrium to development; edited by Zdravko Mlinar and Henry Teune. London, [1978]. pp. 293. *bibliogs. Proceedings of an International Workshop on Comparative Ecological Analysis at Ljubljana in 1976, held under the auspices of the Research Committee for Social Ecology of the International Sociological Association.*

WADDINGTON (CONRAD HAL) The man-made future. New York, 1978. pp. 355. *bibliogs.*

The GLOBAL predicament: ecological perspectives on world order; edited by David W. Orr and Marvin S. Soroos. Chapel Hill, [1979]. pp. 398. *bibliog.*

SOCIAL and ecological systems; edited by P.C. Burnham and R.F. Ellen. London, 1979. pp. 314. *bibliogs. (Association of Social Anthropologists of the Commonwealth. A.S.A. Monographs. 18)*

— Congresses.

INTERNATIONAL MEETING ON HUMAN ECOLOGY, VIENNA, 1975. Proceedings...; edited on behalf of the Society for Human Ecology by Helmut Knötig. St.-Saphorin, [1976]. 2 vols. *bibliogs. In English, French or German.*

— Political aspects.

MACKENZIE (WILLIAM JAMES MILLAR) Biological ideas in politics: an essay on political adaptivity. Harmondsworth, 1978. pp. 93. *(Auckland. University. Sir Douglas Robb Lectures. 1975)*

— Tropics.

UNITED NATIONS EDUCATIONAL, SCIENTIFIC AND CULTURAL ORGANIZATION. 1978. Tropical forest eco-systems: a state-of-knowledge report prepared by Unesco/UNEP/ FAO. Paris, 1978. pp. 683. *bibliogs. (Natural Resources Research. 14)*

HUMAN ENGINEERING.

SINGLETON (W.T.) Introduction to ergonomics. Geneva, World Health Organization, 1972. pp. 145.

HUMAN EVOLUTION.

DARLINGTON (CYRIL DEAN) The little universe of man. London, 1978. pp. 307. *bibliog.*

PFEIFFER (JOHN E.) The emergence of man. 3rd ed. New York, [1978]. pp. 467. *bibliog.*

HUMAN INFORMATION PROCESSING.

STRATEGIES of information processing; edited by Geoffrey Underwood. London, 1978. pp. 455. *bibliog.*

HUMAN POPULATION GENETICS.

MOURANT (ARTHUR ERNEST) and others. The genetics of the Jews. Oxford, 1978. pp. 122. *bibliog.*

— Africa, Subsaharan.

NURSE (G.T.) and JENKINS (T.) Health and the unter-gatherer: biomedical studies on the hunting and gathering populations of southern Africa. Basel, 1977. pp. 126. *bibliog.*

HUMANISM.

The EARTHLY republic: Italian humanists on government and society; edited by Benjamin G. Kohl and Ronald G. Witt. Manchester, [1978]. pp. 337. *bibliog.*

MARXIST humanism and Praxis; edited, with translations, by Gerson S. Sher. New York, 1978. pp. 183.

— 20th century.

EHRENFELD (DAVID) The arrogance of humanism. New York, 1978. pp. 286. *bibliog.*

HUMANITIES

— Bibliography.

INDEX TO SOCIAL SCIENCES AND HUMANITIES PROCEEDINGS; [pd. by] Institute for Scientific Information. q., Ja/Mr 1979(no. 1)- Philadelphia.

— Congresses.

INDEX TO SOCIAL SCIENCES AND HUMANITIES PROCEEDINGS; [pd. by] Institute for Scientific Information. q., Ja/Mr 1979(no. 1)- Philadelphia.

— Periodicals — Indexes.

HARZFELD (LOIS A.) Periodical indexes in the social sciences and humanities: a subject guide. Metuchen, N.J., 1978. pp. 174.

HUMBERSIDE

— Economic policy.

HUMBERSIDE. County Council. Planning Department. Humberside structure plan: annual progress report. a., 1977/78(1st)- [Beverley].

HUMPHREYS (CHRISTMAS).

HUMPHREYS (CHRISTMAS) Both sides of the circle: the autobiography of Christmas Humphreys. London, 1978. pp. 269.

HUNAN, CHINA (PROVINCE)
— **Politics and government.**

McDONALD (ANGUS W.) The urban origins of rural revolution: elites and the masses in Hunan Province, China, 1911-1927. Berkeley, Calif., [1978]. pp. 369. *bibliog.*

HUNDRED YEARS' WAR, 1339-1453.

BURNE (ALFRED HIGGINS) The Crecy war: a military history of the Hundred Years War from 1337 to the peace of Bretigny, 1360. Westport, Conn., 1976. pp. 366. *Reprint of the 1955 edition published in London.*

HUNGARIANS IN CANADA
— **Bibliography.**

SZEPLAKI (JOSEPH) compiler. Hungarians in the United States and Canada: a bibliography: holdings of the Immigration History Research Center of the University of Minnesota; compiled and edited by Joseph Széplaki. [Minneapolis], 1977. pp. 113. *(Minnesota University. Immigration History Research Center. IHRC Ethnic Bibliographies. No. 2)*

HUNGARIANS IN THE UNITED STATES
— **Bibliography.**

SZEPLAKI (JOSEPH) compiler. Hungarians in the United States and Canada: a bibliography: holdings of the Immigration History Research Center of the University of Minnesota; compiled and edited by Joseph Széplaki. [Minneapolis], 1977. pp. 113. *(Minnesota University. Immigration History Research Center. IHRC Ethnic Bibliographies. No. 2)*

HUNGARY
— **Economic conditions.**

HUNGARY. Központi Statisztikai Hivatal. 1971. The development of the national economy in 1970: report, etc. [Budapest], 1971. pp. 21.

GOELLNER (ANDREW B.) The politics of the Hungarian new economic mechanism: the origins and dynamics of the movement towards a socialist market mechanism. 1977 [or rather 1978]. fo. 436. *bibliog. Typescript. Ph.D. (London) thesis: unpublished. This thesis is the property of London University and may not be removed from the Library.*

— **Economic policy.**

ANTAL (ENDRE) Grundlagen und reformpolitische Einordnung des ungarischen Wirtschaftssystems. Berlin, 1978. pp. 170. *bibliog. (Giessen. Universität. Zentrum für Kontinentale Agrar- und Wirtschaftsforschung. Giessener Abhandlungen zur Agrar- und Wirtschaftsforschung des Europäischen Ostens. Band 93) With English summary.*

FRANCE. Direction de la Documentation. La Documentation Française. Notes et Etudes Documentaires. No. 4462. Entreprise et planification socialiste: l'expérience hongroises; [by] Georges Chevallier et Eric Thérenon. [Paris], 1978. pp. 133. *bibliog.*

— **Emigration and immigration.**

SOLYOM-FEKETE (WILLIAM) Travel abroad and emigration under new rules adopted by the government of Hungary. Washington, Library of Congress, 1979. pp. 104.

— **Foreign economic relations.**

Der KLEINSTAAT in der europäischen wirtschaftlichen Zusammenarbeit, aus der Sicht Ungarns und Österreichs; wissenschaftliche Gesamtleitung: Wilhelm Weber. Wien, 1975. pp. 165. *(Österreichisches Ost- und Südosteuropa-Institut. Schriftenreihe. Band 5)*

— **Foreign relations — Yugoslavia.**

TIHANY (LESLIE CHARLES) The Baranya dispute, 1918-1921: diplomacy in the vortex of ideologies. New York, 1978. pp. 138. *bibliog. (East European Quarterly. East European Monographs. 35)*

— **History — 1848-1849, Uprising of.**

DEAK (ISTVAN) The lawful revolution: Louis Kossuth and the Hungarians, 1848-1849. New York, 1979. pp. 415. *bibliog.*

— — **1956, Uprising of.**

The HUNGARIAN Revolution of 1956 in retrospect; edited by Béla K. Király and Paul Jónás. Boulder, 1978. pp. 157. *(East European Quarterly. East European Monographs. 40) (City University of New York. Brooklyn College. Department of History. Studies on Society in Change. No. 6)*

— **Industries.**

HUNGARY. Központi Statisztikai Hivatal. Iparstatisztikai évkönyv. a., 1977(1st)- Budapest.

— **Politics and government.**

POWER, liberty, democracy: speeches and articles of leading Hungarian politicians, 1974-1977. Budapest, 1978. pp. 223.

— **Social conditions.**

SOZIOLOGIE und Gesellschaft in Ungarn: aus dem Ertrag des ersten Jahrzehnts der neueren ungarischen Soziologie; herausgegeben von Bálint Balla. Stuttgart, 1974. 4 vols. (in 1).

HEGEDUS (ANDRÁS) The structure of socialist society; translated by Rudolf Fisher and revised by Peter Szente. London, 1977. pp. 230.

HUNT (JOSEPH McVICKER).

The STRUCTURING of experience; edited by Ina Č. Užgiris and Fredric Weizmann. New York, [1977]. pp. 449. *bibliogs.*

HUNTING
— **Russia — Soviet Far East.**

SUKHOMIROV (GRIGORII ISAKOVICH) Okhotnich'e khoziaistvo Dal'nego Vostoka. Khabarovsk, 1976. pp. 254. *bibliog.*

HUSBAND AND WIFE
— **New Zealand.**

FISHER (ROBERT LLOYD) The Matrimonial Property Act 1976. Wellington, 1977. pp. 187.

HYDERABAD
— **Social history.**

LEONARD (KAREN ISAKSEN) Social history of an Indian caste: the Kayasths of Hyderabad. Berkeley, 1978. pp. 353. *bibliog.*

HYDROLOGY.

INTERMEDIATE TECHNOLOGY DEVELOPMENT GROUP. Technology is not enough: the provision and maintenance of appropriate water supplies;...edited and compiled by Arnold Pacey; [with] Abstracts of thematic papers [of] the United Nations Water Conference. Oxford, 1977. pp. 252. *bibliog. Published as Aqua, vol. 1, no. 1-2, 1977.*

DUNNE (THOMAS) and LEOPOLD (LUNA BERGERE) Water in environmental planning. San Francisco, [1978]. pp. 818. *bibliogs.*

— **Ghana.**

JUNNER (NORMAN ROSS) and HIRST (TOM) The geology and hydrology of the Voltaian basin. Accra, 1946. pp. 51, 4 maps. *(Ghana. Geological Survey. Memoirs. No.8)*

— **United Kingdom.**

NATIONAL WATER COUNCIL [U.K.]. Water industry review, 1978. London, 1978. pp. 99.

— — **Wales.**

WELSH WATER AUTHORITY. Directorate of Resource Planning. Medium term plan, 1978-1983. [Brecon], 1978. 1 vol. (various pagings).

HYGIENE, PUBLIC.

INTERNATIONAL BANK FOR RECONSTRUCTION AND DEVELOPMENT. 1974. Environmental, health, and human ecologic considerations in economic development projects. Washington, 1974. pp. 142. *bibliog.*

WORLD HEALTH: the magazine of the World Health Organization. m. Geneva. *Current issues only kept.*

— **Bibliography.**

CURRENT LITERATURE ON GENERAL HEALTH TOPICS; ([pd. by] Department of Health and Social Security. Library [U.K.]). m. London. *Current issues only kept; a classified selection is pd. later in Studies on community health and personal social services (1972-).*

— **Australia.**

SOCIAL indicators in Australia: health and housing. [Canberra, 1977?]. 2 vols. *bibliogs. Papers presented at a conference at the Research School of Social Sciences, Australian National University, Canberra, 1977.*

— **Brazil.**

SILVA (FERNANDO ANTONIO REZENDE DA) and MAHAR (DENNIS) Saude e previdência social: uma analise econômica. Rio de Janeiro, 1974. pp. 222. *bibliog. (Brazil. Instituto de Planejamento Econômico e Social. Instituto de Pesquisas. Relatorios de Pesquisa. No. 21)*

— **Europe.**

PUBLIC HEALTH IN EUROPE; [pd.by] Regional Office for Europe, World Health Organization. a., 1972(1)- Copenhagen.

— **Malawi.**

SHIRCORE (J.O.) Report on the Nyasaland medical service with special reference to a grant under the Colonial Development Fund. Zomba, Government Printer, 1930. pp. 19.

— **Russia.**

IZUTKIN (ANATOLII MAKSIMOVICH) and TSAREGORODTSEV (GENNADII IVANOVICH) Sotsialisticheskii obraz zhizni i zdorov'e naseleniia v svete reshenii XXV s"ezda KPSS. Moskva, 1977. pp. 232. *bibliog.*

— **Singapore.**

SINGAPORE. Ministry of the Environment. Annual report. a., 1972[1st]- Singapore.

— **South Africa.**

SOUTH AFRICA. Department of Health. Report. a., Jl 1947/D 1952, 1953-1976. Pretoria. *[in English and Afrikaans] Included in SOUTH AFRICA. Parliament. House of Assembly. Votes and proceedings (with Printed annexures)*

— **Underdeveloped areas.**

See UNDERDEVELOPED AREAS — Hygiene, Public.

— **United Kingdom.**

JORDAN (WILLIAM STONE) Community medicine in the United Kingdom: medical education and an emerging specialty within the reorganized National Health Service. New York, [1978]. pp. 310.

SMITH (FRANCIS BARRYMORE) The people's health, 1830-1910. London, [1979]. pp. 436. *bibliog.*

— — Bibliography.

U.K. Department of Health and Social Security. Index of health circulars and notices; chief officer letters; local authority circulars and social service letters. a., 1977- London.

— United States.

FUTURE directions in health care: a new public policy: reports from a conference...; edited by Rick J. Carlson [and] Robert Cunningham. Cambridge, Mass., [1978]. pp. 238.

— — Massachusetts.

MASSACHUSETTS. Metropolitan Area Planning Council. 1967. Hospital and health facilities in eastern Massachusetts. [Boston], 1967. fo. 43.

— — New York.

WOLFE (MARGARET RIPLEY) Lucius Polk Brown and progressive food and drug control: Tennessee and New York City 1908-1920. Lawrence, Kan., [1978]. pp. 194.

— — Tennessee.

WOLFE (MARGARET RIPLEY) Lucius Polk Brown and progressive food and drug control: Tennessee and New York City 1908-1920. Lawrence, Kan., [1978]. pp. 194.

— — Virginia.

SAVITT (TODD L.) Medicine and slavery: the diseases and health care of blacks in antebellum Virginia. Urbana, 1978. pp. 332.

HYPNOTISM.

GORDON (JESSE EMANUEL) ed. Handbook of clinical and experimental hypnosis. New York, [1967]. pp. 653. *bibliogs.*

HYPOTHESIS.

DUBIN (ROBERT) Theory building. rev. ed. New York, [1978]. pp. 304. *bibliog.*

IBM 370 (COMPUTER).

HEBDITCH (DAVID L.) Teleprocessing monitor packages for IBM 370. Manchester, 1978. pp. 89.

ICELAND

— Foreign relations — United Kingdom.

GILCHRIST (Sir ANDREW) Cod wars and how to lose them. Edinburgh, 1977. pp. 122.

— Social conditions.

BJÖRNSSON (SIGURJÓN) and EDELSTEIN (WOLFGANG) Explorations in social inequality: stratification dynamics in social and individual development in Iceland. Berlin, 1977. pp. 172. *bibliog.* (*Max-Planck-Institut für Bildungsforschung. Studien und Berichte. 38*)

ICL 2903 (COMPUTER).

BLEAZARD (G.B.) Teleprocessing monitor packages for ICL 2903/04. Manchester, 1978. pp. 55.

ICL 2904 (COMPUTER).

BLEAZARD (G.B.) Teleprocessing monitor packages for ICL 2903/04. Manchester, 1978. pp. 55.

IDEALISM.

GORDON (PETER) and WHITE (JOHN PONSFORD) Philosophers as educational reformers: the influence of idealism on British educational thought and practice. London, 1979. pp. 314. *bibliog.*

IDEALS (ALGEBRA).

SALLY (JUDITH D.) Numbers of generators of ideals in local rings. New York, [1978]. pp. 93. *bibliog.*

IDENTIFICATION.

IDENTIFICATION evidence: practices and malpractices; a report by JAIL; [prepared by] Martin Walker and Bernadette Brittain. London, [1978]. pp. 115. *bibliog.*

— New Zealand.

NEW ZEALAND. Criminal Law Reform Committee. 1978. Report on identification. Wellington, 1978. pp. 43.

IDEOLOGY.

THEWELEIT (KLAUS) Männerphantasien. Frankfurt am Main, 1977-78. 2 vols. *bibliog.*

HAGOPIAN (MARK N.) Regimes, movements, and ideologies: a comparative introduction to political science. New York, [1978]. pp. 508. *bibliogs.*

MACGREGOR (DAVID EDWARD STEPHEN) Studies in the concept of ideology: from the Hegelian dialectic to western Marxism. 1978. fo. 504. *bibliog.* Typescript. Ph.D. (London) thesis: unpublished. This thesis is the property of London University and may not be removed from the Library.

POLITICS, ideology and the state: papers from the Communist University of London, [9th session, 1977]; edited by Sally Hibbin. London, 1978. pp. 143.

The PSYCHOLOGICAL basis of ideology: readings...; [edited] by Hans J. Eysenck and Glenn D. Wilson. Lancaster, [1978]. pp. 312. *bibliogs.*

BARADAT (LEON P.) Political ideologies: their origins and impact. Englewood Cliffs, 1979. pp. 337. *bibliog.*

HIRST (PAUL QUENTIN) On law and ideology. London, 1979. pp. 181. *bibliog.*

MERQUIOR (JOSE GUILHERME) The veil and the mask: essays on culture and ideology. London, 1979. pp. 161. *bibliog.*

SCHNEIDER (JERROLD E.) Ideological coalitions in Congress. Westport, Conn., 1979. pp. 270. *bibliog.*

SUMNER (COLIN) Reading ideologies: an investigation into the Marxist theory of ideology and law. London, 1979. pp. 313. *bibliog.*

WALFORD (GEORGE W.) Ideologies and their functions: a study in systematic ideology. London, 1979. pp. 163.

ILE-DE-FRANCE

— Industries.

FERNIOT (BERNARD) La décentralisation industrielle. Paris, 1976. pp. 99.

ILLEGITIMACY

— United Kingdom.

U.K. Law Commission. Working Papers. No. 74. Family law: illegitimacy. London, 1979. pp. 159.

ILLINOIS

— Description and travel.

BIRKBECK (MORRIS) Notes on a journey in America from the coast of Virginia to the territory of Illinois;...to which is added: Letters from Illinois. New York, 1971. pp. 163,114. *Reprint of the third edition of the works originally published in London, 1818.*

— Economic history.

KEISER (JOHN H.) Building for the centuries: Illinois, 1865 to 1898. Urbana, [1977]. pp. 386. *bibliog.*

— History.

KEISER (JOHN H.) Building for the centuries: Illinois, 1865 to 1898. Urbana, [1977]. pp. 386. *bibliog.*

— Politics and government.

KEISER (JOHN H.) Building for the centuries: Illinois, 1865 to 1898. Urbana, [1977]. pp. 386. *bibliog.*

— Social history.

KEISER (JOHN H.) Building for the centuries: Illinois, 1865 to 1898. Urbana, [1977]. pp. 386. *bibliog.*

ILLINOIS CENTRAL RAILROAD.

LIGHTNER (DAVID L.) Labor on the Illinois Central Railroad, 1852-1900: the evolution of an industrial environment. New York, 1977. pp. 437. *bibliog.*

ILLITERACY

— America, Latin.

WORLD COUNCIL OF CHURCHES. Commission on the Churches' Participation in Development. Conscientization: [a dossier including separately published articles]. Geneva, 1975. 1 vol. (various pagings). *bibliog.* (*CCPD Documents. 7*)

IMAGINATION.

BRONOWSKI (JACOB) The visionary eye: essays in the arts, literature, and science;.. .selected and edited by Piero E. Ariotti in collaboration with Rita Bronowski. Cambridge, Mass., [1978]. pp. 185.

IMPERIALISM.

FIELDHOUSE (DAVID KENNETH) ed. The theory of capitalist imperialism. London, 1967, repr. 1977. pp. 202. *bibliog.*

OBJECTIVE: JUSTICE; q. magazine covering United Nations activity against apartheid, racial discrimination and colonialism; [pd. by United Nations Office of Public Information]. q., 1970 (v.2)- New York.

The HEART of the Empire: discussions of problems of modern city life in England; [edited by] C.F.G. Masterman; [facsimile reprint of the edition of 1901] edited with an introduction by Bentley B. Gilbert. Brighton, 1973. pp. 415,xlvii.

TESTA (VICTOR) El capital imperialista. Buenos Aires, 1975. pp. 460.

ECKHARDT (WILLIAM) and YOUNG (CHRISTOPHER) Governments under fire: civil conflict and imperialism. New Haven, Conn., [1977]. pp. 379. *bibliog.*

SAU (RANJIT KUMAR) Unequal exchange, imperialism and underdevelopment: an essay on the political economy of world capitalism. Calcutta, [1978]. pp. 202. *bibliog.*

HARRIS (WILLIAM VERNON) War and imperialism in Republican Rome, 327-70 B.C. Oxford, 1979. pp. 293. *bibliog.*

KUBICEK (ROBERT V.) Economic imperialism in theory and practice: the case of South African gold mining finance 1886-1914. Durham, 1979. pp. 239. *bibliog.* (*Duke University. Center for Commonwealth and Comparative Studies. [Publications]. No. 45*)

IMPORT QUOTAS

— Rhodesia.

RHODESIA. Commission of Inquiry into Import Control. 1975. Report; [Albert Rubidge Washington Stumbles, chairman]. [Salisbury], 1975. pp. 48. (*[Command Papers]. 1975. Cmd. R.R. 11*)

— United States.

BOHI (DOUGLAS R.) and RUSSELL (MILTON) Limiting oil imports: an economic history and analysis. Baltimore, [1978]. pp. 356. *Report of a project initiated by Resources for the Future, Inc.*

IMPORT SUBSTITUTION.

AHMAD (JALEEL) Import substitution, trade and development. Greenwich, Conn., [1978]. pp. 128. *bibliog.*

INCAS.

CIEZA DE LEON (PEDRO DE) The Incas; translated by Harriet de Onis; edited, with an introduction, by Victor Wolfgang von Hagen. Norman, 1959. pp. 394. *bibliog.*

INCAS.(Cont.)

GIRON DE VILLASEÑOR (NICOLE) Peru: cronistas indios y mestizos en el siglo XVI; traduccion de Roberto Gomez Ciriza. Mexico, Secretaria de Educacion Publica, 1975. pp. 183. (Sep/Setentas. 199)

INCENTIVES IN INDUSTRY
— Russia.

BARKER (GEOFFREY RUSSELL) Some problems of incentives and labour productivity in Soviet industry: a contribution to the study of the planning of labour in the U.S.S.R. Oxford, [1955?]. pp. 129, xii. (Birmingham. University. Faculty of Commerce and Social Science. Department of Economics and Institutions of the USSR. Monographs on the Soviet Economic System. No. 1)

INCOME.

SIMON (JULIAN LINCOLN) The effects of income on fertility. Chapel Hill, [1974]. pp. 210. bibliog. (North Carolina University. Carolina Population Center. Monographs. [No.] 19)

INTERNATIONAL comparisons of real product and purchasing power: (United Nations International Comparison Project, phase II); produced by the Statistical Office of the United Nations and the World Bank...; published for the World Bank. Baltimore, [1978]. pp. 264.

ORGANISATION FOR ECONOMIC CO-OPERATION AND DEVELOPMENT. Committee on Fiscal Affairs. 1978. The tax/benefit position of selected income groups in OECD member countries, 1972-1976: a report by the Committee, etc. Paris, 1978. pp. 132.

— Mathematical models.

ESTRUP (HECTOR) Essays in the theory of income creation. [Copenhagen], 1977. pp. 261.

— Bahamas.

BAHAMAS. Department of Statistics. 1976. Household income in the Bahamas, 1975. Nassau, [1976?]. pp. 30.

— Belgium.

DELEECK (HERMAN) Ongelijkheden in de welvaartsstaat: opstellen over sociaal beleid: tweede bundel. Antwerpen, [1977]. pp. 319.

— Brazil.

ALMEIDA (ANNA LUIZA OZORIO DE) Distribuição de renda e emprego em serviços. Rio de Janeiro, 1976. pp. 412. bibliog. (Brazil. Instituto de Planejamento Econômico e Social. Instituto de Pesquisas. Relatorios de Pesquisa. No. 34)

LODDER (CELSIUS ANTONIO) Distribuição de renda nas areas metropolitanas. Rio de Janeiro, 1976. pp. 104. bibliog. (Brazil. Instituto de Planejamento Econômico e Social. Instituto de Pesquisas. Relatorios de Pesquisa. No. 31)

MATA (MILTON DA) Concentração de renda, desemprego e pobreza no Brasil. Rio de Janeiro, 1979. pp. 161. bibliog. (Brazil. Instituto de Planejamento Econômico e Social. Instituto de Pesquisas. Relatorios de Pesquisa. No. 41)

— European Economic Community countries.

RIFFAULT (HELENE) and RABIER (JACQUES RENE) The perception of poverty in Europe: report on a public opinion survey carried out in the member countries of the European Community as part of the programme of pilot projects to combat poverty. Brussels, European Communities, 1977. 1 vol. (various pagings). Working document for the Commission of the European Communities.

— France.

Les BENEFICES déclarés par les entrepreneurs individuels non agricoles; [by Philippe Madinier and others]. [Paris, 1974]. pp. 170. (France. Centre d'Etude des Revenus et des Coûts. Documents. No.24)

FRANCE. Centre d'Etude des Revenus et des Coûts. 1977. Les revenus des Français: premier rapport de synthèse; [by René Padieu and others]. [Paris], 1977. pp. 197. (Documents. Nos. 37-38)

— Germany.

KNEBEL (JUERGEN) Koalitionsfreiheit und Gemeinwohl: zur verfassungsrechtlichen Zulässigkeit staatlicher Einwirkung auf die tarifautonome Lohngestaltung. Berlin, 1978. pp. 179. bibliog.

— Japan.

JAPAN. Bureau of Statistics. 1977. Family income and expenditure survey, 1963-1975. [Tokyo], 1977. pp. 508. In English and Japanese.

— Netherlands.

FISELIER (A.A.M.) and KRAFT (H.L.P.R.) Laagstgeklasseerden in Nederland: een beschrijvend onderzoek naar omvang en spreiding van lage inkomens bij diverse typen huishoudens, gerelateerd aan een beperkt aantal relevante variabelen. 's-Gravenhage, 1979. pp. 139. bibliog. (Netherlands. Centraal Bureau voor de Statistiek. Monografieën Volkstelling 1971. 5) With English summary.

— Norway.

NORWAY. Statistiske Centralbyrå. Statistikk over lavinntektsgrupper. a., 1973- Oslo. [in English and Norwegian]

— Russia — Mathematical models.

DIFFERENTSIROVANNYI balans dokhodov i potrebleniia naseleniia. Moskva, 1977. pp. 223. bibliog. (Akademiia Nauk SSSR. Problemy Sovetskoi Ekonomiki)

— United Kingdom.

The CAUSES of poverty; by R.Layard [and others];... background paper to Report No.6: lower incomes. London, 1978. pp. 190. bibliog. (U.K. Royal Commission on the Distribution of Income and Wealth, 1974. Background Papers. No.5) Report No.6 published as British Parliamentary Paper Cmnd. 7175, Session 1977-78.

INCOME ACCOUNTING.

CREEDY (JOHN) The time period and the inequality of earnings. London, [1978]. pp. 26. bibliog. (National Institute of Economic and Social Research. Discussion Papers. No. 15)

TRENDS in managerial and financial accounting: income determination and financial reporting; Cees van Dam, editor. Leiden, 1978. pp. 221. bibliogs. 11 papers from a research seminar 'Decision-making in business', held at Nijenrode, 1976.

INCOME DISTRIBUTION.

GROUP OF EXPERTS ON SOCIAL POLICY AND THE DISTRIBUTION OF INCOME IN THE NATION. Social policy and the distribution of income in the nation :[report and discussion papers of the Group meeting held at United Nations Headquarters from 23 January to 1 February 1967.] (ST/SOA/88). New York, United Nations, 1969. pp. 175.

JAIN (SHAIL) Size distribution of income: a compilation of data. Washington, International Bank for Reconstruction and Development, [1975]. pp. 137. bibliog.

DRESCH (STEPHEN P.) and others. Substituting a value-added tax for the corporate income tax: first-round analysis. Cambridge, Mass., 1977. pp. 213. bibliog. (National Bureau of Economic Research. Fiscal Studies. 15)

NÄSLUND (BERTIL) An analysis of economic size distributions. Berlin, 1977. pp. 100. bibliog.

PEN (JAN) and TINBERGEN (JAN) Naar een rechtvaardiger inkomensverdeling. Amsterdam, 1977. pp. 210. bibliog.

BECKERMAN (WILFRED) Measures of leisure, equality and welfare. Paris, Organisation for Economic Co-operation and Development, 1978. pp. 63.

PERSONAL income distribution...; edited by Wilhelm Krelle [and] Anthony F. Shorrocks. Amsterdam, 1978. pp. 524. bibliogs. Proceedings of a conference held by the International Economic Association at Noordwijk aan Zee, 1977.

RANADIVE (K.R.) Income distribution: the unsolved uzzle. Bombay, 1978. pp. 353.

WOOD (ADRIAN) A theory of pay. Cambridge, 1978. pp. 251. bibliog.

ENGLUND (PETER) Profits and market adjustment: a study in the dynamics of production, productivity and rates of return. Stockholm, 1979. pp. 260. bibliog.

— Mathematical models.

HART (P.E.) Redundant inequalities. London, [1978]. pp. 22. bibliog. (National Institute of Economic and Social Research. Discussion Papers. No. 18)

— America, Latin.

CARNOY (MARTIN) Can educational policy equalise income distribution in Latin America?;...with the collaboration of José Lobo [and others]; a study prepared for the International Labour Office within the framework of the Research Programmes on Income Distribution and Employment and on Education and Employment of the World Employment Programme. Farnborough, [1979]. pp. 110. bibliog.

— Australia.

AUSTRALIA. Commonwealth Bureau of Census and Statistics. 1976- .Income distribution, 1973-74. Canberra, 1976 in progress.

— Bahamas.

BAHAMAS. Department of Statistics. 1976. Household income in the Bahamas, 1975. Nassau, [1976?]. pp. 30.

— France.

FRANCE. Institut National de la Statistique et des Etudes Economiques. Département Population-Ménages. Division des Revenus. 1976. La distribution des revenus en France. Paris, 1976. pp. 143.

— Malaysia.

FREDERICKS (L. J.) and others. Patterns of labour utilization and income distribution in rice double cropping systems: policy implications. Kuala Lumpur, 1977. pp. 66. bibliog. (University of Malaya. Faculty of Economics and Administration. Occasional Papers on Malaysian Socio-Economic Affairs. No. 8)

— Russia.

McAULEY (ALASTAIR) Economic welfare in the Soviet Union: poverty, living standards, and inequality. Madison, [1979]. pp. 389. bibliog.

— Sweden.

SWEDEN. Inrikesdepartementet. Låginkomstutredningen. 1971. Den svenska köpkrafts fördelningen, 1967: betänkande, etc. Stockholm, 1971. pp. 343. (Sweden. Statens Offentliga Utredningar. 1971. 39)

SWEDEN. Statistiska Centralbyrån. Inkomstfördelningen... för hushåll m.m. a., 1976- Stockholm.

SWEDEN. Statistiska Centralbyrån. 1978. Inkomstfördelningen, 1951-1976. Stockholm, 1978. pp. 31. (Statistiska Meddelanden. N/1978/4) With English summary.

— Taiwan.

FORMOSA. Directorate-General of Budget, Accounting and Statistics. Report on the survey of personal income distribution in Taiwan area, Republic of China. a., 1975- Taipei. [in English and Chinese]

— Underdeveloped areas.

See UNDERDEVELOPED AREAS — Income distribution.

— United Kingdom.

TOWNSEND (PETER BRERETON) Trends in the distribution of resources in the United Kingdom 1938-1970. Colchester, 1971. fo. 71.

CITY CAPITAL MARKETS COMMITTEE. Written evidence to the Royal Commission on the Distribution of Income and Wealth. [London], 1975. fo.12.

GOUGH (JULIAN) Housing policy and the distribution of income and wealth in the U.K. Cardiff, 1976. fo.28,ii. bibliog. (Wales. University. University College, Cardiff. Institute of Science and Technology. Research and Discussion Papers in Economics, Finance and Politics. No. 1)

CREEDY (JOHN) Pension schemes and the limits to redistribution. London, [1978]. pp. 22. bibliog. (National Institute of Economic and Social Research. Discussion Papers. No. 24)

— Mathematical models.

HART (P. L.) A cohort analysis of changes in the distribution of incomes, United Kingdom, 1963-73. Reading, 1975. pp. 52. bibliog. (Reading. University. Department of Economics. Discussion Papers in Economics. No. 74)

CREEDY (JOHN) The time period and the inequality of earnings. London, [1978]. pp. 26. bibliog. (National Institute of Economic and Social Research. Discussion Papers. No. 15)

CREEDY (JOHN) and HART (P.E.) Age and the distribution of earnings. London, [1978]. pp. 14,3,2,3,2. bibliog. (National Institute of Economic and Social Research. Discussion Papers. No. 17)

— United States.

NATIONAL BUREAU OF ECONOMIC RESEARCH. Conference on Research in Income and Wealth. Studies in Income and Wealth. vol. 41. The distribution of economic well-being: [papers presented in 1974]; F. Thomas Juster, ed. Cambridge, Mass., 1977. pp. 679. Tables on microfiche (7 cards). Proceedings of a Conference held at the University of Michigan in 1974.

WEALTH redistribution and the income tax...; edited by Arleen A. Leibowitz. Lexington, Mass., [1978]. pp. 130. bibliog. Papers and discussions from a conference sponsored by the Liberty Fund, Jan. 21-23, 1977. Principal paper by Norman B. Ture.

INCOME MAINTENANCE PROGRAMMES

— Canada.

MENDELSON (M.) Author of The administrative cost of income security programs: Ontario and Canada. The administrative cost of income security programs: Ontario and Canada. [Toronto, 1979]. pp. 118. bibliog. (Ontario. Economic Council. Occasional Papers. 9)

— Israel.

DORON (ABRAHAM) and ROTER (RAPHAEL) Low wage earners and low wage subsidies. Jerusalem, Hebrew University Paul Baerwald School of Social Work and National Insurance Institute, Bureau of Research and Planning, 1978. pp. 217. bibliog. First published in Hebrew in 1976.

— United Kingdom.

NORTH TYNESIDE COMMUNITY DEVELOPMENT PROJECT. In and out of work: a study of unemployment, low pay and income maintenance services. [Newcastle-upon-Tyne], 1978. pp. 287.

— United States.

MASTERS (STANLEY H.) and GARFINKEL (IRWIN) Estimating the labor supply effects of income-maintenance alternatives. New York, [1977]. pp. 289. bibliog. (Wisconsin University, Madison. Institute for Research on Poverty. Monograph Series)

SALAMON (LESTER M.) Welfare: the elusive consensus; where we are, how we got there, and what's ahead. New York, [1978]. pp. 257. bibliogs. A report from the Welfare Policy Project of the Ford Foundation and Duke University.

INCOME TAX.

McLURE (CHARLES E.) Must corporate income be taxed twice? Washington, D.C., [1979]. pp. 262. (Brookings Institution. Studies of Government Finance) A report of a conference sponsored by the Fund for Public Policy Research and the Brookings Institution.

— Germany.

GERMANY. Statistisches Reichsamt. Statistik des Deutschen Reichs. Neue Folge. Band 312. Die deutsche Einkommensbesteuerung vor und nach dem Kriege. Berlin, 1925; Osnabrück, 1978. pp. 88. Photographic reprint.

GERMANY. Statistisches Reichsamt. Statistik des Deutschen Reichs. Neue Folge. Band 378. Der Steuerabzug vom Arbeitslohn im Jahre 1928. Berlin, 1931; Osnabrück, 1978. pp. 220. Photographic reprint.

— — North Rhine-Westphalia.

NORTH RHINE-WESTPHALIA. Landesamt für Datenverarbeitung und Statistik. Beiträge zur Statistik des Landes Nordrhein- Westfalen. Heft 404. Steuern vom Einkommen in Nordrhein-Westfalen. Düsseldorf, [1979]. 1 vol. (various pagings).

— Rhodesia.

RHODESIA. Commissioner of Taxes. 1971. Employee's guide to pay as you earn. rev. ed. Salisbury, 1971. pp. 12.

RHODESIA. Commissioner of Taxes. 1971. Employer's guide to the pay as you earn system of tax collection. [Salisbury, 1971]. fo. 24.

RHODESIA. Department of Taxes. 1971. Hints for traders and employees on income tax in Rhodesia. [Salisbury, 1971]. pp. 24.

RHODESIA. Department of Taxes. 1971. Income tax in Rhodesia: information pamphlet setting out the main features of taxation in Rhodesia. Salisbury, 1971. pp. 11.

— — Rates and tables.

RHODESIA. Department of Taxes. 1971. P.A.Y.E.: tax eduction tables issue No. 4: family taxpayers and single persons. [Salisbury, 1971]. 1 vol. (unpaged).

RHODESIA. Department of Taxes. 1971. P.A.Y.E.: tax deduction tables issue No. 4: married women. [Salisbury, 1971]. 1 vol. (unpaged).

— Trinidad and tobago.

TOBY (RICHARD A.) The theory and practice of income tax. London, 1978. pp. 210. bibliog.

— United Kingdom.

POND (CHRIS) A jubilee year for the low paid? London, 1977. fo.4. (Low Pay Unit. Low Pay Papers. No.18)

POND (CHRIS) A social contract for the rich. London, 1977. fo. 6. (Low Pay Unit. Low Pay Papers. No. 16)

U.K. Equal Opportunities Commission. 1977. Income tax and sex discrimination. [Manchester, 1977]. pp. 55.

POND (CHRIS) Crumbs from the master's table?: a checklist on the tax cuts. London, 1978. fo. 8. (Low Pay Unit. Low Pay Papers. No. 22)

TOBY (RICHARD A.) The theory and practice of income tax. London, 1978. pp. 210. bibliog.

U.K. Equal Opportunities Commission. 1979. With all my worldly goods I thee endow...except my tax allowances: the response received by the...Commission to its consultative document Income tax and sex discrimination. [Manchester, 1979]. pp. 61.

— — Foreign income.

SUMPTION (ANTHONY) Taxation of overseas income and gains. 3rd ed. London, 1979. pp. 191.

— — Mathematical models.

CREEDY (JOHN) Income averaging and progressive taxation. London, [1978?]. fo. 13,4,3. bibliog. (National Institute of Economic and Social Research. Discussion Papers. No. 13)

PRICE (R.W.R.) Modelling fiscal policy: the personal income tax system. London, [1978]. pp. 22. bibliog. (National Institute of Economic and Social Research. Discussion Papers. No. 22)

— United States.

WEALTH redistribution and the income tax...; edited by Arleen A. Leibowitz. Lexington, Mass., [1978]. pp. 130. bibliog. Papers and discussions from a conference sponsored by the Liberty Fund, Jan. 21-23, 1977. Principal paper by Norman B. Ture.

— — Foreign income.

McDANIEL (RONALD) and AULT (HUGH J.) Introduction to United States international taxation. Deventer, [1977]. pp. 183. (Erasmus Universiteit Rotterdam. Fiscaal-Economisch Instituut. International Series. no. 2)

INCORPORATED SOCIETY OF AUTHORS, PLAYWRIGHTS, AND COMPOSERS.

BONHAM-CARTER (VICTOR) Authors by profession. London, 1978 in progress. bibliog.

INDEPENDENCE (MATHEMATICS).

BELL (JOHN LANE) Boolean-valued models and independence proofs in set theory. Oxford, 1977. pp. 126. bibliog.

INDEPENDENT REGULATORY COMMISSIONS

— Canada — Ontario.

ONTARIO. Economic Council. 1978. Government regulation. [Toronto], 1978. pp. 275. bibliogs. (Issues and Alternatives, 1978)

— United States.

FREEDMAN (JAMES O.) Crisis and legitimacy: the administrative process and American government. Cambridge, 1978. pp. 324. bibliog.

UNSETTLED questions on regulatory reform;...[by] John W. Barnum [and others]; edited by Paul W. MacAvoy. Washington, [1978]. pp. 33. (American Enterprise Institute for Public Policy Research. AEI Studies. 226)

INDEX NUMBERS (ECONOMICS).

MITCHELL (WESLEY CLAIR) The making and using of index numbers. New York, 1965. pp. 114. Reprint of work first published New York, 1938.

EDEL'GAUZ (GEORGII EVGEN'EVICH) Dostovernost' statisticheskikh pokazatelei. Moskva, 1977. pp. 278.

INDEXATION (ECONOMICS).

KAPLAN (ROBERT S.) Indexing social security: an analysis of the issues. Washington, D.C., [1977]. pp. 67. (American Enterprise Institute for Public Policy Research. AEI Studies. 182)

INDIA.

TEMPLE (Sir RICHARD) Bart., G.C.S.I. India in 1880. London, 1880. pp. 524.

INDIA.(Cont.)

— Administrative and political divisions.

INDIA. Election Commission. 1967. Delimitation of Parliamentary and Assembly Constituencies Order, 1966. [Delhi], 1967. pp. 419.

— Census.

INDIA. Census. Papers. 1972. No.1. Census of India, 1971: Series 1: India...: final population. [Delhi, 1972]. pp. 155.

— — Maps.

INDIA. Census, 1971. Indian census centenary atlas. [Delhi, 1974]. pp. 198.

— Commerce — Denmark.

FELDBAEK (OLE) India trade under the Danish flag, 1772-1808: European enterprise and Anglo-Indian remittance and trade. [Copenhagen], [1969]. pp. 359. *bibliog. (Scandinavian Institute of Asian Studies. Monograph Series. No. 2) Summary in Danish.*

— — Portugal.

DISNEY (ANTHONY R.) Twilight of the pepper empire: Portuguese trade in southwest India in the early seventeenth century. Cambridge, Mass., 1978. pp. 220. *bibliog. (Harvard University. Harvard Historical Studies. vol. 95)*

— Constitution.

INDIA. Constitution. 1977. The constitution of India, as modified up to the 1st February, 1977. [Delhi, 1977]. pp. 324.

INDIA. Constitution. 1978. The constitution of India, as modified up to the 1st August, 1977. [Delhi, 1978]. pp. 443.

— Constitutional history.

BANERJEE (ANIL CHANDRA) The constitutional history of India. Delhi, 1977 in progress. *bibliogs.*

— Defences.

THOMAS (RAJU G.C.) The defence of India: a budgetary perspective of strategy and politics. Delhi, 1978. pp. 245. *bibliogs.*

— Description and travel.

DYSON (KETAKI KUSHARI) A various universe: a study of the journals and memoirs of British men and women in the Indian subcontinent, 1765-1856. Delhi, 1978. pp. 406. *bibliog.*

— Economic conditions.

INDIA'S economic problems: an analytic approach; [edited by] J.S. Uppal. New Delhi, [1975]. pp. 425. *bibliogs.*

SOCIALIST INDIA. Republic Day Number, 1976. The Indira Gandhi decade, 1966-1976. Delhi, 1976. 1 vol. (various pagings). *bibliog.*

INDIA ECONOMIC BULLETIN; [pd. by] Information Service, Embassy of India (Belgium). m., Ag 1978 (v.16, no.8)- Brussels.

CHAUDHURI (PRAMIT) The Indian economy: poverty and development. London, 1978. pp. 279. *bibliog.*

JOHNSON (BASIL LEONARD CLYDE) India: resources and development. London, 1979. pp. 211. *bibliog.*

RAY (RAJAT K.) Industrialization in India: growth and conflict in the private corporate sector 1914-47. Delhi, 1979. pp. 384.

— Economic history.

ESSAYS concerning the socioeconomic history of Brazil and Portuguese India; edited by Dauril Alden and Warren Dean. Gainesville, 1977. pp. 247.

TOMLINSON (BRIAN ROGER) The political economy of the Raj, 1914-1947: the economics of decolonization in India. London, 1979. pp. 199. *bibliog.*

— Economic policy.

VAKIL (CHANDULAL NAGINDAS) and BRAHMANAND (P.R.) Planning for a shortage economy: the Indian experiment. Bombay, 1952. pp. 317.

CHRISTIAN participation in nation-building: the summing up of a corporate study on rapid social change; compiled by M. M. Thomas. Bangalore, 1960. pp. 325. *bibliog.*

SAY not the struggle: essays in honour of A.D. Gorwala; [edited by H.M. Patel]. Delhi, 1976. pp. 328.

SOCIETY and change: essays in honour of Sachin Chaudhuri; edited by K.S. Krishnaswamy [and others]. Bombay, 1977. pp. 327.

CLARKSON (STEPHEN) The Soviet theory of development: India and the third world in marxist-leninist scholarship. Toronto, 1978. pp. 322.

FRANKEL (FRANCINE R.) India's political economy, 1947-1977: the gradual revolution. Princeton, N.J., [1978]. pp. 600. *bibliog.*

INDIA. Planning Commission. 1978. Draft five year plan, 1978-83. [Delhi], 1978. pp. 276.

TYNER (WALLACE EDWARD) Energy resources and economic development in India. Leiden, 1978. pp. 139. *bibliog.*

— Famines.

GANGRADE (KESHARICHAND DASHARATHASA) and DHADDA (SIDDHARAJ) Challenge and response: a study of famines in India. Delhi, 1973. pp. 124.

— Foreign relations.

SOCIALIST INDIA. Republic Day Number, 1976. The Indira Gandhi decade, 1966-1976. Delhi, 1976. 1 vol. (various pagings). *bibliog.*

THOMAS (RAJU G.C.) The defence of India: a budgetary perspective of strategy and politics. Delhi, 1978. pp. 245. *bibliogs.*

— — United Kingdom.

RIZVI (GOWHER) Linlithgow and India: a study of British policy and the political impasse in India, 1936-43. London, 1978. pp. 261. *bibliogs.*

MOORE (ROBIN JAMES) Churchill, Cripps, and India, 1939-1945. Oxford, 1979. pp. 152.

— — United States.

NAYAR (BALDEV RAJ) American geopolitics and India. Columbia, Mo., 1976. pp. 246. *bibliog.*

— History.

BARTON (Sir WILLIAM PELL) The princes of India, with a chapter on Nepal. London, 1934. pp. 327.

— — 1765-1947, British occupation.

SPEAR (THOMAS GEORGE PERCIVAL) The Oxford history of modern India, 1740-1975. 2nd ed. Delhi, 1978. p. 472.

— — — Sources.

The INDIAN nationalist movement, 1885-1947: select documents; edited by B.N. Pandey. London, 1979. pp. 272. *bibliog.*

— — 1857-1858, Sepoy Rebellion.

DOMIN (DOLORES) India in 1857-59: a study in the role of the Sikhs in the people's uprising. Berlin, 1977. pp. 375. *bibliog. (Zentraler Rat für Asien-, Afrika- und Lateinamerikawissenschaften in der DDR. Studien über Asien, Afrika und Lateinamerika. Band 17) Translated from the German by the author.*

— — 1900- .

CONGRESS and the Raj: facets of the Indian struggle, 1917-47; edited by D.A. Low. London, 1977. pp. 513.

JAGAT SINGH. Assessment of emergency: propaganda and reality. New Delhi, 1977. pp. 152.

MANSERGH (PHILIP NICHOLAS SETON) The prelude to partition: concept and aims in Ireland and India. Cambridge, 1978. pp. 62. *(Cambridge. University. Commonwealth Lectures. 1976)*

RIZVI (GOWHER) Linlithgow and India: a study of British policy and the political impasse in India, 1936-43. London, 1978. pp. 261. *bibliogs.*

RUMBOLD (Sir ALGERNON) Watershed in India, 1914-1922. London, 1979. pp. 344. *bibliog.*

— — — Sources.

BIRLA (GHANSHYAM DASS) Bapu: a unique association. Bombay, 1977. 4 vols. *Correspondence between M.K. Gandhi, G.D. Birla, and others, 1924-1947.*

— — 1919-1947.

VOIGT (JOHANNES HERMANN) Indien im Zweiten Weltkrieg. Stuttgart, 1978. pp. 414. *bibliog. (Institut für Zeitgeschichte. Studien zur Zeitgeschichte. Band 11) With English summary.*

— — 1947- .

SOCIALIST INDIA. Republic Day Number, 1976. The Indira Gandhi decade, 1966-1976. Delhi, 1976. 1 vol. (various pagings). *bibliog.*

UNDERGROUND literature during Indian emergency; edited by Sajal Basu. Calcutta, 1978. pp. 242.

— Industries.

JOHNSON (BASIL LEONARD CLYDE) India: resources and development. London, 1979. pp. 211. *bibliog.*

RAY (RAJAT K.) Industrialization in India: growth and conflict in the private corporate sector 1914-47. Delhi, 1979. pp. 384.

— Intellectual life.

CHATTERJI (BANKIM CHANDRA) Bankim on equality: an English translation of Bankim Chandra Chattopadhyay's Bengali article, Samya [with an essay on its background] by M.K. Haldar. Nedlands, W.A., 1974. pp. 38, 124. *(Western Australia, University of. Centre for Asian Studies. Working Papers in Asian Studies. No. 5)*

— Kings and rulers.

BARTON (Sir WILLIAM PELL) The princes of India, with a chapter on Nepal. London, 1934. pp. 327.

RAMUSACK (BARBARA N.) The princes of India in the twilight of empire: dissolution of a patron-client system, 1914-1939. Columbus, [1978]. pp. 322. *bibliog.*

— National Employment Service.

INDIA. Directorate General of Employment and Training. 1977. National Employment Service in India. [Delhi, 1977]. pp. 157.

— National Institute of Rural Development.

INDIA. Department of Rural Development. 1978. National Institute of Rural Development: its growth and achievements. New Delhi, 1978. pp. 24.

— Nationalism.

CHATTERJI (BANKIM CHANDRA) Bankim on equality: an English translation of Bankim Chandra Chattopadhyay's Bengali article, Samya [with an essay on its background] by M.K. Haldar. Nedlands, W.A., 1974. pp. 38, 124. *(Western Australia, University of. Centre for Asian Studies. Working Papers in Asian Studies. No. 5)*

PRASHAD (GANESH) Nehru: a study in colonial liberalism. New Delhi, [1976]. pp. 218. *bibliogs.*

CHOWDHURI (SATYABRATA RAI) Leftist movements in India: 1917-1947. Columbia, 1977. pp. 313. *bibliog.*

KAURA (UMA) Muslims and Indian nationalism: the emergence of the demand for India's partition, 1928-40. Columbia, Mo., 1977. pp. 223. *bibliog.*

The INDIAN nationalist movement, 1885-1947: select documents; edited by B.N. Pandey. London, 1979. pp. 272. *bibliog.*

— Parliament — Biography.

KERALA. Department of Public Relations. 1977. Kerala election reportage, 1977. [Trivandrum], 1977. pp. 96.

— — Elections.

PANTHAM (THOMAS) Political parties and democratic consensus: a study of party organisations in an Indian city. Delhi, 1976. pp. 215. *bibliogs.*

The INCREDIBLE elections: 1977!: A blow-by-blow document as reported in the Indian Express: edited by S.Eevadas Pillai. Bomby, 1977. pp. 439.

— — Lok Sabha.

INDIA. Parliament. Lok Sabha. Secretariat. 1977. Parliament of India: the fifth Lok Sabha, 1971-1977; a study; editor S.L. Shakdher. New Delhi, [1977]. pp. 401.

— — — Elections.

INDIA. Election Commission. 1978. Report on the sixth general election to the House of the People in India, 1977. vol. 2, statistical. [Delhi, 1978]. pp. 519. *In English and Hindi.*

— — Rajya Sabha.

The SECOND chamber: its role in modern legislatures: the twenty-five years of Rajya Sabha; editor: S.S. Bhalerao; published for the Rajya Sabha Secretariat. New Delhi, 1977. pp. 467.

— Politics and government.

BARTON (Sir WILLIAM PELL) The princes of India, with a chapter on Nepal. London, 1934. pp. 327.

The COALITION government: a critical examination of the concept of coalition, the performance of some coalition governments and the future prospects of coalition in India; by Omprakash Deepak [and others]; edited by Saral K. Chatterji. Madras, 1974. pp. 145.

BAKER (CHRISTOPHER JOHN) and WASHBROOK (D.A.) South India: political institutions and political change, 1880-1940. Delhi, 1975. pp. 238.

CENTRE-state relations; by Jacob Eapen [and others]. Bangalore, 1975. pp. 82. *Special issue of 'Religion and Society', vol. 22, no.1, March 1975.*

SOCIETY and religion: essays in honour of M.M. Thomas; edited by Richard W. Taylor. Madras, 1976. pp. 193.

SHAH (GHANSHYAM) Protest movements in two Indian states: a study of the Guyarat and Bihar movements. Delhi, 1977. pp. 171. *bibliogs. (Centre for Social Studies, Surat. Publications. No. 8)*

FRANKEL (FRANCINE R.) India's political economy, 1947-1977: the gradual revolution. Princeton, N.J., [1978]. pp. 600. *bibliog.*

INDIA. Gazetteers Unit. 1978. The gazetteer of India: Indian union. Vol. 4. Administration and public welfare. [New Delhi, 1978]. pp. 812. *bibliog.*

— — 1900- .

The EVOLUTION of Muslim political thought in India...; [edited by] A.M. Zaidi. New Delhi, 1975 in progress.

— — 1919-1947.

BIRLA (GHANSHYAM DASS) Bapu: a unique association. Bombay, 1977. 4 vols. *Correspondence between M.K. Gandhi, G.D. Birla, and others, 1924-1947.*

CHOWDHURI (SATYABRATA RAI) Leftist movements in India: 1917-1947. Columbia, 1977. pp. 313. *bibliog.*

KAURA (UMA) Muslims and Indian nationalism: the emergence of the demand for India's partition, 1928-40. Columbia, Mo., 1977. pp. 223. *bibliog.*

RAMUSACK (BARBARA N.) The princes of India in the twilight of empire: dissolution of a patron-client system, 1914-1939. Columbus, [1978]. pp. 322. *bibliog.*

MOORE (ROBIN JAMES) Churchill, Cripps, and India, 1939-1945. Oxford, 1979. pp. 152.

— — 1947- .

PROBLEMS of Indian democracy; by P.J. Alexander [and others]; (edited by P.D. Devanandan [and] M.M. Thomas). [Bangalore], 1962. pp. 211. *bibliogs. (Christian Institute for the Study of Religion and Society. Social Concerns Series. No. 10)*

SAY not the struggle: essays in honour of A.D. Gorwala; [edited by H.M. Patel]. Delhi, 1976. pp. 328.

SOCIALIST INDIA. Republic Day Number, 1976. The Indira Gandhi decade, 1966-1976. Delhi, 1976. 1 vol. (various pagings). *bibliog.*

DAYAL (JOHN) and BOSE (AJOY) For reasons of state: Delhi under emergency. Delhi, 1977. pp. 239.

GOPAL (RAM) Undemocratic elements in the Indian constitution. Bombay, [1977]. pp. 367.

JAGAT SINGH. Assessment of emergency: propaganda and reality. New Delhi, 1977. pp. 152.

GANI (H.A.) Muslim political issues and national integration. New Delhi, [1978]. pp. 230. *bibliog.*

— Population.

CASSEN (ROBERT H.) India: population, economy, society. London, 1978. pp. 419. *bibliog.*

WEINER (MYRON) Sons of the soil: migration and ethnic conflict in India. Princeton, N.J., [1978]. pp. 383. *bibliogs.*

JOHNSON (BASIL LEONARD CLYDE) India: resources and development. London, 1979. pp. 211. *bibliog.*

— Population policy.

BARNABAS (A.P.) Population control in India: (policy-administration-spread). New Delhi, [1977]. pp. 121. *bibliog.*

INDIA. Department of Family Welfare. 1978. Family welfare programme in India: a brief account. New Delhi, 1978. pp. 22.

— Rural conditions.

RURAL economy and municipal problems of India; by K.P. Bhatnagar [and others]. Kanpur, 1953. pp. 392.

SEN (SUDHIR) Reaping the green revolution: food and jobs for all. New York, [1975]. pp. 397. *bibliog.*

METCALF (THOMAS R.) Land, landlords, and the British Raj: northern India in the nineteenth century. Berkeley, [1979]. pp. 436.

— Social conditions.

O'MALLEY (LEWIS SIDNEY STEWARD) India's social heritage. Oxford, 1934. pp. 194.

CASTE, class and power-structure; by Mumtaz Ali Khan [and others]. Bangalore, 1974. pp. 96. *Special issue of 'Religion and Society', vol. 21, no.3, September 1974.*

INDIA. Gazetteers Unit. 1978. The gazetteer of India: Indian union. Vol. 4. Administration and public welfare. [New Delhi, 1978]. pp. 812. *bibliog.*

MAIN currents in Indian sociology. 3. Cohesion and conflict in modern India; edited by Giri Ray Gupta. New Delhi, [1978]. pp. 324.

RAMUSACK (BARBARA N.) The princes of India in the twilight of empire: dissolution of a patron-client system, 1914-1939. Columbus, [1978]. pp. 322. *bibliog.*

JOHNSON (BASIL LEONARD CLYDE) India: resources and development. London, 1979. pp. 211. *bibliog.*

— — Statistics.

NATIONAL SEMINAR ON SOCIAL STATISTICS, NEW DELHI, 1975. National seminar on social statistics, organized by Central Statistical Organisation: [report and papers presented]. New Delhi, 1977. 2 vols.

— Social history.

ESSAYS concerning the socioeconomic history of Brazil and Portuguese India; edited by Dauril Alden and Warren Dean. Gainesville, 1977. pp. 247.

— Social life and customs.

O'MALLEY (LEWIS SIDNEY STEWARD) India's social heritage. Oxford, 1934. pp. 194.

SCHERMERHORN (RICHARD ALONZO) Ethnic plurality in India. Tucson, [1978]. pp. 369. *bibliogs.*

— Social policy.

CHRISTIAN participation in nation-building: the summing up of a corporate study on rapid social change; compiled by M. M. Thomas. Bangalore, 1960. pp. 325. *bibliog.*

SOCIETY and change: essays in honour of Sachin Chaudhuri; edited by K.S. Krishnaswamy [and others]. Bombay, 1977. pp. 327.

INDIA. Planning Commission. 1978. Draft five year plan, 1978-83. [Delhi], 1978. pp. 276.

INDIA-PAKISTAN CONFLICT, 1971.

INDIA. Ministry of External Affairs. 1972. Bangla Desh and Indo-Pak war: India speaks at the U.N.: speeches by India's External Affairs Minister Shri Swaran Singh and India's Permanent Representative Shri S. Sen at the United Nations. New Delhi, 1972. pp. 129.

INDIAN NATIONAL CONGRESS.

CONGRESS and the Raj: facets of the Indian struggle, 1917-47; edited by D.A. Low. London, 1977. pp. 513.

PANDEY (GYANENDRA) The ascendancy of the Congress in Uttar Pradesh, 1926-34: a study in imperfect mobilization. Delhi, 1978. pp. 245. *bibliog.*

INDIANA

— Economic conditions.

INDIANA'S economic resources and potential...: section III. Transportation; by L.L. Waters [and] Charles Thomas Moore. [Bloomington, Ind.], 1955. fo. 110.

INDIANAPOLIS

— Social history — Sources.

FLETCHER (CALVIN) The diary of Calvin Fletcher, vol.5, 1853-1856, including letters to and from Calvin Fletcher; edited by Gayle Thornbrough [and others]. Indianapolis, 1977. pp. 662.

INDIANS, TREATMENT OF

— America, Latin.

SHERMAN (WILLIAM L.) Forced native labor in sixteenth-century Central America. Lincoln, Neb., 1979. pp. 496. *bibliog.*

— Bolivia.

LEWIS (NORMAN) Eastern Bolivia: the white promised land. Copenhagen, 1978. pp. 27. *(International Work Group for Indigenous Affairs. Documents. 31)*

— Brazil.

MIGLIAZZA (ERNEST C.) The integration of the indigenous peoples of the territory of Roraima, Brazil. Copenhagen, 1978. pp. 29. *bibliog. (International Work Group for Indigenous Affairs. Documents. 32)*

INDIANS, TREATMENT OF (Cont.)

— Guatemala.

GUATEMALA 1978: the massacre at Panzos. Copenhagen, 1978. pp. 58. *(International Work Group for Indigenous Affairs. Documents. 33)*

INDIANS OF CENTRAL AMERICA

— Guatemala.

GUATEMALA 1978: the massacre at Panzos. Copenhagen, 1978. pp. 58. *(International Work Group for Indigenous Affairs. Documents. 33)*

INDIANS OF MEXICO

— Education.

AGUIRRE BELTRAN (GONZALO) Teoria y practica de la educacion indigena. Mexico, Secretaria de Educacion Publica, 1973. pp. 284. *(Sep/Setentas. 64)*

— Medicine.

ROYS (RALPH LOVELAND) The ethno-botany of the Maya; with a new introduction and supplemental bibliography by Sheila Cosminsky. Philadelphia, 1976. pp. 380. *bibliog. (Institute for the Study of Human Issues. ISHI Reprints on Latin America and the Caribbean)* Reprint of the edition of 1931.

— Social conditions.

RECK (GREGORY G.) In the shadow of Tlaloc: life in a Mexican village. Harmondsworth, 1978. pp. 224.

— Wars.

POWELL (PHILIP WAYNE) Mexico's Miguel Caldera: the taming of America's first frontier, 1548-1597. Tucson, 1977. pp. 322. *bibliog.*

INDIANS OF NORTH AMERICA.

BOWDEN (CHARLES) Killing the hidden waters. Austin, [1977]. pp. 174. *bibliog.*

— Legal status, laws, etc.

AMERICAN Indians and the law; edited by Lawrence Rosen. New Brunswick, 1978. pp. 223.

MEDCALF (LINDA) Law and identity: lawyers, native Americans and legal practice. Beverly Hills, [1978]. pp. 211. *bibliog.*

— Urban residence.

SORKIN (ALAN L.) The urban American Indian. Lexington, Mass., [1978]. pp. 158.

— Arizona.

KELLEY (JANE HOLDEN) Yaqui women: contemporary life histories. Lincoln, Neb., [1978]. pp. 265. *bibliog.*

— Canada.

RAY (ARTHUR J.) and FREEMAN (DONALD B.) 'Give us good measure': an economic analysis of relations between the Indians and the Hudson's Bay Company before 1763. Toronto, [1978]. pp. 298. *bibliog.*

— — Reservations.

LITHMAN (YNGVE GEORG) The community apart: a case study of a Canadian Indian reserve community. Stockholm, 1978. pp. 239. *bibliog. (Stockholms Universitet. Socialantropologiska Institutionen. Stockholm Studies in Social Anthropology. 6)*

— — British Columbia — Employment.

KNIGHT (ROLF) Indians at work: an informal history of native Indian labour in British Columbia, 1858-1930. Vancouver, [1978]. pp. 317. *bibliog.*

— — Nova Scotia — Government relations.

NOVA SCOTIA. Tripartite Committee, Indian Affairs. 1975. A guide to Nova Scotia government services for native peoples. [Halifax], 1975. pp. 150.

— New Mexico.

CRAMPTON (CHARLES GREGORY) The Zunis of Cibola. Salt Lake City, [1977]. pp. 201. *bibliog.*

— United States.

AMERICAN ACADEMY OF POLITICAL AND SOCIAL SCIENCE. Annals. vol. 436. American Indians today; special editors of this volume J. Milton Yinger and George Eaton Simpson. Philadelphia, 1978. pp. 211.

— — Government relations — Bibliography.

PRUCHA (FRANCIS PAUL) compiler. United States Indian policy: a critical bibliography. Bloomington, Ind., [1977]. pp. 54. *(Newberry Library Center for the History of the American Indian. Bibliographical Series)*

INDIANS OF SOUTH AMERICA

— Amazon Valley.

WHITTEN (NORMAN E.) Amazonian Ecuador: an ethnic interface in ecological, social and ideological perspectives. Copenhagen, 1978. pp. 80. *bibliog. (International Work Group for Indigenous Affairs. Documents. 34)*

— Bolivia.

APAZA (JULIO TUMIRI) ed. The Indian Liberation and Social Rights Movement in Kollasuyu (Bolivia). Copenhagen, [1978]. pp. 67. *(International Work Group for Indigenous Affairs. Documents. 30)*

LEWIS (NORMAN) Eastern Bolivia: the white promised land. Copenhagen, 1978. pp. 27. *(International Work Group for Indigenous Affairs. Documents. 31)*

— Brazil.

BALDUS (HERBERT) Ensaios de etnologia brasileira. São Paulo, 1937. pp. 346. *bibliog.*

— — Economic conditions.

MIGLIAZZA (ERNEST C.) The integration of the indigenous peoples of the territory of Roraima, Brazil. Copenhagen, 1978. pp. 29. *bibliog. (International Work Group for Indigenous Affairs. Documents. 32)*

— Ecuador.

WHITTEN (NORMAN E.) Amazonian Ecuador: an ethnic interface in ecological, social and ideological perspectives. Copenhagen, 1978. pp. 80. *bibliog. (International Work Group for Indigenous Affairs. Documents. 34)*

INDIVIDUALISM.

FROM contract to community: political theory at the crossroads; edited by Fred R. Dallmayr. New York, [1978]. pp. 172. *Based on a lecture series held at Purdue University's Department of Political Science during the academic year 1974-1975.*

INDOCHINA

— Foreign relations.

MIKHEEV (IURII IAKOVLEVICH) Indokitai: put' k miru: indokitaiskie problemy v svete sovremennogo mezhdunarodnogo prava. Moskva, 1977. pp. 296.

— — United States.

ZASLOFF (JOSEPH JEREMIAH) and BROWN (MACALISTER) Communist Indochina and U.S. foreign policy: postwar realities. Boulder, Colo., 1978. pp. 221. *bibliog.*

— History.

MIKHEEV (IURII IAKOVLEVICH) Indokitai: put' k miru: indokitaiskie problemy v svete sovremennogo mezhdunarodnogo prava. Moskva, 1977. pp. 296.

— Politics and government.

ZASLOFF (JOSEPH JEREMIAH) and BROWN (MACALISTER) Communist Indochina and U.S. foreign policy: postwar realities. Boulder, Colo., 1978. pp. 221. *bibliog.*

INDONESIA.

INDONESIAN NEWS; issued by the Information Department, Embassy of the Republic of Indonesia...London. m. London. *Current issues only kept.*

— Armed forces — Political activity.

CROUCH (HAROLD) The army and politics in Indonesia. Ithaca, 1978. pp. 377. *bibliog.*

— Colonization.

INDONESIA: selected documents on colonialism and nationalism, 1830-1942; edited and translated by Chr. L.M. Penders. St. Lucia, Queensland, 1977. pp. 367.

— Commerce — New Zealand.

NEW ZEALAND. Department of Trade and Industry. Trade Services Division. 1978. Indonesia: [a market profile]. [Wellington, 1978]. fo. 39. *(Background to Exports)*

— Economic conditions.

NEW ZEALAND. Department of Trade and Industry. Trade Services Division. 1978. Indonesia: [a market profile]. [Wellington, 1978]. fo. 39. *(Background to Exports)*

— Economic policy.

INDONESIA. Department of Information. 1974. The second five-year development plan, 1974/5-1978/79. [Jakarta, 1974]. 4 vols.

— Foreign relations — Malaysia.

MACKIE (J.A.C.) Konfrontasi: the Indonesia-Malaysia dispute, 1963-1966. Kuala Lumpur, 1974. pp. 368. *bibliog. Published for the Australian Institute of International Affairs.*

— History — 1798-1942 — Sources.

INDONESIA: selected documents on colonialism and nationalism, 1830-1942; edited and translated by Chr. L.M. Penders. St. Lucia, Queensland, 1977. pp. 367.

— Nationalism.

INDONESIA: selected documents on colonialism and nationalism, 1830-1942; edited and translated by Chr. L.M. Penders. St. Lucia, Queensland, 1977. pp. 367.

— Politics and government.

MACKIE (J.A.C.) Konfrontasi: the Indonesia-Malaysia dispute, 1963-1966. Kuala Lumpur, 1974. pp. 368. *bibliog. Published for the Australian Institute of International Affairs.*

SURYADINATA (LEO) Peranakan Chinese politics in Java, 1917-42. [Singapore, 1976]. pp. 184. *bibliog.*

INDONESIA: selected documents on colonialism and nationalism, 1830-1942; edited and translated by Chr. L.M. Penders. St. Lucia, Queensland, 1977. pp. 367.

CROUCH (HAROLD) The army and politics in Indonesia. Ithaca, 1978. pp. 377. *bibliog.*

— Social policy.

INDONESIA. Department of Information. 1974. The second five-year development plan, 1974/5-1978/79. [Jakarta, 1974]. 4 vols.

INDUSTRIAL AND COMMERCIAL WORKERS' UNION OF AFRICA.

WICKINS (PETER L.) The Industrial and Commercial Workers' Union of Africa. Cape Town, 1978. pp. 222. *bibliog.*

INDUSTRIAL CAPACITY

— United Kingdom.

PANIĆ (M.) Capacity utilisation in UK manufacturing industry. London, National Economic Development Office, 1978. pp. 125. *(Discussion Papers. 5)*

INDUSTRIAL CONCENTRATION

— Mathematical models.

LINDA (REMO) Methodology of concentration analysis applied to the study of industries and markets. [Brussels], European Communities, 1976. pp. 156.

HART (P.E.) Redundant inequalities. London, [1978]. pp. 22. bibliog. *(National Institute of Economic and Social Research. Discussion Papers. No. 18)*

— Belgium.

HALLET (M. JACQUES) Etude sur l'évolution de la concentration dans l'industrie alimentaire en Belgique. [Brussels], Communautés Européennes, 1975. pp. 93.

SOCIÉTÉ STUDIA. Etude sur l'évolution de la concentration dans l'industrie pharmaceutique en Belgique. [Brussels], Communautés Européennes, 1975. pp. 111.

SOCIÉTÉ STUDIA. Etude sur l'évolution de la concentration dans quelques sous- secteurs de l'industrie du textile en Belgique, mise à jour 1968-1972,...laine...coton...bonneterie, etc. [Brussels], Communautés Européennes, 1975. pp. 89.

JACQUEMIN (ALEXIS) and GHELLINCK (ELIZABETH DE) L'évolution de la concentration dans l'industrie de la brasserie et des boissons en Belgique. [Brussels], Communautés Européennes, 1976. pp. 108.

— Denmark.

INSTITUTE FOR FUTURES STUDIES. A study of the evolution of concentration in the Danish food distribution industry, etc. [Brussels], European Communities, 1976. pp. 292.

— France.

BLUNDEN (KATHERINE) Etude sur l'évolution de la concentration dans l'industrie pharmaceutique en France. [Brussels], Communautés Européennes, 1975. pp. 126.

DELANOE (GUIREC) Etude sur l'évolution de la concentration dans l'industrie du textile en France: coton...laine, etc. [Brussels], Communautés Européennes, 1975. pp. 201.

RASTOIN (J.L.) and others. Etude sur l'évolution de la concentration dans l'industrie alimentaire en France...(tableaux de concentration). [Brussels], Communautés Européennes, 1975. 2 vols.(in 1) .

RASTOIN (J.-L.) and others. L'évolution de la concentration dans l'industrie de la brasserie en France. [Brussels], Communautés Européennes, 1975. pp. 99.

BOULET (D.) and LAPORTE (J.P.) Etude sur l'évolution de la concentration dans les industries des boissons et des boissons non alcoolisées en France. [Brussels], Communautés Européennes, 1976. pp. 284.

BOULET (D.) and LAPORTE (J.P.) Etude sur l'évolution de la concentration dans l'industrie des spiritueux en France, etc. [Brussels], Communautés Européennes, 1976. pp. 163.

ETUDE sur l'évolution de la concentration dans la distribution des produits alimentaires en France. [Bruxelles], Communautés Européennes, 1976. pp. 213.

RASTOIN (J.-L.) and others. L'évolution de la concentration dans l'industrie des champagnes et mousseux en France, etc. [Brussels], Communautés Européennes, 1976. pp. 127.

J.R.R.S. INTERNATIONAL. Déconcentration industrielle et productivité [et si on produisait mieux en concentrant moins...; etude réalisée pour le Ministère de l'Industrie, du Commerce et de l'Artisanat. [Paris, 1977]. pp. 113. *(Etudes de Politique Industrielle. 19)*

THALY (SUZANNE) Etude sur l'évolution de la concentration dans l'industrie des pâtes, papiers et cartons en France. [Brussels], Communautés Européennes, 1977. pp. 194.

FRANCE. Ministère de l'Industrie. Service du Traitement de l'Information et des Statistiques Industrielles. 1979. La concentration des entreprises industrielles de 1972 à 1976. Paris, [1979]. pp. 243. *(Traits Fondamentaux du Système Industriel Français. Recueils Statistiques. Publication no. 13)*

— Germany.

BREITENACHER (MICHAEL) Untersuchung zur Konzentrationsentwicklung in ausgewählten Branchen und Produktgruppen der Ernährungsindustrie in Deutschland. [Brussels], Europäischen Gemeinschaften, 1976. pp. 331.

BREITENACHER (MICHAEL) Untersuchung zur Konzentrationsentwicklung in der Getränke Industrie in Deutschland. [Brussels], Europäischen Gemeinschaften, 1976. pp. 156.

GREIPL (ERICH) and WUERL (DIETER) Untersuchung zur Konzentrationsentwicklung in der Nahrungsmitteldistribution in Deutschland. [Brussels], Europäischen Gemeinschaften, 1976. pp. 307.

KIENBAUM UNTERNEHMENSBERATUNG. Untersuchung zur Konzentrationsentwicklung in der Reifenindustrie sowie ein Branchenbild der Kraftfahrzeug-Elektrikindustrie in Deutschland. [Brussels], Europäischen Gemeinschaften, 1976. pp. 190.

KIENBAUM UNTERNEHMENSBERATUNG. Untersuchung zur Konzentrationsentwicklung in verschiedenen Untersektoren der Papier- und Pappeindustrie in Deutschland: Herstellung,...Verarbeitung, etc. [Brussels], Europäischen Gemeinschaften, 1976. pp. 88.

GERMANY (BUNDESREPUBLIK). Monopolkommission. 1978. Fortschreitende Konzentration bei Grossunternehmen: (Hauptgutachten 1976/1977). Baden-Baden, 1978. pp. 659. *(Hauptgutachten. 2)*

— Ireland (Republic).

EIRE. Restrictive Practices Commission. 1976. Report of studies into industrial concentration and mergers in Ireland. Dublin, [1976]. pp. 132. bibliog.

— Italy.

BALLIANO (PIERA) and others. Studio sull'evoluzione della concentrazione nell'industria cotoniera Italiana, etc. [Brussels], Comunità Europee, 1975. pp. 149.

AMADUZZI (ANTONIO) and others. Studio sull'evoluzione della concentrazione industriale in Italia, 1968-1974: pneumatici, candele, accumulatori. [Brussels], Comunità Europee, 1976. pp. 341.

BALLIANO (PIERA) and LANZETTI (RENATO) Studio sull'evoluzione della concentrazione dell'industria cartaria in Italia. [Brussels], Comunità Europee, 1976. pp. 189.

BALLIANO (PIERA) and LANZETTI (RENATO) Studio sull'evoluzione della concentrazione nel settore della costruzione di macchine per l'industria tessile in Italia. [Brussels], Comunità Europee, 1976. pp. 159.

BALLIANO (PIERA) and LANZETTI (RENATO) Studio sull'evoluzione della concentrazione nell'industria delle bevande in Italia. [Brussels], Comunità Europee, 1976. pp. 143.

BALLIANO (PIERA) and MOSINI (FILIPPO) Studio sull'evoluzione della concentrazione nel settore della costruzione di macchine per ufficio in Italia. [Brussels], Comunità Europee, 1976. pp. 149.

BALLIANO (PIERA) and LANZETTI (RENATO) Studio sull'evoluzione della concentrazione dei prodotti alimentari in Italia, etc. [Brussels], Comunità Europee, [1977]. pp. 189.

— Netherlands.

JONG (HENDRIK WOUTER DE) and LANGE (R. DE) A study of the evolution of concentration in the pharmaceutical industry in the Netherlands. [Brussels], European Communities, 1975. pp. 115.

BROUWER (MARIA) and PIJNAPPEL (THEO) A study of the evolution of concentration in the Dutch beverages industry. [Brussels], European Communities, 1976. pp. 149.

BROUWER (W.J.C.) and STEIJN (T.N.) A study of the evolution of concentration in the Dutch paper products industry. [Brussels], European Communities, 1976. pp. 89.

— United Kingdom.

A STUDY of the evolution of concentration in the pharmaceutical industry for the United Kingdom; by...J.B. Heath and [others], etc. [Brussels], European Communities, 1975. pp. 168.

FISHWICK (FRANCIS) A study of the evolution of concentration in the manufacture and supply of tyres, sparking plugs, and motor-vehicle accumulators for the United Kingdom. [Brussels], European Communities, 1977. pp. 119.

UTTON (MICHAEL A.) Diversification and competition. Cambridge, 1979. pp. 113. *(National Institute of Economic and Social Research. Occasional Papers. 31)*

— United States.

KATZ (HAROLD) The decline of competition in the automobile industry, 1920-1940. New York, 1977. pp. 504. bibliog.

INDUSTRIAL DISTRICTS

— United Kingdom — Wales.

PERCIVAL (GEOFFREY) The government's industrial estates in Wales, 1936-1975. [Pontypridd], Welsh Development Agency Information Department, [1978]. 1 vol. (various foliations).

INDUSTRIAL EQUIPMENT LEASES.

CLARK (TOM M.) Leasing. London, [1978]. pp. 307. bibliog.

INDUSTRIAL HYGIENE

— United Kingdom.

EMPLOYMENT MEDICAL ADVISORY SERVICE [U.K.]. Occupational health services: the way ahead. London, H.M.S.O., 1977 repr. 1978. pp. 26. *At head of title: Prevention and health.*

U.K. Equal Opportunities Commission. 1979. Health and safety legislation: should we distinguish between men and women?; report and recommendations of the...Commission. [Manchester], 1979. pp. 153.

— — Bibliography.

U.K. Health and Safety Executive. 1979. Publications catalogue '79. London, 1979. pp. 107.

— United States.

MENDELOFF (JOHN) Regulating safety: an economic and political analysis of occupational safety and health policy. Cambridge, Mass., [1979]. pp. 219. bibliog.

INDUSTRIAL LAWS AND LEGISLATION

— Russia.

ANDRIANOV (NIKOLAI IVANOVICH) Pravovye voprosy deiatel'nosti proizvodstvennykh ob"edinenii. Kiev, 1977. pp. 144.

— Salvador.

SALVADOR. Statutes, etc. 1961. Law for industrial promotion and reforms. San Salvador, [1962 repr. 1970]. pp. 25.

INDUSTRIAL MANAGEMENT.

INDUSTRIAL MANAGEMENT.

PRODUCTIVITY DIGEST: review of literatures on productivity and its related fields; [pd.by] Asian Productivity Organization. q. D 1968(v.4, no.4)- , with gaps (Oc 1969, v.5, no.3; Oc 1970, v.6, no.2, D 1970, v.6, no.3). Tokyo.

TIVEY (LEONARD J.) The politics of the firm. Oxford, 1978. pp. 196. bibliog.

— Japan.

ARAI (SHUNZO) An intersection of East and West: Japanese business management. Tokyo, [1971]. pp. 212.

CLARK (RODNEY C.) The Japanese company. New Haven, 1979. pp. 282. bibliog.

— Russia.

AVDAKOV (IURII KONSTANTINOVICH) and BORODIN (VLADIMIR VASIL'EVICH) USSR: state industry during the transition period. Moscow, 1977. pp. 300. Based on their "Proizvodstvennye ob"edineniia..."

— United States.

KAUFMAN (HERBERT) The forest ranger: a study in administrative behavior. Baltimore, 1960 repr.1967. pp. 259.

INDUSTRIAL ORGANIZATION.

PARENT (JEAN) Les firmes industrielles. Paris, [1975-78]. 2 vols. bibliog.

The BUSINESS system: a bicentennial view; [by] Milton Friedman [and others]. Hanover, N.H., 1977. pp. 91. Symposium to celebrate the 75th anniversary of the Amos Tuck School of Business Administration, Dartmouth College.

NEEDHAM (DOUGLAS) The economics of industrial structure: conduct and performance. London, [1978]. pp. 320. bibliogs.

SHEPHERD (WILLIAM G.) The economics of industrial organization. Englewood Cliffs, N.J. [1979]. pp. 463.

— Research.

RESEARCH needs in work organisation: a Working Party report to the Management and Industrial Relations Committee (of the Social Science Research Council); [Richard Brown chairman]. [London], Social Science Research Council, [1978]. pp. 96.

— France.

FERNIOT (BERNARD) La décentralisation industrielle. Paris, 1976. pp. 99.

— Japan.

SHIMIZU (RYUEI) Appraisal of organization effectiveness: referring mainly to a survey...on 260 firms in Japan. Tokyo, 1978. pp. 89.

— Russia.

ADAMS (JAN S.) Citizen inspectors in the Soviet Union: the People's Control Committee. New York, 1977. pp. 232. bibliog.

OB"EDINENIIA v promyshlennosti; pod redaktsiei Iu.M. Kozlova. Moskva, 1978. pp. 254.

— — Tajikistan.

KLETSEL'MAN (UL'IAN KHAIMOVICH) Formirovanie i razvitie promyshlennykh kompleksov v Tadzhikskoi SSR. Dushanbe, 1977. pp. 70.

— — Ukraine.

GANCHEV (IVAN DMITRIEVICH) Rezervy brigadnogo podriada. Moskva, 1978. pp. 80. (Bibliotechka Profsoiuznogo Aktivista. 31)

— United Kingdom.

SCHUMACHER (CHRISTIAN) The end of an era: calls for new departures. Wellingborough, [1977]. pp. 27. (Scott Bader Commonwealth Centre. Commonwealth Monographs. No.8)

CLOTHING AND ALLIED PRODUCTS INDUSTRY TRAINING BOARD [U.K.]. Self-organised groups: a study of their introduction in one clothing company and what it might mean for others. [Leeds, 1978]. pp. 28.

HULL (DARYLL) The shop stewards' guide to work organisation. Nottingham, 1978. pp. 130.

INDUSTRIAL PROMOTION.

UNIDO NEWSLETTER; [pd. by] United Nations Industrial Development Organization. m,(formerly bi-m.), Je 1967 (no.1)- New York.

— Argentine Republic — Formosa.

FORMOSA (PROVINCE, ARGENTINE REPUBLIC). Ministerio de Economia. 1967. Regimen de promocion y franquicias para las inversiones en la Provincia de Formosa. [Formosa], 1967. pp. 241.

— Australia — New South Wales.

NEW SOUTH WALES. Department of Decentralisation and Development. 1968. The policy and work of the Department of Decentralisation and Development. [Sydney, 1968]. fo. 4.

— Belize.

BELIZE. 1967. Investment opportunities. [Belize City], 1967. pp. 34.

— Canada — Alberta.

ALBERTA. Department of Business Development and Tourism. Annual report. a., 1976/77- Edmonton.

ALBERTA OPPORTUNITY COMPANY. Annual report. a., 1977/78- Edmonton.

— — Newfoundland.

NEWFOUNDLAND AND LABRADOR DEVELOPMENT CORPORATION LTD. Annual report. a., 1976/77- St. John's.

— — Prince Edward Island.

PRINCE EDWARD ISLAND. Department of Industry and Commerce. 1977. Industrial assistance: Prince Edward Island. [Charlottetown, 1977]. pp. 36.

— India — Andhra Pradesh.

ANDHRA PRADESH. State Evaluation Committee. 1967. Study on the working of the rural industries projects in Andhra Pradesh. Hyderabad, [1967]. pp. 41. (Evaluation Studies. No. 25)

— Italy.

ITALY. [Cassa per Opere Straordinarie di Pubblico Interesse nell'Italia Meridionale]. 1978. Rapporto sullo stato di attuazione dei programmi ai sensi della legge 2 maggio 1976 n. 183. [Rome], 1978. 3 vols. (in 1).

— Kenya.

INDUSTRY IN KENYA: newsletter of the Development Finance Company of Kenya. m., current issues only. Nairobi.

— Malawi.

MALAWI. Ministry of Trade, Industry and Tourism. 1973. Industrial promotion in Malawi; a guide for prospective investors. Blantyre, 1973. pp. 23.

— Salvador.

SALVADOR. Statutes, etc. 1961. Law for industrial promotion and reforms. San Salvador, [1962 repr. 1970]. pp. 25.

SALVADOR. Statutes, etc. 1961. Ley de creacion del Instituto Salvadoreño de Fomento Industrial. San Salvador, 1962. pp. 37.

— United Kingdom — Ireland, Northern.

IRELAND, NORTHERN. Department of Commerce. Advances to the Northern Ireland Development Agency...: account of the receipts and payments of the Department of Commerce under schedule 2 to the Industries Development: Northern Ireland Order 1976...together with the report of the Comptroller and Auditor-General thereon. a., 1976/77- Belfast.

— — Scotland.

SCOTLAND. Scottish Economic Planning Department. 1976. Scottish Development Agency: industrial investment guidelines. Edinburgh, 1976. fo. 11, 2.

SCOTTISH DEVELOPMENT AGENCY. Finance and development aid for industry. [Glasgow, 1976?]. pp. (4).

— — Wales.

PERCIVAL (GEOFFREY) The government's industrial estates in Wales, 1936-1975. [Pontypridd], Welsh Development Agency Information Department, [1978]. 1 vol. (various foliations).

INDUSTRIAL PSYCHIATRY.

MISFITS in industry; edited by Pasquale A. Carone [and others]. New York, [1978]. pp. 152. Based on the proceedings of the seventh annual conference on the problems of industrial psychiatric medicine, Stony Brook, 1977.

INDUSTRIAL RELATIONS.

KING (CHARLES D.) Writer on industrial relations, and VALL (MARINUS VAN DE) Models of industrial democracy: consultation, co-determination and workers' management. The Hague, [1978]. pp. 218. bibliog.

MILLS (DANIEL QUINN) Labor-management relations. New York, [1978]. pp. 438.

REYNOLDS (LLOYD GEORGE) Labor economics and abor relations. 7th ed. Englewood Cliffs, [1978]. pp. 651. bibliogs.

INDUSTRIAL relations: a social psychological approach; edited by Geoffrey M. Stephenson and Christopher J. Brotherton. Chichester, [1979]. pp. 412. bibliog.

TOWARDS industrial democracy: Europe, Japan and the United States; edited by Benjamin C. Roberts. London, [1979]. pp. 287.

— Dictionaries and encyclopedias.

MARSH (ARTHUR IVOR) Concise encyclopedia of industrial relations. Farnborough, [1978]. pp. 423. bibliog.

— Africa.

AFRICAN labor history; Peter C.W. Gutkind [and others], editors. Beverly Hills, [1978]. pp. 280. bibliogs.

— Canada.

LEVANT (VICTOR) Capital and labour: partners: two classes - two views. Toronto, 1977. pp. 276. bibliog.

— France.

HAINSWORTH (RAYMOND EDWIN) The trade union movements and labour-management relations in the coal mines of the Nord and Pas-de-Calais departments of France during the depression of 1930-1936. 1978. fo. 587. bibliog. Typescript. Ph.D. (London) thesis: unpublished. This thesis is the property of London University and may not be removed from the Library.

MARSDEN (DAVID) Industrial democracy and industrial control in West Germany, France and Great Britain. [London], 1978. pp. 70. (U.K. Department of Employment. Research Papers. No. 4)

STEARNS (PETER N.) Paths to authority: the middle class and the industrial labor force in France, 1820-48. Urbana, Ill., [1978]. pp. 222. bibliog.

— **Germany.**

MARSDEN (DAVID) Industrial democracy and industrial control in West Germany, France and Great Britain. [London], 1978. pp. 70. *(U.K. Department of Employment. Research Papers. No. 4)*

WALLRAFF (GUENTER) Wallraff: the undesirable journalist; [a selection of articles] translated by Steve Gooch and Paul Knight. London, 1978. pp. 180.

— **Japan.**

CLARK (RODNEY C.) The Japanese company. New Haven, 1979. pp. 282. *bibliog.*

— **Russia.**

VELICHKO (ANATOLII NIKOLAEVICH) and PODMARKOV (VALENTIN GEORGIEVICH) Sotsiolog na predpriiatii. 2nd ed. Moskva, 1976. pp. 240.

PROKOPENKO (VOLODYMYR IVANOVYCH) Pravovye otnosheniia komiteta profsoiuza s administratsiei sotsialisticheskogo predpriiatiia. Kiev, 1977. pp. 159.

— **Senegal.**

BLOCH (PETER C.) Labor relations in Senegal: history, institutions and perspectives. Ann Arbor, Mich., 1978. pp. 41. *bibliog.* *(Michigan University. Center for Research on Economic Development. Discussion Papers. No. 72)*

— **United Kingdom.**

ADVISORY, CONCILIATION AND ARBITRATION SERVICE [U.K.]. Advice on personnel management and industrial relations practices. London, [1977?]. pp. 7.

ANTHONY (PETER) The conduct of industrial relations. London, 1977. pp. 327. *bibliog.*

DEVELOPING employee relations; [by] Peter Warr [and others]. Farnborough, Hants, [1978]. pp. 197.

DROMEY (JACK) and TAYLOR (GRAHAM) of Brent Trades Council. Grunwick: the workers' story. London, 1978. pp. 207.

HULL (DARYLL) The shop stewards' guide to work organisation. Nottingham, 1978. pp. 130.

MARSDEN (DAVID) Industrial democracy and industrial control in West Germany, France and Great Britain. [London], 1978. pp. 70. *(U.K. Department of Employment. Research Papers. No. 4)*

The CONTROL of work; edited by John Purcell and Robin Smith. London, 1979. pp. 184. *bibliogs.*

CROUCH (COLIN) The politics of industrial relations. [London], 1979. pp. 223. *bibliog.*

McCORMICK (BRIAN JOSEPH) Industrial relations in the coal industry. London, 1979. pp. 263. *bibliog.*

— — **Bibliography.**

BAIN (GEORGE SAYERS) and WOOLVEN (GILLIAN B.) compilers. A bibliography of British industrial relations. Cambridge, 1979. pp. 665.

— — **Study and teaching.**

U.K. Social Science Research Council. Bursary scheme. a. London. *Current issues only kept.*

— **United States.**

LEVANT (VICTOR) Capital and labour: partners: two classes - two views. Toronto, 1977. pp. 276. *bibliog.*

MILLS (DANIEL QUINN) Labor-management relations. New York, [1978]. pp. 438.

INDUSTRIAL SAFETY

— **Ireland (Republic).**

EIRE. Department of Labour. Labour inspection: report...of Industrial Inspectorate and General Inspectorate. a., 1977- Dublin.

— **United Kingdom.**

U.K. Equal Opportunities Commission. 1979. Health and safety legislation: should we distinguish between men and women?; report and recommendations of the...Commission. [Manchester], 1979. pp. 153.

— — **Bibliography.**

U.K. Health and Safety Executive. 1979. Publications catalogue '79. London, 1979. pp. 107.

— **United States.**

MENDELOFF (JOHN) Regulating safety: an economic and political analysis of occupational safety and health policy. Cambridge, Mass., [1979]. pp. 219. *bibliog.*

INDUSTRIAL SOCIOLOGY.

SINGELMANN (JOACHIN) From agriculture to services: the transformation of industrial employment. Beverly Hills, [1978]. pp. 175. *bibliog.*

BURRELL (GIBSON) and MORGAN (GARETH) Sociological paradigms and organisational analysis: elements of the sociology of corporate life. London, 1979. pp. 432. *bibliog.*

ETHNICITY at work; edited by Sandra Wallman. London, 1979. pp. 252. *bibliog.*

— **France.**

ROSE (MICHAEL) Servants of post-industrial power?: sociologie du travail in modern France. London, 1979. pp. 226. *bibliog.*

— **Russia.**

VELICHKO (ANATOLII NIKOLAEVICH) and PODMARKOV (VALENTIN GEORGIEVICH) Sotsiolog na predpriiatii. 2nd ed. Moskva, 1976. pp. 240.

INDUSTRIAL STATISTICS.

YEARBOOK OF INDUSTRIAL STATISTICS (formerly Growth of world industry, The); [pd. by] Statistical Office, Department of Economic and Social Affairs, United Nations. [in English and French]. a., 1967 [1st issue]- New York.

ORGANISATION FOR ECONOMIC CO-OPERATION AND DEVELOPMENT. Industrial production. q., 1967-1978(3rd q.); ceased pbln. Paris. *Supplement to* ORGANISATION FOR ECONOMIC CO-OPERATION AND DEVELOPMENT. Main economic indicators. *File includes Historical statistics; 1955/1964, 1955/1971, 1957/1966, 1959/1969, 1966/1975.*

VOLLE (MICHEL) Eléments pour une histoire de la statistique industrielle. Paris, Institut National de la Statistique et des Etudes Economiques, 1978. pp. 373.

ORGANISATION FOR ECONOMIC CO-OPERATION AND DEVELOPMENT. Indicators of industrial activity. q., 1979 [preliminary issue]- Paris. *Supersedes* ORGANISATION FOR ECONOMIC CO-OPERATION AND DEVELOPMENT. Industrial production.

BROWN (C.J.F.) and SHERIFF (TOM D.) De-industrialisation in the UK: background statistics. London, [1979]. pp. 33. *(National Institute of Economic and Social Research. Discussion Papers. No. 23)*

INDUSTRIAL WORKERS OF THE WORLD.

DE CAUX (LEN) The living spirit of the Wobblies. New York, 1978. pp. 156. *bibliog.*

INDUSTRIALIZATION.

HARRISON (FRED) B.A., M.Sc. Marx, economic growth and land taxation. London, 1975. pp. 27. *(Economic and Social Science Research Association. Discussion Papers. No. 2)*

SINGER (HANS WOLFGANG) and STEPHENSON (JULIETTE) The expansion of processing in developing countries and international policy requirements. London, Commonwealth Secretariat, 1978. pp. 80. *bibliog.* *(Commonwealth Economic Papers. No. 10)*

The NEWLY industrialising countries and the adjustment problem; report by a Working Group. London, Foreign and Commonwealth Office, 1979. pp. 57, 39. *(Government Economic Service Working Papers. No. 18)*

INDUSTRIEGEWERKSCHAFT METALL FÜR DIE BUNDESREPUBLIK DEUTSCHLAND.

MEYER (REGINE) Streik und Aussperrung in der Metallindustrie: Analyse der Streikbewegung in Nordwürttemberg-Nordbaden, 1971. Marburg, [1977]. pp. 426. *bibliog.* *(Studiengesellschaft für Sozialgeschichte und Arbeiterbewegung, Marburg. Schriftenreihe für Sozialgeschichte und Arbeiterbewegung. Band 4)*

WEISS (MANFRED) Gewerkschaftliche Vertrauensleute: tarifvertragliche Verbesserungen ihrer Arbeit im Betrieb. Köln, [1978]. pp. 109. *(Otto Brenner Stiftung. Schriftenreihe. 11)*

INDUSTRIES, LOCATION OF.

SPATIAL analysis, industry and the industrial environment: progress in research and applications. Vol. 1. Industrial systems; edited by F.E. Ian Hamilton and G.J.R. Linge. Chichester, [1979]. pp. 289. *bibliog.*

— **Mathematical models.**

CARLINO (GERALD A.) Economics of scale in manufacturing location: theory and measure. Leiden, 1978. pp. 112. *bibliog.*

— **Australia — New South Wales.**

NEW SOUTH WALES. Department of Decentralisation and Development. 1966. Decentralisation: the implications for government and people; by John B. Fuller, Minister for Decentralisation and Development, etc. [Sydney, 1966?]. fo. 11.

NEW SOUTH WALES. Department of Decentralisation and Development. 1967. A new way of life for industry. [Sydney, 1967]. pp. 12.

NEW SOUTH WALES. Department of Decentralisation and Development. 1968. The policy and work of the Department of Decentralisation and Development. [Sydney, 1968]. fo. 4.

— **France.**

FERNIOT (BERNARD) La décentralisation industrielle. Paris, 1976. pp. 99.

J.R.R.S. INTERNATIONAL. Déconcentration industrielle et productivité [et si on produisait mieux en concentrant moins...; etude réalisée pour le Ministère de l'Industrie, du Commerce et de l'Artisanat]. [Paris, 1977]. pp. 113. *(Etudes de Politique Industrielle. 19)*

BACHELARD (PAUL) L'industrialisation de la région Centre: transformations économiques et socio-politiques. [Tours, 1978]. pp. 473. *bibliog.* 19 maps in end pocket.

— **New Zealand.**

THOMSON (JANET) Employment in the suburbs. [Wellington], Town and Country Planning Branch, Ministry of Works, 1969. pp. 8.

TAYLOR (MICHAEL J.) Behavioural considerations in the location of industry in Auckland. [Auckland, Auckland Regional Authority], 1977. pp. 70.

— **Russia.**

BELOUSOV (IVAN IVANOVICH) Osnovy ucheniia ob ekonomicheskom raionirovanii: razmeshchenie i raionirovanie proizvoditel'nykh sil. Moskva, 1976. pp. 320. *bibliog.*

ADAMESKU (ALEKO ALEKSANDROVICH) and BELORUSOV (DMITRII VASIL'EVICH) Razvitie i razmeshchenie proizvoditel'nykh sil SSSR v desiatoi piatiletke. Moskva, 1977. pp. 192.

DOLOTOV (KONSTANTIN ANDREEVICH) and KHARABIBEROV (VIKTOR STEPANOVICH) Mestnaia promyshlennost' i perspektivy ee razvitiia. Moskva, 1977. pp. 192.

INDUSTRIES, LOCATION OF. (Cont.)

METODOLOGICHESKIE i metodicheskie problemy razmeshcheniia otraslei material'nogo proizvodstva. Moskva, 1979. pp. 263. *(Akademiia Nauk SSSR. Problemy Sovetskoi Ekonomiki)*

— — Mathematical models.

PLANIROVANIE razvitiia i razmeshcheniia promyshlennogo proizvodstva: modeli i sistemy. Kiev, 1977. pp. 287. *bibliog.*

— — Ukraine.

PALAMARCHUK (MAKSIM MARTYNOVICH) and others. Mineral'nye resursy i formirovanie promyshlennykh territorial'nykh kompleksov. Kiev, 1978. pp. 219. *bibliog.*

— South Africa.

SOUTH AFRICA. Department of Information. 1968. Taking factories to the people: South Africa's border industry project. [Pretoria, 1968]. pp. 28. *(Fact Paper Series)*

— United Kingdom.

NORTHERN REGION STRATEGY TEAM. Spatial patterns and the development of service industries; (project no. B.1.f). Newcastle-upon-Tyne, 1976. pp. 49. *(Working Papers. No. 8)*

— — Research.

PRIORITIES in industrial location research: report by a working seminar to the S[ocial] S[cience] R[esearch] C[ouncil] 's Human Geography Committee; compiled by P.A. Wood. London, Social Science Research Council, [1978]. pp. 40. *bibliog.*

— United States.

QUANTE (WOLFGANG) The exodus of corporate headquarters from New York city. New York, 1976. pp. 209.

HARPER (ANN K.) The location of the United States steel industry, 1879-1919. New York, 1977. pp. 266. *bibliog.*

INDUSTRIES, SIZE OF.

GORECKI (PAUL KAROL) Economies of scale and efficient plant size in Canadian manufacturing industries. [Ottawa, 1976?]. pp. 111. *bibliog. (Canada. Bureau of Competition Policy. Research Branch. Research Monographs. No. 1)*

NÄSLUND (BERTIL) An analysis of economic size distributions. Berlin, 1977. pp. 100. *bibliog.*

INDUSTRY.

FRANCE. Groupe d'Etudes Prospectives Internationales. 1978. La spécialisation internationale des industries à l'horizon 1985: recherches méthodologiques et scénarios chiffrés à l'échelle mondiale; étude réalisée sous la direction de Michel Courcier [and] Jean Malsot. [Paris, 1978]. pp. 370. *(France. Commissariat Général du Plan. Economie et Planification)*

— Social aspects.

INDUSTRY AND ENVIRONMENT; pd. by the United Nations Environment Programme. q., Oc/D 1978(v.1, no.1)- Paris.

GAMBLING (TREVOR) Beyond the conventions of accounting. London, 1978. pp. 182. *bibliog.*

ETHICAL theory and business; edited by Tom L. Beauchamp, Norman E. Bowie. Englewood Cliffs, N.J., [1979]. pp. 642. *bibliogs.*

— — United Kingdom.

ECONOMIST INTELLIGENCE UNIT. Q[arterly] E[conomic] R[eview] Specials. No. 41. Sponsorship. London, [1977]. pp. 82.

BROWN (DAVID) and HARRISON (MICHAEL J.) A sociology of industrialisation: an introduction. London, 1978. pp. 172. *bibliogs.*

— — United States.

ISSUES in business and society;...[edited by] George A. Steiner [and] John F. Steiner. 2nd ed. New York, [1977]. pp. 560.

ETHICS, free enterprise, and public policy: original essays on moral issues in business; edited by Richard T. de George and Joseph A. Pichler. New York, 1978. pp. 329. *bibliogs.*

POST (JAMES E.) Corporate behavior and social change. Reston, Va., [1978]. pp. 294.

KOCH (FRANK) The new corporate philanthropy: how society and business can profit. New York, [1979]. pp. 305.

INDUSTRY AND EDUCATION.

LUNDGREEN (PETER) Bildung und Wirtschaftswachstum im Industrialisierungsprozess des 19. Jahrhunderts: methodische Ansätze, empirische Studien und internationale Vergleiche. Berlin, [1973]. pp. 182. *bibliog.*

INDUSTRY AND STATE.

KOMOROWSKI (STANISŁAW) Industrial planning. Warsaw, 1976. pp. 91. *(Instytut Gospodarki Krajów Rozwijających Się. Teaching Papers: Advanced Course in National Economic Planning. vol. 23)*

BEDREIGDE democratie?: parlementaire democratie en overheidsbemoeienis in de economie; onder redactie van H. Daudt en E. van der Wolk; met bijdragen van F. Bolkestein [and others]. Assen, 1978. pp. 142.

GALBRAITH (JOHN KENNETH) The new industrial state. 3rd ed. Boston, Mass., 1978. pp. 438.

KINDLEBERGER (CHARLES POOR) Government and international trade. Princeton, 1978. pp. 19. *bibliog. (Princeton University. Department of Economics and Sociology. International Finance Section. Essays in International Finance. No. 129)*

The FUTURE of business: global issues in the 80s and 90s; edited by Max Ways. New York, [1979]. pp. 99.

GOVERNMENT intervention in the developed economy; edited by Peter Maunder. London, [1979]. pp. 226. *bibliogs.*

SCHMALENSEE (RICHARD) The control of natural monopolies. Lexington, Mass., [1979]. pp. 178. *bibliog.*

STATE and economy in contemporary capitalism; edited by Colin Crouch. London, [1979]. pp. 264. *bibliog.*

— Algeria.

La CHARTE communale, la charte de Wilaya [and] la charte de la gestion socialiste des entreprises, et textes réglementaires. Alger, 1979. 1 vol. (pag.var.). *(Algeria. Direction de la Documentation et des Publications. Dossiers Documentaires. 27)* In English and Arabic.

— Canada.

CANADA. Department of Industry, Trade and Commerce. 1973. Industry, Trade and Commerce at your service. Ottawa, 1973. pp. 62.

TRAVES (TOM) The state and enterprise: Canadian manufacturers and the Federal government, 1917-1931. Toronto, [1979]. pp. 175. *Revision of author's thesis, York University.*

— Europe.

BIG business and the state: changing relations in Western Europe; [edited by] Raymond Vernon. Cambridge, Mass., 1974. pp. 310. *bibliog.*

— France.

SCHEMA général d'aménagement de la France: restructuration de l'appareil productif française: prospectives. [Paris], 1976. 2 vols. *(France. Délégation à l'Aménagement du Territoire et à l'Action Régionale. Travaux et Recherches de Prospective. 65-66)*

— Germany.

WEISBROD (BERND) Schwerindustrie in der Weimarer Republik: Interessenpolitik zwischen Stabilisierung und Krise. Wuppertal, [1978]. pp. 552. *bibliog.*

— — Ruhr.

JANKOWSKI (MANFRED DIETER) Public policy in industrial growth: the case of Ruhr mining region, 1776-1865. New York, 1977. pp. 299. *bibliog.*

— Germany, Eastern.

LEPTIN (GERT) and MELZER (MANFRED) Economic reform in East German industry. Oxford, 1978. pp. 200. *(Glasgow. University. Institute of Soviet and East European Studies. Economic Reforms in East European Industry)* Translated from the German by Roger A. Clarke.

— Hungary.

FRANCE. Direction de la Documentation. La Documentation Française. Notes et Etudes Documentaires. No. 4462. Entreprise et planification socialiste: l'expérience hongroises; [by] Georges Chevallier et Eric Thérenon. [Paris], 1978. pp. 133. *bibliog.*

— Rhodesia.

MUSSETT (JACK) The role of private enterprise in a developing economy. Salisbury, 1971. pp. 14. *(Rhodesia. Ministry of Information, Immigration and Tourism. For the Record. No. 13)*

— Sweden.

NICOLIN (CURT) Private industry in a public world. Reading, Mass., [1977]. pp. 127.

— United Kingdom.

The CORPORATE state: reality or myth?; a symposium. London, 1976. pp. 160. *Papers from a symposium organised by the Centre for Studies in Social Policy held in London on 24th September, 1976.*

WEST YORKSHIRE. Metropolitan County Council. Industrial general improvement areas; a report for the Secretary of State for the Environment. [Wakefield, 1976]. fo. 12.

INDUSTRIAL common ownership and co-operative production: report of a seminar held at the Co-operative College, Loughborough, 21 April 1977. [London, Department of Industry, 1977]. pp. 19.

ADVISORY COUNCIL FOR APPLIED RESEARCH AND DEVELOPMENT [U.K.]. Industrial innovation. London, 1978. pp. 43.

BELOFF (MAX) The tide of collectivism: can it be turned? London, 1978. pp. 23. *(Conservative Political Centre. [Publications]. No. 629)*

FREEMAN (CHRISTOPHER) Government policies for industrial innovation. London, 1978. pp. 18. *(London. University. Birkbeck College. Bernal Lectures. 1978)*

OVENDEN (KEITH) The politics of steel. London, 1978. pp. 262. *bibliog.*

INDUSTRIAL STRATEGY STAFF GROUP [U.K.]. Industrial strategy: analysis of sector working party reports; memorandum by the Chairman of the Industrial Strategy Staff Group. London, National Economic Development Office, 1979. pp. 53.

NATIONAL ECONOMIC DEVELOPMENT OFFICE. The state and progress of the industrial strategy: memorandum by the Director General. London, 1979. pp. 5.

U.K. Treasury. 1979. Industrial strategy: memorandum by the Chancellor of the Exchequer and Secretary of State for Industry. [London, 1979]. 1 pamphlet (various pagings).

— United States.

ISSUES in business and society;...[edited by] George A. Steiner [and] John F. Steiner. 2nd ed. New York, [1977]. pp. 560.

GALBRAITH (JOHN KENNETH) The new industrial state. 3rd ed. Boston, Mass., 1978. pp. 438.

OWEN (BRUCE M.) and BRAEUTIGAM (RONALD) The regulation game: strategic uses of the administrative process. Cambridge, Mass., [1978]. pp. 270. *bibliog.*

WEIDENBAUM (MURRAY L.) and DE FINA (ROBERT) The cost of federal regulation of economic activity. Washington, 1978. pp. 33. *(American Enterprise Institute for Public Policy Research. Reprints. No. 88)*

INEQUALITIES (MATHEMATICS).

MITRINOVIC (DRAGOSLAV S.) Analytic inequalities. New York, 1970. pp. 400.

BECKENBACH (EDWIN F.) and BELLMAN (RICHARD ERNEST) Inequalities. Berlin, 1971. pp. 198. *bibliog.*

INFANT PSYCHOLOGY.

BOWER (THOMAS GILLIE RUSSELL) A primer of infant development. San Francisco, [1977]. pp. 187. *bibliog.*

KAGAN (JEROME) and others. Infancy: its place in human development. Cambridge, Mass., 1978. pp. 462. *bibliog.*

INFANTS.

LEWIS (MICHAEL) 1937- , and ROSENBLUM (LEONARD A.) eds. The effect of the infant on its caregiver. New York, [1974]. pp. 264. *bibliogs. The outgrowth of a conference sponsored by Educational Testing Service, Princeton, N.J.*

— Mortality.

U.K. Office of Population Censuses and Surveys. Medical Statistics Division. Social and biological factors in infant mortality. a., 1975/76(3rd)- London.

INFANTS (NEWBORN)

— United Kingdom — Mortality.

NEWCOMBE (ROBERT) Perinatal mortality and low birthweight, 1965-73: an analysis for administrative areas of England and Wales. [London], 1978. pp. 16. *bibliog. (U.K. Office of Population Censuses and Surveys. Occasional Papers. 7)*

INFLATION (FINANCE).

BOURGUES (PAUL) Les salaires sont-ils responsables de l'inflation?; critique de l théorie de l'inflation salariale. [Paris, 1978]. pp. 182.

HAYEK (FRIEDRICH AUGUST) A tiger by the tail: a 40-years' running commentary on Keynesianism...; compiled and introduced by Sudha R. Shenoy with an essay on The outlook for the 1970s: open or repressed inflation?; by F.A. Hayek. 2nd ed. London, 1978. pp. 145. *bibliog. (Institute of Economic Affairs. Hobart Paperbacks. 4)*

SHIN (KILMAN) Inflation, stock price and housing cost: empirical studies. Fairfax, [1978]. pp. 368. *bibliogs.*

PERKINS (JAMES OLIVER NEWTON) The macroeconomic mix to stop stagflation. London, 1979. pp. 193. *bibliog.*

— Mathematical models.

PERSPECTIVES on inflation: models and policies; edited by David F. Heathfield. London, 1979. pp. 238. *bibliogs.*

— America, Latin.

GUZMAN FERRER (MARTIN LUIS) La inflacion y el desarrollo en la America Latina. Mexico, 1976. pp. 653. *bibliog.*

— Canada.

FIRESTONE (OTTO JOHN) Canada's anti-inflation program and Kenneth Galbraith. Ottawa, 1977. pp. 259. *(Ottawa. Université. Collection Sciences Sociales. No. 5)*

— France.

FRANCE. Groupe d'Economie Monétaire Appliquée. 1978. Crédit, change et inflation: rapport du groupe d'économie monétaire appliquée. [Paris, 1978]. 2 vols. *(France. Commissariat Général du Plan. Economie et Planification)*

— Greece.

ZOLOTAS (XENOPHON) Inflation and the monetary target in Greece: an address. Athens, 1978. pp. 27. *bibliog. (Bank of Greece. Papers and Lectures. 38)*

— Netherlands.

BALK (B.M.) and others. Inflatie in Nederland van 1952 tot 1975: een statistische beschrijving van het verloop van 235 reeksen prijsindexcijfers en een analyse van hun samenhang. 's-Gravenhage, 1978. pp. 56. *(Netherlands. Centraal Bureau voor de Statistiek. Statistiche Onderzoekingen. M4) With English summary.*

An INFLATION-adjusted tax system: a summary of the report on the elimination from the Dutch tax system of the distorting effects of inflation; [by] H.J. Hofstra [and others]. The Hague, Government Publishing Office, 1978. pp. 75.

— Nigeria.

NIGERIA. 1975. The attack on inflation: government views on the first report of the Anti-Inflation Task Force. Lagos, 1975. pp. 16. *Bound with the Report.*

NIGERIA. Anti-Inflation Task Force. 1975. First report; [H.M.A. Onitiri, chairman]. Lagos, 1975. pp. 100. *Bound with the Government views on the report.*

— United Kingdom.

ROBBINS (LIONEL CHARLES) Baron Robbins. Against inflation: speeches in the Second Chamber, 1965-1977. London, 1979. pp. 115.

— United States.

CONGRESSIONAL QUARTERLY INC. Continuing energy crisis in America. Washington, D.C., [1975]. pp. 124. *bibliog.*

CONGRESSIONAL QUARTERLY INC. Inflation and unemployment; (senior editor Peter A. Harkness). Washington, D.C., [1975]. pp. 124. *bibliog.*

NEVIS (JOSEPH) The vanishing dollar: a new look at inflation. New York, 1977. pp. 48. *(American Institute for Marxist Studies. Occasional Papers. No. 23)*

BOSWORTH (BARRY) and others. A conversation with the honorable Barry Bosworth: coping with inflation. Washington, [1978]. pp. 26. *(American Enterprise Institute for Public Policy Research. AEI Studies. 215)*

CONTEMPORARY economic problems, 1978: William Fellner, project director [and others]. Washington, D.C., [1978]. pp. 353. *At head of title: American Enterprise Institute.*

The DOLLAR abroad, inflation at home;...[an AEI Public Policy Forum] held on August 31, 1978...[in] Washington; (John Charles Daly, moderator). Washington, [1978]. pp. 27. *(American Enterprise Institute for Public Policy Research. Public Policy Forums. 22)*

MARSHALL (RAY) and others. A conversation with Secretary Ray Marshall: inflation, unemployment and the minimum wage. Washington, [1978]. pp. 27. *(American Enterprise Institute for Public Policy Research. AEI Studies. 224)*

— — Mathematical models.

BERMAN (PETER I.) Inflation and the money supply in the United States, 1956-1977. Lexington, Mass., [1978]. pp. 137. *bibliog.*

INFLATION (FINANCE) AND ACCOUNTING.

KIRKMAN (PATRICK R.A.) Accounting under inflationary conditions. 2nd ed. London, 1974. pp. 300. *bibliogs.*

BAXTER (WILLIAM THREIPLAND) Accounting values and inflation. London, [1975]. pp. 217. *bibliog.*

INFLATION (FINANCE) AND UNEMPLOYMENT.

ELLIS (HOWARD SYLVESTER) Notes on stagflation. Washington, [1978]. pp. 23. *(American Enterprise Institute for Public Policy Research. AEI Studies. 221)*

WEINTRAUB (SIDNEY) b. 1914. Capitalism's inflation and unemployment crisis: beyond monetarism and Keynesianism. Reading, Mass., [1978]. pp. 242.

SIVEN (CLAES-HENRIC) A study in the theory of inflation and unemployment. Amsterdam, 1979. pp. 372. *bibliog.*

INFLUENZA

— United States.

CROSBY (ALFRED W.) Epidemic and peace, 1918. Westport, Conn., 1976. pp. 337. *bibliogs.*

INFORMATION SCIENCE.

UNESCO JOURNAL OF INFORMATION SCIENCE, LIBRARIANSHIP AND ARCHIVE ADMINISTRATION; [pd. by] Unesco. q., Ja/Mr 1979 (v.1, no.1)- Paris. *Supersedes UNESCO BULLETIN FOR LIBRARIES.*

UNISIST NEWSLETTER: programme of international co-operation in scientific and technical information; [pd.by] Unesco. irreg. Paris.

INFORMATION SERVICES

— Canada.

CANADA. Department of Regional Economic Expansion. 1973. Who knows?: hundreds of programs to serve the disadvantaged, but who knows about them? To what extent is failure to communicate information a factor in disadvantage? Ottawa, 1973. pp. 55. *bibliog.*

— United Kingdom.

LLEWELYN-DAVIES WEEKS [AND PARTNERS]. Inner area study: Birmingham: Small Heath Information and Advice Centre. [London], Department of the Environment, [1978]. pp. 46.

— — Scotland.

PAISLEY COMMUNITY DEVELOPMENT PROJECT. The Information and Action Centre; (by Barbara Jackson and Pam Davidson). Paisley, 1978. pp. 30.

INFORMATION STORAGE AND RETRIEVAL SYSTEMS.

GILDERSLEEVE (THOMAS ROBERT) Design of sequential file systems. New York, [1971]. pp. 49.

CONFERENCE ON THE FUTURE ROLE OF COMPUTERISED INFORMATION SERVICES AT THE UNIVERSITY OF LONDON, LONDON, 1977. Proceedings [of the conference organized by the Library Resources Co-ordinating Committee]. London, 1977. pp. 116. *bibliog.*

JAMOUS (HAROUN) and GREMION (PIERRE) L'ordinateur au pouvoir: essai sur les projets de rationalisation du gouvernement des hommes. Paris, [1978]. pp. 254.

CANADA. Treasury Board. Index of federal information banks. a., current issue only. Ottawa. *[in English and French].*

— City planning.

MASON (JIM) Information systems for planning: current designs and applications. London, 1978. pp. 39. *bibliog. (Planning Research Applications Group. PRAG Technical Papers. TP 26)*

INFORMATION STORAGE AND RETRIEVAL SYSTEMS.(Cont.)

— Regional planning.

MASON (JIM) Information systems for planning: current designs and applications. London, 1978. pp. 39. *bibliog.* *(Planning Research Applications Group. PRAG Technical Papers. TP 26)*

INFORMATION THEORY.

KLAPP (ORRIN E.) Opening and closing: strategies of information adaptation in society. Cambridge, 1978. pp. 226. *bibliog.* *(American Sociological Association. Arnold and Caroline Rose Monograph Series in Sociology)*

INGWANE (JULIUS PAUNDE SHIMANGANE).

SITHOLE (NDABANINGI) and INGWANE (JULIUS PAUNDE SHIMANGANE) Frelimo militant: the story of Ingwane from Mozambique, an ordinary, yet extraordinary man, awakened. Nairobi, 1977. pp. 187.

INHERITANCE AND SUCCESSION

— Austria.

GSCHNITZER (FRANZ) Erbrecht. Wien, [1964] repr. 1971. pp. 124.

— New Zealand.

NEW ZEALAND. Property Law and Equity Reform Committee. 1976. The effect of culpable homicide on rights of succession: report... presented to the Minister of Justice in October 1976; [C.P. Hutchinson, chairman]. [Wellington], 1976. pp. 30.

— United States.

ROSENFELD (JEFFREY P.) The legacy of aging: inheritance and disinheritance in social perspective. Norwood, N.J., [1979]. pp. 151. *bibliog.*

— Zambia.

ZAMBIA. Law Development Commission. 1976. Working paper on customary law of succession. Lusaka, [1976?]. pp. 8.

INHERITANCE AND TRANSFER TAX.

GOODMAN (WOLFE D.) International double taxation of estates and inheritances. London, 1978. pp. 277. *bibliog.*

— United Kingdom.

HALLETT (VICTOR GEORGE HENRY) and WARREN (NICHOLAS) Settlements, wills and capital transfer tax. London, 1979. pp. 245.

— United States.

COOPER (GEORGE) A voluntary tax?: new perspectives on sophisticated estate tax avoidance. Washington, D.C., [1979]. pp. 115. *(Reprinted from Columbia Law Review, 1977) (Brookings Institution. Studies of Government Finance. 2nd Series)*

INJUNCTION

— United States.

FISS (OWEN M.) The civil rights injunction. Bloomington, [1978]. pp. 117. *(Indiana University. School of Law. Addison C. Harris Lectures. 1976)*

INLAND NAVIGATION

— Belgium.

BELGIUM. Dienst voor de Scheepvaart. Verslag. a., 1977- Hasselt.

— United Kingdom.

FRAENKEL (PETER) AND PARTNERS. The waterways of the British Waterways Board: a study of operating and maintenance costs. [London], Department of the Environment, 1975 [or rather 1977]. 3 vols. (in 1).

INLAND WATER TRANSPORTATION

— Law and legislation — United States.

AMERICAN ENTERPRISE INSTITUTE FOR PUBLIC POLICY RESEARCH. Legislative Analyses. 95th Congress. No. 12. Waterway user charges. Washington, 1977. pp. 28.

— United States.

ELLET (CHARLES) An essay on the laws of trade, in reference to the works of internal improvement in the United States. New York, 1966. pp. 284. *Reprint of work originally published in Richmond, 1839.*

— — Rates.

AMERICAN ENTERPRISE INSTITUTE FOR PUBLIC POLICY RESEARCH. Legislative Analyses. 95th Congress. No. 12. Waterway user charges. Washington, 1977. pp. 28.

INSTITUTE OF BANKERS.

GREEN (EDWIN) Debtors to their profession: a history of the Institute of Bankers, 1879-1979. London, 1979. pp. 245.

INSTITUTIONAL CARE

— United Kingdom — Scotland.

SCOTLAND. Scottish Education Department. Social Work Services Group. Residential accommodation for children: Scotland. a., 1976/77(1st)- Edinburgh. *Supersedes in part SCOTTISH SOCIAL WORK STATISTICS.*

— — Wales.

U.K. Welsh Office. Residential accommodation for the elderly and younger physically handicapped. a., 1975/76- Cardiff.

INSTRUMENT INDUSTRY

— United Kingdom.

OAKEY (RAYMOND PETER) The British scientific and industrial instruments industry: a study in industrial geography. 1978. fo. 378. *bibliog.* Typescript. Ph.D. (London) thesis: unpublished. Computer program in end pocket. This thesis is the property of London University and may not be removed from the Library.

INSURANCE.

AMERICAN ACADEMY OF POLITICAL AND SOCIAL SCIENCE. Annals. vol. 443. Risk and its treatment; changing societal consequences; special editor of this volume George E. Rejda. Philadelphia, 1979. pp. 202.

— Japan.

NIWATA (NORIAKI) Insurance: its principles and practice in Japan. Tokyo, 1978. pp. 104.

INSURANCE, AGRICULTURAL

— Mauritius.

SUGAR INSURANCE FUND BOARD [MAURITIUS]. Annual report and accounts. a., 1975/76(30th)- Port Louis.

INSURANCE, CREDIT.

ZOLOTAS (XENOPHON) An international loan insurance scheme: a proposal. Athens, 1978. pp. 21. *bibliog. (Bank of Greece. Papers and Lectures. 39)*

INSURANCE, DISASTER

— United States.

KUNREUTHER (HOWARD) Disaster insurance protection: public policy lessons. New York, [1978]. pp. 400.

INSURANCE, EXPORT CREDIT.

UNITED NATIONS. Department of Economic and Social Affairs. Fiscal and Financial Branch. 1967. Export credits and development financing: part one, current practices and problems; part two, national export credit systems. (E/4274) (ST/ECA/95-96). New York, 1967. pp. 122.

INSURANCE, HEALTH

— Canada.

TAYLOR (MALCOLM G.) Health insurance and Canadian public policy: the seven decisions that created the Canadian Health Insurance System. Montreal, [1978]. pp. 473. *bibliog. (Institute of Public Administration of Canada. Canadian Public Administration Series)*

— Europe.

BLANPAIN (JAN) and others. National health insurance and health resources: the European experience. Cambridge, Mass., 1978. pp. 294. *bibliog.*

— United States.

NUMBERS (RONALD L.) Almost persuaded: American physicians and compulsory health insurance, 1912-1920. Baltimore, [1978]. pp. 158. *(Bulletin of the History of Medicine. Henry E. Sigerist Supplements. New Series. No. 1)*

LEE (A.JAMES) Employment, unemployment, and health insurance: behavioral and descriptive analysis of health insurance loss due to unemployment. Cambridge, Mass., [1979]. pp. 150. *bibliog.*

INSURANCE, INVESTMENT GUARANTY.

ZOLOTAS (XENOPHON) The dollar crisis and other papers. Athens, 1979. pp. 69. *bibliog. (Bank of Greece. Papers and Lectures. 41)*

INSURANCE, LIFE

— Mathematics.

GERSHENSON (HARRY) Measurement of mortality. Chicago, 1961 repr. 1972. pp. 340.

JORDAN (CHESTER WALLACE) Society of Actuaries' textbook on life contingencies. 2nd ed. Chicago, [1967] repr. 1975. pp. 390. *bibliog.*

— United Kingdom.

THOMSON (WILLIAM THOMAS) Further suggestions with reference to the amendment of the Joint Stock Companies Registration Act as regards life assurance institutions, contained in a letter to Francis Whitmarsh, Esq., Registrar of joint stock companies. Edinburgh, 1852. pp. 15. *Bound with his On the present position of the life assurance interests, etc. 2nd ed.*

THOMSON (WILLIAM THOMAS) On the present position of the life assurance interests of Great Britain: a letter to the Right Hon. Joseph W. Henley, M. P., President of the Board of Trade. 2nd ed. Edinburgh, 1852. pp. 21.

CLEGG (CYRIL) Friend in deed: the history of a life assurance office from 1858, as the Refuge Friend in Deed Life Assurance and Sick Fund Friendly Society, to 1958, as the Refuge Assurance Company Limited. London, [1958]. pp. 160.

ALLEN (W. GORE) We the undersigned...: a history of the Royal London Mutual Insurance Society Limited and its times, 1861-1961. London, [1961]. pp. 80.

THREADGOLD (A. R.) Personal saving: the impact of life assurance and pension funds. London, 1978. pp. 41. *bibliog. (Bank of England. Discussion Papers. No. 1)*

— United States.

PRITCHETT (BRUCE MICHAEL) A study of capital mobilization: the life insurance industry of the nineteenth century. rev. ed. New York, 1977. pp. 432. *bibliog.*

INSURANCE, PHYSICIANS' LIABILITY.

The ECONOMICS of medical malpractice: (a conference sponsored by the Center for Health Policy Research of the American Enterprise Institute for Public Policy Research); edited by Simon Rottenberg. Washington, D.C., [1978]. pp. 293.

INSURANCE, SOCIAL

See SOCIAL SECURITY.

INSURANCE, UNEMPLOYMENT.

UNEMPLOYMENT insurance: global evidence of its effects on unemployment; proceedings of an international conference held in Vancouver, British Columbia, Canada; edited by Herbert G. Grubel and Michael A. Walker. [Vancouver], 1978. pp. 388. *bibliogs.*

— Australia.

MYERS (DAVID MILTON) Inquiry into unemployment benefit policy and administration: report...for the Minister for Employment and Industrial Relations and the Minister for Social Security. Canberra, 1977. pp. 72.

— Canada.

CANADA. Department of Employment and Immigration. Annual report. a., 1977/78- Ottawa. *[in English and French] Supersedes CANADA. Department of Manpower and Immigration. Annual report and CANADA. Unemployment Insurance Commission. Annual report.*

— United States.

AMERICAN ENTERPRISE INSTITUTE FOR PUBLIC POLICY RESEARCH. Legislative Analyses. 95th Congress. No. 30. Unemployment insurance: reinsurance and cost equalization proposals. Washington, 1978. pp. 44.

— — New Jersey.

NEW JERSEY. Department of Labor and Industry. Division of Planning and Research. 1971. Unemployment insurance in New Jersey, 1936-1970: a statistical handbook. [Trenton], 1971. pp. 48.

INSURANCE COMPANIES

— Norway.

NORWAY. Statistiske Centralbyrå. Kredittmarkedstatistikk: livs- og skadeforsikringsselskaper m.v. a., 1974/1976- Oslo. *[in English and Norwegian] Supersedes in part NORWAY. Statistiske Centralbyrå. Kredittmarkedstatistikk. Balance sheet data in this publication previously included in NORWAY. Statistiske Centralbyrå. Finansinstitutsjoner.*

— South Africa.

SOUTH AFRICA. Bureau of Statistics. 1973. Census of insurance services, 1969-70. [Pretoria, 1973]. pp. 7. *(Reports. No. 04-06-02) In English and Afrikaans.*

— United Kingdom.

THOMSON (WILLIAM THOMAS) Further suggestions with reference to the amendment of the Joint Stock Companies Registration Act as regards life assurance institutions, contained in a letter to Francis Whitmarsh, Esq., Registrar of joint stock companies. Edinburgh, 1852. pp. 15. *Bound with his On the present position of the life assurance interests, etc. 2nd ed.*

THOMSON (WILLIAM THOMAS) On the present position of the life assurance interests of Great Britain: a letter to the Right Hon. Joseph W. Henley, M. P., President of the Board of Trade. 2nd ed. Edinburgh, 1852. pp. 21.

— United States.

PRITCHETT (BRUCE MICHAEL) A study of capital mobilization: the life insurance industry of the nineteenth century. rev. ed. New York, 1977. pp. 432. *bibliog.*

INSURANCE LAW

— United Kingdom.

COLINVAUX (RAOUL PERCY) The law of insurance. 4th ed. London, 1979. pp. 556.

U.K. Law Commission. Working Papers. No. 73. Insurance law: non-disclosure and breach of warranty. London, 1979. pp. 126.

INSURGENCY.

FRIGNANO (GIOVANNI) Teoria della guerra di popolo: (validita e sviluppo della teoria di Lenin e di Mao sulla guerra rivoluzionaria). [Milan, 1977]. pp. 203. *bibliogs.*

INTEGRAL EQUATIONS.

PROESSDORF (SIEGFRIED) Some classes of singular equations; translated by Siegfried Dümmel. Amsterdam, 1978. pp. 417. *bibliog.*

INTEGRAL TRANSFORMS.

SPRINGER (MELVIN DALE) The algebra of random variables. New York, [1979]. pp. 470. *bibliog.*

INTEGRALS, STOCHASTIC.

KUSSMAUL (ALFRED U.) Stochastic integration and generalized martingales. London, [1977]. pp. 163. *bibliog.*

INTEGRATED CIRCUITS

— Social aspects.

GOSLING (WILLIAM) Microcircuits, society and education. London, 1978. pp. 39. *(Council for Educational Technology for the United Kingdom. Occasional Papers. 8)*

INTELLECT.

PHILLIPS (JOHN L.) The origins of intellect: Piaget's theory. 2nd ed. San Francisco, [1975]. pp. 205. *bibliog.*

COULTER (JEFF) The social construction of mind: studies in ethnomethodology and linguistic philosophy. London, 1979. pp. 190.

VERNON (PHILIP EWART) Intelligence: heredity and environment. San Francisco, [1979]. pp. 390. *bibliog.*

INTELLECTUAL PROPERTY (INTERNATIONAL LAW).

EKEDI-SAMNIK (JOSEPH) L'Organisation Mondiale de la Propriété Intellectuelle (OMPI). Bruxelles, 1975. pp. 302. *bibliog.*

INTELLECTUALS

— America, Latin — Political activity.

FERNANDES (FLORESTAN) Circuito fechado: cuatro ensaios sobre o "poder institucional". São Paulo, 1976. pp. 224. *bibliogs.*

— China.

LIN (YU-SHENG) The crisis of Chinese consciousness: radical antitraditionalism in the May Fourth era. Madison, Wis., 1979. pp. 201. *bibliog.*

— Russia.

SOVETSKAIA intelligentsiia: kratkii ocherk istorii, 1917-1975 gg. Moskva, 1977. pp. 318.

INTELLIGENCE LEVELS.

FRANCE. Institut National d'Etudes Démographiques. 1978. Enquête nationale sur le niveau intellectuel des enfants d'âge scolaire. [Paris], 1978. pp. 291. *bibliog. (Travaux et Documents. Cahiers. No. 83)*

INTELLIGENCE SERVICE

— Bibliography.

BLACKSTOCK (PAUL W.) SCHAF (FRANK L.) compilers. Intelligence, espionage, counterespionage, and covert operations: a guide to information sources. Detroit, [1978]. pp. 255.

— Germany.

CHARISIUS (ALBRECHT) and MADER (JULIUS) Nicht länger geheim: Entwicklung, System und Arbeitsweise des imperialistischen deutschen Geheimdienstes. 3rd ed. Berlin, 1978. pp. 771.

— Poland.

WOYTAK (RICHARD A.) On the border of war and peace: Polish intelligence and diplomacy in 1937-1939 and the origins of the ultra secret. Boulder, 1979. pp. 141. *bibliog. (East European Quarterly. East European Monographs. 49)*

— United Kingdom.

KIMCHE (JON) The unfought battle. London, [1968]. pp. 168. *bibliog.*

HINSLEY (FRANCIS HARRY) British intelligence in the Second World War: its influence on strategy and operations. London, H.M.S.O., 1979 in progress. *(U.K. [Cabinet Office]. History of the Second World War)*

— United States.

CONFERENCE ON THE CIA AND WORLD PEACE, YALE UNIVERSITY, 1975. Uncloaking the CIA; Howard Frazier, editor. New York, [1978]. pp. 288.

DIRTY work: the CIA in Western Europe; edited by Philip Agee and Louis Wolf. Secaucus, N.J., [1978]. pp. 734.

QUANTITATIVE approaches to political intelligence: the CIA experience; edited by Richards J. Heuer, Jr. Boulder, Colo., 1978. pp. 181.

STOCKWELL (JOHN) In search of enemies: a CIA story. London, 1978. pp. 285.

THEOHARIS (ATHAN G.) Spying on Americans: political surveillance from Hoover to the Huston Plan. Philadelphia, 1978. pp. 331. *bibliog.*

PERSICO (JOSEPH E.) Piercing the Reich: the penetration of Nazi Germany by OSS agents during World War II. London, 1979. pp. 376.

INTERCULTURAL EDUCATION.

JEFFCOATE (ROBERT) Positive image: towards a multiracial curriculum. London, 1979. pp. 124. *bibliogs.*

INTEREST AND USURY.

KELLOGG (EDWARD) Labor and other capital: the rights of each secured and the wrongs of both eradicated;...and the addition of The true greenback, 1868, by Alexander Campbell. New York, 1971. pp. 298, 48. *Reprint of work originally published in New York, 1849.*

KELLISON (STEPHEN G.) The theory of interest. Homewood, Ill., 1970. pp. 243.

— Japan.

BANK OF JAPAN. Economic Research Department. Special Papers. No. 72. Steps toward flexible interest rates in Japan. Tokyo, 1977. pp. 21.

INTERGOVERNMENTAL FISCAL RELATIONS

— India — Bengal.

MAZUMDAR (DWIJENDRA LAL) A report on some aspects of local finance in their relation to provincial finance in Bengal. Alipore, Bengal Government Press, 1940. pp. 159.

INTERGOVERNMENTAL FISCAL RELATIONS(Cont.)

— Malaysia.

HOLZHAUSEN (WALTER) Federal finance in Malaysia: the theory and problems of federal/state government financial relations in a developing country. Kuala Lumpur, 1974. pp. 196. *bibliog.*

— United Kingdom.

PREST (ALAN RICHMOND) Intergovernmental financial relations in the United Kingdom. Canberra, 1978. pp. 118. *bibliog. (Australian National University. Centre for Research on Federal Financial Relations. Research Monographs. No. 23)*

— United States.

WRIGHT (DEIL S.) Understanding intergovernmental relations: public policy and participants' perspectives in local, state, and national governments. North Scituate, Mass., [1978]. pp. 410.

INTERGOVERNMENTAL MARITIME CONSULTATIVE ORGANIZATION.

IMCO NEWS: the magazine of the Inter-Governmental Maritime Consultative Organization. bi-m., 1977(no.2)- London.

SILVERSTEIN (HARVEY B.) Superships and nation-states: the transnational politics of the Intergovernmental Maritime Consultative Organization. Boulder, Colo., 1978. pp. 251. *bibliog.*

INTERINDUSTRY ECONOMICS.

HUNGARIAN CONFERENCE ON INPUT-OUTPUT TECHNIQUES, 2ND, 197-? Input-output techniques: proceedings of the...Conference...; ([edited by] A. Csepinszky [and others]). Budapest, 1976. pp. 409. *bibliog.*

MORRISON (W.I.) and SMITH (P.N.) Input-output methods in urban and regional planning: a practical guide. London, 1976. pp. 122. *bibliog. (Planning Research Applications Group. PRAG Technical Papers. TP6)*

NORTHERN REGION STRATEGY TEAM. Linkages in the Northern Region. Newcastle-upon-Tyne, 1977. fo. 50. *(Working Papers. No. 6)*

ONG (K.T.) An agriculturally orientated input-output analysis of the Ontario economy. Toronto, 1977. pp. 33. *bibliog. (Ontario. Ministry of Agriculture and Food. Economics Branch. Economic Research)*

AL-ALI (H.M.) and BURDEKIN (R.) An analysis of some aspects of the Scottish economy using input- output techniques. Peterlee, 1978. pp. 47. *(IBM United Kingdom Limited. UK Scientific Centre. [Technical Reports]. 0096)*

BURDEKIN (R.) The construction of the 1973 Scottish input-output tables. Peterlee, 1978. pp. 68. *(IBM United Kingdom Limited. UK Scientific Centre. [Technical Reports]. 0091)*

EIRE. 1978. Input-output tables for 1969. Dublin, 1978. pp. 75.

GLASGOW. University of Strathclyde. Fraser of Allander Institute, and others. Input-output tables for Scotland 1973. Edinburgh, [1978]. pp. 15.

GREECE. Dieuthynsis Ethnikon Logariasmon. 1978. Input-output table of the Greek economy, year 1970. Athens, 1978. pp. 121. *In Greek and English.*

IRESON (RICHARD) and TOMKINS (CYRIL R.) Inter-regional input-output for Wales and the rest of the U.K., 1968. [Cardiff], Welsh Council, [1978]. 1 vol.(various pagings). *bibliog.*

OZEROV (VIKTOR KONSTANTINOVICH) Tempy i proportsii rasshirennogo sotsialisticheskogo vosproizvodstva v SSSR: analiz s ispol'zovaniem ukrupnennoi dinamicheskoi modeli mezhotraslevogo balansa; otvetstvennyi redaktor A.G. Aganbegian. Novosibirsk, 1978. pp. 287.

SINGAPORE. Statistics Department. 1978. Singapore input-output tables, 1973. Singapore, 1978. pp. 137.

THOMSON (J.K.) The framework of industry in Scotland: an analysis of the Scottish input-output table. rev. ed. Edinburgh, 1978. 1 vol. (unpaged).

WOODS (JOHN E.) Mathematical economics. London, 1978. pp. 364. *bibliogs.*

TSUKUI (JINKICHI) and MURAKAMI (YASUSUKE) Turnpike optimality in input-output systems: theory and application for planning. Amsterdam, 1979. pp. 260. *bibliog.*

— Tables.

INTERNATIONAL input-output table Japan-U.S.A., 1970; [by Yasuhiko Torii and others]. Tokyo, [1977]. pp. 205. *(Ajia Keizai Kenkyusho. Statistical Data Series. No. 24). Published as part of a research project organized by the Institute of Developing Economies and the Keio Economic Observatory of Keio University.*

INTERNAL SECURITY

— Canada.

FIDLER (RICHARD) RCMP: the real subversives. Toronto, [1978]. pp. 91. *bibliog.*

— Germany.

SCHWARZE (JOHANNES) Die bayerische Polizei und ihre historische Funktion bei der Aufrechterhaltung der öffentlichen Sicherheit in Bayern von 1919-1933. München, 1977. pp. 292. *bibliog. (Munich. Stadtarchiv. Neue Schriftenreihe. Band 92)*

— United Kingdom.

The TECHNOLOGY of political control; by Carol Ackroyd [and others]. Harmondsworth, 1977. pp. 320.

PINCHER (CHAPMAN) Inside story: a documentary of the pursuit of power. London, 1978. pp. 400.

— United States.

THEOHARIS (ATHAN G.) Spying on Americans: political surveillance from Hoover to the Huston Plan. Philadelphia, 1978. pp. 331. *bibliog.*

INTERNATIONAL, THE.

Die SOZIALISTISCHE Internationale: ihre Geschichte und Politik; von einem Autorenkollektiv unter Leitung von Werner Kowalski und Johannes Glasneck. Berlin, 1977. pp. 304. *bibliog.*

INTERNATIONAL WORKING MEN'S ASSOCIATION. Congress, [5th], The Hague, 1872. The Hague congress of the First International, September 2- 7, 1872: reports and letters. Moscow, [1978]. pp. 701. *(Institut Marksizma-Leninizma. Documents of the First International).*

INTERNATIONALE TAGUNG DER HISTORIKER DER ARBEITERBEWEGUNG, 1975. Einheits- und Volksfrontpolitik, 1935-1939; Klassenkampf und nationale Frage zur Zeit der II. Internationale; [bearbeitet von Hans Hautmann). Wien, 1978. pp. 335. *(Internationale Tagung der Historiker der Arbeiterbewegung. ITH-Tagungsberichte. Band 10)*

McCLELLAN (WOODFORD D.) Revolutionary exiles: the Russians in the First International and the Paris Commune. London, 1979. pp. 266. *bibliog.*

STEININGER (ROLF) Deutschland und die Sozialistische Internationale nach dem Zweiten Weltkrieg: die deutsche Frage, die Internationale und das Problem der Wiederaufnahme der SPD...: Darstellung und Dokumentation. Bonn, [1979]. pp. 433. *bibliog. (Archiv für Sozialgeschichte. Beihefte. 7)*

— Congresses.

VII kongress Kominterna i bor'ba za sozdanie narodnogo fronta v stranakh Tsentral'noi i Iugo-Vostochnoi Evropy. Moskva, 1977. pp. 375.

INTERNATIONAL AGENCIES.

LIMITONE (ANTHONY) The registration of ships by ternational and intergovernmental organizations. Miami, 1971. fo. 28. *(Miami (Florida). University Grant Program. Special Bulletins. 2)*

EUROPEAN COMMUNITIES. Commission. 1977. The European Community, international organisations and multilateral agreements. [Brussels, 1977]. pp. 298.

U.S. policy in international institutions: defining reasonable options in an unreasonable world; edited by Seymour Maxwell Finger and Joseph R. Harbert. Boulder, Colo., [1978]. pp. 489. *bibliog.*

INTERNATIONAL AND MUNICIPAL LAW

— Europe.

BRINKHORST (L.J.) and SCHERMERS (HENRY G.) Judicial remedies in the European Communities: a case book; second revised edition by H.G. Schermers. eventer, 1977. pp. 352.

INTERNATIONAL BANK FOR RECONSTRUCTION AND DEVELOPMENT.

REPORT: news of the World Bank. bi-m. Washington. *Current issues only kept.*

INTERNATIONAL BROADCASTING.

SWANN (Sir MICHAEL MEREDITH) The BBC's external services under threat? London, [1978]. pp. 12.

INTERNATIONAL BROTHERHOOD OF BOILERMAKERS, IRON SHIP BUILDERS, BLACKSMITHS, FORGERS AND HELPERS.

MacINTOSH (ROBERT) Boilermakers in British Columbia. [Vancouver?], 1976. pp. 124.

INTERNATIONAL BROTHERHOOD OF TEAMSTERS, CHAUFFEURS, WAREHOUSEMEN AND HELPERS OF AMERICA.

MOLDEA (DAN E.) The Hoffa wars: teamsters, rebels, politicians and the mob. New York, [1978]. pp. 450.

INTERNATIONAL BUSINESS ENTERPRISES.

WILKINS (MIRA) The emergence of multinational enterprise: American business abroad from the colonial era to 1914. Cambridge, Mass., [1970]. pp. 310. *bibliog.*

LEDOGAR (ROBERT J.) Hungry for profits: U.S. food and drug multinationals in Latin America. New York, [1975]. pp. 206.

NESTLÉ in the developing countries. Vevey, [1975]. pp. 228.

POLITICA economica de las corporaciones multinacionales; [by] Charles D'Argent [and others]. Buenos Aires, [1975]. pp. 253. *bibliog.*

SAMPSON (ANTHONY) The seven sisters: the great oil companies and the world they made. London, 1975. pp. 334.

VARIS (TAPIO) The impact of transnational corporations on communication. Tampere, 1975. fo. 58. *bibliog. (Tampere Peace Research Institute. Research Reports. No. 10)*

CTC REPORTER, THE; [pd. by] United Nations Centre on Transnational Corporations. irreg., D 1976(v.1, no.1)- New York.

BUCKLEY (PETER J.) and CASSON (MARK C.) The future of the multinational enterprise. London, [1976]. pp. 116.

FAJNZYLBER (FERNANDO) and MARTINEZ TARRAGO (TRINIDAD) Las empresas transnacionales: expansión a nivel mundial y proyección en la industria mexicana. México, 1976. pp. 423. *bibliog.*

UNITED NATIONS. Centre on Transnational Corporations. 1976. Transnational corporations: issues involved in the formulation of a code of conduct; report of the Secretariat. (E/C.10/17). New York, 1976. pp. 41.

BENWELL COMMUNITY DEVELOPMENT PROJECT. Multinationals in Tyne and Wear; (compiled by Benwell and North Tyneside Community Development Projects in conjunction with the Tyne Conference of Shop Stewards); (with Amendments). [Newcastle-upon-Tyne, 1977 in progress]. 2 vols. (vol.2 loose- leaf). *bibliog.*

CENTRE D'ETUDES DU DEVELOPPEMENT EN AMERIQUE LATINE. Multinationales et travailleurs au Brésil; [edited by] Paulo Freire. Paris, 1977. pp. 254. *bibliog.*

GERMIDIS (DIMITRIOS A.) ed. Transfer of technology by multinational corporations. Paris, Organisation for Economic Co-operation and Development, 1977. 2 vols. *(Development Centre. Studies)*

ORGANISATION FOR ECONOMIC CO-OPERATION AND DEVELOPMENT. Committee of Experts on Restrictive Business Practices. 1977. Restrictive business practices of multinational enterprises: report of the Committee, etc. Paris, 1977. pp. 78.

SEIDMAN (ANN WILLCOX) and SEIDMAN (NEVA) U.S. multinationals in Southern Africa. Dar es Salaam, 1977. pp. 252. *bibliogs.*

UNITED NATIONS. Centre on Transnational Corporations. 1977. Establishment of a comprehensive information system on transnational corporations: government replies. (ST/CTC/1). New York, 1977. pp. 26.

BARANSON (JACK) Technology and the multinationals: corporate strategies in a changing world economy. Lexington, Mass., [1978]. pp. 170.

BLACK (ROBERT B.) and others. Multinationals in contention: responses at governmental and international levels; a research report from the Conference Board's Public Affairs Research Division. New York, [1978]. pp. 233.

FIELDHOUSE (DAVID KENNETH) Unilever overseas: the anatomy of a multinational, 1895-1965. Stanford, Calif., [1978]. pp. 620. *(Stanford University. Hoover Institution on War, Revolution and Peace. Hoover Institution Publications. 205)*

INTERNATIONAL business in the Pacific Basin; edited by R. Hal Mason. Lexington, Mass. [1978]. pp. 213. *Based on a research symposium held at the University of California, Los Angeles, 1975.*

INTERNATIONALE Monopole; Redaktionskollegium: Christos Fundulis [and others]. Berlin, 1978. pp. 287.

JACQUE (LAURENT L.) Management of foreign exchange risk: theory and praxis. Lexington, Mass., [1978]. pp. 285. *bibliogs.*

PARKER (JOHN EDGAR SAYCE) The economics of innovation: the national and multinational enterprise in technological change. 2nd ed. London, 1978. pp. 396. *bibliogs.*

ROSIE (GEORGE) The Ludwig initiative: a cautionary tale of North Sea oil. Edinburgh, 1978. pp. 147.

SOLOMON (LEWIS D.) Multinational corporations and the emerging world order. Port Washington, N.Y., 1978. pp. 261. *bibliog.*

WEINBERG (PAUL J.) European labor and multinationals. New York, [1978]. pp. 112. *bibliog.*

WHO'S afraid of the multinationals?: a survey of European opinion on multinational corporations; [by] Georges Péninou [and others]. Farnborough, Hants., [1978]. pp. 205. *Survey undertaken for the European Centre for Study and Information on Multinational Corporations.*

BEYNON (HUW) and WAINWRIGHT (HILARY) The workers' report on Vickers. London, 1979. pp. 208. *bibliog.*

CASSON (MARK C.) Alternatives to the multinational enterprise. London, 1979. pp. 116. *bibliog.*

CHANNON (DEREK F.) and JALLAND (MICHAEL) Multinational strategic planning. London, 1979. pp. 344.

HOOD (NEIL) and YOUNG (STEPHEN) The economics of multinational enterprise. London, 1979. pp. 412. *bibliog.*

INTERNATIONAL business in the Middle East: case studies; edited by Ashok Kapoor. Boulder, Colo., 1979. pp. 134. *bibliog.*

The INTERNATIONAL division of labour and multinational companies: [debates from] a symposium organised by the European Centre for Study and Information on Multinational Corporations... summarised by John Robinson; [with] A survey of alternative views; [by] P.K.M. Tharakan. Farnborough, Hants., [1979]. pp. 152.

MARCHAK (PATRICIA) In whose interests: an essay on multinational corporations in a Canadian context. Toronto, [1979]. pp. 317. *bibliog.*

MATHEWSON (G. FRANK) and QUIRIN (G. DAVID) Fiscal transfer pricing in multinational corporations. Toronto, [1979]. pp. 162. *bibliog. (Ontario. Economic Council. Research Studies. 16)*

MATTELART (ARMAND) Multinational corporations and the control of culture: the ideological apparatuses of imperialism; translated from the French by Michael Chanan. Brighton, 1979. pp. 304. *bibliogs.*

MULTINATIONALS and development in black Africa: a case study in the Ivory Coast; by Jean Masini [and others]. Farnborough, [1979]. pp. 181.

NEGANDHI (ANANT R.) Quest for survival and growth: a comparative study of American, European, and Japanese multinationals;...in collaboration with B. R. Baliga. Königstein/Ts., [1979]. pp. 163. *bibliog. (Wissenschaftszentrum Berlin. Sozialwissenschaft und Praxis. Band 1)*

PLASSCHAERT (SYLVAIN R.F.) Transfer pricing and multinational corporations: an overview of concepts, mechanisms and regulations. Farnborough, [1979]. pp. 120. *bibliogs.*

YOUNG (ALEXANDER K.) The Sogo Shosha: Japan's multinational trading companies. Boulder, Colo., 1979. pp. 247. *bibliog.*

— **Directories.**

UNITED NATIONS. Centre on Transnational Corporations. 1977. Transnational corporations: list of company directories and summary of their contents.(ST/CTC/2). New York, 1977. pp. 59.

— **Employees.**

The INTERNATIONAL division of labour and multinational companies: [debates from] a symposium organised by the European Centre for Study and Information on Multinational Corporations... summarised by John Robinson; [with] A survey of alternative views; [by] P.K.M. Tharakan. Farnborough, Hants., [1979]. pp. 152.

— **Law and legislation.**

IJALAYE (DAVID ADEDAYO) The extension of corporate personality in international law. Dobbs Ferry, N.Y., 1978. pp. 354.

— **Research.**

UNITED NATIONS. Centre on Transnational Corporations. 1977. Survey of research on transnational corporations. (ST/CTC/3). [2nd ed.] New York, 1977. pp. 533. *bibliog. Updates mimeographed document E/C.10/12.*

— **Underdeveloped areas.**

See UNDERDEVELOPED AREAS — International business enterprises.

INTERNATIONAL CONFEDERATION OF FREE TRADE UNIONS.

THOMSON (DON) and LARSON (RODNEY) Where were you, brother?: an account of trade union imperialism. London, [1978]. pp. 138. *bibliogs.*

INTERNATIONAL COOPERATION.

GOALS in a global community: the original background papers for Goals for mankind: a report to the Club of Rome; edited by Ervin Laszlo and Judah Bierman. New York, [1977 in progress]. *bibliogs.*

COUNCIL FOR MUTUAL ECONOMIC ASSISTANCE. 1977. Information on the CMEA activities in developing co-operation with the United Nations Economic Commission for Europe in 1976-1977. Moscow, 1977. pp. 13.

HAAS (ERNST BERNARD) and others. Scientists and world order: the uses of technical knowledge in international organizations. Berkeley, Calif., [1977]. pp. 368.

FUJII (TAKASHI) Economic policy co-operation: proposals on formation of international economic policy co-operation and relocation of industry. Tokyo, 1978. pp. 80.

SANDLER (TODD M.) and others. The political economy of public goods and international cooperation. Denver, Colo., [1978]. pp. 98. *bibliog. (Denver. University. Graduate School of International Studies. Monograph Series in World Affairs. vol. 15, no. 3)*

INTERNATIONAL ECONOMIC INTEGRATION.

COUNCIL FOR MUTUAL ECONOMIC ASSISTANCE. 1977. Information on cooperation of the CMEA member countries in planning. Moscow, 1977. pp. 13.

COUNCIL FOR MUTUAL ECONOMIC ASSISTANCE. 1977. Information on the activities of the CMEA in the elaboration of long-term specific programmes of cooperation of the CMEA member countries. Moscow, 1977. pp. 12.

BYSTRICKÝ (RUDOLF) Le droit de l'intégration économique socialiste. Genève, 1979. pp. 471. *bibliog. (Geneva. Graduate Institute of International Studies. Collection de Droit International. 6)*

INTERNATIONAL ECONOMIC RELATIONS.

PAKISTAN. Ministry of Information and Broadcasting. 1967. Pakistan and R[egional] C[o-operation for] D[evelopment]: three years of regional co-operation for development, 1964-1967. [Karachi, 1967!. pp. 48. *bibliog.*

KENWOOD (ALBERT GEORGE) and LOUGHEED (A.L.) The growth of the international economy, 1820-1960: an introductory text. London, 1971. pp. 319. *bibliogs.*

BARAN (PAUL A.) The political economy of growth; with an introduction by R.B. Sutcliffe. Harmondsworth, [1973]. pp. 475.

UNITED NATIONS. Centre for Development Planning, Projections and Policies. 1973. Implementation of the international development strategy: papers for the first over-all review and appraisal of progress during the second United Nations development decade. (E/5267) (ST/ECA/178). New York, 1973. 2 vols. (in 1).

ALGERIA. 1974. Petroleum, raw materials and development: memorandum submitted by Algeria on the occasion of the special session of the United Nations General Assembly, April 1974. [Algiers], 1974. pp. 222.

HELLER (HEINZ ROBERT) International monetary economics. Englewood Cliffs, N.J., [1974]. pp. 230. *bibliogs.*

INTERNATIONAL ECONOMIC RELATIONS.(Cont.)

BERGSTEN (C. FRED) The dilemmas of the dollar: the economics and politics of United States international monetary policy. New York, [1975]. pp. 584.

CAMARA (HELDER) Archbishop of Olinda and Recife. Fraternal appeal to Britain. [London, 1975?]. pp. 4. *(Edwina Mountbatten Memorial Lectures. 1975)*

WORLD inequality: origins and perspectives on the world system; edited by Immanuel Wallerstein. Nottingham, [1975]. pp. 169.

ECONOMIC coercion and the new international economic order; edited by Richard B. Lillich. Charlottesville, Va., [1976]. pp. 401.

NYERERE (JULIUS KAMBARAGE) The economic challenge: dialogue or confrontation. London, [1976]. pp. 12. *Address given to the Royal Commonwealth Society in London in 1975.*

SWEDEN. Finansdepartementet. Långtidsutredningen. 1976. (Långtidsutredningen 1975. Bilaga 1). Den internationella bakgrunden;...[by] Jan Herin [and others]. Stockholm, 1976. pp. 352. *(Sweden. Statens Offentliga Utredningar. 1976.27)*

VELO (DARIO) La crisi economica internazionale e l'alternativa europea: aspetti monetari e finanziari. Milano, 1976. pp. 162. *bibliogs.*

GOALS in a global community: the original background papers for Goals for mankind: a report to the Club of Rome; edited by Ervin Laszlo and Judah Bierman. New York, [1977 in progress]. *bibliogs.*

ECONOMIC issues and national security; edited by Klaus Knorr and Frank N. Trager. New York, [1977]. pp. 330. *biblios. (New York (City). University. National Security Education Program, and National Strategy Information Center. National Security Studies Series. No. 7)*

HAAS (ERNST BERNARD) and others. Scientists and world order: the uses of technical knowledge in international organizations. Berkeley, Calif., [1977]. pp. 368.

U.K. Ministry of Overseas Development. 1977. Challenges of the rich-poor relationship: new imperatives on the international scene; address to Congressional Group for Peace through Law, by Frank Judd M.P., Minister for Overseas Development, Washington, D.C., January 1977. London, [1977]. pp. 10. *(Overseas Development Papers. No.6)*

BETWEEN power and plenty: foreign economic policies of advanced industrial states; edited by Peter J. Katzenstein. Madison, 1978. pp. 344. *Papers presented at a conference held at Harvard University in 1976.*

CARREAU (DOMINIQUE) and others. Droit international économique. Paris, 1978. pp. 513.

CHACHOLIADES (MILTIADES) International trade theory and policy. [2nd ed.] New York, [1978]. pp. 614. *bibliogs. First ed. published in 1973 under title: The pure theory of international trade.*

The FIRST World and the Third World: essays on the new international economic order; edited by Karl Brunner. Rochester, N.Y., [1978]. pp. 272. *bibliog.*

FRANK (ANDRE GUNDER) Dependent accumulation and underdevelopment. London, 1978. pp. 226. *bibliog.*

FRANK (ANDRE GUNDER) World accumulation, 1492-1789. New York, [1978]. pp. 303. *bibliog.*

FUJII (TAKASHI) Economic policy co-operation: proposals on formation of international economic policy co-operation and relocation of industry. Tokyo, 1978. pp. 80.

The GLOBAL political economy of food; edited by Raymond F. Hopkins and Donald J. Puchala. Madison, [1978]. pp. 339. *bibliog. Contents of the Summer 1978 issue of International Organization, (vol. 32, no.3). sponsored by the World Peace Foundation.*

GRIFFIN (KEITH) International inequality and national poverty. London, 1978. pp. 191. *bibliogs.*

INTERNATIONAL economics: comparisons and interdependences: Internationale Wirtschaft: Vergleiche und Interdependenzen;. edited by...F. Levcik; (Festschrift für Franz Nemschak). Wien, 1978. pp. 528. *bibliogs. (Wiener Institut für Internationale Wirtschaftsvergleiche. Studien über Wirtschafts- und Systemvergleiche. Band 9) In English or German.*

MANDEL (ERNEST) The second slump: a marxist analysis of recession in the seventies; translated by Jon Rothschild. London, 1978. pp. 212.

NORENG (ØYSTEIN) Oil politics in the 1980s: patterns of international cooperation. New York, [1978]. pp. 171. *bibliog. (Council on Foreign Relations. 1980s Project Studies)*

ODELL (PETER R.) and VALLENILLA (LUIS) The pressures of oil: a strategy for economic revival. London, 1978. pp. 215.

RICHARDSON (NEIL R.) Foreign policy and economic dependence. Austin, [1978]. pp. 214. *bibliog.*

SHEPHERD (A. ROSS) International economics: a micro-macro approach. Columbus, Ohio, [1978]. pp. 248. *bibliog.*

SOCIAL change in the capitalist world economy; edited by Barbara Hockey Kaplan. Beverly Hills, Calif., [1978]. pp. 239. *bibliogs. (American Sociological Association. Political Economy of the World-System Annuals. vol. 1)*

SOLOMON (LEWIS D.) Multinational corporations and the emerging world order. Port Washington, N.Y., 1978. pp. 261. *bibliog.*

TUMLIR (JAN) National interest and international order. London, [1978]. pp. 21. *(Trade Policy Research Centre. International Issues. No. 4)*

WHITING (D.P.) International trade and payments. Plymouth, 1978. pp. 145.

WRIGGINS (WILLIAM HOWARD) and ADLER-KARLSSON (GUNNAR) Reducing global inequalities. New York, [1978]. pp. 191. *bibliog. (Council on Foreign Relations. 1980s Project Studies)*

The FUTURE of business: global issues in the 80s and 90s; edited by Max Ways. New York, [1979]. pp. 99.

INTERNATIONAL economic policy: theory and evidence; edited by Rudiger Dornbusch and Jacob A. Frenkel. Baltimore, [1979]. pp. 342. *bibliogs. Papers prepared for the Wingspread III Conference on International Economic Policy, Racine, 1977.*

LEVČÍK (FRIEDRICH) and STANKOVSKY (JAN) Industrial cooperation between east and west; translated by Michel Vale. White Plains, N.Y., [1979]. pp. 287. *bibliog.*

MAYRZEDT (HANS M.) Multilaterale Wirtschaftsdiplomatie zwischen westlichen Industriestaaten als Instrument zur Stärkung der multilateralen und liberalen Handelspolitik. Bern, [1979]. pp. 625. *bibliog. (Hochschule St. Gallen. Veröffentlichungen. Schriftenreihe Volkswirtschaft. Band 4)*

SNIDER (DELBERT ARTHUR) Introduction to international economics. 7th ed. Homewood, Ill., 1979. pp. 454. *bibliogs.*

INTERNATIONAL FINANCE.

HELLER (HEINZ ROBERT) International monetary economics. Englewood Cliffs, N.J., [1974]. pp. 230. *bibliogs.*

The INTERNATIONAL monetary system and the developing nations; edited by Danny M. Leipziger. Washington, Agency for International Development, Bureau for Program and Policy Coordination, 1976. pp. 210. *bibliogs.*

VELO (DARIO) La crisi economica internazionale e l'alternativa europea: aspetti monetari e finanziari. Milano, 1976. pp. 162. *bibliogs.*

ARONSON (JONATHAN DAVID) Money and power: banks and the world monetary system. Beverly Hills, [1977]. pp. 224. *bibliog.*

The NEW international monetary system; Robert A. Mundell and Jacques J. Polak, editors. New York, 1977. pp. 244. *Proceedings of a conference held by the I.M.F. in Washington D.C. in 1976, jointly sponsored by Columbia University.*

BIRD (GRAHAM RICHARD) The international monetary system and the less developed countries. London, 1978. pp. 339. *bibliog.*

BROWN (BRENDAN) Money hard and soft on the international currency markets. London, 1978. pp. 183. *bibliog.*

CHRYSTAL (KENNETH ALEXANDER) International money and the future of the S[pecial] D[rawing] R[ight]. Princeton, 1978. pp. 30. *bibliog. (Princeton University. Department of Economics and Sociology. International Finance Section. Essays in International Finance. No. 128)*

DUFEY (GUNTER) and GIDDY (IAN H.) The international money market. Englewood Cliffs, [1978]. pp. 283.

FLEMING (JOHN MARCUS) Essays on economic policy. New York, 1978. pp. 381.

GUNTER (JOHN WADSWORTH) The imbalance of international payments from the viewpoint of the OPEC and other developing countries. Cairo, 1978. pp. 24. *(National Bank of Egypt. Commemoration Lectures Programme)*

JONES (FRANK JOSEPH) Macrofinance: the financial system and the economy. Cambridge, Mass., [1978]. pp. 310. *bibliogs.*

ORGANISATION FOR ECONOMIC CO-OPERATION AND DEVELOPMENT. 1978. Regulations affecting international banking operations of banks and non-banks in France, Germany, the Netherlands, Switzerland, the United Kingdom. Paris, 1978. pp. 108.

ZOLOTAS (XENOPHON) The dollar crisis and other papers. Athens, 1979. pp. 69. *bibliog. (Bank of Greece. Papers and Lectures. 41)*

INTERNATIONAL LABOUR ACTIVITIES.

COUNCIL FOR MUTUAL ECONOMIC ASSISTANCE. 1977. Information on cooperation of state labour bodies of the CMEA member countries in 1976-1977. Moscow, 1977. pp. 6.

THOMSON (DON) and LARSON (RODNEY) Where were you, brother?: an account of trade union imperialism. London, [1978]. pp. 138. *bibliogs.*

WASCHKE (HILDEGARD) Supra-nationale Gewerkschaftspolitik: Ziele und Wege der internationalen Gewerkschaftsbewegung. Köln, [1978]. pp. 60. *bibliog. (Institut der Deutschen Wirtschaft. Beiträge zur Gesellschafts- und Bildungspolitik. 25)*

WEINBERG (PAUL J.) European labor and multinationals. New York, [1978]. pp. 112. *bibliog.*

INTERNATIONAL LAW.

MANUAL of public international law; edited by Max Sørensen. London, 1968 repr. 1978. pp. 930. *bibliogs.*

SOUTH AFRICAN YEARBOOK OF INTERNATIONAL LAW; [pd. by] Institute of Foreign and Comparative Law, University of South Africa. a., 1975(v.1)- Pretoria.

LOMBARDI (ALDO VIRGILIO) Bürgerkrieg und Völkerrecht: die Anwendbarkeit völkerrechtlicher Normen in nicht-zwischenstaatlichen bewaffneten Konflikten. Berlin, 1976. pp. 416. *bibliog.*

TOWARD world order and human dignity: essays in honor of Myres S. McDougal; edited by W. Michael Reisman and Burns H. Weston. New York, [1976]. pp. 603. *bibliog.*

FEL'DMAN (DAVID ISAAKOVICH) and BASKIN (IURII IAKOVLEVICH) Uchenie Kanta i Gegelia o mezhdunarodnom prave i sovremennost'. Kazan', 1977. pp. 127.

VO imia mira: mezhdunarodno-pravovye problemy evropeiskoi bezopasnosti. Moskva, 1977. pp. 191.

ZOLLER (ELISABETH) La bonne foi en droit international public. Paris, [1977]. pp. 392. *bibliog. (Revue Générale de Droit International Public. Publications. Nouvelle série. No. 28)* With English summary.

BOKOR-SZEGÖ (HANNA) The role of the United Nations in international legislation; translated by Dr. Sándor Simon. Amsterdam, 1978. pp. 191. *bibliog.*

CARREAU (DOMINIQUE) and others. Droit international économique. Paris, 1978. pp. 513.

FISHER (ROGER DRUMMER) Points of choice. Oxford, 1978. pp. 89. *(American Society of International Law. International Crises and the Role of Law)*

MAJID (MOHAMED MUNIR BIN ABDUL) Asian and African attitudes to the settlement of international disputes by judicial means. 1978. fo. 379. *bibliog. Typescript. Ph.D. (London) thesis: unpublished. This thesis is the property of London University and may not be removed from the Library.*

BYSTRICKÝ (RUDOLF) Le droit de l'intégration économique socialiste. Genève, 1979. pp. 471. *bibliog. (Geneva. Graduate Institute of International Studies. Collection de Droit International. 6)*

— Bibliography.

MERRILLS (J.G.) compiler. A current bibliography of international law. London, 1978. pp. 277.

— Cases.

GREEN (LESLIE CLAUDE) International law through the cases. 4th ed. Toronto, 1978. pp. 836.

FONTES JURIS GENTIUM. Series A. Sectio 2. Tomus 6. Deutsche Rechtsprechung in völkerrechtlichen Fragen. Decisions of German courts relating to public international law, 1966-1970; bearbeitet im Max-Planck Institut für ausländisches öffentliches Recht und Völkerrecht von Karl Doehring [and others]. Berlin, 1979. pp. 580. *With summaries in English and French.*

HARRIS (DAVID JOHN) Cases and materials on international law. 2nd ed. London, 1979. pp. 829.

— History — Netherlands.

INTERNATIONAL law in the Netherlands; edited by H.F. van Panhuys [and others]. Alphen aan den Rijn, 1978 in progress.

INTERNATIONAL LAW, PRIVATE.

See CONFLICT OF LAWS.

INTERNATIONAL LIQUIDITY.

The NEW international monetary system; Robert A. Mundell and Jacques J. Polak, editors. New York, 1977. pp. 244. *Proceedings of a conference held by the I.M.F. in Washington D.C. in 1976, jointly sponsored by Columbia University.*

INTERNATIONAL MONETARY FUND.

DORMAEL (ARMAND VAN) Bretton Woods: birth of a monetary system. London, 1978. pp. 322.

FABIAN SOCIETY. Fabian Tracts. [No.] 462. The politics of monetarism; [by] Bryan Gould [and others]. London, 1979. pp. 19.

INTERNATIONAL OFFENCES.

LEGAL aspects of international terrorism; edited by Alona E. Evans and John F. Murphy. Lexington, Mass., [1978]. pp. 690.

INTERNATIONAL ORGANIZATION.

WOOLF (LEONARD SIDNEY) ed. The framework of a lasting peace. New York, 1971. pp. 154. *Reprint, with a new introduction, of the work first published London, 1917.*

DIVINE (ROBERT A.) Second chance: the triumph of internationalism in America during World War II. New York, [1967] repr. 1971. pp. 371.

KRATOCHWIL (FRIEDRICH V.) International order and foreign policy: a theoretical sketch of post-war international politics. Boulder, Colo., 1978. pp. 298. *bibliog.*

DEUTSCH (KARL WOLFGANG) Tides among nations. New York, [1979]. pp. 342. *bibliogs.*

The GLOBAL predicament: ecological perspectives on world order; edited by David W. Orr and Marvin S. Soroos. Chapel Hill, [1979]. pp. 398. *bibliog.*

— Study and teaching.

UNITAR NEWS; [pd. by United Nations Institute for Training and Research]. q., New York. *Current issues only kept.*

INTERNATIONAL PEACE BUREAU.

BOOTH (ARTHUR) The International Peace Bureau. Geneva, 1977. pp. 24.

INTERNATIONAL RELATIONS.

SCHELLING (THOMAS CROMBIE) Arms and influence. Westport, Conn., [1966]. pp. 293.

CIENCIALA (ANNA M.) Poland and the Western powers, 1938-1939: a study in the interdependence of Eastern and Western Europe. London, 1968. pp. 310. *bibliog.*

FRANKEL (JOSEPH) National interest. London, 1970. pp. 173. *bibliog.*

JONES (ROY ELLIOTT) Analysing foreign policy: an introduction to some conceptual problems. London, 1970. pp. 157. *bibliogs.*

The EVOLVING United Nations: a prospect for peace?; edited by Kenneth J. Twitchett. New York, 1971. pp. 239. *bibliog.*

NEW ZEALAND FOREIGN AFFAIRS REVIEW; (pd.q.by the Ministry of Foreign Affairs, Wellington). q. (formerly m.), 1973(v.23)- Wellington.

CAPORASO (JAMES A.) The structure and function of European integration. Pacific Palisades, Calif., [1974]. pp. 214. *bibliog.*

KLEIN (ROBERT A.) Sovereign equality among states: the history of an idea. Toronto, [1974]. pp. 198. *bibliog.*

The NATURE of foreign policy: a reader; edited by James Barber and Michael Smith. Edinburgh, 1974. pp. 320. *bibliog.*

STERLING (RICHARD W.) Macropolitics: international relations in a global society. New York, 1974. pp. 648. *bibliog.*

LEBEDEV (NIKOLAI IVANOVICH) A new stage in international relations...; translated by D. Ya Skvirsky and V.M. Schneierson. Oxford, [1976]. pp. 253. *bibliog.*

SMALL states in modern world: the conditions of survival; edited by Peter Worseley and Paschalis Kitromilides. [Nicosia], [1976]. pp. 237. *Papers presented at the "Conference on the Survival of Small Countries," held in Nicosia, 1976, organised by the New Cyprus Association, Cyprus Sociological Association and the Coordinating Committee of Scientific and Cultural Organisations.*

The ORIGINS of the Cold War in Asia; edited by Yonosuke Nagai and Akira Iriye. New York, [1977]. pp. 448. *bibliogs.*

BOYCE (PETER) Foreign affairs for new states: some questions of credentials. New York, 1978. pp. 289. *bibliog.*

CLARKE (MICHAEL) Simulations in the study of international relations. Ormskirk, 1978. pp. 225. *bibliog.*

CLEMENS (WALTER CARL) The U.S.S.R. and global interdependence: alternative futures. Washington, D.C., [1978]. pp. 113. *(American Enterprise Institute for Public Policy Research. AEI Studies. 190)*

CUNY CONFERENCE ON HISTORY AND POLITICS, 2ND, NEW YORK, 1976. Ideology and foreign policy: a global perspective;... [proceedings of the conference]; edited by George Schwab. New York, 1978. pp. 165.

EUROPE and the north-south dialogue; edited by W. Wessels. Paris, [1978]. pp. 78. *(Atlantic Institute. Atlantic Papers. No. 35)*

FISHER (ROGER DRUMMER) Points of choice. Oxford, 1978. pp. 89. *(American Society of International Law. International Crises and the Role of Law)*

FORECASTING in international relations: theory, methods, problems, prospects; edited by Nazli Choucri and Thomas W. Robinson. San Francisco, [1978]. pp. 468. *bibliog.*

HARTMANN (FREDERICK HOWARD) The relations of nations. 5th ed. New York, [1978]. pp. 704. *bibliog.*

INSECURITY!: the spread of weapons in the Indian and Pacific oceans; [edited by] Robert O'Neill. Canberra, 1978. pp. 280. *bibliogs.*

JACOBSEN (KURT) The General Assembly of the United Nations: a quantitative analysis of conflict, inequality, and relevance. Oslo, [1978]. pp. 209. *bibliog.*

JOYNT (CAREY B.) and CORBETT (PERCY ELLWOOD) Theory and reality in world politics. London, 1978. pp. 147. *bibliog.*

KRATOCHWIL (FRIEDRICH V.) International order and foreign policy: a theoretical sketch of post-war international politics. Boulder, Colo., 1978. pp. 298. *bibliog.*

LINKLATER (ANDREW) Obligations beyond the state: the individual, the state and humanity in international theory. 1977 [or rather 1978]. fo. 334. *bibliog. Typescript. Ph.D. (London) thesis: unpublished. This thesis is the property of London University and may not be removed from the Library.*

PARTNERS in tomorrow: strategies for a new international order; edited by Antony J. Dolman and Jan van Ettinger. New York, [1978]. pp. 266.

YARROW (C.H. MIKE) Quaker experiences in international conciliation. New Haven, 1978. pp. 308.

AMERICAN ACADEMY OF POLITICAL AND SOCIAL SCIENCE. Annals. vol. 442. The human dimension of foreign policy: an American perspective; special editor of this volume John Richardson. Philadelphia, 1979. pp. 195.

DEUTSCH (KARL WOLFGANG) Tides among nations. New York, [1979]. pp. 342. *bibliogs.*

FELD (WERNER J.) International relations: a transnational approach. Sherman Oaks, Calif., [1979]. pp. 433. *bibliogs.*

IMPERIALISM, intervention and development; edited by Andrew Mack [and others]. London, [1979]. pp. 393. *bibliogs.*

JONES (ROY ELLIOTT) Principles of foreign policy: the civil state in its world setting. Oxford, 1979. pp. 259. *bibliog.*

SATOW (Sir ERNEST MASON) A guide to diplomatic practice; edited by Lord Gore-Booth; assistant editor Desmond Pakenham. 5th ed. London, [1979]. pp. 544. *bibliog.*

STOESSINGER (JOHN GEORGE) The might of nations: world politics in our time. 6th ed. New York, [1979]. pp. 517. *bibliogs.*

— Bibliography.

INTERNATIONAL relations theory: a bibliography; edited by A.J.R. Groom and C.R. Mitchell. London, 1978. pp. 222.

— Data processing.

EXPLORING competitive arms processes: applications of mathematical modeling and computer simulation in arms policy analysis; editor: W. Ladd Hollist. New York, [1978]. pp. 279.

INTERNATIONAL RELATIONS.(Cont.)

— **Mathematical models.**

EXPLORING competitive arms processes: applications of mathematical modeling and computer simulation in arms policy analysis; editor: W. Ladd Hollist. New York, [1978]. pp. 279.

— **Moral and religious aspects.**

PHILOSOPHY, morality and international affairs; essays edited for the Society for Philosophy and Public Affairs [by] Virginia Held [and others]. New York, 1974. pp. 338.

MORAL claims in world affairs; edited by Ralph Pettman. London, [1979]. pp. 199. *bibliogs.*

— **Research.**

BOULDING (KENNETH EWART) Stable peace. Austin, [1978]. pp. 143.

FALKOWSKI (LAWRENCE S.) Presidents, secretaries of state, and crises in U.S. foreign relations: a model and predictive analysis. Boulder, Colo., 1978. pp. 173.

KAPLAN (MORTON A.) Towards professionalism in international theory: macrosystem analysis. New York, [1979]. pp. 182. *bibliogs.*

— **Study and teaching.**

ATLANTIC INSTITUTE. Statement of purpose and programs. Paris, 1979. pp. 31.

INTERNATIONAL TELECOMMUNICATION UNION.

GARMIER (JACQUES) L'UIT et les télécommunications par satellites. Bruxelles, 1975. pp. 341. *bibliog.*

INTERNATIONAL TELEPHONE AND TELEGRAPH CORPORATION.

GOOLRICK (ROBERT M.) Public policy toward corporate growth: the ITT merger cases. Port Washington, N.Y., [1978]. pp. 212. *bibliog.*

INTERNATIONALISM.

ROSENKO (IVAN ARKHIPOVICH) Internatsional'nye sviazi rabochikh Leningrada, 1921-1937 gg. Leningrad, 1977. pp. 140.

INTERORGANIZATIONAL RELATIONS.

INTERORGANIZATIONAL policy making: limits to coordination and central control; [edited by] Kenneth Hanf and Fritz W. Scharpf. London, [1978]. pp. 373. *bibliogs.*

INTERORGANIZATIONAL relations: selected readings; edited by William M. Evan. Philadelphia, 1978. pp. 442. *bibliogs.*

INTERPERSONAL COMMUNICATION.

STUDIES in the organization of conversational interaction; edited by Jim Schenkein. New York, [1978]. pp. 275. *bibliog.*

INTERPERSONAL RELATIONS.

WILSON (MARY MONICA) For men and elders: change in the relations of generations and of men and women among the Nyakyusa-Ngonde people, 1875-1971. London, [1977]. pp. 209. *bibliog.* 5 appendices in end pocket.

ALMAGOR (URI) Pastoral partners: affinity and bond partners among the Dassanetch of south-west Ethiopia. Manchester, 1978. pp. 258. *bibliog.*

ARGYLE (MICHAEL) The psychology of interpersonal behaviour. 3rd ed. Harmondsworth, 1978. pp. 322. *bibliog.*

KELLEY (HAROLD HARDING) and THIBAUT (JOHN WALTER) Interpersonal relations: a theory of interdependence. New York, [1978]. pp. 341. *bibliog.*

INTERRACIAL ADOPTION

— **Denmark.**

PRUZAN (VITA) Født i udlandet - adopteret i Danmark, etc. København, 1977. pp. 221. *bibliog.* (Socialforskningsinstituttet. Publikationer. 77) With English summary.

INTERVIEWING.

The MEASUREMENT of intrapersonal space by grid technique. Vol. 2. Dimensions of intrapersonal space; edited by Patrick Slater. London, [1977]. pp. 270.

BRADBURN (NORMAN M.) and SUDMAN (SEYMOUR) Improving interview method and questionnaire design; (with the assistance of Edward Blair [and others]). San Francisco, 1979. pp. 214. *bibliog.*

INTUITIONISTIC MATHEMATICS.

DUMMETT (MICHAEL ANTHONY EARDLEY) Elements of intuitionism. Oxford, 1977. pp. 467. *bibliog.*

INVERNIZZI (GAETANO).

ALASIA (FRANCO) Gaetano Invernizzi, dirigente operaio. Milano, [1976]. pp. 243. (Istituto Milanese per la Storia della Resistenza e del Movimento Operaio. Collana di Studi e Biografie)

INVESTMENT BANKING.

CHOWN (JOHN F.) and KELEN (THOMAS F.) Offshore investment centres...; edited by Philip Thorn. London, [1977]. pp. 285.

INVESTMENT OF PUBLIC FUNDS

— **Brazil.**

SILVA (MARIA DA CONCEICÃO) A divida do setor publico brasileiro: seu papel no financiamento dos investimentos publicos. Rio de Janeiro, 1976. pp. 201. *bibliog.* (Brazil. Instituto de Planejamento Econômico e Social. Instituto de Pesquisas. Relatorios de Pesquisa. No. 32)

— **United Kingdom.**

The TEST discount rate and the required rate of return on investment: proceedings of a seminar held at the Civil Service College, Sunningdale, 16/17 June 1978. London, Treasury, 1979. pp. 57. (Government Economic Service Working Papers. No. 22)

— **Yugoslavia.**

BURGER (WILLEM) and others. Self-management and investment control in Yugoslavia: an exploratory investigation. The Hague, [1977]. pp. 336. *bibliog.* (Hague. Institute of Social Studies. Research Report Series. No. 2)

INVESTMENT TRUSTS

— **United Kingdom.**

U.K. Price Commission. 1979. Unit trust management charges: report...following an enquiry commissioned by the Department of Trade. London, 1979. pp. 41.

INVESTMENTS.

CALCUL économique et planification; [report of working party]. Paris, 1973. pp. 110. (France. Commissariat Général du Plan. Economie et Planification)

HONOHAN (PATRICK THOMAS) Uncertainty, portfolio choice and economic fluctuations. 1978. fo. 411. *bibliog.* Typescript. Ph.D. (London) thesis: unpublished. This thesis is the property of London University and may not be removed from the Library.

NICKELL (STEPHEN J.) The investment decisions of firms. Welwyn, 1978. pp. 326. *bibliog.*

RYAN (TERENCE M.) Theory of portfolio selection. London, 1978. pp. 143. *bibliog.*

ENGLUND (PETER) Profits and market adjustment: a study in the dynamics of production, productivity and rates of return. Stockholm, 1979. pp. 260. *bibliog.*

FISCHER (DONALD E.) and JORDAN (RONALD J.) Security analysis and portfolio management. 2nd ed. Englewood Cliffs, N.J., [1979]. pp. 604.

— **Accounting.**

FINANCIAL information requirements for security analysis; edited by A. Rashad Abdel-khalik and Thomas F. Keller. [Durham, N.C., 1979?]. pp. 164. *bibliogs.* Duke Second Accounting Symposium, 1976.

— **Mathematical models.**

NICKELL (STEPHEN J.) The investment decisions of firms. Welwyn, 1978. pp. 326. *bibliog.*

STOCHASTIC dominance: an approach to decision-making under risk; edited by G.A. Whitmore [and] M.C. Findlay. Lexington, Mass., [1978]. pp. 401. *bibliog.*

— **Argentine Republic.**

ALONSO (ALDO) and ETCHEGOYEN (RODOLFO) Analisis de la rentabilidad de inversiones en la empresa argentina. Buenos Aires, [1976]. pp. 168. *bibliogs.* (Federacion Argentina de Consejos Profesionales en Ciencias Economicas. Area: Administracion. Informes.1)

— — **Formosa.**

FORMOSA (PROVINCE, ARGENTINE REPUBLIC). Ministerio de Economia. 1967. Regimen de promocion y franquicias para las inversiones en la Provincia de Formosa. [Formosa], 1967. pp. 241.

— **European Economic Community countries.**

MORGAN (EDWARD VICTOR) and HARRINGTON (RICHARD) Capital markets in the EEC: the sources and uses of medium- and long-term finance. Farnborough, 1977. pp. 495. *bibliog.* Published for the Economists Advisory Group.

— **Salvador.**

INSTITUTO SALVADOREÑO DE FOMENTO INDUSTRIAL. Essentials of laws and regulations related to investments in El Salvador. [San Salvador, 1971?]. pp. 40.

— **Sudan.**

INDUSTRIAL RESEARCH AND CONSULTANCY INSTITUTE [SUDAN]. Industrial investment guide. Khartoum, 1976. pp. 249, ii.

— **Sweden.**

PRASKI (SVERKER) Econometric investment functions and an attempt to evaluate the investment policy in Sweden, 1960-1973. Uppsala, 1978. pp. 131. *bibliog.* (Uppsala. Universitet. Acta Universitatis Upsaliensis. Studia Oeconomica Upsaliensia. 5)

— **Underdeveloped areas.**

See UNDERDEVELOPED AREAS — Investments.

— **United Kingdom.**

DAY (J.G.) and JAMIESON (A.T.) Institutional investment. [London, 1975 repr. 1977-78]. 6 vols. *bibliogs.*

CONFEDERATION OF BRITISH INDUSTRY. Investment lead times in British manufacturing industry: the report of a CBI working party. London, 1978. pp. 48.

NATIONAL ECONOMIC DEVELOPMENT COUNCIL. Brewing Sector Working Group. Investment and efficiency in the brewing industry; report. [London, National Economic Development Office, 1978]. 1 pamphlet (various pagings).

CRAIG (MALCOLM) Successful investment. London, 1979. pp. 188.

REES (R.D.) and MIALL (R.H.C.) The effects of regional policy on manufacturing investment and capital stock within the UK. London, Department of Industry, 1979. pp. 22. (Government Economic Service Working Papers. No. 26)

— — **Mathematical models.**

BEAN (CHARLES R.) An econometric model of manufacturing investment in the UK. London, Treasury, 1979. pp. (39). *bibliog. (Government Economic Service Working Papers. No. 29)*

— **United States.**

STURM (JAMES LESTER) Investing in the United States 1798-1893: upper wealth-holders in a market economy. New York, 1977. pp. 196. *bibliog.*

BLUME (MARSHALL E.) and FRIEND (IRWIN) The changing role of the individual investor. New York, [1978]. pp. 243. *bibliogs.*

DICK (TREVOR J.O.) An economic theory of technological change: the case of patents and the United States railroads 1871-1950. New York, 1978. pp. 145. *bibliog.*

RIFKIN (JEREMY) and BARBER (RANDY) The North will rise again: pensions, politics and power in the 1980s. Boston, Mass., [1978]. pp. 279. *bibliog.*

INVESTMENTS, AMERICAN.

WILKINS (MIRA) The emergence of multinational enterprise: American business abroad from the colonial era to 1914. Cambridge, Mass., [1970]. pp. 310. *bibliog.*

BERGSTEN (C. FRED) An analysis of U.S. foreign direct investment policy and economic development. [Washington], 1976. pp. 114. *bibliog. (United States. Agency for International Development. Bureau for Program and Policy Coordination. A. I.D. Discussion Papers. No. 36)*

FRANK (ROBERT H.) and FREEMAN (RICHARD T.) Distributional consequences of direct foreign investment. New York, 1978. pp. 157. *bibliog.*

KRASNER (STEPHEN D.) Defending the national interest: raw materials investments and U. S. foreign policy. Princeton, N.J., [1978]. pp. 404. *bibliog.*

— **Salvador.**

INSTITUTO SALVADOREÑO DE FOMENTO INDUSTRIAL. The new world of opportunity: El Salvador. [San Salvador, 1971?]. pp. 15.

— **South Africa.**

SEIDMAN (ANN WILLCOX) and SEIDMAN (NEVA) U.S. multinationals in Southern Africa. Dar es Salaam, 1977. pp. 252. *bibliogs.*

INVESTMENTS, BRITISH.

ZALDUENDO (EDUARDO ANDRES) Libras y rieles: las inversiones britanicas para el desarrollo de los ferrocarriles en Argentina, Brasil, Canada e India durante el Siglo XIX. Buenos Aires, [1975]. pp. 595. *bibliog.*

— **Africa, West.**

CONFEDERATION OF BRITISH INDUSTRY. West African visit report: Nigeria, Ivory Coast, Liberia, Senegal. London, 1978. pp. 45. *bibliog.*

INVESTMENTS, FOREIGN.

DAY (J.G.) and JAMIESON (A.T.) Institutional investment. [London, 1975 repr. 1977-78]. 6 vols. *bibliogs.*

CHOWN (JOHN F.) and KELEN (THOMAS F.) Offshore investment centres...; edited by Philip Thorn. London, [1977]. pp. 285.

GOLOSOV (VLADIMIR VIKTOROVICH) Teorii vyvoza kapitala. Moskva, 1977. pp. 224.

CASSON (MARK C.) Alternatives to the multinational enterprise. London, 1979. pp. 116. *bibliog.*

— **Law and legislation — Argentine Republic — Formosa.**

FORMOSA (PROVINCE, ARGENTINE REPUBLIC). Ministerio de Economia. 1967. Regimen de promocion y franquicias para las inversiones en la Provincia de Formosa. [Formosa], 1967. pp. 241.

— **Africa, Subsaharan.**

UNITED NATIONS. Office of Public Information. 1969. Foreign economic interests and decolonization: a report. (OPI/370). New York, 1969. pp. 32.

— **America, Latin.**

PANEL ON FOREIGN INVESTMENT IN LATIN AMERICA, MEDELLÍN, COLOMBIA, 1970. [Report of the] Panel...[held at] Medellín, Colombia, 8-11 June 1970. (ST/ECA/131). New York, United Nations, 1971. pp. 53.

— **Argentine Republic.**

MINSBURG (NAUM) Inversiones extranjeras y dependencia: enfoque historico y actual. Buenos Aires, 1975. pp. 291. *bibliog.*

— **Australia.**

CARR (DAVID WILLIAM) Foreign investment and development in the southwest Pacific with special reference to Australia and Indonesia. New York, [1978]. pp. 197. *bibliog.*

— **Brazil.**

PEREIRA (JOSE EDUARDO DE CARVALHO) Financiamento externo e crescimento econômico no Brasil, 1966/73. Rio de Janeiro, 1974. pp. 273. *bibliog. (Brazil. Instituto de Planejamento Econômico e Social. Instituto de Pesquisas. Relatorios de Pesquisa. No. 27)*

— **Canada.**

AUBIN (HENRY) City for sale. Montréal, [1977]. pp. 401.

PATTISON (JOHN CHARLES) Financial markets and foreign ownership. [Toronto, 1978]. pp. 143. *bibliog. (Ontario. Economic Council. Occasional Papers. 8)*

— **Colombia.**

MATTER (KONRAD) Inversiones extranjeras en la economia colombiana. Medellin, 1977. pp. 407. *bibliog.*

— **East (Near East).**

INTERNATIONAL business in the Middle East: case studies; edited by Ashok Kapoor. Boulder, Colo., 1979. pp. 134. *bibliog.*

— **France.**

FRANCE. Ministère de l'Industrie. Service du Traitement de l'Information et des Statistiques Industrielles. 1978. L'implantation étrangère dans l'industrie au 1er janvier 1976. Paris, [1978]. pp. 183. *(Traits Fondamentaux du Système Industriel Français. Recueils Statistiques. Publication no.9)*

— **Indonesia.**

CARR (DAVID WILLIAM) Foreign investment and development in the southwest Pacific with special reference to Australia and Indonesia. New York, [1978]. pp. 197. *bibliog.*

— **Madagascar.**

MADAGASCAR. Bureau de Développement et de Promotion Industriels. 1968. Guide de l'investisseur; [with 1969 supplement]. [Tananarive], 1968. pp. 87; fo. (4).

— **Mexico.**

FEDER (ERNEST) Agronomist. Strawberry imperialism: an enquiry into the mechanisms of dependency in Mexican agriculture. The Hague, 1977. pp. 199. *(Hague. Institute of Social Studies. Research Report Series. No. 1)*

— **Nigeria.**

TEWSON (GEOFFREY E.) and COTTON (DAVID) Nigeria: business opportunities. London, [1977]. pp. 144.

— **Pacific, The.**

CARR (DAVID WILLIAM) Foreign investment and development in the southwest Pacific with special reference to Australia and Indonesia. New York, [1978]. pp. 197. *bibliog.*

— **Romania.**

HEMY (GEOFFREY W.) Romania: business opportunities. London, [1977]. pp. 193.

— **Singapore.**

YOSHIHARA (KUNIO) Foreign investment and domestic response: a study of Singapore's industrialization. Singapore, [1976]. pp. 263. *bibliog.*

— **South Africa.**

KUBICEK (ROBERT V.) Economic imperialism in theory and practice: the case of South African gold mining finance 1886-1914. Durham, 1979. pp. 239. *bibliog. (Duke University. Center for Commonwealth and Comparative Studies. [Publications]. No. 45)*

— **Uganda.**

UGANDA. Law Reform Commission. 1977. Foreign investment in Uganda; government policy and the law. Entebbe, 1977. pp. 19. *(Law in Action Publication Series. No. 3)*

— **Underdeveloped areas.**

See **UNDERDEVELOPED AREAS - Investments, Foreign.**

— **United States.**

CROWE (KENNETH C.) America for sale. New York, 1978. pp. 297.

FRANK (ROBERT H.) and FREEMAN (RICHARD T.) Distributional consequences of direct foreign investment. New York, 1978. pp. pp. 157. *bibliog.*

INVESTMENTS, JAPANESE.

SEKIGUCHI (SUEO) Japanese direct foreign investment. London, 1979. pp. 153. *bibliogs.*

YOUNG (ALEXANDER K.) The Sogo Shosha: Japan's multinational trading companies. Boulder, Colo., 1979. pp. 247. *bibliog.*

— **Asia, Southeast.**

KATANO (HIKOJI) and others. Japan's direct investment to ASEAN countries. Kobe, [1978]. pp. 152. *bibliog. (Kobe. University. Research Institute for Economics and Business Administration. Kobe Economic and Business Research Series. No. 6)*

YOSHIHARA (KUNIO) Japanese investment in Southeast Asia. Honolulu, [1978]. pp. 230. *bibliog. (Kyoto. University. Center for Southeast Asian Studies. Monographs: English Series. 11)*

INVESTMENTS, SWISS — Underdeveloped areas.

See **UNDERDEVELOPED AREAS — Investments, Swiss.**

IRAN

— **Census.**

IRAN. Census, 1976. National census of population and housing, November 1976: [reports for shahrestans, ostans and total country]. [Tehran, 1978 in progress]. *In English and Persian.*

IRAN(Cont.)

— Economic conditions.

RCD MAGAZINE, THE; [pd. by] Regional Cooperation for Development. q., spring 1974(v.1, no.1)- , with gaps. Tehran.

GRAHAM (ROBERT) Journalist. Iran: the illusion of power. London, [1978]. pp. 228.

HALLIDAY (FRED) Iran: dictatorship and development. Harmondsworth, 1979. pp. 348. *bibliog.*

RCD NEWSLETTER; [pd. by] Information Section, Regional Cooperation for Development. irreg., current issues only. Tehran.

— Economic policy.

PAKISTAN. Ministry of Information and Broadcasting. 1967. Pakistan and R[egional] C[o-operation for] D[evelopment]: three years of regional co-operation for development, 1964-1967. [Karachi, 1967] pp. 48. *bibliog.*

— Foreign relations — Russia.

MOSS (ROBERT) The campaign to destabilise Iran. London, 1978. pp. 18. *(Institute for the Study of Conflict. Conflict Studies. No.101)*

— History.

PROCOPIUS, of Caesarea. History of the wars; (with an English translation by H.B. Dewing). London, 1914-28 repr. 1962-71. 5 vols. *bibliog. Parallel Greek and English texts.*

BAKHASH (SHAUL) Iran: monarchy, bureaucracy and reform under the Qajars: 1858- 1896. London, 1978. pp. 444. *bibliog. (Oxford. University. St. Antony's College. Middle East Centre. St. Antony's Middle East Monographs. No. 8).*

— Politics and government.

BAKHASH (SHAUL) Iran: monarchy, bureaucracy and reform under the Qajars: 1858- 1896. London, 1978. pp. 444. *bibliog. (Oxford. University. St. Antony's College. Middle East Centre. St. Antony's Middle East Monographs. No. 8).*

MOSS (ROBERT) The campaign to destabilise Iran. London, 1978. pp. 18. *(Institute for the Study of Conflict. Conflict Studies. No.101)*

HALLIDAY (FRED) Iran: dictatorship and development. Harmondsworth, 1979. pp. 348. *bibliog.*

IRAQ

— Description and travel.

THESIGER (WILFRED) The Marsh Arabs. Harmondsworth, 1967 repr. 1978. pp. 233. *First published by Longmans, Green, 1964.*

— Economic conditions.

The INTEGRATION of modern Iraq; edited by Abbas Kelidar. London, [1979]. pp. 200.

— Foreign relations.

McLAURIN (RONALD D.) and others. Foreign policy making in the Middle East: domestic influences on policy in Egypt, Iraq, Israel, and Syria. New York, 1977. pp. 313. *bibliog.*

— — United Kingdom.

MEJCHER (HELMUT) Imperial quest for oil: Iraq, 1910-1928. London, 1976. pp. 130. *bibliog. (Oxford. University. St. Antony's College. Middle East Centre. St. Antony's Middle East Monographs. No 6)*

— History.

MEJCHER (HELMUT) Imperial quest for oil: Iraq, 1910-1928. London, 1976. pp. 130. *bibliog. (Oxford. University. St. Antony's College. Middle East Centre. St. Antony's Middle East Monographs. No 6)*

— Politics and government.

BATATU (HANNA) The old social classes and the revolutionary movements of Iraq: a study of Iraq's old landed and commercial classes and of its communists, Ba'thists, and Free Officers. Princeton, [1978]. pp. 1283. *bibliog.*

KHADDURI (MAJID) Socialist Iraq: a study in Iraqi politics since 1968. Washington, D.C., 1978. pp. 265.

The INTEGRATION of modern Iraq; edited by Abbas Kelidar. London, [1979]. pp. 200.

— Social life and customs.

THESIGER (WILFRED) The Marsh Arabs. Harmondsworth, 1967 repr. 1978. pp. 233. *First published by Longmans, Green, 1964.*

IRELAND

— Church history — Sources — Bibliography.

KENNEY (JAMES FRANCIS) The sources for the early history of Ireland: ecclesiastical: an introduction and guide; [reprint of the work first published in 1929, with revisions, addenda and corrigenda by Ludwig Bieler] . New York, 1966 repr. 1979. pp. 815. *bibliogs.*

— Description and travel.

AALEN (F.H.A.) Man and the landscape in Ireland. London, 1978. pp. 343. *bibliog.*

— History.

AALEN (F.H.A.) Man and the landscape in Ireland. London, 1978. pp. 343. *bibliog.*

TIERNEY (MARK) Modern Ireland since 1850. rev. ed. Dublin, 1978. pp. 241.

— — To 1172 — Sources.

KENNEY (JAMES FRANCIS) The sources for the early history of Ireland: ecclesiastical: an introduction and guide; [reprint of the work first published in 1929, with revisions, addenda and corrigenda by Ludwig Bieler] . New York, 1966 repr. 1979. pp. 815. *bibliogs.*

— — 1558-1603.

BERLETH (RICHARD) The twilight Lords. London, 1979. pp. 316. *bibliog.*

— — 1800-1899.

BEW (PAUL) Land and the national question in Ireland, 1858-82. Dublin, 1978. pp. 307.

BRYNN (EDWARD) Crown and castle: British rule in Ireland, 1800-1830. Dublin, 1978. pp. 172. *bibliog.*

— — 1900- .

MANSERGH (PHILIP NICHOLAS SETON) The prelude to partition: concept and aims in Ireland and India. Cambridge, 1978. pp. 62. *(Cambridge. University. Commonwealth Lectures. 1976)*

— — 1910-1921.

CARROLL (FRANCIS M.) American opinion and the Irish question, 1910-23: a study in opinion and policy. Dublin, 1978. pp. 319. *bibliog.*

— Nationalism.

FALIGOT (ROGER) La résistance irlandaise, 1916-1976. Paris, 1977. pp. 339. *bibliog.*

BEW (PAUL) Land and the national question in Ireland, 1858-82. Dublin, 1978. pp. 307.

BRYNN (EDWARD) Crown and castle: British rule in Ireland, 1800-1830. Dublin, 1978. pp. 172. *bibliog.*

CARROLL (FRANCIS M.) American opinion and the Irish question, 1910-23: a study in opinion and policy. Dublin, 1978. pp. 319. *bibliog.*

FALIGOT (ROGER) James Connolly et le mouvement révolutionnaire irlandais. Paris, 1978. pp. 333. *bibliog.*

WATSON (GEORGE) Irish identity and the literary revival: Synge, Yeats, Joyce and O'Casey. London, 1979. pp. 326. *bibliog.*

— Politics and government.

BRYNN (EDWARD) Crown and castle: British rule in Ireland, 1800-1830. Dublin, 1978. pp. 172. *bibliog.*

IRELAND (REPUBLIC)

— Constitution.

CHUBB (BASIL) The constitution and constitutional change in Ireland. Dublin, 1978. pp. 122. *bibliog.*

— Constitutional history.

MAIR (PETER) The break-up of the United Kingdom: the Irish experience of regime change, 1918-49. Glasgow, [1978]. pp. 20. *(Glasgow. University of Strathclyde. Centre for the Study of Public Policy. Studies in Public Policy. No. 13)*

— Department of Finance.

FANNING (RONAN) The Irish Department of Finance, 1922-58. Dublin, [1978]. pp. 707. *bibliog.*

— Economic conditions.

KENNEDY (KIERAN A.) and BRUTON (RICHARD) The Irish economy. Brussels, European Communities, 1975. pp. 168. *bibliog. (European Economic Community. Studies. Economic and Financial Series. 10)*

EIRE. 1978. Input-output tables for 1969. Dublin, 1978. pp. 75.

— Economic policy.

KENNEDY (KIERAN A.) and BRUTON (RICHARD) The Irish economy. Brussels, European Communities, 1975. pp. 168. *bibliog. (European Economic Community. Studies. Economic and Financial Series. 10)*

IRISH economic policy: a review of major issues....; [edited by] B. R. Dowling and J. Durkan. Dublin, 1978. pp. 410. *bibliogs.* At head of title: Economic and Social Research Institute.

EIRE. 1979. Programme for national development, 1978-1981. Dublin, Stationery Office, 1979. pp. 122.

— Executive departments.

FANNING (RONAN) The Irish Department of Finance, 1922-58. Dublin, [1978]. pp. 707. *bibliog.*

— Foreign economic relations.

For related heading see EUROPEAN COMMUNITIES— (Ireland Republic).

— Foreign relations.

See also EUROPEAN COMMUNITIES — Ireland (Republic).

— — United Kingdom.

PECK (JOHN) Dublin from Downing Street. Dublin, 1978. pp. 241.

— Industries.

McALEESE (DERMOT) A profile of grant-aided industry in Ireland. Dublin, Industrial Development Authority, 1977. pp. 92. *bibliog. (Publication Series. Paper 5)*

— Neutrality.

SHARE (BERNARD) The Emergency: neutral Ireland, 1939-1945. Dublin, 1978. pp. 146. *bibliog.*

— Officials and employees — Salaries, allowances, etc.

EIRE. Review Body on Higher Remuneration in the Public Sector. 1978. Reports to Minister for Finance and Minister for the Public Service in the period 13 July to 11 February 1977. [Dublin, 1978]. pp. 273.

— Oireachtas — Elections.

O'LEARY (CORNELIUS) Irish elections, 1918-77: parties, voters and proportional representation. Dublin, 1979. pp. 134.

— Politics and government.

MAIR (PETER) The break-up of the United Kingdom: the Irish experience of regime change, 1918-49. Glasgow, [1978]. pp. 20. *(Glasgow. University of Strathclyde. Centre for the Study of Public Policy. Studies in Public Policy. No. 13)*

O'LEARY (CORNELIUS) Irish elections, 1918-77: parties, voters and proportional representation. Dublin, 1979. pp. 134.

— Social policy.

EIRE. 1979. Programme for national development, 1978-1981. Dublin, Stationery Office, 1979. pp. 122.

IRELAND, NORTHERN

— Assembly — Privileges and immunities.

IRELAND, NORTHERN. Northern Ireland Assembly. Committee of Privileges. 1974. First report...together with the proceedings of the Committee and minutes of evidence and appendices: complaint concerning a letter to a member dated 21st November 1973. Belfast, 1974. pp. 31. *(Northern Ireland Assembly. [Reports and Papers]. 3)*

— — Salaries, pensions, etc.

IRELAND, NORTHERN. Assembly Contributory Pension Fund. Accounts...together with the report of the Comptroller and Auditor-General thereon. a., 1976/77- Belfast.

— Census.

COMPTON (PAUL A.) Northern Ireland: a census atlas. Dublin, 1978. pp. 169. *bibliog.*

— Economic conditions.

PROBERT (BELINDA) Beyond orange and green: the political economy of the Northern Ireland crisis. London, [1978]. pp. 174. *bibliog.*

— History.

McCANN (EAMONN) War and an Irish town. Harmondsworth, 1974. pp. 256.

MILLER (DAVID WILLIAM) Queen's rebels: Ulster loyalism in historical perspective. Dublin, 1978. pp. 194.

MOODY (THEODORE WILLIAM) The Ulster question, 1603-1973. 3rd ed. Dublin, 1978. pp. 134. *bibliog.*

PROBERT (BELINDA) Beyond orange and green: the political economy of the Northern Ireland crisis. London, [1978]. pp. 174. *bibliog.*

— Maps.

COMPTON (PAUL A.) Northern Ireland: a census atlas. Dublin, 1978. pp. 169. *bibliog.*

— Politics and government.

McCANN (EAMONN) War and an Irish town. Harmondsworth, 1974. pp. 256.

FALIGOT (ROGER) La résistance irlandaise, 1916-1976. Paris, 1977. pp. 339. *bibliog.*

SHEANE (MICHAEL) Ulster and its future after the troubles. Stockport, [1977]. pp. 175. *bibliog.*

TROOPS OUT MOVEMENT. Irish news-sheet: chronology Nov. '76-Jun. '77. London, [1977]. pp. 43.

EUROPEAN COURT OF HUMAN RIGHTS. Series A: Judgments and Decisions. [A25]. ...Case of Ireland v. The United Kingdom: 1. Decision of 29 April 1976; 2. Judgment of 18 January 1978. Strasbourg, Council of Europe, 1978. pp. 141 [bis]. *In English and French.*

NORTHERN IRELAND CIVIL RIGHTS ASSOCIATION. "We shall overcome"...; the history of the struggle for civil rights in Northern Ireland 1968-1978. Belfast, [1978?]. pp. 47.

OLIVER (JOHN ANDREW) Working at Stormont: memoirs. Dublin, 1978. pp. 251.

PROBERT (BELINDA) Beyond orange and green: the political economy of the Northern Ireland crisis. London, [1978]. pp. 174. *bibliog.*

EMERSON (PETER J.) Northern Ireland: that sons may bury their fathers. London, 1979. pp. 181.

— — Bibliography.

U.K. Home Office. Library. 1977. Ulster since direct rule: (bibliography compiled by Christine Walker). [London, 1977]. fo. 10. *(Reading lists)*

— Religion.

MILLER (ROBERT L.) Attitudes to work in Northern Ireland. Belfast, 1978. pp. 19. *(Fair Employment Agency for Northern Ireland. Research Papers. 2)*

OSBORNE (ROBERT D.) and MURRAY (RUSSELL C.) Educational qualifications and religious affiliation in Northern Ireland: an examination of G.C.E.'O' and 'A' levels. Belfast, 1978. pp. 42. *bibliog.* *(Fair Employment Agency for Northern Ireland. Research Papers. 3)*

— Social conditions.

EMERSON (PETER J.) Northern Ireland: that sons may bury their fathers. London, 1979. pp. 181.

IRISH AMERICANS.

CARROLL (FRANCIS M.) American opinion and the Irish question, 1910-23: a study in opinion and policy. Dublin, 1978. pp. 319. *bibliog.*

SHORT (K.R.M.) The dynamite war: Irish-American bombers in Victorian Britain. Dublin, 1979. pp. 278. *bibliog.*

IRISH IN LONDON.

LEES (LYNN HOLLEN) Exiles of Erin: Irish migrants in Victorian London. Manchester, 1979. pp. 276. *bibliog.*

IRISH IN THE UNITED KINGDOM.

SHORT (K.R.M.) The dynamite war: Irish-American bombers in Victorian Britain. Dublin, 1979. pp. 278. *bibliog.*

IRISH LITERATURE.

WATSON (GEORGE) Irish identity and the literary revival: Synge, Yeats, Joyce and O'Casey. London, 1979. pp. 326. *bibliog.*

IRISH QUESTION.

McCANN (EAMONN) War and an Irish town. Harmondsworth, 1974. pp. 256.

CARROLL (FRANCIS M.) American opinion and the Irish question, 1910-23: a study in opinion and policy. Dublin, 1978. pp. 319. *bibliog.*

MOODY (THEODORE WILLIAM) The Ulster question, 1603-1973. 3rd ed. Dublin, 1978. pp. 134. *bibliog.*

SHORT (K.R.M.) The dynamite war: Irish-American bombers in Victorian Britain. Dublin, 1979. pp. 278. *bibliog.*

WATSON (GEORGE) Irish identity and the literary revival: Synge, Yeats, Joyce and O'Casey. London, 1979. pp. 326. *bibliog.*

— Public opinion.

ROSE (RICHARD) and others. Is there a concurring majority about Northern Ireland? Glasgow, [1978]. pp. 67. *bibliog.* *(Glasgow. University of Strathclyde. Centre for the Study of Public Policy. Studies in Public Policy. No. 22)*

IRISH REPUBLICAN ARMY.

FALIGOT (ROGER) La résistance irlandaise, 1916-1976. Paris, 1977. pp. 339. *bibliog.*

IRON AND STEEL WORKERS

— United States — New York.

WALKOWITZ (DANIEL J.) Worker city, company town: iron and cotton-worker protest in Troy and Cohoes, New York, 1855-84. Urbana, Ill., [1978]. pp. 292. *bibliog.*

IRON INDUSTRY AND TRADE

— Germany.

SCHINDLER (ROSEMARIE) Die Marktpolitik des Roheisen-Verbandes während der Weimarer Republik. Bielefeld, 1978. pp. 365. *bibliog.*

— United Kingdom.

NORTHERN REGION STRATEGY TEAM. Trends and prospects in major industries: the iron and steel industry. Newcastle-upon-Tyne, 1976. 1 vol. (various foliations). *(Working Papers. No.3)*

— — Statistics.

IRON AND STEEL MONTHLY STATISTICS; pd. by the British Steel Corporation on behalf of the Iron and Steel Statistics Bureau. m., 1956(v.1)- London. *Supersedes British Iron and Steel Federation. Monthly statistical bulletin (1919-1955).*

IRRIGATION

— India.

INDIA. Central Board of Irrigation and Power. 1977. C[entral] B[oard of] I[rrigation and] P[ower] Golden Jubilee, 1927-77: commemorative volume. New Delhi, 1977. pp. 188.

ISLANDS

— Law and legislation.

BOWETT (DEREK WILLIAM) The legal regime of islands in international law. Dobbs Ferry, N.Y., 1979. pp. 337.

SYMMONS (CLIVE RALPH) The maritime zones of islands in international law. The Hague, 1979. pp. 307.

ISLE OF MAN

— Politics and government.

KERMODE (D.G.) Devolution at work: a case study of the Isle of Man. Farnborough, [1979]. pp. 180. *bibliogs.*

ISRAEL

— Commerce — Statistics.

ISRAEL'S FOREIGN TRADE: general summary; [pd. by] Central Bureau of Statistics. a., 1973- Jerusalem. *[in English and Hebrew]*

— Economic policy.

GLASS (MOSES MICHAEL) Die Beeinflussung der israelischen Volkswirtschaft durch die Fiskalpolitik in den Jahren 1960-1974: Versuch einer strukturell-quantitativen Analyse. [Zürich], 1977. pp. 270. *bibliog. Dissertation - Universität Zürich.*

— Emigration and immigration.

IMMIGRATION TO ISRAEL; [pd. by] Central Bureau of Statistics. a., 1973- Jerusalem. *[in English and Hebrew]*

ISRAEL (Cont.)

— Foreign economic relations — South Africa.

STEVENS (RICHARD P.) and ELMESSIRI (ABDELWAHAB M.) eds. Israel and South Africa: the progression of a relationship. New York, [1976]. pp. 214. *bibliog.*

— Foreign relations.

McLAURIN (RONALD D.) and others. Foreign policy making in the Middle East: domestic influences on policy in Egypt, Iraq, Israel, and Syria. New York, 1977. pp. 313. *bibliog.*

ARONSON (SHLOMO) Conflict and bargaining in the Middle East: an Israeli perspective. Baltimore, [1978]. pp. 448. *bibliog.*

NISAN (MORDECHAI) Israel and the territories: a study in control, 1967-1977. Ramat Gan, 1978. pp. 201. *bibliog.*

The LEFT against Zion: communism, Israel and the Middle East; edited by Robert S. Wistrich. London, 1979. pp. 309.

— — America, Latin.

KAUFMAN (EDY) and others. Israel-Latin American relations. New Brunswick, [1979]. pp. 256.

— — South Africa.

STEVENS (RICHARD P.) and ELMESSIRI (ABDELWAHAB M.) eds. Israel and South Africa: the progression of a relationship. New York, [1976]. pp. 214. *bibliog.*

— History — Sources.

The ISRAEL-Arab reader: a documentary history of the Middle East conflict; edited with...comments by Walter Laqueur. 3rd ed. Toronto, 1976. pp. 585. *bibliog.*

— History, Military.

DUPUY (TREVOR N.) Elusive victory: the Arab-Israeli Wars, 1947-1974. London, 1978. pp. 669. *bibliog.*

— Politics and government.

NACHMIAS (DAVID) and ROSENBLOOM (DAVID H.) Bureaucratic culture: citizens and administrators in Israel. London, [1978]. pp. 212. *bibliog.*

GERVASI (FRANK) The life and times of Menahem Begin: rebel to statesman. New York, 1979. pp. 382. *bibliog.*

PERETZ (DON) The government and politics of Israel. Boulder, Colo., [1979]. pp. 219. *bibliog.*

— Population.

ISRAEL. Central Bureau of Statistics. Vital statistics. a., 1972- Jerusalem. *[in English and Hebrew]*

BACHI (ROBERTO) The population of Israel. Jerusalem, [1978?]. pp. 428. *(Committee for International Coordination of National Research in Demography. C.I.C.R.E.D. Series)*

FRIEDLANDER (DOV) and GOLDSCHEIDER (CALVIN) The population of Israel. New York, 1979. pp. 240.

— Statistics, Vital.

ISRAEL. Central Bureau of Statistics. Vital statistics. a., 1972- Jerusalem. *[in English and Hebrew]*

ISRAEL AND THE DIASPORA.

FACKENHEIM (EMIL L.) The Jewish return into history: reflections in the age of Auschwitz and a New Jerusalem. New York, 1978. pp. 296.

ISRAEL-ARAB CONFLICT, 1948- .

MILITARY aspects of the Israeli-Arab conflict; [edited by] Louis Williams. Tel Aviv, [1975]. pp. 265.

The ISRAEL-Arab reader: a documentary history of the Middle East conflict; edited with...comments by Walter Laqueur. 3rd ed. Toronto, 1976. pp. 585. *bibliog.*

DUPUY (TREVOR N.) Elusive victory: the Arab-Israeli Wars, 1947-1974. London, 1978. pp. 669. *bibliog.*

NISAN (MORDECHAI) Israel and the territories: a study in control, 1967-1977. Ramat Gan, 1978. pp. 201. *bibliog.*

O'NEILL (BARD E.) Armed struggle in Palestine: a political-military analysis. Boulder, Colo., 1978. pp. 320.

ISRAEL-ARAB WAR, 1967.

IRAQ. Ministry of Culture and Guidance. Directorate of Public Relations. 1967. Horrors of napalm. Baghdad, 1967. pp. 16.

The ISRAEL-Arab reader: a documentary history of the Middle East conflict; edited with...comments by Walter Laqueur. 3rd ed. Toronto, 1976. pp. 585. *bibliog.*

DUPUY (TREVOR N.) Elusive victory: the Arab-Israeli Wars, 1947-1974. London, 1978. pp. 669. *bibliog.*

— Occupied territories.

ISRAEL. Ministry of Defence. 1968. The military government's civil administration: a concise comprehensive survey, June 1967 - June 1968. Tel Aviv, [1968]. pp. 15.

ISRAEL-ARAB WAR, 1973.

O'BALLANCE (EDGAR) No victor, no vanquished: the Yom Kippur War. San Rafael, Calif., [1978]. pp. 370.

ITALIAN AMERICANS.

GUMINA (DEANNA PAOLI) The Italians of San Francisco, 1850-1930; Gli italiani di San Francisco, 1850-1930. New York, 1978 repr. 1979. pp. 230. *bibliog. Parallel English and Italian texts.*

— Bibliography.

CORDASCO (FRANCESCO) compiler. Italian Americans: a guide to information sources. Detroit, [1978]. pp. 222.

ITALIAN NEWSPAPERS.

ARFE (GAETANO) Storia dell'Avanti! 2nd ed. [Rome, 1977]. pp. 351. *(Istituto Socialista di Studi Storici. Biblioteca Storica)*

ITALIAN PERIODICALS

— Bibliography.

MAJOLO MOLINARI (OLGA) La stampa periodica romana dal 1900 al 1926, scienze morali, storiche e filologiche. Roma, 1977. 2 vols.

ITALY

— Armed forces.

Le FORZE Armate nella società democratica: atti del Seminario di studi, Roma, 16 gennaio 1976. Roma, [1976]. pp. 237.

— — Political activity.

MEDAIL (CESARE) Sotto le stellette: (il movimento dei militari democratici). Torino, [1977]. pp. 104.

— Bibliography.

LANGE (PETER) compiler. Studies on Italy, 1943-1975: select bibliography of American and British materials in political science, economics, sociology and anthropology; with the assistance of Robert Samuels). Torino, 1977. pp. 183.

— Civilization.

MARTINES (LAURO) Power and imagination: city-states in Renaissance Italy. New York, 1979. pp. 368. *bibliog.*

— Constitution.

BAZZICHI (ORESTE) L'organizzazione dello Stato Italiano: rapporti Stato- cittadino. Firenze, 1977. pp. 302.

— Constitutional history.

FROSINI (VITTORIO) Costituzione e società civile. Milano, [1975]. pp. 203. *bibliog.*

— Constitutional law.

LEZIROLI (GIUSEPPE) Aspetti della libertà religiosa, nel quadro dell'attuale sistema di relazione fra Stato e confessioni religiose. Milano, 1977. pp. 240. *bibliog. (Ferrara. Università. Facoltà Giuridica. Pubblicazioni. 2a Serie. 10)*

SCRITTI in onore di Costantino Mortati: aspetti e tendenze del diritto costituzionale. [Milan, 1977]. 4 vols. *(Rome. Università. Istituto di Studi Giuridici. Pubblicazioni. Serie 5. N.22-25)*

La CORTE Costituzionale tra norma giuridica e realtà sociale: bilancio di vent'anni di attività [proceedings of a Convegno di Studio held at Parma in 1976]; a cura di Nicola Occhiocupo. Bologna, [1978]. pp. 528.

— Economic conditions.

GAY (HARRY NELSON) Strenuous Italy: solving a perilous problem. Boston [Mass.], 1927. pp. 217. *bibliog.*

BANCA D'ITALIA. Research Department. Economic papers. irreg., 1977(no. 1)- Roma.

— Economic history.

MONTE (ALFREDO DEL) and GIANNOLA (ADRIANO) Il Mezzogiorno nell'economia italiana. Bologna, [1978]. pp. 405.

— Economic policy.

VANONI (EZIO) Scritti di finanza pubblica e di politica economica; a cura di Antonino Tramontana. Padova, 1976. pp. 219. *(Perugia. Università. Facoltà di Giurisprudenza. Pubblicazioni)*

USCIRE dalla crisi: linee di un programma economico socialista; [by] Bettino Craxi [and others]. Venezia, [1977]. pp. 191.

ZANGIROLAMI (SERGIO) Economia politica marxista e crisi attuale: note per un manuale. Roma, 1977. pp. 187.

ITALY. [Cassa per Opere Straordinarie di Pubblico Interesse nell'Italia Meridionale]. 1978. Rapporto sullo stato di attuazione dei programmi ai sensi della legge 2 maggio 1976 n. 183. [Rome], 1978. 3 vols. (in 1).

— — Mathematical models.

REGIONAL-national econometric modelling with an application to the Italian economy; edited by Murray Brown [and others]. London, [1978]. pp. 203. *bibliogs.*

— Emigration and immigration.

FILIPUZZI (ANGELO) Il dibattito sull'emigrazione: polemiche nazionali e stampa veneta, 1861-1914. Firenze, 1976. pp. 421.

— Executive departments.

BAZZICHI (ORESTE) L'organizzazione dello Stato Italiano: rapporti Stato- cittadino. Firenze, 1977. pp. 302.

ITALY. Istituto Centrale di Statistica. 1978. Cinquanta anni di attività, 1926-1976. Roma, [1978]. pp. 466.

— Foreign economic relations — United States.

Le RELAZIONI economiche fra l'Italia e gli Stati Uniti d'America: esperienze, sviluppi e prospettive; a cura di Franco Tagliarini. Roma, 1976. pp. 227. *In Italian or English.*

— Foreign relations.

NOEL (LEON) Les illusions de Stresa: l'Italie abandonnée à Hitler. Paris, [1975]. pp. 206.

— — **Bibliography.**

LANGE (PETER) compiler. Studies on Italy, 1943-1975: select bibliography of American and British materials in political science, economics, sociology and anthropology; (with the assistance of Robert Samuels). Torino, 1977. pp. 183.

— — **Austria.**

JENKS (WILLIAM ALEXANDER) Francis Joseph and the Italians, 1849-1859. Charlottesville, 1978. pp. 206. *bibliog.*

— — **Germany.**

MICHAELIS (MEIR) Mussolini and the Jews: German-Italian relations and the Jewish question in Italy, 1922-1945. Oxford, 1978. pp. 472. *bibliog.*

SCHREIBER (GERHARD) Revisionismus und Weltmachtstreben: Marineführung und deutsch- italienische Beziehungen, 1919 bis 1944. Stuttgart, 1978. pp. 428. *bibliog. (Militärgeschichtliches Forschungsamt. Beiträge zur Militär- und Kriegsgeschichte. Band 20)*

— — **Sweden.**

EIMER (BIRGITTA) Cavour and Swedish politics. Stockholm, [1978]. pp. 457. *bibliog. (Lund. Universitet. Historiska Institutionen. Lund Studies in International History. 12)*

— **History — 476-1492.**

CELLI (ROBERTO) Studi sui sistemi normativi delle democrazie comunali, secoli 12-15. Firenze, [1976 in progress]. pp. 293. *bibliog.*

— — **1400-1499.**

MALLETT (MICHAEL EDWARD) Mercenaries and their masters: warfare in Renaissance Italy. London, [1974]. pp. 284. *bibliog.*

— — **1789-1870.**

LEONI (FRANCESCO) Storia della controrivoluzione in Italia, 1789-1859. Napoli, [1975]. pp. 347. *bibliog.*

— — **1789-1815.**

TOGNARINI (IVAN) Giacobinismo, rivoluzione, Risorgimento: una messa a punto storiografica. Firenze, 1977. pp. 213.

— — **1815-1870.**

HANCOCK (Sir WILLIAM KEITH) Ricasoli and the Risorgimento in Tuscany. New York, 1969. pp. 320. *bibliog.*

— — **1900- .**

GAY (HARRY NELSON) Strenuous Italy: solving a perilous problem. Boston [Mass.], 1927. pp. 217. *bibliog.*

— — **1914-1945.**

INTERUNIVERSITY CENTRE FOR EUROPEAN STUDIES. International Colloquium, 2nd, 1976. Situations révolutionnaires en Europe, 1917-1922: Allemagne, Italie, Autriche-Hongrie; Revolutionary situations in Europe, 1917-1922: Germany, Italy, Austria-Hungary...edited by Charles L. Bertrand. Montreal, 1977. pp. 251. *bibliog.*

FUCCI (FRANCO) Ali contro Mussolini: i raid aerei antifascisti degli anni trenta. Milano, [1978]. pp. 263. *bibliog.*

ROBERTS (DAVID D.) The syndicalist tradition and Italian fascism. Chapel Hill, N.C., [1979]. pp. 410. *bibliog.*

— — **1937-1945.**

PER una storia della sinistra cristiana: documenti, 1937-1945; a cura di Mario Cocchi e Pio Montesi. Roma, 1975. pp. 278.

— **Industries.**

CONFEDERAZIONE GENERALE DELL'INDUSTRIA ITALIANA. Economia industriale. a., 1976- Roma.

CONFEDERAZIONE GENERALE DELL'INDUSTRIA ITALIANA. Relazione sull'attività confederale. a., 1977- Roma.

— **Istituto Centrale di Statistica.**

ITALY. Istituto Centrale di Statistica. 1978. Cinquanta anni di attività, 1926-1976. Roma, [1978]. pp. 466.

— **Nationalism.**

PERFETTI (FRANCESCO) ed. Il nazionalismo italiano dalle origini alla fusione col fascismo: [an anthology]. Bologna, [1977]. pp. 292. *bibliog.*

— **Parliament.**

LIBERTINI (LUCIO) Quale parlamento?: (osservazioni e proposte sull'istituto parlamentare). Torino, [1977]. pp. 82.

— — **Elections.**

Le ELEZIONI del 20 giugno. Milano, [1976]. pp. 144.

— **Politics and government.**

KOLINSKY (A. MARTIN) Continuity and change in European society: Germany, France and Italy since 1870. London, 1974. pp. 234. *bibliog.*

CHITI (MARIO P.) Partecipazione popolare e pubblica amministrazione. Pisa, 1977. pp. 497. *(Pisa. Università. Istituto Giuridico. Collana. 3)*

— — **Bibliography.**

LANGE (PETER) compiler. Studies on Italy, 1943-1975: select bibliography of American and British materials in political science, economics, sociology and anthropology; (with the assistance of Robert Samuels). Torino, 1977. pp. 183.

— — **476-1268.**

MARTINES (LAURO) Power and imagination: city-states in Renaissance Italy. New York, 1979. pp. 368. *bibliog.*

— — **1268-1559.**

MARTINES (LAURO) Power and imagination: city-states in Renaissance Italy. New York, 1979. pp. 368. *bibliog.*

— — **1789-1900.**

MAZZINI (GIUSEPPE) Scritti politici; a cura di Franco della Peruta. Torino, [1976]. 3 vols. *bibliog.*

— — **1914-1945.**

DELZELL (CHARLES F.) Mussolini's enemies: the Italian anti-fascist resistance. New York, 1974. pp. 620. *bibliog. Reprint of work originally published at Princeton, 1961.*

— — **1922-1945.**

AMENDOLA (GIOVANNI) L'Aventino contro il fascismo: scritti politici, 1924-1926; a cura di Sabato Visco. Milano, 1976. pp. 402.

— — **1937-1945.**

PER una storia della sinistra cristiana: documenti, 1937-1945; a cura di Mario Cocchi e Pio Montesi. Roma, 1975. pp. 278.

— — **1945- .**

GHINI (CELSO) Il terremoto del 15 giugno. Milano, 1976. pp. 282.

FOIS (SERGIO) Sindacati e sistema politico: problematica di un rapporto e implicazioni costituzionali. Milano, 1977. pp. 118.

LEDEEN (MICHAEL ARTHUR) Italy in crisis. Beverly Hills, [1977]. pp. 76. *(Georgetown University. Center for Strategic and International Studies. Washington Papers. vol. 5/43)*

SETTEMBRINI (DOMENICO) La Chiesa nella politica italiana, 1944-1963: alle origini del compromesso storico. [2nd ed.] Milano, 1977. pp. 509.

TOGLIATTI e il Mezzogiorno: atti del convegno tenuto a Bari il 2-3-4 novembre 1975; a cura di Franco De Felice. Roma, 1977. 2 vols.

BARCELLONA (PIETRO) La Repubblica in trasformazione: problemi istituzionali del caso italiano. Bari, [1978]. pp. 222.

— **Presidents — Election.**

ARMAROLI (PAOLO) L'elezione del presidente della repubblica in Italia. Padova, 1977. pp. 416.

— **Rural conditions.**

OTTAVIANI (OBERDAN) Sant'Agata dei Goti: l'informazione mancata; la comunicazione nella società agricola del Mezzogiorno: ricerca in un comune campione. Urbino, [1977]. pp. 319. *bibliog.*

— **Social conditions.**

GAY (HARRY NELSON) Strenuous Italy: solving a perilous problem. Boston [Mass.], 1927. pp. 217. *bibliog.*

— — **Bibliography.**

LANGE (PETER) compiler. Studies on Italy, 1943-1975: select bibliography of American and British materials in political science, economics, sociology and anthropology; (with the assistance of Robert Samuels). Torino, 1977. pp. 183.

— **Statistical services.**

ITALY. Istituto Centrale di Statistica. 1978. Cinquanta anni di attività, 1926-1976. Roma, [1978]. pp. 466.

— **Statistics.**

ITALY. Istituto Centrale di Statistica. 1976. Sommario di statistiche storiche dell' Italia, 1861-1975. Roma, 1976. pp. 187.

IVANOVO (OBLAST')

— **Industries.**

KLIUEV (VLADIMIR GRIGOR'EVICH) Patrioticheskim pochinam - vsemernuiu podderzhku. Moskva, 1978. pp. 78. *(Bibliotechka Profsoiuznogo Aktivista. 36)*

IVORY COAST

— **Economic conditions.**

REVUE ECONOMIQUE ET FINANCIERE IVOIRIENNE; [pd.by] Ministère de l'Economie, des Finances et du Plan [Ivory Coast]. bi-m., Jl 1978(no.1)- Abidjan.

TUINDER (BASTIAAN A. DEN) Ivory Coast: the challenge of success; report of a mission sent to the Ivory Coast...; published for the World Bank. Baltimore, [1978]. pp. 445. *(International Bank for Reconstruction and Development. Country Economic Reports)*

MULTINATIONALS and development in black Africa: a case study in the Ivory Coast; by Jean Masini [and others]. Farnborough, [1979]. pp. 181.

— **Economic policy.**

TUINDER (BASTIAAN A. DEN) Ivory Coast: the challenge of success; report of a mission sent to the Ivory Coast...; published for the World Bank. Baltimore, [1978]. pp. 445. *(International Bank for Reconstruction and Development. Country Economic Reports)*

— — **Mathematical models.**

GOREUX (LOUIS M.) Interdependence in planning: multilevel programming studies of the Ivory Coast; with contributions by Penny Davis and René Vaurs; published for the World Bank. Baltimore, [1978]. pp. 413. *bibliog. (International Bank for Reconstruction and Development. World Bank Research Publications)*

IVYBRIDGE, DEVONSHIRE
— City planning.

GLYN-JONES (ANNE) Village into town: a study of transition in south Devon. [Exeter], Devon County Council and the University of Exeter, [1977]. pp. 88.

— Growth.

GLYN-JONES (ANNE) Village into town: a study of transition in south Devon. [Exeter], Devon County Council and the University of Exeter, [1977]. pp. 88.

JACOBINS.

STUDIEN zu Jakobinismus und Sozialismus; herausgegeben von Hans Pelger. Berlin, [1974]. pp. 271.

TOGNARINI (IVAN) Giacobinismo, rivoluzione, Risorgimento: una messa a punto storiografica. Firenze, 1977. pp. 213.

LINKSRHEINISCHE deutsche Jakobiner: Aufrufe, Reden, Protokolle; Briefe und Schriften, 1794-1801; ([edited by] Axel Kuhn). Stuttgart, [1978]. pp. 353. *bibliog.*

JACOBSSON (PER).

JACOBSSON (ERIN E.) A life for sound money: Per Jacobsson: his biography. Oxford, 1979. pp. 428.

JAMAA MOVEMENT.

DE CRAEMER (WILLY) The Jamaa and the Church: a Bantu Catholic movement in Zaïre. Oxford, 1977. pp. 192. *bibliog.*

JAMAICA
— Description and travel.

BROWN (WILLIAM JOHN) M.P. The land of look-behind. London, 1949. pp. 220.

— Executive departments.

JAMAICA. Ministry of National Mobilisation and Human Resource Development. 1977. The Ministry of National Mobilisation and Human Resource Development: its nature, structure and functions. Kingston, [1977?]. fo. 10.

— Politics and government.

BROWN (WILLIAM JOHN) M.P. The land of look-behind. London, 1949. pp. 220.

JAMAICA. Agency for Public Information. 1977. Government of Jamaica. [Kingston, 1977]. pp. 17.

JAMAICA. Ministry of National Mobilisation and Human Resource Development. 1977. The Ministry of National Mobilisation and Human Resource Development: its nature, structure and functions. Kingston, [1977?]. fo. 10.

BROWN (AGGREY) Color, class, and politics in Jamaica. New Brunswick, N.J., [1979]. pp. 172. *bibliog.*

— Population.

JAMAICA. Department of Statistics. 1974. Population trends and housing needs. [Kingston, 1974]. pp. 43.

— Race relations.

BROWN (AGGREY) Color, class, and politics in Jamaica. New Brunswick, N.J., [1979]. pp. 172. *bibliog.*

— Social conditions.

BROWN (WILLIAM JOHN) M.P. The land of look-behind. London, 1949. pp. 220.

— Social history.

CRATON (MICHAEL) Searching for the invisible man: slaves and plantation life in Jamaica. Cambridge, Mass., 1978. pp. 439.

— Statistics.

FACTS ON JAMAICA; pd. by Department of Statistics, Jamaica. irreg. [Kingston], Jamaica.

JAMES II, King of Great Britain and Ireland.

ASHLEY (MAURICE PERCY) James II. Minneapolis, 1977. pp. 342. *bibliog.*

MILLER (JOHN) Fellow of Gonville and Caius College, Cambridge. James II: a study in kingship. Hove, 1978. pp. 281. *bibliog.*

JAPAN
— Biography.

BIOGRAPHICAL dictionary of Japanese history; supervising editor Seiichi Iwao; translator Burton Watson. Tokyo, 1978. pp. 655. *bibliog.*

— Census.

JAPAN. Census, 1975. 1975 population census of Japan: population counts based on lists of households, October 1, 1975. [Tokyo, 1976]. pp. 50. *In English and Japanese.*

JAPAN. Census, 1975. 1975 population census of Japan: [volume series]. [Tokyo, 1977 in progress]. *In English and Japanese.*

JAPAN. Census, 1975. Commuting population. [Tokyo, 1978]. 1 vol. (various pagings). (*Reference Report Series. No. 1*) *In English and Japanese.*

JAPAN. Census, 1975. Population of major metropolitan areas. [Tokyo, 1979]. 1vol. (various pagings). (*Reference Report Series. No. 2*) *In English and Japanese.*

— Civilization.

JAPAN: a comparative view; edited by Albert M. Craig. Princeton, 1979. pp. 437. *Based on a conference sponsored by the Joint Committee on Japanese Studies of the American Council of Learned Societies and the Social Science Research Council.*

— Commerce.

SAXON (ERIC ALFRED) Japan's food gap and trade in farm products. Canberra, 1977. pp. 63. *bibliog.* (*Australia. Bureau of Agricultural Economics. Occasional Papers. No.42*)

YOUNG (ALEXANDER K.) The Sogo Shosha: Japan's multinational trading companies. Boulder, Colo., 1979. pp. 247. *bibliog.*

— — Asia, Southeast.

KATANO (HIKOJI) and others. Japan's direct investment to ASEAN countries. Kobe, [1978]. pp. 152. *bibliog.* (*Kobe. University. Research Institute for Economics and Business Administration. Kobe Economic and Business Research Series. No. 6*)

— — United States.

INTERNATIONAL input-output table Japan-U.S.A., 1970; [by Yasuhiko Torii and others]. Tokyo, [1977]. pp. 205. (*Ajia Keizai Kenkyusho. Statistical Data Series. No. 24*). *Published as part of a research project organized by the Institute of Developing Economies and the Keio Economic Observatory of Keio University.*

— Defences.

U.S.-JAPAN relations and the security of East Asia: the next decade; edited by Franklin B. Weinstein. Boulder, Colo., [1978]. pp. 318. *bibliog.*

— Economic conditions.

STOKES (HENRY) The Japanese competitor. London, [1976]. pp. 251.

BANK OF JAPAN. Economic Research Department. Special Papers. No. 71. The Japanese economy in 1976: a comprehensive analysis. Tokyo, 1977. pp. 51.

INTERNATIONAL input-output table Japan-U.S.A., 1970; [by Yasuhiko Torii and others]. Tokyo, [1977]. pp. 205. (*Ajia Keizai Kenkyusho. Statistical Data Series. No. 24*). *Published as part of a research project organized by the Institute of Developing Economies and the Keio Economic Observatory of Keio University.*

OLSEN (EDWARD A.) Japan: economic growth, resource scarcity, and environmental constraints. Boulder, Colo., [1978]. pp. 139. *bibliog.*

KAHN (HERMAN) and PEPPER (THOMAS) The Japanese challenge: the success and failure of economic success. New York, [1979]. pp. 162. *bibliog.*

— Economic history.

HALLIDAY (JON) A political history of Japanese capitalism. New York, [1975]. pp. 466. *bibliog.*

SMITH (THOMAS CARLYLE) Nakahara: family farming and population in a Japanese village, 1717-1830. Stanford, 1977. pp. 183. *bibliog.*

REISCHAUER (EDWIN OLDFATHER) and CRAIG (ALBERT MORTON) Japan: tradition and transformation. Boston, Mass., [1978]. pp. 345.

— Economic policy.

KAHN (HERMAN) and PEPPER (THOMAS) The Japanese challenge: the success and failure of economic success. New York, [1979]. pp. 162. *bibliog.*

— Foreign economic relations.

OKITA (SABURO) Essays in Japan and the world economy. Tokyo, 1971. pp. 118. (*Japan Economic Research Center. Center Papers. No. 15*)

YOUNG (ALEXANDER K.) The Sogo Shosha: Japan's multinational trading companies. Boulder, Colo., 1979. pp. 247. *bibliog.*

— — Russia.

MATHIESON (RAYMOND SUCCESS) Japan's role in Soviet economic growth: transfer of technology since 1965. New York, 1979. pp. 277. *bibliog.*

— — United Kingdom.

MUTO (CHOZO) A short history of Anglo-Japanese relations. postwar ed. Tokyo, 1977. pp. 83.

— Foreign opinion.

LEHMANN (JEAN-PIERRE) The image of Japan: from feudal isolation to world power, 1850- 1905. London, 1978. pp. 208.

— Foreign relations.

JAIN (RAJENDRA KUMAR) Japan's postwar peace settlements. Atlantic Highlands, N.J., 1978. pp. 399. *bibliog.*

— Treaties.

JAIN (RAJENDRA KUMAR) Japan's postwar peace settlements. Atlantic Highlands, N.J., 1978. pp. 399. *sbliog.*

— — China.

NOSOV (MIKHAIL GRIGOR'EVICH) Iapono-kitaiskie otnosheniia, 1949-1975. Moskva, 1978. pp. 216. *bibliog.*

— — Germany.

PRESSEISEN (ERNST L.) Germany and Japan: a study in totalitarian diplomacy, 1933-1941. New York, 1969. pp. 368. *bibliog. Reprint of work first published in The Hague, 1958.*

— — Russia.

SSSR - Iaponiia: k 50-letiiu ustanovleniia sovetsko-iaponskikh diplomaticheskikh otnoshenii, 1925-1975. Moskva, 1978. pp. 300.

— — United Kingdom.

MUTO (CHOZO) A short history of Anglo-Japanese relations. postwar ed. Tokyo, 1977. pp. 83.

— — United States.

EMMERSON (JOHN K.) The Japanese thread: a life in the U.S. foreign service. New York, 1978. pp. 465.

U.S.-JAPAN relations and the security of East Asia: the next decade; edited by Franklin B. Weinstein. Boulder, Colo., [1978]. pp. 318. *bibliog.*

The WHALING issue in U.S.-Japan relations; edited by John R. Schmidhauser and George O. Totten III. Boulder, Colo., [1978]. pp. 275.

— History.

NISH (IAN HILL) The story of Japan. London, 1968. pp. 238. *bibliog.*

REISCHAUER (EDWIN OLDFATHER) and CRAIG (ALBERT MORTON) Japan: tradition and transformation. Boston, Mass., [1978]. pp. 345.

— — To 1333.

BROWN (DELMER MYERS) and ISHIDA (ICHIRO) The future and the past: a translation of the Gukansho, an interpretative history of Japan written in 1219. Berkeley, 1979. pp. 479. *bibliog.*

— — 1912-1945.

SHIROYAMA (SABURO) War criminal: the life and death of Hirota Koki; translated by John Bester. Tokyo, 1977. pp. 301. *bibliog.*

— — 1945-52, Allied occupation.

WAR-wasted Asia: letters, 1945-46;... [by] Donald Keene [and others]; (edited by Otis Cary). Tokyo, 1975. pp. 322.

— History, Military.

IENAGA (SABURO) Japan's last war: World War II and the Japanese, 1931-1945. Oxford, 1979. pp. 316.

— Industries.

MONROE (WILBUR F.) and SAKAKIBARA (EISUKE) The Japanese industrial society: organizational, cultural and economic underpinnings. Austin, Tex., [1977]. pp. 74.

— Politics and government.

HALLIDAY (JON) A political history of Japanese capitalism. New York, [1975]. pp. 466. *bibliog.*

TOKAYER (MARVIN) and SWARTZ (MARY SAGMASTER) The Fugu plan: the untold story of the Japanese and the Jews during World War II. New York, 1979. pp. 287.

— Population.

SMITH (THOMAS CARLYLE) Nakahara: family farming and population in a Japanese village, 1717-1830. Stanford, 1977. pp. 183. *bibliog.*

— Religion.

MORIOKA (KIYOMI) Religion in changing Japanese society. Tokyo, 1975. pp. 231. *bibliog.*

— Social history.

LEHMANN (JEAN-PIERRE) The image of Japan: from feudal isolation to world power, 1850-1905. London, 1978. pp. 208.

— Statistical services.

JAPAN. Office of Statistical Standards. 1978. Statistical services in Japan. 1978. [Tokyo], 1978. pp. 200.

JAPANESE IN CANADA.

WARD (W. PETER) White Canada forever: popular attitudes and public policy toward Orientals in British Columbia. Montreal, [1978]. pp. 205.

JAPANESE STUDIES.

PROCEEDINGS OF THE BRITISH ASSOCIATION FOR JAPANESE STUDIES; [pd. by] Centre of Japanese Studies, University of Sheffield. a., 1976 (v.1, pt.2)- Sheffield.

JAVA

— Social life and customs.

MULDER (NIELS) Mysticism and everyday life in contemporary Java: cultural persistence and change. Singapore, [1978]. pp. 150. *bibliog.*

JEFFERSON (THOMAS) President of the United States.

BANNING (LANCE) The Jeffersonian persuasion: evolution of a party ideology. Ithaca, 1978. pp. 307.

JOHNSTONE (ROBERT M.) Jefferson and the Presidency: leadership in the young republic. Ithaca, 1978. pp. 332. *bibliog.*

STUART (REGINALD C.) The half-way pacifist: Thomas Jefferson's view of war. Toronto, [1978]. pp. 93. *bibliog.*

SPIVAK (BURTON) Jefferson's English crisis: commerce, embargo, and the Republican revolution. Charlottesville, Va., 1979. pp. 250.

JERSEY

— History — 1939-1945.

SINEL (L.P.) The German occupation of Jersey: a diary of events from June 1940 to June 1945. London, 1969. pp. 318.

JERUSALEM

— History.

CAMDEN SOCIETY. [Publications]. 4th Series. vol.22. Camden miscellany. vol.27. London, 1979. pp. 248.

— Social conditions.

SIMON (RITA JAMES) Continuity and change: a study of two ethnic communities in Israel. Cambridge, 1978. pp. 180. *bibliog.* (American Sociological Association. Arnold and Caroline Rose Monograph Series in Sociology)

JESUITS IN CHINA.

COOPER (MICHAEL) Rodrigues the interpreter: an early Jesuit in Japan and China. New York, 1974. pp. 416.

JESUITS IN JAPAN.

COOPER (MICHAEL) Rodrigues the interpreter: an early Jesuit in Japan and China. New York, 1974. pp. 416.

JESUS CHRIST

— Biography.

SCOTT (THOMAS) of Mount Pleasant, Ramsgate. English life of Jesus. Ramsgate, 1866-67. 6 pts. (in 1 vol., interleaved with blank pages) *Bound with Prospectus of the English life of Jesus. Privately published.*

— Rationalistic interpretations.

SCOTT (THOMAS) of Mount Pleasant, Ramsgate. English life of Jesus. Ramsgate, 1866-67. 6 pts. (in 1 vol., interleaved with blank pages) *Bound with Prospectus of the English life of Jesus. Privately published.*

JETTISON.

PŁODZIEŃ (STANISŁAW) Lex Rhodia de iactu: studium historyczno-prawne z zakresu rzymskiego prawa handlowo-morskiego. Lublin, 1961. pp. 162. *bibliog.* (Lublin. Katolicki Uniwersytet Lubelski. Towarzystwo Naukowe. Wydział Nauk Społecznych. Rozprawy. 15) *With English summary.*

JEWISH AMERICANS.

PONCINS (LEON DE) Comte, the Younger. State secrets: a documentation of the secret revolutionary mainspring governing Anglo-American politics; translated from the French edition of...Top secret by Timothy Tindal-Robertson. Chulmleigh, Devon, 1975. pp. 191. *bibliog.*

KONVITZ (MILTON RIDVAS) Judaism and the American idea. Ithaca, 1978. pp. 223. *bibliog.*

JEWISH-ARAB RELATIONS.

The ISRAEL-Arab reader: a documentary history of the Middle East conflict; edited with...comments by Walter Laqueur. 3rd ed. Toronto, 1976. pp. 585. *bibliog.*

CHURBA (JOSEPH) The politics of defeat: America's decline in the Middle East. New York, [1977]. pp. 224. *bibliog.*

PALESTINIAN Arabs in Israel: two case studies; [by] Hasan Amun [and others]. London, 1977. pp. 119. *bibliog.*

ARONSON (SHLOMO) Conflict and bargaining in the Middle East: an Israeli perspective. Baltimore, [1978]. pp. 448. *bibliog.*

DUPUY (TREVOR N.) Elusive victory: the Arab-Israeli Wars, 1947-1974. London, 1978. pp. 669. *bibliog.*

HERZOG (CHAIM) Who stands accused?; Israel answers its critics; [speeches at the United Nations]. London, [1978]. pp. 277.

O'NEILL (BARD E.) Armed struggle in Palestine: a political-military analysis. Boulder, Colo., 1978. pp. 320.

FLAPAN (SIMHA) Zionism and the Palestinians. London, [1979]. pp. 361.

KAZZIHA (WALID W.) Palestine in the Arab dilemma. London, [1979]. pp. 111.

ZIONISM, imperialism and racism; edited by A.W. Kayyali. London, 1979. pp. 304.

JEWISH LITERATURE.

GITTLEMAN (SOL) From shtetl to suburbia: the family in Jewish literary imagination. Boston, [Mass.], [1978]. pp. 209. *bibliog.*

JEWISH QUESTION.

WOLFF (SAM DE) Voor het land van belofte: een terugblik op mijn leven. Nijmegen, 1978. pp. 300. *First published in Bussum, 1954.*

HERZOG (CHAIM) Who stands accused?; Israel answers its critics; [speeches at the United Nations]. London, [1978]. pp. 277.

JEWS.

MOURANT (ARTHUR ERNEST) and others. The genetics of the Jews. Oxford, 1978. pp. 122. *bibliog.*

— Colonization.

JEWISH AGENCY. Agricultural Settlement Department and Information Department. 16 years of agricultural settlement in Israel. Jerusalem, 1964. 1 vol. (unpaged).

— History.

ARENDT (HANNAH) The Jew as pariah: Jewish identity and politics in the modern age; edited and with an introduction by Ron H. Feldman. New York, 1978. pp. 288. *bibliog.*

— Identity .

ARENDT (HANNAH) The Jew as pariah: Jewish identity and politics in the modern age; edited and with an introduction by Ron H. Feldman. New York, 1978. pp. 288. *bibliog.*

— Intellectual life.

CUDDIHY (JOHN MURRAY) The ordeal of civility: Freud, Marx, Lévi-Strauss, and the Jewish struggle with modernity. New York, [1974]. pp. 272.

— Legal status, laws, etc. — France.

MALINO (FRANCES) The Sephardic Jews of Bordeaux: assimilation and emancipation in Revolutionary and Napoleonic France. University, Ala., [1978]. pp. 166. *bibliog.*

JEWS.(Cont.)

—— Germany.

ROBINSOHN (HANS) Justiz als politische Verfolgung: die Rechtsprechung in "Rassenschandefällen" beim Landgericht Hamburg 1936-1943. Stuttgart, 1977. pp. 168. *bibliog*. (Vierteljahrshefte für Zeitgeschichte. Schriftenreihe. Nr.35)

— Persecutions.

KLARSFELD (SERGE) Le mémorial de la déportation des Juifs de France. Paris, 1978. ca.600p. *bibliog*.

BANAS (JOSEF) The scapegoats: the exodus of the remnants of Polish jewry. London, 1979. pp. 221.

FEIN (HELEN) Accounting for genocide: national responses and Jewish victimization during the holocaust. London, [1979]. pp. 468. *bibliog*.

— Restoration.

SELECTIVE debates on Palestine; edited by Kadhim Jawad. Baghdad, 1970. pp. 103.

SEGRE (D.V.) Jewish political thought and contemporary politics. [Ramat-Gan, 1978?]. fo.21,3. *(Bar-Ilan University. Department of Political Studies and Center for Jewish Community Studies. Workshop in the Covenant Idea and the Jewish Political Tradition. Working Papers. No. 3)*

FLAPAN (SIMHA) Zionism and the Palestinians. London, [1979]. pp. 361.

WEINSTOCK (NATHAN) Zionism: false messiah; translated and edited by Alan Adler. London, [1979]. pp. 330. *bibliog*. First published as part I of Sionisme contre Israël, Paris, 1969.

ZIONISM, imperialism and racism; edited by A.W. Kayyali. London, 1979. pp. 304.

JEWS IN AUSTRIA.

ROSENKRANZ (HERBERT) Verfolgung und Selbstbehauptung: die Juden in Österreich, 1938-1945. Wien, [1978]. pp. 399. *bibliog*.

JEWS IN EUROPE.

The CATASTROPHE of European Jewry: antecedents, history, reflections: selected papers; edited by Yisrael Gutman and Livia Rothkirchen. Jerusalem, 1976. pp. 757. *bibliog*.

WASSERSTEIN (BERNARD) Britain and the Jews of Europe, 1939-1945. Oxford, 1979. pp. 389. *bibliog*.

JEWS IN FRANCE.

JUSSEM-WILSON (NELLY) Bernard-Lazare: antisemitism and the problem of Jewish identity in late nineteenth-century France. Cambridge, 1978. pp. 348. *bibliog*.

KLARSFELD (SERGE) Le mémorial de la déportation des Juifs de France. Paris, 1978. ca.600p. *bibliog*.

MALINO (FRANCES) The Sephardic Jews of Bordeaux: assimilation and emancipation in Revolutionary and Napoleonic France. University, Ala., [1978]. pp. 166. *bibliog*.

SCHWARZFUCHS (SIMON) Napoleon, the Jews and the Sanhedrin. London, 1979. pp. 218. *bibliog*.

JEWS IN GERMANY.

GAY (PETER) Freud, Jews and other Germans: masters and victims in modernist culture. Oxford, 1978. pp. 289.

JERSCH-WENZEL (STEFI) Juden und "Franzosen" in der Wirtschaft des Raumes Berlin/Brandenburg zur Zeit des Merkantilismus. Berlin, 1978. pp. 290. *bibliog*. (Historische Kommission zu Berlin. Einzelveröffentlichungen. Band 23)

Die JUEDISCHEN Gemeinden in Bayern, 1918-1945: Geschichte und Zerstörung; herausgegeben und bearbeitet von Baruch Z. Ophir und Falk Wiesemann. München, 1979. pp. 525. *bibliog*. Based on the section on Bavaria in Pinkas Hakehillot, Encyclopaedia of Jewish Communities from their Foundation till after the Holocaust, published in Hebrew, Jerusalem 1972.

JEWS IN ITALY.

MICHAELIS (MEIR) Mussolini and the Jews: German-Italian relations and the Jewish question in Italy, 1922-1945. Oxford, 1978. pp. 472. *bibliog*.

JEWS IN JAPAN.

TOKAYER (MARVIN) and SWARTZ (MARY SAGMASTER) The Fugu plan: the untold story of the Japanese and the Jews during World War II. New York, 1979. pp. 287.

JEWS IN LITERATURE.

GITTLEMAN (SOL) From shtetl to suburbia: the family in Jewish literary imagination. Boston, [Mass.], [1978]. pp. 209. *bibliog*.

JEWS IN PALESTINE.

HOROWITZ (DAN) 1928- and LISSAK (MOSHE) Origins of the Israeli polity: Palestine under the Mandate; translated from the Hebrew by Charles Hoffman. Chicago, [1978]. pp. 292. *bibliog*.

JEWS IN POLAND.

RINGELBLUM (EMMANUEL) Polish-Jewish relations during the Second World War; edited...by Joseph Kermish [and] Shmuel Krakowski; translated from Polish by Dafna Allon [and others]. Jerusalem, Yad Vashem, 1974. pp. 330.

BANAS (JOSEF) The scapegoats: the exodus of the remnants of Polish jewry. London, 1979. pp. 221.

JEWS IN RUSSIA.

SOVIET Jewry and the Australian Communist Party: documents. Caulfield, Victoria, [1966]. pp. 79.

SHINDLER (COLIN) Exit visa: detente, human rights and the Jewish emigration movement in the USSR. London, 1978. pp. 291. *bibliog*.

SAWYER (THOMAS E.) The Jewish minority in the Soviet Union. Boulder, 1979. pp. 353. *bibliog*.

JEWS IN SHANGHAI.

TOKAYER (MARVIN) and SWARTZ (MARY SAGMASTER) The Fugu plan: the untold story of the Japanese and the Jews during World War II. New York, 1979. pp. 287.

JEWS IN SPAIN.

MAY (HARRY S.) Francisco Franco: the Jewish connection. Washington, D.C., [1978]. pp. 187. *bibliog*.

JEWS IN THE NETHERLANDS.

WOLFF (SAM DE) Voor het land van belofte: een terugblik op mijn leven. Nijmegen, 1978. pp. 300. *First published in Bussum, 1954.*

JEWS IN THE UNITED KINGDOM.

HOLMES (COLIN) Anti-semitism in British society, 1876-1939. London, 1979. pp. 328. *bibliog*.

JEWS IN THE UNITED STATES.

ZERO population growth - for whom?: differential fertility and minority group survival; edited by Milton Himmelfarb and Victor Baras. Westport, 1978. pp. 213. *Proceedings of a conference held by the American Jewish Committee in 1975, in New York.*

PRATT (NORMA FAIN) Morris Hillquit: a political history of an American Jewish socialist. Westport, Conn., 1979. pp. 272. *bibliog*.

JEYES (JOHN).

PALFREYMAN (DAVID) John Jeyes...: the making of a household name. Thetford, [1977]. pp. 127. *bibliog*.

JEYES SANITARY COMPOUNDS COMPANY.

PALFREYMAN (DAVID) John Jeyes...: the making of a household name. Thetford, [1977]. pp. 127. *bibliog*.

JOB ANALYSIS.

The STUDY of real skills vol. 1. The analysis of practical skills; edited by W.T. Singleton. Lancaster, [1978]. pp. 333. *bibliogs*.

JOB EVALUATION

— Tanzania.

TANGANYIKA. Reviewing Committee on Clerical/Executive and Technical Regrading. 1956. Report; [W. Wenban-Smith, chairman]. Dar es Salaam, 1956. pp. 48.

JOB SATISFACTION

— Europe.

The QUALITY of working life in Western and Eastern Europe; edited by Cary L. Cooper and Enid Mumford. Westport, 1979. pp. 348. *bibliog*.

— United Kingdom.

OLDHAM (MARGARET) Withdrawal from work. Hatfield, 1978. pp. 17. *bibliog*. (Hatfield Polytechnic. School of Social Sciences. Social Sciences Occasional Papers. No. 1)

— United States.

O'TOOLE (JAMES) Work, learning, and the American future. San Francisco, 1977. pp. 238. *bibliog*.

ANDRISANI (PAUL J.) Work attitudes and labor market experience: evidence from the National Longitudinal Surveys. New York, [1978]. pp. 263. *bibliog*.

JOB VACANCIES

— United Kingdom.

U.K. Social Survey. [Reports. New Series]. 1012. Attitudes to the employment service, 1973: a survey carried out for the Department of Employment; [by] Janet Gregory [and] Elizabeth Head. [London, 1977]. pp. 125.

JOFFRE (JOSEPH JACQUES CESAIRE).

JOFFRE (JOSEPH JACQUES CESAIRE) Mémoires du Maréchal Joffre, 1910-1917. Paris, [1932]. 2 vols.

JOHANNESBURG

— Economic conditions.

HART (T.) and BROWETT (J.G.) A multi-variate spatial analysis of the socio-economic structure of Johannesburg, 1970. Johannesburg, 1976. pp. 74. *(Johannesburg. University of the Witwatersrand. Urban and Regional Research Unit. Occasional Papers. No. 13)*

— Social conditions.

HART (T.) and BROWETT (J.G.) A multi-variate spatial analysis of the socio-economic structure of Johannesburg, 1970. Johannesburg, 1976. pp. 74. *(Johannesburg. University of the Witwatersrand. Urban and Regional Research Unit. Occasional Papers. No. 13)*

JOHNSON (JOSHUA).

LONDON. London Record Society. Publications. vol. 15. Joshua Johnson's letterbook, 1771-1774: letters from a merchant in London to his partners in Maryland; edited by Jacob M. Price. London, 1979. pp. 181.

JONOTLA.

RECK (GREGORY G.) In the shadow of Tlaloc: life in a Mexican village. Harmondsworth, 1978. pp. 224.

JORDAN

— Commerce.

MILLHAM (CHARLES B.) and AMERAH (MOHAMMAD S.) Rationalization of imports in Jordan. Amman, 1977. pp. 124. *bibliog*.

— **Economic conditions.**

ROYAL SCIENTIFIC SOCIETY [JORDAN]. Economic Research Department. Economic conditions in Jordan: a report for the first six months of 1974. Amman, 1974. fo. 17.

KANOVSKY (ELIYAHU) The economy of Jordan: the implications of peace in the Middle East. Tel Aviv, 1976. pp. 159. *bibliog.*

— **Politics and government.**

ABDALLAH, King of Jordan. My memoirs completed: al-Takmilah; translated from the Arabic by Harold W. Glidden. London, 1978. pp. 102. *Reprint, with extensive introduction by King Hussein of Jordan of work published in Amman, Jordan, in 1951.*

JOURNALISM

— **Political aspects.**

SEYMOUR-URE (COLIN) The political impact of mass media. London, 1974 repr. 1976. pp. 296. *bibliog.*

JOURNALISM, SOCIALIST

— **Germany.**

RICHTER (ARMIN) Der Ziegelbrenner: das individualanarchistische Kampforgan des frühen B. Traven. Bonn, 1977. pp. 442. *bibliog.*

JOY (C. TURNER).

JOY (C. TURNER) Negotiating while fighting: the diary of Admiral C. Turner Joy at the Korean Armistice Conference; edited and with an introduction by Allan E. Goodman. Stanford, Calif., [1978]. pp. 476. *(Stanford University. Hoover Institution on War, Revolution and Peace. Hoover Institution Publications. 175)*

JOYCE (JAMES AUGUSTINE ALOYSIUS).

WATSON (GEORGE) Irish identity and the literary revival: Synge, Yeats, Joyce and O'Casey. London, 1979. pp. 326. *bibliog.*

JÓZWIAK (FRANCISZEK).

JAKUBOWSKI (ZENON) Franciszek Jóźwiak-Witold: 'zycie i działalność. Warszawa, 1978. pp. 340. *bibliog.*

JUDAISM.

KONVITZ (MILTON RIDVAS) Judaism and the American idea. Ithaca, 1978. pp. 223. *bibliog.*

MARTIN (DAVID ALFRED) The dilemmas of contemporary religion. Oxford, [1978]. pp. 104.

JUDAISM AND STATE.

SEGRE (D.V.) Jewish political thought and contemporary politics. [Ramat-Gan, 1978?]. fo.21,3. *(Bar-Ilan University. Department of Political Studies and Center for Jewish Community Studies. Workshop in the Covenant Idea and the Jewish Political Tradition. Working Papers. No. 3)*

JUDGES

— **Education — United Kingdom.**

U.K. Working Party on Judicial Studies and Information. 1978. Judicial studies and information; report; chairman: Lord Justice Bridge. London, 1978. pp. 44.

— **Australia.**

KERR (Sir JOHN ROBERT) Matters for judgment: an autobiography. London, 1979. pp. 468. *bibliog. First published in Australia in 1978.*

— **France.**

KETTERING (SHARON) Judicial politics and urban revolt in seventeenth-century France: the Parlement of Aix, 1629-1659. Princeton, N.J., [1978]. pp. 370. *bibliog.*

— **Germany.**

FREIER DEUTSCHER GEWERKSCHAFTSBUND. Bundesvorstand. Trade union enemies in judges' robes: a documentation, etc. [Berlin, 1962-63]. 2 vols. (in 1).

— **Italy.**

SINDACATO e magistratura nei conflitti di lavoro; a cura di Tiziano Treu. Bologna, [1975-76]. 2 vols.

— **United Kingdom.**

KEETON (GEORGE WILLIAMS) Harvey the Hasty: a mediaeval Chief Justice. Chichester, [1978]. pp. 178. *bibliog.*

— **United States.**

LEVIN (MARTIN A.) Urban politics and the criminal courts. Chicago, 1977. pp. 332.

JUDGMENTS, FOREIGN

— **United Kingdom — Commonwealth.**

McCLEAN (JOHN DAVID) and PATCHETT (KEITH W.) The recognition and enforcement of judgments and orders and the service of process within the Commonwealth: a further report; (with The reciprocal enforcement of judgments within the Commonwealth: a preliminary report). London, Commonwealth Secretariat, [1978]. pp. 202, 49.

RECOGNITION and enforcement of judgments and orders and the service of process within the Commonwealth: a report of a working meeting held at Basseterre, St. Kitts, 24-26 April 1978. London, Commonwealth Secretariat, [1978]. pp. 354.

JUDICIAL ASSISTANCE

— **France.**

FRANCE. Ministère de la Justice. Direction des Affaires Civiles et du Sceau. 1978. Entraide judiciaire internationale en matière civile, commerciale et administrative: recueil pratique de conventions; (par Louis Chatin). 2nd ed. Paris, 1978. pp. 995.

— **United Kingdom — Commonwealth.**

McCLEAN (JOHN DAVID) and PATCHETT (KEITH W.) The recognition and enforcement of judgments and orders and the service of process within the Commonwealth: a further report; (with The reciprocal enforcement of judgments within the Commonwealth: a preliminary report). London, Commonwealth Secretariat, [1978]. pp. 202, 49.

RECOGNITION and enforcement of judgments and orders and the service of process within the Commonwealth: a report of a working meeting held at Basseterre, St. Kitts, 24-26 April 1978. London, Commonwealth Secretariat, [1978]. pp. 354.

JUDICIAL PROCESS

— **Russia.**

EFFEKTIVNOST' deistviia pravovykh norm. Leningrad, 1977. pp. 143.

JUDICIAL REVIEW

— **United States.**

BALL (HOWARD) Judicial craftsmanship or fiat?: direct overturn by the United States Supreme Court. Westport, Conn., 1978. pp. 160. *bibliog.*

JUDICIAL REVIEW OF ADMINISTRATIVE ACTS

— **Russia.**

LEIDEN. Rijks Universiteit. Documentation Office for East European Law. Law in Eastern Europe. No. 21. The Soviet Procuracy protests, 1937-1973: a collection of translations by Leon Boim...and Glenn G. Morgan. Alphen aan den Rijn, 1978. pp. 603. *bibliog.*

JUSTICE, ADMINISTRATION OF.

SMITH (GORDON B.) The Soviet procuracy and the supervision of administration. Alphen, [1978]. pp. 154. *bibliog. A publication issued by the Documentation Office for East European Law, University of Leyden.*

— **United Kingdom.**

GRIFFITH (JOHN ANEURIN GREY) Administrative law and the judges. London, 1978. pp. 23. *(Haldane Society. Pritt Memorial Lectures. 1978)*

JURISPRUDENCE.

TOWARD world order and human dignity: essays in honor of Myres S. McDougal; edited by W. Michael Reisman and Burns H. Weston. New York, [1976]. pp. 603. *bibliog.*

WORMUTH (FRANCIS DUNHAM) Essays in law and politics; edited by Dalmas H. Nelson and Richard L. Sklar. Port Washington, N.Y., 1978. pp. 274. *bibliog.*

LLOYD (DENNIS) Baron Lloyd of Hampstead. Introduction to jurisprudence; fourth edition [by]...[and] M.D.A. Freeman. London, 1979. pp. 1002.

— **Bibliography.**

DIAS (REGINALD WALTER MICHAEL) A bibliography of jurisprudence. 3rd ed. London, 1979. pp. 453.

JURY

— **United Kingdom.**

BALDWIN (JOHN) Ph.D. and McCONVILLE (MICHAEL) Jury trials. Oxford, 1979. pp. 150. *bibliog.*

HARMAN (HARRIET) and GRIFFITH (JOHN ANEURIN GREY) Justice deserted: the subversion of the jury. London, 1979. pp. 37.

JUSTICE.

FLICK (GEOFFREY A.) Natural justice: principles and practical application. Sydney, 1979. pp. 175. *bibliog.*

JUSTICE, ADMINISTRATION OF.

ACCESS to justice; general editor, Mauro Cappelletti. Alphen aan den Rijn, 1978-79. 4 vols. (in 6). *bibliogs.*

— **Canada — British Columbia.**

LAJEUNESSE (THERESE) Justice councils: a study. Victoria, Justice Planning Unit, 1976. pp. 81.

BRITISH COLUMBIA ASSOCIATION OF JUSTICE COUNCILS. Annual symposium reports. a., 1977(no. 2)- British Columbia.

— — **Ontario.**

ONTARIO. Justice Policy Field. 1976. Justice policy in Ontario. [Toronto], 1976. pp. 67.

— **France.**

FRANCE. Direction de la Documentation. La Documentation Française. Notes et Etudes Documentaires. No.4453. L'organisation judiciaire en France; par Hubert Pinsseau [and] Alain Sierens. 2nd ed. [Paris], 1978. pp. 140.

KAHN-FREUND (Sir OTTO) and others. A source-book on French law: system, methods, outlines of contract. 2nd ed. Oxford, 1979. pp. 550. *bibliog. In French or English.*

— **Germany.**

EUROPEAN COURT OF HUMAN RIGHTS. Publications. Series A: Judgments and Decisions. [A27]. ...König case: 1. Decision of 23 April 1977; 2. Judgment of 28 June 1978. Strasbourg, Council of Europe, 1978. pp. 52bis. *In English and French.*

— **Hong Kong.**

HONG KONG. Judicial Service Commission. Report by the Chairman. a., 1976/77[1st]- Hong Kong.

JUSTICE, ADMINISTRATION OF.(Cont.)

— Iran.

BUTLER (WILLIAM J.) and LEVASSEUR (GEORGES) Human rights and the legal system in Iran. Geneva, 1976. pp. 72. *bibliog.*

— Netherlands.

VEEN (JAC. VAN) Democratisering van het recht?: de werkelijkheid in de paleizen van justitie. Amsterdam, 1977. pp. 133. *bibliog.*

— Russia.

WORTMAN (RICHARD S.) The development of a Russian legal consciousness. Chicago, [1976]. pp. 345. *bibliog.*

HAZARD (JOHN NEWBOLD) and others. The Soviet legal system:...fundamental principles and historical commentary. 3rd ed. Dobbs Ferry, N.Y., 1977. pp. 621. *bibliog. (Columbia University. Parker School of Foreign and Comparative Law. Studies in Foreign and Comparative Law)*

— — White Russia.

MARTINOVICH (IZABELLA IVANOVNA) and PLIUTA (EFIM FEDOTOVICH) Sud i pravosudie v BSSR. Minsk, 1977. pp. 166.

— South Africa.

DUGARD (JOHN) Human rights and the South African legal order. Princeton, N.J., [1978]. pp. 470. *bibliog.*

— Tunisia.

BOURGUIBA (HABIB) Adapting justice to economic and social changes: speech...at the close of the judicial year, at Monastir, on 25th July 1965. [Tunis, Secretariat of State for Information and Orientation, 1965]. pp. 41.

— United Kingdom.

NEWTON (CLIVE RICHARD) General principles of law. 2nd ed. London, 1977. pp. 386.

RADCLIFFE (GEOFFREY REYNOLDS YONGE) and CROSS (ARTHUR GEOFFREY NEALE) Baron Cross of Chelsea. The English legal system; sixth edition by G. J. Hand and D. J. Bentley. London, 1977. pp. 464.

HUMPHREYS (CHRISTMAS) Both sides of the circle: the autobiography of Christmas Humphreys. London, 1978. pp. 269.

KIRALFY (ALBERT KENNETH ROLAND) The English legal system. 6th ed. London, 1978. pp. 297.

SOCIAL work and the courts; edited by Howard Parker. London, 1979. pp. 224. *bibliog.*

JUSTICES OF THE PEACE

— Tanzania.

UNITED REPUBLIC OF TANZANIA. Judiciary. 1964. A guide for justices of the peace: a. assigned to district courts: part 1; b. assigned to primary courts: part 2. Dar es Salaam, [1964?]. pp. 14.

JUSTINIAN I, Emperor of the East.

PROCOPIUS, of Caesarea. History of the wars; (with an English translation by H.B. Dewing). London, 1914-28 repr. 1962-71. 5 vols. *bibliog. Parallel Greek and English texts.*

JUTE INDUSTRY

— United Kingdom.

McDOWALL (STUART) and DRAPER (PAUL) Trade adjustment and the British jute industry: a case study. Glasgow, 1978. pp. 48. *(Glasgow. University of Strathclyde. Fraser of Allander Institute. Research Monographs. No. 5)*

JUVENILE COURTS

— United Kingdom.

ANDERSON (RICHARD) Representation in the juvenile court. London, 1978. pp. 82.

— United States.

SCHLOSSMAN (STEVEN L.) Love and the American delinquent: the theory and practice of progressive juvenile justice, 1825-1920. Chicago, [1977]. pp. 303. *bibliog.*

JUVENILE DELINQUENCY.

HASKELL (MARTIN R.) and YABLONSKY (LEWIS) Crime and delinquency. Chicago, [1978]. pp. 780.

KORNHAUSER (RUTH ROSNER) Social sources of delinquency: an appraisal of analytic models. Chicago, [1978]. pp. 277. *bibliog.*

PEREZ (JOSEPH FRANCIS) The family roots of adolescent delinquency. New York, 1978. pp. 231.

JOHNSON (RICHARD E.) Juvenile delinquency and its origins: an integrated theoretical approach. Cambridge, 1979. pp. 182. *bibliog.*

WADSWORTH (MICHAEL EDWIN JOHN) Roots of delinquency: infancy, adolescence and crime. Oxford, 1979. pp. 150. *bibliog.*

— Mathematical models.

FERGUSSON (DAVID MURRAY) and others. Social background, school performance, adjustment and juvenile offending: a path analytic model. [Wellington], 1976. pp. 26. *bibliog. (Joint Committee on Young Offenders [New Zealand]. Research Unit. Research Reports. No. 5)*

— Belgium.

POTVIN (JEAN PAUL) and TISSEYRE (CHARLES) La police vue par les jeunes. Bruxelles, 1978. pp. 315. *bibliog. (Centre d'Etude de la Délinquance Juvénile. Publications. No. 42)*

— — Statistics.

STATISTIQUES et protection de la jeunesse; Statistieken en jeugdbescherming; [by a] groupe de travail, 1976-1977. Bruxelles, 1977. pp. 97. *(Centre d'Etude de la Délinquance Juvénile. Publications. No. 41) In French or Dutch, with synthesis and conclusion in both languages.*

— Canada.

CRIME and delinquency in Canada; edited by Edmund W. Vaz and Abdul Q. Lodhi. Scarborough, Ont., [1979]. pp. 390.

— — Atlantic Provinces.

LEYTON (ELLIOTT) The myth of delinquency: an anatomy of juvenile nihilism. Toronto, [1979]. pp. 220. *bibliog.*

— France.

REPONSES à la violence... Recherches sur la protection de la jeunesse. Paris, [1977]. pp. 408. *(France. Comité d'Etudes sur la Violence, la Criminalité et la Délinquance. Annexes. 5)*

REPONSES à la violence...Recherches sur les aspects psychologiques et biologiques de la violence. Paris, [1977]. pp. 35,38. *(France. Comité d'Etudes sur la Violence, la Criminalité et la Délinquance. Annexes. 2)*

FRANCE. Direction de la Documentation. La Documentation Française. Notes et Etudes Documentaires. No. 4465. La délinquance des jeunes en France; par Henri Michard. [Paris], 1978. pp. 158. *bibliog.*

— New Zealand.

FERGUSSON (DAVID MURRAY) and others. The effects of race and socio-economic status on juvenile offending statistics. [Wellington, 1975]. pp. 31. *bibliog. (Joint Committee on Young Offenders [New Zealand]. Research Unit. Research Reports. No. 2)*

FERGUSSON (DAVID MURRAY) and others. The prediction of juvenile offending: a New Zealand study. Wellington, 1975. pp. 128. *bibliog. (Joint Committee on Young Offenders [New Zealand]. Research Unit. Research Reports. No. 3)*

— United Kingdom.

INTERMEDIATE treatment in London: a report of a seminar held at the Civil Service College, Sunningdale, on 18/19 March 1977. [London, Department of Health and Social Security, 1977]. pp. 22.

McNEE (Sir DAVID) Crime and the young. [London], 1978. pp. 14. *(National Association of Boys' Clubs. Basil Henriques Memorial Lectures. 1978)*

NATIONAL ASSOCIATION FOR THE CARE AND RESETTLEMENT OF OFFENDERS. The Hammersmith Teenage Project: an experiment in the community care of young offenders. [Chichester], 1978. pp. 56.

— — Scotland.

RUSHFORTH (MONICA) Committal to residential care: a case study in juvenile justice. Edinburgh, 1978. pp. 90. *(Scotland. Scottish Office. Social Research Studies)*

— United States.

SORRENTINO (ANTHONY) Organizing against crime: redeveloping the neighborhood. New York, [1977]. pp. 272. *bibliog.*

VACHSS (ANDREW H.) and BAKAL (YITZHAK) The life-style violent juvenile: the secure treatment approach. Lexington, [1979]. pp. 466.

— — Michigan.

MAX (LAURENCE) and DOWNS (THOMAS) Decentralized delinquency services in Michigan: differential placement and its impact on program effectiveness and cost- effectiveness. [Lansing], 1975. pp. 160. *(Michigan. Department of Social Services. Studies in Welfare Policy. No. 4)*

JUVENILE DETENTION HOMES

— United Kingdom.

NATIONAL ASSOCIATION FOR THE CARE AND RESETTLEMENT OF OFFENDERS. Children and young persons in custody: report of a...working party under the chairmanship of Peter Jay. Chichester, 1977. pp. 80. *bibliog.*

CAWSON (PAT) and MARTELL (MARY) Children referred to closed units. London, 1979. pp. 272. *bibliog. (U.K. Department of Health and Social Security. Research Reports. No. 5)*

JONES (HOWARD) The residential community: a setting for social work. London, 1979. pp. 145.

JUVENILE JUSTICE, ADMINISTRATION OF

— United Kingdom — Scotland.

SCOTLAND. Scottish Education Department. Social Work Services Group. Children's hearings statistics. a., 1976- Edinburgh. *Supersedes in part SCOTTISH SOCIAL WORK STATISTICS.*

— United States.

SCHLOSSMAN (STEVEN L.) Love and the American delinquent: the theory and practice of progressive juvenile justice, 1825-1920. Chicago, [1977]. pp. 303. *bibliog.*

KABYLES.

BOURDIEU (PIERRE) Algeria 1960: The disenchantment of the world; The sense of honour; The Kabyle house or the world reversed; translated by Richard Nice. Cambridge, 1979. pp. 158.

KALINOUSKI (KASTUS').

MAIKHROVICH (AL'FRED STEPANOVICH) Belorusskie revoliutsionnye demokraty: vazhneishie aspekty mirovozzreniia; redaktory N.S. Kupchin, V.M. Konon. Minsk, 1977. pp. 207.

KALINOVSKII (KASTUS').

See **KALINOUSKI (KASTUS').**

KALMYKS.

HOFFMANN (JOACHIM) 1930- . Deutsche und Kalmyken, 1942 bis 1945. Freiburg, [1974]. pp. 214. *bibliog. (Militärgeschichtliches Forschungsamt. Einzelschriften zur Militärischen Geschichte des Zweiten Weltkrieges. 14)*

KALULI (PAPUA NEW GUINEA PEOPLE).

SCHIEFFELIN (EDWARD L.) The sorrow of the lonely and the burning of the dancers. New York, [1976]. pp. 243. *bibliog.*

KAMCHATKA

— History.

MUKHACHEV (BORIS IVANOVICH) Bortsy za vlast' Sovetov na Kamchatke. Petropavlovsk-Kamchatskii, 1977. pp. 110.

KANO (STATE)

— Colonization.

FIKA (ADAMU MOHAMMED) The Kano civil war and British over-rule, 1882-1940. Oxford, [1978]. pp. 307. *bibliog.*

— Foreign relations — United Kingdom.

FIKA (ADAMU MOHAMMED) The Kano civil war and British over-rule, 1882-1940. Oxford, [1978]. pp. 307. *bibliog.*

KANSAS

— History.

JOHNSON (SAMUEL A.) The battle cry of freedom: the New England Emigrant Aid Company in the Kansas Crusade. Westport, Conn., 1977. pp. 357. *bibliog.* Reprint of work originally published Lawrence, Kan., 1954.

KANT (IMMANUEL).

FEL'DMAN (DAVID ISAAKOVICH) and BASKIN (IURII IAKOVLEVICH) Uchenie Kanta i Gegelia o mezhdunarodnom prave i sovremennost'. Kazan', 1977. pp. 127.

WALKER (RALPH CHARLES SUTHERLAND) Kant: the arguments of the philosophers. London, 1978. pp. 201. *bibliog.*

KAPLAN (KAREL).

KAPLAN (KAREL) Dans les archives du comité central: trente ans de secrets du bloc soviétique. [Paris, 1978]. pp. 365.

KARELIA

— History — 1917-1921, Revolution.

MASHEZERSKII (VIKTOR IVANOVICH) Pobeda Velikogo Oktiabria i obrazovanie sovetskoi avtonomii Karelii. Petrozavodsk, 1978. pp. 140.

KARKAR ISLAND (PAPUA NEW GUINEA)

— Social life and customs.

McSWAIN (ROMOLA) The past and future people: tradition and change on a New Guinea island. Melbourne, 1977. pp. 213. *bibliog.*

KASCHAU.

See KOSICE.

KASHMIR QUESTION.

INDIA. Ministry of Information and Broadcasting. Publications Division. 1965. Kashmir answers Pakistan. [Delhi, 1965]. pp. 26, 1 map.

KAUTSKY (KARL).

KAUTSKY: marxistische Vergangenheit der SPD?; ([by] Projekt Klassenanalyse). Westberlin, [1976]. pp. 144.

STEENSON (GARY P.) Karl Kautsky, 1854-1938: Marxism in the classical years. Pittsburgh, [1978]. pp. 308. *bibliog.*

SALVADORI (MASSIMO L.) Karl Kautsky and the socialist revolution, 1880-1938; translated by Jon Rothschild. London, 1979. pp. 375.

KAYASTHS.

LEONARD (KAREN ISAKSEN) Social history of an Indian caste: the Kayasths of Hyderabad. Berkeley, 1978. pp. 353. *bibliog.*

KAYSERI, TURKEY

— Industries.

VELZEN (LEO VAN) Peripheral production in Kayseri, Turkey; translating...of English text by Donald Bloch. Ankara, 1977. pp. 194.

KAZAKSTAN

— Economic history.

IUSUPOV (IL'IAS ISMAILOVICH) Sovetskie dungane v period stroitel'stva sotsializma. Frunze, 1977. pp. 262.

— Nationalism.

NATSIONAL'NYE otnosheniia v SSSR na sovremennom etape: na materialakh respublik Srednei Azii i Kazakhstana. Moskva, 1979. pp. 312.

— Politics and government.

KUNAEV (DINMUKHAMED AKHMEDOVICH) Izbrannye rechi i stat'i, [1965-78]. Moskva, 1978. pp. 511.

— Social life and customs.

SEM'IA i semeinye obriady u narodov Srednei Azii i Kazakhstana. Moskva, 1978. pp. 215.

KENNEDY (JOHN FITZGERALD) President of the United States

— Bibliography.

IRWIN (T.H.) and HALE (HAZEL) compilers. A bibliography of books, newspapers and magazine articles published in English outside the United States of America related to the assassination of John F. Kennedy. Supplement no. 1, 1975- 1977. [Belfast], 1978. pp. 8.

KENYA

— Economic conditions.

PALMER (JOHN CARRINGTON) Entrepreneurs and economic development in a small town in Kenya. 1978. fo. 384. *bibliog.* Typescript. Ph.D. (London) thesis: unpublished. This thesis is the property of London University and may not be removed from the Library.

— Economic policy.

MBITHI (PHILIP M.) and RASMUSSON (RASMUS) Self reliance in Kenya: the case of harambee. Uppsala, 1977. pp. 175. *bibliog.*

KENYA. Ministry of Economic Planning and Community Affairs. 1979. Development plan, 1979-1983. Nairobi, 1979. 2 pts.(in 1 vol.).

— Industries — Directories.

KENYA. Ministry of Finance and Economic Planning. Statistics Division. 1971. Register of manufacturing firms, 1970. [Nairobi], 1971. pp. 125.

— Parliament — Elections.

AMIN (MOHAMED) One man, one vote: a photo-record of Kenya's 1974 general elections;...with text by Peter Moll. Nairobi, 1975. 1 vol. (unpaged).

— Politics and government.

FROST (RICHARD) Race against time: human relations and politics in Kenya before independence. London, 1978. pp. 292. *bibliog.*

— Race relations.

FROST (RICHARD) Race against time: human relations and politics in Kenya before independence. London, 1978. pp. 292. *bibliog.*

— Relations (general) with Botswana.

KHAMA (Sir SERETSE) Dr. Moi in Botswana: speech of welcome by His Excellency the President of Botswana...at a state banquet in honour of the Vice-President of Kenya Dr. Daniel Arap Moi, during his official visit to Botswana in July 1970, and Dr. Moi's reply. [Gaborone, Information Services, 1970]. pp. 9.

— Social conditions.

WOLF (JAN J. DE) Differentiation and integration in Western Kenya: a study of religious innovation and social change among the Bukusu. The Hague, [1977]. pp. 231. *bibliog. (Afrika-Studiecentrum. Change and Continuity in Africa. 10)*

FROST (RICHARD) Race against time: human relations and politics in Kenya before independence. London, 1978. pp. 292. *bibliog.*

PALMER (JOHN CARRINGTON) Entrepreneurs and economic development in a small town in Kenya. 1978. fo. 384. *bibliog.* Typescript. Ph.D. (London) thesis: unpublished. This thesis is the property of London University and may not be removed from the Library.

— Social policy.

MBITHI (PHILIP M.) and RASMUSSON (RASMUS) Self reliance in Kenya: the case of harambee. Uppsala, 1977. pp. 175. *bibliog.*

KENYA. Ministry of Economic Planning and Community Affairs. 1979. Development plan, 1979-1983. Nairobi, 1979. 2 pts.(in 1 vol.).

KEPHART (WILLIAM G.).

MURPHY (LAWRENCE RICHARD) Antislavery in the Southwest: William G. Kephart's mission to New Mexico, 1850-53. El Paso, Tex., [1978]. pp. 55. *(Texas University. Southwestern Studies. Monographs. No. 54)*

KERALA

— Economic conditions.

KERALA. Department of Public Relations. 1975. Kerala forges ahead: U[nited] F[ront] ministry; five years in retrospect. [Trivandrum, 1975]. pp. 83.

KERALA. Bureau of Economics and Statistics. 1977. Progress in two decades, 1956-57 to 1976-77. Trivandrum, 1977. pp. 11.

— — Bibliography.

KERALA. Bureau of Economics and Statistics. 1978. Recent studies by the Bureau of Economics and Statistics, Kerala. [Trivandrum], 1978. pp. 14.

— — Statistics.

KERALA. Bureau of Economics and Statistics. 1975. Basic statistics relating to Kerala economy, 1956-57 to 1973-74. Trivandrum, 1975. pp. 72.

— Economic policy.

KERALA. Planning and Development Department. 1960. The third five year plan: statements. [Trivandrum, 1960]. pp. 199.

KERALA. Department of Public Relations. 1975. Kerala forges ahead: U[nited] F[ront] ministry; five years in retrospect. [Trivandrum, 1975]. pp. 83.

— Industries.

KERALA. Bureau of Economics and Statistics. Industrial Statistics Unit. Annual survey of industries: Kerala State. a., 1973/74(9th)- Trivandrum.

KERALA(Cont.)

— Legislative Assembly — Biography.

KERALA. Department of Public Relations. 1977. Kerala election reportage, 1977. [Trivandrum], 1977. pp. 96.

— Politics and government.

VADAKKAN (JOSEPH) A priest's encounter with revolution: an autobiography. Bangalore, 1974. pp. 159.

KERALA. Department of Public Relations. 1975. Kerala forges ahead: U[nited] F[ront] ministry; five years in retrospect. [Trivandrum, 1975]. pp. 83.

— Population.

KERALA. Demographic Research Centre. 1973. The characteristics of the population of Kerala and the impact of the family planning programme. Trivandrum, 1973. pp. 20. *(Papers. No. 79)*

KERALA. Bureau of Economics and Statistics. Sample registration: Kerala - rural. a., 1975- Trivandrum.

— Social conditions.

KERALA. Department of Public Relations. 1975. Kerala forges ahead: U[nited] F[ront] ministry; five years in retrospect. [Trivandrum, 1975]. pp. 83.

KERALA. Bureau of Economics and Statistics. 1977. Progress in two decades, 1956-57 to 1976-77. Trivandrum, 1977. pp. 11.

— — Bibliography.

KERALA. Bureau of Economics and Statistics. 1978. Recent studies by the Bureau of Economics and Statistics, Kerala. [Trivandrum], 1978. pp. 14.

— Social policy.

KERALA. Planning and Development Department. 1960. The third five year plan: statements. [Trivandrum, 1960]. pp. 199.

KERALA. Department of Public Relations. 1975. Kerala forges ahead: U[nited] F[ront] ministry; five years in retrospect. [Trivandrum, 1975]. pp. 83.

— Statistics, Vital.

KERALA. Bureau of Economics and Statistics. Sample registration: Kerala - rural. a., 1975- Trivandrum.

KERR (Sir JOHN ROBERT).

KERR (Sir JOHN ROBERT) Matters for judgment: an autobiography. London, 1979. pp. 468. *bibliog. First published in Australia in 1978.*

KEYNES (JOHN MAYNARD) 1st Baron Keynes.

HAYEK (FRIEDRICH AUGUST) A tiger by the tail: a 40-years' running commentary on Keynesianism...; compiled and introduced by Sudha R. Shenoy; with an essay on The outlook for the 1970s: open or repressed inflation?; by F.A. Hayek. 2nd ed. London, 1978. pp. 145. *bibliog. (Institute of Economic Affairs. Hobart Paperbacks. 4)*

JOHNSON (ELIZABETH) and JOHNSON (HARRY GORDON) The shadow of Keynes: understanding Keynes, Cambridge and Keynesian economics. Oxford, [1978]. pp. 253.

UNIVERSITY OF KENT AT CANTERBURY. Keynes Seminar, 3rd, 1976. Keynes and laissez-faire; edited by A.P. Thirlwall. London, 1978. pp. 134.

KEYNESIAN ECONOMICS.

ELLIS (HOWARD SYLVESTER) Notes on stagflation. Washington, [1978]. pp. 23. *(American Enterprise Institute for Public Policy Research. AEI Studies. 221)*

KHABAROVSK (KRAI)

— Native races.

BOIKO (VLADIMIR IVANOVICH) Sotsial'noe razvitie narodov Nizhnego Amura; otvetstvennyi redaktor A.P. Okladnikov. Novosibirsk, 1977. pp. 279.

— Social conditions.

BOIKO (VLADIMIR IVANOVICH) Sotsial'noe razvitie narodov Nizhnego Amura; otvetstvennyi redaktor A.P. Okladnikov. Novosibirsk, 1977. pp. 279.

KHAZARS.

DUNLOP (DOUGLAS MORTON) The history of the Jewish Khazars. Princeton, N.J., 1954. pp. 293. *bibliog. (Princeton University. Princeton Oriental Studies. vol. 16)*

KIDNAPPING

— United States.

ALIX (ERNEST KAHLAR) Ransom kidnapping in America, 1874-1974: the creation of a capital crime. Carbondale, [1978]. pp. 222. *bibliog.*

KIM (IL-SUNG).

INTERNATIONAL SEMINAR ON THE JUCHE IDEA, PYONGYANG, 1977. [Proceedings]. Pyongyang, 1977. pp. 763.

AL-MISSURI (MUHAMMAD) Kimilsungism: theory and practice. Pyongyang, 1978. pp. 262.

KING (ERNEST JOSEPH).

KING (ERNEST JOSEPH) and WHITEHILL (WALTER MUIR) Fleet Admiral King: a naval record. New York, 1976. pp. 674. *Reprint of the first edition, published in New York, 1952.*

KING (MARTIN LUTHER).

GARROW (DAVID J.) Protest at Selma: Martin Luther King, Jr., and the Voting Rights Act of 1965. New Haven, 1978. pp. 346.

KINSHIP

— Terminology.

SCHEFFLER (HAROLD WALTER) Australian kin classification. Cambridge, 1978. pp. 567. *bibliog.*

— Andean Group.

ANDEAN kinship and marriage; edited by Ralph Bolton and Enrique Mayer. Washington, D.C., [1977]. pp. 296. *bibliog. (American Anthropologist. Special Publications. No.7)*

— Australia.

SCHEFFLER (HAROLD WALTER) Australian kin classification. Cambridge, 1978. pp. 567. *bibliog.*

— Bengal.

INDEN (RONALD B.) and NICHOLAS (RALPH W.) Kinship in Bengali culture. Chicago, [1977]. pp. 139. *bibliog.*

— China.

BAKER (HUGH D.R.) Chinese family and kinship. London, 1979. pp. 243. *bibliog.*

FREEDMAN (MAURICE) The study of Chinese society: essays by Maurice Freedman; selected and introduced by G. William Skinner. Stanford, 1979. pp. 491. *bibliog.*

— France.

FLANDRIN (JEAN-LOUIS) Families in former times: kinship, household and sexuality...; translated by Richard Southern. Cambridge, 1979. pp. 265. *bibliog.*

— United Kingdom.

TRUMBACH (RANDOLPH) The rise of the egalitarian family: aristocratic kinship and domestic relations in eighteenth-century England. New York, [1978]. pp. 324. *bibliog.*

— Zambia.

WILSON (MARY MONICA) For men and elders: change in the relations of generations and of men and women among the Nyakyusa-Ngonde people, 1875-1971. London, [1977]. pp. 209. *bibliog. 5 appendices in end pocket.*

KIRGHIZIA

— Economic conditions.

KOICHUEV (TURAR KOICHUEVICH) Vosproizvodstvo obshchestvennogo produkta v Kirgizskoi SSR. Frunze, 1977. pp. 112.

— Economic history.

IUSUPOV (IL'IAS ISMAILOVICH) Sovetskie dungane v period stroitel'stva sotsializma. Frunze, 1977. pp. 262.

— History.

KHASANOV (ANVARBEK KHASANOVICH) Narodnye dvizheniia v Kirgizii v period Kokandskogo khanstva. Moskva, 1977. pp. 95.

KIRKBY MANUFACTURING AND ENGINEERING COMPANY.

U.K. Working Party on Kirkby Manufacturing and Engineering Co. Ltd. 1978. Report; [D.C. Hague, chairman]. [London], 1978. fo. 22.

KISSINGER (HENRY ALFRED).

DICKSON (PETER W.) Kissinger and the meaning of history. Cambridge, 1978. pp. 197. *bibliog.*

KLEIN (MELANIE).

SEGAL (HANNA) Klein. [London], 1979. pp. 189. *bibliog.*

KNEE (FRED).

KNEE (FRED) The diary of Fred Knee; [edited by David Englander. Coventry, 1977. pp. 122. *bibliog. (Society for the Study of Labour History. Aids to Research. No.3)*

KNIGHTS OF LABOR.

McLAURIN (MELTON ALONZA) The Knights of Labor in the South. Westport, Conn., 1978. pp. 232. *bibliog.*

KNOWLEDGE, SOCIOLOGY OF.

HOLZNER (BURKART) and MARX (JOHN H.) Knowledge application: the knowledge system in society. Boston, Mass., [1979]. pp. 388. *bibliog.*

SOCIOLOGICAL REVIEW, THE; [published by] University of Keele. Monographs. [No.] 27. On the margins of science: the social construction of rejected knowledge; edited by Roy Wallis. Keele, 1979. pp. 337.

KNOWLEDGE, THEORY OF.

CURRIE (GREGORY PAUL) The objectivism of Frege and Popper: an historical and critical investigation. 1978. fo. 294. *bibliog. Typescript. Ph.D. (London) thesis: unpublished. This thesis is the property of London University and may not be removed from the Library.*

POPPER (Sir KARL RAIMUND) Objective knowledge: an evolutionary approach. rev. ed. Oxford, 1979. pp. 395. *bibliogs.*

RESCHER (NICHOLAS) Cognitive systematization: a systems-theoretic approach to a coherentist theory of knowledge. Oxford, [1979]. pp. 211.

KOENIGSHUETTE.

See KRÓLEWSKA HUTA.

KOKAND KHANATE

— History.

KHASANOV (ANVARBEK KHASANOVICH) Narodnye dvizheniia v Kirgizii v period Kokandskogo khanstva. Moskva, 1977. pp. 95.

KOLAS (IAKUB) pseud.

MAIKHROVICH (AL'FRED STEPANOVICH) Belorusskie revoliutsionnye demokraty: vazhneishie aspekty mirovozzreniia; redaktory N.S. Kupchin, V.M. Konon. Minsk, 1977. pp. 207.

KOLLONTAI (ALEKSANDRA MIKHAILOVNA).

CLEMENTS (BARBARA EVANS) Bolshevik feminist: the life of Aleksandra Kollontai. Bloomington, 1979. pp. 352. bibliog.

KOMI REPUBLIC

— Economic conditions.

EKONOMICHESKIE problemy nauchno-tekhnicheskogo progressa na Severe: na primere promyshlennosti i stroitel'stva Komi ASSR. Moskva, 1977. pp. 128. (Akademiia Nauk SSSR. Problemy Sovetskoi Ekonomiki)

KOMMUNISTISCHER JUGENDVERBAND DEUTSCHLANDS.

JAHNKE (KARL HEINZ) Jungkommunisten im Widerstandskampf gegen den Hitlerfaschismus. Dortmund, 1977. pp. 431. bibliog.

KÖNIG (EBERHARD).

EUROPEAN COURT OF HUMAN RIGHTS. Publications. Series A: Judgments and Decisions. [A27]. ...König case: 1. Decision of 23 April 1977; 2. Judgment of 28 June 1978. Strasbourg, Council of Europe, 1978. pp. 52bis. In English and French.

KORBEL (JOSEF).

CZECHOSLOVAKIA: the heritage of ages past: essays in memory of Josef Korbel; edited by Hans Brisch and Ivan Volgyes. Boulder, 1979. pp. 239. (East European Quarterly. East European Monographs. 51)

KOREA

— Economic conditions.

KOREA: a nation in transition; edited by Se-Jin Kim and Chi-Won Kang. Seoul, 1978. pp. 304. bibliog.

WADE (LARRY L.) and KIM (BYONG SIK) Economic development of South Korea: the political economy of success. New York, [1978]. pp. 270.

HASAN (PARVEZ) and RAO (D.C.) Korea policy issues for long-term development. Baltimore, [1979]. pp. 538. (International Bank for Reconstruction and Development. Country Economic Reports)

— Economic history.

WADE (LARRY L.) and KIM (BYONG SIK) Economic development of South Korea: the political economy of success. New York, [1978]. pp. 270.

— Economic policy.

WADE (LARRY L.) and KIM (BYONG SIK) Economic development of South Korea: the political economy of success. New York, [1978]. pp. 270.

— Foreign relations.

KOREA: a nation in transition; edited by Se-Jin Kim and Chi-Won Kang. Seoul, 1978. pp. 304. bibliog.

— — United States.

WHITE (NATHAN N.) U.S. policy toward Korea: analysis, alternatives and recommendations. Boulder, Colo., 1979. pp. 231.

— Politics and government.

KIM (IL-SUNG) On the building of the people's government. Pyongyang, 1978. 2 vols.

KIM (IL-SUNG) On the work of the United Front: excerpts. Pyongyang, 1978. pp. 208.

KOREA: a nation in transition; edited by Se-Jin Kim and Chi-Won Kang. Seoul, 1978. pp. 304. bibliog.

KOREA, North and South: the deepening crisis; edited by Gavan McCormack and Mark Selden. New York, [1978]. pp. 237. Revised and expanded version of Crisis in Korea.

POLITICS of Korean reunification; edited by Young Hoon Kang and Yong Soon Yim. Seoul, 1978. pp. 250. bibliog.

REES (DAVID) The two Koreas in conflict: a comparative study. London, 1978. pp. 22. (Institute for the Study of Conflict. Conflict Studies. No.94)

— Population.

A STUDY of the Korean population, 1966; [by] Yunshik Chang [and others]. Seoul, 1974. pp. 262. bibliog. (Seoul National University. Population and Development Studies Center. Publication Series. No. 12).

KOREAN REUNIFICATION QUESTION (1945-).

KOREA, North and South: the deepening crisis; edited by Gavan McCormack and Mark Selden. New York, [1978]. pp. 237. Revised and expanded version of Crisis in Korea.

POLITICS of Korean reunification; edited by Young Hoon Kang and Yong Soon Yim. Seoul, 1978. pp. 250. bibliog.

REES (DAVID) The two Koreas in conflict: a comparative study. London, 1978. pp. 22. (Institute for the Study of Conflict. Conflict Studies. No.94)

YIM (YONG SOON) Two Koreas' unification: policy and strategy. Baltimore, 1978. pp. 80. (Maryland University. School of Law. Occasional Papers/Reprints Series in Contemporary Asian Studies. No. 21)

KOREAN WAR, 1950-1953

— Armistices.

JOY (C. TURNER) Negotiating while fighting: the diary of Admiral C. Turner Joy at the Korean Armistice Conference; edited and with an introduction by Allan E. Goodman. Stanford, Calif., [1978]. pp. 476. (Stanford University. Hoover Institution on War, Revolution and Peace. Hoover Institution Publications. 175)

KOREANS IN THE UNITED STATES.

The KOREAN diaspora: historical and sociological studies of Korean immigration and assimilation in North America; Hyung-chan Kim, editor. Santa Barbara, [1977]. pp. 268.

KORNILOV (LAVR GEORGIEVICH).

IVANOV (NIKOLAI IAKOVLEVICH) Kontrrevoliutsiia v Rossii v 1917 godu i ee razgrom. Moskva, 1977. pp. 272.

KORSCH (KARL).

GOODE (PATRICK) Karl Korsch: a study in western marxism. London, 1979. pp. 239. bibliog.

KOSICE

— History.

BORSÁNYI (JULIÁN) Das Rätsel des Bombenangriffs auf Kaschau, 26. Juni 1941: wie wurde Ungarn in den Zweiten Weltkrieg hineingerissen?: e dokumentarischer Bericht. München, 1978. pp. 260. bibliog. (Ungarisches Institut München. Studia Hungarica. 16)

KOSSUTH (LAJOS).

DEAK (ISTVAN) The lawful revolution: Louis Kossuth and the Hungarians, 1848-1849. New York, 1979. pp. 415. bibliog.

KRISHNA.

KRISHNA: myths, rites, and attitudes; edited by Milton Singer. Chicago, 1966. pp. 277. bibliog.

KRÓLEWSKA HUTA

— Coal miners' strike, 1871.

JOŃCZYK (JAN) Der Bergarbeiterstreik im Jahre 1871 in Königshütte auf dem Hintergrund der Lage der Arbeiterklasse in Oberschlesien; übersetzt aus dem Polnischen von Anne-Marie Griese. Bremen, 1977. pp. 63.

KRONSTADT

— History — 1921, Revolt.

LENIN (VLADIMIR IL'ICH) and TROTSKII (LEV DAVYDOVICH) Kronstadt. New York, 1979. pp. 159.

KROPOTKIN (PETR ALEKSEEVICH) Prince.

POLIANSKII (FEDOR IAKOVLEVICH) Kritika ekonomicheskikh teorii anarkhizma. Moskva, 1976. pp. 301.

KRUPSKAIA (NADEZHDA KONSTANTINOVNA).

NADEZHDA Konstantinovna Krupskaia: biografiia. Moskva, 1978. pp. 415. bibliog.

KUBAS.

VANSINA (JAN) The children of Woot: a history of the Kuba peoples. Dawson, 1978. pp. 394. bibliog.

KUEHNE AND NAGEL LIMITED.

HEILBRON (Dame ROSE) and SAMWELL (STANLEY DAVID) Kuehne and Nagel Limited: investigation under section 165(b) of the Companies Act 1948; report. London, H.M.S.O., 1978. 1 vol.(various pagings).

KUOMINTANG.

TONG (TE-KONG) and LI (TSUNG-JEN) The memoirs of Li Tsung-jen. Boulder, Colo., 1979. pp. 636. (Columbia University. East Asian Institute. Studies)

KUPALA (IANKA) pseud.

MAIKHROVICH (AL'FRED STEPANOVICH) Belorusskie revoliutsionnye demokraty: vazhneishie aspekty mirovozzreniia; redaktory N.S. Kupchin, V.M. Konon. Minsk, 1977. pp. 207.

KURANKO (AFRICAN PEOPLE).

JACKSON (MICHAEL) Anthropologist. The Kuranko: dimensions of social reality in a West African society. New York, 1977. pp. 256. bibliog.

KURDS.

Les KURDES et le Kurdistan: la question nationale Kurde au Proche Orient; sous la direction de Gérard Chaliand. Paris, 1978. pp. 354. bibliog.

KURDS IN IRAQ.

ASHIRIAN (SHARAF CHARKIAZOVICH) Natsional'no-demokraticheskoe dvizhenie v Irakskom Kurdistane, 1961-1968. Moskva, 1975. pp. 167. bibliog.

MGOI (SHAKRO KHUDOEVICH) Problema natsional'noi avtonomii kurdskogo naroda v Irakskoi respublike, 1958-1970 gg. Erevan, 1977. pp. 333. bibliog.

KUWAIT

— Economic conditions.

KHOUJA (MOHAMAD W.) and SADLER (PETER G.) The economy of Kuwait: development and role in international finance. London, 1979. pp. 283. bibliog.

KUWAIT (Cont.)

— Foreign economic relations.

KHOUJA (MOHAMAD W.) and SADLER (PETER G.) The economy of Kuwait: development and role in international finance. London, 1979. pp. 283. *bibliog.*

LABOUR AND LABOURING CLASSES.

LANGE (FRIEDRICH ALBERT) Die Arbeiterfrage;...mit Einleitung und Anmerkungen herausgegeben von Fr. Mehring. Berlin, 1910. pp. 176. *Reprint of the work originally published in Duisburg, 1865.*

SOCIAL AND LABOUR BULLETIN; [pd.by] International Labour Office. q., 1974(1/74)- Geneva.

GODSON (ROY) The Kremlin and labor: a study in national security policy. New York, 1977. pp. 79.

KAY (GEOFFREY B.) The economic theory of the working class. London, 1979. pp. 140. *bibliog.*

WORLD OF LABOUR AND DEVELOPMENT, THE: (news and features for the press); issued by the Public Information Branch of the International Labour Office. irreg. Geneva. *Current issues only kept.*

— Abstracts.

U.K. Department of Employment. Work Research Unit. Information system abstracts. m., current issues only. London.

— Bibliography.

MacDOUGALL (IAN) compiler. A catalogue of some labour records in Scotland and some Scots records outside Scotland. Edinburgh, 1978. pp. 598.

— Congresses.

INTERNATIONAL WORKING MEN'S ASSOCIATION. Congress, [5th], The Hague, 1872. The Hague congress of the First International, September 2- 7, 1872: reports and letters. Moscow, [1978]. pp. 701. *(Institut Marksizma-Leninizma. Documents of the First International).*

— Education.

LABOUR EDUCATION; [pd. by] Workers' Education Branch, International Labour Office. 3 a yr., 1978(no. 36)- Geneva.

— — Russia.

RABOCHII klass SSSR na sovremennom etape. vyp.5. Podgotovka i vospitanie kadrov rabochego klassa SSSR v usloviiakh razvitogo sotsializma; otvetstvennye redaktory V.A. Ezhov, V.A. Ovsiankin. Leningrad, 1977. pp. 183.

— — United Kingdom.

HURT (JOHN S.) Elementary schooling and the working classes 1860-1918. London, 1979. pp. 241.

MILLAR (JAMES PRIMROSE MALCOLM) The labour college movement. London, [1979]. pp. 300. *bibliog.*

— History.

IDEOLOGY and the labour movement: essays presented to John Saville; edited by David E. Martin and David Rubinstein. London, [1979]. pp. 276. *bibliogs.*

— Medical care — United States.

BACKGROUND papers on industry's changing role in health care delivery; edited by Richard H. Egdahl. New York, [1977]. pp. 198.

— Research.

U.K. Department of Employment. Work Research Unit. Research register. a., current issue only. London.

— Africa.

AFRICAN labor history; Peter C.W. Gutkind [and others], editors. Beverly Hills, [1978]. pp. 280. *bibliogs.*

— America, Latin.

SPALDING (HOBART A.) Organized labor in Latin America: historical case studies of workers in dependent societies. New York, 1977. pp. 297.

SHERMAN (WILLIAM L.) Forced native labor in sixteenth-century Central America. Lincoln, Neb., 1979. pp. 496. *bibliog.*

— Australia.

WORK AND PEOPLE; [pd. by] Department of Productivity. [Australia]. q., autumn 1975 (v.1, no.1)- Melbourne. *Supersedes PERSONNEL PRACTICE BULLETIN.*

The WORKER in Australia: contributions from research; Allan Bordow, editor; in association with Helen Hurwitz [and others]. St. Lucia, Queensland, [1977]. pp. 301. *bibliogs.*

WHO are our enemies?: racism and the Australian working class; edited by Ann Curthoys and Andrew Markus. Neutral Bay, 1978. pp. 211.

— Austria.

BEWEGUNG und Klasse: Studien zur österreichischen Arbeitergeschichte...; (G. Botz [and others], Hrsg.). Wien, [1978]. pp. 841. *(Ludwig Boltzmann Institut für Geschichte der Arbeiterbewegung. Veröffentlichungen)*

STEINER (HERBERT) 1923- . Karl Marx in Wien: die Arbeiterbewegung zwischen Revolution und Restauration, 1848. Wien, [1978]. pp. 223.

— Brazil.

FAUSTO (BORIS) Trabalho urbano e conflito social, 1890-1920. São Paulo, 1976. pp. 283. *bibliog.*

CENTRE D'ETUDES DU DEVELOPPEMENT EN AMERIQUE LATINE. Multinationales et travailleurs au Brésil; [edited by] Paulo Freire. Paris, 1977. pp. 254. *bibliog.*

— Canada.

LAZARUS (MORDEN) The long winding road: Canadian labour in politics. Vancouver, [1977]. pp. 103. *bibliog.*

BERCUSON (DAVID JAY) Fools and wise men: the rise and fall of the One Big Union. Toronto, [1978]. pp. 300. *bibliog.*

— — Alberta.

ALBERTA. Department of Labour. Annual report. a., 1974/75- Edmonton.

— — Ontario.

SCHULZ (PATRICIA V.) The East York Workers' Association: a response to the great depression. Toronto, [1975]. pp. 74.

— — Quebec.

ROY (JEAN LOUIS) La marche des Québécois: le temps des ruptures, 1945-1960. Ottawa, 1976. pp. 383.

— — Saskatchewan.

SASKATCHEWAN. Department of Labour. Research and Planning Division. Labour trends. a., 1974- Regina.

— China.

WORKERS and workplaces in revolutionary China; edited with an introduction by Stephen Andors. White Plains, 977. pp. 402.

— Czechoslovakia.

BLOOMFIELD (JON) Passive revolution: politics and the Czechoslovak working class, 1945-1948. London, 1979. pp. 290. *bibliog.*

— Europe.

The QUALITY of working life in Western and Eastern Europe; edited by Cary L. Cooper and Enid Mumford. Westport, 1979. pp. 348. *bibliog.*

— France.

ATELIER, L': organe spécial de la classe laborieuse. m., S 1840-Jl 31 1850(nos. 1-36). Paris. *Reprint in 3 v.*

HANOTAUX (GABRIEL) La démocratie et le travail. Paris, 1920. pp. 264.

DURAND (MICHELLE) and HARFF (YVETTE) La qualité de la vie: mouvement écologique, mouvement ouvrier. Paris, [1977]. pp. 258.

— Germany.

ALLGEMEINE DEUTSCHE ARBEITER-ZEITUNG (formerly Arbeiter- Zeitung); hrsg. vom Arbeiterfortbildungsverein in Coburg. w., D 25 1862- Ag 8 1866. Coburg. *1977 reprint in 2 vols.*

GERMANY (BUNDESREPUBLIK). Statistisches Bundesamt. Beruf, Ausbildung und Arbeitsbedingungen der Erwerbstätigen. a., 1975/1976- Wiesbaden. *(Bevölkerung und Erbwerbstätigkeit. Reihe 4.1.2)*

FORSCHUNGEN zur Lage der Arbeiter im Industrialisierungsprozess; herausgegeben von Hans Pohl. Stuttgart, [1978]. pp. 132. *(Arbeitskreis für Moderne Sozialgeschichte. Industrielle Welt. Band 26)*

SCHROEDER (WILHELM HEINZ) Arbeitergeschichte und Arbeiterbewegung: Industriearbeit und Organisationsverhalten im 19. und frühen 20. Jahrhundert. Frankfurt/Main, [1978]. pp. 316. *bibliog.*

— Germany, Eastern.

GRUNDMANN (SIEGFRIED) and others. Zur Entwicklung der Arbeiterklasse und ihrer Struktur in der DDR. Berlin, 1976. pp. 298.

— Italy.

INCHIESTA sulla condizione dei lavoratori in fabbrica; a cura di Nicolò Addario. Torino, [1976]. pp. 196.

MOVIMENTO operaio e cultura alternativa; [by] Vittorio Foa [and others]. Milano, [1976]. pp. 114.

CONGI (GAETANO) L'altra Roma: classe operaia e sviluppo industriale nella capitale. Bari, [1977]. pp. 258.

DONAGGIO (FRANCO) In fabbrica ogni giorno tutti i giorni. Verona, [1977]. pp. 341.

FORBICE (ALDO) Austerità e democrazia operaia: intervista a Giorgio Benvenuto. Milano, [1977]. pp. 196.

MANZINI (GIORGIO) Una vita operaia. Torino, [1977]. pp. 148.

HUNECKE (VOLKER) Arbeiterschaft und industrielle Revolution in Mailand, 1859- 1892: zur Entstehungsgeschichte der italienischen Industrie und Arbeiterbewegung. Göttingen, 1978. pp. 330. *bibliog.*

— Kenya.

LEITNER (KERSTIN) Workers, trade unions and peripheral capitalism in Kenya after independence. Frankfurt am Main, [1977]. pp. 182. *bibliog.*

— Mexico.

GONZALEZ (JOSE MARIA) Del artesanado al socialismo; (seleccion de articulos). Mexico, Secretaria de Educacion Publica, 1974. pp. 182. *(Sep/Setentas. 163)*

CARR (BARRY) El movimiento obrero y la politica en Mexico, 1910-1929; version española de Roberto Gomez Ciriza. Mexico, Secretaria de Educacion Publica, 1976. 2 vols. (in 1) *bibliog. (Sep/Setentas. 256,257)*

TRES estudios sobre el movimiento obrero en Mexico; [by] Jose Luis Reyna [and others]. Mexico, 1976. pp. 202. *bibliogs. (Mexico City. Colegio de Mexico. Jornadas. 80)*

LABOUR AND LABOURING CLASSES.

SCHLAGHECK (JAMES L.) The political, economic and labor climate in Mexico. Philadelphia, [1977]. pp. 164. *(Pennsylvania University. Wharton School of Finance and Commerce. Industrial Research Unit. Multinational Industrial Relations Series. No. 4b)*

VELLINGA (MENNO) Economic development and the dynamics of class: industrialization, power and control in Monterrey, Mexico. Van Gorcum, 1979. pp. 213. *bibliog.*

— Netherlands.

GIELE (JACQUES J.) Arbeidersleven in Nederland 1850-1914. Nijmegen, [1979]. pp. 320.

— Russia.

PRIIMENKO (ALEKSANDR IOSIFOVICH) Legal'nye organizatsii rabochikh Iuga Rossii v period imperializma, 1895 g. -fevral' 1917 g. Kiev, 1977. pp. 163. *bibliog.*

ROSENKO (IVAN ARKHIPOVICH) Internatsional'nye sviazi rabochikh Leningrada, 1921-1937 gg. Leningrad, 1977. pp. 140.

SOTSIAL'NOE razvitie rabochego klassa SSSR: rost chislennosti, kvalifikatsii, blagosostoianiia rabochikh v razvitom sotsialisticheskom obshchestve: istoriko-sotsiologicheskie ocherki. Moskva, 1977. pp. 287.

BOR'BA partii i rabochego klassa za vosstanovlenie i razvitie narodnogo khoziaistva SSSR, 1943-1950 gg. Moskva, 1978. pp. 324.

IASKOVETS (GENNADII ALEKSEEVICH) Pravda i lozh' o rabochem klasse: kritika sovremennoi burzhuaznoi istoriografii Anglii i SShA o roli proletariata v Fevral'skoi i Velikoi Oktiabr'skoi sotsialisticheskoi revoliutsiiakh. Moskva, 1978. pp. 200.

IGLITSKII (ALEKSANDR ALEKSANDROVICH) Sovetskii rabochii klass v usloviiakh nauchno-tekhnicheskoi revoliutsii: kritika burzhuazno-reformistskikh kontseptsii. Moskva, 1978. pp. 124.

LANE (DAVID) and O'DELL (FELICITY ANN) The soviet industrial worker: social class, education and control. Oxford, 1978. pp. 167. *bibliog.*

SANBUROV (VASILII IVANOVICH) Moskovskii "Rabochii soiuz": u istokov proletarskoi bor'by. Moskva, 1978. pp. 133.

SYNDICAT libre en URSS: dossier réuni par le Comité international contre la répression. [Paris, 1978]. pp. 126.

TSYPIN (BORIS LEONIDOVICH) Rabochaia sila i ee osobennosti v period razvitogo sotsialisticheskogo obshchestva: ocherk teorii. Moskva, 1978. pp. 168.

BADIA (LARISA VIKTOROVNA) Akademik A.M. Pankratova - istorik rabochego klassa SSSR. Moskva, 1979. pp. 159.

WORKERS against the Gulag: the new opposition in the Soviet Union; edited by Viktor Haynes and Olga Semyonova. London, 1979. pp. 129.

— — Siberia.

RABOCHII klass Sibiri v period uprocheniia i razvitiia sotsializma 1938-1958 gg.: materialy k "Istorii rabochego klassa Sibiri". Novosibirsk, 1977. pp. 237.

GUSHCHIN (NIKOLAI IAKOVLEVICH) and others. Soiuz rabochego klassa i krest'ianstva Sibiri v period postroeniia sotsializma, 1917-1937 gg. Novosibirsk, 1978. pp. 430.

SOTRUDNICHESTVO rabochikh i krest'ian Sibiri v usloviiakh razvitogo sotsializma: materialy k "Istorii rabochego klassa Sibiri". Novosibirsk, 1978. pp. 158.

— — Turkmenistan.

IAZYKOVA (MAIAGOZEL') Rost rabochego klassa Turkmenistana v 1959-1965 gg.; pod redaktsiei N.V. Atamamedova. Ashkhabad, 1976. pp. 163.

— — Ukraine.

KOVAL' (MIKHAIL VASIL'EVICH) Obshchestvenno-politicheskaia deiatel'nost' trudiashchikhsia Ukrainskoi SSR v period Velikoi Otechestvennoi voiny. Kiev, 1977. pp. 264.

KRAVCHUK (TIKHON NIKANOROVICH) and SLOBODANIUK (ALEKSANDR NIKITOVICH) V sem'e edinoi. Moskva, 1977. pp. 80. *(Bibliotechka Profsoiuznogo Aktivista. 28)*

MAL'KO (OLEH OLEKSIIOVYCH) Robitnychyi klas - trudivnykam sela. Kyïv, 1978. pp. 135.

PONOMAR'OV (ANATOLII PETROVYCH) Suchasna sim'ia i simeinyi pobut robitnykiv Donbasu, 1950-1975. Kyïv, 1978. pp. 143.

SUPRUNENKO (NIKOLAI IVANOVICH) Borot'ba trudiashchykh Ukraïny proty denikinshchyny. Kyïv, 1979. pp. 287.

— Spain.

VILLA (LUIS ENRIQUE DE LA) Los origenes de la Administracion laboral en España. [Madrid, 1969]. pp. 80. *(Escuela Nacional de Administracion Publica [Spain]. Conferencias y Documentos. No. 26)*

RAMOS ESPEJO (ANTONIO) Andalucia: campo de trabajo y represion. Granada, [1978]. pp. 501. *bibliog.*

— Tanzania.

TANGANYIKA. Labour Division. 1950. Specimen tasks for labour employed in agricultural and industrial undertakings. Dar es Salaam, 1950. pp. 5.

— — Statistics.

UNITED REPUBLIC OF TANZANIA. Bureau of Statistics. 1974. N[ational] P[rovident] F[und] statistics 1970/71 with proposals and amendments. Dar es Salaam, 1974. fo. 71.

— Trinidad and Tobago.

RENNIE (BUKKA) The history of the working-class in the 20th century (1919-1956): the Trinidad and Tobago experience. Trinidad, 1973. pp. 167.

— United Kingdom.

FAIRCHILD (EDWIN CHARLES) Labour and the industrial revolution. London, 1923. pp. 222.

POSTGATE (RAYMOND WILLIAM) A pocket history of the British working class. Tillicoultry, 1942 repr. 1943. pp. 99.

MORTON (ARTHUR LESLIE) and TATE (GEORGE KENNETH) The British labour movement, 1770-1920: a history. London, 1956. pp. 313. *bibliog.*

HOBSBAWM (ERIC JOHN ERNEST) Labouring men: studies in the history of labour. London, 1968 repr. 1979. pp. 401.

The AFFLUENT worker in the class structure; [by] John Goldthorpe [and others]. London, 1969. pp. 239. *bibliog.*

HODGKINS (JOHN R.) Over the hills to glory: radicalism in Banburyshire, 1832-1945. Southend, [1978]. pp. 218.

INDEPENDENT collier: the coal miner as archetypal proletarian reconsidered; edited by Royden Harrison. Hassocks, 1978. pp. 276. *bibliog.*

ROBERTS (KENNETH) The working class. London, 1978. pp. 206. *bibliog.*

SEABROOK (JEREMY) What went wrong?: working people and the ideals of the labour movement. London, 1978. pp. 286.

BLACKBURN (ROBERT MARTIN) and MANN (J. MICHAEL) The working class in the labour market. London, 1979. pp. 369. *bibliog.*

CORRIGAN (PAUL) Schooling the Smash Street Kids. London, 1979. pp. 158. *bibliog.*

HOPKINS (ERIC) A social history of the English working classes, 1815-1945. London, 1979. pp. 282. *bibliog.*

WORKING class culture: studies in history and theory; edited by John Clarke [and others]. London, 1979. pp. 301. *bibliog.*

— — Dwellings.

The HISTORY of working class housing: a symposium; edited by Stanley D. Chapman. Totowa, N.J., [1971]. pp. 307. *bibliogs.*

— — Political activity.

CROUCH (COLIN) The politics of industrial relations. [London], 1979. pp. 223. *bibliog.*

CURRIE (ROBERT) Industrial politics. Oxford, 1979. pp. 94.

IDEOLOGY and the labour movement: essays presented to John Saville; edited by David E. Martin and David Rubinstein. London, [1979]. pp. 276. *bibliogs.*

— — Ireland, Northern.

MILLER (ROBERT L.) Attitudes to work in Northern Ireland. Belfast, 1978. pp. 19. *(Fair Employment Agency for Northern Ireland. Research Papers. 2)*

— — Scotland.

ESSAYS in Scottish labour history: a tribute to W.H. Marwick; edited by Ian MacDougall. Edinburgh, [1978]. pp. 265. *bibliogs.*

— — Wales — Dwellings.

LOWE (JEREMY BURMAN) Welsh industrial workers' housing 1775-1875. Cardiff, 1977. pp. 65. *bibliog.*

— United States.

RUBIN (LILLIAN B.) Worlds of pain: life in the working-class family. New York, [1976]. pp. 268.

ESSAYS in Southern labor history...; edited by Gary M. Fink and Merl E. Reed. Westport, Conn., 1977. pp. 275. *bibliogs. Selected papers from the Southern Labor History Conference, Atlanta, 1976.*

SORGE (FRIEDRICH ADOLPH) Labor movement in the United States: a history of the American working class from colonial times to 1890; edited by Philip S. Foner and Brewster Chamberlin; introduction by Philip S. Foner; translated by Brewster Chamberlin and Angela Chamberlin. Westport, Conn., 1977. pp. 394. *Translated articles originally published in German in Die Neue Zeit.*

ANDRISANI (PAUL J.) Work attitudes and labor market experience: evidence from the National Longitudinal Surveys. New York, [1978]. pp. 263. *bibliog.*

CANTOR (MILTON) The divided left: American radicalism, 1900-1975. New York, [1978]. pp. 248. *bibliog.*

HIRSCH (SUSAN E.) Roots of the American working class: the industrialization of crafts in Newark, 1800-1860. [Philadelphia, 1978].

SPENCER (CHARLES) Blue collar: an internal examination of the workplace. 2nd ed. Chicago, 1978. pp. 242.

AMERICAN workingclass culture: explorations in American labor and social history; edited by Milton Cantor. Westport, Conn., 1979. pp. 441.

— — Biography.

BROOKS (THOMAS R.) Clint: a biography of a labor intellectual: Clinton S. Golden. New York, 1978. pp. 377. *bibliog.*

— — New York.

WALKOWITZ (DANIEL J.) Worker city, company town: iron and cotton-worker protest in Troy and Cohoes, New York, 1855-84. Urbana, Ill., [1978]. pp. 292. *bibliog.*

LABOUR CONTRACT

LABOUR CONTRACT
— Russia.

KLENOV (EVGENII ALEKSANDROVICH) Kollektivnyi dogovor: spravochnoe posobie. Moskva, 1977. pp. 80. (Bibliotechka Profsoiuznogo Aktivista. 30)

NEGRU (FEDOR PANTELEEVICH) Nauchno-tekhnicheskii progress i trudovoi dogovor; pod redaktsiei R.Z. Livshitsa. Kishinev, 1977. pp. 95.

LABOUR COSTS
— Canada.

CANADA. Statistics Canada. Labour costs in Canada: trade. a., 1972- Ottawa. *[in English and French]*.

— Italy.

PREDETTI (ADALBERTO) Occupazione, retribuzioni, costo del lavoro in Italia. Milano, [1975]. pp. 265.

LABOUR COURTS
— Canada.

WILLES (JOHN A.) The Ontario Labour Court, 1943-1944. Kingston, Ont., [1979]. pp. 255. *(Kingston, Ontario. Queen's University. Industrial Relations Centre. Research and Current Issues Series. No.37)*

— United Kingdom.

GOODMAN (MICHAEL JACK) Industrial tribunals' procedure. 2nd ed. London, 1979. pp. 127.

LABOUR DISCIPLINE
— Russia.

PRAVOVOE regulirovanie obshchestvennykh otnoshenii. Moskva, 1976. pp. 120.

PIATAKOV (ALEKSANDR VASIL'EVICH) Ukreplenie trudovoi distsipliny: pravovye problemy. Moskva, 1979. pp. 215.

LABOUR DISPUTES
— Germany.

RATIONALISIERUNG und Massenarbeiter: die Kämpfe der norddeutschen Werftarbeiter seit 1945. München, 1973. pp. 157. *bibliog.*

MITSCHERLICH (MATTHIAS) Das Arbeitskampfrecht der Bundesrepublik Deutschland und die Europäische Sozialcharta. Baden-Baden, [1977]. pp. 160. *bibliog.*

— New Zealand.

TURKINGTON (DON) Industrial conflict: a study of three New Zealand industries. Wellington, N.Z., 1976. pp. 324.

— Russia.

SKOBELKIN (VLADIMIR NIKOLAEVICH) Kak rassmatrivaiutsia trudovye spory rabotnika s predpriiatiem. 2nd ed. Voronezh, 1977. pp. 119.

WORKERS against the Gulag: the new opposition in the Soviet Union; edited by Viktor Haynes and Olga Semyonova. London, 1979. pp. 129.

— Spain.

SANZ (JESUS) El movimiento obrero en el Pais Valenciano, 1939-1976. Valencia, 1976. pp. 344.

LABOUR ECONOMICS.

FLEISHER (BELTON MENDEL) Labor economics: theory and evidence. Englewood Cliffs, N.J., [1970]. pp. 304. *bibliog.*

REYNOLDS (LLOYD GEORGE) Labor economics and labor relations. 7th ed. Englewood Cliffs, [1978]. pp. 651. *bibliogs.*

LABOUR EXCHANGES
— India.

INDIA. Directorate General of Employment and Training. 1977. National Employment Service in India. [Delhi, 1977]. pp. 157.

— — Andhra Pradesh.

ANDHRA PRADESH. State Employment Market Information Unit. 1976. Hand-book of employment exchanges statistics, 1964-1974. Hyderabad, 1976. pp. 129.

— United Kingdom.

U.K. Social Survey. [Reports. New Series]. 1012. Attitudes to the employment service, 1973: a survey carried out for the Department of Employment; [by] Janet Gregory [and] Elizabeth Head. [London, 1977]. pp. 125.

U.K. Employment Service Division. 1978. Jobcentres: an evaluation. [London, 1978]. pp. 45.

LABOUR LAWS AND LEGISLATION
— France.

JAMBU-MERLIN (ROGER) Les gens de mer. Paris, 1978. pp. 317.

JAVILLIER (JEAN CLAUDE) Droit du travail: (with Supplement). Paris, 1978. pp. 634.

LYON-CAEN (GERARD) and PELISSIER (JEAN) Les grands arrêts de droit du travail. Paris, 1978. pp. 383.

— Germany.

MITSCHERLICH (MATTHIAS) Das Arbeitskampfrecht der Bundesrepublik Deutschland und die Europäische Sozialcharta. Baden-Baden, [1977]. pp. 160. *bibliog.*

RADÜ (FRIEDRICH WILHELM) Die Konkretisierung der Berufsfreiheit im Arbeitsrecht der Bundesrepublik Deutschland und der Schweiz. Basel, 1978. pp. 171. *bibliog. (Basel. Universität. Juristische Fakultät. Institut für Internationales Recht und Internationale Beziehungen. Schriftenreihe. Heft 26)*

WEISS (MANFRED) Gewerkschaftliche Vertrauensleute: tarifvertragliche Verbesserungen ihrer Arbeit im Betrieb. Köln, [1978]. pp. 109. *(Otto Brenner Stiftung. Schriftenreihe. 11)*

WITTKOWSKI (WOLFRAM) Der Schutz der Arbeitskraft durch das Grundgesetz: zugleich ein Beitrag zum Sozialstaatsprinzip. Frankfurt am Main, 1979. pp. 249. *bibliog.*

— Italy.

L'APPLICAZIONE dello Statuto dei Lavoratori: tendenze ed orientamenti; scritti di C. Assanti [and others]. Milano, 1973 repr. 1975. pp. 374.

SINDACATO e magistratura nei conflitti di lavoro; a cura di Tiziano Treu. Bologna, [1975-76]. 2 vols.

GUALTIEROTTI (PIERO) L'impresa artigiana. Milano, 1977. pp. 465. *bibliog.*

VACCARELLA (ROMANO) Il procedimento di repressione della condotta antisindacale. Milano, [1977]. pp. 244.

BALANDI (GIAN GUIDO) La legge sulla occupazione giovanile. Milano, [1978]. pp. 111.

— Netherlands.

BERG (HARRY VAN DEN) and others. De ontwikkeling van het stakingsrecht in Nederland. Nijmegen, [1978]. pp. 454.

— Russia.

PROKOPENKO (VOLODYMYR IVANOVYCH) Pravovye otnosheniia komiteta profsoiuza s administratsiei sotsialisticheskogo predpriiatiia. Kiev, 1977. pp. 159.

SMOLIARCHUK (VASILII IVANOVICH) Istochniki sovetskogo trudovogo prava. Moskva, 1978. pp. 168.

— Spain.

VILLA (LUIS ENRIQUE DE LA) Los origenes de la Administracion laboral en España. [Madrid, 1969]. pp. 80. *(Escuela Nacional de Administracion Publica [Spain]. Conferencias y Documentos. No. 26)*

— Switzerland.

RADÜ (FRIEDRICH WILHELM) Die Konkretisierung der Berufsfreiheit im Arbeitsrecht der Bundesrepublik Deutschland und der Schweiz. Basel, 1978. pp. 171. *bibliog. (Basel. Universität. Juristische Fakultät. Institut für Internationales Recht und Internationale Beziehungen. Schriftenreihe. Heft 26)*

GROBÉTY (DOMINIQUE) La Suisse aux origines du droit ouvrier: étude du rôle joué par les cantons et la Confédération suisse dans l'élaboration d'un droit ouvrier interne et international au XIXème siècle. Zurich, 1979. pp. 389.

— Tanzania.

UNITED REPUBLIC OF TANZANIA. Statutes, etc. 1964. An Act to provide for the establishment of workers' committees in certain businesses and undertakings, to restrict the powers of employers to dismiss employees summarily and otherwise in relation to the discipline of employees, etc.: (the Security of Employment Act). [Dar es Salaam], 1964. pp. 373-406.

— United Kingdom.

McMULLEN (JEREMY) Rights at work: a workers' guide to employment law. London, 1978. pp. 423.

BUTTERWORTH AND CO., LTD. Employment law handbook; edited by Peter Wallington. London, 1979. pp. 571.

CREIGHTON (WILLIAM BREEN) Working women and the law. London, 1979. pp. 292. *bibliog.*

DAVIES (PAUL LYNDON) and FREEDLAND (MARK ROBERT) Labour law: text and materials. London, [1979]. pp. 766.

HEPPLE (BOB ALEXANDER) and O'HIGGINS (PAUL) Employment law; third edition by B.A. Hepple. London, 1979. pp. 395.

SWEET AND MAXWELL, LIMITED. Labour relations statutes and materials...; advisory editors B.A. Hepple, Paul O'Higgins [and] Lord Wedderburn of Charlton. London, 1979. pp. 675.

— United States.

GETMAN (JULIUS G.) Labor relstions: law, practice and policy. Mineola, N.Y., 1978. pp. 581.

TAYLOR (BENJAMIN J.) and WITNEY (FRED) Labor relations law. 3rd ed. Englewood Cliffs, N.J., 1979. pp. 834. *bibliog.*

— — Rhode Island.

RHODE ISLAND. Statutes, etc. Rhode Island labour laws. Providence, 1955. 1 vol. (various pagings.)

LABOUR LAWS AND LEGISLATION, INTERNATIONAL.

GROBÉTY (DOMINIQUE) La Suisse aux origines du droit ouvrier: étude du rôle joué par les cantons et la Confédération suisse dans l'élaboration d'un droit ouvrier interne et international au XIXème siècle. Zurich, 1979. pp. 389.

LABOUR MOBILITY.

REYNOLDS (LLOYD GEORGE) The structure of labor markets: wages and labor mobility in theory and practice. Westport, Conn., 1951, repr. 1971. pp. 328.

SILVESTRE (JEAN JACQUES) Les inégalités de salaires: marché du travail et croissance économique. [Paris, 1978]. pp. 306.

LABOUR PARTY
— New Zealand.

PAUL (JOHN THOMAS) Humanism in politics: New Zealand Labour Party retrospect. Wellington, 1946. pp. 192.

— United Kingdom.

LABOUR PARTY. Arwyddbyst i'r Cymru newydd. London, [1962?]. pp. 23.

LABOUR PARTY. Signposts to the new Wales:...policy statement for Wales... prepared by a working party including representatives of the National Executive Committee, the Welsh Council of Labour and the Welsh Labour Parliamentary Group. London, [1962?]. pp. 23.

MILIBAND (RALPH) Parliamentary socialism: a study in the politics of labour. 2nd ed. New York, [1972]. pp. 384.

LABOUR COMMITTEE FOR EUROPE. Direct elections to the European Parliament: what the Labour Party should say. London, [1977]. pp. 6.

HATFIELD (MICHAEL) The house the Left built: inside Labour policy-making 1970-75. London, 1978. pp. 272.

LEWIS (W. RUSSELL) Tony Benn: a critical biography. London, 1978. pp. 203.

MICHIE (ALISTAIR) and HOGGART (SIMON) The pact: the inside story of the Lib-Lab government, 1977-8. London, 1978. pp. 183.

MINKIN (LEWIS) The Labour Party conference: a study in the politics of intra- party democracy. London, 1978. pp. 426.

NORTH TYNESIDE COMMUNITY DEVELOPMENT PROJECT. North Shields: working class politics and housing, 1900-1977. [Newcastle-upon-Tyne, 1978]. pp. 72. *(Final Reports. Vol.1)*

TAYLOR (IAN HAMILTON) War and the development of Labour's domestic programme, 1939-45. 1977 [or rather 1978]. fo. 275. *bibliog. Typescript. Ph.D. (London) thesis: unpublished. This thesis is the property of London University and may not be removed from the Library.*

DRUCKER (HENRY MATTHEW) Doctrine and ethos in the Labour Party. London, 1979. pp. 134. *bibliog.*

FABIAN SOCIETY. Fabian Tracts. [No.] 462. The politics of monetarism; [by] Bryan Gould [and others]. London, 1979. pp. 19.

GOYDER (MARK) Socialism tomorrow: fresh thinking for the Labour Party. London, 1979. pp. 32. *(Young Fabian Group. Young Fabian Pamphlets. 49)*

JENKINS (MARK) Bevanism: Labour's high tide: the cold war and the democratic mass movement. Nottingham, 1979. pp. 323. *bibliogs.*

LABOUR PARTY. The Labour way is the better way: the Labour party manifesto 1979. London, [1979]. pp. 40.

McCORMICK (PAUL) Enemies of democracy. London, 1979. pp. 228.

— — Bibliography.

MacDOUGALL (IAN) compiler. A catalogue of some labour records in Scotland and some Scots records outside Scotland. Edinburgh, 1978. pp. 598.

— — History.

PELLING (HENRY MATHISON) A short history of the Labour Party. 6th ed. London, 1978. pp. 184. *bibliogs.*

LABOUR POLICY
— Canada.

OSTRY (SYLVIA) and ZAIDI (MAHMOOD A.) Labour economics in Canada. 3rd ed. Toronto, [1979]. pp. 418.

— France.

FRANCE. Mission pour l'Emploi. 1979. Une politique pour l'emploi au service de l'homme: rapport présenté...par Robert Fabre, etc. Paris, 1979. pp. 179.

— Germany.

KUEHL (JUERGEN) and others. Überlegungen II zu einer vorausschauenden Arbeitsmarktpolitik. Nürnberg, Bundesanstalt für Arbeit, [1978]. pp. 285. *bibliog.*

LABOUR SERVICE
— Hungary.

BRAHAM (RANDOLPH L.) The Hungarian labor service system, 1939-1945. New York, 1977. pp. 159. *bibliog. (East European Quarterly. East European Monographs. 31)*

LABOUR SUPPLY.

INTERNATIONAL LABOUR OFFICE. World Employment Programme. 1978. Research working papers 1974 to 1977. Geneva, 1978. Microfiche [239 cards and index in 2 binders].

LABOUR force participation in low-income countries; edited by Guy Standing and Glen Sheehan, etc. Geneva, International Labour Office, 1978. pp. 338.

ORGANISATION FOR ECONOMIC CO-OPERATION AND DEVELOPMENT. 1978. A medium term strategy for employment and manpower policies. Paris, 1978. pp. 130.

REYNOLDS (LLOYD GEORGE) Labor economics and labor relations. 7th ed. Englewood Cliffs, [1978]. pp. 651. *bibliogs.*

SILVESTRE (JEAN JACQUES) Les inégalités de salaires: marché du travail et croissance économique. [Paris, 1978]. pp. 306.

SINGELMANN (JOACHIN) From agriculture to services: the transformation of industrial employment. Beverly Hills, [1978]. pp. 175. *bibliog.*

UNEMPLOYMENT insurance: global evidence of its effects on unemployment; proceedings of an international conference held in Vancouver, British Columbia, Canada; edited by Herbert G. Grubel and Michael A. Walker. [Vancouver], 1978. pp. 388. *bibliogs.*

KNOX (FRANK) Labour supply in economic development. Farnborough, [1979]. pp. 114. *bibliogs.*

— Bibliography.

BRIGHTON. University of Sussex. Institute of Development Studies. Library. Occasional Guides. No. 12. Labour market backwash and the educational process: an annotated bibliography. Brighton, [1978]. pp. 68.

— Mathematical models.

BARNUM (H.N.) and SQUIRE (LYN) Consistent aggregation of family and hired labor in agricultural production functions. Ann Arbor, Mich., 1978. pp. 12. *(Michigan University. Center for Research on Economic Development. Discussion Papers. No. 73)*

— Africa.

HUMAN resources and African development; edited by Ukandi G. Damachi and Victor P. Diejomaoh. New York, [1978]. pp. 378. *bibliog.*

— America, Latin.

ROGGERO (MARIA ANGELINA) Urbanizacion, industrializacion y crecimiento del sector servicios en America latina. Buenos Aires, [1976]. pp. 139. *bibliog.*

— Australia.

AUSTRALIA. Commonwealth Bureau of Census and Statistics. 1976. Persons aged 15 to 64 years: employment status and period since leaving school, May 1976. Canberra, 1976. pp. 24.

AUSTRALIA. Department of Employment and Industrial Relations. Manpower Programmes Section. 1978. Employment prospects by industry and occupation: a labour market analysis. Canberra, 1978. pp. 206.

AUSTRALIA. Department of Employment and Youth Affairs. Manpower Programmes Section. 1979. Employment prospects by industry and occupation: a labour market analysis. Canberra, 1979. pp. 262.

— Bahamas.

BAHAMAS. Department of Statistics. 1975. The labour force report, 1975. Nassau, 1975. pp. 65.

— Brazil.

ALMEIDA (JOSE) Industrializaçao e emprego no Brasil. Rio de Janeiro, 1974. pp. 139. *(Brazil. Instituto de Planejamento Econômico e Social. Instituto de Pesquisas. Relatorios de Pesquisa. No. 24)*

ALMEIDA (WANDERLY JOSE MANSO DE) Serviços e desenvolvimento econômico no Brazil: aspectos setoriais e suas implicaçoes. Rio de Janeiro, 1974. pp. 127. *(Brazil. Instituto de Planejamento Econômico e Social. Instituto de Pesquisas. Relatorios de Pesquisa. No. 23)*

SOUZA (ALBERTO DE MELLO E) and CASTRO (CLAUDIO DE MOURA) Mão-de-obra industrial no Brasil: mobilidade, treinamento e produtividade. Rio de Janeiro, 1974. pp. 424. *(Brazil. Instituto de Planejamento Econômico e Social. Instituto de Pesquisas. Relatorios de Pesquisa. No. 25)*

ALMEIDA (ANNA LUIZA OZORIO DE) Distribuição de renda e emprego en serviços. Rio de Janeiro, 1976. pp. 412. *bibliog. (Brazil. Instituto de Planejamento Econômico e Social. Instituto de Pesquisas. Relatorios de Pesquisa. No. 34)*

OLIVEIRA (DANIEL A. RIBEIRO DE) Labour supply and employment in Belo Horizonte, Brazil. 1978. fo. 338. *bibliog. Typescript. Ph.D. (London) thesis: unpublished. This thesis is the property of London University and may not be removed from the Library.*

— Canada.

CANADA. Department of Employment and Immigration. Annual report. a., 1977/78- Ottawa. *[in English and French] Supersedes CANADA. Department of Manpower and Immigration. Annual report and CANADA. Unemployment Insurance Commission. Annual report.*

GOYETTE (JEAN-MARIE) and LACHAPELLE (ROBERT) Etude comparative de l'évolution du marché du travail: Québec, Ontario, Canada. [Quebec], 1977. pp. 133. *bibliog.*

OSTRY (SYLVIA) and ZAIDI (MAHMOOD A.) Labour economics in Canada. 3rd ed. Toronto, [1979]. pp. 418.

— — Nova Scotia.

NOVA SCOTIA. Department of Development. Economic Analysis Section. 1977. Employment and gross domestic product by sector, Nova Scotia: 1964-1975 estimated, 1976-1984 projected; highlights, tables, charts and detailed description. Halifax, 1977. fo. 53.

— — Quebec.

QUEBEC (PROVINCE). Office de Planification et de Développement. 1978. Les sièges sociaux et l'emploi au Québec: quelques statistiques partielles. [Québec, 1978]. pp. 64. *bibliog.*

— Denmark.

KJAER (ANDERS) Udstødning fra arbejdsmarkedet: litteratur og begreber, etc. København, 1978. pp. 197. *bibliog. (Socialforskeningsinstituttet. Studier. Nr.36) With English summary.*

— France.

CONTRIBUTIONS à une prospective du travail: présentation et conclusions essentielles du rapport rédigé pour le Commissariat Général du Plan à l'issue des travaux d'un groupe présidé par Yves Chaigneau. [Paris, Commissariat Général du Plan], 1975. fo. 65.

LABOUR SUPPLY.(Cont.)

BUETTNER (OLIVIER) and others. L'emploi salarié tertiaire en France; localisation des activités, hiérarchisation de l'espace. [Paris, 1976]. pp. 156. *(France. Centre d'Etudes de l'Emploi. Cahiers. 10)* With English summary.

DUMARD (JEAN) and LETABLIER (MARIE THERESE) L'emploi industriel en France, fin 1968 - fin 1971: modifications spatiales et structurelles. [Paris, 1976]. pp. 211. *(France. Centre d'Etudes de l'Emploi. Cahiers. 9)* With English summary.

BERTRAND (OLIVIER) and others. L'évolution des emplois et la main-d'oeuvre dans l'industrie automobile: problèmes et perspectives. Paris, 1977. pp. 233. *bibliog*. *(Centre d'Etudes et de Recherches sur les Qualifications. Dossiers. 15)*

CHARLOT (ALAIN) and BECIRSPAHIC (KEMAL) Les universités et le marché du travail: enquête sur les étudiants à la sortie des universités et sur leurs débouchés professionnels. Paris, 1977. pp. 577. *(Centre d'Etudes et de Recherches sur les Qualifications. Dossiers. 14)*

SCHEMA général de l'aménagement de la France: sur l'emploi: premiers dossiers; [by Philippe Barret and others]. Paris, 1977. pp. 208. *(France. Délégation à l'Aménagement du Territoire et a l'Action Régionale. Travaux et Recherches de Prospective. 73)* 16 maps in end pocket.

CHAMBON (BERNARD) Les relations entre l'emploi et la formation professionnelle dans la région Rhône-Alpes: dossier de l'emploi et de la formation professionnelle: emplois d'ouvriers et d'employés qualifiés: département de l'Ain; réalisé...sous la direction de Roland Beltramelli. [Lyons], Etablissement Public Régional Rhône-Alpes, 1978. pp. 121. *bibliog*.

DUCHENE (B.) Un exemple de développement d'un bassin d'emploi: le pays de Lannion. Rennes, Echelon Régional de l'Emploi et du Travail de Rennes, 1978. fo. 176.

Les MARCHES locaux du travail; [by Michel Vernières and others]. Paris, 1978. pp. 139. *bibliog*. *(France. Commissariat Général du Plan. Economie et Planification)*

POMMIER PENEFF (PAULETTE) and others. Population, emploi et formation dans les contrats de pays. [Paris, 1978]. pp. 32. *(France. Délégation à l'Emploi. Politique des Contrats de Pays. Dossiers Techniques)*

SCHEMA général d'aménagement de la France: activités et régions: dynamiques d'une transformation. [Paris, 1978]. pp. 124. *(France. Délégation à l'Aménagement du Territoire et à l'Action Régionale. Travaux et Recherches de Prospective. 75)*

FRANCE. Ministère du Travail et de la Participation. Travail et emploi. q., Je 1979(no.1)- Paris.

FRANCE. Mission pour l'Emploi. 1979. Une politique pour l'emploi au service de l'homme: rapport présenté...par Robert Fabre, etc. Paris, 1979. pp. 179.

SAVREUX (ANNIE) Le bassin d'emploi Le Creusot-Montceau: rôle des primes de développement régional. [Dijon], Echelon Régional de l'Emploi et du Travail de Dijon, 1979. fo. 69.

— Germany.

GERMANY (BUNDESREPUBLIK). Statistisches Bundesamt. Sozialversicherungspflichtig beschäftigte Arbeitnehmer. q and a., Mr 1977- Wiesbaden. *(Bevölkerung und Erwerbstätigkeit. 4.2)*

DEUTSCHES INSTITUT FÜR WIRTSCHAFTSFORSCHUNG. Sonderhefte. [Neue Folge]. 121. Die Entwicklung des Arbeitsplatzangebots in den Arbeitsmarktregionen: Daten für 1961 und 1970, Prognoseergebnisse für 1980...; ([by] Herwig Birg). Berlin, 1978. pp. 152.

— Ghana.

GHANA. Manpower Unit. 1961. Survey of high-level manpower in Ghana, 1960. Accra, 1961. pp. 62.

— Hong Kong.

HONG KONG. Labour Department. 1977. Some facts about employment in Hong Kong. Hong Kong, 1977. pp. 27.

— India.

INDIA. Directorate General of Employment and Training. 1977. Report on the employment pattern of graduates. New Delhi, [1977]. pp. 111.

— — Andhra Pradesh.

ANDHRA PRADESH. State Employment Market Information Unit. 1976. Hand-book of employment exchanges statistics, 1964-1974. Hyderabad, 1976. pp. 129.

— — Maharashtra.

MAHARASHTRA COMMERCIAL AND INDUSTRIAL CONFERENCE, 5TH, BOMBAY, 1972. Development through employment. [Bombay, Maharashtra Economic Development Council, 1972?]. pp. 59.

— Ireland (Republic).

EIRE. Central Statistics Office. 1978. Labour force survey, 1977: first results. Dublin, 1978. pp. 22.

— Italy.

PREDETTI (ADALBERTO) Occupazione, retribuzioni, costo del lavoro in Italia. Milano, [1975]. pp. 265.

— Jamaica — Statistics.

JAMAICA. Department of Statistics. 1978. Employment, earnings and hours in large establishments, 1977. [Kingston, 1978]. pp. 45.

— Malawi.

MALAWI. Manpower and Social Services Section. 1972. Manpower survey, 1971; results of the survey and analysis of requirements, 1971-1980. [Zomba, 1972]. pp. 99.

— Malaysia.

FEDERATION OF MALAYSIA. Department of Statistics. 1977. Report of the labour force survey, April/May 1974. Kuala Lumpur, 1977. 1 vol. (various pagings). In English and Malay.

FREDERICKS (L. J.) and others. Patterns of labour utilization and income distribution in rice double cropping systems: policy implications. Kuala Lumpur, 1977. pp. 66. *bibliog*. *(University of Malaya. Faculty of Economics and Administration. Occasional Papers on Malaysian Socio-Economic Affairs. No. 8)*

— — Mathematical models.

BARNUM (H.N.) and SQUIRE (LYN) Labor heterogeneity and rice production in Malaysia. Ann Arbor, Mich., 1977. pp. 11. *bibliog*. *(Michigan University. Center for Research on Economic Development. Discussion Papers. No. 71)*

— Netherlands.

NETHERLANDS. Centraal Planbureau. 1978. Omvang en samenstelling van het trendmatige arbeidsaanbod tussen 1975 en 2000. 's-Gravenhage, 1978. pp. 77. *(Monografieën. No. 22)*

— New Hebrides.

NEW HEBRIDES. Condominium Bureau of Statistics. 1974. Manpower and employment survey, September 1973: preliminary results. Vila, 1974. pp. 31. *(Statistical Bulletins)* In English and French.

NEW HEBRIDES. Condominium Bureau of Statistics. 1975. Manpower and employment survey. [Vila, 1975]. pp. 126. *(Statistical bulletin. [Publications])*

— New Zealand.

THOMSON (JANET) Employment in the suburbs. [Wellington], Town and Country Planning Branch, Ministry of Works, 1969. pp. 8.

NEW ZEALAND. Department of Labour. Research and Planning Division. 1976. Employment distribution and potential in Hawkes Bay. Wellington, 1976. pp. 44.

— Russia — Mathematical models.

BASALAEVA (NATAL'IA ALEKSEEVNA) Modelirovanie demograficheskikh protsessov i trudovykh resursov. Moskva, 1978. pp. 88. *(Akademiia Nauk SSSR. Problemy Sovetskoi Ekonomiki)*

— Sweden.

SWEDEN. Statistiska Centralbyrån. 1976. Arbetskraftsresurserna 1965-2000: (The labour force resources 1965-2000); [by Karl Martin Sjöstrand and Raili Sjöberg]. Stockholm, 1976. pp. 88. *(Information i Prognosfrågor. 1976.1)*

— Underdeveloped areas.

See UNDERDEVELOPED AREAS — Labour supply.

— United Kingdom.

NORTHERN REGION STRATEGY TEAM. Development of comparable statistics for employment and output, 1948 to date: procedures for adjustment. Newcastle-upon-Tyne, 1975. pp. 67. *(Working Papers. No. 17)*

NORTHERN REGION STRATEGY TEAM. Trends in the structure of occupations in the Northern Region, 1966-1971. Newcastle-upon-Tyne, 1976-77. 2 vols. *(Working Papers. No. 10)*

DOBSON (NEIL) Employment and industry in Greater London: a background document. London, [1977]. pp. 48.

THOMAS (BARRY) and DEATON (DAVID) Labour shortage and economic analysis: a study of occupational labour markets. Oxford, [1977]. pp. 264. *bibliog*. *(Warwick Studies in Industrial Relations)*

WARNES (A.M.) The decentralisation of employment from the larger English cities. London, 1977. pp. 27. *(London. University. King's College. Geography Department. Occasional Papers. No.5)*

MSC REVIEW AND PLAN; [pd.by] Manpower Services Commission [U.K.]. a., 1978(2nd)- London.

DEAN (ANDREW) The labour market in a slow growing economy. London, [1978]. pp. 21. *(National Institute of Economic and Social Research. Discussion Papers. No. 25)*

JOSEPH (Sir KEITH SINJOHN) Conditions for fuller employment. London, 1978. pp. 20.

BLACKBURN (ROBERT MARTIN) and MANN (J. MICHAEL) The working class in the labour market. London, 1979. pp. 369. *bibliog*.

— — Ireland, Northern.

FAIR EMPLOYMENT AGENCY FOR NORTHERN IRELAND. An industrial and occupational profile of the two sections of the population in Northern Ireland: an analysis of the 1971 population census. [Belfast, 1978]. pp. 15. *bibliog*. *([Research Papers. 1])*

— United States.

MASTERS (STANLEY H.) and GARFINKEL (IRWIN) Estimating the labor supply effects of income-maintenance alternatives. New York, [1977]. pp. 289. *bibliog*. *(Wisconsin University, Madison. Institute for Research on Poverty. Monograph Series)*

ANDRISANI (PAUL J.) Work attitudes and labor market experience: evidence from the National Longitudinal Surveys. New York, [1978]. pp. 263. *bibliog*.

— — New Hampshire.

NEW HAMPSHIRE. Department of Employment Security. Economic Analysis and Reports Section. 1972. Growth and decline in New Hampshire industries, 1970 to 1971;...William J. Roy, economist. [Concord], 1972. pp. 22.

NEW HAMPSHIRE. Department of Employment Security. Economic Analysis and Reports Section. 1972. New Hampshire occupations in 1980; prepared by...William J. Roy, economist. [Concord, 1972?]. pp. 76.

LABOUR TURNOVER

— Bibliography.

ARMSTRONG (DOUGLAS) compiler. Labor turnover; a selected bibliography. [Toronto], Ontario Ministry of Labour Research Library, 1975. fo. 12. *Photocopy.*

— Canada — British Columbia.

SUZANNE VEIT AND ASSOCIATES. Labour turnover and community stability: implications for northeast coal development in British Columbia; a report prepared for the Federal/Provincial Manpower Sub-Committee on North East Coal [Development]. [Victoria, B.C.?], 1978. 1 vol. (various pagings) *bibliog.*

— Russia.

ANTOSENKOV (EVGENII GRIGOR'EVICH) and KUPRIIANOVA (ZOIA VASIL'EVNA) Tendentsii v tekuchesti rabochikh kadrov: dinamicheskii aspekt analiza; otvetstvennyi redaktor E.D. Malinin. Novosibirsk, 1977. pp. 253.

— United Kingdom.

OLDHAM (MARGARET) Withdrawal from work. Hatfield, 1978. pp. 17. *bibliog.* (*Hatfield Polytechnic. School of Social Sciences. Social Sciences Occasional Papers. No. 1*)

LABRADOR

— Economic conditions.

LABRADOR RESOURCES ADVISORY COUNCIL. Community priorities for development in Labrador. [Happy Valley, 1978]. 1 vol. (various pagings).

— Economic policy.

LABRADOR RESOURCES ADVISORY COUNCIL. Community priorities for development in Labrador. [Happy Valley, 1978]. 1 vol. (various pagings).

— Social conditions.

LABRADOR RESOURCES ADVISORY COUNCIL. Community priorities for development in Labrador. [Happy Valley, 1978]. 1 vol. (various pagings).

— Social policy.

LABRADOR RESOURCES ADVISORY COUNCIL. Community priorities for development in Labrador. [Happy Valley, 1978]. 1 vol. (various pagings).

LABRIOLA (ANTONIO).

ALOYSIO (FRANCESCO DE) Studi sul pensiero di Antonio Labriola. Assisi, [1976]. pp. 137.

SICILIANI DE CUMIS (NICOLA) Studi su Labriola. Urbino, [1976]. pp. 423.

LACAZE-DUTHIERS (GERARD DE).

DAY (HEM) pseud. [i.e. Marcel DIEU] Gérard de Lacaze-Duthiers, le pacifiste. Paris, 1960. pp. 16.

LA GARDIE (MAGNUS GABRIEL DE).

See DE LA GARDIE (MAGNUS GABRIEL).

LAGOS

— History.

SMITH (ROBERT SYDNEY) The Lagos consulate, 1851-1861. London, 1978. pp. 188. *bibliog.*

LAING (Sir JOHN WILLIAM).

COAD (FREDERICK ROY) Laing: the biography of Sir John W. Laing, C.B.E., 1879- 1978. London, [1979]. pp. 238. *bibliog.*

LAING (RONALD DAVID).

HOWARTH-WILLIAMS (MARTIN) R.D. Laing: his work and its relevance for sociology. London, 1977. pp. 219. *bibliog.*

LAISSEZ-FAIRE.

INDIVIDUAL freedom: selected works of William H. Hutt; edited by Svetozar Pejovich and David Klingaman. Westport, Conn., 1975. pp. 250. *bibliog.*

HAYEK (FRIEDRICH AUGUST) Economic progress in an open society. Seoul, 1978. pp. 53. (*Korea International Economic Institute. Seminar Series. No.16*)

TUMLIR (JAN) National interest and international order. London, [1978]. pp. 21. (*Trade Policy Research Centre. International Issues. No. 4*)

UNIVERSITY OF KENT AT CANTERBURY. Keynes Seminar, 3rd, 1976. Keynes and laissez-faire; edited by A.P. Thirlwall. London, 1978. pp. 134.

ROGGE (BENJAMIN A.) Can capitalism survive? Indianapolis, [1979]. pp. 329.

LAM (STANISLAW).

LAM (STANISŁAW) 'Zycie wśród wielu; przygotował do druku Andrzej Lam. [Warszawa, 1968]. pp. 449.

LAMBETH

— Politics and government.

ROEBUCK (JANET) Urban development in 19th-century London: Lambeth, Battersea and Wandsworth, 1838-1888. London, 1979. pp. 211. *bibliog.*

— Population.

SHANKLAND-COX PARTNERSHIP and INSTITUTE OF COMMUNITY STUDIES. Inner area study: Lambeth: study of intending migrants. [London], Department of the Environment, [1978]. pp. 31.

— Social conditions.

SHANKLAND-COX PARTNERSHIP and INSTITUTE OF COMMUNITY STUDIES. Inner area study: Lambeth: study of intending migrants. [London], Department of the Environment, [1978]. pp. 31.

LANCASHIRE

— History.

BLACKWOOD (B.G.) The Lancashire gentry and the great rebellion, 1640-60. Manchester, 1978. pp. 184. *bibliog.* (*Chetham Society. Remains, Historical and Literary, connected with the Palatine Counties of Lancaster and Chester. 3rd series. vol. 25*)

— — Bibliography.

LANCASHIRE history: historical periods: Norman; Plantagenet; Lancaster and York; Tudor; edited by Sidney Horrocks. Manchester, 1974. pp. 99. (*Joint Committee on the Lancashire Bibliography. Contributions Towards a Lancashire Bibliography. 7*)

LANCASHIRE history: historical period: Stuart; compiled by P. M. Turner; edited by Sidney Horrocks. Manchester, 1976. pp. 122. (*Joint Committee on the Lancashire Bibliography. Contributions Towards a Lancashire Bibliography. 8*)

LANCASHIRE history: historical period: Hanover; compiled by P.M. Turner; edited by Sidney Horrocks. Manchester, 1978. pp. 242. (*Joint Committee on the Lancashire Bibliography. Contributions Towards a Lancashire Bibliography.9*)

LANCASTER UNIVERSITY.

TAYLOR (TOM) CBE, JP. Report of the Taylor enquiry, 8th May - 5th July 1972 [into unrest at Lancaster University]. [Lancaster, 1972]. fo. 17.

LAND REFORM

LAND

See LAND USE.

LAND, NATIONALIZATION OF.

PREUSS (ARTHUR) ed. The fundamental fallacy of socialism: an essay on the question of land-ownership, comprising an authentic account of the famous McGlynn case. 2nd ed. St.Louis, Mo., 1909. pp. 198.

— United Kingdom.

GRIFFITHS (ELDON) Watch out for land nationalization. London, 1978. pp. 23. (*Conservative Political Centre. [Publications]. No. 624*)

LAND AND GENERAL DEVELOPMENTS LIMITED.

NOURSE (MARTIN CHARLES) and DUBUISSON (PETER WILLIAM GROSTETE) Land and General Developments Limited; Napet Securities Limited: investigation under sections 164 and 172 of the Companies Act, 1948; interim and final reports. [London], Department of Trade, 1978. 1 vol. (various pagings)

LAND GRANTS

— Australia — South Australia.

BUXTON (G.L.) South Australian land acts, 1869-1885. Adelaide, Libraries Board of South Australia, 1966. pp. 109. *bibliog.*

LAND REFORM

— Mathematical models.

COHEN (SULEIMAN IBRAHIM) Agrarian structures and agrarian reform: exercises in development theory and policy. Leiden, 1978. pp. 138. *bibliog.*

— America, Latin.

ALEXANDER (ROBERT JACKSON) Agrarian reform in Latin America. New York, [1974]. pp. 118.

REFORMAS agrarias en America Latina: Mexico, Bolivia, Cuba, Chile, Peru; [by] Pedro Negre Rigol [and others]. Buenos Aires, 1976. pp. 103.

LINDQVIST (SVEN) Land and power in South America; translated from the Swedish by Paul Britten Austin. Harmondsworth, 1979. pp. 333. *bibliog.*

— Guatemala.

SOTO (JOSÉ M. AYBAR DE) Dependency and intervention: the case of Guatemala in 1954. Boulder, Colo., 1978. pp. 374. *bibliog.*

— India.

APPU (P.S.) Agrarian structure and rural development. New Delhi, 1975. pp. 34. (*India. Department of Personnel and Administrative Reforms. Training Division. Occasional Papers. No. 7*)

— Ireland (Republic).

EIRE. Inter-departmental Committee on Land Structure Reform. 1977. Interim report. Dublin. 1977. pp. 18.

EIRE. Inter-departmental Committee on Land Structure Reform. 1978. Final report. Dublin, 1978. pp. 105.

— Mexico.

HAMON (JAMES L.) and NIBLO (STEPHEN R.) Precursores de la revolucion agraria en Mexico: las obras de Wistano Luis Orozco y Andres Molina Enriquez; traduccion de Omar Costa Acosta. Mexico, Secretaria de Educacion Publica, 1975. pp. 183. (*Sep/Setentas. 202*)

— Pakistan.

KHAN (MOHAMMAD AYUB) Land reforms: broadcast to the nation...January 24, 1959. Karachi, [Department of Advertising, Films and Publications], 1959. pp. 7.

LAND REFORM (Cont.)

PAKISTAN. Prime Minister. 1977. Address to the nation, Larkana, January 5, 1977: new land reforms. [Islamabad], 1977. pp. 9.

— Peru.

BAYER (DAVID L.) Reforma araria peruana: descapitalizacion del minifundio y formacion de la burguesia rural. Lima, 1975. pp. 83. bibliog. (Universidad Nacional Agraria. Centro de Investigaciones Socio-Economicas. [Publications]. 1)

MATOS MAR (JOSE) Yanaconaje y reforma agraria en el Peru: el caso del valle de Chancay. Lima, 1976. pp. 278. bibliog. (Instituto de Estudios Peruanos. Peru Problema. 15)

— Russia.

GINEV (VLADIMIR NIKOLAEVICH) Agrarnyi vopros i melkoburzhuaznye partii v Rossii v 1917 g.: k istorii bankrotstva neonarodnichestva. Leningrad, 1977. pp. 295.

OKTIABR' i sovetskoe krest'ianstvo, 1917-1927 gg. Moskva, 1977. pp. 295.

— Spain.

ALVAREZ GOMEZ (SANTIAGO) El Partido Comunista y el campo: la evolucion del problema agrario y la posicion de los comunistas. Madrid, [1977]. pp. 265.

— Uganda.

UGANDA. Law Reform Commission. 1977. The Land Reform Decree, 1975, simplified for and explained to the general public. Entebbe, 1977. pp. 48. (Law in Action Publication Series. No. 1)

LAND SETTLEMENT.

SETTLEMENTS; [by] Iain R. Meyer and Richard J. Huggett. London, 1979. pp. 201. (Geography: theory in practice. Book 1)

— Bibliography.

FOOD AND AGRICULTURE ORGANIZATION. Land Tenure and Production Structure Service. 1976. Bibliography on land settlement. Rome, 1976. pp. 146.

— Australia — South Australia.

BUXTON (G.L.) South Australian land acts, 1869-1885. Adelaide, Libraries Board of South Australia, 1966. pp. 109. bibliog.

— United Kingdom — Scotland.

MATHER (ALEXANDER S.) State-aided land settlement in Scotland. Aberdeen, 1978. pp. 34. (Aberdeen. University. Department of Geography. O'Dell Memorial Monographs. No. 6)

LAND SUBDIVISION

— United Kingdom — Scotland.

MATHER (ALEXANDER S.) State-aided land settlement in Scotland. Aberdeen, 1978. pp. 34. (Aberdeen. University. Department of Geography. O'Dell Memorial Monographs. No. 6)

LAND TAX.

See REAL PROPERTY TAX.

LAND TENURE

— Australia — South Australia — Law.

BUXTON (G.L.) South Australian land acts, 1869-1885. Adelaide, Libraries Board of South Australia, 1966. pp. 109. bibliog.

— Germany.

KUCHENBUCH (LUDOLF) Bäuerliche Gesellschaft und Klosterherrschaft im 9. Jahrhundert: Studien zur Sozialstruktur der Familia der Abtei Prüm. Wiesbaden, 1978. pp. 443. bibliog. (Vierteljahrschrift für Sozial- und Wirtschaftsgeschichte. Beihefte. Nr. 66)

— India.

METCALF (THOMAS R.) Land, landlords, and the British Raj: northern India in the nineteenth century. Berkeley, [1979]. pp. 436.

— — Punjab.

PUNJAB (INDIA). Publicity Department. 1950. Rural rehabilitation in East Punjab: a short survey, 1947-48. Simla, [1950]. pp. 36. (East Punjab Pamphlets. No. 5)

— Italy.

MERZARIO (RAUL) Signori e contadini di Calabria: Corigliano Calabro dal XVI al XIX secolo. Milano, 1975. pp. 142. (Università degli Studi della Calabria. Ricerche di Storia ed Economia)

PEZZINO (PAOLO) La riforma agraria in Calabria: intervento pubblico e dinamica sociale in un'area del Mezzogiorno, 1950-1970. Milano, 1977. pp. 253. (Istituto Nazionale per la Storia del Movimento di Liberazione in Italia. [Publications])

— Mexico.

BRADING (DAVID A.) Haciendas and ranchos in the Mexican Bajío, Leon 1700-1860. Cambridge, 1978. pp. 258. bibliog.

— Russia.

PETROV (ALEKSANDR PETROVICH) Kritika fal'sifikatsii agrarno-krest'ianskogo voprosa v trekh russkikh revoliutsiiakh. Moskva, 1977. pp. 399. bibliog.

ZIMIN (ALEKSANDR ALEKSANDROVICH) Krupnaia feodal'naia votchina i sotsial'no-politicheskaia bor'ba v Rossii, konets XV - XVI v. Moskva, 1977. pp. 356.

— — Law.

RIABOV (ALEKSANDR ANDREEVICH) Okhrana prava gosudarstvennoi sobstvennosti na zemliu i prava zemlepol'zovaniia v SSSR. Kazan', 1976. pp. 192.

— Sweden.

REVERA (MARGARETA) Gods och gård, 1650-1680: Magnus Gabriel De la Gardies godsbildning och godsdrift i Västergötland. Uppsala, 1975 in progress. bibliog. (Uppsala. Universitet. Historiska Institutionen. Studia Historica Upsaliensia. 70) With English summary.

— Tunisia.

TUNIS. Statutes, etc. 1958-60. Réforme agraire dans la basse vallée de la Medjerda: loi no. 58/63 du 11 juin 1958...modifiée par la loi no. 6/60 du 26 joillet 1960, etc. [Tunis], Office de la Mise en Valeur de la Vallée de la Medjerda, [1960?]. pp. 15, 16. In French and Arabic.

— Turkey.

MILLER (DUNCAN) and CETIN (IHSAN) Land and man in rural Turkey: a concise view of regional land tenure, land use and land capability. Ankara, 1974. fo. 27. (United States. Agency for International Development. USAID-Ankara. Economic Analysis Staff. Discussion Paper. No. 20)

— United Kingdom.

AGRICULTURAL MORTGAGE CORPORATION and ECONOMIC DEVELOPMENT COMMITTEE FOR THE AGRICULTURAL INDUSTRY. The ownership of land by agricultural landlords in England and Wales; a survey. London, National Economic Development Office, 1977. pp. 26.

ASPINALL (P.) The evolution of urban tenure systems in 19th century cities. Birmingham, 1978. pp. 35,xi,16. (Birmingham. University. Centre for Urban and Regional Studies. Research Memoranda. No. 63)

— — Law.

HARWOOD (MICHAEL) English land law. London, 1975. pp. 510.

RIDDALL (JOHN GERVASE) Introduction to land law. 2nd ed. London, 1979. pp. 403.

— — Ireland.

BEW (PAUL) Land and the national question in Ireland, 1858-82. Dublin, 1978. pp. 307.

LAND TITLES

— Registration and transfer — United States.

SHICK (BLAIR C.) and PLOTKIN (IRVING H.) Torrens in the United States: a legal and economic history and analysis of American land-registration systems. Lexington, Mass., [1978]. pp. 176.

LAND USE.

FABOS (JULIUS GY.) Planning the total landscape: a guide to intelligent land use. Boulder, Colo., [1979]. pp. 181. bibliogs.

RESOURCES and planning; edited by Brian Goodall and Andrew Kirby. Oxford, 1979. pp. 373. bibliogs.

— Bibliography.

U.K. Ministry of Overseas Development. Land Resources Division. Publications list. a., 1977- London.

— Mathematical models.

BATTY (MICHAEL) Paradoxes of science in public policy: the baffling case of land use models. Reading, 1978. pp. 34. bibliog. (Reading. University. Department of Geography. Reading Geographical Papers. No. 69)

— Planning.

DICKINSON (G.C.) and SHAW (M.G.) Monitoring land use change: some theoretical considerations and a workable solution. London, 1977. pp. 42. bibliog. (Planning Research Applications Group. PRAG Technical Papers. TP 20)

— France.

FRANCE. Direction de la Documentation. La Documentation Française. Notes et Etudes Documentaires. Nos. 4,375-4, 377. Les réserves foncières; par Noelle Lenoir. Paris, 1977. pp. 104. bibliog.

— New Zealand.

SEMINAR ON LAND USE PLANNING, WELLINGTON, 1971. Seminar on land use planning: a joint session of the New Zealand Association of Soil Conservators and New Zealand Society of Soil Science, held at the New Zealand Institute of Agricultural Science Conference in August 1971. [Wellington], Ministry of Works for National Water and Soil Conservation Organisation, 1973. pp. 28. bibliogs.

— Rhodesia.

RHODESIA. Information Service. 1965. Land apportionment in Rhodesia. [Salisbury, 1965]. pp. 16. (Information Papers. No. 1)

RHODESIA. Ministry of Information, Immigration and Tourism. 1971. Recent developments in Rhodesia's tribal trust lands. [Salisbury, 1971]. pp. 5.

— South Africa.

FAIR (T.J.D.) The Witwatersrand: its major socio-economic and land use trends, problems and prospects. Johannesburg, 1976. pp. 25. (Johannesburg. University of the Witwatersrand. Urban and Regional Research Unit. Occasional papers. No. 12)

— United Kingdom.

ROYAL INSTITUTUION OF CHARTERED SURVEYORS. The land problem reviewed: an examination of the Community Land Scheme and proposals for the future. [London, 1978]. pp. 53.

— United States — Colorado.

TREGARTHEN (TIMOTHY D.) Food, fuel and shelter: a watershed analysis of land-use trade- offs in a semiarid region. Boulder, Colo., [1978]. pp. 109. bibliog. Report of a conference on the Front Range of Colorado, held at Greeley, Colorado, 1976.

— — Massachusetts.

FABOS (JULIUS GY.) Planning the total landscape: a guide to intelligent land use. Boulder, Colo., [1979]. pp. 181. bibliogs.

LAND USE, RURAL
— Planning — Malaysia.

SENFTLEBEN (WOLFGANG) Background to agricultural land policy in Malaysia. Wiesbaden, [1978]. pp. 347. bibliog. (Hamburg. Institut für Asienkunde. Schriften. Band 44)

— — United Kingdom — Ireland, Northern.

IRELAND, NORTHERN. Department of the Environment. 1978. Policy for the control of development in rural areas. Belfast, 1978. pp. 8.

IRELAND, NORTHERN. Department of the Environment. 1978. Review of rural planning policy; statement by the Department, etc. Belfast, 1978. pp. 8.

REVIEW of rural planning policy; report of the Committee under the chairmanship of W.H. Cockcroft. Belfast, H.M.S.O., [1978]. pp. 41.

— Thailand.

FARMERS in the forest: economic development and marginal agriculture in northern Thailand; edited by Peter Kunstadter [and others]. Honolulu, [1978]. pp. 402. bibliog.

— Turkey.

MILLER (DUNCAN) and CETIN (IHSAN) Land and man in rural Turkey: a concise view of regional land tenure, land use and land capability. Ankara, 1974. fo. 27. (United States. Agency for International Development. USAID-Ankara. Economic Analysis Staff. Discussion Paper. No. 20)

— United Kingdom.

WHITBY (MARTIN CHARLES) and WILLIS (KENNETH G.) Rural resource development: an economic approach. 2nd ed. London, 1978. pp. 303. bibliog.

LAND USE, URBAN.

PEARCE (BARRY J.) and others. Land, planning and the market. Cambridge, 1978. pp. 101. bibliog. (Cambridge. University. Department of Land Economy. Occasional Papers. No. 9)

— Planning.

UNITED NATIONS. Department of Economic and Social Affairs. 1977. Land for human settlements: some legal and economic issues. (ST. ESA/69). New York, 1977. pp. 121.

— Australia — Queensland.

MORETON REGION GROWTH STRATEGY INVESTIGATIONS. Urban land-use and commitment. [Brisbane], Co-ordinator-General's Department and Cities Commission, 1976. 1 vol. (various pagings). bibliog. (Tasks. 2)

— United Kingdom.

DICKINSON (G.C.) and SHAW (M.G.) Monitoring land use change: some theoretical considerations and a workable solution. London, 1977. pp. 42. bibliog. (Planning Research Applications Group. PRAG Technical Papers. TP 20)

ASPINALL (P.) The evolution of urban tenure systems in 19th century cities. Birmingham, 1978. pp. 35,xi,16. (Birmingham. University. Centre for Urban and Regional Studies. Research Memoranda. No. 63)

LANDLORD AND TENANT
— United Kingdom.

An END to private landlordism: a response to the D[epartment] o[f the] E[nvironment] consultation paper on the review of the rent acts, April 1977; (by Benwell Community Development Project and others). [Newcastle-upon-Tyne, Benwell Community Development Project, 1977]. 1 pamphlet (various pagings).

PHILLIPS (MARK) Homelessness and tenants' control: struggles for council housing in Tower Hamlets, 1974-1976. London, 1977. pp. 123.

LEWIS (JOHN ROYSTON) and HOLLAND (JOHN ANTHONY) Landlord and tenant; second edition by C. Burke. Newcastle, 1978. pp. 268.

NATIONAL CONSUMER COUNCIL. Social Policy Unit. Housing policy review: housing management: a tenants' charter: the...Council's response to the Department of the Environment consultation paper. London, [1978]. pp. 18.

— — Scotland.

SCOTLAND. Scottish Development Department. 1977. The review of the rent acts: a consultation paper. [Edinburgh, 1977]. pp. 17.

— United States.

KIM (SUNG BOK) Landlord and tenant in colonial New York: manorial society, 1664-1775. Chapel Hill, N.C. [1978]. pp. 456.

LANDSCAPE.

ARCHAEOLOGY and the landscape: essays for L.V. Grinsell; edited by P.J. Fowler. London, 1972. pp. 263. bibliog.

AALEN (F.H.A.) Man and the landscape in Ireland. London, 1978. pp. 343. bibliog.

POLSKA AKADEMIA NAUK. Instytut Geografii. Geografia Polonica. 38. Rural landscape and settlement evolution in Europe: proceedings of the conference, Warsaw, September 1975; edited by Maria Kiełczewska-Zaleska. Warsaw, 1978. pp. 304. bibliogs. 2 maps in end pocket.

LANDSCAPE PROTECTION.

PRICE (COLIN) Landscape economics. London, 1978. pp. 168. bibliog.

LANGLEY (FRANCIS).

INGRAM (WILLIAM) A London life in the brazen age: Francis Langley, 1548-1602. Cambridge, Mass., 1978. pp. 335.

LANGOS.

TOSH (JOHN) Clan leaders and colonial chiefs in Lango: the political history of an East African stateless society c. 1800-1939. Oxford, 1978. pp. 293. bibliog.

LANGUAGE AND LANGUAGES.

VYGOTSKII (LEV SEMENOVICH) Thought and language; edited and translated by Eugenia Hanfmann and Gertrude Vakar. Cambridge, Mass., 1962. pp. 168. bibliog.

RUHLEN (MERRITT) A guide to the languages of the world. [Stanford, 1976]. pp. 356. bibliogs.

WOLD (ASTRI HEEN) Decoding oral language. London, 1978. pp. 214. bibliog.

— Classification.

VOEGELIN (CHARLES FREDERICK) and VOEGELIN (FLORENCE MARIE ROBINETT) Classification and index of the world's languages. New York, [1977]. pp. 658. bibliog.

— Origins.

LANGUAGE learning by a chimpanzee: the LANA project; edited by Duane M. Rumbaugh. New York, [1977]. pp. 312. bibliogs.

— Study and teaching — Psychological aspects.

SCHUMANN (JOHN H.) The pidginization process: a model for second language acquisition. Rowley, Mass., [1978]. pp. 190. bibliog.

— Variation.

COLLOQUIUM ON NEW WAYS OF ANALYZING VARIATION, 2ND, GEORGETOWN UNIVERSITY, 1973. Analyzing variation in language; papers from the...colloquium...; [edited by] Ralph W. Fasold [and] Roger W. Shuy. Washington, [1975]. pp. 327. bibliogs.

BRIGHT (WILLIAM) Variation and change in language: essays by William Bright. Stanford, 1976. pp. 283. bibliog.

COLLOQUIUM ON NEW WAYS OF ANALYZING VARIATION, 3RD, GEORGETOWN UNIVERSITY, 1974. Studies in language variation: semantics, syntax, phonology, pragmatics, social situations, ethnographic approaches; [edited by] Ralph W. Fasold [and] Roger W. Shuy. Washington, D.C., [1977]. pp. 311. bibliogs.

GAL (SUSAN) Language shift: social determinants of linguistic change in bilingual Austria. New York, [1979]. pp. 20a1. bibliog.

LANGUAGE AND LOGIC.

KEENAN (EDWARD L.) and FALTZ (LEONARD M.) Logical types for natural language. [Los Angeles, 1978]. pp. 338. bibliog. (California University. Occasional Papers in Linguistics. No.3)

LANGUAGES
— Philosophy.

GAZDAR (GERALD) Pragmatics implicature, presupposition, and logical form. New York, [1979]. pp. 186. bibliog.

PLATTS (MARK DE BRETTON) Ways of meaning: an introduction to a philosophy of language. London, 1979. pp. 272. bibliog.

— Physiological aspects.

LANGUAGE development and neurological theory; edited by Sidney J. Segalowitz, Frederic A. Gruber. New York, 1977. pp. 376. bibliogs.

— Political aspects.

LANGUAGE and politics; edited by William M. O'Barr and Jean F. O'Barr. The Hague, [1976]. pp. 506. bibliog.

STEPHENS (MEIC) Linguistic minorities in western Europe. [Llandysul], 1976 repr. 1978. pp. 796. bibliog.

LANGUAGE planning processes; edited by Joan Rubin [and others]. The Hague, [1977]. pp. 288. bibliogs.

GORDON (DAVID CROCKETT) The French language and national identity (1930-1975). The Hague, [1978]. pp. 225. bibliog.

CHOMSKY (NOAM) Language and responsibility: based on conversations with Mitsou Ronat; translated from the French by John Viertel. Hassocks, 1979. pp. 212. bibliog.

SAMPSON (GEOFFREY) Liberty and language. Oxford, 1979. pp. 251. bibliog.

— Psychology.

WOLD (ASTRI HEEN) Decoding oral language. London, 1978. pp. 214. bibliog.

LANGUAGE and social psychology; edited by Howard Giles and Robert N. St. Clair. Oxford, [1979]. pp. 261. bibliog.

LANGUAGES, MODERN
— Study and teaching.

MILLS (ANNE E.) First and second language acquisition in German: a parallel study. Ludwigsburg, 1977. pp. 209. bibliog.

LANSBURY (GEORGE).

BRANSON (NOREEN) Poplarism, 1919-1925: George Lansbury and the councillors' revolt. London, 1979. pp. 242.

LANUSSE (ALEJANDRO AGUSTIN).

LANUSSE (ALEJANDRO AGUSTIN) Mi testimonio. Lima, [1977]. pp. 353.

LARCENY

— United Kingdom.

GRIEW (EDWARD JAMES) The Theft Acts 1968 and 1978. 3rd ed. London, 1978. pp. 219.

LARKFOLD HOLDINGS.

NICHOLLS (DONALD JAMES) and WRIGHT (EDMUND KENNETH) Larkfold Holdings Limited: investigation under section 165(b) of the Companies Act 1948; report. London, H.M.S.O., 1979. pp. (246).

LASSALLE (FERDINAND JOHANN GOTTLIEB).

VAHLTEICH (JULIUS) Ferdinand Lassalle und die Anfänge der deutschen Arbeiterbewegung;...Einleitung zum Nachdruck von Toni Offermann. Berlin, [1978]. pp. 86,xi. *Reprint of work originally published in Munich in 1904.*

STIRNER (HARTMUT) Die Agitation und Rhetorik Ferdinand Lassalles. Marburg, [1979]. pp. 298. *bibliog. (Studiengesellschaft für Sozialgeschichte und Arbeiterbewegung, Marburg. Schriftenreihe für Sozialgeschichte und Arbeiterbewegung. Band 16)*

LATIN AMERICAN FEDERATION.

AMERICA Latina: unidos o dominados; [texts by Bolivar and others]; introduccion y seleccion Norberto Galasso. Buenos Aires, 1975. pp. 166.

LATIN AMERICAN STUDIES.

LATIN American bibliography: a guide to sources of information and research;...edited by Laurence Hallewell. London, 1978. pp. 227.

LATIN POETRY, MEDIEVAL AND MODERN

— Translations into English.

WADDELL (HELEN JANE) Mediaeval Latin lyrics. 5th ed. London, 1948 repr. 1975. pp. 342. *Parallel Latin and English texts.*

LATVIA

— Economic conditions.

GRANTYN' (GAITIS IANOVICH) Chistyi produkt i narodnyi dokhod soiuznoi respubliki: problemy sbalansirovannosti. Riga, 1977. pp. 109. *bibliog.*

NADZINŠ (RAITIS) Latviiskaia SSR: tsifry i fakty. Riga, 1978. pp. 34.

— Politics and government.

PEL'SHE (ARVID IANOVICH) Izbrannye rechi i stat'i, [1940-77]. Moskva, 1978. pp. 671.

— Statistics.

NADZINŠ (RAITIS) Latviiskaia SSR: tsifry i fakty. Riga, 1978. pp. 34.

LAURIER (Sir HENRI CHARLES WILFRID).

See LAURIER (Sir WILFRID).

LAURIER (Sir WILFRID).

CLIPPINGDALE (RICHARD) Laurier: his life and world. Toronto, [1979]. pp. 224. *bibliog.*

LAVIGERIE (CHARLES MARTIAL ALLEMAND-) Cardinal.

See ALLEMAND-LAVIGERIE (CHARLES MARTIAL) Cardinal.

LAVROV (PETR LAVROVICH).

BALKANSKIE strany v novoe i noveishee vremia: sbornik statei. Kishinev, 1977. pp. 178.

UCHENYE ZAPISKI KAFEDR OBSHCHESTVENNYKH NAUK VUZOV LENINGRADA. Filosofiia. vyp.17. Filosofskie i sotsiologicheskie issledovaniia. Leningrad, 1977. pp. 200.

LAW.

SEIDMAN (ROBERT BENJAMIN) The state, law and development. London, [1978]. pp. 483.

— Philosophy.

SECONDAT (CHARLES LOUIS DE) Baron de Montesquieu. The spirit of laws:...a compendium of the first English edition; edited...by David Wallace Carrithers; together with an English translation of An essay on causes affecting minds and characters, 1736-1743. Berkeley, [1977]. pp. 479.

WEBER (MAX) Critique of Stammler;...translated, with an introductory essay, by Guy Oakes. New York, [1977]. pp. 184.

MacCORMICK (DONALD NEIL) Professor. Legal reasoning and legal theory. Oxford, 1978. pp. 298.

PHILOSOPHICAL law: authority, equality, adjudication, privacy; edited by Richard Bronaugh. Westport, Conn., 1978. pp. 208.

EIKEMA HOMMES (HENDRIK JAN VAN) Major trends in the history of legal philosophy. Amsterdam, 1979. pp. 442. *bibliog.*

HARRIS (JAMES WILLIAM) Law and legal science: an inquiry into the concepts "Legal rule" and "Legal system". Oxford, 1979. pp. 174.

— Psychology.

PSYCHOLOGY, law and legal processes; edited by David P. Farrington, Keith Hawkins, Sally M. Lloyd-Bostock. London, 1979. pp. 222. *bibliogs. (U.K. Social Science Research Council. Centre for Socio-Legal Studies. Oxford Socio-Legal Studies)*

— Africa.

SEIDMAN (ROBERT BENJAMIN) The state, law and development. London, [1978]. pp. 483.

— Australia — New South Wales — Public opinion.

TOMASIC (ROMAN ALEXANDER) Lawyers and the community. Sydney, 1978. pp. 318. *bibliog.*

— Botswana.

BOTSWANA. Statutes, etc. 1890-1950. The laws of the Bechuanaland Protectorate, containing the orders-in-council, proclamations and notices made thereunder, in force on the 1st day of January, 1948; (with Amendments to 1950);...prepared...by H.C. Juta. rev. ed. London, 1949. 3 vols.

— China.

SOVETSKIE raiony Kitaia: zakonodatel'stvo Kitaiskoi Sovetskoi Respubliki, 1931-1934. Moskva, 1977. pp. 141.

— Communist countries.

UCHENIE K. Marksa, F. Engel'sa, V.I. Lenina o sotsialisticheskom gosudarstve i prave: istoriia razvitiia i sovremennost'. Moskva, 1978. pp. 431. *Continuation of Marksistsko-leninskoe uchenie o gosudarstve i prave, Moskva, 1977.*

— Europe.

NEW perspectives for a common law of Europe...; contributions. by L. Neville Brown [and others]; edited by Mauro Cappelletti, Florence, 1978. pp. 406. *(European University Institute. Publications. 1) In English or French.*

— European Economic Community countries.

KAPTEYN (PAUL J.G.) and VERLOREN VAN THEMAAT (P.) Introduction to the law of the European Communities, after the accession of new member states. London, 1973. pp. 433. *bibliogs.*

EUROPEAN COMMUNITIES. Court of Justice. Documentation Branch. Synopsis of case-law: the EEC convention of 27 September 1968 on jurisdiction and the enforcement of judgments in civil and commercial matters. a., 1977(no.1)- Luxembourg.

INFORMATION ON THE COURT OF JUSTICE OF THE EUROPEAN COMMUNITIES; [pd. by] Information Office, Court of Justice of the European Communities. q., 1977(4th q.)- Luxembourg.

BRINKHORST (L.J.) and SCHERMERS (HENRY G.) Judicial remedies in the European Communities: a case book; second revised edition by H.G. Schermers. Deventer, 1977. pp. 352.

— France — Sources.

KAHN-FREUND (Sir OTTO) and others. A source-book on French law: system, methods, outlines of contract. 2nd ed. Oxford, 1979. pp. 550. *bibliog. In French or English.*

— Germany.

ANDERBRUEGGE (KLAUS) Völkisches Rechtsdenken: zur Rechtslehre in der Zeit des Nationalsozialismus. Berlin, 1978. pp. 237. *bibliog.*

— Italy — History and criticism.

CELLI (ROBERTO) Studi sui sistemi normativi delle democrazie comunali, secoli 12-15. Firenze, [1976 in progress]. pp. 293. *bibliog.*

— Mexico.

MAYAGOITIA GARZA (ALBERTO) A layman's guide to Mexican law. Albuquerque, 1976 repr. 1977. pp. 131. *bibliog.*

— Netherlands.

INTRODUCTION to Dutch law for foreign lawyers; edited by D.C. Fokkema [and others]: prepared under the auspices of the Netherlands Comparative Law Association. Deventer, 1978. pp. 700. *bibliog.*

— Russia.

PRAVOVOE regulirovanie obshchestvennykh otnoshenii. Moskva, 1976. pp. 120.

PROBLEMY sotsialisticheskoi zakonnosti: respublikanskii mezhvedomstvennyi tematicheskii sbornik. vyp.1. Khar'kov, 1976. pp. 132. *bibliog.*

HAZARD (JOHN NEWBOLD) and others. The Soviet legal system:...fundamental principles and historical commentary. 3rd ed. Dobbs Ferry, N.Y., 1977. pp. 621. *bibliog. (Columbia University. Parker School of Foreign and Comparative Law. Studies in Foreign and Comparative Law)*

PROBLEMY sotsialisticheskoi zakonnosti: respublikanskii mezhvedomstvennyi tematicheskii nauchnyi sbornik. vyp.2. Khar'kov, 1977. pp. 144. *bibliog.*

IAVICH (LEV SAMOILOVICH) Pravo razvitogo sotsialisticheskogo obshchestva: sushchnost' i printsipy. Moskva, 1978. pp. 224.

KUDRIAVTSEV (VLADIMIR NIKOLAEVICH) Pravo i povedenie. Moskva, 1978. pp. 191.

LEIDEN. Rijks Universiteit. Documentation Office for East European Law. Law in Eastern Europe. No. 20. Soviet law after Stalin. Pt.2. Social engineering through law; edited by Donald D. Barry [and others]. Alphen aan den Rijn, 1978. pp. 335.

— — **History and criticism.**

WORTMAN (RICHARD S.) The development of a Russian legal consciousness. Chicago, [1976]. pp. 345. *bibliog.*

CAMERON (GEORGE DANA) The Soviet lawyer and his system: a historical and bibliographic study. Ann Arbor, [1978]. pp. 198. *bibliog. (Michigan University. Bureau of Business Research. Michigan International Business Studies. No.14)*

PLOTNIEK (ANDRIS ADAMOVICH) Stanovlenie i razvitie marksistsko-leninskoi obshchei teorii prava v SSSR, 1917-1936 gg. Riga, 1978. pp. 295.

— — **Interpretation and construction.**

KOMMENTARII sudebnoi praktiki za 1975 god. Moskva, 1976. pp. 223.

KOMMENTARII sudebnoi praktiki za 1976 god. Moskva, 1977. pp. 134.

— **Sweden — Dictionaries and encyclopedias.**

BACKE (TORILD) and others. Kortfattad svensk-engelsk juridisk ordlista: concise Swedish- English glossary of legal terms. Lund, [1973]. pp. 164.

— **Turkey.**

STARR (JUNE) Dispute and settlement in rural Turkey: an ethnography of law. Leiden, 1978. pp. 304. *bibliog.*

— **United Kingdom.**

NEWTON (CLIVE RICHARD) General principles of law. 2nd ed. London, 1977. pp. 386.

DENNING (ALFRED THOMPSON) Baron Denning. The discipline of law. London, 1979. pp. 331.

— — **Dictionaries and encyclopedias.**

MOZLEY (HERBERT NEWMAN) and WHITELEY (GEORGE CECIL) Law dictionary; ninth edition by John B. Saunders. London, 1977. pp. 361.

— — **History and criticism.**

RADCLIFFE (GEOFFREY REYNOLDS YONGE) and CROSS (ARTHUR GEOFFREY NEALE) Baron Cross of Chelsea. The English legal system; sixth edition by G. J. Hand and D. J. Bentley. London, 1977. pp. 464.

LEGAL HISTORY CONFERENCE, 1975. Legal records and the historian: papers presented to the Cambridge Legal History Conference, 7-10 July, 1975, and in Lincoln's Inn Old Hall on 3 July 1974; edited by J.H. Baker. London, 1978. pp. 223. *(Royal Historical Society. Studies in History).*

MEDIEVAL legal records; edited in memory of C.A.F. Meekings; general editors: R.F. Hunnisett [and] J.B. Post. London, H.M.S.O., 1978. pp. 560. *Texts in Latin and Old French with English introductions and notes.*

SELDEN SOCIETY. Publications. vol. 94. The reports of Sir John Spelman. vol.2; edited... by J.H. Baker. London, 1978. pp. 396[238].

BAKER (JOHN HAMILTON) An introduction to English legal history. 2nd ed. London, 1979. pp. 477. *bibliogs.*

WHITE (STEPHEN D.) Sir Edward Coke and "the grievances of the Commonwealth", 1621-1628. Chapel Hill, [1979]. pp. 327. *bibliog.*

— — **Study and teaching.**

WILLIAMS (GLANVILLE LLEWELLYN) Learning the law. 10th ed. London, 1978. pp. 209. *bibliog.*

— — **Commonwealth.**

MEETING OF COMMONWEALTH LAW MINISTERS, WINNIPEG, 1977. Selected memoranda. London, Commonwealth Secretariat, [1978]. pp. 212.

— **United States.**

AMERICAN JOURNAL OF COMPARATIVE LAW, THE. Vol. 26, Supplement, 1978. Law in the U.S.A. in the bicentennial era: reports from the United States of America on topics of major concern as established from the 10th Congress of the International Academy of Comparative Law; [edited by] John N. Hazard [and] Wenceslas J. Wagner. 1978. pp. 529.

— — **History and criticism.**

AMERICAN law and the constitutional order: historical perspectives; edited by Lawrence M. Friedman and Harry N. Scheiber. Cambridge, Mass., 1978. pp. 521.

TACHAU (MARY K. BONSTEEL) Federal courts in the early Republic: Kentucky, 1789-1816. Princeton, N.J., [1978]. pp. 234. *bibliog.*

— — **California — History and criticism.**

POWELL (RICHARD ROY BELDEN) Compromises of conflicting claims: a century of California law; 1760 to 1860. Dobbs Ferry, N.Y., 1977. pp. 332.

LAW, COMPARATIVE.

See COMPARATIVE LAW.

LAW, MOHAMMEDAN.

PEARL (DAVID) A textbook on Muslim law. London, [1979]. pp. 317. *bibliog.*

LAW, PRIMITIVE.

CROSS-EXAMINATIONS: essays in memory of Max Gluckman; edited by P.H. Gulliver. Leiden, 1978. pp. 169.

ROBERTS (SIMON) Order and dispute: an introduction to legal anthropology. Harmondsworth, 1979. pp. 216. *bibliog.*

LAW AND ETHICS.

FULLER (LON L.) The morality of law. 2nd ed. New Haven, 1969 repr. 1978. pp. 262. *(Yale University. Storrs Lectures. 1963)*

RAZ (JOSEPH) The authority of law: essays on law and morality. Oxford, 1979. pp. 292.

LAW AND POLITICS.

WORMUTH (FRANCIS DUNHAM) Essays in law and politics; edited by Dalmas H. Nelson and Richard L. Sklar. Port Washington, N.Y., 1978. pp. 274. *bibliog.*

LAW AND SOCIALISM.

RANKIN (HARRY) Rankin's law: recollections of a radical. Vancouver, [1975]. pp. 220.

PLOTNIEK (ANDRIS ADAMOVICH) Stanovlenie i razvitie marksistsko-leninskoi obshchei teorii prava v SSSR, 1917-1936 gg. Riga, 1978. pp. 295.

EDELMAN (BERNARD) Ownership of the image: elements for a Marxist theory of law; translated by Elizabeth Kingdom. London, 1979. pp. 217.

HIRST (PAUL QUENTIN) On law and ideology. London, 1979. pp. 181. *bibliog.*

MARX and Engels on law; [edited by] Maureen Cain [and] Alan Hunt. London, 1979. pp. 281.

SUMNER (COLIN) Reading ideologies: an investigation into the Marxist theory of ideology and law. London, 1979 pp. 313. *bibliog.*

LAW ENFORCEMENT

— **United Kingdom.**

HOOSON (EMLYN) Law and order in a civilised society. London, 1979. pp. 36.

— **United States.**

REPPETTO (THOMAS A.) The blue parade. New York, 1978. pp. 373. *bibliog.*

REIMAN (JEFFREY H.) The rich get richer and the poor get prison: ideology, class, and criminal justice. New York, [1979]. pp. 214.

LAW IN LEGENDS

— **Mexico.**

CASTILLO FARRERAS (JOSE) Las costumbres y el derecho. Mexico, Secretaria de Educacion Publica, 1973. pp. 183. *bibliog. (Sep/Setentas)*

LAW LIBRARIES.

DANE (JEAN) and THOMAS (PHILIP A.) How to use a law library. London, 1979. pp. 182.

LAW OF LARGE NUMBERS.

RÉVÉSZ (PÁL) The laws of large numbers. New York, 1968. pp. 176. *bibliog.*

LAW REFORM

— **Australia.**

REFORM; [pd. by] Australian Law Reform Commission. q., Ja 1976 (no.1)- Sydney.

— **United Kingdom.**

U.K. Law Commission. Working Papers. No. 73. Insurance law: non-disclosure and breach of warranty. London, 1979. pp. 126.

U.K. Law Commission. Working Papers. No. 74. Family law: illegitimacy. London, 1979. pp. 159.

— **United States.**

HANDLER (JOEL F.) Social movements and the legal system: a theory of law reform and social change. New York, [1978]. pp. 252. *(Wisconsin University, Madison. Institute for Research on Poverty. Monograph Series).*

LAW REPORTS, DIGESTS, ETC.

— **United Kingdom.**

SELDEN SOCIETY. Publications. vol. 94. The reports of Sir John Spelman. vol.2; edited... by J.H. Baker. London, 1978. pp. 396[238].

LAWYERS.

LAWYERS in their social setting...; edited by D.N. MacCormick. Edinburgh, 1976. pp. 227.

GARTH (BRYANT) Neighborhood law firms for the poor: a comparative study of recent developments in legal aid and in the legal profession. Florence, 1978. fo. 470. *bibliog. Typescript.*

— **Directories.**

The INTERNATIONAL law list, 1978. London, 1978. pp. 1139.

— **Discipline.**

NEW ZEALAND. Public and Administrative Law Reform Committee. 1977. Discipline within the legal profession: report...presented to the Minister of Justice, May 1977; [J.F. Northey, chairman]. Wellington, 1977. pp. 21.

— **Australia — New South Wales.**

TOMASIC (ROMAN ALEXANDER) Lawyers and the community. Sydney, 1978. pp. 318. *bibliog.*

LAWYERS.(Cont.)

— Russia.

CAMERON (GEORGE DANA) The Soviet lawyer and his system: a historical and bibliographic study. Ann Arbor, [1978]. pp. 198. *bibliog. (Michigan University. Bureau of Business Research. Michigan International Business Studies. No.14)*

— United Kingdom.

KIRK (HARRY) Portrait of a profession: a history of the solicitor's profession, 1100 to the present day. London, 1976. pp. 218.

LAW SOCIETY. The Royal Commission on Legal Services. Memorandum No. 3. Replies by the Council of the Law Society to the request for evidence from the Law Society by the Royal Commission. London, 1977 in progress.

HAZELL (ROBERT) ed. The Bar on trial. London, 1978. pp. 221. *bibliog.*

— United States.

PFENNIGSTORF (WERNER) and KIMBALL (SPENCER L.) eds. Legal service plans: approaches to regulations. Chicago, 1977. pp. 662.

HANDLER (JOEL F.) and others. Lawyers and the pursuit of legal rights. New York, [1978]. pp. 272. *bibliog. (Wisconsin University, Madison. Institute For Research on Poverty. Poverty Policy Analysis Series)*

MEDCALF (LINDA) Law and identity: lawyers, native Americans and legal practice. Beverly Hills, [1978]. pp. 211. *bibliog.*

WICE (PAUL B.) Criminal lawyers: an endangered species. Beverly Hills, 1978. pp. 233. *bibliog.*

LAZARE (BERNARD).

JUSSEM-WILSON (NELLY) Bernard-Lazare: antisemitism and the problem of Jewish identity in late nineteenth-century France. Cambridge, 1978. pp. 348. *bibliog.*

LEADERSHIP.

BURNS (JAMES MACGREGOR) Leadership. New York, [1978]. pp. 530.

ETHNIC leadership in America; edited by John Higham. Baltimore, [1978]. pp. 214. *(Johns Hopkins University. Department of History. Johns Hopkins Symposia in Comparative History. 9) Based on a symposium held at the Johns Hopkins University in 1976.*

LEADERSHIP in America: consensus, corruption and charisma; edited by Peter Dennis Bathory. New York, [1978]. pp. 200.

LEAGUE OF NATIONS.

JOYCE (JAMES AVERY) Broken star: the story of the League of Nations, 1919-1939. Swansea, 1978. pp. 231.

— Officials and employees.

BARROS (JAMES) Office without power: Secretary-General Sir Eric Drummond, 1919-1933. Oxford, 1979. pp. 423.

LEAGUE OF REVOLUTIONARY BLACK WORKERS.

GESCHWENDER (JAMES A.) Class, race and worker insurgency: the League of Revolutionary Black Workers. Cambridge, 1977. pp. 250. *(American Sociological Association. Arnold and Caroline Rose Monograph Series in Sociology)*

LEARNING, PSYCHOLOGY OF.

WORLD COUNCIL OF CHURCHES. Commission on the Churches' Participation in Development. Conscientization: [a dossier including separately published articles]. Geneva, 1975. 1 vol. (various pagings). *bibliog. (CCPD Documents. 7)*

DONALDSON (MARGARET) Children's minds. London, [1978]. pp. 156. *bibliog.*

ROSENTHAL (TED L.) and ZIMMERMAN (BARRY J.) Social learning and cognition. New York, 1978. pp. 338. *bibliog.*

BRANSFORD (JOHN D.) Human cognition: learning, understanding and remembering. Belmont, Calif., [1979]. pp. 300. *bibliog.*

LEARNING AND SCHOLARSHIP.

BARZUN (JACQUES MARTIN) The house of intellect. Westport, Conn., 1978. pp. 276. *Reprint of the work first published New York, 1959.*

— Europe.

MANDROU (ROBERT) From humanism to science, 1480-1700...; translated by Brian Pearce. Hassocks, 1978. pp. 329. *bibliog.*

LEASES

— United Kingdom.

BIRMINGHAM COMMUNITY DEVELOPMENT PROJECT. Leasehold loopholes. Oxford, 1979. pp. 36. *(Final Reports. No. 5: the Problems of Owner-Occupation in Inner Birmingham)*

LEAST SQUARES.

LINEAR least-squares estimation; edited by Thomas Kailath. Stroudsburg, [1977]. pp. 318.

The MEASUREMENT of intrapersonal space by grid technique. Vol. 2. Dimensions of intrapersonal space; edited by Patrick Slater. London, [1977]. pp. 270.

LEAVE OF ABSENCE.

CENTRE FOR EDUCATIONAL RESEARCH AND INNOVATION. 1978. Alternation between work and education: a study of educational leave of absence at enterprise level. Paris, Organisation for Economic Co-operation and Development, 1978. pp. 97.

— European Economic Community countries.

EUROPEAN ECONOMIC COMMUNITY. Studies. Social Policy Series. 26. Educational leave in member states. Brussels, European Communities, [1976]. pp. 416.

LEBANON

— Foreign relations — France.

SPAGNOLO (JOHN P.) France and Ottoman Lebanon, 1861-1914. London, 1977. pp. 339. *bibliog. (Oxford. University. St. Antony's College. Middle East Centre. St. Antony's Middle East Monographs. No. 7).*

— Religion.

MUSLIM-Christian conflicts: economic, political and social origins; edited by Suad Joseph and Barbara L.K. Pillsbury. Boulder, Colo., 1978. pp. 245. *bibliogs.*

LECA (DOMINIQUE).

LECA (DOMINIQUE) La rupture de 1940. [Paris, 1978]. pp. 353.

LEFEBVRE (GEORGES).

LEFEBVRE (GEORGES) Réflexions sur l'histoire. Paris, 1978. pp. 282.

LEGAL AID.

GARTH (BRYANT) Neighborhood law firms for the poor: a comparative study of recent developments in legal aid and in the legal profession. Florence, 1978. fo. 470. *bibliog.* Typescript.

— America, North.

BRITISH COLUMBIA. Legal Services Commission. Native Programs Division. 1976. Legal services for native peoples of North America. Vancouver, [1976]. pp. 180. *bibliog.*

— Australia.

CASS (MICHAEL) and SACKVILLE (RONALD) Legal needs of the poor. Canberra, 1975. pp. 108. *(Australia. Commission of Inquiry into Poverty. Law and Poverty Series)*

— — Victoria.

FITZGERALD (JEFFREY M.) Poverty and the legal profession in Victoria. Canberra, 1977. pp. 72. *(Australia. Commission of Inquiry into Poverty. Law and Poverty Series)*

— Canada.

RANKIN (HARRY) Rankin's law: recollections of a radical. Vancouver, [1975]. pp. 220.

— United Kingdom.

GRACE (CLIVE) and WILKINSON (PHILIP) Negotiating the law: social work and legal services. London, [1978]. pp. 85.

PARTINGTON (MARTIN) The legal aid means tests: time for a reappraisal; a discussion paper prepared for the Child Poverty Action Group. London, 1978. pp. 37. *(Child Poverty Action Group. Poverty Pamphlets. 34)*

— United States.

PFENNIGSTORF (WERNER) and KIMBALL (SPENCER L.) eds. Legal service plans: approaches to regulations. Chicago, 1977. pp. 662.

HANDLER (JOEL F.) and others. Lawyers and the pursuit of legal rights. New York, [1978]. pp. 272. *bibliog. (Wisconsin University, Madison. Institute For Research on Poverty. Poverty Policy Analysis Series)*

LEGAL ASSISTANCE TO THE POOR

— Australia.

CASS (MICHAEL) and SACKVILLE (RONALD) Legal needs of the poor. Canberra, 1975. pp. 108. *(Australia. Commission of Inquiry into Poverty. Law and Poverty Series)*

LEGAL RESEARCH.

DANE (JEAN) and THOMAS (PHILIP A.) How to use a law library. London, 1979. pp. 182.

— Zambia.

ZAMBIA. Law Development Commission. Annual report. a., 1977- Lusaka.

LEGISLATIVE BODIES.

BLONDEL (JEAN) 1929- . Comparative legislatures. Englewood Cliffs, N.J., [1973]. pp. 173. *bibliog.*

EULAU (HEINZ) and WAHLKE (JOHN CHARLES) The politics of representation: continuities in theory and research. Beverly Hills, [1978]. pp. 312. *bibliog.*

— Upper chambers.

The SECOND chamber: its role in modern legislatures: the twenty-five years of Rajya Sabha; editor: S.S. Bhalerao; published for the Rajya Sabha Secretariat. New Delhi, 1977. pp. 467.

— Europe.

EUROPEAN integration, regional devolution and national parliaments; [by] D. Coombes [and others]. London, 1979. pp. 45. *(Policy Studies Institute. Studies in European Politics. 3)*

— European Economic Community countries.

The EUROPEAN Parliament and the national parliaments; edited by Valentine Herman and Rinus van Schendelen. Farnborough, [1979]. pp. 304. *bibliog.*

— Russia.

LUK'IANOV (ANATOLII IVANOVICH) Razvitie zakonodatel'stva o sovetskikh predstavitel'nykh organakh vlasti: nekotorye voprosy istorii, teorii i praktiki. Moskva, 1978. pp. 351.

LEGISLATORS.

RUBNER (ALEXANDER) The price of a free lunch: the perverse relationship between economists and politicians. London, 1979. pp. 256.

— Austria.

ROSDOLSKY (ROMAN) Die Bauernabgeordneten im konstituierenden österreichischen Reichstag, 1848-1849. Wien, 1976. pp. 234. *bibliog. (Ludwig Boltzmann Institut für Geschichte der Arbeiterbewegung. Materialien zur Arbeiterbewegung. Nr. 5)*

— United Kingdom.

VALLANCE (ELIZABETH M.) Women in the house: a study of women members of Parliament. London, 1979. pp. 212. *bibliog.*

— United States.

TERRY (JANICE J.) Attitudes of United States congressmen toward aid to the Palestinians and arms to Israel. Beirut, [1973]. pp. 78. *(Palestine Research Center. Palestine Essays. No. 37)*

FENNO (RICHARD FRANCIS) Home style: house members in their districts. Boston, Mass., [1978]. pp. 304.

LEGITIMACY OF GOVERNMENTS.

HABERMAS (JUERGEN) Legitimation crisis. London, 1976. pp. 166. *bibliog.*

FREEDMAN (JAMES O.) Crisis and legitimacy: the administrative process and American government. Cambridge, 1978. pp. 324. *bibliog.*

MERQUIOR (JOSE GUILHERME) Legitimacy as a problem: political philosophy and classical sociology. 1978. fo. 409. *bibliog.* Typescript. Ph.D. (London) thesis: unpublished. This thesis is the property of London University and may not be removed from the Library.

LEICESTERSHIRE

— Economic conditions.

LEICESTERSHIRE. County Planning Officer. Leicestershire structure plan: written statement for the City of Leicester and the County of Leicestershire prior to local government re-organisation on 1st April 1974. [Leicester], 1976 repr. 1977. pp. 121. *2 maps in end pocket.*

— Economic policy.

LEICESTERSHIRE. County Planning Officer. Leicestershire structure plan: written statement for the City of Leicester and the County of Leicestershire prior to local government re-organisation on 1st April 1974. [Leicester], 1976 repr. 1977. pp. 121. *2 maps in end pocket.*

— Social conditions.

LEICESTERSHIRE. County Planning Officer. Leicestershire structure plan: written statement for the City of Leicester and the County of Leicestershire prior to local government re-organisation on 1st April 1974. [Leicester], 1976 repr. 1977. pp. 121. *2 maps in end pocket.*

— Social policy.

LEICESTERSHIRE. County Planning Officer. Leicestershire structure plan: written statement for the City of Leicester and the County of Leicestershire prior to local government re-organisation on 1st April 1974. [Leicester], 1976 repr. 1977. pp. 121. *2 maps in end pocket.*

LEIPZIG

— Biography.

BERNDT (HELGA) Eine Dokumentation zum 100. Jahrestag des Sozialistengesetzes, 1878-1890: biographische Skizzen von Leipziger Arbeiterfunktionären. Vaduz/Liechtenstein, 1979. pp. 301.

LEISURE.

BRIGHTBILL (CHARLES K.) and MOBLEY (TONY A.) Education for leisure-centred living. 2nd ed. New York, [1977]. pp. 128.

IOVANE (ANDREA) and PALA (GIANFRANCO) Lavoro salariato e tempo libero: un'analisi dell'economia del tempo. Milano, [1977]. pp. 192. *(Istituto per gli Studi sullo Sviluppo Economico e il Progresso Tecnico. Collana Isvet. n. 32)*

BECKERMAN (WILFRED) Measures of leisure, equality and welfare. Paris, Organisation for Economic Co-operation and Development, 1978. pp. 63.

ROBERTS (KENNETH) Contemporary society and the growth of leisure. London, 1978. pp. 191. *bibliog.*

— Canada.

CANADA. Statistics Canada. Service bulletin: Culture statistics. irreg., current issues only. Ottawa. *[in English and French]*

— Russia.

PATRUSHEV (VASILII DMITRIEVICH) Ispol'zovanie sovokupnogo vremeni obshchestva: problemy balansa vremeni naseleniia. Moskva, 1978. pp. 216. *bibliog.*

— United Kingdom — Bibliography.

PEARSON (LYNN F.) Non work time: a review of the literature. Birmingham, 1978. pp. 66. *bibliog. (Birmingham. University. Centre for Urban and Regional Studies. Research Memoranda. No. 65)*

LEND-LEASE OPERATIONS (1941-1945).

DOUGHERTY (JAMES J.) The politics of wartime aid: American economic assistance to France and French Northwest Africa, 1940-1946. Westport, Conn., 1978. pp. 264. *bibliog.*

LENIN (VLADIMIR IL'ICH).

MAKSIMOV (GRIGORII PETROVICH) The guillotine at work, vol.1: the Leninist counter-revolution. Sanday, 1979. pp. 337. *First published Chicago, 1940.*

LENINISMUS: neue Stufe des wissenschaftlichen Sozialismus?: zum Verhältnis von Marxscher Theorie, Klassenanalyse und revolutionärer Taktik bei W.I. Lenin; ([by] Projekt Klassenanalyse). Westberlin, [1972]. 2 vols. (in 1).

KORONEN (MATVEI MATVEEVICH) V.I. Lenin i Finliandiia. Leningrad, 1977. pp. 311. *bibliog.*

KRASIN (IURII ANDREEVICH) Teoriia sotsialisticheskoi revoliutsii: leninskoe nasledie i sovremennost'. Moskva, 1977. pp. 292.

LENINSKIE traditsii vneshnei politiki Sovetskogo Soiuza; pod redaktsiei A.L. Narochnitskogo. Moskva, 1977. pp. 264.

GOERLITZ (WALTER) Geldgeber der Macht: wie Hitler, Lenin, Mao Tse-tung, Mussolini, Stalin und Tito finanziert wurden. Frankfurt am Main, 1978. pp. 256. *bibliog.*

KLEVCHENIA (ALEKSANDR SEMENOVICH) Ocherki po istorii marksistsko-leninskoi filosofskoi mysli v Pol'she. Minsk, 1978. pp. 198. *bibliog.*

KRITIKA mal'tuzianskikh i neomal'tuzianskikh vzgliadov: Rossiia XIX - nachala XX v. Moskva, 1978. pp. 166.

PLOTNIEK (ANDRIS ADAMOVICH) Stanovlenie i razvitie marksistsko-leninskoi obshchei teorii prava v SSSR, 1917-1936 gg. Riga, 1978. pp. 295.

RIABUSHKIN (TIMON VASIL'EVICH) Leninskoe nasledie i statistika. Moskva, 1978. pp. 266.

SOLOV'EV (OLEG FEDOROVICH) Triumf Lenina i bankrotstvo ego kritikov. Moskva, 1978. pp. 159.

UCHENIE K. Marksa, F. Engel'sa, V.I. Lenina o sotsialisticheskom gosudarstve i prave: istoriia razvitiia i sovremennost'. Moskva, 1978. pp. 431. *Continuation of Marksistsko-leninskoe uchenie o gosudarstve i prave, Moskva, 1977.*

UL'IANOVA (MARIIA IL'INICHNA) O Vladimire Il'iche Lenine i sem'e Ul'ianovykh: vospominaniia, pis'ma, ocherki. Moskva, 1978. pp. 328.

LENINGRAD

— History.

ROSENKO (IVAN ARKHIPOVICH) Internatsional'nye sviazi rabochikh Leningrada, 1921-1937 gg. Leningrad, 1977. pp. 140.

— — 1917-1921, Revolution.

REVOLIUTSIONNYI Petrograd god 1917. Leningrad, 1977. pp. 439.

LEOPOLD II, King of the Belgians.

EMERSON (BARBARA) Leopold II of the Belgians: king of colonialism. London, 1979. pp. 324. *bibliog.*

LESBIANISM.

WYLAND (FRANCIE) Motherhood, lesbianism and child custody. Toronto, 1977. pp. 34.

ETTORRE (ELIZABETH MARY) The sociology of lesbianism: female 'deviance' and female sexuality. 1978. fo. 361. *bibliog.* Typescript. Ph.D. (London) thesis: unpublished. This thesis is the property of London University and may not be removed from the Library.

— United States.

WOLF (DEBORAH GOLEMAN) The lesbian community. Berkeley, [1979]. pp. 196. *bibliog.*

LESOTHO

— Economic conditions.

MAANE (WILLEM) Lesotho: a development challenge;...report...based on the findings of...economic mission[s] to Lesotho in...1973...and... 1974. Washington, International Bank for Reconstruction and Development, 1975. pp. 98. *(Country Economic Reports)*

— Economic policy.

MAANE (WILLEM) Lesotho: a development challenge;...report...based on the findings of...economic mission[s] to Lesotho in...1973...and... 1974. Washington, International Bank for Reconstruction and Development, 1975. pp. 98. *(Country Economic Reports)*

STRØM (GABRIELE WINAI) Development and dependence in Lesotho, the enclave of South Africa. Uppsala, 1978. pp. 189. *bibliog.*

— Foreign economic relations.

STRØM (GABRIELE WINAI) Development and dependence in Lesotho, the enclave of South Africa. Uppsala, 1978. pp. 189. *bibliog.*

— Politics and government.

STRØM (GABRIELE WINAI) Development and dependence in Lesotho, the enclave of South Africa. Uppsala, 1978. pp. 189. *bibliog.*

LEVESQUE (RENE).

DESBARATS (PETER) René: a Canadian in search of a country. Toronto, [1976]. pp. 223.

LEVI-STRAUSS (CLAUDE).

CUDDIHY (JOHN MURRAY) The ordeal of civility: Freud, Marx, Lévi-Strauss, and the Jewish struggle with modernity. New York, [1974]. pp. 272.

SHALVEY (THOMAS) Claude Lévi-Strauss, social psychotherapy and the collective unconscious. Hassocks, [1978?]. pp. 180. *bibliog.*

JENKINS (ALAN) Ph.D. The social theory of Claude Levi-Strauss. London, 1979. pp. 193. *bibliog.*

LEWIS (JOHN LLEWELLYN).

DUBOFSKY (MELVYN) and VAN TINE (WARREN R.) John L. Lewis: a biography. New York, [1977]. pp. 619. *bibliog.*

LEXICOGRAPHERS

— United Kingdom.

MURRAY (KATHERINE MAUD ELISABETH) Caught in the web of words: James A.H. Murray and the Oxford English Dictionary. Oxford, 1979. pp. 386.

LEXICOLOGY.

CHICAGO LINGUISTIC SOCIETY. [Regional Meeting, 14th, 1978]. Papers from the parasession on the lexicon;...edited by Donka Farkas [and others]. Chicago, 1978. pp. 364. *bibliogs.*

LI (TSUNG-JEN).

TONG (TE-KONG) and LI (TSUNG-JEN) The memoirs of Li Tsung-jen. Boulder, Colo., 1979. pp. 636. *(Columbia University. East Asian Institute. Studies)*

LIANG (SHU-MING).

ALITTO (GUY S.) The last Confucian: Liang Shu-ming and the Chinese dilemma of modernity. Berkeley, 1979. pp. 396. *bibliog.*

LIBEL AND SLANDER

— Russia.

LEIDEN. Rijks Universiteit. Documentation Office for East European Law. Law in Eastern Europe. No. 22(1). Copyright, defamation, and privacy in Soviet civil law: De lege lata ac ferenda; by Serge L. Levitsky. Alphen aan den Rijn, 1979. pp. 487.

LIBERAL PARTY

— United Kingdom.

MICHIE (ALISTAIR) and HOGGART (SIMON) The pact: the inside story of the Lib-Lab government, 1977-8. London, 1978. pp. 183.

LIBERAL PARTY. The real fight is for Britain. London, [1979]. pp. 18.

LIBERALISM.

ESSAYS on Russian liberalism; edited, with an introduction by Charles E. Timberlake. Columbia, 1972. pp. 192. *bibliog. Papers presented to the Bi-State (Kansas-Missouri) Slavic Conference in Columbia, Missouri, in November, 1969.*

BRAMSTED (ERNEST KOHN) and MELHUISH (K.J.) eds. Western liberalism: a history in documents from Locke to Croce. London, 1978. pp. 810.

FROM contract to community: political theory at the crossroads; edited by Fred R. Dallmayr. New York, [1978]. pp. 172. *Based on a lecture series held at Purdue University's Department of Political Science during the academic year 1974- 1975.*

LIBERALISM and the modern polity: essays in contemporary political theory; [edited by] Michael J. Gargas McGrath. New York, [1978]. pp. 305. *bibliogs.*

MANSFIELD (HARVEY CLAFLIN) The spirit of liberalism. Cambridge, Mass., 1978. pp. 130. *bibliog.*

MISES (LUDWIG VON) Liberalism: a socio-economic exposition...; translated by Ralph Raico; edited by Arthur Goddard. 2nd ed. Mission, Kan., [1978]. pp. 207. *Published in 1962 under title: The free and prosperous commonwealth.*

PRAGMA: POLITIEKE CLUB VOOR EIGENTIJDS LIBERALISME. Een politieke identiteit voor liberalen. Antwerpen, [1978]. pp. 239.

The RELEVANCE of liberalism...; edited by the staff of the Research Institute on International Change. Boulder, Colo., [1978]. pp. 233. *bibliogs. (Columbia University. Research Institute on International Change. Studies) Product of a conference, held at the Research Institute on International Change, 1976.*

REVEL (JEAN FRANÇOIS) The totalitarian temptation; (translated by David Hapgood). Harmondsworth, 1978. pp. 332.

— America, Latin.

RODRIGUEZ (MARIO) The Cadiz experiment in Central America, 1808 to 1826. Berkeley, [1978]. pp. 316. *bibliog.*

— Europe.

DAHRENDORF (RALF) Intervista sul liberalismo e l'Europa; [translated from the English]; a cura di Vincenzo Ferrari. Roma, 1979. pp. 173.

— Germany.

SHEEHAN (JAMES J.) German liberalism in the nineteenth century. Chicago, 1978. pp. 411. *bibliog.*

— India.

PRASHAD (GANESH) Nehru: a study in colonial liberalism. New Delhi, [1976]. pp. 218. *bibliogs.*

— Italy.

CAMBRIA (RITA) I liberali italiani e il socialismo: il dibattito ideologico nella crisi di fine secolo. Milano, [1974]. pp. 230.

— Mexico.

POWELL (THOMAS GENE) El liberalismo y el campesinado en el centro de Mexico, 1850-1876; traduccion de Roberto Gomez Ciriza. Mexico, Secretaria de Educacion Publica, 1974. pp. 191. *bibliog. (Sep/Setentas. 122)*

— United Kingdom.

CLARKE (PETER) 1942- . Liberals and social democrats. Cambridge, 1978. pp. 344. *bibliog.*

COLLINI (STEFAN) Liberalism and sociology: L. T. Hobhouse and political argument in England, 1880-1914. Cambridge., 1979. pp. 281. *bibliog.*

LIBERIA

— Foreign relations.

SESAY (AMADU) International politics in Africa: a comparative study of the foreign policies of Liberia and Sierra Leone, 1957-73. 1978. fo. 423. *bibliog. Typescript. Ph.D. (London) thesis: unpublished. This thesis is the property of London University and may not be removed from the Library.*

— Politics and government.

SMITH (ROBERT ARTHUR) Deeds not words: a history of the True Whig Party. [Monrovia, 1970]. pp. 62.

LIBERTY.

MACKLEM (MICHAEL) Liberty and the Holy City: the idea of freedom in English history. [Ottawa, 1978]. pp. 210.

SCHUMANN (MAURICE) Angoisse et certitude: de la mort - de la vie - de la liberté. [Paris, 1978]. pp. 204.

LIBERTY and the rule of law: [papers from a conference held in San Francisco in 1976]; edited...by Robert L. Cunningham. College Station, Texas, [1979]. pp. 349.

LIBERTY OF THE PRESS.

The THIRD World and press freedom; edited by Philip C. Horton. New York, [1978]. pp. 253. *bibliog.*

GOREN (DINA) Secrecy and the right to know. Ramat Gan, Israel, 1979. pp. 194. *bibliog.*

— Argentine Republic.

PRENSA, LA. Por defender la libertad. Buenos Aires, 1957. pp. 250. *Reprint of first edition published in Mexico in 1952.*

— Italy.

COEN (FAUSTO) Tre anni di bugie: 328 ordini alla stampa del Minculpop negli anni della guerra. Milano, [1977]. pp. 175.

— Mexico.

REYNA (MARIA DEL CARMEN) ed. La prensa censurada durante el siglo XIX. Mexico, Secretaria de Educacion Publica, 1976. pp. 191. *(Sep/Setentas. 255)*

— Peru.

BELTRAN (PEDRO G.) La verdadera realidad peruana. Madrid, [1976]. pp. 252.

LIBRARIES

— Italy.

TRANIELLO (PAOLO) Regioni e biblioteche in Italia. Milano, [1977]. pp. 293. *bibliog.*

— United Kingdom — Special collections.

LONDON. University. University College. Library. Occasional Publications. No. 1. Manuscript collections in the library of University College, London: a handlist. 2nd ed. London, 1978. pp. 21.

PERCIVAL (JANET) compiler. The Society for the Diffusion of Useful Knowledge, 1826- 1848: a handlist of the society's correspondence and papers. London, 1978. pp. 120. *(London. University College. Library. Occasional Publications. No. 5)*

UNIVERSITY OF ESSEX. Library. Reference Leaflets. No. 6. Guide to material on Russia and the Soviet Union. [Colchester], 1978. pp. 27.

— — Ireland, Northern.

IRELAND, NORTHERN. Department of Education. Education and library boards, grant aided schools, institutions of further education and libraries. a., current issue only. Belfast.

LIBRARIES, GOVERNMENTAL, ADMINISTRATIVE, ETC.

— Australia.

NEW SOUTH WALES. Parliament. Library. 1969. The vital adjunct: parliamentary libraries and their role in Australia. Sydney, 1969. pp. 49. *(Reference Monographs. No. 7)*

LIBRARIES, UNIVERSITY AND COLLEGE

— United Kingdom.

LONDON. University. University College. Library. Occasional Publications. No. 1. Manuscript collections in the library of University College, London: a handlist. 2nd ed. London, 1978. pp. 21.

PERCIVAL (JANET) compiler. The Society for the Diffusion of Useful Knowledge, 1826- 1848: a handlist of the society's correspondence and papers. London, 1978. pp. 120. *(London. University College. Library. Occasional Publications. No. 5)*

HULL. University. Brynmor Jones Library. The Brynmor Jones Library, 1929-1979: short account. Hull, 1979. pp. 36.

LIBRARY ARCHITECTURE

— Fires and fire prevention.

MORRIS (JOHN) Safety engineer. Managing the library fire risk. 2nd ed. Berkeley, 1979. pp. 147. *bibliog.*

LIBRARY RESOURCES ON RUSSIA.

UNIVERSITY OF ESSEX. Library. Reference Leaflets. No. 6. Guide to material on Russia and the Soviet Union. [Colchester], 1978. pp. 27.

LIBRARY SCIENCE.

UNESCO JOURNAL OF INFORMATION SCIENCE, LIBRARIANSHIP AND ARCHIVE ADMINISTRATION; [pd. by] Unesco. q., Ja/Mr 1979 (v.1, no.1)- Paris. *Supersedes UNESCO BULLETIN FOR LIBRARIES.*

LIBYA

— Census.

LIBYA. Census, 1973. Population census: summary data. [Tripoli, 1977]. fo. 32. *In English and Arabic.*

LICENCE SYSTEM

— Ireland (Republic).

EIRE. Restrictive Practices Commission. 1977. Report of study of competition in the licensed drink trade. Dublin, [1977]. fo. 91.

LICENCES

— United Kingdom.

DAWSON (IAN JEFFERIES) and PEARCE (ROBERT A.) Licences relating to the occupation or use of land. London, 1979. pp. 239.

LIEBKNECHT (WILHELM PHILIPP MARTIN CHRISTIAN LUDWIG).

HALTERN (UTZ) Liebknecht und England: zur Publizistik Wilhelm Liebknechts während seines Londoner Exils, 1850-1862. Trier, [1977]. pp. 86. *(Karl-Marx-Haus. Schriften. 18)*

WENDORFF (WERNER) Schule und Bildung in der Politik von Wilhelm Liebknecht: ein Beitrag zur Geschichte der deutschen Arbeiterbewegung im 19. Jahrhundert. Berlin, [1978]. pp. 334. *bibliog.*

LIECHTENSTEIN.

KRANZ (WALTER) ed. The principality of Liechtenstein: a documentary handbook; translated from the German by G.D.C. Martin. 4th ed. [Vaduz], Press and Information Office of the Government of the Principality of Liechtenstein, 1978. pp. 292. *bibliogs.*

— Economic conditions.

KRANZ (WALTER) ed. The Liechtenstein economy; translated from the German by John Anthony Nicholls. [Vaduz], Government Press and Information Office of the Principality of Liechtenstein, 1978. pp. 128.

LIFE.

SCHUMANN (MAURICE) Angoisse et certitude: de la mort - de la vie - de la liberté. [Paris, 1978]. pp. 204.

NAGEL (THOMAS) Mortal questions. Cambridge, 1979. pp. 215.

LIFE SCIENCES

— Mathematical models.

OLINICK (MICHAEL) An introduction to mathematical models in the social and life sciences. Reading, Mass., [1978]. pp. 466. *bibliogs.*

LIFE SPAN, PRODUCTIVE.

HAWLEY (AMOS HENRY) and others. The expectation of working life in peninsular Malaysia, 1970. Kuala Lumpur, 1974. pp. 58. *(Federation of Malaysia. Department of Statistics. Research Papers. No.8) In English and Malay.*

LIGUE COMMUNISTE REVOLUTIONNAIRE.

LIGUE COMMUNISTE REVOLUTIONNAIRE. Oui, le socialisme! Paris, 1978. pp. 397.

LIMANOWSKI (BOLESLAW).

COTTAM (KAZIMIERA JANINA) Boleslaw Limanowski, 1835-1935: a study in socialism and nationalism. Boulder, Colo., 1978. pp. 365. *bibliog. (East European Quarterly. East European Monographs. 41)*

LIN FAMILY.

MESKILL (JOHANNA MENZEL) A Chinese pioneer family: the Lins of Wu-feng, Taiwan, 1729- 1895. Princeton, 1979. pp. 376. *bibliog.*

LINCOLN (ABRAHAM) President of the United States.

BORITT (GÁBOR S.) Lincoln and the economics of the American dream. Memphis, [1978]. pp. 420. *bibliog.*

McCRARY (PEYTON) Abraham Lincoln and reconstruction : the Louisiana experiment. Princeton, N.J., [1978]. pp. 423. *bibliog.*

LINEAR OPERATORS.

SLEEMAN (BRIAN D.) Multiparameter spectral theory in Hilbert space. London, 1978. pp. 118. *bibliogs.*

LINEAR PROGRAMMING.

APPA (GAUTAMKUMAR MANUBHAI) Contributions to linear programming theory: applications to Chebychev and other linear approximation criteria; the 'transportation problem'; and the problem of resolution of degeneracy in linear programming algorithms. 1977 [or rather 1978]. fo.163. *bibliog.* Typescript. Ph.D. (London) thesis: unpublished. This thesis is the property of London University and may not be removed from the Library.

VAJDA (STEVEN) Mathematics of manpower planning. Chichester, [1978]. pp. 206. *bibliog.*

LINEN

— United Kingdom — Scotland.

DURIE (ALASTAIR J.) The Scottish linen industry in the eighteenth century. Edinburgh, 1979. pp. 180. *bibliog.*

LINGUISTIC CHANGE.

ADVANCES in the study of societal multilingualism; edited by Joshua A. Fishman. The Hague, [1978]. pp. 842. *bibliogs.*

LINGUISTICS.

[CHICAGO LINGUISTIC SOCIETY]. CLS book of squibs cumulative index 1968-1977; edited by Samuel E. Fox [and others]. Chicago, Ill., 1977. pp. 174. *bibliogs.*

CHICAGO LINGUISTIC SOCIETY. Regional Meeting, 13th, 1977. Papers...; edited by Woodford A. Beach [and others]. Chicago, Ill., [1977]. pp. 733. *bibliogs.*

JACKENDOFF (RAY S.) X syntax: a study of phrase structure. Cambridge, Mass., [1977]. pp. 248. *bibliog.*

LINGUISTICS at the crossroads; [edited by] Adam Makkai [and others]. Padova, [1977]. pp. 502. *bibliogs.* (Bologna. Università. Centro Interfacoltà di Linguistica Teorica e Applicata. Testi e Studi. 4) Based on the XIth International Congress of Linguists in Bologna, 1972.

LINGUISTIC and literary studies in honor of Archibald A. Hill; edited by Mohammad Ali Jazayery [and others]. The Hague, [1978-79]. 4 vols. *bibliogs.*

CHICAGO LINGUISTIC SOCIETY. Regional Meeting, 14th, 1978. Papers...; edited by Donka Farkas [and others]. Chicago, [1978]. pp. 512. *bibliogs.*

D'AGOSTINO (FREDERICK BRUCE) A philosophical examination of transformational linguistics. 1978. fo. 246. *bibliog.* Typescript. Ph.D. (London) thesis: unpublished. This thesis is the property of London University and may not be removed from the Library.

PAPERS on linguistics and child language; [the] Ruth Hirsch Weir Memorial Volume; edited by Vladimir Honsa [and] M.J. Hardman-de-Bautista. The Hague, [1978]. pp. 298. *bibliogs.*

KRESS (GUNTHER) and HODGE (ROBERT) Language as ideology. London, 1979. pp. 163. *bibliog.*

LIQUOR PROBLEM

— Law and legislation — Australia.

TOMASIC (ROMAN ALEXANDER) Drugs, alcohol and community control. Sydney, 1977. pp. 248. *bibliog. (Law Foundation of New South Wales. Criminal Justice Monograph Series. No.3)*

— South Africa.

VAN DER BURGH (CHRIS) Smoking and drinking patterns of whites: 1975. Pretoria, 1978. pp. 42. *bibliog. (Human Sciences Research Council [South Africa] . Institute for Sociological, Demographic and Criminological Research. Reports. No. S-51)*

— United Kingdom.

CHRISTIAN ECONOMIC AND SOCIAL RESEARCH FOUNDATION. Less to spend: less spent on drink. London, 1978. pp. 9.

LIQUOR TRAFFIC

— Ireland (Republic).

EIRE. Restrictive Practices Commission. 1977. Report of study of competition in the licensed drink trade. Dublin, [1977]. fo. 91.

LIRA PARENTE (MANUEL).

BENTON (PEGGIE) Fight for the drylands: struggle and achievement in Brazil. London, 1977. pp. 188. *First published in 1972.*

LITERATURE

— History and criticism.

LINGUISTIC and literary studies in honor of Archibald A. Hill; edited by Mohammad Ali Jazayery [and others]. The Hague, [1978-79]. 4 vols. *bibliogs.*

LITERATURE, COMPARATIVE.

CASTRO (AMÉRICO) An idea of history; selected essays; translated from the Spanish and edited by Stephen Gilman and Edmund L. King. Columbus, Ohio, [1977]. pp. 343.

LITERATURE, MEDIEVAL.

WILSON (RICHARD MIDDLEWOOD) The lost literature of medieval England. New York, 1969. pp. 272. *First published in 1952.*

LITERATURE AND SOCIETY.

HILL (JOHN EDWARD CHRISTOPHER) Milton and the English Revolution. London, 1977. pp. 541. *bibliog.*

FEINGOLD (RICHARD) Nature and society: later eighteenth-century uses of the pastoral and georgic. Hassocks, 1978. pp. 209.

RICKWORD (EDGELL) Literature in society: essays and opinions (2), 1931-1978; edited by Alan Young. Manchester, [1978]. pp. 332.

SMITH (HENRY NASH) Democracy and the novel: popular resistance to classic American writers. New York, [1978]. pp. 204.

LITERATURE AND SOCIETY.(Cont.)

WEBSTER (FRANK) Sociology and literature: some methodological problems in a variety of approaches to the study of literature. 1978. fo. 295. *bibliog.* Typescript. Ph.D. (London) thesis: unpublished. This thesis is the property of London University and may not be removed from the Library.

WATSON (GEORGE) Irish identity and the literary revival: Synge, Yeats, Joyce and O'Casey. London, 1979. pp. 326. *bibliog.*

ZIPES (JACK) Breaking the magic spell: radical theories of folk and fairy tales. London, 1979. pp. 201.

LITERATURE AND STATE
— Germany.

WIESAND (ANDREAS JOHANNES) and FOHRBECK (KARLA) Literature and the public in the Federal Republic of Germany. Munich, [1976]. pp. 103.

LLANELLI
— Economic history.

SYMONS (MALCOLM V.) Coal mining in the Llanelli area. Llanelli, Borough Council, [1979 in progress]. (Llanelli. Public Library. Local History Research Group Series. No.1)

LOANS, AMERICAN
— France.

SCHRECKER (ELLEN) The hired money: the French debt to the United States, 1917- 1929. New York, 1979. pp. 383. *bibliog.*

LOANS, FOREIGN.

ZOLOTAS (XENOPHON) The dollar crisis and other papers. Athens, 1979. pp. 69. *bibliog.* (Bank of Greece. Papers and Lectures. 41)

— Brazil.

PEREIRA (JOSE EDUARDO DE CARVALHO) Financiamento externo e crescimento econômico no Brasil, 1966/73. Rio de Janeiro, 1974. pp. 273. *bibliog.* (Brazil. Instituto de Planejamento Econômico e Social. Instituto de Pesquisas. Relatorios de Pesquisa. No. 27)

LOANS, MEXICAN
— Colombia.

El EMPRESTITO de Mexico a Colombia; recopilacion de documentos con una introduccion y notas; por Joaquin Ramirez Cabañas. Mexico, 1930. pp. 247. *(Archivo Historico Diplomatico Mexicano. [Serie 1]. Num. 33)*

LOCAL BUDGETS
— United Kingdom.

DANZIGER (JAMES N.) Making budgets: public resource allocation. Beverly Hills, 1978. pp. 254. *bibliog.*

LOCAL ELECTIONS
— Russia.

GRIGOR'EV (VADIM KONSTANTINOVICH) and ZHDANOV (VIKTOR PAVLOVICH) Poriadok provedeniia vyborov v mestnye Sovety deputatov trudiashchikhsia. Moskva, 1977. pp. 79.

LOCAL FINANCE.

HEPWORTH (NOEL PEERS) The finance of local government. 5th ed. London, 1979. pp. 321. *bibliog.*

— Canada — Ontario.

LOCAL GOVERNMENT FINANCE IN ONTARIO; [pd. by] Ministry of Treasury and Economics and Intergovernmental Affairs. a., 1977- Toronto.

— Finland.

FINLAND. Tilastokeskus. Kuntien tulojäämät, siirtomäärärahat, talousarviolainat ja rahastot. a., 1976- Helsinki. [in Finnish and Swedish]

— France.

Le DEVELOPPEMENT des initiatives financières locales et régionales: rapport à Monsieur le Premier Ministre du Groupe de réflexion presidé par Jacques Mayoux. Paris, [1979]. pp. 300.

—New Zealand.

The FINANCING of local authority works: report of the interdepartmental committee. Wellington, Government Printer, 1975. pp. 31.

— Pakistan — Punjab.

PUNJAB (PAKISTAN). Bureau of Statistics. 1975. Public finance statistics of local bodies, the Punjab, 1960-61 to 1974-75. Lahore, [1975]. pp. 46.

— United Kingdom.

U.K. Department of the Environment. 1977. Housing policy review: local authority subsidies: rent rebates and rent allowances: consultation paper. [London, 1977]. pp. 5.

ASSOCIATION OF METROPOLITAN AUTHORITIES. Value for money: local authorities and cost effectiveness. London, [1978]. pp. 19.

U.K. Home Office. 1978. Proposals for replacing section 11 of the Local Government Act 1966: a consultative document: (a new form of grant aid to assist local authorities in meeting the special needs of ethnic minorities). [London], 1978. pp. 11.

LOCAL GOVERNMENT.

TERRITORIAL politics in industrial nations; edited by Sidney Tarrow [and others]. New York, 1978. pp. 328.

— Economic aspects — United Kingdom.

GEARY (K.) Treatment of multiple objectives for programming problems: a review with reference to possible public sector application. London, 1978. pp. 25. *bibliog.* (Planning Research Applications Group. PRAG Technical Papers. TP 25)

— Algeria.

La CHARTE communale, la charte de Wilaya [and] la charte de la gestion socialiste des entreprises, et textes réglementaires. Alger, 1979. 1 vol. (pag.var.). (Algeria. Direction de la Documentation et des Publications. Dossiers Documentaires. 27) In English and Arabic.

— Australia.

AUSTRALIA. Social Welfare Commission. 1976. The role of local government in social welfare. [Canberra], 1976. pp. 84.

PURDIE (DONALD M.) Local government in Australia: reformation or regression? Sydney, 1976. pp. 200. *bibliog.*

— — New South Wales.

NEW SOUTH WALES. Committee of Inquiry into Local Government Areas and Administration. 1974. Report; [C.J. Barnett, chairman]. [Sydney, 1974]. pp. 83.

— Canada.

CANADIAN provincial politics: the party systems of the ten provinces...; edited by Martin Robin. 2nd ed. Scarborough, Ont., [1978]. pp. 316. *bibliogs.*

TINDAL (C.R.) and TINDAL (S.NOBES) Local government in Canada: an introduction. Toronto, [1979]. pp. 159. *bibliog.*

— — Ontario.

ONTARIO. Ministry of Treasury, Economics and Intergovernmental Affairs. 1978. White Paper: government statement on the review of local government in the municipality of metropolitan Toronto. [Toronto], 1978. pp. 61.

— France.

FRANCE. Direction de la Documentation. La Documentation Française. Notes et Etudes Documentaires. No. 4492. Le conseil général; [by] Jean Bourdon. [2nd ed.] [Paris], 1978. pp. 96.

HARDING (ROBERT R.) Anatomy of a power elite: the provincial governors of early modern France. New Haven, 1978. pp. 310. *bibliog.*

LOCAL government in Britain and France: problems and prospects; edited by Jacques Lagroye and Vincent Wright. London, 1979. pp. 244.

— Ghana.

CROOK (RICHARD CHARLES) Local elites and national politics in Ghana: a case study of political centralization and local politics in Offinso, Ashanti (1945-1966). 1977 [or rather 1978]. 2 vols. *bibliog.* Typescript. Ph.D. (London) thesis: unpublished. This thesis is the property of London University and may not be removed from the Library.

— India.

RURAL economy and municipal problems of India; by K.P. Bhatnagar [and others]. Kanpur, 1953. pp. 392.

— Ireland (Republic).

MEGHEN (P.J.) Local government in Ireland; revised by D. Roche. 5th ed. Dublin, 1975. pp. 32.

— Italy.

CASTELLACCI (CLAUDIO) Mani pulite. Milano, [1977]. pp. 175.

— Jamaica.

JAMAICA. Ministry of Local Government. 1974. Report on the reform of local government in Jamaica. [Kingston], 1974. pp. 116. *bibliog.*

— New Zealand.

NEW ZEALAND. Local Government Commission. 1979- [Establishment of regional government]: final scheme[s]. [Wellington,. 1979 in progress].

— Nigeria.

NIGERIA (KWARA STATE). Military Governor, 1968- (Bamigboye). Local government reforms in Kwara State. [Ilorin, 1968]. pp. 17.

NIGERIA (KWARA STATE). Military Governor, 1968- (Bamigboye). Review of local government reforms in Kwara State: phase 2. [Ilorin, 1974]. pp. 7. *Cover title: Towards a progressive local government administration.*

— Rhodesia.

BLOORE (KEITH) Community development and training: a condensation of the Batten report. [Salisbury, Ministry of Internal Affairs, 1967]. pp. 20.

— Russia.

RUSSIA (USSR). Verkhovnyi Sovet. Prezidium. Otdel po Voprosam Raboty Sovetov. 1973. Itogi vyborov i sostav deputatov mestnykh Sovetov deputatov trudiashchikhsia, 1973 g.: statisticheskii sbornik. Moskva, 1973 g. pp. 254.

EREMIN (ALEKSANDR IVANOVICH) Akty mestnykh organov narodnogo kontrolia. Moskva, 1976. pp. 111.

— Tanzania.

TANGANYIKA. 1957. Second interim report on the county council in Tanganyika, 1956- 1957. [Dar es Salaam, 1957]. pp. 17.

— United Kingdom.

ASSOCIATION OF COUNTY COUNCILS. Brief outline of the activities of the Committees of the Association. a., 1975/77- London.

EDDISON (TONY) Local government: management and corporate planning. 2nd ed. Leighton Buzzard, 1975. pp. 225.

SKITT (JOHN) ed. Practical corporate planning in local government. Leighton Buzzard, 1975. pp. 260.

AREA management: objectives and structures; by C.J. Horn [and others]; (area management monitoring project: first interim report);...commissioned by the Department of the Environment. [Birmingham], 1977. pp. 68.

HAM (R.E.) The county and the Kingdom: Sir Herbert Croft and the Elizabethan state. Washington, D.C., [1977]. pp. 304.

TACKLING urban deprivation: the contribution of area-based management; by Tim Mason [and others]; (area management monitoring project);...commissioned by the Department of the Environment. [Birmingham], 1977. pp. 94.

IBM UK SCIENTIFIC CENTRE SEMINAR ON CORPORATE PLANNING IN LOCAL GOVERNMENT, PETERLEE, 1977. Proceedings of the...seminar; edited by B.V. Wagle. Peterlee, 1978. pp. 128. *bibliog.* *(IBM United Kingdom Limited. UK Scientific Centre. [Technical Reports]. 0092)*

IN pursuit of corporate rationality: organisational developments in the post-reorganisation period; by Royston Greenwood [and others]. Birmingham, [1978]. pp. 241,vi.

LEWIS (NORMAN) and GATESHILL (BERNARD) The Commission for Local Administration: a preliminary appraisal. London, 1978. pp. 68. *(Royal Institute of Public Administration. RIPA Studies)*

PAGE (EDWARD) Why should central-local relations in Scotland be any different from those in England? Glasgow, [1978]. fo. 46. *(Glasgow. University of Strathclyde. Centre for the Study of Public Policy. Studies in Public Policy. No. 21)*

POLITICAL leaders in local government; edited by G.W. Jones and Alan Norton. Birmingham, [1978]. pp. 233.

SEELEY (IVOR HUGH) Local government explained. London, 1978. pp. 202. *bibliogs.*

SHEPHERD (JOHN WILLIAM) Education and the urban environment: geographical perspectives on primary school data in inner London. 1977 [or rather 1978]. fo. 273. *bibliog.* Typescript. Ph.D. (London) thesis: unpublished. *This thesis is the property of London University and may not be removed from the Library.*

U.K. Commission for Local Administration in England. Report[s] by the local Ombudsman on investigation[s] into complaint[s]. irreg., Ag 1979- London.

LOCAL government in Britain and France: problems and prospects; edited by Jacques Lagroye and Vincent Wright. London, 1979. pp. 244.

SAUNDERS (PETER) Urban politics: a sociological interpretation. London, 1979. pp. 383. *bibliog.*

U.K. Social Science Research Council. Panel on Central-Local Government Relationships. 1979. Central-local government relationships; report...to the Research Initiatives Board; [G.W. Jones, chairman]. London, [1979]. 1 vol. (various pagings).

— — Scotland.

SCOTLAND. Working Party on Relationships between Health Boards and Local Authorities. 1977. Report; [J.A.M. Mitchell, chairman]. Edinburgh, 1977. pp. 26.

PAGE (EDWARD) Why should central-local relations in Scotland be any different from those in England? Glasgow, [1978]. fo. 46. *(Glasgow. University of Strathclyde. Centre for the Study of Public Policy. Studies in Public Policy. No. 21)*

— United States.

LANCASTER (LANE W.) Government in rural America. 2nd ed. Westport, 1974. pp. 375. *bibliog.* *Reprint of work originally published New York, 1952.*

BURNS (JAMES MACGREGOR) and others. State and local politics: government by the people. 2nd ed. Englewood Cliffs, N.J., [1978]. pp. 289.

TOWN and county: essays on the structure of local government in the American colonies; edited by Bruce C. Daniels. Middletown, Conn., [1978]. pp. 279. *bibliogs.*

ZEIGLER (LUTHER HARMON) and TUCKER (HARVEY J.) The quest for responsive government: an introduction to state and local politics. North Scituate, Mass., [1978]. pp. 337. *bibliogs.*

— — Massachusetts.

MASSACHUSETTS. Department of Community Affairs. 1972. Report...relative to community and environmental development and governmental roles and responsibilities. [Boston], 1972. pp. 39.

LOCAL GOVERNMENT OFFICIALS AND EMPLOYEES

— United Kingdom.

NEW TOWNS STAFF COMMISSION [U.K.]. The first report of the...Commission, 1976-1978; [Philip M. Vine, chairman]. London, H.M.S.O., 1979. pp. 113.

LOCAL RINGS.

SALLY (JUDITH D.) Numbers of generators of ideals in local rings. New York, [1978]. pp. 93. *bibliog.*

LOCAL TAXATION

— Philippine Islands.

PHILIPPINE ISLANDS. Joint Legislative-Executive Tax Commission. 1968. Local taxation. [Manila], 1968. pp. 14.

LOCAL TRANSIT.

PUBLIC transportation: planning, operations, and management; editors George E. Gray, Lester A. Hoel. Englewood Cliffs, N.J., [1979]. pp. 749. *bibliogs.*

LOCKE (JOHN).

LEMOS (RAMON M.) Hobbes and Locke: power and consent. Athens, [1978]. pp. 185.

PARRY (GERAINT BURTON) John Locke. London, 1978. pp. 171. *bibliog.*

LOCKHEED AIRCRAFT CORPORATION.

BOULTON (DAVID) The Lockheed papers. London, 1978. pp. 289.

LOGIC.

LIVELY (JACK) and REES (JOHN COLLWYN) eds. Utilitarian logic and politics: James Mill's Essay on government, Macaulay's critique and the ensuing debate. Oxford, 1978. pp. 270.

LOGIC, SYMBOLIC AND MATHEMATICAL.

HANDBOOK of mathematical logic; edited by Jon Barwise. Amsterdam, 1977 repr. 1978. pp. 1165. *bibliogs.*

MENGER (CARL) Son of Carl Menger the Economist. Selected papers in logic and foundations, didactics, economics. Dordrecht, [1979]. pp. 341. *bibliog.*

LOGUEN (JERMAIN WESLEY).

LOGUEN (JERMAIN WESLEY) The Rev. J. W. Loguen, as a slave and as a freeman: a narrative of real life. [Syracuse, N.Y.], 1859; New York, 1968. pp. 444. *Facsimile reprint. Written in the third person, but apparently by Loguen.*

LOMBARDO TOLEDANO (VICENTE).

KRAUZE (ENRIQUE) Caudillos culturales en la Revolucion mexicana. Mexico, 1976. pp. 340.

LOMBARDY

— Economic history.

ROMANI (MARIO) Aspetti e problemi di storia economica lombarda nei secoli XVIII e XIX: scritti riediti in memoria. Milano, 1977. pp. 572. *(Milan. Università Cattolica del Sacro Cuore. Pubblicazioni. Scienze Storiche. 16)*

— History — Sources.

PROCESSI politici del Senato Lombardo-Veneto, 1815-1851; a cura di Alfredo Grandi. Roma, 1976. pp. 780. *(Istituto per la Storia del Risorgimento Italiano. Pubblicazioni. 2a Serie. Fonti. vol. 67)*

LONDON

— City planning.

CHANGING London; edited by Hugh Clout. Slough, 1978. pp. 151. *bibliogs.*

DOCKLANDS JOINT COMMITTEE. London docklands operational programme, 1978-82. [London], 1978. pp. 86.

LONDON. Greater London Council. The Greater London Council, Covent Garden, GLC action area plan: resolution of adoption, written statement, proposals map. [London, 1978]. pp. 86. *bibliog.*

THAMES TELEVISION. Planning to the people: report of the London Looks Forward project. [London, 1978?]. pp. 128. *Full version of paper 9, London Looks Forward, conference background paper, included in this report.*

— Civic improvement.

THAMES TELEVISION. Planning to the people: report of the London Looks Forward project. [London, 1978?]. pp. 128. *Full version of paper 9, London Looks Forward, conference background paper, included in this report.*

— Description.

CHANGING London; edited by Hugh Clout. Slough, 1978. pp. 151. *bibliogs.*

— Docks.

DOCKLANDS JOINT COMMITTEE. London docklands operational programme, 1978-82. [London], 1978. pp. 86.

— Gilds — Coachmakers' and Coach Harness Makers' Company.

NOCKOLDS (HAROLD) ed. The coachmakers: a history of the Worshipful Company of Coachmakers and Coach Harness Makers, 1677-1977. London, [1977]. pp. 239. *bibliog.*

— — Stationers' Company.

UNWIN (PHILIP) The Stationers' Company 1918-1977: a livery company in the modern world. London, 1978. pp. 144.

— Growth.

ROEBUCK (JANET) Urban development in 19th-century London: Lambeth, Battersea and Wandsworth, 1838-1888. London, 1979. pp. 211. *bibliog.*

— Industries.

DOBSON (NEIL) Employment and industry in Greater London: a background document. London, [1977]. pp. 48.

— Libraries — Special collections.

GARLING (MARGUERITE) compiler. Human rights research guide: library holdings in London on human rights, censorship and freedom of expression. London, 1978. pp. 77. *Compiled for the Writers and Scholars Educational Trust.*

LONDON (Cont.)

— Mayors.

LONDON'S liberties: or, A learned argument of law and reason. Exeter, 1972. pp. 38. *Facsimile reprint of 1st ed., London, 1650.*

— Officials and employees.

LONDON'S liberties: or, A learned argument of law and reason. Exeter, 1972. pp. 38. *Facsimile reprint of 1st ed., London, 1650.*

— Parks.

LONDON. Greater London Council. Intelligence Unit. The future of Alexandra Palace and Park: results of a survey by the GLC Intelligence Unit. [London, 1974]. pp. 35. *(Greater London Research. Research Reports. No. 16)*

— Politics and government.

LONDON'S liberties: or, A learned argument of law and reason. Exeter, 1972. pp. 38. *Facsimile reprint of 1st ed., London, 1650.*

MARSHALL (Sir FRANK) The Marshall inquiry on Greater London; report to the Greater London Council. [London], Greater London Council, 1978. pp. 134.

— Recreational activities.

LONDON. Greater London Council. Intelligence Unit. The future of Alexandra Palace and Park: results of a survey by the GLC Intelligence Unit. [London, 1974]. pp. 35. *(Greater London Research. Research Reports. No. 16)*

— Social conditions.

TRISTAN (FLORA) Promenades dans Londres; ou, L'aristocratie et les prolétaire anglais; édition établie et commentée par François Bédarida. Paris, 1978. pp. 358. *(Paris. Université de Paris I (Panthéon-Sorbonne). Centre d'Histoire du Syndicalisme. Collection) Reprint of 1840 ed.*

ROBINS (DAVID) and COHEN (PHILIP) 1944- . Knuckle sandwich: growing up in the working-class city. Harmondsworth, 1978. pp. 203.

FISHMAN (WILLIAM JOHN) The streets of East London. London, 1979. pp. 139. *bibliog.*

— Social history.

FISHMAN (WILLIAM JOHN) The streets of East London. London, 1979. pp. 139. *bibliog.*

— Stock Exchange.

LONDON. Stock Exchange. Evidence to the Committee to Review the Functioning of Financial Institutions: the role and functioning of the Stock Exchange. [London, 1978]. pp. 60.

— Theatres.

INGRAM (WILLIAM) A London life in the brazen age: Francis Langley, 1548-1602. Cambridge, Mass., 1978. pp. 335.

— Transit systems.

JACKSON (ALAN ARTHUR) London's local railways. Newton Abbot, 1978 repr. 1979. pp. 384. *bibliog.*

BARMAN (CHRISTIAN) The man who built London Transport: a biography of Frank Pick. Newton Abbot, [1979]. pp. 287.

LONDON CAPITAL GROUP.

SHERRARD (MICHAEL) and DAVISON (IAN HAY) London Capital Group Limited, formerly British Bangladesh Trust Limited: investigation under section 165b of the Companies Act 1948; report. London, H.M.S.O., 1977. pp. 376.

LONDON STATIONERS' COMPANY.

UNWIN (PHILIP) The Stationers' Company 1918-1977: a livery company in the modern world. London, 1978. pp. 144.

LONDON UNIVERSITY

— Libraries.

CONFERENCE ON THE FUTURE ROLE OF COMPUTERISED INFORMATION SERVICES AT THE UNIVERSITY OF LONDON, LONDON, 1977. Proceedings [of the conference organized by the Library Resources Co-ordinating Committee]. London, 1977. pp. 116. *bibliog.*

LONGSHOREMEN

— New Zealand.

TURKINGTON (DON) Industrial conflict: a study of three New Zealand industries. Wellington, N.Z., 1976. pp. 324.

LOPEZ MICHELSEN (ALFONSO).

GOMEZ BUENDIA (HERNANDO) Alfonso Lopez Michelsen: un examen critico de su pensamiento y de su obra de gobierno. Bogota, 1978. pp. 367.

LOS ANGELES

— Description.

ORD (EDWARD OTHO CRESAP) The city of the angels and the city of the saints; or, A trip to Los Angeles and San Bernardino in 1856;...edited by Neal Harlow. San Marino, 1978. pp. 56. *bibliog.*

— Early maps.

HARLOW (NEAL) Maps and surveys of the pueblo lands of Los Angeles. Los Angeles, 1976. pp. 169. *bibliog. Two maps in end pocket.*

— History.

HARLOW (NEAL) Maps and surveys of the pueblo lands of Los Angeles. Los Angeles, 1976. pp. 169. *bibliog. Two maps in end pocket.*

SINGLETON (GREGORY H.) Religion in the city of angels: American protestant culture and urbanization, Los Angeles, 1850-1930. [London, 1979]. pp. 262. *bibliog.*

— Water supply.

OSTROM (VINCENT) Water and politics: a study of water policies and administration in the development of Los Angeles. Los Angeles, 1953. pp. 297. *bibliog. Reprint, New York, 1972.*

LOTTA CONTINUA.

LOTTA CONTINUA. Congresso, 2, 1976. [Proceedings]. Roma, [1976]. pp. 316.

LOTTERIES

— Canada.

LOTO CANADA. Annual report. a., 1977/78 [1st]- Ottawa.

LOUIS XI, King of France.

KENDALL (PAUL MURRAY) Louis XI: "the universal spider". London, 1971. pp. 464. *bibliog.*

LOUIS XIV, King of France.

GOUBERT (PIERRE) Louis XIV and twenty million Frenchmen; translated from the French by Anne Carter. New York, [1966]. pp. 350. *bibliog.*

LOUISIANA

— History.

McCRARY (PEYTON) Abraham Lincoln and reconstruction : the Louisiana experiment. Princeton, N.J., [1978]. pp. 423. *bibliog.*

— — Sources.

FITZPATRICK (JOHN) c.1737-1791. The merchant of Manchac: the letterbooks of John Fitzpatrick, 1768-1790; edited with an introduction by Margaret Fisher Dalrymple. Baton Rouge, [1978]. pp. 451. *bibliog.*

LUBBE (MARINUS VAN DER).

REED (DOUGLAS) The burning of the Reichstag. London, 1934. pp. 352.

LÜBKE (HEINRICH).

See LUEBKE (HEINRICH).

LUCERNE (CANTON)

— Economic history.

WICKI (HANS) Bevölkerung und Wirtschaft des Kantons Luzern im 18. Jahrhundert. Luzern, 1979. pp. 666. *bibliog. (Lucerne (Canton). Staatsarchiv. Luzerner Historische Veröffentlichungen. Band 9)*

— Population.

WICKI (HANS) Bevölkerung und Wirtschaft des Kantons Luzern im 18. Jahrhundert. Luzern, 1979. pp. 666. *bibliog. (Lucerne (Canton). Staatsarchiv. Luzerner Historische Veröffentlichungen. Band 9)*

LUDLOW (EDMUND).

CAMDEN SOCIETY. [Publications]. 4th Series. vol. 21. A voyce from the watch tower; ([by] Edmund Ludlow); part five, 1660-1662; edited by A.B. Worden. London, 1978. pp. 70.

LUDWIG BOLTZMANN INSTITUT FÜR GESCHICHTE DER ARBEITERBEWEGUNG.

RUECKBLICK und Ausschau: (10 Jahre Ludwig Boltzmann Institut für Geschichte der Arbeiterbewegung; [by] Karl R. Stadler [and others]). Wien, 1978. pp. 139. *bibliog. (Ludwig Boltzmann Institut für Geschichte der Arbeiterbewegung. Materialien zur Arbeiterbewegung. Nr. 12)*

LUEBKE (HEINRICH).

QUARTA (HUBERT GEORG) Heinrich Lübke: Zeugnisse eines Lebens; Versuch einer biographischen Darstellung. Buxheim/Allgäu, 1978. pp. 253. *bibliog.*

LUHMANN (NIKLAS).

FEBBRAJO (ALBERTO) Funzionalismo strutturale e sociologia del diritto nell'opera di Niklas Luhmann. Milano, 1975. pp. 226. *bibliog. (Milan. Università. Istituto di Filosofia e Sociologia del Diritto. Studi di Sociologia del Diritto. 2)*

LUKÁCS (GEORG).

DIALOG und Kontroverse mit Georg Lukács: der Methodenstreit deutscher sozialistischer Schriftsteller; (herausgegeben von Werner Mittenzwei). Leipzig, 1975. pp. 475.

APITZSCH (URSULA) Gesellschaftstheorie und Ästhetik bei Georg Lukacs bis 1933. Stuttgart-Bad Cannstatt, 1977. pp. 206. *bibliog.*

HERMANN (ISTVÁN) Die Gedankenwelt von Georg Lukács; (Übersetzung aus dem Ungarischen: Endre Kiss). Budapest, 1978. pp. 403.

KILMINSTER (RICHARD) Praxis and method: a sociological dialogue with Lukács, Gramsci and the early Frankfurt school. London, 1979. pp. 334. *bibliog.*

LUMBERING

— Canada.

MACKAY (DONALD) Journalist. The lumberjacks. Toronto, [1978]. pp. 319. *bibliog.*

LUMBERMEN

— Canada.

MACKAY (DONALD) Journalist. The lumberjacks. Toronto, [1978]. pp. 319. *bibliog.*

LUMIERE [MADAGASCAR].

MARON (CLAUDE) L'hebdomadaire Lumière à Madagascar de 1935 à 1972. Aix-Marseille, 1977. pp. 295. bibliog. (Université d'Aix-Marseille III. Faculté de Droit et de Science Politique.Travaux et Mémoires. 28)

LUMUMBA (PATRICE).

HEINZ (G.) and DONNAY (H.) Lumumba Patrice: les cinquante derniers jours de sa vie. Paris, 1976. pp. 196. *Endpocket contains two sound discs of speeches by Lumumba.*

LUNGS

— Cancer.

REPORT on a second retrospective mortality study in North-East England;...[by] G. Dean [and others]. London, 1977-78. 2 pts. (in 1 vol.). bibliogs. (Tobacco Research Council. Research Papers. 14) *Report of the first study published as Research Paper 8.*

LUOS (NILOTIC TRIBE).

PARKIN (DAVID J.) The cultural definition of political response: lineal destiny among the Luo. London, 1978. pp. 347. bibliog.

LUTSEVICH (IVAN DAMINIKAVICH).

See KUPALA (IANKA) pseud.

LUXEMBURG (ROSA).

ROSA Luxemburg: die Krise des Marxismus; ([by] Projekt Klassenanalyse). Westberlin, [1975]. pp. 171.

KIRSCH (HANS CHRISTIAN) Rosa L.: die Geschichte der Rosa Luxemburg und ihrer Zeit.. .; ([by] Frederik Hetmann [pseud.]). Weinheim, 1976 repr. 1977. pp. 308. bibliog.

CAMPANELLA (MIRIAM) Economia e stato in Rosa Luxemburg. Bari, [1977]. pp. 196.

LUXEMBURG (ROSA) The letters of Rosa Luxemburg; edited with an introduction by Stephen Eric Bronner. Boulder, 1978. pp. 259.

LUYIAS.

WIPPER (AUDREY) Rural rebels: a study of two protest movements in Kenya. Nairobi, 1977. pp. 363. bibliog.

MACAO

— Commerce — Statistics.

MACAO. Serviços de Estatistica. Boletim mensal do comercio externo. m., Ja 1977(no. 1)- Macau. *[in English and Portuguese]*

MACARTHUR (DOUGLAS).

MANCHESTER (WILLIAM) American Caesar: Douglas MacArthur, 1880-1964. London, 1979. pp. 793.

MACCHIAVELLI (NICCOLO).

STUDIES on Machiavelli; edited by Myron P. Gilmore. Firenze, [1972]. pp. 415. *In English or Italian. Includes most of the papers presented at a seminar at I Tatti in 1969 organized by the Harvard University Center for Italian Renaissance Studies.*

MACDONALD (JAMES RAMSAY).

TRACEY (HERBERT TREVOR) From Doughty Street to Downing Street: the Rt. Hon. J. Ramsay MacDonald, M.P.; a biographical study. 3rd ed. London, 1924. pp. 103.

McDOUGAL (MYRES SMITH).

TOWARD world order and human dignity: essays in honor of Myres S. McDougal; edited by W. Michael Reisman and Burns H. Weston. New York, [1976]. pp. 603. bibliog.

MACEDONIAN QUESTION.

MACDERMOTT (MERCIA) Freedom or death: the life of Gotsé Delchev. London, 1978. pp. 405. bibliog.

McGLYNN (EDWARD).

PREUSS (ARTHUR) ed. The fundamental fallacy of socialism: an essay on the question of land-ownership, comprising an authentic account of the famous McGlynn case. 2nd ed. St.Louis, Mo., 1909. pp. 198.

MACHINE-TOOLS

— Trade and manufacture — United Kingdom.

JONES (D.T.) Plant size and efficiency in the production of metalworking machine tools. London, [1978]. pp. 26. bibliog. (National Institute of Economic and Social Research. Discussion Papers. No. 19)

MACHLUP (FRITZ).

BREADTH and depth in economics: Fritz Machlup: the man and his ideas; edited by Jacob S. Dreyer. Lexington, Mass., [1978]. pp. 316. bibliog.

MACLEAN (JOHN).

MACLEAN (JOHN) Socialist. In the rapids of revolution: essays, articles and letters 1902- 23; edited and with an introduction and commentaries by Nan Milton. London, 1978. pp. 256.

MADAGASCAR

— Economic conditions.

MADAGASCAR. Bureau de Développement et de Promotion Industriels. 1968. Guide de l'investisseur; [with 1969 supplement]. [Tananarive], 1968. pp. 87; fo. (4).

MADHYA BHARAT

— Economic conditions.

MADHYA BHARAT. 1952. The economy of Madhya Bharat. Indore, 1952. pp. 4.

— Economic policy.

MADHYA BHARAT. 1952. The five year plan of Madhya Bharat (1951-56). Indore, 1952. pp. 4.

— Social policy.

MADHYA BHARAT. 1952. The five year plan of Madhya Bharat (1951-56). Indore, 1952. pp. 4.

MADHYA PRADESH

— Economic policy.

MADHYA PRADESH. Planning and Development Department. 1971. Fourth five year plan of Madhya Pradesh: mid-term appraisal. [Bhopal, 1971]. pp. 113.

— Social policy.

MADHYA PRADESH. Planning and Development Department. 1971. Fourth five year plan of Madhya Pradesh: mid-term appraisal. [Bhopal, 1971]. pp. 113.

MADRAS

— Economic conditions.

MADRAS. Finance Department. 1976. Tamil Nadu: an economic appraisal, 1976. Madras, 1976. pp. 223.

— Economic policy.

MADRAS. 1964. Third five year plan, Madras state: mid-term review. [Madras, 1964]. pp. 137.

— Politics and government.

MUTHULAKSHMI REDDY (S.) My experience as a legislator. Madras, [imprint], 1930. pp. 246.

— Population.

INDIA. Census, 1971. Series 19. Tamil Nadu: portrait of population; [by] K. Chockalingam. [Delhi, 1978]. pp. 159.

— Social policy.

MADRAS. 1964. Third five year plan, Madras state: mid-term review. [Madras, 1964]. pp. 137.

MAGDEBURG

— Economic history.

LANDWIRTSCHAFT und Kapitalismus: zur Entwicklung der ökonomischen und sozialen Verhältnisse in der Magdeburger Börde...; herausgegeben von Hans-Jürgen Rach und Bernhard Weissel. Berlin, 1978-79. 2 vols. bibliogs. (Akademie der Wissenschaften der DDR. Zentralinstitut für Geschichte. Veröffentlichungen zur Volkskunde und Kulturgeschichte. Band 66)

MAGIC.

SKORUPSKI (JOHN) Symbol and theory: a philosophical study of theories of religion in social anthropology. Cambridge, 1976. pp. 265. bibliog.

— Europe.

BRONOWSKI (JACOB) Magic, science and civilization. New York, 1978. pp. 88. (Columbia University. Bampton Lectures in America. No. No. 20)

MAHARASHTRA

— Economic policy.

MAHARASHTRA COMMERCIAL AND INDUSTRIAL CONFERENCE, 5TH, BOMBAY, 1972. Development through employment. [Bombay, Maharashtra Economic Development Council, 1972?]. pp. 59.

MAIZE

— Malawi.

MALAWI. Agro-Economic Survey. 1972. Agro-economic survey: 9th report: Lake Chilwa: a sample farm management survey among rice and maize growers at the northern end of Lake Chilwa in Kasupe district, Malawi; prepared by T.W. Bieze. Zomba, 1972. fo. 63.

MALAWI. Agro-Economic Survey. 1973. Agro-economic survey: 11th report: Mbawa: a sample farm management survey among oriental tobacco, maize and groundnut growers in the Mbawa area in the southern part of Mzimba district, Malawi, with special reference to oriental tobacco; prepared by T.W. Bieze. Lilongwe, 1973. fo. 87. bibliog.

MAKHNO (NESTOR).

ARSHINOV (PETR ANDREEVICH) History of the Makhnovist movement (1918-1921)...; translated by Lorraine and Fredy Perlman. Detroit, 1974. pp. 284.

MALACCA, STRAIT OF.

LEIFER (MICHAEL) Malacca, Singapore and Indonesia. Alphen aan den Rijn, 1978. pp. 217. bibliog.

MALAGASY NEWSPAPERS.

MARON (CLAUDE) L'hebdomadaire Lumière à Madagascar de 1935 à 1972. Aix-Marseille, 1977. pp. 295. bibliog. (Université d'Aix-Marseille III. Faculté de Droit et de Science Politique.Travaux et Mémoires. 28)

MALATESTA FAMILY.

JONES (P.J.) The Malatesta of Rimini and the papal state. London, 1974. pp. 372. bibliog.

MALAWI

— Administrative and political divisions.

MALAWI. Electoral Commission on Delimitation of Constituencies. 1973. The second report...19th March, 1973; [N.D. Kwenje, chairman]. Zomba, 1973. pp. 25, 1 map. *1st report out of print.*

MALAWI(Cont.)

— Commerce — Tanzania.

TANGANYIKA. 1954. Report on a survey of inter-territorial trade between Tanganyika and Northern Rhodesia and Nyasaland. [Dar es Salaam, 1954]. pp. 30.

— Economic conditions.

MALAWI. Economic Planning Division. 1971. Developing Malawi. Zomba, 1971. pp. 76. *bibliog.*

MALAWI. Department of Information. 1975. The economic development of Malawi since independence. [Blantyre, 1975]. pp. 23.

WILLIAMS (T. DAVID) Malawi: the politics of despair. Ithaca, 1978. pp. 339. *bibliog.*

— Economic history.

MALAWI. Department of Information. 1968. 10 years of progress: a review of development in Malawi. [Blantyre, 1968]. pp. 28.

— Economic policy.

MALAWI. Economic Planning Division. 1971. Developing Malawi. Zomba, 1971. pp. 76. *bibliog.*

— Politics and government.

BANDA (HASTINGS KAMUZU) His Excellency the Life President's speeches: mass rally at Chingale, Zomba district, August 22, 1976. [Blantyre, Department of Information, 1976?]. pp. 9.

BANDA (HASTINGS KAMUZU) His Excellency the Life President's speeches: Kamuzu Day celebrations, Kamuzu stadium and Sanjika Palace, Blantyre, May 15, 1978. [Blantyre, Department of Information, 1978?]. pp. 9.

WILLIAMS (T. DAVID) Malawi: the politics of despair. Ithaca, 1978. pp. 339. *bibliog.*

— Social policy.

MALAWI. Economic Planning Division. 1971. Developing Malawi. Zomba, 1971. pp. 76. *bibliog.*

MALAWI HOUSING CORPORATION.

MALAWI HOUSING CORPORATION. Annual reports and accounts. a., 1977- Blantyre.

MALAYA

— History.

RUBIN (ALFRED P.) Piracy, paramountcy and protectorates. Kuala Lumpur, 1974. pp. 179. *bibliog.*

CHIN (KEE ONN) Malaya upside down. 3rd ed. Singapore, 1976. pp. 202.

MALAYSIA

— Census.

FEDERATION OF MALAYSIA. Census, 1970. 1970 general report: population census of Malaysia. Kuala Lumpur, 1975-77. 2 vols. *In Malay and English.*

— Commerce — New Zealand.

NEW ZEALAND. Department of Trade and Industry. Trade Services Division. 1978. Malaysia: [a market profile]. [Wellington. 1978?]. fo. 45. *(Background to Export)*

— Constitution.

The CONSTITUTION of Malaysia: its development, 1957-1977; edited by Tun Mohamed Suffian [and others]. Kuala Lumpur, 1978. pp. 425.

— Constitutional history.

The CONSTITUTION of Malaysia: its development, 1957-1977; edited by Tun Mohamed Suffian [and others]. Kuala Lumpur, 1978. pp. 425.

— Economic conditions.

NEW ZEALAND. Department of Trade and Industry. Trade Services Division. 1978. Malaysia: [a market profile]. [Wellington. 1978?]. fo. 45. *(Background to Export)*

— Economic history.

FEDERATION OF MALAYSIA. Department of Information. 1967. Ten years of achievement: a review of Malaysia's 10 years of achievements in the economic field, based on a Radio Malaysia broadcast commemorating the 10th Merdeka Anniversary. [Kuala Lumpur, 1967]. 1 pamphlet (unpaged).

— Foreign relations.

PATHMANATHAN (MURUGESU) Conflict management in Southeast Asia: a neutralized Malaysia? Kuala Lumpur, 1977. pp. 32,4. *(University of Malaya. Faculty of Economics and Administration. Occasional Papers on Malaysian Socio- Economic Affairs. No. 7)*

— — Indonesia.

MACKIE (J.A.C.) Konfrontasi: the Indonesia-Malaysia dispute, 1963-1966. Kuala Lumpur, 1974. pp. 368. *bibliog. Published for the Australian Institute of International Affairs.*

— History.

EMERSON (RUPERT) Malaysia: a study in direct and indirect rule. Kuala Lumpur, [1964]. pp. 536. *Reprint of work first published in 1937.*

— Industries.

KHERA (HARCHARAN SINGH) The oil palm industry of Malaysia: an economic study. Kuala Lumpur, 1976. pp. 354. *bibliog.*

— Parliament.

MUSOLF (LLOYD DARYL) and SPRINGER (J. FREDERICK) Malaysia's parliamentary system: representative politics and policymaking in a divided society. Boulder, Colo., 1979. pp. 143. *bibliog.*

— Politics and government.

ISSUES in contemporary Malaysia; [by] Chandriah Appa Rao [and others]; edited by Bruce Ross-Larson. Kuala Lumpur, 1977. pp. 188.

BEDLINGTON (STANLEY S.) Malaysia and Singapore: the building of new states. Ithaca, 1978. pp. 285. *bibliog.*

PUTHUCHEARY (MAVIS) The politics of administration: the Malaysian experience. Kuala Lumpur, 1978. pp. 170. *bibliog.*

MUSOLF (LLOYD DARYL) and SPRINGER (J. FREDERICK) Malaysia's parliamentary system: representative politics and policymaking in a divided society. Boulder, Colo., 1979. pp. 143. *bibliog.*

— Race relations.

MOHAMAD (MAHATHIR BIN) The Malay dilemma. Singapore, 1970. pp. 188.

— Relations (general) with other countries.

FEDERATION OF MALAYSIA. Department of Information Services. 1968. Another successful tour: (the Razak touch). [Kuala Lumpur, 1968?]. pp. 56.

— Social conditions — Statistics.

FEDERATION OF MALAYSIA. Department of Statistics. Social statistics bulletin: peninsular Malaysia. a., 1969/1971- Kuala Lumpur. *[in English and Malay]*

— Statistics, Vital.

HIRSCHMAN (CHARLES) and TAN KAH JOO (EDWARD) Evaluation of mortality date in the vital statistics of West Malaysia. Kuala Lumpur, 1971. pp. 28, 26. *(Federation of Malaysia. Department of Statistics. Research Papers. No.5) In English and Malay.*

FEDERATION OF MALAYSIA. Department of Statistics. 1974. Abridged life tables, Malaysia 1970. Kuala Lumpur, 1974. pp. 116. *In English and Malay.*

MALINOVSKII (ROMAN).

ELWOOD (RALPH CARTER) Roman Malinovsky: a life without a cause. Newtonville, Mass., 1977. pp. 107. *bibliog.*

MALINOWSKI (BRONISLAW).

MALINOWSKI (BRONISLAW) The ethnography of Malinowski: the Trobriand Islands, 1915- 18; edited by Michael W. Young. London, 1979. pp. 254. *bibliog.*

MALLESON (NICOLAS BORRELL).

STUDENTS in need: essays in memory of Nicolas Malleson. Guildford, 1978. pp. 230. *bibliogs. (Society for Research into Higher Education. Occasional Papers)*

MALMEDY MASSACRE, 1944-1945.

WEINGARTNER (JAMES J.) Crossroads of death: the story of the Malmédy massacre and trial. Berkeley, [1979]. pp. 274. *bibliog.*

MALNUTRITION — Underdeveloped areas.

See UNDERDEVELOPED AREAS — Malnutrition.

MALPRACTICE

— United States.

The MEDICAL malpractice dilemma; (a Round Table held on December 15, 1976...); John Charles Daly, moderator, etc. Washington, [1977]. pp. 46. *(American Enterprise Institute for Public Policy Research. Round Tables)*

MALRAUX (CLARA).

MALRAUX (CLARA) Et pourtant j'étais libre. Paris, [1979]. pp. 262. *(Le bruit de nos pas. 6)*

MALT DISTILLERS ASSOCIATION OF SCOTLAND.

WEIR (RONALD B.) The history of the Malt Distillers' Association of Scotland. [York?, 1974?]. pp. 177.

MALTA

— Economic conditions.

GRECH (JOHN C.) Threads of dependence. Msida, Malta, 1978. pp. 200. *bibliog.*

— Economic policy.

JOINT STEERING COMMITTEE FOR MALTA. Timetable for the new Malta; [Lord Robens of Woldingham, chairman]. Valletta, [1968]. pp. (8).

MALTHUS (THOMAS ROBERT).

JAMES (PATRICIA) Population Malthus: his life and times. London, 1979. pp. 524.

MALTHUSIANISM.

KRITIKA mal'tuzianskikh i neomal'tuzianskikh vzgliadov: Rossiia XIX - nachala XX v. Moskva, 1978. pp. 166.

MALVA (CONSTANT).

MALVA (CONSTANT) Ma nuit au jour le jour. Paris, 1978. pp. 203.

MAN.

HELLER (AGNES) Renaissance man;...translated from the Hungarian by Richard E. Allen. London, 1978. pp. 481.

— Animal nature.

MIDGLEY (MARY) Beast and man: the roots of human nature. Hassocks, 1979. pp. 377. *bibliog.*

— Influence of climate.

SECONDAT (CHARLES LOUIS DE) Baron de Montesquieu. The spirit of laws:...a compendium of the first English edition; edited...by David Wallace Carrithers; together with an English translation of An essay on causes affecting minds and characters, 1736-1743. Berkeley, [1977]. pp. 479.

— Influence of environment.

GOULD (PETER R.) and WHITE (RODNEY) Mental maps. Harmondsworth, [1974]. pp. 203. *bibliog.*

GEOGRAPHIES of the mind: essays in historical geosophy in honor of John Kirtland Wright; edited by David Lowenthal and Martyn J. Bowden. New York, 1976. pp. 263. *bibliog.*

HEREDITY and environment; edited by A.H. Halsey. London, 1977. pp. 337. *bibliog.*

The BIOLOGY of high-altitude peoples; edited by P.T. Baker. Cambridge, 1978. pp. 357. *bibliogs. (International Council of Scientific Unions. International Biological Programme. 14)*

EXTINCTION and survival in human populations; edited by Charles D. Laughlin, Jr., and Ivan A. Brady. New York, 1978. pp. 327. *bibliog.*

FARBSTEIN (JAY) and KANTROWITZ (MIN) People in places: experiencing, using, and changing the built environment. Englewood Cliffs, N.J., [1978]. pp. 182.

SOCIAL and ecological systems; edited by P.C. Burnham and R.F. Ellen. London, 1979. pp. 314. *bibliogs. (Association of Social Anthropologists of the Commonwealth. A.S.A. Monographs. 18)*

— Influence on nature.

DETWYLER (THOMAS R.) ed. Man's impact on environment. New York, [1971]. pp. 731. *bibliogs.*

MAN and the ecosphere. San Francisco, 1971. pp. 307. *bibliog. Readings from Scientific American.*

— Origins.

NAPIER (JOHN RUSSELL) The roots of mankind. London, 1971. pp. 240. *bibliog.*

MAN (THEOLOGY).

TOURNIER (PAUL) The violence inside. London, 1978. pp. 201.

MAN, PREHISTORIC.

PFEIFFER (JOHN E.) The emergence of man. 3rd ed. New York, [1978]. pp. 467. *bibliog.*

— United Kingdom.

BRADLEY (RICHARD) 1946- . The prehistoric settlement of Britain. London, 1978. pp. 155.

MANAGEMENT.

DAVIES (C.J.) Problems in urban management. Birmingham, 1976. pp. 115. *bibliog. (Birmingham. University. Institute of Local Government Studies. Development Administration Group. Case Studies in Development Administration. vol. 3)*

CENTRE FOR INTERFIRM COMPARISON. Management policies and practices and business performance. Colchester, [1977]. 3 vols.

REVIEW COMMITTEE FOR THE OXFORD REGION. Report on the management functions of the regional and area health authorities: discussion document; [G.J. Roberts, chairman]. [Oxford, Oxford Regional Health Authority], 1977. pp. (38).

BOWER (JOSEPH L.) and CHRISTENSON (CHARLES J.) Public management: text and cases. Homewood, Ill., 1978. pp. 653.

KING (WILLIAM R.) and CLELAND (DAVID I.) Strategic planning and policy. New York, [1978]. pp. 374. *bibliogs.*

MANAGEMENT of financial resources in the National Health Service; (a report prepared...by a research team at the Centre for Industrial Economic and Business Research, University of Warwick: [John Perrin and others]). London, 1978. pp. 258. *(U.K. Royal Commission on the National Health Service, 1976. Research Papers. No.2)*

MILLER (P.A.) Lecturer in business administration, and others. Management in South Africa: an introductory text. Cape Town, 1978. pp. 214.

U.K. Civil Service Department. 1979. Guide for new managers. London, 1979. pp. 34. *First issued as a CSD departmental publication in 1975.*

WREN (DANIEL A.) The evolution of management thought. 2nd ed. New York, [1979]. pp. 598. *bibliog.*

— Data processing.

BRESLIN (JUDSON) and TASHENBERG (C. BRADLEY) Distributed processing systems: end of the mainframe era? New York, [1978]. pp. 228.

— Mathematical models.

TAPIERO (CHARLES S.) Managerial planning: an optimum and stochastic control approach. New York, [1977]. 2 vols. *bibliogs.*

— Study and teaching — United Kingdom.

U.K. Social Science Research Council. Bursary scheme. a. London. *Current issues only kept.*

MANAGEMENT GAMES.

HENDERSON (THOMAS A.) and FOSTER (JOHN L.) Urban policy game: a simulation of urban politics. New York, [1978]. pp. 137.

MANAGEMENT INFORMATION SYSTEMS.

EIN-DOR (PHILLIP) and SEGEV (ELI) Managing management information systems. Lexington, Mass., [1978]. pp. 191. *bibliogs.*

THIERAUF (ROBERT J.) Distributed processing systems. Englewood Cliffs, N.J., [1978]. pp. 305. *bibliogs.*

MANAGERIAL ACCOUNTING.

ACCOUNTING for managerial decision making...; editors: Don T. DeCoster [and others]. 2nd ed. Santa Barbara, [1978]. pp. 438. *bibliogs.*

MANAGERIAL ECONOMICS.

KOUTSOGIANNES (A.) Modern microeconomics. 2nd ed. London, 1979. pp. 581. *bibliog.*

MANAKHA

— Social conditions.

GERHOLM (TOMAS) Market, mosque and mafraj: social inequality in a Yemeni town. [Stockholm, 1977]. pp. 217. *bibliog. (Stockholms Universitet. Socialantropologiska Institutionen. Stockholm Studies in Social Anthropology. 4)*

MANCHESTER

— City planning.

MANCHESTER AND SALFORD INNER CITY PARTNERSHIP COMMITTEE. New life for the inner cities: the inner area programme 1979/80. [Manchester], 1979. 1 vol. (various pagings).

— Dwellings.

ELLIOTT (MARGARET) Writer on Housing. Shifting patterns in multi-occupation. Bristol, Social Science Research Council Research Unit on Ethnic Relations, [1978]. pp. 53. *(Working Papers on Ethnic Relations. No. 11)*

— Foreign population.

ELLIOTT (MARGARET) Writer on Housing. Shifting patterns in multi-occupation. Bristol, Social Science Research Council Research Unit on Ethnic Relations, [1978]. pp. 53. *(Working Papers on Ethnic Relations. No. 11)*

— Growth.

WIRTH (JOHN D.) and JONES (ROBERT L.) Writer on international studies, eds. Manchester and São Paulo: problems of rapid urban growth. Stanford, 1978. pp. 234. *Edited version of papers given at a conference sponsored by the Center for Latin American Studies of Stanford University in April 1977.*

— Race relations.

WARD (ROBIN W.) Where race didn't divide: some reflections on slum clearance in Moss Side. [Bristol, Social Science Research Council Research Unit on Ethnic Relations, 1976]. fo. 19.

— Social conditions.

MANCHESTER AND SALFORD INNER CITY PARTNERSHIP RESEARCH GROUP. Manchester and Salford inner area study. [Manchester, Department of the Environment North West Regional Office, 1978]. pp. 60.

— Social policy.

MANCHESTER AND SALFORD INNER CITY PARTNERSHIP COMMITTEE. New life for the inner cities: the inner area programme 1979/80. [Manchester], 1979. 1 vol. (various pagings).

MANCHESTER SHIP CANAL.

GRANT (RODERICK) The great canal. London, [1978]. pp. 156. *bibliog.*

MANCHESTER UNIVERSITY.

KELLY (THOMAS) M.A., Ph.D., F.R.Hist.S. Outside the walls: sixty years of university extension at Manchester, 1886-1946. Manchester, 1950. pp. 124.

MANCHURIA

— History.

IENAGA (SABURO) Japan's last war: World War II and the Japanese, 1931-1945. Oxford, 1979. pp. 316.

MANGABEIRA (OTAVIO).

MANGABEIRA (OTAVIO) Discursos parlamentares; seleção e introdução de Josephat Marinho. Brasilia, 1978. pp. 557. *(Brazil. Congresso. Câmara dos Deputados. Perfis Parlamentares. 10)*

MANIN (DANIELE).

GINSBORG (PAUL) Daniele Manin and the Venetian revolution of 1848-49. Cambridge, 1979. pp. 417. *bibliog.*

MANITOBA

— Government publications — Bibliography.

TOOTH (JOHN) ed. Looking for Manitoba government publications: an annotated bibliography of books and pamphlets. Winnipeg, 1978. pp. 264.

— History — Bibliography.

CANADA. National Library of Canada. 1970. Manitoba authors. Ottawa, 1970. 1 vol. (unpaged). *In English and French.*

MANNERS AND CUSTOMS.

ELIAS (NORBERT) The civilizing process: the history of manners; translated by Edmund Jephcott. Oxford, 1978. pp. 314.

MANORS

— United States.

KIM (SUNG BOK) Landlord and tenant in colonial New York: manorial society, 1664-1775. Chapel Hill, N.C. [1978]. pp. 456.

MANPOWER

— India — Kerala.

KERALA. Bureau of Economics and Statistics. 1978. Man power studies. vol. 1. Trivandrum, 1978. pp. 321.

MANPOWER POLICY.

BIEDENKOPF (KURT H.) and MIEGEL (MEINHARD) Wege aus der Arbeitslosigkeit: Arbeitsmarktpolitik in der sozialen Marktwirtschaft. Stuttgart, 1978. pp. 111. *(Institut für Wirtschafts- und Gesellschaftspolitik. IWG Impulse. Band 1)*

ORGANISATION FOR ECONOMIC CO-OPERATION AND DEVELOPMENT. 1978. A medium term strategy for employment and manpower policies. Paris, 1978. pp. 130.

— Mathematical models.

VAJDA (STEVEN) Mathematics of manpower planning. Chichester, [1978]. pp. 206. *bibliog.*

BARTHOLOMEW (DAVID JOHN) and FORBES (ANDREW F.) Statistical techniques for manpower planning. Chichester, [1979]. pp. 288. *bibliog.*

— Egypt.

UNITED ARAB REPUBLIC. Institute of National Planning. 1966. Manpower planning in the United Arab Republic. [Cairo, 1966]. pp. (182). *bibliog.*

— Sudan.

EL JACK (AHMED H.) and ALI TAHA (ABDEL RAHMAN E.) An evaluation of human resources planning in the Sudan: 1960- 1975. Khartoum, 1974. fo. 21. *(Economic and Social Research Council [Sudan]. Bulletins. No. 7)*

— Underdeveloped areas.

See UNDERDEVELOPED AREAS — Manpower policy.

— United Kingdom.

NATIONAL ECONOMIC DEVELOPMENT OFFICE and MANPOWER SERVICES COMMISSION [U.K.]. Case studies in company manpower planning; a joint OMSC/NEDO report. London, 1978. pp. 64. *bibliog.*

— United States.

SQUIRES (GREGORY D.) Education and jobs: the imbalancing of the social machinery. New Brunswick, N.J., [1979]. pp. 235. *bibliog.*

MANUEL II, King of Portugal.

BENTON (RUSSELL E.) The downfall of a king: Dom Manuel II of Portugal. Washington, [1977]. pp. 238. *bibliog.*

MANUFACTURERS

— France.

STEARNS (PETER N.) Paths to authority: the middle class and the industrial labor force in France, 1820-48. Urbana, Ill., [1978]. pp. 222. *bibliog.*

MANUFACTURES.

SPATIAL analysis, industry and the industrial environment: progress in research and applications. Vol. 1. Industrial systems; edited by F.E. Ian Hamilton and G.J.R. Linge. Chichester, [1979]. pp. 289. *bibliog.*

MANUSCRIPTS

— United Kingdom — Catalogues.

NORTHAMPTONSHIRE RECORD SOCIETY. [Publications]. vol. 28. The cartularies and registers of Peterborough Abbey; by Janet D. Martin. [Northampton], 1978. pp. 52.

MANUTIUS (ALDUS).

LOWRY (MARTIN) The world of Aldus Manutius: business and scholarship in Renaissance Venice. Oxford, [1979]. pp. 350. *bibliog.*

MAO (TSE-TUNG).

IASHCHENKO (GEORGII NIKOLAEVICH) Ideologicheskaia bor'ba v KNR, 1957-1964. Moskva, 1977. pp. 107. *bibliog.*

GOERLITZ (WALTER) Geldgeber der Macht: wie Hitler, Lenin, Mao Tse-tung, Mussolini, Stalin und Tito finanziert wurden. Frankfurt am Main, 1978. pp. 256. *bibliog.*

CORRIGAN (PHILIP R.D.) and others. For Mao: essays in historical materialism. London, 1979. pp. 207. *bibliog.*

WILSON (RICHARD GARRATT) Mao: the people's emperor. London, 1979. pp. 480. *bibliog.*

MAORIS

— Education.

BEST (ELSDON) The Maori school of learning: its objects, methods, and ceremonial. Wellington, [1923] repr. 1959. pp. 31. *(New Zealand. Dominion Museum. Monographs. No. 6)*

— Health and hygiene.

POPE (JAMES H.) Health for the Maori: a manual for use in native schools. 3rd ed, Wellington, Government Printer, 1901. pp. 152.

— Psychology.

BEST (ELSDON) Spiritual and mental concepts of the Maori. Wellington, [1922] repr. 1954. pp. 57. *(New Zealand. Dominion Museum. Monographs. No. 2)*

BEST (ELSDON) The Maori school of learning: its objects, methods, and ceremonial. Wellington, [1923] repr. 1959. pp. 31. *(New Zealand. Dominion Museum. Monographs. No. 6)*

— Religion.

BEST (ELSDON) Some aspects of Maori myth and religion. Wellington, [1922] repr. 1954. pp. 43. *(New Zealand. Dominion Museum. Monographs. No. 1)*

BEST (ELSDON) Spiritual and mental concepts of the Maori. Wellington, [1922] repr. 1954. pp. 57. *(New Zealand. Dominion Museum. Monographs. No. 2)*

MARCUSE (HERBERT).

BREUER (STEFAN) Die Krise der Revolutionstheorie: negative Vergesellschaftung und Arbeitsmetaphysik bei Herbert Marcuse. Frankfurt am Main, [1977]. pp. 308. *bibliog.*

MARIHUANA.

De BETEKENIS en de gevolgen van cannabis-gebruik. ['s-Gravenhage, 1969]. pp. 82. *(Netherlands. Ministerie van Sociale Zaken. Verslagen en Mededelingen betreffende de Volksgezondheid. 1969. 2)*

AULD (JOHN RICHARD MANSON) Deviant behaviour and social change: the case of marijuana use. 1978. fo. 340. *bibliog.* Typescript. Ph.D. (London) thesis: unpublished. *This thesis is the property of London University and may not be removed from the Library.*

MARINE RESOURCES.

OCEAN science: readings from Scientific American; with introductions by H.W. Menard. San Francisco, [1977]. pp. 307. *bibliog.*

— Law and legislation.

ECKERT (ROSS D.) The enclosure of ocean resources: economics and the law of the sea. Stanford, Calif., [1979]. pp. 390. *bibliog.*

MARITIME LAW.

ECKERT (ROSS D.) The enclosure of ocean resources: economics and the law of the sea. Stanford, Calif., [1979]. pp. 390. *bibliog.*

— Asia, Southeast.

LEE (YONG LENG) Southeast Asia and the law of the sea: some preliminary observations on the political geography of Southeast Asian seas. Singapore, [1978]. pp. 44. *bibliog.*

— France.

JAMBU-MERLIN (ROGER) Les gens de mer. Paris, 1978. pp. 317.

— United Kingdom.

GRIME (ROBERT PETER) Shipping law. London, 1978. ıpp. 261.

MARK (Sir ROBERT).

MARK (Sir ROBERT) In the office of constable. London, 1978. pp. 320.

MARKETING.

DAWSON (JOHN ALAN) The marketing environment. London, [1979]. pp. 379. *bibliogs.*

MARKETS.

NORDIN (CHRISTINA) A comparative study of markets in France and Sweden: methodological problems in market system research and attempt at a model; and, Le marché forain: un milieu d'achat apprécié mais peu connu. [Göteborg, 1977]. pp. 5,18. *bibliogs. (Göteborgs Universitet. Geografiska Institutioner. Meddelanden. Ser. B. Nr. 62)*

ENGLUND (PETER) Profits and market adjustment: a study in the dynamics of production, productivity and rates of return. Stockholm, 1979. pp. 260. *bibliog.*

MARKOV PROCESSES.

CHUNG (KAI LAI) Markov chains, with stationary transition probabilities. 2nd ed. Berlin, 1967. pp. 301. *bibliog.*

ADVANCED SEMINAR ON MARKOV DECISION, AMSTERDAM, 1976. Markov decision theory; proceedings of the...seminar...; edited by H.C. Tijms and J. Wessels. Amsterdam, 1977. pp. 220. *bibliogs. (Mathematical Centre. Tracts. [No.] 93)*

PORT (SIDNEY C.) and STONE (CHARLES JOEL) Brownian motion and classical potential theory. New York, 1978. pp. 236. *bibliog.*

WHITE (DOUGLAS JOHN) Finite dynamic programming: an approach to finite Markov decision processes. Chichester, [1978]. pp. 204. *bibliog.*

WILLIAMS (DAVID) 1938- . Diffusions, Markov processes and martingales. vol.1. Foundations. Chichester, [1979]. pp. 237. *bibliog.*

MARLBOROUGH (JOHN CHURCHILL) 1st Duke of.

See CHURCHILL (JOHN) 1st Duke of Marlborough.

MARRIAGE

— Andean Group.

ANDEAN kinship and marriage; edited by Ralph Bolton and Enrique Mayer. Washington, D.C., [1977]. pp. 296. *bibliog. (American Anthropologist. Special Publications. No.7)*

— **France.**

ROUSSEL (LOUIS) Demographer, and BOURGUIGNON (ODILE) Générations nouvelles et mariage traditionnel: enquête auprès de jeunes de 18-30 ans. [Paris], 1978. pp. 283. *(France. Institut National d'Etudes Démographiques. Travaux et Documents. Cahiers. No. 86)*

— **India.**

INDIA. Census. Papers. 1977. No 4. Census of India, 1971: Series 1: India...: female age at marriage: an analysis of 1971 census data. [Delhi, 1977]. pp. 40.

NAIR (P.T.) Marriage and dowry in India. Calcutta, 1978. pp. 205. *bibliog.*

— **Singapore.**

HASSAN (RIAZ) Interethnic marriage in Singapore: a study in interethnic relations. Singapore, 1974. pp. 85. *bibliog. (Institute of Southeast Asian Studies. Occasional Papers. No. 21)*

— **United Kingdom.**

COLEMAN (DAVID ANWYLL) Sociological, demographic and genetical aspects of the geographical origins of marriage partners since 1920. 1978. fo. 550. *bibliog.* Typescript. Ph.D.(London) thesis: unpublished. *This thesis is the property of London University and may not be removed from the Library.*

LEETE (RICHARD) Changing patterns of family formation and dissolution in England and Wales, 1964-76. London, 1979. pp. 130. *bibliog. (U.K. Office of Population Censuses and Surveys. Studies on Medical and Population Subjects. No. 39)*

U.K. Social Survey. [Reports. New Series]. 1080. Family formation 1976: a survey carried out on behalf of Population Statistics Division 1 of the Office of Population Censuses and Surveys of a sample of women, both single and ever married, aged 16-49 in Great Britain; [by] Karen Dunnell. London, 1979. pp. 117.

— **United States — California.**

CALIFORNIA. Department of Health. 1977. Marriage and marriage dissolution in California: marriages and final decrees of dissolution of marriage, judgment of nullity and legal separation, 1966-1973. [Sacramento], 1977. pp. 110. *bibliog.*

MARRIAGE CUSTOMS AND RITES, HINDU.

NAIR (P.T.) Marriage and dowry in India. Calcutta, 1978. pp. 205. *bibliog.*

MARRIAGE GUIDANCE

— **United Kingdom.**

U.K. Working Party on Marriage Guidance. 1979. Marriage matters: a consultative document; [H.W. Stotesbury, chairman]. London, 1979. pp. 146.

MARRIAGE LAW

— **Germany.**

ROBINSOHN (HANS) Justiz als politische Verfolgung: die Rechtsprechung in "Rassenschandefällen" beim Landgericht Hamburg 1936-1943. Stuttgart, 1977. pp. 168. *bibliog. (Vierteljahrshefte für Zeitgeschichte. Schriftenreihe. Nr.35)*

MARRIED WOMEN

— **Belgium.**

DOOGHE (GILBERT) and VANDERLEYDEN (L.) Bejaarden en hun levensvoldoening: een empirisch onderzoek bij weduwen en gehuwde vrouwen. Antwerp, 1978. pp. 132. *bibliog. (Centre d'Etude de la Population et de la Famille [Belgium]. Studies en Dokumenten. 10)*

MARSEILLE

— **Social conditions.**

MAURICE (MARC) and DELOMENIE (DOMINIQUE) Mode de vie et espaces sociaux: processus d'urbanisation et différenciation sociale dans deux zones urbaines de Marseille. Paris, [1976]. pp. 223. *bibliog.*

MARTIAL LAW

— **Rhodesia.**

RHODESIA. Ministry of Information, Immigration and Tourism. 1978. Martial law in Rhodesia 1978: how it will affect people in their daily lives. [Salisbury, 1978]. pp. 8.

MARTIN DU GARD (ROGER).

JOUEJATI (RAFIC) The quest for total peace: the political thought of Roger Martin du Gard. London, 1977. pp. 111. *bibliog.*

MARTINGALES (MATHEMATICS).

KUSSMAUL (ALFRED U.) Stochastic integration and generalized martingales. London, [1977]. pp. 163. *bibliog.*

CHOW (YUAN-SHIH) and TEICHER (HENRY) Probability theory: independence, interchangeability, martingales. New York, [1978]. pp. 455. *bibliogs.*

PROBABILITY on Banach spaces; edited by James Kuelbs. New York, [1978]. pp. 521. *bibliog.*

WILLIAMS (DAVID) 1938- . Diffusions, Markov processes and martingales. vol.1. Foundations. Chichester, [1979]. pp. 237. *bibliog.*

MARX (KARL).

CUDDIHY (JOHN MURRAY) The ordeal of civility: Freud, Marx, Lévi-Strauss, and the Jewish struggle with modernity. New York, [1974]. pp. 272.

KUCZYNSKI (JUERGEN) Studien zu einer Geschichte der Gesellschaftswissenschaften. Berlin, 1975-78. 10 vols.

HARRISON (FRED) B.A., M.Sc. Marx, economic growth and land taxation. London, 1975. pp. 27. *(Economic and Social Science Research Association. Discussion Papers. No. 2)*

MOLNÁR (MIKLÓS) Marx, Engels et la politique internationale. Paris, 1975. pp. 385. *bibliog.*

JAGUIN (AURELIANO) Il geroglifico sociale: forze produttive e strutture di classe in Marx. Bari, [1976]. pp. 462.

MARX-ENGELS JAHRBUCH; hrsg. vom Institut für Marxismus- Leninismus (Berlin). a., [1977] (no.1)- Berlin.

BRAVO (GIAN MARIO) ed. Da Weitling a Marx: la Lega dei Comunisti; [a collection of documents]. Milano, [1977]. pp. 307. *bibliog.*

SHEVTSOV (IVAN SEMENOVICH) Voprosy metodologii "Kapitala" K. Marksa. Kazan', 1977. pp. 104.

BENSON (LESLIE) Proletarians and parties: five essays in social class. London, 1978. pp. 194. *bibliog.*

GOULD (CAROL C.) Marx's social ontology: individuality and community in Marx's theory of social reality. Cambridge, Mass., [1978]. pp. 208. *bibliog.*

HORNUNG (KLAUS) Der faszinierende Irrtum: Karl Marx und die Folgen. Freiburg im Breisgau, 1978. pp. 160. *bibliog.*

KARL Marx und Friedrich Engels: ihr Leben und ihre Zeit; (Herausgeber:...Karl-Heinz Mahlert, Leitung). Berlin, [1978]. pp. 352.

LAUFNER (RICHARD) and KOENIG (KARL LUDWIG) Bruno Bauer, Karl Marx und Trier: ein unbekannter Brief von Bruno Bauer an Karl Marx und radikale Vormärzliteratur in der Stadtbibliothek Trier. Trier, [1978]. pp. 28. *(Karl-Marx-Haus. Schriften. 20)*

McCARTHY (TIMOTHY) Marx and the proletariat: a study in social theory. Westport, 1978. pp. 102 *bibliog.*

MARXIAN ECONOMICS.

MARX' Verhaftung und Ausweisung, Brüssel, Februar/März 1848; ([edited by] Bert Andréas). Trier, [1978]. pp. 148. *bibliog. (Karl-Marx-Haus. Schriften. 22)*

ROSE (MARGARET A.) Reading the young Marx and Engels: poetry, parody and the censor. London, 1978. pp. 165. *bibliog.*

ROTH (MIKE) and ELDRED (MICHAEL) Guide to Marx's "Capital". London, 1978. pp. 127. *(Conference of Socialist Economists. CSE Books)*

SEIGEL (JERROLD E.) Marx's fate: the shape of a life. Princeton, [1978]. pp. 451.

STEINER (HERBERT) 1923- . Karl Marx in Wien: die Arbeiterbewegung zwischen Revolution und Restauration, 1848. Wien, [1978]. pp. 223.

UCHENIE K. Marksa, F. Engel'sa, V.I. Lenina o sotsialisticheskom gosudarstve i prave: istoriia razvitiia i sovremennost'. Moskva, 1978. pp. 431. *Continuation of Marksistsko-leninskoe uchenie o gosudarstve i prave, Moskva, 1977.*

...UNSRER Partei einen Sieg erringen: Studien zur Entstehungs- und Wirkungsgeschichte des "Kapitals" von Karl Marx: ein Sammelband; (wissenschaftliche Redaktion: Roland Nietzold [and others]). Berlin, [1978]. pp. 272.

VOLPE (GALVANO DELLA) Rousseau and Marx. London, 1978. pp. 206.

ZANDER (JUERGEN) Das Problem der Beziehung Max Webers zu Karl Marx. Frankfurt/Main, [1978]. pp. 179. *bibliog.*

ISSUES in Marxist philosophy; edited by John Mepham and David Hillel Ruben. Brighton, 1979. 3 vols. *bibliogs.*

MAAREK (GÉRARD) An introduction to Karl Marx's Das Kapital: a study in formalisation...; (translated by Mansel Evans). Oxford, 1979. pp. 233. *bibliog.*

RADDATZ (FRITZ J.) Karl Marx: a political biography. London, 1979. pp. 335. *bibliog.*

— **Bibliography.**

EUBANKS (CECIL L.) compiler. Karl Marx and Friedrich Engels: an analytical bibliography. New York, 1977. pp. 163.

GRIN (TSILIA IOSIFOVNA) compiler. K. Marks, F. Engel's i revoliutsionnaia Rossiia: k 160- letiiu so dnia rozhdeniia K. Marksa: rekomendatel'nyi ukazatel' literatury; nauchnyi redaktor S.S. Volk. Moskva, 1978. pp. 95.

MARXIAN ECONOMICS.

DVA podrazdeleniia obshchestvennogo produkta: metodologiia deleniia; pod redaktsiei A.I. Zalkinda. Moskva, 1976. pp. 191. *bibliog.*

POLIANSKII (FEDOR IAKOVLEVICH) Kritika ekonomicheskikh teorii anarkhizma. Moskva, 1976. pp. 301.

KAPITALISTISCHE Ausbeutung heute: Autorenkollektiv DR-UdSSR; (verantwortliche Redaktion: Günter Fabiunke [and others]). Berlin, [1977]. pp. 264.

LUKINOV (IVAN ILLARIONOVICH) Vosproizvodstvo i tseny. Moskva, 1977. pp. 431.

SAWER (MARIAN) Marxism and the question of the Asiatic mode of production. The Hague, 1977. pp. 252. *bibliog. (International Institute of Social History. Studies in Social History. [No.] 3)*

SHCHERBINA (VLADIMIR FEDOROVICH) Problemy dialekticheskikh protivorechii v ekonomike sotsializma. Leningrad, 1977. pp. 112.

VOITSEKHOVSKII (VIKTOR ALEKSANDROVICH) Sistema ekonomicheskikh zakonov razvitogo sotsializma. Minsk, 1977. pp. 270.

AMIN (SAMIR) The law of value and historical materialism...; (translated by Brian Pearce). New York, [1978]. pp. 133.

MARXIAN ECONOMICS.(Cont.)

BOCCARA (PAUL) Sur la mise en mouvement du "Capital": premiers essais. [Paris, 1978]. pp. 334.

CLARKSON (STEPHEN) The Soviet theory of development: India and the third world in marxist-leninist scholarship. Toronto, 1978. pp. 322.

GESCHICHTE der politischen Ökonomie: Grundriss; (herausgegeben von Herbert Meissner). Frankfurt am Main, 1978. pp. 683.

MANDEL (ERNEST) The second slump: a marxist analysis of recession in the seventies; translated by Jon Rothschild. London, 1978. pp. 212.

POKRYTAN (ANATOLII KARPOVICH) Istoricheskoe i logicheskoe v ekonomicheskoi teorii sotsializma. Moskva, 1978. pp. 248.

ROTH (MIKE) and ELDRED (MICHAEL) Guide to Marx's "Capital". London, 1978. pp. 127. *(Conference of Socialist Economists. CSE Books)*

SHAW (WILLIAM HARRY) Marx's theory of history. Stanford, 1978. pp. 202. *bibliog.*

...UNSRER Partei einen Sieg erringen: Studien zur Entstehungs- und Wirkungsgeschichte des "Kapitals" von Karl Marx: ein Sammelband; (wissenschaftliche Redaktion: Roland Nietzold [and others]). Berlin, [1978]. pp. 272.

WEISS (OTTO GEORGES) Critique de "l'économie marxiste traditionnelle". [Paris, 1978]. pp. 295. *bibliog.*

DESAI (MEGHNAD J.) Marxian economics. Oxford, [1979]. pp. 265. *bibliog.*

ELLMAN (MICHAEL JOHN) Socialist planning. Cambridge, 1979. pp. 300. *bibliog.*

FINE (BENJAMIN JOLLY) and HARRIS (LAURENCE) Rereading Capital. London, 1979. pp. 184. *bibliog.*

KAY (GEOFFREY B.) The economic theory of the working class. London, 1979. pp. 140. *bibliog.*

MAAREK (GÉRARD) An introduction to Karl Marx's Das Kapital: a study in formalisation...; (translated by Mansel Evans). Oxford, 1979. pp. 233. *bibliog.*

ROUSSEAS (STEPHEN W.) Capitalism and catastrophe: a critical appraisal of the limits to capitalism. Cambridge, 1979. pp. 139. *bibliog.*

SAYER (DEREK) Marx's method: ideology, science and critique in "Capital". Hassocks, 1979. pp. 197. *bibliog.*

SENSAT (JULIUS) Habermas and Marxism: an appraisal. Beverly Hills, [1979]. pp. 176. *bibliog.*

MARXISM.

LENINISMUS: neue Stufe des wissenschaftlichen Sozialismus?: zum Verhältnis von Marxscher Theorie, Klassenanalyse und revolutionärer Taktik bei W.I. Lenin; ([by] Projekt Klassenanalyse). Westberlin, [1972]. 2 vols. (in 1).

LEONHARD (WOLFGANG) Three faces of Marxism: the political concepts of Soviet ideology, Maoism, and humanist Marxism; (translated [from the German] by Ewald Osers). New York, [1974]. pp. 497. *bibliog.*

MARXIXME-léninisme et psychanalysme?sic!. Paris, 1975. pp. 162. *(Groupe Yenan. Cahiers Yenan. No. 1)*

ESERCITO e società borghese: l'istituzione militare nell'analisi marxista; a cura di Fabrizio Battistelli. Roma, 1976. pp. 336. *bibliog.*

GAVIN (WILLIAM J.) and BLAKELEY (THOMAS J.) Russia and America: a philosophical comparison: development and change of outlook from the 19th to the 20th century. Dordrecht, [1976]. pp. 114. *(Freiburg (Switzerland). Universität. Ost-Europa Institut. Sovietica. vol. 38)*

JAGUIN (AURELIANO) Il geroglifico sociale: forze produttive e strutture di classe in Marx. Bari, [1976]. pp. 462.

MARX (KARL) and ENGELS (FRIEDRICH) The German ideology; translated from the German. 3rd ed. Moscow, 1976. pp. 711. *bibliog.*

MORRA (GIANFRANCO) Marxismo e religione. Milano, 1976 repr. 1977. pp. 317.

WIELENGA (BASTIAAN) Marxist views on India in historical perspective. Madras, 1976. pp. 155. *(Christian Institute for the Study of Religion and Society. Studies on Indian Marxism. No. 2)*

MARX-ENGELS JAHRBUCH; hrsg. vom Institut für Marxismus- Leninismus (Berlin). a., [1977] (no.1)- Berlin.

BANFI (ANTONIO) La crisi della civiltà borghese e il marxismo; introduzione, scelta e note a cura di Giovanni Mari. Firenze, 1977. pp. 346. *bibliog.*

FÖLDESI (TAMÁS) Grundlagen der Beweistheorie der marxistischen Philosophie; (aus dem Ungarischen übersetzt von Maria Bondy). Köln, 1977. pp. 480.

GIORGETTI (GIORGIO) Capitalismo e agricoltura in Italia. Roma, 1977. pp. 591.

GLUCKSMANN (ANDRE) Les maîtres penseurs. Paris, [1977]. pp. 323.

METODOLOGICHESKIE problemy istorii filosofii i obshchestvennoi mysli. Moskva, 1977. pp. 360. *bibliog.*

PEERY (SUE) ed. Outline for the study of Marxism-Leninism; prepared under the direction of the National Education Committee, Communist Labor Party of the United States of North America. Chicago, [1977]. pp. 190. *bibliogs.*

SOCIETÀ, politica e stato in Hegel, Marx e Gramsci; [by] Remo Bodei [and others]. Padova, 1977. pp. 111.

UCHENYE ZAPISKI KAFEDR OBSHCHESTVENNYKH NAUK VUZOV LENINGRADA. Filosofiia. vyp.17. Filosofskie i sotsiologicheskie issledovaniia. Leningrad, 1977. pp. 200.

"ANTI-Diuring" F. Engel'sa i sovremennost'. Moskva, 1978. pp. 192. *bibliog.*

BOCCARA (PAUL) Sur la mise en mouvement du "Capital": premiers essais. [Paris, 1978]. pp. 334.

COE (SAMUEL P.) Contemporary psychology in Marx and Engels. New York, 1978. pp. 53. *(American Institute for Marxist Studies. Occasional Papers. No. 26)*

COHEN (G.A.) Karl Marx's theory of history: a defence. Oxford, 1978. pp. 369. *bibliog.*

COMMUNIST WORKERS' MOVEMENT. Why Paul Foot should be a socialist: the case against the Socialist Workers' Party. Liverpool, 1978. pp. 198.

DAVIS (HORACE BANCROFT) Toward a Marxist theory of nationalism. New York, [1978]. pp. 294. *bibliog.*

FLECHTHEIM (OSSIP KURT) Von Marx bis Kolakowski: Sozialismus oder Untergang in der Barbarei? Köln, [1978]. pp. 286.

GOMBIN (RICHARD) The radical tradition: a study in modern revolutionary thought; translated by Rupert Swyer. London, 1978. pp. 153. *bibliog.*

HORNUNG (KLAUS) Der faszinierende Irrtum: Karl Marx und die Folgen. Freiburg im Breisgau, 1978. pp. 160. *bibliog.*

JENSEN (KENNETH MARTIN) Beyond Marx and Mach: Aleksandr Bogdanov's philosophy of living experience. Dordrecht, [1978]. pp. 189. *bibliog. (Freiburg (Switzerland). Universität. Ost- Europa Institut. Sovietica. vol. 41)*

KLEVCHENIA (ALEKSANDR SEMENOVICH) Ocherki po istorii marksistsko-leninskoi filosofskoi mysli v Pol'she. Minsk, 1978. pp. 198. *bibliog.*

KOŁAKOWSKI (LESZEK) Main currents of Marxism: its rise, growth, and dissolution;... translated from the Polish by P.S. Falla. Oxford, 1978. 3 vols. *bibliogs.*

LEONHARD (WOLFGANG) Was ist Kommunismus?: Wandlungen einer Ideologie. [Munich], 1978. pp. 271. *bibliog.*

MACGREGOR (DAVID EDWARD STEPHEN) Studies in the concept of ideology: from the Hegelian dialectic to western Marxism. 1978. fo. 504. *bibliog.* Typescript. Ph.D. (London) thesis: unpublished. This thesis is the property of London University and may not be removed from the Library.

MARTIN (DAVID ALFRED) The dilemmas of contemporary religion. Oxford, [1978]. pp. 104.

MARX: sociology/social change/capitalism; edited by Donald McQuarie. London, 1978. pp. 327. *bibliogs.*

MARXIST humanism and Praxis; edited, with translations, by Gerson S. Sher. New York, 1978. pp. 183.

MOLYNEUX (JOHN) Marxism and the party. London, 1978. pp. 192.

NOVACK (GEORGE) Polemics in Marxist philosophy. New York, [1978]. pp. 344. *bibliog.*

NYILAS (JÓZSEF) Marxist approach to the problems of appropriate technology. Budapest, 1978. pp. 48. *(Hungarian Scientific Council for World Economy. [Publications]. Trends in World Economy. No. 26)*

PANNEKOEK (ANTON) and GORTER (HERMAN) Pannekoek and Gorter's Marxism; (edited and introduced by D. A. Smart). London, 1978. pp. 176.

PLOTNIEK (ANDRIS ADAMOVICH) Stanovlenie i razvitie marksistsko-leninskoi obshchei teorii prava v SSSR, 1917-1936 gg. Riga, 1978. pp. 295.

PONZIO (AUGUSTO) Marxismo, scienza e problema dell'uomo, con un'intervista dell'autore ad Adam Schaff. Verona, [1978]. pp. 270.

RAMM (HARTMUT) The Marxism of Régis Debray: between Lenin and Guevara. Lawrence, Kan., [1978]. pp. 240. *bibliog.*

SARUP (MADAN) Marxism and education. London, 1978. pp. 224.

VOLODIN (ALEKSANDR IVANOVICH) "Anti-Diuring" F.Engel'sa i obshchestvennaia mysl' Rossii XIX veka: istoriko-filosofskie ocherki. Moskva, 1978. pp. 252.

VYGODSKII (VITALII SOLOMONOVICH) Das Werden der ökonomischen Theorie von Marx und der wissenschaftliche Kommunismus; (aus dem Russischen übersetzt von G. Rieske). Berlin, 1978. pp. 312.

BLANK (FRANK VON) Rote Werwölfe: Volksfront gegen die Völker Europas. Rosenheim, [1979]. pp. 192.

EDDY (WILLIAM HENRY CHARLES) Understanding Marxism: an approach through dialogue. Oxford, 1979. pp. 157. *bibliog.*

GOODE (PATRICK) Karl Korsch: a study in western marxism. London, 1979. pp. 239. *bibliog.*

GRUJIĆ (PREDRAG M.) Von Marx bis Berlinguer: klassischer Marxismus und Eurokommunismus. Würzburg, [1979]. pp. 126.

HIRST (PAUL QUENTIN) On law and ideology. London, 1979. pp. 181. *bibliog.*

ISSUES in Marxist philosophy; edited by John Mepham and David Hillel Ruben. Brighton, 1979. 3 vols. *bibliogs.*

MARX and Engels on law; [edited by] Maureen Cain [and] Alan Hunt. London, 1979. pp. 281.

PARKIN (FRANK IORWETH) Marxism and class theory: a bourgeois critique. London, 1979. pp. 217. *bibliog.*

SENSAT (JULIUS) Habermas and Marxism: an appraisal. Beverly Hills, [1979]. pp. 176. *bibliog.*

SUMNER (COLIN) Reading ideologies: an investigation into the Marxist theory of ideology and law. London, 1979. pp. 313. *bibliog.*

TOWARD a Marxist anthropology: problems and perspectives; editor, Stanley Diamond. The Hague, [1979]. pp. 492. *bibliogs.*

ULAM (ADAM BRUNO) The unfinished revolution: marxism and communism in the modern world. rev. ed. Boulder, Colo., 1979. pp. 287.

— **Dictionaries and encyclopedias.**

MARXISTISCH-leninistisches Wörterbuch der Philosophie; herausgegeben von Georg Klaus und Manfred Buhr. new ed. Reinbek bei Hamburg, 1975 repr. 1977-79. 3 vols.

MARXISM AND SOCIAL SCIENCES.

MARX (KARL) Selected writings in sociology and social philosophy; edited with an introduction and notes by T.B. Bottomore and Maximilien Rubel..., translated by T.B. Bottomore. Harmondsworth, 1963. pp. 272.

COX (TERENCE M.) Rural sociology in the Soviet Union: its history and basic concepts. London, [1979]. pp. 106. *bibliog.*

TOWARD a Marxist anthropology: problems and perspectives; editor, Stanley Diamond. The Hague, [1979]. pp. 492. *bibliogs.*

MARYLAND

— **Economic history.**

CONFERENCE ON MARYLAND HISTORY, 1ST., ANNAPOLIS, 1974. Law, society and politics in early Maryland; (proceedings...); edited by Aubrey C. Land [and others]. Baltimore, [1977]. pp. 350. *(Maryland. Hall of Records Commission. Studies in Maryland History and Culture)*

— **History.**

CONFERENCE ON MARYLAND HISTORY, 1ST., ANNAPOLIS, 1974. Law, society and politics in early Maryland; (proceedings...); edited by Aubrey C. Land [and others]. Baltimore, [1977]. pp. 350. *(Maryland. Hall of Records Commission. Studies in Maryland History and Culture)*

— **Politics and government.**

RISJORD (NORMAN K.) Chesapeake politics 1781-1800. New York, 1978. pp. 715. *bibliog.*

— **Social history.**

CONFERENCE ON MARYLAND HISTORY, 1ST., ANNAPOLIS, 1974. Law, society and politics in early Maryland; (proceedings...); edited by Aubrey C. Land [and others]. Baltimore, [1977]. pp. 350. *(Maryland. Hall of Records Commission. Studies in Maryland History and Culture)*

MASARYK (THOMAS GARRIGUE).

FUNDA (OTAKAR A.) Thomas Garrigue Masaryk: sein philosophisches, religiöses und politisches Denken. Bern, [1978]. pp. 268. *bibliog.*

MASHONA.

OLIVEIRA (CARLOS MANUEL GRAÇA RAMOS DE) Os Tauaras de vale do Zambeze. [Lisboa], Junta de Investigações Cientificas do Ultramar, 1976. pp. 120. *bibliog. Includes summary in English.*

MASS MEDIA.

The USES of mass communications: current perspectives on gratifications research; Jay G. Blumler and Elihu Katz, editors. Beverly Hills, [1974]. pp. 318. *bibliogs.*

COMMUNICATION research: a half-century appraisal; edited by Daniel Lerner and Lyle M. Nelson. Honolulu, [1977]. pp. 348. *bibliog.*

HOGGART (RICHARD) The mass media: a new colonialism? London, [1978]. pp. 6. *(Standard Telephones and Cables. Communication Lectures. 1978)*

— **Political aspects — South Africa.**

CHIMUTENGWENDE (CHENHAMO C.) South Africa: the press and the politics of liberation. London, 1978. pp. 197. *bibliog.*

— — **United Kingdom.**

SEYMOUR-URE (COLIN) The political impact of mass media. London, 1974 repr. 1976. pp. 296. *bibliog.*

SWANN (Sir MICHAEL MEREDITH) Are the lamps going out? London, [1977]. pp. 15. *(Claysmore Lectures. 1977)*

— — — **Ireland, Northern.**

ETHNICITY and the media: an analysis of media reporting in the United Kingdom, Canada and Ireland. Paris, United Nations Educational, Scientific and Cultural Organization, 1977. pp. 376. *bibliogs.*

— — **United States.**

SIMMONS (STEVEN J.) The fairness doctrine and the media. Berkeley, [1978]. pp. 285. *bibliog.*

— **Psychological aspects.**

CASSATA (MARY B.) and ASANTE (MOLEFI K.) Mass communication: principles and practices. New York, [1979]. pp. 360. *bibliog.*

— **Social aspects.**

WILSON (DAVID) Science correspondent. The communicators and society. Oxford, 1968. pp. 121. *bibliog.*

CASSATA (MARY B.) and ASANTE (MOLEFI K.) Mass communication: principles and practices. New York, [1979]. pp. 360. *bibliog.*

— — **United States.**

DEVIANCE and mass media; edited by Charles Winick. Beverly Hills, [1978]. pp. 309. *bibliogs.*

— **Underdeveloped areas.**

See UNDERDEVELOPED AREAS — Mass media.

— **United Kingdom — Scotland.**

HEADLINES: the media in Scotland; edited by David Hutchison. Edinburgh, 1978. pp. 112. *bibliog.*

— **United States.**

PEMBER (DON R.) Mass media in America. 2nd ed. Chicago, [1977]. pp. 389.

MASS MEDIA AND LITERATURE

— **Germany.**

WIESAND (ANDREAS JOHANNES) and FOHRBECK (KARLA) Literature and the public in the Federal Republic of Germany. Munich, [1976]. pp. 103.

MASS MEDIA AND RACE RELATIONS.

RACE as news; introduction by James D. Halloran; two general studies on attitude change by Otto Klineberg and Colette Guillaumin and a study of the British national press by Paul Hartmann, Charles Husband and Jean Clark. Paris, The Unesco Press, 1974. pp. 173. *bibliog.*

MASSACHUSETTS

— **Politics and government.**

HOERDER (DIRK) Crowd action in revolutionary Massachusetts, 1765-1780. New York, [1977]. pp. 394.

MASSACHUSETTS LOCAL INITIATIVE PROGRAM.

PRAGER (AUDREY) Job creation in the community: an evaluation of locally initiated employment projects in Massachusetts. Cambridge, Mass., [1977]. pp. 175.

MASSIF CENTRAL.

FRANCE. Délégation à l'Aménagement du Territoire et à l'Action Régionale. 1978. Le Massif Central: [forests; by J. le Ray and others]. [Paris, 1978]. pp. 126. *(Massif Central. Dossiers. 4)*

FRANCE. Mission des Villes du Massif Central. 1979. Le Massif Central: politique des villes et des pays. Paris, [1979]. pp. 112. *(France. Délégation à l'Aménagement du Territoire et à l'Action Régionale. Massif Central. Dossiers. 5)*

MATABELE.

RASMUSSEN (R. KENT) Migrant kingdom: Mzilikazi's Ndebele in South Africa. London, 1978. pp. 262. *bibliog.*

MATERIALISM.

MARX (KARL) and ENGELS (FRIEDRICH) The German ideology; translated from the German. 3rd ed. Moscow, 1976. pp. 711. *bibliog.*

MATERNAL AND INFANT WELFARE.

KLAUS (MARSHALL H.) and KENNELL (JOHN H.) Maternal-infant bonding: (the impact of early separation or loss on family development). Saint Louis, 1976. pp. 260. *bibliog.*

MATHEMATICAL ANALYSIS.

MITRINOVIC (DRAGOSLAV S.) Analytic inequalities. New York, 1970. pp. 400.

BEALS (RICHARD) Advanced mathematical analysis: periodic functions and distributions, complex analysis, Laplace transform and applications. New York, [1973]. pp. 230. *bibliog.*

MATHEMATICAL MODELS.

MATHEMATICAL modelling; edited by J.G. Andrews and R.R. McLone. London, 1976. pp. 260. *bibliog.*

OLINICK (MICHAEL) An introduction to mathematical models in the social and life sciences. Reading, Mass., [1978]. pp. 466. *bibliogs.*

ROBERTS (PETER C.) Modelling large systems: (limits to growth revisited). London, 1978. pp. 120. *bibliog. (Operational Research Society. ORASA Texts. No. 4)*

MATHEMATICAL OPTIMIZATION.

ADBY (P.R.) and DEMPSTER (M.A.H.) Introduction to optimization methods. London, 1974 repr. 1978. pp. 204. *bibliog.*

ZIEMBA (W.T.) and VICKSON (R.G.) eds. Stochastic optimization models in finance. New York, [1975]. pp. 719. *bibliogs.*

EKELAND (IVAR) and TEMAM (ROGER) Convex analysis and variational problems. Amsterdam, 1976. pp. 402. *bibliog.*

LAWLER (EUGENE L.) Combinatorial optimization: networks and matroids. New York, [1976]. pp. 374.

NEUSTADT (L.W.) Optimization: a theory of necessary conditions. Princeton, N.J., 1976. pp. 424. *bibliog.*

KOO (DELIA) Elements of optimization with applications in economics and business. New York, [1977]. pp. 220. *bibliog.*

MURATA (YASUO) Mathematics for stability and optimization of economic systems. New York, 1977. pp. 418. *bibliog.*

DINAMICHESKAIA i veroiatnostnaia optimizatsiia ekonomiki; otvetstvennyi redaktor K.K. Val'tukh. Novosibirsk, 1978. pp. 368. *(Akademiia Nauk SSSR. Sibirskoe Otdelenie. Institut Ekonomiki i Organizatsii Promyshlennogo Proizvodstva. Problemy Narodnokhoziaistvennogo Optimuma. [vyp. 5])*

WOLFE (MICHAEL ANTHONY) Numerical methods for unconstrained optimization: an introduction. New York, 1978. pp. 312. *bibliog.*

MATHEMATICAL STATISTICS.

MATHEMATICAL STATISTICS.

BARNETT (VIC) Comparative statistical inference. London, [1973] repr. 1975. pp. 287. *bibliogs.*

KAGAN (ABRAM MEEROVICH) and others. Characterization problems in mathematical statistics. New York, [1973]. pp. 499. *bibliog.*

CHAMBERS (JOHN M.) Computational methods for data analysis. New York, [1977]. pp. 268. *bibliog.*

McNEIL (DONALD R.) Interactive data analysis: a practical primer. New York, [1977]. pp. 186.

ALLEN (ARNOLD O.) Probability, statistics and queueing theory: with computer science applications. New York, 1978. pp. 390.

MOORE (RICHARD W.) Introduction to the use of computer packages for statistical analyses. Englewood Cliffs, N.J., [1978]. pp. 115.

FRASER (DONALD ALEXANDER STUART) Inference and linear models. New York, [1979]. pp. 297. *bibliogs.*

JENKINS (GWILYM M.) Practical experiences with modelling and forecasting time series. St. Helier, 1979. pp. 146.

— Tables, etc.

CRC handbook of tables for probability and statistics;...editor William H. Beyer. 2nd ed. Cleveland, Ohio, 1968 repr. 1976. pp. 642.

MATHEMATICS.

VON NEUMANN (JOHN) Collected works; general editor: A.H. Taub. New York, 1961-63. 6 vols. *bibliogs. Reprinted 1976; papers mainly in English, but some in German or Hungarian.*

DOERRIE (HEINRICH) 100 great problems of elementary mathematics: their history and solution; translated by David Antin. New York, [1965]. pp. 393.

DIEUDONNÉ (JEAN) Panorama des mathématiques pures: le choix bourbachique. [Paris, 1977]. pp. 302. *bibliog.*

GARDING (LARS) Encounter with mathematics. New York, [1977]. pp. 270.

WHIPKEY (KENNETH L.) and others. The power of mathematics: applications to management and the social sciences. New York, [1978]. pp. 452.

— Philosophy.

WITTGENSTEIN (LUDWIG) Remarks on the foundation of mathematics; (edited by G.H. von Wright [and others]; translated by G.E.M. Anscombe). 3rd ed. Oxford, 1978. pp. 444.

MENGER (CARL) Son of Carl Menger the Economist. Selected papers in logic and foundations, didactics, economics. Dordrecht, [1979]. pp. 341. *bibliog.*

— Study and teaching.

MENGER (CARL) Son of Carl Menger the Economist. Selected papers in logic and foundations, didactics, economics. Dordrecht, [1979]. pp. 341. *bibliog.*

MATRIMONIAL ACTIONS

— United Kingdom.

PASSINGHAM (BERNARD) Law and practice in matrimonial causes; third edition by B. Passingham and Caroline Harmer. London, 1979. pp. 529.

— — Ireland, Northern.

IRELAND, NORTHERN. Supreme Court. 1979. Rules of the Supreme Court, Northern Ireland, 1979. [Belfast, 1979]. 1 vol. (loose-leaf). *Issued as Statutory Rules of Northern Ireland.*

MATROIDS.

LAWLER (EUGENE L.) Combinatorial optimization: networks and matroids. New York, [1976]. pp. 374.

MATURATION (PSYCHOLOGY).

GUBRIUM (JABER F.) and BUCKHOLDT (DAVID R.) Toward maturity: the social processing of human development. San Francisco, 1977. pp. 224. *bibliog.*

MAUDE (H.E.)

The CHANGING Pacific: essays in honour of H.E. Maude; edited by Niel Gunson. Melbourne, 1978. pp. 351. *bibliog.*

MAUDLING (REGINALD).

MAUDLING (REGINALD) Memoirs. London, 1978. pp. 285.

MAURITIUS

— Economic conditions.

MAURITIUS. 1978. The fruits of political and social democracy: 10th anniversary of the independence of Mauritius. [Port Louis, Government Printer, 1978]. pp. 33.

MAURITIUS. Ministry of Information and Broadcasting. 1978. Glanures. [Port Louis, 1978]. pp. 43.

MANNICK (A.R.) Mauritius: the development of a plural society. Nottingham, 1979. pp. 174. *bibliog.*

— Foreign relations.

MAURITIUS. Ministry of Information and Broadcasting. 1978. Glanures. [Port Louis, 1978]. pp. 43.

— Full employment policies.

SEMINAIRE SUR LE CHOMAGE, PORT LOUIS, 1971. Séminaire sur le chômage: [report]. Port Louis, Ministère de l'Information, 1971. pp. 12. *Issue of Inforama: bulletin d'information et de documentation. Vol. 10, No. 7.*

— Politics and government.

MAURITIUS. 1978. The fruits of political and social democracy: 10th anniversary of the independence of Mauritius. [Port Louis, Government Printer, 1978]. pp. 33.

MAURITIUS. Ministry of Information and Broadcasting. 1978. Glanures. [Port Louis, 1978]. pp. 43.

MANNICK (A.R.) Mauritius: the development of a plural society. Nottingham, 1979. pp. 174. *bibliog.*

— Social conditions.

MAURITIUS. 1978. The fruits of political and social democracy: 10th anniversary of the independence of Mauritius. [Port Louis, Government Printer, 1978]. pp. 33.

MANNICK (A.R.) Mauritius: the development of a plural society. Nottingham, 1979. pp. 174. *bibliog.*

MAYA LITERATURE

— History and criticism.

LEON-PORTILLA (MIGUEL) Pre-Columbian literatures of Mexico. Norman, 1969. pp. 191.

MAYAGUEZ CRISIS, 1975.

SIMMONS (ROBERT R.) The Pueblo, EC-121, and Mayaguez incidents: some continuities and changes. Baltimore, 1978. pp. 51. *(Maryland University. School of Law. Occasional Papers/Reprints Series in Contemporary Asian Studies. No.20)*

MAYAS.

WEAVER (MURIEL PORTER) The Aztecs, Maya, and their predecessors. New York, 1972. pp. 347. *bibliog. (Northwestern University. Studies in Archaeology)*

— Medicine.

ROYS (RALPH LOVELAND) The ethno-botany of the Maya; with a new introduction and supplemental bibliography by Sheila Cosminsky. Philadelphia, 1976. pp. 380. *bibliog. (Institute for the Study of Human Issues. ISHI Reprints on Latin America and the Caribbean) Reprint of the edition of 1931.*

MAZAHUA INDIANS.

IWANSKA (ALICJA) Purgatorio y utopia: una aldea de los indigenas mazahuas; (traduccion de Hector David Torres). Mexico, Secretaria de Educacion Publica, 1972. pp. 204. *(Sep/Setentas. 41)*

MARGOLIES (BARBARA LUISE) Princes of the earth: subcultural diversity in a Mexican municipality. Washington, [1975]. pp. 179. *bibliog. (American Anthropological Association. Special Publications. [New Series]. No. 2)*

MEAD (MARGARET).

MEAD (MARGARET) Letters from the field, 1925-1975. New York, [1977]. pp. 343. *bibliog.*

MEASURE THEORY.

PFANZAGL (J.) and PIERLO (W.) Compact systems of sets. Berlin, 1966. pp. 48. *bibliog.*

DE BARRA (G.) Introduction to measure theory. New York, 1974. pp. 287. *bibliog.*

PARTHASARATHY (K.R.) Introduction to probability and measure. Delhi, 1977. pp. 312. *bibliog.*

MEAT

— Prices — France.

FRANCE. Centre d'Etude des Revenus et des Coûts. 1977. L'évolution du prix des viandes depuis une quinzaine d'années; [by Bruno de Lasteyrie and Jean-Jacques Malpot]. [Paris], 1977. pp. 207. *(Documents. No. 39-40)*

MEAT INDUSTRY AND TRADE

— New Zealand.

TURKINGTON (DON) Industrial conflict: a study of three New Zealand industries. Wellington, N.Z., 1976. pp. 324.

— United Kingdom.

PERREN (RICHARD) The meat trade in Britain, 1840-1914. London, 1978. pp. 258.

MEDIATION AND CONCILIATION, INDUSTRIAL

— Australia.

AUSTRALIA. Department of Labor and Immigration. 1974. Conciliation and arbitration in Australia. Canberra, 1974. pp. 32.

— United Kingdom.

ADVISORY, CONCILIATION AND ARBITRATION SERVICE [U.K.]. An industrial relations service to industry. London, [1977]. pp. 7.

ADVISORY, CONCILIATION AND ARBITRATION SERVICE [U.K.]. The ACAS role: (the ACAS role in conciliation, arbitration and mediation). [London, 1979]. pp. 24. *An extract from the ACAS annual report 1978.*

ADVISORY, CONCILIATION AND ARBITRATION SERVICE [U.K.]. Conciliation in complaints by individuals to industrial tribunals: the ACAS role. [London, 1979]. pp. 15. *An extract from the ACAS annual report 1978.*

MEDICAL CARE.

NAAR sociale indicatoren op het terrein van de volksgezondheid; [by J.H.W. van den Berg and others]. Rijswijk, 1976. fo.44. *bibliog. (Netherlands. Sociaal en Cultureel Planbureau. SCP-Cahiers. No.7)*

CAMPBELL (ALASTAIR V.) Medicine, health and justice: the problem of priorities. Edinburgh, [1978]. pp. 100. *bibliog.*

FRY (JOHN) F.R.C.S. A new approach to medicine: principles and priorities in health care. Baltimore, [1978]. pp. 154. *bibliogs.*

STEPHEN (WILLIAM JOHN) An analysis of primary medical care: an international study. Cambridge, 1979. pp. 401. *bibliog.*

— Czechoslovakia.

ŠTICH (ZDENĚK) Health care in Czechoslovakia. Praha, 1954. pp. 69.

— Denmark.

NORD-LARSEN (MOGENS) and HULTCRANTZ (ELISABETH) Sundhedsvaesenet i tre geografiske områder: en undersøgelse af sudhedsvaesenet og dele af den sociale sektor på grundlag af de offentligt tilgaengelige oplysninger. København, 1977. pp. 176. *(Socialforskningsinstituttet. Meddelelser. 21)*

— Europe.

WORLD HEALTH ORGANIZATION. Regional Office for Europe. 1975. Health services in Europe. 2nd ed. Copenhagen, 1975. pp. 299.

BLANPAIN (JAN) and others. National health insurance and health resources: the European experience. Cambridge, Mass., 1978. pp. 294. *bibliog.*

— Netherlands.

POLL (CH. A.) and others. Het verhaal van een vijftigjarige: bijdragen tot de geschiedenis van de gezondheidszorg in Schiedam. Schiedam, 1978. pp. 118.

— Sweden.

SWEDISH medical care in the 1980's; ways and means: report from a study tour of today's planning for the future, etc; [by Ragnar Berfenstam and others]. [Stockholm, Sjukvårdens och Socialvårdens Planerings- och Rationaliseringsinstitut, 1973]. pp. 66.

— Underdeveloped areas.

See UNDERDEVELOPED AREAS — Medical care.

— United Kingdom.

STIMSON (GERALD VIVIAN) and STIMSON (CAROL) Health rights handbook: a guide to medical care. Dorchester, 1978. pp. 179.

SIMPSON (ROBIN) Access to primary care. London, 1979. pp. 62. *bibliog.* (U.K. Royal Commission on the National Health Service, 1976. Research Papers. No.6)

— — Wales.

WELSH CONSUMER COUNCIL. Getting primary care on the NHS: a sample survey carried out in the Merthyr and Cynon Valley Health District of parents of children under 10 and people aged over 60. Cardiff, 1979. pp. 43, 22.

— United States.

EQUITY in health services: empirical analyses in social policy; edited by Ronald Andersen [and others]. Cambridge, Mass., [1975]. pp. 295. *bibliog.*

BROWN (JACK HAROLD UPTON) The politics of health care. Cambridge, Mass., [1978]. pp. 153. *bibliog.*

FUTURE directions in health care: a new public policy: reports from a conference...; edited by Rick J. Carlson [and] Robert Cunningham. Cambridge, Mass., [1978]. pp. 238.

ROEMER (MILTON IRWIN) Social medicine: the advance of organized health services in America. New York, [1978]. pp. 560. *bibliogs.*

SLOAN (FRANK A.) and others. Private physicians and public programs. Lexington, Mass., [1978]. pp. 173.

MEDICAL CARE, COST OF.

CULLIS (JOHN G.) and WEST (PETER A.) The economics of health: an introduction. Oxford, 1979. pp. 309. *bibliogs.*

— Australia.

AUSTRALIA. Hospitals and Health Services Commission. 1978. A discussion paper on paying for health care: a review of the financing of health services in Australia and a discussion of possible alternative arrangements. Canberra, 1978. pp. 149. *bibliog.*

— Canada.

BARER (M.L.) and others. Controlling health care costs by direct charges to patients: snare or delusion? [Toronto, 1979]. pp. 126. *bibliog.* (Ontario. Economic Council. Occasional Papers. 10)

— United States.

HELMS (ROBERT B.) Regulating the cost of health care: can we learn from experience? Washington, 1978. pp. 11. *(American Enterprise Institute for Public Policy Research. Reprints. No. 85)*

MEDICAL ECONOMICS.

WORKING GROUP ON THE ROLE OF HEALTH ECONOMICS IN NATIONAL HEALTH PLANNING AND POLICY-MAKING. The role of health economics in national health planning and policy- making; report on a working group [held in] Cologne, 7-10 June 1977. Copenhagen, World Health Organization, Regional Office for Europe, 1978. pp. 31.

CULLIS (JOHN G.) and WEST (PETER A.) The economics of health: an introduction. Oxford, 1979. pp. 309. *bibliogs.*

ECONOMICS and health planning; edited by Kenneth Lee. London, [1979]. pp. 195. *bibliog.*

— United Kingdom.

The ECONOMICS of medical care; edited by M.M. Hauser. London, 1972. pp. 334.

— United States.

RORTY (JAMES) American medicine mobilizes. New York, [1939]. pp. 358.

FELDSTEIN (PAUL J.) Health associations and the demand for legislation: the political economy of health. Cambridge, Mass., [1977]. pp. 255.

CAPITAL INVESTMENT CONFERENCE, UNIVERSITY OF PITTSBURGH, 1976. Health care capital: competition and control; editors: Gordon K. Macleod, Mark Perlman. Cambridge, Mass., [1978]. pp. 412.

MEDICAL ETHICS.

WORLD HEALTH ORGANIZATION. 1976. Health aspects of human rights: with special reference to developments in biology and medicine. Geneva, 1976. pp. 48.

AMERICAN ACADEMY OF POLITICAL AND SOCIAL SCIENCE. Annals. vol. 437. Medical ethics and social change; special editor of this volume Bernard Barber. Philadelphia, 1978. pp. 201.

CAMPBELL (ALASTAIR V.) Medicine, health and justice: the problem of priorities. Edinburgh, [1978]. pp. 100. *bibliog.*

MEDICAL FEES

— United States.

SLOAN (FRANK A.) and others. Private physicians and public programs. Lexington, Mass., [1978]. pp. 173.

MEDICAL POLICY

MEDICAL INNOVATIONS.

PACKARD (VANCE OAKLEY) The people shapers. London, 1978. pp. 395. *bibliog.*

— United Kingdom.

YOUNGSON (ALEXANDER JOHN) The scientific revolution in Victorian medicine. London, 1979. pp. 237.

MEDICAL JURISPRUDENCE.

GRADWOHL (RUTHERFORD BIRCHARD HAYES) Legal medicine; edited by Francis E. Camps [and others]. 3rd ed. Bristol, 1976. pp. 717.

MEDICAL LAWS AND LEGISLATION.

WORLD HEALTH ORGANIZATION. 1967. Equivalence of medical qualifications and the practice of medicine: a survey of existing legislation. Geneva, 1967. pp. 47. *Originally published in International Digest of Health Legislation, v. 18, 1967.*

MEDICAL PERSONNEL.

WORLD HEALTH ORGANIZATION. 1967. Equivalence of medical qualifications and the practice of medicine: a survey of existing legislation. Geneva, 1967. pp. 47. *Originally published in International Digest of Health Legislation, v. 18, 1967.*

HEALTH manpower planning: principles, methods, issues; edited by T.L. Hall...and A. Mejía, etc. Geneva, World Health Organization, 1978. pp. 311.

— Canada.

CANADA. Statistics Canada. Compendium of selected health manpower statistics. a., 1976(1st)- Ottawa. *[in English and French]*

— Europe.

WORLD HEALTH ORGANIZATION. Regional Office for Europe. 1975. Health services in Europe. 2nd ed. Copenhagen, 1975. pp. 299.

— United Kingdom.

HEALTH services: their nature and organization, and the role of patients, doctors, nurses, and the complementary professions; editor Elliott Jaques, with members of the Brunel Health Services Organization Research Unit. London, 1978. pp. 346. *bibliog. A report of the main findings arising from the Brunel Health Services Organization Research Unit.*

PARKHOUSE (JAMES) Medical manpower in Britain. Edinburgh, 1979. pp. 144. *bibliogs.*

MEDICAL PERSONNEL AND PATIENT

— United Kingdom.

STIMSON (GERALD VIVIAN) and STIMSON (CAROL) Health rights handbook: a guide to medical care. Dorchester, 1978. pp. 179.

MEDICAL POLICY

— Europe.

BLANPAIN (JAN) and others. National health insurance and health resources: the European experience. Cambridge, Mass., 1978. pp. 294. *bibliog.*

— Germany.

BEAVAN (G.N.D.) Social policy in West Germany: the case of the medical profession. [Coventry, 1978?]. pp. 40. *bibliog.* (University of Warwick. Department of Politics. Working Papers. No. 21)

— Sweden.

SWEDISH medical care in the 1980's; ways and means: report from a study tour of today's planning for the future, etc; [by Ragnar Berfenstam and others]. [Stockholm, Sjukvårdens och Socialvårdens Planerings- och Rationaliseringsinstitut, 1973]. pp. 66.

MEDICAL POLICY(Cont.)

— United States.

EQUITY in health services: empirical analyses in social policy; edited by Ronald Andersen [and others]. Cambridge, Mass., [1975]. pp. 295. *bibliog.*

BROWN (JACK HAROLD UPTON) The politics of health care. Cambridge, Mass., [1978]. pp. 153. *bibliog.*

FUTURE directions in health care: a new public policy: reports from a conference...; edited by Rick J. Carlson [and] Robert Cunningham. Cambridge, Mass., [1978]. pp. 238.

STRICKLAND (STEPHEN P.) Research and the health of Americans. Lexington, Mass., [1978]. pp. 162.

MEDICAL RESEARCH

— United States.

HEALTH services research and RD in perspective; edited by E. Evelyn Flook and Paul J. Sanazaro. Ann Arbor, Mich., [1973]. pp. 311. *bibliog.*

STRICKLAND (STEPHEN P.) Research and the health of Americans. Lexington, Mass., [1978]. pp. 162.

MEDICAL SOCIETIES

— United States.

FELDSTEIN (PAUL J.) Health associations and the demand for legislation: the political economy of health. Cambridge, Mass., [1977]. pp. 255.

MEDICAL STATISTICS.

KRAMER (MORTON) Applications of mental health statistics: uses in mental health programmes of statistics derived from psychiatric services and selected vital and morbidity records. Geneva, World Health Organization, 1969. pp. 112. *bibliog.*

MEDICI FAMILY.

HALE (JOHN RIGBY) Florence and the Medici: the pattern of control. London, [1977]. pp. 208. *bibliog.*

MEDICINE

— History.

FOUCAULT (MICHEL) The birth of the clinic: an archaeology of medical perception; translated from the French by A. M. Sheridan. London, 1976. pp. 215. *bibliog.*

DOWLING (HARRY FILMORE) Fighting infection: conquests of the twentieth century. Cambridge, Mass., [1977]. pp. 339. *bibliog.*

— Study and teaching — United Kingdom.

JORDAN (WILLIAM STONE) Community medicine in the United Kingdom: medical education and an emerging specialty within the reorganized National Health Service. New York, [1978]. pp. 310.

— Germany.

BEAVAN (G.N.D.) Social policy in West Germany: the case of the medical profession. [Coventry, 1978?]. pp. 40. *bibliog. (University of Warwick. Department of Politics. Working Papers. No. 21)*

— Netherlands.

POLL (CH. A.) and others. Het verhaal van een vijftigjarige: bijdragen tot de geschiedenis van de gezondheidszorg in Schiedam. Schiedam, 1978. pp. 118.

— United Kingdom — History.

YOUNGSON (ALEXANDER JOHN) The scientific revolution in Victorian medicine. London, 1979. pp. 237.

— United States.

RORTY (JAMES) American medicine mobilizes. New York, [1939]. pp. 358.

MEDICINE, MAGIC, MYSTIC AND SPAGIRIC.

LAGARRIGA ATTIAS (ISABEL) Medicina tradicional y espiritualismo: los espiritualistas trinitarios marianos de Jalapa, Veracruz. Mexico, Secretaria de Educacion Publica, 1975. pp. 158. *bibliog. (Sep/Setentas. 191)*

MEDICINE, PREVENTIVE.

WORLD HEALTH ORGANIZATION. Regional Office for Europe. 1975. Health services in Europe. 2nd ed. Copenhagen, 1975. pp. 299.

DOWLING (HARRY FILMORE) Fighting infection: conquests of the twentieth century. Cambridge, Mass., [1977]. pp. 339. *bibliog.*

GRAY (JOHN ARMSTRONG MUIR) Man against disease: preventive medicine. Oxford, 1979. pp. 192. *bibliog.*

MEDICINE, PSYCHOSOMATIC.

TOTMAN (RICHARD) Social causes of illness. London, 1979. pp. 263. *bibliog.*

MEDICINE, STATE

— Bibliography.

CURRENT LITERATURE ON HEALTH SERVICES; [pd. by] Department of Health and Social Security Library [U.K.]. m. London. *Current issues only kept; a classified selection is pd. later in Studies on Community health and personal social services/ (1972-).*

— Czechoslovakia.

ŠTICH (ZDENĚK) Health care in Czechoslovakia. Praha, 1954. pp. 69.

— Europe.

BLANPAIN (JAN) and others. National health insurance and health resources: the European experience. Cambridge, Mass., 1978. pp. 294. *bibliog.*

— South Africa.

SOUTH AFRICA. Department of Health. Report. a., Jl 1947/D 1952, 1953-1976. Pretoria. *[in English and Afrikaans] Included in SOUTH AFRICA. Parliament. House of Assembly. Votes and proceedings (with Printed annexures)*

— United Kingdom.

CONFEDERATION OF HEALTH SERVICE EMPLOYEES. Memorandum of evidence to the Royal Commission on the National Health Service. Banstead, Surrey, 1977. pp. 82.

OFFICE OF HEALTH ECONOMICS. [Studies in Current Health Problems]. No. 58. The reorganised NHS. London, [1977]. pp. 35. *bibliog.*

U.K. Equal Opportunities Commission. 1977. Evidence to the Royal Commission on the National Health Service. [Manchester], 1977. fo.11.

BUXTON (MARTIN J.) and KLEIN (RUDOLF EWALD) Allocating health resources: a commentary on the report of the Resource Allocation Working Party. London, 1978. pp. 27. *(U.K. Royal Commission on the National Health Service, 1976. Research Papers. No.3)*

JORDAN (WILLIAM STONE) Community medicine in the United Kingdom: medical education and an emerging specialty within the reorganized National Health Service. New York, [1978]. pp. 310.

MANAGEMENT of financial resources in the National Health Service; (a report prepared...by a research team at the Centre for Industrial Economic and Business Research, University of Warwick: [John Perrin and others]). London, 1978. pp. 258. *(U.K. Royal Commission on the National Health Service, 1976. Research Papers. No.2)*

NAVARRO (VICENTE) Class struggle, the state and medicine: an historical and contemporary analysis of the medical sector in Great Britain. London, 1978. pp. 156. *bibliog.*

SCOTTISH CONSERVATIVE WOMEN'S ORGANISATION. How well is the health service?: a report of the findings of a survey, etc. [Edinburgh], [1978?]. pp. 8.

SKRIMSHIRE (ANGELA) Area disadvantage, social class and the health service: a pilot study of variation between areas in reported sickness and in the experience of receiving general practice care. Oxford, 1978. pp. 69. *bibliog.*

WANDSWORTH COUNCIL FOR COMMUNITY RELATIONS. Asians and the health service: a directory of measures implemented by area health authorities to meet the needs of the Asian community. London, 1978. pp. 30.

BROWN (RONALD GORDON SCLATER) Reorganising the National Health Service: a case study in administrative change. Oxford, 1979. pp. 232. *bibliog.*

PROSPECTS for the National Health; edited by Paul Atkinson [and others]. London, [1979]. pp. 218. *bibliog.*

TRADES UNION CONGRESS. Conference, 1978. Report of the...conference...to mark the 30th anniversary of the establishment of the National Health Service. London, [1979?]. pp. 48.

U.K. Royal Commission on the National Health Service, 1976. A service for patients: conclusions and recommendations of the Royal Commission's report; [Sir Alec Merrison, chairman] , London, 1979. pp. 42. *Full report of the Commission published as British Parliamentary Paper Cmnd. 7615, Session 1979/80.*

WIDGERY (DAVID) Health in danger: the crisis in the National Health Service. London, 1979. pp. 178. *bibliog.*

— — Bibliography.

U.K. Department of Health and Social Security. Index of health circulars and notices; chief officer letters; local authority circulars and social service letters. a., 1977- London.

MATHERS (NANCY M.) compiler. National Health Service: bibliography. Leeds, 1978. fo. 34.

SHRIGLEY (SHEILA M.) compiler. Selected official publications on the National Health Service. London, 1978. pp. 9. *(U.K. Department of Health and Social Security. Library. Bibliography Series. B23)*

— — Wales.

U.K. Steering Committee on Resource Allocations in Wales. 1977. Report; [W.J. Griffiths, chairman]. [Cardiff, 1977]. pp. 219.

U.K. Steering Committee on Resource Allocations in Wales. 1978. The distribution of resources to health authorities in Wales; second report of the Steering Committee; [W.J. Griffiths, chairman]. [Cardiff], 1977 [or rather 1978]. pp. 52.

— United States.

NUMBERS (RONALD L.) Almost persuaded: American physicians and compulsory health insurance, 1912-1920. Baltimore, [1978]. pp. 158. *(Bulletin of the History of Medicine. Henry E. Sigerist Supplements. New Series. No. 1)*

SLOAN (FRANK A.) and others. Private physicians and public programs. Lexington, Mass., [1978]. pp. 173.

MEDICINE AND PSYCHOLOGY.

RACHMAN (STANLEY) and PHILIPS (CLARE) Psychology and medicine. Harmondsworth, 1978. pp. 205. *First published in London, 1975.*

MEDINA ECHAVARRIA (JOSE).

SOLARI (ALDO E.) ed. Poder y desarrollo: America Latina; estudios sociologicos en homenaje a Jose Medina Echavarria. Mexico, 1977. pp. 429.

MEDITATIONS.

SURTEES SOCIETY. Publications. vol. 190. The meditations of Lady Elizabeth Delaval, written between 1662 and 1671; edited by Douglas G. Greene. Gateshead, 1978. pp. 223.

MEDITERRANEAN

— Commerce — European Economic Community countries.

EUROPEAN COMMUNITIES. Statistical Office. EC trade with the: ACP states: South Mediterranean states. q., 1978 (preliminary issue)- Luxembourg. *[in Community languages]*

— Foreign relations — European Economic Community countries.

PETIT-LAURENT (PHILIPPE) Les fondements politiques des engagements de la Communauté Européenne en Méditerranée. Paris, [1976]. pp. 168. *bibliog.* (Paris. Université de Paris II. Travaux et Recherches. Série Science Politique. 7)

— — Russia.

SAUL (NORMAN E.) Russia and the Mediterranean, 1797-1807. Chicago, 1970. pp. 268. *bibliog.*

— History.

HESS (ANDREW C.) The forgotten frontier: a history of the sixteenth-century Ibero-African frontier. Chicago, 1978. pp. 278. *bibliog.* (Chicago. University. Center for Middle Eastern Studies. Publications. 10)

MEGHALAYA

— Appropriations and expenditures.

MEGHALAYA. Planning Department. Annual plan: a plan and budget link. a., 1976/77- Shillong.

— Economic policy.

MEGHALAYA. Planning Department. Annual plan: a plan and budget link. a., 1976/77- Shillong.

MEGHALAYA. Planning Department. Draft annual plan. a., 1976/77- Shillong.

MEGHALAYA. Planning Department. Review of the implementation of development schemes and programmes: supplement to the budget. a., 1976/77- Shillong.

— Legislative Assembly — Rules and practice.

MEGHALAYA. Legislative Assembly. Secretariat. 1978. Rules of procedure and conduct of business in Meghalaya Legislative Assembly, modified up to December 1977. Shillong, 1978. pp. 165.

— Social policy.

MEGHALAYA. Planning Department. Annual plan: a plan and budget link. a., 1976/77- Shillong.

MEGHALAYA. Planning Department. Draft annual plan. a., 1976/77- Shillong.

MEGHALAYA. Planning Department. Review of the implementation of development schemes and programmes: supplement to the budget. a., 1976/77- Shillong.

MEINHOF (ULRIKE MARIE).

BECKER (JILLIAN) Hitler's children. rev. ed. London, 1978. pp. 415. *bibliog.*

MEININGEN (ERNST MUELLER-).

See MUELLER-MEININGEN (ERNST).

MELBOURNE

— Charities.

LIFFMAN (MICHAEL) Power for the poor: the Family Centre Project: an experiment in self-help. Sydney, 1978. pp. 160. *bibliog.*

MEMORY.

BURSEN (HOWARD ALEXANDER) Dismantling the memory machine: a philosophical investigation of machine theories of memory. Dordrecht, [1978]. pp. 157. *bibliog.*

CONFERENCE ON PERSPECTIVES ON MEMORY RESEARCH, UNIVERSITY OF UPPSALA, 1977. Perspectives on memory research: essays in honor of Uppsala University's 500th anniversary: edited by Lars-Göran Nilsson. Hillsdale, N.J., 1979. pp. 400. *bibliog.*

MEMORY IN CHILDREN.

PERSPECTIVES on the development of memory and cognition; edited by Robert V. Kail [and] John W. Hagen. Hillsdale, 1977. pp. 498. *bibliogs.*

MEMORY development in children; edited by Peter A. Ornstein. Hillsdale, N.J., 1978. pp. 280. *bibliogs.*

MEN.

RED COLLECTIVE. The politics of sexuality in capitalism. London, 1973 repr. 1978. pp. 146.

MENCKEN (HENRY LOUIS).

DOUGLAS (GEORGE H.) H.L. Mencken: critic of American life. Hamden, Conn., 1978. pp. 248. *bibliog.*

MENHENIOTT (STEPHEN).

U.K. Social Work Service. 1978. Report...into certain aspects of the management of the case of Stephen Menheniott. London, 1978. pp. 48.

MENTAL HEALTH LAWS

— United States.

WILSON (JOHN PASLEY) The rights of adolescents in the mental health system. Lexington, Mass., [1978]. pp. 321.

MENTAL HEALTH PERSONNEL.

GERSHON (MICHAEL) and BILLER (HENRY B.) The other helpers: paraprofessionals and nonprofessionals in mental health. Lexington, Mass., [1977]. pp. 268. *bibliog.*

— United Kingdom — Scotland.

TIBBITT (JOHN E.) Social workers as mental health officers. Edinburgh, 1978. pp. 41. (Scotland. Scottish Office. Social Research Studies)

MENTAL HEALTH SERVICES

— Europe — Evaluation.

WORKING GROUP ON THE FUTURE OF MENTAL HOSPITALS. The future of mental hospitals: report on a working group [held in] Mannheim, 2-5 November 1976. Copenhagen, World Health Organization, Regional Office for Europe, 1978. pp. 68.

— Underdeveloped areas.

See UNDERDEVELOPED AREAS — Mental health services.

— United Kingdom.

NEW methods of mental health care; edited by Molly Meacher. Oxford, 1979. pp. 233. *bibliogs.*

MENTAL HYGIENE.

KRAMER (MORTON) Applications of mental health statistics: uses in mental health programmes of statistics derived from psychiatric services and selected vital and morbidity records. Geneva, World Health Organization, 1969. pp. 112. *bibliog.*

MENTAL ILLNESS.

SIEGLER (MIRIAM) and OSMOND (HUMPHRY) Models of madness, models of medicine. New York, [1974]. pp. 287. *bibliog.*

TROWER (PETER) and others. Social skills and mental health. London, 1978. pp. 306. *bibliogs.*

MENTAL TESTS.

CRONBACH (LEE JOSEPH) Essentials of psychological testing. 3rd ed. New York, [1970]. pp. 752. *bibliog.*

SIMON (BRIAN) Intelligence, psychology and education: a Marxist critique. rev. ed. London, [1971]. pp. 286.

MENTALLY HANDICAPPED.

BEHAVIOUR modification with the severely retarded...; edited by C.C. Kiernan and F. Peter Woodford. Amsterdam, 1975. pp. 332. *bibliogs.* (Institute for Research into Mental and Multiple Handicap. Study Groups. No. 8)

— Care and treatment — United kingdom.

FABIAN SOCIETY. Fabian Tracts. [No.] 460. A family service for the mentally handicapped; [by] Walter Jaehnig. London, 1979. pp. 24.

— Education — United States.

SARASON (SEYMOUR BERNARD) and DORIS (JOHN) Educational handicap, public policy, and social history: a broadened perspective on mental retardation. New York, [1979]. pp. 460. *bibliog.*

— Institutional care — United Kingdom.

NATIONAL DEVELOPMENT GROUP FOR THE MENTALLY HANDICAPPED [U.K.]. Helping mentally handicapped people in hospital; a report to the Secretary of State for Social Services...; chairman: P. Mittler. [London, Department of Health and Social Security, 1978]. pp. 136. *bibliog.*

— United Kingdom — Ireland, Northern.

IRELAND, NORTHERN. Department of Health and Social Services. 1978. Services for the mentally handicapped in Northern Ireland: policy and objectives. Belfast, 1978. pp. 33.

— — Scotland.

MENTAL DISORDER PROGRAMME PLANNING GROUP [SCOTLAND]. A better life: report on services for the mentally handicapped in Scotland; a report by a Programme Planning Group of the Scottish Health Service Planning Council and the Advisory Council on Social Work; [D.A. Peters, chairman of the Sub-Committee]. Edinburgh, H.M.S.O., 1979. pp. 119.

MENTALLY HANDICAPPED CHILDREN

— Care and treatment.

BALDWIN (VICTOR L.) and others. Isn't it time he outgrew this?; or, A training program for parents of retarded children. Springfield, Ill., 1973 repr. 1976. pp. 209.

— Family relationships.

BALDWIN (VICTOR L.) and others. Isn't it time he outgrew this?; or, A training program for parents of retarded children. Springfield, Ill., 1973 repr. 1976. pp. 209.

MENTALLY ILL

— Care and treatment.

ALTERNATIVES to mental hospital treatment; edited by Leonard I. Stein and Mary Ann Test. New York, [1978]. pp. 327. *bibliogs. Papers from the Conference on Alternatives to Mental Hospital Treatment, Madison, Wis., 1975.*

— — United Kingdom.

SCULL (ANDREW T.) Museums of madness: the social organization of insanity in nineteenth-century England. London, 1979. pp. 275.

— Family relationships.

PEREZ (JOSEPH FRANCIS) The family roots of adolescent delinquency. New York, 1978. pp. 231.

— Rehabilitation.

TROWER (PETER) and others. Social skills and mental health. London, 1978. pp. 306. *bibliogs.*

— New Zealand.

NEW ZEALAND. Department of Health. National Health Statistics Centre. 1979. Survey of occupied psychiatric hospital beds and psychiatric day and outpatients, 1976. Wellington, 1979. pp. 74. *(Department of Health. Special Report Series. No. 55)*

MERCENARY TROOPS.

MALLETT (MICHAEL EDWARD) Mercenaries and their masters: warfare in Renaissance Italy. London, [1974]. pp. 284. *bibliog.*

MERCHANT MARINE

— Russia.

FRANCE. Direction de la Documentation. La Documentation Française. Notes et Etudes Documentaires. No. 4479-4480. La marine soviétique; [by] Claude Huan [and] Jürgen Rohwer. [Paris], 1978. pp. 157.

MERCHANTS

— Argentine Republic — Buenos Aires.

SOCOLOW (SUSAN MIGDEN) The merchants of Buenos Aires 1778-1810: family and commerce. Cambridge, 1978. pp. 253. *bibliog.*

— United States.

FITZPATRICK (JOHN) c.1737-1791. The merchant of Manchac: the letterbooks of John Fitzpatrick, 1768-1790; edited with an introduction by Margaret Fisher Dalrymple. Baton Rouge, [1978]. pp. 451. *bibliog.*

MERCHANTS, FOREIGN

— United Kingdom.

LONDON. London Record Society. Publications. vol. 15. Joshua Johnson's letterbook, 1771-1774: letters from a merchant in London to his partners in Maryland; edited by Jacob M. Price. London, 1979. pp. 181.

MERKEL (GARLIEB).

See MERKELIS (GARLIBS).

MERKELIS (GARLIBS).

MILLER (VISVARIS OTTOVICH) and MEL'KISIS (EDGAR ADAMOVICH) Politikopravovye vzgliady Garliba Merkelia. Moskva, 1977. pp. 160.

MERSEYSIDE

— Social conditions.

WEBBER (RICHARD J.) and SHAW (M.G.) The social characteristics of residential neighbourhoods: Merseyside. London, 1978. pp. 126. *(Planning Research Applications Group. PRAG Technical Papers. TP 24)*

METAL TRADE

— Sweden.

OHLSSON (LENNART) Metallmanufakturindustrin: produktions förutsättningar och specialisering i internationell jämförelse, etc. Stockholm, 1973. pp. 186. *(Sweden. Statens Offentliga Utredningar. 1973. 30) With English summary.*

METAL WORKERS

— Germany.

STREIK-NACHRICHTEN des Metallarbeiterstreiks in Schleswig- Holstein; [pd. by] Industriegewerkschaft Metall für die Bundesrepublik Deutschland. irreg., Oc 25 1956 - F 14 1957(nos. 1-80). Hamburg. *Reprint in 1 v.*

KOMMUNISTISCHER BUND WESTDEUTSCHLAND. Ortsgruppe Bremen. Der Streik der Metallarbeiter, Bremen, März 74: Analyse und Dokumentation. Heidelberg, 1974. pp. 118.

MEYER (REGINE) Streik und Aussperrung in der Metallindustrie: Analyse der Streikbewegung in Nordwürttemberg-Nordbaden, 1971. Marburg, [1977]. pp. 426. *bibliog. (Studiengesellschaft für Sozialgeschichte und Arbeiterbewegung, Marburg. Schriftenreihe für Sozialgeschichte und Arbeiterbewegung. Band 4)*

METAMATHEMATICS.

SCHUETTE (KURT) Proof theory; translation from the German by J.N. Crossley. Berlin, 1977. pp. 299. *bibliog.*

MÉTAYER SYSTEM

— Peru.

MATOS MAR (JOSE) Yanaconaje y reforma agraria en el Peru: el caso del valle de Chancay. Lima, 1976. pp. 278. *bibliog. (Instituto de Estudios Peruanos. Peru Problema. 15)*

METCALFE (FRANCIS JAMES).

METCALFE (FRANCIS JAMES) Colliers and I; or, Thirty years' work among Derbyshire colliers. Manchester, 1903. pp. 218.

METEOROLOGY

— Canada — British Columbia.

WON (THORNE K.) Meteorology in British Columbia: a centennial review, (1871- 1971). Vancouver, Canadian Meteorological Service, 1971. pp. 48.

— United States.

BURNABY (ANDREW) Travels through the middle settlements in North America in the years 1759 and 1760, with observations upon the state of the colonies. New York, 1970. pp. 265. *Reprint of the third edition, London, 1798.*

METHANE INDUSTRY

— Italy.

GIORGIO (MARIO) La sconfitta del Subappennino Dauno. Matera, [1977]. pp. 101.

METRIC SYSTEM.

— Canada.

CANADA. Department of Consumer and Corporate Affairs. 1972. Metrication: a guide for consumers. Ottawa, 1972. pp. 24. *(Consumer Research Reports. No. 2)*

CANADA. Department of Consumer and Corporate Affairs. 1973. Metrication: a guide for producers of packaged goods. 2nd ed. Ottawa, 1973. pp. 12. *(Consumer Research Reports. No. 4)*

METROPOLITAN AREAS.

HEALTH care in big cities; edited by Leslie H.W. Paine. New York, 1978. pp. 368.

FABOS (JULIUS GY.) Planning the total landscape: a guide to intelligent land use. Boulder, Colo., [1979]. pp. 181. *bibliogs.*

— Canada — Alberta.

ALBERTA. Task Force on Urbanization and the Future. 1972. Choices for metropolitan growth. [Edmonton, 1972]. pp. 22. *bibliog.*

— South Africa.

BROWETT (J.G.) and HART (T.) Projections of the urban population of the southern P[retoria] W[itwatersrand] V[ereeniging] [conurbation] for the years 1980, 1990 and 2000. Johannesburg, 1978. pp. 135. *bibliog. (Johannesburg. University of the Witwatersrand. Urban and Regional Research Unit. Occasional Papers. No. 19)*

— United Kingdom.

WARNES (A.M.) The decentralisation of employment from the larger English cities. London, 1977. pp. 27. *(London. University. King's College. Geography Department. Occasional Papers. No.5)*

METROPOLITAN GOVERNMENT.

SCHECTER (STEPHEN BENJAMIN) The politics of urban liberation. Montreal, [1978]. pp. 203. *bibliogs.*

— United Kingdom.

SAUNDERS (PETER) Urban politics: a sociological interpretation. London, 1979. pp. 383. *bibliog.*

— United States.

GOODALL (LEONARD E.) and SPRENGEL (DONALD P.) The American metropolis. 2nd ed. Columbus, Ohio, [1975]. pp. 277. *bibliogs.*

MEXICAN AMERICANS.

The CHICANOS: Mexican American voices; edited by Ed Ludwig and James Santibañez. Harmondsworth, 1971. pp. 286. *bibliog.*

GARCIA (F. CHRIS) and DE LA GARZA (RUDOLPH O.) The Chicano political experience: three perspectives. North Scituate, Mass., [1977]. pp. 205.

HIRSCH (HERBERT) and GUTIERREZ (ARMANDO) Learning to be militant: ethnic identity and the development of political militance in a Chicano community. San Francisco, 1977. pp. 146.

VIGIL (MAURILIO) Chicano politics. Washington, D.C., [1978]. pp. 368. *bibliogs.*

STEINER (STAN) The Mexican Americans. London, 1979. pp. 19. *bibliog. (Minority Rights Group. Reports. No.39)*

MEXICO.

MEXICO. Secretaria de la Presidencia. 1976. Mexico a vuelo de pajaro. Mexico, 1976. pp. 259.

— Armed forces.

LOZOYA (JORGE ALBERTO) El ejercito mexicano. 2nd ed. Mexico, 1976. pp. 156. *bibliog. (Mexico City. Colegio de Mexico. Jornadas. 65)*

— Biography.

CAMP (RODERIC AI) Mexican political biographies, 1935-1975. Tucson, Ariz., [1976 repr. 1978]. pp. 468. *bibliog.*

— Economic conditions.

AUTHORITARIANISM in Mexico; [edited by] José Luis Reyna and Richard S. Weinert. Philadelphia, [1977]. pp. 241. *bibliogs. (Center for Inter-American Relations. Inter-American Politics Series. vol. 2)*

SCHLAGHECK (JAMES L.) The political, economic and labor climate in Mexico. Philadelphia, [1977]. pp. 164. *(Pennsylvania University. Wharton School of Finance and Commerce. Industrial Research Unit. Multinational Industrial Relations Series. No. 4b)*

BRADING (DAVID A.) Haciendas and ranchos in the Mexican Bajío, Leon 1700-1860. Cambridge, 1978. pp. 258. *bibliog.*

VELLINGA (MENNO) Economic development and the dynamics of class: industrialization, power and control in Monterrey, Mexico. Van Gorcum, 1979. pp. 213. *bibliog.*

— **Economic history.**

BRADING (DAVID A.) Haciendas and ranchos in the Mexican Bajío, Leon 1700-1860. Cambridge, 1978. pp. 258. *bibliog.*

— **Economic policy.**

SOLIS M. (LEOPOLDO) Planes de desarrollo economico y social en Mexico. Mexico, Secretaria de Educacion Publica, 1975. pp. 197. *(Sep/Setentas. 215)*

— **Foreign relations.**

MEXICO. Secretaria de la Presidencia. 1976. Documentos de la gira. Mexico, 1976. pp. 413. *Speeches and agreements made during Presidential tour of countries in America, Africa, 8 July-22 August, 1975.*

MEXICO. Secretaria de la Presidencia. 1976. Mision de paz. Mexico, 1976. pp. 391. *Press reports of Presidential tour to America, Africa and Asia, 8 July-22 August, 1975.*

— — **United States.**

GARCIA CANTU (GASTON) Las invasiones norteamericanas en Mexico. Mexico, 1971 repr. 1975. pp. 362.

GILDERHUS (MARK T.) Diplomacy and revolution: U.S.-Mexican relations under Wilson and Carranza. Tucson, Ariz., [1977]. pp. 159. *bibliog.*

— **History.**

MEXICO CITY. Colegio de Mexico. Centro de Estudios Historicos. Historia general de Mexico. Mexico, 1977. 4 vols.

— — **Sources.**

El EMPRESTITO de Mexico a Colombia; recopilacion de documentos con una introduccion y notas; por Joaquin Ramirez Cabañas. Mexico, 1930. pp. 247. *(Archivo Historico Diplomatico Mexicano. [Serie 1]. Num. 33)*

— — **1910-1946.**

FLORES MAGON (RICARDO) Land and liberty: anarchist influences in the Mexican Revolution. Sanday, 1977. pp. 156. *bibliog.*

— — **1910-1929, Revolution.**

CARR (BARRY) El movimiento obrero y la politica en Mexico, 1910-1929; version española de Roberto Gomez Ciriza. Mexico, Secretaria de Educacion Publica, 1976. 2 vols. (in 1) *bibliog. (Sep/Setentas. 256,257)*

— **Industries.**

FAJNZYLBER (FERNANDO) and MARTINEZ TARRAGO (TRINIDAD) Las empresas transnacionales: expansión a nivel mundial y proyección en la industria mexicana. México, 1976. pp. 423. *bibliog.*

— **Native races.**

LOMBARDO TOLEDANO (VICENTE) El problema del indio; seleccion de textos de Marcela Lombardo; con una introduccion de Gonzalo Aguirre Beltran. Mexico, Secretaria de Educacion Publica. 1973. pp. 207. *bibliog. (Sep/Setentas. 114)*

— **Politics and government.**

CAMP (RODERIC AI) Mexican political biographies, 1935-1975. Tucson, Ariz., [1976 repr. 1978]. pp. 468. *bibliog.*

AUTHORITARIANISM in Mexico; [edited by] José Luis Reyna and Richard S. Weinert. Philadelphia, [1977]. pp. 241. *bibliogs. (Center for Inter-American Relations. Inter-American Politics Series. vol. 2)*

JOHNSON (KENNETH F.) Mexican democracy: a critical view. rev. ed. New York, [1978]. pp. 267. *bibliog.*

— **Religion.**

COSTELOE (MICHAEL P.) Church and state in independent Mexico: a study of the patronage debate, 1821-1857. London, 1978. pp. 207. *bibliog. (Royal Historical Society. Studies in History)*

— **Rural conditions.**

DEWALT (BILLIE R.) Modernization in a Mexican ejido: a study in economic adaption. Cambridge, 1979. pp. 303. *bibliog.*

FRANK (ANDRE GUNDER) Mexican agriculture, 1521-1630: transformation of the mode of production. Cambridge, 1979. pp. 91. *bibliog.*

— **Social policy.**

SOLIS M. (LEOPOLDO) Planes de desarrollo economico y social en Mexico. Mexico, Secretaria de Educacion Publica, 1975. pp. 197. *(Sep/Setentas. 215)*

— **Statistics.**

NACIONAL FINANCIERA. Statistics on the Mexican economy. Mexico, 1977. pp. 452.

MIAO PEOPLE.

SUWANBUBPA (ARAN) Hill tribe development and welfare programmes in Northern Thailand. Singapore, 1976. pp. 93.

MICHAEL III PALAEOLOGUS, Emperor of the East.

GEANAKOPLOS (DENO JOHN) Emperor Michael Palaeologus and the west, 1258-1282: a study in Byzantine-Latin relations. Hamden, Conn., 1973. pp. 434. *bibliog. First published in Cambridge, Massachusetts, in 1959.*

MICHELSEN (ALFONSO LOPEZ).

See LOPEZ MICHELSEN (ALFONSO).

MICROCOMPUTERS.

BEIZER (BORIS) Micro-analysis of computer system performance. New York, [1978]. pp. 404. *bibliog.*

McKEONE (DERMOT H.) Small computers for business and industry. Farnborough, Hants., [1979]. pp. 209.

MICROELECTRONICS.

U.K. Central Policy Review Staff. 1978. Social and employment implications of microelectronics; paper. [London], 1978. pp. 24.

MICRONESIA

— **Foreign relations — United States.**

NUFER (HAROLD F.) Micronesia under American rule: an evaluation of the strategic trusteeship, 1947-77. Hicksville, N.Y., [1978]. pp. 245.

MICROPROCESSORS.

CHIPS with everything: microprocessor technology, its applications and implications: proceedings of the Interlab symposium..., London, 16th June 1977. [London], Department of Industry, London and South East Regional Office, [1978]. pp. 80.

MID GLAMORGAN

— **Economic conditions.**

MID GLAMORGAN. [County Planning Department]. Mid Glamorgan county structure plan:...report of survey. [Cardiff], 1977. 13 vols. (in 1).

— **Economic policy.**

MID GLAMORGAN. [County Planning Department]. Mid Glamorgan county structure plan: draft written statement, January, 1978. [Cardiff], 1978. pp. 210.

MID GLAMORGAN. [County Planning Department]. Mid Glamorgan county structure plan: guide to the plan, January 1978. [Cardiff], 1978. pp. 29.

MID GLAMORGAN. [County Planning Department]. Mid Glamorgan county structure plan: report of public participation and consultations, October 1978. [Cardiff], 1978. pp. 146.

MID GLAMORGAN. [County Planning Department]. Mid Glamorgan county structure plan: written statement, October, 1978. [Cardiff], 1978. pp. 253.

— **Social conditions.**

MID GLAMORGAN. [County Planning Department]. Mid Glamorgan county structure plan:...report of survey. [Cardiff], 1977. 13 vols. (in 1).

— **Social policy.**

MID GLAMORGAN. [County Planning Department]. Mid Glamorgan county structure plan: draft written statement, January, 1978. [Cardiff], 1978. pp. 210.

MID GLAMORGAN. [County Planning Department]. Mid Glamorgan county structure plan: guide to the plan, January 1978. [Cardiff], 1978. pp. 29.

MID GLAMORGAN. [County Planning Department]. Mid Glamorgan county structure plan: report of public participation and consultations, October 1978. [Cardiff], 1978. pp. 146.

MID GLAMORGAN. [County Planning Department]. Mid Glamorgan county structure plan: written statement, October, 1978. [Cardiff], 1978. pp. 253.

MIDDLE AGES.

THRUPP (SYLVIA LETTICE) Society and history: essays...; edited by Raymond Grew and Nicholas H. Steneck. Ann Arbor, [1977]. pp. 363. *bibliog.*

— **Economic conditions.**

DOEHAERD (RENEE) The early Middle Ages in the West: economy and society; translated by W.G. Deakin. Amsterdam, 1978. pp. 307. *bibliog.*

— **Social conditions.**

DUBY (GEORGES) The chivalrous society; translated by Cynthia Postan. London, 1977. pp. 246.

FOURQUIN (GUY) The anatomy of popular rebellion in the Middle Ages...; translated by Anne Chesters. Amsterdam, 1978. pp. 181. *bibliog.*

MIDDLE CLASSES.

BANFI (ANTONIO) La crisi della civiltà borghese e il marxismo; introduzione, scelta e note a cura di Giovanni Mari. Firenze, 1977. pp. 346. *bibliog.*

— **Egypt.**

BINDER (LEONARD) In a moment of enthusiasm: political power and the second stratum in Egypt. Chicago, [1978]. pp. 437. *bibliog.*

— **France.**

STEARNS (PETER N.) Paths to authority: the middle class and the industrial labor force in France, 1820-48. Urbana, Ill., [1978]. pp. 222. *bibliog.*

— **India — Goa, Daman and Diu.**

GOA, DAMAN AND DIU. General Statistics Department. 1967. Report on the middle class family living survey in Panaji town, 1964-65. [Panaji], 1967. pp. 85.

MIDDLE CLASSES.(Cont.)

— United Kingdom.

The MIDDLE class in politics; edited by John Garrard and others. Farnborough, Hants, [1978]. pp. 373. *bibliog. Based on a conference held at the University of Salford in 1977.*

HAMMERTON (A. JAMES) Emigrant gentlewomen: genteel poverty and female emigration, 1830-1914. London, [1979]. pp. 220. *bibliog.*

MIDWIVES

— United Kingdom.

DONNISON (JEAN ELIZABETH) Midwives and medical men: a history of inter-professional rivalries and women's rights. London, 1977. pp. 250. *bibliog.*

— United States.

LITOFF (JUDY BARRETT) American midwives: 1860 to the present. Westport, Conn., 1978. pp. 197. *bibliog.*

MIGRANT LABOUR

— Europe.

GENDT (RIEN VAN) and GARCIA PASSIGLI (G.) Return migration and reintegration services. Paris, Organisation for Economic Co-operation and Development, 1977. pp. 64.

MIGRANT women speak; interviews presented by Jean Guyot [and others]. London, 1978. pp. 164. *bibliog.*

— United Kingdom.

LEESON (R.A.) Travelling brothers: the six centuries' road from craft fellowship to trade unionism. London, 1979. pp. 348. *bibliog.*

— United States.

PIORE (MICHAEL J.) Birds of passage: migrant labor and industrial societies. Cambridge, 1979. pp. 229. *bibliog.*

MIGRATION, INTERNAL.

REYNOLDS (LLOYD GEORGE) The structure of labor markets: wages and labor mobility in theory and practice. Westport, Conn., 1951, repr. 1971. pp. 328.

HUMAN migration: patterns and policies; edited by William H. McNeill and Ruth S. Adams. Bloomington, [1978]. pp. 442. *Proceedings of a conference held in 1976 by the Midwest Council of the American Academy of Arts and Sciences and Indiana University, at New Haven, Indiana.*

— Brazil.

MATA (MILTON DA) and others. Migrações internas no Brasil: aspectos econômicos e demograficos. Rio de Janeiro, 1973. pp. 217. *bibliog. (Brazil. Instituto de Planejamento Econômico e Social. Instituto de Pesquisas. Relatorios de Pesquisa. No. 19)*

— France.

ATELIER PARISIEN D'URBANISME. Service de Politique Urbaine. Les migrations de la population de Paris entre 1962 et 1968: (rapport préliminaire); d'après les travaux préliminaires de Eliane Jaulerry. [Paris], 1971. fo. 18.

— India.

WEINER (MYRON) Sons of the soil: migration and ethnic conflict in India. Princeton, N.J., [1978]. pp. 383. *bibliogs.*

— Indonesia.

HARDJONO (J.M.) Transmigration in Indonesia. Kuala Lumpur, 1977. pp. 116. *bibliog.*

— Nigeria.

PEACE (ADRIAN J.) Choice, class and conflict: a study of Southern Nigerian factory workers. Brighton, 1979. pp. 204. *bibliog.*

— Papua New Guinea.

CHANGE and movement: readings on internal migration in Papua New Guinea; [edited by] R.J. May. Canberra, 1977. pp. 284. *bibliog.*

— Poland.

PROBLEMY migracji wewnętrznych w Polsce i ZSRR; praca zbiorowa pod redakcją Antoniego Kuklińskiego i Aleksandra Łukaszewicza. Warszawa, 1978. pp. 251.

— Russia.

PROBLEMY migracji wewnętrznych w Polsce i ZSRR; praca zbiorowa pod redakcją Antoniego Kuklińskiego i Aleksandra Łukaszewicza. Warszawa, 1978. pp. 251.

— United Kingdom.

KENNETT (STEPHEN) Census data and migration analysis: an appraisal. London, 1978. pp. 16. *biblig.*

LONDON. University. London School of Economics and Political Science. Graduate School of Geography. Discussion Papers. No. 66. The differential migration of socio-economic groups, 1966-71; [by] Stephen Kennett and Bill Randolph. London, 1978. pp. 56. *bibliog.*

— United States.

VICKERY (WILLIAM EDWARD) The economics of the negro migration, 1900-1960. New York, 1977. pp. 223. *bibliog.*

MIHAILOVIC (DRAGOLJUB).

COMMITTEE FOR A FAIR TRIAL FOR DRAJA MIHAILOVICH. Commission of Inquiry. Patriot or traitor: the case of General Mihailovich; proceedings and report of the commission. Stanford, Calif., [1978]. pp. 499. *(Stanford University. Hoover Institution on War, Revolution and Peace. Hoover Institution Publications. 191)*

MILAN (CITY)

— Economic history.

HUNECKE (VOLKER) Arbeiterschaft und industrielle Revolution in Mailand, 1859-1892: zur Entstehungsgeschichte der italienischen Industrie und Arbeiterbewegung. Göttingen, 1978. pp. 330. *bibliog.*

MILAN (DUCHY)

— Economic history.

ROMANI (MARIO) Aspetti e problemi di storia economica lombarda nei secoli XVIII e XIX: scritti riediti in memoria. Milano, 1977. pp. 572. *(Milan. Università Cattolica del Sacro Cuore. Pubblicazioni. Scienze Storiche. 16)*

— History.

CORIO (BERNARDINO) Storia di Milano: a cura di Anna Morisi Guerra. Torino, 1978. 2 vols.

MILITARISM

— France.

PELLETIER (ROBERT) and RAVET (SERGE) Le mouvement des soldats: les comités de soldats et l'antimilitarisme révolutionnaire. Paris, 1976. pp. 199.

— Germany.

[SCHREINER (ALBERT)] Hitler rearms: an exposure of Germany's war plans; edited by Dorothy Woodman. London, 1934. pp. 336. *Translation of Hitler treibt zum Krieg.*

MILITARY ART AND SCIENCE

— History.

DIXON (NORMAN F.) On the psychology of military incompetence. London, 1976. pp. 447. *bibliog.*

MILITARY ASSISTANCE, AMERICAN.

LEFEVER (ERNEST WARREN) Nuclear arms in the Third World: U.S. policy dilemma. Washington, D.C., [1979]. pp. 154.

— Angola.

STOCKWELL (JOHN) In search of enemies: a CIA story. London, 1978. pp. 285.

— Israel.

TERRY (JANICE J.) Attitudes of United States congressmen toward aid to the Palestinians and arms to Israel. Beirut, [1973]. pp. 78. *(Palestine Research Center. Palestine Essays. No. 37)*

MILITARY ASSISTANCE, GERMAN

— South Africa.

CERVENKA (ZDENEK) and ROGERS (BARBARA) The nuclear axis: secret collaboration between West Germany and South Africa. London, 1978. pp. 464.

MILITARY ASSISTANCE, RUSSIAN

— China.

SEMENOV (GEORGII GAVRILOVICH) Tri goda v Pekine: zapiski voennogo sovetnika. Moskva, 1978. pp. 296.

MILITARY BASES, AMERICAN.

COTTRELL (ALVIN J.) and MOORER (THOMAS H.) U.S. overseas bases: problems of projecting American military power abroad. Beverly Hills, [1977]. pp. 66. *bibliog. (Georgetown University. Center for Strategic and International Studies. Washington Papers. vol. 5/47)*

MILITARY GOVERNMENT.

— Underdeveloped areas.

See UNDERDEVELOPED AREAS — Military government.

MILITARY HISTORY.

DIXON (NORMAN F.) On the psychology of military incompetence. London, 1976. pp. 447. *bibliog.*

MILITARY POLICY.

SCHELLING (THOMAS CROMBIE) Arms and influence. Westport, Conn., [1966]. pp. 293.

HALPERIN (MORTON H.) Contemporary military strategy. new ed. London, 1972. pp. 149. *bibliog.*

SIVARD (RUTH LEGER) World military and social expenditures, 1977. Leesburg, Va., [1977]. pp. 31.

INTERNATIONAL perceptions of the superpower military balance; edited by Donald C. Daniel. New York, [1978]. pp. 198. *bibliogs.*

RESTRAINTS on war: studies in the limitation of armed conflict; edited by Michael Howard. Oxford, 1979. pp. 173. *bibliog.*

— Data processing.

EXPLORING competitive arms processes: applications of mathematical modeling and computer simulation in arms policy analysis; editor: W. Ladd Hollist. New York, [1978]. pp. 279.

— Mathematical models.

EXPLORING competitive arms processes: applications of mathematical modeling and computer simulation in arms policy analysis; editor: W. Ladd Hollist. New York, [1978]. pp. 279.

MILITARY SERVICE, COMPULSORY

— United States.

BROOKE (EDWARD W.) and NUNN (SAM) An all-volunteer force for the United States? Washington, [1977]. pp. 18. *(American Enterprise Institute for Public Policy Research. AEI Defense Reviews. [Vol. 1]. No. 5)*

BASKIR (LAWRENCE M.) and STRAUSS (WILLIAM A.) Chance and circumstance: the draft, the war, and the Vietnam generation. New York, 1978. pp. 312. *bibliog.*

MILIUTIN (NIKOLAI ALEKSEEVICH).

LINCOLN (W. BRUCE) Nikolai Miliutin: an enlightened Russian bureaucrat. Newtonville, Mass., 1977. pp. 130. *bibliog.*

MILK

— Prices — Australia.

LONGSON (IAN) Market milk pricing in Australia. [Perth], Department of Agriculture, 1975. pp. 35.

MILK TRADE

— Australia.

LONGSON (IAN) Market milk pricing in Australia. [Perth], Department of Agriculture, 1975. pp. 35.

MILL (JAMES).

LIVELY (JACK) and REES (JOHN COLLWYN) eds. Utilitarian logic and politics: James Mill's Essay on government, Macaulay's critique and the ensuing debate. Oxford, 1978. pp. 270.

MILLENNIUM.

WIPPER (AUDREY) Rural rebels: a study of two protest movements in Kenya. Nairobi, 1977. pp. 363. *bibliog.*

— History of doctrines.

OLIVER (WILLIAM HALDANE) Prophets and millennialists: the uses of biblical prophecy in England from the 1790s to the 1840s. Auckland, 1978. pp. 269. *bibliog.*

HARRISON (JOHN FLETCHER CLEWS) The second coming: popular millenarianism, 1780-1850. London, 1979. pp. 277. *bibliog.*

LAMONT (WILLIAM MONTGOMERIE) Richard Baxter and the millennium: Protestant imperialism and the English revolution. London, 1979. pp. 340.

MILLS (CHARLES WRIGHT).

KOROVIN (VLADISLAV FEDOROVICH) Osnovnye problemy "novoi sotsiologii" Raita Millsa [i.e. Wright Mills]. Moskva, 1977. pp. 95. *bibliog.*

MILTON (JOHN).

HILL (JOHN EDWARD CHRISTOPHER) Milton and the English Revolution. London, 1977. pp. 541. *bibliog.*

MIND AND BODY.

POPPER (Sir KARL RAIMUND) and ECCLES (Sir JOHN CAREW) The self and its brain. Berlin, [1977]. pp. 597. *bibliogs.*

WILKES (KATHLEEN V.) Physicalism. London, 1978. pp. 142.

MINERAL INDUSTRIES

— Australia — New South Wales.

NEW SOUTH WALES. Department of Mines. 1967. The mineral wealth of New South Wales. [Sydney, 1967]. pp. (16).

— Brazil.

BRAZIL. Conselho Nacional de Estatistica. Laboratorio de Estatistica. 1959. Numeros indices das quantidades e dos preços do produtor de 22 produtos da industria extrativa mineral nos anos de 1950 a 1958. Rio de Janeiro, [1959?]. fo. 13. *(Estudos sôbre as Quantidades e os Preços das Mercadorias Produzidas ou Negociadas. No. 88)*

— Canada — New Brunswick.

NEW BRUNSWICK. Office of the Economic Advisor. 1975. Mining. [Fredericton], 1975. fo.62. *(New Brunswick Industry Profiles. No.10)*

— Italy — Sardinia.

SARDINIA. Consiglio Regionale. Commissione Permanente Industria e Commercio - Dogane. 1969. Indagine nelle zone minerarie...: relazione, etc. [Cagliari, 1969]. pp. 308.

— United States.

NETSCHERT (BRUCE CARLTON) The mineral foreign trade of the United States in the twentieth century: a study in mineral economics. New York, 1977. pp. 465. *bibliog.*

MINERS

— Africa, Central.

PERRINGS (CHARLES) Black mineworkers in Central Africa: industrial strategies and the evolution of an African proletariat in the copperbelt 1911-41. London, 1979. pp. 302. *bibliog.*

— Canada.

MACMILLAN (JAMES A.) and others. Human resources in Canadian mining: a preliminary analysis. Kingston, Ont., [1977]. pp. 176. *(Kingston, Ontario. Queen's University. Centre for Resource Studies. National Impact of Mining Series. 4)*

— United Kingdom.

ARNOT (ROBERT PAGE) The miners: one union, one industry: a history of the National Union of Mineworkers, 1939-46. London, 1979. pp. 212.

MINES AND MINERAL RESOURCES.

CROWSON (PHILLIP) Non-fuel minerals and foreign policy. London, [1977]. 2 vols. *(Royal Institute of International Affairs. British Foreign Policy to 1985)*

ALEXANDERSSON (GUNNAR) and KLEVEBRING (BJÖRN-IVAR) World resources: energy, metals, minerals; studies in economic and political geography. Berlin, 1978. pp. 248. *bibliog.*

— Atlases.

DIXON (COLIN J.) Atlas of economic mineral deposits. London, 1979. pp. 143. *bibliog.*

— Canada — British Columbia.

GUNN (ANGUS M.) Minerals in British Columbia. [Victoria], Ministry of Mines and Petroleum Resources, [1978]. pp. 71.

— — New Brunswick.

NEW BRUNSWICK. Mines Division. 1978. New Brunswick's mineral industry, 1977. [Fredericton, 1978]. pp. 191. *(Topical Reports. 78-1)*

— — Newfoundland.

NEWFOUNDLAND. Mineral Development Division. Report of activities. a., 1974- , with gap(1975). St. John's.

— — Nova Scotia.

NOVA SCOTIA. Department of Mines. 1974. A brief history of mining and geology in Nova Scotia. [Halifax, 1974?]. 1 vol. (unpaged).

NOVA SCOTIA. Department of Development. Economics and Statistics Division. 1975. Mining industry profile and impact study. [Halifax], 1975. fo. 86.

NOVA SCOTIA. Department of Mines. 1976. Geology, minerals and mining in Nova Scotia. Halifax, [1976]. 1 pamphlet (unpaged). *bibliog. (Information Series. No.1)*

— Russia — Ukraine.

PALAMARCHUK (MAKSIM MARTYNOVICH) and others. Mineral'nye resursy i formirovanie promyshlennykh territorial'nykh kompleksov. Kiev, 1978. pp. 219. *bibliog.*

— South Africa.

DICKASON (G.B.) Cornish immigrants to South Africa: the Cousin Jacks' contribution to the development of mining and commerce, 1820-1920. Cape Town, 1978. pp. 122. *bibliog.*

ECONOMIST INTELLIGENCE UNIT. Q[uarterly] E[conomic] R[eview] Specials. No. 59. Mineral supplies from South Africa: their place in world resources; by W.C.J. van Rensburg. London, 1978. pp. 64.

MINIATURE COMPUTERS.

BRESLIN (JUDSON) and TASHENBERG (C. BRADLEY) Distributed processing systems: end of the mainframe era? New York, [1978]. pp. 228.

McKEONE (DERMOT H.) Small computers for business and industry. Farnborough, Hants., [1979]. pp. 209.

MINING ENGINEERS

— Poland.

JAROS (JERZY) Dzieje polskiej kadry technicznej w górnictwie, 1136-1976. Warszawa, 1978. pp. 296. *bibliog. With Russian and English summaries.*

MINING INDUSTRY AND FINANCE

— Colombia.

COLOMBIA. Departamento Administrativo Nacional de Estadistica. Censo de Minas y Canteras, 1969. Censo de minas y canteras, 1969. Bogota, [1969?]. pp. 18.

— Zambia.

MINING AND DEVELOPMENT CORPORATION [ZAMBIA]. An outline of the new structure for the mining industry in Zambia. Lusaka, 1970. pp. 23.

MINNESOTA UNIVERSITY.

GANDHI (RAJNIKANT SURESH) Locals and cosmopolitans of Little India: a sociological study of the Indian student community at Minnesota, U.S.A. Bombay, 1974. pp. 216. *bibliog.*

MINORITIES.

The MULTINATIONAL society: papers of the Ljubljana Seminar; William F. Mackey [and] Albert Verdoodt, editors. Rowley, Mass., [1975]. pp. 388. *bibliogs.*

WORLD minorities...; edited by Georgina Ashworth. Sunbury, Middx., 1977 in progress.

MINORITIES in history; edited by A.C. Hepburn. London, 1978. pp. 251. *Papers read before the Thirteenth Irish Conference of Historians at the New University of Ulster, 1977.*

TAJFEL (HENRI) The social psychology of minorities. London, 1978. pp. 20. *bibliog. (Minority Rights Group. Reports. No. 38)*

The FUTURE of cultural minorities; edited by Antony E. Alcock [and others]. London, 1979. pp. 221.

— Education.

RACE, education and identity; edited by Gajendra K. Verma and Christopher Bagley. London, 1979. pp. 268. *bibliog.*

— — United Kingdom.

EDWARDS (V.K.) The West Indian language issue in British schools: challenges and responses. London, 1979. pp. 168. *bibliog.*

MINORITIES.(Cont.)

JEFFCOATE (ROBERT) Positive image: towards a multiracial curriculum. London, 1979. pp. 124. *bibliogs.*

— — United States.

BRESNICK (DAVID) and others. Black white green red: the politics of education in ethnic America. New York, [1978]. pp. 166. *bibliog.*

— Employment — United States.

MANGUM (GARTH LEROY) and SENINGER (STEPHEN F.) Coming of age in the ghetto: a dilemma of youth unemployment. Baltimore, [1978]. pp. 114. *bibliog.*

— Housing — United Kingdom.

ETHNIC minorities and the public and voluntary services: housing; text of paper given to Institute of Social Welfare seminar, University of Nottingham, 18 March 1976. [Bristol, Social Science Research Council Research Unit on Ethnic Relations, 1976]. fo. 10.

WARD (ROBIN W.) Where race didn't divide: some reflections on slum clearance in Moss Side. [Bristol, Social Science Research Council Research Unit on Ethnic Relations, 1976]. fo. 19.

CLARK (DAVID) Immigrant responses to the British housing market: a case study in the West Midlands conurbation. Bristol, Social Science Research Council Research Unit on Ethnic Relations, [1977]. pp. 65. *bibliog. (Working Papers on Ethnic Relations. No. 7)*

U.K. Commission for Racial Equality. 1977. Housing need among ethnic minorities: comments on the consultative document on housing policy presented to Parliament by the Secretary of State for the Environment and the Secretary of State for Wales. London, 1977. pp. 9.

BARR (ALAN) Housing improvement and the multi-racial community: a report on action and research strategies in Oldham C[ommunity] D[evelopment] P[roject]. [York], 1978. pp. 99. *(Papers in Community Studies. No. 16)*

ELLIOTT (MARGARET) Writer on Housing. Shifting patterns in multi-occupation. Bristol, Social Science Research Council Research Unit on Ethnic Relations, [1978]. pp. 53. *(Working Papers on Ethnic Relations. No. 11)*

FLETT (HAZEL) Black council tenants in Birmingham. Bristol, Social Science Research Council Research Unit on Ethnic Relations, [1979]. pp. 79. *bibliog. (Working Papers on Ethnic Relations. No. 12)*

— Canada.

KRAUTER (JOSEPH F.) and DAVIS (MORRIS) Minority Canadians: ethnic groups. Toronto, [1978]. pp. 120.

UKRAINIAN Canadians, multiculturalism, and separation: an assessment: proceedings of a conference sponsored by the Canadian Institute of Ukrainian Studies,...Edmonton...1977; edited by Manoly R. Lupul. Edmonton, 1978. pp. 177.

— Europe.

STEPHENS (MEIC) Linguistic minorities in western Europe. [Llandysul], 1976 repr. 1978. pp. 796. *bibliog.*

— India.

SCHERMERHORN (RICHARD ALONZO) Ethnic plurality in India. Tucson, [1978]. pp. 369. *bibliogs.*

— Indonesia.

SURYADINATA (LEO) The Chinese minority in Indonesia. Singapore, 1978. pp. 175.

— Iraq.

MGOI (SHAKRO KHUDOEVICH) Problema natsional'noi avtonomii kurdskogo naroda v Irakskoi respublike, 1958-1970 gg. Erevan, 1977. pp. 333. *bibliog.*

— Russia.

AZRAEL (JEREMY RICHARD) Emergent nationality problems in the USSR. Santa Monica, 1977. pp. 33. *(Rand Corporation. [Rand Reports]. 2172)*

LISETSKII (ANATOLII MIKHAILOVICH) Voprosy natsional'noi politiki KPSS v usloviiakh razvitogo sotsializma: na materialakh Moldavskoi SSR. Kishinev, 1977. pp. 159.

NATIONALITIES and nationalism in the USSR: a Soviet dilemma; a joint symposium sponsored by the Center for Strategic and International Studies, Georgetown University, and the Institute for Sino-Soviet Studies, the George Washington University...1976; edited by Carl A. Linden and Dimitri K. Simes. Washington, D.C., 1977. pp. 61.

CARRÈRE D'ENCAUSSE (HÉLÈNE) L'empire éclaté: la révolte des nations en U.R.S.S. [Paris, 1978]. pp. 314. *bibliog.*

SOVIET nationality policies and practices; edited by Jeremy R. Azrael. New York, [1978]. pp. 393. *bibliogs.*

NATSIONAL'NYE otnosheniia v SSSR na sovremennom etape: na materialakh respublik Srednei Azii i Kazakhstana. Moskva, 1979. pp. 312.

— — Siberia.

DEMIDOV (VIKTOR ALEKSANDROVICH) Oktiabr' i natsional'nyi vopros v Sibiri, 1917-1923 gg. Novosibirsk, 1978. pp. 367.

— — Soviet Central Asia.

DAVLIATKADAMOV (KHUSHKADAM DAVLIATKADAMOVICH) Sotsial'no-klassovye osnovy sblizheniia sotsialisticheskikh natsii. Dushanbe, 1976. pp. 172.

— United Kingdom.

KANNAN (C.T.) Cultural adaptation of Asian immigrants: first and second generation. Greenford, 1978. pp. 246. *bibliog.*

— — Bibliography.

MADAN (RAJ) compiler. Coloured minorities in Great Britain: a comprehensive bibliography, 1970-1977. London, 1979. pp. 199.

— United States.

The ETHNIC experience in Pennsylvania; edited and with an introduction by John E. Bodnar. Lewisburg, [1973]. pp. 330.

ESSAYS and data on American ethnic groups; edited by Thomas Sowell. [Washington, 1978]. pp. 418.

ETHNIC leadership in America; edited by John Higham. Baltimore, [1978]. pp. 214. *(Johns Hopkins University. Department of History. Johns Hopkins Symposia in Comparative History. 9) Based on a symposium held at the Johns Hopkins University in 1976.*

ZERO population growth - for whom?: differential fertility and minority group survival; edited by Milton Himmelfarb and Victor Baras. Westport, 1978. pp. 213. *Proceedings of a conference held by the American Jewish Committee in 1975, in New York.*

DINNERSTEIN (LEONARD) and others. Natives and strangers: ethnic groups and the building of America. New York, 1979. pp. 333. *bibliog.*

— — Political activity.

PAVLAK (THOMAS JAMES) Ethnic identification and political behavior. San Francisco, 1976. pp. 108. *bibliog.*

— Yugoslavia.

NATIONS and nationalities of Yugoslavia. Beograd, 1974. pp. 549. *bibliog.*

MINORITY BUSINESS ENTERPRISES

— United States.

GLOVER (ROBERT W.) Minority enterprise in construction. New York, 1977. pp. 174. *bibliog.*

MINORITY WOMEN

— Europe.

MIGRANT women speak; interviews presented by Jean Guyot [and others]. London, 1978. pp. 164. *bibliog.*

MISCEGENATION

— Singapore.

HASSAN (RIAZ) Interethnic marriage in Singapore: a study in interethnic relations. Singapore, 1974. pp. 85. *bibliog. (Institute of Southeast Asian Studies. Occasional Papers. No. 21)*

MISCONDUCT IN OFFICE

— India.

INDIA. Shah Commission of Inquiry. 1978. Interim (and final) report(s); [J.C.Shah, chairman]. [Delhi], 1978. 3 vols. (in 1).

MISES (LUDWIG VON).

SYMPOSIUM ON THE ECONOMICS OF LUDWIG VON MISES, ATLANTA, 1974. The economics of Ludwig von Mises: toward a critical reappraisal; edited...by Laurence S. Moss. Kansas City, [1976]. pp. 129. *bibliog.*

MISSIONARIES

— Rhodesia.

RHODESIA. Ministry of Information, Immigration and Tourism. 1978. The murder of missionaries in Rhodesia. [Salisbury, 1978]. pp. 27.

MISSIONS

— Tunisia.

O'DONNELL (JOSEPH DEAN) Lavigerie in Tunisia: the interplay of imperialist and missionary. Athens, Ga., [1979]. pp. 300. *bibliog.*

— United Kingdom.

STUART (JOHN) Writer on Christian missions. Fifty years of the Costers' Mission and its founder W. J. Orsman, J.P. London, [1911]. pp. 122.

MISSISSIPPI

— Race relations.

COHN (DAVID LEWIS) Where I was born and raised. Notre Dame, 1967. pp. 380. *Part 1 of this book was published in 1935 under the title God shakes creation.*

MISSOURI

— Economic conditions.

MISSOURI ECONOMIC REVIEW: including new and expanding industries; [pd. by] Missouri Division of Commerce and Industrial Development. a., 1972- Jefferson City, Missouri.

MITSKEVICH (KANSTANTSIN MIKHAILAVICH).

See KOLAS (IAKUB) pseud.

MITTERRAND (FRANÇOIS).

MITTERRAND (FRANÇOIS) L'abeille et l'architecte: chronique. [Paris, 1978]. pp. 403.

MIXTEC LITERATURE

— History and criticism.

LEON-PORTILLA (MIGUEL) Pre-Columbian literatures of Mexico. Norman, 1969. pp. 191.

MLADOCESKÁ STRANA.

See NÁRODNÍ STRANA SVOBODOMYSLNÁ.

MOBILE COMMUNICATION SYSTEMS.

COMMUNICATIONS for a mobile society: an assessment of new technology; edited by Raymond Bowers [and others]. Beverly Hills, [1978]. pp. 427.

MOBILE HOMES
— United Kingdom.

U.K. Department of the Environment. 1977. Report of the mobile homes review; a study carried out within the Department of the Environment. London, 1977. pp. 38.

MODENA (PROVINCE)
— History.

La RESISTENZA nelle campagne modenesi. Modena, 1976. pp. 405. *(Istituto Storico della Resistenza in Modena e Provincia. Quaderni. 11)*

MODULES (ALGEBRA).

NORTHCOTT (DOUGLAS GEOFFREY) Finite free resolutions. Cambridge, 1976. pp. 271. *bibliog.*

MOHAMMEDAN COUNTRIES
— Population.

WOMEN'S status and fertility in the Muslim world; edited by James Allman. New York, [1978]. pp. 378. *bibliog.*

— Social conditions.

TURNER (BRYAN STANLEY) Marx and the end of Orientalism. London, 1978. pp. 98. *bibliog.*

— Social life and customs.

MUSLIM peoples: a world ethnographic survey; edited by Richard V. Weekes. Westport, Conn., 1978. pp. 546. *bibliogs.*

MOHAMMEDAN EMPIRE.

WATT (WILLIAM MONTGOMERY) and CACHIA (PIERRE) A history of Islamic Spain. Edinburgh, 1965. pp. 210. *bibliog.*

MOHAMMEDANISM.

GREEN (ARNOLD H.) The Tunisian ulama, 1873-1915: social structure and response to ideological currents. Leiden, 1978. pp. 324. *bibliog. (Social, Economic and Political Studies of the Middle East. vol. 22)*

MUSLIM-Christian conflicts: economic, political and social origins; edited by Suad Joseph and Barbara L.K. Pillsbury. Boulder, Colo., 1978. pp. 245. *bibliogs.*

MOHAMMEDANISM AND ECONOMICS.

GRAN (PETER) Islamic roots of capitalism: Egypt, 1760-1840. Austin, [1979]. pp. 278. *bibliog. (Texas University. Center for Middle Eastern Studies. Modern Middle Eastern Series. No. 4)*

MOHAMMEDANISM AND POLITICS.

WARBURG (GABRIEL) Islam, nationalism and communism in a traditional society: the case of Sudan. London, 1978. pp. 253. *bibliog.*

MOHAMMEDANISM IN AFRICA.

NAUDE (J.A.) Islam in Africa. Braamfontein, 1978. pp. 8. *(South African Institute of International Affairs. Occasional Papers)*

MOHAMMEDANS IN INDIA.

The EVOLUTION of Muslim political thought in India...; [edited by] A.M. Zaidi. New Delhi, 1975 in progress.

KAURA (UMA) Muslims and Indian nationalism: the emergence of the demand for India's partition, 1928-40. Columbia, Mo., 1977. pp. 223. *bibliog.*

GANI (H.A.) Muslim political issues and national integration. New Delhi, [1978]. pp. 230. *bibliog.*

MOHAMMEDANS IN MOROCCO.

MOROCCO. Service Central des Statistiques. 1961. La consommation et les dépenses des ménages Marocains Musulmans: résultats de l'enquête 1959-60; (rédigée par [P.] Dubois). [Rabat], 1961. pp. 206.

MOHAMMEDANS IN NIGERIA.

GBADAMOSI (T.G.O.) The growth of Islam among the Yoruba, 1841-1908. London, 1978. pp. 265. *bibliog.*

MOHAMMEDANS IN PAKISTAN.

HUSSAIN (ASAF) Elite politics in an ideological state: the case of Pakistan. Folkestone, 1979. pp. 212. *bibliog.*

MOHAMMEDANS IN RUSSIA.

BENNIGSEN (ALEXANDRE) and WIMBUSH (S. ENDERS) Muslim national communism in the Soviet Union: a revolutionary strategy for the colonial world. Chicago, [1979]. pp. 267. *bibliog. (Chicago. University. Center for Middle Eastern Studies. Publications. 11)*

MOHAMMEDANS IN SOUTH AFRICA.

DESAI (BARNEY) and MARNEY (CARDIFF) The killing of the Imam. London, 1978. pp. 146.

MOHAMMEDANS IN SPAIN.

WATT (WILLIAM MONTGOMERY) and CACHIA (PIERRE) A history of Islamic Spain. Edinburgh, 1965. pp. 210. *bibliog.*

BURCKHARDT (TITUS) Moorish culture in Spain; translated by Alisa Jaffa. London, [1972]. pp. 219. *bibliog.*

MOHAMMEDANS IN TUNISIA.

GREEN (ARNOLD H.) The Tunisian ulama, 1873-1915: social structure and response to ideological currents. Leiden, 1978. pp. 324. *bibliog. (Social, Economic and Political Studies of the Middle East. vol. 22)*

MOLDAVIA
— Nationalism.

ESAULENKO (ALEKSANDR SERGEEVICH) Sotsialisticheskaia revoliutsiia v Moldavii i politicheskii krakh burzhuaznogo natsionalizma, 1917-1918. Kishinev, 1977. pp. 212. *bibliog.*

MOLDAVIAN REPUBLIC
— Economic history.

SOTSIALISTICHESKOE i kommunisticheskoe stroitel'stvo v Moldavskoi SSR: voprosy istorii; mezhvuzovskii sbornik. Kishinev, 1978. pp. 89.

— Economic policy — Mathematical models.

KOZHUKHAR' (PAVEL VASIL'EVICH) Voprosy kompleksnogo planirovaniia khoziaistva soiuznoi respubliki. Moskva, 1979. pp. 179. *bibliog. (Akademiia Nauk SSSR. Problemy Sovetskoi Ekonomiki)*

— History — Sources.

SOVETSKOE stroitel'stvo v levoberezhnykh raionakh Moldavii, 1921-1924: sbornik dokumentov i materialov; redaktsionnaia kollegiia B.K. Vizer [and others]. Kishinev, 1977. pp. 378.

— — 1917-1921, Revolution.

ESAULENKO (ALEKSANDR SERGEEVICH) Sotsialisticheskaia revoliutsiia v Moldavii i politicheskii krakh burzhuaznogo natsionalizma, 1917-1918. Kishinev, 1977. pp. 212. *bibliog.*

— Nationalism.

LISETSKII (ANATOLII MIKHAILOVICH) Voprosy natsional'noi politiki KPSS v usloviiakh razvitogo sotsializma: na materialakh Moldavskoi SSR. Kishinev, 1977. pp. 159.

MOLINA ENRIQUEZ (ANDRES).

HAMON (JAMES L.) and NIBLO (STEPHEN R.) Precursores de la revolucion agraria en Mexico: las obras de Wistano Luis Orozco y Andres Molina Enriquez; traduccion de Omar Costa Acosta. Mexico, Secretaria de Educacion Publica, 1975. pp. 183. *(Sep/Setentas. 202)*

MOLTKE (HELMUTH JAMES VON) Graf.

FINKER (KURT) Graf Moltke und der Kreisauer Kreis. Berlin, [1978]. pp. 336. *bibliog.*

MOMBASA
— Politics and government.

STREN (RICHARD E.) Housing the urban poor in Africa: policy, politics and bureaucracy in Mombasa. Berkeley, Calif., [1978]. pp. 330. *bibliog. (California University. Institute of International Studies. Research Series. No. 34)*

— Social conditions.

STREN (RICHARD E.) Housing the urban poor in Africa: policy, politics and bureaucracy in Mombasa. Berkeley, Calif., [1978]. pp. 330. *bibliog. (California University. Institute of International Studies. Research Series. No. 34)*

MOMMSEN (THEODOR).

KUCZYNSKI (JUERGEN) Studien zu einer Geschichte der Gesellschaftswissenschaften. Berlin, 1975-78. 10 vols.

MONARCHY.

BENDIX (REINHARD) Kings or people: power and the mandate to rule. Berkeley, 1978. pp. 692.

MONASTERIES
— France.

EVANS (JOAN) Monastic life at Cluny 910-1157. Hamden, Conn., 1968. pp. 137. *bibliog. Reprint of work first published in 1931.*

HUNT (NOREEN) Cluny under Saint Hugh 1049-1109. Notre Dame, Ind., 1968. pp. 228. *bibliog.*

SUGER, Abbot of Saint-Denis, 1081-1151. Abbot Suger on the abbey church of St. Denis and its art treasures; edited...by Erwin Panofsky; second edition by Gerda Panofsky-Soergel. 2nd ed. Princeton, [1979]. pp. 285. *bibliog.*

— Russia.

ZIMIN (ALEKSANDR ALEKSANDROVICH) Krupnaia feodal'naia votchina i sotsial'no-politicheskaia bor'ba v Rossii, konets XV - XVI v. Moskva, 1977. pp. 356.

— United Kingdom.

NORTHAMPTONSHIRE RECORD SOCIETY. [Publications]. vol. 28. The cartularies and registers of Peterborough Abbey; by Janet D. Martin. [Northampton], 1978. pp. 52.

MONASTICISM AND RELIGIOUS ORDERS
— Rules.

BENEDICT, Saint, Abbot of Monte Cassino. The rule of Saint Benedict. London, 1978. pp. 79.

MONETARY POLICY.

ECONOMETRIC studies of macro and monetary relations; edited by Alan A. Powell and Ross A. Williams. Amsterdam, 1973. pp. 358. *bibliog. Papers presented at the second Australasian Conference of Econometricians held at Monash University, 1971.*

SZASZ (ANDRE) Monetary policy and exchange rate stability. Amsterdam, [1978?]. pp. 33. *(Nederlandsche Bank. Reprints. No. 39)*

CARGILL (THOMAS F.) Money, the financial system, and monetary policy. Englewood Cliffs, [1979]. pp. 552. *bibliogs.*

MONETARY POLICY.(Cont.)

FABIAN SOCIETY. Fabian Tracts. [No.] 462. The politics of monetarism; [by] Bryan Gould [and others]. London, 1979. pp. 19.

PERKINS (JAMES OLIVER NEWTON) The macroeconomic mix to stop stagflation. London, 1979. pp. 193. *bibliog.*

VANE (HOWARD R.) and THOMPSON (JOHN L.) Monetarism: theory, evidence and policy. Oxford, 1979. pp. 200. *bibliogs.*

— Africa.

NANA-SINKAM (SAMUEL C.) Monetary integration and theory of optimum currency areas in Africa. The Hague, [1978]. pp. 315. *bibliog.*

— France.

FRANCE. Groupe d'Economie Monétaire Appliquée. 1978. Crédit, change et inflation: rapport du groupe d'économie monétaire appliquée. [Paris, 1978]. 2 vols. *(France. Commissariat Général du Plan. Economie et Planification)*

— Greece.

ZOLOTAS (XENOPHON) Inflation and the monetary target in Greece: an address. Athens, 1978. pp. 27. *bibliog.* *(Bank of Greece. Papers and Lectures. 38)*

— New Zealand.

NICHOLL (P.W.E.) New Zealand monetary policy in the 1970s: analysis and perspective. Wellington, 1977. pp. 22. *bibliog.* *(Reserve Bank of New Zealand. Research Papers. No.23)*

— Switzerland.

LEUTWILER (FRITZ) Swiss monetary and exchange rate policy in an inflationary world; translated [from the German] by Herbert Zassenhaus. Washington, [1978]. pp. 14. *(American Enterprise Institute for Public Policy Research. AEI Studies. 218)*

— United Kingdom.

CRAVEN (B.) Recent developments in British monetary policy. [Newcastle], 1977. fo. 42. *bibliog.* *(Newcastle-upon-Tyne Polytechnic. Department of Economics. Occasional Papers. No. 1)*

GOWLAND (DAVID) Monetary policy and credit control: the U.K. experience. London, [1978]. pp. 219.

HOCKLEY (GRAHAM CHARLES) Public finance: an introduction. rev. ed. London, 1979. pp. 448. *bibliog.*

— — Mathematical models.

SAVAGE (DAVID) The monetary sector of the NIESR model: preliminary results. London, [1978]. pp. 24. *bibliog.* *(National Institute of Economic and Social Research. Discussion Papers. No.21)*

— United States.

HYMAN (SIDNEY) Marriner S. Eccles: private entrepreneur and public servant. Stanford, Calif., 1976. pp. 456.

SUTTON (ANTONY C.) The war on gold. Sandton, South Africa, 1977. pp. 238. *bibliog.*

ECKSTEIN (OTTO) The great recession, with a postscript on stagflation. Amsterdam, 1978. pp. 213.

MILLER (RANDALL J.) The regional impact of monetary policy in the United States. Lexington, Mass., [1978]. pp. 155. *bibliogs.*

REDISTRIBUTION through the financial system: the grants economics of money and credit; [edited by] Kenneth E. Boulding and Thomas Frederick Wilson. New York, [1978]. pp. 301. *bibliogs.*

TIMBERLAKE (RICHARD HENRY) The origins of central banking in the United States. Cambridge, Mass., 1978. pp. 272. *bibliog.*

COCHRAN (JOHN A.) Money, banking, and the economy. 4th ed. New York, [1979]. pp. 588. *bibliogs.*

MONETARY UNIONS.

VLERICK (ANDRE J.) European monetary union. [Brussels], Ministry of Foreign Affairs, External Trade and Cooperation in Development, 1972. pp. 14. *(Memo from Belgium. No. 153)*

NANA-SINKAM (SAMUEL C.) Monetary integration and theory of optimum currency areas in Africa. The Hague, [1978]. pp. 315. *bibliog.*

MONEY.

[CARRER (LUIGI) ed.] Notizie mercantili delle monete e de'cambi; [extracts from works by Francesco Dino di Iacopo, Bernardo Davanzati, Giovanni Botero, and John Locke]. Venezia, [imprint], 1840. pp. 226. *(Biblioteca Classica Italiana di Scienza, Lettere ed Arti. Classe 5, vol. 6)*

The INTERNATIONAL monetary system and the developing nations; edited by Danny M. Leipziger. Washington, Agency for International Development, Bureau for Program and Policy Coordination, 1976. pp. 210. *bibliogs.*

BROWN (BRENDAN) Money hard and soft on the international currency markets. London, 1978. pp. 183. *bibliog.*

EBELING (RICHARD M.) ed. The Austrian theory of the trade cycle and other essays; by Ludwig von Mises [and others]. New York, 1978. pp. 44. *(Centre for Libertarian Studies. Occasional Papers Series. 8)*

HANSON (JOHN LLOYD) Monetary theory and practice. 6th ed. Plymouth, 1978. pp. 338.

HAYEK (FRIEDRICH AUGUST) Denationalisation of money: the argument refined: an analysis of the theory and practice of concurrent currencies. 2nd ed. London, 1978. pp. 144. *bibliog.* *(Institute of Economic Affairs. Hobart Papers. 70)*

LINDHOLM (RICHARD WADSWORTH) Money management and institutions. Totowa, N.J., 1978. pp. 434. *bibliogs.*

NAGATANI (KEIZO) Monetary theory. Amsterdam, 1978. pp. 299. *bibliogs.*

SMELT (SIMON JONATHAN) Money as a social phenomenon. 1978. fo. 408. *bibliog. Typescript.* Ph.D. (London) thesis: unpublished. This thesis is the property of London University and may not be removed from the Library.

THOMAS (LLOYD BREWSTER) Money, banking, and economic activity. Englewood Cliffs, N.J., [1979]. pp. 626.

— Congresses — Bretton Woods International Monetary Conference, 1944.

DORMAEL (ARMAND VAN) Bretton Woods: birth of a monetary system. London, 1978. pp. 322.

— Psychological aspects.

SMELT (SIMON JONATHAN) Money as a social phenomenon. 1978. fo. 408. *bibliog. Typescript.* Ph.D. (London) thesis: unpublished. This thesis is the property of London University and may not be removed from the Library.

— Africa, East.

BLUMENTHAL (ERWIN) Tanganyika - East Africa: the present monetary system and its future; report to the Government of Tanganyika. Dar es Salaam, Government Printer, 1963. pp. 76.

— Argentine Republic.

SEGRETI (CARLOS S.A.) Moneda y politica en la primera mitad del siglo XIX: contribucion al estudio de la historia de la moneda argentina. Tucuman, 1975. pp. 269.

— Brazil.

PELAEZ (CARLOS MANUEL) and SUZIGAN (WILSON) Historia monetaria do Brasil: analise da politica, comportamento e instituições monetarias. Rio de Janeiro, 1976. pp. 487. *(Brazil. Instituto de Planejamento Econômico e Social. Instituto de Pesquisas. Monografias. No.23)*

— Communist countries.

LIUBSKII (MIKHAIL SERGEEVICH) and others. Valiutnye i kreditnye otnosheniia stran SEV. Moskva, 1978. pp. 160.

— European Economic Community countries.

BANKER RESEARCH UNIT. Banking and sources of finance in the European Community; edited by Philip Thorn [and] Jean M. Lack. London, 1977. pp. 313.

— Russia.

ROGOVA (OL'GA LEONIDOVNA) Denezhnoe obrashchenie i kratkosrochnyi kredit: issledovanie sviazei i proportsii. Moskva, 1978. pp. 158.

— Underdeveloped areas.

See UNDERDEVELOPED AREAS — Money.

— United Kingdom.

HOCKLEY (GRAHAM CHARLES) Public finance: an introduction. rev. ed. London, 1979. pp. 448. *bibliog.*

— — Mathematical models.

A FINANCIAL sector for the Treasury model. Part 1. The model of the domestic monetary system; by Peter Spencer and Colin Mowl. Part 2. The model of external capital flows; by Rachel Lomax and Michael Denham. London, Treasury, 1978. pp. 115. *bibliogs.* *(Government Economic Service Working Papers. No. 17)*

— — Wales.

JONES (REG CHAMBERS) Arian: the story of money and banking in Wales. Swansea, 1978. pp. 170. *bibliog.*

— United States.

COCHRAN (JOHN A.) Money, banking, and the economy. 4th ed. New York, [1979]. pp. 588. *bibliogs.*

MONEY SUPPLY.

CRAVEN (B.) The theory of the optimum supply of money: some empirical evidence. [Newcastle], 1977. fo. 15. *bibliog.* *(Newcastle-upon-Tyne Polytechnic. Department of Economics. Occasional Papers. No.2)*

HAYEK (FRIEDRICH AUGUST) Denationalisation of money: the argument refined: an analysis of the theory and practice of concurrent currencies. 2nd ed. London, 1978. pp. 144. *bibliog.* *(Institute of Economic Affairs. Hobart Papers. 70)*

— United States.

BERMAN (PETER I.) Inflation and the money supply in the United States, 1956-1977. Lexington, Mass., [1978]. pp. 137. *bibliog.*

MONGOLIA

— Economic conditions.

MATVEEVA (GALINA SERGEEVNA) Sozdanie material'no-tekhnicheskoi bazy sotsializma v MNR. Moskva, 1978. pp. 278. *bibliog.*

— Industries.

GERBOVA (ANGELINA ANATOL'EVNA) and SHURUBOVICH (ALEKSEI VIKTOROVICH) Razvitie promyshlennosti MNR na sovremennom etape. Moskva, 1978. pp. 114. *bibliog.*

MONMOUTH'S REBELLION, 1685.

EARLE (PETER) Monmouth's rebels: the road to Sedgemoor, 1685. London, [1977]. pp. 236.

MONOPOLIES.

TESTA (VICTOR) El capital imperialista. Buenos Aires, 1975. pp. 460.

INTERNATIONALE Monopole; Redaktionskollegium: Christos Fundulis [and others]. Berlin, 1978. pp. 287.

SCHMALENSEE (RICHARD) The control of natural monopolies. Lexington, Mass., [1979]. pp. 178. *bibliog.*

MONOTHEISM.

GUTKIND (ERICH) The absolute collective: a philosophical attempt to overcome our broken state;...translated from the original German text by Marjorie Gabain. London, 1937. pp. 120.

MONTAGU (Lady MARY WORTLEY).

[SYMONDS (EMILY MORSE)] Lady Mary Wortley Montagu and her times; by George Paston, [pseud.]. London, 1907. pp. 559.

MONTE ALBAN, MEXICO.

BLANTON (RICHARD E.) Monte Albán: settlement patterns at the ancient Zapotec capital. New York, [1978]. pp. 451. *bibliog. Map in end pocket.*

MONTREAL

— Climate.

POWE (NORMAN N.) The climate of Montreal. Ottawa, Queen's Printer, 1969 [or rather 1970]. pp. 51. *bibliog. (Climatological Studies. No. 15)*

— Economic conditions.

AUBIN (HENRY) City for sale. Montréal, [1977]. pp. 401.

— Growth.

AUBIN (HENRY) City for sale. Montréal, [1977]. pp. 401.

MONTREAL COLONIZATION RAILWAY.

YOUNG (BRIAN J.) Promoters and politicians: the North-Shore Railways in the history of Quebec, 1854-85. Toronto, [1978]. pp. 193. *bibliog.*

MORAL CONDITIONS.

DAVISON (IAN) b. 1939. Values, ends, and society. St. Lucia, [1977]. pp. 257. *bibliog.*

MORENO BACA (JESUS).

KRAUZE (ENRIQUE) Caudillos culturales en la Revolucion mexicana. Mexico, 1976. pp. 340.

MORMONS AND MORMONISM.

HILL (DONNA) Joseph Smith: the first Mormon. Garden City, 1977. pp. 527. *bibliog.*

MORTALITY.

GERSHENSON (HARRY) Measurement of mortality. Chicago, 1961 repr. 1972. pp. 340.

HIRSCHMAN (CHARLES) and TAN KAH JOO (EDWARD) Evaluation of mortality date in the vital statistics of West Malaysia. Kuala Lumpur, 1971. pp. 28, 26. *(Federation of Malaysia. Department of Statistics. Research Papers. No.5) In English and Malay.*

BRUNEEL (CLAUDE) La mortalité dans les campagnes: le duché de Brabant aux XVIIe et XVIIIe siècles. Louvain, 1977. pp. 777. *bibliog. (Louvain. Université. Recueil de Travaux d'Histoire et de Philologie. 6e Série. Fasc. 10)*

— Tables.

OSWALD (R.R.) Report on Bahamas life tables 1962-1964 and 1969-1971. Nassau, Department of Statistics, [1973]. pp. 36.

U.K. Office of Population Censuses and Surveys. Medical Statistics Division. Social and biological factors in infant mortality. a., 1975/76(3rd)- London.

— United Kingdom — Tables.

U.K. Office of Population Censuses and Surveys. Medical Statistics Division. 1977. Mortality surveillance, 1968-1975, England and Wales: deaths and rates by A-list cause, sex and age group. [London, 1977]. 1 vol. (unfoliated).

U.K. Office of Population Censuses and Surveys. Medical Statistics Division. 1978. Mortality surveillance, 1968-1976, England and Wales: deaths and rates by A-list cause, sex and age group: microfiche version. [London, 1978]. Microfiche (1 card) and accompanying booklet.

MORTGAGES

— United Kingdom.

MAYES (DAVID G.) The property boom: the effects of building society behaviour on house prices. Oxford, 1979. pp. 146. *bibliog.*

MOSCOW

— Economic conditions — Mathematical models.

CHISTIAKOV (EVGENII GAVRILOVICH) and SEMENOV (AL'BERT KONSTANTINOVICH) Balansovye modeli khoziaistva goroda. Moskva, 1977. pp. 192. *bibliog.*

— Politics and government.

GORODSKOE KHOZIAISTVO MOSKVY: (ezhemesiachnyi zhurnal Ispolkoma Moskovskogo Gorodskogo Soveta Deputatov Trudiashchikhsia). m., Ap 1953 (1953: 4)- , with gap (My 1966). Moskva.

SANBUROV (VASILII IVANOVICH) Moskovskii "Rabochii soiuz": u istokov proletarskoi bor'by. Moskva, 1978. pp. 133.

MOTHER AND CHILD.

LEWIS (MICHAEL) 1937- , and ROSENBLUM (LEONARD A.) eds. The effect of the infant on its caregiver. New York, [1974]. pp. 264. *bibliogs. The outgrowth of a conference sponsored by Educational Testing Service, Princeton, N.J.*

SOCIAL development in childhood: day-care programs and research; edited by Roger A. Webb. Baltimore, [1977]. pp. 196. *bibliogs. Papers from the 4th Hyman Blumberg Symposium on Research in Early Childhood Education, held Mar. 7-9, 1974.*

WYLAND (FRANCIE) Motherhood, lesbianism and child custody. Toronto, 1977. pp. 34.

MOTHERS.

OAKLEY (ANN) Becoming a mother. Oxford, 1979. pp. 328.

— Employment — Canada.

CANADA. Women's Bureau. 1970. Working mothers and their child-care arrangements. Ottawa, 1970. pp. 58.

— — United Kingdom.

HEWITT (MARGARET) Wives and mothers in Victorian industry. Westport, Conn., 1975. pp. 245. *bibliog. Reprint of work originally published London, 1958.*

NURSERY ACTION GROUP and BENWELL COMMUNITY DEVELOPMENT PROJECT. Work and play in Benwell. [Newcastle-upon-Tyne, 1977?]. pp. 29.

MOTON (ROBERT RUSSA).

MOTON (ROBERT RUSSA) Finding a way out: an autobiography. [Garden City, N.Y.], 1920; New York, 1969. pp. 296. *Facsimile reprint.*

MOTOR BUS LINES

— Zambia.

ZAMBIA. Central Statistical Office. 1972. Report on passenger road transport in Zambia, 1971. Lusaka, [1972?]. pp. 37.

MOTOR TRUCKS

— Law and legislation — United States.

DAVIS (GRANT MILLER) and DILLARD (JOHN E.) Increasing motor carrier productivity: an empirical analysis. New York, [1977]. pp. 128. *bibliog.*

MOVIMENTO SOCIALE ITALIANO.

ROSENBAUM (PETRA) Neofaschismus in Italien. Frankfurt, [1975]. pp. 117. *bibliog.*

MOVING PICTURES.

SARRIS (ANDREW) Politics and cinema. New York, 1978. pp. 215.

— Censorship — United Kingdom.

DEFENCE OF LITERATURE AND THE ARTS SOCIETY. Evidence to the Committee on Obscenity and Film Censorship. London, 1978. pp. 13.

— Social aspects — Hong Kong.

JARVIE (IAN CHARLES) Window on Hong Kong: a sociological study of the Hong Kong film industry and its audience. Hong Kong, 1977. pp. 223. *bibliog. (Hong Kong. University. Centre of Asian Studies. Occasional Papers and Monographs. No. 22)*

— Germany.

TAYLOR (RICHARD TRUEMAN) Film propaganda: Soviet Russia and Nazi Germany. London, [1979]. pp. 265. *bibliog.*

— Russia.

TAYLOR (RICHARD TRUEMAN) Film propaganda: Soviet Russia and Nazi Germany. London, [1979]. pp. 265. *bibliog.*

MOVING PICTURES IN PROPAGANDA.

TAYLOR (RICHARD TRUEMAN) Film propaganda: Soviet Russia and Nazi Germany. London, [1979]. pp. 265. *bibliog.*

MUELLER-MEININGEN (ERNST).

REIMANN (JOACHIM) Ernst Müller-Meiningen senior und der Linksliberalismus in seiner Zeit: zur Biographie eines bayerischen und deutschen Politikers, 1866-1944. München, 1968. pp. 305. *bibliog. (Munich. Stadtarchiv. Neue Schriftenreihe. Band 27)*

MUENZENBERG (WILLY).

GROSS (BABETTE) Willi Münzenberg: a political biography;...translated by Marian Jackson. [East Lansing], 1974. pp. 337.

MULTILINGUALISM.

ADVANCES in the study of societal multilingualism; edited by Joshua A. Fishman. The Hague, [1978]. pp. 842. *bibliogs.*

MULTIVARIATE ANALYSIS.

PURI (MADAN LAL) and SEN (PRANAB KUMAR) Nonparametric statistics in multivariate analysis. New York, [1971]. pp. 440. *bibliog.*

JOHNSON (NORMAN LLOYD) and KOTZ (SAMUEL) Distributions in statistics: continuous multivariate distributions. New York, [1972]. pp. 333. *bibliog.*

GNANADESIKAN (R.) Methods for statistical data analysis of multivariate observations. New York, [1977]. pp. 311. *bibliog.*

MULTIVARIATE ANALYSIS.(Cont.)

MAXWELL (ALBERT ERNEST) Multivariate analysis in behavioural research. London, 1977. pp. 164. *bibliog.*

GOODMAN (LEO A.) Analyzing qualitative/categorical data: log-linear models and latent-structure analysis;...Jay Magidson, editor. Cambridge, Mass., [1978]. pp. 471. *bibliogs.*

KSHIRSAGAR (ANANT M.) Multivariate analysis. New York, [1978?]. pp. 533. *bibliogs.*

WEBBER (RICHARD J.) Parliamentary constituencies: a socio-economic classification. [London], 1978. pp. 58. *(U.K. Office of Population Censuses and Surveys. Occasional Papers. 13)*

— Bibliography.

ANDERSON (THEODORE WILBUR) and others, compilers. A bibliography of multivariate statistical analysis. Huntington, N.Y., 1977. pp. 642.

— Graphic methods.

EVERITT (BRIAN S.) Graphical techniques for multivariate data. London, 1978. pp. 117. *bibliog.*

MUN (ADRIEN ALBERT MARIE DE) Comte.

MARTIN (BENJAMIN F.) Count Albert de Mun: paladin of the Third Republic. Chapel Hill, [1978]. pp. 367.

MUN (ALBERT DE) Comte.

See MUN (ADRIEN ALBERT MARIE DE) Comte.

MUNICH

— Politics and government.

SCHNEIDER (LUDWIG M.) Die populäre Kritik an Staat und Gesellschaft in München, 1886-1914: ein Beitrag zur Vorgeschichte der Münchner Revolution von 1918/19. München, 1975. pp. 425. *bibliog. (Munich. Stadtarchiv. Neue Schriftenreihe. Band 81)*

— Social history.

SCHNEIDER (LUDWIG M.) Die populäre Kritik an Staat und Gesellschaft in München, 1886-1914: ein Beitrag zur Vorgeschichte der Münchner Revolution von 1918/19. München, 1975. pp. 425. *bibliog. (Munich. Stadtarchiv. Neue Schriftenreihe. Band 81)*

MUNICH FOUR-POWER AGREEMENT, 1938.

WOYTAK (RICHARD A.) On the border of war and peace: Polish intelligence and diplomacy in 1937-1939 and the origins of the ultra secret. Boulder, 1979. pp. 141. *bibliog. (East European Quarterly. East European Monographs. 49)*

MUNICIPAL BUDGETS

— United States.

HENDERSON (THOMAS A.) and FOSTER (JOHN L.) Urban policy game: a simulation of urban politics. New York, [1978]. pp. 137.

MUNICIPAL CORPORATIONS

— Canada — Nova Scotia.

NOVA SCOTIA. Statutes, etc. 1979. Towns Act: 1979 office consolidation. Halifax, 1979. pp. 66.

MUNICIPAL FINANCE.

BURCHELL (ROBERT WILLIAM) and LISTOKIN (DAVID) The fiscal impact handbook: estimating local costs and revenues of land development. New Brunswick, [1978]. pp. 480. *bibliog.*

— Canada — Nova Scotia.

NOVA SCOTIA. Department of Municipal Affairs. 1979. Fiscal justice: proposals for a new municipal grant system. Halifax, 1979. pp. 33.

— Germany.

GERMANY. Statistisches Reichsamt. Statistik des Deutschen Reichs. Neue Folge. Band 387. Kommunale Finanzwirtschaft: Ausgaben und Einnahmen der Gemeinden nach Grössenklassen sowie der Gemeindeverbände für die Rechnungsjahre 1913/14 und 1925/26 bis 1928/29. Berlin, 1931; Osnabrück, 1978. pp. 647. *Photographic reprint.*

MUNICIPAL GOVERNMENT.

ANASTASSOPOULOS (J.P.) and others. La gestion des grandes métropoles: étude comparée de douze agglomérations étrangères;...préface de Pierre Christian Taittinger. Paris, La Documentation Française, [1978]. pp. 176. *bibliog.*

HENDERSON (THOMAS A.) and FOSTER (JOHN L.) Urban policy game: a simulation of urban politics. New York, [1978]. pp. 137.

SCHECTER (STEPHEN BENJAMIN) The politics of urban liberation. Montreal, [1978]. pp. 203. *bibliogs.*

— Canada.

PLUNKETT (THOMAS J.) and BETTS (GEORGE M.) The management of Canadian urban government: a basic text for a course in urban management. Kingston, Ontario, [1978]. pp. 304. *bibliog.*

TINDAL (C.R.) and TINDAL (S.NOBES) Local government in Canada: an introduction. Toronto, [1979]. pp. 159. *bibliog.*

— — New Brunswick.

NEW BRUNSWICK. Task Force on Non-Incorporated Areas in New Brunswick. 1976. Report; [E.G. Allen, chairman]. [Fredericton], 1976. pp. 103.

— Netherlands.

BERGE (J.B.J.M. TEN) Decentraliseren met commissies: binnengemeentelijke organisatiestructuren op basis van artikel 61 gemeentewet. 's-Gravenhage, 1978. pp. 343. *bibliog.*

— Russia.

KIZEVETTER (ALEKSANDR ALEKSANDROVICH) Posadskaia obshchina v Rossii XVIII stoletiia...; with a new introduction by Gilbert Rozman, Princeton University. Newtonville, Mass., 1978. pp. 810. *bibliog. Xerographic reprint of 1st ed., Moscow, 1903, with additional new title page.*

— Underdeveloped areas.

See UNDERDEVELOPED AREAS — Municipal government.

— United Kingdom.

FRASER (DEREK) Power and authority in the Victorian city. Oxford, 1979. pp. 190. *bibliog.*

— United States.

The AGE of urban reform: new perspectives on the progressive era; [edited by] Michael H. Ebner and Eugene M. Tobin. Port Washington, N.Y., 1977. pp. 213. *bibliog.*

FOX (KENNETH) Better city government: innovation in American urban politics, 1850-1937. Philadelphia, 1977. pp. 222.

LINEBERRY (ROBERT L.) and SHARKANSKY (IRA) Urban politics and public policy. 3rd ed. New York, [1978]. pp. 421. *bibliogs.*

MUNICIPAL GOVERNMENT BY COMMISSION.

RICE (BRADLEY ROBERT) Progressive cities: the commission government movement in America, 1901-1920. Austin, Tex., [1977]. pp. 160. *bibliog.*

MUNICIPAL HOME RULE

— United States.

FOX (KENNETH) Better city government: innovation in American urban politics, 1850-1937. Philadelphia, 1977. pp. 222.

MUNICIPAL OWNERSHIP

— United Kingdom.

HOPPÉ (MALCOLM) Direct labour: how councils waste our money. [London, 1978]. pp. 11.

MUNICIPAL RESEARCH

— United Kingdom.

U.K. Department of the Environment. Library. 1978. Urban and regional research: a directory of organisations; eited by W.W. Helps. [London], 1978. pp. 78. *bibliogs. (Information Series. No. 30)*

MUNICIPAL SERVICES

— Canada — New Brunswick.

NEW BRUNSWICK. Department of Municipal Affairs. Annual report. a., 1955- , with gaps. Fredericton.

— — Prince Edward Island.

PRINCE EDWARD ISLAND. Department of Municipal Affairs. Annual report. a., 1971- Charlottetown.

— — Saskatchewan.

SASKATCHEWAN. Department of Municipal Affairs. Annual report. a., 1977/78- Regina.

— Underdeveloped areas.

See UNDERDEVELOPED AREAS — Municipal services.

— United Kingdom.

URBAN PROGRAMME RESEARCH. Working Papers. 4. Urban programme decision making: the phase 7 exercise. Leeds, [1974?]. fo. 42.

— United States.

DIMOND (PAUL R.) and others. A dilemma of local government: discrimination in the provision of public services. Lexington, Mass., [1978]. pp. 319. *bibliogs.*

MUNITIONS

— Belgium.

GAIER (CLAUDE) L'industrie et le commerce des armes dans les anciennes principautés belges du XIIIme à la fin du XVme siècle. Paris, 1973. pp. 395. *bibliog. (Liège. Université. Faculté de Philosophie et Lettres. Bibliothèque. Fasc. 202)*

— Russia.

INTERNATIONAL INSTITUTE FOR STRATEGIC STUDIES. Adelphi Papers. No. 147, 148. Decision-making in Soviet weapons procurement; by Arthur J. Alexander. London, 1978-79. pp. 64.

— United Kingdom.

EVANS (HAROLD) Vickers: against the odds, 1956-1977. London, [1978]. pp. 287.

FREEDMAN (LAWRENCE DAVID) Arms production in the United Kingdom: problems and prospects. London, [1978]. pp. 50. *(Royal Institute of International Affairs. British Foreign Policy to 1985)*

MURDER

— United Kingdom.

MORRIS (TERENCE PATRICK) and BLOM-COOPER (LOUIS JACQUES) Murder in England and Wales since 1957. [London], 1979. pp. 16.

MURRAY (Sir JAMES AUGUSTUS HENRY).

MURRAY (KATHERINE MAUD ELISABETH) Caught in the web of words: James A.H. Murray and the Oxford English Dictionary. Oxford, 1979. pp. 386.

MUSEUMS

— Canada.

CANADA. Statistics Canada. Culture statistics: museums, art galleries and related institutions, large institutions. a., 1976(1st)- Ottawa. *[in English and French]*

MUSIC-HALLS (VARIETY-THEATRES, CABARETS, ETC.).

— United Kingdom.

CHESHIRE (D.F.) Music hall in Britain. Rutherford, N.J., 1974. pp. 112. *bibliog.*

MUSSOLINI (BENITO).

GOERLITZ (WALTER) Geldgeber der Macht: wie Hitler, Lenin, Mao Tse-tung, Mussolini, Stalin und Tito finanziert wurden. Frankfurt am Main, 1978. pp. 256. *bibliog.*

MICHAELIS (MEIR) Mussolini and the Jews: German-Italian relations and the Jewish question in Italy, 1922-1945. Oxford, 1978. pp. 472. *bibliog.*

MUTHULAKSHMI REDDY (S.).

MUTHULAKSHMI REDDY (S.) My experience as a legislator. Madras, [imprint], 1930. pp. 246.

MUTINY

— United Kingdom.

EDWARDS (DUDLEY) The soldiers' revolt. Nottingham, [1978]. pp. 22. *(Spokesman, The. Pamphlets. No.62)*

MUZOREWA (ABEL TENDEKAI).

MUZOREWA (ABEL TENDEKAI) Rise up and walk: an autobiography. London, 1978. pp. 289.

MYSORE

— Economic conditions.

KARNATAKA TO-DAY: basic facts; [pd. by] Bureau of Economics and Statistics [Mysore]. a., 1974/75 (1st)- Bangalore.

MYSORE. Directorate of Information and Publicity. 1976. 20 point economic programme: achievements; a new era. [Bangalore, 1976]. pp. 30.

— Economic history.

HETTNE (BJØRN) The political economy of indirect rule: Mysore, 1881-1947. London, 1978. pp. 402. *bibliog. (Scandinavian Institute of Asian Studies. Monograph Series. No. 32)*

— Economic policy.

MYSORE. Directorate of Information and Publicity. 1976. 20 point economic programme: achievements; a new era. [Bangalore, 1976]. pp. 30.

— Officials and employees — Salaries, allowances, etc.

MYSORE. Pay Commission. 1976. Report; [A. Narayana Pai, commissioner]. [Bangalore], 1976. pp. 453. *bibliog.*

— Politics and government.

HETTNE (BJØRN) The political economy of indirect rule: Mysore, 1881-1947. London, 1978. pp. 402. *bibliog. (Scandinavian Institute of Asian Studies. Monograph Series. No. 32)*

— Social conditions.

KARNATAKA TO-DAY: basic facts; [pd. by] Bureau of Economics and Statistics [Mysore]. a., 1974/75 (1st)- Bangalore.

MYSORE. Directorate of Information and Publicity. 1976. 20 point economic programme: achievements; a new era. [Bangalore, 1976]. pp. 30.

— Social policy.

MYSORE. Directorate of Information and Publicity. 1976. 20 point economic programme: achievements; a new era. [Bangalore, 1976]. pp. 30.

MYSTICISM

— Mohammedanism — Indonesia.

MULDER (NIELS) Mysticism and everyday life in contemporary Java: cultural persistence and change. Singapore, [1978]. pp. 150. *bibliog.*

— Indonesia.

MULDER (NIELS) Mysticism and everyday life in contemporary Java: cultural persistence and change. Singapore, [1978]. pp. 150. *bibliog.*

MYTHOLOGY.

MIDDLETON (JOHN) ed. Myth and cosmos: readings in mythology and symbolism. Austin, Tex., [1967]. pp. 368. *bibliog.*

LÉVI-STRAUSS (CLAUDE) Myth and meaning. London, 1978. pp. 54. *(Canadian Broadcasting Corporation. Massey Lectures. 1977)*

MYTHOLOGY, INDIAN.

KRISHNA: myths, rites, and attitudes; edited by Milton Singer. Chicago, 1966. pp. 277. *bibliog.*

MYTHOLOGY, MAORI.

BEST (ELSDON) Some aspects of Maori myth and religion. Wellington, [1922] repr. 1954. pp. 43. *(New Zealand. Dominion Museum. Monographs. No. 1)*

MZILIKAZI, King of the Matabele.

RASMUSSEN (R. KENT) Migrant kingdom: Mzilikazi's Ndebele in South Africa. London, 1978. pp. 262. *bibliog.*

NAHUAS

— Social conditions.

RECK (GREGORY G.) In the shadow of Tlaloc: life in a Mexican village. Harmondsworth, 1978. pp. 224.

NAMES, GEOGRAPHICAL

— United Kingdom.

GELLING (MARGARET) The place-names of Berkshire. Cambridge, 1973. 3 vols. *(English Place-Name Society. [Publications]. vols. 49- 51) With folder of maps in end paper of second volume.*

GELLING (MARGARET) Signposts to the past: place-names and the history of England. London, 1978 repr. 1979. pp. 256. *bibliog.*

NAMES, PERSONAL

— United Kingdom — Scotland.

BLACK (GEORGE FRASER) The surnames of Scotland: their origin, meaning, and history. New York, 1946 repr. 1979. pp. 838. *bibliog.*

NAPALM.

IRAQ. Ministry of Culture and Guidance. Directorate of Public Relations. 1967. Horrors of napalm. Baghdad, 1967. pp. 16.

NAPET SECURITIES.

NOURSE (MARTIN CHARLES) and DUBUISSON (PETER WILLIAM GROSTETE) Land and General Developments Limited; Napet Securities Limited: investigation under sections 164 and 172 of the Companies Act, 1948; interim and final reports. [London], Department of Trade, 1978. 1 vol. (various pagings)

NAPLES

— Social conditions.

BELMONTE (THOMAS) The broken fountain. New York, 1979. pp. 151.

NAPOLEON I, Emperor of the French.

PURYEAR (VERNON JOHN) Napoleon and the Dardanelles. Berkeley, 1951. pp. 437. *bibliog.*

GEYL (PIETER) Napoleon for and against; translated from the Dutch by Olive Renier. Harmondsworth, 1965. pp. 431. *First published in Great Britain in 1949.*

COLLINS (IRENE) Napoleon and his parliaments, 1800-1815. London, 1979. pp. 193. *bibliog.*

SCHWARZFUCHS (SIMON) Napoleon, the Jews and the Sanhedrin. London, 1979. pp. 218. *bibliog.*

NARAYAN (JAYAPRAKASH).

BARIK (RADHAKANTA) Politics of the JP movement. New Delhi, 1977. pp. 120. *bibliog.*

NARAYANA (SREE).

THOMAS (DANIEL) Sree Narayana Guru. Bangalore, 1965. pp. 42. *(Christian Institute for the Study of Religion and Society. Pamphlets of Religion)*

NARCOTIC ADDICTS

— United Kingdom.

STATISTICS OF THE MISUSE OF DRUGS IN THE UNITED KINGDOM (formerly Statistics of drug addiction and drug offences in the United Kingdom); [pd. by] Home Office. a., 1973- London.

NARCOTIC HABIT.

De BETEKENIS en de gevolgen van cannabis-gebruik. ['s-Gravenhage, 1969]. pp. 82. *(Netherlands. Ministerie van Sociale Zaken. Verslagen en Mededelingen betreffende de Volksgezondheid. 1969. 2)*

NARCOTIC LAWS.

WORLD HEALTH ORGANIZATION. 1962. Treatment of drug addicts: a survey of existing legislation. Geneva, 1962. pp. 46. *bibliog. Originally published in International Digest of Health Legislation, v.13, 1962.*

NARCOTICS, CONTROL OF.

UNITED NATIONS. Office of Public Information. 1972. The United Nations and the fight against drug abuse. New York, 1972. pp. 30.

— United States.

DRUGS, crime and politics; edited...by Arnold S. Trebach. New York, 1978. pp. 178. *bibliogs.*

NÁRODNÍ STRANA SVOBODOMYSLNÁ.

GARVER (BRUCE M.) The Young Czech party, 1874-1901, and the emergence of a multi- party system. ew Haven, 1978. pp. 568. *bibliog. (Yale University. Yale Historical Publications. Miscellany. 111)*

NARODNO-SOTSIALISTICHESKAIA (TRUDOVAIA) PARTIIA.

GINEV (VLADIMIR NIKOLAEVICH) Agrarnyi vopros i melkoburzhuaznye partii v Rossii v 1917 g.: k istorii bankrotstva neonarodnichestva. Leningrad, 1977. pp. 295.

NATAL

— Biography.

DEANE (DEE SHIRLEY) Black South Africans: a Who's who: 57 profiles of Natal's leading blacks. Cape Town, 1978. pp. 210.

NATIONAL ARCHIVES AND RECORDS SERVICE.

McCOY (DONALD RICHARD) The National Archives: America's ministry of documents, 1934- 1968. Chapel Hill, [1978]. pp. 437. *bibliog.*

NATIONAL AWAMI PARTY.

PAKISTAN. Supreme Court. 1975. Rejoinder...to written statement of Abdul Wali Khan, president of defunct National Awami Party, in reference by Islamic Republic of Pakistan on dissolution of National Awami Party. [Islamabad], 1975. pp. 79.

NATIONAL CHARACTERISTICS, AMERICAN.

The NATIONAL purpose reconsidered; Dona Baron, editor. New York, 1978. pp. 139.

NATIONAL CHARACTERISTICS, BRITISH.

JENKINS (DANIEL T.) The British: their identity and their religion. London, 1975. pp. 201.

NATIONAL CHARACTERISTICS, LATIN AMERICAN.

NIDA (EUGENE A.) Understanding Latin Americans, with special reference to religious values and movements. South Pasadena, Calif., 1974 repr. 1976. pp. 165. *bibliog.*

NATIONAL COUNCIL OF LABOUR COLLEGES.

MILLAR (JAMES PRIMROSE MALCOLM) The labour college movement. London, [1979]. pp. 300. *bibliog.*

NATIONAL FRONT.

BILLIG (MICHAEL) Fascists: a social psychological view of the National Front. London, 1978. pp. 393. *bibliog. (European Association of Experimental Social Psychology. European Monographs in Social Psychology. 15)*

NATIONAL FRONT. It's our country: let's win it back: the manifesto of the National Front. [London], 1979. pp. 68.

NATIONAL GUARDIAN.

BELFRAGE (CEDRIC) and ARONSON (JAMES) Something to guard: the stormy life of the National Guardian, 1948-1967. New York, 1978. pp. 362.

NATIONAL INCOME

— Accounting.

UNITED NATIONS. Statistical Office. Statistical Papers. Series F. No.22. The feasibility of welfare-oriented measures to supplement the national accounts and balances: a technical report. (ST/ESA/STAT/SER.F/22). New York, 1977. pp. 71.

— Finland — Accounting.

FINLAND. Tilastokeskus. Kansantalouden tilinpito. q., 1977(4th q.)- Helsinki. *[in Finnish and Swedish with English summary and table headings].*

— France — Accounting.

FRANCE. Institut National de la Statistique et des Etudes Economiques. Les comptes régionaux des ménages...: les comptes régionaux des administrations publiques locales, etc. a., 1973- Paris.

— Germany — Accounting.

GESAMTREPRODUKTIONSPROZESS der BRD, 1950-1975: Kritik der volkswirtschaftlichen Gesamtrechnung; ([by] Projekt Klassenanalyse). Westberlin, [1976]. pp. 320.

— Ghana.

SINGAL (M.S.) and NARTEY (J.D.N.) Sources and methods of estimation of national income at current prices in Ghana. Accra, Central Bureau of Statistics, 1971. pp. 117. *bibliog.*

— India — Goa, Daman and Diu — Accounting.

GOA, DAMAN AND DIU. Bureau of Economics, Statistics and Evaluation. Standard supporting tables for the regional accounts. irreg., 1970-71/1975-76- Panaji.

— Malaysia — Accounting.

RAO (V.V. BHANOJI) National accounts of West Malaysia 1947-1971. Singapore, 1976. pp. 109. *bibliog.*

— Russia — Latvia.

GRANTYN' (GAITIS IANOVICH) Chistyi produkt i narodnyi dokhod soiuznoi respubliki: problemy sbalansirovannosti. Riga, 1977. pp. 109. *bibliog.*

— Spain — Accounting.

SCHWARTZ (PEDRO) ed. El producto nacional de España en el siglo XX: seleccion de textos. Madrid, Instituto de Estudios Fiscales, 1977. pp. 690.

— Tanzania — Accounting.

UNITED REPUBLIC OF TANZANIA. Bureau of Statistics. 1971. National accounts of Tanzania, 1966 to 1968: sources and methods. Dar es Salaam, 1971. pp. 118.

— United Kingdom — Accounting.

U.K. Central Statistical Office. 1978. Personal sector balance sheets and current developments in Inland Revenue estimates of personal wealth. London, 1978. pp. 51. *(Studies in Official Statistics. No. 35)*

— — Mathematical models.

MATTHEWS (K.G.P.) A monetary model of nominal income determination for the U.K. London, 1977. pp. 22. *bibliog. (National Institute of Economic and Social Research. Discussion Papers. No. 16)*

— United States.

NATIONAL BUREAU OF ECONOMIC RESEARCH. Conference on Research in Income and Wealth. Studies in Income and Wealth. vol. 41. The distribution of economic well-being: [papers presented in 1974]; F. Thomas Juster, ed. Cambridge, Mass., 1977. pp. 679. *Tables on microfiche (7 cards). Proceedings of a Conference held at the University of Michigan in 1974.*

NATIONAL INSTITUTE OF EDUCATION.

SPROULL (LEE) and others. Organizing an anarchy: belief, bureaucracy, and politics in the National Institute of Education. Chicago, 1978. pp. 282. *bibliog.*

NATIONAL PARKS AND RESERVES

— United Kingdom.

EXMOOR NATIONAL PARK COMMITTEE. Exmoor National Park plan; ([with] Supplement). Dulverton, 1977. 2 pts. (in 1 vol.) *bibliog.*

NATIONAL SOCIALISM.

[SCHREINER (ALBERT)] Hitler rearms: an exposure of Germany's war plans; edited by Dorothy Woodman. London, 1934. pp. 336. *Translation of Hitler treibt zum Krieg.*

HITLER (ADOLF) Mein Kampf...: unexpurgated edition; [translated and annotated by James Murphy]. London, [1939]. pp. 584. *Published in 18 parts by Hutchinson and Co.*

SCHWARZ (ROBERT) 1921- . "Sozialismus" der Propaganda: das Werben des "Völkischen Beobachters" um die österreichische Arbeiterschaft, 1938/1939; mit einer Einleitung von Gerhard Botz, etc. Wien, 1975. pp. 159. *bibliog. (Ludwig Boltzmann Institut für Geschichte der Arbeiterbewegung. Materialien zur Arbeiterbewegung. Nr.2)*

BAYERN in der NS-Zeit...; herausgegeben von Martin Broszat [and others]. München, 1977 in progress. *bibliog.*

SCHOLDER (KLAUS) Die Kirchen und das Dritte Reich. Frankfurt/M, 1977 in progress. *bibliog.*

THEWELEIT (KLAUS) Männerphantasien. Frankfurt am Main, 1977-78. 2 vols. *bibliog.*

ENGELMANN (BERNT) Einig gegen Recht und Freiheit: deutsches Anti- Geschichtsbuch, 2. Teil. Frankfurt am Main, 1977. pp. 296. *bibliog.*

GOEBBELS (JOSEPH) Tagebücher, 1945: die letzten Aufzeichnungen; Einführung: Rolf Hochhuth; (Redaktion: Peter Stadelmayer). Hamburg, [1977]. pp. 608.

STEINBERG (MICHAEL STEPHEN) Sabers and brown shirts: the German students' path to National Socialism, 1918-1935. Chicago, 1977. pp. 237. *bibliog.*

TEPPE (KARL) Provinz, Partei, Staat: zur provinziellen Selbstverwaltung im Dritten Reich, untersucht am Beispiel Westfalens. Münster in Westfalen, 1977. pp. 300. *bibliog. (Historische Kommission für Westfalen. Veröffentlichungen. 38)*

WINKLER (DOERTE) Frauenarbeit im "Dritten Reich". Hamburg, 1977. pp. 253. *bibliog.*

ANDERBRUEGGE (KLAUS) Völkisches Rechtsdenken: zur Rechtslehre in der Zeit des Nationalsozialismus. Berlin, 1978. pp. 237. *bibliog.*

ARETZ (JUERGEN) Katholische Arbeiterbewegung und Nationalsozialismus: der Verband katholischer Arbeiter- und Knappenvereine Westdeutschlands, 1923-1945. Mainz, [1978]. pp. 252. *bibliog. (Kommission für Zeitgeschichte. Veröffentlichungen. Reihe B: Forschungen. Band 25)*

BOESCHENSTEIN (HERMANN) Vor unsern Augen: Aufzeichnungen über das Jahrzehnt 1935- 1945. Bern, 1978. pp. 334.

BOTZ (GERHARD) Wien vom "Anschluss" zum Krieg: nationalsozialistische Machtübernahme und politisch-soziale Umgestaltung am Beispiel der Stadt Wien, 1938/39; mit einem einleitenden Beitrag von Karl R. Stadler. Wien, [1978]. pp. 646. *bibliog.*

BRODER (HENRYK M.) Deutschland erwacht; mit Beiträgen von: Ossip K. Flechtheim [and others]. Köln, 1978. pp. 135.

COOPER (MATTHEW) The German Army, 1933-1945: its political and military failure. London, 1978. pp. 598. *bibliog.*

Die FRAU im Dritten Reich: eine Dokumentation; von Gertrud Scholtz-Klink. Tübingen, [1978]. pp. 546.

HENTSCHEL (VOLKER) Weimars letzte Monate: Hitler und der Untergang der Republik. Düsseldorf, [1978 repr. 1979]. pp. 180. *bibliog.*

MOSSE (GEORGE L.) and LEDEEN (MICHAEL ARTHUR) Nazism: a historical and comparative analysis of National Socialism;...an interview with Michael A. Ledeen. New Brunswick, N.J., [1978]. pp. 134.

Der NATIONALSOZIALISTISCHE Alltag: so lebte man unter Hitler; ([edited by] George L. Mosse; aus dem Englischen von Renate Becker. Königstein/Ts., 1978. pp. 389.

NATIONALSOZIALISTISCHE Aussenpolitik; herausgegeben von Wolfgang Michalka. Darmstadt, 1978. pp. 579. *bibliog.*

ROSENKRANZ (HERBERT) Verfolgung und Selbstbehauptung: die Juden in Österreich, 1938-1945. Wien, [1978]. pp. 399. *bibliog.*

SCHAAP (KLAUS) Die Endphase der Weimarer Republik im Freistaat Oldenburg, 1928-1933. Düsseldorf, [1978]. pp. 313. *bibliog. (Germany (Bundesrepublik). Kommission für Geschichte des Parlamentarismus und der Politischen Parteien. Beiträge zur Geschichte des Parlamentarismus und der Politischen Parteien. Band 61)*

SLAPNICKA (HARRY) Oberösterreich - als es "Oberdonau" hiess, 1938-1945. Linz, 1978. pp. 513. *bibliog. (Upper Austria. Landesarchiv. Beiträge zur Zeitgeschichte Oberösterreichs. 5)*

SOHN-RETHEL (ALFRED) Economy and class structure of German fascism...; translated [from the German] by Martin Sohn-Rethel. London, 1978. pp. 159.

WAS verschweigt Fest?: Analysen und Dokumente zum Hitler- Film von J.C. Fest; ([edited by] Jörg Berlin [and others]). Köln, [1978]. pp. 217.

HERZSTEIN (ROBERT EDWIN) The war that Hitler won: the most infamous propaganda campaign in history. London, 1979. pp. 491. *bibliog.*

KOGON (EUGEN) Der SS-Staat: das System der deutschen Konzentrationslager. München, 1979. pp. 431.

POOL (JAMES) and POOL (SUZANNE) Who financed Hitler: the secret funding of Hitler's rise to power, 1919-1933. London, 1979. pp. 535. *bibliog.*

STAEGLICH (WILHELM) Der Auschwitz-Mythos: Legende oder Wirklichkeit?: eine kritische Bestandsaufnahme. Tübingen, 1979. pp. 467. *bibliog.* (*Institut für Deutsche Nachkriegsgeschichte. Veröffentlichungen. Band 9*)

NATIONAL UNION OF MINEWORKERS.

ARNOT (ROBERT PAGE) The miners: one union, one industry: a history of the National Union of Mineworkers, 1939-46. London, 1979. pp. 212.

NATIONALISM.

FRANKEL (JOSEPH) National interest. London, 1970. pp. 173. *bibliog.*

CURCIO (CARLO) Nazione e autodecisione dei popoli: due idee nella storia. Milano, [1977]. pp. 396.

DEUTSCH (KARL WOLFGANG) Tides among nations. New York, [1979]. pp. 342. *bibliogs.*

The NEW nationalism: implications for transatlantic relations; edited by Werner Link, Werner J. Feld. New York, 1979. pp. 165. *bibliogs. Papers given at the annual conference of the Committee on Atlantic Studies, Luxembourg, 1977.*

SMITH (ANTHONY DAVID STEPHEN) Nationalism in the twentieth century. Oxford, 1979. pp. 257. *bibliog.*

NATIONALISM AND SOCIALISM.

DAVIS (HORACE BANCROFT) Toward a Marxist theory of nationalism. New York, [1978]. pp. 294. *bibliog.*

INTERNATIONALE TAGUNG DER HISTORIKER DER ARBEITERBEWEGUNG, 1975. Einheits- und Volksfrontpolitik, 1935-1939; Klassenkampf und nationale Frage zur Zeit der II. Internationale; (bearbeitet von Hans Hautmann). Wien, 1978. pp. 335. (*Internationale Tagung der Historiker der Arbeiterbewegung. ITH-Tagungsberichte. Band 10*)

BENNIGSEN (ALEXANDRE) and WIMBUSH (S. ENDERS) Muslim national communism in the Soviet Union: a revolutionary strategy for the colonial world. Chicago, [1979]. pp. 267. *bibliog.* (*Chicago. University. Center for Middle Eastern Studies. Publications. 11*)

NATIONALKOMITEE FREIES DEUTSCHLAND.

Die FRONT war überall: (Erlebnisse und Berichte vom Kampf des Nationalkomitees "Freies Deutschland"; herausgegeben von Else und Bernt von Kügelgen). 2nd ed. Berlin, 1978. pp. 507. *bibliog.*

NATIVE RACES

— Law and legislation.

BENNETT (GORDON IRVINE) Aboriginal rights in international law. London, 1978. pp. 88. *bibliog.* (*Royal Anthropological Institute of Great Britain and Ireland. Occasional Papers. No. 37*)

NATURAL LAW.

SIBLEY (MULFORD QUICKERT) Nature and civilization: some implications for politics. Itasca, Ill., [1977]. pp. 319. *bibliogs.*

LEMOS (RAMON M.) Hobbes and Locke: power and consent. Athens, [1978]. pp. 185.

NATURAL RESOURCES.

MUKERJEE (RADHAKAMAL) Races, lands, and food: a program for world subsistence. New York, 1946. pp. 107.

NATURAL RESOURCES FORUM; ([pd.by] Department of Economic and Social Affairs) United Nations. [in English, French and Spanish]. irreg., 1971 (v.1., no.1)- New York.

NATURAL resources for a democratic society: public participation in decision-making; edited by Albert E. Utton [and others]. Boulder, 1976. pp. 236. (*Reprinted from Natural Resources Journal, vol.16, 1976. no. 1*)

BROWN (LESTER RUSSELL) Redefining national security. Washington, 1977. pp. 46. (*Worldwatch Institute. Worldwatch Papers. No. 14*)

RAJAN (MANNARASWAMIGHALA SREERANGA) Sovereignty over natural resources. Atlantic Highlands, 1978. pp. 176.

RESOURCES for an uncertain future: papers presented at a forum marking the 25th anniversary of Resources for the Future, October 13, 1977, Washington, D.C.; Charles J. Hitch, editor. Baltimore, [1978]. pp. 105.

GILLAND (BERNARD) The next seventy years: population, food and resources. Tunbridge Wells, 1979. pp. 133. *bibliog.*

The GLOBAL predicament: ecological perspectives on world order; edited by David W. Orr and Marvin S. Soroos. Chapel Hill, [1979]. pp. 398. *bibliog.*

LECOMBER (RICHARD) The economics of natural resources. London, 1979. pp. 247. *bibliog.*

— Canada.

FEDERALISM: central/regional relations. Edinburgh, [1975?]. 1 vol. (various foliations). (*Edinburgh. University. Centre of Canadian Studies. Seminar Papers. No. 1*)

— — Alberta.

ALBERTA. Department of Business Development and Tourism. Industry and resources. a., 1978/79- Edmonton.

— North Sea.

The EFFECTIVE management of resources: the international politics of the North Sea; edited by C.M. Mason. London, 1979. pp. 268. *bibliogs.*

— Russia.

NATURAL resources of the Soviet Union: their use and renewal; edited by I.P. Gerasimov [and others]; translated from the Russian by Jacek I. Romanowski; English edition edited by W. A. Douglas Jackson. San Francisco, [1971]. pp. 349. *bibliogs.*

— — Buryat Republic.

PROBLEMY osvoeniia severa Buriatskoi ASSR. Novosibirsk, 1978. pp. 109.

— Underdeveloped areas.

See UNDERDEVELOPED AREAS — Natural resources.

— United States — Alaska.

WEEDEN (ROBERT B.) Alaska: promises to keep. Boston, Mass., 1978. pp. 254.

NATURAL SELECTION.

SEXUAL selection and The descent of man 1871-1971; edited by Bernard Campbell. London, 1972. pp. 378. *bibliogs.*

NATURE AND NURTURE.

HEREDITY and environment; edited by A.H. Halsey. London, 1977. pp. 337. *bibliog.*

VERNON (PHILIP EWART) Intelligence: heredity and environment. San Francisco, [1979]. pp. 390. *bibliog.*

NATURE CONSERVATION

— United States — New Jersey.

CAVANAUGH (CAM) Saving the Great Swamp: the people, the power brokers, and an urban wilderness. Frenchtown, N.J., [1978]. pp. 240.

NATURE IN LITERATURE.

FEINGOLD (RICHARD) Nature and society: later eighteenth-century uses of the pastoral and georgic. Hassocks, 1978. pp. 209.

NAVAL ARCHITECTURE.

EMMERSON (GEORGE S.) John Scott Russell: a great Victorian engineer and naval architect. London, [1977]. pp. 342. *bibliog.*

NAVAL STRATEGY.

NEW strategic factors in the North Atlantic; edited by Christoph Bertram and Johan Jørgen Holst. Oslo, [1977]. pp. 193. (*Norsk Utenrikspolitisk Institutt. Norwegian Foreign Policy Studies. Nr. 21*)

NDEBELE.

See MATABELE.

NEAVE (AIREY).

NEAVE (AIREY) Nuremberg: a personal record of the trial of the major Nazi war criminals. London, 1978. pp. 348.

NECHAEV (SERGEI GENNADIEVICH).

POMPER (PHILIP) Sergei Nechaev. New Brunswick, [1979]. pp. 273. *bibliog.*

NECKER (JACQUES).

HARRIS (ROBERT D.) Necker: reform statesman of the ancien régime. Berkeley, Calif., [1979]. pp. 259. *bibliog.*

NEGLIGENCE

— United Kingdom.

BINGHAM (RICHARD) The modern cases on negligence. 3rd ed. London, 1978. pp. 724.

NEGOTIATION.

NEGOTIATIONS: social-psychological perspectives; edited by Daniel Druckman. Beverly Hills, [1977]. pp. 416. *bibliogs.*

The NEGOTIATION process: theories and applications; editor I. William Zartman. Beverly Hills, Calif., [1978]. pp. 240. *bibliog.*

STRAUSS (ANSELM LEONARD) Negotiations: varieties, contexts, processes, and social order. San Francisco, 1978. pp. 275. *bibliog.*

NEHRU (JAWAHARLAL).

LAMB (BEATRICE PITNEY) The Nehrus of India: three generations of leadership. New York, [1967]. pp. 276. *bibliog.*

PRASHAD (GANESH) Nehru: a study in colonial liberalism. New Delhi, [1976]. pp. 218. *bibliogs.*

NEHRU (MOTILAL).

LAMB (BEATRICE PITNEY) The Nehrus of India: three generations of leadership. New York, [1967]. pp. 276. *bibliog.*

NEIGHBOURHOOD GOVERNMENT

— United Kingdom.

AREA management: objectives and structures; by C.J. Horn [and others]; (area management monitoring project: first interim report);...commissioned by the Department of the Environment. [Birmingham], 1977. pp. 68.

NEIGHBOURHOOD GOVERNMENT(Cont.)

HUMBLE (STEPHEN) and TALBOT (JENNIFER) Neighbourhood councils in England: a report to the Department of the Environment. Birmingham, 1977. pp. 146, vii.

TACKLING urban deprivation: the contribution of area-based management; by Tim Mason [and others]; (area management monitoring project);...commissioned by the Department of the Environment. [Birmingham], 1977. pp. 94.

A VOICE for your neighbourhood: the neighbourhood council; [R.M. Knowles, chairman of the Advisory Group]. [London], Department of the Environment, [1977]. pp. 32.

LLEWELYN-DAVIES WEEKS [AND PARTNERS]. Inner area study: Birmingham: Small Heath Community Federation: a study in local influence. [London], Department of the Environment, [1978]. pp. 43.

NEIGHBOURLINESS.

AGE CONCERN ENGLAND. Action Guides. Street warden schemes. Mitcham, [1977]. pp. 16.

NEPAL

— Economic conditions.

EVALUATION of a regional development strategy: a case study in the Kathmandu growth zone; by Wolfgang Zehender [and others]. Berlin, 1975. pp. 143.

— Economic policy.

NEPAL. Department of Publicity. 1967. The developing Nepal. [Kathmandu], 1967. pp. 31.

— Population.

GABORIEAU (MARC) Le Népal et ses populations. [Paris, 1978]. pp. 312. *bibliog.*

— Social policy.

NEPAL. Department of Publicity. 1967. The developing Nepal. [Kathmandu], 1967. pp. 31.

NERVOUS SYSTEM, AUTONOMIC.

VAN TOLLER (C.) The nervous body: an introduction to the autonomic nervous system and behaviour. Chichester, [1979]. pp. 176. *bibliogs.*

NESTLÉ.

NESTLÉ in the developing countries. Vevey, [1975]. pp. 228.

NETHERLANDS

— Aerial photographs.

LUCHTATLAS van Nederland; onder auspiciën van het Koninklijk Nederlands Aardrijkskundig Genootschap. Bussum, [1978]. pp. 229. *bibliog.*

— Census.

BERENDS (A.B.) and BOELMANS-KLEINJAN (A.C.) Beroepsarbeid door vrouwen in Nederland: een benadering vanuit de plaats van de vrouw in gezin en huishouden. 's-Gravenhage, 1979. pp. 165. *bibliog. (Netherlands. Centraal Bureau voor de Statistiek. Monografieën Volkstelling 1971. 7) With English summary.*

FISELIER (A.A.M.) and KRAFT (H.L.P.R.) Laagstgeklasseerden in Nederland: een beschrijvend onderzoek naar omvang en spreiding van lage inkomens bij diverse typen huishoudens, gerelateerd aan een beperkt aantal relevante variabelen. 's-Gravenhage, 1979. pp. 139. *bibliog. (Netherlands. Centraal Bureau voor de Statistiek. Monografieën Volkstelling 1971. 5) With English summary.*

De POSITIE van jongeren ten opzichte van het ouderlijk gezin: een analyse op basis van de volkstelling 1971; [by] L.H. Boerma [and others]. 's-Gravenhage, 1979. pp. 67. *bibliog. (Netherlands. Centraal Bureau voor de Statistiek. Monografieën Volkstelling 1971. 10) With English summary.*

— Civilization.

DEMEY (J.) De historische twee-eenheid der Nederlanden: bestendige kloof in toenadering. Nijmegen, [1978]. pp. 214. *bibliogs.*

— Colonies.

EMERSON (RUPERT) Malaysia: a study in direct and indirect rule. Kuala Lumpur, [1964]. pp. 536. *Reprint of work first published in 1937.*

— Commerce — United States.

WINTER (PIETER JAN VAN) American finance and Dutch investment, 1780-1805; with an epilogue to 1840;...English adaptation of the revised version of the original Dutch edition...by James C. Riley. New York, 1977. 2 vols. *bibliog.*

— Economic history.

VRIES (JOHAN DE) The Netherlands economy in the twentieth century: an examination of the most characteristic features in the period 1900-1970. Assen, 1978. pp. 135. *bibliog.*

— Economic policy.

IDENBURG (RIENK) Spotlight on the future: how 20,000,000 Dutchmen will live in 40, 000 square kilometres. 2nd rev. ed. The Hague, Government Publishing Office, 1971. pp. 72.

DOEL (HANS VAN DEN) Het biefstuk-socialisme en de economie. Utrecht, 1978. pp. 176.

VRIES (JOHAN DE) The Netherlands economy in the twentieth century: an examination of the most characteristic features in the period 1900-1970. Assen, 1978. pp. 135. *bibliog.*

— Emigration and immigration.

STOKVIS (PIETER RUDOLF DEGENHARD) De Nederlandse trek naar Amerika, 1846-1847. Leiden, 1977. pp. 251. *bibliog. (Leiden. Rijks Universiteit. Leidse Historische Reeks. Deel 21) With summary in English.*

— Foreign economic relations — Thailand.

SMITH (GEORGE VINAL) The Dutch in seventeenth-century Thailand. Detroit, [1977]. pp. 203. *bibliog. (Northern Illinois University. Center for Southeast Asian Studies. Special Reports. No. 16)*

— Foreign relations.

The FOREIGN policy of the Netherlands; edited by J.H. Leurdijk. Alphen aan den Rijn, 1978. pp. 356. *bibliog.*

NEDERLANDS buitenlandse politiek: heden en verleden; (met bijdragen van E.H. van der Beugel [and others]). Baarn, [1978]. pp. 123.

— History.

DEMEY (J.) De historische twee-eenheid der Nederlanden: bestendige kloof in toenadering. Nijmegen, [1978]. pp. 214. *bibliogs.*

— — 1648-1714.

ROWEN (HERBERT H.) John de Witt, grand pensionary of Holland, 1625-1672. Princeton, N.J., [1978]. pp. 948. *bibliog.*

— — 1940-1945, German occupation.

GROEN (KOOS) 'Er heerst orde en rust...': chaotisch Nederland tussen september 1944 en december 1945. Nijmegen, [1979]. pp. 208. *7 inch record: Authentiek historische geluidsfragmenten, in end pocket.*

— History, Local — Bibliography.

HERWIJNEN (G. VAN) compiler. Bibliografie van de stedengeschiedenis van Nederland;...met medewerking van W.G. van der Moer [and others]. Leiden, 1978. pp. 355.

— Maps.

LUCHTATLAS van Nederland; onder auspiciën van het Koninklijk Nederlands Aardrijkskundig Genootschap. Bussum, [1978]. pp. 229. *bibliog.*

— Politics and government.

GRIBLING (J.P.) Willem Hubert Nolens, 1860-1931: uit het leven van een priester-staatsman. Assen, 1978. pp. 377. *With German and French summaries.*

ZIJLSTRA (JELLE) Gesprekken en geschriften; samengesteld door G. Puchinger met bijdrage van W. Drees. Naarden, [1978]. pp. 383.

— Population.

POPULATION and family in the Low Countries, II; edited by H. G. Moors [and others]. Leiden, 1978. pp. 153. *bibliogs. (Nederlands Interuniversitair Demografisch Instituut and Centre d'Etude de la Population et de la Famille [Belgium]. Publications. vol. 6)*

— Social history.

AALBERS (P.G.) Het einde van de horigheid in Twente en Oost-Gelderland, 1795- 1850. Zutphen, 1979. pp. 284. *bibliog.*

— — Sources.

GIELE (JACQUES J.) Arbeidersleven in Nederland 1850-1914. Nijmegen, [1979]. pp. 320.

— Social policy.

MEIJER (WIM) Welzijnsbeleid: een keuze voor verandering van de maatschappij. Alphen aan den Rijn, 1978. pp. 182.

— Statistics, Vital.

NETHERLANDS. Centraal Bureau voor de Statistiek. 1974. Regionale huwelijksvruchtbaarheidsverschillen, 1959/1961, 1967/1968, 1971/1972. 's-Gravenhage, 1974. pp. 21. *Map transparency and list of economic-geographical regions in end pocket.*

NETTLAU (MAX).

ROCKER (RUDOLF) Max Nettlau: Leben und Werk des Historikers vergessener sozialer Bewegungen; Einleitung von Rudolf de Jong. Berlin, 1978. pp. 336. *bibliog.*

NETWORK ANALYSIS (PLANNING).

LAWLER (EUGENE L.) Combinatorial optimization: networks and matroids. New York, [1976]. pp. 374.

MINIEKA (EDWARD) Optimization algorithms for networks and graphs. New York, [1978]. pp. 356. *bibliogs.*

NEUROPSYCHIATRY.

BROWN (JASON) Mind, brain, and consciousness: the neuropsychology of cognition. New York, 1977. pp. 190. *bibliog.*

NEUROPSYCHOLOGY.

BURSEN (HOWARD ALEXANDER) Dismantling the memory machine: a philosophical investigation of machine theories of memory. Dordrecht, [1978]. pp. 157. *bibliog.*

VAN TOLLER (C.) The nervous body: an introduction to the autonomic nervous system and behaviour. Chichester, [1979]. pp. 176. *bibliogs.*

NEUROSES.

EYSENCK (HANS JÜRGEN) The dynamics of anxiety and hysteria: an experimental application of modern learning theory to psychiatry. London, 1957. pp. 311. *bibliog.*

NEUTRALITY.

The NONALIGNED movement in world politics; [edited by A.W. Singham]. Westport, Conn., [1977]. pp. 273. *Papers prepared for the Howard Conference on Non-Alignment, held at Howard University, 1976.*

SCHWEITZER (MICHAEL) Dauernde Neutralität und europäische Integration. Wien, 1977. pp. 347. *bibliog.*

NEW BRIGHTON ASSOCIATION FOOTBALL AND ATHLETIC CLUB COMPANY.

RANKIN (ANDREW) and WHITE (THOMAS) F.C.A. New Brighton Association Football and Athletic Club Company Limited: investigation under section 165b of the Companies Act, 1948; report. London, H.M.S.O., 1977. pp. 112.

NEW BRUNSWICK

— Department of Municipal Affairs.

NEW BRUNSWICK. Department of Municial Affairs. Annual report. a., 1955- , with gaps. Fredericton.

— Executive departments.

NEW BRUNSWICK. Department of Municial Affairs. Annual report. a., 1955- , with gaps. Fredericton.

— Legislative Assembly — Elections.

NEW BRUNSWICK. Chief Electoral Office. 1975. Twenty-eighth general election 1974; report of the Chief Electoral Officer. [Fredericton, 1975?]. pp. 151, 1 map. *In English and French.*

NEW CALEDONIA

— Census.

NEW CALEDONIA. Census, 1976. Résultats statistiques du recensement général de la population de la Nouvelle-Calédonie, 23 avril 1976. Paris, [1977]. pp. 56.

— Statistics.

NEW CALEDONIA. Service de la Statistique. Bulletin de statistique. q., Jl/S 1972 - Ja/Mr 1973; ceased pbln. Noumea.

NEW DEMOCRATIC PARTY (CANADA).

HURMUSES (PAUL) Power without glory: the rise and fall of the NDP government in British Columbia. Vancouver, [1976]. pp. 146.

NEW ENGLAND

— Social history.

AXTELL (JAMES L.) The school upon a hill: education and society in colonial New England. New Haven, Conn., 1974. pp. 298.

NEW ENGLAND EMIGRANT AID COMPANY.

JOHNSON (SAMUEL A.) The battle cry of freedom: the New England Emigrant Aid Company in the Kansas Crusade. Westport, Conn., 1977. pp. 357. *bibliog. Reprint of work originally published Lawrence, Kan., 1954.*

NEW HAMPSHIRE

— Industries.

NEW HAMPSHIRE. Department of Employment Security. Economic Analysis and Reports Section. 1972. Growth and decline in New Hampshire industries, 1970 to 1971;. ..William J. Roy, economist. [Concord], 1972. pp. 22.

— Occupations.

NEW HAMPSHIRE. Department of Employment Security. Economic Analysis and Reports Section. 1972. New Hampshire occupations in 1980; prepared by...William J. Roy, economist. [Concord, 1972?]. pp. 76.

NEW HARMONY, INDIANA

— History.

MACDONALD (DONALD) Captain. The diaries of Donald Macdonald 1824-1826; with an introduction by Caroline Dale Snedeker. Clifton, N.J., 1973. pp. 379. *(Indiana Historical Society. Publications. vol. 14. no. 2) Reprint of work first published Indianapolis, 1942.*

NEW JERSEY

— Occupations.

HIRSCH (SUSAN E.) Roots of the American working class: the industrialization of crafts in Newark, 1800-1860. [Philadelphia, 1978].

NEW MEXICO

— Description and travel.

COOKE (PHILIP ST. GEORGE) and others. Exploring southwestern trails, 1846-1854;...edited by Ralph P. Bieber...in collaboration with Averam B. Bender. Glendale, 1938; Philadelphia, 1974. pp. 383. *Facsimile reprint.*

NEW SOUTH WALES

— Administrative and political divisions.

NEW SOUTH WALES. Bureau of Census and Statistics. 1969. Statistical divisions and subdivisions of New South Wales for publication of official statistics from January, 1970. Sydney, [1969]. pp. 12, 1 map.

— Economic policy.

NEW SOUTH WALES. Premier's Department. Southern Tablelands Regional Development Committee. 1965. Supplementary report...on the possible future development of the southern tablelands region of N.S.W. [Goulburn], 1965. pp. 48.

— Executive departments.

NEW SOUTH WALES. Department of Decentralisation and Development. 1968. The policy and work of the Department of Decentralisation and Development. [Sydney, 1968]. fo. 4.

NEW SPAIN (VICEROYALTY)

— Economic history.

BARBOSA RAMIREZ (A. RENE) La estructura economica de la Nueva España, 1519-1810. Mexico, 1971 repr. 1977. pp. 259. *bibliog.*

NEW TOWNS.

INTERNATIONAL urban growth policies: new-town contributions; Gideon Golany, editor. New York, [1978]. pp. 460.

— Canada — British Columbia.

SUZANNE VEIT AND ASSOCIATES. Labour turnover and community stability: implications for northeast coal development in British Columbia; a report prepared for the Federal/Provincial Manpower Sub-Committee on North East Coal [Development]. [Victoria, B.C.?], 1978. 1 vol. (various pagings) *bibliog.*

— France.

RUBENSTEIN (JAMES M.) The French new towns. Baltimore, [1978]. pp. 165.

— Hong Kong.

HONG KONG. New Territories Development Department. 1976. Hong Kong's new towns: Tsuen Wan. Hong Kong, [1976?]. pp. 49.

— United Kingdom.

NEW towns: the British experience; edited by Hazel Evans. London, 1972. pp. 196. *bibliog.*

NORTHERN REGION STRATEGY TEAM. New towns in the Northern Region. Newcastle-upon-Tyne, 1977. fo. 82. *(Working Papers. No. 7)*

NEW TOWNS STAFF COMMISSION [U.K.]. The first report of the...Commission, 1976-1978; [Philip M. Vine, chairman]. London, H.M.S.O., 1979. pp. 113.

NEW YEAR.

KUROCHKIN (OLEKSANDR VOLODYMYROVYCH) Novorichni sviata ukraïntsiv: tradytsiï i suchasnist'. Kyïv, 1978. pp. 191.

NEW YORK (CITY)

— Economic conditions.

AULETTA (KEN) The streets were paved with gold. New York, [1979]. pp. 345.

— Economic Development Council.

See ECONOMIC DEVELOPMENT COUNCIL OF NEW YORK CITY.

— Executive departments.

ROGERS (DAVID) Can business management save the cities?: the case of New York. New York, [1978]. pp. 276.

— History.

VAN DER ZEE (HENRI) and VAN DER ZEE (BARBARA) A sweet and alien land: the story of Dutch New York. London, 1978. pp. 560. *bibliog.*

— Lodging houses.

SIEGAL (HARVEY A.) Outposts of the forgotten: socially terminal people in slum hotels and single room occupancy tenements. New Brunswick, N.J., [1978]. pp. 211. *bibliog.*

— Politics and government.

HERSHKOWITZ (LEO) Tweed's New York: another look. Garden City, N.Y., 1978. pp. 409. *bibliog.*

ROGERS (DAVID) Can business management save the cities?: the case of New York. New York, [1978]. pp. 276.

AULETTA (KEN) The streets were paved with gold. New York, [1979]. pp. 345.

— Poor.

SIEGAL (HARVEY A.) Outposts of the forgotten: socially terminal people in slum hotels and single room occupancy tenements. New Brunswick, N.J., [1978]. pp. 211. *bibliog.*

— Riots.

WEINBAUM (PAUL OWEN) Mobs and demagogues: the New York response to collective violence in the early nineteenth century. [London, 1979]. pp. 194. *bibliog.*

— Social policy.

EICHNER (ALFRED S.) and BRECHER (CHARLES) Controlling social expenditures: the search for output measures. Montclair, 1979. pp. 210. *bibliogs.*

NEW YORK (STATE)

— Census.

NEW YORK (STATE). Census, 1865. Census of the state of New York for 1865. Albany, 1867. pp. 743.

— Description and travel.

FOWLER (JOHN) Traveller. Journal of a tour through the State of New York in the year 1830 with remarks on agriculture in those parts most eligible for settlers. New York, 1970. pp. 333. *Reprint of work first published London, 1831.*

— Economic conditions.

LABOR-MANAGEMENT CONFERENCE ON THE BUSINESS CLIMATE AND JOBS IN NEW YORK STATE, BUFFALO, 1975. New York state's economic crisis: jobs, income and economic growth; proceedings and commentary from the...conference...; edited by Felician F. Foltman and Peter D. McClelland. Ithaca, N.Y., 1977. pp. 213.

The DECLINING Northeast: demographic and economic analyses; edited by Benjamin Chinitz. New York, [1978]. pp. 182. *bibliogs.*

NEW YORK (STATE)(Cont.)

— Economic policy.

LABOR-MANAGEMENT CONFERENCE ON THE BUSINESS CLIMATE AND JOBS IN NEW YORK STATE, BUFFALO, 1975. New York state's economic crisis: jobs, income and economic growth; proceedings and commentary from the...conference...; edited by Felician F. Foltman and Peter D. McClelland. Ithaca, N.Y., 1977. pp. 213.

— Politics and government.

MORGAN (DAVID R.) The capitol press corps: newsmen and the governing of New York State. Westport, Conn., 1978. pp. 177. *bibliog.*

— Population.

The DECLINING Northeast: demographic and economic analyses; edited by Benjamin Chinitz. New York, [1978]. pp. 182. *bibliogs.*

NEW ZEALAND.

NEW ZEALAND QUARTERLY: a New Zealand government publication; [pd. by] High Commissioner for New Zealand, London. q., S 1978(no.1)- London.

— Commerce — Germany, Eastern.

NEW ZEALAND. Department of Trade and Industry. Trade Services Division. 1978. German Democratic Republic: [a market profile]. [Wellington, 1978]. fo. 34. *(Background to Export)*

— — Indonesia.

NEW ZEALAND. Department of Trade and Industry. Trade Services Division. 1978. Indonesia: [a market profile]. [Wellington, 1978]. fo. 39. *(Background to Exports)*

— — Malaysia.

NEW ZEALAND. Department of Trade and Industry. Trade Services Division. 1978. Malaysia: [a market profile]. [Wellington. 1978?]. fo. 45. *(Background to Export)*

— — Papua New Guinea.

NEW ZEALAND. Department of Trade and Industry. Trade Services Division. 1978. Papua New Guinea: [a market profile]. [Wellington, 1978?]. fo. 38. *(Background to Export)*

— — United States.

NEW ZEALAND. Department of Trade and Industry. Trade Services Division. 1979. West coast U.S.A.: [a market profile]. [Wellington, 1979]. fo. 63. *(Background to Export)*

— — Venezuela.

NEW ZEALAND. Department of Trade and Industry. Trade Services Division. 1978. Venezuela: [a market profile]. [Wellington, 1978]. fo.39. *(Background to Export)*

— East Coast Planning Council.

NEW ZEALAND. Ministry of Works and Development. 1975. The East Coast Planning Council. [Wellington, 1975]. pp. 11.

— Economic conditions.

NEW ZEALAND. Planning Council. 1977. A moment of truth. Wellington, [1977]. fo. 7.

NEW ZEALAND GEOGRAPHY CONFERENCE, 9TH, DUNEDIN, 1977. Proceedings of the...conference; edited by T.J. Hearn and R.P. Hargreaves. Dunedin, 1977. pp. 133. *bibliogs. (New Zealand Geographical Society. Conference Series. No. 9)*

FRANKLIN (S.H.) Trade, growth and anxiety: New Zealand beyond the welfare state. Wellington, 1978. pp. 402. *bibliogs.*

NEW ZEALAND. Economic Monitoring Group. 1978. New Zealand's economic trends and policies: report...to the New Zealand Planning Council; [Donald T. Brash, chairman] . Wellington, 1978. pp. 49. *(Reports. No.1)*

NEW ZEALAND. Planning Council. 1978. Planning perspectives 1978-1983. [Wellington], 1978. pp. 103.

— — Mathematical models.

MORGAN (G.H.T.) and others. Topics in econometric model research. Wellington, 1978. pp. 48. *bibliogs. (Reserve Bank of New Zealand. Research Papers. No.24)*

— Economic policy.

NEW ZEALAND. Planning Council. 1977. A moment of truth. Wellington, [1977]. fo. 7.

NEW ZEALAND. Economic Monitoring Group. 1978. New Zealand's economic trends and policies: report...to the New Zealand Planning Council; [Donald T. Brash, chairman] . Wellington, 1978. pp. 49. *(Reports. No.1)*

NEW ZEALAND. Planning Council. 1978. Planning perspectives 1978-1983. [Wellington], 1978. pp. 103.

— Emigration and immigration.

NEW ZEALAND. Immigration Division. 1978. Immigration and New Zealand: a statement of current immigration policy. [Wellington, 1978]. pp. 15.

— — Bibliography.

NEW ZEALAND. Department of Labour. Research and Planning Division. 1978. Immigration and immigrants: a bibliography; a bibliography of the historical, demographic, social and economic aspects of immigration to and immigrants in New Zealand. 2nd interim ed. Wellington, 1978. pp. 79.

— Foreign economic relations — European Economic Community countries.

NEW ZEALAND. Planning Council. 1978. New Zealand and the European Community. Wellington, 1978. pp. 82.

— Foreign population — Bibliography.

NEW ZEALAND. Department of Labour. Research and Planning Division. 1978. Immigration and immigrants: a bibliography; a bibliography of the historical, demographic, social and economic aspects of immigration to and immigrants in New Zealand. 2nd interim ed. Wellington, 1978. pp. 79.

— Foreign relations.

NEW ZEALAND FOREIGN AFFAIRS REVIEW; (pd.q.by the Ministry of Foreign Affairs, Wellington). q. (formerly m.), 1973(v.23)- Wellington.

See also EUROPEAN ECONOMIC COMMUNITY — New Zealand.

— Government publications.

NEW ZEALAND. Department of Statistics. 1977. Catalogue of New Zealand statistics. 4th ed. [Wellington], 1977 in progress. 1 loose leaf folder.

— History — Sources.

MANDER JONES (PHYLLIS) compiler. Manuscripts in the British Isles relating to Australia, New Zealand and the Pacific. Honolulu, [1972]. pp. 697.

— Parliament.

NEW ZEALAND. General Assembly. House of Representatives. 1973. The parliament of New Zealand and Parliament House...; prepared by H.N. Dollimore. Rev. ed. [Wellington], 1973. pp. 70.

The REFORM of Parliament: contributions by Alan Robinson and papers presented in his memory concerning the New Zealand Parliament; edited by Sir John Marshall. Wellington, New Zealand Institute of Public Administration, 1978. pp. 238. *bibliog.*

— Politics and government.

PAUL (JOHN THOMAS) Humanism in politics: New Zealand Labour Party retrospect. Wellington, 1946. pp. 192.

POLITICS in New Zealand: a reader; edited by Stephen Levine. Sydney, 1978. pp. 437.

— Social conditions.

NEW ZEALAND GEOGRAPHY CONFERENCE, 9TH, DUNEDIN, 1977. Proceedings of the...conference; edited by T.J. Hearn and R.P. Hargreaves. Dunedin, 1977. pp. 133. *bibliogs. (New Zealand Geographical Society. Conference Series. No. 9)*

NEW ZEALAND. Planning Council. 1978. Planning perspectives 1978-1983. [Wellington], 1978. pp. 103.

NEW ZEALAND. Planning Council. 1979. The welfare state?: social policy in the 1980's. Wellington, 1979. pp. 113.

— — Statistics.

NEW ZEALAND. Department of Statistics. 1977. Social trends in New Zealand. [Wellington, 1977]. pp. 193.

— Social policy.

SOCIAL welfare and New Zealand society; edited by A.D. Trlin. Wellington, 1977. pp. 235. *bibliogs.*

FRANKLIN (S.H.) Trade, growth and anxiety: New Zealand beyond the welfare state. Wellington, 1978. pp. 402. *bibliogs.*

NEW ZEALAND. Planning Council. 1978. Planning perspectives 1978-1983. [Wellington], 1978. pp. 103.

NEW ZEALAND. Planning Council. 1979. The welfare state?: social policy in the 1980's. Wellington, 1979. pp. 113.

— Statistics — Bibliography.

NEW ZEALAND. Department of Statistics. 1977. Catalogue of New Zealand statistics. 4th ed. [Wellington], 1977 in progress. 1 loose leaf folder.

— Statistics, Vital.

NEW ZEALAND. Department of Health. National Health Statistics Centre. 1976. A review of mortality rates of children aged between one and under five years, in New Zealand and in selected countries, 1972. Wellington, [1976]. pp. 6.

NEW ZEALAND. Department of Health. National Health Statistics Centre. 1978. A review of mortality rates of children aged between 1 and under 5 years, in New Zealand and in selected countries, 1972-74. Wellington, [1978]. pp. 6.

NEWARK, NEW JERSEY.

HIRSCH (SUSAN E.) Roots of the American working class: the industrialization of crafts in Newark, 1800-1860. [Philadelphia, 1978].

NEWCASTLE-UPON-TYNE

— Commerce.

BENWELL COMMUNITY DEVELOPMENT PROJECT. Storing up trouble: warehousing and distribution in west Newcastle. Newcastle-upon-Tyne, 1978. pp. 44. *(Final Report Series. No. 1)*

— Industries.

BENWELL: news and views from Benwell Community Project. Special issue on employment and industry, April 1977: (the costs of industrial change). Newcastle-upon-Tyne, Benwell Community Development Project], 1977. pp. 16.

BENWELL COMMUNITY DEVELOPMENT PROJECT. Permanent unemployment. Newcastle-upon-Tyne, 1978. pp. 80. *(Final Report Series. No. 2)*

— **Stores, shopping centres, etc.**

BENWELL COMMUNITY DEVELOPMENT PROJECT. From blacksmiths to white elephants: (Benwell's changing shops). Newcastle-upon-Tyne, 1979. pp. 72. *(Final Report Series. No. 7)*

NEWFOUNDLAND

— **Social life and customs.**

WIDDOWSON (JOHN D.A.) If you don't be good: verbal social control in Newfoundland. St. John's, 1977. pp. 345. *bibliog. (St. John's. Memorial University of Newfoundland. Institute of Social and Economic Research. Newfoundland Social and Economic Papers. No. 21)*

NEWFOUNDLAND AND LABRADOR

— **Statistics.**

NEWFOUNDLAND. Central Statistical Services. Historical statistics of Newfoundland and Labrador. irreg., Oc 1970(v. 1, no. 1)- St. John's. *File includes supplement.*

NEWFOUNDLAND AND LABRADOR DEVELOPMENT CORPORATION.

NEWFOUNDLAND AND LABRADOR DEVELOPMENT CORPORATION LTD. Annual report. a., 1976/77- St. John's.

NEWHAM

— **Industries.**

CANNING TOWN COMMUNITY DEVELOPMENT PROJECT. How important are industrial rates? [London, 1976?]. pp. 27.

NEWMAN (JOHN HENRY) Cardinal.

NEWMAN and Gladstone: centennial essays; edited by James D. Bastable. Dublin, 1978. pp. 324. *bibliogs. Selection of papers presented at the International Newman Conference, Dublin, 1975.*

NEWS AGENCIES.

INDIA. Committee on News Agencies. 1977. Report; [Kuldip Nayar, chairman]. [Delhi], 1977. pp. 165.

NEWSPAPER PUBLISHING

— **Canada.**

CANADA. Statistics Canada. Culture statistics: newspapers and periodicals. a., 1976/1977(1st)- Ottawa. *[in English and French]*

— **United Kingdom.**

JENKINS (SIMON) Journalist. Newspapers: the power and the money. London, 1979. pp. 130. *bibliog.*

— — **History.**

WILLIAMS (KEITH) The English newspaper: an illustrated history to 1900. London, [1977]. pp. 128. *bibliog.*

NEWSPAPER READING.

EVENING NEWSPAPER ADVERTISING BUREAU. ENAB regional readership surveys: East Anglian ITV area. London, [1964]. 1 vol. (various pagings).

EVENING NEWSPAPER ADVERTISING BUREAU. ENAB regional readership surveys: Midland ITV area. London, [1964]. 1 vol. (various pagings).

EVENING NEWSPAPER ADVERTISING BUREAU. ENAB regional readership surveys: Northern (Lancashire) ITV area. London, [1964]. 1 vol. (various pagings).

EVENING NEWSPAPER ADVERTISING BUREAU. ENAB regional readership surveys: Southern area. London, [1964]. 1 vol. (various pagings).

EVENING NEWSPAPER ADVERTISING BUREAU. ENAB regional readership surveys: Wales and the West ITV area. London, [1964]. 1 vol. (various pagings).

EVENING NEWSPAPER ADVERTISING BUREAU. Evening newspaper readership: a summary of ENAB regional readership surveys. London, 1964. pp. 12.

NEWTON CHAMBERS AND COMPANY.

GRINYER (PETER HUGH) and SPENDER (J.C.) Turnaround: managerial recipes for strategic success; the fall and rise of the Newton Chambers group. London, 1979. pp. 211.

NGONDE (AFRICAN TRIBE).

WILSON (MARY MONICA) For men and elders: change in the relations of generations and of men and women among the Nyakyusa-Ngonde people, 1875-1971. London, [1977]. pp. 209. *bibliog. 5 appendices in end pocket.*

NICARAGUA

— **Politics and government.**

CRAWLEY (EDUARDO) Dictators never die: a portrait of Nicaragua and the Samoza dynasty. London, 1979. pp. 180. *bibliog.*

NICOLAS (JEAN).

MARTIN (HENRI JEAN) and LECOCQ (M.) Les registres du libraire Nicolas, 1645-1668. Genève, 1977. 2 vols. *bibliog. (Paris. Ecole Pratique des Hautes Etudes. Section des Sciences Historiques et Philologiques. Centre de Recherches d'Histoire et de Philologie. Publications. 6. Histoire et Civilisation du Livre. 10)*

NICOLE (LEON).

REY (MICHEL) Genève 1930-1933: la révolution de Léon Nicole. Berne, [1978]. pp. 309. *bibliog.*

NIEDZIALKOWSKI (MIECZYSLAW).

TOMICKI (JAN) Mieczysław Niedziałkowski. Warszawa, 1978. pp. 98.

NIETZSCHE (FRIEDRICH WILHELM).

STERN (JOSEPH PETER) A study of Nietzsche. Cambridge, 1979. pp. 220. *bibliog.*

NIGER

— **Economic conditions — Statistics.**

FRANCE. Ministère de la Coopération. Service des Etudes et Questions Internationales. 1978. Niger...: données statistiques sur les activités économiques, culturelles et sociales. Paris, 1978. pp. 155.

— **Social conditions — Statistics.**

FRANCE. Ministère de la Coopération. Service des Etudes et Questions Internationales. 1978. Niger...: données statistiques sur les activités économiques, culturelles et sociales. Paris, 1978. pp. 155.

NIGERIA

— **Armed forces — Political activity.**

ODETOLA (THEOPHILUS OLATUNDE) Military politics in Nigeria: economic development and political stability. New Brunswick, [1978]. pp. 179.

— **Commerce.**

NORTHUP (DAVID) Trade without rulers: pre-colonial economic development in south- eastern Nigeria. Oxford, 1978. pp. 269. *bibliog.*

— **Economic conditions.**

NIGERIA. 1968. Focus on the states. [Lagos, 1968?]. pp. 29.

NIGERIA (KWARA STATE). Information Division. 1968. Kwara State. rev. ed. [Ilorin, 1968]. pp. 42.

TEWSON (GEOFFREY E.) and COTTON (DAVID) Nigeria: business opportunities. London, [1977]. pp. 144.

BIERSTEKER (THOMAS J.) Distortion or development?: contending perspectives on the multinational corporation. Cambridge, Mass., [1978]. pp. 199. *bibliog.*

ODETOLA (THEOPHILUS OLATUNDE) Military politics in Nigeria: economic development and political stability. New Brunswick, [1978]. pp. 179.

— **Economic policy.**

NIGERIA. High Commission, London. 1971. Why Nigeria?: a businessman's guide to development in Nigeria between 1970 and 1974. [London, 1971?]. pp. 32.

NIGERIA (WESTERN STATE). 1975. Western State programme of the third national development plan, 1975-80. [Ibadan, 1975?]. pp. 209.

— **Executive departments.**

NIGERIA (KWARA STATE). Information Division. 1972. Kwara State of Nigeria, April 1969-December 1971: summary of the activities and achievements of the Kwara State military government. [Ilorin, 1972]. pp. 68. *Cover title: Your government at work.*

— **Foreign relations.**

CAMPBELL (R. KEITH) Nigerian foreign policy and the Economic Community of West African states (ECOWAS). Braamfontein, 1978. pp. 10. *bibliog. (South African Institute of International Affairs. Occasional Papers)*

NIGERIA and the world: readings in Nigerian foreign policy; edited by Dr. A. Bolaji Akinyemi. Ibadan, 1978. pp. 152. *bibliog. Papers presented at a conference organized by the Nigerian Institute of International Affairs, Lagos, 1976.*

WAYAS (JOSEPH) Nigeria's leadership role in Africa. London, 1979. pp. 132.

— **History.**

GOLDIE (Sir GEORGE DASHWOOD TAUBMAN) Empire builder extraordinary: Sir George Goldie, his philosophy of government and empire; [selected articles, letters, etc.; edited by] D.J.M. Muffett. Douglas, 1978. pp. 334. *bibliog.*

SMITH (ROBERT SYDNEY) The Lagos consulate, 1851-1861. London, 1978. pp. 188. *bibliog.*

— — **1967-1970, Civil War.**

OBSERVER TEAM TO NIGERIA. Nigeria: international observers team reports: final report of the first phase from October 5 to December 10 by the Organization of African Unity observers in Nigeria. [London, Nigerian High Commission, 1969]. pp. 5.

OBSERVER TEAM TO NIGERIA. Nigeria: international observer teams reports: fourth interim report of the personal representation of the United Nations Secretary-General. [London, Nigerian High Commission, 1969]. pp. 5.

OBSERVER TEAM TO NIGERIA. Nigeria: international observers teams reports: report on activities of the representatives of Canada, Poland, Sweden and the United Kingdom during the period November 24, 1968, to January 13, 1969. [London, Nigerian High Commission, 1969]. pp. (3).

— **Industries.**

TEWSON (GEOFFREY E.) and COTTON (DAVID) Nigeria: business opportunities. London, [1977]. pp. 144.

— **Nationalism.**

OLUSANYA (G.O.) The unfinished task. Lagos, 1978. pp. 17. *(Lagos. University. Inaugural Lecture Series)*

— **Officials and employees.**

NIGERIA. Public Service Review Commission. 1974. Main report; [J.O. Udoji, chairman]. Lagos, 1974. pp. 228.

— — **Salaries, allowances, etc.**

NIGERIA. Public Service Review Panel. 1975. Main report; [Akintola Williams, chairman]. Lagos, 1975. pp. 347. *Bound with the Government's views on the report.*

NIGERIA(Cont.)

NIGERIA. 1975. The public service of Nigeria: Government views on the report of the Public Service Review Panel. Lagos, 1975. pp. 31. *Bound with the Report.*

— Politics and government.

NIGERIA (KWARA STATE). Information Division. 1968. Kwara State. rev. ed. [Ilorin, 1968]. pp. 42.

NIGERIA (LAGOS STATE). Information Division. 1968. Togetherness in Lagos State. [Lagos, 1968]. pp. 16.

NIGERIA (KWARA STATE). Information Division. 1972. Kwara State of Nigeria, April 1969-December 1971: summary of the activities and achievements of the Kwara State military government. [Ilorin, 1972]. pp. 68. *Cover title: Your government at work.*

ODETOLA (THEOPHILUS OLATUNDE) Military politics in Nigeria: economic development and political stability. New Brunswick, [1978]. pp. 179.

OLUSANYA (G.O.) The unfinished task. Lagos, 1978. pp. 17. *(Lagos. University. Inaugural Lecture Series)*

— Religion.

GBADAMOSI (T.G.O.) The growth of Islam among the Yoruba, 1841-1908. London, 1978. pp. 265. *bibliog.*

— Social policy.

NIGERIA (WESTERN STATE). 1975. Western State programme of the third national development plan, 1975-80. [Ibadan, 1975?]. pp. 209.

NIGERIA (OYO STATE)

— Public Service Commission.

NIGERIA (OYO STATE). Public Service Commission. Report. a., 1976/77(1st)- [Ibadan]. *Supersedes in part* NIGERIA (WESTERN STATE). *Public Service Commission. Report.*

NIGERIAN COUNCIL FOR SCIENCE AND TECHNOLOGY.

NIGERIAN COUNCIL FOR SCIENCE AND TECHNOLOGY. The Nigerian Council for Science and Technology: inaugural brochure. Lagos, 1970. pp. 22.

NIKOPOL'

— Industries.

GANCHEV (IVAN DMITRIEVICH) Rezervy brigadnogo podriada. Moskva, 1978. pp. 80. *(Bibliotechka Profsoiuznogo Aktivista. 31)*

NIN (ANDRES).

NIN (ANDRES) Por la unificacion marxista. Madrid, [1978]. pp. 623. *bibliog.*

NIUE

— Census.

NEW ZEALAND. Department of Justice. 1973. Census of population and dwellings, Niue Island, 1971. [Alofi], 1973. pp. 48.

NIXON (RICHARD MILHOUS) President of the United States.

CONGRESSIONAL QUARTERLY INC. Nixon: the fifth year of his presidency. Washington, D.C., [1974]. pp. 74,191.

NIXON (RICHARD MILHOUS) President of the United States. The memoirs of Richard Nixon. London, 1978. pp. 1120.

NIXON (RICHARD MILHOUS) President of the United States. The Nixon presidential press conferences; introduction by Helen Thomas; [edited by George W. Johnson]. London, 1978. pp. 419.

NJÁLL THORGEIRSSON, c.930-1011.

The STORY of Burnt Njal; translated by Sir George Webbe Dasent. London, [1957?] repr. 1971. pp. 336. *bibliog.*

NOBEL PRIZES.

ZUCKERMAN (HARRIET) Scientific elite: Nobel laureates in the United States. New York, [1977]. pp. 335. *bibliog.*

NOISE CONTROL.

ORGANISATION FOR ECONOMIC CO-OPERATION AND DEVELOPMENT. Ad Hoc Group on Noise Abatement Policies. 1978. Reducing noise in OECD countries: a report of the Ad Hoc Group, etc. Paris, 1978. pp. 113.

NOLENS (WILLEM HUBERT).

GRIBLING (J.P.) Willem Hubert Nolens, 1860-1931: uit het leven van een priester-staatsman. Assen, 1978. pp. 377. *With German and French summaries.*

NOMADS.

PASTORAL production and society; Production pastorale et société: proceedings of the international meeting on nomadic pastoralism...Paris 1-3 Dec. 1976; edited by...l'Equipe écologie et anthropologie des sociétés pastorales. Cambridge, 1979. pp. 493. *bibliogs. In English or French.*

NONFERROUS METAL INDUSTRIES.

ATKINS (M.H.) and LOWE (J.F.) The economics of pollution control in the non-ferrous metals industry. Oxford, [1979]. pp. 177.

SCHMITZ (CHRISTOPHER J.) World non-ferrous metal production and prices, 1700-1976. London, 1979. pp. 432. *bibliog.*

NONLINEAR THEORIES.

STUDIES in nonlinear estimation; [including papers given at a seminar at Princeton University in 1974]; edited by Stephen M. Goldfeld and Richard E. Quandt. Cambridge, Mass., [1976]. pp. 278. *bibliog.*

NONPARAMETRIC STATISTICS.

PURI (MADAN LAL) and SEN (PRANAB KUMAR) Nonparametric statistics in multivariate analysis. New York, [1971]. pp. 440. *bibliog.*

NONTARIFF TRADE BARRIERS.

HILLMAN (JIMMYE S.) Nontariff agricultural trade barriers. Lincoln, Neb., [1978]. pp. 236. *bibliog.*

GENERAL AGREEMENT ON TARIFFS AND TRADE. 1979. The Tokyo Round of multilateral trade negotiations: report by the Director-General of GATT. Geneva, 1979. pp. 196.

NONVERBAL COMMUNICATION.

ACTION, gesture and symbol: the emergence of language; edited by Andrew Lock. London, 1978. pp. 588. *bibliog.*

NONVIOLENCE.

STRATEGIES against violence: design for non-violent change; edited by Israel W. Charny. Boulder, Colo., 1978. pp. 417. *bibliogs.*

HOPE (MARJORIE) and YOUNG (JAMES) 1916- . The struggle for humanity: agents of nonviolent change in a violent world. Maryknoll, 1979. pp. 305. *bibliog.*

NORD (DEPARTMENT)

— History.

PIERRARD (PIERRE) Histoire du Nord: Flandre, Artois, Hainaut, Picardie. [Paris, 1978]. pp. 404. *bibliog.*

NORDISK RÅD.

ØRVIK (NILS) and BJØL (ERLING) The Scandinavian allies and the European Community. Kingston, Ont., 1978. pp. 98. *(Kingston, Ontario. Queen's University. Centre for International Relations. European Studies Series. No. 1/78)*

NORFOLK

— Economic policy.

NORFOLK. County Council. County structure plan: draft written statement for consultation. [Norwich], 1976. pp. 141.

— Social policy.

NORFOLK. County Council. County structure plan: draft written statement for consultation. [Norwich], 1976. pp. 141.

NORMANDY

— Economic conditions.

DONNEES ECONOMIQUES ET SOCIALES DE BASSE-NORMANDIE: analyse trimestrielle; [pd. by] Service Régionale [de] Caen, Institut National de la Statistique et des Etudes Economiques. q., 1977(no. 1)- Caen.

— Social conditions.

DONNEES ECONOMIQUES ET SOCIALES DE BASSE-NORMANDIE: analyse trimestrielle; [pd. by] Service Régionale [de] Caen, Institut National de la Statistique et des Etudes Economiques. q., 1977(no. 1)- iCaen.

NORMANS IN ITALY.

CURTIS (EDMUND) Roger of Sicily and the Normans in Lower Italy, 1016-1154. New York, 1973. pp. 483. *Reprint of 1912, New York, ed.*

NORTH ATLANTIC REGION

— Politics and government.

The NEW nationalism: implications for transatlantic relations; edited by Werner Link, Werner J. Feld. New York, 1979. pp. 165. *bibliogs. Papers given at the annual conference of the Committee on Atlantic Studies, Luxembourg, 1977.*

NORTH ATLANTIC TREATY ORGANIZATION.

STEINBRUNER (JOHN D.) The cybernetic theory of decision: new dimensions of political analysis. Princeton, N.J. [1974]. pp. 366. *bibliog.*

STOCKHOLM INTERNATIONAL PEACE RESEARCH INSTITUTE. Tactical nuclear weapons: European perspectives; [edited by Frank Barnaby]. London, 1978. pp. 371.

JORDAN (ROBERT S.) Political leadership in NATO: a study in multinational diplomacy. Boulder, Colo., 1979. pp. 316.

The NEW nationalism: implications for transatlantic relations; edited by Werner Link, Werner J. Feld. New York, 1979. pp. 165. *bibliogs. Papers given at the annual conference of the Committee on Atlantic Studies, Luxembourg, 1977.*

NORTH ATLANTIC TREATY ORGANIZATION. Information Service. [Press releases]. irreg. Bruxelles. *Current issues only kept.*

— Bibliography.

GORDON (COLIN) compiler. The Atlantic Alliance; a bibliography. London, 1978. pp. 216.

NORTH CAROLINA

— Politics and government.

RISJORD (NORMAN K.) Chesapeake politics 1781-1800. New York, 1978. pp. 715. *bibliog.*

NORTH DEVON RAILWAY COMPANY.

HOOPER (BRIAN MICHAEL) and BUTTIMER (JAMES MICHAEL) North Devon Railway Company Limited; Words in Action Limited: investigations under section 165b of the Companies Act, 1948; reports. London, Department of Trade, 1979. 1 vol. (various pagings).

NORTH HOLLAND

— Economic history.

BOER (DICK EDWARD HERMAN DE) Graaf en grafiek: sociale en economische ontwikkelingen in het middeleeuwse 'Noordholland' tussen [c.] 1345 en [c.] 1415. Leiden, 1978. pp. 395. *bibliog. Proefschrift (Doctor in de Letteren) - Rijksuniversiteit te Leiden. With English summary.*

— Population.

BOER (DICK EDWARD HERMAN DE) Graaf en grafiek: sociale en economische ontwikkelingen in het middeleeuwse 'Noordholland' tussen [c.] 1345 en [c.] 1415. Leiden, 1978. pp. 395. *bibliog. Proefschrift (Doctor in de Letteren) - Rijksuniversiteit te Leiden. With English summary.*

NORTH ISLINGTON HOUSING RIGHTS PROJECT.

SHELTER. Street by street: improvement and tenant control in Islington: North Islington Housing Rights Project. London, [1977]. pp. 64.

NORTH RHINE-WESTPHALIA

— Industries.

NORTH RHINE-WESTPHALIA. Landesamt für Datenverarbeitung und Statistik. Beiträge zur Statistik des Landes Nordrhein- Westfalen. Heft 388. Investitionen der Industrie in Nordrhein- Westfalen 1966 bis 1975. Düsseldorf, 1978. pp. 169.

NORTH SHIELDS

— Industries.

NORTH TYNESIDE COMMUNITY DEVELOPMENT PROJECT. North Shields: living with industrial change. [Newcastle-upon-Tyne, 1978]. pp. 187. *(Final Reports. Vol.2)*

NORTH SHORE RAILWAY (QUEBEC).

YOUNG (BRIAN J.) Promoters and politicians: the North-Shore Railways in the history of Quebec, 1854-85. Toronto, [1978]. pp. 193. *bibliog.*

NORTH WALES QUARRYMEN'S UNION.

WILLIAMS (J. ROOSE) Quarryman's champion: the life and activities of William John Parry of Coetmor. Denbigh, [imprint, 1978]. pp. 258.

NORTH-WEST FRONTIER PROVINCE

— Economic conditions.

NORTH-WEST FRONTIER PROVINCE. Administration report. a., 1901/03-1938/39, with gap(1931/32). Peshawar.

— Politics and government.

NORTH-WEST FRONTIER PROVINCE. Administration report. a., 1901/03-1938/39, with gap(1931/32). Peshawar.

— Social conditions.

NORTH-WEST FRONTIER PROVINCE. Administration report. a., 1901/03-1938/39, with gap(1931/32). Peshawar.

NORTHEAST BOUNDARY OF THE UNITED STATES.

JONES (HOWARD) 1940- . To the Webster-Ashburton Treaty: a study in Anglo- American relations, 1783-1843. Chapel Hill, [1977]. pp. 251. *bibliog.*

NORTHERN IRELAND CIVIL RIGHTS ASSOCIATION.

NORTHERN IRELAND CIVIL RIGHTS ASSOCIATION. "We shall overcome"...; the history of the struggle for civil rights in Northern Ireland 1968-1978. Belfast, [1978?]. pp. 47.

NORTHERN STANDARD REGION (UNITED KINGDOM)

— Industries.

NORTHERN REGION STRATEGY TEAM. Development of comparable statistics for employment and output, 1948 to date: procedures for adjustment. Newcastle-upon-Tyne, 1975. pp. 67. *(Working Papers. No. 17)*

NORTHERN REGION STRATEGY TEAM. Changes in the corporate structure of manufacturing industry in the Northern Region; (project A.9). Newcastle-upon-Tyne, 1976. pp. 41. *(Working Papers. [No.5])*

NORTHERN REGION STRATEGY TEAM. Linkages in the Northern Region. Newcastle-upon-Tyne, 1977. fo. 50. *(Working Papers. No. 6)*

— Occupations.

NORTHERN REGION STRATEGY TEAM. Trends in the structure of occupations in the Northern Region, 1966-1971. Newcastle-upon-Tyne, 1976-77. 2 vols. *(Working Papers. No. 10)*

NORTHMEN.

OLRIK (AXEL) Viking civilization; revised...by Hans Ellekilde. New York, 1971. pp. 246. *bibliog. Reprint of work first published 1930.*

NORTHUMBERLAND

— Economic history.

McCORD (NORMAN) North East England: an economic and social history. London, 1979. pp. 267.

— Social history.

McCORD (NORMAN) North East England: an economic and social history. London, 1979. pp. 267.

NORWAY

— Economic conditions.

STENSTADVOLD (KJELL) Regional and structural effects of North Sea oil in Norway. Bergen, 1977. fo. 55. *bibliog. (Norges Handelshøyskole and Bergen. Universitet. Geography Department. Meddelelser. No.37)*

WETTERGREEN (KJELL) Konjunkturbølger fra utlandet i Norsk økonomi: international cycles in the Norwegian economy. Oslo, 1978. pp. 138. *(Norway. Statistiske Centralbyrå. Samfunnsøkonomiske Studier. 36)*

— Emigration and immigration.

NORWAY. Statistiske Centralbyrå. 1977. Inn- og utvandring for Norge, 1958-1975, etc. Oslo, 1977. pp. 92. *(Statistiske Analyser. 33) With English summary.*

— Government publications — Bibliography.

FORTEGNELSE over Norges offisielle statistikk og andre publikasjoner utgitt av Statistisk Sentralbyrå 1828-1976: Catalogue of Norwegian official statistics and other publications published by the Central Bureau of Statistics 1828-1976. Oslo, Statistisk Sentralbyrå, 1978. pp. 196. *(Norges Offisielle Statistikk. Rekke A.957)*

— History — 1940-1945, German occupation.

WORM-MÜLLER (JACOB S.) Norway revolts against the Nazis. 2nd ed. London, 1941. pp. 152.

WALKER (ROY) A people who loved peace: the Norwegian struggle against Nazism. London, 1946. pp. 111. *bibliog.*

— Population.

NORWAY. Statistiske Centralbyrå. 1978. Historiske tabeller over folkemengde, giftermål og dødsfall, 1911-1976: Historical tables on population, marriages and deaths, 1911-1976. Oslo, 1978. pp. 130.

— Statistics.

NORWAY. Statistiske Centralbyrå. 1978. Historisk statistikk, 1978; historical statistics, 1978. Oslo, 1978. pp. 650. *(Norges Offisielle Statistikk. Rekke 12.291)*

— — Bibliography.

FORTEGNELSE over Norges offisielle statistikk og andre publikasjoner utgitt av Statistisk Sentralbyrå 1828-1976: Catalogue of Norwegian official statistics and other publications published by the Central Bureau of Statistics 1828-1976. Oslo, Statistisk Sentralbyrå, 1978. pp. 196. *(Norges Offisielle Statistikk. Rekke A.957)*

— Vital statistics.

NORWAY. Statistiske Centralbyrå. 1978. Historiske tabeller over folkemengde, giftermål og dødsfall, 1911-1976: Historical tables on population, marriages and deaths, 1911-1976. Oslo, 1978. pp. 130.

NOSKE (GUSTAV).

SCHROEDER (HANS CHRISTOPH) Gustav Noske und die Kolonialpolitik des Deutschen Kaiserreichs. Berlin, [1979]. pp. 107.

NOVA SCOTIA

— Department of Development.

NOVA SCOTIA. Department of Development. Annual report. a., 1976/77- Halifax.

— Economic conditions.

SOUTH WESTERN NOVA SCOTIA STUDY TEAM. The economic and social base of south western Nova Scotia: a study prepared for Nova Scotia Department of Municipal Affairs. [Halifax, 1977]. pp. 208. *bibliog.*

NOVA SCOTIA ECONOMY, THE:...year end review and...outlook; [pd. by] Economic Analysis Section, Department of Development. a., 1978- Halifax.

— Economic policy.

NOVA SCOTIA. Department of Development. Annual report. a., 1976/77- Halifax.

— Executive departments.

NOVA SCOTIA. Department of Development. Annual report. a., 1976/77- Halifax.

— Politics and government.

NOVA SCOTIA. General Assembly. House of Assembly. 1979. The Nova Scotia legislature. Halifax, 1979. 1 vol. (unpaged). *bibliog.*

— Population.

NOVA SCOTIA. Department of Municipal Affairs. Community Planning Division. 1978. Population changes in Nova Scotia, 1971-1976. [Halifax], 1978. fo. 19.

— Social conditions.

SOUTH WESTERN NOVA SCOTIA STUDY TEAM. The economic and social base of south western Nova Scotia: a study prepared for Nova Scotia Department of Municipal Affairs. [Halifax, 1977]. pp. 208. *bibliog.*

NOVGOROD

— Antiquities.

RYBINA (ELENA ALEKSANDROVNA) Arkheologicheskie ocherki istorii novgorodskoi torgovli X-XIV vv. Moskva, 1978. pp. 167. *bibliog.*

NOVGOROD (Cont.)

— Commerce.

RYBINA (ELENA ALEKSANDROVNA) Arkheologicheskie ocherki istorii novgorodskoi torgovli X-XIV vv. Moskva, 1978. pp. 167. *bibliog.*

NUCLEAR FUELS.

WONDER (EDWARD F.) Nuclear fuel and American foreign policy: multilateralization for uranium enrichment. Boulder, Colo., 1977. pp. 72.

AHMED (S. BASHEER) Nuclear fuel and energy policy. Lexington, Mass., [1979]. pp. 158. *bibliog.*

NUCLEAR NONPROLIFERATION.

CERVENKA (ZDENEK) and ROGERS (BARBARA) The nuclear axis: secret collaboration between West Germany and South Africa. London, 1978. pp. 464.

NUFFIELD FOUNDATION SCIENCE TEACHING PROJECT.

WARING (MARY) Social pressures and curriculum innovation: a study of the Nuffield Foundation Science Teaching Project. London, 1979. pp. 263. *bibliog.*

NUMBERS, RANDOM.

NEWMAN (THOMAS GERALD) and ODELL (PATRICK L.) The generation of random variates. London, 1971. pp. 88. *bibliog.*

NUMERICAL ANALYSIS.

CARNAHAN (BRICE) and others. Applied numerical methods. New York, 1969. pp. 604. *bibliog.*

CHAMBERS (JOHN M.) Computational methods for data analysis. New York, [1977]. pp. 268. *bibliog.*

NUNES MACHADO (FRANCISCO).

NUNES MACHADO (FRANCISCO) Discursos parlamentares; seleção e introdução de Vamireh Chacon. Brasilia, 1978. pp. 201. *(Brazil. Congresso. Câmara dos Deputados. Perfis Parlamentares. 3)*

NUREMBERG

— Economic history.

GOEMMELL (RAINER) Wachstum und Konjunktur der Nürnberger Wirtschaft, 1815-1914. [Stuttgart, 1978]. pp. 242. *bibliog.*

NURSES AND NURSING

— United Kingdom — Ireland, Northern.

IRELAND, NORTHERN. Nursing Service Study Group. 1977. Report on the feasibility of achieving economies and increased efficiency in the hospital and community nursing service; [D. McCullough, chairman]. [Belfast], 1977. pp. (67).

NUTRITION.

PAG BULLETIN: (international review of action to improve world protein nutrition); [pd. by] Protein-Calorie Advisory Group of the United Nations System. irreg., 1971(no.11)- , with gap (1972: v.2, no.3). New York.

FOOD AND NUTRITION; [pd. q. by the Nutrition Division of] Food and Agriculture Organization of the United Nations. q., 1975(v.1, no.1)- Rome.

U.K. Department of Health and Social Security. 1978. Eating for health: a discussion booklet prepared by the health departments of Great Britain and Northern Ireland. London, 1978. pp. 83. *bibliog. At head of title: Prevention and health.*

NUTRITION POLICY.

FOOD, health and farming: reports of panels on the implications for U.K. agriculture; edited by C.J. Robbins. rev. ed. Reading, 1978. pp. 119. *bibliogs. (Reading. University. Centre for Agricultural Strategy. CAS Papers. 7)*

NUTRITION and national policy; [edited by] Beverly Winikoff. Cambridge, Mass., [1978]. pp. 580.

— Underdeveloped areas.

See UNDERDEVELOPED AREAS — Nutrition policy.

NYAKYUSAS.

WILSON (MARY MONICA) For men and elders: change in the relations of generations and of men and women among the Nyakyusa-Ngonde people, 1875-1971. London, [1977]. pp. 209. *bibliog. 5 appendices in end pocket.*

OASES.

WILKINSON (JOHN CRAVEN) Problems of oasis development. Oxford, 1978. pp. 40. *bibliog. (Oxford. University. School of Geography. Research Papers. No.20)*

OBERWART

— Languages.

GAL (SUSAN) Language shift: social determinants of linguistic change in bilingual Austria. New York, [1979]. pp. 20a1. *bibliog.*

OBSCENITY (LAW)

— United Kingdom.

DEFENCE OF LITERATURE AND THE ARTS SOCIETY. Evidence to the Committee on Obscenity and Film Censorship. London, 1978. pp. 13.

ROBERTSON (GEOFFREY) Obscenity: an account of censorship laws and their enforcement in England and Wales. London, [1979]. pp. 364.

OBSTETRICS.

DONNISON (JEAN ELIZABETH) Midwives and medical men: a history of inter-professional rivalries and women's rights. London, 1977. pp. 250. *bibliog.*

O'CASEY (SEAN).

WATSON (GEORGE) Irish identity and the literary revival: Synge, Yeats, Joyce and O'Casey. London, 1979. pp. 326. *bibliog.*

OCCUPATIONAL MOBILITY

— United States.

DE JONG (PETER) Patterns on intergenerational occupational mobility of American females. San Francisco, 1977. pp. 138. *bibliog.*

FEATHERMAN (DAVID L.) and HAUSER (ROBERT MASON) Opportunity and change. New York, [1978]. pp. 572. *bibliog.*

LEIGH (DUANE E.) An analysis of the determinants of occupational upgrading. New York, [1978]. pp. 185. *bibliog. (Wisconsin University, Madison. Institute for Research on Poverty. Monograph Series)*

OCCUPATIONAL PRESTIGE

— Finland.

ALESTALO (MATTI) and UUSITALO (HANNU) Occupational prestige and its determinants: the case of Finland. Helsinki, 1978. pp. 54. *(Helsinki. Yliopisto. Research Group for Comparative Sociology. Research Reports. No. 20)*

OCCUPATIONAL TRAINING

— France.

POMMIER PENEFF (PAULETTE) and others. Population, emploi et formation dans les contrats de pays. [Paris, 1978]. pp. 32. *(France. Délégation à l'Emploi. Politique des Contrats de Pays. Dossiers Techniques)*

— Russia.

RABOCHII klass SSSR na sovremennom etape. vyp.5. Podgotovka i vospitanie kadrov rabochego klassa SSSR v usloviiakh razvitogo sotsializma; otvetstvennye redaktory V.A. Ezhov, V.A. Ovsiankin. Leningrad, 1977. pp. 183.

— United Kingdom.

COMMUNITY RELATIONS COMMISSION and RUNNYMEDE TRUST. Industrial training boards and race relations: a discussion paper. London, 1977. pp. 30, (26). *bibliog.*

INDUSTRIAL TRAINING RESEARCH UNIT. Widening employment opportunities: a summary report of an evaluation study of the wider opportunities courses; carried out by the Industrial Training Research Unit for the Training Services Agency; (written by Roger Mottram). Cambridge, 1977. pp. 40. *(Publications. TR 10)*

NORTHERN REGION STRATEGY TEAM. Industrial training in the Northern Region. Newcastle-upon-Tyne, 1977. pp. 114. *(Technical Reports. No. 17)*

BAYLEY (L.P.) The work experience programme; a report by...[the] former director of the programme. London, Manpower Services Commission, [1978]. 1 vol. (various pagings).

ZIDERMAN (ADRIAN) Manpower training: theory and policy. London, 1978. pp. 90. *bibliog.*

U.K. Department of Education and Science. 1979. 16-18: education and training for 16-18 year olds: a consultative paper. [London, 1979]. pp. 16.

— United States.

LEIGH (DUANE E.) An analysis of the determinants of occupational upgrading. New York, [1978]. pp. 185. *bibliog. (Wisconsin University, Madison. Institute for Research on Poverty. Monograph Series)*

OCCUPATIONS.

MILLER (GALE) Odd jobs: the world of deviant work. Englewood Cliffs, N.J., [1978]. pp. 260. *bibliog.*

COXON (ANTHONY PETER MACMILLAN) and JONES (CHARLES L.) Class and hierarchy: the social meaning of occupations. London, 1979. pp. 217. *bibliog.*

DAVIS (HOWARD H.) Beyond class images: explorations in the structure of social consciousness. London, [1979]. pp. 213. *bibliog.*

— Classification.

FRANCE. Institut National de la Statistique et des Etudes Economiques. 1962. Code des catégories socio-professionnelles; (code[s] no[s.] 3 [-6] du recensement de la population de 1962). 4th ed. Paris, 1962. 1 vol. (various pagings).

OCEAN BOTTOM.

RAMBERG (BENNETT) The seabed arms control negotiations: a study of multilateral arms control conference diplomacy. Denver, [1978]. pp. 135. *bibliog. (Denver. University. Graduate School of International Studies. Monograph Series in World Affairs. vol. 15, no. 2)*

OCEAN ENGINEERING.

JANE'S ocean technology: fourth edition (1979-80); edited by Robert L. Trillo. London, [1979]. pp. 824.

OCEAN MINING.

JANE'S ocean technology: fourth edition (1979-80); edited by Robert L. Trillo. London, [1979]. pp. 824.

OCEANOGRAPHIC RESEARCH.

McQUILLIN (R.) and ARDUS (D.A.) Exploring the geology of shelf seas. London, 1977. pp. 234. *bibliog.*

OCEANOGRAPHIC RESEARCH SHIPS.

JANE'S ocean technology: fourth edition (1979-80); edited by Robert L. Trillo. London, [1979]. pp. 824.

OCEANOGRAPHY.

WEYL (PETER K.) Oceanography: an introduction to the marine environment. New York, [1970]. pp. 535. *bibliogs.*

OCEAN science: readings from Scientific American; with introductions by H.W. Menard. San Francisco, [1977]. pp. 307. *bibliog.*

SHEPARD (FRANCIS P.) Geological oceanography: evolution of coasts, continental margins, and the deep-sea floor. New York, [1977]. pp. 214. *bibliogs.*

OCEAN yearbook 1; edited by Elisabeth Mann Borgese and Norton Ginsburg. Chicago, 1978. pp. 890.

OCEANOGRAPHY; [by] Charles L. Drake [and others]. New York, [1978]. pp. 447. *bibliog.*

O'CONNOR (CHARLES YELVERTON).

TAUMAN (MERAB) The chief: C.Y. O'Connor. Nedlands, 1978. pp. 290.

OFFA, King of Angel.

CHAMBERS (RAYMOND WILSON) Beowulf: an introduction to the study of the poem with a discussion of the stories of Offa and Finn;...with a supplement by C.L. Wrenn. 3rd ed. Cambridge, 1959 repr. 1972. pp. 628. *bibliogs.*

OFFA, King of the Mercians, d.796.

CHAMBERS (RAYMOND WILSON) Beowulf: an introduction to the study of the poem with a discussion of the stories of Offa and Finn;...with a supplement by C.L. Wrenn. 3rd ed. Cambridge, 1959 repr. 1972. pp. 628. *bibliogs.*

OFFA SAGA.

CHAMBERS (RAYMOND WILSON) Beowulf: an introduction to the study of the poem with a discussion of the stories of Offa and Finn;...with a supplement by C.L. Wrenn. 3rd ed. Cambridge, 1959 repr. 1972. pp. 628. *bibliogs.*

OFFENCES AGAINST PROPERTY
— Russia.

PANOV (NIKOLAI IVANOVICH) Ugolovnaia otvetstvennost' za prichinenie imushchestvennogo ushcherba putem obmana ili zloupotrebleniia doveriem. Khar'kov, 1977. pp. 127. *bibliog.*

— United Kingdom — Ireland, Northern.

IRELAND, NORTHERN. Committee to Review the Principles and Operation of the Criminal Injuries to Property (Compensation Act) (Northern Ireland) 1971. 1976. Report...; chairman: Sir James Waddell. Belfast, [1976]. pp. 63.

OFFICE EQUIPMENT AND SUPPLIES INDUSTRY
— Italy.

BALLIANO (PIERA) and MOSINI (FILIPPO) Studio sull'evoluzione della concentrazione nel settore della costruzione di macchine per ufficio in Italia. [Brussels], Comunità Europee, 1976. pp. 149.

OFFICES
— Location.

SPATIAL patterns of office growth and location; [edited by] P. W. Daniels. Chichester, [1979]. pp. 414. *bibliogs.*

— — Canada — Quebec.

QUEBEC (PROVINCE). Office de Planification et de Développement. 1978. Les sièges sociaux et l'emploi au Québec: quelques statistiques partielles. [Québec, 1978]. pp. 64. *bibliog.*

— — United Kingdom.

NORTHERN REGION STRATEGY TEAM. Spatial patterns and the development of office activities; (project no. B.1.f). Newcastle-upon-Tyne, 1976. pp. 54. (*Working Papers. [No. 9]*)

OFFICIAL SECRETS.

MATHEWS (ANTHONY S.) The darker reaches of government: access to information about public administration in the United States, Britain and South Africa. Berkeley, 1978. pp. 245. *bibliogs.*

ADMINISTRATIVE secrecy in developed countries; edited by Donald C. Rowat. London, 1979. pp. 364.

GOREN (DINA) Secrecy and the right to know. Ramat Gan, Israel, 1979. pp. 194. *bibliog.*

U.K. Civil Service Department. 1979. Disclosure of official information: a report on overseas practice. London, 1979. pp. 54, 150. *bibliog.*

— United Kingdom.

PINCHER (CHAPMAN) Inside story: a documentary of the pursuit of power. London, 1978. pp. 400.

OFFSHORE OIL INDUSTRY
— Law and legislation.

KETO (DAVID B.) Law and offshore oil development: the North Sea experience. New York, [1978]. pp. 123.

— Licences — United Kingdom.

U.K. Department of Energy. 1976. UK offshore petroleum production licensing: fifth round: a consultative document. [London, 1976]. pp. (9).

— North Sea.

U.K. Department of Energy. 1978. Offshore oil policy; note. [London, 1978]. pp. 11. (*Energy Commission [U.K.]. Papers. No. 19*)

U.K. OFFSHORE OPERATORS ASSOCIATION. Exploration and development of U.K. continental shelf oil; the inter-dependence of government policies and industry effort in optimising the potential benefits of U.K. continental shelf oil;... with an Annex entitled Exploration and development activity: a critical factor in oil depletion policy. [London], 1978. 1 vol. (various pagings). (*Energy Commission [U.K.]. Papers. No. 17*)

OHIO
— Historical geography.

SMITH (THOMAS H.) The mapping of Ohio. [Kent, Ohio], [1977]. pp. 252. *bibliogs.*

— Maps.

SMITH (THOMAS H.) The mapping of Ohio. [Kent, Ohio], [1977]. pp. 252. *bibliogs.*

OHIO VALLEY
— Manufactures.

LIPPINCOTT (ISAAC) A history of manufactures in the Ohio Valley to the year 1860. New York, 1914; Philadelphia, 1974. pp. 214. *bibliog.* Facsimile reprint.

OIL INDUSTRIES.

SAMPSON (ANTHONY) The seven sisters: the great oil companies and the world they made. London, 1975. pp. 334.

OLD AGE
— Home care services — United States.

BALZANO (MICHAEL P.) Federalizing meals-on-wheels: private sector loss or gain? Washington, [1979]. pp. 41. (*American Enterprise Institute for Public Policy Research. Special Analyses. No. 79-1*)

OLD AGE

— Belgium.

DOOGHE (GILBERT) and VANDERLEYDEN (L.) Bejaarden en hun levensvoldoening: een empirisch onderzoek by weduwen en gehuwde vrouwen. Antwerp, 1978. pp. 132. *bibliog.* (*Centre d'Etude de la Population et de la Famille [Belgium]. Studies en Dokumenten. 10*)

— France — Statistics.

CHASSERIAUX-JAULERRY (ELIANE) La population âgée de Paris en 1968: (situation et perspectives). [Paris], Atelier Parisien d'Urbanisme, 1971. pp. 118.

— Hong Kong.

HONG KONG. Working Party on the Future Needs of the Elderly. 1973. Services for the elderly: report; (with Summary); [Strachan Heppell, chairman]. Hong Kong, [1973]. 2 pts.

— New Zealand.

NEW ZEALAND. Department of Statistics. 1977. Survey of persons aged 65 years and over, 1973-74. [Wellington, 1977]. pp. 59.

— Switzerland — Dwellings.

Das WOHNPROBLEM der pflegebeduerftigen Betagten im Kanton Thurgau: Bericht der vom Regierungsrat eingesetzten Studienkommission...vom 14. März 1969; [Rudolf Vogler, chairman]. [Frauenfeld, 1969]. fo.40. *4 maps in end-pocket.*

— United Kingdom.

HEARNDEN (ROBERT) and FUJISHIN (BARRY S.) Members of old peoples' clubs: needs and services: a survey in West Bromwich;...with the assistance of Greta Sumner. Birmingham, 1974. pp. 132. *bibliog.* (*Birmingham. University. Centre for Urban and Regional Studies. Research Memoranda. No. 35*)

AGE CONCERN ENGLAND. Research Unit. Profiles of the elderly. Vols. 1-4. London, 1977-78. 4 pts (in 1). (*Age Concern England. Research Publications*)

BUTCHER (HUGH) and CROSBIE (DAVID) Pensioned off...: a study of elderly people in Cleator Moor. [York, 1977]. pp. 118. (*Papers in Community Studies. No. 15*)

ABRAMS (MARK ALEXANDER) Beyond three-score and ten: a first report on a survey of the elderly. London, 1978. pp. 63.

An AGEING population: a reader and sourcebook; edited by Vida Carver and Penny Liddiard. Sevenoaks, [1978]. pp. 434. *bibliogs.*

SOUTH EAST THAMES REGIONAL HEALTH AUTHORITY. Strategies and guidelines for the care of elderly people. [Croydon], 1978. pp. 71.

STEVENSON (OLIVE) Ageing: a professional perspective. London, 1978. pp. 12. *bibliog.* (*Age Concern England. Occasional Papers*)

U.K. Department of Health and Social Security. 1978. A happier old age: a discussion document on elderly people in our society. London, 1978. pp. 44.

— — Care and hygiene.

CHAPMAN (PAUL) Unmet needs and the delivery of care: a study of the utilisation of social services by old people. [London], 1979. pp. 110. (*Social Administration Research Trust. Occasional Papers on Social Administration. No. 61*)

— — Dwellings.

U.K. Department of the Environment. 1976. Housing for old people: a consultation paper. [London], 1976. pp. 8.

AGE CONCERN GREATER LONDON. Housing Working Party. Housing advice for the elderly. London, [1977]. pp. 36.

GRAY (MUIR) Building for our future: housing problems of the elderly: a prescription for change. London, 1977. pp. 20. *bibliog.* (*Age Concern England. Occasional Papers*)

OLD AGE (Cont.)

LLEWELYN-DAVIES WEEKS [AND PARTNERS]. Inner area study: Birmingham: home environment of the elderly disabled. [London], Department of the Environment, [1978]. pp. 19.

— United States.

JUSTICE and older Americans; [edited by] Marlene A. Young Rifai. Lexington, Mass., [1977]. pp. 201.

ACHENBAUM (W. ANDREW) Old age in the new land: the American experience since 1790. Baltimore, [1978]. pp. 237. *bibliog.*

KASSCHAU (PATRICIA L.) Aging and social policy: leadership planning. New York, 1978. pp. 419.

— — Nutrition.

BALZANO (MICHAEL P.) Federalizing meals-on-wheels: private sector loss or gain? Washington, [1979]. pp. 41. *(American Enterprise Institute for Public Policy Research. Special Analyses. No. 79-1)*

OLD AGE ASSISTANCE

— United Kingdom.

AGE CONCERN ENGLAND. Action Guides. Street warden schemes. Mitcham, [1977]. pp. 16.

AGE CONCERN ENGLAND. Policy Publications. No. 2. Age Concern policy: focus on the future. London, 1977. pp. 29.

AGE CONCERN ENGLAND. Action Guides. Transport schemes. Mitcham, 1978. pp. 15. *bibliog.*

HEBDITCH (SIMON) Age Concern: the national policy. London, [1978]. pp. 20.

POLITICAL party priorities for the elderly; report of a discussion...at [the] Four Nations Conference, Harrogate, November 1977; [edited by Pat Healy]. London, [1978]. pp. 20.

U.K. Department of Health and Social Security. 1978. A happier old age: a discussion document on elderly people in our society. London, 1978. pp. 44.

CHAPMAN (PAUL) Unmet needs and the delivery of care: a study of the utilisation of social services by old people. [London], 1979. pp. 110. *(Social Administration Research Trust. Occasional Papers on Social Administration. No. 61)*

— United States.

KASSCHAU (PATRICIA L.) Aging and social policy: leadership planning. New York, 1978. pp. 419.

OLD AGE HOMES

— New Zealand.

NEW ZEALAND. Department of Health. National Health Statistics Centre. 1979. Bed occupation survey 1976: public, private and maternity hospital patients and old people's homes. Wellington, 1979. pp. 47. *(Department of Health. Special Report Series. No. 54)*

— United Kingdom.

GIBBERD (KATHLEEN) Home for life: residential care: what alternatives? London, 1977. pp. 16. *(Age Concern England. Occasional Papers)*

OLD AGE PENSIONS

— Canada.

CANADA. Department of National Health and Welfare. Old Age Security Division. 1971. Your old age pension: a program of the government of Canada. Ottawa, 1971. pp. 8, 8. *In English and French.*

— — Quebec.

REGIMES DE RETRAITE AU QUEBEC, LES [sub-titles vary]; [pd. by] Actuarial Branch, Pension Plan. irreg., 1973(no.2)- Québec. *Each issue contains specialized article which is in English and French.*

— Russia.

KARTSKHIIA (AMIRAN ANDREEVICH) Pensionnoe obespechenie po starosti. Moskva, 1978. pp. 134.

— United Kingdom.

PILCH (MICHAEL) and WOOD (VICTOR) Pension schemes: a guide to principles and practice. Farnborough, Hants., [1979]. pp. 277. *bibliog.*

— United States.

KLEILER (FRANK M.) Can we afford early retirement? Baltimore, [1978]. pp. 163. *bibliog.*

OLDENBURG

— History.

SCHAAP (KLAUS) Die Endphase der Weimarer Republik im Freistaat Oldenburg, 1928-1933. Düsseldorf, [1978]. pp. 313. *bibliog. (Germany (Bundesrepublik). Kommission für Geschichte des Parlamentarismus und der Politischen Parteien. Beiträge zur Geschichte des Parlamentarismus und der Politischen Parteien. Band 61)*

— Politics and government.

MEYENBERG (RUEDIGER) SPD in der Provinz: empirische Untersuchung...von SPD- Mitgliedern am Beispiel des Unterbezirks Oldenburg, Oldb. Frankfurt, [1978]. pp. 282. *bibliog.*

OLDHAM

— Race relations.

BARR (ALAN) Housing improvement and the multi-racial community: a report on action and research strategies in Oldham C[ommunity] D[evelopment] P[roject]. [York], 1978. pp. 99. *(Papers in Community Studies. No. 16)*

— Social policy.

CORINA (LEWIS) and others. Oldham C[ommunity] D[evelopment] P[roject]: the final report. [York], 1979. pp. 86. *bibliog. (Papers in Community Studies. No. 23)*

OLDS (RANSOM ELI).

MAY (GEORGE SMITH) R.E. Olds: auto industry pioneer. Grand Rapids, Mich., [1977]. pp. 458.

OLEA Y LEYVA (TEOFILO).

KRAUZE (ENRIQUE) Caudillos culturales en la Revolucion mexicana. Mexico, 1976. pp. 340.

OLIVER (JOHN ANDREW).

OLIVER (JOHN ANDREW) Working at Stormont: memoirs. Dublin, 1978. pp. 251.

OMBUDSMAN.

STACEY (FRANK ARTHUR) Ombudsmen compared. Oxford, 1978. pp. 256. *bibliog.*

— Belgium.

IMPE (HERMAN VAN) An ombudsman or parliamentary commissioner: an appointment being considered in Belgium. [Brussels], Ministry of Foreign Affairs, External Trade and Cooperation in Development, 1972. pp. 9. *(Memo from Belgium. No.149-150)*

— Canada — Ontario.

ONTARIO. Ombudsman. Report. s-a., 1975/76(1st)- Toronto.

— Israel.

KERBER (NATHALIE MARGUERITE) The Israeli ombudsman. [rev. ed.] [Jerusalem, State Comptroller's Office, 1976 . pp. 97. *bibliog.*

— Russia.

LEIDEN. Rijks Universiteit. Documentation Office for East European Law. Law in Eastern Europe. No. 21. The Soviet Procuracy protests, 1937-1973: a collection of translations by Leon Boim...and Glenn G. Morgan. Alphen aan den Rijn, 1978. pp. 603. *bibliog.*

— United Kingdom.

LEWIS (NORMAN) and GATESHILL (BERNARD) The Commission for Local Administration: a preliminary appraisal. London, 1978. pp. 68. *(Royal Institute of Public Administration. RIPA Studies)*

U.K. Commission for Local Administration in England. Report[s] by the local Ombudsman on investigation[s] into complaint[s]. irreg., Ag 1979- London.

ONE BIG UNION.

BERCUSON (DAVID JAY) Fools and wise men: the rise and fall of the One Big Union. Toronto, [1978]. pp. 300. *bibliog.*

ONEIDA COMMUNITY.

DAILY Journal of Oneida Community. vols. 1-3 [and] The O. C. Daily. vols. 4-5. Philadelphia, 1975. 1 vol. (unpaged). *Reprint of 2 newspapers first published 1866 and 1868.*

ONTARIO

— Climate.

TOSINE (TONU P.) The physical base for agriculture in central Canada. Toronto, 1978. pp. 59. *bibliog. (Ontario. Ministry of Agriculture and Food. Economics Branch. Economics Information)*

— Diplomatic and consular service.

ONTARIO. Ontario House, London. 1978. A history of Ontario House; (researched and compiled by George D. Taylor). [Toronto, 1978?]. 1 vol. (unpaged).

— Economic conditions.

ONTARIO. Royal Commission on the Northern Environment. 1978. Issues report; [E.P. Hartt, commissioner]. Toronto, 1978. pp. 275.

SAWYER (JOHN A.) and others. The Ontario economy, 1978-1987. [Toronto, Ontario Economic Council, 1978]. pp. 150. *bibliog.*

— Economic policy.

ONTARIO. Ministry of Treasury, Economics and Intergovernmental Affairs. 1978. Northwestern Ontario: a strategy for development. [Toronto], 1978. pp. 98.

ONTARIO. Royal Commission on the Northern Environment. 1978. Issues report; [E.P. Hartt, commissioner]. Toronto, 1978. pp. 275.

SAWYER (JOHN A.) and others. The Ontario economy, 1978-1987. [Toronto, Ontario Economic Council, 1978]. pp. 150. *bibliog.*

— Executive departments.

ONTARIO. Justice Policy Field. 1976. Justice policy in Ontario. [Toronto], 1976. pp. 67.

— Industries.

ONG (K.T.) An agriculturally orientated input-output analysis of the Ontario economy. Toronto, 1977. pp. 33. *bibliog. (Ontario. Ministry of Agriculture and Food. Economics Branch. Economic Research)*

— Population.

ONTARIO. Regional Planning Branch. 1976. Ontario's changing population. [Toronto], 1976. 2 vols. *bibliogs.*

ONTARIO. Central Statistical Services Division. 1978. Ontario: 1977 population estimates by five-year age groups and sex for counties, planning regions and centres of 10,000 population and over. [Toronto], 1978. fo. 25.

ONTARIO. Central Statistical Services Division. 1978. Ontario: revised population estimates by five-year age group and sex for counties and planning regions, 1971-1976. [Toronto], 1978. pp. 96.

— Social conditions.

ONTARIO. Royal Commission on the Northern Environment. 1978. Issues report; [E.P. Hartt, commissioner]. Toronto, 1978. pp. 275.

— Social policy.

ONTARIO. Ministry of Treasury, Economics and Intergovernmental Affairs. 1978. Northwestern Ontario: a strategy for development. [Toronto], 1978. pp. 98.

ONTARIO. Royal Commission on the Northern Environment. 1978. Issues report; [E.P. Hartt, commissioner]. Toronto, 1978. pp. 275.

ONTOLOGY.

GOULD (CAROL C.) Marx's social ontology: individuality and community in Marx's theory of social reality. Cambridge, Mass., [1978]. pp. 208. *bibliog.*

OPEN AND CLOSED SHOP

— Law and legislation — United Kingdom.

[U.K. Department of Employment]. 1979. Working paper for consultations on proposed industrial relations legislation: closed shop. [London, 1979]. fo. (4).

— United Kingdom.

CHURCH OF ENGLAND. National Assembly. Board for Social Responsibility. Industrial Committee. Understanding closed shops: a Christian enquiry into compulsory trade union membership. London, [1977]. pp. 31. *bibliog.* (Church of England. National Assembly. Board for Social Responsibility. Occasional Papers)

OPEN SPACES

— New Zealand.

NEW ZEALAND. Ministry of Works and Development. Town and Country Planning Division. 1977. Public open space in New Zealand cities. [Wellington], 1977. pp. 29.

OPERATIONS RESEARCH.

EISELT (HORST A.) and FRAJER (HELMUT VON) Operations research handbook: standard algorithms and methods with examples. London, 1977. pp. 398. *bibliog.*

BOOTHROYD (HYLTON) Articulate intervention. London, 1978. pp. 154. *bibliog.* (Operational Research Society. ORASA Texts. No. 1)

MERCER (ALAN) and others. Operational distribution research: innovative case studies. London, 1978. pp. 196. *bibliog.* (Operational Research Society. ORASA Texts. No.2)

THESEN (ARNE) Computer methods in operations research. New York, 1978. pp. 268. *bibliogs.*

INTERNATIONAL CONFERENCE ON OPERATIONAL RESEARCH. 8th Conference, Toronto, 1978. Operational research '78: proceedings...; edited by K.B. Haley. Amsterdam, 1979. pp. 1114. *bibliog.*

— Bibliography.

ZAREMBA (JOSEPH M.) compiler. Mathematical economics and operations research: a guide to information sources. Detroit, [1978]. pp. 606.

OPPOSITION (POLITICAL SCIENCE).

HOFMANN (HEINZ) Mehrparteiensystem ohne Opposition: die nichtkommunistischen Partein in der DDR, Polen, der Tschechoslowakei und Bulgarien. Bern, 1976. pp. 130. *bibliog.*

OPPOSITION in Eastern Europe; edited by Rudolf L. Tökés. London, 1979. pp. 306.

OPTICAL TRADE

— Russia.

IVANOV (NIKOLAI IVANOVICH) Aleksandr L'vovich Gershun, 1868-1915. Leningrad, 1976. pp. 135. *bibliog.* (Akademiia Nauk SSSR. Nauchno-Bibliograficheskaia Seriia)

ORAL COMMUNICATION.

ATKINSON (JOHN MAXWELL) and DREW (PAUL) Order in court: the organisation of verbal interaction in judicial settings. London, 1979. pp. 275. *bibliog.* (U.K. Social Science Research Council. Centre for Socio-Legal Studies. Oxford Socio-Legal Studies)

ORANGE FREE STATE

— Government publications — Bibliography.

EALES (MARJORY) compiler. An annotated guide to the pre-union government publications of the Orange Free State, 1854-1910. Boston, Mass., [1976]. pp. 523.

ORANGE RIVER.

SOUTH AFRICA. Department of Information. 1968. Orange River project. [Pretoria, 1968]. pp. 48. (Fact Paper Series)

ORDER STATISTICS

— Bibliography.

HARTER (H. LEON) compiler. A chronological annotated bibliography on order statistics. vol. 1: pre-1950. Wright-Patterson Air Force Base, Ohio, Air Force Flight Dynamics Laboratory, [1978]. fo. 515.

OREGON UNIVERSITY.

The OREGON experiment; [by] Christopher Alexander [and others]. New York, 1975. pp. 190. (Center for Environmental Structure. Center for Environmental Structure Series. vol.3)

ORGANIC AGRICULTURE.

OELHAF (ROBERT C.) Organic agriculture: economic and ecological comparisons with conventional methods. Montclair, N.J., [1978]. pp. 271. *bibliog.*

ORGANISATION COMMUNE DES REGIONS SAHARIENNES.

FRANCE. Organisation Commune des Régions Sahariennes. 1962. O.C.R.S. Paris, 1962. 1 vol. (various pagings).

ORGANISATION MONDIALE DE LA PROPRIETE INTELLECTUELLE.

See WORLD INTELLECTUAL PROPERTY ORGANIZATION.

ORGANIZATION.

MARCH (JAMES GARDNER) and SIMON (HERBERT ALEXANDER) Organizations. New York, [1958]. pp. 262. *bibliog.*

PUGH (DEREK SALMAN) and HININGS (C.R.) eds. Organizational structure: extensions and replications: the Aston programme II. Farnborough, 1976 repr. 1978. pp. 192. *bibliog.*

ORGANIZATIONAL behaviour in its context: the Aston programme III; edited by D.S. Pugh [and] R.L. Payne. Farnborough, Hants., [1977]. pp. 188. *bibliog.*

SHCHIGLIK (ARON ISAAKOVICH) Zakonomernosti stanovleniia i razvitiia obshchestvennykh organizatsii v SSSR: politiko-pravovoe issledovanie. Moskva, 1977. pp. 253.

SCHUMAN (DAVID) The ideology of form: the influence of organizations in America. Lexington, Mass., [1978]. pp. 196.

BRAKEL (ARIE) Gelijk is niet gelijk: over het veranderen van organisaties. Meppel, [1979]. pp. 344. *bibliog. Proefschrift - Doctor in de Sociale Wetenschappen - Erasmus Universiteit Rotterdam. With English summary.*

BURRELL (GIBSON) and MORGAN (GARETH) Sociological paradigms and organisational analysis: elements of the sociology of corporate life. London, 1979. pp. 432. *bibliog.*

CLEGG (STEWART) The theory of power and organization. London, 1979. pp. 176. *bibliog.*

PRESTHUS (ROBERT V.) The organizational society. rev.ed. London, 1979. pp. 288.

SMITH (GILBERT) Social work and the sociology of organizations. rev. ed. London, 1979. pp. 108. *bibliog.*

ORGANIZATION OF THE PETROLEUM EXPORTING COUNTRIES.

WYANT (FRANK R.) The United States, OPEC, and multinational oil. Lexington, Mass., [1977]. pp. 214. *bibliog.*

ANDREASIAN (RUBEN NAPOLEONOVICH) and KAZIUKOV (ALEKSANDR DMITRIEVICH) OPEK v mire nefti. Moskva, 1978. pp. 232. *bibliog.*

EZZATI (ALI) World energy markets and OPEC stability. Lexington, Mass., [1978]. pp. 205. *bibliog.*

GUNTER (JOHN WADSWORTH) The imbalance of international payments from the viewpoint of the OPEC and other developing countries. Cairo, 1978. pp. 24. (National Bank of Egypt. Commemoration Lectures Programme)

NORENG (ØYSTEIN) Oil politics in the 1980s: patterns of international cooperation. New York, [1978]. pp. 171. *bibliog.* (Council on Foreign Relations. 1980s Project Studies)

ORGANIZATIONAL BEHAVIOUR.

MANGHAM (IAIN LESLIE) Interactions and interventions in organizations. Chichester, [1978]. pp. 150. *bibliog.*

ORGANIZATIONAL CHANGE.

GUEST (ROBERT HENRY) and others. Organizational change through effective leadership. Englewood Cliffs, N.J., [1977]. pp. 184. *bibliog.*

ORGANIZATION development in public administration...; edited by Robert T. Golembiewski and William B. Eddy. New York, [1978] in progress. *bibligs.*

MANGHAM (IAIN LESLIE) Interactions and interventions in organizations. Chichester, [1978]. pp. 150. *bibliog.*

ORGANIZED CRIME

— United States.

CHAMBLISS (WILLIAM J.) On the take: from petty crooks to presidents. Bloomington, 1978. pp. 269.

ORIENTAL STUDIES

— Russia.

OBSHCHESTVENNO-politicheskaia mysl' v Povolzh'e v XIX - nachale XX vv. Kazan', 1977. pp. 272.

ORKNEY ISLANDS

— Economic conditions.

FENTON (ALEXANDER) The Northern isles: Orkney and Shetland. Edinburgh, [1978]. pp. 721.

— Social life and customs.

FENTON (ALEXANDER) The Northern isles: Orkney andShetland. Edinburgh, [1978]. pp. 721.

ORLETON (ADAM).
See ADAM, of Orleton, Bishop of Winchester.

OROZCO (WISTANO LUIS).
HAMON (JAMES L.) and NIBLO (STEPHEN R.) Precursores de la revolucion agraria en Mexico: las obras de Wistano Luis Orozco y Andres Molina Enriquez; traduccion de Omar Costa Acosta. Mexico, Secretaria de Educacion Publica, 1975. pp. 183. *(Sep/Setentas. 202)*

ORPHANS AND ORPHAN ASYLUMS
— United Kingdom.

WAGNER (GILLIAN) Barnardo. London, [1979]. pp. 344. *bibliog.*

ORSMAN (WILLIAM JAMES).
STUART (JOHN) Writer on Christian missions. Fifty years of the Costers' Mission and its founder W. J. Orsman, J.P. London, [1911]. pp. 122.

OSCAR II (SHIP).
KRAFT (BARBARA S.) The peace ship: Henry Ford's pacifist adventure in the First World War. New York, [1978]. pp. 367. *bibliog.*

OUTDOOR RECREATION.
SCHECTER (MORDECHAI) and LUCAS (ROBERT C.) Simulation of recreational use for park and wilderness management. Baltimore, [1978]. pp. 220. *bibliogs.*

OUTER SPACE
— Research.

O'NEILL (GERARD K.) The high frontier: human colonies in space. London, 1977. pp. 288. *bibliog.*

OVAMBOS.
TOETEMEYER (GERHARD) Namibia old and new: traditional and modern leaders in Ovamboland. London, [1978]. pp. 257. *bibliog.*

OVERLAND JOURNEYS TO THE PACIFIC.
FARAGHER (JOHN MACK) Women and men on the overland trail. New Haven, 1979. pp. 281. *bibliog. (Yale University. Yale Historical Publications. Miscellany. 121)*

UNRUH (JOHN DAVID) The plains across: the overland emigrants and the Trans- Mississippi West, 1840-60. Urbana, 1979. pp. 565. *bibliog.*

OVERPRODUCTION.
MANDEL (ERNEST) The second slump: a marxist analysis of recession in the seventies; translated by Jon Rothschild. London, 1978. pp. 212.

OWEN (ROBERT).
PODMARKOV (VALENTIN GEORGIEVICH) Robert Ouen [i.e. Owen] - gumanist i myslitel'. Moskva, 1976. pp. 128. *bibliog. (Akademiia Nauk SSSR. Seriia "Biografii i Memuary")*

PACIFIC, THE.
INSECURITY!: the spread of weapons in the Indian and Pacific oceans; [edited by] Robert O'Neill. Canberra, 1978. pp. 280. *bibliogs.*

— Commerce.

INTERNATIONAL business in the Pacific Basin; edited by R. Hal Mason. Lexington, Mass. [1978]. pp. 213. *Based on a research symposium held at the University of California, Los Angeles, 1975.*

— Foreign relations — United States.

WILEY (PETER) Vietnam and the Pacific rim strategy. Boston, Mass., [c.1972]. pp. 22. *bibliog. Reprinted from the Leviathan of June 1969.*

— History.

The CHANGING Pacific: essays in honour of H.E. Maude; edited by Niel Gunson. Melbourne, 1978. pp. 351. *bibliog.*

— — Sources.

MANDER JONES (PHYLLIS) compiler. Manuscripts in the British Isles relating to Australia, New Zealand and the Pacific. Honolulu, [1972]. pp. 697.

— Relations (general) with Europe.

RALSTON (CAROLINE) Grass huts and warehouses: Pacific beach communities of the nineteenth century. Canberra, 1977. pp. 268. *bibliog.*

— Social life and customs.

RALSTON (CAROLINE) Grass huts and warehouses: Pacific beach communities of the nineteenth century. Canberra, 1977. pp. 268. *bibliog.*

The CHANGING Pacific: essays in honour of H.E. Maude; edited by Niel Gunson. Melbourne, 1978. pp. 351. *bibliog.*

— Statistics.

QUARTERLY BULLETIN OF STATISTICS FOR ASIA AND THE PACIFIC (formerly Quarterly Bulletin of Statistics for Asia and the Far East) ([pd.by] Economic and Social Commission for Asia and the Pacific) United Nations. q., S 1971(v.1, no.1)- Bangkok.

SOUTH PACIFIC COMMISSION. Statistical bulletin. [in English and French]. irreg., 1972(no.1)- Noumea.

PACIFIC SETTLEMENT OF INTERNATIONAL DISPUTES.
MAJID (MOHAMED MUNIR BIN ABDUL) Asian and African attitudes to the settlement of international disputes by judicial means. 1978. fo. 379. *bibliog.* Typescript. Ph.D. (London) thesis: unpublished. This thesis is the property of London University and may not be removed from the Library.

LOCKHART (CHARLES) Bargaining in international conflicts. New York, 1979. pp. 205. *bibliog.*

PACIFISM.
DAY (HEM) pseud. [i.e. Marcel DIEU] Gérard de Lacaze-Duthiers, le pacifiste. Paris, 1960. pp. 16.

ANGLICAN PACIFIST FELLOWSHIP. Annual report. a., 1977/78- Oxford.

LITHERLAND (ALAN) War under judgement. New Malden, [1978]. pp. 57.

QUIDDE (LUDWIG) Der deutsche Pazifismus während des Weltkrieges 1914-1918; aus dem Nachlass Ludwig Quiddes herausgegeben von Karl Holl unter Mitwirkung von Helmut Donat. Boppard am Rhein, 1979. pp. 416. *bibliog. (Germany (Bundesrepublik). Bundesarchiv. Schriften. 23)*

PADERBORN
— Economic history.

HEGGEN (ALFRED) Staat und Wirtschaft im Fürstentum Paderborn im 18. Jahrhundert. Paderborn, [1978]. pp. 174. *bibliog. (Verein für Geschichte und Altertumskunde Westfalen. Abteilung Paderborn. Studien und Quellen zur Westfälischen Geschichte. Band 17)*

PAEA
— Social conditions.

FAGES (JEAN) Punaauia-Paea: contact ville-campagne et croissance urbaine de la côte ouest de Tahiti. Paris, 1975. pp. 111. *bibliog. (France. Office de la Recherche Scientifique et Technique Outre-Mer. Travaux et Documents. No. 41)*

PAIN.
NEAL (HELEN) The politics of pain. New York, [1978]. pp. 222. *bibliog.*

PAINTING, NETHERLANDISH.
PANOFSKY (ERWIN) Early Netherlandish painting: its origins and character. New York, 1971. 2 vols. *bibliog. (Harvard University. Charles Eliot Norton Lectures. 1947-1948)* First published in Cambridge, Mass., in 1953.

PAKISTAN.
SULERI (ZIAUDDIN AHMAD) Whither Pakistan? London, [1949]. pp. 96.

— Boundaries — Afghanistan.

PAZHWAK (RAHMAN) An article on Pakhtunistan, a new state in central Asia. London, Royal Afghan Embassy, [1960]. pp. 28.

— Economic conditions.

RCD MAGAZINE, THE; [pd. by] Regional Cooperation for Development. q., spring 1974(v.1, no.1)- , with gaps. Tehran.

PAKISTAN. Directorate of Films and Publications. 1978. From stagnation to economic recovery; [summary of Pakistan Economic Survey for 1977-78]. [Islamabad, 1978]. pp. 18.

PAKISTAN. Planning Division. Economic Research Section. 1978. Abstracts of research studies. [Karachi?], 1978. fo. 46.

RCD NEWSLETTER; [pd. by] Information Section, Regional Cooperation for Development. irreg., current issues only. Tehran.

— Economic policy.

PAKISTAN. Ministry of Information and Broadcasting. 1967. Pakistan and R[egional] C[o-operation for] D[evelopment]: three years of regional co-operation for development, 1964-1967. [Karachi, 1967!]. pp. 48. *bibliog.*

PAKISTAN. Ministry of Finance, Planning and Economic Affairs. 1975. Address at a press conference held in Islamabad on June 8, 1975, by Mohammad Hanif etc. [Islamabad, 1975]. pp. 8.

PAKISTAN. Economic Publicity Wing. 1978. Planning for prosperity in Pakistan. [Islamabad, 1978]. pp. 41.

— Foreign relations.

PAKISTAN. Prime Minister. 1976. Bilateralism: new directions, [by] Zulfikar Ali Bhutto. Islamabad, [1976?]. pp. 76.

— — China.

PAKISTAN. Department of Films and Publications. 1978. New era of Pak-China friendship. [Islamabad, 1978]. pp. 53.

— Politics and government.

JINNAH (MOHAMED ALI) Speeches as Governor-General of Pakistan, 1947-1948. [Karachi, 194-]. pp. 176.

PAKISTAN. Supreme Court. 1975. Rejoinder...to written statement of Abdul Wali Khan, president of defunct National Awami Party, in reference by Islamic Republic of Pakistan on dissolution of National Awami Party. [Islamabad], 1975. pp. 79.

PAKISTAN. Prime Minister. 1977. Address at the joint session of the National Assembly and the Senate, April 28, 1977. Islamabad, 1977. pp. 24.

BEG (AZIZ) Battle of ballot or war of attrition: (perils of polls in Pakistan). Islamabad, [1978]. pp. 243.

PAKISTAN. Supreme Court. 1978. Order...on application by Zulfikar Ali Bhutto, Rawalpindi, May 20, 1978. Rawalpindi, 1978. pp. 15.

PUNJAB (PAKISTAN). High Court. 1978. Summary of judgement in murder trial: state vs Zulfikar Ali Bhutto and others. [Lahore, 1978?]. pp. 23.

HUSSAIN (ASAF) Elite politics in an ideological state: the case of Pakistan. Folkestone, 1979. pp. 212. *bibliog.*

— **Population.**

PAKISTAN. Census, 1972-73. Housing, economic and demographic survey, 1973. volume 2. Islamabad, [197-]. 5 pts.

PAKISTAN. Population Planning Council. 1976. World fertility survey: Pakistan fertility survey: first report. [Islamabad], 1976. 1 vol. (various pagings). *bibliog.*

— **Rural conditions.**

ALBRECHT (HERBERT) Economist. Living conditions of rural families in Pakistan...; translated by V. June Hager. Saarbrücken, 1976. pp. 265. *bibliog.*

— **Social conditions.**

PAKISTAN. Planning Division. Economic Research Section. 1978. Abstracts of research studies. [Karachi?], 1978. fo. 46.

— **Social policy.**

PAKISTAN. Economic Publicity Wing. 1978. Planning for prosperity in Pakistan. [Islamabad, 1978]. pp. 41.

PAKISTANIS IN THE UNITED KINGDOM.

ANWAR (MUHAMMAD) The myth of the return: Pakistanis in Britain. London, 1979. pp. 278. *bibliog.*

PALESTINE

— **Economic conditions.**

FINEGOLD (JULIAN LEWIS) British economic policy in Palestine, 1920-1948. 1979. fo. 241. *bibliog.* Typescript. Ph.D. (London) thesis: unpublished. *This thesis is the property of London University and may not be removed from the Library.*

— **Foreign economic relations — United Kingdom.**

FINEGOLD (JULIAN LEWIS) British economic policy in Palestine, 1920-1948. 1979. fo. 241. *bibliog.* Typescript. Ph.D. (London) thesis: unpublished. *This thesis is the property of London University and may not be removed from the Library.*

— **History — 1917-1948.**

BEGIN (MENACHEM) The revolt. rev. ed. New York, [1977]. pp. 386.

— — **1929-1948.**

BETHELL (NICHOLAS WILLIAM) 4th Baron Bethell. The Palestine triangle: the struggle between the British, the Jews and the Arabs, 1935-48. London, 1979. pp. 384. *bibliog.*

— **History, Local.**

COHEN (AMNON) and LEWIS (BERNARD) Population and revenue in the towns of Palestine in the sixteenth century. Princeton, N.J., [1978]. pp. 199. *bibliog.*

— **Politics and government.**

HOROWITZ (DAN) 1928- and LISSAK (MOSHE) Origins of the Israeli polity: Palestine under the Mandate; translated from the Hebrew by Charles Hoffman. Chicago, [1978]. pp. 292. *bibliog.*

TOWARDS a socialist republic of Palestine; edited by Fouzi el- Asmar [and others]. London, 1978. pp. 209. *Based on discussions held in Europe in 1976.*

WEINSTOCK (NATHAN) Zionism: false messiah; translated and edited by Alan Adler. London, [1979]. pp. 330. *bibliog. First published as part I of Sionisme contre Israël, Paris, 1969.*

— **Population.**

COHEN (AMNON) and LEWIS (BERNARD) Population and revenue in the towns of Palestine in the sixteenth century. Princeton, N.J., [1978]. pp. 199. *bibliog.*

PALESTINIAN ARABS.

ABDALLAH, King of Jordan. My memoirs completed: al-Takmilah; translated from the Arabic by Harold W. Glidden. London, 1978. pp. 102. *Reprint, with extensive introduction by King Hussein of Jordan of work published in Amman, Jordan, in 1951.*

The PALESTINIANS and the Middle East conflict; [edited by] Gabriel Ben-Dor. Ramat Gan, 1978. pp. 575. *bibliog. Proceedings of an international conference held at the Institute of Middle Eastern Studies, University of Haifa, 1976.*

KAZZIHA (WALID W.) Palestine in the Arab dilemma. London, [1979]. pp. 111.

— **Israel.**

PALESTINIAN Arabs in Israel: two case studies; [by] Hasan Amun [and others]. London, 1977. pp. 119. *bibliog.*

O'NEILL (BARD E.) Armed struggle in Palestine: a political-military analysis. Boulder, Colo., 1978. pp. 320.

SIMON (RITA JAMES) Continuity and change: a study of two ethnic communities in Israel. Cambridge, 1978. pp. 180. *bibliog.* (American Sociological Association. Arnold and Caroline Rose Monograph Series in Sociology)

SMOOHA (SAMMY) and CIBULSKI (ORA) Social research on Arabs in Israel, 1948-1977: trends and an annotated bibliography. Ramat Gan, 1978. pp. 148.

ZUREIK (ELIA T.) The Palestinians in Israel: a study in internal colonialism. London, 1979. pp. 249.

PALM OIL INDUSTRY.

KHERA (HARCHARAN SINGH) The oil palm industry of Malaysia: an economic study. Kuala Lumpur, 1976. pp. 354. *bibliog.*

PANAFRICANISM.

GHANA. Prime Minister. 1959. Conférence des peuples africains: discours prononcés par le premier ministre du Ghana à l'ouverture et à la clôture le 8 et le 13 décembre, 1958. Accra, [1959]. pp. 13.

MOSES (WILSON JEREMIAH) The golden age of black nationalism, 1850-1925. Hamden, 1978. pp. 345. *bibliog.*

PANAMA

— **Foreign relations — United States.**

LOWENTHAL (ABRAHAM F.) and others. A new treaty for Panama? Washington, [1977]. pp. 34. (American Enterprise Institute for Public Policy Research. AEI Defense Reviews. [Vol. 1]. No. 4)

VALDES (EDUARDO) The roots of the problem: a positive approach to the Panama Canal issue. New York, [1977]. pp. 66.

— **Politics and government.**

GILHODES (PIERRE) Paysans de Panama. [Paris, 1978]. pp. 303. *bibliog.*

PANAMA CANAL.

LOWENTHAL (ABRAHAM F.) and others. A new treaty for Panama? Washington, [1977]. pp. 34. (American Enterprise Institute for Public Policy Research. AEI Defense Reviews. [Vol. 1]. No. 4)

McCULLOUGH (DAVID G.) The path between the seas: the creation of the Panama Canal, 1870-1914. New York, [1977]. pp. 698. *bibliog.*

VALDES (EDUARDO) The roots of the problem: a positive approach to the Panama Canal issue. New York, [1977]. pp. 66.

PANARE INDIANS.

DUMONT (JEAN PAUL) The headman and I: ambiguity and ambivalence in the fieldworking experience. Austin, [1978]. pp. 211. *bibliog.*

PANKHURST (ESTELLE SYLVIA).

PANKHURST (RICHARD KEIR PETHICK) Sylvia Pankhurst: artist and crusader. New York, [1979]. pp. 224.

PANKRATOVA (ANNA MIKHAILOVNA).

BADIA (LARISA VIKTOROVNA) Akademik A.M. Pankratova - istorik rabochego klassa SSSR. Moskva, 1979. pp. 159.

PANNEKOEK (ANTON).

PANNEKOEK (ANTON) and GORTER (HERMAN) Pannekoek and Gorter's Marxism; (edited and introduced by D. A. Smart). London, 1978. pp. 176.

PANSLAVISM.

ORTON (LAWRENCE D.) The Prague Slav Congress of 1848. Boulder, 1978. pp. 187. *bibliog.* (East European Quarterly. East European Monographs. 46) (Columbia University. East Central European Studies)

PANZOS

— **Massacre, 1978.**

GUATEMALA 1978: the massacre at Panzos. Copenhagen, 1978. pp. 58. (International Work Group for Indigenous Affairs. Documents. 33)

PAPACY

— **History.**

HOLMES (J. DEREK) The triumph of the Holy See: a short history of the Papacy in the nineteenth century. London, 1978. pp. 306. *bibliog.*

PAPAL STATES

— **History.**

CARAVALE (MARIO) and CARACCIOLO (ALBERTO) Lo Stato Pontificio da Martino V a Pio IX. Torino, [1978]. pp. 793. *bibliog.* (Storia d'Italia, diretta da Giuseppe Galasso. vol. 14)

PAPER MAKING AND TRADE.

FOOD AND AGRICULTURE ORGANIZATION. Pulp and paper capacities: survey. a., 1977/1982- Rome. *[in English, French and Spanish]*

— **France.**

THALY (SUZANNE) Etude sur l'évolution de la concentration dans l'industrie des pâtes, papiers et cartons en France. [Brussels], Communautés Européennes, 1977. pp. 194.

— **Germany.**

KIENBAUM UNTERNEHMENSBERATUNG. Untersuchung zur Konzentrationsentwicklung in verschiedenen Untersektoren der Papier- und Pappeindustrie in Deutschland: Herstellung,...Verarbeitung, etc. [Brussels], Europäischen Gemeinschaften, 1976. pp. 88.

— **Italy.**

BALLIANO (PIERA) and LANZETTI (RENATO) Studio sull'evoluzione della concentrazione dell'industria cartaria in Italia. [Brussels], Comunità Europee, 1976. pp. 189.

PAPER MAKING AND TRADE.(Cont.)

— United Kingdom.

TILLMANNS (MARTIN) Bridge Hall Mills: three centuries of paper and cellulose film manufacture. Tisbury, 1978. pp. 219. *bibliog.*

PAPER MONEY.

KELLOGG (EDWARD) Labor and other capital: the rights of each secured and the wrongs of both eradicated;...and the addition of The true greenback, 1868, by Alexander Campbell. New York, 1971. pp. 298, 48. *Reprint of work originally published in New York, 1849.*

PAPER PRODUCTS.

BROUWER (W.J.C.) and STEIJN (T.N.) A study of the evolution of concentration in the Dutch paper products industry. [Brussels], European Communities, 1976. pp. 89.

PAPUA NEW GUINEA

— Commerce.

PAPUA NEW GUINEA. Bureau of Statistics. Statistical bulletin: import price indexes. q., Je 1976- Port Moresby.

— — New Zealand.

NEW ZEALAND. Department of Trade and Industry. Trade Services Division. 1978. Papua New Guinea: [a market profile]. [Wellington, 1978?]. fo. 38. *(Background to Export)*

— Economic conditions.

BALDWIN (GEORGE B.) Papua New Guinea: its economic situation and prospects for development; report of a mission sent to Papua New Guinea by the World Bank, etc. Washington, International Bank for Reconstruction and Development, [1978]. pp. 223. *bibliog.* *(Country Economic Reports)*

NEW ZEALAND. Department of Trade and Industry. Trade Services Division. 1978. Papua New Guinea: [a market profile]. [Wellington, 1978?]. fo. 38. *(Background to Export)*

— Economic policy.

BALDWIN (GEORGE B.) Papua New Guinea: its economic situation and prospects for development; report of a mission sent to Papua New Guinea by the World Bank, etc. Washington, International Bank for Reconstruction and Development, [1978]. pp. 223. *bibliog.* *(Country Economic Reports)*

— Statistics.

PAPUA NEW GUINEA. Bureau of Statistics. Summary of statistics. a., 1970/71- Konedobu.

PAPUA NEW GUINEA. Bureau of Statistics. Abstract of statistics. q., D 1973- Konedobu. *Each issue contains figures for the last 3 yrs. Supersedes its Quarterly summary of statistics (Je 1959 - D 1970). File includes current issues of its m. Economic indicators, until superseded by the Abstract.*

PARAGUAY

— Economic conditions.

PARAGUAY. Embassy (U.K.). Trade Centre. 1971. Paraguay today: information handbook. London, [1971?]. pp. 50.

— Economic history.

WHITE (RICHARD ALAN) Paraguay's autonomous revolution, 1810-1840. Albuquerque, [1978]. pp. 295. *bibliog.*

— History.

WHITE (RICHARD ALAN) Paraguay's autonomous revolution, 1810-1840. Albuquerque, [1978]. pp. 295. *bibliog.*

PARAMILITARY FORCES

— Austria.

KOCH (HANNSJOACHIM WOLFGANG) Der deutsche Bürgerkrieg: eine Geschichte der deutschen und österreichischen Freikorps, 1918-1923. Berlin, [1978]. pp. 487. *bibliog.*

— Germany.

THEWELEIT (KLAUS) Männerphantasien. Frankfurt am Main, 1977-78. 2 vols. *bibliog.*

KOCH (HANNSJOACHIM WOLFGANG) Der deutsche Bürgerkrieg: eine Geschichte der deutschen und österreichischen Freikorps, 1918-1923. Berlin, [1978]. pp. 487. *bibliog.*

PARDON

— United Kingdom.

ROLPH (C.H.) pseud. [i.e. Cecil Rolph HEWITT) The Queen's pardon. London, 1978. pp. 173.

PARENT AND CHILD.

KLAUS (MARSHALL H.) and KENNELL (JOHN H.) Maternal-infant bonding: (the impact of early separation or loss on family development). Saint Louis, 1976. pp. 260. *bibliog.*

WOODS (PETER) The divided school. London, 1979. pp. 310.

— Law.

The CHILD and the courts: [essays; edited by] Ian F.G. Baxter and Mary A. Eberts. Toronto, 1978. pp. 429.

— France.

FRANCE. Délégation à la Condition Féminine. 1978. Attitudes et comportements des parents envers le problème de l'orientation scolaire. [Paris], 1978. pp. 70.

— New Zealand.

NEW ZEALAND. Social Development Council. 1977. Bringing up children in New Zealand: can we do better? [Wellington], 1977. pp. 30. *bibliog.*

PARENTE (MANUEL LIRA).

See LIRA PARENTE (MANUEL).

PARIS

— Growth.

ATELIER PARISIEN D'URBANISME. Vingt ans d'évolution de Paris: données statistiques 1954- 1975, Paris et arrondissements: population, logement, ménages. Paris, [1976?]. 1 vol. (unfoliated).

— History — 1871, Commune.

IMAGES of the Commune; edited by James A. Leith. Montreal, 1978. pp. 349.

McCLELLAN (WOODFORD D.) Revolutionary exiles: the Russians in the First International and the Paris Commune. London, 1979. pp. 266. *bibliog.*

— Industries.

ATELIER PARISIEN D'URBANISME. Service de Politique Urbaine. L'évolution récente de l'industrie parisienne. [Paris], 1971. 3 vols. *bibliog. Tome 2 has 3 maps in end pocket.*

— Occupations.

HAUMONT (BERNARD) Le tertiaire financier à Paris. [Paris], 1968. 2 vols.

QUIVAUX (ROBERT) Le tertiaire public et semi-public dans l'agglomération et la région parisiennes;... sous la direction du Professeur Jean Bastié. [Paris], Atelier Parisien d'Urbanisme, [1969?]. pp. 84.

— Population.

ATELIER PARISIEN D'URBANISME. Service de Politique Urbaine. La population de Paris; (par Michel Lallemand [and others] sous la direction de Joël Herbulot). [Paris], 1969-70. 3 vols.

ATELIER PARISIEN D'URBANISME. Service de Politique Urbaine. Les migrations de la population de Paris entre 1962 et 1968: (rapport préliminaire); d'après les travaux préliminaires de Eliane Jaulerry. [Paris], 1971. fo. 18.

CHASSERIAUX-JAULERRY (ELIANE) La population âgée de Paris en 1968: (situation et perspectives). [Paris], Atelier Parisien d'Urbanisme, 1971. pp. 118.

ATELIER PARISIEN D'URBANISME. Vingt ans d'évolution de Paris: données statistiques 1954- 1975, Paris et arrondissements: population, logement, ménages. Paris, [1976?]. 1 vol. (unfoliated).

COUTRAS (J.) L'évolution récente de la population parisienne. Paris, Atelier Parisien d'Urbanisme, 1976. fo. 54.

COUTRAS (J.) La structure par âges de la population parisienne en 1975 et sa récente évolution. Paris, Atelier Parisien d'Urbanisme, 1977. fo.25.

— Statistics.

ATELIER PARISIEN D'URBANISME. Vingt ans d'évolution de Paris: données statistiques 1954- 1975, Paris et arrondissements: population, logement, ménages. Paris, [1976?]. 1 vol. (unfoliated).

PARIS (REGION).

La FRANCE des villes; (sous la direction de Jacqueline Beaujeu-Garnier [and others]): vol. 1. Le Bassin parisien. [Paris, La Documentation Française, 1978]. pp. 221.

PARK (ROBERT EZRA).

RAUSHENBUSH (WINIFRED) Robert E. Park: biography of a sociologist. Durham, N.C., 1979. pp. 206. *bibliog.*

PARKS.

SCHECTER (MORDECHAI) and LUCAS (ROBERT C.) Simulation of recreational use for park and wilderness management. Baltimore, [1978]. pp. 220. *bibliogs.*

PARMA (PROVINCE)

— Social history.

SERENI (UMBERTO) Il movimento cooperativo a Parma tra riformismo e sindacalismo. Bari, [1977]. pp. 326.

PAROLE

— United States.

McCLEARY (RICHARD) Dangerous men: the sociology of parole. Beverly Hills, [1978]. pp. 181. *bibliog.*

PARRY (JOHN WILLIAM).

WILLIAMS (J. ROOSE) Quarryman's champion: the life and activities of William John Parry of Coetmor. Denbigh, [imprint, 1978]. pp. 258.

PARSONS (TALCOTT).

SCHUTZ (ALFRED) and PARSONS (TALCOTT) The theory of social action: the correspondence of Alfred Schutz and Talcott Parsons; edited by Richard Grathoff. Bloomington, [1978]. pp. 145. *bibliog.*

PART-TIME EMPLOYMENT

— United Kingdom.

HURSTFIELD (JENNIFER) The part-time trap: part-time workers in Britain today. London, 1978. pp. 86. *(Low Pay Unit. Low Pay Pamphlets. No. 9)*

— **United States.**

NOLLEN (STANLEY D.) and others. Permanent part-time employment: the manager's perspective. New York, 1978. pp. 212. *bibliog.*

PARTI QUÉBÉCOIS.

DUPONT (PIERRE) How Levesque won;...translated by Sheila Fischman. Toronto, 1977. pp. 136.

SAYWELL (JOHN T.) The rise of the Parti québécois, 1967-76. Toronto, 1977. pp. 174.

LÉVESQUE (RENÉ) My Québec; [translated by] Gaynor Fitzpatrick. Toronto, [1978]. pp. 191.

PARTI SOCIALISTE UNIFIE.

HAUSS (CHARLES) The new left in France: the Unified Socialist Party. Westport, Conn., 1978. pp. 283. *bibliog.*

PARTIDO DEMOCRATA POPULAR.

CAMUÑAS SOLIS (IGNACIO) Partido Democrata Popular. Bilbao, 1977. pp. 125.

PARTIJ VAN DE ARBEID.

DEMOKRATISCH-socialisme in Nederland: over de beginselen van de P[artij] v[an] d[e] A[rbeid]. Amsterdam, 1977. pp. 283.

Een VERJONGINGSKUUR voor de Partij van de Arbeid: (opkomst, ontwikkeling en betekenis van Nieuw Links); [by] Bertus Boivin [and others]. Deventer, 1978. pp. 124. *bibliog. (Studie- en Documentatiecentrum Nederlandse Politieke Partijen te Groningen. Cahiers Nederlandse Politiek)*

PARTIT SOCIALISTA DE CATALUNYA.

PARTIT SOCIALISTA DE CATALUNYA. P.S.C.: Partit Socialista de Catalunya; documentos aprobados en su Congreso Constituyente, celebrado el 1 de noviembre de 1976. Barcelona, [1977]. pp. 175.

PARTITION, TERRITORIAL.

MANSERGH (PHILIP NICHOLAS SETON) The prelude to partition: concept and aims in Ireland and India. Cambridge, 1978. pp. 62. *(Cambridge. University. Commonwealth Lectures. 1976)*

PARTITO POPOLARE ITALIANO.

TRONCONI (GABRIELLA MEDRI) Giovanni Braschi e il partito popolare nel forlivese. Roma, [1975]. pp. 194. *bibliog.*

PARTITO RADICALE (ITALY).

MORABITO (FABIO) La sfida radicale. Milano, [1977]. pp. 219. *bibliog.*

PARTNERSHIP

— **United Kingdom.**

LINDLEY (NATHANIEL) Baron Lindley. On the law of partnership; fourteenth edition by Ernest H. Scamell and R. C. I'Anson Banks. London, 1979. pp. 1068.

— — **Taxation.**

RAY (EDWARD E.) Partnership taxation. 2nd ed. London, 1978. pp. 416.

PASCAL (COMPUTER PROGRAM LANGUAGE).

GROGONO (PETER) Programming in PASCAL. Reading, Mass., [1978] repr. 1979. pp. 359.

KIEBURTZ (RICHARD B.) Structured programming and problem-solving with PASCAL. Englewood Cliffs, N.J., [1978]. pp. 365.

PASSIVE RESISTANCE

— **India.**

DESAI (MAHADEV) The story of Bardoli: being a history of the Bardoli Satyagraha of 1928 and its sequel. Ahmedabad, 1929. pp. 363.

— **United States.**

The POWER of the people: active nonviolence in the United States; edited and produced by Robert Cooney and Helen Michalowski. Culver City, [1977]. pp. 240. *bibliog.*

PATENT LICENCES

— **European Economic Community countries.**

CAWTHRA (BRUCE ILLINGWORTH) Patent licensing in Europe. London, 1978. pp. 256. *bibliog.*

PATENTS

— **Germany.**

HUNDERT Jahre Patentamt: Festschrift herausgegeben vom Deutschen Patentamt. München, 1977. pp. 476.

— **United States.**

DICK (TREVOR J.O.) An economic theory of technological change: the case of patents and the United States railroads 1871-1950. New York, 1978. pp. 145. *bibliog.*

PATHANS IN PAKISTAN.

PAZHWAK (RAHMAN) An article on Pakhtunistan, a new state in central Asia. London, Royal Afghan Embassy, [1960]. pp. 28.

PATRIOTISM

— **United Kingdom.**

KARSTEN (PETER) Patriot-heroes in England and America: political symbolism and changing values over three centuries. Madison, Wis., 1978. pp. 257.

— **United States.**

KARSTEN (PETER) Patriot-heroes in England and America: political symbolism and changing values over three centuries. Madison, Wis., 1978. pp. 257.

PATRON AND CLIENT.

FRIENDS, followers, and factions: a reader in political clientelism; edited by Steffen W. Schmidt [and others]. Berkley, [1977]. pp. 512. *bibliogs.*

PATRONAGE, POLITICAL.

FRIENDS, followers, and factions: a reader in political clientelism; edited by Steffen W. Schmidt [and others]. Berkley, [1977]. pp. 512. *bibliogs.*

— **United Kingdom.**

HOLLAND (PHILIP WELSBY) and FALLON (MICHAEL) The quango explosion: public bodies and ministerial patronage. London, 1978. pp. 28. *(Conservative Political Centre. [Publications]. No. 627)*

SHERMAN (ALFRED V.) The newest profession. [London, 1978]. pp. 16.

PAWNBROKING

— **Italy.**

CAPECCHI (ILVO) and GAI (LUCIA) Il Monte della Pietà a Pistoia e le sue origini. Firenze, 1976. pp. 263. *(Deputazione di Storia Patria per la Toscana. Biblioteca Storica Toscana. 17)*

PEA (ENRICO).

SALVESTRONI (SIMONETTA) Enrico Pea: fra anarchia e integrazione. Firenze, 1976. pp. 168. *bibliogs.*

PEACE.

WOOLF (LEONARD SIDNEY) ed. The framework of a lasting peace. New York, 1971. pp. 154. *Reprint, with a new introduction, of the work first published London, 1917.*

GALTUNG (JOHAN) Peace: research, education, action; essays in peace research. Copenhagen, 1975. pp. 406. *(International Peace Research Institute. PRIO Monographs. No.4)*

FRIEDENSRAT DER DEUTSCHEN DEMOKRATISCHEN REPUBLIK. Dokumente der Weltfriedensbewegung: Oktober 1962 bis Dezember 1974. [Wittenberg, imprint], 1976. pp. 320.

GALTUNG (JOHAN) Peace, war and defence; essays in peace research. Copenhagen, 1976. pp. 472. *(International Peace Research Institute. PRIO Monographs. No.5)*

PROBLEMELE păcii şi ale războiului în condiţiile revoluţiei ştiinţifice şi tehnice: necesitatea istorică a dezarmării: sesiunea ştiinţifică din 21 ianuarie 1977. Bucureşti, 1977. pp. 488. *With English, French, German, Italian, Russian and Spanish tables of contents and identifications of authors.*

GALLIE (WALTER BRYCE) Philosophers of peace and war: Kant, Clausewitz, Marx, Engels and Tolstoy. Cambridge, 1978 repr. 1979. pp. 147. *bibliog.*

STRATEGIES against violence: design for non-violent change; edited by Israel W. Charny. Boulder, Colo., 1978. pp. 417. *bibliogs.*

UNITED Nations peace-keeping: legal essays; edited by A. Cassese. Alphen aan den Rijn, 1978. pp. 255.

YARROW (C.H. MIKE) Quaker experiences in international conciliation. New Haven, 1978. pp. 308.

BREZHNEV (LEONID IL'ICH) Peace, détente, and Soviet-American relations: a collection of public statements. New York, [1979]. pp. 235.

— **Research.**

BOULDING (KENNETH EWART) Stable peace. Austin, [1978]. pp. 143.

— **Social aspects.**

GALTUNG (JOHAN) Peace and social structure; essays in peace research. Copenhagen, 1978. pp. 564. *(International Peace Research Institute. PRIO Monographs. No.7)*

— **Societies.**

DEBENEDETTI (CHARLES) Origins of the modern American peace movement, 1915-1929. New York, [1978]. pp. 281. *bibliog.*

PEACHEY PROPERTY CORPORATION.

KIDWELL (RAYMOND INCLEDON) and SAMWELL (STANLEY DAVID) Peachey Property Corporation Limited: investigation under section 165(b) of the Companies Act 1948; report. London, H.M.S.O., 1979. pp. (205).

PEANUTS

— **Malawi.**

MALAWI. Agro-Economic Survey. 1972. Agro-economic survey: 10th report: Malimba groundnut growers in Nsanje south: a survey among Malimba, Gambia, groundnut growers in the southern part of Nsanje district, Malawi; prepared by T.W. Bieze. Zomba, 1972. fo. 14.

MALAWI. Agro-Economic Survey. 1973. Agro-economic survey: 11th report: Mbawa: a sample farm management survey among oriental tobacco, maize and groundnut growers in the Mbawa area in the southern part of Mzimba district, Malawi, with special reference to oriental tobacco; prepared by T.W. Bieze. Lilongwe, 1973. fo. 87. *bibliog.*

PEARL HARBOR, ATTACK ON, 1941.

BARTLETT (BRUCE R.) Cover-up: the politics of Pearl Harbor, 1941-1946. New Rochelle, [1978]. pp. 189. *bibliog.*

PEARSON (LESTER BOWLES).

STURSBERG (PETER) Lester Pearson and the dream of unity. Toronto, 1978. pp. 456.

PEASANT UPRISINGS.

RURAL protest: peasant movements and social change; edited by Henry A. Landsberger. London, 1974. pp. 430.

PEASANTRY.

PEASANT society: a reader; edited by Jack M. Potter [and others]. Boston, Mass., [1967]. pp. 453. *bibliog.*

— America, Latin.

LINDQVIST (SVEN) Land and power in South America; translated from the Swedish by Paul Britten Austin. Harmondsworth, 1979. pp. 333. *bibliog.*

— Brazil.

VELHO (OTAVIO GUILHERME) Capitalismo autoritario e campesinato: um estudo comparativo a partir da fronteira em movimento. São Paulo, 1976. pp. 261. *bibliog.*

— China.

SU (JING) and LUN (LUO) Landlord and labor in late imperial China: case studies from Shandong...; translated from the Chinese with an introduction by Endymion Wilkinson. Cambridge, Mass., 1978. pp. 310. *bibliog.* (*Harvard University. East Asian Research Center. Harvard East Asian Monographs. 80*)

— Europe.

BLUM (JEROME) The end of the old order in rural Europe. Princeton, 1978. pp. 505. *bibliog.*

— France.

CONTRIBUTIONS à l'histoire paysanne de la révolution française; sous la direction d'Albert Soboul. [Paris, 1977]. pp. 407.

— Germany.

KUCHENBUCH (LUDOLF) Bäuerliche Gesellschaft und Klosterherrschaft im 9. Jahrhundert: Studien zur Sozialstruktur der Familia der Abtei Prüm. Wiesbaden, 1978. pp. 443. *bibliog.* (*Vierteljahrschrift für Sozial- und Wirtschaftsgeschichte. Beihefte. Nr. 66*)

— Haiti.

LUNDAHL (MATS) Peasants and poverty: a study of Haiti. London, 1979. pp. 699. *bibliog.*

— Italy.

MERZARIO (RAUL) Signori e contadini di Calabria: Corigliano Calabro dal XVI al XIX secolo. Milano, 1975. pp. 142. (*Università degli Studi della Calabria. Ricerche di Storia ed Economia*)

ZANGHERI (RENATO) Agricoltura e contadini nella storia d'Italia: discussioni e ricerche. Torino, [1977]. pp. 290.

— Mexico.

POWELL (THOMAS GENE) El liberalismo y el campesinado en el centro de Mexico, 1850-1876; traduccion de Roberto Gomez Ciriza. Mexico, Secretaria de Educacion Publica, 1974. pp. 191. *bibliog.* (*Sep/Setentas. 122*)

SALAMINI (HEATHER FOWLER) Agrarian radicalism in Veracruz, 1920-38. Lincoln, Neb., [1978]. pp. 239. *bibliog.*

DEWALT (BILLIE R.) Modernization in a Mexican ejido: a study in economic adaption. Cambridge, 1979. pp. 303. *bibliog.*

— Panama.

GILHODES (PIERRE) Paysans de Panama. [Paris, 1978]. pp. 303. *bibliog.*

— Peru.

LEWELLEN (TED) Peasants in transition: the changing economy of the Peruvian Aymara: a general systems approach. Boulder, Colo., [1978]. pp. 195. *bibliog.*

PEASANT cooperation and capitalist expansion in central Peru; edited by Norman Long and Bryan R. Roberts. Austin, [1978]. pp. 349. *bibliog.*

— Romania.

LAPADATU (AUREL) Über die Genesis der rumänischen Agrargesellschaft bis zum Aufgang des 18. Jahrhunderts, etc. Köln, 1978. pp. 142. *bibliog.*

— Russia.

OKTIABR' i sovetskoe krest'ianstvo, 1917-1927 gg. Moskva, 1977. pp. 295.

PETROV (ALEKSANDR PETROVICH) Kritika fal'sifikatsii agrarno-krest'ianskogo voprosa v trekh russkikh revoliutsiiakh. Moskva, 1977. pp. 399. *bibliog.*

FAILEVIC (MAURICE) and LA ROCHEFOUCAULD (JEAN DOMINIQUE DE) 1788: luttes révolutionnaires pour une propriété paysanne. [Paris, 1978]. pp. 303.

HARRISON (MARK) Peasant economy, subordinate Marxism and the struggle for socialised agriculture in the USSR in the 1920s. Coventry, 1978. pp. 22. (*University of Warwick. Department of Economics. Warwick Economic Research Papers. No. 131*)

GILL (GRAEME JOSEPH) Peasants and government in the Russian revolution. London, 1979. pp. 233. *bibliog.*

The POLITICS of rural Russia, 1905-1914; edited by Leopold H. Haimson. Bloomington, [1979]. pp. 309. (*Columbia University. Russian Institute. Studies*)

— — Russia (RSFSR).

CHERNOBAEV (ANATOLII ALEKSANDROVICH) Kombed. Moskva, 1978. pp. 127. *bibliog.*

— — Siberia.

PROBLEMY istorii sovetskoi sibirskoi derevni. Novosibirsk, 1977. pp. 302.

GUSHCHIN (NIKOLAI IAKOVLEVICH) and others. Soiuz rabochego klassa i krest'ianstva Sibiri v period postroeniia sotsializma, 1917-1937 gg. Novosibirsk, 1978. pp. 430.

SOTRUDNICHESTVO rabochikh i krest'ian Sibiri v usloviiakh razvitogo sotsializma: materialy k "Istorii rabochego klassa Sibiri". Novosibirsk, 1978. pp. 158.

— — Ukraine.

KHMIL' (IVAN VASYL'OVYCH) Trudiashche selianstvo Ukraïny v borot'bi za vladu Rad. Kyïv, 1977. pp. 199.

LESHCHENKO (MYKOLA NYKYFOROVYCH) Ukraïns'ke selo v revoliutsiï, 1905-1907 rr. Kyïv, 1977. pp. 360.

HRYNIV (OLEH IVANOVYCH) and NIKONENKO (VASYL' MYKOLAIOVYCH) Kolhospne selianstvo: zrostannia sotsial'noï aktyvnosti. Kyïv, 1978. pp. 128.

— Scandinavia.

ØSTERUD (ØYVIND) Agrarian structure and peasant politics in Scandinavia: a comparative study of rural response to economic change. Oslo, [1978]. pp. 278. *bibliog.*

— Sweden.

MARTINIUS (STURE) Peasant destinies: the history of 552 Swedes born 1810-12. Stockholm, 1977. pp. 154. *bibliog.* (*Stockholms Universitet. Acta Universitatis Stockholmiensis. Stockholm Studies in Economic History. 3*)

— Tunisia.

VALENSI (LUCETTE) Fellahs tunisiens: l'économie rurale et la vie des campagnes au 18e et 19e siécles. Paris, [1977]. pp. 421. *bibliog.* (*Paris. Ecole des Hautes Etudes en Sciences Sociales. Centre de Recherches Historiques. Civilisations et Sociétés. 45*)

— United Kingdom — Scotland.

CARTER (IAN) Farmlife in northeast Scotland, 1840-1914: the poor man's country. Edinburgh, [1979]. pp. 258. *bibliog.*

— Vietnam.

POPKIN (SAMUEL L.) The rational peasant: the political economy of rural society in Vietnam. Berkeley, 1979. pp. 306. *bibliog.*

PEASE (JOSEPH).

BELL (JOHN HYSLOP) British folks and British India fifty years ago: Joseph Pease and his contemporaries, containing letters by Thomas Clarkson,...and others. London, [1891]. pp. 207.

PEATMEN

— Netherlands.

HOEK (SIETSE VAN DER) Hopend op een vrijer leven: Drentse veenarbeiders/sters verhalen. 's-Gravenhage, 1978 repr. 1979. pp. 89. *bibliog.*

PECK (JOHN).

PECK (JOHN) Dublin from Downing Street. Dublin, 1978. pp. 241.

PEIXOTO (CARLOS).

PEIXOTO (CARLOS) Discursos parlamentares; seleção, introdução e comentarios de David V. Fleischer. Brasilia, 1978. pp. 759. *bibliog.* (*Brazil. Congresso. Câmara dos Deputados. Perfis Parlamentares. 2*)

PENAL COLONIES, BRITISH.

RUDÉ (GEORGE E.) Protest and punishment: the story of the social and political protesters transported to Australia 1788-1868. Oxford, 1978. pp. 270. *bibliog.*

PENINSULAR WAR, 1807-1814.

GLOVER (MICHAEL) Wellington's army in the Peninsula, 1808-1814. Vancouver, [1977]. pp. 192. *bibliog.*

PENNSYLVANIA

— Economic policy.

DUANE (WILLIAM JOHN) Letters addressed to the people of Pennsylvania respecting the internal improvement of the commonwealth by means of roads and canals. Philadelphia, 1811; New York, 1968. pp. 125.

— Foreign population.

The ETHNIC experience in Pennsylvania; edited and with an introduction by John E. Bodnar. Lewisburg, [1973]. pp. 330.

— History.

COCHRAN (THOMAS CHILDS) Pennsylvania: a bicentennial history. New York, [1978]. pp. 207. *bibliog.*

PENOLOGY

— United States.

McCLEARY (RICHARD) Dangerous men: the sociology of parole. Beverly Hills, [1978]. pp. 181. *bibliog.*

PENSION TRUSTS

— United States.

RIFKIN (JEREMY) and BARBER (RANDY) The North will rise again: pensions, politics and power in the 1980s. Boston, Mass., [1978]. pp. 279. *bibliog.*

PENSIONS

— Canada — Manitoba.

An INQUIRY into the future of public and private pension plans: proceedings of a seminar sponsored by the Manitoba Economic Development Advisory Board; compiled and edited by John McGuire. Winnipeg, 1976. pp. 54.

— Denmark.

HÜBBE (PER) Invalidepensionistundersøgelserne 4. Ansogere til invalide pension...; Surveys of disability pensioners 4. Applicants for disability pensions, etc. København, 1978. pp. 175. *bibliog. (Socialforskningsinstituttet. Publikationer. 84) With English summary.*

HÜBBE (PER) and WESTERGÅRD (POUL) Invalidepensionistundersøgelserne 3. Materiale og metoder; Surveys of disability pensioners 3. Material and methods. København, 1978. pp. 216. *bibliog. (Socialforskningsinstituttet. Publikationer. 83) With English summary.*

HÜBBE (PER) Invalidepensionistundersøgelserne 5. Forhold efter første ansøgning; Surveys of disability pensioners 5. Situation after the first application. København, 1979. pp. 167. *bibliog. (Socialforskningsinstituttet. Publikationer. 85) With English summary.*

— Mauritius.

ABEL-SMITH (BRIAN) and LYNES (TONY ALFRED) Report....on a national pension scheme for Mauritius. Port Louis, Government Printer, 1976. pp. 30.

— United Kingdom.

NATIONAL ASSOCIATION OF PENSION FUNDS. Survey of occupational pension schemes. a., 1977- Croydon.

CREEDY (JOHN) An analysis of government pension schemes. London, [1978]. pp. 23,3,6. *bibliog. (National Institute of Economic and Social Research. Discussion Papers. No. 20)*

CREEDY (JOHN) Pension schemes and the limits to redistribution. London, [1978]. pp. 22. *bibliog. (National Institute of Economic and Social Research. Discussion Papers. No. 24)*

THREADGOLD (A. R.) Personal saving: the impact of life assurance and pension funds. London, 1978. pp. 41. *bibliog. (Bank of England. Discussion Papers. No. 1)*

U.K. Equal Opportunities Commission. 1978. Equalising the pension age. [London], 1978. pp. 43.

U.K. Government Actuary's Department. 1978. Occupational pension schemes, 1975; fifth survey. London, 1978. pp. 113. *bibliog.*

PENTECOSTAL CHURCHES

— United States.

ANDERSON (ROBERT MAPES) Vision of the disinherited: the making of American Pentecostalism. New York, 1979. pp. 334. *bibliog.*

PENTECOSTALISM.

HOWE (GARY NIGEL) Pentecostalism, Umbanda and the Brazilian socio-economic order: from 1945 to the present day. 1978. fo. 409. *bibliog.* Typescript. Ph.D. (London) thesis: unpublished. *This thesis is the property of London University and may not be removed from the Library.*

PENTRICH

— History.

STEVENS (JOHN) Journalist. England's last revolution: Pentrich 1817. Hartington, [1977]. pp. 167. *bibliog.*

PEONAGE

— United States.

NOVAK (DANIEL A.) The wheel of servitude: black forced labor after slavery. Lexington, Ky., [1978]. pp. 126. *bibliog.*

PEPPER.

DISNEY (ANTHONY R.) Twilight of the pepper empire: Portuguese trade in southwest India in the early seventeenth century. Cambridge, Mass., 1978. pp. 220. *bibliog. (Harvard University. Harvard Historical Studies. vol. 95)*

PERAK

— History.

ANDAYA (BARBARA WATSON) Perak, the abode of grace: a study of an eighteenth-century Malay state. Kuala Lumpur, 1979. pp. 444. *bibliog.*

PERCEPTION.

LIVESLEY (WILLIAM JOHN) and BROMLEY (DENNIS BASIL) Person perception in childhood and adolescence. London, [1973]. pp. 320. *bibliog.*

RELPH (EDWARD) Place and placelessness. London, [1976]. pp. 156. *bibliog.*

— Testing.

O'CONNOR (NEIL) and HERMELIN (BEATE) Seeing and hearing and space and time. London, 1978. pp. 157. *bibliog.*

PERFORMANCE.

NORTON (DAVID P.) and RAU (KENNETH G.) A guide to EDP performance management, systems development, computer performance operations. Wellesley, Mass., [1978]. pp. 310. *bibliog.*

PERFORMING ARTS

— Canada.

CANADA. Statistics Canada. Culture statistics: performing arts. a., 1976(1st)- Ottawa. *[in English and French].*

— South Africa.

SOUTH AFRICA. Department of Information. 1969. Performing arts in South Africa. [Pretoria, 1969]. 1 vol. (unpaged).

PERIODICALS

— Bibliography.

PARIS. Université. Bibliothèque de Documentation Internationale Contemporaine. Liste des périodiques en cours reçus par la bibliothèque. a., 1978(5th)- Nanterre.

IRREGULAR serials and annuals: an international directory...1978- 1979. 5th ed. New York, [1978]. pp. 1396. *bibliog.*

EUROPEAN COMMUNITIES. Bibliothèque [Luxembourg]. List of periodicals. a. Luxembourg. *Current issue only kept.*

— — Union lists.

BRITISH UNION CATALOGUE OF PERIODICALS:...new periodical titles; edited for the National Central Library. q., with a. cumulation, Mr 1964(no.1[covering 1960-])- London. *Incorporates World list of scientific periodicals (1900-1950).*

— Indexes.

EUROPEAN COMMUNITIES. Bibliothèque [Luxembourg]. Articles sélectionnés. [in French, German, Italian and Dutch]. irreg. Luxembourg. *Current issues only kept.*

PERIODICALS, PUBLISHING OF.

WENBAN-SMITH (HUGH B.) Magazine publishing: a case of joint products. London, Price Commission, 1978. pp. 18. *(Government Economic Service Working Papers. No. 16)*

— Canada.

CANADA. Statistics Canada. Culture statistics: newspapers and periodicals. a., 1976/1977(1st)- Ottawa. *[in English and French]*

PERKINS (MAXWELL EVARTS).

BERG (A. SCOTT) Max Perkins: editor of genius. London, 1979. pp. 498.

PERKINS (WILLIAM MAXWELL EVARTS).

See PERKINS (MAXWELL EVARTS).

PERNAMBUCO

— History.

LEVINE (ROBERT M.) Pernambuco in the Brazilian federation, 1889-1937. Stanford, Calif., 1978. pp. 236. *bibliog.*

PERON (JUAN DOMINGO).

CHAVEZ (FERMIN) Peron y el peronismo en la historia contemporanea. Buenos Aires, [1975].

MARTINEZ CONSTANZO (PEDRO SANTOS) La nueva Argentina, 1946-1955. Buenos Aires, [1976]. 2 vols. *bibliog.*

PERPETUITIES

— United Kingdom — Scotland.

STAIR SOCIETY. [Publications]. 31. Perpetuities in Scots law; by Robert Burgess. Edinburgh, 1979. pp. 231.

PERROUX (FRANÇOIS).

HOMMAGE à François Perroux; (by Maurice Allais and others). Grenoble, 1978. pp. 748. *bibliog. In French or English.*

PERSONAL PROPERTY.

SMITH (THOMAS BROUN) Property problems in sale. Calcutta, 1978. pp. 232. *(Calcutta. University. Tagore Law Lectures. 1977)*

PERSONAL SPACE.

INSEL (PAUL M.) and LINDGREN (HENRY CLAY) Too close for comfort: the psychology of crowding. Englewood Cliffs, [1978]. pp. 180. *bibliog.*

PERSONALITY.

MISCHEL (WALTER) Introduction to personality. 2nd ed. New York, [1976]. pp. 575. *bibliog.*

BROMLEY (DENNIS BASIL) Personality description in ordinary language. London, [1977]. pp. 278. *bibliog.*

NEW perspectives in personal construct theory; edited by D. Bannister. London, 1977. pp. 355. *bibliogs.*

PERVIN (LAWRENCE AARON) Current controversies and issues in personality. New York, [1978]. pp. 313. *bibliog.*

ADAMS-WEBBER (J.R.) Personal construct theory: concepts and applications. Chichester, [1979]. pp. 239. *bibliog.*

JOHN PAUL II., Pope [Karol WOJTYŁA]. The acting person; translated from the Polish by Andrzej Potocki; this definitive text of the work established in collaboration with the author by Anna-Teresa Tymieniecka. Dordrecht, [1979]. pp. 367. *(Analecta Husserliana. vol. 10)*

PERSONALITY, DISORDERS OF.

PERSONALITY, DISORDERS OF.

CLARIDGE (GORDON) Personality and arousal: a psychophysiological study of psychiatric disorder. Oxford, [1967]. pp. 274. *bibliog.*

PERSONALITY TESTS.

The MEASUREMENT of intrapersonal space by grid technique. Vol. 2. Dimensions of intrapersonal space; edited by Patrick Slater. London, [1977]. pp. 270.

PERSONAL construct psychology, 1977; edited by Fay Fransella. London, 1978. pp. 274. *Based on papers given at the Second International Congress on Personal Construct Theory held at Oxford in July 1977.*

PERSONNEL MANAGEMENT.

MISFITS in industry; edited by Pasquale A. Carone [and others]. New York, [1978]. pp. 152. *Based on the proceedings of the seventh annual conference on the problems of industrial psychiatric medicine, Stony Brook, 1977.*

— Abstracts.

U.K. Department of Employment. Work Research Unit. Information system abstracts. m., current issues only. London.

— Australia.

WORK AND PEOPLE; [pd. by] Department of Productivity. [Australia]. q., autumn 1975 (v.1, no.1)- Melbourne. *Supersedes PERSONNEL PRACTICE BULLETIN.*

— United Kingdom.

ADVISORY, CONCILIATION AND ARBITRATION SERVICE [U.K.]. Advice on personnel management and industrial relations practices. London, [1977?]. pp. 7.

— United States.

STAHL (OSCAR GLENN) Public personnel administration. 7th ed. New York, [1976]. pp. 575. *bibliog.*

PERSONNEL management in government: politics and process; [by] Jay M. Shafritz [and others]. New York, [1978]. pp. 305. *bibliogs.*

PERSONNEL RECORDS

— United States.

ON record: files and dossiers in American life; edited by Stanton Wheeler. New Brunswick, N.J., [1976]. pp. 449.

PERSONNEL RESEARCH.

U.K. Department of Employment. Work Research Unit. Research register. a., current issue only. London.

PERSONS (INTERNATIONAL LAW).

IJALAYE (DAVID ADEDAYO) The extension of corporate personality in international law. Dobbs Ferry, N.Y., 1978. pp. 354.

PERSONS (LAW)

— Canada — Quebec.

QUEBEC (PROVINCE). Civil Code Revision Office. Committee on the Law on Persons and on the Family. 1974-75. Report on the family; [Claire L'Heureux-Dubé, présidente] . Montréal, 1974-75. 2 pts. *(Quebec (Province). Civil Code Revision Office. [Reports]. 26, 36) In English and French.*

QUEBEC (PROVINCE). Civil Code Revision Office. Committee on Legal Personality. 1976. Report on legal personality; [Yves Caron, président]. Montréal, 1976. pp. 86. *(Quebec (Province). Civil Code Revision Office. [Reports]. 43)*

PERU

— Armed forces.

CAMPBELL (LEON G.) The military and society in colonial Peru, 1750-1810. Philadelphia, 1978. pp. 254. *bibliog.*

— Description and travel.

CIEZA DE LEON (PEDRO DE) The Incas; translated by Harriet de Onis; edited, with an introduction, by Victor Wolfgang von Hagen. Norman, 1959. pp. 394. *bibliog.*

— Economic conditions.

INFORME demografico Peru - 1970; preparado por el Centro de Estudios de Poblacion y Desarrollo (CEPD). Lima, 1972. pp. 408.

LÓPEZ SORIA (JOSÉ IGNACIO) El modo de producción en el Perú y otros ensayos. Lima, 1977. pp. 152.

PEASANT cooperation and capitalist expansion in central Peru; edited by Norman Long and Bryan R. Roberts. Austin, [1978]. pp. 349. *bibliog.*

— Economic history.

ESTEVES (LUIS) Apuntes para la historia economica del Peru. Lima, 1882 repr. 1971. pp. 159. *Facsimile reprint.*

CARAVEDO MOLINARI (BALTAZAR) Clases, lucha politica y gobierno en el Peru (1919-1933). Lima, 1977. pp. 124.

LÓPEZ SORIA (JOSÉ IGNACIO) El modo de producción en el Perú y otros ensayos. Lima, 1977. pp. 152.

— — Sources.

MACERA (PABLO) ed. Historía economica peruana: documentos. Lima, 1975. pp. 320.

— Economic policy.

BELTRAN (PEDRO G.) La verdadera realidad peruana. Madrid, [1976]. pp. 252.

STEPAN (ALFRED C.) The state and society: Peru in comparative perspective. Princeton, [1978]. pp. 348. *bibliog.*

— History.

CHIRINOS SOTO (ENRIQUE) Historia de la Republica: 1821-Peru-1978. Lima, [1977]. pp. 504. *bibliog.*

— — To 1820.

GIRON DE VILLASEÑOR (NICOLE) Peru: cronistas indios y mestizos en el siglo XVI; traduccion de Roberto Gomez Ciriza. Mexico, Secretaria de Educacion Publica, 1975. pp. 183. *(Sep/Setentas. 199)*

— — To 1548.

CIEZA DE LEON (PEDRO DE) The Incas; translated by Harriet de Onis; edited, with an introduction, by Victor Wolfgang von Hagen. Norman, 1959. pp. 394. *bibliog.*

— — 1548-1820.

CAMPBELL (LEON G.) The military and society in colonial Peru, 1750-1810. Philadelphia, 1978. pp. 254. *bibliog.*

— Industries.

PERU. Direccion General de Asuntos Financieros. 1976. La actividad del Banco Industrial del Peru: el fomento del desarrollo industrial en provincias, 1970-1974. Lima, 1976. 3 vols. (in 1).

— Politics and government.

PERU hoy; por Fernando Fuenzalida Vollmar [and others]. Mexico, 1971 repr. 1975. pp. 366.

BELTRAN (PEDRO G.) La verdadera realidad peruana. Madrid, [1976]. pp. 252.

BAELLA TUESTA (ALFONSO) Que pasa? Lima, [1977]. pp. 400. *Reprint of editorials from El Tiempo, 31 October 1975 - 2 September, 1977.*

CARAVEDO MOLINARI (BALTAZAR) Clases, lucha politica y gobierno en el Peru (1919-1933). Lima, 1977. pp. 124.

HAYA DE LA TORRE (VICTOR RAUL) Obras completas. Lima, [1977]. 7 vols.

STEPAN (ALFRED C.) The state and society: Peru in comparative perspective. Princeton, [1978]. pp. 348. *bibliog.*

— Population.

INFORME demografico Peru - 1970; preparado por el Centro de Estudios de Poblacion y Desarrollo (CEPD). Lima, 1972. pp. 408.

MACERA (PABLO) ed. Poblacion rural en haciendas, 1876. Lima, 1976. pp. 82.

— Rural conditions.

PEASANT cooperation and capitalist expansion in central Peru; edited by Norman Long and Bryan R. Roberts. Austin, [1978]. pp. 349. *bibliog.*

— Social conditions.

PERU hoy; por Fernando Fuenzalida Vollmar [and others]. Mexico, 1971 repr. 1975. pp. 366.

— Social policy.

STEPAN (ALFRED C.) The state and society: Peru in comparative perspective. Princeton, [1978]. pp. 348. *bibliog.*

PERUGIA

— History.

BLANSHEI (SARAH RUBIN) Perugia, 1260-1340: conflict and change in a medieval Italian urban society. Philadelphia, 1976. pp. 128. *bibliog. (American Philosophical Society. Transactions. New Series. vol. 66. Pt. 2)*

PESSOA (EPITACIO).

PESSOA (EPITACIO) Discursos parlamentares; seleção e introdução, Jose Octavio. Brasilia, 1978. pp. 453. *(Brazil. Congresso. Câmara dos Deputados. Perfis Parlamentares. 7)*

PESTICIDES.

PESTICIDES and human welfare; edited by D.L. Gunn and J.G.R. Stevens. Oxford, 1976 repr. 1978. pp. 278. *bibliogs.*

PETAIN (HENRI PHILIPPE BENONI OMER JOSEPH).

MICHEL (HENRI) Pétain et le régime de Vichy. [Paris, 1978]. pp. 128. *bibliog.*

PETERBOROUGH ABBEY.

NORTHAMPTONSHIRE RECORD SOCIETY. [Publications]. vol. 28. The cartularies and registers of Peterborough Abbey; by Janet D. Martin. [Northampton], 1978. pp. 52.

PETROLEUM.

HENRY (J.T.) The early and later history of petroleum; with authentic facts in regard to its development in western Pennsylvania. Philadelphia, 1873; New York, 1970. pp. 607.

— Prices.

SVERIGES INDUSTRIFÖRBUND. Economic Affairs Directorate. The Nordic economic outlook: a survey prepared [by Eva Christina Horwitz]...; [with] special studies [by various authors]. [Stockholm], 1975. pp. 86.

— — India.

INDIA. Oil Prices Committee. 1977. Report; [K.S. Krishnaswamy, chairman]. [Delhi, 1977]. pp. 269.

— — United States.

MAURIZI (ALEX R.) and KELLY (THOM) Prices and consumer information: the benefits from posting retail gasoline prices. Washington, D.C., [1978]. pp. 76. *(American Enterprise Institute for Public Policy Research. AEI Studies. 193)*

PETROLEUM IN SUBMERGED LANDS

— Canada — Newfoundland.

SCARLETT (MAURICE) ed. Consequences of offshore oil and gas: Norway, Scotland and Newfoundland; a selection of background papers prepared for a colloquium (November, 1974) on the potential impact on the province of future commercial oil/gas discovery offshore Newfoundland. St. John's, Nfld., 1977. pp. 264. *(St. John's. Memorial University of Newfoundland. Institute of Social and Economic Research. Newfoundland Social and Economic Papers. No.6)*

— North Sea.

MARSHALL (ELIZABETH) Shetland's oil era. Lerwick, Shetland Islands Council, Research and Development Department, [1977]. pp. 73. *bibliog.*

ABERDEEN. University. Department of Political Economy. The economic impact of North Sea oil on Scotland; final report to the Scottish Economic Planning Department on a study conducted within the Department of Political Economy, the University of Aberdeen, 1973-77. Edinburgh, H.M.S.O., 1978. pp. 101.

BARNES (MICHAEL CECIL JOHN) and others. U.K. oil and natural gas depletion. [London, 1978]. pp. 4. *(Energy Commission [U.K.]. Papers. No. 20)*

JOHNSON (CHRISTOPHER) 1931- . North Sea energy wealth 1965-1985: oil and gas in the British and Norwegian economies. London, [1978]. 2 vols. *bibliog.*

KETO (DAVID B.) Law and offshore oil development: the North Sea experience. New York, [1978]. pp. 123.

MARSHALL (ELIZABETH) Shetland's oil era: phase 2. Lerwick, Shetland Islands Council, Research and Development Department, [1978]. pp. 107. *bibliog.*

ROSIE (GEORGE) The Ludwig initiative: a cautionary tale of North Sea oil. Edinburgh, 1978. pp. 147.

U.K. OFFSHORE OPERATORS ASSOCIATION. Exploration and development of U.K. continental shelf oil; the inter-dependence of government policies and industry effort in optimising the potential benefits of U.K. continental shelf oil;... with an Annex entitled Exploration and development activity: a critical factor in oil depletion policy. [London], 1978. 1 vol. (various pagings). *(Energy Commission [U.K.]. Papers. No. 17)*

The EFFECTIVE management of resources: the international politics of the North Sea; edited by C.M. Mason. London, 1979. pp. 268. *bibliogs.*

— Norway.

SCARLETT (MAURICE) ed. Consequences of offshore oil and gas: Norway, Scotland and Newfoundland; a selection of background papers prepared for a colloquium (November, 1974) on the potential impact on the province of future commercial oil/gas discovery offshore Newfoundland. St. John's, Nfld., 1977. pp. 264. *(St. John's. Memorial University of Newfoundland. Institute of Social and Economic Research. Newfoundland Social and Economic Papers. No.6)*

— United Kingdom — Scotland.

SCARLETT (MAURICE) ed. Consequences of offshore oil and gas: Norway, Scotland and Newfoundland; a selection of background papers prepared for a colloquium (November, 1974) on the potential impact on the province of future commercial oil/gas discovery offshore Newfoundland. St. John's, Nfld., 1977. pp. 264. *(St. John's. Memorial University of Newfoundland. Institute of Social and Economic Research. Newfoundland Social and Economic Papers. No.6)*

PETROLEUM INDUSTRY AND TRADE.

SELECTED DOCUMENTS OF THE INTERNATIONAL PETROLEUM INDUSTRY; [pd.by] Organization of the Petroleum Exporting Countries. a., 1967- Vienna.

ALGERIA. 1974. Petroleum, raw materials and development: memorandum submitted by Algeria on the occasion of the special session of the United Nations General Assembly, April 1974. [Algiers], 1974. pp. 222.

SAMPSON (ANTHONY) The seven sisters: the great oil companies and the world they made. London, 1975. pp. 334.

GROSSLING (BERNARDO F.) Window on oil; a survey of world petroleum sources. London, [1976]. pp. 140. *bibliog.*

WYANT (FRANK R.) The United States, OPEC, and multinational oil. Lexington, Mass., [1977]. pp. 214. *bibliog.*

EZZATI (ALI) World energy markets and OPEC stability. Lexington, Mass., [1978]. pp. 205. *bibliog.*

NORENG (ØYSTEIN) Oil politics in the 1980s: patterns of international cooperation. New York, [1978]. pp. 171. *bibliog. (Council on Foreign Relations. 1980s Project Studies)*

ODELL (PETER R.) and VALLENILLA (LUIS) The pressures of oil: a strategy for economic revival. London, 1978. pp. 215.

ODELL (PETER R.) Oil and world power. 5th ed. Harmondsworth, 1979. pp. 271. *bibliog.*

— America, Latin.

LATIN America and Caribbean oil report;...[edited by] Bryan Cooper [and others]. London, 1979. pp. 327.

— Arab countries.

ECONOMIC coercion and the new international economic order; edited by Richard B. Lillich. Charlottesville, Va., [1976]. pp. 401.

FRANCE. Direction de la Documentation. La Documentation Française. Notes et Etudes Documentaires. No. 4481. Pétrole et développement au Moyen-Orient; [by] Mahmoud Montazer-Zohour. [Paris], 1978. pp. 96.

— Argentine Republic.

MONTEMAYOR (MARIANO) Proyeccion latinoamericana de la politica petrolera nacional. Buenos Aires, 1958. pp. 79.

— Canada.

SMITH (PHILIP) 1925- . The treasure-seekers: the men who built Home Oil. Toronto, [1978]. pp. 310.

— — British Columbia.

BRITISH COLUMBIA. Energy Commission. 1977. 1977 petroleum and natural gas price and incentives hearing. [Vancouver], 1977. pp. 99.

— Caribbean area.

LATIN America and Caribbean oil report;...[edited by] Bryan Cooper [and others]. London, 1979. pp. 327.

— China.

HARDY (RANDALL W.) China's oil future: a case of modest expectations. Boulder, Colo., 1978. pp. 148.

— Europe, Eastern.

PARK (DANIEL) Oil and gas in COMECON countries. London, 1979. pp. 240. *bibliog.*

— European Economic Community countries.

EUROPEAN COMMUNITIES. Commission. 1975. Report by the Commission on the behaviour of the oil companies in the Community during the period from October 1973 to March 1974. Brussels, 1975. pp. 168. *(European Economic Community. Studies. Competition: Approximation of Legislation Series. 26)*

— Indonesia.

[UNITED STATES. Embassy (Indonesia)]. Indonesia's petroleum sector. [Jakarta], 1979. fo. 72. *Photocopy.*

— Iraq.

IRAQ OIL NEWS BULLETIN; [pd.by] Ministry of Oil. irreg., My 1979(no.41)- Baghdad.

— Mexico.

BERMUDEZ (ANTONIO J.) La politica petrolera mexicana. Mexico, 1976. pp. 124.

— Norway.

STENSTADVOLD (KJELL) Regional and structural effects of North Sea oil in Norway. Bergen, 1977. fo. 55. *bibliog. (Norges Handelshøyskole and Bergen. Universitet. Geography Department. Meddelelser. No.37)*

JOHNSON (CHRISTOPHER) 1931- . North Sea energy wealth 1965-1985: oil and gas in the British and Norwegian economies. London, [1978]. 2 vols. *bibliog.*

— Qatar.

EL MALLAKH (RAGAEI) Qatar: development of an oil economy. London, [1979]. pp. 183. *bibliogs.*

— United Kingdom.

HAMILTON (ADRIAN) North Sea impact: off-shore oil and the British economy. London, 1978. pp. 191.

JOHNSON (CHRISTOPHER) 1931- . North Sea energy wealth 1965-1985: oil and gas in the British and Norwegian economies. London, [1978]. 2 vols. *bibliog.*

— — Scotland.

MARSHALL (ELIZABETH) Shetland's oil era. Lerwick, Shetland Islands Council, Research and Development Department, [1977]. pp. 73. *bibliog.*

MARSHALL (ELIZABETH) Shetland's oil era: phase 2. Lerwick, Shetland Islands Council, Research and Development Department, [1978]. pp. 107. *bibliog.*

TURNOCK (DAVID) The new Scotland. Newton Abbot, [1979]. pp. 168. *bibliog.*

— United States.

HENRY (J.T.) The early and later history of petroleum; with authentic facts in regard to its development in western Pennsylvania. Philadelphia, 1873; New York, 1970. pp. 607.

WYANT (FRANK R.) The United States, OPEC, and multinational oil. Lexington, Mass., [1977]. pp. 214. *bibliog.*

BOHI (DOUGLAS R.) and RUSSELL (MILTON) Limiting oil imports: an economic history and analysis. Baltimore, [1978]. pp. 356. *Report of a project initiated by Resources for the Future, Inc.*

CONFERENCE ON HORIZONTAL DIVESTITURE IN THE OIL INDUSTRY, WASHINGTON, 1977. Horizontal divestiture in the oil industry: proceedings of a conference addressing the question: should oil companies be prohibited from owning nonpetroleum energy resources?; edited by Edward J. Mitchell. Washington, D.C., [1978]. pp. 111. *(American Enterprise Institute for Public Policy Research. AEI Symposia. 78E)*

PETROLEUM INDUSTRY AND TRADE.(Cont.)

KAUFMAN (BURTON IRA) The oil cartel case: a documentary study of antitrust activity in the Cold War era. Westport, Conn., 1978. pp. 217.

— Venezuela.

RODRIGUEZ GALLAD (IRENE) El petroleo en la historiografia venezolana. Caracas, 1974. pp. 261. bibliog.

PETROLEUM PRODUCTS
— Prices — Canada — British Columbia.

BRITISH COLUMBIA. Energy Commission. l977. 1977 petroleum and natural gas price and incentives hearing. [Vancouver], 1977. pp. 99.

— — India.

NATIONAL COUNCIL OF APPLIED ECONOMIC RESEARCH. The impact of the price rise in petroleum based agricultural inputs on the production of wheat and rice in India; a study prepared for the Commonwealth Secretariat;...[directed by] I.Z. Bhatty. London, Commonwealth Secretariat, [1976]. pp. 74. (Commonwealth Economic Papers. No. 6)

— — United States.

CONGRESSIONAL QUARTERLY INC. Continuing energy crisis in America. Washington, D.C., [1975]. pp. 124. bibliog.

PETROVSKII (GRIGORII IVANOVICH).

VOSPOMINANIIA o G.I. Petrovskom. Moskva, 1978. pp. 215. bibliog.

PHARMACY
— United Kingdom — History.

BRITISH SOCIETY FOR THE HISTORY OF PHARMACY. Transactions. vol. 1. no. 4. [Articles on the history of pharmacy]. Edinburgh, 1977. pp. 67.

PHENOMENOLOGY.

RELPH (EDWARD) Place and placelessness. London, [1976]. pp. 156. bibliog.

JOHN PAUL II., Pope [Karol WOJTYŁA]. The acting person; translated from the Polish by Andrzej Potocki; this definitive text of the work established in collaboration with the author by Anna-Teresa Tymieniecka. Dordrecht, [1979]. pp. 367. (Analecta Husserliana. vol. 10)

PHILADELPHIA
— Commerce.

GOLDSTEIN (JONATHAN) Philadelphia and the China trade, 1682-1846: commercial, cultural and attitudinal effects. University Park, Pa., [1978]. pp. 121. bibliog.

— Economic conditions — Mathematical models.

GLICKMAN (NORMAN J.) Econometric analysis of regional systems: explorations in model building and policy analysis. New York, [1977]. pp. 210. bibliog.

PHILANTHROPISTS
— United Kingdom.

POPE (NORRIS) Dickens and charity. London, 1978. pp. 303.

PHILBY (HAROLD ADRIAN RUSSELL).

SEALE (PATRICK) and McCONVILLE (MAUREEN) Philby: the long road to Moscow. rev. ed. Harmondsworth, 1978. pp. 349.

PHILIPPINE ISLANDS
— Economic conditions.

PHILIPPINE PROGRESS: business and economic information pd. by the Board of Investments in cooperation with the Development Bank of the Philippines. q., 1970-1975 (v.4-9). Makati. Superseded by PHILIPPINE INDUSTRY AND INVESTMENT.

NEDA MIDYEAR REPORT ON THE ECONOMY; [pd. by] National Economic and Development Authority [Philippine Islands]. s-a., 1973- Manila.

NEDA JOURNAL OF DEVELOPMENT; pd. every semester by the National Economic and Development Authority [Philippine Islands]. s-a., 1974 (v.1)- Manila..

— Economic policy.

PALMER (INGRID) The new rice in the Philippines (UNRISD Report No. 75.2) (UNRISD/75/C.38). Geneva, United Nations Research Institute for Social Development, 1975. pp. 200. bibliog. ([Studies on the Green Revolution. No. 10])

— History — 1899-1901, Insurrection.

WELCH (RICHARD E.) Response to imperialism: the United States and the Philippine-American War, 1899-1902. Chapel Hill, [1979]. pp. 215. bibliog.

— Population.

QUEZON CITY. University of the Philippines. Population Institute. Population of the Philippines;... Mercedes B. Concepcion, editor. Manila, [1977]. pp. 152. bibliogs. (Committee for International Coordination of National Research in Demography. C.I.C.R.E.D. Series)

— Statistics, Vital.

PHILIPPINE ISLANDS. National Census and Statistics Office. Vital statistics report. a., 1974- Manila.

PHILIPS GLOEILAMPENFABRIEKEN,

TEULINGS (AD) Philips: geschiedenis en praktijk van een wereldconcern. Amsterdam, 1977. pp. 325. bibliog.

PHILLIPS (Sir LIONEL).

PHILLIPS (Sir LIONEL) All that glittered: selected correspondence...1890-1924; [edited by] Maryna Fraser and Alan Jeeves. Cape Town, 1977. pp. 428. bibliog.

PHILOLOGY
— Study and teaching.

BLEICH (DAVID) Subjective criticism. Baltimore, Md., [1978]. pp. 309.

PHILOSOPHERS
— Germany.

LIPTON (DAVID R.) Ernst Cassirer: the dilemma of a liberal intellectual in Germany, 1914-1933. Toronto, [1978]. pp. 212. bibliog.

PHILOSOPHICAL ANTHROPOLOGY.

SCHUMANN (MAURICE) Angoisse et certitude: de la mort - de la vie - de la liberté. [Paris, 1978]. pp. 204.

JOHN PAUL II., Pope [Karol WOJTYŁA]. The acting person; translated from the Polish by Andrzej Potocki; this definitive text of the work established in collaboration with the author by Anna-Teresa Tymieniecka. Dordrecht, [1979]. pp. 367. (Analecta Husserliana. vol. 10)

MIDGLEY (MARY) Beast and man: the roots of human nature. Hassocks, 1979. pp. 377. bibliog.

PHILOSOPHY.

FEINBERG (JOEL) Social philosophy. Englewood Cliffs, [1973]. pp. 126. bibliog.

WADDINGTON (CONRAD HAL) Tools for thought. St. Albans, 1977. pp. 250. bibliog.

BRONOWSKI (JACOB) Magic, science and civilization. New York, 1978. pp. 88. (Columbia University. Bampton Lectures in America. No. No. 20)

MILL (JOHN STUART) Collected works of John Stuart Mill. vol.10. Essays on philosophy and the classics; editor of the text J.M. Robson; introduction by F.E. Sparshott. Toronto, [1978]. pp. 578. bibliog.

NOVACK (GEORGE) Polemics in Marxist philosophy. New York, [1978]. pp. 344. bibliog.

CASSIRER (ERNST) Symbol, myth, and culture: essays and lectures of Ernst Cassirer, 1935-1945; edited by Donald Phillip Verene. New Haven, 1979. pp. 304.

ISSUES in Marxist philosophy; edited by John Mepham and David Hillel Ruben. Brighton, 1979. 3 vols. bibliogs.

— Dictionaries and encyclopedias.

MARXISTISCH-leninistisches Wörterbuch der Philosophie; herausgegeben von Georg Klaus und Manfred Buhr. new ed. Reinbek bei Hamburg, 1975 repr. 1977-79. 3 vols.

— History.

KUCZYNSKI (JUERGEN) Studien zu einer Geschichte der Gesellschaftswissenschaften. Berlin, 1975-78. 10 vols.

— — Methodology.

METODOLOGICHESKIE problemy istorii filosofii i obshchestvennoi mysli. Moskva, 1977. pp. 360. bibliog.

PHILOSOPHY, AMERICAN.

GAVIN (WILLIAM J.) and BLAKELEY (THOMAS J.) Russia and America: a philosophical comparison: development and change of outlook from the 19th to the 20th century. Dordrecht, [1976]. pp. 114. (Freiburg (Switzerland). Universität. Ost-Europa Institut. Sovietica. vol. 38)

KUKLICK (BRUCE) The rise of American philosophy: Cambridge, Massachusetts, 1860-1930. New Haven, 1977. pp. 674. bibliog.

PHILOSOPHY, ANCIENT.

KIRK (GEOFFREY STEPHEN) and RAVEN (JOHN EARLE) The presocratic philosophers: a critical history with a selection of texts. Cambridge, 1957 repr. 1975. pp. 487. bibliog.

PHILOSOPHY, AZERBAIJANI.

MAMEDOV (SHEIDABEK FARADZHIEVICH) Mirza-Fatali Akhundov. Moskva, 1978. pp. 166. bibliog.

PHILOSOPHY, GERMAN.

GLUCKSMANN (ANDRE) Les maîtres penseurs. Paris, [1977]. pp. 323.

PHILOSOPHY, ITALIAN.

The EARTHLY republic: Italian humanists on government and society; edited by Benjamin G. Kohl and Ronald G. Witt. Manchester, [1978]. pp. 337. bibliog.

PHILOSOPHY, MEDIEVAL.

HELLER (AGNES) Renaissance man;...translated from the Hungarian by Richard E. Allen. London, 1978. pp. 481.

PHILOSOPHY, MODERN.

SPANN (OTHMAR) Gesamtausgabe; Herausgeber: Walter Heinrich [and others]. Graz, 1963-79. 21 vols. bibliogs.

KUCZYNSKI (JUERGEN) Studien zu einer Geschichte der Gesellschaftswissenschaften. Berlin, 1975-78. 10 vols.

GLUCKSMANN (ANDRE) Les maîtres penseurs. Paris, [1977]. pp. 323.

HUME (DAVID) the Historian. A treatise of human nature; edited, with an analytical index, by L.A. Selby-Bigge; second edition with text revised and variant readings by P.H. Nidditch. Oxford, 1978. pp. 743.

— History.

RANDALL (JOHN HERMAN) the Younger. Philosophy after Darwin: chapters for The career of philosophy, vol. 3, and other essays;...edited by Beth J. Singer. New York, 1977. pp. 352.

PHILOSOPHY, POLISH.

KLEVCHENIA (ALEKSANDR SEMENOVICH) Ocherki po istorii marksistsko-leninskoi filosofskoi mysli v Pol'she. Minsk, 1978. pp. 198. *bibliog.*

LIEBICH (ANDRE) Between ideology and utopia: the politics and philosophy of August Cieszkowski. Dordrecht, [1979]. pp. 390. *(Freiburg (Switzerland). Universität. Ost-Europa Institut. Sovietica. vol. 39)*

PHILOSOPHY, RENAISSANCE.

The EARTHLY republic: Italian humanists on government and society; edited by Benjamin G. Kohl and Ronald G. Witt. Manchester, [1978]. pp. 337. *bibliog.*

HELLER (AGNES) Renaissance man;...translated from the Hungarian by Richard E. Allen. London, 1978. pp. 481.

MANDROU (ROBERT) From humanism to science, 1480-1700...; translated by Brian Pearce. Hassocks, 1978. pp. 329. *bibliog.*

KOENIGSBERGER (DOROTHY) Renaissance man and creative thinking: a history of concepts of harmony, 1400-1700. Hassocks, [1979]. pp. 282. *bibliogs.*

PHILOSOPHY, RUSSIAN.

GAVIN (WILLIAM J.) and BLAKELEY (THOMAS J.) Russia and America: a philosophical comparison: development and change of outlook from the 19th to the 20th century. Dordrecht, [1976]. pp. 114. *(Freiburg (Switzerland). Universität. Ost-Europa Institut. Sovietica. vol. 38)*

UCHENYE ZAPISKI KAFEDR OBSHCHESTVENNYKH NAUK VUZOV LENINGRADA. Filosofiia. vyp.17. Filosofskie i sotsiologicheskie issledovaniia. Leningrad, 1977. pp. 200.

JENSEN (KENNETH MARTIN) Beyond Marx and Mach: Aleksandr Bogdanov's philosophy of living experience. Dordrecht, [1978]. pp. 189. *bibliog. (Freiburg (Switzerland). Universität. Ost- Europa Institut. Sovietica. vol. 41)*

ROZVYTOK prohresyvnoï filosofs'koï dumky rosiis'koho, ukraïns'koho ta bilorus'koho narodiv u XVII-XVIII st. Kyïv, 1978. pp. 167. *With brief Russian summary.*

PHILOSOPHY, UKRAINIAN.

ROZVYTOK prohresyvnoï filosofs'koï dumky rosiis'koho, ukraïns'koho ta bilorus'koho narodiv u XVII-XVIII st. Kyïv, 1978. pp. 167. *With brief Russian summary.*

PHILOSOPHY, WHITE RUSSIAN.

ROZVYTOK prohresyvnoï filosofs'koï dumky rosiis'koho, ukraïns'koho ta bilorus'koho narodiv u XVII-XVIII st. Kyïv, 1978. pp. 167. *With brief Russian summary.*

PHILOSOPHY, YUGOSLAV.

MARXIST humanism and Praxis; edited, with translations, by Gerson S. Sher. New York, 1978. pp. 183.

PHOTOGRAMMETRY.

SYMPOSIUM ON PHOTO INTERPRETATION, DELFT, 1962. Transactions...; edited by Commission VII, International Society for Photogrammetry. Delft, [1963?]. pp. 533. *bibliogs. (International Society for Photogrammetry. International Archives of Photogrammetry. vol. 14). In English, French or German.*

PHOTOGRAPHIC INTERPRETATION.

SYMPOSIUM ON PHOTO INTERPRETATION, DELFT, 1962. Transactions...; edited by Commission VII, International Society for Photogrammetry. Delft, [1963?]. pp. 533. *bibliogs. (International Society for Photogrammetry. International Archives of Photogrammetry. vol. 14). In English, French or German.*

PHYSICAL ANTHROPOLOGY.

In earlier volumes of this Bibliography similar material is entered under SOMATOLOGY.

BIOLOGICAL anthropology: readings from Scientific American with introductions by Solomon H. Katz. San Francisco, [1975 repr. 1977]. pp. 494. *bibliog.*

NURSE (G.T.) and JENKINS (T.) Health and the hunter-gatherer: biomedical studies on the hunting and gathering populations of southern Africa. Basel, 1977. pp. 126. *bibliog.*

The BIOLOGY of high-altitude peoples; edited by P.T. Baker. Cambridge, 1978. pp. 357. *bibliogs. (International Council of Scientific Unions. International Biological Programme. 14)*

PHYSICAL DISTRIBUTION OF GOODS.

MERCER (ALAN) and others. Operational distribution research: innovative case studies. London, 1978. pp. 196. *bibliog. (Operational Research Society. ORASA Texts. No. 2)*

MURPHY (G.J.) Transport and distribution. 2nd ed. London, 1978. pp. 300.

PHYSICAL GEOGRAPHY.

PRESS (FRANK) and SIEVER (RAYMOND) Earth. 2nd ed. San Francisco, [1978]. pp. 649. *bibliogs.*

— Africa, West.

UDO (REUBEN K.) A comprehensive geography of West Africa. Ibadan, 1978. pp. 304. *bibliog.*

— Europe, Eastern.

POUNDS (NORMAN JOHN GREVILLE) Eastern Europe. London, 1969. pp. 912. *bibliogs.*

— Russia.

DEWDNEY (JOHN CHRISTOPHER) A geography of the Soviet Union. 3rd ed. Oxford, 1979. pp. 175. *bibliog.*

— South Africa.

VAN DER MERWE (SANDRA) The environment of South African business. Cape Town, 1976. pp. 324. *bibliogs.*

PHYSICALLY HANDICAPPED

— Education — United Kingdom.

MOHR (DIANA H.) Research monograph on adult education and the physically handicapped person. London, [1977]. pp. 143. *bibliog.*

— United Kingdom.

SOCIAL SERVICES RESEARCH AND INTELLIGENCE UNIT [PORTSMOUTH]. Occasional Papers. No. 6. A community's perception of the physically disabled; [by] G. Williams. Portsmouth, 1979. fo. 20.

PHYSICALLY HANDICAPPED CHILDREN

— Care and treatment — United Kingdom — Wales.

WELSH COUNCIL. Problems of physically-handicapped children in Wales. [Cardiff], 1978. pp. (42).

PHYSICIAN AND PATIENT.

BRADSHAW (JOHN S.) Doctors on trial. London, 1978. pp. 320.

PHYSICIANS.

BRADSHAW (JOHN S.) Doctors on trial. London, 1978. pp. 320.

— Malpractice.

The ECONOMICS of medical malpractice: (a conference sponsored by the Center for Health Policy Research of the American Enterprise Institute for Public Policy Research); edited by Simon Rottenberg. Washington, D.C., [1978]. pp. 293.

— Sierra Leone.

SIERRA LEONE. Committee to Consider the Medical Salaries and Private Practice. 1954. Report on medical salaries and private practice; [T.C. Luke, chairman]. Freetown, 1954. pp. 15. *(Sierra Leone. Sessional Papers. 1954. No.3)*

— United Kingdom — Supply and demand.

MAYNARD (ALAN K.) and WALKER (ARTHUR) Doctor manpower 1975-2000: alternative forecasts and their resource implications. London, 1978. pp. 60. *bibliog. (U.K. Royal Commission on the National Health Service, 1976. Research Papers. No.4)*

U.K. Department of Health and Social Security. 1978. Medical manpower: the next twenty years; a discussion paper. London, 1978 repr. 1979. pp. 84.

— United States.

NUMBERS (RONALD L.) Almost persuaded: American physicians and compulsory health insurance, 1912-1920. Baltimore, [1978]. pp. 158. *(Bulletin of the History of Medicine. Henry E. Sigerist Supplements. New Series. No. 1)*

PHYSICISTS

— United States.

KEVLES (DANIEL J.) The physicists: the history of a scientific community in modern America. New York, [1979]. pp. 489. *bibliog.*

PHYSICS

— Philosophy.

DUHEM (PIERRE) To save the phenomena: an essay on the idea of physical theory from Plato to Galileo;...with an introductory essay by Stanley L. Jaki. Chicago, 1969. pp. 120.

BOLTZMANN (LUDWIG) Theoretical physics and philosophical problems: selected writings [translated from the German by Paul Foulkes]; edited by Brian McGuinness. Dordrecht, [1974]. pp. 280. *bibliog.*

— United States.

KEVLES (DANIEL J.) The physicists: the history of a scientific community in modern America. New York, [1979]. pp. 489. *bibliog.*

PIAGET (JEAN).

PHILLIPS (JOHN L.) The origins of intellect: Piaget's theory. 2nd ed. San Francisco, [1975]. pp. 205. *bibliog.*

PIAGET, psychology and education: papers in honour of Jean Piaget; edited by Ved P. Varma and Philip Williams. London, [1976]. pp. 233. *bibliog.*

PICARDY

— History.

PIERRARD (PIERRE) Histoire du Nord: Flandre, Artois, Hainaut, Picardie. [Paris, 1978]. pp. 404. *bibliog.*

PICHETA (VLADIMIR IVANOVICH).

SLAVIANE v epokhu feodalizma: k stoletiiu akademika V.I. Pichety. Moskva, 1978. pp. 343.

PICK (FRANK).

BARMAN (CHRISTIAN) The man who built London Transport: a biography of Frank Pick. Newton Abbot, [1979]. pp. 287.

PICKETING
— United Kingdom.

[U.K. Department of Employment]. 1979. Working paper for consultations on proposed industrial relations legislation: picketing. [London, 1979]. fo. (4).

PIDGIN ENGLISH.

PIDGINS and creoles: current trends and prospects; [papers presented at the pidgin and creole interest group session which met at the Georgetown University Round Table on Languages and Linguistics in 1972]; edited by David DeCamp [and] Ian F. Hancock. Washington, [1974]. pp. 137. *bibliogs.*

SCHUMANN (JOHN H.) The pidginization process: a model for second language acquisition. Rowley, Mass., [1978]. pp. 190. *bibliog.*

PIDGIN LANGUAGES.

PIDGIN and creole linguistics; edited by Albert Valdman. Bloomington, [1977]. pp. 399. *bibliogs.*

PIERCE FAMILY.

McGOVERN (JAMES R.) Yankee family. New Orleans, 1975. pp. 191.

PIOCH (KARL).

PIOCH (KARL) Nie im Abseits. Berlin, [1978]. pp. 204.

PISTOIA
— Economic history.

CAPECCHI (ILVO) and GAI (LUCIA) Il Monte della Pietà a Pistoia e le sue origini. Firenze, 1976. pp. 263. *(Deputazione di Storia Patria per la Toscana. Biblioteca Storica Toscana. 17)*

PLAGUE
— United Kingdom.

The PLAGUE reconsidered: a new look at its origins and effects in 16th and 17th century England; [edited by Paul Slack]. Matlock, [1977]. pp. 145. *(Local Population Studies. Supplements. 4) Published by Local Population Studies in association with the...Cambridge Group for the History of Population and Social Structure.*

PLANNING.

CAMHIS (MATHIEU MARIOS) Planning theory and philosophy: a comparative analysis. 1977. fo. 313. *bibliog. Typescript. Ph.D. (London) thesis: unpublished. This thesis is the property of London University and may not be removed from the Library.*

KING (WILLIAM R.) and CLELAND (DAVID I.) Strategic planning and policy. New York, [1978]. pp. 374. *bibliogs.*

LONDON. University. London School of Economics and Political Science. Graduate School of Geography. Discussion Papers. No. 69. Measures of spatial opportunity: the use of urban images in constructing subjective indicators of spatial opportunity; [by] Lefteris Tsoulouvis. London, 1978. pp. 58. *bibliog.*

ELLMAN (MICHAEL JOHN) Socialist planning. Cambridge, 1979. pp. 300. *bibliog.*

PLANTATION LIFE
— Jamaica.

CRATON (MICHAEL) Searching for the invisible man: slaves and plantation life in Jamaica. Cambridge, Mass., 1978. pp. 439.

— United States.

ROARK (JAMES L.) Master without slaves: Southern planters in the Civil War and Reconstruction. New York, [1977]. pp. 273. *bibliog.*

REVISITING Blassingame's The slave community: the scholars respond; edited by Al-Tony Gilmore. Westport, Conn., 1978. pp. 204.

VAN DEBURG (WILLIAM L.) The slave drivers: black agricultural labor supervisors in the antebellum South. Westport, 1979. pp. 202.

PLANTATIONS
— Brazil.

VELHO (OTAVIO GUILHERME) Capitalismo autoritario e campesinato: um estudo comparativo a partir da fronteira em movimento. São Paulo, 1976. pp. 261. *bibliog.*

— Peru.

MACERA (PABLO) Las plantaciones azucareras en el Peru, 1821-1875. Lima, 1974. pp. 167.

PLASTICS INDUSTRY AND TRADE
— Zambia.

ZAMBIA. Central Statistical Office. 1976. Chemicals, rubber and plastics industries. Lusaka, 1976. pp. 64. *(Industry Monographs. No.5)*

PLATO.

WOOD (ELLEN MEIKSINS) and WOOD (NEAL) Class ideology and ancient political theory: Socrates, Plato and Aristotle in social context. Oxford, 1978. pp. 275. *bibliog.*

PLAY.

BRUNER (JEROME SEYMOUR) and others, eds. Play: its role in development and evolution. Harmondsworth, 1976, repr. 1978. pp. 716. *bibliogs.*

DUVERGER (CHRISTIAN) L'esprit du jeu chez les Aztèques. Paris, 1978. pp. 298. *bibliog. (Paris. Ecole des Hautes Etudes en Sciences Sociales. Centre de Recherches Historiques. Civilisations et Sociétés. 59)*

PLEKHANOV (GEORGII VALENTINOVICH).

IOVCHUK (MIKHAIL TRIFONOVICH) and KURBATOVA (IRINA NIKOLAEVNA) Plekhanov. Moskva, 1977. pp. 351. *bibliog.*

PLEKHANOV (GEORGII VALENTINOVICH) Ob ateizme i religii v istorii obshchestva i kul'tury: izbrannye proizvedeniia i izvlecheniia iz trudov. Moskva, 1977. pp. 355.

PLEKHANOV (GEORGII VALENTINOVICH) Estetika i sotsiologiia iskusstva: [sbornik statei, 1897-1913]. Moskva, 1978. 2 vols. *With introductory article by M. Lifshits.*

PLURALISM (SOCIAL SCIENCES).

INTERGROUP accommodation in plural societies: a selection of conference papers with special reference to the Republic of South Africa; edited by Nic Rhoodie. London, 1978. pp. 482. *Twenty-three of the twenty-six papers in this volume were presented at the International Conference on Intergroup Accommodation in Plural Societies, Cape Town, 1977.*

WESSON (ROBERT GALE) State systems: international pluralism, politics, and culture. New York, [1978]. pp. 296. *bibliog.*

POINT PROCESSES.

SNYDER (DONALD LEE) Random point processes. New York, [1975]. pp. 485. *bibliogs.*

POKROVSKII (MIKHAIL NIKOLAEVICH).

ENTEEN (GEORGE M.) The Soviet scholar-bureaucrat: M.N. Pokrovskii and the Society of Marxist Historians. University Park, Penn., 1978. pp. 236. *bibliog.*

POLAND
— Economic conditions.

SOCIAL structure and change: Finland and Poland: comparative perspective; edited by Erik Allardt and Włodzimierz Wesołowski. Warszawa, 1978. pp. 392.

— Economic history.

MIŚ (WŁADYSŁAW) Od wojny do pokoju: gospodarka Polski w latach 1944-1946. Warszawa, 1978. pp. 355. *bibliog.*

— Emigration and immigration.

MURDZEK (BENJAMIN P.) Emigration in Polish social-political thought, 1870-1914. Boulder, Colo., 1977. pp. 396. *bibliog. (East European Quarterly. East European Monographs. 33)*

— Foreign relations.

CIENCIALA (ANNA M.) Poland and the Western powers, 1938-1939: a study in the interdependence of Eastern and Western Europe. London, 1968. pp. 310. *bibliog.*

— — United States.

LUKAS (RICHARD C.) The strange allies: the United States and Poland, 1941-1945. Knoxville, Tenn., [1978]. pp. 230. *bibliog.*

— History.

INTERNATIONAL CONGRESS OF HISTORICAL SCIENCES, 11TH, STOCKHOLM, 1960. Poland at the XIth International Congress of Historical Sciences in Stockholm. Warszawa, 1960. pp. 337.

— — 1864-1918.

MURDZEK (BENJAMIN P.) Emigration in Polish social-political thought, 1870-1914. Boulder, Colo., 1977. pp. 396. *bibliog. (East European Quarterly. East European Monographs. 33)*

— — 1939-1945, Occupation.

SZAROTA (TOMASZ) Okupowanej Warszawy dzień powszedni: studium historyczne. 2nd ed. Warszawa, 1978. pp. 706. *bibliog.*

— — 1945- .

MAGIERSKA (ANNA) Ziemie zachodnie i północne w 1945 roku: kształtowanie się podstaw polityki integracyjnej państwa polskiego. Warszawa, 1978. pp. 306. *bibliog.*

— Intellectual life.

LAM (STANISŁAW) 'Zycie wśród wielu; przygotował do druku Andrzej Lam. [Warszawa, 1968]. pp. 449.

— Maps.

BREU (JOSEF) ed. Atlas der Donauländer; Atlas of the Danubian countries. Wien, 1970 in progress.

— Nationalism.

COTTAM (KAZIMIERA JANINA) Boleslaw Limanowski, 1835-1935: a study in socialism and nationalism. Boulder, Colo., 1978. pp. 365. *bibliog. (East European Quarterly. East European Monographs. 41)*

— Politics and government.

SCAEVOLA, pseud. A study in forgery: (the Lublin Committee and its rule over Poland). London, [1945]. pp. 123.

SOCIAL structure and change: Finland and Poland: comparative perspective; edited by Erik Allardt and Włodzimierz Wesołowski. Warszawa, 1978. pp. 392.

— Population.

VOSPROIZVODSTVO naseleniia sotsialisticheskikh stran: na primere Sovetskogo Soiuza i Pol'shi; pod redaktsiei D.I. Valenteia i M. Liatukha. Moskva, 1977. pp. 360.

— **Relations (general) with Russia.**

TSYBENKO (ELENA ZAKHAROVNA) Iz istorii pol'sko-russkikh literaturnykh sviazei XIX-XX vv. Moskva, 1978. pp. 280.

— **Relations (general) with the United Kingdom.**

LIPOŃSKI (WOJCIECH) Polska a Brytania, 1801-1830: próby politycznego i cywilizacyjnego dźwignięcia kraju w oparciu o Wielką Brytanię. Poznań, 1978. pp. 195. *(Poznań. Uniwersytet. Seria Filologia Angielska. Nr. 11)* With English and French summaries.

— **Social conditions.**

SOCIAL structure and change: Finland and Poland: comparative perspective; edited by Erik Allardt and Włodzimierz Wesołowski. Warszawa, 1978. pp. 392.

— **Statistics.**

POLAND. Główny Urząd Statystyczny. 1964. Polska w liczbach, 1944-1964. Warszawa, 1964. pp. 130.

POLES IN CANADA.

PAMIĘTNIKI imigrantów polskich w Kanadzie: wybór pamiętników nadesłanych na konkurs Kanadyjsko-Polskiego Instytutu Badawczego w 1972 r.; Memoirs of Polish immigrants in Canada; edited by Benedykt Heydenkorn. Toronto, 1975-77. 2 vols. *(Canadian-Polish Research Institute. Studies. 10, 12)*

POLES IN FOREIGN COUNTRIES.

MURDZEK (BENJAMIN P.) Emigration in Polish social-political thought, 1870-1914. Boulder, Colo., 1977. pp. 396. *bibliog. (East European Quarterly. East European Monographs. 33)*

POLES IN FRANCE.

COLLOQUE DE RECHERCHE HISTORIQUE, PARIS, 1975. La Pologne et la France dans la guerre et la résistance de 1939 à 1945. Paris, Secrétariat d'Etat aux Anciens Combattants, [1978]. pp. 235.

POLES IN GDANSK.

DRZYCIMSKI (ANDRZEJ) Polacy w Wolnym Mieście Gdańsku, 1920-1933: polityka Senatu gdańskiego wobec ludnosci polskiej. Wrocław, 1978. pp. 367. *bibliog.* With English summary.

POLICE

— **Family relationships.**

NIEDERHOFFER (ARTHUR) and NIEDERHOFFER (ELAINE) The police family: from station house to ranch house. Lexington, Mass., [1978]. pp. 220.

— **Canada.**

FIDLER (RICHARD) RCMP: the real subversives. Toronto, [1978]. pp. 91. *bibliog.*

— **Europe.**

FOWLER (NORMAN) After the riots: the police in Europe. London, 1979. pp. 197.

— **Germany.**

SCHWARZE (JOHANNES) Die bayerische Polizei und ihre historische Funktion bei der Aufrechterhaltung der öffentlichen Sicherheit in Bayern von 1919-1933. München, 1977. pp. 292. *bibliog. (Munich. Stadtarchiv. Neue Schriftenreihe. Band 92)*

— **Italy.**

ISMAN (FABIO) I forzati dell'ordine: l'Italia delle molte polizie. Venezia, 1977. pp. 159. *bibliog.*

— **United Kingdom.**

The TECHNOLOGY of political control; by Carol Ackroyd [and others]. Harmondsworth, 1977. pp. 320.

MARK (Sir ROBERT) In the office of constable. London, 1978. pp. 320.

HAIN (PETER) and others. Policing the police. London, 1979 in progress.

TOBIAS (JOHN JACOB) Crime and police in England, 1700-1900. London, 1979. pp. 194.

WHITAKER (BENJAMIN CHARLES GEORGE) The police in society. London, 1979. pp. 351. *bibliog.*

— **United States.**

POLICE accountability: performance measures and unionism; edited by Richard C. Larson. Lexington, Mass., [1978]. pp. 211. *(Innovative Resource Planning in Urban Public Safety Systems. [Publications]. vol. 2)*

REPPETTO (THOMAS A.) The blue parade. New York, 1978. pp. 373. *bibliog.*

SHERMAN (LAWRENCE W.) Scandal and reform: controlling police corruption. Berkeley, Calif., [1978]. pp. 273.

POLICE, POLITICAL AND SECRET

— **Germany.**

MAJEWSKI (RYSZARD) Waffen SS: mity i rzeczywistość. Wrocław, 1977. pp. 302. *bibliog.*

SYDNOR (CHARLES W.) Soldiers of destruction: the SS Death's Head Division, 1933-1945. Princeton, N.J., [1977]. pp. 371. *bibliog.*

GRABER (G.S.) History of the SS. London, 1978. pp. 244.

POLICE POWER

— **United Kingdom.**

U.K. Commission for Racial Equality. 1978. Evidence and recommendations to the Royal Commission on Criminal Procedure. [London], 1978. pp. 48.

U.K. Home Office. 1978. Evidence to the Royal Commission on Criminal Procedure: memorandum no. 4: the law and procedures relating to the detention and treatment of persons in police custody. London, 1978. pp. 51.

U.K. [Home Office]. Metropolitan Police Force. 1978. The Royal Commission on Criminal Procedure:...written evidence of the Commissioner of Police of the Metropolis. London, 1978. 2 pts.

POLICE PSYCHOLOGY.

NIEDERHOFFER (ARTHUR) and NIEDERHOFFER (ELAINE) The police family: from station house to ranch house. Lexington, Mass., [1978]. pp. 220.

POLICE QUESTIONING

— **United Kingdom.**

MORRIS (PAULINE J.) Police interrogation in England and Wales: a critical review of the literature prepared for the Royal Commission on Criminal Procedure. 1978. pp. 82. *bibliog. Photocopy of typescript: unpublished.*

U.K. Home Office. 1978. Evidence to the Royal Commission on Criminal Procedure: memorandum no. 5: the law and procedures relating to the questioning of persons in the investigation of crime. London, 1978. pp. 74.

U.K. Home Office. Circulars. No. 89/1978. Judges' rules and administrative directions to the police. 2nd ed. London, 1978. pp. 11.

POLICE SERVICES FOR JUVENILES

— **Belgium.**

POTVIN (JEAN PAUL) and TISSEYRE (CHARLES) La police vue par les jeunes. Bruxelles, 1978. pp. 315. *bibliog. (Centre d'Etude de la Délinquance Juvénile. Publications. No. 42)*

POLICY SCIENCES.

HOFFERBERT (RICHARD I.) The study of public policy. Indianapolis, [1974]. pp. 275.

RAHMAN (MOHAMED AL-UDEID ABDEL) Public administration as an applied off-shoot of social sciences. Khartoum, 1974. fo. 26. *(Economic and Social Research Council [Sudan]. Bulletins. No. 8)*

HOOD (CHRISTOPHER C.) The limits of administration. London, [1976]. pp. 213.

ANDERSON (JAMES E.) and others. Public policy and politics in America. North Scituate, [1978]. pp. 434. *bibliogs.*

BATTY (MICHAEL) Paradoxes of science in public policy: the baffling case of land use models. Reading, 1978. pp. 34. *bibliog. (Reading. University. Department of Geography. Reading Geographical Papers. No. 69)*

CALABRESI (GUIDO) and BOBBITT (PHILIP) Tragic choices. New York, [1978]. pp. 252. *bibliog.*

COMPARING public policies: new concepts and methods; Douglas E. Ashford, editor. Beverly Hills, [1978]. pp. 254. *bibliogs.*

EDMUNDS (STAHRL) Alternative U.S. futures: a policy analysis of individual choices in a political economy. Santa Monica, [1978]. pp. 217. *bibliog.*

JENKINS (W.I.) Policy analysis: a political and organizational perspective. New York, 1978. pp. 278. *bibliog.*

NATIONALIZING government public policies in America; Theodore J. Lowi, Alan Stone, editors. Beverly Hills, [1978]. pp. 454.

POLICY research; edited by Amitai Etzioni. Leiden, 1978. pp. 171. *bibliogs.*

PUBLIC goods and public policy; edited by William Loehr and Todd Sandler. Beverly Hills, [1978]. pp. 240. *bibliogs.*

SCHELLING (THOMAS CROMBIE) Micromotives and macrobehavior. New York, [1978]. pp. 252. *(Pennsylvania University. Fels Center of Government. Fels Lectures on Public Policy Analysis)*

STRAUSSMAN (JEFFREY D.) The limits of technocratic politics. New Brunswick, [1978]. pp. 164. *bibliog.*

CHANDLER (MARSHA) and CHANDLER (WILLIAM M.) Public policy and provincial politics. Toronto, [1979]. pp.325. *bibliog.*

CHERNS (ALBERT B.) Using the social sciences. London, 1979. pp. 502. *bibliog.*

NACHMIAS (DAVID) Public policy evaluation: approaches and methods. New York, [1979]. pp. 195. *bibliog.*

NAGEL (STUART S.) and NEEF (MARIAN) Policy analysis in social science research. Beverly Hills, [1979]. pp. 240. *bibliog.*

RHODES (R.A.W.) Public administration and policy analysis: recent developments in Britain and America. Farnborough, [1979]. pp. 122.

— **Mathematical models.**

GEARY (K.) Treatment of multiple objectives for programming problems: a review with reference to possible public sector application. London, 1978. pp. 25. *bibliog. (Planning Research Applications Group. PRAG Technical Papers. TP 25)*

— **Study and teaching.**

LETWIN (WILLIAM) On the study of public policy. London, 1979. pp. 33. *Inaugural lecture delivered at the London School of Economics on 16 February 1978.*

POLISH AMERICANS.

BAKER (T. LINDSAY) The first Polish Americans: Silesian settlements in Texas. College Station, 1979. pp. 268. *bibliog.*

POLISH AMERICANS.(Cont.)

WROBEL (PAUL) Our way: family, parish, and neighborhood in a Polish-American community. Notre Dame, Ind., [1979]. pp. 192.

POLISH LITERATURE

— History and criticism.

TSYBENKO (ELENA ZAKHAROVNA) Iz istorii pol'sko-russkikh literaturnykh sviazei XIX-XX vv. Moskva, 1978. pp. 280.

POLITICAL CRIMES AND OFFENCES.

PEARSON (GEOFFREY) The deviant imagination: psychiatry, social work and social change. London, 1975. pp. 258. *bibliog.*

— Italy.

PROCESSI politici del Senato Lombardo-Veneto, 1815-1851; a cura di Alfredo Grandi. Roma, 1976. pp. 780. *(Istituto per la Storia del Risorgimento Italiano. Pubblicazioni. 2a Serie. Fonti. vol. 67)*

— United States.

ROEBUCK (JULIAN B.) and WEEBER (STANLEY C.) Political crime in the United States: analyzing crime by and against government. New York, [1978]. pp. 244. *bibliog.*

POLITICAL ETHICS.

PUBLIC and private morality; edited by Stuart Hampshire. Cambridge, 1978. pp. 143.

POLITICAL ORATORY

— France.

LABBE (DOMINIQUE) Le discours communiste. [Paris, 1977]. pp. 204.

POLITICAL PARTICIPATION.

JELFS (MARTIN) Manual for action: (techniques to enable groups engaged in action for change to increase their effectiveness). London, [1977]. 1 vol. (various pagings). *bibliog. Prepared for Action Resources Group.*

FISCHER (GEORGE) Ways to self rule: beyond Marxism and anarchism. New York, [1978]. pp. 244. *bibliog.*

SCHECTER (STEPHEN BENJAMIN) The politics of urban liberation. Montreal, [1978]. pp. 203. *bibliogs.*

VERBA (SIDNEY) and others. Participation and political equality: a seven-nation comparison. Cambridge, 1978. pp. 394. *bibliog.*

— America, Latin.

POLITICAL participation in Latin America;...edited by John A. Booth and Mitchell A. Seligson. New York, 1978-79. 2 vols. *bibliog.*

— Botswana.

A COMPARATIVE study of political involvement in three African states: Botswana, Ghana and Kenya; by John D. Holm [and others]. Syracuse, N.Y., 1978. pp. 141. *(Syracuse University. Maxwell Graduate School of Citizenship and Public Affairs. Foreign and Comparative Studies. African Series. 30)*

— China.

RADDOCK (DAVID M.) Political behavior of adolescents in China: the Cultural Revolution in Kwangchow. Tucson, [1977]. pp. 242. *bibliog. (Association for Asian Studies. Monographs. 32)*

— Germany.

CONRADT (DAVID P.) The German polity. New York, [1978]. pp. 235. *bibliog.*

— Ghana.

A COMPARATIVE study of political involvement in three African states: Botswana, Ghana and Kenya; by John D. Holm [and others]. Syracuse, N.Y., 1978. pp. 141. *(Syracuse University. Maxwell Graduate School of Citizenship and Public Affairs. Foreign and Comparative Studies. African Series. 30)*

— India.

CHRISTIAN participation in nation-building: the summing up of a corporate study on rapid social change; compiled y M. M. Thomas. Bangalore, 1960. pp. 325. *bibliog.*

— Italy.

CHITI (MARIO P.) Partecipazione popolare e pubblica amministrazione. Pisa, 1977. pp. 497. *(Pisa. Università. Istituto Giuridico. Collana. 3)*

— Jamaica.

BROWN (AGGREY) Color, class, and politics in Jamaica. New Brunswick, N.J., [1979]. pp. 172. *bibliog.*

— Kenya.

A COMPARATIVE study of political involvement in three African states: Botswana, Ghana and Kenya; by John D. Holm [and others]. Syracuse, N.Y., 1978. pp. 141. *(Syracuse University. Maxwell Graduate School of Citizenship and Public Affairs. Foreign and Comparative Studies. African Series. 30)*

— Russia.

ADAMS (JAN S.) Citizen inspectors in the Soviet Union: the People's Control Committee. New York, 1977. pp. 232. *bibliog.*

— United States.

COBB (ROGER W.) and ELDER (CHARLES D.) Participation in American politics: the dynamics of agenda-building. Baltimore, 1977. pp. 182. *bibliog.*

ANTICIPATORY democracy: people in the politics of the future; edited by Clement Bezold. New York, [1978]. pp. 405. *bibliog.*

GOLDENBERG (I. IRA) Oppression and social intervention: essays on the human condition and the problems of change. Chicago, [1978]. pp. 213. *bibliog.*

WELLSTONE (PAUL DAVID) How the rural poor got power: narrative of a grass-roots organizer. Amherst, Mass., 1978. pp. 227.

JEFFRIES (JOHN W.) Testing the Roosevelt coalition: Connecticut society and politics in the era of World War II. Knoxville, [1979]. pp. 312.

POLITICAL PARTIES.

FACTION politics: political parties and factionalism in comparative perspective; Frank P. Belloni [and] Dennis C. Beller, editors. Santa Barbara, [1978]. pp. 471. *bibliogs.*

POLITICAL parties: development and decay; edited by Louis Maisel and Joseph Cooper. Beverly Hills, [1978]. pp. 344. *bibliogs.*

— Africa.

BIENEN (HENRY) Armies and parties in Africa. New York, [1978]. pp. 278. *bibliogs.*

— Argentine Republic.

CIRIA (ALBERTO) Partidos y poder en la Argentina moderna, 1930-1946. 3rd ed. Buenos Aires, 1975. pp. 414. *bibliog.*

— Canada.

CANADIAN provincial politics: the party systems of the ten provinces...; edited by Martin Robin. 2nd ed. Scarborough, Ont., [1978]. pp. 316. *bibliogs.*

— Czechoslovakia.

See also **NÁRODNÍ STRANA SVOBODOMYSLNÁ.**

— Dutch Guiana.

DEW (EDWARD) The difficult flowering of Surinam: ethnicity and politics in a plural society. The Hague, 1978. pp. 234. *bibliog.*

— Europe.

SEILER (DANIEL L.) Les partis politiques en Europe. [Paris, 1978]. pp. 128. *bibliog.*

— Europe, Eastern.

HOFMANN (HEINZ) Mehrparteiensystem ohne Opposition: die nichtkommunistischen Partein in der DDR, Polen, der Tschechoslowakei und Bulgarien. Bern, 1976. pp. 130. *bibliog.*

— European Economic Community countries.

POLITICAL parties in the European community; edited by Stanley Henig. London, 1979. pp. 314. *bibliogs.*

— France.

CHARLOT (JEAN) Les partis politiques en France. [Paris], Ministère des Affaires Etrangères, Service d'Information et de Presse, [1978]. pp. 62. *bibliog.*

HAUSS (CHARLES) The new left in France: the Unified Socialist Party. Westport, Conn., 1978. pp. 283. *bibliog.*

— Germany.

PARTEIPROGRAMME; herausgegeben und erläutert von Ingomar Reinartz. München, 1976 repr.1979. pp. 285.

MUELLER (TERESA) Die Haltung der Parteien zu den Problemen von Strafe und Strafvollzug. Frankfurt am Main, [1977]. pp. 355. *bibliog.*

CONRADT (DAVID P.) The German polity. New York, [1978]. pp. 235. *bibliog.*

EINHEIT der Nation: Diskussionen und Konzeptionen zur Deutschlandpolitik der grossen Parteien seit 1945; ([by] Wolfgang Benz [and others]). Stuttgart-Bad Cannstatt, [1978]. pp. 399. *bibliog.*

LUDEWIG (HANS ULRICH) Arbeiterbewegung und Aufstand: eine Untersuchung zum Verhalten der Arbeiterparteien in den Aufstandsbewegungen der frühen Weimarer Republik, 1920-1923. Husum, [1978]. pp. 267. *bibliog.*

— — Ruhr.

PIETSCH (HARTMUT) Militärregierung, Bürokratie und Sozialisierung: zur Entwicklung des politischen Systems in den Städten des Ruhrgebietes, 1945 bis 1948. Duisburg, 1978. pp. 358. *bibliog. (Duisburg. Stadtarchiv. Duisburger Forschungen. Band 26)*

— India.

PROBLEMS of Indian democracy; by P.J. Alexander [and others]; edited by P.D. Devanandan [and] M.M. Thomas). [Bangalore], 1962. pp. 211. *bibliogs. (Christian Institute for the Study of Religion and Society. Social Concerns Series. No. 10)*

The COALITION government: a critical examination of the concept of coalition, the performance of some coalition governments and the future prospects of coalition in India; by Omprakash Deepak [and others]; edited by Saral K. Chatterji. Madras, 1974. pp. 145.

PANTHAM (THOMAS) Political parties and democratic consensus: a study of party organisations in an Indian city. Delhi, 1976. pp. 215. *bibliogs.*

— — Uttar Pradesh.

U.P. politics and elections; by B. Jhunjhunwala [and others] Bangalore, 1974. pp. 99. *Special issue of 'Religion and Society', vol. 21, no. 2, June 1974.*

— Netherlands.

GRIBLING (J.P.) Willem Hubert Nolens, 1860-1931: uit het leven van een priester-staatsman. Assen, 1978. pp. 377. *With German and French summaries.*

— Sardinia.

MANCONI (FRANCESCO) and others. Storia dei partiti popolari in Sardegna, 1890-1926; a cura di Luigi Berlinguer. Roma, 1977. pp. 462.

— Scandinavia.

BERGLUND (STEN) and LINDSTRÖM (ULF) The Scandinavian party system(s): a comparative study. Lund, [1978]. pp. 202. *bibliog.*

— Spain.

RAMIREZ (PEDRO J.) Asi se ganaron las elecciones. Barcelona, 1977. pp. 372.

— United Kingdom.

HANHAM (HAROLD JOHN) Elections and party management: politics in the time of Disraeli and Gladstone. new ed. Hassocks, [1978]. pp. 468. *bibliog.*

SACK (JAMES J.) The Grenvillites, 1801-29: party politics and factionalism in the age of Pitt and Liverpool. Urbana, [1979]. pp. 244. *bibliog.*

— United States.

EMERGING coalitions in American politics; [by] Jack Bass [and others]; Seymour Martin Lipset, editor. San Francisco, 1978. pp. 524. *bibliog.*

LADD (EVERETT CARLL) Where have all the voters gone?: the fracturing of America's political parties. New York, [1978]. pp. 86.

LIPSET (SEYMOUR MARTIN) and RAAB (EARL) The politics of unreason: right-wing extremism in America, 1790- 1977. 2nd ed. Chicago, [1978]. pp. 581.

PARTIES and elections in an anti-party age: American politics and the crisis of confidence; edited with an introduction by Jeff Fishel. Bloomington, [1978]. pp. 350.

VOPROSY metodologii i istorii istoricheskoi nauki. vyp.2. Moskva, 1978. pp. 206.

WILLIAMS (R. HAL) Years of decision: American politics in the 1890s. New York, [1978]. pp. 219. *bibliog.*

— — Maryland.

RISJORD (NORMAN K.) Chesapeake politics 1781-1800. New York, 1978. pp. 715. *bibliog.*

— — States.

RISJORD (NORMAN K.) Chesapeake politics 1781-1800. New York, 1978. pp. 715. *bibliog.*

POLITICAL PRISONERS

— Chile.

CHILE COMMITTEE FOR HUMAN RIGHTS. Chile's secret prisoners. London, [1977]. pp. 40.

— Guatemala.

AMNESTY INTERNATIONAL. Schweizer Sektion. Situation in Guatemala. Bern, [1973?]. pp. 27. *bibliog.*

— Morocco.

AMNESTY INTERNATIONAL. Briefing Papers. No.13. Morocco. [London], 1977. pp. 15.

— Peru.

SEOANE CORRALES (JUAN) Hombres y rejas. [Lima], 1977. pp. 293.

— Russia.

SSYLKA i obshchestvenno-politicheskaia zhizn' v Sibiri, XVIII - nachalo XX v. Novosibirsk, 1978. pp. 332.

— — Personal narratives.

SHAVISHVILI (FEDOR AMBAKOVICH) Tsarskaia katorga: vospominaniia byvshego politkatorzhanina; perevod s gruzinskogo N. Mikava. Tbilisi, 1977. pp. 198.

— Singapore.

AMNESTY INTERNATIONAL. Briefing Papers. No.1. Singapore. 2nd ed. [London], 1978. pp. 12.

— South Africa.

DESAI (BARNEY) and MARNEY (CARDIFF) The killing of the Imam. London, 1978. pp. 146.

POLITICAL PSYCHOLOGY.

THEWELEIT (KLAUS) Männerphantasien. Frankfurt am Main, 1977-78. 2 vols. *bibliog.*

JUDGEMENT and decision in public policy formation; eited by Kenneth R. Hammond. Boulder, Colo., [1978]. pp. 175. *bibliog. (American Association for the Adavancement of Science. Selected Symposia Series. 1)*

POLITICAL SATIRE, AMERICAN.

McCARTHY (EUGENE J.) and KILPATRICK (JAMES JACKSON) A political bestiary: viable alternatives, impressive mandates, and other fables; illustrated by Jeff MacNelly. New York, 1978. pp. 90.

POLITICAL SCIENCE.

MURRAY (ALEXANDER RAINY MACLEAN) An introduction to political philosophy. London, 1953. pp. 240.

HUNTINGTON (SAMUEL PHILLIPS) Political order in changing societies. New Haven, [1968]. pp. 488.

FEINBERG (JOEL) Social philosophy. Englewood Cliffs, [1973]. pp. 126. *bibliog.*

FITZGERALD (ROSS) ed. Human needs and politics. Rushcutters Bay, N.S.W., [1977]. pp. 278. *bibliog.*

ROSE (RICHARD) Governing and ungovernability: a sceptical inquiry. Glasgow, [1977]. pp. 29. *(Glasgow. University of Strathclyde. Centre for the Study of Public Policy. Studies in Public Policy. No. 1)*

ROSE (RICHARD) and PETERS (B. GUY) The political consequences of economic overload: on the possibility of political bankruptcy. Glasgow, 1977. pp. 27,5. *bibliog. (Glasgow. University of Strathclyde. Centre for the Study of Public Policy. Studies in Public Policy. No. 4)*

SECONDAT (CHARLES LOUIS DE) Baron de Montesquieu. The spirit of laws:...a compendium of the first English edition; edited...by David Wallace Carrithers; together with an English translation of An essay on causes affecting minds and characters, 1736-1743. Berkeley, [1977]. pp. 479.

WIKSE (JOHN R.) About possession: the self as private property. University Park, Pa., [1977]. pp. 169. *bibliog.*

ARON (RAYMOND) Politics and history: selected essays...; collected, translated, and edited by Miriam Bernheim Conant. New York, [1978]. pp. 274.

LINKLATER (ANDREW) Obligations beyond the state: the individual, the state and humanity in international theory. 1977 [or rather 1978]. fo. 334. *bibliog. Typescript. Ph.D. (London) thesis: unpublished. This thesis is the property of London University and may not be removed from the Library.*

LIVELY (JACK) and REES (JOHN COLLWYN) eds. Utilitarian logic and politics: James Mill's Essay on government, Macaulay's critique and the ensuing debate. Oxford, 1978. pp. 270.

MACKENZIE (WILLIAM JAMES MILLAR) Biological ideas in politics: an essay on political adaptivity. Harmondsworth, 1978. pp. 93. *(Auckland. University. Sir Douglas Robb Lectures. 1975)*

MILL (JOHN STUART) Collected works of John Stuart Mill. vol.10. Essays on philosophy and the classics; editor of the text J.M. Robson; introduction by F.E. Sparshott. Toronto, [1978]. pp. 578. *bibliog.*

WOOD (ELLEN MEIKSINS) and WOOD (NEAL) Class ideology and ancient political theory: Socrates, Plato and Aristotle in social context. Oxford, 1978. pp. 275. *bibliog.*

WORMUTH (FRANCIS DUNHAM) Essays in law and politics; edited by Dalmas H. Nelson and Richard L. Sklar. Port Washington, N.Y., 1978. pp. 274. *bibliog.*

CADART (JACQUES) Institutions politiques et droit constitutionnel. 2nd ed. Paris, 1979 in progress.

CASSIRER (ERNST) Symbol, myth, and culture: essays and lectures of Ernst Cassirer, 1935-1945; edited by Donald Phillip Verene. New Haven, 1979. pp. 304.

PHILOSOPHY, politics and society: fifth series; a collection edited by Peter Laslett and James Fishkin. Oxford, 1979. pp. 312.

POLITICAL anthropology: the state of the art; editors S. Lee Seaton, Henri J.M. Claessen. The Hague, [1979]. pp. 411. *bibliogs.*

WALFORD (GEORGE W.) Ideologies and their functions: a study in systematic ideology. London, 1979. pp. 163.

— Decision making.

STEINBRUNER (JOHN D.) The cybernetic theory of decision: new dimensions of political analysis. Princeton, N.J. [1974]. pp. 366. *bibliog.*

INTERNATIONAL CONFERENCE ON SYSTEMS MODELLING IN DEVELOPING COUNTRIES, BANGKOK, 1978. Systems models for decision making; edited by Nawaz Sharif, Pakorn Adulbhan. Bangkok, 1978. pp. 433. *bibliogs.*

— Dictionaries and encyclopedias.

BECK (REINHART) Sachwörterbuch der Politik. Stuttgart, [1977]. pp. 1003.

— History.

SABINE (GEORGE HOLLAND) A history of political theory; revised by Thomas Landon Thorson. 4th ed. Hinsdale, Ill., [1973]. pp. 871. *bibliogs.*

PER una storia del moderno concetto di politica: genesi e sviluppo della separazione tra "politico" e "sociale"; [by] A. Biral [and others]. Padova, 1977. pp. 331.

BENDIX (REINHARD) Kings or people: power and the mandate to rule. Berkeley, 1978. pp. 692.

SEGRE (D.V.) Jewish political thought and contemporary politics. [Ramat-Gan, 1978?]. fo.21,3. *(Bar-Ilan University. Department of Political Studies and Center for Jewish Community Studies. Workshop in the Covenant Idea and the Jewish Political Tradition. Working Papers. No. 3)*

SKINNER (QUENTIN) The foundations of modern political thought. Cambridge, 1978. 2 vols. *bibliog.*

BARADAT (LEON P.) Political ideologies: their origins and impact. Englewood Cliffs, 1979. pp. 337. *bibliog.*

— — Sources.

BRAMSTED (ERNEST KOHN) and MELHUISH (K.J.) eds. Western liberalism: a history in documents from Locke to Croce. London, 1978. pp. 810.

— — Europe.

DUNN (JOHN) Western political theory in the face of the future. Cambridge, 1979. pp. 120.

— — France.

RIALS (STEPHANE) Les idées politiques du Président Georges Pompidou. Paris, [1977]. pp. 192. *bibliog. (Paris. Université de Paris II. Travaux et Recherches. Série Science Politique. 9)*

— — Germany.

SONTHEIMER (KURT) Antidemokratisches Denken in der Weimarer Republik: die politischen Ideen des deutschen Nationalismus zwischen 1918 und 1933. München, 1978. pp. 331. *bibliog.*

POLITICAL SCIENCE.(Cont.)

— — India.

The EVOLUTION of Muslim political thought in India...; [edited by] A.M. Zaidi. New Delhi, 1975 in progress.

— — Italy.

The EARTHLY republic: Italian humanists on government and society; edited by Benjamin G. Kohl and Ronald G. Witt. Manchester, [1978]. pp. 337. *bibliog.*

— — Russia.

OBSHCHESTVENNO-politicheskaia mysl' v Povolzh'e v XIX - nachale XX vv. Kazan', 1977. pp. 272.

VOLODIN (ALEKSANDR IVANOVICH) "Anti-Diuring" F.Engel'sa i obshchestvennaia mysl' Rossii XIX veka: istoriko-filosofskie ocherki. Moskva, 1978. pp. 252.

— — — Latvia.

MILLER (VISVARIS OTTOVICH) and MEL'KISIS (EDGAR ADAMOVICH) Politikopravovye vzgliady Garliba Merkelia. Moskva, 1977. pp. 160.

— — United Kingdom.

BARKER (RODNEY STEVEN) Political ideas in modern Britain. London, 1978. pp. 246. *bibliog.*

CLARKE (PETER) 1942- . Liberals and social democrats. Cambridge, 1978. pp. 344. *bibliog.*

LEMOS (RAMON M.) Hobbes and Locke: power and consent. Athens, [1978]. pp. 185.

MACKLEM (MICHAEL) Liberty and the Holy City: the idea of freedom in English history. [Ottawa, 1978]. pp. 210.

PARRY (GERAINT BURTON) John Locke. London, 1978. pp. 171. *bibliog.*

DALY (JAMES) Sir Robert Filmer and English political thought. Toronto, [1979]. pp. 212. *bibliog.*

— — United States.

COFFEY (JOHN W.) Political realism in American thought. Lewisburg, [1977]. pp. 217. *bibliog.*

FOWLER (ROBERT BOOTH) Believing skeptics: American political intellectuals, 1945-1964. Westport, 1978. pp. 317. *bibliog.*

KONVITZ (MILTON RIDVAS) Judaism and the American idea. Ithaca, 1978. pp. 223. *bibliog.*

SCHUMAN (DAVID) The ideology of form: the influence of organizations in America. Lexington, Mass., [1978]. pp. 196.

— Mathematical models.

GAME theory and political science; edited by Peter C. Ordeshook. New York, 1978. pp. 627. *bibliogs. Papers based on a Mathematical Social Science Board sponsored Conference on Game Theory and Political Science, Hyannis, 1977.*

— Methodology.

DANFORD (JOHN W.) Wittgenstein and political philosophy: a reexamination of the foundations of social science. Chicago, [1978]. pp. 265. *bibliog.*

GAME theory and political science; edited by Peter C. Ordeshook. New York, 1978. pp. 627. *bibliogs. Papers based on a Mathematical Social Science Board sponsored Conference on Game Theory and Political Science, Hyannis, 1977.*

POLITICAL SOCIOLOGY.

HUNTINGTON (SAMUEL PHILLIPS) Political order in changing societies. New Haven, [1968]. pp. 488.

Les DOMINATIONS socio-politiques dans le monde, [by] Michel Rocard [and others]. Paris, [1975]. pp. 147. *bibliog. (Institut Oecuménique pour le Développement des Peuples. Cahiers. 2)*

BLONDEL (JEAN) 1929- . Voters, parties, and leaders: the social fabric of British politics. rev. ed. Harmondsworth, [1977]. pp. 271. *bibliog.*

FRIENDS, followers, and factions: a reader in political clientelism; edited by Steffen W. Schmidt [and others]. Berkley, [1977]. pp. 512. *bibliogs.*

MICHELAT (GUY) and SIMON (MICHEL) Classe, religion et comportement politique. Paris, [1977]. pp. 498.

BOTTOMORE (THOMAS BURTON) Political sociology. London, 1979. pp. 176. *bibliog.*

POLITICIANS

— France.

LECOMTE (BERNARD) and SAUVAGE (CHRISTIAN) Les Giscardiens. [Paris, 1978]. pp. 217.

— United States — Georgia.

WATTS (EUGENE J.) The social bases of city politics: Atlanta, 1865-1903. Westport, Conn., 1978. pp. 188. *bibliog.*

POLITICS AND EDUCATION

— United States.

BRESNICK (DAVID) and others. Black white green red: the politics of education in ethnic America. New York, [1978]. pp. 166. *bibliog.*

POLITICS AND LITERATURE.

BUTT (JOHN) Writer on Spanish literature. Writers and politics in modern Spain. London, 1978. pp. 76. *bibliog.*

POLITICS IN MOVING PICTURES.

SARRIS (ANDREW) Politics and cinema. New York, 1978. pp. 215.

POLLUTION.

MAN and the ecosphere. San Francisco, 1971. pp. 307. *bibliog. Readings from Scientific American.*

HOLDGATE (M.W.) A perspective of environmental pollution. Cambridge, 1979. pp. 278. *bibliog.*

— Economic aspects.

ENVIRONMENTAL improvement through economic incentives; [by] Frederick R. Anderson [and others]. Baltimore, [1977]. pp. 195. *A joint project of Resources for the Future and the Environmental Law Institute.*

FRIENDS OF THE EARTH. Progress as if survival mattered: a handbook for a conserver society, by Friends of the Earth; edited by Hugh Nash. San Francisco, [1977]. pp. 319. *bibliog.*

ORGANISATION FOR ECONOMIC CO-OPERATION AND DEVELOPMENT. Environment Directorate. 1977. Pollution control costs in the primary aluminium industry. Paris, 1977. pp. 151. *bibliog.*

MILLS (EDWIN S.) The economics of environmental quality. New York, [1978]. pp. 304. *bibliogs.*

ATKINS (M.H.) and LOWE (J.F.) The economics of pollution control in the non-ferrous metals industry. Oxford, [1979]. pp. 177.

— — Mathematical models.

COUPE (BERNARD EDDY MARIE GHISLAIN) Regional economic structure and environmental pollution: an application of interregional models. Leiden, 1977. pp. 166. *bibliog.*

— — Netherlands.

NETHERLANDS. Centraal Planbureau. 1977. Economic consequences of pollution control. The Hague, 1977. pp. 142. *(Monografieën. No. 20a)*

— — United States.

CURRENT issues in U.S. environmental policy; [edited by] Paul R. Portney. Baltimore, [1978]. pp. 207.

— — — Illinois.

CARIS (SUSAN) Community attitudes toward pollution. Chicago, Ill., 1978. pp. 211. *bibliog. (Chicago. University. Department of Geography. Research Papers. No. 188)*

— Law and legislation.

ENLOE (CYNTHIA H.) The politics of pollution in a comparative perspective: ecology and power in four nations. New York, [1975]. pp. 342.

ENVIRONMENTAL pollution and individual rights: an international symposium; edited by Stephen C. McCaffrey...and Robert E. Lutz. Deventer, 1978. pp. 213. *Four tables in pocket.*

— United Kingdom.

NORTHERN REGION STRATEGY TEAM. Pollution and dereliction in the Northern Region. Newcastle-upon-Tyne, 1976. fo. (102). *(Technical Reports. No. 18)*

U.K. Department of the Environment. Digest of environmental pollution statistics. a., 1978(no.1)- London.

MACRORY (RICHARD BRABAZON) and ZABA (B.) The Control of Pollution Act explained. London, 1978. pp. 87. *bibliog. (Friends of the Earth. FOE Publications)*

U.K. Central Unit on Environmental Pollution, 1978. Pollution control in Great Britain: how it works: a review of legislative and administrative procedures. 2nd ed. London, 1978. pp. 107. *bibliog. (Pollution Papers. No.9)*

POLSKI KOMITET WYZWOLENIA NARODWEGO.

SCAEVOLA, pseud. A study in forgery: (the Lublin Committee and its rule over Poland). London, [1945]. pp. 123.

POMPIDOU (GEORGES).

RIALS (STEPHANE) Les idées politiques du Président Georges Pompidou. Paris, [1977]. pp. 192. *bibliog. (Paris. Université de Paris II. Travaux et Recherches. Série Science Politique. 9)*

PONDICHERRY

— Population.

INDIA. Census, 1971. Series 30. Portrait of population: Pondicherry; [by] K. Chockalingam. [Delhi, 1978]. pp. 185.

POOR.

HARRINGTON (MICHAEL) b. 1928. The vast majority: a journey to the world's poor. New York, [1977]. pp. 281. *bibliog.*

— America, Latin.

POLITICAL participation in Latin America;...edited by John A. Booth and Mitchell A. Seligson. New York, 1978-79. 2 vols. *bibliog.*

— Australia.

LIFELONG education and poor people: three studies. Canberra, 1976. pp. 71. *bibliog. (Australia. Commission of Inquiry into Poverty. Poverty and Education Series)*

PODDER (NRIPESH) The economic circumstances of the poor. Canberra, 1978. pp. 81. *(Australia. Commission of Inquiry into Poverty. Consumers and Clients Series)*

— — Victoria.

FITZGERALD (JEFFREY M.) Poverty and the legal profession in Victoria. Canberra, 1977. pp. 72. *(Australia. Commission of Inquiry into Poverty. Law and Poverty Series)*

— Bangladesh.

OSMANI (SIDDIQUR RAHMAN) Economic inequality and group welfare: theory and application to Bangladesh. 1978. fo. 329. *bibliog. Typescript. Ph.D. (London) thesis: unpublished. This thesis is the property of London University and may not be removed from the Library.*

— Brazil.

MATA (MILTON DA) Concentração de renda, desemprego e pobreza no Brasil. Rio de Janeiro, 1979. pp. 161. *bibliog. (Brazil. Instituto de Planejamento Econômico e Social. Instituto de Pesquisas. Relatorios de Pesquisa. No. 41)*

— Canada.

CLARK (SAMUEL DELBERT) The new urban poor. Toronto, [1978]. pp. 169.

— Europe.

LIS (CATHARINA) and SOLY (HUGO) Poverty and capitalism in pre-industrial Europe. Hassocks, 1979. pp. 267. *bibliog.*

— India.

CHAUDHURI (PRAMIT) The Indian economy: poverty and development. London, 1978. pp. 279. *bibliog.*

— Israel.

DORON (ABRAHAM) and ROTER (RAPHAEL) Low wage earners and low wage subsidies. Jerusalem, Hebrew University Paul Baerwald School of Social Work and National Insurance Institute, Bureau of Research and Planning, 1978. pp. 217. *bibliog. First published in Hebrew in 1976.*

— Italy — Naples.

BELMONTE (THOMAS) The broken fountain. New York, 1979. pp. 151.

— Netherlands.

FISELIER (A.A.M.) and KRAFT (H.L.P.R.) Laagstgeklasseerden in Nederland: een beschrijvend onderzoek naar omvang en spreiding van lage inkomens bij diverse typen huishoudens, gerelateerd aan een beperkt aantal relevante variabelen. 's-Gravenhage, 1979. pp. 139. *bibliog. (Netherlands. Centraal Bureau voor de Statistiek. Monografieën Volkstelling 1971. 5) With English summary.*

— United Kingdom.

WEDGE (PETER) and PROSSER (HILARY) Born to fail? London, 1973 repr. 1977. pp. 64.

The CAUSES of poverty; by R.Layard [and others];... background paper to Report No.6: lower incomes. London, 1978. pp. 190. *bibliog. (U.K. Royal Commission on the Distribution of Income and Wealth, 1974. Background Papers. No.5) Report No.6 published as British Parliamentary Paper Cmnd. 7175, Session 1977-78.*

NORTH TYNESIDE COMMUNITY DEVELOPMENT PROJECT. In and out of work: a study of unemployment, low pay and income maintenance services. [Newcastle-upon-Tyne], 1978. pp. 287.

LAWLESS (PAUL) Urban deprivation and government initiative. London, 1979. pp. 251. *bibliog.*

TREBLE (JAMES H.) Urban poverty in Britain 1830-1914. London, 1979. pp. 216.

— — Ireland, Northern.

EVASON (EILEEN) Family poverty in Northern Ireland. London, 1978. pp. 36. *(Child Poverty Action Group. Poverty Research Series. 6)*

— United States.

GRØNBJERG (KIRSTEN A.) and others. Poverty and social change. Chicago, [1978]. pp. 248. *bibliog.*

OSTER (SHARON M.) and others. The definition and measurement of poverty. Boulder, Colo., 1978. 2 vols. *bibliog.*

TREND (M.G.) Housing allowances for the poor: a social experiment. Boulder, Colo., [1978]. pp. 369. *bibliog.*

— — Bibliography.

OSTER (SHARON M.) and others. The definition and measurement of poverty. Boulder, Colo., 1978. 2 vols. *bibliog.*

— — Michigan.

CARTER (REGINALD) and NELL (CATHY) Family planning services provided to AFDC recipients in Michigan, January-June 1974. [Lansing], 1975. pp. 92. *bibliog. (Michigan. Department of Social Services. Studies in Welfare Policy. No. 6)*

SMITH (VERNON K.) and HOWITT (GARY A.) The economic status of Michigan AFDC families: an analysis of income and benefit receipt. [Lansing], 1976. pp. 54. *(Michigan. Department of Social Services. Studies in Welfare Policy. No. 8)*

POOR AS CONSUMERS

— United Kingdom.

NATIONAL CONSUMER COUNCIL. Means tests in local authority social services: who needs them?; discussion paper based on the report of a workshop. London, 1978. pp. 31.

RICHARDSON (PAUL) Fuel poverty: a study of fuel expenditure among low income council tenants. [York], 1978. pp. 56. *(Papers in Community Studies. No. 20)*

POOR FAMILY.

McGOVERN (JAMES R.) Yankee family. New Orleans, 1975. pp. 191.

POOR LAWS

— United Kingdom.

COWHERD (RAYMOND GIBSON) Political economists and the English Poor Laws: a historical study of the influence of classical economics on the formation of social welfare policy. Athens, Ohio, [1977]. pp. 300. *bibliog.*

STEWART (PATRICIA) Poor law administration at Abingdon, Berkshire, before 1834. 1978. fo. 154. *bibliog. Typescript. M.Sc. (Econ.) (London) thesis: unpublished. This thesis is the property of London University and may not be removed from the Library.*

POPLAR

— Politics and government.

BRANSON (NOREEN) Poplarism, 1919-1925: George Lansbury and the councillors' revolt. London, 1979. pp. 242.

POPPER (Sir KARL RAIMUND).

JOHANSSON (INGVAR) A critique of Karl Popper's methodology. Stockholm, [1975]. pp. 210. *bibliog.*

CURRIE (GREGORY PAUL) The objectivism of Frege and Popper: an historical and critical investigation. 1978. fo. 294. *bibliog. Typescript. Ph.D. (London) thesis: unpublished. This thesis is the property of London University and may not be removed from the Library.*

WILKINS (BURLEIGH TAYLOR) Has history any meaning: a critique of Popper's philosophy of history. Hassocks, [1978]. pp. 251.

POPPER-LYNKEUS (JOSEF).

BELKE (INGRID) Die sozialreformerischen Ideen von Josef Popper-Lynkeus, 1838-1921, im Zusammenhang mit allgemeinen Reformbestrebungen des Wiener Bürgertums um die Jahrhundertwende. Tübingen, 1978. pp. 296. *bibliog.*

POPULAR CULTURE.

CHANEY (DAVID C.) Fictions and ceremonies: representations of popular experience. London, 1979. pp. 156. *bibliog.*

POPULAR FRONTS.

BERG (CHARLES) Communist and JUST (STEPHANE) Fronts populaires d'hier et d'aujourd'hui. [Paris, 1977]. pp. 445.

INTERNATIONALE TAGUNG DER HISTORIKER DER ARBEITERBEWEGUNG, 1975. Einheits- und Volksfrontpolitik, 1935-1939; Klassenkampf und nationale Frage zur Zeit der II. Internationale; (bearbeitet von Hans Hautmann). Wien, 1978. pp. 335. *(Internationale Tagung der Historiker der Arbeiterbewegung. ITH-Tagungsberichte. Band 10)*

BLANK (FRANK VON) Rote Werwölfe: Volksfront gegen die Völker Europas. Rosenheim, [1979]. pp. 192.

POPULATION.

HANSEN (ALVIN HARVEY) Economic stabilization in an unbalanced world. New York, 1971. pp. 384. *Reprint of work originally published in New York, 1932.*

HIGGINS (EDWARD) A study of some norms and values pertaining to fertility in an urban white population. [Johannesburg], 1960. pp. 266. *bibliog. Dissertation presented to the University of the Witwatersrand for the degree of Master of Arts, 1960.*

POPULATION NEWSLETTER; issued by the Population Division of the Department of Economic and Social Affairs, United Nations. q., Ap 1968 (no.1)- New York.

NOTAS DE POBLACION: revista latinoamericana de demografia; [pd. by] Centro Latinoamericano de Demografia. 3 a yr., Ap 1973 (año 1, v.1)- Santiago.

POPULATION mobility and residential change; edited by W.A.V. Clark and Eric G. Moore. Evanston, Ill., 1978. pp. 281. *bibliogs. (Northwestern University. Studies in Geography. No. 25)*

GILLAND (BERNARD) The next seventy years: population, food and resources. Tunbridge Wells, 1979. pp. 133. *bibliog.*

— Atlases.

ATLAS of world population history, by Colin McEvedy and Richard Jones. Harmondsworth, 1978. pp. 368. *bibliog.*

— History.

ATLAS of world population history, by Colin McEvedy and Richard Jones. Harmondsworth, 1978. pp. 368. *bibliog.*

— Societies — Directories.

TRZYNA (THADDEUS C.) and SMITH (JOAN DICKSON) Population: an international directory of organizations and information resources. Claremont, Calif., 1976. pp. 132.

— Statistics.

GLASS (DAVID VICTOR) compiler. The development of population statistics: a collective reprint of materials concerning the history of census taking and vital registration in England and Wales. Farnborough, 1973. pp. 348.

ATLAS of world population history, by Colin McEvedy and Richard Jones. Harmondsworth, 1978. pp. 368. *bibliog.*

POPULATION BIOLOGY.

LEWIS (EDWIN R.) Network models in population biology. New York, 1977. pp. 402. *bibliog.*

POPULATION COUNCIL.

POPULATION COUNCIL. The Population Council: a chronicle of the first twenty-five years, 1952-1977. New York, [1978]. pp. 210.

POPULATION FORECASTING.

POPULATION FORECASTING.

ARAB-OGLY (EDVARD ARTUROVICH) Demograficheskie i ekologicheskie prognozy: kritika sovremennykh burzhuaznykh kontseptsii; Demographic and ecological forecasts: critical survey of modern bourgeois conceptions. Moskva, 1978. pp. 319. *With Russian and English tables of contents.*

— **Bangladesh.**

BANGLADESH. Bureau of Statistics. 1976. Population projection of Bangladesh by age and sex from 1960 to 2005 A.D. [Dacca], 1976. pp. 57. *(Population and Demographic Research Series. No.1)*

— **Canada.**

CANADA. Statistics Canada. Estimates of population for Canada and the provinces. a., Je 1977- Ottawa. *[in English and French]*

— — **Nova Scotia.**

COFFEY (WILLIAM J.) Nova Scotia population, household, family and labour force projections, 1977-1986; prepared for Nova Scotia [Department of] Development. [Halifax], 1979. fo. 87. *bibliog.*

— — **Ontario.**

FOOT (DAVID K.) Public policy and future population in Ontario. [Toronto, 1979]. pp. 57. *bibliog. (Ontario. Economic Council. Discussion Paper Series)*

— **South Africa.**

BROWETT (J.G.) and HART (T.) Projections of the urban population of the southern P[retoria] W[itwatersrand] V[ereeniging] [conurbation] for the years 1980, 1990 and 2000. Johannesburg, 1978. pp. 135. *bibliog. (Johannesburg. University of the Witwatersrand. Urban and Regional Research Unit. Occasional Papers. No. 19)*

— **Turkey.**

TUNCER (BARAN) The impact of population growth on the Turkish economy. [Ankara, 1968]. pp. 66.

— **United Kingdom.**

EAST ANGLIA ECONOMIC PLANNING COUNCIL. Future population of East Anglia; a report. [London, 1978]. pp. 52. *bibliog.*

— — **Wales.**

U.K. Welsh Office. 1978. 1976 based home population projections for the counties of Wales. [Cardiff], 1978. pp. 30.

POPULATION POLICY.

SRIKANTAN (K.S.) The family planning program in the socioeconomic context. New York, [1977]. pp. 240.

DIXON (RUTH B.) Rural women at work: strategies for development in South Asia. Baltimore, [1978]. pp. 227. *bibliog.*

FOOD and population: priorities in decision making...; edited by T.Dams [and others]. Farnborough, [1978]. pp. 192. *bibliogs. Report of a meeting of the International Conference of Agricultural Economists, Nairobi, 1976.*

— **Moral and religious aspects.**

POPULATION policy and ethics: the American experience; edited by Robert M. Veatch. New York, [1977]. pp. 501. *bibliogs. A project of the Research Group on Ethics and Population of the Institute of Society, Ethics and the Life Sciences.*

POPULATION RESEARCH.

CENTRE D'ETUDE DE LA POPULATION ET DE LA FAMILLE. Annual report. a., 1976- Brussels.

RESEARCH IN POPULATION ECONOMICS: an annual compilation of research. a., 1978(no. 1)- Greenwich, Connecticut.

RESEARCH IN POPULATION ECONOMICS: an annual compilation of research. a., 1978(no. 1)- Greenwich, Connecticut.

CONFERENCE ON SOCIAL DEMOGRAPHY, MADISON, 1975. Social demography; edited by Karl E. Taeuber, Larry L. Bumpass, James A. Sweet. New York, [1978]. pp. 336. *bibliogs.*

— **Directories.**

TRZYNA (THADDEUS C.) and SMITH (JOAN DICKSON) Population: an international directory of organizations and information resources. Claremont, Calif., 1976. pp. 132.

— **United States.**

POPULATION COUNCIL. The Population Council: a chronicle of the first twenty-five years, 1952-1977. New York, [1978]. pp. 210.

POPULISM

— **Russia.**

GINEV (VLADIMIR NIKOLAEVICH) Agrarnyi vopros i melkoburzhuaznye partii v Rossii v 1917 g.: k istorii bankrotstva neonarodnichestva. Leningrad, 1977. pp. 295.

— **United States.**

KLEPPER (ROBERT) The economic bases for agrarian protest movements in the United States, 1870-1900. New York, 1978. pp. 378. *bibliog. Originally presented as a thesis, University of Chicago, 1973.*

PORT OF SPAIN

— **City planning.**

TRINIDAD AND TOBAGO. Town and Country Planning Division. 1973. Planning for development: east Port-of-Spain draft redevelopment plan. [Port of Spain], 1973. pp. 71. *bibliog. (Development Planning Series. T1.2)*

PORTUGAL

— **Colonies.**

UNITED NATIONS. Office of Public Information. 1970. A principle in torment, II. The United Nations and Portuguese administered territories. New York, 1970. pp. 60.

ESSAYS concerning the socioeconomic history of Brazil and Portuguese India; edited by Dauril Alden and Warren Dean. Gainesville, 1977. pp. 247.

— **Commerce — India.**

DISNEY (ANTHONY R.) Twilight of the pepper empire: Portuguese trade in southwest India in the early seventeenth century. Cambridge, Mass., 1978. pp. 220. *bibliog. (Harvard University. Harvard Historical Studies. vol. 95)*

— **Economic conditions.**

ALMEIDA (CARLOS) and BARRETO (ANTONIO) Capitalismo e emigração em Portugal. Lisboa, 1976. pp. 329. *bibliog. Reprint, with new preface, of work first published in 1970.*

ROSA (EUGENIO) Portugal: dois anos de revolução na economia. Lisboa, 1976. pp. 346.

PLANEAMENTO; [pd. by] Departamento Central de Planeamento [Portugal]. 3 a yr., Je 1978(v.1, no.1)- Lisboa.

BAKLANOFF (ERIC NICOLAS) The economic transformation of Spain and Portugal. New York, 1978. pp. 211. *bibliog.*

— **Emigration and immigration.**

ALMEIDA (CARLOS) and BARRETO (ANTONIO) Capitalismo e emigração em Portugal. Lisboa, 1976. pp. 329. *bibliog. Reprint, with new preface, of work first published in 1970.*

— **Foreign economic relations.**

See also EUROPEAN COMMUNITIES — Portugal.

— **Foreign relations.**

See also EUROPEAN COMMUNITIES — Portugal.

— **History — 1910, Revolution.**

BENTON (RUSSELL E.) The downfall of a king: Dom Manuel II of Portugal. Washington, [1977]. pp. 238. *bibliog.*

— **Industries.**

PEREIRA (JOÃO MARTINS) Industria, ideologia e quotidiano: ensaio sobre o capitalismo em Portugal. Porto, 1974. pp. 254.

PORTUGAL. Instituto Nacional de Estatistica. Divisão de Estatisticas Industriais. Industria transformadora: informação trimestral de conjuntura: relatorio de sintese. q., 1977 (ano 1, no. 1/2)- Lisboa.

PORTUGAL. Instituto Nacional de Estatistica. Serviços Centrais. 1977. Recenseamento industrial 1972. [Lisbon, 1977]. 4 vols. (in 1) *Data covers Portugal by distritos and concelhos, Azores and Madeira.*

PORTUGUESE IN ANGOLA.

BENDER (GERALD J.) Angola under the Portuguese: the myth and the reality. London, 1978. pp. 287. *bibliog.*

PORTUGUESE IN GUYANA.

WAGNER (MICHAEL JOHN) Structural pluralism and the Portuguese in nineteenth century British Guiana: a study in historical geography. Montreal, 1975. pp. 346. *Microfiche copy.*

POSITIVISM.

MISES (LUDWIG VON) The ultimate foundation of economic science: an essay on method. 2nd ed. Kansas City, [1978]. pp. 148.

POSTAL SERVICE

— **Austria.**

KAINZ (CHRISTINE) Post in Österreich 1945-1946: Daten und Fakten, zusammengestellt unter Benützung zeitgenössischer Quellen. Wien, Bundesministerium für Verkehr, Generaldirektion für die Post- und Telegraphenverwaltung, 1978. pp. 90.

— **Canada.**

DAVIDSON (JOE) and DEVERELL (JOHN) Joe Davidson. Toronto, 1978. pp. 192.

— **Germany — Employees.**

AUSBEUTUNG: ich arbeite bei der Post; Hrsg. Klaus Kolb. Berlin, [1972]. pp. 144.

— **United Kingdom.**

U.K. Post Office. Public Affairs Division. Public affairs background briefing. irreg., D 1978- London.

— **United States — Laws and regulations.**

FOWLER (DOROTHY GANFIELD) Unmailable: Congress and the Post Office. Athens, Ga., [1977]. pp. 266. *bibliog.*

POTTERS

— **United Kingdom.**

BURCHILL (FRANK) and ROSS (RICHARD) A history of the potter's union. Stoke-on-Trent, 1977. pp. 292. *bibliog.*

POUJADE (PIERRE).

POUJADE (PIERRE) A l'heure de la colère. [Paris, 1977]. pp. 253.

POULTRY
— Bangladesh.

BANGLADESH. Bureau of Statistics. 1976. Report on the survey of livestock and poultry in the rural areas of Bangladesh, 1970. Dacca, 1976. pp. 40. (Agricultural Statistics Papers. No.2)

POVERTY.

PLUM (WERNER) Industrialization and mass poverty: points from two centuries of debate; translated from the German by Lux Furtmüller. Bonn-Bad Godesberg, [1977]. pp. 213. bibliog. (Friedrich-Ebert Stiftung. Forschungsinstitut. Social and Cultural Aspects of Industrialization)

RIFFAULT (HELENE) and RABIER (JACQUES RENE) The perception of poverty in Europe: report on a public opinion survey carried out in the member countries of the European Community as part of the programme of pilot projects to combat poverty. Brussels, European Communities, 1977. 1 vol. (various pagings). *Working document for the Commission of the European Communities.*

POVERTY RESEARCH.

SOCIAL security research: the definition and measurement of poverty: papers of a seminar sponsored by DHSS and organised by the Policy Studies Institute, D[epartment of] H[ealth and] S[ocial] S[ecurity]. London, H.M.S.O., 1979. pp. 162.

— United Kingdom.

SOCIAL security research: the definition and measurement of poverty: papers and report of a seminar sponsored by DHSS and organised by the Policy Studies Institute, D[epartment of] H[ealth and] S[ocial] S[ecurity]. London, H.M.S.O., 1979. pp. 162.

POWELL (JOHN ENOCH).

LEWIS (ROY) Enoch Powell: principle in politics. London, 1979. pp. 272.

POWER (SOCIAL SCIENCES).

PARENTI (MICHAEL) Power and the powerless. New York, [1974]. pp. 238. bibliogs.

BENDIX (REINHARD) Kings or people: power and the mandate to rule. Berkeley, 1978. pp. 692.

GOLDENBERG (I. IRA) Oppression and social intervention: essays on the human condition and the problems of change. Chicago, [1978]. pp. 213. bibliog.

KRAUS (WOLFGANG) Kultur und Macht: die Verwandlung der Wünsche. München, 1978. pp. 156. bibliog.

CHOROVER (STEPHAN L.) From genesis to genocide: the meaning of human nature and the power of behavior control. Cambridge, Mass., [1979]. pp. 238.

CLEGG (STEWART) The theory of power and organization. London, 1979. pp. 176. bibliog.

WELSH (WILLIAM A.) Leaders and elites. New York, 1979. pp. 209.

POWER OF ATTORNEY
— Canada.

MANITOBA. Law Reform Commission. 1974. Report on special, enduring powers of attorney. [Winnipeg], 1974. pp. 28. (Reports. 14)

POWER RESOURCES.

DICERTO (JOSEPH J.) The electric wishing well: the solution to the energy crisis. New York, [1976]. pp. 317. bibliog.

DARMSTADTER (JOEL) and others. How industrial societies use energy: a comparative analysis. Baltimore, [1977]. pp. 282.

ENERGY: global prospects, 1985-2000: report of the Workshop on Alternative Energy Strategies: a project sponsored by the Massachusetts Institute of Technology. New York, [1977]. pp. 291.

UNITED States and world energy resources: prospects and priorities...; edited by Ragaei El Mallakh and Carl McGuire. Boulder, Colo., [1977]. pp. 272. *Proceedings of the third international conference of the International Research Center for Energy and Economic Development held at Boulder, Colorado, 1976.*

ALEXANDERSSON (GUNNAR) and KLEVEBRING (BJÖRN-IVAR) World resources: energy, metals, minerals; studies in economic and political geography. Berlin, 1978. pp. 248. bibliog.

CHANDLER (GEOFFREY) The international energy prospect. [London?, 1978?]. pp. 10.

MIHAILOVITCH (LIOUBOMIR) and PLUCHART (JEAN JACQUES) Energie mondiale: les nouvelles stratégies. Paris, [1978]. pp. 288. bibliog.

SLESSER (MALCOLM) Energy in the economy. London, 1978. pp. 164. bibliog.

BLAIR (PETER D.) Multiobjective regional energy planning: application to the energy park concept. Boston, Mass., [1979]. pp. 163. bibliog.

INTERNATIONAL ENERGY AGENCY. 1979. Workshops on energy supply and demand. Paris, 1978 [or rather 1979]. pp. 501. bibliogs.

— Research — Sweden.

SWEDEN. Industridepartementet. Energiprogramkommittén. 1974. Energiforskning: program för forskning och utveckling: betänkande avgivet av Energiprogramkommittén. Stockholm, 1974. pp. 225. bibliog. (Sweden. Statens Offentliga Utredningar. 1974.72)

— Canada.

CANADA. Statistics Canada. Quarterly report on energy supply-demand in Canada. q., 1976(1st)- Ottawa. *[in English and French] 1976 and 1977 pd. as annuals.*

— Europe.

SIMEONS (CHARLES) Energy research and development programmes in western Europe. Amsterdam, 1978. pp. 323. bibliog.

— Europe, Eastern.

PARK (DANIEL) Oil and gas in COMECON countries. London, 1979. pp. 240. bibliog.

— European Economic Community countries.

EUROPEAN COMMUNITIES. Statistical Office. Energy: press notice. [in French]. m. Luxembourg. *Current issues only kept.*

— India.

INDIA. Central Board of Irrigation and Power. 1977. C[entral] B[oard of] I[rrigation and] P[ower] Golden Jubilee, 1927-77: commemorative volume. New Delhi, 1977. pp. 188.

— Italy.

Una STRATEGIA per lo sviluppo energetico italiano; [by] G. Cozzi [and others]. Milano, [1977]. pp. 356.

— Pakistan.

SHERMAN (MICHEL M.) Household use of energy in Pakistan. Islamabad, United States Agency for International Development, 1978. 1 vol. (various foliations).

— Philippine Islands.

ENERGY DEVELOPMENT BOARD [PHILIPPINE ISLANDS]. Annual report. a., 1976- Manila.

— Russia — Siberia.

TOPLIVNO-energeticheskii kompleks Sibiri: sostoianie i napravleniia razvitiia. Novosibirsk, 1978. pp. 255.

— Sweden.

SWEDEN. Industridepartementet. Energiprogramkommittén. 1974. Energiforskning: expertmaterial utarbetat på uppdrag av Energiprogramkommittén. Avdelning A. Utvinning av energiråvaror och industriell energiproduktion. Stockholm, 1974. pp. 482. (Sweden. Statens Offentliga Utredningar. 1974. 73)

— United Kingdom.

A SYMPOSIUM on renewable sources of energy and how far they might be made to meet Britain's energy needs; held [in] ... London on...16th June 1976 [by the Royal Society of Arts; chairman Lord Avebury]. London, [1976]. pp. 137. bibliogs. Looseleaf.

WATT COMMITTEE ON ENERGY. Deployment of national resources in the provision of energy in the United Kingdom, 1975-2025. London, [1977]. pp. 60. (Watt Committee on Energy. Reports. No. 2)

WATT COMMITTEE ON ENERGY. Energy research and development in the United Kingdom. London, [1977]. pp. 68. (Watt Committee on Energy. Reports. No. 1)

RAY (GEORGE F.) Energy and transport: problems of medium-term assessment: a post-mortem on the Energy and Inland Transport chapters of The British economy in 1975. London, 1978. pp. 31. (National Institute of Economic and Social Research. Discussion Papers. No. 14)

WATT COMMITTEE ON ENERGY. The rational use of energy. London, 1978. pp. 71. (Watt Committee on Energy. Reports. No. 3)

U.K. Central Office of Information. Reference Division. Reference Pamphlets. 124. British industry today: energy. 5th ed. London, 1979. pp. 32. bibliog.

— — Bibliography.

U.K. Department of Energy. Library. Publications in print. a., 1978- London.

— United States.

CONGRESSIONAL QUARTERLY INC. Continuing energy crisis in America. Washington, D.C., [1975]. pp. 124. bibliog.

NATIONAL ACADEMY OF SCIENCES. Academy Forum, 1977. Coal as an energy resource: conflict and consensus. Washington, 1977. pp. 326.

GORDON (RICHARD L.) Coal in the U.S. energy market: history and prospects. Lexington, Mass., [1978]. pp. 224. bibliog.

ENERGY future: report of the energy project at the Harvard Business School. New York, [1979]. pp. 353.

PHILLIPS (OWEN M.) The last chance energy book. Baltimore, 1979. pp. 142.

PRAGMATICS.

COLLOQUIUM ON NEW WAYS OF ANALYZING VARIATION, 3RD, GEORGETOWN UNIVERSITY, 1974. Studies in language variation: semantics, syntax, phonology, pragmatics, social situations, ethnographic approaches; [edited by] Ralph W. Fasold [and] Roger W. Shuy. Washington, D.C., [1977]. pp. 311. bibliogs.

GAZDAR (GERALD) Pragmatics implicature, presupposition, and logical form. New York, [1979]. pp. 186. bibliog.

PREČAN (VILÉM).

PREČAN (VILÉM) Die sieben Jahre von Prag, 1969-1976: Briefe und Dokumente aus der Zeit der "Normalisierung"; übersetzt von Ilse Löffler. Frankfurt am Main, 1978. pp. 254.

PREDATION (BIOLOGY).

HASSELL (MICHAEL P.) The dynamics of arthropod predator-prey systems. Princeton, N.J., 1978. pp. 237. *bibliog.*

PRESIDENTS.

MOULIN (RICHARD) Le présidentialisme et la classification des régimes politiques. Paris, 1978. pp. 389. *bibliog.*

NUECHTERLEIN (DONALD EDWIN) National interests and Presidential leadership: the setting of priorities. Boulder, Colo., 1978. pp. 246.

PRESS

— **Africa.**

BARTON (FRANK) The press of Africa: persecution and perseverance. London, 1979. pp. 304. *bibliog.*

— **France.**

FRANCE. Direction de la Documentation. La Documentation Française. Notes et Etudes Documentaires. No. 4469. La presse française; par Pierre Albert avec la collaboration de Christine Leteinturier. [Paris], 1978. pp. 158. *bibliog.*

— **Germany.**

WIESAND (ANDREAS JOHANNES) and FOHRBECK (KARLA) Literature and the public in the Federal Republic of Germany. Munich, [1976]. pp. 103.

— **Italy.**

FILIPUZZI (ANGELO) Il dibattito sull'emigrazione: polemiche nazionali e stampa veneta, 1861-1914. Firenze, 1976. pp. 421.

— **Madagascar.**

MARON (CLAUDE) L'hebdomadaire Lumière à Madagascar de 1935 à 1972. Aix-Marseille, 1977. pp. 295. *bibliog. (Université d'Aix-Marseille III. Faculté de Droit et de Science Politique.Travaux et Mémoires. 28)*

— **Mexico.**

REYNA (MARIA DEL CARMEN) ed. La prensa censurada durante el siglo XIX. Mexico, Secretaria de Educacion Publica, 1976. pp. 191. *(Sep/Setentas. 255)*

— **Underdeveloped areas.**

See UNDERDEVELOPED AREAS — Press.

— **United Kingdom.**

BEHIND the headlines - the business of the British press: readings in the economics of the press; edited by Harry Henry. London, 1978. pp. 240.

The BRITISH press: a manifesto; edited by James Curran. London, 1978. pp. 339. *bibliog.*

— **United States.**

HOHENBERG (JOHN) A crisis for the American press. New York, 1978. pp. 316.

PRESS AND POLITICS.

RIGHTER (ROSEMARY) Whose news?: politics, the press and the third world. London, 1978. pp. 272. *bibliog.*

— **Africa.**

BARTON (FRANK) The press of Africa: persecution and perseverance. London, 1979. pp. 304. *bibliog.*

— **Czechoslovakia.**

KAPLAN (FRANK L.) Winter into spring: the Czechoslovak press and the reform movement, 1963-1968. New York, 1977. pp. 208. *bibliog. (East European Quarterly. East European Monographs. 29)*

— **Germany.**

SCHOSSER (ERICH) Presse und Landtag in Bayern von 1850 bis 1918. München, 1968. pp. 127. *bibliog. (Munich. Stadtarchiv. Neue Schriftenreihe. Band 22)*

— **Nigeria.**

OMU (FRED I.A.) Press and politics in Nigeria, 1880-1937. London, 1978. pp. 290. *bibliog. (Ibadan. University. Department of History. Ibadan History Series)*

— **Russia.**

METTIG (VOLKER) Russische Presse und Sozialistengesetz: die deutsche Sozialdemokratie und die Entstehung des Sozialistengesetzes aus russischer Sicht, 1869-1878. Bonn, [1979]. pp. 476. *bibliog. (Friedrich-Ebert-Stiftung. Forschungsinstitut. Reihe: Politik- und Gesellschaftsgeschichte. Band 4)*

— — **Ukraine.**

SOLDATENKO (VALERII FEDOROVICH) Tribuna proletarskogo internatsionalizma. Kiev, 1977. pp. 183.

— **South Africa.**

CHIMUTENGWENDE (CHENHAMO C.) South Africa: the press and the politics of liberation. London, 1978. pp. 197. *bibliog.*

PRESS LAW

— **Europe, Eastern.**

RÉVÉSZ (LÁSZLÓ) Die uniforme Presse in Osteuropa: eine vergleichende presserechtliche Studie. Freiburg, [1977]. pp. 160. *(Freiburg (Switzerland). Universität. Institut für Journalistik. Öffentliche Soziale Kommunikationen. Werkpapiere. 7)*

PRESSURE GROUPS.

MOODIE (GRAEME COCHRANE) and STUDDERT-KENNEDY (GERALD) Opinions, publics and pressure groups: an essay on vox populi and representative government. London, 1970. pp. 115.

STOCKTON (BAYARD) and JANKE (PETER F.) Nuclear power: protest and violence. London, 1978. pp. 20. *bibliog. (Institute for the Study of Conflict. Conflict Studies. No.102)*

— **European Economic Community countries.**

AVERYT (WILLIAM F.) Agropolitics in the European Community: interest groups and the common agricultural policy. New York, 1977. pp. 128. *bibliog.*

— **Germany.**

BAMBERG (HANS DIETER) Die Deutschland-Stiftung e.V.: Studien über Kräfte der "demokratischen Mitte" und des Konservatismus in der Bundesrepublik Deutschland. Meisenheim am Glan, 1978. pp. 563. *bibliog.*

— **United Kingdom.**

WOOTTON (JOHN GRAHAM GEORGE) Pressure politics in contemporary Britain. Lexington, Mass., [1978]. pp. 256.

— — **Directories.**

DIRECTORY of pressure groups and representative associations; [edited by] Peter Shipley. 2nd ed. Epping, 1979. pp. 123.

— **United States.**

FELDSTEIN (PAUL J.) Health associations and the demand for legislation: the political economy of health. Cambridge, Mass., [1977]. pp. 255.

The POWER of the people: active nonviolence in the United States; edited and produced by Robert Cooney and Helen Michalowski. Culver City, [1977]. pp. 240. *bibliog.*

GARSON (G. DAVID) Group theories of politics. Beverly Hills, [1978]. pp. 215. *bibliogs.*

LIPSET (SEYMOUR MARTIN) and RAAB (EARL) The politics of unreason: right-wing extremism in America, 1790- 1977. 2nd ed. Chicago, [1978]. pp. 581.

PRESTIGE.

GOODE (WILLIAM J.) The celebration of heroes: prestige as a social control system. Berkeley, [1978]. pp. 407.

PRESUMPTIONS (LAW)

— **Russia.**

OIGENZIKHT (VIKTOR ARKAD'EVICH) Prezumptsii v sovetskom grazhdanskom prave. Dushanbe, 1976. pp. 190.

PRICE INDEXES

— **Bahamas.**

BAHAMAS. Department of Statistics. 1975. The Grand Bahama household budgetary survey and retail price index report. Nassau, [1975?]. fo.60.

— **European Economic Community countries.**

EUROPEAN COMMUNITIES. Statistical Office. EC-index of producer prices of agricultural products. bi-m., 1978(no. 4/5)- Luxembourg. *[in Community languages]*

— **India.**

INDIA. Office of the Economic Adviser. 1977. A note on the revised index numbers of wholesale prices in India; 1970-71 equals 100. Delhi, [1977]. pp. 98.

— **Jamaica.**

JAMAICA. Department of Statistics. 1978. Consumer price indices: percentage movements, 1970-1978. [Kingston, 1978]. pp. 211.

— **Netherlands.**

BALK (B.M.) and others. Inflatie in Nederland van 1952 tot 1975: een statistische beschrijving van het verloop van 235 reeksen prijsindexcijfers en een analyse van hun samenhang. 's-Gravenhage, 1978. pp. 56. *(Netherlands. Centraal Bureau voor de Statistiek. Statistische Onderzoekingen. M4) With English summary.*

— **Pakistan.**

PAKISTAN. Statistical Division. 1974. Consumer price index numbers, July 1970 to December 1973. Karachi, [1974]. pp. 71.

— **Papua New Guinea.**

PAPUA NEW GUINEA. Bureau of Statistics. Statistical bulletin: import price indexes. q., Je 1976- Port Moresby.

PRICE POLICY.

MAURIZI (ALEX R.) and KELLY (THOM) Prices and consumer information: the benefits from posting retail gasoline prices. Washington, D.C., [1978]. pp. 76. *(American Enterprise Institute for Public Policy Research. AEI Studies. 193)*

— **United States.**

KOTTKE (FRANK JOSEPH) The promotion of price competition where sellers are few. Lexington, Mass., [1978]. pp. 227. *bibliogs.*

PRICE REGULATION.

STABILIZING world commodity markets: analysis, practice, and policy; edited by F. Gerard Adams and Sonia A. Klein. Lexington, Mass., [1978]. pp. 335. *bibliogs. Representative selection of papers presented at a conference held at Airlie, Va., 1977, and sponsored by the Ford Foundation.*

— **United Kingdom.**

U.K. Department of Prices and Consumer Protection. 1978. Prices policy: a review of the secondary legislation on prices: the Government's proposals. [London, 1978]. fo. 11,2.

GRIBBIN (J.D.) The role of competition in the 1977 Price Commission Act. London, Price Commision, 1979. pp. (34). *(Government Economic Service Working Papers. No. 21)*

U.K. Department of Prices and Consumer Protection. 1979. The government's prices policy. London, 1979. fo. 7.

PRICES.

SQUIRE (LYN) and TAK (HERMAN G. VAN DER) Economic analysis of projects...; published for the World Bank. Baltimore, [1975]. pp. 153. *bibliog. (International Bank for Reconstruction and Development. World Bank Research Publications)*

DRESCH (STEPHEN P.) and others. Substituting a value-added tax for the corporate income tax: first-round analysis. Cambridge, Mass., 1977. pp. 213. *bibliog. (National Bureau of Economic Research. Fiscal Studies. 15)*

WATSON (DONALD STEVENSON) Price theory and its uses. 4th ed. Boston, Mass., [1977]. pp. 445. *bibliogs.*

WILLNER (JOHAN) Costs of production, values and prices. Åbo, 1978. pp. 146. *bibliog. (Åbo. Akademi. Acta Academiae Aboensis. Humaniora. 55.2)*

— Australia.

AUSTRALIAN trade practices: readings; edited by J.P. Nieuwenhuysen. 2nd ed. London, 1976. pp. 317. *bibliog.*

— France.

FRANCE. Centre d'Etude des Revenus et des Coûts. 1978. Connaissances et opinions des Français sur les prix: ce qu'ils perçoivent des évolutions de prix: analyse de résultats d'enquêtes 1970, 1972, 1974, 1976; [by] Raymond Jaulent and Jacques Antoine. [Paris], 1978. pp. 152. *(Documents. Nos. 43-44)*

— India — Orissa.

ORISSA. State Civil Supplies Price Enquiry Committee. 1969. Final report; Radhanath Rath, chairman. Cuttack, 1969. pp. 150.

— Nigeria.

NIGERIA (OYO STATE). Ministry of Finance and Economic Development. Statistics Division. Digest of price statistics. a., 1977- Ibadan.

— Russia.

LUKINOV (IVAN ILLARIONOVICH) Vosproizvodstvo i tseny. Moskva, 1977. pp. 431.

— United States.

SHIELDS (ROGER ELWOOD) Economic growth with price deflation, 1873-1896. New York, 1977. pp. 346. *bibliog.*

PRIMATES

— Behaviour.

JOLLY (ALISON) The evolution of primate behavior. New York, [1972]. pp. 397. *bibliog.*

— Evolution.

JOLLY (ALISON) The evolution of primate behavior. New York, [1972]. pp. 397. *bibliog.*

PRINCE EDWARD ISLAND

— Department of Municipal Affairs.

PRINCE EDWARD ISLAND. Department of Municipal Affairs. Annual report. a., 1971- Charlottetown.

— Executive departments.

PRINCE EDWARD ISLAND. Department of Municipal Affairs. Annual report. a., 1971- Charlottetown.

PRINTERS

— India — Maharashtra.

MAHARASHTRA. Minimum Wages Committee for Employment in Printing and Allied Trades. 1965. Report...1964; [P.G. Kher, chairman]. [Bombay, 1965]. pp. 58.

PRINTING

— History — Italy.

LOWRY (MARTIN) The world of Aldus Manutius: business and scholarship in Renaissance Venice. Oxford, [1979]. pp. 350. *bibliog.*

— — Poland.

ALEKSIEWICZ (ANNA) Drukarstwo w Rzeczypospolitej Krakowskiej i Galicji Zachodniej w latach 1815-1860. Warszawa, 1976. pp. 179. *bibliog. (Wrocław. Uniwersytet. Acta Universitatis Wratislaviensis. No. 300. Bibliotekoznawstwo. 8) With German summary.*

PRINTING, PUBLIC

— Trinidad and Tobago.

WEEKES (LESLIE O.) 1st hundred years, 1873-1973. [Port of Spain, Government Printing Office, 1974]. pp. 50.

PRISON ADMINISTRATION

— United Kingdom.

NEALE (KENNETH) Her Majesty's Commissioners, 1878-1978: a centenary essay. [London], Home Office, 1978. pp. 71.

PRISON PSYCHOLOGY.

PAWEŁCZYŃSKA (ANNA) Values and violence in Auschwitz: a sociological analysis; translated with an introduction by Catherine S. Leach. Berkeley, 1979. pp. 170.

PRISON SENTENCES.

SHORT (RENÉE) The care of long-term prisoners. London, 1979. pp. 163. *bibliog.*

PRISONERS.

SHORT (RENÉE) The care of long-term prisoners. London, 1979. pp. 163. *bibliog.*

— United Kingdom.

U.K. Home Office. 1977. Prisons and the prisoner: the work of the prison service in England and Wales. London, 1977. pp. 188.

PRISONERS OF WAR

— United States.

UNITED STATES. Sanitary Commission. 1864. Narrative of privations and sufferings of United States officers and soldiers while prisoners of war in the hands of the rebel authorities. Being the report of a commission of inquiry, appointed by the United States Sanitary Commission. With an appendix containing the testimony. Philadelphia, 1864. pp. 283.

PRISONERS OF WAR, JAPANESE.

CARR-GREGG (CHARLOTTE) Japanese prisoners of war in revolt: the outbreaks at Featherston and Cowra during World War II. St. Lucia, Qld., [1978]. pp. 225. *bibliog.*

PRISONS.

MELOSSI (DARIO) and PAVARINI (MASSIMO) Carcere e fabbrica: alle origini del sistema penitenziario (16- 19 secolo). Bologna, [1977]. pp. 252. *(La Questione Criminale. Quaderni. 1)*

— Canada.

CANADA. Statistics Canada. Penitentiary statistics. a., 1975- Ottawa. *[in English and French]*

— Israel.

COMMITTEE FOR THE DEFENCE OF POLITICAL PRISONERS IN ISRAEL. Prisoners and prisons in Israel. Umm al-Fahm, [1978]. pp. 49. *bibliog.*

— Peru.

SEOANE CORRALES (JUAN) Hombres y rejas. [Lima], 1977. pp. 293.

— United Kingdom.

U.K. Home Office. 1977. Prisons and the prisoner: the work of the prison service in England and Wales. London, 1977. pp. 188.

EDWARDS (AMY) The prison system in England and Wales, 1878-1978. [London, Home Office, 1978]. pp. 13. *bibliog.*

IGNATIEFF (MICHAEL) A just measure of pain: the penitentiary in the industrial revolution, 1750-1850. London, 1978. pp. 257.

FITZGERALD (MIKE) and SIM (JOE) British prisons. Oxford, 1979. pp. 165. *bibliog.*

— — Scotland.

MURRAY (ANNE) Reforming Scottish prisons: a task for the assembly. [Glasgow, 1979]. pp. 24. *bibliog. (Scottish Council of Fabian Societies. Scottish Fabian Research Papers. 3)*

— United States — California.

CALIFORNIA. Legislature. Senate Subcommittee on Civil Disorder. 1974. Executive session...: gang violence in penal institutions. Los Angeles, 1974. pp. 104.

PRIVACY, RIGHT OF.

BOWER (ROBERT) and DE GASPARIS (PRISCILLA) Ethics in social research: protecting the interests of human subjects. New York, [1978]. pp. 227. *bibliog.*

WILSON (SUANNA J.) Confidentiality in social work: issues and principles. New York, [1978]. pp. 274. *bibliog.*

— Canada — Ontario.

FLAHERTY (DAVID) Research and statistical uses of Ontario government personal data. [Toronto], 1979. pp. 188. *(Ontario. Commission on Freedom of Information and Individual Privacy. Research Publications. 5)*

— Russia.

LEIDEN. Rijks Universiteit. Documentation Office for East European Law. Law in Eastern Europe. No. 22(1). Copyright, defamation, and privacy in Soviet civil law: De lege lata ac ferenda; by Serge L. Levitsky. Alphen aan den Rijn, 1979. pp. 487.

— South Africa.

McQUOID-MASON (DAVID JAN) The law of privacy in South Africa. Cape Town, 1978. pp. 272. *bibliog.*

— United Kingdom.

CENSUSES, surveys and privacy; edited by Martin Bulmer. London, 1979. pp. 279. *bibliog.*

— United States.

ON record: files and dossiers in American life; edited by Stanton Wheeler. New Brunswick, N.J., [1976]. pp. 449.

PRIVATE COMPANIES

— United Kingdom.

JORDAN DATAQUEST LTD. Britain's top 1000 private companies, 1977. London, [1978]. pp. 111.

PROBABILITIES.

KEILSON (JULIAN) Green's function methods in probability theory. London, 1965. pp. 220.

PROBABILITIES.(Cont.)

LAMPERTI (JOHN) Probability: a survey of the mathematical theory. New York, 1966. pp. 150. *bibliog.*

PFANZAGL (J.) and PIERLO (W.) Compact systems of sets. Berlin, 1966. pp. 48. *bibliog.*

FELLER (WILLIAM) An introduction to probability theory and its applications. New York, [1968-71]. 2 vols. *Volume one is of the 3rd ed., volume two of the 2nd.*

STATISTICAL inference under order restrictions: the theory and application of isotonic regression; [by] R.E. Barlow [and others]. Chichester, 1972 repr. 1978. pp. 388. *bibliog.*

CHUNG (KAI LAI) A course in probability theory. 2nd ed. New York, [1974]. pp. 365. *bibliog.*

CONFERENCE ON FOUNDATIONAL QUESTIONS IN STATISTICAL INFERENCE, AARHUS, 1973. Proceedings...; editors Ole Barndorff-Nielsen [and others]. Aarhus, 1974. pp. 371. *(Aarhus. Universitet. Department of Theoretical Statistics. Memoirs. No. 1)*

JOHNSON (NORMAN LLOYD) and KOTZ (SAMUEL) Urn models and their application: an approach to modern discrete probability theory. New York, [1977]. pp. 402. *bibliogs.*

PARTHASARATHY (K.R.) Introduction to probability and measure. Delhi, 1977. pp. 312. *bibliog.*

ALLEN (ARNOLD O.) Probability, statistics and queueing theory: with computer science applications. New York, 1978. pp. 390.

BRANCHING processes; edited by Anatole Joffe and Peter Ney. New York, [1978]. pp. 322. *bibliogs. Papers presented at a conference held in Quebec, August 11-20, 1976 under the sponsorship of the Centre de Recherches Mathématiques of the Université de Montréal and the National Research Council of Canada.*

CHOW (YUAN-SHIH) and TEICHER (HENRY) Probability theory: independence, interchangeability, martingales. New York, [1978]. pp. 455. *bibliogs.*

PROBABILITY on Banach spaces; edited by James Kuelbs. New York, [1978]. pp. 521. *bibliog.*

FRASER (DONALD ALEXANDER STUART) Inference and linear models. New York, [1979]. pp. 297. *bibliogs.*

UNCERTAIN outcomes; edited by C.R. Bell. Lancaster, [1979]. pp. 204. *bibliogs.*

— Tables, etc.

CRC handbook of tables for probability and statistics;...editor William H. Beyer. 2nd ed. Cleveland, Ohio, 1968 repr. 1976. pp. 642.

PROBATION

— Canada — Ontario.

RENNER (JOHN C.) The adult probationer in Ontario. [Toronto], Ministry of Correctional Services, [1978]. 1 vol. (various pagings).

RENNER (JOHN C.) The juvenile probationer in Ontario. [Toronto], Ministry of Correctional Services, [1978]. 1 vol. (various pagings).

— United Kingdom.

THORPE (JENNIFER) Social inquiry reports: a survey; a Home Office Research Unit report. London, 1979. pp. 52. *bibliog. (U.K. Home Office. Home Office Research Studies. No. 48)*

PROBATION OFFICERS

— Norway.

COPING and cooperation;...some views of an interchange course for probation officers and social workers from the South East of England and Norway in 1977; edited by Thelma Wilson [and others]. London, [1978]. pp. 85.

— United Kingdom.

COPING and cooperation;...some views of an interchange course for probation officers and social workers from the South East of England and Norway in 1977; edited by Thelma Wilson [and others]. London, [1978]. pp. 85.

PROBLEM SOLVING.

SPIVACK (GEORGE) and others. The problem-solving approach to adjustment. San Francisco, 1976. pp. 318. *bibliog.*

KIEBURTZ (RICHARD B.) Structured programming and problem-solving with PASCAL. Englewood Cliffs, N.J., [1978]. pp. 365.

PROCESS

— United Kingdom — Commonwealth.

McCLEAN (JOHN DAVID) and PATCHETT (KEITH W.) The recognition and enforcement of judgments and orders and the service of process within the Commonwealth: a further report; (with The reciprocal enforcement of judgments within the Commonwealth: a preliminary report). London, Commonwealth Secretariat, [1978]. pp. 202, 49.

RECOGNITION and enforcement of judgments and orders and the service of process within the Commonwealth: a report of a working meeting held at Basseterre, St. Kitts, 24-26 April 1978. London, Commonwealth Secretariat, [1978]. pp. 354.

PRODUCE TRADE.

HILLMAN (JIMMYE S.) Nontariff agricultural trade barriers. Lincoln, Neb., [1978]. pp. 236. *bibliog.*

— European Economic Community countries.

EUROPEAN COMMUNITIES. Statistical Office. Purchase prices of the means of production, (formerly Purchase prices of agriculture). q., 1977(v.1 no.1)- Luxembourg. *[in Community languages].*

PRODUCTION (ECONOMIC THEORY).

JUNIUS (T.) Shephard technologies and neoclassical production functions. Leiden, 1977. pp. 128. *bibliog. (Tilburg. Katholieke Hogeschool. Tilburg Institute of Economics. Tilburg Studies in Econometrics. vol. 2)*

SAWER (MARIAN) Marxism and the question of the Asiatic mode of production. The Hague, 1977. pp. 252. *bibliog. (International Institute of Social History. Studies in Social History. [No.] 3)*

DOLL (JOHN P.) and ORAZEM (FRANK) Production economics: theory with applications. Columbus, Ohio, [1978]. pp. 406. *bibliogs.*

PRODUCTION economics: a dual approach to theory and applications; ...editors Melvyn Fuss and Daniel McFadden. Amsterdam, 1978. 2 vols. *bibliogs.*

— Mathematical models.

POLISH-SOVIET REGIONAL SCIENCE SEMINAR, 1ST, SZYMBARK, 1973. Economic models in regional development and planning; edited by Marek Jerczyński [and] Mark K. Bandman. Warszawa, 1976. pp. 181. *bibliogs.*

PRODUCTION FUNCTIONS (ECONOMIC THEORY).

BARNUM (H.N.) and SQUIRE (LYN) Labor heterogeneity and rice production in Malaysia. Ann Arbor, Mich., 1977. pp. 11. *bibliog. (Michigan University. Center for Research on Economic Development. Discussion Papers. No. 71)*

NZIRAMASANGA (MUDZIVIRI) Production from an exhaustible resource under government control in an LDC. Ann Arbor, Michigan, 1977. pp. 17. *bibliog. (Michigan University. Center for Research on Economic Development. Discussion Papers. No. 70)*

BARNUM (H.N.) and SQUIRE (LYN) Consistent aggregation of family and hired labor in agricultural production functions. Ann Arbor, Mich., 1978. pp. 12. *(Michigan University. Center for Research on Economic Development. Discussion Papers. No. 73)*

PRODUCTIVITY.

PRODUCTIVITY DIGEST: review of literatures on productivity and its related fields; [pd.by] Asian Productivity Organization. q. D 1968(v.4, no.4)- , with gaps (Oc 1969, v.5, no.3; Oc 1970, v.6, no.2, D 1970, v.6, no.3). Tokyo.

— Brazil.

BOISIER (SERGIO) and others. Desenvolvimento regional e urbano: diferenciais de produtividade e salarios industriais. Rio de Janeiro, 1973. pp. 151. *(Brazil. Instituto de Planejamento Econômico e Social. Instituto de Pesquisas. Relatorios de Pesquisa. No.15)*

— France.

BROST (FRANZ FRIEDRICH) and VILLOT (JEAN GERARD) Analyse comparative de l'évolution structurelle des systèmes productifs français et ouest-allemands: une étude statistique pour la période de 1960 à 1974. Frankfurt am Main, [1978]. pp. 259. *bibliog.*

— Germany.

BROST (FRANZ FRIEDRICH) and VILLOT (JEAN GERARD) Analyse comparative de l'évolution structurelle des systèmes productifs français et ouest-allemands: une étude statistique pour la période de 1960 à 1974. Frankfurt am Main, [1978]. pp. 259. *bibliog.*

— Ireland (Republic).

COGAN (D.J.) The Irish services sector: a study of productive efficiency. Dublin, Stationery Office, 1978. pp. 244. *bibliog.*

— Italy.

MARZI (GRAZIELLA) and VARRI (PAOLO) Variazioni di produttività nell'economia italiana, 1959-1967: un'applicazione dello schema di Sraffa. Bologna, [1977]. pp. 129. *bibliog.*

— Russia.

BARKER (GEOFFREY RUSSELL) Some problems of incentives and labour productivity in Soviet industry: a contribution to the study of the planning of labour in the U.S.S.R. Oxford, [1955?]. pp. 129, xii. *(Birmingham. University. Faculty of Commerce and Social Science. Department of Economics and Institutions of the USSR. Monographs on the Soviet Economic System. No. 1)*

CHERNIAVSKII (VASILII OSIPOVICH) Voprosy effektivnosti i optimal'nosti. Moskva, 1977. pp. 171. *(Akademiia Nauk SSSR. Problemy Sovetskoi Ekonomiki)*

EKONOMICHESKAIA effektivnost' obshchestvennogo proizvodstva v period razvitogo sotsializma: metodologicheskie voprosy. Moskva, 1977. pp. 359. *(Akademiia Nauk SSSR. Problemy Sovetskoi Ekonomiki)*

NAZAROV (MIKHAIL GEORGIEVICH) Proizvoditel'nost' truda: izmerenie, analiz, rezervy. Moskva, 1977. pp. 207.

ABALKIN (LEONID IVANOVICH) Konechnye narodnokhoziaistvennye rezul'taty: sushchnost', pokazateli, puti povysheniia. Moskva, 1978. pp. 151.

BARANOV (ALEKSANDR ALEKSEEVICH) Intensivnoe sotsialisticheskoe proizvodstvo. Moskva, 1978. pp. 349. *bibliog.*

— United States.

ABERNATHY (WILLIAM J.) The productivity dilemma: roadblock to innovation in the automobile industry. Baltimore, [1978]. pp. 267. *bibliog.*

PROFESSIONAL EDUCATION

— Belgium.

INSTITUT BELGE D'INFORMATION ET DE DOCUMENTATION. Le monde des professions. [Brussels, 1968]. pp. 143.

— United Kingdom.

BUTLER (RICHARD AUSTEN) Baron Butler of Saffron Walden. The responsibilities of education. London, 1968. pp. 162. *bibliog. The inaugural P.D. Leake lecture. Includes appendix on the educational and training requirements of professional bodies.*

PROFESSIONS

— Canada.

The PROFESSIONS and public policy; edited by Philip Slayton and Michael J. Trebilcock. Toronto, [1978]. pp. 346. *Conference held October 15-16, 1976, and sponsored by the Law and Economics Program of the University of Toronto Faculty of Law.*

— — Quebec.

DUSSAULT (RENÉ) and BORGEAT (LOUIS) Reform of the professions in Quebec. Quebec, [1976]. pp. 71. *English version of article originally published in Revue du Barreau, vol. 34, no.3, May 1974.*

— South Africa.

DE KLERK (DANIEL) The profitability of occupations pursued by highly qualified persons in 1975. Pretoria, 1976. pp. 59. *bibliog. (Human Sciences Research Council [South Africa]. Institute for Manpower Research. Reports. No. MM-60)*

— United States.

HUMMER (PATRICIA M.) The decade of elusive promise: professional women in the United States, 1920-1930. [London, 1979]. pp. 182. *bibliog.*

PROFIT.

TUCKER (GEORGE) The laws of wages, profits and rent investigated. New York, 1964. pp. 189. *Reprint of the work first published Philadelphia, 1837.*

NEW challenges to the role of profit...; edited by Benjamin M. Friedman. Lexington, Mass., [1978]. pp. 127. *(Harvard University. Graduate School of Business Administration. John Diebold Lectures. 1976)*

ENGLUND (PETER) Profits and market adjustment: a study in the dynamics of production, productivity and rates of return. Stockholm, 1979. pp. 260. *bibliog.*

— France.

DELESTRE (HENRI) and MAIRESSE (JACQUES) La rentabilité des sociétés privées en France de 1956 à 1975. Paris, Institut National de la Statistique et des Etudes Economiques, 1978. pp. 154.

KING (MERVYN A.) and MAIRESSE (JACQUES) Profitability in Britain and France: a comparative study, 1956- 1975. Paris, Institut National de la Statistique et des Etudes Economiques, 1978. pp. 80.

— United Kingdom.

KING (MERVYN A.) and MAIRESSE (JACQUES) Profitability in Britain and France: a comparative study, 1956- 1975. Paris, Institut National de la Statistique et des Etudes Economiques, 1978. pp. 80.

PROFIT SHARING

— United Kingdom.

MORSE (GEOFFREY K.) and WILLIAMS (DAVID) Solicitor. Profit sharing: legal aspects of employee share schemes. London, 1979. pp. 224.

PROGRAMME BUDGETING

— Mathematical models.

GEARY (K.) Treatment of multiple objectives for programming problems: a review with reference to possible public sector application. London, 1978. pp. 25. *bibliog. (Planning Research Applications Group. PRAG Technical Papers. TP 25)*

— Canada.

CANADA. Treasury Board. Program performance measurement. a., 1979- Ottawa. *[in English and French]*

— United States.

PALMER (GREGORY) The McNamara strategy and the Vietnam war: program budgeting in the Pentagon, 1960-1968. Westport, Conn., [1978]. pp. 169. *bibliog.*

PROGRAMMING (ELECTRONIC COMPUTERS).

NATIONAL CONFERENCE ON SOFTWARE ENGINEERING, 1ST, WASHINGTON, 1975. Proceedings of the...Conference...sponsored by the National Bureau of Standards and the IEEE Computer Society. New York, [1975]. pp. 94.

FREEMAN (PETER) and WASSERMAN (ANTHONY I.) Tutorial on software design techniques. 2nd ed. Long Beach, Calif., [1977]. pp. 288. *bibliog.*

FINDLAY (WILLIAM) and WATT (DAVID A.) Pascal: an introduction to methodical programming. London, 1978 repr. 1979. pp. 306.

INTERNATIONAL CONFERENCE ON SOFTWARE ENGINEERING, 3RD, ATLANTA, 1978. Proceedings [of the]...conference. New York, [1978]. pp. 341. *bibliogs. Sponsored by the IEEE Computer Society, the National Bureau of Standards, and Association for Computing Machinery.*

PROGRAMMING methodology...; edited by David Gries. New York, [1978]. pp. 437. *bibliog.*

VAN TASSEL (DENNIS) Program style, design, efficiency, debugging, and testing. 2nd ed. Englewood Cliffs, N.J., [1978]. pp. 323. *bibliogs.*

PROGRESS.

PROGRESUL istoric şi contemporaneitatea. Bucureşti, 1976. pp. 538. *With English, French, German and Russian tables of contents.*

PROGRESSIVISM (U.S. POLITICS).

The AGE of urban reform: new perspectives on the progressive era; [edited by] Michael H. Ebner and Eugene M. Tobin. Port Washington, N.Y., 1977. pp. 213. *bibliog.*

WOLFE (MARGARET RIPLEY) Lucius Polk Brown and progressive food and drug control: Tennessee and New York City 1908-1920. Lawrence, Kan., [1978]. pp. 194.

PROOF THEORY.

FÖLDESI (TAMÁS) Grundlagen der Beweistheorie der marxistischen Philosophie; (aus dem Ungarischen übersetzt von Maria Bondy). Köln, 1977. pp. 480.

SCHUETTE (KURT) Proof theory; translation from the German by J.N. Crossley. Berlin, 1977. pp. 299. *bibliog.*

PROPAGANDA, BRITISH.

BALFOUR (MICHAEL) Propaganda in war, 1939-1945: organisations, policies and publics in Britain and Germany. London, 1979. pp. 520. *bibliog.*

PROPAGANDA, COMMUNIST.

AKADEMIIA OBSHCHESTVENNYKH NAUK. Kafedra Teorii i Metodov Ideologicheskoi Raboty. Voprosy Teorii i Metodov Ideologicheskoi Raboty. vyp.9. Problemy kompleksnogo podkhoda k ideologicheskoi rabotes; Propaganda preimushchestv sotsializma v usloviiakh sovremennoi ideologicheskoi bor'by. Moskva, 1978. pp. 280.

PROPAGANDA, GERMAN.

BALFOUR (MICHAEL) Propaganda in war, 1939-1945: organisations, policies and publics in Britain and Germany. London, 1979. pp. 520. *bibliog.*

HERZSTEIN (ROBERT EDWIN) The war that Hitler won: the most infamous propaganda campaign in history. London, 1979. pp. 491. *bibliog.*

TAYLOR (RICHARD TRUEMAN) Film propaganda: Soviet Russia and Nazi Germany. London, [1979]. pp. 265. *bibliog.*

PROPAGANDA, RUSSIAN.

TAYLOR (RICHARD TRUEMAN) Film propaganda: Soviet Russia and Nazi Germany. London, [1979]. pp. 265. *bibliog.*

PROPERTY.

DAY (J.G.) and JAMIESON (A.T.) Institutional investment. [London, 1975 repr. 1977-78]. 6 vols. *bibliogs.*

SCHMID (ALFRED ALLAN) Property, power, and public choice: an inquiry into law and economics. New York, [1978]. pp. 316. *bibliog.*

— Austria.

GSCHNITZER (FRANZ) Sachenrecht. Wien, 1968. pp. 237.

— European Economic Community countries.

GRAVENHORST (WULF) and others. The law of property in the European Community. Brussels, European Communities, [1976]. pp. 305. *(European Economic Community. Studies. Competition: Approximation of Legislation Series. 27)*

PROPERTY TAX

— Canada — Ontario.

ONTARIO. Commission on the Reform of Property Taxation in Ontario. 1977. Report; [Willis L. Blair, chairman]. [Toronto, 1977]. pp. 143.

BIRD (RICHARD MILLER) and SLACK (N. ENID) Residential property tax relief in Ontario. Toronto, [1978]. pp. 188. *bibliog. (Ontario. Economic Council. Research Studies. 15)*

— France.

FRANCE. Commission d'Etude d'un Prélèvement sur les Fortunes. 1979. Rapport...; membres de la Commission, Gabriel Ventejol [and others]. Paris, 1979. 3 vols. *bibliog.*

— Germany.

GERMANY. Statistisches Reichsamt. Statistik des Deutschen Reichs. Neue Folge. Band 365. Statistik der Einheitswerte für den ersten Hauptfeststellungszeitraum, 1925-1927. Berlin, 1930; Osnabrück, 1978. pp. 341. *Photographic reprint.*

GERMANY. Statistisches Reichsamt. Statistik des Deutschen Reichs. Neue Folge. Band 392. Statistik der Einheitswerte für den zweiten Hauptfeststellungszeitraum, 1928-1930. Berlin, 1931; Osnabrück, 1978. pp. 231. *Photographic reprint.*

— Switzerland — Bern (Canton).

BERN (CANTON). Amt für Statistik. 1978. Eidg. Abstimmung vom 4. Dezember 1977 im Kanton Bern: Reichtumsteuer-Initiative, etc. Bern, 1978. pp. 74. *(Beiträge zur Statistik des Kantons Bern. Politische Statistik. Reihe F. Heft 5) In French and German.*

PROSECUTION

— United Kingdom.

U.K. Home Office. 1978. Evidence to the Royal Commission on Criminal Procedure: memorandum no. 8: the prosecution process. London, 1978. pp. 52.

PROSTITUTION

— United Kingdom.

SION (ABRAHAM A.) Prostitution and the law. London, 1977. pp. 160. *bibliog.*

FINNEGAN (FRANCES) Poverty and prostitution: a study of Victorian prostitutes in York. Cambridge, 1979. pp. 231. *bibliog.*

PROTECTORATES.

RUBIN (ALFRED P.) Piracy, paramountcy and protectorates. Kuala Lumpur, 1974. pp. 179. *bibliog.*

PROTEINS.

PAG BULLETIN: (international review of action to improve world protein nutrition); [pd. by] Protein-Calorie Advisory Group of the United Nations System. irreg., 1971(no.11)- , with gap (1972: v.2, no.3). New York.

PROTESTANT CHURCHES

— United States.

PRIMER (BEN) Protestants and American business methods. [London, 1979]. pp. 223. *bibliog.*

SINGLETON (GREGORY H.) Religion in the city of angels: American protestant culture and urbanization, Los Angeles, 1850-1930. [London, 1979]. pp. 262. *bibliog.*

PROTESTANTISM AND CAPITALISM.

PRIMER (BEN) Protestants and American business methods. [London, 1979]. pp. 223. *bibliog.*

PROTESTANTS IN AUSTRIA.

FLOREY (GERHARD) Geschichte der Salzburger Protestanten und ihrer Emigration, 1731/32. Wien, [1977]. pp. 276. *bibliog.*

PROTESTANTS IN LATIN AMERICA

— Bibliography.

SINCLAIR (JOHN H.) compiler. Protestantism in Latin America: a bibliographical guide, etc. [2nd ed.] South Pasadena, Calif., [1976]. pp. 415.

PROTESTANTS IN NORTHERN IRELAND.

MILLER (DAVID WILLIAM) Queen's rebels: Ulster loyalism in historical perspective. Dublin, 1978. pp. 194.

PROTESTANTS IN THE UNITED STATES.

GREVEN (PHILIP J.) The protestant temperament: patterns of child-rearing, religious experience, and the self in early America. New York, 1977. pp. 431.

PROUDHON (PIERRE JOSEPH).

RAPPOPORT (CHARLES) P.J. Proudhon et le socialisme scientifique, 1809-1909. Paris, [191-]. pp. 48.

HYAMS (EDWARD SOLOMON) Pierre Joseph Proudhon: his revolutionary life, mind and works. London, 1979. pp. 304.

PRUEM

— Social history.

KUCHENBUCH (LUDOLF) Bäuerliche Gesellschaft und Klosterherrschaft im 9. Jahrhundert: Studien zur Sozialstruktur der Familia der Abtei Prüm. Wiesbaden, 1978. pp. 443. *bibliog. (Vierteljahrschrift für Sozial- und Wirtschaftsgeschichte. Beihefte. Nr. 66)*

PRÜM.

See PRUEM.

PRUSSIA

— Dictionaries and encyclopedias.

PRUSSIA. Staatsministerium. Pressestelle. 1932. Preussen, 1932: Politik in Stichworten. [2nd ed.] Berlin, 1932. pp. 159.

— Economic history.

MITTENZWEI (INGRID) Preussen nach dem Siebenjährigen Krieg: Auseinandersetzungen zwischen Bürgertum und Staat um die Wirtschaftspolitik. Berlin, 1979. pp. 266. *bibliog. (Akademie der Wissenschaften der DDR. Zentralinstitut für Geschichte. Schriften. Band 62)*

— History.

KAPLAN (HERBERT HAROLD) Russia and the outbreak of the Seven Years' War. Berkeley, 1968. pp. 165. *bibliog.*

KOCH (HANNSJOACHIM WOLFGANG) A history of Prussia. London, 1978. pp. 326. *bibliog.*

— — 1740-1786, Frederick II, the Great.

REDDAWAY (WILLIAM FIDDIAN) Frederick the Great and the rise of Prussia. New York, 1904; New York, 1969. pp. 368.

— Politics and government.

PRUSSIA. Staatsministerium. Pressestelle. 1932. Preussen, 1932: Politik in Stichworten. [2nd ed.] Berlin, 1932. pp. 159.

— Social history.

LAGE und Kampf der Landarbeiter im ostelbischen Preussen, vom Anfang des 19. Jahrhunderts bis zur Novemberrevolution 1918/19...: Quellen; Einleitung: Hans Hübner; Auswahl und Bearbeitung: Hans Hübner und Heinz Kathe. Vaduz, 1977. 2 vols. *(Akademie der Wissenschaften der DDR. Zentralinstitut für Geschichte. Archivalische Forschungen zur Geschichte der Deutschen Arbeiterbewegung. Band 8)*

SCHISSLER (HANNA) Preussische Agrargesellschaft im Wandel: wirtschaftliche, gesellschaftliche und politische Transformationsprozesse von 1763 bis 1847. Göttingen, 1978. pp. 285. *bibliog.*

PSYCHIATRIC CLINICS

— United Kingdom.

PINSENT (ELLEN FRANCES) The mental health services in Oxford city, Oxfordshire and Berkshire. Oxford, 1937. pp. 87.

PSYCHIATRIC HOSPITALS.

ALTERNATIVES to mental hospital treatment; edited by Leonard I. Stein and Mary Ann Test. New York, [1978]. pp. 327. *bibliogs. Papers from the Conference on Alternatives to Mental Hospital Treatment, Madison, Wis., 1975.*

— Europe.

WORKING GROUP ON THE FUTURE OF MENTAL HOSPITALS. The future of mental hospitals: report on a working group [held in] Mannheim, 2-5 November 1976. Copenhagen, World Health Organization, Regional Office for Europe, 1978. pp. 68.

— United Kingdom.

PINSENT (ELLEN FRANCES) The mental health services in Oxford city, Oxfordshire and Berkshire. Oxford, 1937. pp. 87.

SCULL (ANDREW T.) Museums of madness: the social organization of insanity in nineteenth-century England. London, 1979. pp. 275.

— — Statistics.

DAVIES (HYWEL) Admissions of residents of Greater London to psychiatric hospitals and units, 1974 and 1975. London, [1978]. pp. 93. *(London. Greater London Council. Research Memoranda. 535)*

— — Scotland.

STATE Hospital, Carstairs: report of public local inquiry into circumstances surrounding the escape of two patients on 30 November 1976 and into security and other arrangements at the hospital; (presented to the Secretary of State for Scotland by Sheriff Principal R. Reid). Edinburgh, H.M.S.O., 1977. pp. 73.

— — Wales — Statistics.

U.K. Welsh Office. Mental illness and mental handicap: hospitals and units in Wales: statistics (formerly Statistics of psychiatric hospitals in Wales). a., 1973/1974(1st)- Cardiff.

PSYCHIATRIC SOCIAL WORK

— United Kingdom — Scotland.

TIBBITT (JOHN E.) Social workers as mental health officers. Edinburgh, 1978. pp. 41. *(Scotland. Scottish Office. Social Research Studies)*

PSYCHIATRY.

EYSENCK (HANS JÜRGEN) The dynamics of anxiety and hysteria: an experimental application of modern learning theory to psychiatry. London, 1957. pp. 311. *bibliog.*

SIEGLER (MIRIAM) and OSMOND (HUMPHRY) Models of madness, models of medicine. New York, [1974]. pp. 287. *bibliog.*

HOWARTH-WILLIAMS (MARTIN) R.D. Laing: his work and its relevance for sociology. London, 1977. pp. 219. *bibliog.*

PINSENT (ELLEN FRANCES) The mental health services in Oxford city, Oxfordshire and Berkshire. Oxford, 1937. pp. 87.

PSYCHOANALYSIS.

MARXISME-léninisme et psychanalysme (sic). Paris, 1975. pp. 162. *(Groupe Yenan, Cahiers Yenan. No. 1)*

BOCOCK (ROBERT) Freud and modern society: an outline and analysis of Freud's sociology. New York, 1978. pp. 200. *bibliog.*

RYCROFT (CHARLES) The innocence of dreams. London, 1979. pp. 184.

SEGAL (HANNA) Klein. [London], 1979. pp. 189. *bibliog.*

PSYCHOBIOLOGY.

REYNOLDS (VERNON) The biology of human action. San Francisco, [1976]. pp. 269. *bibliog.*

PSYCHOLINGUISTICS.

VYGOTSKII (LEV SEMENOVICH) Thought and language; edited and translated by Eugenia Hanfmann and Gertrude Vakar. Cambridge, Mass., 1962. pp. 168. *bibliog.*

LANGUAGE learning and thought; edited by John Macnamara. New York, 1977. pp. 296. *bibliogs.*

MENYUK (PAULA) Language and maturation. Cambridge, Mass., [1977]. pp. 180. *bibliog.*

ACTION, gesture and symbol: the emergence of language; edited by Andrew Lock. London, 1978. pp. 588. *bibliog.*

DE VILLIERS (JILL G.) and DE VILLIERS (PETER A.) Language acquisition. Cambridge, Mass., 1978. pp. 312. *bibliog.*

MERINGER (RUDOLF) and MAYER (CARL) Versprechen und verlesen: eine psychologisch-linguistische Studie; new edition with an introductory article by Anne Cutler and David Fay. Amsterdam, 1978. pp. 207.

PSYCHOLINGUISTICS series. 2. Structures and processes; [by] N.V. Smith [and others]. London, 1979. pp. 187. *bibliogs.*

— **Bibliography.**

ABRAHAMSEN (ADELE A.) compiler. Child language: an interdisciplinary guide to theory and research. Baltimore, [1977]. pp. 381. bibliogs.

— **Congresses.**

STIRLING PSYCHOLOGY OF LANGUAGE CONFERENCE, UNIVERSITY OF STIRLING, 1976. Recent advances in the psychology of language: (proceedings of the...Conference...sponsored by the NATO Special Program Panel on Human Factors); edited by Robin N. Campbell and Philip T. Smith. New York, 1978. 2 vols. bibliogs. (North Atlantic Treaty Organization. NATO Conference Series. Series III: Human Factors. vol.4)

PSYCHOLOGICAL WARFARE.

OWEN (DAVID) b. 1939. Battle of wits: a history of psychology and deception in modern warfare. London, 1978. pp. 207.

PSYCHOLOGY.

NEW horizons in psychology, 1; edited by Brian M. Foss. Harmondsworth, 1966 repr. 1977. pp. 448. bibliog.

RACHMAN (STANLEY) and PHILIPS (CLARE) Psychology and medicine. Harmondsworth, 1978. pp. 205. *First published in London, 1975.*

COE (SAMUEL P.) Contemporary psychology in Marx and Engels. New York, 1978. pp. 53. (American Institute for Marxist Studies. Occasional Papers. No. 26)

PERSONAL construct psychology, 1977; edited by Fay Fransella. London, 1978. pp. 274. *Based on papers given at the Second International Congress on Personal Construct Theory held at Oxford in July 1977.*

MAUSS (MARCEL) Sociology and psychology: essays; translated by Ben Brewster. London, 1979. pp. 135. bibliog.

WICKELGREN (WAYNE A.) Cognitive psychology. Englewood Cliffs, N.J., [1979]. pp. 436. bibliog.

— **Mathematical models.**

THEORY construction and data analysis in the behavioral sciences: a volume in honor of Louis Guttman; [edited by] Samuel Shye. San Francisco, 1978. pp. 426. bibliog.

— **Methodology.**

WOHLWILL (JOACHIM F.) The study of behavioral development. New York, 1973. pp. 413. bibliog.

PSYCHOLOGY, EXPERIMENTAL.

BINET (ALFRED) The experimental psychology of Alfred Binet: selected papers; edited by Robert H. Pollack and Margaret W. Brenner; translated by Frances K. Zetland [and] Claire Ellis. New York, [1969]. pp. 235. bibliog.

PSYCHOLOGY, FORENSIC.

PSYCHOLOGY, law and legal processes; edited by David P. Farrington, Keith Hawkins, Sally M. Lloyd-Bostock. London, 1979. pp. 222. bibliogs. (U.K. Social Science Research Council. Centre for Socio-Legal Studies. Oxford Socio-Legal Studies)

PSYCHOLOGY, INDUSTRIAL.

ORGANIZATIONAL behaviour in its context: the Aston programme III; edited by D.S. Pugh [and] R.L. Payne. Farnborough, Hants., [1977]. pp. 188. bibliog.

MISFITS in industry; edited by Pasquale A. Carone [and others]. New York, [1978]. pp. 152. *Based on the proceedings of the seventh annual conference on the problems of industrial psychiatric medicine, Stony Brook, 1977.*

INDUSTRIAL relations: a social psychological approach; edited by Geoffrey M. Stephenson and Christopher J. Brotherton. Chichester, [1979]. pp. 412. bibliog.

PSYCHOLOGY, MILITARY.

SHIBUTANI (TAMOTSU) The derelicts of company K: a sociological study of demoralization. Berkeley, Calif., [1978]. pp. 455. bibliog.

PSYCHOLOGY, PATHOLOGICAL.

EYSENCK (HANS JÜRGEN) The dynamics of anxiety and hysteria: an experimental application of modern learning theory to psychiatry. London, 1957. pp. 311. bibliog.

PSYCHOPATHIC disorders and their assessment; edited by Michael Craft. Oxford, [1966]. pp. 320. bibliog.

CLECKLEY (HERVEY MILTON) The mask of sanity: an attempt to clarify some issues about the so-called psychopathic personality. 5th ed. Saint Louis, 1976. pp. 471. bibliog.

PSYCHOLOGY, RELIGIOUS.

ECCLESIASTICAL HISTORY SOCIETY. Summer Meeting, 16th, and Winter Meeting, 17th, 197-. Religious motivation: biographical and sociological problems for the church historian: papers read at the...meeting[s]...; edited by Derek Baker. Oxford, 1978. pp. 516. (Studies in Church History. vol.15)

PSYCHOMETRICS.

MAXWELL (ALBERT ERNEST) Multivariate analysis in behavioural research. London, 1977. pp. 164. bibliog.

The MEASUREMENT of intrapersonal space by grid technique. Vol. 2. Dimensions of intrapersonal space; edited by Patrick Slater. London, [1977]. pp. 270.

NEW perspectives in personal construct theory; edited by D. Bannister. London, 1977. pp. 355. bibliogs.

ADAMS-WEBBER (J.R.) Personal construct theory: concepts and applications. Chichester, [1979]. pp. 239. bibliog.

ALLEN (MARY J.) and YEN (WENDY M.) Introduction to measurement theory. Monterey, Calif., [1979]. pp. 310. bibliog.

PSYCHOTHERAPY.

HALEY (JAY) Strategies of psychotherapy. New York, [1963]. pp. 204. bibliog.

PUBLIC CONTRACTS

— **United States.**

HOLTZ (HERMAN) Government contracts: proposalmanship and winning strategies. New York, [1979]. pp. 288.

PUBLIC GOODS.

ESSAYS in public economics: the Kiryat Anavim papers; edited by Agnar Sandmo. Lexington, Mass., [1978]. pp. 367. bibliogs. *Papers of a conference held at Kibbutz Kiryat Anavim, 1975.*

KINDLEBERGER (CHARLES POOR) Government and international trade. Princeton, 1978. pp. 19. bibliog. (Princeton University. Department of Economics and Sociology. International Finance Section. Essays in International Finance. No. 129)

PUBLIC goods and public policy; edited by William Loehr and Todd Sandler. Beverly Hills, [1978]. pp. 240. bibliogs.

SANDLER (TODD M.) and others. The political economy of public goods and international cooperation. Denver, Colo., [1978]. pp. 98. bibliog. (Denver. University. Graduate School of International Studies. Monograph Series in World Affairs. vol. 15, no. 3)

BROWNING (EDGAR K.) and BROWNING (JACQUELENE M.) Public finance and the price system. New York, [1979]. pp. 464. bibliogs.

PUBLIC HEALTH ADMINISTRATION

— **Argentine Republic.**

ESCUDE (CARLOS) Aspectos ocultos de la salud en la Argentina: la productividad de los recursos del sector. Buenos Aires, 1976. pp. 131.

PUBLIC HEALTH PERSONNEL

— **Education — Europe.**

WORKING GROUP ON THE CONTINUING EDUCATION OF HEALTH PERSONNEL. Continuing education of health personnel: report on a working group [held in] Dublin, 18-21 October, 1976. Copenhagen, World Health Organization, Regional Office for Europe, 1977. pp. 29.

— **United States.**

WOLFE (MARGARET RIPLEY) Lucius Polk Brown and progressive food and drug control: Tennessee and New York City 1908-1920. Lawrence, Kan., [1978]. pp. 194.

PUBLIC HEALTH RESEARCH

— **India.**

WORLD HEALTH ORGANIZATION. 1968. The Central Public Health Engineering Research Institute, Nagpur, India: report prepared for the Government of India by the World Health Organization acting. ..for the United Nations Development Programme. Geneva, 1968. pp. 56.

PUBLIC HOUSING

— **United Kingdom.**

FIELD (FRANK) 1942- . Do we need council houses? London, [1975]. pp. 16. (Catholic Housing Aid Society. Occasional Papers. 2)

GRIFFITHS (PETRA) Homes fit for heroes; a Shelter report on council housing. London, 1975. pp. 74.

GORRIE (DONALD) Tenants' cooperatives. Manchester, [1977?]. pp. 15.

NATIONAL CONSUMER COUNCIL. Social Policy Unit. Access, allocation and transfers in council housing: the... Council's response to the Department of the Environment consultation paper. London, 1977. pp. 34.

The SALE of council houses: papers presented at a one-day conference on the sale of council houses...on 5th October 1976; edited by John English and Colin Jones. Glasgow, 1977. pp. 100. bibliogs. (Glasgow. University. Department of Economic and Social Research. Discussion Papers in Social Research. No.18)

RICHARDSON (ANN WICKENDEN) The politics of participation: a study of schemes for tenant participation in council housing management. 1978. fo. 430. bibliog. *Typescript. Ph.D. (London) thesis: unpublished. This thesis is the property of London University and may not be removed from the Library.*

U.K. Housing Services Advisory Group. 1978. Allocation of council housing; [T.L. Jones, chairman]. [London, 1978]. pp. 76.

U.K. Housing Services Advisory Group. 1978. The housing of one-parent families; [T.L. Jones, chairman]. [London, 1978]. pp. 25.

MERRETT (STEPHEN) State housing in Britain. London, 1979. pp. 376. bibliog.

— — **Rent.**

DOWNEY (PATRICIA) Rent arrears in local authority housing: a discussion paper. [London], Department of the Environment, [1978]. pp. 18. bibliog. (HDD Occasional Papers. 78/1)

— — **Birmingham.**

FLETT (HAZEL) Black council tenants in Birmingham. Bristol, Social Science Research Council Research Unit on Ethnic Relations, [1979]. pp. 79. bibliog. (Working Papers on Ethnic Relations. No. 12)

PUBLIC HOUSING(Cont.)

— — London.

PHILLIPS (MARK) Homelessness and tenants' control: struggles for council housing in Tower Hamlets, 1974-1976. London, 1977. pp. 123.

A STREET door of our own; a short history of life on an LCC estate by local people from the Honor Oak estate. London, 1977. pp. 48.

— — Newcastle-upon-Tyne.

BENWELL COMMUNITY DEVELOPMENT PROJECT. Pendower: whatever happened to the homes for the heroes; (a joint report from Benwell C.D.P. and Newcastle Housing Department). [Newcastle-upon-Tyne, 1977]. pp. 16.

BENWELL COMMUNITY DEVELOPMENT PROJECT. Slums on the drawing board. Newcastle-upon-Tyne, 1978. pp. 47. *(Final Report Series. No. 4)*

— — North Tyneside.

NORTH TYNESIDE COMMUNITY DEVELOPMENT PROJECT. North Shields: working class politics and housing, 1900-1977. [Newcastle-upon-Tyne, 1978]. pp. 72. *(Final Reports. Vol.1)*

— — Scotland — Clydebank — Rent.

O'BRIEN (FREDERICK WILLIAM FITZGERALD) Report...on the local inquiry in relation to the implementation by Clydebank Town Council of Parts 2 and 4 of the Housing, Financial Provisions, Scotland, Act 1972. Edinburgh, H.M.S.O., [1973]. pp. 9.

— — — Dunfermline — Rent.

TAYLOR (ROBERT RICHARDSON) Report...on the local inquiry in relation to the implementation by Dunfermline Town Council of Parts 2 and 4 of the Housing, Financial Provisions, Scotland, Act 1972. Edinburgh, H.M.S.O., [1973]. pp. 7.

— — — Falkirk — Rent.

JAUNCEY (C.E.) Report...on the local inquiry in relation to the implementation by Falkirk Town Council of Parts 2 and 4 of the Housing, Financial Provisions, Scotland, Act 1972. Edinburgh, H.M.S.O., [1972]. pp. 7.

— — — Glasgow — Rent.

MACDONALD (IAN ALEXANDER) Report...on the local inquiry in relation to the implementation by Glasgow Corporation of Parts 2 and 4 of the Housing, Financial Provisions, Scotland, Act 1972. Edinburgh, H.M.S.O., [1972]. pp. 10.

— — — Kilmarnock — Rent.

CAMERON (KENNETH JOHN) Report...on the local inquiry in relation to the implementation by Kilmarnock Town Council of Parts 2 and 4 of the Housing, Financial Provisions, Scotland, Act 1972. Edinburgh, H.M.S.O., [1973]. pp. 9.

— — — Kirkcaldy — Rent.

MAXWELL (PETER) Lord. Report...on the local inquiry in relation to the implementation by Kirkcaldy Town Council of Parts 2 and 4 of the Housing, Financial Provisions, Scotland, Act 1972. Edinburgh, H.M.S.O., [1972]. pp. 8.

— — — Lanark — Rent.

ROSS (DONALD MACARTHUR) Report...on the local inquiry in relation to the implementation by Lanark County Council of Parts 2 and 4 of the Housing, Financial Provisions, Scotland, Act 1972. Edinburgh, H.M.S.O., [1972]. pp. 10.

— — — Midlothian — Rent.

MACDONALD (IAN ALEXANDER) Report...on the local inquiry in relation to the implementation by Midlothian County Council of Parts 2 and 4 of the Housing, Financial Provisions, Scotland, Act 1972. Edinburgh, H.M.S.O., [1973]. pp. 13.

— — — Paisley.

PAISLEY COMMUNITY DEVELOPMENT PROJECT. Against eviction; (by Barbara Jackson [and others]). [Paisley, 1978]. pp. (91).

PAISLEY COMMUNITY DEVELOPMENT PROJECT. Housing allocations and social segregation; (by John English). Paisley, 1978. pp. 22.

PAISLEY COMMUNITY DEVELOPMENT PROJECT. A profile of Ferguslie Park; (by John English). [Paisley, 1978]. pp. 22.

PAISLEY COMMUNITY DEVELOPMENT PROJECT. Westmarch action group: a fight for improvements; (by Barbara Jackson). [Paisley, 1978]. pp. 59.

— United States — Chicago.

BOWLY (DEVEREUX) The poorhouse: subsidized housing in Chicago, 1895-1976. Carbondale, Ill., [1978]. pp. 254. *bibliog.*

PUBLIC MEETINGS

— United Kingdom.

GOLDSMITH (MICHAEL) and SAUNDERS (PETER) Participation through public meetings: the case in Cheshire. [London], 1976. pp. 30. *(Linked Research Project into Public Participation in Structure Planning. Interim Research Papers. 9)*

PUBLIC OPINION.

MOODIE (GRAEME COCHRANE) and STUDDERT-KENNEDY (GERALD) Opinions, publics and pressure groups: an essay on vox populi and representative government. London, 1970. pp. 115.

OSKAMP (STUART) Attitudes and opinions. Englewood Cliffs, [1977]. pp. 466. *bibliogs.*

— America, Latin.

REID (JOHN TURNER) Spanish American images of the United States, 1790-1960. Gainesville, 1977. pp. 298. *bibliog.*

— France.

REPONSES à la violence...Recherches sur l'urbanisation, l'habitat et la violence. Paris, [1977]. pp. 424. *bibliog. (France. Comité d'Etudes sur la Violence, la Criminalité et la Délinquance. Annexes. 3)*

— Germany.

WIPPERMANN (KLAUS W.) Politische Propaganda und staatsbürgerliche Bildung: die Reichszentrale für Heimatdienst in der Weimarer Republik. Köln, [1976]. pp. 584. *bibliog.*

— Ireland (Republic).

ROSE (RICHARD) and others. Is there a concurring majority about Northern Ireland? Glasgow, [1978]. pp. 67. *bibliog. (Glasgow. University of Strathclyde. Centre for the Study of Public Policy. Studies in Public Policy. No. 22)*

— United Kingdom.

CLARKE (FRANCIS GORDON) The land of contrarieties: British attitudes to the Australian colonies, 1828-1835. Melbourne, 1977. pp. 223. *bibliog.*

AUGHEY (ARTHUR) Conservative party attitudes towards the Common Market. Hull, 1978. fo. 29. *(Hull. University. Department of Politics. Hull Papers in Politics. No. 2)*

HAMPTON (WILLIAM) and WALKER (RAYMOND) The individual citizen and public participation: a survey of individual written response in Teesside. [London], 1978. pp. 24. *(Linked Research Project into Public Participation in Structure Planning. Interim Research Papers. 13)*

ROSE (RICHARD) and others. Is there a concurring majority about Northern Ireland? Glasgow, [1978]. pp. 67. *bibliog. (Glasgow. University of Strathclyde. Centre for the Study of Public Policy. Studies in Public Policy. No. 22)*

STRINGER (PETER) Tuning in to the public: survey before participation. [London], 1978. pp. 44. *(Linked Research Project into Public Participation in Structure Planning. Interim Research Papers. 14)*

SOCIAL SERVICES RESEARCH AND INTELLIGENCE UNIT [PORTSMOUTH]. Occasional Papers. No. 6. A community's perception of the physically disabled; [by] G. Williams. Portsmouth, 1979. fo. 20.

— — Ireland, Northern.

ROSE (RICHARD) and others. Is there a concurring majority about Northern Ireland? Glasgow, [1978]. pp. 67. *bibliog. (Glasgow. University of Strathclyde. Centre for the Study of Public Policy. Studies in Public Policy. No. 22)*

— — Wales.

BOLLOM (CHRIS) Attitudes and second homes in rural Wales. Cardiff, 1978. pp. 126. *(Wales. University. Board of Celtic Studies. Social Science Monographs. No. 3)*

— United States.

CHISMAN (FORREST P.) Attitude psychology and the study of public opinion. University Park, Pa., [1976]. pp. 253. *bibliog.*

CARTER (PURVIS M.) Congressional and public reaction to Wilson's Caribbean policy, 1913-1917. New York, [1977]. pp. 164. *bibliog.*

AMERICAN appraisals of Soviet Russia, 1917-1977; edited, with an introduction and commentaries, by Eugene Anschel. Metuchen, N.J., 1978. pp. 386. *bibliog.*

MACDOWELL (MICHAEL ALAN) Public understanding of economic policies: the tax cuts of 1962 and 1964. New York, 1978. pp. 321. *bibliog.*

PUBLIC OPINION POLLS.

OSKAMP (STUART) Attitudes and opinions. Englewood Cliffs, [1977]. pp. 466. *bibliogs.*

SONQUIST (JOHN A.) and DUNKELBERG (WILLIAM C.) Survey and opinion research: procedures for processing and analysis. Englewood Cliffs, N.J., [1977]. pp. 502. *bibliog.*

PUBLIC PROSECUTORS

— Russia.

NOVIKOV (SAVELII GRIGOR'EVICH) Prokurorskaia sistema v SSSR. Moskva, 1977. pp. 168.

PUBLIC RECORDS

— United States.

ON record: files and dossiers in American life; edited by Stanton Wheeler. New Brunswick, N.J., [1976]. pp. 449.

PUBLIC RELATIONS

— Police.

POTVIN (JEAN PAUL) and TISSEYRE (CHARLES) La police vue par les jeunes. Bruxelles, 1978. pp. 315. *bibliog. (Centre d'Etude de la Délinquance Juvénile. Publications. No. 42)*

PUBLIC SERVICE

— United States.

PUBLIC employee unions: a study of the crisis in public sector labor relations; A. Lawrence Chickering, editor. San Francisco, [1976]. pp. 248. *bibliog.*

PUBLIC SPEAKING.

WALKER (G.E.M.) "Speech!": a simple guide to the platform. London, [1933]. pp. 95.

PUBLIC UTILITIES.

CREW (MICHAEL A.) and KLEINDORFER (PAUL R.) Public utility economics. London, 1979. pp. 246. *bibliog.*

SCHMALENSEE (RICHARD) The control of natural monopolies. Lexington, Mass., [1979]. pp. 178. *bibliog.*

PUBLICITY (LAW)

— United States.

BERKSON (LARRY CHARLES) The Supreme Court and its publics: the communication of policy decisions. Lexington, Mass., 1978. pp. 145.

PUBLISHERS AND PUBLISHING

— Canada — Statistics.

CANADA. Statistics Canada. Culture statistics: book publishing: a cultural analysis. a., 1975(1st)- Ottawa. *[in English and French]*

CANADA. Statistics Canada. Culture statistics: book publishing: an industry analysis. a., 1975(1st)- Ottawa. *[in English and French]*

CANADA. Statistics Canada. Culture statistics: book publishing: text books. a., 1975(1st)- Ottawa. *[in English and French]*

— Germany.

GERMANY (BUNDESREPUBLIK). Statistisches Bundesamt. Verlagswesen. quadrennial, 1972. Wiesbaden. *(Unternehmen und Arbeitsstätten. Reihe 1.5.3) Superseded by* GERMANY (BUNDESREPUBLIK). *Statistisches Bundesamt. Kostenstruktur im Grosshandel bei Buch- u.ä. Verlagen.*

GERMANY (BUNDESREPUBLIK). Statistisches Bundesamt. Kostenstruktur im Grosshandel bei Buch- u.ä. Verlagen. quadrennial, 1976- Wiesbaden. *(Unternehmen und Arbeitsstätten. Reihe 1.2.1) Supersedes* GERMANY (BUNDESREPUBLIK). *Statistisches Bundesamt. Verlagswesen and* GERMANY (BUNDESREPUBLIK). *Statistisches Bundesamt. Grosshandel.*

— Poland.

LAM (STANISŁAW) 'Zycie wśród wielu; przygotował do druku Andrzej Lam. [Warszawa, 1968]. pp. 449.

— Russia.

PRAVOVOE regulirovanie obshchestvennykh otnoshenii. Moskva, 1976. pp. 120.

— United Kingdom.

WORKERS' PUBLICATIONS LIMITED. Rules of the Workers' Publications Limited. London, [1926]. pp. 23.

WORKERS' PUBLICATIONS LIMITED. Committee of Management. Report. London, [1927]. pp. 12.

CENTERPRISE TRUST. Local publishing and local culture: an account of the work of the Centerprise publishing project, 1972-1977. London, [1977]. pp. 22.

PUEA (TE).

See PUEA HERANGI (TE).

PUEA HERANGI (TE).

KING (MICHAEL) Writer on Maoris. Te Puea: a biography. Auckland, [1977]. pp. 331. *bibliog.*

PUEBLO CRISIS, 1968.

SIMMONS (ROBERT R.) The Pueblo, EC-121, and Mayaguez incidents: some continuities and changes. Baltimore, 1978. pp. 51. *(Maryland University. School of Law. Occasional Papers/Reprints Series in Contemporary Asian Studies. No.20)*

PUERTO RICO

— Economic policy.

GOLDSMITH (WILLIAM W.) and VIETORISZ (THOMAS) A new development strategy for Puerto Rico: technological autonomy, human resources, a parallel economy. Ithaca, N.Y., 1978. pp. 105.

— Politics and government.

CABRANES (JOSÉ A.) Citizenship and the American Empire: notes on the legislative history of the United States citizenship of Puerto Ricans. New Haven, 1979. pp. 101. *Reprinted from University of Pennsylvania Law Review, 1978*

PUGLIA

— History.

DILIO (MARIO) Puglia antifascista. Bari, [1977]. pp. 320. *bibliog.*

PUNAAUIA

— Social conditions.

FAGES (JEAN) Punaauia-Paea: contact ville-campagne et croissance urbaine de la côte ouest de Tahiti. Paris, 1975. pp. 111. *bibliog. (France. Office de la Recherche Scientifique et Technique Outre-Mer. Travaux et Documents. No. 41)*

PUNISHMENT.

MANNHEIM (HERMANN) Group problems in crime and punishment, and other studies in criminology and criminal law. 2nd ed. Montclair, N.J., 1971. pp. 328.

VAN DEN HAAG (ERNEST) Punishing criminals: concerning a very old and painful question. New York, [1975]. pp. 283. *bibliog.*

— Europe.

WEISSER (MICHAEL R.) Crime and punishment in early modern Europe. Hassocks, 1979. pp. 193. *bibliog.*

— Germany.

MUELLER (TERESA) Die Haltung der Parteien zu den Problemen von Strafe und Strafvollzug. Frankfurt am Main, [1977]. pp. 355. *bibliog.*

— United Kingdom.

U.K. Home Office. 1978. The sentence of the court: a handbook for courts on the treatment of offenders. 3rd ed. London, 1978. pp. 90. *bibliog.*

PUNJAB (INDIA)

— Commerce.

PUNJAB (INDIA). Economic and Statistical Organisation. 1976. Report on the distributive trade survey relating to urban areas of Punjab. Chandigarh, 1976. pp. 206. *(Publications. No. 218)*

— Economic conditions.

PUNJAB (INDIA). Economic and Statistical Organisation. 1974. Compendium of the evaluation studies in Punjab. (Volume 2), 1970-71 to 1972-73. Chandigarh, [1974]. pp. 401. *(Publications. No. 200)*

— Economic policy.

PUNJAB (INDIA). Planning Department. 1965. Preliminary memorandum on the fourth five-year plan, Punjab State. Chandigarh, [1965]. pp. 70.

— Social conditions.

PUNJAB (INDIA). Economic and Statistical Organisation. 1974. Compendium of the evaluation studies in Punjab. (Volume 2), 1970-71 to 1972-73. Chandigarh, [1974]. pp. 401. *(Publications. No. 200)*

— Social policy.

PUNJAB (INDIA). Planning Department. 1965. Preliminary memorandum on the fourth five-year plan, Punjab State. Chandigarh, [1965]. pp. 70.

— Vidhan Sabha — Elections.

PUNJAB (INDIA). Chief Electoral Officer. 1974. Report on the general election to the Punjab Vidhan Sabha, 1972. Chandigarh, 1974. pp. 79.

PURCHASING POWER.

INTERNATIONAL comparisons of real product and purchasing power: (United Nations International Comparison Project, phase II); produced by the Statistical Office of the United Nations and the World Bank...; published for the World Bank. Baltimore, [1978]. pp. 264.

— Sweden.

SWEDEN. Inrikesdepartementet. Låginkomstutredningen. 1971. Den svenska köpkrafts fördelningen, 1967: betänkande, etc. Stockholm, 1971. pp. 343. *(Sweden. Statens Offentliga Utredningar. 1971. 39)*

PURITANS.

EMERSON (EVERETT) Puritanism in America, 1620-1750. Boston, [Mass.], 1977. pp. 180. *bibliog.*

SLATER (PETER GREGG) Children in the New England mind in death and in life. Hamden, Conn., 1977. pp. 248. *bibliog.*

STANNARD (DAVID E.) The Puritan way of death: a study in religion, culture and social change. New York, 1977. pp. 236.

PUT AND CALL TRANSACTIONS.

BRODY (EUGENE D.) and BLISS (BETSY L.) Odds-on investing: survival and success in the new stock market. New York, [1978]. pp. 238.

PYTHAGORAS.

GORMAN (PETER) Pythagoras: a life. London, 1979. pp. 216. *bibliog.*

QATAR

— Economic conditions.

QATAR MONETARY AGENCY. Monetary and financial report. a., 1977(1st)- Doha. *[in English and Arabic]*

QATAR NATIONAL BANK S.A.Q. Annual report and accounts. a., 1977- Doha. *[in English and Arabic]*

EL MALLAKH (RAGAEI) Qatar: development of an oil economy. London, [1979]. pp. 183. *bibliogs.*

QATAR NATIONAL BANK S.A.Q.

QATAR NATIONAL BANK S.A.Q. Annual report and accounts. a., 1977- Doha. *[in English and Arabic]*

QUALITY CONTROL.

DOBBEN DE BRUYN (CORNELIS SIMON VAN) Cumulative sum tests: theory and practice. London, 1968. pp. 82. *bibliog.*

BURR (IRVING W.) Elementary statistical quality control. New York, [1979]. pp. 413. *bibliog.*

QUARRIES AND QUARRYING

— United Kingdom — Wales.

WILLIAMS (J. ROOSE) Quarryman's champion: the life and activities of William John Parry of Coetmor. Denbigh, [imprint], 1978]. pp. 258.

QUEBEC (PROVINCE)

— Administrative and political divisions.

QUEBEC (PROVINCE). Commission Permanente de la Réforme des Districts Electoraux. 1972. Rapport; [F. Drouin, président]. [Québec, 1972]. pp. 226.

— Assemblée Nationale.

DESCHENES (GASTON) Organisation et fonctionnement de l'Assemblée nationale; préfacé et révisé par Jean-Noël Lavoie. Quebec, 1976. pp. 63. *bibliog. (Quebec (Province). Assemblé Nationale. Vie Parlementaire.1)*

QUEBEC (PROVINCE)(Cont.)

— — Elections.

QUEBEC (PROVINCE). Président Général des Elections. 1977. Elections 1976: résultats officiels élections générales 15 novembre 1976, élection partielle 30e législature. [Québec, 1977]. pp. 490.

— Economic conditions.

OSE; [pd. by] Opération Solidarité Economique, Québec (Province). m., D 1978 (v.1,no.4)- Québec.

— — Bibliography.

BIBLIOGRAPHIE POLITIQUE DU QUEBEC; [pd. by] Legislative Library. a., 1973/74- Quebec.

— Emigration and immigration.

ALACOQUE (ROGER) Les importés: essai-témoignage sur l'immigration au Québec. [Québec, 1977]. pp. 126.

LAVOIE (YOLANDE) L'émigration des Québécois aux Etats-Unis de 1840 à 1930. Québec, [1979]. pp. 57. bibliog. (Quebec (Province). Conseil de la Langue Française. Etudes et Documents)

— Foreign economic relations — European Economic Community countries.

VALASKAKIS (KIMON) "L'option Europe": analyse de la plausibilité d'une association Québec/Canada/Europe; préparé pour le compte du Ministère des Affaires Intergouvernementales du Québec. [Québec, 1979]. pp. 176.

— — Scandinavia.

TELLIER (LUC-NORMAND) Etude des possibilités de rapprochement économique entre le Québec, le Canada et les pays scandinaves; préparé pour le compte du Ministère des Affaires Intergouvernementales du Québec. [Québec, 1979]. pp. 139. bibliog.

— Government publications.

THERIAULT (YVON) Les publications parlementaires du Québec depuis 1792. Quebec, 1976. pp. 37. bibliog. (Quebec (Province). Assemblée Nationale. Vie Parlementaire.2)

— History.

BASHAM (RICHARD DALTON) Crisis in blanc and white: urbanization and ethnic identity in French Canada. Boston, Mass., [1978]. pp. 287. bibliog.

LÉVESQUE (RENÉ) My Québec; [translated by] Gaynor Fitzpatrick. Toronto, [1978]. pp. 191.

UKRAINIAN Canadians, multiculturalism, and separation: an assessment: proceedings of a conference sponsored by the Canadian Institute of Ukrainian Studies,...Edmonton...1977; edited by Manoly R. Lupul. Edmonton, 1978. pp. 177.

— Languages.

MALLEA (JOHN R.) ed. Quebec's language policies: background and response. Quebec, 1977. pp. 313. (Quebec. Université Laval. Centre International de Recherche sur le Bilinguisme. Travaux. A.13)

QUEBEC (PROVINCE). Department of Cultural Development. 1977. Québec's policy on the French language. [Quebec], 1977. pp. 109.

— — Law and legislation.

QUEBEC (PROVINCE). Statutes, etc. 1977. Bill 101: charter of the French language. Québec, 1977. pp. 45.

— Nationalism.

LIGUE OUVRIERE REVOLUTIONNAIRE. Socialisme et libération nationale: la lutte contre l'Etat canadien. [Montréal, 1978]. pp. 109.

UKRAINIAN Canadians, multiculturalism, and separation: an assessment: proceedings of a conference sponsored by the Canadian Institute of Ukrainian Studies,...Edmonton...1977; edited by Manoly R. Lupul. Edmonton, 1978. pp. 177.

— Politics and government.

DUPONT (PIERRE) How Levesque won;...translated by Sheila Fischman. Toronto, 1977. pp. 136.

SAYWELL (JOHN T.) The rise of the Parti québécois, 1967-76. Toronto, 1977. pp. 174.

FULLERTON (DOUGLAS H.) The dangerous delusion: Quebec's independence obsession, as seen by former adviser to René Lévesque and Jean Lesage. Toronto, [1978]. pp. 240.

LÉVESQUE (RENÉ) My Que-bbec; [translated by] Gaynor Fitzpatrick. Toronto, [1978]. pp. 191.

MILNER (HENRY) Politics in the new Quebec. Toronto, [1978]. pp. 257. bibliog.

O'NEILL (PIERRE) and BENJAMIN (JACQUES) Les mandarins du pouvoir au Québec de Jean Lesage à René Lévesque. Montréal, 1978. pp. 285.

— — Bibliography.

BIBLIOGRAPHIE POLITIQUE DU QUEBEC; [pd. by] Legislative Library. a., 1973/74- Quebec.

— Social conditions — Bibliography.

BIBLIOGRAPHIE POLITIQUE DU QUEBEC; [pd. by] Legislative Library. a., 1973/74- Quebec.

QUEBEC, MONTREAL, OTTAWA AND OCCIDENTAL RAILWAY.

YOUNG (BRIAN J.) Promoters and politicians: the North-Shore Railways in the history of Quebec, 1854-85. Toronto, [1978]. pp. 193. bibliog.

QUEENSLAND

— Economic conditions.

BEREZOVSKY (C.A.) The relative dependence of the Queensland economy on the rural sector. [Brisbane], Marketing Services Branch, Department of Primary Industries, 1975. pp. 61. bibliog.

— Population.

QUEENSLAND. Commonwealth Bureau of Census and Statistics. Queensland Office. 1973. Population growth within the Brisbane statistical division, 1856- 1971. Brisbane, [1973]. pp. 33.

QUESTIONNAIRES.

DILLMAN (DON A.) Mail and telephone surveys: the total design method. New York, [1978]. pp. 325. bibliog.

BRADBURN (NORMAN M.) and SUDMAN (SEYMOUR) Improving interview method and questionnaire design; (with the assistance of Edward Blair [and others]). San Francisco, 1979. pp. 214. bibliog.

QUEUEING THEORY.

ALLEN (ARNOLD O.) Probability, statistics and queueing theory: with computer science applications. New York, 1978. pp. 390.

QWAQWA

— Economic conditions.

SOUTH AFRICA. Bureau for Economic Research re Bantu Development. 1978. Qwaqwa:...economic revue [sic], etc. Pretoria, [1978]. pp. 74. bibliog. In English and Afrikaans.

RABIES

— Europe.

CONFERENCE ON THE SURVEILLANCE AND CONTROL OF RABIES, 2ND, FRANKFURT-AM-MAIN, 1977. Surveillance and control of rabies; report, etc. Copenhagen, World Health Organization, Regional Office for Europe, 1978. pp. 69. bibliog.

WORLD HEALTH ORGANIZATION. Regional Office for Europe. 1978. Directory of services for rabies prevention and control in the European region. Copenhagen, 1978. pp. 99. In English, French, German and Russian.

RACE.

KATZ (JUDY H.) White awareness: handbook for anti-racism training. Norman, [1978]. pp. 211. bibliog.

RACE AWARENESS.

PAVLAK (THOMAS JAMES) Ethnic identification and political behavior. San Francisco, 1976. pp. 108. bibliog.

BURKEY (RICHARD M.) Ethnic and racial groups: the dynamics of dominance. Menlo Park, Calif., [1978]. pp. 510. bibliog.

KATZ (JUDY H.) White awareness: handbook for anti-racism training. Norman, [1978]. pp. 211. bibliog.

ETHNICITY at work; edited by Sandra Wallman. London, 1979. pp. 252. bibliog.

RACE DISCRIMINATION.

STONE (JOHN) D. Phil. Race, ethnicity, and social change: readings in the sociology of race and ethnic relations. North Scituate, Mass., [1977]. pp. 399. bibliog.

AGAINST racism, apartheid and colonialism: documents published by the GDR, 1949-1977; [edited by Alfred Babing]. Berlin, 1978. pp. 664. Facing title page: GDR Institute for International Politics and Economics; GDR Committee for the Decade of Action to Combat Racism and Racial Discrimination.

KATZ (JUDY H.) White awareness: handbook for anti-racism training. Norman, [1978]. pp. 211. bibliog.

— Law and legislation — South Africa.

HORRELL (MURIEL) compiler. Laws affecting race relations in South Africa, to the end of 1976. Johannesburg, 1978. pp. 529.

— — United Kingdom.

HEWITT (PATRICIA) and others. A practical guide to the Race Relations Act. London, [1978]. pp. 48. (National Council for Civil Liberties. Know Your Rights Series. No. 1)

— Africa, Subsaharan.

ETHNICITY in modern Africa; edited by Brian M. du Toit. Boulder, Colo., 1978. pp. 319. bibliog.

— Australia.

WHO are our enemies?: racism and the Australian working class; edited by Ann Curthoys and Andrew Markus. Neutral Bay, 1978. pp. 211.

MARKUS (ANDREW) Fear and hatred: purifying Australia and California, 1850-1901. Sydney, 1979. pp. 95.

— Malaysia.

MOHAMAD (MAHATHIR BIN) The Malay dilemma. Singapore, 1970. pp. 188.

— South Africa.

AFRICAN perspectives on South Africa: a collection of speeches, articles and documents; edited by Hendrik W. van der Merwe [and others]. Stanford, 1978. pp. 612. (Stanford University. Hoover Institution on War, Revolution and Peace. Hoover Institution Publications 176)

QUISLINGS or realists?: a documentary study of "Coloured" politics in South Africa; [edited by] Pierre Hugo. Johannesburg, 1978. pp. 744.

BIKO (STEVEN) The testimony of Steve Biko; [edited by Millard Arnold]. London, 1979. pp. 298.

— **United Kingdom.**

NATIONAL CONFERENCE OF COMMUNITY RELATIONS COUNCILS, LEICESTER, 1977. Conference report: strategy statement, speeches, etc. London, Commission for Racial Equality, 1977. pp. 43.

U.K. Commission for Racial Equality. 1978. Evidence and recommendations to the Royal Commission on Criminal Procedure. [London], 1978. pp. 48.

WILSON (MAGGIE) White student, black world: (a handbook for action against racism) . Oxford, [1978]. pp. 97. *bibliog.*

JEFFCOATE (ROBERT) Positive image: towards a multiracial curriculum. London, 1979. pp. 124. *bibliogs.*

— **United States.**

BRAXTON (BERNARD) Sexual, racial and political faces of corruption: a view on the high cost of institutional evils. Washington, [1977]. pp. 278. *bibliog.*

— — **California.**

MARKUS (ANDREW) Fear and hatred: purifying Australia and California, 1850-1901. Sydney, 1979. pp. 95.

RACE PROBLEMS.

See RACE RELATIONS.

RACE QUESTION.

See RACE RELATIONS.

RACE RELATIONS.

OBJECTIVE: JUSTICE; q. magazine covering United Nations activity against apartheid, racial discrimination and colonialism; [pd. by United Nations Office of Public Information]. q., 1970 (v.2)- New York.

BANTON (MICHAEL PARKER) Rational choice: a theory of racial and ethnic relations. Bristol, Social Science Research Council Research Unit on Ethnic Relations, [1977]. pp. 68. *bibliog.* *(Working Papers on Ethnic Relations. No. 8)*

See also RACE DISCRIMINATION; RACISM; and subdivision Race relations under names of regions, countries, cities, etc.

RACE RELATIONS AND THE PRESS.

RACE as news; introduction by James D. Halloran; two general studies on attitude change by Otto Klineberg and Colette Guillaumin and a study of the British national press by Paul Hartmann, Charles Husband and Jean Clark. Paris, The Unesco Press, 1974. pp. 173. *bibliog.*

— **Canada.**

ETHNICITY and the media: an analysis of media reporting in the United Kingdom, Canada and Ireland. Paris, United Nations Educational, Scientific and Cultural Organization, 1977. pp. 376. *bibliogs.*

— **United Kingdom.**

RACE as news; introduction by James D. Halloran; two general studies on attitude change by Otto Klineberg and Colette Guillaumin and a study of the British national press by Paul Hartmann, Charles Husband and Jean Clark. Paris, The Unesco Press, 1974. pp. 173. *bibliog.*

ETHNICITY and the media: an analysis of media reporting in the United Kingdom, Canada and Ireland. Paris, United Nations Educational, Scientific and Cultural Organization, 1977. pp. 376. *bibliogs.*

RACISM

See also RACE DISCRIMINATION; RACE RELATIONS.

— **Europe.**

MOSSE (GEORGE L.) Toward the final solution: a history of European racism. London, 1978. pp. 277.

— **South Africa.**

MULLER (HILGARD) Why apartheid?; (an address to a joint meeting of the Royal African Society and the Royal Commonwealth Society on November 15, 1962). London, Department of Information, South African Embassy, 1962. pp. 15. *(Reports on the State of South Africa. No. 23)*

REPORTS ON THE STATE OF SOUTH AFRICA. No. 26. You be the judge. London, Department of Information, South African Embassy, 1964. pp. (4).

LUTTIG (HENDRIK GERHARDUS) South Africa faces the future; (an address given...to the South Africa Society at the Royal Society of Arts, London, on May 12, 1967). [London, Department of Information, South African Embassy, 1967]. pp. 14. *(Reports on the State of South Africa. No. 32)*

SOUTH AFRICA. Information Service of South Africa, New York. 1967. Setting the record straight. New York, [1967]. pp. 24.

UNITED NATIONS. Office of Public Information. 1969. Action against apartheid. (OPI/364). New York, [1969]. pp. 31.

RUBIN (LESLIE) Apartheid in practice. (OPI/428). [New York], United Nations, 1971. pp. 70.

— **United Kingdom.**

RACISM and political action in Britain; edited by Robert Miles and Annie Phizacklea. London, 1979. pp. 246. *bibliogs. Papers from the Conference on Racism and Political Action in Britain, held by the Social Science Research Council Research Unit on Ethnic Relations, 1977.*

RADIATION

— **Dosage.**

TAYLOR (F.E.) and WEBB (G.A.M.) Radiation exposure of the UK population. Harwell, National Radiological Protection Board, 1978. pp. 86, fo.(13). *bibliog.* *([Publications]. R77)*

RADICALISM

— **America, North.**

SATIN (MARK IVOR) New age politics: healing self and society: the emerging new alternative to Marxism and liberalism. West Vancouver, 1978. pp. 240. *bibliog.*

— **Canada.**

BENOIT (JACQUES) Journalist. L'extrême gauche. Ottawa, 1977. pp. 137.

— **Germany.**

APO und Gewerkschaften: von der Kooperation zum Bruch; herausgegeben von Gudrun Küsel. Berlin, [1978]. pp. 188.

— **Mexico.**

SALAMINI (HEATHER FOWLER) Agrarian radicalism in Veracruz, 1920-38. Lincoln, Neb., [1978]. pp. 239. *bibliog.*

— **Russia.**

OBSHCHESTVENNO-politicheskaia mysl' v Povolzh'e v XIX - nachale XX vv. Kazan', 1977. pp. 272.

PLEKHANOV (GEORGII VALENTINOVICH) Estetika i sotsiologiia iskusstva: [sbornik statei, 1897-1913]. Moskva, 1978. 2 vols. *With introductory article by M. Lifshits.*

VOLODIN (ALEKSANDR IVANOVICH) "Anti-Diuring" F.Engel'sa i obshchestvennaia mysl' Rossii XIX veka: istoriko-filosofskie ocherki. Moskva, 1978. pp. 252.

— — **White Russia.**

MAIKHROVICH (AL'FRED STEPANOVICH) Belorusskie revoliutsionnye demokraty: vazhneishie aspekty mirovozzreniia; redaktory N.S. Kupchin, V.M. Konon. Minsk, 1977. pp. 207.

— **United Kingdom.**

BOUCHIER (DAVID LESLIE) Idealism and revolution: new ideologies of liberation in Britain and the United States. London, 1978. pp. 190. *bibliog.*

HODGKINS (JOHN R.) Over the hills to glory: radicalism in Banburyshire, 1832-1945. Southend, [1978]. pp. 218.

TOOHEY (ROBERT E.) Liberty and empire: British radical solutions to the American problem, 1774-1776. Lexington, [1978]. pp. 210. *bibliog.*

GOODWIN (ALBERT) The friends of liberty: the English democratic movement in the age of the French revolution. London, 1979. pp. 594. *bibliog.*

PROTHERO (IORWERTH J.) Artisans and politics in early nineteenth-century London: John Gast and his times. Folkestone, 1979. pp. 418. *bibliog.*

SIMPKIN (MICHAEL) Trapped within welfare: surviving social work. London, 1979. pp. 168.

— **United States.**

BONE (CHRISTOPHER) The disinherited children: a study of the New Left and the generation gap. New York, [1977]. pp. 183. *bibliogs.*

WOLFE (TOM) Mauve gloves and madmen, clutter and vine: and other stories, sketches and essays. Toronto, 1977. pp. 214.

BOUCHIER (DAVID LESLIE) Idealism and revolution: new ideologies of liberation in Britain and the United States. London, 1978. pp. 190. *bibliog.*

CANTOR (MILTON) The divided left: American radicalism, 1900-1975. New York, [1978]. pp. 248. *bibliog.*

DELEON (DAVID) The American as anarchist: reflections on indigenous radicalism. Baltimore, 1978. pp. 242. *bibliog.*

RADICALS

— **United Kingdom — Biography.**

BIOGRAPHICAL dictionary of modern British radicals;...edited by Joseph O. Baylen and Norbert J. Gossman. Hassocks, 1979 in progress. *bibliogs.*

RADIO BROADCASTING

— **Europe, Eastern.**

PAULU (BURTON) Radio and television broadcasting in Eastern Europe. Minneapolis, 1974. pp. 592.

— **Russia.**

PAULU (BURTON) Radio and television broadcasting in Eastern Europe. Minneapolis, 1974. pp. 592.

— **United Kingdom.**

CURRAN (Sir CHARLES J.) A seamless robe: broadcasting: philosophy and practice. London, 1979. pp. 358.

WOOD (ROBERT) 1903- . A world in your ear: the broadcasting of an era, 1923-64. London, 1979. pp. 194.

RAHMAN (MUJIBUR).

SHEIKH Mujib: a commemorative anthology; edited by Abdul Gaffar Choudhury. London, 1977. pp. 72.

RAILWAYS

RAILWAYS
— Finance.

ZALDUENDO (EDUARDO ANDRES) Libras y rieles: las inversiones britanicas para el desarrollo de los ferrocarriles en Argentina, Brasil, Canada e India durante el Siglo XIX. Buenos Aires, [1975]. pp. 595. *bibliog.*

— America — Societies.

PAN-AMERICAN RAILWAY CONGRESS. 13th Congress, 1975. Informe de la Comision Permanente;...1968-1975. Buenos Aires, 1975. pp. 80.

— Canada — History.

YOUNG (BRIAN J.) Promoters and politicians: the North-Shore Railways in the history of Quebec, 1854-85. Toronto, [1978]. pp. 193. *bibliog.*

— France.

CHESNAIS (MICHEL) Le renouveau du chemin de fer: échanges ferroviaires et système de transport. Paris, 1979. pp. 341. *bibliog.*

— Ghana — Employees.

JEFFRIES (RICHARD) Class, power and ideology in Ghana: the railwaymen of Sekondi. Cambridge, 1978. pp. 244. *bibliog.* (Cambridge. University. African Studies Centre. African Studies Series. 22)

— Mexico.

COATSWORTH (JOHN H.) Crecimiento contra desarrollo: el impacto economico de los ferrocarriles en el porfiriato. Mexico, Secretaria de Educacion Publica, 1976. 2 vols. (in 1). *bibliog.* (Sep/Setentas. 271-272)

— Peru — History.

DIEZ CANSECO (JESUS ANTONIO) Para la historia patria: el ferrocarril de Arequipa y el Gral. Don Pedro Diez Canseco. Arequipa, 1921. pp. 52. *2 fold. leaves.*

— Russia — History.

METZER (JACOB) Some economic aspects of railroad development in Tsarist Russia. New York, 1977. pp. 138. *bibliog.*

— Switzerland — Bern (Canton).

CHATELAIN (RENE) Die Produktivität der bernischen Privatbahnen: Vergleich und Entwicklung 1909 bis 1967. Bern. 1978. 1 vol. (various pagings). *bibliog. (Bern (Canton). Amt fur Statistik. Beiträge zur Statistik des Kantons Bern. Produktionsstatistik. Reihe C. Heft 5)*

— United Kingdom — Management.

PARKER (PETER) b. 1924. A way to run a railway. London, 1978. pp. 19. (London. University. Birkbeck College. Haldane Memorial Lectures. 41)

— — Maps.

BRITISH railways pre-grouping atlas and gazetteer. London, 1976. pp. 84.

BAKER (STUART K.) Rail atlas of Britain. Oxford, 1978. pp. 107. *Maps drawn by Paul Karan.*

— — Ireland — Maps.

HAJDUCKI (STEPHEN MAXWELL) A railway atlas of Ireland. Newton Abbot, 1974. pp. 62. *bibliog.*

— — London.

JACKSON (ALAN ARTHUR) London's local railways. Newton Abbot, 1978 repr. 1979. pp. 384. *bibliog.*

— United States.

MARTIN (ALBRO) James J. Hill and the opening of the Northwest. New York, 1976. pp. 676.

— — Employees.

LIGHTNER (DAVID L.) Labor on the Illinois Central Railroad, 1852-1900: the evolution of an industrial environment. New York, 1977. pp. 437. *bibliog.*

— — History.

POOR (HENRY VARNUM) History of the railroads and canals of the United States of America. New York, 1970. pp. 612. *Reprint of work originally published in New York, 1860.*

FOGEL (ROBERT WILLIAM) Railroads and American economic growth: essays in econometric history. Baltimore, 1964. pp. 296. *bibliog.*

DICK (TREVOR J.O.) An economic theory of technological change: the case of patents and the United States railroads 1871-1950. New York, 1978. pp. 145. *bibliog.*

— Zambia — Accidents.

ZAMBIA. Board of Inquiry into the Railway Accidents at Kalibu on 1st September, 1967, and Kaniki on 10th September, 1967. 1968. Report; [B.A. Doyle, chairman]. Lusaka, 1968. pp. 14, 4 plans.

RAIN FOREST ECOLOGY.

UNITED NATIONS EDUCATIONAL, SCIENTIFIC AND CULTURAL ORGANIZATION. 1978. Tropical forest eco-systems: a state-of-knowledge report prepared by Unesco/UNEP/ FAO. Paris, 1978. pp. 683. *bibliogs. (Natural Resources Research. 14)*

RAINSFORD (GEORGE).

CAMDEN SOCIETY. [Publications]. 4th Series. vol.22. Camden miscellany. vol.27. London, 1979. pp. 248.

RAJASTHAN
— Economic policy.

RAJASTHAN. Directorate of Economics and Statistics. 1975. Fourth plan progress report, 1969-74. Jaipur, [1975]. pp. 99.

— Social policy.

RAJASTHAN. Directorate of Economics and Statistics. 1975. Fourth plan progress report, 1969-74. Jaipur, [1975]. pp. 99.

RAJAWELLA PRODUCE HOLDINGS.

STANLEY (RONALD ARTHUR TERENCE) and BUTTIMER (JAMES MICHAEL) Rajawella Produce Holdings Limited: investigation under section 165b of the Companies Act 1948; report . [London], Department of Trade, 1978. 1 vol. (various pagings).

RANDOM VARIABLES.

GALAMBOS (JANOS) The asymptotic theory of extreme order statistics. New York, [1978]. pp. 352. *bibliog.*

SPRINGER (MELVIN DALE) The algebra of random variables. New York, [1979]. pp. 470. *bibliog.*

RANKIN (HARRY).

RANKIN (HARRY) Rankin's law: recollections of a radical. Vancouver, [1975]. pp. 220.

RAS TAFARI MOVEMENT.

MILES (ROBERT) Between two cultures?: the case of Rastafarianism. Bristol, Social Science Reseach Council Research Unit on Ethnic Relations, [1978]. pp. 34. *bibliog. (Working Papers on Ethnic Relations. No. 10)*

PLUMMER (JOHN) Movement of Jah people. Birmingham, 1978. pp. 72.

RASKOLNIKS.

IWANIEC (EUGENIUSZ) Z dziejów staroobrzędowców na ziemiach polskich XVII-XX w. Warszawa, 1977. pp. 295. *bibliog. (Białystok. Białostockie Towarzystwo Naukowe. Prace. Nr.23) With Russian and English summaries.*

RASPAIL (FRANÇOIS VINCENT).

VERMOREL (AUGUSTE JEAN MARIE) Mr F.V. Raspail. [Paris, 1869]. pp. 35.

RATIONALISM.

ELSTER (JON) Ulysses and the Sirens. Cambridge, 1979. pp. 193.

RATIONALITY; edited by Bryan R. Wilson. Oxford, 1979. pp. 275. *bibliog.*

RAW MATERIALS
— Africa, Subsaharan.

SOUTHERN Africa: the politics of raw materials; a selection of papers delivered at a conference of the Foreign Affairs Association at...Hamburg...1977; edited by Cas de Villiers. Pretoria, [1977]. pp. 132. *bibliogs.*

— Underdeveloped areas.

See UNDERDEVELOPED AREAS — Raw materials.

RAY-O-VAC FEDERAL UNION.

ZIEGER (ROBERT H.) Madison's battery workers, 1934-1952: a history of Federal Labor Union 19587. Ithaca, N.Y., 1977. pp. 126. *bibliog.* (Cornell University. New York State School of Industrial and Labor Relations. ILR Paperbacks. No. 16)

RAZAK BIN HUSSEIN (TUN ABDUL).

FEDERATION OF MALAYSIA. Department of Information Services. 1968. Another successful tour: (the Razak touch). [Kuala Lumpur, 1968?]. pp. 56.

REACTOR FUEL REPROCESSING.

TOWN AND COUNTRY PLANNING ASSOCIATION. Planning and plutonium: evidence of the Town and Country Planning Association to the public inquiry into an oxide reprocessing plant at Windscale. London, 1978. pp. 110. *bibliogs.*

READERSHIP SURVEYS
— United Kingdom.

EVENING NEWSPAPER ADVERTISING BUREAU. ENAB regional readership surveys: East Anglian ITV area. London, [1964]. 1 vol. (various pagings).

EVENING NEWSPAPER ADVERTISING BUREAU. ENAB regional readership surveys: Midland ITV area. London, [1964]. 1 vol. (various pagings).

EVENING NEWSPAPER ADVERTISING BUREAU. ENAB regional readership surveys: Northern (Lancashire) ITV area. London, [1964]. 1 vol. (various pagings).

EVENING NEWSPAPER ADVERTISING BUREAU. ENAB regional readership surveys: Southern area. London, [1964]. 1 vol. (various pagings).

EVENING NEWSPAPER ADVERTISING BUREAU. ENAB regional readership surveys: Wales and the West ITV area. London, [1964]. 1 vol. (various pagings).

EVENING NEWSPAPER ADVERTISING BUREAU. Evening newspaper readership: a summary of ENAB regional readership surveys. London, 1964. pp. 12.

REAL ESTATE AGENTS

— United Kingdom.

HATCH (J.C.S.) Estate agents as urban gatekeepers: [a talk given to the] B[ritish] S[ociological] A[ssociation] Urban Sociology Group, University of Stirling, 6th October 1973. [Bristol, Social Science Research Council Research Unit on Ethnic Relations, 1973]. fo. 19.

REAL ESTATE BUSINESS

— Canada.

AUBIN (HENRY) City for sale. Montréal, [1977]. pp. 401.

REAL ESTATE DEVELOPMENT

— United Kingdom.

LAND availability: a study of land with residential planning permission: final report of a consultants' study for the Department of the Environment and the Housing Research Foundation. [London], Economist Intelligence Unit, 1978. pp. 82.

REAL PROPERTY

— Prices.

PEARCE (BARRY J.) and others. Land, planning and the market. Cambridge, 1978. pp. 101. *bibliog. (Cambridge. University. Department of Land Economy. Occasional Papers. No. 9)*

— Valuation.

BAUM (ANDREW) Writer on estate management and MACKMIN (DAVID) The income approach to property valuation. London, 1979. pp. 205. *bibliog.*

— Canada — Ontario — Valuation.

LENTZ (GARY) Rural real estate values in southern Ontario, 1971. Toronto, 1974. pp. 17. *(Ontario. Ministry of Agriculture and Food. Economics Branch. Economics Information)*

— Italy — Florence.

HERLIHY (DAVID) and KLAPISCH-ZUBER (CHRISTIANE) Les Toscans et leurs familles: une étude du catasto florentin de 1427. [Paris, 1978]. pp. 703. *bibliog.*

— United Kingdom.

HARWOOD (MICHAEL) English land law. London, 1975. pp. 510.

RIDDALL (JOHN GERVASE) Introduction to land law. 2nd ed. London, 1979. pp. 403.

REAL PROPERTY TAX.

HARRISON (FRED) B.A., M.Sc. Marx, economic growth and land taxation. London, 1975. pp. 27. *(Economic and Social Science Research Association. Discussion Papers. No. 2)*

— India — Bombay.

DESAI (MAHADEV) The story of Bardoli: being a history of the Bardoli Satyagraha of 1928 and its sequel. Ahmedabad, 1929. pp. 363.

— United Kingdom.

U.K. Board of Inland Revenue. 1978. Development land tax. [London, 1978]. pp. 94.

REALISM.

COFFEY (JOHN W.) Political realism in American thought. Lewisburg, [1977]. pp. 217. *bibliog.*

REALISM IN LITERATURE.

BISZTRAY (GEORGE) Marxist models of literary realism. New York, 1978. pp. 247. *bibliog.*

REASONING (PSYCHOLOGY).

ELSTER (JON) Ulysses and the Sirens. Cambridge, 1979. pp. 193.

RECIDIVISTS

— United States.

McCLEARY (RICHARD) Dangerous men: the sociology of parole. Beverly Hills, [1978]. pp. 181. *bibliog.*

RECLAMATION OF LAND

— United Kingdom.

U.K. Department of the Environment. Planning Land Use Policy Division. 1979. Derelict land reclamation: summary of local authority returns for 1st April 1976-31st March 1978. London, 1979. pp. 36.

RECLUS (ELISEE).

DAY (HEM) pseud. [i.e. Marcel DIEU] Elisée Reclus en Belgique: sa vie, son activité, 1894-1905. Paris, 1956. pp. 32.

FLEMING (MARIE) The anarchist way to socialism: Elisée Reclus and nineteenth-century European anarchism. London, 1979. pp. 299. *bibliog.*

RECONSTRUCTION (1914-1939)

— Russia.

SPARGO (JOHN) Russia as an American problem. New York, 1920. pp. 444.

RECONSTRUCTION (1939-1951).

CHILDS (JOHN LAWRENCE) and COUNTS (GEORGE SYLVESTER) America, Russia and the Communist Party in the postwar world. New York, [1943]. pp. 92.

RECONSTRUCTION (UNITED STATES).

ROARK (JAMES L.) Master without slaves: Southern planters in the Civil War and Reconstruction. New York, [1977]. pp. 273. *bibliog.*

BELZ (HERMAN) Emancipation and equal rights: politics and constitutionalism in the Civil War era. New York, [1978]. pp. 171.

DONALD (DAVID) Liberty and union. Lexington, Mass., [1978]. pp. 323.

McCRARY (PEYTON) Abraham Lincoln and reconstruction: the Louisiana experiment. Princeton, N.J., [1978]. pp. 423. *bibliog.*

NOVAK (DANIEL A.) The wheel of servitude: black forced labor after slavery. Lexington, Ky., [1978]. pp. 126. *bibliog.*

OUBRE (CLAUDE F.) Forty acres and a mule: the Freedmen's Bureau and black land ownership. Baton Rouge, [1978]. pp. 212. *bibliog.*

RECREATION AND STATE

— Hong Kong.

COUNCIL FOR RECREATION AND SPORT [HONG KONG]. Report. a., 1973/75- Hong Kong.

RECURSIVE PROGRAMMING.

MODELLING economic change: the recursive programming approach; [edited by] Richard H. Day and Alessandro Cigno. Amsterdam, 1978. pp. 447. *bibliog.*

RECYCLING (WASTE, ETC.).

GRACE (RICHARD) and FISHER (JONATHAN) Beverage containers: re-use or recycling. Paris, Organisation for Economic Co-operation and Development, 1978. pp. 159. *bibliog.*

RED CROSS.

BUERKLER-GIUSSANI (LUISA) Die rechtliche Stellung der Rotkreuzformationen nach schweizerischem Recht und nach Völkerrecht. Zürich, 1979. pp. 177. *bibliog.*

— Switzerland.

BUERKLER-GIUSSANI (LUISA) Die rechtliche Stellung der Rotkreuzformationen nach schweizerischem Recht und nach Völkerrecht. Zürich, 1979. pp. 177. *bibliog.*

RED INTERNATIONAL OF LABOUR UNIONS.

NIN (ANDRES) Las organizaciones obreras internacionales. Madrid, [1977]. pp. 304.

REDDY (S. MUTHULAKSHMI).

See MUTHULAKSHMI REDDY (S.).

REFERENCE BOOKS

— History.

POULTON (HELEN J.) and HOWLAND (MARGUERITE S.) compilers. The historian's handbook: a descriptive guide to reference works. Norman, Okla., 1972 repr. 1974. pp. 304.

REFERENDUM

— Canada — Quebec.

QUEBEC (PROVINCE). Ministry of Electoral and Parliamentary Reform. 1977. Consulting the people of Quebec; [by] Robert Burns, etc. [Quebec], 1977. pp. 27.

— Germany.

GERMANY. Statistisches Reichsamt. Statistik des Deutschen Reichs. Neue Folge. Band 332. Volksbegehren und Volksentscheid "Enteignung der Fürstenvermögen". Anhang: Die Vorabstimmung in Hannover am 18.Mai 1924. Berlin, 1926; Osnabrück, 1978. pp. 38. *Photographic reprint.*

— Ireland (Republic).

O'LEARY (CORNELIUS) Irish elections, 1918-77: parties, voters and proportional representation. Dublin, 1979. pp. 134.

— Switzerland — Bern (Canton).

BERN (CANTON). Amt für Statistik. 1978. Eidg. Abstimmung vom 12. Juni 1977 im Kanton Bern: Umsatzsteuer, direkte Bundessteuer, etc. Bern, 1978. pp. 72. *(Beiträge zur Statistik des Kantons Bern. Politische Statistik. Reihe F. Heft 4) In French and German.*

BERN (CANTON). Amt für Statistik. 1978. Eidg. Abstimmung vom 4. Dezember 1977 im Kanton Bern: Reichtumsteuer-Initiative, etc. Bern, 1978. pp. 74. *(Beiträge zur Statistik des Kantons Bern. Politische Statistik. Reihe F. Heft 5) In French and German.*

REFORM CLUB.

WOODBRIDGE (GEORGE) The Reform Club, 1836-1978: a history from the club's records. London, 1978. pp. 185. *bibliog.*

REFORMATION

— Germany.

STRAUSS (GERALD) Luther's house of learning: indoctrination of the young in the German Reformation. Baltimore, 1978. pp. 390.

REFORMATORIES

— United Kingdom — Scotland.

RUSHFORTH (MONICA) Committal to residential care: a case study in juvenile justice. Edinburgh, 1978. pp. 90. *(Scotland. Scottish Office. Social Research Studies)*

REFUGE ASSURANCE COMPANY.

CLEGG (CYRIL) Friend in deed: the history of a life assurance office from 1858, as the Refuge Friend in Deed Life Assurance and Sick Fund Friendly Society, to 1958, as the Refuge Assurance Company Limited. London, [1958]. pp. 160.

REFUGEES.

PEOPLE FOR PROGRESS: Les Hommes du progrès; [pd.by] Intergovernmental Committee for European Migration. [in English and French]. irreg., 1967(3)- Geneva.

UNHCR; [pd. by] United Nations High Commissioner for Refugees. 6 a yr., Jl 1972(no.1)- Geneva. *Supersedes HCR bulletin (Ja/Mr 1968 - Ap/Je 1972).*

REFUGEES, AUSTRIAN.

GOLDNER (FRANZ) Die österreichische Emigration, 1938 bis 1945. 2nd ed. Wien, [1977]. pp. 364. *bibliog.*

REFUGEES, POLITICAL

— India — Punjab.

PUNJAB (INDIA). Publicity Department. 1950. Rural rehabilitation in East Punjab: a short survey, 1947-48. Simla, [1950]. pp. 36. *(East Punjab Pamphlets. No. 5)*

REFUGEES, RELIGIOUS.

FLOREY (GERHARD) Geschichte der Salzburger Protestanten und ihrer Emigration, 1731/32. Wien, [1977]. pp. 276. *bibliog.*

REFUGEES IN AFRICA.

CHRISTIAN AID. Refugees: Africa's challenge; a special report. London, 1978. pp. 72.

REFUSE COLLECTORS

— United States — San Francisco.

PERRY (STEWART E.) Sociologist. San Francisco scavengers: dirty work and the pride of ownership. Berkeley, [1978]. pp. 236.

REGIONAL COOPERATION FOR DEVELOPMENT.

RCD MAGAZINE, THE; [pd. by] Regional Cooperation for Development. q., spring 1974(v.1, no.1)- , with gaps. Tehran.

RCD NEWSLETTER; [pd. by] Information Section, Regional Cooperation for Development. irreg., current issues only. Tehran.

REGIONAL ECONOMICS.

STOEHR (WALTER) Regional development experiences and prospects in Latin America. Paris, [1975]. pp. 186. *bibliog.*

ARMSTRONG (HARVEY) and TAYLOR (JIM) Regional economic policy and its analysis. Oxford, 1978. pp. 335. *bibliog.*

SPATIAL interaction theory and planning models: (papers presented at an international research conference in Båstad, Sweden... 1977); edited by Anders Karlqvist [and others]. Amsterdam, 1978. pp. 388.

MILLER (ROBERTA BALSTAD) City and hinterland: a case study of urban growth and regional development. Westport, Conn., 1979. pp. 179.

REGIONAL policy: past experience and new directions; edited by Duncan Maclennan and John B. Parr. Oxford, 1979. pp. 334. *bibliogs. (Glasgow. University. Social and Economic Research Studies. 6)*

— Mathematical models.

COUPE (BERNARD EDDY MARIE GHISLAIN) Regional economic structure and environmental pollution: an application of interregional models. Leiden, 1977. pp. 166. *bibliog.*

GLICKMAN (NORMAN J.) Econometric analysis of regional systems: explorations in model building and policy analysis. New York, [1977]. pp. 210. *bibliog.*

GUNNARSON (JAN) Production systems and hierarchies of centres: the relationship between spatial and economic structures. Leiden, 1977. pp. 140. *bibliog.*

ALARCÓN-RIVERO (JORGE) A two region model on the basis of Yugoslav statistical data. The Hague, [1978]. pp. 105. *bibliog. (Hague. Institute of Social Studies. Research Report Series. No.3)*

REGIONAL-national econometric modelling with an application to the Italian economy; edited by Murray Brown [and others]. London, [1978]. pp. 203. *bibliogs.*

— Europe.

UNDERDEVELOPED Europe: studies in core-periphery relations; edited by Dudley Seers [and others]. Hassocks, 1979. pp. 325. *bibliogs.*

— Russia.

NEVELEV (ALEKSANDR MIKHAILOVICH) and GOL'TSBERG (MAKS ABRAMOVICH) Territorial'noe planirovanie material'nykh resursov. Moskva, 1978. pp. 152. *bibliog.*

REGIONAL PLANNING.

CAMHIS (MATHIEU MARIOS) Planning theory and philosophy: a comparative analysis. 1977. fo. 313. *bibliog.* Typescript. Ph.D. (London) thesis: unpublished. This thesis is the property of London University and may not be removed from the Library.

CHADWICK (GEORGE F.) A systems view of planning: towards a theory of the urban and regional planning process. 2nd ed. Oxford, [1978]. pp. 432. *bibliogs.*

DUNNE (THOMAS) and LEOPOLD (LUNA BERGERE) Water in environmental planning. San Francisco, [1978]. pp. 818. *bibliogs.*

HAMEL (JACQUES) Evaluation of alternative plans in regional planning: a critique and extension of ordinal methods. 1978. fo. 289. *bibliogs.* Typescript. Ph.D. (London) thesis: unpublished. This thesis is the property of London University and may not be removed from the Library.

REGIONAL policy: past experience and new directions; edited by Duncan Maclennan and John B. Parr. Oxford, 1979. pp. 334. *bibliogs. (Glasgow. University. Social and Economic Research Studies. 6)*

RESOURCES and planning; edited by Brian Goodall and Andrew Kirby. Oxford, 1979. pp. 373. *bibliogs.*

U.K. Department of the Environment. Library. Bulletin. fortn. London. *Current issues only kept.*

— Bibliography.

BODDAERT (JACQUELINE) compiler. Bibliographie sélective: aménagement du territoire, environnement, urbanisme. 3rd ed. Paris, Délégation à l'Aménagement du Territoire et à l'Action Régionale, 1978. pp. 38.

— Congresses.

URBAN, regional and national planning (UNRENAP): proceedings of the IFAC Workshop, Kyoto, Japan, 5-6 August 1977; edited by T. Hasegawa and K. Inoue. Oxford, 1978. pp. 233.

— Mathematical models.

MORRISON (W.I.) and SMITH (P.N.) Input-output methods in urban and regional planning: a practical guide. London, 1976. pp. 122. *bibliog. (Planning Research Applications Group. PRAG Technical Papers. TP6)*

POLISH-SOVIET REGIONAL SCIENCE SEMINAR, 1ST, SZYMBARK, 1973. Economic models in regional development and planning; edited by Marek Jerczyński [and] Mark K. Bandman. Warszawa, 1976. pp. 181. *bibliogs.*

HAMEL (JACQUES) Evaluation of alternative plans in regional planning: a critique and extension of ordinal methods. 1978. fo. 289. *bibliogs.* Typescript. Ph.D. (London) thesis: unpublished. This thesis is the property of London University and may not be removed from the Library.

JOINT IBM/IIASA CONFERENCE, VIENNA, 1977. Models for regional planning and policy-making; proceedings of the ...conference; ...edited by A. Straszak [and] B.V. Wagle. [Peterlee, 1978?]. pp. 371. *bibliogs. (IBM United Kingdom Limited. UK Scientific Centre. [Technical Reports]. 0097)*

— Research — United Kingdom.

U.K. Department of the Environment. Library. 1978. Urban and regional research: a directory of organisations; edited by W.W. Helps. [London], 1978. pp. 78. *bibliogs. (Information Series. No. 30)*

— Africa.

DIFFERENCIATION régionale et régionalisation en Afrique francophone et à Madagascar: journées de travail de Yaoundé, 9-12 octobre 1972. Paris, 1974. pp. 325. *bibliog. (France. Office de la Recherche Scientifique et Technique Outre-Mer. Travaux et Documents. No. 39)*

— America, Latin.

LATIN American urban researchs; [series editors] Francine F. Rabinovitz and Felicity M. Trueblood. Beverly Hills, [1971 in progress]. *bibliog.*

STOEHR (WALTER) Regional development experiences and prospects in Latin America. Paris, [1975]. pp. 186. *bibliog.*

— Asia — Congresses.

GROWTH pole strategy and regional development policy: Asian experience and alternative approaches; edited by Fu-Chen Lo... and Kamal Salih...; published for the United Nations Centre for Regional Development, etc. Oxford, 1978. pp. 274.

— Australia.

AUSTRALIA. Department of Urban and Regional Development. 1975. The inter-relation of manufacturing industry policy and urban and regional development policy: a discussion paper based on a submission to the Committee to Advise on Policies for Manufacturing Industry, Jackson Committee. [Canberra], 1975. pp. 109.

— — Queensland.

QUEENSLAND. Department of the Co-ordinator-General of Public Works. 1975. State of regional planning, public works organization and environmental control in Queensland. [Brisbane, 1975?]. pp. 16.

MORETON REGION GROWTH STRATEGY INVESTIGATIONS. Urban land-use and commitment. [Brisbane], Co-ordinator-General's Department and Cities Commission, 1976. 1 vol. (various pagings). *bibliog. (Tasks. 2)*

— Brazil.

PLANEJAMENTO regional: metodos e aplicação ao caso brasileiro;...Paulo Roberto Haddad, editor. Rio de Janeiro, 1974. pp. 244. *bibliog. (Brazil. Instituto de Planejamento Econômico e Social. Instituto de Pesquisas. Monografias. No. 8)*

— Canada — Alberta.

ALBERTA. Task Force on Urbanization and the Future. 1972. Task committee reports. [Edmonton, 1972]. pp. 91.

NORTHERN ALBERTA DEVELOPMENT COUNCIL. Economic development of northern Alberta: position paper. [Edmonton], 1977. pp. 15.

— — Newfoundland.

NEWFOUNDLAND. Provincial Planning Office. 1976. St. John's urban region regional plan. [St. John's, 1976]. fo. 49. *1 map in end pocket.*

REGIONAL PLANNING.

— Nova Scotia.

LANG (R.S.) Nova Scotia municipal and regional planning in the seventies: report/evaluation of the Town Planning Act review...; prepared and published under an agreement between the Nova Scotia Department of Municipal Affairs and Central Mortgage and Housing Corporation. [Halifax], 1972. pp. 470.

— Ontario.

ONTARIO. Ministry of Treasury, Economics and Intergovernmental Affairs. 1978. Northwestern Ontario: a strategy for development. [Toronto], 1978. pp. 98.

— Colombia.

REVISTA DE PLANEACION Y DESARROLLO; publicada por el Departamento Nacional de Planeación,...Colombia. [articles in English or Spanish]. q., 1969 (v.1)- Bogota.

— France.

REMOND (BRUNO) Les OREAM et l'aménagement du territoire, 1966-76. [Paris, Documentation Française, 1977]. pp. 215. *bibliog.* *11 maps in end pocket.*

TRANSPORTS et aménagement du territoire: réflexions sur le rééquilibrage Est-Ouest; [by Philippe Andre and others; edited by Pierre Henri Derycke and Alain Plaud]. Paris, Délégation à l'Aménagement du Territoire et à l'Action Régionale, 1977. pp. 102. *bibliog.*

HOUSE (JOHN WILLIAM) France: an applied geography. London, 1978. pp. 478. *bibliogs.*

CONFERENCE NATIONALE D'AMENAGEMENT DU TERRITOIRE, VICHY, 1978. Nouvelles orientations pour l'aménagement de la France. Paris, La Documentation Française, 1979. pp. 258.

— Germany.

GERMANY (BUNDESREPUBLIK). Bundesforschungsanstalt für Landeskunde und Raumordnung. Informationen zur Raumentwicklung. m., Ja 1973 (Heft 1)- Bonn-Bad Godesberg. *Supersedes Rundbrief des Instituts für Landeskunde [of which the Library has no file] and Informationen; [pd. by] Institut für Raumordnung (N 1950 - 1973).*

— Nepal.

EVALUATION of a regional development strategy: a case study in the Kathmandu growth zone; by Wolfgang Zehender [and others]. Berlin, 1975. pp. 143.

— New Zealand.

NEW ZEALAND. Ministry of Works and Development. 1975. The East Coast Planning Council. [Wellington, 1975]. pp. 11.

NEW ZEALAND. Planning Council. 1977. Regional options. Wellington, 1977. fo. 10.

NEW ZEALAND. Department of Trade and Industry. 1978. The regional development programme. [Wellington, 1978]. pp. 16.

— Russia.

BELOUSOV (IVAN IVANOVICH) Osnovy ucheniia ob ekonomicheskom raionirovanii: razmeshchenie i raionirovanie proizvoditel'nykh sil. Moskva, 1976. pp. 320. *bibliog.*

— South Africa.

DAVIES (WILLIAM J.) Principal distributional and structural characteristics of the Border Region and some internal implications of the national regional development policy. Port Elizabeth, S.A., 1976. pp. 122. *(University of Port Elizabeth. Institute for Planning Research. Research Reports. No. 16) With summaries in English and Afrikaans.*

— Switzerland.

BRUGGER (ERNST A.) and HAEBERLING (GEORGE) Abbau regionaler Ungleichgewichte: föderalistischer Ausgleich durch Raumordnungspolitik: Ansprüche und konkrete Möglichkeiten im Kanton Zürich. Zürich, 1978. 3 vols. *bibliog.*

— Trinidad and Tobago.

TRINIDAD AND TOBAGO. Town and Country Planning Division. 1975. Planning for development: the San Fernando region preliminary draft development plan. [Port of Spain], 1975. pp. 83. *(Development Planning Series. T7)*

— United Kingdom.

PLANNING IN DURHAM; (pd. by the Durham County Planning Department). a., 1970(no.1)- Durham.

BERKSHIRE. Planning Department. Berkshire: record of planning policies. [Reading, Berks.], 1973. pp. 28.

BERKSHIRE. Planning Department. East Berkshire structure plan: issues report. [Reading, Berks., 1974]. pp. 39.

CLEVELAND [COUNTY]. Planning Department. Cleveland (Hartlepool) structure plan: report of survey: draft document for consultation: stud[ies]. Middlesbrough, 1975. 19 pts. (in 1 vol.).

ESSEX. County Planning Department. Development plan scheme [1975]. [Chelmsford], 1975. pp. 88.

HEREFORD AND WORCESTER [COUNTY]. Planning Department and WEST MIDLANDS. County Council. Worcestershire structure plan, 1975, for the former administrative County of Worcestershire and those parts of the former administrative County of Worcestershire transferred to the West Midlands County on 1 April 1974. [Worcester], 1975. pp. 108.

BERKSHIRE. Planning Department. Central Berkshire structure plan: report of survey. [Reading, Berks.], 1976. pp. 260.

BERKSHIRE. Planning Department. The first structure plan for West Berkshire: consultation document. [Reading, Berks.], 1976. pp. 141.

CAMBRIDGESHIRE. County Planning Department. Cambridgeshire structure plan: report of survey: consultation draft. Cambridge, 1976. pp. 160.

LEICESTERSHIRE. County Planning Officer. Leicestershire structure plan: written statement for the City of Leicester and the County of Leicestershire prior to local government re-organisation on 1st April 1974. [Leicester], 1976 repr. 1977. pp. 121. *2 maps in end pocket.*

NORFOLK. County Council. County structure plan: draft written statement for consultation. [Norwich], 1976. pp. 141.

HUMBERSIDE. County Council. Planning Department. Humberside structure plan: annual progress report. a., 1977/78(1st)- [Beverley].

CLEVELAND [COUNTY]. Planning Department. Cleveland (Hartlepool) structure plan: report of survey. [Middlesbrough], 1977-78. 2 vols. *(Reports. No. 115)*

HAMPSHIRE. County Council. (North East Hampshire structure plan): report of survey: summary and conclusions; ([with] Supplement). [Winchester], 1977-8. 2 pts. (in 1 vol.)

BERKSHIRE. Planning Department. Central Berkshire structure plan: consultation document. [Reading, Berks.], 1977. pp. 169.

BERKSHIRE. Planning Department. East Berkshire structure plan: consultation document. [Reading, Berks.], 1977. pp. 151.

BERKSHIRE. Planning Department. West Berkshire structure plan, submitted to the Secretary of State for the Environment, August 1977. [Reading, Berks., 1977]. pp. 109.

CAMBRIDGESHIRE. County Planning Department. Cambridgeshire structure plan: Cambridge sub-area: report of the joint study team. Cambridge, 1977. pp. 77.

CAMBRIDGESHIRE. County Planning Department. Cambridgeshire structure plan: draft written statement. Cambridge, 1977. pp. 182.

CAMBRIDGESHIRE. County Planning Department. Cambridgeshire structure plan: report on alternative strategies. Cambridge, 1977. pp. 74.

CAMBRIDGESHIRE. County Planning Department. Cambridgeshire structure plan: supplement to report of survey: consultation draft. Cambridge, 1977. pp. 93.

CLEVELAND [COUNTY]. [Planning Department]. Cleveland (East Cleveland) structure plan. [Middlesbrough], 1974 [or rather 1977]. pp. 199. *Map in end pocket.*

CLEVELAND [COUNTY]. [Planning Department]. Cleveland (West Cleveland) structure plan. [Middlesbrough], 1974 [or rather 1977]. pp. 193. *Map in end pocket.*

CLEVELAND [COUNTY]. [Planning Department]. Teesside structure plan. [Middlesbrough], 1977. pp. 235. *Map in end pocket.*

DURHAM (COUNTY). County Council. County structure plan: report of survey. vol. 2. Resolving the issues. [Durham], 1977. pp. 145.

EAST Anglia regional strategy: monitoring report no. 1. [London, Department of the Environment], 1977. pp. 64.

ESSEX. County Planning Department. Development plan scheme [1977]. [Chelmsford], 1977. pp. 72. *Looseleaf.*

HAMPSHIRE. County Council. (North East Hampshire structure plan): choice and policy. [Winchester], 1977. pp. 38.

LEICESTERSHIRE. County Planning Officer. Structure plan for Rutland: report of survey. Leicester, 1977. pp. 144.

LEICESTERSHIRE. County Planning Officer. Structure plan for Rutland: written statement. Leicester, 1977. pp. 64.

WEST YORKSHIRE. Metropolitan County Council. Structure plan: report of survey; [part 1], December 1977. [Wakefield], 1977. 2 vols.

WEST YORKSHIRE. Metropolitan County Council. Structure plan: written statement: consultation draft, October 1977. Wakefield, 1977. 1 vol. (various pagings). *Folding map in end pocket.*

WORRALL (A.R.) Heathrow sub-regional study: (the first draft of a thesis). [1977]. fo. 106. *bibliog.*

BEDFORDSHIRE. County Council. County structure plan: annual monitory report. a., 1978- Bedford.

ASHCROFT (BRIAN) The evaluation of regional economic policy: the case of the United Kingdom. Glasgow, [1978]. pp. 72,3,6. *bibliog. (Glasgow. University of Strathclyde. Centre for the Study of Public Policy. Studies in Public Policy. No. 12)*

BERKSHIRE. Planning Department. Central Berkshire structure plan, submitted to the Secretary of State for the Environment, June 1978. [Reading, Berks., 1978]. pp. 119.

BERKSHIRE. Planning Department. East Berkshire structure plan, submitted to the Secretary of State for the Environment, June 1978. [Reading, Berks., 1978]. pp. 115.

BERKSHIRE. Planning Department. West Berkshire structure plan: monitoring process report. [Reading, Berks.], 1978. pp. 41.

CLEVELAND [COUNTY]. Planning Department. Cleveland (Hartlepool) structure plan: written statement. [Middlesbrough], 1978. pp. 285. *(Reports. No. 114) Map in ed pocket.*

REGIONAL PLANNING.(Cont.)

DURHAM (COUNTY). County Council. County structure plan: report of survey. vol. 3. Choosing the policies; ([with] Supplement: City of Durham: choosing the policies). [Durham], 1978. 2 vols. (in 1).

EAST SUSSEX. Planning Department. County structure plan 1978, as approved by the Secretary of State for the Environment, May 1978. Lewes, 1978. pp. 86.

EAST SUSSEX. Planning Department. County structure plan [1978]: first alteration; ([with] County structure plan [1978]: first alteration: report of survey). Lewes, 1978. 2 pts. (in 1 vol.).

EAST SUSSEX. Planning Department. The altered county structure plan 1978: the approved county structure plan 1978 as amended by the County Council in the submitted first alteration: informal draft. Lewes, 1978. pp. 121.

HAMPSHIRE. County Council. Mid Hampshire structure plan, submitted 1978. [Winchester], 1978. pp. 121. *Map in end pocket.*

HAMPSHIRE. County Council. North East Hampshire structure plan, submitted 1978. [Winchester], 1978. pp. 108. *Map in end pocket.*

PICKVANCE (CHRISTOPHER GEOFFREY) Policies as chameleons: an interpretation of regional policy and office policy in Britain. Canterbury, 1978. fo. 48. *bibliog.*

U.K. Department of the Environment. 1978. Strategic plan for the South East: review: government statement, 1978. London, 1978. pp. 37.

WEST YORKSHIRE. Metropolitan County Council. Structure plan: report of survey; part 2, December 1978. [Wakefield], 1978. 1 vol. (various pagings).

CAMBRIDGESHIRE. County Planning Department. Cambridgeshire structure plan: supplement to report of survey. Cambridge, 1979. pp. 176.

CAMBRIDGESHIRE. County Planning Department. Cambridgeshire structure plan: written statement. Cambridge, 1979. pp. 197.

DURHAM (COUNTY). County Council. Durham county structure plan: (written statement). Durham, [1979]. pp. 194. *Map in end pocket.*

— — Citizen participation.

CLEVELAND [COUNTY]. County Council. Cleveland (Teesside) structure plan, Cleveland (East Cleveland) structure plan, Cleveland (West Cleveland) structure plan: examination in public, June 1975: County Council statement. [Middlesbrough], 1975. fo 84, xxxiii.

OPINION RESEARCH CENTRE. A report on a survey of public attitudes in connection with the preparation of the structure plan; prepared for West Yorkshire Metropolitan County Council. London, 1975. pp. 99, 25.

BOADEN (NOEL) and WALKER (RAYMOND) Sample surveys and public participation. [London], 1976. pp. 29. *(Linked Research Project into Public Participation in Structure Planning. Interim Research Papers. 10)*

CLEVELAND [COUNTY]. Planning Department. (Cleveland (Hartlepool) structure plan): public participation, stage 1. [Middlesborough], 1976. pp. 33,x. *(Reports. No. 61)*

CLEVELAND [COUNTY]. Planning Department. (Cleveland (Hartlepool) structure plan): public participation, stage 2. [Middlesbrough], 1976. pp. 91. *(Reports. No. 79)*

GOLDSMITH (MICHAEL) and SAUNDERS (PETER) Participation through public meetings: the case in Cheshire. [London], 1976. pp. 30. *(Linked Research Project into Public Participation in Structure Planning. Interim Research Papers. 9)*

HAMPTON (WILLIAM) and BEALE (WENDY) Methods of approaching groups in South Yorkshire. [London], 1976. pp. 51. *(Linked Research Project into Public Participation in Structure Planning. Interim Research Papers. 11)*

BERKSHIRE. Planning Department. West Berkshire structure plan: report of public participation. [Reading, Berks.], 1977. 1 vol. (various pagings).

BERKSHIRE. Planning Department. Central Berkshire structure plan: report of public participation. [Reading, Berks.], 1978. pp. 113.

BERKSHIRE. Planning Department. East Berkshire structure plan: report of public participation. [Reading, Berks.], 1978. pp. 67,40.

CLEVELAND [COUNTY]. Planning Department. Cleveland (East Cleveland) structure plan: proposals for alterations. [Middlesbrough], 1978. 3 pts. (in 1 vol.). *(Reports. Nos. 125-127)*

CLEVELAND [COUNTY]. Planning Department. (Cleveland (Hartlepool) structure plan): public participation, stage 3: public and formal consultations. [Middlesbrough], 1978. 1 vol. (various pagings). *(Reports. No. 100)*

CLEVELAND [COUNTY]. Planning Department. (Cleveland (Hartlepool) structure plan): public participation, stage 3: response and recommended changes. [Middlesbrough], 1978. pp. 164. *(Reports. No. 101)*

CLEVELAND [COUNTY]. Planning Department. Cleveland (West Cleveland) structure plan: proposals for alterations. [Middlesbrough], 1978. 3 pts. (in 1 vol.) *(Reports. Nos. 128-130)*

CLEVELAND [COUNTY]. Planning Department. Teesside structure plan: proposals for alterations. [Middlesbrough], 1978. 3 pts. (in 1 vol.). *(Reports. Nos. 122-124)*

URHAM (COUNTY). County Council. Durham county structure plan: (public participation: aims stage). [Durham, 1978?]. pp. 161. *(Technical Papers. No. 25)*

DURHAM (COUNTY). County Council. Durham county structure plan: (public participation: survey stage). [Durham, 1978?]. pp. 168. *(Technical Papers. No. 23)*

HAMPSHIRE. County Council. Mid Hampshire structure plan: report on publicity and consultations. [Winchester], 1978. 3 vols. (in 1).

HAMPSHIRE. County Council. (North East Hampshire structure plan): report on publicity and consultations; ([with] Representations [and] Technical comments). [Winchester], 1978. 3 vols. (in 1).

HAMPTON (WILLIAM) and WALKER (RAYMOND) The individual citizen and public participation: a survey of individual written response in Teesside. [London], 1978. pp. 24. *(Linked Research Project into Public Participation in Structure Planning. Interim Research Papers. 13)*

STRINGER (PETER) Tuning in to the public: survey before participation. [London], 1978. pp. 44. *(Linked Research Project into Public Participation in Structure Planning. Interim Research Papers. 14)*

CAMBRIDGESHIRE. County Planning Department. Cambridgeshire structure plan: report on public participation and consultations. Cambridge, 1979. pp. 60, 89.

COMMUNITY involvement and leisure; edited by John T. Haworth. London, [1979]. pp. 205.

DURHAM (COUNTY). County Council. Durham county structure plan: comments on "Choosing the policies". [Durham], 1979. pp. 132.

DURHAM (COUNTY). County Council. Durham county structure plan: (public participation: policy stage). [Durham, 1979?]. pp. 172. *(Technical Papers. No. 26)*

— — Ireland, Northern.

IRELAND, NORTHERN. Department of the Environment. 1979. North east area plan: written statement: comprising Coleraine, Ballymoney and Moyle district areas. Belfast, 1979. pp. 82. *6 maps in end pocket.*

— — Wales.

MID GLAMORGAN. [County Planning Department]. Mid Glamorgan county structure plan: draft written statement, January, 1978. [Cardiff], 1978. pp. 210.

MID GLAMORGAN. [County Planning Department]. Mid Glamorgan county structure plan: guide to the plan, January 1978. [Cardiff], 1978. pp. 29.

MID GLAMORGAN. [County Planning Department]. Mid Glamorgan county structure plan: written statement, October, 1978. [Cardiff], 1978. pp. 253.

— — — Citizen participation.

MID GLAMORGAN. [County Planning Department]. Mid Glamorgan county structure plan: report of public participation and consultations, October 1978. [Cardiff], 1978. pp. 146.

— — West Midlands.

SMITH (BARBARA M.D.) Industry in metropolitan area plans: proposals and experience in the West Midlands County area. Birmingham, 1977. pp. 148. *(Birmingham. University. Centre for Urban and Regional Studies. Research Memoranda. No.62)*

— United States.

REVITALIZING the Northeast; edited by George Sternlieb and James W. Hughes. New Brunswick, N.J., [1978]. pp. 443. *bibliogs.*

MILLER (ROBERTA BALSTAD) City and hinterland: a case study of urban growth and regional development. Westport, Conn., 1979. pp. 179.

REGIONALISM.

BIRMINGHAM. University. Centre for Urban and Regional Studies. Papers in urban and regional studies. Birmingham. 1977 in progress.

DE BLIJ (HARM J.) Geography: regions and concepts; with a chapter by Stephen S. Birdsall. 2nd ed. New York, [1978]. pp. 593.

— Belgium.

TINDEMANS (LEO) Regionalised Belgium: transition from the nation-state to the multinational state. [Brussels], Ministry of Foreign Affairs, External Trade and Cooperation in Development, 1972. pp. 15. *(Memo from Belgium. No. 151-152)*

— Brazil.

LEVINE (ROBERT M.) Pernambuco in the Brazilian ederation, 1889-1937. Stanford, Calif., 1978. pp. 236. *bibliog.*

— Canada.

RAWLYK (GEORGE A.) and others. Regionalism in Canada: flexible federalism or fractured nation? Scarborough, Ont., [1979]. pp. 244. *bibliog.*

— Europe.

EUROPEAN integration, regional devolution and national parliaments; [by] D. Coombes [and others]. London, 1979. pp. 45. *(Policy Studies Institute. Studies in European Politics. 3)*

— European Economic Community countries.

REGIONAL problems and policies in the European Community: a bibliography; general editor: Kevin Allen. Farnborough, Hants., [1978]. 2 vols.

— Italy.

TRANIELLO (PAOLO) Regioni e biblioteche in Italia. Milano, [1977]. pp. 293. *bibliog.*

— United Kingdom.

PAGE (EDWARD) Michael Hechter's internal colonial thesis: some theoretical and methodological problems. Glasgow, [1977]. pp. 30,3. *(Glasgow. University of Strathclyde. Centre for the Study of Public Policy. Studies in Public Policy. No. 9)*

REGRESSION ANALYSIS.

STATISTICAL inference under order restrictions: the theory and application of isotonic regression; [by] R.E. Barlow [and others]. Chichester, 1972 repr. 1978. pp. 388. *bibliog.*

MOSTELLER (CHARLES FREDERICK) and TUKEY (JOHN W.) Data analysis and regression: a second course in statistics. Reading, Mass., [1977]. pp. 588.

REHABILITATION.

UNITED NATIONS. Department of Economic and Social Affairs. 1976. Comparative study on legislation, organization and administration of rehabilitation services for the disabled: prepared jointly by the United Nations, the International Labour Organisation and the World Health Organization. (ST/ESA/28). New York, 1976. pp. 183.

— Costs.

HAMMERMAN (SUSAN R.) Rehabilitation for the disabled: the social and economic implications of investments for this purpose. (ST/ESA/35). New York, United Nations, 1977. pp. 70.

— Australia.

LE SUEUR (EDDIE J.) The Australia Government Rehabilitation Service. Canberra, 1977. pp. 108. *(Australia. Commission of Inquiry into Poverty. Social/Medical Aspects of Poverty Series)*

REHABILITATION OF CRIMINALS
— United Kingdom.

CORDEN (JOHN) and others. After prison: a study of the post-release experiences of discharged prisoners. [York, 1978]. pp. 93. *(Papers in Community Studies. No. 21)*

REHABILITATION OF JUVENILE DELINQUENTS.

WALD (KAREN) Children of Che: childcare and education in Cuba. Palo Alto, Calif., [1978]. pp. 399.

— United Kingdom.

NATIONAL ASSOCIATION FOR THE CARE AND RESETTLEMENT OF OFFENDERS. The Hammersmith Teenage Project: an experiment in the community care of young offenders. [Chichester], 1978. pp. 56.

— United States.

VACHSS (ANDREW H.) and BAKAL (YITZHAK) The life-style violent juvenile: the secure treatment approach. Lexington, [1979]. pp. 466.

— — Michigan.

MAX (LAURENCE) and DOWNS (THOMAS) Decentralized delinquency services in Michigan: differential placement and its impact on program effectiveness and cost- effectiveness. [Lansing], 1975. pp. 160. *(Michigan. Department of Social Services. Studies in Welfare Policy. No. 4)*

REICHSZENTRALE FÜR HEIMATDIENST.

WIPPERMANN (KLAUS W.) Politische Propaganda und staatsbürgerliche Bildung: die Reichszentrale für Heimatdienst in der Weimarer Republik. Köln, [1976]. pp. 584. *bibliog.*

REID (LOREN).

REID (LOREN) Hurry home Wednesday: growing up in a small Missouri town, 1905-1921. Columbia, 1978. pp. 291.

REIMS
— History.

HUNT (LYNN AVERY) Revolution and urban politics in provincial France: Troyes and Reims, 1786-1790. Stanford, Ca., 1978. pp. 187. *bibliog.*

REINSURANCE.

CARTER (ROBERT LEWIS) Reinsurance. Brentford, 1979. pp. 590. *bibliog.*

RELIGION.

OFFICIAL and popular religion: analysis of a theme for religious studies; edited by Pieter Hendrik Vrijhof and Jacques Waardenburg. The Hague, [1979]. pp. 739. *bibliog.*

— History.

PLEKHANOV (GEORGII VALENTINOVICH) Ob ateizme i religii v istorii obshchestva i kul'tury: izbrannye proizvedeniia i izvlecheniia iz trudov. Moskva, 1977. pp. 355.

ELIADE (MIRCEA) A history of religious ideas; translated by Willard R. Trask. London, 1979 in progress. *bibliog.*

RELIGION, PRIMITIVE.

SKORUPSKI (JOHN) Symbol and theory: a philosophical study of theories of religion in social anthropology. Cambridge, 1976. pp. 265. *bibliog.*

RELIGION AND POLITICS.

MICHELAT (GUY) and SIMON (MICHEL) Classe, religion et comportement politique. Paris, [1977]. pp. 498.

RELIGION AND SCIENCE.

WHITE (LYNN T.) Medieval religion and technology: collected essays. Berkeley, Calif., [1978]. pp. 360. *(California University. Center for Medieval and Renaissance Studies. Publications. 13)*

RELIGION AND SOCIOLOGY.

IDENTITY and religion: international cross-cultural approaches; edited by Hans Mol. London, [1978]. pp. 246. *bibliog.*

KOBETSKII (VLADIMIR DMITRIEVICH) Sotsiologicheskoe izuchenie religioznosti i ateizma. Leningrad, 1978. pp. 118. *bibliog.*

MARTIN (DAVID ALFRED) The dilemmas of contemporary religion. Oxford, [1978]. pp. 104.

REED (BRUCE) The dynamics of religion: process and movement in Christian churches. London, 1978. pp. 235. *bibliog.*

OFFICIAL and popular religion: analysis of a theme for religious studies; edited by Pieter Hendrik Vrijhof and Jacques Waardenburg. The Hague, [1979]. pp. 739. *bibliog.*

RELIGION AND STATE
— Asia.

RELIGION and the legitimation of power in South Asia; edited by Bardwell L. Smith. Leiden, 1978. pp. 186. *bibliogs.*

— Brazil.

CHRISTO (CARLOS ALBERTO LIBANIO) Letters from a prisoner of conscience...; translated by John Drury. Guildford, 1978. pp. 241.

— Russia.

BOURDEAUX (MICHAEL) White book on restrictions of religion in the USSR. Brussels, [1977?]. pp. 66.

RELIGION and modernization in the Soviet Union; edited by Dennis J. Dunn. Boulder, Colo., 1977. pp. 412.

BABRIS (PETER J.) Silent churches: persecution of religions in the Soviet- dominated areas. Arlington Heights, Ill., 1978. pp. 531. *bibliog.*

RELIGIONS.

LESSA (WILLIAM ARMAND) and VOGT (EVON ZARTMAN) eds. Reader in comparative religion: an anthropological approach. 4th ed. New York, [1979]. pp. 488. *bibliog.*

RELIGIOUS BIOGRAPHY.

The BIOGRAPHICAL process: studies in the history and psychology of religion; edited by Frank E. Reynolds and Donald Capps. The Hague, [1976]. pp. 436. *bibliog.*

ECCLESIASTICAL HISTORY SOCIETY. Summer Meeting, 16th, and Winter Meeting, 17th, 197-. Religious motivation: biographical and sociological problems for the church historian: papers read at the...meeting[s]...; edited by Derek Baker. Oxford, 1978. pp. 516. *(Studies in Church History. vol.15)*

RELIGIOUS FILMS
— Germany.

SCHMITT (HEINER) Kirche und Film: kirchliche Filmarbeit in Deutschland von ihren Anfängen bis 1945. Boppard am Rhein, 1979. pp. 382. *(Germany (Bundesrepublik). Bundesarchiv. Schriften. 26)*

RELIGIOUS LIBERTY
— Italy.

LEZIROLI (GIUSEPPE) Aspetti della libertà religiosa, nel quadro dell'attuale sistema di relazione fra Stato e confessioni religiose. Milano, 1977. pp. 240. *bibliog. (Ferrara. Università. Facoltà Giuridica. Pubblicazioni. 2a Serie. 10)*

— Russia.

BOURDEAUX (MICHAEL) and others, eds. Religious liberty in the Soviet Union: W[orld] C[ouncil of] C[hurches] and USSR: a post-Nairobi documentation. West Wickham, Kent, [1976]. pp. 96. *(Centre for the Study of Religion and Communism. Keston Books. No.7)*

RELIGIOUS THOUGHT
— United States.

GREVEN (PHILIP J.) The protestant temperament: patterns of child-rearing, religious experience, and the self in early America. New York, 1977. pp. 431.

RELOCATION (HOUSING)
— South Africa.

MAASDORP (GAVIN G.) and PILLAY (P. NESEN) Urban relocation and racial segregation: the case of Indian South Africans. Durban, 1977. pp. 206. *bibliog. (Natal University. Department of Economics. Research Monographs)*

REMAND HOMES
— United Kingdom — Scotland.

WALTER (J.A.) Sent away: a study of young offenders in care. Farnborough, Hants., [1978]. pp. 178. *biblog. Published in association with the Institute of Medical Sociology, University of Aberdeen.*

RENAISSANCE.

DEBUS (ALLEN G.) Man and nature in the Renaissance. Cambridge, 1978. pp. 159.

RENEGOTIATION OF GOVERNMENT CONTRACTS
— United States.

AMERICAN ENTERPRISE INSTITUTE FOR PUBLIC POLICY RESEARCH. Legislative Analyses. 95th Congress. No. 10. The Renegotiation Reform Act of 1977. Washington, 1977. pp. 21.

RENT.

TUCKER (GEORGE) The laws of wages, profits and rent investigated. New York, 1964. pp. 189. *Reprint of the work first published Philadelphia, 1837.*

RENT CONTROL

— India — Punjab.

PUNJAB (INDIA). Statutes, etc. 1949-59. The East Punjab Urban Rent Restriction Act, 1949,...as adapted and amended up to 30th September, 1959. Chandigarh, 1959. pp. 14.

— United Kingdom.

LAW CENTRES' WORKING GROUP. Rent Act 1978?...: submissions to the Department of the Environment's review of the Rent Acts. London, 1977. pp. 84.

ARDEN (ANDREW) Housing: security and rent control. London, 1978. pp. 231. *bibliogs.*

— — Scotland.

SCOTLAND. Scottish Development Department. 1977. The review of the rent acts: a consultation paper. [Edinburgh, 1977]. pp. 17.

RENT SUBSIDIES

— United Kingdom.

U.K. Department of the Environment. 1977. Housing policy review: local authority subsidies: rent rebates and rent allowances: consultation paper. [London, 1977]. pp. 5.

— — Scotland.

JAUNCEY (C.E.) Report...on the local inquiry in relation to the implementation by Falkirk Town Council of Parts 2 and 4 of the Housing, Financial Provisions, Scotland, Act 1972. Edinburgh, H.M.S.O., [1972]. pp. 7.

MACDONALD (IAN ALEXANDER) Report...on the local inquiry in relation to the implementation by Glasgow Corporation of Parts 2 and 4 of the Housing, Financial Provisions, Scotland, Act 1972. Edinburgh, H.M.S.O., [1972]. pp. 10.

MAXWELL (PETER) Lord. Report...on the local inquiry in relation to the implementation by Kirkcaldy Town Council of Parts 2 and 4 of the Housing, Financial Provisions, Scotland, Act 1972. Edinburgh, H.M.S.O., [1972]. pp. 8.

ROSS (DONALD MACARTHUR) Report...on the local inquiry in relation to the implementation by Lanark County Council of Parts 2 and 4 of the Housing, Financial Provisions, Scotland, Act 1972. Edinburgh, H.M.S.O., [1972]. pp. 10.

CAMERON (KENNETH JOHN) Report...on the local inquiry in relation to the implementation by Kilmarnock Town Council of Parts 2 and 4 of the Housing, Financial Provisions, Scotland, Act 1972. Edinburgh, H.M.S.O., [1973]. pp. 9.

MACDONALD (IAN ALEXANDER) Report...on the local inquiry in relation to the implementation by Midlothian County Council of Parts 2 and 4 of the Housing, Financial Provisions, Scotland, Act 1972. Edinburgh, H.M.S.O., [1973]. pp. 13.

O'BRIEN (FREDERICK WILLIAM FITZGERALD) Report...on the local inquiry in relation to the implementation by Clydebank Town Council of Parts 2 and 4 of the Housing, Financial Provisions, Scotland, Act 1972. Edinburgh, H.M.S.O., [1973]. pp. 9.

TAYLOR (ROBERT RICHARDSON) Report...on the local inquiry in relation to the implementation by Dunfermline Town Council of Parts 2 and 4 of the Housing, Financial Provisions, Scotland, Act 1972. Edinburgh, H.M.S.O., [1973]. pp. 7.

REPARATION.

MEINERS (ROGER EVERT) Victim compensation: economic, legal, and political aspects. Lexington, Mass., [1978]. pp. 123. *bibliog.*

REPERTORY GRID TECHNIQUE.

RYLE (ANTHONY) Frames and cages: the repertory grid approach to human understanding. London, [1975]. pp. 148. *bibliog.*

PERSONAL construct psychology, 1977; edited by Fay Fransella. London, 1978. pp. 274. *Based on papers given at the Second International Congress on Personal Construct Theory held at Oxford in July 1977.*

REPRESENTATIVE GOVERNMENT AND REPRESENTATION.

MOODIE (GRAEME COCHRANE) and STUDDERT-KENNEDY (GERALD) Opinions, publics and pressure groups: an essay on vox populi and representative government. London, 1970. pp. 115.

EULAU (HEINZ) and WAHLKE (JOHN CHARLES) The politics of representation: continuities in theory and research. Beverly Hills, [1978]. pp. 312. *bibliog.*

FISCHER (GEORGE) Ways to self rule: beyond Marxism and anarchism. New York, [1978]. pp. 244. *bibliog.*

KARDELJ (EDVARD) Democracy and socialism; translated by Margot and Boško Milosavljević. London, [1978]. pp. 244.

ZEIGLER (LUTHER HARMON) and TUCKER (HARVEY J.) The quest for responsive government: an introduction to state and local politics. North Scituate, Mass., [1978]. pp. 337. *bibliogs.*

— Fiji.

FIJI. Royal Commission appointed for the purpose of considering and making recommendations as to the most appropriate method of electing members to, and representing the people of Fiji in, the House of Representatives, 1975. Report; [Harry Street, chairman]. [Suva], 1975. pp. 29. *(Fiji. Parliament. Parliamentary Papers. 1975. No. 24)*

— United States.

BANNING (LANCE) The Jeffersonian persuasion: evolution of a party ideology. Ithaca, 1978. pp. 307.

REPUBLICAN PARTY (UNITED STATES).

BANNING (LANCE) The Jeffersonian persuasion: evolution of a party ideology. Ithaca, 1978. pp. 307.

McKINNEY (GORDON B.) Southern mountain Republicans 1865-1900: politics and the Appalachian community. Chapel Hill, N.C., [1978]. pp. 277. *bibliog.*

REPUBLICANISM IN SPAIN.

BEN-AMI (SHLOMO) The origins of the Second Republic in Spain. Oxford, [1978]. pp. 356. *bibliog.*

RESEARCH

— Economic aspects.

PROBLEMY ekonomiki nauki. Erevan, 1977. pp. 267.

SCIENCE, technology, and economic development: a historical and comparative study; edited by William Beranek, Jr. [and] Gustav Ranis. New York, [1978]. pp. 347. *bibliogs.*

— Canada.

CANADA. Statistics Canada. Service bulletin: Science statistics. irreg., current issues only Ottawa. *[in English and French]*

— European Economic Community countries — Finance.

EUROPEAN COMMUNITIES. Statistical Office. Government financing of research and development (formerly Public expenditure on research and development). a., 1974/76- Luxembourg. *[in Community languages]*

— Ireland (Republic).

RESEARCH AND DEVELOPMENT IN IRELAND; [pd. by] National Science Council. a., 1974- Dublin.

— Russia — Economic aspects.

VEGER (LEONID LEONIDOVICH) and MATEVOSOV (IURII DAVIDOVICH) Ekonomicheskii effekt nauchnykh issledovanii. Erevan, 1977. pp. 145.

— United Kingdom.

DEVELOPMENT STUDIES: register of research in the United Kingdom; [pd. by] Institute of Development Studies at the University of Sussex. bien., 1977/78- Brighton.

NORRIS (GRAEME) Justifying research and teaching objectives in universities. Farnborough, [1979]. pp. 219. *bibliogs.*

— United States.

The STATE of science and research: some new indicators; [edited by] Nestor E. Terleckyj. Boulder, [1977]. pp. 201. *bibliogs.*

RESEARCH, INDUSTRIAL

— Management.

KAY (NEIL M.) The innovating firm: a behavioural theory of corporate R D. London, 1979. pp. 266. *bibliog.*

— Statistical methods.

DANIEL (CUTHBERT) Applications of statistics to industrial experimentation. New York, [1976]. pp. 294. *bibliog.*

RESEARCH GRANTS

— United Kingdom.

U.K. Social Science Research Council. Bursary scheme. a. London. *Current issues only kept.*

U.K. Social Science Research Council. Postgraduate studentships in the social sciences. a. London. *Current issue only kept.*

RESIDENTIAL MOBILITY.

POPULATION mobility and residential change; edited by W.A.V. Clark and Eric G. Moore. Evanston, Ill., 1978. pp. 281. *bibliogs. (Northwestern University. Studies in Geography. No. 25)*

— United Kingdom.

CROSBY (CHARLES) Intra-urban migration: a study of residential mobility in the Clarksfield and Glodwick districts of Oldham. [York], 1978. pp. 78. *bibliog. (Papers in Community Studies. No. 17)*

— United States.

REES (P.H.) Residential patterns in American cities: 1960. Chicago, 1979. pp. 405. *bibliog. (Chicago. Unversity. Department of Geography. Research Papers. No. 189)*

RESONANCE.

AWOJOBI (A.O.) Beyond resonance. Lagos, 1977. pp. 20. *bibliog. (Lagos. University. Inaugural Lecture Series)*

RESONANT VIBRATION

— Mathematical models.

AWOJOBI (A.O.) Beyond resonance. Lagos, 1977. pp. 20. *bibliog. (Lagos. University. Inaugural Lecture Series)*

RESTAURANTS, LUNCH ROOMS, ETC.

— United States.

WYCKOFF (D. DARYL) and SASSER (W. EARL) The chain-restaurant industry. Lexington, Mass., [1978]. pp. 188.

RESTITUTION

— United Kingdom.

GOFF (Sir ROBERT LIONEL ARCHIBALD) and JONES (GARETH HYWEL) The law of restitution. 2nd ed. London, 1978. pp. 614. *bibliog.*

JONES (GARETH) Anglo-American trends in restitution: lecture given in the auditorium of the University of Amsterdam on Friday 16th December 1977, etc. Deventer, 1978. pp. 14.

RESTRAINT OF TRADE.

ORGANISATION FOR ECONOMIC CO-OPERATION AND DEVELOPMENT. Committee of Experts on Restrictive Business Practices. 1978. Restrictive business practices relating to trademarks. Paris, 1978. pp. 76.

— Germany.

GERMANY (BUNDESREPUBLIK). Monopolkommission. 1977. Missbräuche der Nachfragemacht und Möglichkeiten zu ihrer Kontrolle im Rahmen des Gesetzes gegen Wettbewerbsbeschränkungen. Baden-Baden, 1977. pp. 166. *(Sondergutachten. Band 7)*

— Ireland (Republic).

EIRE. Restrictive Practices Commission. 1977. Report of study of competition in the licensed drink trade. Dublin, [1977]. fo. 91.

RETAIL TRADE.

TUCKER (KENNETH ARTHUR) Concentration and costs in retailing. Farnborough, [1978]. pp. 175. *bibliog.*

— Accounting.

MOSCARELLO (LOUIS C.) and others. Retail accounting and financial control. 4th ed. New York, [1976]. pp. 511.

— Finland.

FINLAND. Tilastokeskus. Vähittäiskaupan toimipaikat. a., 1974- Helsinki. *[in Finnish and Swedish]*

— India — Punjab.

PUNJAB (INDIA). Economic and Statistical Organisation. 1976. Report on the distributive trade survey relating to urban areas of Punjab. Chandigarh, 1976. pp. 206. *(Publications. No. 218)*

— Portugal.

PORTUGAL. Instituto Nacional de Estatística. 1979- . 1977 recenseamento à distribuição e serviços: Portugal: [provisional results]. Lisboa, [1979 in progress].

— Sweden.

SWEDEN. Finansdepartementet. Långtidsutredningen. 1975. (Långtidsutredningen 1975. Bilaga 4). Varuhandeln, 1975- 1980;...rapport av Handelns Utredningsinstitut. Stockholm, 1975. pp. 44. *(Sweden. Statens Offentliga Utredningar. 1975.97)*

SWEDEN. Statistiska Centralbyrån. Regional omsättning inom parti- och detaljhandel samt vissa tjänstenäringar. a., 1976- Stockholm. *[in Swedish with English summary]*

— United Kingdom.

DAWSON (JOHN ALAN) and KIRBY (DAVID) Small scale retailing in the UK. Farnborough, [1979]. pp. 173. *bibliogs.*

RETIREMENT.

IMPLICATIONS for social security of research on aging and retirement: report of round table meeting, The Hague, 27-29 April 1976. Geneva, 1977. pp. 74. *(International Social Security Association. Studies and Research. No.9)*

— Denmark.

HILLESTRØM (KARSTEN) and KOCH-NIELSEN (INGER) Ønsker om fleksibel pensionsalder og nedsat arbejdstid. København, 1977. pp. 55. *(Socialforskningsinstituttet. Meddelelser. 23)*

OLSEN (HENNING) and HANSEN (GERT) Aeldres arbejdsophør: rapport nr. 2 fra forløbsundersøgelsen af de aeldre, etc. København, 1977. pp. 203. *bibliog. (Socialforskningsinstituttet. Publikationer. 79) With English summary.*

— United States.

KLEILER (FRANK M.) Can we afford early retirement? Baltimore, [1978]. pp. 163. *bibliog.*

REVENUE

— Pakistan.

FAROOQ (DANIAL M.) A note on domestic sources of government revenues: who collects what in Pakistan. Islamabad, United States Agency for International Development, 1977. fo. 21. *bibliog.*

REVIVALS

— United Kingdom.

CARWARDINE (RICHARD) Transatlantic revivalism: popular evangelicalism in Britain and America, 1790-1865. Westport, [1978]. pp. 249. *bibliog.*

— United States.

CARWARDINE (RICHARD) Transatlantic revivalism: popular evangelicalism in Britain and America, 1790-1865. Westport, [1978]. pp. 249. *bibliog.*

McLOUGHLIN (WILLIAM GERALD) Revivals, awakenings, and reform: an essay on religion and social change in America, 1607-1977. Chicago, [1978]. pp. 239. *bibliog.*

HAMMOND (JOHN L.) The politics of benevolence: revival religion and American voting behavior. Norwood, N.J., [1979]. pp. 243. *bibliog.*

REVOLUTIONISTS.

REJAI (MOSTAFA) and PHILLIPS (KAY) Leaders of revolution. Beverly Hills, [1979]. pp. 243. *bibliog.*

— Canada.

FLANAGAN (THOMAS) Louis 'David' Riel: 'prophet of the new world'. Toronto, [1979]. pp. 216.

— France.

VERMOREL (AUGUSTE JEAN MARIE) Mr F.V. Raspail. [Paris, 1869]. pp. 35.

— Germany.

TAMPKE (JÜRGEN) The Ruhr and revolution: the revolutionary movement in the Rhenish-Westphalian industrial region, 1912-1919. London, [1979]. pp. 209. *bibliog.*

— Iraq.

BATATU (HANNA) The old social classes and the revolutionary movements of Iraq: a study of Iraq's old landed and commercial classes and of its communists, Ba'thists, and Free Officers. Princeton, [1978]. pp. 1283. *bibliog.*

— Russia.

TROITSKII (NIKOLAI ALEKSEEVICH) Tsarskie sudy protiv revoliutsionnoi Rossii: politicheskie protsessy, 1871-1880 gg. Saratov, 1976. pp. 408.

SERGE (VICTOR) pseud. [i.e. Viktor L'vovich KIBAL'CHICH]. Mémoires d'un révolutionnaire, 1901-1941. Paris, [1978]. pp. 444. *bibliog. Text, first published 1951, revised and corrected by author.*

ACTON (EDWARD) Alexander Herzen and the role of the intellectual revolutionary. Cambridge, 1979. pp. 194. *bibliog.*

McCLELLAN (WOODFORD D.) Revolutionary exiles: the Russians in the First International and the Paris Commune. London, 1979. pp. 266. *bibliog.*

POMPER (PHILIP) Sergei Nechaev. New Brunswick, [1979]. pp. 273. *bibliog.*

SEGAL (RONALD MICHAEL) The tragedy of Leon Trotsky. London, 1979. pp. 446. *bibliog.*

REVOLUTIONS.

BREUER (STEFAN) Die Krise der Revolutionstheorie: negative Vergesellschaftung und Arbeitsmetaphysik bei Herbert Marcuse. Frankfurt am Main, [1977]. pp. 308. *bibliog.*

FRIGNANO (GIOVANNI) Teoria della guerra di popolo: (validita e sviluppo della teoria di Lenin e di Mao sulla guerra rivoluzionaria). [Milan, 1977]. pp. 203. *bibliogs.*

INTERUNIVERSITY CENTRE FOR EUROPEAN STUDIES. International Colloquium, 2nd, 1976. Situations révolutionnaires en Europe, 1917-1922: Allemagne, Italie, Autriche-Hongrie; Revolutionary situations in Europe, 1917-1922: Germany, Italy, Austria-Hungary...edited by Charles L. Bertrand. Montreal, 1977. pp. 251. *bibliog.*

KAESLER (DIRK) Revolution und Veralltäglichung: eine Theorie postrevolutionärer Prozesse. München, [1977]. pp. 311. *bibliog.*

KRASIN (IURII ANDREEVICH) Teoriia sotsialisticheskoi revoliutsii: leninskoe nasledie i sovremennost'. Moskva, 1977. pp. 292.

RIFORME e rivoluzione nella storia contemporanea; [by] Aldo Zanardo [and others]; a cura di Guido Quazza. Torino, [1977]. pp. 342.

CHERTKOV (VIKTOR PETROVICH) Dialektika revoliutsionnogo protsessa. Moskva, 1978. pp. 144.

CONTOGIORGIS (GEORGES D.) La théorie des révolutions chez Aristote. Paris, 1978. pp. 288. *bibliog.*

GOMBIN (RICHARD) The radical tradition: a study in modern revolutionary thought; translated by Rupert Swyer. London, 1978. pp. 153. *bibliog.*

TILLY (CHARLES) From mobilization to revolution. Reading, Mass., [1978]. pp. 349. *bibliog.*

VERNON (RICHARD ANTHONY) Commitment and change: Georges Sorel and the idea of revolution. Toronto, [1978]. pp. 148. *bibliog.*

REJAI (MOSTAFA) and PHILLIPS (KAY) Leaders of revolution. Beverly Hills, [1979]. pp. 243. *bibliog.*

— Africa.

AKE (CLAUDE) Revolutionary pressures in Africa. London, 1978. pp. 109.

— Chad.

BUIJTENHUIJS (ROBERT) Le Frolinat et les révoltes populaires du Tchad, 1965-1976. The Hague, [1978]. pp. 526. *bibliog. (Afrika-Studiecentrum. Change and Continuity in Africa)*

— China.

DIRLIK (ARIF) Revolution and history: the origins of Marxist historiography in China, 1919-1937. Berkeley, Calif., [1978]. pp. 299. *bibliog.*

McDONALD (ANGUS W.) The urban origins of rural revolution: elites and the masses in Hunan Province, China, 1911-1927. Berkeley, Calif., [1978]. pp. 369. *bibliog.*

SKOCPOL (THEDA) States and social revolutions: a comparative analysis of France, Russia, and China. Cambridge, 1979. pp. 407. *bibliog.*

REVOLUTIONS.(Cont.)

— Ethiopia.

OTTAWAY (MARINA) and OTTAWAY (DAVID) Ethiopia: empire in revolution. New York, 1978. pp. 250.

— Europe, Eastern.

VELIKII Oktiabr' i revoliutsii 40-kh godov v stranakh Tsentral'noi i Iugo-Vostochnoi Evropy: opyt sravnitel'nogo izucheniia sotsial'no-ekonomicheskikh preobrazovanii v revoliutsionnom protsesse. Moskva, 1977. pp. 541.

IZ istorii Velikogo Oktiabria i posleduiushchikh sotsialisticheskikh revoliutsii: sbornik statei. Moskva, 1978. pp. 542.

— France.

SKOCPOL (THEDA) States and social revolutions: a comparative analysis of France, Russia, and China. Cambridge, 1979. pp. 407. *bibliog.*

— Russia.

SKOCPOL (THEDA) States and social revolutions: a comparative analysis of France, Russia, and China. Cambridge, 1979. pp. 407. *bibliog.*

RHINE PROVINCE

— Politics and government.

LINKSRHEINISCHE deutsche Jakobiner: Aufrufe, Reden, Protokolle; Briefe und Schriften, 1794-1801; [edited by] Axel Kuhn. Stuttgart, [1978]. pp. 353. *bibliog.*

TAMPKE (JÜRGEN) The Ruhr and revolution: the revolutionary movement in the Rhenish-Westphalian industrial region, 1912-1919. London, [1979]. pp. 209. *bibliog.*

RHINE VALLEY

— Separatist movement, 1918-1924.

McDOUGALL (WALTER A.) France's Rhineland diplomacy, 1914-1924: the last bid for a balance of power in Europe. Princeton, [1978]. pp. 420. *bibliog.*

RHODES (CECIL JOHN).

VINDEX, pseud. [i.e. F. VERSCHOYLE] Cecil Rhodes: his political life and speeches, 1881-1900. London, 1900. pp. 864.

RHODESIA.

RHODESIA. Ministry of Information, Immigration and Tourism. 1977. Rhodesia in brief: some basic facts about Rhodesia. [Salisbury, 1977?]. pp. 79.

— Administrative and political divisions.

RHODESIA. Delimitation Commission. 1978. Report; [H.N. Macdonald, chairman]. Salisbury, 1978. pp. 15. *(Rhodesia. [Sessional Papers]. 1978. C.S.R. 18)* 3 maps in end pocket.

— Census.

RHODESIA. Census, 1969. Census of population, 1969. Salisbury, [1973?]. pp. 210. *1 map, 4 forms in end pocket.*

— Constitution.

RHODESIA. Ministry of Information, Immigration and Tourism. 1978. Rhodesia constitutional agreement, 3rd March 1978. [Salisbury, 1978]. pp. 6. *(For the Record. No. 44)*

— Description and travel.

RHODESIA. Department of Information. Production Services Branch. 1970. Rhodesian scene 1970. Salisbury, 1970. pp. 25.

— Economic conditions.

RHODESIA. Ministry of Finance. 1970. Outlook for the 1970s; by the Minister of Finance, the Hon. J.J. Wrathall. [Salisbury, 1970]. pp. 6. *(Rhodesia. Ministry of Information, Immigration and Tourism. For the Record. No. 11)*

RHODESIA. Ministry of Information, Immigration and Tourism. 1971. Opportunities for development. [Salisbury, 1971]. pp. 7.

— Economic policy.

RHODESIA. Ministry of Information, Immigration and Tourism. 1971. Rhodesia's tribal areas: the need for rapid economic expansion. [Salisbury, 1971]. pp. 4.

— Foreign relations — United Kingdom.

MACDONALD (HECTOR NORMAN) A judge's thoughts..., 30th May, 1970. [Salisbury, 1970]. pp. 5. *(Rhodesia. Ministry of Information, Immigration and Tourism. For the Record. No. 12)*

— Frontier troubles.

RHODESIA. Ministry of Information, Immigration and Tourism. 1977. Aggression: a Rhodesian viewpoint. [Salisbury, 1977]. pp. 18.

— History.

DI PERNA (ANTHONY) A right to be proud: the struggle for self-government and the roots of white nationalism in Rhodesia, 1890-1922. Bulawayo, 1978. pp. 245. *bibliog.*

DUPONT (CLIFFORD W.). The reluctant president: the memoirs of...Clifford Dupont. Bulawayo, 1978. pp. 246.

— Nationalism.

DI PERNA (ANTHONY) A right to be proud: the struggle for self-government and the roots of white nationalism in Rhodesia, 1890-1922. Bulawayo, 1978. pp. 245. *bibliog.*

MUZOREWA (ABEL TENDEKAI) Rise up and walk: an autobiography. London, 1978. pp. 289.

— Native races.

RHODESIA. Ministry of Information, Immigration and Tourism. 1969. A people's progress. [Salisbury, 1969]. 1 pamphlet (unpaged).

PARTRIDGE (MARK) Minister speaks on community development and the urban African;.. .text of an address by the Minister of Local Government and Housing...to the Associate Member Council of the Associated Members of Commerce of Rhodesia. [Salisbury, 1972]. fo.9. *(Rhodesia. Ministry of Information, Immigration and Tourism. Press Statements) Xerox copy.*

— Officials and employees — Salaries, allowances, etc.

RHODESIA. Committee on Ministerial and Parliamentary Salaries and Allowances. 1975. Report; [L.K.S. Wilson, chairman]. Salisbury, 1975. pp. 25.

— Politics and government.

RHODESIA. Parliament. House of Assembly. Report[s of Committees and Select Committees]. Salisbury, 1958 to date.

UNITED NATIONS. Office of Public Information. 1969. A principle in torment, I. The United Nations and Southern Rhodesia. New York, 1969. pp. 71.

GALE (WILLIAM DANIEL) The years between: 1923-1973: half a century of responsible government in Rhodesia. Salisbury, [1973]. pp. 68.

RHODESIA. Judge President. 1975. An assessment of the present situation and an appeal to South Africans to come and see for themselves. [Salisbury], 1975. pp. 8. *(Rhodesia. Ministry of Information and Tourism. For the Record. No. 29)*

RHODESIA. Ministry of Information, Immigration and Tourism. 1977. Safeguards for a settlement: Rhodesia government policy statement. [Salisbury, 1977]. pp. 2.

BERLYN (PHILLIPPA) The quiet man: a biography of the Hon. Ian Douglas Smith, I.D., Prime Minister of Rhodesia. Salisbury, Rhodesia, 1978. pp. 256.

CATHOLIC INSTITUTE FOR INTERNATIONAL RELATIONS. Rhodesia: after the internal settlement. London, [1978]. pp. 25.

HILLS (DENIS) Rebel people. London, 1978. pp. 248.

INTERNATIONAL DEFENCE AND AID FUND. Fact Papers on Southern Africa. No. 6. Smith's settlement: events in Zimbabwe since 3rd March 1978. London, 1978. pp. 37.

RHODESIA. Ministry of Foreign Affairs. Information Section. 1978. Ten questions on the Rhodesian settlement. [Salisbury, 1978]. fo. 7.

RHODESIA. Ministry of Information, Immigration and Tourism. 1978. Rhodesia constitutional agreement, 3rd March 1978. [Salisbury, 1978]. pp. 6. *(For the Record. No. 44)*

RHODESIA. Prime Minister. 1978. Prime Minister's broadcast to the nation, Sunday, 12th March, 1978. [Salisbury, 1978]. pp. 6. *(Rhodesia. Ministry of Information, Immigration and Tourism. For the Record. No. 45)*

— Social life and customs.

RHODESIA. Ministry of Information, Immigration and Tourism. 1969. The man - and his ways: an introduction to the customs and beliefs of Rhodesia's African people. [Salisbury, 1969 repr. 1970]. pp. 43.

RHODESIA AND NYASALAND, FEDERATION OF

— Native races.

FEDERATION OF RHODESIA AND NYASALAND. Federal Information Department. 1959. The Federation of Rhodesia and Nyasaland: the facts. Salisbury, 1959. pp. 38.

FEDERATION OF RHODESIA AND NYASALAND. Federal Information Department. 1960. Success stories: African achievement in Rhodesia and Nyasaland. Salisbury, 1960. pp. 36.

— Politics and government.

FEDERATION OF RHODESIA AND NYASALAND. Federal Information Department. 1959. The Federation of Rhodesia and Nyasaland: the facts. Salisbury, 1959. pp. 38.

RHÔNE-ALPES

— Economic conditions.

FAURE (SUZANNE) Pour comprendre l'économie de Rhône-Alpes, ouvrage réalisé pour l'Etablissement Public Régional...avec la collaboration de l'INSEE...Direction Régionale du Travail. [Lyon], 1978. pp. 175. *bibliog. Map in end pocket.*

— Industries.

RHONE-ALPES 1985: une région s'interroge sur son avenir industriel; [by R. Benguigui and others]. [Paris, 1978]. pp. 223. *(France. Ministère de l'Industrie, du Commerce et de l'Artisanat. Etudes de Politique Industrielle. 22)*

RICASOLI (BETTINO) Barone.

HANCOCK (Sir WILLIAM KEITH) Ricasoli and the Risorgimento in Tuscany. New York, 1969. pp. 320. *bibliog.*

RICE

— India.

SEN (SUDHIR) Land and its problems. volume 1. Some regional investigations with a special study on paddy cultivation. Santiniketan, 1943. pp. 166. *(Visva-Bharati University. Economic Research Publications. No. 3)*

NATIONAL COUNCIL OF APPLIED ECONOMIC RESEARCH. The impact of the price rise in petroleum based agricultural inputs on the production of wheat and rice in India; a study prepared for the Commonwealth Secretariat;...[directed by] I.Z. Bhatty. London, Commonwealth Secretariat, [1976]. pp. 74. *(Commonwealth Economic Papers. No. 6)*

— Indonesia.

PALMER (INGRID) The new rice in Indonesia. (UNRISD Reports. No. 77.1) (UNRISD/76/C.44). Geneva, United Nations Research Institute for Social Development, 1976. pp. 198. ([Studies on the Green Revolution. No. 15.])

— Malawi.

MALAWI. Agro-Economic Survey. 1972. Agro-economic survey: 9th report: Lake Chilwa: a sample farm management survey among rice and maize growers at the northern end of Lake Chilwa in Kasupe district, Malawi; prepared by T.W. Bieze. Zomba, 1972. fo. 63.

— Malaysia.

BARNUM (H.N.) and SQUIRE (LYN) Labor heterogeneity and rice production in Malaysia. Ann Arbor, Mich., 1977. pp. 11. bibliog. (Michigan University. Center for Research on Economic Development. Discussion Papers. No. 71)

FREDERICKS (L. J.) and others. Patterns of labour utilization and income distribution in rice double cropping systems: policy implications. Kuala Lumpur, 1977. pp. 66. bibliog. (University of Malaya. Faculty of Economics and Administration. Occasional Papers on Malaysian Socio-Economic Affairs. No. 8)

— Mauritius.

LUTCHMEENARAIDOO (KESHAWA) Rice production: review and prospects. [Port Louis, Ministry of Agriculture and Natural Resources and the Environment, 1975]. pp. 48, 1 map. bibliog.

— Philippine Islands.

PALMER (INGRID) The new rice in the Philippines (UNRISD Report No. 75.2) (UNRISD/75/C.38). Geneva, United Nations Research Institute for Social Development, 1975. pp. 200. bibliog. ([Studies on the Green Revolution. No. 10])

RICE (Sir CECIL SPRING).

WELLS (SHERRILL PERKINS BROWN) The influence of Sir Cecil Spring Rice and Sir Edward Grey on the shaping of Anglo-American relations, 1913-1916. 1978. fo. 416. bibliog. Typescript. Ph.D. (London) thesis: unpublished. This thesis is the property of London University and may not be removed from the Library.

RIDDELL (GEORGE ALLARDICE) 1st Baron Riddell.

RIDDELL (GEORGE ALLARDICE) 1st Baron Riddell. More pages from my diary, 1908-1914. London, 1934. pp. 238.

RIEL (LOUIS).

FLANAGAN (THOMAS) Louis 'David' Riel: 'prophet of the new world'. Toronto, [1979]. pp. 216.

RIEL REBELLION, 1885.

FLANAGAN (THOMAS) Louis 'David' Riel: 'prophet of the new world'. Toronto, [1979]. pp. 216.

RIGHT AND LEFT (POLITICAL SCIENCE).

LIPSET (SEYMOUR MARTIN) and RAAB (EARL) The politics of unreason: right-wing extremism in America, 1790- 1977. 2nd ed. Chicago, [1978]. pp. 581.

RIGHT OF PROPERTY

— United Kingdom — London.

CANT (D. H.) Squatting and private property rights: an analysis of the effects of squatting seen in the context of a theory about how increased activity by the state affects the way change comes about in our society. London, 1976 repr. 1978. pp. 71. bibliog. (London. University. University College. Bartlett School of Architecture and Planning. Town Planning Discussion Papers. No. 24)

RIGHT OF REPLY

— Europe.

Das GEGENDARSTELLUNGSRECHT in Europa: Möglichkeiten der Harmonisierung; (The right of reply in Europe: possibilities of harmonization); herausgegeben...von Martin Löffler [and others]. München, 1974. pp. 335. (Deutsche Studiengesellschaft für Publizistik. Schriftenreihe. Band 11) In English, French and German.

RIJEKA

— History.

LEDEEN (MICHAEL ARTHUR) The first duce: D'Annunzio at Fiume. Baltimore, [1977]. pp. 225.

RIMINI

— Politics and government.

JONES (P.J.) The Malatesta of Rimini and the papal state. London, 1974. pp. 372. bibliog.

RINGS (ALGEBRA).

BEHRENS (ERNST-AUGUST) Ring theory; translated [from the German] by Clive Reis. New York, 1972. pp. 320. bibliog.

GOODEARL (K.R.) Von Neumann regular rings. London, 1979. pp. 369. bibliog.

RIO DE JANEIRO (CITY)

— Population.

ARAUJO (ALOISIO BARBOSA DE) Aspectos fiscais das areas metropolitanas. Rio de Janeiro, 1974. pp. 125. (Brazil. Instituto de Planejamento Econômico e Social. Instituto de Pesquisas. Monografias. No. 15)

RIOT CONTROL.

WEINBAUM (PAUL OWEN) Mobs and demagogues: the New York response to collective violence in the early nineteenth century. [London, 1979]. pp. 194. bibliog.

RIOTS

— South Africa.

KANE-BERMAN (JOHN) Soweto: black revolt, white reaction. Johannesburg, 1978 repr. 1979. pp. 268.

— United Kingdom.

U.K. Home Office. 1812-55. British 19th century riots and disturbances: HO 40/1-59; Home Office, Correspondence and Papers, Disturbances, 1812-1855. v.p., 1812-55. Microfilm : 46 reels. (U.K. Public Record Office. Public Records of Great Britain. Series 5) Means of reference on reel 1.

— United States.

HOERDER (DIRK) Crowd action in revolutionary Massachusetts, 1765-1780. New York, [1977]. pp. 394.

RISK.

HONOHAN (PATRICK THOMAS) Uncertainty, portfolio choice and economic fluctuations. 1978. fo. 411. bibliog. Typescript. Ph.D. (London) thesis: unpublished. This thesis is the property of London University and may not be removed from the Library.

UNCERTAINTY in economics: readings and exercises; edited by Peter Diamond, Michael Rothschild. New York, [1978]. pp. 574. bibliogs.

AMERICAN ACADEMY OF POLITICAL AND SOCIAL SCIENCE. Annals. vol. 443. Risk and its treatment; changing societal consequences; special editor of this volume George E. Rejda. Philadelphia, 1979. pp. 202.

— Mathematical models.

FOLDES (LUCIEN P.) Optimal saving and risk in continuous time with constant returns. [new ed.] London, 1978. pp. 60. bibliog. (Papers on Capital and Risk. No. 1)

RISK (INSURANCE).

SEAL (HILARY LATHAM) Survival probabilities: the goal of risk theory. Chichester, [1978]. pp. 103. bibliog.

RITES AND CEREMONIES.

ESSAYS on the ritual of social relations...; edited by Max Gluckman. Manchester, 1962. pp. 190. bibliog.

The INTERPRETATION of ritual: essays in honour of A.I. Richards; edited by J.S. La Fontaine. London, 1972. pp. 296. bibliog.

— New Guinea.

RUBEL (PAULA G.) and ROSMAN (ABRAHAM) Your own pigs you may not eat: a comparative study of New Guinea societies. Chicago, 1978. pp. 368. bibliog.

— Yugoslavia.

VODANOVICH (IVANICA MARY) The structure of roles and their ritual in a Yugoslav community. 1978. fo. 313. bibliog. Typescript. Ph.D. (London) thesis: unpublished. This thesis is the property of London University and may not be removed from the Library.

RIVADAVIA (BERNARDINO).

FRIZZI DE LONGONI (HAYDEE E.) Rivadavia y la economia argentina. Buenos Aires, [1947 repr. 1976]. pp. 209. bibliog.

RIVERS

— Regulation.

PRINCIPLES of river engineering: the non-tidal alluvial river; editorial board: P.Ph. Jansen [and others]. London, 1979. pp. 509. bibliog.

RIVERS (WILLIAM HALSE RIVERS).

SLOBODIN (RICHARD) W.H.R. Rivers; [includes selections from his writings]. New York, 1978. pp. 295. bibliog.

ROAD PLANNING

— United Kingdom — Citizen participation.

TYME (JOHN) Motorways versus democracy: public inquiries into road proposals and their political significance. London, 1978. pp. 166.

ROAD TRANSPORT WORKERS

— United Kingdom.

TRANSPORT TRAINING: the newspaper of the Road Transport Industry Training Board. m. Wembley. Current issues only kept.

ROADS

— Environmental aspects — United Kingdom.

DE HAMEL (BRUNO) Roads and the environment. London, H.M.S.O., 1976. pp. 10.

— Australia — Western Australia.

UREN (MALCOLM JOHN LEGGOE) and PARRICK (F.) Servant of the state: the history of the Main Roads Department 1926-1976. abridged ed. [Perth], Commissioner of Main Roads, 1976. pp. 44. bibliog.

— India — Bihar.

BAHL (M.L.) Development of roads in Bihar, 1947-1955. Patna, [Public Relations Department], 1955. pp. 47.

— United Kingdom.

TAYLOR (CHRISTOPHER) 1935- . Roads and tracks of Britain. London, 1979. pp. 210.

— — Wales.

ROADS IN WALES; [pd. by] Welsh Office. a., 1978(1st)- Cardiff.

ROADS (Cont.)

— United States — Pennsylvania.

DUANE (WILLIAM JOHN) Letters addressed to the people of Pennsylvania respecting the internal improvement of the commonwealth by means of roads and canals. Philadelphia, 1811; New York, 1968. pp. 125.

ROADSIDE IMPROVEMENT.

TEK HAI. The landscaping and amenity treatment of highways in town and country. 1962. fo. 20. *(London. University. London School of Economics and Political Science. Rees Jeffreys Studentship for Research into Transport. 1962-63) Typescript: unpublished. With volume of photographs bound in.*

ROBERTSON (Sir DENNIS HOLME).

PRESLEY (JOHN R.) Robertsonian economics: an examination of the work of Sir D.H. Robertson on industrial fluctuation. London, 1979. pp. 320.

ROBUST STATISTICS.

HUBER (PETER J.) Robust statistical procedures. Philadelphia, [1977]. pp. 56. *bibliog. (Conference Board of the Mathematical Sciences. Regional Conference Series in Applied Mathematics. No. 27)*

ROCHDALE

— City planning.

TYM (ROGER) AND ASSOCIATES, and others. Time for industry: evaluation of the Rochdale industrial improvement area, for the Department of the Environment. London, H.M.S.O., 1979. 1 vol. (various pagings).

— Foreign population.

ANWAR (MUHAMMAD) The myth of the return: Pakistanis in Britain. London, 1979. pp. 278. *bibliog.*

— Industries.

TYM (ROGER) AND ASSOCIATES, and others. Time for industry: evaluation of the Rochdale industrial improvement area, for the Department of the Environment. London, H.M.S.O., 1979. 1 vol. (various pagings).

RODRIGUES (JOÃO).

COOPER (MICHAEL) Rodrigues the interpreter: an early Jesuit in Japan and China. New York, 1974. pp. 416.

RODRIGUEZ DE FRANCIA (JOSE GASPAR).

VAZQUEZ (JOSE ANTONIO) ed. El Doctor Francia visto y oido por sus contemporaneos. Buenos Aires, 1975. pp. 420.

ROGER II, King of Sicily.

CURTIS (EDMUND) Roger of Sicily and the Normans in Lower Italy, 1016-1154. New York, 1973. pp. 483. *Reprint of 1912, New York, ed.*

ROHEISEN-VERBAND.

SCHINDLER (ROSEMARIE) Die Marktpolitik des Roheisen-Verbandes während der Weimarer Republik. Bielefeld, 1978. pp. 365. *bibliog.*

ROLAND-HOLST (HENRIETTE).

HERMAN Gorter en Henriette Roland Holst in hun tijd; (samengesteld en verzorgd door het Nederlands Letterkundig Museum en Documentatiecentrum). Amsterdam, 1978. pp. 135.

ROLLS-ROYCE.

LLOYD (IAN) Rolls-Royce: the growth of a firm. London, 1978. pp. 164.

ROMAGNA

— Politics and government.

TRONCONI (GABRIELLA MEDRI) Giovanni Braschi e il partito popolare nel forlivese. Roma, [1975]. pp. 194. *bibliog.*

ROMANCE LANGUAGES

— Syntax.

HARRIS (MARTIN) The evolution of French syntax: a comparative approach. London, 1978. pp. 268. *bibliog.*

ROMANIA

— Economic conditions.

HEMY (GEOFFREY W.) Romania: business opportunities. London, [1977]. pp. 193.

— Economic policy.

RAFAEL (EDGAR R.) "Entwicklungsland" Rumänien: zur Geschichte der "Umdefinierung" eines sozialistischen Staates. München, 1977. pp. 145. *bibliog. (Munich. Südost-Institut München. Untersuchungen zur Gegenwartskunde Südosteuropas. 12)*

— Foreign relations.

ROMANIA. 1946. Roumania at the peace conference. Paris, 1946. pp. 145, 6 maps.

BRAUN (AUREL) Romanian foreign policy since 1965: the political and military limits of autonomy. New York, [1978]. pp. 217. *bibliog.*

— — Russia.

SHEVIAKOV (ALEKSEI ALEKSEEVICH) Sovetsko-rumynskie otnosheniia i problema evropeiskoi bezopasnosti, 1932-1939. Moskva, 1977. pp. 382.

— Historiography.

GIURESCU (CONSTANTIN C.) Probleme controversate în istoriografia română. [București, 1977]. pp. 176.

— History.

SETON-WATSON (ROBERT WILLIAM) A history of the Roumanians: from Roman times to the completion of unity. [Hamden, Conn.], 1963. pp. 596. *bibliog. Reprint of work first published in 1934.*

The INDEPENDENCE of Romania; edited by Ștefan Pascu. București, 1977. pp. 263. *bibliog. (Academia Republicii Socialiste România. Sectia de Științe Istorice, Filozofice și Economico-Juridice. Bibliotheca Historica Romaniae. Monographies. 18)*

— Industries.

HEMY (GEOFFREY W.) Romania: business opportunities. London, [1977]. pp. 193.

— Military policy.

PROBLEMELE păcii și ale războiului în condițiile revoluției științifice și tehnice: necesitatea istorică a dezarmării: sesiunea științifică din 21 ianuarie 1977. București, 1977. pp. 488. *With English, French, German, Italian, Russian and Spanish tables of contents and identifications of authors.*

BRAUN (AUREL) Romanian foreign policy since 1965: the political and military limits of autonomy. New York, [1978]. pp. 217. *bibliog.*

— Nationalism.

The INDEPENDENCE of Romania; edited by Ștefan Pascu. București, 1977. pp. 263. *bibliog. (Academia Republicii Socialiste România. Sectia de Științe Istorice, Filozofice și Economico-Juridice. Bibliotheca Historica Romaniae. Monographies. 18)*

— Politics and government.

MUȘAT (MIRCEA) and ARDELEANU (ION) La vie politique en Roumanie, 1918-1921. [București], 1978. pp. 259. *(Akademia Republicii Socialiste România. Sectia de Științe Istorice, Filozofice și Economico-Juridice. Bibliotheca Historica Romaniae. Monographies. 19)*

— Social history.

SOCIAL change in Romania, 1860-1940: a debate on development in a European nation; Kenneth Jowitt, editor. Berkeley, Calif., [1978]. pp. 207. *(California University. Institute of International Studies. Research Series. No.36) Based on a conference held by the Institute.*

ROME (CITY)

— Bibliography.

MAJOLO MOLINARI (OLGA) La stampa periodica romana dal 1900 al 1926, scienze morali, storiche e filologiche. Roma, 1977. 2 vols.

— History.

BRENTANO (ROBERT) Rome before Avignon: a social history of thirteenth-century Rome. London, 1974. pp. 340.

— Industries.

CONGI (GAETANO) L'altra Roma: classe operaia e sviluppo industriale nella capitale. Bari, [1977]. pp. 258.

— Politics and government.

ARGAN (GIULIO CARLO) Un'idea di Roma: intervista di Mino Monicelli. Roma, 1979. pp. 117.

— Social conditions.

CONGI (GAETANO) L'altra Roma: classe operaia e sviluppo industriale nella capitale. Bari, [1977]. pp. 258.

— Social history.

BRENTANO (ROBERT) Rome before Avignon: a social history of thirteenth-century Rome. London, 1974. pp. 340.

— Statistics.

ROME. Ufficio di Statistica e Censimento. Bollettino statistico. m., 1959 - S 1968, with gap (My 1965). Roma.

ROME, ANCIENT

— Civilization.

BROWN (PETER ROBERT LAMONT) The world of late antiquity: from Marcus Aurelius to Muhammad. London, 1976. pp. 216. *bibliog.*

— Economic history.

WALBANK (FRANK WILLIAM) The awful revolution: the decline of the Roman Empire in the West. Liverpool, 1969 repr. 1978. pp. 139. *bibliogs.*

— Foreign relations.

HARRIS (WILLIAM VERNON) War and imperialism in Republican Rome, 327-70 B.C. Oxford, 1979. pp. 293. *bibliog.*

— History.

JONES (ARNOLD HUGH MARTIN) The decline of the ancient world. London, 1978. pp. 414.

— — 510-30 B.C., Republic.

CRAWFORD (MICHAEL HEWSON) The Roman Republic. [London], 1978. pp. 224. *bibliog.*

HARRIS (WILLIAM VERNON) War and imperialism in Republican Rome, 327-70 B.C. Oxford, 1979. pp. 293. *bibliog.*

— — 30 B.C. — 476 A.D., Empire.

WALBANK (FRANK WILLIAM) The awful revolution: the decline of the Roman Empire in the West. Liverpool, 1969 repr. 1978. pp. 139. *bibliogs.*

— Politics and government.

JONES (ARNOLD HUGH MARTIN) The decline of the ancient world. London, 1978. pp. 414.

— Religion.

LIEBESCHUETZ (JOHN HUGO WOLFGANG GIDEON) Continuity and change in Roman religion. Oxford, 1979. pp. 359. *bibliog.*

— Social history.

WALBANK (FRANK WILLIAM) The awful revolution: the decline of the Roman Empire in the West. Liverpool, 1969 repr. 1978. pp. 139. *bibliogs.*

ROOSEVELT (FRANKLIN DELANO) President of the United States.

FEIS (HERBERT) Churchill, Roosevelt, Stalin: the war they waged and the peace they sought. 2nd ed. Princeton, N.J., 1967 repr. 1974. pp. 702.

KIMBALL (WARREN F.) ed. Franklin D. Roosevelt and the world crisis, 1937-1945. Lexington, Mass., [1973]. pp. 297. *bibliog.* (Amherst College. Department of American Studies. Problems in American Civilization)

BARTLETT (BRUCE R.) Cover-up: the politics of Pearl Harbor, 1941-1946. New Rochelle, [1978]. pp. 189. *bibliog.*

KINSELLA (WILLIAM E.) Leadership in isolation: FDR and the origins of the Second World War. Boston, Mass., [1978]. pp. 282. *bibliog.*

DALLEK (ROBERT) Franklin D. Roosevelt and American foreign policy, 1932-1945. New York, 1979. pp. 657. *bibliog.*

ROSSI (GIOVANNI).

GOSI (ROSELLINA) Il socialismo utopistico: Giovanni Rossi e la colonia anarchica Cecilia. Milano, [1977]. pp. 179. *bibliog.*

ROTE ARMEE FRAKTION.

BECKER (JILLIAN) Hitler's children. rev. ed. London, 1978. pp. 415. *bibliog.*

ROTTWEIL

— Economic history.

WEISSER (LOTHAR) Rottweils Wirtschaft und Gesellschaft vom Ende der Reichsstadtzeit bis zum Ersten Weltkrieg. Rottweil, 1978. pp. 303. *bibliog.* (Rottweil. Stadtarchiv. Veröffentlichungen. Band 4)

ROUSSEAU (JEAN JACQUES).

VOLPE (GALVANO DELLA) Rousseau and Marx. London, 1978. pp. 206.

ROYAL ASIATIC COMPANY OF DENMARK.

FELDBAEK (OLE) India trade under the Danish flag, 1772-1808: European enterprise and Anglo-Indian remittance and trade. [Copenhagen], [1969]. pp. 359. *bibliog.* (Scandinavian Institute of Asian Studies. Monograph Series. No. 2) Summary in Danish.

ROYAL LONDON MUTUAL INSURANCE SOCIETY.

ALLEN (W. GORE) We the undersigned...: a history of the Royal London Mutual Insurance Society Limited and its times, 1861-1961. London, [1961]. pp. 80.

RUBBER INDUSTRY AND TRADE

— Malaysia.

BARLOW (COLIN) The natural rubber industry: its development, technology, and economy in Malaysia. Kuala Lumpur, 1978. pp. 500. *bibliog.*

— Zambia.

ZAMBIA. Central Statistical Office. 1976. Chemicals, rubber and plastics industries. Lusaka, 1976. pp. 64. (Industry Monographs. No.5)

RUHR

— Economic policy.

JANKOWSKI (MANFRED DIETER) Public policy in industrial growth: the case of Ruhr mining region, 1776-1865. New York, 1977. pp. 299. *bibliog.*

— Foreign population.

KLESSMANN (CHRISTOPH) Polnische Bergarbeiter im Ruhrgebiet, 1870-1945: soziale Integration und nationale Subkultur einer Minderheit in der deutschen Industriegesellschaft. Göttingen, 1978. pp. 306. *bibliog.*

— History.

TAMPKE (JÜRGEN) The Ruhr and revolution: the revolutionary movement in the Rhenish-Westphalian industrial region, 1912-1919. London, [1979]. pp. 209. *bibliog.*

— Politics and government.

PIETSCH (HARTMUT) Militärregierung, Bürokratie und Sozialisierung: zur Entwicklung des politischen Systems in den Städten des Ruhrgebietes, 1945 bis 1948. Duisburg, 1978. pp. 358. *bibliog.* (Duisburg. Stadtarchiv. Duisburger Forschungen. Band 26)

TAMPKE (JÜRGEN) The Ruhr and revolution: the revolutionary movement in the Rhenish-Westphalian industrial region, 1912-1919. London, [1979]. pp. 209. *bibliog.*

RULE OF LAW.

LIBERTY and the rule of law: [papers from a conference held in San Francisco in 1976]; edited...by Robert L. Cunningham. College Station, Texas, [1979]. pp. 349.

RURAL DEVELOPMENT.

RONDINELLI (DENNIS A.) and RUDDLE (KENNETH) Urbanization and rural development: a spatial policy for equitable growth. New York, [1978]. pp. 221. *bibliog.*

INTERNATIONAL CONFERENCE ON ECONOMIC ANALYSIS IN THE DESIGN OF NEW TECHNOLOGY FOR SMALL FARMERS, 1975. Economics and the design of small-farmer technology; edited by Alberto Valdés [and iothers]. Ames, 1979. pp. 211. *bibliog.*

— Africa.

The ROOTS of rural poverty in central and southern Africa; edited by Robin Palmer and Neil Parsons. Berkeley, Calif., 1977. pp. 430. *bibliogs.*

— Asia.

DIXON (RUTH B.) Rural women at work: strategies for development in South Asia. Baltimore, [1978]. pp. 227. *bibliog.*

— China.

ULLERICH (CURTIS) Rural employment and manpower problems in China. New York, [1979]. pp. 130. *bibliog.*

— France.

Le COMMERCE et l'artisanat dans les zones rurales, 1976-1977: une politique expérimentale; [by C. Herrault and others]. [Paris, 1976]. pp. 27. *bibliog.* (France. Ministère de l'Industrie du Commerce et de l'Artisanat. Programmes et Bilans. 1)

FRANCE. Ministère du Commerce et de l'Artisanat. 1978. Le commerce et l'artisanat dans les zones rurales: étude de vingt actions expérimentales. [Paris], 1978. pp. 64. (Programmes et Bilans. 2)

— India.

TAGORE (RONENDRA MOHAN) Rural reconstruction. Calcutta, [1937?]. pp. 76.

BATTERSBY (OLWEN) Samanway Vidapith: the Marr-Munning ashram. London, [1974?]. pp. 14. (Marr-Munning Trust. Edwina Mountbatten Papers. No. 4)

INDIA. Department of Rural Development. 1978. Drought prone areas programme. New Delhi, 1978. pp. 19.

INDIA. Department of Rural Development. 1978. National Institute of Rural Development: its growth and achievements. New Delhi, 1978. pp. 24.

INDIA. Department of Rural Development. 1979. Rural development programme: participation of industrial/business houses. New Delhi, [1979]. pp. 86.

— Ireland (Republic).

COMMINS (P.) and others. Rural areas: change and development. Dublin, Stationery Office, [1978]. pp. 184. *bibliog.* (National Economic and Social Council [Eire]. [Reports]. No.41)

— Jamaica.

JAMAICA. Ministry of Agriculture. 1973. Green paper on agricultural development strategy. [Kingston, 1973]. pp. 46.

— Norfolk Island.

AUSTRALIA. Bureau of Agricultural Economics. 1978. The prospects for rural development on Norfolk Island. Canberra, 1978. pp. 20. (Occasional Papers. No. 46)

— Pakistan.

LYVERS (F. KENNETH) and AUCHTER (EDMUND L.) Rural development: a suggested role for I[ntegrated] R[ural] D[evelopment] P[rogram]; a discussion paper on rural development in Pakistan. Islamabad. United States Agency for International Development, 1978. fo. 12.

— Poland — Silesia.

HAINES (MICHAEL R.) Economic-demographic interrelations in developing agricultural regions: a case study of Prussian Upper Silesia, 1840-1914. New York, 1977. pp. 499. *bibliogs.*

— Rhodesia.

BLOORE (KEITH) Community development and training: a condensation of the Batten report. [Salisbury, Ministry of Internal Affairs, 1967]. pp. 20.

— Thailand.

FARMERS in the forest: economic development and marginal agriculture in northern Thailand; edited by Peter Kunstadter [and others]. Honolulu, [1978]. pp. 402. *bibliog.*

— Underdeveloped areas.

See UNDERDEVELOPED AREAS — Rural development.

— United Kingdom.

PHILIP (ALAN BUTT) and others. A new deal for rural Britain. London, 1978. pp. 24.

RURAL transport and country planning; edited by Roy Cresswell. Glasgow, 1978. pp. 197. *bibliogs. Proceedings of the Conference held at the University of Nottingham, in March 1977 organised...by the Construction Industry Conference Centre Limited.*

RURAL deprivation and planning; edited by J. Martin Shaw. Norwich, [1979]. pp. 207. *bibliogs.*

— United States.

DANBOM (DAVID B.) The resisted revolution: urban America and the industrialization of agriculture, 1900-1930. Ames, Iowa, 1979. pp. 195. *bibliog.*

RURAL FAMILIES

— China.

PARISH (WILLIAM L.) and WHYTE (MARTIN KING) Village and family in contemporary China. Chicago, [1978]. pp. 419. *bibliog.*

RURAL GEOGRAPHY.

RURAL GEOGRAPHY.

CHISHOLM (MICHAEL) Rural settlement and land use: an essay in location. 3rd ed. London. 1979. pp. 189. *bibliog.*

RURAL HEALTH SERVICES

— United Kingdom.

HAYNES (R.M.) and BENTHAM (C.G.) Community hospitals and rural accessibility. Farnborough, [1979]. pp. 200. *bibliog.*

RURAL POOR

— Africa.

The ROOTS of rural poverty in central and southern Africa; edited by Robin Palmer and Neil Parsons. Berkeley, Calif., 1977. pp. 430. *bibliogs.*

— United Kingdom.

RURAL poverty: poverty, deprivation and planning in rural areas; [papers based on drafts presented at a conference organized by the Child Poverty Action Group in Colchester in 1977]; edited by Alan Walker. London, 1978. pp.117. *(Child Poverty Action Group. Poverty Pamphlets. 37)*

— United States.

EMPLOYMENT, income, and welfare in the rural South; by Brian Rungeling [and others]. New York, 1977. pp. 355. *bibliog.*

MERTZ (PAUL E.) New Deal policy and southern rural poverty. Baton Rouge, [1978]. pp. 279. *bibliog.*

WELLSTONE (PAUL DAVID) How the rural poor got power: narrative of a grass-roots organizer. Amherst, Mass., 1978. pp. 227.

RURAL-URBAN MIGRATION

— Bolivia.

PRESTON (DAVID ANTHONY) Farmers and towns: rural-urban relations in highland Bolivia. Norwich, [1978]. pp. 196. *bibliog.*

— Brazil.

MATA (MILTON DA) and others. Migrações internas no Brasil: aspectos econômicos e demograficos. Rio de Janeiro, 1973. pp. 217. *bibliog. (Brazil. Instituto de Planejamento Econômico e Social. Instituto de Pesquisas. Relatorios de Pesquisa. No. 19)*

— Cameroun.

MARGUERAT (Y.) Analyse numérique des migrations vers les villes du Cameroun. Paris, 1975. pp. 107. *(France. Office de la Recherche Scientifique et Technique Outre-Mer. Travaux et Documents. No.40)*

— Canada.

CLARK (SAMUEL DELBERT) The new urban poor. Toronto, [1978]. pp. 169.

— Mexico.

UGALDE (ANTONIO) The urbanization process of a poor Mexican neighborhood. Austin, 1974. pp. 68. *bibliog. (Texas University. Institute of Latin American Studies. Special Publications)*

— New Hebrides.

BONNEMAISON (JOEL) Système de migration et croissance urbaine à Port-Vila et Luganville, Nouvelles-Hébrides. Paris, 1977. pp. 97. *bibliog. (France. Office de la Recherche Scientifique et Technique Outre-Mer. Travaux et Documents. No. 60)*

— Nigeria.

PEACE (ADRIAN J.) Choice, class and conflict: a study of Southern Nigerian factory workers. Brighton, 1979. pp. 204. *bibliog.*

— Papua New Guinea.

CHANGE and movement: readings on internal migration in Papua New Guinea; [edited by] R.J. May. Canberra, 1977. pp. 284. *bibliog.*

— Senegal.

EXODE rural et urbanisation au Sénégal: sociologie de la migration des Serer de Niakhar vers Dakar en 1970; [by] Bernard Lacombe [and others]. Paris, 1977. pp. 207. *(France. Office de la Recherche Scientifique et Technique Outre-Mer. Travaux et Documents. No. 73)*

— Sierra Leone.

HARRELL-BOND (BARBARA E.) and others. Community leadership and the transformation of Freetown (1801- 1976). The Hague, [1978]. pp. 416. *bibliog.*

— Tahiti.

FAGES (JEAN) Punaauia-Paea: contact ville-campagne et croissance urbaine de la côte ouest de Tahiti. Paris, 1975. pp. 111. *bibliog. (France. Office de la Recherche Scientifique et Technique Outre-Mer. Travaux et Documents. No. 41)*

— United Kingdom.

U.K. Department of the Environment. 1977. The causes of rural depopulation: review of research. [London], 1977. pp. 127. *bibliog.*

— United States.

PIORE (MICHAEL J.) Birds of passage: migrant labor and industrial societies. Cambridge, 1979. pp. 229. *bibliog.*

RURAL WOMEN

— Employment — Asia.

DIXON (RUTH B.) Rural women at work: strategies for development in South Asia. Baltimore, [1978]. pp. 227. *bibliog.*

— Malawi.

MALAWI. Agro-Economic Survey. 1972. The work done by rural women in Malawi; [by] Barbara A. Clark. Zomba, 1972. fo. 13.

— United States.

JUSTER (NORTON) So sweet to labor: rural women in America, 1865-1895. New York, 1979. pp. 293. *bibliog.*

RUSSELL (BERTRAND ARTHUR WILLIAM) 3rd Earl Russell.

UCHENYE ZAPISKI KAFEDR OBSHCHESTVENNYKH NAUK VUZOV LENINGRADA. Filosofiia. vyp.17. Filosofskie i sotsiologicheskie issledovaniia. Leningrad, 1977. pp. 200.

KOLESNIKOV (ANATOLII SERGEEVICH) Svobodomyslie Bertrana Rassela [i.e. Bertrand Russell]. Moskva, 1978. pp. 133. *bibliog.*

BERTRAND Russell memorial volume; edited by George W. Roberts. London, 1979. pp. 488.

SAINSBURY (R.M.) Russell. London, 1979. pp. 348. *bibliog.*

RUSSELL (JOHN SCOTT).

EMMERSON (GEORGE S.) John Scott Russell: a great Victorian engineer and naval architect . London, [1977] . pp. 342. *bibliog.*

RUSSIA.

DVADTSATYI VEK: obshchestvenno-politicheskii i literaturnyi al'manakh; izbrannye materialy iz samizdatnogo zhurnala "xx-i vek". irreg., 1976(no. 1)- London.

AMERICAN appraisals of Soviet Russia, 1917-1977; edited, with an introduction and commentaries, by Eugene Anschel. Metuchen, N.J., 1978. pp. 386. *bibliog.*

— Armed forces.

SPIELMANN (KARL F.) Analyzing Soviet strategic arms decisions. Boulder, Colo., [1978]. pp. 184. *bibliog.*

SOVIET military power and performance; edited by John Erickson and E.J. Feuchtwanger. London, 1979. pp. 219.

— — Political activity.

GOLUB (PAVEL AKIMOVICH) Bol'sheviki i armiia v trekh revoliutsiiakh. Moskva, 1977. pp. 320.

BATALOV (ALEKSANDR NIKOLAEVICH) Bor'ba bol'shevikov za armiiu v Sibiri, 1916 - fevral' 1918. Novosibirsk, 1978. pp. 285.

COLTON (TIMOTHY J.) Commissars, commanders, and civilian authority: the structure of Soviet military politics. Cambridge, Mass., 1979. pp. 365. *(Harvard University. Russian Research Center. Studies. 79)*

— — Procurement.

INTERNATIONAL INSTITUTE FOR STRATEGIC STUDIES. Adelphi Papers. No. 147, 148. Decision-making in Soviet weapons procurement; by Arthur J. Alexander. London, 1978-79. pp. 64.

— Army — History.

GOLUB (PAVEL AKIMOVICH) Bol'sheviki i armiia v trekh revoliutsiiakh. Moskva, 1977. pp. 320.

— — — Sources.

VOENNO-revoliutsionnye komitety deistvuiushchei armii, 25 oktiabria 1917 g. - mart 1918 g. Moskva, 1977. pp. 659.

— Bibliography.

JONES (DAVID LEWIS) compiler. Books in English on the Soviet Union, 1917-73: a bibliography. New York, 1975. pp. 331.

UNIVERSITY OF ESSEX. Library. Reference Leaflets. No. 6. Guide to material on Russia and the Soviet Union. [Colchester], 1978. pp. 27.

— Boundaries — China.

ROBINSON (THOMAS W.) The Sino-Soviet border dispute: background, development and the March 1969 clashes. Santa Monica, Ca., 1970. pp. 74. *(Rand Corporation. Research Memoranda. 6171)*

ROBINSON (THOMAS W.) The border negotiations and the future of Sino-Soviet-American relations. [Santa Monica, Calif., 1971]. pp. 48. *(Rand Corporation. [Papers]. 4661)*

GINSBURGS (GEORGE) and PINKELE (CARL F.) The Sino-Soviet territorial dispute, 1949-64. New York, [1978]. pp. 145. *bibliog.*

— Civilization.

GAVIN (WILLIAM J.) and BLAKELEY (THOMAS J.) Russia and America: a philosophical comparison: development and change of outlook from the 19th to the 20th century. Dordrecht, [1976]. pp. 114. *(Freiburg (Switzerland). Universität. Ost-Europa Institut. Sovietica. vol. 38)*

— Colonies — America, North.

TIKHMENEV (PETR ALEKSANDROVICH) A history of the Russian-American Company; translated and edited by Richard A. Pierce and Alton S. Donnelly. Seattle, 1978. pp. 522.

— Commerce.

ARKHIPOV (VLADIMIR ANDREEVICH) and MOROZOV (LEONID FEDOROVICH) Bor'ba protiv kapitalisticheskikh elementov v promyshlennosti i torgovle, 20-e - nachalo 30-kh godov. Moskva, 1978. pp. 263. *bibliog.*

RUSSIA.

— **Constitution.**

FRANCE. Direction de la Documentation. La Documentation Française. Notes et Etudes Documentaires. Nos. 4,493-4, 494. La constitution de l'URSS, 7 octobre 1977: texte et commentaires; [by] Michel Lesage. Paris, 1978. pp. 142. *bibliog.*

SOVETSKOE gosudarstvo v usloviiakh razvitogo sotsialisticheskogo obshchestva. Moskva, 1978. pp. 327.

— **Constitutional history.**

RIGBY (THOMAS HENRY RICHARD) Lenin's government: Sovnarkom, 1917-1922. Cambridge, 1979. pp. 320. *bibliog.* (National Association for Soviet and East European Studies. Soviet and East European Studies)

— **Constitutional law.**

METODY i formy gosudarstvennogo upravleniia. Moskva, 1977. pp. 334.

LUK'IANOV (ANATOLII IVANOVICH) Razvitie zakonodatel'stva o sovetskikh predstavitel'nykh organakh vlasti: nekotorye voprosy istorii, teorii i praktiki. Moskva, 1978. pp. 351.

— **Defences.**

HAGEN (LAWRENCE S.) Civil defence: the case for reconsideration. Kingston, Ont., 1977. pp. 88. *bibliog.* (Kingston, Ontario. Queen's University. Center for International Relations. National Security Series. No. 7/77).

— **Description and travel.**

KIRILOV (IVAN KIRILOVICH) Tsvetushchee sostoianie Vserossiiskogo gosudarstva; [edited by] B.A. Rybakov [and others]. Moskva, 1977. pp. 443. *First published 1727. This edition in modern orthography with introduction and foreword, the former with English summary.*

VANE (FRANCES ANNE EMILY) Marchioness of Londonderry. Russian journal of Lady Londonderry, 1836-7; edited by W.A.L. Seaman and J.R. Sewell. London, [1973]. pp. 185.

DEWDNEY (JOHN CHRISTOPHER) A geography of the Soviet Union. 3rd ed. Oxford, 1979. pp. 175. *bibliog.*

— **Economic conditions.**

FINANSOVAIA GAZETA (formerly Ekonomicheskaia zhizn'); [pd.by] Ministerstvo Finansov [Russia (USSR)]. d., N 11 1918 - Je 13 1941, with gaps. Moskva.

SPARGO (JOHN) Russia as an American problem. New York, 1920. pp. 444.

NEARING (SCOTT) and HARDY (JACK) Economic organization of the Soviet Union. New York, 1927 repr. 1929. pp. 245.

NATURAL resources of the Soviet Union: their use and renewal; edited by I.P. Gerasimov [and others]; translated from the Russian by Jacek I. Romanowski; English edition edited by W. A. Douglas Jackson. San Francisco, [1971]. pp. 349. *bibliogs.*

AGENTSTVO PECHATI NOVOSTI. USSR '75: Novosti Press Agency Year Book. Moscow, 1974. pp. 288.

AGENTSTVO PECHATI NOVOSTI. USSR '76: Novosti Press Agency Year Book. Moscow, 1976. pp. 252.

DVA podrazdeleniia obshchestvennogo produkta: metodologiia deleniia; pod redaktsiei A.I. Zalkinda. Moskva, 1976. pp. 191. *bibliog.*

ADAMESKU (ALEKO ALEKSANDROVICH) and BELORUSOV (DMITRII VASIL'EVICH) Razvitie i razmeshchenie proizvoditel'nykh sil SSSR v desiatoi piatiletke. Moskva, 1977. pp. 192.

ANCHISHKIN (IVAN ALEKSANDROVICH) Ekonomicheskie usloviia rosta blagosostoianiia sovetskogo naroda. Moskva, 1977. pp. 199.

EKONOMICHESKAIA effektivnost' obshchestvennogo proizvodstva v period razvitogo sotsializma: metodologicheskie voprosy. Moskva, 1977. pp. 359. (Akademiia Nauk SSSR. Problemy Sovetskoi Ekonomiki)

KAMAEV (VLADIMIR DOROFEEVICH) Razvitoi sotsializm: tempy i kachestvo ekonomicheskogo rosta. Moskva, 1977. pp. 210.

LUKINOV (IVAN ILLARIONOVICH) Vosproizvodstvo i tseny. Moskva, 1977. pp. 431.

VOITSEKHOVSKII (VIKTOR ALEKSANDROVICH) Sistema ekonomicheskikh zakonov razvitogo sotsializma. Minsk, 1977. pp. 270.

PRAVDA: organ tsentralvnogo komiteta KPSS. a., Ja 1 1978- Moskva.

ERMOLOVICH (LIDIIA LUKINICHNA) Sovershenstvovanie ekonomicheskogo analiza effektivnosti proizvodstva. Minsk, 1978. pp. 119.

The FUTURE of the Soviet economy, 1978-1985: edited by Holland Hunter; contributors: David W. Carey [and others]. Boulder, Colo., [1978]. pp. 177. *bibliogs.*

OSNOVNYE napravleniia razvitiia ekonomiki zrelogo sotsializma. Kiev, 1978. pp. 174.

RAZVITIE sotsialisticheskogo material'nogo proizvodstva. Leningrad, 1978. pp. 148.

RAZVITOI sotsializm. Moskva, 1978. pp. 432.

The SOVIET Union and East Europe into the 1980's: multidisciplinary perspectives: [papers from a conference held at Laval University, May 1976]; edited by Simon McInnes, William McGrath and Peter J. Potichnyj. [Ontario, 1978]. pp. 340. *bibliog.*

VECHKANOV (VASILII SERGEEVICH) Mera effektivnosti sotsialisticheskogo vosproizvodstva: voprosy teorii i metodologii. Moskva, 1978. pp. 188.

DEWDNEY (JOHN CHRISTOPHER) A geography of the Soviet Union. 3rd ed. Oxford, 1979. pp. 175. *bibliog.*

KRYLOV (KONSTANTIN ARKAD'EVICH) The Soviet economy: how it really works. Lexington, [1979]. pp. 255.

McAULEY (ALASTAIR) Economic welfare in the Soviet Union: poverty, living standards, and inequality. Madison, [1979]. pp. 389. *bibliog.*

— — **Mathematical models.**

STAROVSKII (VLADIMIR NIKONOVICH) Teoriia i praktika sovetskoi gosudarstvennoi statistiki: sbornik nauchnykh trudov. Moskva, 1977. pp. 296.

OZEROV (VIKTOR KONSTANTINOVICH) Tempy i proportsii rasshirennogo sotsialisticheskogo vosproizvodstva v SSSR: analiz s ispol'zovaniem ukrupnen.ioi dinamicheskoi modeli mezhotraslevogo balansa; otvetstvennyi redaktor A.G. Aganbegian. Novosibirsk, 1978. pp. 287.

— **Economic history.**

GIMPEL'SON (EFIM GILEVICH) Velikii Oktiabr' i stanovlenie Sovetskoi sistemy upravleniia narodnym khoziaistvom, noiabr' 1917 - 1920 gg. Moskva, 1977. pp. 310.

METZER (JACOB) Some economic aspects of railroad development in Tsarist Russia. New York, 1977. pp. 138. *bibliog.*

BETTELHEIM (CHARLES) Class struggles in the USSR: second period, 1923-1930; translated by Brian Pearce. Hassocks, 1978. pp. 640. *bibliog.*

BOR'BA partii i rabochego klassa za vosstanovlenie i razvitie narodnogo khoziaistva SSSR, 1943-1950 gg. Moskva, 1978. pp. 324.

RYNDZIUNSKII (PAVEL GRIGOR'EVICH) Utverzhdenie kapitalizma v Rossii, 1850-1880 gg. Moskva, 1978. pp. 295.

NOVE (ALEXANDER) Political economy and Soviet socialism. London, 1978. pp. 249. *bibliog.*

— **Economic policy.**

AVDAKOV (IURII KONSTANTINOVICH) and BORODIN (VLADIMIR VASIL'EVICH) USSR: state industry during the transition period. Moscow, 1977. pp. 300. *Based on their "Proizvodstvennye ob"edineniia..."*

RAZVITIE ekonomiki SSSR v desiatoi piatiletke; pod redaktsiei F.I. Kotova, I.I. Prostiakova. Moskva, 1977. pp. 175.

ABALKIN (LEONID IVANOVICH) Konechnye narodnokhoziaistvennye rezul'taty: sushchnost', pokazateli, puti povysheniia. Moskva, 1978. pp. 151.

BARANOV (ALEKSANDR ALEKSEEVICH) Intensivnoe sotsialisticheskoe proizvodstvo. Moskva, 1978. pp. 349. *bibliog.*

The FUTURE of the Soviet economy, 1978-1985: edited by Holland Hunter; contributors: David W. Carey [and others]. Boulder, Colo., [1978]. pp. 177. *bibliogs.*

HAFFNER (FRIEDRICH) Systemkonträre Beziehungen in der sowjetischen Planwirtschaft: ein Beitrag zur Theorie der mixed economy. Berlin, 1978. pp. 300. *bibliog.* (Berlin. Freie Universität. Osteuropa-Institut. Wirtschaftswissenschaftliche Veröffentlichungen. Band 37)

KATSENELINBOIGEN (ARON IOSIFOVICH) Studies in Soviet economic planning. White Plains, N.Y., [1978]. pp. 228.

ELLMAN (MICHAEL JOHN) Socialist planning. Cambridge, 1979. pp. 300. *bibliog.*

KRYLOV (KONSTANTIN ARKAD'EVICH) The Soviet economy: how it really works. Lexington, [1979]. pp. 255.

NOVE (ALEXANDER) Political economy and Soviet socialism. London, 1978. pp. 249. *bibliog.*

— — **Mathematical models.**

CHERNIAVSKII (VASILII OSIPOVICH) Voprosy effektivnosti i optimal'nosti. Moskva, 1977. pp. 171. (Akademiia Nauk SSSR. Problemy Sovetskoi Ekonomiki)

DINAMICHESKAIA i veroiatnostnaia optimizatsiia ekonomiki; otvetstvennyi redaktor K.K. Val'tukh. Novosibirsk, 1978. pp. 368. (Akademiia Nauk SSSR. Sibirskoe Otdelenie. Institut Ekonomiki i Organizatsii Promyshlennogo Proizvodstva. Problemy Narodnokhoziaistvennogo Optimuma. [vyp. 5])

MODELI sotsial'no-ekonomicheskikh protsessov i sotsial'noe planirovanie. Moskva, 1979. pp. 213. *bibliog.* (Akademiia Nauk SSSR. Problemy Sovetskoi Ekonomiki)

— **Foreign economic relations.**

MAKSIMOVA (MARGARITA MATVEEVNA) SSSR i mezhdunarodnoe ekonomicheskoe sotrudnichestvo. Moskva, 1977. pp. 196.

— — **China.**

SLADKOVSKII (MIKHAIL IOSIFOVICH) Istoriia torgovo-ekonomicheskikh otnoshenii SSSR s Kitaem, 1917-1974. Moskva, 1977. pp. 368. *bibliog.*

— — **Japan.**

MATHIESON (RAYMOND SUCCESS) Japan's role in Soviet economic growth: transfer of technology since 1965. New York, 1979. pp. 277. *bibliog.*

— — **Sweden.**

EKONOMICHESKIE sviazi mezhdu Rossiei i Shvetsiei v XVII v.: dokumenty iz sovetskikh arkhivov; Ekonomiska förbindelser mellan Sverige och Ryssland under 1600-talet: dokument ur Svenska arkiv; redaktsionnaia kollegiia A. Attman [and others]. Moskva, 1978. pp. 296. *In Russian or Swedish.*

— **Foreign opinion, American.**

AMERICAN appraisals of Soviet Russia, 1917-1977; edited, with an introduction and commentaries, by Eugene Anschel. Metuchen, N.J., 1978. pp. 386. *bibliog.*

RUSSIA.(Cont.)

— Foreign relations.

SPARGO (JOHN) Russia as an American problem. New York, 1920. pp. 444.

ZILLIACUS (KONNI) the Younger. A new birth of freedom?: world communism after Stalin. London, 1957. pp. 286.

ROBINSON (THOMAS W.) The border negotiations and the future of Sino-Soviet-American relations. [Santa Monica, Calif., 1971]. pp. 48. *(Rand Corporation. [Papers]. 4661)*

HALPERIN (MORTON H.) Contemporary military strategy. new ed. London, 1972. pp. 149. *bibliog.*

ULAM (ADAM BRUNO) Expansion and coexistence: Soviet foreign policy, 1917-73. 2nd ed. New York, 1974. pp. 797.

LEBEDEV (NIKOLAI IVANOVICH) A new stage in international relations...; translated by D. Ya Skvirsky and V.M. Schneierson. Oxford, [1976]. pp. 253. *bibliog.*

LENINSKIE traditsii vneshnei politiki Sovetskogo Soiuza; pod redaktsiei A.L. Narochnitskogo. Moskva, 1977. pp. 264.

SIMES (DIMITRI K.) Detente and conflict: Soviet foreign policy, 1972-1977. Beverly Hills, [1977]. pp. 64. *bibliog. (Georgetown University. Center for Strategic and International Studies. Washington Papers. vol. 5/44)*

VO imia mira: mezhdunarodno-pravovye problemy evropeiskoi bezopasnosti. Moskva, 1977. pp. 191.

YANOV (ALEXANDER) Détente after Brezhnev: the domestic roots of Soviet foreign policy; translation by Robert Kessler. Berkeley, [1977]. pp. 87. *(California University. Institute of International Studies. Policy Papers in International Affairs. No. 2)*

PRAVDA: organ centralvnogo komiteta KPSS. a., Ja 1 1978- Moskva.

BREZHNEV (LEONID IL'ICH) Mir sotsializma - torzhestvo velikikh idei: (rechi, stat'i i vystupleniia za period 1964-1978 gg.). Moskva, 1978. pp. 656.

CLEMENS (WALTER CARL) The U.S.S.R. and global interdependence: alternative futures. Washington, D.C., [1978]. pp. 113. *(American Enterprise Institute for Public Policy Research. AEI Studies. 190)*

LABOUR PARTY. Cold peace: Soviet power and Western security. [London], 1978. pp. 54.

SOVIET foreign policy: its social and economic conditions; edited by Egbert Jahn. London, 1978. pp. 159. *Translated from the German.*

The SOVIET threat: myths and realities; edited by Grayson Kirk and Nils Wessell. New York, 1978. pp. 182.

VNESHNEPOLITICHESKAIA programma XXV s"ezda KPSS v deistvii. Kiev, 1978. pp. 307.

BREZHNEV (LEONID IL'ICH) Peace, détente, and

— — Africa, Subsaharan.

WALKER (Sir WALTER) The bear at the back door: the Soviet threat to the West's lifeline in Africa. Richmond, Surrey, 1978. pp. 246.

— — America, Latin.

BARTLEY (RUSSELL H.) Imperial Russia and the struggle for Latin American independence, 1808-1828. Austin, [1978]. pp. 236. *bibliog. (Texas University. Institute of Latin American Studies. Latin American Monographs. No. 43)*

— — China.

MIDDLETON (DREW) The duel of the giants: China and Russia in Asia. New York, 1978. pp. 241.

RUEBENSAAL (JACK DWIGHT) The impact of the Sino-Soviet dispute on the Afro-Asian People's Solidarity Organization. 1978. fo.237. *bibliog. Typescript. M.Phil. (London)thesis: unpublished. This thesis is the property of London University and may not be removed from the Library.*

— — Cuba.

LEVESQUE (JACQUES) The USSR and the Cuban revolution: Soviet ideological and strategical perspectives 1959-77; translated from the French by Deanna Drendel Leboeuf. New York, [1978]. pp. 215. *bibliog.*

— — Czechoslovakia.

KAPLAN (KAREL) Dans les archives du comité central: trente ans de secrets du bloc soviétique. [Paris, 1978]. pp. 365.

VALENTA (JIRI) Soviet intervention in Czechoslovakia, 1968: anatomy of a decision. Baltimore, [1979]. pp. 208. *bibliog.*

— — East (Near East).

FREEDMAN (ROBERT OWEN) Soviet policy toward the Middle East since 1970. rev. ed. New York, 1978. pp. 373. *bibliog.*

HEIKAL (MOHAMED) Sphinx and commissar: the rise and fall of Soviet influence in the Arab world. London, 1978. pp. 303.

KASS (ILANA) Soviet involvement in the Middle East: policy formulation, 1966-1973. Boulder, 1978. pp. 273.

The LIMITS to power: Soviet policy in the Middle East; edited by Yaacov Ro'i. London, [1979]. pp. 376. *bibliogs.*

— — Egypt.

HEIKAL (MOHAMED) Sphinx and commissar: the rise and fall of Soviet influence in the Arab world. London, 1978. pp. 303.

DAWISHA (KAREN) Soviet foreign policy towards Egypt. London, 1979. pp. 271.

— — Europe.

— — Iran.

MOSS (ROBERT) The campaign to destabilise Iran. London, 1978. pp. 18. *(Institute for the Study of Conflict. Conflict Studies. No.101)*

— — Japan.

SSSR - Iaponiia: k 50-letiiu ustanovleniia sovetsko-iaponskikh diplomaticheskikh otnoshenii, 1925-1975. Moskva, 1978. pp. 300.

— — Mediterranean.

SAUL (NORMAN E.) Russia and the Mediterranean, 1797-1807. Chicago, 1970. pp. 268. *bibliog.*

— — Romania.

SHEVIAKOV (ALEKSEI ALEKSEEVICH) Sovetsko-rumynskie otnosheniia i problema evropeiskoi bezopasnosti, 1932-1939. Moskva, 1977. pp. 382.

— — Sweden.

ROGINSKII (VADIM VADIMOVICH) Shvetsiia i Rossiia: soiuz 1812 goda. Moskva, 1978. pp. 175. *bibliog.*

— — United States.

CHILDS (JOHN LAWRENCE) and COUNTS (GEORGE SYLVESTER) America, Russia and the Communist Party in the postwar world. New York, [1943]. pp. 92.

McNEILL (WILLIAM HARDY) America, Britain and Russia: their co-operation and conflict, 1941-1946. New York, [1976]. pp. 819. *Reprint of work originally published as one volume of the Survey of International Affairs, London, 1953.*

HALLE (LOUIS JOSEPH) The cold war as history. New York, [1967]. pp. 434. *bibliog.*

UNITED STATES. United States Information Service. 1973. "To build peace": a summary of agreements and statements during the visit to the United States of General Secretary Leonid Brezhnev of the Soviet Union, June 18-25, 1973. [Washington, 1973?]. pp. 36.

COX (ARTHUR MACY) The dynamics of détente: how to end the arms race. New York, [1976]. pp. 256. *bibliog.*

BACKER (JOHN H.) The decision to divide Germany: American foreign policy in transition. Durham, N.C., 1978. pp. 212. *bibliog.*

COLLINS (JOHN M.) Imbalance of power: an analysis of shifting U.S.-Soviet military strengths. San Rafael, Calif., [1978]. pp. 316. *Includes: Net assessment appraisal, by Anthony H. Cordesman.*

CONTAINMENT: documents on American policy and strategy, 1945- 1950; [edited by] Thomas H. Etzold and John Lewis Gaddis. New York, 1978. pp. 449.

DIMENSIONS of detente; edited by Della W. Sheldon. New York, 1978. pp. 221.

INTERNATIONAL perceptions

RUSSIA.(Cont.)

— **Historiography.**

MARUSHKIN (BORIS IL'ICH) and others. Tri revoliutsii v Rossii i burzhuaznaia istoriografiia. Moskva, 1977. pp. 279. *bibliog.*

TSAMUTALI (ALEKSEI NIKOLAEVICH) Bor'ba techenii v russkoi istoriografii vo vtoroi polovine XIX veka. Leningrad, 1977. pp. 256.

AKTUAL'NYE problemy sovetskoi istoriografii pervoi russkoi revoliutsii: sbornik statei. Moskva, 1978. pp. 317.

ENTEEN (GEORGE M.) The Soviet scholar-bureaucrat: M.N. Pokrovskii and the Society of Marxist Historians. University Park, Penn., 1978. pp. 236. *bibliog.*

ZOLOTAREV (VLADIMIR ANTONOVICH) Russko-turetskaia voina, 1877-1878 gg.: v otechestvennoi istoriografii kontsa XIX - nachala XX v. Moskva, 1978. pp. 144. *bibliog.*

— **History.**

VERNADSKII (GEORGII VLADIMIROVICH) A history of Russia. New Haven, 1943 in progress. *bibliog.* Vols. 1-4 by G.V. Vernadskii and M. Karpovich.

— — **1689-1800.**

KAPLAN (HERBERT HAROLD) Russia and the outbreak of the Seven Years' War. Berkeley, 1968. pp. 165. *bibliog.*

— — **1773-1775, Rebellion of Pugachev.**

ALEXANDER (JOHN T.) Emperor of the Cossacks: Pugachev and the frontier Jacquerie of 1773-1775. Lawrence, Kan., 1973. pp. 245.

— — **1800-1899.**

CRANKSHAW (EDWARD) The shadow of the Winter Palace: the drift to revolution, 1825- 1917. Harmondsworth, 1976. pp. 509. *bibliog.*

— — **1894-1917.**

CRANKSHAW (EDWARD) The shadow of the Winter Palace: the drift to revolution, 1825- 1917. Harmondsworth, 1976. pp. 509. *bibliog.*

— — **1900- .**

SALISBURY (HARRISON EVANS) Russia in revolution, 1900-1930. London, 1978. pp. 287.

BREZHNEV (LEONID IL'ICH) How it was: the war and post-war reconstruction in the Soviet Union. Oxford, 1979. pp. 115. *Translation of his "Malaia zemlia" and "Vozrozhdenie".*

— — **1905, Revolution of.**

GOLUB (PAVEL AKIMOVICH) Bol'sheviki i armiia v trekh revoliutsiiakh. Moskva, 1977. pp. 320.

KLIUEVA (ANNA DANILOVNA) Partiia bol'shevikov i pervoi russkoi revoliutsii 1905-1907 gg. Moskva, 1977. pp. 255.

MARUSHKIN (BORIS IL'ICH) and others. Tri revoliutsii v Rossii i burzhuaznaia istoriografii. Moskva, 1977. pp. 279. *bibliog.*

PETROV (ALEKSANDR PETROVICH) Kritika fal'sifikatsii agrarno-krest'ianskogo voprosa v trekh russkikh revoliutsiiakh. Moskva, 1977. pp. 399. *bibliog.*

AKTUAL'NYE problemy sovetskoi istoriografii pervoi russkoi revoliutsii: sbornik statei. Moskva, 1978. pp. 317.

— — **1917, February Revolution.**

IASKOVETS (GENNADII ALEKSEEVICH) Pravda i lozh' o rabochem klasse: kritika sovremennoi burzhuaznoi istoriografii Anglii i SShA o roli proletariata v Fevral'skoi i Velikoi Oktiabr'skoi sotsialisticheskoi revoliutsiiakh. Moskva, 1978. pp. 200.

— — **1917- .**

BETTELHEIM (CHARLES) Class struggles in the USSR: second period, 1923-1930; translated by Brian Pearce. Hassocks, 1978. pp. 640. *bibliog.*

GILBERT (MARTIN) Soviet history atlas. London, 1979. pp. 83. *bibliog. Originally published as part of Russian history atlas by same author, 1972 - this edition enlarged and up-dated.*

— — **1917-1921, Revolution.**

PRICE (MORGAN PHILIPS) War and revolution in Asiatic Russia. London, 1918. pp. 296.

ARSHINOV (PETR ANDREEVICH) History of the Makhnovist movement (1918-1921)...; translated by Lorraine and Fredy Perlman. Detroit, 1974. pp. 284.

GOLUB (PAVEL AKIMOVICH) Bol'sheviki i armiia v trekh revoliutsiiakh. Moskva, 1977. pp. 320.

IVANOV (NIKOLAI IAKOVLEVICH) Kontrrevoliutsiia v Rossii v 1917 godu i ee razgrom. Moskva, 1977. pp. 272.

KENEZ (PETER) Civil war in South Russia, 1919-1920: the defeat of the Whites. Berkeley, [1977]. pp. 378. *bibliog.*

PETROV (ALEKSANDR PETROVICH) Kritika fal'sifikatsii agrarno-krest'ianskogo voprosa v trekh russkikh revoliutsiiakh. Moskva, 1977. pp. 399. *bibliog.*

ARTEM'EV (SERGEI ARTEM'EVICH) Partiia bol'shevikov i Sovety rabochikh i soldatskikh deputatov v 1917 g., iiul'-oktiabr'. Moskva, 1978. pp. 214.

KONEV (ALEKSANDR MIKHAILOVICH) Krasnaia gvardiia na zashchite Oktiabria. Moskva, 1978. pp. 223.

MAWDSLEY (EVAN) The Russian Revolution and the Baltic fleet: war and politics, February 1917-April 1918. London, 1978. pp. 213. *bibliog.*

MEDVEDEV (ROI ALEKSANDROVICH) La révolution d'Octobre: faits et réflexions. Paris, 1978. pp. 240.

NOSACH (VIKTOR IVANOVICH) Profsoiuzy Sovetskoi Rossii v gody grazhdanskoi voiny, 1918-1920. Moskva, 1978. pp. 215.

SALISBURY (HARRISON EVANS) Russia in revolution, 1900-1930. London, 1978. pp. 287.

DUKES (PAUL) Ph.D. October and the world: perspectives on the Russian revolution. London, 1979. pp. 224.

GILL (GRAEME JOSEPH) Peasants and government in the Russian revolution. London, 1979. pp. 233. *bibliog.*

— — — **Foreign participation.**

KOPYLOV (VLADIMIR ROMANOVICH) Zarubezhnye internatsionalisty v Oktiabr'skoi revoliutsii, 1917- 1918. Moskva, 1977. pp. 213.

— — — **Foreign public opinion.**

VELIKII Oktiabr' i revoliutsii 40-kh godov v stranakh Tsentral'noi i Iugo-Vostochnoi Evropy: opyt sravnitel'nogo izucheniia sotsial'no-ekonomicheskikh preobrazovanii v revoliutsionnom protsesse. Moskva, 1977. pp. 541.

IZ istorii Velikogo Oktiabria i posleduiushchikh sotsialisticheskikh revoliutsii: sbornik statei. Moskva, 1978. pp. 542.

VELIKAIA Oktiabr'skaia sotsialisticheskaia revoliutsiia i strany Zapadnoi Evropy. Moskva, 1978. pp. 219.

— — — **Historiography.**

ISTORICHESKII opyt Velikogo Oktiabria i kritika burzhuaznoi is- toriografii. Moskva, 1977. pp. 375.

MARUSHKIN (BORIS IL'ICH) and others. Tri revoliutsii v Rossii i burzhuaznaia istoriografiia. Moskva, 1977. pp. 279. *bibliog.*

IASKOVETS (GENNADII ALEKSEEVICH) Pravda i lozh' o rabochem klasse: kritika sovremennoi burzhuaznoi istoriografii Anglii i SShA o roli proletariata v Fevral'skoi i Velikoi Oktiabr'skoi sotsialisticheskoi revoliutsiiakh. Moskva, 1978. pp. 200.

— — — **Personal narratives.**

USPENSKII (PETR DEMIANOVICH) Letters from Russia, 1919. London, 1978. pp. 59.

— — — **Sources.**

VOENNO-revoliutsionnye komitety deistvuiushchei armii, 25 oktiabria 1917 g. - mart 1918 g. Moskva, 1977. pp. 659.

— — **1918-1920, Allied intervention.**

MARGVELASHVILI (VLADIMIR I.) Iz istorii angliiskoi okkupatsii Adzharii, 1918-1920 gg. Batumi, 1973. pp. 52.

GOLDHURST (RICHARD) The midnight war: the American intervention in Russia, 1918- 1920. New York, 1978. pp. 288. *bibliog.*

— — **1925-1953.**

COATES (KEN) The case of Nikolai Bukharin. Nottingham, 1978. pp. 104. *bibliogs.*

— — **1941-1945, German occupation.**

SYDNOR (CHARLES W.) Soldiers of destruction: the SS Death's Head Division, 1933-1945. Princeton, N.J., [1977]. pp. 371. *bibliog.*

— — **1953-1964.**

MEISSNER (BORIS) Russland unter Chruschtschow. München, 1960. pp. 699. *(Deutsche Gesellschaft für Auswärtige Politik. Forschungsinstitut. Dokumente und Berichte. Band 15)*

— **History, Naval.**

MAWDSLEY (EVAN) The Russian Revolution and the Baltic fleet: war and politics, February 1917-April 1918. London, 1978. pp. 213. *bibliog.*

GORSHKOV (S.G.) The sea power of the state. Oxford, 1979. pp. 290.

— **Industries.**

KISLIAKOV (BORIS IOSIFOVICH) Legkaia promyshlennost' v deviatoi piatiletke. Moskva, 1976. pp. 143.

AVDAKOV (IURII KONSTANTINOVICH) and BORODIN (VLADIMIR VASIL'EVICH) USSR: state industry during the transition period. Moscow, 1977. pp. 300. *Based on their "Proizvodstvennye ob"edineniia..."*

DOLOTOV (KONSTANTIN ANDREEVICH) and KHARABIBEROV (VIKTOR STEPANOVICH) Mestnaia promyshlennost' i perspektivy ee razvitiia. Moskva, 1977. pp. 192.

EKONOMIKA legkoi promyshlennosti; pod obshchei redaktsiei V.V. Osmolovskogo i V.G. Khriapchenkova. Minsk, 1977. pp. 279.

ARKHIPOV (VLADIMIR ANDREEVICH) and MOROZOV (LEONID FEDOROVICH) Bor'ba protiv kapitalisticheskikh elementov v promyshlennosti i torgovle, 20-e - nachalo 30-kh godov. Moskva, 1978. pp. 263. *bibliog.*

OB"EDINENIIA v promyshlennosti; pod redaktsiei Iu.M. Kozlova. Moskva, 1978. pp. 254.

— — **Mathematical models.**

PLANIROVANIE razvitiia i razmeshcheniia promyshlennogo proizvodstva: modeli i sistemy. Kiev, 1977. pp. 287. *bibliog.*

— **Intellectual life.**

LUKIN (IURII ANDREEVICH) Mnogogrannaia sotsialisticheskaia kul'tura: XXV s"ezd KPSS o glavnykh napravleniiakh kul'turnoi politiki partii. Moskva, 1977. pp. 155.

RUSSIA.(Cont.)

— Maps.

BREU (JOSEF) ed. Atlas der Donauländer; Atlas of the Danubian countries. Wien, 1970 in progress.

GILBERT (MARTIN) Soviet history atlas. London, 1979. pp. 83. *bibliog. Originally published as part of Russian history atlas by same author, 1972 - this edition enlarged and up-dated.*

— Military policy.

RUSSIA (USSR). Ministerstvo Oborony. 1977. Voina i armiia: filosofsko-sotsiologicheskii ocherk; pod redaktsiei D.A. Volkogonova [and others]. Moskva, 1977. pp. 415. *bibliog.*

BRAUN (AUREL) Romanian foreign policy since 1965: the political and military limits of autonomy. New York, [1978]. pp. 217. *bibliog.*

COLLINS (JOHN M.) Imbalance of power: an analysis of shifting U.S.-Soviet military strengths. San Rafael, Calif., [1978]. pp. 316. *Includes: Net assessment appraisal, by Anthony H. Cordesman.*

LABOUR PARTY. Cold peace: Soviet power and Western security. [London], 1978. pp. 54.

SPIELMANN (KARL F.) Analyzing Soviet strategic arms decisions. Boulder, Colo., [1978]. pp. 184. *bibliog.*

— Militia.

KONEV (ALEKSANDR MIKHAILOVICH) Krasnaia gvardiia na zashchite Oktiabria. Moskva, 1978. pp. 223.

— Nationalism.

AZRAEL (JEREMY RICHARD) Emergent nationality problems in the USSR. Santa Monica, 1977. pp. 33. *(Rand Corporation. [Rand Reports]. 2172)*

DASHDAMIROV (AFRAND FIRUDINOV) Sovetskii narod: nekotorye filosofsko-sotsiologicheskie problemy edinstva novoi istoricheskoi obshchnosti. Baku, 1977. pp. 156.

NATIONALITIES and nationalism in the USSR: a Soviet dilemma; a joint symposium sponsored by the Center for Strategic and International Studies, Georgetown University, and the Institute for Sino-Soviet Studies, the George Washington University...1976; edited by Carl A. Linden and Dimitri K. Simes. Washington, D.C., 1977. pp. 61.

CARRÈRE D'ENCAUSSE (HÉLÈNE) L'empire éclaté: la révolte des nations en U.R.S.S. [Paris, 1978]. pp. 314. *bibliog.*

SOVIET nationality policies and practices; edited by Jeremy R. Azrael. New York, [1978]. pp. 393. *bibliogs.*

NATSIONAL'NYE otnosheniia v SSSR na sovremennom etape: na materialakh respublik Srednei Azii i Kazakhstana. Moskva, 1979. pp. 312.

— Navy.

FRANCE. Direction de la Documentation. La Documentation Française. Notes et Etudes Documentaires. No. 4479-4480. La marine soviétique; [by] Claude Huan [and] Jürgen Rohwer. [Paris], 1978. pp. 157.

— Occupations.

ZANIATOST' v nebol'shikh gorodakh: ekonomiko-demograficheskii aspekt; pod redaktsiei A.E. Kotliara. Moskva, 1978. pp. 207.

— Politics and government.

AGENTSTVO PECHATI NOVOSTI. USSR '75: Novosti Press Agency Year Book. Moscow, 1974. pp. 288.

AGENTSTVO PECHATI NOVOSTI. USSR '76: Novosti Press Agency Year Book. Moscow, 1976. pp. 252.

KOSITSYN (ALEKSANDR PAVLOVICH) Sotsializm i gosudarstvo. Moskva, 1976. pp. 144.

PRAVOVOE regulirovanie obshchestvennykh otnoshenii. Moskva, 1976. pp. 120.

YANOV (ALEXANDER) Détente after Brezhnev: the domestic roots of Soviet foreign policy; translation by Robert Kessler. Berkeley, [1977]. pp. 87. *(California University. Institute of International Studies. Policy Papers in International Affairs. No. 2)*

RAZVITOI sotsializm. Moskva, 1978. pp. 432.

RUKOVODIASHCHAIA i organizuiushchaia rol' KPSS v period razvitogo sotsializma. Leningrad, 1978. pp. 304.

SOVETSKOE gosudarstvo v usloviiakh razvitogo sotsialisticheskogo obshchestva. Moskva, 1978. pp. 327.

SOVIET nationality policies and practices; edited by Jeremy R. Azrael. New York, [1978]. pp. 393. *bibliogs.*

The SOVIET Union and East Europe into the 1980's: multidisciplinary perspectives: [papers from a conference held at Laval University, May 1976]; edited by Simon McInnes, William McGrath and Peter J. Potichnyj. [Ontario, 1978]. pp. 340. *bibliog.*

HOUGH (JERRY F.) and FAINSOD (MERLE) How the Soviet Union is governed. Cambridge, Mass., 1979. pp. 679. *An extensively revised and enlarged ed. by J.F. Hough of M. Fainsod's How Russia is ruled.*

MASNATA (ALBERT) Le monde marxiste soviétique par lui-même: connaître et juger. Lausanne, 1979. pp. 90. *(Lausanne. Université. Centre de Recherches Européennes. Publications. 4. L'Europe et les Pays Tiers)*

NOVE (ALEXANDER) Political economy and Soviet socialism. London, 1978. pp. 249. *bibliog.*

— — Bibliography.

GRIN (TSILIA IOSIFOVNA) compiler. K. Marks, F. Engel's i revoliutsionnaia Rossiia: k 160- letiiu so dnia rozhdeniia K. Marksa: rekomendatel'nyi ukazatel' literatury; nauchnyi redaktor S.S. Volk. Moskva, 1978. pp. 95.

— — 1800-1899.

ESSAYS on Russian liberalism; edited, with an introduction by Charles E. Timberlake. Columbia, 1972. pp. 192. *bibliog. Papers presented to the Bi-State (Kansas-Missouri) Slavic Conference in Columbia, Missouri, in November, 1969.*

CHERNUKHA (VALENTINA GRIGOR'EVNA) Vnutrenniaia politika tsarizma s serediny 50-kh do nachala 80-kh gg. XIX v.; pod redaktsiei R.Sh. Gnelina. Leningrad, 1978. pp. 248.

— — 1894-1917.

ANWEILER (OSKAR) The soviets: the Russian workers, peasants and soldiers councils, 1905-1921; translated by Ruth Hein. New York, 1974. pp. 337. *bibliog.*

The POLITICS of rural Russia, 1905-1914; edited by Leopold H. Haimson. Bloomington, [1979]. pp. 309. *(Columbia University. Russian Institute. Studies)*

— — 1917- .

HAMMER (DARRELL P.) USSR: the politics of oligarchy. New York, [1974]. pp. 452. *bibliog.*

ADAMS (JAN S.) Citizen inspectors in the Soviet Union: the People's Control Committee. New York, 1977. pp. 232. *bibliog.*

RESHETAR (JOHN STEPHEN) The Soviet polity: government and politics in the U.S.S.R. 2nd ed. New York, [1978]. pp. 413. *bibliog.*

SOVIET society and the Communist Party; edited by Karl W. Ryavec; contributors, Karl W. Ryavec [and others]. Amherst, Mass., 1978. pp. 220.

BELLIS (PAUL) Marxism and the U.S.S.R.: the theory of proletarian dictatorship and the Marxist analysis of Soviet society. London, 1979. pp. 267. *bibliog.*

WHITE (STEPHEN) Lecturer in politics. Political culture and Soviet politics. London, 1979. pp. 234. *bibliog.*

— — 1917-1936.

MAKSIMOV (GRIGORII PETROVICH) The guillotine at work, vol.1: the Leninist counter-revolution. Sanday, 1979. pp. 337. *First published Chicago, 1940.*

SERGE (VICTOR) pseud. [i.e. Viktor L'vovich KIBAL'CHICH]. Mémoires d'un révolutionnaire, 1901-1941. Paris, [1978]. pp. 444. *bibliog. Text, first published 1951, revised and corrected by author.*

ANWEILER (OSKAR) The soviets: the Russian workers, peasants and soldiers councils, 1905-1921; translated by Ruth Hein. New York, 1974. pp. 337. *bibliog.*

MAWDSLEY (EVAN) The Russian Revolution and the Baltic fleet: war and politics, February 1917-April 1918. London, 1978. pp. 213. *bibliog.*

The DEBATE on Soviet power: minutes of the All-Russian Central Executive Committee of Soviets: second convocation, October 1917-January 1918; translated and edited by John L.H. Keep. Oxford, 1979. pp. 465. *bibliog.*

DUKES (PAUL) Ph.D. October and the world: perspectives on the Russian revolution. London, 1979. pp. 224.

GILL (GRAEME JOSEPH) Peasants and government in the Russian revolution. London, 1979. pp. 233. *bibliog.*

RIGBY (THOMAS HENRY RICHARD) Lenin's government: Sovnarkom, 1917-1922. Cambridge, 1979. pp. 320. *bibliog. (National Association for Soviet and East European Studies. Soviet and East European Studies)*

— — 1936- .

PEL'SHE (ARVID IANOVICH) Izbrannye rechi i stat'i, [1940-77]. Moskva, 1978. pp. 671.

— — 1953- .

ZILLIACUS (KONNI) the Younger. A new birth of freedom?: world communism after Stalin. London, 1957. pp. 286.

TARSCHYS (DANIEL) The Soviet political agenda: problems and priorities, 1950-1970. London, 1979. pp. 217. *bibliog.*

— — 1964- .

BREZHNEV (LEONID IL'ICH) Ob aktual'nykh problemakh partiinogo stroitel'stva: (rechi, stat'i i vystupleniia s 1964 po oktiabr' 1976 g.). 2nd ed. Moskva, 1976. pp. 775.

FRANCE. Direction de la Documentation. La Documentation Française. Notes et Etudes Documentaires. Nos. 4467-4468. L'URSS et l'Europe de l'Est en 1977; [by Thomas Schreiber and others]. [Paris], 1978 in progress. *bibliog.*

KUNAEV (DINMUKHAMED AKHMEDOVICH) Izbrannye rechi i stat'i, [1965-78]. Moskva, 1978. pp. 511.

— Population.

PANKRAT'EVA (NINA VIKTOROVNA) Naselenie i sotsialisticheskoe vosproizvodstvo; pod redaktsiei A. Ia. Boiarskogo. Moskva, 1977. pp. 223.

VOSPROIZVODSTVO naseleniia sotsialisticheskikh stran: na primere Sovetskogo Soiuza i Pol'shi; pod redaktsiei D.I. Valenteia i M. Liatukha. Moskva, 1977. pp. 360.

— — Mathematical models.

STAROVSKII (VLADIMIR NIKONOVICH) Teoriia i praktika sovetskoi gosudarstvennoi statistiki: sbornik nauchnykh trudov. Moskva, 1977. pp. 296.

BASALAEVA (NATAL'IA ALEKSEEVNA) Modelirovanie demograficheskikh protsessov i trudovykh resursov. Moskva, 1978. pp. 88. *(Akademiia Nauk SSSR. Problemy Sovetskoi Ekonomiki)*

— Relations (general) with Bulgaria.

ULUNIAN (AKOP ARUTIUNOVICH) Aprel'skoe vosstanie 1876 goda v Bolgarii i Rossiia: ocherki. Moskva, 1978. pp. 214. *bibliog. With English table of contents.*

— Relations (general) with Finland.

KORONEN (MATVEI MATVEEVICH) V.I. Lenin i Finliandiia. Leningrad, 1977. pp. 311. *bibliog.*

BARTEN'EV (T.) and KOMISSAROV (IU.) SSSR - Finliandiia: orientiry sotrudnichestva. Moskva, 1978. pp. 118.

— Relations (general) with Latin America.

SOVIET historians on Latin America: recent scholarly contributions; edited and translated by Russell H. Bartley. Madison, 1978. pp. 345. *bibliog.* (*Conference on Latin American History. Publications. No.5*)

— Relations (general) with other countries.

ROSENKO (IVAN ARKHIPOVICH) Internatsional'nye sviazi rabochikh Leningrada, 1921-1937 gg. Leningrad, 1977. pp. 140.

— Relations (general) with Poland.

TSYBENKO (ELENA ZAKHAROVNA) Iz istorii pol'sko-russkikh literaturnykh sviazei XIX-XX vv. Moskva, 1978. pp. 280.

— Relations (general) with Slovakia.

CHURKINA (ISKRA VASIL'EVNA) Slovenskoe natsional'no-osvoboditel'noe dvizhenie v XIX v. i Rossiia. Moskva, 1978. pp. 392.

— Relations (general) with the Balkan States.

BALKANSKIE strany v novoe i noveishee vremia: sbornik statei. Kishinev, 1977. pp. 178.

— Relations (general) with the United States.

LARSON (THOMAS B.) Soviet-American rivalry. New York, [1978]. pp. 308. *bibliog.*

— Religion.

RELIGION and modernization in the Soviet Union; edited by Dennis J. Dunn. Boulder, Colo., 1977. pp. 412.

KOBETSKII (VLADIMIR DMITRIEVICH) Sotsiologicheskoe izuchenie religioznosti i ateizma. Leningrad, 1978. pp. 118. *bibliog.*

— Rural conditions.

COX (TERENCE M.) Rural sociology in the Soviet Union: its history and basic concepts. London, [1979]. pp. 106. *bibliog.*

The POLITICS of rural Russia, 1905-1914; edited by Leopold H. Haimson. Bloomington, [1979]. pp. 309. (*Columbia University. Russian Institute. Studies*)

— Social conditions.

AGENTSTVO PECHATI NOVOSTI. USSR '75: Novosti Press Agency Year Book. Moscow, 1974. pp. 288.

AGENTSTVO PECHATI NOVOSTI. USSR '76: Novosti Press Agency Year Book. Moscow, 1976. pp. 252.

IZUTKIN (ANATOLII MAKSIMOVICH) and TSAREGORODTSEV (GENNADII IVANOVICH) Sotsialisticheskii obraz zhizni i zdorov'e naseleniia v svete reshenii XXV s"ezda KPSS. Moskva, 1977. pp. 232. *bibliog.*

SEMENOV (VADIM SERGEEVICH) Dialektika razvitiia sotsial'noi struktury sovetskogo obshchestva. Moskva, 1977. pp. 215.

SOTSIALISTICHESKII obraz zhizni i voprosy ideologicheskoi raboty: po materialam Vsesoiuznoi nauchno-prakticheskoi konferentsii v Kieve, 18-20 maia 1977 g. Moskva, 1977. pp. 383.

PRAVDA: organ tsentral'nogo komiteta KPSS. a., Ja 1 1978- Moskva.

BAILES (KENDALL E.) Technology and society under Lenin and Stalin: origins of the Soviet technical intelligentsia, 1917-1941. Princeton, 1978. pp. 469. *bibliog.* (*Columbia University. Russian Institute. Studies*)

KEHAYAN (NINA) and KEHAYAN (JEAN) Rue du Prolétaire rouge: deux communistes français en URSS. Paris, 1978. pp. 223.

RAZVITOI sotsializm. Moskva, 1978. pp. 432.

— Statistical services.

STAROVSKII (VLADIMIR NIKONOVICH) Teoriia i praktika sovetskoi gosudarstvennoi statistiki: sbornik nauchnykh trudov. Moskva, 1977. pp. 296.

RUSSIAN-AMERICAN COMPANY.

TIKHMENEV (PETR ALEKSANDROVICH) A history of the Russian-American Company; translated and edited by Richard A. Pierce and Alton S. Donnelly. Seattle, 1978. pp. 522.

RUSSIAN GERMAN AMERICANS.

KOCH (FRED C.) The Volga Germans in Russia and the Americas, from 1763 to the present. University Park, Pa., 1977. pp. 365. *bibliog.*

RUSSIAN GERMANS IN AMERICA.

KOCH (FRED C.) The Volga Germans in Russia and the Americas, from 1763 to the present. University Park, Pa., 1977. pp. 365. *bibliog.*

RUSSIAN LITERATURE.

DVADTSATYI VEK: obshchestvenno-politicheskii i literaturnyi al'manakh; izbrannye materialy iz samizdatnogo zhurnala "xx-i vek". irreg., 1976(no. 1)- London.

— Congresses.

S"EZD PISATELEI RSFSR, 4-yi, 1975. Chetvertyi s"ezd pisatelei RSFSR, 15-18 dekabria 1975 g.: stenograficheskii otchet. Moskva, 1977. pp. 384.

— History and criticism.

LITERATURNO-kriticheskie raboty dekabristov. Moskva, 1978. pp. 381.

TSYBENKO (ELENA ZAKHAROVNA) Iz istorii pol'sko-russkikh literaturnykh sviazei XIX-XX vv. Moskva, 1978. pp. 280.

RUSSIAN PERIODICALS.

ULUNIAN (AKOP ARUTIUNOVICH) Aprel'skoe vosstanie 1876 goda v Bolgarii i Rossiia: ocherki. Moskva, 1978. pp. 214. *bibliog. With English table of contents.*

— Bibliography.

RUSSIA (USSR). Vsesoiuznaia Knizhnaia Palata. 1977. Letopis' periodicheskikh i prodolzhaiushchikhsia izdanii, 1971- 1975. ch.1. Zhurnaly. Moskva, 1977. pp. 152.

— Indexes.

MASANOV (IURII IVANOVICH) and others, compilers. Ukazateli soderzhaniia russkikh zhurnalov i prodolzhaiushchikhsia izdanii 1755-1970 gg.; with a new introduction and additional items published from 1971 through to 1979 by P.H. Clendenning, etc. Newtonville, Mass., 1979. pp. 439. *Xerographic reprint of 1st ed., Moscow, 1975, with additional new title page.*

RUSSIANS IN CHINA.

SEMENOV (GEORGII GAVRILOVICH) Tri goda v Pekine: zapiski voennogo sovetnika. Moskva, 1978. pp. 296.

RUSSIANS IN POLAND.

IWANIEC (EUGENIUSZ) Z dziejów staroobrzędowców na ziemiach polskich XVII-XX w. Warszawa, 1977. pp. 295. *bibliog.* (*Białystok. Białostockie Towarzystwo Naukowe. Prace. Nr.23*) *With Russian and English summaries.*

RUSSIANS IN THE BURYAT REPUBLIC.

BOLONEV (FIRS FEDOSOVICH) Narodnyi kalendar' semeiskikh Zabaikal'ia, vtoraia polovina XIX - nachalo XX v.; otvetstvennyi redaktor E.A. Ashchepkov. Novosibirsk, 1978. pp. 159.

RUSSO-GERMAN TREATY, 1939.

UEBERSCHAER (GERD R.) Hitler und Finnland, 1939-1941: die deutsch-finnischen Beziehungen während des Hitler-Stalin-Paktes. Wiesbaden, 1978. pp. 376. *bibliog.*

RUSSO-JAPANESE WAR, 1904-1905.

ISTORIIA russko-iaponskoi voiny, 1904-1905 gg.; pod redaktsiei I. I.Rostunova. Moskva, 1977. pp. 383. *bibliog.*

RUSSO-TURKISH WAR, 1877-1878.

K stoletiiu russko-turetskoi voiny 1877-1878 godov; pod redaktsiei V. Maamiagi. Tallin, 1977. pp. 120.

RUSSKO-turetskaia voina 1877-1878. Moskva, 1977. pp. 263.

ZOLOTAREV (VLADIMIR ANTONOVICH) Russko-turetskaia voina, 1877-1878 gg.: v otechestvennoi istoriografii kontsa XIX - nachala XX v. Moskva, 1978. pp. 144. *bibliog.*

RUTLAND

— Economic conditions.

LEICESTERSHIRE. County Planning Officer. Structure plan for Rutland: report of survey. Leicester, 1977. pp. 144.

LEICESTERSHIRE. County Planning Officer. Structure plan for Rutland: written statement. Leicester, 1977. pp. 64.

— Economic policy.

LEICESTERSHIRE. County Planning Officer. Structure plan for Rutland: written statement. Leicester, 1977. pp. 64.

— Social conditions.

LEICESTERSHIRE. County Planning Officer. Structure plan for Rutland: report of survey. Leicester, 1977. pp. 144.

LEICESTERSHIRE. County Planning Officer. Structure plan for Rutland: written statement. Leicester, 1977. pp. 64.

— Social policy.

LEICESTERSHIRE. County Planning Officer. Structure plan for Rutland: written statement. Leicester, 1977. pp. 64.

RYKOV (ALEKSEI IVANOVICH).

VAGANOV (FEDOR MIKHAILOVICH) Pravyi uklon v VKP(b) i ego razgrom, 1928-1930 gg. 2nd ed. Moskva, 1977. pp. 328.

SAAR TERRITORY

— Foreign relations — France.

SAARGEBIET. Treaties. 1953. Die neuen Staatsverträge zwischen Frankreich und dem Saarland: Text der am 20. Mai 1953 in Paris unterzeichneten Verträge mit Anlagen und Zusatzprotokollen in den beiden amtlichen Sprachen. Saarbrücken, [1953?]. pp. 215. *In German and French.*

SABAH

— Foreign relations — United Kingdom.

TARLING (NICHOLAS) Sulu and Sabah: a study of British policy towards the Philippines and North Borneo from the late eighteenth century. Kuala Lumpur, 1978. pp. 385. *bibliog.*

SABAH(Cont.)

— Politics and government.

ROSS-LARSON (BRUCE) The politics of federalism: Syed Kechik in East Malaysia. Singapore, 1976. pp. 240.

SABOTAGE

— Bibliography.

SHEA (MARNIE) compiler. Sabotage and pilferage: a selected bibliography. [Toronto], Ontario Ministry of Labour Research Library, 1975. fo. 5. *Photocopy.*

SACRAMENTO-SAN JOAQUIN DELTA.

JACKSON (W. TURRENTINE) and PATERSON (ALAN M.) The Sacramento-San Joaquin Delta: the evolution and implementation of water policy: an historical perspective. Davis, Calif., 1977. pp. 192. *(California University. Water Resources Center. Contributions. No. 163)*

SAHARA

— Economic conditions.

FRANCE. Organisation Commune des Régions Sahariennes. 1962. O.C.R.S. Paris, 1962. 1 vol. (various pagings).

SAIGON

— Social conditions.

THOMAS (LIZ) Dust of life: children of the Saigon streets. London, 1978. pp. 199.

ST. ANDREWS UNIVERSITY.

CAMERON (JOHN) Lord Cameron. The fabric of a university. Edinburgh, 1961. pp. 32. *(St. Andrews University. Dow Lectures. 1960)*

ST. BARTHOLOMEW'S DAY, MASSACRE OF, 1572.

SUTHERLAND (NICOLA MARY) The massacre of St. Bartholomew and the European conflict, 1559-1572. London, 1973. pp. 373. *bibliog.*

ST. HELENS

— Economic history.

FORMAN (CHARLES) Author of Industrial town. Industrial town: self portrait of St. Helens in the 1920s. London, 1978. pp. 272.

— Industries.

FORMAN (CHARLES) Author of Industrial town. Industrial town: self portrait of St. Helens in the 1920s. London, 1978. pp. 272.

ST. JOHN'S

— Politics and government.

NEWFOUNDLAND. Royal Commission on the City of St. John's Act. 1969-70. Interim (and final) report and recommendations; [Edmund J. Phelan, chairman]. [St. John's], 1969-70. 2 vols.

SAINTSIMONIANISM.

VOILQUIN (SUZANNE) Souvenirs d'une fille du peuple; ou, La Saint-simonienne en Égypte. Paris, 1978. pp. 406.

SALES.

SMITH (THOMAS BROUN) Property problems in sale. Calcutta, 1978. pp. 232. *(Calcutta. University. Tagore Law Lectures. 1977)*

SALES TAX

— Switzerland — Bern (Canton).

BERN (CANTON). Amt für Statistik. 1978. Eidg. Abstimmung vom 12. Juni 1977 im Kanton Bern: Umsatzsteuer, direkte Bundessteuer, etc. Bern, 1978. pp. 72. *(Beiträge zur Statistik des Kantons Bern. Politische Statistik. Reihe F. Heft 4) In French and German.*

SALFORD

— City planning.

MANCHESTER AND SALFORD INNER CITY PARTNERSHIP COMMITTEE. New life for the inner cities: the inner area programme 1979/80. [Manchester], 1979. 1 vol. (various pagings).

— Social conditions.

MANCHESTER AND SALFORD INNER CITY PARTNERSHIP RESEARCH GROUP. Manchester and Salford inner area study. [Manchester, Department of the Environment North West Regional Office, 1978]. pp. 60.

— Social policy.

MANCHESTER AND SALFORD INNER CITY PARTNERSHIP COMMITTEE. New life for the inner cities: the inner area programme 1979/80. [Manchester], 1979. 1 vol. (various pagings).

SALISBURY, RHODESIA

— Politics and government.

RHODESIA. Ministry of Local Government and Housing. 1970. Government proposals for a Greater Salisbury unitary authority. [Salisbury, 1970]. pp. 14.

SALT INDUSTRY AND TRADE

— Bangladesh.

BANGLADESH. Small Industries Corporation. 1966. Survey of salt manufacturing units in East Pakistan. [Dacca, 1966]. pp. 34.

— India.

AGGARWAL (SHUGAN CHAND) The salt industry in India. 3rd rev. ed. Delhi, Controller of Publications, 1976. pp. 913.

SALTWATER ENCROACHMENT

— United States.

JACKSON (W. TURRENTINE) and PATERSON (ALAN M.) The Sacramento-San Joaquin Delta: the evolution and implementation of water policy: an historical perspective. Davis, Calif., 1977. pp. 192. *(California University. Water Resources Center. Contributions. No. 163)*

SALVADOR

— Economic conditions.

INSTITUTO SALVADOREÑO DE FOMENTO INDUSTRIAL. Profile of El Salvador. [San Salvador, 1968]. pp. 31.

— Economic policy.

SALVADOR. Ministerio de Planificacion y Coordinacion del Desarrollo Economico y Social. 1978. Plan nacional: bienestar para todos, 1978-1982. [San Salvador], 1978. pp. 229. *3 folded tables at end.*

— Politics and government.

MOLINA (ARTURO ARMANDO) Ideario politico democratico del señor Presidente de la Republica. San Salvador, [1974]. pp. 90.

LATIN AMERICA BUREAU. Violence and fraud in El Salvador: a report on current political events in El Salvador. London, 1977. pp. 44.

— Social policy.

SALVADOR. Ministerio de Planificacion y Coordinacion del Desarrollo Economico y Social. 1978. Plan nacional: bienestar para todos, 1978-1982. [San Salvador], 1978. pp. 229. *3 folded tables at end.*

SALVATION ARMY.

COUTTS (FREDERICK) Bread for my neighbour: an appreciation of the social influence of William Booth. London, 1978. pp. 192. *bibliog.*

SALVEMINI (GAETANO).

BUETLER (HUGO) Gaetano Salvemini und die italienische Politik vor dem Ersten Weltkrieg. Tübingen, 1978. pp. 498. *bibliog. (Deutsches Historisches Institut in Rom. Bibliothek. Band 50)*

SALZBURG

— Emigration and immigration.

FLOREY (GERHARD) Geschichte der Salzburger Protestanten und ihrer Emigration, 1731/32. Wien, [1977]. pp. 276. *bibliog.*

SAMANWAY VIDAPITH.

BATTERSBY (OLWEN) Samanway Vidapith: the Marr-Munning ashram. London, [1974?]. pp. 14. *(Marr-Munning Trust. Edwina Mountbatten Papers. No. 4)*

SAMARITANS.

SAMARITANS. Answers to suicide presented by the Samaritans to Chad Varah on the occasion of the twenty-fifth anniversary of their founding. London, 1978. pp. 277.

SAMPLING (STATISTICS).

LEWIS (THEODORE GYLE) Distribution sampling for computer simulation. Lexington, Mass., [1975]. pp. 150. *bibliog.*

CONTRIBUTIONS to survey sampling and applied statistics: papers in honor of H.O. Hartley; edited by H.A. David. New York, 1978. pp. 318. *bibliog.*

JESSEN (RAYMOND J.) Statistical survey techniques. New York, [1978]. pp. 520. *bibliogs.*

— Tables.

HALD (ANDERS H.) and MØLLER (UFFE) Statistical tables for sampling inspection by attributes. Copenhagen, 1977. pp. 65.

SAMUELSON (PAUL ANTHONY).

WONG (STANLEY) The foundations of Paul Samuelson's revealed preference theory: a study by the method of rational reconstruction. London, 1978. pp. 148. *bibliog.*

SAN ANDRÉS

— Social life and customs.

WARREN (KAY B.) The symbolism of subordination: Indian identity in a Guatemalan town. Austin, [1978]. pp. 209. *bibliog.*

SAN BERNARDINO, CALIFORNIA

— Description.

ORD (EDWARD OTHO CRESAP) The city of the angels and the city of the saints; or, A trip to Los Angeles and San Bernardino in 1856;...edited by Neal Harlow. San Marino, 1978. pp. 56. *bibliog.*

SAN FELIPE DEL PROGRESO, MEXICO

— Social conditions.

MARGOLIES (BARBARA LUISE) Princes of the earth: subcultural diversity in a Mexican municipality. Washington, [1975]. pp. 179. *bibliog. (American Anthropological Association. Special Publications. [New Series]. No. 2)*

— Social history.

MARGOLIES (BARBARA LUISE) Princes of the earth: subcultural diversity in a Mexican municipality. Washington, [1975]. pp. 179. *bibliog. (American Anthropological Association. Special Publications. [New Series]. No. 2)*

SAN FRANCISCO

— Foreign population.

GUMINA (DEANNA PAOLI) The Italians of San Francisco, 1850-1930; Gli italiani di San Francisco, 1850-1930. New York, 1978 repr. 1979. pp. 230. *bibliog. Parallel English and Italian texts.*

SAN LUIS POTOSI

— Rural conditions.

BAZANT (JAN) Cino haciendas mexicanas: tres siglos de vida rural en San Luis Potosi, 1600-1910. Mexico, 1975. pp. 226. *(Mexico City. Colegio de Mexico. Centro de Estudios Historicos. Nueva Serie. 20)*

SANCHEZ (FEDERICO) pseud.

See SEMPRUN (JORGE).

SANT'AGATA DEI GOTI

— Social conditions.

OTTAVIANI (OBERDAN) Sant'Agata dei Goti: l'informazione mancata; la comunicazione nella società agricola del Mezzogiorno: ricerca in un comune campione. Urbino, [1977]. pp. 319. *bibliog.*

SANTALS.

ARCHER (WILLIAM GEORGE) The hill of flutes: life, love and poetry in tribal India: a portrait of the Santals. London, 1974. pp. 375. *bibliog.*

SANTANDER (SPAIN)

— Rural conditions.

FREEMAN (SUSAN TAX) The Pasiegos: Spaniards in no man's land. Chicago, [1979]. pp. 291. *bibliog.*

SÃO PAULO (CITY)

— Growth.

SÃO Paulo: growth and poverty; a report from the São Paulo Justice and Peace Commission. London, 1978. pp. 128.

WIRTH (JOHN D.) and JONES (ROBERT L.) Writer on international studies, eds. Manchester and São Paulo: problems of rapid urban growth. Stanford, 1978. pp. 234. *Edited version of papers given at a conference sponsored by the Center for Latin American Studies of Stanford University in April 1977.*

— Poor.

SÃO Paulo: growth and poverty; a report from the São Paulo Justice and Peace Commission. London, 1978. pp. 128.

— Population.

ARAUJO (ALOISIO BARBOSA DE) Aspectos fiscais das areas metropolitanas. Rio de Janeiro, 1974. pp. 125. *(Brazil. Instituto de Planejamento Econômico e Social. Instituto de Pesquisas. Monografias. No. 15)*

SÃO TOME E PRINCIPE

— Maps.

RODRIGUES (FRANCISCO MANUEL DE CARVALHO) S. Tome e Principe sob o ponto de vista agrícola. Lisboa, 1974. pp. 180; 25 plates. *bibliog. (Portugal. Junta de Investigações Científicas do Ultramar. Estudos, Ensaios e Documentos. 130) 3 maps in end pocket.*

SAPIR-WHORF HYPOTHESIS.

UNIVERSALISM versus relativism in language and thought...;[edited by] Rik Pinxten. The Hague, [1976]. pp. 310. *bibliogs. Proceedings of a colloquium on the Sapir-Whorf hypotheses.*

SARAIVA (JOSE ANTÔNIO).

SARAIVA (JOSE ANTÔNIO) Discursos parlamentares; seleção e introdução, Alvaro Valle. Brasilia, 1978. pp. 661. *(Brazil. Congresso. Câmara dos Deputados. Perfis Parlamentares. 4)*

SARAWAK

— Kings and rulers.

CRISSWELL (COLIN N.) Rajah Charles Brooke, monarch of all he surveyed. Kuala Lumpur, 1978. pp. 253. *bibliog.*

— Politics and government.

ROSS-LARSON (BRUCE) The politics of federalism: Syed Kechik in East Malaysia. Singapore, 1976. pp. 240.

SARDINIA

— Rural conditions.

ANGIONI (GIULIO) Sa laurera: il lavoro contadino in Sardegna. Cagliari, [1976]. pp. 294.

SARGAN (J.D.).

ENDERWICK (PETER) An examination of the Sargan method of wage leadership identification. Bradford, [1978?]. fo. 26. *bibliog. (University of Bradford. Management Centre. Occasional Papers. No. 7702)*

SARKAR (PRABHAT RANJAN).

BATRA (RAVEENDRA NATH) The downfall of capitalism and communism: a new study of history. London, 1978. pp. 283.

SARTRE (JEAN PAUL).

STACK (GEORGE J.) Sartre's philosophy of social existence. St. Louis, [1977]. pp. 149.

SASKATCHEWAN

— Department of Municipal Affairs.

SASKATCHEWAN. Department of Municipal Affairs. Annual report. a., 1977/78- Regina.

— Executive departments.

SASKATCHEWAN. Department of Municipal Affairs. Annual report. a., 1977/78- Regina.

— Government publications — Bibliography.

CHECKLIST OF SASKATCHEWAN GOVERNMENT PUBLICATIONS; [pd. by] Legislative Library. a., 1977- Regina.

SATIRE, RUSSIAN.

ZINOV'EV (ALEKSANDR ALEKSANDROVICH) Svetloe budushchee. [Lausanne, 1978]. pp. 231.

SATISFACTION.

POMMER (E.J.) and PRAAG (C.S. VAN) Satisfactie en leefsituatie. Rijswijk, 1978. 1 vol. (various pagings). *bibliog. (Netherlands. Sociaal en Cultureel Planbureau. SCP-Cahiers. No. 13) With English summary.*

SAUDI ARABIA

— Biography.

WHO's who in Saudi Arabia, 1978-79; (edited by M. Samir Sarhan). Jeddah, [1978]. pp. 309.

— Economic conditions.

AL-FARSY (FOUAD) Saudi Arabia: a case study in development. London, 1978. pp. 220. *bibliog.*

CLERON (JEAN PAUL) Saudi Arabia 2000: a strategy for growth. London, 1978. pp. 168. *bibliog.*

— Economic policy.

CLERON (JEAN PAUL) Saudi Arabia 2000: a strategy for growth. London, 1978. pp. 168. *bibliog.*

CRANE (ROBERT DICKSON) Planning the future of Saudi Arabia: a model for achieving national priorities. New York, [1978]. pp. 241.

— Politics and government.

AL-FARSY (FOUAD) Saudi Arabia: a case study in development. London, 1978. pp. 220. *bibliog.*

— Statistics.

SAUDI ARABIA. Central Department of Statistics. The statistical indicator. a., 1976(1st issue)- Riyadh. *[in Arabic and English].*

SAVING AND INVESTMENT.

VICKERS (DOUGLAS WILLIAM) Financial markets in the capitalist process. Philadelphia, 1978. pp. 180.

— Mathematical models.

FOLDES (LUCIEN P.) Optimal saving and risk in continuous time with constant returns. [new ed.] London, 1978. pp. 60. *bibliog. (Papers on Capital and Risk. No. 1)*

— European Economic Community countries.

MORGAN (EDWARD VICTOR) and HARRINGTON (RICHARD) Capital markets in the EEC: the sources and uses of medium- and long-term finance. Farnborough, 1977. pp. 495. *bibliog. Published for the Economists Advisory Group.*

— Germany.

SAMUELS (J.M.) and McMAHON (P.C.) Savings and investment in the United Kingdom and West Germany. Farnborough, Hants., [1978]. pp. 135.

— Mexico.

CAMBRIDGE. University. Centre of Latin American Studies. Working Papers. No. 30. Patterns of saving and investment in Mexico, 1939-76; by E.V.K. Fitzgerald. Cambridge, 1977. pp. 58. *bibliog.*

— United Kingdom.

SAMUELS (J.M.) and McMAHON (P.C.) Savings and investment in the United Kingdom and West Germany. Farnborough, Hants., [1978]. pp. 135.

THREADGOLD (A. R.) Personal saving: the impact of life assurance and pension funds. London, 1978. pp. 41. *bibliog. (Bank of England. Discussion Papers. No. 1)*

— United States.

HENDERSHOTT (PATRIC H.) and others. Understanding capital markets. Lexington, Mass., [1977]. 2 vols. *bibliogs.*

SAMETZ (ARNOLD WILLIAM) Prospects for capital formation and capital markets: financial requirements over the next decade. Lexington, Mass., [1978]. pp. 145. *bibliog.*

SAVINGS BANKS

— United Kingdom.

TAYLOR (EDWARD) of Rochdale. Savings banks: ought Government to make good past losses in savings banks?; the opinion of eminent writers and authorities on the security of savings banks and the claim of the depositors stated. London, Longman, 1853. pp. 15. *The head-title reads The Rochdale savings bank depositors' case, and an argument for their claim on Government.*

SCANDINAVIA

— Antiquities.

SHETELIG (HAAKON) and FALK (HJALMAR) Scandinavian archaeology. New York, 1978. pp. 458.

— Defences.

BERGQUIST (MATS) Trends and changes in Nordic security: a Swedish view. n.p. [1978]. fo. 20. *Photocopy of typescript.*

SCANDINAVIA (Cont.)

— Economic conditions.

SVERIGES INDUSTRIFÖRBUND. Economic Affairs Directorate. The Nordic economic outlook: a survey prepared [by Eva Christina Horwitz]...; [with] special studies [by various authors]. [Stockholm], 1975. pp. 86.

— Foreign economic relations — Canada.

TELLIER (LUC-NORMAND) Etude des possibilités de rapprochement économique entre le Québec, le Canada et les pays scandinaves; préparé pour le compte du Ministère des Affaires Intergouvernementales du Québec. [Québec, 1979]. pp. 139. *bibliog.*

— — — Quebec.

TELLIER (LUC-NORMAND) Etude des possibilités de rapprochement économique entre le Québec, le Canada et les pays scandinaves; préparé pour le compte du Ministère des Affaires Intergouvernementales du Québec. [Québec, 1979]. pp. 139. *bibliog.*

— — European Economic Community countries.

ØRVIK (NILS) and BJØL (ERLING) The Scandinavian allies and the European Community. Kingston, Ont., 1978. pp. 98. *(Kingston, Ontario. Queen's University. Centre for International Relations. European Studies Series. No. 1/78)*

— Foreign relations — South Africa.

WINQUIST (ALAN H.) Scandinavians and South Africa: their impact on the cultural, social and economic development of pre-1902 South Africa. Cape Town, 1978. pp. 268. *bibliog.*

— History.

TURVILLE-PETRE (G.) The heroic age of Scandinavia. Westport, Conn., 1976. pp. 196. *bibliog. Reprint of work first published in London in 1951.*

FOL (JEAN JACQUES) Les pays nordiques aux XIXe et XXe siècles. Paris, [1977]. pp. 327. *bibliog.*

— Rural conditions.

ØSTERUD (ØYVIND) Agrarian structure and peasant politics in Scandinavia: a comparative study of rural response to economic change. Oslo, [1978]. pp. 278. *bibliog.*

SCANDINAVIANS IN SOUTH AFRICA.

WINQUIST (ALAN H.) Scandinavians and South Africa: their impact on the cultural, social and economic development of pre-1902 South Africa. Cape Town, 1978. pp. 268. *bibliog.*

SCHIEDAM

— Hospitals.

POLL (CH. A.) and others. Het verhaal van een vijftigjarige: bijdragen tot de geschiedenis van de gezondheidszorg in Schiedam. Schiedam, 1978. pp. 118.

SCHISM, THE GREAT WESTERN, 1378-1417.

CROWDER (C.M.D.) compiler. Unity, heresy and reform, 1378-1460: the conciliar response to the Great Schism. London, 1977. pp. 212. *bibliog.*

SCHIZOPHRENIA.

CHAPMAN (LOREN J.) and CHAPMAN (JEAN P.) Disordered thought in schizophrenia. Englewood Cliffs, [1973]. pp. 359. *bibliogs.*

SCHIZOPHRENIA: towards a new synthesis; edited by J.K. Wing. London, 1978. pp. 291. *bibliog.*

SCHLESWIG-HOLSTEIN

— Economic conditions.

SCHLESWIG-HOLSTEIN. Statistisches Landesamt. 1977. Lange Reihen zur Bevölkerungs- und Wirtschaftsentwicklung Schleswig-Holsteins, 1950-1975. Kiel, 1977. pp. 99.

— Population.

SCHLESWIG-HOLSTEIN. Statistisches Landesamt. 1977. Lange Reihen zur Bevölkerungs- und Wirtschaftsentwicklung Schleswig-Holsteins, 1950-1975. Kiel, 1977. pp. 99.

— Statistics.

SCHLESWIG-HOLSTEIN. Statistisches Landesamt. 1967. Beiträge zur historischen Statistik Schleswig-Holsteins. Kiel, 1967. pp. 202.

SCHOLARLY PUBLISHING

— United Kingdom.

MANN (PETER HENRY) Author-publisher relationships in scholarly publishing. London, 1978. pp. 79. *bibliog. (British Library. Research and Development Department. Reports. 5416)*

SCHOLARSHIPS

— Directories.

The GRANTS register, 1979-1981; editor Roland Turner. London, [1978]. pp. 798.

SCHOOL, CHOICE OF.

COONS (JOHN E.) and SUGARMAN (STEPHEN D.) Education by choice: the case for family control. Berkeley, Calif., [1978]. pp. 249. *bibliog.*

SCHOOL ATTENDANCE

— Australia.

ROSIER (MALCOLM J.) Early school leavers in Australia: family, school and personal determinants of the decision of 16-year-old Australians to remain at school or to leave. Stockholm, [1978]. pp. 198. *bibliog. (International Association for the Evaluation of Educational Achievement. IEA Monograph Studies. No. 7)*

— Canada — Ontario.

ONTARIO. Commission on Declining School Enrolments in Ontario. 1978. Implications of declining enrolment for the schools of Ontario: a statement of effects and solutions: final report; [R.W.B. Jackson, commissioner]. Toronto, 1978. pp. 331.

SCHOOL BOARDS

— United Kingdom — Ireland, Northern.

IRELAND, NORTHERN. Department of Education. Education and library boards, grant aided schools, institutions of further education and libraries. a., current issue only. Belfast.

SCHOOL CHILDREN

— Food.

DAVIES (BLEDDYN PRYCE) and REDDIN (MIKE) Universality, selectivity, and effectiveness in social policy. London, 1978. pp. 264. *bibliog.*

— Australia.

ROSIER (MALCOLM J.) Early school leavers in Australia: family, school and personal determinants of the decision of 16-year-old Australians to remain at school or to leave. Stockholm, [1978]. pp. 198. *bibliog. (International Association for the Evaluation of Educational Achievement. IEA Monograph Studies. No. 7)*

— France.

FRANCE. Institut National d'Etudes Démographiques. 1978. Enquête nationale sur le niveau intellectuel des enfants d'âge scolaire. [Paris], 1978. pp. 291. *bibliog. (Travaux et Documents. Cahiers. No. 83)*

SCHOOL DISCIPLINE.

FRANCIS (PAUL) Beyond control?: a study of discipline in the comprehensive school. London, 1975. pp. 184.

METZ (MARY HAYWOOD) Classrooms and corridors: the crisis of authority in desegregated secondary schools. Berkeley, Calif., [1978]. pp. 275. *bibliog.*

SCHOOL DISTRICTS

— United States.

PUBLIC participation in local school districts: the dissatisfaction theory of democracy; edited by Frank W. Lutz [and] Laurence Iannaccone. Lexington, Mass., [1978]. pp. 135. *bibliogs.*

SCHOOL INTEGRATION

— United Kingdom.

JEFFCOATE (ROBERT) Positive image: towards a multiracial curriculum. London, 1979. pp. 124. *bibliogs.*

— United States.

METZ (MARY HAYWOOD) Classrooms and corridors: the crisis of authority in desegregated secondary schools. Berkeley, Calif., [1978]. pp. 275. *bibliog.*

WILLIE (CHARLES VERT) The sociology of urban education: desegregation and integration. Lexington, Mass., [1978]. pp. 184. *bibliogs.*

SCHOOL MANAGEMENT AND ORGANIZATION

YATES (ALFRED) The organization of schooling: a study of educational grouping practices. London, 1971. pp. 104. *bibliog.*

— New Zealand.

EDUCATIONAL DEVELOPMENT CONFERENCE, NEW ZEALAND, 1974. Working Party on Organisation and Administration. Organisation and administration of education. Wellington, [Government Printer], 1974. pp. 175.

SCHOOL SOCIAL WORK

— United Kingdom.

ROBINSON (MARGARET) Schools and social work. London, 1978. pp. 268.

— — Scotland.

PAISLEY COMMUNITY DEVELOPMENT PROJECT. Social work in the primary school; (by Rosemary Watson). [Paisley, 1978]. pp. 161.

SCHOOLS

— Bangladesh.

BANGLADESH. Planning Commission. Manpower Section. 1974. An educational geography of Bangladesh: locational availability against ideal requirement. [Dacca], 1974. pp. 142.

— Canada — Newfoundland and Labrador.

NEWFOUNDLAND. Task Force on Education. 1978. Perspectives on declining enrolments in the schools of Newfoundland and Labrador: interim report. St. John's, 1978. pp. (173).

— Germany.

GERMANY (BUNDESREPUBLIK). Statistisches Bundesamt. Allgemeines Schulwesen. a., 1976- Wiesbaden. *(Bildung und Kultur. Reihe 1.)*

— United Kingdom.

U.K. Central Office of Information. Reference Division. Reference Pamphlets. 156. Schools in Britain. London, 1978. pp. 56. *bibliog.*

— — Ireland, Northern.

IRELAND, NORTHERN. Department of Education. Education and library boards, grant aided schools, institutions of further education and libraries. a., current issue only. Belfast.

— **United States.**

NASAW (DAVID) Schooled to order: a social history of public schooling in the United States. New York, 1979. pp. 303. *bibliog.*

SCHUTZ (ALFRED).

SCHUTZ (ALFRED) and PARSONS (TALCOTT) The theory of social action: the correspondence of Alfred Schutz and Talcott Parsons; edited by Richard Grathoff. Bloomington, [1978]. pp. 145. *bibliog.*

SCHWERIN VON KROSIGK (LUTZ) Graf.

SCHWERIN VON KROSIGK (LUTZ) Graf. Memoiren. Stuttgart, [1977]. pp. 340.

SCIENCE.

SCIENCE, technology, and economic development: a historical and comparative study; edited by William Beranek, Jr. [and] Gustav Ranis. New York, [1978]. pp. 347. *bibliogs.*

SOCIOLOGICAL REVIEW, THE; [published by] University of Keele. Monographs. [No.] 27. On the margins of science: the social construction of rejected knowledge; edited by Roy Wallis. Keele, 1979. pp. 337.

— **History.**

KUHN (THOMAS SAMUEL) The essential tension: selected studies in scientific tradition and change. Chicago, [1977]. pp. 366.

DEBUS (ALLEN G.) Man and nature in the Renaissance. Cambridge, 1978. pp. 159.

— — **Europe.**

BRONOWSKI (JACOB) Magic, science and civilization. New York, 1978. pp. 88. *(Columbia University. Bampton Lectures in America. No. No. 20)*

— — **United States.**

KOHLSTEDT (SALLY GREGORY) The formation of the American scientific community: the American Association for the Advancement of Science, 1848-60. Urbana, Ill., [1976]. pp. 330. *bibliog.*

— **Mathematical models.**

BENDER (CARL M.) and ORSZAG (STEVEN A.) Advanced mathematical methods for scientists and engineers. New York, [1978]. pp. 593. *bibliog.*

— **Methodology.**

DUBIN (ROBERT) Theory building. rev. ed. New York, [1978]. pp. 304. *bibliog.*

MITROFF (IAN I.) and KILMANN (RALPH H.) Methodological approaches to social science. San Francisco, 1978. pp. 150. *bibliog.*

— **Philosophy.**

HESSE (MARY B.) The structure of scientific inference. London, 1974. pp. 309.

BRONOWSKI (JACOB) A sense of the future: essays in natural philosophy; selected and edited by Piero E. Ariotti. Cambridge, Mass., 1977. pp. 286. *bibliog.*

KUHN (THOMAS SAMUEL) The essential tension: selected studies in scientific tradition and change. Chicago, [1977]. pp. 366.

DUBIN (ROBERT) Theory building. rev. ed. New York, [1978]. pp. 304. *bibliog.*

FEYERABEND (PAUL K.) Science in a free society. London, 1978. pp. 221.

STENT (GUNTHER SIEGMUND) Paradoxes of progress. San Francisco, [1978]. pp. 231. *bibliogs.*

ZIMAN (JOHN MICHAEL) Reliable knowledge: an exploration of the grounds for belief in science. Cambridge, 1978. pp. 197.

— **Social aspects.**

GOWING (MARGARET MARY) Science and politics. London, [1977]. pp. 16. *(London. University. Birkbeck College. Bernal Lectures. 1977)*

HAAS (ERNST BERNARD) and others. Scientists and world order: the uses of technical knowledge in international organizations. Berkeley, Calif., [1977]. pp. 368.

BODINGTON (STEPHEN) Science and social action. London, [1978]. pp. 192.

SOCIOLOGY of science; [edited by] Jerry Gaston. San Francisco, 1978. pp. 226. *bibliogs.*

STENT (GUNTHER SIEGMUND) Paradoxes of progress. San Francisco, [1978]. pp. 231. *bibliogs.*

MULKAY (MICHAEL J.) Science and the sociology of knowledge. London, 1979. pp. 132. *bibliog.*

— — **Russia.**

LUBRANO (LINDA L.) Soviet sociology of science. Columbus, 1976. pp. 102. *bibliog.*

— **Study and teaching.**

WARING (MARY) Social pressures and curriculum innovation: a study of the Nuffield Foundation Science Teaching Project. London, 1979. pp. 263. *bibliog.*

— — **United Kingdom.**

JENKINS (E.W.) From Armstrong to Nuffield: studies in twentieth-century science education in England and Wales. London, [1979]. pp. 318. *bibliogs.*

NORRIS (GRAEME) Justifying research and teaching objectives in universities. Farnborough, [1979]. pp. 219. *bibliogs.*

— **Canada.**

CANADA. Statistics Canada. Service bulletin: Science statistics. irreg., current issues only Ottawa. *[in English and French]*

— **China.**

SCIENCE and technology in the People's Republic of China. Paris, Organisation for Economic Co-operation and Development, 1977. pp. 216.

— **Russia.**

LUBRANO (LINDA L.) Soviet sociology of science. Columbus, 1976. pp. 102. *bibliog.*

PROBLEMY ekonomiki nauki. Erevan, 1977. pp. 267.

— — **Kirghizia.**

KARAKEEV (KURMAN-GALI KARAKEEVICH) Velikii Oktiabr' i nauka Kirgizstana. Frunze, 1977. pp. 229.

— **Underdeveloped areas.**

See UNDERDEVELOPED AREAS— Science.

— **United Kingdom — Political aspects.**

GOWING (MARGARET MARY) Science and politics. London, 1977. pp. 16. *(London. University. Birkbeck College. Bernal Lectures. 1977)*

— **United States.**

The STATE of science and research: some new indicators; [edited by] Nestor E. Terleckyj. Boulder, [1977]. pp. 201. *bibliogs.*

SCIENCE, MEDIEVAL.

WHITE (LYNN T.) Medieval religion and technology: collected essays. Berkeley, Calif., [1978]. pp. 360. *(California University. Center for Medieval and Renaissance Studies. Publications. 13)*

SCIENCE AND CIVILIZATION.

BRONOWSKI (JACOB) Magic, science and civilization. New York, 1978. pp. 88. *(Columbia University. Bampton Lectures in America. No. No. 20)*

BRONOWSKI (JACOB) The visionary eye: essays in the arts, literature, and science;.. .selected and edited by Piero E. Ariotti in collaboration with Rita Bronowski. Cambridge, Mass., [1978]. pp. 185.

HOLZNER (BURKART) and MARX (JOHN H.) Knowledge application: the knowledge system in society. Boston, Mass., [1979]. pp. 388. *bibliog.*

SCIENCE AND STATE.

GOWING (MARGARET MARY) Science and politics. London, [1977]. pp. 16. *(London. University. Birkbeck College. Bernal Lectures. 1977)*

BATTY (MICHAEL) Paradoxes of science in public policy: the baffling case of land use models. Reading, 1978. pp. 34. *bibliog. (Reading. University. Department of Geography. Reading Geographical Papers. No. 69)*

— **America, Latin.**

SABATO (JORGE A.) ed. El pensamiento latinoamericano en la problematica ciencia-tecnologia-desarrollo-dependencia. Buenos Aires, [1975]. pp. 349.

— **Nigeria.**

NIGERIAN COUNCIL FOR SCIENCE AND TECHNOLOGY. The Nigerian Council for Science and Technology: inaugural brochure. Lagos, 1970. pp. 22.

SCIENTIFIC APPARATUS AND INSTRUMENTS.

OAKEY (RAYMOND PETER) The British scientific and industrial instruments industry: a study in industrial geography. 1978. fo. 378. *bibliog.* Typescript. Ph.D. (London) thesis: unpublished. Computer program in end pocket. This thesis is the property of London University and may not be removed from the Library.

SCIENTISTS

— **Russia.**

The SCIENTIFIC intelligentsia in the USSR: structure and dynamics of personnel; edited by D.M. Gvishiani, S.R. Mikulinsky, S.A. Kugel. Moscow, 1976. pp. 247.

— **United Kingdom.**

WERSKEY (GARY) The visible college. London, 1978. pp. 376.

— **United States.**

ZUCKERMAN (HARRIET) Scientific elite: Nobel laureates in the United States. New York, [1977]. pp. 335. *bibliog.*

SCIENTOLOGY.

MALKO (GEORGE) Scientology: the now religion. New York, 1970. pp. 205.

SCOTLAND

— **Church history.**

DRUMMOND (ANDREW L.) and BULLOCH (JAMES) Ph.D., D.D. The church in late Victorian Scotland, 1874-1900. Edinburgh, 1978. pp. 342. *bibliog.*

MAKEY (WALTER H.) The church of the Covenant, 1637-1651: revolution and social change in Scotland. Edinburgh, [1979]. pp. 216. *bibliog.*

— **Economic conditions.**

ABERDEEN. University. Department of Political Economy. The economic impact of North Sea oil on Scotland; final report to the Scottish Economic Planning Department on a study conducted within the Department of Political Economy, the University of Aberdeen, 1973-77. Edinburgh, H.M.S.O., 1978. pp. 101.

SCOTLAND (Cont.)

GLASGOW. University of Strathclyde. Fraser of Allander Institute, and others. Input-output tables for Scotland 1973. Edinburgh, [1978]. pp. 15.

— — Mathematical models.

AL-ALI (H.M.) and BURDEKIN (R.) An analysis of some aspects of the Scottish economy using input- output techniques. Peterlee, 1978. pp. 47. *(IBM United Kingdom Limited. UK Scientific Centre. [Technical Reports]. 0096)*

BURDEKIN (R.) The construction of the 1973 Scottish input-output tables. Peterlee, 1978. pp. 68. *(IBM United Kingdom Limited. UK Scientific Centre. [Technical Reports]. 0091)*

— Economic history.

GIBB (ANDREW DEWAR) Scotland in eclipse. London, 1930. pp. 200.

LENMAN (BRUCE) An economic history of modern Scotland, 1660-1976. London, 1977. pp. 288. *bibliog.*

CARTER (IAN) Farmlife in northeast Scotland, 1840-1914: the poor man's country. Edinburgh, [1979]. pp. 258. *bibliog.*

— Economic policy.

HOGWOOD (BRIAN W.) The primacy of politics in the economic policy of Scottish government. Glasgow, [1978]. pp. 35. *(Glasgow. University of Strathclyde. Centre for the Study of Public Policy. Studies in Public Policy. No. 14)*

— Executive departments.

POTTINGER (GEORGE) The Secretaries of State for Scotland, 1926-76. Edinburgh, [1979]. pp. 214. *bibliog.*

— History — 1603-1707.

STEVENSON (DAVID) Historian. Revolution and counter-revolution in Scotland, 1644-1651. London, 1977. pp. 283. *bibliog. (Royal Historical Society. Studies in History)*

— — 1707, The Union.

RILEY (PATRICK WILLIAM JOSEPH) The union of England and Scotland: a study in Anglo-Scottish politics of the eighteenth century. Manchester, [1978]. pp. 351. *bibliogs.*

— Industries.

SCOTTISH COUNCIL (DEVELOPMENT AND INDUSTRY). Review of the industrial situation in Scotland. Edinburgh, [1977?]. pp. 13.

THOMSON (J.K.) The framework of industry in Scotland: an analysis of the Scottish input-output table. rev. ed. Edinburgh, 1978. 1 vol. (unpaged).

TURNOCK (DAVID) The new Scotland. Newton Abbot, [1979]. pp. 168. *bibliog.*

— Intellectual life.

RENDALL (JANE) The origins of the Scottish Enlightenment. London, 1978. pp. 257. *bibliog.*

— Nationalism.

GIBB (ANDREW DEWAR) Scotland in eclipse. London, 1930. pp. 200.

BRAND (JACK) The national movement in Scotland. London, 1978. pp. 330.

STUART (JAMES GIBB) The mind benders: the gradual revolution and Scottish independence. Glasgow, 1978. pp. 180. *bibliog.*

— Politics and government.

FEDERALISM: central/regional relations. Edinburgh, [1975?]. 1 vol. (various foliations). *(Edinburgh. University. Centre of Canadian Studies. Seminar Papers. No. 1)*

SCOTLAND. Scottish Economic Planning Department. 1976. Scottish Development Agency: industrial investment guidelines. Edinburgh, 1976. fo. 11, 2.

HOGWOOD (BRIAN W.) The primacy of politics in the economic policy of Scottish government. Glasgow, [1978]. pp. 35. *(Glasgow. University of Strathclyde. Centre for the Study of Public Policy. Studies in Public Policy. No. 14)*

PAGE (EDWARD) Why should central-local relations in Scotland be any different from those in England? Glasgow, [1978]. fo. 46. *(Glasgow. University of Strathclyde. Centre for the Study of Public Policy. Studies in Public Policy. No. 21)*

BOOTH (SIMON) The Scottish executive: departmental and ministerial structure. [Glasgow, 1979]. pp. 15. *bibliog. (Scottish Council of Fabian Societies. Scottish Fabian Research Papers. 4)*

CRAIG (CAROL) and GILMORE (SHEILA) Women and the Scottish assembly. [Glasgow, 1979]. pp. 15. *(Scottish Council of Fabian Societies. Scottish Fabian Research Papers. 2)*

KEATING (MICHAEL) Fabian. The structure of the Scottish assembly. [Glasgow, 1979]. pp. 15. *(Scottish Council of Fabian Societies. Scottish Fabian Research Papers. 5)*

MURRAY (ANNE) Reforming Scottish prisons: a task for the assembly. [Glasgow, 1979]. pp. 24. *bibliog. (Scottish Council of Fabian Societies. Scottish Fabian Research Papers. 3)*

SCOTLAND: the framework for change; [edited by] Donald I. Mackay. Edinburgh, 1979. pp. 196.

— Rural conditions.

TURNOCK (DAVID) The new Scotland. Newton Abbot, [1979]. pp. 168. *bibliog.*

— Social history.

RENDALL (JANE) The origins of the Scottish Enlightenment. London, 1978. pp. 257. *bibliog.*

— Social life and customs.

GIBB (ANDREW DEWAR) Scotland in eclipse. London, 1930. pp. 200.

SCOTT (DRED).

FEHRENBACHER (DON EDWARD) The Dred Scott case: its significance in American law and politics. New York, 1978. pp. 741.

SCOTTISH LABOUR PARTY.

DRUCKER (HENRY MATTHEW) Breakaway: the Scottish Labour Party. Edinburgh, [1978]. pp. 157. *bibliog.*

SCULPTURE, GOTHIC.

MUELLER (THEODOR) 1905- . Sculpture in the Netherlands, Germany, France, and Spain, 1400 to 1500. Harmondsworth, 1966. pp. 262,192 plates. *bibliog.*

SCULPTURE, RENAISSANCE.

MUELLER (THEODOR) 1905- . Sculpture in the Netherlands, Germany, France, and Spain, 1400 to 1500. Harmondsworth, 1966. pp. 262,192 plates. *bibliog.*

SEA LEVEL

— Irish Sea.

TOOLEY (M.J.) Sea-level changes: North-West England during the Flandrian stage. Oxford, 1978. pp. 232. *bibliog.*

SEAMEN

— France.

JAMBU-MERLIN (ROGER) Les gens de mer. Paris, 1978. pp. 317.

SEARCHES AND SEIZURES

— United States.

HIRSCHEL (J. DAVID) Fourth amendment rights. Lexington, Mass., [1979]. pp. 158. *bibliog.*

SECRET SERVICE

— Russia.

DEACON (RICHARD) The British connection: Russia's manipulation of British individuals and institutions. London, 1979. pp. 291. *bibliog.*

— United States.

THEOHARIS (ATHAN G.) Spying on Americans: political surveillance from Hoover to the Huston Plan. Philadelphia, 1978. pp. 331. *bibliog.*

SECTS.

WALLIS (ROY) Salvation and protest: studies of social and religious movements. New York, 1979. pp. 231.

— Russia.

BELOV (ANATOLII VASIL'EVICH) Sekty, sektantstvo, sektanty. Moskva, 1978. pp. 151. *(Akademiia Nauk SSSR. Nauchno-Ateisticheskaia Seriia)*

— — Buryat Republic.

BOLONEV (FIRS FEDOSOVICH) Narodnyi kalendar' semeiskikh Zabaikal'ia, vtoraia polovina XIX - nachalo XX v.; otvetstvennyi redaktor E.A. Ashchepkov. Novosibirsk, 1978. pp. 159.

SECURITIES.

GIFFEN (Sir ROBERT) Stock exchange securities: an essay on the general causes of fluctuations in their price. London, 1877. pp. 163.

DAY (J.G.) and JAMIESON (A.T.) Institutional investment. [London, 1975 repr. 1977-78]. 6 vols. *bibliogs.*

HONOHAN (PATRICK THOMAS) Uncertainty, portfolio choice and economic fluctuations. 1978. fo. 411. *bibliog.* Typescript. Ph.D. (London) thesis: unpublished. *This thesis is the property of London University and may not be removed from the Library.*

FINANCIAL information requirements for security analysis; edited by A. Rashad Abdel-khalik and Thomas F. Keller. [Durham, N.C., 1979?]. pp. 164. *bibliogs.* Duke Second Accounting Symposium, 1976.

— United Kingdom.

KING (J.R.) Realisations and accruals of capital gains, with particular reference to company securities. London, Inland Revenue, 1978. pp. 29. *(Government Economic Service Working Papers. No. 15)*

HILLIARD (B.C.) Exchange flows and the gilt-edged security market: a causality study. London, 1979. pp. 31. *bibliog. (Bank of England. Discussion Papers. No. 2)*

— United States.

The DEREGULATION of the banking and securities industries; edited by Lawrence G. Goldberg, Lawrence J. hite. Lexington, Mass., [1979]. pp. 356. *Papers of a conference sponsored by the Salomon Brothers Center for the Study of Financial Institutions.*

— — Mathematical models.

SOLDOFSKY (ROBERT MELVIN) and MAX (DALE F.) Holding period yields and risk-premium curves for long-term marketable securities, 1910-1976. New York, 1978. pp. 81. *bibliog. (New York (City). University. Salomon Brothers Center for the Study of Financial Institutions. Monograph Series in Finance and Economics. 1978. No. 2)*

— — New York.

KEENAN (W. MICHAEL) Profile of the New York based security industry. New York, 1977. pp. 69. *(New York (City). University. Salomon Brothers Center for the Study o Financial Institutions. Monograph Series in Finance and Economics. 1977. No. 3)*

SECURITIES, TAX-EXEMPT

— United States — Mathematical models.

HENDERSHOTT (PATRIC H.) and KOCH (TIMOTHY W.) An empirical analysis of the market for tax-exempt securities: estimates and forecasts. New York, 1977. pp. 72. *bibliog.* (New York (City). University. Salomon Brothers Center for the Study of Financial Institutions. Monograph Series in Finance and Economics. 1977. No. 4)

SECURITY (LAW)

— India.

INDIA. Banking Laws Committee. 1978. Report on personal property security law; [P.V. Rajamannar, chairman]. [Delhi, 1978]. pp. 407,2.

INDIA. Banking Laws Committee. 1978. Report on real property security law; [P.V. Rajamannar, chairman]. [Delhi, 1978]. pp. 356,4.

SECURITY, INTERNATIONAL.

BROWN (LESTER RUSSELL) Redefining national security. Washington, 1977. pp. 46. *(Worldwatch Institute. Worldwatch Papers. No. 14)*

VO imia mira: mezhdunarodno-pravovye problemy evropeiskoi bezopasnosti. Moskva, 1977. pp. 191.

CRITCHLEY (JULIAN) Warning and response: a study of surprise attack in the twentieth century and an analysis of its lessons for the future. London, 1978. pp. 123.

JOHANSEN (ROBERT C.) Toward a dependable peace: a proposal for an appropriate security system. New York, [1978]. pp. 58.

LABOUR PARTY. Cold peace: Soviet power and Western security. [London], 1978. pp. 54.

MENAUL (STEWART WILLIAM BLACKER) Salt II: the Eurostrategic imbalance. London, 1979. pp. 17. *(Institute for the Study of Conflict. Conflict Studies. No.104)*

NEGOTIATING security: an arms control reader; edited by William H. Kincade and Jeffrey D. Porro. Washington, D.C., [1979]. pp. 321. *bibliog.*

SECURITY SYSTEMS

— United Kingdom.

U.K. Home Office. 1979. The private security industry: a discussion paper. London, 1979. pp. 31.

SEDGWICK (THEODORE).

SEDGWICK (THEODORE) Public and private economy...in three parts, 1836-1839 with an introduction: Theodore Sedgwick: from federalism to Jacksonianism, by Joseph Dorfman. Clifton, N. J., 1974. pp. 490. *Reprint of work originally published in New York, 1836-1839.*

SEGREGATION

— United States.

The AGE of segregation: race relations in the South, 1890-1945; essays by Derrick Bell [and others]; edited by Robert Haws. Jackson, Miss., 1978. pp. 156.

SEIPEL (IGNAZ).

RENNHOFER (FRIEDRICH) Ignaz Seipel: Mensch und Staatsmann; eine biographische Dokumentation. Wien, 1978. pp. 800. *bibliog.*

SELF.

POPPER (Sir KARL RAIMUND) and ECCLES (Sir JOHN CAREW) The self and its brain. Berlin, [1977]. pp. 597. *bibliogs.*

WIKSE (JOHN R.) About possession: the self as private property. University Park, Pa., [1977]. pp. 169. *bibliog.*

SELF-DEFENCE (INTERNATIONAL LAW).

TAOKA (RYOICHI) The right of self-defence in international law. Osaka, [1978]. pp. 195. *(Osaka University of Economics and Law. Institute of Legal Study. Legal Research Series. No. 1)*

SELF-DETERMINATION, NATIONAL.

CURCIO (CARLO) Nazione e autodecisione dei popoli: due idee nella storia. Milano, [1977]. pp. 396.

SELF-EMPLOYED

— France.

Les BENEFICES déclarés par les entrepreneurs individuels non agricoles; [by Philippe Madinier and others]. [Paris, 1974]. pp. 170. *(France. Centre d'Etude des Revenus et des Coûts. Documents. No.24)*

SELF-HELP GROUPS.

JELFS (MARTIN) Manual for action: (techniques to enable groups engaged in action for change to increase their effectiveness). London, [1977]. 1 vol. (various pagings). *bibliog. Prepared for Action Resources Group.*

SELF MEDICATION

— United States.

MEDICINE without doctors: home health care in American history; edited by Guenter B. Risse [and others]. New York, 1977. pp. 124. *bibliogs.*

SELF-PERCEPTION.

ALVERSON (HOYT) Mind in the heart of darkness: value and self-identity among the Tswana of southern Africa. New Haven, 1978. pp. 299. *bibliog.*

SEMANTICS.

GEORGETOWN UNIVERSITY ROUND TABLE ON LANGUAGES AND LINGUISTICS, 1976. Semantics: theory and application; Clea Rameh, editor. Washington, D.C., [1976]. pp. 279. *bibliogs.*

KEENAN (EDWARD L.) and FALTZ (LEONARD M.) Logical types for natural language. [Los Angeles, 1978]. pp. 338. *bibliog. (California University. Occasional Papers in Linguistics. No.3)*

SEMANTIC factors in cognition; edited by John W. Cotton, Roberta L. Klatzky. Hillsdale, N.J., 1978. pp. 239. *Papers presented at a conference held on May 26 and 27, 1976 at the University of California, Santa Barbara.*

SEMENOV (GEORGII GAVRILOVICH).

SEMENOV (GEORGII GAVRILOVICH) Tri goda v Pekine: zapiski voennogo sovetnika. Moskva, 1978. pp. 296.

SEMIOTICS.

HAWKES (TERENCE) Structuralism and semiotics. London, 1977. pp. 192. *bibliog.*

SEMPRUN (JORGE).

SEMPRUN (JORGE) Autobiographie de Federico Sánchez; traduit de l'espagnol par Claude et Carmen Durand. Paris, 1978. pp. 319.

SENEGAL

— Economic conditions.

PROSPECTIVE du développement en Afrique Noire: un scénario, le Sénégal; sous la direction de Louis- Vincent Thomas. Bruxelles, [1978]. pp. 191.

UNION GENERALE DES TRAVAILLEURS SENEGALAIS EN FRANCE. Notre Afrique: débats sur le tiers monde. Paris, 1978. pp. 123.

— Economic policy.

PROSPECTIVE du développement en Afrique Noire: un scénario, le Sénégal; sous la direction de Louis- Vincent Thomas. Bruxelles, [1978]. pp. 191.

— Social conditions.

MAINTENANCE sociale et changement économique au Sénégal. 2. Pratique du travail et rééquilibres sociaux en milieu Serer; [by] B. Delpech [and others]. Paris, 1974. pp. 155. *bibliog. (France. Office de la Recherche Scientifique et Technique Outre-Mer. Travaux et Documents. No. 34) Vol. 1 published as Travaux et Documents. No. 15.*

SENTENCES (CRIMINAL PROCEDURE)

— United Kingdom.

U.K. Home Office. 1978. The sentence of the court: a handbook for courts on the treatment of offenders. 3rd ed. London, 1978. pp. 90. *bibliog.*

THOMAS (DAVID ARTHUR) Principles of sentencing: the sentencing policy of the Court of Appeal, Criminal Division. 2nd ed. London, 1979. pp. 410. *(Cambridge. University. Institute of Criminology. Cambridge Studies in Criminology. vol. 27)*

— United States.

LEVIN (MARTIN A.) Urban politics and the criminal courts. Chicago, 1977. pp. 332.

SEPHARDIM.

MALINO (FRANCES) The Sephardic Jews of Bordeaux: assimilation and emancipation in Revolutionary and Napoleonic France. University, Ala., [1978]. pp. 166. *bibliog.*

SEQUENTIAL MACHINE THEORY.

CONWAY (JOHN HORTON) Regular algebra and finite machines. London, 1971. pp. 147.

SERBIA

— History.

DRAGNICH (ALEX N.) The development of parliamentary government in Serbia. New York, 1978. pp. 138. *(East European Quarterly. East European Monographs. 44)*

— Politics and government.

DRAGNICH (ALEX N.) The development of parliamentary government in Serbia. New York, 1978. pp. 138. *(East European Quarterly. East European Monographs. 44)*

SERERS.

MAINTENANCE sociale et changement économique au Sénégal. 2. Pratique du travail et rééquilibres sociaux en milieu Serer; [by] B. Delpech [and others]. Paris, 1974. pp. 155. *bibliog. (France. Office de la Recherche Scientifique et Technique Outre-Mer. Travaux et Documents. No. 34) Vol. 1 published as Travaux et Documents. No. 15.*

SERFDOM

— Netherlands.

AALBERS (P.G.) Het einde van de horigheid in Twente en Oost-Gelderland, 1795- 1850. Zutphen, 1979. pp. 284. *bibliog.*

SERGE (VICTOR) pseud.

SERGE (VICTOR) pseud. [i.e. Viktor L'vovich KIBAL'CHICH]. Mémoires d'un révolutionnaire, 1901-1941. Paris, [1978]. pp. 444. *bibliog. Text, first published 1951, revised and corrected by author.*

SERVANTS

— France.

GUIRAL (PIERRE) and THUILLIER (GUY) La vie quotidienne des domestiques en France au XIXe siècle. [Paris, 1978]. pp. 281. *bibliog.*

— United States.

KATZMAN (DAVID M.) Seven days a week: women and domestic service in industrializing America. New York, 1978. pp. 374. *bibliog.*

SERVICE INDUSTRIES.

SERVICE INDUSTRIES.

SINGELMANN (JOACHIN) From agriculture to services: the transformation of industrial employment. Beverly Hills, [1978]. pp. 175. *bibliog.*

— America, Latin.

ROGGERO (MARIA ANGELINA) Urbanizacion, industrializacion y crecimiento del sector servicios en America latina. Buenos Aires, [1976]. pp. 139. *bibliog.*

— Brazil.

ALMEIDA (WANDERLY JOSE MANSO DE) Serviços e desenvolvimento econômico no Brazil: aspectos setoriais e suas implicaçoes. Rio de Janeiro, 1974. pp. 127. *(Brazil. Instituto de Planejamento Econômico e Social. Instituto de Pesquisas. Relatorios de Pesquisa. No. 23)*

ALMEIDA (ANNA LUIZA OZORIO DE) Distribuição de renda e emprego en serviços. Rio de Janeiro, 1976. pp. 412. *bibliog. (Brazil. Instituto de Planejamento Econômico e Social. Instituto de Pesquisas. Relatorios de Pesquisa. No. 34)*

— France.

BUETTNER (OLIVIER) and others. L'emploi salarié tertiaire en France; localisation des activités, hiérarchisation de l'espace. [Paris, 1976]. pp. 156. *(France. Centre d'Etudes de l'Emploi. Cahiers. 10) With English summary.*

SCHEMA général d'aménagement de la France: activités et régions: dynamiques d'une transformation. [Paris, 1978]. pp. 124. *(France. Délégation à l'Aménagement du Territoire et à l'Action Régionale. Travaux et Recherches de Prospective. 75)*

— India — Punjab.

PUNJAB (INDIA). Economic and Statistical Organisation. 1976. Report on the distributive trade survey relating to urban areas of Punjab. Chandigarh, 1976. pp. 206. *(publications. No. 218)*

— Ireland (Republic).

COGAN (D.J.) The Irish services sector: a study of productive efficiency. Dublin, Stationery Office, 1978. pp. 244. *bibliog.*

— Japan.

EMI (KOICHI) Essays on the service industry and social security in Japan. Tokyo, [1978]. pp. 186. *(Tokyo. Hitotsubashi University. Institute of Economic Research. Economic Research Series. No. 17)*

— Portugal.

PORTUGAL. Instituto Nacional de Estatística. 1979- . 1977 recenseamento à distribuição e serviços: Portugal: [provisional results]. Lisboa, [1979 in progress].

— Russia.

KOMPLEKSNYI plan razvitiia sfery obsluzhivaniia naseleniia; pod redaktsiei V.M. Rutgaizera. Moskva, 1977. pp. 231.

— Sweden.

SWEDEN. Statistiska Centralbyrån. Regional omsättning inom parti- och detaljhandel samt vissa tjänstenäringar. a., 1976- Stockholm. *[in Swedish with English summary]*

— United Kingdom.

NORTHERN REGION STRATEGY TEAM. Spatial patterns and the development of service industries; (project no. B.1.f). Newcastle-upon-Tyne, 1976. pp. 49. *(Working Papers. No. 8)*

CHANNON (DEREK F.) The service industries: strategy, structure and financial performance. London, 1978. pp. 292.

SET THEORY.

BELL (JOHN LANE) Boolean-valued models and independence proofs in set theory. Oxford, 1977. pp. 126. *bibliog.*

KICKERT (WALTER J.M.) Fuzzy theories on decision-making: a critical review. Leiden, 1978. pp. 182. *bibliog.*

SETTLEMENTS (LAW)

— United Kingdom — Taxation.

HALLETT (VICTOR GEORGE HENRY) and WARREN (NICHOLAS) Settlements, wills and capital transfer tax. London, 1979. pp. 245.

SEVEN YEARS' WAR, 1756-1763.

KAPLAN (HERBERT HAROLD) Russia and the outbreak of the Seven Years' War. Berkeley, 1968. pp. 165. *bibliog.*

SEWING MACHINE INDUSTRY

— United States.

DAVIES (ROBERT BRUCE) Peacefully working to conquer the world: Singer sewing machines in foreign markets, 1854-1920. [New York], 1976. pp. 390. *bibliog.*

SEX.

SEXUAL selection and The descent of man 1871-1971; edited by Bernard Campbell. London, 1972. pp. 378. *bibliogs.*

FOUCAULT (MICHEL) The history of sexuality: vol. 1: an introduction; translated from the French by Robert Hurley. London, 1979. pp. 168. *Translation first published in 1978.*

SEX (BIOLOGY).

HUMAN sexuality: a comparative and developmental perspective; Herant A. Katchadourian, editor. Berkeley, [1979]. pp. 358. *bibliog.*

SEX (PSYCHOLOGY).

SEXUAL behavior in the human female; [by] Alfred C. Kinsey [and others]. Philadelphia, [1953]. pp. 842. *bibliog.*

WALKER (KENNETH MACFARLANE) and FLETCHER (PETER) pseud. [i.e. Alfred Brinson Woods FLETCHER] Sex and society. Harmondsworth, 1955. pp. 251.

KLEIN (VIOLA) The feminine character: history of an ideology. 2nd ed. London, 1971. pp. 202. *bibliog.*

SEX and age as principles of social differentiation; edited by J. S. La Fontaine. London, 1978. pp. 188. *bibliogs. (Association of Social Anthropologists of the Commonwealth. A.S.A. Monographs. 17)*

HUMAN sexuality: a comparative and developmental perspective; Herant A. Katchadourian, editor. Berkeley, [1979]. pp. 358. *bibliog.*

SEX AND LAW

— United Kingdom.

SION (ABRAHAM A.) Prostitution and the law. London, 1977. pp. 160. *bibliog.*

HONORÉ (TONY) Sex law. London, 1978. pp. 200. *bibliog.*

The LAW and sexuality: how to cope with the law if you're not 100 per cent conventionally heterosexual; [by] Steve Cohen [and others]. Manchester, 1978. pp. 175.

SEX CRIMES.

SEXUAL assault of children and adolescents; [by] Ann Wolbert Burgess [and others]. Lexington, Mass., [1978]. pp. 245.

The VICTIMIZATION of women; edited by Jane Roberts Chapman and Margaret Gates. Beverly Hills, [1978]. pp. 282. *bibliogs.*

— New Zealand.

NEW ZEALAND. Criminal Law Reform Committee. 1977. Report on the position of young witnesses in cases involving a sexual offence. Wellington, 1977. pp. 8.

— United Kingdom.

U.K. Policy Advisory Committee on Sexual Offences. 1979. Working party [sic., i.e. paper] on the age of consent in relation to sexual offences; [Lord Justice Waller, chairman]. London, 1979. pp. 31.

SEX CUSTOMS.

RED COLLECTIVE. The politics of sexuality in capitalism. London, 1973 repr. 1978. pp. 146.

HUMAN sexuality: a comparative and developmental perspective; Herant A. Katchadourian, editor. Berkeley, [1979]. pp. 358. *bibliog.*

— United States.

BARKER-BENFIELD (G.J.) The horrors of the half-known life: male attitudes toward women and sexuality in nineteenth century America. New York, 1977. pp. 352.

SEX DISCRIMINATION

— France.

FRANCE. Secrétariat d'Etat à la Condition Féminine. 1976. Cent mesures pour les femmes; présentées par Françoise Giroud. Paris, [1976]. pp. 196.

— United Kingdom.

E.O.C. RESEARCH BULLETIN; [pd. by] Equal Opportunities Commission. q., winter 1978/79(v.1, no.1)- Manchester.

EOC NEWS; pd. by Equal Opportunities Commission. bi-m., Mr 1978- Manchester.

SEX DISCRIMINATION AGAINST WOMEN

— Law and legislation — United States.

WOMEN'S rights and the law: the impact of the ERA on State laws; [by] Barbara A. Brown [and others]; edited...by Hazel Greenberg. New York, 1977. pp. 433. *bibliog.*

— United Kingdom.

U.K. Equal Opportunities Commission. 1977. Income tax and sex discrimination. [Manchester, 1977]. pp. 55.

SACHS (ALBIE) and WILSON (JOAN HOFF) Sexism and the law: a study of male beliefs and legal bias in Britain and the United States. Oxford, 1978. pp. 257. *bibliog.*

U.K. Equal Opportunities Commission. 1979. With all my worldly goods I thee endow...except my tax allowances: the response received by the...Commission to its consultative document Income tax and sex discrimination. [Manchester, 1979]. pp. 61.

— United States.

BAER (JUDITH A.) The chains of protection: the judicial response to women's labor legislation. Westport, Conn., 1978. pp. 238. *bibliog.*

SACHS (ALBIE) and WILSON (JOAN HOFF) Sexism and the law: a study of male beliefs and legal bias in Britain and the United States. Oxford, 1978. pp. 257. *bibliog.*

SEX DISCRIMINATION IN EDUCATION

— United Kingdom.

BYRNE (EILEEN M.) Women and education. London, 1978. pp. 285. *bibliog.*

DEEM (ROSEMARY) Women and schooling. London, 1978. pp. 170. *bibliog.*

SEX DISCRIMINATION IN EMPLOYMENT

— Law and legislation — United States.

BAER (JUDITH A.) The chains of protection: the judicial response to women's labor legislation. Westport, Conn., 1978. pp. 238. *bibliog.*

— United Kingdom.

DEEM (ROSEMARY) Women and schooling. London, 1978. pp. 170. *bibliog.*

U.K. Equal Opportunities Commission. 1978. Equalising the pension age. [London], 1978. pp. 43.

— United States.

BENOKRAITIS (NIJOLE V.) and FEAGIN (JOE R.) Affirmative action and equal opportunity: action, inaction, reaction. Boulder, Colo., 1978. pp. 255. *bibliog.*

SEX ROLE.

FILENE (PETER GABRIEL) Him/her/self: sex roles in modern America. New York, 1976. pp. 326. *bibliog.*

BARKER-BENFIELD (G.J.) The horrors of the half-known life: male attitudes toward women and sexuality in nineteenth century America. New York, 1977. pp. 352.

NEW ZEALAND. Social Development Council. 1977. Housework and caring work: can men do better? [Wellington], 1977. 1 vol. (various pagings). *bibliog.*

DUNCAN (BEVERLEY) and DUNCAN (OTIS DUDLEY) Sex typing and social roles: a research report. New York, [1978]. pp. 389.

GIELE (JANET ZOLLINGER) Women and the future: changing sex roles in modern America. New York, [1978]. pp. 386. *bibliog.*

SCANZONI (JOHN H.) Sex roles, women's work and marital conflict: a study of family change. Lexington, Mass., [1978]. pp. 175. *bibliog.*

SEX and age as principles of social differentiation; edited by J. S. La Fontaine. London, 1978. pp. 188. *bibliogs.* (*Association of Social Anthropologists of the Commonwealth. A.S.A. Monographs. 17*)

SIMON (RITA JAMES) Continuity and change: a study of two ethnic communities in Israel. Cambridge, 1978. pp. 180. *bibliog.* (*American Sociological Association. Arnold and Caroline Rose Monograph Series in Sociology*)

HUMAN sexuality: a comparative and developmental perspective; Herant A. Katchadourian, editor. Berkeley, [1979]. pp. 358. *bibliog.*

SEX roles and social policy: a complex social science equation; edited by Jean Lipman-Blumen and Jessie Bernard. London, [1979]. pp. 404. *bibliogs.*

SEXUAL PERVERSION.

PLUMMER (KENNETH JOHN) Sexual stigma: an interactionist account. London, 1975. pp. 258. *bibliog.*

SEYDEWITZ (MAX).

SEYDEWITZ (MAX) Es hat sich gelohnt zu leben: Lebenserinnerungen eines alten Arbeiterfunktionärs. Berlin, 1976-78. 2 vols. *bibliog.*

SHABA

— Religion.

DE CRAEMER (WILLY) The Jamaa and the Church: a Bantu Catholic movement in Zaïre. Oxford, 1977. pp. 192. *bibliog.*

SHAVISHVILI (FEDOR AMBAKOVICH).

SHAVISHVILI (FEDOR AMBAKOVICH) Tsarskaia katorga: vospominaniia byvshego politkatorzhanina; perevod s gruzinskogo N. Mikava. Tbilisi, 1977. pp. 198.

SHAW (GEORGE BERNARD).

HACKETT (J.P.) Shaw: George versus Bernard. London, 1937. pp. 216.

SHEEP

— Barbados.

PATTERSON (HAROLD C.) and NURSE (JAMES O. J.) A survey on sheep production in Barbados, 1972. [Bridgetown], Ministry of Agriculture, Science and Technology, 1974. pp. 37.

SHEFFIELD

— Schools.

PARSONS (CHERYL) Schools in an urban community: a study of Carbrook, 1870-1965. London, 1978. pp. 155. *bibliog.*

SHETLAND ISLANDS

— Economic conditions.

MARSHALL (ELIZABETH) Shetland's oil era. Lerwick, Shetland Islands Council, Research and Development Department, [1977]. pp. 73. *bibliog.*

FENTON (ALEXANDER) The Northern isles: Orkney and Shetland. Edinburgh, [1978]. pp. 721.

MARSHALL (ELIZABETH) Shetland's oil era: phase 2. Lerwick, Shetland Islands Council, Research and Development Department, [1978]. pp. 107. *bibliog.*

— Social life and customs.

FENTON (ALEXANDER) The Northern isles: Orkney and Shetland. Edinburgh, [1978]. pp. 721.

SHIFTING CULTIVATION

— Thailand.

FARMERS in the forest: economic development and marginal agriculture in northern Thailand; edited by Peter Kunstadter [and others]. Honolulu, [1978]. pp. 402. *bibliog.*

SHINOHATA, JAPAN.

DORE (RONALD PHILIP) Shinohata: a portrait of a Japanese village. London, 1978. pp. 322.

SHIPBUILDING

— European Economic Community countries.

EUROPEAN COMMUNITIES. Commission. 1978. Reorganization of the Community shipbuilding industry: communication...sent to the Council on 9 December 1977. [Brussels, 1978]. pp. 21. (*Bulletin of the European Communities. Supplements. [1977/7]*)

— United Kingdom.

BRITISH SHIPBUILDERS. Report and accounts. a., 1977/78(1st)- London.

NORTHERN REGION STRATEGY TEAM. Trends and prospects in the shipbuilding and heavy engineering industries. Newcastle-upon-Tyne, 1977. pp. 247. (*Working Papers. No. 11*)

POLLARD (SIDNEY) and ROBERTSON (PAUL) The British shipbuilding industry, 1870-1914. Cambridge, Mass., 1979. pp. 312. *bibliog.* (*Harvard University. Harvard Studies in Business History. 30*)

— — Government ownership.

HOGWOOD (BRIAN W.) Government and shipbuilding: the politics of industrial change. Farnborough, [1979]. pp. 302. *bibliog.*

SHIPBUILDING WORKERS

— France.

SABATINI (ANDREE) Les problèmes d'emploi et la restructuration dans la réparation navale Marseillaise. Marseille, Echelon Régional de l'Emploi et du Travail de Marseille, 1978. fo. 50.

— Germany.

RATIONALISIERUNG und Massenarbeiter: die Kämpfe der norddeutschen Werftarbeiter seit 1945. München, 1973. pp. 157. *bibliog.*

SHIPPING.

IMCO NEWS: the magazine of the Inter-Governmental Maritime Consultative Organization. bi-m., 1977(no.2)- London.

BOEHME (HANS) Restraints on competition in world shipping. London, 1978. pp. 85. (*Trade Policy Research Centre. Thames Essays. No. 15*)

— Directories.

FAIRPLAY world shipping year book 1979. London, [1978]. pp. 772.

— Maps.

LLOYD'S maritime atlas, including a comprehensive list of ports and shipping places of the world. 10th ed. London, 1975. pp. 160.

— France.

FRANCE. Département des Statistiques des Transports. 1976. Système d'information sur les transports de marchandises: comment évaluer la part du trafic maritime né de notre commerce extérieur qui échappe aux ports français. Paris, 1976. pp. 38.

SHIPS

— Cargo.

U.K. Standing Advisory Committee on the Carriage of Dangerous Goods in Ships. 1978- . Carriage of dangerous goods in ships; report..., 1978: the Blue Book; (with Amendments); [R. K. Roberts, chairman]. 3rd ed. London, 1978 in progress. 1 vol.(loose-leaf)

— Registration and transfer.

LIMITONE (ANTHONY) The registration of ships by international and intergovernmental organizations. Miami, 1971. fo. 28. (*Miami (Florida). University Grant Program. Special Bulletins. 2*)

SHIPYARDS

— United Kingdom.

POLLARD (SIDNEY) and ROBERTSON (PAUL) The British shipbuilding industry, 1870-1914. Cambridge, Mass., 1979. pp. 312. *bibliog.* (*Harvard University. Harvard Studies in Business History. 30*)

SHOP STEWARDS

— Germany.

WEISS (MANFRED) Gewerkschaftliche Vertrauensleute: tarifvertragliche Verbesserungen ihrer Arbeit im Betrieb. Köln, [1978]. pp. 109. (*Otto Brenner Stiftung. Schriftenreihe. 11*)

— United Kingdom.

FOX (ALAN) Socialism and shop floor power. London, 1978. pp. 20. (*Fabian Society. Research Series. [No.] 338*)

HULL (DARYLL) The shop stewards' guide to work organisation. Nottingham, 1978. pp. 130.

SHOP STEWARDS (Cont.)

MOORE (RONALD JAMES) The motivation, attitudes, interests and satisfactions of shop stewards in a cross-section of industrial occupations in Hertfordshire, 1971-1974. 1978. fo. 549. *bibliog. Typescript. Ph.D. (London) thesis: unpublished. Appendices 6,7 and 8 in end pocket. This thesis is the property of London University and may not be removed from the Library.*

SHVERNIK (NIKOLAI MIKHAILOVICH).

MEL'CHIN (ANATOLII IVANOVICH) Nikolai Mikhailovich Shvernik: biograficheskii ocherk. Moskva, 1977. pp. 223. *bibliog.*

SIBERIA

— Commerce.

DUDUKALOV (VIKTOR IVANOVICH) Deiatel'nost' partiinykh organizatsii Sibiri po razvitiiu sovetskoi torgovli v pervye gody nepa, 1921-1923 gg. Tomsk, 1976. pp. 185. *bibliog.*

— Constitutional history.

AGALAKOV (VIKTOR TROFIMOVICH) Sovety Sibiri, 1917-1918 gg. Novosibirsk, 1978. pp. 255.

SHISHKIN (VLADIMIR IVANOVICH) Revoliutsionnye komitety Sibiri v gody grazhdanskoi voiny, avgust 1919 - mart 1921 g. Novosibirsk, 1978. pp. 333.

— Economic history.

PROBLEMY istorii sovetskoi sibirskoi derevni. Novosibirsk, 1977. pp. 302.

RABOCHII klass Sibiri v period uprocheniia i razvitiia sotsializma 1938-1958 gg.: materialy k "Istorii rabochego klassa Sibiri". Novosibirsk, 1977. pp. 237.

GUSHCHIN (NIKOLAI IAKOVLEVICH) and others. Soiuz rabochego klassa i krest'ianstva Sibiri v period postroeniia sotsializma, 1917-1937 gg. Novosibirsk, 1978. pp. 430.

— Exiles.

SSYLKA i obshchestvenno-politicheskaia zhizn' v Sibiri, XVIII - nachalo XX v. Novosibirsk, 1978. pp. 332.

— History — 1917-1921, Revolution.

AGALAKOV (VIKTOR TROFIMOVICH) Sovety Sibiri, 1917-1918 gg. Novosibirsk, 1978. pp. 255.

BATALOV (ALEKSANDR NIKOLAEVICH) Bor'ba bol'shevikov za armiiu v Sibiri, 1916 - fevral' 1918. Novosibirsk, 1978. pp. 285.

DEMIDOV (VIKTOR ALEKSANDROVICH) Oktiabr' i natsional'nyi vopros v Sibiri, 1917-1923 gg. Novosibirsk, 1978. pp. 367.

GUSHCHIN (NIKOLAI IAKOVLEVICH) and others. Soiuz rabochego klassa i krest'ianstva Sibiri v period postroeniia sotsializma, 1917-1937 gg. Novosibirsk, 1978. pp. 430.

SHISHKIN (VLADIMIR IVANOVICH) Revoliutsionnye komitety Sibiri v gody grazhdanskoi voiny, avgust 1919 - mart 1921 g. Novosibirsk, 1978. pp. 333.

— Industries.

KHALBAEV (MAKSIM NIKOLAEVICH) Industrial'noe razvitie natsional'nykh raionov Sibiri, 1959- 1970. Novosibirsk, 1978. pp. 256.

— Nationalism.

DEMIDOV (VIKTOR ALEKSANDROVICH) Oktiabr' i natsional'nyi vopros v Sibiri, 1917-1923 gg. Novosibirsk, 1978. pp. 367.

— Politics and government.

MOLETOTOV (IVAN AFANAS'EVICH) Sibkraikom: partiinoe stroitel'stvo v Sibiri, 1924-1930 gg.; otvetstvennyi redaktor B.M. Shereshevskii. Novosibirsk, 1978. pp. 366. *bibliog.*

— Population.

VOROB'EV (VLADIMIR VASIL'EVICH) Naselenie Vostochnoi Sibiri: sovremennaia dinamika i voprosy prognozirovaniia; otvetstvennyi redaktor V.B. Sochava. Novosibirsk, 1977. pp. 160. *bibliog.*

SICILY

— Economic history.

RESTIFO (GIUSEPPE) Sottosviluppo e lotte popolari in Sicilia, 1943-1974. Cosenza, 1976. pp. 214.

— History — 1016-1194.

CURTIS (EDMUND) Roger of Sicily and the Normans in Lower Italy, 1016-1154. New York, 1973. pp. 483. *Reprint of 1912, New York, ed.*

— Social history.

RESTIFO (GIUSEPPE) Sottosviluppo e lotte popolari in Sicilia, 1943-1974. Cosenza, 1976. pp. 214.

SICK.

TOTMAN (RICHARD) Social causes of illness. London, 1979. pp. 263. *bibliog.*

— United Kingdom.

STIMSON (GERALD VIVIAN) and STIMSON (CAROL) Health rights handbook: a guide to medical care. Dorchester, 1978. pp. 179.

SIERRA LEONE.

SIERRA LEONE. Chief Commissioner's Office. 1949. Sierra Leone Protectorate handbook, 1949. [Bo], 1949. pp. 40.

— Economic history.

SIERRA LEONE. Government Information Services. 1971. Sierra Leone: ten years of independence, 1961-1971. [Freetown, 1971]. pp. 53.

— Foreign relations.

SESAY (AMADU) International politics in Africa: a comparative study of the foreign policies of Liberia and Sierra Leone, 1957-73. 1978. fo. 423. *bibliog. Typescript. Ph.D. (London) thesis: unpublished. This thesis is the property of London University and may not be removed from the Library.*

— Legislative Council.

SIERRA LEONE. Legislative Council. Select Committee...to consider Proposals for a Reconstituted Legislative Council in Sierra Leone. 1948. Report; [Ragnar Hyne, chairman]. Freetown, 1948. pp. 4. *(Sierra Leone. Sessional Papers. 1948. No. 7)*

— Politics and government.

ABRAHAM (ARTHUR) Mende government and politics under colonial rule: a historical study of political change in Sierra Leone, 1890-1937. Freetown, Sierra Leone, 1978. pp. 330. *bibliog.*

— Social life and customs.

GERVIS (PEARCE) Sierra Leone story. London, 1956. pp. 250. *First published by Cassell in 1952.*

SIGHT.

GREGORY (RICHARD LANGTON) Eye and brain: the psychology of seeing. 3rd ed. London, 1977. pp. 256. *bibliog.*

SIGN LANGUAGE.

SIGN language of the deaf: psychological, linguistic, and sociological perspectives; edited by I.M. Schlesinger and Lila Namir. New York, 1978. pp. 380. *bibliog.*

SIKHS.

DOMIN (DOLORES) India in 1857-59: a study in the role of the Sikhs in the people's uprising. Berlin, 1977. pp. 375. *bibliog. (Zentraler Rat für Asien-, Afrika- und Lateinamerikawissenschaften in der DDR. Studien über Asien, Afrika und Lateinamerika. Band 17) Translated from the German by the author.*

SILESIA

— Population, Rural.

HAINES (MICHAEL R.) Economic-demographic interrelations in developing agricultural regions: a case study of Prussian Upper Silesia, 1840-1914. New York, 1977. pp. 499. *bibliogs.*

SILVER MINES AND MINING

— Canada — British Columbia.

TRIMBLE (WILLIAM JOSEPH) The mining advance into the Inland Empire;...with an introduction...by Rodman W. Paul. New York, 1972. pp. 254. *bibliog. (Wisconsin University, Madison. Bulletins. History Series. vol. 3, no. 2) Reprint of work originally published Madison, Wis., 1914.*

— United States.

TRIMBLE (WILLIAM JOSEPH) The mining advance into the Inland Empire;...with an introduction...by Rodman W. Paul. New York, 1972. pp. 254. *bibliog. (Wisconsin University, Madison. Bulletins. History Series. vol. 3, no. 2) Reprint of work originally published Madison, Wis., 1914.*

SIMULATION METHODS.

MIHRAM (G. ARTHUR) Simulation: statistical foundations and methodology. New York, 1972. pp. 526. *bibliog.*

KLEIJNEN (JACK P.C.) Statistical techniques in simulation. New York, [1974-75]. 2 vols. *bibliogs.*

CLARKE (MICHAEL) Simulations in the study of international relations. Ormskirk, 1978. pp. 225. *bibliog.*

HENDERSON (THOMAS A.) and FOSTER (JOHN L.) Urban policy game: a simulation of urban politics. New York, [1978]. pp. 137.

ROBERTS (PETER C.) Modelling large systems: (limits to growth revisited). London, 1978. pp. 120. *bibliog. (Operational Research Society. ORASA Texts. No. 4)*

SINGAPORE

— Commerce.

SINGAPORE. Sessional Papers. 1958. Cmd. 3. The external trade and balance of payments of Singapore, 1956. [Singapore, 1958]. pp. 13.

— Economic conditions.

The FUTURE of Singapore: the global city; edited by Wee Teong-Boo. [Singapore, 1977]. pp. 219. *Includes papers delivered at the seminar "Political and economic trends in Singapore", 1975, organized by the Democratic Socialist Club, University of Singapore.*

GOH (KENG SWEE) The practice of economic growth. Singapore, [1977]. pp. 265. *bibliog.*

— Foreign relations.

WILAIRAT (KAWIN) Singapore's foreign policy: the first decade. Singapore, 1975. pp. 105. *(Institute of Southeast Asian Studies. Field Report Series. No. 10)*

— Government publications — Bibliography.

LEONG (ALICE) compiler. Select list of Singapore parliamentary papers, 1948-1976. Singapore, 1977. pp. 44.

— Industries.

YOSHIHARA (KUNIO) Foreign investment and domestic response: a study of Singapore's industrialization. Singapore, [1976]. pp. 263. *bibliog.*

SINGAPORE. Statistics Department. 1978. Singapore input-output tables, 1973. Singapore, 1978. pp. 137.

— **Ministry of the Environment.**

SINGAPORE. Ministry of the Environment. Annual report. a., 1972[1st]- Singapore.

— **Politics and government.**

The FUTURE of Singapore: the global city; edited by Wee Teong-Boo. [Singapore, 1977]. pp. 219. *Includes papers delivered at the seminar "Political and economic trends in Singapore", 1975, organized by the Democratic Socialist Club, University of Singapore.*

GOH (KENG SWEE) The practice of economic growth. Singapore, [1977]. pp. 265. *bibliog.*

BEDLINGTON (STANLEY S.) Malaysia and Singapore: the building of new states. Ithaca, 1978. pp. 285. *bibliog.*

— **Population.**

SINGAPORE. Ministry of Health. 1977. Population and trends. Singapore, 1977. pp. 88.

— **Social conditions.**

KUO (EDDIE C.Y.) Families under economic stress: the Singapore experience. [Singapore, 1976]. pp. 72. *bibliog. (Institute of Southeast Asian Studies. Field Reports. No. 11)*

The FUTURE of Singapore: the global city; edited by Wee Teong-Boo. [Singapore, 1977]. pp. 219. *Includes papers delivered at the seminar "Political and economic trends in Singapore", 1975, organized by the Democratic Socialist Club, University of Singapore.*

GOH (KENG SWEE) The practice of economic growth. Singapore, [1977]. pp. 265. *bibliog.*

WILSON (H.E.) Social engineering in Singapore: educational policies and social change, 1819-1972. Singapore. [1978]. pp. 300. *bibliog.*

— **Statistical services.**

NSC STATISTICAL NEWS; [pd. by] National Statistical Commission [Singapore]. irreg., 1978(v.1, no.1)- Singapore.

— **Statistics.**

NSC STATISTICAL NEWS; [pd. by] National Statistical Commission [Singapore]. irreg., 1978(v.1, no.1)- Singapore.

SINGER SEWING MACHINE COMPANY.

DAVIES (ROBERT BRUCE) Peacefully working to conquer the world: Singer sewing machines in foreign markets, 1854-1920. [New York], 1976. pp. 390. *bibliog.*

SINGLE PARENT FAMILY.

SCHLESINGER (BENJAMIN) The one-parent family: perspectives and annotated bibliography. 4th ed. Toronto, [1978]. pp. 224. *bibliog.*

— **Netherlands.**

NEDERLANDSE GEZINSRAAD. De sociale en de economische positie van weduwnaars met kinderen. 's-Gravenhage, 1973. pp. 47. *bibliog.*

— **United Kingdom.**

HAMILL (LYNNE) An explanation of the increase in female one parent families receiving supplementary benefit. London, Department of Health and Social Security, 1978. pp. 21. *(Government Economic Service Working Papers. No. 14)*

U.K. Housing Services Advisory Group. 1978. The housing of one-parent families; [T.L. Jones, chairman]. [London, 1978]. pp. 25.

NIXON (JACQUELINE MARY) Fatherless families on family income supplement: FIS. London, 1979. pp. 241. *(U.K. Department of Health and Social Security. Research Reports. No. 4)*

— — **Ireland, Northern.**

IRELAND, NORTHERN. Inter-departmental Committee on Family Problems. 1977. Family problems: a commentary on the implementation in Northern Ireland of the recommendations of the Finer report on one parent families and of the report of the Select Committee on Violence in Marriage. [Belfast], 1977. fo. 11.

— **United States.**

CASSETTY (JUDITH) Child support and public policy: securing support from absent fathers. Lexington, Mass., [1978]. pp. 171.

SINKING FUNDS
— **United Kingdom.**

U.K. Air Travel Reserve Fund Agency. Report and accounts. a., 1975/76[1st]- London.

SKILLED LABOUR.

La QUALIFICATION du travail: de quoi parle-t-on?; [by Alain d'Iribarne and others]. [Paris, 1978]. pp. 203. *bibliog. (France. Commissariat Général du Plan. Economie et Planification)*

— **Australia.**

SALTER (MOIRA JOAN) Studies in the immigration of the highly skilled. Canberra, 1978. pp. 208. *bibliog. (Academy of the Social Sciences in Australia. Immigrants in Australia. 7)*

— **United Kingdom.**

CROSSICK (GEOFFREY) An artisan elite in Victorian society: Kentish London, 1840- 1880. London, [1978]. pp. 306.

— **United States.**

HIRSCH (SUSAN E.) Roots of the American working class: the industrialization of crafts in Newark, 1800-1860. [Philadelphia, 1978].

SLATER (JAMES DERRICK).

RAW (CHARLES) Slater Walker: an investigation of a financial phenomenon. London, 1977. pp. 368.

SLATER WALKER (FIRM).

RAW (CHARLES) Slater Walker: an investigation of a financial phenomenon. London, 1977. pp. 368.

SLAVE TRADE
— **Africa, West.**

EVERAERT (JOHN G.) De Franse slavenhandel: organisatie, conjunctuur en sociaal milieu van de driehoekshandel, 1763-1793. Brussel, 1978. pp. 461. *bibliog. (Academie voor Wetenschappen, Letteren en Schone Kunsten van België. Verhandelingen. Klasse der Letteren. Jaargang 40. Nr. 87) With summary in French.*

— **Antilles.**

EVERAERT (JOHN G.) De Franse slavenhandel: organisatie, conjunctuur en sociaal milieu van de driehoekshandel, 1763-1793. Brussel, 1978. pp. 461. *bibliog. (Academie voor Wetenschappen, Letteren en Schone Kunsten van België. Verhandelingen. Klasse der Letteren. Jaargang 40. Nr. 87) With summary in French.*

— **France.**

EVERAERT (JOHN G.) De Franse slavenhandel: organisatie, conjunctuur en sociaal milieu van de driehoekshandel, 1763-1793. Brussel, 1978. pp. 461. *bibliog. (Academie voor Wetenschappen, Letteren en Schone Kunsten van België. Verhandelingen. Klasse der Letteren. Jaargang 40. Nr. 87) With summary in French.*

— **Nigeria.**

NORTHUP (DAVID) Trade without rulers: pre-colonial economic development in south- eastern Nigeria. Oxford, 1978. pp. 269. *bibliog.*

— **United Kingdom.**

LEVEEN (E. PHILIP) British slave trade suppression policies, 1821-1865. New York, 1977. pp. 186. *bibliog.*

SLAVERY.

VOGT (JOSEPH) Ancient slavery and the ideal of man; translated by Thomas Wiedemann. Cambridge, Mass., 1975. pp. 227. *bibliog.*

VOPROSY metodologii i istorii istoricheskoi nauki. vyp.2. Moskva, 1978. pp. 206.

SLAVERY IN AFRICA.

SLAVERY in Africa: historical and anthropological perspectives; edited by Suzanne Miers and Igor Kopytoff. Madison, Wis., [1977]. pp. 473. *bibliogs.*

SLAVERY IN BRAZIL.

TAYLOR (KIT SIMS) Sugar and the underdevelopment of northeastern Brazil, 1500-1970. Gainesville, Fla., 1978. pp. 167. *bibliog. (Florida University. Monographs. Social Sciences. No. 63)*

SLAVERY IN INDIA
— **Anti-slavery movements.**

BELL (JOHN HYSLOP) British folks and British India fifty years ago: Joseph Pease and his contemporaries, containing letters by Thomas Clarkson,...and others. London, [1891]. pp. 207.

SLAVERY IN JAMAICA.

CRATON (MICHAEL) Searching for the invisible man: slaves and plantation life in Jamaica. Cambridge, Mass., 1978. pp. 439.

SLAVERY IN LATIN AMERICA.

SHERMAN (WILLIAM L.) Forced native labor in sixteenth-century Central America. Lincoln, Neb., 1979. pp. 496. *bibliog.*

SLAVERY IN THE CARIBBEAN AREA.

MINTZ (SIDNEY WILFRED) and PRICE (RICHARD) Anthropological approach to the Afro-American past: a Caribbean perspective. Philadelphia, [1976]. pp. 64. *bibliog. (Institute for the Study of Human Issues. ISHI Occasional Papers in Social Change. No. 2)*

SLAVERY IN THE UNITED STATES.

BIBB (HENRY) Narrative of the life and adventures of Henry Bibb, an American slave, written by himself. New York, 1850; New York, 1969. pp. 204. *Facsimile reprint.*

STEWARD (AUSTIN) Twenty-two years a slave, and forty years a freeman; embracing correspondence of several years, while president of Wilberforce Colony, London, Canada West. [Rochester, N.Y.], 1856; New York, 1968. pp. 360. *Facsimile reprint.*

[BROWNE (MARTHA)] Autobiography of a female slave. [New York], 1857; New York, 1969. pp. 401. *Facsimile reprint. Probably a fictional account.*

LOGUEN (JERMAIN WESLEY) The Rev. J. W. Loguen, as a slave and as a freeman: a narrative of real life. [Syracuse, N.Y.], 1859; New York, 1968. pp. 444. *Facsimile reprint. Written in the third person, but apparently by Loguen.*

HENRY (HOWELL MEADOES) The police control of the slave in South Carolina: a dissertation submitted to the Faculty of Vanderbilt University, etc. New York, 1968. pp. 216. *bibliog. Reprint of work originally published in Emory, Va., in 1914.*

DEGLER (CARL N.) Place over time: the continuity of Southern distinctiveness. Baton Rouge, [1977]. pp. 138. *(Louisiana State University. Walter Lynwood Fleming Lectures in Southern History. 1976)*

ROARK (JAMES L.) Master without slaves: Southern planters in the Civil War and Reconstruction. New York, [1977]. pp. 273. *bibliog.*

SLAVERY IN THE UNITED STATES.(Cont.)

COOPER (WILLIAM JAMES) The South and the politics of slavery, 1828-1856. Baton Rouge, [1978]. pp. 401. *bibliog.*

RABOTEAU (ALBERT J.) Slave religion: the "invisible institution" in the antebellum South. New York, 1978. pp. 382.

REVISITING Blassingame's The slave community: the scholars respond; edited by Al-Tony Gilmore. Westport, Conn., 1978. pp. 204.

SAVITT (TODD L.) Medicine and slavery: the diseases and health care of blacks in antebellum Virginia. Urbana, 1978. pp. 332.

WRIGHT (GAVIN) The political economy of the cotton South: households, markets, and wealth in the nineteenth century. New York, [1978]. pp. 205. *bibliog.*

AMERICAN negro slavery: a modern reader...; edited by Allen Weinstein [and others]. 3rd ed. New York, 1979. pp. 317. *bibliog.*

HUGGINS (NATHAN IRVIN) Black Odyssey: the ordeal of slavery in America. London, 1979. pp. 250. *bibliog.*

PERDUE (THEDA) Slavery and the evolution of Cherokee society, 1540-1866. Knoxville, 1979. pp. 207. *bibliog.*

VAN DEBURG (WILLIAM L.) The slave drivers: black agricultural labor supervisors in the antebellum South. Westport, 1979. pp. 202.

— **Antislavery movements.**

LOGUEN (JERMAIN WESLEY) The Rev. J. W. Loguen, as a slave and as a freeman: a narrative of real life. [Syracuse, N.Y.], 1859; New York, 1968. pp. 444. *Facsimile reprint. Written in the third person, but apparently by Loguen.*

JOHNSON (SAMUEL A.) The battle cry of freedom: the New England Emigrant Aid Company in the Kansas Crusade. Westport, Conn., 1977. pp. 357. *bibliog. Reprint of work originally published Lawrence, Kan., 1954.*

DILLON (MERTON LYNN) The abolitionists: the growth of a dissenting minority. De Kalb, 1974 repr. 1975. pp. 298. *bibliog.*

MURPHY (LAWRENCE RICHARD) Antislavery in the Southwest: William G. Kephart's mission to New Mexico, 1850-53. El Paso, Tex., [1978]. pp. 55. *(Texas University. Southwestern Studies. Monographs. No. 54)*

WALKER (PETER F.) Moral choices: memory, desire, and imagination in nineteenth- century American abolition. Baton Rouge, [1978]. pp. 387. *bibliog.*

— **Controversial literature.**

CHRISTY (DAVID) Cotton is king: or the culture of cotton and its relation to agriculture, manufactures and commerce. 2nd ed. Clifton, N. J., 1975. pp. 298. *Reprint of work originally published New York, 1856.*

— **Emancipation.**

OUBRE (CLAUDE F.) Forty acres and a mule: the Freedmen's Bureau and black land ownership. Baton Rouge, [1978]. pp. 212. *bibliog.*

— **Insurrections, etc.**

CARROLL (JOSEPH CEPHAS) Slave insurrections in the United States, 1800-1865. New York, [1968]. pp. 229. *bibliogs. Reprint of work originally published in Boston, Mass., 1938.*

— **Law.**

FEHRENBACHER (DON EDWARD) The Dred Scott case: its significance in American law and politics. New York, 1978. pp. 741.

SLAVERY IN THE WEST INDIES.

BUCKLEY (ROGER NORMAN) Slaves in red coats: the British West India regiments, 1795- 1815. New Haven, 1979. pp. 210. *bibliog.*

SLAVS

— **History.**

SLAVIANE v epokhu feodalizma: k stoletiiu akademika V.I. Pichety. Moskva, 1978. pp. 343.

SLOPES (PHYSICAL GEOGRAPHY).

CARSON (MICHAEL ANTHONY) and KIRKBY (M.J.) Hillslope form and process. London, 1972 repr. 1975. pp. 475. *bibliog.*

— **United Kingdom.**

HAIGH (MARTIN J.) Evolution of slopes on artificial landforms: Blaenavon, U.K. Chicago, 1978. pp. 293. *bibliog. (Chicago. University. Department of Geography. Research Papers. No. 183)*

SLOVAK LITERATURE

— **History and criticism.**

KOVIJANIĆ (RISTO) Štúdie z dejín juhoslovansko-slovenských vztahov; [translated from the Serbo-Croat by Ján Siracký]. Martin, [1976]. pp. 141.

SLOVAKIA

— **History.**

VNUK (FRANTIŠEK) This is Dr. Jozef Tiso, President of the Slovak Republic. 3rd ed. Cambridge, Ont., 1977. pp. 83.

— **Intellectual life.**

KOVIJANIĆ (RISTO) Štúdie z dejín juhoslovansko-slovenských vztahov; [translated from the Serbo-Croat by Ján Siracký]. Martin, [1976]. pp. 141.

— **Nationalism.**

CHURKINA (ISKRA VASIL'EVNA) Slovenskoe natsional'no-osvoboditel'noe dvizhenie v XIX v. i Rossiia. Moskva, 1978. pp. 392.

— **Relations (general) with Russia.**

CHURKINA (ISKRA VASIL'EVNA) Slovenskoe natsional'no-osvoboditel'noe dvizhenie v XIX v. i Rossiia. Moskva, 1978. pp. 392.

— **Relations (general) with Yugoslavia.**

KOVIJANIĆ (RISTO) Štúdie z dejín juhoslovansko-slovenských vztahov; [translated from the Serbo-Croat by Ján Siracký]. Martin, [1976]. pp. 141.

SLOW LEARNING CHILDREN.

BALDWIN (VICTOR L.) and others. Isn't it time he outgrew this?; or, A training program for parents of retarded children. Springfield, Ill., 1973 repr. 1976. pp. 209.

SLUMS

— **Denmark — Frederiksberg.**

PLOVSING (JAN) Boligforbedringer og beboerønsker: sanering af en karré på Frederiksberg. København, 1977. pp. 94. *bibliog. (Socialforskningsinstituttet. Meddelelser. 22)*

— **Underdeveloped areas.**

See UNDERDEVELOPED AREAS — Slums.

— **United Kingdom — Manchester.**

WARD (ROBIN W.) Where race didn't divide: some reflections on slum clearance in Moss Side. [Bristol, Social Science Research Council Research Unit on Ethnic Relations, 1976]. fo. 19.

— — **Newcastle-upon-Tyne.**

BENWELL COMMUNITY DEVELOPMENT PROJECT. Slums on the drawing board. Newcastle-upon-Tyne, 1978. pp. 47. *(Final Report Series. No. 4)*

SMALL BUSINESS

— **Australia.**

JOHNS (BRIAN LESLIE) and others. Small business in Australia: problems and prospects. Sydney, 1978. pp. 204. *bibliogs.*

— **Europe — Finance.**

UNION DES INDUSTRIES DE LA COMMUNAUTÉ EUROPÉENNE. Committee for the Study of the Problems of Small and Medium-Sized Industrial Enterprises. Working Group on Financing. Small and medium-sized enterprises: a report, conclusions and recommendations in respect of their financing;...rapporteur [of the group], J. Turner. n.p., 1978. pp. 247.

— **India — Finance.**

SEMINAR ON FINANCING OF SMALL-SCALE INDUSTRIES IN INDIA, HYDERABAD, 1959. Report of proceedings ([and] background papers). Bombay, [1960?]. 2 vols.

— — **Bengal, West.**

WEST BENGAL. Bureau of Applied Economics and Statistics. 1974. Economic survey of small industries, 1965 and 1966, West Bengal. No. 2. Report on food manufacturing industries. [Calcutta], 1974. pp. 127.

— — **Meghalaya.**

MEGHALAYA. Directorate of Economics and Statistics. 1976. Report on detailed survey of small scale industrial units in the urban areas of Meghalaya, 1972-73. Shillong, [1976]. pp. 57.

— **Malaysia — Finance.**

LIM (CHEE PENG) Financing the development of small industry in Malaysia. Kuala Lumpur, 1977. pp. 57. *(University of Malaya. Faculty of Economics and Administration. Occasional Papers on Malaysian Socio-Economic Affairs. No. 6)*

— **Sweden.**

JÖNSSON (BENGT) and WADENSJÖ (ESKIL) Industriell miljö i Halland: (en undersökning om de mindre och medelstora företagens problem och utvecklingsbetingelser). [Falkenberg, imprint, 1972]. pp. 176. *bibliog.*

— **Turkey.**

VELZEN (LEO VAN) Peripheral production in Kayseri, Turkey; translating...of English text by Donald Bloch. Ankara, 1977. pp. 194.

— **United Kingdom.**

SMALL FIRMS IN INNER CITIES CONFERENCE, HOLME PIERREPONT, NOTTINGHAM, 1977. Conference report. [Nottingham, 1978]. pp. 27.

SMALL GROUPS.

DYNAMICS of group decisions; edited by Hermann Brandstätter and others. Beverly Hills, [1978]. pp. 276. *bibliogs.*

The SMALL group in political science: the last two decades of development; edited by Robert T. Golembiewski. Athens, [1978]. pp. 519. *bibliogs.*

SMALL HOLDINGS

— **Malawi.**

MALAWI. Agro-Economic Survey. 1972. Agro-economic survey: 9th report: Lake Chilwa: a sample farm management survey among rice and maize growers at the northern end of Lake Chilwa in Kasupe district, Malawi; prepared by T.W. Bieze. Zomba, 1972. fo. 63.

MALAWI. Agro-Economic Survey. 1972. Agro-economic survey: 10th report: Malimba groundnut growers in Nsanje south: a survey among Malimba, Gambia, groundnut growers in the southern part of Nsanje district, Malawi; prepared by T.W. Bieze. Zomba, 1972. fo. 14.

MALAWI. Agro-Economic Survey. 1973. Agro-economic survey: 11th report: Mbawa: a sample farm management survey among oriental tobacco, maize and groundnut growers in the Mbawa area in the southern part of Mzimba district, Malawi, with special reference to oriental tobacco; prepared by T.W. Bieze. Lilongwe, 1973. fo. 87. *bibliog.*

MALAWI. Agro-Economic Survey. 1978. Agro-economic survey: report no. 24: Thiwi-Lifidzi: a farm management survey of smallholder rural farmers in the Thiwi- Lifidzi area of Dedza district, Malawi. Lilongwe, 1978. fo. 97.

SMITH (ADAM).

WINCH (DONALD NORMAN) Adam Smith's politics: an essay in historiographic revision. Cambridge, 1978. pp. 206. *bibliog.*

ADAM Smith and modern political economy: bicentennial essays on The wealth of nations; edited by Gerald P. O'Driscoll. Ames, Iowa, 1979. pp. 181. *(California University. Harry Girvetz Memorial Lectures. 1976)*

SMITH (IAN DOUGLAS).

BERLYN (PHILLIPPA) The quiet man: a biography of the Hon. Ian Douglas Smith, I.D., Prime Minister of Rhodesia. Salisbury, Rhodesia, 1978. pp. 256.

SMITH (JOSEPH).

HILL (DONNA) Joseph Smith: the first Mormon. Garden City, 1977. pp. 527. *bibliog.*

SMOKE PREVENTION.

OBERMEYER (HENRY) Stop that smoke. New York, 1933. pp. 289. *bibliog.*

SMOKING.

WORLD HEALTH ORGANIZATION. 1976. Legislative action to combat smoking around the world: a survey of existing legislation. Geneva, 1976. pp. 27. *bibliog. Originally published in International Digest of Health Legislation, v. 27, 1976.*

REPORT on a second retrospective mortality study in North-East England;...[by] G. Dean [and others]. London, 1977-78. 2 pts. (in 1 vol.). *bibliogs. (Tobacco Research Council. Research Papers. 14) Report of the first study published as Research Paper 8.*

— South Africa.

VAN DER BURGH (CHRIS) Smoking and drinking patterns of whites: 1975. Pretoria, 1978. pp. 42. *bibliog. (Human Sciences Research Council [South Africa]. Institute for Sociological, Demographic and Criminological Research. Reports. No. S-51)*

SNOW HILL NORMAL AND INDUSTRIAL INSTITUTE, SNOW HILL, ALABAMA.

EDWARDS (WILLIAM JAMES) Twenty-five years in the black belt. Boston, Mass., 1918; Westport, Conn., 1970. pp. 143. *Facsimile reprint.*

SOBHUZA II, king of Swaziland.

KUPER (HILDA) Sobhuza II, ngwenyama and king of Swaziland: the story of an hereditary ruler and his country. London, 1978. pp. 363. *bibliog.*

SOCCER

— United Kingdom — Scotland.

SCOTLAND. Working Group on Football Crowd Behaviour. 1977. Report; [Frank McElhone, chairman]. Edinburgh, 1977. pp. 41.

SOCIAL ACTION.

JELFS (MARTIN) Manual for action: (techniques to enable groups engaged in action for change to increase their effectiveness). London, [1977]. 1 vol. (various pagings). *bibliog. Prepared for Action Resources Group.*

GOLDENBERG (I. IRA) Oppression and social intervention: essays on the human condition and the problems of change. Chicago, [1978]. pp. 213. *bibliog.*

SOCIAL ADJUSTMENT.

TROWER (PETER) and others. Social skills and mental health. London, 1978. pp. 306. *bibliogs.*

SOCIAL BEHAVIOUR IN ANIMALS.

TINBERGEN (NICHOLAS) The animal in its world: explorations of an ethologist, 1932-1972. London, 1972-73. 2 vols. *bibliogs.*

RUSE (MICHAEL) Sociobiology: sense or nonsense? Dordrecht, 1979. pp. 231. *bibliog.*

SOCIAL CASE WORK.

FRIEND (JEANNETTE G.) and HAGGARD (ERNEST ALEXANDER) Work adjustment in relation to family background: a conceptual basis for counseling; a report of an investigation sponsored by the Family Society of Greater Boston. Stanford, 1948. pp. 150. *bibliog. (American Psychological Association. Applied Psychology Monographs. No. 16)*

REES (STUART) Social work face to face: clients' and social workers' perceptions of the content and outcomes of their meetings. London, 1978. pp. 154. *bibliog.*

REID (WILLIAM J.) The task-centered system. New York, 1978. pp. 354. *bibliog.*

WILSON (SUANNA J.) Confidentiality in social work: issues and principles. New York, [1978]. pp. 274. *bibliog.*

SOCIAL CASE WORK REPORTING.

HALLETT (CHRISTINE) and STEVENSON (OLIVE) Case conferences: a study of interprofessional communication concerning children at risk. Keele, 1977 repr. 1978. pp. 71.

SOCIAL CASE WORK WITH CHILDREN.

HALLETT (CHRISTINE) and STEVENSON (OLIVE) Case conferences: a study of interprofessional communication concerning children at risk. Keele, 1977 repr. 1978. pp. 71.

U.K. Social Work Service. 1978. Report...into certain aspects of the management of the case of Stephen Menheniott. London, 1978. pp. 48.

SOCIAL CHANGE.

The FAMILY and change; edited by John N. Edwards. New York, [1969]. pp. 492. *bibliog.*

ACKOFF (RUSSELL LINCOLN) Redesigning the future: a systems approach to societal problems. New York, [1974]. pp. 260.

TERLECKYJ (NESTOR E.) Improvements in the quality of life: estimates of possibilities in the United States, 1974-1983. Washington, D.C., 1975. pp. 285.

CANT (D. H.) Squatting and private property rights: an analysis of the effects of squatting seen in the context of a theory about how increased activity by the state affects the way change comes about in our society. London, 1976 repr. 1978. pp. 71. *bibliog. (London. University. University College. Bartlett School of Architecture and Planning. Town Planning Discussion Papers. No. 24)*

BENDIX (REINHARD) Nation-building and citizenship: studies of our social changing order. Berkeley, 1977. pp. 449.

RESEARCH SEMINAR IN ARCHAEOLOGY AND RELATED SUBJECTS. Meeting, London, [1976?]. The evolution of social systems; (proceedings of a meeting of the...seminar); edited by J. Friedman and M.J. Rowlands. London, 1977. pp. 562.

SOCIETY and change: essays in honour of Sachin Chaudhuri; edited by K.S. Krishnaswamy [and others]. Bombay, 1977. pp. 327.

WILLIAMS (ROBIN MURPHY) Mutual accommodation: ethnic conflict and cooperation. Minneapolis, [1977]. pp. 458. *bibliog.*

SOCIAL CHOICE.

WILSON (MARY MONICA) For men and elders: change in the relations of generations and of men and women among the Nyakyusa-Ngonde people, 1875-1971. London, [1977]. pp. 209. *bibliog. 5 appendices in end pocket.*

AMERICAN ACADEMY OF POLITICAL AND SOCIAL SCIENCE. Annals. vol. 437. Medical ethics and social change; special editor of this volume Bernard Barber. Philadelphia, 1978. pp. 201.

BENDER (THOMAS) Community and social change in America. New Brunswick, [1978]. pp. 159.

GRØNBJERG (KIRSTEN A.) and others. Poverty and social change. Chicago, [1978]. pp. 248. *bibliog.*

HANDLER (JOEL F.) Social movements and the legal system: a theory of law reform and social change. New York, [1978]. pp. 252. *(Wisconsin University, Madison. Institute for Research on Poverty. Monograph Series).*

LASZLO (ERVIN) The inner limits of mankind: heretical reflections on today's values, culture, and politics. Oxford, 1978. pp. 78.

MEAD (MARGARET) Culture and commitment: the new relationships between the generations in the 1970s. [rev. ed.] New York, 1978. pp. 178. *bibliog.*

MIEMOIS (KARL JOHAN) Changes in the social structure of the Swedish-speaking population of Finland, 1950-1970. Helsinki, 1978. pp. 37. *bibliog. (Helsinki. Yliopisto. Research Group for Comparative Sociology. Research Reports. No. 19)*

PARKIN (DAVID J.) The cultural definition of political response: lineal destiny among the Luo. London, 1978. pp. 347. *bibliog.*

SOCIAL change in Romania, 1860-1940: a debate on development in a European nation; Kenneth Jowitt, editor. Berkeley, Calif., [1978]. pp. 207. *(California University. Institute of International Studies. Research Series. No.36) Based on a conference held by the Institute.*

SOCIAL structure and change: Finland and Poland: comparative perspective; edited by Erik Allardt and Włodzimierz Wesołowski. Warszawa, 1978. pp. 392.

STRATEGIES against violence: design for non-violent change; edited by Israel W. Charny. Boulder, Colo., 1978. pp. 417. *bibliogs.*

TEUNE (HENRY) and MLINAR (ZDRAVKO) The developmental logic of social systems. Beverly Hills, [1978]. pp. 175.

VODANOVICH (IVANICA MARY) The structure of roles and their ritual in a Yugoslav community. 1978. fo. 313. *bibliog. Typescript. Ph.D. (London) thesis: unpublished. This thesis is the property of London University and may not be removed from the Library.*

BELL (DANIEL) The cultural contradictions of capitalism. 2nd ed. London, 1979. pp. 301.

HOLZNER (BURKART) and MARX (JOHN H.) Knowledge application: the knowledge system in society. Boston, Mass., [1979]. pp. 388. *bibliog.*

MARSDEN (LORNA R.) and HARVEY (EDWARD B.) Fragile federation: social change in Canada. Toronto, [1979]. pp. 242. *bibliog.*

PEETERS (PETER) Can we avoid a third world war around 2010?: the political, social and economic past and future of humanity. London, 1979. pp. 266.

ROSZAK (THEODORE) Person/planet: the creative disintegration of industrial society. London, 1979. pp. 347. *bibliog.*

SOCIAL CHOICE.

DECISION theory and social ethics: issues in social choice; edited by Hans W. Gottinger and Werner Leinfellner. Dordrecht, [1978]. pp. 329. *bibliogs.*

MIZUTANI (SHIGEAKI) Collective choice and extended orderings. 1978. fo. 104. *bibliog. Typescript. M.Phil. (London) thesis: unpublished. This thesis is the property of London University and may not be removed from the Library.*

SOCIAL CHOICE.(Cont.)

PATTANAIK (PRASANTA KUMAR) Strategy and group choice. Amsterdam, 1978. pp. 213. *bibliog.*

SCHELLING (THOMAS CROMBIE) Micromotives and macrobehavior. New York, [1978]. pp. 252. (*Pennsylvania University. Fels Center of Government. Fels Lectures on Public Policy Analysis*)

SOCIAL CLASSES.

GIDDENS (ANTHONY) The class structure of the advanced societies. London, 1973. pp. 336. *bibliog.*

Les DOMINATIONS socio-politiques dans le monde, [by] Michel Rocard [and others]. Paris, [1975]. pp. 147. *bibliog.* (*Institut Oecuménique pour le Développement des Peuples. Cahiers. 2*)

MICHELAT (GUY) and SIMON (MICHEL) Classe, religion et comportement politique. Paris, [1977]. pp. 498.

BENSON (LESLIE) Proletarians and parties: five essays in social class. London, 1978. pp. 194. *bibliog.*

DRAYER (EDWARD HARRY) Problems in the analysis of social prestige, with special reference to aristocracy at six formative periods. 1978. fo. 407. *bibliog.* Typescript. Ph.D. (London) thesis: unpublished. This thesis is the property of London University and may not be removed from the Library.

SOCIALE stratificatie: op weg naar empirisch-theoretisch stratificatieonderzoek in Nederland; onder redactie van Jules L. Peschar en Wout C. Ultee. Deventer, [1978]. pp. 170. *bibliog.* (*Mens en Maatschappij. Boekafleveringen. 1978*)

COXON (ANTHONY PETER MACMILLAN) and JONES (CHARLES L.) Class and hierarchy: the social meaning of occupations. London, 1979. pp. 217. *bibliog.*

PARKIN (FRANK IORWETH) Marxism and class theory: a bourgeois critique. London, 1979. pp. 217. *bibliog.*

WALLERSTEIN (IMMANUEL) The capitalist world-economy. Cambridge, 1979. pp. 305. *bibliogs.*

WESOŁOWSKI (WŁODZIMIERZ) Classes, strata and power; translated and with an introduction by George Kolankiewicz. London, 1979. pp. 159. *bibliog.*

— Africa.

AKE (CLAUDE) Revolutionary pressures in Africa. London, 1978. pp. 109.

— Europe.

BLUM (JEROME) The end of the old order in rural Europe. Princeton, 1978. pp. 505. *bibliog.*

— Finland.

SOCIAL structure and change: Finland and Poland: comparative perspective; edited by Erik Allardt and Włodzimierz Wesołowski. Warszawa, 1978. pp. 392.

— Iceland.

BJÖRNSSON (SIGURJÓN) and EDELSTEIN (WOLFGANG) Explorations in social inequality: stratification dynamics in social and individual development in Iceland. Berlin, 1977. pp. 172. *bibliog.* (*Max-Planck-Institut für Bildungsforschung. Studien und Berichte. 38*)

— Iraq.

BATATU (HANNA) The old social classes and the revolutionary movements of Iraq: a study of Iraq's old landed and commercial classes and of its communists, Ba'thists, and Free Officers. Princeton, [1978]. pp. 1283. *bibliog.*

— Jamaica.

BROWN (AGGREY) Color, class, and politics in Jamaica. New Brunswick, N.J., [1979]. pp. 172. *bibliog.*

— Mexico.

VELLINGA (MENNO) Economic development and the dynamics of class: industrialization, power and control in Monterrey, Mexico. Van Gorcum, 1979. pp. 213. *bibliog.*

— Peru.

CARAVEDO MOLINARI (BALTAZAR) Clases, lucha politica y gobierno en el Peru (1919-1933). Lima, 1977. pp. 124.

— Poland.

SOCIAL structure and change: Finland and Poland: comparative perspective; edited by Erik Allardt and Włodzimierz Wesołowski. Warszawa, 1978. pp. 392.

— Russia.

The FAMILY in imperial Russia: new lines of historical research; [papers presented at a symposium held at the University of Illinois, Urbana-Champaign, Oct. 1976]; edited by David L. Ransel. Urbana, 1978. pp. 342. *bibliog.*

— — Soviet Central Asia.

DAVLIATKADAMOV (KHUSHKADAM DAVLIATKADAMOVICH) Sotsial'no-klassovye osnovy sblizheniia sotsialisticheskikh natsii. Dushanbe, 1976. pp. 172.

— Spain.

NUÑEZ ASTRAIN (LUIS C.) Clases sociales en Euskadi. San Sebastian, [1977]. pp. 217.

— United Kingdom.

The AFFLUENT worker in the class structure; [by] John Goldthorpe [and others]. London, 1969. pp. 239. *bibliog.*

BAUER (PETER TAMAS) Class on the brain: the cost of a British obsession. London, 1978. pp. 15.

NAVARRO (VICENTE) Class struggle, the state and medicine: an historical and contemporary analysis of the medical sector in Great Britain. London, 1978. pp. 156. *bibliog.*

SKRIMSHIRE (ANGELA) Area disadvantage, social class and the health service: a pilot study of variation between areas in reported sickness and in the experience of receiving general practice care. Oxford, 1978. pp. 69. *bibliog.*

MORRIS (ROBERT JOHN) Class and class consciousness in the Industrial Revolution 1780-1850. Edinburgh, 1979. pp. 79. *bibliog.* (*Economic History Society. Studies in Economic and Social History*)

REX (JOHN ARDERNE) and TOMLINSON (SALLY) Colonial immigrants in a British city: a class analysis. London, 1979. pp. 357. *bibliog.*

— — Scotland.

DAVIS (HOWARD H.) Beyond class images: explorations in the structure of social consciousness. London, [1979]. pp. 213. *bibliog.*

— United States.

MIDWEST MARXIST SCHOLARS CONFERENCE, 2ND, UNIVERSITY OF MINNESOTA, 1977. Social class in the contemporary United States; Gerald Erickson and Harold L. Schwartz, editors. Minneapolis, [1977]. pp. 101.

BEEGHLEY (LEONARD) Social stratification in America: a critical analysis of theory and research. Santa Monica, Calif., [1978]. pp. 381. *bibliog.*

COLEMAN (RICHARD P.) and others. Social standing in America: new dimensions of class. New York, 1978. pp. 353. *bibliog.*

GESCHWENDER (JAMES A.) Racial stratification in America. Dubuque, Iwa, [1978]. pp. 282. *bibliogs.*

— — Alabama.

WIENER (JONATHAN M.) Social origins of the new South: Alabama, 1860-1885. Baton Rouge, [1978]. pp. 247.

— Yemen.

GERHOLM (TOMAS) Market, mosque and mafraj: social inequality in a Yemeni town. [Stockholm, 1977]. pp. 217. *bibliog.* (*Stockholms Universitet. Socialantropologiska Institutionen. Stockholm Studies in Social Anthropology. 4*)

SOCIAL CONDITIONS.

ROBERTS (KENNETH) Contemporary society and the growth of leisure. London, 1978. pp. 191. *bibliog.*

— Statistics.

WORLD STATISTICS IN BRIEF; [pd. by] Statistical Office [United Nations]. a., 1977(2nd)- New York.

SOCIAL CONFLICT.

BURTON (JOHN W.) Conflict as a function of change. London, [1966]. pp. 31. *bibliog.* Reprinted from Ciba Foundation Symposium on conflict in society, 1966.

ECKHARDT (WILLIAM) and YOUNG (CHRISTOPHER) Governments under fire: civil conflict and imperialism. New Haven, Conn., [1977]. pp. 379. *bibliog.*

FOURQUIN (GUY) The anatomy of popular rebellion in the Middle Ages...; translated by Anne Chesters. Amsterdam, 1978. pp. 181. *bibliog.*

SIMAI (MIHÁLY) Developing countries and international class conflicts. Budapest, 1979. pp. 57. (*Magyar Tudományos Akadémia. Afro-Azsiai Kutató Központ. Studies on Developing Countries. No. 79*)

— Italy.

ROSSI (MARIO G.) Le origini del partito cattolico: movimento cattolico e lotta di classe nell'Italia liberale. Roma, 1977. pp. 466.

— Kenya.

LEITNER (KERSTIN) Workers, trade unions and peripheral capitalism in Kenya after independence. Frankfurt am Main, [1977]. pp. 182. *bibliog.*

— Russia.

BETTELHEIM (CHARLES) Class struggles in the USSR: second period, 1923-1930; translated by Brian Pearce. Hassocks, 1978. pp. 640. *bibliog.*

— United States.

COBB (ROGER W.) and ELDER (CHARLES D.) Participation in American politics: the dynamics of agenda-building. Baltimore, 1977. pp. 182. *bibliog.*

SOCIAL CONTROL.

The TECHNOLOGY of political control; by Carol Ackroyd [and others]. Harmondsworth, 1977. pp. 320.

GOODE (WILLIAM J.) The celebration of heroes: prestige as a social control system. Berkeley, [1978]. pp. 407.

WIENER (A.) Magnificent myth: patterns of control in post-industrial society. Oxford, [1978]. pp. 413. *bibliogs.*

CHOROVER (STEPHAN L.) From genesis to genocide: the meaning of human nature and the power of behavior control. Cambridge, Mass., [1979]. pp. 238.

DITTON (JASON) Contrology: beyond the new criminology. London, 1979. pp. 124. *bibliog.*

SOCIAL DARWINISM.

WILSON (EDWARD OSBORNE) On human nature. Cambridge, Mass., 1978. pp. 260.

SOCIAL DEMOCRATIC PARTY (GERMANY).

VAHLTEICH (JULIUS) Ferdinand Lassalle und die Anfänge der deutschen Arbeiterbewegung;...Einleitung zum Nachdruck von Toni Offermann. Berlin, [1978]. pp. 86,xi. *Reprint of work originally published in Munich in 1904.*

KRUEGER (HANS) Stadtrat, and BAADE (FRITZ) Sozialdemokratische Agrarpolitik: Erläuterungen zum sozialdemokratischen Agrarprogramm. Berlin, [1927]. pp. 99.

KERN (ERICH) pseud. [i.e. Erich Knud KERNMAYR] SPD ohne Maske: eine politische Dokumentation. new ed. Rosenheim, 1976. pp. 96.

HUSTER (ERNST ULRICH) Die Politik der SPD, 1945-1950. Frankfurt/Main, [1978]. pp. 232. *bibliog.*

MEYENBERG (RUEDIGER) SPD in der Provinz: empirische Untersuchung...von SPD- Mitgliedern am Beispiel des Unterbezirks Oldenburg, Oldb. Frankfurt, [1978]. pp. 282. *bibliog.*

MILITARISMUS und Opportunismus gegen die Novemberrevolution; ([edited by] Lothar Berthold [and] Helmut Neef). 2nd ed. Frankfurt am Main, 1978. pp. 468.

ROVAN (JOSEPH) Histoire de la social-démocratie allemande. Paris, [1978]. pp. 527. *bibliog.*

WENDORFF (WERNER) Schule und Bildung in der Politik von Wilhelm Liebknecht: ein Beitrag zur Geschichte der deutschen Arbeiterbewegung im 19. Jahrhundert. Berlin, [1978]. pp. 334. *bibliog.*

STEININGER (ROLF) Deutschland und die Sozialistische Internationale nach dem Zweiten Weltkrieg: die deutsche Frage, die Internationale und das Problem der Wiederaufnahme der SPD...: Darstellung und Dokumentation. Bonn, [1979]. pp. 433. *bibliog. (Archiv für Sozialgeschichte. Beihefte. 7)*

— **History.**

BRAUNTHAL (GERARD) Socialist labor and politics in Weimar Germany: the General Federation of German Trade Unions. Hamden, Conn., 1978. pp. 253. *bibliog.*

ELSAESSER (KONRAD) Die badische Sozialdemokratie, 1890 bis 1914: zum Zusammenhang von Bildung und Organisation. Marburg, [1978]. pp. 323. *bibliog. (Studiengesellschaft für Sozialgeschichte und Arbeiterbewegung, Marburg. Schriftenreihe für Sozialgeschichte und Arbeiterbewegung. Band 14)*

FISCH (GERHARD) and KRAUSE (FRITZ) Writer on politics. SPD und KPD, 1945/46: Einheitsbestrebungen der Arbeiterparteien, dargestellt an Beispielen aus Südhessen. Frankfurt am Main, 1978. pp. 169. *bibliog.*

MILLER (SUSANNE) Die Bürde der Macht: die deutsche Sozialdemokratie, 1918- 1920. Düsseldorf, [1978]. pp. 532. *bibliog. (Germany (Bundesrepublik). Kommission für Geschichte des Parlamentarismus und der Politischen Parteien. Beiträge zur Geschichte des Parlamentarismus und der Politischen Parteien. Band 63)*

OTT (ERICH) Die Wirtschaftskonzeption der SPD nach 1945. Marburg, [1978]. pp. 298. *bibliog. (Studiengesellschaft für Sozialgeschichte und Arbeiterbewegung, Marburg. Schriftenreihe für Sozialgeschichte und Arbeiterbewegung. Band 12)*

BELLERS (JUERGEN) Reformpolitik und EWG-Strategie der SPD: die innen- und aussenpolitischen Faktoren der europapolitischen Integrationswilligkeit einer Oppositionspartei, 1957-63. München, [1979]. pp. 570. *bibliog.*

HIRSCHFELDER (HEINRICH) Die bayerische Sozialdemokratie, 1864-1914. Erlangen, 1979. 2 vols.(in 1). *bibliog.*

METTIG (VOLKER) Russische Presse und Sozialistengesetz: die deutsche Sozialdemokratie und die Entstehung des Sozialistengesetzes aus russischer Sicht, 1869-1878. Bonn, [1979]. pp. 476. *bibliog. (Friedrich-Ebert-Stiftung. Forschungsinstitut. Reihe: Politik- und Gesellschaftsgeschichte. Band 4)*

SOCIAL DEMOCRATIC PARTY (RUSSIA).

TROTSKII (LEV DAVYDOVICH) Nos tâches politiques. Paris, 1970. pp. 256.

KLIUEVA (ANNA DANILOVNA) Partiia bol'shevikov v pervoi russkoi revoliutsii 1905-1907 gg. Moskva, 1977. pp. 255.

VOENNO-revoliutsionnye komitety deistvuiushchei armii, 25 oktiabria 1917 g. - mart 1918 g. Moskva, 1977. pp. 659.

BATALOV (ALEKSANDR NIKOLAEVICH) Bor'ba bol'shevikov za armiiu v Sibiri, 1916 - fevral' 1918. Novosibirsk, 1978. pp. 285.

— **History.**

GOLUB (PAVEL AKIMOVICH) Bol'sheviki i armiia v trekh revoliutsiiakh. Moskva, 1977. pp. 320.

ARTEM'EV (SERGEI ARTEM'EVICH) Partiia bol'shevikov i Sovety rabochikh i soldatskikh deputatov v 1917 g., iiul'-oktiabr'. Moskva, 1978. pp. 214.

SANBUROV (VASILII IVANOVICH) Moskovskii "Rabochii soiuz": u istokov proletarskoi bor'by. Moskva, 1978. pp. 133.

— **Periodicals.**

SOLDATENKO (VALERII FEDOROVICH) Tribuna proletarskogo internatsionalizma. Kiev, 1977. pp. 183.

SOCIAL ETHICS.

DAVISON (IAN) b. 1939. Values, ends, and society. St. Lucia, [1977]. pp. 257. *bibliog.*

DECISION theory and social ethics: issues in social choice; edited by Hans W. Gottinger and Werner Leinfellner. Dordrecht, [1978]. pp. 329. *bibliogs.*

ETHICS, free enterprise, and public policy: original essays on moral issues in business; edited by Richard T. de George and Joseph A. Pichler. New York, 1978. pp. 329. *bibliogs.*

SOCIAL EVOLUTION.

BOULDING (KENNETH EWART) Ecodynamics: a new theory of societal evolution. Beverly Hills, [1978]. pp. 367. *bibliog.*

DARLINGTON (CYRIL DEAN) The little universe of man. London, 1978. pp. 307. *bibliog.*

EXTINCTION and survival in human populations; edited by Charles D. Laughlin, Jr., and Ivan A. Brady. New York, 1978. pp. 327. *bibliog.*

SOCIAL GROUP WORK.

NEW YORK (CITY). Youth Board. Youth Board Monographs. No. 4. Reaching the group: an analysis of group work methods used with teenagers. New York, 1956. pp. 75.

LEVINE (BARUCH) Fundamentals of group treatment. Northbrook, Ill., [1967]. pp. 94. *bibliog.*

DOUGLAS (TOM) Basic groupwork. London, 1978. pp. 196. *bibliog.*

REID (WILLIAM J.) The task-centered system. New York, 1978. pp. 354. *bibliog.*

SOCIAL GROUPS.

DIFFERENTIATION between social groups: studies in the social psychology of intergroup relations; edited by Henri Tajfel. London, 1978. pp. 474. *bibliog. (European Association of Experimental Social Psychology. European Monographs in Social Psychology. 14)*

SHIBUTANI (TAMOTSU) The derelicts of company K: a sociological study of demoralization. Berkeley, Calif., [1978]. pp. 455. *bibliog.*

SOCIAL HISTORY.

The FAMILY in history; edited by Charles E. Rosenberg. [Philadelphia, 1975 repr. 1978]. pp. 207.

LEON (PIERRE) Histoire économique et sociale du monde. Paris, [1977-78]. 6 vols. *bibliog.*

MAJOR social issues: a multidisciplinary view; edited by J. Milton Yinger and Stephen J. Cutler. New York, [1978]. pp. 575. *bibliog.*

COLEBROOK (JOAN) Innocents of the west: travels through the sixties. New York, [1979]. pp. 454.

— **Methodology.**

STINCHCOMBE (ARTHUR LEONARD) Theoretical methods in social history. New York, [1978]. pp. 130. *bibliog.*

SOCIAL INDICATORS.

NAAR sociale indicatoren op het terrein van de volksgezondheid; [by] J.H.W. van den Berg and others]. Rijswijk, 1976. fo.44. *bibliog. (Netherlands. Sociaal en Cultureel Planbureau. SCP-Cahiers. No.7)*

UNITED NATIONS. Statistical Office. Statistical Papers. Series M. No.63. Social indicators: preliminary guidelines and illustrative series. (ST/ESA/STAT/SER.M/63). New York, 1978. pp. 134.

LUSTGRAAF (R.E. VAN DE) and HUIGSLOOT (P.C.M.) Sociale indicatoren, een bewuste keuze? Rijswijk, 1979. fo. 114. *bibliog. (Netherlands. Sociaal en Cultureel Planbureau. SCP-Cahiers. No. 16) With English summary.*

— **Australia.**

SOCIAL indicators in Australia: health and housing. [Canberra, 1977?]. 2 vols. *bibliogs. Papers presented at a conference at the Research School of Social Sciences, Australian National University, Canberra, 1977.*

— **Fiji Islands.**

SOCIAL INDICATORS FOR FIJI; [pd. by] Bureau of Statistics, Fiji. a., N1972(no.1)- Suva.

— **France — Picardy.**

OBSERVATOIRE ECONOMIQUE DE PICARDIE. Indicateurs économiques et sociaux. a., 1978- Amiens.

— **United Kingdom.**

HAKIM (C.) Census-based area profiles: a review. [London], 1977. pp. 14. *bibliog. (U.K. Office of Population Censuses and Surveys. Occasional Papers. 2)*

HAKIM (C.) Social and community indicators from the census. [London], 1978. pp. 80. *bibliog. (U.K. Office of Population Censuses and Surveys. Occasional Papers. 5)*

LONDON. University. London School of Economics and Political Science. Graduate School of Geography. Discussion Papers. No. 69. Measures of spatial opportunity: the use of urban images in constructing subjective indicators of spatial opportunity; [by] Lefteris Tsoulouvis. London, 1978. pp. 58. *bibliog.*

WEBBER (RICHARD J.) Parliamentary constituencies: a socio-economic classification. [London], 1978. pp. 58. *(U.K. Office of Population Censuses and Surveys. Occasional Papers. 13)*

SOCIAL INSTITUTIONS.

COMMONS (JOHN ROGERS) A sociological view of sovereignty: [articles from the American Journal of Sociology, 1899-1900); with an introductory essay, John R. Commons' general theory of institutions, by Joseph Dorfman. New York, 1965 repr. 1967. pp. 109. *bibliog.*

DURKHEIM (EMILE) On institutional analysis; edited, translated and with an introduction by Mark Traugott. Chicago, [1978]. pp. 276. *bibliog.*

— **United States.**

GOLDENBERG (I. IRA) Oppression and social intervention: essays on the human condition and the problems of change. Chicago, [1978]. pp. 213. *bibliog.*

JANOWITZ (MORRIS) The last half-century: societal change and politics in America. Chicago, [1978]. pp. 583.

SOCIAL INTERACTION.

BERNE (ERIC LENNARD) Games people play: the psychology of human relationships. Harmondsworth, 1968. pp. 173.

SOCIAL INTERACTION.(Cont.)

BLUMER (HERBERT) Symbolic interactionism: perspective and method. Englewood Cliffs, N.J., [1969]. pp. 208.

GUBRIUM (JABER F.) and BUCKHOLDT (DAVID R.) Toward maturity: the social processing of human development. San Francisco, 1977. pp. 224. *bibliog.*

ARGYLE (MICHAEL) The psychology of interpersonal behaviour. 3rd ed. Harmondsworth, 1978. pp. 322. *bibliog.*

GRAHAM (JEAN ANN) Aspects of gaze, facial expression and gesture in dyadic interactions. 1978. fo. 433. *bibliog.* Typescript. Ph.D. (London) thesis: unpublished. This thesis is the property of London University and may not be removed from the Library.

MANGHAM (IAIN LESLIE) Interactions and interventions in organizations. Chichester, [1978]. pp. 150. *bibliog.*

WALSTER (ELAINE) and others. Equity: theory and research. Boston, Mass., [1978]. pp. 312. *bibliog.*

ROCK (PAUL ELLIOT) The making of symbolic interactionism. London, 1979. pp. 268. *bibliog.*

SOCIAL JUSTICE.

WALSTER (ELAINE) and others. Equity: theory and research. Boston, Mass., [1978]. pp. 312. *bibliog.*

SOCIAL LEGISLATION

— Europe.

MITSCHERLICH (MATTHIAS) Das Arbeitskampfrecht der Bundesrepublik Deutschland und die Europäische Sozialcharta. Baden-Baden, [1977]. pp. 160. *bibliog.*

— United Kingdom.

BROOKE (ROSALIND) Law, justice and social policy. London, [1979]. pp. 136.

SOCIAL MEDICINE.

PARSONS (TALCOTT) Action theory and the human condition. New York, [1978]. pp. 464. *bibliogs. Collected essays.*

— United States.

ROEMER (MILTON IRWIN) Social medicine: the advance of organized health services in America. New York, [1978]. pp. 560. *bibliogs.*

SOCIAL MOBILITY.

INVESTIGATING social mobility; [by] Leonard Broom [and others]. [Canberra, 1977]. pp. 220. *bibliog.*

CONFERENCE ON SOCIAL DEMOGRAPHY, MADISON, 1975. Social demography; edited by Karl E. Taeuber, Larry L. Bumpass, James A. Sweet. New York, [1978]. pp. 336. *bibliogs.*

SOCIAL mobility in comparative perspective; edited by Włodzimierz Wesołowski [and others]. Wrocław, 1978. pp. 319. *bibliogs.*

SOCIALE stratificatie: op weg naar empirisch-theoretisch stratificatieonderzoek in Nederland; onder redactie van Jules L. Peschar en Wout C. Ultee. Deventer, [1978]. pp. 170. *bibliog.* (Mens en Maatschappij. Boekafleveringen. 1978)

DAHRENDORF (RALF) Lebenschancen: Anläufe zur sozialen und politischen Theorie. Frankfurt am Main, 1979. pp. 240.

— India.

WEINER (MYRON) Sons of the soil: migration and ethnic conflict in India. Princeton, N.J., [1978]. pp. 383. *bibliogs.*

— Sweden.

MARTINIUS (STURE) Peasant destinies: the history of 552 Swedes born 1810-12. Stockholm, 1977. pp. 154. *bibliog.* (Stockholms Universitet. Acta Universitatis Stockholmiensis. Stockholm Studies in Economic History. 3)

— United States.

COLEMAN (RICHARD P.) and others. Social standing in America: new dimensions of class. New York, 1978. pp. 353. *bibliog.*

FEATHERMAN (DAVID L.) and HAUSER (ROBERT MASON) Opportunity and change. New York, [1978]. pp. 572. *bibliog.*

KIRK (GORDON W.) The promise of American life: social mobility in a nineteenth century immigrant community, Holland, Michigan, 1847-1894. Philadelphia, 1978. pp. 164. *bibliog.* (American Philosophical Society. Memoirs. vol. 124)

SOCIAL MOVEMENTS.

FOURQUIN (GUY) The anatomy of popular rebellion in the Middle Ages...; translated by Anne Chesters. Amsterdam, 1978. pp. 181. *bibliog.*

TILLY (CHARLES) From mobilization to revolution. Reading, Mass., [1978]. pp. 349. *bibliog.*

WALLIS (ROY) Salvation and protest: studies of social and religious movements. New York, 1979. pp. 231.

— Kenya.

WIPPER (AUDREY) Rural rebels: a study of two protest movements in Kenya. Nairobi, 1977. pp. 363. *bibliog.*

— United States.

HANDLER (JOEL F.) Social movements and the legal system: a theory of law reform and social change. New York, [1978]. pp. 252. *(Wisconsin University, Madison. Institute for Research on Poverty. Monograph Series).*

SOCIAL PARTICIPATION.

COMMUNITY involvement and leisure; edited by John T. Haworth. London, [1979]. pp. 205.

— Germany.

RASCHKE (PETER) Vereine und Verbände: zur Organisation von Interessen in der Bundesrepublik Deutschland. München, [1978]. pp. 272. *bibliog.*

SOCIAL PERCEPTION.

SOCIAL SERVICES RESEARCH AND INTELLIGENCE UNIT [PORTSMOUTH]. Occasional Papers. No. 6. A community's perception of the physically disabled; [by] G. Williams. Portsmouth, 1979. fo. 20.

SOCIAL POLICY.

INTERNATIONAL SOCIAL DEVELOPMENT REVIEW; [pd. by] (Department of Economic and Social Affairs), United Nations. irreg., 1968 (no.1)- New York. *Supersedes its Housing, building and planning (N 1948 - Ja 1960), its Population bulletin of the United Nations (D 1951 - 1963), and its International social service review (Ja 1956 - Ap 1963).*

GROUP OF EXPERTS ON SOCIAL POLICY AND THE DISTRIBUTION OF INCOME IN THE NATION. Social policy and the distribution of income in the nation :[report and discussion papers of the Group meeting held at United Nations Headquarters from 23 January to 1 February 1967.] (ST/SOA/88). New York, United Nations, 1969. pp. 175.

UNITED NATIONS. Department of Economic and Social Affairs. 1970. Social welfare planning in the context of national development plans. (ST/SOA/99). New York, 1970. pp. 92.

COLLETTE (JEAN MICHEL) L'allocation des ressources dans les secteurs sociaux: étude sur les systèmes de décision. Paris, 1975. pp. 130. *bibliog.*

ROSE (RICHARD) Governing and ungovernability: a sceptical inquiry. Glasgow, [1977]. pp. 29. *(Glasgow. University of Strathclyde. Centre for the Study of Public Policy. Studies in Public Policy. No. 1)*

ROSE (RICHARD) and PETERS (B. GUY) The political consequences of economic overload: on the possibility of political bankruptcy. Glasgow, 1977. pp. 27,5. *bibliog.* *(Glasgow. University of Strathclyde. Centre for the Study of Public Policy. Studies in Public Policy. No. 4)*

SIVARD (RUTH LEGER) World military and social expenditures, 1977. Leesburg, Va., [1977]. pp. 31.

CALABRESI (GUIDO) and BOBBITT (PHILIP) Tragic choices. New York, [1978]. pp. 252. *bibliog.*

RULE (JAMES B.) Insight and social betterment: a preface to applied social science. New York, 1978. pp. 205.

INTRODUCING social policy; edited by David C. Marsh. London, 1979. pp. 286. *bibliogs.*

— Congresses.

INTERNATIONAL ECONOMIC ASSOCIATION. Conference, 1976, Urbino. Econometric contributions to public policy: proceedings of a conference...; edited by Richard Stone and William Peterson. London, 1978. pp. 474. *bibliogs.*

— Mathematical models.

KLAASSEN (LEONARDUS HENDRIK) and others. Spatial systems: a general introduction. Farnborough, [1979]. pp. 165. *bibliog.*

MODELI sotsial'no-ekonomicheskikh protsessov i sotsial'noe planirovanie. Moskva, 1979. pp. 213. *bibliog.* (Akademiia Nauk SSSR. Problemy Sovetskoi Ekonomiki)

SOCIAL PROBLEMS.

INTERNATIONAL SOCIAL DEVELOPMENT REVIEW; [pd. by] (Department of Economic and Social Affairs), United Nations. irreg., 1968 (no.1)- New York. *Supersedes its Housing, building and planning (N 1948 - Ja 1960), its Population bulletin of the United Nations (D 1951 - 1963), and its International social service review (Ja 1956 - Ap 1963).*

ACKOFF (RUSSELL LINCOLN) Redesigning the future: a systems approach to societal problems. New York, [1974]. pp. 260.

SEVERY (LAWRENCE J.) and others. A contemporary introduction to social psychology. New York, [1976]. pp. 462. *bibliog.*

EUGENICS SOCIETY. Annual Symposium, 14th, 1978. Perimeters of social repair: proceedings...; edited by W.H.G. Armytage and John Peel. London, 1978. pp. 157. *bibliogs.*

GORDON (LEONARD) Sociologist, and HARVEY (PATRICIA ATCHISON) Sociology and American social issues. Boston, Mass., [1978]. pp. 548. *bibliogs.*

MAJOR social issues: a multidisciplinary view; edited by J. Milton Yinger and Stephen J. Cutler. New York, [1978]. pp. 575. *bibliog.*

ROBERTS (RON E.) Social problems: human possibilities. Saint Louis, 1978. pp. 310. *bibliogs.*

RULE (JAMES B.) Insight and social betterment: a preface to applied social science. New York, 1978. pp. 205.

HASTINGS (WILLIAM M.) How to think about social problems: a primer for citizens. New York, 1979. pp. 251. *bibliog.*

PALEN (J. JOHN) Social problems. New York, [1979]. pp. 625. *bibliog.*

SOCIAL problems and the city: geographical perspectives; edited by David T. Herbert and David M. Smith. Oxford, 1979. pp. 2717. *bibliogs.*

SOCIAL PSYCHOLOGY.

BICKMAN (LEONARD) and HENCHY (THOMAS) eds. Beyond the laboratory: field research in social psychology. New York, [1972]. pp. 340. *bibliogs.*

BERKOWITZ (LEONARD) A survey of social psychology. Hinsdale, Ill., [1975]. pp. 580.

SOCIAL behaviour and experience: multiple perspectives; edited by Hedy Brown and Richard Stevens. Sevenoaks, [1975]. pp. 627. *bibliogs.*

SEVERY (LAWRENCE J.) and others. A contemporary introduction to social psychology. New York, [1976]. pp. 462. *bibliog.*

SPIVACK (GEORGE) and others. The problem-solving approach to adjustment. San Francisco, 1976. pp. 318. *bibliog.*

THEWELEIT (KLAUS) Männerphantasien. Frankfurt am Main, 1977-78. 2 vols. *bibliog.*

CONTEMPORARY issues in social psychology; edited by John C. Brigham and Lawrence S. Wrightsman. 3rd ed. Monterey, [1977]. pp. 367.

GOODMAN (ARNOLD ABRAHAM) Baron Goodman. How much paternalism? [Colchester], 1977. pp. 19. *(University of Essex. Noel Buxton Lectures. 1977)*

SOCIAL rules and social behaviour; edited by Peter Collett. Oxford, [1977]. pp. 185. *bibliog.*

EVANS (ELLIS D.) and McCANDLESS (BOYD R.) Children and youth: psychosocial development. 2nd ed. New York, [1978]. pp. 568. *bibliogs.*

INTRODUCING social psychology; edited by Henri Tajfel and Colin Fraser. Harmondsworth, 1978. pp. 490. *bibliog.*

SHIBUTANI (TAMOTSU) The derelicts of company K: a sociological study of demoralization. Berkeley, Calif., [1978]. pp. 455. *bibliog.*

STREUFERT (SIEGFRIED) and STREUFERT (SUSAN C.) Behavior in the complex environment. New York, 1978. pp. 316. *bibliogs.*

WALSTER (ELAINE) and others. Equity: theory and research. Boston, Mass., [1978]. pp. 312. *bibliog.*

BETTELHEIM (BRUNO) Surviving and other essays. New York, 1979. pp. 432.

BRAKEL (ARIE) Gelijk is niet gelijk: over het veranderen van organisaties. Meppel, [1979]. pp. 344. *bibliog. Proefschrift - Doctor in de Sociale Wetenschappen - Erasmus Universiteit Rotterdam. With English summary.*

FERNANDEZ (RONALD) and BARRILE (LEO) The promise of sociology. 2nd ed. New York, 1979. pp. 596.

PRESTHUS (ROBERT V.) The organizational society. rev.ed. London, 1979. pp. 288.

SOCIAL REFORMERS.

HOPE (MARJORIE) and YOUNG (JAMES) 1916- . The struggle for humanity: agents of nonviolent change in a violent world. Maryknoll, 1979. pp. 305. *bibliog.*

— Canada.

RUDÉ (GEORGE E.) Protest and punishment: the story of the social and political protesters transported to Australia 1788-1868. Oxford, 1978. pp. 270. *bibliog.*

— United Kingdom.

RUDÉ (GEORGE E.) Protest and punishment: the story of the social and political protesters transported to Australia 1788-1868. Oxford, 1978. pp. 270. *bibliog.*

SOCIAL ROLE.

BERNE (ERIC LENNARD) Games people play: the psychology of human relationships. Harmondsworth, 1968. pp. 173.

LIGHT (PAUL) The development of social sensitivity: a study of social aspects of role-taking in young children. Cambridge, 1979. pp. 123. *bibliog.*

SOCIAL SCIENCE RESEARCH.

LOUGHBOROUGH UNIVERSITY OF TECHNOLOGY. Centre for Utilisation of Social Science Research. Papers on social science utilisation. Monograph 1. Loughborough, 1972. pp. 171. *bibliogs.*

CONFERENCE ON SOCIAL SCIENCE RESEARCH ON DEVELOPMENT, BELLAGIO, 1974. The social sciences and development: papers presented at a Conference...on the financing of social science research for development, February 12-16, 1974. [Washington, International Bank for Reconstruction and Development, 1974]. pp. 238. *bibliogs.*

SONQUIST (JOHN A.) and DUNKELBERG (WILLIAM C.) Survey and opinion research: procedures for processing and analysis. Englewood Cliffs, N.J., [1977]. pp. 502. *bibliog.*

BOWER (ROBERT) and DE GASPARIS (PRISCILLA) Ethics in social research: protecting the interests of human subjects. New York, [1978]. pp. 227. *bibliog.*

INSIDE the whale: ten personal accounts of social research; edited by Colin Bell and S. Encel. Rushcutters Bay, N.S.W., [1978]. pp. 269. *bibliogs.*

COOK (THOMAS D.) and CAMPBELL (DONALD THOMAS) Quasi-experimentation: design and analysis issues for field settings. Chicago, [1979]. pp. 405. *bibliog.*

NAGEL (STUART S.) and NEEF (MARIAN) Policy analysis in social science research. Beverly Hills, [1979]. pp. 240. *bibliog.*

SOCIAL research: principles and procedures; edited by John Bynner and Keith M. Stribley. New York, 1979. pp. 354. *bibliogs.*

— America, Latin.

KAPLAN (MARCOS) La investigacion latinoamericana en ciencias sociales. Mexico, 1973. pp. 86. *(Mexico City. Colegio de Mexico. Jornadas. 74)*

— United Kingdom.

PERRY (NORMAN H.) The organisation of social science research in the United Kingdom. London, Social Science Research Council Survey Unit, [1975]. pp. (133). *(Occasional Papers in Survey Research. 6)*

BOVAIRD (TONY) and others, compilers. Inlogov register of research: 1978 mid year update, April 1978. Birmingham, 1978. pp. 71.

CENSUSES, surveys and privacy; edited by Martin Bulmer. London, 1979. pp. 279. *bibliog.*

— United States.

DIENER (EDWARD) and CRANDALL (RICK) Ethics in social and behavioral research. Chicago, 1978. pp. 266. *bibliog.*

QUANTITATIVE approaches to political intelligence: the CIA experience; edited by Richards J. Heuer, Jr. Boulder, Colo., 1978. pp. 181.

SOCIAL SCIENCES.

INTERNATIONAL SOCIAL SCIENCE JOURNAL (formerly International social science bulletin); [pd.by] Unesco. q., 1949(v. 1)- Paris.

SPANN (OTHMAR) Gesamtausgabe; Herausgeber: Walter Heinrich [and others]. Graz, 1963-79. 21 vols. *bibliogs.*

GUIZART (MAURICE) Science sociale selon la pensée de Hippolyte Colins. Paris, [1971]. pp. 75.

RAHMAN (MOHAMED AL-UDEID ABDEL) Public administration as an applied off-shoot of social sciences. Khartoum, 1974. fo. 26. *(Economic and Social Research Council [Sudan]. Bulletins. No. 8)*

KUHN (ALFRED) The logic of social systems: [a unified, deductive, system-based approach to social science]. San Francisco, 1976. pp. 534. *bibliog.*

BOULDING (KENNETH EWART) and others. The social system of the planet Earth: preliminary edition. Reading, Mass., [1977]. pp. 196. *bibliog.*

BAUMAN (ZYGMUNT) Hermeneutics and social science: approaches to understanding. London, 1978. pp. 263.

BEEHLER (RODGER) and DRENGSON (ALAN R.) eds. The philosophy of society. London, 1978. pp. 437. *bibliog.*

STRUCTURE, consciousness, and history; edited by Richard Harvey Brown [and] Stanford M. Lyman. Cambridge, 1978. pp. 284.

CHERNS (ALBERT B.) Using the social sciences. London, 1979. pp. 502. *bibliog.*

The FOUNDING fathers of social science; edited by Timothy Raison; revised edition by Paul Barker. rev. ed. London, 1979. pp. 319. *bibliogs. Articles first published in New Society.*

— Bibliography.

INDEX TO SOCIAL SCIENCES AND HUMANITIES PROCEEDINGS; [pd. by] Institute for Scientific Information. q., Ja/Mr 1979(no. 1)- Philadelphia.

UNITED NATIONS. Library. Current bibliographical information. [in English and French]. s-m. New York. *Current issues only kept. Supersedes its New publications in the...Library [of which the Library has no file], and its Current issues: a selected bibliography on subjects of concern to the United Nations (1965-1970, with gaps).*

— Congresses.

INDEX TO SOCIAL SCIENCES AND HUMANITIES PROCEEDINGS; [pd. by] Institute for Scientific Information. q., Ja/Mr 1979(no. 1)- Philadelphia.

— Dictionaries and encyclopedias.

FOULQUIE (PAUL) Vocabulaire des sciences sociales. Paris, [1978]. pp. 378. *bibliog.*

— History.

KUCZYNSKI (JUERGEN) Studien zu einer Geschichte der Gesellschaftswissenschaften. Berlin, 1975-78. 10 vols.

— — Methodology.

METODOLOGICHESKIE problemy istorii filosofii i obshchestvennoi mysli. Moskva, 1977. pp. 360. *bibliog.*

— Indexes.

SOCIAL SCIENCES CITATION INDEX; [pd.by] Institute for Scientific Information. a., (with periodic cumulations). 1976- Philadelphia. *File includes Guide and Journal List, Citation Index, Corporate Index, Source Index and Permuterm Subject Index.*

— Mathematical models.

DOREIAN (PATRICK) and HUMMON (NORMAN P.) Modeling social processes. New York, 1976. pp. 172. *bibliog.*

OLINICK (MICHAEL) An introduction to mathematical models in the social and life sciences. Reading, Mass., [1978]. pp. 466. *bibliogs.*

THEORY construction and data analysis in the behavioral sciences: a volume in honor of Louis Guttman; [edited by] Samuel Shye. San Francisco, 1978. pp. 426. *bibliog.*

— Mathematics.

WHIPKEY (KENNETH L.) and others. The power of mathematics: applications to management and the social sciences. New York, [1978]. pp. 452.

— Methodology.

MITROFF (IAN I.) and KILMANN (RALPH H.) Methodological approaches to social science. San Francisco, 1978. pp. 150. *bibliog.*

PAPINEAU (DAVID) For science in the social sciences. London, 1978. pp. 201.

RULE (JAMES B.) Insight and social betterment: a preface to applied social science. New York, 1978. pp. 205

SCHUTZ (ALFRED) and PARSONS (TALCOTT) The theory of social action: the correspondence of Alfred Schutz and Talcott Parsons; edited by Richard Grathoff. Bloomington, [1978]. pp. 145. *bibliog.*

SOCIAL SCIENCES.(Cont.)

STRUCTURE, consciousness, and history; edited by Richard Harvey Brown [and] Stanford M. Lyman. Cambridge, 1978. pp. 284.

POLISH essays in the methodology of the social sciences; edited by Jerzy J. Wiatr. Dordrecht, [1979]. pp. 260. *(Boston Colloquium for the Philosophy of Science. Boston Studies in the Philosophy of Science. vol. 29)*

RATIONALITY; edited by Bryan R. Wilson. Oxford, 1979. pp. 275. *bibliog.*

SOCIAL research: principles and procedures; edited by John Bynner and Keith M. Stribley. New York, 1979. pp. 354. *bibliogs.*

— Periodicals — Indexes.

HARZFELD (LOIS A.) Periodical indexes in the social sciences and humanities: a subject guide. Metuchen, N.J., 1978. pp. 174.

— Philosophy.

PRATT (VERNON) The philosophy of the social sciences. London, 1978. pp. 189. *bibliog.*

— Statistical methods.

HORTON (RAYMOND L.) The general linear model: data analysis in the social and behavioral sciences. New York, [1978]. pp. 274. *bibliog.*

DEMYSTIFYING social statistics; edited by John Irvine [and others]. London, 1979. pp. 390. *bibliogs.*

— — Dictionaries.

INTERNATIONAL encyclopedia of statistics; edited by William H. Kruskal and Judith M. Tanur. New York, [1978]. 2 vols. *bibliogs.*

— Study and teaching — United Kingdom.

U.K. Social Science Research Council. Postgraduate studentships in the social sciences. a. London. *Current issue only kept.*

SOCIAL SCIENCES AND ETHICS.

DIENER (EDWARD) and CRANDALL (RICK) Ethics in social and behavioral research. Chicago, 1978. pp. 266. *bibliog.*

SOCIAL SCIENTISTS.

KUCZYNSKI (JUERGEN) Studien zu einer Geschichte der Gesellschaftswissenschaften. Berlin, 1975-78. 10 vols.

— United States.

AMERICAN men and women of science: social and behavioral sciences. 13th ed. New York, 1978. pp. 1545.

SOCIAL scientists as advocates: views from the applied disciplines; edited by George H. Weber and George J. McCall. Beverly Hills, [1978]. pp. 215. *bibliogs. Contributions from a symposium of the Society for Applied Anthropology held in San Diego, 1977.*

SOCIAL SCIENTISTS IN GOVERNMENT

— United States.

STRAUSSMAN (JEFFREY D.) The limits of technocratic politics. New Brunswick, [1978]. pp. 164. *bibliog.*

SOCIAL SECURITY.

METHODS of evaluating the effectiveness of social security programmes: report of research conference Vienna, 10-13 September 1975. Geneva, 1976. pp. 107. *bibliog. (International Social Security Association. Studies and Research. No. 8)*

IMPLICATIONS for social security of research on aging and retirement: report of round table meeting, The Hague, 27-29 April 1976. Geneva, 1977. pp. 74. *(International Social Security Association. Studies and Research. No.9)*

ORGANISATION FOR ECONOMIC CO-OPERATION AND DEVELOPMENT. Committee on Fiscal Affairs. 1978. The tax/benefit position of selected income groups in OECD member countries, 1972-1976: a report by the Committee, etc. Paris, 1978. pp. 132.

AMERICAN ACADEMY OF POLITICAL AND SOCIAL SCIENCE. Annals. vol. 443. Risk and its treatment; changing societal consequences; special editor of this volume George E. Rejda. Philadelphia, 1979. pp. 202.

— Australia.

AUSTRALIA. Department of Social Services. 1970. Social services handbook. [Canberra], 1970. pp. 96.

SOCIAL SECURITY QUARTERLY; (pd. for the Australian Department of Social Security). q., winter 1973[1st issue]- Canberra.

AUSTRALIA. Department of Social Security. 1973. Commonwealth social services: statistical summary, 1963 to 1972. Canberra, [1973?]. fo. 21. *Photocopy.*

— Belgium.

BELGIUM. Ministère de la Prévoyance Sociale. Secrétariat Général. 1977. Aperçu de la sécurité social en Belgique. [Brussels], 1977. pp. 296. *bibliog. (Etudes Juridiques)*

DELEECK (HERMAN) Ongelijkheden in de welvaartsstaat: opstellen over sociaal beleid: tweede bundel. Antwerpen, [1977]. pp. 319.

— Bolivia.

SEGURIDAD SOCIAL: organo oficial de la Caja Nacional de Seguridad Social [Bolivia]. irreg., Ja/Mr 1960-Ja/Mr 1965 (año 21, no. 237/239- año 24, no. 251). with gap (no.246). La Paz.

— Brazil.

SILVA (FERNANDO ANTONIO REZENDE DA) and MAHAR (DENNIS) Saude e previdência social: uma analise econômica. Rio de Janeiro, 1974. pp. 222. *bibliog. (Brazil. Instituto de Planejamento Econômico e Social. Instituto de Pesquisas. Relatorios de Pesquisa. No. 21)*

— Cyprus.

CYPRUS. Ministry of Labour and Social Insurance. Statistics and Research Section. 1971. Report on the sample survey of the 1968/1969 social insurance cards. Nicosia, 1971. pp. 78.

— Denmark.

KNUDSEN (RITA) De kontante ydelsers størrelse, 1978; (with an English summary) The size of social cash payments, 1978. København, 1979. pp. 137 *(Socialforskningsinstituttet. Publikationer. 88)*

— France.

FRANCE. Ministère de l'Agriculture et du Développement Rural. 1974. Pour les professions agricoles un régime autonome et décentralisé de protection sociale. [Paris, 1974]. pp. 115. *(Bulletin d'Information. Numéros spéciaux) Cover title: Point 74: la protection sociale agricole.*

— Germany.

GERMANY (BUNDESREPUBLIK). Statistisches Bundesamt. Sozialversicherungspflichtig beschäftigte Arbeitnehmer. q and a., Mr 1977- Wiesbaden. *(Bevölkerung und Erwerbstätigkeit. 4.2)*

— Japan.

EMI (KOICHI) Essays on the service industry and social security in Japan. Tokyo, [1978]. pp. 186. *(Tokyo. Hitotsubashi University. Institute of Economic Research. Economic Research Series. No. 17)*

— Tanzania.

UNITED REPUBLIC OF TANZANIA. Statutes, etc. 1964. The National Provident Fund Act, 1964. [Dar es Salaam], 1964. pp. 217-242.

— Trinidad and Tobago.

TRINIDAD AND TOBAGO. 1969. Social security in Trinidad and Tobago: the introduction of the national insurance scheme. [Port-of-Spain], 1969. pp. 8.

— United Kingdom.

U.K. Department of Health and Social Security. [Circulars] irreg., Jl 7 1976 (no. 142)-, with gaps. London.

U.K. Supplementary Benefits Commission. [Circulars]. irreg., Oc 25 1978(no. 349)- London.

HAMILL (LYNNE) An explanation of the increase in female one parent families receiving supplementary benefit. London, Department of Health and Social Security, 1978. pp. 21. *(Government Economic Service Working Papers. No. 14)*

McCLEMENTS (LESLIE D.) The economics of social security. London, 1978. pp. 239.

SMEE (CLIVE H.) and STERN (JON) The unemployed in a period of high unemployment: some notes on characteristics and benefit status. [London], Department of Health and Social Security, 1978. pp. 30. *(Government Economic Service Working Papers. No. 11)*

U.K. Department of Health and Social Security. 1978. Social assistance: a review of the supplementary benefits scheme in Great Britain. [London], 1978. pp. 127.

U.K. Supplementary Benefits Commission. 1978. Take-up of supplementary benefits. London, 1978. pp. 31. *(Supplementary Benefits Administration Papers. 7)*

NIXON (JACQUELINE MARY) Fatherless families on family income supplement: FIS. London, 1979. pp. 241. *(U.K. Department of Health and Social Security. Research Reports. No. 4)*

U.K. Social Survey. [Reports. New Series]. 1043. Social security claimants: a survey amongst the customers of a local social security office carried out on behalf of the Department of Health and Social Security; [by] Jane Ritchie and Paul Wilson. [London], 1979. pp. 72.

U.K. Supplementary Benefits Commission. 1979. Response of the...Commission to Social assistance: a review of the supplementary benefits scheme in Great Britain. London, 1979. pp. 42. *(Supplementary Benefits Administration Papers. 9)*

— — Research.

SOCIAL security research: the definition and measurement of poverty: papers and report of a seminar sponsored by DHSS and organised by the Policy Studies Institute, D[epartment of] H[ealth and] S[ocial] S[ecurity]. London, H.M.S.O., 1979. pp. 162.

— — Ireland, Northern.

FAMILY BENEFITS AND PENSIONS IN NORTHERN IRELAND; [pd. by] Department of Health and Social Services. a., 1977- Belfast.

— United States.

KAPLAN (ROBERT S.) Indexing social security: an analysis of the issues. Washington, D.C., [1977]. pp. 67. *(American Enterprise Institute for Public Policy Research. AEI Studies. 182)*

MITCHELL (WILLIAM C.) The popularity of social security: a paradox in public choice. Washington, [1977]. pp. 21. *(American Enterprise Institute for Public Policy Research. AEI Studies. 179)*

PENNER (RUDOLPH GERHARD) Social security financing proposals. Washington, [1977]. pp. 29. *(American Enterprise Institute for Public Policy Research. Special Analyses. No. 77-1)*

DERTHICK (MARTHA) Policymaking for social security. Washington, D.C., [1979]. pp. 446.

— — Michigan.

SMITH (VERNON K.) and HOWITT (GARY A.) The economic status of Michigan AFDC families: an analysis of income and benefit receipt. [Lansing], 1976. pp. 54. *(Michigan. Department of Social Services. Studies in Welfare Policy. No. 8)*

SOCIAL SECURITY COURTS

— United Kingdom.

U.K. Department of Health and Social Security. 1977. Supplementary benefit appeal tribunals: a guide to procedure. London, 1977. pp. 53.

SOCIAL SERVICE.

RADICAL social work; edited by Roy Bailey and Mike Brake. London, 1975. pp. 170. *bibliog.*

TITMUSS (RICHARD MORRIS) Commitment to welfare. 2nd ed. London, 1976. pp. 272. *bibliogs.*

EUGENICS SOCIETY. Annual Symposium, 14th, 1978. Perimeters of social repair: proceedings...; edited by W.H.G. Armytage and John Peel. London, 1978. pp. 157. *bibliogs.*

MACAROV (DAVID) The design of social welfare. New York, 1978. pp. 303. *bibliog.*

JORDAN (WILLIAM) Helping in social work. London, 1979. pp. 150.

PINKER (ROBERT ARTHUR) The idea of welfare. London, 1979. pp. 276. *bibliog.*

SMITH (GILBERT) Social work and the sociology of organizations. rev. ed. London, 1979. pp. 108. *bibliog.*

— Research — United Kingdom.

PINKER (ROBERT ARTHUR) Research priorities in the personal social services: a report to the Research Initiatives Board, Social Science Research Council. London, Social Science Research Council, 1978. pp. 107.

— Societies, etc.

SOCIAL service organisations; editor-in-chief Peter Romanofsky: advisory editor Clarke A. Chambers. Westport, Conn., 1978. 2 vols.

— Asia.

INTERNATIONAL FEDERATION OF SOCIAL WORKERS. Regional Conference for Asia, Bangkok, 1967. Report...; theme: action programmes of social work organizations in meeting present and emerging social welfare problems in changing Asia. [Bangkok], Department of Public Welfare, Government of Thailand, 1968. pp. 75.

— Australia.

AUSTRALIA. Department of Social Services. 1970. Social services handbook. [Canberra], 1970. pp. 96.

AUSTRALIA. Social Welfare Commission. 1976. The role of local government in social welfare. [Canberra], 1976. pp. 84.

The DELIVERY of welfare services. Canberra, 1977. pp. 147. *(Australia. Commission of Inquiry into Poverty. Consumers and Clients Series)*

— — Statistics.

AUSTRALIA. Department of Social Security. 1973. Commonwealth social services: statistical summary, 1963 to 1972. Canberra, [1973?]. fo. 21. *Photocopy.*

— Canada — Quebec.

QUEBEC (PROVINCE). Conseil des Affaires Sociales et de la Famille. 1974. Contribution à une politique des affaires sociales et de la famille: les propositions et recommandations du Conseil des Affaires Sociales et de la Famille. [Québec], 1974. pp. 85.

— European Economic Community countries.

FABIAN SOCIETY. Fabian Tracts. [No.] 461. Creating a caring Community; [by] Roy Manley [and others]. London, 1979. pp. 28.

— Germany, Eastern.

LIVING in security: a report from the GDR. Berlin, 1978. pp. 64. *At foot of title page: Panorama DDR.*

— India — Andhra Pradesh.

ANDHRA PRADESH. Department of Social Welfare. 1975. Note on the activities of the Social Welfare Department. Hyderabad, [1975?]. fo. 50.

— Netherlands.

MEIJER (WIM) Welzijnsbeleid: een keuze voor verandering van de maatschappij. Alphen aan den Rijn, 1978. pp. 182.

MICHIELSE (H.C.M.) De burger als andragoog: een geschiedenis van 125 jaar welzijnswerk, 1848-1972. 2nd ed. Amsterdam, [1978]. pp. 292.

— New Zealand.

NEW ZEALAND COUNCIL OF SOCIAL SERVICE. Sharing social responsibility: report...on desirable roles and directions in social service development. [Wellington], 1978. pp. 80,6.

— Sudan.

NATIONAL COUNCIL FOR SOCIAL WELFARE [SUDAN]. Second All African Seminar on Social Welfare: theme: relating social justice and participation to development and welfare: institutional challenges and responses; country paper from Sudan by Director General, N[ational] C[ouncil for] S[ocial] W[elfare]. Khartoum, 1977. fo. 11.

— Thailand.

SUWANBUBPA (ARAN) Hill tribe development and welfare programmes in Northern Thailand. Singapore, 1976. pp. 93.

— United Kingdom.

U.K. Department of Health and Social Security. Local authority personal social services: summary of planning returns. a., 1976-77/1979-80- London.

GLAMPSON (ANN) and others. A guide to the assessment of community needs and resources. London, 1975 repr. 1977. pp. 80. *bibliog. (National Institute for Social Work. Papers. No. 1)*

ROBSON (WILLIAM ALEXANDER) Welfare state and welfare society: illusion and reality. London, 1976, repr. 1977. pp. 184.

SPECHT (HARRY) The Community Development Project: national and local strategies for improving the delivery of services. London, 1976. pp. 70. *bibliog. (National Institute for Social Work. Papers. No. 2)*

TAYLOR (MARILYN) and others. Principles and practice of community work in a British town. London, 1976. pp. 81. *(Young Volunteer Force Foundation. Community and Youth Work Papers)*

YOUNGHUSBAND (Dame EILEEN LOUISE) Social work in Britain: 1950-1975: a follow-up study. London, 1978 in progress. *bibliog.*

COLLABORATION in community care: a discussion document; [Dame Albertine Winner, chairman of the Working Party]. London, H.M.S.O., 1978. pp. 64. *bibliog.*

LEATHARD (AUDREY MARY) The development of family planning services in Britain. 1977 [or rather 1978]. fo. 564. *bibliog.* Typescript. Ph.D. (London) thesis: unpublished. This thesis is the property of London University and may not be removed from the Library.

NATIONAL CONSUMER COUNCIL. Means tests in local authority social services: who needs them?; discussion paper based on the report of a workshop. London, 1978. pp. 31.

SOCIAL SETTLEMENTS

RODGERS (BARBARA N.) Human well-being: challenges for the 1980s: social, economic and political action. London, 1978. pp. 25. *bibliog. Report written on behalf of the United Kingdom National Committee of the International Council on Social Welfare for the XIX International Conference on Social Welfare, Jerusalem, 1978.*

CHAPMAN (PAUL) Unmet needs and the delivery of care: a study of the utilisation of social services by old people. [London], 1979. pp. 110. *(Social Administration Research Trust. Occasional Papers on Social Administration. No. 61)*

HENRIQUES (URSULA R.Q.) Before the welfare state: social administration in early industrial Britain. London, 1979. pp. 294. *bibliog.*

— — Bibliography.

U.K. Department of Health and Social Security. Index of health circulars and notices; chief officer letters; local authority circulars and social service letters. a., 1977- London.

— — Field work.

SOCIAL service teams: the practitioner's view. London, H.M.S.O., 1978. pp. 421.

— — Scotland.

SCOTLAND. Scottish Education Department. Social Work Services Group. Home care services: day care establishments: day services: Scotland. a., 1976/77(1st)- Edinburgh. *Supersedes in part SCOTTISH SOCIAL WORK STATISTICS.*

— United States.

BLACK heritage in social welfare, 1860-1930; compiled and edited by Edyth L. Ross. Metuchen, N.J., 1978. pp. 488. *bibliogs.*

EVALUATION and accountability in human service programs...; edited by William C. Sze [and] June G. Hopps. 2nd ed. Cambridge, Mass., [1978]. pp. 222. *bibliog.*

EVALUATION of human service programs; edited by C. Clifford Attkisson [and others]. New York, 1978. pp. 492. *bibliogs.*

LEIBY (JAMES) A history of social welfare and social work in the United States. New York, 1978. pp. 426. *bibliog.*

TRATTNER (WALTER I.) From poor law to welfare state: a history of social welfare in America. 2nd ed. London, [1979]. pp. 290. *bibliogs.*

— — Directories.

SOCIAL service organisations; editor-in-chief Peter Romanofsky: advisory editor Clarke A. Chambers. Westport, Conn., 1978. 2 vols.

— — Michigan.

DAHLKE (SHERYL L.) and SAVAGE (E. LYNN) General assistance in Michigan: a profile of program and recipient characteristics. [Lansing], 1975. pp. 200. *(Michigan. Department of Social Services. Studies in Welfare Policy. No. 5)*

SOCIAL SERVICE AND RACE RELATIONS

— United Kingdom.

MULTI-racial Britain: the social services response: Association of Directors of Social Services and the Commission for Racial Equality: a Working Party report; [Tom White, chairman]. London, Commission for Racial Equality, 1978. pp. 81.

SOCIAL SETTLEMENTS

— United States.

LEIGHTY (CHESTER R.) People working together. New York, 1960. pp. 28.

SOCIAL STATUS.

COLEMAN (RICHARD P.) and others. Social standing in America: new dimensions of class. New York, 1978. pp. 353. *bibliog.*

DRAYER (EDWARD HARRY) Problems in the analysis of social prestige, with special reference to aristocracy at six formative periods. 1978. fo. 407. *bibliog. Typescript. Ph.D. (London) thesis: unpublished. This thesis is the property of London University and may not be removed from the Library.*

GOODE (WILLIAM J.) The celebration of heroes: prestige as a social control system. Berkeley, [1978]. pp. 407.

SOCIAL STRUCTURE.

GIDDENS (ANTHONY) The class structure of the advanced societies. London, 1973. pp. 336. *bibliog.*

PARENTI (MICHAEL) Power and the powerless. New York, [1974]. pp. 238. *bibliogs.*

HEGEDUS (ANDRÁS) The structure of socialist society; translated by Rudolf Fisher and revised by Peter Szente. London, 1977. pp. 230.

ADAPTATION and symbolism: essays on social organization; presented to Sir Raymond Firth...; edited by Karen Ann Watson-Gegeo and S. Lee Seaton. Honolulu, [1978]. pp. 228. *bibliogs.*

BEEGHLEY (LEONARD) Social stratification in America: a critical analysis of theory and research. Santa Monica, Calif., [1978]. pp. 381. *bibliog.*

BOULDING (KENNETH EWART) Ecodynamics: a new theory of societal evolution. Beverly Hills, [1978]. pp. 367. *bibliog.*

MAIN currents in Indian sociology. 3. Cohesion and conflict in modern India; edited by Giri Ray Gupta. New Delhi, [1978]. pp. 324.

SOCIAL system and tradition in southern Africa: essays in honour of Eileen Krige; edited by John Argyle [and] Eleanor Preston-Whyte. Cape Town, 1978. pp. 251. *bibliogs.*

DYER (EVERETT D.) The American family: variety and change. New York, [1979]. pp. 478. *bibliogs.*

WESOŁOWSKI (WŁODZIMIERZ) Classes, strata and power; translated and with an introduction by George Kolankiewicz. London, 1979. pp. 159. *bibliog.*

SOCIAL SURVEYS.

WORLD FERTILITY SURVEY. Occasional Papers. Voorburg, 1973 in progress.

WORLD FERTILITY SURVEY. Basic Documentation. Voorburg, 1975 in progress.

WORLD FERTILITY SURVEY. Technical Bulletins. Voorburg, 1976 in progress.

WORLD FERTILITY SURVEY. Scientific Reports. Voorburg, 1977 in progress.

SONQUIST (JOHN A.) and DUNKELBERG (WILLIAM C.) Survey and opinion research: procedures for processing and analysis. Englewood Cliffs, N.J., [1977]. pp. 502. *bibliog.*

DILLMAN (DON A.) Mail and telephone surveys: the total design method. New York, [1978]. pp. 325. *bibliog.*

GARDNER (GODFREY) Social surveys for social planners. Milton Keynes, 1978. pp. 165. *bibliog.*

ORENSTEIN (ALAN) and PHILLIPS (WILLIAM R.F.) Understanding social research: an introduction. Boston, Mass., 1978. pp. 428.

BRADBURN (NORMAN M.) and SUDMAN (SEYMOUR) Improving interview method and questionnaire design; (with the assistance of Edward Blair [and others]). San Francisco, 1979. pp. 214. *bibliog.*

— Israel.

SIMON (RITA JAMES) Continuity and change: a study of wo ethnic communities in Israel. Cambridge, 1978. pp. 180. *bibliog. (American Sociological Association. Arnold and Caroline Rose Monograph Series in Sociology)*

— Netherlands.

WELCKER (J.M.) Heren en arbeiders in de vroege Nederlandse arbeidersbeweging, 1870-1914. Amsterdam, 1978. pp. 681. *bibliog. (International Institute of Social History. De Nederlandse Arbeidersbeweging. 3) With summary in English.*

— United Kingdom.

BOADEN (NOEL) and WALKER (RAYMOND) Sample surveys and public participation. [London], 1976. pp. 29. *(Linked Research Project into Public Participation in Structure Planning. Interim Research Papers. 10)*

GOLDSMITH (MICHAEL) and SAUNDERS (PETER) Participation through public meetings: the case in Cheshire. [London], 1976. pp. 30. *(Linked Research Project into Public Participation in Structure Planning. Interim Research Papers. 9)*

HAMPTON (WILLIAM) and BEALE (WENDY) Methods of approaching groups in South Yorkshire. [London], 1976. pp. 51. *(Linked Research Project into Public Participation in Structure Planning. Interim Research Papers. 11)*

U.K. Social Survey. Methodology Unit. Survey methodology bulletin. q., Mr 1978(no.2)- London. *No.1, internal document, not generally distributed.*

HAMPTON (WILLIAM) and WALKER (RAYMOND) The individual citizen and public participation: a survey of individual written response in Teesside. [London], 1978. pp. 24. *(Linked Research Project into Public Participation in Structure Planning. Interim Research Papers. 13)*

STRINGER (PETER) Tuning in to the public: survey before participation. [London], 1978. pp. 44. *(Linked Research Project into Public Participation in Structure Planning. Interim Research Papers. 14)*

SOCIAL SYSTEMS.

KUHN (ALFRED) The logic of social systems: [a unified, deductive, system-based approach to social science]. San Francisco, 1976. pp. 534. *bibliog.*

MILLER (JAMES GRIER) Living systems. New York, 1978. pp. 1102. *bibliog.*

TEUNE (HENRY) and MLINAR (ZDRAVKO) The developmental logic of social systems. Beverly Hills, [1978]. pp. 175.

COMMUNICATION and control in society; edited by Klaus Krippendorff. New York, [1979]. pp. 529. *bibliogs.*

SOCIAL VALUES.

SATIN (MARK IVOR) New age politics: healing self and society: the emerging new alternative to Marxism and liberalism. West Vancouver, 1978. pp. 240. *bibliog.*

SOCIAL WORK ADMINISTRATION

— United Kingdom.

FALK (NICHOLAS) and LEE (JAMES) Planning the social services. Farnborough, Hants., [1978]. pp. 113.

SOCIAL WORK AS A PROFESSION.

HAINES (JOHN) Skills and methods in social work. London, 1975. pp. 227. *bibliog.*

RADICAL social work; edited by Roy Bailey and Mike Brake. London, 1975. pp. 170. *bibliog.*

JORDAN (WILLIAM) Helping in social work. London, 1979. pp. 150.

SOCIAL WORK EDUCATION.

KENDALL (KATHERINE A.) Reflections on social work education, 1950-1978. New York, [1978]. pp. 201. *bibliog.*

— India.

INDIA. Department of Social Welfare. 1977. Handbook on social work education facilities in India. [Delhi, 1977]. pp. 103.

— United Kingdom.

SOCIAL service teams: the practitioner's view. London, H.M.S.O., 1978. pp. 421.

SOCIAL WORK WITH ALCOHOLICS

— United States.

REGIER (MARILYN C.) Social policy in action: perspectives on the implementation of alcoholism reforms. Lexington, Mass., [1979]. pp. 177. *bibliog.*

SOCIAL WORK WITH CHILDREN

— United Kingdom.

NATIONAL ASSOCIATION FOR THE CARE AND RESETTLEMENT OF OFFENDERS. The Hammersmith Teenage Project: an experiment in the community care of young offenders. [Chichester], 1978. pp. 56.

SOCIAL WORK WITH DELINQUENTS AND CRIMINALS.

PEARSON (GEOFFREY) The deviant imagination: psychiatry, social work and social change. London, 1975. pp. 258. *bibliog.*

SOCIAL WORK WITH MINORITIES

— United Kingdom.

LLEWELYN-DAVIES WEEKS [AND PARTNERS]. Inner area study: Birmingham: Birmingham Community Relations Council: Small Heath fieldworker. [London], Department of the Environment, [1978]. pp. 38.

SOCIAL WORK WITH THE AGED

— United Kingdom.

An AGEING population: a reader and sourcebook; edited by Vida Carver and Penny Liddiard. Sevenoaks, [1978]. pp. 434. *bibliogs.*

SOCIAL WORK WITH YOUTH

— Belgium.

STATISTIQUES et protection de la jeunesse; Statistieken en jeugdbescherming; [by a] groupe de travail, 1976-1977. Bruxelles, 1977. pp. 97. *(Centre d'Etude de la Délinquance Juvénile. Publications. No. 41) In French or Dutch, with synthesis and conclusion in both languages.*

— United Kingdom.

ROBINS (DAVID) and COHEN (PHILIP) 1944- . Knuckle sandwich: growing up in the working-class city. Harmondsworth, 1978. pp. 203.

SOCIAL WORKERS.

HAINES (JOHN) Skills and methods in social work. London, 1975. pp. 227. *bibliog.*

JORDAN (WILLIAM) Helping in social work. London, 1979. pp. 150.

— Australia — Western Australia.

WESTERN AUSTRALIA. Committee into Social Welfare Manpower. 1974. A study of social welfare manpower in Western Australia. [Perth]. 1974. pp. 144. *bibliog.*

— Norway.

COPING and cooperation;...some views of an interchange course for probation officers and social workers from the South East of England and Norway in 1977; edited by Thelma Wilson [and others]. London, [1978]. pp. 85.

— **United Kingdom.**

COPING and cooperation;...some views of an interchange course for probation officers and social workers from the South East of England and Norway in 1977; edited by Thelma Wilson [and others]. London, [1978]. pp. 85.

GRACE (CLIVE) and WILKINSON (PHILIP) Negotiating the law: social work and legal services. London, [1978]. pp. 85.

ROBINSON (MARGARET) Schools and social work. London, 1978. pp. 268.

SIMPKIN (MICHAEL) Trapped within welfare: surviving social work. London, 1979. pp. 168.

SOCIAL work and the courts; edited by Howard Parker. London, 1979. pp. 224. *bibliog.*

— — **Scotland.**

SCOTLAND. Scottish Education Department. Social Work Services Group. Staff of Scottish social work departments. a., 1978(no.1)- Edinburgh.

TIBBITT (JOHN E.) Social workers as mental health officers. Edinburgh, 1978. pp. 41. *(Scotland. Scottish Office. Social Research Studies)*

SOCIALISM.

MARBIE (EUGENE) Pour comprendre le socialisme. Paris, [1944]. pp. 102.

STUDIEN zu Jakobinismus und Sozialismus; herausgegeben von Hans Pelger. Berlin, [1974]. pp. 271.

'DEMOKRATISCHER Sozialismus': Schein und Wirklichkeit; ([by the] Institut für Gesellschaftswissenschaften beim ZK der SED). Frankfurt am Main, 1975. pp. 180.

INTERNATIONAL SEMINAR ON THE JUCHE IDEA, PYONGYANG, 1977. [Proceedings]. Pyongyang, 1977. pp. 763.

MIDWEST MARXIST SCHOLARS CONFERENCE, 1ST, UNIVERSITY OF MINNESOTA, 1976. Marxism and new left ideology; Ileana Rodríguez and William L. Rowe, editors. Minneapolis, [1977]. pp. 102.

FLECHTHEIM (OSSIP KURT) Von Marx bis Kolakowski: Sozialismus oder Untergang in der Barbarei? Köln, [1978]. pp. 286.

REVEL (JEAN FRANÇOIS) The totalitarian temptation; (translated by David Hapgood). Harmondsworth, 1978. pp. 332.

STUART (JAMES GIBB) The mind benders: the gradual revolution and Scottish independence. Glasgow, 1978. pp. 180. *bibliog.*

EDDY (WILLIAM HENRY CHARLES) Understanding Marxism: an approach through dialogue. Oxford, 1979. pp. 157. *bibliog.*

LUARD (DAVID EVAN TRANT) Socialism without the state. London, 1979. pp. 184.

SACHSSE (HANS) Was ist Sozialismus?: zur Naturphilosophie der Gesellschaft. München, [1979]. pp. 155. *bibliog.*

STEPHENS (JOHN D.) The transition from capitalism to socialism. London, 1979. pp. 231. *bibliog.*

— **Congresses.**

INTERNATIONAL WORKING MEN'S ASSOCIATION. Congress, [5th], The Hague, 1872. The Hague congress of the First International, September 2- 7, 1872: reports and letters. Moscow, [1978]. pp. 701. *(Institut Marksizma-Leninizma. Documents of the First International.)*

— **History.**

INTERNATIONALE TAGUNG DER HISTORIKER DER ARBEITERBEWEGUNG, 1974. Arbeiterbewegung und Faschismus; Der Februar 1934 in Österreich; (bearbeitet von Gerhard Botz). Wien, 1976. pp. 464. *(Internationale Tagung der Historiker der Arbeiterbewegung. ITH-Tagungsberichte. Band 9)*

MEYER (AHLRICH) Frühsozialismus: Theorien der sozialen Bewegung, 1789-1848. Freiburg, [1977]. pp. 405. *bibliog.*

INTERNATIONALE TAGUNG DER HISTORIKER DER ARBEITERBEWEGUNG, 1975. Einheits- und Volksfrontpolitik, 1935-1939; Klassenkampf und nationale Frage zur Zeit der II. Internationale; (bearbeitet von Hans Hautmann). Wien, 1978. pp. 335. *(Internationale Tagung der Historiker der Arbeiterbewegung. ITH-Tagungsberichte. Band 10)*

KOŁAKOWSKI (LESZEK) Main currents of Marxism: its rise, growth, and dissolution;... translated from the Polish by P.S. Falla. Oxford, 1978. 3 vols. *bibliogs.*

LUEBBE (PETER) Kommunismus und Sozialdemokratie: eine Streitschrift. Berlin, [1978]. pp. 299.

SALVADORI (MASSIMO L.) Karl Kautsky and the socialist revolution, 1880-1938; translated by Jon Rothschild. London, 1979. pp. 375.

— **Periodicals.**

ARFE (GAETANO) Storia dell'Avanti! 2nd ed. [Rome, 1977]. pp. 351. *(Istituto Socialista di Studi Storici. Biblioteca Storica.)*

— **Study and teaching.**

STUDIES in socialist pedagogy; edited by Theodore Mills Norton and Bertell Ollman. New York, [1978]. pp. 405. *bibliog.*

SOCIALISM AND EDUCATION.

STUDIES in socialist pedagogy; edited by Theodore Mills Norton and Bertell Ollman. New York, [1978]. pp. 405. *bibliog.*

CASTLES (STEPHEN) and WÜSTENBERG (WIEBKE) The education of the future: an introduction to the theory and practice of socialist education. London, 1979. pp. 220. *bibliog.*

— **Germany.**

ELSAESSER (KONRAD) Die badische Sozialdemokratie, 1890 bis 1914: zum Zusammenhang von Bildung und Organisation. Marburg, [1978]. pp. 323. *bibliog. (Studiengesellschaft für Sozialgeschichte und Arbeiterbewegung, Marburg. Schriftenreihe für Sozialgeschichte und Arbeiterbewegung. Band 14)*

SOCIALISM AND THE ARTS.

PLEKHANOV (GEORGII VALENTINOVICH) Art and society and other papers in historical materialism. New York, [1974]. pp. 187.

PLEKHANOV (GEORGII VALENTINOVICH) Estetika i sotsiologiia iskusstva: [sbornik statei, 1897-1913]. Moskva, 1978. 2 vols. *With introductory article by M. Lifshits.*

SOCIALISM AND YOUTH.

NEUGEBAUER (WOLFGANG) Die sozialdemokratische Jugendbewegung in Österreich 1894-1945. [Vienna, 1969]. 2 vols. *bibliog. Vol. 2 lacks pages 8, 14, 31, 121, 173, 288, 334, 369 and 372.*

FRANCHI (PAOLO) Nuove generazioni, democrazia, socialismo. Roma, 1977. pp. 177.

I COMUNISTI e la questione giovanile: atti della sessione del Comitato centrale del Partito comunista italiano, Roma, 14-16 marzo 1977. Roma, 1977. pp. 378.

Il P.C.I. e la questione giovanile: [an anthology]; a cura di Walter Veltroni. Roma, 1977. pp. 353.

GESCHICHTE der Freien Deutschen Jugend: Chronik; (Redaktionskollegium: K.H. Jahnke [and others]; Autoren: W. Arlt [and others]). 2nd ed. Berlin, 1978. pp. 391.

SOCIALISM IN ARAB COUNTRIES.

AMIN (SAMIR) The Arab nation; translated [from the French] by Michael Pallis. London, 1978. pp. 116.

SOCIALISM IN AUSTRIA.

NEUGEBAUER (WOLFGANG) Die sozialdemokratische Jugendbewegung in Österreich 1894-1945. [Vienna, 1969]. 2 vols. *bibliog. Vol. 2 lacks pages 8, 14, 31, 121, 173, 288, 334, 369 and 372.*

BEWEGUNG und Klasse: Studien zur österreichischen Arbeiterbewegung...; (G. Botz [and others], Hrsg.). Wien, [1978]. pp. 841. *(Ludwig Boltzmann Institut für Geschichte der Arbeiterbewegung. Veröffentlichungen)*

GARDINER (MURIEL) and BUTTINGER (JOSEPH) Damit wir nicht vergessen: unsere Jahre 1934-1947 in Wien, Paris und New York. Wien, [1978]. pp. 168. *bibliog.*

RUECKBLICK und Ausschau: (10 Jahre Ludwig Boltzmann Institut für Geschichte der Arbeiterbewegung; [by] Karl R. Stadler [and others]). Wien, 1978. pp. 139. *bibliog. (Ludwig Boltzmann Institut für Geschichte der Arbeiterbewegung. Materialien zur Arbeiterbewegung. Nr. 12)*

WEST (FRANZ) Die Linke im Ständestaat Österreich: Revolutionäre Sozialisten und Kommunisten, 1934-1938. Wien, [1978]. pp. 353. *(Ludwig Boltzmann Institut für Geschichte der Arbeiterbewegung. Schriftenreihe. 8)*

POLLAK (WALTER) 1912-1977. Sozialismus in Österreich: von der Donaumonarchie bis zur Ära Kreisky. Wien, 1979. pp. 319.

SOCIALISM IN BULGARIA.

DIMITR Blagoev - vydaiushchiisia teoretik i revoliutsioner: sbornik statei k 120-letiiu so dnia rozhdeniia; [perevod s bolgarskogo]. Moskva, 1977. pp. 303.

SOCIALISM IN CANADA.

RANKIN (HARRY) Rankin's law: recollections of a radical. Vancouver, [1975]. pp. 220.

BENOIT (JACQUES) Journalist. L'extrême gauche. Ottawa, 1977. pp. 137.

PENNER (NORMAN) The Canadian left: a critical analysis. Scarborough, Ont., [1977]. pp. 287. *bibliog.*

LIGUE OUVRIERE REVOLUTIONNAIRE. Socialisme et libération nationale: la lutte contre l'Etat canadien. [Montréal, 1978]. pp. 109.

SOCIALISM IN CUBA.

HANSEN (JOSEPH) Marxist. Dynamics of the Cuban revolution: the Trotskyist view. New York, [1978]. pp. 393.

SOCIALISM IN CZECHOSLOVAKIA.

MLYNAR (ZDENEK) Nachtfrost: Erfahrungen auf dem Weg vom realen zum menschlichen Sozialismus. Köln, 1978. pp. 366.

SOCIALISM IN EASTERN EUROPE.

BAHRO (RUDOLF) The alternative in Eastern Europe; translated by David Fernbach. [London], 1978. pp. 463.

POWER and opposition in post-revolutionary societies; translated from the French by Patrick Camiller and the Italian by Jon Rothschild. London, 1979. pp. 281. *bibliogs. Papers of a conference organised by Il Manifesto and held in Venice, 1977.*

SOCIALISM IN EASTERN GERMANY.

ARNOLD (KARL HEINZ) Socialist economy - aim and strategy. Berlin, 1977. pp. 64. *At foot of title page: Panorama DDR.*

The GDR today. Dresden, 1977. pp. 175.

SOCIALISM IN EASTERN GERMANY. (Cont.)

LIVING in security: a report from the GDR. Berlin, 1978. pp. 64. *At foot of title page: Panorama DDR.*

SOCIALIST life and its values: aspects of advanced socialist society in the GDR. Berlin, 1978. pp. 87. *At foot of title page: Panorama DDR.*

SOCIALISM IN ETHIOPIA.

OTTAWAY (MARINA) and OTTAWAY (DAVID) Ethiopia: empire in revolution. New York, 1978. pp. 250.

SOCIALISM IN EUROPE.

ESPERIENZE riformiste in Europa: il socialismo tra il 1919 e il 1934; [by] Giorgio Galli [and others]. Napoli, [1976]. pp. 306. *bibliogs.*

EUROCOMMUNISM and Eurosocialism: the left confronts modernity; edited by Bernard E. Brown. New York, [1979]. pp. 408.

EUROSOZIALISMUS: die demokratische Alternative; herausgegeben von Gerhard Kiersch und Reimund Seidelmann. Köln, [1979]. pp. 267. *(Hochschulinitiative Demokratischer Sozialismus. Basis Arbeitsergebnisse)*

SOCIALISM IN FRANCE.

ATELIER, L': organe spécial de la classe laborieuse. m., S 1840-Jl 31 1850(nos. 1-36). Paris. *Reprint in 3 v.*

HANOTAUX (GABRIEL) La démocratie et le travail. Paris, 1920. pp. 264.

LIGUE COMMUNISTE REVOLUTIONNAIRE. Oui, le socialisme! Paris, 1978. pp. 397.

JUDT (TONY) Socialism in Provence, 1871-1914: a study in the origins of the modern French left. Cambridge, 1979. pp. 370. *bibliog.*

SOCIALISM IN GERMANY.

ALLGEMEINE DEUTSCHE ARBEITER-ZEITUNG (formerly Arbeiter- Zeitung); hrsg. vom Arbeiterfortbildungsverein in Coburg. w., D 25 1862- Ag 8 1866. Coburg. *1977 reprint in 2 vols.*

PLESS (PHILIPP) Der Wille zur Tat: Gewerkschaften als gesellschaftsverändernde Kraft: Reden und Aufsätze; herausgegeben von Rudolf Schneider. Berlin, [1973]. pp. 182. *bibliog.*

STUDIEN zu Jakobinismus und Sozialismus; herausgegeben von Hans Pelger. Berlin, [1974]. pp. 271.

BRD: Klassen, Analysen, etc.; ([by] Projekt Klassenanalyse). Westberlin, [1975]. pp. 226.

MARX (KARL) and ENGELS (FRIEDRICH) The German ideology; translated from the German. 3rd ed. Moscow, 1976. pp. 711. *bibliog.*

LEIN (ALBRECHT) Antifaschistische Aktion 1945: die "Stunde Null" in Braunschweig. Göttingen, [1978]. pp. 480. *bibliog. (Göttingen. Universität. Seminar für die Wissenschaft von der Politik. Göttinger Politikwissenschaftliche Forschungen. Band 2)*

LUDEWIG (HANS ULRICH) Arbeiterbewegung und Aufstand: eine Untersuchung zum Verhalten der Arbeiterparteien in den Aufstandsbewegungen der frühen Weimarer Republik, 1920-1923. Husum, [1978]. pp. 267. *bibliog.*

ROVAN (JOSEPH) Histoire de la social-démocratie allemande. Paris, [1978]. pp. 527. *bibliog.*

SOCIALISM IN GUYANA.

GUYANA. Prime Minister. 1975. Onward to socialism: Prime Minister's address to the nation on the occasion of the celebration of the fifth anniversary of the Co-operative Republic of Guyana...February 23, 1975. [Georgetown, 1975]. pp. 20.

GUYANA. Prime Minister. 1976. On the road to socialism; [address by...L.F.S. Burnham on the occasion of the celebration of the sixth anniversary of the Co- operative Republic of Guyana...February 22, 1976]. [Georgetown, 1976]. pp. 24.

GUYANA. Prime Minister. 1976. The pursuit of perfection; [address to the nation by L.F.S. Burnham on the occasion of the 10th anniversary of independence, National Park, May 25, 1976]. [Georgetown, 1976]. pp. 44.

SOCIALISM IN INDIA.

MAHAJAN (V.S.) b. 1923. Socialistic pattern in India: an assessment. New Delhi, 1974. pp. 151. *bibliog.*

CHOWDHURI (SATYABRATA RAI) Leftist movements in India: 1917-1947. Columbia, 1977. pp. 313. *bibliog.*

SOCIALISM IN IRELAND.

FALIGOT (ROGER) James Connolly et le mouvement révolutionnaire irlandais. Paris, 1978. pp. 333. *bibliog.*

SOCIALISM IN ITALY.

CAMBRIA (RITA) I liberali italiani e il socialismo: il dibattito ideologico nella crisi di fine secolo. Milano, [1974]. pp. 230.

CAGGIA (CARLO) Cronache fra due secoli: lotte politiche e sociali dal 1896 al 1909 in una città del Salento attraverso la stampa socialista. [Napoli, 1976]. pp. 179.

Il SOCIALISMO dal basso: le autonomie locali nella transizione al socialismo; [by] Francesco De Martino [and others]. Venezia, 1976. pp. 392.

HUNECKE (VOLKER) Arbeiterschaft und industrielle Revolution in Mailand, 1859- 1892: zur Entstehungsgeschichte der italienischen Industrie und Arbeiterbewegung. Göttingen, 1978. pp. 330. *bibliog.*

SOCIALISM IN KOREA.

INTERNATIONAL SEMINAR ON THE JUCHE IDEA, PYONGYANG, 1977. [Proceedings]. Pyongyang, 1977. pp. 763.

AL-MISSURI (MUHAMMAD) Kimilsungism: theory and practice. Pyongyang, 1978. pp. 262.

KIM (IL-SUNG) On the building of the people's government. Pyongyang, 1978. 2 vols.

SOCIALISM IN LITERATURE.

INGLE (STEPHEN) Socialist thought in imaginative literature. London, 1979. pp. 211.

SOCIALISM IN POLAND.

COTTAM (KAZIMIERA JANINA) Boleslaw Limanowski, 1835-1935: a study in socialism and nationalism. Boulder, Colo., 1978. pp. 365. *bibliog. (East European Quarterly. East European Monographs. 41)*

KLEVCHENIA (ALEKSANDR SEMENOVICH) Ocherki po istorii marksistsko-leninskoi filosofskoi mysli v Pol'she. Minsk, 1978. pp. 198. *bibliog.*

SOCIALISM IN RUSSIA.

TROTSKII (LEV DAVYDOVICH) Nos tâches politiques. Paris, 1970. pp. 256.

— Bibliography.

GRIN (TSILIA IOSIFOVNA) compiler. K. Marks, F. Engel's i revoliutsionnaia Rossiia: k 160- letiiu so dnia rozhdeniia K. Marksa: rekomendatel'nyi ukazatel' literatury; nauchnyi redaktor S.S. Volk. Moskva, 1978. pp. 95.

SOCIALISM IN SUBSAHARAN AFRICA.

SOCIALISM in Sub-Saharan Africa: a new assessment; edited by Carl G. Rosberg and Thomas M. Callaghy. Berkeley, [1979]. pp. 426. *bibliog. (California University. Institute of International Studies. Research Series. No.38)*

SOCIALISM IN SWEDEN.

LIMITS of the welfare state: critical views on post-war Sweden; edited by John Fry. Farnborough, Hants., [1979]. pp. 234. *Selection of articles, in English translation, which originally appeared in Zenit and other Swedish periodicals.*

SOCIALISM IN TANZANIA.

BOESEN (JANNIK) and others. Ujamaa: socialism from above. Uppsala, 1977. pp. 186.

TOWARDS socialism in Tanzania; edited by Bismarck U. Mwansasu and Cranford Pratt. Toronto, 1979. pp. 243.

SOCIALISM IN THE NETHERLANDS.

WOLFF (SAM DE) Voor het land van belofte: een terugblik op mijn leven. Nijmegen, 1978. pp. 300. *First published in Bussum, 1954.*

DOEL (HANS VAN DEN) Het biefstuk-socialisme en de economie. Utrecht, 1978. pp. 176.

SOCIALISM IN THE UNITED KINGDOM.

OYSTON (HENRY GIFFORD) Socialism and the drink evil: a series of brotherhood addresses. London, [1909]. pp. 127.

SOCIALISM the British way...: the socialist experiment carried out in Great Britain by the Labour government of 1945; by Evan F.M. Durbin [and others]; edited by Donald Munro. London, [1948]. pp. 345.

MILIBAND (RALPH) Parliamentary socialism: a study in the politics of labour. 2nd ed. New York, [1972]. pp. 384.

COMMUNITY DEVELOPMENT PROJECT. Political Economy Collective. C[ommunity] D[evelopment] P[roject]: community work or class politics. [North Shields, 1976]. pp. 8.

KNEE (FRED) The diary of Fred Knee; [edited] by David Englander. Coventry, 1977. pp. 122. *bibliog. (Society for the Study of Labour History. Aids to Research. No.3)*

CLARKE (PETER) 1942- . Liberals and social democrats. Cambridge, 1978. pp. 344. *bibliog.*

COMMUNIST WORKERS' MOVEMENT. Why Paul Foot should be a socialist: the case against the Socialist Workers' Party. Liverpool, 1978. pp. 198.

MACLEAN (JOHN) Socialist. In the rapids of revolution: essays, articles and letters 1902- 23; edited and with an introduction and commentaries by Nan Milton. London, 1978. pp. 256.

MALMGREEN (GAIL) Neither bread nor roses: Utopian feminists and the English working class, 1800-1850. Brighton, 1978. pp. 44.

SEABROOK (JEREMY) What went wrong?: working people and the ideals of the labour movement. London, 1978. pp. 286.

WERSKEY (GARY) The visible college. London, 1978. pp. 376.

BENN (ANTHONY NEIL WEDGWOOD) Arguments for socialism [based on miscellaneous writings]; edited by Chris Mullin. London, 1979. pp. 206.

DRUCKER (HENRY MATTHEW) Doctrine and ethos in the Labour Party. London, 1979. pp. 134. *bibliog.*

GOYDER (MARK) Socialism tomorrow: fresh thinking for the Labour Party. London, 1979. pp. 32. *(Young Fabian Group. Young Fabian Pamphlets. 49)*

HARDY (DENNIS) Alternative communities in nineteenth century England. London, 1979. pp. 268. *bibliog.*

JENKINS (MARK) Bevanism: Labour's high tide: the cold war and the democratic mass movement. Nottingham, 1979. pp. 323. *bibliogs.*

PIERSON (STANLEY) British socialists: the journey from fantasy to politics. Cambridge, Mass., 1979. pp. 403.

SOCIALISM IN THE UNITED STATES.

BONE (CHRISTOPHER) The disinherited children: a study of the New Left and the generation gap. New York, [1977]. pp. 183. *bibliogs.*

SORGE (FRIEDRICH ADOLPH) Labor movement in the United States: a history of the American working class from colonial times to 1890; edited by Philip S.Foner and Brewster Chamberlin; introduction by Philip S. Foner; translated by Brewster Chamberlin and Angela Chamberlin. Westport, Conn., 1977. pp. 394. *Translated articles originally published in German in Die Neue Zeit.*

BECKWITH (BURNHAM PUTNAM) Liberal socialism applied: the applied welfare economics of a liberal socialist economy. Palo Alto, [1978]. pp. 331.

CANTOR (MILTON) The divided left: American radicalism, 1900-1975. New York, [1978]. pp. 248. *bibliog.*

GREEN (JAMES R.) Grass-roots socialism: radical movements in the Southwest, 1895- 1943. Baton Rouge, [1978]. pp. 450.

PRATT (NORMA FAIN) Morris Hillquit: a political history of an American Jewish socialist. Westport, Conn., 1979. pp. 272. *bibliog.*

SERETAN (L. GLEN) Daniel DeLeon: the odyssey of an American Marxist. Cambridge, Mass., 1979. pp. 302. *bibliog.*

SOCIALISM IN VIETNAM.

THÂNHKHÔI (LÊ) Socialisme et développement au Viêt Nam. [Paris, 1978]. pp. 323. *bibliog. (Paris. Université de Paris I (Panthéon- Sorbonne). Institut d'Etude du Développement Economique et Social. Collection Tiers Monde)*

SOCIALISM IN YUGOSLAVIA.

KARDELJ (EDVARD) Democracy and socialism; translated by Margot and Boško Milosavljević. London, [1978]. pp. 244.

SOCIALIST PARTY (ARGENTINE REPUBLIC).

WALTER (RICHARD J.) The Socialist Party of Argentina, 1890-1930. Austin, [1977]. pp. 284. *bibliog. (Texas University. Institute of Latin American Studies. Latin American Monographs. No. 42)*

SOCIALIST PARTY (AUSTRIA).

BEWEGUNG und Klasse: Studien zur österreichischen Arbeitergeschichte...; (G. Botz [and others], Hrsg.). Wien, [1978]. pp. 841. *(Ludwig Boltzmann Institut für Geschichte der Arbeiterbewegung. Veröffentlichungen)*

DUCZYNSKA (ILONA) Workers in arms: the Austrian Schutzbund and the civil war of 1934. New York, [1978]. pp. 256. *bibliog. An abridged version of Der demokratische Bolschewik, published in Munich, 1945.*

HOLTMANN (EVERHARD) Zwischen Unterdrückung und Befriedung: sozialistische Arbeiterbewegung und autoritäres Regime in Österreich, 1933- 1938. Wien, [1978]. pp. 328. *bibliog. (Theodor-Körner-Stiftungsfonds, and Leopold- Kunschak-Preis. Wissenschaftliche Kommission zur Erforschung der Österreichischen Geschichte der Jahre 1918 bis 1938. Studien und Quellen zur Österreichischen Zeitgeschichte. Band 1)*

KAUFMANN (FRITZ) Sozialdemokratie in Österreich: Idee und Geschichte einer Partei von 1889 bis zur Gegenwart. Wien, [1978]. pp. 598. *bibliog.*

WEST (FRANZ) Die Linke im Ständestaat Österreich: Revolutionäre Sozialisten und Kommunisten, 1934-1938. Wien, [1978]. pp. 353. *(Ludwig Boltzmann Institut für Geschichte der Arbeiterbewegung. Schriftenreihe. 8)*

— History.

INTERNATIONALE TAGUNG DER HISTORIKER DER ARBEITERBEWEGUNG, 1974. 100 Jahre sozialdemokratischer Parteitag, Neudörfl, 1974; (bearbeitet von Josef Weidenholzer). Wien, 1976. pp. 133. *(Internationale Tagung der Historiker der Arbeiterbewegung. ITH-Tagungsberichte. Band 8)*

INTERNATIONALE TAGUNG DER HISTORIKER DER ARBEITERBEWEGUNG, 1974. Arbeiterbewegung und Faschismus; Der Februar 1934 in Österreich; (bearbeitet von Gerhard Botz). Wien, 1976. pp. 464. *(Internationale Tagung der Historiker der Arbeiterbewegung. ITH-Tagungsberichte. Band 9)*

POLLAK (WALTER) 1912-1977. Sozialismus in Österreich: von der Donaumonarchie bis zur Ära Kreisky. Wien, 1979. pp. 319.

SOCIALIST PARTY (CHILE).

El PROCESO chileno: pensamiento teorico y politico del P. Socialista de Chile; [by] Alejandro Chelen [and others] . Buenos Aires, 1974. pp. 175.

SOCIALIST PARTY (FRANCE).

GROSSHEIM (HEINRICH) Sozialisten in der Verantwortung: die französischen Sozialisten und Gewerkschafter im ersten Weltkrieg, 1914-17. Bonn, [1978]. pp. 286. *bibliog. (Friedrich-Ebert-Stiftung. Forschungsinstitut. Schriftenreihe. Band 140)*

CODDING (GEORGE ARTHUR) and SAFRAN (WILLIAM) Ideology and politics: the Socialist Party of France. Boulder, Colo., [1979]. pp. 280. *bibliog.*

SOCIALIST PARTY (POLAND).

WIĘCH (KAZIMIERZ) Polska Partia Socjalistyczna, 1918-1921. Warszawa, 1978. pp. 459. *bibliog.*

GŁOWACKI (BOGDAN) Polityka Polskiej Partii Socjalistycznej, 1929-1933. Warszawa, 1979. pp. 345. *bibliog.*

SOCIALIST PARTY (SPAIN).

JULIA (SANTOS) La izquierda del PSOE, 1935-1936. Madrid, 1977. pp. 328. *bibliog.*

PARTIDO SOCIALISTA OBRERO ESPAÑOL. PSOE en sus documentos, 1879-1977. Madrid, 1977. pp. 285. *bibliog.*

SOCIALIST PARTY (UNITED STATES).

GREEN (JAMES R.) Grass-roots socialism: radical movements in the Southwest, 1895- 1943. Baton Rouge, [1978]. pp. 450.

SOCIALIST REVOLUTIONARY PARTY (RUSSIA).

GINEV (VLADIMIR NIKOLAEVICH) Agrarnyi vopros i melkoburzhuaznye partii v Rossii v 1917 g.: k istorii bankrotstva neonarodnichestva. Leningrad, 1977. pp. 295.

— History.

HILDERMEIER (MANFRED) Die Sozialrevolutionäre Partei Russlands: Agrarsozialismus und Modernisierung im Zarenreich, 1900-1914. Köln, [1978]. pp. 458. *bibliog.*

SOCIALISTS

— Germany.

BERNDT (HELGA) Eine Dokumentation zum 100. Jahrestag des Sozialistengesetzes, 1878-1890: biographische Skizzen von Leipziger Arbeiterfunktionären. Vaduz/Liechtenstein, 1979. pp. 301.

— Poland.

COTTAM (KAZIMIERA JANINA) Boleslaw Limanowski, 1835-1935: a study in socialism and nationalism. Boulder, Colo., 1978. pp. 365. *bibliog. (East European Quarterly. East European Monographs. 41)*

— United States.

PRATT (NORMA FAIN) Morris Hillquit: a political history of an American Jewish socialist. Westport, Conn., 1979. pp. 272. *bibliog.*

SOCIALISTS, JEWISH.

PRATT (NORMA FAIN) Morris Hillquit: a political history of an American Jewish socialist. Westport, Conn., 1979. pp. 272. *bibliog.*

SOCIALIZATION.

AXTELL (JAMES L.) The school upon a hill: education and society in colonial New England. New Haven, Conn., 1974. pp. 298.

The DEVELOPMENT of social understanding; edited by Joseph Glick and K. Alison Clarke-Stewart. New York, [1978]. pp. 288. *bibliogs.*

ISSUES in childhood social development; edited by Harry McGurk. London, 1978. pp. 270. *bibliogs.*

O'DELL (FELICITY ANN) Socialisation through children's literature: the Soviet example. Cambridge, 1978. pp. 278. *bibliog. (National Association for Soviet and East European Studies. Soviet and East European Studies)*

ROSENTHAL (TED L.) and ZIMMERMAN (BARRY J.) Social learning and cognition. New York, 1978. pp. 338. *bibliog.*

LIGHT (PAUL) The development of social sensitivity: a study of social aspects of role-taking in young children. Cambridge, 1979. pp. 123. *bibliog.*

SOCIALLY HANDICAPPED.

LEWIS (MICHAEL) 1937- . The culture of inequality. Amherst, 1978. pp. 207.

— United Kingdom.

HAKIM (C.) Census-based area profiles: a review. [London], 1977. pp. 14. *bibliog. (U.K. Office of Population Censuses and Surveys. Occasional Papers. 2)*

TACKLING urban deprivation: the contribution of area-based management; by Tim Mason [and others]; (area management monitoring project);...commissioned by the Department of the Environment. [Birmingham], 1977. pp. 94.

CROSS (CRISPIN PATRIC ROBERT) Ethnic minorities in the inner city: the ethnic dimension in urban deprivation in England. London, Commission for Racial Equality, 1978. pp. 183. *bibliog.*

— — Research.

U.K. Joint Working Party on Transmitted Deprivation. 1977. Third report; [D. Robinson, chairman]. [London, 1977]. pp. 12, vii.

— — Scotland.

PAISLEY COMMUNITY DEVELOPMENT PROJECT. A profile of Ferguslie Park; (by John English). [Paisley, 1978]. pp. 22.

SOCIALLY HANDICAPPED CHILDREN

— Education — Denmark.

NORD-LARSEN (MOGENS) Tabere i skolen, 7 år efter: Losers in school, 7 years later. København, 1977. pp. 166. *bibliog. (Socialforskningsinstituttet. Publikationer. 80) With English summary.*

— United Kingdom.

WEDGE (PETER) and PROSSER (HILARY) Born to fail? London, 1973 repr. 1977. pp. 64.

SOCIEDAD NACIONAL DE AGRICULTURA.

CARRIERE (JEAN) The "Sociedad Nacional de Agricultura" in Chilean politics: 1932-1970. 1978. fo. 235. *bibliog.* Typescript. Ph.D. (London) thesis: unpublished. *This thesis is the property of London University and may not be removed from the Library.*

SOCIETE DU CANADA.

MIQUELON (DALE) Dugard of Rouen: French trade to Canada and the West Indies, 1729-1770. Montreal, [1978]. pp. 282. *bibliog.*

SOCIETY FOR THE DIFFUSION OF USEFUL KNOWLEDGE.

PERCIVAL (JANET) compiler. The Society for the Diffusion of Useful Knowledge, 1826- 1848: a handlist of the society's correspondence and papers. London, 1978. pp. 120. *(London. University College. Library. Occasional Publications. No. 5)*

SOCIOBIOLOGY.

WILSON (EDWARD OSBORNE) On human nature. Cambridge, Mass., 1978. pp. 260.

RUSE (MICHAEL) Sociobiology: sense or nonsense? Dordrecht, 1979. pp. 231. *bibliog.*

SOCIOLINGUISTICS.

SOCIOCULTURAL dimensions of language use; edited by Mary Sanches and Ben G. Blount. New York, [1975]. pp. 404. *bibliogs.*

LANGUAGE and politics; edited by William M. O'Barr and Jean F. O'Barr. The Hague, [1976]. pp. 506. *bibliog.*

UNIVERSALISM versus relativism in language and thought...;[edited by] Rik Pinxten. The Hague, [1976]. pp. 310. *bibliogs. Proceedings of a colloquium on the Sapir-Whorf hypotheses.*

COLLOQUIUM ON NEW WAYS OF ANALYZING VARIATION, 3RD, GEORGETOWN UNIVERSITY, 1974. Studies in language variation: semantics, syntax, phonology, pragmatics, social situations, ethnographic approaches; [edited by] Ralph W. Fasold [and] Roger W. Shuy. Washington, D.C., [1977]. pp. 311. *bibliogs.*

LANGUAGE planning processes; edited by Joan Rubin [and others]. The Hague, [1977]. pp. 288. *bibliogs.*

LANGUAGE, ethnicity and intergroup relations; edited by Howard Giles. London, 1977. pp. 370. *bibliog.*

ADVANCES in the study of societal multilingualism; edited by Joshua A. Fishman. The Hague, [1978]. pp. 842. *bibliogs.*

CHURCHILL (LINDSEY) Questioning strategies in sociolinguistics. Rowley, Mass., 1978. pp. 161. *bibliog.*

GREGORY (MICHAEL J.) and CARROLL (SUSANNE) Language and situation: language varieties and their social contexts. London, 1978. pp. 113. *bibliog.*

HALLIDAY (MICHAEL ALEXANDER KIRKWOOD) Language as social semiotic: the social interpretation of language and meaning. London, 1978. pp. 256. *bibliog.*

INTERNATIONAL CONGRESS OF ANTHROPOLOGICAL AND ETHNOLOGICAL SCIENCES. 9th Congress, 1973. Language and society: anthropological issues; [papers and discussion of a session of the congress]; edited by William C. McCormack [and] Stephen A. Wurm. The Hague, [1979]. pp. 771. *bibliog.*

LANGUAGE and social psychology; edited by Howard Giles and Robert N. St. Clair. Oxford, [1979]. pp. 261. *bibliog.*

SOCIOLOGICAL JURISPRUDENCE.

SOCIOLOGY of law: selected readings; edited by Vilhelm Aubert. Harmondsworth, 1969 repr. 1977. pp. 367. *bibliog.*

FEBBRAJO (ALBERTO) Funzionalismo strutturale e sociologia del diritto nell'opera di Niklas Luhmann. Milano, 1975. pp. 226. *bibliog. (Milan. Università. Istituto di Filosofia e Sociologia del Diritto. Studi di Sociologia del Diritto. 2)*

LAWYERS in their social setting...; edited by D.N. MacCormick. Edinburgh, 1976. pp. 227.

EUROPEAN YEARBOOK IN LAW AND SOCIOLOGY. a., 1977 (1st)- The Hague.

RESEARCH IN LAW AND SOCIOLOGY: an annual compilation of research. a., 1978(v.1)- Connecticut.

GRACE (CLIVE) and WILKINSON (PHILIP) Sociological inquiry and legal phenomena. London, 1978. pp. 307. *bibliog.*

KUDRIAVTSEV (VLADIMIR NIKOLAEVICH) Pravo i povedenie. Moskva, 1978. pp. 191.

NONET (PHILIPPE) and SELZNICK (PHILIP) Law and society in transition: toward responsive law. New York, [1978]. pp. 122.

RECHT und Gesellschaft: Festschrift für Helmut Schelsky zum 65. Geburtstag; herausgegeben von Friedrich Kaulbach und Werner Krawietz. Berlin, [1978]. pp. 839. *bibliog.*

SOCIAL system and legal process; [edited by] Harry M. Johnson. San Francisco, [1978]. pp. 352. *bibliogs. (Sociological Inquiry. 1977)*

INTERNATIONALE VEREINIGUNG FÜR RECHTS- UND SOZIALPHILOSOPHIE. Kongress, 1977. Law and the future of society: a selection of papers...; edited by F. C. Hutley [and others]. Wiesbaden, 1979. pp. 371. *(Archiv für Rechts- und Sozialphilosophie. Beihefte. Neue Folge. Nr. 11). In various languages.*

LAW and society: (readings in the sociology of law); edited by C.M. Campbell [and] Paul Wiles. Oxford, 1979. pp. 310.

SOCIOLOGICAL RESEARCH.

RILEY (MATILDA WHITE) Sociological research; vol.1; a case approach. New York, [1963]. pp. 777. *bibliog.*

ORENSTEIN (ALAN) and PHILLIPS (WILLIAM R.F.) Understanding social research: an introduction. Boston, Mass., 1978. pp. 428.

CONTEMPORARY issues in theory and research: a metasociological perspective; edited by William E. Snizek [and others]. Westport, Conn., 1979. pp. 298. *bibliog.*

SOCIOLOGISTS.

The FOUNDING fathers of social science; edited by Timothy Raison; revised edition by Paul Barker. rev. ed. London, 1979. pp. 319. *bibliogs. Articles first published in New Society.*

— United Kingdom.

BANKS (JOSEPH AMBROSE) and WEBB (DAVID) Ideas or people: the vocational dilemma for sociology graduates. London, [1977]. pp. 111.

— United States.

The HIDDEN professoriate: credentialism, professionalism, and the tenure crisis; edited by Arthur S. Wilke. Westport, Conn., [1979]. pp. 290. *bibliog.*

SOCIOLOGY.

MACIVER (ROBERT MORRISON) Society: a textbook of sociology. New York, 1937 repr. 1947. pp. 596. *bibliog. A rewriting, with substantive additions, of the author's earlier work, Society: its structure and changes.*

HUMAN person, society and state; edited by P.D. Devanandan [and] M.M.Thomas. Bangalore, 1957. pp. 140.

SPANN (OTHMAR) Gesamtausgabe; Herausgeber: Walter Heinrich [and others]. Graz, 1963-79. 21 vols. *bibliogs.*

MARX (KARL) Selected writings in sociology and social philosophy; edited with an introduction and notes by T.B. Bottomore and Maximilien Rubel..., translated by T.B. Bottomore. Harmondsworth, 1963. pp. 272.

MAX Weber and sociology today; edited by Otto Stammer; translated by Kathleen Morris. Oxford, 1971. pp. 256. *Transactions of the 15th German Sociological Congress held in Heidelberg.*

THOMPSON (KENNETH) Sociologist and TUNSTALL (JEREMY) eds. Sociological perspectives: selected readings. Harmondsworth, 1971 repr. 1977. pp. 592. *bibliogs.*

JARVIE (IAN CHARLES) Concepts and society. London, 1972. pp. 214. *bibliog.*

KOROVIN (VLADISLAV FEDOROVICH) Osnovnye problemy "novoi sotsiologii" Raita Millsa [i.e. Wright Mills]. Moskva, 1977. pp. 95. *bibliog.*

READINGS in introductory sociology; [edited by] Dennis H. Wrong, Harry L. Gracey. 3rd ed. New York, [1977]. pp. 564. *bibliogs.*

SOCIETY and change: essays in honour of Sachin Chaudhuri; edited by K.S. Krishnaswamy [and others]. Bombay, 1977. pp. 327.

TOURAINE (ALAIN) La société invisible: regards 1974-1976. Paris, 1977. pp. 289.

WEBER (MAX) Critique of Stammler;...translated, with an introductory essay, by Guy Oakes. New York, [1977]. pp. 184.

BOCOCK (ROBERT) Freud and modern society: an outline and analysis of Freud's sociology. New York, 1978. pp. 200. *bibliog.*

LEE (ALFRED McCLUNG) Sociology for whom? New York, 1978. pp. 236.

MARSLAND (DAVID) Sociological explorations in the service of youth. Leicester, [1978]. pp. 251. *bibliog.*

MARX: sociology/social change/capitalism; edited by Donald McQuarie. London, 1978. pp. 327. *bibliogs.*

OLSEN (MARVIN ELLIOTT) The process of social organization: power in social systems. 2nd ed. New York, [1978]. pp. 415. *bibliogs.*

PAPINEAU (DAVID) For science in the social sciences. London, 1978. pp. 201.

PARSONS (TALCOTT) Action theory and the human condition. New York, [1978]. pp. 464. *bibliogs. Collected essays.*

STINCHCOMBE (ARTHUR LEONARD) Theoretical methods in social history. New York, [1978]. pp. 130. *bibliog.*

WEBSTER (FRANK) Sociology and literature: some methodological problems in a variety of approaches to the study of literature. 1978. fo. 295. *bibliog. Typescript. Ph.D. (London) thesis: unpublished. This thesis is the property of London University and may not be removed from the Library.*

WILSON (EDWARD OSBORNE) On human nature. Cambridge, Mass., 1978. pp. 260.

BURRELL (GIBSON) and MORGAN (GARETH) Sociological paradigms and organisational analysis: elements of the sociology of corporate life. London, 1979. pp. 432. *bibliog.*

CONTEMPORARY issues in theory and research: a metasociological perspective; edited by William E. Snizek [and others]. Westport, Conn., 1979. pp. 298. *bibliog.*

DAHRENDORF (RALF) Lebenschancen: Anläufe zur sozialen und politischen Theorie. Frankfurt am Main, 1979. pp. 240.

FERNANDEZ (RONALD) and BARRILE (LEO) The promise of sociology. 2nd ed. New York, 1979. pp. 596.

HASTINGS (WILLIAM M.) How to think about social problems: a primer for citizens. New York, 1979. pp. 251. *bibliog.*

MAUSS (MARCEL) Sociology and psychology: essays; translated by Ben Brewster. London, 1979. pp. 135. *bibliog.*

PALEN (J. JOHN) Social problems. New York, [1979]. pp. 625. *bibliog.*

PERSPECTIVES in sociology; edited by E.C. Cuff and G.C.F. Payne. London, 1979. pp. 205. *bibliogs.*

SMITH (GILBERT) Social work and the sociology of organizations. rev. ed. London, 1979. pp. 108. *bibliog.*

SOCIOLOGICAL economics; edited by Louis Lévy-Garboua. London, [1979]. pp. 306. *bibliogs. Papers presented at a seminar held in Paris, 1977, sponsored by the Centre National de la Recherche Scientifique, Maison des Sciences de l'Homme and the National Science Foundation.*

— Congresses.

SOCIOLOGICAL ASSOCIATION OF IRELAND. Annual Conference, 1st, Dublin, 1974 and 4th, Ballymascanlon, 1977. Proceedings...; edited by A.E.C.W. Spencer and H. Tovey. Belfast, 1978. pp. 74. *bibliogs.*

SOCIOLOGICAL ASSOCIATION OF IRELAND. Annual Conference, 3rd, Dublin, 1976. Proceedings...; edited by A.E.C.W. Spencer [and others]. Belfast, 1977. pp. 50.

— History.

ROSSIDES (DANIEL W.) The history and nature of sociological theory. Boston, Mass., [1978]. pp. 567.

BOTTOMORE (THOMAS BURTON) and NISBET (ROBERT ALEXANDER) eds. A history of sociological analysis. London, 1979. pp. 717. *bibliogs.*

The FOUNDING fathers of social science; edited by Timothy Raison; revised edition by Paul Barker. rev. ed. London, 1979. pp. 319. *bibliogs. Articles first published in New Society.*

PERSPECTIVES in sociology; edited by E.C. Cuff and G.C.F. Payne. London, 1979. pp. 205. *bibliogs.*

— — China.

WONG (SIU-LUN) Sociology and socialism in contemporary China. London, 1979. pp. 147. *bibliog.*

— Methodology.

BLUMER (HERBERT) Symbolic interactionism: perspective and method. Englewood Cliffs, N.J., [1969]. pp. 208.

KRITIKA sovremennoi burzhuaznoi teoreticheskoi sotsiologii. Moskva, 1977. pp. 279.

OSIPOV (GENNADII VASIL'EVICH) and ANDREEV (E.P.) Metody izmereniia v sotsiologii. Moskva, 1977. pp. 183. *bibliog.*

DURKHEIM (EMILE) On institutional analysis; edited, translated and with an introduction by Mark Traugott. Chicago, [1978]. pp. 276. *bibliog.*

ORENSTEIN (ALAN) and PHILLIPS (WILLIAM R.F.) Understanding social research: an introduction. Boston, Mass., 1978. pp. 428.

TURNER (JONATHAN H.) The structure of sociological theory. Rev. ed. Homewood, Ill., 1978. pp. 446.

BASH (HARRY H.) Sociology, race and ethnicity: a critique of American ideological intrusions upon sociological theory. New York, [1979]. pp. 252. *bibliog.*

— Philosophy.

SMITH (CHARLES W.) 1938- . A critique of sociological reasoning: an essay in philosophical sociology. Oxford, [1979]. pp. 155. *bibliog.*

— Study and teaching — Spain.

SOLARI (ALDO E.) ed. Poder y desarrollo: America Latina; estudios sociológicos en homenaje a Jose Medina Echavarria. Mexico, 1977. pp. 429.

— Hungary.

SOZIOLOGIE und Gesellschaft in Ungarn: aus dem Ertrag des ersten Jahrzehnts der neueren ungarischen Soziologie; herausgegeben von Bálint Balla. Stuttgart, 1974. 4 vols. (in 1).

— United Kingdom.

COLLINI (STEFAN) Liberalism and sociology: L. T. Hobhouse and political argument in England, 1880-1914. Cambridge, 1979. pp. 281. *bibliog.*

— United States.

DU BOIS (WILLIAM EDWARD BURGHARDT) W.E.B. Du Bois on sociology and the Black community; edited... by Dan S. Green and Edwin D. Driver. Chicago, 1978. pp. 320. *bibliog.*

GORDON (LEONARD) Sociologist, and HARVEY (PATRICIA ATCHISON) Sociology and American social issues. Boston, Mass., [1978]. pp. 548. *bibliogs.*

SOCIOLOGY, CHRISTIAN.

ECCLESIASTICAL HISTORY SOCIETY. Summer Meeting, 16th, and Winter Meeting, 17th, 197-. Religious motivation: biographical and sociological problems for the church historian: papers read at the...meeting[s]...; edited by Derek Baker. Oxford, 1978. pp. 516. *(Studies in Church History. vol.15)*

ACQUAVIVA (SABINO SAMELE) The decline of the sacred in industrial society; translated by Patricia Lipscomb. Oxford, 1979. pp. 289. *bibliog.*

SOCIOLOGY, MILITARY.

ESERCITO e società borghese: l'istituzione militare nell'analisi marxista; a cura di Fabrizio Battistelli. Roma, 1976. pp. 336. *bibliog.*

The POLITICS of antipolitics: the military in Latin America; edited by Brian Loveman and Thomas M. Davies. Lincoln, Nebr., [1978]. pp. 309.

SOCIOLOGY, RURAL.

PEASANT society: a reader; edited by Jack M. Potter [and others]. Boston, Mass., [1967]. pp. 453. *bibliog.*

RAMBAUD (PLACIDE) Sociologie rurale: recueil de textes. Paris, [1976]. pp. 325. *bibliog. (Paris. Ecole des Hautes Etudes en Sciences Sociales. Textes de Sciences Sociales. 16)*

COX (TERENCE M.) Rural sociology in the Soviet Union: its history and basic concepts. London, [1979]. pp. 106. *bibliog.*

LEWIS (G.J.) Rural communities. London, 1979. pp. 255. *bibliog.*

SOCIOLOGY, URBAN.

MAURICE (MARC) and DELOMENIE (DOMINIQUE) Mode de vie et espaces sociaux: processus d'urbanisation et différenciation sociale dans deux zones urbaines de Marseille. Paris, [1976]. pp. 223. *bibliog.*

SOCIAL areas in cities; edited by D.T. Herbert and R.J. Johnston. London, [1976]. 2 vols. *bibliogs.*

DAGNAUD (MONIQUE) Le mythe de la qualité de la vie et la politique urbaine en France: enquête sur l'idéologie urbaine de l'élite technocratique et politique, 1945-1975. Paris, [1978]. pp. 326. *bibliog.*

KILMARTIN (LESLIE) and THORNS (DAVID C.) Cities unlimited: the sociology of urban development in Australia and New Zealand. Sydney, 1978. pp. 195. *bibliog.*

WILSON (ROBERT A.) of Delaware University and SCHULZ (DAVID A.) Urban sociology. Englewood Cliffs, [1978]. pp. 368.

COUSINS (ALBERT N.) and NAGPAUL (HANS) Urban life: the sociology of cities and urban society. New York, [1979]. pp. 608. *bibliog.*

REES (P.H.) Residential patterns in American cities: 1960. Chicago, 1979. pp. 405. *bibliog. (Chicago. Unversity. Department of Geography. Research Papers. No. 189)*

TREBLE (JAMES H.) Urban poverty in Britain 1830-1914. London, 1979. pp. 216.

SOCIOLOGY AS A PROFESSION.

BANKS (JOSEPH AMBROSE) and WEBB (DAVID) Ideas or people: the vocational dilemma for sociology graduates. London, [1977]. pp. 111.

SOCRATES.

WOOD (ELLEN MEIKSINS) and WOOD (NEAL) Class ideology and ancient political theory: Socrates, Plato and Aristotle in social context. Oxford, 1978. pp. 275. *bibliog.*

SANTAS (GERASIMOS XENOPHON) Socrates: philosophy in Plato's early dialogues. London, 1979. pp. 343. *bibliog.*

SOFT DRINK INDUSTRY

— Belgium.

JACQUEMIN (ALEXIS) and GHELLINCK (ELIZABETH DE) L'évolution de la concentration dans l'industrie de la brasserie et des boissons en Belgique. [Brussels], Communautés Européennes, 1976. pp. 108.

— France.

BOULET (D.) and LAPORTE (J.P.) Etude sur l'évolution de la concentration dans les industries des boissons et des boissons non alcoolisées en France. [Brussels], Communautés Européennes, 1976. pp. 284.

— Germany.

BREITENACHER (MICHAEL) Untersuchung zur Konzentrationsentwicklung in der Getränke Industrie in Deutschland. [Brussels], Europäischen Gemeinschaften, 1976. pp. 156.

— Italy.

BALLIANO (PIERA) and LANZETTI (RENATO) Studio sull'evoluzione della concentrazione nell'industria delle bevande in Italia. [Brussels], Comunità Europee, 1976. pp. 143.

— Netherlands.

BROUWER (MARIA) and PIJNAPPEL (THEO) A study of the evolution of concentration in the Dutch beverages industry. [Brussels], European Communities, 1976. pp. 149.

SOGAS.

MWAMULA-LUBANDI (E.D.) Transitional socio-economic clan relations among Basoga. [Uppsala], 1978. pp. 182. *bibliog.*

SOIL EROSION

— Fiji.

FIJI. Department of Agriculture. 1955. Soil erosion and its control in Fiji; by C.E. Whitehead. Sura, [1955]. pp. (52). *(Bulletins. No. 28)*

— New Zealand.

NEW ZEALAND. Ministry of Works and Development. 1975. The East Coast Planning Council. [Wellington, 1975]. pp. 11.

SOIL SURVEYS

— Canada.

TOSINE (TONU P.) The physical base for agriculture in central Canada. Toronto, 1978. pp. 59. *bibliog. (Ontario. Ministry of Agriculture and Food. Economics Branch. Economics Information)*

— Philippine Islands.

SOIL survey of Cebu province, Philippines;...by Alfredo Barrera [and others]. Manila, 1954. pp. 134. *bibliog. (Philippine Islands. Department of Agriculture and Natural Resources. Soil Reports. No. 17) Map in end pocket.*

— United Kingdom.

FURNESS (R.R.) Soils of Cheshire. Harpenden, 1978. pp. 240. *bibliog. (U.K. Soil Survey of Great Britain. Bulletins. No. 6) Map in end pocket.*

CARROLL (D.M.) and others. Soils of South and West Yorkshire. Harpenden, 1979. pp. 201. *bibliog. (U.K. Soil Survey of Great Britain. Bulletins. No. 7)*

SOLDIERS

— Family relationships.

MILITARY families: adaptation to change; edited by Edna J. Hunter and D. Stephen Nice. New York, [1978]. pp. 278. *bibliog.*

SOLDIERS(Cont.)

— France.

PELLETIER (ROBERT) and RAVET (SERGE) Le mouvement des soldats: les comités de soldats et l'antimilitarisme révolutionnaire. Paris, 1976. pp. 199.

— United Kingdom.

U.K. Social Survey. [Reports. New Series]. 1060. Army welfare; a survey carried out for the Army Welfare Inquiry Committee, Ministry of Defence; [by] Malcolm Wilders. London, 1977. pp. 28.

BUCKLEY (ROGER NORMAN) Slaves in red coats: the British West India regiments, 1795- 1815. New Haven, 1979. pp. 210. *bibliog.*

SOLIDARITY.

DURKHEIM (EMILE) On institutional analysis; edited, translated and with an introduction by Mark Traugott. Chicago, [1978]. pp. 276. *bibliog.*

SOLZHENITSYN (ALEKSANDR ISAEVICH).

MEDVEDEV (ROI ALEKSANDROVICH) Political essays. Nottingham, 1976. pp. 151.

SOMALI REPUBLIC.

WAR SOMALI SIDIHI; [pd. by] Information Office, Somaliland Protectorate. fortn., Jl 31 1954-N 1 1958 (no. 41 - no. 152), with gaps; ceased pbln. Hargeisa.

SOMALILAND NEWS; [pd. by] Information Office, Somaliland Protectorate. w., (formerly fortn.,). N 24 1958-D 12 1960 (no.1, special issue - no. 96), with gaps. Hargeisa. *[articles in English and Arabic] Incorporates WAR SOMALI SIDIHI.*

DAWN; [pd. by] Ministry of Information and National Guidance, Somali Republic. w., Ap 24 1970-Ja 19 1973(no. 23 - no.176, last issue), with gaps. Mogadishu.

SOMATOLOGY.

See PHYSICAL ANTHROPOLOGY.

SOMOZA FAMILY.

CRAWLEY (EDUARDO) Dictators never die: a portrait of Nicaragua and the Samoza dynasty. London, 1979. pp. 180. *bibliog.*

SOPORE

— Economic conditions.

INDIA. Office of the Director of Census Operations, Jamma and Kashmir. 1970. A pilot town study of Sopore, Tehsil Sopore, District Baramulla; field investigation and draft by J. Kay Nanda; editor J.N. Zutshi. [Delhi, 1970]. pp. 157.

— Social conditions.

INDIA. Office of the Director of Census Operations, Jamma and Kashmir. 1970. A pilot town study of Sopore, Tehsil Sopore, District Baramulla; field investigation and draft by J. Kay Nanda; editor J.N. Zutshi. [Delhi, 1970]. pp. 157.

SOREL (GEORGES).

VERNON (RICHARD ANTHONY) Commitment and change: Georges Sorel and the idea of revolution. Toronto, [1978]. pp. 148. *bibliog.*

SOUTH AFRICA.

REPORTS ON THE STATE OF SOUTH AFRICA. No. 27. South Africa today: a brief glimpse at Africa's most stable and progressive country. London, Department of Information, South African Embassy, 1964. 1 pamphlet (unpaged).

— Appropriations and expenditures.

SOUTH AFRICA. Bureau of Statistics. Expenditure of the central government. a., 1970/1977(1st)- Pretoria. *[in English and Afrikaans] File includes Statistical news release. Expenditure of the central government.*

— Commerce.

DICKASON (G.B.) Cornish immigrants to South Africa: the Cousin Jacks' contribution to the development of mining and commerce, 1820-1920. Cape Town, 1978. pp. 122. *bibliog.*

— Constitution.

SOUTH AFRICA. Constitution. 1961-67. Republic of South Africa Constitution Act, No. 32 of 1961, as amended... [to] 1967. [Pretoria, 1967]. pp. 95. *In English and Afrikaans.*

CONFERENCE ON CONSTITUTIONAL MODELS AND CONSTITUTIONAL CHANGE IN SOUTH AFRICA, UNIVERSITY OF NATAL, 1978. Constitutional change in South Africa: proceedings...; edited by John Benyon. Pietermaritzburg, 1978. pp. 297.

— Defences.

SOUTH Africa in world strategy: special survey. London, Department of Information, South African Embassy, 1969. pp. 21.

GELDENHUYS (DEON) South Africa's search for security since the Second World War. Braamfontein, 1978. pp. 19. *(South African Institute of International Affairs. Occasional Papers)*

GRUNDY (KENNETH W.) Defense legislation and communal politics: the evolution of a white South African nation as reflected in the controversy over the assignment of armed forces abroad, 1912-1976. Athens, Ohio, 1978. pp. 51. *(Ohio University. Center for International Studies. Papers in International Studies. Africa Series. No. 33)*

— Department of Information.

SOUTH AFRICA. Commission of Inquiry into Alleged Irregularities in the former Department of Information. 1978. Report; [R.P.B. Erasmus, chairman] (R.P. 113/1978). in SOUTH AFRICA. Parliament. House of Assembly. Votes and proceedings; (with Printed annexures).

— Description and travel.

ALLEN (VIVIEN) Lady trader: a biography of Mrs. Sarah Heckford. London, 1979. pp. 243.

— Economic conditions.

SOUTH AFRICA. Information Service of South Africa, New York, 1975. Prospects and progress in South Africa. [5th ed.] New York, [1975]. pp. 153. *bibliog.*

DAVIES (WILLIAM J.) Principal distributional and structural characteristics of the Border Region and some internal implications of the national regional development policy. Port Elizabeth, S.A., 1976. pp. 122. *(University of Port Elizabeth. Institute for Planning Research. Research Reports. No. 16) With summaries in English and Afrikaans.*

DEVELOPMENT STUDIES ON SOUTHERN AFRICA: journal of the Bureau for Economic Research: Co-operation and Development. q., Oc 1978 (v.1, no.1)- Pretoria.

ALVERSON (HOYT) Mind in the heart of darkness: value and self-identity among the Tswana of southern Africa. New Haven, 1978. pp. 299. *bibliog.*

TURNER (RICHARD) The eye of the needle: toward participatory democracy in South Africa. Maryknoll, 1978. pp. 173.

— Economic policy.

DAVIES (WILLIAM J.) Principal distributional and structural characteristics of the Border Region and some internal implications of the national regional development policy. Port Elizabeth, S.A., 1976. pp. 122. *(University of Port Elizabeth. Institute for Planning Research. Research Reports. No. 16) With summaries in English and Afrikaans.*

VAN DER MERWE (SANDRA) The environment of South African business. Cape Town, 1976. pp. 324. *bibliogs.*

— Executive departments.

SOUTH AFRICA. Department of Health. Report. a., Jl 1947/D 1952, 1953-1976. Pretoria. *[in English and Afrikaans] Included in SOUTH AFRICA. Parliament. House of Assembly. Votes and proceedings (with Printed annexures)*

SOUTH AFRICA. Commission of Inquiry into Alleged Irregularities in the former Department of Information. 1978. Report; [R.P.B. Erasmus, chairman] (R.P. 113/1978). in SOUTH AFRICA. Parliament. House of Assembly. Votes and proceedings; (with Printed annexures).

— Foreign economic relations — Germany.

CERVENKA (ZDENEK) and ROGERS (BARBARA) The nuclear axis: secret collaboration between West Germany and South Africa. London, 1978. pp. 464.

— — Israel.

STEVENS (RICHARD P.) and ELMESSIRI (ABDELWAHAB M.) eds. Israel and South Africa: the progression of a relationship. New York, [1976]. pp. 214. *bibliog.*

— — United States.

SEIDMAN (ANN WILLCOX) and SEIDMAN (NEVA) U.S. multinationals in Southern Africa. Dar es Salaam, 1977. pp. 252. *bibliogs.*

— Foreign opinion.

GANN (LEWIS H.) and DUIGNAN (PETER) South Africa: war, revolution or peace? Stanford, [1978]. pp. 85. *(Stanford University. Hoover Institution on War, Revolution and Peace. Hoover Institution Publications. 199)*

— Foreign relations.

OLIVIER (G.C.) Suid-Afrika se buitelandse beleid. Pretoria, 1977. pp. 236. *bibliog.*

GELDENHUYS (DEON) South Africa's search for security since the Second World War. Braamfontein, 1978. pp. 19. *(South African Institute of International Affairs. Occasional Papers)*

INTERNATIONAL pressures and political change in South Africa: (papers in a symposium...held at the University of Natal in August 1977 under the auspices of the Department of History and Political Science and the South African Institute of International Affairs); edited by F. McA. Clifford- Vaughan. Cape Town, 1978. pp. 109.

SOUTH AFRICA. 1978. South West Africa/Namibia: the South African government's response to the U.N. Secretary-General's report on the implementation of the Western proposal: the government's statement of 20 September 1978; and, An analysis by André du Pisani. Braamfontein, 1978. pp. 9. *(South African Institute of International Affairs. Occasional Papers)*

GELDENHUYS (DEON) The neutral option and sub-continental solidarity: a consideration of Foreign Minister Pik Botha's Zürich statement of 7 March 1979. Braamfontein, 1979. pp. 13. *(South African Institute of International Affairs. Occasional Papers)*

— — Israel.

STEVENS (RICHARD P.) and ELMESSIRI (ABDELWAHAB M.) eds. Israel and South Africa: the progression of a relationship. New York, [1976]. pp. 214. *bibliog.*

— — Scandinavia.

WINQUIST (ALAN H.) Scandinavians and South Africa: their impact on the cultural, social and economic development of pre-1902 South Africa. Cape Town, 1978. pp. 268. *bibliog.*

SOUTH AFRICA.

— — Transkei.

VENTER (DENIS) The Republic of Transkei: two years of independence, 1976-1978. Braamfontein, 1979. pp. 9. *(South African Institute of International Affairs. Occasional Papers)*

— — United States.

SPRING (MARTIN C.) Confrontation: the approaching crisis between the United States and South Africa. Sandton, 1977. pp. 181.

GANN (LEWIS H.) and DUIGNAN (PETER) South Africa: war, revolution or peace? Stanford, [1978]. pp. 85. *(Stanford University. Hoover Institution on War, Revolution and Peace. Hoover Institution Publications. 199)*

— Government publications — Bibliography.

SOUTH AFRICA. Division of Library Services. 1978. Bibliography of South African government publications. Vol. 2. Department of Agricultural Technical Services, Department of Agricultural Economics and Marketing publications: 1910- 1972. Pretoria, 1978. pp. 610.

— History.

MULLER (C.F.J.) ed. Five hundred years: a history of South Africa. 2nd ed. Pretoria, 1975. pp. 542. *bibliog.*

WINQUIST (ALAN H.) Scandinavians and South Africa: their impact on the cultural, social and economic development of pre-1902 South Africa. Cape Town, 1978. pp. 268. *bibliog.*

ALLEN (VIVIEN) Lady trader: a biography of Mrs. Sarah Heckford. London, 1979. pp. 243.

BLACK leaders in Southern African history; edited by Christopher Saunders. London, 1979. pp. 160.

— — Bibliography.

PRETORIA. State Library. Publications françaises concernant l'Afrique du Sud: bibliographie des livres et fascicules jusqu'à l'année 1935; French publications on South Africa: a bibliography of books and pamphlets to the year 1935; edited by M.M. Boshoff. Pretoria, 1978. pp. 163. *(Bibliographies. No. 20) In French and English.*

— Industries.

INDUSTRIAL DEVELOPMENT CORPORATION OF SOUTH AFRICA. [Handbook]. Johannesburg, 1975. pp. 118.

VAN DER MERWE (SANDRA) The environment of South African business. Cape Town, 1976. pp. 324. *bibliogs.*

SOUTH AFRICA. Bureau of Statistics. 1977- . Census of manufacturing, 1972. [Pretoria, 1977 in progress]. *(Reports. Nos. 10-21-28, etc.) In English and Afrikaans.*

— Manufactures.

SOUTH AFRICA. Bureau of Statistics. 1977- . Census of manufacturing, 1972. [Pretoria, 1977 in progress]. *(Reports. Nos. 10-21-28, etc.) In English and Afrikaans.*

— Nationalism.

GRUNDY (KENNETH W.) Defense legislation and communal politics: the evolution of a white South African nation as reflected in the controversy over the assignment of armed forces abroad, 1912-1976. Athens, Ohio, 1978. pp. 51. *(Ohio University. Center for International Studies. Papers in International Studies. Africa Series. No. 33)*

— Native races.

SOUTH AFRICA. Department of Information. 1968. Taking factories to the people: South Africa's border industry project. [Pretoria, 1968]. pp. 28. *(Fact Paper Series)*

CILLIE (PIET) Vision of the seventies: evolving relationships in southern Africa. [London, Department of Information, South African Embassy, 1969]. pp. (7). *Reprinted from January 1969 Report from South Africa.*

The SQUATTER problem in the Western Cape: some causes and remedies; by George Ellis [and others]. Johannesburg, [1977]. pp. 119.

— Neutrality.

GELDENHUYS (DEON) The neutral option and sub-continental solidarity: a consideration of Foreign Minister Pik Botha's Zürich statement of 7 March 1979. Braamfontein, 1979. pp. 13. *(South African Institute of International Affairs. Occasional Papers)*

— Politics and government.

FARRELLY (MICHAEL JAMES) The settlement after the war in South Africa. London, 1900. pp. 321.

VINDEX, pseud. [i.e. F. VERSCHOYLE] Cecil Rhodes: his political life and speeches, 1881-1900. London, 1900. pp. 864.

VAN DER MERWE (SANDRA) The environment of South African business. Cape Town, 1976. pp. 324. *bibliogs.*

CLOETE (JACOBUS JOHANNES NICOLAAS) South African public administration: selected readings; Suid-Afrikaanse publieke administrasie: uitgesoekte leesstukke. Pretoria, 1977. pp. 326. *In English or Afrikaans, the latter with an English summary.*

VORSTER (BALTHAZAR JOHANNES) Select speeches; edited by O. Geyser. Bloemfontein, 1977. pp. 363. *bibliog.*

BOTHA (P. ROELF) South Africa: plan for the future: a basis for dialogue. Johannesburg, 1978. pp. 250. *bibliog.*

GANN (LEWIS H.) and DUIGNAN (PETER) South Africa: war, revolution or peace? Stanford, [1978]. pp. 85. *(Stanford University. Hoover Institution on War, Revolution and Peace. Hoover Institution Publications. 199)*

The GOVERNMENT and politics of South Africa; edited by Anthony de Crespigny and Robert Schrire. Cape Town, 1978. pp. 260. *bibliog.*

INTERNATIONAL pressures and political change in South Africa: (papers in a symposium...held at the University of Natal in August 1977 under the auspices of the Department of History and Political Science and the South African Institute of International Affairs); edited by F. McA. Clifford- Vaughan. Cape Town, 1978. pp. 109.

STARCKE (ANNA) Survival; taped interviews with South Africa's power élite. Cape Town, 1978. pp. 217.

TURNER (RICHARD) The eye of the needle: toward participatory democracy in South Africa. Maryknoll, 1978. pp. 173.

VILJOEN (STEPHANUS PETRUS DU TOIT) Whither South Africa? Braamfontein, 1978. pp. 12. *(South African Institute of International Affairs. Occasional Papers)*

BIKO (STEVEN) The testimony of Steve Biko; [edited by Millard Arnold]. London, 1979. pp. 298.

BLACK leaders in Southern African history; edited by Christopher Saunders. London, 1979. pp. 160.

MAGUBANE (BERNARD MAKHOSEZWE) The political economy of race and class in South Africa. New York, [1979]. pp. 364.

— Population.

HIGGINS (EDWARD) A study of some norms and values pertaining to fertility in an urban white population. [Johannesburg], 1960. pp. 266. *bibliog. Dissertation presented to the University of the Witwatersrand for the degree of Master of Arts, 1960.*

LÖTTER (JOHANN MORGENDALL) and VAN TONDER (JAN LOUIS) Aspects of fertility of Indian South Africans. Pretoria, 1975. pp. 37. *bibliog. (Human Sciences Research Council [South Africa]. Institute for Sociological, Demographic and Criminological Research. Reports. No. S-40)*

— Race relations.

MULLER (HILGARD) Why apartheid?; (an address to a joint meeting of the Royal African Society and the Royal Commonwealth Society on November 15, 1962). London, Department of Information, South African Embassy, 1962. pp. 15. *(Reports on the State of South Africa. No. 23)*

REPORTS ON THE STATE OF SOUTH AFRICA. No. 26. You be the judge. London, Department of Information, South African Embassy, 1964. pp. (4).

LUTTIG (HENDRIK GERHARDUS) South Africa faces the future; (an address given...to the South Africa Society at the Royal Society of Arts, London, on May 12, 1967). [London, Department of Information, South African Embassy, 1967]. pp. 14. *(Reports on the State of South Africa. No. 32)*

SOUTH AFRICA. Information Service of South Africa, New York. 1967. Setting the record straight. New York, [1967]. pp. 24.

UNITED NATIONS. Office of Public Information. 1969. Action against apartheid. (OPI/364). New York, [1969]. pp. 31.

RUBIN (LESLIE) Apartheid in practice. (OPI/428). [New York], United Nations, 1971. pp. 70.

SMEDLEY (LINDA NORA) and GROENEWALD (DIRK CORNELIS) The Chinese community in South Africa: phase 1: background and attitudes of the white population group towards the Chinese minority group. Pretoria, 1976. pp. 103. *bibliog. (Human Sciences Research Council [South Africa]. Institute for Sociological, Demographic and Criminological Research. Reports. No. S-44)*

AFRICAN perspectives on South Africa: a collection of speeches, articles and documents; edited by Hendrik W. van der Merwe [and others]. Stanford, 1978. pp. 612. *(Stanford University. Hoover Institution on War, Revolution and Peace. Hoover Institution Publications 176)*

AGAINST racism, apartheid and colonialism: documents published by the GDR, 1949-1977; [edited by Alfred Babing]. Berlin, 1978. pp. 664. *Facing title page: GDR Institute for International Politics and Economics; GDR Committee for the Decade of Action to Combat Racism and Racial Discrimination.*

DESAI (BARNEY) and MARNEY (CARDIFF) The killing of the Imam. London, 1978. pp. 146.

GANN (LEWIS H.) and DUIGNAN (PETER) South Africa: war, revolution or peace? Stanford, [1978]. pp. 85. *(Stanford University. Hoover Institution on War, Revolution and Peace. Hoover Institution Publications. 199)*

GERHART (GAIL M.) Black Power in South Africa: the evolution of an ideology. Berkeley, Calif., [1978]. pp. 364. *bibliog.*

HORRELL (MURIEL) compiler. Laws affecting race relations in South Africa, to the end of 1976. Johannesburg, 1978. pp. 529.

KANE-BERMAN (JOHN) Soweto: black revolt, white reaction. Johannesburg, 1978 repr. 1979. pp. 268.

QUISLINGS or realists?: a documentary study of "Coloured" politics in South Africa; [edited by] Pierre Hugo. Johannesburg, 1978. pp. 744.

TURNER (RICHARD) The eye of the needle: toward participatory democracy in South Africa. Maryknoll, 1978. pp. 173.

VILJOEN (STEPHANUS PETRUS DU TOIT) Whither South Africa? Braamfontein, 1978. pp. 12. *(South African Institute of International Affairs. Occasional Papers)*

BIKO (STEVEN) The testimony of Steve Biko; [edited by Millard Arnold]. London, 1979. pp. 298.

BLACK leaders in Southern African history; edited by Christopher Saunders. London, 1979. pp. 160.

HERBSTEIN (DENIS) White man, we want to talk to you. London, 1979. pp. 270.

SOUTH AFRICA.(Cont.)

MAGUBANE (BERNARD MAKHOSEZWE) The political economy of race and class in South Africa. New York, [1979]. pp. 364.

— Bibliography.

SCHOLTZ (P.L.) and others, compilers. A select bibliography on race relations at the Cape, 1652-1795: a guide for historical research. Bellville, South Africa, [1977]. pp. 132.

— Relations (general) with Subsaharan Africa.

CILLIE (PIET) Vision of the seventies: evolving relationships in southern Africa. [London, Department of Information, South African Embassy, 1969]. pp. (7). *Reprinted from January 1969 Report from South Africa.*

— Social conditions.

AFRICAN perspectives on South Africa: a collection of speeches, articles and documents; edited by Hendrik W. van der Merwe [and others]. Stanford, 1978. pp. 612. *(Stanford University. Hoover Institution on War, Revolution and Peace. Hoover Institution Publications 176)*

LEVER (HENRY) South African society. Johannesburg, 1978. pp. 312. *bibliogs.*

MAGUBANE (BERNARD MAKHOSEZWE) The political economy of race and class in South Africa. New York, [1979]. pp. 364.

— Social policy.

VAN DER MERWE (SANDRA) The environment of South African business. Cape Town, 1976. pp. 324. *bibliogs.*

— Statistics, Vital.

SOUTH AFRICA. Bureau of Statistics. Report on births: South Africa. a., 1972/1974(2nd)- Pretoria. *[in English and Afrikaans]*

SOUTH AFRICAN WAR, 1899-1902.

FARRELLY (MICHAEL JAMES) The settlement after the war in South Africa. London, 1900. pp. 321.

SOUTH AUSTRALIA

— Economic conditions.

SOUTH AUSTRALIA. Industrial Development Division. 1972. South Australia: patterns of progress. [Adelaide], 1972. pp. 96. *Pamphlet in end pocket: South Australia: the facts behind the state.*

— Social conditions.

SOUTH AUSTRALIA. Industrial Development Division. 1972. South Australia: patterns of progress. [Adelaide], 1972. pp. 96. *Pamphlet in end pocket: South Australia: the facts behind the state.*

SOUTH EAST STANDARD REGION (UNITED KINGDOM)

— Economic policy.

U.K. Department of the Environment. 1978. Strategic plan for the South East: review: government statement, 1978. London, 1978. pp. 37.

— Social policy.

U.K. Department of the Environment. 1978. Strategic plan for the South East: review: government statement, 1978. London, 1978. pp. 37.

SOUTH WEST AFRICA

— Economic conditions.

THOMAS (WOLFGANG H.) Economic development in Namibia: towards acceptable development strategies for independent Namibia. Munich, [1978]. pp. 367. *bibliog. Summary in German.*

TOETEMEYER (GERHARD) Namibia old and new: traditional and modern leaders in Ovamboland. London, [1978]. pp. 257. *bibliog.*

— History.

UNITED NATIONS. Office of Public Information. 1971. A principle in torment, III. The United Nations and Namibia. New York, 1971. pp. 44.

— International status.

POSSONY (STEFAN THOMAS) South Africa, the Hague decision and the United Nations; (from an address to the Commonwealth Club, San Francisco, 4 November 1966). [London, Department of Information, South African Embassy], 1967]. pp. 10. *(Reports on the State of South Africa. No.31)*

— Nationalism.

UNITED NATIONS. Office of Public Information. 1971. A principle in torment, III. The United Nations and Namibia. New York, 1971. pp. 44.

— Politics and government.

BOTHA (ANDRIES) SWAPO: dialogue or conflict? Sandton, South Africa, 1977. pp. 30.

SOUTH AFRICA. 1978. South West Africa/Namibia: the South African government's response to the U.N. Secretary-General's report on the implementation of the Western proposal: the government's statement of 20 September 1978; and, An analysis by André du Pisani. Braamfontein, 1978. pp. 9. *(South African Institute of International Affairs. Occasional Papers)*

THOMAS (WOLFGANG H.) Economic development in Namibia: towards acceptable development strategies for independent Namibia. Munich, [1978]. pp. 367. *bibliog. Summary in German.*

TOETEMEYER (GERHARD) Namibia old and new: traditional and modern leaders in Ovamboland. London, [1978]. pp. 257. *bibliog.*

— Social conditions.

TOETEMEYER (GERHARD) Namibia old and new: traditional and modern leaders in Ovamboland. London, [1978]. pp. 257. *bibliog.*

— Statistics.

GERMANY (BUNDESREPUBLIK). Statistisches Bundesamt. Länderkurzbericht: Namibia: Südwestafrika. a., 1978- Wiesbaden.

SOUTH WEST AFRICAN PEOPLE'S ORGANIZATION.

BOTHA (ANDRIES) SWAPO: dialogue or conflict? Sandton, South Africa, 1977. pp. 30.

SOUTHERN STATES

— Economic conditions.

EMPLOYMENT of blacks in the South: a perspective on the 1960s; edited by Ray Marshall and Virgil L. Christian, Jr. Austin, [1978]. pp. 247. *bibliogs.*

— Economic history.

GRAY (LEWIS CECIL) and THOMPSON (ESTHER KATHERINE) History of agriculture in the southern United States to 1860. Gloucester, Mass., 1958. 2 vols. *bibliog. First published in 1933.*

WRIGHT (GAVIN) The political economy of the cotton South: households, markets, and wealth in the nineteenth century. New York, [1978]. pp. 205. *bibliog.*

— History.

DEGLER (CARL N.) Place over time: the continuity of Southern distinctiveness. Baton Rouge, [1977]. pp. 138. *(Louisiana State University. Walter Lynwood Fleming Lectures in Southern History. 1976)*

The AGE of segregation: race relations in the South, 1890-1945; essays by Derrick Bell [and others]; edited by Robert Haws. Jackson, Miss., 1978. pp. 156.

O'BRIEN (MICHAEL) The idea of the American South, 1920-1941. Baltimore, [1979]. pp. 273. *(Johns Hopkins University. Studies in Historical and Political Science. Series 97. No. 1)*

— Race relations.

SOUTHERN SOCIETY FOR THE PROMOTION OF THE STUDY OF RACE CONDITIONS AND PROBLEMS IN THE SOUTH. Annual Conference, 1st, 1900. Race problems of the south: report of the proceedings of the... conference...at Montgomery, Alabama, etc. [Richmond, Va.], 1900; New York, 1969. pp. 240. *bibliog. Facsimile reprint.*

MATHEWS (DONALD G.) Religion in the Old South. Chicago, [1977]. pp. 274. *bibliog.*

The AGE of segregation: race relations in the South, 1890-1945; essays by Derrick Bell [and others]; edited by Robert Haws. Jackson, Miss., 1978. pp. 156.

— Rural conditions.

EMPLOYMENT, income, and welfare in the rural South; by Brian Rungeling [and others]. New York, 1977. pp. 355. *bibliog.*

— Social history.

DEGLER (CARL N.) Place over time: the continuity of Southern distinctiveness. Baton Rouge, [1977]. pp. 138. *(Louisiana State University. Walter Lynwood Fleming Lectures in Southern History. 1976)*

O'BRIEN (MICHAEL) The idea of the American South, 1920-1941. Baltimore, [1979]. pp. 273. *(Johns Hopkins University. Studies in Historical and Political Science. Series 97. No. 1)*

SOUTHWARK

— Almshouses.

CHARLES Hopton and the founding of the almshouses. [London, 1977]. pp. 32.

SOVEREIGNTY.

COMMONS (JOHN ROGERS) A sociological view of sovereignty: [articles from the American Journal of Sociology, 1899-1900]; with an introductory essay, John R. Commons' general theory of institutions, by Joseph Dorfman. New York, 1965 repr. 1967. pp. 109. *bibliog.*

KLEIN (ROBERT A.) Sovereign equality among states: the history of an idea. Toronto, [1974]. pp. 198. *bibliog.*

KRAUTHEIM (ULRIKE) Die Souveränitätskonzeption in den englischen Verfassungskonflikten des 17. Jahrhunderts: eine Studie zur Rezeption der Lehre Bodins in England, etc. Frankfurt am Main, [1977]. pp. 597. *bibliog.*

RAJAN (MANNARASWAMIGHALA SREERANGA) Sovereignty over natural resources. Atlantic Highlands, 1978. pp. 176.

SOVIET CENTRAL ASIA

— Nationalism.

DAVLIATKADAMOV (KHUSHKADAM DAVLIATKADAMOVICH) Sotsial'no-klassovye osnovy sblizheniia sotsialisticheskikh natsii. Dushanbe, 1976. pp. 172.

NATSIONAL'NYE otnosheniia v SSSR na sovremennom etape: na materialakh respublik Srednei Azii i Kazakhstana. Moskva, 1979. pp. 312.

— Social life and customs.

SEM'IA i semeinye obriady u narodov Srednei Azii i Kazakhstana. Moskva, 1978. pp. 215.

SOVIETS

— Germany.

MATERNA (INGO) Der Vollzugsrat der Berliner Arbeiter- und Soldatenräte, 1918/19. Berlin, 1978. pp. 294. *bibliog.*

— Russia.

ANWEILER (OSKAR) The soviets: the Russian workers, peasants and soldiers councils, 1905-1921; translated by Ruth Hein. New York, 1974. pp. 337. *bibliog.*

ARTEM'EV (SERGEI ARTEM'EVICH) Partiia bol'shevikov i Sovety rabochikh i soldatskikh deputatov v 1917 g., iiul'-oktiabr'. Moskva, 1978. pp. 214.

LUK'IANOV (ANATOLII IVANOVICH) Razvitie zakonodatel'stva o sovetskikh predstavitel'nykh organakh vlasti: nekotorye voprosy istorii, teorii i praktiki. Moskva, 1978. pp. 351.

The DEBATE on Soviet power: minutes of the All-Russian Central Executive Committee of Soviets: second convocation, October 1917-January 1918; translated and edited by John L.H. Keep. Oxford, 1979. pp. 465. *bibliog.*

— — Armenia.

EL'CHIBEKIAN (AMBARTSUM MELKONOVICH) Ot revkomov k Sovetam: sozdanie Sovetov v Armenii. Erevan, 1978. pp. 144.

— — Siberia.

AGALAKOV (VIKTOR TROFIMOVICH) Sovety Sibiri, 1917-1918 gg. Novosibirsk, 1978. pp. 255.

SHISHKIN (VLADIMIR IVANOVICH) Revoliutsionnye komitety Sibiri v gody grazhdanskoi voiny, avgust 1919 - mart 1921 g. Novosibirsk, 1978. pp. 333.

— — Ukraine.

KHMIL' (IVAN VASYL'OVYCH) Trudiashche selianstvo Ukraïny v borot'bi za vladu Rad. Kyïv, 1977. pp. 199.

SPACE AND TIME.

TIMING space and spacing time; edited by Tommy Carlstein [and others]. London, 1978. 3 vols. *bibliogs.*

SPACE COLONIES.

O'NEILL (GERARD K.) The high frontier: human colonies in space. London, 1977. pp. 288. *bibliog.*

SPACE IN ECONOMICS.

SPATIAL interaction theory and planning models: (papers presented at an international research conference in Båstad, Sweden... 1977); edited by Anders Karlqvist [and others]. Amsterdam, 1978. pp. 388.

— Mathematical models.

GUNNARSON (JAN) Production systems and hierarchies of centres: the relationship between spatial and economic structures. Leiden, 1977. pp. 140. *bibliog.*

SPACE LAW.

RUBANOV (AVGUST AFANAS'EVICH) Mezhdunarodnaia kosmichesko-pravovaia imushchestvennaia otvetstvennost'. Moskva, 1977. pp. 268.

VERESHCHETIN (VLADLEN STEPANOVICH) Mezhdunarodnoe sotrudnichestvo v kosmose: pravovye voprosy. Moskva, 1977. pp. 264. *bibliog.*

SPACE PERCEPTION.

GOULD (PETER R.) and WHITE (RODNEY) Mental maps. Harmondsworth, [1974]. pp. 203. *bibliog.*

TUAN (YI-FU) Space and place: the perspective of experience. London, 1977. pp. 235. *bibliog.*

SPACE SCIENCES.

BRANDT (JOHN C.) and MARAN (STEPHEN P.) The new astronomy and space science reader. San Francisco, [1977]. pp. 371. *bibliogs.*

— International cooperation.

O'NEILL (GERARD K.) The high frontier: human colonies in space. London, 1977. pp. 288. *bibliog.*

STOCKHOLM INTERNATIONAL PEACE RESEARCH INSTITUTE. Outer space: battlefield of the future?; [written by Bhupendra M. Jasani]. London, 1978. pp. 202. *bibliog.*

SPAIN

— Appropriations and expenditures.

BELTRAN VILLALVA (MIGUEL) Ideologias y gasto publico en España, 1814-1860. [Madrid], Instituto de Estudios Fiscales, [1977]. pp. 522. *bibliog.*

— Church history.

COLOQUIO DE PAU, 8TH, 1977. La crisis del estado español 1898-1936; [by] Manuel Tuñón de Lara [and others]. Madrid, 1978. pp. 533. *Colloquium held at the Centro de Investigaciones Hispánicas, Universidad de Pau.*

— Civilization.

CHEJNE (ANWAR G.) Muslim Spain: its history and culture. Minneapolis, [1974]. pp. 559. *bibliog.*

CASTRO (AMÉRICO) An idea of history; selected essays; translated from the Spanish and edited by Stephen Gilman and Edmund L. King. Columbus, Ohio, [1977]. pp. 343.

— Colonies.

CAMPBELL (LEON G.) The military and society in colonial Peru, 1750-1810. Philadelphia, 1978. pp. 254. *bibliog.*

— — History.

NEWSON (LINDA A.) Aboriginal and Spanish colonial Trinidad: a study in culture contact. London, 1976. pp. 268. *bibliog.*

— Economic conditions.

SPAIN. Oficina de Coordinacion y Programacion Economica. Documentacion Economica. No. 37. Evolucion de la economia española en el año 1962; (and Anejos). Madrid, 1963. 2 pts.

SPAIN. Oficina de Coordinacion y Programacion Economica. Documentacion Economica. No. 43. Evolucion de la economia española en el año 1963; (and Anejos). Madrid, 1964. 2 pts.

GARCIA DELGADO (JOSE LUIS) and SEGURA (JULIO) Reformismo y crisis economica: la herencia de la dictadura. Madrid, [1977]. pp. 159. *bibliog.*

SCHWARTZ (PEDRO) ed. El producto nacional de España en el siglo XX: seleccion de textos. Madrid, Instituto de Estudios Fiscales, 1977. pp. 690.

BAKLANOFF (ERIC NICOLAS) The economic transformation of Spain and Portugal. New York, 1978. pp. 211. *bibliog.*

— Economic history.

BERNECKER (WALTHER L.) Anarchismus und Bürgerkrieg: zur Geschichte der sozialen Revolution in Spanien, 1936-1939. Hamburg, 1978. pp. 372. *bibliog.* With English summary.

HARRISON (ROBERT JOSEPH) An economic history of modern Spain. Manchester, [1978]. pp. 187. *bibliog.*

— Economic policy.

CASADO RAIGON (JOSE MARIA) La politica de accion regional en España: los polos de desarrollo y especial referencia al caso de Cordoba. Sevilla, 1977. pp. 227. *bibliog.*

GARCIA DELGADO (JOSE LUIS) and SEGURA (JULIO) Reformismo y crisis economica: la herencia de la dictadura. Madrid, [1977]. pp. 159. *bibliog.*

— Foreign relations — Argentine Republic.

FRABOSCHI (ROBERTO O.) La Comision regia española al Rio de la Plata, 1820-1821. Buenos Aires, 1945. pp. 57,xx. *(Buenos Aires. Universidad. Instituto de Investigaciones Historicas. Publicaciones. No. 89)*

— — United Kingdom.

SMITH (LAWRENCE BARTLAM) Spain and Britain 1715-19: the Jacobite issue. 1977 [or rather 1978]. fo.361. *bibliog.* Typescript. Ph.D. (London) thesis: unpublished. *This thesis is the property of London University and may not be removed from the Library.*

— — United States.

CORTADA (JAMES W.) Two nations over time: Spain and the United States, 1776- 1977. Westport, Conn., 1978. pp. 305. *bibliog.*

— History.

CASTRO (AMÉRICO) An idea of history; selected essays; translated from the Spanish and edited by Stephen Gilman and Edmund L. King. Columbus, Ohio, [1977]. pp. 343.

MAY (HARRY S.) Francisco Franco: the Jewish connection. Washington, D.C., [1978]. pp. 187. *bibliog.*

— — 711-1516.

WATT (WILLIAM MONTGOMERY) and CACHIA (PIERRE) A history of Islamic Spain. Edinburgh, 1965. pp. 210. *bibliog.*

BURCKHARDT (TITUS) Moorish culture in Spain; translated by Alisa Jaffa. London, [1972]. pp. 219. *bibliog.*

— — 711-1492, Arab period.

CHEJNE (ANWAR G.) Muslim Spain: its history and culture. Minneapolis, [1974]. pp. 559. *bibliog.*

LOMAX (DEREK W.) The reconquest of Spain. London, 1978. pp. 212. *bibliog.*

— — 1516-1700, House of Austria.

HESS (ANDREW C.) The forgotten frontier: a history of the sixteenth-century Ibero- African frontier. Chicago, 1978. pp. 278. *bibliog.* *(Chicago. University. Center for Middle Eastern Studies. Publications. 10)*

— — 1700-1746, Philip V.

SMITH (LAWRENCE BARTLAM) Spain and Britain 1715-19: the Jacobite issue. 1977 [or rather 1978]. fo.361. *bibliog.* Typescript. Ph.D. (London) thesis: unpublished. *This thesis is the property of London University and may not be removed from the Library.*

— — 1814-1868, Bourbon Restoration.

MARICHAL (CARLOS) Spain, 1834-1844: a new society. London, [1977]. pp. 232. *bibliog.*

— — 1886-1931.

PRESTON (PAUL) The coming of the Spanish Civil War: reform, reaction and revolution in the Second Republic, 1931-1936. London, 1978. pp. 264. *bibliog.*

— — 1900- .

RAMIREZ (LUIS) Franco: la obsesión de ser, la obsesión de poder. Paris, 1976. pp. 324.

ALBA (VÍCTOR) Transition in Spain: from Franco to democracy. New Brunswick, [1978]. pp. 333. *bibliog.* Translated by Barbara Lotito.

COLOQUIO DE PAU, 8TH, 1977. La crisis del estado español 1898-1936; [by] Manuel Tuñón de Lara [and others]. Madrid, 1978. pp. 533. *Colloquium held at the Centro de Investigaciones Hispánicas, Universidad de Pau.*

— — 1923-1930, Dictatorship.

BEN-AMI (SHLOMO) The origins of the Second Republic in Spain. Oxford, [1978]. pp. 356. *bibliog.*

SPAIN (Cont.)

—— 1931, Revolution.

BEN-AMI (SHLOMO) The origins of the Second Republic in Spain. Oxford, [1978]. pp. 356. *bibliog.*

—— 1931-1939, Republic.

MONTERO (JOSE R.) La CEDA: el catolicismo social y politico en la II republica. Madrid, Ediciones de la Revista de Trabajo, Ministerio de Trabajo, [1977]. 2 vols. *bibliog.*

COLOQUIO DE PAU, 8TH, 1977. La crisis del estado español 1898-1936; [by] Manuel Tuñón de Lara [and others]. Madrid, 1978. pp. 533. *Colloquium held at the Centro de Investigaciones Hispánicas, Universidad de Pau.*

PRESTON (PAUL) The coming of the Spanish Civil War: reform, reaction and revolution in the Second Republic, 1931-1936. London, 1978. pp. 264. *bibliog.*

—— 1936-1939, Civil War.

GARCIA (FELIX) Colectivizaciones campesinas y obreras en la Revolucion española. Bilbao, 1977. pp. 266. *bibliog.*

BERNECKER (WALTHER L.) Anarchismus und Bürgerkrieg: zur Geschichte der sozialen Revolution in Spanien, 1936-1939. Hamburg, 1978. pp. 372. *bibliog.* With English summary.

BOLLOTEN (BURNETT) The Spanish revolution: the left and the struggle for power during the Civil War. Chapel Hill, N.C., [1979]. pp. 665. *bibliog.*

——— Foreign participation, German.

OVEN (WILFRED VON) Hitler und der Spanische Bürgerkrieg: Mission und Schicksal der Legion Condor. Tübingen, [1978]. pp. 557.

——— Personal narratives.

AGUIRRE Y LECUBE (JOSÉ ANTONIO DE) Freedom was flesh and blood. London, 1945. pp. 288.

OVEN (WILFRED VON) Hitler und der Spanische Bürgerkrieg: Mission und Schicksal der Legion Condor. Tübingen, [1978]. pp. 557.

—— 1939-1975.

CARR (RAYMOND) and FUSI (JUAN PABLO) Spain: dictatorship to democracy. London, 1979. pp. 282.

—— 1975- .

MENGES (CONSTANTINE) Spain: the struggle for democracy today. Beverly Hills, [1978]. pp. 80. *bibliog.* (Georgetown University. Center for Strategic and International Studies. Washington Papers. vol. 6/58)

CARR (RAYMOND) and FUSI (JUAN PABLO) Spain: dictatorship to democracy. London, 1979. pp. 282.

— Intellectual life.

COLOQUIO DE PAU, 8TH, 1977. La crisis del estado español 1898-1936; [by] Manuel Tuñón de Lara [and others]. Madrid, 1978. pp. 533. *Colloquium held at the Centro de Investigaciones Hispánicas, Universidad de Pau.*

— Officials and employees.

ANSON OLIART (FRANCISCO) Tipos y valores en funcionarios españoles. [Madrid], Escuela Nacional de Administracion Publica, 1967. pp. 98. (*Coleccion Alcala. 2*)

— Politics and government.

MARICHAL (CARLOS) Spain, 1834-1844: a new society. London, [1977]. pp. 232. *bibliog.*

ARANGO (ERGASTO RAMÓN) The Spanish political system: Franco's legacy. Boulder, [1978]. pp. 293. *bibliogs.*

COLOQUIO DE PAU, 8TH, 1977. La crisis del estado español 1898-1936; [by] Manuel Tuñón de Lara [and others]. Madrid, 1978. pp. 533. *Colloquium held at the Centro de Investigaciones Hispánicas, Universidad de Pau.*

MENGES (CONSTANTINE) Spain: the struggle for democracy today. Beverly Hills, [1978]. pp. 80. *bibliog.* (Georgetown University. Center for Strategic and International Studies. Washington Papers. vol. 6/58)

PRESTON (PAUL) The coming of the Spanish Civil War: reform, reaction and revolution in the Second Republic, 1931-1936. London, 1978. pp. 264. *bibliog.*

—— Anecdotes, facetiae, satire, etc.

VAZQUEZ MONTALBAN (MANUEL) Como liquidaron el franquismo en dieciseis meses y un dia. Barcelona, 1977. pp. 311.

— Population.

MIGUEL (AMANDO DE) La piramide social española. Barcelona, [1977]. pp. 297.

— Relations (general) with North Africa.

HESS (ANDREW C.) The forgotten frontier: a history of the sixteenth-century Ibero-African frontier. Chicago, 1978. pp. 278. *bibliog.* (Chicago. University. Center for Middle Eastern Studies. Publications. 10)

— Social history.

BERNECKER (WALTHER L.) Anarchismus und Bürgerkrieg: zur Geschichte der sozialen Revolution in Spanien, 1936-1939. Hamburg, 1978. pp. 372. *bibliog.* With English summary.

BOASE (ROGER) The troubadour revival: a study of social change and traditionalism in late medieval Spain. London, 1978. pp. 219. *bibliog.*

— Statistics — Bibliography.

CONSORCIO DE INFORMACION Y DOCUMENTACION DE CATALUÑA. Inventario de estadisticas de España: analisis documental de las publicaciones editadas desde 1960; (with Actualizacion 1978). Barcelona, 1975-78. 2 pts. (in 1 vol.).

SPANISH LITERATURE

— History and criticism.

BUTT (JOHN) Writer on Spanish literature. Writers and politics in modern Spain. London, 1978. pp. 76. *bibliog.*

SPANISH SAHARA

— Nationalism.

MERCER (JOHN) The Sahrawis of Western Sahara. London, 1979. pp. 24. *bibliog.* (Minority Rights Group. Reports. No. 40)

— Politics and government.

MERCER (JOHN) The Sahrawis of Western Sahara. London, 1979. pp. 24. *bibliog.* (Minority Rights Group. Reports. No. 40)

SPANN (OTHMAR).

SPANN (OTHMAR) Gesamtausgabe; Herausgeber: Walter Heinrich [and others]. Graz, 1963-79. 21 vols. *bibliogs.*

SPARTA

— History.

HAMILTON (CHARLES DANIEL) Sparta's bitter victories: politics and diplomacy in the Corinthian war. Ithaca, 1979. pp. 346. *bibliog.*

SPATIAL ANALYSIS (STATISTICS).

KLAASSEN (LEONARDUS HENDRIK) and others. Spatial systems: a general introduction. Farnborough, [1979]. pp. 165. *bibliog.*

SPEARS (Sir EDWARD LOUIS).

SPEARS (Sir EDWARD LOUIS) Fulfilment of a mission: the Spears mission to Syria and Lebanon 1941-1944. Hamden, Conn., 1977. pp. 311.

SPECIAL DRAWING RIGHTS.

CHRYSTAL (KENNETH ALEXANDER) International money and the future of the S[pecial] D[rawing] R[ight]. Princeton, 1978. pp. 30. *bibliog.* (Princeton University. Department of Economics and Sociology. International Finance Section. Essays in International Finance. No. 128)

SPECTRAL THEORY (MATHEMATICS).

SLEEMAN (BRIAN D.) Multiparameter spectral theory in Hilbert space. London, 1978. pp. 118. *bibliogs.*

SPECULATION.

BERTOCCI (SILVIO) Dossier Baia Domizia: uno scandalo democristiano. Roma, 1977. pp. 180.

BRODY (EUGENE D.) and BLISS (BETSY L.) Odds-on investing: survival and success in the new stock market. New York, [1978]. pp. 238.

SPEECH.

WOLD (ASTRI HEEN) Decoding oral language. London, 1978. pp. 214. *bibliog.*

SPEECH, DISORDERS OF.

MERINGER (RUDOLF) and MAYER (CARL) Versprechen und verlesen: eine psychologisch-linguistische Studie; new edition with an introductory article by Anne Cutler and David Fay. Amsterdam, 1978. pp. 207.

SPEECH DISORDERS IN CHILDREN.

BLOOM (LOIS) and LAHEY (MARGARET) Language development and language disorders. New York, [1978]. pp. 689. *bibliog.*

DE VILLIERS (JILL G.) and DE VILLIERS (PETER A.) Language acquisition. Cambridge, Mass., 1978. pp. 312. *bibliog.*

DEVELOPMENTAL dysphasia; edited by Maria A. Wyke. London, 1978. pp. 179. *bibliogs.*

SPEECH PERCEPTION.

LANGUAGE development and neurological theory; edited by Sidney J. Segalowitz, Frederic A. Gruber. New York, 1977. pp. 376. *bibliogs.*

WOLD (ASTRI HEEN) Decoding oral language. London, 1978. pp. 214. *bibliog.*

SPEER (ALBERT).

ALBERT Speer: Kontroversen um ein deutsches Phänomen; ([edited by] Adelbert Reif). München, [1978]. pp. 501. *bibliog.*

SPEIDEL (HANS).

SPEIDEL (HANS) Aus unserer Zeit: Erinnerungen. Frankfurt/M, 1977. pp. 512.

SPENDINGS TAX

— Sweden.

LODIN (SVEN OLOF) Progressive expenditure tax - an alternative? A report of the 1972 Government Commission on Taxation. Stockholm, 1978. pp. 278. *bibliog.*

SPIRITUALISM.

SPIRIT mediumship and society in Africa...; edited by John Beattie and John Middleton. New York, 1969. pp. 310. *bibliogs.*

SPORTS.

AMERICAN ACADEMY OF POLITICAL AND SOCIAL SCIENCE. Annals. vol. 445. Contemporary issues in sport; special editor of this volume James H. Frey. Philadelphia, 1979. pp. 222.

McINTOSH (PETER CHISHOLM) Fair play: ethics in sport and education. London, 1979. pp. 213. *bibliog.*

— **Economic aspects — United Kingdom.**

ECONOMIST INTELLIGENCE UNIT. Q[arterly] E[conomic] R[eview] Specials. No. 41. Sponsorship. London, [1977]. pp. 82.

— **Social aspects.**

COAKLEY (JAY J.) Sport in society: issues and controversies. Saint Louis, 1978. pp. 349. *bibliog.*

LOY (JOHN W.) and others. Sport and social systems: a guide to the analysis, problems and literature. Reading, Mass., [1978]. pp. 447. *bibliog.*

SNYDER (ELDON E.) and SPREITZER (ELMER A.) Social aspects of sport. Englewood Cliffs, [1978]. pp. 214. *bibliog.*

— **Communist countries.**

SPORT under communism: the U.S.S.R., Czechoslovakia, the G.D. R., China, Cuba; James Riordan, editor. London, [1978]. pp. 177.

— **United States.**

AMERICAN ACADEMY OF POLITICAL AND SOCIAL SCIENCE. Annals. vol. 445. Contemporary issues in sport; special editor of this volume James H. Frey. Philadelphia, 1979. pp. 222.

SPORTS AND STATE

— **Hong Kong.**

COUNCIL FOR RECREATION AND SPORT [HONG KONG]. Report. a., 1973/75- Hong Kong.

— **United Kingdom — Wales.**

SPORTS COUNCIL FOR WALES. Annual report. a., 1972/73(1st)- Cardiff.

SQUATTERS

— **Kenya.**

HENNING (PETER H.) The urban popular economy and informal sector productions. Ann Arbor, Mich., 1978. pp. 67. *(Michigan University. Center for Research on Economic Development. Discussion Papers. No. 69)*

— **South Africa.**

The SQUATTER problem in the Western Cape: some causes and remedies; by George Ellis [and others]. Johannesburg, [1977]. pp. 119.

— **Turkey.**

YÜCEL (ASUMAN) The squatter areas and their employment problems with special reference to the city of Ankara. [Ankara], State Planning Organization, 1969 [or rather 1970]. fo. 68. *bibliog.*

— **Underdeveloped areas.**

See UNDERDEVELOPED AREAS — Squatters.

— **United Kingdom.**

PARIS (CHRIS T.) and POPPLESTONE (GERRY) compilers. Squatting: a bibliography. London, 1978. pp. 8. *bibliog. (Centre for Environmental Studies. Occasional Papers. No. 3)*

— — **London.**

CANT (D. H.) Squatting and private property rights: an analysis of the effects of squatting seen in the context of a theory about how increased activity by the state affects the way change comes about in our society. London, 1976 repr. 1978. pp. 71. *bibliog. (London. University. University College. Bartlett School of Architecture and Planning. Town Planning Discussion Papers. No. 24)*

— **Zambia.**

PASTEUR (DAVID) The management of squatter upgrading: a case study of organisation, procedures and participation. Farnborough, [1979]. pp. 232. *bibliog.*

SRI LANKA

— **Biography.**

DHANAPALA (D.B.) Among those present. Colombo, 1962. pp. 212.

— **History.**

BROHIER (RICHARD LESLIE) Links between Sri Lanka and the Netherlands: a book of Dutch Ceylon. Colombo, [1978?]. pp. 165. *bibliog.*

— **Parliament — Elections.**

SRI LANKA. Department of Elections. 1978. Report on the general election to the second National State Assembly of Sri Lanka, eighth parliamentary general election, 21st July, 1977. Colombo, 1978. pp. 115. *(Sri Lanka. Parliament. Sessional Papers. 1978. No. 4.*

— **Population.**

SRI LANKA. Department of Census and Statistics. Bulletin on vital statistics. a., 1976(4th)- Colombo.

— **Religion.**

MALALGODA (KITSIRI) Buddhism in Sinhalese society, 1750-1900: a study of religious revival and change. Berkeley, 1976. pp. 300. *bibliog.*

— **Statistics, Vital.**

SRI LANKA. Department of Census and Statistics. Bulletin on vital statistics. a., 1976(4th)- Colombo.

SRI LANKA. Department of Census and Statistics. 1978. Life tables, 1970-1972: Sri Lanka. Colombo, [1978]. 1 vol. (various pagings).

STAFFORDSHIRE

— **Economic history.**

SHERLOCK (ROBERT) The industrial archaeology of Staffordshire: [a survey made on behalf of Staffordshire County Council]. Newton Abbot, [1976]. pp. 216. *bibliog.*

STAGNATION (ECONOMICS).

WEINTRAUB (SIDNEY) b. 1914. Capitalism's inflation and unemployment crisis: beyond monetarism and Keynesianism. Reading, Mass., [1978]. pp. 242.

STALIN (IOSIF VISSARIONOVICH).

FEIS (HERBERT) Churchill, Roosevelt, Stalin: the war they waged and the peace they sought. 2nd ed. Princeton, N.J., 1967 repr. 1974. pp. 702.

HINGLEY (RONALD) Joseph Stalin: man and legend. London, 1974. pp. 482. *bibliog.*

GOERLITZ (WALTER) Geldgeber der Macht: wie Hitler, Lenin, Mao Tse-tung, Mussolini, Stalin und Tito finanziert wurden. Frankfurt am Main, 1978. pp. 256. *bibliog.*

STAMMLER (RUDOLF).

WEBER (MAX) Critique of Stammler;...translated, with an introductory essay, by Guy Oakes. New York, [1977]. pp. 184.

STANDARD FRUIT AND STEAMSHIP COMPANY.

KARNES (THOMAS L.) Tropical enterprise: the Standard Fruit and Steamship Company in Latin America. Baton Rouge, [1978]. pp. 332. *bibliog.*

STATE, THE.

KAPLAN (MARCOS) Formacion del Estado nacional en America Latina. Buenos Aires, 1969 repr. 1976. pp. 356. *bibliog.*

REGIERBARKEIT: Studien zu ihrer Problematisierung...; herausgegeben von Wilhelm Hennis [and others]. Stuttgart, [1977 in progress]. pp. 314.

CAPOGRASSI (GIUSEPPE) Riflessioni sull'autorità e la sua crisi...; a cura di Mario D'Addio. Milano, [1977]. pp. 290.

SECONDAT (CHARLES LOUIS DE) Baron de Montesquieu. The spirit of laws:...a compendium of the first English edition; edited...by David Wallace Carrithers; together with an English translation of An essay on causes affecting minds and characters, 1736-1743. Berkeley, [1977]. pp. 479.

BENDIX (REINHARD) Kings or people: power and the mandate to rule. Berkeley, 1978. pp. 692.

FROM contract to community: political theory at the crossroads; edited by Fred R. Dallmayr. New York, [1978]. pp. 172. *Based on a lecture series held at Purdue University's Department of Political Science during the academic year 1974- 1975.*

HOWARD (MICHAEL ELIOT) War and the nation state. Oxford, 1978. pp. 19. *An inaugural lecture delivered before Oxford University on 18 November 1977.*

POLITICS, ideology and the state: papers from the Communist University of London, [9th session, 1977]; edited by Sally Hibbin. London, 1978. pp. 143.

POULANTZAS (NICOS) State, power, socialism. London, 1978. pp. 269.

STEPAN (ALFRED C.) The state and society: Peru in comparative perspective. Princeton, [1978]. pp. 348. *bibliog.*

FRY (GEOFFREY KINGDON) The growth of government: the development of ideas about the role of the state and the machinery and functions of government in Britain since 1780. London, 1979. pp. 295. *bibliog.*

STATE and economy in contemporary capitalism; edited by Colin Crouch. London, [1979]. pp. 264. *bibliog.*

STATE ENCOURAGEMENT OF SCIENCE, LITERATURE AND ART

— **United Kingdom.**

The ARTS: the way forward; a Conservative discussion paper. London, 1978. pp. 39. *(Conservative Political Centre. [Publications]. No. 630)*

STATE FARMS

— **Russia — Siberia.**

TONAEVSKAIA (NELLI SERGEEVNA) Rabochie sovkhozov Zapadnoi Sibiri, 1959-1965 gg.; otvetstvennyi redaktor V.T. Aniskov. Novosibirsk, 1978. pp. 191.

STATE GOVERNMENTS

— **United States.**

HOLT (CHARLES FRANK) The role of state government in the nineteenth century American economy, 1820-1902: a quantitative study. New York, 1977. pp. 325. *bibliog. Originally presented as a thesis, Purdue University, 1970.*

BURNS (JAMES MACGREGOR) and others. State and local politics: government by the people. 2nd ed. Englewood Cliffs, N.J., [1978]. pp. 289.

ZEIGLER (LUTHER HARMON) and TUCKER (HARVEY J.) The quest for responsive government: an introduction to state and local politics. North Scituate, Mass., [1978]. pp. 337. *bibliogs.*

STATE RIGHTS.

CENTRE-state relations; by Jacob Eapen [and others]. Bangalore, 1975. pp. 82. *Special issue of 'Religion and Society', vol. 22, no.1, March 1975.*

STATES, SMALL.

STATES, SMALL.

SMALL states in modern world: the conditions of survival; edited by Peter Worseley and Paschalis Kitromilides. [Nicosia], [1976]. pp. 237. *Papers presented at the "Conference on the Survival of Small Countries," held in Nicosia, 1976, organised by the New Cyprus Association, Cyprus Sociological Association and the Coordinating Committee of Scientific and Cultural Organisations.*

The SATELLITE state in the 17th and 18th centuries: [papers from a conference held at the University of Bergen, 1-4 September, 1977]; edited by Ståle Dyrvik [and others]. Bergen, [1979]. pp. 192.

STATESMEN.

GOVERNMENTS and leaders: an approach to comparative politics; [by] Edward Feit, contributing editor [and others]. Boston, [Mass., 1978]. pp. 552. *bibliogs.*

— United Kingdom.

KARSTEN (PETER) Patriot-heroes in England and America: political symbolism and changing values over three centuries. Madison, Wis., 1978. pp. 257.

SHRAPNEL (NORMAN) The performers. London, 1978. pp. 213.

STATISTICAL DECISION.

STOCHASTIC dominance: an approach to decision-making under risk; edited by G.A. Whitmore [and] M.C. Findlay. Lexington, Mass., [1978]. pp. 401. *bibliog.*

STATISTICS.

STATISTICS and urban planning....; edited by Ken Williams. London, [1975]. pp. 189. *Based on papers presented at the 8th general meeting of the International Association of Municipal Statisticians, held at Helsinki, 1972.*

NATIONAL SEMINAR ON SOCIAL STATISTICS, NEW DELHI, 1975. National seminar on social statistics, organized by Central Statistical Organisation: [report and papers presented]. New Delhi, 1977. 2 vols.

JESSEN (RAYMOND J.) Statistical survey techniques. New York, [1978]. pp. 520. *bibliogs.*

— Bibliography.

PIEPER (F.C.) compiler. SISCIS: subject index to sources of comparative international statistics. Beckenham, 1978. pp. 745.

— Charts, tables, etc.

MARDIA (K.V.) and ZEMROCH (P.J.) Tables of the F- and related distributions with algorithms. London, 1978. pp. 256. *bibliog.*

— Data processing.

COMPSTAT SYMPOSIUM, 2ND., BERLIN, 1976. Compstat 1976; proceedings in computational statistics;... edited by Johannes Gordesch [and] Peter Naeve. Wien, 1976. pp. 496. *bibliogs.*

— Dictionaries.

INTERNATIONAL encyclopedia of statistics; edited by William H. Kruskal and Judith M. Tanur. New York, [1978]. 2 vols. *bibliogs.*

— History.

KENDALL (Sir MAURICE GEORGE) and PLACKETT (ROBERT LEWIS) eds. Studies in the history of statistics and probability. vol. 2. London, [1977]. pp. 488. *bibliogs.*

PEARSON (KARL) The history of statistics in the 17th and 18th centuries against the changing background of intellectual, scientific and religious thought; lectures...given at University College, London... 1921-1933; edited by E.S. Pearson. London, [1978]. pp. 744.

—— Russia.

RIABUSHKIN (TIMON VASIL'EVICH) Leninskoe nasledie i statistika. Moskva, 1978. pp. 266.

— Indexes.

PIEPER (F.C.) compiler. SISCIS: subject index to sources of comparative international statistics. Beckenham, 1978. pp. 745.

— Theory, methods, etc.

REVISTA BRASILEIRA DE ESTATISTICA: (orgão oficial do IBGE [Instituto Brazileiro de Geografia e Estatistica, Brazil] e Sociedade Brasileira de Estatistica). q., 1940 (ano 1)- , with gaps (nos. 11, 16, 106). Rio de Janeiro.

HALD (ANDERS H.) Statistical tables and formulas. New York, 1952. pp. 97.

DAVID (HERBERT ARON) The method of paired comparisons. London, 1963 repr. 1969. pp. 124. *bibliog.*

DOBBEN DE BRUYN (CORNELIS SIMON VAN) Cumulative sum tests: theory and practice. London, 1968. pp. 82. *bibliog.*

RAHMAN (N.A.) A course in theoretical statistics. London, 1968. pp. 542.

CZECHOSLOVAKIA. Federální Statistický Úřad. Statistická revue sborník. irreg., 1970(no. 1)- , with gap (no. 3). Praha. *[in Czech with summaries in English and Russian]*

DAVID (FLORENCE NIGHTINGALE) A first course in statistics. 2nd ed. London, 1971. pp. 228.

ASHTON (WINIFRED DIANA) The logit transformation with special reference to its uses in bioassay. London, 1972. pp. 88. *bibliog.*

HABER (AUDREY) and RUNYON (RICHARD PORTER) General statistics. 2nd ed. London, [1973]. pp. 401.

KLEIJNEN (JACK P.C.) Statistical techniques in simulation. New York, [1974-75]. 2 vols. *bibliogs.*

CONFERENCE ON FOUNDATIONAL QUESTIONS IN STATISTICAL INFERENCE, AARHUS, 1973. Proceedings...; editors Ole Barndorff-Nielsen [and others]. Aarhus, 1974. pp. 371. *(Aarhus. Universitet. Department of Theoretical Statistics. Memoirs. No. 1)*

BICKEL (PETER J.) and DOKSUM (KJELL A.) Mathematical statistics: basic ideas and selected topics. San Francisco, [1977]. pp. 492. *bibliogs.*

MOSTELLER (CHARLES FREDERICK) and TUKEY (JOHN W.) Data analysis and regression: a second course in statistics. Reading, Mass., [1977]. pp. 588.

STAROVSKII (VLADIMIR NIKONOVICH) Teoriia i praktika sovetskoi gosudarstvennoi statistiki: sbornik nauchnykh trudov. Moskva, 1977. pp. 296.

UNITED NATIONS. Statistical Office. Statistical Papers. Series F. No.22. The feasibility of welfare-oriented measures to supplement the national accounts and balances: a technical report. (ST/ESA/STAT/SER.F/22). New York, 1977. pp. 71.

CONTRIBUTIONS to survey sampling and applied statistics: papers in honor of H.O. Hartley; edited by H.A. David. New York, 1978. pp. 318. *bibliog.*

FREEDMAN (DAVID) and others. Instructor's manual for statistics. New York, [1978]. pp. 135.

HORTON (RAYMOND L.) The general linear model: data analysis in the social and behavioral sciences. New York, [1978]. pp. 274. *bibliog.*

KIRK (ROGER E.) Introductory statistics. Monterey, Calif., [1978]. pp. 438. *bibliog.*

UNITED NATIONS. Statistical Office. Statistical Papers. Series M. No.63. Social indicators: preliminary guidelines and illustrative series. (ST/ESA/STAT/SER.M/63). New York, 1978. pp. 134.

BURR (IRVING W.) Elementary statistical quality control. New York, [1979]. pp. 413. *bibliog.*

DEMYSTIFYING social statistics; edited by John Irvine [and others]. London, 1979. pp. 390. *bibliogs.*

STAUNTON (HARVEY DE).

KEETON (GEORGE WILLIAMS) Harvey the Hasty: a mediaeval Chief Justice. Chichester, [1978]. pp. 178. *bibliog.*

STEEL

— Prices — Europe.

STEGEMANN (KLAUS F.) Price competition and output adjustment in the European steel market. Tübingen, [1977]. pp. 359. *bibliog. (Kiel. Universität. Institut für Weltwirtschaft. Kieler Studien. 147)*

STEEL INDUSTRY AND TRADE.

MUELLER (HANS) Ph.D. and KAWAHITO (KIYOSHI) Steel industry economics: a comparative analysis of structure, conduct and performance. New York, 1978. pp. 63.

— Statistics.

INTERNATIONAL STEEL STATISTICS: world tables; [pd. by] British Steel Corporation. a., 1970[1st]- London. *Replaces in part its Statistical handbook (1966-1969).*

— Europe.

STEGEMANN (KLAUS F.) Price competition and output adjustment in the European steel market. Tübingen, [1977]. pp. 359. *bibliog. (Kiel. Universität. Institut für Weltwirtschaft. Kieler Studien. 147)*

— United Kingdom.

OVENDEN (KEITH) The politics of steel. London, 1978. pp. 262. *bibliog.*

— United States.

HARPER (ANN K.) The location of the United States steel industry, 1879-1919. New York, 1977. pp. 266. *bibliog.*

STEPHEN, King of England.

GESTA Stephani; edited and translated by K.R. Potter; with new introduction and notes by R.H.C. Davis. Oxford, 1976. pp. 249.

DAVIS (RALPH HENRY CARLESS) King Stephen, 1135-1154. London, 1977. pp. 162.

STERILIZATION (BIRTH CONTROL).

KERALA. Demographic Research Centre. 1977. A study of sterilised persons in Kerala, 1971-74. Trivandrum, 1977. pp. 30.

STEWARD (AUSTIN).

STEWARD (AUSTIN) Twenty-two years a slave, and forty years a freeman; embracing correspondence of several years, while president of Wilberforce Colony, London, Canada West. [Rochester, N.Y.], 1856; New York, 1968. pp. 360. *Facsimile reprint.*

STOCHASTIC DIFFERENTIAL EQUATIONS.

ARNOLD (LUDWIG) Stochastic differential equations: theory and applications. New York, [1974]. pp. 228. *bibliog.*

STOCHASTIC PROCESSES.

STOCHASTIC analysis: a tribute to the memory of Rollo Davidson; edited by D.G. Kendall and E.F. Harding. London, [1973]. pp. 465. *bibliogs.*

ZIEMBA (W.T.) and VICKSON (R.G.) eds. Stochastic optimization models in finance. New York, [1975]. pp. 719. *bibliogs.*

LAMPERTI (JOHN) Stochastic processes: a survey of the mathematical theory. New York, [1977]. pp. 266. *bibliog.*

LINEAR least-squares estimation; edited by Thomas Kailath. Stroudsburg, [1977]. pp. 318.

BARTLETT (MAURICE STEVENSON) An introduction to stochastic processes, with special reference to methods and applications. 3rd ed. Cambridge, 1978. pp. 388. *bibliog.*

ENGEN (S.) Stochastic abundance models with emphasis on biological communities and species diversity. London, 1978. pp. 126. *bibliog.*

GALAMBOS (JANOS) The asymptotic theory of extreme order statistics. New York, [1978]. pp. 352. *bibliog.*

IBRAGIMOV (IL'DAR ABDULOVICH) and ROZANOV (IURII ANATOL'EVICH) Gaussian random processes; translated by A.B. Aries. New York, [1978]. pp. 275. *bibliog.*

STOCHASTIC dominance: an approach to decision-making under risk; edited by G.A. Whitmore [and] M.C. Findlay. Lexington, Mass., [1978]. pp. 401. *bibliog.*

STOCK AND STOCK BREEDING

— **Environmental aspects — United Kingdom.**

FARM AND FOOD SOCIETY. Evidence presented to the Royal Commission on Environmental Pollution on environmental pollution by modern methods of livestock production...; with a brief report concerning other aspects of pollution by agriculture. London, 1977. pp. 39.

— **Bangladesh.**

BANGLADESH. Bureau of Statistics. 1976. Report on the survey of livestock and poultry in the rural areas of Bangladesh, 1970. Dacca, 1976. pp. 40. (*Agricultural Statistics Papers. No.2*)

— **Botswana.**

G.P. McGOWAN AND ASSOCIATES. A study of drought relief and contingency measures relating to the livestock sector of Botswana: final report. volume 1. Executive report;...carried out for the government of Botswana. Albury, 1979. pp. 70, 4 maps.

— **Russia — Bashkir Republic.**

GUBAIDULLIN (MANSUR SADYKOVICH) Ekonomicheskie problemy razvitiia zhivotnovodstva v usloviiakh nauchno-tekhnicheskogo progressa: na primere Bashkirskoi ASSR. Moskva, 1978. pp. 144. (*Akademiia Nauk SSSR. Problemy Sovetskoi Ekonomiki*)

STOCK EXCHANGE.

GIFFEN (Sir ROBERT) Stock exchange securities: an essay on the general causes of fluctuations in their price. London, 1877. pp. 163.

BRODY (EUGENE D.) and BLISS (BETSY L.) Odds-on investing: survival and success in the new stock market. New York, [1978]. pp. 238.

EKHOLM (BO-GÖRAN) Determinanter för transaktionsbeteendet på aktiemarknaden: Determinants of transaction behaviour on the stock market. Helsingfors, 1978. pp. 378. *bibliog.* (*Svenska Handelshögskolan. Ekonomi och Samhälle. Nr. 27*) With English summary.

— **United Kingdom.**

HAMILTON (JAMES DUNDAS) Stockbroking today. 2nd ed. London, 1979. pp. 276. *bibliog.*

HILLIARD (B.C.) Exchange flows and the gilt-edged security market: a causality study. London, 1979. pp. 31. *bibliog.* (*Bank of England. Discussion Papers. No. 2*)

STOCK OWNERSHIP

— **United Kingdom.**

ERRITT (M.J.) and others. The ownership of company shares: a survey for 1975. London, 1979. pp. 73. (*U.K. Central Statistical Office. Studies in Official Statistics. No. 34*)

STOCKHOLDERS

— **Finland.**

EKHOLM (BO-GÖRAN) Determinanter för transaktionsbeteendet på aktiemarknaden: Determinants of transaction behaviour on the stock market. Helsingfors, 1978. pp. 378. *bibliog.* (*Svenska Handelshögskolan. Ekonomi och Samhälle. Nr. 27*) With English summary.

— **United States.**

BLUME (MARSHALL E.) and FRIEND (IRWIN) The changing role of the individual investor. New York, [1978]. pp. 243. *bibliogs.*

STOCKS

— **Prices.**

RICHARDS (PAUL H.) U.K. and European share price behaviour: the evidence. London, 1979. pp. 294. *bibliog.*

STONE-CECH COMPACTIFICATION.

WALKER (RUSSELL C.) The Stone-Čech compactification. New York, 1974. pp. 332. *bibliog.*

STONEHENGE.

U.K. Social Survey. [Reports. New Series]. 1127. Restrictions at Stonehenge: the reactions of visitors to limitations in access; report of a survey carried out...for the Department of Environment; [by] Sheila Bainbridge. London, 1979. pp. 36.

STRAEHL (WOLFGANG).

GRANDJONC (JACQUES) and WERNER (MICHAEL) Wolfgang Strähls "Briefe eines Schweizers aus Paris", 1835: zur Geschichte des Bundes der Geächteten in der Schweiz und zur Rezeption Heines unter deutschen Handwerkern in Paris. Trier, [1978]. pp. 85. *bibliog.* (*Karl-Marx-Haus. Schriften. 21*)

STRÄHL (WOLFGANG).

See STRAEHL (WOLFGANG).

STRAITS

— **Pacific, The.**

LEIFER (MICHAEL) Malacca, Singapore and Indonesia. Alphen aan den Rijn, 1978. pp. 217. *bibliog.*

STRAITS QUESTION.

PURYEAR (VERNON JOHN) Napoleon and the Dardanelles. Berkeley, 1951. pp. 437. *bibliog.*

STRASSER (GREGOR).

KISSENKOETTER (UDO) Gregor Strasser und die NSDAP. Stuttgart, [1978]. pp. 220. *bibliog.* (*Vierteljahrshefte für Zeitgeschichte. Schriftenreihe. Nr. 37*)

STRATEGY.

HALPERIN (MORTON H.) Contemporary military strategy. new ed. London, 1972. pp. 149. *bibliog.*

DIXON (NORMAN F.) On the psychology of military incompetence. London, 1976. pp. 447. *bibliog.*

BOOTH (KEN) Strategy and ethnocentrism. London, [1979]. pp. 191. *bibliogs.*

STRAUSS (FRANZ JOSEF).

ZIERER (OTTO) Franz Josef Strauss: Lebensbild. München, [1978]. pp. 400.

STRAWBERRIES.

FEDER (ERNEST) Agronomist. Strawberry imperialism: an enquiry into the mechanisms of dependency in Mexican agriculture. The Hague, 1977. pp. 199. (*Hague. Institute of Social Studies. Research Report Series. No. 1*)

STRIKES AND LOCKOUTS.

STREAM MEASUREMENTS

— **United Kingdom — Mathematical models.**

LONDON. University. London School of Economics and Political Science. Graduate School of Geography. Discussion Papers. No. 71. Flow depth monitoring in an ephemeral channel and its relationship to channel changes; [by] Geoff Butcher and John Thornes. London, 1978. pp. 26. *bibliog.*

STRESA CONFERENCE, 1935.

NOEL (LEON) Les illusions de Stresa: l'Italie abandonnée à Hitler. Paris, [1975]. pp. 206.

STRESEMANN (GUSTAV).

GERMANY. Reichskanzlei. 1923. Die Kabinette Stresemann I u. II: 13. August bis 6. Oktober 1923; 6. Oktober bis 30. November 1923; bearbeitet von Karl Dietrich Erdmann und Martin Vogt. Boppard am Rhein, [1978]. 2 vols. *bibliog.* (*Akten der Reichskanzlei. Weimarer Republik*)

STRESS (PHYSIOLOGY).

STRESS at work; edited by Cary L. Cooper and Roy Payne. Chichester, [1978]. pp. 293. *bibliogs.*

STRESS (PSYCHOLOGY).

CONFERENCE ON STRESSFUL LIFE EVENTS: THEIR NATURE AND EFFECTS, NEW YORK, 1973. Stressful life events: their nature and effects; edited by Barbara Snell Dohrenwend [and] Bruce P. Dohrenwend. New York, [1974]. pp. 340. *bibliogs.*

KLAPP (ORRIN E.) Opening and closing: strategies of information adaptation in society. Cambridge, 1978. pp. 226. *bibliog.* (*American Sociological Association. Arnold and Caroline Rose Monograph Series in Sociology*)

STRESS at work; edited by Cary L. Cooper and Roy Payne. Chichester, [1978]. pp. 293. *bibliogs.*

STRIKES AND LOCKOUTS.

STACHKI: istoriia i sovremennost'. Moskva, 1978. pp. 344.

SEMINAR ON THIRD WORLD STRIKES, THE HAGUE, 1977. Papers on third world strikes submitted to a Seminar..., Institute of Social Studies, The Hague; with introduction by Peter Waterman. Zug, Switzerland, 1979. 11 fiches. *The introduction, with list of contents, is in pamphlet form and is shelved with the microfiches.*

— **Austria.**

GRUBER (RONALD) and HOERZINGER (MANFRED) ... bis der Preistreiberpakt fällt: der Massenstreik der österreichischen Arbeiter im September/Oktober 1950. Wien, [1975]. pp. 136.

— **Brazil.**

FAUSTO (BORIS) Trabalho urbano e conflito social, 1890-1920. São Paulo, 1976. pp. 283. *bibliog.*

— **France.**

RAMIN (ALAIN) Le lock-out et le chômage technique. Paris, 1977. pp. 375. *bibliog.*

WRITING on the wall: May 1968: a documentary anthology; edited by Vladimir Fišera; translated from the French. London, 1978. pp. 327. *bibliog.*

— **Germany.**

STREIK-NACHRICHTEN des Metallarbeiterstreiks in Schleswig-Holstein; [pd. by] Industriegewerkschaft Metall für die Bundesrepublik Deutschland. irreg., Oc 25 1956 - F 14 1957(nos. 1-80). Hamburg. *Reprint in 1 v.*

SPONTANE Streiks, 1973: Krise der Gewerkschaftspolitik; ([by] Redaktionskollektiv "Express"). Offenbach, 1974. pp. 160. (*Sozialistisches Büro. Reihe Betrieb und Gewerkschaften*).

STRIKES AND LOCKOUTS.(Cont.)

MEYER (REGINE) Streik und Aussperrung in der Metallindustrie: Analyse der Streikbewegung in Nordwürttemberg-Nordbaden, 1971. Marburg, [1977]. pp. 426. *bibliog. (Studiengesellschaft für Sozialgeschichte und Arbeiterbewegung, Marburg. Schriftenreihe für Sozialgeschichte und Arbeiterbewegung. Band 4)*

— **Italy.**

La FABBRICA diffusa: scontro di classe nei servizi e nel territorio, lavoro nero, lotte degli ospedalieri, lotte delle donne a Padova. Milano, [1977]. pp. 134.

— **Netherlands.**

BERG (HARRY VAN DEN) and others. De ontwikkeling van het stakingsrecht in Nederland. Nijmegen, [1978]. pp. 454.

— **Sweden.**

STOLPE (STAFFAN) Persberg 1869: dokument kring en av Sveriges första strejker uppsatta efter poetiska principer. [Stockholm, 1977]. pp. 137.

— **Underdeveloped areas.**

See UNDERDEVELOPED AREAS — Strikes and lockouts.

— **United Kingdom.**

STRIKES in Britain: a research study of industrial stoppages in the United Kingdom; by C.T.B. Smith [and others]. [London], 1978. pp. 180. *(U.K. Department of Employment. Manpower Papers. No. 15)*

WHITE (JOSEPH L.) The limits of trade union militancy: the Lancashire textile workers, 1910-1914. Westport, Conn., 1978. pp. 258. *bibliog.*

— **United States.**

RUSSELL (FRANCIS) 1910- . A city in terror: the 1919 Boston police strike. Harmondsworth, 1977. pp. 256. *bibliog. First published in 1975 by Viking Press.*

ESSAYS in Southern labor history...; edited by Gary M. Fink and Merl E. Reed. Westport, Conn., 1977. pp. 275. *bibliogs. Selected papers from the Southern Labor History Conference, Atlanta, 1976.*

See also HOMESTEAD STRIKE, 1892.

— — **Kentucky.**

HEVENER (JOHN W.) Which side are you on?: the Harlan County coal miners, 1931- 1939. Urbana, [1978]. pp. 216. *bibliogs.*

STRUCTURAL ANTHROPOLOGY.

JENKINS (ALAN) Ph.D. The social theory of Claude Levi-Strauss. London, 1979. pp. 193. *bibliog.*

STRUCTURALISM.

LÉVI-STRAUSS (CLAUDE) Myth and meaning. London, 1978. pp. 54. *(Canadian Broadcasting Corporation. Massey Lectures. 1977)*

STRUCTURALISM (LITERARY ANALYSIS).

HAWKES (TERENCE) Structuralism and semiotics. London, 1977. pp. 192. *bibliog.*

STRUCTURED PROGRAMMING.

KIEBURTZ (RICHARD B.) Structured programming and problem-solving with PASCAL. Englewood Cliffs, N.J., [1978]. pp. 365.

YOURDON (EDWARD) and CONSTANTINE (LARRY L.) Structured design: fundamentals of a discipline of computer program and systems design. 2nd ed. New York, [1978]. pp. 446. *bibliogs.*

STUDENT ASPIRATIONS.

LITTLE (ANGELA) The occupational and educational expectations of students in developed and developing countries. Brighton, 1978. pp. 70. *bibliog. (Brighton. University of Sussex. Institute of Development Studies. Research Reports)*

STUDENTS

— **Attitudes.**

STUDENTS, values, and politics: a crosscultural comparison; [by] Otto Klineberg [and others]. New York, [1979]. pp. 342. *bibliog.*

— **Health and hygiene.**

STUDENTS in need: essays in memory of Nicolas Malleson. Guildford, 1978. pp. 230. *bibliogs. (Society for Research into Higher Education. Occasional Papers)*

— **Political activity.**

STUDENTS, values, and politics: a crosscultural comparison; [by] Otto Klineberg [and others]. New York, [1979]. pp. 342. *bibliog.*

— **Psychology.**

STUDENTS in need: essays in memory of Nicolas Malleson. Guildford, 1978. pp. 230. *bibliogs. (Society for Research into Higher Education. Occasional Papers)*

— **Belgium.**

VANDEKERCKHOVE (LIEVEN) and HUYSE (LUCIEN) In de buitenbaan: arbeiderskinderen, universitair onderwijs en sociale ongelijkheid. 2nd ed. Antwerpen, [1977]. pp. 207. *bibliog.*

— **France.**

CHARLOT (ALAIN) and BECIRSPAHIC (KEMAL) Les universités et le marché du travail: enquête sur les étudiants à la sortie des universités et sur leurs débouchés professionnels. Paris, 1977. pp. 577. *(Centre d'Etudes et de Recherches sur les Qualifications. Dossiers. 14)*

— — **Political activity.**

WRITING on the wall: May 1968: a documentary anthology; edited by Vladimir Fišera; translated from the French. London, 1978. pp. 327. *bibliog.*

— **Germany — Political activity.**

STEINBERG (MICHAEL STEPHEN) Sabers and brown shirts: the German students' path to National Socialism, 1918-1935. Chicago, 1977. pp. 237. *bibliog.*

APO und Gewerkschaften: von der Kooperation zum Bruch; herausgegeben von Gudrun Küsel. Berlin, [1978]. pp. 188.

— **India — Political activity.**

SHAH (GHANSHYAM) Protest movements in two Indian states: a study of the Guyarat and Bihar movements. Delhi, 1977. pp. 171. *bibliogs. (Centre for Social Studies, Surat. Publications. No. 8)*

— **Norway.**

KOBBERSTAD (TOR) Studenter, kandidater og ressursforbruk ved universiteter og høgskoler fram til 1990, etc. [Oslo], 1972. pp. 92. *(Utredninger om Forskning og Høyere Utdanning. 1972.5)*

— **United Kingdom.**

U.K. Social Survey. [Reports. New Series]. 1039. Undergraduate income and expenditure: a survey commissioned by the Department of Education and Science and the Scottish Education Department of undergraduates' and trainee teachers' sources of income and patterns of expenditure for the academic year 1974/5; [by] Peter Bush [and] Susan Dight. London, 1979. pp. 70.

WOODS (PETER) The divided school. London, 1979. pp. 310.

— **Yugoslavia.**

PERVAN (RALPH) Tito and the students: the university and the university student in self-managing Yugoslavia. Nedlands, W.A., 1978. pp. 239. *bibliog.*

STUDENTS, FOREIGN

— **United Kingdom.**

GRANTLEY (DAVID) Practical training in Britain of students from the developing countries. London, [1973?]. pp. 7. *(Marr-Munning Trust. Edwina Mountbatten Papers. No. 3)*

STUDENTS' SOCIETIES

— **Germany.**

STEINBERG (MICHAEL STEPHEN) Sabers and brown shirts: the German students' path to National Socialism, 1918-1935. Chicago, 1977. pp. 237. *bibliog.*

SUBCONSCIOUSNESS.

SHALVEY (THOMAS) Claude Lévi-Strauss, social psychotherapy and the collective unconscious. Hassocks, [1978?]. pp. 180. *bibliog.*

SUBCONTRACTING.

SALLEZ (ALAIN) Polarisation et sous-traitance: conditions du développement régional. Paris, 1972. pp. 237. *bibliog.*

SUBMARINE GEOLOGY.

SHEPARD (FRANCIS P.) Geological oceanography: evolution of coasts, continental margins, and the deep-sea floor. New York, [1977]. pp. 214. *bibliogs.*

SUBSIDIES

— **Australia — New South Wales.**

NEW SOUTH WALES. Department of Decentralisation and Development. 1967. Direct assistance to industry in decentralized areas. Sydney, [1967]. pp. 3.

— **Canada.**

CANADA. Statutes, etc. 1969. Office consolidation of the Regional Development Incentives Act, 1968-69, c.56 and the Regional Development Incentives Regulations, P.C. 1969,1571. Ottawa, 1969. pp. 19.

— **Ireland (Republic).**

McALEESE (DERMOT) A profile of grant-aided industry in Ireland. Dublin, Industrial Development Authority, 1977. pp. 92. *bibliog. (Publication Series. Paper 5)*

— **Italy.**

ITALY. [Cassa per Opere Straordinarie di Pubblico Interesse nell'Italia Meridionale]. 1978. Rapporto sullo stato di attuazione dei programmi ai sensi della legge 2 maggio 1976 n. 183. [Rome], 1978. 3 vols. (in 1).

— **Salvador.**

SALVADOR. Statutes, etc. 1970. Export Development Law. [San Salvador], 1971. fo. 16.

— **United Kingdom.**

REES (R.D.) and MIALL (R.H.C.) The effects of regional policy on manufacturing investment and capital stock within the UK. London, Department of Industry, 1979. pp. 22. *(Government Economic Service Working Papers. No. 26)*

SUBSTITUTION (ECONOMICS).

MINFORD (ANTHONY PATRICK LESLIE) Substitution effects, speculation and exchange rate stability. Amsterdam, 1978. pp. 222. *bibliog.*

SUBURBS

— New Zealand.

THOMSON (JANET) Employment in the suburbs. [Wellington], Town and Country Planning Branch, Ministry of Works, 1969. pp. 8.

— United Kingdom.

YOUNG (KENNETH GEORGE) and KRAMER (JOHN) Strategy and conflict in metropolitan housing: suburbia versus the Greater London Council, 1965-75. London, 1978. pp. 306.

SUBVERSIVE ACTIVITIES.

STOCKTON (BAYARD) and JANKE (PETER F.) Nuclear power: protest and violence. London, 1978. pp. 20. bibliog. (Institute for the Study of Conflict. Conflict Studies. No.102)

— Canada.

FIDLER (RICHARD) RCMP: the real subversives. Toronto, [1978]. pp. 91. bibliog.

— Iran.

MOSS (ROBERT) The campaign to destabilise Iran. London, 1978. pp. 18. (Institute for the Study of Conflict. Conflict Studies. No.101)

— Malaysia.

FEDERATION OF MALAYSIA. 1971. The resurgence of armed communism in west Malaysia. Kuala Lumpur, 1971. pp. 30.

— United Kingdom.

DEACON (RICHARD) The British connection: Russia's manipulation of British individuals and institutions. London, 1979. pp. 291. bibliog.

— Venezuela.

VENEZUELA. Oficina Central de Informacion. 1967. Six years of aggression. [Caracas, 1967]. pp. 95.

SUCCESS.

TRESEMER (DAVID WARD) Fear of success. New York, [1977]. pp. 245. bibliog.

SUDAN

— Armed forces — Political activity.

ABDEL-RAHIM (MUDDATHIR) Changing patterns of civilian-military relations in the Sudan. Uppsala, 1978. pp. 32. (Nordiska Afrikainstitutet. Research Reports. No. 46)

— Department of Labour — Officials and employees.

ELARABI (ALI) Traditionalism and modernity in the Sudanese bureaucracy: an empirical study in the Sudan Department of Labour. [Khartoum, 1976]. fo. 45. (Institute of Public Administration [Sudan]. Occasional Papers)

— Economic conditions.

INDUSTRIAL RESEARCH AND CONSULTANCY INSTITUTE [SUDAN]. Industrial investment guide. Khartoum, 1976. pp. 249, ii.

— Economic policy.

SUDAN NEWS. Special Issues. The Sudan ten year plan of economic development. London, Sudan Embassy, [1961?]. fo. 17.

ALI (MOHAMED ABDEL RAHMAN) Fiscal and monetary policies and employment in the Sudan. Khartoum, 1974. fo. 37. (Economic and Social Research Council [Sudan]. Bulletins. No. 6) Cover title reads: Survey of contemporary theories of government expenditure.

— History.

WARBURG (GABRIEL) Islam, nationalism and communism in a traditional society: the case of Sudan. London, 1978. pp. 253. bibliog.

— Officials and employees — Salaries, allowances, etc.

SUDAN. 1951. Memorandum on the recommendations of the Unclassified Staff Wages Commission. Khartoum, 1951. pp. 25.

— Politics and government.

The SOUTHERN Front memorandum to O.A.U. on Afro-Arab conflict in the Sudan. Accra, 1965. 1 vol. (unpaged).

— Social policy.

SUDAN NEWS. Special Issues. The Sudan ten year plan of economic development. London, Sudan Embassy, [1961?]. fo. 17.

SUFFRAGE

— United Kingdom.

WALKER (ERNESTEIN) Struggle for the reform of Parliament, 1853-1867. New York, [1977]. pp. 212. bibliog.

SUGAR

— Manufacture and refining — Jamaica.

JAMAICA. Sugar Industry Enquiry Commission. 1967. Report; [John Mordecai, chairman]. [Kingston], 1967. pp. 233.

— — Pakistan.

ANWAR (ABDUL AZIZ) and KHAN (MUHAMMAD AHMAD) Introductory report on the socio-economic benefits of sugar industry in West Pakistan...; project co-ordinator: H.A. Syed. [Lahore, Boards of Economic Inquiry, Lahore and Peshawar], 1962. pp. 70.

— Statistics.

INTERNATIONAL SUGAR ORGANIZATION. Statistical bulletin. m. (sometime q.), 1937(v.1)- ; susp. pbln. 1942-1945. London.

— Taxation — United Kingdom.

RUSSELL (JOHN) 1st Earl Russell. Speech...in the House of Commons, on Friday, May 7, 1841: ways and means; sugar duties, etc. [London, Ridgway, 1841?]. pp. 15.

SUGAR GROWING

— Jamaica.

JAMAICA. Sugar Industry Enquiry Commission. 1967. Report; [John Mordecai, chairman]. [Kingston], 1967. pp. 233.

— Pakistan.

ANWAR (ABDUL AZIZ) and KHAN (MUHAMMAD AHMAD) Introductory report on the socio-economic benefits of sugar industry in West Pakistan...; project co-ordinator: H.A. Syed. [Lahore, Boards of Economic Inquiry, Lahore and Peshawar], 1962. pp. 70.

— Peru.

MACERA (PABLO) Las plantaciones azucareras en el Peru, 1821-1875. Lima, 1974. pp. 167.

SUGAR TRADE

— Brazil.

TAYLOR (KIT SIMS) Sugar and the underdevelopment of northeastern Brazil, 1500-1970. Gainesville, Fla., 1978. pp. 167. bibliog. (Florida University. Monographs. Social Sciences. No. 63)

— Mauritius.

SUGAR INSURANCE FUND BOARD [MAURITIUS]. Annual report and accounts. a., 1975/76(30th)- Port Louis.

SUGER, Abbot of Saint-Denis.

SUGER, Abbot of Saint-Denis, 1081-1151. Abbot Suger on the abbey church of St. Denis and its art treasures; edited...by Erwin Panofsky; second edition by Gerda Panofsky-Soergel. 2nd ed. Princeton, [1979]. pp. 285. bibliog.

SUGGESTION SYSTEMS

— Russia — Russia (RSFSR).

KLIUEV (VLADIMIR GRIGOR'EVICH) Patrioticheskim pochinam - vsemernuiu podderzhku. Moskva, 1978. pp. 78. (Bibliotechka Profsoiuznogo Aktivista. 36)

SUICIDE.

SAMARITANS. Answers to suicide presented by the Samaritans to Chad Varah on the occasion of the twenty-fifth anniversary of their founding. London, 1978. pp. 277.

SULU

— Foreign relations — United Kingdom.

TARLING (NICHOLAS) Sulu and Sabah: s study of British policy towards the Philippines and North Borneo from the late eighteenth century. Kuala Lumpur, 1978. pp. 385. bibliog.

SUMMER HOMES

— United Kingdom — Scotland.

DARTINGTON AMENITY RESEARCH TRUST. Second homes in Scotland; a report to Countryside Commission for Scotland, Scottish Tourist Board, Highlands and Islands Development Board, Scottish Development Department. Totnes, 1977. pp. 88. bibliog. (Publications. No. 22)

SUN (YAT-SEN).

BARLOW (JEFFREY G.) Sun Yat-Sen and the French, 1900-1908. Berkeley, [1979]. pp. 93. (California University. Center for Chinese Studies. China Research Monographs. No.14)

SUPERVISION OF SOCIAL WORKERS.

PETTES (DOROTHY E.) Staff and student supervision: a task-centred approach. London, 1979. pp. 159. bibliogs. (National Institute for Social Work Training. National Institute Social Services Library. 34)

SUPPLY AND DEMAND.

DECAILLOT (M.) and others. Besoins et mode de production: du capitalisme en crise au socialisme. [Paris, 1977]. pp. 285.

GERMANY (BUNDESREPUBLIK). Monopolkommission. 1977. Missbräuche der Nachfragemacht und Möglichkeiten zu ihrer Kontrolle im Rahmen des Gesetzes gegen Wettbewerbsbeschränkungen. Baden-Baden, 1977. pp. 166. (Sondergutachten. Band 7)

BHATTACHARYYA (D.K.) Demand for financial assets: an econometric study of the U.K. personal sector. Farnborough, [1978]. pp. 197. bibliogs.

— Mathematical models.

BARANOVA (LIANA IAKOVLEVNA) and LEVIN (ALEKSANDR IVANOVICH) Modelirovanie i prognozirovanie sprosa naseleniia. Moskva, 1978. pp. 208.

SURREALISM.

ROSEMONT (FRANKLIN) André Breton and the first principles of surrealism. London, 1978. pp. 147.

SURREY

— Social life and customs.

CONNELL (JOHN) 1946- . The end of tradition: country life in central Surrey. London, 1978. pp. 231.

SURVIVORS' BENEFITS

— Israel.

ISRAEL. Ministry of Defence. Rehabilitation Department. 1968. Rehabilitation programs and benefits for disabled veterans and dependents. [Tel Aviv], 1968. pp. 20.

SWABIA

— Emigration and immigration.

HACKER (WERNER) Auswanderungen aus Oberschwaben im 17. und 18. Jahrhundert, archivalisch dokumentiert. Stuttgart, [1977]. pp. 799. *bibliog.*

SWAZILAND

— History.

KUPER (HILDA) Sobhuza II, ngwenyama and king of Swaziland: the story of an hereditary ruler and his country. London, 1978. pp. 363. *bibliog.*

SWEATING SYSTEM.

BYTHELL (DUNCAN) The sweated trades: outwork in nineteenth-century Britain. London, 1978. pp. 287.

SWEDEN

— Commercial policy.

SWEDEN. Finansdepartementet. Långtidsutredningen. 1976. (Långtidsutredningen 1975. Bilaga 2). Sveriges export 1975- 1980;...rapport av Konjunkturinstitutet. Stockholm, 1976. pp. 117. *(Sweden. Statens Offentliga Utredningar. 1976. 22)*

— Economic conditions.

BERGMAN (LARS) Energy and economic growth in Sweden: an analysis of historical trends and present choices. Stockholm, [1977]. pp. 321. *bibliog.*

— Economic policy.

SWEDEN. Finansdepartementet. Långtidsutredningen. 1975. Långtidsutredningen 1975: huvudrapport; [by] Finansdepartementets Ekonomiska Avdelning. Stockholm, 1975. pp. 387. *(Sweden. Statens Offentliga Utredningar. 1975.89)*

SWEDEN. Finansdepartementet. Långtidsutredningen. 1975. (Långtidsutredningen 1975. Bilaga 5). Den offentliga sektorn 1975-1980: visst underlagsmaterial. [Stockholm, 1976]. pp. 90. *(Sweden. Finansdepartementet. Ds. Fi. 1976:1)*

SWEDEN. Finansdepartementet. Långtidsutredningen. 1976. (Långtidsutredningen 1975. Bilaga 1). Den internationella bakgrunden;...[by] Jan Herin [and others]. Stockholm, 1976. pp. 352. *(Sweden. Statens Offentliga Utredningar. 1976.27)*

SWEDEN. Finansdepartementet. Långtidsutredningen. 1976. The Swedish economy 1975-1980: a translation of the main report of the 1975 medium term survey; [by the] Economic Department, Ministry of Finance. Stockholm, 1976. pp. 358.

LIMITS of the welfare state: critical views on post-war Sweden; edited by John Fry. Farnborough, Hants., [1979]. pp. 234. *Selection of articles, in English translation, which originally appeared in Zenit and other Swedish periodicals.*

— — Mathematical models.

The IMPORTANCE of technology and the permanence of structure in industrial growth: proceedings of a symposium at IUI, Stockholm, July 18-19, 1977; [edited by] Bo Carlsson [and others]. Stockholm, 1978. pp. 237. *bibliogs. (Industriens Utredningsinstitut. IUI Conference Reports. 1978:2)*

— Foreign economic relations — Germany.

WITTMANN (KLAUS) Schwedens Wirtschaftsbeziehungen zum Dritten Reich, 1933-1945. München, 1978. pp. 479. *bibliog. (Hamburg. Hansische Universität. Studien zur Modernen Geschichte. Band 23)*

— — Russia.

EKONOMICHESKIE sviazi mezhdu Rossiei i Shvetsiei v XVII v.: dokumenty iz sovetskikh arkhivov; Ekonomiska förbindelser mellan Sverige och Ryssland under 1600-talet: dokument ur Svenska arkiv; redaktsionnaia kollegiia A. Attman [and others]. Moskva, 1978. pp. 296. *In Russian or Swedish.*

— Foreign relations — Germany.

KARLSSON (RUNE) Så stoppades tysktågen: den tysktågen: den tyska transiteringstrafiken i svensk politik, 1942-1943. Stockholm, 1974. pp. 363. *bibliog. With English summary.*

— — Italy.

EIMER (BIRGITTA) Cavour and Swedish politics. Stockholm, [1978]. pp. 457. *bibliog. (Lund. Universitet. Historiska Institutionen. Lund Studies in International History. 12)*

— — Russia.

ROGINSKII (VADIM VADIMOVICH) Shvetsiia i Rossiia: soiuz 1812 goda. Moskva, 1978. pp. 175. *bibliog.*

— History — 1905- .

KARLSSON (RUNE) Så stoppades tysktågen: den tysktågen: den tyska transiteringstrafiken i svensk politik, 1942-1943. Stockholm, 1974. pp. 363. *bibliog. With English summary.*

— Industries.

LINDSTRÖM (SVERKER) and NORDIN (STEN) Vem äger storföretagen? [Stockholm, 1977]. pp. 202. *bibliog.*

The IMPORTANCE of technology and the permanence of structure in industrial growth: proceedings of a symposium at IUI, Stockholm, July 18-19, 1977; [edited by] Bo Carlsson [and others]. Stockholm, 1978. pp. 237. *bibliogs. (Industriens Utredningsinstitut. IUI Conference Reports. 1978:2)*

— Neutrality.

KARLSSON (RUNE) Så stoppades tysktågen: den tysktågen: den tyska transiteringstrafiken i svensk politik, 1942-1943. Stockholm, 1974. pp. 363. *bibliog. With English summary.*

— Population.

SWEDEN. Statistiska Centralbyrån. 1979. Lägenheter och hushåll enligt folk- och bostadsräkningarna 1965, 1970 och 1975 kommunvis enligt indelningen 1976-01-01; Dwellings and households according to the 1965, 1970 and 1975 population and housing censuses, by communes, etc. Stockholm, 1979. pp. 76. *(Statistiska Meddelanden. Be 1979: 6) With English summary.*

— Social policy.

SWEDEN. Finansdepartementet. Långtidsutredningen. 1975. (Långtidsutredningen 1975. Bilaga 5). Den offentliga sektorn 1975-1980: visst underlagsmaterial. [Stockholm, 1976]. pp. 90. *(Sweden. Finansdepartementet. Ds. Fi. 1976:1)*

LIMITS of the welfare state: critical views on post-war Sweden; edited by John Fry. Farnborough, Hants., [1979]. pp. 234. *Selection of articles, in English translation, which originally appeared in Zenit and other Swedish periodicals.*

SWEDES IN ETHIOPIA.

HALLDIN NORBERG (VIVECA) Swedes in Haile Selassie's Ethiopia, 1924-1952: a study in early development co-operation. Uppsala, 1977. pp. 317. *bibliog. (Uppsala. Universitet. Historiska Institutionen. Studia Historica Upsaliensia. 92)*

SWEDES IN FINLAND.

ALLARDT (ERIK) Finland's Swedish speaking minority. Helsinki, 1977. pp. 21. *bibliog. (Helsinki. Yliopisto. Research Group for Comparative Sociology. Research Reports. No. 17)*

MIEMOIS (KARL JOHAN) Changes in the social structure of the Swedish-speaking population of Finland, 1950-1970. Helsinki, 1978. pp. 37. *bibliog. (Helsinki. Yliopisto. Research Group for Comparative Sociology. Research Reports. No. 19)*

SWITZERLAND

— Constitution.

TOTALREVISION der Bundesverfassung-Notwendigkeit oder Wunschtraum?; der Entwurf der Expertenkommission im Spiegel ihrer Mitglieder. Zürich, 1978. pp. 253. *(Schweizerischer Aufklärungs Dienst. Schriften des SAD. 15) In French and German.*

ZEITSCHRIFT FÜR SCHWEIZERISCHES RECHT. Band 119, 1978. Totalrevision der Bundesverfassung - zur Diskussion gestellt. Basel, 1979. pp. 300. *In French or German.*

—Constitutional law.

MASTRONARDI (PHILIPPE) Der Verfassungsgrundsatz der Menschenwürde in der Schweiz: ein Beitrag zu Theorie und Praxis der Grundrechte. Berlin, 1978. pp. 331. *bibliog.*

— Economic conditions.

KUENG (EMIL) The secret of Switzerland's economic success; translated [from the German] by Eric Schiff. Washington, [1978]. pp. 10. *(American Enterprise Institute for Public Policy Research. AEI Studies. 219)*

— Economic policy.

KUENG (EMIL) The secret of Switzerland's economic success; translated [from the German] by Eric Schiff. Washington, [1978]. pp. 10. *(American Enterprise Institute for Public Policy Research. AEI Studies. 219)*

— Emigration and immigration.

BORY-LUGON (VALERIE) Immigration et zénophobie dans la société suisse. Lausanne, 1977. pp. 117. *bibliog.*

— Foreign economic relations.

ZIEGLER (JEAN) Switzerland exposed...; translated from the French by Rosemary Sheed Middleton. London, 1978. pp. 173.

— Neutrality.

ZIEGLER (JEAN) Switzerland exposed...; translated from the French by Rosemary Sheed Middleton. London, 1978. pp. 173.

— Parliament — Rules and practice.

ZURKIRCHEN (JOSEF) Die Instrumente des parlamentarischen Vorstosses: ein Beitrag zum Schweizerischen Parlamentsrecht. Zürich, 1979. pp. 211. *bibliog.*

— Politics and government.

AUBERT (JEAN FRANCOIS) Exposé des institutions politiques de la Suisse à partir de quelques affaires controversées. Lausanne, [1978]. pp. 317.

ZIEGLER (JEAN) Switzerland exposed...; translated from the French by Rosemary Sheed Middleton. London, 1978. pp. 173.

SYED KECHIK.

ROSS-LARSON (BRUCE) The politics of federalism: Syed Kechik in East Malaysia. Singapore, 1976. pp. 240.

SYMBOLIC INVERSION.

FORMS OF SYMBOLIC INVERSION SYMPOSIUM, TORONTO, 1972. The reversible world: symbolic inversion in art and society; edited...by Barbara A. Babcock. Ithaca, N.Y., 1978. pp. 302. *bibliogs.*

SYMBOLISM.

MIDDLETON (JOHN) ed. Myth and cosmos: readings in mythology and symbolism. Austin, Tex., [1967]. pp. 368. *bibliog.*

TURNER (VICTOR WITTER) Dramas, fields, and metaphors: symbolic action in human society; [essays]. Ithaca, 1974. pp. 309. *bibliogs.*

SKORUPSKI (JOHN) Symbol and theory: a philosophical study of theories of religion in social anthropology. Cambridge, 1976. pp. 265. *bibliog.*

SYNDICALISM.

WEBB (SIDNEY) 1st Baron Passfield, and WEBB (BEATRICE) What syndicalism means: an examination of the origin and motives of the movement with an analysis of its proposals for the control of industry. London, 1912. pp. 19. *Published as a supplement to The Crusade.*

— Canada — Quebec.

ROY (JEAN LOUIS) La marche des Québécois: le temps des ruptures, 1945-1960. Ottawa, 1976. pp. 383.

— France.

JOUHAUX (LEON) Le syndicalisme: ce qu'il est, ce qu'il doit être. [Paris, 1937]. pp. 47.

PELLETIER (ROBERT) and RAVET (SERGE) Le mouvement des soldats: les comités de soldats et l'antimilitarisme révolutionnaire. Paris, 1976. pp. 199.

ZYLBERBERG-HOCQUARD (MARIE HELENE) Féminisme et syndicalisme en France. Paris, 1978. pp. 199.

— Germany.

VOGEL (ANGELA) Der deutsche Anarcho-Syndikalismus: Genese und Theorie einer vergessenen Bewegung. Berlin, 1977. pp. 312. *bibliog.*

— Italy.

FURIOZZI (GIAN BIAGIO) Il sindacalismo rivoluzionario italiano. Milano, [1977]. pp. 127. *bibliog.*

ROBERTS (DAVID D.) The syndicalist tradition and Italian fascism. Chapel Hill, N.C., [1979]. pp. 410. *bibliog.*

SYNGE (JOHN MILLINGTON).

WATSON (GEORGE) Irish identity and the literary revival: Synge, Yeats, Joyce and O'Casey. London, 1979. pp. 326. *bibliog.*

SYRIA

— Central Bureau of Statistics.

SYRIA. Statutes, etc. 1968. Décret législatif no. 87 du 6.7.1968, portant création d'un Bureau Central de Statistiques. [Damas, 1968]. fo.5.

— Commerce.

SYRIA. Ministry of Economy and Foreign Trade. 1972. Notes sur le commerce extérieur de la Syrie durant les dernières années; par Daoud Haydo; (with Foreign trade statistics). Damas, Syrian Documentation Papers, 1972. fo. 24; 47. *In French and English.*

— Conseil Supérieur de Planification.

SYRIA. Statutes, etc. 1968. Décret législatif no. 81 du 6 juin 1968, portant création du Conseil Supérieur de Planification. [Damas, 1968]. fo. 2.

— Economic policy.

SYRIA. Ministry of Economy and Foreign Trade. 1972. Fundamental features of the strategy of the third five-year plan (1971-1975) for economic and social development in Syria; by Abdallah El-Azmeh. Damascus, Syrian Documentation Papers, 1972. fo.30.

SYRIA. Statutes, etc. 1977. Fourth five year economic and social development plan of the Syrian Arab Republic; 1976-1980. Damascus, [1977]. pp. 263. (*Office Arabe de Presse et de Documentation. Série Documents. 1127*)

— Executive departments.

SYRIA. Statutes, etc. 1968. Décret législatif no. 81 du 6 juin 1968, portant création du Conseil Supérieur de Planification. [Damas, 1968]. fo. 2.

SYRIA. Statutes, etc. 1968. Décret législatif no. 86 du 2.7.1968, portant création d'un Organisme d'Etat pour la Planification. [Damas, 1968]. fo. 7.

SYRIA. Statutes, etc. 1968. Décret législatif no. 87 du 6.7.1968, portant création d'un Bureau Central de Statistiques. [Damas, 1968]. fo.5.

— Foreign relations.

McLAURIN (RONALD D.) and others. Foreign policy making in the Middle East: domestic influences on policy in Egypt, Iraq, Israel, and Syria. New York, 1977. pp. 313. *bibliog.*

— Organisme d'Etat pour la Planification.

SYRIA. Statutes, etc. 1968. Décret législatif no. 86 du 2.7.1968, portant création d'un Organisme d'Etat pour la Planification. [Damas, 1968]. fo. 7.

— Politics and government.

DAM (NIKOLAOS VAN) The struggle for power in Syria: sectarianism, regionalism and tribalism in politics, 1961-1978. London, [1979]. pp. 147. *bibliog.*

— Social policy.

SYRIA. Statutes, etc. 1977. Fourth five year economic and social development plan of the Syrian Arab Republic; 1976-1980. Damascus, [1977]. pp. 263. (*Office Arabe de Presse et de Documentation. Série Documents. 1127*)

SYSTEM ANALYSIS.

CHURCHMAN (CHARLES WEST) The design of inquiring systems: basic concepts of systems and organization. New York, [1971]. pp. 288. *bibliog.*

BERLINSKI (DAVID J.) On systems analysis: an essay concerning the limitations of some mathematical methods in the social, political, and biological sciences. Cambridge, Mass., 1976 repr. 1977. pp. 186.

GILDERSLEEVE (THOMAS ROBERT) Successful data processing system analysis. Englewood Cliffs, [1978]. pp. 309.

BLAIR (PETER D.) Multiobjective regional energy planning: application to the energy park concept. Boston, Mass., [1979]. pp. 163. *bibliog.*

SYSTEM THEORY.

CHURCHMAN (CHARLES WEST) The design of inquiring systems: basic concepts of systems and organization. New York, [1971]. pp. 288. *bibliog.*

ACKOFF (RUSSELL LINCOLN) Redesigning the future: a systems approach to societal problems. New York, [1974]. pp. 260.

MILLER (JAMES GRIER) Living systems. New York, 1978. pp. 1102. *bibliog.*

TAEGLICHE RUNDSCHAU.

POEHLS (JOACHIM) Die "Tägliche Rundschau" und die Zerstörung der Weimarer Republik, 1930 bis 1933. Münster, 1975. 2 vols. (in 1). *bibliog.* (*Münster in Westfalen. Westfälische Wilhelms- Universität. Institut für Publizistik. Arbeiten. Band 14*)

TAFT (WILLIAM HOWARD) President of the United States.

SCHOLES (WALTER V.) and SCHOLES (MARIE V.) The foreign policies of the Taft administration. Columbia, [1970]. pp. 259. *bibliog.*

TAIPING REBELLION, 1850-1864.

COMPILATION GROUP FOR THE "HISTORY OF MODERN CHINA" SERIES. The Taiping revolution. Peking, 1976. pp. 188.

TAIWAN

— Foreign relations.

TWO Chinese states: U.S. foreign policy and interests; edited by Ramon H. Myers. Stanford, [1978]. pp. 81. (*Stanford University. Hoover Institution on War, Revolution and Peace. Hoover Institution Publications. 200*)

— — United States.

CLOUGH (RALPH N.) Island China. Cambridge, Mass., 1978. pp. 264. *bibliog.*

— Industries.

FORMOSA. Ministry of Economic Affairs. Report on industrial and commercial surveys. a., 1976(no.9)- Taipei. *[in English and Chinese]*

— Politics and government.

BATE (H. MACLEAR) Report from Formosa. London, 1952. pp. 210.

HUANG (MAB) Intellectual ferment for political reforms in Taiwan, 1971-1973. Ann Arbor, 1976. pp. 131. (*Michigan University. Center for Chinese Studies. Michigan Papers in Chinese Studies. No. 28*)

— Social conditions.

HUANG (MAB) Intellectual ferment for political reforms in Taiwan, 1971-1973. Ann Arbor, 1976. pp. 131. (*Michigan University. Center for Chinese Studies. Michigan Papers in Chinese Studies. No. 28*)

— Social history.

MESKILL (JOHANNA MENZEL) A Chinese pioneer family: the Lins of Wu-feng, Taiwan, 1729- 1895. Princeton, 1979. pp. 376. *bibliog.*

TAJIKISTAN

— Industries.

KLETSEL'MAN (UL'IAN KHAIMOVICH) Formirovanie i razvitie promyshlennykh kompleksov v Tadzhikskoi SSR. Dushanbe, 1977. pp. 70.

TANZANIA

— Commerce — Malawi.

TANGANYIKA. 1954. Report on a survey of inter-territorial trade between Tanganyika and Northern Rhodesia and Nyasaland. [Dar es Salaam, 1954]. pp. 30.

— — Zambia.

TANGANYIKA. 1954. Report on a survey of inter-territorial trade between Tanganyika and Northern Rhodesia and Nyasaland. [Dar es Salaam, 1954]. pp. 30.

— Constitution.

UNITED REPUBLIC OF TANZANIA. Constitution. 1965. An Act to make provision consequential upon the enactment of the interim constitution of Tanzania, 1965 and for connected matters, and to repeal and amend certain laws. [Dar es Salaam], 1965. pp. 277-283.

UNITED REPUBLIC OF TANZANIA. Constitution. 1965. The interim constitution of Tanzania, 1965. [Dar es Salaam], 1965. pp. 207-268.

UNITED REPUBLIC OF TANZANIA. Constitution. 1965. The interim constitution of Tanzania, 1965: (Bill). [Dar es Salaam], 1965. pp. 66.

— Economic conditions — Bibliography.

UNITED REPUBLIC OF TANZANIA. Bureau of Statistics. 1975. A bibliography of economic and statistical publications on Tanzania, 1975. Dar es Salaam, 1975. fo. 19.

— Economic policy.

TOWARDS socialism in Tanzania; edited by Bismarck U. Mwansasu and Cranford Pratt. Toronto, 1979. pp. 243.

TANZANIA(Cont.)

— Foreign relations.

NNOLI (OKWUDIBA) Self reliance and foreign policy in Tanzania: the dynamics of the diplomacy of a new state, 1961 to 1971. New York, [1978]. pp. 340. *bibliog.*

NYERERE (JULIUS KAMBARAGE) Tanzania rejects western domination of Africa: statement...to foreign envoys accredited to Tanzania, June 8, 1978. Dar es Salaam, 1978. pp. 8.

— History.

ILIFFE (JOHN) A modern history of Tanganyika. Cambridge, 1979. pp. 616. *bibliog. (Cambridge. University. African Studies Centre. African Studies Series. 25)*

— Officials and employees.

TANGANYIKA. Reviewing Committee on Clerical/Executive and Technical Regrading. 1956. Report; [W. Wenban-Smith, chairman]. Dar es Salaam, 1956. pp. 48.

— Politics and government.

TOWARDS socialism in Tanzania; edited by Bismarck U. Mwansasu and Cranford Pratt. Toronto, 1979. pp. 243.

TARIFFS.

GENERAL AGREEMENT ON TARIFFS AND TRADE. 1979. The Tokyo Round of multilateral trade negotiations: report by the Director-General of GATT. Geneva, 1979. pp. 196.

ROM (MICHAEL) The role of tariff quotas in commercial policy. London, 1979. pp. 258. *bibliog.*

— Australia.

AUSTRALIA. Department of Overseas Trade. 1976. Australian tariff preferences for developing countries. Canberra, 1976. pp. 22.

AUSTRALIA. Department of Overseas Trade. 1976. Information on the operation of the Australian generalised system of preferences in 1974/75. [Canberra, 1976]. 1 pamphlet (various pagings).

AUSTRALIAN trade practices: readings; edited by J.P. Nieuwenhuysen. 2nd ed. London, 1976. pp. 317. *bibliog.*

TASHKENT

— Politics and government.

OCHERKI istorii Tashkentskoi gorodskoi partiinoi organizatsii. Tashkent, 1976. pp. 446.

TASMANIA

— Economic conditions.

TASMANIA. Directorate of Industrial Development and Trade. Research Section. 1975. Tasmania: a businessman's handbook: information about investment in Tasmania. [7th ed.] Hobart, 1975. pp. 111.

— Government publications — Bibliography.

TASMANIAN OFFICIAL PUBLICATIONS; [pd. by] State Library of Tasmania. q., 1972-1976 (v. 1-5); ceased pbln. Hobart. *From 1977- information on Tasmanian official publications included in AUSTRALIAN GOVERNMENT PUBLICATIONS.*

TAX ADMINISTRATION AND PROCEDURE

— Rhodesia.

RHODESIA. Commissioner of Taxes. 1971. Employee's guide to pay as you earn. rev. ed. Salisbury, 1971. pp. 12.

RHODESIA. Commissioner of Taxes. 1971. Employer's guide to the pay as you earn system of tax collection. [Salisbury, 1971]. fo. 24.

TAX CREDITS

— France.

LAFOURCADE (JEAN) Avantages fiscaux de développement régional. Paris, [1970]. pp. 115. *bibliog.*

— United Kingdom.

VINCE (PHILIP) To each according...; Liberal tax credit proposals. London, 1979. pp. 28.

TAX INCIDENCE

— United States.

CATSAMBAS (THANOS) Regional impacts of federal fiscal policy: theory and estimation of economic incidence. Lexington, Mass., [1978]. pp. 135. *bibliog.*

TAX PLANNING

— United Kingdom.

LAWTON (PHILIP) and SUMPTION (ANTHONY) Tax and tax planning. 8th ed. London, 1979. pp. 199.

TAX REVENUE ESTIMATING.

BURCHELL (ROBERT WILLIAM) and LISTOKIN (DAVID) The fiscal impact handbook: estimating local costs and revenues of land development. New Brunswick, [1978]. pp. 480. *bibliog.*

— Mathematical models.

PRICE (R.W.R.) Modelling fiscal policy: the personal income tax system. London, [1978]. pp. 22. *bibliog. (National Institute of Economic and Social Research. Discussion Papers. No. 22)*

TAXATION.

SINGER (NEIL M.) Public microeconomics: an introduction to government finance. 2nd ed. Boston, Mass., [1976]. pp. 447.

JAMES (SIMON R.) and NOBES (CHRISTOPHER) The economics of taxation. Oxford, 1978. pp. 310. *bibliogs.*

ORGANISATION FOR ECONOMIC CO-OPERATION AND DEVELOPMENT. Committee on Fiscal Affairs. 1978. The tax/benefit position of selected income groups in OECD member countries, 1972-1976: a report by the Committee, etc. Paris, 1978. pp. 132.

CURRENT issues in fiscal policy; edited by S.T. Cook and P.M. Jackson. Oxford, 1979. pp. 230. *bibliog.*

— History.

NEURRISSE (ANDRE) Histoire de l'impôt. [Paris, 1978]. pp. 128. *bibliog.*

— Denmark.

DENMARK. Skattedepartementet. 1979. Direct taxation in Denmark: a brief survey. 3rd ed. [Copenhagen, 1979]. pp. 65.

— France — Law.

TIXIER (GILBERT) and GEST (GUY) Droit fiscal. 2nd ed. Paris, 1978. pp. 535.

— Hong Kong.

HO (H.C.Y.) The fiscal system of Hong Kong. London, [1979]. pp. 182. *bibliogs.*

— India — Law.

INDIA. Direct Tax Laws Committee. 1978. Final report; [C.C. Chokshi, chairman]. [Delhi], 1978. pp. 253.

— Netherlands.

DUTCH business law: legal, accounting and tax aspects of business in the Netherlands; by Steven R. Schuit [and others]. Deventer, 1978. pp. 567.

An INFLATION-adjusted tax system: a summary of the report on the elimination from the Dutch tax system of the distorting effects of inflation; [by] H.J. Hofstra [and others]. The Hague, Government Publishing Office, 1978. pp. 75.

— Pakistan.

PAKISTAN. Finance Division. 1977. Taxation structure of Pakistan. [Islamabad], 1977. pp. 57.

— — Punjab.

PUNJAB (PAKISTAN). Bureau of Statistics. 1974. Census of provincial taxes in the Punjab, 1961-62 to 1973-74. Lahore, [1974]. pp. 24.

— Palestine — History.

COHEN (AMNON) and LEWIS (BERNARD) Population and revenue in the towns of Palestine in the sixteenth century. Princeton, N.J., [1978]. pp. 199. *bibliog.*

— Spain.

CANSECO CANSECO (JOSE EMILIO) Politica fiscal de España: estudio de la politica economica publica española desde el plan de estabilizacion. Madrid, Instituto de Estudios Fiscales, 1978. pp. 691. *bibliog.*

— Switzerland — Bern (Canton).

BERN (CANTON). Amt für Statistik. 1978. Eidg. Abstimmung vom 12. Juni 1977 im Kanton Bern: Umsatzsteuer, direkte Bundessteuer, etc. Bern, 1978. pp. 72. *(Beiträge zur Statistik des Kantons Bern. Politische Statistik. Reihe F. Heft 4) In French and German.*

— Underdeveloped areas.

See UNDERDEVELOPED AREAS — Taxation.

— United Kingdom.

POND (CHRIS) The wages free fall: a submission to the chancellor and the TUC. London, 1977. fo. 8. *(Low Pay Unit. Low Pay Papers. No. 14)*

BROWN (CHARLES VICTOR) and others. Tax reform in the United Kingdom. London, [1978]. pp. 32. *bibliog. (Economics Association. Occasional Papers)*

JAMES (SIMON R.) and NOBES (CHRISTOPHER) The economics of taxation. Oxford, 1978. pp. 310. *bibliogs.*

LAWTON (PHILIP) and SUMPTION (ANTHONY) Tax and tax planning. 8th ed. London, 1979. pp. 199.

— — Law.

PINSON (BARRY) On revenue law: comprising income tax, capital gains tax, development land tax, etc. 12th ed. London, 1978. pp. 647.

ROWLAND'S tax guide, 1978-79; [edited by] Nigel Eastaway [and] David Trill. 2nd ed. London, 1979. pp. [576].

— United States.

SINGER (NEIL M.) Public microeconomics: an introduction to government finance. 2nd ed. Boston, Mass., [1976]. pp. 447.

AMERICAN ENTERPRISE INSTITUTE FOR PUBLIC POLICY RESEARCH. Legislative Analyses. 95th Congress. No. 28. The administration's 1978 tax package. Washington, 1978. pp. 48.

MACDOWELL (MICHAEL ALAN) Public understanding of economic policies: the tax cuts of 1962 and 1964. New York, 1978. pp. 321. *bibliog.*

TAX policies in the 1979 budget: highlights of a conference [held at] Washington, D.C., February 27, 1978; edited by Rudolph G. Penner. Washington, [1978]. pp. 66.

UNITED STATES. Statutes, etc. 1954-1977. Internal revenue code (of 1954): income, estate and gift tax provisions, including 1977 amendments. Chicago, 1978. pp. [2162].

TAXATION, DOUBLE.

ORGANISATION FOR ECONOMIC COOPERATION AND DEVELOPMENT. Committee on Fiscal Affairs. 1977. Model double taxation Convention on income and on capital: report of the...Committee, etc. Paris, 1977. pp. 216.

CARROLL (MITCHELL BENEDICT) Global perspectives of an international tax lawyer. Hicksville, N.Y., [1978]. pp. 151.

GOODMAN (WOLFE D.) International double taxation of estates and inheritances. London, 1978. pp. 277. *bibliog.*

— United Kingdom.

NEWMAN (JOHN A.) United Kingdom double tax treaties. London, 1979. pp. 128.

TAXATION, EXEMPTION FROM

— France.

LAFOURCADE (JEAN) Avantages fiscaux de développement régional. Paris, [1970]. pp. 115. *bibliog.*

— Salvador.

SALVADOR. Statutes, etc. 1970. Export Development Law. [San Salvador], 1971. fo. 16.

— United Kingdom.

WILLIS (J.R.M.) and HARDWICK (PETER J.W.) Tax expenditures in the United Kingdom. London, 1978. pp. 107.

TAXATION, PAPAL.

LUNT (WILLIAM EDWARD) Accounts rendered by papal collectors in England, 1317-1378; transcribed with annotations and introduction by William E. Lunt; edited with additions and revisions by Edgar B. Graves. Philadelphia, 1968. pp. 579. *(American Philosophical Society. Memoirs. vol. 70)*

TAXATION OF ALIENS

— United States.

McDANIEL (RONALD) and AULT (HUGH J.) Introduction to United States international taxation. Deventer, [1977]. pp. 183. *(Erasmus Universiteit Rotterdam. Fiscaal-Economisch Instituut. International Series. no. 2)*

TAXATION OF BONDS, SECURITIES, ETC.

— United Kingdom.

ORHNIAL (ANTONY J. H.) Estimates of marginal tax rates for dividends and bond interest 1970- 75. London, 1977. pp. 18. *bibliog. (Papers on Capital and Risk. No. 5)*

TAXICABS

— Zambia.

ZAMBIA. Central Statistical Office. 1972. Report on passenger road transport in Zambia, 1971. Lusaka, [1972?]. pp. 37.

TEA

— Statistics.

INTERNATIONAL TEA COMMITTEE. Bulletin of statistics (formerly Monthly bulletin of statistics). a., with s-a. suppl. (formerly m.), 1936(v.1)- ; susp. pbln. 1942-1945, and 1956. London.

TEA MACHINERY.

TULL (D.W.) Tea looks forward: (plans for the modernisation and rationalisation of tea production and manufacture). [London], 1951. pp. 38.

TULL (D.W.) Tea progresses. [London], 1955. pp. 57.

TEA TRADE

— India.

DUNCAN (WALTER) AND GOODRICKE. The Duncan Group: being a short history of Duncan Brothers and Co. Ltd., Calcutta and Walter Duncan and Goodricke Ltd., London, 1859-1959. London, 1959. pp. 184. *The first ten chapters were originally printed for private circulation in 1931.*

— Pakistan.

DUNCAN (WALTER) AND GOODRICKE. The Duncan Group: being a short history of Duncan Brothers and Co. Ltd., Calcutta and Walter Duncan and Goodricke Ltd., London, 1859-1959. London, 1959. pp. 184. *The first ten chapters were originally printed for private circulation in 1931.*

TEACHER-STUDENT RELATIONSHIPS.

METZ (MARY HAYWOOD) Classrooms and corridors: the crisis of authority in desegregated secondary schools. Berkeley, Calif., [1978]. pp. 275. *bibliog.*

WOODS (PETER) The divided school. London, 1979. pp. 310.

TEACHERS

— Salaries, pensions, etc.

ZABALZA-MARTI (ANTONIO) and others. The economics of teacher supply. Cambridge, 1979. pp. 280. *bibliog.*

— Supply and demand.

ZABALZA-MARTI (ANTONIO) and others. The economics of teacher supply. Cambridge, 1979. pp. 280. *bibliog.*

— Canada.

CANADA. Statistics Canada. Educational staff of community colleges and vocational schools. a., 1976/77- Ottawa. *[in English and French]* Supersedes CANADA. Statistics Canada. Educational staff in community colleges and CANADA. Statistics Canada. Educational staff in public trade schools and similar institutions.

— Germany.

STOEHR (WOLFGANG) Lehrer und Arbeiterbewegung: Entstehung und Politik der ersten Gewerkschaftsorganisation der Lehrer in Deutschland, 1920 bis 1923. Marburg, [1978]. 2 vols. *bibliog. (Studiengesellschaft für Sozialgeschichte und Arbeiterbewegung, Marburg. Schriftenreihe für Sozialgeschichte und Arbeiterbewegung. Band 13)*

— Sierra Leone.

SIERRA LEONE. Commission of Enquiry into Conditions of Service of Teachers. 1949. Report; [A.L. Binns, commissioner]. Freetown, 1949. pp. 6. *(Sierra Leone. Sessional Papers. 1949. No. 3)*

— United Kingdom.

PIPER (DAVID WARREN) and GLATTER (RON) The changing university: a report on the Staff Development in Universities programme 1972/4. Windsor, 1977. pp. 410. *bibliog.*

GRACE (GERALD) Teachers, ideology and control: a study in urban education. London, 1978. pp. 264. *bibliog.*

ROBINSON (MARGARET) Schools and social work. London, 1978. pp. 268.

WOODS (PETER) The divided school. London, 1979. pp. 310.

— United States — Political activity.

PROFESSORS, politicians and public policy; (a Round Table held on July 29 1977...); John Charles Daly, moderator, etc. Washington, [1977]. pp. 38. *(American Enterprise Institute for Public Policy Research. Round Tables)*

— — Tenure.

The HIDDEN professoriate: credentialism, professionalism, and the tenure crisis; edited by Arthur S. Wilke. Westport, Conn., [1979]. pp. 290. *bibliog.*

TEACHERS, TRAINING OF

— Malawi.

MALAWI. Ministry of Education. Planning Section. 1965. Education project, International Development Association: secondary technical education and teacher training. [Zomba, 1965]. pp. 202.

— United Kingdom.

TEACHER education for a multi-cultural society: (the report of a joint working party of the Community Relations Commission and the Association of Teachers in Colleges and Departments of Education; [Beryl Paston-Brown, chairman]). 2nd ed. London, Commission for Racial Equality, 1978. pp. 71.

TEACHERS' COLLEGES

— United Kingdom.

HENCKE (DAVID) Colleges in crisis: the reorganization of teacher training 1971-7. Harmondsworth, 1978. pp. 140. *bibliog.*

TEACHERS' UNIONS

— Germany.

STOEHR (WOLFGANG) Lehrer und Arbeiterbewegung: Entstehung und Politik der ersten Gewerkschaftsorganisation der Lehrer in Deutschland, 1920 bis 1923. Marburg, [1978]. 2 vols. *bibliog. (Studiengesellschaft für Sozialgeschichte und Arbeiterbewegung, Marburg. Schriftenreihe für Sozialgeschichte und Arbeiterbewegung. Band 13)*

TEAK.

MAHAPHOL (S.) Teak in Thailand. Bangkok, 1954. pp. 31. *bibliog. (Thailand. Forest Department. [Publications]. No. R. 16)*

TECHNICAL ASSISTANCE.

WILSON (Sir HAROLD) The first Edwina Mountbatten Memorial Lecture. London, [1973?]. 1 pamphlet (unpaged). *(Marr-Munning Trust. Edwina Mountbatten Papers. No. 1)*

GOULET (DENIS) The uncertain promise: value conflicts in technology transfer. New York, [1977]. pp. 320. *bibliog.*

ZEYLSTRA (WILLEM GUSTAAF) Aid or development: the relevance of development aid to problems of developing countries. 2nd ed. Leyden, 1977. pp. 269. *bibliog.*

BELL (JOHN LAMBERTON) And the crowd is still hungry. Glasgow, 1978. pp. 22. *Rectorial address delivered in the University of Glasgow in 1978.*

EXCHANGE of expertise: the counterpart system in the new international order; edited by Irving J. Spitzberg, Jr. Boulder, Colo., [1978]. pp. 257. *bibliogs.*

HOOLE (FRANCIS W.) Evaluation research and development activities. Beverly Hills, [1978]. pp. 205. *bibliog.*

DAHLBERG (KENNETH A.) Beyond the green revolution: the ecology and politics of global agricultural development. New York, [1979]. pp. 256. *bibliog.*

TECHNICAL ASSISTANCE, AMERICAN.

LOWTHER (KEVIN) and LUCAS (C. PAYNE) Keeping Kennedy's promise: the Peace Corps: unmet hope of the new frontier. Boulder, [1978]. pp. 153. *bibliog.*

TECHNICAL ASSISTANCE, BRITISH.

U.K. 1978. Science and technology for development: the British national paper for the United Nations Conference on Science and Technology for Development, 1979. [London, 1978]. 1 pamphlet (unpaged). *bibliog.*

TECHNICAL ASSISTANCE, FRENCH

TECHNICAL ASSISTANCE, FRENCH
— Africa.

FRANCE. Ministère de la Coopération. Service des Etudes [Economiques] et [des] Questions Internationales. 1978. La coopération scientifique et technique entre la France et les pays d'Afrique noire et de l'Océan Indien. Paris, 1978. pp. 80. *(Etudes et Documents. No. 34)*

— Indian Ocean Region.

FRANCE. Ministère de la Coopération. Service des Etudes [Economiques] et [des] Questions Internationales. 1978. La coopération scientifique et technique entre la France et les pays d'Afrique noire et de l'Océan Indien. Paris, 1978. pp. 80. *(Etudes et Documents. No. 34)*

TECHNICAL ASSISTANCE IN AFRICA.

ARNOLD (GUY) Aid in Africa. London, 1979. pp. 240. *bibliog.*

TECHNICAL ASSISTANCE IN ASIA.

TECHNICAL CO-OPERATION UNDER THE COLOMBO PLAN: report of the Colombo Plan Council for Technical Co-operation in South and South-East Asia...Colombo Plan Bureau. a., 1967/8- [Colombo]. *Supersedes a report of the same title pd. in London (1952, 1953/4-1966/7).*

TECHNICAL EDUCATION
— Brazil.

SOUZA (ALBERTO DE MELLO E) and CASTRO (CLAUDIO DE MOURA) Mão-de-obra industrial no Brasil: mobilidade, treinamento e produtividade. Rio de Janeiro, 1974. pp. 424. *(Brazil. Instituto de Planejamento Econômico e Social. Instituto de Pesquisas. Relatorios de Pesquisa. No. 25)*

— Italy.

EMMA (ROSANNA) and MOSCATI (ROBERTO) La fabbrica dei disoccupati: scuola e occupazione giovanile in una inchiesta sugli Istituti Tecnici Industriali nel mezzogiorno. Torino, 1976. pp. 293.

— Malawi.

MALAWI. Ministry of Education. Planning Section. 1965. Education project, International Development Association: secondary technical education and teacher training. [Zomba, 1965]. pp. 202.

— Russia — Soviet Far East.

DEREVIANKO (ALEKSEI PANTELEVICH) Inzhenerno-tekhnicheskie kadry Dal'nego Vostoka SSSR, 1959- 1965 gg. Moskva, 1978. pp. 150.

— United Kingdom.

BUTLER (RICHARD AUSTEN) Baron Butler of Saffron Walden. The responsibilities of education. London, 1968. pp. 162. *bibliog. The inaugural P.D. Leake lecture. Includes appendix on the educational and training requirements of professional bodies.*

— United States.

EDUCATING for careers: policy issues in a time of change; edited by Thomas F. Powers with the assistance of John R. Swinton. University Park, Pa., [1977]. pp. 190. *Based on a symposium held in 1976 at the Pennsylvania State University.*

TECHNOLOGICAL INNOVATIONS.

The BUSINESS system: a bicentennial view; [by] Milton Friedman [and others]. Hanover, N.H., 1977. pp. 91. *Symposium to celebrate the 75th anniversary of the Amos Tuck School of Business Administration, Dartmouth College.*

BINSWANGER (HANS P.) and RUTTAN (VERNON WESLEY) Induced innovation: technology, institutions, and development. Baltimore, [1978]. pp. 423.

DICK (TREVOR J.O.) An economic theory of technological change: the case of patents and the United States railroads 1871-1950. New York, 1978. pp. 145. *bibliog.*

HOPE-SIMPSON (JACYNTH) The making of the machine age. London, 1978. pp. 216. *bibliog.*

PARKER (JOHN EDGAR SAYCE) The economics of innovation: the national and multinational enterprise in technological change. 2nd ed. London, 1978. pp. 396. *bibliogs.*

DAVIES (STEPHEN) The diffusion of process innovations. Cambridge, 1979. pp. 193. *bibliog.*

INDUSTRIAL innovation: technology, policy, diffusion; edited by Michael J. Baker. London, 1979. pp. 464. *bibliogs.*

— Social aspects.

GOURVITCH (ALEXANDER) Survey of economic theory on technological change and employment. New York, 1966. pp. 252. *Reprint of work first published Philadelphia, 1940.*

— — Mexico.

DEWALT (BILLIE R.) Modernization in a Mexican ejido: a study in economic adaption. Cambridge, 1979. pp. 303. *bibliog.*

— — Russia.

METODOLOGICHESKIE voprosy opredeleniia sotsial'no-ekonomicheskoi effektivnosti novoi tekhniki. Moskva, 1977. pp. 230. *(Akademiia Nauk SSSR. Problemy Sovetskoi Ekonomiki)*

— — United Kingdom.

FREEMAN (CHRISTOPHER) Government policies for industrial innovation. London, 1978. pp. 18. *(London. University. Birkbeck College. Bernal Lectures. 1978)*

— America, Latin.

TECHNOLOGICAL progress in Latin America: the prospects for overcoming dependency; edited by James H. Street and Dilmus D. James. Boulder, Colo., 1979. pp. 257.

— Arab countries.

TECHNOLOGY transfer and change in the Arab world: the proceedings of a seminar of the United Nations Economic Commission for Western Asia organized by the Natural Resources, Science and Technology Division, Beirut, 9-14 October 1977; edited by A.B. Zahlan with the assistance of Rosemarie Said Zahlan. Oxford, 1978. pp. 506. *bibliogs.*

— Brazil.

DIFUSÃO de inovações na industria brasileira: três estudos de caso; [edited by] Jose Tavares de Araujo Jr. Rio de Janeiro, 1976. pp. 246. *bibliog. (Brazil. Instituto de Planejamento Econômico e Social. Instituto de Pesquisas. Monografias. No.24)*

— Russia.

NEGRU (FEDOR PANTELEEVICH) Nauchno-tekhnicheskii progress i trudovoi dogovor; pod redaktsiei R.Z. Livshitsa. Kishinev, 1977. pp. 95.

PAP'IAN (ZAVEN TELEMAKOVICH) KPSS i glavnye napravleniia nauchno-tekhnicheskoi politiki na sovremennom etape. Erevan, 1977. pp. 199.

ZYKOV (IURII ANATOL'EVICH) and SLETOVA (TAT'IANA LEONIDOVNA) Kompleksnye programmy nauchno-tekhnicheskogo progressa: metodologicheskie voprosy formirovaniia i realisatsii. Moskva, 1977. pp. 160. *(Akademiia Nauk SSSR. Problemy Sovetskoi Ekonomiki)*

DOZORTSEV (VIKTOR ABRAMOVICH) Zakonodatel'stvo i nauchno-tekhnicheskii progress. Moskva, 1978. pp. 191.

IGLITSKII (ALEKSANDR ALEKSANDROVICH) Sovetskii rabochii klass v usloviiakh nauchno-tekhnicheskoi revoliutsii: kritika burzhuazno-reformistskikh kontseptsii. Moskva, 1978. pp. 124.

— — Komi Republic.

EKONOMICHESKIE problemy nauchno-tekhnicheskogo progressa na Severe: na primere promyshlennosti i stroitel'stva Komi ASSR. Moskva, 1977. pp. 128. *(Akademiia Nauk SSSR. Problemy Sovetskoi Ekonomiki)*

— — Ukraine.

EFFEKTIVNOST' novoi tekhniki: na primere promyshlennosti Ukrainskoi SSR. Kiev, 1977. pp. 199.

— Sweden.

The IMPORTANCE of technology and the permanence of structure in industrial growth: proceedings of a symposium at IUI, Stockholm, July 18-19, 1977; [edited by] Bo Carlsson [and others]. Stockholm, 1978. pp. 237. *bibliogs. (Industriens Utredningsinstitut. IUI Conference Reports. 1978:2)*

— Underdeveloped areas.

See UNDERDEVELOPED AREAS — Technological innovations.

— United Kingdom.

ADVISORY COUNCIL FOR APPLIED RESEARCH AND DEVELOPMENT [U.K.]. Industrial innovation. London, 1978. pp. 43.

— United States.

WATERS (JOSEPH PAUL) Technological acceleration and the Great Depression. New York, 1977. pp. 250. *bibliog.*

TECHNOLOGISTS
— Russia.

BAILES (KENDALL E.) Technology and society under Lenin and Stalin: origins of the Soviet technical intelligentsia, 1917-1941. Princeton, 1978. pp. 469. *bibliog. (Columbia University. Russian Institute. Studies)*

TECHNOLOGY.

CLAUDON (MICHAEL P.) International trade and technology: models of dynamic comparative advantage. Washington, D.C., [1977]. pp. 179. *bibliog.*

SCIENCE, technology, and economic development: a historical and comparative study; edited by William Beranek, Jr. [and] Gustav Ranis. New York, [1978]. pp. 347. *bibliogs.*

— History.

PACEY (ARNOLD) The maze of ingenuity: ideas and idealism in the development of technology. New York, 1975. pp. 350. *bibliog.*

HOPE-SIMPSON (JACYNTH) The making of the machine age. London, 1978. pp. 216. *bibliog.*

WHITE (LYNN T.) Medieval religion and technology: collected essays. Berkeley, Calif., [1978]. pp. 360. *(California University. Center for Medieval and Renaissance Studies. Publications. 13)*

— International cooperation.

GRANGER (JOHN V.) Technology and international relations. San Francisco, [1979]. pp. 202. *bibliogs.*

— Social aspects.

PACEY (ARNOLD) The maze of ingenuity: ideas and idealism in the development of technology. New York, 1975. pp. 350. *bibliog.*

HAAS (ERNST BERNARD) and others. Scientists and world order: the uses of technical knowledge in international organizations. Berkeley, Calif., [1977]. pp. 368.

HOPE-SIMPSON (JACYNTH) The making of the machine age. London, 1978. pp. 216. *bibliog.*

STANLEY (MANFRED) The technological conscience: survival and dignity in an age of expertise. New York, [1978]. pp. 281. *bibliog.*

DIRECTING technology: policies for promotion and control; edited by Ron Johnston and Philip Gummett. London, [1979]. pp. 271. *bibliogs.*

JENKINS (CLIVE) and SHERMAN (BARRIE) The collapse of work. London, 1979. pp. 181.

— — **Communist countries.**

NYILAS (JÓZSEF) Marxist approach to the problems of appropriate technology. Budapest, 1978. pp. 48. *(Hungarian Scientific Council for World Economy. [Publications]. Trends in World Economy. No. 26)*

— — **Russia.**

BAILES (KENDALL E.) Technology and society under Lenin and Stalin: origins of the Soviet technical intelligentsia, 1917-1941. Princeton, 1978. pp. 469. *bibliog. (Columbia University. Russian Institute. Studies)*

— **America, Latin.**

TECHNOLOGICAL progress in Latin America: the prospects for overcoming dependency; edited by James H. Street and Dilmus D. James. Boulder, Colo., 1979. pp. 257.

— **Brazil.**

FIGUEIREDO (NUNO FIDELINO DE) A transferência de tecnologia no desenvolvimento industrial do Brasil. Rio de Janeiro, 1972. pp. 360. *(Brazil. Instituto de Planejamento Econômico e Social. Instituto de Pesquisas. Monografias. No. 7)*

— **China.**

SCIENCE and technology in the People's Republic of China. Paris, Organisation for Economic Co-operation and Development, 1977. pp. 216.

— **Underdeveloped areas.**

See UNDERDEVELOPED AREAS — Technology.

TECHNOLOGY AND CIVILIZATION.

HOLZNER (BURKART) and MARX (JOHN H.) Knowledge application: the knowledge system in society. Boston, Mass., [1979]. pp. 388. *bibliog.*

TECHNOLOGY AND ETHICS.

WHITE (LYNN T.) Medieval religion and technology: collected essays. Berkeley, Calif., [1978]. pp. 360. *(California University. Center for Medieval and Renaissance Studies. Publications. 13)*

TECHNOLOGY AND LAW.

ZENIN (IVAN ALEKSANDROVICH) Nauka i tekhnika v grazhdanskom prave. Moskva, 1977. pp. 208.

DOZORTSEV (VIKTOR ABRAMOVICH) Zakonodatel'stvo i nauchno-tekhnicheskii progress. Moskva, 1978. pp. 191.

TECHNOLOGY AND STATE.

DIRECTING technology: policies for promotion and control; edited by Ron Johnston and Philip Gummett. London, [1979]. pp. 271. *bibliogs.*

GRANGER (JOHN V.) Technology and international relations. San Francisco, [1979]. pp. 202. *bibliogs.*

— **America, Latin.**

FERRER (ALDO) Tecnologia y politica economica en America Latina. Buenos Aires, 1974. pp. 132. *bibliog.*

SABATO (JORGE A.) ed. El pensamiento latinoamericano en la problematica ciencia-tecnologia-desarrollo-dependencia. Buenos Aires, [1975]. pp. 349.

— **Nigeria.**

NIGERIAN COUNCIL FOR SCIENCE AND TECHNOLOGY. The Nigerian Council for Science and Technology: inaugural brochure. Lagos, 1970. pp. 22.

TECHNOLOGY TRANSFER.

SABATO (JORGE A.) ed. El pensamiento latinoamericano en la problematica ciencia-tecnologia-desarrollo-dependencia. Buenos Aires, [1975]. pp. 349.

GERMIDIS (DIMITRIOS A.) ed. Transfer of technology by multinational corporations. Paris, Organisation for Economic Co-operation and Development, 1977. 2 vols. *(Development Centre. Studies)*

GOULET (DENIS) The uncertain promise: value conflicts in technology transfer. New York, [1977]. pp. 320. *bibliog.*

INDUSTRIAL policies and technology transfers between East and West; edited by C.T. Saunders. Wien, 1977. pp. 316. *(Wiener Institut Für Internationale Wirtschaftsvergleiche. East-West European Economic Interaction. Workshop Papers. vol.3)*

TECHNOLOGY for development; [edited] by Ann Kestenbaum. rev. ed. London, 1977. pp. 97.

BARANSON (JACK) Technology and the multinationals: corporate strategies in a changing world economy. Lexington, Mass., [1978]. pp. 170.

GRECH (JOHN C.) Threads of dependence. Msida, Malta, 1978. pp. 200. *bibliog.*

JEREMY (DAVID JOHN) The transmission of cotton and woollen manufacturing technologies between Britain and the U.S.A. from 1790 to the 1830s. 1978. fo. 344. *bibliog.* Typescript. Ph.D. (London) thesis: unpublished. This thesis is the property of London University and may not be removed from the Library.

TECHNOLOGY transfer and change in the Arab world: the proceedings of a seminar of the United Nations Economic Commission for Western Asia organized by the Natural Resources, Science and Technology Division, Beirut, 9-14 October 1977; edited by A.B. Zahlan with the assistance of Rosemarie Said Zahlan. Oxford, 1978. pp. 506. *bibliogs.*

CASSON (MARK C.) Alternatives to the multinational enterprise. London, 1979. pp. 116. *bibliog.*

MATHIESON (RAYMOND SUCCESS) Japan's role in Soviet economic growth: transfer of technology since 1965. New York, 1979. pp. 277. *bibliog.*

TEES RIVER.

CLEVELAND [COUNTY]. Planning Department. Preparing a plan for the River Tees: a summary of the River Tees plan report of survey. [Middlesbrough], 1976. pp. xi. *(Reports. No. 71)*

CLEVELAND [COUNTY]. [Planning Department]. River Tees plan: report of survey. [Middlesbrough], 1976. pp. 46, xxv. *(Reports. No. 70)*

CLEVELAND [COUNTY]. Planning Department. River Tees plan: report of survey: public participation report. [Middlesbrough], 1976. pp. 97. *(Reports. No. 78)*

CLEVELAND [COUNTY]. Planning Department. Cleveland County Council River Tees plan for recreation and amenity. Middlesbrough, 1978. pp. 71. *(Reports. No. 121)*

CLEVELAND [COUNTY]. Planning Department. River Tees plan for recreation and amenity: report on public participation of draft written statement. [Middlesbrough], 1978. fo.71 *(Reports. No. 105) Publicity material (3 items) in end pocket.*

TEESSIDE

— **Economic conditions.**

TEESSIDE. County Borough Council. Teesside structure plan: report of survey, 1972. [Middlesbrough], 1972. pp. 303.

— **Economic policy.**

CLEVELAND [COUNTY]. County Council. Cleveland (Teesside) structure plan, Cleveland (East Cleveland) structure plan, Cleveland (West Cleveland) structure plan: examination in public, June 1975: County Council statement. [Middlesbrough], 1975. fo 84, xxxiii.

CLEVELAND [COUNTY]. [Planning Department]. Teesside structure plan. [Middlesbrough], 1977. pp. 235. *Map in end pocket.*

CLEVELAND [COUNTY]. Planning Department. Teesside structure plan: proposals for alterations. [Middlesbrough], 1978. 3 pts. (in 1 vol.). *(Reports. Nos. 122-124)*

— **Social conditions.**

TEESSIDE. County Borough Council. Teesside structure plan: report of survey, 1972. [Middlesbrough], 1972. pp. 303.

— **Social policy.**

CLEVELAND [COUNTY]. County Council. Cleveland (Teesside) structure plan, Cleveland (East Cleveland) structure plan, Cleveland (West Cleveland) structure plan: examination in public, June 1975: County Council statement. [Middlesbrough], 1975. fo 84, xxxiii.

CLEVELAND [COUNTY]. [Planning Department]. Teesside structure plan. [Middlesbrough], 1977. pp. 235. *Map in end pocket.*

CLEVELAND [COUNTY]. Planning Department. Teesside structure plan: proposals for alterations. [Middlesbrough], 1978. 3 pts. (in 1 vol.). *(Reports. Nos. 122-124)*

TELECOMMUNICATION.

YEARBOOK OF COMMON CARRIER TELECOMMUNICATION STATISTICS AND TELECOMMUNICATION STATISTICS; [pd. by] the International Telecommunication Union. a., 1974- Genève. *[In English, French and Spanish]. From 1974 - incorporates TELECOMMUNICATION STATISTICS.*

GARMIER (JACQUES) L'UIT et les télécommunications par satellites. Bruxelles, 1975. pp. 341. *bibliog.*

MARTIN (JAMES THOMAS) The wired society. Englewood Cliffs, N.J., [1978]. pp. 300.

MATTELART (ARMAND) Multinational corporations and the control of culture: the ideological apparatuses of imperialism; translated from the French by Michael Chanan. Brighton, 1979. pp. 304. *bibliogs.*

— **Social aspects.**

McGILLEM (CLARE D.) and McLAUCHLAN (WILLIAM P.) Hermes bound: the policy and technology of telecommunications. West Lafayette, Ind., 1978. pp. 284. *bibliog.*

— **Australia.**

AUSTRALIAN TELECOMMUNICATIONS COMMISSION. Annual report. a., 1975/76(1st)- Canberra. *Included in AUSTRALIA. Parliament. [Parliamentary papers], which see.*

— **United Kingdom.**

CRIPPS (FRANCIS) and GODLEY (WYNNE) The planning of telecommunications in the United Kingdom. Cambridge, 1978. pp. 76.

— **United States.**

GALLAGHER (EDWARD A.) Getting the message across: the story of Western Union International, Inc. New York, 1971. pp. 24. *(Newcomen Society in North America. Newcomen Addresses. 1971)*

COMMUNICATIONS for tomorrow: policy perspectives for the 1980s; edited by Glen O. Robinson. New York, [1978]. pp. 526. *First report of the Project on Communications Policy of the Program on Communications and Society of the Aspen Institute for Humanistic Studies.*

TELEGRAPH

TELEGRAPH
— United States.
STEHMAN (JONAS WARREN) The financial history of the American Telephone and Telegraph Company. New York, 1967. pp. 339. *bibliog. Reprint of work originally published Boston, 1925.*

TELEPHONE
— History.
FIELD (KATE) ed. The history of Bell's telephone. London, 1878. pp. 71.

— Sweden — Apparatus and supplies.
L.M. Ericsson 100 years; [by] Artur Attman [and others]. [Stockholm?, 1977]. 3 vols.

— United States.
STEHMAN (JONAS WARREN) The financial history of the American Telephone and Telegraph Company. New York, 1967. pp. 339. *bibliog. Reprint of work originally published Boston, 1925.*

TELEVISION BROADCASTING.
McARTHUR (COLIN) Television and history. London, 1978. pp. 60. *(British Film Institute. Television Monographs. 8)*

TELEVISION: ideology and exchange; edited by John Caughie. London, 1978. pp. 93. *bibliog. (British Film Institute. Television Monographs. 9)*

— Australia.
AUSTRALIA. Australian Broadcasting Tribunal. 1977. Television and the public...; research report based on a survey conducted in Melbourne in 1977. Canberra, 1977. pp. 31.

— Canada.
PEERS (FRANK W.) The public eye: television and the politics of Canadian broadcasting, 1952-1968. Toronto, [1979]. pp. 459. *bibliog.*

— Europe, Eastern.
PAULU (BURTON) Radio and television broadcasting in Eastern Europe. Minneapolis, 1974. pp. 592.

— Russia.
PAULU (BURTON) Radio and television broadcasting in Eastern Europe. Minneapolis, 1974. pp. 592.

— United Kingdom.
CURRAN (Sir CHARLES J.) A seamless robe: broadcasting: philosophy and practice. London, 1979. pp. 358.

TELEVISION IN POLITICS.
TELEVISION: ideology and exchange; edited by John Caughie. London, 1978. pp. 93. *bibliog. (British Film Institute. Television Monographs. 9)*

— Europe.
TELEVISION and political life: studies in six European countries; edited by Anthony Smith. London, 1979. pp. 261. *bibliog.*

TELEVISION INDUSTRY WORKERS
— United Kingdom.
SEGLOW (PETER) Trade unionism in television: a case study in the development of white collar militancy. Farnborough, [1978]. pp. 287.

TEMPERANCE.
OYSTON (HENRY GIFFORD) Socialism and the drink evil: a series of brotherhood addresses. London, [1909]. pp. 127.

TEMPLE (HENRY JOHN) 3rd Viscount Palmerston.
KREIN (DAVID F.) The last Palmerston government: foreign policy, domestic politics, and the genesis of "splendid isolation". Ames, Iowa, 1978. pp. 252. *bibliog.*

TEMPLES, BUDDHIST.
SENEVIRATNE (H.L.) Rituals of the Kandyan State. Cambridge, 1978. pp. 190. *bibliog.*

TEMPORARY EMPLOYMENT.
ALBEDA (W.) and others. Temporary work in modern society: a comparative study of the International Institute for Temporary Work, on request of the Fondation Internationale pour la Promotion de l'Etude du Travail Temporaire. [The Hague], 1978. 2 vols.

TENDER OFFERS (SECURITIES).
AULD (ROBIN ERNEST) and others. Ashbourne Investments Limited: investigation under sections 164 and 172 of the Companies Act 1948; report. London, H.M.S.O., 1979. pp. 602.

TENNESSEE
— Race relations.
LAMON (LESTER C.) Black Tennesseans 1900-1930. Knoxville, [1977]. pp. 320.

TERMINAL CARE.
STODDARD (SANDOL) The hospice movement: a better way of caring for the dying. London, 1979. pp. 266. *bibliog.*

TERRITORIAL WATERS.
FRANCE. Direction de la Documentation. La Documentation Française. Notes et Etudes Documentaires. No. 4451-4452. Les états et la mer: le nationalisme maritime; [by] Laurent Lucchini [and] Michel Voelckel. [Paris], 1978. pp. 463.

GREENWICH FORUM CONFERENCE, 3RD, GREENWICH, 1977. Britain and the sea: the 200 mile zone and its implications; [papers] edited by D.C. Watt. London, [1979]. pp. 45. *bibliogs.*

SYMMONS (CLIVE RALPH) The maritime zones of islands in international law. The Hague, 1979. pp. 307.

— United Kingdom.
GREENWICH FORUM CONFERENCE, 3RD, GREENWICH, 1977. Britain and the sea: the 200 mile zone and its implications; [papers] edited by D.C. Watt. London, [1979]. pp. 45. *bibliogs.*

TERRORISM.
TERRORISM: interdisciplinary perspectives; edited, with an introduction by Yonah Alexander and Seymour Maxwell Finger. New York, [1977]. pp. 377. *bibliog.*

CRELINSTEN (RONALD D.) and others. Terrorism and criminal justice: an international perspective. Lexington, Mass., [1978]. pp. 131. *Based on a conference held in 1976 in Rochester, Michigan.*

INTERNATIONAL terrorism in the contemporary world; edited by Marius H. Livingston [and others]. Westport, [1978]. pp. 522. *bibliog. Based on the 1976 Glassboro State College International Symposium.*

LEGAL aspects of international terrorism; edited by Alona E. Evans and John F. Murphy. Lexington, Mass., [1978]. pp. 690.

DOBSON (CHRISTOPHER) and PAYNE (RONALD) The weapons of terror: international terrorism at work. London, 1979. pp. 216. *bibliog.*

The POLITICS of terrorism; edited by Michael Stohl. New York, 1979. pp. 419. *bibliog.*

SHORT (K.R.M.) The dynamite war: Irish-American bombers in Victorian Britain. Dublin, 1979. pp. 278. *bibliog.*

TEN years of terrorism: collected views; editorial team, Jennifer Shaw [and others]. London, 1979. pp. 192.

TERRORISM: theory and practice; edited by Yonah Alexander [and others]. Boulder, Colo., 1979. pp. 280. *bibliog.*

The TERRORISM reader: a historical anthology; edited by Walter Laqueur. London, 1979. pp. 291. *bibliog.*

— European Economic Community countries.
FLETCHER-COOKE (CHARLES FLETCHER) Terrorism and the European Community. [Eastbourne], 1979. pp. 18.

— Germany.
BAUMANN (MICHAEL) Wie alles anfing: how it all began; translated by Helene Ellenbogen and Wayne Parker. Vancouver, [1977]. pp. 121.

BECKER (JILLIAN) Hitler's children. rev. ed. London, 1978. pp. 415. *bibliog.*

RADVANYI (MIKLOS) Anti-terrorist legislation in the Federal Republic of Germany. Washington, Library of Congress, 1979. pp. 143.

— Italy.
PISANO (VITTORFRANCO S.) Contemporary Italian terrorism: analysis and countermeasures. Washington, Library of Congress, 1979. pp. 185. *bibliog.*

— Rhodesia.
RHODESIA. Ministry of Information, Immigration and Tourism. 1978. Massacre of the innocents. [Salisbury, 1978]. pp. 39.

RHODESIA. Ministry of Information, Immigration and Tourism. 1978. The murder of missionaries in Rhodesia. [Salisbury, 1978]. pp. 27.

— United Kingdom.
STOKE NEWINGTON FIVE SOLIDARITY COMMITTEE. Release the five; statement of the...committee. London, [1973?]. pp. 8.

— Yugoslavia.
CLISSOLD (STEPHEN) Croat separatism: nationalism, dissidence and terrorism. London, 1979. pp. 21. *(Institute for the Study of Conflict. Conflict Studies. No.103)*

TEXAS
— Description and travel.
COOKE (PHILIP ST. GEORGE) and others. Exploring southwestern trails, 1846-1854;...edited by Ralph P. Bieber...in collaboration with Averam B. Bender. Glendale, 1938; Philadelphia, 1974. pp. 383. *Facsimile reprint.*

— Economic conditions.
CAMPBELL (RANDOLPH B.) and LOWE (RICHARD) Wealth and power in antebellum Texas. College Station, [1977]. pp. 183. *bibliog.*

DYNAMICS of growth: an economic profile of Texas; edited by Louis J. Rodriguez. Austin, [1978]. pp. 314. *bibliog.*

— History.
BAKER (T. LINDSAY) The first Polish Americans: Silesian settlements in Texas. College Station, 1979. pp. 268. *bibliog.*

TEXTILE INDUSTRY AND FABRICS
— Belgium.
SOCIÉTÉ STUDIA. Etude sur l'évolution de la concentration dans quelques sous- secteurs de l'industrie du textile en Belgique, mise à jour 1968-1972,...laine...coton...bonneterie, etc. [Brussels], Communautés Européennes, 1975. pp. 89.

— France.

DELANOE (GUIREC) Etude sur l'évolution de la concentration dans l'industrie du textile en France: coton...laine, etc. [Brussels], Communautés Européennes, 1975. pp. 201.

— Russia — Russia (RSFSR).

KLIUEV (VLADIMIR GRIGOR'EVICH) Patrioticheskim pochinam - vsemernuiu podderzhku. Moskva, 1978. pp. 78. *(Bibliotechka Profsoiuznogo Aktivista. 36)*

— Turkey.

AYDIN (SEMIH) and others. Textile sector. Istanbul, 1978. pp. 50,50,85. *(Türkiye Sinaî Kalkinma Bankasi. Sector Research Publications. No.20)*

— United Kingdom — Ireland, Northern.

MESSENGER (BETTY) Picking up the linen threads: a study in industrial folklore. Austin, [1975]. pp. 265. *bibliog.*

— United States.

BAGNALL (WILLIAM R.) The textile industries of the United States, including sketches and notices of cotton, woolen, silk and linen manufactures in the colonial period. New York, 1971. pp. 660. *Reprint, with new index, of vol. 1, 1639-1810, originally published in Cambridge, Mass., 1893; no more published.*

TEXTILE MACHINERY.

BALLIANO (PIERA) and LANZETTI (RENATO) Studio sull'evoluzione della concentrazione nel settore della costruzione di macchine per l'industria tessile in Italia. [Brussels], Comunità Europee, 1976. pp. 159.

TEXTILE WORKERS

— United Kingdom.

WHITE (JOSEPH L.) The limits of trade union militancy: the Lancashire textile workers, 1910-1914. Westport, Conn., 1978. pp. 258. *bibliog.*

— — Ireland, Northern.

MESSENGER (BETTY) Picking up the linen threads: a study in industrial folklore. Austin, [1975]. pp. 265. *bibliog.*

— United States — New York.

WALKOWITZ (DANIEL J.) Worker city, company town: iron and cotton-worker protest in Troy and Cohoes, New York, 1855-84. Urbana, Ill., [1978]. pp. 292. *bibliog.*

THAILAND

— Economic conditions.

THAILAND: roots of conflict; edited by Andrew Turton [and others]. Nottingham, 1978. pp. 196.

— Foreign economic relations — Netherlands.

SMITH (GEORGE VINAL) The Dutch in seventeenth-century Thailand. Detroit, [1977]. pp. 203. *bibliog. (Northern Illinois University. Center for Southeast Asian Studies. Special Reports. No. 16)*

— Foreign relations.

VIRAPHOL (SARASIN) Directions in Thai foreign policy. Singapore, 1976. pp. 69. *(Institute of Southeast Asian Studies. Occasional Papers. No. 40)*

THAILAND: roots of conflict; edited by Andrew Turton [and others]. Nottingham, 1978. pp. 196.

— Forest policy.

SAMAPUDDHI (KRIT) The forests of Thailand and forestry programs. [2nd ed.] Bangkok, 1957. pp. 35. *bibliog. (Thailand. Forest Department. [Publications]. No. R.20)*

— Government publications — Bibliography.

NATIONAL LIBRARY OF THAILAND. List of Thai government publications covering the years 1954, 1955, 1956. Bangkok, 1958. pp. 31.

— Parliament — Elections.

SANGCHAI (SOMPORN) Some observations on the elections and coalition formation in Thailand, 1976. Singapore, 1976. fo. 51. *(Institute of Southeast Asian Studies. Occasional Papers. No. 43)*

— Politics and government.

SANGCHAI (SOMPORN) Coalition behaviour in modern Thai politics. Singapore, 1976. fo. 26. *(Institute of Southeast Asian Studies. Occasional Papers. No. 41)*

THAILAND: roots of conflict; edited by Andrew Turton [and others]. Nottingham, 1978. pp. 196.

— Population.

THAILAND. Manpower Planning Division. 1972. Population growth in Thailand. 2nd ed. [Bangkok], 1972. pp. 42.

— Social conditions.

SHARP (LAURISTON W.) and HANKS (LUCIEN MASON) Bang Chan: social history of a rural community in Thailand. Ithaca, 1978. pp. 314. *bibliog.*

THAILAND: roots of conflict; edited by Andrew Turton [and others]. Nottingham, 1978. pp. 196.

THALIDOMIDE.

SUFFER the children: the story of thalidomide; [by] Phillip Knightley [and others]. London, 1979. pp. 309. *bibliog.*

THATCHER (MARGARET).

THATCHER (MARGARET) and HARRIS (KENNETH) Margaret Thatcher talks to the Observer; interviewed by Kenneth Harris. London, [1979]. pp. 13.

THEATRE

— Censorship — United Kingdom.

DEFENCE OF LITERATURE AND THE ARTS SOCIETY. Evidence to the Committee on Obscenity and Film Censorship. London, 1978. pp. 13.

THEOLOGY.

DUSSEL (ENRIQUE) History and the theology of liberation: a Latin American perspective...; translated by John Drury. New York, [1976]. pp. 189. *bibliog.*

THEOLOGY, CATHOLIC.

NEWMAN and Gladstone: centennial essays; edited by James D. Bastable. Dublin, 1978. pp. 324. *bibliogs. Selection of papers presented at the International Newman Conference, Dublin, 1975.*

THEORY (PHILOSOPHY).

McCARTHY (THOMAS A.) The critical theory of Jürgen Habermas. Cambridge, Mass., [1978]. pp. 466. *bibliog.*

THERAPEUTIC COMMUNITY.

THERAPEUTIC communities: reflections and progress; edited by R. D. Hinshelwood and Nick Manning. London, 1979. pp. 336. *bibliog.*

THIRTY YEARS WAR, 1618-1648.

BENECKE (GERHARD) ed. Germany in the Thirty Years War. London, 1978. pp. 108. *bibliog.*

POLISENSKÝ (J.V.) War and society in Europe, 1618-1648; with the collaboration of Frederick Snider. Cambridge, 1978. pp. 261. *bibliog.*

— Economic aspects.

FRANZ (GUENTHER) Der Dreissigjährige Krieg und das deutsche Volk: Untersuchungen zur Bevölkerungs- und Agrargeschichte. 4th ed. Stuttgart, 1979. pp. 140.

THORPE (JEREMY).

CHESTER (LEWIS) and others. Jeremy Thorpe: a secret life. [Glasgow], 1979. pp. 384.

THORPE (JEREMY) and others, defendants. The Thorpe committal; [by] Peter Chippindale and David Leigh. London, 1979. pp. 190.

THORPE (JOHN JEREMY).

See THORPE (JEREMY).

THOUGHT AND THINKING.

RADFORD (JOHN) and BURTON (ANDREW) Thinking: its nature and development. Chichester, [1974]. pp. 440. *bibliog.*

LANGUAGE learning and thought; edited by John Macnamara. New York, 1977. pp. 296. *bibliogs.*

ARENDT (HANNAH) The life of the mind. London, 1978. 2 vols.

DE BONO (EDWARD FRANCIS CHARLES PUBLIUS) Lateral thinking: a textbook of creativity. Harmondsworth, 1978. pp. 260.

COULTER (JEFF) The social construction of mind: studies in ethnomethodology and linguistic philosophy. London, 1979. pp. 190.

THURINGIA

— Population.

ASTEL (KARL) and WEBER (ERNA) Die Kinderzahl der 29000 politischen Leiter des Gaues Thüringen der NSDAP und die Ursachen der ermittelten Fortpflanzungshäufigkeit; 4. Untersuchung über die unterschiedliche Fortpflanzung in Thüringen (aus dem Thüringischen Landesamt für Rassewesen, Weimar und Jena). Berlin, 1943. pp. 187.

TIBET

— History.

BOGOSLOVSKII (VASILII ALEKSEEVICH) Tibetskii raion KNR, 1949-1976. Moskva, 1978. pp. 199. *bibliog.*

TICINO

— Constitution.

TICINO (CANTON). Constitution. 1967. Costituzione della Repubblica e Cantone del Ticino del 4 luglio 1830 (riordinata il 29 ottobre 1967). [Bellinzona?, 1970?]. pp. 12.

TIMBER

— Canada — British Columbia.

BRITISH COLUMBIA. Royal Commission on Forest Resources. 1976. Synopsis of timber rights and forest policy in British Columbia: report...; Peter H. Pearse, commissioner. Victoria, 1976. pp. 55.

— Thailand.

SUVARNASUDDHI (KHID) Some commercial timbers of Thailand: their properties and uses. [Bangkok], Royal Forest Department, 1950 repr. 1954. pp. 52.

TIME ALLOCATION SURVEYS

— Russia.

PATRUSHEV (VASILII DMITRIEVICH) Ispol'zovanie sovokupnogo vremeni obshchestva: problemy balansa vremeni naseleniia. Moskva, 1978. pp. 216. *bibliog.*

TIME SERIES ANALYSIS.

BLOOMFIELD (PETER) Fourier analysis of time series: an introduction. Nex York, [1976]. pp. 258. *bibliog.*

TIME SERIES ANALYSIS.(Cont.)

ÖLLER (LARS ERIK) Time series analysis of Finnish foreign trade. Helsinki, 1978. 1 vol.(various pagings). bibliog. (Suomen Tilastoseura. Tilastotieteellisiä Tutkimuksia. 3)

JENKINS (GWILYM M.) Practical experiences with modelling and forecasting time series. St. Helier, 1979. pp. 146.

TIMISKAMING

— History.

MITCHELL (ELAINE ALLAN) Fort Timiskaming and the fur trade. Toronto, [1977]. pp. 306. bibliog.

TIN.

INTERNATIONAL TIN COUNCIL. Notes on tin. m. (formerly bi-m), Ja/F 1960 (no.30)- London.

— Statistics.

INTERNATIONAL TIN COUNCIL. Monthly statistical bulletin. m., Ap 1957(v.1, no.1)- London. Supersedes International Tin Study Group. Statistical bulletin (1948 - Mr 1957).

TIN STATISTICS; pd. by the International Tin Council. a., 1963/1973[1st issue]- London.

TIN MINES AND MINING

— United Kingdom — Cornwall.

JENKIN (ALFRED KENNETH HAMILTON) Wendron tin. Helston, 1978. pp. 64.

TISO (JOZEF).

VNUK (FRANTIŠEK) This is Dr. Jozef Tiso, President of the Slovak Republic. 3rd ed. Cambridge, Ont., 1977. pp. 83.

TITO (JOSIP BROZ).

GOERLITZ (WALTER) Geldgeber der Macht: wie Hitler, Lenin, Mao Tse-tung, Mussolini, Stalin und Tito finanziert wurden. Frankfurt am Main, 1978. pp. 256. bibliog.

TOBACCO

— Malawi.

MALAWI. Agro-Economic Survey. 1973. Agro-economic survey: 11th report: Mbawa: a sample farm management survey among oriental tobacco, maize and groundnut growers in the Mbawa area in the southern part of Mzimba district, Malawi, with special reference to oriental tobacco; prepared by T.W. Bieze. Lilongwe, 1973. fo. 87. bibliog.

TOBACCO MANUFACTURE AND TRADE.

COMMONWEALTH SECRETARIAT. Tobacco quarterly. q., Ja 1979- London.

— United Kingdom.

LONDON. London Record Society. Publications. vol. 15. Joshua Johnson's letterbook, 1771-1774: letters from a merchant in London to his partners in Maryland; edited by Jacob M. Price. London, 1979. pp. 181.

— United States.

LONDON. London Record Society. Publications. vol. 15. Joshua Johnson's letterbook, 1771-1774: letters from a merchant in London to his partners in Maryland; edited by Jacob M. Price. London, 1979. pp. 181.

TOGLIATTI (PALMIRO).

TOGLIATTI e il Mezzogiorno: atti del convegno tenuto a Bari il 2-3-4 novembre 1975; a cura di Franco De Felice. Roma, 1977. 2 vols.

TOGO

— Economic conditions.

FRANCE. Ministère de la Coopération. Sous-Direction des Etudes Economiques et de la Planification. 1976. Togo: données statistiques sur les activités économiques, culturelles et sociales. Paris, 1976. pp. 157.

— History.

KNOLL (ARTHUR J.) Togo under imperial Germany, 1884-1914: a case study in colonial rule. Stanford, Calif., [1978]. pp. 224. bibliog. (Stanford University. Hoover Institution on War, Revolution and Peace. Hoover Institution Publications. 190)

— Social conditions.

FRANCE. Ministère de la Coopération. Sous-Direction des Etudes Economiques et de la Planification. 1976. Togo: données statistiques sur les activités économiques, culturelles et sociales. Paris, 1976. pp. 157.

— Statistics.

FRANCE. Ministère de la Coopération. Sous-Direction des Etudes Economiques et de la Planification. 1976. Togo: données statistiques sur les activités économiques, culturelles et sociales. Paris, 1976. pp. 157.

TOKYO ROUND, 1973-1979.

GENERAL AGREEMENT ON TARIFFS AND TRADE. 1979. The Tokyo Round of multilateral trade negotiations: report by the Director-General of GATT. Geneva, 1979. pp. 196.

TOLERATION.

NUNN (CLYDE Z.) and others. Tolerance for nonconformity: a national survey of Americans' changing commitment to civil liberties. San Francisco, 1978. pp. 212. bibliog.

TOLLER (ERNST).

TOLLER (ERNST) I was a German: an autobiography;...translated by Edward Crankshaw. London, 1934. pp. 298.

TOMSKII (MIKHAIL PAVLOVICH).

VAGANOV (FEDOR MIKHAILOVICH) Pravyi uklon v VKP(b) i ego razgrom, 1928-1930 gg. 2nd ed. Moskva, 1977. pp. 328.

TOPOLOGY.

PFANZAGL (J.) and PIERLO (W.) Compact systems of sets. Berlin, 1966. pp. 48. bibliog.

TORONTO

— Politics and government.

ONTARIO. Ministry of Treasury, Economics and Intergovernmental Affairs. 1978. White Paper: government statement on the review of local government in the municipality of metropolitan Toronto. [Toronto], 1978. pp. 61.

TORRENS SYSTEM

— United States.

SHICK (BLAIR C.) and PLOTKIN (IRVING H.) Torrens in the United States: a legal and economic history and analysis of American land-registration systems. Lexington, Mass., [1978]. pp. 176.

TORTS.

FLEMING (JOHN GUNTHER) An introduction to the law of torts. Oxford, 1967 repr. 1979. pp. 230.

FLEMING (JOHN GUNTHER) The law of torts. 5th ed. Sydney, 1977. pp. 729.

— United Kingdom.

HEYDON (JOHN DYSON) Economic torts. 2nd ed. London, 1978. pp. 144.

WEIR (TONY) A casebook on tort. 4th ed. London, 1979. pp. 584.

WINFIELD (Sir PERCY HENRY) and JOLOWICZ (JOHN ANTHONY) On tort; eleventh edition by W.V.H. Rogers. London, 1979. pp. 718.

— United States.

SHAPO (MARSHALL S.) The duty to act: tort law, power and public policy. Austin, [1977]. pp. 203.

TORTURE

— South Africa.

DESAI (BARNEY) and MARNEY (CARDIFF) The killing of the Imam. London, 1978. pp. 146.

— Uruguay.

AMNESTY INTERNATIONAL. Uruguay: deaths under torture, 1975-77. London, 1978. pp. 12.

TORY ISLAND

— Social life and customs.

FOX (ROBIN) The Tory Islanders: a people of the Celtic fringe. Cambridge, 1978. pp. 210. bibliog.

TOTALITARIANISM.

CHIPPINDALE (PETER) and HARRIMAN (ED) Juntas unitede' London, [1978]. pp. 144.

REVEL (JEAN FRANÇOIS) The totalitarian temptation; (translated by David Hapgood). Harmondsworth, 1978. pp. 332.

TOURIST TRADE.

ROBINSON (HARRY) A geography of tourism. Plymouth, [1976]. pp. 478. bibliog.

— Canada — Alberta.

ALBERTA. Department of Business Development and Tourism. Annual report. a., 1976/77- Edmonton.

— — Ontario.

ONTARIO. Ministry of Industry and Tourism. 1977. Framework for opportunity: a guide for tourism development in Ontario/Canada. [Toronto, 1977]. pp. 25.

— European Economic Community countries.

WORKING GROUP OF THE NATIONAL TOURIST ORGANISATIONS OF THE EUROPEAN ECONOMIC COMMUNITIES. The economic significance of tourism within the European Community; a report;...prepared by J.H. Haughton [and others]. [London], British Tourist Authority, 1975. pp. 48.

WORKING GROUP OF THE NATIONAL TOURIST ORGANISATIONS OF THE EUROPEAN ECONOMIC COMMUNITIES. The economic significance of tourism within the European Community; a second report;...prepared by M.J. O'Donoghue [and others]. London, British Tourist Authority, 1977. pp. 24.

— New Zealand.

NEW ZEALAND. Tourism Advisory Council. 1978. Report...to the Minister of Tourism; [R.W. Baird, chairman]. Wellington, 1978. pp. 72.

— Sicily.

SICILY. Statutes, etc. 1967. Provvedimenti per lo sviluppo dell'economia turistica nella regione Siciliana: legge regionale 12 aprile 1967, no. 46. [Palermo, 1967]. pp. 63.

— Spain.

SPAIN. Direccion General de Promocion del Turismo. 1970. Turismo 1969. [Madrid, 1970]. pp. 231.

TRADE UNIONS.

TRADE AND PROFESSIONAL ASSOCIATIONS

— Germany.

SCHINDLER (ROSEMARIE) Die Marktpolitik des Roheisen-Verbandes während der Weimarer Republik. Bielefeld, 1978. pp. 365. *bibliog.*

— United Kingdom.

GREEN (EDWIN) Debtors to their profession: a history of the Institute of Bankers, 1879-1979. London, 1979. pp. 245.

TRADE MARKS.

ORGANISATION FOR ECONOMIC CO-OPERATION AND DEVELOPMENT. Committee of Experts on Restrictive Business Practices. 1978. Restrictive business practices relating to trademarks. Paris, 1978. pp. 76.

TRADE REGULATION

— Australia.

AUSTRALIAN trade practices: readings; edited by J.P. Nieuwenhuysen. 2nd ed. London, 1976. pp. 317. *bibliog.*

— United Kingdom.

GRIBBIN (J.D.) The post-war revival of competition as industrial policy. London, Price Commission, 1978. pp. 58, 2. *(Government Economic Service Working Papers. No. 19)*

NATIONAL ECONOMIC DEVELOPMENT OFFICE. Competition policy; including a research annex by Alan Hughes: Competition policy and economic performance in the UK. London, 1978. pp. 102.

— United States.

OWEN (BRUCE M.) and BRAEUTIGAM (RONALD) The regulation game: strategic uses of the administrative process. Cambridge, Mass., [1978]. pp. 270. *bibliog.*

TRADE UNIONS.

INTERNATIONALE TAGUNG DER HISTORIKER DER ARBEITERBEWEGUNG, 1974. Arbeiterbewegung und Faschismus; Der Februar 1934 in Österreich; (bearbeitet von Gerhard Botz). Wien, 1976. pp. 464. *(Internationale Tagung der Historiker der Arbeiterbewegung. ITH-Tagungsberichte. Band 9)*

WASCHKE (HILDEGARD) Supra-nationale Gewerkschaftspolitik: Ziele und Wege der internationalen Gewerkschaftsbewegung. Köln, [1978]. pp. 60. *bibliog. (Institut der Deutschen Wirtschaft. Beiträge zur Gesellschafts- und Bildungspolitik. 25)*

—Bibliography.

BULLETIN DU CENTRE D'HISTOIRE DU SYNDICALISME; [pd. by] Centre d'Histoire du Syndicalisme, Université de Paris. a., 1976/77(no.1)- Paris.

— Government employees — United States — California.

CROUCH (WINSTON WINFORD) Organized civil servants: public employer-employee relations in California. Berkeley, [1978]. pp. 302. *bibliog.*

— Africa.

AFRICAN labor history; Peter C.W. Gutkind [and others], editors. Beverly Hills, [1978]. pp. 280. *bibliogs.*

ANANABA (WOGU) The trade union movement in Africa: promise and performance. London, [1979]. pp. 248. *bibliog.*

— America, Latin.

SPALDING (HOBART A.) Organized labor in Latin America: historical case studies of workers in dependent societies. New York, 1977. pp. 297.

— Asia.

ASIA-FIET REGIONAL TRADE SECTION CONFERENCE, PENANG, 1975. Regional trade section conference for ASIA-FIET affiliates;... sponsored by the Friedrich Naumann-Stiftung,...[the] Deutsche Angestellten Gewerkschaft [and by ASIA-FIET]. [Petaling Jaya, 1976?]. pp. 57.

— Australia.

AUSTRALIAN TRADE UNION TRAINING AUTHORITY. Annual report. a., 1975/76(1st)- Canberra. *Included in AUSTRALIA. Parliament. [Parliamentary papers].*

— Austria.

RUECKBLICK und Ausschau: (10 Jahre Ludwig Boltzmann Institut für Geschichte der Arbeiterbewegung; [by] Karl R. Stadler [and others]). Wien, 1978. pp. 139. *bibliog. (Ludwig Boltzmann Institut für Geschichte der Arbeiterbewegung. Materialien zur Arbeiterbewegung. Nr. 12)*

— Botswana.

KHAMA (Sir SERETSE) Trade unions in Botswana: address...at Botswana Trade Union Education Centre's cornerstone ceremony, Saturday, July 10th 1971. Gaborone, 1971. pp. 9.

KHAMA (Sir SERETSE) Address...during the inauguration of the first delegates conference of the Botswana Federation of Trade Unions at the town hall, Gaborone, on Saturday, 2nd April, 1977. Gaborone, 1977. pp. 7.

— Canada.

VERNER (COOLIE) and DICKINSON (GARY) Union education in Canada: a report of the educational activities of labour organizations...; submitted to the Canadian Labour Congress and the Canada Department of Labour. Vancouver, Adult Research Centre, University of British Columbia, 1974. pp. 224.

LAZARUS (MORDEN) The long winding road: Canadian labour in politics. Vancouver, [1977]. pp. 103. *bibliog.*

BERCUSON (DAVID JAY) Fools and wise men: the rise and fall of the One Big Union. Toronto, [1978]. pp. 300. *bibliog.*

A CHRISTIAN union in labour's wasteland; edited by Edward Vanderkloet. Toronto, 1978. pp. 139. *bibliog.*

DAVIDSON (JOE) and DEVERELL (JOHN) Joe Davidson. Toronto, 1978. pp. 192.

— — British Columbia.

MacINTOSH (ROBERT) Boilermakers in British Columbia. [Vancouver?], 1976. pp. 124.

— Denmark.

LANDSORGANISATIONEN I DANMARK. The Danish trade union movement. Copenhagen, [1968?]. pp. 28.

— Europe.

WEINBERG (PAUL J.) European labor and multinationals. New York, [1978]. pp. 112. *bibliog.*

The QUALITY of working life in Western and Eastern Europe; edited by Cary L. Cooper and Enid Mumford. Westport, 1979. pp. 348. *bibliog.*

— European Economic Community countries.

TRADE UNION NEWS FROM THE EUROPEAN COMMUNITY; [pd. by] European Communities Press and Information...London. q., autumn 1969 (no.1)- London. *Supersedes Trade union news.*

TRADE UNION INFORMATION: Fortn. jl. for trade unions produced by the [European] Community's Trade Union Division, Information Directorate-General. fortn. Brussels. *Current issues only kept.*

— France.

FRANCE. Direction de la Documentation. La Documentation Française. Notes et Etudes Documentaires. Nos. 4488-4489. Institutions représentatives du personnel dans l'entreprise; par Albert Arseguel. [Paris], 1978. pp. 175. *bibliog.*

HAINSWORTH (RAYMOND EDWIN) The trade union movements and labour-management relations in the coal mines of the Nord and Pas-de-Calais departments of France during the depression of 1930-1936. 1978. fo. 587. *bibliog.* Typescript. Ph.D. (London) thesis: unpublished. *This thesis is the property of London University and may not be removed from the Library.*

— Germany.

SEIDEL (RICHARD) The trade union movement of Germany...; including a section on the non-manual workers' trade union movement, by Bernhard Göring. Amsterdam, 1928. pp. 157. *(International Federation of Trade Unions. International Trade Union Library. Nos. 7-8)*

PIRKER (THEO) Die blinde Macht: die Gewerkschaftsbewegung in Westdeutschland. Berlin, 1979. 2 vols (in 1). *Reprint, with new introduction, of work originally published Munich, 1960.*

FREIER DEUTSCHER GEWERKSCHAFTSBUND. Bundesvorstand. Trade union enemies in judges' robes: a documentation, etc. [Berlin, 1962-63). 2 vols. (in 1).

ARBEITERVERTRETER in den Betriebsrat: Dokumentation und Auseinandersetzung um eine ausserordentliche Betriebsratswahl 1973 bei Krone, Westberlin, etc. Berlin, [1973]. pp. 122. *(Internationale Marxistische Diskussion. Arbeitspapiere. No. 13)*

PLESS (PHILIPP) Der Wille zur Tat: Gewerkschaften als gesellschaftsverändernde Kraft: Reden und Aufsätze; herausgegeben von Rudolf Schneider. Berlin, [1973]. pp. 182. *bibliog.*

BEDINGUNGEN und Prinzipien revolutionärer Gewerkschaftspolitik; herausgegeben von linken Gewerkschaftern in der IG Chemie. Berlin, [1974]. pp. 100. *(Internationale Marxistische Diskussion. Arbeitspapiere. No. 14)*

ENGELHARDT (ULRICH) "Nur vereinigt sind wir stark": die Anfänge der deutschen Gewerkschaftsbewegung, 1862/63 bis 1869/70. Stuttgart, 1977. 2 vols. *bibliog. (Arbeitskreis für Moderne Sozialgeschichte. Industrielle Welt. Band 23)*

MEYER (REGINE) Streik und Aussperrung in der Metallindustrie: Analyse der Streikbewegung in Nordwürttemberg-Nordbaden, 1971. Marburg, [1977]. pp. 426. *bibliog. (Studiengesellschaft für Sozialgeschichte und Arbeiterbewegung, Marburg. Schriftenreihe für Sozialgeschichte und Arbeiterbewegung. Band 4)*

WEISS-HARTMANN (ANNE) Der Freie Gewerkschaftsbund Hessen, 1945-1949. Marburg, 1977 repr. 1978. pp. 417. *bibliog. (Studiengesellschaft für Sozialgeschichte und Arbeiterbewegung, Marburg. Schriftenreihe für Sozialgeschichte und Arbeiterbewegung. Band 2)*

APO und Gewerkschaften: von der Kooperation zum Bruch; herausgegeben von Gudrun Küsel. Berlin, [1978]. pp. 188.

BRAUNTHAL (GERARD) Socialist labor and politics in Weimar Germany: the General Federation of German Trade Unions. Hamden, Conn., 1978. pp. 253. *bibliog.*

GEWERKSCHAFTSPOLITIK in der Krise: kritisches Gewerkschaftsjahrbuch 1977/78; (Otto Jacobi [and others], Hg.). Berlin, [1978]. pp. 223. *bibliogs.*

INSTITUT FÜR MARXISTISCHE STUDIEN UND FORSCHUNGEN. DGB wohin?: Dokumente zur Programm-Diskussion; eingeleitet von Frank Deppe. Frankfurt am Main, [1978]. pp. 280. *bibliog.*

SCHARPF (FRITZ W.) Autonome Gewerkschaften und staatliche Wirtschaftspolitik: Probleme einer Verbändegesetzgebung. Köln, [1978]. pp. 50. *(Otto Brenner Stiftung. Schriftenreihe. 12)*

TRADE UNIONS.(Cont.)

SCHROEDER (WILHELM HEINZ) Arbeitergeschichte und Arbeiterbewegung: Industriearbeit und Organisationsverhalten im 19. und frühen 20. Jahrhundert. Frankfurt/Main, [1978]. pp. 316. *bibliog.*

STOEHR (WOLFGANG) Lehrer und Arbeiterbewegung: Entstehung und Politik der ersten Gewerkschaftsorganisation der Lehrer in Deutschland, 1920 bis 1923. Marburg, [1978]. 2 vols. *bibliog. (Studiengesellschaft für Sozialgeschichte und Arbeiterbewegung, Marburg. Schriftenreihe für Sozialgeschichte und Arbeiterbewegung. Band 13)*

WEISS (GERHARD) Die ÖTV: Politik und gesellschaftspolitische Konzeptionen der Gewerkschaft Ö[ffentliche Dienste], T[ransport und] V[erkehr] von 1966 bis 1976. Marburg, 1978. pp. 533. *bibliog. (Studiengesellschaft für Sozialgeschichte und Arbeiterbewegung, Marburg. Schriftenreihe für Sozialgeschichte und Arbeiterbewegung. Band 7)*

DEPPE (FRANK) Autonomie und Integration: Materialien zur Gewerkschaftsanalyse. Marburg, [1979]. pp. 243. *(Studiengesellschaft für Sozialgeschichte und Arbeiterbewegung, Marburg. Schriftenreihe für Sozialgeschichte und Arbeiterbewegung. Band 9)*

WIEDENHOFER (HARALD) Probleme gewerkschaftlicher Interessenvertretung: das Beispiel der Gewerkschaft Nahrung, Genuss, Gaststätten. Bonn, [1979]. pp. 166. *bibliog. (Friedrich-Ebert-Stiftung. Forschungsinstitut. Reihe: Arbeit. Band 3)*

— — Officials and employees.

HOCHGUERTEL (GERHARD) and STIEGLER (BARBARA) Die Aufgaben des DGB an der Basis: zum Berufsbild des DGB-Sekretärs. Bonn, [1978]. pp. 238. *bibliog. (Friedrich-Ebert-Stiftung. Forschungsinstitut. Reihe: Arbeit)*

— Germany, Eastern.

BIERMANN (WOLFGANG) Demokratisierung in der DDR?: ökonomische Notwendigkeiten, Herrschaftsstrukturen, Rolle der Gewerkschaften, 1961-1977. Köln, [1978]. pp. 170. *bibliog.*

SIMON (GUENTER) Ohne sie geht nichts: Gewerkschaften im Alltag der DDR. Frankfurt am Main, [1979]. pp. 171.

— Ghana.

JEFFRIES (RICHARD) Class, power and ideology in Ghana: the railwaymen of Sekondi. Cambridge, 1978. pp. 244. *bibliog. (Cambridge. University. African Studies Centre. African Studies Series. 22)*

— India — Officials and employees.

REINDORP (JULIAN) Leaders and leadership in the trade unions in Bangalore. Madras, [1971]. pp. 239. *(Christian Institute for the Study of Religion and Society. Social Research Series. No. 7)*

— Italy.

FOIS (SERGIO) Sindacati e sistema politico: problematica di un rapporto e implicazioni costituzionali. Milano, 1977. pp. 118.

FORBICE (ALDO) Austerità e democrazia operaia: intervista a Giorgio Benvenuto. Milano, [1977]. pp. 196.

LAMA (LUCIANO) Il sindacato nella crisi italiana. Roma, 1977. pp. 301.

PISTILLO (MICHELE) Giuseppe Di Vittorio, 1944-1957: la costruzione della CGIL; la lotta per la rinascita del paese e l'unità dei lavoratori. Roma, 1977. pp. 361.

— — Law.

TREU (TIZIANO) Condotta antisindacale e atti discriminatori. Milano, [1974]. pp. 213.

SINDACATO e magistratura nei conflitti di lavoro; a cura di Tiziano Treu. Bologna, [1975-76]. 2 vols.

VACCARELLA (ROMANO) Il procedimento di repressione della condotta antisindacale. Milano, [1977]. pp. 244.

— Kenya.

LEITNER (KERSTIN) Workers, trade unions and peripheral capitalism in Kenya after independence. Frankfurt am Main, [1977]. pp. 182. *bibliog.*

— Mexico.

TRES estudios sobre el movimiento obrero en Mexico; [by] Jose Luis Reyna [and others]. Mexico, 1976. pp. 202. *bibliogs. (Mexico City. Colegio de Mexico. Jornadas. 80)*

— Netherlands.

WELCKER (J.M.) Heren en arbeiders in de vroege Nederlandse arbeidersbeweging, 1870-1914. Amsterdam, 1978. pp. 681. *bibliog. (International Institute of Social History. De Nederlandse Arbeidersbeweging. 3) With summary in English.*

— Nigeria.

NIGERIAN labour archive, (1943-1975): collection [of] Chief o.A. Fagbenro Beyioku. Zug, Switzerland, 1978. 62 fiches.

— Papua New Guinea.

PLOWMAN (DAVID) Trade unions in Papua New Guinea: progress, problems, prospects. Kensington, N.S.W., 1978. pp. 23. *bibliog. (New South Wales, University of. Department of Industrial Relations. [Working Papers])*

— Peru.

BLAKE (WALTER) El sindicalismo libre en el Peru. Lima, 1975. pp. 70. *bibliog. (Pontificia Universidad Catolica del Peru. Taller de Estudios Urbano Industriales. Estudios Sindicales. No.2)*

— Poland.

JOŃCZYK (JAN) Der Bergarbeiterstreik im Jahre 1871 in Königshütte auf dem Hintergrund der Lage der Arbeiterklasse in Oberschlesien; übersetzt aus dem Polnischen von Anne-Marie Griese. Bremen, 1977. pp. 63.

KOŁODZIEJ (EDWARD) Komunistycna Partia Robotnicza Polski w ruchu zawodowym, 1918- 1923. Warszawa, 1978. pp. 254. *bibliog.*

— Russia.

PRIIMENKO (ALEKSANDR IOSIFOVICH) Legal'nye organizatsii rabochikh Iuga Rossii v period imperializma, 1895 g. -fevral' 1917 g. Kiev, 1977. pp. 163. *bibliog.*

NOSACH (VIKTOR IVANOVICH) Profsoiuzy Sovetskoi Rossii v gody grazhdanskoi voiny, 1918-1920. Moskva, 1978. pp. 215.

SYNDICAT libre en URSS: dossier réuni par le Comité international contre la répression. [Paris, 1978]. pp. 126.

— — Congresses.

VSESOIUZNYI TSENTRAL'NYI SOVET PROFESSIONAL'NYKH SOIUZOV. S"ezd, 16- yi, 1977. Materialy XVI s"ezda professional'nykh soiuzov SSSR. Moskva, 1977. pp. 176.

— — Ukraine.

KRAVCHUK (TIKHON NIKANOROVICH) and SLOBODANIUK (ALEKSANDR NIKITOVICH) V sem'e edinoi. Moskva, 1977. pp. 80. *(Bibliotechka Profsoiuznogo Aktivista. 28)*

— South Africa.

WICKINS (PETER L.) The Industrial and Commercial Workers' Union of Africa. Cape Town, 1978. pp. 222. *bibliog.*

— Syria — Law.

SYRIA. Statutes, etc. 1968. Loi sur l'organisation syndicale: (décret législatif no. 84 du 26 juin 1968). [Damas, 1968]. fo. 19.

— United Kingdom.

MORTON (ARTHUR LESLIE) and TATE (GEORGE KENNETH) The British labour movement, 1770-1920: a history. London, 1956. pp. 313. *bibliog.*

BURCHILL (FRANK) and ROSS (RICHARD) A history of the potter's union. Stoke-on-Trent, 1977. pp. 292. *bibliog.*

KNEE (FRED) The diary of Fred Knee; [edited by David Englander. Coventry, 1977. pp. 122. *bibliog. (Society for the Study of Labour History. Aids to Research. No.3)*

HODGKINS (JOHN R.) Over the hills to glory: radicalism in Banburyshire, 1832-1945. Southend, [1978]. pp. 218.

JOHNSON (PAUL) Britain's own road to serfdom. London, 1978. pp. 15. *(Conservative Political Centre. [Publications]. No. 633)*

MOORE (RONALD JAMES) The motivation, attitudes, interests and satisfactions of shop stewards in a cross-section of industrial occupations in Hertfordshire, 1971-1974. 1978. fo. 549. *bibliog.* Typescript. Ph.D. (London) thesis: unpublished. Appendices 6,7 and 8 in end pocket. This thesis is the property of London University and may not be removed from the Library.

MORAN (MICHAEL) Trade unions and politics: past patterns, future problems. Hull, 1978. fo. 10. *bibliog. (Hull. University. Department of Politics. Hull Papers in Politics. No. 4)*

SEGLOW (PETER) Trade unionism in television: a case study in the development of white collar militancy. Farnborough, [1978]. pp. 287.

SHRIMSLEY (ANTHONY) The new establishment: an inquiry into who really governs Britain in 1978. [London], 1978. pp. 44.

WHITE (JOSEPH L.) The limits of trade union militancy: the Lancashire textile workers, 1910-1914. Westport, Conn., 1978. pp. 258. *bibliog.*

ARNOT (ROBERT PAGE) The miners: one union, one industry: a history of the National Union of Mineworkers, 1939-46. London, 1979. pp. 212.

The CONTROL of work; edited by John Purcell and Robin Smith. London, 1979. pp. 184. *bibliogs.*

The ECONOMY, the government and trade union responsibilities; joint statement by the TUC and the government. London, 1979. pp. 12.

JENKINS (CLIVE) and SHERMAN (BARRIE) White-collar unionism: the rebellious salariat. London, 1979. pp. 174.

LEESON (R.A.) Travelling brothers: the six centuries' road from craft fellowship to trade unionism. London, 1979. pp. 348. *bibliog.*

MARSH (ARTHUR IVOR) Trade union handbook: a guide and directory to the structure, membership, policy and personnel of the British trade unions. Farnborough, Hants., [1979]. pp. 369. *bibliog.*

TRADES UNION CONGRESS. The economy, the government and trade union responsibilities: joint statement by the TUC and the government. London, H.M.S.O., 1979. pp. 20.

TRADES UNION CONGRESS. TUC guides: negotiating procedures: conduct of disputes: union organisation. London, 1979. pp. 24.

— — Bibliography.

MARSH (ARTHUR IVOR) Trade union handbook: a guide and directory to the structure, membership, policy and personnel of the British trade unions. Farnborough, Hants., [1979]. pp. 369. *bibliog.*

— — Directories.

MARSH (ARTHUR IVOR) Trade union handbook: a guide and directory to the structure, membership, policy and personnel of the British trade unions. Farnborough, Hants., [1979]. pp. 369. *bibliog.*

— — Law.

KIDNER (RICHARD) Trade union law. London, 1979. pp. 343.

— — Officials and employees.

SHERMAN (ALFRED V.) The newest profession. [London, 1978]. pp. 16.

— — Political activity.

CURRIE (ROBERT) Industrial politics. Oxford, 1979. pp. 294.

PROTHERO (IORWERTH J.) Artisans and politics in early nineteenth-century London: John Gast and his times. Folkestone, 1979. pp. 418. *bibliog.*

TAYLOR (WINIFRED ANN) and FYRTH (HUBERT JIM) Political action. London, 1979. pp. 121.

— — Voting.

[U.K. Department of Employment. 1979. Working paper for consultations on proposed industrial relations legislation: support from public funds for union ballots. (London, 1979). fo. (3).

— — Scotland.

ESSAYS in Scottish labour history: a tribute to W.H. Marwick; edited by Ian MacDougall. Edinburgh, [1978]. pp. 265. *bibliogs.*

— — Wales.

WILLIAMS (J. ROOSE) Quarryman's champion: the life and activities of William John Parry of Coetmor. Denbigh, [imprint, 1978]. pp. 258.

— United States.

BRANDEIS (LOUIS DEMBITZ) Business: a profession. New York, 1971. pp. 327. *Reprint of work originally published Boston, 1914.*

PUBLIC employee unions: a study of the crisis in public sector labor relations; A. Lawrence Chickering, editor. San Francisco, [1976]. pp. 248. *bibliog.*

DUBOFSKY (MELVYN) and VAN TINE (WARREN R.) John L. Lewis: a biography. New York, [1977]. pp. 619. *bibliog.*

ESSAYS in Southern labor history...; edited by Gary M. Fink and Merl E. Reed. Westport, Conn., 1977. pp. 275. *bibliogs. Selected papers from the Southern Labor History Conference, Atlanta, 1976.*

SORGE (FRIEDRICH ADOLPH) Labor movement in the United States: a history of the American working class from colonial times to 1890; edited by Philip S. Foner and Brewster Chamberlin; introduction by Philip S. Foner; translated by Brewster Chamberlin and Angela Chamberlin. Westport, Conn., 1977. pp. 394. *Translated articles originally published in German in Die Neue Zeit.*

ZIEGER (ROBERT H.) Madison's battery workers, 1934-1952: a history of Federal Labor Union 19587. Ithaca, N.Y., 1977. pp. 126. *bibliog. (Cornell University. New York State School of Industrial and Labor Relations. ILR Paperbacks. No. 16)*

BROOKS (THOMAS R.) Clint: a biography of a labor intellectual: Clinton S. Golden. New York, 1978. pp. 377. *bibliog.*

DE CAUX (LEN) The living spirit of the Wobblies. New York, 1978. pp. 156. *bibliog.*

KENNEALLY (JAMES J.) Women and American trade unions. St. Albans, Vt., [1978]. pp. 240.

MOLDEA (DAN E.) The Hoffa wars: teamsters, rebels, politicians and the mob. New York, [1978]. pp. 450.

POLICE accountability: performance measures and unionism; edited by Richard C. Larson. Lexington, Mass., [1978]. pp. 211. *(Innovative Resource Planning in Urban Public Safety Systems. [Publications]. vol. 2)*

RIFKIN (JEREMY) and BARBER (RANDY) The North will rise again: pensions, politics and power in the 1980s. Boston, Mass., [1978]. pp. 279. *bibliog.*

— — Afro-American membership.

NATIONAL URBAN LEAGUE. Department of Research and Investigations. Negro membership in American labor unions. [New York], 1930; New York, 1969. pp. 180. *Facsimile reprint.*

— — Political activity.

SCOTT (JACK) Yankee unions, go home!: how the AFL helped the U.S. build an empire in Latin America. Vancouver, [1978]. pp. 287. *bibliog.*

— — California.

GALARZA (ERNESTO) Farm workers and agri-business in California, 1947-1960. Notre Dame, [1977]. pp. 405.

— — Kentucky.

HEVENER (JOHN W.) Which side are you on?: the Harlan County coal miners, 1931-1939. Urbana, [1978]. pp. 216. *bibliogs.*

— — Southern States.

McLAURIN (MELTON ALONZA) The Knights of Labor in the South. Westport, Conn., 1978. pp. 232. *bibliog.*

TRADE UNIONS, CATHOLIC

— Germany.

ARETZ (JUERGEN) Katholische Arbeiterbewegung und Nationalsozialismus: der Verband katholischer Arbeiter- und Knappenvereine Westdeutschlands, 1923-1945. Mainz, [1978]. pp. 252. *bibliog. (Kommission für Zeitgeschichte. Veröffentlichungen. Reihe B: Forschungen. Band 25)*

TRADE UNIONS AND COMMUNISM.

GODSON (ROY) The Kremlin and labor: a study in national security policy. New York, 1977. pp. 79.

NIN (ANDRES) Las organizaciones obreras internacionales. Madrid, [1977]. pp. 304.

TRAFFIC ENGINEERING.

LANE (ROBERT) and others. Analytical transport planning. London, 1971 repr. 1974. pp. 283.

INTERNATIONAL SYMPOSIUM ON TRANSPORTATION AND TRAFFIC THEORY, 7TH, KYOTO, 1977. Proceedings...; edited by Tsuna Sasaki and Takeo Yamaoka. Kyoto, [1977?]. pp. 941.

TRAFFIC ESTIMATION

— United Kingdom.

U.K. Department of Transport. 1978. National traffic forecasts: (interim memorandum). [London, 1978]. pp. (18), fo. (10).

— United States — Massachusetts.

MASSACHUSETTS. Metropolitan Area Planning Council. 1967. Affluence and mobility: a discussion of the automobile and the future of the Boston region. [Boston], 1967. fo. 13. *(Working Papers. 2)*

TRAFFIC OFFENCES

— New Zealand.

PARSONS (K.R.) Violence on the road: a logical extension to the subculture of violence thesis? [Wellington], 1978. pp. 148. *bibliog. (New Zealand. Department of Justice. Research Section. Research Series. No. 6)*

TRAMPS

— United Kingdom.

BERRY (CHARLES ACKERMAN) Gentleman of the road. London, 1978. pp. 216.

TRANSFER PRICING.

MATHEWSON (G. FRANK) and QUIRIN (G. DAVID) Fiscal transfer pricing in multinational corporations. Toronto, [1979]. pp. 162. *bibliog. (Ontario. Economic Council. Research Studies. 16)*

PLASSCHAERT (SYLVAIN R.F.) Transfer pricing and multinational corporations: an overview of concepts, mechanisms and regulations. Farnborough, [1979]. pp. 120. *bibliogs.*

TRANSFORMATIONS (MATHEMATICS).

CAMPBELL (STEPHEN LA VERN) and MEYER (CARL DEAN) Generalized inverses of linear transformations. London, 1979. pp. 272. *bibliog.*

TRANSHUMANCE

— Spain.

FREEMAN (SUSAN TAX) The Pasiegos: Spaniards in no man's land. Chicago, [1979]. pp. 291. *bibliog.*

TRANSIENTS, RELIEF OF.

LEESON (R.A.) Travelling brothers: the six centuries' road from craft fellowship to trade unionism. London, 1979. pp. 348. *bibliog.*

TRANSKEI

— Boundaries.

VENTER (DENIS) The Republic of Transkei: two years of independence, 1976-1978. Braamfontein, 1979. pp. 9. *(South African Institute of International Affairs. Occasional Papers)*

— Economic policy.

VENTER (DENIS) The Republic of Transkei: two years of independence, 1976-1978. Braamfontein, 1979. pp. 9. *(South African Institute of International Affairs. Occasional Papers)*

— Foreign relations — South Africa.

VENTER (DENIS) The Republic of Transkei: two years of independence, 1976-1978. Braamfontein, 1979. pp. 9. *(South African Institute of International Affairs. Occasional Papers)*

— Politics and government.

VENTER (DENIS) The Republic of Transkei: two years of independence, 1976-1978. Braamfontein, 1979. pp. 9. *(South African Institute of International Affairs. Occasional Papers)*

TRANSPARENT PAPER LIMITED.

TILLMANNS (MARTIN) Bridge Hall Mills: three centuries of paper and cellulose film manufacture. Tisbury, 1978. pp. 219. *bibliog.*

TRANSPLANTATION OF ORGANS, TISSUES, ETC.

— Law and Legislation.

WORLD HEALTH ORGANIZATION. 1969. Use of human tissues and organs for therapeutic purposes: a survey of existing legislation. Geneva, 1969. pp. 22. *bibliog. Originally published in International Digest of Health Legislation, v. 20, 1969.*

TRANSPORTATION.

KOBE (SUSUMU) Transport modes and technologies for development. (ST/ECA/127). New York, United Nations, 1970. pp. 147.

LANE (ROBERT) and others. Analytical transport planning. London, 1971 repr. 1974. pp. 283.

— Bibliography.

UNIVERSITIES TRANSPORT STUDY GROUP. Occasional Publications. No. 1. Doctoral theses in transport from Great Britain: first issue, 1960-1975; edited by Howard R. Kirby. London, 1977. pp. 24.

TRANSPORTATION.(Cont.)

UNIVERSITIES TRANSPORT STUDY GROUP. Occasional Publications. No. 3. Publications and working papers in transport from British universities and polytechnics: first issue, 1974-1976; edited by Howard R. Kirby. London, 1977. pp. 52.

— Congresses.

INTERNATIONAL SYMPOSIUM ON TRANSPORTATION AND TRAFFIC THEORY, 7TH, KYOTO, 1977. Proceedings...; edited by Tsuna Sasaki and Takeo Yamaoka. Kyoto, [1977?]. pp. 941.

UNIVERSITIES TRANSPORT STUDY GROUP. Occasional Publications. No. 2. Annual conferences of the Universities Transport Study Group: first issue, 1969-1978; edited by Howard R. Kirby. London, 1977. pp. 22.

WORLD CONFERENCE ON TRANSPORT RESEARCH, 3RD, ROTTERDAM, 1977. Transport decisions in an age of uncertainty: proceedings of the.. .Conference...organized by the Netherlands Institute of Transport; edited by Evert J. Visser. The Hague, [1977]. pp. 657. *In English or French.*

— Decision making.

WORLD CONFERENCE ON TRANSPORT RESEARCH, 3RD, ROTTERDAM, 1977. Transport decisions in an age of uncertainty: proceedings of the.. .Conference...organized by the Netherlands Institute of Transport; edited by Evert J. Visser. The Hague, [1977]. pp. 657. *In English or French.*

— Energy consumption — Sweden.

SWEDEN. Industridepartementet. Energiprogramkommittén. 1974. Energiforskning: expertmaterial utarbetat av uppdrag av Energiprogramkommittén. Avdelning C. Energianvändning för transporter och samfärdsel. Stockholm, 1974. pp. 77. *bibliog. (Sweden. Statens Offentliga Utredningar. 1974. 75)*

— Argentine Republic — Laws and regulations.

BELTRAME (JOSE) La coordinacion de los transportes nacionales, Ley No. 12,346: comentario y antecedentes parlamentarios. Buenos Aires, 1937. pp. 401.

— Asia.

TRANSPORT AND COMMUNICATIONS BULLETIN FOR ASIA AND THE PACIFIC (formerly TRANSPORT AND COMMUNICATIONS BULLETIN FOR ASIA AND THE FAR EAST previously Transport bulletin); ([pd.by] Economic and Social Commission for Asia and the Pacific) United Nations. irreg., Oc 1951(v.1, no.4)- with gaps. New York (formerly Bangkok).

— Australia.

AUSTRALIA. Bureau of Transport Economics. 1978. An approach to developing transport improvement proposals. Canberra, 1978. pp. 128. *bibliog. (Occasional Papers. 24)*

AUSTRALIA. Bureau of Transport Economics. 1978. A review of transport and development in Australia. Canberra, 1978. pp. 131.

— — Passenger traffic.

MANNING (IAN) The journey to work. Sydney, 1978. pp. 194. *bibliog.*

— Canada — Alberta — Passenger traffic.

ALBERTA. Department of Transportation. Transportation Planning and Services Division. 1977. Alberta regional passenger transportation study. [Edmonton], 1977. fo. 228. *1 map in end pocket.*

— European Economic Community countries.

GWILLIAM (KENNETH MASON) and others. Coordination of investments in transport infrastructures: analysis, recommendations, procedures; study drawn up at the request of the Commission of the European Communities, etc. Brussels, European Communities, 1973. pp. 85. *(European Economic Community. Studies. Transport Series. 3)*

— France.

COMMENT économiser l'énergie dans les transports: (étude interministerielle de rationalisation des choix budgetaires); [by] (Pierre Merlin). Paris, La Documentation Française, 1976. 2 vols (in 1).

BERNADET (MAURICE) and JOLY (GILLES) Le secteur des transports. Paris, 1978. pp. 336. *bibliogs.*

— — Lyons.

FRANCE. Direction Départementale de l'Equipement du Rhône. 1974. Etude préliminaire d'infrastructures de transport de l'agglomeration Lyonnaise. [Lyons, 1974]. pp. 102. *bibliog.*

— Israel.

ISRAEL. Central Bureau of Statistics. Quarterly transport statistics. q., Ja 1974(v.1, no.1)- Jerusalem. *[in English and Hebrew]*

— Netherlands.

NEW developments in modelling travel demand and urban systems: some results of recent Dutch research; edited by G.R.M. Jansen [and others]. Farnborough, [1979]. pp. 403. *bibligs. Papers presented at the fifth Transportation Planning Research Colloquium, The Hague, 1978.*

— Pacific, The.

TRANSPORT AND COMMUNICATIONS BULLETIN FOR ASIA AND THE PACIFIC (formerly TRANSPORT AND COMMUNICATIONS BULLETIN FOR ASIA AND THE FAR EAST previously Transport bulletin); ([pd.by] Economic and Social Commission for Asia and the Pacific) United Nations. irreg., Oc 1951(v.1, no.4)- with gaps. New York (formerly Bangkok).

— Russia.

DANILOV (SERGEI KONSTANTINOVICH) Ekonomicheskaia geografiia transporta SSSR. Moskva, 1977. pp. 376.

— — White Russia.

NIKITENKO (VIKTOR GRIGOR'EVICH) and GUTSEV (EVGENII GAVRILOVICH) Transport v narodnokhoziaistvennom komplekse BSSR; nauchnyi redaktor V.I. Drits. Minsk, 1978. pp. 144.

— Sudan — Statistics.

SUDAN. Ministry of Finance, Planning and National Economy. Transport and Communication Section. Transport statistical bulletin. a., 1975(2nd)- Khartoum.

— Tanzania.

UNITED REPUBLIC OF TANZANIA. Information Services Division. Tanzania: transport and communications. Dar es Salaam, 1979. pp. 16.

— — Statistics.

UNITED REPUBLIC OF TANZANIA. Bureau of Statistics. 1977. Transport statistics, 1968-1976. Dar es Salaam, 1977. fo. 42.

— United Kingdom.

RAY (GEORGE F.) Energy and transport: problems of medium-term assessment: a post- mortem on the Energy and Inland Transport chapters of The British economy in 1975. London, 1978. pp. 31. *(National Institute of Economic and Social Research. Discussion Papers. No. 14)*

AVON. County Council. Transport policies and programme: submission. a., 1979/80- Bristol.

BUCKINGHAMSHIRE. County Council. Transport policies and programme. a., 1979/80- [Aylesbury].

RURAL transport problems in Britain; papers and discussion; report of a symposium...organised by the Transport Geography Study Group of the Institute of British Geographers in... 1978 at...Bangor; editors, David A. Halsall [and] Brian J. Turton. [London], 1979. pp. 216. *bibliogs.*

— — Passenger traffic.

U.K. Licensing Authority for Public Service Vehicles: East Midland Traffic Area. Notices and proceedings. fortn., Mr 2 1948 - D 16 1949 (nos.466-510). Nottingham.

RURAL transport and accessibility; [by] M.J. Moseley [and others];...final report to the Department of the Environment. Norwich, 1977. 2 vols. (in 1). *bibliog.*

RURAL transport and country planning; edited by Roy Cresswell. Glasgow, 1978. pp. 197. *bibligs. Proceedings of the Conference held at the University of Nottingham, in March 1977 organised...by the Construction Industry Conference Centre Limited.*

SHROPSHIRE. County Council. Public transport plan. a., 1979/1984- Shrewsbury.

U.K. Department of Transport. 1979. National travel survey: 1975/6 report. [London, 1979. pp. 189.

— — Statistics.

MUNBY (DENYS LAWRENCE) Inland transport statistics, Great Britain, 1900-1970;... edited and completed by A.H. Watson. Oxford, 1978 in progress. *bibliogs.*

— — Wales.

GLAMORGAN-GLYNCORRWG COMMUNITY DEVELOPMENT PROJECT. The transport needs of Abercregan. Port Talbot, [1973]. fo. (20).

— United States — Rates.

ELLET (CHARLES) An essay on the laws of trade, in reference to the works of internal improvement in the United States. New York, 1966. pp. 284. *Reprint of work originally published in Richmond, 1839.*

— — Indiana.

INDIANA'S economic resources and potential...: section III. Transportation; by L.L. Waters [and] Charles Thomas Moore. [Bloomington, Ind.], 1955. fo. 110.

— Zambia — Passenger traffic.

ZAMBIA. Central Statistical Office. 1972. Report on passenger road transport in Zambia, 1971. Lusaka, [1972?]. pp. 37.

TRANSPORTATION, AUTOMOTIVE

— Licences — United Kingdom.

U.K. Committee of Inquiry into Operators' Licensing. 1979. Road haulage operators' licensing: report of the independent committee of inquiry; chairman: Christopher Foster. London, 1979. pp. 162.

— Research.

INTERNATIONAL ROAD FEDERATION. A report covering an international survey of current research and development on roads and road transport prepared for the Federal Highway Administration; (prepared... in cooperation with the Organization for Economic Cooperation and Development and the Transportation Research Board). Washington, D.C., 1978. pp. 566. *Cover title: 1978 world survey of current research and development on roads and road transport.*

— France — Freight.

FRANCE. Département des Statistiques des Transports. Enquête sur l'utilisation des véhicules de transport routier de marchandises: véhicules de 3 tonnes et plus de charge utile. a., 1975[covers 1966-1975]- Paris.

— United Kingdom.

U.K. Licensing Authority for Public Service Vehicles: East Midland Traffic Area. Notices and proceedings. fortn., Mr 2 1948 - D 16 1949 (nos.466-510). Nottingham.

— — Freight.

U.K. Committee of Inquiry into Operators' Licensing. 1979. Road haulage operators' licensing: report of the independent committee of inquiry; chairman: Christopher Foster. London, 1979. pp. 162.

— United States — Freight.

DAVIS (GRANT MILLER) and DILLARD (JOHN E.) Increasing motor carrier productivity: an empirical analysis. New York, [1977]. pp. 128. *bibliog.*

TRANSPORTATION AND STATE

— France.

TRANSPORTS et aménagement du territoire: réflexions sur le rééquilibrage Est-Ouest; [by Philippe Andre and others; edited by Pierre Henri Derycke and Alain Plaud]. Paris, Délégation à l'Aménagement du Territoire et à l'Action Régionale, 1977. pp. 102. *bibliog.*

FRANCE. Commission d'Etude sur l'Avenir des Transports Terrestres. 1978. Orientations pour les transports terrestres: rapport à M. le Premier Ministre présenté par Pierre Guillaumat. Paris, 1978. pp. 155.

FRANCE. Groupe Interministériel de Coordination. 1978. Transports et aménagement du territoire: schémas régionaux de transports: rapport. [Paris, 1978]. pp. 59.

— United Kingdom.

STARKIE (DAVID NICHOLAS MARTIN) Transportation planning, policy and analysis. Oxford, 1976. pp. 147. *bibliog.*

— United States.

LEVINE (HARVEY A.) National transportation policy: a study of studies. Lexington, Mass., [1978]. pp. 185.

TRANSPORTATION PLANNING.

EVALUER la politique des transports; [by] Eddy Bloy [and others]. Paris, 1977. pp. 103.

O'SULLIVAN (PATRICK MICHAEL) and others. Transport network planning. London, [1979]. pp. 187. *bibliog.*

PUBLIC transportation: planning, operations, and management; editors George E. Gray, Lester A. Hoel. Englewood Cliffs, N.J., [1979]. pp. 749. *bibliogs.*

— France.

FRANCE. Commission d'Etude sur l'Avenir des Transports Terrestres. 1978. Orientations pour les transports terrestres: rapport à M. le Premier Ministre présenté par Pierre Guillaumat. Paris, 1978. pp. 155.

— United Kingdom.

STARKIE (DAVID NICHOLAS MARTIN) Transportation planning, policy and analysis. Oxford, 1976. pp. 147. *bibliog.*

RURAL transport and country planning; edited by Roy Cresswell. Glasgow, 1978. pp. 197. *bibliogs. Proceedings of the Conference held at the University of Nottingham, in March 1977 organised...by the Construction Industry Conference Centre Limited.*

TRANSVAAL

— History.

ALLEN (VIVIEN) Lady trader: a biography of Mrs. Sarah Heckford. London, 1979. pp. 243.

— Politics and government.

FARRELLY (MICHAEL JAMES) The settlement after the war in South Africa. London, 1900. pp. 321.

TRAVEL AGENTS

— Fiji.

FIJI. Bureau of Statistics. 1973. A report on the survey of the hotel industry and the travel agencies in Fiji. Suva, 1973. fo. (14).

— United Kingdom.

AIR TRANSPORT AND TRAVEL INDUSTRY TRAINING BOARD [U.K.]. Manpower in travel, 1977-1980. [Staines, 1979?]. pp. 34.

TRAVEL RESEARCH

— Mathematical models.

DAOR (ERELLA SIEW) An analytical technique for designing a trip generation model with reference to London. 1978. fo. 236. *Typescript. M.Phil. (London) thesis: unpublished. This thesis is the property of London University and may not be removed from the Library.*

TRAVEL TIME (TRAFFIC ENGINEERING).

BRUZELIUS (NILS) The value of travel time: theory and measurement. London, [1979]. pp. 222. *bibliog.*

TRAVEN (BRUNO).

RICHTER (ARMIN) Der Ziegelbrenner: das individualanarchistische Kampforgan des frühen B. Traven. Bonn, 1977. pp. 442. *bibliog.*

TREASON

— United Kingdom.

BELLAMY (JOHN G.) The Tudor law of treason: an introduction. London, 1979. pp. 305.

TREATIES

— Ratification.

SMETS (PAUL F.) Les traités internationaux devant le Parlement, 1945-1955. Bruxelles, 1978. pp. 565. *bibliog. (Centre Interuniversitaire de Droit Public. Travaux et Etudes. 14)*

TREATY-MAKING POWER

— Belgium.

SMETS (PAUL F.) Les traités internationaux devant le Parlement, 1945-1955. Bruxelles, 1978. pp. 565. *bibliog. (Centre Interuniversitaire de Droit Public. Travaux et Etudes. 14)*

TRENCHARD (HUGH MONTAGUE) 1st Viscount Trenchard.

BOYLE (ANDREW) Trenchard. London, 1962. pp. 768. *bibliog.*

TRIALS (CONSPIRACY)

— United Kingdom.

STOKE NEWINGTON FIVE SOLIDARITY COMMITTEE. Release the five; statement of the...committee. London, [1973?]. pp. 8.

CHESTER (LEWIS) and others. Jeremy Thorpe: a secret life. [Glasgow], 1979. pp. 384.

THORPE (JEREMY) and others, defendants. The Thorpe committal; [by] Peter Chippindale and David Leigh. London, 1979. pp. 190.

TRIALS (POLITICAL CRIMES AND OFFENCES)

— Germany.

TRADITIONEN deutscher Justiz: politische Prozesse, 1914-1932: ein Lesebuch zur Geschichte der Weimarer Republik; herausgegeben von Kurt Kreiler, etc. Berlin, [1978]. pp. 310. *bibliog.*

— Russia.

TROITSKII (NIKOLAI ALEKSEEVICH) Tsarskie sudy protiv revoliutsionnoi Rossii: politicheskie protsessy, 1871-1880 gg. Saratov, 1976. pp. 408.

— South Africa.

SOUTH AFRICAN INSTITUTE OF RACE RELATIONS. Research Department. Security and related trials in South Africa, July 1976-May 1977. Johannesburg, [1977]. pp. 77.

TRIALS (TREASON)

— Yugoslavia.

COMMITTEE FOR A FAIR TRIAL FOR DRAJA MIHAILOVICH. Commission of Inquiry. Patriot or traitor: the case of General Mihailovich; proceedings and report of the commission. Stanford, Calif., [1978]. pp. 499. *(Stanford University. Hoover Institution on War, Revolution and Peace. Hoover Institution Publications. 191)*

TRIBAL GOVERNMENT

— Rhodesia.

RHODESIA. Ministry of Information, Immigration and Tourism. 1971. Recent developments in Rhodesia's tribal trust lands. [Salisbury, 1971]. pp. 5.

RHODESIA. Ministry of Information, Immigration and Tourism. 1971. Rhodesia's tribal areas: the need for rapid economic expansion. [Salisbury, 1971]. pp. 4.

TRIBES AND TRIBAL SYSTEM

— Africa, East.

KESBY (JOHN D.) The cultural regions of East Africa. London, [1977]. pp. 320. *bibliog.*

— Africa, Subsaharan.

ETHNICITY in modern Africa; edited by Brian M. du Toit. Boulder, Colo., 1978. pp. 319. *bibliog.*

— India.

ARCHER (WILLIAM GEORGE) The hill of flutes: life, love and poetry in tribal India: a portrait of the Santals. London, 1974. pp. 375. *bibliog.*

— — Assam.

BAHADUR (K.P.) Caste, tribes and culture of India: Assam. Delhi, 1977. pp. 137.

— Sierra Leone.

HARRELL-BOND (BARBARA E.) and others. Community leadership and the transformation of Freetown (1801-1976). The Hague, [1978]. pp. 416. *bibliog.*

— Uganda.

TOSH (JOHN) Clan leaders and colonial chiefs in Lango: the political history of an East African stateless society c. 1800-1939. Oxford, 1978. pp. 293. *bibliog.*

TRILATERAL COMMISSION.

GOLDRING (MAURICE) Démocratie, croissance zéro. [Paris, 1978]. pp. 187.

TRINIDAD AND TOBAGO

— Constitution.

TRINIDAD AND TOBAGO. Constitution. 1974. The constitution of Trinidad and Tobago. [Port of Spain], 1974. pp. 100.

TRINIDAD AND TOBAGO. Constitution Commission. 1974. Minority report; [by M.G. Sinanan]. [Port of Spain], 1974. pp. 13.

TRINIDAD AND TOBAGO. Constitution. 1975. Draft constitution of Trinidad and Tobago, 1975. [Port of Spain], 1975. pp. 80.

— History.

RENNIE (BUKKA) The history of the working-class in the 20th century (1919-1956): the Trinidad and Tobago experience. Trinidad, 1973. pp. 167.

NEWSON (LINDA A.) Aboriginal and Spanish colonial Trinidad: a study in culture contact. London, 1976. pp. 268. *bibliog.*

TRINIDAD AND TOBAGO (Cont.)

— Industries.

TRINIDAD AND TOBAGO. Central Statistical Office. 1978. Business surveys, 1974/75. [Port of Spain, 1978]. pp. 82.

— Nationalism.

RENNIE (BUKKA) The history of the working-class in the 20th century (1919-1956): the Trinidad and Tobago experience. Trinidad, 1973. pp. 167.

— Officials and employees — Salaries, allowances, etc.

TRINIDAD AND TOBAGO. Salaries Commission. 1975. Second interim report; [Mitra Sinanan, chairman]. [Port of Spain, 1975]. pp. 5.

TRIP LENGTH

— Mathematical models.

DAOR (ERELLA SIEW) An analytical technique for designing a trip generation model with reference to London. 1978. fo. 236. *Typescript. M.Phil. (London) thesis: unpublished. This thesis is the property of London University and may not be removed from the Library.*

TRISTAN (FLORA).

TRISTAN (FLORA) Promenades dans Londres; ou, L'aristocratie et les prolétaire anglais; édition établie et commentée par François Bédarida. Paris, 1978. pp. 358. *(Paris. Université de Paris I (Panthéon-Sorbonne). Centre d'Histoire du Syndicalisme. Collection) Reprint of 1840 ed.*

TROPICAL CROPS.

COMMONWEALTH SECRETARIAT. Fruit and tropical products. s-a., D 1978(no.1)- London.

— Brazil.

BRAZIL. Conselho Nacional de Estatistica. Laboratorio de Estatistica. 1960. Numeros indices das quantidades e dos preços do produtor de 15 produtos da industria extrativa vegetal nos anos de 1950 a 1958. Rio de Janeiro, [1960?]. fo. 13. *(Estudos sôbre as Quantidades e os Preços das Mercadorias Produzidas ou Negociadas. No. 92)*

TROPICS

— Diseases and hygiene.

KAMARCK (ANDREW M.) The tropics and economic development: a provocative inquiry into the poverty of nations...; published for the World Bank. Baltimore, [1976]. pp. 113. *bibliog.*

— Economic conditions.

KAMARCK (ANDREW M.) The tropics and economic development: a provocative inquiry into the poverty of nations...; published for the World Bank. Baltimore, [1976]. pp. 113. *bibliog.*

TROTSKII (LEV DAVYDOVICH).

TROTSKII (LEV DAVYDOVICH) Nos tâches politiques. Paris, 1970. pp. 256.

SEGAL (RONALD MICHAEL) The tragedy of Leon Trotsky. London, 1979. pp. 446. *bibliog.*

TROYES

— History.

HUNT (LYNN AVERY) Revolution and urban politics in provincial France: Troyes and Reims, 1786-1790. Stanford, Ca., 1978. pp. 187. *bibliog.*

TRUDEAU (PIERRE ELLIOTT).

RADWANSKI (GEORGE) Trudeau. Toronto, [1978]. pp. 372. *bibliog.*

SOMERVILLE (DAVID) Trudeau revealed by his actions and words. Richmond Hill, Ont., 1978. pp. 225.

TRUDOVAIA NARODNO-SOTSIALISTICHESKAIA PARTIIA.

See NARODNO-SOTSIALISTICHESKAIA (TRUDOVAIA) PARTIIA.

TRUE WHIG PARTY.

SMITH (ROBERT ARTHUR) Deeds not words: a history of the True Whig Party. [Monrovia, 1970]. pp. 62.

TRUJILLO MOLINA (RAFAEL LEONIDAS).

DIEDERICH (BERNARD) Trujillo: the death of the goat. Boston, Mass., 1978. pp. 265.

TRUST TERRITORIES

— Oceania.

NUFER (HAROLD F.) Micronesia under American rule: an evaluation of the strategic trusteeship, 1947-77. Hicksville, N.Y., [1978]. pp. 245.

TRUSTS, INDUSTRIAL

— United States.

BRANDEIS (LOUIS DEMBITZ) Business: a profession. New York, 1971. pp. 327. *Reprint of work originally published Boston, 1914.*

KAUFMAN (BURTON IRA) The oil cartel case: a documentary study of antitrust activity in the Cold War era. Westport, Conn., 1978. pp. 217.

KOTTKE (FRANK JOSEPH) The promotion of price competition where sellers are few. Lexington, Mass., [1978]. pp. 227. *bibliogs.*

TRUSTS AND TRUSTEES

— United Kingdom.

RIDDALL (JOHN GERVASE) Law of trusts. London, 1977. pp. 375.

PARKER (DAVID BERKELEY) and MELLOWS (ANTHONY ROGER) The modern law of trusts. 4th ed. London, 1979. pp. 428.

PETTIT (PHILIP HENRY) Equity and the law of trusts. 4th ed. London, 1979. pp. 594.

TSWANA (BANTU TRIBE).

CHIRENJE (J. MUTERO) A history of Northern Botswana, 1850-1910. Rutherford, N.J., 1977. pp. 316. *bibliog.*

ALVERSON (HOYT) Mind in the heart of darkness: value and self-identity among the Tswana of southern Africa. New Haven, 1978. pp. 299. *bibliog.*

TUCUMAN (PROVINCE)

— Economic conditions.

CARBONELL (ROBERTO) Tucuman como polo de desarrollo regional. San Miguel de Tucuman, [1973]. pp. 180.

— Economic policy.

CARBONELL (ROBERTO) Tucuman como polo de desarrollo regional. San Miguel de Tucuman, [1973]. pp. 180.

TUMOURS IN CHILDREN.

WORKING GROUP ON CHILD CANCER CONTROL. Child cancer control: report on a working group [held in] Prague, 25-28 April 1977. Copenhagen, World Health Organization, Regional Office for Europe, 1978. pp. 39.

TUNISIA

— Constitution.

TUNIS. Constitution. 1959-76. Constitution de la République Tunisienne. [Tunis, 1976]. pp. 46.

— Economic history.

VALENSI (LUCETTE) Fellahs tunisiens: l'économie rurale et la vie des campagnes au 18e et 19e siécles. Paris, [1977]. pp. 421. *bibliog. (Paris. Ecole des Hautes Etudes en Sciences Sociales. Centre de Recherches Historiques. Civilisations et Sociétés. 45)*

— Economic policy.

TUNIS. Secrétariat d'Etat à l'Information. 1976. Tunisia moves ahead. Tunis, [1976]. pp. 351.

— Politics and government.

BOURGUIBA (HABIB) Electoral campaign speeches, October 26-November 5, 1959. [Tunis, Secretariat of State for Information, 1960]. pp. 100. *(Publications)*

TUNIS. Secrétariat d'Etat à l'Information. 1976. Tunisia moves ahead. Tunis, [1976]. pp. 351.

GREEN (ARNOLD H.) The Tunisian ulama, 1873-1915: social structure and response to ideological currents. Leiden, 1978. pp. 324. *bibliog. (Social, Economic and Political Studies of the Middle East. vol. 22)*

O'DONNELL (JOSEPH DEAN) Lavigerie in Tunisia: the interplay of imperialist and missionary. Athens, Ga., [1979]. pp. 300. *bibliog.*

— Rural conditions.

VALENSI (LUCETTE) Fellahs tunisiens: l'économie rurale et la vie des campagnes au 18e et 19e siécles. Paris, [1977]. pp. 421. *bibliog. (Paris. Ecole des Hautes Etudes en Sciences Sociales. Centre de Recherches Historiques. Civilisations et Sociétés. 45)*

— Social policy.

TUNIS. Secrétariat d'Etat à l'Information. 1976. Tunisia moves ahead. Tunis, [1976]. pp. 351.

TURKESTAN

— History — 1917-1921, Revolution.

INOIATOV (KHAMID SHARAPOVICH) Pobeda Sovetskoi vlasti v Turkestane. Moskva, 1978. pp. 364. *bibliog.*

TURKEY

— Census.

TURKEY. Census, 1975. Census of population, (26.10.1975) by administrative division: province, district, sub-district and village, muhtarlik, population. Ankara, 1977. 1 vol. (various pagings). *(Istatistik Umum Müdürlügü. Yayinlar. No. 813) In English and Turkish.*

— Economic conditions.

TUNCER (BARAN) The impact of population growth on the Turkish economy. [Ankara, 1968]. pp. 66.

RCD MAGAZINE, THE; [pd. by] Regional Cooperation for Development. q., spring 1974(v.1, no.1)- , with gaps. Tehran.

TURKIYE IŞ BANKASI. Economic report. a., 1977- [Ankara].

HATIBOĞLU (ZEYYAT) An unconventional analysis of Turkish economy: an essay on economic development. Istanbul, 1978. pp. 312.

RCD NEWSLETTER; [pd. by] Information Section, Regional Cooperation for Development. irreg., current issues only. Tehran.

— Economic policy.

PAKISTAN. Ministry of Information and Broadcasting. 1967. Pakistan and R[egional] C[o-operation for] D[evelopment]: three years of regional co-operation for development, 1964-1967. [Karachi, 1967]. pp. 48. *bibliog.*

HATIBOĞLU (ZEYYAT) An unconventional analysis of Turkish economy: an essay on economic development. Istanbul, 1978. pp. 312.

— Foreign relations — Europe.

VAUGHAN (DOROTHY MARGARET) Europe and the Turk: a pattern of alliances, 1350-1700. Liverpool, 1954; New York, 1976. pp. 305. *bibliog. Facsimile reprint.*

— — Germany.

WEBER (FRANK G.) The evasive neutral: Germany, Britain and the quest for a Turkish alliance in the Second World War. Columbia, Mo., 1979. pp. 244. *bibliog.*

— — United Kingdom.

WEBER (FRANK G.) The evasive neutral: Germany, Britain and the quest for a Turkish alliance in the Second World War. Columbia, Mo., 1979. pp. 244. *bibliog.*

— — United States.

STERN (LAURENCE) The wrong horse: the politics of intervention and the failure of American diplomacy. New York, [1977]. pp. 170.

— History.

SHAW (STANFORD JAY) and SHAW (EZEL KURAL) History of the Ottoman Empire and modern Turkey. Cambridge, 1976-77. 2 vols. *bibliog.*

— Population.

TUNCER (BARAN) The impact of population growth on the Turkish economy. [Ankara, 1968]. pp. 66.

TURNOVER (BUSINESS)

— Sweden.

SWEDEN. Statistiska Centralbyrån. Regional omsättning inom parti- och detaljhandel samt vissa tjänstenäringar. a., 1976- Stockholm. *[in Swedish with English summary]*

TUSCANY

— Politics and government.

HANCOCK (Sir WILLIAM KEITH) Ricasoli and the Risorgimento in Tuscany. New York, 1969. pp. 320. *bibliog.*

TUSKEGEE NORMAL AND INDUSTRIAL INSTITUTE.

THRASHER (MAX BENNETT) Tuskegee: its story and its work. Boston, Mass., 1901; New York, 1969. pp. 215. *Facsimile reprint.*

TWEED (WILLIAM MARCY).

HERSHKOWITZ (LEO) Tweed's New York: another look. Garden City, N.Y., 1978. pp. 409. *bibliog.*

TWENTIETH CENTURY

— Forecasts.

DROUIN (MARIE JOSÉE) and BRUCE-BRIGGS (B.) Canada has a future. Toronto, [1978]. pp. 282. *Published for the Hudson Institute of Canada.*

DE BONO (EDWARD FRANCIS CHARLES PUBLIUS) Future positive. London, 1979. pp. 234.

PEETERS (PETER) Can we avoid a third world war around 2010?: the political, social and economic past and future of humanity. London, 1979. pp. 266.

TWENTY-FIRST CENTURY

— Forecasts.

ABLER (RONALD) and others. Human geography in a shrinking world. North Scituate, Mass., [1975]. pp. 307. *bibliogs.*

WADDINGTON (CONRAD HAL) The man-made future. New York, 1978. pp. 355. *bibliogs.*

PEETERS (PETER) Can we avoid a third world war around 2010?: the political, social and economic past and future of humanity. London, 1979. pp. 266.

TYNE AND WEAR

— Industries.

BENWELL COMMUNITY DEVELOPMENT PROJECT. Multinationals in Tyne and Wear; (compiled by Benwell and North Tyneside Community Development Projects in conjunction with the Tyne Conference of Shop Stewards); (with Amendments). [Newcastle-upon-Tyne, 1977 in progress]. 2 vols. (vol.2 loose- leaf). *bibliog.*

TYNESIDE

— Economic history.

BENWELL COMMUNITY DEVELOPMENT PROJECT. The making of a ruling class: two centuries of capital development on Tyneside. Newcastle-upon-Tyne, 1978. pp. 121. *(Final Report Series. No. 6)*

TYPOLOGY (LINGUISTICS).

SYNTACTIC typology: studies in the phenomenology of language; edited by Winfred P. Lehmann. Austin, [1978]. pp. 463. *bibliog.*

TYPOLOGY (PSYCHOLOGY).

ANSON OLIART (FRANCISCO) Tipos y valores en funcionarios españoles. [Madrid], Escuela Nacional de Administracion Publica, 1967. pp. 98. *(Coleccion Alcala. 2)*

LOUDEN (DELROY M.) West Indian adolescents in school: towards a typology of behaviour patterns. [Bristol, Social Science Research Council Research Unit on Ethnic Relations, 1976?]. fo. 14.

TYRER (ANTHONY M.).

EUROPEAN COURT OF HUMAN RIGHTS. Publications. Series A: Judgments and Decisions. [A26]. ... Tyrer case: judgment of 25 April 1978. Strasbourg, Council of Europe, 1978. pp. 32bis. *In English and French.*

TYRES

— Germany.

KIENBAUM UNTERNEHMENSBERATUNG. Untersuchung der Konzentrationsentwicklung in der Reifenindustrie sowie ein Branchenbild der Kraftfahrzeug-Elektrikindustrie in Deutschland. [Brussels], Europäischen Gemeinschaften, 1976. pp. 190.

— Italy.

AMADUZZI (ANTONIO) and others. Studio sull'evoluzione della concentrazione industriale in Italia, 1968-1974: pneumatici, candele, accumulatori. [Brussels], Comunità Europee, 1976. pp. 341.

TZELTAL INDIANS.

ARIAS (JACINTO) El mundo numinoso de los mayas: estructura y cambios contemporaneos; traduccion de Jorge Ferreiro Santana. Mexico, Secretaria de Educacion Publica, 1975. pp. 146. *bibliog. (Sep/Setentas. 188)*

TZOTZIL INDIANS.

ARIAS (JACINTO) El mundo numinoso de los mayas: estructura y cambios contemporaneos; traduccion de Jorge Ferreiro Santana. Mexico, Secretaria de Educacion Publica, 1975. pp. 146. *bibliog. (Sep/Setentas. 188)*

HAVILAND (JOHN BEARD) Gossip, reputation, and knowledge in Zinacantan. Chicago, 1977. pp. 260. *bibliog.*

UGANDA

— History.

STEINHART (EDWARD I.) Conflict and collaboration: the kingdoms of western Uganda, 1890- 1907. Princeton, N.J., [1977]. pp. 311. *bibliog.*

— Officials and employees — Salaries, allowances, etc.

UGANDA. Public Service Salaries Commission. 1974. Report..., 1973-1974; under the chairmanship of John Bikangaga. [Kampala, 1974?]. pp. 351,188.

— Politics and government.

KYEMBA (HENRY) State of blood: the inside story of Idi Amin. London, 1977. pp. 288.

UKRAINE

— Economic conditions.

PALAMARCHUK (MAKSIM MARTYNOVICH) Ekonomicheskaia geografiia Ukrainskoi SSR s osnovami teorii: posobie dlia uchitelia. Kiev, 1977. pp. 311. *bibliog.*

— Economic history — Chronology.

LITOPYS komunistychnoho budivnytstva: khronika naivazhlyvishykh podii v Ukraïns'kii RSR, 1971-1975. Kyïv, 1977. pp. 431.

— History — 1905, Revolution of.

LESHCHENKO (MYKOLA NYKYFOROVYCH) Ukraïns'ke selo v revoliutsiï, 1905-1907 rr. Kyïv, 1977. pp. 360.

— — 1917-1921, Revolution.

ARSHINOV (PETR ANDREEVICH) History of the Makhnovist movement (1918-1921)...; translated by Lorraine and Fredy Perlman. Detroit, 1974. pp. 284.

BOROT'BA za vladu Rad na Ukraïni. Kyïv, 1977. pp. 199.

KHMIL' (IVAN VASYL'OVYCH) Trudiashche selianstvo Ukraïny v borot'bi za vladu Rad. Kyïv, 1977. pp. 199.

SOLDATENKO (VALERII FEDOROVICH) Tribuna proletarskogo internatsionalizma. Kiev, 1977. pp. 183.

SUPRUNENKO (NIKOLAI IVANOVICH) Borot'ba trudiashchykh Ukraïny proty denikinshchyny. Kyïv, 1979. pp. 287.

— — — Foreign participation.

MEL'NYCHENKO (VOLODYMYR IUKHYMOVYCH) Diial'nist' inozemnykh komunistychnykh hrup na Ukraïni, 1918- 1920. Kyïv, 1977. pp. 208.

— Industries.

EFFEKTIVNOST' novoi tekhniki: na primere promyshlennosti Ukrainskoi SSR. Kiev, 1977. pp. 199.

PALAMARCHUK (MAKSIM MARTYNOVICH) and others. Mineral'nye resursy i formirovanie promyshlennykh territorial'nykh kompleksov. Kiev, 1978. pp. 219. *bibliog.*

VIDBUDOVA i rozvytok sotsialistychnoï industriï Ukraïns'koï RSR: period budivnytstva rozvynutoho sotsializmu. Kyïv, 1978. pp. 227. *bibliog.*

— Politics and government.

KOVAL' (MIKHAIL VASIL'EVICH) Obshchestvenno-politicheskaia deiatel'nost' trudiashchikhsia Ukrainskoi SSR v period Velikoi Otechestvennoi voiny. Kiev, 1977. pp. 264.

— Population.

VOSPROIZVODSTVO naseleniia v usloviiakh razvitogo sotsializma: na primere Ukrainskoi SSR. Kiev, 1978. pp. 243.

UKRAINE (Cont.)

— Social life and customs.

KUROCHKIN (OLEKSANDR VOLODYMYROVYCH) Novorichni sviata ukraïntsiv: tradytsiï i suchasnist'. Kyïv, 1978. pp. 191.

UKRAINIANS IN CANADA.

UKRAINIAN Canadians, multiculturalism, and separation: an assessment: proceedings of a conference sponsored by the Canadian Institute of Ukrainian Studies,...Edmonton...1977; edited by Manoly R. Lupul. Edmonton, 1978. pp. 177.

UL'IANOV FAMILY.

UL'IANOVA (MARIIA IL'INICHNA) O Vladimire Il'iche Lenine i sem'e Ul'ianovykh: vospominaniia, pis'ma, ocherki. Moskva, 1978. pp. 328.

UMBANDA (CULTUS).

HOWE (GARY NIGEL) Pentecostalism, Umbanda and the Brazilian socio-economic order: from 1945 to the present day. 1978. fo. 409. *bibliog. Typescript. Ph.D. (London) thesis: unpublished. This thesis is the property of London University and may not be removed from the Library.*

UNCERTAINTY.

UNCERTAINTY in economics: readings and exercises; edited by Peter Diamond, Michael Rothschild. New York, [1978]. pp. 574. *bibliogs.*

HEY (JOHN DENIS) Uncertainty in microeconomics. Oxford, 1979. pp. 261. *bibliog.*

MENGER (CARL) Son of Carl Menger the Economist. Selected papers in logic and foundations, didactics, economics. Dordrecht, [1979]. pp. 341. *bibliog.*

UNCERTAIN outcomes; edited by C.R. Bell. Lancaster, [1979]. pp. 204. *bibliogs.*

UNDERDEVELOPED AREAS.

TRENDS IN DEVELOPING COUNTRIES; [pd.by] World Bank Group. a., S 1968- Washington, D.C. *Not pd. 1972.*

HARRINGTON (MICHAEL) b. 1928. The vast majority: a journey to the world's poor. New York, [1977]. pp. 281. *bibliog.*

The CHANGING face of the third world: regional and national studies; edited by József Nyilas. Leyden, 1978. pp. 431. *Based on Korunk világgazdasága, vol. 3.*

GEOGRAPHY and development: a world regional approach; edited by Don R. Hoy. New York, [1978]. pp. 728.

RIGHTER (ROSEMARY) Whose news?: politics, the press and the third world. London, 1978. pp. 272. *bibliog.*

— Agricultural research.

FOOD AND AGRICULTURE ORGANIZATION. Current Agricultural Research Information System. 1978. Agricultural research in developing countries. Rome, 1978. 3 vols.

— Agriculture.

SEN (SUDHIR) A richer harvest: new horizons for developing countries. New York, [1974]. pp. 573. *bibliog.*

UNITED NATIONS RESEARCH INSTITUTE FOR SOCIAL DEVELOPMENT. UNRISD Reports. No. 74.1. The social and economic implications of large-scale introduction of new varieties of foodgrain: summary of conclusions of a global research project. (UNRISD 74/27). Geneva, 1974. pp. 55. *([Studies on the Green Revolution. No. 6])*

DAHLBERG (KENNETH A.) Beyond the green revolution: the ecology and politics of global agricultural development. New York, [1979]. pp. 256. *bibliog.*

GRIFFIN (KEITH) The political economy of agrarian change: an essay on the green revolution. 2nd ed. London, [1979]. pp. 268.

— Armed forces — Political activity.

The MILITARY and security in the Third World: domestic and international impacts; edited by Sheldon W. Simon. Boulder, Colo., [1978]. pp. 348. *bibliogs.*

— Balance of payments.

BIRD (GRAHAM RICHARD) The international monetary system and the less developed countries. London, 1978. pp. 339. *bibliog.*

GUNTER (JOHN WADSWORTH) The imbalance of international payments from the viewpoint of the OPEC and other developing countries. Cairo, 1978. pp. 24. *(National Bank of Egypt. Commemoration Lectures Programme)*

KRUEGER (ANNE O.) Foreign trade regimes and economic development: liberalization attempts and consequences. Cambridge, Mass., 1978. pp. 310. *bibliogs. (National Bureau of Economic Research. Special Conference Series on Foreign Trade Regimes and Economic Development. vol. 10)*

— Birth control.

CUCA (ROBERTO) and PIERCE (CATHERINE S.) Experiments in family planning: lessons from the developing world; foreword by Bernard Berelson; published for the World Bank. Baltimore, [1978]. pp. 261. *bibliog. (International Bank for Reconstruction and Development. World Bank Research Publications)*

— Capital.

FITZGERALD (EDMUND VALPY KNOX) Public sector investment planning for developing countries. London, 1978. pp. 200. *bibliog.*

— Children — Nutrition.

FOOD and nutrition policy in a changing world; edited by Jean Mayer and Johanna T. Dwyer. New York, 1979. pp. 300. *bibliogs.*

— Cities and towns.

U.K. Ministry of Overseas Development. Study Group on Urban Poverty. 1979. Urban poverty: report; [E.C. Burr, chairman]. London, [1979]. pp. 44. *(Overseas Development Papers. No. 19)*

— Commerce.

TRADE IN MANUFACTURES OF DEVELOPING COUNTRIES AND TERRITORIES: review; ([pd. by] United Nations Conference on Trade and Development). a., 1968 [1st issue]- New York.

ROUND TABLE ON EXPORT CREDIT AS A MEANS OF PROMOTING EXPORTS FROM DEVELOPING COUNTRIES, NEW YORK, 1969. Report of the Round Table...[held at] New York 24 to 28 March 1969. (E/4661)(ST/ECA/116). New York, United Nations, 1969. pp. 27.

— — European Economic Community countries.

McQUEEN (MATTHEW) Britain, the EEC and the developing world. London, 1977. pp. 119. *bibliog.*

— Commercial policy.

DONGES (JUERGEN B.) and MUELLER-OHLSEN (LOTTE) Aussenwirtschaftsstrategien und Industrialisierung in Entwicklungsländern. Tübingen, [1978]. pp. 239. *bibliog. (Kiel. Universität. Institut für Weltwirtschaft. Kieler Studien. 157)*

— Commercial products.

The COMMON fund: papers prepared for Commonwealth Technical Group. London, Commonwealth Secretariat, 1977. 2 vols. *bibliog. (Commonwealth Economic Papers. No. 8)*

COMMONWEALTH TECHNICAL GROUP ON THE COMMON FUND. The common fund: report of the Commonwealth Technical Group; [Lord Campbell of Eskan, chairman]. London, Commonwealth Secretariat, 1977. pp. 84.

MICHALOPOULOS (CONSTANTINE) U.S. commodity trade policy and the developing countries. [Washington], 1977. pp. 40. *(United States. Agency for International Development. Bureau for Program and Policy Coordination. A.I.D. Discussion Papers. No. 37)*

— Cooperative societies.

TORRES (JAMES F.) Success in smallness: a self-help plan for developing countries. [River Falls, Wis., 1978]. pp. 54.

— Debts, External.

DESHAYES (HENRY) L'endettement des pays en développement. Paris, 1978. pp. 120. *(France. Ministère de la Coopération. Service des Etudes [Economiques] et [des] Questions Internationales. Etudes et Documents. No. 33)*

PARSONS (CHRISTOPHER) Finance for development or survival?: the debt crisis of developing countries. London, 1978. pp. 27. *(Fabian Society. Research Series. [No.] 336)*

ABBOTT (GEORGE C.) International indebtedness and the developing countries. London, 1979. pp. 312. *bibliog.*

— Economic conditions.

BARAN (PAUL A.) The political economy of growth; with an introduction by R.B. Sutcliffe. Harmondsworth, [1973]. pp. 475.

UNITED NATIONS. Centre for Development Planning, Projections and Policies. 1973. Implementation of the international development strategy: papers for the first over-all review and appraisal of progress during the second United Nations development decade. (E/5267) (ST/ECA/178). New York, 1973. 2 vols. (in 1.)

SINGER (HANS WOLFGANG) The strategy of international development: essays in the economics of backwardness; edited by Sir Alec Cairncross and Mohinder Puri. London, 1975. pp. 248. *bibliog.*

MORAWETZ (DAVID) Twenty-five years of economic development 1950 to 1975. Washington, D.C., International Bank for Reconstruction and Development, 1977. pp. 125.

NZIRAMASANGA (MUDZIVIRI) Production from an exhaustible resource under government control in an LDC. Ann Arbor, Michigan, 1977. pp. 17. *bibliog. (Michigan University. Center for Research on Economic Development. Discussion Papers. No. 70)*

TECHNOLOGY for development; [edited] by Ann Kestenbaum. rev. ed. London, 1977. pp. 97.

COLMAN (DAVID) and NIXSON (F.I.) Economics of change in less developed countries. Oxford, [1978]. pp. 309. *bibliogs.*

FRANK (ANDRE GUNDER) Dependent accumulation and underdevelopment. London, 1978. pp. 226. *bibliog.*

GHATAK (SUBRATA) Development economics. London, 1978. pp. 269. *bibliog.*

GRIFFIN (KEITH) International inequality and national poverty. London, 1978. pp. 191. *bibliogs.*

The NEW economics of the less developed countries: changing perceptions in the North-South dialogue; edited by Nake M. Kamrany. Boulder, Colo., [1978]. pp. 346. *bibliogs.*

SAU (RANJIT KUMAR) Unequal exchange, imperialism and underdevelopment: an essay on the political economy of world capitalism. Calcutta, [1978]. pp. 202. *bibliog.*

SCIENCE, technology and economic growth in developing countries; edited by G.E. Skorov; translated [from the Russian] by Jenny Warren. Oxford, 1978. pp. 211.

TAXATION and economic development; edited by J.F.J. Toye. London, 1978. pp. 299. *bibliogs.*

The THIRD world: premises of U.S. policy; [edited by] W. Scott Thompson. San Francisco, [1978]. pp. 332. *bibliog.*

UNDERDEVELOPMENT to developing economies; edited by S.P. Singh. Bombay, 1978. pp. 551.

APPROPRIATE technologies for Third World development: proceedings of a conference held by the International Economic Association at Teheran, Iran; edited by Austin Robinson. London, 1979. pp. 417. *bibliog.*

DEVELOPMENT theory: four critical studies; edited by David Lehmann. London, 1979. pp. 106. *bibliog.*

LLOYD (PETER CUTT) Slums of hope: shanty towns of the Thirld World. Harmondsworth, 1979. pp. 246. *bibliog.*

ROXBOROUGH (IAN) Theories of underdevelopment. London, 1979. pp. 175. *bibliog.*

The THIRD world: problems and perspectives; edited by Alan B. Mountjoy. New York, 1979. pp. 165. *bibliog.*

— — **Mathematical models.**

VERNARDAKIS (NIKOS) Econometric models for the developing economies: a case study of Greece. Farnborough, Hants., [1978]. pp. 143. *bibliog.*

— **Economic policy.**

NYERERE (JULIUS KAMBARAGE) The rational choice;...address delivered at Sudanese Socialist Union headquarters, Khartoum, 2nd January, 1973. [Dar es Salaam, Government Printer, 1972]. pp. 13.

UNITED NATIONS. Centre for Development Planning, Projections and Policies. 1973. Implementation of the international development strategy: papers for the first over-all review and appraisal of progress during the second United Nations development decade. (E/5267) (ST/ECA/178). New York, 1973. 2 vols. (in 1).

CLARKSON (STEPHEN) The Soviet theory of development: India and the third world in marxist-leninist scholarship. Toronto, 1978. pp. 322.

DONGES (JUERGEN B.) and MUELLER-OHLSEN (LOTTE) Aussenwirtschaftsstrategien und Industrialisierung in Entwicklungsländern. Tübingen, [1978]. pp. 239. *bibliog.* (Kiel. Universität. Institut für Weltwirtschaft. Kieler Studien. 157)

KRUEGER (ANNE O.) Foreign trade regimes and economic development: liberalization attempts and consequences. Cambridge, Mass., 1978. pp. 310. *bibliogs.* (National Bureau of Economic Research. Special Conference Series on Foreign Trade Regimes and Economic Development. vol. 10)

UNDERDEVELOPMENT to developing economies; edited by S.P. Singh. Bombay, 1978. pp. 551.

WRIGGINS (WILLIAM HOWARD) and ADLER-KARLSSON (GUNNAR) Reducing global inequalities. New York, [1978]. pp. 191. *bibliog.* (Council on Foreign Relations. 1980s Project Studies)

— **Education.**

WORLD COUNCIL OF CHURCHES. Commission on the Churches' Participation in Development. Conscientization: [a dossier including separately published articles]. Geneva, 1975. 1 vol. (various pagings). *bibliog.* (CCPD Documents. 7)

COMMONWEALTH COUNCIL FOR EDUCATIONAL ADMINISTRATION. Regional Conference, 3rd, Dacca, 1977. Education for development; proceedings of the...conference, etc. [London, 1977]. pp. 114. *bibliogs.* (Commonwealth Foundation. Occasional Papers. No. 44)

— **Education, Rural.**

LEARNING and living: education for rural families in developing countries; (edited) from the contributions of L.C. Arulpragasam. ..[and others] by John Higgs and Philip Mbithi. Rome, Food and Agriculture Organization, 1977. pp. 72.

— **Elections.**

SENFTLEBEN (WOLFGANG) Studies in electoral geography. Taipei, 1977. pp. 113. *bibliog.*

— **Export premiums.**

BALASSA (BELA A.) and SHARPSTON (MICHAEL) Export subsidies by developing countries: issues of policy. Geneva, 1977. pp. 61. *(Geneva. Graduate Institute of International Studies, and Trade Policy Research Centre. Commercial Policy Issues. 2)*

— **Finance.**

FINANCE AND DEVELOPMENT (formerly The Fund and Bank review): a publication of the International Monetary Fund and the World Bank Group. q., Je 1964(v.1, no.1)- Washington.

The INTERNATIONAL monetary system and the developing nations; edited by Danny M. Leipziger. Washington, Agency for International Development, Bureau for Program and Policy Coordination, 1976. pp. 210. *bibliogs.*

BIRD (GRAHAM RICHARD) The international monetary system and the less developed countries. London, 1978. pp. 339. *bibliog.*

BRETON (JEAN MARIE) Le contrôle d'état sur le continent africain: contribution à une théorie des contrôles administratifs et financiers dans les pays en voie de développement. Paris, 1978. pp. 532. *bibliog.*

— **Food supply.**

SEN (SUDHIR) A richer harvest: new horizons for developing countries. New York, [1974]. pp. 573. *bibliog.*

STEVENS (CHRISTOPHER ANTHONY) Food aid and the developing world: four African case studies. London, [1979]. pp. 224. *bibliog.*

— **Foreign economic relations.**

UNITED NATIONS. Centre for Development Planning, Projections and Policies. 1973. Implementation of the international development strategy: papers for the first over-all review and appraisal of progress during the second United Nations development decade. (E/5267) (ST/ECA/178). New York, 1973. 2 vols. (in 1).

ALGERIA. 1974. Petroleum, raw materials and development: memorandum submitted by Algeria on the occasion of the special session of the United Nations General Assembly, April 1974. [Algiers], 1974. pp. 222.

SINGER (HANS WOLFGANG) The strategy of international development: essays in the economics of backwardness; edited by Sir Alec Cairncross and Mohinder Puri. London, 1975. pp. 248. *bibliog.*

ECONOMIC coercion and the new international economic order; edited by Richard B. Lillich. Charlottesville, Va., [1976]. pp. 401.

ATLANTIC COUNCIL OF THE UNITED STATES. The Atlantic Council Working Group on the United States and the Developing Countries. The United States and the developing countries. Boulder, Colo., [1977]. pp. 150.

U.K. Ministry of Overseas Development. 1977. Challenges of the rich-poor relationship: new imperatives on the international scene; address to Congressional Group for Peace through Law, by Frank Judd M.P., Minister for Overseas Development, Washington, D.C., January 1977. London, [1977]. pp. 10. *(Overseas Development Papers. No.6)*

EUROPE and the north-south dialogue; edited by W. Wessels. Paris, [1978]. pp. 78. *(Atlantic Institute. Atlantic Papers. No. 35)*

EXCHANGE of expertise: the counterpart system in the new international order; edited by Irving J. Spitzberg, Jr. Boulder, Colo., [1978]. pp. 257. *bibliogs.*

The FIRST World and the Third World: essays on the new international economic order; edited by Karl Brunner. Rochester, N.Y., [1978]. pp. 272. *bibliog.*

FRANK (ANDRE GUNDER) Dependent accumulation and underdevelopment. London, 1978. pp. 226. *bibliog.*

GRIFFIN (KEITH) International inequality and national poverty. London, 1978. pp. 191. *bibliogs.*

UNDERDEVELOPED AREAS.

The NEW economics of the less developed countries: changing perceptions in the North-South dialogue; edited by Nake M. Kamrany. Boulder, Colo., [1978]. pp. 346. *bibliogs.*

RICHARDSON (NEIL R.) Foreign policy and economic dependence. Austin, [1978]. pp. 214. *bibliog.*

SAU (RANJIT KUMAR) Unequal exchange, imperialism and underdevelopment: an essay on the political economy of world capitalism. Calcutta, [1978]. pp. 202. *bibliog.*

— — **France.**

Le DEFI économique de tiers monde; rapport du groupe de travail animé par Yves Berthelot et Gérard Tardy; préface par Michel Albert; [with] Annexes. Paris, La Documentation Française, [1978]. 2 vols. *bibliog.*

— **Foreign exchange.**

BIRD (GRAHAM RICHARD) The international monetary system and the less developed countries. London, 1978. pp. 339. *bibliog.*

KRUEGER (ANNE O.) Foreign trade regimes and economic development: liberalization attempts and consequences. Cambridge, Mass., 1978. pp. 310. *bibliogs.* (National Bureau of Economic Research. Special Conference Series on Foreign Trade Regimes and Economic Development. vol. 10)

— **Foreign relations.**

The NONALIGNED movement in world politics; [edited by A.W. Singham]. Westport, Conn., [1977]. pp. 273. *Papers prepared for the Howard Conference on Non-Alignment, held at Howard University, 1976.*

BOYCE (PETER) Foreign affairs for new states: some questions of credentials. New York, 1978. pp. 289. *bibliog.*

The MILITARY and security in the Third World: domestic and international impacts; edited by Sheldon W. Simon. Boulder, Colo., [1978]. pp. 348. *bibliogs.*

RICHARDSON (NEIL R.) Foreign policy and economic dependence. Austin, [1978]. pp. 214. *bibliog.*

— — **United States.**

The THIRD world: premises of U.S. policy; [edited by] W. Scott Thompson. San Francisco, [1978]. pp. 332. *bibliog.*

— **Foreign trade promotion.**

INTERNATIONAL TRADE FORUM; [pd.by] International Trade Centre UNCTAD/GATT. q., D 1964(v.1, no.1)- ; with gaps (Ap-D 1973, v.9, nos. 2-4; 1974 v.10). Geneva. *File includes q. suppl., Ag 1965(no.1)-Supersedes General Agreement on Tariffs and Trade. Developments in commercial policy (Ja/Je 1960 - Ja/Je 1963).*

— **Government business enterprises.**

FITZGERALD (EDMUND VALPY KNOX) Public sector investment planning for developing countries. London, 1978. pp. 200. *bibliog.*

— **Government ownership.**

NZIRAMASANGA (MUDZIVIRI) Production from an exhaustible resource under government control in an LDC. Ann Arbor, Michigan, 1977. pp. 17. *bibliog.* (Michigan University. Center for Research on Economic Development. Discussion Papers. No. 70)

The NATIONALISATION of multinationals in peripheral economies; edited by Julio Faundez and Sol Picciotto. London, 1978. pp. 238.

— **Housing.**

HABITAT FOUNDATION NEWS; [pd. by] United Nations Habitat and Human Settlements Foundation. q., Je 1977(no.2)- Nairobi.

PAYNE (GEOFFREY K.) Urban housing in the Third World. London, 1977. pp. 242. *bibliog.*

UNDERDEVELOPED AREAS.(Cont.)

PASTEUR (DAVID) The management of squatter upgrading: a case study of organisation, procedures and participation. Farnborough, [1979]. pp. 232. *bibliog.*

— **Housing policy.**

SHANKLAND-COX PARTNERSHIP. Third world urban housing: aspirations, resources, programmes, projects; a report prepared for the Overseas Division, Building Research Establishment, UK...from a study financed by Ministry of Overseas Development. Watford, Building Research Establishment, [1978]. pp. 249.

— **Hygiene, Public.**

ALTERNATIVE approaches to meeting basic health needs in developing countries: a joint UNICEF/WHO study; edited by V. Djukanovic [and] E.P. Mach, etc. Geneva, World Health Organization, 1975. pp. 116.

— **Income distribution.**

HENNING (PETER H.) The urban popular economy and informal sector productions. Ann Arbor, Mich., 1978. pp. 67. *(Michigan University. Center for Research on Economic Development. Discussion Papers. No. 69)*

— **Industries.**

TRADE IN MANUFACTURES OF DEVELOPING COUNTRIES AND TERRITORIES: review; ([pd. by] United Nations Conference on Trade and Development). a., 1968 [1st issue]- New York.

UNDP BUSINESS BULLETIN; pd.by the United Nations Development Programme. m., Jl 1974[1st]- New York. *Supersedes in part Pre-investment news (Ja 1967 - Ap/Mr 1974).*

— **International business enterprises.**

NESTLÉ in the developing countries. Vevey, [1975]. pp. 228.

LALL (SANJAYA) Developing countries and multinational corporations: effects on host countries' welfare and the role of government policy. London, Commonwealth Secretariat, [1976]. pp. 65. *bibliog. (Commonwealth Economic Papers. No. 5)*

BIERSTEKER (THOMAS J.) Distortion or development?: contending perspectives on the multinational corporation. Cambridge, Mass., [1978]. pp. 199. *bibliog.*

FIELDHOUSE (DAVID KENNETH) Unilever overseas: the anatomy of a multinational, 1895-1965. Stanford, Calif., [1978]. pp. 620. *(Stanford University. Hoover Institution on War, Revolution and Peace. Hoover Institution Publications. 205)*

The NATIONALISATION of multinationals in peripheral economies; edited by Julio Faundez and Sol Picciotto. London, 1978. pp. 238.

SOLOMON (LEWIS D.) Multinational corporations and the emerging world order. Port Washington, N.Y., 1978. pp. 261. *bibliog.*

— **Investments.**

U.K. Ministry of Overseas Development. 1977. A guide to the economic appraisal of projects in developing countries. rev. ed. London, 1977. pp. 160. *bibliog.*

— **Investments, Foreign.**

PANEL ON FOREIGN INVESTMENT IN DEVELOPING COUNTRIES, AMSTERDAM, 1969. Report on a meeting [of the Panel] held at Amsterdam from 16-20 February 1969. (E/4654)(ST/ECA/117). New York, United Nations, 1969. pp. 57.

BERGSTEN (C. FRED) An analysis of U.S. foreign direct investment policy and economic development. [Washington], 1976. pp. 114. *bibliog. (United States. Agency for International Development. Bureau for Program and Policy Coordination. A. I.D. Discussion Papers. No. 36)*

— **Investments, Swiss.**

ZIEGLER (JEAN) Switzerland exposed...; translated from the French by Rosemary Sheed Middleton. London, 1978. pp. 173.

— **Labour supply.**

LABOUR force participation in low-income countries; edited by Guy Standing and Glen Sheehan, etc. Geneva, International Labour Office, 1978. pp. 338.

— **Malnutrition.**

FOOD and nutrition policy in a changing world; edited by Jean Mayer and Johanna T. Dwyer. New York, 1979. pp. 300. *bibliogs.*

SCHOFIELD (SUE) Development and the problems of village nutrition. London, [1979]. pp. 174. *bibliog.*

— **Manpower policy.**

MATHESON (ROSS) People development in developing countries. New York, 1978. pp. 246.

— **Mass media.**

SUSSMAN (LEONARD R.) Mass news media and the third world challenge. Beverly Hills, [1977]. pp. 80. *bibliog. (Georgetown University. Center for Strategic and International Studies. Washington Papers. vol. 5/46)*

HOGGART (RICHARD) The mass media: a new colonialism? London, [1978]. pp. 6. *(Standard Telephones and Cables. Communication Lectures. 1978)*

— **Medical care.**

ALTERNATIVE approaches to meeting basic health needs in developing countries: a joint UNICEF/WHO study; edited by V. Djukanovic [and] E.P. Mach, etc. Geneva, World Health Organization, 1975. pp. 116.

— **Mental health services.**

SEMINAR ON THE ORGANIZATION OF MENTAL HEALTH SERVICES, ADDIS ABABA, 1973. Mental health services in developing countries: papers presented at...[the] Seminar...27 November to 4 December 1973; edited by T.A. Baasher [and others], etc. Geneva, World Health Organization, 1975. pp. 132.

— **Military government.**

The MILITARY and security in the Third World: domestic and international impacts; edited by Sheldon W. Simon. Boulder, Colo., [1978]. pp. 348. *bibliogs.*

— **Military policy.**

LEFEVER (ERNEST WARREN) Nuclear arms in the Third World: U.S. policy dilemma. Washington, D.C., [1979]. pp. 154.

— **Money.**

The INTERNATIONAL monetary system and the developing nations; edited by Danny M. Leipziger. Washington, Agency for International Development, Bureau for Program and Policy Coordination, 1976. pp. 210. *bibliogs.*

— **Municipal government.**

DAVIES (C.J.) Problems in urban management. Birmingham, 1976. pp. 115. *bibliog. (Birmingham. University. Institute of Local Government Studies. Development Administration Group. Case Studies in Development Administration. vol. 3)*

— **Municipal services.**

DAVIES (C.J.) Urban services. Birmingham, 1976. pp. 132. *bibliog. (Birmingham. University. Institute of Local Government Studies. Development Administration Group. Case Studies in Development Administration. vol. 2)*

— **Natural resources.**

RAJAN (MANNARASWAMIGHALA SREERANGA) Sovereignty over natural resources. Atlantic Highlands, 1978. pp. 176.

— **Nutrition policy.**

FOOD and nutrition policy in a changing world; edited by Jean Mayer and Johanna T. Dwyer. New York, 1979. pp. 300. *bibliogs.*

SCHOFIELD (SUE) Development and the problems of village nutrition. London, [1979]. pp. 174. *bibliog.*

— **Politics and government.**

BRETON (JEAN MARIE) Le contrôle d'état sur le continent africain: contribution à une théorie des contrôles administratifs et financiers dans les pays en voie de développement. Paris, 1978. pp. 532. *bibliog.*

INTERNATIONAL CONFERENCE ON SYSTEMS MODELLING IN DEVELOPING COUNTRIES, BANGKOK, 1978. Systems models for decision making; edited by Nawaz Sharif, Pakorn Adulbhan. Bangkok, 1978. pp. 433. *bibliogs.*

The THIRD world: premises of U.S. policy; [edited by] W. Scott Thompson. San Francisco, [1978]. pp. 332. *bibliog.*

— **Population.**

POPULATION problems and Catholic responsibility...; edited by L.H. Janssen. Rotterdam, 1975. pp. 196. *(Tilburg. Katholieke Hogeschool. Tilburg Institute of Development Research. Studies on Development Research. 2) Proceedings of the international symposium on population problems in developing countries and worldwide Catholic responsibility.*

— **Press.**

The THIRD World and press freedom; edited by Philip C. Horton. New York, [1978]. pp. 253. *bibliog.*

— **Raw materials.**

ALGERIA. 1974. Petroleum, raw materials and development: memorandum submitted by Algeria on the occasion of the special session of the United Nations General Assembly, April 1974. [Algiers], 1974. pp. 222.

SINGER (HANS WOLFGANG) and STEPHENSON (JULIETTE) The expansion of processing in developing countries and international policy requirements. London, Commonwealth Secretariat, 1978. pp. 80. *bibliog. (Commonwealth Economic Papers. No. 10)*

— **Rural conditions — Bibliography.**

BRIGHTON. University of Sussex. Institute of Development Studies. Village Studies Programme. Village studies: data analysis and bibliography;...compiled by Mick Moore [and others]; edited by Claire M. Lambert. Epping, afterwards London, 1976-78. 2 vols.

— **Rural development.**

INTER-UNIVERSITY COUNCIL FOR HIGHER EDUCATION OVERSEAS. Rural development overseas: first thoughts on the co-operative role of British universities and polytechnics: report of a working party, etc. London, 1976. pp. 35. *bibliog.*

— **Science.**

AVAKOV (RACHIK MAMIKONOVICH) Razvivaiushchiesia strany: nauchno-tekhnicheskaia revoliutsiia i problema nezavisimosti. Moskva, 1976. pp. 295. *(Akademiia Nauk SSSR. Institut Mirovoi Ekonomiki i Mezhdunarodnykh Otnoshenii. Ekonomika i Politika Razvivaiushchikhsia Stran)*

— — **Social aspects.**

TECHNOLOGY for development; [edited] by Ann Kestenbaum. rev. ed. London, 1977. pp. 97.

SCIENCE, technology and economic growth in developing countries; edited by G.E. Skorov; translated [from the Russian] by Jenny Warren. Oxford, 1978. pp. 211.

— **Slums.**

LLOYD (PETER CUTT) Slums of hope: shanty towns of the Thirld World. Harmondsworth, 1979. pp. 246. *bibliog.*

— Social conditions.

BIGO (PIERRE) The Church and third world revolution. Maryknoll, N.Y., 1977. pp. 316.

TECHNOLOGY for development; [edited] by Ann Kestenbaum. rev. ed. London, 1977. pp. 97.

HOOGVELT (ANKIE M.M.) The sociology of developing societies. 2nd ed. London, 1978. pp. 209. *bibliog.*

MATHESON (ROSS) People development in developing countries. New York, 1978. pp. 246.

RONDINELLI (DENNIS A.) and RUDDLE (KENNETH) Urbanization and rural development: a spatial policy for equitable growth. New York, [1978]. pp. 221. *bibliog.*

SCIENCE, technology and economic growth in developing countries; edited by G.E. Skorov; translated [from the Russian] by Jenny Warren. Oxford, 1978. pp. 211.

— Social conflict.

SIMAI (MIHÁLY) Developing countries and international class conflicts. Budapest, 1979. pp. 57. *(Magyar Tudományos Akadémia. Afro-Azsiai Kutató Központ. Studies on Developing Countries. No. 79)*

— Social policy.

INTERNATIONAL SOCIAL DEVELOPMENT REVIEW; [pd. by] (Department of Economic and Social Affairs), United Nations. irreg., 1968 (no.1)- New York. *Supersedes its Housing, building and planning (N 1948 - Ja 1960), its Population bulletin of the United Nations (D 1951 - 1963), and its International social service review (Ja 1956 - Ap 1963).*

NYERERE (JULIUS KAMBARAGE) The rational choice;...address delivered at Sudanese Socialist Union headquarters, Khartoum, 2nd January, 1973. [Dar es Salaam, Government Printer, 1972]. pp. 13.

— Squatters.

LLOYD (PETER CUTT) Slums of hope: shanty towns of the Third World. Harmondsworth, 1979. pp. 246. *bibliog.*

— Statistics.

IMPROVEMENT of development statistics: report of a group of experts meeting on 1-3 December 1975. Geneva, United Nations Research Institute for Social Development, 1976. pp. 43. *(UNRISD Reports. No. 76. 4)*

— Strikes and lockouts.

SEMINAR ON THIRD WORLD STRIKES, THE HAGUE, 1977. Papers on third world strikes submitted to a Seminar..., Institute of Social Studies, The Hague; with introduction by Peter Waterman. Zug, Switzerland, 1979. 11 fiches. *The introduction, with list of contents, is in pamphlet form and is shelved with the microfiches.*

— Taxation.

NGAOSYVATHN (PHEUIPHANH) Le rôle de l'impôt dans les pays en voie de développement: appréciation de l'influence exercée par les structures économiques et socio-politiques sur le prélèvement fiscal. Paris, 1978. pp. 316. *bibliog.*

TAXATION and economic development; edited by J.F.J. Toye. London, 1978. pp. 299. *bibliogs.*

— Technological innovations.

AVAKOV (RACHIK MAMIKONOVICH) Razvivaiushchiesia strany: nauchno-tekhnicheskaia revoliutsiia i problema nezavisimosti. Moskva, 1976. pp. 295. *(Akademiia Nauk SSSR. Institut Mirovoi Ekonomiki i Mezhdunarodnykh Otnoshenii. Ekonomika i Politika Razvivaiushchikhsia Stran)*

— Technology.

APPROPRIATE technologies for Third World development: proceedings of a conference held by the International Economic Association at Teheran, Iran; edited by Austin Robinson. London, 1979. pp. 417. *bibliog.*

— — Social aspects.

TECHNOLOGY for development; [edited] by Ann Kestenbaum. rev. ed. London, 1977. pp. 97.

SCIENCE, technology and economic growth in developing countries; edited by G.E. Skorov; translated [from the Russian] by Jenny Warren. Oxford, 1978. pp. 211.

— Urbanization.

RONDINELLI (DENNIS A.) and RUDDLE (KENNETH) Urbanization and rural development: a spatial policy for equitable growth. New York, [1978]. pp. 221. *bibliog.*

— Villages.

SCHOFIELD (SUE) Development and the problems of village nutrition. London, [1979]. pp. 174. *bibliog.*

— — Bibliography.

BRIGHTON. University of Sussex. Institute of Development Studies. Village Studies Programme. Village studies: data analysis and bibliography;...compiled by Mick Moore [and others]; edited by Claire M. Lambert. Epping, afterwards London, 1976-78. 2 vols.

— Wages.

McDIARMID (ORVILLE JOHN) Unskilled labor for development: its economic cost...; published for the World Bank. Baltimore, [1977]. pp. 206. *bibliog. (International Bank for Reconstruction and Development. World Bank Research Publications)*

— Water resources development.

WATER in a developing world: the management of a critical response; edited by Albert E. Utton and Ludwik Teclaff. Boulder, Colo., 1978. pp. 282. *bibliog.*

— — Social aspects.

WATER and society: conflicts in development. Part 1. The social and ecological effects of water development in developing countries; editor Carl Widstrand. Oxford, 1978. pp. 406. *bibliogs.*

— Water supply.

PASTEUR (DAVID) The Metroville water supply exercise: a case study in project appraisal and implementation in a large scale infrastructure project. Birmingham, 1976. pp. 33. *(Birmingham. University. Institute of Local Government Studies. Development Administration Group. Case Studies in Development Administration. vol. 1)*

WATER in a developing world: the management of a critical response; edited by Albert E. Utton and Ludwik Teclaff. Boulder, Colo., 1978. pp. 282. *bibliog.*

UNDERGROUND LITERATURE

— India.

UNDERGROUND literature during Indian emergency; edited by Sajal Basu. Calcutta, 1978. pp. 242.

— United Kingdom — Directories.

NOYCE (JOHN LEONARD) compiler. The directory of British alternative periodicals, 1965-1974. Hassocks, Sussex, 1979. pp. 359.

UNEMPLOYED.

HANSEN (ALVIN HARVEY) Economic stabilization in an unbalanced world. New York, 1971. pp. 384. *Reprint of work originally published in New York, 1932.*

SVERIGES INDUSTRIFÖRBUND. Economic Affairs Directorate. The Nordic economic outlook: a survey prepared [by Eva Christina Horwitz]...; [with] special studies [by various authors]. [Stockholm], 1975. pp. 86.

CAPITAL shortage and unemployment in the world economy: symposium 1977; edited by Herbert Giersch. Tübingen, [1978]. pp. 348. *bibliogs.*

UNEMPLOYMENT insurance: global evidence of its effects on unemployment; proceedings of an international conference held in Vancouver, British Columbia, Canada; edited by Herbert G. Grubel and Michael A. Walker. [Vancouver], 1978. pp. 388. *bibliogs.*

JENKINS (CLIVE) and SHERMAN (BARRIE) The collapse of work. London, 1979. pp. 181.

SIVEN (CLAES-HENRIC) A study in the theory of inflation and unemployment. Amsterdam, 1979. pp. 372. *bibliog.*

— Australia.

MYERS (DAVID MILTON) Inquiry into unemployment benefit policy and administration: report...for the Minister for Employment and Industrial Relations and the Minister for Social Security. Canberra, 1977. pp. 72.

— Brazil.

MATA (MILTON DA) Concentração de renda, desemprego e pobreza no Brasil. Rio de Janeiro, 1979. pp. 161. *bibliog. (Brazil. Instituto de Planejamento Econômico e Social. Instituto de Pesquisas. Relatorios de Pesquisa. No. 41)*

— Denmark.

MØLLER (IVER HORNEMANN) Ungdomsarbejdsløshed. København, 1978. pp. 55. *bibliog. (Socialforskningsinstituttet, Meddelelser. 25)*

— India — Assam.

ASSAM. Directorate of National Employment Service. 1963. Report on urban and rural unemployment in Assam, 1961. Shillong, [1963]. pp. 11, fo. 4.

— Mauritius.

SEMINAIRE SUR LE CHOMAGE, PORT LOUIS, 1971. Séminaire sur le chômage: [report]. Port Louis, Ministère de l'Information, 1971. pp. 12. *Issue of Inforama: bulletin d'information et de documentation. Vol. 10, No. 7.*

— Sudan.

ALI (MOHAMED ABDEL RAHMAN) Fiscal and monetary policies and employment in the Sudan. Khartoum, 1974. fo. 37. *(Economic and Social Research Council [Sudan]. Bulletins. No. 6) Cover title reads: Survey of contemporary theories of government expenditure.*

— United Kingdom.

HILL (J.M.M.) The social and psychological impact of unemployment: a pilot study. London, 1977. fo. 51. *bibliog.*

BENWELL COMMUNITY DEVELOPMENT PROJECT. Permanent unemployment. Newcastle-upon-Tyne, 1978. pp. 80. *(Final Report Series. No. 2)*

NORTH TYNESIDE COMMUNITY DEVELOPMENT PROJECT. In and out of work: a study of unemployment, low pay and income maintenance services. [Newcastle-upon-Tyne], 1978. pp. 287.

SCOTT (MAURICE FITZGERALD) and LASLETT (ROBERT A.) Can we get back to full employment? London, 1978. pp. 148. *bibliog. Based on two papers presented at a seminar held at Nuffield College, Oxford, in 1977.*

SMEE (CLIVE H.) and STERN (JON) The unemployed in a period of high unemployment: some notes on characteristics and benefit status. [London], Department of Health and Social Security, 1978. pp. 30. *(Government Economic Service Working Papers. No. 11)*

CASSON (MARK C.) Youth unemployment. London, 1979. pp. 141. *bibliog.*

NEEDHAM (BARRIE) Guidelines for a local employment study. Farnborough, Hants., [1979]. pp. 111.

— — Scotland.

PAISLEY COMMUNITY DEVELOPMENT PROJECT. Concentrated unemployment and a local initiative; (by Mike Martin). Paisley, 1978. pp. 47.

UNEMPLOYED.(Cont.)

— United States.

GOURVITCH (ALEXANDER) Survey of economic theory on technological change and employment. New York, 1966. pp. 252. *Reprint of work first published Philadelphia, 1940.*

CONGRESSIONAL QUARTERLY INC. Inflation and unemployment; (senior editor Peter A. Harkness). Washington, D.C., [1975]. pp. 124. *bibliog.*

MANGUM (GARTH LEROY) and SENINGER (STEPHEN F.) Coming of age in the ghetto: a dilemma of youth unemployment. Baltimore, [1978]. pp. 114. *bibliog.*

MARSHALL (RAY) and others. A conversation with Secretary Ray Marshall: inflation, unemployment and the minimum wage. Washington, [1978]. pp. 27. *(American Enterprise Institute for Public Policy Research. AEI Studies. 224)*

LEE (A.JAMES) Employment, unemployment, and health insurance: behavioral and descriptive analysis of health insurance loss due to unemployment. Cambridge, Mass., [1979]. pp. 150. *bibliog.*

— — Massachusetts.

PRAGER (AUDREY) Job creation in the community: an evaluation of locally initiated employment projects in Massachusetts. Cambridge, Mass., [1977]. pp. 175.

UNILEVER LIMITED.

FIELDHOUSE (DAVID KENNETH) Unilever overseas: the anatomy of a multinational, 1895-1965. Stanford, Calif., [1978]. pp. 620. *(Stanford University. Hoover Institution on War, Revolution and Peace. Hoover Institution Publications. 205)*

UNITED ARAB REPUBLIC

— Constitution.

UNITED ARAB REPUBLIC. Constitution. 1958. The provisional constitution of the U.A.R. [Cairo?], 1958. fo. 7.

UNITED KINGDOM

— Administrative and political divisions.

CLARKE (IAN) The great boundaries scandal. London, 1979. pp. 31. *(Conservative Political Centre. [Publications]. No. 635)*

— Air Travel Reserve Fund Agency.

U.K.Air Travel Reserve Fund Agency. Report and accounts. a., 1975/76[1st]- London.

— Antiquities.

ARCHAEOLOGY and the landscape: essays for L.V. Grinsell; edited by P.J. Fowler. London, 1972. pp. 263. *bibliog.*

BRADLEY (RICHARD) 1946- . The prehistoric settlement of Britain. London, 1978. pp. 155.

The EFFECT of man on the landscape: the lowland zone; edited by S. Limbrey and J.G. Evans. London, 1978. pp. 153. *bibliogs. (Council for British Archaeology. Research Reports. No. 21) Papers of a conference held at the University of Reading, 1975.*

STEANE (JOHN M.) and DIX (BRIAN F.) Peopling past landscapes: a handbook introducing archaeological fieldwork techniques in rural areas. London, 1978. pp. 94. *bibliog.*

— Appropriations and expenditures.

OUTRAM (QUENTIN) The significance of public expenditure plans. [London], 1975. pp. 105. *bibliog. (Centre for Studies in Social Policy. Working Papers)*

ROBINSON (ANN) Parliament and public spending: the Expenditure Committee of the House of Commons, 1970-76. London, 1978. pp. 184. *bibliog.*

JUTSUM (CAROLYN) and WALKER (GRAEME) Public expenditure 1977-78: outturn compared with plan. London, Treasury, 1979. pp. 27. *(Government Economic Service Working Papers. No. 28)*

— Armed forces — Pay, allowances, etc.

U.K. Review Body on Armed Forces Pay. 1979. Eighth report, 1979. London, 1979. pp. 24. *Reports 1-7 published in British Parliamentary Papers.*

— Army.

The TECHNOLOGY of political control; by Carol Ackroyd [and others]. Harmondsworth, 1977. pp. 320.

— — Colonial forces.

BUCKLEY (ROGER NORMAN) Slaves in red coats: the British West India regiments, 1795- 1815. New Haven, 1979. pp. 210. *bibliog.*

— — History.

GLOVER (MICHAEL) Wellington's army in the Peninsula, 1808-1814. Vancouver, [1977]. pp. 192. *bibliog.*

— — Social services.

U.K. Social Survey. [Reports. New Series]. 1060. Army welfare; a survey carried out for the Army Welfare Inquiry Committee, Ministry of Defence; [by] Malcolm Wilders. London, 1977. pp. 28.

— Census.

HAKIM (C.) Census-based area profiles: a review. [London], 1977. pp. 14. *bibliog. (U.K. Office of Population Censuses and Surveys. Occasional Papers. 2)*

HAKIM (C.) Data dissemination for the population census. [London], 1978. pp. 62. *(U.K. Office of Population Censuses and Surveys. Occasional Papers. 11)*

AKIM (C.) Social and community indicators from the census. [London], 1978. pp. 80. *bibliog. (U.K. Office of Population Censuses and Surveys. Occasional Papers. 5)*

KENNETT (STEPHEN) Census data and migration analysis: an appraisal. London, 1978. pp. 16. *biblig.*

U.K. Social Survey. [Reports. New Series]. 1074. Ethnic origins 1(-3): an experiment in the use of a direct question about ethnicity, for the census; [by] Ken Sillitoe. [London], 1978. 3 pts. (in 1 vol.). *(U.K. Office of Population Censuses and Surveys. Occasional Papers. 8-10). 6 forms in end pocket.*

— — Bibliography.

HAKIM (C.) Census data and analysis: a selected bibliography. [London], 1978. pp. 30. *(U.K. Office of Population Censuses and Surveys. Occasional Papers. 6)*

— — 1971.

U.K. Census, 1971. Census, 1971: Great Britain; as constituted on 1st April 1974 for England and Wales and 16th May 1975 for Scotland: migration tables, 10 per cent sample. London, 1978. pp. 304.

U.K. Census, 1971. Census, 1971: Great Britain: country of birth supplementary tables, 10 per cent sample. London, 1978. 2 pts. (in 1 vol.)

U.K. Census, 1971. Census, 1971: England and Wales: general report. London, 1979 in progress.

U.K. Census, 1971. Census, 1971: England and Wales: fertility tables. London, 1979. 3 vols.(in 1).

— — 1981.

LONDON. University. London School of Economics and Political Science. Graduate School of Geography. Discussion Papers. No. 70. Exploding the myth of rapidly expanding urban systems in Britain: implications for the adoption of functional areas in the 1981 census; [by] Stephen Kennett. London, 1978. pp. 20. *bibliog.*

— Charity Commission.

TOMPSON (RICHARD S.) The Charity Commission and the age of reform. London, 1979. pp. 379. *bibliog.*

— Church history.

CONFERENCE ON CHRISTIANITY IN ROMAN AND SUB-ROMAN BRITAIN, NOTTINGHAM, 1967. Christianity in Britain, 300-700; papers presented to the conference...; edited by M.W. Barley and R.P.C. Hanson. Leicester, 1968. pp. 221.

CURRIE (ROBERT) and others. Churches and churchgoers: patterns of church growth in the British Isles since 1700. Oxford, 1977. pp. 244.

CARWARDINE (RICHARD) Transatlantic revivalism: popular evangelicalism in Britain and America, 1790-1865. Westport, [1978]. pp. 249. *bibliog.*

KENT (JOHN) 1923- . Holding the fort: studies in Victorian revivalism. London, 1978. pp. 381.

— Colonial Office.

SAINTY (JOHN CHRISTOPHER) Colonial Office officials: officials of the Secretary of State for War 1794-1801, of the Secretary of State for War and Colonies 1801-54 and of the Secretary of State for Colonies 1854-70. London, 1976. pp. 52. *(London. University. Institute of Historical Research. Office-Holders in Modern Britain. 6)*

GANN (LEWIS H.) and DUIGNAN (PETER) The rulers of British Africa, 1870-1914. London, [1978]. pp. 406. *bibliog.*

— Commerce.

PASS (CHRISTOPHER L.) and SPARKES (JOHN R.) Trade and growth: a study of the U.K. in the world economy. London, 1977. pp. 129. *bibliog.*

DAVIS (RALPH) Professor of Economic History, Leicester University. The industrial revolution and British overseas trade. Leicester, 1979. pp. 135.

The NEWLY industrialising countries and the adjustment problem; report by a Working Group. London, Foreign and Commonwealth Office, 1979. pp. 57, 39. *(Government Economic Service Working Papers. No. 18)*

— — Europe.

EXPORTING to western Europe, 1977: case studies; a B[ritish] O[verseas] T[rade] B[oard] national conference, November 29, 1977,...Wembley. [London], British Overseas Trade Board, [1977]. pp. 52.

— — Germany.

KRAWEHL (OTTO ERNST) Hamburgs Schiffs- und Warenverkehr mit England und den englischen Kolonien, 1814-1860. Köln, 1977. pp. 536. *bibliog. With summary and table of contents in English.*

— — Spain — Castile.

CHILDS (WENDY R.) Anglo-Castilian trade in the later Middle Ages. Manchester, 1978. pp. 264. *bibliog.*

— — United States.

LONDON. London Record Society. Publications. vol. 15. Joshua Johnson's letterbook, 1771-1774: letters from a merchant in London to his partners in Maryland; edited by Jacob M. Price. London, 1979. pp. 181.

— Commercial policy.

LEVEEN (E. PHILIP) British slave trade suppression policies, 1821-1865. New York, 1977. pp. 186. *bibliog.*

McDOWALL (STUART) and DRAPER (PAUL) Trade adjustment and the British jute industry: a case study. Glasgow, 1978. pp. 48. *(Glasgow. University of Strathclyde. Fraser of Allander Institute. Research Monographs. No. 5)*

— Commonwealth Office.

GARNER (JOE) The Commonwealth Office, 1925-68. London, 1978. pp. 474. *bibliog.*

— Constitution.

G. (R.) A copy of a letter from an officer of the army in Ireland. Exeter, 1974. pp. 23. *Facsimile reprint of 1st ed., London, 1656.*

PEELE (GILLIAN) Change, decay and the British constitution. Hull, 1978. fo. 12. *(Hull. University. Department of Politics. Hull Papers in Politics. No. 1)*

— Constitutional history.

HUGHES (DOROTHY) A study of social and constitutional tendencies in the early years of Edward III, as illustrated more especially by the events connected with the ministerial inquiries of 1340 and the following years. Philadelphia, 1978. pp. 245. *bibliog. Reprint of work originally published London, 1915.*

KRAUTHEIM (ULRIKE) Die Souveränitätskonzeption in den englischen Verfassungskonflikten des 17. Jahrhunderts: eine Studie zur Rezeption der Lehre Bodins in England, etc. Frankfurt am Main, [1977]. pp. 597. *bibliog.*

— Constitutional law.

PHILLIPS (OWEN HOOD) Constitutional and administrative law; sixth edition by O.H. Phillips and Paul Jackson. London, 1978. pp. 746.

YARDLEY (DAVID CHARLES MILLER) Introduction to British constitutional law. 5th ed. London, 1978. pp. 168.

KEIR (Sir DAVID LINDSAY) and LAWSON (FREDERICK HARRY) Cases in constitutional law; sixth edition by F.H. Lawson and D.J. Bentley. Oxford, 1979. pp. 550.

— Defences.

BELLINI (JAMES) and PATTIE (GEOFFREY) A new world role for the medium power: the British opportunity. London, 1977. pp. 121.

LABOUR PARTY. Study Group on Defence Expenditure, the Arms Trade and Alternative Employment. Sense about defence: the report of the...Study Group; [Ian Mikardo, chairman]. Appendices 3-17. London, [1977?]. 1 vol. (various pagings).

SMART (IAN) The future of the British nuclear deterrent: technical, economic and strategic issues. London, [1977]. pp. 82. *(Royal Institute of International Affairs. British Foreign Policy to 1985)*

BONDI (Sir HERMANN) Defence and the citizen. London, 1978. pp. 8. *(David Davies Memorial Institute of International Studies. Annual Memorial Lectures. 1978)*

HODGSON (ROBIN GRANVILLE) and BANKS (ROBERT GEORGE) Britain's home-defence gamble. London, [1978]. pp. 31. *bibliog. (Conservative Political Centre. [Publications]. No. 628)*

— Department of Education and Science.

PILE (Sir WILLIAM DENNIS) The Department of Education and Science. London, 1979. pp. 247. *(Royal Institute of Public Administration. New Whitehall Series. No. 16)*

— Department of the Environment.

DRAPER (PAUL) Creation of the D.O.E.: (a study of the merger of three departments to form the Department of the Environment). London, 1977. pp. 239. *(U.K. Civil Service Department. Civil Service Studies. No. 4)*

— Description and travel.

DEFOE (DANIEL) A tour through the whole island of Great Britain. rev ed. London, 1962 repr. 1974. pp. 437.

OSIPOV (VLADIMIR DMITRIEVICH) Britaniia glazami russkogo. Moskva, 1976. pp. 208.

CAMDEN SOCIETY. [Publications]. 4th Series. vol.22. Camden miscellany. vol.27. London, 1979. pp. 248.

— Diplomatic and consular service.

INTERCHANGE between the home civil service and the diplomatic service; report of a Working Group; [Sir John Herbecq, chairman]. [London], Civil Service Department, 1978. pp. 17.

— Economic conditions.

NATIONAL INSTITUTE OF ECONOMIC AND SOCIAL RESEARCH. The United Kingdom economy. Brussels, European Communities, 1975. pp. 155. *bibliog. (European Economic Community. Studies. Economic and Financial Series. 9)*

NORTHERN REGION STRATEGY TEAM. Future trends and prospects in the United Kingdom economy; interim draft report; (project no.A.5.a). Newcastle-upon-Tyne, 1976. 1 vol. (various pagings). *([Working Papers. No.2])*

PAGE (EDWARD) Michael Hechter's internal colonial thesis: some theoretical and methodological problems. Glasgow, [1977]. pp. 30,3. *(Glasgow. University of Strathclyde. Centre for the Study of Public Policy. Studies in Public Policy. No. 9)*

PASS (CHRISTOPHER L.) and SPARKES (JOHN R.) Trade and growth: a study of the U.K. in the world economy. London, 1977. pp. 129. *bibliog.*

BHATTACHARYYA (D.K.) Demand for financial assets: an econometric study of the U.K. personal sector. Farnborough, [1978]. pp. 197. *bibliogs.*

DEANE (PHYLLIS) and COLE (W.A.) British economic growth 1688-1959: trends and structure. 2nd ed. Cambridge, 1978. pp. 350. *bibliog. (Cambridge. University. Department of Applied Economics. Monographs. 8)*

HAMILTON (ADRIAN) North Sea impact: off-shore oil and the British economy. London, 1978. pp. 191.

PREST (ALAN RICHMOND) Intergovernmental financial relations in the United Kingdom. Canberra, 1978. pp. 118. *bibliog. (Australian National University. Centre for Research on Federal Financial Relations. Research Monographs. No. 23)*

BLACK (JOHN) Economist. The economics of modern Britain: an introduction to macroeconomics. Oxford, 1979. pp. 272. *bibliog.*

DE-INDUSTRIALISATION; edited by Frank Blackaby. London, 1979. pp. 275. *bibliogs. (National Institute of Economic and Social Research. Economic Policy Papers. 2)*

KEEGAN (WILLIAM) and PENNANT-REA (RUPERT) Who runs the economy?: control and influence in British economic policy. London, 1979. pp. 235. *bibliog.*

KNOX (FRANK) Labour supply in economic development. Farnborough, [1979]. pp. 114. *bibliogs.*

— — Mathematical models.

NATIONAL Institute model II;... [by] George Fane [and others]. London, [1977]. 4 vols. *(National Institute of Economic and Social Research. Discussion Papers. No. 10)*

ORMEROD (P.A.) The structure and properties of the NIESR model of the UK economy. London, 1977. pp. 28. *(National Institute of Economic and Social Research. Discussion Papers. No. 4) Paper presented to the Academic Panel of H.M. Treasury in 1977.*

— — Statistics.

BROWN (C.J.F.) and SHERIFF (TOM D.) De-industrialisation in the UK: background statistics. London, [1979]. pp. 33. *(National Institute of Economic and Social Research. Discussion Papers. No. 23)*

— Economic history.

FAIRCHILD (EDWIN CHARLES) Labour and the industrial revolution. London, 1923. pp. 222.

SAYERS (RICHARD SIDNEY) A history of economic change in England, 1880-1939. Oxford, 1967. pp. 179. *bibliog.*

DEANE (PHYLLIS) and COLE (W.A.) British economic growth 1688-1959: trends and structure. 2nd ed. Cambridge, 1978. pp. 350. *bibliog. (Cambridge. University. Department of Applied Economics. Monographs. 8)*

DONKIN (ROBIN A.) The Cistercians: studies in the geography of medieval England and Wales. Toronto, 1978. pp. 242. *bibliog. (Pontifical Institute of Mediaeval Studies. Studies and Texts. 38)*

MILLER (EDWARD) M.A. and HATCHER (JOHN) Medieval England: rural society and economic change 1086-1348. London, 1978. pp. 302. *bibliog.*

JULIAN (MARK ROBERT) English economic legislation 1660-1714. 1979. fo. 376. *bibliog. Typescript. M.Phil. (London) thesis: unpublished. This thesis is the property of London University and may not be removed from the Library.*

PAWSON (ERIC) The early industrial revolution: Britain in the eighteenth century. New York, 1979. pp. 233. *bibliog.*

PRE-INDUSTRIAL England: geographical essays; edited with an introduction by John Patten. Folkstone, [1979]. pp. 245. *bibliogs.*

The SEARCH for wealth and stability: essays in economic and social history presented to M.W. Flinn; edited by T.C. Smout. London, 1979. pp. 291.

WALKER (JAMES) 1898- . British economic and social history, 1700-1977;...revised by C.W. Munn. 2nd ed. Plymouth, 1979. pp. 448.

— Economic policy.

MOSLEY (Sir OSWALD ERNALD) The greater Britain. new ed. London, [1934]. pp. 191.

SOCIALISM the British way...: the socialist experiment carried out in Great Britain by the Labour government of 1945; by Evan F.M. Durbin [and others]; edited by Donald Munro. London, [1948]. pp. 345.

NATIONAL INSTITUTE OF ECONOMIC AND SOCIAL RESEARCH. The United Kingdom economy. Brussels, European Communities, 1975. pp. 155. *bibliog. (European Economic Community. Studies. Economic and Financial Series. 9)*

ASHCROFT (BRIAN) The evaluation of regional economic policy: the case of the United Kingdom. Glasgow, [1978]. pp. 72,3,6. *bibliog. (Glasgow. University of Strathclyde. Centre for the Study of Public Policy. Studies in Public Policy. No. 12)*

BELOFF (MAX) The tide of collectivism: can it be turned? London, 1978. pp. 23. *(Conservative Political Centre. [Publications]. No. 629)*

BRITISH economic policy, 1960-74; F. T. Blackaby (editor). Cambridge, 1978. pp. 687. *bibliog. (National Institute of Economic and Social Research. Economic and Social Studies. 31)*

The COMING confrontation: will the open society survive to 1989?; [by] W.H. Chaloner [and others]. London, 1978. pp. 250. *bibliogs. (Institute of Economic Affairs. Hobart Paperbacks. 12)*

COSTELLO (MICK) Cut the dole queues: smash the 5 per cent limit: win a 35 hour week: expand social services. London, [1978?]. pp. 18.

The ECONOMICS of politics;...[by] James M. Buchanan [and others]. [London], 1978. pp. 192. *bibliogs. (Institute of Economic Affairs. Readings. 18)*

GOWLAND (DAVID) Monetary policy and credit control: the U.K. experience. London, [1978]. pp. 219.

HARROD (DOMINICK) The politics of economics. London, 1978. pp. 80. *Based on a series of six radio programmes, first broadcast by the BBC 1977/78.*

JOSEPH (Sir KEITH SINJOHN) Conditions for fuller employment. London, 1978. pp. 20.

NATIONAL CONSUMER COUNCIL. Real money, real choice: consumer priorities in economic policy: a document for discussion. London, 1978. pp. 68.

TRADES UNION CONGRESS. Industrial strategy: a checklist for trade union representatives. London, 1978. pp. 7.

UNITED KINGDOM (Cont.)

TRADES UNION CONGRESS and LABOUR PARTY. Liaison Committee. Into the eighties: an agreement. London, 1978. pp. 16.

[U.K. Department of Industry. 1978.] Regional development programme, United Kingdom, 1978-1980. [London, 1978]. pp. 91.

WHITBY (MARTIN CHARLES) and WILLIS (KENNETH G.) Rural resource development: an economic approach. 2nd ed. London, 1978. pp. 303. *bibliog.*

ALLEN (GEORGE CYRIL) British industry and economic policy. London, 1979. pp. 220. *bibliog.*

The CASE for private enterprise; editor: Cecil Turner. London, 1979. pp. 111.

COMPETITION policy, profitability and growth; [by] D.P. O'Brien. London, 1979. pp. 154. *bibliog.*

FABIAN SOCIETY. Fabian Tracts. [No.] 462. The politics of monetarism; [by] Bryan Gould [and others]. London, 1979. pp. 19.

GOUGH (IAN) The political economy of the welfare state. London, 1979. pp. 196.

KEEGAN (WILLIAM) and PENNANT-REA (RUPERT) Who runs the economy?: control and influence in British economic policy. London, 1979. pp. 235. *bibliog.*

SHERIFF (TOM D.) A deindustrialised Britain? London, 1979. pp. 23. *(Fabian Society. Research Series. [No.] 341)*

SMITH (TREVOR) Liberal. The politics of the corporate economy. Oxford, 1979. pp. 229. *bibliog.*

TRADES UNION CONGRESS. The economy, the government and trade union responsibilities: joint statement by the TUC and the government. London, H.M.S.O., 1979. pp. 20.

— **Emigration and immigration.**

HAMMERTON (A. JAMES) Emigrant gentlewomen: genteel poverty and female emigration, 1830- 1914. London, [1979]. pp. 220. *bibliog.*

REX (JOHN ARDERNE) and TOMLINSON (SALLY) Colonial immigrants in a British city: a class analysis. London, 1979. pp. 357. *bibliog.*

— **Executive departments.**

CROSS (JOHN ARTHUR) British public administration. London, 1970. pp. 190. *bibliogs.*

U.K. Civil Service Department. Directory of paid public appointments made by ministers. irreg., 1976- London.

SAINTY (JOHN CHRISTOPHER) Colonial Office officials: officials of the Secretary of State for War 1794-1801, of the Secretary of State for War and Colonies 1801-54 and of the Secretary of State for Colonies 1854-70. London, 1976. pp. 52. *(London. University. Institute of Historical Research. Office-Holders in Modern Britain. 6)*

DRAPER (PAUL) Creation of the D.O.E.: (a study of the merger of three departments to form the Department of the Environment). London, 1977. pp. 239. *(U.K. Civil Service Department. Civil Service Studies. No. 4)*

U.K. Home Office. 1977. The Home Office. [London, 1977]. fo. 29. Photocopy.

BAKER (JOHN FLEETWOOD) Baron Baker. Enterprise versus bureaucracy: the development of structural air- raid precautions during the 2nd World War. Oxford, 1978. pp. 123.

CLARKE (Sir RICHARD WILLIAM BARNES) Public expenditure, management and controls: the development of the Public Expenditure Survey Committee (PESC). London, 1978. pp. 212.

COLLINGE (J.M.) Navy Board officials, 1660-1832. London, 1978. pp. 153. *(London. University. Institute of Historical Research. Office-Holders in Modern Britain.7)*

KYNASTON (DAVID) The Secretary of State. Lavenham, 1978. pp. 177. *bibliog.*

McLAINE (IAN) Ministry of morale: home front morale and the Ministry of Information in World War II. London, 1979. pp. 325. *bibliog.*

PEDEN (G.C.) British rearmament and the Treasury: 1932-1939. Edinburgh, 1979. pp. 227. *bibliog.*

PILE (Sir WILLIAM DENNIS) The Department of Education and Science. London, 1979. pp. 247. *(Royal Institute of Public Administration. New Whitehall Series. No. 16)*

POTTINGER (GEORGE) The Secretaries of State for Scotland, 1926-76. Edinburgh, [1979]. pp. 214. *bibliog.*

— **Expenditure Committee of the House of Commons.**

ROBINSON (ANN) Parliament and public spending: the Expenditure Committee of the House of Commons, 1970-76. London, 1978. pp. 184. *bibliog.*

— **Foreign economic relations.**

CAMARA (HELDER) Archbishop of Olinda and Recife. Fraternal appeal to Britain. [London, 1975?]. pp. 4. *(Edwina Mountbatten Memorial Lectures. 1975)*

CROWSON (PHILLIP) Non-fuel minerals and foreign policy. London, [1977]. 2 vols. *(Royal Institute of International Affairs. British Foreign Policy to 1985)*

PASS (CHRISTOPHER L.) and SPARKES (JOHN R.) Trade and growth: a study of the U.K. in the world economy. London, 1977. pp. 129. *bibliog.*

See also EUROPEAN ECONOMIC COMMUNITY — United Kingdom.

— — **Africa.**

BANGURA (YUSUF) The politics of economic relations between Britain and Commonwealth Africa, 1951-1975. 1978. fo. 526. *bibliog.* Typescript. Ph.D. (London) thesis: unpublished. This thesis is the property of London University and may not be removed from the Library.

— — **East (Far East).**

STEEDS (DAVID) and NISH (IAN HILL) compilers. China, Japan and 19th century Britain; [commentaries on British parliamentary papers]. Dublin, [1977]. pp. 136. *bibliog.*

— — **Japan.**

MUTO (CHOZO) A short history of Anglo-Japanese relations. postwar ed. Tokyo, 1977. pp. 83.

— — **Palestine.**

FINEGOLD (JULIAN LEWIS) British economic policy in Palestine, 1920-1948. 1979. fo. 241. *bibliog.* Typescript. Ph.D. (London) thesis: unpublished. This thesis is the property of London University and may not be removed from the Library.

— **Foreign opinion.**

OSIPOV (VLADIMIR DMITRIEVICH) Britaniia glazami russkogo. Moskva, 1976. pp. 208.

— **Foreign population.**

ETHNIC minorities and the public and voluntary services: housing; text of paper given to Institute of Social Welfare seminar, University of Nottingham, 18 March 1976. [Bristol, Social Science Research Council Research Unit on Ethnic Relations, 1976]. fo. 10.

U.K. Commission for Racial Equality. 1977. Housing need among ethnic minorities: comments on the consultative document on housing policy presented to Parliament by the Secretary of State for the Environment and the Secretary of State for Wales. London, 1977. pp. 9.

CROSS (CRISPIN PATRIC ROBERT) Ethnic minorities in the inner city: the ethnic dimension in urban deprivation in England. London, Commission for Racial Equality, 1978. pp. 183. *bibliog.*

U.K. Census, 1971. Census, 1971: Great Britain: country of birth supplementary tables, 10 per cent sample. London, 1978. 2 pts. (in 1 vol.)

U.K. Commission for Racial Equality. 1978. Ethnic minorities in Britain: statistical background. London, 1978 repr. 1979. pp. 37.

U.K. Social Survey. [Reports. New Series]. 1074. Ethnic origins 1(-3): an experiment in the use of a direct question about ethnicity, for the census; [by] Ken Sillitoe. [London], 1978. 3 pts. (in 1 vol.). *(U.K. Office of Population Censuses and Surveys. Occasional Papers. 8-10).* 6 forms in end pocket.

— **Foreign relations.**

BRITISH AND FOREIGN STATE PAPERS; compiled and ed. in the Library and Records Department of the Foreign and Commonwealth Office, etc. irreg., 1812/1814(v.1)- , with gap (v.21, pt. 2). London. *Indexes: 1871/1873(v.64); 1873/1900(v.93); 1900/1921(v. 115); 1922/1934(v.138). Incorporates from v.116 Hertslet's commercial treaties (1840-1925)*

DILKS (DAVID) Appeasement revisited. Leeds, 1972. pp. 29. *Inaugural lecture in the University of Leeds Review, vol. 15, no.1, May 1972.*

NOEL (LEON) Les illusions de Stresa: l'Italie abandonnée à Hitler. Paris, [1975]. pp. 206.

PONCINS (LEON DE) Comte, the Younger. State secrets: a documentation of the secret revolutionary mainspring governing Anglo-American politics; translated from the French edition of...Top secret by Timothy Tindal-Robertson. Chulmleigh, Devon, 1975. pp. 191. *bibliog.*

CROWSON (PHILLIP) Non-fuel minerals and foreign policy. London, [1977]. 2 vols. *(Royal Institute of International Affairs. British Foreign Policy to 1985)*

BARKER (ELISABETH) Churchill and Eden at war. London, 1978. pp. 346. *bibliog.*

HAYES (PAUL M.) The twentieth century, 1880-1939. New York, 1978. pp. 343. *bibliog.*

KREIN (DAVID F.) The last Palmerston government: foreign policy, domestic politics, and the genesis of "splendid isolation". Ames, Iowa, 1978. pp. 252. *bibliog.*

LISKA (GEORGE) Career of empire: America and imperial expansion over land and sea. Baltimore, [1978]. pp. 360. *(Washington Center of Foreign Policy Research. Studies in International Affairs)*

ORDE (ANNE) Great Britain and international security, 1920-1926. London, 1978. pp. 244. *bibliog. (Royal Historical Society. Studies in History)*

U.K. Foreign and Commonwealth Office. 1978. British policy towards the United Nations. London, 1978. pp. 39. *(Foreign Policy Documents. No. 26)*

WASSERSTEIN (BERNARD) Britain and the Jews of Europe, 1939-1945. Oxford, 1979. pp. 389. *bibliog.*

See also EUROPEAN ECONOMIC COMMUNITY — United Kingdom; UNITED NATIONS—United Kingdom.

— — **Asia.**

INGRAM (EDWARD) The beginning of the great game in Asia, 1828-1834. Oxford, 1979. pp. 361. *bibliog.*

— — **Balkan States.**

MILLMAN (RICHARD) Britain and the Eastern question, 1875-1878. Oxford, 1979. pp. 613. *bibliog.*

— — **China.**

GRAHAM (GERALD SANDFORD) The China station: war and diplomacy, 1830-1860. Oxford, 1978. pp. 444. *bibliog.*

OSTRIKOV (PETR IVANOVICH) Imperialisticheskaia politika Anglii v Kitae v 1900-1914 godakh. Moskva, 1978. pp. 227. *bibliog.*

UNITED KINGDOM (Cont.)

—— East (Far East).

STEEDS (DAVID) and NISH (IAN HILL) compilers. China, Japan and 19th century Britain; [commentaries on British parliamentary papers]. Dublin, [1977]. pp. 136. *bibliog.*

—— France.

LECA (DOMINIQUE) La rupture de 1940. [Paris, 1978]. pp. 353.

THOMAS (R.T.) Britain and Vichy: the dilemma of Anglo-French relations, 1940-42. London, 1979. pp. 230. *bibliog.*

—— Germany.

YOUNG (ARTHUR PRIMROSE) The 'X' documents; edited by Sidney Aster. London, 1974. pp. 253. *bibliog.*

—— Iceland.

GILCHRIST (Sir ANDREW) Cod wars and how to lose them. Edinburgh, 1977. pp. 122.

—— India.

RIZVI (GOWHER) Linlithgow and India: a study of British policy and the political impasse in India, 1936-43. London, 1978. pp. 261. *bibliogs.*

MOORE (ROBIN JAMES) Churchill, Cripps, and India, 1939-1945. Oxford, 1979. pp. 152.

—— Iraq.

MEJCHER (HELMUT) Imperial quest for oil: Iraq, 1910-1928. London, 1976. pp. 130. *bibliog. (Oxford. University. St. Antony's College. Middle East Centre. St. Antony's Middle East Monographs. No. 6)*

—— Ireland (Republic).

PECK (JOHN) Dublin from Downing Street. Dublin, 1978. pp. 241.

—— Japan.

MUTO (CHOZO) A short history of Anglo-Japanese relations. postwar ed. Tokyo, 1977. pp. 83.

—— Nigeria —— Kano (State).

FIKA (ADAMU MOHAMMED) The Kano civil war and British over-rule, 1882-1940. Oxford, [1978]. pp. 307. *bibliog.*

—— Rhodesia.

MACDONALD (HECTOR NORMAN) A judge's thoughts..., 30th May, 1970. [Salisbury, 1970]. pp. 5. *(Rhodesia. Ministry of Information, Immigration and Tourism. For the Record. No. 12)*

—— Sabah.

TARLING (NICHOLAS) Sulu and Sabah: s study of British policy towards the Philippines and North Borneo from the late eighteenth century. Kuala Lumpur, 1978. pp. 385. *bibliog.*

—— Spain.

SMITH (LAWRENCE BARTLAM) Spain and Britain 1715-19: the Jacobite issue. 1977 [or rather 1978]. fo.361. *bibliog.* Typescript. Ph.D. (London) thesis: unpublished. This thesis is the property of London University and may not be removed from the Library.

—— Sulu.

TARLING (NICHOLAS) Sulu and Sabah: s study of British policy towards the Philippines and North Borneo from the late eighteenth century. Kuala Lumpur, 1978. pp. 385. *bibliog.*

—— Turkey.

WEBER (FRANK G.) The evasive neutral: Germany, Britain and the quest for a Turkish alliance in the Second World War. Columbia, Mo., 1979. pp. 244. *bibliog.*

—— United States.

JONES (HOWARD) 1940- . To the Webster-Ashburton Treaty: a study in Anglo-American relations, 1783-1843. Chapel Hill, [1977]. pp. 251. *bibliog.*

WELLS (SHERRILL PERKINS BROWN) The influence of Sir Cecil Spring Rice and Sir Edward Grey on the shaping of Anglo-American relations, 1913-1916. 1978. fo. 416. *bibliog.* Typescript. Ph.D. (London) thesis: unpublished. This thesis is the property of London University and may not be removed from the Library.

— Full employment policies.

NEEDHAM (BARRIE) Guidelines for a local employment study. Farnborough, Hants., [1979]. pp. 111.

— Gentry.

BLACKWOOD (B.G.) The Lancashire gentry and the great rebellion, 1640-60. Manchester, 1978. pp. 184. *bibliog. (Chetham Society. Remains, Historical and Literary, connected with the Palatine Counties of Lancaster and Chester. 3rd series. vol. 25)*

— Government publications.

PEMBERTON (JOHN EDWARD) British official publications. 2nd ed. Oxford, 1973 repr. 1974. pp. 328.

STEEDS (DAVID) and NISH (IAN HILL) compilers. China, Japan and 19th century Britain; [commentaries on British parliamentary papers]. Dublin, [1977]. pp. 136. *bibliog.*

U.K. Treasury. 1979. Guide to public sector financial information. No.1, 1979; editors: part 1: P.R. Money; part 2: E.A. Thomas. London, 1979. pp. 108. *bibliog.*

—— Bibliography.

U.K. Department of Industry. Common Services Library. Bibliographical Services. Publications: a list of documents issued by the Departments of Industry, Trade, Prices and Consumer Protection, Energy and their associated bodies, and not available from H.M.S.O. a., 1976(1st)- London.

U.K. Department of Health and Social Security. Index of health circulars and notices; chief officer letters; local authority circulars and social service letters. a., 1977- London.

U.K. Ministry of Overseas Development. Land Resources Division. Publications list. a., 1977- London.

U.K. Department of Energy. Library. Publications in print. a., 1978- London.

SHRIGLEY (SHEILA M.) compiler. Selected official publications on the National Health Service. London, 1978. pp. 9. *(U.K. Department of Health and Social Security. Library. Bibliography Series. B23)*

U.K. Health and Safety Executive. 1979. Publications catalogue '79. London, 1979. pp. 107.

U.K. Stationery Office. Sectional lists. irreg., current issue only. London.

— Historical geography.

DODGSHON (R.A.) and BUTLIN (ROBIN A.) eds. An historical geography of England and Wales. London, 1978. pp. 450. *bibliogs.*

DONKIN (ROBIN A.) The Cistercians: studies in the geography of medieval England and Wales. Toronto, 1978. pp. 242. *bibliog. (Pontifical Institute of Mediaeval Studies. Studies and Texts. 38)*

— History.

BRABAZON (REGINALD) 12th Earl of Meath. Memories of the twentieth century. London, 1924. pp. 310.

TREVELYAN (GEORGE MACAULAY) English social history: a survey of six centuries from Chaucer to Queen Victoria. [new ed.] London, [1978]. pp. 555. *bibliog.*

CAMDEN SOCIETY. [Publications]. 4th Series. vol.22. Camden miscellany. vol.27. London, 1979. pp. 248.

—— 55 B.C. - 449 A.D., Roman period.

CONFERENCE ON CHRISTIANITY IN ROMAN AND SUB-ROMAN BRITAIN, NOTTINGHAM, 1967. Christianity in Britain, 300-700; papers presented to the conference...; edited by M.W. Barley and R.P.C. Hanson. Leicester, 1968. pp. 221.

—— 449-1066, Anglo-Saxon period.

ROBINSON (JOSEPH ARMITAGE) The times of Saint Dunstan. Oxford, 1923 repr. 1969. pp. 188. *(Oxford. University. Ford Lectures. 1922)*

CONFERENCE ON CHRISTIANITY IN ROMAN AND SUB-ROMAN BRITAIN, NOTTINGHAM, 1967. Christianity in Britain, 300-700; papers presented to the conference...; edited by M.W. Barley and R.P.C. Hanson. Leicester, 1968. pp. 221.

BROOKE (CHRISTOPHER NUGENT LAWRENCE) The Saxon and Norman Kings. London, 1978. pp. 224. *bibliog.*

SAWYER (PETER HAYES) From Roman Britain to Norman England. New York, [1978]. pp. 294. *bibliog.*

——— Sources.

The ANGLO-Saxon Chronicle; translated and edited by G.N. Garmonsway. London, 1972 repr. 1975. pp. 295.

—— 1066-1485, Medieval period —— Bibliography.

WILKINSON (BERTIE) compiler. The high Middle Ages in England, 1154-1377. Cambridge, 1978. pp. 130. *bibliog. (Conference on British Studies. Bibliographical Handbooks)*

——— Sources.

MEDIEVAL legal records; edited in memory of C.A.F. Meekings; general editors: R.F. Hunnisett [and] J.B. Post. London, H.M.S.O., 1978. pp. 560. *Texts in Latin and Old French with English introductions and notes.*

—— 1066-1154, Norman period.

DAVIS (RALPH HENRY CARLESS) King Stephen, 1135-1154. London, 1977. pp. 162.

BROOKE (CHRISTOPHER NUGENT LAWRENCE) The Saxon and Norman Kings. London, 1978. pp. 224. *bibliog.*

SAWYER (PETER HAYES) From Roman Britain to Norman England. New York, [1978]. pp. 294. *bibliog.*

——— Sources.

The ANGLO-Saxon Chronicle; translated and edited by G.N. Garmonsway. London, 1972 repr. 1975. pp. 295.

GESTA Stephani; edited and translated by K.R. Potter; with new introduction and notes by R.H.C. Davis. Oxford, 1976. pp. 249.

—— 1300-1399.

HUGHES (DOROTHY) A study of social and constitutional tendencies in the early years of Edward III, as illustrated more especially by the events connected with the ministerial inquiries of 1340 and the following years. Philadelphia, 1978. pp. 245. *bibliog.* Reprint of work originally published London, 1915.

HAINES (ROY MARTIN) The church and politics in fourteenth-century England: the career of Adam Orleton, c.1275-1345. Cambridge, 1978. pp. 303. *bibliog.*

FRYDE (NATALIE) The tyranny and fall of Edward II, 1321-1326. Cambridge, 1979. pp. 301. *bibliog.*

—— 1485-1603, Tudors.

The ENGLISH commonwealth, 1547-1640: essays in politics and society presented to Joel Hurstfield; edited by Peter Clark (and others). Leicester, 1979. pp. 274. *bibliog.*

PRITCHARD (ARNOLD) Catholic loyalism in Elizabethan England. London, 1979. pp. 243. *bibliog.*

UNITED KINGDOM (Cont.)

— — 1603-1714, Stuarts.

ASHLEY (MAURICE PERCY) England in the seventeenth century. new ed. London, 1978. pp. 275. *bibliog.*

BLACKWOOD (B.G.) The Lancashire gentry and the great rebellion, 1640-60. Manchester, 1978. pp. 184. *bibliog. (Chetham Society. Remains, Historical and Literary, connected with the Palatine Counties of Lancaster and Chester. 3rd series. vol. 25)*

PURITANS and revolutionaries: essays in seventeenth-century history presented to Christopher Hill; edited by Donald Pennington and Keith Thomas. Oxford, 1978. pp. 149. *bibliog.*

RILEY (PATRICK WILLIAM JOSEPH) The union of England and Scotland: a study in Anglo-Scottish politics of the eighteenth century. Manchester, [1978]. pp. 351. *bibliogs.*

— — 1603-1649, Early Stuarts.

ASHTON (ROBERT) The English Civil War: Conservatism and Revolution, 1603-1649. London, [1978]. pp. 453. *bibliog.*

The ENGLISH commonwealth, 1547-1640: essays in politics and society presented to Joel Hurstfield; edited by Peter Clark (and others). Leicester, 1979. pp. 274. *bibliog.*

— — 1642-1649, Civil War.

HOLMES (CLIVE) The Eastern Association in the English civil war. London, 1974. pp. 322. *bibliog.*

— — — Historiography.

RICHARDSON (ROGER CHARLES) The debate on the English Revolution. London, 1977. pp. 195. *bibliog.*

— — 1660-1688, Restoration.

The RESTORED monarchy, 1660-1688; edited by J.R. Jones. London, 1979. pp. 232. *bibliog.*

— — — Sources.

CAMDEN SOCIETY. [Publications]. 4th Series. vol. 21. A voyce from the watch tower; ([by] Edmund Ludlow); part five, 1660-1662; edited by A.B. Worden. London, 1978. pp. 370.

— — 1714-1837.

OWEN (JOHN BERESFORD) The eighteenth century, 1714-1815. London, [1974]. pp. 365. *bibliog.*

— — 1714-1760.

SMITH (LAWRENCE BARTLAM) Spain and Britain 1715-19: the Jacobite issue. 1977 [or rather 1978]. fo.361. *bibliog.* Typescript. Ph.D. (London) thesis: unpublished. *This thesis is the property of London University and may not be removed from the Library.*

— — 1760-1820.

BROOKE (JOHN) 1920- . King George III. London, [1972]. pp. 411.

EMSLEY (CLIVE) British society and the French wars, 1793-1815. London, 1979. pp. 216. *bibliog.*

— — 1800-1899.

CLARKE (FRANCIS GORDON) The land of contrarieties: British attitudes to the Australian colonies, 1828-1835. Melbourne, 1977. pp. 223. *bibliog.*

FOX (ROBERT BARCLAY) Barclay Fox's journal; edited by R.L. Brett. London, 1979. pp. 426.

The SEARCH for wealth and stability: essays in economic and social history presented to M.W. Flinn; edited by T.C. Smout. London, 1979. pp. 291.

— — — Sources.

U.K. Home Office. 1812-55. British 19th century riots and disturbances: HO 40/1-59; Home Office, Correspondence and Papers, Disturbances, 1812-1855. v.p., 1812-55. Microfilm : 46 reels. *(U.K. Public Record Office. Public Records of Great Britain. Series 5) Means of reference on reel 1.*

— — 1800-1837.

STEVENS (JOHN) Journalist. England's last revolution: Pentrich 1817. Hartington, [1977]. pp. 167. *bibliog.*

— — 1837-1901.

READ (DONALD) England 1868-1914: the age of urban democracy. London, [1979]. pp. 530. *bibliog.*

— — 1900- .

HAYES (PAUL M.) The twentieth century, 1880-1939. New York, 1978. pp. 343. *bibliog.*

LLOYD (TREVOR OWEN) Empire to welfare state: English history, 1906-1967. 2nd ed. Oxford, 1979. pp. 511. *bibliog.*

PEDEN (G.C.) British rearmament and the Treasury: 1932-1939. Edinburgh, 1979. pp. 227. *bibliog.*

COOK (CHRISTOPHER PIERS) and WEEKS (JEFFREY) compilers. Sources in British political history, 1900-1951: compiled for the British Library of Political and Economic Science; vol. 5. London, 1978. pp. 221.

— — 1900-1914.

RIDDELL (GEORGE ALLARDICE) 1st Baron Riddell. More pages from my diary, 1908-1914. London, 1934. pp. 238.

READ (DONALD) England 1868-1914: the age of urban democracy. London, [1979]. pp. 530. *bibliog.*

— — 1910-1936.

NATIONAL government 1931: extracts from the 'Times' January to October 1931; introduced and edited by Colin Bell. London, 1975. pp. 209. *bibliog.*

— History, Military.

PEDEN (G.C.) British rearmament and the Treasury: 1932-1939. Edinburgh, 1979. pp. 227. *bibliog.*

— History, Naval.

GRAHAM (GERALD SANDFORD) The China station: war and diplomacy, 1830-1860. Oxford, 1978. pp. 444. *bibliog.*

— Home Office.

U.K. Home Office. 1977. The Home Office. [London, 1977]. fo. 29. *Photocopy.*

— Industries.

LITTLECHILD (STEPHEN CHARLES) Change rules, O.K.? Birmingham, 1977. pp. 23. *Inaugural lecture given at the University of Birmingham in 1977.*

RAW (CHARLES) Slater Walker: an investigation of a financial phenomenon. London, 1977. pp. 368.

BROWN (DAVID) and HARRISON (MICHAEL J.) A sociology of industrialisation: an introduction. London, 1978. pp. 172. *bibliogs.*

IRESON (RICHARD) and TOMKINS (CYRIL R.) Inter-regional input-output for Wales and the rest of the U.K., 1968. [Cardiff], Welsh Council, [1978]. 1 vol.(various pagings). *bibliog.*

KING (MERVYN A.) and MAIRESSE (JACQUES) Profitability in Britain and France: a comparative study, 1956- 1975. Paris, Institut National de la Statistique et des Etudes Economiques, 1978. pp. 80.

THOMAS (W.A.) The finance of British industry, 1918-1976. London, 1978. pp. 351. *bibliog.*

U.K. Business Statistics Office. 1978. Historical record of the census of production, 1907 to 1970. [London, 1978]. pp. 402, lxv. *bibliog.*

U.K. Inner Cities Directorate. 1978. Industry in the inner city: case studies in mixed-use development. [London, 1978]. pp. 39.

ALLEN (GEORGE CYRIL) British industry and economic policy. London, 1979. pp. 220. *bibliog.*

BROWN (C.J.F.) and SHERIFF (TOM D.) De-industrialisation in the UK: background statistics. London, [1979]. pp. 33. *(National Institute of Economic and Social Research. Discussion Papers. No. 23)*

DAVIS (RALPH) Professor of Economic History, Leicester University. The industrial revolution and British overseas trade. Leicester, 1979. pp. 135.

DE-INDUSTRIALISATION; edited by Frank Blackaby. London, 1979. pp. 275. *bibliogs. (National Institute of Economic and Social Research. Economic Policy Papers. 2)*

PAWSON (ERIC) The early industrial revolution: Britain in the eighteenth century. New York, 1979. pp. 233. *bibliog.*

SHERIFF (TOM D.) A deindustrialised Britain? London, 1979. pp. 23. *(Fabian Society. Research Series. [No.] 341)*

— — Classification.

NORTHERN REGION STRATEGY TEAM. Development of comparable statistics for employment and output, 1948 to date: procedures for adjustment. Newcastle-upon-Tyne, 1975. pp. 67. *(Working Papers. No. 17)*

— Intellectual life.

WILLEY (BASIL) The seventeenth-century background: studies in the thought of the age in relation to poetry and religion. London, 1979. pp. 284.

— Kings and rulers.

BROOKE (JOHN) 1920- . King George III. London, [1972]. pp. 411.

BROOKE (CHRISTOPHER NUGENT LAWRENCE) The Saxon and Norman Kings. London, 1978. pp. 224. *bibliog.*

KARSTEN (PETER) Patriot-heroes in England and America: political symbolism and changing values over three centuries. Madison, Wis., 1978. pp. 257.

FRYDE (NATALIE) The tyranny and fall of Edward II, 1321-1326. Cambridge, 1979. pp. 301. *bibliog.*

— Military policy.

BELLINI (JAMES) and PATTIE (GEOFFREY) A new world role for the medium power: the British opportunity. London, 1977. pp. 121.

— Ministry of Home Security.

BAKER (JOHN FLEETWOOD) Baron Baker. Enterprise versus bureaucracy: the development of structural air-raid precautions during the 2nd World War. Oxford, 1978. pp. 123.

— Ministry of Information.

McLAINE (IAN) Ministry of morale: home front morale and the Ministry of Information in World War II. London, 1979. pp. 325. *bibliog.*

— Moral conditions.

WARD (WILLIAM) Author of "How can I help England?". How can I help England?; and other addresses on the relationship of Christianity to social and political problems of today. London, 1906. pp. 168.

— Nationalism.

JENKINS (DANIEL T.) The British: their identity and their religion. London, 1975. pp. 201.

UNITED KINGDOM (Cont.)

— Navy Board — Officials and employees.

COLLINGE (J.M.) Navy Board officials, 1660-1832. London, 1978. pp. 153. *(London. University. Institute of Historical Research. Office-Holders in Modern Britain. 7)*

— Nobility.

TRUMBACH (RANDOLPH) The rise of the egalitarian family: aristocratic kinship and domestic relations in eighteenth-century England. New York, [1978]. pp. 324. *bibliog.*

PHILLIPS (GREGORY D.) The diehards: aristocratic society and politics in Edwardian England. Cambridge, Mass., 1979. pp. 228. *bibliog. (Harvard University. Harvard Historical Studies. vol. 96)*

— Officials and employees.

SAINTY (JOHN CHRISTOPHER) Colonial Office officials: officials of the Secretary of State for War 1794-1801, of the Secretary of State for War and Colonies 1801-54 and of the Secretary of State for Colonies 1854-70. London, 1976. pp. 52. *(London. University. Institute of Historical Research. Office-Holders in Modern Britain. 6)*

See also the subdivision Officials and employees under the names of government departments and offices.

— Parliament.

RAISON (TIMOTHY) Power and Parliament. Oxford, [1979]. pp. 122.

— — Elections.

HANHAM (HAROLD JOHN) Elections and party management: politics in the time of Disraeli and Gladstone. new ed. Hassocks, [1978]. pp. 468. *bibliog.*

CRUICKSHANKS (EVELINE) Political untouchables: the Tories and the '45. London, 1979. pp. 166. *bibliog.*

— — History.

WALKER (ERNESTEIN) Struggle for the reform of Parliament, 1853-1867. New York, [1977]. pp. 212. *bibliog.*

FLICK (CARLOS) The Birmingham Political Union and the movements for reform in Britain, 1830-1839. Hamden, Conn., 1978. pp. 206. *bibliog.*

EDWARDS (Sir JOHN GORONWY) The second century of the English parliament. Oxford, 1979. pp. 90. *(Oxford. University. Ford Lectures. 1960/61)*

RUSSELL (CONRAD) Parliaments and English politics, 1621-1629. Oxford, 1979. pp. 453.

— — House of Commons.

NORTON (PHILIP) The House of Commons in the 1970s: three views on reform. Hull, 1978. fo. 15. *(Hull. University. Department of Politics. Hull Papers in Politics. No. 3)*

STOBAUGH (BEVERLY PARKER) Women and Parliament, 1918-1970. New York, [1978]. pp. 152. *bibliog.*

The HOUSE of Commons in the twentieth century: essays by members of the Study of Parliament Group; edited by S.A. Walkland. Oxford, 1979. pp. 649.

MARSDEN (PHILIP) The officers of the Commons, 1363-1978. London, H.M.S.O., 1979. pp. 262. *bibliog.*

VALLANCE (ELIZABETH M.) Women in the house: a study of women members of Parliament. London, 1979. pp. 212. *bibliog.*

— — — History.

JULIAN (MARK ROBERT) English economic legislation 1660-1714. 1979. fo. 376. *bibliog.* Typescript. M.Phil. *(London) thesis: unpublished. This thesis is the property of London University and may not be removed from the Library.*

— — House of Lords.

CONSERVATIVE REVIEW COMMITTEE [ON THE FUTURE OF THE HOUSE OF LORDS]. The House of Lords: the report of the...Committee; [the Lord Home of the Hirsel, chairman]. London, 1978. pp. 63. *bibliog.*

LIBERAL PARTY. Reform of the House of Lords. London, 1978. pp. 5.

McCAHILL (MICHAEL W.) Order and equipoise: the peerage and the House of Lords, 1783-1806. London, 1978. pp. 256. *bibliog. (Royal Historical Society. Studies in History)*

UNDERHILL (NICHOLAS) The Lord Chancellor. Lavenham, 1978. pp. 180. *bibliog.*

PHILLIPS (GREGORY D.) The diehards: aristocratic society and politics in Edwardian England. Cambridge, Mass., 1979. pp. 228. *bibliog. (Harvard University. Harvard Historical Studies. vol. 96)*

STEVENS (ROBERT BOCKING) Law and politics: the House of Lords as a judicial body, 1800-1976. London, 1979. pp. 701. *bibliog.*

— — Officials and employees.

MARSDEN (PHILIP) The officers of the Commons, 1363-1978. London, H.M.S.O., 1979. pp. 262. *bibliog.*

— Politics and government.

PENNAN (JOHN SIMPSON) The irresistible movement of democracy. New York, 1923. pp. 729.

CROSS (JOHN ARTHUR) British public administration. London, 1970. pp. 190. *bibliogs.*

PAGE (EDWARD) Why should central-local relations in Scotland be any different from those in England? Glasgow, [1978]. fo. 46. *(Glasgow. University of Strathclyde. Centre for the Study of Public Policy. Studies in Public Policy. No. 21)*

PINCHER (CHAPMAN) Inside story: a documentary of the pursuit of power. London, 1978. pp. 400.

POLITICAL leaders in local government; edited by G.W. Jones and Alan Norton. Birmingham, [1978]. pp. 233.

BROWN (RUPERT GEOFFREY STUART) and STEEL (D.R.) The administrative process in Britain. 2nd ed. London, 1979. pp. 352. *bibliog.*

FRY (GEOFFREY KINGDON) The growth of government: the development of ideas about the role of the state and the machinery and functions of government in Britain since 1780. London, 1979. pp. 295. *bibliog.*

HOGWOOD (BRIAN W.) Government and shipbuilding: the politics of industrial change. Farnborough, [1979]. pp. 302. *bibliog.*

The HOUSE of Commons in the twentieth century: essays by members of the Study of Parliament Group; edited by S.A. Walkland. Oxford, 1979. pp. 649.

RICHARDSON (J.J.) and JORDAN (A.G.) Governing under pressure: the policy process in a post-parliamentary democracy. Oxford, 1979. pp. 212. *bibliog.*

SAUNDERS (PETER) Urban politics: a sociological interpretation. London, 1979. pp. 383. *bibliog.*

U.K. Social Science Research Council. Panel on Central-Local Government Relationships. 1979. Central-local government relationships; report...to the Research Initiatives Board; [G.W. Jones, chairman]. London, [1979]. 1 vol. (various pagings).

— — Research.

JONES (J. BARRY) A register of research into United Kingdom politics. Glasgow, 1978. pp. 23. *(Glasgow. University of Strathclyde. Centre for the Study of Public Policy. Studies in Public Policy. No. 23)*

— — Sources.

COOK (CHRISTOPHER PIERS) and WEEKS (JEFFREY) compilers. Sources in British political history, 1900-1951: compiled for the British Library of Political and Economic Science; vol. 5. London, 1978. pp. 221.

— — 1485-1603.

HAM (R.E.) The county and the Kingdom: Sir Herbert Croft and the Elizabethan state. Washington, D.C., [1977]. pp. 304.

WILLIAMS (PENRY) The Tudor regime. Oxford, 1979. pp. 486.

— — 1603-1714.

G. (R.) A copy of a letter from an officer of the army in Ireland. Exeter, 1974. pp. 23. *Facsimile reprint of 1st ed., London, 1656.*

HAM (R.E.) The county and the Kingdom: Sir Herbert Croft and the Elizabethan state. Washington, D.C., [1977]. pp. 304.

KARSTEN (PETER) Patriot-heroes in England and America: political symbolism and changing values over three centuries. Madison, Wis., 1978. pp. 257.

— — 1603-1649.

WHITE (STEPHEN D.) Sir Edward Coke and "the grievances of the Commonwealth", 1621-1628. Chapel Hill, [1979]. pp. 327. *bibliog.*

— — 1660-1714.

JULIAN (MARK ROBERT) English economic legislation 1660-1714. 1979. fo. 376. *bibliog.* Typescript. M.Phil. *(London) thesis: unpublished. This thesis is the property of London University and may not be removed from the Library.*

— — 1700-1799.

TOOHEY (ROBERT E.) Liberty and empire: British radical solutions to the American problem, 1774-1776. Lexington, [1978]. pp. 210. *bibliog.*

— — 1800-1899.

ASPECTS of government in nineteenth-century Britain; [by] Valerie Cromwell [and others]. Dublin, [1978]. pp. 134. *bibliogs.*

FLICK (CARLOS) The Birmingham Political Union and the movements for reform in Britain, 1830-1839. Hamden, Conn., 1978. pp. 206. *bibliog.*

The MIDDLE class in politics; edited by John Garrard and others. Farnborough, Hants, [1978]. pp. 373. *bibliog. Based on a conference held at the University of Salford in 1977.*

— — 1800-1837.

SACK (JAMES J.) The Grenvillites, 1801-29: party politics and factionalism in the age of Pitt and Liverpool. Urbana, [1979]. pp. 244. *bibliog.*

— — 1837-1901.

MACKINTOSH (Sir ALEXANDER) The story of Mr. Chamberlain's life. London, 1914. pp. 144.

GLADSTONE (WILLIAM EWART) Autobiographical memoranda, 1845-1866; edited by John Brooke and Mary Sorensen. London, 1978. pp. 292. *(U.K. Historical Manuscripts Commission. The Prime Ministers' Papers. W.E. Gladstone. 3)*

HANHAM (HAROLD JOHN) Elections and party management: politics in the time of Disraeli and Gladstone. new ed. Hassocks, [1978]. pp. 468. *bibliog.*

HAWKINS (ANGUS B.) A forgotten crisis: Gladstone and finance during the 1850's. London, 1978. fo. 39. *(London. University. London School of Economics and Political Science. Gladstone Memorial Trust Prize Essays. 1978)* Typescript.

UNITED KINGDOM (Cont.)

KREIN (DAVID F.) The last Palmerston government: foreign policy, domestic politics, and the genesis of "splendid isolation". Ames, Iowa, 1978. pp. 252. *bibliog.*

ROBERTS (DAVID) Assistant Professor of History at Dartmouth College. Paternalism in early Victorian England. London, 1979. pp. 337. *bibliog.*

— — 1900- .

MILIBAND (RALPH) Parliamentary socialism: a study in the politics of labour. 2nd ed. New York, [1972]. pp. 384.

NATIONAL government 1931: extracts from the 'Times' January to October 1931; introduced and edited by Colin Bell. London, 1975. pp. 209. *bibliog.*

The MIDDLE class in politics; edited by John Garrard and others. Farnborough, Hants, [1978]. pp. 373. *bibliog. Based on a conference held at the University of Salford in 1977.*

— — 1901-1918.

MACKINTOSH (Sir ALEXANDER) The story of Mr. Chamberlain's life. London, 1914. pp. 144.

RIDDELL (GEORGE ALLARDICE) 1st Baron Riddell. More pages from my diary, 1908-1914. London, 1934. pp. 238.

PHILLIPS (GREGORY D.) The diehards: aristocratic society and politics in Edwardian England. Cambridge, Mass., 1979. pp. 228. *bibliog. (Harvard University. Harvard Historical Studies. vol. 96)*

— — 1918-1945.

BERKELEY (HUMPHRY) The myth that will not die: the formation of the National Government, 1931. London, [1978]. pp. 143.

ORDE (ANNE) Great Britain and international security, 1920-1926. London, 1978. pp. 244. *bibliog. (Royal Historical Society. Studies in History)*

TAYLOR (IAN HAMILTON) War and the development of Labour's domestic programme, 1939-45. 1977 [or rather 1978]. fo. 275. *bibliog.* Typescript. Ph.D. (London) thesis: unpublished. *This thesis is the property of London University and may not be removed from the Library.*

— — 1945- .

SOCIALISM the British way...: the socialist experiment carried out in Great Britain by the Labour government of 1945; by Evan F.M. Durbin [and others]; edited by Donald Munro. London, [1948]. pp. 345.

The MODERNIZATION of British government; edited by William Thornhill. London, 1975. pp. 322.

The CORPORATE state: reality or myth?; a symposium. London, 1976. pp. 160. *Papers from a symposium organised by the Centre for Studies in Social Policy held in London on 24th September, 1976.*

SMITH (BRIAN CLIVE) Policy-making in British government: an analysis of power and rationality. London, 1976. pp. 210. *bibliog.*

BLONDEL (JEAN) 1929- . Voters, parties, and leaders: the social fabric of British politics. rev. ed. Harmondsworth, [1977]. pp. 271. *bibliog.*

CONSERVATIVE AND UNIONIST PARTY. The campaign guide, 1977; [edited by Anthony Greenland]. London, [1977]. pp. 789.

GOODMAN (ARNOLD ABRAHAM) Baron Goodman. How much paternalism? [Colchester], 1977. pp. 19. *(University of Essex. Noel Buxton Lectures. 1977)*

JENKINS (ROY HARRIS) The quest for national satisfaction. Birmingham, 1977. pp. 11. *(Birmingham. University. Baggs Memorial Lectures. 1977)*

BARKER (RODNEY STEVEN) Political ideas in modern Britain. London, 1978. pp. 246. *bibliog.*

The COMING confrontation: will the open society survive to 1989?; [by] W.H. Chaloner [and others]. London, 1978. pp. 250. *bibliogs. (Institute of Economic Affairs. Hobart Paperbacks. 12)*

JOHNSON (PAUL) Britain's own road to serfdom. London, 1978. pp. 15. *(Conservative Political Centre. [Publications]. No. 633)*

LABOUR PARTY. Good for Britain: Labour's record in government. London, [1978]. pp. 37.

LABOUR PARTY. National Executive Committee. Statements to annual conference. London, [1978]. pp. 67.

LEWIS (W. RUSSELL) Tony Benn: a critical biography. London, 1978. pp. 203.

MAUDLING (REGINALD) Memoirs. London, 1978. pp. 285.

MICHIE (ALISTAIR) and HOGGART (SIMON) The pact: the inside story of the Lib-Lab government, 1977-8. London, 1978. pp. 183.

PEELE (GILLIAN) Change, decay and the British constitution. Hull, 1978. fo. 12. *(Hull. University. Department of Politics. Hull Papers in Politics. No. 1)*

STEEL (DAVID) 1938- . A new majority for a new parliament. London, [1978]. pp. 12. *Speech...at the...assembly of the Liberal Party, Southport, 1978.*

STUART (JAMES GIBB) The mind benders: the gradual revolution and Scottish independence. Glasgow, 1978. pp. 180. *bibliog.*

TRADES UNION CONGRESS and LABOUR PARTY. Liaison Committee. Into the eighties: an agreement. London, 1978. pp. 16.

BENN (ANTHONY NEIL WEDGWOOD) Arguments for socialism [based on miscellaneous writings]; edited by Chris Mullin. London, 1979. pp. 206.

BRITISH politics today: a students' guide; edited by Bill Jones and Dennis Kavanagh. Manchester, [1979]. pp. 145. *bibliog.*

LIBERAL PARTY. The real fight is for Britain. London, [1979]. pp. 18.

RAISON (TIMOTHY) Power and Parliament. Oxford, [1979]. pp. 122.

SKED (ALAN) and COOK (CHRISTOPHER PIERS) Post-war Britain: a political history. Brighton, 1979. pp. 394. *bibliog.*

THATCHER (MARGARET) and HARRIS (KENNETH) Margaret Thatcher talks to the Observer; interviewed by Kenneth Harris. London, [1979]. pp. 13.

— Population.

DEMOGRAPHIC change and social policy: the uncertain future; edited by Martin Buxton and Edward Craven. London, [1976]. pp. 87.

GOTTFRIED (ROBERT S.) Epidemic disease in fifteenth century England: the medical response and the demographic consequences. Leicester, 1978. pp. 262. *bibliog.*

U.K. Census, 1971. Census, 1971: Great Britain; as constituted on 1st April 1974 for England and Wales and 16th May 1975 for Scotland: migration tables, 10 per cent sample. London, 1978. pp. 304.

WACHTER (KENNETH W.) and others. Statistical studies of historical social structure. New York, [1978]. pp. 229. *bibliog.*

WILLIAMS (ROBERT MICHAEL) British population. 2nd ed. London, 1978. pp. 130. *bibliog.*

KELSALL (ROGER KEITH) Population. 4th ed. London, 1979. pp. 136. *bibliog.*

— Public Expenditure Survey Committee.

CLARKE (Sir RICHARD WILLIAM BARNES) Public expenditure, management and controls: the development of the Public Expenditure Survey Committee (PESC). London, 1978. pp. 212.

— Race relations.

WARD (ROBIN W.) Ugandan Asians in Britain: some local variations in the potential for resettlement; paper presented [to] (Seminar [on] Ugandan Asians, London, 2 December 1976). [Bristol], Social Science Research Council Research Unit on Ethnic Relations, [1976?]. fo. (11).

COMMUNITY RELATIONS COMMISSION and RUNNYMEDE TRUST. Industrial training boards and race relations: a discussion paper. London, 1977. pp. 30, (26). *bibliog.*

NATIONAL CONFERENCE OF COMMUNITY RELATIONS COUNCILS, LEICESTER, 1977. Conference report: strategy statement, speeches, etc. London, Commission for Racial Equality, 1977. pp. 43.

CROSS (CRISPIN PATRIC ROBERT) Ethnic minorities in the inner city: the ethnic dimension in urban deprivation in England. London, Commission for Racial Equality, 1978. pp. 183. *bibliog.*

FIVE views of multi-racial Britain; talks on race relations broadcast by BBC TV. London, 1978. pp. 80.

FIVE views of multi-racial Britain; talks on race relations broadcast by BBC TV; (by John Rex and others). 2nd ed. London, Commission for Racial Equality, 1978. pp. 77.

PEARN (M.A.) Employment testing and the goal of equal opportunity: the American experience. [London], 1978. pp. 38.

TAVISTOCK INSTITUTE OF HUMAN RELATIONS. Application of race relations policy in the civil service. London, H.M.S.O., 1978. pp. 275.

U.K. Home Office. 1978. Proposals for replacing section 11 of the Local Government Act 1966: a consultative document: (a new form of grant aid to assist local authorities in meeting the special needs of ethnic minorities). [London], 1978. pp. 11.

JEFFCOATE (ROBERT) Positive image: towards a multiracial curriculum. London, 1979. pp. 124. *bibliogs.*

RACISM and political action in Britain; edited by Robert Miles and Annie Phizacklea. London, 1979. pp. 246. *bibliogs. Papers from the Conference on Racism and Political Action in Britain, held by the Social Science Research Council Research Unit on Ethnic Relations, 1977.*

— Relations (general) with Poland.

LIPOŃSKI (WOJCIECH) Polska a Brytania, 1801-1830: próby politycznego i cywilizacyjnego dźwignięcia kraju w oparciu o Wielką Brytanię. Poznań, 1978. pp. 195. *(Poznań. Uniwersytet. Seria Filologia Angielska. Nr. 11) With English and French summaries.*

— Relations (general) with the East (Near East).

SEARIGHT (SARAH) The British in the Middle East. rev. ed. London, 1979. pp. 290. *bibliog.*

— Religion.

JENKINS (DANIEL T.) The British: their identity and their religion. London, 1975. pp. 201.

— Rural conditions.

USHER (RUFUS) Essays on the dwellings of the poor, and other subjects. 2nd ed. London, 1877. pp. 143.

RURAL transport and accessibility; [by] M.J. Moseley [and others];...final report to the Department of the Environment. Norwich, 1977. 2 vols. (in 1). *bibliog.*

RURAL poverty: poverty, deprivation and planning in rural areas; [papers based on drafts presented at a conference organized by the Child Poverty Action Group in Colchester in 1977]; edited by Alan Walker. London, 1978. pp. 117. *(Child Poverty Action Group. Poverty Pamphlets. 37)*

WHITBY (MARTIN CHARLES) and WILLIS (KENNETH G.) Rural resource development: an economic approach. 2nd ed. London, 1978. pp. 303. *bibliog.*

RURAL deprivation and planning; edited by J. Martin Shaw. Norwich, [1979]. pp. 207. *bibliogs.*

— Secretary of State.

KYNASTON (DAVID) The Secretary of State. Lavenham, 1978. pp. 177. *bibliog.*

SEDGEMORE (BRIAN) Mr Secretary of State: [a novel]. London, 1978. pp. 154.

— Social conditions.

TRISTAN (FLORA) Promenades dans Londres; ou, L'aristocratie et les prolétaire anglais; édition établie et commentée par François Bédarida. Paris, 1978. pp. 358. *(Paris. Université de Paris I (Panthéon-Sorbonne). Centre d'Histoire du Syndicalisme. Collection) Reprint of 1840 ed.*

WARD (WILLIAM) Author of "How can I help England?". How can I help England?; and other addresses on the relationship of Christianity to social and political problems of today. London, 1906. pp. 168.

The HEART of the Empire: discussions of problems of modern city life in England; [edited by] C.F.G. Masterman; [facsimile reprint of the edition of 1901] edited with an introduction by Bentley B. Gilbert. Brighton, 1973. pp. 415,xlvii.

WEDGE (PETER) and PROSSER (HILARY) Born to fail? London, 1973 repr. 1977. pp. 64.

BLONDEL (JEAN) 1929- . Voters, parties, and leaders: the social fabric of British politics. rev. ed. Harmondsworth, [1977]. pp. 271. *bibliog.*

ROBERTS (KENNETH) The working class. London, 1978. pp. 206. *bibliog.*

SEABROOK (JEREMY) What went wrong?: working people and the ideals of the labour movement. London, 1978. pp. 286.

WEBBER (RICHARD J.) Parliamentary constituencies: a socio-economic classification. [London], 1978. pp. 58. *(U.K. Office of Population Censuses and Surveys. Occasional Papers. 13)*

ROBERTS (DAVID) Assistant Professor of History at Dartmouth College. Paternalism in early Victorian England. London, 1979. pp. 337. *bibliog.*

SOCIAL problems and the city: geographical perspectives; edited by David T. Herbert and David M. Smith. Oxford, 1979. pp. 2717. *bibliogs.*

WORKING class culture: studies in history and theory; edited by John Clarke [and others]. London, 1979. pp. 301. *bibliog.*

— Social history.

OPEN UNIVERSITY. Arts A322 [Course Team]. Block 3, units 9-12. English urban history, 1500-1780: the traditional community under stress; ([with] Supplementary material). Milton Keynes, 1977. 2 pts. (in 1 vol.) *bibliogs.*

OPEN UNIVERSITY. Arts A322 [Course Team]. Block 4, units 13-16. English urban history, 1500-1780: the rise of the new urban society. Milton Keynes, 1977. pp. 120. *bibliogs.*

THRUPP (SYLVIA LETTICE) Society and history: essays...; edited by Raymond Grew and Nicholas H. Steneck. Ann Arbor, [1977]. pp. 363. *bibliog.*

FEINGOLD (RICHARD) Nature and society: later eighteenth-century uses of the pastoral and georgic. Hassocks, 1978. pp. 209.

GIROUARD (MARK) Life in the English country house: a social and architectural history. New Haven, 1978. pp. 344.

LONGMAN atlas of modern British history: a visual guide to British society and politics, 1700-1970; compiled by Chris Cook and John Stevenson. London, 1978. pp. 208. *bibliog.*

MACFARLANE (ALAN DONALD JAMES) The origins of English individualism: the family, property and social transition. Oxford, [1978]. pp. 216. *bibliog.*

MILLER (EDWARD) M.A. and HATCHER (JOHN) Medieval England: rural society and economic change 1086-1348. London, 1978. pp. 302. *bibliog.*

POPE (NORRIS) Dickens and charity. London, 1978. pp. 303.

PURITANS and revolutionaries: essays in seventeenth-century history presented to Christopher Hill; edited by Donald Pennington and Keith Thomas. Oxford, 1978. pp. 149. *bibliog.*

TREVELYAN (GEORGE MACAULAY) English social history: a survey of six centuries from Chaucer to Queen Victoria. [new ed.] London, [1978]. pp. 555. *bibliog.*

EMSLEY (CLIVE) British society and the French wars, 1793-1815. London, 1979. pp. 216. *bibliog.*

MORRIS (ROBERT JOHN) Class and class consciousness in the Industrial Revolution 1780-1850. Edinburgh, 1979. pp. 79. *bibliog. (Economic History Society. Studies in Economic and Social History)*

The SEARCH for wealth and stability: essays in economic and social history presented to M.W. Flinn; edited by T.C. Smout. London, 1979. pp. 291.

WALKER (JAMES) 1898- . British economic and social history, 1700-1977;...revised by C.W. Munn. 2nd ed. Plymouth, 1979. pp. 448.

— — Sources.

FARINGTON (JOSEPH) The diary of Joseph Farington; edited by Kenneth Garlick and Angus Macintyre. New Haven, 1978 in progress. *(Paul Mellon Centre for Studies in British Art. Studies in British Art)*

— Social life and customs.

BURN (JAMES DAWSON) The autobiography of a beggar boy;...edited with an introduction by David Vincent. London, [1978]. pp. 205. *bibliog. Reprint of the first edition published in London, 1855.*

FOX (ROBERT BARCLAY) Barclay Fox's journal; edited by R.L. Brett. London, 1979. pp. 426.

— Social policy.

The HEART of the Empire: discussions of problems of modern city life in England; [edited by] C.F.G. Masterman; [facsimile reprint of the edition of 1901] edited with an introduction by Bentley B. Gilbert. Brighton, 1973. pp. 415,xlvii.

DEMOGRAPHIC change and social policy: the uncertain future; edited by Martin Buxton and Edward Craven. London, [1976]. pp. 87.

ROBSON (WILLIAM ALEXANDER) Welfare state and welfare society: illusion and reality. London, 1976, repr. 1977. pp. 184.

TITMUSS (RICHARD MORRIS) Commitment to welfare. 2nd ed. London, 1976. pp. 272. *bibliogs.*

COWHERD (RAYMOND GIBSON) Political economists and the English Poor Laws: a historical study of the influence of classical economics on the formation of social welfare policy. Athens, Ohio, [1977]. pp. 300. *bibliog.*

BELOFF (MAX) The tide of collectivism: can it be turned? London, 1978. pp. 7. *(Conservative Political Centre. [Publications]. No. 629)*

DAVIES (BLEDDYN PRYCE) and REDDIN (MIKE) Universality, selectivity, and effectiveness in social policy. London, 1978. pp. 264. *bibliog.*

EDWARDS (JOHN) Author of A study in access, and BATLEY (RICHARD) The politics of positive discrimination: an evaluation of the Urban Programme, 1967-77. London, 1978. pp. 287. *bibliog.*

PICKVANCE (CHRISTOPHER GEOFFREY) Policies as chameleons: an interpretation of regional policy and office policy in Britain. Canterbury, 1978. fo. 48. *bibliog.*

UNITED KINGDOM (Cont.)

RODGERS (BARBARA N.) Human well-being: challenges for the 1980s: social, economic and political action. London, 1978. pp. 25. *bibliog. Report written on behalf of the United Kingdom National Committee of the International Council on Social Welfare for the XIX International Conference on Social Welfare, Jerusalem, 1978.*

SIMKINS (JEAN) and TICKNER (VINCENT) Whose benefit: an examination of the existing system of cash benefits and related provisions for intrinsically handicapped adults and their families. London, [1978]. pp. 245. *bibliog.*

TRADES UNION CONGRESS and LABOUR PARTY. Liaison Committee. Into the eighties: an agreement. London, 1978. pp. 16.

U.K. Central Policy Review Staff. 1978. Housing and social policies: some interactions; report. London, 1978. pp. 50.

INTRODUCING social policy; edited by David C. Marsh. London, 1979. pp. 286. *bibliogs.*

LAWLESS (PAUL) Urban deprivation and government initiative. London, 1979. pp. 251. *bibliog.*

McKAY (DAVID H.) and COX (ANDREW W.) The politics of urban change. London, 1979. pp. 297. *bibliog.*

ROBERTS (DAVID) Assistant Professor of History at Dartmouth College. Paternalism in early Victorian England. London, 1979. pp. 337. *bibliog.*

SIMPKIN (MICHAEL) Trapped within welfare: surviving social work. London, 1979. pp. 168.

— Statistics, Medical.

U.K. Office of Population Censuses and Surveys. Morbidity statistics from general practice: second national study. a., 1971/72- London.

— Statistics, Vital.

GLASS (DAVID VICTOR) compiler. The development of population statistics: a collective reprint of materials concerning the history of census taking and vital registration in England and Wales. Farnborough, 1973. pp. 348.

U.K. Office of Population Censuses and Surveys. Medical Statistics Division. Social and biological factors in infant mortality. a., 1975/76(3rd)- London.

U.K. Office of Population Censuses and Surveys. Medical Statistics Division. 1977. Mortality surveillance, 1968-1975, England and Wales: deaths and rates by A-list cause, sex and age group. [London, 1977]. 1 vol. (unfoliated).

PRESSAT (ROLAND) Statistical demography;...translated and adapted by Damien A. Courtney. London, 1978. pp. 150.

U.K. Office of Population Censuses and Surveys. Medical Statistics Division. 1978. Mortality surveillance, 1968-1976, England and Wales: deaths and rates by A-list cause, sex and age group: microfiche version. [London, 1978]. Microfiche (1 card) and accompanying booklet.

— Treasury.

PEDEN (G.C.) British rearmament and the Treasury: 1932-1939. Edinburgh, 1979. pp. 227. *bibliog.*

— Voting registers.

U.K. Working Party on the Electoral Register. 1978. Report; [J.E. Hayzelden, chairman]. London, 1978. pp. 38.

— Commonwealth.

NYERERE (JULIUS KAMBARAGE) The economic challenge: dialogue or confrontation. London, [1976]. pp. 12. *Address given to the Royal Commonwealth Society in London in 1975.*

MANSERGH (PHILIP NICHOLAS SETON) The prelude to partition: concept and aims in Ireland and India. Cambridge, 1978. pp. 62. *(Cambridge. University. Commonwealth Lectures. 1976)*

UNITED KINGDOM (Cont.)

WINDEYER (Sir WILLIAM JOHN VICTOR) Australia in the Commonwealth. London, 1978. pp. 32. *(Cambridge. University. Commonwealth Lectures. 1977)*

COMMONWEALTH CURRENTS; pd. by Commonwealth Secretariat. irreg., current issues only. London.

—— History.

BRABAZON (REGINALD) 12th Earl of Meath. Memories of the twentieth century. London, 1924. pp. 310.

GANN (LEWIS H.) and DUIGNAN (PETER) The rulers of British Africa, 1870-1914. London, [1978]. pp. 406. *bibliog.*

—— Politics and government.

HANCOCK (Sir WILLIAM KEITH) Empire in the changing world. New York, 1943. pp. 186.

ABRAHAM (ARTHUR) Mende government and politics under colonial rule: a historical study of political change in Sierra Leone, 1890-1937. Freetown, Sierra Leone, 1978. pp. 330. *bibliog.*

GARNER (JOE) The Commonwealth Office, 1925-68. London, 1978. pp. 474. *bibliog.*

COOK (CHRISTOPHER PIERS) and PAXTON (JOHN) Commonwealth political facts. London, 1979. pp. 293.

—— Societies, etc.

COMMONWEALTH SECRETARIAT. Information Division. Commonwealth organisations: a handbook of official and unofficial organisation active in the Commonwealth. 2nd ed. London, 1979. pp. 125. *bibliog.*

UNITED MINE WORKERS OF AMERICA.

DUBOFSKY (MELVYN) and VAN TINE (WARREN R.) John L. Lewis: a biography. New York, [1977]. pp. 619. *bibliog.*

UNITED NATIONS.

DIVINE (ROBERT A.) Second chance: the triumph of internationalism in America during World War II. New York, [1967] repr. 1971. pp. 371.

HUMAN rights: a compilation of international instruments of the United Nations. (A/CONF.32/4). New York, United Nations, 1967. pp. 94.

UNITED NATIONS. Office of Public Information. 1968. The United Nations and human rights. New York, 1968. pp. 93.

UNITED NATIONS. Office of Public Information. 1969. A principle in torment, I. The United Nations and Southern Rhodesia. New York, 1969. pp. 71.

UNITED NATIONS. Office of Public Information. 1970. A principle in torment, II. The United Nations and Portuguese administered territories. New York, 1970. pp. 60.

The EVOLVING United Nations: a prospect for peace?; edited by Kenneth J. Twitchett. New York, 1971. pp. 239. *bibliog.*

UNITED NATIONS. Office of Public Information. 1971. A principle in torment, III. The United Nations and Namibia. New York, 1971. pp. 44.

BELGIUM. Ministère des Affaires Etrangères, du Commerce Extérieur et de la Coopération au Développement. 1972. Stability through co-operation; by Pierre Harmel, Minister for Foreign Affairs: (speech made...at the 27th session of the United Nations General Assembly in New York, 5 October 1972). [Brussels], 1972. pp. 12. *(Memo from Belgium. No. 154-155)*

UNITED NATIONS. Office of Public Information. 1972. The United Nations and the fight against drug abuse. New York, 1972. pp. 30.

HUMAN rights: a compilation of international instruments of the United Nations. (ST/HR/1). [2nd ed.] New York, United Nations, 1973. pp. 106.

BOKOR-SZEGÖ (HANNA) The role of the United Nations in international legislation; translated by Dr. Sándor Simon. Amsterdam, 1978. pp. 191. *bibliog.*

HAGUE. International Court of Justice. [Series D.] Acts and Documents concerning the Organization of the Court. No. 4. Charter of the United Nations, statute and rules of Court and other documents. [4th. ed.] [The Hague], 1978. pp. 268. *In English and French.*

HUMAN rights: a compilation of international instruments. (ST/HR/1/Rev.1). [3rd ed.] New York, United Nations, 1978. pp. 132.

JACOBSEN (KURT) The General Assembly of the United Nations: a quantitative analysis of conflict, inequality, and relevance. Oslo, [1978]. pp. 209. *bibliog.*

RAJAN (MANNARASWAMIGHALA SREERANGA) Sovereignty over natural resources. Atlantic Highlands, 1978. pp. 176.

U.S. policy in international institutions: defining reasonable options in an unreasonable world; edited by Seymour Maxwell Finger and Joseph R. Harbert. Boulder, Colo., [1978]. pp. 489. *bibliog.*

LUARD (DAVID EVAN TRANT) The United Nations: how it works and what it does. London, 1979. pp. 187. *bibliog.*

STOESSINGER (JOHN GEORGE) The might of nations: world politics in our time. 6th ed. New York, [1979]. pp. 517. *bibliogs.*

FACTS; issued by the Centre for Economic and Social Information/OPI (United Nations). irreg. New York. *Current issues only kept.*

UNITAR NEWS; [pd. by United Nations Institute for Training and Research]. q., New York. *Current issues only kept.*

UNITED NATIONS. Information Service. Press releases. irreg., current issue only. Geneva.

— Armed forces.

ABI-SAAB (GEORGES) The United Nations operation in the Congo 1960-1964. Oxford, 1978. pp. 206. *Published under the auspices of the American Society of International Law.*

UNITED Nations peace-keeping: legal essays; edited by A. Cassese. Alphen aan den Rijn, 1978. pp. 255.

— Bibliography.

HUEFNER (KLAUS) and NAUMANN (JENS) compilers. The United Nations system: international bibliography; Das System der Vereinten Nationen: internationale Bibliographie. München, 1977-79. 4 vols. *Contents: vols. 2A and B. Learned journals, 1965-(1975). vols. 3A and B. Monographs and articles in collective volumes, 1965-(1975). Contents list, introductory matter and headings in English and German.*

— Economic assistance.

UNDP BUSINESS BULLETIN; pd.by the United Nations Development Programme. m., Jl 1974[1st]- New York. *Supersedes in part Pre-investment news (Ja 1967 - Ap/Mr 1974).*

FACTS; issued by the Centre for Economic and Social Information/OPI (United Nations). irreg. New York. *Current issues only kept.*

— Secretariat.

CARNEGIE ENDOWMENT FOR INTERNATIONAL PEACE. United Nations Studies. 11. The secretariat of the United Nations; by Sydney D. Bailey. rev. ed. Westport, Conn., 1978. pp. 128. *bibliog. Reprint of the revised edition of 1964.*

— Botswana.

BOTSWANA. President, 1966- (Khama). Address to the General Assembly of the United Nations... September 1969. Gaborone, [1969]. pp. (7).

— China.

KIM (SAMUEL S.) China, the United Nations and world order. Princeton, 1979. pp. 581. *bibliog.*

— South Africa.

POSSONY (STEFAN THOMAS) South Africa, the Hague decision and the United Nations; (from an address to the Commonwealth Club, San Francisco, 4 November 1966). [London, Department of Information, South African Embassy, 1967]. pp. 10. *(Reports on the State of South Africa. No.31)*

SOUTH AFRICA. Information Service of South Africa, New York. 1967. Setting the record straight. New York, [1967]. pp. 24.

— United Kingdom.

U.K. Foreign and Commonwealth Office. 1978. British policy towards the United Nations. London, 1978. pp. 39. *(Foreign Policy Documents. No. 26)*

— Zaire.

RHODESIA. Ministry of Information, Immigration and Tourism. 1978. The United Nations in central Africa, 1961-62: a review of United Nations military achievement in Central Africa, in the light of proposed activity of the United Nations in Rhodesia. [Salisbury, 1978]. pp. 16.

UNITED NATIONS CONFERENCE ON TRADE AND DEVELOPMENT.

RHYNE (CHARLES S.) and others. Law-making activities of the United Nations Conference on Trade and Development. Washington, D.C., 1976. pp. 120.

UNITED NATIONS. Conference on Trade and Development, 4th, Nairobi, 1976. Proceedings of the...Conference..., fourth session, Nairobi, 5- 31 May 1976. (TD/218). New York, 1977-78. 3 vols. (in 1).

UNITED NATIONS ECONOMIC COMMISSION FOR EUROPE.

COUNCIL FOR MUTUAL ECONOMIC ASSISTANCE. 1977. Information on the CMEA activities in developing co-operation with the United Nations Economic Commission for Europe in 1976-1977. Moscow, 1977. pp. 13.

UNITED NATIONS EDUCATIONAL, SCIENTIFIC AND CULTURAL ORGANIZATION.

MYLONAS (DENIS) La genèse de l'Unesco: la Conférence des Ministres alliés de l'Education (1942-1945). Bruxelles, 1976. pp. 495. *bibliog.*

HOGGART (RICHARD) An idea and its servants: UNESCO from within. London, 1978. pp. 220. *bibliog.*

UNITED NATIONS INDUSTRIAL DEVELOPMENT ORGANIZATION.

UNIDO NEWSLETTER; [pd. by] United Nations Industrial Development Organization. m.,(formerly bi-m.), Je 1967 (no.1)- New York.

UNITED STATES

— Air Force — Weapons systems.

CULVER (JOHN C.) and McLUCAS (JOHN L.) Prospects for the strategic bomber: two views. Washington, [1978]. pp. 24. *(American Enterprise Institute for Public Policy Research. AEI Defense Reviews. Vol. 2. No. 1)*

— Appropriations and expenditures.

HOLT (CHARLES FRANK) The role of state government in the nineteenth century American economy, 1820-1902: a quantitative study. New York, 1977. pp. 325. *bibliog. Originally presented as a thesis, Purdue University, 1970.*

SINGER (NEIL M.) Public microeconomics: an introduction to government finance. 2nd ed. Boston, Mass., [1976]. pp. 447.

UNITED STATES

CATSAMBAS (THANOS) Regional impacts of federal fiscal policy: theory and estimation of economic incidence. Lexington, Mass., [1978]. pp. 135. *bibliog.*

WEIDENBAUM (MURRAY L.) and DE FINA (ROBERT) The cost of federal regulation of economic activity. Washington, 1978. pp. 33. *(American Enterprise Institute for Public Policy Research. Reprints. No. 88)*

— Armed forces.

COULAM (ROBERT F.) Illusions of choice: the F-111 and the problem of weapons acquisition reform. Princeton, [1977]. pp. 432. *bibliog.*

BLECHMAN (BARRY M.) and KAPLAN (STEPHEN S.) Force without war: U.S. armed forces as a political instrument. Washington, D.C., [1978]. pp. 584. *bibliog.*

SHIBUTANI (TAMOTSU) The derelicts of company K: a sociological study of demoralization. Berkeley, Calif., [1978]. pp. 455. *bibliog.*

— — Foreign service.

TREVERTON (GREGORY F.) The dollar drain and American forces in Germany: managing the political economics of alliance. Athens, Ohio, [1978]. pp. 226. *bibliog.*

— — Recruiting, enlistment, etc.

BROOKE (EDWARD W.) and NUNN (SAM) An all-volunteer force for the United States? Washington, [1977]. pp. 18. *(American Enterprise Institute for Public Policy Research. AEI Defense Reviews. [Vol. 1]. No. 5)*

— Army — Military life.

MILITARY families: adaptation to change; edited by Edna J. Hunter and D. Stephen Nice. New York, [1978]. pp. 278. *bibliog.*

— — Sanitary affairs.

UNITED STATES. Sanitary Commission. Bulletin. fortn., N 1 1863 - Ag 1 1865(v.1, no.1 - v.3, no.40) Washington.

UNITED STATES. Sanitary Commission. 1866. Documents of the U.S. Sanitary Commission. No[s]. 1-[95]. New York, 1866. 2 vols.

— Biography.

AMERICAN men and women of science: social and behavioral sciences. 13th ed. New York, 1978. pp. 1545.

WHITE (THEODORE HAROLD) In search of history: a personal adventure. London, [1978]. pp. 561.

— Bureau of Refugees, Freedmen, and Abandoned Lands.

OUBRE (CLAUDE F.) Forty acres and a mule: the Freedmen's Bureau and black land ownership. Baton Rouge, [1978]. pp. 212. *bibliog.*

— Census.

UNITED STATES. Census, 1790. Population schedules of the first census of the United States, 1790. [Washington, 1907-08]. Microfilm: 3 reels.

— Church history.

CARWARDINE (RICHARD) Transatlantic revivalism: popular evangelicalism in Britain and America, 1790-1865. Westport, [1978]. pp. 249. *bibliog.*

McLOUGHLIN (WILLIAM GERALD) Revivals, awakenings, and reform: an essay on religion and social change in America, 1607-1977. Chicago, [1978]. pp. 239. *bibliog.*

PRIMER (BEN) Protestants and American business methods. [London, 1979]. pp. 223. *bibliog.*

— Civilization.

GABRIEL (RALPH HENRY) American values: continuity and change. Westport, Conn., 1974. pp. 230. *bibliog.*

GAVIN (WILLIAM J.) and BLAKELEY (THOMAS J.) Russia and America: a philosophical comparison: development and change of outlook from the 19th to the 20th century. Dordrecht, [1976]. pp. 114. *(Freiburg (Switzerland). Universität. Ost-Europa Institut. Sovietica. vol. 38)*

WOLFE (TOM) Mauve gloves and madmen, clutter and vine: and other stories, sketches and essays. Toronto, 1977. pp. 214.

DOUGLAS (GEORGE H.) H.L. Mencken: critic of American life. Hamden, Conn., 1978. pp. 248. *bibliog.*

McLOUGHLIN (WILLIAM GERALD) Revivals, awakenings, and reform: an essay on religion and social change in America, 1607-1977. Chicago, [1978]. pp. 239. *bibliog.*

The NATIONAL purpose reconsidered; Dona Baron, editor. New York, 1978. pp. 139.

— Commerce.

ELLET (CHARLES) An essay on the laws of trade, in reference to the works of internal improvement in the United States. New York, 1966. pp. 284. *Reprint of work originally published in Richmond, 1839.*

SURVEY OF CURRENT BUSINESS; [pd. by] United States Department of Commerce, Office of Business Economics. m. (with w. suppl.) Jl 1921 (no.1)- , with gap (D 1929). Washington. *File includes bien. suppl., Business statistics, and w. suppls. to 1964, afterwards only kept currently.*

CLAUDER (ANNA CORNELIA) American commerce as affected by the wars of the French Revolution and Napoleon, 1793-1812. Clifton, N. J., 1972. pp. 264. *bibliog. Reprint of work originally published Philadelphia, 1932.*

EDWARDS (PAUL KENNETH) The southern urban negro as a consumer. New York, 1932; New York, 1969. pp. 323. *bibliog. Facsimile reprint.*

DAVIES (ROBERT BRUCE) Peacefully working to conquer the world: Singer sewing machines in foreign markets, 1854-1920. [New York], 1976. pp. 390. *bibliog.*

NETSCHERT (BRUCE CARLTON) The mineral foreign trade of the United States in the twentieth century: a study in mineral economics. New York, 1977. pp. 465. *bibliog.*

— — China.

GOLDSTEIN (JONATHAN) Philadelphia and the China trade, 1682-1846: commercial, cultural and attitudinal effects. University Park, Pa., [1978]. pp. 121. *bibliog.*

— — Japan.

INTERNATIONAL input-output table Japan-U.S.A., 1970; [by Yasuhiko Torii and others]. Tokyo, [1977]. pp. 205. *(Ajia Keizai Kenkyusho. Statistical Data Series. No. 24). Published as part of a research project organized by the Institute of Developing Economies and the Keio Economic Observatory of Keio University.*

— — Netherlands.

WINTER (PIETER JAN VAN) American finance and Dutch investment, 1780-1805; with an epilogue to 1840;...English adaptation of the revised version of the original Dutch edition...by James C. Riley. New York, 1977. 2 vols. *bibliog.*

— — New Zealand.

NEW ZEALAND. Department of Trade and Industry. Trade Services Division. 1979. West coast U.S.A.: [a market profile]. [Wellington, 1979]. fo. 63. *(Backgound to Export)*

— — United Kingdom.

LONDON. London Record Society. Publications. vol. 15. Joshua Johnson's letterbook, 1771-1774: letters from a merchant in London to his partners in Maryland; edited by Jacob M. Price. London, 1979. pp. 181.

— Commercial policy.

MICHALOPOULOS (CONSTANTINE) U.S. commodity trade policy and the developing countries. [Washington], 1977. pp. 40. *(United States. Agency for International Development. Bureau for Program and Policy Coordination. A.I.D. Discussion Papers. No. 37)*

TODER (ERIC J.) and others. Trade policy and the U.S. automobile industry. New York, 1978. pp. 243. *(Charles River Associates. Research Reports).*

— Congress.

VOORHIS (JERRY) Confessions of a congressman. Westport, Conn., 1970. pp. 365. *Reprint of work originally published Garden City, 1947.*

BIOGRAPHICAL directory of the United States executive branch, 1774-1977; Robert Sobel, editor in chief. Westport, 1977. pp. 503.

FOWLER (DOROTHY GANFIELD) Unmailable: Congress and the Post Office. Athens, Ga., [1977]. pp. 266. *bibliog.*

HOLT (PAT M.) The War Powers Resolution: the role of Congress in U.S. armed intervention. Washington, D.C., [1978]. pp. 48. *(American Enterprise Institute for Public Policy Research. AEI Studies. 197)*

SCHNEIDER (JERROLD E.) Ideological coalitions in Congress. Westport, Conn., 1979. pp. 270. *bibliog.*

— — Elections.

CONGRESSIONAL QUARTERLY INC. Electing Congress: timely reports to keep journalists, scholars and the public abreast of developing issues, events and trends. Washington, 1978. pp. 216. *bibliog.*

— — House of Representatives.

FENNO (RICHARD FRANCIS) Home style: house members in their districts. Boston, Mass., [1978]. pp. 304.

LEGISLATIVE reform: the policy impact; edited by Leroy N. Rieselbach. Lexington, Mass., [1978]. pp. 259. *bibliog.*

— — — Committees.

SHEPSLE (KENNETH A.) The giant jigsaw puzzle: Democratic committee assignments in the modern House. Chicago, [1978]. pp. 333. *bibliog.*

— — Senate.

PLATT (ALAN) The U.S. Senate and strategic arms policy, 1969-1977. Boulder, Colo., [1978]. pp. 129. *bibliog.*

POPOVA (EVGENIIA IVANOVNA) Amerikanskii senat i vneshniaia politika, 1969-1974. Moskva, 1978. pp. 232.

— — Constitution — Amendments.

GRIMES (ALAN PENDLETON) Democracy and the amendments to the Constitution. Lexington, Mass., [1978]. pp. 190.

— — 4th Amendment.

HIRSCHEL (J. DAVID) Fourth amendment rights. Lexington, Mass., [1979]. pp. 158. *bibliog.*

— Constitutional history.

AMERICAN law and the constitutional order: historical perspectives; edited by Lawrence M. Friedman and Harry N. Scheiber. Cambridge, Mass., 1978. pp. 521.

LEGISLATIVE reform: the policy impact; edited by Leroy N. Rieselbach. Lexington, Mass., [1978]. pp. 259. *bibliog.*

— Constitutional law.

GRIMES (ALAN PENDLETON) Democracy and the amendments to the Constitution. Lexington, Mass., [1978]. pp. 190.

TRIBE (LAURENCE H.) American constitutional law. Mineola, N.Y., 1978. pp. 1202.

UNITED STATES (Cont.)

—Defences.

HAGEN (LAWRENCE S.) Civil defence: the case for reconsideration. Kingston, Ont., 1977. pp. 88. *bibliog. (Kingston, Ontario. Queen's University. Center for International Relations. National Security Series. No. 7/77).*

YANARELLA (ERNEST J.) The missile defense controversy: strategy, technology, and politics, 1955-1972. Lexington, [1977]. pp. 236.

BINKIN (MARTIN) and others. Shaping the defense civilian workforce: economics, politics, and national security. Washington, D.C., [1978]. pp. 113.

DIVINE (ROBERT A.) Blowing on the wind: the nuclear test ban debate, 1954-1960. New York, 1978. pp. 393. *bibliog.*

— Department of State.

DE CONDE (ALEXANDER) The American Secretary of State: an interpretation. Westport, 1975. pp. 182. *bibliog.*

WEST (RACHEL) The Department of State on the eve of the First World War. Athens, Ga., [1978]. pp. 183. *bibliog.*

— Description and travel.

BURNABY (ANDREW) Travels through the middle settlements in North America in the years 1759 and 1760, with observations upon the state of the colonies. New York, 1970. pp. 265. *Reprint of the third edition, London, 1798.*

BIRKBECK (MORRIS) Notes on a journey in America from the coast of Virginia to the territory of Illinois;...to which is added: Letters from Illinois. New York, 1971. pp. 163,114. *Reprint of the third edition of the works originally published in London, 1818.*

FEARON (HENRY BRADSHAW) Sketches of America: a narrative of a journey of five thousand miles through the eastern and western states of America. 2nd ed. New York, 1970. pp. 454. *Reprint of work originally published at London, 1818.*

BREMER (FREDRIKA) The homes of the new world: impressions of America;... translated by Mary Howitt. New York, 1853; New York, 1968. 2 vols. *Facsimile reprint.*

MACDONALD (DONALD) Captain. The diaries of Donald Macdonald 1824-1826; with an introduction by Caroline Dale Snedeker. Clifton, N.J., 1973. pp. 379. *(Indiana Historical Society. Publications. vol. 14. no. 2) Reprint of work first published Indianapolis, 1942.*

— Diplomatic and consular service.

ETHERIDGE (LLOYD S.) A world of men: the private sources of American foreign policy. Cambridge, Mass., [1978]. pp. 178. *bibliog.*

— Economic conditions.

[BLODGET (SAMUEL)] Economica: a statistical manual for the United States of America. New York, 1964. pp. 202,xiv. *Facsimile reprint of the original printed in Washington for the author in 1806.*

BALDWIN (LOAMMI) Thoughts on the study of political economy as connected with the population, industry and paper currency of the United States;... to which is added an appendix, Dry docks, etc. New York, 1968. pp. 105. *Reprint of work first published in Cambridge, Mass., 1809, with appendix of articles first published in the Columbian Centinel, 1804.*

FEARON (HENRY BRADSHAW) Sketches of America: a narrative of a journey of five thousand miles through the eastern and western states of America. 2nd ed. New York, 1970. pp. 454. *Reprint of work originally published at London, 1818.*

SEDGWICK (THEODORE) Public and private economy...in three parts, 1836-1839 with an introduction: Theodore Sedgwick: from federalism to Jacksonianism, by Joseph Dorfman. Clifton, N. J., 1974. pp. 490. *Reprint of work originally published in New York, 1836-1839.*

BRANDEIS (LOUIS DEMBITZ) Business: a profession. New York, 1971. pp. 327. *Reprint of work originally published Boston, 1914.*

INTERNATIONAL input-output table Japan-U.S.A., 1970; [by Yasuhiko Torii and others]. Tokyo, [1977]. pp. 205. *(Ajia Keizai Kenkyusho. Statistical Data Series. No. 24). Published as part of a research project organized by the Institute of Developing Economies and the Keio Economic Observatory of Keio University.*

ALBIN (PETER S.) Progress without poverty: socially responsible economic growth. New York, [1978]. pp. 229. *bibliog.*

CONTEMPORARY economic problems, 1978: William Fellner, project director [and others]. Washington, D.C., [1978]. pp. 353. *At head of title: American Enterprise Institute.*

The DECLINING Northeast: demographic and economic analyses; edited by Benjamin Chinitz. New York, [1978]. pp. 182. *bibliogs.*

ECKSTEIN (OTTO) The great recession, with a postscript on stagflation. Amsterdam, 1978. pp. 213.

HOW energy affects the economy; edited by A. Bradley Askin. Lexington, Mass., [1978]. pp. 133. *bibliogs.*

REVITALIZING the Northeast; edited by George Sternlieb and James W. Hughes. New Brunswick, N.J., [1978]. pp. 443. *bibliogs.*

RIFKIN (JEREMY) and BARBER (RANDY) The North will rise again: pensions, politics and power in the 1980s. Boston, Mass., [1978]. pp. 279. *bibliog.*

SHIN (KILMAN) Inflation, stock price and housing cost: empirical studies. Fairfax, [1978]. pp. 368. *bibliogs.*

AGLIETTA (MICHEL) A theory of capitalist regulation: the U.S. experience; translated by David Fernbach. London, 1979. pp. 390.

NEW ZEALAND. Department of Trade and Industry. Trade Services Division. 1979. West coast U.S.A.: [a market profile]. [Wellington, 1979]. fo. 63. *(Background to Export)*

PETERSEN (RODNEY) The philosophy of a peasant. Heber Springs, Ark., [1979]. pp. 554.

— Economic history.

BOWDEN (WITT) The industrial history of the United States. New York, 1967. pp. 511. *bibliog. Reprint of work originally published in New York, 1930.*

NORTH (DOUGLASS CECIL) The economic growth of the United States 1790-1860. New York, [1966]. pp. 304. *bibliog. First published in 1961.*

FOGEL (ROBERT WILLIAM) Railroads and American economic growth: essays in econometric history. Baltimore, 1964. pp. 296. *bibliog.*

SCHEIBER (HARRY N.) and others. American economic history. New York, [1976]. pp. 514. *bibliogs. A comprehensive revision of the earlier work by Harold Underwood Faulkner.*

JONES (ALICE HANSON) American colonial wealth: documents and methods. 2nd ed. New York, 1977. 3 vols.

SHIELDS (ROGER ELWOOD) Economic growth with price deflation, 1873-1896. New York, 1977. pp. 346. *bibliog.*

WATERS (JOSEPH PAUL) Technological acceleration and the Great Depression. New York, 1977. pp. 250. *bibliog.*

WINTER (PIETER JAN VAN) American finance and Dutch investment, 1780-1805; with an epilogue to 1840;...English adaptation of the revised version of the original Dutch edition...by James C. Riley. New York, 1977. 2 vols. *bibliog.*

BORITT (GÁBOR S.) Lincoln and the economics of the American dream. Memphis, [1978]. pp. 420. *bibliog.*

DETHLOFF (HENRY C.) Americans and free enterprise. Englewood Cliffs, [1979]. pp. 336. *bibliogs.*

— Economic policy.

BALDWIN (LOAMMI) Thoughts on the study of political economy as connected with the population, industry and paper currency of the United States;... to which is added an appendix, Dry docks, etc. New York, 1968. pp. 105. *Reprint of work first published in Cambridge, Mass., 1809, with appendix of articles first published in the Columbian Centinel, 1804.*

NORTH (DOUGLASS CECIL) The economic growth of the United States 1790-1860. New York, [1966]. pp. 304. *bibliog. First published in 1961.*

HOLT (CHARLES FRANK) The role of state government in the nineteenth century American economy, 1820-1902: a quantitative study. New York, 1977. pp. 325. *bibliog. Originally presented as a thesis, Purdue University, 1970.*

CONGRESSIONAL QUARTERLY INC. Inflation and unemployment; (senior editor Peter A. Harkness). Washington, D.C., [1975]. pp. 124. *bibliog.*

FISHLOW (ALBERT) The mature neighbor policy: a new United States economic policy for Latin America. Berkeley, [1977?]. pp. 56. *bibliog. (California University. Institute of International Studies. Policy Papers in International Affairs. No. 3).*

ALBIN (PETER S.) Progress without poverty: socially responsible economic growth. New York, [1978]. pp. 229. *bibliog.*

ANDERSON (JAMES E.) and others. Public policy and politics in America. North Scituate, [1978]. pp. 434. *bibliogs.*

BAROODY (WILLIAM J.) The critical choices we face. Washington, 1978. pp. 8. *(American Enterprise Institute for Public Policy Research. Reprints. No. 89)*

BECKWITH (BURNHAM PUTNAM) Liberal socialism applied: the applied welfare economics of a liberal socialist economy. Palo Alto, [1978]. pp. 331.

CONNALLY (JOHN) and others. A conversation with John Connally of Texas. Washington, [1978]. pp. 26. *(American Enterprise Institute for Public Policy Research. AEI Studies. 230)*

CONSERVATION and the changing direction of economic growth; edited by Bernhard J. Abrahamsson. Boulder, Colo., 1978. pp. 151. *bibliogs. Revisions of papers presented at a conference, sponsored by the Rocky Mountain Oil and Gas Association and the Denver Research Institute.*

CONTEMPORARY economic problems, 1978: William Fellner, project director [and others]. Washington, D.C., [1978]. pp. 353. *At head of title: American Enterprise Institute.*

ECONOMIC advice and executive policy: recommendations from past members of the Council of Economic Advisers; edited by Werner Sichel. New York, 1978. pp. 113.

EDMUNDS (STAHRL) Alternative U.S. futures: a policy analysis of individual choices in a political economy. Santa Monica, [1978]. pp. 217. *bibliog.*

GALBRAITH (JOHN KENNETH) The new industrial state. 3rd ed. Boston, Mass., 1978. pp. 438.

MACDOWELL (MICHAEL ALAN) Public understanding of economic policies: the tax cuts of 1962 and 1964. New York, 1978. pp. 321. *bibliog.*

MERTZ (PAUL E.) New Deal policy and southern rural poverty. Baton Rouge, [1978]. pp. 279. *bibliog.*

NATIONALIZING government public policies in America; Theodore J. Lowi, Alan Stone, editors. Beverly Hills, [1978]. pp. 454.

PLANNING, politics, and the public interest; edited by Walter Goldstein. New York, 1978. pp. 202.

REVITALIZING the Northeast; edited by George Sternlieb and James W. Hughes. New Brunswick, N.J., [1978]. pp. 443. *bibliogs.*

UNITED STATES(Cont.)

SEMINAR in economic policy with Gerald R. Ford. Washington, [1978]. pp. 14. *(American Enterprise Institute for Public Policy Research. AEI Studies. 186)*

WEIDENBAUM (MURRAY L.) and DE FINA (ROBERT) The cost of federal regulation of economic activity. Washington, 1978. pp. 33. *(American Enterprise Institute for Public Policy Research. Reprints. No. 88)*

NACHMIAS (DAVID) Public policy evaluation: approaches and methods. New York, [1979]. pp. 195. *bibliog.*

SCHIFF (IRWIN A.) The biggest con: how the government is fleecing you. Hamden, Conn., [1979]. pp. 368.

— Emigration and immigration.

BROMWELL (WILLIAM JEREMY) History of immigration to the United States, exhibiting the number, sex, age, occupation, and country of birth of passengers arriving from foreign countries by sea, 1819 to 1855. New York, 1969. pp. 225. *Reprint of work originally published New York, 1856.*

SCHACHTER (JOSEPH) Capital value and relative wage effects of immigration into the United States, 1870-1930. New York, 1977. pp. 125. *bibliog. Facsimile reprint of Ph.D. thesis, City University of New York, submitted in 1969.*

PAVLAK (THOMAS JAMES) Ethnic identification and political behavior. San Francisco, 1976. pp. 108. *bibliog.*

DINNERSTEIN (LEONARD) and REIMERS (DAVID M.) Ethnic Americans: a history of immigration and assimilation. New York, 1977. pp. 184. *bibliog.*

The KOREAN diaspora: historical and sociological studies of Korean immigration and assimilation in North America; Hyung-chan Kim, editor. Santa Barbara, [1977]. pp. 268. *bibliog.*

STOKVIS (PIETER RUDOLF DEGENHARD) De Nederlandse trek naar Amerika, 1846-1847. Leiden, 1977. pp. 251. *bibliog. (Leiden. Rijks Universiteit. Leidse Historische Reeks. Deel 21) With summary in English.*

NAMIAS (JUNE) First generation: in the words of twentieth-century American immigrants. Boston, Mass., 1978. pp. 234. *bibliog.*

PIORE (MICHAEL J.) Birds of passage: migrant labor and industrial societies. Cambridge, 1979. pp. 229. *bibliog.*

— Executive departments.

KAUFMAN (HERBERT) The forest ranger: a study in administrative behavior. Baltimore, 1960 repr.1967. pp. 259.

DAVIS (JAMES WARREN) An introduction to public administration: politics, policy, and bureaucracy. New York, [1974]. pp. 336. *bibliog.*

WOLL (PETER) American bureaucracy. 2nd ed. New York, [1977]. pp. 260.

BINKIN (MARTIN) and others. Shaping the defense civilian workforce: economics, politics, and national security. Washington, D.C., [1978]. pp. 113.

WEST (RACHEL) The Department of State on the eve of the First World War. Athens, Ga., [1978]. pp. 183. *bibliog.*

PEMBERTON (WILLIAM ERWIN) Bureaucratic politics: executive reorganization during the Truman administration. Columbia, Mo., 1979. pp. 262. *bibliog.*

— Foreign economic relations.

ATLANTIC COUNCIL OF THE UNITED STATES. The Atlantic Council Working Group on the United States and the Developing Countries. The United States and the developing countries. Boulder, Colo. [1977]. pp. 150.

DOBSON (JOHN M.) America's ascent: the United States becomes a great power, 1880-1914. DeKalb, I11, [1978]. pp. 251. *bibliog.*

KRASNER (STEPHEN D.) Defending the national interest: raw materials investments and U. S. foreign policy. Princeton, N.J., [1978]. pp. 404. *bibliog.*

— — America, Latin.

FISHLOW (ALBERT) The mature neighbor policy: a new United States economic policy for Latin America. Berkeley, [1977?]. pp. 56. *bibliog. (California University. Institute of International Studies. Policy Papers in International Affairs. No. 3).*

— — Canada.

CUFF (ROBERT D.) and GRANATSTEIN (JACK LAWRENCE) American dollars - Canadian prosperity: Canadian-American economic relations, 1945-1950. Toronto, 1978. pp. 286. *bibliog.*

FRANK (HELMUT J.) and SCHANZ (JOHN J.) U.S.-Canadian energy trade: a study of changing relationships. Boulder, [1978]. pp. 136.

— — Caribbean Area.

PALMER (RANSFORD W.) Caribbean dependence on the United States economy. New York, [1979]. pp. 173. *bibliog.*

— — Europe.

KAISER (KARL) Europe and the United States: the future of the relationship. Washington, 1973. pp. 146.

— — Italy.

Le RELAZIONI economiche fra l'Italia e gli Stati Uniti d'America: esperienze, sviluppi e prospettive; a cura di Franco Tagliarini. Roma, 1976. pp. 227. *In Italian or English.*

— — South Africa.

SEIDMAN (ANN WILLCOX) and SEIDMAN (NEVA) U.S. multinationals in Southern Africa. Dar es Salaam, 1977. pp. 252. *bibliogs.*

— Foreign opinion, French.

STRAUSS (DAVID) Historian. Menace in the West: the rise of French anti-Americanism in modern times. Westport, Conn., 1978. pp. 317. *bibliog.*

— Foreign opinion, Latin American.

REID (JOHN TURNER) Spanish American images of the United States, 1790-1960. Gainesville, 1977. pp. 298. *bbliog.*

— Foreign opinion, Russian.

SCHWARTZ (MORTON) Soviet perceptions of the United States. Berkeley, [1978]. pp. 216. *bibliog.*

— Foreign population.

DINNERSTEIN (LEONARD) and REIMERS (DAVID M.) Ethnic Americans: a history of immigration and assimilation. New York, 1977. pp. 184. *bibliog.*

ESSAYS and data on American ethnic groups; edited by Thomas Sowell. [Washington, 1978]. pp. 418.

— Foreign relations.

ESSAYS in history and international relations: in honor of George Hubbard Blakeslee; edited by Dwight E. Lee and George E. McReynolds. Port Washington, N.Y., [1949]. pp. 324. *bibliog.*

HALLE (LOUIS JOSEPH) Civilization and foreign policy: an inquiry for Americans. New York, [1952]. pp. 277.

FINLETTER (THOMAS KNIGHT) Power and policy: US foreign policy and military power in the hydrogen age. New York, [1954]. pp. 408.

FOSDICK (DOROTHY) Common sense and world affairs. New York, [1955]. pp. 207.

LINK (ARTHUR STANLEY) Wilson the diplomatist: a look at his major foreign policies. New York, 1974. pp. 165. *First published 1957.*

DIVINE (ROBERT A.) Second chance: the triumph of internationalism in America during World War II. New York, [1967] repr. 1971. pp. 371.

KOLKO (GABRIEL) The roots of American foreign policy: an analysis of power and purpose. Boston, [1969]. pp. 166.

SCHOLES (WALTER V.) and SCHOLES (MARIE V.) The foreign policies of the Taft administration. Columbia, [1970]. pp. 259. *bibliog.*

SMITH (DANIEL MALLOY) Aftermath of war: Bainbridge Colby and Wilsonian diplomacy, 1920-1921. Philadelphia, 1970. pp. 173. *bibliog. (American Philosophical Society. Memoirs. vol. 80)*

ROBINSON (THOMAS W.) The border negotiations and the future of Sino-Soviet-American relations. [Santa Monica, Calif., 1971]. pp. 48. *(Rand Corporation. [Papers]. 4661)*

HALPERIN (MORTON H.) Contemporary military strategy. new ed. London, 1972. pp. 149. *bibliog.*

KIMBALL (WARREN F.) ed. Franklin D. Roosevelt and the world crisis, 1937-1945. Lexington, Mass., [1973]. pp. 297. *bibliog. (Amherst College. Department of American Studies. Problems in American Civilization)*

The NEW era in American foreign policy; John H. Gilbert, editor. New York, [1973]. pp. 214. *Based on papers presented at a symposium held in 1972 at North Carolina State University.*

SCHOLES (WALTER V.) ed. United States diplomatic history. Vol.2. Readings for the twentieth century. Boston, Mass., [1973]. pp. 312.

CLYMER (KENTON J.) John Hay: the gentleman as diplomat. Ann Arbor, [1975]. pp. 314. *bibliog.*

PONCINS (LEON DE) Comte, the Younger. State secrets: a documentation of the secret revolutionary mainspring governing Anglo-American politics; translated from the French edition of...Top secret by Timothy Tindal-Robertson. Chulmleigh, Devon, 1975. pp. 191. *bibliog.*

WONDER (EDWARD F.) Nuclear fuel and American foreign policy: multilateralization for uranium enrichment. Boulder, Colo., 1977. pp. 72.

BLECHMAN (BARRY M.) and KAPLAN (STEPHEN S.) Force without war: U.S. armed forces as a political instrument. Washington, D.C., [1978]. pp. 584. *bibliog.*

DEBENEDETTI (CHARLES) Origins of the modern American peace movement, 1915-1929. New York, [1978]. pp. 281. *bibliog.*

DICKSON (PETER W.) Kissinger and the meaning of history. Cambridge, 1978. pp. 197. *bibliog.*

DOBSON (JOHN M.) America's ascent: the United States becomes a great power, 1880-1914. DeKalb, I11, [1978]. pp. 251. *bibliog.*

FALKOWSKI (LAWRENCE S.) Presidents, secretaries of state, and crises in U.S. foreign relations: a model and predictive analysis. Boulder, Colo., 1978. pp. 173.

HOFFMAN (STANLEY HARRY) Primacy or world order: American foreign policy since the Cold War. New York, [1978]. pp. 331. *bibliogs.*

KIERNAN (V.G.) America: the new imperialism: from white settlement to world hegemony. London, 1978. pp. 304. *bibliog.*

KINSELLA (WILLIAM E.) Leadership in isolation: FDR and the origins of the Second World War. Boston, Mass., [1978]. pp. 282. *bibliog.*

KRASNER (STEPHEN D.) Defending the national interest: raw materials investments and U. S. foreign policy. Princeton, N.J., [1978]. pp. 404. *bibliog.*

LISKA (GEORGE) Career of empire: America and imperial expansion over land and sea. Baltimore, [1978]. pp. 360. *(Washington Center of Foreign Policy Research. Studies in International Affairs)*

NUECHTERLEIN (DONALD EDWIN) National interests and Presidential leadership: the setting of priorities. Boulder, Colo., 1978. pp. 246.

UNITED STATES (Cont.)

PARSONS (EDWARD B.) Wilsonian diplomacy: Allied-American rivalries in war and peace. St. Louis, Miss., [1978]. pp. 213. *bibliog.*

PLATT (ALAN) The U.S. Senate and strategic arms policy, 1969-1977. Boulder, Colo., [1978]. pp. 129. *bibliog.*

POPOVA (EVGENIIA IVANOVNA) Amerikanskii senat i vneshniaia politika, 1969-1974. Moskva, 1978. pp. 232.

RAVENAL (EARL C.) Never again: learning from America's foreign policy failures. Philadelphia, 1978. pp. 153. *bibliog.*

U.S. policy in international institutions: defining reasonable options in an unreasonable world; edited by Seymour Maxwell Finger and Joseph R. Harbert. Boulder, Colo., [1978]. pp. 489. *bibliog.*

WEST (RACHEL) The Department of State on the eve of the First World War. Athens, Ga., [1978]. pp. 183. *bibliog.*

WHITE (THEODORE HAROLD) In search of history: a personal adventure. London, [1978]. pp. 561.

AMERICAN ACADEMY OF POLITICAL AND SOCIAL SCIENCE. Annals. vol. 442. The human dimension of foreign policy: an American perspective; special editor of this volume John Richardson. Philadelphia, 1979. pp. 195.

DALLEK (ROBERT) Franklin D. Roosevelt and American foreign policy, 1932-1945. New York, 1979. pp. 657. *bibliog.*

MOYNIHAN (DANIEL PATRICK) A dangerous place. London, 1979. pp. 297.

SPIVAK (BURTON) Jefferson's English crisis: commerce, embargo, and the Republican revolution. Charlottesville, Va., 1979. pp. 250.

— — **America, Latin.**

SCOTT (JACK) Yankee unions, go home!: how the AFL helped the U.S. build an empire in Latin America. Vancouver, [1978]. pp. 287. *bibliog.*

— — **Angola.**

STOCKWELL (JOHN) In search of enemies: a CIA story. London, 1978. pp. 285.

— — **Asia.**

UNITED States foreign policy in Asia: an appraisal; edited by Yung-Hwan Jo. Santa Barbara, [1978]. pp. 488. *bibliogs.*

JAPAN, Korea, and China: American perceptions and policies; [by] William Watts. Lexington, Mass., [1979]. pp. 154.

— — **Cambodia.**

SHAWCROSS (WILLIAM) Sideshow: Kissinger, Nixon and the destruction of Cambodia. London, 1979. pp. 467. *bibliog.*

— — **Canada.**

PRESTON (RICHARD ARTHUR) The defence of the undefended border: planning for war in North America, 1867-1939. Montreal, 1977. pp. 300.

— — **Caribbean Area.**

CARTER (PURVIS M.) Congressional and public reaction to Wilson's Caribbean policy, 1913-1917. New York, [1977]. pp. 164. *bibliog.*

MARTIN (JOHN BARTLOW) U.S. policy in the Caribbean. Boulder, Colo., [1978]. pp. 420. *bibliog. A Twentieth Century Fund essay.*

— — **China.**

SYMPOSIUM ON CHINESE-AMERICAN RELATIONS, 1976. Our China prospects; [proceedings of the] symposium...; edited by John K. Fairbank. Philadelphia, 1977. pp. 51. (*American Philosophical Society. Memoirs. vol. 121*)

CLOUGH (RALPH N.) Island China. Cambridge, Mass., 1978. pp. 264. *bibliog.*

DRAGON and eagle: United States-China relations; past and future; edited by Michel Oksenberg, Robert B. Oxnam. New York, [1978]. pp. 384. *bibliog.*

TWO Chinese states: U.S. foreign policy and interests; edited by Ramon H. Myers. Stanford, [1978]. pp. 81. (*Stanford University. Hoover Institution on War, Revolution and Peace. Hoover Institution Publications. 200*)

FAIRBANK (JOHN KING) The United States and China. 4th ed. Cambridge, Mass., 1979. pp. 606. *bibliog.*

SCHALLER (MICHAEL) The U.S. crusade in China, 1938-1945. New York, 1979. pp. 364. *bibliog.*

— — **Czechoslovakia.**

ULLMAN (WALTER) The United States in Prague, 1945-1948. New York, 1978. pp. 205. *bibliog. (East European Quarterly. East European Monographs. 36).*

— — **East (Near East).**

CHURBA (JOSEPH) The politics of defeat: America's decline in the Middle East. New York, [1977]. pp. 224. *bibliog.*

CONGRESSIONAL QUARTERLY INC. The Middle East: U.S. policy, Israel, oil and the Arabs. 3rd ed. Washington, D.C., [1977]. pp. 196.

QUANDT (WILLIAM B.) Decade of decisions: American policy toward the Arab-Israeli conflict, 1967-1976. Berkeley, [1977]. pp. 313. *bibliog.*

— — **Europe.**

KAISER (KARL) Europe and the United States: the future of the relationship. Washington, 1973. pp. 146.

BAILEY (THOMAS ANDREW) The Marshall Plan summer: an eyewitness report on Europe and the Russians in 1947. Stanford, Calif., [1977]. pp. 246.

DEPORTE (ANTON WILLIAM) Europe between the superpowers: the enduring balance. New Haven, 1979. pp. 256. *bibliog.*

LEFFLER (MELVYN P.) The elusive quest: America's pursuit of European stability and French security, 1919-1933. Chapel Hill, [1979]. pp. 409. *bibliog.*

— — **France.**

DUROSELLE (JEAN BAPTISTE) France and the United States: from the beginnings to the present...; (translated by Derek Coltman). Chicago, 1978. pp. 276. *bibliog.*

STRAUSS (DAVID) Historian. Menace in the West: the rise of French anti-Americanism in modern times. Westport, Conn., 1978. pp. 317. *bibliog.*

SULLIVAN (MARIANNA P.) France's Vietnam policy: a study in French-American relations. Westport, Conn., 1978. pp. 165. *bibliog.*

LEFFLER (MELVYN P.) The elusive quest: America's pursuit of European stability and French security, 1919-1933. Chapel Hill, [1979]. pp. 409. *bibliog.*

— — **Germany.**

TREVERTON (GREGORY F.) The dollar drain and American forces in Germany: managing the political economics of alliance. Athens, Ohio, [1978]. pp. 226. *bibliog.*

— — **Greece.**

STERN (LAURENCE) The wrong horse: the politics of intervention and the failure of American diplomacy. New York, [1977]. pp. 170.

AMEN (MICHAEL MARK) American foreign policy in Greece, 1944/1949: economic, military and institutional aspects. Frankfurt am Main, 1978. pp. 310.

— — **Guatemala.**

SOTO (JOSÉ M. AYBAR DE) Dependency and intervention: the case of Guatemala in 1954. Boulder, Colo., 1978. pp. 374. *bibliog.*

— — **India.**

NAYAR (BALDEV RAJ) American geopolitics and India. Columbia, Mo., 1976. pp. 246. *bibliog.*

— — **Indochina.**

ZASLOFF (JOSEPH JEREMIAH) and BROWN (MACALISTER) Communist Indochina and U.S. foreign policy: postwar realities. Boulder, Colo., 1978. pp. 221. *bibliog.*

— — **Japan.**

EMMERSON (JOHN K.) The Japanese thread: a life in the U.S. foreign service. New York, 1978. pp. 465.

U.S.-JAPAN relations and the security of East Asia: the next decade; edited by Franklin B. Weinstein. Boulder, Colo., [1978]. pp. 318. *bibliog.*

The WHALING issue in U.S.-Japan relations; edited by John R. Schmidhauser and George O. Totten III. Boulder, Colo., [1978]. pp. 275.

— — **Korea.**

WHITE (NATHAN N.) U.S. policy toward Korea: analysis, alternatives and recommendations. Boulder, Colo., 1979. pp. 231.

— — **Mexico.**

GARCIA CANTU (GASTON) Las invasiones norteamericanas en Mexico. Mexico, 1971 repr. 1975. pp. 362.

GILDERHUS (MARK T.) Diplomacy and revolution: U.S.-Mexican relations under Wilson and Carranza. Tucson, Ariz., [1977]. pp. 159. *bibliog.*

— — **Micronesia.**

NUFER (HAROLD F.) Micronesia under American rule: an evaluation of the strategic trusteeship, 1947-77. Hicksville, N.Y., [1978]. pp. 245.

— — **Pacific, The.**

WILEY (PETER) Vietnam and the Pacific rim strategy. Boston, Mass., [c.1972]. pp. 22. *bibliog. Reprinted from the Lviathan of June 1969.*

— — **Panama.**

LOWENTHAL (ABRAHAM F.) and others. A new treaty for Panama? Washington, [1977]. pp. 34. (*American Enterprise Institute for Public Policy Research. AEI Defense Reviews. [Vol. 1]. No. 4*)

VALDES (EDUARDO) The roots of the problem: a positive approach to the Panama Canal issue. New York, [1977]. pp. 66.

— — **Poland.**

LUKAS (RICHARD C.) The strange allies: the United States and Poland, 1941-1945. Knoxville, Tenn., [1978]. pp. 230. *bibliog.*

— — **Russia.**

CHILDS (JOHN LAWRENCE) and COUNTS (GEORGE SYLVESTER) America, Russia and the Communist Party in the postwar world. New York, [1943]. pp. 92.

McNEILL (WILLIAM HARDY) America, Britain and Russia: their co-operation and conflict, 1941-1946. New York, [1976]. pp. 819. *Reprint of work originally published as one volume of the Survey of International Affairs, London, 1953.*

HALLE (LOUIS JOSEPH) The cold war as history. New York, [1967]. pp. 434. *bibliog.*

UNITED STATES (Cont.)

UNITED STATES. United States Information Service. 1973. "To build peace": a summary of agreements and statements during the visit to the United States of General Secretary Leonid Brezhnev of the Soviet Union, June 18-25, 1973. [Washington, 1973?]. pp. 36.

COX (ARTHUR MACY) The dynamics of détente: how to end the arms race. New York, [1976]. pp. 256. bibliog.

BACKER (JOHN H.) The decision to divide Germany: American foreign policy in transition. Durham, N.C., 1978. pp. 212. bibliog.

COLLINS (JOHN M.) Imbalance of power: an analysis of shifting U.S.-Soviet military strengths. San Rafael, Calif., [1978]. pp. 316. Includes: Net assessment appraisal, by Anthony H. Cordesman.

CONTAINMENT: documents on American policy and strategy, 1945- 1950; [edited by] Thomas H. Etzold and John Lewis Gaddis. New York, 1978. pp. 449.

DIMENSIONS of detente; edited by Della W. Sheldon. New York, 1978. pp. 221.

INTERNATIONAL perceptions of the superpower military balance; edited by Donald C. Daniel. New York, [1978]. pp. 198. bibliogs.

SCHWARTZ (MORTON) Soviet perceptions of the United States. Berkeley, [1978]. pp. 216. bibliog.

BREZHNEV (LEONID IL'ICH) Peace, détente, and Soviet-American relations: a collection of public statements. New York, [1979]. pp. 235.

SIVACHEV (NIKOLAI VASIL'EVICH) and IAKOVLEV (NIKOLAI NIKOLAEVICH) Russia and the United States; translated by Olga Adler Titelbaum. Chicago, 1979. pp. 301.

STERN (PAULA) Water's edge: domestic politics and the making of American foreign policy. Westport, Conn., 1979. pp. 265. bibliog.

— — South Africa.

SPRING (MARTIN C.) Confrontation: the approaching crisis between the United States and South Africa. Sandton, 1977. pp. 181.

GANN (LEWIS H.) and DUIGNAN (PETER) South Africa: war, revolution or peace? Stanford, [1978]. pp. 85. (Stanford University. Hoover Institution on War, Revolution and Peace. Hoover Institution Publications. 199)

— — Spain.

CORTADA (JAMES W.) Two nations over time: Spain and the United States, 1776- 1977. Westport, Conn., 1978. pp. 305. bibliog.

— — Taiwan.

CLOUGH (RALPH N.) Island China. Cambridge, Mass., 1978. pp. 264. bibliog.

— — Turkey.

STERN (LAURENCE) The wrong horse: the politics of intervention and the failure of American diplomacy. New York, [1977]. pp. 170.

— — Underdeveloped areas.

The THIRD world: premises of U.S. policy; [edited by] W. Scott Thompson. San Francisco, [1978]. pp. 332. bibliog.

— — United Kingdom.

JONES (HOWARD) 1940- . To the Webster-Ashburton Treaty: a study in Anglo- American relations, 1783-1843. Chapel Hill, [1977]. pp. 251. bibliog.

WELLS (SHERRILL PERKINS BROWN) The influence of Sir Cecil Spring Rice and Sir Edward Grey on the shaping of Anglo- American relations, 1913-1916. 1978. fo. 416. bibliog. Typescript. Ph.D. (London) thesis: unpublished. This thesis is the property of London University and may not be removed from the Library.

— — Vietnam.

VIETNAM (DEMOCRATIC REPUBLIC). Commission for Investigation on the American Imperialists' War Crimes in Vietnam. 1966. The U.S. war of aggression in Vietnam: a crime against the Vietnamese people, against peace and humanity. [Hanoi?], 1966. pp. 47. Photocopy.

LEWY (GUENTER) America in Vietnam. New York, 1978. pp. 540. bibliog.

GELB (LESLIE H.) and BETTS (RICHARD K.) The irony of Vietnam: the system worked. Washington, D.C., [1979]. pp. 387. bibliog.

— Foreign relations administration.

ETHERIDGE (LLOYD S.) A world of men: the private sources of American foreign policy. Cambridge, Mass., [1978]. pp. 178. bibliog.

FALKOWSKI (LAWRENCE S.) Presidents, secretaries of state, and crises in U.S. foreign relations: a model and predictive analysis. Boulder, Colo., 1978. pp. 173.

— Forest Service.

KAUFMAN (HERBERT) The forest ranger: a study in administrative behavior. Baltimore, 1960 repr.1967. pp. 259.

— Full employment policies.

CREATING jobs: public employment programs and wage subsidies: a study sponsored jointly by the Institute for Research on Poverty and the Brookings Institution; John L. Palmer, editor. Washington, D.C., [1978]. pp. 379. (Brookings Institution. Studies in Social Economics) (Wisconsin University, Madison. Institute for Research on Poverty. Monograph Series) Based on a conference held in 1977.

— Government publications — Indexes.

LESTER (DANIEL W.) and others, compilers. Cumulative title index to United States public documents, 1789- 1976. Arlington, Va., 1979 in progress.

— Governors.

SABATO (LARRY) Goodbye to good-time Charlie: the American governor transformed, 1950-1975. Lexington, Mass., [1978]. pp. 283. bibliog.

— — Biography.

BIOGRAPHICAL directory of the governors of the United States, 1789-1978; edited by Robert Sobel and John Raimo. Westport, Conn., [1978]. 4 vols.

— Historiography.

BERINGER (RICHARD E.) Historical analysis: contemporary approaches to Clio's craft. New York, [1978]. ppi 317.

— History.

I.S.R.P. COLLECTIVE. America: 200th anniversary. Long Kesh, 1976. pp. 68.

TOWARD a new view of America; essays in honor of Arthur C. Cole; edited by Hans L. Trefousse. [New York, 1977]. pp. 230.

JEFFREYS-JONES (RHODRI) Violence and reform in American history. New York, 1978. pp. 242. bibliog.

KIERNAN (V.G.) America: the new imperialism: from white settlement to world hegemony. London, 1978. pp. 304. bibliog.

— — 1775-1783, Revolution.

FERLING (JOHN E.) The Loyalist mind: Joseph Galloway and the American Revolution. University Park, [1977]. pp. 157. bibliog.

The SOUTHERN experience in the American Revolution; edited by Jeffrey J. Crow and Larry E. Tise. Chapel Hill, [1978]. pp. 310.

— — — Foreign public opinion.

TOOHEY (ROBERT E.) Liberty and empire: British radical solutions to the American problem, 1774-1776. Lexington, [1978]. pp. 210. bibliog.

— — 1783-1865.

CLAUDER (ANNA CORNELIA) American commerce as affected by the wars of the French Revolution and Napoleon, 1793-1812. Clifton, N. J., 1972. pp. 264. bibliog. Reprint of work originally published Philadelphia, 1932.

— — 1789-1801, Constitutional period.

BASSETT (JOHN SPENCER) The federalist system, 1789-1801. New York, 1969. pp. 327. bibliog. Reprint of work originally published New York, 1906.

— — 1800-1899.

DONALD (DAVID) Liberty and union. Lexington, Mass., [1978]. pp. 323.

PESSEN (EDWARD) Jacksonian America: society, personality, and politics. rev. ed. Homewood, Ill., 1978. pp. 379.

— — 1812, War of.

BABCOCK (KENDRIC CHARLES) The rise of American nationality, 1811-1819. New York, 1906; New York, 1969. pp. 339. bibliog. Facsimile reprint.

— — 1845-1848, War with Mexico.

COOKE (PHILIP ST. GEORGE) and others. Exploring southwestern trails, 1846-1854;...edited by Ralph P. Bieber...in collaboration with Averam B. Bender. Glendale, 1938; Philadelphia, 1974. pp. 383. Facsimile reprint.

— — 1861-1865, Civil War.

UNITED STATES. Sanitary Commission. Bulletin. fortn., N 1 1863 - Ag 1 1865(v.1, no.1 - v.3, no.40) Washington.

ROARK (JAMES L.) Master without slaves: Southern planters in the Civil War and Reconstruction. New York, [1977]. pp. 273. bibliog.

ADAMS (MICHAEL C.C.) Our masters the rebels: a speculation on Union military failure in the east, 1861-1865. Cambridge, Mass., 1978. pp. 256.

ESCOTT (PAUL D.) After secession: Jefferson Davis and the failure of confederate nationalism. Baton Rouge, [1978]. pp. 295. bibliog.

— — — Causes.

DONALD (DAVID) Liberty and union. Lexington, Mass., [1978]. pp. 323.

— — — Prisoners and prisons.

UNITED STATES. Sanitary Commission. 1864. Narrative of privations and sufferings of United States officers and soldiers while prisoners of war in the hands of the rebel authorities. Being the report of a commission of inquiry, appointed by the United States Sanitary Commission. With an appendix containing the testimony. Philadelphia, 1864. pp. 283.

— — — Sources.

[HOPLEY (CATHERINE COOPER)] Life in the South from the commencement of the war; by a blockaded British subject; being a social history of those who took part in the battles...from the spring of 1860 to August 1862. London, 1863; New York, 1971. 2 vols.

— — 1898, War of.

WELCH (RICHARD E.) Response to imperialism: the United States and the Philippine-American War, 1899-1902. Chapel Hill, [1979]. pp. 215. bibliog.

— — 1898-1945.

ABRAMS (RICHARD M.) The burdens of progress, 1900-1929. Glenview, Ill., [1978]. pp. 199. bibliog.

UNITED STATES (Cont.)

— — 1900- .

ROTHSTEIN (ARTHUR) The depression years as photographed. New York, [1978]. pp. 119.

SNOWMAN (DANIEL) America since 1920. London, 1978. pp. 246.

WHITE (THEODORE HAROLD) In search of history: a personal adventure. London, [1978]. pp. 561.

JEFFRIES (JOHN W.) Testing the Roosevelt coalition: Connecticut society and politics in the era of World War II. Knoxville, [1979]. pp. 312.

— — 1945- .

BASKIR (LAWRENCE M.) and STRAUSS (WILLIAM A.) Chance and circumstance: the draft, the war, and the Vietnam generation. New York, 1978. pp. 312. *bibliog.*

PALMER (DAVE RICHARD) Summons of the trumpet: U.S.-Vietnam in perspective. San Rafael, [1978]. pp. 277.

SHARP (ULYSSES S. GRANT) Strategy for defeat: Vietnam in retrospect. San Rafael, Calif., [1978]. pp. 324.

— History, Military.

MANCHESTER (WILLIAM) American Caesar: Douglas MacArthur, 1880-1964. London, 1979. pp. 793.

— History, Naval.

IN peace and war: interpretations of American naval history, 1775-1978; edited by Kenneth J. Hagan. Westport, Conn., 1978. pp. 368. *bibliogs.*

— Industries.

GOURVITCH (ALEXANDER) Survey of economic theory on technological change and employment. New York, 1966. pp. 252. *Reprint of work first published Philadelphia, 1940.*

GALBRAITH (JOHN KENNETH) The new industrial state. 3rd ed. Boston, Mass., 1978. pp. 438.

— Intellectual life.

COMMAGER (HENRY STEELE) The empire of reason: how Europe imagined and America realized the enlightenment. Garden City, 1978. pp. 381.

— Military policy.

FINLETTER (THOMAS KNIGHT) Power and policy: US foreign policy and military power in the hydrogen age. New York, [1954]. pp. 408.

BLECHMAN (BARRY M.) and KAPLAN (STEPHEN S.) Force without war: U.S. armed forces as a political instrument. Washington, D.C., [1978]. pp. 584. *bibliog.*

COLLINS (JOHN M.) Imbalance of power: an analysis of shifting U.S.-Soviet military strengths. San Rafael, Calif., [1978]. pp. 316. *Includes: Net assessment appraisal, by Anthony H. Cordesman.*

CONGRESS and arms control; edited by Alan Platt and Lawrence D. Weiler. Boulder, Colo., [1978]. pp. 227.

PALMER (GREGORY) The McNamara strategy and the Vietnam war: program budgeting in the Pentagon, 1960-1968. Westport, Conn., [1978]. pp. 169. *bibliog.*

PLATT (ALAN) The U.S. Senate and strategic arms policy, 1969-1977. Boulder, Colo., [1978]. pp. 129. *bibliog.*

— Moral conditions.

BOYER (PAUL S.) Urban masses and moral order in America, 1820-1920. Cambridge, Mass., 1978. pp. 387. *bibliogs.*

WASSERSTROM (RICHARD ALAN) ed. Today's moral problems. 2nd ed. New York, [1979]. pp. 623. *bibliogs.*

— National Recovery Administration — Codes.

PIDGEON (MARY ELIZABETH) Women in the economy of the United States of America; [with] Employed women under N.R.A. codes. New York, 1975. 1 vol. (various pagings). *Reprint of works published in Washington D.C., 1937 and 1935.*

— National security.

CONTAINMENT: documents on American policy and strategy, 1945- 1950; [edited by] Thomas H. Etzold and John Lewis Gaddis. New York, 1978. pp. 449.

UNITED States national security policy in the decade ahead; edited by James E. Dornan, Jr. London, [1978]. pp. 304. *bibliogs.*

— Officials and employees.

PUBLIC employee unions: a study of the crisis in public sector labor relations; A. Lawrence Chickering, editor. San Francisco, [1976]. pp. 248. *bibliog.*

STAHL (OSCAR GLENN) Public personnel administration. 7th ed. New York, [1976]. pp. 575. *bibliog.*

See also the subdivision Officials and employees under the names of government departments and offices.

— Peace Corps.

LOWTHER (KEVIN) and LUCAS (C. PAYNE) Keeping Kennedy's promise: the Peace Corps: unmet hope of the new frontier. Boulder, [1978]. pp. 153. *bibliog.*

— Politics and government.

PENNAN (JOHN SIMPSON) The irresistible movement of democracy. New York, 1923. pp. 729.

MILLETT (JOHN DAVID) Organization for the public service. Princeton, [1966]. pp. 159.

GABRIEL (RALPH HENRY) American values: continuity and change. Westport, Conn., 1974. pp. 230. *bibliog.*

ANDERSON (JAMES E.) and others. Public policy and politics in America. North Scituate, [1978]. pp. 434. *bibliogs.*

CRISES of political development in Europe and the United States; edited by Raymond Grew; contributors: David D. Bien [and others]. Princeton, [1978]. pp. 434. *bibliogs.*

EMERGING coalitions in American politics; [by] Jack Bass [and others]; Seymour Martin Lipset, editor. San Francisco, 1978. pp. 524. *bibliog.*

GORDON (GEORGE J.) Public administration in America. New York, [1978]. pp. 470. *bibliogs.*

RIOT, rout, and tumult: readings in American social and political violence; edited by Roger Lane and John J. Turner. Westport, Conn., 1978. pp. 399. *bibliog.*

SCHUMAN (DAVID) The ideology of form: the influence of organizations in America. Lexington, Mass., [1978]. pp. 196.

TOWN and county: essays on the structure of local government in the American colonies; edited by Bruce C. Daniels. Middletown, Conn., [1978]. pp. 279. *bibliogs.*

— — 1607-1783, Colonial period.

KARSTEN (PETER) Patriot-heroes in England and America: political symbolism and changing values over three centuries. Madison, Wis., 1978. pp. 257.

— — 1783-1865.

BABCOCK (KENDRIC CHARLES) The rise of American nationality, 1811-1819. New York, 1906; New York, 1969. pp. 339. *bibliog. Facsimile reprint.*

BROUSSARD (JAMES H.) The Southern Federalists, 1800-1816. Baton Rouge, [1978]. pp. 438. *bibliog.*

JOHNSTONE (ROBERT M.) Jefferson and the Presidency: leadership in the young republic. Ithaca, 1978. pp. 332. *bibliog.*

KARSTEN (PETER) Patriot-heroes in England and America: political symbolism and changing values over three centuries. Madison, Wis., 1978. pp. 257.

SPIVAK (BURTON) Jefferson's English crisis: commerce, embargo, and the Republican revolution. Charlottesville, Va., 1979. pp. 250.

— — 1800-1899.

KLEPPNER (PAUL) The third electoral system, 1853-1892: parties, voters and political cultures. Chapel Hill, N.C., [1979]. pp. 424. *bibliog.*

— — 1815-1861.

PESSEN (EDWARD) Jacksonian America: society, personality, and politics. rev. ed. Homewood, Ill., 1978. pp. 379.

— — 1865-1898.

WILLIAMS (R. HAL) Years of decision: American politics in the 1890s. New York, [1978]. pp. 219. *bibliog.*

— — 1900- .

EISENHOWER (DWIGHT DAVID) President of the United States. The papers of Dwight David Eisenhower...; Alfred D. Chandler ([and] Louis Galambos) editor[s]. Baltimore, [1970 in progress]. *bibliogs.*

CRANE (PHILIP M.) The sum of good government. Ottawa, Ill., [1976]. pp. 214. *bibliog.*

JANOWITZ (MORRIS) The last half-century: societal change and politics in America. Chicago, [1978]. pp. 583.

— — 1901-1953.

VOORHIS (JERRY) Confessions of a congressman. Westport, Conn., 1970. pp. 365. *Reprint of work originally published Garden City, 1947.*

ALLSWANG (JOHN M.) The New Deal and American politics: a study in political change. New York, [1978]. pp. 155. *bibliog.*

— — 1945- .

EISENHOWER (DWIGHT DAVID) President of the United States. The papers of Dwight David Eisenhower...; Alfred D. Chandler ([and] Louis Galambos) editor[s]. Baltimore, [1970 in progress]. *bibliogs.*

DAVIS (JAMES WARREN) An introduction to public administration: politics, policy, and bureaucracy. New York, [1974]. pp. 336. *bibliog.*

HOFFERBERT (RICHARD I.) The study of public policy. Indianapolis, [1974]. pp. 275.

COBB (ROGER W.) and ELDER (CHARLES D.) Participation in American politics: the dynamics of agenda-building. Baltimore, 1977. pp. 182. *bibliog.*

WOLL (PETER) American bureaucracy. 2nd ed. New York, [1977]. pp. 260.

AMERICAN politics and public policy; edited by Walter Dean Burnham and Martha Wagner Weinberg. Cambridge, Mass., [1978]. pp. 418. *(Massachusetts Institute of Technology. MIT Studies in American Politics and Public Policy. 4)*

BAROODY (WILLIAM J.) The critical choices we face. Washington, 1978. pp. 8. *(American Enterprise Institute for Public Policy Research. Reprints. No. 89)*

CONGRESSIONAL QUARTERLY INC. Electing Congress: timely reports to keep journalists, scholars and the public abreast of developing issues, events and trends. Washington, 1978. pp. 216. *bibliog.*

CONNALLY (JOHN) and others. A conversation with John Connally of Texas. Washington, [1978]. pp. 26. *(American Enterprise Institute for Public Policy Research. AEI Studies. 230)*

UNITED STATES (Cont.)

FENNO (RICHARD FRANCIS) Home style: house members in their districts. Boston, Mass., [1978]. pp. 304.

FOWLER (ROBERT BOOTH) Believing skeptics: American political intellectuals, 1945-1964. Westport, 1978. pp. 317. *bibliog.*

HOROWITZ (IRVING LOUIS) and LIPSET (SEYMOUR MARTIN) Dialogues on American politics. Oxford, 1978. pp. 199. *bibliog.*

MILLER (WILLIAM LEE) Yankee from Georgia: the emergence of Jimmy Carter. New York, [1978]. pp. 247.

NATIONALIZING government public policies in America; Theodore J. Lowi, Alan Stone, editors. Beverly Hills, [1978]. pp. 454.

The NEW American political system; [by] Samuel H. Beer [and others]; edited by Anthony King. Washington, D.C., [1978]. pp. 407. *(American Enterprise Institute for Public Policy Research. AEI Studies. 213)*

NIXON (RICHARD MILHOUS) President of the United States. The memoirs of Richard Nixon. London, 1978. pp. 1120.

NIXON (RICHARD MILHOUS) President of the United States. The Nixon presidential press conferences; introduction by Helen Thomas; [edited by George W. Johnson]. London, 1978. pp. 419.

PARTIES and elections in an anti-party age: American politics and the crisis of confidence; edited with an introduction by Jeff Fishel. Bloomington, [1978]. pp. 350.

PEMBERTON (WILLIAM ERWIN) Bureaucratic politics: executive reorganization during the Truman administration. Columbia, Mo., 1979. pp. 262. *bibliog.*

PETERSEN (RODNEY) The philosophy of a peasant. Heber Springs, Ark., [1979]. pp. 554.

SCHNEIDER (JERROLD E.) Ideological coalitions in Congress. Westport, Conn., 1979. pp. 270. *bibliog.*

— Population.

POPULATION policy and ethics: the American experience; edited by Robert M. Veatch. New York, [1977]. pp. 501. *bibliogs. A project of the Research Group on Ethics and Population of the Institute of Society, Ethics and the Life Sciences.*

The ECONOMIC consequences of slowing population growth; edited by Thomas J. Espenshade and William J. Serow. New York, 1978. pp. 288. *bibliog.*

ZERO population growth - for whom?: differential fertility and minority group survival; edited by Milton Himmelfarb and Victor Baras. Westport, 1978. pp. 213. *Proceedings of a conference held by the American Jewish Committee in 1975, in New York.*

— Population policy.

POPULATION policy analysis: issues in American politics; edited by Michael E. Kraft and Marke Schneider. Lexington, Mass., [1978]. pp. 204. *bibliogs.*

— Presidents.

EGGER (ROWLAND ANDREWS) The President of the United States. 2nd ed. New York, [1972]. pp. 198. *bibliog.*

BIOGRAPHICAL directory of the United States executive branch, 1774-1977; Robert Sobel, editor in chief. Westport, 1977. pp. 503.

KARSTEN (PETER) Patriot-heroes in England and America: political symbolism and changing values over three centuries. Madison, Wis., 1978. pp. 257.

MILLER (WILLIAM LEE) Yankee from Georgia: the emergence of Jimmy Carter. New York, [1978]. pp. 247.

THOMAS (SUNNY) Jimmy Carter: from peanuts to presidency. Cornwall, Ont., [1978]. pp. 101.

— — Election.

POMPER (GERALD M.) and others. The election of 1976: reports and interpretations; Marlene M. Pomper, editor. New York, [1977]. pp. 184.

BRAMS (STEVEN J.) The Presidential election game. New Haven, 1978. pp. 242.

PAGE (BENJAMIN I.) Choices and echoes in Presidential elections: rational man and electoral democracy. Chicago, [1978]. pp. 336.

— — Succession — Bibliography.

TOMPKINS (DOROTHY LOUISE CAMPBELL) compiler. Selection of the vice president; [a bibliography]. Berkeley, 1974. pp. 26. *(California University. Institute of Governmental Studies. Public Policy Bibliographies. No. 6)*

— Public works.

ELLET (CHARLES) An essay on the laws of trade, in reference to the works of internal improvement in the United States. New York, 1966. pp. 284. *Reprint of work originally published in Richmond, 1839.*

ICKES (HAROLD LECLAIRE) Back to work: the story of P.W.A. New York, 1973. pp. 276. *Reprint of work first published New York, 1935.*

— Public Works Administration.

ICKES (HAROLD LECLAIRE) Back to work: the story of P.W.A. New York, 1973. pp. 276. *Reprint of work first published New York, 1935.*

— Race relations.

SOUTHERN SOCIETY FOR THE PROMOTION OF THE STUDY OF RACE CONDITIONS AND PROBLEMS IN THE SOUTH. Annual Conference, 1st, 1900. Race problems of the south: report of the proceedings of the... conference...at Montgomery, Alabama, etc. [Richmond, Va.], 1900; New York, 1969. pp. 240. *bibliog. Facsimile reprint.*

MOTON (ROBERT RUSSA) Finding a way out: an autobiography. [Garden City, N.Y.], 1920; New York, 1969. pp. 296. *Facsimile reprint.*

PAVLAK (THOMAS JAMES) Ethnic identification and political behavior. San Francisco, 1976. pp. 108. *bibliog.*

MELENDY (HOWARD BRETT) Asians in America: Filipinos, Koreans, and East Indians. Boston, Mass., [1977]. pp. 340. *bibliog.*

WILLIAMS (ROBIN MURPHY) Mutual accommodation: ethnic conflict and cooperation. Minneapolis, [1977]. pp. 458. *bibliog.*

BURKEY (RICHARD M.) Ethnic and racial groups: the dynamics of dominance. Menlo Park, Calif., [1978]. pp. 510. *bibliog.*

GESCHWENDER (JAMES A.) Racial stratification in America. Dubuque, Iwa, [1978]. pp. 282. *bibliogs.*

BASH (HARRY H.) Sociology, race and ethnicity: a critique of American ideological intrusions upon sociological theory. New York, [1979]. pp. 252. *bibliog.*

WROBEL (PAUL) Our way: family, parish, and neighborhood in a Polish-American community. Notre Dame, Ind., [1979]. pp. 192.

— Relations (general) with Cuba.

BENJAMIN (JULES ROBERT) The United States and Cuba: hegemony and dependent development, 1880-1934. Pittsburgh, [1977]. pp. 266. *bibliog.*

— Relations (general) with Eastern Europe.

EAST Central European perceptions of early America; edited by Béla K. Király and George Barany. Lisse, 1977. pp. 139. *(City University of New York. Brooklyn College. Department of History. Studies on Society in Change. No. 5)*

— Relations (general) with Latin America.

REID (JOHN TURNER) Spanish American images of the United States, 1790-1960. Gainesville, 1977. pp. 298. *bibliog.*

— Relations (general) with Russia.

LARSON (THOMAS B.) Soviet-American rivalry. New York, [1978]. pp. 308. *bibliog.*

— Relations (general) with the Dominican Republic.

GLEIJESES (PIERO) The Dominican crisis: the 1965 constitutionalist revolt and American intervention...; translated by Lawrence Lipson. Baltimore, [1978]. pp. 460. *bibliog.*

— Religion.

WUTHNOW (ROBERT) Experimentation in American religion: the new mysticisms and their implications for the churches. Berkeley, [1978]. pp. 221.

ELLWOOD (ROBERT S.) Alternative altars: unconventional and eastern spirituality in America. Chicago, [1979]. pp. 192.

— Rural conditions.

MERTZ (PAUL E.) New Deal policy and southern rural poverty. Baton Rouge, [1978]. pp. 279. *bibliog.*

DANBOM (DAVID B.) The resisted revolution: urban America and the industrialization of agriculture, 1900-1930. Ames, Iowa, 1979. pp. 195. *bibliog.*

— Social conditions.

ACKOFF (RUSSELL LINCOLN) Redesigning the future: a systems approach to societal problems. New York, [1974]. pp. 260.

TERLECKYJ (NESTOR E.) Improvements in the quality of life: estimates of possibilities in the United States, 1974-1983. Washington, D.C., 1975. pp. 285.

RUBIN (LILLIAN B.) Worlds of pain: life in the working-class family. New York, [1976]. pp. 268.

KENISTON (KENNETH) and others. All our children: the American family under pressure. New York, [1977]. pp. 255. *Published under the auspices of the Carnegie Council on Children, Carnegie Corporation of New York.*

WOLFE (TOM) Mauve gloves and madmen, clutter and vine: and other stories, sketches and essays. Toronto, 1977. pp. 214.

ALBIN (PETER S.) Progress without poverty: socially responsible economic growth. New York, [1978]. pp. 229. *bibliog.*

AMERICAN ACADEMY OF POLITICAL AND SOCIAL SCIENCE. Annals. vol. 435. America in the seventies: some social indicators; special editor of this volume Conrad Taeuber. Philadelphia, 1978. pp. 354.

APPLIED anthropology in America; [edited by] Elizabeth M. Eddy and William L. Partridge. New York, 1978. pp. 484. *bibliog.*

BEEGHLEY (LEONARD) Social stratification in America: a critical analysis of theory and research. Santa Monica, Calif., [1978]. pp. 381. *bibliog.*

FEATHERMAN (DAVID L.) and HAUSER (ROBERT MASON) Opportunity and change. New York, [1978]. pp. 572. *bibliog.*

GORDON (LEONARD) Sociologist, and HARVEY (PATRICIA ATCHISON) Sociology and American social issues. Boston, Mass., [1978]. pp. 548. *bibliogs.*

HOROWITZ (IRVING LOUIS) and LIPSET (SEYMOUR MARTIN) Dialogues on American politics. Oxford, 1978. pp. 199. *bibliog.*

LEWIS (MICHAEL) 1937- . The culture of inequality. Amherst, 1978. pp. 207.

UNITED STATES (Cont.)

ROBERTS (RON E.) Social problems: human possibilities. Saint Louis, 1978. pp. 310. *bibliogs.*

RULE (JAMES B.) Insight and social betterment: a preface to applied social science. New York, 1978. pp. 205.

HASTINGS (WILLIAM M.) How to think about social problems: a primer for citizens. New York, 1979. pp. 251. *bibliog.*

PALEN (J. JOHN) Social problems. New York, [1979]. pp. 625. *bibliog.*

PETERSEN (RODNEY) The philosophy of a peasant. Heber Springs, Ark., [1979]. pp. 554.

WATSON (JAMES WREFORD) Social geography of the United States. London, 1979. pp. 290. *bibliogs.*

— Social history.

DAVIS (GLENN) Childhood and history in America. New York, [1976]. pp. 281. *bibliogs.*

The POWER of the people: active nonviolence in the United States; edited and produced by Robert Cooney and Helen Michalowski. Culver City, [1977]. pp. 240. *bibliog.*

The AMERICAN family in social-historical perspective;...Michael Gordon, editor. 2nd ed. New York, [1978]. pp. 580. *bibliogs.*

BENDER (THOMAS) Community and social change in America. New Brunswick, [1978]. pp. 159.

JANOWITZ (MORRIS) The last half-century: societal change and politics in America. Chicago, [1978]. pp. 583.

— Social life and customs.

BREMER (FREDRIKA) The homes of the new world: impressions of America;... translated by Mary Howitt. New York, 1853; New York, 1968. 2 vols. *Facsimile reprint.*

[HOPLEY (CATHERINE COOPER)] Life in the South from the commencement of the war; by a blockaded British subject; being a social history of those who took part in the battles...from the spring of 1860 to August 1862. London, 1863; New York, 1971. 2 vols.

FILENE (PETER GABRIEL) Him/her/self: sex roles in modern America. New York, 1976. pp. 326. *bibliog.*

WOLFE (TOM) Mauve gloves and madmen, clutter and vine: and other stories, sketches and essays. Toronto, 1977. pp. 214.

— Social policy.

ANDERSON (JAMES E.) and others. Public policy and politics in America. North Scituate, [1978]. pp. 434. *bibliogs.*

BAROODY (WILLIAM J.) The critical choices we face. Washington, 1978. pp. 8. *(American Enterprise Institute for Public Policy Research. Reprints. No. 89)*

CHILD care and public policy: studies of the economic issues; edited by Philip K. Robins, Samuel Weiner. Lexington, Mass., [1978]. pp. 237. *bibliog.*

GRØNBJERG (KIRSTEN A.) and others. Poverty and social change. Chicago, [1978]. pp. 248. *bibliog.*

KASSCHAU (PATRICIA L.) Aging and social policy: leadership planning. New York, 1978. pp. 419.

LEIBY (JAMES) A history of social welfare and social work in the United States. New York, 1978. pp. 426. *bibliog.*

NATIONALIZING government public policies in America; Theodore J. Lowi, Alan Stone, editors. Beverly Hills, [1978]. pp. 454.

SALAMON (LESTER M.) Welfare: the elusive consensus; where we are, how we got there, and what's ahead. New York, [1978]. pp. 257. *bibliogs. A report from the Welfare Policy Project of the Ford Foundation and Duke University.*

SOCIAL scientists as advocates: views from the applied disciplines; edited by George H. Weber and George J. McCall. Beverly Hills, [1978]. pp. 215. *bibliogs.* Contributions from a symposium of the Society for Applied Anthropology held in San Diego, 1977.

EICHNER (ALFRED S.) and BRECHER (CHARLES) Controlling social expenditures: the search for output measures. Montclair, 1979. pp. 210. *bibliogs.*

NACHMIAS (DAVID) Public policy evaluation: approaches and methods. New York, [1979]. pp. 195. *bibliog.*

SARASON (SEYMOUR BERNARD) and DORIS (JOHN) Educational handicap, public policy, and social history: a broadened perspective on mental retardation. New York, [1979]. pp. 460. *bibliog.*

TRATTNER (WALTER I.) From poor law to welfare state: a history of social welfare in America. 2nd ed. London, [1979]. pp. 290. *bibliog.*

— Statistics.

[BLODGET (SAMUEL)] Economica: a statistical manual for the United States of America. New York, 1964. pp. 202,xiv. *Facsimile reprint of the original printed in Washington for the author in 1806.*

WALKER (FRANCIS AMASA) Discussions in economics and statistics; edited by Davis R. Dewey; with an introduction by Joseph Dorfman. New York, 1971. 2 vols. *Reprint of work first published New York, 1899.*

— Vice presidents.

BIOGRAPHICAL directory of the United States executive branch, 1774-1977; Robert Sobel, editor in chief. Westport, 1977. pp. 503.

— — Bibliography.

TOMPKINS (DOROTHY LOUISE CAMPBELL) compiler. Selection of the vice president; [a bibliography]. Berkeley, 1974. pp. 26. *(California University. Institute of Governmental Studies. Public Policy Bibliographies. No. 6)*

UNIVERSAL NEGRO IMPROVEMENT ASSOCIATION.

BURKETT (RANDALL K.) Garveyism as a religious movement: the institutionalization of black civil religion. Metuchen, 1978. pp. 216. *(American Theological Library Association. ATLA Monograph Series. No.13)*

UNIVERSALS (LINGUISTICS).

JOSEPH (BRIAN DANIEL) Morphology and universals in syntactic change: evidence from medieval and modern Greek. Bloomington, Ind., 1978. pp. 293. *bibliog.*

UNIVERSALS of human language; [papers based on work of the Stanford Project on Language Universals]; edited by Joseph H. Greenberg. Stanford, 1978. 4 vols. *bibliogs.*

UNIVERSITIES AND COLLEGES

— Administration — New Zealand.

EDUCATIONAL DEVELOPMENT CONFERENCE, NEW ZEALAND, 1974. Working Party on Organisation and Administration. Organisation and administration of education. Wellington, [Government Printer], 1974. pp. 175.

— America, Latin.

FERNANDES (FLORESTAN) Circuito fechado: cuatro ensaios sobre o "poder institucional". São Paulo, 1976. pp. 224. *bibliog.*

SOLARI (ALDO E.) ed. Poder y desarrollo: America Latina; estudios sociologicos en homenaje a Jose Medina Echavarria. Mexico, 1977. pp. 429.

— Europe.

SOLARI (ALDO E.) ed. Poder y desarrollo: America Latina; estudios sociologicos en homenaje a Jose Medina Echavarria. Mexico, 1977. pp. 429.

— European Economic Community countries.

HIGHER EDUCATION IN THE EUROPEAN COMMUNITY: a handbook for students; [pd. by] Directorate-General for Research, Science and Education, [European Communities]. irreg., current issue only. Brussels.

— France.

FRANCE. Direction de la Documentation. La ocumentation Française. Notes et Etudes Documentaires. Nos. 4,424-4, 427. Les institutions universitaires françaises: situation actuelle; par Isabel Boussard [and others]. [Paris], 1977. pp. 124. *bibliog.*

COHEN (HABIBA S.) Elusive reform: the French universities, 1968-1978. Boulder, Colo., 1978. pp. 280. *bibliog.*

— Nigeria.

GOWON (YAKUBU) Vital role for universities; [two significant addresses...on university occasions]. [Lagos, 1973?]. pp. 18.

— Norway.

KOBBERSTAD (TOR) Studenter, kandidater og ressursforbruk ved universiteter og høgskoler fram til 1990, etc. [Oslo], 1972. pp. 92. *(Utredninger om Forskning og Høyere Utdanning. 1972.5)*

— Peru.

PERU hoy; por Fernando Fuenzalida Vollmar [and others]. Mexico, 1971 repr. 1975. pp. 366.

— Russia.

VOPROSY metodiki prepodavaniia istorii KPSS v universitete: mezhvuzovskii sbornik. Leningrad, 1978. pp. 150.

— Scandinavia — Administration.

ENDERUD (HARALD GJESSING) Four faces of leadership in an academic organization: a study of joint decision making in a Scandinavian university. København, 1977. pp. 484. *bibliog. (Copenhagen. Handelshøjskolen. Skriftraekke O. 7)*

— South Africa.

BUDLENDER (GEOFF) Looking forward: the university in a democratic South Africa. Cape Town, 1978. pp. 23. *(Cape Town. University. T.B. Davie Memorial Lectures. 19)*

— — Directories.

STIMIE (CHRISTIAAN MATTHYS) and GEGGUS (CAROLINE) University education in the Republic of South Africa. [rev. ed.] Pretoria, 1976. pp. 302. *(Human Sciences Research Council [South Africa]. Institute for Information and Special Services. Reports. No. IN-28)*

— United Kingdom.

SWANN (Sir MICHAEL MEREDITH) Certainty and purpose: a university dilemma. London, 1978. pp. 16. *(London. University. Bedford College. Stevenson Lectures. 1977-78)*

— — Ireland, Northern.

IRELAND, NORTHERN. Department of Education. Education and library boards, grant aided schools, institutions of further education and libraries. a., current issue only. Belfast.

— United States.

The UNIVERSITY and the state: what role for government in higher education?: edited by Sidney Hook [and others]. New York, [1978]. pp. 296. *bibliogs.*

— Yugoslavia.

PERVAN (RALPH) Tito and the students: the university and the university student in self-managing Yugoslavia. Nedlands, W.A., 1978. pp. 239. *bibliog.*

UNIVERSITY EXTENSION

— United Kingdom.

KELLY (THOMAS) M.A., Ph.D., F.R.Hist.S. Outside the walls: sixty years of university extension at Manchester, 1886-1946. Manchester, 1950. pp. 124.

UNMARRIED MOTHERS

— United Kingdom.

HAMILL (LYNNE) An explanation of the increase in female one parent families receiving supplementary benefit. London, Department of Health and Social Security, 1978. pp. 21. *(Government Economic Service Working Papers. No. 14)*

UNSKILLED LABOUR.

McDIARMID (ORVILLE JOHN) Unskilled labor for development: its economic cost...; published for the World Bank. Baltimore, [1977]. pp. 206. *bibliog.* *(International Bank for Reconstruction and Development. World Bank Research Publications)*

UPPER AUSTRIA

— History — 1938-1945.

SLAPNICKA (HARRY) Oberösterreich - als es "Oberdonau" hiess, 1938-1945. Linz, 1978. pp. 513. *bibliog.* *(Upper Austria. Landesarchiv. Beiträge zur Zeitgeschichte Oberösterreichs. 5)*

UPPER CLASSES

— United Kingdom.

BENWELL COMMUNITY DEVELOPMENT PROJECT. The making of a ruling class: two centuries of capital development on Tyneside. Newcastle-upon-Tyne, 1978. pp. 121. *(Final Report Series. No. 6)*

GIROUARD (MARK) Life in the English country house: a social and architectural history. New Haven, 1978. pp. 344.

UPPER SILESIAN QUESTION.

PRZEWŁOCKI (JAN) Stosunek mocarstw zachodnioeuropejskich do problemów Górnego Śląska w latach 1918-1939. Warszawa, 1978. pp. 254. *bibliog.*

UPPER VOLTA

— Commerce.

UPPER VOLTA. Ministère des Finances et du Commerce. 1972. Qu'est-ce que le Ministère des Finances et du Commerce? Ouagadougou, 1972. pp. 112. *(Opération Portes Ouvertes. Documents. 1)*

— Executive departments.

UPPER VOLTA. Ministère des Finances et du Commerce. 1972. Qu'est-ce que le Ministère des Finances et du Commerce? Ouagadougou, 1972. pp. 112. *(Opération Portes Ouvertes. Documents. 1)*

— Ministère des Finances et du Commerce.

UPPER VOLTA. Ministère des Finances et du Commerce. 1972. Qu'est-ce que le Ministère des Finances et du Commerce? Ouagadougou, 1972. pp. 112. *(Opération Portes Ouvertes. Documents. 1)*

UPPSALA

— Social history.

UPPSALA: samhällsgeografiska studier; redigerade av Maj Aldskogius. Uppsala, 1977. pp. 176. *bibliogs.* *(Uppsala. Universitet. Kulturgeografiska Institutionen. Geografiska Regionstudier. Nr. 12)*

URAL REGION

— History — 1917-1921, Revolution.

TAGIROV (INDUS RIZAKOVICH) Revoliutsionnaia bor'ba i natsional'no-osvoboditel'noe dvizhenie v Povolzh'e i na Urale, fevral' - iiul' 1917 goda. Kazan', 1977. pp. 216.

URANIUM.

WONDER (EDWARD F.) Nuclear fuel and American foreign policy: multilateralization for uranium enrichment. Boulder, Colo., 1977. pp. 72.

URANIUM INDUSTRY

— Canada.

WILLIAMS (R.M.) and LITTLE (H.W.) Canadian uranium resource and production capability. Ottawa, 1973. pp. 23. *(Canada. Mineral Resources Division. Mineral [Information] Bulletins. 140)*

— United States.

AHMED (S. BASHEER) Nuclear fuel and energy policy. Lexington, Mass., [1979]. pp. 158. *bibliog.*

URBAN ECONOMICS.

HENDERSON (J. VERNON) Economic theory and the cities. New York, 1977. pp. 238. *bibliog.*

SPATIAL interaction theory and planning models: (papers presented at an international research conference in Båstad, Sweden... 1977); edited by Anders Karlqvist [and others]. Amsterdam, 1978. pp. 388.

ZANIATOST' v nebol'shikh gorodakh: ekonomiko-demograficheskii aspekt; pod redaktsiei A.E. Kotliara. Moskva, 1978. pp. 207.

CENTRAL city economic development; edited by Benjamin Chinitz. Cambridge, Mass., [1979]. pp. 198. *bibliogs.*

TOLLEY (GEORGE STANFORD) and others. Urban growth policy in a market economy. New York, 1979. pp. 220. *bibliogs.*

— Mathematical models.

CHISTIAKOV (EVGENII GAVRILOVICH) and SEMENOV (AL'BERT KONSTANTINOVICH) Balansovye modeli khoziaistva goroda. Moskva, 1977. pp. 192. *bibliog.*

HENNING (PETER H.) The urban popular economy and informal sector productions. Ann Arbor, Mich., 1978. pp. 67. *(Michigan University. Center for Research on Economic Development. Discussion Papers. No. 69)*

URBAN RENEWAL

— United Kingdom.

EDWARDS (JOHN) Author of A study in access, and BATLEY (RICHARD) The politics of positive discrimination: an evaluation of the Urban Programme, 1967-77. London, 1978. pp. 287. *bibliog.*

McLOUGHLIN (PETE) Regional policy and the inner areas: a study of planners' attitudes. Reading, 1978. pp. 26. *bibliog.* *(Reading. University. Department of Geography. Reading Geographical Papers. No. 64)*

SAVING our cities: freeing enterprise in the inner areas; [by] George Bailey [and others]. London, [1978]. pp. 15.

tBAN deprivation and the inner city; edited by Colin Jones. London, [1979]. pp. 218. *bibliogs.*

— — Citizen participation.

BERESFORD (PETER) and BERESFORD (SUZIE) A say in the future: planning, participation and meeting social need: a new approach: North Battersea: a case study. London, 1978. pp. 210. *bibliog.* *(Battersea Community Action. Reports. No.1)*

— — Cost effectiveness.

U.K. Department of the Environment. Economics, Urban and Regional Division. 1978. The economic assessment of housing renewal schemes. [London], 1978. pp. 60. *(Improvement Research Notes. 78-4)*

— — Leamington.

ALLISON (LINCOLN) Southtown: the politics and practicalities of urban decay. [Coventry], 1978. pp. 22. *(University of Warwick. Department of Politics. Working Papers. No. 20)*

URBAN TRANSPORTATION.

PUBLIC transportation: planning, operations, and management; editors George E. Gray, Lester A. Hoel. Englewood Cliffs, N.J., [1979]. pp. 749. *bibliogs.*

— Mathematical models.

DAOR (ERELLA SIEW) An analytical technique for designing a trip generation model with reference to London. 1978. fo. 236. Typescript. M.Phil. (London) thesis: unpublished. This thesis is the property of London University and may not be removed from the Library.

— Australia.

MANNING (IAN) The journey to work. Sydney, 1978. pp. 194. *bibliog.*

— France.

FRANCE. Département des Statistiques des Transports. Enquête annuelle d'entreprise: entreprises et réseaux urbains. a., 1976- Paris.

— Netherlands.

NEW developments in modelling travel demand and urban systems: some results of recent Dutch research; edited by G.R.M. Jansen [and others]. Farnborough, [1979]. pp. 403. *bibliogs.* Papers presented at the fifth Transportation Planning Research Colloquium, The Hague, 1978.

— United Kingdom.

BARMAN (CHRISTIAN) The man who built London Transport: a biography of Frank Pick. Newton Abbot, [1979]. pp. 287.

URBAN TRANSPORTATION POLICY

— Russia.

WHITE (PAUL M.) Planning of urban transport systems in the Soviet Union: a policy analysis. Birmingham, 1978. pp. 34,2. *bibliog.* *(Birmingham. University. Centre for Urban and Regional Studies. Research Memoranda. No. 66)*

URBANIZATION.

POLSKA AKADEMIA NAUK. Instytut Geografii. Geografia Polonica. 39. Urbanization and settlement system; edited by Kazimierz Dziewonski. Warsaw, 1978. pp. 240. *bibliogs.*

COUSINS (ALBERT N.) and NAGPAUL (HANS) Urban life: the sociology of cities and urban society. New York, [1979]. pp. 608. *bibliog.*

— America, Latin.

QUIJANO (ANÍBAL) Dependencia, urbanización y cambio social en Latinoamerica. Lima, 1977. pp. 242.

— Canada.

CLARK (SAMUEL DELBERT) The new urban poor. Toronto, [1978]. pp. 169.

—— Quebec.

BASHAM (RICHARD DALTON) Crisis in blanc and white: urbanization and ethnic identity in French Canada. Boston, Mass., [1978]. pp. 287. *bibliog.*

— Finland.

NORDISK HISTORIKERMØDE, 1977. Urbaniseringsprosessen i Norden:...det XVII. nordiske historikermøte, Trondheim 1977; redigert av Grethe Authén Blom. Oslo, [1977]. 3 vols. *bibliogs.* In various Scandinavian languages.

URBANIZATION.(Cont.)

— Iceland.

NORDISK HISTORIKERMØDE, 1977. Urbaniseringsprosessen i Norden:...det XVII. nordiske historikermøte, Trondheim 1977; redigert av Grethe Authén Blom. Oslo, [1977]. 3 vols. *bibliogs. In various Scandinavian languages.*

— India.

RAO (V.L.S. PRAKASA) Some aspects of urbanization in South India. [Delhi, 1973]. pp. 37. *(India. Census, 1961. Vol. 1. Monographs. No. 12)*

— Mexico.

UGALDE (ANTONIO) The urbanization process of a poor Mexican neighborhood. Austin, 1974. pp. 68. *bibliog. (Texas University. Institute of Latin American Studies. Special Publications)*

— Scandinavia.

NORDISK HISTORIKERMØDE, 1977. Urbaniseringsprosessen i Norden:...det XVII. nordiske historikermøte, Trondheim 1977; redigert av Grethe Authén Blom. Oslo, [1977]. 3 vols. *bibliogs. In various Scandinavian languages.*

— Underdeveloped areas.

See UNDERDEVELOPED AREAS — Urbanization.

— United Kingdom.

OPEN UNIVERSITY. Arts A322 [Course Team]. Block 3, units 9-12. English urban history, 1500-1780: the traditional community under stress; ([with] Supplementary material). Milton Keynes, 1977. 2 pts. (in 1 vol.) *bibliogs.*

OPEN UNIVERSITY. Arts A322 [Course Team]. Block 4, units 13-16. English urban history, 1500-1780: the rise of the new urban society. Milton Keynes, 1977. pp. 120. *bibliogs.*

— United States.

BOYER (PAUL S.) Urban masses and moral order in America, 1820-1920. Cambridge, Mass., 1978. pp. 387. *bibliogs.*

CENTRAL city economic development; edited by Benjamin Chinitz. Cambridge, Mass., [1979]. pp. 198. *bibliogs.*

COUSINS (ALBERT N.) and NAGPAUL (HANS) Urban life: the sociology of cities and urban society. New York, [1979]. pp. 608. *bibliog.*

URUGUAY

— Commerce.

URUGUAY IMPORTACION-EXPORTACION: (analisis estadistico); [pd. by] Centro de Estadisticas Nacionales y Comercio Internacional del Uruguay. a., 1969 13 ed.)- Montevideo.

— Politics and government.

AMNESTY INTERNATIONAL. Uruguay: deaths under torture, 1975-77. London, 1978. pp. 12.

USTIUG (KRAI)

— Population, Rural.

VLASOVA (IRINA VLADIMIROVNA) Sel'skoe rasselenie v Ustiuzhskom krae v XVIII - pervoi chetverti XX v. Moskva, 1976. pp. 119.

UTILITARIANISM.

LIVELY (JACK) and REES (JOHN COLLWYN) eds. Utilitarian logic and politics: James Mill's Essay on government, Macaulay's critique and the ensuing debate. Oxford, 1978. pp. 270.

UTOPIAS.

DAILY Journal of Oneida Community. vols. 1-3 [and] The O. C. Daily. vols. 4-5. Philadelphia, 1975. 1 vol. (unpaged). *Reprint of 2 newspapers first published 1866 and 1868.*

EGERTON (JOHN) Historian. Visions of Utopia: Nashoba, Rugby, Ruskin and the new communities in Tennessee's past. Knoxville, [1977]. pp. 95. *bibliog.*

MALMGREEN (GAIL) Neither bread nor roses: Utopian feminists and the English working class, 1800-1850. Brighton, 1978. pp. 44.

HARDY (DENNIS) Alternative communities in nineteenth century England. London, 1979. pp. 268. *bibliog.*

— Bibliography.

NEGLEY (GLENN ROBERT) compiler. Utopian literature: a bibliography with a supplementary listing of works influential in Utopian thought. Lawrence, Kan., [1977]. pp. 228.

UTTAR PRADESH

— Nationalism.

PANDEY (GYANENDRA) The ascendancy of the Congress in Uttar Pradesh, 1926-34: a study in imperfect mobilization. Delhi, 1978. pp. 245. *bibliog.*

— Politics and government.

U.P. politics and elections; by B. Jhunjhunwala [and others] Bangalore, 1974. pp. 99. *Special issue of 'Religion and Society', vol. 21, no. 2, June 1974.*

PANDEY (GYANENDRA) The ascendancy of the Congress in Uttar Pradesh, 1926-34: a study in imperfect mobilization. Delhi, 1978. pp. 245. *bibliog.*

UZBEKISTAN

— History.

KHASANOV (ANVARBEK KHASANOVICH) Narodnye dvizheniia v Kirgizii v period Kokandskogo khanstva. Moskva, 1977. pp. 95.

VADAKKAN (JOSEPH).

VADAKKAN (JOSEPH) A priest's encounter with revolution: an autobiography. Bangalore, 1974. pp. 159.

VAJIRAVUDH, King of Thailand.

VELLA (WALTER FRANCIS) Chaiyoe': King Vajiravudh and the development of Thai nationalism. Honolulu, [1978]. pp. 348. *bibliog.*

VALENCIA

— Economic history.

CASEY (JAMES) The Kingdom of Valencia in the seventeenth century. Cambridge, 1979. pp. 271. *bibliog.*

— History.

CASEY (JAMES) The Kingdom of Valencia in the seventeenth century. Cambridge, 1979. pp. 271. *bibliog.*

VALUE.

LANTZ (PIERRE) Valeur et richesse: aux marges de l'économie politique, une approche de l'idée de nature. Paris, 1977. pp. 458. *bibliog.*

AKADEMIIA NAUK SSSR. Nauchnyi Sovet po Probleme "Ekonomicheskie Zakonomernosti Razvitiia Sotsializma i Ego Pererastaniia v Kommunizm". Potrebitel'naia stoimost' produktov truda pri sotsializme: materialy nauchnoi sessii. Moskva, 1978. pp. 247.

AMIN (SAMIR) The law of value and historical materialism...; (translated by Brian Pearce). New York, [1978]. pp. 133.

YOUNG (JEFFREY T.) Classical theories of value: from Smith to Sraffa. Boulder, Colo., 1978. pp. 129. *bibliog.*

LANGHOLM (ODD) Price and value in the Aristotelian tradition: a study in scholastic economic sources. Bergen, [1979]. pp. 175. *bibliog.*

VALUE ADDED TAX.

DRESCH (STEPHEN P.) and others. Substituting a value-added tax for the corporate income tax: first-round analysis. Cambridge, Mass., 1977. pp. 213. *bibliog. (National Bureau of Economic Research. Fiscal Studies. 15)*

— Belgium.

INSTITUT BELGE D'INFORMATION ET DE DOCUMENTATION. Les prix: [taxe sur la valeur ajoutée]. [Brussels, 1970]. pp. 32.

— Brazil.

SILVA (FERNANDO ANTONIO REZENDE DA) and SILVA (MARIA DA CONCEIÇÃO) O sistema tributario e as desigualdades regionais: uma analise da recente controversia sobre o ICM. Rio de Janeiro, 1974. pp. 42. *bibliog. (Brazil. Instituto de Planejamento Econômico e Social. Instituto de Pesquisas. Monografias. No. 13)*

VALUES.

GRIER (PHILIP TODD) Marxist ethical theory in the Soviet Union. Dordrecht, 1978. pp. 276. *bibliog. (Freiburg (Switzerland). Universität. Ost- Europa Institut. Sovietica. vol. 40)*

VANDALISM

— United Kingdom.

RESEARCH BUREAU LIMITED. Combatting vandalism: a study to provide information for a possible publicity campaign. [London], Home Office, [1977?]. pp. 13.

TACKLING vandalism; edited by R.V.G. Clarke; contributors: F. J. Gladstone, A. Sturman, Sheena Wilson; a Home Office Research Unit report. London, 1978. pp. 88. *bibliog. (U.K. Home Office. Home Office Research Studies. No. 47)*

U.K. Central Policy Review Staff. 1978. Vandalism; a note. London, 1978. pp. 26.

VANDALS.

PROCOPIUS, of Caesarea. History of the wars; (with an English translation by H.B. Dewing). London, 1914-28 repr. 1962-71. 5 vols. *bibliog. Parallel Greek and English texts.*

VANSITTART (ROBERT GILBERT) 1st Baron Vansittart.

ROSE (NORMAN ANTHONY) Vansittart: study of a diplomat. London, 1978. pp. 308. *bibliog.*

VASCONCELOS (ZACARIAS DE GOIS E).

VASCONCELOS (ZACARIAS DE GOIS E) Discursos parlamentares; seleção e introdução de Alberto Venancio Filho. Brasilia, 1979. pp. 588. *(Brazil. Congresso. Câmara dos Deputados. Perfis Parlamentares. 9)*

VASQUEZ DEL MERCADO (ALBERTO).

KRAUZE (ENRIQUE) Caudillos culturales en la Revolucion mexicana. Mexico, 1976. pp. 340.

VAUCLUSE (DEPARTMENT).

FRANCE. Direction de la Documentation. La Documentation Française. Notes et Etudes Documentaires. Nos. 4475-4476. Les départements français. 84. Vaucluse, Provence-Alpes- Côte d'Azur; [by Jacques Brian and others]. [Paris], 1978. pp. 150.

VEGETABLES

— Australia — Marketing.

WEISSEL (D.A.) and WHITTINGHAM (R.B.) Price information in the fresh fruit and vegetable industries in Australia: an exploratory analysis of its effectiveness of transmission. Canberra, 1978. pp. 46. *(Australia. Bureau of Agricultural Economics. Occasional Papers. No.47)*

— **European Economic Community countries.**

EUROPEAN COMMUNITIES. Statistical Office. Selling prices of vegetable products. bi-m., 1978(no.5)- Luxembourg. *[in Community languages]*

VENDEAN WAR, 1793-1800.

LEWIS (GWYNNE) The second Vendée: the continuity of counter-revolution in the Department of the Gard, 1789-1815. Oxford, 1978. pp. 250. *bibliog.*

VENEREAL DISEASES

— **Europe.**

SYMPOSIUM ON THE SURVEILLANCE AND CONTROL OF SEXUALLY TRANSMITTED DISEASES, VIENNA, 1976. The surveillance and control of sexually transmitted diseases; report, etc. Copenhagen, World Health Organization, Regional Office for Europe, 1977. pp. 79. *bibliogs.*

VENEZIA

— **Emigration and immigration.**

FILIPUZZI (ANGELO) Il dibattito sull'emigrazione: polemiche nazionali e stampa veneta, 1861-1914. Firenze, 1976. pp. 421.

— **History — Sources.**

PROCESSI politici del Senato Lombardo-Veneto, 1815-1851; a cura di Alfredo Grandi. Roma, 1976. pp. 780. *(Istituto per la Storia del Risorgimento Italiano. Pubblicazioni. 2a Serie. Fonti. vol. 67)*

RELAZIONI dei rettori veneti in terraferma; a cura dell'Istituto di Storia Economica dell'Università di Trieste. Milano, 1977-78. 4 vols.

VENEZUELA

— **Bibliography.**

LOMBARDI (JOHN V.) and others, compilers. Venezuelan history: a comprehensive working bibliography. Boston, Mass., [1977]. pp. 530.

— **Census.**

VENEZUELA. Census, 1961. IX censo nacional de poblacion: poblacion urbana, intermedia y rural; censos de 1961, 1950, 1941 y 1936. Caracas, 1962. pp. 87.

— **Commerce — New Zealand.**

NEW ZEALAND. Department of Trade and Industry. Trade Services Division. 1978. Venezuela: [a market profile]. [Wellington, 1978]. fo.39. *(Background to Export)*

— **Economic conditions.**

NEW ZEALAND. Department of Trade and Industry. Trade Services Division. 1978. Venezuela: [a market profile]. [Wellington, 1978]. fo.39. *(Background to Export)*

— **Economic history — Historiography.**

RODRIGUEZ GALLAD (IRENE) El petroleo en la historiografia venezolana. Caracas, 1974. pp. 261. *bibliog.*

— **Economic policy.**

VENEZUELA. Oficina Central de Coordinacion y Planificacion. 1973. Notas para la evaluacion de la obra de gobierno, 1969-1973. [Caracas], 1973. fo. 91.

— **Foreign relations — Cuba.**

VENEZUELA. Oficina Central de Informacion. 1967. Six years of aggression. [Caracas, 1967]. pp. 95.

— **History — Bibliography.**

LOMBARDI (JOHN V.) and others, compilers. Venezuelan history: a comprehensive working bibliography. Boston, Mass., [1977]. pp. 530.

— **Politics and government.**

VENEZUELA. Oficina Central de Coordinacion y Planificacion. 1973. Notas para la evaluacion de la obra de gobierno, 1969-1973. [Caracas], 1973. fo. 91.

— **Social policy.**

VENEZUELA. Oficina Central de Coordinacion y Planificacion. 1973. Notas para la evaluacion de la obra de gobierno, 1969-1973. [Caracas], 1973. fo. 91.

VENICE

— **City planning — Data processing.**

FOOT (DAVID H.S.) and others. Urban models II: a model of Venice. Reading, 1978. pp. 41. *bibliog. (Reading. University. Department of Geography. Reading Geographical Papers. No. 66)*

— — **Mathematical models.**

FOOT (DAVID H.S.) and others. Urban models II: a model of Venice. Reading, 1978. pp. 41. *bibliog. (Reading. University. Department of Geography. Reading Geographical Papers. No. 66)*

— **Civic improvement.**

FOOT (DAVID H.S.) and others. Urban models II: a model of Venice. Reading, 1978. pp. 41. *bibliog. (Reading. University. Department of Geography. Reading Geographical Papers. No. 66)*

— **History.**

GINSBORG (PAUL) Daniele Manin and the Venetian revolution of 1848-49. Cambridge, 1979. pp. 417. *bibliog.*

VERBAND DER UNABHÄNGIGEN.

RIEDLSPERGER (MAX E.) The lingering shadow of Nazism: the Austrian Independence Party Movement since 1945. Boulder, Colo., 1978. pp. 214. *bibliog. (East European Quarterly. East European Monographs. 42)*

VERBAND KATHHOLISCHER ARBEITER- UND KNAPPENVEREINE WEST- DEUTSCHLANDS.

ARETZ (JUERGEN) Katholische Arbeiterbewegung und Nationalsozialismus: der Verband katholischer Arbeiter- und Knappenvereine Westdeutschlands, 1923-1945. Mainz, [1978]. pp. 252. *bibliog. (Kommission für Zeitgeschichte. Veröffentlichungen. Reihe B: Forschungen. Band 25)*

VETERINARY MEDICINE

— **Canada.**

A NATIONAL statement by the faculties of agriculture and veterinary medicine at Canadian universities. [Ottawa, Science Council of Canada, 1974?]. pp. 22.

VICKERS LIMITED.

EVANS (HAROLD) Vickers: against the odds, 1956-1977. London, [1978]. pp. 287.

BEYNON (HUW) and WAINWRIGHT (HILARY) The workers' report on Vickers. London, 1979. pp. 208. *bibliog.*

VICTIMS OF CRIME.

MEINERS (ROGER EVERT) Victim compensation: economic, legal, and political aspects. Lexington, Mass., [1978]. pp. 123. *bibliog.*

See also **ABUSED WIVES.**

— **Canada.**

WALLER (IRVIN) and OKIHIRO (NORMAN) Burglary: the victim and the public. Toronto, [1978]. pp. 190. *bibliog. (Toronto. University. Centre of Criminology. Canadian Studies in Criminology. 4)*

VICTOR VERSTER PRISON.

SOUTH AFRICA. Department of Prisons. 1968. Victor Verster prison complex. [Pretoria, 1968]. 1 pamphlet (unpaged).

VIENNA

— **Civilization.**

MAY (ARTHUR JAMES) Vienna in the age of Franz Josef. Norman, Okla., [1966]. pp. 154. *bibliog.*

— **History.**

MAY (ARTHUR JAMES) Vienna in the age of Franz Josef. Norman, Okla., [1966]. pp. 154. *bibliog.*

BOTZ (GERHARD) Wien vom "Anschluss" zum Krieg: nationalsozialistische Machtübernahme und politisch-soziale Umgestaltung am Beispiel der Stadt Wien, 1938/39; mit einem einleitenden Beitrag von Karl R. Stadler. Wien, [1978]. pp. 646. *bibliog.*

STEINER (HERBERT) 1923- . Karl Marx in Wien: die Arbeiterbewegung zwischen Revolution und Restauration, 1848. Wien, [1978]. pp. 223.

WIEN 1938; [by the Kommission Wien 1938; edited by Felix Czeike]. Wien, 1978. pp. 326. *bibliog. (Vienna. Verein für Geschichte der Stadt Wien. Forschungen und Beiträge zur Wiener Stadtgeschichte. Band 2)*

— **Intellectual life.**

MAY (ARTHUR JAMES) Vienna in the age of Franz Josef. Norman, Okla., [1966]. pp. 154. *bibliog.*

VIETNAM

— **Economic conditions.**

NGUYEN TIEN HUNG (G.) Economic developments of socialist Vietnam, 1955-80. New York, 1977. pp. 193.

THÂNHKHÔI (LÊ) Socialisme et développement au Viêt Nam. [Paris, 1978]. pp. 323. *bibliog. (Paris. Université de Paris I (Panthéon- Sorbonne). Institut d'Etude du Développement Economique et Social. Collection Tiers Monde)*

— **Economic policy.**

NGUYEN TIEN HUNG (G.) Economic developments of socialist Vietnam, 1955-80. New York, 1977. pp. 193.

— **Foreign relations — France.**

SULLIVAN (MARIANNA P.) France's Vietnam policy: a study in French-American relations. Westport, Conn., 1978. pp. 165. *bibliog.*

— — **United States.**

VIETNAM (DEMOCRATIC REPUBLIC). Commission for Investigation on the American Imperialists' War Crimes in Vietnam. 1966. The U.S. war of aggression in Vietnam: a crime against the Vietnamese people, against peace and humanity. [Hanoi?], 1966. pp. 47. Photocopy.

LEWY (GUENTER) America in Vietnam. New York, 1978. pp. 540. *bibliog.*

GELB (LESLIE H.) and BETTS (RICHARD K.) The irony of Vietnam: the system worked. Washington, D.C., [1979]. pp. 387. *bibliog.*

— **Population.**

VIETNAM (REPUBLIC). National Institute of Statistics. 1973. Population survey in rural areas in Vietnam, 1971. [Saigon], 1973. pp. 40. *In English and Vietnamese.*

— **Rural conditions.**

POPKIN (SAMUEL L.) The rational peasant: the political economy of rural society in Vietnam. Berkeley, 1979. pp. 306. *bibliog.*

VIETNAM (Cont.)

— Social conditions.

THÂNHKHÔI (LÊ) Socialisme et développement au Viêt Nam. [Paris, 1978]. pp. 323. *bibliog.* (*Paris. Université de Paris I (Panthéon- Sorbonne). Institut d'Etude du Développement Economique et Social. Collection Tiers Monde*)

VIETNAMESE WARS, 1945-1975.

VIETNAM (DEMOCRATIC REPUBLIC). Commission for Investigation on the American Imperialists' War Crimes in Vietnam. 1966. The U.S. war of aggression in Vietnam: a crime against the Vietnamese people, against peace and humanity. [Hanoi?], 1966. pp. 47. Photocopy.

VIETNAM (REPUBLIC). Ministry of Foreign Affairs. 1969. The peace negotiations and the communist aggression. Saigon, 1969. pp. 30.

WILEY (PETER) Vietnam and the Pacific rim strategy. Boston, Mass., [c.1972]. pp. 22. *bibliog. Reprinted from the Leviathan of June 1969.*

BASKIR (LAWRENCE M.) and STRAUSS (WILLIAM A.) Chance and circumstance: the draft, the war, and the Vietnam generation. New York, 1978. pp. 312. *bibliog.*

LEWY (GUENTER) America in Vietnam. New York, 1978. pp. 540. *bibliog.*

PALMER (DAVE RICHARD) Summons of the trumpet: U.S.-Vietnam in perspective. San Rafael, [1978]. pp. 277.

PALMER (GREGORY) The McNamara strategy and the Vietnam war: program budgeting in the Pentagon, 1960-1968. Westport, Conn., [1978]. pp. 169. *bibliog.*

SHARP (ULYSSES S. GRANT) Strategy for defeat: Vietnam in retrospect. San Rafael, Calif., [1978]. pp. 324.

A SHORT history of the Vietnam War; edited by Allan R. Millett. Bloomington, [1978]. pp. 169. *bibliog.*

GELB (LESLIE H.) and BETTS (RICHARD K.) The irony of Vietnam: the system worked. Washington, D.C., [1979]. pp. 387. *bibliog.*

— Personal narratives, British.

THOMAS (LIZ) Dust of life: children of the Saigon streets. London, 1978. pp. 199.

— Protest movements — United States.

HALSTEAD (FRED) Out nowe': a participant's account of the American movement against the Vietnam war. New York, 1978. pp. 759.

VIKINGS.

BRØNDSTED (JOHANNES) The Vikings. Harmondsworth, 1978 pp. 347. *bibliog.*

VILLAGE COMMUNITIES

— India.

BATTERSBY (OLWEN) Bhoodan-Gramden: the gentle revolution. London, [1973?]. pp. 8. (*Marr-Munning Trust. Edwina Mountbatten Papers. No. 2*)

BATTERSBY (OLWEN) Samanway Vidapith: the Marr-Munning ashram. London, [1974?]. pp. 14. (*Marr-Munning Trust. Edwina Mountbatten Papers. No. 4*)

VILLAGES

— Bibliography.

BRIGHTON. University of Sussex. Institute of Development Studies. Village Studies Programme. Village studies: data analysis and bibliography;...compiled by Mick Moore [and others]; edited by Claire M. Lambert. Epping, afterwards London, 1976-78. 2 vols.

— China.

PARISH (WILLIAM L.) and WHYTE (MARTIN KING) Village and family in contemporary China. Chicago, [1978]. pp. 419. *bibliog.*

— Denmark.

MOGENSEN (GUNNAR VIBY) and others. Småbyer i landdistrikter; (with an English summary) Villages in rural areas: population development and living conditions. København, 1979. pp. 421. *bibliog.* (*Socialforskningsinstituttet. Publikationer. 86*)

— Japan.

DORE (RONALD PHILIP) Shinohata: a portrait of a Japanese village. London, 1978. pp. 322.

— Thailand.

SHARP (LAURISTON W.) and HANKS (LUCIEN MASON) Bang Chan: social history of a rural community in Thailand. Ithaca, 1978. pp. 314. *bibliog.*

— Underdeveloped areas.

See UNDERDEVELOPED AREAS — Villages.

VIOLENCE.

TOURNIER (PAUL) The violence inside. London, 1978. pp. 201.

VIOLENCE and responsibility: the individual, the family and society; [edited by] Robert L. Sadoff. New York, [1978]. pp. 139.

TERRORISM: theory and practice; edited by Yonah Alexander [and others]. Boulder, Colo., 1979. pp. 280. *bibliog.*

— Bibliography.

FRANCE. Comité d'Etudes sur la Violence, la Criminalité et la Délinquance. 1977. Réponses à la violence...Documentation du comité. Paris, [1977]. pp. 397. *bibliog.* (*Annexes. 8*)

— France.

FRANCE. Comité d'Etudes sur la Violence, la Criminalité et la Délinquance. 1977. Réponses à la violence... Auditions du comité. Paris, [1977]. pp. 233. (*Annexes. 7*)

FRANCE. Comité d'Etudes sur la Violence, la Criminalité et la Délinquance. 1977. Réponses à la violence...Documentation du comité. Paris, [1977]. pp. 397. *bibliog.* (*Annexes. 8*)

I.F.O.P. Réponses à la violence...Trois études générales. Paris, [1977]. pp. 165. (*France. Comité d'Etudes sur la Violence, la Criminalité et la Délinquance. Annexes. 1*)

REPONSES à la violence...Recherches sur l'urbanisation, l'habitat et la violence. Paris, [1977]. pp. 424. *bibliog.* (*France. Comité d'Etudes sur la Violence, la Criminalité et la Délinquance. Annexes. 3*)

REPONSES à la violence... Recherches sur la protection de la jeunesse. Paris, [1977]. pp. 408. (*France. Comité d'Etudes sur la Violence, la Criminalité et la Délinquance. Annexes. 5*)

REPONSES à la violence... Recherches sur la violence et l'économie. Paris, [1977]. pp. 457. (*France. Comité d'Etudes sur la Violence, la Criminalité et la Délinquance. Annexes. 4*)

REPONSES à la violence...Recherches sur les aspects pénaux et pénitentiaires. Paris, [1977]. pp. 202. *bibliog.* (*France. Comité d'Etudes sur la Violence, la Criminalité et la Délinquance. Annexes. 6*)

REPONSES à la violence...Recherches sur les aspects psychologiques et biologiques de la violence. Paris, [1977]. pp. 35,38. (*France. Comité d'Etudes sur la Violence, la Criminalité et la Délinquance. Annexes. 2*)

— Germany.

LUDEWIG (HANS ULRICH) Arbeiterbewegung und Aufstand: eine Untersuchung zum Verhalten der Arbeiterparteien in den Aufstandsbewegungen der frühen Weimarer Republik, 1920-1923. Husum, [1978]. pp. 267. *bibliog.*

— Poland.

PAWEŁCZYŃSKA (ANNA) Values and violence in Auschwitz: a sociological analysis; translated with an introduction by Catherine S. Leach. Berkeley, 1979. pp. 170.

— United States.

JEFFREYS-JONES (RHODRI) Violence and reform in American history. New York, 1978. pp. 242. *bibliog.*

RIOT, rout, and tumult: readings in American social and political violence; edited by Roger Lane and John J. Turner. Westport, Conn., 1978. pp. 399. *bibliog.*

VIOLENCE and responsibility: the individual, the family and society; [edited by] Robert L. Sadoff. New York, [1978]. pp. 139.

WEINBAUM (PAUL OWEN) Mobs and demagogues: the New York response to collective violence in the early nineteenth century. [London, 1979]. pp. 194. *bibliog.*

VIOLENCE IN MASS MEDIA.

DEVIANCE and mass media; edited by Charles Winick. Beverly Hills, [1978]. pp. 309. *bibliogs.*

VIRGINIA

— Economic conditions.

VIRGINIA ECONOMIC REVIEW, THE: a pbln. of the Virginia Division of Industrial Development. irreg., D 1971- Richmond, Va.

—Politics and government.

RISJORD (NORMAN K.) Chesapeake politics 1781-1800. New York, 1978. pp. 715. *bibliog.*

VISUAL PERCEPTION.

DAVIDOFF (JULES B.) Differences in visual perception: the individual eye. St. Albans, 1975. pp. 231. *bibliog.*

VITAL STATISTICS.

PRESSAT (ROLAND) Statistical demography;...translated and adapted by Damien A. Courtney. London, 1978. pp. 150.

VITTORIO (GIUSEPPE DI).

PISTILLO (MICHELE) Giuseppe Di Vittorio, 1944-1957: la costruzione della CGIL; la lotta per la rinascita del paese e l'unità dei lavoratori. Roma, 1977. pp. 361.

VOCATIONAL EDUCATION

— European Economic Community countries.

VOCATIONAL TRAINING INFORMATION BULLETIN; [pd.by] Commission of the European Communities, Directorate-General for Social Affairs, Vocational Guidance and Training Division. q., Jl 1974(no.1)- Bruxelles. *Incorporates Documentation pédagogique, of which the Library has no file.*

— Finland.

FINLAND. Tilastokeskus. Ammatilliset oppilaitokset. a., 1977- Helsinki. *[in Finnish and Swedish with English summary and table headings]*

— France.

FRANCE. Comité du Travail Féminin. 1976. La formation professionnelle continue des femmes;...mise à jour: juillet 1976. [Paris, Centre pour le Développement de l'Information sur la Formation Permanente, 1976]. pp. 68.

FRANCE. Commission sur l'Avenir de la Formation. 1976. L'avenir de la formation: rapport, etc. 2nd ed. [Paris], 1976. pp. 75.

CHAMBON (BERNARD) Les relations entre l'emploi et la formation professionnelle dans la région Rhône-Alpes: dossier de l'emploi et de la formation professionnelle: emplois d'ouvriers et d'employés qualifiés: département de l'Ain; réalisé...sous la direction de Roland Beltramelli. [Lyons], Etablissement Public Régional Rhône-Alpes, 1978. pp. 121. bibliog.

FRANCE. Délégation à la Condition Féminine. 1978. Attitudes et comportements des parents envers le problème de l'orientation scolaire. [Paris], 1978. pp. 70.

— India.

INDIA. National Review Committee on Higher Secondary Education with Special Reference to Vocationalisation. 1978. Learning to do: towards a learning and working society: report.. .; [M.S. Adiseshiah, chairman]. New Delhi, 1978. pp. 60.

— Russia.

RABOCHII klass SSSR na sovremennom etape. vyp.5. Podgotovka i vospitanie kadrov rabochego klassa SSSR v usloviiakh razvitogo sotsializma; otvetstvennye redaktory V.A. Ezhov, V.A. Ovsiankin. Leningrad, 1977. pp. 183.

— United States.

EDUCATING for careers: policy issues in a time of change; edited by Thomas F. Powers with the assistance of John R. Swinton. University Park, Pa., [1977]. pp. 190. *Based on a symposium held in 1976 at the Pennsylvania State University.*

VOCATIONAL GUIDANCE.

FRIEND (JEANNETTE G.) and HAGGARD (ERNEST ALEXANDER) Work adjustment in relation to family background: a conceptual basis for counseling; a report of an investigation sponsored by the Family Society of Greater Boston. Stanford, 1948. pp. 150. bibliog. *(American Psychological Association. Applied Psychology Monographs. No. 16)*

— Belgium.

INSTITUT BELGE D'INFORMATION ET DE DOCUMENTATION. Le monde des professions. [Brussels, 1968]. pp. 143.

— Russia — Siberia.

KONSTANTINOVSKII (DAVID L'VOVICH) Dinamika professional'nykh orientatsii molodezhi Sibiri: opyt sotsiologicheskogo issledovaniia. Novosibirsk, 1977. pp. 174. bibliog.

— Singapore.

VOCATIONAL GUIDANCE STEERING COMMITTEE [SINGAPORE]. Sea careers. Singapore, Government Printing Office, [1968]. pp. 69.

— United Kingdom — Ireland, Northern.

OPPORTUNITIES at sixteen; report of a study group; [Derek Birley, chairman]. Belfast, H.M.S.O., 1978. pp. 110. bibliog.

— United States.

EDUCATING for careers: policy issues in a time of change; edited by Thomas F. Powers with the assistance of John R. Swinton. University Park, Pa., [1977]. pp. 190. *Based on a symposium held in 1976 at the Pennsylvania State University.*

VOCATIONAL QUALIFICATIONS.

The STUDY of real skills vol. 1. The analysis of practical skills; edited by W.T. Singleton. Lancaster, [1978]. pp. 333. bibliogs.

VOEGELIN (ERIC HERMAN WILHELM).

ERIC Voegelin's search for order in history; edited by Stephen A. McKnight. Baton Rouge, [1978]. pp. 209. bibliog.

VOELKISCHER BEOBACHTER.

SCHWARZ (ROBERT) 1921- . "Sozialismus" der Propaganda: das Werben des "Völkischen Beobachters" um die österreichische Arbeiterschaft, 1938/1939; mit einer Einleitung von Gerhard Botz, etc. Wien, 1975. pp. 159. bibliog. *(Ludwig Boltzmann Institut für Geschichte der Arbeiterbewegung. Materialien zur Arbeiterbewegung. Nr.2)*

VOILQUIN (SUZANNE).

VOILQUIN (SUZANNE) Souvenirs d'une fille du peuple; ou, La Saint-simonienne en Égypte. Paris, 1978. pp. 406.

VOLGA BASIN

— History — 1917-1921, Revolution.

TAGIROV (INDUS RIZAKOVICH) Revoliutsionnaia bor'ba i natsional'no-osvoboditel'noe dvizhenie v Povolzh'e i na Urale, fevral' - iiul' 1917 goda. Kazan', 1977. pp. 216.

— Politics and government.

OBSHCHESTVENNO-politicheskaia mysl' v Povolzh'e v XIX - nachale XX vv. Kazan', 1977. pp. 272.

VOLGOGRAD (OBLAST')

— Politics and government.

OCHERKI istorii Volgogradskoi organizatsii KPSS. Volgograd, 1977. pp. 703.

VÖLKISCHER BEOBACHTER.

See VOELKISCHER BEOBACHTER.

VOLTAIRE (FRANÇOIS MARIE AROUET DE).

SIVOLAP (INESSA IVANOVNA) Sotsial'nye idei Vol'tera. Moskva, 1978. pp. 284. bibliog.

VOLUNTEER WORKERS IN SOCIAL SERVICE.

LEAT (DIANA) Towards a definition of volunteer involvement. Berkhamsted, [1977]. pp. 27. bibliog.

— Canada — Quebec.

QUEBEC (PROVINCE). Conseil des Affaires Sociales et de la Famille. 1978. La question de la promotion des initiatives volontaires dans le domaine des affaires sociales au Québec. [Quebec, 1978]. pp. 27. *(Etudes et Avis)*

— Israel.

KRAMER (RALPH M.) The voluntary service agency in Israel. Berkeley, [1976]. pp. 94. bibliog. *(California University. Institute of International Studies. Research Series. No.26)*

— United Kingdom.

U.K. 1978. The government and the voluntary sector: a consultative document. [London, 1978]. pp. 53.

VOORHIS (JERRY).

VOORHIS (JERRY) Confessions of a congressman. Westport, Conn., 1970. pp. 365. *Reprint of work originally published Garden City, 1947.*

VORSTER (BALTHAZAR JOHANNES).

VORSTER (BALTHAZAR JOHANNES) Select speeches; edited by O. Geyser. Bloemfontein, 1977. pp. 363. bibliog.

VOTERS, REGISTRATION OF

— United States.

GARROW (DAVID J.) Protest at Selma: Martin Luther King, Jr., and the Voting Rights Act of 1965. New Haven, 1978. pp. 346.

VOTING

— Japan.

FLANAGAN (SCOTT C.) and RICHARDSON (BRADLEY M.) Japanese electoral behavior: social cleavages, social networks and partisanship. London, [1977]. pp. 93. bibliog.

— United States.

CHISMAN (FORREST P.) Attitude psychology and the study of public opinion. University Park, Pa., [1976]. pp. 253. bibliog.

ALLSWANG (JOHN M.) The New Deal and American politics: a study in political change. New York, [1978]. pp. 155. bibliog.

HADLEY (ARTHUR TWINING) 1924- . The empty polling booth. Englewood Cliffs, [1978]. pp. 179. bibliog.

PAGE (BENJAMIN I.) Choices and echoes in Presidential elections: rational man and electoral democracy. Chicago, [1978]. pp. 336.

KLEPPNER (PAUL) The third electoral system, 1853-1892: parties, voters and political cultures. Chapel Hill, N.C., [1979]. pp. 424. bibliog.

VOWELS.

NEAREY (TERRANCE MICHAEL) Phonetic feature systems for vowels. Bloomington, Ind., 1978. pp. 200. bibliog.

WAFD PARTY.

DEEB (MARIUS) Party politics in Egypt: the Wafd and its rivals, 1919-1939. London, 1979. pp. 451. bibliog.

WAGE-PRICE POLICY.

PERKINS (JAMES OLIVER NEWTON) The macroeconomic mix to stop stagflation. London, 1979. pp. 193. bibliog.

— Botswana.

KHAMA (Sir SERETSE) Address...during the inauguration of the first delegates conference of the Botswana Federation of Trade Unions at the town hall, Gaborone, on Saturday, 2nd April, 1977. Gaborone, 1977. pp. 7.

— Fiji.

FIJI. Ministry of Commerce, Industry and Co-operatives. 1973. Prices and incomes policy for Fiji. Suva, 1973. fo. 26.

— United Kingdom.

POND (CHRIS) The wages free fall: a submission to the chancellor and the TUC. London, 1977. fo. 8. *(Low Pay Unit. Low Pay Papers. No. 14)*

— United States.

CANADA. Food Prices Review Board. 1974. Food price trends in Canada and the United States: report with special reference to the U.S. price and income control program. [Ottawa], 1974. pp. 26,26. *In English and French.*

BOSWORTH (BARRY) and others. A conversation with the honorable Barry Bosworth: coping with inflation. Washington, [1978]. pp. 26. *(American Enterprise Institute for Public Policy Research. AEI Studies. 215)*

WAGES.

TUCKER (GEORGE) The laws of wages, profits and rent investigated. New York, 1964. pp. 189. *Reprint of the work first published Philadelphia, 1837.*

REYNOLDS (LLOYD GEORGE) The structure of labor markets: wages and labor mobility in theory and practice. Westport, Conn., 1951, repr. 1971. pp. 328.

BOURGUES (PAUL) Les salaires sont-ils responsables de l'inflation?; critique de l théorie de l'inflation salariale. [Paris, 1978]. pp. 182.

WAGES.(Cont.)

SILVESTRE (JEAN JACQUES) Les inégalités de salaires: marché du travail et croissance économique. [Paris, 1978]. pp. 306.

WOOD (ADRIAN) A theory of pay. Cambridge, 1978. pp. 251. *bibliog.*

— Dismissal wage — Brazil.

ALMEIDA (WANDERLY JOSE MANSO DE) and CHAUTARD (JOSE LUIZ) FGTS: uma politica de bem-estar social. Rio de Janeiro, 1976. pp. 159. *(Brazil. Instituto de Planejamento Econômico e Social. Instituto de Pesquisas. Relatorios de Pesquisa. No. 30)*

— Exemption — Canada.

PUCKETT (THOMAS COLLIN) Wage garnishment: a study of the problem in a Canadian metropolis. 1978. fo. 443. *bibliog. Typescript. Ph.D. (London) thesis: unpublished. Copy of questionnaire in end pocket. This thesis is the property of London University and may not be removed from the Library.*

— Minimum wage — Canada — British Columbia.

BRITISH COLUMBIA. Board of Industrial Relations. 1969. Summary of orders and regulations made pursuant to Male Minimum Wage Act, Female Minimum Wage Act, Annual and General Holidays Act, Hours of Work Act, Payment of Wages Act; compiled as at May 31, 1969. [Victoria], 1969. pp. 52.

— — India — Maharashtra.

MAHARASHTRA. Minimum Wages Committee for Employment in Printing and Allied Trades. 1965. Report...1964; [P.G. Kher, chairman]. [Bombay, 1965]. pp. 58.

MAHARASHTRA. Minimum Wages Committee for Employment in Glass Industry. 1970. Report...1969; [Adam Adil, chairman]. [Bombay, 1970]. pp. 50.

— — Tanzania.

TANGANYIKA. Non-Plantation Agricultural Workers Minimum Wages Board. 1963. Report; [F. Mfundo, chairman]. Dar es Salaam, 1963. pp. 15.

— — United States.

PIDGEON (MARY ELIZABETH) Women in the economy of the United States of America; [with] Employed women under N.R.A. codes. New York, 1975. 1 vol. (various pagings). *Reprint of works published in Washington D.C., 1937 and 1935.*

MARSHALL (RAY) and others. A conversation with Secretary Ray Marshall: inflation, unemployment and the minimum wage. Washington, [1978]. pp. 27. *(American Enterprise Institute for Public Policy Research. AEI Studies. 224)*

— Asia.

McDIARMID (ORVILLE JOHN) Unskilled labor for development: its economic cost...; published for the World Bank. Baltimore, [1977]. pp. 206. *bibliog. (International Bank for Reconstruction and Development. World Bank Research Publications)*

— Australia.

AUSTRALIA. Commonwealth Bureau of Census and Statistics. Earnings and hours of employees. a., 1977- Canberra.

— Brazil.

WERNECK (DOROTHEA FONSECA FURQUIM) Emprego e salarios na industria de construção. Rio de Janeiro, 1978. pp. 160. *bibliog. (Brazil. Instituto de Planejamento Econômico e Social. Instituto de Pesquisas. Relatorios de Pesquisa. No. 40)*

— Canada.

OSTRY (SYLVIA) and ZAIDI (MAHMOOD A.) Labour economics in Canada. 3rd ed. Toronto, [1979]. pp. 418.

— — Newfoundland.

TRADE DISPUTE BOARD [NEWFOUNDLAND]. Settlement of Trade Dispute Board appointed under the Defence, control and conditions of employment and disputes settlement, regulations, 1941, for the settlement of a dispute between the Employers' Association and the Longshoremen's Protective Union of St. John's. St. John's, Office of the King's Printer, 1942. pp. 62.

— France.

FRANCE. Centre d'Etude des Revenus et des Coûts. 1976. Dispersion et disparités de salaires en France au cours des vingt dernières années; [by Véronique Schloesing and Jean-Pierre Treuil]. Paris, 1976. pp. 162. *(Documents. No. 25-26)*

— Germany.

GERMANY. Statistisches Reichsamt. Statistik des Deutschen Reichs. Neue Folge. Band 293. Lohn- und Gehaltserhebung vom Februar 1920. Berlin, 1921; Osnabrück, 1977. pp. 438. *Photographic reprint.*

— Hong Kong.

HONG KONG. Labour Department. 1977. Some facts about employment in Hong Kong. Hong Kong, 1977. pp. 27.

— Israel.

DORON (ABRAHAM) and ROTER (RAPHAEL) Low wage earners and low wage subsidies. Jerusalem, Hebrew University Paul Baerwald School of Social Work and National Insurance Institute, Bureau of Research and Planning, 1978. pp. 217. *bibliog. First published in Hebrew in 1976.*

— Italy.

PREDETTI (ADALBERTO) Occupazione, retribuzioni, costo del lavoro in Italia. Milano, [1975]. pp. 265.

— Jamaica — Statistics.

JAMAICA. Department of Statistics. 1978. Employment, earnings and hours in large establishments, 1977. [Kingston, 1978]. pp. 45.

— Poland.

OPLATA truda pri sotsializme: voprosy teorii i praktiki; Płaca w ustroju socjalistycznym: zagadnienia teorii i praktyki. Moskva, 1977. pp. 207.

— Russia.

OPLATA truda pri sotsializme: voprosy teorii i praktiki; Płaca w ustroju socjalistycznym: zagadnienia teorii i praktyki. Moskva, 1977. pp. 207.

LUTOKHINA (ELEONORA ALEKSEEVNA) Zarabotnaia plata: zakonomernosti i problemy formirovaniia; redaktor G.T. Kovalevskii. Minsk, 1978. pp. 215.

— South Africa.

DE KLERK (DANIEL) The profitability of occupations pursued by highly qualified persons in 1975. Pretoria, 1976. pp. 59. *bibliog. (Human Sciences Research Council [South Africa] . Institute for Manpower Research. Reports. No. MM-60)*

DE KLERK (DANIEL) The wage structure of highly qualified white men as at 1 March, 1977. Pretoria, 1977. pp. 65. *(Human Sciences Research Council [South Africa]. Istitute for Manpower Research. Research Findings. M-N-48) In English and Afrikaans.*

RAEDEL (FRITZ E.) Progress or exploitation? Cape Town, 1978. pp. 55. *Translated from the German.*

— Tanzania.

UNITED REPUBLIC OF TANZANIA. Bureau of Statistics. 1974. N[ational] P[rovident] F[und] statistics 1970/71 with proposals and amendments. Dar es Salaam, 1974. fo. 71.

— Underdeveloped areas.

See UNDERDEVELOPED AREAS — Wages.

— United Kingdom.

POND (CHRIS) A jubilee year for the low paid? London, 1977. fo.4. *(Low Pay Unit. Low Pay Papers. No.18)*

POND (CHRIS) A social contract for the rich. London, 1977. fo. 6. *(Low Pay Unit. Low Pay Papers. No. 16)*

ENDERWICK (PETER) An examination of the Sargan method of wage leadership identification. Bradford, [1978?]. fo. 26. *bibliog. (University of Bradford. Management Centre. Occasional Papers. No. 7702)*

HURSTFIELD (JENNIFER) The part-time trap: part-time workers in Britain today. London, 1978. pp. 86. *(Low Pay Unit. Low Pay Pamphlets. No. 9)*

POND (CHRIS) Crumbs from the master's table?: a checklist on the tax cuts. London, 1978. fo. 8. *(Low Pay Unit. Low Pay Papers. No. 22)*

THOMAS (CERI) and ERLAM (ANDREW) Unequal portions: a survey of pay in the hotel and catering industry. London, 1978. pp. 18. *(Low Pay Unit. Low Pay Papers. No.23)*

— United States.

SCHACHTER (JOSEPH) Capital value and relative wage effects of immigration into the United States, 1870-1930. New York, 1977. pp. 125. *bibliog. Facsimile reprint of Ph.D. thesis, City University of New York, submitted in 1969.*

WALES

— Administrative and political divisions.

U.K. Local Government Boundary Commission for Wales. 1979- . Review of district electoral arrangements: draft proposals. [Cardiff, 1979 in progress].

— Church history.

LEWIS (HOWELL ELVET) Nonconformity in Wales. London, 1904. pp. 117. *(National Council of the Evangelical Free Churches. Eras of Nonconformity. 4)*

— Economic conditions.

WELSH ECONOMIC BULLETIN: a quarterly summary of Welsh facts and figures; [pd. by] Welsh Office. q., Ja/Mr 1975- , with gap (Oc/D 1975, Ja/Mr 1976) Cardiff.

— Economic policy.

LABOUR PARTY. Arwyddbyst i'r Cymru newydd. London, [1962?]. pp. 23.

LABOUR PARTY. Signposts to the new Wales:...policy statement for Wales... prepared by a working party including representatives of the National Executive Committee, the Welsh Council of Labour and the Welsh Labour Parliamentary Group. London, [1962?]. pp. 23.

— Foreign population.

BOLLOM (CHRIS) Attitudes and second homes in rural Wales. Cardiff, 1978. pp. 126. *(Wales. University. Board of Celtic Studies. Social Science Monographs. No. 3)*

— History.

WILLIAMS (GLANMOR) Religion, language, and nationality in Wales: historical essays. Cardiff, [1979]. pp. 252. *bibliog.*

— Industries.

IRESON (RICHARD) and TOMKINS (CYRIL R.) Inter-regional input-output for Wales and the rest of the U.K., 1968. [Cardiff], Welsh Council, [1978]. 1 vol.(various pagings). *bibliog.*

— **Population.**

U.K. Welsh Office. Planning Services Division. 1977. Wales population change, 1971-1976. [Cardiff], 1977. pp. (28). (*Occasional Papers. No. 5*)

— **Religion.**

WILLIAMS (GLANMOR) Religion, language, and nationality in Wales: historical essays. Cardiff, [1979]. pp. 252. *bibliog.*

—**Social policy.**

LABOUR PARTY. Arwyddbyst i'r Cymru newydd. London, [1962?]. pp. 23.

LABOUR PARTY. Signposts to the new Wales:...policy statement for Wales... prepared by a working party including representatives of the National Executive Committee, the Welsh Council of Labour and the Welsh Labour Parliamentary Group. London, [1962?]. pp. 23.

WALKER (PETER) M.P.

RAW (CHARLES) Slater Walker: an investigation of a financial phenomenon. London, 1977. pp. 368.

WALLIS AND FUTUNA ISLANDS

— **Census.**

WALLIS AND FUTUNA ISLANDS. Census, 1976. Résultats du recensement de la population de Wallis et Futuna, 26 mars 1976; [edited by Jean Paul Colliez]. Paris, [1978]. pp. 172.

WALLONIA

— **Economic conditions.**

La WALLONIE et l'Europe; troisième Colloque sur la Politique Régionale organisé par le Centre d'Etudes Européennes. Louvain, 1977. pp. 238. (*Groupe de Sociologie Wallone. Les Dossiers Wallons*)

— **Social conditions.**

La WALLONIE et l'Europe; troisième Colloque sur la Politique Régionale organisé par le Centre d'Etudes Européennes. Louvain, 1977. pp. 238. (*Groupe de Sociologie Wallone. Les Dossiers Wallons*)

WALLRAFF (GUENTER).

WALLRAFF (GUENTER) Wallraff: the undesirable journalist; [a selection of articles] translated by Steve Gooch and Paul Knight. London, 1978. pp. 180.

WALVIS BAY

— **History.**

WILKEN (J.J.J.) and FOX (G.J.) The history of the port and settlement of Walvis Bay, 1878-1978. Johannesburg, 1978. pp. 197. *bibliog.*

WANDSWORTH

— **Politics and government.**

ROEBUCK (JANET) Urban development in 19th-century London: Lambeth, Battersea and Wandsworth, 1838-1888. London, 1979. pp. 211. *bibliog.*

WAR.

BURTON (JOHN W.) Conflict as a function of change. London, [1966]. pp. 31. *bibliog. Reprinted from Ciba Foundation Symposium on conflict in society, 1966.*

WEEDE (ERICH) Weltpolitik und Kriegsursachen im 20. Jahrhundert: eine quantitativ-empirische Studie. München, 1975. pp. 438. *bibliog. With English summary.*

PROBLEMELE păcii şi ale războiului în condiţiile revoluţiei ştiinţifice şi tehnice: necesitatea istorică a dezarmării: sesiunea ştiinţifică din 21 ianuarie 1977. Bucureşti, 1977. pp. 488. *With English, French, German, Italian, Russian and Spanish tables of contents and identifications of authors.*

RUSSIA (USSR). Ministerstvo Oborony. 1977. Voina i armiia: filosofsko-sotsiologicheskii ocherk; pod redaktsiei D.A. Volkogonova [and others]. Moskva, 1977. pp. 415. *bibliog.*

COOK (CHRISTOPHER PIERS) and STEVENSON (JOHN) Historian. The atlas of modern warfare; research editor: Stephen Brooks. London, [1978]. pp. 191.

HOWARD (MICHAEL ELIOT) War and the nation state. Oxford, 1978. pp. 19. *An inaugural lecture delivered before Oxford University on 18 November 1977.*

STUART (REGINALD C.) The half-way pacifist: Thomas Jefferson's view of war. Toronto, [1978]. pp. 93. *bibliog.*

TAYLOR (ALAN JOHN PERCIVALE) How wars begin. London, 1979. pp. 180.

— **Moral aspects.**

LITHERLAND (ALAN) War under judgement. New Malden, [1978]. pp. 57.

— **Psychological aspects.**

OWEN (DAVID) b. 1939. Battle of wits: a history of psychology and deception in modern warfare. London, 1978. pp. 207.

WAR (INTERNATIONAL LAW).

RESTRAINTS on war: studies in the limitation of armed conflict; edited by Michael Howard. Oxford, 1979. pp. 173. *bibliog.*

WAR, MARITIME (INTERNATIONAL LAW).

OTTMUELLER (ROLF) Die Anwendung von Seekriegsrecht in militärischen Konflikten seit 1945. Hamburg, 1978. pp. 375. *bibliog.* (*Hamburg. Hansische Universität. Institut für Internationale Angelegenheiten. Das geltende Seekriegsrecht in Einzeldarstellungen. Band 10*) *With summary in English.*

WAR AND EMERGENCY POWERS

— **India.**

DAYAL (JOHN) and BOSE (AJOY) For reasons of state: Delhi under emergency. Delhi, 1977. pp. 239.

— **United States.**

HOLT (PAT M.) The War Powers Resolution: the role of Congress in U.S. armed intervention. Washington, D.C., [1978]. pp. 48. (*American Enterprise Institute for Public Policy Research. AEI Studies. 197*)

WAR AND MORALS.

PASKINS (BARRIE) and DOCKRILL (MICHAEL LAWRENCE) The ethics of war. London, 1979. pp. 332. *bibliog.*

WAR AND SOCIALISM.

GROSSHEIM (HEINRICH) Sozialisten in der Verantwortung: die französischen Sozialisten und Gewerkschafter im ersten Weltkrieg, 1914-17. Bonn, [1978]. pp. 286. *bibliog.* (*Friedrich-Ebert-Stiftung. Forschungsinstitut. Schriftenreihe. Band 140*)

LIDER (JULIAN) The political and military laws of war: an analysis of Marxist-Leninist concepts. Farnborough, 1979. pp. 266. *bibliog.* (*Utrikespolitiska Institutet. Swedish Studies in International Relations. 9*)

WAR CRIMES

— **Trials — Germany.**

NEAVE (AIREY) Nuremberg: a personal record of the trial of the major Nazi war criminals. London, 1978. pp. 348.

WEINGARTNER (JAMES J.) Crossroads of death: the story of the Malmédy massacre and trial. Berkeley, [1979]. pp. 274. *bibliog.*

WAR GAMES.

BREWER (GARRY D.) and SHUBIK (MARTIN) The war game: a critique of military problem solving. Cambridge, Mass., 1979. pp. 385.

WAREHOUSES

— **United Kingdom.**

BENWELL COMMUNITY DEVELOPMENT PROJECT. Storing up trouble: warehousing and distribution in west Newcastle. Newcastle-upon-Tyne, 1978. pp. 44. (*Final Report Series. No. 1*)

WARRANTY

— **United Kingdom.**

U.K. Law Commission. Working Papers. No. 73. Insurance law: non-disclosure and breach of warranty. London, 1979. pp. 126.

WARSAW

— **History.**

SZAROTA (TOMASZ) Okupowanej Warszawy dzień powszedni: studium historyczne. 2nd ed. Warszawa, 1978. pp. 706. *bibliog.*

WARSAW, PACT OF, 1955.

ZIEGER (GOTTFRIED) Der Warschauer Pakt. Hannover, Niedersächsische Landeszentrale für Politische Bildung, 1974. pp. 124.

WARWICKSHIRE

— **Economic history.**

SKIPP (VICTOR HENRY THOMAS) Crisis and development: an ecological case study of the Forest of Arden, 1570-1674. Cambridge, 1978. pp. 132.

— **Population.**

SKIPP (VICTOR HENRY THOMAS) Crisis and development: an ecological case study of the Forest of Arden, 1570-1674. Cambridge, 1978. pp. 132.

— **Social history.**

SKIPP (VICTOR HENRY THOMAS) Crisis and development: an ecological case study of the Forest of Arden, 1570-1674. Cambridge, 1978. pp. 132.

WARYAGHAR (BERBER PEOPLE).

HART (DAVID MONTGOMERY) The Aith Waryaghar of the Moroccan Rif: an ethnography and history. Tucson, Ariz., [1976]. pp. 556. *bibliog.* (*Wenner-Gren Foundation for Anthropological Research. Viking Fund Publications in Anthropology. No. 55*)

WASHINGTON (BOOKER TALIAFERRO).

THRASHER (MAX BENNETT) Tuskegee: its story and its work. Boston, Mass., 1901; New York, 1969. pp. 215. *Facsimile reprint.*

WASHINGTON, DURHAM

— **Growth.**

HOLE (WINIFRED VERE) and others. Washington New Town: the early years. London, H.M.S.O., 1979. pp. 149.

WASHINGTON, TREATY OF, 1842.

JONES (HOWARD) 1940- . To the Webster-Ashburton Treaty: a study in Anglo-American relations, 1783-1843. Chapel Hill, [1977]. pp. 251. *bibliog.*

WASTE LANDS

— **United Kingdom.**

NORTHERN REGION STRATEGY TEAM. Pollution and dereliction in the Northern Region. Newcastle-upon-Tyne, 1976. fo. (102). (*Technical Reports. No. 18*)

WASTE PRODUCTS.

WASTE PRODUCTS.

GRACE (RICHARD) and FISHER (JONATHAN) Beverage containers: re-use or recycling. Paris, Organisation for Economic Co-operation and Development, 1978. pp. 159. *bibliog.*

WATER

— Purification.

WORKING GROUP ON TREATMENT AGENTS AND PROCESSES FOR DRINKING-WATER AND THEIR EFFECTS ON HEALTH. Treatment agents and processes for drinking-water and their effects on health: report on a working group [held in] Brussels, 6-9 December 1977. Copenhagen, World Health Organization, Regional Office for Europe, 1978. pp. 22. *bibliog.*

— Waste.

UNITED NATIONS. Economic Commission for Europe. Committee on Water Problems. 1976. Principles and methods for the provision of economic incentives in water supply and waste disposal systems, including the fixing of charges: a report, etc. (ECE/WATER/16). New York, 1976. pp. 25.

WATER, UNDERGROUND

— United States.

BOWDEN (CHARLES) Killing the hidden waters. Austin, [1977]. pp. 174. *bibliog.*

WATER MILLS

— United Kingdom.

SOMERVELL (JOHN) Water-power mills of South Westmorland, on the Kent, Bela and Gilpin and their tributaries. Kendal, 1930. pp. 138.

WATER POWER

— United Kingdom.

SOMERVELL (JOHN) Water-power mills of South Westmorland, on the Kent, Bela and Gilpin and their tributaries. Kendal, 1930. pp. 138.

WATER POWER ELECTRIC PLANTS

— France.

FRANCE. Commission d'Etude de la Production d'Electricité d'Origine Hydraulique et Marémotrice. 1976. La production d'électricité d'origine hydraulique: rapport Paris, 1976. pp. 120. *(France. Ministère de l'Industrie et de la Recherche. Les Dossiers de l'Energie. 9)*

— Malawi.

MALAWI. Electricity Supply Commission. 1971. Malawi's Hydro-Electric Resources. [Blantyre, 1971]. pp. (7).

WATER QUALITY MANAGEMENT.

SEMINAR ON LONG-TERM PLANNING OF WATER MANAGEMENT, ZLATNI PIASATZI, 1976. Proceedings of the Seminar...17-22 May 1976. (ECE/WATER/15). New York, United Nations, 1976. 3 vols. (in 1).

REES (JUDITH ANNE) The management of urban domestic water services: studies in Australia and in England and Wales. 1978. fo. 368. *bibliog.* Typescript. Ph.D. (London) thesis: unpublished. This thesis is the property of London University and may not be removed from the Library.

WATER RESOURCES DEVELOPMENT.

SEMINAR ON LONG-TERM PLANNING OF WATER MANAGEMENT, ZLATNI PIASATZI, 1976. Proceedings of the Seminar...17-22 May 1976. (ECE/WATER/15). New York, United Nations, 1976. 3 vols. (in 1).

REES (JUDITH ANNE) The management of urban domestic water services: studies in Australia and in England and Wales. 1978. fo. 368. *bibliog.* Typescript. Ph.D. (London) thesis: unpublished. This thesis is the property of London University and may not be removed from the Library.

— Citizen participation — United Kingdom.

CLEVELAND [COUNTY]. Planning Department. River Tees plan: report of survey: public participation report. [Middlesbrough], 1976. pp. 97. *(Reports. No. 78)*

CLEVELAND [COUNTY]. Planning Department. River Tees plan for recreation and amenity: report on public participation of draft written statement. [Middlesbrough], 1978. fo.71 *(Reports. No. 105) Publicity material (3 items) in end pocket.*

— Social aspects.

FITZSIMMONS (STEPHEN J.) and SALAMA (OVADIA) Man and water: a social report. Boulder, Colo., 1977. pp. 428. *bibliog.*

— China.

GREER (CHARLES) Water management in the Yellow River basin of China. Austin, [1979]. pp. 174. *bibliog.*

— Latin America.

SELECTED water management issues in Latin American agriculture; edited by Pierre R. Crosson [and others]. Baltimore, [1978]. pp. 190. *bibliog.*

— South Africa.

SOUTH AFRICA. Department of Information. 1968. Orange River project. [Pretoria, 1968]. pp. 48. *(Fact Paper Series)*

— Underdeveloped areas.

See UNDERDEVELOPED AREAS — Water resources development.

— United States.

JACKSON (W. TURRENTINE) and PATERSON (ALAN M.) The Sacramento-San Joaquin Delta: the evolution and implementation of water policy: an historical perspective. Davis, Calif., 1977. pp. 192. *(California University. Water Resources Center. Contributions. No. 163)*

WATER SUPPLY.

SEMINAR ON LONG-TERM PLANNING OF WATER MANAGEMENT, ZLATNI PIASATZI, 1976. Proceedings of the Seminar...17-22 May 1976. (ECE/WATER/15). New York, United Nations, 1976. 3 vols. (in 1).

UNITED NATIONS. Economic Commission for Europe. Committee on Water Problems. 1976. Principles and methods for the provision of economic incentives in water supply and waste disposal systems, including the fixing of charges: a report, etc. (ECE/WATER/16). New York, 1976. pp. 25.

INTERMEDIATE TECHNOLOGY DEVELOPMENT GROUP. Technology is not enough: the provision and maintenance of appropriate water supplies;...edited and compiled by Arnold Pacey; [with] Abstracts of thematic papers [of] the United Nations Water Conference. Oxford, 1977. pp. 252. *bibliog.* Published as Aqua, vol. 1, no. 1-2, 1977.

— Brazil.

ALMEIDA (WANDERLY JOSE MANSO DE) Abastecimento de agua à população urbana: una avaliação do PLANASA. Rio de Janeiro, 1977. pp. 136. *(Brazil. Instituto de Planejamento Econômico e Social. Instituto de Pesquisas. Relatorios de Pesquisa. No. 37)*

— India — Punjab.

PUNJAB (INDIA). Economic and Statistical Organisation. 1976. Evaluation report on the survey of rural water supply schemes in Punjab. Chandigarh, [1976]. pp. 81. *(Publications. No. 256)*

— Malawi.

NYASALAND. [Legislative Council]. Sessional Papers. 1930. No. 5. Colonial Development Fund: scheme for investigation of water supplies. [Zomba], 1930. pp. 5.

— Underdeveloped areas.

See UNDERDEVELOPED AREAS — Water supply.

— United Kingdom.

OKUN (DANIEL A.) Regionalization of water management: a revolution in England and Wales. London, [1977]. pp. 377. *bibliogs.*

NATIONAL WATER COUNCIL [U.K.]. Water industry review, 1978. London, 1978. pp. 99.

PORTER (ELIZABETH) Water management in England and Wales. Cambridge, 1978. pp. 178. *bibliog.*

WATER SUPPLY, AGRICULTURAL

— Latin America.

SELECTED water management issues in Latin American agriculture; edited by Pierre R. Crosson [and others]. Baltimore, [1978]. pp. 190. *bibliog.*

WEALTH.

LANTZ (PIERRE) Valeur et richesse: aux marges de l'économie politique, une approche de l'idée de nature. Paris, 1977. pp. 458. *bibliog.*

HARRISON (ALAN JAMES) The distribution of wealth in ten countries;...background paper to Report No. 7: fourth report on the standing reference. London, 1979. pp. 77. *bibliog. (U.K. Royal Commission on the Distribution of Income and Wealth, 1974. Background Papers. No. 7) Report No.7 published as British Parliamentary Paper Cmnd. 7595, Session 1979-80.*

HUTTON (JOHN) The mystery of wealth: political economy - its development and impact on world events. Cheltenham, 1979. pp. 412. *bibliog.*

— East (Near East).

DUNCAN (ANDREW) Money rush. London, 1979. pp. 384. *bibliog.*

— Germany.

ENGELMANN (BERNT) Das Reich zerfiel, die Reichen blieben: Deutschlands Geld- und Machtelite; mit Rangliste der 500 grossen alten Vermögen. München, 1975 repr.1978. pp. 402. *bibliog.*

— United Kingdom.

TOWNSEND (PETER BRERETON) Trends in the distribution of resources in the United Kingdom 1938-1970. Colchester, 1971. fo. 71.

CITY CAPITAL MARKETS COMMITTEE. Written evidence to the Royal Commission on the Distribution of Income and Wealth. [London], 1975. fo.12.

GOUGH (JULIAN) Housing policy and the distribution of income and wealth in the U.K. Cardiff, 1976. fo.28,ii. *bibliog. (Wales. University. University College, Cardiff. Institute of Science and Technology. Research and Discussion Papers in Economics, Finance and Politics. No. 1)*

CREEDY (JOHN) Pension schemes and the limits to redistribution. London, [1978]. pp. 22. *bibliog. (National Institute of Economic and Social Research. Discussion Papers. No. 24)*

U.K. Central Statistical Office. 1978. Personal sector balance sheets and current developments in Inland Revenue estimates of personal wealth. London, 1978. pp. 51. *(Studies in Official Statistics. No. 35)*

The WEALTH report; edited by Frank Field. London, 1979. pp. 196. *bibliog.*

— United States.

JONES (ALICE HANSON) American colonial wealth: documents and methods. 2nd ed. New York, 1977. 3 vols.

STURM (JAMES LESTER) Investing in the United States 1798-1893: upper wealth-holders in a market economy. New York, 1977. pp. 196. *bibliog.*

WEALTH redistribution and the income tax...; edited by Arleen A. Leibowitz. Lexington, Mass., [1978]. pp. 130. *bibliog. Papers and discussions from a conference sponsored by the Liberty Fund, Jan. 21-23, 1977. Principal paper by Norman B. Ture.*

— — Texas.

CAMPBELL (RANDOLPH B.) and LOWE (RICHARD) Wealth and power in antebellum Texas. College Station, [1977]. pp. 183. *bibliog.*

WEAPONS SYSTEMS.

INSECURITY!: the spread of weapons in the Indian and Pacific oceans; [edited by] Robert O'Neill. Canberra, 1978. pp. 280. *bibliogs.*

WEBER (MAX).

MAX Weber and sociology today; edited by Otto Stammer; translated by Kathleen Morris. Oxford, 1971. pp. 256. *Transactions of the 15th German Sociological Congress held in Heidelberg.*

BENSON (LESLIE) Proletarians and parties: five essays in social class. London, 1978. pp. 194. *bibliog.*

ZANDER (JUERGEN) Das Problem der Beziehung Max Webers zu Karl Marx. Frankfurt/Main, [1978]. pp. 179. *bibliog.*

WEDGWOOD (JOSIAH CLEMENT) 1st Baron Wedgwood.

WEDGWOOD (JOSIAH CLEMENT) 1st Baron Wedgwood. Memoirs of a fighting life. London, 1940. pp. 256.

WEITLING (WILHELM).

BRAVO (GIAN MARIO) ed. Da Weitling a Marx: la Lega dei Comunisti; [a collection of documents]. Milano, [1977]. pp. 307. *bibliog.*

WELCH GRAPE JUICE COMPANY.

CHAZANOF (WILLIAM) Welch's grape juice: from corporation to co-operative. New York, [1977]. pp. 407. *bibliog.*

WELFARE ECONOMICS.

COWHERD (RAYMOND GIBSON) Political economists and the English Poor Laws: a historical study of the influence of classical economics on the formation of social welfare policy. Athens, Ohio, [1977]. pp. 300. *bibliog.*

BECKWITH (BURNHAM PUTNAM) Liberal socialism applied: the applied welfare economics of a liberal socialist economy. Palo Alto, [1978]. pp. 331.

MEIJER (WIM) Welzijnsbeleid: een keuze voor verandering van de maatschappij. Alphen aan den Rijn, 1978. pp. 182.

OSMANI (SIDDIQUR RAHMAN) Economic inequality and group welfare: theory and application to Bangladesh. 1978. fo. 329. *bibliog. Typescript. Ph.D. (London) thesis: unpublished. This thesis is the property of London University and may not be removed from the Library.*

SALAMON (LESTER M.) Welfare: the elusive consensus; where we are, how we got there, and what's ahead. New York, [1978]. pp. 257. *bibliogs. A report from the Welfare Policy Project of the Ford Foundation and Duke University.*

SANDLER (TODD M.) and others. The political economy of public goods and international cooperation. Denver, Colo., [1978]. pp. 98. *bibliog. (Denver. University. Graduate School of International Studies. Monograph Series in World Affairs. vol. 15, no. 3)*

SCHMID (ALFRED ALLAN) Property, power, and public choice: an inquiry into law and economics. New York, [1978]. pp. 316. *bibliog.*

The VALUATION of social cost; edited by David W. Pearce. London, 1978. pp. 197. *bibliogs.*

PINKER (ROBERT ARTHUR) The idea of welfare. London, 1979. pp. 276. *bibliog.*

WELFARE STATE.

ROBSON (WILLIAM ALEXANDER) Welfare state and welfare society: illusion and reality. London, 1976, repr. 1977. pp. 184.

DELEECK (HERMAN) Ongelijkheden in de welvaartsstaat: opstellen over sociaal beleid: tweede bundel. Antwerpen, [1977]. pp. 319.

SOCIAL welfare and New Zealand society; edited by A.D. Trlin. Wellington, 1977. pp. 235. *bibliogs.*

GRØNBJERG (KIRSTEN A.) and others. Poverty and social change. Chicago, [1978]. pp. 248. *bibliog.*

FRY (GEOFFREY KINGDON) The growth of government: the development of ideas about the role of the state and the machinery and functions of government in Britain since 1780. London, 1979. pp. 295. *bibliog.*

HARRIS (RALPH) and SELDON (ARTHUR) Over-ruled on welfare: the increasing desire for choice in education and medicine and its frustration by 'representative' government. London, 1979. pp. 249. *bibliog.*

KRAUSS (MELVYN B.) The new protectionism: the welfare state and international trade. Oxford, [1979]. pp. 119. *bibliogs.*

LIMITS of the welfare state: critical views on post-war Sweden; edited by John Fry. Farnborough, Hants., [1979]. pp. 234. *Selection of articles, in English translation, which originally appeared in Zenit and other Swedish periodicals.*

POST-INDUSTRIAL society: proceedings of an international symposium held in Uppsala from 22 to 25 March 1977 to mark the occasion of the 500th anniversary of Uppsala University; edited by Bo Gustafsson. London, [1979]. pp. 238. *bibliogs.*

WELFARE WORK IN INDUSTRY

— Netherlands.

KOOPMANS (R.R.) Deprivatie en arbeids problematiek in het bijzonder van werknemers uit probleemgezinnen. 's-Gravenhage, Ministerie van Cultuur, Recreatie en Maatschappelijk Werk, 1970. pp. 64.

WELLESLEY (ARTHUR) 1st Duke of Wellington.

GLOVER (MICHAEL) Wellington's army in the Peninsula, 1808-1814. Vancouver, [1977]. pp. 192. *bibliog.*

WEST, THE

— History.

HARDEMAN (NICHOLAS PERKINS) Wilderness calling: the Hardeman family in the American westward movement, 1750-1900. Knoxville, [1977]. pp. 357. *bibliog.*

LARSEN (LAWRENCE HAROLD) The urban West at the end of the frontier. Lawrence, [1978]. pp. 173. *bibliog.*

WEST INDIAN LITERATURE

— History and criticism.

GRIFFITHS (GARETH) A double exile: African and West Indian writing between two cultures. London, 1978. pp. 205. *bibliog.*

WEST INDIANS IN THE UNITED KINGDOM.

LOUDEN (DELROY M.) West Indian adolescents in school: towards a typology of behaviour patterns. [Bristol, Social Science Research Council Research Unit on Ethnic Relations, 1976?]. fo. 14.

U.K. Commission for Racial Equality. 1977. Education of ethnic minorities: comments on the consultative document issued by the Department of Education and Science on the report on the West Indian community issued by the Select Committee on Race Relations and Immigration. London, 1977. pp. 6. *(Occasional Papers. No. 1)*

LEACH (BRIDGET) Youth and spatial poverty: activity space patterns of black and white young people in Leeds. Bristol, Social Science Research Council Research Unit on Ethnic Relations, [1978]. pp. 78. *bibliog. (Working Papers on Ethnic Relations. No. 9)*

MILES (ROBERT) Between two cultures?: the case of Rastafarianism. Bristol, Social Science Reseach Council Research Unit on Ethnic Relations, [1978]. pp. 34. *bibliog. (Working Papers on Ethnic Relations. No. 10)*

EDWARDS (V.K.) The West Indian language issue in British schools: challenges and responses. London, 1979. pp. 168. *bibliog.*

FONER (NANCY) Jamaica farewell: Jamaican migrants in London. London, 1979. pp. 262. *bibliog.*

REX (JOHN ARDERNE) and TOMLINSON (SALLY) Colonial immigrants in a British city: a class analysis. London, 1979. pp. 357. *bibliog.*

WEST INDIES

— Commerce — France.

MIQUELON (DALE) Dugard of Rouen: French trade to Canada and the West Indies, 1729-1770. Montreal, [1978]. pp. 282. *bibliog.*

WEST MIDLANDS

— Bibliography.

SMITH (BARBARA M.D.) and MACDONALD (MORAG) compilers. A bibliographic profile of the West Midlands county in the 1970s. Birmingham, 1978. pp. 188. *(Birmingham. University. Centre for Urban and Regional Studies. Re~earch Memoranda. No. 61)*

— Economic policy.

SMITH (BARBARA M.D.) Industry in metropolitan area plans: proposals and experience in the West Midlands County area. Birmingham, 1977. pp. 148. *(Birmingham. University. Centre for Urban and Regional Studies. Research Memoranda. No.62)*

— Foreign population.

CLARK (DAVID) Immigrant responses to the British housing market: a case study in the West Midlands conurbation. Bristol, Social Science Research Council Research Unit on Ethnic Relations, [1977]. pp. 65. *bibliog. (Working Papers on Ethnic Relations. No. 7)*

— Industries.

SMITH (BARBARA M.D.) Industry in metropolitan area plans: proposals and experience in the West Midlands County area. Birmingham, 1977. pp. 148. *(Birmingham. University. Centre for Urban and Regional Studies. Research Memoranda. No.62)*

WEST YORKSHIRE

— Economic conditions.

WEST YORKSHIRE. Metropolitan County Council. Structure plan: report of survey; [part 1], December 1977. [Wakefield], 1977. 2 vols.

WEST YORKSHIRE. Metropolitan County Council. Structure plan: report of survey; part 2, December 1978. [Wakefield], 1978. 1 vol. (various pagings).

— Economic policy.

OPINION RESEARCH CENTRE. A report on a survey of public attitudes in connection with the preparation of the structure plan; prepared for West Yorkshire Metropolitan County Council. London, 1975. pp. 99, 25.

WEST YORKSHIRE. Metropolitan County Council. Structure plan: report of survey; [part 1], December 1977. [Wakefield], 1977. 2 vols.

WEST YORKSHIRE. Metropolitan County Council. Structure plan: written statement: consultation draft, October 1977. Wakefield, 1977. 1 vol. (various pagings). *Folding map in end pocket.*

WEST YORKSHIRE (Cont.)

WEST YORKSHIRE. Metropolitan County Council. Structure plan: report of survey; part 2, December 1978. [Wakefield], 1978. 1 vol. (various pagings).

— Industries.

WEST YORKSHIRE. Metropolitan County Council. Industrial general improvement areas; a report for the Secretary of State for the Environment. [Wakefield, 1976]. fo. 12.

— Social conditions.

WEST YORKSHIRE. Metropolitan County Council. Structure plan: report of survey; [part 1], December 1977. [Wakefield], 1977. 2 vols.

WEST YORKSHIRE. Metropolitan County Council. Structure plan: report of survey; part 2, December 1978. [Wakefield], 1978. 1 vol. (various pagings).

— Social policy.

OPINION RESEARCH CENTRE. A report on a survey of public attitudes in connection with the preparation of the structure plan; prepared for West Yorkshire Metropolitan County Council. London, 1975. pp. 99, 25.

WEST YORKSHIRE. Metropolitan County Council. Structure plan: report of survey; [part 1], December 1977. [Wakefield], 1977. 2 vols.

WEST YORKSHIRE. Metropolitan County Council. Structure plan: written statement: consultation draft, October 1977. Wakefield, 1977. 1 vol. (various pagings). *Folding map in end pocket.*

WEST YORKSHIRE. Metropolitan County Council. Structure plan: report of survey; part 2, December 1978. [Wakefield], 1978. 1 vol. (various pagings).

WESTERN AUSTRALIA

— Economic conditions.

WESTERN AUSTRALIA. 1970. Progress: a report by the government of Western Australia: 1968-71. [Perth, 1970]. pp. 208.

WESTERN AUSTRALIA. 1975. Review of performance: first year in government. [Perth?], 1975. pp. 13.

WESTERN AUSTRALIA. 1976. Achievement: a record of the Western Australian Liberal N[ational] C[ountry] P[arty] government, 1974-1977. [Perth, 1976?]. pp. 37.

— Executive departments.

UREN (MALCOLM JOHN LEGGOE) and PARRICK (F.) Servant of the state: the history of the Main Roads Department 1926-1976. abridged ed. [Perth], Commissioner of Main Roads, 1976. pp. 44. *bibliog.*

— Government publications — Bibliography.

OFFICIAL PUBLICATIONS OF WESTERN AUSTRALIA; [pd. by] Parliamentary Library of Western Australia. q., Ja/Je 1973(v.1, no.1)- Perth.

— Main Roads Department.

UREN (MALCOLM JOHN LEGGOE) and PARRICK (F.) Servant of the state: the history of the Main Roads Department 1926-1976. abridged ed. [Perth], Commissioner of Main Roads, 1976. pp. 44. *bibliog.*

— Politics and government.

WESTERN AUSTRALIA. 1975. Review of performance: first year in government. [Perth?], 1975. pp. 13.

— Social conditions.

WESTERN AUSTRALIA. 1970. Progress: a report by the government of Western Australia: 1968-71. [Perth, 1970]. pp. 208.

WESTERN AUSTRALIA. 1975. Review of performance: first year in government. [Perth?], 1975. pp. 13.

WESTERN AUSTRALIA. 1976. Achievement: a record of the Western Australian Liberal N[ational] C[ountry] P[arty] government, 1974-1977. [Perth, 1976?]. pp. 37.

— Statistics.

WESTERN AUSTRALIA. Commonwealth Bureau of Census and Statistics. Western Australian Office. Monthly statistical summary. m., Jl 1978- Perth.

WESTERN UNION INTERNATIONAL.

GALLAGHER (EDWARD A.) Getting the message across: the story of Western Union International, Inc. New York, 1971. pp. 24. *(Newcomen Society in North America. Newcomen Addresses. 1971)*

WESTMINSTER ABBEY.

HARVEY (BARBARA F.) Westminster Abbey and its estates in the Middle Ages. Oxford, 1977. pp. 499. *bibliog.*

WESTMORLAND

— Economic history.

SOMERVELL (JOHN) Water-power mills of South Westmorland, on the Kent, Bela and Gilpin and their tributaries. Kendal, 1930. pp. 138.

WESTPHALIA

— History.

TAMPKE (JÜRGEN) The Ruhr and revolution: the revolutionary movement in the Rhenish-Westphalian industrial region, 1912-1919. London, [1979]. pp. 209. *bibliog.*

— Politics and government.

TEPPE (KARL) Provinz, Partei, Staat: zur provinziellen Selbstverwaltung im Dritten Reich, untersucht am Beispiel Westfalens. Münster in Westfalen, 1977. pp. 300. *bibliog. (Historische Kommission für Westfalen. Veröffentlichungen. 38)*

TAMPKE (JÜRGEN) The Ruhr and revolution: the revolutionary movement in the Rhenish-Westphalian industrial region, 1912-1919. London, [1979]. pp. 209. *bibliog.*

WHALING.

HOHMAN (ELMO PAUL) The American whaleman: a study of life and labor in the whaling industry. New York, 1928; Clifton, N.J., 1972. pp. 355. *bibliog.*

— Japan.

The WHALING issue in U.S.-Japan relations; edited by John R. Schmidhauser and George O. Totten III. Boulder, Colo., [1978]. pp. 275.

WHEAT

— Australia — Transportation.

AUSTRALIA. Bureau of Transport Economics. 1978. Transportation of the Australian wheat harvest. Canberra, 1978. pp. 157.

— India.

NATIONAL COUNCIL OF APPLIED ECONOMIC RESEARCH. The impact of the price rise in petroleum based agricultural inputs on the production of wheat and rice in India; a study prepared for the Commonwealth Secretariat;...[directed by] I.Z. Bhatty. London, Commonwealth Secretariat, [1976]. pp. 74. *(Commonwealth Economic Papers. No. 6)*

WHISKY

— United Kingdom — Scotland.

WEIR (RONALD B.) The history of the Malt Distillers' Association of Scotland. [York?, 1974?]. pp. 177.

WHITE (ANDREW DICKSON).

ALTSCHULER (GLENN C.) Andrew D. White: educator, historian, diplomat. Ithaca, 1979. pp. 300. *bibliog.*

WHITE (THEODORE HAROLD).

WHITE (THEODORE HAROLD) In search of history: a personal adventure. London, [1978]. pp. 561.

WHITE COLLAR CRIMES

— United States.

BEQUAI (AUGUST) White-collar crime: a 20th-century crisis. Lexington, Mass., [1978]. pp. 187. *bibliog.*

EDELHERTZ (HERBERT) and WALSH (MARILYN) The white-collar challenge to nuclear safeguards. Lexington, Mass., [1978]. pp. 101.

WHITE COLLAR WORKERS

— United Kingdom.

JENKINS (CLIVE) and SHERMAN (BARRIE) White-collar unionism: the rebellious salariat. London, 1979. pp. 174.

WHITE RUSSIA

— Economic conditions.

MIKHAILOVA (IRINA ALEKSEEVNA) Materialoemkost' obshchestvennogo proizvodstva BSSR; pod redaktsiei M.N. Shatokhinoi. Minsk, 1978. pp. 167.

— Economic history.

RAZVITIE otraslei narodnogo khoziaistva Belorussii: istoriko- geograficheskie ocherki; pod redaktsiei V.P. Borodinoi, V.A. Zhuchkevicha, N.T. Romanovskogo. Minsk, 1978. pp. 191.

— History — 1917-1921, Revolution — Foreign participation.

KENEZ (PETER) Civil war in South Russia, 1919-1920: the defeat of the Whites. Berkeley, [1977]. pp. 378. *bibliog.*

WHOLESALE TRADE

— European Economic Community countries.

EUROPEAN ECONOMIC COMMUNITY. Studies. Commerce and Distribution Series. 1. Market structures and conditions of competition in the wholesale trade in the countries of the EEC; summary of a study carried out by IFO-Economic Research Institute, etc. Brussels, 1976. pp. 39.

— Finland.

FINLAND. Tilastokeskus. Tukkukaupan toimipaikat. a., 1974- Helsinki. *[in Finnish and Swedish]*

— Germany.

GERMANY (BUNDESREPUBLIK). Statistisches Bundesamt. Grosshandel. quadrennial, 1972. Wiesbaden. *(Unternehmen und Arbeitsstätten. Reihe 1.5.1)* Superseded by GERMANY (BUNDESREPUBLIK). Statistisches Bundesamt. Kostenstruktur im Grosshandel, bei Buch- u.ä. Verlagen.

GERMANY (BUNDESREPUBLIK). Statistisches Bundesamt. Kostenstruktur im Grosshandel bei Buch- u.ä. Verlagen. quadrennial, 1976- Wiesbaden. *(Unternehmen und Arbeitsstätten. Reihe 1.2.1)* Supersedes GERMANY (BUNDESREPUBLIK). Statistisches Bundesamt. Verlagswesen and GERMANY (BUNDESREPUBLIK). Statistisches Bundesamt. Grosshandel.

— India — Punjab.

PUNJAB (INDIA). Economic and Statistical Organisation. 1976, Report on the distributive trade survey relating to urban areas of Punjab. Chandigarh, 1976, pp. 206. *(Publications. No. 218)*

— Norway.

NORWAY. Statistiske Centralbyrå. 1978. Innkjøp og omsetning i engroshandelen, etc. Oslo, 1978. pp. 81. *(Statistiske Analyser. 34)* With English summary.

WOMEN.

— Portugal.

PORTUGAL. Instituto Nacional de Estatística. 1979- . 1977 recenseamento à distribuição e serviços: Portugal: [provisional results]. Lisboa, [1979 in progress].

— Sweden.

SWEDEN. Finansdepartementet. Långtidsutredningen. 1975. (Långtidsutredningen 1975. Bilaga 4). Varuhandeln, 1975- 1980;...rapport av Handelns Utredningsinstitut. Stockholm, 1975. pp. 44. *(Sweden. Statens Offentliga Utredningar. 1975.97)*

SWEDEN. Statistiska Centralbyrån. Regional omsättning inom parti- och detaljhandel samt vissa tjänstenäringar. a., 1976- Stockholm. *[in Swedish with English summary]*

— United Kingdom.

U.K. Business Statistics Office. 1979. Wholesaling and dealing, (1974). London, [1979]. pp. 142. *(Business monitor: Service and distributive series. SD 26)*

WIDOWS

— Belgium.

DOOGHE (GILBERT) and VANDERLEYDEN (L.) Bejaarden en hun levensvoldoening: een empirisch onderzoek by weduwen en gehuwde vrouwen. Antwerp, 1978. pp. 132. *bibliog. (Centre d'Etude de la Population et de la Famille [Belgium]. Studies en Dokumenten. 10)*

WIFE ABUSE.

— United Kingdom.

FREEMAN (MICHAEL D.A.) Violence in the home. Farnborough, [1979]. pp. 257. *bibliogs.*

WIFE ABUSE VICTIMS.

See ABUSED WIVES.

WILBERFORCE NEGRO COLONY, MIDDLESEX COUNTY, ONTARIO.

STEWARD (AUSTIN) Twenty-two years a slave, and forty years a freeman; embracing correspondence of several years, while president of Wilberforce Colony, London, Canada West. [Rochester, N.Y.], 1856; New York, 1968. pp. 360. *Facsimile reprint.*

WILDERNESS AREAS.

SCHECTER (MORDECHAI) and LUCAS (ROBERT C.) Simulation of recreational use for park and wilderness management. Baltimore, [1978]. pp. 220. *bibliogs.*

WILLIAMS (SAMUEL MAY).

HENSON (MARGARET SWETT) Samuel May Williams: early Texas entrepreneur. College Station, Tex., [1976]. pp. 190. *bibliog.*

WILLS

— United Kingdom.

HALLETT (VICTOR GEORGE HENRY) and WARREN (NICHOLAS) Settlements, wills and capital transfer tax. London, 1979. pp. 245.

WILSON (THOMAS WOODROW) President of the United States.

LINK (ARTHUR STANLEY) Wilson the diplomatist: a look at his major foreign policies. New York, 1974. pp. 165. *First published 1957.*

SMITH (DANIEL MALLOY) Aftermath of war: Bainbridge Colby and Wilsonian diplomacy, 1920-1921. Philadelphia, 1970. pp. 173. *bibliog. (American Philosophical Society. Memoirs. vol. 80)*

CARTER (PURVIS M.) Congressional and public reaction to Wilson's Caribbean policy, 1913-1917. New York, [1977]. pp. 164. *bibliog.*

GILDERHUS (MARK T.) Diplomacy and revolution: U.S.-Mexican relations under Wilson and Carranza. Tucson, Ariz., [1977]. pp. 159. *bibliog.*

HOOVER (HERBERT CLARK) and WILSON (THOMAS WOODROW) Two peacemakers in Paris: the Hoover-Wilson post-armistice letters, 1918-1920; edited and with commentaries by Francis William O'Brien. College Station, [1978]. pp. 254. *bibliog.*

PARSONS (EDWARD B.) Wilsonian diplomacy: Allied-American rivalries in war and peace. St. Louis, Miss., [1978]. pp. 213. *bibliog.*

WINE AND WINE MAKING

— France.

BOULET (D.) and LAPORTE (J.P.) Etude sur l'évolution de la concentration dans les industries des boissons et des boissons non alcoolisées en France. [Brussels], Communautés Européennes, 1976. pp. 284.

RASTOIN (J.-L.) and others. L'évolution de la concentration dans l'industrie des champagnes et mousseux en France, etc. [Brussels], Communautés Européennes, 1976. pp. 127.

FALUDY (ANDREW) The crisis in the Languedoc wine trade. Brighton, 1977. pp. 38. *bibliog.*

— Germany.

BREITENACHER (MICHAEL) Untersuchung zur Konzentrationsentwicklung in der Getränke Industrie in Deutschland. [Brussels], Europäischen Gemeinschaften, 1976. pp. 156.

— Italy.

BALLIANO (PIERA) and LANZETTI (RENATO) Studio sull'evoluzione della concentrazione nell'industria delle bevande in Italia. [Brussels], Comunità Europee, 1976. pp. 143.

WINFREY FAMILY.

NEWTON (DAVID) Men of mark: makers of East Midland Allied Press. Peterborough, 1977. pp. 239.

WITCHCRAFT.

PARRINDER (EDWARD GEOFFREY SIMONS) Witchcraft. Harmondsworth, 1958. pp. 208. *bibliog.*

WITOLD (FRANCISZEK JÓZWIAK-) pseud.

See JÓZWIAK (FRANCISZEK).

WITT (JOHAN DE).

ROWEN (HERBERT H.) John de Witt, grand pensionary of Holland, 1625-1672. Princeton, N.J., [1978]. pp. 948. *bibliog.*

WITTGENSTEIN (LUDWIG).

DANFORD (JOHN W.) Wittgenstein and political philosophy: a reexamination of the foundations of social science. Chicago, [1978]. pp. 265. *bibliog.*

INTERNATIONAL WITTGENSTEIN SYMPOSIUM, 2ND, 1977. Wittgenstein and his impact on contemporary thought: proceedings . ..29th August to 4th September 1977, Kirchberg/Wechsel, Austria; editors: Elisabeth Leinfellner [and others]: Wittgenstein und sein Einfluss auf die gegenwärtige Philosophie: Akten, etc. Vienna, 1978. pp. 550. *(Wittgenstein-Gesellschaft. Schriftenreihe) In English or German.*

WITWATERSRAND

— Economic conditions.

FAIR (T.J.D.) The Witwatersrand: its major socio-economic and land use trends, problems and prospects. Johannesburg, 1976. pp. 25. *(Johannesburg. University of the Witwatersrand. Urban and Regional Research Unit. Occasional papers. No. 12)*

— Social conditions.

FAIR (T.J.D.) The Witwatersrand: its major socio-economic and land use trends, problems and prospects. Johannesburg, 1976. pp. 25. *(Johannesburg. University of the Witwatersrand. Urban and Regional Research Unit. Occasional papers. No. 12)*

WIVES

See also ABUSED WIVES.

— Employment — United Kingdom.

HEWITT (MARGARET) Wives and mothers in Victorian industry. Westport, Conn., 1975. pp. 245. *bibliog. Reprint of work originally published London, 1958.*

HAMILL (LYNNE) Wives as sole and joint breadwinners. London, Department of Health and Social Security, 1978. pp. 19, 18. *(Government Economic Service Working Papers. No. 13)*

WOLFF (SAM DE).

WOLFF (SAM DE) Voor het land van belofte: een terugblik op mijn leven. Nijmegen, 1978. pp. 300. *First published in Bussum, 1954.*

WOMEN.

RED COLLECTIVE. The politics of sexuality in capitalism. London, 1973 repr. 1978. pp. 146.

UNITED NATIONS DECADE FOR WOMEN 1976-1985: equality, development and peace. Bulletin. q., 1978(no.1)- New York.

MEIJER-WICHMANN (CLARA) Vrouw en maatschappij;...met een inleiding van Henriette Roland tlst-van der Schalk. Nijmegen, 1978. pp. 248. *bibliog. Reprint of the edition of 1936 with some additional material.*

— Employment

AGASSI (JUDITH BUBER) The characteristics of typical women's jobs and the attitudes of women to those jobs: a comparative multinational study. [n.p., 1978]. pp. 495.

BENMOUYAL-ACOCA (VIVIANE) Le retour des femmes sur le marché du travail: rapport d'étude. [Québec], 1978. pp. 195. *bibliog. (Quebec (Province). Department of Labour and Manpower. Direction Générale de la Recherche. Etudes et Recherches. 2)*

FEMINISM and materialism: women and modes of production; edited by Annette Kuhn and AnnMarie Wolpe. London, 1978. pp. 328. *bibliogs.*

SCANZONI (JOHN H.) Sex roles, women's work and marital conflict: a study of family change. Lexington, Mass., [1978]. pp. 175. *bibliog.*

TILLY (LOUISE) and SCOTT (JOAN WALLACH) Women, work, and family. New York, [1978]. pp. 274. *bibliog.*

— — Canada.

ARMSTRONG (PAT) and ARMSTRONG (HUGH) The double ghetto: Canadian women and their segregated work. Toronto, [1978]. pp. 199. *bibliog.*

— — — Alberta.

ALBERTA. Department of Manpower and Labour. Research Division. 1972. Women in the labour force: Alberta. Edmonton, 1972. pp. 20.

— — — Nova Scotia.

NOVA SCOTIA. Department of Labour. Economics and Research Division. 1976. Working women in Nova Scotia, fall, 1976. [Halifax], 1976. fo. 13. *(Information Bulletins)*

— — Germany.

WINKLER (DOERTE) Frauenarbeit im "Dritten Reich". Hamburg, 1977. pp. 253. *bibliog.*

WOMEN.(Cont.)

— — India.

INDIA. Labour Bureau. 1978. Study on employment of women in selected industries, 1977. Chandigarh, [1978]. pp. 32, 9.

— — Italy.

CUTRUFELLI (MARIA ROSA) Operaie senza fabbrica: inchiesta sul lavoro a domicilio. Roma, 1977. pp. 150. *bibliog.*

— — Netherlands.

NETHERLANDS. Commissie. Arbeidspositie Vrouwen en Meisjes. 1972. Adviezen, 1970-1972. 's-Gravenhage, 1972. pp. 24. *(Netherlands. Ministerie van Sociale Zaken. Verslagen en Rapporten: Sociale Zaken. 1972.2)*

BERENDS (A.B.) and BOELMANS-KLEINJAN (A.C.) Beroepsarbeid door vrouwen in Nederland: een benadering vanuit de plaats van de vrouw in gezin en huishouden. 's-Gravenhage, 1979. pp. 165. *bibliog.* *(Netherlands. Centraal Bureau voor de Statistiek. Monografieën Volkstelling 1971. 7) With English summary.*

— — United Kingdom.

[SIMKINS (MAUD ELLEN)] Mixed herbs: a working woman's remonstrance against the suffrage agitation; by M.E.S. [i.e. Maud Ellen Simkins]. London, 1908. pp. 158.

WOOD (ETHEL MARY) Mainly for men. London, 1943. pp. 126. *Written at the request of the Committee on Woman Power.*

HOLCOMBE (LEE) Victorian ladies at work: middle-class working women in England and Wales, 1850-1914. Hamden, Conn., 1973. pp. 253.

JAMES (SELMA) Women, the unions and work; or, What is not to be done; and, The perspective of winning. London, [1976]. pp. 32.

UNION PLACE COMMUNITY RESOURCE CENTRE. As things are: women, work and family in South London. London, 1976. pp. 52. *Reprint of 4 articles appearing in 1975 and 1976 in Knuckle.*

HURSTFIELD (JENNIFER) The part-time trap: part-time workers in Britain today. London, 1978. pp. 86. *(Low Pay Unit. Low Pay Pamphlets. No. 9)*

NORTH TYNESIDE COMMUNITY DEVELOPMENT PROJECT. North Shields: women's work. [Newcastle-upon-Tyne, 1978]. pp. 86. *(Final Reports. Vol.5)*

CREIGHTON (WILLIAM BREEN) Working women and the law. London, 1979. pp. 292. *bibliog.*

FIT work for women; edited by Sandra Burman. London, [1979]. pp. 201. *bibliogs. Papers from interdisciplinary seminars organised at Oxford University throughout the academic year, 1977-78.*

U.K. Equal Opportunities Commission. 1979. Health and safety legislation: should we distinguish between men and women?; report and recommendations of the...Commission. [Manchester], 1979. pp. 153.

— — United States.

PIDGEON (MARY ELIZABETH) Women in the economy of the United States of America; [with] Employed women under N.R.A. codes. New York, 1975. 1 vol. (various pagings). *Reprint of works published in Washington D.C., 1937 and 1935.*

CALIFORNIA. Employment Data and Research Division. 1974. Women at work in California;...prepared by Kathryn S. Karrer. [Sacramento], 1974. pp. 41. *bibliog.*

CLASS, sex and the woman worker; edited by Milton Cantor and Bruce Laurie. Westport, Conn., 1977. pp. 253.

DE JONG (PETER) Patterns on intergenerational occupational mobility of American females. San Francisco, 1977. pp. 138. *bibliog.*

BAER (JUDITH A.) The chains of protection: the judicial response to women's labor legislation. Westport, Conn., 1978. pp. 238. *bibliog.*

DUNCAN (BEVERLEY) and DUNCAN (OTIS DUDLEY) Sex typing and social roles: a research report. New York, [1978]. pp. 389.

GIELE (JANET ZOLLINGER) Women and the future: changing sex roles in modern America. New York, [1978]. pp. 386. *bibliog.*

HARRIS (BARBARA J.) Beyond her sphere: women and the professions in American history. Westport, Conn., 1978. pp. 212. *bibliog.*

KENNEALLY (JAMES J.) Women and American trade unions. St. Albans, Vt., [1978]. pp. 240.

MOTT (FRANK L.) Women, work, and family: dimensions of change in American society. Lexington, Mass., [1978]. pp. 152. *bibliog.*

SHAEFFER (RUTH GILBERT) and AXEL (HELEN) Improving job opportunities for women: a chartbook focusing on the progress in business. New York, [1978]. pp. 87. *(National Industrial Conference Board. Conference Board Reports. No. 744)*

HUMMER (PATRICIA M.) The decade of elusive promise: professional women in the United States, 1920-1930. [London, 1979]. pp. 182. *bibliog.*

— History.

The NEGLECTED majority: essays in Canadian women's history; edited by Susan Mann Trofimenkoff and Alison Prentice. Toronto, [1977]. pp. 192. *bibliog.*

KATZMAN (DAVID M.) Seven days a week: women and domestic service in industrializing America. New York, 1978. pp. 374. *bibliog.*

LATIN American women: historical perspectives; edited by Asunción Lavrin. Westport, Conn., [1978]. pp. 343. *bibliogs.*

TILLY (LOUISE) and SCOTT (JOAN WALLACH) Women, work, and family. New York, [1978]. pp. 274. *bibliog.*

CAMPBELL (BARBARA KUHN) The "liberated" woman of 1914: prominent women in the progressive era. [London, 1979]. pp. 220. *bibliogs.*

HAMMERTON (A. JAMES) Emigrant gentlewomen: genteel poverty and female emigration, 1830- 1914. London, [1979]. pp. 220. *bibliog.*

SCHRAMM (SARAH SLAVIN) Plow women rather than reapers: an intellectual history of feminism in the United States. Metuchen, N.J., 1979. pp. 441. *bibliog.*

— Legal status, laws, etc. — Ireland (Republic).

MARTIN (JANET) The essential guide for women in Ireland. Galway, [1977]. pp. 141.

— — United Kingdom.

SACHS (ALBIE) and WILSON (JOAN HOFF) Sexism and the law: a study of male beliefs and legal bias in Britain and the United States. Oxford, 1978. pp. 257. *bibliog.*

— — United States.

WOMEN'S rights and the law: the impact of the ERA on State laws; [by] Barbara A. Brown [and others]; edited...by Hazel Greenberg. New York, 1977. pp. 433. *bibliog.*

SACHS (ALBIE) and WILSON (JOAN HOFF) Sexism and the law: a study of male beliefs and legal bias in Britain and the United States. Oxford, 1978. pp. 257. *bibliog.*

— Psychology.

SEXUAL behavior in the human female; [by] Alfred C. Kinsey [and others]. Philadelphia, [1953]. pp. 842. *bibliog.*

KLEIN (VIOLA) The feminine character: history of an ideology. 2nd ed. London, 1971. pp. 202. *bibliog.*

BREEN (DANA) The birth of a first child: towards an understanding of femininity. London, 1975. pp. 262. *bibliog.*

WOMEN united, women divided: cross-cultural perspectives on female solidarity; edited by Patricia Caplan and Janet M. Bujra. London, 1978. pp. 288. *bibliogs.*

— Social conditions.

FRIEDAN (BETTY) The feminine mystique. London, 1971. pp. 410. *bibliog.*

IZMENENIE polozheniia zhenshchiny i sem'ia: [sbornik statei]. Moskva, 1977. pp. 214.

ARMSTRONG (PAT) and ARMSTRONG (HUGH) The double ghetto: Canadian women and their segregated work. Toronto, [1978]. pp. 199. *bibliog.*

FEMINISM and materialism: women and modes of production; edited by Annette Kuhn and AnnMarie Wolpe. London, 1978. pp. 328. *bibliogs.*

GIELE (JANET ZOLLINGER) Women and the future: changing sex roles in modern America. New York, [1978]. pp. 386. *bibliog.*

KATZMAN (DAVID M.) Seven days a week: women and domestic service in industrializing America. New York, 1978. pp. 374. *bibliog.*

LATIN American women: historical perspectives; edited by Asunción Lavrin. Westport, Conn., [1978]. pp. 343. *bibliogs.*

MOTT (FRANK L.) Women, work, and family: dimensions of change in American society. Lexington, Mass., [1978]. pp. 152. *bibliog.*

RUPP (LEILA J.) Mobilizing women for war: German and American propaganda, 1939- 1945. Princeton, [1978]. pp. 243. *bibliog.*

SAFFIOTI (HELEIETH I.B.) Women in class society...; translated from the Portuguese by Michael Vale. New York, [1978]. pp. 378. *bibliog.*

WILSON (AMRIT) Finding a voice: Asian women in Britain. London, [1978]. pp. 179.

WOMEN united, women divided: cross-cultural perspectives on female solidarity; edited by Patricia Caplan and Janet M. Bujra. London, 1978. pp. 288. *bibliogs.*

CAMPBELL (BARBARA KUHN) The "liberated" woman of 1914: prominent women in the progressive era. [London, 1979]. pp. 220. *bibliogs.*

FIT work for women; edited by Sandra Burman. London, [1979]. pp. 201. *bibliogs. Papers from interdisciplinary seminars organised at Oxford University throughout the academic year, 1977-78.*

HOLLIS (PATRICIA) Women in public, 1850-1900: documents of the Victorian women's movement. London, 1979. pp. 331.

SEX roles and social policy: a complex social science equation; edited by Jean Lipman-Blumen and Jessie Bernard. London, [1979]. pp. 404. *bibliogs.*

DUNCAN (BEVERLEY) and DUNCAN (OTIS DUDLEY) Sex typing and social roles: a research report. New York, [1978]. pp. 389.

— Suffrage.

WHITTICK (ARNOLD) Woman into citizen. London, 1979. pp. 327. *bibliog. Introduction by Helvi Sipilä, Assistant Secretary-general for Social Development and Humanitarian Affairs of the United Nations.*

— — United Kingdom.

[SIMKINS (MAUD ELLEN)] Mixed herbs: a working woman's remonstrance against the suffrage agitation; by M.E.S. [i.e. Maud Ellen Simkins]. London, 1908. pp. 158.

OWEN (HAROLD) Woman adrift: the menace of suffragism. London, [1912]. pp. 333.

LIDDINGTON (JILL) and NORRIS (JILL) One hand tied behind us: the rise of the women's suffrage movement. London, 1978. pp. 304. *bibliog.*

STOBAUGH (BEVERLY PARKER) Women and Parliament, 1918-1970. New York, [1978]. pp. 152. *bibliog.*

— America, Latin.

ELU DE LEÑERO (MARIA DEL CARMEN) ed. La mujer en America Latina. Mexico, Secretaria de Educacion Publica, 1975. 2 vols. (in 1) bibliogs. *(Sep/Setentas. 211-212) Contains some of the papers presented at the conference "Perspectivas Femeninas en Investigacion Social en America Latina", Buenos Aires, 1974.*

LATIN American women: historical perspectives; edited by Asunción Lavrin. Westport, Conn., [1978]. pp. 343. *bibliogs.*

— Australia.

TEALE (RUTH) ed. Colonial Eve: sources on women in Australia, 1788-1914. Melbourne, 1978. pp. 288. *bibliog.*

— Austria.

TIDL (MARIE) Frauen im Widerstand: Frauen im Kampf gegen Faschismus und Krieg. [Vienna, 1978]. pp. 52. *bibliog.*

— Belgium.

BOGAERT (G. VAN DEN) Profiel van de vrouw in Belgie: een doorlichting van de relatie- en gezinsvorming en de maatschappelijke achtergrond van de vrouw. Antwerpen, 1978. pp. 161. *bibliog. (Centre d'Etude de la Population et de la Famille [Belgium]. Studies en Dokumenten. 9)*

— Brazil.

SAFFIOTI (HELEIETH I.B.) Women in class society...; translated from the Portuguese by Michael Vale. New York, [1978]. pp. 378. *bibliog.*

— Canada.

The NEGLECTED majority: essays in Canadian women's history; edited by Susan Mann Trofimenkoff and Alison Prentice. Toronto, [1977]. pp. 192. *bibliog.*

— — Alberta.

ALBERTA. Citizens' Advisory Board. 1972. An interim report on the status of women in Alberta, made in 1972. [Edmonton, 1972]. pp. 45.

— — Nova Scotia.

NOVA SCOTIA. Task Force on the Status of Women. 1976. Herself: report of the Task Force...; [Mairi St. John Macdonald, chairperson]. Halifax, 1976. pp. 91.

— Communist countries.

JANCAR (BARBARA WOLFE) Women under communism. Baltimore, [1978]. pp. 291. *bibliog.*

— France.

FRANCE. Secrétariat d'Etat à la Condition Féminine. 1976. Cent mesures pour les femmes; présentées par Françoise Giroud. Paris, [1976]. pp. 196.

FEMMES et immigrées: l'insertion des femmes immigrées en France; [by Isabel Taboada Leonetti [and others]. [Paris, 1978]. pp. 286. *(France. Direction de la Population et des Migrations. Migrations et Sociétés. 4)*

— Germany.

Die FRAU im Dritten Reich: eine Dokumentation; von Gertrud Scholtz-Klink. Tübingen, [1978]. pp. 546.

— India.

INDIA. Women's Welfare Division. 1975. Women in India: a compendium of programmes. New Delhi, 1975. pp. 118.

— Ireland (Republic).

EIRE. Women's Representative Committee. 1976. Progress report on the implementation of the recommendations in the rport of the Commission on the Status of Women. Dublin, 1976. pp. 57.

— Netherlands.

MEIJER-WICHMANN (CLARA) Vrouw en maatschappij;...met een inleiding van Henriette Roland Holst-van der Schalk. Nijmegen, 1978. pp. 248. *bibliog. Reprint of the edition of 1936 with some additional material.*

— Russia.

IANKOVA (ZOIA ALEKSEEVNA) Sovetskaia zhenshchina: sotsial'nyi portret. Moskva, 1978. pp. 159.

— Trinidad and Tobago.

TRINIDAD AND TOBAGO. National Commission on the Status of Women. 1978. Final report; [E. Bourne-Hollands, chairman]. [Port of Spain, 1978]. pp. 79.

— United Kingdom.

LYTTELTON (MARY KATHLEEN) Women and their work. London, 1901. pp. 152.

WOOD (ETHEL MARY) Mainly for men. London, 1943. pp. 126. *Written at the request of the Committee on Woman Power.*

HAMMERTON (A. JAMES) Emigrant gentlewomen: genteel poverty and female emigration, 1830- 1914. London, [1979]. pp. 220. *bibliog.*

U.K. Social Survey. [Reports. New Series]. 1080. Family formation 1976: a survey carried out on behalf of Population Statistics Division 1 of the Office of Population Censuses and Surveys of a sample of women, both single and ever married, aged 16-49 in Great Britain; [by] Karen Dunnell. London, 1979. pp. 117.

— United States.

FRIEDAN (BETTY) The feminine mystique. London, 1971. pp. 410. *bibliog.*

BARKER-BENFIELD (G.J.) The horrors of the half-known life: male attitudes toward women and sexuality in nineteenth century America. New York, 1977. pp. 352.

MOTT (FRANK L.) Women, work, and family: dimensions of change in American society. Lexington, Mass., [1978]. pp. 152. *bibliog.*

ROBINSON (LILLIAN S.) Sex, class, and culture. Bloomington, [1978]. pp. 349.

CAMPBELL (BARBARA KUHN) The "liberated" woman of 1914: prominent women in the progressive era. [London, 1979]. pp. 220. *bibliogs.*

FARAGHER (JOHN MACK) Women and men on the overland trail. New Haven, 1979. pp. 281. *bibliog. (Yale University. Yale Historical Publications. Miscellany. 121)*

SCHRAMM (SARAH SLAVIN) Plow women rather than reapers: an intellectual history of feminism in the United States. Metuchen, N.J., 1979. pp. 441. *bibliog.*

— — Crimes against.

BRAXTON (BERNARD) Sexual, racial and political faces of corruption: a view on the high cost of institutional evils. Washington, [1977]. pp. 278. *bibliog.*

WOMEN, MOHAMMEDAN.

WOMEN in the Muslim world; edited by Lois Beck and Nikki Keddie. Cambridge, Mass., 1978. pp. 698.

WOMEN'S status and fertility in the Muslim world; edited by James Allman. New York, [1978]. pp. 378. *bibliog.*

WOMEN AND SOCIALISM.

SPARGO (JOHN) Socialism and motherhood. New York, 1914. pp. 128.

EASTMAN (CRYSTAL) On women and revolution; edited by Blanche Wiesen Cook. New York, 1978. pp. 388.

SAFFIOTI (HELEIETH I.B.) Women in class society...; translated from the Portuguese by Michael Vale. New York, [1978]. pp. 378. *bibliog.*

SOCIALIST women: European socialist feminism in the nineteenth and early twentieth centuries; edited by Marilyn J. Boxer and Jean H. Quataert. New York, [1978]. pp. 260. *bibliog.*

SOWERWINE (CHARLES) Les femmes et le socialisme: un siècle d'histoire. [Paris, 1978]. pp. 286. *bibliog. Bibliography on microfiche in endpocket.*

WOMEN ARTISTS

— United Kingdom.

PANKHURST (RICHARD KEIR PETHICK) Sylvia Pankhurst: artist and crusader. New York, [1979]. pp. 224.

WOMEN IN COMMUNITY DEVELOPMENT

— United Kingdom.

UNION PLACE COMMUNITY RESOURCE CENTRE. As things are: women, work and family in South London. London, 1976. pp. 52. *Reprint of 4 articles appearing in 1975 and 1976 in Knuckle.*

WOMEN IN LITERATURE.

CUNNINGHAM (GAIL) The new woman and the Victorian novel. London, 1978. pp. 172. *bibliog.*

WOMEN IN MEDICINE.

DONNISON (JEAN ELIZABETH) Midwives and medical men: a history of inter-professional rivalries and women's rights. London, 1977. pp. 250. *bibliog.*

U.K. Equal Opportunities Commission. 1977. Evidence to the Royal Commission on the National Health Service. [Manchester], 1977. fo.11.

WOMEN IN POLITICS.

STOBAUGH (BEVERLY PARKER) Women and Parliament, 1918-1970. New York, [1978]. pp. 152. *bibliog.*

— Canada — Alberta.

ALBERTA STATUS OF WOMEN ACTION COMMITTEE. Political involvement handbook for Alberta women; prepared...for the Alberta Women's Bureau. [Edmonton], 1978. fo.79. *Photocopy.*

— United Kingdom.

VALLANCE (ELIZABETH M.) Women in the house: a study of women members of Parliament. London, 1979. pp. 212. *bibliog.*

WOMEN IN PUBLIC LIFE.

COUDENHOVE-KALERGI (RICHARD NICOLAUS) Count. Die europäische Mission der Frau. Zürich, [1953]. pp. 43.

WOMEN IN RURAL DEVELOPMENT

— Rhodesia.

SMITH (LANCE BALES) Leadership training for women in community development. [Salisbury, 1969]. pp. 8. *(Rhodesia. Ministry of Information, Immigration and Tourism. For the Record. No. 5)*

WOMEN IN TRADE UNIONS

— United Kingdom.

JAMES (SELMA) Women, the unions and work; or, What is not to be done; and, The perspective of winning. London, [1976]. pp. 32.

UNION PLACE COMMUNITY RESOURCE CENTRE. As things are: women, work and family in South London. London, 1976. pp. 52. *Reprint of 4 articles appearing in 1975 and 1976 in Knuckle.*

WOMEN IN TRADE UNIONS(Cont.)

— United States.

KENNEALLY (JAMES J.) Women and American trade unions. St. Albans, Vt., [1978]. pp. 240.

WOMEN PRISONERS

— Canada — British Columbia.

KIRKALDY (ANNE D.) Incarcerated women in British Columbia provincial institutions. [Victoria], Corrections Branch, 1978. pp. 102.

WOMEN TEACHERS

— United Kingdom.

DEEM (ROSEMARY) Women and schooling. London, 1978. pp. 170. *bibliog.*

WOMEN'S HEALTH SERVICES

— United Kingdom.

U.K. Equal Opportunities Commission. 1977. Evidence to the Royal Commission on the National Health Service. [Manchester], 1977. fo.11.

WOMEN'S RIGHTS.

SOUTHAMPTON WOMEN'S LIBERATION. Pent-up. [Southampton, 1972]. pp. 40.

SCHRAMM (SARAH SLAVIN) Plow women rather than reapers: an intellectual history of feminism in the United States. Metuchen, N.J., 1979. pp. 441. *bibliog.*

WHITTICK (ARNOLD) Woman into citizen. London, 1979. pp. 327. *bibliog.* Introduction by Helvi Sipilä, Assistant Secretary-general for Social Development and Humanitarian Affairs of the United Nations.

— Ireland (Republic).

MARTIN (JANET) The essential guide for women in Ireland. Galway, [1977]. pp. 141.

— United Kingdom — Scotland.

CRAIG (CAROL) and GILMORE (SHEILA) Women and the Scottish assembly. [Glasgow, 1979]. pp. 15. *(Scottish Council of Fabian Societies. Scottish Fabian Research Papers. 2)*

— United States.

BRAXTON (BERNARD) Sexual, racial and political faces of corruption: a view on the high cost of institutional evils. Washington, [1977]. pp. 278. *bibliog.*

GIELE (JANET ZOLLINGER) Women and the future: changing sex roles in modern America. New York, [1978]. pp. 386. *bibliog.*

HARRIS (BARBARA J.) Beyond her sphere: women and the professions in American history. Westport, Conn., 1978. pp. 212. *bibliog.*

HERSH (BLANCHE GLASSMAN) The slavery of sex: feminist-abolitionists in America. Urbana, Ill., [1978]. pp. 280. *bibliog.*

WOOD.

U.K. Forestry Commission. 1978. The wood production outlook in Britain: a review. [Edinburgh], 1977 [or rather 1978]. fo. 111. *bibliog.*

— United Kingdom.

U.K. Forestry Commission. 1978. The wood production outlook in Britain: a review. [Edinburgh], 1977 [or rather 1978]. fo. 111. *bibliog.*

WOOD (ROBERT) 1903- .

WOOD (ROBERT) 1903- . A world in your ear: the broadcasting of an era, 1923-64. London, 1979. pp. 194.

WOOD AS FUEL.

TILLMAN (DAVID A.) Wood as an energy resource. New York, 1978. pp. 252.

WOOD-PULP INDUSTRY.

FOOD AND AGRICULTURE ORGANIZATION. Pulp and paper capacities: survey. a., 1977/1982- Rome. *[in English, French and Spanish]*

WOOD-USING INDUSTRIES

— Thailand.

RATANAPRASIDHI (METH) Forest industries and forestry of Thailand. Bangkok, 1963. fo. 31. *(Thailand. Forest Department. [Publications]. No. R. 59)*

WOOL TRADE AND INDUSTRY.

COMMONWEALTH SECRETARIAT. Wool statistics. a., 1977/78(31st)- London. *1948-1976(1st-29th) pd. as a. supplement to WOOL INTELLIGENCE.*

JEREMY (DAVID JOHN) The transmission of cotton and woollen manufacturing technologies between Britain and the U.S.A. from 1790 to the 1830s. 1978. fo. 344. *bibliog.* Typescript. Ph.D. (London) thesis: unpublished. This thesis is the property of London University and may not be removed from the Library.

COMMONWEALTH SECRETARIAT. Wool quarterly. q., Ja 1979(v.1, no.1)- London.

WOOLF (LEONARD SIDNEY).

LEHMANN (JOHN) Thrown to the Woolfs. London, [1978]. pp. 164.

WOOLF (VIRGINIA).

LEHMANN (JOHN) Thrown to the Woolfs. London, [1978]. pp. 164.

WORCESTERSHIRE

— Economic policy.

HEREFORD AND WORCESTER [COUNTY]. Planning Department and WEST MIDLANDS. County Council. Worcestershire structure plan, 1975, for the former administrative County of Worcestershire and those parts of the former administrative County of Worcestershire transferred to the West Midlands County on 1 April 1974. [Worcester], 1975. pp. 108.

— Social policy.

HEREFORD AND WORCESTER [COUNTY]. Planning Department and WEST MIDLANDS. County Council. Worcestershire structure plan, 1975, for the former administrative County of Worcestershire and those parts of the former administrative County of Worcestershire transferred to the West Midlands County on 1 April 1974. [Worcester], 1975. pp. 108.

WORDS IN ACTION LIMITED.

HOOPER (BRIAN MICHAEL) and BUTTIMER (JAMES MICHAEL) North Devon Railway Company Limited; Words in Action Limited: investigations under section 165b of the Companies Act, 1948; reports. London, Department of Trade, 1979. 1 vol. (various pagings).

WORK.

STAHLEDER (HELMUTH) Arbeit in der mittelalterlichen Gesellschaft. München, 1972. pp. 317. *bibliog. (Munich. Stadtarchiv. Neue Schriftenreihe. Band 59)*

DURAND (MICHELLE) and HARFF (YVETTE) La qualité de la vie: mouvement écologique, mouvement ouvrier. Paris, [1977]. pp. 258.

— Psychological aspects.

O'TOOLE (JAMES) Work, learning, and the American future. San Francisco, 1977. pp. 238. *bibliog.*

MILLER (ROBERT L.) Attitudes to work in Northern Ireland. Belfast, 1978. pp. 19. *(Fair Employment Agency for Northern Ireland. Research Papers. 2)*

STRESS at work; edited by Cary L. Cooper and Roy Payne. Chichester, [1978]. pp. 293. *bibliogs.*

WORK DESIGN.

SCHUMACHER (CHRISTIAN) The end of an era: calls for new departures. Wellingborough, [1977]. pp. 27. *(Scott Bader Commonwealth Centre. Commonwealth Monographs. No.8)*

GUEST (DAVID) and others. Job design and the psychology of boredom;...a paper presented at the nineteenth International Congress of Applied Psychology, Munich, August 1978. London, Department of Employment, Work Research Unit, [1979]. pp. 10. *bibliog.*

WORK ENVIRONMENT

— Europe.

The QUALITY of working life in Western and Eastern Europe; edited by Cary L. Cooper and Enid Mumford. Westport, 1979. pp. 348. *bibliog.*

WORK GROUPS

— United Kingdom.

SCHUMACHER (CHRISTIAN) The end of an era: calls for new departures. Wellingborough, [1977]. pp. 27. *(Scott Bader Commonwealth Centre. Commonwealth Monographs. No.8)*

WORK RELIEF

— United States.

CREATING jobs: public employment programs and wage subsidies: a study sponsored jointly by the Institute for Research on Poverty and the Brookings Institution; John L. Palmer, editor. Washington, D.C., [1978]. pp. 379. *(Brookings Institution. Studies in Social Economics) (Wisconsin University. Madison. Institute for Research on Poverty. Monograph Series) Based on a conference held in 1977.*

— — Massachusetts.

PRAGER (AUDREY) Job creation in the community: an evaluation of locally initiated employment projects in Massachusetts. Cambridge, Mass., [1977]. pp. 175.

WORKMEN'S COMPENSATION

— Pakistan.

PAKISTAN. Statutes, etc. 1923-54. The Workmen's Compensation Act, 1923...as modified up to the 30th September, 1954. Karachi, 1954. pp. 32.

— United Kingdom.

SMITH (PETER F.) Industrial injuries benefits. London, 1978. pp. 183.

MUNKMAN (JOHN HENRY) Employer's liability at common law. 9th ed. London, 1979. pp. 653.

WORKS COUNCILS.

OAKESHOTT (ROBERT) The case for workers' co-ops. London, 1978. pp. 272.

— Czechoslovakia.

WORKERS' councils in Czechoslovakia, 1968-9: documents and essays; edited with an introduction by Vladimir Fišera. London, 1978. pp. 199.

— Europe.

KOLVENBACH (WALTER) Employee councils in European companies. Kluwer, 1978. pp. 334.

— Germany.

ARBEITERVERTRETER in den Betriebsrat: Dokumentation und Auseinandersetzung um eine ausserordentliche Betriebsratswahl 1973 bei Krone, Westberlin, etc. Berlin, [1973]. pp. 122. *(Internationale Marxistische Diskussion. Arbeitspapiere. No. 13)*

ERFAHRUNGEN in der Betriebsrats- und Gewerkschaftsarbeit; Herausgeber: Gruppe Arbeiterpolitik. Bremen, 1973. pp. 48.

— Netherlands.

NETHERLANDS. Ministerie van Sociale Zaken. 1973. De wet op de ondernemingsraden: een beknopte gids voor de praktijk; (with Wettekst). 's-Gravenhage, 1973. 2 pts.

WORLD COUNCIL OF CHURCHES.

BOURDEAUX (MICHAEL) and others, eds. Religious liberty in the Soviet Union: W[orld] C[ouncil of] C[hurches] and USSR: a post-Nairobi documentation. West Wickham, Kent, [1976]. pp. 96. *(Centre for the Study of Religion and Communism. Keston Books. No.7)*

HUDSON (DARRIL) The World Council of Churches in international affairs. Leighton Buzzard, Beds., 1977. pp. 336.

AUSTIN (GEORGE) World Council of Churches' Programme to Combat Racism. London, 1979. pp. 20. *bibliog. (Institute for the Study of Conflict. Conflict Studies. No. 105)*

WORLD DISARMAMENT CONFERENCE.

NOEL-BAKER (PHILIP JOHN) Baron Noel-Baker. The first world disarmament conference, 1932-1933, and why it failed. Oxford, 1979. pp. 147.

WORLD FERTILITY SURVEY.

WORLD FERTILITY SURVEY. Annual report. a., 1972/75 (1st issue)- Voorburg.

WORLD INTELLECTUAL PROPERTY ORGANIZATION.

EKEDI-SAMNIK (JOSEPH) L'Organisation Mondiale de la Propriété Intellectuelle (OMPI). Bruxelles, 1975. pp. 302. *bibliog.*

WORLD PEACE COUNCIL.

FRIEDENSRAT DER DEUTSCHEN DEMOKRATISCHEN REPUBLIK. Dokumente der Weltfriedensbewegung: Oktober 1962 bis Dezember 1974. [Wittenberg, imprint], 1976. pp. 320.

WORLD POLITICS.

BYRNES (JAMES FRANCIS) Speaking frankly. New York, [1947]. pp. 324.

HALLE (LOUIS JOSEPH) Civilization and foreign policy: an inquiry for Americans. New York, [1952]. pp. 277.

McNEILL (WILLIAM HARDY) America, Britain and Russia: their co-operation and conflict, 1941-1946. New York, [1976]. pp. 819. *Reprint of work originally published as one volume of the Survey of International Affairs, London, 1953.*

FOSDICK (DOROTHY) Common sense and world affairs. New York, [1955]. pp. 207.

HALLE (LOUIS JOSEPH) The cold war as history. New York, [1967]. pp. 434. *bibliog.*

MOLNÁR (MIKLÓS) Marx, Engels et la politique internationale. Paris, 1975. pp. 385. *bibliog.*

PONCINS (LEON DE) Comte, the Younger. State secrets: a documentation of the secret revolutionary mainspring governing Anglo-American politics; translated from the French edition of...Top secret by Timothy Tindal-Robertson. Chulmleigh, Devon, 1975. pp. 191. *bibliog.*

WEEDE (ERICH) Weltpolitik und Kriegsursachen im 20. Jahrhundert: eine quantitativ-empirische Studie. München, 1975. pp. 438. *bibliog. With English summary.*

WORLD inequality: origins and perspectives on the world system; edited by Immanuel Wallerstein. Nottingham, [1975]. pp. 169.

PROGRESUL istoric și contemporaneitatea. București, 1976. pp. 538. *With English, French, German and Russian tables of contents.*

ECONOMIC issues and national security; edited by Klaus Knorr and Frank N. Trager. New York, [1977]. pp. 330. *bibliogs. (New York (City). University. National Security Education Program, and National Strategy Information Center. National Security Studies Series. No. 7)*

HUDSON (DARRIL) The World Council of Churches in international affairs. Leighton Buzzard, Beds., 1977. pp. 336.

The NONALIGNED movement in world politics; [edited by A.W. Singham]. Westport, Conn., [1977]. pp. 273. *Papers prepared for the Howard Conference on Non-Alignment, held at Howard University, 1976.*

The ORIGINS of the Cold War in Asia; edited by Yonosuke Nagai and Akira Iriye. New York, [1977]. pp. 448. *bibliogs.*

XXV s″ezd KPSS o sovremennom mirovom revoliutsionnom protsesse. Kiev, 1978. pp. 191.

BARZEL (RAINER) Auf dem Drahtseil. München, [1978]. pp. 247.

BREZHNEV (LEONID IL'ICH) Mir sotsializma - torzhestvo velikikh idei: (rechi, stat'i i vystupleniia za period 1964-1978 gg.). Moskva, 1978. pp. 656.

HARTMANN (FREDERICK HOWARD) The relations of nations. 5th ed. New York, [1978]. pp. 704. *bibliog.*

HOFFMAN (STANLEY HARRY) Primacy or world order: American foreign policy since the Cold War. New York, [1978]. pp. 331. *bibliogs.*

KREISKY (BRUNO) Die Zeit, in der wir leben: Betrachtungen zur internationalen Politik; herausgegeben von Manuel Lucbert. Wien, [1978]. pp. 207.

LARSON (THOMAS B.) Soviet-American rivalry. New York, [1978]. pp. 308. *bibliog.*

The ORIGINS of the cold war and contemporary Europe; edited with an introduction by Charles S. Maier. New York, 1978. pp. 254. *bibliog.*

SOCIAL change in the capitalist world economy; edited by Barbara Hockey Kaplan. Beverly Hills, Calif., [1978]. pp. 239. *bibliogs. (American Sociological Association. Political Economy of the World-System Annuals. vol. 1)*

The SOVIET threat: myths and realities; edited by Grayson Kirk and Nils Wessell. New York, 1978. pp. 182.

THATCHER (MARGARET) The sinews of foreign policy. London, 1978. pp. 12.

ANGELL (ROBERT COOLEY) The quest for world order. Michigan, [1979]. pp. 186. *bibliog.*

BARROS (JAMES) Office without power: Secretary-General Sir Eric Drummond, 1919-1933. Oxford, 1979. pp. 423.

DEPORTE (ANTON WILLIAM) Europe between the superpowers: the enduring balance. New Haven, 1979. pp. 256. *bibliog.*

KIM (SAMUEL S.) China, the United Nations and world order. Princeton, 1979. pp. 581. *bibliog.*

MOYNIHAN (DANIEL PATRICK) A dangerous place. London, 1979. pp. 297.

STOESSINGER (JOHN GEORGE) The might of nations: world politics in our time. 6th ed. New York, [1979]. pp. 517. *bibliogs.*

WORLD WAR, 1939-1945.

DOUGLAS (ROY) The advent of war, 1939-40. London, 1978. pp. 167.

MASTNY (VOJTECH) Russia's road to the cold war: diplomacy, warfare, and the politics of communism, 1941-1945. New York, 1979. pp. 409. *bibliog.*

— Aerial operations.

WOOD (DEREK) and DEMPSTER (DEREK) The narrow margin: the Battle of Britain and the rise of air power, 1930-40. Westport, Conn., [1961]. pp. 536.

— Aerial operations, German.

GALLAND (ADOLF) The first and the last: the German fighter force in World War II. London, 1955 repr. 1973. pp. 368.

— Aerial operations, Russian.

BORSÁNYI (JULIÁN) Das Rätsel des Bombenangriffs auf Kaschau, 26. Juni 1941: wie wurde Ungarn in den Zweiten Weltkrieg hineingerissen?: e dokumentarischer Bericht. München, 1978. pp. 260. *bibliog. (Ungarisches Institut München. Studia Hungarica. 16)*

— Campaigns.

GUDERIAN (HEINZ) Panzer leader:...translated from the German by Constantine Fitzgibbon. London, 1974 repr. 1979. pp. 528. *First published in Great Britain in 1952.*

— — France.

GANT (ROLAND) How like a wilderness. London, 1946. pp. 160.

SYDNOR (CHARLES W.) Soldiers of destruction: the SS Death's Head Division, 1933-1945. Princeton, N.J., [1977]. pp. 371. *bibliog.*

LUCAS (JAMES) Germany's elite panzer force: Grossdeutschland. London, 1978. pp. 152. *bibliog.*

— — Pacific.

IENAGA (SABURO) Japan's last war: World War II and the Japanese, 1931-1945. Oxford, 1979. pp. 316.

— — Russia.

HOFFMANN (JOACHIM) 1930- . Deutsche und Kalmyken, 1942 bis 1945. Freiburg, [1974]. pp. 214. *bibliog. (Militärgeschichtliches Forschungsamt. Einzelschriften zur Militärischen Geschichte des Zweiten Weltkrieges. 14)*

SYDNOR (CHARLES W.) Soldiers of destruction: the SS Death's Head Division, 1933-1945. Princeton, N.J., [1977]. pp. 371. *bibliog.*

LUCAS (JAMES) Germany's elite panzer force: Grossdeutschland. London, 1978. pp. 152. *bibliog.*

— Causes.

THORNE (CHRISTOPHER) The approach of war, 1938-1939. London, 1967 repr. 1977. pp. 232. *bibliog.*

KIMCHE (JON) The unfought battle. London, [1968]. pp. 168. *bibliog.*

DILKS (DAVID) Appeasement revisited. Leeds, 1972. pp. 29. *Inaugural lecture in the University of Leeds Review, vol. 15, no.1, May 1972.*

YOUNG (ARTHUR PRIMROSE) The 'X' documents; edited by Sidney Aster. London, 1974. pp. 253. *bibliog.*

BAUMONT (MAURICE) The origins of the Second World War; translated by Simone de Couvreur Ferguson. New Haven, 1978. pp. 327.

BORSÁNYI (JULIÁN) Das Rätsel des Bombenangriffs auf Kaschau, 26. Juni 1941: wie wurde Ungarn in den Zweiten Weltkrieg hineingerissen?: e dokumentarischer Bericht. München, 1978. pp. 260. *bibliog. (Ungarisches Institut München. Studia Hungarica. 16)*

IRVING (DAVID J.) The war path: Hitler's Germany, 1933-9. London, [1978]. pp. 301.

KINSELLA (WILLIAM E.) Leadership in isolation: FDR and the origins of the Second World War. Boston, Mass., [1978]. pp. 282. *bibliog.*

— Censorship — Italy.

COEN (FAUSTO) Tre anni di bugie: 328 ordini alla stampa del Minculpop negli anni della guerra. Milano, [1977]. pp. 175.

— Collaborationists — France.

DESANTI (DOMINIQUE) Drieu la Rochelle: le séducteur mystifié. Paris, 1978. pp. 476. *bibliog.*

WORLD WAR, 1939-1945.(Cont.)

— — Russia.

HOFFMANN (JOACHIM) 1930- . Deutsche und Kalmyken, 1942 bis 1945. Freiburg, [1974]. pp. 214. *bibliog. (Militärgeschichtliches Forschungsamt. Einzelschriften zur Militärischen Geschichte des Zweiten Weltkrieges. 14)*

— Congresses.

BIRSE (ARTHUR HERBERT) Memoirs of an interpreter. London, 1967. pp. 254.

— Counterfeit money.

HOETTL (WILHELM) Hitler's paper weapon;...translated from the German by Basil Creighton. London, 1955. pp. 187.

— Cryptography.

WINTERBOTHAM (F.W.) The Ultra secret. London, 1974. pp. 199.

WOYTAK (RICHARD A.) On the border of war and peace: Polish intelligence and diplomacy in 1937-1939 and the origins of the ultra secret. Boulder, 1979. pp. 141. *bibliog. (East European Quarterly. East European Monographs. 49)*

— Diplomatic history.

BYRNES (JAMES FRANCIS) Speaking frankly. New York, [1947]. pp. 324.

BIRSE (ARTHUR HERBERT) Memoirs of an interpreter. London, 1967. pp. 254.

FEIS (HERBERT) Churchill, Roosevelt, Stalin: the war they waged and the peace they sought. 2nd ed. Princeton, N.J., 1967 repr. 1974. pp. 702.

KIMCHE (JON) The unfought battle. London, [1968]. pp. 168. *bibliog.*

YOUNG (ARTHUR PRIMROSE) The 'X' documents; edited by Sidney Aster. London, 1974. pp. 253. *bibliog.*

SPEARS (Sir EDWARD LOUIS) Fulfilment of a mission: the Spears mission to Syria and Lebanon 1941-1944. Hamden, Conn., 1977. pp. 311.

BARKER (ELISABETH) Churchill and Eden at war. London, 1978. pp. 346. *bibliog.*

LUKAS (RICHARD C.) The strange allies: the United States and Poland, 1941-1945. Knoxville, Tenn., [1978]. pp. 230. *bibliog.*

UEBERSCHAER (GERD R.) Hitler und Finnland, 1939-1941: die deutsch-finnischen Beziehungen während des Hitler-Stalin-Paktes. Wiesbaden, 1978. pp. 376. *bibliog.*

THOMAS (R.T.) Britain and Vichy: the dilemma of Anglo-French relations, 1940-42. London, 1979. pp. 230. *bibliog.*

WEBER (FRANK G.) The evasive neutral: Germany, Britain and the quest for a Turkish alliance in the Second World War. Columbia, Mo., 1979. pp. 244. *bibliog.*

— Economic aspects — Australia.

AUSTRALIA. Australian War Memorial. Australia in the War of 1939-1945. Series. 4.4. War economy, 1942-1945; by S.J. Butlin and C.B. Schedvin. Canberra, [1977]. pp. 817.

— — Germany.

WITTMANN (KLAUS) Schwedens Wirtschaftsbeziehungen zum Dritten Reich, 1933-1945. München, 1978. pp. 479. *bibliog. (Hamburg. Hansische Universität. Studien zur Modernen Geschichte. Band 23)*

— — Poland.

MIŚ (WŁADYSŁAW) Od wojny do pokoju: gospodarka Polski w latach 1944-1946. Warszawa, 1978. pp. 355. *bibliog.*

— Governments in exile.

Die FRONT war überall: (Erlebnisse und Berichte vom Kampf des Nationalkomitees "Freies Deutschland"; herausgegeben von Else und Bernt von Kügelgen). 2nd ed. Berlin, 1978. pp. 507. *bibliog.*

— Jews.

MORSE (ARTHUR D.) While six million died. London, [1968]. pp. 420.

The CATASTROPHE of European Jewry: antecedents, history, reflections: selected papers; edited by Yisrael Gutman and Livia Rothkirchen. Jerusalem, 1976. pp. 757. *bibliog.*

BAUER (YEHUDA) The holocaust in historical perspective. Seattle, [1978]. pp. 181.

TOKAYER (MARVIN) and SWARTZ (MARY SAGMASTER) The Fugu plan: the untold story of the Japanese and the Jews during World War II. New York, 1979. pp. 287.

— Peace.

ROMANIA. 1946. Roumania at the peace conference. Paris, 1946. pp. 145, 6 maps.

BYRNES (JAMES FRANCIS) Speaking frankly. New York, [1947]. pp. 324.

BALKANSKIE strany v novoe i noveishee vremia: sbornik statei. Kishinev, 1977. pp. 178.

BACKER (JOHN H.) The decision to divide Germany: American foreign policy in transition. Durham, N.C., 1978. pp. 212. *bibliog.*

— Personal narratives, American.

WAR-wasted Asia: letters, 1945-46;... [by] Donald Keene [and others]; (edited by Otis Cary). Tokyo, 1975. pp. 322.

— Personal narratives, Basque.

AGUIRRE Y LECUBE (JOSÉ ANTONIO DE) Freedom was flesh and blood. London, 1945. pp. 288.

— Personal narratives, British.

GANT (ROLAND) How like a wilderness. London, 1946. pp. 160.

SPEARS (Sir EDWARD LOUIS) Fulfilment of a mission: the Spears mission to Syria and Lebanon 1941-1944. Hamden, Conn., 1977. pp. 311.

— Personal narratives, German.

GUDERIAN (HEINZ) Panzer leader:...translated from the German by Constantine Fitzgibbon. London, 1974 repr. 1979. pp. 528. *First published in Great Britain in 1952.*

— Personal narratives, Yugoslav.

DJILAS (MILOVAN) Wartime; translated [from the Serbo-Croat] by Michael B. Petrovich. New York, [1977]. pp. 470.

— Prisoners and prisons, Australian.

CARR-GREGG (CHARLOTTE) Japanese prisoners of war in revolt: the outbreaks at Featherston and Cowra during World War II. St. Lucia, Qld., [1978]. pp. 225. *bibliog.*

— Prisoners and prisons, British.

SULLIVAN (MATTHEW BARRY) Thresholds of peace: four hundred thousand German prisoners and the people of Britain, 1944-1948. London, 1979. pp. 420. *bibliog.*

— Prisoners and prisons, German.

GANT (ROLAND) How like a wilderness. London, 1946. pp. 160.

— Prisoners and prisons, New Zealand.

CARR-GREGG (CHARLOTTE) Japanese prisoners of war in revolt: the outbreaks at Featherston and Cowra during World War II. St. Lucia, Qld., [1978]. pp. 225. *bibliog.*

— Propaganda.

RUPP (LEILA J.) Mobilizing women for war: German and American propaganda, 1939- 1945. Princeton, [1978]. pp. 243. *bibliog.*

BALFOUR (MICHAEL) Propaganda in war, 1939-1945: organisations, policies and publics in Britain and Germany. London, 1979. pp. 520. *bibliog.*

HERZSTEIN (ROBERT EDWIN) The war that Hitler won: the most infamous propaganda campaign in history. London, 1979. pp. 491. *bibliog.*

McLAINE (IAN) Ministry of morale: home front morale and the Ministry of Information in World War II. London, 1979. pp. 325. *bibliog.*

TAYLOR (RICHARD TRUEMAN) Film propaganda: Soviet Russia and Nazi Germany. London, [1979]. pp. 265. *bibliog.*

— Psychological aspects.

OWEN (DAVID) b. 1939. Battle of wits: a history of psychology and deception in modern warfare. London, 1978. pp. 207.

SHIBUTANI (TAMOTSU) The derelicts of company K: a sociological study of demoralization. Berkeley, Calif., [1978]. pp. 455. *bibliog.*

McLAINE (IAN) Ministry of morale: home front morale and the Ministry of Information in World War II. London, 1979. pp. 325. *bibliog.*

— Public opinion — United Kingdom.

U.K. Home Intelligence Unit. 1940-44. The British people and World War II: Home Intelligence reports on opinion and morale, 1940-1944. Brighton, [1979]. Microfilm: 4 reels.

— Regimental histories — Germany — Panzerdivision Grossdeutschland.

LUCAS (JAMES) Germany's elite panzer force: Grossdeutschland. London, 1978. pp. 152. *bibliog.*

— Reparations.

BACKER (JOHN H.) The decision to divide Germany: American foreign policy in transition. Durham, N.C., 1978. pp. 212. *bibliog.*

— Secret service — Germany.

STEPHAN (ENNO) Spies in Ireland;...translated from the German by Arthur Davidson. London, 1963. pp. 311. *bibliog.*

— — United States.

PERSICO (JOSEPH E.) Piercing the Reich: the penetration of Nazi Germany by OSS agents during World War II. London, 1979. pp. 376.

— Sources.

EISENHOWER (DWIGHT DAVID) President of the United States. The papers of Dwight David Eisenhower...; Alfred D. Chandler ([and] Louis Galambos) editor[s]. Baltimore, [1970 in progress]. *bibliogs.*

— Territorial questions — Poland.

MAGIERSKA (ANNA) Ziemie zachodnie i północne w 1945 roku: kształtowanie się podstaw polityki integracyjnej państwa polskiego. Warszawa, 1978. pp. 306. *bibliog.*

— Transportation.

ROHDE (HORST) Das deutsche Wehrmachttransportwesen im Zweiten Weltkrieg: Entstehung, Organisation, Aufgaben. Stuttgart, 1971. pp. 439. *bibliog. (Militärgeschichtliches Forschungsamt. Beiträge zur Militär- und Kriegsgeschichte. Band 12)*

— Underground movements — Austria.

ZEUGEN des Widerstandes: eine Dokumentation über die Opfer des Nationalsozialismus in Nord-,Ost- und Südtirol von 1938 bis 1945; bearbeitet von Johann Holzner [and others] . Innsbruck, [1977]. pp. 112.

WORLD WAR, 1939-1945.(Cont.)

KONRAD (HELMUT) Widerstand an Donau und Moldau: KPÖ und KSČ zur Zeit des Hitler-Stalin-Paktes. Wien, [1978]. pp. 348. *bibliog. (Ludwig Boltzmann Institut für Geschichte der Arbeiterbewegung. Veröffentlichungen)*

TIDL (MARIE) Frauen im Widerstand: Frauen im Kampf gegen Faschismus und Krieg. [Vienna, 1978]. pp. 52. *bibliog.*

WIDERSTAND und Verfolgung im Burgenland, 1934-1945: eine Dokumentation; Auswahl, Bearbeitung und Zusammenstellung: Wolfgang Neugebauer; unter Mitarbeit von Erica Fischer [and others]. Wien, Österreichischer Bundesverlag, [1979]. pp. 487.

— — Czechoslovakia.

DOLEŽAL (JIŘÍ) and KŘEN (JAN) eds. Czechoslovakia's fight: documents on the resistance movement of the Czechoslovak people, 1938-1945. Prague, 1964. pp. 210.

KONRAD (HELMUT) Widerstand an Donau und Moldau: KPÖ und KSČ zur Zeit des Hitler-Stalin-Paktes. Wien, [1978]. pp. 348. *bibliog. (Ludwig Boltzmann Institut für Geschichte der Arbeiterbewegung. Veröffentlichungen)*

— — France.

COLLOQUE DE RECHERCHE HISTORIQUE, PARIS, 1975. La Pologne et la France dans la guerre et la résistance de 1939 à 1945. Paris, Secrétariat d'Etat aux Anciens Combattants, [1978]. pp. 235.

DEBU-BRIDEL (JACQUES) De Gaulle et le CNR. Paris, [1978]. pp. 278. *bibliog.*

— — Italy.

DELZELL (CHARLES F.) Mussolini's enemies: the Italian anti-fascist resistance. New York, 1974. pp. 620. *bibliog.* Reprint of work originally published at Princeton, 1961.

PER una storia della sinistra cristiana: documenti, 1937-1945; a cura di Mario Cocchi e Pio Montesi. Roma, 1975. pp. 278.

ALASIA (FRANCO) Gaetano Invernizzi, dirigente operaio. Milano, [1976]. pp. 243. *(Istituto Milanese per la Storia della Resistenza e del Movimento Operaio. Collana di Studi e Biografie)*

La RESISTENZA nelle campagne modenesi. Modena, 1976. pp. 405. *(Istituto Storico della Resistenza in Modena e Provincia. Quaderni. 11)*

DILIO (MARIO) Puglia antifascista. Bari, [1977]. pp. 320. *bibliog.*

— — Poland.

COLLOQUE DE RECHERCHE HISTORIQUE, PARIS, 1975. La Pologne et la France dans la guerre et la résistance de 1939 à 1945. Paris, Secrétariat d'Etat aux Anciens Combattants, [1978]. pp. 235.

— — Yugoslavia.

DJILAS (MILOVAN) Wartime; translated [from the Serbo-Croat] by Michael B. Petrovich. New York, [1977]. pp. 470.

— Women.

TIDL (MARIE) Frauen im Widerstand: Frauen im Kampf gegen Faschismus und Krieg. [Vienna, 1978]. pp. 52. *bibliog.*

— Women's work.

WOOD (ETHEL MARY) Mainly for men. London, 1943. pp. 126.

GERSDORFF (URSULA VON) Frauen im Kriegsdienst, 1914-1945. Stuttgart, 1969. pp. 572. *bibliog. (Militärgeschichtliches Forschungsamt. Beiträge zur Militär- und Kriegsgeschichte. Band 11)*

RUPP (LEILA J.) Mobilizing women for war: German and American propaganda, 1939- 1945. Princeton, [1978]. pp. 243. *bibliog.*

— Africa, North.

DOUGHERTY (JAMES J.) The politics of wartime aid: American economic assistance to France and French Northwest Africa, 1940-1946. Westport, Conn., 1978. pp. 264. *bibliog.*

— China.

SCHALLER (MICHAEL) The U.S. crusade in China, 1938-1945. New York, 1979. pp. 364. *bibliog.*

— France.

KIMCHE (JON) The unfought battle. London, [1968]. pp. 168. *bibliog.*

DOUGHERTY (JAMES J.) The politics of wartime aid: American economic assistance to France and French Northwest Africa, 1940-1946. Westport, Conn., 1978. pp. 264. *bibliog.*

— Germany.

GALLAND (ADOLF) The first and the last: the German fighter force in World War II. London, 1955 repr. 1973. pp. 368.

KIMCHE (JON) The unfought battle. London, [1968]. pp. 168. *bibliog.*

GOEBBELS (JOSEPH) Tagebücher, 1945: die letzten Aufzeichnungen; Einführung: Rolf Hochhuth; (Redaktion: Peter Stadelmayer). Hamburg, [1977]. pp. 608.

SPEIDEL (HANS) Aus unserer Zeit: Erinnerungen. Frankfurt/M, 1977. pp. 512.

COOPER (MATTHEW) The German Army, 1933-1945: its political and military failure. London, 1978. pp. 598. *bibliog.*

Die FRONT war überall: (Erlebnisse und Berichte vom Kampf des Nationalkomitees "Freies Deutschland"; herausgegeben von Else und Bernt von Kügelgen). 2nd ed. Berlin, 1978. pp. 507. *bibliog.*

LUCAS (JAMES) Germany's elite panzer force: Grossdeutschland. London, 1978. pp. 152. *bibliog.*

— Hungary.

BORSÁNYI (JULIÁN) Das Rätsel des Bombenangriffs auf Kaschau, 26. Juni 1941: wie wurde Ungarn in den Zweiten Weltkrieg hineingerissen?: e dokumentarischer Bericht. München, 1978. pp. 260. *bibliog. (Ungarisches Institut München. Studia Hungarica. 16)*

— India.

VOIGT (JOHANNES HERMANN) Indien im Zweiten Weltkrieg. Stuttgart, 1978. pp. 414. *bibliog. (Institut für Zeitgeschichte. Studien zur Zeitgeschichte. Band 11)* With English summary.

— Ireland (Republic).

STEPHAN (ENNO) Spies in Ireland;...translated from the German by Arthur Davidson. London, 1963. pp. 311. *bibliog.*

SHARE (BERNARD) The Emergency: neutral Ireland, 1939-1945. Dublin, 1978. pp. 146. *bibliog.*

— Lebanon.

SPEARS (Sir EDWARD LOUIS) Fulfilment of a mission: the Spears mission to Syria and Lebanon 1941-1944. Hamden, Conn., 1977. pp. 311.

— Malaya.

CHIN (KEE ONN) Malaya upside down. 3rd ed. Singapore, 1976. pp. 202.

— Netherlands.

GROEN (KOOS) 'Er heerst orde en rust...': chaotisch Nederland tussen september 1944 en december 1945. Nijmegen, [1979]. pp. 208. 7 inch record: Authentiek historische geluidsfragmenten, in end pocket.

— Norway.

WALKER (ROY) A people who loved peace: the Norwegian struggle against Nazism. London, 1946. pp. 111. *bibliog.*

— Poland.

SCAEVOLA, pseud. A study in forgery: (the Lublin Committee and its rule over Poland). London, [1945]. pp. 123.

— Romania.

ROMANIA. 1946. Roumania at the peace conference. Paris, 1946. pp. 145, 6 maps.

— Russia — Russia (RSFSR).

SHUSHKIN (NIKOLAI NIKITICH) and ULITIN (S.D.) Soiuz rabochikh i krest'ian v Velikoi Otechestvennoi voine: na materialakh respublik i oblastei Severo-Zapada RSFSR. Leningrad, 1977. pp. 182.

— — Ukraine.

KOVAL' (MIKHAIL VASIL'EVICH) Obshchestvenno-politicheskaia deiatel'nost' trudiashchikhsia Ukrainskoi SSR v period Velikoi Otechestvennoi voiny. Kiev, 1977. pp. 264.

— Scandinavia.

NOSKOV (ANATOLII MIKHAILOVICH) Skandinavskii platsdarm vo vtoroi mirovoi voine. Moskva, 1977. pp. 247. *bibliog.*

— Sweden.

KARLSSON (RUNE) Så stoppades tysktågen: den tysktågen: den tyska transiteringstrafiken i svensk politik, 1942-1943. Stockholm, 1974. pp. 363. *bibliog.* With English summary.

— Syria.

SPEARS (Sir EDWARD LOUIS) Fulfilment of a mission: the Spears mission to Syria and Lebanon 1941-1944. Hamden, Conn., 1977. pp. 311.

— United Kingdom.

KIMCHE (JON) The unfought battle. London, [1968]. pp. 168. *bibliog.*

BARKER (ELISABETH) Churchill and Eden at war. London, 1978. pp. 346. *bibliog.*

HINSLEY (FRANCIS HARRY) British intelligence in the Second World War: its influence on strategy and operations. London, H.M.S.O., 1979 in progress. *(U.K. [Cabinet Office]. History of the Second World War)*

McLAINE (IAN) Ministry of morale: home front morale and the Ministry of Information in World War II. London, 1979. pp. 325. *bibliog.*

U.K. Home Intelligence Unit. 1940-44. The British people and World War II: Home Intelligence reports on opinion and morale, 1940-1944. Brighton, [1979]. Microfilm: 4 reels.

— — Jersey.

SINEL (L.P.) The German occupation of Jersey: a diary of events from June 1940 to June 1945. London, 1969. pp. 318.

— United States.

MORSE (ARTHUR D.) While six million died. London, [1968]. pp. 420.

RUSSETT (BRUCE MARTIN) No clear and present danger: a skeptical view of the United States entry into World War II. New York, 1972. pp. 111.

— Upper Austria.

SLAPNICKA (HARRY) Oberösterreich - als es "Oberdonau" hiess, 1938-1945. Linz, 1978. pp. 513. *bibliog. (Upper Austria. Landesarchiv. Beiträge zur Zeitgeschichte Oberösterreichs. 5)*

WORSHIPFUL COMPANY OF COACHMAKERS AND COACH HARNESS MAKERS.

NOCKOLDS (HAROLD) ed. The coachmakers: a history of the Worshipful Company of Coachmakers and Coach Harness Makers, 1677-1977. London, [1977]. pp. 239. *bibliog.*

YANOAMA INDIANS.

MIGLIAZZA (ERNEST C.) The integration of the indigenous peoples of the territory of Roraima, Brazil. Copenhagen, 1978. pp. 29. *bibliog. (International Work Group for Indigenous Affairs. Documents. 32)*

YAQUI INDIANS.

KELLEY (JANE HOLDEN) Yaqui women: contemporary life histories. Lincoln, Neb., [1978]. pp. 265. *bibliog.*

YEATS (WILLIAM BUTLER).

WATSON (GEORGE) Irish identity and the literary revival: Synge, Yeats, Joyce and O'Casey. London, 1979. pp. 326. *bibliog.*

YEMEN

— History.

STOOKEY (ROBERT W.) Yemen: the politics of the Yemen Arab Republic. Boulder, Colo., 1978. pp. 322. *bibliog.*

YORK

— Social conditions.

FINNEGAN (FRANCES) Poverty and prostitution: a study of Victorian prostitutes in York. Cambridge, 1979. pp. 231. *bibliog.*

YORKSHIRE, WEST.

See WEST YORKSHIRE.

YORUBAS.

ARONSON (DAN R.) The city is our farm: seven migrant Ijebu Yoruba families. Cambridge, Mass., [1978]. pp. 208. *bibliog.*

GBADAMOSI (T.G.O.) The growth of Islam among the Yoruba, 1841-1908. London, 1978. pp. 265. *bibliog.*

YOUNG (ARTHUR PRIMROSE).

YOUNG (ARTHUR PRIMROSE) The 'X' documents; edited by Sidney Aster. London, 1974. pp. 253. *bibliog.*

YOUNG COMMUNIST LEAGUE

— Russia.

SLAVNYI put' leninskogo komsomola: istoriia VLKSM. 2nd ed. Moskva, 1978. pp. 590.

— — Congresses.

VSESOIUZNYI LENINSKII KOMMUNISTICHESKII SOIUZ MOLODEZHI. S"ezd, 18- yi, 1978. XVIII s"ezd Vsesoiuznogo Leninskogo Kommunisticheskogo Soiuza Molodezhi 25-28 aprelia 1978 g.: stenograficheskii otchet. Moskva, 1978. 2 vols.

— — Ukraine.

KOMMUNISTICHESKAIA PARTIIA UKRAINY. Tsentral'nyi Komitet. Plenum, noiabr', 1977. Materialy, etc. Kiev, 1977. pp. 52.

YOUNG CZECH PARTY.

See NÁRODNÍ STRANA SVOBODOMYSLNÁ.

YOUTH.

GILLIS (JOHN R.) Youth and history: tradition and change in European age relations, 1770-present. New York, [1974]. pp. 232. *bibliog.*

IS anyone there?; edited by Monica Dickens and Rosemary Sutcliff. [Harmondsworth, 1978]. pp. 204.

MARSLAND (DAVID) Sociological explorations in the service of youth. Leicester, [1978]. pp. 251. *bibliog.*

— Employment — Australia.

SCHOOL leavers: choice and opportunity. Canberra, 1977. pp. 116. *bibliogs. (Australia. Commission of Inquiry into Poverty. Poverty and Education Series)*

— — Canada — Quebec.

GIRARD (MICHEL) and others. Les jeunes Québécois et le travail: rapport d'étape. [Québec, 1978]. pp. 204. *bibliog. (Québec (Province). Office de Planification et de Développement. Collection Etudes et Recherches)*

— — Denmark.

HILLESTRØM (KARSTEN) and REDDER (K. W.) Ungdomsarbejdsløshed i Århus kommune. København, 1977. pp. 145. *bibliog. (Socialforskningsinstituttet. Meddelelser. 20)*

MØLLER (IVER HORNEMANN) Ungdomsarbejdsløshed. København, 1978. pp. 55. *bibliog. (Socialforskningsinstituttet, Meddelelser. 25)*

— — France.

DEBRAND (JEAN CLAUDE) Le chômage des jeunes: formation et recherche d'un emploi dans l'A.L.E. de Dijon. Dijon, Echelon Régional de l'Emploi de Dijon, 1977. fo. 74.

Les JEUNES et le premier emploi; document préparé par Anne Marie Métailié et Jean Marie Thiveaud: [proceedings and papers of a conference held by the] Association des Ages. Paris, [1978]. pp. 544.

— — Italy.

EMMA (ROSANNA) and MOSCATI (ROBERTO) La fabbrica dei disoccupati: scuola e occupazione giovanile in una inchiesta sugli Istituti Tecnici Industriali nel mezzogiorno. Torino, 1976. pp. 293.

I GIOVANI ad elevato livello di istruzione e i mercati del lavoro in Italia; di Andrea Cafarelli [and others]. Milano, [1977]. pp. 166.

BALANDI (GIAN GUIDO) La legge sulla occupazione giovanile. Milano, [1978]. pp. 111.

— — Netherlands.

NETHERLANDS. Arbeidsinspectie. 1973. Jeugdige werknemers werkzaam in vestigingen met 20 of meer personen: gegevens uit de personeelsenquêtes over 1970 en 1972. 's-Gravenhage. 1973. pp. 29. *(Netherlands. Ministerie van Sociale Zaken. Verslagen en Rapporten: Sociale Zaken. 1973.5)*

— — Russia — Siberia.

KONSTANTINOVSKII (DAVID L'VOVICH) Dinamika professional'nykh orientatsii molodezhi Sibiri: opyt sotsiologicheskogo issledovaniia. Novosibirsk, 1977. pp. 174. *bibliog.*

— — United Kingdom.

SMITH (BARBARA M.D.) Youth employment in Birmingham in 1972: an exploration of the statistics and their implications. Birmingham, 1975. fo. 92. *bibliog. (Birmingham. University. Centre for Urban and Regional Studies. Research Memoranda. No. 45)*

BALL (COLIN) Community service and the young unemployed. Leicester, 1977. pp. 24.

U.K. Commission for Racial Equality. 1978. Looking for work: black and white school leavers in Lewisham; a short report of a survey carried out for the Commission for Racial Equality in conjunction with Lewisham Borough Council and Lewisham Council for Community Relations. London, 1978. pp. 16. *bibliog.*

CASSON (MARK C.) Youth unemployment. London, 1979. pp. 141. *bibliog.*

— — — Ireland, Northern.

OSBORNE (ROBERT D.) and MURRAY (RUSSELL C.) Educational qualifications and religious affiliation in Northern Ireland: an examination of G.C.E.'O' and 'A' levels. Belfast, 1978. pp. 42. *bibliog. (Fair Employment Agency for Northern Ireland. Research Papers. 3)*

— Institutional care — Denmark.

LIHME (BENNY) and PALSVIG (KURT) Effekten af behandling på børne- og ungdomshjem: en analyse af foreliggende undersøgelser, etc. København, 1977. pp. 387. *bibliog. (Socialforskningsinstituttet. Publikationer. 78)* With English summary.

—Austria.

NEUGEBAUER (WOLFGANG) Die sozialdemokratische Jugendbewegung in Österreich 1894-1945. [Vienna, 1969]. 2 vols. *bibliog.* Vol. 2 lacks pages 8, 14, 31, 121, 173, 288, 334, 369 and 372.

— Belgium.

STATISTIQUES et protection de la jeunesse; Statistieken en jeugdbescherming; [by a] groupe de travail, 1976-1977. Bruxelles, 1977. pp. 97. *(Centre d'Etude de la Délinquance Juvénile. Publications. No. 41)* In French or Dutch, with synthesis and conclusion in both languages.

— Canada — Alberta — Bibliography.

JAQUE (MERVYN H.) compiler. Research on youth: an annotated bibliography of selected current reports. [Edmonton], Youth Development Division, 1976. fo. 24.

— China.

The RUSTICATION of urban youth in China: a social experiment; edited by Peter J. Seybolt. White Plains, 1977. pp. 199.

— — Political activity.

RADDOCK (DAVID M.) Political behavior of adolescents in China: the Cultural Revolution in Kwangchow. Tucson, [1977]. pp. 242. *bibliog. (Association for Asian Studies. Monographs. 32)*

— Germany, Eastern — Political activity.

GESCHICHTE der Freien Deutschen Jugend: Chronik; (Redaktionskollegium: K.H. Jahnke [and others]; Autoren: W. Arlt [and others]). 2nd ed. Berlin, 1978. pp. 391.

— Hungary.

HUNGARY. Embassy (U.K.). Press Section. 1971. Young Hungary. London, 1971. pp. 64.

— Italy.

I COMUNISTI e la questione giovanile: atti della sessione del Comitato centrale del Partito comunista italiano, Roma, 14-16 marzo 1977. Roma, 1977. pp. 378.

Il P.C.I. e la questione giovanile: [an anthology]; a cura di Walter Veltroni. Roma, 1977. pp. 353.

— — Political activity.

FRANCHI (PAOLO) Nuove generazioni, democrazia, socialismo. Roma, 1977. pp. 177.

— Korea.

KIM (IL-SUNG) On the work with children and youth. Pyongyang, 1978. pp. 375.

— **Netherlands.**

NETHERLANDS. Centraal Bureau voor de Statistiek. 1977- . De Nederlandse jeugd: een inventarisatie van statistische gegevens. 's- Gravenhage, 1977 in progress.

De POSITIE van jongeren ten opzichte van het ouderlijk gezin: een analyse op basis van de volkstelling 1971; [by] L.H. Boerma [and others]. 's-Gravenhage, 1979. pp. 67. bibliog. (Netherlands. Centraal Bureau voor de Statistiek. Monografieën Volkstelling 1971. 10) With English summary.

— **Seychelles.**

YOUTH in nation building: report of a Seychelles national seminar, February 1978. [London], Commonwealth Secretariat, [1978]. pp. 113.

— **United Kingdom.**

LEACH (BRIDGET) Youth and spatial poverty: activity space patterns of black and white young people in Leeds. Bristol, Social Science Research Council Research Unit on Ethnic Relations, [1978]. pp. 78. bibliog. (Working Papers on Ethnic Relations. No. 9)

WILLIS (PAUL E.) Profane culture. London, 1978. pp. 212.

— — **Recreation.**

ROBINS (DAVID) and COHEN (PHILIP) 1944- . Knuckle sandwich: growing up in the working-class city. Harmondsworth, 1978. pp. 203.

— **United States.**

NEW YORK (CITY). Youth Board. Youth Board Monographs. No. 4. Reaching the group: an analysis of group work methods used with teenagers. New York, 1956. pp. 75.

— — **Political activity.**

BONE (CHRISTOPHER) The disinherited children: a study of the New Left and the generation gap. New York, [1977]. pp. 183. bibliogs.

YOUTH VOLUNTEERS IN COMMUNITY DEVELOPMENT

— **United Kingdom.**

BALL (COLIN) Community service and the young unemployed. Leicester, 1977. pp. 24.

YUGOSLAVIA

— **Church history.**

ALEXANDER (STELLA) Church and state in Yugoslavia since 1945. Cambridge, 1979. pp. 351. bibliog. (National Association for Soviet and East European Studies. Soviet and East European Studies)

— **Economic conditions — Mathematical models.**

ALARCÓN-RIVERO (JORGE) A two region model on the basis of Yugoslav statistical data. The Hague, [1978]. pp. 105. bibliog. (Hague. Institute of Social Studies. Research Report Series. No.3)

— **Foreign relations — Hungary.**

TIHANY (LESLIE CHARLES) The Baranya dispute, 1918-1921: diplomacy in the vortex of ideologies. New York, 1978. pp. 138. bibliog. (East European Quarterly. East European Monographs. 35)

— — **Russia.**

DEDIJER (VLADIMIR) The battle Stalin lost: memoirs of Yugoslavia, 1948-1953. Nottingham, 1978. pp. 341.

— **History.**

DEDIJER (VLADIMIR) The battle Stalin lost: memoirs of Yugoslavia, 1948-1953. Nottingham, 1978. pp. 341.

— **Nationalism.**

NATIONS and nationalities of Yugoslavia. Beograd, 1974. pp. 549. bibliog.

— **Politics and government.**

The BELGRADE revisionist clique - renegades from Marxism- Leninism and agents of imperialism. Tirana, 1964. pp. 325.

DODER (DUSKO) The Yugoslavs. New York, [1978]. pp. 256. bibliog.

KARDELJ (EDVARD) Democracy and socialism; translated by Margot and Boško Milosavljević. London, [1978]. pp. 244.

CLISSOLD (STEPHEN) Croat separatism: nationalism, dissidence and terrorism. London, 1979. pp. 21. (Institute for the Study of Conflict. Conflict Studies. No.103)

— **Population.**

ROGERS (ANDREI) The aggregation problem in demography. Ljubljana, 1967. 2 pts. (in 1 vol.). bibliog. Appendix entitled An analysis of the aggregation problem in demography: data for Yugoslavia; by Silvo Kranjec and Andrei Rogers. A study of the American- Yugoslav Project in Regional and Urban Planning Studies.

— **Relations (general) with Slovakia.**

KOVIJANIĆ (RISTO) Štúdie z dejín juhoslovansko-slovenských vztahov; [translated from the Serbo-Croat by Ján Siracký]. Martin, [1976]. pp. 141.

— **Social conditions.**

DODER (DUSKO) The Yugoslavs. New York, [1978]. pp. 256. bibliog.

YUGOSLAVS IN SLOVAKIA.

KOVIJANIĆ (RISTO) Štúdie z dejín juhoslovansko-slovenských vztahov; [translated from the Serbo-Croat by Ján Siracký]. Martin, [1976]. pp. 141.

ZAIRE

— **History.**

ABI-SAAB (GEORGES) The United Nations operation in the Congo 1960-1964. Oxford, 1978. pp. 206. Published under the auspices of the American Society of International Law.

RHODESIA. Ministry of Information, Immigration and Tourism. 1978. The United Nations in central Africa, 1961-62: a review of United Nations military achievement in Central Africa, in the light of proposed activity of the United Nations in Rhodesia. [Salisbury, 1978]. pp. 16.

— **Politics and government.**

ABI-SAAB (GEORGES) The United Nations operation in the Congo 1960-1964. Oxford, 1978. pp. 206. Published under the auspices of the American Society of International Law.

RHODESIA. Ministry of Information, Immigration and Tourism. 1978. The United Nations in central Africa, 1961-62: a review of United Nations military achievement in Central Africa, in the light of proposed activity of the United Nations in Rhodesia. [Salisbury, 1978]. pp. 16.

ZAMBIA

— **Administrative and political divisions.**

ZAMBIA. Local Government Electoral Commission. 1970. Report on the delimitation of council areas into wards...; [Thomas Pickett, chairman]. Lusaka, 1970. pp. 22.

— **Census.**

ZAMBIA. Central Statistical Office. 1977. The census mapping project: an outline. Lusaka, 1977. 1 vol. (various foliations).

— **Commerce — Tanzania.**

TANGANYIKA. 1954. Report on a survey of inter-territorial trade between Tanganyika and Northern Rhodesia and Nyasaland. [Dar es Salaam, 1954]. pp. 30.

— **Constitution.**

FEDERATION OF RHODESIA AND NYASALAND. [High Commission, London] . 1961. Proposals for onstitution change in Northern Rhodesia (Cmd. 1295). [London, 1961]. fo. 7.

— **Department of Industrial Participatory Democracy.**

ZAMBIA. Department of Industrial Participatory Democracy. Annual report. a., 1976- Lusaka.

— **Economic conditions.**

UNITED NATIONAL INDEPENDENCE PARTY [ZAMBIA]. National Council. The nation is you: addresses to, and resolutions of, the National Council of the United National Independence Party at Mulungushi Hall, Lusaka, 4th to 6th March, 1972. [Lusaka, Government Printer, 1972]. pp. 72.

NATIONAL CONFERENCE ON POPULATION AND DEVELOPMENT, LUSAKA, 1974. Report [of the conference organised by the] Extra-Mural Studies Department, University of Zambia. Lusaka, [1975?]. fo. 80.

— **Economic policy.**

UNITED NATIONAL INDEPENDENCE PARTY [ZAMBIA]. National Council. The nation is you: addresses to, and resolutions of, the National Council of the United National Independence Party at Mulungushi Hall, Lusaka, 4th to 6th March, 1972. [Lusaka, Government Printer, 1972]. pp. 72.

UNITED NATIONAL INDEPENDENCE PARTY [ZAMBIA]. National Council. 'A nation of equals': the Kabwe declaration: addresses to the National Council of the United National Independence Party at the Hindu Hall, Kabwe, 1-3 December, 1972. [Lusaka, 1973]. pp. 88.

— **Executive departments.**

ZAMBIA. Department of Industrial Participatory Democracy. Annual report. a., 1976- Lusaka.

— **Foreign relations.**

HALL (RICHARD) Zambia, 1890-1964: the colonial period. new ed. London, 1976. pp. 225. bibliog.

— **History.**

HALL (RICHARD) Zambia, 1890-1964: the colonial period. new ed. London, 1976. pp. 225. bibliog.

— **Politics and government.**

UNITED NATIONAL INDEPENDENCE PARTY [ZAMBIA]. National Council. The nation is you: addresses to, and resolutions of, the National Council of the United National Independence Party at Mulungushi Hall, Lusaka, 4th to 6th March, 1972. [Lusaka, Government Printer, 1972]. pp. 72.

ZAMBIA. National Commission on the Establishment of a One- Party Participatory Democracy in Zambia. 1972. Report; [M. Mainza Chona, chairman]. Lusaka, 1972. pp. 72.

UNITED NATIONAL INDEPENDENCE PARTY [ZAMBIA]. National Council. 'A nation of equals': the Kabwe declaration: addresses to the National Council of the United National Independence Party at the Hindu Hall, Kabwe, 1-3 December, 1972. [Lusaka, 1973]. pp. 88.

— **Population.**

NATIONAL CONFERENCE ON POPULATION AND DEVELOPMENT, LUSAKA, 1974. Report [of the conference organised by the] Extra-Mural Studies Department, University of Zambia. Lusaka, [1975?]. fo. 80.

ZAMBIA(Cont.)

— Social conditions.

NATIONAL CONFERENCE ON POPULATION AND DEVELOPMENT, LUSAKA, 1974. Report [of the conference organised by the] Extra-Mural Studies Department, University of Zambia. Lusaka, [1975?]. fo. 80.

ZAPOTEC INDIANS.

WHITECOTTON (JOSEPH W.) The Zapotecs: princes, priests, and peasants. Norman, [1977]. pp. 338. *bibliog.*

ZARPAZO.

BUITRAGO SALAZAR (EVELIO) Zarpazo the bandit: memoirs of an undercover agent of the Colombian Army;...translated by M. Murray Lasley; edited.. .by Russell W. Ramsey. University, Ala., [1977]. pp. 169.

ZIEGELBRENNER, DER.

RICHTER (ARMIN) Der Ziegelbrenner: das individualanarchistische Kampforgan des frühen B. Traven. Bonn, 1977. pp. 442. *bibliog.*

ZIJLSTRA (JELLE).

ZIJLSTRA (JELLE) Gesprekken en geschriften; samengesteld door G. Puchinger met bijdrage van W. Drees. Naarden, [1978]. pp. 383.

ZINACANTAN, MEXICO

— Social life and customs.

HAVILAND (JOHN BEARD) Gossip, reputation, and knowledge in Zinacantan. Chicago, 1977. pp. 260. *bibliog.*

ZONING LAW

— United States.

AFTER Mount Laurel: the new suburban zoning; edited by Jerome G. Rose and Robert E. Rothman. New Brunswick, N.J., [1977]. pp. 354.

ZUERICH (CANTON)

— Constitution.

ZUERICH (CANTON). Regierungsrat. 1969. Unser Kanton Zürich: hundert Jahre Staatsverfassung 1869-1969. [Zürich, 1969]. pp. 23.

— Economic history.

SALZMANN (MARTIN) Die Wirtschaftskrise im Kanton Zürich, 1845 bis 1848, etc. Bern, [1978]. pp. 399. *bibliog.*

— Economic policy.

BRUGGER (ERNST A.) and HAEBERLING (GEORGE) Abbau regionaler Ungleichgewichte: föderalistischer Ausgleich durch Raumordnungspolitik: Ansprüche und konkrete Möglichkeiten im Kanton Zürich. Zürich, 1978. 3 vols. *bibliog.*

ZUERICH (CITY)

— Statistics.

ZUERCHER STATISTISCHE NACHRICHTEN: [pd. by] Statistisches Amt der Stadt Zürich. 4 a yr., 1957 (Jg.37, Heft 3)- Zurich.

ZUÑI INDIANS.

CRAMPTON (CHARLES GREGORY) The Zunis of Cibola. Salt Lake City, [1977]. pp. 201. *bibliog.*

List of subject headings used
in the Bibliography
arranged under topics

TABLE OF SUBJECT SUB-DIVISIONS

SUBJECT SUB-DIVISIONS UNDER NAMES OF CONTINENTS, COUNTRIES, STATES OR TOWNS

Works on the following subjects, if confined to a particular geographical area, are entered not under subject, but under the name of the country, etc., with the subject sub-division.

Administrative and political divisions
Air force
Annexation
Antiquities
Appropriations and expenditures
Armed forces
Army

Bibliography
Bio-bibliography
Biography
Boundaries

Capital
Census
Centennial celebrations, etc
Charters, grants, privileges
Church history
City planning
Civilization
Claims
Climate
Clubs
Colonies
Colonization
Commerce
Commercial policy
Commercial treaties
Constitution
Constitutional conventions
Constitutional history
Constitutional laws
Courts and courtiers

Defences
Description and travel
Dictionaries and encyclopaedias
Diplomatic and consular service
Directories
Discovery and exploration

Economic conditions
Economic history
Economic integration
Economic policy

Emigration and immigration
Executive departments
Exiles

Fairs
Famines
Foreign economic relations
Foreign opinion
Foreign population
Foreign relations
Foreign relations — Treaties
Foreign relations administration

Gazeteers
Genealogy
Gentry
Government property
Government publications
Government vessels
Governors

Historic houses, etc.
Historical geography
History
History, Local
History, Military
History, Naval

Industries
Intellectual life
International status

Kings and rulers

Languages
Learned institutions and societies

Manufactures
Maps
Military policy
Militia
Moral conditions

Nationalism
Native races

Navy
Neutrality
Nobility

Occupations
Officials and employees

Parliament (Congress, Nationalrat, etc.)
Peerage
Politics and government
Population
Presidents
Public buildings
Public lands
Public works

Race relations
Registers
Relations (general) with (country)
Relations (military) with (country)
Religion
Religion and mythology
Rural conditions

Sanitary affairs
Seal
Semi-centennial celebrations, etc.
Social conditions
Social history
Social life and customs
Social policy
Statistics
Statistics, Medical
Statistics, Vital
Surveys

Territorial expansion
Territories and possessions
Tornadoes

Vice-Presidents
Voting registers

Year-books

SUBJECT SUB-DIVISIONS USED ONLY UNDER NAMES OF CITIES OR TOWNS

Works on the following matters, if confined to a particular region or country, are entered under the subject, with local sub-division, if confined to a particular city or town, under the name of the city or town, with subject sub-division.

Almshouses and workhouses
Ambulance service
Amusements

Benevolent and moral institutions
 and societies
Bridges
Buildings

Cemeteries
Charities
Civic improvement
Clubs

Description
Docks

Earthquake
Evening and continuation schools
Exhibitions
Fires and fire prevention

Fortifications

Gilds
Growth

Harbour
Hospitals
Hotels, taverns, etc.

Libraries
Lodging-houses

Markets
Massacre
Music-halls (Variety-theatres,
 cabarets, etc.)

Office buildings

Parks
Police
Poor
Port

Porters
Prisons and reformatories
Public laundries

Rapid transit
Recreation areas
Recreational activities
Riots

Schools
Sewerage
Stock Exchange (Beurs, Bourse, etc.)
Street cleaning
Streets
Suburbs and environs
Synagogues

Theatres
Transit systems

Water-supply

AGRICULTURE (including ANIMAL AND PLANT INDUSTRIES)

General.

AGRICULTURAL ASSISTANCE, NORWEGIAN
AGRICULTURAL COLONIES
AGRICULTURAL CREDIT
AGRICULTURAL EDUCATION
AGRICULTURAL EXPERIMENT STATIONS
AGRICULTURAL GEOGRAPHY.
AGRICULTURAL INDUSTRIES
AGRICULTURAL INNOVATIONS.
AGRICULTURAL PRICE SUPPORTS
AGRICULTURAL PRICES.
AGRICULTURAL RESEARCH
AGRICULTURE.
AGRICULTURE, COOPERATIVE
AGRICULTURE AND STATE.
ANIMAL INDUSTRY.
ANIMAL PRODUCTS.
ANIMALS, HABITS AND BEHAVIOUR OF.
COCONUT INDUSTRY
COMMUNICATION IN AGRICULTURE.
COOPERATIVE MARKETING OF FARM PRODUCE
COTTON GROWING
CROP YIELDS.
DAIRYING
DOUBLE CROPPING
FARM EQUIPMENT.
FARM INCOME
FARM LIFE
FARM MANAGEMENT.
FARM OWNERSHIP
FARM PRODUCE
FARM TENANCY
FARMS
FARMS, COLLECTIVE
FARMS, SIZE OF.
FERTILIZERS AND MANURES
FOREST MANAGEMENT
FOREST POLICY.
FOREST PRODUCTS
FORESTS AND FORESTRY
FRUIT TRADE.
FUR TRADE
GRAIN TRADE.
GREEN REVOLUTION.
HIDES AND SKINS INDUSTRY.
HILL FARMING
HORTICULTURE
HUNTING
IRRIGATION
LAND SETTLEMENT.
ORGANIC AGRICULTURE.
PALM OIL INDUSTRY.
PESTICIDES.
PLANTATIONS
PRODUCE TRADE.
SHIFTING CULTIVATION
SMALL HOLDINGS
SOIL SURVEYS
STATE FARMS
STOCK AND STOCK BREEDING
SUGAR GROWING
TROPICAL CROPS.
VETERINARY MEDICINE
WATER SUPPLY, AGRICULTURAL

Particular animals and animal products.

BEEF
BEEF CATTLE
CHIMPANZEES.
EGGS
MEAT
MILK
POULTRY
SHEEP

Particular crops and plant products.

ALLSPICE.
COCOA
COFFEE
FRUIT
GINGER.
GRAIN.
MAIZE
MARIHUANA.
PEANUTS
PEPPER.
RICE
STRAWBERRIES.
SUGAR
TEA
TEAK.
TIMBER
TOBACCO
VEGETABLES
WHEAT
WOOD.

Fisheries.

BRITISH FISHERIES SOCIETY.
FISHERIES.
FISHERY LAW AND LEGISLATION
FISHERY MANAGEMENT.
FISHERY PRODUCTS
FISHING BOATS
FISHING VILLAGES
WHALING.

BIBLIOGRAPHY AND GENERAL WORKS.

ABSTRACTING AND INDEXING SERVICES.
AFRICAN STUDIES
AKADEMIE DER WISSENSCHAFTEN DER DDR.
ANTIQUARIAN BOOKSELLERS
ARCHIVES.
BIBLIOGRAPHICAL SERVICES.
BIBLIOGRAPHY
BIBLIOGRAPHY, NATIONAL
BOOKS
BOOKSELLERS AND BOOKSELLING
BRITISH LIBRARY OF POLITICAL AND ECONOMIC SCIENCE.
CATALOGUES, LIBRARY.
COLLEGE LIBRARIANS
DEUTSCHE AKADEMIE DER WISSENSCHAFTEN ZU BERLIN.
DISSERTATIONS, ACADEMIC
ENCYCLOPEDIAS AND DICTIONARIES.
GOVERNMENT PUBLICATIONS.
HUMANITIES
INFORMATION SERVICES
LAW LIBRARIES.
LEGAL RESEARCH.
LIBRARIES
LIBRARIES, GOVERNMENTAL, ADMINISTRATIVE, ETC.
LIBRARIES, UNIVERSITY AND COLLEGE
LIBRARY ARCHITECTURE
LIBRARY RESOURCES ON RUSSIA.
LIBRARY SCIENCE.
MUSEUMS
NATIONAL ARCHIVES AND RECORDS SERVICE.
PERIODICALS
PRINTING, PUBLIC
READERSHIP SURVEYS
REFERENCE BOOKS
SCHOLARLY PUBLISHING
SOCIETY FOR THE DIFFUSION OF USEFUL KNOWLEDGE.

BIOGRAPHY.

ABAELARDUS (PETRUS).
ABDALLAH, King of Jordan.
ADAM, of Orleton, Bishop of Winchester.
ADORNO (THEODOR WIESENGRUND).
AGUIRRE Y LECUBE (JOSÉ ANTONIO DE).
AKHUNDOV (MIRZA FATALI).
ALENCAR (JOSE DE).
ALLEMAND-LAVIGERIE (CHARLES MARTIAL) Cardinal.
ALLENDE (SALVADOR).
ALTHUSSER (LOUIS).
AMIN (IDI).
ANDRÁSSY (GYULA) Gróf.
ANDRONICUS II PALAEOLOGUS, Emperor of the East.
ANNUNZIO (GABRIELE D').
ARISTOTLE.
ARONSON (JAMES).
BAADER (ANDREAS).
BABEUF (FRANÇOIS NOEL).
BAHRO (RUDOLF).
BAHUSHEVICH (FRANTSISHAK).
BAKUNIN (MIKHAIL ALEKSANDROVICH).
BANDA (HASTINGS KAMUZU).
BARDINI (VITTORIO).
BARNARDO (THOMAS JOHN).
BARTH (KARL).
BAUER (BRUNO).
BAXTER (RICHARD).
BEGIN (MENACHEM).
BELFRAGE (CEDRIC).
BELL (ALEXANDER GRAHAM).
BEN-GURION (DAVID).
BENN (ANTHONY NEIL WEDGWOOD).
BENTHAM (JEREMY).
BENTHAM (THOMAS) Bishop of Lichfield and Coventry.
BERARD (ARMAND).
BERDIAEV (NIKOLAI ALEKSANDROVICH).
BERNSTEIN (EDUARD).
BERRY (CHARLES ACKERMAN).
BEVAN (ANEURIN).
BHAVE (VINOBA).
BHUTTO (ZULFIKAR ALI).
BIBB (HENRY).
BIKO (STEVEN).
BIRSE (ARTHUR HERBERT).
BISMARCK-SCHOENHAUSEN (OTTO EDUARD LEOPOLD VON) Prince.
BLADEN (VINCENT WHEELER).
BLAGOEV (DIMITUR).
BLASSINGAME (JOHN W.).
BODIN (JEAN).
BOESCHENSTEIN (HERMANN).
BOGDANOV (ALEKSANDR ALEKSANDROVICH) pseud.
BOOTH (WILLIAM).
BOOTHBY (ROBERT JOHN GRAHAM) Baron Boothby.
BORGIA FAMILY.
BOSANQUET (BERNARD).
BOURBAKI (NICOLAS).
BOURGUIBA (HABIB).
BRABAZON (REGINALD) 12th Earl of Meath.
BRACKEN (BRENDAN) Viscount Bracken of Christchurch.
BRAHMS (JOHANNES).
BRASCHI (GIOVANNI).
BRETON (ANDRE).
BREZHNEV (LEONID IL'ICH).
BRIGHT (JOHN).
BRONFMAN FAMILY.
BROOKE (Sir CHARLES ANTHONI) Rajah of Sarawak.
BROWN (LUCIUS POLK).
BRYDGES (CHARLES JOHN).
BUITRAGO SALAZAR (EVELIO).

BIOGRAPHY (Cont.)

BUKHARIN (NIKOLAI IVANOVICH).
BUKOVSKII (VLADIMIR KONSTANTINOVICH).
BURKE (EDMUND).
BURN (JAMES DAWSON).
BUSTAMANTE (Sir ALEXANDER).
BUTTINGER (JOSEPH).
CALDERA (MIGUEL).
CALVIN (JEAN).
CAMARA (HELDER) Archbishop of Olinda and Recife.
CAMPOS (FRANCISCO LUIS DA SILVA).
CAPRIVI (LEO VON) Graf.
CARLYLE (THOMAS).
CARRANZA (VENUSTIANO).
CARROLL (JOHN) Archbishop of Baltimore.
CARTER (JAMES EARL) President of the United States.
CASO (ALFONSO).
CASSIRER (ERNST).
CASTRO LEAL (ANTONIO).
CAVOUR (CAMILLO BENSO DI) Conte.
CHAIANOV (ALEKSANDR VASIL'EVICH).
CHAMBERLAIN (JOSEPH).
CHARLES, Duke of Burgundy, called the Bold.
CHARLES, the Great.
CHATTERJI (BANKIM CHANDRA).
CHOMSKY (NOAM).
CHRISTO (CARLOS ALBERTO LIBANIO).
CHURCHILL (JOHN) 1st Duke of Marlborough.
CHURCHILL (Sir WINSTON LEONARD SPENCER).
CIESZKOWSKI (AUGUST VON) Graf.
CLARK (JOE).
CLEAVER (ELDRIDGE).
CLEMENCEAU (GEORGES EUGENE BENJAMIN).
COHN (DAVID LEWIS).
COKE (Sir EDWARD).
COLBY (BAINBRIDGE).
COLE (ARTHUR CHARLES).
COLINS (JEAN GUILLAUME CESAR ALEXANDRE HIPPOLYTE).
COLUMBUS (CHRISTOPHER).
COMINES (PHILIPPE DE).
CONNOLLY (JAMES).
CROFT (Sir HERBERT).
CUNNINGHAME-GRAHAM (ROBERT BONTINE).
DALEY (RICHARD J.).
DAVIDSON (JOE).
DAVIS (JEFFERSON).
DE BLANK (JOOST) Archbishop of Capetown.
DEBRAY (REGIS).
DE CLEYRE (VOLTAIRINE).
DEFOE (DANIEL).
DE LA GARDIE (MAGNUS GABRIEL).
DELAVAL (Lady ELIZABETH).
DELČEV (GOCE).
DE LEON (DANIEL).
DENIKIN (ANTON IVANOVICH).
DESAI (MORARJI RANCHHODRI).
DESCARTES (RENE).
DEWEY (JOHN).
DICKENS (CHARLES).
DIEDERICHS (GEORG).
DILTHEY (WILHELM).
DJILAS (MILOVAN).
DREXEL (JOSEPH EDUARD).
DRIEU LA ROCHELLE (PIERRE).
DRUMMOND (JAMES ERIC) 16th Earl of Perth.
DUBČEK (ALEXANDER).
DUEHRING (EUGEN KARL).
DUGARD (ROBERT).
DULLES (JOHN FOSTER).
DUNCAN (JONATHAN) 1756-1811.
DUNSTAN, Saint, Archbishop of Canterbury.
DU PLESSIS (ARMAND JEAN) Cardinal, Duc de Richelieu.
DUPONT (CLIFFORD W.).
DURKHEIM (EMILE).
DZERZHINSKII (FELIKS EDMUNDOVICH).
EASTMAN (ELAINE GOODALE).
EASTMAN (MAX).
ECCLES (MARRINER STODDARD).
EDEN (ROBERT ANTHONY) 1st Earl of Avon.
EDWARD II, King of England.
EDWARDS (WILLIAM JAMES).
EGERTON (FRANCIS) 3rd Duke of Bridgewater.
EINAUDI (LUIGI).
EINSTEIN (ALBERT).
EISENHOWER (DWIGHT DAVID) President of the United States.
ELEANOR, Queen Consort of Henry II, King of England.
EMERSON (RALPH WALDO).
EMMERSON (JOHN K.).
ENGELS (FRIEDRICH).
ERASMUS (DESIDERIUS).
FALKENHAUSEN (ALEXANDER VON).
FARIA (GILBERTO DE LIMA AZEVEDO SOUZA FERREIRA AMADO DE).
FARINGTON (JOSEPH).
FERRER Y GUARDIA (FRANCISCO).
FEST (JOACHIM).
FIGUEIREDO (AFONSO CELSO DE ASSIS) Visconde de Ouro Preto.
FILMER (Sir ROBERT).
FISHER (Sir RONALD AYLMER).
FITZPATRICK (JOHN).
FLAVELLE (Sir JOSEPH WESLEY).
FLETCHER (CALVIN).
FONTOURA (JOÃO NEVES DE).
FOOT (PAUL).
FORD (HENRY).
FORNANDER (ABRAHAM).
FOURIER (FRANÇOIS CHARLES MARIE).
FOX (Sir STEPHEN).
FRANCIS JOSEPH I, Emperor of Austria.
FRANCO BAHAMONDE (FRANCISCO).
FREDERICK II, called the Great, King of Prussia.
FREGE (GOTTLOB).
FREIRE (PAULO).
FREUD (SIGMUND).
FROEBEL (JULIUS).
FUERSTENBERG (WILHELM EGON) Graf von, Cardinal.
FULLERTON (DOUGLAS H.).
GAITSKELL (HUGH TODD-NAYLOR).
GALBRAITH (JOHN KENNETH).
GALILEI (GALILEO).
GALLAND (ADOLF).
GALLIENI (JOSEPH SIMON).
GALLOWAY (JOSEPH).
GANDHI (INDIRA).
GANDHI (MOHANDAS KARAMCHAND).
GARDINER (MURIEL).
GARVEY (MARCUS).
GAST (JOHN).
GAULLE (CHARLES DE).
GEORGE I, King of Great Britain and Ireland.
GEORGE III, King of Great Britain and Ireland.
GEORGE (DAVID LLOYD) 1st Earl Lloyd George.
GEORGE (HENRY).
GERSHUN (ALEKSANDR L'VOVICH).
GILCHRIST (Sir ANDREW).
GIRARD (STEPHEN).
GISCARD D'ESTAING (VALERY).
GLADSTONE (WILLIAM EWART).
GOBETTI (PIERO).
GODWIN (MARY).
GOEBBELS (JOSEPH).
GOERDELER (CARL FRIEDRICH).
GOLDEN (CLINTON STRONG).
GOLDIE (Sir GEORGE DASHWOOD TAUBMAN).
GOMEZ MORIN (MANUEL).
GORDON (GEORGE HAMILTON) 4th Earl of Aberdeen.
GORTER (HERMAN).
GORWALA (ASTAD DINSHAW).
GRAMSCI (ANTONIO).
GRANELLI (GIUSEPPE).
GRENVILLE FAMILY.
GREWE (WILHELM GEORG).
GREY (EDWARD) 1st Viscount Grey of Fallodon.
GROMYKO (ANDREI ANDREEVICH).
GUDERIAN (HEINZ).
GURO MAHARAJ JI.
GUTTMAN (LOUIS).
HABERMAS (JUERGEN).
HABSBURG FAMILY.
HAMILTON (ALEXANDER).
HAMILTON (PEGGY) Lady.
HANCOCK (WALTER).
HANSLICK (EDUARD).
HARDEMAN FAMILY.
HARON (ABDULLA).
HARRINGTON (JAMES).
HARRISON (PAT).
HAUSHOFER (KARL).
HAY (JOHN).
HAYA DE LA TORRE (VICTOR RAUL).
HAYEK (FRIEDRICH AUGUST).
HECKFORD (SARAH).
HEGEL (GEORG WILHELM FRIEDRICH).
HEIDEGGER (MARTIN).
HILBERT (DAVID).
HILL (JAMES JEROME).
HILLQUIT (MORRIS).
HILLS (DENIS).
HINCMARUS, Bishop of Laon.
HIROTA (KOKI).
HITLER (ADOLF).
HOBBES (THOMAS).
HOBHOUSE (LEONARD TRELAWNEY).
HOEGNER (WILHELM).
HOFFA (JAMES RIDDLE).
HOOVER (HERBERT CLARK) President of the United States.
HOPE (VICTOR ALEXANDER JOHN) 2nd Marquess of Linlithgow.
HOPTON (CHARLES).
HUGENBERG (ALFRED).
HUGH, Saint, Abbot of Cluny.
HUMPHREYS (CHRISTMAS).
HUNT (JOSEPH McVICKER).
INGWANE (JULIUS PAUNDE SHIMANGANE).
INVERNIZZI (GAETANO).
JACOBSSON (PER).
JAMES II, King of Great Britain and Ireland.
JEFFERSON (THOMAS) President of the United States.
JEYES (JOHN).
JOFFRE (JOSEPH JACQUES CESAIRE).
JOHNSON (JOSHUA).
JOY (C. TURNER).
JOYCE (JAMES AUGUSTINE ALOYSIUS).
JÓŹWIAK (FRANCISZEK).
JUSTINIAN I, Emperor of the East.
KALINOUSKI (KASTUS').
KANT (IMMANUEL).
KAPLAN (KAREL).
KAUTSKY (KARL).
KENNEDY (JOHN FITZGERALD) President of the United States.
KEPHART (WILLIAM G.).
KERR (Sir JOHN ROBERT).
KEYNES (JOHN MAYNARD) 1st Baron Keynes.
KIM (IL-SUNG).
KING (ERNEST JOSEPH).
KING (MARTIN LUTHER).
KISSINGER (HENRY ALFRED).
KLEIN (MELANIE).
KNEE (FRED).
KOLAS (IAKUB) pseud.

BIOGRAPHY(Cont.)

KOLLONTAI (ALEKSANDRA MIKHAILOVNA).
KÖNIG (EBERHARD).
KORBEL (JOSEF).
KORNILOV (LAVR GEORGIEVICH).
KORSCH (KARL).
KOSSUTH (LAJOS).
KROPOTKIN (PETR ALEKSEEVICH) Prince.
KRUPSKAIA (NADEZHDA KONSTANTINOVNA).
KUPALA (IANKA) pseud.
LABRIOLA (ANTONIO).
LACAZE-DUTHIERS (GERARD DE).
LAING (Sir JOHN WILLIAM).
LAING (RONALD DAVID).
LAM (STANISŁAW).
LANGLEY (FRANCIS).
LANSBURY (GEORGE).
LANUSSE (ALEJANDRO AGUSTIN).
LASSALLE (FERDINAND JOHANN GOTTLIEB).
LAURIER (Sir WILFRID).
LAVROV (PETR LAVROVICH).
LAZARE (BERNARD).
LECA (DOMINIQUE).
LEFEBVRE (GEORGES).
LENIN (VLADIMIR IL'ICH).
LEOPOLD II, King of the Belgians.
LEVESQUE (RENE).
LEVI-STRAUSS (CLAUDE).
LEWIS (JOHN LLEWELLYN).
LI (TSUNG-JEN).
LIANG (SHU-MING).
LIEBKNECHT (WILHELM PHILIPP MARTIN CHRISTIAN LUDWIG).
LIMANOWSKI (BOLESLAW).
LIN FAMILY.
LINCOLN (ABRAHAM) President of the United States.
LIRA PARENTE (MANUEL).
LOCKE (JOHN).
LOGUEN (JERMAIN WESLEY).
LOMBARDO TOLEDANO (VICENTE).
LOPEZ MICHELSEN (ALFONSO).
LOUIS XI, King of France.
LOUIS XIV, King of France.
LUBBE (MARINUS VAN DER).
LUDLOW (EDMUND).
LUEBKE (HEINRICH).
LUHMANN (NIKLAS).
LUKÁCS (GEORG).
LUMUMBA (PATRICE).
LUXEMBURG (ROSA).
MACARTHUR (DOUGLAS).
MACCHIAVELLI (NICCOLO).
MACDONALD (JAMES RAMSAY).
McDOUGAL (MYRES SMITH).
McGLYNN (EDWARD).
MACHLUP (FRITZ).
MACLEAN (JOHN).
MAKHNO (NESTOR).
MALATESTA FAMILY.
MALINOVSKII (ROMAN).
MALINOWSKI (BRONISLAW).
MALLESON (NICOLAS BORRELL).
MALRAUX (CLARA).
MALTHUS (THOMAS ROBERT).
MALVA (CONSTANT).
MANGABEIRA (OTAVIO).
MANIN (DANIELE).
MANUEL II, King of Portugal.
MANUTIUS (ALDUS).
MAO (TSE-TUNG).
MARCUSE (HERBERT).
MARK (Sir ROBERT).
MARTIN DU GARD (ROGER).
MARX (KARL).
MASARYK (THOMAS GARRIGUE).
MAUDE (H.E.).
MAUDLING (REGINALD).
MEAD (MARGARET).
MEDICI FAMILY.
MEDINA ECHAVARRIA (JOSE).
MEINHOF (ULRIKE MARIE).
MENCKEN (HENRY LOUIS).
MENHENIOTT (STEPHEN).
MERKELIS (GARLIBS).
METCALFE (FRANCIS JAMES).
MICHAEL III PALAEOLOGUS, Emperor of the East.
MIHAILOVIC (DRAGOLJUB).
MILIUTIN (NIKOLAI ALEKSEEVICH).
MILL (JAMES).
MILLS (CHARLES WRIGHT).
MILTON (JOHN).
MISES (LUDWIG VON).
MITTERRAND (FRANÇOIS).
MOLINA ENRIQUEZ (ANDRES).
MOLTKE (HELMUTH JAMES VON) Graf.
MOMMSEN (THEODOR).
MONTAGU (Lady MARY WORTLEY).
MORENO BACA (JESUS).
MOTON (ROBERT RUSSA).
MUELLER-MEININGEN (ERNST).
MUENZENBERG (WILLY).
MUN (ADRIEN ALBERT MARIE DE) Comte.
MURRAY (Sir JAMES AUGUSTUS HENRY).
MUSSOLINI (BENITO).
MUTHULAKSHMI REDDY (S.).
MUZOREWA (ABEL TENDEKAI).
MZILIKAZI, King of the Matabele.
NAPOLEON I, Emperor of the French.
NARAYAN (JAYAPRAKASH).
NARAYANA (SREE).
NEAVE (AIREY).
NECHAEV (SERGEI GENNADIEVICH).
NECKER (JACQUES).
NEHRU (JAWAHARLAL).
NEHRU (MOTILAL).
NETTLAU (MAX).
NEWMAN (JOHN HENRY) Cardinal.
NICOLAS (JEAN).
NICOLE (LEON).
NIEDZIAŁKOWSKI (MIECZYSŁAW).
NIETZSCHE (FRIEDRICH WILHELM).
NIN (ANDRES).
NIXON (RICHARD MILHOUS) President of the United States.
NJÁLL THORGEIRSSON, c. 930-1011.
NOLENS (WILLEM HUBERT).
NOSKE (GUSTAV).
NUNES MACHADO (FRANCISCO).
O'CASEY (SEAN).
O'CONNOR (CHARLES YELVERTON).
OFFA, King of Angel.
OFFA, King of the Mercians, d.796.
OLDS (RANSOM ELI).
OLEA Y LEYVA (TEOFILO).
OLIVER (JOHN ANDREW).
OROZCO (WISTANO LUIS).
ORSMAN (WILLIAM JAMES).
OWEN (ROBERT).
PANKHURST (ESTELLE SYLVIA).
PANKRATOVA (ANNA MIKHAILOVNA).
PANNEKOEK (ANTON).
PARK (ROBERT EZRA).
PARRY (JOHN WILLIAM).
PARSONS (TALCOTT).
PEA (ENRICO).
PEARSON (LESTER BOWLES).
PEASE (JOSEPH).
PECK (JOHN).
PEIXOTO (CARLOS).
PERKINS (MAXWELL EVARTS).
PERON (JUAN DOMINGO).
PERROUX (FRANÇOIS).
PESSOA (EPITACIO).
PETAIN (HENRI PHILIPPE BENONI OMER JOSEPH).
PETROVSKII (GRIGORII IVANOVICH).
PHILBY (HAROLD ADRIAN RUSSELL).
PHILLIPS (Sir LIONEL).
PIAGET (JEAN).
PICHETA (VLADIMIR IVANOVICH).
PICK (FRANK).
PIERCE FAMILY.
PIOCH (KARL).
PLATO.
PLEKHANOV (GEORGII VALENTINOVICH).
POKROVSKII (MIKHAIL NIKOLAEVICH).
POMPIDOU (GEORGES).
POOR FAMILY.
POPPER (Sir KARL RAIMUND).
POPPER-LYNKEUS (JOSEF).
POUJADE (PIERRE).
POWELL (JOHN ENOCH).
PREČAN (VILÉM).
PROUDHON (PIERRE JOSEPH).
PUEA HERANGI (TE).
PYTHAGORAS.
RAHMAN (MUJIBUR).
RAINSFORD (GEORGE).
RANKIN (HARRY).
RASPAIL (FRANÇOIS VINCENT).
RAZAK BIN HUSSEIN (TUN ABDUL).
RECLUS (ELISEE).
REID (LOREN).
RHODES (CECIL JOHN).
RICASOLI (BETTINO) Barone.
RICE (Sir CECIL SPRING).
RIDDELL (GEORGE ALLARDICE) 1st Baron Riddell.
RIEL (LOUIS).
RIVADAVIA (BERNARDINO).
RIVERS (WILLIAM HALSE RIVERS).
ROBERTSON (Sir DENNIS HOLME).
RODRIGUES (JOÃO).
RODRIGUEZ DE FRANCIA (JOSE GASPAR).
ROGER II, King of Sicily.
ROLAND-HOLST (HENRIETTE).
ROOSEVELT (FRANKLIN DELANO) President of the United States.
ROSSI (GIOVANNI).
ROUSSEAU (JEAN JACQUES).
RUSSELL (BERTRAND ARTHUR WILLIAM) 3rd Earl Russell.
RUSSELL (JOHN SCOTT).
RYKOV (ALEKSEI IVANOVICH).
SALVEMINI (GAETANO).
SAMUELSON (PAUL ANTHONY).
SARAIVA (JOSE ANTÔNIO).
SARGAN (J.D.).
SARKAR (PRABHAT RANJAN).
SARTRE (JEAN PAUL).
SCHUTZ (ALFRED).
SCHWERIN VON KROSIGK (LUTZ) Graf.
SCOTT (DRED).
SEDGWICK (THEODORE).
SEIPEL (IGNAZ).
SEMENOV (GEORGII GAVRILOVICH).
SEMPRUN (JORGE).
SERGE (VICTOR) pseud.
SEYDEWITZ (MAX).
SHAVISHVILI (FEDOR AMBAKOVICH).
SHAW (GEORGE BERNARD).
SHVERNIK (NIKOLAI MIKHAILOVICH).
SLATER (JAMES DERRICK).
SMITH (ADAM).
SMITH (IAN DOUGLAS).
SMITH (JOSEPH).
SOBHUZA II, King of Swaziland.
SOCRATES.
SOLZHENITSYN (ALEKSANDR ISAEVICH).
SOMOZA FAMILY.
SOREL (GEORGES).
SPANN (OTHMAR).
SPEARS (Sir EDWARD LOUIS).
SPEER (ALBERT).
SPEIDEL (HANS).
STALIN (IOSIF VISSARIONOVICH).
STAMMLER (RUDOLF).
STAUNTON (HARVEY DE).
STEPHEN, King of England.
STEWARD (AUSTIN).
STRAEHL (WOLFGANG).

371

BIOGRAPHY (Cont.)

STRASSER (GREGOR).
STRAUSS (FRANZ JOSEF).
STRESEMANN (GUSTAV).
SUGER, Abbot of Saint-Denis.
SUN (YAT-SEN).
SYED KECHIK.
SYNGE (JOHN MILLINGTON).
TAFT (WILLIAM HOWARD) President of the United States.
TEMPLE (HENRY JOHN) 3rd Viscount Palmerston.
THATCHER (MARGARET).
THORPE (JEREMY).
TISO (JOZEF).
TITO (JOSIP BROZ).
TOGLIATTI (PALMIRO).
TOLLER (ERNST).
TOMSKII (MIKHAIL PAVLOVICH).
TRAVEN (BRUNO).
TRENCHARD (HUGH MONTAGUE) 1st Viscount Trenchard.
TRISTAN (FLORA).
TROTSKII (LEV DAVYDOVICH).
TRUDEAU (PIERRE ELLIOTT).
TRUJILLO MOLINA (RAFAEL LEONIDAS).
TWEED (WILLIAM MARCY).
TYRER (ANTHONY M.).
UL'IANOV FAMILY.
VADAKKAN (JOSEPH).
VAJIRAVUDH, King of Thailand.
VANSITTART (ROBERT GILBERT) 1st Baron Vansittart.
VASCONCELOS (ZACARIAS DE GOIS E).
VASQUEZ DEL MERCADO (ALBERTO).
VITTORIO (GIUSEPPE DI).
VOEGELIN (ERIC HERMAN WILHELM).
VOILQUIN (SUZANNE).
VOLTAIRE (FRANÇOIS MARIE AROUET DE).
VOORHIS (JERRY).
VORSTER (BALTHAZAR JOHANNES).
WALKER (PETER) M.P.
WALLRAFF (GUENTER).
WASHINGTON (BOOKER TALIAFERRO).
WEBER (MAX).
WEDGWOOD (JOSIAH CLEMENT) 1st Baron Wedgwood.
WEITLING (WILHELM).
WELLESLEY (ARTHUR) 1st Duke of Wellington.
WHITE (ANDREW DICKSON).
WHITE (THEODORE HAROLD).
WILLIAMS (SAMUEL MAY).
WILSON (THOMAS WOODROW) President of the United States.
WINFREY FAMILY.
WITT (JOHAN DE).
WITTGENSTEIN (LUDWIG).
WOLFF (SAM DE).
WOOD (ROBERT) 1903- .
WOOLF (LEONARD SIDNEY).
WOOLF (VIRGINIA).
YEATS (WILLIAM BUTLER).
YOUNG (ARTHUR PRIMROSE).
ZARPAZO.
ZIJLSTRA (JELLE).

COMMERCE AND INDUSTRY.

General.

ABILITY.
ACCOUNTING.
ADVERTISING.
AFRO-AMERICANS AS CONSUMERS.
ALCOHOLISM AND EMPLOYMENT.
APPRENTICES
ARBITRATION, INDUSTRIAL
ARBITRATION AND AWARD, INTERNATIONAL.
AUCTIONS.
AUDITING.
BALANCE OF TRADE
BIG BUSINESS
BOOKKEEPING.
BUSINESS.
BUSINESS CYCLES.
BUSINESS ETHICS.
BUSINESS FORECASTING.
BUSINESS RELOCATION
CENTRAL AMERICAN COMMON MARKET.
CENTRAL BUSINESS DISTRICTS.
COMMERCE.
COMMERCE, PRIMITIVE.
COMMERCIAL AGENTS
COMMERCIAL FINANCE COMPANIES
COMMERCIAL POLICY.
COMMODITY CONTROL.
COMMODITY EXCHANGES.
COMMUNICATION IN MANAGEMENT.
CONSOLIDATION AND MERGER OF CORPORATIONS
CONSUMER EDUCATION.
CONSUMERS.
CONSUMERS' PREFERENCES
CONTRACTS, LETTING OF.
CONTROLLERSHIP.
COOPERATION.
COOPERATIVE SOCIETIES.
CORPORATE DIVESTITURE
CORPORATE PLANNING.
CORPORATIONS.
CORPORATIONS, AMERICAN
CORPORATIONS, FOREIGN
CORPORATIONS, JAPANESE.
CORPORATIONS, PUBLIC
DECENTRALIZATION IN MANAGEMENT
DEPARTMENT STORES
EAST-WEST TRADE (1945-).
EFFICIENCY, INDUSTRIAL.
EMPLOYEE MORALE.
EMPLOYEE RIGHTS
EMPLOYEE THEFT
EMPLOYEES, DISMISSAL OF
EMPLOYEES, REPORTING TO.
EMPLOYEES, TRAINING OF
EMPLOYEES' MAGAZINES, HANDBOOKS, ETC.
EMPLOYEES' REPRESENTATION IN MANAGEMENT.
EMPLOYMENT FORECASTING.
EMPLOYMENT SUBSIDIES
EMPLOYMENT TESTING
EXPORT CREDIT.
EXPORT MARKETING.
FACTORIES
FACTORY INSPECTION
FIRMS.
FLOOR SPACE, INDUSTRIAL.
FOOD PRICES
FOREIGN TRADE PROMOTION
FOREIGN TRADE REGULATION.
FREE TRADE AND PROTECTION.
GOVERNMENT BUSINESS ENTERPRISES.
HANDICRAFT
HAZARDOUS SUBSTANCES
HOLDING COMPANIES
IMPORT QUOTAS
IMPORT SUBSTITUTION.
INCENTIVES IN INDUSTRY
INDUSTRIAL CAPACITY
INDUSTRIAL CONCENTRATION
INDUSTRIAL DISTRICTS
INDUSTRIAL EQUIPMENT LEASES.
INDUSTRIAL HYGIENE
INDUSTRIAL MANAGEMENT.
INDUSTRIAL ORGANIZATION.
INDUSTRIAL PROMOTION.
INDUSTRIAL PSYCHIATRY.
INDUSTRIAL RELATIONS.
INDUSTRIAL SAFETY
INDUSTRIAL SOCIOLOGY.
INDUSTRIAL STATISTICS.
INDUSTRIALIZATION.
INDUSTRIES, LOCATION OF.
INDUSTRIES, SIZE OF.
INDUSTRY.
INDUSTRY AND EDUCATION.
INDUSTRY AND STATE.
INFLATION (FINANCE) AND ACCOUNTING.
INTERNATIONAL BUSINESS ENTERPRISES.
LICENCE SYSTEM
MANAGEMENT.
MANAGEMENT GAMES.
MANAGEMENT INFORMATION SYSTEMS.
MANAGERIAL ACCOUNTING.
MANUFACTURERS
MANUFACTURES.
MARKETING.
MARKETS.
MEDIATION AND CONCILIATION, INDUSTRIAL
METRIC SYSTEM.
MINORITY BUSINESS ENTERPRISES
NONTARIFF TRADE BARRIERS.
OFFICES
ORGANIZATION OF THE PETROLEUM EXPORTING COUNTRIES.
PATENTS
PERSONNEL MANAGEMENT.
PERSONNEL RECORDS
PERSONNEL RESEARCH.
POOR AS CONSUMERS
POWER RESOURCES.
PRIVATE COMPANIES
PRODUCTIVITY.
PROFESSIONS
PROTESTANTISM AND CAPITALISM.
PUBLIC CONTRACTS
PUBLIC UTILITIES.
QUALITY CONTROL.
RAW MATERIALS
RENEGOTIATION OF GOVERNMENT CONTRACTS
RESEARCH, INDUSTRIAL
RETAIL TRADE.
SABOTAGE
SERVICE INDUSTRIES.
SMALL BUSINESS
SUGGESTION SYSTEMS
TOKYO ROUND, 1973-1979.
TRADE MARKS.
TRADE REGULATION
TURNOVER (BUSINESS)
UNITED NATIONS CONFERENCE ON TRADE AND DEVELOPMENT.
VOCATIONAL GUIDANCE.
VOCATIONAL QUALIFICATIONS.
WELFARE WORK IN INDUSTRY
WHOLESALE TRADE
WOOD AS FUEL.
WORK.
WORK DESIGN.
WORK ENVIRONMENT
WORK GROUPS
WORK RELIEF
WORKMEN'S COMPENSATION

Occupations and professions.

ACCOUNTANTS
AFRO-AMERICAN LAWYERS.
AFRO-AMERICAN PHYSICIANS.
AGRICULTURAL LABOURERS
ALLIED MENTAL HEALTH PERSONNEL.
ARTISANS
AUDITORS
AUTOMOBILE INDUSTRY WORKERS
BANKERS
BOILER-MAKERS
BUSINESSMEN.
CAPITALISTS AND FINANCIERS

COMMERCE AND INDUSTRY

CITY PLANNERS
CIVIL ENGINEERS
COAL MINERS
CONSTRUCTION WORKERS
CONSULTING ENGINEERS
CROFTERS
DIPLOMATS
DIPLOMATS, AMERICAN
DOCK WORKERS
ENGINEERS
EXECUTIVES.
FARMERS
FISHERMEN
FOREST RANGERS
GLASS WORKERS
HEALTH OFFICERS
IRON AND STEEL WORKERS
JUDGES
LAWYERS.
LONGSHOREMEN
LUMBERMEN
MEDICAL PERSONNEL.
MENTAL HEALTH PERSONNEL.
MERCHANTS
MERCHANTS, FOREIGN
METAL WORKERS
MIDWIVES
MINERS
MINING ENGINEERS
MISSIONARIES
PEATMEN
PHYSICIANS.
PHYSICISTS
POLITICIANS
POTTERS
PRINTERS
PROBATION OFFICERS
PUBLIC HEALTH PERSONNEL
PUBLIC PROSECUTORS
REAL ESTATE AGENTS
REFUSE COLLECTORS
ROAD TRANSPORT WORKERS
SCIENTISTS
SEAMEN
SELF-EMPLOYED
SERVANTS
SHIPBUILDING WORKERS
SOCIAL SCIENTISTS.
SOCIAL WORK AS A PROFESSION.
SOCIAL WORKERS.
SOCIOLOGISTS.
SOCIOLOGY AS A PROFESSION.
TEACHERS
TECHNOLOGISTS
TELEVISION INDUSTRY WORKERS
TEXTILE WORKERS
TRAVEL AGENTS
WOMEN ARTISTS
WOMEN IN MEDICINE.

Particular firms, trades and industries.

AEROPLANE INDUSTRY AND TRADE
ALBERTA OPPORTUNITY COMPANY.
ALUMINIUM INDUSTRY AND TRADE.
AMERICAN TELEPHONE AND TELEGRAPH COMPANY.
ASHBOURNE INVESTMENTS.
ATOMIC ENERGY INDUSTRIES
ATOMIC POWER INDUSTRY
ATOMIC POWER-PLANTS
AUTOMOBILE INDUSTRY AND TRADE.
BAHAMAS ELECTRICITY CORPORATION.
BAKERS AND BAKERIES
BEVERAGES.
BIBBY (J.) AND SONS.
BIRMINGHAM AND MIDLAND CANAL CARRYING COMPANY.
BOOK INDUSTRIES AND TRADE
BOTTLES.
BRAYHEAD LIMITED.
BREWING INDUSTRIES
BRITISH AEROSPACE.
BRITISH AIRWAYS.
BRITISH LEYLAND.
BRITISH SHIPBUILDERS.
BUILDING
BUILDING FITTINGS
BUILDING MATERIALS INDUSTRY
BUILDING TRADES
BURNHOLME AND FORDER LIMITED.
CARRIAGE AND WAGON MAKING
CATERERS AND CATERING
CATHEDRALS
CENTERPRISE TRUST.
CENTRAL AND SHERWOOD.
CHEMICAL INDUSTRIES
CLOCK AND WATCH MAKING
CLOTHING TRADE
COAL
COAL MINES AND MINING
COAL TRADE
COCA-COLA COMPANY.
COCONUT INDUSTRY
COFFEE TRADE.
COKE INDUSTRY
CONSTRUCTION INDUSTRY.
COPPER INDUSTRY AND TRADE.
COPPERSMITHING
COTTAGE INDUSTRIES
COTTON MANUFACTURE.
COTTON TRADE
COURT LINE LIMITED.
CROMARTY PETROLEUM COMPANY.
DEBENHAMS LIMITED.
DEVELOPMENT FINANCE COMPANY OF KENYA.
DISTILLING INDUSTRIES
DRUG TRADE.
DUN (R.G.) AND COMPANY.
DUNCAN (WALTER) AND GOODRICKE.
EAST MIDLAND ALLIED PRESS.
EGG TRADE
ELECTERMINATIONS LIMITED.
ELECTRIC INDUSTRIES
ELECTRIC POWER PLANTS
ELECTRIC POWER TRANSMISSION
ELECTRICITY SUPPLY
ELECTRONIC INDUSTRIES.
ENGINEERING
ERICSSON (L.M.) TELEFONAKTIEBOLAGET.
FIBRES.
FLETCHERS' BAKERIES.
FLOUR-MILLS
FOOD INDUSTRY AND TRADE
FRUIT TRADE.
FUR TRADE
GOLD MINES AND MINING
GRAIN TRADE.
HARNESS MAKING AND TRADE
HAW PAR BROTHERS INTERNATIONAL.
HIDES AND SKINS INDUSTRY.
HOME OIL COMPANY.
HOTELS, TAVERNS, ETC.
INSTRUMENT INDUSTRY
INTERNATIONAL TELEPHONE AND TELEGRAPH CORPORATION.
IRON INDUSTRY AND TRADE
JEYES SANITARY COMPOUNDS COMPANY.
JUTE INDUSTRY
KIRKBY MANUFACTURING AND ENGINEERING COMPANY.
KUEHNE AND NAGEL LIMITED.
LAND AND GENERAL DEVELOPMENTS LIMITED.
LARKFOLD HOLDINGS.
LINEN
LIQUOR TRAFFIC
LOCKHEED AIRCRAFT CORPORATION.
LONDON CAPITAL GROUP.
LONDON STATIONERS' COMPANY.
LUMBERING
MACHINE-TOOLS
MALAWI HOUSING CORPORATION.
MALT DISTILLERS ASSOCIATION OF SCOTLAND.
MEAT INDUSTRY AND TRADE
METAL TRADE
METHANE INDUSTRY
MILK TRADE
MINERAL INDUSTRIES
MINES AND MINERAL RESOURCES.
MINING INDUSTRY AND FINANCE
MUNITIONS
NAPET SECURITIES.
NESTLÉ.
NEW BRIGHTON ASSOCIATION FOOTBALL AND ATHLETIC CLUB COMPANY.
NEWFOUNDLAND AND LABRADOR DEVELOPMENT CORPORATION.
NEWS AGENCIES.
NEWTON CHAMBERS AND COMPANY.
NONFERROUS METAL INDUSTRIES.
NORTH DEVON RAILWAY COMPANY.
NUCLEAR FUELS.
OFFICE EQUIPMENT AND SUPPLIES INDUSTRY
OFFSHORE OIL INDUSTRY
OIL INDUSTRIES.
OPTICAL TRADE
PALM OIL INDUSTRY.
PAPER MAKING AND TRADE.
PAPER PRODUCTS.
PEACHEY PROPERTY CORPORATION.
PERIODICALS, PUBLISHING OF.
PETROLEUM.
PETROLEUM IN SUBMERGED LANDS
PETROLEUM INDUSTRY AND TRADE.
PETROLEUM PRODUCTS
PHILIPS GLOEILAMPENFABRIEKEN, N.V.
PLASTICS INDUSTRY AND TRADE
PRINTING
PRODUCE TRADE.
QUARRIES AND QUARRYING
RAJAWELLA PRODUCE HOLDINGS.
REACTOR FUEL REPROCESSING.
REAL ESTATE BUSINESS
REAL ESTATE DEVELOPMENT
RESTAURANTS, LUNCH ROOMS, ETC.
ROHEISEN-VERBAND.
ROLLS-ROYCE.
RUBBER INDUSTRY AND TRADE
SALT INDUSTRY AND TRADE
SECURITY SYSTEMS
SEWING MACHINE INDUSTRY
SHIPBUILDING
SHIPYARDS
SILVER MINES AND MINING
SINGER SEWING MACHINE COMPANY.
SLATER WALKER (FIRM).
SOFT DRINK INDUSTRY
STANDARD FRUIT AND STEAMSHIP COMPANY.
STEEL
STEEL INDUSTRY AND TRADE.
SUGAR TRADE
TEA MACHINERY.
TEA TRADE
TEXTILE INDUSTRY AND FABRICS
TEXTILE MACHINERY.
TIN.
TIN MINES AND MINING
TOBACCO MANUFACTURE AND TRADE.
TOURIST TRADE.
TRANSPARENT PAPER LIMITED.
TYRES
UNILEVER LIMITED.
URANIUM.
URANIUM INDUSTRY
VICKERS LIMITED.
WATER POWER ELECTRIC PLANTS
WELCH GRAPE JUICE COMPANY.

COMMERCE AND INDUSTRY (Cont.)

WESTERN UNION INTERNATIONAL.
WHISKY
WINE AND WINE MAKING
WOOD-PULP INDUSTRY.
WOOD-USING INDUSTRIES
WOOL TRADE AND INDUSTRY.
WORDS IN ACTION LIMITED.
WORSHIPFUL COMPANY OF COACHMAKERS AND COACH HARNESS MAKERS.

ECONOMICS.

see also AGRICULTURE; COMMERCE AND INDUSTRY; FINANCE; TRANSPORT

ABSENTEEISM (LABOUR).
ALIEN LABOUR
ALIEN LABOUR, AFRICAN
ALIEN LABOUR, MEXICAN
ALIEN LABOUR, POLISH
ALLGEMEINER DEUTSCHER GEWERKSCHAFTSBUND.
AMERICAN FEDERATION OF LABOR.
AMERICAN INSTITUTE FOR FREE LABOR DEVELOPMENT.
ANDEAN GROUP.
ASSOCIATION OF SOUTHEAST ASIAN NATIONS.
ATOMIC ENERGY.
AUSTRIAN SCHOOL OF ECONOMISTS.
BHOODAN MOVEMENT.
BIRTH CONTROL.
CANADIAN UNION OF POSTAL WORKERS.
CAPITALISM.
CARIBBEAN COMMUNITY.
CERAMIC AND ALLIED TRADES UNION.
CHRISTIAN LABOUR ASSOCIATION OF CANADA.
CHRISTIANITY AND ECONOMICS.
CHURCH AND LABOUR
COHORT ANALYSIS.
COLLECTIVE BARGAINING.
COMPETITION.
COMPETITION, INTERNATIONAL.
COMPULSORY LICENSING OF PATENTS
CONFEDERAZIONE GENERALE ITALIANA DEL LAVORO.
CONSERVATION OF NATURAL RESOURCES.
CONSUMPTION (ECONOMICS).
COST AND STANDARD OF LIVING
COST EFFECTIVENESS.
COSTS, INDUSTRIAL.
COUNCIL FOR MUTUAL ECONOMIC ASSISTANCE.
COUNTERPART FUNDS.
CRISES.
DEMOGRAPHY.
DEUTSCHER GEWERKSCHAFTSBUND.
DIFFUSION OF INNOVATIONS.
DISCRIMINATION IN EMPLOYMENT
DISTRIBUTION (ECONOMIC THEORY).
DIVERSIFICATION IN INDUSTRY
EAST YORK WORKERS' ASSOCIATION.
ECOLOGY.
ECONOMIC ASSISTANCE.
ECONOMIC ASSISTANCE, AMERICAN.
ECONOMIC ASSISTANCE, BRITISH.
ECONOMIC ASSISTANCE, DOMESTIC
ECONOMIC ASSISTANCE, EUROPEAN.
ECONOMIC ASSISTANCE, FRENCH.
ECONOMIC ASSISTANCE, RUSSIAN.
ECONOMIC ASSISTANCE IN AFRICA.
ECONOMIC COMMUNITY OF WEST AFRICAN STATES.
ECONOMIC CONDITIONS.
ECONOMIC COUNCILS
ECONOMIC DEVELOPMENT.
ECONOMIC DEVELOPMENT COUNCIL OF NEW YORK CITY.
ECONOMIC FORECASTING.
ECONOMIC HISTORY.
ECONOMIC INDICATORS.
ECONOMIC LEGISLATION
ECONOMIC POLICY.
ECONOMIC RESEARCH
ECONOMIC STABILIZATION.
ECONOMIC SURVEYS.
ECONOMIC ZONING
ECONOMICS.
ECONOMICS, COMPARATIVE.
ECONOMICS, MATHEMATICAL.
ECONOMICS, PRIMITIVE.
ECONOMISTS.
EMPLOYMENT (ECONOMIC THEORY)
ENERGY
ENERGY CONSERVATION
ENERGY CONSUMPTION.
ENERGY INDUSTRIES
ENERGY POLICY.
ENTREPRENEUR.
ENVIRONMENTAL POLICY.
ENVIRONMENTAL PROTECTION.
EQUAL PAY FOR EQUAL WORK.
EQUILIBRIUM (ECONOMICS).
EUROPEAN ECONOMIC COMMUNITY.
EUROPEAN REGIONAL DEVELOPMENT FUND.
EXTERNALITIES (ECONOMICS).
FAMILY ALLOWANCES
FERTILITY, HUMAN.
FOOD CONSERVATION.
FOOD CONSUMPTION.
FOOD SUPPLY.
FREIE LEHRERGEWERKSCHAFT DEUTSCHLANDS.
FREIER GEWERKSCHAFTSBUND HESSEN.
FUEL.
FULL EMPLOYMENT POLICIES
GAS, NATURAL.
GAS, NATURAL, IN SUBMERGED LANDS
GENERAL AGREEMENT ON TARIFFS AND TRADE.
GEOGRAPHY, ECONOMIC.
GEWERKSCHAFT NAHRUNG, GENUSS, GASTSTÄTTEN.
GEWERKSCHAFT ÖFFENTLICHE DIENSTE, TRANSPORT UND VERKEHR.
GOVERNMENT OWNERSHIP.
GOVERNMENT PURCHASING
GROSS DOMESTIC PRODUCT
GROSS NATIONAL PRODUCT.
GRUNWICK STRIKE, 1976.
HOLLOWAY TENANT COOPERATIVE.
HOME ECONOMICS.
HOME LABOUR
HOMESTEAD STRIKE, 1892.
HOURS OF LABOUR
HOUSE BUYING.
HOUSING.
HOUSING, COOPERATIVE
HOUSING MANAGEMENT.
HOUSING POLICY.
HOUSING REHABILITATION
HOUSING SUBSIDIES
HOUSING SURVEYS.
INCOME.
INCOME ACCOUNTING.
INCOME DISTRIBUTION.
INCOME MAINTENANCE PROGRAMMES
INDEX NUMBERS (ECONOMICS).
INDEXATION (ECONOMICS).
INDUSTRIAL AND COMMERCIAL WORKERS' UNION OF AFRICA.
INDUSTRIAL WORKERS OF THE WORLD.
INDUSTRIEGEWERKSCHAFT METALL FÜR DIE BUNDESREPUBLIK DEUTSCHLAND.
INTEREST AND USURY.
INTERINDUSTRY ECONOMICS.
INTERNATIONAL CONFEDERATION OF FREE TRADE UNIONS.
INTERNATIONAL COOPERATION.
INTERNATIONAL ECONOMIC INTEGRATION.
INTERNATIONAL ECONOMIC RELATIONS.
INTERNATIONAL LABOUR ACTIVITIES.
JOB ANALYSIS.
JOB EVALUATION
JOB SATISFACTION
JOB VACANCIES
KEYNESIAN ECONOMICS.
KNIGHTS OF LABOR.
LABOUR AND LABOURING CLASSES.
LABOUR CONTRACT
LABOUR COSTS
LABOUR DISCIPLINE
LABOUR DISPUTES
LABOUR ECONOMICS.
LABOUR EXCHANGES
LABOUR MOBILITY.
LABOUR POLICY
LABOUR SERVICE
LABOUR SUPPLY.
LABOUR TURNOVER
LAISSEZ-FAIRE.
LAND, NATIONALIZATION OF.
LAND REFORM
LAND SETTLEMENT.
LAND SUBDIVISION
LAND TENURE
LAND USE.
LAND USE, RURAL
LAND USE, URBAN.
LEASES
LIFE SPAN, PRODUCTIVE.
MALTHUSIANISM.
MANAGERIAL ECONOMICS.
MANORS
MANPOWER
MANPOWER POLICY.
MARXIAN ECONOMICS.
MASSACHUSETTS LOCAL INITIATIVE PROGRAM.
MEDICAL CARE, COST OF.
MEDICAL ECONOMICS.
MÉTAYER SYSTEM
METROPOLITAN AREAS.
MIGRANT LABOUR
MIGRATION, INTERNAL.
MOHAMMEDANISM AND ECONOMICS.
MONOPOLIES.
MUNICIPAL OWNERSHIP
MUNICIPAL SERVICES
NATIONAL UNION OF MINEWORKERS.
NATURAL RESOURCES.
NOISE CONTROL.
NONLINEAR THEORIES.
NORTH ISLINGTON HOUSING RIGHTS PROJECT.
NORTH WALES QUARRYMEN'S UNION.
OCCUPATIONAL MOBILITY
OCCUPATIONAL PRESTIGE
OCCUPATIONAL TRAINING
OLD AGE PENSIONS
ONE BIG UNION.
OPEN AND CLOSED SHOP
ORGANISATION COMMUNE DES REGIONS SAHARIENNES.
ORGANIZATIONAL CHANGE.
OVERPRODUCTION.
PART-TIME EMPLOYMENT
PENSION TRUSTS
PENSIONS
PICKETING
POLLUTION.
POPULATION.
POPULATION COUNCIL.
POPULATION POLICY.

FINANCE

POPULATION RESEARCH.
PRICE INDEXES
PRICE POLICY.
PRICE REGULATION.
PRICES.
PRODUCTION (ECONOMIC THEORY).
PRODUCTION FUNCTIONS (ECONOMIC THEORY).
PROFIT.
PROFIT SHARING
PROPERTY.
PUBLIC GOODS.
PUBLIC HOUSING
PUBLIC SERVICE
PURCHASING POWER.
RAY-O-VAC FEDERAL UNION.
REAL PROPERTY
RECYCLING (WASTE, ETC.).
REGIONAL COOPERATION FOR DEVELOPMENT.
REGIONAL ECONOMICS.
RENT.
RENT CONTROL
RENT SUBSIDIES
RESIDENTIAL MOBILITY.
RESTRAINT OF TRADE.
RETIREMENT.
RIGHT OF PROPERTY
RURAL DEVELOPMENT.
SEX DISCRIMINATION AGAINST WOMEN
SEX DISCRIMINATION IN EMPLOYMENT
SHOP STEWARDS
SKILLED LABOUR.
SPACE IN ECONOMICS.
STAGNATION (ECONOMICS).
STERILIZATION (BIRTH CONTROL).
STRIKES AND LOCKOUTS.
SUBCONTRACTING.
SUBSIDIES
SUBSTITUTION (ECONOMICS).
SUPPLY AND DEMAND.
SWEATING SYSTEM.
SYNDICALISM.
TEACHERS' UNIONS
TECHNICAL ASSISTANCE.
TECHNICAL ASSISTANCE, AMERICAN.
TECHNICAL ASSISTANCE, BRITISH.
TECHNICAL ASSISTANCE, FRENCH
TECHNICAL ASSISTANCE IN AFRICA.
TECHNICAL ASSISTANCE IN ASIA.
TEMPORARY EMPLOYMENT.
TRADE AND PROFESSIONAL ASSOCIATIONS
TRADE UNIONS.
TRADE UNIONS, CATHOLIC
TRADE UNIONS AND COMMUNISM.
TRANSFER PRICING.
TRANSIENTS, RELIEF OF.
TRUSTS, INDUSTRIAL
UNCERTAINTY.
UNDERDEVELOPED AREAS.
UNEMPLOYED.
UNITED MINE WORKERS OF AMERICA.
UNITED NATIONS ECONOMIC COMMISSION FOR EUROPE.
UNITED NATIONS INDUSTRIAL DEVELOPMENT ORGANIZATION.
UNSKILLED LABOUR.
URBAN ECONOMICS.
URBAN RENEWAL
VALUE.
VERBAND KATHOLISCHER ARBEITER- UND KNAPPENVEREINE WESTDEUTSCHLANDS
WAGE-PRICE POLICY.
WAGES.
WASTE LANDS
WASTE PRODUCTS.
WEALTH.
WELFARE ECONOMICS.
WHITE COLLAR WORKERS
WOMEN IN TRADE UNIONS

WORKS COUNCILS.
WORLD FERTILITY SURVEY.

EDUCATION.

General.

ABILITY GROUPING IN EDUCATION.
AFRO-AMERICAN STUDENTS
AGRICULTURAL EDUCATION
CHILDREN OF IMMIGRANTS
CITIZENS' ADVISORY COMMITTEES IN EDUCATION
CLASSROOM MANAGEMENT.
COLLEGE ADMINISTRATORS
COLLEGE COSTS
COMMUNIST EDUCATION
COMMUNITY AND SCHOOL.
DISCRIMINATION IN EDUCATION.
EAST INDIAN STUDENTS IN THE UNITED STATES.
EDUCATION.
EDUCATION, COMPARATIVE.
EDUCATION, COOPERATIVE
EDUCATION, ELEMENTARY
EDUCATION, HIGHER.
EDUCATION, PRESCHOOL.
EDUCATION, SECONDARY.
EDUCATION, URBAN
EDUCATION AND STATE.
EDUCATION OF ADULTS.
EDUCATION OF CHILDREN.
EDUCATION OF PRISONERS
EDUCATION OF WOMEN
EDUCATIONAL ACCOUNTABILITY
EDUCATIONAL ASSISTANCE, BRITISH.
EDUCATIONAL EQUALIZATION.
EDUCATIONAL INNOVATIONS.
EDUCATIONAL LAW AND LEGISLATION
EDUCATIONAL PLANNING.
EDUCATIONAL PSYCHOLOGY.
EDUCATIONAL RESEARCH
EDUCATIONAL SOCIOLOGY.
EXAMINATIONS
FEDERAL AID TO HIGHER EDUCATION
GRADUATES
HEALTH EDUCATION
HIGHER EDUCATION AND STATE
HOME AND SCHOOL.
ILLITERACY
INDUSTRY AND EDUCATION.
INTERCULTURAL EDUCATION.
JAPANESE STUDIES.
LATIN AMERICAN STUDIES.
LEARNING AND SCHOLARSHIP.
LEAVE OF ABSENCE.
NONVERBAL COMMUNICATION.
NUFFIELD FOUNDATION SCIENCE TEACHING PROJECT.
ORIENTAL STUDIES
POLITICS AND EDUCATION
PROFESSIONAL EDUCATION
SCHOLARSHIPS
SCHOOL, CHOICE OF.
SCHOOL ATTENDANCE
SCHOOL BOARDS
SCHOOL CHILDREN
SCHOOL DISCIPLINE.
SCHOOL DISTRICTS
SCHOOL INTEGRATION
SCHOOL MANAGEMENT AND ORGANIZATION
SCHOOL SOCIAL WORK
SCHOOLS
SEX DISCRIMINATION IN EDUCATION
SOCIAL WORK EDUCATION.
SOCIALISM AND EDUCATION.
STUDENT ASPIRATIONS.
STUDENTS
STUDENTS, FOREIGN
STUDENTS' SOCIETIES

TEACHER-STUDENT RELATIONSHIPS.
TEACHERS, TRAINING OF
TEACHERS' COLLEGES
TECHNICAL EDUCATION
UNITED NATIONS EDUCATIONAL, SCIENTIFIC AND CULTURAL ORGANIZATION.
UNIVERSITIES AND COLLEGES
UNIVERSITY EXTENSION
VOCATIONAL EDUCATION
WOMEN TEACHERS

Educational institutions.

FOURAH BAY COLLEGE
HULL UNIVERSITY.
LANCASTER UNIVERSITY.
LONDON UNIVERSITY
MANCHESTER UNIVERSITY.
MINNESOTA UNIVERSITY.
NATIONAL COUNCIL OF LABOUR COLLEGES.
NATIONAL INSTITUTE OF EDUCATION.
OREGON UNIVERSITY.
ST. ANDREWS UNIVERSITY.
SNOW HILL NORMAL AND INDUSTRIAL INSTITUTE, SNOW HILL, ALABAMA.
TUSKEGEE NORMAL AND INDUSTRIAL INSTITUTE.

FINANCE.

General.

AGRICULTURAL CREDIT
BALANCE OF PAYMENTS.
BANKS AND BANKING.
BANKS AND BANKING, AMERICAN.
BANKS AND BANKING, CENTRAL
BANKS AND BANKING, COOPERATIVE
BANKS AND BANKING, INTERNATIONAL.
BUDGET.
BUILDING AND LOAN ASSOCIATIONS
CAPITAL.
CAPITAL BUDGET
CAPITAL GAINS TAX
CAPITAL INVESTMENTS.
CAPITAL MOVEMENTS
CAPITAL STOCK
COINAGE
COMMERCIAL FINANCE COMPANIES
CONSUMER COOPERATIVES
COST ACCOUNTING
COUNTERFEITS AND COUNTERFEITING
CREDIT
CUSTOMS UNIONS.
DEBTS, EXTERNAL
DEBTS, PUBLIC
DEVELOPMENT BANKS
DEVELOPMENT CREDIT CORPORATIONS.
DISCOUNT
DIVIDENDS
DOLLAR.
EUROBOND MARKET.
EURODOLLAR MARKET.
EXPENDITURES, PUBLIC.
EXPORT CREDIT.
FEDERAL RESERVE BANKS.
FEES, PROFESSIONAL
FINANCE.
FINANCIAL INSTITUTIONS.
FINANCIAL INSTITUTIONS, INTERNATIONAL.
FINANCIAL STATEMENTS.
FLOW OF FUNDS
FOREIGN EXCHANGE.
FOREIGN EXCHANGE PROBLEM.
FRIENDLY SOCIETIES
GOLD.
GOVERNMENT SPENDING POLICY.

FINANCE (Cont.)

GRANTS-IN-AID
INCOME TAX.
INFLATION (FINANCE).
INFLATION (FINANCE) AND ACCOUNTING.
INFLATION (FINANCE) AND UNEMPLOYMENT.
INHERITANCE AND TRANSFER TAX.
INSTITUTE OF BANKERS.
INSURANCE.
INSURANCE, AGRICULTURAL
INSURANCE, CREDIT.
INSURANCE, DISASTER
INSURANCE, EXPORT CREDIT.
INSURANCE, HEALTH
INSURANCE, INVESTMENT GUARANTY.
INSURANCE, LIFE
INSURANCE, PHYSICIANS' LIABILITY.
INSURANCE, UNEMPLOYMENT.
INSURANCE COMPANIES
INTERGOVERNMENTAL FISCAL RELATIONS
INTERNATIONAL FINANCE.
INTERNATIONAL LIQUIDITY.
INTERNATIONAL MONETARY FUND.
INVESTMENT BANKING.
INVESTMENT OF PUBLIC FUNDS
INVESTMENT TRUSTS
INVESTMENTS.
INVESTMENTS, AMERICAN.
INVESTMENTS, BRITISH.
INVESTMENTS, FOREIGN.
INVESTMENTS, JAPANESE.
LAND GRANTS
LOANS, AMERICAN
LOANS, FOREIGN.
LOANS, MEXICAN
LOCAL BUDGETS
LOCAL FINANCE.
LOCAL TAXATION
MEDICAL FEES
MONETARY POLICY.
MONETARY UNIONS.
MONEY.
MONEY SUPPLY.
MORTGAGES
MUNICIPAL BUDGETS
MUNICIPAL FINANCE.
NATIONAL INCOME
PAPER MONEY.
PAWNBROKING
PROGRAMME BUDGETING
PROPERTY TAX
PUT AND CALL TRANSACTIONS.
REAL PROPERTY TAX.
REFUGE ASSURANCE COMPANY.
REINSURANCE.
RESEARCH GRANTS
REVENUE
RISK.
RISK (INSURANCE).
ROYAL LONDON MUTUAL INSURANCE SOCIETY.
SALES TAX
SAVING AND INVESTMENT.
SAVINGS BANKS
SECURITIES.
SECURITIES, TAX-EXEMPT
SINKING FUNDS
SPECIAL DRAWING RIGHTS.
SPECULATION.
SPENDINGS TAX
STOCK EXCHANGE.
STOCK OWNERSHIP
STOCKHOLDERS
STOCKS
TARIFFS.
TAX ADMINISTRATION AND PROCEDURE
TAX CREDITS
TAX INCIDENCE
TAX REVENUE ESTIMATING.
TAXATION.

TAXATION, DOUBLE.
TAXATION, EXEMPTION FROM
TAXATION, PAPAL.
TAXATION OF ALIENS
TAXATION OF BONDS, SECURITIES, ETC.
TENDER OFFERS (SECURITIES).
VALUE ADDED TAX.

Banks, exchanges, etc.

BANCA D'ITALIA.
BANCO INDUSTRIAL DEL PERU.
BANK FUER GEMEINWIRTSCHAFT.
CENTRAL BANK OF KENYA.
EUROPEAN INVESTMENT BANK.
GIRARD BANK.
INTERNATIONAL BANK FOR RECONSTRUCTION AND DEVELOPMENT.
QATAR NATIONAL BANK S.A.Q.

GEOGRAPHY, GEOLOGY AND METEOROLOGY.

General.

AERIAL PHOTOGRAMMETRY.
AGRICULTURAL GEOGRAPHY.
ANTARCTIC REGIONS.
ANTHROPOGEOGRAPHY.
ARCTIC REGIONS
ARID REGIONS
ATLANTIC, THE
CARTOGRAPHY
CENTRAL PLACES
CONTINENTAL SHELF.
DAMS
DESERTIFICATION
DISCOVERIES (IN GEOGRAPHY).
DRAINAGE.
DROUGHTS
ECOLOGY.
EPHEMERAL STREAMS.
EUROPEAN ECONOMIC COMMUNITY ASSOCIATED COUNTRIES
FLOOD CONTROL.
FLOOD DAMAGE PREVENTION.
FLOODS
GEOGRAPHICAL PERCEPTION.
GEOGRAPHY.
GEOGRAPHY, ECONOMIC.
GEOGRAPHY, HISTORICAL
GEOGRAPHY, POLITICAL.
GEOLOGY.
GEOLOGY, ECONOMIC.
GEOLOGY, STRATIGRAPHIC
GEOMORPHOLOGY.
GEOPHYSICS.
HUMAN ECOLOGY.
LANDSCAPE.
LANDSCAPE PROTECTION.
MAN.
MARINE RESOURCES.
METEOROLOGY
MINES AND MINERAL RESOURCES.
MOHAMMEDAN COUNTRIES
NAMES, GEOGRAPHICAL
NATIONAL PARKS AND RESERVES
NATURE CONSERVATION
NORTH ATLANTIC REGION
OASES.
OCEANOGRAPHY.
OPEN SPACES
PHOTOGRAMMETRY.
PHOTOGRAPHIC INTERPRETATION.
PHYSICAL GEOGRAPHY.
RAIN FOREST ECOLOGY.
RECLAMATION OF LAND
RIVERS
RURAL GEOGRAPHY.

SALTWATER ENCROACHMENT
SEA LEVEL
SLOPES (PHYSICAL GEOGRAPHY).
SOIL EROSION
SOIL SURVEYS
SPACE AND TIME.
SPACE PERCEPTION.
STRAITS
STREAM MEASUREMENTS
SUBMARINE GEOLOGY.
TROPICS
WATER
WATER, UNDERGROUND
WATER QUALITY MANAGEMENT.
WATER RESOURCES DEVELOPMENT.
WATER SUPPLY.
WILDERNESS AREAS.

Individual countries and places

Africa

ADDIS ABABA
AFRICA
AFRICA, CENTRAL
AFRICA, EAST
AFRICA, NORTH
AFRICA, SUBSAHARAN
AFRICA, WEST
ALGERIA
ANGOLA
ARAB COUNTRIES
BENIN
BOPHUTHATSWANA
BOTSWANA
BOUAKE
CAPE OF GOOD HOPE
CHAD
CHIRADZULU
CONGO (BRAZZAVILLE)
DAR ES SALAAM
DAURA
EGYPT.
ETHIOPIA
FORT-LAMY
FREETOWN
GAMBIA
GHANA
IVORY COAST
JOHANNESBURG
KANO (STATE)
KENYA
LAGOS
LANGOS.
LESOTHO
LIBERIA
LIBYA
LUMIERE [MADAGASCAR].
MADAGASCAR
MALAWI
MAURITIUS
MOMBASA
NATAL
NIGER
NIGERIA
NIGERIA (OYO STATE)
ORANGE FREE STATE
ORANGE RIVER.
QWAQWA
RHODESIA.
RHODESIA AND NYASALAND, FEDERATION OF
SAHARA
SALISBURY, RHODESIA
SÃO TOME E PRINCIPE
SENEGAL
SHABA
SIERRA LEONE.
SOMALI REPUBLIC.
SOUTH AFRICA.
SOUTH WEST AFRICA

GEOGRAPHY, GEOLOGY AND METEOROLOGY

SPANISH SAHARA
SUDAN
SWAZILAND
TANZANIA
TOGO
TRANSKEI
TRANSVAAL
TUNISIA
UGANDA
UPPER VOLTA
WALVIS BAY
WITWATERSRAND
ZAIRE
ZAMBIA

America, Latin.

AMAZON VALLEY
AMERICA
AMERICA, LATIN.
ARGENTINE REPUBLIC
BAHAMAS
BARBADOS
BELIZE.
BOLIVIA
BRAZIL.
BUENOS AIRES
CARIBBEAN AREA
CHILE
CHOCO
CIUDAD JUAREZ
COLOMBIA
CORDOBA (PROVINCE, ARGENTINE REPUBLIC)
COSTA RICA
CUBA
CURAÇAO
DOMINICA
DOMINICAN REPUBLIC
DUTCH GUIANA
ECUADOR
FRENCH GUIANA
GUATEMALA
GUYANA.
HAITI.
JAMAICA
JONOTLA.
MEXICO.
MONTE ALBAN, MEXICO.
NEW SPAIN (VICEROYALTY)
NICARAGUA
PANAMA
PANZOS
PARAGUAY
PERNAMBUCO
PERU
PORT OF SPAIN
PUERTO RICO
RIO DE JANEIRO (CITY)
SALVADOR
SAN ANDRÉS
SAN FELIPE DEL PROGRESO, MEXICO
SAN LUIS POTOSI
SÃO PAULO (CITY)
TRINIDAD AND TOBAGO
TUCUMAN (PROVINCE)
URUGUAY
VENEZUELA
WEST INDIES
ZINACANTAN, MEXICO

America, North.

ALABAMA
ALASKA
ALBERTA
AMERICA
APPALACHIAN MOUNTAINS.
ATLANTA
BOSTON, MASSACHUSETTS
BRITISH COLUMBIA
BUFFALO CREEK
CALIFORNIA
CANADA.
CHICAGO
CINCINNATI
CONNECTICUT
CRYSTAL CITY
DELAWARE
DETROIT
FAIRBANKS
GILMAN CITY
GREAT PLAINS
GREAT SWAMP.
GREENLAND
HOLLAND, MICHIGAN
ILLINOIS
INDIANA
INDIANAPOLIS
KANSAS
LABRADOR
LOS ANGELES
LOUISIANA
MANITOBA
MARYLAND
MASSACHUSETTS
MISSISSIPPI
MISSOURI
MONTREAL
NEW BRUNSWICK
NEW ENGLAND
NEW HAMPSHIRE
NEW HARMONY, INDIANA
NEW JERSEY
NEW MEXICO
NEW YORK (CITY)
NEW YORK (STATE)
NEWARK, NEW JERSEY.
NEWFOUNDLAND
NEWFOUNDLAND AND LABRADOR
NORTH CAROLINA
NOVA SCOTIA
OHIO
OHIO VALLEY
ONTARIO
PENNSYLVANIA
PHILADELPHIA
PRINCE EDWARD ISLAND
QUEBEC (PROVINCE)
SACRAMENTO-SAN JOAQUIN DELTA.
ST. JOHN'S
SAN BERNARDINO, CALIFORNIA
SAN FRANCISCO
SASKATCHEWAN
SOUTHERN STATES
TENNESSEE
TEXAS
TIMISKAMING
TORONTO
UNITED STATES
VIRGINIA
WEST, THE

Asia.

AFGHANISTAN.
ANDHRA PRADESH
ARAB COUNTRIES
ARABIA
ARMENIA
ARUNPUR
ASIA
ASIA, SOUTHEAST
ASSAM
BALUCHISTAN.
BANDA ISLANDS
BANG CHAN.
BANGLADESH.
BARODA
BENARES
BENGAL

BENGAL, WEST
BHUTAN
BIHAR
BOMBAY (STATE)
BORNEO.
BURYAT REPUBLIC
CALCUTTA
CAMBODIA
CHINA.
CYPRUS.
DELHI (UNION TERRITORY)
EAST (FAR EAST)
EAST (NEAR EAST)
GOA, DAMAN AND DIU
GUJARAT
HONG KONG
HUNAN, CHINA (PROVINCE)
HYDERABAD
INDIA.
INDOCHINA
INDONESIA.
IRAN
IRAQ
ISRAEL
JAPAN
JAVA
JERUSALEM
JORDAN
KAMCHATKA
KAYSERI, TURKEY
KAZAKSTAN
KERALA
KHABAROVSK (KRAI)
KIRGHIZIA
KOKAND KHANATE
KOREA
KUWAIT
LEBANON
MACAO
MADHYA BHARAT
MADHYA PRADESH
MADRAS
MAHARASHTRA
MALACCA, STRAIT OF.
MALAYA
MALAYSIA
MANAKHA
MANCHURIA
MEGHALAYA
MONGOLIA
MYSORE
NEPAL
NORTH-WEST FRONTIER PROVINCE
PAKISTAN.
PALESTINE
PERAK
PHILIPPINE ISLANDS
PONDICHERRY
PUNJAB (INDIA)
QATAR
RAJASTHAN
RUSSIA.
SABAH
SAIGON
SAMANWAY VIDAPITH.
SARAWAK
SAUDI ARABIA
SHINOHATA, JAPAN.
SIBERIA
SINGAPORE
SOPORE
SOVIET CENTRAL ASIA
SRI LANKA
SULU
SYRIA
TAIWAN
TAJIKISTAN
TASHKENT
THAILAND
TIBET
TURKESTAN
TURKEY

GEOGRAPHY, GEOLOGY AND METEOROLOGY (Cont.)

UNITED ARAB REPUBLIC
UTTAR PRADESH
UZBEKISTAN
VIETNAM
YEMEN

Australia and Oceania.

AUCKLAND
AUSTRALIA
BRISBANE
FIJI.
HAWAIIAN ISLANDS
KARKAR ISLAND (PAPUA NEW GUINEA)
MELBOURNE
MICRONESIA
NEW CALEDONIA
NEW SOUTH WALES
NEW ZEALAND.
NIUE
PACIFIC, THE.
PAEA
PAPUA NEW GUINEA
PUNAAUIA
QUEENSLAND
SOUTH AUSTRALIA
TASMANIA
WALLIS AND FUTUNA ISLANDS
WESTERN AUSTRALIA

Europe.

AARGAU (CANTON)
ADYGEI
ADZHARIA
AIX-EN-PROVENCE.
ALBANIA
AMSTERDAM
ANDALUSIA
AQUITAINE
ARTOIS
ASTURIAS
AUSTRIA
AUSTRIA-HUNGARY
AZERBAIJAN
AZORES
BADEN
BADEN-WUERTTEMBERG
BALKAN STATES
BALTIC STATES
BARANYA
BAS-RHIN (DEPARTMENT).
BASEL (CITY)
BASEL-LAND (CANTON)
BASHKIR REPUBLIC
BASQUE PROVINCES
BASSE-NORMANDIE
BAVARIA
BELGIUM
BERLIN
BESSARABIA
BOCHUM
BONNIERES
BORDEAUX
BRABANT (DUCHY)
BRANDENBURG
BREMEN
BRUNSWICK
BRUSSELS
BULGARIA
BURGUNDY
CALABRIA
CASTILE
CAUCASUS
CHAMPAGNE-ARDENNE
CHARENTE (DEPARTMENT).
CIUDAD REAL (CITY)
CIUDAD REAL (PROVINCE)
COLOGNE
CORDOBA (CITY)
CORIGLIANO
CROATIA
CUESMES
CZECHOSLOVAKIA
DAGHESTAN
DANUBE VALLEY
DENMARK
DONETS BASIN
DRENTHE
DUISBURG
EMILIA-ROMAGNA
ESTONIA
EUROPE
EUROPE, EASTERN.
EUROPEAN ECONOMIC COMMUNITY
   COUNTRIES.
FERRARA (PROVINCE)
FINLAND.
FLANDERS
FLORENCE
FOGGIA (PROVINCE)
FRANCE
FRIULI-VENEZIA GIULIA
GALATINA
GALICIA (SPAIN)
GARD
GDAŃSK
GENEVA (CANTON)
GERMANY.
GERMANY, EASTERN
GOTHENBURG
GREECE
HAGUE
HAINAUT
HALLAND
HAMBURG
HANOVER
HAUT-RHIN (DEPARTMENT).
HAUTE-LOIRE (DEPARTMENT).
HAUTE-SAVOIE.
HESSE
HUNGARY
ICELAND
ILE-DE-FRANCE
IRELAND (REPUBLIC)
ITALY
IVANOVO (OBLAST')
KARELIA
KOMI REPUBLIC
KOŠICE
KRÓLEWSKA HUTA
KRONSTADT
LATVIA
LEIPZIG
LENINGRAD
LIECHTENSTEIN.
LOMBARDY
LUCERNE (CANTON)
MAGDEBURG
MALTA
MARSEILLE
MASSIF CENTRAL.
MEDITERRANEAN
MILAN (CITY)
MILAN (DUCHY)
MODENA (PROVINCE)
MOLDAVIA
MOLDAVIAN REPUBLIC
MOSCOW
MUNICH
NAPLES
NETHERLANDS
NIKOPOL'
NORD (DEPARTMENT)
NORMANDY
NORTH HOLLAND
NORTH RHINE-WESTPHALIA
NORWAY
NOVGOROD
NUREMBERG
OBERWART
OLDENBURG
PADERBORN
PARIS
PARIS (REGION).
PARMA (PROVINCE)
PERUGIA
PICARDY
PISTOIA
POLAND
PORTUGAL
PRUEM
PRUSSIA
PUGLIA
REIMS
RHINE PROVINCE
RHINE VALLEY
RHÔNE-ALPES
RIJEKA
RIMINI
ROMAGNA
ROMANIA
ROME (CITY)
ROTTWEIL
RUHR
RUSSIA.
SAAR TERRITORY
SALZBURG
SANT'AGATA DEI GOTI
SANTANDER (SPAIN)
SARDINIA
SCANDINAVIA
SCHIEDAM
SCHLESWIG-HOLSTEIN
SERBIA
SICILY
SILESIA
SLOVAKIA
SPAIN
SWABIA
SWEDEN
SWITZERLAND
THURINGIA
TICINO
TROYES
TUSCANY
UKRAINE
UPPER AUSTRIA
UPPSALA
URAL REGION
USTIUG (KRAI)
VALENCIA
VAUCLUSE (DEPARTMENT).
VENEZIA
VENICE
VIENNA
VOLGA BASIN
VOLGOGRAD (OBLAST')
WALLONIA
WARSAW
WESTPHALIA
WHITE RUSSIA
YUGOSLAVIA
ZUERICH (CANTON)
ZUERICH (CITY)

United Kingdom.

AFAN VALLEY
BANBURY
BATH
BATLEY
BATTERSEA
BEDFORDSHIRE
BELFAST
BERKSHIRE
BIRMINGHAM
BLACKHEATH
BRISTOL
BURTON-UPON-TRENT
CAMBRIDGE
CAMBRIDGESHIRE
CANNING TOWN

HISTORY

CANVEY ISLAND.
CHESHIRE
CLEATOR MOOR
CLEVELAND, UNITED KINGDOM
CLYRO, WALES
CORNWALL
CUMBRIA
DARLINGTON
DEVONSHIRE
DURHAM (CITY)
DURHAM (COUNTY)
EAST ANGLIA
EAST KILBRIDE
EAST SUSSEX
ESSEX
EXMOOR NATIONAL PARK.
GLASGOW
HACKNEY
HAMPSHIRE
HAMPSTEAD HEATH
HEREFORDSHIRE
HUMBERSIDE
IRELAND
IRELAND, NORTHERN
ISLE OF MAN
IVYBRIDGE, DEVONSHIRE
JERSEY
LAMBETH
LANCASHIRE
LEICESTERSHIRE
LLANELLI
LONDON
MANCHESTER
MERSEYSIDE
MID GLAMORGAN
NEWCASTLE-UPON-TYNE
NEWHAM
NORFOLK
NORTH SHIELDS
NORTHERN STANDARD REGION (UNITED KINGDOM)
NORTHUMBERLAND
OLDHAM
ORKNEY ISLANDS
PENTRICH
POPLAR
ROCHDALE
RUTLAND
ST. HELENS
SALFORD
SCOTLAND
SHEFFIELD
SHETLAND ISLANDS
SOUTH EAST STANDARD REGION (UNITED KINGDOM)
SOUTHWARK
STAFFORDSHIRE
SURREY
TEES RIVER.
TEESSIDE
TORY ISLAND
TYNE AND WEAR
TYNESIDE
UNITED KINGDOM
WALES
WANDSWORTH
WARWICKSHIRE
WASHINGTON, DURHAM
WEST MIDLANDS
WEST YORKSHIRE
WESTMORLAND
WORCESTERSHIRE
YORK

HISTORY.

General.

ANTISEMITISM
ARCHAEOLOGY, MEDIEVAL.
CHURCH HISTORY.
CITIES AND TOWNS, MEDIEVAL
CIVILIZATION.
CIVILIZATION, MEDIEVAL.
CIVILIZATION, MODERN.
CIVILIZATION, MOHAMMEDAN.
CIVILIZATION, OCCIDENTAL.
CONCENTRATION CAMPS
CONDOTTIERI.
CRUSADES.
FORECASTING.
GEOGRAPHY, HISTORICAL
HISTORIANS.
HISTORICAL FILMS.
HISTORICAL SOCIOLOGY.
HISTORIOGRAPHY.
HISTORY.
HISTORY, MODERN
HISTORY, UNIVERSAL.
MANNERS AND CUSTOMS.
MIDDLE AGES.
MILITARY HISTORY.
PEASANT UPRISINGS.
PROGRESS.
RIOTS
SERFDOM
SOCIAL HISTORY.
TWENTIETH CENTURY
TWENTY-FIRST CENTURY

International (including wars).

BERLIN, TREATY OF, 1878.
BRITAIN, BATTLE OF, 1940.
CHINESE-JAPANESE WAR, 1937-1945.
CONGRESS OF BERLIN, 1878.
CONGRESS OF VIENNA.
CRIMEAN WAR, 1853-1856
EC-121 CRISIS, 1969.
EUROPEAN WAR, 1914-1918
FRANCO-GERMAN WAR, 1870-1871.
HUNDRED YEARS WAR, 1339-1453.
INDIA-PAKISTAN CONFLICT, 1971.
ISRAEL-ARAB CONFLICT, 1948- .
ISRAEL-ARAB WAR, 1967.
ISRAEL-ARAB WAR, 1973.
KOREAN WAR, 1950-1953
LEND-LEASE OPERATIONS (1941-1945).
MALMEDY MASSACRE, 1944-1945.
MAYAGUEZ CRISIS, 1975.
MUNICH FOUR-POWER AGREEMENT, 1938.
PEARL HARBOR, ATTACK ON, 1941.
PENINSULAR WAR, 1807-1814.
PRISONERS OF WAR
PRISONERS OF WAR, JAPANESE.
PUEBLO CRISIS, 1968.
RECONSTRUCTION (1914-1939)
RECONSTRUCTION (1939-1951).
RUSSO-GERMAN TREATY, 1939.
RUSSO-JAPANESE WAR, 1904-1905.
RUSSO-TURKISH WAR, 1877-1878.
SEVEN YEARS' WAR, 1756-1763.
SOUTH AFRICAN WAR, 1899-1902.
STRAITS QUESTION.
STRESA CONFERENCE, 1935.
THIRTY YEARS WAR, 1618-1648.
VENDEAN WAR, 1793-1800.
VIETNAMESE WARS, 1945-1975.
WARSAW, PACT OF, 1955.
WASHINGTON, TREATY OF, 1842.
WORLD WAR, 1939-1945.

American territories.

AMERICAN LOYALISTS.
CONFEDERATE STATES OF AMERICA
CROWDS.
FRONTIER AND PIONEER LIFE
HACIENDAS
NORTHEAST BOUNDARY OF THE UNITED STATES.
OVERLAND JOURNEYS TO THE PACIFIC.
RECONSTRUCTION (UNITED STATES).
RIEL REBELLION, 1885.

Asiatic territories.

BOXERS.
JEWISH-ARAB RELATIONS.
JEWISH QUESTION.
KASHMIR QUESTION.
KOREAN REUNIFICATION QUESTION (1945-).
TAIPING REBELLION, 1850-1864.

European territories.

BERLIN QUESTION (1945-).
BRONZE AGE
BYZANTINE EMPIRE
CARLOVINGIANS.
CONFEDERACION ESPAÑOLA DE DERECHAS AUTONOMAS.
EASTERN QUESTION (BALKAN).
FEUDALISM.
GERMAN REUNIFICATION QUESTION (1949-).
GREECE, ANCIENT
HOLOCAUST, JEWISH (1939-1945).
HOLY ROMAN EMPIRE
JACOBINS.
MACEDONIAN QUESTION.
MOHAMMEDAN EMPIRE.
NATIONALKOMITEE "FREIES DEUTSCHLAND".
PAPAL STATES
POLSKI KOMITET WYZWOLENIA NARODWEGO.
REFORMATION
RENAISSANCE.
ROME, ANCIENT
ST. BARTHOLOMEW'S DAY, MASSACRE OF, 1572.
SPARTA
UPPER SILESIAN QUESTION.

United Kingdom.

CHRISTIAN ANTIQUITIES
COVENANTERS.
COVENT GARDEN.
CULLODEN, BATTLE OF, 1746.
HOME RULE
IRISH QUESTION.
IRISH REPUBLICAN ARMY.
MANUSCRIPTS
MONMOUTH'S REBELLION, 1685.
NAMES, PERSONAL
STONEHENGE.
WESTMINSTER ABBEY.

Colonial companies.

DUTCH EAST INDIA COMPANY.
DUTCH WEST INDIA COMPANY.
EAST INDIA COMPANY.
HUDSON'S BAY COMPANY.
ROYAL ASIATIC COMPANY OF DENMARK.
RUSSIAN-AMERICAN COMPANY.
SOCIETE DU CANADA.

LANGUAGE, LITERATURE AND THE ARTS

Language.

AFRIKAANS LANGUAGE.
ANTHROPOLOGICAL LINGUISTICS.
BILINGUALISM.
BIOLINGUISTICS.
COMPETENCE AND PERFORMANCE (LINGUISTICS).
CREOLE DIALECTS.
ENGLISH LANGUAGE
ENGLISH PHILOLOGY
FRENCH LANGUAGE.
FRENCH LANGUAGE IN CANADA.
GAELIC LANGUAGE.
GENERATIVE GRAMMAR.
GERMAN LANGUAGE
GRAMMAR, COMPARATIVE AND GENERAL
GREEK LANGUAGE
LANGUAGE AND LANGUAGES.
LANGUAGE AND LOGIC.
LANGUAGES
LANGUAGES, MODERN
LEXICOGRAPHERS
LEXICOLOGY.
LINGUISTIC CHANGE.
LINGUISTICS.
MULTILINGUALISM.
PHILOLOGY
PIDGIN ENGLISH.
PIDGIN LANGUAGES.
PRAGMATICS.
PSYCHOLINGUISTICS.
ROMANCE LANGUAGES
SAPIR-WHORF HYPOTHESIS.
SEMANTICS.
SEMIOTICS.
SOCIOLINGUISTICS.
SPEECH.
SPEECH, DISORDERS OF.
SPEECH PERCEPTION.
TYPOLOGY (LINGUISTICS).
UNIVERSALS (LINGUISTICS).
VOWELS.

Literature.

AFRICA IN LITERATURE.
AFRICAN LITERATURE
AFRIKAANS LITERATURE.
AMERICAN FICTION
AMERICAN LITERATURE
AMERICAN PERIODICALS.
ANGLO-SAXON LITERATURE.
ARABIC LITERATURE.
AUSTRALIAN PERIODICALS
AUTHORS, AFRICAN.
AUTHORS, AMERICAN.
AUTHORS, ENGLISH.
AUTHORS, GERMAN.
AUTHORS, WEST INDIAN.
AUTHORS AND PUBLISHERS
AUTHORS AND READERS.
AZTEC LITERATURE
BEOWULF.
BIOGRAPHY.
CANADIAN LITERATURE
CHILDREN'S LITERATURE, RUSSIAN.
COMMUNISM AND LITERATURE.
CRITICISM.
CZECH NEWSPAPERS.
ENGLISH FICTION
ENGLISH LITERATURE
ENGLISH NEWSPAPERS.
ENGLISH PERIODICALS
ENGLISH POETRY.
ESTONIAN LITERATURE
FINNESBURH.
FORMALISM (RUSSIAN LITERATURE).
FRENCH POETRY
GERMAN LITERATURE
GERMAN NEWSPAPERS.
GERMAN PERIODICALS.
IRISH LITERATURE.
ITALIAN NEWSPAPERS.
ITALIAN PERIODICALS
JEWISH LITERATURE.
JEWS IN LITERATURE.
LATIN POETRY, MEDIEVAL AND MODERN
LAW IN LEGENDS
LITERATURE
LITERATURE, COMPARATIVE.
LITERATURE, MEDIEVAL.
LITERATURE AND SOCIETY.
LITERATURE AND STATE
MALAGASY NEWSPAPERS.
MASS MEDIA AND LITERATURE
MAYA LITERATURE
MIXTEC LITERATURE
NATIONAL GUARDIAN.
NATURE IN LITERATURE.
NEWSPAPER PUBLISHING
NEWSPAPER READING.
OFFA SAGA.
POLISH LITERATURE
POLITICS AND LITERATURE.
PRESS
RACE RELATIONS AND THE PRESS.
REALISM IN LITERATURE.
RUSSIAN LITERATURE.
RUSSIAN PERIODICALS.
SATIRE, RUSSIAN.
SLOVAK LITERATURE
SOCIALISM IN LITERATURE.
SPANISH LITERATURE
STRUCTURALISM (LITERARY ANALYSIS).
SURREALISM.
TAEGLICHE RUNDSCHAU.
UNDERGROUND LITERATURE
VOELKISCHER BEOBACHTER.
WEST INDIAN LITERATURE
WOMEN IN LITERATURE.
ZIEGELBRENNER, DER.

The Arts.

AESTHETICS.
ARCHITECTURE
ARCHITECTURE, ANGLO-SAXON.
ARCHITECTURE, CARLOVINGIAN.
ARCHITECTURE, ROMANESQUE.
ARCHITECTURE AND SOCIETY.
ART
ART, CARLOVINGIAN.
ART, ENGLISH.
ART, MODERN
ART, RENAISSANCE.
ART AND SOCIETY.
ART AND STATE
ART COMMISSIONS
ART PATRONAGE
ARTISTS, EUROPEAN.
ARTS.
ARTS AND SOCIETY.
COMMUNISM AND THE ARTS.
FEDERAL AID TO THE ARTS
IMAGINATION.
INCORPORATED SOCIETY OF AUTHORS, PLAYWRIGHTS, AND COMPOSERS.
PAINTING, NETHERLANDISH.
PERFORMING ARTS
POPULAR CULTURE.
PUBLIC SPEAKING.
RELIGIOUS FILMS
SCULPTURE, GOTHIC.
SCULPTURE, RENAISSANCE.
SOCIALISM AND THE ARTS.
STATE ENCOURAGEMENT OF SCIENCE, LITERATURE AND ART
THEATRE
WOMEN ARTISTS

LAW (including INTERNATIONAL LAW).

General.

APPELLATE PROCEDURE
BAIL
CHILDREN AS WITNESSES
COMPARATIVE LAW.
CONDUCT OF COURT PROCEEDINGS
COURT RECORDS
COURT RULES
COURTS
CUSTOMARY LAW.
ETHNOLOGICAL JURISPRUDENCE.
GOVERNMENT LAWYERS
IDENTIFICATION.
JUDICIAL ASSISTANCE
JUDICIAL PROCESS
JUDICIAL REVIEW
JURISPRUDENCE.
JURY
JUSTICE.
JUSTICE, ADMINISTRATION OF.
JUSTICES OF THE PEACE
JUVENILE COURTS
JUVENILE JUSTICE, ADMINISTRATION OF
LAW.
LAW AND ETHICS.
LAW AND POLITICS.
LAW AND SOCIALISM.
LAW LIBRARIES.
LAW REFORM
LAW REPORTS, DIGESTS, ETC.
LEGAL AID.
LEGAL ASSISTANCE TO THE POOR
LEGAL RESEARCH.
NATURAL LAW.
ORAL COMMUNICATION.
PRESUMPTIONS (LAW)
PUBLICITY (LAW)
RIGHT OF REPLY
RULE OF LAW.
SEARCHES AND SEIZURES
SEX AND LAW
SOCIAL LEGISLATION
SOCIOLOGICAL JURISPRUDENCE.
TECHNOLOGY AND LAW.

Public law.

ABORTION.
ADMINISTRATIVE COURTS
ADMINISTRATIVE LAW
ADMINISTRATIVE RESPONSIBILITY
BILL DRAFTING.
BREAD.
CENSORSHIP
CITIZENSHIP
CITY PLANNING AND REDEVELOPMENT LAW
COMPENSATION (LAW)
CONSTITUTIONAL COURTS
CONSTITUTIONAL LAW.
DETENTION OF PERSONS
ECONOMIC LEGISLATION
EDUCATIONAL LAW AND LEGISLATION
ELECTION LAW
EMIGRATION AND IMMIGRATION LAW
EMINENT DOMAIN
ENVIRONMENTAL LAW.
FISHERY LAW AND LEGISLATION
JUDICIAL REVIEW OF ADMINISTRATIVE ACTS
LEGITIMACY OF GOVERNMENTS.

LICENCES
MARTIAL LAW
MEDICAL JURISPRUDENCE.
MEDICAL LAWS AND LEGISLATION.
MENTAL HEALTH LAWS
MUNICIPAL CORPORATIONS
NARCOTIC LAWS.
OBSCENITY (LAW)
POLITICAL CRIMES AND OFFENCES.
POOR LAWS
PRESS LAW
RESTITUTION
ZONING LAW

Civil law and procedure.

ADOPTION
AGE OF CONSENT
ATTACHMENT AND GARNISHMENT.
CHARITABLE USES, TRUSTS AND FOUNDATIONS
CIVIL LAW
CIVIL PROCEDURE.
DAMAGES
DEBTOR AND CREDITOR
DOMESTIC ANIMALS
DOMESTIC RELATIONS
EQUITY
ESTATE PLANNING
FREEDOM OF ASSOCIATION
GUARDIAN AND WARD
HUSBAND AND WIFE
ILLEGITIMACY
INHERITANCE AND SUCCESSION
INHERITANCE AND TRANSFER TAX.
INJUNCTION
LAND TITLES
LANDLORD AND TENANT
LIBEL AND SLANDER
MARRIAGE LAW
MATRIMONIAL ACTIONS
NEGLIGENCE
PERPETUITIES
PERSONAL PROPERTY.
PERSONS (LAW)
PROCESS
SECURITY (LAW)
SETTLEMENTS (LAW)
TAX PLANNING
TORRENS SYSTEM
TORTS.
TRUSTS AND TRUSTEES
WILLS

Commercial, industrial and labour laws.

AGENCY (LAW)
ANTITRUST LAW
ARBITRATION AND AWARD.
BANKING LAW
BUSINESS LAW
CARRIERS
COMMERCIAL LAW
CONSUMER CREDIT
CONSUMER PROTECTION.
CONTRACTS
COPYRIGHT
CORN LAWS
CORPORATION LAW
DESIGN PROTECTION
DISCRIMINATION IN EMPLOYMENT
FREE CHOICE OF EMPLOYMENT
INDUSTRIAL LAWS AND LEGISLATION
INSURANCE LAW
LABOUR COURTS
LABOUR LAWS AND LEGISLATION
PARTNERSHIP
PATENT LICENCES
POWER OF ATTORNEY
PUBLIC CONTRACTS

SALES.
SOCIAL SECURITY COURTS
WARRANTY

Criminal law and procedure.

ALIBI
CRIMINAL COURTS
CRIMINAL JUSTICE, ADMINISTRATION OF.
CRIMINAL LAW.
CRIMINAL LIABILITY
CRIMINAL PROCEDURE
EVIDENCE, CRIMINAL
FRAUD
FRAUDULENT CONVEYANCES
HOMICIDE
LARCENY
OFFENCES AGAINST PROPERTY
PARDON
PAROLE
PROSECUTION
SENTENCES (CRIMINAL PROCEDURE)
SEX CRIMES.
TREASON
TRIALS (CONSPIRACY)
TRIALS (POLITICAL CRIMES AND OFFENCES)
TRIALS (TREASON)

Ecclesiastical law.

ECCLESIASTICAL COURTS

Foreign law.

ADAT LAW
LAW, MOHAMMEDAN.
LAW, PRIMITIVE.

Conflict of laws, civil and criminal.

CONFLICT OF LAWS
JUDGMENTS, FOREIGN

International law.

ALIENS
ARBITRATION, INTERNATIONAL.
ASTRONAUTICS
ASYLUM, RIGHT OF.
CIVIL RIGHTS (INTERNATIONAL LAW).
CIVIL WAR.
CONTIGUOUS ZONES (MARITIME LAW).
CONTRACTS, MARITIME
COURT OF JUSTICE OF THE EUROPEAN COMMUNITIES.
GOOD FAITH (LAW).
INTELLECTUAL PROPERTY (INTERNATIONAL LAW).
INTERGOVERNMENTAL MARITIME CONSULTATIVE ORGANIZATION.
INTERNATIONAL AND MUNICIPAL LAW
INTERNATIONAL LAW.
ISLANDS
JETTISON.
LABOUR LAWS AND LEGISLATION, INTERNATIONAL.
MARITIME LAW.
NATIVE RACES
PERSONS (INTERNATIONAL LAW).
SELF-DEFENCE (INTERNATIONAL LAW).
SPACE LAW.
TERRITORIAL WATERS.
TREATIES
TREATY-MAKING POWER
WAR (INTERNATIONAL LAW).

MATHEMATICS AND STATISTICS

WAR, MARITIME (INTERNATIONAL LAW).
WAR CRIMES
WORLD INTELLECTUAL PROPERTY ORGANIZATION.

MATHEMATICS AND STATISTICS.

ALGEBRA.
ALGEBRA, BOOLEAN.
ALGEBRA, HOMOLOGICAL.
ALGEBRAIC NUMBER THEORY.
ALGEBRAS, LINEAR.
ALGORITHMS.
ANALYSIS OF VARIANCE.
APPROXIMATION THEORY.
ASYMPTOTIC EXPANSIONS.
BANACH SPACES.
BASIC (COMPUTER PROGRAM LANGUAGE).
BAYESIAN STATISTICAL DECISION THEORY.
BRANCHING PROCESSES.
BUSINESS MATHEMATICS.
CALCULUS.
CALCULUS, DIFFERENTIAL.
CALCULUS OF VARIATIONS.
CATASTROPHES (MATHEMATICS).
CENSUS.
CENTRAL LIMIT THEOREM.
CENTRAL LIMIT THEORY.
CLUSTER ANALYSIS.
COMBINATORIAL ANALYSIS
COMPUTER ARCHITECTURE.
COMPUTER INTERFACES.
COMPUTER NETWORKS.
COMPUTER PROGRAMS.
COMPUTER SIMULATION.
COMPUTERS.
CONIC SECTIONS.
CONTINGENCY TABLES.
CONTROL THEORY.
CONVERGENCE.
CONVEX FUNCTIONS.
CORRELATION (STATISTICS).
CRIMINAL STATISTICS
CYBERNETICS.
DATA BASE MANAGEMENT.
DEBUGGING IN COMPUTER SCIENCE.
DIFFERENCE EQUATIONS.
DIFFERENTIAL EQUATIONS.
DIFFERENTIAL EQUATIONS, PARTIAL.
DIFFERENTIAL TOPOLOGY.
DIFFUSION PROCESSES.
DIGITAL COMPUTER SIMULATION.
DISCRIMINANT ANALYSIS.
DISTRIBUTION (PROBABILITY THEORY).
ECONOMICS, MATHEMATICAL.
ELECTRONIC DATA PROCESSING.
ELECTRONIC DATA PROCESSING DEPARTMENTS
ELECTRONIC DIGITAL COMPUTERS.
ENGINEERING MATHEMATICS.
EQUATIONS.
EQUILIBRIUM.
ESTIMATION THEORY.
EXPERIMENTAL DESIGN.
EXTREME VALUE THEORY.
FACTOR ANALYSIS.
FERMAT'S THEOREM.
FINITE ELEMENT METHOD.
FIXED POINT THEOREMS (TOPOLOGY).
FOUR-COLOUR PROBLEM.
FOURIER ANALYSIS.
FREQUENCY CURVES.
FUNCTIONAL ANALYSIS.
FUNCTIONAL EQUATIONS.
FUNCTIONS.
FUNCTIONS, HYPERGEOMETRIC.
GAMES, THEORY OF.
GEOMETRIC PROBABILITIES.
GEOMETRY.

MATHEMATICS AND STATISTICS (Cont.)

GEOMETRY, AFFINE.
GRAPH THEORY.
GREEN'S FUNCTIONS.
HILBERT SPACE.
HOMOLOGY THEORY.
IBM 370 (COMPUTER).
ICL 2903 (COMPUTER).
ICL 2904 (COMPUTER).
IDEALS (ALGEBRA).
INDEPENDENCE (MATHEMATICS).
INDUSTRIAL STATISTICS.
INEQUALITIES (MATHEMATICS).
INFORMATION STORAGE AND RETRIEVAL SYSTEMS.
INTEGRAL EQUATIONS.
INTEGRAL TRANSFORMS.
INTEGRALS, STOCHASTIC.
INTUITIONISTIC MATHEMATICS.
LAW OF LARGE NUMBERS.
LEAST SQUARES.
LINEAR OPERATORS.
LINEAR PROGRAMMING.
LOCAL RINGS.
LOGIC, SYMBOLIC AND MATHEMATICAL.
MARKOV PROCESSES.
MARTINGALES (MATHEMATICS).
MATHEMATICAL ANALYSIS.
MATHEMATICAL MODELS.
MATHEMATICAL OPTIMIZATION.
MATHEMATICAL STATISTICS.
MATHEMATICS.
MATROIDS.
MEASURE THEORY.
MEDICAL STATISTICS.
METAMATHEMATICS.
MICROCOMPUTERS.
MINIATURE COMPUTERS.
MODULES (ALGEBRA).
MORTALITY.
MULTIVARIATE ANALYSIS.
NETWORK ANALYSIS (PLANNING).
NONPARAMETRIC STATISTICS.
NUMBERS, RANDOM.
NUMERICAL ANALYSIS.
ORDER STATISTICS
PASCAL (COMPUTER PROGRAM LANGUAGE).
PERFORMANCE.
POINT PROCESSES.
POPULATION BIOLOGY.
POPULATION FORECASTING.
PROBABILITIES.
PROBLEM SOLVING.
PROGRAMMING (ELECTRONIC COMPUTERS).
PROOF THEORY.
QUEUEING THEORY.
RANDOM VARIABLES.
RECURSIVE PROGRAMMING.
REGRESSION ANALYSIS.
RINGS (ALGEBRA).
ROBUST STATISTICS.
SAMPLING (STATISTICS).
SEQUENTIAL MACHINE THEORY.
SET THEORY.
SIMULATION METHODS.
SPATIAL ANALYSIS (STATISTICS).
SPECTRAL THEORY (MATHEMATICS).
STATISTICAL DECISION.
STATISTICS.
STOCHASTIC DIFFERENTIAL EQUATIONS.
STOCHASTIC PROCESSES.
STONE-ČECH COMPACTIFICATION.
STRUCTURED PROGRAMMING.
SYSTEM ANALYSIS.
SYSTEM THEORY.
TIME SERIES ANALYSIS.
TOPOLOGY.
TRANSFORMATIONS (MATHEMATICS).
VITAL STATISTICS.

MILITARY AND NAVAL SCIENCE.

AERONAUTICS, MILITARY
AEROPLANES, MILITARY.
AIR POWER.
AIR RAID SHELTERS
AIRCRAFT CARRIERS.
ARMAMENTS.
ARMIES.
ARTIFICIAL SATELLITES.
ATOMIC WEAPONS.
ATTACK AND DEFENCE (MILITARY SCIENCE).
BIOLOGICAL WARFARE.
BOMBERS.
CHEMICAL WARFARE.
CIVIL SUPREMACY OVER THE MILITARY
DEFENCES, NATIONAL.
DESERTION, MILITARY
EXSERVICEMEN
GUIDED MISSILES.
MERCENARY TROOPS.
MILITARISM
MILITARY ART AND SCIENCE
MILITARY ASSISTANCE, AMERICAN.
MILITARY ASSISTANCE, GERMAN
MILITARY ASSISTANCE, RUSSIAN
MILITARY BASES, AMERICAN.
MILITARY HISTORY.
MILITARY POLICY.
MILITARY SERVICE, COMPULSORY
MUNITIONS
MUTINY
NAPALM.
NAVAL ARCHITECTURE.
NAVAL STRATEGY.
NUCLEAR NONPROLIFERATION.
PARAMILITARY FORCES
PRISONERS OF WAR
PSYCHOLOGICAL WARFARE.
PSYCHOLOGY, MILITARY.
SOCIOLOGY, MILITARY.
SOLDIERS
STRATEGY.
SURVIVORS' BENEFITS
WAR.
WAR GAMES.
WEAPONS SYSTEMS.

PHILOSOPHY AND RELIGION.

Philosophy.

ACT (PHILOSOPHY).
ALIENATION (PHILOSOPHY).
ALTRUISM.
ANIMISM.
ATOMISM.
BUSINESS ETHICS.
COMMUNIST ETHICS.
COUNTERFACTUALS (LOGIC).
CRITICISM (PHILOSOPHY).
ENLIGHTENMENT.
ETHICS.
FREE WILL AND DETERMINISM.
GOOD AND EVIL.
HUMANISM.
HYPOTHESIS.
IDEALISM.
IDEOLOGY.
KNOWLEDGE, THEORY OF.
LANGUAGE AND LOGIC.
LAW AND ETHICS.
LIFE.
MATERIALISM.
MEDICAL ETHICS.
ONTOLOGY.
PHENOMENOLOGY.
PHILOSOPHERS
PHILOSOPHICAL ANTHROPOLOGY.
PHILOSOPHY.
PHILOSOPHY, AMERICAN.
PHILOSOPHY, ANCIENT.
PHILOSOPHY, AZERBAIJANI.
PHILOSOPHY, GERMAN.
PHILOSOPHY, ITALIAN.
PHILOSOPHY, MEDIEVAL.
PHILOSOPHY, MODERN.
PHILOSOPHY, POLISH.
PHILOSOPHY, RENAISSANCE.
PHILOSOPHY, RUSSIAN.
PHILOSOPHY, UKRAINIAN.
PHILOSOPHY, WHITE RUSSIAN.
PHILOSOPHY, YUGOSLAV.
PLATO.
POLITICAL ETHICS.
POSITIVISM.
PRAGMATICS.
RATIONALISM.
REALISM.
SOCIAL ETHICS.
SOCIAL SCIENCES AND ETHICS.
STRUCTURALISM.
TECHNOLOGY AND ETHICS.
THEORY (PHILOSOPHY).
UTILITARIANISM.
VALUES.
WAR AND MORALS.

Religion.

AFRO-AMERICAN CLERGY.
ANGLICAN PACIFIST FELLOWSHIP.
ATHEISM.
BENEDICTINES.
BIBLE.
BISHOPS
BLACK THEOLOGY.
BUDDHA AND BUDDHISM
BUDDHIST RITES AND CEREMONIES
CALENDAR, RUSSIAN SECTARIAN.
CATHOLIC CHURCH.
CATHOLIC CHURCH IN BRAZIL.
CATHOLIC CHURCH IN COMMUNIST COUNTRIES.
CATHOLIC CHURCH IN EUROPE.
CATHOLIC CHURCH IN FRANCE.
CATHOLIC CHURCH IN IRELAND.
CATHOLIC CHURCH IN ITALY.
CATHOLIC CHURCH IN SPAIN.
CATHOLIC CHURCH IN THE NETHERLANDS.
CATHOLIC CHURCH IN THE UNITED KINGDOM.
CATHOLIC CHURCH IN THE UNITED STATES.
CATHOLICS IN ITALY.
CATHOLICS IN THE UNITED KINGDOM.
CATHOLICS IN THE UNITED STATES.
CHILDREN (CHRISTIAN THEOLOGY).
CHRISTIAN ANTIQUITIES
CHRISTIAN LABOUR ASSOCIATION OF CANADA.
CHRISTIANITY.
CHRISTIANITY AND ECONOMICS.
CHRISTIANITY AND INTERNATIONAL AFFAIRS.
CHRISTIANITY AND OTHER RELIGIONS.
CHRISTIANITY AND POLITICS.
CHRISTIANS IN INDIA.
CHRISTIANS IN THE NEAR EAST.
CHURCH AND LABOUR
CHURCH AND RACE RELATIONS.
CHURCH AND SOCIAL PROBLEMS.
CHURCH AND STATE
CHURCH AND STATE IN GERMANY.
CHURCH AND STATE IN ITALY.
CHURCH AND STATE IN MALAWI.
CHURCH AND STATE IN MEXICO.
CHURCH AND STATE IN SPAIN.

POLITICAL SCIENCE, POLITICS AND GOVERNMENT

CHURCH AND STATE IN TUNISIA.
CHURCH AND STATE IN YUGOSLAVIA.
CHURCH HISTORY.
CHURCH LANDS
CHURCH OF ENGLAND.
CHURCH OF ENGLAND IN AMERICA.
CISTERCIANS.
CISTERCIANS IN THE UNITED KINGDOM.
CLERGY
CLUNIACS IN FRANCE.
COMMUNISM AND CHRISTIANITY.
COMMUNISM AND ISLAM.
COMMUNISM AND RELIGION.
CONCILIAR THEORY.
CONFUCIUS AND CONFUCIANISM.
CONVERSION
COUNCILS AND SYNODS.
COUNTER-REFORMATION.
COVENANTERS.
CRUSADES.
CULTS
DEATH.
DEVOTIO MODERNA.
DISSENTERS, RELIGIOUS
DIVINE LIGHT MISSION.
DOMINICANS.
DUTCH REFORMED CHURCH IN AFRICA.
EVANGELICAL REVIVAL.
EVANGELICALISM.
EXPERIENCE (RELIGION).
FRIENDS, SOCIETY OF.
GOD.
HISTORY (THEOLOGY).
ISRAEL AND THE DIASPORA.
JAMAA MOVEMENT.
JESUITS IN CHINA.
JESUITS IN JAPAN.
JESUS CHRIST
JUDAISM.
JUDAISM AND STATE.
KRISHNA.
MAN (THEOLOGY).
MEDITATIONS.
MILLENNIUM.
MISSIONS
MOHAMMEDANISM.
MOHAMMEDANISM AND ECONOMICS.
MOHAMMEDANISM AND POLITICS.
MOHAMMEDANISM IN AFRICA.
MOHAMMEDANS IN INDIA.
MOHAMMEDANS IN MOROCCO.
MOHAMMEDANS IN NIGERIA.
MOHAMMEDANS IN PAKISTAN.
MOHAMMEDANS IN RUSSIA.
MOHAMMEDANS IN SOUTH AFRICA.
MOHAMMEDANS IN SPAIN.
MOHAMMEDANS IN TUNISIA.
MONASTERIES
MONASTICISM AND RELIGIOUS ORDERS
MONOTHEISM.
MORMONS AND MORMONISM.
MYSTICISM
MYTHOLOGY.
MYTHOLOGY, INDIAN.
MYTHOLOGY, MAORI.
ONEIDA COMMUNITY.
PAPACY
PENTECOSTAL CHURCHES
PENTECOSTALISM.
PETERBOROUGH ABBEY.
PROTESTANT CHURCHES
PROTESTANTISM AND CAPITALISM.
PROTESTANTS IN AUSTRIA.
PROTESTANTS IN LATIN AMERICA
PROTESTANTS IN NORTHERN IRELAND.
PROTESTANTS IN THE UNITED STATES.
PSYCHOLOGY, RELIGIOUS.
PURITANS.
RAS TAFARI MOVEMENT.
RASKOLNIKS.
REFORMATION
REFUGEES, RELIGIOUS.

RELIGION.
RELIGION, PRIMITIVE.
RELIGION AND POLITICS.
RELIGION AND SCIENCE.
RELIGION AND SOCIOLOGY.
RELIGION AND STATE
RELIGIONS.
RELIGIOUS BIOGRAPHY.
RELIGIOUS FILMS
RELIGIOUS LIBERTY
RELIGIOUS THOUGHT
REVIVALS
SALVATION ARMY.
SCHISM, THE GREAT WESTERN, 1378-1417.
SCIENTOLOGY.
SECTS.
SOCIOLOGY, CHRISTIAN.
SPIRITUALISM.
TEMPLES, BUDDHIST.
THEOLOGY.
THEOLOGY, CATHOLIC.
TRADE UNIONS, CATHOLIC
UMBANDA (CULTUS).
UNIVERSAL NEGRO IMPROVEMENT
   ASSOCIATION.
WOMEN, MOHAMMEDAN.
WORLD COUNCIL OF CHURCHES.

POLITICAL SCIENCE, POLITICS AND GOVERNMENT.

General.

ABUSE OF ADMINISTRATIVE POWER
ADMINISTRATION.
ADMINISTRATIVE AGENCIES
ADMINISTRATIVE AND POLITICAL
   DIVISIONS.
ADMINISTRATIVE PROCEDURE
AFFIRMATIVE ACTION PROGRAMMES
AGRICULTURE AND STATE.
ALIENS
ANARCHISM AND ANARCHISTS.
ANTISEMITISM
ARMS CONTROL.
ART AND STATE
ASSASSINATION
ATOMIC WEAPONS AND DISARMAMENT.
AUTHORITARIANISM.
AUTHORITY.
BALANCE OF POWER.
BOUNDARIES.
BUREAUCRACY.
CABINET MINISTERS
CENTRE PARTIES
CHILDREN AND POLITICS.
CHRISTIANITY AND INTERNATIONAL
   AFFAIRS.
CHRISTIANITY AND POLITICS.
CHURCH AND STATE
CHURCH AND STATE IN GERMANY.
CHURCH AND STATE IN ITALY.
CHURCH AND STATE IN MALAWI.
CHURCH AND STATE IN MEXICO.
CHURCH AND STATE IN SPAIN.
CHURCH AND STATE IN TUNISIA.
CHURCH AND STATE IN YUGOSLAVIA.
CIVIL RIGHTS.
CIVIL SERVICE.
CIVIL SUPREMACY OVER THE MILITARY
COALITION (SOCIAL SCIENCES).
COALITION GOVERNMENTS
COLLECTIVISM.
COLONIES.
COLONIES IN AFRICA.
COLONIES IN ASIA.
COMMISSIONS OF INQUIRY
COMMUNISM.
COMMUNISM AND ANTHROPOLOGY.
COMMUNISM AND CHRISTIANITY.
COMMUNISM AND CULTURE.

COMMUNISM AND ISLAM.
COMMUNISM AND LITERATURE.
COMMUNISM AND RELIGION.
COMMUNISM AND SCIENCE.
COMMUNISM AND SOCIAL SCIENCES.
COMMUNISM AND SOCIETY.
COMMUNISM AND THE ARTS.
COMMUNISM AND ZIONISM.
COMMUNIST EDUCATION
COMMUNIST ETHICS.
COMMUNIST REVISIONISM.
COMMUNIST STATE.
COMMUNIST STRATEGY.
COMMUNISTIC SETTLEMENTS
CONFLICT OF INTERESTS (PUBLIC
   OFFICE)
CONSERVATISM.
CORPORATE STATE.
CORRUPTION (IN POLITICS).
DECENTRALIZATION IN GOVERNMENT
DELEGATED LEGISLATION
DEMOCRACY.
DETENTE.
DICTATORSHIP OF THE PROLETARIAT.
DIPLOMACY.
DIPLOMATIC AND CONSULAR SERVICE.
DIPLOMATIC NEGOTIATIONS IN
   INTERNATIONAL DISPUTES.
DISARMAMENT.
DISCRIMINATION.
DISSENTERS.
EDUCATION AND STATE.
ELECTIONS.
EMIGRATION AND IMMIGRATION.
EMPLOYEE-MANAGEMENT RELATIONS
   IN GOVERNMENT
ESPIONAGE
ESPIONAGE, GERMAN
ESPIONAGE, RUSSIAN
EUROPEAN FEDERATION.
EXECUTIVE POWER.
FASCISM.
FEDERAL GOVERNMENT.
FREEDOM OF INFORMATION.
FREEDOM OF MOVEMENT
GEOGRAPHY, POLITICAL.
GOVERNMENT, COMPARATIVE.
GOVERNMENT AND THE PRESS.
GOVERNMENT CONSULTANTS.
GOVERNMENT EXECUTIVES
GOVERNMENT INFORMATION.
GOVERNMENT PUBLICITY
HIGHER EDUCATION AND STATE
HISTORICAL MATERIALISM.
IDEOLOGY.
IMPERIALISM.
INDEPENDENT REGULATORY
   COMMISSIONS
INDIVIDUALISM.
INDUSTRY AND STATE.
INSURGENCY.
INTELLECTUALS
INTELLIGENCE SERVICE
INTERNAL SECURITY
INTERNATIONAL AGENCIES.
INTERNATIONAL COOPERATION.
INTERNATIONAL OFFENCES.
INTERNATIONAL ORGANIZATION.
INTERNATIONAL RELATIONS.
INTERNATIONALISM.
INTERORGANIZATIONAL RELATIONS.
JOURNALISM, SOCIALIST
JUDAISM AND STATE.
LATIN AMERICAN FEDERATION.
LAW AND POLITICS.
LAW AND SOCIALISM.
LEGISLATIVE BODIES.
LEGISLATORS.
LEGITIMACY OF GOVERNMENTS.
LIBERALISM.
LIBERTY.
LITERATURE AND STATE

POLITICAL SCIENCE, POLITICS AND GOVERNMENT (Cont.)

LOCAL ELECTIONS
LOCAL GOVERNMENT.
LOCAL GOVERNMENT OFFICIALS AND EMPLOYEES
LOGIC.
MARXISM.
MARXISM AND SOCIAL SCIENCES.
METROPOLITAN GOVERNMENT.
MIDDLE CLASSES.
MILITARISM
MILITARY POLICY.
MISCONDUCT IN OFFICE
MOHAMMEDANISM AND POLITICS.
MONARCHY.
MOVING PICTURES IN PROPAGANDA.
MUNICIPAL GOVERNMENT.
MUNICIPAL GOVERNMENT BY COMMISSION.
MUNICIPAL HOME RULE
NATIONALISM.
NATIONALISM AND SOCIALISM.
NEIGHBOURHOOD GOVERNMENT
NEUTRALITY.
OCEAN BOTTOM.
OFFICIAL SECRETS.
OMBUDSMAN.
OPPOSITION (POLITICAL SCIENCE).
PACIFIC SETTLEMENT OF INTERNATIONAL DISPUTES.
PACIFISM.
PARTITION, TERRITORIAL.
PASSIVE RESISTANCE
PATRIOTISM
PATRON AND CLIENT.
PATRONAGE, POLITICAL.
PEACE.
PICKETING
POLICE, POLITICAL AND SECRET
POLICY SCIENCES.
POLITICAL CRIMES AND OFFENCES.
POLITICAL ETHICS.
POLITICAL ORATORY
POLITICAL PARTICIPATION.
POLITICAL PARTIES.
POLITICAL PRISONERS
POLITICAL PSYCHOLOGY.
POLITICAL SCIENCE.
POLITICAL SOCIOLOGY.
POLITICS AND EDUCATION
POLITICS AND LITERATURE.
POLITICS IN MOVING PICTURES.
POPULAR FRONTS.
POPULISM
POWER (SOCIAL SCIENCES).
PRESIDENTS.
PRESS AND POLITICS.
PRESSURE GROUPS.
PRIVACY, RIGHT OF.
PROTECTORATES.
PUBLIC RECORDS
PUBLIC SERVICE
RADICALISM
RADICALS
REALISM.
REFERENDUM
REFUGEES.
REFUGEES, AUSTRIAN.
REFUGEES, POLITICAL
REFUGEES, RELIGIOUS.
REGIONALISM.
RELIGION AND POLITICS.
RELIGION AND STATE
RELIGIOUS LIBERTY
REPRESENTATIVE GOVERNMENT AND REPRESENTATION.
REVOLUTIONISTS.
REVOLUTIONS.
RIGHT AND LEFT (POLITICAL SCIENCE).
SAINTSIMONIANISM.
SCIENCE AND STATE.
SECRET SERVICE
SECURITY, INTERNATIONAL.
SELF-DETERMINATION, NATIONAL.
SOCIAL SCIENTISTS IN GOVERNMENT
SOCIALISM.
SOCIALISM AND EDUCATION.
SOCIALISM AND THE ARTS.
SOCIALISM AND YOUTH.
SOCIALISM IN LITERATURE.
SOCIALISTS
SOCIALISTS, JEWISH.
SOVEREIGNTY.
SOVIETS
SPORTS AND STATE
STATE, THE.
STATE ENCOURAGEMENT OF SCIENCE, LITERATURE AND ART
STATE GOVERNMENTS
STATE RIGHTS.
STATES, SMALL.
STATESMEN.
SUBVERSIVE ACTIVITIES.
SUFFRAGE
TECHNOLOGY AND STATE
TELEVISION IN POLITICS.
TERRORISM.
TOLERATION.
TORTURE
TOTALITARIANISM.
TRADE UNIONS AND COMMUNISM.
TRIBAL GOVERNMENT
TRUST TERRITORIES
UTOPIAS.
VIOLENCE.
VOTERS, REGISTRATION OF
VOTING
WAR.
WAR AND EMERGENCY POWERS
WAR AND SOCIALISM.
WOMEN AND SOCIALISM.
WOMEN IN POLITICS.
WORLD DISARMAMENT CONFERENCE.
WORLD POLITICS.

Particular countries, nationalities, parties, organizations, etc.

AFRICAN NATIONAL CONGRESS (SOUTH AFRICA).
AFRIKANER-BROEDERBOND.
AFRO-ASIAN PEOPLE'S SOLIDARITY ORGANIZATION.
ALIANZA POPULAR REVOLUCIONARIA AMERICANA.
ALLIANCE PARTY.
AMERICAN LOYALISTS.
AMNESTY INTERNATIONAL.
ANGLICAN PACIFIST FELLOWSHIP.
ANTIFASCHISTISCHE AKTION.
ANTINAZI MOVEMENT.
ASSOCIATION OF COUNTY COUNCILS.
ATLANTIC COMMUNITY
ATLANTIC INSTITUTE FOR INTERNATIONAL AFFAIRS.
BIRMINGHAM POLITICAL UNION.
BLACK NATIONALISM
BLACK POWER.
BUND DER GEÄCHTETEN.
CHARTISM.
COMMUNES (CHINA).
COMMUNIST COUNTRIES
COMMUNIST PARTIES.
COMMUNIST PARTY
COMMUNISTS
CONSERVATIVE PARTY (UNITED KINGDOM).
DECEMBRISTS.
DEMOCRATIC PARTY (UNITED STATES).
DEUTSCHE DEMOKRATISCHE PARTEI.
DEUTSCHLAND-STIFTUNG.
ECOLOGY PARTY
EUROPEAN COMMUNITIES.
EUROPEAN CONVENTION ON HUMAN RIGHTS.
EUROPEAN ECONOMIC COMMUNITY.
EUROPEAN PARLIAMENT.
FABIAN SOCIETY.
FEDERAL PARTY.
FLEMISH MOVEMENT.
FREIE DEMOKRATISCHE PARTEI.
FRENTE DE LIBERTAÇÃO DE MOÇAMBIQUE.
FROLINAT.
FRONT DE LIBERATION NATIONALE.
INDIAN NATIONAL CONGRESS.
INTERNATIONAL, THE.
INTERNATIONAL PEACE BUREAU.
KOMMUNISTISCHER JUGENDVERBAND DEUTSCHLANDS.
KUOMINTANG.
LABOUR PARTY
LEAGUE OF NATIONS.
LIBERAL PARTY
LIGUE COMMUNISTE RÉVOLUTIONNAIRE.
LOTTA CONTINUA.
LUDWIG BOLTZMANN INSTITUT FÜR GESCHICHTE DER ARBEITERBEWEGUNG.
MOVIMENTO SOCIALE ITALIANO.
NÁRODNÍ STRANA SVOBODOMYSLNÁ.
NARODNO-SOTSIALISTICHESKAIA (TRUDOVAIA) PARTIIA.
NATIONAL AWAMI PARTY.
NATIONAL FRONT.
NATIONAL SOCIALISM.
NEW DEMOCRATIC PARTY (CANADA).
NORDISK RÅD.
NORTH ATLANTIC TREATY ORGANIZATION.
NORTHERN IRELAND CIVIL RIGHTS ASSOCIATION.
PANAFRICANISM.
PANSLAVISM.
PARTI QUÉBÉCOIS.
PARTI SOCIALISTE UNIFIE.
PARTIDO DEMOCRATA POPULAR.
PARTIJ VAN DE ARBEID.
PARTIT SOCIALISTA DE CATALUNYA.
PARTITO POPOLARE ITALIANO.
PARTITO RADICALE (ITALY).
POLITICAL SATIRE, AMERICAN.
PROGRESSIVISM (U.S. POLITICS).
PROPAGANDA, BRITISH.
PROPAGANDA, COMMUNIST.
PROPAGANDA, GERMAN.
PROPAGANDA, RUSSIAN.
RED CROSS.
RED INTERNATIONAL OF LABOUR UNIONS.
REFUGEES IN AFRICA.
REGIONAL COOPERATION FOR DEVELOPMENT.
REICHSZENTRALE FÜR HEIMATDIENST.
REPUBLICAN PARTY (UNITED STATES).
REPUBLICANISM IN SPAIN.
SCOTTISH LABOUR PARTY.
SOCIAL DEMOCRATIC PARTY (GERMANY).
SOCIAL DEMOCRATIC PARTY (RUSSIA).
SOCIALISM IN ARAB COUNTRIES.
SOCIALISM IN AUSTRIA.
SOCIALISM IN BULGARIA.
SOCIALISM IN CANADA.
SOCIALISM IN CUBA.
SOCIALISM IN CZECHOSLOVAKIA.
SOCIALISM IN EASTERN EUROPE.
SOCIALISM IN EASTERN GERMANY.
SOCIALISM IN ETHIOPIA.
SOCIALISM IN EUROPE.
SOCIALISM IN FRANCE.
SOCIALISM IN GERMANY.
SOCIALISM IN INDIA.
SOCIALISM IN IRELAND.

PUBLIC HEALTH AND MEDICINE

SOCIALISM IN ITALY.
SOCIALISM IN KOREA.
SOCIALISM IN POLAND.
SOCIALISM IN RUSSIA.
SOCIALISM IN SUBSAHARAN AFRICA.
SOCIALISM IN SWEDEN.
SOCIALISM IN TANZANIA.
SOCIALISM IN THE NETHERLANDS.
SOCIALISM IN THE UNITED KINGDOM.
SOCIALISM IN THE UNITED STATES.
SOCIALISM IN VIETNAM.
SOCIALISM IN YUGOSLAVIA.
SOCIALIST PARTY (ARGENTINE REPUBLIC).
SOCIALIST PARTY (AUSTRIA).
SOCIALIST PARTY (CHILE).
SOCIALIST PARTY (FRANCE).
SOCIALIST PARTY (POLAND).
SOCIALIST PARTY (SPAIN).
SOCIALIST PARTY (UNITED STATES).
SOCIALIST REVOLUTIONARY PARTY (RUSSIA).
SOCIEDAD NACIONAL DE AGRICULTURA.
SOUTH WEST AFRICAN PEOPLE'S ORGANIZATION.
TRILATERAL COMMISSION.
TRUE WHIG PARTY.
UNITED NATIONS.
VERBAND DER UNABHÄNGIGEN.
WAFD PARTY.
WORLD PEACE COUNCIL.
YOUNG COMMUNIST LEAGUE

PSYCHOLOGY.

ADOLESCENT PSYCHOLOGY.
AGE (PSYCHOLOGY).
ANXIETY.
ATTITUDE (PSYCHOLOGY).
ATTITUDE CHANGE.
BEHAVIOUR MODIFICATION.
BEHAVIOURISM (PSYCHOLOGY).
BOREDOM.
BRAIN.
CEREBRAL DOMINANCE.
CHILD DEVELOPMENT.
CHILD PSYCHIATRY.
CHILD PSYCHOLOGY.
CHOICE (PSYCHOLOGY).
COGNITION.
COGNITION (CHILD PSYCHOLOGY).
COMMUNITY PSYCHOLOGY.
COMPREHENSION.
CREATIVE ABILITY.
CRISIS INTERVENTION (PSYCHIATRY).
CROWDING STRESS.
DECISION-MAKING.
DECISION-MAKING, GROUP.
DEPRESSION, MENTAL.
DEVELOPMENTAL PSYCHOLOGY.
DREAMS.
EDUCATIONAL PSYCHOLOGY.
EGO (PSYCHOLOGY).
ENVIRONMENTAL PSYCHOLOGY.
FEAR.
GERIATRIC PSYCHIATRY
GROUP PSYCHOTHERAPY.
HELPLESSNESS (PSYCHOLOGY).
HEREDITY.
HUMAN BEHAVIOUR.
HUMAN INFORMATION PROCESSING.
HYPNOTISM.
INDUSTRIAL PSYCHIATRY.
INFANT PSYCHOLOGY.
INTELLECT.
INTELLIGENCE LEVELS.
LEARNING, PSYCHOLOGY OF.
MATURATION (PSYCHOLOGY).
MEDICINE AND PSYCHOLOGY.
MEMORY.

MEMORY IN CHILDREN.
MENTAL TESTS.
MIND AND BODY.
NATURE AND NURTURE.
NEGOTIATION.
NEUROPSYCHOLOGY.
PERCEPTION.
PERSONAL SPACE.
PERSONALITY.
PERSONALITY, DISORDERS OF.
PERSONALITY TESTS.
POLITICAL PSYCHOLOGY.
PRISON PSYCHOLOGY.
PSYCHOANALYSIS.
PSYCHOBIOLOGY.
PSYCHOLINGUISTICS.
PSYCHOLOGICAL WARFARE.
PSYCHOLOGY.
PSYCHOLOGY, EXPERIMENTAL.
PSYCHOLOGY, FORENSIC.
PSYCHOLOGY, INDUSTRIAL.
PSYCHOLOGY, MILITARY.
PSYCHOLOGY, PATHOLOGICAL.
PSYCHOLOGY, RELIGIOUS.
PSYCHOMETRICS.
PSYCHOTHERAPY.
REASONING (PSYCHOLOGY).
REPERTORY GRID TECHNIQUE.
SELF.
SELF-PERCEPTION.
SEX (PSYCHOLOGY).
SIGHT.
SOCIAL PSYCHOLOGY.
SPEECH, DISORDERS OF.
SPEECH DISORDERS IN CHILDREN.
STRESS (PSYCHOLOGY).
SUBCONSCIOUSNESS.
SUCCESS.
THOUGHT AND THINKING.
TYPOLOGY (PSYCHOLOGY).
VISUAL PERCEPTION.
WORK.

PUBLIC HEALTH AND MEDICINE.

AMBULATORY MEDICAL CARE.
APHASIA.
AUTISM.
BIRTH WEIGHT, LOW
BRAIN DAMAGE.
BRONCHITIS.
CANCER
CENTRAL PUBLIC HEALTH ENGINEERING RESEARCH INSTITUTE.
CHILDBIRTH.
CHILDREN, FIRSTBORN.
COMMUNICABLE DISEASES.
COMMUNITY HEALTH SERVICES.
COMMUNITY HEALTH SERVICES FOR THE AGED.
COMMUNITY MENTAL HEALTH SERVICES.
CONSCIOUSNESS.
CONTRACEPTION
DEVELOPMENTALLY DISABLED CHILDREN.
DIET
DISEASES
DISINFECTION AND DISINFECTANTS.
DRINKING WATER
DRUGS.
EMERGENCY MEDICAL SERVICES.
EPIDEMICS
EUTHANASIA.
EXSERVICEMEN, DISABLED
FAMILY PSYCHOTHERAPY.
FOLK MEDICINE
FOOD ADULTERATION AND INSPECTION
FOOD CONTAMINATION
GENETIC ENGINEERING.
GERIATRIC NURSING.

HEALTH BOARDS
HEALTH EDUCATION
HEALTH PLANNING.
HEALTH SERVICES ADMINISTRATION.
HEALTH SURVEYS.
HOME ACCIDENTS
HOSPITAL CARE
HOSPITAL PATIENTS
HOSPITALS
HUMAN ENGINEERING.
HYGIENE, PUBLIC.
INDUSTRIAL HYGIENE
INFANTS (NEWBORN)
INFLUENZA
LUNGS
MALPRACTICE
MATERNAL AND INFANT WELFARE.
MEDICAL CARE.
MEDICAL CARE, COST OF.
MEDICAL ECONOMICS.
MEDICAL ETHICS.
MEDICAL FEES
MEDICAL INNOVATIONS.
MEDICAL JURISPRUDENCE.
MEDICAL LAWS AND LEGISLATION.
MEDICAL PERSONNEL AND PATIENT
MEDICAL POLICY
MEDICAL RESEARCH
MEDICAL SOCIETIES
MEDICAL STATISTICS.
MEDICINE
MEDICINE, MAGIC, MYSTIC AND SPAGIRIC.
MEDICINE, PREVENTIVE.
MEDICINE, PSYCHOSOMATIC.
MEDICINE, STATE
MEDICINE AND PSYCHOLOGY.
MENTAL HEALTH LAWS
MENTAL HEALTH SERVICES
MENTAL HYGIENE.
MENTAL ILLNESS.
MENTALLY ILL
NARCOTIC ADDICTS
NARCOTIC HABIT.
NERVOUS SYSTEM, AUTONOMIC.
NEUROPSYCHIATRY.
NEUROSES.
NURSES AND NURSING
NUTRITION.
NUTRITION POLICY.
OBSTETRICS.
PAIN.
PHARMACY
PHYSICALLY HANDICAPPED
PHYSICALLY HANDICAPPED CHILDREN
PHYSICIAN AND PATIENT.
PLAGUE
PROTEINS.
PSYCHIATRIC CLINICS
PSYCHIATRIC HOSPITALS.
PSYCHIATRIC SOCIAL WORK
PSYCHIATRY.
PSYCHOLOGY, PATHOLOGICAL.
PSYCHOTHERAPY.
PUBLIC HEALTH ADMINISTRATION
PUBLIC HEALTH RESEARCH
RABIES
RADIATION
RURAL HEALTH SERVICES
SCHIZOPHRENIA.
SELF MEDICATION
SICK.
SMOKING.
SOCIAL MEDICINE.
STRESS (PHYSIOLOGY).
TERMINAL CARE.
THALIDOMIDE.
TRANSPLANTATION OF ORGANS, TISSUES, ETC.
TUMOURS IN CHILDREN.
VENEREAL DISEASES
WOMEN IN MEDICINE.

PUBLIC HEALTH AND MEDICINE (Cont.)

WOMEN'S HEALTH SERVICES

SCIENCE AND TECHNOLOGY.

ADAPTATION (BIOLOGY).
AIR
ALTITUDE, INFLUENCE OF.
AMERICAN ASSOCIATION FOR THE ADVANCEMENT OF SCIENCE.
ANIMAL COMMUNICATION.
ANIMAL POPULATIONS
ARCHAEOLOGY, INDUSTRIAL.
ARTHROPODA.
ARTIFICIAL INTELLIGENCE.
ASTRONOMY.
ATOMIC BOMB.
AUTOMATIC CONTROL.
AUTOMATION
BIOLOGICAL ASSAY.
BIOLOGICAL SYSTEMS.
BIOLOGICAL WARFARE.
BIOLOGY
BOTANY
BOTANY, MEDICAL
CHEMICAL WARFARE.
COMMUNISM AND SCIENCE.
COMPUTER GRAPHICS.
COMPUTER OUTPUT MICROFILM DEVICES.
COSMOLOGY.
DESIGN, INDUSTRIAL.
DYNAMIC PROGRAMMING.
EARTH SCIENCES.
ENVIRONMENTAL ENGINEERING.
ENVIRONMENTAL IMPACT ANALYSIS.
ENVIRONMENTAL IMPACT STATEMENTS.
HYDROLOGY.
INFORMATION SCIENCE.
INTEGRATED CIRCUITS
LIFE SCIENCES
MICROELECTRONICS.
MICROPROCESSORS.
MOBILE COMMUNICATION SYSTEMS.
NATURAL SELECTION.
NIGERIAN COUNCIL FOR SCIENCE AND TECHNOLOGY.
NOBEL PRIZES.
NUFFIELD FOUNDATION SCIENCE TEACHING PROJECT.
OCEAN ENGINEERING.
OCEAN MINING.
OCEANOGRAPHIC RESEARCH.
OPERATIONS RESEARCH.
OUTER SPACE
PHYSICS
PREDATION (BIOLOGY).
PRIMATES
RELIGION AND SCIENCE.
RESEARCH
RESONANCE.
RESONANT VIBRATION
SCIENCE.
SCIENCE, MEDIEVAL.
SCIENCE AND CIVILIZATION.
SCIENCE AND STATE.
SCIENTIFIC APPARATUS AND INSTRUMENTS.
SEX.
SEX (BIOLOGY).
SMOKE PREVENTION.
SOCIAL BEHAVIOUR IN ANIMALS.
SPACE COLONIES.
SPACE SCIENCES.
TECHNOLOGICAL INNOVATIONS.
TECHNOLOGY.
TECHNOLOGY AND CIVILIZATION.
TECHNOLOGY AND ETHICS.
TECHNOLOGY AND LAW.
TECHNOLOGY AND STATE.
TECHNOLOGY TRANSFER.
WATER MILLS

WATER POWER

SOCIOLOGY, ANTHROPOLOGY AND ETHNOLOGY.

General.

ABOLITIONISTS.
ABORTION.
ABUSED WIVES
ACCULTURATION.
ADOLESCENCE.
ADOPTION
AGE GROUPS.
AGING.
ALCOHOL AND CHILDREN
ALCOHOL AND YOUTH
ALCOHOLICS ANONYMOUS.
ALCOHOLISM
ALIENATION (SOCIAL PSYCHOLOGY).
AMERICANIZATION.
ANIMALS, TREATMENT OF
ANTHROPOLOGICAL LINGUISTICS.
ANTHROPOLOGY.
APARTMENT HOUSES
ARCHAEOLOGY.
ARCHITECTURE, DOMESTIC.
ARCHITECTURE AND SOCIETY.
ARISTOCRACY.
ART AND SOCIETY.
ARTS AND SOCIETY.
ASSIMILATION (SOCIOLOGY).
ASSISTANCE IN EMERGENCIES
ASSOCIATIONS, INSTITUTIONS, ETC.
ATOMIC POWER.
ATTRIBUTION (SOCIAL PSYCHOLOGY).
BLIND
BRIBERY
BRIGANDS AND ROBBERS
BRITISH BROADCASTING CORPORATION.
BURGLARY
CALENDAR, RUSSIAN SECTARIAN.
CANNIBALISM.
CAPITAL PUNISHMENT
CASTE
CATTLE STEALING.
CHARITIES
CHILD ABUSE.
CHILD DEVELOPMENT.
CHILD MOLESTING.
CHILD WELFARE.
CHILDLESSNESS
CHILDREN.
CHILDREN AND POLITICS.
CHILDREN OF WORKING MOTHERS
CHILDREN'S ACCIDENTS
CHILDREN'S RIGHTS.
CHRONOLOGY, MAORI.
CHURCH AND RACE RELATIONS.
CHURCH AND SOCIAL PROBLEMS.
CITIES AND TOWNS.
CITIES AND TOWNS, MEDIEVAL
CITY PLANNING.
COLONIZATION.
COMMERCE, PRIMITIVE.
COMMUNICATION.
COMMUNICATIONS RESEARCH.
COMMUNISM AND ANTHROPOLOGY.
COMMUNISM AND CULTURE.
COMMUNISM AND SOCIAL SCIENCES.
COMMUNISM AND SOCIETY.
COMMUNITY.
COMMUNITY AND SCHOOL.
COMMUNITY CENTRES
COMMUNITY DEVELOPMENT.
COMMUNITY DEVELOPMENT, URBAN
COMMUNITY HEALTH SERVICES FOR THE AGED.
COMMUNITY LIFE.
COMMUNITY ORGANIZATION.
CONCENTRATION CAMPS

CONCUBINAGE
CONDUCT OF LIFE.
CONFIDENTIAL COMMUNICATIONS.
CONFLICT OF GENERATIONS.
CONJUGAL VIOLENCE.
CONVERSATION.
CONVICT LABOUR.
CORPORAL PUNISHMENT
COUNSELLING.
COUNTRY HOMES
CRIME AND AGE.
CRIME AND CRIMINALS.
CRIME FORECASTING
CRIME PREVENTION.
CRIMINAL BEHAVIOUR, PREDICTION OF.
CRIMINAL STATISTICS
CULTURAL PROPERTY, PROTECTION OF.
CULTURE.
CULTURE CONFLICT.
CUSTODY OF CHILDREN.
DAY NURSERIES
DEAF
DEUTSCHER WERKBUND.
DEUTSCHES AUSLAND-INSTITUT.
DEVIANT BEHAVIOUR.
DISABILITY EVALUATION.
DISASTER RELIEF
DISASTERS
DISCRIMINATION IN HOUSING
DISSENTERS.
DIVORCE
DRINKING CUSTOMS
DRUG ABUSE
DRUG ABUSE AND CRIME.
DWELLINGS
ELITE.
ENDOWMENTS.
EQUALITY.
ETHNIC ATTITUDES.
ETHNIC GROUPS.
ETHNICITY.
ETHNOBOTANY.
ETHNOCENTRISM.
ETHNOLOGICAL JURISPRUDENCE.
ETHNOLOGY.
EUGENICS.
EVALUATION RESEARCH (SOCIAL ACTION PROGRAMMES).
EVICTION
EVOLUTION.
EXPERIENCE.
EXSERVICEMEN
EXSERVICEMEN, DISABLED
FACIAL EXPRESSION.
FAMILY.
FAMILY PLANNING ASSOCIATION.
FAMILY RESEARCH.
FAMILY SIZE.
FAMILY SOCIAL WORK
FATHER-SEPARATED CHILDREN.
FEDERAL-CITY RELATIONS
FEMINISM.
FIRE DEPARTMENTS
FISHING VILLAGES
FOLK LORE
FOLK LORE, MAORI.
FOLK LORE OF CHILDREN.
FOLK MEDICINE
FOOD (IN RELIGION, FOLK-LORE, ETC.).
FOOD HABITS.
FOOD RELIEF
FOOTBALL
FORCED LABOUR
FORD FOUNDATION.
FOREIGN NEWS.
FREEDMEN IN THE UNITED STATES.
FREEMASONS
FRONTIER AND PIONEER LIFE
FUNCTIONAL ANALYSIS (SOCIAL SCIENCES).
FUNERAL RITES AND CEREMONIES
GANGS

SOCIOLOGY, ANTHROPOLOGY AND ETHNOLOGY

GENIUS.
GESTURE.
GOSSIP.
GOVERNMENT AND THE PRESS.
GROUP RELATIONS TRAINING.
GUERRILLAS.
HANDICAPPED.
HANDICAPPED CHILDREN.
HERMENEUTICS.
HISTORICAL FILMS.
HOLIDAYS
HOME HELPS.
HOMELESSNESS
HOMOSEXUALITY.
HUMAN EVOLUTION.
HUMAN POPULATION GENETICS.
INDIANS, TREATMENT OF
INDUSTRIAL SOCIOLOGY.
INFANTS.
INFORMATION THEORY.
INSTITUTIONAL CARE
INTERNATIONAL BROADCASTING.
INTERPERSONAL COMMUNICATION.
INTERPERSONAL RELATIONS.
INTERRACIAL ADOPTION
INTERVIEWING.
JOURNALISM
JUVENILE DELINQUENCY.
JUVENILE DETENTION HOMES
KIDNAPPING
KINSHIP
KNOWLEDGE, SOCIOLOGY OF.
LAW ENFORCEMENT
LEADERSHIP.
LEAGUE OF REVOLUTIONARY BLACK WORKERS.
LEGAL ASSISTANCE TO THE POOR
LEISURE.
LESBIANISM.
LIBERTY OF THE PRESS.
LIQUOR PROBLEM
LITERATURE AND SOCIETY.
LOTTERIES
MAGIC.
MAN, PREHISTORIC.
MARIHUANA.
MARRIAGE
MARRIAGE CUSTOMS AND RITES, HINDU.
MARRIAGE GUIDANCE
MARRIED WOMEN
MARXISM AND SOCIAL SCIENCES.
MASS MEDIA.
MASS MEDIA AND LITERATURE
MASS MEDIA AND RACE RELATIONS.
MATERNAL AND INFANT WELFARE.
MEDICINE, MAGIC, MYSTIC AND SPAGIRIC.
MEN.
MENTALLY HANDICAPPED.
MENTALLY HANDICAPPED CHILDREN
MIDDLE CLASSES.
MINORITIES.
MINORITY WOMEN
MISCEGENATION
MOBILE HOMES
MORAL CONDITIONS.
MOTHER AND CHILD.
MOTHERS.
MOVING PICTURES.
MUNICIPAL RESEARCH
MURDER
MUSIC-HALLS (VARIETY-THEATRES, CABARETS, ETC.).
NARCOTIC ADDICTS
NARCOTIC HABIT.
NARCOTICS, CONTROL OF.
NATIONAL CHARACTERISTICS, AMERICAN.
NATIONAL CHARACTERISTICS, BRITISH.
NATIONAL CHARACTERISTICS, LATIN AMERICAN.
NATIONAL PARKS AND RESERVES
NEIGHBOURLINESS.
NEW ENGLAND EMIGRANT AID COMPANY.
NEW TOWNS.
NEW YEAR.
NOMADS.
NONVIOLENCE.
OCCUPATIONS.
OLD AGE
OLD AGE ASSISTANCE
OLD AGE HOMES
ORGANIZATION.
ORGANIZATIONAL BEHAVIOUR.
ORGANIZED CRIME
ORPHANS AND ORPHAN ASYLUMS
OUTDOOR RECREATION.
OVERLAND JOURNEYS TO THE PACIFIC.
PARENT AND CHILD.
PARKS.
PEASANTRY.
PENAL COLONIES, BRITISH.
PENOLOGY
PEONAGE
PHILANTHROPISTS
PHILOSOPHICAL ANTHROPOLOGY.
PHYSICAL ANTHROPOLOGY.
PLANNING.
PLANTATION LIFE
PLAY.
PLURALISM (SOCIAL SCIENCES).
POLICE
POLICE POWER
POLICE PSYCHOLOGY.
POLICE QUESTIONING
POLICE SERVICES FOR JUVENILES
POLITICAL SOCIOLOGY.
POOR.
POPULAR CULTURE.
POVERTY.
POVERTY RESEARCH.
POWER (SOCIAL SCIENCES).
PRESTIGE.
PRISON ADMINISTRATION
PRISON PSYCHOLOGY.
PRISON SENTENCES.
PRISONERS.
PRISONS.
PRIVACY, RIGHT OF.
PROBATION
PROSTITUTION
PSYCHIATRIC SOCIAL WORK
PUBLIC HOUSING
PUBLIC MEETINGS
PUBLIC OPINION.
PUBLIC OPINION POLLS.
PUBLIC RELATIONS
PUNISHMENT.
QUESTIONNAIRES.
RACE.
RACE AWARENESS.
RACE DISCRIMINATION.
RACE RELATIONS.
RACE RELATIONS AND THE PRESS.
RACISM
RECIDIVISTS
RECREATION AND STATE
REFORM CLUB.
REFORMATORIES
REGIONAL PLANNING.
REHABILITATION.
REHABILITATION OF CRIMINALS
REHABILITATION OF JUVENILE DELINQUENTS.
RELIGION, PRIMITIVE.
RELIGION AND SOCIOLOGY.
RELOCATION (HOUSING)
REMAND HOMES
REPARATION.
RETIREMENT.
RIOT CONTROL.
RITES AND CEREMONIES.
ROTE ARMEE FRAKTION.
RURAL FAMILIES
RURAL POOR
RURAL WOMEN
RURAL-URBAN MIGRATION
SAMARITANS.
SATISFACTION.
SCHOOL SOCIAL WORK
SEGREGATION
SELF-HELP GROUPS.
SEX AND LAW
SEX CUSTOMS.
SEX DISCRIMINATION
SEX DISCRIMINATION AGAINST WOMEN
SEX ROLE.
SEXUAL PERVERSION.
SIGN LANGUAGE.
SINGLE PARENT FAMILY.
SLAVE TRADE
SLAVERY.
SLAVERY IN AFRICA.
SLAVERY IN BRAZIL.
SLAVERY IN INDIA
SLAVERY IN JAMAICA.
SLAVERY IN LATIN AMERICA.
SLAVERY IN THE CARIBBEAN AREA.
SLAVERY IN THE UNITED STATES.
SLAVERY IN THE WEST INDIES.
SLOW LEARNING CHILDREN.
SLUMS
SMALL GROUPS.
SOCCER
SOCIAL ACTION.
SOCIAL ADJUSTMENT.
SOCIAL CASE WORK.
SOCIAL CASE WORK REPORTING.
SOCIAL CASE WORK WITH CHILDREN.
SOCIAL CHANGE.
SOCIAL CHOICE.
SOCIAL CLASSES.
SOCIAL CONDITIONS.
SOCIAL CONFLICT.
SOCIAL CONTROL.
SOCIAL DARWINISM.
SOCIAL ETHICS.
SOCIAL EVOLUTION.
SOCIAL GROUP WORK.
SOCIAL GROUPS.
SOCIAL HISTORY.
SOCIAL INDICATORS.
SOCIAL INSTITUTIONS.
SOCIAL INTERACTION.
SOCIAL JUSTICE.
SOCIAL LEGISLATION
SOCIAL MOBILITY.
SOCIAL MOVEMENTS.
SOCIAL PARTICIPATION.
SOCIAL PERCEPTION.
SOCIAL POLICY.
SOCIAL PROBLEMS.
SOCIAL PSYCHOLOGY.
SOCIAL REFORMERS.
SOCIAL ROLE.
SOCIAL SCIENCE RESEARCH.
SOCIAL SCIENCES.
SOCIAL SCIENCES AND ETHICS.
SOCIAL SCIENTISTS.
SOCIAL SECURITY.
SOCIAL SERVICE.
SOCIAL SERVICE AND RACE RELATIONS
SOCIAL SETTLEMENTS
SOCIAL STATUS.
SOCIAL STRUCTURE.
SOCIAL SURVEYS.
SOCIAL SYSTEMS.
SOCIAL VALUES.
SOCIAL WORK ADMINISTRATION
SOCIAL WORK EDUCATION.
SOCIAL WORK WITH ALCOHOLICS
SOCIAL WORK WITH CHILDREN
SOCIAL WORK WITH DELINQUENTS AND CRIMINALS.

SOCIOLOGY, ANTHROPOLOGY AND ETHNOLOGY (Cont.)

SOCIAL WORK WITH MINORITIES
SOCIAL WORK WITH THE AGED
SOCIAL WORK WITH YOUTH
SOCIALISM AND YOUTH.
SOCIALIZATION.
SOCIALLY HANDICAPPED.
SOCIALLY HANDICAPPED CHILDREN
SOCIOBIOLOGY.
SOCIOLINGUISTICS.
SOCIOLOGICAL JURISPRUDENCE.
SOCIOLOGICAL RESEARCH.
SOCIOLOGISTS.
SOCIOLOGY.
SOCIOLOGY, CHRISTIAN.
SOCIOLOGY, MILITARY.
SOCIOLOGY, RURAL.
SOCIOLOGY, URBAN.
SOLIDARITY.
SPORTS.
SPORTS AND STATE
SQUATTERS
STRUCTURAL ANTHROPOLOGY.
SUBURBS
SUICIDE.
SUMMER HOMES
SUPERVISION OF SOCIAL WORKERS.
SYMBOLIC INVERSION.
SYMBOLISM.
TELEVISION BROADCASTING.
TEMPERANCE.
TERRORISM.
THERAPEUTIC COMMUNITY.
TIME ALLOCATION SURVEYS
TRAMPS
TRANSHUMANCE
TRIBES AND TRIBAL SYSTEM
UNDERDEVELOPED AREAS.
UNIVERSAL NEGRO IMPROVEMENT
   ASSOCIATION.
UNMARRIED MOTHERS
UPPER CLASSES
URBAN RENEWAL
URBANIZATION.
VANDALISM
VICTIMS OF CRIME.
VICTOR VERSTER PRISON.
VILLAGE COMMUNITIES
VILLAGES
VIOLENCE.
VIOLENCE IN MASS MEDIA.
VOLUNTEER WORKERS IN SOCIAL
   SERVICE.
WELFARE STATE.
WHITE COLLAR CRIMES
WIDOWS
WIFE ABUSE
WILBERFORCE NEGRO COLONY,
   MIDDLESEX COUNTY, ONTARIO.
WITCHCRAFT.
WIVES
WOMEN.
WOMEN, MOHAMMEDAN.
WOMEN AND SOCIALISM.
WOMEN IN COMMUNITY DEVELOPMENT
WOMEN IN LITERATURE.
WOMEN IN PUBLIC LIFE.
WOMEN IN RURAL DEVELOPMENT
WOMEN PRISONERS
WOMEN'S RIGHTS.
YOUTH.
YOUTH VOLUNTEERS IN COMMUNITY
   DEVELOPMENT

Particular races, tribes and nationalities.

AETAS (PHILIPPINE NIGRITOS).
AFRICANS IN FRANCE.
AFRO-AMERICAN FAMILIES.
AFRO-AMERICAN YOUTH.
AFRO-AMERICANS.
AMERICANS IN THE FAR EAST.
ARAUCANIAN INDIANS.
ARAWAK INDIANS.
ASIATICS IN THE UNITED KINGDOM.
ASIATICS IN THE UNITED STATES.
AUSTRALIAN ABORIGINES.
AUSTRIANS IN THE UNITED KINGDOM
AUSTRIANS IN THE UNITED STATES.
AYMARA INDIANS.
AZTECS.
BANTUS.
BLACKS
BOERS.
BRITISH IN BENIN.
BRITISH IN INDIA.
BRITISH IN THE NEAR EAST.
BRITISH IN WEST AFRICA.
BUKUSU.
BULGARIANS IN MACEDONIA.
CAKCHIKEL INDIANS.
CARIB INDIANS.
CHEROKEE INDIANS.
CHICHIMECS.
CHIMBUS.
CHINESE IN AFRICA.
CHINESE IN AUSTRALIA.
CHINESE IN CANADA.
CHINESE IN INDONESIA.
CHINESE IN PAPUA NEW GUINEA.
CHINESE IN SINGAPORE.
CHINESE IN SOUTH AFRICA.
CHINESE IN SOUTHEAST ASIA.
CHINESE IN THE UNITED STATES.
COLOURED PEOPLE (SOUTH AFRICA).
CORNISH IN SOUTH AFRICA.
DAKOTA INDIANS.
DASANETCH (AFRICAN PEOPLE).
DUNGANS.
DUSUNS.
DUTCH IN INDONESIA.
DUTCH IN SRI LANKA.
DUTCH IN THE UNITED STATES.
EAST INDIANS IN CANADA.
EAST INDIANS IN FIJI.
EAST INDIANS IN NATAL.
EAST INDIANS IN SOUTH AFRICA.
EAST INDIANS IN THE UNITED
   KINGDOM.
EAST INDIANS IN THE UNITED STATES.
ESKIMOS.
EUROPEANS IN ASIA.
EUROPEANS IN SOUTH AFRICA.
EUROPEANS IN SUBSAHARAN AFRICA.
EUROPEANS IN THE PACIFIC.
FINNISH AMERICANS.
FRENCH CANADIANS.
FRENCH IN GERMANY.
FULAHS.
GERMANIC TRIBES.
GERMANS IN EASTERN EUROPE.
GERMANS IN FOREIGN COUNTRIES.
GERMANS IN HUNGARY.
GERMANS IN RUSSIA.
GONDS.
GOTHS IN ITALY.
GUAYAQUI INDIANS.
GUSII.
HAUSAS.
HOPI INDIANS.
HUNGARIANS IN CANADA
HUNGARIANS IN THE UNITED STATES
INCAS.
INDIANS OF CENTRAL AMERICA
INDIANS OF MEXICO
INDIANS OF NORTH AMERICA.
INDIANS OF SOUTH AMERICA
IRISH AMERICANS.
IRISH IN LONDON.
IRISH IN THE UNITED KINGDOM.
ITALIAN AMERICANS.
JAPANESE IN CANADA.
JEWISH AMERICANS.
JEWS.
JEWS IN AUSTRIA.
JEWS IN EUROPE.
JEWS IN FRANCE.
JEWS IN GERMANY.
JEWS IN ITALY.
JEWS IN JAPAN.
JEWS IN PALESTINE.
JEWS IN POLAND.
JEWS IN RUSSIA.
JEWS IN SHANGHAI.
JEWS IN SPAIN.
JEWS IN THE NETHERLANDS.
JEWS IN THE UNITED KINGDOM.
JEWS IN THE UNITED STATES.
KABYLES.
KALMYKS.
KALULI (PAPUA NEW GUINEA PEOPLE).
KAYASTHS.
KHAZARS.
KOREANS IN THE UNITED STATES.
KUBAS.
KURANKO (AFRICAN PEOPLE).
KURDS.
KURDS IN IRAQ.
LUOS (NILOTIC TRIBE).
LUYIAS.
MAORIS
MASHONA.
MATABELE.
MAYAS.
MAZAHUA INDIANS.
MEXICAN AMERICANS.
MIAO PEOPLE.
NAHUAS
NGONDE (AFRICAN TRIBE).
NORMANS IN ITALY.
NORTHMEN.
NYAKYUSAS.
OVAMBOS.
PAKISTANIS IN THE UNITED KINGDOM.
PALESTINIAN ARABS.
PANARE INDIANS.
PATHANS IN PAKISTAN.
POLES IN CANADA.
POLES IN FOREIGN COUNTRIES.
POLES IN FRANCE.
POLES IN GDAŃSK.
POLISH AMERICANS.
PORTUGUESE IN ANGOLA.
PORTUGUESE IN GUYANA.
RUSSIAN GERMAN AMERICANS.
RUSSIAN GERMANS IN AMERICA.
RUSSIANS IN CHINA.
RUSSIANS IN POLAND.
RUSSIANS IN THE BURYAT REPUBLIC.
SANTALS.
SCANDINAVIANS IN SOUTH AFRICA.
SEPHARDIM.
SERERS.
SIKHS.
SLAVS
SOGAS.
SWEDES IN ETHIOPIA.
SWEDES IN FINLAND.
TSWANA (BANTU TRIBE).
TZELTAL INDIANS.
TZOTZIL INDIANS.
UKRAINIANS IN CANADA.
VANDALS.
VIKINGS
WARYAGHAR (BERBER PEOPLE).
WEST INDIANS IN THE UNITED
   KINGDOM.
YANOAMA INDIANS.
YAQUI INDIANS.
YORUBAS.
YUGOSLAVS IN SLOVAKIA.
ZAPOTEC INDIANS.
ZUÑI INDIANS.

TRANSPORT AND COMMUNICATIONS.

General.

AERONAUTICS
AERONAUTICS, COMMERCIAL.
AIR LINES
AIRPORTS
ARTIFICIAL SATELLITES IN
   TELECOMMUNICATION.
AUTOMOBILE OWNERSHIP.
AUTOMOBILES
AUTOMOBILES, STEAM.
BROADCASTING
BROADCASTING POLICY
CANALS
CITY TRAFFIC
COMMUNICATION AND TRAFFIC.
COMMUTERS
COMMUTING
CONCORDE (JET TRANSPORTS).
DRY-DOCKS.
FISHING BOATS
FREIGHT AND FREIGHTAGE.
FREIGHT FORWARDERS
HARBOURS
HAZARDOUS SUBSTANCES
HIGHWAY RESEARCH.
INLAND NAVIGATION
INLAND WATER TRANSPORTATION
INTERNATIONAL TELECOMMUNICATION
   UNION.
LOCAL TRANSIT.
MERCHANT MARINE
MOTOR BUS LINES
MOTOR TRUCKS
OCEANOGRAPHIC RESEARCH SHIPS.
PHYSICAL DISTRIBUTION OF GOODS.
POSTAL SERVICE
RADIO BROADCASTING
RAILWAYS
ROAD PLANNING
ROADS
ROADSIDE IMPROVEMENT.
SHIPPING.
SHIPS
TAXICABS
TELECOMMUNICATION.
TELEGRAPH
TELEPHONE
TRAFFIC ENGINEERING.
TRAFFIC ESTIMATION
TRAFFIC OFFENCES
TRANSPORTATION.
TRANSPORTATION, AUTOMOTIVE
TRANSPORTATION AND STATE
TRANSPORTATION PLANNING.
TRAVEL RESEARCH
TRAVEL TIME (TRAFFIC ENGINEERING).
TRIP LENGTH
URBAN TRANSPORTATION.
URBAN TRANSPORTATION POLICY
WAREHOUSES

Individual undertakings, etc.

BAGDAD RAILWAY.
ILLINOIS CENTRAL RAILROAD.
MANCHESTER SHIP CANAL.
MONTREAL COLONIZATION RAILWAY.
NORTH SHORE RAILWAY (QUEBEC).
OSCAR II (SHIP).
PANAMA CANAL.
QUEBEC, MONTREAL, OTTAWA AND
   OCCIDENTAL RAILWAY.

Ref
Z
7161
L84
v.37
1979

APR 2 1981